The STANDARD
CALIFORNIA CODES
6-in-2™

VOLUME 1

CIVIL—CIVIL PROCEDURE—EVIDENCE—FAMILY—PROBATE

Selected Provisions of the Government Code

VOLUME 2

CALIFORNIA RULES OF COURT

With The

RULES OF PROFESSIONAL CONDUCT

RULES & POLICY DECLARATIONS OF THE
COMMISSION ON JUDICIAL PERFORMANCE

2009 EDITION

As revised by Legislative Enactments
up to and including the
second year of the
2007–2008 Regular Session
and Rules of Court changes
issued by the Judicial Council
through November 24, 2008

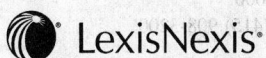 LexisNexis

QUESTIONS ABOUT THIS PUBLICATION?

For questions about the **Editorial Content** appearing in these volumes or reprint permission, please call:

Katie Solomon at .... 1-800-424-0651 EXT. 3251
Email: .... katie.k.solomon@lexisnexis.com
Kathleen Hoover at .... 1-800-446-3410 EXT. 5203
Email: .... kathleen.hoover@lexisnexis.com
or e-mail at .... CalCodes@lexisnexis.com
FOR 2009 UPDATES TO THE RULES OF COURT, please call .... 1-800-424-0651 EXT. 3466

For assistance with replacement pages, shipments, billing or other customer service matters, please call:

Customer Services Department at .... (800) 833-9844
Outside the United States and Canada, please call .... (518) 487-3000
Fax number .... (518) 487-3584
Customer Service Website .... http://www.lexisnexis.com/custserv/

For information on other Matthew Bender Publications, please call
Your account manager .... (800) 223-1940
Outside the United States and Canada, please call .... (518) 487-3000

ISBN 978-1-4224-5357-5 (HB)
ISBN 978-1-4224-5407-7 (SB)

MATTHEW◆BENDER

Editorial Offices
744 Broad Street, Newark, NJ 07102 (973) 820-2000
201 Mission St., San Francisco, CA 94105-1831 (415) 908-3200
www.lexis.com

PREFACE TO VOLUME 2

This 2009 Edition of the Standard California Codes incorporates all changes required by legislative enactments up to and including the second year of the 2007–2008 Regular Session and Rules of Court changes received by the Judicial Council through November 24, 2008.

This Edition gives the legislative history of each rule. Amendments made in 2008 are highlighted by printing in boldface type all matter added to a rule and indicating by a figure within brackets, such as [1], each point of deletion. The deleted matter is then shown by footnotes keyed to the corresponding figures. Where changes are extensive, the former rule may be reprinted in full.

The following reproduction of Rule 5.10, as amended effective January 1, 2007, clearly illustrates the "stressed amendment" feature:

> **Rule 5.10. Definitions and use of terms.**
> As used in this division, unless the context or subject matter otherwise requires, **the following definitions apply**:
> [1] **(1)** "Family Code" means that code enacted by chapter 162 of the Statutes of 1992 and any subsequent amendments to that code.
> [2] **(2)** "Proceeding" means a proceeding under the Family Code for dissolution of marriage, nullity of marriage, legal separation, custody and support of minor children, or actions under the Domestic Violence Prevention Act, the Uniform Parentage Act, the Uniform Child Custody Jurisdiction and Enforcement Act, or the Uniform Interstate Family Support Act; local child support agency actions under the Family [3] **Code**; and contempt proceedings relating to family law or local child support agency actions.
> [4] **(3)** "Property" includes assets and obligations.
> [5]
> **Adopted** Jan. 1, 1970; **amended** Jan. 1, 1994; Jan. 1, 1999; **renumbered** from Rule 1201 and **amended** Jan. 1, 2003; **amended** Jan. 1, 2007.
> **Rule 5.10. 2006 Deletes.** [1] (a) [2] (b) "Party," "petitioner," "respondent," "plaintiff," "defendant," "other parent," or any other designation of a party includes such party's attorney of record. When a notice or other paper is required to be given or served on a party, such notice or service must be given to or made on the party's attorney of record if the party has an attorney of record. (c) [3] code [4] (d) [5] (e) "Serve and file" means that a paper filed in a court is to be accompanied by proof of prior service in a manner permitted by law of a copy of the paper on each party appearing in the proceeding.

To read Rule 5.10 as amended, you read the section as printed, omitting the bracketed figures "[1]" through "[5]":

> **Rule 5.10. Definitions and use of terms.**
> As used in this division, unless the context or subject matter otherwise requires, **the following definitions apply**:
> **(1)** "Family Code" means that code enacted by chapter 162 of the Statutes of 1992 and any subsequent amendments to that code.
> **(2)** "Proceeding" means a proceeding under the Family Code for dissolution of marriage, nullity of marriage, legal separation, custody and support of minor children, or actions under the Domestic Violence Prevention Act, the Uniform Parentage Act, the Uniform Child Custody Jurisdiction and Enforcement Act, or the Uniform Interstate Family Support Act; local child support agency actions under the Family **Code**; and contempt proceedings relating to family law or local child support agency actions.

(3) "Property" includes assets and obligations.

To reconstruct the rule as it read before being amended, you read the rule as printed, omitting the words in boldface type and inserting the words appearing in the footnote under Rule 5.10 and referred to by the "[1]" through "[5]" in the rule:

Rule 5.10. Definitions and use of terms.

As used in this division, unless the context or subject matter otherwise requires:

(a) "Family Code" means that code enacted by chapter 162 of the Statutes of 1992 and any subsequent amendments to that code.

(b) "Party," "petitioner," "respondent," "plaintiff," "defendant," "other parent," or any other designation of a party includes such party's attorney of record. When a notice or other paper is required to be given or served on a party, such notice or service must be given to or made on the party's attorney of record if the party has an attorney of record.

(c) "Proceeding" means a proceeding under the Family Code for dissolution of marriage, nullity of marriage, legal separation, custody and support of minor children, or actions under the Domestic Violence Prevention Act, the Uniform Parentage Act, the Uniform Child Custody Jurisdiction and Enforcement Act, or the Uniform Interstate Family Support Act; local child support agency actions under the Family code; and contempt proceedings relating to family law or local child support agency actions.

(d) "Property" includes assets and obligations.

(e) "Serve and file" means that a paper filed in a court is to be accompanied by proof of prior service in a manner permitted by law of a copy of the paper on each party appearing in the proceeding.

In presenting this Edition of the Standard California Codes, we wish to acknowledge with gratitude the many helpful suggestions received from users of our Codes, and to express the hope that this Edition will serve effectively the needs of bench and bar alike.

THE PUBLISHER

CALIFORNIA
RULES OF COURT

2009 EDITION

Rules of practice and procedure promulgated by the Judicial Council and the Supreme Court with amendments received from November 24, 2007 through November 24, 2008.

PREFACE

The California Rules of Court includes all rules of practice and procedure adopted by the Judicial Council and the Supreme Court pursuant to the authority contained in California Constitution, Article VI, Section 6, and in various code sections. The Council originally adopted rules for the superior courts, the Supreme Court, and the courts of appeal shortly after its organization in 1926, and later adopted rules for the appellate departments of the superior court. In 1943, new rules on appeal to the Supreme Court and courts of appeal were adopted. These rules were renumbered and combined into the California Rules of Court adopted April 1, 1962. Since that date the rules have continued, with yearly changes and additions, in the same general form.

On June 30, 2006, the Judicial Council of California approved a major reorganization of the California Rules of Court, a group of more than 1,000 rules and 47 standards of judicial administration that govern state court policy and procedure. The reorganization, effective January 1, 2007, involves a major restructuring, reordering, and renumbering of the rules and standards to make them clearer, better organized, and easier to read. "The changes to the California Rules of Court are part of a larger, historic effort to make the law clearer, more accessible, and user-friendly," said Chief Justice Ronald M. George, chair of the 28-member council, the administrative policymaking body of state courts. "This major rules reorganization joins the ranks of other successful efforts to improve public understanding of the courts, such as the Judicial Council's plain English jury instructions and plain-language court forms for self-represented litigants," the Chief Justice continued.

The effective dates of amendments subsequent to the adoption of each rule that appears in this edition of the Standard California Codes are indicated in chronological order following each subdivision of a rule that has been amended.

A table of disposition follows on pages xi-lxviii.

THE PUBLISHER

PREFACE

The California Rules of Court include all rules of practice and procedure adopted by the Judicial Council and the Supreme Court pursuant to the authority contained in California Constitution, Article VI, Section 6, and in various code sections. The Council originally adopted rules for the superior courts, the Supreme Court, and the courts of appeal shortly after its reorganization in 1926, and later adopted rules for the appellate departments of the superior court. In 1943, new rules on appeal to the Supreme Court and courts of appeal were adopted. These rules were renumbered and combined into the California Rules of Court adopted April 1, 1962. Since that date the rules have continued, with yearly changes and additions, in the same general form.

On June 30, 2006, the Judicial Council of California approved a major reorganization of the California Rules of Court: a group of more than 1,000 rules and 47 standards of judicial administration that govern state court policy and procedure. The reorganization, effective January 1, 2007, involves a major restructuring, reordering, and renumbering of the rules and standards to make them clearer, better organized, and easier to read. "The changes to the California Rules of Court are part of a larger historic effort to make the law clearer, more accessible, and user friendly," said Chief Justice Ronald M. George, chair of the 28-member council, the administrative policymaking body of state courts. "This major rules reorganization joins the ranks of other successful efforts to improve public understanding of the courts, such as the Judicial Council's plain-English jury instructions and plain-language court forms for self-represented litigants," the Chief Justice continued.

The effective dates of amendments subsequent to the adoption of each rule that appears in this edition of the Standard California Codes are indicated in chronological order following each subdivision of a rule that has been amended.

A table of disposition follows on pages xi-lxviii.

THE PUBLISHER

Table Showing Changes Received From the Judicial Council
From November 24, 2007 Through November 24, 2008

Rule	Effect	Date
1.6(15)	Amended	July 1, 2008
1.31(e)	Amended	Jan. 1, 2009
1.35(e)	Amended	Jan. 1, 2009
1.45(a)	Amended	July 1, 2008
2.260(f)(1)	Amended	Jan. 1, 2009
2.306(d), (e)	Amended	July 1, 2008
2.400(a)	Amended	Jan. 1, 2009
2.810(a)	Amended	Jan. 1, 2009
2.812(c)	Amended	Jan. 1, 2009
2.812(d)	Relettered to (e) / Adopted	Jan. 1, 2009
2.812(e)	Relettered to (f) / Relettered from (d)	Jan. 1, 2009
2.812(f)	Relettered to (g) / Relettered from (e)	Jan. 1, 2009
2.812(g)	Relettered from (f)	Jan. 1, 2009
3.61(6)	Amended	Jan. 1, 2009
3.220 Hdg	Amended	Jan. 1, 2009
3.220(a)	Amended	Jan. 1, 2009
Ch. 3 Hdg (comm w/3.670)	Amended	July 1, 2008
Ch. 4 Hdg (comm w/3.740)	Adopted	July 1, 2008
3.740(b)	Amended	Jan. 1, 2009
Ch. 4 Hdg (comm w/3.750)	Renumbered to Ch. 5	July 1, 2008
Ch. 5 Hdg (comm w/3.750)	Renumbered from Ch. 4	July 1, 2008
Ch. 5 Hdg (comm w/3.760)	Renumbered to Ch. 6	July 1, 2008
Ch. 6 Hdg (comm w/3.760)	Renumbered from Ch. 5	July 1, 2008
3.769(h) Hdg	Amended	Jan. 1, 2009
3.769(h)	Amended	Jan. 1, 2009
3.770(a)	Amended	Jan. 1, 2009
3.851(a)(1)	Amended	Jan. 1, 2009
Art. 3 (comm w/3.865)	Adopted	July 1, 2009
3.865	Amended & Renumbered to 3.868 / Adopted	July 1, 2009
3.865 Adv. Comment	Adopted	July 1, 2009
3.866	Amended & Renumbered to 3.867 / Adopted	July 1, 2009
3.866 Adv. Comment	Adopted	July 1, 2009
3.867	Amended & Renumbered to 3.871 / Amended & Renumbered from 3.866	July 1, 2009
3.867 Adv. Comment	Renumbered to 3.871 Adv. Comment / Adopted	July 1, 2009
3.868	Amended & Renumbered to 3.872 / Amended & Renumbered from 3.865	July 1, 2009
3.869	Adopted	July 1, 2009
3.869 Adv. Comment	Adopted	July 1, 2009
3.870	Renumbered to 3.890 / Adopted	July 1, 2009
3.870 Adv. Comment	Adopted	July 1, 2009
3.871	Renumbered to 3.891 / Amended & Renumbered from 3.867	July 1, 2009
3.871 Adv. Comment	Renumbered from 3.867 Adv. Comment	July 1, 2009
3.872	Renumbered to 3.892 / Amended & Renumbered from 3.868	July 1, 2009
3.872 Adv. Comment	Adopted	July 1, 2009
3.873	Renumbered to 3.893	July 1, 2009
3.874	Renumbered to 3.894	July 1, 2009
3.875	Renumbered to 3.895	July 1, 2009
3.876	Renumbered to 3.896	July 1, 2009
3.877	Renumbered to 3.897	July 1, 2009
3.878	Renumbered to 3.898	July 1, 2009
3.890	Renumbered from 3.870	July 1, 2009
3.891	Renumbered from 3.871	July 1, 2009
3.892	Renumbered from 3.872	July 1, 2009
3.893	Renumbered from 3.873	July 1, 2009
3.894	Renumbered from 3.874	July 1, 2009
3.895	Renumbered from 3.875	July 1, 2009
3.896	Renumbered from 3.876	July 1, 2009
3.897	Renumbered from 3.877	July 1, 2009
3.898	Renumbered from 3.878	July 1, 2009
Ch. 3 Hdg (comm w/3.1020)	Repealed	Jan. 1, 2009
3.1020	Renumbered to 3.1345	Jan. 1, 2009
3.1025	Renumbered to 3.1346	Jan. 1, 2009
3.1030	Renumbered to 3.1348	Jan. 1, 2009
3.1112(e)	Amended	July 1, 2008
3.1320(i)	Amended	Jan. 1, 2009
3.1327	Adopted	Jan. 1, 2009
3.1342(a)	Amended	Jan. 1, 2009
Art. 4 (comm w/3.1345)	Adopted	Jan. 1, 2009
3.1345	Renumbered from 3.1020	Jan. 1, 2009
3.1346	Renumbered from 3.1025	Jan. 1, 2009
3.1347	Adopted	Jan. 1, 2009
3.1348	Renumbered from 3.1030	Jan. 1, 2009
Art. 4 (comm w/3.1350)	Renumbered to Art. 5 (comm w/3.1350)	Jan. 1, 2009

Rule	Effect	Date	Rule	Effect	Date
Art. 5 (comm w/3.1350)	Renumbered from Art. 4 (comm w/3.1350)	Jan. 1, 2009	7.552(d)–(f)	Amended	Mar. 1, 2008
			7.553	Adopted	Mar. 1, 2008
3.1350(c)	Amended	Jan. 1, 2009	7.1011	Adopted	Jan. 1, 2009
3.1350(e)	Amended	Jan. 1, 2009	7.1012	Amended	Jan. 1, 2009
3.1350(h)	Amended	July 1, 2008	7.1061	Adopted	Jan. 1, 2009
3.1351	Adopted	July 1, 2008	7.1062(a), (b)	Amended	Jan. 1, 2009
Art. 5 (comm w/3.1360)	Renumbered to Art. 6 (comm w/3.1360)	Jan. 1, 2009	7.1062(c)	Amended	July 1, 2008
			7.1062(d), (e)	Amended	Jan. 1, 2009
Art. 6 (comm w/3.1360)	Renumbered from Art. 5 (comm w/3.1360)	Jan. 1, 2009	Ch. 23 Hdg (comm w/7.1101)	Adopted	Jan. 1, 2008
			7.1101	Adopted	Jan. 1, 2008
3.1362(d), (e)	Amended	Jan. 1, 2009	7.1101(a)(7)	Adopted	Jan. 1, 2009
3.1385(b)	Amended	Jan. 1, 2009	7.1101(b)	Amended	Jan. 1, 2009
3.1385(d), (e)	Adopted	Jan. 1, 2009	7.1101(e), (f)	Amended	Jan. 1, 2009
3.1702(b)(2)	Amended	Jan. 1, 2009	7.1101(h) Hdg	Amended	Jan. 1, 2009
3.1702(c)	Amended	July 1, 2008	7.1101(h)	Amended	Jan. 1, 2009
4.115(a)	Amended	Jan. 1, 2008	8.18 Adv. Comment	Amended	Jan. 1, 2009
4.115(b)	Adopted	Jan. 1, 2008	8.25(b)(2)	Amended	Jan. 1, 2009
4.115 Adv. Comment	Adopted	Jan. 1, 2008	8.25 Adv. Comment	Amended	Jan. 1, 2009
4.201 Adv. Comment	Adopted	Jan. 1, 2008	8.32(b)(1)	Amended	July 1, 2008
4.405 Adv. Comment	Amended	Jan. 1, 2008	8.32(d) Hdg	Amended	July 1, 2008
4.420(b)	Amended	Jan. 1, 2008	8.32(d)	Amended	July 1, 2008
4.420(d)	Amended	Jan. 1, 2008	8.112(d)(3)	Amended	Jan. 1, 2009
4.428	Amended	Jan. 1, 2008	8.130(f)	Amended	July 1, 2008
4.433(b)	Amended	Jan. 1, 2008	8.200(c)(3)	Relettered to (c)(4) / Adopted	Jan. 1, 2009
4.437 Adv. Comment	Amended	Jan. 1, 2008	8.200(c)(4)	Relettered to (c)(5) / Relettered from (c)(3)	Jan. 1, 2009
4.551(a)(1)	Amended	Jan. 1, 2009			
Ch. 6 Hdg (comm w/5.275)	Amended	Jan. 1, 2009	8.200(c)(5)	Relettered to (c)(6) / Relettered from (c)(4)	Jan. 1, 2009
5.275(j)	Amended	Jan. 1, 2009			
5.324(j)	Amended	July 1, 2008	8.200(c)(6)	Amended & Relettered to (c)(7) / Relettered from (c)(5)	Jan. 1, 2009
5.505	Adopted	Jan. 1, 2009			
5.505 Adv. Comment	Adopted	Jan. 1, 2009			
5.552(b) Hdg	Amended	Jan. 1, 2009	8.200(c)(7)	Amended & Relettered from (c)(6)	Jan. 1, 2009
5.552(b)	Amended	Jan. 1, 2009			
5.552(d) Hdg	Amended	Jan. 1, 2009	8.200 Adv. Comment	Amended	Jan. 1, 2009
5.552(d), (e)	Amended	Jan. 1, 2009	8.208(d)	Amended	Jan. 1, 2009
5.552(f)	Repealed / Relettered from (g)	Jan. 1, 2009	8.208(e)(2)	Amended	Jan. 1, 2009
			8.216(b)(2)	Amended	Jan. 1, 2009
5.552(g)	Relettered to (f) / Relettered from (h)	Jan. 1, 2009	8.252(a)(2)	Relettered to (a)(3) / Adopted	Jan. 1, 2009
5.552(h)	Relettered to (g) / Relettered from (i)	Jan. 1, 2009	8.252(a)(3)	Relettered from (a)(2)	Jan. 1, 2009
			8.264(b)	Amended	Jan. 1, 2009
5.552(i)	Relettered to (h)	Jan. 1, 2009	8.264 Adv. Comment	Amended	Mar. 1, 2009
5.552 Adv. Comment	Repealed	Jan. 1, 2009	8.268(b)(1)	Amended	Jan. 1, 2009
5.553	Adopted	Jan. 1, 2009	8.272 Adv. Comment	Amended	Jan. 1, 2009
5.570(a)(4), (5)	Amended	Jan. 1, 2009	8.278 Adv. Comment	Amended	Jan. 1, 2009
5.600(f)(2)	Amended	Jan. 1, 2009	8.312(d)	Amended	Jan. 1, 2009
5.640(a) Hdg	Amended	Jan. 1, 2009	8.312 Adv. Comment	Amended	Jan. 1, 2009
5.640(b) Hdg	Amended	Jan. 1, 2009	8.361	Adopted	Jan. 1, 2009
5.640(b)	Amended	Jan. 1, 2009	8.361 Adv. Comment	Adopted	Jan. 1, 2009
5.640(c)(1), (5), (9)	Amended	Jan. 1, 2009	8.366	Amended	Jan. 1, 2009
5.640(h)	Amended	Jan. 1, 2009	8.366 Adv. Comment	Adopted	Jan. 1, 2009
5.645(c)	Amended	Jan. 1, 2009	8.380(a)	Amended	Jan. 1, 2009
5.690(c)(1)	Amended	Jan. 1, 2009	8.380(a)(2)	Amended & Relettered to (b)	Jan. 1, 2009
5.725 Hdg	Amended	Jan. 1, 2009			
5.725(a)	Amended	Jan. 1, 2009	8.380(a)(3)	Amended & Relettered to (c)	Jan. 1, 2009
5.725(e)(1)	Amended	Jan. 1, 2009			
5.772(h)	Amended	Jan. 1, 2009	8.380(b)	Repealed / Amended & Relettered from (a)(2)	Jan. 1, 2009
7.151(a)–(c)	Amended	Mar. 1, 2008			
7.151(e)	Amended	Mar. 1, 2008			
7.151(g) Hdg	Amended	Mar. 1, 2008			
7.151(g)	Amended	Mar. 1, 2008	8.380(c)	Repealed / Amended &	
7.552 Hdg	Amended	Mar. 1, 2008			
7.552 Intro ¶	Adopted	Mar. 1, 2008			
7.552(a)	Amended	Mar. 1, 2008			

Rule	Effect	Date	Rule	Effect	Date
	Relettered from		8.488	Adopted	Jan. 1, 2009
	(a)(3)	Jan. 1, 2009	8.488 Adv. Comment	Adopted	Jan. 1, 2009
8.380(d)	Repealed	Jan. 1, 2009	8.489	Adopted	Jan. 1, 2009
8.380 Adv. Comment	Amended &		Ch. 7 (comm w/8.490)	Amended &	
	Renumbered to			Renumbered to Ch.	
	8.385 Adv.			8 (comm w/8.495)	Jan. 1, 2009
	Comment	Jan. 1, 2009	8.490	Amended &	
8.384(a)	Repealed /			Renumbered to	
	Amended &			8.486 / Adopted	Jan. 1, 2009
	Relettered from		8.490 Adv. Comment	Amended &	
	(b)(1), (2), (6)	Jan. 1, 2009		Renumbered to	
8.384(b)(1)	Amended &			8.486 Adv.	
	Relettered to (a)(1) /			Comment /	
	Amended &			Adopted	Jan. 1, 2009
	Relettered from		8.491–8.493	Adopted	Jan. 1, 2009
	(b)(3)	Jan. 1, 2009	8.494	Renumbered to 8.495	Jan. 1, 2009
8.384(b)(2)	Amended &		Ch. 8 (comm w/8.495)	Amended &	
	Relettered to (a)(2) /			Renumbered from	
	Amended &			Ch. 7 (comm	
	Relettered from			w/8.490)	Jan. 1, 2009
	(b)(4)	Jan. 1, 2009	8.495	Renumbered from	
8.384(b)(3)	Amended &			8.494	Jan. 1, 2009
	Relettered to (b)(1) /		Ch. 8 (comm w/8.500)	Renumbered to Ch. 9	
	Amended &			(comm w/8.500)	Jan. 1, 2009
	Relettered from		Ch. 9 (comm w/8.500)	Renumbered from Ch.	
	(b)(5)	Jan. 1, 2009		8 (comm w/8.500)	Jan. 1, 2009
8.384(b)(4)	Amended &		8.500(e)	Amended	Jan. 1, 2009
	Relettered to		8.500 Adv. Comment	Amended	Jan. 1, 2009
	(b)(2)	Jan. 1, 2009	8.504(b)(5)	Relettered to (b)(6) /	
8.384(b)(5)	Amended &			Adopted	Jan. 1, 2009
	Relettered to		8.504(b)(6)	Relettered to (b)(7) /	
	(b)(3)	Jan. 1, 2009		Relettered from	
8.384(b)(6)	Relettered to (a)(3)	Jan. 1, 2009		(b)(5)	Jan. 1, 2009
8.384(b)(7)	Amended &		8.504(b)(7)	Relettered from (b)(6)	Jan. 1, 2009
	Relettered to (c)	Jan. 1, 2009	8.504(e)(1), (2)	Amended	Jan. 1, 2009
8.384(b)(8)	Amended &		8.520(c)(1), (2)	Amended	Jan. 1, 2009
	Relettered to (d)		8.520(f)(4)	Relettered to (f)(5) /	
8.384(c)	Amended &			Adopted	Jan. 1, 2009
	Relettered from		8.520(f)(5)	Relettered to (f)(6) /	
	(b)(7)	Jan. 1, 2009		Relettered from	
8.384(d)	Amended &			(f)(4)	Jan. 1, 2009
	Relettered from		8.520(f)(6)	Relettered to (f)(7) /	
	(b)(8)	Jan. 1, 2009		Relettered from	
8.385	Adopted	Jan. 1, 2009		(f)(5)	Jan. 1, 2009
8.385 Adv. Comment	Amended &		8.520(f)(7)	Amended &	
	Renumbered from			Relettered to (f)(8) /	
	8.380 Adv.			Relettered from	
	Comment	Jan. 1, 2009		(f)(6)	Jan. 1, 2009
8.386	Amended &		8.520(f)(8)	Amended &	
	Renumbered to			Relettered from	
	8.387 / Adopted	Jan. 1, 2009		(f)(7)	Jan. 1, 2009
8.387	Amended &		8.544	Amended	July 1, 2008
	Renumbered from		8.544 Adv. Comment	Amended	July 1, 2008
	8.386	Jan. 1, 2009	8.552(b)	Amended	Jan. 1, 2009
8.387 Adv. Comment	Adopted	Jan. 1, 2009	8.552 Adv. Comment	Amended	Jan. 1, 2009
8.450(a)	Amended	Jan. 1, 2009	Ch. 9 (comm w/8.600)	Amended &	
8.454(a)	Amended	Jan. 1, 2009		Renumbered to Ch.	
Ch. 7 (comm w/8.485)	Adopted	Jan. 1, 2009		10 (comm w/8.600)	Jan. 1, 2009
8.485	Adopted	Jan. 1, 2009	Ch. 10 (comm		
8.486	Amended &		w/8.600)	Amended &	
	Renumbered from			Renumbered from	
	8.490	Jan. 1, 2009		Ch. 9 (comm	
8.486 Adv. Comment	Amended &			w/8.600)	Jan. 1, 2009
	Renumbered from		Div. 2 Hdg (comm		
	8.490 Adv.		w/8.700)	Repealed	Jan. 1, 2009
	Comment	Jan. 1, 2009	Ch. 1 Hdg (comm		
8.487	Adopted	Jan. 1, 2009	w/8.700)	Repealed	Jan. 1, 2009
8.487 Adv. Comment	Adopted	Jan. 1, 2009	8.700–8.709	Repealed	Jan. 1, 2009

Rule	Effect	Date
Ch. 2 Hdg (comm w/8.750)	Repealed	Jan. 1, 2009
8.750–8.773	Repealed	Jan. 1, 2009
Ch. 3 Hdg (comm w/8.780)	Repealed	Jan. 1, 2009
8.780–8.793	Repealed	Jan. 1, 2009
Div. 2 Hdg (comm w/8.800)	Adopted	Jan. 1, 2009
Div. 2 Adv. Comment (comm w/8.800)	Adopted	Jan. 1, 2009
Ch. 1 Hdg (comm w/8.800)	Adopted	Jan. 1, 2009
8.800–8.817	Adopted	Jan. 1, 2009
Ch. 2 Hdg (comm w/8.820)	Adopted	Jan. 1, 2009
Art. 1 Hdg (comm w/8.820)	Adopted	Jan. 1, 2009
8.820–8.825	Adopted	Jan. 1, 2009
Art. 2 Hdg (comm w/8.830)	Adopted	Jan. 1, 2009
8.830–8.843	Adopted	Jan. 1, 2009
Ch. 3 Hdg (comm w/8.850)	Adopted	Jan. 1, 2009
Art. 1 Hdg (comm w/8.850)	Adopted	Jan. 1, 2009
8.850–8.855	Adopted	Jan. 1, 2009
Art. 2 Hdg (comm w/8.860)	Adopted	Jan. 1, 2009
8.860–8.873	Adopted	Jan. 1, 2009
Ch. 4 Hdg (comm w/8.880)	Adopted	Jan. 1, 2009
8.880–8.882	Adopted	Jan. 1, 2009
8.882(b)	Relettered to (c) / Adopted	Jan. 1, 2009
8.882(c)	Amended & Relettered to (d) / Relettered from (b)	Jan. 1, 2009
8.882(d)	Amended & Relettered to (e) / Amended & Relettered from (c)	Jan. 1, 2009
8.882(e)	Amended & Relettered from (d)	Jan. 1, 2009
8.883	Adopted	Jan. 1, 2009
8.884	Adopted	Jan. 1, 2009
8.884(b)(3)	Amended	Jan. 1, 2009
8.885–8.891	Adopted	Jan. 1, 2009
Div. 3 Hdg (comm w/8.900)	Transferred (comm w/8.950)	Jan. 1, 2009
Ch. 5 Hdg (comm w/8.900)	Adopted	Jan. 1, 2009
Art. 1 Hdg (comm w/8.900)	Adopted	Jan. 1, 2009
8.900	Renumbered to 8.950 / Adopted	Jan. 1, 2009
8.900 Adv. Comment	Adopted	Jan. 1, 2009
8.901	Adopted	Jan. 1, 2009
8.901 Adv. Comment	Adopted	Jan. 1, 2009
8.902	Renumbered to 8.952 / Adopted	Jan. 1, 2009
8.903	Adopted	Jan. 1, 2009
8.903 Adv. Comment	Adopted	Jan. 1, 2009
8.904	Renumbered to 8.954 / Adopted	Jan. 1, 2009
8.904 Adv. Comment	Adopted	Jan. 1, 2009
8.907	Renumbered to 8.957	Jan. 1, 2009
Art. 2 Hdg (comm w/8.910)	Adopted	Jan. 1, 2009
8.910	Renumbered to 8.960 / Adopted	Jan. 1, 2009
8.911	Adopted	Jan. 1, 2009
8.912	Adopted	Jan. 1, 2009
8.913	Renumbered to 8.963 / Adopted	Jan. 1, 2009
8.913 Adv. Comment	Adopted	Jan. 1, 2009
8.914	Adopted	Jan. 1, 2009
8.914 Adv. Comment	Adopted	Jan. 1, 2009
8.915	Adopted	Jan. 1, 2009
8.915 Adv. Comment	Adopted	Jan. 1, 2009
8.916	Renumbered to 8.966 / Adopted	Jan. 1, 2009
8.916 Adv. Comment	Adopted	Jan. 1, 2009
8.917	Adopted	Jan. 1, 2009
8.917 Adv. Comment	Adopted	Jan. 1, 2009
	Amended	Jan. 1, 2009
8.918	Adopted	Jan. 1, 2009
8.919	Adopted	Jan. 1, 2009
8.919 Adv. Comment	Adopted	Jan. 1, 2009
	Amended	Jan. 1, 2009
8.920–8.923	Adopted	Jan. 1, 2009
Art. 3 Hdg (comm w/8.925)	Adopted	Jan. 1, 2009
8.925–8.929	Adopted	Jan. 1, 2009
8.929 Adv. Comment	Adopted	Jan. 1, 2009
Ch. 6 Hdg (comm w/8.930)	Adopted	Jan. 1, 2009
8.930	Adopted	Jan. 1, 2009
8.930 Adv. Comment	Adopted	Jan. 1, 2009
8.931	Adopted	Jan. 1, 2009
8.931(b)	Amended	Jan. 1, 2009
8.931 Adv. Comment	Adopted	Jan. 1, 2009
8.932–8.936	Adopted	Jan. 1, 2009
8.950	Renumbered from 8.900	Jan. 1, 2009
8.952	Renumbered from 8.902	Jan. 1, 2009
8.954	Renumbered from 8.904	Jan. 1, 2009
8.957	Renumbered from 8.907	Jan. 1, 2009
8.960	Renumbered from 8.910	Jan. 1, 2009
8.963	Renumbered from 8.913	Jan. 1, 2009
8.966	Renumbered from 8.916	Jan. 1, 2009
8.1018 Hdg	Amended	Jan. 1, 2009
8.1018(a)	Relettered to (b) / Adopted	Jan. 1, 2009
8.1018(b)	Relettered to (c) / Relettered from (a)	Jan. 1, 2009
8.1018(c)	Relettered to (d) / Relettered from (b)	Jan. 1, 2009
8.1018(d)	Relettered from (c)	Jan. 1, 2009
8.1018 Adv. Comment	Adopted	Jan. 1, 2009
8.1105(b)	Amended	July 23, 2008
9.6	Amended	June 1, 2007
9.11(a)–(c)	Amended	Jan. 1, 2009
9.23	Adopted	Apr. 1, 2007
10.106	Adopted	July 1, 2008
10.172	Adopted	Jan. 1, 2009
10.172 Adv. Comment	Adopted	Jan. 1, 2009
10.173	Adopted	Jan. 1, 2009
10.461(e)	Amended	Aug. 15, 2008

Rule	Effect	Date	Rule	Effect	Date
10.461 Adv. Comment	Amended	Aug. 15, 2008		8 / Renumbered	
10.462(c)	Amended	July 1, 2008		to Ch. 10	Jan. 1, 2008
10.462(f)	Amended	Aug. 15, 2008	Ch. 10 Hdg (comm		
10.462 Adv. Comment	Amended	Aug. 15, 2008	w/10.870)	Renumbered from Ch.	
10.468	Adopted	Jan. 1, 2008		9 / Renumbered	
10.478	Adopted	Jan. 1, 2008		to Ch. 11	Jan. 1, 2008
10.481(a)	Amended	Jan. 1, 2008	Ch. 11 Hdg (comm		
10.481(b)	Amended	Jan. 1, 2008	w/10.900)	Renumbered from Ch.	
10.491(f)	Amended	July 1, 2008		10 / Renumbered	
10.613(d)(1)	Amended	Jan. 1, 2009		to Ch. 12	Jan. 1, 2008
10.660(a)	Amended	Oct. 24, 2008	Ch. 12 Hdg (comm		
10.701(d)	Amended	July 1, 2008	w/10.950)	Renumbered from Ch.	
Ch. 7 Hdg (comm				11/ Renumbered	
w/10.776)	Adopted	Jan. 1, 2008		to Ch. 13	Jan. 1, 2008
10.776	Adopted	Jan. 1, 2008	Ch. 13 Hdg (comm		
10.777	Adopted	Jan. 1, 2008	w/10.950)	Renumbered from	
Ch. 7 Hdg (comm				Ch. 12	Jan. 1, 2008
w/10.780)	Renumbered to Ch. 8	Jan. 1, 2008	Ch. 14 Hdg (comm		
10.781(c)	Adopted	July 1, 2009	w/10.960)	Adopted	July 1, 2008
10.781 Adv. Comment	Adopted	July 1, 2009	Ch. 2 Hdg (comm		
Ch. 8 Hdg (comm			w/10.1100)	Adopted	Jan. 1, 2009
w/10.800)	Renumbered from Ch.		10.1100	Adopted	Jan. 1, 2009
	7 / Renumbered		10.1100 Adv. Comment	Adopted	Jan. 1, 2009
	to Ch. 9	Jan. 1, 2008	10.1104	Adopted	Jan. 1, 2009
10.820(e)	Amended	Jan. 1, 2009	10.1104 Adv. Comment	Adopted	Jan. 1, 2009
Ch. 9 Hdg (comm			10.1108	Adopted	Jan. 1, 2009
w/10.851)	Renumbered from Ch.				

Standards of Judicial Administration

Standard	Effect	Date
10.16	Amended	July 1, 2008
10.40	Repealed	Jan. 1, 2009

Appendices

Appendix	Effect	Date
A	Amended	Feb. 13, 2008, Mar. 1, 2008, Apr. 1, 2008, July 1, 2008, July 24, 2008, Jan. 1, 2009, July 1, 2009

Supplement to the California Rules of Court

Supreme Court Policies Regarding Cases Arising From Judgments of Death

Policy	Effect	Date
3:2-2.1	Amended	Jan. 1, 2008

Payment Guidelines for Appointed Counsel Representing Indigent Criminal Appellants in the California Supreme Court

Guideline	Effect	Date
Part II A	Amended	Oct. 1, 2007
Part III B	Amended	Oct. 1, 2007, July 23, 2008
Part III C	Amended	July 23, 2008, Aug. 27, 2008

Guidelines for Fixed Fee Appointments, on Optional Basis, to Automatic Appeals and Related Habeas Corpus Proceedings in the California Supreme Court

Guideline	Effect	Date
Introduction	Amended	Oct. 1, 2007
1	Amended	Oct. 1, 2007
1.1	Amended	Oct. 1, 2007
1.2	Amended	Oct. 1, 2007
2	Amended	Jan. 1, 2008
10	Amended	Oct. 1, 2007

Court of Appeal—Second Appellate District

Local Rules

Rule	Effect	Date
5	Adopted	May 5, 2008

Internal Operating Practices and Procedures

IOPPs	Effect	Date
IOPPs	Amended	Jan. 1, 2008

Court of Appeal—Third Appellate District

Local Rules

Order	Effect	Date
Miscellaneous Order 2008-001	Adopted	Jan. 2, 2008

Court of Appeal—Fourth Appellate District

Internal Operating Practices and Procedures, Division One

IOPP	Effect	Date
VI	Amended	Jan. 1, 2008

Internal Operating Practices and Procedures, Division Three

IOPP	Effect	Date
SECTIONS III, IV	Amended	Jan. 1, 2008

Court of Appeal—Sixth Appellate District

Internal Operating Practices and Procedures

IOPP	Effect	Date
II	Amended	Jan. 1, 2008

California Rules of Court Reorganization
(Effective January 1, 2007)
(From former number to new number)

Old Rule Number	New Rule Number	Rule Title
1	8.100	~~Taking~~ Filing the appeal
2	8.104	Time to appeal
3	8.108	~~Extensions of~~ Extending the time to appeal
4	8.130	Reporter's transcript
5	8.120	Clerk's transcript
5.1	8.124	Appendixes instead of clerk's transcript
5.2	8.128	Superior court file instead of clerk's transcript
6	8.134	Agreed statement
7	8.137	Settled statement
8	8.140	Failure to procure the record
9	8.144	Form of the record
10	8.147	Record in multiple or later appeals in same case
11	8.150	Filing ~~and lending~~ the record
12	8.155	Augmenting and correcting the record
12.5	8.160	Sealed records
13	8.200	Briefs by parties and amici curiae
14	8.204	Contents and form of briefs
14.5	8.208	Certificate of Interested Entities or Persons
15	8.212	Service and filing of briefs
16	8.216	Appeals in which a party is both appellant and respondent
17	8.220	Failure to file a brief
18	8.224	Transmitting exhibits
19	8.240	Calendar preference
20	8.244	Settlement, abandonment, voluntary dismissal, and compromise
21	8.248	Prehearing conference
22	8.252	Judicial notice; findings and evidence on appeal
23	8.256	Oral argument and submission of the cause
24	8.264	Filing, finality, and modification of decision
25	8.268	Rehearing
26	8.272	Remittitur
27	8.276	Costs and sanctions
28	8.500	Petition for review
28.1	8.504	Form and contents of petition, answer, and reply
28.2	8.512	Ordering review
29	8.516	Issues on review
29.1	8.520	Briefs by parties and amici curiae; judicial notice
29.2	8.524	Oral argument and submission of the cause
29.3	8.528	Disposition ~~of causes~~
29.4	8.532	Filing, finality, and modification of decision
29.5	8.536	Rehearing
29.6	8.540	Remittitur
29.7	8.544	Costs and sanctions
29.8	8.548	Decision on request of a court of another jurisdiction
29.9	8.552	Transfer for decision
30	8.304	~~Taking~~ Filing the appeal; certificate of probable cause
30.1	8.308	Time to appeal
30.2	8.312	Stay of execution and release on appeal
30.3	8.316	Abandoning the appeal
31	8.320	Normal record; exhibits
31.1	8.324	Application in superior court for addition to normal record
31.2	8.328	Sealed records
31.3	8.332	Juror-identifying information
32	8.336	Preparing, certifying, and sending the record

Old Rule Number	New Rule Number	Rule Title
32.1	8.340	Augmenting or correcting the record in the Court of Appeal
32.2	8.344	Agreed statement
32.3	8.346	Settled statement
33	8.360	Briefs by parties and amici curiae
33.1	8.366	Hearing and decision in the Court of Appeal
33.2	8.368	Hearing and decision in the Supreme Court
33.3	8.508	Petition for review to exhaust state remedies
34	8.600	In general
34.1	8.610	Contents and form of the record
34.2	8.613	Preparing and certifying the record of preliminary proceedings
35	8.616	Preparing the trial record
35.1	8.619	Certifying the trial record for completeness
35.2	8.622	Certifying the trial record for accuracy
35.3	8.625	Certifying the record in pre-1997 trials
36	8.630	Briefs by parties and amici curiae
36.1	8.634	Transmitting exhibits; augmenting the record in the Supreme Court
36.2	8.638	Oral argument and submission of the cause
36.3	8.642	Filing, finality, and modification of decision; rehearing; remittitur
37	8.400	Appeals in juvenile cases generally
37.1	8.404	Record on appeal
37.2	8.408	Preparing, sending, augmenting, and correcting the record
37.3	8.412	Briefs by parties and amici curiae
37.4	8.416	Appeals from all terminations of parental rights; dependency appeals in Orange, Imperial, and San Diego Counties
38	8.450	Notice of intent to file writ petition to review order setting hearing under Welfare and Institutions Code section 366.26
38.1	8.452	Writ petition to review order setting hearing under Welfare and Institutions Code section 366.26 and rule 1436.5 5.600
38.2	8.454	Notice of intent to file writ petition under Welfare and Institutions Code section 366.28 to review order designating specific placement of a dependent child after termination of parental rights
38.3	8.456	Writ petition under Welfare and Institutions Code section 366.28 and rule 1436.5 5.600 to review order designating specific placement of a dependent child after termination of parental rights
38.4	8.470	Hearing and decision in the Court of Appeal
38.5	8.472	Hearing and decision in the Supreme Court
38.6	8.474	Procedures and data
39	8.480	Appeal from order establishing conservatorship
39.1	8.482	Appeal from judgment authorizing conservator to consent to sterilization of conservatee
39.2	8.388	Appeal from order granting relief by writ of habeas corpus
40	8.10	Definitions and use of terms
40.1	8.25	Service and filing
40.2	Repealed	Recycled paper
40.5	8.32	Notice of change of address or telephone number
41	8.54	Motions in the reviewing court
42	8.57	Motions before the record is filed
43	8.50	Applications in the reviewing court
44	8.40	Form, number, and cover of documents filed in the reviewing court of filed documents
44.5	8.29	Service on nonparty public officer or agency
45	8.60	Extending and shortening time
45.1	8.66	Appellate emergencies Extending time because of public emergency
45.5	8.63	Policies and factors governing extensions of time
46	8.18	Documents violating rules not to be filed
46.5	8.23	Sanctions to compel compliance
47	10.1008	Courts of Appeal with more than one division
47.1	10.1000	Transfer of causes
48	8.36	Substituting parties; substituting or withdrawing attorneys
49	8.112	Petition for writ of supersedeas

Rules of Court

Old Rule Number	New Rule Number	Rule Title
212	Repealed; divided into 3.720–3.730	~~Case management conference; meet and confer requirement; and case management order~~
213	3.734	Assignment to one judge for all or limited purposes
214	3.735	Management of short cause cases
222	3.1380	Mandatory settlement conferences
224	3.650	Duty to notify court and others of stay
225	3.1385	Duty to notify court and others of settlement of entire case
226	10.910	Assigned cases to be tried or dismissed—notification to presiding judge
227	2.30	Sanctions ~~in respect to rules~~ <u>for rules violations in civil cases</u>
227.1	10.950	Role of presiding judge, supervising judge, criminal division, and master calendar department in courts having more than three judges
227.2	10.951	Duties of supervising judge of the criminal division
227.8	10.952	Meeting ~~respecting~~ <u>concerning</u> the criminal court system
227.10	10.953	Procedures for disposition of cases before the preliminary hearing
228	3.1540	Examination of prospective jurors in civil cases
229	2.1055	Proposed jury instructions
230	3.1580	Request for special findings by jury
231	2.1030	Communications from or with jury
232	3.1590	Announcement of tentative decision, statement of decision, and judgment
232.5	3.1591	Statement of decision, judgment, and motion for new trial following bifurcated trial
233	Repealed	~~Family law rules~~
234	3.1806	Notation of written instrument of rendition of judgment
235	2.20	<u>Application for an</u> orders extending time
236	3.1602	Hearing of motion to vacate judgment
236.5	3.1600	Notice of intention to move for new trial—~~time for service and filing of memorandum~~
243	2.400	Court records
243.1	2.550	Sealed records
243.2	2.551	Procedures for filing records under seal
243.3	2.580	Request for delayed public disclosure
243.4	2.585	Confidential in-camera proceedings
243.5	2.570	Filing False Claims Act records under seal
243.6	2.571	Procedures for filing records <u>under seal</u> in a False Claims Act cases ~~under seal~~
243.7	2.572	~~Motion~~ <u>Ex parte application</u> for an extension of time
243.8	2.573	Unsealing of records and management of False Claims Act cases
243.9	2.1040	Electronic recordings offered in evidence—~~transcripts~~
243.10	Repealed	~~Definition of temporary judge~~
243.11	2.810	Temporary judges appointed by the trial courts
243.12	2.811	Court appointment of temporary judges
243.13	2.812	Requirements for court appointment of an attorney to serve as a temporary judge
243.14	2.813	Contents of training programs
243.15	2.814	Appointment of temporary judge
243.17	2.815	Continuing education
243.18 (1727)	2.816	Stipulation to court-appointed temporary judge
243.19	2.817	Disclosures to the parties
243.20	2.818	Disqualifications and limitations
243.21	2.819	Continuing duty to disclose and disqualify
243.30	2.830	Temporary judges requested by the parties
243.31 (244)	2.831	Temporary judge—stipulation, order, oath, assignment, disclosure, and disqualification
243.32	2.832	Compensation
243.33	2.833	Notices, use of court facilities, and order for hearing site
243.34	2.834	Motions or applications to be heard by the court
244.1	Repealed; divided into 3.900–3.910	~~Reference by agreement~~

Old Rule Number	New Rule Number	Rule Title
244.2	Repealed; divided into 3.920–3.927	Reference by order
245.5	Repealed	Superior court sessions held at municipal and justice court locations under Government Code section 69753
251	5.590	Notification of appeal rights in juvenile cases
270	3.1370	Emancipation of minors
298	3.670	Telephone appearance
299	10.505	Judicial robes
301	3.1100	Applicabilitytion
303	3.1103	Definitions and construction
307	Repealed	Assignment of matters
309	3.1109	Notice of determination of submitted matters
311	3.1110	General format
312	3.1112	Motions, demurrers, and other pleadings
313	3.1113	Memorandum of points and authorities
314	3.1114	Applications, motions, and petitions not requiring a supporting memorandum
315	3.1115	Miscellaneous papers Declarations
316	3.1116	Deposition testimony as an exhibit
317	3.1300	Time for filing and service of motion papers
319	3.1302	Place and manner of filing
321	3.1304	Time of hearing
323	3.1306	Evidence at hearing
324	3.1308	Tentative rulings
324.5	3.1310	Report of proceedings on motions
325	3.1320	Demurrers
326	3.1326	Motions for change of venue
327	3.1324	Amended pleadings and amendments to pleadings
329	3.1322	Motions to strike
330	3.1382	Good faith settlement and dismissal
331	3.1000	Format of supplemental and further discovery
333	3.1010	Oral depositions by telephone, videoconference, or other remote electronic means
335	3.1020	Format of discovery motions
337	3.1025	Service of motion papers on nonparty deponent
341	3.1030	Sanctions for failure to provide discovery
342	3.1350	Motion for summary judgment or summary adjudication
343	3.1352	Objections to evidence
345	3.1354	Form of Written objections to evidence
347	3.1140	Lodging of record in administrative mandate cases
354	Repealed	Receivership rules
355	3.1142	Stay of driving license suspension
359	3.1150	Preliminary injunctions and bonds
361	3.1151	Requirements for injunction in certain cases
363	3.1152	Civil harassment and workplace violence
364	3.1153	Minors may appear without counsel to seeking specified restraining orders
367	3.350	Consolidation of cases
369	3.1360	Motion to grant lien on cause of action
371	3.1330	Motion concerning arbitration
372	3.1340	Motion for discretionary dismissal after two years for delay in prosecution
373	3.1342	Motion to dismiss for delay in prosecution
375	3.1332	Motion or application for continuance of trial
375.1	3.1335	Motion or application to advance, specially set, or reset trial date
376	3.1362	Motion to be relieved as counsel
378	3.1384	Petition for approval of the compromise of a claim of a minor or incompetent person; order for deposit of funds; and petition for withdrawal
379	Repealed; divided into 3.1200–3.1207	Ex parte applications and orders
381	3.1130	Bonds and undertakings
383	3.1390	Service and filing of notice of entry of dismissal

Old Rule Number	New Rule Number	Rule Title
385	2.200	Service and filing of notice of change of address
388	3.1800	Default judgments
389	3.1804	Periodic payment of judgments against public entities
391	3.1312	Preparation of order
804	3.300	Notice of related case
805	10.821	Acceptance of checks and other negotiable paper
810	10.810	Court operations
813	10.630	~~Reciprocal agreement and exchange assignment defined~~ Reporting of reciprocal assignment orders
820	Repealed	~~Motion to dismiss~~
825	2.900	Submission of a cause in a trial court
826	2.1100	Notice when statute or regulation declared unconstitutional
828	4.210	Traffic court—trial by written declaration
830	Repealed	~~Trial settings~~
851	4.104	Procedures and eligibility criteria for attending traffic violator school
855	2.1050	Judicial Council jury instructions
858	2.1004	Scheduling accommodations for jurors
859	2.1006	Deferral of jury service
860	2.1008	~~Granting~~ Excuses from jury service
861	2.1002	Length of juror service
862	2.1010	Juror motion to set aside sanctions imposed by default
870	3.1700	Prejudgment costs
870.2	3.1702	Claiming attorney fees
870.4	3.2000	Unlawful detainer—supplemental costs
875	3.1802	Inclusion of interest in judgment
890	Repealed	~~Court reporting services in civil cases—municipal and justice courts~~
891	2.956	Court reporting services in civil cases~~—superior court departments generally~~
892	2.958	Assessing fee for official reporter
935	9.60	Review of determinations by the Commission on Judicial Performance
936	9.61	Proceedings involving public or private admonishment, censure, removal, or retirement of a judge of the Supreme Court
950	9.5	Definitions
950.5	9.6	Roll of attorneys ~~of persons~~ admitted to practice
951	9.10	Authority of the State Bar Court
951.5	9.12	Standard of review for State Bar Court Review Department
952	9.13	Review of State Bar Court decisions
952.5	9.14	Petitions for review by the Chief Trial Counsel
952.6	9.15	Petitions for review by the Committee of Bar Examiners; grounds for review; confidentiality
953	9.18	Effective date of disciplinary orders and decisions
953.5	9.17	Remand with instructions
954	9.16	Grounds for review of State Bar Court decisions in the Supreme Court
955	9.20	Duties of disbarred, resigned, or suspended attorneys
956	9.19	Conditions attached to reprovals
957	9.30	Law school study in schools other than those accredited by the examining committee
958	9.31	Minimum continuing legal education
960	9.21	Resignations of members of the State Bar with disciplinary charges pending
961	9.11	State Bar Court judges
962	9.22	Suspension of members of the State Bar for failure to comply with judgment or order for child or family support
963	Repealed	~~Interim Special Regulatory Fee for Attorney Discipline~~
964	9.45	Registered legal services attorneys
965	9.46	Registered in-house counsel
966	9.47	Attorneys practicing law temporarily in California as part of litigation
967	9.48	~~Non-litigating~~ Nonlitigating attorneys temporarily in California to provide legal services
970	10.501	Judicial education
976	8.1105	Publication of appellate opinions
976.1	8.1110	Partial publication

Old Rule Number	New Rule Number	Rule Title
977	8.1115	Citation of opinions
978	8.1120	Requesting publication of unpublished opinions
979	8.1125	Requesting depublication of published opinions
980	1.150	Photographing, recording, and broadcasting in court
980.4	2.950	Sequential list of reporters
980.5	2.952	Electronic recording as official record of proceedings
980.6	2.954	Specifications for electronic recording equipment
981	10.613	Local court rules—adopting, filing, distributing, and maintaining
981.1	3.20	Preemption of local rules
982.9	2.150	Authorization for computer-generated or typewritten forms for proof of service of summons and complaint
983	9.40	Counsel *pro hac vice*
983.1	9.41	Appearances by military counsel
983.2	9.42	Certified law students
983.4	9.43	Out-of-state attorney arbitration counsel
983.5	9.35	California Rules of Court [Certifying Certified legal specialists]
984	2.891	Periodic review of court interpreter skills and professional conduct
984.1	2.892	Guidelines for approval of certification programs for interpreters for deaf and hard-of-hearing persons
984.2	2.893	Appointment of noncertified interpreters in criminal cases and juvenile delinquency proceedings
984.3	2.894	Reports on appointments of certified and registered interpreters and noncertified and nonregistered interpreters in courts
984.4	2.890	Professional conduct for interpreters
985	Repealed; divided into 3.50–3.63	Permission to proceed without paying court fees and costs (in forma pauperis)
986	3.1900	Notice of renewal of judgment
987	1.11	Holiday falling on a Saturday or Sunday
988	9.44	Registered foreign legal consultant
989	2.1058	Use of gender-neutral language in jury instructions
989.1	10.503	Use of recycled paper by all courts
989.2	10.611	Nondiscrimination in court appointments
989.3	1.100	Requests for accommodations by persons with disabilities
989.5	10.504	Smoking policy for trial and appellate courts prohibited in all courts
991	Repealed	Trial court coordination implementation
996	10.400	Judicial Branch Statistical Information System (JBSIS)
999.1	10.870	Trial court automation standards
4.100	4.100	Arraignments
4.101	4.101	Bail in criminal cases
4.102	4.102	Uniform bail and penalty schedules—traffic, boating, fish and game, forestry, public utilities, parks and recreation, business licensing
4.103	4.103	Notice to appear forms
4.110	4.110	Time limits for criminal proceedings on information or indictment
4.111	4.111	Pretrial motions in criminal cases
4.112	4.112	Readiness conference
4.113	4.113	Motions and grounds for continuance of criminal case set for trial
4.114	4.114	Certification pursuant to under Penal Code section 859a
4.115	4.115	Criminal case assignment
4.116	4.116	Certification to juvenile court
4.117	4.117	Qualifications for appointed trial counsel in capital cases
4.150	4.150	Change of venue; application and general provisions
4.151	4.151	Motion for change of venue
4.152	4.152	Selection of court and trial judge
4.153	4.153	Order on change of venue
4.154	4.154	Proceedings in the receiving court
4.155	4.155	Guidelines for reimbursement of costs in change of venue cases—criminal cases
4.200	4.200	Pre–voir dire conference in criminal cases
4.201	4.201	Voir dire in criminal cases
4.300	4.300	Commitments to nonpenal institutions

Rules of Court

Old Rule Number	New Rule Number	Rule Title
5.102	5.102	Parties to proceeding
5.104	5.104	Other causes of action
5.106	5.106	Injunctive relief and reservation of jurisdiction
5.108	5.108	Pleadings
5.110	5.110	Summons; restraining order
5.112	5.112	Continuing jurisdiction
5.114	5.114	Alternative relief
5.116	5.116	Stipulation for judgment
5.118	5.118	Application for court order
5.120	5.120	Appearance
5.121	5.121	Motion to quash proceeding or responsive relief
5.122	5.122	Default
5.124	5.124	Request for default
5.126	5.126	Alternate date of valuation
5.128	5.128	Financial declaration
5.130	5.130	Summary dissolution
5.134	5.134	Notice of entry of judgment
5.136	5.136	Completion of notice of entry of judgment
5.140	5.140	Implied procedures
5.150	5.150	Joinder of persons claiming interest
5.152	5.152	"Claimant" defined
5.154	5.154	Persons who may seek joinder
5.156	5.156	Form of joinder application
5.158	5.158	Determination on joinder
5.160	5.160	Pleading rules applicable
5.162	5.162	Joinder of employee pension benefit plan
5.175	5.175	Bifurcation of issues
5.180	5.180	Interlocutory appeals
5.210	5.210	Court-connected child custody mediation
5.215	5.215	Domestic violence protocol for Family Court Services
5.220	5.220	Court-ordered child custody evaluations
5.225	5.225	Education, training, and experience standards for court-appointed child custody investigators and evaluators
5.230	5.230	Domestic violence training standards for court-appointed child custody investigators and evaluators
5.235	5.235	Ex parte communication in child custody proceedings
5.275	5.275	Standards for computer software to assist in determining support
5.300	5.300	Purpose, authority, and definitions
5.305	5.305	Hearing of matters by a judge under Family Code sections 4251(a) and 4252(b)(7)
5.310	5.310	Use of existing family law forms
5.311	5.311	Implementation of new and revised governmental forms by local child support agencies
5.315	5.315	Memorandum of points and authorities
5.320	5.320	Attorney of record in support actions under title IV-D of the Social Security Act
5.324	5.324	Telephone appearance in title IV-D hearings and conferences
5.325	5.325	Procedures for clerk's handling of combined summons and complaint
5.330	5.330	Procedures for child support case registry form
5.335	5.335	Procedures for hearings on interstate income withholding orders
5.340	5.340	Judicial education for child support commissioners
5.350	5.350	Procedures for hearings to set aside voluntary declarations of paternity when no previous action has been filed
5.355	5.355	Minimum standards of training for court clerk staff whose assignment includes title IV-D child support cases
5.360	5.360	Appearance by local child support agency
5.365	5.365	Procedure for consolidation of child support orders
5.370	5.370	Party designation in interstate and intrastate orders
5.375	5.375	Procedure for a support obligor to file a motion regarding mistaken identity
5.400	5.400	Contact after adoption agreement

Rules of Court

Old Rule Number	New Rule Number	Rule Title
1446	5.678	Findings in support of detention; factors to consider; reasonable efforts; detention alternatives
1447	5.680	Detention rehearings; prima facie hearings
1448	5.662	Child Abuse Prevention and Treatment Act (CAPTA) guardian ad litem for a child subject to a juvenile dependency petition
1449	5.682	Commencement of jurisdiction hearing— ~~advice~~ advisement of trial rights; admission; no contest; submission
1450	5.684	Contested hearing on petition
1451	5.686	Continuance pending disposition hearing
1452	5.688	Failure to cooperate with services (§ 360(b))
1455	5.690	General conduct of disposition hearing
1456	5.695	Orders of the court
1457	5.700	Order determining custody (§§ 304, 361.2, 362.4)
1459	5.705	Setting a hearing under section 366.26
1460	5.710	Six-month review hearing
1461	5.715	Twelve-month review hearing
1462	5.720	Eighteen-month review hearing
1463	5.725	Selection of permanent plan (§ 366.26)
1463.1	5.726	Prospective adoptive parent designation (§ 366.26(n))
1463.3	5.727	Proposed removal (§ 366.26(n))
1463.5	5.728	Emergency removal (§ 366.26(n))
1464	5.730	Adoption
1465	5.735	Legal guardianship
1466	5.740	Hearings subsequent to a permanent plan (§§ 366.26, 366.3, 391)
1471	5.752	Initial hearing; detention hearings; time limit on custody; setting jurisdiction hearing
1472	5.754	Commencement of initial hearing—explanation, ~~advice~~ advisement, admission
1473	5.756	Conduct of detention hearing
1474	5.758	Requirements for detention; prima facie case
1475	5.760	Detention hearing; report; grounds; determinations; findings; orders; factors to consider for detention; restraining orders
1476	5.762	Detention rehearings~~; prima facie hearings~~
1479	5.663	Responsibilities of children's counsel in delinquency proceedings (~~Welf. & Inst. Code,~~ §§ 202, 265, 633, 634, 634.6, 679, 700)
1480	5.766	General provisions
1481	5.768	Report of probation officer
1482	5.770	Conduct of fitness hearing under section 707(a)(1)
1483	5.772	Conduct of fitness hearing under sections 707(a)(2) and 707(c)
1485	5.774	Setting petition for hearing—detained and nondetained cases; waiver of hearing
1486	5.776	Grounds for continuance of jurisdiction hearing
1487	5.778	Commencement of hearing on section 601 or section 602 petition; right to counsel; ~~advice~~ advisement of trial rights; admission, no contest
1488	5.780	Contested hearing on section 601 or section 602 petition
1489	5.782	Continuance pending disposition hearing
1492	5.785	General conduct of hearing
1493	5.790	Orders of the court
1494	5.795	Required determinations
1494.5	5.805	California Department of Corrections and Rehabilitation, Division of Juvenile Justice, commitments
1495	5.800	Deferred entry of judgment
1496	5.810	Reviews, hearings, and permanency planning ~~hearings~~
1496.2	5.815	Appointment of legal guardians for wards of the juvenile court; modification or termination of guardianship
1496.3	5.820	Termination of parental rights for child in foster care for 15 of the last 22 months
1496.5	5.825	Freeing wards for adoption
1497	5.830	Sealing records
1498	5.645	Mental health or condition of child; court procedures
1499	5.650	Appointment of responsible adult as educational representative
1499.5	5.652	Access to pupil records for truancy purposes

Rules of Court

Old Rule Number	New Rule Number	Rule Title
1620.2	3.852	Definitions
1620.3	3.853	Voluntary participation and self-determination
1620.4	3.854	Confidentiality
1620.5	3.855	Impartiality, conflicts of interest, disclosure, and withdrawal
1620.6	3.856	Competence
1620.7	3.857	Quality of mediation process
1620.8	3.858	Marketing
1620.9	3.859	Compensation and gifts
1621	3.860	Attendance sheet and agreement to disclose
1622	3.865	Complaint procedure required
1622.1	3.866	Designation of person to receive inquiries and complaints
1622.2	3.867	Confidentiality of complaint procedures, information, and records
1622.3	3.868	Disqualification from subsequently serving as an adjudicator
1630	3.870	Applicabilitytion
1631	3.871	Actions subject to mediation
1632	3.872	Panels of mediators
1633	3.873	Selection of mediators
1634	3.874	Appearance at mediation sessions
1635	3.875	Filing of statement by mediator
1636	Repealed	Return of unresolved case to active status
1637	3.876	Coordination with Trial Court Delay Reduction Act
1638	3.877	Statistical information
1639	3.878	Educational material
1701	3.2100	Compliance with fictitious business name laws
1702	3.2102	Substituted service
1703	3.2104	Defendant's claim
1704	3.2106	Venue challenge
1705	3.2108	Form of judgment
1706	3.2110	Role of clerk in assisting small claims litigants
1725	3.2120	Advisor assistance
1726	Repealed	Temporary judges in small claims cases
1800	3.400	Definition
1810	3.401	Complex case designation
1811	3.402	Complex case counterdesignations
1812	3.403	Action by court
1830	3.751	Electronic service
1850	3.760	Applicabilitytion
1851	3.761	Form of complaint
1852	3.762	Case conference
1853	3.763	Conference order
1854	3.764	Motion to certify or decertify a class or amend or modify an order certifying a class
1855	3.765	Class action order
1856	3.766	Notice to class members
1857	3.767	Orders in the conduct of class actions
1858	3.768	Discovery from unnamed class members
1859	3.769	Settlement of class actions
1860	3.770	Dismissal of class actions
1861	3.771	Judgment
1900	3.1175	Ex parte application for appointment of receiver
1901	3.1176	Confirmation of ex parte appointment of receiver
1902	3.1177	Nomination of receivers
1902.5	3.1178	Amount of undertakings
1903	3.1179	The receiver
1904	3.1180	Employment of attorney
1905	3.1181	Receiver's inventory
1906	3.1182	Monthly reports
1907	3.1183	Interim fees and objections
1908	3.1184	Receiver's final account and report
2001	Repealed	Authority

Rules of Court

Old Rule Number	New Rule Number	Rule Title
2002	2.300	Applicabilitytion
2003	2.301	Definitions
2004	2.302	Compliance with the rules 201 and 501 on the form and format of papers
2005	2.303	Filing through fax filing agency
2006	2.304	Direct filing
2007	2.305	Requirements for signatures on documents
2008	2.306	Service of papers by facsimile fax transmission
2009	Repealed	Facsimile Transmission Cover Sheet
2050	2.250	Definitions
2051	Repealed	Authority and purpose
2052	2.252	Documents that may be filed electronically
2053	2.253	Court order requiring electronic filing and service
2054	2.254	Responsibilities of court
2055	2.255	Contracts with electronic filing service providers
2056	2.256	Responsibilities of electronic filer
2057	2.257	Requirements for signatures on documents
2058	2.258	Payment of filing fees
2059	2.259	Actions by court on receipt of electronic filing
2060	2.260	Electronic service
2061	2.261	Authorization for courts to continue modifying forms for the purpose of electronic filing and forms generation
2070	2.500	Statement of purpose
2071	2.501	Authority and applicability Application and scope
2072	2.502	Definitions
2073	2.503	Public access
2074	2.504	Limitations and conditions
2075	2.505	Contracts with vendors
2076	2.506	Fees for electronic access
2077	2.507	Electronic access to court calendars, indexes, and registers of actions
2201	10.651	Purpose
2202	10.652	Definitions
2203	10.653	Right and obligation to meet and confer
2204	10.654	Scope of representation
2205	10.655	Governing court employee labor relations
2206	10.656	Transition provisions
2207	10.657	Construction
2208	10.658	Interpretation
2209	10.659	Other provisions
2210	Repealed	Effective date
2211	10.660	Enforcement of agreements—petitions (Gov. Code, §§ 71639.5 and 71825.2)
6.1	10.1	Authority, duties, and goals of the Judicial Council
6.2	10.2	Judicial Council membership and terms
6.3	10.3	Nonvoting members
6.4	10.4	Nominations and appointments to the Judicial Council
6.5	10.5	Notice and agenda of council meetings
6.6	10.6	Judicial Council meetings
6.10	10.10	Judicial Council internal committees
6.11	10.11	Executive and Planning Committee
6.12	10.12	Policy Coordination and Liaison Committee
6.13	10.13	Rules and Projects Committee
6.14	10.14	Litigation Management Committee
6.15	10.15	Interim Court Facilities Panel
6.20	10.20	Proposals for new or amended rules, standards, or forms; rule-making process in general
6.21	10.21	Proposals from members of the public for changes to rules, standards, or forms
6.22	10.22	Rule-making procedures
6.30	10.30	Judicial Council advisory committees
6.31	10.31	Advisory committee membership and terms
6.32	10.32	Nominations and appointments to advisory committees
6.33	10.33	Advisory committee meetings

Old Rule Number	New Rule Number	Rule Title
6.34	10.34	Duties and responsibilities of advisory committees
6.40	10.40	Appellate Advisory Committee
6.41	10.41	Civil and Small Claims Advisory Committee
6.42	10.42	Criminal Law Advisory Committee
6.43	10.43	Family and Juvenile Law Advisory Committee
6.44	10.44	Probate and Mental Health Advisory Committee
6.45	10.45	Trial Court Budget Working Group
6.46	10.46	Trial Court Presiding Judges Advisory Committee
6.48	10.48	Court Executives Advisory Committee
6.49	10.49	Conference of Court Executives
6.50	10.50	Governing Committee of the Center for Judicial Education and Research
6.51	10.51	Court Interpreters Advisory Panel
6.52	10.52	Administrative Presiding Justices Advisory Committee
6.53	10.53	Court Technology Advisory Committee
6.54	10.54	Traffic Advisory Committee
6.55	10.55	Access and Fairness Advisory Committee
6.56	10.56	Collaborative Justice Courts Advisory Committee
6.57	10.57	Judicial Service Advisory Committee
6.58	10.58	Advisory Committee on Civil Jury Instructions
6.59	10.59	Advisory Committee on Criminal Jury Instructions
6.60	10.71	Court Facilities Transitional Task Force
6.70	10.70	Task forces
6.80	10.80	Administrative Director of the Courts
6.81	10.81	Administrative Office of the Courts
6.101	10.101	Role of the Judicial Council and Administrative Office of the Courts
6.102	10.102	Acceptance of gifts
6.103	10.103	Limitation on intrabranch contracting
6.104	10.104	Limitation on contracting with former employees
6.105	10.105	Allocation of new fee, fine, and forfeiture revenue
6.150	10.180	Court facilities standards
6.151	10.502	Judicial sabbatical pilot program
6.170	10.170	Working Group on Court Security
6.171	10.171	Working Group on Court Security Fiscal Guidelines
6.180	10.181	Court facilities policies, procedures, and standards
6.181	10.182	Operation and maintenance of court facilities
6.182	10.183	Decision making on transfer of responsibility for trial court facilities
6.183	10.184	Acquisition, space programming, construction, and design of court facilities
6.201	10.201	Claim and litigation procedure
6.202	10.202	Claims and litigation management
6.203	10.203	Contractual indemnification
6.301	10.301	Ethics training for Judicial Council members and judicial branch employees
6.302	10.350	Workers' compensation program
6.601	10.601	Superior court management
6.602	10.602	Selection and term of presiding judge
6.603	10.603	Authority and duties of presiding judge
6.605	10.605	Executive committee
6.608	10.608	Duties of all judges
6.609	10.700	Role of subordinate judicial officers
6.610	10.610	Duties of court executive officer
6.620	10.620	Public access to administrative decisions of trial courts
6.650	10.670	Trial court personnel plans
6.655	10.703	Complaints against subordinate judicial officers
6.660	10.701	Qualifications and education of subordinate judicial officers
6.661	10.761	Regional Court Interpreter Employment Relations Committees
6.662	10.762	Cross-assignments for court interpreter employees
6.665	10.702	Subordinate judicial officers: practice of law
6.700	10.800	Superior court budgeting
6.701	10.801	Superior court budget procedures
6.702	10.802	Maintenance of and public access to budget and management information
6.703	10.820	Acceptance of credit cards by ~~trial~~ the superior courts

California Standards of Judicial Administration

Former Section	New Standard	Title
4.6	10.31	~~Accuracy of~~ Master jury list
6	8.1	Memorandum opinions
7	10.40	Court security
7.5	10.41	Court sessions at or near state penal institutions
8	3.25	Examination of prospective jurors in civil cases
8.5	4.30	Examination of prospective jurors in criminal cases
8.6	2.25	Uninterrupted jury selection
8.9	2.20	Trial management standards
10.5	4.40	~~Municipal and justice court~~ Traffic infraction procedures
10.6	4.41	Courtesy notice—traffic procedures
10.7	4.42	Traffic infraction trial scheduling ~~—round-table discussions~~
11	Repealed	~~Calendar management review~~
11.5	Repealed	~~Date certain for trial~~
14	2.30	Judicial comment on verdict or mistrial
16.5	Repealed	~~Temporary judges hearing small claims cases~~
17	10.50	Selection of regular grand jury
17.5	10.55	Local ~~policies~~ program on waste reduction and recycling
18	2.10	Procedures for determining the need for an interpreter and a preappearance interview
18.1	2.11	Interpreted proceedings—instructing participants on procedure
19	3.10	Complex civil litigation
20.5	5.11	Guidelines for appointment of counsel for minors when time with or responsibility for the minor is disputed
20.6	5.10	Guidelines for determining payment for costs of appointed counsel for children in family court
21	3.1	Appearance by telephone
22	Repealed	~~Tentative rulings in law and motion matters~~
24	5.40	Juvenile court matters
24.5	5.45	Resource guidelines for child abuse and neglect cases
25	10.10	Judicial branch education
25.1	10.11	General judicial education standards
25.2	10.12	Judicial education for judicial officers in particular judicial assignments
25.3	10.13	Judicial education curricula provided in particular judicial assignments
25.4	10.14	Judicial education for judges hearing a capital cases
25.6	10.15	General court employee education standards
26.2	5.20	Uniform standards of practice for providers of supervised visitation
28	Repealed	~~Trial court coordination plan (Gov. Code, §68112)~~
29	Repealed	~~Methods of trial court coordination~~
30	10.17	Trial court performance standards
32	10.70	Implementation and coordination of mediation and other alternative dispute resolution (ADR) programs
32.1	10.71	Alternative dispute resolution (ADR) committees
33	10.70	Alternative dispute resolution (ADR) committees and criteria for referring cases to dispute resolution neutrals
34	10.80	Court records management standards
35	10.16	Model code of ethics for court employees
36	4.10	Guidelines for diversion drug court programs
39	10.5	The role of the judiciary in the community
40	7.10	Settlements or judgments in certain civil cases involving minors or persons with disabilities

California Rules of Court Reorganization
(Effective January 1, 2007)
(From new number to former number)

Title 1. Rules Applicable to All Courts

New Rule Number	Old Rule Number	Rule Title
Repealed		~~Introductory Statement~~ (came before title 1)
		Chapter 1. Preliminary Rules
1.1	New	The California Rules of Court
1.2	New	Title
1.3	New	Authority
1.4	New	Contents of the rules
1.5	New; (a) based on 53(b)	Construction of rules and standards
1.6	200.1	Definitions and use of terms
		Chapter 2. Timing and Holidays
1.10	200.3	Time for actions
1.11	987	Holiday falling on a Saturday or Sunday
		Chapter 3. Service and Filing
1.20	New	Filing
1.21	New	Service
1.22	New	Recycled paper
		Chapter 4. Judicial Council Forms
1.30	201.1	Judicial Council forms
1.31	New; based on 201.1(b)	Mandatory forms
1.35	New; based on 201.1(c)	Optional forms
1.40	New; based on 201.1(d)	Statutory references on forms
1.41	New; based on 201.1(e)	Proofs of service on forms
1.42	New; based on 201.1(f)	Forms not to be rejected
1.43	New; based on 201.1(h)	Legibility
1.44	New; based on 201.1(i)	Electronically produced forms
1.45	201.2	Judicial Council pleading forms
		Chapter 5. Accommodations
1.100	989.3	Requests for accommodations by persons with disabilities
		Chapter 6. Public Access to Court Proceedings
1.150	980	Photographing, recording, and broadcasting in court

Title 2. Trial Court Rules

New Rule Number	Old Rule Number	Rule Title
		Division 1. General Provisions
		Chapter 1. Title and Application
2.1	New	Title
2.2	200	Application
		Chapter 2. Definitions and Scope of Rules
2.3	New	Definitions
Repealed	200.2	~~Construction of terms~~
2.10	New	Scope of rules [Reserved]
Repealed	233	~~Family law rules~~

Rules of Court

New Rule Number	Old Rule Number	Rule Title
4.408	4.408	Criteria not exclusive; sequence not significant
4.409	4.409	Consideration of criteria
4.410	4.410	General objectives in sentencing
4.411	4.411	Presentence investigations and reports
4.411.5	4.411.5	Probation officer's presentence investigation report
4.412	4.412	Reasons:—agreement to punishment as an adequate reason and as abandonment of certain claims
4.413	4.413	Probation eligibility when probation is limited
4.414	4.414	Criteria affecting probation
4.420	4.420	Selection of base term of imprisonment
4.421	4.421	Circumstances in aggravation
4.423	4.423	Circumstances in mitigation
4.424	4.424	Consideration of applicability of section 654
4.425	4.425	Criteria affecting concurrent or consecutive sentences
4.426	4.426	Violent sex crimes
4.428	4.428	Criteria affecting imposition of enhancements
4.431	4.431	Proceedings at sentencing to be reported
4.433	4.433	Matters to be considered at time set for sentencing
4.435	4.435	Sentencing upon revocation of probation
4.437	4.437	Statements in aggravation and mitigation
4.447	4.447	Limitations on enhancements
4.451	4.451	Sentence consecutive to indeterminate term or to term in other jurisdiction
4.452	4.452	Determinate sentence consecutive to prior determinate sentence
4.453	4.453	Commitments to nonpenal institutions
4.470	4.470	Notification of appeal rights in felony cases
4.472	4.472	Determination of presentence custody time credit
4.480	4.480	Judge's statement under section 1203.01
		Division 6. Postconviction and Writs
		Chapter 1. Postconviction
4.510	4.510	Reverse remand
		Chapter 2. Habeas Corpus
4.550	4.550	Habeas corpus application and definitions
4.551	4.551	Habeas corpus proceedings
4.552	4.552	Habeas corpus jurisdiction
		Division 7. Miscellaneous
4.601	4.601	Judicial determination of factual innocence form

Title 5. Family and Juvenile Rules

New Rule Number	Old Rule Number	Rule Title
5.1	New	Title
		Division 1. Family Rules
		Chapter 1. General Provisions
5.5	New	Division title
5.10	5.10	Definitions and use of terms
Repealed	5.11	Construction of terms
5.15	5.15	Extensions of time
Repealed	5.16	Holidays
5.20	5.20	Applicability of rules
5.21	5.21	General law applicable
5.22	5.22	Other proceedings
5.25	5.25	Status of family law and domestic violence forms
5.26	5.26	Use of forms in nonfamily law proceedings
5.27	5.27	Use of interstate forms
5.28	5.28	Domestic partnerships
5.30	5.30	Judicial education for family court judicial officers
5.35	5.35	Minimum standards for the Office of the Family Law Facilitator
5.70	5.70	Nondisclosure of attorney assistance in preparation of court documents

Title 7. Probate Rules

Title 8. Appellate Rules

New Rule Number	Old Rule Number	Rule Title
8.787	186	Extensions of time and relief from default
8.788	187	Settlement of statement or transcript
8.789	187.5	Experimental rule on use of recordings to facilitate settlement of statements
8.790	188	Abandonment of appeal
8.791	189	Additions to record
8.792	190	Hearings and dismissals
8.793	191	Remittiturs
		Division 3. Trial of Small Claims Cases on Appeal
8.900	151	~~Scope~~ Application
8.902	156	Definitions
8.904	152	Filing ~~notice of~~ the appeal
8.907	153	Record on appeal
8.910	154	Continuances
8.913	155	Abandonment, dismissal, and judgment for failure to bring to trial
8.916	157	Examination of witnesses
		Division 4. Transfer of Appellate Division Cases to the Court of Appeal
8.1000	61	~~Scope of rules~~ Application
8.1002	62	Transfer authority
8.1005	63	Certification
8.1008	64	Transfer
8.1010	65	Record on transfer
8.1012	66	Briefs
8.1014	67	Proceedings in the appellate division after certification
8.1016	68	Disposition of transferred case
8.1018	69	Remittitur
		Division 5. Publication of Appellate Opinions
8.1100	New	Authority
8.1105	976	Publication of appellate opinions
8.1110	976.1	Partial publication
8.1115	977	Citation of opinions
8.1120	978	Requesting publication of unpublished opinions
8.1125	979	Requesting depublication of published opinions
Repealed	40.2	~~Recycled paper~~
Repealed	51	~~Substitute trial judge~~

Title 9. Rules on Law Practice, Attorneys, and Judges

New Rule Number	Old Rule Number	Rule Title
		Division 1. General Provisions
9.1	New	Title
9.2	New	Source
		Division 2. Attorney Admission and Disciplinary Proceedings and Review of State Bar Proceedings
		Chapter 1. General Provisions
9.5	950	Definitions
9.6	950.5	Roll of attorneys ~~of persons~~ admitted to practice
		Chapter 2. Attorney Disciplinary Proceedings
9.10	951	Authority of the State Bar Court
9.11	961	State Bar Court judges
9.12	951.5	Standard of review for State Bar Court Review Department
9.13	952	Review of State Bar Court decisions
9.14	952.5	Petitions for review by the Chief Trial Counsel
9.15	952.6	Petitions for review by the Committee of Bar Examiners; grounds for review; confidentiality
9.16	954	Grounds for review of State Bar Court decisions in the Supreme Court
9.17	953.5	Remand with instructions
9.18	953	Effective date of disciplinary orders and decisions
9.19	956	Conditions attached to reprovals
9.20	955	Duties of disbarred, resigned, or suspended attorneys

Title 10. Judicial Administration Rules

California Standards of Judicial Administration

Disposition Table
Appellate Rules 8.700–8.793
(Effective January 1, 2009)
Numerically by Old Rule Numbers

Current Rule	Revised Rule
8.700	8.802(d)
8.701(a)	10.1100(a)
8.701(b)	10.1100(b)
8.701(c)	10.1100(c)
8.701(d)	10.1100(d)
8.702	10.1108
8.703, paragraph 1	10.1104(b)
8.703, paragraph 2	10.1104(a)
8.704(a)	8.885(a) and 8.929(a)
8.704(b)	8.881, 8.885(b), 8.926, and 8.929(b)
8.705(a)	8.808(a)
8.705(b)	8.808(b)
8.706(a)	8.882(a)(1), (2), (3), and (5) and 8.927(a)(1), (2), (3), and (5)
8.706(b)	8.882(d)
8.706(c)	8.883(a) and (b) and 8.928(a) and (b)
8.706(d)	8.883(c) and 8.928(c)
8.706(e)	8.882(c)(1), (2) and (4) and 8.882(d) and 8.927(c)(1), (2) and (4) and 8.928(d)
8.706(f)	8.882(c)(3) and 8.927(c)(3)
8.706(g)	DELETED
8.706(h)	DELETED
8.707(a)	8.886(a)
8.707(b)	8.887(a)
8.707(c)	8.887(c)
8.708(a)(1)	8.888(a)(1)
8.708(a)(2)	DELETED
8.708(b)	8.888(b)
8.708(c)(1)	8.889(a)(1)
8.708(c)(2)	8.889(b)(1)
8.708(c)(3)	8.889(b)(1) and (2)
8.708(c)(4)	8.889(b)(1) and (3)
8.708(c)(5)	8.889(d)
8.708(d)	8.889(c)
8.709	8.888(c)
8.750(a)	8.821(a)(1) and (2)
8.750(b)	8.821(d)
8.750(c)	8.821(b)(1)
8.750(d)	8.821(b)(1)
8.750(e)	8.821(e)
8.751(a)	8.822(a)
8.751(b)	8.822(b)
8.751(c)	8.822(c)
8.752(a)	8.823(b) and (b)(1)
8.752(b)	8.823(c)
8.752(c)	8.823(f)
8.752(d)	DELETED
8.753(a)	8.831 and 8.834(a)(4), (b)(1), and (c)(2)
8.753(b)	8.834(a)(2) and (3) and (c)(3)
8.753(c)	8.834(b)(2)
8.753(d)	8.834(c)(1) and (4) and (d)(1) and (2)
8.753(e)	8.834(e)
8.754(a)	8.831

Current Rule	Revised Rule
8.754(b)	8.832(b)(1)
8.754(c)	8.832(c)(3)
8.754(d)	8.832(d)(1)
8.754(e)	DELETED
8.754(f)	DELETED
8.755(a)	8.836(b)
8.755(b)	8.831 and 8.836(c)
8.756(a)	8.831 and 8.837(b)(1) and (c)
8.756(b)	DELETED
8.756(c)	8.837(d)(1) and (3), (e), and (f)
8.757	DELETED
8.758(a)	8.838(a)
8.758(b)	8.838(b)
8.758(c)	8.838(c)
8.759	8.840
8.760	8.839
8.761(a)	8.841(a)
8.761(b)	8.841(b)
8.761(c)	8.841(b)
8.762(a)	8.825(b)(1), (2), (4), and (5) and (d)(2) and (3)
8.762(b)	8.825(b)(1) and (2)
8.762(c)	8.842(b)(1)
8.762(d)	8.825(b)(3)
8.762(e)	8.825(c)
8.763	DELETED
8.764(a)	8.891(a)
8.764(b)	8.891(b)
8.764(c)	8.891(d)
8.764(d)	8.891(c)
8.764(e)	8.891(e)
8.765(1)	8.802(c)(1), (2), and (3)
8.765(2)	8.804(21) and (22)
8.765(3)	8.804(11) and (12)
8.765(4)	8.802(b)(1) and (2)
8.765(5)	8.804(13)
8.765(6)	8.804(18)
8.765(7)	8.804(23)
8.765(8)	DELETED
8.765(9)	8.804(8)
8.765(10)	DELETED
8.765(11)	DELETED
8.765(12)	8.802(c)(4)
8.766	8.806
8.767(a)	8.810(a)
8.767(b)	8.810(b)
8.767(c)	8.810(c)
8.767(d)	8.813
8.768(a)	8.814(a)
8.768(b)	8.814(b) and (c)
8.769, paragraph 1	8.824(a), (c), and (d)(1)
8.769, paragraph 2	8.824(d)(2)
8.770	DELETED
8.771	8.830(b)
8.772(a)	8.800, 8.802(a), and 8.820
8.772(b)	8.812
8.773(a)	8.890(b)(1)
8.773(b)	8.890(c)(1)
8.773(c)	8.890(c)(3)
8.773(d)	8.890(c)(2)
8.780(a)	DELETED
8.780(b)	8.800, 8.850, and 8.900

Current Rule	Revised Rule
8.781	DELETED, see 8.804
8.782(a), paragraph 1	8.852(a) and 8.901(a)
8.782(a), paragraph 2	8.853(a) and 8.902(a)
8.782(a), paragraph 3	8.853(d) and 8.902(d)
8.782(a), paragraph 4	8.853(c) and 8.902(c)
8.782(b)	8.852(b)(1), (2), and (6) and 8.901(b)(1), (2) and (6)
8.783	8.860(a) and 8.910(a)
8.783(a)(1)	8.861(1) and 8.912(1)
8.783(a)(2)	8.861(2) and 8.912(2)
8.783(a)(3)	8.861(4)
8.783(a)(4)	8.912(4) and 8.861(6) and (7)
8.783(a)(5)	8.912(6) and 8.861(9)
8.783(a)(6)	8.861(2) and 8.912(2)
8.783(a)(7)	8.861(3) and 8.912(3)
8.783(a)(8)	8.861(8) and 8.912(5)
8.783(a)(9)	8.912(8) and 8.861(11)
8.783(a)(10)	DELETED, see 8.860(a)(2) and 8.910(a)(2)
8.783(a)(11)	DELETED, see 8.870 and 8.921
8.783(a)(12)	8.867 and 8.920
8.783(b)	8.913(b) and (d) and 8.862(b) and (d)
8.784(a)	8.837(c)(2)(B), 8.860(a)(2), 8.869(c)(2)(B), 8.910(a)(2), and 8.916(c)(2)(B)
8.784(b)	8.837(c)(2), 8.837(c)(2)(A) and (C), 8.869(c), 8.869(c)(2)(A) and (C), 8.916(c) and 8.916(c)(2)(A) and (C)
8.784(c)	8.837(c)(2)(D) and 8.869(c)(2)(D)
8.784(d)	8.869(b)(1) and 8.916(b)(1)
8.785	8.869(d)(1) and 8.916(d)(1)
8.786(a)	8.851(a)
8.786(b)	8.851(b)
8.786(c)	8.851(c)
8.787(a)	8.810(b) and (c), 8.869(g), and 8.916(g)
8.787(b)	8.812
8.788, paragraph 1	8.869(d)(3) and 8.916(d)(3)
8.788, paragraph 2	8.869(d)(4) and (5) and (f) and 8.916(d)(4) and (5) and (f)
8.788, paragraph 3	DELETED, see 8.872 and 8.922
8.789(a)	DELETED
8.789(b)	DELETED
8.789(c)	DELETED
8.789(d)	8.869(b)(1) and 8.916(b)(1)
8.789(e)	DELETED
8.789(f), paragraph 1	8.869(d)(1) and 8.916(d)(1)
8.789(f), paragraph 2	DELETED
8.789(g), paragraph 1	DELETED
8.789(g), paragraph 2	8.869(d)(2) and (4) and 8.916(d)(2) and (4)
8.789(g), paragraph 3	8.869(d)(4) and 8.916(d)(4)
8.789(h)	8.869(f) and 8.916(f)
8.789(i)	DELETED
8.789(j)	8.863 and 8.914
8.789(k)	8.873(c)
8.789(*l*)	DELETED
8.789(m)	DELETED
8.790	8.855(a) and (b)
8.791	8.873(c) and 8.923(c)
8.792	8.880 and 8.881
8.793(a)	8.880 and 8.890(b)(1)
8.793(b)	8.890(c)(1)
8.793(c)	8.890(c)(3)
8.793(d)	8.890(c)(2)

Disposition Table
Appellate Rules 8.800–8.936 and 10.1100–10.1108
(Effective January 1, 2009)
Numerically by Revised Rule Number

Revised Rule	Current Rule
8.823(g)	NEW
8.824(a)	8.769, paragraph 1
8.824(b)	NEW
8.824(c)	8.769, paragraph 1
8.824(d)(1)	8.769, paragraph 1
8.824(d)(2)	8.769, paragraph 2
8.825(a)	NEW
8.825(b)(1) and (2)	8.762(a) and (b)
8.825(b)(3)	8.762(d)
8.825(b)(4) and (5)	8.762(a)
8.825(c)	8.762(e)
8.830(a)	NEW
8.830(b)	8.771
8.831	8.753(a), 8.754(a), 8.755(b), and 8.756(a)
8.832(a)	8.754(d)
8.832(b)(1)	8.754(b)
8.832(b)(2)	NEW
8.832(b)(3)	NEW
8.832(c)(1) and (2)	NEW
8.832(c)(3)	8.754(c)
8.832(d)(1)	8.754(d)
8.832(d)(2)	8.762(a)
8.833	NEW
8.834(a)(1)	NEW
8.834(a)(2)	8.753(b)
8.834(a)(3)	8.753(b)
8.834(a)(4)	8.753(a)
8.834(b)(1)	8.753(a)
8.834(b)(2)	8.753(c)
8.834(c)(1)	8.753(d)
8.834(c)(2)	8.753(a)
8.834(c)(3)	8.753(b)
8.834(c)(4)	8.753(d)
8.834(d)(1)	8.753(d)
8.834(d)(2)	8.753(d)
8.834(d)(3)	8.762(a)
8.834(e)	8.753(e)
8.835	NEW
8.836(a)	NEW
8.836(b)	8.755(a)
8.836(c)	8.755(b)
8.837(a)	NEW
8.837(b)(1)	8.756(a)
8.837(b)(2)	NEW
8.837(c)(1)	8.756(a)
8.837(c)(2)	8.756(a) and 8.784(b)
8.837(c)(2)(A)	8.784(b)
8.837(c)(2)(B)	8.784(a)
8.837(c)(2)(C)	8.784(b)
8.837(c)(2)(D)	8.784(c)
8.837(d)(1)	8.756(c)
8.837(d)(2)	NEW
8.837(d)(3)	8.756(c)
8.837(d)(4), (5), and (6)	NEW
8.837(e)	8.756(c)
8.837(f)	8.756(c)
8.838(a)	8.758(a)
8.838(b)	8.758(b)
8.838(c)	8.758(c)
8.839	8.760
8.840	8.759

Revised Rule	Current Rule
8.841(a)	8.761(a)
8.841(b)	8.761(b) and (c)
8.841(c)	NEW
8.841(d)	NEW
8.842(a)	NEW
8.842(b)(1)	8.762(c)
8.842(b)(2)	NEW
8.850	8.780(b)
8.851(a)	8.786(a)
8.851(b)	8.786(b)
8.851(c)	8.786(c)
8.852(a)	8.782(a), paragraph 1
8.852(b)(1) and (2)	8.782(b)
8.852(b)(3), (4), and (5)	NEW
8.852(b)(6)	8.782(b)
8.853(a)	8.782(a), paragraph 2
8.853(b)	NEW
8.853(c)	8.782(a), paragraph 4
8.853(d)	8.782(a), paragraph 3
8.853(e)	NEW
8.854	NEW
8.855(a)	8.790
8.855(b)	8.790
8.855(c)	NEW
8.860(a)	8.783
8.860(b)	NEW
8.861(1)	8.783(a)(1)
8.861(2)	8.783(a)(2) and (6)
8.861(3)	8.783(a)(7)
8.861(4)	8.783(a)(3)
8.861(5)	NEW
8.861(6)	8.783(a)(4)
8.861(7)	8.783(a)(4)
8.861(8)	8.783(a)(8)
8.861(9)	8.783(a)(5)
8.861(10)	NEW
8.861(11)	8.783(a)(9)
8.861(12)	NEW
8.862(a)	NEW
8.862(b)	8.783(b)
8.862(c)	NEW
8.862(d)	8.783(b)
8.863	8.789(j)
8.864	NEW
8.865	NEW
8.866	NEW
8.867	8.783(a)(12)
8.868	NEW
8.869(a)	NEW
8.869(b)(1)	8.784(d) and 8.789(d)
8.869(b)(2) and (3)	NEW
8.869(c)(1)	8.756(a)
8.869(c)(2)	8.756(a) and 8.784(b)
8.869(c)(2)(A)	8.784(b)
8.869(c)(2)(B)	8.784(a)
8.869(c)(2)(C)	8.784(b)
8.869(c)(2)(D)	8.784(c)
8.869(d)(1)	8.785 and 8.789(f), paragraph 1
8.869(d)(2)	8.789(g), paragraph 2
8.869(d)(3)	8.788, paragraph 1

Revised Rule	Current Rule
8.869(d)(4)	8.788, paragraph 2 and 8.789(g), paragraphs 2 and 3
8.869(d)(5)	8.788, paragraph 2
8.869(d)(6)	NEW
8.869(e)	NEW
8.869(f)	8.788, paragraph 2 and 8.789(h)
8.869(g)	8.787(a)
8.870	NEW
8.871	NEW
8.872	NEW
8.873(a)	NEW
8.873(b)	NEW
8.873(c)	8.789(k) and 8.791
8.880	8.792 and 8.793
8.881	8.704(b) and 8.792
8.882(a)(1), (2), and (3)	8.706(a)
8.882(a)(4)	NEW
8.882(a)(5)	8.706(a)
8.882(b)	NEW
8.882(c)	NEW
8.882(d)	8.706(b)
8.882(c)(1) and (2)	8.706(e)
8.882(c)(3)	8.706(f)
8.882(c)(4)	8.706(e)
8.883(a)	8.706(c)
8.883(b)	8.706(c)
8.883(c)	8.706(d)
8.883(d)	8.706(e)
8.884	NEW
8.885(a)	8.704(a)
8.885(b)	8.704(b)
8.885(c)	NEW
8.885(d)	NEW
8.886(a)	8.707(a)
8.886(b)	NEW
8.887(a)	8.707(b)
8.887(b)	NEW
8.887(c)	8.707(c)
8.888(a)(1)	8.708(a)(1)
8.888(a)(2) and (3)	NEW
8.888(b)	8.708(b)
8.888(c)	8.709
8.889(a)(1)	8.708(c)(1)
8.889(a)(2)	NEW
8.889(b)(1)	8.708(c)(2), (3), and (4)
8.889(b)(2)	8.708(c)(3)
8.889(b)(3)	8.708(c)(4)
8.889(b)(4)	NEW
8.889(c)	8.708(d)
8.889(d)	8.708(c)(5)
8.890(a)	NEW
8.890(b)(1)	8.773(a) and 8.793(a)
8.890(b)(2)	NEW
8.890(c)(1)	8.773(b) and 8.793(b)
8.890(c)(2)	8.773(d) and 8.793(d)
8.890(c)(3)	8.773(c) and 8.793(c)
8.8890(d)	NEW
8.891(a)	8.764(a)
8.891(b)	8.764(b)
8.891(c)	8.764(d)
8.891(d)	8.764(c)

Revised Rule	Current Rule
8.891(e)	8.764(e)
8.900	8.780(b)
8.901(a)	8.782(a), paragraph 1
8.901(b)(1) and (2)	8.782(b)
8.901(b)(3), (4), and (5)	NEW
8.901(b)(6)	8.782(b)
8.902(a)	8.782(a), paragraph 2
8.902(b)	NEW
8.902(c)	8.782(a), paragraph 4
8.902(d)	8.782(a), paragraph 3
8.902(e)	NEW
8.903	NEW
8.904(a)	8.790
8.904(b)	8.790
8.904(c)	NEW
8.910(a)	8.783
8.910(b)	NEW
8.911	NEW
8.912(1)	8.783(a)(1)
8.912(2)	8.783(a)(2) and (6)
8.912(3)	8.783(a)(7)
8.912(4)	8.783(a)(4)
8.912(5)	8.783(a)(8)
8.912(6)	8.783(a)(5)
8.912(7)	NEW
8.912(8)	8.783(a)(9)
8.912(9)	NEW
8.913(a)	NEW
8.913(b)	8.783(b)
8.913(c)	NEW
8.913(d)	8.783(b)
8.914	8.789(j)
8.915	NEW
8.916(a)	NEW
8.916(b)(1)	8.784(d) and 8.789(d)
8.916(b)(2) and (3)	NEW
8.916(c)(1)	8.756(a)
8.916(c)(2)	8.756(a) and 8.784(b)
8.916(c)(2)(A)	8.784(b)
8.916(c)(2)(B)	8.784(a)
8.916(c)(2)(C)	8.784(b)
8.916(d)(1)	8.785 and 8.789(f), paragraph 1
8.916(d)(2)	8.789(g), paragraph 2
8.916(d)(3)	8.788, paragraph 1
8.916(d)(4)	8.788, paragraph 2 and 8.789(g), paragraphs 2 and 3
8.916(d)(5)	8.788, paragraph 2
8.916(d)(6)	NEW
8.916(e)	NEW
8.916(f)	8.788, paragraph 2 and 8.789(h)
8.916(g)	8.787(a)
8.917	NEW
8.918	NEW
8.919	NEW
8.920	8.783(a)(12)
8.921	NEW
8.922	NEW
8.923(a)	NEW
8.923(b)	NEW
8.923(c)	8.789(k) and 8.791
8.925	NEW

Revised Rule	Current Rule
8.926	8.704(b)
8.927(a)(1), (2), and (3)	8.706(a)
8.927(a)(4)	NEW
8.927(a)(5)	8.706(a)
8.927(b)	NEW
8.927(c)(1) and (2)	8.706(e)
8.927(c)(3)	8.706(f)
8.927(c)(4)	8.706(e)
8.928(a)	8.706(c)
8.928(b)	8.706(c)
8.928(c)	8.706(d)
8.928(d)	8.706(e)
8.929(a)	8.704(a)
8.929(b)	8.704(b)
8.929(c)	NEW
8.929(d)	NEW
8.930	NEW
8.931	NEW
8.932	NEW
8.933	NEW
8.934	NEW
8.935	NEW
8.936	NEW
10.1100(a)	8.701(a)
10.1100(b)	8.701(b)
10.1100(c)	8.701(c)
10.1100(d)	8.701(d)
10.1104(a)	8.703, paragraph 2
10.1104(b)	8.703, paragraph 1
10.1108	8.702

CONTENTS

Rules

Rules

Rules of Court

Rules

**Ethics Standards for Neutral Arbitrators in Contractual
Arbitration**

Appendix A. Judicial Council Legal Forms List

**Appendix B. Liability Limits of a Parent or Guardian Having
Custody and Control of a Minor for the Torts of a Minor**

**Appendix C. Guidelines for the Operation of Family Law
Information Centers and Family Law Facilitator Offices**

Supplement to the California Rules of Court
 California Code of Judicial Ethics
 Internal Operating Practices and Procedures of the California
  Supreme Court
 Supreme Court Policies Regarding Cases Arising From

Rules

CALIFORNIA
RULES OF COURT

[Approved June 30, 2006. Effective January 1, 2007.]

[References are to *California Forms of Pleading and Practice* (Matthew Bender); *California Class Actions Practice and Procedure* (Matthew Bender); Matthew Bender® Practice Guide: California Debt Collection and Enforcement of Judgments; Matthew Bender® Practice Guide: California Pretrial Civil Procedure; Matthew Bender® Practice Guide: California Trial and Post-Trial Civil Procedure; Judicial Council of California Civil Jury Instructions (Matthew Bender, Official Publisher); Judicial Council of California Criminal Jury Instructions (Matthew Bender, Official Publisher); Witkin's *Summary of California Law*, 10th Ed.]

TITLE 1
Rules Applicable to All Courts

Chapter 1
Preliminary Rules

Rule 1.1.   The California Rules of Court

These rules are entitled the California Rules of Court.
Rule 1.1 adopted effective January 1, 2007.

Ref.: Cal. Fms Pl. & Pr., Ch. 425, "Pretrial Proceedings."

Rule 1.2.   Title

The rules in this title of the California Rules of Court may be referred to as the Rules Applicable to All Courts.
Rule 1.2 adopted effective January 1, 2007.

Rule 1.3.   Authority

The rules in the California Rules of Court are adopted by the Judicial Council of California under the authority of article VI, section 6, of the Constitution of the State of California, unless otherwise indicated. The rules in division 5 of title 8 and in title 9 were adopted by the Supreme Court.

Rule 1.3 amended effective January 1, 2008; adopted effective January 1, 2007.

Rule 1.4.   Contents of the rules

(a) The titles

The California Rules of Court includes the following titles:

(1) Title 1. Rules Applicable to All Courts;

(2) Title 2. Trial Court Rules;

(3) Title 3. Civil Rules;

(4) Title 4. Criminal Rules;

(5) Title 5. Family and Juvenile Rules;

(6) Title 6. [Reserved];

(7) Title 7. Probate Rules;

(8) Title 8. Appellate Rules;

(9) Title 9. Rules on Law Practice, Attorneys, and Judges; and

(10) Title 10. Judicial Administration Rules.

(Subd (a) adopted effective January 1, 2007.)

(b) Standards of Judicial Administration

The California Rules of Court includes the Standards of Judicial Administration adopted by the Judicial Council.

(Subd (b) adopted effective January 1, 2007.)

(c) Ethics Standards for Neutral Arbitrators in Contractual Arbitrations

The California Rules of Court includes Ethics Standards for Neutral Arbitrators in Contractual Arbitrations adopted by the Judicial Council under the authority of Code of Civil Procedure section 1281.85.

(Subd (c) repealed and relettered effective January 1, 2008; adopted as subd (d) effective January 1, 2007.)

(d) The appendixes

The California Rules of Court includes the following appendixes:

(1) Appendix A. Judicial Council Legal Forms List;

(2) Appendix B. Liability Limits of a Parent or Guard-

ian Having Custody and Control of a Minor for the Torts of a Minor; and

(3) Appendix C. Guidelines for the Operation of Family Law Information Centers and Family Law Facilitator Offices.

(Subd (d) relettered effective January 1, 2008; adopted as subd (e) effective January 1, 2007.)

Rule 1.4 amended effective January 1, 2008; adopted effective January 1, 2007.

Rule 1.5.   Construction of rules and standards

(a) Construction

The rules and standards of the California Rules of Court must be liberally construed to ensure the just and speedy determination of the proceedings that they govern.

(Subd (a) adopted effective January 1, 2007.)

(b) Terminology

As used in the rules and standards:

(1) "Must" is mandatory;

(2) "May" is permissive;

(3) "May not" means not permitted to;

(4) "Will" expresses a future contingency or predicts action by a court or person in the ordinary course of events, but does not signify a mandatory duty; and

(5) "Should" expresses a preference or a nonbinding recommendation.

(Subd (b) adopted effective January 1, 2007.)

(c) Standards

Standards are guidelines or goals recommended by the Judicial Council. The nonbinding nature of standards is indicated by the use of "should" in the standards instead of the mandatory "must" used in the rules.

(Subd (c) adopted effective January 1, 2007.)

(d) Construction of additional terms

In the rules:

(1) Each tense (past, present, or future) includes the others;

(2) Each gender (masculine, feminine, or neuter) includes the others; and

(3) Each number (singular or plural) includes the other.

(Subd (d) adopted effective January 1, 2007.)

Rule 1.5 adopted effective January 1, 2007.

Ref.: Cal. Fms Pl. & Pr., Ch. 3, "Abatement of Actions," Ch. 40, "Appeal: An Overview," Ch. 45, "Appeal: Motion Procedure," Ch. 206, "Demurrers and Motions for Judgment on the Pleadings," Ch. 372, "Motions and Orders"; MB Prac. Guide: Cal. Pretrial Proc., §§11.03, 11.17[2], 26.39.

Rule 1.6.   Definitions and use of terms

As used in the California Rules of Court, unless the context or subject matter otherwise requires:

(1) "Action" includes special proceeding.

(2) "Case" includes action or proceeding.

(3) "Civil case" means a case prosecuted by one party against another for the declaration, enforcement, or protection of a right or the redress or prevention of a wrong. Civil cases include all cases except criminal cases and petitions for habeas corpus.

(4) "General civil case" means all civil cases except probate, guardianship, conservatorship, juvenile, and family law proceedings (including proceedings under divi-

sions 6–9 of the Family Code, Uniform Parentage Act, Domestic Violence Prevention Act, and Uniform Interstate Family Support Act; freedom from parental custody and control proceedings; and adoption proceedings), small claims proceedings, unlawful detainer proceedings, and "other civil petitions" described in (5).

(5) "Civil petitions" that are not general civil cases include petitions to prevent civil harassment, elder abuse, and workplace violence; petitions for name change; election contest petitions; and petitions for relief from late claims.

(6) "Unlimited civil cases" and "limited civil cases" are defined in Code of Civil Procedure section 85 et seq.

(7) "Criminal case" means a proceeding by which a party charged with a public offense is accused and prosecuted for the offense.

(8) "Rule" means a rule of the California Rules of Court.

(9) "Local rule" means every rule, regulation, order, policy, form, or standard of general application adopted by a court to govern practice and procedure in that court or by a judge of the court to govern practice or procedure in that judge's courtroom.

(10) "Chief Justice" and "presiding justice" include the Acting Chief Justice and the acting presiding justice, respectively.

(11) "Presiding judge" includes the acting presiding judge or the judicial officer designated by the presiding judge.

(12) "Judge" includes, as applicable, a judge of the superior court, a commissioner, or a temporary judge.

(13) "Temporary judge" means an active or inactive member of the State Bar of California who, under article VI, section 21 of the California Constitution and these rules, serves or expects to serve as a judge once, sporadically, or regularly on a part-time basis under a separate court appointment for each period of service or each case heard.

(14) "Person" includes a corporation or other legal entity as well as a natural person.

(15) "Party" is a person appearing in an action. [1] **Parties include both self-represented persons and persons** represented by an attorney of record. "Party," "plaintiff," "People of the State of California," "applicant," "petitioner," "defendant," "respondent," "other parent," or any other designation of a party includes the party's attorney of record.

(16) "Attorney" means a member of the State Bar of California.

(17) "Counsel" means an attorney.

(18) "Sheriff" includes marshal.

(19) "Service" means service in the manner prescribed by a statute or rule.

(20) "Memorandum" means a written document containing: a statement of facts; a concise statement of the law, evidence, and arguments relied on; and a discussion of the statutes, cases, rules, and other legal sources relied on in support of the position advanced.

(21) "Declaration" includes "affidavit."

(22) "Recycled" as applied to paper means "recycled printing and writing paper" as defined by section 12209 of the Public Contract Code.

(23) "California Courts Web Site" means the Web site established by the Judicial Council that includes news and information, reference materials, rules and forms, and a self-help center. The address is: *www.courtinfo.ca.gov.*

Rule 1.6 amended effective July 1, 2008; adopted as rule 200.1 effective January 1, 2003; previously amended and renumbered effective January 1, 2007; previously amended effective July 1, 2007.

Rule 1.6. 2008 Deletes. [1] A party may be self-represented or

Ref.: Cal. Fms Pl. & Pr., Ch. 1, "New Developments," Ch. 26, "Answers," Ch. 123, "Complaints and Cross Complaints," Ch. 206, "Demurrers and Motions for Judgment on the Pleadings," Ch. 372, "Motions and Orders," Ch. 375, "Motions to Strike: Pleadings," Ch. 376, "Motions to Strike: Anti-SLAPP," Ch. 425, "Pretrial Proceedings"; MB Prac. Guide: Cal. Pretrial Proc., §§7.06[1], 7.32, 11.03, 23.04[1][a], [b], 26.18, 26.20, 26.39, 27.25, 27.27[1]; MB Prac. Guide: Cal. Trial & Post-Trial Civ. Proc., §4.10.

Chapter 2
Timing and Holidays

Rule 1.10. Time for actions
Rule 1.11. Holiday falling on a Saturday or Sunday

Rule 1.10. Time for actions

(a) Computation of time

The time in which any act provided by these rules is to be performed is computed by excluding the first day and including the last, unless the last day is a Saturday, Sunday, or other legal holiday, and then it is also excluded.

(Subd (a) amended effective January 1, 2007.)

(b) Holidays

Unless otherwise provided by law, if the last day for the performance of any act that is required by these rules to be performed within a specific period of time falls on a Saturday, Sunday, or other legal holiday, the period is extended to and includes the next day that is not a holiday.

(Subd (b) amended effective January 1, 2007.)

(c) Extending or shortening time

Unless otherwise provided by law, the court may extend or shorten the time within which a party must perform any act under the rules.

(Subd (c) amended effective January 1, 2007.)

Rule 1.10 amended and renumbered effective January 1, 2007; adopted as rule 200.3 effective January 1, 2003.

Ref.: Cal. Fms Pl. & Pr., Ch. 524, "Shortening and Extension of Time," Ch. 529, "Statement of Decision."

Rule 1.11. Holiday falling on a Saturday or Sunday

When a judicial holiday specified by Code of Civil Procedure section 135 falls on a Saturday, the courts must observe the holiday on the preceding Friday. When a judicial holiday specified by Code of Civil Procedure section 135 falls on a Sunday, the courts must observe the holiday on the following Monday.

Rule 1.11 amended and renumbered effective January 1, 2007; adopted as rule 987 effective January 1, 1986, operative January 1, 1989.

Chapter 3
Service and Filing

Rule 1.20. Filing
Rule 1.21. Service
Rule 1.22. Recycled paper

Rule 1.20. Filing

(a) Effective date of filing

Unless otherwise provided, a document is deemed filed on the date it is received by the court clerk.

(Subd (a) lettered effective January 1, 2008; adopted as unlettered subd effective January 1, 2007.)

(b) Protection of privacy

(1) Scope

The requirements of this subdivision that parties or their attorneys must not include, or must redact, certain identifiers from documents or records filed with the court do not apply to documents or records that by court order or operation of law are filed in their entirety either confidentially or under seal.

(2) Exclusion or redaction of identifiers

To protect personal privacy and other legitimate interests, parties and their attorneys must not include, or must redact where inclusion is necessary, the following identifiers from all pleadings and other papers filed in the court's public file, whether filed in paper or electronic form, unless otherwise provided by law or ordered by the court:

(A) Social security numbers. If an individual's social security number is required in a pleading or other paper filed in the public file, only the last four digits of that number may be used.

(B) Financial account numbers. If financial account numbers are required in a pleading or other paper filed in the public file, only the last four digits of these numbers may be used.

(3) Responsibility of the filer

The responsibility for excluding or redacting identifiers identified in (b)(2) from all documents filed with the court rests solely with the parties and their attorneys. The court clerk will not review each pleading or other paper for compliance with this provision.

(4) Confidential reference list

If the court orders on a showing of good cause, a party filing a document containing identifiers listed in (b)(2) may file, along with the redacted document that will be placed in the public file, a reference list. The reference list is confidential. A party filing a confidential reference list must use *Confidential Reference List of Identifiers* (form MC-120) for that purpose. The confidential list must identify each item of redacted information and specify an appropriate reference that uniquely corresponds to each item of redacted information listed. All references in the case to the redacted identifiers included in the confidential reference list will be understood to refer to the corresponding complete identifier. A party may amend its reference list as of right.

(Subd (b) adopted effective January 1, 2008.)

Rule 1.20 amended effective January 1, 2008; adopted effective January 1, 2007.

Ref.: Cal. Fms Pl. & Pr., Ch. 1, "New Developments," Ch. 26, "Answers," Ch. 95, "Banks, Deposits, and Checks," Ch. 123, "Complaints and Cross Complaints," Ch. 206, "Demurrers and Motions for Judgment on the Pleadings," Ch. 253, "Escrows," Ch. 316, "Joint Tenancy and Tenancy in Common," Ch. 385, "Negotiable Instruments," Ch. 417, "Points and Authorities," Ch. 515, "Securities and Franchise Regulation."

Rule 1.21.   Service

(a) Service on a party or attorney

Whenever a document is required to be served on a party, the service must be made on the party's attorney if the party is represented.

(Subd (a) amended effective January 1, 2007.)

(b) "Serve and file"

As used in these rules, unless a statute or rule provides for a different method for filing or service, a requirement to "serve and file" a document means that a copy of the document must be served on the attorney for each party separately represented, on each self-represented party, and on any other person or entity when required by statute, rule, or court order, and that the document and a proof of service of the document must be filed with the court.

(Subd (b) amended effective January 1, 2007.)

(c) "Proof of service"

As used in these rules, "proof of service" means a declaration stating that service has been made as provided in (a) and (b). If the proof of service names attorneys for separately represented parties, it must also state which party or parties each of the attorneys served is representing.

(Subd (c) adopted effective January 1, 2007.)

Rule 1.21 amended effective January 1, 2007; adopted effective January 1, 2007.

Ref.: Cal. Fms Pl. & Pr., Ch. 206, "Demurrers and Motions for Judgment on the Pleadings," Ch. 324, "Jurisdiction: Subject Matter Jurisdiction," Ch. 372, "Motions and Orders," Ch. 518, "Service of Summons and Papers"; MB Prac. Guide: Cal. Pretrial Proc., §§11.03, 11.16[4], 26.10[3], 26.39, 27.25, 27.27[1].

Rule 1.22.   Recycled paper

(a) Use of recycled paper required

Recycled paper, as defined in rule 1.6, must be used for all original papers filed with the trial and appellate courts and for all copies of papers, documents, and exhibits, whether filed with the courts or served on other parties.

(Subd (a) adopted effective January 1, 2007.)

(b) Certification

Whenever the use of recycled paper is required by these rules, the attorney, party, or other person filing or serving a document certifies, by the act of filing or service, that the document was produced on paper purchased as recycled.

(Subd (b) adopted effective January 1, 2007.)

Rule 1.22 adopted effective January 1, 2007.

Ref.: MB Prac. Guide: Cal. Pretrial Proc., §7.06[1].

Chapter 4
Judicial Council Forms

Rule 1.30. Judicial Council forms
Rule 1.31. Mandatory forms

Rule 1.35. Optional forms
Rule 1.37. Use of forms
Rule 1.40. Statutory references on forms
Rule 1.41. Proofs of service on forms
Rule 1.42. Forms not to be rejected
Rule 1.43. Legibility
Rule 1.44. Electronically produced forms
Rule 1.45. Judicial Council pleading forms

Rule 1.30.   Judicial Council forms

(a) Application

The rules in this chapter apply to Judicial Council forms.

(Subd (a) adopted effective January 1, 2007.)

(b) Mandatory or optional forms

Judicial Council forms are either mandatory or optional.

(Subd (b) relettered effective January 1, 2007; adopted as subd (a) effective January 1, 2003.)

Rule 1.30 amended and renumbered effective January 1, 2007; adopted as rule 982 effective November 10, 1969; previously amended effective November 23, 1969, July 1, 1970, November 23, 1970, January 1, 1971, January 1, 1972, March 4, 1972, July 1, 1972, March 7, 1973, January 1, 1975, July 1, 1975, July 1, 1976, January 1, 1977, July 1, 1977, January 1, 1978, October 1, 1978, January 1, 1979, July 1, 1980, January 1, 1981, July 1, 1983, July 1, 1988, January 1, 1997, and January 1, 2006; amended and renumbered as rule 201.1 effective January 1, 2003.

Ref.: Cal. Fms Pl. & Pr., Ch. 2, "Procedural Guide for Civil Actions," Ch. 174, "Costs and Attorney's Fees," Ch. 205, "Defaults and Default Judgments," Ch. 220, "Dissolution of Marriage: Master Procedural Guide," Ch. 221, "Dissolution of Marriage: Procedure," Ch. 249, "Employment Law: Termination and Discipline," Ch. 254, "Executions and Enforcement of Judgments," Ch. 276, "Garnishment," Ch. 290A, "Guardianship and Conservatorship: Asset Management and Investment," Ch. 294, "Homesteads," Ch. 318, "Judgments," Ch. 362, "Mental Suffering and Emotional Distress," Ch. 364, "Minors: Claims and Property of Minors," Ch. 377, "Name, Change of," Ch. 380, "Negligence," Ch. 411, "Patents and Inventions," Ch. 447, "Probate: Statutory Notice Requirements," Ch. 451, "Probate: Inventory and Appraisal," Ch. 454, "Probate: Claims Against the Estate," Ch. 517, "Self-Service Storage Facilities," Ch. 518, "Service of Summons and Papers," Ch. 526, "Small Claims"; MB Prac. Guide: Cal. Trial & Post-Trial Civ. Proc., §§12.27, 12.29, 12.43, 12.44; W. Cal. Sum., 10 "Parent and Child" §§445, 712.

Rule 1.31.   Mandatory forms

(a) Use of mandatory forms and acceptance for filing

Forms adopted by the Judicial Council for mandatory use are forms prescribed under Government Code section 68511. Wherever applicable, they must be used by all parties and must be accepted for filing by all courts. In some areas, alternative mandatory forms have been adopted.

(Subd (a) adopted effective January 1, 2007.)

(b) List of mandatory forms

Each mandatory Judicial Council form is identified as mandatory by an asterisk (*) on the list of Judicial Council forms in Appendix A to the California Rules of Court. The list is available on the California Courts Web site at *www.courtinfo.ca.gov/forms.*

(Subd (b) adopted effective January 1, 2007.)

(c) Identification of mandatory forms

Forms adopted by the Judicial Council for mandatory use bear the words "Form Adopted for Mandatory Use,"

"Mandatory Form," or "Form Adopted for Alternative Mandatory Use" in the lower left corner of the first page.

(Subd (c) adopted effective January 1, 2007.)

(d) Words on forms

Publishers and courts reprinting a mandatory Judicial Council form in effect before July 1, 1999, must add the words "Mandatory Form" to the bottom of the first page.

(Subd (d) adopted effective January 1, 2007.)

(e) No alteration of forms

Except as provided in rule 5.504, concerning court orders in juvenile court proceedings, and rule 7.101.5, concerning court orders in proceedings under the Probate Code, courts may not [1] require the **use of an** altered [2] **mandatory Judicial Council form** in place of the Judicial Council form. **However, a judicial officer may modify a Judicial Council form order as necessary or appropriate to adjudicate a particular case.**

(Subd (e) amended effective January 1, 2009; adopted effective January 1, 2007; previously amended effective January 1, 2007.)

Rule 1.31(e). 2008 Deletes. [1] alter a mandatory Judicial Council form and [2] form's use

(f) No colored forms

Courts may not require that any mandatory Judicial Council form be submitted on any color of paper other than white.

(Subd (f) adopted effective January 1, 2007.)

(g) Orders not on mandatory forms

An otherwise legally sufficient court order for which there is a mandatory Judicial Council form is not invalid or unenforceable because the order is not prepared on a Judicial Council form or the correct Judicial Council form.

(Subd (g) adopted effective January 1, 2007.)

Rule 1.31 amended effective January 1, 2009; adopted effective January 1, 2007; previously amended effective January 1, 2007.

Ref.: Cal. Fms Pl. & Pr., Ch. 26, "Answers," Ch. 42, "Appeal: Notice of Appeal," Ch. 115, "Civil Rights: Employment Discrimination," Ch. 119, "Claim and Delivery," Ch. 137, "Continuing Duties During Litigation," Ch. 196, "Discovery: Requests for Admissions," Ch. 205, "Defaults and Default Judgments," Ch. 212, "Dismissal," Ch. 220, "Dissolution of Marriage: Master Procedural Guide," Ch. 254, "Executions and Enforcement of Judgments," Ch. 258, "Family Law Enforcement: General Enforcement Principles and Remedies," Ch. 259, "Family Law Enforcement: Special Remedies for Support Enforcement," Ch. 264, "Fax Filing and Service of Papers," Ch. 280, "Guardianship and Conservatorship: Appointment of Guardians," Ch. 281, "Guardianship and Conservatorship: Appointment of Conservators," Ch. 282, "Guardianship and Conservatorship: Temporary Guardians and Conservators," Ch. 284, "Guardianship and Conservatorship: Notice," Ch. 285, "Guardianship and Conservatorship: Care of Ward or Conservatee," Ch. 286, "Guardianship and Conservatorship: Inventory and Appraisal," Ch. 290A, "Guardianship and Conservatorship: Asset Management and Investment," Ch. 317, "Judges," Ch. 328, "Juvenile Courts: Dependency Proceedings," Ch. 345A, "Limited Civil Cases," Ch. 364, "Minors: Claims and Property of Minors," Ch. 377, "Name, Change of," Ch. 441, "Probate: Disposition Without Administration," Ch. 442, "Probate: Initiating Probate Administration," Ch. 526, "Small Claims"; MB Prac. Guide: Cal. Debt Collection & Enforcement of Judgments, §§3.29, 3.30, 7.42, 8.65–8.68, 8.77, 9.45, 10.46, 11.07[1], 11.55, 13.10[3], 16.79, 17.51, 21.22[2], 21.29, 21.30, 21.33, 21.35–21.38, 21.40–21.42; MB Prac. Guide: Cal. Pretrial Proc., §§3.38A, 6.64B, 7.26[4][b], 8.04, 8.43, 8.45, 8.46, 14.12, 14.23, 14.34, 19.46, 19.55, 20.06[2], 20.07[1], 20.13[4], 20.15[2][b], [3][b], [4][b], [5][b], 20.19[3][a], 20.23[2], [4][b], 20.25[3], 20.28–20.31, 20.33–20.37, 27.52, 36.30, 36.31, 39.18, 39.19; MB Prac. Guide: Cal. Trial & Post-Trial Civ. Proc., §7.06[2][e]; W. Cal. Sum., 10 "Parent and Child" §564.

Rule 1.35. Optional forms

(a) Use of optional forms and acceptance for filing

Forms approved by the Judicial Council for optional use, wherever applicable, may be used by parties and must be accepted for filing by all courts.

(Subd (a) adopted effective January 1, 2007.)

(b) List of optional forms

Each optional Judicial Council form appears without an asterisk (*) on the list of Judicial Council forms in Appendix A to the California Rules of Court. The list is available on the California Courts Web site at *www.courtinfo.ca.gov/forms.*

(Subd (b) adopted effective January 1, 2007.)

(c) Identification of optional forms

Forms approved by the Judicial Council for optional use bear the words "Form Approved for Optional Use" or "Optional Form" in the lower left corner of the first page.

(Subd (c) adopted effective January 1, 2007.)

(d) Words on forms

Publishers and courts reprinting an optional Judicial Council form in effect before July 1, 1999, must add the words "Optional Form" to the bottom of the first page.

(Subd (d) adopted effective January 1, 2007.)

(e) No alteration of forms

Courts may not [1] require the **use of an** altered [2] **optional Judicial Council form** in place of the Judicial Council form. **However, a judicial officer may modify a Judicial Council form order as necessary or appropriate to adjudicate a particular case.**

(Subd (e) amended effective January 1, 2009; adopted effective January 1, 2007.)

Rule 1.35(e). 2008 Deletes. [1] alter an optional Judicial Council form and [2] form's use

(f) No colored forms

Courts may not require that any optional Judicial Council form be submitted on any color of paper other than white.

(Subd (f) adopted effective January 1, 2007.)

Rule 1.35 amended effective January 1, 2009; adopted effective January 1, 2007.

Ref.: Cal. Fms Pl. & Pr., Ch. 26, "Answers," Ch. 40, "Appeal: An Overview," Ch. 42, "Appeal: Notice of Appeal," Ch. 44, "Appeal: Preparing and Filing the Record," Ch. 48, "Appeal: Abandonment, Dismissal, and Stipulated Reversal," Ch. 50, "Appeal: Briefs," Ch. 53, "Appeal: Remittitur and Costs on Appeal," Ch. 99, "Birth and Death, Establishing the Fact of," Ch. 115, "Civil Rights: Employment Discrimination," Ch. 137, "Continuing Duties During Litigation," Ch. 140, "Contracts," Ch. 194, "Discovery: Interrogatories," Ch. 196, "Discovery: Requests for Admissions," Ch. 220, "Dissolution of Marriage: Master Procedural Guide," Ch. 221, "Dissolution of Marriage: Procedure," Ch. 249, "Employment Law: Termination and Discipline," Ch. 280, "Guardianship and Conservatorship: Appointment of Guardians," Ch. 284, "Guardianship and Conservatorship: Notice," Ch. 286, "Guardianship and Conservatorship: Inventory and Appraisal," Ch. 292, "Habeas Corpus," Ch. 304, "Insane and Other Incompetent Persons," Ch. 317, "Judges," Ch. 318, "Judgments," Ch. 328, "Juvenile Courts: Dependency Proceedings," Ch. 377, "Name, Change of," Ch. 380, "Negligence," Ch. 393, "Oil and Gas," Ch. 447, "Probate: Statutory Notice Requirements," Ch. 518, "Service of Summons and Papers," Ch. 524, "Shortening and Extension of Time," Ch. 526, "Small Claims," Ch. 573, "Vexatious Litigants"; MB Prac. Guide: Cal. Debt Collection & Enforcement of Judgments, §§6.36–6.38, 8.72–8.76, 8.79, 8.81–8.84, 10.46A, 11.39[1], 11.59, 16.07[2], 16.13, 16.20, 16.69, 16.72[2], 16.73–16.75, 16.79, 16.80, 17.57, 21.31, 22.08[5][b], 24.11[1], 24.28, 25.17, 25.18; MB Prac. Guide: Cal. Pretrial Proc., §§3.38B–3.38D, 7.04[1], 14.12, 14.23, 14.34, 19.41–19.45, 19.47 19.52, 19.54, 20.08[1], 20.09[1], 20.19[3][b], [4][a], 25.11[1][a], 25.23, 25.25, 27.47A, 27.48, 27.50, 27.51, 32.04[3], 32.26A; MB Prac. Guide: Cal. Trial & Post-Trial Civ. Proc., §§6.34, 19.33, 26.39.

Rule 1.37.   Use of forms

A person serving and filing a Judicial Council form must use the current version of the form adopted or approved by the council, unless a rule in the California Rules of Court allows the use of a different form.
Rule 1.37 adopted effective January 1, 2007.

Ref.: W. Cal. Sum., 10 "Parent and Child" §445.

Rule 1.40.   Statutory references on forms

The references to statutes and rules at the bottom of Judicial Council forms are advisory only. The presence or absence of a particular reference is not a ground for rejecting a form otherwise applicable in the action or proceeding for the purpose presented.
Rule 1.40 adopted effective January 1, 2007.

Rule 1.41.   Proofs of service on forms

Proofs of service are included on some Judicial Council forms solely for the convenience of the parties. A party may use an included proof of service or any other proper proof of service.
Rule 1.41 adopted effective January 1, 2007.

Rule 1.42.   Forms not to be rejected

A court must not reject for filing a Judicial Council form for any of the following reasons:

(1) The form lacks the preprinted title and address of the court;

(2) The form lacks the name of the clerk;

(3) The preprinted title and address of another court or its clerk's name is legibly modified;

(4) The form lacks the court's local form number;

(5) The form lacks any other material added by a court, unless the material is required by the Judicial Council;

(6) The form is printed by a publisher or another court;

(7) The form is imprinted with the name or symbol of the publisher, unless the name or symbol replaces or obscures any material on the printed form;

(8) The form is legibly and obviously modified to correct a code section number or to comply with the law under which the form is filed; or

(9) The form is not the latest version of the form adopted or approved by the Judicial Council.
Rule 1.42 amended effective January 1, 2007; adopted effective January 1, 2007.

Ref.: Cal. Fms Pl. & Pr., Ch. 181, "Death and Survival Actions."

Rule 1.43.   Legibility

A Judicial Council form filed must be a true copy of the original form and must be as legible as a printed form.

Rule 1.43 adopted effective January 1, 2007.

Ref.: Cal. Fms Pl. & Pr., Ch. 123, "Complaints and Cross Complaints."

Rule 1.44.   Electronically produced forms

A party or attorney may file a duplicate of a Judicial Council form produced by a computer and a printer or similar device with a resolution of at least 300 dots per inch.
Rule 1.44 adopted effective January 1, 2007.

Ref.: Cal. Fms Pl. & Pr., Ch. 123, "Complaints and Cross Complaints"; MB Prac. Guide: Cal. Pretrial Proc., §7.04[2].

Rule 1.45.   Judicial Council pleading forms

(a) Pleading forms

The forms listed under the "Pleading" heading on the list of Judicial Council forms in Appendix A to the California Rules of Court [1] are approved by the Judicial Council.
(Subd (a) amended effective July 1, 2008; previously amended effective July 1, 1999, January 1, 2005, and January 1, 2007.)

Rule 1.45(a).   2008 Deletes. [1] (forms 982.1(1)–982.1(95))

(b) Cause of action forms

Any approved cause of action form may be attached to any approved form of complaint or cross-complaint.
(Subd (b) adopted effective January 1, 1982.)

(c) Other causes of action

A cause of action for which no form has been approved may be prepared in the format prescribed by the rules in chapter 1 of division 2 of title 2 and attached to any approved form of complaint or cross-complaint. Each paragraph within a cause of action must be numbered consecutively beginning with one. Each paragraph number must be preceded with one or more identifying letters derived from the title of the cause of action.
(Subd (c) amended effective January 1, 2007; adopted effective January 1, 1982; previously amended effective January 1, 2003.)
Rule 1.45 amended effective July 1, 2008; adopted as rule 982.1 effective January 1, 1982; previously amended effective July 1, 1995, July 1, 1996, January 1, 1997, July 1, 1999, and January 1, 2005; previously amended and renumbered as rule 201.2 effective January 1, 2003; previously amended and renumbered effective January 1, 2007.

Ref.: Cal. Fms Pl. & Pr., Ch. 16, "Airplanes and Airports," Ch. 26, "Answers," Ch. 58, "Assault and Battery," Ch. 83, "Automobiles: Bringing the Action," Ch. 121, "Common Counts," Ch. 123, "Complaints and Cross Complaints," Ch. 140, "Contracts," Ch. 177, "Damages," Ch. 181, "Death and Survival Actions," Ch. 269, "Fraud and Deceit," Ch. 300, "Indemnity and Contribution," Ch. 333, "Landlord and Tenant: Eviction Actions," Ch. 349, "Literary Property and Copyright," Ch. 362, "Mental Suffering and Emotional Distress," Ch. 367A, "Minors: Tort Actions," Ch. 380, "Negligence," Ch. 391, "Nuisance," Ch. 402, "Partnerships: Actions Between General Partners or Partnership and Third Parties," Ch. 411, "Patents and Inventions," Ch. 415, "Physicians: Medical Malpractice"; MB Prac. Guide: Cal. Debt Collection & Enforcement of Judgments, §§6.07[1], 6.37; MB Prac. Guide: Cal. Pretrial Proc., §§7.04[1], [3][b], [c], [4], 14.12, 14.23, 14.34.

Chapter 5
Accommodations

Rule 1.100.   Requests for accommodations by persons with disabilities

(a) Definitions

As used in this rule:

(1) "Persons with disabilities" means individuals covered by California Civil Code section 51 et seq.; the Americans With Disabilities Act of 1990 (42 U.S.C. §12101 et seq.); or other applicable state and federal laws. This definition includes persons who have a physical or mental impairment that limits one or more of the major life activities, have a record of such an impairment, or are regarded as having such an impairment.

(2) "Applicant" means any lawyer, party, witness, juror, or other person with an interest in attending any proceeding before any court of this state.

(3) "Accommodations" means actions that result in court services, programs, or activities being readily accessible to and usable by persons with disabilities. Accommodations may include making reasonable modifications in policies, practices, and procedures; furnishing, at no charge, to persons with disabilities, auxiliary aids and services, equipment, devices, materials in alternative formats, readers, or certified interpreters for persons with hearing impairments; relocating services or programs to accessible facilities; or providing services at alternative sites. Although not required where other actions are effective in providing access to court services, programs, or activities, alteration of existing facilities by the responsible entity may be an accommodation.

(Subd (a) repealed, amended, and relettered effective January 1, 2007; adopted as subd (b) effective January 1, 1996; previously amended effective January 1, 2006.)

(b) Policy

It is the policy of the courts of this state to ensure that persons with disabilities have equal and full access to the judicial system. To ensure access to the courts for persons with disabilities, each superior and appellate court must delegate at least one person to be the ADA coordinator, also known as the access coordinator, or designee to address requests for accommodations. This rule is not intended to impose limitations or to invalidate the remedies, rights, and procedures accorded to persons with disabilities under state or federal law.

(Subd (b) adopted effective January 1, 2007.)

(c) Process for requesting accommodations

The process for requesting accommodations is as follows:

(1) Requests for accommodations under this rule may be presented ex parte on a form approved by the Judicial Council, in another written format, or orally. Requests must be forwarded to the ADA coordinator, also known as the access coordinator, or designee, within the time frame provided in (c)(3).

(2) Requests for accommodations must include a description of the accommodation sought, along with a statement of the impairment that necessitates the accommodation. The court, in its discretion, may require the applicant to provide additional information about the impairment.

(3) Requests for accommodations must be made as far in advance as possible, and in any event must be made no fewer than 5 court days before the requested implementation date. The court may, in its discretion, waive this requirement.

(4) The court must keep confidential all information of the applicant concerning the request for accommodation, unless confidentiality is waived in writing by the applicant or disclosure is required by law. The applicant's identity and confidential information may not be disclosed to the public or to persons other than those involved in the accommodation process. Confidential information includes all medical information pertaining to the applicant, and all oral or written communication from the applicant concerning the request for accommodation.

(Subd (c) amended effective January 1, 2007; previously amended effective January 1, 2006.)

(d) Permitted communication

Communications under this rule must address only the accommodation requested by the applicant and must not address, in any manner, the subject matter or merits of the proceedings before the court.

(Subd (d) amended effective January 1, 2006.)

(e) Response to accommodation request

The court must respond to a request for accommodation as follows:

(1) The court must consider, but is not limited by, California Civil Code section 51 et seq., the provisions of the Americans With Disabilities Act of 1990, and other applicable state and federal laws in determining whether to provide an accommodation or an appropriate alternative accommodation.

(2) The court must inform the applicant in writing, as may be appropriate, and if applicable, in an alternative format, of the following:

(A) That the request for accommodation is granted or denied, in whole or in part, and if the request for accommodation is denied, the reason therefor; or that an alternative accommodation is granted;

(B) The nature of the accommodation to be provided, if any; and

(C) The duration of the accommodation to be provided.

(Subd (e) amended effective January 1, 2007; previously amended effective January 1, 2006.)

(f) Denial of accommodation request

A request for accommodation may be denied only when the court determines that:

(1) The applicant has failed to satisfy the requirements of this rule;

(2) The requested accommodation would create an undue financial or administrative burden on the court; or

(3) The requested accommodation would fundamentally alter the nature of the service, program, or activity.

(Subd (f) amended effective January 1, 2007; previously amended effective January 1, 2006.)

(g) Review procedure

(1) An applicant or any participant in the proceeding in which an accommodation request has been denied or granted may seek review of a determination made by nonjudicial court personnel within 10 days of the date of the response by submitting, in writing, a request for review to the presiding judge or designated judicial officer.

(2) An applicant or any participant in the proceeding in which an accommodation request has been denied or granted may seek review of a determination made by a presiding judge or another judicial officer within 10 days of the date of the notice of determination by filing a

petition for extraordinary relief in a court of superior jurisdiction.

(Subd (g) amended effective January 1, 2006.)

(h) Duration of accommodations

The accommodation by the court must be provided for the duration indicated in the response to the request for accommodation and must remain in effect for the period specified. The court may provide an accommodation for an indefinite period of time, for a limited period of time, or for a particular matter or appearance.

(Subd (h) amended effective January 1, 2006.)

Rule 1.100 amended and renumbered effective January 1, 2007; adopted as rule 989.3 effective January 1, 1996; previously amended effective January 1, 2006.

Ref.: Cal. Fms Pl. & Pr., Ch. 112, "Civil Rights: Government-Funded Programs and Activities," Ch. 322, "Juries and Jury Selection," Ch. 329, "Juvenile Courts: Delinquency Proceedings," Ch. 395, "Parties."

Chapter 6
Public Access to Court Proceedings

Rule 1.150.   Photographing, recording, and broadcasting in court

(a) Introduction

The judiciary is responsible for ensuring the fair and equal administration of justice. The judiciary adjudicates controversies, both civil and criminal, in accordance with established legal procedures in the calmness and solemnity of the courtroom. Photographing, recording, and broadcasting of courtroom proceedings may be permitted as circumscribed in this rule if executed in a manner that ensures that the fairness and dignity of the proceedings are not adversely affected. This rule does not create a presumption for or against granting permission to photograph, record, or broadcast court proceedings.

(Subd (a) adopted effective January 1, 1997.)

(b) Definitions

As used in this rule:

(1) "Media coverage" means any photographing, recording, or broadcasting of court proceedings by the media using television, radio, photographic, or recording equipment.

(2) "Media" or "media agency" means any person or organization engaging in news gathering or reporting and includes any newspaper, radio or television station or network, news service, magazine, trade paper, in-house publication, professional journal, or other news-reporting or news-gathering agency.

(3) "Court" means the courtroom at issue, the courthouse, and its entrances and exits.

(4) "Judge" means the judicial officer or officers assigned to or presiding at the proceeding, except as provided in (e)(1) if no judge has been assigned.

(5) "Photographing" means recording a likeness, regardless of the method used, including by digital or photographic methods. As used in this rule, photographing does not include drawings or sketchings of the court proceedings.

(6) "Recording" means the use of any analog or digital device to aurally or visually preserve court proceedings. As used in this rule, recording does not include handwritten notes on the court record, whether by court reporter or by digital or analog preservation.

(7) "Broadcasting" means a visual or aural transmission or signal, by any method, of the court proceedings, including any electronic transmission or transmission by sound waves.

(Subd (b) amended effective January 1, 2007; adopted as subd (a) effective July 1, 1984; previously amended and relettered as subd (b) effective January 1, 1997; previously amended effective January 1, 2006.)

(c) Photographing, recording, and broadcasting prohibited

Except as provided in this rule, court proceedings may not be photographed, recorded, or broadcast. This rule does not prohibit courts from photographing or videotaping sessions for judicial education or publications and is not intended to apply to closed-circuit television broadcasts solely within the courthouse or between court facilities if the broadcasts are controlled by the court and court personnel.

(Subd (c) amended effective January 1, 2006; adopted effective January 1, 1997.)

(d) Personal recording devices

The judge may permit inconspicuous personal recording devices to be used by persons in a courtroom to make sound recordings as personal notes of the proceedings. A person proposing to use a recording device must obtain advance permission from the judge. The recordings must not be used for any purpose other than as personal notes.

(Subd (d) amended effective January 1, 2007; adopted as subd (c) effective July 1, 1984; previously amended and relettered as subd (d) effective January 1, 1997; previously amended effective January 1, 2006.)

(e) Media coverage

Media coverage may be permitted only on written order of the judge as provided in this subdivision. The judge in his or her discretion may permit, refuse, limit, or terminate media coverage. This rule does not otherwise limit or restrict the right of the media to cover and report court proceedings.

(1) *Request for order*

The media may request an order on *Media Request to Photograph, Record, or Broadcast* (form MC-500). The form must be filed at least five court days before the portion of the proceeding to be covered unless good cause is shown. A completed, proposed order on *Order on Media Request to Permit Coverage* (form MC-510) must be filed with the request. The judge assigned to the proceeding must rule on the request. If no judge has been assigned, the request will be submitted to the judge supervising the calendar department, and thereafter be ruled on by the judge assigned to the proceeding. The clerk must promptly notify the parties that a request has been filed.

(2) *Hearing on request*

The judge may hold a hearing on the request or may rule on the request without a hearing.

(3) *Factors to be considered by the judge*

In ruling on the request, the judge is to consider the following factors:

(A) The importance of maintaining public trust and confidence in the judicial system;

(B) The importance of promoting public access to the judicial system;

(C) The parties' support of or opposition to the request;

(D) The nature of the case;

(E) The privacy rights of all participants in the proceeding, including witnesses, jurors, and victims;

(F) The effect on any minor who is a party, prospective witness, victim, or other participant in the proceeding;

(G) The effect on the parties' ability to select a fair and unbiased jury;

(H) The effect on any ongoing law enforcement activity in the case;

(I) The effect on any unresolved identification issues;

(J) The effect on any subsequent proceedings in the case;

(K) The effect of coverage on the willingness of witnesses to cooperate, including the risk that coverage will engender threats to the health or safety of any witness;

(L) The effect on excluded witnesses who would have access to the televised testimony of prior witnesses;

(M) The scope of the coverage and whether partial coverage might unfairly influence or distract the jury;

(N) The difficulty of jury selection if a mistrial is declared;

(O) The security and dignity of the court;

(P) Undue administrative or financial burden to the court or participants;

(Q) The interference with neighboring courtrooms;

(R) The maintenance of the orderly conduct of the proceeding; and

(S) Any other factor the judge deems relevant.

(4) *Order permitting media coverage*

The judge ruling on the request to permit media coverage is not required to make findings or a statement of decision. The order may incorporate any local rule or order of the presiding or supervising judge regulating media activity outside of the courtroom. The judge may condition the order permitting media coverage on the media agency's agreement to pay any increased court-incurred costs resulting from the permitted media coverage (for example, for additional court security or utility service). Each media agency is responsible for ensuring that all its media personnel who cover the court proceeding know and follow the provisions of the court order and this rule.

(5) *Modified order*

The order permitting media coverage may be modified or terminated on the judge's own motion or on application to the judge without the necessity of a prior hearing or written findings. Notice of the application and any modification or termination ordered under the application must be given to the parties and each media agency permitted by the previous order to cover the proceeding.

(6) *Prohibited coverage*

The judge may not permit media coverage of the following:

(A) Proceedings held in chambers;

(B) Proceedings closed to the public;

(C) Jury selection;

(D) Jurors or spectators; or

(E) Conferences between an attorney and a client, witness, or aide; between attorneys; or between counsel and the judge at the bench.

(7) *Equipment and personnel*

The judge may require media agencies to demonstrate that proposed personnel and equipment comply with this rule. The judge may specify the placement of media personnel and equipment to permit reasonable media coverage without disruption of the proceedings.

(8) *Normal requirements for media coverage of proceedings*

Unless the judge in his or her discretion orders otherwise, the following requirements apply to media coverage of court proceedings:

(A) One television camera and one still photographer will be permitted.

(B) The equipment used may not produce distracting sound or light. Signal lights or devices to show when equipment is operating may not be visible.

(C) An order permitting or requiring modification of existing sound or lighting systems is deemed to require that the modifications be installed, maintained, and removed without public expense or disruption of proceedings.

(D) Microphones and wiring must be unobtrusively located in places approved by the judge and must be operated by one person.

(E) Operators may not move equipment or enter or leave the courtroom while the court is in session, or otherwise cause a distraction.

(F) Equipment or clothing must not bear the insignia or marking of a media agency.

(9) *Media pooling*

If two or more media agencies of the same type request media coverage of a proceeding, they must file a joint statement of agreed arrangements. If they are unable to agree, the judge may deny media coverage by that type of media agency.

(Subd (e) amended effective January 1, 2007; adopted as subd (b) effective July 1, 1984; previously amended and relettered as subd (e) effective January 1, 1997; previously amended effective January 1, 2006.)

(f) Sanctions

Any violation of this rule or an order made under this rule is an unlawful interference with the proceedings of the court and may be the basis for an order terminating media coverage, a citation for contempt of court, or an order imposing monetary or other sanctions as provided by law.

(Subd (f) amended and relettered as subd (f) effective January 1, 1997; adopted as subd (e) effective July 1, 1984.)

Rule 1.150 amended and renumbered effective January 1, 2007; adopted as rule 980 effective July 1, 1984; previously amended effective January 1, 1997, and January 1, 2006.

Ref.: Cal. Fms Pl. & Pr., Ch. 372, "Motions and Orders," Ch. 551, "Trial"; MB Prac. Guide: Cal. Pretrial Proc., §§26.03, 26.06[4]; MB Prac. Guide: Cal. Trial & Post-Trial Civ. Proc., §§2.40[1], [2], 2.41–2.43, 2.44[1]–[8], 2.45[2][c], [d], [3][a]–[c], [5][e], [f], 2.47, 2.48[1]–[3], 2.49[1], [3], [4], 2.50, 2.51, 2.52[1], [2], 2.53, 2.60, 2.61, 4.19[1][b].

Chapter 7
Form and Format of Papers

Chapter 7 adopted effective January 1, 2008.

Rule 1.200. Format of citations

Citations to cases and other authorities in all documents filed in the courts must be in the style established by either the *California Style Manual* or *The Bluebook: A Uniform System of Citation*, at the option of the party filing the document. The same style must be used consistently throughout the document.

Rule 1.200 adopted effective January 1, 2008.

Ref.: Cal. Fms Pl. & Pr., Ch. 417, "Points and Authorities."

TITLE 2
Trial Court Rules

Division 1
General Provisions

Chapter 1
Title and Application

Rule 2.1.   Title

The rules in this title may be referred to as the Trial Court Rules.

Rule 2.1 adopted effective January 1, 2007.

Ref.: Cal. Fms Pl. & Pr., Ch. 474C, "Procedures in Reviewing Agency Decisions," Ch. 510, "Sanctions"; MB Prac. Guide: Cal. Pretrial Proc., §§23.02, 35.07[1][a].

Rule 2.2.   Application

The Trial Court Rules apply to all cases in the superior courts unless otherwise specified by a rule or statute.

Rule 2.2 amended and renumbered effective January 1, 2007; adopted as rule 200 effective January 1, 2001; previously amended effective January 1, 2002, and January 1, 2003.

Ref.: Cal. Fms Pl. & Pr., Ch. 471B, "Licensing by Public Agencies."

Chapter 2
Definitions and Scope of Rules

Rule 2.3.   Definitions

As used in the Trial Court Rules, unless the context or subject matter otherwise requires:

(1) "Court" means the superior court;

(2) "Papers" includes all documents, except exhibits and copies of exhibits, that are offered for filing in any case, but does not include Judicial Council and local court forms, records on appeal in limited civil cases, or briefs filed in appellate divisions; and

(3) "Written," "writing," "typewritten," and "typewriting" include other methods equivalent in legibility to typewriting.

Rule 2.3 adopted effective January 1, 2007.

Ref.: Cal. Fms Pl. & Pr., Ch. 26, "Answers," Ch. 123, "Complaints and Cross Complaints," Ch. 474C, "Procedures in Reviewing Agency Decisions," Ch. 482, "Quieting Title."

Rule 2.10.   Scope of rules [Reserved]

Rule 2.10 adopted effective January 1, 2007.

Chapter 3
Timing

Rule 2.20.   Application for an order extending time

(a) Application—to whom made

An application for an order extending the time within which any act is required by law to be done must be heard and determined by the judge before whom the matter is pending; provided, however, that in case of the inability, death, or absence of such judge, the application may be heard and determined by another judge of the same court.

(Subd (a) amended effective January 1, 2007.)

(b) Disclosure of previous extensions

An application for an order extending time must disclose in writing the nature of the case and what extensions, if any, have previously been granted by order of court or stipulation of counsel.

(Subd (b) amended effective January 1, 2007.)

(c) Filing and service

An order extending time must be filed immediately and copies served within 24 hours after the making of the order or within such other time as may be fixed by the court.

(Subd (c) amended effective January 1, 2007.)

Rule 2.20 amended and renumbered effective January 1, 2007; adopted as rule 235 effective January 1, 1949.

Ref.: Cal. Fms Pl. & Pr., Ch. 168, "Corporations: Derivative Actions," Ch. 193, "Discovery: Depositions," Ch. 194, "Discovery: Interrogatories," Ch. 206, "Demurrers and Motions for Judgment on the Pleadings," Ch. 333, "Landlord and Tenant: Eviction Actions," Ch. 372, "Motions and Orders," Ch. 524, "Shortening and Extension of Time"; MB Prac. Guide: Cal. Pretrial Proc., §§27.21[2]–[4], 27.23.

Chapter 4
Sanctions

Rule 2.30. Sanctions for rules violations in civil cases

(a) Application
This sanctions rule applies to the rules in the California Rules of Court relating to general civil cases, unlawful detainer cases, probate proceedings, civil proceedings in the appellate division of the superior court, and small claims cases.

(Subd (a) amended effective January 1, 2004; adopted effective July 1, 2001.)

(b) Sanctions
In addition to any other sanctions permitted by law, the court may order a person, after written notice and an opportunity to be heard, to pay reasonable monetary sanctions to the court or an aggrieved person, or both, for failure without good cause to comply with the applicable rules. For the purposes of this rule, "person" means a party, a party's attorney, a witness, and an insurer or any other individual or entity whose consent is necessary for the disposition of the case. If a failure to comply with an applicable rule is the responsibility of counsel and not of the party, any penalty must be imposed on counsel and must not adversely affect the party's cause of action or defense thereto.

(Subd (b) amended effective January 1, 2007; adopted as untitled subdivision effective January 1, 1985; amended and relettered effective July 1, 2001; previously amended effective January 1, 1994, and January 1, 2004.)

(c) Notice and procedure
Sanctions must not be imposed under this rule except on noticed motion by the party seeking sanctions or on the court's own motion after the court has provided notice and an opportunity to be heard. A party's motion for sanctions must (1) state the applicable rule that has been violated, (2) describe the specific conduct that is alleged to have violated the rule, and (3) identify the attorney, law firm, party, witness, or other person against whom sanctions are sought. The court on its own motion may issue an order to show cause that must (1) state the applicable rule that has been violated, (2) describe the specific conduct that appears to have violated the rule, and (3) direct the attorney, law firm, party, witness, or other person to show cause why sanctions should not be imposed against them for violation of the rule.

(Subd (c) amended effective January 1, 2007; adopted effective July 1, 2001; previously amended effective January 1, 2004.)

(d) Award of expenses
In addition to the sanctions awardable under (b), the court may order the person who has violated an applicable rule to pay to the party aggrieved by the violation that party's reasonable expenses, including reasonable attorney's fees and costs, incurred in connection with the motion for sanctions or the order to show cause.

(Subd (d) amended effective January 1, 2007; adopted effective July 1, 2001; previously amended effective January 1, 2004.)

(e) Order
An order imposing sanctions must be in writing and must recite in detail the conduct or circumstances justifying the order.

(Subd (e) amended effective January 1, 2004; adopted effective July 1, 2001.)

Rule 2.30 amended and renumbered effective January 1, 2007; adopted as rule 227 effective January 1, 1985; previously amended effective January 1, 1994, July 1, 2001, and January 1, 2004.

Ref.: Cal. Fms Pl. & Pr., Ch. 32, "Contractual Arbitration: Agreements and Compelling Arbitration," Ch. 123, "Complaints and Cross Complaints," Ch. 125, "Consolidation, Severance, and Coordination of Actions," Ch. 174, "Costs and Attorney's Fees," Ch. 192, "Discovery: Sanctions for Discovery Misuse," Ch. 220, "Dissolution of Marriage: Master Procedural Guide," Ch. 417, "Points and Authorities," Ch. 425, "Pretrial Proceedings," Ch. 510, "Sanctions," Ch. 552, "Trial Court Delay Reduction"; MB Prac. Guide: Cal. Pretrial Proc., §§6.17[2][b], 7.05, 7.20[4], 23.04[3], 23.13, 23.16, 23.17[3], 35.02, 35.03[3], 35.07[1][a]–[d], [2][d], 35.14[7], 37.26; MB Prac. Guide: Cal. Trial & Post-Trial Civ. Proc., §§4.05[2], 4.07[1].

Division 2
Papers and Forms to Be Filed

Chap. 1.   Papers. Rules 2.100–2.119.
Chap. 2.   General Rules on Forms. Rules 2.130–2.141.
Chap. 3.   Other Forms. Rule 2.150.

Chapter 1
Papers

Rule 2.100. Form and format of papers presented for filing in the trial courts
Rule 2.101. Use of recycled paper; certification by attorney or party
Rule 2.102. One-sided paper
Rule 2.103. Quality, color, and size of paper
Rule 2.104. Printing; type size
Rule 2.105. Type style
Rule 2.106. Color of print
Rule 2.107. Margins
Rule 2.108. Spacing and numbering of lines
Rule 2.109. Page numbering
Rule 2.110. Footer
Rule 2.111. Format of first page
Rule 2.112. Separate causes of action, counts, and defenses
Rule 2.113. Binding
Rule 2.114. Exhibits
Rule 2.115. Hole punching
Rule 2.116. Changes on face of paper
Rule 2.117. Conformed copies of papers
Rule 2.118. Acceptance of papers for filing
Rule 2.119. Exceptions for forms

Rule 2.100. Form and format of papers presented for filing in the trial courts

(a) Preemption of local rules
The Judicial Council has preempted local rules relating to the form and format of papers to be filed in the trial courts. No trial court, or any division or branch of a trial

court, may enact or enforce any local rule concerning the form or format of papers.

(Subd (a) adopted effective January 1, 2007.)

(b) Rules prescribe form and format

The rules in this chapter prescribe the form and format of papers to be filed in the trial courts.

(Subd (b) adopted effective January 1, 2007.)

Rule 2.100 amended and renumbered effective January 1, 2007; adopted as rule 201 effective January 1, 1949; previously amended effective April 1, 1962, May 1, 1962, July 1, 1964, January 1, 1966, July 1, 1969, July 1, 1971, January 1, 1973, July 1, 1974, January 1, 1976, January 1, 1978, May 6, 1978, January 1, 1984, April 1, 1990, July 1, 1990, January 1, 1992, July 1, 1992, January 1, 1993, July 1, 1993, January 1, 1994, January 1, 1998, January 1, 1999, July 1, 1999, July 1, 2000, January 1, 2001, January 1, 2003, and January 1, 2006.

Ref.: Cal. Fms Pl. & Pr., Ch. 16, "Airplanes and Airports," Ch. 26, "Answers," Ch. 38, "Reference," Ch. 45, "Appeal: Motion Procedure," Ch. 83, "Automobiles: Bringing the Action," Ch. 108, "Captions and Introductions," Ch. 123, "Complaints and Cross Complaints," Ch. 125, "Consolidation, Severance, and Coordination of Actions," Ch. 177, "Damages," Ch. 209, "Dentists," Ch. 221, "Dissolution of Marriage: Procedure," Ch. 264, "Fax Filing and Service of Papers," Ch. 317, "Judges," Ch. 345A, "Limited Civil Cases," Ch. 358, "Mandate and Prohibition," Ch. 380, "Negligence," Ch. 391, "Nuisance," Ch. 417, "Points and Authorities," Ch. 441, "Probate: Disposition Without Administration," Ch. 460, "Products Liability," Ch. 471B, "Licensing by Public Agencies," Ch. 474C, "Procedures in Reviewing Agency Decisions," Ch. 482, "Quieting Title," Ch. 518, "Service of Summons and Papers," Ch. 548, "Title Insurance"; MB Prac. Guide: Cal. Pretrial Proc., §§7.01, 7.03, 7.04[3][c], [4], 7.05, 7.16, 7.17, 7.24, 8.36[3], 11.03, 11.15[3], 14.12, 14.22, 14.24, 16.03, 16.04[1][a], 26.43[5][b], [c], 27.34[2][b], [5][d], 38.03, 38.19; MB Prac. Guide: Cal. Trial & Post-Trial Civ. Proc., §§16.03, 16.07[1][b].

Rule 2.101.   Use of recycled paper; certification by attorney or party

(a) Use of recycled paper

Recycled paper must be used for the following:

(1) All original papers filed with the court and all copies of papers, documents, and exhibits, whether filed with the court or served on other parties; and

(2) The original record on appeal from a limited civil case, any brief filed with the court in a matter to be heard in the appellate division, and all copies of such documents, whether filed with the court or served on other parties.

(b) Certification

Whenever recycled paper must be used under the rules in this chapter, the attorney, party, or other person filing or serving a document certifies, by the act of filing or service, that the document was produced on paper purchased as recycled.

Rule 2.101 adopted effective January 1, 2007.

Ref.: Cal. Fms Pl. & Pr., Ch. 26, "Answers," Ch. 123, "Complaints and Cross Complaints," Ch. 455, "Probate: Sale of Estate Property"; MB Prac. Guide: Cal. Pretrial Proc., §7.06[1].

Rule 2.102.   One-sided paper

On papers, only one side of each page may be used.

Rule 2.102 adopted effective January 1, 2007.

Ref.: Cal. Fms Pl. & Pr., Ch. 417, "Points and Authorities"; MB Prac. Guide: Cal. Pretrial Proc., §7.06[1].

Rule 2.103.   Quality, color, and size of paper

All papers must be on opaque, unglazed paper, white or unbleached, of standard quality not less than 20-pound weight, 8½ by 11 inches.

Rule 2.103 adopted effective January 1, 2007.

Ref.: Cal. Fms Pl. & Pr., Ch. 123, "Complaints and Cross Complaints"; MB Prac. Guide: Cal. Pretrial Proc., §7.06[1].

Rule 2.104.   Printing; type size

All papers must be printed or typewritten or be prepared by a photocopying or other duplication process that will produce clear and permanent copies equally as legible as printing in type not smaller than 12 points.

Rule 2.104 adopted effective January 1, 2007.

Ref.: Cal. Fms Pl. & Pr., Ch. 333, "Landlord and Tenant: Eviction Actions," Ch. 537, "Summary Judgment"; MB Prac. Guide: Cal. Pretrial Proc., §§7.06[2], 38.17, 38.25[2], 38.33[2].

Rule 2.105.   Type style

The typeface must be essentially equivalent to Courier, Times New Roman, or Arial.

Rule 2.105 adopted effective January 1, 2007.

Ref.: MB Prac. Guide: Cal. Pretrial Proc., §7.06[2].

Rule 2.106.   Color of print

The color of print must be black or blue-black.

Rule 2.106 adopted effective January 1, 2007.

Ref.: Cal. Fms Pl. & Pr., Ch. 26, "Answers," Ch. 123, "Complaints and Cross Complaints"; MB Prac. Guide: Cal. Pretrial Proc., §7.06[2].

Rule 2.107.   Margins

The left margin of each page must be at least one inch from the left edge of the paper and the right margin at least ½ inch from the right edge of the paper.

Rule 2.107 adopted effective January 1, 2007.

Ref.: MB Prac. Guide: Cal. Pretrial Proc., §7.06[4].

Rule 2.108.   Spacing and numbering of lines

The spacing and numbering of lines on a page must be as follows:

(1) The lines on each page must be one and one-half spaced or double-spaced and numbered consecutively.

(2) Descriptions of real property may be single-spaced.

(3) Footnotes, quotations, and printed forms of corporate surety bonds and undertakings may be single-spaced and have unnumbered lines if they comply generally with the space requirements of rule 2.111.

(4) Line numbers must be placed at the left margin and separated from the text of the paper by a vertical column of space at least ⅕ inch wide or a single or double vertical line. Each line number must be aligned with a line of type, or the line numbers must be evenly spaced vertically on the page. Line numbers must be consecutively numbered, beginning with the number 1 on each page. There must be at least three line numbers for every vertical inch on the page.

Rule 2.108 adopted effective January 1, 2007.

Ref.: Cal. Fms Pl. & Pr., Ch. 26, "Answers," Ch. 123, "Complaints and Cross Complaints," Ch. 124, "Condominiums and Other Common Interest Developments," Ch. 318, "Judgments," Ch. 397, "Partition," Ch. 417, "Points and Authorities," Ch. 482, "Quieting Title," Ch. 537, "Summary Judgment"; MB Prac. Guide: Cal. Pretrial Proc., §§7.06[3], [5], 38.17, 38.25[2], 38.33[2].

Rule 2.109.   Page numbering

Each page must be numbered consecutively at the bottom unless a rule provides otherwise for a particular type of document.

Rule 2.109 adopted effective January 1, 2007.

Ref.: Cal. Fms Pl. & Pr., Ch. 123, "Complaints and Cross Complaints," Ch. 417, "Points and Authorities"; MB Prac. Guide: Cal. Pretrial Proc., §7.06[6].

Rule 2.110.   Footer

(a) Location

Except for exhibits, each paper filed with the court must bear a footer in the bottom margin of each page, placed below the page number and divided from the rest of the document page by a printed line.

(b) Contents

The footer must contain the title of the paper (examples: "Complaint," "XYZ Corp.'s Motion for Summary Judgment") or some clear and concise abbreviation.

(c) Type size

The title of the paper in the footer must be in at least 10-point type.

Rule 2.110 adopted effective January 1, 2007.

Ref.: Cal. Fms Pl. & Pr., Ch. 26, "Answers," Ch. 123, "Complaints and Cross Complaints," Ch. 206, "Demurrers and Motions for Judgment on the Pleadings," Ch. 394, "Parent and Child," Ch. 417, "Points and Authorities"; MB Prac. Guide: Cal. Pretrial Proc., §7.06[8].

Rule 2.111.   Format of first page

The first page of each paper must be in the following form:

(1) In the space commencing 1 inch from the top of the page with line 1, to the left of the center of the page, the name, office address or, if none, residence address or mailing address (if different), telephone number, fax number and e-mail address (if available), and State Bar membership number of the attorney for the party in whose behalf the paper is presented, or of the party if he or she is appearing in person. The inclusion of a fax number or e-mail address on any document does not constitute consent to service by fax or e-mail unless otherwise provided by law.

(2) In the first 2 inches of space between lines 1 and 7 to the right of the center of the page, a blank space for the use of the clerk.

(3) On line 8, at or below 3⅓ inches from the top of the paper, the title of the court.

(4) Below the title of the court, in the space to the left of the center of the page, the title of the case. In the title of the case on each initial complaint or cross-complaint, the name of each party must commence on a separate line beginning at the left margin of the page. On any subsequent pleading or paper, it is sufficient to provide a short title of the case (1) stating the name of the first party on each side, with appropriate indication of other parties, and (2) stating that a cross-action or cross-actions are involved (e.g., "and Related Cross-action"), if applicable.

(5) To the right of and opposite the title, the number of the case.

(6) Below the number of the case, the nature of the paper and, on all complaints and petitions, the character of the action or proceeding. In a case having multiple parties, any answer, response, or opposition must specifically identify the complaining, propounding, or moving party and the complaint, motion, or other matter being answered or opposed.

(7) Below the nature of the paper or the character of the action or proceeding, the name of the judge and department, if any, to which the case is assigned.

(8) Below the nature of the paper or the character of the action or proceeding, the word "Referee:" followed by the name of the referee, on any paper filed in a case pending before a referee appointed under Code of Civil Procedure section 638 or 639.

(9) On the complaint, petition, or application filed in a limited civil case, below the character of the action or proceeding, the amount demanded in the complaint, petition, or application, stated as follows: "Amount demanded exceeds $10,000" or "Amount demanded does not exceed $10,000," as required by Government Code section 70613.

(10) In the caption of every pleading and every other paper filed in a limited civil case, the words "Limited Civil Case," as required by Code of Civil Procedure section 422.30(b).

(11) If a case is reclassified by an amended complaint, cross-complaint, amended cross-complaint, or other pleading under Code of Civil Procedure section 403.020 or 403.030, the caption must indicate that the action or proceeding is reclassified by this pleading. If a case is reclassified by stipulation under Code of Civil Procedure section 403.050, the title of the stipulation must state that the action or proceeding is reclassified by this stipulation. The caption or title must state that the case is a limited civil case reclassified as an unlimited civil case, or an unlimited civil case reclassified as a limited civil case, or other words to that effect.

Rule 2.111 amended effective January 1, 2008; adopted effective January 1, 2007.

Ref.: Cal. Fms Pl. & Pr., Ch. 1, "New Developments," Ch. 6, "Accord and Satisfaction," Ch. 12C, "Adoptions: Adults and Married Minors," Ch. 21, "Amended and Supplemental Pleadings," Ch. 23, "Animals: Civil Liability," Ch. 24, "Animals: Liens," Ch. 25, "Annulment (Nullity) of Marriage and Related Spousal Rights," Ch. 26, "Answers," Ch. 32, "Contractual Arbitration: Agreements and Compelling Arbitration," Ch. 33, "Contractual Arbitration: Appointment of Arbitrator and Conduct of Proceeding," Ch. 34, "Contractual Arbitration: Judicial Review," Ch. 38, "Reference," Ch. 60, "Assignments," Ch. 72, "Attorney Practice and Ethics," Ch. 77, "Auctions and Auctioneers," Ch. 83, "Automobiles: Bringing the Action," Ch. 88, "Automobiles: Automobile Insurance," Ch. 88A, "Automobiles: Uninsured Motorist Claims," Ch. 89, "Automobiles: Sales and Financing Under the Rees-Levering Act," Ch. 90, "Automobiles: Vehicle Leasing Act," Ch. 91, "Automobiles: Actions Involving Defects and Repairs," Ch. 108, "Captions and Introductions," Ch. 110, "Churches and Religious Organizations," Ch. 115, "Civil Rights: Employment Discrimination," Ch. 123, "Complaints and Cross Complaints," Ch. 127, "Consumer Contracts and Loans," Ch. 140, "Contracts," Ch. 162, "Corporations: Issuance of Shares," Ch. 167, "Corporations: Directors and Management," Ch. 182, "Declaratory Relief," Ch. 206, "Demurrers and Motions for Judgment on the Pleadings," Ch. 221, "Dissolution of Marriage:

Rules of Court

Procedure," Ch. 264, "Fax Filing and Service of Papers," Ch. 333, "Landlord and Tenant: Eviction Actions," Ch. 345A, "Limited Civil Cases," Ch. 346, "Limited Liability Companies," Ch. 361, "Mechanics' Liens," Ch. 372, "Motions and Orders," Ch. 374, "Motions to Reconsider and Renewed Motions," Ch. 458C, "Probate: Preliminary Distribution and Partial Allowance of Compensation," Ch. 460, "Products Liability," Ch. 464, "Public Entities and Officers: California Tort Claims Act," Ch. 470C, "Public Records Act," Ch. 474C, "Procedures in Reviewing Agency Decisions," Ch. 484, "Radio and Television," Ch. 518, "Service of Summons and Papers," Ch. 526, "Small Claims," Ch. 527, "Social Services," Ch. 551, "Trial," Ch. 569, "Vendor and Purchaser of Real Property"; MB Prac. Guide: Cal. Pretrial Proc., §§6.15[2][c], 7.03, 7.06[3], 7.07[1], [2], 7.08[1], [2][a], [b], [d]–[g], 7.13[1][a], 7.35, 8.50, 15.09, 15.10[1], 15.11[2], 26.46, 27.34[3], [6][a], 34.13, 34.48; MB Prac. Guide: Cal. Trial & Post-Trial Civ. Proc., §§2.17[5][e], 3.08.

Rule 2.112. Separate causes of action, counts, and defenses

Each separately stated cause of action, count, or defense must specifically state:

(1) Its number (e.g., "first cause of action");

(2) Its nature (e.g., "for fraud");

(3) The party asserting it if more than one party is represented on the pleading (e.g., "by plaintiff Jones"); and

(4) The party or parties to whom it is directed (e.g., "against defendant Smith").

Rule 2.112 adopted effective January 1, 2007.

Ref.: Cal. Fms Pl. & Pr., Ch. 26, "Answers," Ch. 83, "Automobiles: Bringing the Action," Ch. 84, "Automobiles: Responding to the Action," Ch. 108, "Captions and Introductions," Ch. 123, "Complaints and Cross Complaints," Ch. 140, "Contracts," Ch. 182, "Declaratory Relief," Ch. 206, "Demurrers and Motions for Judgment on the Pleadings," Ch. 213, "Documents of Title," Ch. 308, "Insurance," Ch. 380, "Negligence," Ch. 391, "Nuisance," Ch. 421, "Premises Liability," Ch. 429, "Privacy," Ch. 460, "Products Liability," Ch. 548, "Title Insurance," Ch. 562, "Trusts: Resulting Trusts," Ch. 565, "Unfair Competition," Ch. 575, "Waters"; MB Prac. Guide: Cal. Pretrial Proc., §§7.03, 7.12[1], 7.35, 14.12, 14.18[5].

Rule 2.113. Binding

Each paper must consist entirely of original pages without riders and must be firmly bound together at the top.

Rule 2.113 adopted effective January 1, 2007.

Ref.: MB Prac. Guide: Cal. Pretrial Proc., §7.06[6].

Rule 2.114. Exhibits

Exhibits may be fastened to pages of the specified size and, when prepared by a machine copying process, must be equal to typewritten material in legibility and permanency of image.

Rule 2.114 adopted effective January 1, 2007.

Ref.: Cal. Fms Pl. & Pr., Ch. 26, "Answers," Ch. 123, "Complaints and Cross Complaints"; MB Prac. Guide: Cal. Pretrial Proc., §7.06[6].

Rule 2.115. Hole punching

Each paper presented for filing must contain two prepunched normal-sized holes, centered 2½ inches apart and ⅝ inch from the top of the paper.

Rule 2.115 adopted effective January 1, 2007.

Ref.: Cal. Fms Pl. & Pr., Ch. 123, "Complaints and Cross Complaints"; MB Prac. Guide: Cal. Pretrial Proc., §7.06[7].

Rule 2.116. Changes on face of paper

Any addition, deletion, or interlineation to a paper must be initialed by the clerk or judge at the time of filing.

Rule 2.116 adopted effective January 1, 2007.

Ref.: Cal. Fms Pl. & Pr., Ch. 123, "Complaints and Cross Complaints"; MB Prac. Guide: Cal. Pretrial Proc., §7.21.

Rule 2.117. Conformed copies of papers

All copies of papers served must conform to the original papers filed, including the numbering of lines, pagination, additions, deletions, and interlineations.

Rule 2.117 adopted effective January 1, 2007.

Ref.: Cal. Fms Pl. & Pr., Ch. 123, "Complaints and Cross Complaints," Ch. 206, "Demurrers and Motions for Judgment on the Pleadings"; MB Prac. Guide: Cal. Pretrial Proc., §§7.16, 7.22.

Rule 2.118. Acceptance of papers for filing

(a) Papers not in compliance

The clerk of the court must not accept for filing or file any papers that do not comply with the rules in this chapter, except the clerk must not reject a paper for filing solely on the ground that:

(1) It is handwritten or hand-printed; or

(2) The handwriting or hand printing on the paper is in a color other than black or blue-black.

(b) Absence of fax number or e-mail address

The clerk must not reject a paper for filing solely on the ground that it does not contain an attorney's or a party's fax number or e-mail address on the first page.

(c) Filing of papers for good cause

For good cause shown, the court may permit the filing of papers that do not comply with the rules in this chapter.

Rule 2.118 adopted effective January 1, 2007.

Ref.: Cal. Fms Pl. & Pr., Ch. 38, "Reference," Ch. 123, "Complaints and Cross Complaints," Ch. 108, "Captions and Introductions," Ch. 206, "Demurrers and Motions for Judgment on the Pleadings"; MB Prac. Guide: Cal. Pretrial Proc., §§7.07[1], 7.17.

Rule 2.119. Exceptions for forms

Except as provided elsewhere in the California Rules of Court, the rules in this chapter do not apply to Judicial Council forms, local court forms, or forms for juvenile dependency proceedings produced by the California State Department of Social Services Child Welfare Systems Case Management System.

Rule 2.119 adopted effective January 1, 2007.

Advisory Committee Comment

The California Department of Social Services (CDSS) has begun to distribute a new, comprehensive, computerized case management system to county welfare agencies. This system is not able to exactly conform to Judicial Council format in all instances. However, item numbering on the forms will remain the same. The changes allow CDSS computer-generated Judicial Council forms to be used in juvenile court proceedings.

Ref.: MB Prac. Guide: Cal. Trial & Post-Trial Civ. Proc., §16.07[1][b].

Chapter 2
General Rules on Forms

Rule 2.130. Application
Rule 2.131. Recycled paper
Rule 2.132. True copy certified
Rule 2.133. Hole punching
Rule 2.134. Forms longer than one page
Rule 2.135. Filing of handwritten or hand-printed forms
Rule 2.140. Judicial Council forms
Rule 2.141. Local court forms

Rule 2.130.   Application

The rules in this chapter apply to Judicial Council forms, local court forms, and all other official forms to be filed in the trial courts.

Rule 2.130 adopted effective January 1, 2007.

Rule 2.131.   Recycled paper

All forms and copies of forms filed with the court must use recycled paper as defined in rule 1.6.

Rule 2.131 adopted effective January 1, 2007.

Ref.: W. Cal. Sum., 10 "Parent and Child" §445.

Rule 2.132.   True copy certified

A party or attorney who files a form certifies by filing the form that it is a true copy of the form.

Rule 2.132 adopted effective January 1, 2007.

Ref.: Cal. Fms Pl. & Pr., Ch. 123, "Complaints and Cross Complaints"; MB Prac. Guide: Cal. Pretrial Proc., §7.04[2].

Rule 2.133.   Hole punching

All forms must contain two prepunched normal-sized holes, centered 2½ inches apart and ⅝ inch from the top of the form.

Rule 2.133 adopted effective January 1, 2007.

Rule 2.134.   Forms longer than one page

(a) Single side may be used

If a form is longer than one page, the form may be printed on sheets printed only on one side even if the original has two sides to a sheet.

(Subd (a) adopted effective January 1, 2007.)

(b) Two-sided forms must be tumbled

If a form is filed on a sheet printed on two sides, the reverse side must be rotated 180 degrees (printed head to foot).

(Subd (b) adopted effective January 1, 2007.)

(c) Multiple-page forms must be bound

If a form is longer than one page, it must be firmly bound at the top.

(Subd (c) adopted effective January 1, 2007.)

Rule 2.134 adopted effective January 1, 2007.

Ref.: W. Cal. Sum., 10 "Parent and Child" §445.

Rule 2.135.   Filing of handwritten or hand-printed forms

The clerk must not reject for filing or refuse to file any Judicial Council or local court form solely on the ground that:

(1) It is completed in handwritten or hand-printed characters; or

(2) The handwriting or hand-printing is a color other than blue-black or black.

Rule 2.135 amended and renumbered effective January 1, 2007; adopted as rule 201.4 effective January 1, 2003.

Rule 2.140.   Judicial Council forms

Judicial Council forms are governed by the rules in this chapter and chapter 4 of title 1.

Rule 2.140 adopted effective January 1, 2007.

Rule 2.141.   Local court forms

Local court forms are governed by the rules in this chapter and rules 10.613 and 10.614.

Rule 2.141 adopted effective January 1, 2007.

Chapter 3
Other Forms

Rule 2.150.   Authorization for computer-generated or typewritten forms for proof of service of summons and complaint

(a) Computer-generated or typewritten forms; conditions

Notwithstanding the adoption of mandatory form *Proof of Service of Summons* (form POS-010), a form for proof of service of a summons and complaint prepared entirely by word processor, typewriter, or similar process may be used for proof of service in any applicable action or proceeding if the following conditions are met:

(1) The form complies with the rules in chapter 1 of this division except as otherwise provided in this rule, but numbered lines are not required.

(2) The left, right, and bottom margins of the proof of service must be at least ½ inch. The top margin must be at least ¾ of an inch. The typeface must be Times New Roman, Courier, Arial, or an equivalent typeface not smaller than 9 points. Text must be single-spaced and a blank line must precede each main numbered item.

(3) The title and all the text of form POS-010 that is not accompanied by a check box must be copied word for word except for any instructions, which need not be copied. In addition, the optional text describing the particular method of service used must be copied word for word, except that the check boxes must not be copied. Any optional text not describing such service need not be included.

(4) The Judicial Council number of the *Proof of Service of Summons* must be typed as follows either in the left margin of the first page opposite the last line of text or at the bottom of each page: "Judicial Council form POS-010."

(5) The text of form POS-010 must be copied in the same order as it appears on the printed form using the same item numbers. A declaration of diligence may be attached to the proof of service or inserted as item 5b(5).

(6) Areas marked "For Court Use" must be copied in the same general locations and occupy approximately the same amount of space as on the printed form.

(7) The telephone number of the attorney or party must appear flush with the left margin and below the attorney's or party's address.

(8) The name of the court must be flush with the left margin. The address of the court is not required.

(9) Material that would have been typed onto the printed form must be typed with each line indented 3 inches from the left margin.

(Subd (a) amended effective January 1, 2007; previously amended effective July 1, 1985, January 1, 1986, January 1, 1987, July 1, 1999, January 1, 2004, and July 1, 2004.)

(b) Compliance with rule

The act of filing a computer-generated or typewritten form under this rule constitutes a certification by the party or attorney filing the form that it complies with this rule and is a true and correct copy of the form to the extent required by this rule.

(Subd (b) amended effective January 1, 2004; previously amended effective July 1, 1985, January 1, 1987, January 1, 1988, and July 1, 1999; relettered effective January 1, 1986.)

Rule 2.150 amended and renumbered effective January 1, 2007; adopted as rule 982.9; previously amended effective January 1, 1989, July 1, 1999, January 1, 2004, and July 1, 2004.

Advisory Committee Comment

This rule is intended to permit process servers and others to prepare their own shortened versions of *Proof of Service of Summons* (form POS-010) containing only the information that is relevant to show the method of service used.

Ref.: Cal. Fms Pl. & Pr., Ch. 220, "Dissolution of Marriage: Master Procedural Guide," Ch. 518, "Service of Summons and Papers"; MB Prac. Guide: Cal. Pretrial Proc., §§8.07, 8.36[3], 8.45.

Division 3
Filing and Service

Chap. 1. General Provisions. Rules 2.200, 2.210.
Chap. 2. Filing and Service by Electronic Means. Rules 2.250–2.261.
Chap. 3. Filing and Service by Fax. Rules 2.300–2.306.

Chapter 1
General Provisions

Rule 2.200. Service and filing of notice of change of address
Rule 2.210. Drop box for filing documents

Rule 2.200. Service and filing of notice of change of address

A party or attorney whose address changes while an action is pending must serve on all parties and file a written notice of the change of address.

Rule 2.200 amended and renumbered effective January 1, 2007; adopted as rule 385 effective January 1, 1984.

Ref.: Cal. Fms Pl. & Pr., Ch. 72, "Attorney Practice and Ethics," Ch. 108, "Captions and Introductions," Ch. 123, "Complaints and Cross Complaints," Ch. 137, "Continuing Duties During Litigation," Ch. 372, "Motions and Orders," Ch. 518, "Service of Summons and Papers"; MB Prac. Guide: Cal. Pretrial Proc., §7.07[1].

Rule 2.210. Drop box for filing documents

(a) Use of drop box

Whenever a clerk's office filing counter is closed at any time between 8:30 a.m. and 4:00 p.m. on a court day, the court must provide a drop box for depositing documents to be filed with the clerk. A court may provide a drop box during other times.

(b) Documents deemed filed on day of deposit

Any document deposited in a court's drop box up to and including 4:00 p.m. on a court day is deemed to have been deposited for filing on that day. A court may provide for same-day filing of a document deposited in its drop box after 4:00 p.m. on a court day. If so, the court must give notice of the deadline for same-day filing of a document deposited in its drop box.

(c) Documents deemed filed on next court day

Any document deposited in a court's drop box is deemed to have been deposited for filing on the next court day if:

(1) It is deposited on a court day after 4:00 p.m. or after the deadline for same-day filing if a court provides for a later time; or

(2) It is deposited on a judicial holiday.

(Subd (c) amended effective January 1, 2007.)

(d) Date and time documents deposited

A court must have a means of determining whether a document was deposited in the drop box by 4:00 p.m., or after the deadline for same-day filing if a court provides for a later time, on a court day.

Rule 2.210 amended and renumbered effective January 1, 2007; adopted as rule 201.6 effective January 1, 2005.

Advisory Committee Comment

The notice required by (b) may be provided by the same means a court provides notice of its clerk's office hours. The means of providing notice may include the following: information on the court's Web site, a local rule provision, a notice in a legal newspaper, a sign in the clerk's office, or a sign near the drop box.

Ref.: Cal. Fms Pl. & Pr., Ch. 518, "Service of Summons and Papers"; MB Prac. Guide: Cal. Pretrial Proc., §§7.18, 26.44[1].

Chapter 2
Filing and Service by Electronic Means

Rule 2.250. Definitions
Rule 2.252. Documents that may be filed electronically
Rule 2.253. Court order requiring electronic service or filing
Rule 2.254. Responsibilities of court
Rule 2.255. Contracts with electronic filing service providers
Rule 2.256. Responsibilities of electronic filer
Rule 2.257. Requirements for signatures on documents
Rule 2.258. Payment of filing fees
Rule 2.259. Actions by court on receipt of electronic filing
Rule 2.260. Electronic service
Rule 2.261. Authorization for courts to continue modifying forms for the purpose of electronic filing and forms generation

Rule 2.250. Definitions

As used in this chapter, unless the context otherwise requires:

(1) "Close of business" is 5 p.m. or any other time on a court day at which the court stops accepting documents for filing at its filing counter, whichever is earlier. The court must provide notice of its close-of-business time electronically. The court may give this notice in any additional manner it deems appropriate.

(2) A "document" is a pleading, a paper, a declaration, an exhibit, or another filing submitted by a party or by an agent of a party on the party's behalf. A document may be in paper or electronic form.

(3) An "electronic filer" is a party filing a document in electronic form directly with the court, by an agent, or through an electronic filing service provider.

(4) "Electronic filing" is the electronic transmission to a court of a document in electronic form.

(5) An "electronic filing service provider" is a person or entity that receives an electronic filing from a party for retransmission to the court. In submission of filings, the electronic filing service provider does so on behalf of the electronic filer and not as an agent of the court.

(6) "Electronic service" is the electronic transmission of a document to a party's electronic notification address, either directly or through an electronic filing service provider, for the purpose of effecting service.

(7) "Regular filing hours" are the hours during which a court accepts documents for filing.

(8) "Electronic notification address" of a party means the electronic address at or through which the party has authorized electronic service.

Rule 2.250 amended effective January 1, 2008; adopted as rule 2050 effective January 1, 2003; previously amended effective January 1, 2006; previously amended and renumbered effective January 1, 2007.

Ref.: Cal. Fms Pl. & Pr., Ch. 50, "Appeal: Briefs," Ch. 190, "Discovery: Scope, Regulation, and Timing," Ch. 518, "Service of Summons and Papers"; MB Prac. Guide: Cal. Pretrial Proc., §§27.29, 27.35[1], [3][b], [k], [m], [4][f].

Rule 2.252.   Documents that may be filed electronically

(a) In general

A court may permit electronic filing of a document in any action or proceeding unless the rules in this chapter or other legal authority expressly prohibit electronic filing.

(Subd (a) amended effective January 1, 2007.)

(b) Original documents

In a proceeding that requires the filing of an original document, an electronic filer may file a scanned copy of a document if the original document is then filed with the court within 10 calendar days.

(c) Application for waiver of court fees and costs

The court may permit electronic filing of an application for waiver of court fees and costs in any proceeding in which the court accepts electronic filings.

(Subd (c) amended effective January 1, 2007.)

(d) Orders and judgments

The court may electronically file any notice, order, minute order, judgment, or other document prepared by the court.

(e) Effect of document filed electronically

(1) A document that the court or a party files electronically under the rules in this chapter has the same legal effect as a document in paper form.

(2) Filing a document electronically does not alter any filing deadline.

(Subd (e) amended effective January 1, 2007.)

Rule 2.252 amended and renumbered effective January 1, 2007; adopted as rule 2052 effective January 1, 2003.

Ref.: Cal. Fms Pl. & Pr., Ch. 190, "Discovery: Scope, Regulation, and Timing," Ch. 518, "Service of Summons and Papers"; MB Prac. Guide: Cal. Pretrial Proc., §§8.10, 27.35[3][a]–[d], [j].

Rule 2.253.   Court order requiring electronic service or filing

(a) Court order

The court may, on the motion of any party or on its own motion, after finding that such an order would not cause undue hardship or significant prejudice to any party, order all parties in any class action, a consolidated action, a group of actions, a coordinated action, or an action that is complex under rule 3.403 to:

(1) Serve all documents electronically, except when personal service is required by statute or rule;

(2) File all documents electronically; or

(3) Serve and file all documents electronically, except when personal service is required by statute or rule.

(Subd (a) amended effective January 1, 2008; previously amended effective January 1, 2007.)

(b) Additional provisions of order

The court's order may also provide that:

(1) Documents previously filed in paper form may be resubmitted in electronic form; and

(2) When the court sends confirmation of filing to all parties, receipt of the confirmation constitutes service of the filing if the filed document is available electronically.

(Subd (b) relettered and amended effective January 1, 2008; adopted as part of subd (a) effective January 1, 2003.)

(c) Filing in paper form

When it is not feasible for a party to convert a document to electronic form by scanning, imaging, or another means, a court may allow that party to serve, file, or serve and file the document in paper form.

(Subd (c) relettered and amended effective January 1, 2008; adopted as subd (b) effective January 1, 2003.)

Rule 2.253 amended effective January 1, 2008; adopted as rule 2053 effective January 1, 2003; previously amended and renumbered effective January 1, 2007.

Ref.: Cal. Fms Pl. & Pr., Ch. 1, "New Developments," Ch. 190, "Discovery: Scope, Regulation, and Timing," Ch. 518, "Service of Summons and Papers"; MB Prac. Guide: Cal. Pretrial Proc., §27.35[5].

Rule 2.254.   Responsibilities of court

(a) Internet-accessible system

(1) Except as provided in (2), a court that orders electronic filing must permit filing over the Internet by means designed to ensure the security and integrity of an Internet transmission.

(2) The court may decide not to permit service and filing over the Internet if the court determines that doing so would facilitate the management of a particular action or proceeding and would not cause undue prejudice to any party.

(Subd (a) amended effective January 1, 2007.)

(b) Publication of electronic filing requirements

Each court that permits electronic filing must publish, in both electronic and print formats, the court's electronic filing requirements.

(Subd (b) amended effective January 1, 2007.)

(c) Problems with electronic filing

If the court is aware of a problem that impedes or precludes electronic filing during the court's regular filing hours, it must promptly take reasonable steps to provide notice of the problem.

(Subd (c) amended effective January 1, 2007.)

(d) Public access to electronically filed documents

Except as provided in rules 2.250–2.260 and 2.500–2.506, an electronically filed document is a public document at the time it is filed unless it is sealed under rule 2.551(b) or made confidential by law.

(Subd (d) amended effective January 1, 2007.)

Rule 2.254 amended and renumbered effective January 1, 2007; adopted as rule 2054 effective January 1, 2003.

Ref.: Cal. Fms Pl. & Pr., Ch. 518, "Service of Summons and Papers"; MB Prac. Guide: Cal. Pretrial Proc., §27.35[2][a].

Rule 2.255.   Contracts with electronic filing service providers

(a) Right to contract

(1) A court may contract with one or more electronic filing service providers to furnish and maintain an electronic filing system for the court.

(2) If the court contracts with an electronic filing service provider, it may require electronic filers to transmit the documents to the provider.

(3) If there is a single provider or an in-house system, it must accept filing from other electronic filing service providers to the extent it is compatible with them.

(Subd (a) amended effective January 1, 2007.)

(b) Provisions of contract

The court's contract with an electronic filing service provider may allow the provider to charge electronic filers a reasonable fee in addition to the court's filing fee. The contract may also allow the electronic filing service provider to make other reasonable requirements for use of the electronic filing system.

(c) Transmission of filing to court

An electronic filing service provider must promptly transmit any electronic filing, with the applicable filing fee, to the court.

(d) Confirmation of receipt and filing of document

(1) An electronic filing service provider must promptly send to an electronic filer confirmation of the receipt of any document that the filer has transmitted to the provider for filing with the court.

(2) The electronic filing service provider must send its confirmation to the filer's electronic notification address and must indicate the date and time of receipt, in accordance with rule 2.259(a).

(3) After reviewing the documents, the court must promptly transmit to the electronic filing service provider and the electronic filer the court's confirmation of filing or notice of rejection of filing, in accordance with rule 2.259.

(Subd (d) amended effective January 1, 2007.)

(e) Ownership of information

All contracts between the court and electronic filing service providers must acknowledge that the court is the owner of the contents of the filing system and has the exclusive right to control the system's use.

(Subd (e) amended effective January 1, 2007.)

Rule 2.255 amended and renumbered effective January 1, 2007; adopted as rule 2055 effective January 1, 2003.

Advisory Committee Comment

The Court Technology Advisory Committee recommends that electronic filing service providers comply with the technical standards specified on the California Courts Web site at *www.courtinfo.ca.gov/programs/efiling/.* The committee anticipates that these rules may be amended to require compliance with the California Electronic Filing Technical Standards once the standards are sufficiently developed.

Ref.: Cal. Fms Pl. & Pr., Ch. 518, "Service of Summons and Papers"; MB Prac. Guide: Cal. Pretrial Proc., §§8.07, 27.35[3][k].

Rule 2.256.   Responsibilities of electronic filer

(a) Conditions of filing

Each electronic filer agrees to, and must:

(1) Comply with any court requirements designed to ensure the integrity of electronic filing and to protect sensitive personal information;

(2) Furnish information the court requires for case processing;

(3) Take all reasonable steps to ensure that the filing does not contain computer code, including viruses, that might be harmful to the court's electronic filing system and to other users of that system;

(4) Furnish one or more electronic notification addresses, in the manner specified by the court, at which the electronic filer agrees to accept service; and

(5) Immediately provide the court and all parties with any change to the electronic filer's electronic notification address.

(Subd (a) amended effective January 1, 2007.)

(b) Format of documents to be filed electronically

A document that is filed electronically with the court must be in a format specified by the court unless it cannot be created in that format. The format adopted by a court must meet the following requirements:

(1) The software for creating and reading documents must be in the public domain or generally available at a reasonable cost.

(2) By January 1, 2010, any format adopted by the court must allow for full text searching. Documents not available in a format that permits full text searching must be scanned or imaged as required by the court, unless the court orders that scanning or imaging would be unduly burdensome. By January 1, 2010, such scanning or imaging must allow for full text searching to the extent feasible.

(3) The printing of documents must not result in the loss of document text, format, or appearance.

If a document is filed electronically under the rules in this chapter and cannot be formatted to be consistent with a formatting rule elsewhere in the California Rules of Court, the rules in this chapter prevail.

(Subd (b) amended effective January 1, 2008; previously amended effective January 1, 2006.)

Rule 2.256 amended effective January 1, 2008; adopted as rule 2056 effective January 1, 2003; previously amended effective

January 1, 2006; previously amended and renumbered effective January 1, 2007.

Ref.: Cal. Fms Pl. & Pr., Ch. 190, "Discovery: Scope, Regulation, and Timing," Ch. 518, "Service of Summons and Papers"; MB Prac. Guide: Cal. Pretrial Proc., §27.35[2][b], [3][e].

Rule 2.257. Requirements for signatures on documents

(a) Documents signed under penalty of perjury

When a document to be filed electronically provides for a signature under penalty of perjury, the following applies:

(1) The document is deemed signed by the declarant if, before filing, the declarant has signed a printed form of the document.

(2) By electronically filing the document, the electronic filer certifies that (1) has been complied with and that the original, signed document is available for inspection and copying at the request of the court or any other party.

(3) At any time after the document is filed, any other party may serve a demand for production of the original signed document. The demand must be served on all other parties but need not be filed with the court.

(4) Within five days of service of the demand under (3), the party on whom the demand is made must make the original signed document available for inspection and copying by all other parties.

(5) At any time after the document is filed, the court may order the filing party to produce the original signed document in court for inspection and copying by the court. The order must specify the date, time, and place for the production and must be served on all parties.

(Subd (a) amended effective January 1, 2007.)

(b) Documents not signed under penalty of perjury

If a document does not require a signature under penalty of perjury, the document is deemed signed by the party if the document is filed electronically.

(Subd (b) amended effective January 1, 2007.)

(c) Documents requiring signatures of opposing parties

When a document to be filed electronically, such as a stipulation, requires the signatures of opposing parties, the following procedure applies:

(1) The party filing the document must obtain the signatures of all parties on a printed form of the document.

(2) The party filing the document must maintain the original, signed document and must make it available for inspection and copying as provided in (a)(2). The court and any other party may demand production of the original signed document in the manner provided in (a)(3)–(5).

(3) By electronically filing the document, the electronic filer indicates that all parties have signed the document and that the filer has the signed original in his or her possession.

(Subd (c) amended effective January 1, 2007.)

(d) Digital signature

A party is not required to use a digital signature on an electronically filed document.

(e) Judicial signatures

If a document requires a signature by a court or a judicial officer, the document may be electronically signed in any manner permitted by law.

(Subd (e) adopted effective January 1, 2008.)

Rule 2.257 amended effective January 1, 2008; adopted as rule 2057 effective January 1, 2003; previously amended and renumbered effective January 1, 2007.

Ref.: Cal. Fms Pl. & Pr., Ch. 1, "New Developments," Ch. 190, "Discovery: Scope, Regulation, and Timing," Ch. 372, "Motions and Orders," Ch. 518, "Service of Summons and Papers"; MB Prac. Guide: Cal. Pretrial Proc., §27.35[3][f]–[i], [4][g].

Rule 2.258. Payment of filing fees

(a) Use of credit cards and other methods

A court may permit the use of credit cards, debit cards, electronic fund transfers, or debit accounts for the payment of filing fees associated with electronic filing, as provided in Government Code section 6159, rule 10.820, and other applicable law. A court may also authorize other methods of payment.

(Subd (a) amended effective January 1, 2007.)

(b) Fee waivers

Eligible persons may seek a waiver of court fees and costs, as provided in Government Code section 68511.3, rule 2.252(c), and division 2 of title 3 of these rules.

(Subd (b) amended effective January 1, 2007.)

Rule 2.258 amended and renumbered effective January 1, 2007; adopted as rule 2058 effective January 1, 2003.

Ref.: Cal. Fms Pl. & Pr., Ch. 518, "Service of Summons and Papers"; MB Prac. Guide: Cal. Pretrial Proc., §27.35[3][j].

Rule 2.259. Actions by court on receipt of electronic filing

(a) Confirmation of receipt and filing of document

(1) *Confirmation of receipt*

When a court receives an electronically submitted document, the court must promptly send the electronic filer confirmation of the court's receipt of the document, indicating the date and time of receipt. A document is considered received at the date and time the confirmation of receipt is created.

(2) *Confirmation of filing*

If the document received by the court under (1) complies with filing requirements and all required filing fees have been paid, the court must promptly send the electronic filer confirmation that the document has been filed. The filing confirmation must indicate the date and time of filing and is proof that the document was filed on the date and at the time specified. The filing confirmation must also specify:

(A) Any transaction number associated with the filing;

(B) The titles of the documents as filed by the court; and

(C) The fees assessed for the filing.

(3) *Transmission of confirmations*

The court must send receipt and filing confirmation to the electronic filer at the electronic notification address the filer furnished to the court under rule 2.256(a)(4). The court must maintain a record of all receipt and filing confirmations.

(4) *Filer responsible for verification*

In the absence of the court's confirmation of receipt and filing, there is no presumption that the court received and filed the document. The electronic filer is responsible for verifying that the court received and filed any document that the electronic filer submitted to the court electronically.

(Subd (a) amended effective January 1, 2008; previously amended effective January 1, 2007.)

(b) Notice of rejection of document for filing

If the clerk does not file a document because it does not comply with applicable filing requirements or because the required filing fee has not been paid, the court must promptly send notice of the rejection of the document for filing to the electronic filer. The notice must state the reasons that the document was rejected for filing.

(Subd (b) amended effective January 1, 2007.)

(c) Document filed after close of business

A document that is filed electronically with the court after the close of business is deemed to have been filed on the next court day.

(Subd (c) amended effective January 1, 2007.)

(d) Delayed delivery

If a technical problem with a court's electronic filing system prevents the court from accepting an electronic filing during its regular filing hours on a particular court day, and the electronic filer demonstrates that he or she attempted to electronically file the document on that day, the court must deem the document as filed on that day. This subdivision does not apply to the filing of a complaint or any other initial pleading in an action or proceeding.

(Subd (d) amended effective January 1, 2007.)

(e) Endorsement

(1) The court's endorsement of a document electronically filed must contain the following: "Electronically filed by Superior Court of California, County of _____, on _____ (date)," followed by the name of the court clerk.

(2) The endorsement required under (1) has the same force and effect as a manually affixed endorsement stamp with the signature and initials of the court clerk.

(3) A complaint or another initial pleading in an action or proceeding that is filed and endorsed electronically may be printed and served on the defendant or respondent in the same manner as if it had been filed in paper form.

(Subd (e) amended effective January 1, 2007.)

(f) Issuance of electronic summons

(1) On the electronic filing of a complaint, a petition, or another document that must be served with a summons, the court may transmit a summons electronically to the electronic filer.

(2) The electronically transmitted summons must contain an image of the court's seal and the assigned case number.

(3) Personal service of the printed form of a summons transmitted electronically to the electronic filer has the same legal effect as personal service of a copy of an original summons.

(Subd (f) amended effective January 1, 2007.)

Rule 2.259 amended effective January 1, 2008; adopted as rule 2059 effective January 1, 2003; previously amended and renumbered effective January 1, 2007.

Ref.: Cal. Fms Pl. & Pr., Ch. 518, "Service of Summons and Papers"; MB Prac. Guide: Cal. Pretrial Proc., §§8.10, 27.35[3][*l*]–[p].

Rule 2.260.   Electronic service

(a) Consent to electronic service

(1) When a notice may be served by mail, express mail, overnight delivery, or fax transmission, electronic service of the notice is permitted when authorized by these rules.

(2) A party indicates that the party agrees to accept electronic service by:

(A) Filing and serving a notice that the party accepts electronic service. The notice must include the electronic notification address at which the party agrees to accept service; or

(B) Electronically filing any document with the court. The act of electronic filing is evidence that the party agrees to accept service at the electronic notification address the party has furnished to the court under rule 2.256(a)(4).

(3) A party that has consented to electronic service under (2) and has used an electronic filing service provider to file and serve documents in a case consents to service on that electronic filing service provider as the designated agent for service for the party in the case, until such time as the party designates a different agent for service.

(Subd (a) amended effective January 1, 2008; previously amended effective January 1, 2007.)

(b) Maintenance of electronic service lists

By January 1, 2009, or before if possible, a court that permits electronic filing in a case must maintain and make available electronically to the parties an electronic service list that contains the parties' current electronic notification addresses, as provided by the parties that have filed electronically in the case.

(Subd (b) adopted effective January 1, 2008.)

(c) Service by the parties

Notwithstanding (b), parties are responsible for electronic service on all other parties in the case. A party may serve documents electronically directly, by an agent, or through a designated electronic filing service provider.

(Subd (c) adopted effective January 1, 2008.)

(d) Change of electronic notification address

(1) A party whose electronic notification address changes while the action or proceeding is pending must promptly file a notice of change of address electronically with the court and must serve this notice electronically on all other parties.

(2) A party's election to contract with an electronic filing service provider to electronically file and serve documents or to receive electronic service of documents on the party's behalf does not relieve the party of its duties under (1).

(3) An electronic notification address is presumed valid for a party if the party files electronic documents with the court from that address and has not filed and served notice that the address is no longer valid.

(Subd (d) repealed and adopted effective January 1, 2008.)

(e) When service is complete

(1) Electronic service is complete at the time of transmission.

(2) If a document is served electronically, any period of notice, or any right or duty to act or respond within a specified period or on a date certain after service of the document, is extended by two court days.

(3) The extension under (2) does not extend the time for filing:

(A) A notice of intent to move for a new trial;

(B) A notice of intent to move to vacate the judgment under Code of Civil Procedure section 663a; or

(C) A notice of appeal.

(4) Service that occurs after the close of business is deemed to have occurred on the next court day.

(Subd (e) relettered effective January 1, 2008; adopted as subd (b) effective January 1, 2003; previously amended effective January 1, 2007.)

(f) Proof of service

(1) Proof of electronic service may be by any of the methods provided in Code of Civil Procedure section 1013(a), except that the proof of service must state:

(A) The electronic notification address of the person making the service, in [1] **addition to** that person's residence or business address;

(B) The date and time of the electronic service, instead of the date and place of deposit in the mail;

(C) The name and electronic notification address of the person served, in place of that person's name and address as shown on the envelope; and

(D) That the document was served electronically and the transmission was reported as complete and without error, in place of the statement that the envelope was sealed and deposited in the mail with postage fully prepaid.

(2) Proof of electronic service may be in electronic form and may be filed electronically with the court.

(3) Under rule 3.1300(c), proof of service of the moving papers must be filed at least five calendar days before the hearing.

(4) The party filing the proof of service must maintain the printed form of the document bearing the declarant's original signature and must make the document available for inspection and copying on the request of the court or any party to the action or proceeding in which it is filed, in the manner provided in rule 2.257(a).

(Subd (f) amended effective January 1, 2009; adopted as subd (c) effective January 1, 2003; previously amended effective January 1, 2007; previously relettered effective January 1, 2008.)

Rule 2.260(f).   2008 Deletes. [1] place of

(g) Electronic service by court

The court may electronically serve any notice, order, judgment, or other document issued by the court in the same manner that parties may serve documents by electronic service.

(Subd (g) relettered effective January 1, 2008; adopted as subd (e) effective January 1, 2003; previously amended effective January 1, 2007.)

Rule 2.260 amended effective January 1, 2009; adopted as rule 2060 effective January 1, 2003; previously amended and renumbered effective January 1, 2007; previously amended effective January 1, 2008.

Ref.: Cal. Fms Pl. & Pr., Ch. 190, "Discovery: Scope, Regulation, and Timing," Ch. 518, "Service of Summons and Papers"; MB Prac. Guide: Cal. Pretrial Proc., §§12.06[2][d], 27.03, 27.04[2], 27.07[3], [4], 27.35[4][a]–[g].

Rule 2.261.   Authorization for courts to continue modifying forms for the purpose of electronic filing and forms generation

Courts that participated in pilot projects for electronic filing and forms generation under former rule 981.5 are authorized to continue to modify Judicial Council forms for the purpose of accepting electronic filing or providing electronic generation of court documents provided that the modification of the forms is consistent with the rules in this chapter.

Rule 2.261 amended and renumbered effective January 1, 2007; adopted as rule 2061 effective July 1, 2004.

Chapter 3
Filing and Service by Fax

Rule 2.300.   Application

(a) Proceedings to which rules apply

The rules in this chapter apply to civil, probate, and family law proceedings in all trial courts. Rule 5.522 applies to fax filing in juvenile law proceedings.

(Subd (a) amended and lettered effective January 1, 2007; adopted as part of unlettered subd effective March 1, 1992.)

(b) Documents that may not be issued by fax

Notwithstanding any provision in the rules in this chapter, no will, codicil, bond, or undertaking may be filed by fax nor may a court issue by fax any document intended to carry the original seal of the court.

(Subd (b) amended and lettered effective January 1, 2007; adopted as part of unlettered subd effective March 1, 1992.)

Rule 2.300 amended and renumbered effective January 1, 2007; adopted as rule 2002 effective March 1, 1992; previously amended effective January 1, 1999.

Ref.: Cal. Fms Pl. & Pr., Ch. 206, "Demurrers and Motions for Judgment on the Pleadings," Ch. 264, "Fax Filing and Service of Papers," Ch. 518, "Service of Summons and Papers"; MB Prac. Guide: Cal. Pretrial Proc., §§11.03, 27.02, 27.34[5][a], [b].

Rule 2.301.   Definitions

As used in this chapter, unless the context otherwise requires:

(1) "Fax" is an abbreviation for "facsimile" and refers, as indicated by the context, to facsimile transmission or to a document so transmitted.

(2) "Fax transmission" means the transmission of a document by a system that encodes a document into electrical signals, transmits these electrical signals over a telephone line, and reconstructs the signals to print a duplicate of the original document at the receiving end.

(3) "Fax machine" means a machine that can send a facsimile transmission using the international standard for scanning, coding, and transmission established for Group 3 machines by the Consultative Committee of International Telegraphy and Telephone of the International

Telecommunications Union (CCITT),[1] in regular resolution. Any fax machine used to send documents to a court under rule 2.305 must send at an initial transmission speed of no less than 4800 baud and be able to generate a transmission record. "Fax machine" includes a fax modem that is connected to a personal computer.

(4) "Fax filing" means the fax transmission of a document to a court that accepts such documents.

(5) "Service by fax" means the transmission of a document to a party or the attorney for a party under the rules in this chapter.

(6) "Transmission record" means the document printed by the sending fax machine, stating the telephone number of the receiving fax machine, the number of pages sent, the transmission time and date, and an indication of any errors in transmission.

(7) "Fax filing agency" means an entity that receives documents by fax for processing and filing with the court.
Rule 2.301 amended and renumbered effective January 1, 2007; adopted as rule 2003 effective March 1, 1992.

Ref.: Cal. Fms Pl. & Pr., Ch. 95, "Banks, Deposits, and Checks," Ch. 137, "Continuing Duties During Litigation," Ch. 264, "Fax Filing and Service of Papers," Ch. 290H, "Guardianship and Conservatorship: Termination of Guardianships and Conservatorships"; MB Prac. Guide: Cal. Pretrial Proc., §27.34[1], [2][a].

Rule 2.302. Compliance with the rules on the form and format of papers

The document used for transmitting a fax must comply with the rules in division 2, chapter 1 of this title regarding form or format of papers. Any exhibit that exceeds 8-½ by 11 inches must be reduced in size to not more than 8-½ by 11 inches before it is transmitted. The court may require the filing party to file the original of an exhibit that the party has filed by fax.
Rule 2.302 amended and renumbered effective January 1, 2007; adopted as rule 2004 effective March 1, 1992.

Ref.: Cal. Fms Pl. & Pr., Ch. 264, "Fax Filing and Service of Papers"; MB Prac. Guide: Cal. Pretrial Proc., §27.34[2][b].

Rule 2.303. Filing through fax filing agency

(a) Transmission of document for filing

A party may transmit a document by fax to a fax filing agency for filing with any trial court. The agency acts as the agent of the filing party and not as an agent of the court.

(b) Duties of fax filing agency

The fax filing agency that receives a document for filing must:

(1) Prepare the document so that it complies with the rules in division 2, chapter 1 of this title and any other requirements for filing with the court;

(2) Physically transport the document to the court; and

(3) File the document with the court, paying any applicable filing fee.
(Subd (b) amended effective January 1, 2007.)

(c) Requirement of advance arrangements

A fax filing agency is not required to accept papers for filing from any party unless appropriate arrangements for payment of filing fees and service charges have been made in advance of any transmission to the agency. If an agency receives a document from a party with whom it does not have prior arrangements, the agency may discard the document without notice to the sender.
(Subd (c) amended effective January 1, 2007.)

(d) Confidentiality

A fax filing agency must keep all documents transmitted to it confidential except as provided in the rules in this chapter.
(Subd (d) amended effective January 1, 2007.)

(e) Certification

A fax filing agency, by filing a document with the court, certifies that it has complied with the rules in this chapter and that the document filed is the full and unaltered fax-produced document received by it. The agency is not required to give any additional certification.
(Subd (e) amended effective January 1, 2007.)

(f) Notation of fax filing

Each document filed by a fax filing agency must contain the phrase "By fax" immediately below the title of the document.
(Subd (f) amended effective January 1, 2007.)
Rule 2.303 amended and renumbered effective January 1, 2007; adopted as rule 2005 effective March 1, 1992.

Ref.: Cal. Fms Pl. & Pr., Ch. 264, "Fax Filing and Service of Papers"; MB Prac. Guide: Cal. Pretrial Proc., §27.34[5][d].

Rule 2.304. Direct filing

(a) Courts in which applicable

A party may file by fax directly to any court that, by local rule, has provided for direct fax filing. The local rule must state that direct fax filing may be made under the rules in this chapter and must provide the fax telephone number for filings and specific telephone numbers for any departments to which fax filings should be made directly. The court must also accept agency filings under rule 2.303.
(Subd (a) amended effective January 1, 2007.)

(b) Mandatory cover sheet

A party filing a document directly by fax must use the *Facsimile Transmission Cover Sheet (Fax Filing)* (form MC-005). The cover sheet must be the first page transmitted, to be followed by any special handling instructions needed to ensure that the document will comply with local rules. Neither the cover sheet nor the special handling instructions are to be filed in the case. The court must ensure that any credit card information on the cover sheet is not publicly disclosed. The court is not required to keep a copy of the cover sheet.
(Subd (b) amended effective January 1, 2007.)

(c) Notation of fax filing

Each document transmitted for direct filing with the court must contain the phrase "By fax" immediately below the title of the document.
(Subd (c) amended effective January 1, 2007.)

(d) Presumption of filing

[1] Recommendations T.4 and T.30, Volume VII—Facsimile VII.3, CCITT Red Book, Malaga-Torremolinos, 1984, U.N. Bookstore Code ITU 6731.

A party filing by fax must cause the transmitting fax machine to print a transmission record of each filing by fax. If the document transmitted to the court by fax machine is not filed with the court because of (1) an error in the transmission of the document to the court that was unknown to the sending party or (2) a failure to process the document after it has been received by the court, the sending party may move the court for an order filing the document nunc pro tunc. The motion must be accompanied by the transmission record and a proof of transmission in the following form:

"At the time of transmission I was at least 18 years of age and not a party to this legal proceeding. On (date) _____ at (time) _____, I transmitted to the (court name) _____ the following documents (name) _____ by fax machine, under California Rules of Court, rule 2.304. The court's fax telephone number that I used was (fax telephone number) _____. The fax machine I used complied with rule 2.301 and no error was reported by the machine. Under rule 2.304, I caused the machine to print a transmission record of the transmission, a copy of which is attached to this declaration.

"I declare under penalty of perjury under the laws of the State of California that the foregoing is true and correct."

(Subd (d) amended effective January 1, 2007.)

(e) Payment of fees by credit card

(1) *Credit or debit card payments*

The court may permit credit cards, debit cards, electronic funds transfers, or debit accounts to be used to pay filing fees for fax filings made directly with the court, as provided in Government Code section 6159, rule 10.820, and other applicable laws. The cover sheet for these filings must include (1) the credit or debit card account number to which the fees may be charged, (2) the signature of the cardholder authorizing the charging of the fees, and (3) the expiration date of the credit or debit card.

(2) *Rejection of charge*

If the charge is rejected by the credit or debit card issuing company, the court must proceed in the same manner as under Code of Civil Procedure section 411.20 relating to returned checks. This provision does not prevent a court from seeking authorization for the charge before the filing and rejecting the filing if the charge is not approved by the issuing company.

(3) *Amount of charge*

The amount charged is the applicable filing fee plus any fee or discount imposed by the card issuer or draft purchaser.

(Subd (e) amended effective January 1, 2007.)

(f) Filing fee accounts

If a court so provides in its local rule establishing a direct fax filing program, an account may be used to pay for documents filed by fax by an attorney or party who has established an account with the court before filing a paper by fax. The court may require the deposit in advance of an amount not to exceed $1,000, or the court may agree to bill the attorney or party not more often than monthly.

(Subd (f) amended effective January 1, 2007.)

Rule 2.304 amended and renumbered effective January 1, 2007; adopted as rule 2006 effective March 1, 1992; previously amended effective July 1, 2006.

Ref.: Cal. Fms Pl. & Pr., Ch. 1, "New Developments," Ch. 264, "Fax Filing and Service of Papers," Ch. 317, "Judges," Ch. 537, "Summary Judgment"; MB Prac. Guide: Cal. Pretrial Proc., §§27.29, 27.34[5][c], [d], 27.52.

Rule 2.305.   Requirements for signatures on documents

(a) Possession of original document

A party who files or serves a signed document by fax under the rules in this chapter represents that the original signed document is in the party's possession or control.

(Subd (a) amended effective January 1, 2007.)

(b) Demand for original; waiver

At any time after filing or service of a signed fax document, any other party may serve a demand for production of the original physically signed document. The demand must be served on all other parties but not filed with the court.

(Subd (b) amended effective January 1, 2007.)

(c) Examination of original

If a demand for production of the original signed document is made, the parties must arrange a meeting at which the original signed document can be examined.

(Subd (c) amended effective January 1, 2007.)

(d) Fax signature as original

Notwithstanding any provision of law to the contrary, including Evidence Code sections 255 and 260, a signature produced by fax transmission is deemed to be an original.

(Subd (d) amended effective January 1, 2007.)

Rule 2.305 amended and renumbered effective January 1, 2007; adopted as rule 2007 effective March 1, 1992.

Ref.: Cal. Fms Pl. & Pr., Ch. 264, "Fax Filing and Service of Papers"; MB Prac. Guide: Cal. Pretrial Proc., §27.34[4][a], [b].

Rule 2.306.   Service of papers by fax transmission

(a) Service by fax

(1) *Agreement of parties required*

Service by fax transmission is permitted only if the parties agree and a written confirmation of that agreement is made.

(2) *Service on last-given fax number*

Any notice or other document to be served must be transmitted to a fax machine maintained by the person on whom it is served at the fax machine telephone number as last given by that person on any document that the party has filed in the case and served on the party making service.

(Subd (a) amended and lettered effective January 1, 2007; adopted as part of subd (b) effective March 1, 1992.)

(b) Service lists

(1) *Duties of first-named plaintiff or petitioner*

In a case in which the parties have agreed to service by fax, the plaintiff or petitioner named first in the complaint or petition, in addition to its responsibilities under rule 3.254, must:

(A) Maintain a current list of the parties that includes their fax numbers for service of notice on each party; and

(B) Furnish a copy of the list on request to any party or the court.

(2) *Duties of each party*

In a case in which the parties have agreed to service by fax, each party, in addition to its responsibilities under rule 3.254, must:

(A) Furnish the first-named plaintiff or petitioner with the party's current fax number for service of notice when it first appears in the action; and

(B) If the party serves an order, notice, or pleading on a party that has not yet appeared in the action, serve a copy of the service list under (1) at the same time that the order, notice, or pleading is served.

(Subd (b) adopted effective January 1, 2008.)

(c) Transmission of papers by court

A court may serve any notice by fax in the same manner that parties may serve papers by fax.

(Subd (c) relettered effective January 1, 2008; adopted as subd (b) effective January 1, 2007.)

(d) Notice period extended

Except as provided in [1] (e), any prescribed period of notice and any right or duty to do any act or make any response within any prescribed period or on a date certain after the service of a document served by fax transmission is extended by two court days.

(Subd (d) amended effective July 1, 2008; adopted as part of subd (b) effective March 1, 1992; previously amended and lettered as subd (c) effective January 1, 2007; previously relettered as subd (d) effective January 1, 2008.)

Rule 2.306(d).   2008 Deletes. [1] (d)

(e) Extension inapplicable to certain motions

The extension provided in [1] (d) does not apply to extend the time for the filing of:

(1) A notice of intent to move for new trial;

(2) A notice of intent to move to vacate a judgment under Code of Civil Procedure section 663; or

(3) A notice of appeal.

(Subd (e) amended effective July 1, 2008; adopted as part of subd (b) effective March 1, 1992; previously amended and lettered as subd (d) effective January 1, 2007; previously relettered as subd (e) effective January 1, 2008.)

Rule 2.306(e).   2008 Deletes. [1] (c)

(f) Availability of fax

A party or attorney agreeing to accept service by fax must make his or her fax machine generally available for receipt of served documents between the hours of 9 a.m. and 5 p.m. on days that are not court holidays under Code of Civil Procedure section 136. This provision does not prevent the party or attorney from sending other documents by means of the fax machine or providing for normal repair and maintenance of the fax machine during these hours.

(Subd (f) relettered effective January 1, 2008; adopted as subd (c) effective March 1, 1992; previously amended and relettered as subd (e) effective January 1, 2007.)

(g) When service complete

Service by fax is complete on transmission of the entire document to the receiving party's fax machine. Service that is completed after 5 p.m. is deemed to have occurred on the next court day. Time is extended as provided by this rule.

(Subd (g) relettered effective January 1, 2008; adopted as subd (d) effective March 1, 1992; previously amended effective July 1, 1997; previously amended and relettered as subd (f) effective January 1, 2007.)

(h) Proof of service by fax

Proof of service by fax may be made by any of the methods provided in Code of Civil Procedure section 1013(a), except that:

(1) The time, date, and sending fax machine telephone number must be used instead of the date and place of deposit in the mail;

(2) The name and fax machine telephone number of the person served must be used instead of the name and address of the person served as shown on the envelope;

(3) A statement that the document was sent by fax transmission and that the transmission was reported as complete and without error must be used instead of the statement that the envelope was sealed and deposited in the mail with the postage thereon fully prepaid;

(4) A copy of the transmission report must be attached to the proof of service and the proof of service must declare that the transmission report was properly issued by the sending fax machine; and

(5) Service of papers by fax is ineffective if the transmission does not fully conform to these provisions.

(Subd (h) relettered effective January 1, 2008; adopted as subd (e) effective March 1, 1992; previously amended effective July 1, 1997, and May 1, 1998; previously amended and relettered as subd (g) effective January 1, 2007.)

Rule 2.306 amended effective July 1, 2008; adopted as rule 2008 effective March 1, 1992; previously amended effective July 1, 1997, May 1, 1998, and January 1, 2008; previously amended and renumbered effective January 1, 2007.

Ref.: Cal. Fms Pl. & Pr., Ch. 1, "New Developments," Ch. 206, "Demurrers and Motions for Judgment on the Pleadings," Ch. 264, "Fax Filing and Service of Papers," Ch. 518, "Service of Summons and Papers"; MB Prac. Guide: Cal. Pretrial Proc., §§27.29, 27.34[3], [5][b], [6][a], [b], [d], [e].

Division 4
Court Records

Chap. 1.   General Provisions. Rule 2.400.
Chap. 2.   Public Access to Electronic Trial Court Records. Rules 2.500–2.507.
Chap. 3.   Sealed Records. Rules 2.550, 2.551.
Chap. 4.   Records in False Claims Act Cases. Rules 2.570–2.573.
Chap. 5.   Other Sealed or Closed Records. Rules 2.580, 2.585.

Chapter 1
General Provisions

Rule 2.400.   Court records

(a) Removal of papers

Only the clerk may remove and replace papers in the court's files. Unless otherwise ordered by the court, filed papers may only be inspected by the public in the office of the clerk and released to [1] authorized court personnel **or an attorney of record** for use in a court facility. No original papers filed with the clerk may be used in any location other than a court facility, unless so ordered by the presiding judge.

(Subd (a) amended effective January 1, 2009; previously amended effective July 1, 1993, January 1, 2007, and January 1, 2008.)

Rule 2.400(a). 2008 Deletes. [1] a court officer or

(b) Original papers filed with the clerk; duplicate papers for temporary judge or referee

In a case pending before a temporary judge or referee, whether privately compensated or not, a party must tender and the clerk must accept for filing all original papers accompanied by the required fee within the time limits specified by law. The filing party must provide a filed-stamped copy to the temporary judge or referee of each paper relevant to the issues before the temporary judge or referee. When the paper may be filed without payment of a fee, instead of a filed-stamped copy, the filing party may use a true copy of the paper accompanied by a declaration about the date of its filing.

(Subd (b) amended effective January 1, 2007; adopted effective July 1, 1993.)

(c) Return of exhibits

(1) The clerk must not release any exhibit except on order of the court. The clerk must require a signed receipt for a released exhibit.

(2) If proceedings are conducted by a temporary judge or a referee outside of court facilities, the temporary judge or referee must keep all exhibits and deliver them, properly marked, to the clerk at the conclusion of the proceedings, unless the parties file a written stipulation that the exhibits may be disposed of otherwise. On request of the temporary judge or referee, the clerk must deliver exhibits to the possession of the temporary judge or referee, who must not release them to any person other than the clerk. Exhibits in the possession of the temporary judge or referee must be made available during business hours for inspection by any person within a reasonable time after request.

(Subd (c) amended effective January 1, 2007; adopted as subd (b) effective January 1, 1949; previously amended and relettered effective July 1, 1993.)
Rule 2.400 amended effective January 1, 2009; adopted as rule 243 effective January 1, 1949; previously amended and renumbered effective January 1, 2007; previously amended effective July 1, 1993, and January 1, 2008.

Ref.: Cal. Fms Pl. & Pr., Ch. 38, "Reference"; MB Prac. Guide: Cal. Pretrial Proc., §§25.10[1], 25.11[2][a]–[c].

Chapter 2
Public Access to Electronic Trial Court Records

Rule 2.500. Statement of purpose
Rule 2.501. Application and scope
Rule 2.502. Definitions
Rule 2.503. Public access
Rule 2.504. Limitations and conditions
Rule 2.505. Contracts with vendors
Rule 2.506. Fees for electronic access
Rule 2.507. Electronic access to court calendars, indexes, and registers of actions

Rule 2.500. Statement of purpose

(a) Intent

The rules in this chapter are intended to provide the public with reasonable access to trial court records that are maintained in electronic form, while protecting privacy interests.

(b) Benefits of electronic access

Improved technologies provide courts with many alternatives to the historical paper-based record receipt and retention process, including the creation and use of court records maintained in electronic form. Providing public access to trial court records that are maintained in electronic form may save the courts and the public time, money, and effort and encourage courts to be more efficient in their operations. Improved access to trial court records may also foster in the public a more comprehensive understanding of the trial court system.

(c) No creation of rights

The rules in this chapter are not intended to give the public a right of access to any record that they are not otherwise entitled to access. The rules do not create any right of access to records that are sealed by court order or confidential as a matter of law.

(Subd (c) amended effective January 1, 2007.)
Rule 2.500 amended and renumbered effective January 1, 2007; adopted as rule 2070 effective July 1, 2002.

Advisory Committee Comment

The rules in this chapter acknowledge the benefits that electronic court records provide but attempt to limit the potential for unjustified intrusions into the privacy of individuals involved in litigation that can occur as a result of remote access to electronic court records. The proposed rules take into account the limited resources currently available in the trial courts. It is contemplated that the rules may be modified to provide greater electronic access as the courts' technical capabilities improve and with the knowledge gained from the experience of the courts in providing electronic access under these rules.

Ref.: MB Prac. Guide: Cal. Pretrial Proc., §8.07.

Rule 2.501. Application and scope
(a) Application

The rules in this chapter apply only to trial court records.

(Subd (a) amended and relettered effective January 1, 2007; adopted as subd (b) effective July 1, 2002.)

(b) Access by parties and attorneys

The rules in this chapter apply only to access to court records by the public. They do not limit access to court records by a party to an action or proceeding, by the attorney of a party, or by other persons or entities that are entitled to access by statute or rule.

(Subd (b) amended and relettered effective January 1, 2007; adopted as subd (c) effective July 1, 2002.)
Rule 2.501 amended and renumbered effective January 1, 2007; adopted as rule 2017 effective July 1, 2002.

Rule 2.502. Definitions

As used in this chapter, the following definitions apply:

(1) "Court record" is any document, paper, or exhibit filed by the parties to an action or proceeding; any order or judgment of the court; and any item listed in Government Code section 68151(a), excluding any reporter's transcript for which the reporter is entitled to receive a fee for any copy. The term does not include the personal notes or

preliminary memoranda of judges or other judicial branch personnel.

(2) "Electronic record" is a computerized court record, regardless of the manner in which it has been computerized. The term includes both a document that has been filed electronically and an electronic copy or version of a record that was filed in paper form. The term does not include a court record that is maintained only on microfiche, paper, or any other medium that can be read without the use of an electronic device.

(3) "The public" means an individual, a group, or an entity, including print or electronic media, or the representative of an individual, a group, or an entity.

(4) "Electronic access" means computer access to court records available to the public through both public terminals at the courthouse and remotely, unless otherwise specified in the rules in this chapter.

Rule 2.502 amended and renumbered effective January 1, 2007; adopted as rule 2072 effective July 1, 2002.

Rule 2.503. Public access

(a) General right of access

All electronic records must be made reasonably available to the public in some form, whether in electronic or in paper form, except those that are sealed by court order or made confidential by law.

(Subd (a) amended effective January 1, 2007.)

(b) Electronic access required to extent feasible

A court that maintains the following records in electronic form must provide electronic access to them, both remotely and at the courthouse, to the extent it is feasible to do so:

(1) Registers of actions (as defined in Gov. Code, § 69845), calendars, and indexes in all cases; and

(2) All records in civil cases, except those listed in (c)(1)–(8).

(Subd (b) amended effective January 1, 2008; previously amended effective July 1, 2004, and January 1, 2007.)

(c) Courthouse electronic access only

A court that maintains the following records in electronic form must provide electronic access to them at the courthouse, to the extent it is feasible to do so, but may provide remote electronic access only to the records governed by (b):

(1) Records in a proceeding under the Family Code, including proceedings for dissolution, legal separation, and nullity of marriage; child and spousal support proceedings; child custody proceedings; and domestic violence prevention proceedings;

(2) Records in a juvenile court proceeding;

(3) Records in a guardianship or conservatorship proceeding;

(4) Records in a mental health proceeding;

(5) Records in a criminal proceeding;

(6) Records in a civil harassment proceeding under Code of Civil Procedure section 527.6;

(7) Records in a workplace violence prevention proceeding under Code of Civil Procedure section 527.8; and

(8) Records in an elder or dependent adult abuse prevention proceeding under Welfare and Institutions Code section 15657.03.

(Subd (c) amended effective January 1, 2008; previously amended effective July 1, 2004, and January 1, 2007.)

(d) "Feasible" defined

As used in this rule, the requirement that a court provide electronic access to its electronic records "to the extent it is feasible to do so" means that a court is required to provide electronic access to the extent it determines it has the resources and technical capacity to do so.

(Subd (d) amended effective January 1, 2007.)

(e) Remote electronic access allowed in extraordinary criminal cases

Notwithstanding (c)(5), the presiding judge of the court, or a judge assigned by the presiding judge, may exercise discretion, subject to (e)(1), to permit electronic access by the public to all or a portion of the public court records in an individual criminal case if (1) the number of requests for access to documents in the case is extraordinarily high and (2) responding to those requests would significantly burden the operations of the court. An individualized determination must be made in each case in which such remote electronic access is provided.

(1) In exercising discretion under (e), the judge should consider the relevant factors, such as:

(A) The privacy interests of parties, victims, witnesses, and court personnel, and the ability of the court to redact sensitive personal information;

(B) The benefits to and burdens on the parties in allowing remote electronic access, including possible impacts on jury selection; and

(C) The burdens on the court in responding to an extraordinarily high number of requests for access to documents.

(2) The court should, to the extent feasible, redact the following information from records to which it allows remote access under (e): driver license numbers; dates of birth; social security numbers; Criminal Identification and Information and National Crime Information numbers; addresses and phone numbers of parties, victims, witnesses, and court personnel; medical or psychiatric information; financial information; account numbers; and other personal identifying information. The court may order any party who files a document containing such information to provide the court with both an original unredacted version of the document for filing in the court file and a redacted version of the document for remote electronic access. No juror names or other juror identifying information may be provided by remote electronic access. This subdivision does not apply to any document in the original court file; it applies only to documents that are available by remote electronic access.

(3) Five days' notice must be provided to the parties and the public before the court makes a determination to provide remote electronic access under this rule. Notice to the public may be accomplished by posting notice on the court's Web site. Any person may file comments with the court for consideration, but no hearing is required.

(4) The court's order permitting remote electronic access must specify which court records will be available by remote electronic access and what categories of information are to be redacted. The court is not required to make findings of fact. The court's order must be posted on the court's Web site and a copy sent to the Judicial Council.

(Subd (e) amended effective January 1, 2007; adopted effective January 1, 2005.)

(f) Access only on a case-by-case basis

The court may only grant electronic access to an electronic record when the record is identified by the number of the case, the caption of the case, or the name of a party, and only on a case-by-case basis. This case-by-case limitation does not apply to the court's electronic records of a calendar, register of actions, or index.

(Subd (f) amended effective January 1, 2007; adopted as subd (e) effective July 1, 2002; previously relettered effective January 1, 2005.)

(g) Bulk distribution

The court may provide bulk distribution of only its electronic records of a calendar, register of actions, and index. "Bulk distribution" means distribution of all, or a significant subset, of the court's electronic records.

(Subd (g) amended effective January 1, 2007; adopted as subd (f) effective July 1, 2002; previously relettered effective January 1, 2005.)

(h) Records that become inaccessible

If an electronic record to which the court has provided electronic access is made inaccessible to the public by court order or by operation of law, the court is not required to take action with respect to any copy of the record that was made by the public before the record became inaccessible.

(Subd (h) relettered effective January 1, 2005; adopted as subd (g) effective July 1, 2002.)

(i) Off-site access

Courts should encourage availability of electronic access to court records at public off-site locations.

(Subd (i) relettered effective January 1, 2005; adopted as subd (h) effective July 1, 2002.)

Rule 2.503 amended effective January 1, 2008; adopted as rule 2073 effective July 1, 2002; previously amended effective July 1, 2004, and January 1, 2005; previously amended and renumbered effective January 1, 2007.

Advisory Committee Comment

The rule allows a level of access by the public to all electronic records that is at least equivalent to the access that is available for paper records and, for some types of records, is much greater. At the same time, it seeks to protect legitimate privacy concerns.

Subdivision (c). This subdivision excludes certain records (those other than the register, calendar, and indexes) in specified types of cases (notably criminal, juvenile, and family court matters) from remote electronic access. The committee recognized that while these case records are public records and should remain available at the courthouse, either in paper or electronic form, they often contain sensitive personal information. The court should not publish that information over the Internet. However, the committee also recognized that the use of the Internet may be appropriate in certain criminal cases of extraordinary public interest where information regarding a case will be widely disseminated through the media. In such cases, posting of selected nonconfidential court records, redacted where necessary to protect the privacy of the participants, may provide more timely and accurate information regarding the court proceedings, and may relieve substantial burdens on court staff in responding to individual requests for documents and information. Thus, under subdivision (e), if the presiding judge makes individualized determinations in a specific case, certain records in criminal cases may be made available over the Internet.

Subdivisions (f), (g). These subdivisions limit electronic access to records (other than the register, calendars, or indexes) to a case-by-case basis and prohibit bulk distribution of those records. These limitations are based on the qualitative difference between obtaining information from a specific case file and obtaining bulk information that may be manipulated to compile personal information culled from any document, paper, or exhibit filed in a lawsuit. This type of aggregate information may be exploited for commercial or other purposes unrelated to the operations of the courts, at the expense of privacy rights of individuals.

Courts must send a copy of the order permitting remote electronic access in extraordinary criminal cases to: Secretariat, Executive Office Programs Division, Administrative Office of the Courts, 455 Golden Gate Avenue, San Francisco, CA 94102-3688 or secretariat@jud.ca.gov.

Rule 2.504.   Limitations and conditions

(a) Means of access

A court that maintains records in electronic form must provide electronic access to those records by means of a network or software that is based on industry standards or is in the public domain.

(Subd (a) amended effective January 1, 2007.)

(b) Official record

Unless electronically certified by the court, a trial court record available by electronic access is not the official record of the court.

(Subd (b) amended effective January 1, 2007.)

(c) Conditions of use by persons accessing records

A court may condition electronic access to its records on:

(1) The user's consent to access the records only as instructed by the court; and

(2) The user's consent to the court's monitoring of access to its records.

The court must give notice of these conditions, in any manner it deems appropriate. The court may deny access to a member of the public for failure to comply with either of these conditions of use.

(Subd (c) amended effective January 1, 2007.)

(d) Notices to persons accessing records

The court must give notice of the following information to members of the public accessing its records electronically, in any manner it deems appropriate:

(1) The identity of the court staff member to be contacted about the requirements for accessing the court's records electronically.

(2) That copyright and other proprietary rights may apply to information in a case file, absent an express grant of additional rights by the holder of the copyright or other proprietary right. This notice must advise the public that:

(A) Use of such information in a case file is permissible only to the extent permitted by law or court order; and

(B) Any use inconsistent with proprietary rights is prohibited.

(3) Whether electronic records are the official records of the court. The notice must describe the procedure and any fee required for obtaining a certified copy of an official record of the court.

(4) That any person who willfully destroys or alters any court record maintained in electronic form is subject to the penalties imposed by Government Code section 6201.

(Subd (d) amended effective January 1, 2007.)

(e) Access policy

The court must post a privacy policy on its public-access Web site to inform members of the public accessing its electronic records of the information it collects regarding access transactions and the uses that the court may make of the collected information.

(Subd (e) amended effective January 1, 2007.)

Rule 2.504 amended and renumbered effective January 1, 2007; adopted as rule 2074 effective July 1, 2002.

Rule 2.505. Contracts with vendors

(a) Contract must provide access consistent with rules

The court's contract with a vendor to provide public access to its electronic records must be consistent with the rules in this chapter and must require the vendor to provide public access to court records and to protect the confidentiality of court records as required by law or by court order.

(Subd (a) amended and lettered effective January 1, 2007; adopted as part of unlettered subd effective July 1, 2002.)

(b) Contract must provide that court owns the records

Any contract between the court and a vendor to provide public access to the court's electronic records must provide that the court is the owner of these records and has the exclusive right to control their use.

(Subd (b) amended and lettered effective January 1, 2007; adopted as part of unlettered subd effective July 1, 2002.)

Rule 2.505 amended and renumbered effective January 1, 2007; adopted as rule 2075 effective July 1, 2002.

Rule 2.506. Fees for electronic access

(a) Court may impose fees

The court may impose fees for the costs of providing public access to its electronic records, under Government Code section 68150(h). On request, the court must provide the public with a statement of the costs on which these fees are based.

(Subd (a) amended and lettered effective January 1, 2007; adopted as part of unlettered subd effective July 1, 2002.)

(b) Fees of vendor must be reasonable

To the extent that public access to a court's electronic records is provided exclusively through a vendor, the court must ensure that any fees the vendor imposes for the costs of providing access are reasonable.

(Subd (b) lettered effective January 1, 2007; adopted as part of unlettered subd effective July 1, 2002.)

Rule 2.506 amended and renumbered effective January 1, 2007; adopted as rule 2076 effective July 1, 2002.

Rule 2.507. Electronic access to court calendars, indexes, and registers of actions

(a) Intent

This rule specifies information to be included in and excluded from the court calendars, indexes, and registers of actions to which public access is available by electronic means under rule 2.503(b). To the extent it is feasible to do so, the court must maintain court calendars, indexes, and registers of actions available to the public by electronic means in accordance with this rule.

(Subd (a) amended effective January 1, 2007.)

(b) Minimum contents for electronically accessible court calendars, indexes, and registers of actions

(1) The electronic court calendar must include:

(A) Date of court calendar;

(B) Time of calendared event;

(C) Court department number;

(D) Case number; and

(E) Case title (unless made confidential by law).

(2) The electronic index must include:

(A) Case title (unless made confidential by law);

(B) Party names (unless made confidential by law);

(C) Party type;

(D) Date on which the case was filed; and

(E) Case number.

(3) The register of actions must be a summary of every proceeding in a case, in compliance with Government Code section 69845, and must include:

(A) Date case commenced;

(B) Case number;

(C) Case type;

(D) Case title (unless made confidential by law);

(E) Party names (unless made confidential by law);

(F) Party type;

(G) Date of each activity; and

(H) Description of each activity.

(Subd (b) amended effective January 1, 2007.)

(c) Information that must be excluded from court calendars, indexes, and registers of actions

The following information must be excluded from a court's electronic calendar, index, and register of actions:

(1) Social security number;

(2) Any financial information;

(3) Arrest warrant information;

(4) Search warrant information;

(5) Victim information;

(6) Witness information;

(7) Ethnicity;

(8) Age;

(9) Gender;

(10) Government-issued identification card numbers (i.e., military);

(11) Driver's license number; and

(12) Date of birth.

(Subd (c) amended effective January 1, 2007.)

Rule 2.507 amended and renumbered effective January 1, 2007; adopted as rule 2077 effective July 1, 2003.

Chapter 3
Sealed Records

Rule 2.550. Sealed records
Rule 2.551. Procedures for filing records under seal

Rule 2.550. Sealed records

(a) Application

(1) Rules 2.550–2.551 apply to records sealed or proposed to be sealed by court order.

(2) These rules do not apply to records that are required to be kept confidential by law.

(3) These rules do not apply to discovery motions and records filed or lodged in connection with discovery motions or proceedings. However, the rules do apply to discovery materials that are used at trial or submitted as a basis for adjudication of matters other than discovery motions or proceedings.

(Subd (a) amended effective January 1, 2007.)

(b) Definitions

As used in this chapter:

(1) "Record." Unless the context indicates otherwise, "record" means all or a portion of any document, paper, exhibit, transcript, or other thing filed or lodged with the court.

(2) "Sealed." A "sealed" record is a record that by court order is not open to inspection by the public.

(3) "Lodged." A "lodged" record is a record that is temporarily placed or deposited with the court, but not filed.

(Subd (b) amended effective January 1, 2007.)

(c) Court records presumed to be open

Unless confidentiality is required by law, court records are presumed to be open.

(d) Express factual findings required to seal records

The court may order that a record be filed under seal only if it expressly finds facts that establish:

(1) There exists an overriding interest that overcomes the right of public access to the record;

(2) The overriding interest supports sealing the record;

(3) A substantial probability exists that the overriding interest will be prejudiced if the record is not sealed;

(4) The proposed sealing is narrowly tailored; and

(5) No less restrictive means exist to achieve the overriding interest.

(Subd (d) amended effective January 1, 2004.)

(e) Content and scope of the order

(1) An order sealing the record must:

(A) Specifically state the facts that support the findings; and

(B) Direct the sealing of only those documents and pages, or, if reasonably practicable, portions of those documents and pages, that contain the material that needs to be placed under seal. All other portions of each document or page must be included in the public file.

(2) Consistent with Code of Civil Procedure sections 639 and 645.1, if the records that a party is requesting be placed under seal are voluminous, the court may appoint a referee and fix and allocate the referee's fees among the parties.

(Subd (e) amended effective January 1, 2007; previously amended effective January 1, 2004.)

Rule 2.550 amended and renumbered effective January 1, 2007; adopted as rule 243.1 effective January 1, 2001; previously amended effective January 1, 2004.

Advisory Committee Comment

This rule and rule 2.551 provide a standard and procedures for courts to use when a request is made to seal a record. The standard is based on *NBC Subsidiary (KNBC-TV), Inc. v. Superior Court* (1999) 20 Cal.4th 1178. These rules apply to civil and criminal cases. They recognize the First Amendment right of access to

documents used at trial or as a basis of adjudication. The rules do not apply to records that courts must keep confidential by law. Examples of confidential records to which public access is restricted by law are records of the family conciliation court (Family Code, § 1818(b)), in forma pauperis applications (Cal. Rules of Court, rule 985(h)), and search warrant affidavits sealed under *People v. Hobbs* (1994) 7 Cal.4th 948. The sealed records rules also do not apply to discovery proceedings, motions, and materials that are not used at trial or submitted to the court as a basis for adjudication. (See *NBC Subsidiary, supra,* 20 Cal.4th at pp. 1208–1209, fn. 25.)

Rule 2.550(d)–(e) is derived from *NBC Subsidiary.* That decision contains the requirements that the court, before closing a hearing or sealing a transcript, must find an "overriding interest" that supports the closure or sealing, and must make certain express findings. (*Id.* at pp. 1217–1218.) The decision notes that the First Amendment right of access applies to records filed in both civil and criminal cases as a basis for adjudication. (*Id.* at pp. 1208–1209, fn. 25.) Thus, the *NBC Subsidiary* test applies to the sealing of records.

NBC Subsidiary provides examples of various interests that courts have acknowledged may constitute "overriding interests." (See *id.* at p. 1222, fn. 46.) Courts have found that, under appropriate circumstances, various statutory privileges, trade secrets, and privacy interests, when properly asserted and not waived, may constitute "overriding interests." The rules do not attempt to define what may constitute an "overriding interest," but leave this to case law.

Ref.: Cal. Fms Pl. & Pr., Ch. 38, "Reference," Ch. 44, "Appeal: Preparing and Filing the Record," Ch. 190, "Discovery: Scope, Regulation, and Timing," Ch. 221, "Dissolution of Marriage: Procedure," Ch. 551, "Trial"; MB Prac. Guide: Cal. Trial & Post-Trial Civ. Proc., §§1.11, 2.11[1], [2], 2.12, 2.13, 2.14[1]–[5], 2.17[3][a], [b], [6], 2.18[1], [2], 2.19[1], [4][b], 2.20[1], [2], [5], 2.24[5], [6], 2.29[1], [2], 2.56, 2.57, 4.19[2][b], 11.52, 11.54[2][a]; MB Prac. Guide: Cal. Pretrial Proc., §37.31[2][f].

Rule 2.551.   Procedures for filing records under seal

(a) Court approval required

A record must not be filed under seal without a court order. The court must not permit a record to be filed under seal based solely on the agreement or stipulation of the parties.

(Subd (a) amended effective January 1, 2007.)

(b) Motion or application to seal a record

(1) *Motion or application required*

A party requesting that a record be filed under seal must file a motion or an application for an order sealing the record. The motion or application must be accompanied by a memorandum and a declaration containing facts sufficient to justify the sealing.

(2) *Service of motion or application*

A copy of the motion or application must be served on all parties that have appeared in the case. Unless the court orders otherwise, any party that already possesses copies of the records to be placed under seal must be served with a complete, unredacted version of all papers as well as a redacted version.

(3) *Procedure for party not intending to file motion or application*

(A) A party that files or intends to file with the court, for the purposes of adjudication or to use at trial, records produced in discovery that are subject to a confidentiality agreement or protective order, and does not intend to request to have the records sealed, must:

(i) Lodge the unredacted records subject to the confidentiality agreement or protective order and any pleadings, memorandums, declarations, and other documents that disclose the contents of the records, in the manner stated in (d);

(ii) File copies of the documents in (i) that are redacted so that they do not disclose the contents of the records that are subject to the confidentiality agreement or protective order; and

(iii) Give written notice to the party that produced the records that the records and the other documents lodged under (i) will be placed in the public court file unless that party files a timely motion or application to seal the records under this rule.

(B) If the party that produced the documents and was served with the notice under (A)(iii) fails to file a motion or an application to seal the records within 10 days or to obtain a court order extending the time to file such a motion or an application, the clerk must promptly remove all the documents in (A)(i) from the envelope or container where they are located and place them in the public file. If the party files a motion or an application to seal within 10 days or such later time as the court has ordered, these documents are to remain conditionally under seal until the court rules on the motion or application and thereafter are to be filed as ordered by the court.

(4) *Lodging of record pending determination of motion or application*

The party requesting that a record be filed under seal must lodge it with the court under (d) when the motion or application is made, unless good cause exists for not lodging it or the record has previously been lodged under (3)(A)(i). Pending the determination of the motion or application, the lodged record will be conditionally under seal.

(5) *Redacted and unredacted versions*

If necessary to prevent disclosure, any motion or application, any opposition, and any supporting documents must be filed in a public redacted version and lodged in a complete version conditionally under seal.

(6) *Return of lodged record*

If the court denies the motion or application to seal, the clerk must return the lodged record to the submitting party and must not place it in the case file unless that party notifies the clerk in writing within 10 days after the order denying the motion or application that the record is to be filed.

(Subd (b) amended effective January 1, 2007; previously amended effective January 1, 2004.)

(c) References to nonpublic material in public records

A record filed publicly in the court must not disclose material contained in a record that is sealed, conditionally under seal, or subject to a pending motion or an application to seal.

(Subd (c) amended effective January 1, 2004.)

(d) Procedure for lodging of records

(1) A record that may be filed under seal must be put in an envelope or other appropriate container, sealed in the envelope or container, and lodged with the court.

(2) The envelope or container lodged with the court must be labeled "CONDITIONALLY UNDER SEAL."

(3) The party submitting the lodged record must affix to the envelope or container a cover sheet that:

(A) Contains all the information required on a caption page under rule 2.111; and

(B) States that the enclosed record is subject to a motion or an application to file the record under seal.

(4) On receipt of a record lodged under this rule, the clerk must endorse the affixed cover sheet with the date of its receipt and must retain but not file the record unless the court orders it filed.

(Subd (d) amended effective January 1, 2007; previously amended effective January 1, 2004.)

(e) Order

(1) If the court grants an order sealing a record, the clerk must substitute on the envelope or container for the label required by (d)(2) a label prominently stating "SEALED BY ORDER OF THE COURT ON *(DATE)*," and must replace the cover sheet required by (d)(3) with a filed-endorsed copy of the court's order.

(2) The order must state whether—in addition to records in the envelope or container—the order itself, the register of actions, any other court records, or any other records relating to the case are to be sealed.

(3) The order must state whether any person other than the court is authorized to inspect the sealed record.

(4) Unless the sealing order provides otherwise, it prohibits the parties from disclosing the contents of any materials that have been sealed in any subsequently filed records or papers.

(Subd (e) amended effective January 1, 2007; previously amended effective January 1, 2004.)

(f) Custody of sealed records

Sealed records must be securely filed and kept separate from the public file in the case.

(Subd (f) amended effective January 1, 2004.)

(g) Custody of voluminous records

If the records to be placed under seal are voluminous and are in the possession of a public agency, the court may by written order direct the agency instead of the clerk to maintain custody of the original records in a secure fashion. If the records are requested by a reviewing court, the trial court must order the public agency to deliver the records to the clerk for transmission to the reviewing court under these rules.

(h) Motion, application, or petition to unseal records

(1) A sealed record must not be unsealed except on order of the court.

(2) A party or member of the public may move, apply, or petition, or the court on its own motion may move, to unseal a record. Notice of any motion, application, or petition to unseal must be filed and served on all parties in the case. The motion, application, or petition and any opposition, reply, and supporting documents must be filed in a public redacted version and a sealed complete version if necessary to comply with (c).

(3) If the court proposes to order a record unsealed on its own motion, the court must mail notice to the parties stating the reason therefor. Any party may serve and file an opposition within 10 days after the notice is mailed or within such time as the court specifies. Any other party

may file a response within 5 days after the filing of an opposition.

(4) In determining whether to unseal a record, the court must consider the matters addressed in rule 2.550(c)–(e).

(5) The order unsealing a record must state whether the record is unsealed entirely or in part. If the court's order unseals only part of the record or unseals the record only as to certain persons, the order must specify the particular records that are unsealed, the particular persons who may have access to the record, or both. If, in addition to the records in the envelope or container, the court has previously ordered the sealing order, the register of actions, or any other court records relating to the case to be sealed, the unsealing order must state whether these additional records are unsealed.

(Subd (h) amended effective January 1, 2007; previously amended effective January 1, 2004.)

Rule 2.551 amended and renumbered effective January 1, 2007; adopted as rule 243.2 effective January 1, 2001; previously amended effective January 1, 2004.

Ref.: Cal. Fms Pl. & Pr., Ch. 38, "Reference," Ch. 44, "Appeal: Preparing and Filing the Record," Ch. 221, "Dissolution of Marriage: Procedure," Ch. 372, "Motions and Orders," Ch. 518, "Service of Summons and Papers," Ch. 551, "Trial"; MB Prac. Guide: Cal. Pretrial Proc., §37.31[2][f]; MB Prac. Guide: Cal. Trial & Post-Trial Civ. Proc., §§2.11[1], [2], 2.14[2], 2.15, 2.17[1], [2], [3][a], [b], [5][a]–[g], 2.19[3], 2.20[3]–[5], 2.21[1], [2], 2.22[1]–[3], 2.24[1], [2], [3][a], [4][a], [b], [5], 2.25[1], [3], 2.26, 2.29[2], 2.56, 2.57, 4.19[2][b].

Chapter 4
Records in False Claims Act Cases

Rule 2.570. Filing False Claims Act records under seal
Rule 2.571. Procedures for filing records under seal in a False Claims Act case
Rule 2.572. Ex parte application for an extension of time
Rule 2.573. Unsealing of records and management of False Claims Act cases

Rule 2.570. Filing False Claims Act records under seal

(a) Application

Rules 2.570–2.573 apply to records initially filed under seal pursuant to the False Claims Act, Government Code section 12650 et seq. As to these records, rules 2.550–2.551 on sealed records do not apply.

(Subd (a) amended effective January 1, 2007.)

(b) Definitions

As used in this chapter, unless the context or subject matter otherwise requires:

(1) "Attorney General" means the Attorney General of the State of California.

(2) "Prosecuting authority" means the county counsel, city attorney, or other local government official charged with investigating, filing, and conducting civil legal proceedings on behalf of or in the name of a particular political subdivision.

(3) *"Qui tam* plaintiff" means a person who files a complaint under the False Claims Act.

(4) The definitions in Government Code section 12650 apply to the rules in this chapter.

(Subd (b) amended effective January 1, 2007.)

(c) Confidentiality of records filed under the False Claims Act

Records of actions filed by a *qui tam* plaintiff must initially be filed as confidential and under seal as required by Government Code section 12652(c). Until the seal is lifted, the records in the action must remain under seal, except to the extent otherwise provided in this rule.

(d) Persons permitted access to sealed records in a False Claims Act case

(1) *Public access prohibited*

As long as the records in a False Claims Act case are under seal, public access to the records in the case is prohibited. The prohibition on public access applies not only to filed documents but also to electronic records that would disclose information about the case, including the identity of any plaintiff or defendant.

(2) *Information on register of actions*

As long as the records in a False Claims Act case are under seal, only the information concerning filed records contained on the confidential cover sheet prescribed under rule 2.571(c) may be entered into the register of actions that is accessible to the public.

(3) *Parties permitted access to the sealed court file*

As long as the records in a False Claims Act case are under seal, the only parties permitted access to the court file are:

(A) The Attorney General;

(B) A prosecuting authority for the political subdivision on whose behalf the action is brought, unless the political subdivision is named as a defendant; and

(C) A prosecuting authority for any other political subdivision interested in the matter whose identity has been provided to the court by the Attorney General.

(4) *Parties not permitted access to the sealed court file*

As long as records in a False Claims Act case are under seal, no defendant is permitted to have access to the court records or other information concerning the case. Defendants not permitted access include any political subdivision that has been named as a defendant in a False Claims Act action.

(5) Qui tam *plaintiff's limited access to sealed court file*

The *qui tam* plaintiff in a False Claims Act case may have access to all documents filed by the *qui tam* plaintiff and to such other documents as the court may order.

(Subd (d) amended effective January 1, 2007.)

Rule 2.570 amended and renumbered effective January 1, 2007; adopted as rule 243.5 effective July 1, 2002.

Rule 2.571. Procedures for filing records under seal in a False Claims Act case

(a) No sealing order required

On the filing of an action under the False Claims Act, the complaint, motions for extensions of time, and other papers filed with the court must be kept under seal. Under Government Code section 12652, no order sealing these records is necessary.

(Subd (a) amended effective January 1, 2007.)

(b) Filing a False Claims Act case in a county where filings are accepted in multiple locations

In a county where complaints in civil cases may be filed in more than one location, the presiding judge must designate one particular location where all filings in False Claims Act cases must be made.

(Subd (b) amended effective January 1, 2007.)

(c) Special cover sheet omitting names of the parties

In a False Claims Act case, the complaint and every other paper filed while the case is under seal must have a completed *Confidential Cover Sheet—False Claims Action* (form MC-060) affixed to the first page.

(Subd (c) amended effective January 1, 2007.)

(d) Filing of papers under seal

When the complaint or other paper in a False Claims Act case is filed under seal, the clerk must stamp both the cover sheet and the caption page of the paper.

(Subd (d) amended effective January 1, 2007.)

(e) Custody of sealed records

Records in a False Claims Act case that are confidential and under seal must be securely filed and kept separate from the public file in the case.

(Subd (e) amended effective January 1, 2007.)

Rule 2.571 amended and renumbered effective January 1, 2007; adopted as rule 243.6 effective July 1, 2002.

Rule 2.572. Ex parte application for an extension of time

A party in a False Claims Act case may apply under the ex parte rules in title 3 for an extension of time under Government Code section 12652.

Rule 2.572 amended and renumbered effective January 1, 2007; adopted as rule 243.7 effective July 1, 2002.

Rule 2.573. Unsealing of records and management of False Claims Act cases

(a) Expiration or lifting of seal

(1) Records in a False Claims Act case to which public access has been prohibited under Government Code section 12652(c) must remain under seal until the Attorney General and all local prosecuting authorities involved in the action have notified the court of their decision to intervene or not intervene.

(2) The Attorney General and all local prosecuting authorities involved in the action must give the notice required under (1) within 60 days of the filing of the complaint or before an order extending the time to intervene has expired, unless a new motion to extend time to intervene is pending, in which case the seal remains in effect until a ruling is made on the motion.

(Subd (a) amended effective January 1, 2007.)

(b) Coordination of state and local authorities

The Attorney General and all local prosecuting authorities must coordinate their activities to provide timely and effective notice to the court that:

(1) A political subdivision or subdivisions remain interested in the action and have not yet determined whether to intervene; or

(2) The seal has been extended by the filing or grant of a motion to extend time to intervene, and therefore the seal has not expired.

(Subd (b) amended effective January 1, 2007.)

(c) Designation of lead local prosecuting authority

In a False Claims Act case in which the Attorney General is not involved or has declined to intervene and local prosecuting authorities remain interested in the action, the court may designate a lead prosecuting authority to keep the court apprised of whether all the prosecuting authorities have either intervened or declined to intervene, and whether the seal is to be lifted.

(d) Order unsealing record

The Attorney General or other prosecuting authority filing a notice of intervention or nonintervention must submit a proposed order indicating the documents that are to be unsealed or to remain sealed.

(e) Case management

(1) *Case management conferences*

The court, at the request of the parties or on its own motion, may hold a conference at any time in a False Claims Act case to determine what case management is appropriate for the case, including the lifting or partial lifting of the seal, the scheduling of trial and other events, and any other matters that may assist in managing the case.

(2) *Exemption from case management rules*

Cases under the False Claims Act are exempt from rule 3.110 and the case management rules in title 3, division 7, but are subject to such case management orders as the court may issue.

(Subd (e) amended effective January 1, 2007.)

Rule 2.573 amended and renumbered effective January 1, 2007; adopted as rule 243.8 effective July 1, 2002.

Ref.: Cal. Fms Pl. & Pr., Ch. 372, "Motions and Orders."

Chapter 5
Other Sealed or Closed Records

Rule 2.580. Request for delayed public disclosure
Rule 2.585. Confidential in-camera proceedings

Rule 2.580. Request for delayed public disclosure

In an action in which the prejudgment attachment remedy under Code of Civil Procedure section 483.010 et seq. is sought, if the plaintiff requests at the time a complaint is filed that the records in the action or the fact of the filing of the action be made temporarily unavailable to the public under Code of Civil Procedure section 482.050, the plaintiff must file a declaration stating one of the following:

(1) "This action is on a claim for money based on contract against a defendant who is not a natural person. The claim is not secured within the meaning of Code of Civil Procedure section 483.010(b)."—or—

(2) "This action is on a claim for money based on contract against a defendant who is a natural person. The claim arises out of the defendant's conduct of a trade, business, or profession, and the money, property, or services were not used by the defendant primarily for personal, family, or household purposes. The claim is not secured within the meaning of Code of Civil Procedure section 483.010(b)."

Rule 2.580 renumbered effective January 1, 2007; adopted as rule 243.3 effective January 1, 2001.

Ref.: Cal. Fms Pl. & Pr., Ch. 44, "Appeal: Preparing and Filing the Record," Ch. 62, "Attachment," Ch. 551, "Trial"; MB Prac. Guide: Cal. Trial & Post-Trial Civ. Proc., §§2.27, 2.28.

Rule 2.585.   Confidential in-camera proceedings

(a) Minutes of proceedings

If a confidential in-camera proceeding is held in which a party is excluded from being represented, the clerk must include in the minutes the nature of the hearing and only such references to writings or witnesses as will not disclose privileged information.

(b) Disposition of examined records

Records examined by the court in confidence under (a), or copies of them, must be filed with the clerk under seal and must not be disclosed without court order.

Rule 2.585 renumbered effective January 1, 2007; adopted as rule 243.4 effective January 1, 2001.

Ref.: Cal. Fms Pl. & Pr., Ch. 551, "Trial."

Division 5
Venue and Sessions

Chap. 1.   Venue [Reserved]. Rule 2.700.
Chap. 2.   Sessions [Reserved].

Chapter 1
Venue
[Reserved]

Rule 2.700.   Intracounty venue [Reserved]

Rule 2.700 adopted effective January 1, 2007.

Chapter 2
Sessions
[Reserved]

Division 6
Appointments by the Court or Agreement of the Parties

Chap. 1.   Court-Appointed Temporary Judges. Rules 2.810–2.819.
Chap. 2.   Temporary Judges Requested by the Parties. Rules 2.830–2.834.
Chap. 3.   Referees [Reserved].
Chap. 4.   Court Interpreters. Rules 2.890–2.894.

Chapter 1
Court-Appointed Temporary Judges

Rule 2.810. Temporary judges appointed by the trial courts

Rule 2.811. Court appointment of temporary judges
Rule 2.812. Requirements for court appointment of an attorney to serve as a temporary judge
Rule 2.813. Contents of training programs
Rule 2.814. Appointment of temporary judge
Rule 2.815. Continuing education
Rule 2.816. Stipulation to court-appointed temporary judge
Rule 2.817. Disclosures to the parties
Rule 2.818. Disqualifications and limitations
Rule 2.819. Continuing duty to disclose and disqualify

Rule 2.810.   Temporary judges appointed by the trial courts

(a) Scope of rules

Rules 2.810–2.819 apply to attorneys who serve as court-appointed temporary judges in the trial courts. The rules do not apply to subordinate judicial officers [1] or to attorneys designated by the courts to serve as temporary judges at the parties' request.

(Subd (a) amended effective January 1, 2009; previously amended effective January 1, 2007.)

Rule 2.810(a).   2008 Deletes. [1] , to retired judicial officers appointed by the courts to serve as temporary judges,

(b) Definition of "court-appointed temporary judge"

A "court-appointed temporary judge" means an attorney who has satisfied the requirements for appointment under rule 2.812 and has been appointed by the court to serve as a temporary judge in that court.

(Subd (b) amended effective January 1, 2007.)

(c) Appointment of attorneys as temporary judges

Trial courts may appoint an attorney as a temporary judge only if the attorney has satisfied the requirements of rule 2.812.

(Subd (c) amended effective January 1, 2007.)

(d) Exception for extraordinary circumstances

A presiding judge may appoint an attorney who is qualified under 2.812(a), but who has not satisfied the other requirements of that rule, only in case of extraordinary circumstances. Any appointment under this subdivision based on extraordinary circumstances must be made before the attorney serves as a temporary judge, must be recorded for reporting purposes under rule 10.742(c)(3), and must not last more than 10 court days in a three-year period.

(Subd (d) amended effective January 1, 2007.)
Rule 2.810 amended effective January 1, 2009; adopted as rule 243.11 effective July 1, 2006; previously amended and renumbered effective January 1, 2007.

Ref.: Cal. Fms Pl. & Pr., Ch. 1, "New Developments," Ch. 317, "Judges," Ch. 526, "Small Claims."

Rule 2.811.   Court appointment of temporary judges

(a) Purpose of court appointment

The purpose of court appointment of attorneys as temporary judges is to assist the public by providing the court with a panel of trained, qualified, and experienced attorneys who may serve as temporary judges at the discretion of the court if the court needs judicial assistance that it cannot provide using its full-time judicial officers.

(b) Appointment and service discretionary

Court-appointed attorneys are appointed and serve as temporary judges solely at the discretion of the presiding judge.

(c) No employment relationship

Court appointment and service of an attorney as a temporary judge do not establish an employment relationship between the court and the attorney.

(d) Responsibility of the presiding judge for appointments

The appointment of attorneys to serve as temporary judges is the responsibility of the presiding judge, who may designate another judge or committee of judges to perform this responsibility. In carrying out this responsibility, the presiding judge is assisted by a Temporary Judge Administrator as prescribed by rule 10.743.

(Subd (d) amended effective January 1, 2007.)

Rule 2.811 amended and renumbered effective January 1, 2007; adopted as rule 243.12 effective July 1, 2006.

Ref.: Cal. Fms Pl. & Pr., Ch. 317, "Judges."

Rule 2.812.   Requirements for court appointment of an attorney to serve as a temporary judge

(a) Experience required for appointment and service

The presiding judge may not appoint an attorney to serve as a temporary judge unless the attorney has been admitted to practice as a member of the State Bar of California for at least 10 years before the appointment. However, for good cause, the presiding judge may permit an attorney who has been admitted to practice for at least 5 years to serve as a temporary judge.

(b) Conditions for appointment by the court

The presiding judge may appoint an attorney to serve as a temporary judge only if the attorney:

(1) Is a member in good standing of the State Bar and has no disciplinary action pending;

(2) Has not pled guilty or no contest to a felony, or has not been convicted of a felony that has not been reversed;

(3) Has satisfied the education and training requirements in (c);

(4) Has satisfied all other general conditions that the court may establish for appointment of an attorney as a temporary judge in that court; and

(5) Has satisfied any additional conditions that the court may require for an attorney to be appointed as a temporary judge for a particular assignment or type of case in that court.

(c) Education and training requirements

The presiding judge may appoint an attorney to serve as a temporary judge only if the following minimum training requirements are satisfied:

(1) *Mandatory training on bench conduct and demeanor*

Before appointment, the attorney must have attended and successfully completed, within the previous three years, a course of at least 3 [1] **hours'** duration on the subjects identified in rule 2.813(a) approved by the court in which the attorney will serve. This course must be taken in person and be taught by a qualified judicial officer [2].

(2) *Mandatory training in ethics*

Before appointment, the attorney must have attended and successfully completed, within the previous three years, a course of at least 3 [3] **hours'** duration on the

subjects identified in rule 2.813(b) approved by the court in which the attorney will serve. This course may be taken by any means approved by the court, including in-person, by broadcast with participation, or online.

(3) *Substantive training*

Before appointment, the attorney must have attended and successfully completed, within the previous three years, a course on the substantive law in each subject area in which the attorney will serve as a temporary judge. These courses may be taken by any means approved by the court, including in-person, by broadcast with participation, or online. The substantive courses have the following minimum requirements:

(A) *Small claims*

An attorney serving as a temporary judge in small claims cases must have attended and successfully completed, within the previous three years, a course of at least 3 [4] **hours'** duration on the subjects identified in rule 2.813(c) approved by the court in which the attorney will serve.

(B) *Traffic*

An attorney serving as a temporary judge in traffic cases must have attended and completed, within the previous three years, a course of at least 3 [5] **hours'** duration on the subjects identified in rule 2.813(d) approved by the court in which the attorney will serve.

(C) *Other subject areas*

If the court assigns attorneys to serve as temporary judges in other substantive areas such as civil law, family law, juvenile law, unlawful detainers, or case management, the court must determine what additional training is required and what additional courses are required before an attorney may serve as a temporary judge in each of those subject areas. The training required in each area must be of at least 3 [6] **hours'** duration. The court may also require that an attorney possess additional years of practical experience in each substantive area before being assigned to serve as a temporary judge in that subject area.

(D) *Settlement*

An attorney need not be a temporary judge to assist the court in settlement conferences. However, an attorney assisting the court with settlement conferences who performs any judicial function, such as entering a settlement on the record under Code of Civil Procedure section 664.6, must be a qualified temporary judge who has satisfied the training requirements under (c)(1) and (c)(2) of this rule.

(E) The substantive training requirements in (3)(A)–(C) do not apply to courts in which temporary judges are used fewer than 10 times altogether in a calendar year.

(Subd (c) amended effective January 1, 2009; previously amended effective January 1, 2007.)

Rule 2.812(c).   2008 Deletes. [1] hours **[2]** or other person approved by the Administrative Office of the Courts **[3]** hours **[4]** hours **[5]** hours **[6]** hours

(d) Requirements for retired judicial officers

Commencing five years after the retired judicial officer last served in a judicial position either as a full-time judicial officer or as an assigned judge, a retired judicial officer serving as a temporary judge must satisfy all the education and training requirements of this rule. However, a retired judicial officer serving as a temporary judge in a small claims case must satisfy all the requirements of Code of Civil Procedure section 116.240(b) and the rules in this chapter before serving in the case.

(Subd (d) adopted effective January 1, 2009.)

(e) Additional requirements

The presiding judge in each court should establish additional experience and training requirements for temporary judges beyond the minimum requirements provided in this rule if it is feasible for the court to do so.

(Subd (e) relettered effective January 1, 2009; adopted as subd (d) effective July 1, 2006.)

(f) Records of attendance

A court that uses temporary judges must maintain records verifying that each attorney who serves as a temporary judge in that court has attended and successfully completed the courses required under this rule.

(Subd (f) relettered effective January 1, 2009; adopted as subd (e) effective July 1, 2006.)

(g) Application and appointment

To serve as a temporary judge, an attorney must complete the application required under rule 10.744, must satisfy the requirements prescribed in this rule, and must satisfy such other requirements as the court appointing the attorney in its discretion may determine are appropriate.

(Subd (g) relettered effective January 1, 2009; adopted as subd (f) effective July 1, 2006.)

Rule 2.812 amended effective January 1, 2009; adopted as rule 243.13 effective July 1, 2006; previously amended and renumbered effective January 1, 2007.

Advisory Committee Comment

The goal of this rule is to ensure that attorneys who serve as court-appointed temporary judges are qualified and properly trained.

Subdivision (a). If a court determines that there is good cause under (a) to appoint an attorney with less than 10 years of practice as a temporary judge, the attorney must still satisfy the other requirements of the rule before being appointed.

Subdivision (b). "Good standing" means that the attorney is currently eligible to practice law in the State of California. An attorney in good standing may be either an active or a voluntarily inactive member of the State Bar. The rule does not require that an attorney be an active member of the State Bar to serve as a court-appointed temporary judge. Voluntarily inactive members may be appointed as temporary judges if the court decides to appoint them.

Subdivision (c). A court may use attorneys who are not temporary judges to assist in the settlement of cases. For example, attorneys may work under the presiding judge or individual judges and may assist them in settling cases. However, these attorneys may not perform any judicial functions such as entering a settlement on the record under Code of Civil Procedure section 664.6. Settlement attorneys who are not temporary judges are not required to satisfy the requirements of these rules, but must satisfy any requirements established by the court for attorneys who assist in the settlement of cases.

Ref.: Cal. Fms Pl. & Pr., Ch. 317, "Judges," Ch. 526, "Small Claims."

Rule 2.813.   Contents of training programs

(a) Bench conduct

Before the court may appoint an attorney to serve as a temporary judge in any type of case, the attorney must have received training under rule 2.812(c)(1) in the following subjects:

(1) Bench conduct, demeanor, and decorum;

(2) Access, fairness, and elimination of bias; and

(3) Adjudicating cases involving self-represented parties.

(Subd (a) amended effective January 1, 2007.)

(b) Ethics

Before the court may appoint an attorney to serve as a temporary judge in any type of case, the attorney must have received ethics training under rule 2.812(c)(2) in the following subjects:

(1) Judicial ethics generally;

(2) Conflicts;

(3) Disclosures, disqualifications, and limitations on appearances; and

(4) Ex parte communications.

(Subd (b) amended effective January 1, 2007.)

(c) Small claims

Before the court may appoint an attorney to serve as a temporary judge in small claims cases, the attorney must have received training under rule 2.812(c)(3)(A) in the following subjects:

(1) Small claims procedures and practices;

(2) Consumer sales;

(3) Vehicular sales, leasing, and repairs;

(4) Credit and financing transactions;

(5) Professional and occupational licensing;

(6) Tenant rent deposit law;

(7) Contract, warranty, tort, and negotiable instruments law; and

(8) Other subjects deemed appropriate by the presiding judge based on local needs and conditions.

In addition, an attorney serving as a temporary judge in small claims cases must be familiar with the publications identified in Code of Civil Procedure section 116.930.

(Subd (c) amended effective January 1, 2007.)

(d) Traffic

Before the court may appoint an attorney to serve as a temporary judge in traffic cases, the attorney must have received training under rule 2.812(c)(3)(B) in the following subjects:

(1) Traffic court procedures and practices;

(2) Correctable violations;

(3) Discovery;

(4) Driver licensing;

(5) Failure to appear;

(6) Mandatory insurance;

(7) Notice to appear citation forms;

(8) Red-light enforcement;

(9) Sentencing and court-ordered traffic school;

(10) Speed enforcement;

(11) Settlement of the record;

(12) Uniform bail and penalty schedules;

(13) Vehicle registration and licensing; and

(14) Other subjects deemed appropriate by the presiding judge based on local needs and conditions.

(Subd (d) amended effective January 1, 2007.)

Rule 2.813 amended and renumbered effective January 1, 2007; adopted as rule 243.14 effective July 1, 2006.

Advisory Committee Comment

The purpose of this rule is to ensure that all court-appointed temporary judges have proper training in bench conduct and demeanor, ethics, and each substantive area in which they adjudicate cases. Each court is responsible for approving the training and instructional materials for the temporary judges appointed by that court. The training in bench conduct and demeanor must be in person, but in other areas each court may determine the approved method or methods by which the training is provided. The methods may include in-person courses, broadcasts with participation, and online courses. Courts may offer MCLE credit for courses that they provide and may approve MCLE courses provided by others as satisfying the substantive training requirements under this rule. Courts may work together with other courts, or may cooperate on a regional basis, to develop and provide training programs for court-appointed temporary judges under this rule.

Ref.: Cal. Fms Pl. & Pr., Ch. 317, "Judges," Ch. 526, "Small Claims."

Rule 2.814. Appointment of temporary judge

An attorney may serve as a temporary judge for the court only after the court has issued an order appointing him or her to serve. Before serving, the attorney must subscribe the oath of office and must certify that he or she is aware of and will comply with applicable provisions of canon 6 of the Code of Judicial Ethics and the California Rules of Court.

Rule 2.814 renumbered effective January 1, 2007; adopted as rule 243.15 effective July 1, 2006.

Ref.: Cal. Fms Pl. & Pr., Ch. 317, "Judges," Ch. 526, "Small Claims."

Rule 2.815. Continuing education

(a) Continuing education required

Each attorney appointed as a temporary judge must attend and successfully complete every three years a course on bench conduct and demeanor, an ethics course, and a course in each substantive area in which the attorney will serve as a temporary judge. The courses must cover the same subjects and be of the same duration as the courses prescribed in rule 2.812(c). These courses must be approved by the court that appoints the attorney.

(Subd (a) amended effective January 1, 2007.)

(b) Records of attendance

A court that uses temporary judges must maintain records verifying that each attorney who serves as a temporary judge in that court has attended and successfully completed the courses required under this rule.

Rule 2.815 amended and renumbered effective January 1, 2007; adopted as rule 243.17 effective July 1, 2006.

Ref.: Cal. Fms Pl. & Pr., Ch. 317, "Judges," Ch. 526, "Small Claims."

Rule 2.816. Stipulation to court-appointed temporary judge

(a) Application

This rule governs a stipulation for a matter to be heard by a temporary judge when the court has appointed and assigned an attorney to serve as a temporary judge in that court.

(Subd (a) adopted effective July 1, 2006.)

(b) Contents of notice

Before the swearing in of the first witness at a small claims hearing, before the entry of a plea by the defendant at a traffic arraignment, or before the commencement of any other proceeding, the court must give notice to each party that:

(1) A temporary judge will be hearing the matters for that calendar;

(2) The temporary judge is a qualified member of the State Bar and the name of the temporary judge is provided; and

(3) The party has a right to have the matter heard before a judge, commissioner, or referee of the court.

(Subd (b) amended and relettered effective July 1, 2006; adopted as subd (a) effective January 1, 2001.)

(c) Form of notice

The court may give the notice in (b) by either of the following methods:

(1) A conspicuous sign posted inside or just outside the courtroom, accompanied by oral notification or notification by videotape or audiotape by a court officer on the day of the hearing; or

(2) A written notice provided to each party.

(Subd (c) amended and relettered effective July 1, 2006; adopted as subd (b) effective January 1, 2001.)

(d) Methods of stipulation

After notice has been given under (a) and (b), a party stipulates to a court-appointed temporary judge by either of the following:

(1) The party is deemed to have stipulated to the attorney serving as a temporary judge if the party fails to object to the matter being heard by the temporary judge before the temporary judge begins the proceeding; or

(2) The party signs a written stipulation agreeing that the matter may be heard by the temporary judge.

(Subd (d) amended effective January 1, 2007; adopted effective July 1, 2006.)

(e) Application or motion to withdraw stipulation

An application or motion to withdraw a stipulation for the appointment of a temporary judge must be supported by a declaration of facts establishing good cause for permitting the party to withdraw the stipulation. In addition:

(1) The application or motion must be heard by the presiding judge or a judge designated by the presiding judge.

(2) A declaration that a ruling by a temporary judge is based on an error of fact or law does not establish good cause for withdrawing a stipulation.

(3) The application or motion must be served and filed, and the moving party must mail or deliver a copy to the presiding judge.

(4) If the application or motion for withdrawing the stipulation is based on grounds for the disqualification of, or limitation of the appearance by, the temporary judge first learned or arising after the temporary judge has made one or more rulings, but before the temporary judge has completed judicial action in the proceeding, the temporary judge, unless the disqualification or termination is waived, must disqualify himself or herself. But in the absence of good cause, the rulings the temporary judge has made up to that time must not be set aside by the judicial officer or temporary judge who replaces the temporary judge.

(Subd (e) amended effective January 1, 2007; adopted effective July 1, 2006.)

Rule 2.816 amended and renumbered effective January 1, 2007; adopted as rule 1727 effective January 1, 2001; previously amended and renumbered as rule 243.18 effective July 1, 2006.

Ref.: Cal. Fms Pl. & Pr., Ch. 317, "Judges," Ch. 526, "Small Claims"; MB Prac. Guide: Cal. Pretrial Proc., §§22.15, 22.22A, 28.08[4].

Rule 2.817.   Disclosures to the parties

A temporary judge must make all disclosures required under the Code of Judicial Ethics.

Rule 2.817 renumbered effective January 1, 2007; adopted as rule 243.19 effective July 1, 2006.

Ref.: Cal. Fms Pl. & Pr., Ch. 317, "Judges."

Rule 2.818.   Disqualifications and limitations

(a) Code of Judicial Ethics

A temporary judge must disqualify himself or herself as a temporary judge in proceedings as provided under the Code of Judicial Ethics.

(Subd (a) lettered effective July 1, 2006; adopted as unlettered subd effective July 1, 2006.)

(b) Limitations on service

In addition to being disqualified as provided in (a), an attorney may not serve as a court-appointed temporary judge:

(1) If the attorney, in any type of case, is appearing on the same day in the same courthouse as an attorney or as a party;

(2) If the attorney, in the same type of case, is presently a party to any action or proceeding in the court; or

(3) If, in a family law or unlawful detainer case, one party is self-represented and the other party is represented by an attorney or is an attorney.

For good cause, the presiding judge may waive the limitations established in this subdivision.

(Subd (b) adopted effective July 1, 2006.)

(c) Waiver of disqualifications or limitations

(1) After a temporary judge who has determined himself or herself to be disqualified under the Code of Judicial Ethics or prohibited from serving under (b) has disclosed the basis for his or her disqualification or limitation on the record, the parties and their attorneys may agree to waive the disqualification or limitation and the temporary judge may accept the waiver. The temporary judge must not seek to induce a waiver and must avoid any effort to discover which attorneys or parties favored or opposed a waiver. The waiver must be in writing, must recite the basis for the disqualification or limitation, and must state that it was knowingly made. The waiver is effective only when signed by all parties and their attorneys and filed in the record.

(2) No waiver is permitted where the basis for the disqualification is any of the following:

(A) The temporary judge has a personal bias or prejudice concerning a party;

(B) The temporary judge has served as an attorney in the matter in controversy; or

(C) The temporary judge has been a material witness in the controversy.

(Subd (c) adopted effective July 1, 2006.)

(d) Late discovery of grounds for disqualification or limitation

In the event that grounds for disqualification or limitation are first learned of or arise after the temporary judge has made one or more rulings in a proceeding, but before the temporary judge has completed judicial action in the proceeding, the temporary judge, unless the disqualification or limitation is waived, must disqualify himself or herself. But in the absence of good cause, the rulings the temporary judge has made up to that time must not be set aside by the judicial officer or temporary judge who replaces the temporary judge.

(Subd (d) amended effective January 1, 2007; adopted effective July 1, 2006.)

(e) Notification of the court

Whenever a temporary judge determines himself or herself to be disqualified or limited from serving, the temporary judge must notify the presiding judge or the judge designated by the presiding judge of his or her withdrawal and must not further participate in the proceeding, unless his or her disqualification or limitation is waived by the parties as provided in (c).

(Subd (e) adopted effective July 1, 2006.)

(f) Requests for disqualifications

A party may request that a temporary judge withdraw on the ground that he or she is disqualified or limited from serving. If a temporary judge who should disqualify himself or herself or who is limited from serving in a case fails to withdraw, a party may apply to the presiding judge under rule 2.816(e) of the California Rules of Court for a withdrawal of the stipulation. The presiding judge or the judge designated by the presiding judge must determine whether good cause exists for granting withdrawal of the stipulation.

(Subd (f) amended effective January 1, 2007; previously adopted effective July 1, 2006.)

Rule 2.818 amended and renumbered effective January 1, 2007; adopted as rule 243.20 effective July 1, 2006; previously amended effective July 1, 2006.

Advisory Committee Comment

Subdivision (a) indicates that the rules concerning the disqualification of temporary judges are provided in the Code of Judicial Ethics. Subdivision (b) establishes additional limitations that prohibit attorneys from serving as court-appointed temporary judges under certain specified circumstances. Under subdivisions (c)–(e), the provisions of Code of Civil Procedure section 170.3 on waiver of disqualifications, the effect of late discovery of the grounds of disqualification, and notification of disqualification of judicial officers are made applicable to temporary judges. Under subdivision (f), requests for disqualification are handled as withdrawals of the stipulation to a temporary judge and are ruled on by the presiding judge. This procedure is different from that for seeking the disqualification of a judge under Code of Civil Procedure section 170.3.

Ref.: Cal. Fms Pl. & Pr., Ch. 317, "Judges"; MB Prac. Guide: Cal. Pretrial Proc., §§22.15, 22.17, 22.18[10], 22.22A.

Rule 2.819.   Continuing duty to disclose and disqualify

A temporary judge has a continuing duty to make disclosures, to disqualify himself or herself, and to limit his or her service as provided under the Code of Judicial Ethics.

Rule 2.819 renumbered effective January 1, 2007; adopted as rule 243.21 effective July 1, 2006.

Ref.: Cal. Fms Pl. & Pr., Ch. 317, "Judges."

Chapter 2
Temporary Judges Requested by the Parties

Rule 2.830. Temporary judges requested by the parties
Rule 2.831. Temporary judge—stipulation, order, oath, assignment, disclosure, and disqualification
Rule 2.832. Compensation
Rule 2.833. Notices, use of court facilities, and order for hearing site
Rule 2.834. Motions or applications to be heard by the court

Rule 2.830. Temporary judges requested by the parties

(a) Application

Rules 2.830–2.834 apply to attorneys designated as temporary judges under article VI, section 21 of the California Constitution at the request of the parties rather than by prior appointment of the court, including privately compensated temporary judges and attorneys who serve as temporary judges pro bono at the request of the parties.

(Subd (a) amended effective January 1, 2007.)

(b) Definition

"Privately compensated" means that the temporary judge is paid by the parties.

(c) Limitation

These rules do not apply to subordinate judicial officers or to attorneys who are appointed by the court to serve as temporary judges for the court.

Rule 2.830 amended and renumbered effective January 1, 2007; adopted as rule 243.30 effective July 1, 2006.

Ref.: Cal. Fms Pl. & Pr., Ch. 1, "New Developments," Ch. 317, "Judges," Ch. 526, "Small Claims."

Rule 2.831. Temporary judge—stipulation, order, oath, assignment, disclosure, and disqualification

(a) Stipulation

When the parties request that an attorney be designated by the court to serve as a temporary judge on a case, the stipulation of the parties that a case may be tried by a temporary judge must be in writing and must state the name and office address of the member of the State Bar agreed on. The stipulation must be submitted for approval to the presiding judge or the judge designated by the presiding judge.

(Subd (a) amended effective July 1, 2006; previously amended and relettered effective July 1, 1993; previously amended effective January 1, 2001, and July 1, 2001.)

(b) Order, oath, and certification

The order designating the temporary judge must be signed by the presiding judge or the presiding judge's designee and refer to the stipulation. The stipulation and order must then be filed. The temporary judge must take and subscribe the oath of office and certify that he or she is aware of and will comply with applicable provisions of canon 6 of the Code of Judicial Ethics and the California Rules of Court.

(Subd (b) amended effective July 1, 2006; previously amended and relettered effective July 1, 1993; previously amended effective July 1, 2001.)

(c) When the temporary judge may proceed The temporary judge may proceed with the hearing, trial, and determination of the cause after the stipulation, order, oath, and certification have been filed.

(Subd (c) amended and relettered effective July 1, 2006; formerly adopted as subd (b).)

(d) Disclosure to the parties

In addition to any other disclosure required by law, no later than five days after designation as a temporary judge or, if the temporary judge is not aware of his or her designation or of a matter subject to disclosure at that time, as soon as practicable thereafter, a temporary judge must disclose to the parties any matter subject to disclosure under the Code of Judicial Ethics.

(Subd (d) amended effective July 1, 2006; adopted as subd (c) effective July 1, 2001; previously amended and relettered effective July 1, 2006.)

(e) Disqualification

In addition to any other disqualification required by law, a temporary judge requested by the parties and designated by the court under this rule must disqualify himself or herself as provided under the Code of Judicial Ethics.

(Subd (e) amended and relettered effective July 1, 2006; adopted as subd (c) effective July 1, 1993; previously amended and relettered as subd (d) effective July 1, 2001.)

(f) Motion to withdraw stipulation

A motion to withdraw a stipulation for the appointment of a temporary judge must be supported by a declaration of facts establishing good cause for permitting the party to withdraw the stipulation, and must be heard by the presiding judge or a judge designated by the presiding judge. A declaration that a ruling is based on error of fact or law does not establish good cause for withdrawing a stipulation. Notice of the motion must be served and filed, and the moving party must mail or deliver a copy to the temporary judge. If the motion to withdraw the stipulation is based on grounds for the disqualification of the temporary judge first learned or arising after the temporary judge has made one or more rulings, but before the temporary judge has completed judicial action in the proceeding, the provisions of rule 2.816(e)(4) apply. If a motion to withdraw a stipulation is granted, the presiding judge must assign the case for hearing or trial as promptly as possible.

(Subd (f) amended effective January 1, 2007; adopted as subd (f) effective July 1, 1993; previously amended and relettered as subd (g) effective July 1, 2001, and as subd (f) effective July 1, 2006.)

Rule 2.831 amended and renumbered effective January 1, 2007; adopted as rule 244 effective January 1, 1999; previously amended effective April 1, 1962, July 1, 1981, July 1, 1987, July 1, 1993, July 1, 1995, January 1, 2001, and July 1, 2001; previously amended and renumbered as rule 243.31 effective July 1, 2006.

Ref.: Cal. Fms Pl. & Pr., Ch. 317, "Judges," Ch. 327, "Juvenile Courts: Jurisdiction and General Procedures," Ch. 526, "Small Claims"; MB Prac. Guide: Cal. Pretrial Proc., §§22.15, 22.17, 22.22A; W. Cal. Sum., 10 "Parent and Child" §466.

Rule 2.832. Compensation

A temporary judge selected by the parties may not be compensated by the parties unless the parties agree in writing on a rate of compensation that they will pay.

Rule 2.832 renumbered effective January 1, 2007; adopted as rule 243.32 effective July 1, 2006.

Ref.: Cal. Fms Pl. & Pr., Ch. 317, "Judges."

Rule 2.833.   Notices, use of court facilities, and order for hearing site

(a) Posting of notice regarding proceeding before privately compensated judge

For all matters pending before privately compensated temporary judges, the clerk must post a notice in the courthouse indicating the case name and number as well as the telephone number of a person to contact to arrange for attendance at any proceeding that would be open to the public if held in a courthouse.

(b) Use of court facilities, court personnel, and summoned jurors

A party who has elected to use the services of a privately compensated judge is deemed to have elected to proceed outside the courtroom. Court facilities, court personnel, and summoned jurors may not be used in proceedings pending before a privately compensated judge except on a finding by the presiding judge that their use would further the interests of justice.

(c) Order the appropriate hearing site

The presiding judge, on request of any person or on the judge's own motion, may order that a case before a privately compensated temporary judge must be heard at a site easily accessible to the public and appropriate for seating those who have made known their plan to attend hearings. The request must be made by letter with reasons stated and must be accompanied by a declaration that a copy of the request was mailed to each party, to the temporary judge, and to the clerk for placement in the file. The order may require that notice of trial or of other proceedings be given to the requesting person directly. The granting of an order for an accessible and appropriate hearing site is not a ground for withdrawal of a stipulation.

Rule 2.833 renumbered effective January 1, 2007; adopted as rule 243.33 effective July 1, 2006.

Ref.: Cal. Fms Pl. & Pr., Ch. 317, "Judges."

Rule 2.834.   Motions or applications to be heard by the court

(a) Motion or application to seal records

A motion or application to seal records in a cause before a privately compensated temporary judge must be filed with the court and must be served on all parties, the temporary judge, and any person or organization that has made known their intention to attend the hearing. The motion or application must be heard by the trial court judge to whom the case is assigned or, if the case has not been assigned, by the presiding judge. Rules 2.550–2.551 on sealed records apply to motions or applications filed under this rule.

(Subd (a) amended effective January 1, 2007.)

(b) Motion for leave to file complaint for intervention

A motion for leave to file a complaint for intervention in a cause before a privately compensated temporary judge must be filed with the court and served on all parties and the temporary judge. The motion must be heard by the trial court judge to whom the case is assigned or, if the case has

not been assigned, by the presiding judge. If intervention is allowed, the case must be returned to the trial court docket unless all parties stipulate in the manner prescribed in rule 2.831(a) to proceed before the temporary judge.

(Subd (b) amended effective January 1, 2007.)

Rule 2.834 amended and renumbered effective January 1, 2007; adopted as rule 243.34 effective July 1, 2006.

Ref.: Cal. Fms Pl. & Pr., Ch. 317, "Judges"; MB Prac. Guide: Cal. Pretrial Proc., §31.07[2].

Chapter 3
Referees
[Reserved]

Chapter 4
Court Interpreters

Rule 2.890. Professional conduct for interpreters
Rule 2.891. Periodic review of court interpreter skills and professional conduct
Rule 2.892. Guidelines for approval of certification programs for interpreters for deaf and hard-of-hearing persons
Rule 2.893. Appointment of noncertified interpreters in criminal cases and juvenile delinquency proceedings
Rule 2.894. Reports on appointments of certified and registered interpreters and noncertified and nonregistered interpreters

Rule 2.890.   Professional conduct for interpreters

(a) Representation of qualifications

An interpreter must accurately and completely represent his or her certifications, training, and relevant experience.

(Subd (a) amended effective January 1, 2007.)

(b) Complete and accurate interpretation

An interpreter must use his or her best skills and judgment to interpret accurately without embellishing, omitting, or editing. When interpreting for a party, the interpreter must interpret everything that is said during the entire proceedings. When interpreting for a witness, the interpreter must interpret everything that is said during the witness's testimony.

(Subd (b) amended effective January 1, 2007.)

(c) Impartiality and avoidance of conflicts of interest

(1) Impartiality

An interpreter must be impartial and unbiased and must refrain from conduct that may give an appearance of bias.

(2) Disclosure of conflicts

An interpreter must disclose to the judge and to all parties any actual or apparent conflict of interest. Any condition that interferes with the objectivity of an interpreter is a conflict of interest. A conflict may exist if the interpreter is acquainted with or related to any witness or party to the action or if the interpreter has an interest in the outcome of the case.

(3) Conduct

An interpreter must not engage in conduct creating the appearance of bias, prejudice, or partiality.

(4) Statements

An interpreter must not make statements to any person about the merits of the case until the litigation has concluded.

(Subd (c) amended effective January 1, 2007.)

(d) Confidentiality of privileged communications

An interpreter must not disclose privileged communications between counsel and client to any person.

(Subd (d) amended effective January 1, 2007.)

(e) Giving legal advice

An interpreter must not give legal advice to parties and witnesses, nor recommend specific attorneys or law firms.

(Subd (e) amended effective January 1, 2007.)

(f) Impartial professional relationships

An interpreter must maintain an impartial, professional relationship with all court officers, attorneys, jurors, parties, and witnesses.

(Subd (f) amended effective January 1, 2007.)

(g) Continuing education and duty to the profession

An interpreter must, through continuing education, maintain and improve his or her interpreting skills and knowledge of procedures used by the courts. An interpreter should seek to elevate the standards of performance of the interpreting profession.

(Subd (g) amended effective January 1, 2007.)

(h) Assessing and reporting impediments to performance

An interpreter must assess at all times his or her ability to perform interpreting services. If an interpreter has any reservation about his or her ability to satisfy an assignment competently, the interpreter must immediately disclose that reservation to the court or other appropriate authority.

(Subd (h) amended effective January 1, 2007.)

(i) Duty to report ethical violations

An interpreter must report to the court or other appropriate authority any effort to impede the interpreter's compliance with the law, this rule, or any other official policy governing court interpreting and legal translating.

(Subd (i) amended effective January 1, 2007.)

Rule 2.890 amended and renumbered effective January 1, 2007; adopted as rule 984.4 effective January 1, 1999.

Ref.: Cal. Fms Pl. & Pr., Ch. 551, "Trial"; MB Prac. Guide: Cal. Trial & Post-Trial Civ. Proc., §§8.10, 8.19[1], [3][b].

Rule 2.891. Periodic review of court interpreter skills and professional conduct

Each trial court must establish a procedure for biennial, or more frequent, review of the performance and skills of each court interpreter certified under Government Code section 68560 et seq. The court may designate a review panel, which must include at least one person qualified in the interpreter's language. The review procedure may include interviews, observations of courtroom performance, rating forms, and other evaluation techniques.

Rule 2.891 amended and renumbered effective January 1, 2007; adopted as rule 984 effective July 1, 1979; previously amended effective January 1, 1996.

Ref.: Cal. Fms Pl. & Pr., Ch. 551, "Trial."

Rule 2.892. Guidelines for approval of certification programs for interpreters for deaf and hard-of-hearing persons

Each organization, agency, or educational institution that administers tests for certification of court interpreters

for deaf and hard-of-hearing persons under Evidence Code section 754 must comply with the guidelines adopted by the Judicial Council effective February 21, 1992, and any subsequent revisions, and must hold a valid, current approval by the Judicial Council to administer the tests as a certifying organization. The guidelines are stated in the *Judicial Council Guidelines for Approval of Certification Programs for Interpreters for Deaf and Hard-of-Hearing Persons,* published by the Administrative Office of the Courts.

Rule 2.892 amended and renumbered effective January 1, 2007; adopted as rule 984.1 effective January 1, 1994.

Ref.: Cal. Fms Pl. & Pr., Ch. 551, "Trial."

Rule 2.893. Appointment of noncertified interpreters in criminal cases and juvenile delinquency proceedings

(a) Application

This rule applies to trial court proceedings in criminal cases and juvenile delinquency proceedings under Welfare and Institutions Code section 602 et seq. in which the court determines that an interpreter is required.

(Subd (a) amended effective January 1, 2007.)

(b) Appointment of noncertified interpreters

An interpreter who is not certified by the Judicial Council to interpret a language designated by the Judicial Council under Government Code section 68560 et seq. may be appointed under Government Code section 68561(c) in a proceeding if:

(1) *Noncertified interpreter provisionally qualified*

(A) The presiding judge of the court, or other judicial officer designated by the presiding judge:

(i) Finds the noncertified interpreter to be provisionally qualified following the *Procedures and Guidelines to Appoint a Noncertified Interpreter in Criminal and Juvenile Delinquency Proceedings (Designated Languages)* (form IN-100); and

(ii) Signs an order allowing the interpreter to be considered for appointment on *Qualifications of a Noncertified Interpreter* (form IN-110); and

(B) The judge in the proceeding finds on the record that:

(i) Good cause exists to appoint the noncertified interpreter; and

(ii) The interpreter is qualified to interpret the proceeding, following procedures adopted by the Judicial Council (see forms IN-100, IN-110, and IN-120).

(C) Each order of the presiding judge under (b)(1) finding a noncertified interpreter to be provisionally qualified and allowing the interpreter to be considered for appointment in a proceeding is for a six-month period.

(2) *Noncertified interpreter not provisionally qualified*

(A) To prevent burdensome delay or in other unusual circumstances, at the request of the defendant, or of the minor in a juvenile delinquency proceeding, the judge in the proceeding may appoint a noncertified interpreter who is not provisionally qualified under (b)(1) to interpret a brief, routine matter provided the judge, on the record:

(i) Indicates that the defendant or minor has waived the appointment of a certified interpreter and the appointment of an interpreter found provisionally qualified by the presiding judge;

(ii) Finds that good cause exists to appoint an interpreter who is neither certified nor provisionally qualified; and

(iii) Finds that the interpreter is qualified to interpret that proceeding.

(B) The findings and appointment under (b)(2)(A) made by the judge in the proceeding are effective only in that proceeding. The appointment must not be extended to subsequent proceedings without an additional waiver, findings, and appointment.

(Subd (b) amended effective January 1, 2007; previously amended effective January 1, 2007.)

(c) Limit on appointment of noncertified interpreters

(1) A noncertified interpreter allowed to be appointed under (b) may not interpret in the trial courts for more than any four 6-month periods, except that:

(A) In counties with a population greater than 80,000, a noncertified interpreter of Spanish may be allowed to interpret for no more than any two 6-month periods.

(B) A noncertified interpreter may be allowed to interpret beyond four 6-month periods, or two 6-month periods for an interpreter of Spanish under (A), if the judge in the proceeding makes a specific finding on the record in each case in which the interpreter is sworn that good cause exists to appoint the interpreter notwithstanding that he or she has failed to achieve Judicial Council certification.

(2) Except as provided in (3), each six-month period under (1) begins on the date a presiding judge signs an order under (b)(1)(A)(ii) allowing the noncertified interpreter to be considered for appointment.

(3) If an interpreter is provisionally qualified under (b)(1) in more than one court at the same time, each six-month period runs concurrently for purposes of determining the maximum periods allowed in this subdivision.

(Subd (c) amended effective January 1, 2007.)

(d) Waiver of certified interpreter or objection to noncertified interpreter

(1) If after a diligent search a certified interpreter is not available in a criminal case or in a juvenile delinquency proceeding, the judge in the proceeding must inform the defendant or the minor that:

(A) The proposed interpreter is not certified;

(B) The court has found good cause to appoint a noncertified interpreter; and

(C) The court has found the proposed interpreter to be qualified to interpret in the proceeding.

(2) If the defendant or minor objects to the appointment of the proposed interpreter or waives the appointment of a certified interpreter, the objection or waiver must be on the record.

(Subd (d) amended effective January 1, 2007.)

(e) Court record

The minute order or docket must record the information in (1) or (2) below for each proceeding requiring the appointment of an interpreter:

(1) *Certified interpreters*

For each certified interpreter, the following information must be recorded:

(A) The name of the interpreter;

(B) The language to be interpreted;

(C) The fact that the interpreter is certified to interpret in the language to be interpreted; and

(D) Whether the interpreter was administered the interpreter's oath or has an oath on file with the court (only certified interpreters may have an oath on file).

(2) *Noncertified interpreters*

For each noncertified interpreter, the following information must be recorded:

(A) The name of the interpreter;

(B) The language to be interpreted;

(C) The fact that the interpreter was administered the interpreter's oath;

(D) The fact that the interpreter is not certified to interpret in the language to be interpreted;

(E) Whether a *Certification of Unavailability of Certified Interpreters* (form IN-120) for the language to be interpreted is on file for this date with the court administrator;

(F) The court's finding that good cause exists for the court to appoint a noncertified interpreter;

(G) The court's finding that the interpreter is qualified to interpret in the proceeding;

(H) If applicable, the court's finding under (c)(1)(B) that good cause exists for the court to appoint a noncertified interpreter beyond the time allowed in (c); and

(I) If applicable, the objection or waiver of the defendant or minor under (d).

(Subd (e) amended effective January 1, 2007.)

Rule 2.893 amended effective January 1, 2007; adopted as rule 984.2 effective January 1, 1996; previously amended and renumbered effective January 1, 2007.

Ref.: Cal. Fms Pl. & Pr., Ch. 329, "Juvenile Courts: Delinquency Proceedings"; MB Prac. Guide: Cal. Trial & Post-Trial Civ. Proc., §8.37.

Rule 2.894. Reports on appointments of certified and registered interpreters and noncertified and nonregistered interpreters

Each superior court must report to the Judicial Council on:

(1) The appointment of certified and registered interpreters under Government Code section 71802, as required by the Administrative Office of the Courts; and

(2) The appointment of noncertified interpreters of languages designated under Government Code section 68562(a), and registered and nonregistered interpreters of nondesignated languages.

Rule 2.894 amended and renumbered effective January 1, 2007; adopted as rule 984.3 effective January 1, 1996; previously amended effective March 1, 2003.

Division 7
Proceedings

Chap. 1.   General Provisions. Rule 2.900.

Chap. 2.   Records of Proceedings. Rules 2.950–2.958.

Chapter 1
General Provisions

Rule 2.900.   Submission of a cause in a trial court

(a) Submission

A cause is deemed submitted in a trial court when either of the following first occurs:

(1) The date the court orders the matter submitted; or

(2) The date the final paper is required to be filed or the date argument is heard, whichever is later.

(Subd (a) amended effective January 1, 2007.)

(b) Vacating submission

The court may vacate submission only by issuing an order served on the parties stating reasons constituting good cause and providing for resubmission.

(c) Pendency of a submitted cause

A submitted cause is pending and undetermined unless the court has announced its tentative decision or the cause is terminated. The time required to finalize a tentative decision is not time in which the cause is pending and undetermined. For purposes of this rule only, a motion that has the effect of vacating, reconsidering, or rehearing the cause will be considered a separate and new cause and will be deemed submitted as provided in (a).

(Subd (c) amended effective January 1, 2007.)

Rule 2.900 amended and renumbered effective January 1, 2007; adopted as rule 825 effective January 1, 1989.

Ref.: MB Prac. Guide: Cal. Trial & Post-Trial Civ. Proc., §§5.36[1], 19.13, 19.15, 19.16[2], [3].

Chapter 2
Records of Proceedings

Rule 2.950. Sequential list of reporters
Rule 2.952. Electronic recording as official record of proceedings
Rule 2.954. Specifications for electronic recording equipment
Rule 2.956. Court reporting services in civil cases
Rule 2.958. Assessing fee for official reporter

Rule 2.950.   Sequential list of reporters

During any reported court proceeding, the clerk must keep a sequential list of all reporters working on the case, indicating the date the reporter worked and the reporter's name, business address, and Certified Shorthand Reporter license number. If more than one reporter reports a case during one day, the information pertaining to each reporter must be listed with the first reporter designated "A," the second designated "B," etc. If reporter "A" returns during the same day, that reporter will be designated as both reporter "A" and reporter "C" on the list. The list of reporters may be kept in an electronic database maintained by the clerk; however, a hard copy must be available to members of the public within one working day of a request for the list of reporters.

Rule 2.950 amended and renumbered effective January 1, 2007; adopted as rule 980.4 effective July 1, 1991.

Ref.: W. Cal. Sum., 10 "Parent and Child" §712.

Rule 2.952.   Electronic recording as official record of proceedings

(a) Application

This rule applies when a court has ordered proceedings to be electronically recorded on a device of a type approved by the Judicial Council or conforming to specifications adopted by the Judicial Council.

(Subd (a) amended effective January 1, 2007; previously amended effective January 1, 1990.)

(b) Definitions

As used in this rule, the following definitions apply:

(1) "Reel" means an individual reel or cassette of magnetic recording tape or a comparable unit of the medium on which an electronic recording is made.

(2) "Monitor" means any person designated by the court to operate electronic recording equipment and to make appropriate notations to identify the proceedings recorded on each reel, including the date and time of the recording. The trial judge, a courtroom clerk, or a bailiff may be the monitor, but when recording is of sound only, a separate monitor without other substantial duties is recommended.

(Subd (b) amended effective January 1, 2007; previously amended effective January 1, 1990.)

(c) Reel numbers

Each reel must be distinctively marked with the date recorded, the department number of the court, if any, and, if possible, a serial number.

(Subd (c) amended effective January 1, 2007; previously amended effective January 1, 1990.)

(d) Certificate of monitor

As soon as practicable after the close of each day's court proceedings, the monitor must execute a certificate for each reel recorded during the day, stating:

(1) That the person executing the certificate was designated by the court as monitor;

(2) The number or other identification assigned to the reel;

(3) The date of the proceedings recorded on that reel;

(4) The titles and numbers of actions and proceedings, or portions thereof, recorded on the reel, and the general nature of the proceedings; and

(5) That the recording equipment was functioning normally, and that all of the proceedings in open court between designated times of day were recorded, except for such matters as were expressly directed to be "off the record" or as otherwise specified.

(Subd (d) amended effective January 1, 2007; previously amended effective January 1, 1990.)

(e) Two or more monitors

If two or more persons acted as monitors during the recording of a single reel, each monitor must execute a certificate as to the portion of the reel that he or she monitored. The certificate of a person other than a judge, clerk, or deputy clerk of the court must be in the form of an affidavit or declaration under penalty of perjury.

(Subd (e) lettered effective January 1, 2007; adopted as part of subd (d) effective January 1, 1976.)

(f) Storage

The monitor's certificate, the recorded reel, and the monitor's notes must be retained and safely stored by the clerk in a manner that will permit their convenient retrieval and use.

(Subd (f) amended and relettered effective January 1, 2007; adopted as subd (e) effective January 1, 1976.)

(g) Transcripts

(1) Written transcripts of electronic recordings may be made by or under the direction of the clerk or a person designated by the court. The person making the transcript must execute a declaration under penalty of perjury that:

(A) Identifies the reel or reels transcribed, or the portions thereof, by reference to the numbers assigned thereto and, where only portions of a reel are transcribed, by reference to index numbers or other means of identifying the portion transcribed; and

(B) States that the transcript is a full, true, and correct transcript of the identified reel or reels or the designated portions thereof.

(2) The transcript must conform, as nearly as possible, to the requirements for a reporter's transcript as provided for in these rules.

(Subd (g) amended and relettered effective January 1, 2007; adopted as subd (f) effective January 1, 1976.)

(h) Use of transcripts

A transcript prepared and certified under (g), and accompanied by a certified copy of the monitor's certificate pertaining to each reel transcribed, is prima facie a true and complete record of the oral proceedings it purports to cover, and satisfies any requirement in the California Rules of Court or in any statute for a reporter's transcript of oral proceedings.

(Subd (h) amended and relettered effective January 1, 2007; adopted as subd (g) effective January 1, 1976.)

(i) Original reels

A reviewing court may order the transmittal to it of the original reels containing electronic recordings of proceedings being reviewed by it, or electronic copies of them.

(Subd (i) relettered effective January 1, 2007; adopted as subd (h) effective January 1, 1976; previously amended effective January 1, 1990.)

(j) Record on appeal

(1) *Stipulation and approval of record without transcription*

On stipulation of the parties approved by the reviewing court, the original reels or electronic copies of them may be transmitted as the record of oral proceedings without being transcribed, in which case the reels or copies satisfy the requirements in the California Rules of Court or in any statute for a reporter's transcript.

(2) *Request for preparation of transcript*

In the absence of a stipulation and approval under (1), the appellant must, within 10 days after filing a notice of appeal in a civil case, serve and file with the clerk directions indicating the portions of the oral proceedings to be transcribed and must, at the same time, deposit with the clerk the approximate cost computed as specified in rule 8.130. Other steps necessary to complete preparation of the record on appeal must be taken following, as nearly as possible, the procedures in rules 8.120 and 8.130.

(3) *Preparation of transcript*

On receiving directions to have a transcript prepared, the clerk may have the material transcribed by a court employee, but should ordinarily send the reels in question

to a professional recording service that has been certified by the federal court system or the Administrative Office of the Courts or verified by the clerk to be skilled in producing transcripts.

(Subd (j) amended and relettered effective January 1, 2007; adopted as subd (i) effective January 1, 1990; previously amended effective January 1, 1993.)

Rule 2.952 amended and renumbered effective January 1, 2007; adopted as rule 980.5 effective January 1, 1976; previously amended effective January 1, 1990, and January 1, 1993.

Ref.: Cal. Fms Pl. & Pr., Ch. 44, "Appeal: Preparing and Filing the Record," Ch. 551, "Trial."

Rule 2.954.   Specifications for electronic recording equipment

(a) Specifications mandated

Electronic recording equipment used in making the official verbatim record of oral courtroom proceedings must conform to the specifications in this rule.

(Subd (a) amended effective January 1, 2007.)

(b) Sound recording only

The following specifications for electronic recording devices and appurtenant equipment apply when only sound is to be recorded:

(1) *Mandatory specifications*

(A) The device must be capable of simultaneously recording at least four separate channels or "tracks," each of which has a separate playback control so that any one channel separately or any combination of channels may be played back.

(B) The device must not have an operative erase head.

(C) The device must have a digital counter or comparable means of logging and locating the place on a reel where specific proceedings were recorded.

(D) Earphones must be provided for monitoring the recorded signal.

(E) The signal going to the earphones must come from a separate playback head, so that the monitor will hear what has actually been recorded on the tape.

(F) The device must be capable of recording at least two hours without interruption. This requirement may be satisfied by a device that automatically switches from one recording deck to another at the completion of a reel of tape of less than two hours in duration.

(G) A separate visual indicator of signal level must be provided for each recording channel.

(H) The appurtenant equipment must include at least four microphones, which should include one at the witness stand, one at the bench, and one at each counsel table. In the absence of unusual circumstances, all microphones must be directional (cardioid).

(I) A loudspeaker must be provided for courtroom playback.

(2) *Recommended features*

The following features are recommended, but not required:

(A) The recording level control should be automatic rather than manual.

(B) The device should be equipped to prevent recording over a previously recorded segment of tape.

(C) The device should give a warning signal at the end of a reel of tape.

(Subd (b) amended effective January 1, 2007.)

(c) Audio-and-video recording

The following specifications for electronic audio-video recording devices and appurtenant equipment apply when audio and video are to be recorded simultaneously.

(1) *Mandatory specifications*

The system must include:

(A) At least five charge-coupled-device color video cameras in fixed mounts, equipped with lenses appropriate to the courtroom. Cameras must conform to EIA standard, accept C-mount lenses, have 2000 lux sensitivity at f4.0 at 3200 degrees Kelvin so as to produce an adequate picture with 30 lux minimum illumination and an f1.4 lens, and be approximately 2.6″ × 2.4″ × 8.0.″

(B) At least eight phase-coherent cardioid (directional) microphones, Crown PCC-160 or equivalent, appropriately placed.

(C) At least two VHS videotape recorders with hi-fi sound on video, specially modified to record 4 channels of audio (2 linear channels with Dolby noise reduction and 2 hi-fi sound on video channels), capable of recording up to 6 hours on T-120 cassettes, modified to prevent automatic rewind at end of tape, and wired for remote control. The two recorders must simultaneously record the same audio and video signals, as selected by the audio-video mixer.

(D) A computer-controlled audio-video mixer and switching system that:

(i) Automatically selects for the VCRs the signal from the video camera that is associated with the active microphone; and

(ii) Compares microphone active signal to ambient noise signal so that microphones are recorded only when a person is speaking, and so that only the microphone nearest a speaker is active, thus minimizing recording of ambient noise.

(E) A sound system that serves both as a sound reinforcement system while recording is in progress, and as a playback amplification system, integrated with other components to minimize feedback.

(F) A time-date generator that is active and records at all times the system is recording.

(G) A color monitor.

(H) Appropriate cables, distribution amplifiers, switches, and the like.

(I) The system must produce:

(i) A signal visible to the judge, the in-court clerk, and counsel indicating that the system is recording;

(ii) An audible signal at end-of-tape or if the tape jams while the controls are set to record; and

(iii) Blanking of the judge's bench monitor when the system is not actually recording.

(2) *Recommended features*

The system should normally include:

(A) A chambers camera and microphone or microphones that, when in use, will override any signals originating in the courtroom, and that will be inactivated when not in use.

(B) Two additional videocassette recorders that will produce tapes with the same video and audio as the main two, but may have fewer channels of sound, for the use of parties in cases recorded.

(Subd (c) amended effective January 1, 2007.)

(d) Substantial compliance

A sound or video and sound system that substantially conforms to these specifications is approved if the deviation does not significantly impair a major function of the system. Subdivision (c)(1)(D)(ii) of this rule describes a specification from which deviation is permissible, if the system produces adequate sound quality.

(Subd (d) amended effective January 1, 2007.)

(e) Previous equipment

The Administrative Director of the Courts is authorized to approve any electronic recording devices and equipment acquired before the adoption or amendment of this rule that has been found by the court to produce satisfactory recordings of proceedings.

(Subd (e) amended effective January 1, 2007.)

Rule 2.954 amended and renumbered effective January 1, 2007; adopted as rule 980.6 effective January 1, 1990.

Ref.: Cal. Fms Pl. & Pr., Ch. 551, "Trial."

Rule 2.956.   Court reporting services in civil cases

(a) Statutory reference; application

This rule is adopted solely to effectuate the statutory mandate of Government Code sections 68086(a)–(b) and must be applied so as to give effect to these sections. It applies to trial courts.

(Subd (a) amended effective January 1, 2007; previously amended effective January 31, 1997.)

(b) Notice of availability; parties' request

(1) *Local policy to be adopted and posted*

Each trial court must adopt and post in the clerk's office a local policy enumerating the departments in which the services of official court reporters are normally available, and the departments in which the services of official court reporters are not normally available during regular court hours. If the services of official court reporters are normally available in a department only for certain types of matters, those matters must be identified in the policy.

(2) *Publication of policy*

The court must publish its policy in a newspaper if one is published in the county. Instead of publishing the policy, the court may:

(A) Send each party a copy of the policy at least 10 days before any hearing is held in a case; or

(B) Adopt the policy as a local rule.

(3) *Requests for official court reporter for civil trials and notices to parties*

Unless the court's policy states that all courtrooms normally have the services of official court reporters available for civil trials, the court must require that each party file a statement before the trial date indicating whether the party requests the presence of an official court reporter. If a party requests the presence of an official court reporter and it appears that none will be available, the clerk must notify the party of that fact as soon as possible before the trial. If the services of official court reporters are normally available in all courtrooms, the clerk must notify the parties to a civil trial as soon as possible if it appears that those services will not be available.

(4) *Notice of nonavailability of court reporter for nontrial matters*

If the services of an official court reporter will not be available during a hearing on law and motion or other nontrial matters in civil cases, that fact must be noted on the court's official calendar.

(Subd (b) amended effective January 1, 2007.)

(c) Party may procure reporter

If the services of an official court reporter are not available for a hearing or trial in a civil case, a party may arrange for the presence of a certified shorthand reporter to serve as an official pro tempore reporter. It is that party's responsibility to pay the reporter's fee for attendance at the proceedings, but the expense may be recoverable as part of the costs, as provided by law.

(d) No additional charge if party arranges for reporter

If a party arranges and pays for the attendance of a certified shorthand reporter at a hearing in a civil case because of the unavailability of the services of an official court reporter, none of the parties may be charged the reporter's attendance fee provided for in Government Code sections 68086(a)(1) or (b)(1).

(Subd (d) amended effective January 1, 2007.)

(e) Definitions

As used in this rule and in Government Code section 68086:

(1) "Civil case" includes all matters other than criminal and juvenile matters.

(2) "Official reporter" and "official reporting services" both include an official court reporter or official reporter as those phrases are used in statutes, including Code of Civil Procedure sections 269 and 274c and Government Code section 69941; and include an official reporter pro tempore as the phrase is used in Government Code section 69945 and other statutes, whose fee for attending and reporting proceedings is paid for by the court or the county, and who attends court sessions as directed by the court, and who was not employed to report specific causes at the request of a party or parties. "Official reporter" and "official reporting services" do not include official reporters pro tempore employed by the court expressly to report only criminal, or criminal and juvenile, matters. "Official reporting services" include electronic recording equipment operated by the court to make the official verbatim record of proceedings where it is permitted.

(Subd (e) amended effective January 1, 2007.)

Rule 2.956 amended and renumbered effective January 1, 2007; adopted as rule 891 effective January 1, 1994; previously amended effective January 31, 1997.

Ref.: Cal. Fms Pl. & Pr., Ch. 551, "Trial."

Rule 2.958.   Assessing fee for official reporter

The half-day fee to be charged under Government Code section 68086 for the services of an official reporter must be established by the trial court as follows: for a proceeding or portion of a proceeding in which a certified shorthand reporter is used, the fee is equal to the average salary and benefit costs of the reporter, plus indirect costs of up to 18 percent of salary and benefits. For purposes of this rule, the daily salary is determined by dividing the average annual salary of temporary and full-time reporters by 225 workdays.

Rule 2.958 amended and renumbered effective January 1, 2007; adopted as rule 892 effective January 1, 1994; previously

amended effective January 31, 1997, August 17, 2003, January 1, 2004, and July 1, 2004.

Ref.: Cal. Fms Pl. & Pr., Ch. 551, "Trial."

Division 8
Trials

Chapter 1
Jury Service

Rule 2.1000.   Jury service [Reserved]

Rule 2.1000 adopted effective January 1, 2007.

Rule 2.1002.   Length of juror service

(a) Purpose

This rule implements Government Code section 68550, which is intended to make jury service more convenient and alleviate the problem of potential jurors refusing to appear for jury duty by shortening the time a person would be required to serve to one day or one trial. The exemptions authorized by the rule are intended to be of limited scope and duration, and they must be applied with the goal of achieving full compliance throughout the state as soon as possible.

(Subd (a) amended effective January 1, 2007.)

(b) Definitions

As used in this rule:

(1) "Trial court system" means all the courts of a county.

(2) "One trial" means jury service provided by a citizen after being sworn as a trial juror.

(3) "One day" means the hours of one normal court working day (the hours a court is open to the public for business).

(4) "On call" means all same-day notice procedures used to inform prospective jurors of the time they are to report for jury service.

(5) "Telephone standby" means all previous-day notice procedures used to inform prospective jurors of their date to report for service.

(Subd (b) amended effective January 1, 2007.)

(c) One-day/one-trial

Each trial court system must implement a juror management program under which a person has fulfilled his or her jury service obligation when the person has:

(1) Served on one trial until discharged;

(2) Been assigned on one day to one or more trial departments for jury selection and served through the completion of jury selection or until excused by the jury commissioner;

(3) Attended court but was not assigned to a trial department for selection of a jury before the end of that day;

(4) Served one day on call; or

(5) Served no more than five court days on telephone standby.

(Subd (c) amended effective January 1, 2007.)

(d) Exemption

(1) *Good cause*

The Judicial Council may grant an exemption from the requirements of this rule for a specified period of time if the trial court system demonstrates good cause by establishing that:

(A) The cost of implementing a one-day/one-trial system is so high that the trial court system would be unable to provide essential services to the public if required to implement such a system; or

(B) The requirements of this rule cannot be met because of the size of the population in the county compared to the number of jury trials.

(2) *Application*

Any application for exemption from the requirements of this rule must be submitted to the Judicial Council no later than September 1, 1999. The application must demonstrate good cause for the exemption sought and must include either:

(A) A plan to fully comply with this rule by a specified date; or

(B) An alternative plan that would advance the purposes of this rule to the extent possible, given the conditions in the county.

(3) *Decision*

If the council finds good cause, it may grant an exemption for a limited period of time and on such conditions as it deems appropriate to further the purposes of this rule.

(Subd (d) amended effective January 1, 2007.)

Rule 2.1002 amended and renumbered effective January 1, 2007; adopted as rule 861 effective July 1, 1999.

Rule 2.1004. Scheduling accommodations for jurors

(a) Accommodations for all jurors

The jury commissioner should accommodate a prospective juror's schedule by granting a prospective juror's request for a one-time deferral of jury service. If the request for a deferral is made under penalty of perjury in writing or through the court's established electronic means, and in accordance with the court's local procedure, the jury commissioner should not require the prospective juror to appear at court to make the request in person.

(b) Scheduling accommodations for peace officers

If a prospective juror is a peace officer, as defined by Penal Code section 830.5, the jury commissioner must make scheduling accommodations on application of the peace officer stating the reason a scheduling accommodation is necessary. The jury commissioner must establish

procedures for the form and timing of the application. If the request for special accommodations is made under penalty of perjury in writing or through the court's established electronic means, and in accordance with the court's local procedure, the jury commissioner must not require the prospective juror to appear at court to make the request in person.

(Subd (b) amended effective January 1, 2007.)

Rule 2.1004 amended and renumbered effective January 1, 2007; adopted as rule 858 effective January 1, 2005.

Ref.: Cal. Fms Pl. & Pr., Ch. 322, "Juries and Jury Selection."

Rule 2.1006. Deferral of jury service

A mother who is breastfeeding a child may request that jury service be deferred for up to one year, and may renew that request as long as she is breastfeeding. If the request is made in writing, under penalty of perjury, the jury commissioner must grant it without requiring the prospective juror to appear at court.

Rule 2.1006 renumbered effective January 1, 2007; adopted as rule 859 effective July 1, 2001.

Ref.: Cal. Fms Pl. & Pr., Ch. 322, "Juries and Jury Selection."

Rule 2.1008. Excuses from jury service

(a) Duty of citizenship

Jury service, unless excused by law, is a responsibility of citizenship. The court and its staff must employ all necessary and appropriate means to ensure that citizens fulfill this important civic responsibility.

(Subd (a) amended effective January 1, 2007.)

(b) Principles

The following principles govern the granting of excuses from jury service by the jury commissioner on grounds of undue hardship under Code of Civil Procedure section 204:

(1) No class or category of persons may be automatically excluded from jury duty except as provided by law.

(2) A statutory exemption from jury service must be granted only when the eligible person claims it.

(3) Deferring jury service is preferred to excusing a prospective juror for a temporary or marginal hardship.

(4) Inconvenience to a prospective juror or an employer is not an adequate reason to be excused from jury duty, although it may be considered a ground for deferral.

(Subd (b) amended effective January 1, 2007.)

(c) Requests to be excused from jury service

All requests to be excused from jury service that are granted for undue hardship must be put in writing by the prospective juror, reduced to writing, or placed on the court's record. The prospective juror must support the request with facts specifying the hardship and a statement why the circumstances constituting the undue hardship cannot be avoided by deferring the prospective juror's service.

(Subd (c) amended effective January 1, 2007.)

(d) Reasons for excusing a juror because of undue hardship

An excuse on the ground of undue hardship may be granted for any of the following reasons:

(1) The prospective juror has no reasonably available means of public or private transportation to the court.

(2) The prospective juror must travel an excessive distance. Unless otherwise established by statute or local rule, an excessive distance is reasonable travel time that exceeds one-and-one-half hours from the prospective juror's home to the court.

(3) The prospective juror will bear an extreme financial burden. In determining whether to excuse the prospective juror for this reason, consideration must be given to:

(A) The sources of the prospective juror's household income;

(B) The availability and extent of income reimbursement;

(C) The expected length of service; and

(D) Whether service can reasonably be expected to compromise the prospective juror's ability to support himself or herself or his or her dependents, or so disrupt the economic stability of any individual as to be against the interests of justice.

(4) The prospective juror will bear an undue risk of material injury to or destruction of the prospective juror's property or property entrusted to the prospective juror, and it is not feasible to make alternative arrangements to alleviate the risk. In determining whether to excuse the prospective juror for this reason, consideration must be given to:

(A) The nature of the property;

(B) The source and duration of the risk;

(C) The probability that the risk will be realized;

(D) The reason alternative arrangements to protect the property cannot be made; and

(E) Whether material injury to or destruction of the property will so disrupt the economic stability of any individual as to be against the interests of justice.

(5) The prospective juror has a physical or mental disability or impairment, not affecting that person's competence to act as a juror, that would expose the potential juror to undue risk of mental or physical harm. In any individual case, unless the person is aged 70 years or older, the prospective juror may be required to furnish verification or a method of verification of the disability or impairment, its probable duration, and the particular reasons for the person's inability to serve as a juror.

(6) The prospective juror's services are immediately needed for the protection of the public health and safety, and it is not feasible to make alternative arrangements to relieve the person of those responsibilities during the period of service as a juror without substantially reducing essential public services.

(7) The prospective juror has a personal obligation to provide actual and necessary care to another, including sick, aged, or infirm dependents, or a child who requires the prospective juror's personal care and attention, and no comparable substitute care is either available or practical without imposing an undue economic hardship on the prospective juror or person cared for. If the request to be excused is based on care provided to a sick, disabled, or infirm person, the prospective juror may be required to furnish verification or a method of verification that the person being cared for is in need of regular and personal care.

(Subd (d) amended effective January 1, 2007.)

(e) Excuse based on previous jury service

A prospective juror who has served on a grand or trial jury or was summoned and appeared for jury service in any state or federal court during the previous 12 months must be excused from service on request. The jury commissioner, in his or her discretion, may establish a longer period of repose.

(Subd (e) amended effective January 1, 2007.)

Rule 2.1008 amended and renumbered effective January 1, 2007; adopted as rule 860 effective July 1, 1997.

Ref.: Cal. Fms Pl. & Pr., Ch. 322, "Juries and Jury Selection," Ch. 551, "Trial"; MB Prac. Guide: Cal. Trial & Post-Trial Civ. Proc., §§6.05[1], 6.19.

Rule 2.1010.   [Effective Until January 1, 2010] Juror motion to set aside sanctions imposed by default

(a) Motion

A prospective juror against whom sanctions have been imposed by default under Code of Civil Procedure section 209 may move to set aside the default. The motion must be brought no later than 60 days after sanctions have been imposed.

(b) Contents of motion

A motion to set aside sanctions imposed by default must contain a short and concise statement of the reasons the prospective juror was not able to attend when summoned for jury duty and any supporting documentation.

(c) Judicial Council form may be used

A motion to set aside sanctions imposed by default may be made by completing and filing *Juror's Motion to Set Aside Sanctions and Order* (form MC-070).

(Subd (c) amended effective January 1, 2007.)

(d) Hearing

The court may decide the motion with or without a hearing.

(Subd (d) amended effective January 1, 2007.)

(e) Good cause required

If the motion demonstrates good cause, a court must set aside sanctions imposed against a prospective juror.

(f) Continuing obligation to serve

Nothing in this rule relieves a prospective juror of the obligation of jury service.

(g) Notice to juror

The court must provide a copy of this rule to the prospective juror against whom sanctions have been imposed.

(h) Sunset date

This rule is effective until January 1, 2010.

(Subd (h) amended effective January 1, 2007.)

Rule 2.1010 amended and renumbered effective January 1, 2007; adopted as rule 862 effective January 1, 2005.

Ref.: Cal. Fms Pl. & Pr., Ch. 322, "Juries and Jury Selection."

Chapter 2
Conduct of Trial

Rule 2.1030. Communications from or with jury
Rule 2.1031. Juror note-taking
Rule 2.1032. Juror notebooks in complex civil cases
Rule 2.1033. Juror questions
Rule 2.1034. Statements to the jury panel

Rule 2.1035. Preinstruction
Rule 2.1036. Assisting the jury at impasse

Rule 2.1030. Communications from or with jury

(a) Preservation of written jury communications

The trial judge must preserve and deliver to the clerk for inclusion in the record all written communications, formal or informal, received from the jury or from individual jurors or sent by the judge to the jury or individual jurors, from the time the jury is sworn until it is discharged.

(Subd (a) amended and lettered effective January 1, 2007; adopted as part of unlettered subd effective January 1, 1990.)

(b) Recording of oral jury communications

The trial judge must ensure that the reporter, or any electronic recording system used instead of a reporter, records all oral communications, formal or informal, received from the jury or from individual jurors or communicated by the judge to the jury or individual jurors, from the time the jury is sworn until it is discharged.

(Subd (b) amended and lettered effective January 1, 2007; adopted as part of unlettered subd effective January 1, 1990.)
Rule 2.1030 amended and renumbered effective January 1, 2007; adopted as rule 231 effective January 1, 1990.

Rule 2.1031. Juror note-taking

Jurors must be permitted to take written notes in all civil and criminal trials. At the beginning of a trial, a trial judge must inform jurors that they may take written notes during the trial. The court must provide materials suitable for this purpose.
Rule 2.1031 adopted effective January 1, 2007.

Advisory Committee Comment

Several cautionary jury instructions address jurors' note-taking during trial and use of notes in deliberations. (See CACI Nos. 102, 5010 and CALCRIM Nos. 102, 202.)

Ref.: Cal. Fms Pl. & Pr., Ch. 322, "Juries and Jury Selection," Ch. 326, "Jury Instructions"; MB Prac. Guide: Cal. Trial & Post-Trial Civ. Proc., §17.08[1]; CACI Nos. 102, 5010 (Matthew Bender); CALCRIM Nos. 102, 202 (Matthew Bender).

Rule 2.1032. Juror notebooks in complex civil cases

A trial judge should encourage counsel in complex civil cases to include key documents, exhibits, and other appropriate materials in notebooks for use by jurors during trial to assist them in performing their duties.
Rule 2.1032 adopted effective January 1, 2007.

Advisory Committee Comment

While this rule is intended to apply to complex civil cases, there may be other types of civil cases in which notebooks may be appropriate or useful. Resources, including guidelines for use and recommended notebook contents, are available in *Bench Handbook: Jury Management* (CJER, rev. 2006, p. 59).

Ref.: Cal. Fms Pl. & Pr., Ch. 322, "Juries and Jury Selection"; MB Prac. Guide: Cal. Trial & Post-Trial Civ. Proc., §17.08[5].

Rule 2.1033. Juror questions

A trial judge should allow jurors to submit written questions directed to witnesses. An opportunity must be given to counsel to object to such questions out of the presence of the jury.
Rule 2.1033 adopted effective January 1, 2007.

Advisory Committee Comment

See CACI No. 112 and CALCRIM No. 106. Resources, including a model admonition and a sample form for jurors to use to submit questions to the court, are available in *Bench Handbook: Jury Management* (CJER, rev. 2006, pp. 60–62).

Ref.: Cal. Fms Pl. & Pr., Ch. 322, "Juries and Jury Selection," Ch. 326, "Jury Instructions"; MB Prac. Guide: Cal. Trial & Post-Trial Civ. Proc., §§17.05[2], 17.10, 17.16, 17.17[3]; CACI Nos. 101, 112 (Matthew Bender); CALCRIM No. 106 (Matthew Bender).

Rule 2.1034. Statements to the jury panel

Prior to the examination of prospective jurors, the trial judge may, in his or her discretion, permit brief opening statements by counsel to the panel.
Rule 2.1034 adopted effective January 1, 2007.

Advisory Committee Comment

This statement is not a substitute for opening statements. Its purpose is to place voir dire questions in context and to generate interest in the case so that prospective jurors will be less inclined to claim marginal hardships.

Ref.: Cal. Fms Pl. & Pr., Ch. 322, "Juries and Jury Selection"; MB Prac. Guide: Cal. Trial & Post-Trial Civ. Proc., §17.05[4].

Rule 2.1035. Preinstruction

Immediately after the jury is sworn, the trial judge may, in his or her discretion, preinstruct the jury concerning the elements of the charges or claims, its duties, its conduct, the order of proceedings, the procedure for submitting written questions for witnesses as set forth in rule 2.1033 if questions are allowed, and the legal principles that will govern the proceeding.
Rule 2.1035 adopted effective January 1, 2007.

Ref.: Cal. Fms Pl. & Pr., Ch. 322, "Juries and Jury Selection," Ch. 326, "Jury Instructions"; MB Prac. Guide: Cal. Trial & Post-Trial Civ. Proc., §17.05[2]; CACI No. 101 (Matthew Bender); CALCRIM Nos. 100, 101 (Matthew Bender).

Rule 2.1036. Assisting the jury at impasse

(a) Determination

After a jury reports that it has reached an impasse in its deliberations, the trial judge may, in the presence of counsel, advise the jury of its duty to decide the case based on the evidence while keeping an open mind and talking about the evidence with each other. The judge should ask the jury if it has specific concerns which, if resolved, might assist the jury in reaching a verdict.

(Subd (a) adopted effective January 1, 2007.)

(b) Possible further action

If the trial judge determines that further action might assist the jury in reaching a verdict, the judge may:

(1) Give additional instructions;

(2) Clarify previous instructions;

(3) Permit attorneys to make additional closing arguments; or

(4) Employ any combination of these measures.

(Subd (b) adopted effective January 1, 2007.)
Rule 2.1036 adopted effective January 1, 2007.

Advisory Committee Comment

See Judicial Council CACI No. 5013 and Judicial Council CALCRIM No. 3550.

Ref.: Cal. Fms Pl. & Pr., Ch. 322, "Juries and Jury Selection," Ch. 326, "Jury Instructions"; MB Prac. Guide: Cal. Trial & Post-Trial Civ. Proc., §17.39[1]; CACI No. 5013 (Matthew Bender).

Chapter 3
Testimony and Evidence

Rule 2.1040. Electronic recordings offered in evidence

(a) Transcript of electronic recording

Unless otherwise ordered by the trial judge, a party offering into evidence an electronic sound or sound-and-video recording must tender to the court and to opposing parties a typewritten transcript of the electronic recording. The transcript must be marked for identification. A duplicate of the transcript, as defined in Evidence Code section 260, must be filed by the clerk and must be part of the clerk's transcript in the event of an appeal. Any other recording transcript provided to the jury must also be marked for identification, and a duplicate must be filed by the clerk and made part of the clerk's transcript in the event of an appeal.

(Subd (a) amended and lettered effective January 1, 2003.)

(b) Transcription by court reporter not required

Unless otherwise ordered by the trial judge, the court reporter need not take down or transcribe an electronic recording that is admitted into evidence.

(Subd (b) amended and lettered effective January 1, 2003.)

Rule 2.1040 amended and renumbered effective January 1, 2007; adopted as rule 203.5 effective July 1, 1988; previously amended effective January 1, 1997; amended and renumbered as rule 243.9 effective January 1, 2003.

Ref.: Cal. Fms Pl. & Pr., Ch. 221, "Dissolution of Marriage: Procedure"; W. Cal. Sum., 10 "Parent and Child" §713.

Chapter 4
Jury Instructions

Rule 2.1050. Judicial Council jury instructions
Rule 2.1055. Proposed jury instructions
Rule 2.1058. Use of gender-neutral language in jury instructions

Rule 2.1050. Judicial Council jury instructions

(a) Purpose

The California jury instructions approved by the Judicial Council are the official instructions for use in the state of California. The goal of these instructions is to improve the quality of jury decision making by providing standardized instructions that accurately state the law in a way that is understandable to the average juror.

(b) Accuracy

The Judicial Council endorses these instructions for use and makes every effort to ensure that they accurately state existing law. The articulation and interpretation of California law, however, remains within the purview of the Legislature and the courts of review.

(c) Public access

The Administrative Office of the Courts must provide copies and updates of the approved jury instructions to the public on the California Courts Web site. The Administrative Office of the Courts may contract with an official publisher to publish the instructions in both paper and electronic formats. The Judicial Council intends that the instructions be freely available for use and reproduction by parties, attorneys, and the public, except as limited by this subdivision. The Administrative Office of the Courts may take steps necessary to ensure that publication of the instructions by commercial publishers does not occur without its permission, including, without limitation, ensuring that commercial publishers accurately publish the Judicial Council's instructions, accurately credit the Judicial Council as the source of the instructions, and do not claim copyright of the instructions. The Administrative Office of the Courts may require commercial publishers to pay fees or royalties in exchange for permission to publish the instructions. As used in this rule, "commercial publishers" means entities that publish works for sale, whether for profit or otherwise.

(Subd (c) amended effective January 1, 2007; previously amended effective August 26, 2005.)

(d) Updating and amendments

The Judicial Council instructions will be regularly updated and maintained through its advisory committees on jury instructions. Amendments to these instructions will be circulated for public comment before publication. Trial judges and attorneys may submit for the advisory committees' consideration suggestions for improving or modifying these instructions or creating new instructions, with an explanation of why the change is proposed. Suggestions should be sent to the Administrative Office of the Courts, Office of the General Counsel.

(e) Use of instructions

Use of the Judicial Council instructions is strongly encouraged. If the latest edition of the jury instructions approved by the Judicial Council contains an instruction applicable to a case and the trial judge determines that the jury should be instructed on the subject, it is recommended that the judge use the Judicial Council instruction unless he or she finds that a different instruction would more accurately state the law and be understood by jurors. Whenever the latest edition of the Judicial Council jury instructions does not contain an instruction on a subject on which the trial judge determines that the jury should be instructed, or when a Judicial Council instruction cannot be modified to submit the issue properly, the instruction given on that subject should be accurate, brief, understandable, impartial, and free from argument.

(Subd (e) amended effective August 26, 2005.)

Rule 2.1050 amended and renumbered effective January 1, 2007; adopted as rule 855 effective September 1, 2003; previously amended effective August 26, 2005.

Ref.: Cal. Fms Pl. & Pr., Ch. 1, "New Developments," Ch. 247, "Eminent Domain and Inverse Condemnation," Ch. 326, "Jury Instructions," Ch. 460, "Products Liability," Ch. 551, "Trial"; MB Prac. Guide: Cal. Trial & Post-Trial Civ. Proc., §§1.09, 16.02–16.04, 16.06[1], [2][b], 16.07[3], 16.27–16.30, 17.03, 17.27, 18.09[2], 18.11, 18.16, 18.44, 18.45.

Rule 2.1055. Proposed jury instructions

(a) Application

(1) This rule applies to proposed jury instructions that a party submits to the court, including:

(A) "Approved jury instructions," meaning jury instructions approved by the Judicial Council of California; and

(B) "Special jury instructions," meaning instructions from other sources, those specially prepared by the party, or approved instructions that have been substantially modified by the party.

(2) This rule does not apply to the form or format of the instructions presented to the jury, which is a matter left to the discretion of the court.

(Subd (a) amended effective August 26, 2005; previously amended effective January 1, 2003, and January 1, 2004.)

(b) Form and format of proposed instructions

(1) All proposed instructions must be submitted to the court in the form and format prescribed for papers in the rules in division 2 of this title.

(2) Each set of proposed jury instructions must have a cover page, containing the caption of the case and stating the name of the party proposing the instructions, and an index listing all the proposed instructions.

(3) In the index, approved jury instructions must be identified by their reference numbers and special jury instructions must be numbered consecutively. The index must contain a checklist that the court may use to indicate whether the instruction was:

(A) Given as proposed;

(B) Given as modified;

(C) Refused; or

(D) Withdrawn.

(4) Each set of proposed jury instructions must be bound loosely.

(Subd (b) amended effective January 1, 2007; previously amended effective July 1, 1988, January 1, 2003, and January 1, 2004.)

(c) Format of each proposed instruction

Each proposed instruction must:

(1) Be on a separate page or pages;

(2) Include the instruction number and title of the instruction at the top of the first page of the instruction; and

(3) Be prepared without any blank lines or unused bracketed portions, so that it can be read directly to the jury.

(Subd (c) amended effective January 1, 2004; previously amended effective July 1, 1988, April 1, 1962, and January 1, 2003.)

(d) Citation of authorities

For each special instruction, a citation of authorities that support the instruction must be included at the bottom of the page. No citation is required for approved instructions.

(Subd (d) adopted effective January 1, 2004.)

(e) Form and format are exclusive

No local court form or rule for the filing or submission of proposed jury instructions may require that the instructions be submitted in any manner other than as prescribed by this rule.

(Subd (e) adopted effective January 1, 2004.)

Rule 2.1055 amended and renumbered effective January 1, 2007; adopted as rule 229 effective January 1, 1949; previously amended effective April 1, 1962, July 1, 1988, January 1, 2003, January 1, 2004, and August 26, 2005.

Advisory Committee Comment

This rule does not preclude a judge from requiring the parties in an individual case to transmit the jury instructions to the court electronically.

Ref.: Cal. Fms Pl. & Pr., Ch. 44, "Appeal: Preparing and Filing the Record," Ch. 326, "Jury Instructions," Ch. 551, "Trial"; MB Prac. Guide: Cal. Trial & Post-Trial Civ. Proc., §§1.09, 16.02–16.04, 16.06[1], [2][a], [c], 16.07[1][a]–[h], [3], 16.09[3], 16.17.

Rule 2.1058. Use of gender-neutral language in jury instructions

All instructions submitted to the jury must be written in gender-neutral language. If standard jury instructions (*CALCRIM* and *CACI*) are to be submitted to the jury, the court or, at the court's request, counsel must recast the instructions as necessary to ensure that gender-neutral language is used in each instruction.

Rule 2.1058 amended and renumbered effective January 1, 2007; adopted as rule 989 effective January 1, 1991.

Ref.: MB Prac. Guide: Cal. Trial & Post-Trial Civ. Proc., §16.08[1].

Division 9
Judgments

Rule 2.1100. Notice when statute or regulation declared unconstitutional

Within 10 days after a court has entered judgment in a contested action or special proceeding in which the court has declared unconstitutional a state statute or regulation, the prevailing party, or as otherwise ordered by the court, must mail a copy of the judgment and a notice of entry of judgment to the Attorney General and file a proof of service with the court.

Rule 2.1100 amended and renumbered effective January 1, 2007; adopted as rule 826 effective January 1, 1999.

Ref.: Cal. Fms Pl. & Pr., Ch. 318, "Judgments"; MB Prac. Guide: Cal. Trial & Post-Trial Civ. Proc., §§26.25, 26.29.

TITLE 3
Civil Rules

Division 1
General Provisions

Chapter 1
Preliminary Rules

Rule 3.1. Title

The rules in this title may be referred to as the Civil Rules.

Rule 3.1 adopted effective January 1, 2007.

Ref.: Cal. Fms Pl. & Pr., Ch. 425, "Pretrial Proceedings"; MB Prac. Guide: Cal. Pretrial Proc., §23.02.

Chapter 2
Scope of the Civil Rules

Rule 3.10. Application

Rule 3.20. Preemption of local rules

Rule 3.10. Application

The Civil Rules apply to all civil cases in the superior courts, including general civil, family, juvenile, and pro-bate cases, unless otherwise provided by a statute or rule in the California Rules of Court.

Rule 3.10 adopted effective January 1, 2007.

Rule 3.20. Preemption of local rules

(a) Fields occupied

The Judicial Council has preempted all local rules relating to pleadings, demurrers, ex parte applications, motions, discovery, provisional remedies, and the form and format of papers. No trial court, or any division or branch of a trial court, may enact or enforce any local rule concerning these fields. All local rules concerning these fields are null and void unless otherwise permitted or required by a statute or a rule in the California Rules of Court.

(Subd (a) amended effective January 1, 2007; adopted as untitled subd effective July 1, 1997; previously amended effective July 1, 2000.)

(b) Application

This rule applies to all matters identified in (a) except:

(1) Trial and post-trial proceedings including but not limited to motions in limine (see rule 3.112(f));

(2) Proceedings under Code of Civil Procedure sections 527.6, 527.7, and 527.8; the Family Code; the Probate Code; the Welfare and Institutions Code; and the Penal Code and all other criminal proceedings;

(3) Eminent domain proceedings; and

(4) Local court rules adopted under the Trial Court Delay Reduction Act.

(Subd (b) amended effective January 1, 2007; adopted effective

July 1, 2000; previously amended effective July 1, 2000, and January 1, 2002.)

Rule 3.20 amended and renumbered effective January 1, 2007; adopted as rule 302 effective July 1, 1997; amended and renumbered as rule 981.1 effective July 1, 2000; previously amended effective January 1, 2002.

Ref.: Cal. Fms Pl. & Pr., Ch. 120, "Class Actions," Ch. 190, "Discovery: Scope, Regulation, and Timing," Ch. 206, "Demurrers and Motions for Judgment on the Pleadings," Ch. 220, "Dissolution of Marriage: Master Procedural Guide," Ch. 264, "Fax Filing and Service of Papers," Ch. 303, "Injunctions," Ch. 317, "Judges," Ch. 321, "Judicial Notice," Ch. 372, "Motions and Orders," Ch. 406, "Partnerships: Dissolution," Ch. 417, "Points and Authorities," Ch. 425, "Pretrial Proceedings," Ch. 486, "Receivers," Ch. 537, "Summary Judgment"; Cal. Class Actions Prac. & Proc., §2.01; MB Prac. Guide: Cal. Pretrial Proc., §§11.15[3], 12.06[5], 18.02, 23.11[1], 26.01, 26.28, 26.43[5][b], 27.34[2][b]; MB Prac. Guide: Cal. Trial & Post-Trial Civ. Proc., §4.23.

Chapter 3
Attorneys

Rule 3.35. Definition of limited scope representation; application of rules

Rule 3.36. Notice of limited scope representation and application to be relieved as attorney

Rule 3.37. Nondisclosure of attorney assistance in preparation of court documents

Rule 3.35. Definition of limited scope representation; application of rules

(a) Definition

"Limited scope representation" is a relationship between an attorney and a person seeking legal services in which they have agreed that the scope of the legal services will be limited to specific tasks that the attorney will perform for the person.

(Subd (a) adopted effective January 1, 2007.)

(b) Application

Rules 3.35 through 3.37 apply to limited scope representation in civil cases, except in family law cases. Rules 5.70 and 5.71 apply to limited scope representation in family law cases.

(Subd (b) adopted effective January 1, 2007.)

(c) Types of limited scope representation

These rules recognize two types of limited scope representation:

(1) *Noticed representation*

Rule 3.36 provides procedures for cases in which an attorney and a party notify the court and other parties of the limited scope representation.

(2) *Undisclosed representation*

Rule 3.37 applies to cases in which the limited scope representation is not disclosed.

(Subd (c) adopted effective January 1, 2007.)

Rule 3.35 adopted effective January 1, 2007.

Ref.: Cal. Fms Pl. & Pr., Ch. 72, "Attorney Practice and Ethics"; MB Prac. Guide: Cal. Pretrial Proc., §§3.11, 3.12, 3.13[2][a]–[c], 3.38A–3.38C; W. Cal. Sum., 11 "Husband and Wife" §74.

Rule 3.36. Notice of limited scope representation and application to be relieved as attorney

(a) Notice of limited scope representation

A party and an attorney may provide notice of their agreement to limited scope representation by serving and filing a *Notice of Limited Scope Representation* (form MC-950).

(Subd (a) adopted effective January 1, 2007.)

(b) Notice and service of papers

After the notice in (a) is received and until either a substitution of attorney or an order to be relieved as attorney is filed and served, papers in the case must be served on both the attorney providing the limited scope representation and the client.

(Subd (b) adopted effective January 1, 2007.)

(c) Procedures to be relieved as counsel on completion of representation

Notwithstanding rule 3.1362, an attorney who has completed the tasks specified in the *Notice of Limited Scope Representation* (form MC-950) may use the procedures in this rule to request that he or she be relieved as attorney in cases in which the attorney has appeared before the court as an attorney of record and the client has not signed a *Substitution of Attorney—Civil* (form MC-050).

(Subd (c) adopted effective January 1, 2007.)

(d) Application

An application to be relieved as attorney on completion of limited scope representation under Code of Civil Procedure section 284(2) must be directed to the client and made on the *Application to Be Relieved as Attorney on Completion of Limited Scope Representation* (form MC-955).

(Subd (d) adopted effective January 1, 2007.)

(e) Filing and service of application

The application to be relieved as attorney must be filed with the court and served on the client and on all other parties or attorneys for parties in the case. The client must also be served with a blank *Objection to Application to Be Relieved as Attorney on Completion of Limited Scope Representation* (form MC-956).

(Subd (e) adopted effective January 1, 2007.)

(f) No objection

If no objection is served and filed with the court within 15 days from the date that the *Application to Be Relieved as Attorney on Completion of Limited Scope Representation* (form MC-955) is served on the client, the attorney making the application must file an updated form MC-955 indicating the lack of objection, along with a proposed *Order on Application to Be Relieved as Attorney on Completion of Limited Scope Representation* (form MC-958). The clerk must then forward the order for judicial signature.

(Subd (f) adopted effective January 1, 2007.)

(g) Objection

If an objection to the application is served and filed within 15 days, the clerk must set a hearing date on the *Objection to Application to Be Relieved as Attorney on Completion of Limited Scope Representation* (form MC-956). The hearing must be scheduled no later than 25 days from the date the objection is filed. The clerk must send the notice of the hearing to the parties and the attorney.

(Subd (g) adopted effective January 1, 2007.)

(h) Service of the order

If no objection is served and filed and the proposed order is signed under (f), the attorney who filed the *Application to Be Relieved as Attorney on Completion of Limited Scope Representation* (form MC-955) must serve a copy of the signed order on the client and on all parties or the attorneys for all parties who have appeared in the case. The court may delay the effective date of the order relieving the attorney until proof of service of a copy of the signed order on the client has been filed with the court.

(Subd (h) adopted effective January 1, 2007.)
Rule 3.36 adopted effective January 1, 2007.

Ref.: Cal. Fms Pl. & Pr., Ch. 72, "Attorney Practice and Ethics," Ch. 372, "Motions and Orders"; MB Prac. Guide: Cal. Pretrial Proc., §§3.11, 3.13[2][a], [b], 3.27[1], 3.29[7], 3.30[4][a]–[c], 3.38A, 26.10[3].

Rule 3.37. Nondisclosure of attorney assistance in preparation of court documents

(a) Nondisclosure

In a civil proceeding, an attorney who contracts with a client to draft or assist in drafting legal documents, but not to make an appearance in the case, is not required to disclose within the text of the documents that he or she was involved in preparing the documents.

(Subd (a) adopted effective January 1, 2007.)

(b) Attorney's fees

If a litigant seeks a court order for attorney's fees incurred as a result of document preparation, the litigant must disclose to the court information required for a proper determination of the attorney's fees, including:

(1) The name of the attorney who assisted in the preparation of the documents;

(2) The time involved or other basis for billing;

(3) The tasks performed; and

(4) The amount billed.

(Subd (b) adopted effective January 1, 2007.)

(c) Application of rule

This rule does not apply to an attorney who has made a general appearance in a case.

(Subd (c) adopted effective January 1, 2007.)
Rule 3.37 adopted effective January 1, 2007.

Ref.: Cal. Fms Pl. & Pr., Ch. 72, "Attorney Practice and Ethics"; MB Prac. Guide: Cal. Pretrial Proc., §3.13[2][a], [c].

Division 2
Waiver of Fees and Costs

Rule 3.50.   Application

The rules in this division govern applications for an order to proceed in forma pauperis—that is, without paying court fees and costs because of the applicant's financial condition.

Rule 3.50 adopted effective January 1, 2007.

Ref.: Cal. Fms Pl. & Pr., Ch. 40, "Appeal: An Overview," Ch. 42, "Appeal: Notice of Appeal," Ch. 44, "Appeal: Preparing and Filing the Record," Ch. 92, "Automobiles: Drivers' Licenses," Ch. 174, "Costs and Attorney's Fees," Ch. 220, "Dissolution of Marriage: Master Procedural Guide," Ch. 527, "Social Services," Ch. 551, "Trial"; MB Prac. Guide: Cal. Pretrial Proc., §§7.16, 7.44.

Rule 3.51.   Method of application and filing of papers

(a) Mandatory application forms

An application to proceed in forma pauperis must be made on *Application for Waiver of Court Fees and Costs* (form FW-001). An application for waiver of additional court fees and costs under rule 3.62 must be made on *Application for Waiver of Additional Court Fees and Costs* (form FW-002). The clerk must provide either form without charge to any person who requests it or indicates that he or she is unable to pay any court fee or cost.

(Subd (a) amended effective January 1, 2007.)

(b) Other forms

No applicant may be required to complete any form as part of his or her application under this rule other than forms adopted by the Judicial Council, except as authorized by Government Code section 68511.3(e)(1). Upon receipt of an application, the clerk must immediately file the application and any pleading or other paper presented by the applicant.

Rule 3.51 amended effective January 1, 2007; adopted effective January 1, 2007.

Ref.: Cal. Fms Pl. & Pr., Ch. 40, "Appeal: An Overview," Ch. 174, "Costs and Attorney's Fees," Ch. 474C, "Procedures in Reviewing Agency Decisions"; MB Prac. Guide: Cal. Pretrial Proc., §7.26[4][b], [c].

Rule 3.52.   Eligibility

(a) Mandatory

The court must grant an application to proceed in forma pauperis and must waive payment of court fees and costs listed in rule 3.61, and must waive payment of those additional court fees and costs listed in rule 3.62 that the court finds necessary, if the applicant meets the standards of eligibility established by Government Code section 68511.3(a)(6)(A) or (a)(6)(B).

(b) Discretionary

Except for an order required under (a), the court may make an order granting an application to proceed in forma pauperis under Government Code section 68511.3 or otherwise. The order may waive payment of part or all of the fees and costs and may provide that a lien exists on any money recovered by the applicant for any waived fees and costs, which shall be deemed to be taxable costs.

Rule 3.52 adopted effective January 1, 2007.

Ref.: Cal. Fms Pl. & Pr., Ch. 2, "Procedural Guide for Civil Actions," Ch. 174, "Costs and Attorney's Fees," Ch. 221, "Dissolution of Marriage: Procedure"; MB Prac. Guide: Cal. Pretrial Proc., §7.26[4][a].

Rule 3.53.   Verification of financial condition

(a) Reasonable efforts to verify financial condition

The court may authorize the clerk of the court, a county financial officer, or other appropriate county officer to make reasonable efforts to verify an applicant's financial condition. The reasonable efforts to verify must not include requiring all applicants to submit documentation to support the information contained in their applications except as authorized by Government Code section 68511.3(b)(1) and (e)(1).

(b) Additional documentation

Additional documentation of an applicant's financial condition may be required only if the applicant failed to provide the information required by the application form or if the court has good reason to doubt the truthfulness of the factual allegations in the application. If the applicant is required to submit additional documentation of his or her financial condition, the court or person authorized under (a) must:

(1) Inform the applicant of the information in the application that is insufficient or that the court believes may not be truthful;

(2) Inform the applicant of the specific type or types of documentation the applicant must submit;

(3) Require the applicant to submit only documentation that the applicant has in his or her possession or can obtain with reasonable efforts; and

(4) Require the applicant to submit only enough documentation as is necessary to clarify or prove the truthfulness of the factual allegations in the application.

Rule 3.53 adopted effective January 1, 2007.

Ref.: Cal. Fms Pl. & Pr., Ch. 174, "Costs and Attorney's Fees"; MB Prac. Guide: Cal. Pretrial Proc., §7.26[4][b].

Rule 3.54.   Determination without regard to pleading or paper submitted for filing

The court must determine an application to proceed in forma pauperis without regard to the applicant's pleading or other paper filed, if any.

Rule 3.54 adopted effective January 1, 2007.

Ref.: Cal. Fms Pl. & Pr., Ch. 174, "Costs and Attorney's Fees."

Rule 3.55.   Effect of denial of application; time for payment of fees

If an application is denied, any paper filed without payment of fees is ineffective unless the fees are paid within 10 days after notice is given by the clerk under rule 3.56. If the fees are paid more than 10 days after that notice was given, the date the applicant's pleading or other paper was originally presented to the clerk is the date for determining whether the action or proceeding was commenced within the period provided by law.

Rule 3.55 adopted effective January 1, 2007.

Ref.: Cal. Fms Pl. & Pr., Ch. 174, "Costs and Attorney's Fees."

Rule 3.56.   Procedure for determining application

The procedure for determining an application is as follows:

(1) The court must consider and determine the application as required by Government Code section 68511.3.

(2) An order determining an application to proceed in forma pauperis must be made on *Order on Application for Waiver of Court Fees and Costs* (form FW-003).

(3) An order denying an application to proceed in forma pauperis, in whole or in part, must include a statement of the reasons for the denial as required by Government Code section 68511.3.

(4) The clerk must immediately mail or deliver a copy of the order to the attorney for the applicant or, if no attorney, to the applicant if the application is not granted in full and, if the application is denied, to each other party who has appeared in the action or proceeding.

(5) The court may delegate to the clerk in writing the authority to grant applications to proceed in forma pauperis that meet the standards of eligibility in Government Code section 68511.3(a)(6)(A) or (a)(6)(B). The court may not delegate authority to deny an application.

Rule 3.56 amended effective January 1, 2007; adopted effective January 1, 2007.

Ref.: Cal. Fms Pl. & Pr., Ch. 174, "Costs and Attorney's Fees."

Rule 3.57.   Application granted unless acted on by the court

The application to proceed in forma pauperis is deemed granted unless acted on by the court within five court days after it is filed. If the application is deemed granted under this provision, the clerk must execute a *Notice of Waiver of Court Fees and Costs* (form FW-005) five court days after the application is filed.

Rule 3.57 amended effective January 1, 2007; adopted effective January 1, 2007.

Ref.: Cal. Fms Pl. & Pr., Ch. 174, "Costs and Attorney's Fees"; MB Prac. Guide: Cal. Pretrial Proc., §7.26[4][b].

Rule 3.58.   Hearing on application

(a) Notice of hearing

If the court determines that there is substantial evidentiary conflict concerning the applicant's eligibility to proceed in forma pauperis, the clerk must immediately give the applicant at least 10 days' written notice of a hearing.

(Subd (a) adopted effective January 1, 2007.)

(b) Confidentiality of hearing

To ensure confidentiality of the applicant's financial information, the hearing must be held in private and the court must exclude all persons except authorized court personnel, the applicant, those present with the applicant's consent, and any witness being examined.

(Subd (b) amended effective January 1, 2008; adopted effective January 1, 2007)

Rule 3.58 amended effective January 1, 2008; adopted effective January 1, 2007.

Ref.: Cal. Fms Pl. & Pr., Ch. 174, "Costs and Attorney's Fees"; MB Prac. Guide: Cal. Pretrial Proc., §7.26[4][b].

Rule 3.59.   Changed circumstances

(a) Duty to notify court of changed circumstances

A person whose application to proceed in forma pauperis has been granted must promptly notify the court of any changed financial circumstances affecting his or her ability to pay court fees and costs.

(Subd (a) adopted effective January 1, 2007.)

(b) Reconsideration by court

The court may not reconsider a successful applicant's eligibility to proceed in forma pauperis before the final determination of the case except in connection with an application for waiver of additional court fees and costs under rule 3.62 or in accordance with Government Code section 68511.3(d).

(Subd (b) adopted effective January 1, 2007.)

(c) Authorization to determine if condition has changed

The court may authorize the clerk of the court, the county financial officer, or another appropriate county officer to determine whether a successful applicant's financial condition has changed, enabling the applicant to pay all or a portion of the fees and costs that were waived, in the following manner:

(1) The authorized officer must notify the applicant personally or in writing that the applicant must complete and file a new application to proceed in forma pauperis.

(2) The notice under (1) must be accompanied by a blank application form.

(3) No applicant may be required to submit a new completed application more frequently than once every four months.

(4) The authorized clerk or county officer must review the new application. If the clerk or officer determines that the applicant's financial condition has changed, the court may order the applicant to pay a sum in a manner that the court believes is compatible with the applicant's financial ability.

(Subd (c) adopted effective January 1, 2007.)

Rule 3.59 adopted effective January 1, 2007.

Ref.: Cal. Fms Pl. & Pr., Ch. 174, "Costs and Attorney's Fees"; MB Prac. Guide: Cal. Pretrial Proc., §7.26[4][c].

Rule 3.60.   Confidentiality

No person may have access to an application to proceed in forma pauperis except the court and authorized court personnel, persons authorized to verify the information under rules 3.53 and 3.59(c) and under Government Code section 68511.3, and any person authorized by the applicant. No person may reveal any information contained in the application except as authorized by law.

Rule 3.60 amended effective January 1, 2008; adopted effective January 1, 2007.

Ref.: Cal. Fms Pl. & Pr., Ch. 174, "Costs and Attorney's Fees"; MB Prac. Guide: Cal. Pretrial Proc., §7.26[4][b]; MB Prac. Guide: Cal. Trial & Post-Trial Civ. Proc., §2.14[2].

Rule 3.61.   Court fees and costs waived by initial application

Court fees and costs that must be waived upon granting an application to proceed in forma pauperis include:

(1) Clerk's fees for filing papers;

(2) Clerk's fees for reasonably necessary certification and copying;

(3) Clerk's fees for issuance of process and certificates;

(4) Clerk's fees for transmittal of papers;

(5) Court-appointed interpreter's fees for parties in small claims actions;

(6) Sheriff's and marshal's fees under article 7 of **chapter 2 of part 3 of division 2 of** title 3 [1] of the Government Code **(commencing with section 26720);**

(7) Reporter's fees for attendance at hearings and trials held within 60 days of the date of the order granting the application;

(8) The fee for a telephone appearance under Government Code section 68070.1(c); and

(9) Clerk's fees for preparing, certifying, and transmitting the clerk's transcript on appeal. A party proceeding in forma pauperis must specify with particularity the documents to be included in the clerk's transcript on appeal.

Rule 3.61 amended effective January 1, 2009; adopted effective January 1, 2007.

Rule 3.61.   2008 Deletes. [1] of division 2

Ref.: Cal. Fms Pl. & Pr., Ch. 40, "Appeal: An Overview," Ch. 44, "Appeal: Preparing and Filing the Record," Ch. 174, "Costs and Attorney's Fees," Ch. 474C, "Procedures in Reviewing Agency Decisions"; MB Prac. Guide: Cal. Pretrial Proc., §7.26[4][c].

Rule 3.62.   Additional court fees and costs waived

The court fees and costs that may be waived upon granting an application include:

(1) Jury fees and expenses;

(2) Court-appointed interpreter's fees for witnesses;

(3) Witness fees of peace officers whose attendance is reasonably necessary for prosecution or defense of the case;

(4) Reporter's fees for attendance at hearings and trials held more than 60 days after the date of the order granting the application;

(5) Witness fees of court-appointed experts; and

(6) Other fees or expenses as itemized in the application.

Rule 3.62 adopted effective January 1, 2007.

Ref.: Cal. Fms Pl. & Pr., Ch. 174, "Costs and Attorney's Fees"; MB Prac. Guide: Cal. Pretrial Proc., §7.26[4][c].

Rule 3.63.   Posting notice

Each trial court must post in a conspicuous place near the filing window or counter a notice, 8½ by 11 inches or larger, advising litigants in English and Spanish that they may ask the court to waive court fees and costs. The notice must be substantially as follows:

"NOTICE: If you are unable to pay fees and costs, ask the court to permit you to proceed without paying them. Ask the clerk for the *Information Sheet on Waiver of Court Fees and Costs* and the *Application for Waiver of Court Fees and Costs.*"

Rule 3.63 adopted effective January 1, 2007.

Division 3
Filing and Service

Chap. 1.   Filing. Rule 3.100.
Chap. 2.   Time for Service. Rule 3.110.
Chap. 3.   Papers to Be Served. Rules 3.220–3.222.
Chap. 4.   Miscellaneous. Rules 3.250–3.254.

Chapter 1
Filing

Rule 3.100.   Payment of filing fees by credit or debit card

A party may pay a filing fee by credit or debit card provided the court is authorized to accept payment by this method under Government Code section 6159, rule 10.820, and other applicable law.

Rule 3.100 adopted effective January 1, 2007.

Ref.: Cal. Fms Pl. & Pr., Ch. 290D, "Guardianship and Conservatorship: Actions Against Guardians, Conservators, and Sureties"; MB Prac. Guide: Cal. Pretrial Proc., §14.24.

Chapter 2
Time for Service

Rule 3.110.   Time for service of complaint, cross-complaint, and response

(a) Application

This rule applies to the service of pleadings in civil cases except for collections cases under rule 3.740(a), unlawful detainer actions, proceedings under the Family Code, and other proceedings for which different service requirements are prescribed by law.

(Subd (a) amended effective July 1, 2007; previously amended effective January 1, 2007.)

(b) Service of complaint

The complaint must be served on all named defendants and proofs of service on those defendants must be filed with the court within 60 days after the filing of the complaint. When the complaint is amended to add a defendant, the added defendant must be served and proof of service must be filed within 30 days after the filing of the amended complaint.

(c) Service of cross-complaint

A cross-complaint against a party who has appeared in the action must be accompanied by proof of service of the cross-complaint at the time it is filed. If the cross-complaint adds new parties, the cross-complaint must be served on all parties and proofs of service on the new parties must be filed within 30 days of the filing of the cross-complaint.

(d) Timing of responsive pleadings

The parties may stipulate without leave of court to one 15-day extension beyond the 30-day time period prescribed for the response after service of the initial complaint.

(e) Modification of timing; application for order extending time

The court, on its own motion or on the application of a party, may extend or otherwise modify the times provided in (b)–(d). An application for a court order extending the time to serve a pleading must be filed before the time for service has elapsed. The application must be accompanied by a declaration showing why service has not been completed, documenting the efforts that have been made to complete service, and specifying the date by which service is proposed to be completed.

(Subd (e) amended effective January 1, 2007.)

(f) Failure to serve

If a party fails to serve and file pleadings as required under this rule, and has not obtained an order extending time to serve its pleadings, the court may issue an order to show cause why sanctions shall not be imposed.

(Subd (f) amended effective January 1, 2007.)

(g) Request for entry of default

If a responsive pleading is not served within the time limits specified in this rule and no extension of time has been granted, the plaintiff must file a request for entry of default within 10 days after the time for service has elapsed. The court may issue an order to show cause why sanctions should not be imposed if the plaintiff fails to timely file the request for the entry of default.

(Subd (g) amended effective January 1, 2007.)

(h) Default judgment

When a default is entered, the party who requested the entry of default must obtain a default judgment against the defaulting party within 45 days after the default was entered, unless the court has granted an extension of time. The court may issue an order to show cause why sanctions should not be imposed if that party fails to obtain entry of judgment against a defaulting party or to request an extension of time to apply for a default judgment within that time.

(Subd (h) amended effective January 1, 2007.)

(i) Order to show cause

Responsive papers to an order to show cause issued under this rule must be filed and served at least 5 calendar days before the hearing.

(Subd (i) amended effective January 1, 2007.)

Rule 3.110 amended effective July 1, 2007; adopted as rule 201.7 effective July 1, 2002; previously amended and renumbered effective January 1, 2007.

Ref.: Cal. Fms Pl. & Pr., Ch. 1, "New Developments," Ch. 123, "Complaints and Cross Complaints," Ch. 125, "Consolidation, Severance, and Coordination of Actions," Ch. 346, "Limited Liability Companies," Ch. 425, "Pretrial Proceedings," Ch. 518, "Service of Summons and Papers"; MB Prac. Guide: Cal. Debt Collection & Enforcement of Judgments, §§7.10, 7.12[1], [2]; MB Prac. Guide: Cal. Pretrial Proc., §§1.05, 7.28–7.31, 8.07, 8.08[1][a]–[c], 8.36[1], [2], 9.03, 9.06[2], 9.41, 16.13[5], 16.14, 36.13.

Chapter 3
Papers to Be Served

Rule 3.220. Case cover sheet
Rule 3.221. Information about alternative dispute resolution
Rule 3.222. Papers to be served on cross-defendants

Rule 3.220.   Case cover sheet
(a) Cover sheet required

The first paper filed in an action or proceeding must be accompanied by a case cover sheet as required in (b). The cover sheet must be on a form prescribed by the Judicial Council and must be filed in addition to any cover sheet required by local court rule. If the plaintiff indicates on the cover sheet that the case is complex under rule 3.400 et seq. **or a collections case under rule 3.740**, the plaintiff must serve a copy of the cover sheet with the complaint. In all other cases, the plaintiff is not required to serve the cover sheet. The cover sheet is used for statistical purposes and may affect the assignment of a complex case.

(Subd (a) amended effective January 1, 2009; previously amended effective January 1, 2000, January 1, 2002, and January 1, 2007.)

(b) List of cover sheets

(1) *Civil Case Cover Sheet* (form CM-010) must be filed in each civil action or proceeding, except those filed in small claims court or filed under the Probate Code, Family Code, or Welfare and Institutions Code.

(2) [**Note:** Case cover sheets will be added for use in additional areas of the law as the data collection program expands.]

(Subd (b) amended effective January 1, 2007; previously amended effective July 1, 2002, and July 1, 2003.)

(c) Failure to provide cover sheet

If a party that is required to provide a cover sheet under this rule or a similar local rule fails to do so or provides a defective or incomplete cover sheet at the time the party's first paper is submitted for filing, the clerk of the court must file the paper. Failure of a party or a party's counsel to file a cover sheet as required by this rule may subject that party, its counsel, or both, to sanctions under rule 2.30.

(Subd (c) amended effective January 1, 2007; adopted effective January 1, 2002.)

Rule 3.220 amended effective January 1, 2009; adopted as rule 982.2 effective July 1, 1996; previously amended and renumbered as rule 201.8 effective July 1, 2002, and as rule 3.220 effective January 1, 2007; previously amended effective January 1, 2000, January 1, 2002, and July 1, 2003.

Ref.: Cal. Fms Pl. & Pr., Ch. 2, "Procedural Guide for Civil Actions," Ch. 26, "Answers," Ch. 123, "Complaints and Cross Complaints," Ch. 333, "Landlord and Tenant: Eviction Actions," Ch. 345A, "Limited Civil Cases," Ch. 358, "Mandate and Prohibition," Ch. 425, "Pretrial Proceedings"; MB Prac. Guide: Cal. Pretrial Proc., §§7.16, 7.20[1]–[4], 7.43, 7.44, 14.25, 23.04[3].

Rule 3.221. Information about alternative dispute resolution

(a) Court to provide information package

Each court must make available to the plaintiff, at the time the complaint is filed in all general civil cases, an alternative dispute resolution (ADR) information package that includes, at a minimum, all of the following:

(1) General information about the potential advantages and disadvantages of ADR and descriptions of the principal ADR processes. The Administrative Office of the Courts has prepared model language that the courts may use to provide this information.

(2) Information about the ADR programs available in that court, including citations to any applicable local court rules and directions for contacting any court staff responsible for providing parties with assistance regarding ADR.

(3) In counties that are participating in the Dispute Resolution Programs Act (DRPA), information about the availability of local dispute resolution programs funded under the DRPA. This information may take the form of a list of the applicable programs or directions for contacting the county's DRPA coordinator.

(4) An ADR stipulation form that parties may use to stipulate to the use of an ADR process.

(Subd (a) amended effective January 1, 2007; previously amended effective July 1, 2002.)

(b) Court may make package available on Web site

A court may make the ADR information package available on its Web site as long as paper copies are also made available in the clerk's office.

(Subd (b) adopted effective July 1, 2002.)

(c) Plaintiff to serve information package

In all general civil cases, the plaintiff must serve a copy of the ADR information package on each defendant together with the complaint. Cross-complainants must serve a copy of the ADR information package on any new parties to the action together with the cross-complaint.

(Subd (c) amended effective January 1, 2007; adopted as subd (b) effective January 1, 2001; previously amended and relettered effective July 1, 2002.)

Rule 3.221 amended and renumbered effective January 1, 2007; adopted as rule 1590.1 effective January 1, 2001; previously amended and renumbered as rule 201.9 effective July 1, 2002.

Ref.: Cal. Fms Pl. & Pr., Ch. 2, "Procedural Guide for Civil Actions," Ch. 30, "Using Alternative Dispute Resolution," Ch. 32, "Contractual Arbitration: Agreements and Compelling Arbitration," Ch. 36, "Judicial Arbitration," Ch. 37, "Judicially Mandated Civil Action Mediation," Ch. 123, "Complaints and Cross Complaints," Ch. 425, "Pretrial Proceedings," Ch. 518, "Service of Summons and Papers"; MB Prac. Guide: Cal. Pretrial Proc., §§6.10[1][a], 7.28, 7.32, 16.13[4], 24.04[1][c], 24.43, 24.52[2], 24.64.

Rule 3.222. Papers to be served on cross-defendants

A cross-complainant must serve a copy of the complaint or, if it has been amended, the most recently amended complaint and any answers thereto on cross-defendants who have not previously appeared.

Rule 3.222 amended and renumbered effective January 1, 2007; adopted as rule 202 effective January 1, 1985; previously amended effective January 1, 2003.

Ref.: Cal. Fms Pl. & Pr., Ch. 2, "Procedural Guide for Civil Actions," Ch. 123, "Complaints and Cross Complaints," Ch. 460, "Products Liability," Ch. 518, "Service of Summons and Papers"; MB Prac. Guide: Cal. Pretrial Proc., §16.13[3].

Chapter 4
Miscellaneous

Rule 3.250. Limitations on the filing of papers

(a) Papers not to be filed

The following papers, whether offered separately or as attachments to other documents, may not be filed unless they are offered as relevant to the determination of an issue in a law and motion proceeding or other hearing or are ordered filed for good cause:

(1) Subpoena;

(2) Subpoena duces tecum;

(3) Deposition notice, and response;

(4) Notice to consumer or employee, and objection;

(5) Notice of intention to record testimony by audio or video tape;

(6) Notice of intention to take an oral deposition by telephone, videoconference, or other remote electronic means;

(7) Agreement to set or extend time for deposition, agreement to extend time for response to discovery requests, and notice of these agreements;

(8) Interrogatories, and responses or objections to interrogatories;

(9) Demand for production or inspection of documents, things, and places, and responses or objections to demand;

(10) Request for admissions, and responses or objections to request;

(11) Agreement for physical and mental examinations;

(12) Demand for delivery of medical reports, and response;

(13) Demand for exchange of expert witnesses;

(14) Demand for production of discoverable reports and writings of expert witnesses;

(15) List of expert witnesses whose opinion a party intends to offer in evidence at trial and declaration;

(16) Statement that a party does not presently intend to offer the testimony of any expert witness;

(17) Declaration for additional discovery;

(18) Stipulation to enlarge the scope of number of discovery requests from that specified by statute, and notice of the stipulation;

(19) Demand for bill of particulars or an accounting, and response;

(20) Request for statement of damages, and response, unless it is accompanied by a request to enter default and is the notice of special and general damages;

(21) Notice of deposit of jury fees;

(22) Notice to produce party, agent, or tangible things before a court, and response; and

(23) Offer to compromise, unless accompanied by an original proof of acceptance and a written judgment for the court's signature and entry of judgment.

(Subd (a) amended effective January 1, 2003; previously amended effective January 1, 2001.)

(b) Retaining originals of papers not filed

Unless the paper served is a response, the party who serves a paper listed in (a) must retain the original with the original proof of service affixed. The original of a response must be served, and it must be retained by the person upon whom it is served. All original papers must be retained until six months after final disposition of the case, unless the court on motion of any party and for good cause shown orders the original papers preserved for a longer period.

(Subd (b) amended effective January 1, 2007; amended effective January 1, 2003.)

(c) Papers defined

As used in this rule, papers include printed forms furnished by the clerk, but do not include notices filed and served by the clerk.

Rule 3.250 amended and renumbered effective January 1, 2007; adopted as rule 201.5 effective July 1, 1987; previously amended effective January 1, 2001, and January 1, 2003.

Ref.: Cal. Fms Pl. & Pr., Ch. 85, "Automobiles: Discovery," Ch. 121, "Common Counts," Ch. 190, "Discovery: Scope, Regulation, and Timing," Ch. 193, "Discovery: Depositions," Ch. 194, "Discovery: Interrogatories," Ch. 195, "Discovery: Inspection of Tangible Evidence," Ch. 196, "Discovery: Requests for Admissions," Ch. 197, "Discovery: Physical and Mental Examinations," Ch. 198, "Discovery: Exchange of Expert Witness Information," Ch. 482, "Quieting Title," Ch. 518, "Service of Summons and Papers."

Rule 3.252. Service of papers on the clerk when a party's address is unknown

(a) Service of papers

When service is made under Code of Civil Procedure section 1011(b) and a party's residence address is unknown, the notice or papers delivered to the clerk, or to the judge if there is no clerk, must be enclosed in an envelope addressed to the party in care of the clerk or the judge.

(Subd (a) amended and lettered effective January 1, 2003.)

(b) Information on the envelope

The back of the envelope delivered under (a) must bear the following information:

"Service is being made under Code of Civil Procedure section 1011(b) on a party whose residence address is unknown."

[Name of party whose residence address is unknown]

[Case name and number]

(Subd (b) amended and lettered effective January 1, 2003.)

Rule 3.252 renumbered effective January 1, 2007; adopted as rule 202.5 effective July 1, 1997; previously amended effective January 1, 2003.

Ref.: Cal. Fms Pl. & Pr., Ch. 518, "Service of Summons and Papers"; MB Prac. Guide: Cal. Pretrial Proc., §27.36.

Rule 3.254. List of parties

(a) Duties of first-named plaintiff or petitioner

If more than two parties have appeared in a case and are represented by different counsel, the plaintiff or petitioner named first in the complaint or petition must:

(1) Maintain a current list of the parties and their addresses for service of notice on each party; and

(2) Furnish a copy of the list on request to any party or the court.

(Subd (a) amended and lettered effective January 1, 2007; adopted as part of unlettered subd effective July 1, 1984.)

(b) Duties of each party

Each party must:

(1) Furnish the first-named plaintiff or petitioner with its current address for service of notice when it first appears in the action;

(2) Furnish the first-named plaintiff or petitioner with any changes in its address for service of notice; and

(3) If it serves an order, notice, or pleading on a party who has not yet appeared in the action, serve a copy of the list required under (a) at the same time as the order, notice, or pleading is served.

(Subd (b) amended and lettered effective January 1, 2007; adopted as part of unlettered subd effective July 1, 1984.)
Rule 3.254 amended and renumbered effective January 1, 2007; adopted as rule 387 effective July 1, 1984; previously amended and renumbered as rule 202.7 effective January 1, 2003.

Ref.: Cal. Fms Pl. & Pr., Ch. 2, "Procedural Guide for Civil Actions," Ch. 137, "Continuing Duties During Litigation," Ch. 264, "Fax Filing and Service of Papers," Ch. 518, "Service of Summons and Papers"; MB Prac. Guide: Cal. Pretrial Proc., §§27.25, 27.26.

Division 4
Parties and Actions

Chap. 1. [Reserved].
Chap. 2. Joinder of Parties [Reserved].
Chap. 3. Related Cases. Rule 3.300.
Chap. 4. Consolidated Cases. Rule 3.350.
Chap. 5. Complex Cases. Rules 3.400–3.403.
Chap. 6. Coordination of Noncomplex Actions. Rule 3.500.
Chap. 7. Coordination of Complex Actions. Rules 3.501–3.550.

Chapter 1
[Reserved]

Chapter 2
Joinder of Parties
[Reserved]

Chapter 3
Related Cases

Rule 3.300. Related cases

(a) Definition of "related case"

A pending civil case is related to another pending civil case, or to a civil case that was dismissed with or without prejudice, or to a civil case that was disposed of by judgment, if the cases:

(1) Involve the same parties and are based on the same or similar claims;

(2) Arise from the same or substantially identical transactions, incidents, or events requiring the determination of the same or substantially identical questions of law or fact;

(3) Involve claims against, title to, possession of, or damages to the same property; or

(4) Are likely for other reasons to require substantial duplication of judicial resources if heard by different judges.

(Subd (a) adopted effective January 1, 2007.)

(b) Duty to provide notice

Whenever a party in a civil action knows or learns that the action or proceeding is related to another action or proceeding pending, dismissed, or disposed of by judgment in any state or federal court in California, the party must serve and file a Notice of Related Case.

(Subd (b) amended and relettered effective January 1, 2007; adopted as part of subd (a) effective January 1, 1996; previously amended effective January 1, 2007.)

(c) Contents of the notice

The Notice of Related Case must:

(1) List all civil cases that are related by court, case name, case number, and filing date;

(2) Identify the case that has the earliest filing date and the court and department in which that case is pending; and

(3) Describe the manner in which the cases are related.

(Subd (c) repealed and adopted effective January 1, 2007.)

(d) Service and filing of notice

The Notice of Related Case must be filed in all pending cases listed in the notice and must be served on all parties in those cases.

(Subd (d) adopted effective January 1, 2007.)

(e) Time for service

The Notice of Related Case must be served and filed as soon as possible, but no later than 15 days after the facts concerning the existence of related cases become known.

(Subd (e) adopted effective January 1, 2007.)

(f) Continuing duty to provide notice

The duty under (b)–(e) is a continuing duty that applies when a party files a case with knowledge of a related action or proceeding, and that applies thereafter whenever a party learns of a related action or proceeding.

(Subd (f) amended and relettered effective January 1, 2007; adopted as part of subd (a) effective January 1, 1996; previously adopted as subd (b) effective January 1, 2007.)

(g) Response

Within 5 days after service on a party of a Notice of Related Case, the party may serve and file a response supporting or opposing the notice. The response must state why one or more of the cases listed in the notice are not related or why other good cause exists for the court not to transfer the cases to or from a particular court or department. The response must be filed in all pending cases listed in the notice and must be served on all parties in those cases.

(Subd (g) amended and relettered effective January 1, 2007; adopted as subd (c) effective January 1, 1996; previously amended and relettered subd (d) effective January 1, 2007.)

(h) Judicial action

(1) *Related cases pending in one superior court*

If all the related cases have been filed in one superior court, the court, on notice to all parties, may order that the cases, including probate and family law cases, be related and may assign them to a single judge or department. In a superior court where there is a master calendar, the presiding judge may order the cases related. In a court in which cases are assigned to a single judge or department, cases may be ordered related as follows:

(A) Where all the cases listed in the notice are unlimited civil cases, or where all the cases listed in the notice are limited civil cases, the judge who has the earliest filed case must determine whether the cases must be ordered related and assigned to his or her department;

(B) Where the cases listed in the notice include both unlimited and limited civil cases, the judge who has the earliest filed unlimited civil case must determine whether the cases should be ordered related and assigned to his or her department;

(C) Where the cases listed in the notice contain a probate or family law case, the presiding judge or a judge designated by the presiding judge must determine whether the cases should be ordered related and, if so, to which judge or department they should be assigned;

(D) In the event that any of the cases listed in the notice are not ordered related under (A), (B), or (C), any party in any of the cases listed in the notice may file a motion to have the cases related. The motion must be filed with the presiding judge or the judge designated by the presiding judge; and

(E) If the procedures for relating pending cases under this rule do not apply, the procedures under Code of Civil Procedure section 1048 and rule 3.350 must be followed to consolidate cases pending in the same superior court.

(2) *Related cases pending in different superior courts*

(A) If the related cases are pending in more than one superior court on notice to all parties, the judge to whom the earliest filed case is assigned may confer informally with the parties and with the judges to whom each related case is assigned, to determine the feasibility and desirability of joint discovery orders and other informal or formal means of coordinating proceedings in the cases.

(B) If it is determined that related cases pending in different superior courts should be formally coordinated, the procedures in Code of Civil Procedure section 403 and rule 3.500 must be followed for noncomplex cases, and the procedures in Code of Civil Procedure section 404 et seq. and rules 3.501 et seq. must be followed for complex cases.

(3) *Complex cases*

The provisions in (1) of this subdivision do not apply to cases that have been designated as complex by the parties or determined to be complex by the court.

(Subd (h) amended effective January 1, 2008; adopted as subd (d) effective January 1, 1996; previously amended and relettered as subd (e) effective January 1, 2007.)

(i) Ruling on related cases

The court, department, or judge issuing an order relating cases under this rule must either:

(1) File a notice of the order in all pending cases and serve a copy of the notice on all parties listed in the Notice of Related Case; or

(2) Direct counsel for a party to file the notice in all pending cases and serve a copy on all parties.

(Subd (i) adopted effective January 1, 2007.)

(j) Cases not ordered related

If for any reason a case is not ordered related under this rule, that case will remain assigned to the court, judge, or department where it was pending at the time of the filing and service of the Notice of Related Case.

(Subd (j) adopted effective January 1, 2007.)

(k) Exception

A party is not required to serve and file Notice of Related Case under this rule if another party has already filed a notice and served all parties under this rule on the same case.

(Subd (k) adopted effective January 1, 2007.)

Rule 3.300 amended effective January 1, 2008; adopted as rule 804 effective January 1, 1996; previously amended and renumbered effective January 1, 2007.

Ref.: Cal. Fms Pl. & Pr., Ch. 1, "New Developments," Ch. 2, "Procedural Guide for Civil Actions," Ch. 3, "Abatement of

Actions," Ch. 123, "Complaints and Cross Complaints," Ch. 125, "Consolidation, Severance, and Coordination of Actions," Ch. 137, "Continuing Duties During Litigation"; MB Prac. Guide: Cal. Pretrial Proc., §§7.16, 7.25, 16.02, 32.01, 32.03, 32.04[1], [2][a], [b], [3], 32.05, 32.06[1][a]–[d], [2]–[4], 32.26A, 39.10[5][c].

Chapter 4
Consolidated Cases

Rule 3.350.   Consolidation of cases

(a) Requirements of motion

(1) A notice of motion to consolidate must:

(A) List all named parties in each case, the names of those who have appeared, and the names of their respective attorneys of record;

(B) Contain the captions of all the cases sought to be consolidated, with the lowest numbered case shown first; and

(C) Be filed in each case sought to be consolidated.

(2) The motion to consolidate:

(A) Is deemed a single motion for the purpose of determining the appropriate filing fee, but memorandums, declarations, and other supporting papers must be filed only in the lowest numbered case;

(B) Must be served on all attorneys of record and all nonrepresented parties in all of the cases sought to be consolidated; and

(C) Must have a proof of service filed as part of the motion.

(Subd (a) amended effective January 1, 2007; adopted effective July 1, 1999.)

(b) Lead case

Unless otherwise provided in the order granting the motion to consolidate, the lowest numbered case in the consolidated case is the lead case.

(Subd (b) amended effective January 1, 2007; adopted effective July 1, 1999.)

(c) Order

An order granting or denying all or part of a motion to consolidate must be filed in each case sought to be consolidated. If the motion is granted for all purposes including trial, any subsequent document must be filed only in the lead case.

(Subd (c) amended effective January 1, 2007; adopted effective July 1, 1999.)

(d) Caption and case number

All documents filed in the consolidated case must include the caption and case number of the lead case, followed by the case numbers of all of the other consolidated cases.

(Subd (d) amended effective January 1, 2007; adopted effective July 1, 1999.)

Rule 3.350 amended and renumbered effective January 1, 2007; adopted as rule 367 effective January 1, 1984; previously amended effective July 1, 1999.

Ref.: Cal. Fms Pl. & Pr., Ch. 125, "Consolidation, Severance, and Coordination of Actions"; MB Prac. Guide: Cal. Pretrial Proc., §§1.07, 1.09, 32.01, 32.06[1][c], 32.07[1], 32.09[1], 32.10[1], 32.11, 32.12, 32.17[4], 32.29.

Chapter 5
Complex Cases

Rule 3.400. Definition

Rule 3.401. Complex case designation
Rule 3.402. Complex case counterdesignations
Rule 3.403. Action by court

Rule 3.400. Definition

(a) Definition

A "complex case" is an action that requires exceptional judicial management to avoid placing unnecessary burdens on the court or the litigants and to expedite the case, keep costs reasonable, and promote effective decision making by the court, the parties, and counsel.

(b) Factors

In deciding whether an action is a complex case under (a), the court must consider, among other things, whether the action is likely to involve:

(1) Numerous pretrial motions raising difficult or novel legal issues that will be time-consuming to resolve;

(2) Management of a large number of witnesses or a substantial amount of documentary evidence;

(3) Management of a large number of separately represented parties;

(4) Coordination with related actions pending in one or more courts in other counties, states, or countries, or in a federal court; or

(5) Substantial postjudgment judicial supervision.

(Subd (b) amended effective January 1, 2007.)

(c) Provisional designation

Except as provided in (d), an action is provisionally a complex case if it involves one or more of the following types of claims:

(1) Antitrust or trade regulation claims;

(2) Construction defect claims involving many parties or structures;

(3) Securities claims or investment losses involving many parties;

(4) Environmental or toxic tort claims involving many parties;

(5) Claims involving mass torts;

(6) Claims involving class actions; or

(7) Insurance coverage claims arising out of any of the claims listed in (c)(1) through (c)(6).

(Subd (c) amended effective January 1, 2007.)

(d) Court's discretion

Notwithstanding (c), an action is not provisionally complex if the court has significant experience in resolving like claims involving similar facts and the management of those claims has become routine. A court may declare by local rule that certain types of cases are or are not provisionally complex under this subdivision.

(Subd (d) amended effective January 1, 2007.)
Rule 3.400 amended and renumbered effective January 1, 2007; adopted as rule 1800 effective January 1, 2000.

Ref.: Cal. Fms Pl. & Pr., Ch. 2, "Procedural Guide for Civil Actions," Ch. 26, "Answers," Ch. 123, "Complaints and Cross Complaints," Ch. 125, "Consolidation, Severance, and Coordination of Actions," Ch. 168, "Corporations: Derivative Actions," Ch. 425, "Pretrial Proceedings," Ch. 460, "Products Liability," Ch. 551, "Trial"; MB Prac. Guide: Cal. Pretrial Proc., §§7.20[1], 23.04[1][f], 23.12[1], 32.08[1], 32.14[1], 32.15[2], 32.16[2], 32.18[1], 32.19[3], 32.33, 32.39.

Rule 3.401. Complex case designation

A plaintiff may designate an action as a complex case by filing and serving with the initial complaint the *Civil Case Cover Sheet* (form CM-010) marked to indicate that the action is a complex case.

Rule 3.401 renumbered effective January 1, 2007; adopted as rule 1810 effective January 1, 2000; previously amended effective July 1, 2002, and July 1, 2004.

Ref.: Cal. Fms Pl. & Pr., Ch. 425, "Pretrial Proceedings"; MB Prac. Guide: Cal. Pretrial Proc., §§14.25, 23.12[1].

Rule 3.402. Complex case counterdesignations

(a) Noncomplex counterdesignation

If a *Civil Case Cover Sheet* (form CM-010) designating an action as a complex case has been filed and served and the court has not previously declared the action to be a complex case, a defendant may file and serve no later than its first appearance a counter *Civil Case Cover Sheet* (form CM-010) designating the action as not a complex case. The court must decide, with or without a hearing, whether the action is a complex case within 30 days after the filing of the counterdesignation.

(Subd (a) amended effective January 1, 2007; previously amended effective July 1, 2004.)

(b) Complex counterdesignation

A defendant may file and serve no later than its first appearance a counter *Civil Case Cover Sheet* (form CM-010) designating the action as a complex case. The court must decide, with or without a hearing, whether the action is a complex case within 30 days after the filing of the counterdesignation.

(Subd (b) amended effective January 1, 2007; previously amended effective July 1, 2004.)

(c) Joint complex designation

A defendant may join the plaintiff in designating an action as a complex case.

Rule 3.402 amended and renumbered effective January 1, 2007; adopted as rule 1811 effective January 1, 2000; previously amended effective July 1, 2004.

Ref.: Cal. Fms Pl. & Pr., Ch. 2, "Procedural Guide for Civil Actions," Ch. 26, "Answers," Ch. 425, "Pretrial Proceedings"; MB Prac. Guide: Cal. Pretrial Proc., §§14.12, 14.25, 23.04[1][f], 23.12[1].

Rule 3.403. Action by court

(a) Decision on complex designation

Except as provided in rule 3.402, if a *Civil Case Cover Sheet* (form CM-010) that has been filed and served designates an action as a complex case or checks a case type described as provisionally complex civil litigation, the court must decide as soon as reasonably practicable, with or without a hearing, whether the action is a complex case.

(Subd (a) amended effective January 1, 2007; previously amended effective July 1, 2004.)

(b) Court's continuing power

With or without a hearing, the court may decide on its own motion, or on a noticed motion by any party, that a civil action is a complex case or that an action previously declared to be a complex case is not a complex case.

Rule 3.403 amended effective January 1, 2007; adopted as rule 1812 effective January 1, 2000; previously amended effective July 1, 2004; previously amended and renumbered effective January 1, 2007.

Ref.: Cal. Fms Pl. & Pr., Ch. 2, "Procedural Guide for Civil Actions," Ch. 190, "Discovery: Scope, Regulation, and Timing," Ch. 425, "Pretrial Proceedings," Ch. 518, "Service of Summons and Papers"; MB Prac. Guide: Cal. Pretrial Proc., §§23.12[1], 27.35[5].

Chapter 6
Coordination of Noncomplex Actions

Rule 3.500. Transfer and consolidation of noncomplex common-issue actions filed in different courts

(a) Application

This rule applies when a motion under Code of Civil Procedure section 403 is filed requesting transfer and consolidation of noncomplex cases involving a common issue of fact or law filed in different courts.

(Subd (a) amended and lettered effective January 1, 2007; adopted as unlettered subd effective September 21, 1996.)

(b) Preliminary step

A party that intends to file a motion under Code of Civil Procedure section 403 must first make a good-faith effort to obtain agreement of all parties to each case to the proposed transfer and consolidation.

(Subd (b) amended and relettered effective January 1, 2007; adopted as subd (a) effective September 21, 1996.)

(c) Motion and hearing

A motion to transfer an action under Code of Civil Procedure section 403 must conform to the requirements generally applicable to motions, and must be supported by a declaration stating facts showing that:

(1) The actions are not complex;

(2) The moving party has made a good-faith effort to obtain agreement to the transfer and consolidation from all parties to the actions; and

(3) The moving party has notified all parties of their obligation to disclose to the court any information they may have concerning any other motions requesting transfer of any case that would be affected by the granting of the motion before the court.

(Subd (c) amended and relettered effective January 1, 2007; adopted as subd (b) effective September 21, 1996.)

(d) Findings and order

If the court orders that the case or cases be transferred from another court, the order must specify the reasons supporting a finding that the transfer will promote the ends of justice, with reference to the following standards:

(1) The actions are not complex;

(2) Whether the common question of fact or law is predominating and significant to the litigation;

(3) The convenience of the parties, witnesses, and counsel;

(4) The relative development of the actions and the work product of counsel;

(5) The efficient utilization of judicial facilities and staff resources;

(6) The calendar of the courts;

(7) The disadvantages of duplicative and inconsistent rulings, orders, or judgments; and

(8) The likelihood of settlement of the actions without further litigation should coordination be denied.

(Subd (d) amended and relettered effective January 1, 2007; adopted as subd (c) effective September 21, 1996.)

(e) Moving party to provide copies of order

If the court orders that the case or cases be transferred from another court, the moving party must promptly serve the order on all parties to each case and send it to the Judicial Council and to the presiding judge of the court from which each case is to be transferred.

(Subd (e) amended and relettered effective January 1, 2007; adopted as subd (d) effective September 21, 1996.)

(f) Moving party to take necessary action to complete transfer and consolidation

If the court orders a case or cases transferred, the moving party must promptly take all appropriate action necessary to assure that the transfer takes place and that proceedings are initiated in the other court or courts to complete consolidation with the case pending in that court.

(Subd (f) amended and relettered effective January 1, 2007; adopted as subd (3) effective September 21, 1996.)

(g) Conflicting orders

The coordination staff in the Administrative Office of the Courts must review all transfer orders submitted under (e) and must promptly confer with the presiding judges of any courts that have issued conflicting orders under Code of Civil Procedure section 403. The presiding judges of those courts must confer with each other and with the judges who have issued the orders to the extent necessary to resolve the conflict. If it is determined that any party to a case has failed to disclose information concerning pending motions, the court may, after a duly noticed hearing, find that the party's failure to disclose is an unlawful interference with the processes of the court.

(Subd (g) amended and relettered effective January 1, 2007; adopted as subd (f) effective September 21, 1996.)

(h) Alternative disposition of motion

If after considering the motion the judge determines that the action or actions pending in another court should not be transferred to the judge's court but instead all the actions that are subject to the motion to transfer should be transferred and consolidated in another court, the judge may order the parties to prepare, serve, and file a motion to have the actions transferred to the appropriate court.

(Subd (h) amended and relettered effective January 1, 2007; adopted as subd (g) effective September 21, 1996.)
Rule 3.500 amended and renumbered effective January 1, 2007; adopted as rule 1500 effective September 21, 1996.

Ref.: Cal. Fms Pl. & Pr., Ch. 125, "Consolidation, Severance, and Coordination of Actions"; MB Prac. Guide: Cal. Pretrial Proc., §§32.01, 32.06[2], 32.14[1], [2], 32.16[2], [4], [7], 32.17[2], [3], [5], 32.33, 32.34.

Chapter 7
Coordination of Complex Actions

Art. 4.   Pretrial and Trial Rules for Complex Coordinated
Actions. Rules 3.540–3.545.
Art. 5.   Administration of Coordinated Complex Actions.
Rule 3.550.

Article 1
General Provisions

Rule 3.501. Definitions
Rule 3.502. Complex case—determination
Rule 3.503. Requests for extensions of time or to shorten time
Rule 3.504. General law applicable
Rule 3.505. Appellate review
Rule 3.506. Liaison counsel

Rule 3.501.   Definitions

As used in this chapter, unless the context or subject matter otherwise requires:

(1) "Action" means any civil action or proceeding that is subject to coordination or that affects an action subject to coordination.

(2) "Add-on case" means an action that is proposed for coordination, under Code of Civil Procedure section 404.4, with actions previously ordered coordinated.

(3) "Assigned judge" means any judge assigned by the Chair of the Judicial Council or by a presiding judge authorized by the Chair of the Judicial Council to assign a judge under Code of Civil Procedure section 404 or 404.3, including a "coordination motion judge" and a "coordination trial judge."

(4) "Clerk," unless otherwise indicated, means any person designated by an assigned judge to perform any clerical duties required by the rules in this chapter.

(5) "Coordinated action" means any action that has been ordered coordinated with one or more other actions under chapter 3 (commencing with section 404) of title 4 of part 2 of the Code of Civil Procedure and the rules in this chapter.

(6) "Coordination attorney" means an attorney in the Administrative Office of the Courts appointed by the Chair of the Judicial Council to perform such administrative functions as may be appropriate under the rules in this chapter, including but not limited to the functions described in rules 3.524 and 3.550.

(7) "Coordination motion judge" means an assigned judge designated under Code of Civil Procedure section 404 to determine whether coordination is appropriate.

(8) "Coordination proceeding" means any procedure authorized by chapter 3 (commencing with section 404) of title 4 of part 2 of the Code of Civil Procedure and by the rules in this chapter.

(9) "Coordination trial judge" means an assigned judge designated under Code of Civil Procedure section 404.3 to hear and determine coordinated actions.

(10) "Expenses" means all necessary costs that are reimbursable under Code of Civil Procedure section 404.8, including the compensation of the assigned judge and other necessary judicial officers and employees, the costs of any necessary travel and subsistence determined under rules of the State Board of Control, and all necessarily incurred costs of facilities, supplies, materials, and telephone and mailing expenses.

(11) "Included action" means any action or proceeding included in a petition for coordination.

(12) "Liaison counsel" means an attorney of record for a party to an included action or a coordinated action who has been appointed by an assigned judge to serve as representative of all parties on a side with the following powers and duties, as appropriate:

(A) To receive on behalf of and promptly distribute to the parties for whom he or she acts all notices and other documents from the court;

(B) To act as spokesperson for the side that he or she represents at all proceedings set on notice before trial, subject to the right of each party to present individual or divergent positions; and

(C) To call meetings of counsel for the purpose of proposing joint action.

(13) "Party" includes all parties to all included actions or coordinated actions, and the word "party," "petitioner," or any other designation of a party includes that party's attorney of record. When a notice or other paper is required to be given or served on a party, the notice or paper must be given to or served on the party's attorney of record, if any.

(14) "Petition for coordination" means any petition, motion, application, or request for coordination of actions submitted to the Chair of the Judicial Council or to a coordination trial judge under rule 3.544.

(15) "Remand" means to return a coordinated action or a severable claim or issue in a coordinated action from a coordination proceeding to the court in which the action was pending at the time the coordination of that action was ordered. If a remanded action or claim had been transferred by the coordination trial judge under rule 3.543 from the court in which the remanded action or claim was pending, the remand must include the retransfer of that action or claim to that court.

(16) "Serve and file" means that a paper filed in a court must be accompanied by proof of prior service of a copy of the paper on each party required to be served under the rules in this chapter.

(17) "Serve and submit" means that a paper to be submitted to an assigned judge under the rules in this chapter must be submitted to that judge at a designated court address. Every paper so submitted must be accompanied by proof of prior service on each party required to be served under the rules in this chapter. If there is no assigned judge or if the paper is of a type included in rule 3.511(a), the paper must be submitted to the Chair of the Judicial Council.

(18) "Side" means all parties to an included or a coordinated action who have a common or substantially similar interest in the issues, as determined by the assigned judge for the purpose of appointing liaison counsel or of allotting peremptory challenges in jury selection, or for any other appropriate purpose. Except as defined in rule 3.515, a side may include less than all plaintiffs or all defendants.

(19) "Transfer" means to remove a coordinated action or severable claim in that action from the court in which it is pending to any other court under rule 3.543, without removing the action or claim from the coordination proceeding. "Transfer" includes "retransfer."

Rule 3.501 amended and renumbered effective January 1, 2007; adopted as rule 1501 effective January 1, 1974; previously amended effective July 1, 1974, and January 1, 2005.

Ref.: Cal. Fms Pl. & Pr., Ch. 120, "Class Actions," Ch. 125, "Consolidation, Severance, and Coordination of Actions," Ch. 317, "Judges"; MB Prac. Guide: Cal. Pretrial Proc., §§32.01, 32.06[2], 32.20[10], 33.02.

Rule 3.502. Complex case—determination

The court must consider rule 3.400 et seq. in determining whether a case is or is not a complex case within the meaning of Code of Civil Procedure sections 403 and 404.

Rule 3.502 amended and renumbered effective January 1, 2007; adopted as rule 1501.1 effective September 21, 1996; previously amended effective January 1, 2000; previously amended and renumbered as rule 1502 effective January 1, 2005.

Ref.: Cal. Fms Pl. & Pr., Ch. 125, "Consolidation, Severance, and Coordination of Actions"; MB Prac. Guide: Cal. Pretrial Proc., §§32.14[1], 32.15[2], 32.18[1], 32.19[3], 32.33, 32.39.

Rule 3.503. Requests for extensions of time or to shorten time

(a) Assigned judge may grant request

The assigned judge, on terms that are just, may shorten or extend the time within which any act is permitted or required to be done by a party. Unless otherwise ordered, any motion or application for an extension of time to perform an act required by these rules must be served and submitted in accordance with rule 3.501(17).

(Subd (a) amended effective January 1, 2007; adopted as part of unlettered subd effective January 1, 1974; previously amended and lettered effective January 1, 2005.)

(b) Stipulation requires consent of assigned judge

A stipulation for an extension of time for the filing and service of documents required by the rules in this chapter requires approval of the assigned judge.

(Subd (b) amended and lettered effective January 1, 2005; adopted as part of unlettered subd effective January 1, 1974.)

(c) Extension does not extend time for bringing action to trial

Nothing in this rule extends the time within which a party must bring an action to trial under Code of Civil Procedure section 583.310.

(Subd (c) adopted effective January 1, 2005.)

Rule 3.503 amended and renumbered effective January 1, 2007; adopted as rule 1503 effective January 1, 1974; previously amended effective January 1, 2005.

Ref.: Cal. Fms Pl. & Pr., Ch. 125, "Consolidation, Severance, and Coordination of Actions."

Rule 3.504. General law applicable

(a) General law applicable

Except as otherwise provided in the rules in this chapter, all provisions of law applicable to civil actions generally apply to an action included in a coordination proceeding.

(Subd (a) amended effective January 1, 2005.)

(b) Rules prevail over conflicting general provisions of law

To the extent that the rules in this chapter conflict with provisions of law applicable to civil actions generally, the rules in this chapter prevail, as provided by Code of Civil Procedure section 404.7.

(Subd (b) amended and lettered effective January 1, 2005; adopted as part of subd (a) effective January 1, 1974.)

(c) Manner of proceeding may be prescribed by assigned judge

If the manner of proceeding is not prescribed by chapter 3 (commencing with section 404) of title 4 of part 2 of the Code of Civil Procedure or by the rules in this chapter, or if the prescribed manner of proceeding cannot, with reasonable diligence, be followed in a particular coordination proceeding, the assigned judge may prescribe any suitable manner of proceeding that appears most consistent with those statutes and rules.

(Subd (c) amended and relettered effective January 1, 2005; adopted as subd (b) effective January 1, 1974.)

(d) Specification of applicable local rules

At the beginning of a coordination proceeding, the assigned judge must specify, subject to rule 3.20, any local court rules to be followed in that proceeding, and thereafter all parties must comply with those rules. Except as otherwise provided in the rules in this chapter or as directed by the assigned judge, the local rules of the court designated in the order appointing the assigned judge apply in all respects if they would otherwise apply without reference to the rules in this chapter.

(Subd (d) amended effective January 1, 2007; adopted as subd (c) effective January 1, 1974; previously amended and relettered effective January 1, 2005.)

Rule 3.504 amended and renumbered effective January 1, 2007; adopted as rule 1504 effective January 1, 1974; previously amended effective January 1, 2005.

Ref.: Cal. Fms Pl. & Pr., Ch. 125, "Consolidation, Severance, and Coordination of Actions."

Rule 3.505. Appellate review

(a) Coordination order to specify reviewing court

If the actions to be coordinated are within the jurisdiction of more than one reviewing court, the coordination motion judge must select and the order granting a petition for coordination must specify, in accordance with Code of Civil Procedure section 404.2, the court having appellate jurisdiction of the coordinated actions.

(Subd (a) amended and lettered effective January 1, 2005; adopted as part of unlettered subd effective January 1, 1974.)

(b) Court for review of order granting or denying coordination

A petition for a writ relating to an order granting or denying coordination may be filed, subject to the provisions of rule 10.1000, in any reviewing court having jurisdiction under the rules applicable to civil actions generally.

(Subd (b) amended effective January 1, 2007; adopted as part of unlettered subd effective January 1, 1974; previously amended and lettered effective January 1, 2005.)

Rule 3.505 amended and renumbered effective January 1, 2007; adopted as rule 1505 effective January 1, 1974; previously amended effective January 1, 2005.

Ref.: Cal. Fms Pl. & Pr., Ch. 125, "Consolidation, Severance, and Coordination of Actions."

Rule 3.506. Liaison counsel

(a) Selection and appointment

An assigned judge may at any time request that the parties on each side of the included or coordinated actions select one or more of the attorneys of record on that side for appointment as liaison counsel, and may appoint liaison counsel if the parties are unable to agree.

(Subd (a) amended effective January 1, 2005.)

(b) Duration of appointment by coordination motion judge

Unless otherwise stipulated to or directed by an assigned judge, the appointment of a liaison counsel by a coordination motion judge terminates on the final determination of the issue whether coordination is appropriate. For good cause shown, the coordination motion judge, on the court's own motion or on the motion of any party, may remove previously appointed counsel as liaison counsel.

(Subd (b) amended and lettered effective January 1, 2005; adopted as part of subd (a) effective January 1, 1974.)

(c) Service on party that has requested special notice

Except as otherwise directed by the assigned judge, any party that has made a written request for special notice must be served with a copy of any document thereafter served on the party's liaison counsel.

(Subd (c) amended effective January 1, 2007; adopted as subd (b) effective January 1, 1974.) amended and relettered effective January 1, 2005.)

Rule 3.506 amended and renumbered effective January 1, 2007; adopted as rule 1506 effective January 1, 1974; previously amended effective January 1, 2005.)

Ref.: Cal. Fms Pl. & Pr., Ch. 125, "Consolidation, Severance, and Coordination of Actions"; MB Prac. Guide: Cal. Pretrial Proc., §32.20[10].

Article 2
Procedural Rules Applicable to All Complex Coordination Proceedings

Rule 3.510. Service of papers

(a) Proof of service

Except as otherwise provided in the rules in this chapter, all papers filed or submitted must be accompanied by proof of prior service on all other parties to the coordination proceeding, including all parties appearing in all included actions and coordinated actions. Service and proof of such service must be made as provided for in civil actions generally.

(Subd (a) amended and lettered effective January 1, 2005; adopted as part of unlettered subd effective January 1, 1974.)

(b) Service on liaison counsel

Except as provided in rule 3.506(c), any party for whom liaison counsel has been designated may be served by serving the liaison counsel.

(Subd (b) amended effective January 1, 2007; adopted as part of unlettered subd effective January 1, 1974; previously amended and lettered effective January 1, 2005.)

(c) Effect of failure to serve

Failure to serve any defendant with a copy of the summons and of the complaint, or failure to serve any party with any other paper or order as required by the rules in this chapter, will not preclude the coordination of the actions, but the unserved defendant or party may assert the failure to serve as a basis for appropriate relief.

(Subd (c) amended and lettered effective January 1, 2005; adopted as part of unlettered subd effective January 1, 1974.)

Rule 3.510 amended and renumbered effective January 1, 2007; adopted as rule 1510 effective January 1, 1974; previously amended effective January 1, 2005.)

Ref.: Cal. Fms Pl. & Pr., Ch. 125, "Consolidation, Severance, and Coordination of Actions," Ch. 212, "Dismissal"; MB Prac. Guide: Cal. Pretrial Proc., §§32.18[2], 32.20[3][c].

Rule 3.511. Papers to be submitted to the Chair of the Judicial Council

(a) Types of papers

A copy of the following papers must be submitted to the Chair of the Judicial Council at the Judicial Council's San Francisco office:

(1) Petition for coordination, including a petition for coordination of add-on cases;

(2) Notice of submission of petition for coordination, along with the caption page of the original action;

(3) Order assigning coordination motion judge, if made by a presiding judge;

(4) Order assigning coordination trial judge, if made by a presiding judge;

(5) Notice of opposition;

(6) Response in opposition to or in support of a petition for coordination;

(7) Motion for a stay order;

(8) Notice of hearing on petition;

(9) Order granting or denying coordination, including coordination of add-on cases;

(10) Order of remand;

(11) Order of transfer;

(12) Order terminating a coordination proceeding in whole or in part;

(13) Order dismissing an included or coordinated action;

(14) Notice of appeal; and

(15) Notice of disposition of appeal.

(Subd (a) adopted effective January 1, 2005.)

(b) Obligation of party

The papers listed in (a) are to be submitted by the party that filed or submitted and served the papers or that was directed to give notice of entry of the order. Notice of submission must be filed with the court as part of the proof of service.

(Subd (b) adopted effective January 1, 2005.)

Rule 3.511 amended and renumbered effective January 1, 2007; adopted as rule 1511 effective January 1, 1974; previously amended effective January 1, 2005.

Ref.: Cal. Fms Pl. & Pr., Ch. 125, "Consolidation, Severance, and Coordination of Actions"; MB Prac. Guide: Cal. Pretrial Proc., §§32.18[1], [2], 32.20[3][c], 32.21[1].

Rule 3.512. Electronic submission of documents to the Chair of the Judicial Council

(a) Documents that may be submitted electronically

Any paper listed in rule 3.511(a) may be submitted electronically to coordination@jud.ca.gov.

(Subd (a) amended effective January 1, 2008; previously amended effective January 1, 2007.)

(b) Responsibilities of party submitting documents electronically

A party submitting a document electronically must:

(1) Take all reasonable steps to ensure that the submission does not contain computer code, including viruses, that might be harmful to the Judicial Council's electronic system and to other users of that system; and

(2) Furnish one or more electronic notification addresses and immediately provide any change to his or her electronic notification addresses.

(c) Format of documents to be submitted electronically

A document that is submitted electronically must meet the following requirements:

(1) The software for creating and reading the document must be in the public domain or generally available at a reasonable cost; and

(2) The printing of documents must not result in the loss of document text, format, or appearance.

(d) Signature on documents under penalty of perjury

(1) When a document to be submitted electronically requires a signature under penalty of perjury, the document is deemed signed by the declarant if, before submission, the declarant has signed a printed form of the document.

(2) By electronically submitting the document, the party submitting it indicates that he or she has complied with subdivision (d)(1) of this rule and that the original, signed document is available for review and copying at the request of the court or any party.

(3) At any time after the document is submitted, any other party may serve a demand for production of the original signed document. The demand must be served on all other parties but need not be filed with the court.

(4) Within five days of service of the demand, the party on whom the demand is made must make the original signed document available for review and copying by all other parties.

(e) Signature on documents not under penalty of perjury

If a document does not require a signature under penalty of perjury, the document is deemed signed by the party if the document is submitted electronically.

(f) Digital signature

A party is not required to use a digital signature on an electronically submitted document.

Rule 3.512 amended effective January 1, 2008; adopted as rule 1511.5 effective July 1, 2005; previously amended and renumbered effective January 1, 2007.

Ref.: Cal. Fms Pl. & Pr., Ch. 125, "Consolidation, Severance, and Coordination of Actions"; MB Prac. Guide: Cal. Pretrial Proc., §§32.18[1], 32.20[3][c], [4][b], [c], 32.21[1].

Rule 3.513. Service of memorandums and declarations

Unless otherwise provided in the rules in this chapter or directed by the assigned judge, all memorandums and declarations in support of or opposition to any petition, motion, or application must be served and submitted at least nine court days before any hearing on the matter at issue.

Rule 3.513 amended effective January 1, 2007; adopted as rule 1512 effective January 1, 1974; previously amended effective January 1, 2005; previously amended and renumbered effective January 1, 2007.

Ref.: Cal. Fms Pl. & Pr., Ch. 125, "Consolidation, Severance, and Coordination of Actions"; MB Prac. Guide: Cal. Pretrial Proc., §§32.16[5], 32.20[4][d].

Rule 3.514. Evidence presented at court hearings

All factual matters to be heard on any petition for coordination, or on any other petition, motion, or application under the rules in this chapter, must be initially presented and heard on declarations, answers to interrogatories or requests for admissions, depositions, or matters judicially noticed. Oral testimony will not be permitted at a hearing except as the assigned judge may permit to resolve factual issues shown by the declarations, responses to discovery, or matters judicially noticed to be in dispute. Only parties that have submitted a petition or motion, or a written response or opposition to a petition or motion, will be permitted to appear at the hearing, except the assigned judge may permit other parties to appear, on a showing of good cause.

Rule 3.514 renumbered effective January 1, 2007; adopted as rule 1513 effective January 1, 1974; previously amended effective January 1, 2005.

Ref.: Cal. Fms Pl. & Pr., Ch. 125, "Consolidation, Severance, and Coordination of Actions"; MB Prac. Guide: Cal. Pretrial Proc., §§32.16[6], [8], 32.20[8].

Rule 3.515. Motions and orders for a stay

(a) Motion for stay

Any party may file a motion for an order under Code of Civil Procedure section 404.5 staying the proceedings in any action being considered for, or affecting an action being considered for, coordination, or the court may stay the proceedings on its own motion. The motion for a stay may be included with a petition for coordination or may be served and submitted to the Chair of the Judicial Council and the coordination motion judge by any party at any time prior to the determination of the petition.

(Subd (a) amended effective January 1, 2005.)

(b) Contents of motion

A motion for a stay order must:

(1) List all known pending related cases;

(2) State whether the stay order should extend to any such related case; and

(3) Be supported by a memorandum and by declarations establishing the facts relied on to show that a stay order is necessary and appropriate to effectuate the purposes of coordination.

(Subd (b) amended and lettered effective January 1, 2005; adopted as part of subd (a) effective January 1, 1974.)

(c) Service requirements for certain motions for stay orders

If the action to be stayed is not included in the petition for coordination or any response to that petition, the motion for a stay order and all supporting documents must be served on each party to the action to be stayed and any such party may serve and submit opposition to the motion for a stay order.

(Subd (c) amended and lettered effective January 1, 2005; adopted as part of subd (a) effective January 1, 1974.)

(d) Opposition to motion for stay order

Any memorandums and declarations in opposition to a motion for a stay order must be served and submitted within 10 days after service of the motion.

(Subd (d) amended and lettered effective January 1, 2005; adopted as part of subd (a) effective January 1, 1974.)

(e) Hearing on motion for stay order

A stay order may be issued with or without a hearing. A party filing a motion for a stay order or opposition thereto may request a hearing to determine whether the stay order should be granted. A request for hearing should be made at the time the requesting party files the motion or opposition. If the coordination motion judge grants the request for a hearing, the requesting party must provide notice.

(Subd (e) amended and lettered effective January 1, 2005; adopted as part of subd (a) effective January 1, 1974.)

(f) Determination of motion for stay order

In ruling on a motion for a stay order, the assigned judge must determine whether the stay will promote the ends of justice, considering the imminence of any trial or other proceeding that might materially affect the status of the action to be stayed, and whether a final judgment in that action would have a res judicata or collateral estoppel effect with regard to any common issue of the included actions.

(Subd (f) amended and relettered effective January 1, 2005; adopted as subd (e) effective January 1, 1974.)

(g) Issuance of stay order and termination of stay

If a stay order is issued, the party that requested the stay must serve and file a copy of the order in each included action that is stayed. Thirty or more days following issuance of the stay order, any party that is subject to the stay order may move to terminate the stay.

(Subd (g) amended and relettered effective January 1, 2005; adopted as subd (b) effective January 1, 1974.)

(h) Effect of stay order

Unless otherwise specified in the order, a stay order suspends all proceedings in the action to which it applies. A stay order may be limited by its terms to specified proceedings, orders, motions, or other phases of the action to which the order applies.

(Subd (h) amended and relettered effective January 1, 2005; adopted as subd (c) effective January 1, 1974.)

(i) Effect of absence of stay order

In the absence of a stay order, a court receiving an order assigning a coordination motion judge may continue to exercise jurisdiction over the included action for purposes of all pretrial and discovery proceedings, but no trial may be commenced and no judgment may be entered in that action unless trial of the action had commenced before the assignment of the coordination motion judge.

(Subd (i) amended and relettered effective January 1, 2005; adopted as subd (d) effective January 1, 1974; previously amended effective July 1, 1974.)

(j) Effect of stay order on dismissal for lack of prosecution

The time during which any stay of proceedings is in effect under the rules in this chapter must not be included in determining whether the action stayed should be dismissed for lack of prosecution under chapter 1.5 (§ 583.110 et seq.) of title 8 of part 2 of the Code of Civil Procedure.

(Subd (j) amended and relettered effective January 1, 2005; adopted as subd (f) effective January 1, 1974; previously amended effective January 1, 1986.)

Rule 3.515 renumbered effective January 1, 2007; adopted as rule 1514 effective January 1, 1974; previously amended effective July 1, 1974, January 1, 1986, and January 1, 2005.

Ref.: Cal. Fms Pl. & Pr., Ch. 125, "Consolidation, Severance, and Coordination of Actions," Ch. 212, "Dismissal"; MB Prac. Guide: Cal. Pretrial Proc., §§32.18[2], 32.20[2][d], [5][a]–[f], 40.03[1], 40.14[2].

Rule 3.516.   Motions under Code of Civil Procedure section 170.6

A party making a peremptory challenge by motion or affidavit of prejudice regarding an assigned judge must submit it in writing to the assigned judge within 20 days after service of the order assigning the judge to the coordination proceeding. All plaintiffs or similar parties in the included or coordinated actions constitute a side and all defendants or similar parties in such actions constitute a side for purposes of applying Code of Civil Procedure section 170.6.

Rule 3.516 renumbered effective January 1, 2007; adopted as rule 1515 effective January 1, 1974; previously amended effective June 19, 1982, and January 1, 2005.

Ref.: Cal. Fms Pl. & Pr., Ch. 125, "Consolidation, Severance, and Coordination of Actions," Ch. 317, "Judges"; Cal. Class Actions Prac. & Proc., §9.01[2]; MB Prac. Guide: Cal. Pretrial Proc., §§22.09[8], 22.11[1], 32.18[1], [2], 32.20[7], 32.21[4].

Article 3
Petitions and Proceedings for Coordination of Complex Actions

Rule 3.520. Motions filed in the trial court
Rule 3.521. Petition for coordination
Rule 3.522. Notice of submission of petition for coordination
Rule 3.523. Service of notice of submission on party
Rule 3.524. Order assigning coordination motion judge
Rule 3.525. Response in opposition to petition for coordination
Rule 3.526. Response in support of petition for coordination
Rule 3.527. Notice of hearing on petition for coordination
Rule 3.528. Separate hearing on certain coordination issues
Rule 3.529. Order granting or denying coordination
Rule 3.530. Site of coordination proceedings
Rule 3.531. Potential add-on case
Rule 3.532. Petition for coordination when cases already ordered coordinated

Rule 3.520.   Motions filed in the trial court

(a) General requirements

A motion filed in the trial court under this rule must specify the matters required by rule 3.521(a) and must be made in the manner provided by law for motions in civil actions generally.

(Subd (a) amended effective January 1, 2007; previously amended effective January 1, 1983, and January 1, 2005.)

(b) Permission to submit a petition for coordination

(1) *Request for permission to submit coordination petition*

If a direct petition is not authorized by Code of Civil Procedure section 404, a party may request permission from the presiding judge of the court in which one of the included actions is pending to submit a petition for coordination to the Chair of the Judicial Council. The request must be made by noticed motion accompanied by a proposed order. The proposed order must state that the moving party has permission to submit a petition for coordination to the Chair of the Judicial Council under rules 3.521–3.523.

(2) *Order to be prepared*

If permission to submit a petition is granted, the moving party must serve and file the signed order and submit it to the Chair of the Judicial Council.

(3) *Stay permitted pending preparation of petition*

To provide sufficient time for a party to submit a petition, the presiding judge may stay all related actions pending in that court for a reasonable time not to exceed 30 calendar days.

(Subd (b) amended effective January 1, 2007; previously amended effective January 1, 1983, January 1, 2005, and July 1, 2006.)

Rule 3.520 amended and renumbered effective January 1, 2007; adopted as rule 1520 effective January 1, 1974; previously amended effective January 1, 1983, January 1, 2005, and July 1, 2006.

Ref.: Cal. Fms Pl. & Pr., Ch. 125, "Consolidation, Severance, and Coordination of Actions," Ch. 372, "Motions and Orders"; MB Prac. Guide: Cal. Pretrial Proc., §§32.18[1], [2], 32.20[2][a]–[d], 32.35–32.38.

Rule 3.521. Petition for coordination

(a) Contents of petition

A request submitted to the Chair of the Judicial Council for the assignment of a judge to determine whether the coordination of certain actions is appropriate, or a request that a coordination trial judge make such a determination concerning an add-on case, must be designated a "Petition for Coordination" and may be made at any time after filing of the complaint. The petition must state whether a hearing is requested and must be supported by a memorandum and declarations showing:

(1) The name of each petitioner or, when the petition is submitted by a presiding or sole judge, the name of each real party in interest, and the name and address of each party's attorney of record, if any;

(2) The names of the parties to all included actions, and the name and address of each party's attorney of record, if any;

(3) If the party seeking to submit a petition for coordination is a plaintiff, whether the party's attorney has served the summons and complaint on all parties in all included actions in which the attorney has appeared;

(4) For each included action, the complete title and case number, the date the complaint was filed, and the title of the court in which the action is pending;

(5) The complete title and case number of any other action known to the petitioner to be pending in a court of this state that shares a common question of fact or law with the included actions, and a statement of the reasons for not including the other action in the petition for coordination or a statement that the petitioner knows of no other actions sharing a common question of fact or law;

(6) The status of each included action, including the status of any pretrial or discovery motions or orders in that action, if known to petitioner;

(7) The facts relied on to show that each included action meets the coordination standards specified in Code of Civil Procedure section 404.1; and

(8) The facts relied on in support of a request that a particular site or sites be selected for a hearing on the petition for coordination.

(Subd (a) amended effective January 1, 2005.)

(b) Submit proof of filing and service

Within five court days of submitting the petition for coordination, the petitioner must submit to the Chair of the Judicial Council proof of filing of the notice of submission of petition required by rule 3.522, and proof of service of the notice of submission of petition and of the petition required by rule 3.523.

(Subd (b) amended effective January 1, 2007; previously amended effective January 1, 2005, and January 1, 2007.)

(c) Copies of pleadings in lieu of proof by declaration

In lieu of proof by declaration of any fact required by (a)(2), (4), (7), and (8), a certified or endorsed copy of the respective pleadings may be attached to the petition for coordination, provided that the petitioner specifies with particularity the portions of the pleadings that are relied on to show the fact.

(Subd (c) amended effective January 1, 2005.)

(d) Effect of imminent trial date

The imminence of a trial in any action otherwise appropriate for coordination may be a ground for summary denial of a petition for coordination, in whole or in part.

(Subd (d) amended effective January 1, 2005.)

Rule 3.521 amended effective January 1, 2007; adopted as rule 1521 effective January 1, 1974; previously amended effective January 1, 2005; previously amended and renumbered effective January 1, 2007.

Ref.: Cal. Fms Pl. & Pr., Ch. 125, "Consolidation, Severance, and Coordination of Actions"; MB Prac. Guide: Cal. Pretrial Proc., §§32.18[1], 32.19[4], 32.20[1], [3][a]–[c], [4][a], 32.36, 32.39.

Rule 3.522. Notice of submission of petition for coordination

(a) Contents of notice of submission

In each included action, the petitioner must file a "Notice of Submission of Petition for Coordination" and the petition for coordination. Each notice must bear the title of the court in which the notice is to be filed and the title and case number of each included action that is pending in that court. Each notice must include:

(1) The date that the petition for coordination was submitted to the Chair of the Judicial Council;

(2) The name and address of the petitioner's attorney of record;

(3) The title and case number of each included action to which the petitioner is a party and the title of the court in which each action is pending; and

(4) The statement that any written opposition to the petition must be submitted and served at least nine court days before the hearing date.

(Subd (a) amended effective January 1, 2007; adopted as part of unlettered subd effective January 1, 1974; previously amended and lettered effective January 1, 2005; previously amended effective January 1, 2006.)

(b) Copies of notice

The petitioner must submit the notice and proof of filing in each included action to the Chair of the Judicial Council within five court days of submitting the petition for coordination.

(Subd (b) amended effective January 1, 2007; adopted as part of unlettered subd effective January 1, 1974; previously amended and lettered effective January 1, 2005.)

Rule 3.522 amended and renumbered effective January 1, 2007; adopted as rule 1522 effective January 1, 1974; previously amended effective January 1, 2005, and January 1, 2006.

Ref.: Cal. Fms Pl. & Pr., Ch. 125, "Consolidation, Severance, and Coordination of Actions"; MB Prac. Guide: Cal. Pretrial Proc., §§32.18[1], 32.20[3][c], 32.36, 32.39, 32.40.

Rule 3.523.   Service of notice of submission on party

The petitioner must serve the notice of submission of petition for coordination that was filed in each included action, the petition for coordination, and supporting documents on each party appearing in each included action and submit the notice to the Chair of the Judicial Council within five court days of submitting the petition for coordination.

Rule 3.523 amended effective January 1, 2007; adopted as rule 1523 effective January 1, 1974; previously amended effective January 1, 2005; previously amended and renumbered effective January 1, 2007.

Ref.: Cal. Fms Pl. & Pr., Ch. 125, "Consolidation, Severance, and Coordination of Actions"; MB Prac. Guide: Cal. Pretrial Proc., §§32.20[3][c], 32.36, 32.39.

Rule 3.524.   Order assigning coordination motion judge

(a) Contents of order

An order by the Chair of the Judicial Council assigning a coordination motion judge to determine whether coordination is appropriate, or authorizing the presiding judge of a court to assign the matter to judicial officers of the court to make the determination in the same manner as assignments are made in other civil cases, must include the following:

(1) The special title and number assigned to the coordination proceeding; and

(2) The court address for submitting all subsequent documents to be considered by the coordination motion judge.

(Subd (a) amended and lettered effective January 1, 2005; adopted as part of unlettered subd effective January 1, 1974.)

(b) Service of order

The petitioner must serve the order described in (a) on each party appearing in an included action and send it to each court in which an included action is pending with directions to the clerk to file the order in the included action.

(Subd (b) amended and lettered effective January 1, 2005; adopted as part of unlettered subd effective January 1, 1974.)

Rule 3.524 renumbered effective January 1, 2007; adopted as rule 1524 effective January 1, 1974; previously amended effective January 1, 2005.

Ref.: Cal. Fms Pl. & Pr., Ch. 125, "Consolidation, Severance, and Coordination of Actions"; MB Prac. Guide: Cal. Pretrial Proc., §32.20[6][a], [b].

Rule 3.525.   Response in opposition to petition for coordination

Any party to an included action that opposes coordination may serve and submit a memorandum and declarations in opposition to the petition. Any response in opposition must be served and filed at least nine court days before the date set for hearing.

Rule 3.525 amended effective January 1, 2007; adopted as rule 1525 effective January 1, 1974; previously amended effective January 1, 2005; previously amended and renumbered effective January 1, 2007.

Ref.: Cal. Fms Pl. & Pr., Ch. 125, "Consolidation, Severance, and Coordination of Actions"; MB Prac. Guide: Cal. Pretrial Proc., §§32.18[2], 32.20[4][c], [9][c], 32.42.

Rule 3.526.   Response in support of petition for coordination

Any party to an included action that supports coordination may serve and submit a written statement in support of the petition. Any response in support must be served and filed at least nine court days before the date set for hearing. If a party that supports coordination does not support the particular site or sites requested by the petitioner for the hearing on the petition for coordination, that party may request that a different site or sites be selected and include in his or her response the facts relied on in support thereof.

Rule 3.526 amended effective January 1, 2007; adopted as rule 1526 effective January 1, 1974; previously amended effective January 1, 2005; previously amended and renumbered effective January 1, 2007.

Ref.: Cal. Fms Pl. & Pr., Ch. 125, "Consolidation, Severance, and Coordination of Actions"; MB Prac. Guide: Cal. Pretrial Proc., §§32.20[4][b], 32.41.

Rule 3.527.   Notice of hearing on petition for coordination

(a) Timing and notice of hearing

The coordination motion judge must set a hearing date on a petition for coordination within 30 days of the date of the order assigning the coordination motion judge. When a coordination motion judge is assigned to decide a petition for coordination that lists additional included actions sharing a common question of law or fact with included actions in a petition for coordination already pending before the judge, the judge may continue the hearing date on the first petition no more than 30 calendar days in order to hear both petitions at the same time. The petitioner must provide notice of the hearing to each party appearing in an included action. If the coordination motion judge determines that a party that should be served with notice of the petition for coordination has not been served with notice, the coordination motion judge must order the petitioner to promptly serve that party. If the coordination motion judge determines that a hearing is not required under (b), the hearing date must be vacated and notice provided to the parties.

(Subd (a) amended and relettered effective January 1, 2005; adopted as subd (b) effective January 1, 1974.)

(b) Circumstances in which hearing required

A hearing must be held to decide a petition for coordination if a party opposes coordination. A petition for coordination may not be denied unless a hearing has been held.

(Subd (b) adopted effective January 1, 2005.)

(c) Report to the Chair of the Judicial Council

If the petition for coordination has not been decided within 30 calendar days after the hearing, the coordination motion judge must promptly submit to the Chair of the Judicial Council a written report describing:

(1) The present status of the petition for coordination proceeding;

(2) Any factors or circumstances that may have caused undue or unanticipated delay in the decision on the petition for coordination; and

(3) Any stay orders that are in effect.

(Subd (c) amended effective January 1, 2005.)

Rule 3.527 renumbered effective January 1, 2007; adopted as rule 1527 effective January 1, 1974; previously amended effective January 1, 2005.

Ref.: Cal. Fms Pl. & Pr., Ch. 125, "Consolidation, Severance, and Coordination of Actions"; MB Prac. Guide: Cal. Pretrial Proc., §§32.18[1], [2], 32.20[9][a]–[c].

Rule 3.528. Separate hearing on certain coordination issues

When a petition for coordination may be disposed of on the determination of a specified issue or issues, without a hearing on all issues raised by the petition and any opposition, the assigned judge may order that the specified issue or issues be heard and determined before a hearing on the remaining issues.

Rule 3.528 renumbered effective January 1, 2007; adopted as rule 1528 effective January 1, 1974; previously amended effective January 1, 2005.

Ref.: Cal. Fms Pl. & Pr., Ch. 125, "Consolidation, Severance, and Coordination of Actions"; MB Prac. Guide: Cal. Pretrial Proc., §§32.18[2], 32.20[4][b], [c], [6][b].

Rule 3.529. Order granting or denying coordination

(a) Filing, service, and submittal

When a petition for coordination is granted or denied, the petitioner must promptly file the order in each included action, serve it on each party appearing in an included action, and submit it to the Chair of the Judicial Council.

(Subd (a) amended effective January 1, 2007; previously amended effective January 1, 2005.)

(b) Stay of further proceedings

When an order granting coordination is filed in an included action, all further proceedings in that action are automatically stayed, except as directed by the coordination trial judge or by the coordination motion judge under (c). The stay does not preclude the court in which the included action is pending from accepting and filing papers with proof of submission of a copy to the assigned

judge or from exercising jurisdiction over any severable claim that has not been ordered coordinated.

(Subd (b) amended effective January 1, 2005.)

(c) Authority of coordination motion judge pending assignment of coordination trial judge

After a petition for coordination has been granted and before a coordination trial judge has been assigned, the coordination motion judge may for good cause make any appropriate order as the ends of justice may require but may not commence a trial or enter judgment in any included action. Good cause includes a showing of an urgent need for judicial action to preserve the rights of a party pending assignment of a coordination trial judge.

(Subd (c) amended effective January 1, 2005.)

(d) Order denying coordination

The authority of a coordination motion judge over an included action terminates when an order denying a petition for coordination is filed in the included action and served on the parties to the action. A stay ordered by the coordination motion judge terminates 10 days after the order denying coordination is filed.

(Subd (d) amended effective January 1, 2005.)

Rule 3.529 amended and renumbered effective January 1, 2007; adopted as rule 1529 effective January 1, 1974; previously amended effective June 19, 1982, and January 1, 2005.

Ref.: Cal. Fms Pl. & Pr., Ch. 125, "Consolidation, Severance, and Coordination of Actions"; MB Prac. Guide: Cal. Pretrial Proc., §§32.18[1], 32.21[1]–[3].

Rule 3.530. Site of coordination proceedings

(a) Recommendation by coordination motion judge

If a petition for coordination is granted, the coordination motion judge must, in the order granting coordination, recommend to the Chair of the Judicial Council a particular superior court for the site of the coordination proceedings.

(b) Factors to consider

The coordination motion judge may consider any relevant factors in making a recommendation for the site of the coordination proceedings, including the following:

(1) The number of included actions in particular locations;

(2) Whether the litigation is at an advanced stage in a particular court;

(3) The efficient use of court facilities and judicial resources;

(4) The locations of witnesses and evidence;

(5) The convenience of the parties and witnesses;

(6) The parties' principal places of business;

(7) The office locations of counsel for the parties; and

(8) The ease of travel to and availability of accommodations in particular locations.

Rule 3.530 renumbered effective January 1, 2007; adopted as rule 1530 effective January 1, 2005.

Ref.: Cal. Fms Pl. & Pr., Ch. 125, "Consolidation, Severance, and Coordination of Actions"; MB Prac. Guide: Cal. Pretrial Proc., §§32.20[4][b], [c], 32.21[3].

Rule 3.531. Potential add-on case

(a) Notice

Any party to an included action in a pending petition for coordination must promptly provide notice of any potential add-on cases in which that party is also named or in which that party's attorney has appeared. The party must submit notice to the coordination motion judge and the Chair of the Judicial Council and serve it on each party appearing in the included actions in the pending petition and each party appearing in the potential add-on cases.

(b) Stipulation or order

By stipulation of all parties or order of the coordination motion judge, each potential add-on case will be deemed an included action for purposes of the hearing on the petition for coordination.

Rule 3.531 renumbered effective January 1, 2007; adopted as rule 1531 effective January 1, 2005.

Ref.: Cal. Fms Pl. & Pr., Ch. 125, "Consolidation, Severance, and Coordination of Actions"; MB Prac. Guide: Cal. Pretrial Proc., §32.20[4][e], [9][a].

Rule 3.532.   Petition for coordination when cases already ordered coordinated

(a) Assignment of coordination trial judge

If it appears that included actions in a petition for coordination share a common question of law or fact with cases already ordered coordinated, the Chair of the Judicial Council may assign the petition to the coordination trial judge for the existing coordinated cases to decide the petition as a request to coordinate an add-on case under rule 3.544.

(Subd (a) amended effective January 1, 2007.)

(b) Order

The coordination trial judge's order must specify that the request to coordinate an add-on case is either granted or denied.

(c) Filing and service

The petitioner must promptly file the order in each included action, serve it on each party appearing in an included action, and submit a copy to the Chair of the Judicial Council.

(Subd (c) amended effective January 1, 2007.)

(d) Cases added on and right to peremptory challenge

If the coordination trial judge grants the petition, the included actions will be coordinated as add-on cases and the right to file a peremptory challenge under Code of Civil Procedure section 170.6 will be limited by rule 3.516.

(Subd (d) amended effective January 1, 2007.)

(e) Assignment of coordination motion judge if cases not added on

If the coordination trial judge denies the petition as a request to coordinate an add-on case under rule 3.544, the Chair of the Judicial Council must assign a coordination motion judge to determine whether coordination is appropriate under rule 3.524.

(Subd (e) amended effective January 1, 2007.)

Rule 3.532 amended and renumbered effective January 1, 2007; adopted as rule 1532 effective January 1, 2005.

Ref.: Cal. Fms Pl. & Pr., Ch. 125, "Consolidation, Severance, and Coordination of Actions"; MB Prac. Guide: Cal. Pretrial Proc., §§32.20[6][a], 32.21[4], 32.22[3].

Article 4
Pretrial and Trial Rules for Complex Coordinated Actions

Rule 3.540. Order assigning coordination trial judge
Rule 3.541. Duties of the coordination trial judge
Rule 3.542. Remand of action or claim
Rule 3.543. Transfer of action or claim
Rule 3.544. Add-on cases
Rule 3.545. Termination of coordinated action

Rule 3.540.   Order assigning coordination trial judge

(a) Assignment by the Chair of the Judicial Council

When a petition for coordination is granted, the Chair of the Judicial Council must either assign a coordination trial judge to hear and determine the coordinated actions or authorize the presiding judge of a court to assign the matter to judicial officers of the court in the same manner as assignments are made in other civil cases, under Code of Civil Procedure section 404.3. The order assigning a coordination trial judge must designate an address for submission of papers to that judge.

(Subd (a) amended and lettered effective January 1, 2005; adopted as part of unlettered subd effective January 1, 1974.)

(b) Powers of coordination trial judge

Immediately on assignment, the coordination trial judge may exercise all the powers over each coordinated action that are available to a judge of the court in which that action is pending.

(Subd (b) amended effective January 1, 2007; adopted as part of unlettered subd effective January 1, 1974; previously amended and lettered effective January 1, 2005.)

(c) Filing and service of copies of assignment order

The petitioner must file the assignment order in each coordinated action and serve it on each party appearing in each action. Every paper filed in a coordinated action must be accompanied by proof of submission of a copy of the paper to the coordination trial judge at the designated address. A copy of the assignment order must be included in any subsequent service of process on any defendant in the action.

(Subd (c) amended and lettered effective January 1, 2005; adopted as part of unlettered subd effective January 1, 1974.)

Rule 3.540 amended and renumbered effective January 1, 2007; adopted as rule 1540 effective January 1, 1974; previously amended effective January 1, 2005.

Ref.: Cal. Fms Pl. & Pr., Ch. 125, "Consolidation, Severance, and Coordination of Actions"; MB Prac. Guide: Cal. Pretrial Proc., §§32.18[1], 32.21[1], [3].

Rule 3.541.   Duties of the coordination trial judge

(a) Initial case management conference

The coordination trial judge must hold a case management conference within 45 days after issuance of the assignment order. Counsel and all self-represented persons must attend the conference and be prepared to discuss all matters specified in the order setting the conference. At any time following the assignment of the coordination trial judge, a party may serve and submit a proposed agenda for the conference and a proposed form of order covering such matters of procedure and discovery as may be appropriate. At the conference, the judge may:

(1) Appoint liaison counsel under rule 3.506;

(2) Establish a timetable for filing motions other than discovery motions;

(3) Establish a schedule for discovery;

(4) Provide a method and schedule for the submission of preliminary legal questions that might serve to expedite the disposition of the coordinated actions;

(5) In class actions, establish a schedule, if practicable, for the prompt determination of matters pertinent to the class action issue;

(6) Establish a central depository or depositories to receive and maintain for inspection by the parties evidentiary material and specified documents that are not required by the rules in this chapter to be served on all parties; and

(7) Schedule further conferences if appropriate.

(Subd (a) amended effective January 1, 2007; previously amended effective January 1, 2005.)

(b) Management of proceedings by coordination trial judge

The coordination trial judge must assume an active role in managing all steps of the pretrial, discovery, and trial proceedings to expedite the just determination of the coordinated actions without delay. The judge may, for the purpose of coordination and to serve the ends of justice:

(1) Order any coordinated action transferred to another court under rule 3.543;

(2) Schedule and conduct hearings, conferences, and a trial or trials at any site within this state that the judge deems appropriate with due consideration to the convenience of parties, witnesses, and counsel; to the relative development of the actions and the work product of counsel; to the efficient use of judicial facilities and resources; and to the calendar of the courts; and

(3) Order any issue or defense to be tried separately and before trial of the remaining issues when it appears that the disposition of any of the coordinated actions might thereby be expedited.

(Subd (b) amended effective January 1, 2007; previously amended effective January 1, 2005.)

Rule 3.541 amended and renumbered effective January 1, 2007; adopted as rule 1541 effective January 1, 1974; previously amended effective January 1, 2005.

Ref.: Cal. Fms Pl. & Pr., Ch. 125, "Consolidation, Severance, and Coordination of Actions"; Cal. Class Actions Prac. & Proc., §§2.02[5], 9.01[3]; MB Prac. Guide: Cal. Pretrial Proc., §§32.18[1], 32.19[1], 32.22[2], [3].

Rule 3.542.   Remand of action or claim

The coordination trial judge may at any time remand a coordinated action or any severable claim or issue in that action to the court in which the action was pending at the time the coordination of that action was ordered. Remand may be made on the stipulation of all parties or on the basis of evidence received at a hearing on the court's own motion or on the motion of any party to any coordinated action. No action or severable claim or issue in that action may be remanded over the objection of any party unless the evidence demonstrates a material change in the circumstances that are relevant to the criteria for coordination under Code of Civil Procedure section 404.1. If the order of remand requires that the action be transferred, the provisions of rule 3.543(c)–(e) are applicable to the transfer. A remanded action is no longer part of the coordination proceedings for purposes of the rules in this chapter.

Rule 3.542 amended and renumbered effective January 1, 2007; adopted as rule 1542 effective January 1, 1974; previously amended effective January 1, 2005, and July 1, 2006.

Ref.: MB Prac. Guide: Cal. Pretrial Proc., §32.22[3].

Rule 3.543.   Transfer of action or claim

(a) Court may transfer coordinated action

The coordination trial judge may order any coordinated action or severable claim in that action transferred from the court in which it is pending to another court for a specified purpose or for all purposes. Transfer may be made by the court on its own motion or on the motion of any party to any coordinated action.

(Subd (a) amended effective January 1, 2005.)

(b) Hearing on motion to transfer

If a party objects to the transfer, the court must hold a hearing on at least 10 days' written notice served on all parties to that action. At any hearing to determine whether an action or claim should be transferred, the court must consider the convenience of parties, witnesses, and counsel; the relative development of the actions and the work product of counsel; the efficient use of judicial facilities and resources; the calendar of the courts; and any other relevant matter.

(Subd (b) amended effective January 1, 2007; adopted as part of subd (a) effective January 1, 1974; previously amended and lettered effective January 1, 2005.)

(c) Order transferring action

The order transferring the action or claim must designate the court to which the action is transferred and must direct that a copy of the order of transfer be filed in each coordinated action. The order must indicate whether the action remains part of the coordination proceedings for purposes of the rules in this chapter.

(Subd (c) amended and lettered effective January 1, 2005; adopted as part of subd (b) effective January 1, 1974.)

(d) Duties of transferor and transferee courts

(1) Duty of transferor court

The clerk of the court in which the action was pending must immediately prepare and transmit to the court to which the action is transferred a certified copy of the order of transfer and of the pleadings and proceedings in the transferred action and must serve a copy of the order of transfer on each party appearing in that action.

(2) Duty of transferee court

The court to which the action is transferred must file the action as if the action had been commenced in that court. No fees may be required for such transfer by either court.

(3) Transmission of papers

If it is necessary to have any of the original pleadings or other papers in the transferred action before the coordination trial judge, the clerk of the court from which the action was transferred must, on written request of a party to that action or of the coordination trial judge, transmit such papers or pleadings to the court to which the action is transferred and must retain a certified copy.

(Subd (d) amended effective January 1, 2007; adopted as part of subd (b) effective January 1, 1974; previously amended and lettered effective January 1, 2005.)

(e) Transferee court to exercise jurisdiction

On receipt of a transfer order, the court to which the action is transferred may exercise jurisdiction over the action in accordance with the orders and directions of the coordination trial judge, and no other court may exercise jurisdiction over that action except as provided in this rule.

(Subd (e) amended and lettered effective January 1, 2005; adopted as part of subd (b) effective January 1, 1974.)

Rule 3.543 amended and renumbered effective January 1, 2007; adopted as rule 1543 effective January 1, 1974; previously amended effective January 1, 2005.

Ref.: Cal. Fms Pl. & Pr., Ch. 125, "Consolidation, Severance, and Coordination of Actions"; MB Prac. Guide: Cal. Pretrial Proc., §32.22[3].

Rule 3.544.   Add-on cases

(a) Request to coordinate add-on case

A request to coordinate an add-on case must comply with the requirements of rules 3.520 through 3.523, except that the request must be submitted to the coordination trial judge under Code of Civil Procedure section 404.4, with proof of mailing of one copy to the Chair of the Judicial Council and proof of service as required by rule 3.510.

(Subd (a) amended effective January 1, 2007; previously amended effective January 1, 2005.)

(b) Opposition to request to coordinate an add-on case

Within 10 days after the service of a request, any party may serve and submit a notice of opposition to the request. Thereafter, within 15 days after submitting a notice of opposition, the party must serve and submit a memorandum and declarations in opposition to the request. Failure to serve and submit a memorandum and declarations in opposition may be a ground for granting the request to coordinate an add-on case.

(Subd (b) amended and lettered effective January 1, 2005; adopted as part of subd (a) effective January 1, 1974.)

(c) Hearing on request to coordinate an add-on case

The coordination trial judge may order a hearing on a request to coordinate an add-on case under rules 3.527 and 3.528 and may allow the parties to serve and submit additional written materials in support of or opposition to the request. In deciding the request to coordinate, the court must consider the relative development of the actions and the work product of counsel, in addition to any other relevant matter. An application for an order staying the add-on case must be made to the coordination trial judge under rule 3.515.

(Subd (c) amended effective January 1, 2007; adopted as subd (b) effective January 1, 1974; previously amended and relettered effective January 1, 2005.)

(d) Order on request to coordinate an add-on case

If no party has filed a notice of opposition within the time required under (b), the coordination trial judge may enter an order granting or denying the request without a hearing. An order granting or denying a request to coordinate an add-on case must be prepared and served

under rule 3.529, and an order granting such request automatically stays all further proceedings in the add-on case under rule 3.529.

(Subd (d) amended effective January 1, 2007; adopted as subd (c) effective January 1, 1974; previously amended and relettered effective January 1, 2005.)

Rule 3.544 amended and renumbered effective January 1, 2007; adopted as rule 1544 effective January 1, 1974; previously amended effective January 1, 2005.

Ref.: Cal. Fms Pl. & Pr., Ch. 125, "Consolidation, Severance, and Coordination of Actions"; MB Prac. Guide: Cal. Pretrial Proc., §§32.21[4], 32.22[3].

Rule 3.545.   Termination of coordinated action

(a) Coordination trial judge may terminate action

The coordination trial judge may terminate any coordinated action by settlement or final dismissal, summary judgment, or judgment, or may transfer the action so that it may be dismissed or otherwise terminated in the court where it was pending when coordination was ordered.

(Subd (a) amended and lettered effective January 1, 2005; adopted as part of unlettered subd effective January 1, 1974.)

(b) Copies of order dismissing or terminating action and judgment

A certified copy of the order dismissing or terminating the action and of any judgment must be transmitted to:

(1) The clerk of the court in which the action was pending when coordination was ordered, who shall promptly enter any judgment and serve notice of entry of the judgment on all parties to the action and on the Chair of the Judicial Council; and

(2) The appropriate clerks for filing in each pending coordinated action.

(Subd (b) amended and lettered effective January 1, 2005; adopted as part of unlettered subd effective January 1, 1974.)

(c) Judgment in coordinated action

The judgment entered in each coordinated action must bear the title and case number assigned to the action at the time it was filed.

(Subd (c) amended and lettered effective January 1, 2005; adopted as part of unlettered subd effective January 1, 1974.)

(d) Proceedings in trial court after judgment

Until the judgment in a coordinated action becomes final or until a coordinated action is remanded, all further proceedings in that action to be determined by the trial court must be determined by the coordination trial judge. Thereafter, unless otherwise ordered by the coordination trial judge, all such proceedings must be conducted in the court where the action was pending when coordination was ordered. The coordination trial judge must also specify the court in which any ancillary proceedings will be heard and determined. For purposes of this rule, a judgment is final when it is no longer subject to appeal.

(Subd (d) amended and lettered effective January 1, 2005; adopted as part of unlettered subd effective January 1, 1974.)

Rule 3.545 renumbered effective January 1, 2007; adopted as rule 1545 effective January 1, 1974; previously amended effective January 1, 2005.

Ref.: Cal. Fms Pl. & Pr., Ch. 125, "Consolidation, Severance, and Coordination of Actions"; MB Prac. Guide: Cal. Pretrial Proc., §32.22[3].

Article 5
Administration of Coordinated Complex Actions

Rule 3.550. General administration by the Administrative Office of the Courts

(a) Coordination attorney

Except as otherwise provided in the rules in this chapter, all necessary administrative functions under this chapter will be performed at the direction of the Chair of the Judicial Council by a coordination attorney in the Administrative Office of the Courts.

(Subd (a) amended effective January 1, 2007; previously amended effective January 1, 2005.)

(b) Duties of coordination attorney

The coordination attorney must at all times maintain:

(1) A list of active and retired judges who are qualified and currently available to conduct coordination proceedings; and

(2) A register of all coordination proceedings and a file for each proceeding, for public inspection during regular business hours at the San Francisco office of the Judicial Council.

(Subd (b) amended and lettered effective January 1, 2005; previously adopted as part of subd (a) effective January 1, 2005.)

(c) Coordination proceeding title and case number

The coordination attorney must assign each coordination proceeding a special title and coordination proceeding number. Thereafter all papers in that proceeding must bear that title and number.

(Subd (c) amended and relettered effective January 1, 2005; adopted as subd (b) effective January 1, 1974.)

Rule 3.550 amended and renumbered effective January 1, 2007; adopted as rule 1550 effective January 1, 1974; previously amended effective January 1, 2005.

Ref.: Cal. Fms Pl. & Pr., Ch. 125, "Consolidation, Severance, and Coordination of Actions."

Division 5
Venue
[Reserved]

Division 6
Proceedings

Chap. 1.   General Provisions [Reserved].
Chap. 2.   Stay of Proceedings. Rule 3.650.
Chap. 3.   Hearings, Conferences, and Proceedings. Rule 3.670.

Chapter 1
General Provisions
[Reserved]

Chapter 2
Stay of Proceedings

Rule 3.650. Duty to notify court and others of stay

(a) Notice of stay

The party who requested or caused a stay of a proceeding must immediately serve and file a notice of the stay and attach a copy of the order or other document showing that the proceeding is stayed. If the person who requested or caused the stay has not appeared, or is not subject to the jurisdiction of the court, the plaintiff must immediately file a notice of the stay and attach a copy of the order or other document showing that the proceeding is stayed. The notice of stay must be served on all parties who have appeared in the case.

(b) When notice must be provided

The party responsible for giving notice under (a) must provide notice if the case is stayed for any of the following reasons:

(1) An order of a federal court or a higher state court;

(2) Contractual arbitration under Code of Civil Procedure section 1281.4;

(3) Arbitration of attorney fees and costs under Business and Professions Code section 6201; or

(4) Automatic stay caused by a filing in another court, including a federal bankruptcy court.

(Subd (b) amended effective January 1, 2007.)

(c) Contents of notice

The notice must state whether the case is stayed with regard to all parties or only certain parties. If it is stayed with regard to only certain parties, the notice must specifically identify those parties. The notice must also state the reason that the case is stayed.

(Subd (c) amended effective January 1, 2006.)

(d) Notice that stay is terminated or modified

When a stay is vacated, is no longer in effect, or is modified, the party who filed the notice of the stay must immediately serve and file a notice of termination or modification of stay. If that party fails to do so, any other party in the action who has knowledge of the termination or modification of the stay must serve and file a notice of termination or modification of stay. Once one party in the action has served and filed a notice of termination or modification of stay, other parties in the action are not required to do so.

(Subd (d) amended effective January 1, 2006.)

Rule 3.650 amended and renumbered effective January 1, 2007; adopted as rule 224 effective January 1, 2004; previously amended effective January 1, 2006.

Ref.: Cal. Fms Pl. & Pr., Ch. 1, "New Developments," Ch. 2, "Procedural Guide for Civil Actions," Ch. 32, "Contractual Arbitration: Agreements and Compelling Arbitration," Ch. 43, "Appeal: Stay of Proceedings," Ch. 137, "Continuing Duties During Litigation"; MB Prac. Guide: Cal. Debt Collection & Enforcement of Judgments, §§3.04[2], 3.10[3], 3.29, 3.30; MB Prac. Guide: Cal. Pretrial Proc., §§6.09, 6.17[2][b], 6.64A, 6.64B, 30.04[1][b], 32.03, 32.06A[1], [2].

Chapter 3
Hearings, Conferences, and Proceedings

Chapter 3 amended effective July 1, 2008.

Rule 3.670.   Telephone appearance

(a) Policy favoring telephone appearances

The intent of this rule is to promote uniformity in the practices and procedures relating to telephone appearances in civil cases. To improve access to the courts and reduce litigation costs, courts should permit parties, to the extent feasible, to appear by telephone at appropriate conferences, hearings, and proceedings in civil cases.

(Subd (a) adopted effective January 1, 2008.)

(b) Application

This rule applies to all general civil cases as defined in rule 1.6 and to unlawful detainer and probate proceedings.

(Subd (b) relettered effective January 1, 2008; previously repealed and adopted as subd (a) effective July 1, 1998; previously amended effective January 1, 1999, January 1, 2001, January 1, 2003, and January 1, 2007.)

(c) General provision authorizing parties to appear by telephone

Except as provided in (e)(2), a party may appear by telephone at the following conferences, hearings, and proceedings:

(1) Case management conferences, provided the party has made a good faith effort to meet and confer and has timely served and filed a case management statement before the conference date;

(2) Trial setting conferences;

(3) Hearings on law and motion, except motions in limine;

(4) Hearings on discovery motions;

(5) Status conferences, including conferences to review the status of an arbitration or a mediation; and

(6) Hearings to review the dismissal of an action.

(Subd (c) amended and relettered effective January 1, 2008; previously repealed and adopted as subd (b) effective July 1, 1998; previously amended effective July 1, 1999, and January 1, 2003.)

(d) Required personal appearances

Except as provided in (e)(3), a personal appearance is required for hearings, conferences, and proceedings not listed in (c), including the following:

(1) Trials and hearings at which witnesses are expected to testify;

(2) Hearings on temporary restraining orders;

(3) Settlement conferences;

(4) Trial management conferences;

(5) Hearings on motions in limine; and

(6) Hearings on petitions to confirm the sale of property under the Probate Code.

In addition, except as provided in (e)(3), a personal appearance is required for the following persons:

(7) Applicants seeking an ex parte order, except when the applicant is seeking an order:

(A) For permission to file a memorandum in excess of the applicable page limits;

(B) For an extension of time to serve pleadings;

(C) To set hearing dates on alternative writs and orders to show cause; or

(D) By stipulation of the parties;

(8) Persons ordered to appear to show cause why sanctions should not be imposed for violation of a court order or a rule; or

(9) Persons ordered to appear in an order or citation issued under the Probate Code.

At the proceedings under (7), (8), and (9), parties who are not required to appear in person under this rule may appear by telephone.

(Subd (d) amended and relettered effective January 1, 2008; adopted as subd (c) effective July 1, 1998; previously amended effective July 1, 2002, and January 1, 2003.)

(e) Court discretion to modify rule

(1) *Policy favoring telephone appearances in civil cases*

In exercising its discretion under this provision, the court should consider the general policy favoring telephone appearances in civil cases.

(2) *Court may require personal appearances*

The court may require a party to appear in person at a hearing, conference, or proceeding listed in (c) if the court determines on a hearing-by-hearing basis that a personal appearance would materially assist in the determination of the proceedings or in the effective management or resolution of the particular case.

(3) *Court may permit appearances by telephone*

The court may permit a party to appear by telephone at a hearing, conference, or proceeding under (d) if the court determines that a telephone appearance is appropriate.

(Subd (e) adopted effective January 1, 2008.)

(f) Need for personal appearance

If, at any time during a hearing, conference, or proceeding conducted by telephone, the court determines that a personal appearance is necessary, the court may continue the matter and require a personal appearance.

(Subd (f) adopted effective January 1, 2008.)

(g) Notice by party

(1) A party choosing to appear by telephone at a hearing, conference, or proceeding under this rule must either:

(A) Place the phrase "Telephone Appearance" below the title of the moving, opposing, or reply papers; or

(B) At least three court days before the appearance, notify the court and all other parties of the party's intent to appear by telephone. If the notice is oral, it must be given either in person or by telephone. If the notice is in writing, it must be given by filing a "Notice of Intent to Appear by Telephone" with the court at least three court days before the appearance and by serving the notice at the same time on all other parties by personal delivery, fax transmission, express mail, or other means reasonably calculated to ensure delivery to the parties no later than the close of the next business day.

(2) If after receiving notice from another party as provided under (1) a party that has not given notice also decides to appear by telephone, the party may do so by notifying the court and all other parties that have appeared in the action, no later than noon on the court day before the appearance, of its intent to appear by telephone.

(3) If a party that has given notice that it intends to appear by telephone under (1) subsequently chooses to appear in person, the party must so notify the court and all other parties that have appeared in the action, by telephone, at least two court days before the appearance.

(4) The court, on a showing of good cause, may permit a party to appear by telephone at a conference, hearing, or proceeding even if the party has not given the notice required under (1) or (2) and may permit a party to appear in person even if the party has not given the notice required in (3).

(Subd (g) amended and relettered effective January 1, 2008; adopted as subd (d) effective July 1, 1998; previously amended effective January 1, 1999, July 1, 1999, January 1, 2003, and January 1, 2007.)

(h) Notice by court

After a party has requested a telephone appearance under (g), if the court requires the personal appearance of the party, the court must give reasonable notice to all parties before the hearing and may continue the hearing if necessary to accommodate the personal appearance. The court may direct the court clerk, a court-appointed vendor, a party, or an attorney to provide the notification. In courts using a telephonic tentative ruling system for law and motion matters, court notification that parties must appear in person may be given as part of the court's tentative ruling on a specific law and motion matter if that notification is given one court day before the hearing.

(Subd (h) amended and relettered effective January 1, 2008; adopted as subd (e) effective July 1, 1998; previously amended effective January 1, 1999, and January 1, 2003.)

(i) Private vendor; charges for service

A court may provide teleconferencing for court appearances by entering into a contract with a private vendor. The contract may provide that the vendor may charge the party appearing by telephone a reasonable fee, specified in the contract, for its services.

(Subd (i) relettered effective January 1, 2008; adopted as subd (f) effective July 1, 1998; previously amended effective January 1, 2003.)

(j) Audibility and procedure

The court must ensure that the statements of participants are audible to all other participants and the court staff and that the statements made by a participant are identified as being made by that participant.

(Subd (j) amended and relettered effective January 1, 2008; adopted as subd (f) effective March 1, 1988; previously relettered as subd (c) effective January 1, 1989, and as subd (g) effective July 1, 1998; previously amended effective January 1, 2003, and January 1, 2007.)

(k) Reporting

All proceedings involving telephone appearances must be reported to the same extent and in the same manner as if the participants had appeared in person.

(Subd (k) relettered effective January 1, 2008; adopted as subd (h) effective July 1, 1998; previously amended effective January 1, 2003.)

(l) Conference call provider

A court, by local rule, may designate a particular conference call provider that must be used for telephone appearances.

(Subd (l) relettered effective January 1, 2008; adopted as subd (i) effective July 1, 1998; previously amended effective January 1, 1999, and January 1, 2003.)

(m) Information on telephone appearances

The court must publish notice providing parties with the particular information necessary for them to appear by telephone at conferences, hearings, and proceedings in that court under this rule.

(Subd (m) amended and relettered effective January 1, 2008; adopted as subd (j) effective March 1, 1998; previously amended effective January 1, 2003, and January 1, 2007.)

Rule 3.670 amended effective January 1, 2008; adopted as rule 298 effective March 1, 1988; previously amended effective January 1, 1989, July 1, 1998, January 1, 1999, July 1, 1999, January 1, 2001, July 1, 2002, and January 1, 2003; previously amended and renumbered effective January 1, 2007.

Ref.: Cal. Fms Pl. & Pr., Ch. 2, "Procedural Guide for Civil Actions," Ch. 206, "Demurrers and Motions for Judgment on the Pleadings," Ch. 212, "Dismissal," Ch. 220, "Dissolution of Marriage: Master Procedural Guide," Ch. 259, "Family Law Enforcement: Special Remedies for Support Enforcement," Ch. 372, "Motions and Orders," Ch. 417, "Points and Authorities," Ch. 425, "Pretrial Proceedings," Ch. 537, "Summary Judgment"; MB Prac. Guide: Cal. Pretrial Proc., §§11.26, 11.27[2], 23.08[5], [6], 26.01, 26.18, 26.20–26.22, 26.39, 26.43[8], 26.46, 26.51, 26.56, 26.59[2], 26.69; MB Prac. Guide: Cal. Trial & Post-Trial Civ. Proc., §§4.07[1], 4.10; W. Cal. Sum., 10 "Parent and Child" §303.

Division 7
Civil Case Management

Chap. 1.   General Provisions. Rule 3.700.

Chap. 2.   Differential Case Management. Rules 3.710–3.715.

Chap. 3.   Case Management. Rules 3.720–3.735.

Chap. 4.   Management of Collections Cases. Rules 3.740, 3.741.

Chap. 5.   Management of Complex Cases. Rules 3.750, 3.751.

Chap. 6.   Management of Class Actions. Rules 3.760–3.771.

Chapter 1
General Provisions

Rule 3.700. Scope and purpose of the case management rules

The rules in this division are to be construed and administered to secure the fair, timely, and efficient disposition of every civil case. The rules are to be applied in a fair, practical, and flexible manner so as to achieve the ends of justice.

Rule 3.700 amended and renumbered effective January 1, 2007; adopted as rule 204 effective January 1, 2004.

Ref.: Cal. Fms Pl. & Pr., Ch. 317, "Judges," Ch. 425, "Pretrial Proceedings."

Chapter 2
Differential Case Management

Rule 3.713. Delay reduction goals
Rule 3.714. Differentiation of cases to achieve goals
Rule 3.715. Case evaluation factors

Rule 3.710. Authority

The rules in this chapter implement Government Code section 68603(c) under the Trial Court Delay Reduction Act of 1990.

Rule 3.710 amended and renumbered effective January 1, 2007; adopted as rule 2101 effective July 1, 1991; previously amended and renumbered as rule 205 effective July 1, 2002.

Ref.: Cal. Fms Pl. & Pr., Ch. 425, "Pretrial Proceedings," Ch. 552, "Trial Court Delay Reduction"; MB Prac. Guide: Cal. Pretrial Proc., §9.41.

Rule 3.711. Local court rules

Each court must adopt local rules on differential case management as provided in this chapter consistent with the rules on case management in chapter 3 of this division and standard 2.1 of the California Standards of Judicial Administration.

Rule 3.711 amended and renumbered effective January 1, 2007; adopted as rule 2102 effective July 1, 1991; previously amended effective January 1, 1994, and January 1, 2000; previously amended and renumbered as rule 206 effective July 1, 2002.

Rule 3.712. Application and exceptions

(a) Application

The rules in this chapter apply to all general civil cases filed in the trial courts except those specified in (b), (c), and (d).

(Subd (a) amended effective July 1, 2007; previously amended effective January 1, 1994, July 1, 2002, and January 1, 2007.)

(b) Uninsured motorist cases

To allow for arbitration of the plaintiff's claim, the rules in this chapter do not apply to a case designated by the court as "uninsured motorist" until 180 days after the designation.

(Subd (b) amended and relettered effective January 1, 2007; adopted as subd (c) effective July 1, 1991; previously amended effective July 1, 2002.)

(c) Coordinated cases

The rules in this chapter do not apply to any case included in a petition for coordination. If the petition is granted, the coordination trial judge may establish a case progression plan for the cases, which may be assigned for review under the case management rules in chapter 3 of this division or, after appropriate findings, for treatment as an exceptional case.

(Subd (c) amended and relettered effective January 1, 2007; adopted as subd (d) effective July 1, 1991; previously amended effective July 1, 2002.)

(d) Collections cases

The rules in this chapter do not apply to a collections case, as defined in rule 3.740(a), unless a defendant files a responsive pleading.

(Subd (d) adopted effective July 1, 2007.)

Rule 3.712 amended effective July 1, 2007; adopted as rule 2103 effective July 1, 1991; previously amended and renumbered as rule 207 effective July 1, 2002, and amended and renumbered effective January 1, 2007; previously amended effective January 1, 1994.

Ref.: Cal. Fms Pl. & Pr., Ch. 425, "Pretrial Proceedings," Ch. 552, "Trial Court Delay Reduction"; MB Prac. Guide: Cal. Pretrial Proc., §§23.03, 23.04[1][a], [h], [i], [2].

Rule 3.713. Delay reduction goals

(a) Case management goals

The rules in this chapter are adopted to advance the goals of Government Code section 68607 and standard 2.1 of the California Standards of Judicial Administration.

(Subd (a) amended effective January 1, 2007; previously amended effective July 1, 2002.)

(b) Case disposition time goals

The goal of the court is to manage general civil cases from filing to disposition as provided under standard 2.2 of the California Standards of Judicial Administration.

(Subd (b) amended effective January 1, 2007; previously amended effective January 1, 1994, July 1, 2002, and January 1, 2004.)

(c) Judges' responsibility

It is the responsibility of judges to achieve a just and effective resolution of each general civil case through active management and supervision of the pace of litigation from the date of filing to disposition.

(Subd (c) amended effective July 1, 2002.)

Rule 3.713 amended and renumbered effective January 1, 2007; adopted as rule 2104 effective July 1, 1991; previously amended and renumbered as rule 208 effective July 1, 2003; previously amended effective January 1, 1994, and January 1, 2004.

Rule 3.714. Differentiation of cases to achieve goals

(a) Evaluation and assignment

The court must evaluate each case on its own merits as provided in rule 3.715, under procedures adopted by local court rules. After evaluation, the court must:

(1) Assign the case to the case management program for review under the case management rules in chapter 3 of this division for disposition under the case disposition time goals in (b) of this rule;

(2) Exempt the case as an exceptional case under (c) of this rule from the case disposition time goals specified in rule 3.713(b) and monitor it with the goal of disposing of it within three years; or

(3) Assign the case under (d) of this rule to a local case management plan for disposition within six to nine months after filing.

(Subd (a) amended effective January 1, 2007; previously amended effective July 1, 2002, and January 1, 2004.)

(b) Civil case disposition time goals

Civil cases assigned for review under the case management rules in chapter 3 of this division should be managed so as to achieve the following goals:

(1) *Unlimited civil cases*

The goal of each trial court should be to manage unlimited civil cases from filing so that:

(A) 75 percent are disposed of within 12 months;

(B) 85 percent are disposed of within 18 months; and

(C) 100 percent are disposed of within 24 months.

(2) *Limited civil cases*

The goal of each trial court should be to manage limited civil cases from filing so that:

(A) 90 percent are disposed of within 12 months;

(B) 98 percent are disposed of within 18 months; and

(C) 100 percent are disposed of within 24 months.

(3) *Individualized case management*

The goals in (1) and (2) are guidelines for the court's disposition of all unlimited and limited civil cases filed in that court. In managing individual civil cases, the court must consider each case on its merits. To enable the fair and efficient resolution of civil cases, each case should be set for trial as soon as appropriate for that individual case consistent with rule 3.729.

(Subd (b) amended effective January 1, 2007; previously amended effective July 1, 2002, and January 1, 2004.)

(c) Exemption of exceptional cases

(1) The court may in the interest of justice exempt a general civil case from the case disposition time goals under rule 3.713(b) if it finds the case involves exceptional circumstances that will prevent the court and the parties from meeting the goals and deadlines imposed by the program. In making the determination, the court is guided by rules 3.715 and 3.400.

(2) If the court exempts the case from the case disposition time goals, the court must establish a case progression plan and monitor the case to ensure timely disposition consistent with the exceptional circumstances, with the goal of disposing of the case within three years.

(Subd (c) amended effective January 1, 2007; adopted as subd (d) effective July 1, 1991; previously amended effective January 1, 2000, and July 1, 2002; previously amended and relettered as subd (c) effective January 1, 2004.)

(d) Local case management plan for expedited case disposition

(1) For expedited case disposition, the court may by local rule adopt a case management plan that establishes a goal for disposing of appropriate cases within six to nine months after filing. The plan must establish a procedure to identify the cases to be assigned to the plan.

(2) The plan must be used only for uncomplicated cases amenable to early disposition that do not need a case management conference or review or similar event to guide the case to early resolution.

(Subd (d) amended and relettered effective January 1, 2004; adopted as subd (e) effective July 1, 1991; previously amended effective January 1, 1994, and July 1, 2002.)

Rule 3.714 amended and renumbered effective January 1, 2007; adopted as rule 2105 effective July 1, 1991; amended and renumbered as rule 209 effective July 1, 2002; previously amended effective January 1, 1994, January 1, 2000, and January 1, 2004.

Ref.: Cal. Fms Pl. & Pr., Ch. 136, "Continuances," Ch. 418, "Pollution and Environmental Matters," Ch. 425, "Pretrial Proceedings," Ch. 552, "Trial Court Delay Reduction"; MB Prac. Guide: Cal. Pretrial Proc., §§23.03, 23.04[1][a], [c], [d], [f], 23.12[3], 30.02.

Rule 3.715.   Case evaluation factors

(a) Time estimate

In applying rule 3.714, the court must estimate the maximum time that will reasonably be required to dispose of each case in a just and effective manner. The court must consider the following factors and any other information the court deems relevant, understanding that no one factor or set of factors will be controlling and that cases may have unique characteristics incapable of precise definition:

(1) Type and subject matter of the action;

(2) Number of causes of action or affirmative defenses alleged;

(3) Number of parties with separate interests;

(4) Number of cross-complaints and the subject matter;

(5) Complexity of issues, including issues of first impression;

(6) Difficulty in identifying, locating, and serving parties;

(7) Nature and extent of discovery anticipated;

(8) Number and location of percipient and expert witnesses;

(9) Estimated length of trial;

(10) Whether some or all issues can be arbitrated or resolved through other alternative dispute resolution processes;

(11) Statutory priority for the issues;

(12) Likelihood of review by writ or appeal;

(13) Amount in controversy and the type of remedy sought, including measures of damages;

(14) Pendency of other actions or proceedings that may affect the case;

(15) Nature and extent of law and motion proceedings anticipated;

(16) Nature and extent of the injuries and damages;

(17) Pendency of underinsured claims; and

(18) Any other factor that would affect the time for disposition of the case.

(Subd (a) amended and lettered effective January 1, 2007; adopted as untitled subd effective July 1, 1991.)

Rule 3.715 amended and renumbered effective January 1, 2007; adopted as rule 2106 effective July 1, 1991; previously amended and renumbered as rule 210 effective July 1, 2002.

Ref.: Cal. Fms Pl. & Pr., Ch. 425, "Pretrial Proceedings," Ch. 552, "Trial Court Delay Reduction"; MB Prac. Guide: Cal. Pretrial Proc., §§23.04[1][a], [f], 23.05.

Chapter 3
Case Management

Rule 3.720. Application
Rule 3.721. Case management review
Rule 3.722. Case management conference
Rule 3.723. Additional case management conferences
Rule 3.724. Duty to meet and confer
Rule 3.725. Case Management Statement
Rule 3.726. Stipulation to alternative dispute resolution
Rule 3.727. Subjects to be considered at the case management conference
Rule 3.728. Case management order
Rule 3.729. Setting the trial date
Rule 3.730. Case management order controls
Rule 3.734. Assignment to one judge for all or limited purposes
Rule 3.735. Management of short cause cases

Rule 3.720.   Application

The rules in this chapter prescribe the procedures for the management of all applicable court cases. These rules may be referred to as "the case management rules."

Rule 3.720 adopted effective January 1, 2007.

Ref.: Cal. Fms Pl. & Pr., Ch. 21, "Amended and Supplemental Pleadings," Ch. 36, "Judicial Arbitration," Ch. 37, "Judicially Mandated Civil Action Mediation," Ch. 87, "Automobiles: Trial,"

Ch. 351, "Long-Term Health and Residential Care," Ch. 425, "Pretrial Proceedings," Ch. 552, "Trial Court Delay Reduction"; MB Prac. Guide: Cal. Pretrial Proc., §§6.07[1], 23.03, 23.04[1][a], [c], 23.08[1], 34.15.

Rule 3.721. Case management review

In every general civil case except complex cases and cases exempted under rules 3.712(b)–(d), 3.714(c)–(d), 3.735(b), 2.573(e), and 3.740(c), the court must review the case no later than 180 days after the filing of the initial complaint.

Rule 3.721 amended effective July 1, 2007; adopted effective January 1, 2007.

Ref.: Cal. Fms Pl. & Pr., Ch. 84, "Automobiles: Responding to the Action," Ch. 425, "Pretrial Proceedings"; MB Prac. Guide: Cal. Pretrial Proc., §§23.03, 23.08[1], 24.45; MB Prac. Guide: Cal. Trial & Post-Trial Civ. Proc., §4.07[1].

Rule 3.722. Case management conference

(a) The initial conference

In each case, the court must set an initial case management conference to review the case. At the conference, the court must review the case comprehensively and decide whether to assign the case to an alternative dispute resolution process, whether to set the case for trial, and whether to take action regarding any of the other matters identified in rules 3.727 and 3.728. The initial case management conference should generally be the first case management event conducted by court order in each case, except for orders to show cause.

(Subd (a) adopted effective January 1, 2007.)

(b) Notice of the initial conference

Notice of the date of the initial case management conference must be given to all parties no later than 45 days before the conference, unless otherwise ordered by the court. The court may provide by local rule for the time and manner of giving notice to the parties.

(Subd (b) adopted effective January 1, 2007.)

(c) Preparation for the conference

At the conference, counsel for each party and each self-represented party must appear by telephone or personally as provided in rule 3.670; must be familiar with the case; and must be prepared to discuss and commit to the party's position on the issues listed in rules 3.724 and 3.727.

(Subd (c) amended effective January 1, 2008; adopted effective January 1, 2007.)

(d) Case management order without appearance

If, based on its review of the written submissions of the parties and such other information as is available, the court determines that appearances at the conference are not necessary, the court may issue a case management order and notify the parties that no appearance is required.

(Subd (d) adopted effective January 1, 2007.)

(e) Option to excuse attendance at initial conferences in limited civil cases

By local rule the court may provide that counsel and self-represented parties are not to attend an initial case management conference in limited civil cases unless ordered to do so by the court.

(Subd (e) adopted effective January 1, 2007.)

Rule 3.722 amended effective January 1, 2008; adopted effective January 1, 2007.

Ref.: Cal. Fms Pl. & Pr., Ch. 2, "Procedural Guide for Civil Actions," Ch. 36, "Judicial Arbitration," Ch. 84, "Automobiles: Responding to the Action," Ch. 87, "Automobiles: Trial," Ch. 196, "Discovery: Requests for Admissions," Ch. 425, "Pretrial Proceedings"; MB Prac. Guide: Cal. Pretrial Proc., §§23.06, 23.08[2], [5]–[7], 23.09, 23.11[1], 24.45; MB Prac. Guide: Cal. Trial & Post-Trial Civ. Proc., §§4.07[1], 4.08.

Rule 3.723. Additional case management conferences

The court on its own motion may order, or a party or parties may request, that an additional case management conference be held at any time. A party should be required to appear at an additional conference only if an appearance is necessary for the effective management of the case. In determining whether to hold an additional conference, the court must consider each case individually on its own merits.

Rule 3.723 adopted effective January 1, 2007.

Advisory Committee Comment

Regarding additional case management conferences, in many civil cases one initial conference and one other conference before trial will be sufficient. But in other cases, including complicated or difficult cases, the court may order an additional case management conference or conferences if that would promote the fair and efficient administration of the case.

Ref.: Cal. Fms Pl. & Pr., Ch. 425, "Pretrial Proceedings"; MB Prac. Guide: Cal. Pretrial Proc., §23.08[8].

Rule 3.724. Duty to meet and confer

Unless the court orders another time period, no later than 30 calendar days before the date set for the case management conference, the parties must meet and confer, in person or by telephone, to consider each of the issues identified in rule 3.727 and, in addition, to consider the following:

(1) Resolving any discovery disputes and setting a discovery schedule;

(2) Identifying and, if possible, informally resolving any anticipated motions;

(3) Identifying the facts and issues in the case that are uncontested and may be the subject of stipulation;

(4) Identifying the facts and issues in the case that are in dispute;

(5) Determining whether the issues in the case can be narrowed by eliminating any claims or defenses by means of a motion or otherwise;

(6) Determining whether settlement is possible;

(7) Identifying the dates on which all parties and their attorneys are available or not available for trial, including the reasons for unavailability; and

(8) Other relevant matters.

Rule 3.724 adopted effective January 1, 2007.

Ref.: Cal. Fms Pl. & Pr., Ch. 2, "Procedural Guide for Civil Actions," Ch. 30, "Using Alternative Dispute Resolution," Ch. 36, "Judicial Arbitration," Ch. 425, "Pretrial Proceedings"; MB Prac. Guide: Cal. Pretrial Proc., §§1.06, 23.06, 23.08[3][d], [4], [7], 23.20[1], 24.03[1], [2], 24.04[1][c], 24.43, 24.46, 34.15; MB Prac. Guide: Cal. Trial & Post-Trial Civ. Proc., §4.07[1].

Rule 3.725. Case Management Statement

(a) Timing of statement

No later than 15 calendar days before the date set for the case management conference or review, each party must file a case management statement and serve it on all other parties in the case.

(b) Joint statement

In lieu of each party's filing a separate case management statement, any two or more parties may file a joint statement.

(c) Contents of statement

Parties must use the mandatory *Case Management Statement* (form CM-110). All applicable items on the form must be completed.

Rule 3.725 adopted effective January 1, 2007.

Ref.: Cal. Fms Pl. & Pr., Ch. 2, "Procedural Guide for Civil Actions," Ch. 30, "Using Alternative Dispute Resolution," Ch. 36, "Judicial Arbitration," Ch. 37, "Judicially Mandated Civil Action Mediation," Ch. 84, "Automobiles: Responding to the Action," Ch. 87, "Automobiles: Trial," Ch. 322, "Juries and Jury Selection," Ch. 425, "Pretrial Proceedings," Ch. 481, "Public Works"; MB Prac. Guide: Cal. Pretrial Proc., §§23.06, 23.08[3][a], 23.20[1], 23.22, 23.34, 23.37[1], [2], 23.43, 23.58, 24.03[1], [2], 24.43, 24.46; MB Prac. Guide: Cal. Trial & Post-Trial Civ. Proc., §§4.07[1], 5.16[2].

Rule 3.726. Stipulation to alternative dispute resolution

If all parties agree to use an alternative dispute resolution (ADR) process, they must jointly complete the ADR stipulation form provided for under rule 3.221 and file it with the court.

Rule 3.726 adopted effective January 1, 2007.

Ref.: Cal. Fms Pl. & Pr., Ch. 2, "Procedural Guide for Civil Actions," Ch. 30, "Using Alternative Dispute Resolution," Ch. 32, "Contractual Arbitration: Agreements and Compelling Arbitration," Ch. 36, "Judicial Arbitration," Ch. 37, "Judicially Mandated Civil Action Mediation"; MB Prac. Guide: Cal. Pretrial Proc., §§6.10[1][a], 24.04[1][c], 24.43, 24.46, 24.64.

Rule 3.727. Subjects to be considered at the case management conference

In any case management conference or review conducted under this chapter, the parties must address, if applicable, and the court may take appropriate action with respect to, the following:

(1) Whether there are any related cases;

(2) Whether all parties named in the complaint or cross-complaint have been served, have appeared, or have been dismissed;

(3) Whether any additional parties may be added or the pleadings may be amended;

(4) Whether, if the case is a limited civil case, the economic litigation procedures under Code of Civil Procedure section 90 et seq. will apply to it or the party intends to bring a motion to exempt the case from these procedures;

(5) Whether any other matters (e.g., the bankruptcy of a party) may affect the court's jurisdiction or processing of the case;

(6) Whether the parties have stipulated to, or the case should be referred to, judicial arbitration in courts having a judicial arbitration program or to any other form of alternative dispute resolution (ADR) process and, if so, the

date by which the judicial arbitration or other ADR process must be completed;

(7) Whether an early settlement conference should be scheduled and, if so, on what date;

(8) Whether discovery has been completed and, if not, the date by which it will be completed;

(9) What discovery issues are anticipated;

(10) Whether the case should be bifurcated or a hearing should be set for a motion to bifurcate under Code of Civil Procedure section 598;

(11) Whether there are any cross-complaints that are not ready to be set for trial and, if so, whether they should be severed;

(12) Whether the case is entitled to any statutory preference and, if so, the statute granting the preference;

(13) Whether a jury trial is demanded, and, if so, the identity of each party requesting a jury trial;

(14) If the trial date has not been previously set, the date by which the case will be ready for trial and the available trial dates;

(15) The estimated length of trial;

(16) The nature of the injuries;

(17) The amount of damages, including any special or punitive damages;

(18) Any additional relief sought;

(19) Whether there are any insurance coverage issues that may affect the resolution of the case; and

(20) Any other matters that should be considered by the court or addressed in its case management order.

Rule 3.727 adopted effective January 1, 2007.

Ref.: Cal. Fms Pl. & Pr., Ch. 2, "Procedural Guide for Civil Actions," Ch. 30, "Using Alternative Dispute Resolution," Ch. 36, "Judicial Arbitration," Ch. 37, "Judicially Mandated Civil Action Mediation," Ch. 84, "Automobiles: Responding to the Action," Ch. 322, "Juries and Jury Selection," Ch. 425, "Pretrial Proceedings," Ch. 481, "Public Works"; MB Prac. Guide: Cal. Pretrial Proc., §§1.06, 23.08[7], 23.09, 23.10[2], 23.37[2], 23.43, 24.04[1][c], 24.45, 34.03[1], [2]; MB Prac. Guide: Cal. Trial & Post-Trial Civ. Proc., §§4.07[1], 4.19[3], 5.12, 5.13, 5.16[1], [3].

Rule 3.728. Case management order

The case management conference must be conducted in the manner provided by local rule. The court must enter a case management order setting a schedule for subsequent proceedings and otherwise providing for the management of the case. The order may include appropriate provisions, such as:

(1) Referral of the case to judicial arbitration or other alternative dispute resolution process;

(2) A date for completion of the judicial arbitration process or other alternative dispute resolution process if the case has been referred to such a process;

(3) In the event that a trial date has not previously been set, a date certain for trial if the case is ready to be set for trial;

(4) Whether the trial will be a jury trial or a nonjury trial;

(5) The identity of each party demanding a jury trial;

(6) The estimated length of trial;

(7) Whether all parties necessary to the disposition of the case have been served or have appeared;

(8) The dismissal or severance of unserved or not-appearing defendants from the action;

(9) The names and addresses of the attorneys who will try the case;

(10) The date, time, and place for a mandatory settlement conference as provided in rule 3.1380;

(11) The date, time, and place for the final case management conference before trial if such a conference is required by the court or the judge assigned to the case;

(12) The date, time, and place of any further case management conferences or review; and

(13) Any additional orders that may be appropriate, including orders on matters listed in rules 3.724 and 3.727.

Rule 3.728 adopted effective January 1, 2007.

Ref.: Cal. Fms Pl. & Pr., Ch. 36, "Judicial Arbitration," Ch. 425, "Pretrial Proceedings"; MB Prac. Guide: Cal. Pretrial Proc., §§23.08[1], 23.09, 23.10[2], 23.14, 23.37[1], 23.43, 23.59, 24.04[1][c], 34.15; MB Prac. Guide: Cal. Trial & Post-Trial Civ. Proc., §§4.07[1], [2], 4.08, 5.12, 5.13, 5.16[1], [3].

Rule 3.729. Setting the trial date

In setting a case for trial, the court, at the initial case management conference or at any other proceeding at which the case is set for trial, must consider all the facts and circumstances that are relevant. These may include:

(1) The type and subject matter of the action to be tried;

(2) Whether the case has statutory priority;

(3) The number of causes of action, cross-actions, and affirmative defenses that will be tried;

(4) Whether any significant amendments to the pleadings have been made recently or are likely to be made before trial;

(5) Whether the plaintiff intends to bring a motion to amend the complaint to seek punitive damages under Code of Civil Procedure section 425.13;

(6) The number of parties with separate interests who will be involved in the trial;

(7) The complexity of the issues to be tried, including issues of first impression;

(8) Any difficulties in identifying, locating, or serving parties;

(9) Whether all parties have been served and, if so, the date by which they were served;

(10) Whether all parties have appeared in the action and, if so, the date by which they appeared;

(11) How long the attorneys who will try the case have been involved in the action;

(12) The trial date or dates proposed by the parties and their attorneys;

(13) The professional and personal schedules of the parties and their attorneys, including any conflicts with previously assigned trial dates or other significant events;

(14) The amount of discovery, if any, that remains to be conducted in the case;

(15) The nature and extent of law and motion proceedings anticipated, including whether any motions for summary judgment will be filed;

(16) Whether any other actions or proceedings that are pending may affect the case;

(17) The amount in controversy and the type of remedy sought;

(18) The nature and extent of the injuries or damages, including whether these are ready for determination;

(19) The court's trial calendar, including the pendency of other trial dates;

(20) Whether the trial will be a jury or a nonjury trial;

(21) The anticipated length of trial;

(22) The number, availability, and locations of witnesses, including witnesses who reside outside the county, state, or country;

(23) Whether there have been any previous continuances of the trial or delays in setting the case for trial;

(24) The achievement of a fair, timely, and efficient disposition of the case; and

(25) Any other factor that would significantly affect the determination of the appropriate date of trial.

Rule 3.729 adopted effective January 1, 2007.

Ref.: Cal. Fms Pl. & Pr., Ch. 425, "Pretrial Proceedings"; MB Prac. Guide: Cal. Pretrial Proc., §1.06.

Rule 3.730. Case management order controls

The order issued after the case management conference or review controls the subsequent course of the action or proceeding unless it is modified by a subsequent order.

Rule 3.730 adopted effective January 1, 2007.

Ref.: Cal. Fms Pl. & Pr., Ch. 2, "Procedural Guide for Civil Actions," Ch. 425, "Pretrial Proceedings"; MB Prac. Guide: Cal. Pretrial Proc., §§23.07, 23.10[1]; MB Prac. Guide: Cal. Trial & Post-Trial Civ. Proc., §4.07[1].

Rule 3.734. Assignment to one judge for all or limited purposes

The presiding judge may, on the noticed motion of a party or on the court's own motion, order the assignment of any case to one judge for all or such limited purposes as will promote the efficient administration of justice.

Rule 3.734 amended and renumbered effective January 1, 2007; adopted as rule 213 effective January 1, 1985; previously amended effective July 1, 2002.

Ref.: Cal. Fms Pl. & Pr., Ch. 551, "Trial"; MB Prac. Guide: Cal. Pretrial Proc., §§23.03, 23.04[4].

Rule 3.735. Management of short cause cases

(a) Short cause case defined

A short cause case is a civil case in which the time estimated for trial by all parties or the court is five hours or less. All other civil cases are long cause cases.

(Subd (a) amended effective January 1, 2007.)

(b) Exemption for short cause case and setting of case for trial

The court may order, upon the stipulation of all parties or the court's own motion, that a case is a short cause case exempted from the requirements of case management review and set the case for trial.

(c) Mistrial

If a short cause case is not completely tried within five hours, the judge may declare a mistrial or, in the judge's discretion, may complete the trial. In the event of a mistrial, the case will be treated as a long cause case and must promptly be set either for a new trial or for a case management conference.

Rule 3.735 amended and renumbered effective January 1, 2007; adopted as rule 214 effective July 1, 2002.

Ref.: Cal. Fms Pl. & Pr., Ch. 84, "Automobiles: Responding to the Action," Ch. 425, "Pretrial Proceedings," Ch. 551, "Trial"; MB Prac. Guide: Cal. Pretrial Proc., §§23.04[1][e], 23.11[2].

Chapter 4
Management of Collections Cases

Chapter 4 adopted effective July 1, 2008.

Rule 3.740. Collections cases
Rule 3.741. Settlement of collections case

Rule 3.740. Collections cases

(a) **Definition**

"Collections case" means an action for recovery of money owed in a sum stated to be certain that is not more than $25,000, exclusive of interest and attorney fees, arising from a transaction in which property, services, or money was acquired on credit. A collections case does not include an action seeking any of the following:

(1) Tort damages;

(2) Punitive damages;

(3) Recovery of real property;

(4) Recovery of personal property; or

(5) A prejudgment writ of attachment.

(Subd (a) adopted effective July 1, 2007.)

(b) *Civil Case Cover Sheet*

If a case meets the definition in (a), a plaintiff must check the case type box on the *Civil Case Cover Sheet* (form CM-010) to indicate that the case is a collections case under rule 3.740 **and serve the *Civil Case Cover Sheet* (form CM-010) with the initial complaint**.

(Subd (b) amended effective January 1, 2009; adopted effective July 1, 2007.)

(c) **Exemption from general time-for-service requirement and case management rules**

A collections case is exempt from:

(1) The time-for-service requirement of rule 3.110(b); and

(2) The case management rules that apply to all general civil cases under rules 3.712–3.715 and 3.721–3.730, unless a defendant files a responsive pleading.

(Subd (c) adopted effective July 1, 2007.)

(d) **Time for service**

The complaint in a collections case must be served on all named defendants, and proofs of service on those defendants must be filed, or the plaintiff must obtain an order for publication of the summons, within 180 days after the filing of the complaint.

(Subd (d) adopted effective July 1, 2007.)

(e) **Effect of failure to serve within required time**

If proofs of service on all defendants are not filed or the plaintiff has not obtained an order for publication of the summons within 180 days after the filing of the complaint, the court may issue an order to show cause why reasonable monetary sanctions should not be imposed. If proofs of service on all defendants are filed or an order for publication of the summons is filed at least 10 court days before the order to show cause hearing, the court must continue the hearing to 360 days after the filing of the complaint.

(Subd (e) adopted effective July 1, 2007.)

(f) **Effect of failure to obtain default judgment within required time**

If proofs of service of the complaint are filed or service by publication is made and defendants do not file responsive pleadings, the plaintiff must obtain a default judgment within 360 days after the filing of the complaint. If the plaintiff has not obtained a default judgment by that time, the court must issue an order to show cause why reasonable monetary sanctions should not be imposed. The order to show cause must be vacated if the plaintiff obtains a default judgment at least 10 court days before the order to show cause hearing.

(Subd (f) adopted effective July 1, 2007.)

Rule 3.740 amended effective January 1, 2009; adopted effective July 1, 2007.

Ref.: Cal. Fms Pl. & Pr., Ch. 1, "New Developments," Ch. 205, "Defaults and Default Judgments," Ch. 425, "Pretrial Proceedings," Ch. 518, "Service of Summons and Papers"; MB Prac. Guide: Cal. Pretrial Proc., §§7.29, 8.36[1], 23.03, 23.04[1][i], 37.26.

Rule 3.741. Settlement of collections case

If the plaintiff or other party seeking affirmative relief in a case meeting the definition of "collections case" in rule 3.740(a) files a notice of settlement under rule 3.1385, including a conditional settlement, the court must vacate all hearing, case management conference, and trial dates.

Rule 3.741 adopted effective July 1, 2007.

Ref.: MB Prac. Guide: Cal. Pretrial Proc., §37.26.

Chapter 5
Management of Complex Cases

Chapter 5 renumbered effective July 1, 2008; adopted as chapter 4 effective January 1, 2007.

Rule 3.750. Initial case management conference
Rule 3.751. Electronic service

Rule 3.750. Initial case management conference

(a) **Timing of conference**

The court in a complex case should hold an initial case management conference with all parties represented at the earliest practical date.

(b) **Subjects for consideration**

At the conference, the court should consider the following subjects:

(1) Whether all parties named in the complaint or cross-complaint have been served, have appeared, or have been dismissed;

(2) Whether any additional parties may be added or the pleadings may be amended;

(3) The deadline for the filing of any remaining pleadings and service of any additional parties;

(4) Whether severance, consolidation, or coordination with other actions is desirable;

(5) The schedule for discovery proceedings to avoid duplication and whether discovery should be stayed until all parties have been brought into the case;

(6) The schedule for settlement conferences or alternative dispute resolution;

(7) Whether to appoint liaison or lead counsel;

(8) The date for the filing of any dispositive motions;

(9) The creation of preliminary and updated lists of the persons to be deposed and the subjects to be addressed in each deposition;

(10) The exchange of documents and whether to establish an electronic document depository;

(11) Whether a special master should be appointed and the purposes for such appointment;

(12) Whether to establish a case-based Web site and other means to provide a current master list of addresses and telephone numbers of counsel; and

(13) The schedule for further conferences.

(c) Objects of conference

Principal objects of the initial case management conference are to expose at an early date the essential issues in the litigation and to avoid unnecessary and burdensome discovery procedures in the course of preparing for trial of those issues.

(d) Meet and confer requirement

The court may order counsel to meet privately before the initial case management conference to discuss the items specified in (a) and to prepare a joint statement of matters agreed upon, matters on which the court must rule at the conference, and a description of the major legal and factual issues involved in the litigation.

Rule 3.750 adopted effective January 1, 2007.

Ref.: MB Prac. Guide: Cal. Pretrial Proc., §23.12[2A][a]–[c].

Rule 3.751.   Electronic service

The court may provide in a case management order that documents filed electronically in a central electronic depository available to all parties are deemed served on all parties.

Rule 3.751 renumbered effective January 1, 2007; adopted as rule 1830 effective January 1, 2000.

Ref.: MB Prac. Guide: Cal. Pretrial Proc., §23.12[2A][b].

Chapter 6
Management of Class Actions

Chapter 6 renumbered effective July 1, 2008; adopted as chapter 5 effective January 1, 2007.

Rule 3.760.   Application

(a) Class actions

The rules in this chapter apply to each class action brought under Civil Code section 1750 et seq. or Code of Civil Procedure section 382 until the court finds the action is not maintainable as a class action or revokes a prior class certification.

(Subd (a) amended effective January 1, 2007.)

(b) Relief from compliance with rules

The court, on its own motion or on motion of any named party, may grant relief from compliance with the rules in this chapter in an appropriate case.

(Subd (b) amended effective January 1, 2007.)

Rule 3.760 amended and renumbered effective January 1, 2007; adopted as rule 1850 effective January 1, 2002.

Ref.: Cal. Fms Pl. & Pr., Ch. 120, "Class Actions"; Cal. Class Actions Prac. & Proc., §§1.02, 2.01, 2.02[2], 9.01[1], 22.04; MB Prac. Guide: Cal. Pretrial Proc., §33.01.

Rule 3.761.   Form of complaint

(a) Caption of pleadings

A complaint for or against a class party must include in the caption the designation "CLASS ACTION." This designation must be in capital letters on the first page of the complaint, immediately below the case number but above the description of the nature of the complaint.

(b) Heading and class action allegations

The complaint in a class action must contain a separate heading entitled "CLASS ACTION ALLEGATIONS," under which the plaintiff describes how the requirements for class certification are met.

Rule 3.761 renumbered effective January 1, 2007; adopted as rule 1851 effective January 1, 2002.

Ref.: Cal. Fms Pl. & Pr., Ch. 108, "Captions and Introductions," Ch. 120, "Class Actions," Ch. 123, "Complaints and Cross Complaints"; Cal. Class Actions Prac. & Proc., §§2.02[3], 6.02[1], 20.03[1], 21.01[2][a][ii], [iii], 22.04; MB Prac. Guide: Cal. Pretrial Proc., §33.10[1], [2].

Rule 3.762.   Case conference

(a) Purpose

One or more conferences between the court and counsel for the parties may be held to discuss class issues, conduct and scheduling of discovery, scheduling of hearings, and other matters. No evidence may be presented at the conference, but counsel must be fully prepared to discuss class issues and must possess authority to enter into stipulations.

(b) Notice by the parties

Notice of the conference may be given by any party. If notice is given by a named plaintiff, notice must be served on all named parties to the action. If notice is given by a defendant, notice must be served only on the parties who have appeared. Within 10 calendar days after receipt of the notice, the plaintiff must serve a copy on each named party who has not appeared in the action and must file a declaration of service. If the plaintiff is unable to serve any party, the plaintiff must file a declaration stating the reasons for failure of service.

(Subd (b) amended effective January 1, 2007.)

(c) Notice by the court

The court may give notice of the conference to the plaintiff. Within 10 calendar days after receipt of the notice given by the court, the plaintiff must serve a copy of the notice on all parties who have been served in the action, whether they have appeared or not, and must file a declaration of service. If the plaintiff is unable to serve any party, the plaintiff must file a declaration stating the reasons for failure of service.

(Subd (c) amended effective January 1, 2007.)

(d) Timing of notice

The notice must be filed and served on the parties at least 20 calendar days before the scheduled date of the conference.

(Subd (d) amended effective January 1, 2007.)

(e) Timing of conference

A conference may be held at any time after the first defendant has appeared. Before selecting a conference date, the party noticing the conference must:

(1) Obtain prior approval from the clerk of the department assigned to hear the class action; and

(2) Make reasonable efforts to accommodate the schedules of all parties entitled to receive notice under (b).

(Subd (e) amended effective January 1, 2007.)

Rule 3.762 amended and renumbered effective January 1, 2007; adopted as rule 1852 effective January 1, 2002.

Ref.: Cal. Fms Pl. & Pr., Ch. 120, "Class Actions"; Cal. Class Actions Prac. & Proc., §§2.02[4], [5], [10], 20.03[2], [3], 21.02[2][a], [b][ii], 21.04[2][a], 22.04; MB Prac. Guide: Cal. Pretrial Proc., §§33.12, 33.13, 33.44; MB Prac. Guide: Cal. Trial & Post-Trial Civ. Proc., §4.04.

Rule 3.763.   Conference order

At the conclusion of the conference, the court may make an order:

(1) Approving any stipulations of the parties;

(2) Establishing a schedule for discovery;

(3) Setting the date for the hearing on class certification;

(4) Setting the dates for any subsequent conferences; and

(5) Addressing any other matters related to management of the case.

Rule 3.763 renumbered effective January 1, 2007; adopted as rule 1853 effective January 1, 2002.

Ref.: Cal. Fms Pl. & Pr., Ch. 120, "Class Actions"; Cal. Class Actions Prac. & Proc., §§2.02[5], [10], 20.03[2], [3], 21.02[2][b][ii], 22.04; MB Prac. Guide: Cal. Pretrial Proc., §33.14; MB Prac. Guide: Cal. Trial & Post-Trial Civ. Proc., §4.04.

Rule 3.764.   Motion to certify or decertify a class or amend or modify an order certifying a class

(a) Purpose

Any party may file a motion to:

(1) Certify a class;

(2) Determine the existence of and certify subclasses;

(3) Amend or modify an order certifying a class; or

(4) Decertify a class.

(b) Timing of motion, hearing, extension, deferral

A motion for class certification should be filed when practicable. In its discretion, the court may establish a deadline for the filing of the motion, as part of the case conference or as part of other case management proceedings. Any such deadline must take into account discovery proceedings that may be necessary to the filing of the motion.

(c) Format and filing of motion

(1) *Time for service of papers*

Notice of a motion to certify or decertify a class or to amend or modify a certification order must be filed and served on all parties to the action at least 28 calendar days before the date appointed for hearing. Any opposition to the motion must be served and filed at least 14 calendar days before the noticed or continued hearing, unless the court for good cause orders otherwise. Any reply to the opposition must be served and filed at least 5 calendar days before the noticed or continued date of the hearing, unless the court for good cause orders otherwise. The provisions of Code of Civil Procedure section 1005 otherwise apply.

(2) *Length of papers*

An opening or responding memorandum filed in support of or in opposition to a motion for class certification must not exceed 20 pages. A reply memorandum must not exceed 15 pages. The provisions of rule 3.1113 otherwise apply.

(3) *Documents in support*

The documents in support of a motion for class certification consist of the notice of motion; a memorandum; evidence in support of the motion in the form of declarations of counsel, class representatives, or other appropriate declarants; and any requests for judicial notice.

(4) *Documents in opposition*

The documents in opposition to the motion consist of the opposing party's memorandum; the opposing party's evidence in opposition to the motion, including any declarations of counsel or other appropriate declarants; and any requests for judicial notice.

(Subd (c) amended effective January 1, 2007.)

(d) Presentation of evidence

Evidence to be considered at the hearing must be presented in accordance with rule 3.1306.

(Subd (d) amended effective January 1, 2007.)

(e) Stipulations

The parties should endeavor to resolve any uncontroverted issues by written stipulation before the hearing. If all class issues are resolved by stipulation of the named parties and approved by the court before the hearing, no hearing on class certification is necessary.

Rule 3.764 amended and renumbered effective January 1, 2007; adopted as rule 1854 effective January 1, 2002.

Ref.: Cal. Fms Pl. & Pr., Ch. 120, "Class Actions"; Cal. Class Actions Prac. & Proc., §§2.02[6], 6.01, 6.04, 6.18[1], 20.03[3]–[6], 21.02[2][a], [b][ii], 21.04[2][a], 22.04; MB Prac. Guide: Cal. Pretrial Proc., §§33.15, 33.16[1][a], [2][a]–[d], 33.18, 33.22[4][c], [5], 33.27[1][a]–[c], 33.28[1], 33.44.

Rule 3.765.   Class action order

(a) Class described

An order certifying, amending, or modifying a class must contain a description of the class and any subclasses.

(b) Limited issues and subclasses

When appropriate, an action may be maintained as a class action limited to particular issues. A class may be divided into subclasses.

Rule 3.765 renumbered effective January 1, 2007; adopted as rule 1855 effective January 1, 2002.

Ref.: Cal. Fms Pl. & Pr., Ch. 120, "Class Actions"; Cal. Class Actions Prac. & Proc., §§2.02[7], 3.02[3], 6.13, 20.03[3], 21.02[2][b][ii], 22.04; MB Prac. Guide: Cal. Pretrial Proc., §33.44.

Rule 3.766. Notice to class members

(a) Party to provide notice

If the class is certified, the court may require either party to notify the class of the action in the manner specified by the court.

(b) Statement regarding class notice

The class proponent must submit a statement regarding class notice and a proposed notice to class members. The statement must include the following items:

(1) Whether notice is necessary;

(2) Whether class members may exclude themselves from the action;

(3) The time and manner in which notice should be given;

(4) A proposal for which parties should bear the costs of notice; and,

(5) If cost shifting or sharing is proposed under subdivision (4), an estimate of the cost involved in giving notice.

(c) Order

Upon certification of a class, or as soon thereafter as practicable, the court must make an order determining:

(1) Whether notice to class members is necessary;

(2) Whether class members may exclude themselves from the action;

(3) The time and manner of notice;

(4) The content of the notice; and

(5) The parties responsible for the cost of notice.

(d) Content of class notice

The content of the class notice is subject to court approval. If class members are to be given the right to request exclusion from the class, the notice must include the following:

(1) A brief explanation of the case, including the basic contentions or denials of the parties;

(2) A statement that the court will exclude the member from the class if the member so requests by a specified date;

(3) A procedure for the member to follow in requesting exclusion from the class;

(4) A statement that the judgment, whether favorable or not, will bind all members who do not request exclusion; and

(5) A statement that any member who does not request exclusion may, if the member so desires, enter an appearance through counsel.

(e) Manner of giving notice

In determining the manner of the notice, the court must consider:

(1) The interests of the class;

(2) The type of relief requested;

(3) The stake of the individual class members;

(4) The cost of notifying class members;

(5) The resources of the parties;

(6) The possible prejudice to class members who do not receive notice; and

(7) The res judicata effect on class members.

(f) Court may order means of notice

If personal notification is unreasonably expensive or the stake of individual class members is insubstantial, or if it appears that all members of the class cannot be notified personally, the court may order a means of notice reasonably calculated to apprise the class members of the pendency of the action—for example, publication in a newspaper or magazine; broadcasting on television, radio, or the Internet; or posting or distribution through a trade or professional association, union, or public interest group.

(Subd (f) lettered effective January 1, 2007; adopted as part of subd (e) effective January 1, 2002.)

Rule 3.766 amended and renumbered effective January 1, 2007; adopted as rule 1856 effective January 1, 2002.

Ref.: Cal. Fms Pl. & Pr., Ch. 120, "Class Actions"; Cal. Class Actions Prac. & Proc., §§2.02[8], 8.01, 8.03[1], 8.05[1], [5], 8.06[2], 8.08[1], [2], 8.09, 20.03[3], [6], 21.04[2], 21.05[2][b], 21.06[2][b], [d][iii], 22.04; MB Prac. Guide: Cal. Pretrial Proc., §§33.21, 33.22[1]–[3], [4][a], [5], 33.23[1], [2], 33.48.

Rule 3.767. Orders in the conduct of class actions

(a) Court orders

In the conduct of a class action, the court may make orders that:

(1) Require that some or all of the members of the class be given notice in such manner as the court may direct of any action in the proceeding, or of their opportunity to seek to appear and indicate whether they consider the representation fair and adequate, or of the proposed extent of the judgment;

(2) Impose conditions on the representative parties or on intervenors;

(3) Require that the pleadings be amended to eliminate allegations as to representation of absent persons, and that the action proceed accordingly;

(4) Facilitate the management of class actions through consolidation, severance, coordination, bifurcation, intervention, or joinder; and

(5) Address similar procedural matters.

(Subd (a) amended effective January 1, 2007.)

(b) Altered or amended orders

The orders may be altered or amended as necessary.

(Subd (b) amended effective January 1, 2007.)

Rule 3.767 amended and renumbered effective January 1, 2007; adopted as rule 1857 effective January 1, 2002.

Ref.: Cal. Fms Pl. & Pr., Ch. 120, "Class Actions"; Cal. Class Actions Prac. & Proc., §§2.02[5], [9], 6.14, 21.02[2][a], [b][ii], 21.03[2][a], [b][ii], 22.04; MB Prac. Guide: Cal. Pretrial Proc., §33.45.

Rule 3.768. Discovery from unnamed class members

(a) Types of discovery permitted

The following types of discovery may be sought, through service of a subpoena and without a court order, from a member of a class who is not a party representative or who has not appeared:

(1) An oral deposition;

(2) A written deposition; and

(3) A deposition for production of business records and things.

(b) Motion for protective order

A party representative, deponent, or other affected person may move for a protective order to preclude or limit the discovery.

(c) Interrogatories require court order

A party may not serve interrogatories on a member of a class who is not a party representative or who has not appeared, without a court order.

(d) Determination by court

In deciding whether to allow the discovery requested under (a) or (c), the court must consider, among other relevant factors:

(1) The timing of the request;

(2) The subject matter to be covered;

(3) The materiality of the information being sought;

(4) The likelihood that class members have such information;

(5) The possibility of reaching factual stipulations that eliminate the need for such discovery;

(6) Whether class representatives are seeking discovery on the subject to be covered; and

(7) Whether discovery will result in annoyance, oppression, or undue burden or expense for the members of the class.

(Subd (d) amended effective January 1, 2007.)

Rule 3.768 amended and renumbered effective January 1, 2007; adopted as rule 1858 effective January 1, 2002.

Ref.: Cal. Fms Pl. & Pr., Ch. 194, "Discovery: Interrogatories"; Cal. Class Actions Prac. & Proc., §§2.02[10], 6.03, 22.04.

Rule 3.769.   Settlement of class actions

(a) Court approval after hearing

A settlement or compromise of an entire class action, or of a cause of action in a class action, or as to a party, requires the approval of the court after hearing.

(Subd (a) amended effective January 1, 2007.)

(b) Attorney's fees

Any agreement, express or implied, that has been entered into with respect to the payment of attorney's fees or the submission of an application for the approval of attorney's fees must be set forth in full in any application for approval of the dismissal or settlement of an action that has been certified as a class action.

(Subd (b) amended effective January 1, 2007.)

(c) Preliminary approval of settlement

Any party to a settlement agreement may serve and file a written notice of motion for preliminary approval of the settlement. The settlement agreement and proposed notice to class members must be filed with the motion, and the proposed order must be lodged with the motion.

(Subd (c) amended effective January 1, 2007.)

(d) Order certifying provisional settlement class

The court may make an order approving or denying certification of a provisional settlement class after the preliminary settlement hearing.

(e) Order for final approval hearing

If the court grants preliminary approval, its order must include the time, date, and place of the final approval hearing; the notice to be given to the class; and any other matters deemed necessary for the proper conduct of a settlement hearing.

(f) Notice to class of final approval hearing

If the court has certified the action as a class action, notice of the final approval hearing must be given to the class members in the manner specified by the court. The notice must contain an explanation of the proposed settlement and procedures for class members to follow in filing written objections to it and in arranging to appear at the settlement hearing and state any objections to the proposed settlement.

(Subd (f) amended effective January 1, 2007.)

(g) Conduct of final approval hearing

Before final approval, the court must conduct an inquiry into the fairness of the proposed settlement.

(h) Judgment and retention of jurisdiction to enforce

If the court approves the settlement agreement after the final approval hearing, the court must make and enter judgment. The judgment must include a provision for the retention of the court's jurisdiction over the parties to enforce the terms of the judgment. **The court may not enter an order dismissing the action at the same time as, or after, entry of judgment.**

(Subd (h) amended effective January 1, 2009.)

Rule 3.769 amended effective January 1, 2009; adopted as rule 1859 effective January 1, 2002; previously amended and renumbered effective January 1, 2007.

Ref.: Cal. Fms Pl. & Pr., Ch. 120, "Class Actions," Ch. 372, "Motions and Orders"; Cal. Class Actions Prac. & Proc., §§2.02[11], 14.01, 20.03[7], 22.04; MB Prac. Guide: Cal. Pretrial Proc., §§33.30, 33.31[1]–[5], [6][a], [b], 33.32[1]–[4], 33.42.

Rule 3.770.   Dismissal of class actions

(a) Court approval of dismissal

A dismissal of an entire class action, or of any party or cause of action in a class action, requires court approval. **The court may not grant a request to dismiss a class action if the court has entered judgment following final approval of a settlement.** Requests for dismissal must be accompanied by a declaration setting forth the facts on which the party relies. The declaration must clearly state whether consideration, direct or indirect, is being given for the dismissal and must describe the consideration in detail.

(Subd (a) amended effective January 1, 2009; adopted as untitled subd effective January 1, 1984; previously amended and lettered as subd (a) effective January 1, 2002; previously amended effective January 1, 2007.)

(b) Hearing on request for dismissal

The court may grant the request without a hearing. If the request is disapproved, notice of tentative disapproval must be sent to the attorneys of record. Any party may seek, within 15 calendar days of the service of the notice of tentative disapproval, a hearing on the request. If no hearing is sought within that period, the request for dismissal will be deemed denied.

(Subd (b) amended effective January 1, 2007; adopted as untitled subd effective January 1, 1984; previously amended and lettered as subd (b) effective January 1, 2002.)

(c) Notice to class of dismissal

If the court has certified the class, and notice of the pendency of the action has been provided to class members, notice of the dismissal must be given to the class in the manner specified by the court. If the court has not ruled on class certification, or if notice of the pendency of the action has not been provided to class members in a case in which such notice was required, notice of the proposed dismissal may be given in the manner and to those class members specified by the court, or the action may be dismissed without notice to the class members if the court finds that the dismissal will not prejudice them.

(Subd (c) amended effective January 1, 2007; adopted effective January 1, 2002.)

Rule 3.770 amended effective January 1, 2009; adopted as rule 365 effective January 1, 1984; previously amended and renumbered as rule 1860 effective January 1, 2002, and as rule 3.770 effective January 1, 2007.

Ref.: Cal. Fms Pl. & Pr., Ch. 120, "Class Actions," Ch. 212, "Dismissal"; Cal. Class Actions Prac. & Proc., §§2.02[12], 6.18[2], 20.03[8], 21.03[2][a], 21.08[2][b], [c][ii], 22.04; MB Prac. Guide: Cal. Pretrial Proc., §§33.25, 33.29[2][a]–[d], 33.45, 33.49, 39.10[5][h], [k].

Rule 3.771. Judgment

(a) Class members to be included in judgment

The judgment in an action maintained as a class action must include and describe those whom the court finds to be members of the class.

(Subd (a) amended and lettered effective January 1, 2007; adopted as unlettered subd effective January 1, 2002.)

(b) Notice of judgment to class

Notice of the judgment must be given to the class in the manner specified by the court.

(Subd (b) amended and lettered effective January 1, 2007; adopted as unlettered subd effective January 1, 2002.)

Rule 3.771 amended and renumbered effective January 1, 2007; adopted as rule 1861 effective January 1, 2002.

Ref.: Cal. Fms Pl. & Pr., Ch. 120, "Class Actions"; Cal. Class Actions Prac. & Proc., §§2.02[13], 22.04.

Division 8
Alternative Dispute Resolution

Chap. 1.   General Provisions. Rule 3.800.

Chap. 2.   Judicial Arbitration. Rules 3.810–3.830.

Chap. 3.   General Rules Relating to Mediation of Civil Cases. Rules 3.850–3.872.

Chap. 4.   Civil Action Mediation Program Rules [Effective Until July 1, 2009]. Rules 3.870–3.878.

Chap. 4.   Civil Action Mediation Program Rules [Effective July 1, 2009]. Rules 3.890–3.898.

Chapter 1
General Provisions

Rule 3.800.   Definitions

As used in this division:

(1) "Alternative dispute resolution process" or "ADR process" means a process, other than formal litigation, in which a neutral person or persons resolve a dispute or assist parties in resolving their dispute.

(2) "Mediation" means a process in which a neutral person or persons facilitate communication between disputants to assist them in reaching a mutually acceptable agreement. As used in this division, mediation does not include a settlement conference under rule 3.1380.

Rule 3.800 amended and renumbered effective January 1, 2007; adopted as rule 1580 effective January 1, 2001; previously amended effective July 1, 2002.

Ref.: Cal. Fms Pl. & Pr., Ch. 30, "Using Alternative Dispute Resolution," Ch. 32, "Contractual Arbitration: Agreements and Compelling Arbitration," Ch. 36, "Judicial Arbitration," Ch. 37, "Judicially Mandated Civil Action Mediation," Ch. 123, "Complaints and Cross Complaints"; MB Prac. Guide: Cal. Pretrial Proc., §6.04.

Chapter 2
Judicial Arbitration

Rule 3.810. Application
Rule 3.811. Cases subject to and exempt from arbitration
Rule 3.812. Assignment to arbitration
Rule 3.813. Arbitration program administration
Rule 3.814. Panels of arbitrators
Rule 3.815. Selection of the arbitrator
Rule 3.816. Disqualification for conflict of interest
Rule 3.817. Arbitration hearings; notice; when and where held
Rule 3.818. Continuances
Rule 3.819. Arbitrator's fees
Rule 3.820. Communication with the arbitrator
Rule 3.821. Representation by counsel; proceedings when party absent
Rule 3.822. Discovery
Rule 3.823. Rules of evidence at arbitration hearing
Rule 3.824. Conduct of the hearing
Rule 3.825. The award
Rule 3.826. Trial after arbitration
Rule 3.827. Entry of award as judgment
Rule 3.828. Vacating judgment on award
Rule 3.829. Settlement of case
Rule 3.830. Arbitration not pursuant to rules

Rule 3.810.   Application

The rules in this chapter (commencing with this rule) apply if Code of Civil Procedure, part 3, title 3, chapter 2.5 (commencing with section 1141.10) is in effect.

Rule 3.810 amended and renumbered effective January 1, 2007; adopted as rule 1600.1 effective January 1, 1988; previously amended effective July 1, 1999, and January 1, 2000; previously amended and renumbered as rule 1600 effective January 1, 2004.

Ref.: Cal. Fms Pl. & Pr., Ch. 2, "Procedural Guide for Civil Actions," Ch. 36, "Judicial Arbitration," Ch. 212, "Dismissal"; MB Prac. Guide: Cal. Pretrial Proc., §§6.07[1], 24.04[2][a], 24.64.

Rule 3.811.   Cases subject to and exempt from arbitration

(a) Cases subject to arbitration

Except as provided in (b), the following cases must be arbitrated:

(1) In each superior court with 18 or more authorized judges, all unlimited civil cases where the amount in controversy does not exceed $50,000 as to any plaintiff;

(2) In each superior court with fewer than 18 authorized judges that so provides by local rule, all unlimited civil cases where the amount in controversy does not exceed $50,000 as to any plaintiff;

(3) All limited civil cases in courts that so provide by local rule;

(4) Upon stipulation, any limited or unlimited civil case in any court, regardless of the amount in controversy; and

(5) Upon filing of an election by all plaintiffs, any limited or unlimited civil case in any court in which each plaintiff agrees that the arbitration award will not exceed $50,000 as to that plaintiff.

(Subd (a) amended effective January 1, 2004.)

(b) Cases exempt from arbitration

The following cases are exempt from arbitration:

(1) Cases that include a prayer for equitable relief that is not frivolous or insubstantial;

(2) Class actions;

(3) Small claims cases or trials de novo on appeal from the small claims court;

(4) Unlawful detainer proceedings;

(5) Family Law Act proceedings except as provided in Family Code section 2554;

(6) Any case otherwise subject to arbitration that is found by the court not to be amenable to arbitration on the ground that arbitration would not reduce the probable time and expense necessary to resolve the litigation;

(7) Any category of cases otherwise subject to arbitration but excluded by local rule as not amenable to arbitration on the ground that, under the circumstances relating to the particular court, arbitration of such cases would not reduce the probable time and expense necessary to resolve the litigation; and

(8) Cases involving multiple causes of action or a cross-complaint if the court determines that the amount in controversy as to any given cause of action or cross-complaint exceeds $50,000.

(Subd (b) adopted effective January 1, 2004.)

Rule 3.811 renumbered effective January 1, 2007; adopted as rule 1600 effective July 1, 1979; previously amended effective January 1, 1982, January 1, 1986, January 1, 1988, and July 1, 1999; previously amended and renumbered as rule 1601 effective January 1, 2004.

Ref.: Cal. Fms Pl. & Pr., Ch. 2, "Procedural Guide for Civil Actions," Ch. 36, "Judicial Arbitration"; MB Prac. Guide: Cal. Pretrial Proc., §§24.03[1], [2], 24.04[1][a], 24.05[1], [2][c], 24.06, 24.49, 24.64, 28.07[1].

Rule 3.812. Assignment to arbitration

(a) Stipulations to arbitration

When the parties stipulate to arbitration, the case must be set for arbitration forthwith. The stipulation must be filed no later than the time the initial case management statement is filed, unless the court orders otherwise.

(Subd (a) amended effective January 1, 2004; previously amended effective July 1, 1979, January 1, 1999, and January 1, 2003.)

(b) Plaintiff election for arbitration

Upon written election of all plaintiffs to submit a case to arbitration, the case must be set for arbitration forthwith, subject to a motion by defendant for good cause to delay the arbitration hearing. The election must be filed no later than the time the initial case management statement is filed, unless the court orders otherwise.

(Subd (b) amended effective January 1, 2004; adopted effective July 1, 1979; previously amended effective January 1, 1982, January 1, 1986, January 1, 1988, and January 1, 2003.)

(c) Cross-actions

A case involving a cross-complaint where all plaintiffs have elected to arbitrate must be removed from the list of cases assigned to arbitration if, upon motion of the cross-complainant made within 15 days after notice of the election to arbitrate, the court determines that the amount in controversy relating to the cross-complaint exceeds $50,000.

(Subd (c) amended effective January 1, 2004; adopted as part of subd (b) effective July 1, 1979; amended and lettered effective January 1, 2003.)

(d) Case management conference

Absent a stipulation or an election by all plaintiffs to submit to arbitration, cases must be set for arbitration when the court determines that the amount in controversy does not exceed $50,000. The amount in controversy must be determined at the first case management conference or review under the rules on case management in division 7 of this title that takes place after all named parties have appeared or defaulted.

(Subd (d) amended effective January 1, 2007; adopted as subd (c) effective July 1, 1976; previously amended effective July 1, 1979, January 1, 1982, and January 1, 2004; previously amended and relettered effective January 1, 2003.)

Rule 3.812 amended and renumbered effective January 1, 2007; adopted as rule 1601 effective July 1, 1976; previously amended effective July 1, 1979, January 1, 1982, January 1, 1985, January 1, 1986, January 1, 1988, January 1, 1991, and January 1, 2003; previously amended and renumbered as rule 1602 effective January 1, 2004.

Ref.: Cal. Fms Pl. & Pr., Ch. 36, "Judicial Arbitration," Ch. 37, "Judicially Mandated Civil Action Mediation"; MB Prac. Guide: Cal. Pretrial Proc., §§24.03[1], [2], 24.05[1], [2][a]–[c], 24.08[1], 24.64–24.66.

Rule 3.813. Arbitration program administration

(a) Arbitration administrator

The presiding judge must designate the ADR administrator selected under rule 10.783 to serve as arbitration administrator. The arbitration administrator must supervise the selection of arbitrators for the cases on the arbitration hearing list, generally supervise the operation of the arbitration program, and perform any additional duties delegated by the presiding judge.

(Subd (a) amended effective January 1, 2007; previously amended effective January 1, 2004.)

(b) Responsibilities of ADR committee

The ADR committee established under rule 10.783 is responsible for:

(1) Appointing the panels of arbitrators provided for in rule 3.814;

(2) Removing a person from a panel of arbitrators;

(3) Establishing procedures for selecting an arbitrator not inconsistent with these rules or local court rules; and

(4) Reviewing the administration and operation of the arbitration program periodically and making recommendations to the Judicial Council as the committee deems appropriate to improve the program, promote the ends of justice, and serve the needs of the community.

(Subd (b) amended effective January 1, 2007; adopted as subd (d) effective July 1, 1976; previously amended and relettered as subd (b) effective January 1, 2004.)

Rule 3.813 amended and renumbered effective January 1, 2007; adopted as rule 1603 effective July 1, 1976; previously amended July 1, 1979, July 1, 1999, and January 1, 2004.

Ref.: Cal. Fms Pl. & Pr., Ch. 36, "Judicial Arbitration," Ch. 317, "Judges."

Rule 3.814. Panels of arbitrators

(a) Creation of panels

Every court must have a panel of arbitrators for personal injury cases, and such additional panels as the presiding judge may, from time to time, determine are needed.

(Subd (a) amended effective January 1, 2004; previously amended effective July 1, 1979, and July 1, 2001.)

(b) Composition of panels

The panels of arbitrators must be composed of active or inactive members of the State Bar, retired court commissioners who were licensed to practice law before their appointment as commissioners, and retired judges. A former California judicial officer is not eligible for the panel of arbitrators unless he or she is an active or inactive member of the State Bar.

(Subd (b) amended effective January 1, 2007; previously amended effective July 1, 1979, January 1, 1996, July 1, 2001, and January 1, 2004.)

(c) Responsibilities of ADR committee

The ADR committee is responsible for determining the size and composition of each panel of arbitrators. The personal injury panel, to the extent feasible, must contain an equal number of those who usually represent plaintiffs and those who usually represent defendants.

(Subd (c) amended effective January 1, 2004; previously amended effective July 1, 2001.)

(d) Service on panel

Each person appointed serves as a member of a panel of arbitrators at the pleasure of the ADR committee. A person may be on arbitration panels in more than one county. An appointment to a panel is effective when the person appointed:

(1) Agrees to serve;

(2) Certifies that he or she is aware of and will comply with applicable provisions of canon 6 of the Code of Judicial Ethics and these rules; and

(3) Files an oath or affirmation to justly try all matters submitted to him or her.

(Subd (d) amended effective January 1, 2004; previously amended effective January 1, 1996, and July 1, 2001.)

(e) Panel lists

Lists showing the names of panel arbitrators available to hear cases must be available for public inspection in the ADR administrator's office.

(Subd (e) amended effective January 1, 2007; previously amended effective July 1, 2001, and January 1, 2004.)

Rule 3.814 amended and renumbered effective January 1, 2007; adopted as rule 1604 effective July 1, 1976; previously amended effective July 1, 1979, January 1, 1996, July 1, 2001, and January 1, 2004.

Ref.: Cal. Fms Pl. & Pr., Ch. 36, "Judicial Arbitration"; MB Prac. Guide: Cal. Pretrial Proc., §§24.07, 24.08[2][a].

Rule 3.815. Selection of the arbitrator

(a) Selection by stipulation

By stipulation, the parties may select any person to serve as arbitrator. If the parties select a person who is not on the court's arbitration panel to serve as the arbitrator, the stipulation will be effective only if:

(1) The selected person completes a written consent to serve and the oath required of panel arbitrators under these rules; and

(2) Both the consent and the oath are attached to the stipulation.

A stipulation may specify the maximum amount of the arbitrator's award. The stipulation to an arbitrator must be served and filed no later than 10 days after the case has been set for arbitration under rule 3.812.

(Subd (a) amended effective January 1, 2007; adopted effective January 1, 2004.)

(b) Selection absent stipulation or local procedures

If the arbitrator has not been selected by stipulation and the court has not adopted local rules or procedures for the selection of the arbitrator as permitted under (c), the arbitrator will be selected as follows:

(1) Within 15 days after a case is set for arbitration under rule 3.812, the administrator must determine the number of clearly adverse sides in the case; in the absence of a cross-complaint bringing in a new party, the administrator may assume there are two sides. A dispute as to the number or identity of sides must be decided by the presiding judge in the same manner as disputes in determining sides entitled to peremptory challenges of jurors.

(2) The administrator must select at random a number of names equal to the number of sides, plus one, and mail the list of randomly selected names to counsel for the parties.

(3) Each side has 10 days from the date of mailing to file a rejection, in writing, of no more than one name on the list; if there are two or more parties on a side, they must join in the rejection of a single name.

(4) Promptly on the expiration of the 10-day period, the administrator must appoint, at random, one of the persons on the list whose name was not rejected, if more than one name remains.

(5) The administrator must assign the case to the arbitrator appointed and must give notice of the appointment to the arbitrator and to all parties.

(Subd (b) amended effective January 1, 2007; adopted as subd (a) effective July 1, 1976; previously amended effective July 1, 1979, January 1, 1982, and January 1, 1984; previously amended and relettered as subd (b) effective January 1, 2004.)

(c) Local selection procedures

Instead of the procedure in (b), a court that has an arbitration program may, by local rule or by procedures adopted by its ADR committee, establish any fair method of selecting an arbitrator that:

(1) Affords each side an opportunity to challenge at least one listed arbitrator peremptorily; and

(2) Ensures that an arbitrator is appointed within 30 days from the submission of a case to arbitration.

The local rule or procedure may require that all steps leading to the selection of the arbitrator take place during or immediately following the case management conference or review under the rules on case management in division 7 of this title at which the court determines the amount in controversy and the suitability of the case for arbitration.

(Subd (c) amended effective January 1, 2007; adopted effective January 1, 2004.)

(d) Procedure if first arbitrator declines to serve

If the first arbitrator selected declines to serve, the administrator must vacate the appointment of the arbitrator and may either:

(1) Return the case to the top of the arbitration hearing list, restore the arbitrator's name to the list of those available for selection to hear cases, and appoint a new arbitrator; or

(2) Certify the case to the court.

(Subd (d) amended and relettered effective January 1, 2004; adopted as subd (b) effective July 1, 1976; previously amended effective January 1, 1991, and January 1, 1994.)

(e) Procedure if second arbitrator declines to serve or hearing is not timely held

If the second arbitrator selected declines to serve or if the arbitrator does not complete the hearing within 90 days after the date of the assignment of the case to him or her, including any time due to continuances granted under rule 3.818, the administrator must certify the case to the court.

(Subd (e) amended effective January 1, 2007; adopted as subd (c) effective July 1, 1976; previously amended effective January 1, 1991; previously amended and relettered effective January 1, 2004.)

(f) Cases certified to court

If a case is certified to the court under either (d) or (e), the court must hold a case management conference. If the inability to hold an arbitration hearing is due to the neglect or lack of cooperation of a party who elected or stipulated to arbitration, the court may set the case for trial and may make any other appropriate orders. In all other circumstances, the court may reassign the case to arbitration or make any other appropriate orders to expedite disposition of the case.

(Subd (f) amended effective January 1, 2007; adopted as part of subd (c) effective July 1, 1976; previously amended and relettered as subd (f) effective January 1, 2004.)

Rule 3.815 amended and renumbered effective January 1, 2007; adopted as rule 1605 effective July 1, 1976; previously amended effective July 1, 1979, January 1, 1982; January 1, 1984, January 1, 1991, January 1, 1994, and January 1, 2004.

Ref.: Cal. Fms Pl. & Pr., Ch. 32, "Contractual Arbitration: Agreements and Compelling Arbitration," Ch. 36, "Judicial Arbitration"; MB Prac. Guide: Cal. Pretrial Proc., §§24.07, 24.08[1], [2][b]–[e], 24.09[1], [2], 24.10[1][a], 24.67.

Rule 3.816. Disqualification for conflict of interest

(a) Arbitrator's duty to disqualify himself or herself

The arbitrator must determine whether any cause exists for disqualification upon any of the grounds set forth in Code of Civil Procedure section 170.1 governing the disqualification of judges. If any member of the arbitrator's law firm would be disqualified under subdivision (a)(2) of section 170.1, the arbitrator is disqualified. Unless the ground for disqualification is disclosed to the parties in writing and is expressly waived by all parties in writing, the arbitrator must promptly notify the administrator of any known ground for disqualification and another arbitrator must be selected as provided in rule 3.815.

(Subd (a) amended effective January 1, 2007; previously amended effective July 1, 1979, July 1, 1990, July 1, 2001, January 1, 2004, and July 1, 2004.)

(b) Disclosures by arbitrator

In addition to any other disclosure required by law, no later than five days before the deadline for parties to file a motion for disqualification of the arbitrator under Code of Civil Procedure section 170.6 or, if the arbitrator is not aware of his or her appointment or of a matter subject to disclosure at that time, as soon as practicable thereafter, an arbitrator must disclose to the parties:

(1) Any matter subject to disclosure under subdivisions (D)(5)(a) and (D)(5)(b) of canon 6 of the Code of Judicial Ethics; and

(2) Any significant personal or professional relationship the arbitrator has or has had with a party, attorney, or law firm in the instant case, including the number and nature of any other proceedings in the past 24 months in which the arbitrator has been privately compensated by a party, attorney, law firm, or insurance company in the instant case for any services, including service as an attorney, expert witness, or consultant or as a judge, referee, arbitrator, mediator, settlement facilitator, or other alternative dispute resolution neutral.

(Subd (b) amended effective January 1, 2008; adopted effective July 1, 2001; previously amended effective January 1, 2007.)

(c) Request for disqualification

A copy of any request by a party for the disqualification of an arbitrator under Code of Civil Procedure section 170.1 or 170.6 must be sent to the ADR administrator.

(Subd (c) amended effective January 1, 2007; adopted as subd (b) effective July 1, 1976; previously amended and relettered effective July 1, 2001; previously amended effective July 1, 1979, July 1, 1990, and January 1, 2004.)

(d) Arbitrator's failure to disqualify himself or herself

On motion of any party, made as promptly as possible under Code of Civil Procedure sections 170.1 and 1141.18(d) and before the conclusion of arbitration proceedings, the appointment of an arbitrator to a case must be vacated if the court finds that:

(1) The party has demanded that the arbitrator disqualify himself or herself;

(2) The arbitrator has failed to do so; and

(3) Any of the grounds specified in section 170.1 exists.

The ADR administrator must return the case to the top of the arbitration hearing list and appoint a new arbitrator. The disqualified arbitrator's name must be returned to the list of those available for selection to hear cases, unless the court orders that the circumstances of the disqualification be reviewed by the ADR administrator, the ADR committee, or the presiding judge for appropriate action.

(Subd (d) amended effective January 1, 2007; adopted as subd (c) effective January 1, 1994; previously amended and relettered effective July 1, 2001; previously amended effective January 1, 2004.)

Rule 3.816 amended effective January 1, 2008; adopted as rule 1606 effective July 1, 1976; previously amended effective July 1, 1979, July 1, 1990, January 1, 1994, July 1, 2001, January 1, 2004, and July 1, 2004; previously amended and renumbered effective January 1, 2007.

Ref.: Cal. Fms Pl. & Pr., Ch. 36, "Judicial Arbitration"; MB Prac. Guide: Cal. Pretrial Proc., §§24.07, 24.10[1][a]–[c], [3], 24.68.

Rule 3.817. Arbitration hearings; notice; when and where held

(a) Setting hearing; notice

Within 15 days after the appointment of the arbitrator, the arbitrator must set the time, date, and place of the arbitration hearing and notify each party and the administrator in writing of the time, date, and place set.

(Subd (a) amended and lettered effective January 1, 2004; adopted as part of unlettered subd effective July 1, 1976.)

(b) Date of hearing; limitations

Except upon the agreement of all parties and the arbitrator, the arbitration hearing date must not be set:

(1) Earlier than 30 days after the date the arbitrator sends the notice of the hearing under (a); or

(2) On Saturdays, Sundays, or legal holidays.

(Subd (b) amended and lettered effective January 1, 2004; adopted as part of unlettered subd effective July 1, 1976.)

(c) Hearing completion deadline

The hearing must be scheduled so as to be completed no later than 90 days from the date of the assignment of the case to the arbitrator, including any time due to continuances granted under rule 3.818.

(Subd (c) amended effective January 1, 2007; adopted as part of unlettered subd effective July 1, 1976; previously amended and relettered effective January 1, 2004.)

(d) Hearing location

The hearing must take place in appropriate facilities provided by the court or selected by the arbitrator.

(Subd (d) amended effective January 1, 2004.)

Rule 3.817 amended and renumbered effective January 1, 2007; adopted as rule 1611 effective July 1, 1976; previously amended effective July 1, 1979, and January 1, 1992; previously amended and renumbered as rule 1607 effective January 1, 2004.

Ref.: Cal. Fms Pl. & Pr., Ch. 36, "Judicial Arbitration"; MB Prac. Guide: Cal. Pretrial Proc., §§24.12, 24.13.

Rule 3.818. Continuances

(a) Stipulation to continuance; consent of arbitrator

Except as provided in (c), the parties may stipulate to a continuance in the case, with the consent of the assigned arbitrator. An arbitrator must consent to a request for a continuance if it appears that good cause exists. Notice of the continuance must be sent to the ADR administrator.

(Subd (a) amended effective January 1, 2004; previously amended effective January 1, 1984, and January 1, 1992.)

(b) Court grant of continuance

If the arbitrator declines to give consent to a continuance, upon the motion of a party and for good cause shown, the court may grant a continuance of the arbitration hearing. In the event the court grants the motion, the party who requested the continuance must notify the arbitrator and the arbitrator must reschedule the hearing, giving notice to all parties to the arbitration proceeding.

(Subd (b) amended effective January 1, 2007; previously amended effective July 1, 1979, and January 1, 2004.)

(c) Limitation on length of continuance

An arbitration hearing must not be continued to a date later than 90 days after the assignment of the case to the arbitrator, including any time due to continuances granted under this rule, except by order of the court upon the motion of a party as provided in (b).

(Subd (c) amended effective January 1, 2004; previously amended effective January 1, 1991 and January 1, 1994.)

Rule 3.818 amended and renumbered effective January 1, 2007; adopted as rule 1607 effective July 1, 1976; previously amended effective July 1, 1979, January 1, 1984, January 1, 1991, January 1, 1992, and January 1, 1994; previously amended and renumbered as rule 1608 effective January 1, 2004.

Ref.: Cal. Fms Pl. & Pr., Ch. 36, "Judicial Arbitration"; MB Prac. Guide: Cal. Pretrial Proc., §§24.09[2], 24.11, 24.14[1], [2].

Rule 3.819. Arbitrator's fees

(a) Filing of award or notice of settlement required

The arbitrator's award must be timely filed with the clerk of the court under rule 3.825(b) or a notice of settlement must have been filed before a fee may be paid to the arbitrator.

(Subd (a) amended effective January 1, 2007; previously amended effective July 1, 1979, and January 1, 2004.)

(b) Exceptions for good cause

On the arbitrator's verified ex parte application, the court may for good cause authorize payment of a fee:

(1) If the arbitrator devoted a substantial amount of time to a case that was settled without a hearing; or

(2) If the award was not timely filed.

(Subd (b) amended effective January 1, 2004; previously amended effective July 1, 1979, and January 1, 1987.)

(c) Arbitrator's fee statement

The arbitrator's fee statement must be submitted to the administrator promptly upon the completion of the arbitrator's duties and must set forth the title and number of the cause arbitrated, the date of the arbitration hearing, and the date the award or settlement was filed.

(Subd (c) amended effective January 1, 2007; previously amended effective July 1, 1979, and January 1, 2004.)

Rule 3.819 amended and renumbered effective January 1, 2007; adopted as rule 1608 effective July 1, 1976; previously amended effective July 1, 1979, and January 1, 1987; previously amended and renumbered as rule 1609 effective January 1, 2004.

Ref.: Cal. Fms Pl. & Pr., Ch. 36, "Judicial Arbitration."

Rule 3.820. Communication with the arbitrator

(a) Disclosure of settlement offers prohibited

No disclosure of any offers of settlement made by any party may be made to the arbitrator prior to the filing of the award.

(Subd (a) amended and relettered effective January 1, 2004; adopted as part of unlettered subd effective July 1, 1976.)

(b) Ex parte communication prohibited

An arbitrator must not initiate, permit, or consider any ex parte communications or consider other communications made to the arbitrator outside the presence of all of the parties concerning a pending arbitration, except as follows:

(1) An arbitrator may communicate with a party in the absence of other parties about administrative matters, such as setting the time and place of hearings or making other arrangements for the conduct of the proceedings, as long as the arbitrator reasonably believes that the communication will not result in a procedural or tactical advantage for any party. When such a discussion occurs, the arbitrator must promptly inform the other parties of the communi-

cation and must give the other parties an opportunity to respond before making any final determination concerning the matter discussed.

(2) An arbitrator may initiate or consider any ex parte communication when expressly authorized by law to do so.

(Subd (b) amended effective January 1, 2007; adopted as part of unlettered subd effective July 1, 1976; previously amended and lettered effective January 1, 2004.)

Rule 3.820 amended and renumbered effective January 1, 2007; adopted as rule 1609 effective July 1, 1976; previously amended and renumbered as rule 1610 effective January 1, 2004.

Ref.: Cal. Fms Pl. & Pr., Ch. 36, "Judicial Arbitration"; MB Prac. Guide: Cal. Pretrial Proc., §24.16[1], [2].

Rule 3.821. Representation by counsel; proceedings when party absent

(a) Representation by counsel

A party to the arbitration has a right to be represented by an attorney at any proceeding or hearing in arbitration, but this right may be waived. A waiver of this right may be revoked, but if revoked, the other party is entitled to a reasonable continuance for the purpose of obtaining counsel.

(Subd (a) amended effective January 1, 2004.)

(b) Proceedings when party absent

The arbitration may proceed in the absence of any party who, after due notice, fails to be present and to obtain a continuance. An award must not be based solely on the absence of a party. In the event of a default by defendant, the arbitrator must require the plaintiff to submit such evidence as may be appropriate for the making of an award.

(Subd (b) amended effective January 1, 2007; previously amended effective January 1, 2004.)

Rule 3.821 amended and renumbered effective January 1, 2007; adopted as rule 1610 effective July 1, 1976; previously amended and renumbered as rule 1611 effective January 1, 2004.

Ref.: Cal. Fms Pl. & Pr., Ch. 36, "Judicial Arbitration"; MB Prac. Guide: Cal. Pretrial Proc., §§24.18, 24.19.

Rule 3.822. Discovery

(a) Right to discovery

The parties to the arbitration have the right to take depositions and to obtain discovery, and to that end may exercise all of the same rights, remedies, and procedures, and are subject to all of the same duties, liabilities, and obligations as provided in part 4, title 3, chapter 3 of the Code of Civil Procedure, except as provided in (b).

(Subd (a) amended and lettered effective January 1, 2007; adopted as part of unlettered subd effective July 1, 1976.)

(b) Completion of discovery

All discovery must be completed not later than 15 days before the date set for the arbitration hearing unless the court, upon a showing of good cause, makes an order granting an extension of the time within which discovery must be completed.

(Subd (b) amended and lettered effective January 1, 2007; adopted as part of unlettered subd effective July 1, 1976.)

Rule 3.822 amended and renumbered effective January 1, 2007; adopted as rule 1612 effective July 1, 1976; previously amended effective July 1, 1979, and January 1, 2004.

Ref.: Cal. Fms Pl. & Pr., Ch. 32, "Contractual Arbitration: Agreements and Compelling Arbitration," Ch. 36, "Judicial Arbitration," Ch. 190, "Discovery: Scope, Regulation, and Timing," Ch. 425, "Pretrial Proceedings"; MB Prac. Guide: Cal. Pretrial Proc., §§24.11, 24.15[1].

Rule 3.823. Rules of evidence at arbitration hearing

(a) Presence of arbitrator and parties

All evidence must be taken in the presence of the arbitrator and all parties, except where any of the parties has waived the right to be present or is absent after due notice of the hearing.

(Subd (a) amended effective January 1, 2004.)

(b) Application of civil rules of evidence

The rules of evidence governing civil cases apply to the conduct of the arbitration hearing, except:

(1) *Written reports and other documents*

Any party may offer written reports of any expert witness, medical records and bills (including physiotherapy, nursing, and prescription bills), documentary evidence of loss of income, property damage repair bills or estimates, police reports concerning an accident that gave rise to the case, other bills and invoices, purchase orders, checks, written contracts, and similar documents prepared and maintained in the ordinary course of business.

(A) The arbitrator must receive them in evidence if copies have been delivered to all opposing parties at least 20 days before the hearing.

(B) Any other party may subpoena the author or custodian of the document as a witness and examine the witness as if under cross-examination.

(C) Any repair estimate offered as an exhibit, and the copies delivered to opposing parties, must be accompanied by:

(i) A statement indicating whether or not the property was repaired, and, if it was, whether the estimated repairs were made in full or in part; and

(ii) A copy of the receipted bill showing the items of repair made and the amount paid.

(D) The arbitrator must not consider any opinion as to ultimate fault expressed in a police report.

(2) *Witness statements*

The written statements of any other witness may be offered and must be received in evidence if:

(A) They are made by declaration under penalty of perjury;

(B) Copies have been delivered to all opposing parties at least 20 days before the hearing; and

(C) No opposing party has, at least 10 days before the hearing, delivered to the proponent of the evidence a written demand that the witness be produced in person to testify at the hearing. The arbitrator must disregard any portion of a statement received under this rule that would be inadmissible if the witness were testifying in person, but the inclusion of inadmissible matter does not render the entire statement inadmissible.

(3) *Depositions*

(A) The deposition of any witness may be offered by any party and must be received in evidence, subject to objections available under Code of Civil Procedure section 2025.410, notwithstanding that the deponent is not "unavailable as a witness" within the meaning of Evidence Code section 240 and no exceptional circumstances exist, if:

(i) The deposition was taken in the manner provided for by law or by stipulation of the parties and within the time provided for in these rules; and

(ii) Not less than 20 days before the hearing the proponent of the deposition delivered to all opposing parties notice of intention to offer the deposition in evidence.

(B) The opposing party, upon receiving the notice, may subpoena the deponent and, at the discretion of the arbitrator, either the deposition may be excluded from evidence or the deposition may be admitted and the deponent may be further cross-examined by the subpoenaing party. These limitations are not applicable to a deposition admissible under the terms of Code of Civil Procedure section 2025.620.

(Subd (b) amended effective January 1, 2008; previously amended effective July 1, 1979, January 1, 1984, January 1, 1988, July 1, 1990, January 1, 2004, and January 1, 2007.)

(c) Subpoenas

(1) *Compelling witnesses to appear*

The attendance of witnesses at arbitration hearings may be compelled through the issuance of subpoenas as provided in the Code of Civil Procedure, in section 1985 and elsewhere in part 4, title 3, chapters 2 and 3. It is the duty of the party requesting the subpoena to modify the form of subpoena so as to show that the appearance is before an arbitrator and to give the time and place set for the arbitration hearing.

(2) *Adjournment or continuances*

At the discretion of the arbitrator, nonappearance of a properly subpoenaed witness may be a ground for an adjournment or continuance of the hearing.

(3) *Contempt*

If any witness properly served with a subpoena fails to appear at the arbitration hearing or, having appeared, refuses to be sworn or to answer, proceedings to compel compliance with the subpoena on penalty of contempt may be had before the superior court as provided in Code of Civil Procedure section 1991 for other instances of refusal to appear and answer before an officer or commissioner out of court.

(Subd (c) amended effective January 1, 2007; previously amended effective July 1, 1979, and January 1, 2004.)

(d) Delivery of documents

For purposes of this rule, "delivery" of a document or notice may be accomplished manually or by mail in the manner provided by Code of Civil Procedure section 1013. If service is by mail, the times prescribed in this rule for delivery of documents, notices, and demands are increased by five days.

(Subd (d) amended effective January 1, 2004; adopted effective January 1, 1988.)

Rule 3.823 amended effective January 1, 2008; adopted as rule 1613 effective July 1, 1976; previously amended effective July 1, 1979, January 1, 1984, January 1, 1988, July 1, 1990, and January 1, 2004; previously amended and renumbered effective January 1, 2007.

Ref.: Cal. Fms Pl. & Pr., Ch. 32, "Contractual Arbitration: Agreements and Compelling Arbitration," Ch. 36, "Judicial Arbitration"; MB Prac. Guide: Cal. Pretrial Proc., §§24.11,

24.20[1], [2][a]–[c], [3][a], [b], [4][a]–[c], [5][a], [b], 24.69, 24.70.

Rule 3.824. Conduct of the hearing

(a) Arbitrator's powers

The arbitrator has the following powers; all other questions arising out of the case are reserved to the court:

(1) To administer oaths or affirmations to witnesses;

(2) To take adjournments upon the request of a party or upon his or her own initiative when deemed necessary;

(3) To permit testimony to be offered by deposition;

(4) To permit evidence to be offered and introduced as provided in these rules;

(5) To rule upon the admissibility and relevancy of evidence offered;

(6) To invite the parties, on reasonable notice, to submit arbitration briefs;

(7) To decide the law and facts of the case and make an award accordingly;

(8) To award costs, not to exceed the statutory costs of the suit; and

(9) To examine any site or object relevant to the case.

(Subd (a) amended effective January 1, 2007; previously amended effective January 1, 2004.)

(b) Record of proceedings

(1) *Arbitrator's record*

The arbitrator may, but is not required to, make a record of the proceedings.

(2) *Record not subject to discovery*

Any records of the proceedings made by or at the direction of the arbitrator are deemed the arbitrator's personal notes and are not subject to discovery, and the arbitrator must not deliver them to any party to the case or to any other person, except to an employee using the records under the arbitrator's supervision or pursuant to a subpoena issued in a criminal investigation or prosecution for perjury.

(3) *No other record*

No other record may be made, and the arbitrator must not permit the presence of a stenographer or court reporter or the use of any recording device at the hearing, except as expressly permitted by (1).

(Subd (b) amended effective January 1, 2007; previously amended effective January 1, 2004.)

Rule 3.824 amended and renumbered effective January 1, 2007; adopted as rule 1614 effective July 1, 1976; previously amended effective January 1, 2004.

Ref.: Cal. Fms Pl. & Pr., Ch. 32, "Contractual Arbitration: Agreements and Compelling Arbitration," Ch. 36, "Judicial Arbitration"; MB Prac. Guide: Cal. Pretrial Proc., §24.21[1].

Rule 3.825. The award

(a) Form and content of the award

(1) *Award in writing*

The award must be in writing and signed by the arbitrator. It must determine all issues properly raised by the pleadings, including a determination of any damages and an award of costs if appropriate.

(2) *No findings or conclusions required*

The arbitrator is not required to make findings of fact or conclusions of law.

(Subd (a) amended effective January 1, 2007; previously amended effective January 1, 2004.)

(b) Filing the award or amended award

(1) *Time for filing the award*

Within 10 days after the conclusion of the arbitration hearing, the arbitrator must file the award with the clerk, with proof of service on each party to the arbitration. On the arbitrator's application in cases of unusual length or complexity, the court may allow up to 20 additional days for the filing and service of the award.

(2) *Amended award*

Within the time for filing the award, the arbitrator may file and serve an amended award.

(Subd (b) amended effective January 1, 2007; previously amended effective January 1, 1995, and January 1, 2004.)

Rule 3.825 amended and renumbered effective January 1, 2007; adopted as rule 1615 effective July 1, 1976; previously amended effective January 1, 1983, January 1, 1985, January 1, 1995, January 1, 2003, and January 1, 2004.

Ref.: Cal. Fms Pl. & Pr., Ch. 36, "Judicial Arbitration," Ch. 174, "Costs and Attorney's Fees."

Rule 3.826. Trial after arbitration

(a) Request for trial; deadline

Within 30 days after the arbitration award is filed with the clerk of the court, a party may request a trial by filing with the clerk a request for trial, with proof of service of a copy upon all other parties appearing in the case. A request for trial filed after the parties have been served with a copy of the award by the arbitrator, but before the award has been filed with the clerk, is valid and timely filed. The 30-day period within which to request trial may not be extended.

(Subd (a) amended effective January 1, 2007; previously amended effective January 1, 1985, July 1, 1990, and January 1, 2004.)

(b) Prosecution of the case

If a party makes a timely request for a trial, the case must proceed as provided under an applicable case management order. If no pending order provides for the prosecution of the case after a request for a trial after arbitration, the court must promptly schedule a case management conference.

(Subd (b) amended effective January 1, 2007; previously amended effective January 1, 2004.)

(c) References to arbitration during trial prohibited

The case must be tried as though no arbitration proceedings had occurred. No reference may be made during the trial to the arbitration award, to the fact that there had been arbitration proceedings, to the evidence adduced at the arbitration hearing, or to any other aspect of the arbitration proceedings, and none of the foregoing may be used as affirmative evidence, or by way of impeachment, or for any other purpose at the trial.

(Subd (c) amended effective January 1, 2004.)

(d) Costs after trial

In assessing costs after the trial, the court must apply the standards specified in Code of Civil Procedure section 1141.21.

(Subd (d) amended effective January 1, 2007; previously amended effective July 1, 1979, and January 1, 2004.)

Rule 3.826 amended and renumbered effective January 1, 2007; adopted as rule 1616 effective July 1, 1976; previously amended effective July 1, 1979, July 1, 1990, and January 1, 2004.

Ref.: Cal. Fms Pl. & Pr., Ch. 32, "Contractual Arbitration: Agreements and Compelling Arbitration," Ch. 36, "Judicial Arbitration," Ch. 425, "Pretrial Proceedings"; MB Prac. Guide: Cal. Pretrial Proc., §§24.33, 24.34[1], 24.35, 24.37[1], [2], 24.40[1], 24.41, 24.42[2][c], 24.73–24.75.

Rule 3.827. Entry of award as judgment

(a) Entry of award as judgment by clerk

The clerk must enter the award as a judgment immediately upon the expiration of 30 days after the award is filed if no party has, during that period, served and filed a request for trial as provided in these rules.

(b) Notice of entry of judgment

Promptly upon entry of the award as a judgment, the clerk must mail notice of entry of judgment to all parties who have appeared in the case and must execute a certificate of mailing and place it in the court's file in the case.

(c) Effect of judgment

The judgment so entered has the same force and effect in all respects as, and is subject to all provisions of law relating to, a judgment in a civil case or proceeding, except that it is not subject to appeal and it may not be attacked or set aside except as provided in rule 3.828. The judgment so entered may be enforced as if it had been rendered by the court in which it is entered.

Rule 3.827 adopted effective January 1, 2007.

Ref.: Cal. Fms Pl. & Pr., Ch. 36, "Judicial Arbitration"; MB Prac. Guide: Cal. Pretrial Proc., §24.29[1]–[3].

Rule 3.828. Vacating judgment on award

(a) Motion to vacate

A party against whom a judgment is entered under an arbitration award may, within six months after its entry, move to vacate the judgment on the ground that the arbitrator was subject to a disqualification not disclosed before the hearing and of which the arbitrator was then aware, or upon one of the grounds set forth in Code of Civil Procedure sections 473 or 1286.2(a)(1), (2), and (3), and on no other grounds.

(b) Notice and grounds for granting motion

The motion must be heard upon notice to the adverse parties and to the arbitrator, and may be granted only upon clear and convincing evidence that the grounds alleged are true, and that the motion was made as soon as practicable after the moving party learned of the existence of those grounds.

Rule 3.828 adopted effective January 1, 2007.

Ref.: Cal. Fms Pl. & Pr., Ch. 36, "Judicial Arbitration"; MB Prac. Guide: Cal. Pretrial Proc., §§24.31[1]–[3], 24.33, 24.38[1], 24.71, 24.72.

Rule 3.829. Settlement of case

If a case is settled, each plaintiff or other party seeking affirmative relief must notify the arbitrator and the court as required in rule 3.1385.

Rule 3.829 amended and renumbered effective January 1, 2007; adopted as rule 1618 effective January 1, 1992; previously amended effective January 1, 2004.

Ref.: Cal. Fms Pl. & Pr., Ch. 36, "Judicial Arbitration."

Rule 3.830. Arbitration not pursuant to rules

These rules do not prohibit the parties to any civil case

or proceeding from entering into arbitration agreements under part 3, title 9 of the Code of Civil Procedure. Neither the ADR committee nor the ADR administrator may take any part in the conduct of an arbitration under an agreement not in conformity with these rules except that the administrator may, upon joint request of the parties, furnish the parties to the agreement with a randomly selected list of at least three names of members of the appropriate panel of arbitrators.

Rule 3.830 amended and renumbered effective January 1, 2007; adopted as rule 1617 effective July 1, 1976; previously amended effective January 1, 2004.

Chapter 3
General Rules Relating to Mediation of Civil Cases

Art. 1. [Reserved].
Art. 2. Rules of Conduct for Mediators in Court-Connected Mediation Programs for Civil Cases. Rules 3.850–3.868.
Art. 3. Requirements for Addressing Complaints About Court-Program Mediators. Rules 3.865–3.872.

Article 1
[Reserved]

Article 2
Rules of Conduct for Mediators in Court-Connected Mediation Programs for Civil Cases

Rule 3.850. Purpose and function
Rule 3.851. Application
Rule 3.852. Definitions
Rule 3.853. Voluntary participation and self-determination
Rule 3.854. Confidentiality
Rule 3.855. Impartiality, conflicts of interest, disclosure, and withdrawal
Rule 3.856. Competence
Rule 3.857. Quality of mediation process
Rule 3.858. Marketing
Rule 3.859. Compensation and gifts
Rule 3.860. Attendance sheet and agreement to disclosure
Rule 3.865. Complaint procedure required
Rule 3.866. Designation of person to receive inquiries and complaints
Rule 3.867. Confidentiality of complaint procedures, information, and records
Rule 3.868. Disqualification from subsequently serving as an adjudicator

Rule 3.850.   Purpose and function
(a) Standards of conduct

The rules in this article establish the minimum standards of conduct for mediators in court-connected mediation programs for general civil cases. These rules are intended to guide the conduct of mediators in these programs, to inform and protect participants in these mediation programs, and to promote public confidence in the mediation process and the courts. For mediation to be effective, there must be broad public confidence in the

integrity and fairness of the process. Mediators in court-connected programs are responsible to the parties, the public, and the courts for conducting themselves in a manner that merits that confidence.

(Subd (a) amended effective January 1, 2007.)

(b) Scope and limitations

These rules are not intended to:

(1) Establish a ceiling on what is considered good practice in mediation or discourage efforts by courts, mediators, or others to educate mediators about best practices;

(2) Create a basis for challenging a settlement agreement reached in connection with mediation; or

(3) Create a basis for a civil cause of action against a mediator.

(Subd (b) amended effective January 1, 2007.)

Rule 3.850 amended and renumbered effective January 1, 2007; adopted as rule 1620 effective January 1, 2003.

Ref.: Cal. Fms Pl. & Pr., Ch. 31, "Mediation," Ch. 37, "Judicially Mandated Civil Action Mediation."

Rule 3.851.   Application
(a) Circumstances applicable

The rules in this article apply to mediations in which a mediator:

(1) Has agreed to be included on a superior court's list or panel of mediators for general civil cases and is notified by the court or the parties that he or she has been selected to mediate a case within that court's mediation program; [1] **or**

(2) Has agreed to mediate a general civil case pending in a superior court after being notified by the court or the parties that he or she was recommended, selected, or appointed by that court or will be compensated by that court to mediate a case within that court's mediation program.

(Subd (a) amended effective January 1, 2009; previously amended effective January 1, 2007.)

Rule 3.851(a).   2008 Deletes. [1] and
(b) Application to listed firms

If a court's panel or list includes firms that provide mediation services, all mediators affiliated with a listed firm are required to comply with the rules in this article when they are notified by the court or the parties that the firm was selected from the court list to mediate a general civil case within that court's mediation program.

(Subd (b) amended effective July 1, 2007; previously amended effective January 1, 2007.)

(c) Time of applicability

Except as otherwise provided in these rules, the rules in this article apply from the time the mediator agrees to mediate a case until the end of the mediation in that case.

(Subd (c) amended effective January 1, 2007.)

(d) Inapplicability to judges

The rules in this article do not apply to judges or other judicial officers while they are serving in a capacity in which they are governed by the Code of Judicial Ethics.

(Subd (d) amended effective January 1, 2007.)

(e) Inapplicability to settlement conferences

The rules in this article do not apply to settlement conferences conducted under rule 3.1380.

(Subd (e) amended effective January 1, 2007.)

Rule 3.851 amended effective January 1, 2009; adopted as rule 1620.1 effective January 1, 2003; previously amended and renumbered effective January 1, 2007; previously amended effective July 1, 2007.

Advisory Committee Comment

Subdivision (d). Although these rules do not apply to them, judicial officers who serve as mediators in their courts' mediation programs are nevertheless encouraged to be familiar with and observe these rules when mediating, particularly the rules concerning subjects not covered in the Code of Judicial Ethics such as voluntary participation and self-determination.

Ref.: Cal. Fms Pl. & Pr., Ch. 37, "Judicially Mandated Civil Action Mediation."

Rule 3.852. Definitions

As used in this article, unless the context or subject matter requires otherwise:

(1) "Mediation" means a process in which a neutral person or persons facilitate communication between the disputants to assist them in reaching a mutually acceptable agreement.

(2) "Mediator" means a neutral person who conducts a mediation.

(3) "Participant" means any individual, entity, or group, other than the mediator taking part in a mediation, including but not limited to attorneys for the parties.

(4) "Party" means any individual, entity, or group taking part in a mediation that is a plaintiff, a defendant, a cross-complainant, a cross-defendant, a petitioner, a respondent, or an intervenor in the case.

Rule 3.852 amended and renumbered effective January 1, 2007; adopted as rule 1620.2 effective January 1, 2003.

Advisory Committee Comment

The definition of "mediator" in this rule departs from the definition in Evidence Code section 1115(b) in that it does not include persons designated by the mediator to assist in the mediation or to communicate with a participant in preparation for the mediation. However, these definitions are applicable only to these rules of conduct and do not limit or expand mediation confidentiality under the Evidence Code or other law.

The definition of "participant" includes insurance adjusters, experts, and consultants as well as the parties and their attorneys.

Ref.: Cal. Fms Pl. & Pr., Ch. 37, "Judicially Mandated Civil Action Mediation."

Rule 3.853. Voluntary participation and self-determination

A mediator must conduct the mediation in a manner that supports the principles of voluntary participation and self-determination by the parties. For this purpose a mediator must:

(1) Inform the parties, at or before the outset of the first mediation session, that any resolution of the dispute in mediation requires a voluntary agreement of the parties;

(2) Respect the right of each participant to decide the extent of his or her participation in the mediation, including the right to withdraw from the mediation at any time; and

(3) Refrain from coercing any party to make a decision or to continue to participate in the mediation.

Rule 3.853 amended and renumbered effective January 1, 2007; adopted as rule 1620.3 effective January 1, 2003.

Advisory Committee Comment

Voluntary participation and self-determination are fundamental principles of mediation that apply both to mediations in which the parties voluntarily elect to mediate and to those in which the parties are required to go to mediation in a mandatory court mediation program or by court order. Although the court may order participants to attend mediation, a mediator may not mandate the extent of their participation in the mediation process or coerce any party to settle the case.

After informing the parties of their choices and the consequences of those choices, a mediator can invoke a broad range of approaches to assist the parties in reaching an agreement without offending the principles of voluntary participation and self-determination, including (1) encouraging the parties to continue participating in the mediation when it reasonably appears to the mediator that the possibility of reaching an uncoerced, consensual agreement has not been exhausted and (2) suggesting that a party consider obtaining professional advice (for example, informing an unrepresented party that he or she may consider obtaining legal advice). Conversely, examples of conduct that violate the principles of voluntary participation and self-determination include coercing a party to continue participating in the mediation after the party has told the mediator that he or she wishes to terminate the mediation, providing an opinion or evaluation of the dispute in a coercive manner or over the objection of the parties, using abusive language, and threatening to make a report to the court about a party's conduct at the mediation.

Ref.: Cal. Fms Pl. & Pr., Ch. 31, "Mediation," Ch. 37, "Judicially Mandated Civil Action Mediation."

Rule 3.854. Confidentiality

(a) Compliance with confidentiality law

A mediator must, at all times, comply with the applicable law concerning confidentiality.

(b) Informing participants of confidentiality

At or before the outset of the first mediation session, a mediator must provide the participants with a general explanation of the confidentiality of mediation proceedings.

(c) Confidentiality of separate communications; caucuses

If, after all the parties have agreed to participate in the mediation process and the mediator has agreed to mediate the case, a mediator speaks separately with one or more participants out of the presence of the other participants, the mediator must first discuss with all participants the mediator's practice regarding confidentiality for separate communications with the participants. Except as required by law, a mediator must not disclose information revealed in confidence during such separate communications unless authorized to do so by the participant or participants who revealed the information.

(d) Use of confidential information

A mediator must not use information that is acquired in confidence in the course of a mediation outside the mediation or for personal gain.

Rule 3.854 renumbered effective January 1, 2007; adopted as rule 1620.4 effective January 1, 2003.

Advisory Committee Comment

Subdivision (a). The general law concerning mediation confidentiality is found in Evidence Code sections 703.5 and 1115–1128 and in cases interpreting those sections. (See, e.g., *Foxgate Homeowners' Association, Inc. v. Bramalea California, Inc.* (2001) 26 Cal.4th 1; *Rinaker v. Superior Court* (1998) 62

Cal.App.4th 155; and *Gilbert v. National Corp. for Housing Partnerships* (1999) 71 Cal.App.4th 1240.)

Ref.: Cal. Fms Pl. & Pr., Ch. 31, "Mediation," Ch. 37, "Judicially Mandated Civil Action Mediation."

Rule 3.855. Impartiality, conflicts of interest, disclosure, and withdrawal

(a) Impartiality

A mediator must maintain impartiality toward all participants in the mediation process at all times.

(b) Disclosure of matters potentially affecting impartiality

(1) A mediator must make reasonable efforts to keep informed about matters that reasonably could raise a question about his or her ability to conduct the proceedings impartially, and must disclose these matters to the parties. These matters include:

(A) Past, present, and currently expected interests, relationships, and affiliations of a personal, professional, or financial nature; and

(B) The existence of any grounds for disqualification of a judge specified in Code of Civil Procedure section 170.1.

(2) A mediator's duty to disclose is a continuing obligation, from the inception of the mediation process through its completion. Disclosures required by this rule must be made as soon as practicable after a mediator becomes aware of a matter that must be disclosed. To the extent possible, such disclosures should be made before the first mediation session, but in any event they must be made within the time required by applicable court rules or statutes.

(Subd (b) amended effective January 1, 2007.)

(c) Proceeding if there are no objections or questions concerning impartiality

Except as provided in (f), if, after a mediator makes disclosures, no party objects to the mediator and no participant raises any question or concern about the mediator's ability to conduct the mediation impartially, the mediator may proceed.

(Subd (c) amended effective January 1, 2007.)

(d) Responding to questions or concerns concerning impartiality

If, after a mediator makes disclosures or at any other point in the mediation process, a participant raises a question or concern about the mediator's ability to conduct the mediation impartially, the mediator must address the question or concern with the participants. Except as provided in (f), if, after the question or concern is addressed, no party objects to the mediator, the mediator may proceed.

(Subd (d) amended effective January 1, 2007.)

(e) Withdrawal or continuation upon party objection concerning impartiality

In a two-party mediation, if any party objects to the mediator after the mediator makes disclosures or discusses a participant's question or concern regarding the mediator's ability to conduct the mediation impartially, the mediator must withdraw. In a mediation in which there are more than two parties, the mediator may continue the mediation with the nonobjecting parties, provided that doing so would not violate any other provision of these rules, any law, or any local court rule or program guideline.

(f) Circumstances requiring mediator recusal despite party consent

Regardless of the consent of the parties, a mediator either must decline to serve as mediator or, if already serving, must withdraw from the mediation if:

(1) The mediator cannot maintain impartiality toward all participants in the mediation process; or

(2) Proceeding with the mediation would jeopardize the integrity of the court or of the mediation process.

Rule 3.855 amended and renumbered effective January 1, 2007; adopted as rule 1620.5 effective January 1, 2003.

Advisory Committee Comment

Subdivision (b). This subdivision is intended to provide parties with information they need to help them determine whether a mediator can conduct the mediation impartially. A mediator's overarching duty under this subdivision is to make a "reasonable effort" to identify matters that, in the eyes of a reasonable person, could raise a question about the mediator's ability to conduct the mediation impartially, and to inform the parties about those matters. What constitutes a "reasonable effort" to identify such matters varies depending on the circumstances, including whether the case is scheduled in advance or received on the spot, and the information about the participants and the subject matter that is provided to the mediator by the court and the parties.

The interests, relationships, and affiliations that a mediator may need to disclose under (b)(1)(A) include: (1) prior, current, or currently expected service as a mediator in another mediation involving any of the participants in the present mediation; (2) prior, current, or currently expected business relationships or transactions between the mediator and any of the participants; and (3) the mediator's ownership of stock or any other significant financial interest involving any participant in the mediation. Currently expected interests, relationships, and affiliations may include, for example, an intention to form a partnership or to enter into a future business relationship with one of the participants in the mediation.

Although (b)(1) specifies interests, relationships, affiliations, and matters that are grounds for disqualification of a judge under Code of Civil Procedure section 170.1, these are only examples of common matters that reasonably could raise a question about a mediator's ability to conduct the mediation impartially and, thus, must be disclosed. The absence of particular interests, relationships, affiliations, and section 170.1 matters does not necessarily mean that there is no matter that could reasonably raise a question about the mediator's ability to conduct the mediation impartially. A mediator must make determinations concerning disclosure on a case-by-case basis, applying the general criteria for disclosure under (b)(1).

Attorney mediators should be aware that under the section 170.1 standard, they may need to make disclosures when an attorney in their firm is serving or has served as a lawyer for any of the parties in the mediation. Section 170.1 does not specifically address whether a mediator must disclose when another member of the mediator's dispute resolution services firm is providing or has provided services to any of the parties in the mediation. Therefore, a mediator must evaluate such circumstances under the general criteria for disclosure under (b)(1)—that is, is it a matter that, in the eyes of a reasonable person, could raise a question about the mediator's ability to conduct the mediation impartially?

If there is a conflict between the mediator's obligation to maintain confidentiality and the mediator's obligation to make a disclosure, the mediator must determine whether he or she can make a general disclosure of the circumstance without revealing any confidential information, or must decline to serve.

Ref.: Cal. Fms Pl. & Pr., Ch. 31, "Mediation," Ch. 37, "Judicially Mandated Civil Action Mediation."

Rule 3.856. Competence

(a) Compliance with court qualifications

A mediator must comply with experience, training, educational, and other requirements established by the court for appointment and retention.

(b) Truthful representation of background

A mediator has a continuing obligation to truthfully represent his or her background to the court and participants. Upon a request by any party, a mediator must provide truthful information regarding his or her experience, training, and education.

(c) Informing court of public discipline and other matters

A mediator must also inform the court if:

(1) Public discipline has been imposed on the mediator by any public disciplinary or professional licensing agency;

(2) The mediator has resigned his or her membership in the State Bar or another professional licensing agency while disciplinary or criminal charges were pending;

(3) A felony charge is pending against the mediator;

(4) The mediator has been convicted of a felony or of a misdemeanor involving moral turpitude; or

(5) There has been an entry of judgment against the mediator in any civil action for actual fraud or punitive damages.

(d) Assessment of skills; withdrawal

A mediator has a continuing obligation to assess whether or not his or her level of skill, knowledge, and ability is sufficient to conduct the mediation effectively. A mediator must decline to serve or withdraw from the mediation if the mediator determines that he or she does not have the level of skill, knowledge, or ability necessary to conduct the mediation effectively.

Rule 3.856 renumbered effective January 1, 2007; adopted as rule 1620.6 effective January 1, 2003.

Advisory Committee Comment

Subdivision (d). No particular advanced academic degree or technical or professional experience is a prerequisite for competence as a mediator. Core mediation skills include communicating clearly, listening effectively, facilitating communication among all participants, promoting exploration of mutually acceptable settlement options, and conducting oneself in a neutral manner.

A mediator must consider and weigh a variety of issues in order to assess whether his or her level of skill, knowledge, and ability is sufficient to make him or her effective in a particular mediation. Issues include whether the parties (1) were involved or had input in the selection of the mediator; (2) had access to information about the mediator's background or level of skill, knowledge, and ability; (3) have a specific expectation or perception regarding the mediator's level of skill, knowledge, and ability; (4) have expressed a preference regarding the style of mediation they would like or expect; or (5) have expressed a desire to discuss legal or other professional information, to hear a personal evaluation of or opinion on a set of facts as presented, or to be made aware of the interests of persons who are not represented in mediation.

Ref.: Cal. Fms Pl. & Pr., Ch. 37, "Judicially Mandated Civil Action Mediation."

Rule 3.857. Quality of mediation process

(a) Diligence

A mediator must make reasonable efforts to advance the mediation in a timely manner. If a mediator schedules a mediation for a specific time period, he or she must keep that time period free of other commitments.

(b) Procedural fairness

A mediator must conduct the mediation proceedings in a procedurally fair manner. "Procedural fairness" means a balanced process in which each party is given an opportunity to participate and make uncoerced decisions. A mediator is not obligated to ensure the substantive fairness of an agreement reached by the parties.

(c) Explanation of process

In addition to the requirements of rule 3.853 (voluntary participation and self-determination), rule 3.854(a) (confidentiality), and (d) of this rule (representation and other professional services), at or before the outset of the mediation the mediator must provide all participants with a general explanation of:

(1) The nature of the mediation process;

(2) The procedures to be used; and

(3) The roles of the mediator, the parties, and the other participants.

(Subd (c) amended effective January 1, 2007.)

(d) Representation and other professional services

A mediator must inform all participants, at or before the outset of the first mediation session, that during the mediation he or she will not represent any participant as a lawyer or perform professional services in any capacity other than as an impartial mediator. Subject to the principles of impartiality and self-determination, a mediator may provide information or opinions that he or she is qualified by training or experience to provide.

(e) Recommending other services

A mediator may recommend the use of other services in connection with a mediation and may recommend particular providers of other services. However, a mediator must disclose any related personal or financial interests if recommending the services of specific individuals or organizations.

(f) Nonparticipants' interests

A mediator may bring to the attention of the parties the interests of others who are not participating in the mediation but who may be affected by agreements reached as a result of the mediation.

(g) Combining mediation with other ADR processes

A mediator must exercise caution in combining mediation with other alternative dispute resolution (ADR) processes and may do so only with the informed consent of the parties and in a manner consistent with any applicable law or court order. The mediator must inform the parties of the general natures of the different processes and the consequences of revealing information during any one process that might be used for decision making in another process, and must give the parties the opportunity to select another neutral for the subsequent process. If the parties consent to a combination of processes, the mediator must clearly inform the participants when the transition from one process to another is occurring.

(h) Settlement agreements

Consistent with (d), a mediator may present possible settlement options and terms for discussion. A mediator may also assist the parties in preparing a written settlement agreement, provided that in doing so the mediator confines the assistance to stating the settlement as determined by the parties.

(Subd (h) amended effective January 1, 2007.)

(i) Discretionary termination and withdrawal

A mediator may suspend or terminate the mediation or withdraw as mediator when he or she reasonably believes the circumstances require it, including when he or she suspects that:

(1) The mediation is being used to further illegal conduct;

(2) A participant is unable to participate meaningfully in negotiations; or

(3) Continuation of the process would cause significant harm to any participant or a third party.

(j) Manner of withdrawal

When a mediator determines that it is necessary to suspend or terminate a mediation or to withdraw, the mediator must do so without violating the obligation of confidentiality and in a manner that will cause the least possible harm to the participants.

Rule 3.857 amended and renumbered effective January 1, 2007; adopted as rule 1620.7 effective January 1, 2003.

Advisory Committee Comment

Subdivision (c). The explanation of the mediation process should include a description of the mediator's style of mediation.

Subdivision (d). Subject to the principles of impartiality and self-determination, and if qualified to do so, a mediator may (1) discuss a party's options, including a range of possible outcomes in an adjudicative process; (2) offer a personal evaluation of or opinion on a set of facts as presented, which should be clearly identified as a personal evaluation or opinion; or (3) communicate the mediator's opinion or view of what the law is or how it applies to the subject of the mediation, provided that the mediator does not also advise any participant about how to adhere to the law or on what position the participant should take in light of that opinion.

One question that frequently arises is whether a mediator's assessment of claims, defenses, or possible litigation outcomes constitutes legal advice or the practice of law. Similar questions may arise when accounting, architecture, construction, counseling, medicine, real estate, or other licensed professions are relevant to a mediation. This rule does not determine what constitutes the practice of law or any other licensed profession. A mediator should be cautious when providing any information or opinion related to any field for which a professional license is required, in order to avoid doing so in a manner that may constitute the practice of a profession for which the mediator is not licensed, or in a manner that may violate the regulations of a profession that the mediator is licensed to practice. A mediator should exercise particular caution when discussing the law with unrepresented parties and should inform such parties that they may seek independent advice from a lawyer.

Subdivision (i). Subdivision (i)(2) is not intended to establish any new responsibility or diminish any existing responsibilities that a mediator may have, under the Americans With Disabilities Act or other similar law, to attempt to accommodate physical or mental disabilities of a participant in mediation.

Ref.: Cal. Fms Pl. & Pr., Ch. 37, "Judicially Mandated Civil Action Mediation."

Rule 3.858.　Marketing

(a) Truthfulness

A mediator must be truthful and accurate in marketing his or her mediation services. A mediator is responsible for ensuring that both his or her own marketing activities and any marketing activities carried out on his or her behalf by others comply with this rule.

(b) Representations concerning court approval

A mediator may indicate in his or her marketing materials that he or she is a member of a particular court's panel or list but, unless specifically permitted by the court, must not indicate that he or she is approved, endorsed, certified, or licensed by the court.

(c) Promises, guarantees, and implications of favoritism

In marketing his or her mediation services, a mediator must not:

(1) Promise or guarantee results; or

(2) Make any statement that directly or indirectly implies bias in favor of one party or participant over another.

(d) Solicitation of business

A mediator must not solicit business from a participant in a mediation proceeding while that mediation is pending.

Rule 3.858 renumbered effective January 1, 2007; adopted as rule 1620.8 effective January 1, 2003.

Advisory Committee Comment

Subdivision (d). This rule is not intended to prohibit a mediator from accepting other employment from a participant while a mediation is pending, provided that there was no express solicitation of this business by the mediator and that accepting that employment does not contravene any other provision of these rules, including the obligations to maintain impartiality, confidentiality, and the integrity of the process. If other employment is accepted from a participant while a mediation is pending, however, the mediator may be required to disclose this to the parties under rule 3.855.

This rule also is not intended to prohibit a mediator from engaging in general marketing activities. General marketing activities include, but are not limited to, running an advertisement in a newspaper and sending out a general mailing (either of which may be directed to a particular industry or market).

Ref.: Cal. Fms Pl. & Pr., Ch. 37, "Judicially Mandated Civil Action Mediation."

Rule 3.859.　Compensation and gifts

(a) Compliance with law

A mediator must comply with any applicable requirements concerning compensation established by statute or the court.

(b) Disclosure of and compliance with compensation terms

Before commencing the mediation, the mediator must disclose to the parties in writing any fees, costs, or charges to be paid to the mediator by the parties. A mediator must abide by any agreement that is reached concerning compensation.

(c) Contingent fees

The amount or nature of a mediator's fee must not be made contingent on the outcome of the mediation.

(Subd (c) amended effective January 1, 2007.)

(d) Gifts and favors

A mediator must not at any time solicit or accept from or give to any participant or affiliate of a participant any gift, bequest, or favor that might reasonably raise a question concerning the mediator's impartiality.

Rule 3.859 amended and renumbered effective January 1, 2007; adopted as rule 1620.9 effective January 1, 2003.

Advisory Committee Comment

Subdivision (b). It is good practice to put mediation fee agreements in writing, and mediators are strongly encouraged to do so; however, nothing in this rule is intended to preclude enforcement of a compensation agreement for mediation services that is not in writing.

Subdivision (d). Whether a gift, bequest, or favor "might reasonably raise a question concerning the mediator's impartiality" must be determined on a case-by-case basis. This subdivision is not intended to prohibit a mediator from accepting other employment from any of the participants, consistent with rule 3.858(d).

Ref.: Cal. Fms Pl. & Pr., Ch. 37, "Judicially Mandated Civil Action Mediation."

Rule 3.860. Attendance sheet and agreement to disclosure

(a) Attendance sheet

In each mediation to which these rules apply under rule 3.851(a), the mediator must request that all participants in the mediation complete an attendance sheet stating their names, mailing addresses, and telephone numbers; retain the attendance sheet for at least two years; and submit it to the court on request.

(Subd (a) amended effective January 1, 2007.)

(b) Agreement to disclosure

The mediator must agree, in each mediation to which these rules apply under rule 3.851(a), that if an inquiry or a compliant is made about the conduct of the mediator, mediation communications may be disclosed solely for purposes of a complaint procedure conducted pursuant to rule 3.865 to address that complaint or inquiry.

(Subd (b) amended effective January 1, 2007.)

Rule 3.860 amended and renumbered effective January 1, 2007; adopted as rule 1621 effective January 1, 2006.

Ref.: Cal. Fms Pl. & Pr., Ch. 37, "Judicially Mandated Civil Action Mediation."

Rule 3.865. [Renumbered to Rule 3.868 Effective July 1, 2009] Complaint procedure required

(a) Court procedures required

Each superior court that makes a list of mediators available to litigants in general civil cases or that recommends, selects, appoints, or compensates a mediator to mediate any general civil case pending in the court must establish procedures for receiving, investigating, and resolving complaints that mediators who are on the court's list or who are recommended, selected, appointed, or compensated by the court failed to comply with the rules for conduct of mediators set forth in this article, when applicable.

(Subd (a) amended effective January 1, 2007; previously amended effective January 1, 2006.)

(b) Actions court may take

The court may impose additional mediation training requirements on a mediator, reprimand a mediator, remove a mediator from the court's panel or list, or otherwise prohibit a mediator from receiving future mediation referrals from the court if the mediator fails to comply with the

rules of conduct for mediators in this article, when applicable.

(Subd (b) amended effective January 1, 2007; previously amended effective January 1, 2006.)

Rule 3.865 amended and renumbered to rule 3.868 effective July 1, 2009; adopted as rule 1622 effective January 1, 2003; previously amended effective January 1, 2006; previously amended effective January 1, 2007.

2008 Note: Another Rule 3.865, effective July 1, 2009, follows in Article 3.

Ref.: Cal. Fms Pl. & Pr., Ch. 37, "Judicially Mandated Civil Action Mediation."

Rule 3.866. [Renumbered to Rule 3.867 Effective July 1, 2009] Designation of person to receive inquiries and complaints

In each superior court that is required to establish a complaint procedure under rule 3.865, the presiding judge must designate a person who is knowledgeable about mediation to receive and coordinate the investigation of any inquiries or complaints about the conduct of mediators who are subject to rule 3.865.

Rule 3.866 amended and renumbered to rule 3.867 effective July 1, 2009; adopted as rule 1622.1 effective January 1, 2006; previously amended and renumbered effective January 1, 2007.

2008 Note: Another Rule 3.866, effective July 1, 2009, follows in Article 3.

Ref.: Cal. Fms Pl. & Pr., Ch. 37, "Judicially Mandated Civil Action Mediation."

Rule 3.867. [Renumbered to Rule 3.871 Effective July 1, 2009] Confidentiality of complaint procedures, information, and records

(a) This rule's requirement that rule 3.865 complaint procedures be confidential is intended to:

(1) Preserve the confidentiality of mediation communications as required by Evidence Code sections 1115–1128;

(2) Promote cooperation in the reporting, investigation, and resolution of complaints about mediators on court panels; and

(3) Protect mediators against damage to their reputations that might result from unfounded complaints against them.

(Subd (a) amended effective January 1, 2007.)

(b) All procedures for receiving, investigating, and resolving inquiries or complaints about the conduct of mediators must be designed to preserve the confidentiality of mediation communications, including but not limited to the confidentiality of any communications between the mediator and individual mediation participants or subgroups of mediation participants.

(c) All communications, inquiries, complaints, investigations, procedures, deliberations, and decisions about the conduct of a mediator under rule 3.865 must occur in private and must be kept confidential. No information or records concerning the receipt, investigation, or resolution of an inquiry or a complaint under rule 3.865 may be open to the public or disclosed outside the course of the rule 3.865 complaint procedure except as provided in (d) or as otherwise required by law.

(Subd (c) amended effective January 1, 2007.)

(d) The presiding judge or a person designated by the presiding judge for this purpose may, in his or her discretion, authorize the disclosure of information or records concerning rule 3.865 complaint procedures that do not reveal any mediation communications, including the name of a mediator against whom action has been taken under rule 3.865, the action taken, and the general basis on which the action was taken. In determining whether to authorize the disclosure of information or records under this subdivision, the presiding judge or designee should consider the purposes of the confidentiality of rule 3.865 complaint procedures stated in (a)(2) and (a)(3).

(Subd (d) amended effective January 1, 2007.)

(e) In determining whether the disclosure of information or records concerning rule 3.865 complaint procedures is required by law, courts should consider the purposes of the confidentiality of rule 3.865 complaint procedures stated in (a). Before the disclosure of records concerning procedures under rule 3.865 is ordered, notice should be given to any person whose mediation communications may be revealed.

(Subd (e) amended effective January 1, 2007.)

Rule 3.867 amended and renumbered to rule 3.871 effective July 1, 2009; adopted as rule 1622.2 effective January 1, 2006; previously amended and renumbered effective January 1, 2007; previously amended effective January 1, 2008.

Advisory Committee Comment

See Evidence Code sections 1115 and 1119 concerning the scope and types of mediation communications protected by mediation confidentiality.

Subdivision (b). Private meetings, or "caucuses," between a mediator and subgroups of participants are common in court-connected mediations, and it is frequently understood that these communications will not be disclosed to other participants in the mediation. (See Cal. Rules of Court, rule 3.854(c).) It is important to protect the confidentiality of these communications in rule 3.865 complaint procedures, so that one participant in the mediation does not learn what another participant discussed in confidence with the mediator.

Subdivisions (c)–(e). The provisions of (c)–(e) that authorize the disclosure of information and records related to rule 3.865 complaint procedures do not create any new exceptions to mediation confidentiality. Information and records about rule 3.865 complaint procedures that would reveal mediation communications should only be publicly disclosed consistent with the statutes and case law governing mediation confidentiality.

Evidence Code sections 915 and 1040 establish procedures and criteria for deciding whether information acquired in confidence by a public employee in the course of his or her duty is subject to disclosure. These sections may be applicable or helpful in determining whether the disclosure of information or records acquired by judicial officers, court staff, and other persons while receiving, investigating, or resolving complaints under rule 3.865 is required by law or should be authorized in the discretion of the presiding judge.

2008 Note: Another Rule 3.867, effective July 1, 2009, follows in Article 3.

Ref.: Cal. Fms Pl. & Pr., Ch. 37, "Judicially Mandated Civil Action Mediation."

Rule 3.868. [Renumbered to Rule 3.872 Effective July 1, 2009] Disqualification from subsequently serving as an adjudicator

A person who has participated in or received information about the receipt, investigation or resolution of an inquiry or a complaint under rule 3.865 must not subsequently hear or determine any contested issue of law, fact, or procedure concerning the dispute that was the subject of the underlying mediation or any other dispute that arises from the mediation, as a judge, an arbitrator, a referee, or a juror, or in any other adjudicative capacity, in any court action or proceeding.

Rule 3.868 amended and renumbered to rule 3.872 effective July 1, 2009; adopted as rule 1622.3 effective January 1, 2006; previously amended and renumbered effective January 1, 2007.

2008 Note: Another Rule 3.868, effective July 1, 2009, follows in Article 3.

Ref.: Cal. Fms Pl. & Pr., Ch. 37, "Judicially Mandated Civil Action Mediation."

Article 3
Requirements for Addressing Complaints About Court-Program Mediators
[Effective July 1, 2009]

Title 3, Civil Rules—Division 8, Alternative Dispute Resolution—Chapter 3, General Rules Relating to Mediation of Civil Cases—Article 3, Requirements for Addressing Complaints About Court-Program Mediators adopted effective July 1, 2009.

Rule 3.865. Application and purpose
Rule 3.866. Definitions
Rule 3.867. Complaint coordinator
Rule 3.868. Complaint procedure required
Rule 3.869. General requirements for complaint procedures and complaint proceedings
Rule 3.870. Permissible court actions on complaints
Rule 3.871. Confidentiality of complaint proceedings, information, and records
Rule 3.872. Disqualification from subsequently serving as an adjudicator

Rule 3.865. [Effective July 1, 2009]
Application and purpose

The rules in this article apply to each superior court that makes a list of mediators available to litigants in general civil cases or that recommends, selects, appoints, or compensates a mediator to mediate any general civil case pending in that court. These rules are intended to promote the resolution of complaints that mediators in court-connected mediation programs for civil cases may have violated a provision of the rules of conduct for such mediators in article 2. They are intended to help courts promptly resolve any such complaints in a manner that is respectful and fair to the complainant and the mediator and consistent with the California mediation confidentiality statutes.

Rule 3.865 adopted effective July 1, 2009.

Advisory Committee Comment

As used in this article, complaint means a written communication presented to a court's complaint coordinator indicating that a mediator may have violated a provision of the rules of conduct for mediators in article 2.

Complaints about mediators are relatively rare. To ensure the quality of court mediation panels and public confidence in the mediation process and the courts, it is, nevertheless, important to ensure that any complaints that do arise are resolved through procedures that are consistent with California mediation confidentiality statutes (Evid. Code, §§ 703.5 and 1115 et seq.), as well as fair and respectful to the interested parties.

The requirements and procedures in this article do not abrogate or limit a court's inherent or other authority, in its sole and absolute discretion, to determine who may be included on or removed from a court list of mediators; to approve or revoke a mediator's eligibility to be recommended, selected, appointed, or compensated by the court; or to follow other procedures or take other actions to ensure the quality of mediators who serve in the court's mediation program in contexts other than when addressing a complaint. The failure to follow a requirement or procedure in this article will not invalidate any action taken by the court in addressing a complaint.

2008 Note: Another Rule 3.865, effective until July 1, 2009, precedes in Article 2.

Rule 3.866.   [Effective July 1, 2009] Definitions

As used in this article, unless the context or subject matter requires otherwise:

(1) "The rules of conduct" means rules 3.850–3.860 of the California Rules of Court in article 2.

(2) "Court-program mediator" means a person subject to the rules of conduct under rule 3.851.

(3) "Inquiry" means an unwritten communication presented to the court's complaint coordinator indicating that a mediator may have violated a provision of the rules of conduct.

(4) "Complaint" means a written communication presented to the court's complaint coordinator indicating that a mediator may have violated a provision of the rules of conduct.

(5) "Complainant" means the person who makes or presents a complaint.

(6) "Complaint coordinator" means the person designated by the presiding judge under rule 3.867(a) to receive complaints and inquiries about the conduct of mediators.

(7) "Complaint committee" means a committee designated or appointed to investigate and make recommendations concerning complaints under rule 3.869(d)(2).

(8) "Complaint procedure" means a procedure for presenting, receiving, reviewing, responding to, investigating, and acting on any inquiry or complaint.

(9) "Complaint proceeding" means all of the proceedings that take place as part of a complaint procedure concerning a specific inquiry or complaint.

(10) "Mediation communication" means any statement that is made or any writing that is prepared for the purpose of, in the course of, or pursuant to a mediation or a mediation consultation, as defined in Evidence Code section 1115, and includes any communications, negotiations, and settlement discussions between participants in the course of a mediation or a mediation consultation.

Rule 3.866 adopted effective July 1, 2009.

Advisory Committee Comment

Paragraph (2). Under rule 3.851, the rules of conduct apply when a mediator, or a firm with which a mediator is affiliated, has agreed to be included on a superior court's list or panel of mediators for general civil cases and is notified by the court or the parties that he or she has been selected to mediate a case within that court's mediation program or when a mediator has agreed to mediate a general civil case after being notified that he or she was recommended, selected, or appointed by a court, or will be compensated by a court, to mediate a case within a court's mediation program.

Paragraphs (3) and (4). The distinction between "inquiries" and "complaints" is significant because some provisions of this

article apply only to complaints (i.e., written communications presented to the court's complaint coordinator indicating that a mediator may have violated a provision of the rules of conduct) and not to inquiries.

2008 Note: Another Rule 3.866, effective until July 1, 2009, precedes in Article 2.

Rule 3.867.   [Effective July 1, 2009] Complaint coordinator

(a) Designation of the complaint coordinator

[1] The presiding judge must designate a person who is knowledgeable about mediation to [2] **serve as the complaint coordinator**.

(Subd (a) amended and lettered effective July 1, 2009; adopted as unlettered subd effective January 1, 2006.)

Rule 3.867(a).   2008 Deletes. [1] In each superior court that is required to establish a complaint procedure under rule 3.865, [2] receive and coordinate the investigation of any inquiries or complaints about the conduct of mediators who are subject to rule 3.865

(b) Identification of the complaint coordinator

The court must make the complaint coordinator's identity and contact information readily accessible to litigants and the public.

(Subd (b) adopted effective July 1, 2009.)

Rule 3.867 amended and renumbered effective July 1, 2009; adopted as rule 1622.1 effective January 1, 2006; previously amended and renumbered as rule 3.866 effective January 1, 2007.

Advisory Committee Comment

The alternative dispute resolution program administrator appointed under rule 10.783(a) may also be appointed as the complaint coordinator if that person is knowledgeable about mediation.

2008 Note: Another Rule 3.867, effective until July 1, 2009, precedes in Article 2.

Ref.: Cal. Fms Pl. & Pr., Ch. 37, "Judicially Mandated Civil Action Mediation."

Rule 3.868.   [Effective July 1, 2009] Complaint procedure required

[1]

Each [2] **court** to which this article applies under rule 3.865 must establish [3] **a complaint procedure by local rule of court that is consistent with this article**.

(Subd (a) amended and unlettered effective July 1, 2009; adopted as subd (a) effective January 1, 2003; previously amended effective January 1, 2006, and January 1, 2007.)

Rule 3.868(a).   2008 Deletes. [1] (a) Court procedures required [2] superior court that makes a list of mediators available to litigants in general civil cases or that recommends, selects, appoints, or compensates a mediator to mediate any general civil case pending in the [3] procedures for receiving, investigating, and resolving complaints that mediators who are on the court's list or who are recommended, selected, appointed, or compensated by the court failed to comply with the rules for conduct of mediators set forth in this article, when applicable

(b) Actions court may take [Repealed]

(Subd (b) repealed effective July 1, 2009; previously amended effective January 1, 2006 and January 1, 2007.)

Rule 3.868 amended and renumbered effective July 1, 2009; adopted as rule 1622 effective January 1, 2003; previously amended effective January 1, 2006; previously amended and renumbered as rule 3.865 effective January 1, 2007.

2008 Note: Another Rule 3.868, effective until July 1, 2009, precedes in Article 2.

Ref.: Cal. Fms Pl. & Pr., Ch. 37, "Judicially Mandated Civil Action Mediation."

Rule 3.869.   [Effective July 1, 2009] General requirements for complaint procedures and complaint proceedings

(a) Submission and referral of inquiries and complaints to the complaint coordinator

All inquiries and complaints should be submitted or referred to the complaint coordinator.

(Subd (a) adopted effective July 1, 2009.)

(b) Acknowledgment of complaint

The complaint coordinator must send the complainant a written acknowledgment that the court has received the complaint.

(Subd (b) adopted effective July 1, 2009.)

(c) Preliminary review and disposition of complaints

The complaint coordinator must conduct a preliminary review of all complaints to determine whether the complaint can be informally resolved or closed, or whether the complaint warrants investigation.

(Subd (c) adopted effective July 1, 2009.)

(d) Procedure for complaints not resolved through the preliminary review

The following procedures are required only if a complaint is not resolved or closed through the preliminary review.

(1) *Mediator's notice and opportunity to respond*

The mediator must be given notice of the complaint and an opportunity to respond.

(2) *Investigation and recommendation*

(A) Except as provided in (B), the complaint must be investigated and a recommendation concerning court action on the complaint must be made by either an individual who has experience as a mediator and who is familiar with the rules of conduct stated in article 2 or a complaint committee that has at least one such individual as a member.

(B) A court with eight or fewer authorized judges may waive the requirement in (A) for participation by an individual who has experience as a mediator in conducting the investigation and making the recommendation if the court cannot find a suitable qualified individual to perform the functions described in (A) or for other grounds of hardship.

(3) *Final decision*

The final decision on the complaint must be made by the presiding judge or his or her designee, who must not be the complaint coordinator or an individual who investigated the complaint before its submission for final decision.

(Subd (d) adopted effective July 1, 2009.)

(e) Notice of final action

(1) The court must send the complainant notice of the final action taken by the court on the complaint.

(2) If the complaint was not closed during the preliminary review, the court must send notice of the final action to the mediator.

(Subd (e) adopted effective July 1, 2009.)

(f) Promptness

The court must process complaints promptly at all stages.

(Subd (f) adopted effective July 1, 2009.)

(g) Records of complaints

The court should maintain sufficient information about each complaint and its disposition to identify any history or patterns of complaints submitted under these rules.

(Subd (g) adopted effective July 1, 2009.)

Rule 3.869 adopted effective July 1, 2009.

Advisory Committee Comment

The Administrative Office of the Courts has developed model local rules that satisfy the requirements of this rule. These model local rules were developed with input from judicial officers, court administrators, alternative dispute resolution (ADR) program administrators, court-program mediators, and public commentators and are designed so that they can be readily adapted to the circumstances of individual courts and specific complaints. Courts are encouraged to adopt rules that follow the model rules, to the extent feasible. Courts can obtain copies of these model rules from civil ADR program staff at the Administrative Office of the Courts.

Subdivision (a). Coordination of inquiries and complaints by a person knowledgeable about mediation is important to help ensure that the requirements of this article are followed and that mediation confidentiality is preserved.

Subdivision (c). Courts are encouraged to resolve inquiries and complaints about mediators using the simplest, least formal procedures that are appropriate under the circumstances, provided that they meet the requirements stated in this article.

Most complaints can be appropriately resolved during the preliminary review stage of the complaint process, through informal discussions between or among the complaint coordinator, the complainant, and the mediator. Although complaint coordinators are not required to communicate with the mediator during the preliminary review, they are encouraged to consider doing so. For example, some complaints may arise from a misunderstanding of the mediator's role or from behavior that would not violate the standards of conduct. These types of complaints might appropriately be addressed by providing the complainant with additional information or by informing the mediator that certain behavior was upsetting to a mediation participant.

The circumstances under which a complaint coordinator might informally resolve or close a complaint include, for example, when (1) the complaint is withdrawn; (2) no violation of the rules of conduct appears to have occurred; (3) the alleged violation of the rules of conduct is very minor and the mediator has provided an acceptable explanation or response; and (4) the complainant, the mediator, and the complaint coordinator have agreed on a resolution. In determining whether to close a complaint, the complaint coordinator might also consider whether there are or have been other complaints about the mediator.

Subdivision (d). At the investigation and recommendation stage, all courts are encouraged to consider using a complaint committee comprised of members with a variety of backgrounds, including at least one person with experience as a mediator, to investigate and make recommendations concerning those rare complaints that are not resolved during the preliminary review.

Courts are also encouraged to have a judicial officer who is knowledgeable about mediation, or a committee that includes another person who is knowledgeable about mediation, make the final decision on complaints that are not resolved through the preliminary review.

Rule 3.870. [Effective July 1, 2009] Permissible court actions on complaints

After an investigation has been conducted, the presiding judge or his or her designee may do one or more of the following:

(1) Direct that no action be taken on the complaint;

(2) Counsel, admonish, or reprimand the mediator;

(3) Impose additional training requirements as a condition of the mediator remaining on the court's panel or list;

(4) Suspend the mediator from the court's panel or list or otherwise temporarily prohibit the mediator from receiving future mediation referrals from the court; or

(5) Remove the mediator from the court's panel or list or otherwise prohibit the mediator from receiving future mediation referrals from the court.

Rule 3.870 adopted effective July 1, 2009.

Advisory Committee Comment

This rule does not abrogate or limit any existing legal right or duty of the court to take other actions, including interim suspension of a mediator pending final action by the court on a complaint.

2008 Note: Another Rule 3.870, effective until July 1, 2009, follows in Chapter 4.

Rule 3.871. [Effective July 1, 2009] Confidentiality of complaint proceedings, information, and records

(a) **Intent**

This [1] **rule is** intended to:

(1) Preserve the confidentiality of mediation communications as required by Evidence Code sections 1115–1128;

(2) Promote cooperation in the reporting, investigation, and resolution of complaints about **court-program** mediators [2]; and

(3) Protect mediators against damage to their reputations that might result from **the disclosure of** unfounded complaints against them.

(Subd (a) amended effective July 1, 2009; previously amended effective January 1, 2007.)

Rule 3.871(a). 2008 Deletes. [1] rule's requirement that rule 3.865 complaint procedures be confidential is **[2]** on court panels

(b) **Preserving the confidentiality of mediation communications**

All **complaint** procedures [1] **and complaint proceedings** must be designed [2] **and conducted in a manner that preserves** the confidentiality of mediation communications, including but not limited to the confidentiality of any communications between the mediator and individual mediation participants or subgroups of mediation participants.

(Subd (b) amended effective July 1, 2009.)

Rule 3.871(b). 2008 Deletes. [1] for receiving, investigating, and resolving inquiries or complaints about the conduct of mediators **[2]** to preserve

(c) **Confidentiality of complaint proceedings**

All [1] **complaint proceedings** must occur in private and must be kept confidential. No information or records concerning the receipt, investigation, or resolution of an inquiry or a complaint [2] may be open to the public or

disclosed outside the course of the [3] **complaint proceeding** except as provided in (d) or as otherwise required by law.

(Subd (c) amended effective July 1, 2009; previously amended effective January 1, 2007.)

Rule 3.871(c). 2008 Deletes. [1] communications, inquiries, complaints, investigations, procedures, deliberations, and decisions about the conduct of a mediator under rule 3.865 **[2]** under rule 3.865 **[3]** rule 3.865 complaint procedure

(d) **Authorized disclosures**

After the decision on a complaint, the presiding judge, or a person [1] **whom** the presiding judge [2] **designates to do so, may** authorize the **public** disclosure of information or records concerning [3] **the complaint proceeding** that do not reveal any mediation communications [4]. **The disclosures that may be authorized under this subdivision include** the name of a mediator against whom action has been taken under rule [5] **3.870,** the action taken, and the general basis on which the action was taken. In determining whether to authorize the disclosure of information or records under this subdivision, the presiding judge or **the** designee should consider the purposes of the confidentiality of [6] **complaint proceedings** stated in (a)(2) and (a)(3).

(Subd (d) amended effective July 1, 2009; previously amended effective January 1, 2007.)

Rule 3.871(d). 2008 Deletes. [1] designated by **[2]** for this purpose may, in his or her discretion, **[3]** rule 3.865 complaint procedures **[4]**, including **[5]** 3.865 **[6]** rule 3.865 complaint procedures

(e) **Disclosures required by law**

In determining whether the disclosure of information or records concerning [1] **a complaint proceeding** is required by law, courts should consider the purposes of the confidentiality of [2] **complaint proceedings** stated in (a). [3] **If it appears that** the disclosure of **information or** records concerning [4] **a complaint proceeding that would reveal mediation communications is required by law, before the information or records are disclosed,** notice should be given to any person whose mediation communications may **thereby** be revealed.

(Subd (e) amended effective July 1, 2009; previously amended effective January 1, 2007.)

Rule 3.871(e). 2008 Deletes. [1] rule 3.865 complaint procedures **[2]** rule 3.865 complaint procedures **[3]** Before **[4]** procedures under rule 3.865 is ordered

Rule 3.871 amended and renumbered effective July 1, 2009; adopted as rule 1622.2 effective January 1, 2006; previously amended and renumbered as rule 3.867 effective January 1, 2007.

Advisory Committee Comment

Under rule 3.866(9), the complaint proceedings covered by this rule include proceedings to address inquiries as well as complaints (i.e., to unwritten as well as written communications indicating that a mediator may have violated a provision of the rules of conduct).

Subdivision (a). See Evidence Code sections 1115 and 1119 concerning the scope and types of mediation communications protected by mediation confidentiality. Rule 3.871 is intended to supplement the confidentiality of mediation communications established by the Evidence Code by ensuring that disclosure of information or records about a complaint proceeding does not reveal confidential mediation communications. Rule 3.871 is not intended to supersede or abrogate the confidentiality of mediation communications established by the Evidence Code.

Subdivision (b). Private meetings, or "caucuses," between a mediator and subgroups of participants are common in court-connected mediations, and it is frequently understood that these communications will not be disclosed to other participants in the mediation. (See Cal. Rules of Court, rule 3.854(c).) It is important to protect the confidentiality of these communications in complaint proceedings so that one participant in the mediation does not learn what another participant discussed in confidence with the mediator without the consent of the participants in the caucus communication.

Subdivisions (c)–(e). The provisions of (c)–(e) that authorize the disclosure of information and records related to complaint proceedings do not create any new exceptions to mediation confidentiality. Although public disclosure of information and records about complaint proceedings that do not reveal mediation communications may be authorized under (d), information and records that *would* reveal mediation communications may be publicly disclosed only as required by law (e.g., in response to a subpoena or court order) and consistent with the statutes and case law governing mediation confidentiality. A person who is knowledgeable about California's mediation confidentiality laws should determine whether the disclosure of mediation communications is required by law.

Evidence Code sections 915 and 1040 establish procedures and criteria for deciding whether information acquired in confidence by a public employee in the course of his or her duty is subject to disclosure. These sections may be applicable or helpful in determining whether the disclosure of information or records acquired by judicial officers, court staff, and other persons in the course of a complaint proceeding is required by law or should be authorized in the discretion of the presiding judge.

2008 Note: Another Rule 3.871, effective until July 1, 2009, follows in Chapter 4.

Ref.: Cal. Fms Pl. & Pr., Ch. 37, "Judicially Mandated Civil Action Mediation."

Rule 3.872. [Effective July 1, 2009] Disqualification from subsequently serving as an adjudicator

A person who has participated in **a complaint proceeding or otherwise** received information about the [1] **substance of a complaint, other than information that is publicly disclosed under rule 3.871(d),** must not subsequently hear or determine any contested issue of law, fact, or procedure concerning the dispute that was the subject of the underlying mediation or any other dispute that arises from the mediation, as a judge, an arbitrator, a referee, or a juror, or in any other adjudicative capacity, in any court action or proceeding.

Rule 3.872 amended and renumbered effective July 1, 2009; adopted as rule 1622.3 effective January 1, 2006; previously amended and renumbered as rule 3.868 effective January 1, 2007.

Rule 3.872. 2008 Deletes. [1] receipt, investigation or resolution of an inquiry or a complaint under rule 3.865

Advisory Committee Comment

Persons who participated in a complaint proceeding are prohibited from subsequently adjudicating the dispute that was the subject of the underlying mediation or any other dispute that arises from the mediation because they may have learned of confidential mediation communications that were disclosed in the complaint proceeding or may have been influenced by what transpired in that proceeding. Because the information that can be disclosed publicly under rule 3.871(d) is limited and excludes mediation communications, it is unnecessary to disqualify persons who received only publicly disclosed information from subsequently adjudicating the dispute.

2008 Note: Another Rule 3.872, effective until July 1, 2009, follows in Chapter 4.

Chapter 4
Civil Action Mediation Program Rules
[Effective Until July 1, 2009]

Rule 3.870. [Renumbered to Rule 3.890 Effective July 1, 2009] Application

The rules in this chapter implement the Civil Action Mediation Act, Code of Civil Procedure section 1775 et seq. Under section 1775.2, they apply in the Superior Court of California, County of Los Angeles and in other courts that elect to apply the act.

Rule 3.870 renumbered to rule 3.890 effective July 1, 2009; adopted as rule 1630 effective March 1, 1994; previously amended and renumbered effective January 1, 2007.

2008 Note: Another Rule 3.870, effective July 1, 2009, precedes in Article 3.

Ref.: Cal. Fms Pl. & Pr., Ch. 31, "Mediation," Ch. 37, "Judicially Mandated Civil Action Mediation," Ch. 222, "Dissolution of Marriage: Property Division and Valuation"; MB Prac. Guide: Cal. Pretrial Proc., §24.01.

Rule 3.871. [Renumbered to Rule 3.891 Effective July 1, 2009] Actions subject to mediation

(a) Actions that may be submitted to mediation

The following actions may be submitted to mediation under these provisions:

(1) *By court order*

Any action in which the amount in controversy, independent of the merits of liability, defenses, or comparative negligence, does not exceed $50,000 for each plaintiff. The court must determine the amount in controversy under Code of Civil Procedure section 1775.5. Determinations to send a case to mediation must be made by the court after consideration of the expressed views of the parties on the amenability of the case to mediation. The court must not require the parties or their counsel to personally appear in court for a conference held solely to determine whether to send their case to mediation.

(2) *By stipulation*

Any other action, regardless of the amount of controversy, in which all parties stipulate to such mediation. The stipulation must be filed not later than 90 days before trial unless the court permits a later time.

(Subd (a) amended effective January 1, 2007.)

(b) Case-by-case determination

Amenability of a particular action for mediation must be determined on a case-by-case basis, rather than categorically.

(Subd (b) amended effective January 1, 2007.)

Rule 3.871 renumbered to rule 3.891 effective July 1, 2009; adopted as rule 1631 effective March 1, 1994; previously amended and renumbered effective January 1, 2007.

2008 Note: Another Rule 3.871, effective July 1, 2009, precedes in Article 3.

Ref.: Cal. Fms Pl. & Pr., Ch. 37, "Judicially Mandated Civil Action Mediation"; MB Prac. Guide: Cal. Pretrial Proc., §§24.43, 24.48, 24.51, 24.52[1], [2], 24.64, 28.07[2].

Rule 3.872. [Renumbered to Rule 3.892 Effective July 1, 2009] Panels of mediators

Each court, in consultation with local bar associations, ADR providers, and associations of providers, must identify persons who may be appointed as mediators. The court must consider the criteria in standard 10.72 of the Standards of Judicial Administration and California Code of Regulations, title 16, section 3622, relating to the Dispute Resolution Program Act.

Rule 3.872 renumbered to rule 3.892 effective July 1, 2009; adopted as rule 1632 effective March 1, 1994; previously amended and renumbered effective January 1, 2007.

2008 Note: Another Rule 3.872, effective July 1, 2009, precedes in Article 3.

Ref.: Cal. Fms Pl. & Pr., Ch. 37, "Judicially Mandated Civil Action Mediation."

Rule 3.873. [Renumbered to Rule 3.893 Effective July 1, 2009] Selection of mediators

The parties may stipulate to any mediator, whether or not the person selected is among those identified under rule 3.872, within 15 days of the date an action is submitted to mediation. If the parties do not stipulate to a mediator, the court must promptly assign a mediator to the action from those identified under rule 3.872.

Rule 3.873 renumbered to rule 3.893 effective July 1, 2009; adopted as rule 1633 effective March 1, 1994; previously amended and renumbered effective January 1, 2007.

Ref.: Cal. Fms Pl. & Pr., Ch. 37, "Judicially Mandated Civil Action Mediation"; MB Prac. Guide: Cal. Pretrial Proc., §§24.43, 24.53.

Rule 3.874. [Renumbered to Rule 3.894 Effective July 1, 2009] Attendance, participant lists, and mediation statements

(a) Attendance

(1) All parties and attorneys of record must attend all mediation sessions in person unless excused or permitted to attend by telephone as provided in (3). If a party is not a natural person, a representative of that party with authority to resolve the dispute or, in the case of a governmental entity that requires an agreement to be approved by an elected official or a legislative body, a representative with authority to recommend such agreement, must attend all mediation sessions in person, unless excused or permitted to attend by telephone as provided in (3).

(2) If any party is insured under a policy of insurance that provides or may provide coverage for a claim that is a subject of the action, a representative of the insurer with authority to settle or recommend settlement of the claim must attend all mediation sessions in person, unless excused or permitted to attend by telephone as provided in (3).

(3) The mediator may excuse a party, attorney, or representative from the requirement to attend a mediation session under (1) or (2) or permit attendance by telephone. The party, attorney, or representative who is excused or permitted to attend by telephone must promptly send a letter or an electronic communication to the mediator and to all parties confirming the excuse or permission.

(4) Each party may have counsel present at all mediation sessions that concern the party.

(Subd (a) amended and lettered effective January 1, 2007; adopted as untitled subd effective March 1, 1994.)

(b) Participant lists and mediation statements

(1) At least five court days before the first mediation session, each party must serve a list of its mediation participants on the mediator and all other parties. The list must include the names of all parties, attorneys, representatives of a party that is not a natural person, insurance representatives, and other persons who will attend the mediation with or on behalf of that party. A party must promptly serve a supplemental list if the party subsequently determines that other persons will attend the mediation with or on behalf of the party.

(2) The mediator may request that each party submit a short mediation statement providing information about the issues in dispute and possible resolutions of those issues and other information or documents that may appear helpful to resolve the dispute.

(Subd (b) adopted effective January 1, 2007.)

Rule 3.874 renumbered to rule 3.894 effective July 1, 2009; adopted as rule 1634 effective March 1, 1994; previously amended and renumbered effective January 1, 2007; previously amended effective January 1, 2007.

Ref.: Cal. Fms Pl. & Pr., Ch. 37, "Judicially Mandated Civil Action Mediation"; MB Prac. Guide: Cal. Pretrial Proc., §§24.43, 24.56[1][a]–[c], [2], [4][a].

Rule 3.875. [Renumbered to Rule 3.895 Effective July 1, 2009] Filing of statement by mediator

Within 10 days after conclusion of the mediation, the mediator must file a statement on *Statement of Agreement or Nonagreement* (form ADR-100), advising the court whether the mediation ended in full agreement or nonagreement as to the entire case or as to particular parties in the case.

Rule 3.875 renumbered to rule 3.895 effective July 1, 2009; adopted as rule 1635 effective March 1, 1994; previously amended and renumbered effective January 1, 2007.

Ref.: Cal. Fms Pl. & Pr., Ch. 37, "Judicially Mandated Civil Action Mediation"; MB Prac. Guide: Cal. Pretrial Proc., §§24.43, 24.59.

Rule 3.876. [Renumbered to Rule 3.896 Effective July 1, 2009] Coordination with Trial Court Delay Reduction Act

(a) Effect of mediation on time standards

Submission of an action to mediation under the rules in this chapter does not affect time periods specified in the

Trial Court Delay Reduction Act (Gov. Code, § 68600 et seq.), except as provided in this rule.

(Subd (a) amended effective January 1, 2007.)

(b) Exception to delay reduction time standards

On written stipulation of the parties filed with the court, the court may order an exception of up to 90 days to the delay reduction time standards to permit mediation of an action. The court must coordinate the timing of the exception period with its delay reduction calendar.

(Subd (b) amended effective January 1, 2007.)

(c) Time for completion of mediation

Mediation must be completed within 60 days of a reference to a mediator, but that period may be extended by the court for up to 30 days on a showing of good cause.

(Subd (c) amended and lettered effective January 1, 2007; adopted as part of subd (b) effective March 1, 1994.)

(d) Restraint in discovery

The parties should exercise restraint in discovery while a case is in mediation. In appropriate cases to accommodate that objective, the court may issue a protective order under Code of Civil Procedure section 2017(c) and related provisions.

(Subd (d) amended and lettered effective January 1, 2007; adopted as part of subd (b) effective March 1, 1994.)

Rule 3.876 renumbered to rule 3.896 effective July 1, 2009; adopted as rule 1637 effective March 1, 1994; previously amended and renumbered effective January 1, 2007.

Ref.: Cal. Fms Pl. & Pr., Ch. 37, "Judicially Mandated Civil Action Mediation"; MB Prac. Guide: Cal. Pretrial Proc., §§1.03, 24.43, 24.57, 24.58, 24.62.

Rule 3.877. [Renumbered to Rule 3.897 Effective July 1, 2009] Statistical information

(a) Quarterly information reports

Each court must submit quarterly to the Judicial Council pertinent information on:

(1) The cost and time savings afforded by mediation;

(2) The effectiveness of mediation in resolving disputes;

(3) The number of cases referred to mediation;

(4) The time cases were in mediation; and

(5) Whether mediation ended in full agreement or nonagreement as to the entire case or as to particular parties in the case.

(Subd (a) amended effective January 1, 2007; previously amended effective February 9, 1999.)

(b) Submission of reports to the Judicial Council

The information required by this rule must be submitted to the Judicial Council either on the *Statement of Agreement or Nonagreement* (form ADR-100) and *ADR Information Form* (form ADR-101) or as an electronic database that includes, at a minimum, all of the information required on these forms. The format of any electronic database used to submit this information must be approved by the Administrative Office of the Courts.

(Subd (b) amended and lettered effective January 1, 2007; adopted as part of subd (a) effective March 1, 1994.)

(c) Parties and mediators to supply information

Each court must require parties and mediators, as appropriate, to supply pertinent information for the reports required under this rule.

(Subd (c) amended and relettered effective January 1, 2007; adopted as subd (b) effective March 1, 1994.)

(d) Alternative reporting method

On request, a court may report cases in mediation under the rules in this chapter under the appropriate reporting methods for cases stayed for contractual arbitration.

(Subd (d) amended and relettered effective January 1, 2007; adopted as subd (c) effective March 1, 1994.)

Rule 3.877 renumbered to rule 3.897 effective July 1, 2009; adopted as rule 1638 effective March 1, 1994; previously amended effective February 9, 1999; previously amended and renumbered effective January 1, 2007.

Ref.: Cal. Fms Pl. & Pr., Ch. 37, "Judicially Mandated Civil Action Mediation."

Rule 3.878. [Renumbered to Rule 3.898 Effective July 1, 2009] Educational material

Each court must make available educational material, adopted by the Judicial Council, or from other sources, describing available ADR processes in the community.

Rule 3.878 renumbered to rule 3.898 effective July 1, 2009; adopted as rule 1639 effective March 1, 1994; amended and renumbered effective January 1, 2007.

Chapter 4
Civil Action Mediation Program Rules
[Effective July 1, 2009]

Rule 3.890. Application
Rule 3.891. Actions subject to mediation
Rule 3.892. Panels of mediators
Rule 3.893. Selection of mediators
Rule 3.894. Attendance, participant lists, and mediation statements
Rule 3.895. Filing of statement by mediator
Rule 3.896. Coordination with Trial Court Delay Reduction Act
Rule 3.897. Statistical information
Rule 3.898. Educational material

Rule 3.890. [Effective July 1, 2009] Application

The rules in this chapter implement the Civil Action Mediation Act, Code of Civil Procedure section 1775 et seq. Under section 1775.2, they apply in the Superior Court of California, County of Los Angeles and in other courts that elect to apply the act.

Rule 3.890 renumbered effective July 1, 2009; adopted as rule 1630 effective March 1, 1994; previously amended and renumbered as rule 3.870 effective January 1, 2007.

Ref.: Cal. Fms Pl. & Pr., Ch. 31, "Mediation," Ch. 37, "Judicially Mandated Civil Action Mediation," Ch. 222, "Dissolution of Marriage: Property Division and Valuation"; MB Prac. Guide: Cal. Pretrial Proc., §24.01.

Rule 3.891. [Effective July 1, 2009] Actions subject to mediation

(a) Actions that may be submitted to mediation

The following actions may be submitted to mediation under these provisions:

(1) *By court order*

Any action in which the amount in controversy, independent of the merits of liability, defenses, or comparative negligence, does not exceed $50,000 for each plaintiff. The court must determine the amount in controversy under Code of Civil Procedure section 1775.5. Determinations to send a case to mediation must be made by the court after consideration of the expressed views of the parties on the amenability of the case to mediation. The court must not require the parties or their counsel to personally appear in court for a conference held solely to determine whether to send their case to mediation.

(2) By stipulation

Any other action, regardless of the amount of controversy, in which all parties stipulate to such mediation. The stipulation must be filed not later than 90 days before trial unless the court permits a later time.

(Subd (a) amended effective January 1, 2007.)

(b) Case-by-case determination

Amenability of a particular action for mediation must be determined on a case-by-case basis, rather than categorically.

(Subd (b) amended effective January 1, 2007.)

Rule 3.891 renumbered effective July 1, 2009; adopted as rule 1631 effective March 1, 1994; previously amended and renumbered as rule 3.871 effective January 1, 2007.

Ref.: Cal. Fms Pl. & Pr., Ch. 37, "Judicially Mandated Civil Action Mediation"; MB Prac. Guide: Cal. Pretrial Proc., §§24.43, 24.48, 24.51, 24.52[1], [2], 24.64, 28.07[2].

Rule 3.892.   [Effective July 1, 2009] Panels of mediators

Each court, in consultation with local bar associations, ADR providers, and associations of providers, must identify persons who may be appointed as mediators. The court must consider the criteria in standard 10.72 of the Standards of Judicial Administration and California Code of Regulations, title 16, section 3622, relating to the Dispute Resolution Program Act.

Rule 3.892 renumbered effective July 1, 2009; adopted as rule 1632 effective March 1, 1994; previously amended and renumbered as rule 3.872 effective January 1, 2007.

Ref.: Cal. Fms Pl. & Pr., Ch. 37, "Judicially Mandated Civil Action Mediation."

Rule 3.893.   [Effective July 1, 2009] Selection of mediators

The parties may stipulate to any mediator, whether or not the person selected is among those identified under rule 3.872, within 15 days of the date an action is submitted to mediation. If the parties do not stipulate to a mediator, the court must promptly assign a mediator to the action from those identified under rule 3.872.

Rule 3.893 renumbered effective July 1, 2009; adopted as rule 1633 effective March 1, 1994; previously amended and renumbered as rule 3.873 effective January 1, 2007.

Ref.: Cal. Fms Pl. & Pr., Ch. 37, "Judicially Mandated Civil Action Mediation"; MB Prac. Guide: Cal. Pretrial Proc., §§24.43, 24.53.

Rule 3.894.   [Effective July 1, 2009] Attendance, participant lists, and mediation statements

(a) Attendance

(1) All parties and attorneys of record must attend all mediation sessions in person unless excused or permitted to attend by telephone as provided in (3). If a party is not a natural person, a representative of that party with authority to resolve the dispute or, in the case of a governmental entity that requires an agreement to be approved by an elected official or a legislative body, a representative with authority to recommend such agreement, must attend all mediation sessions in person, unless excused or permitted to attend by telephone as provided in (3).

(2) If any party is insured under a policy of insurance that provides or may provide coverage for a claim that is a subject of the action, a representative of the insurer with authority to settle or recommend settlement of the claim must attend all mediation sessions in person, unless excused or permitted to attend by telephone as provided in (3).

(3) The mediator may excuse a party, attorney, or representative from the requirement to attend a mediation session under (1) or (2) or permit attendance by telephone. The party, attorney, or representative who is excused or permitted to attend by telephone must promptly send a letter or an electronic communication to the mediator and to all parties confirming the excuse or permission.

(4) Each party may have counsel present at all mediation sessions that concern the party.

(Subd (a) amended and lettered effective January 1, 2007; adopted as untitled subd effective March 1, 1994.)

(b) Participant lists and mediation statements

(1) At least five court days before the first mediation session, each party must serve a list of its mediation participants on the mediator and all other parties. The list must include the names of all parties, attorneys, representatives of a party that is not a natural person, insurance representatives, and other persons who will attend the mediation with or on behalf of that party. A party must promptly serve a supplemental list if the party subsequently determines that other persons will attend the mediation with or on behalf of the party.

(2) The mediator may request that each party submit a short mediation statement providing information about the issues in dispute and possible resolutions of those issues and other information or documents that may appear helpful to resolve the dispute.

(Subd (b) adopted effective January 1, 2007.)

Rule 3.894 renumbered effective July 1, 2009; adopted as rule 1634 effective March 1, 1994; previously amended and renumbered as rule 3.874 effective January 1, 2007.

Ref.: Cal. Fms Pl. & Pr., Ch. 37, "Judicially Mandated Civil Action Mediation"; MB Prac. Guide: Cal. Pretrial Proc., §§24.43, 24.56[1][a]–[c], [2], [4][a].

Rule 3.895.   [Effective July 1, 2009] Filing of statement by mediator

Within 10 days after conclusion of the mediation, the mediator must file a statement on *Statement of Agreement or Nonagreement* (form ADR-100), advising the court whether the mediation ended in full agreement or nonagreement as to the entire case or as to particular parties in the case.

Rule 3.895 renumbered effective July 1, 2009; adopted as rule 1635 effective March 1, 1994; previously amended and renumbered as rule 3.875 effective January 1, 2007.

Ref.: Cal. Fms Pl. & Pr., Ch. 37, "Judicially Mandated Civil Action Mediation"; MB Prac. Guide: Cal. Pretrial Proc., §§24.43, 24.59.

Rule 3.896.   [Effective July 1, 2009]
Coordination with Trial Court Delay Reduction Act

(a) Effect of mediation on time standards

Submission of an action to mediation under the rules in this chapter does not affect time periods specified in the Trial Court Delay Reduction Act (Gov. Code, § 68600 et seq.), except as provided in this rule.

(Subd (a) amended effective January 1, 2007.)

(b) Exception to delay reduction time standards

On written stipulation of the parties filed with the court, the court may order an exception of up to 90 days to the delay reduction time standards to permit mediation of an action. The court must coordinate the timing of the exception period with its delay reduction calendar.

(Subd (b) amended effective January 1, 2007.)

(c) Time for completion of mediation

Mediation must be completed within 60 days of a reference to a mediator, but that period may be extended by the court for up to 30 days on a showing of good cause.

(Subd (c) amended and lettered effective January 1, 2007; adopted as part of subd (b) effective March 1, 1994.)

(d) Restraint in discovery

The parties should exercise restraint in discovery while a case is in mediation. In appropriate cases to accommodate that objective, the court may issue a protective order under Code of Civil Procedure section 2017(c) and related provisions.

(Subd (d) amended and lettered effective January 1, 2007; adopted as part of subd (b) effective March 1, 1994.)

Rule 3.896 renumbered effective July 1, 2009; adopted as rule 1637 effective March 1, 1994; previously amended and renumbered as rule 3.876 effective January 1, 2007.

Ref.: Cal. Fms Pl. & Pr., Ch. 37, "Judicially Mandated Civil Action Mediation"; MB Prac. Guide: Cal. Pretrial Proc., §§1.03, 24.43, 24.57, 24.58, 24.62.

Rule 3.897.   [Effective July 1, 2009] Statistical information

(a) Quarterly information reports

Each court must submit quarterly to the Judicial Council pertinent information on:

(1) The cost and time savings afforded by mediation;

(2) The effectiveness of mediation in resolving disputes;

(3) The number of cases referred to mediation;

(4) The time cases were in mediation; and

(5) Whether mediation ended in full agreement or nonagreement as to the entire case or as to particular parties in the case.

(Subd (a) amended effective January 1, 2007; previously amended effective February 9, 1999.)

(b) Submission of reports to the Judicial Council

The information required by this rule must be submitted to the Judicial Council either on the *Statement of Agreement or Nonagreement* (form ADR-100) and *ADR Information Form* (form ADR-101) or as an electronic database that includes, at a minimum, all of the informa-

tion required on these forms. The format of any electronic database used to submit this information must be approved by the Administrative Office of the Courts.

(Subd (b) amended and lettered effective January 1, 2007; adopted as part of subd (a) effective March 1, 1994.)

(c) Parties and mediators to supply information

Each court must require parties and mediators, as appropriate, to supply pertinent information for the reports required under this rule.

(Subd (c) amended and relettered effective January 1, 2007; adopted as subd (b) effective March 1, 1994.)

(d) Alternative reporting method

On request, a court may report cases in mediation under the rules in this chapter under the appropriate reporting methods for cases stayed for contractual arbitration.

(Subd (d) amended and relettered effective January 1, 2007; adopted as subd (c) effective March 1, 1994.)

Rule 3.897 renumbered effective July 1, 2009; adopted as rule 1638 effective March 1, 1994; previously amended effective February 9, 1999; previously amended and renumbered as rule 3.877 effective January 1, 2007.

Ref.: Cal. Fms Pl. & Pr., Ch. 37, "Judicially Mandated Civil Action Mediation."

Rule 3.898.   [Effective July 1, 2009]
Educational material

Each court must make available educational material, adopted by the Judicial Council, or from other sources, describing available ADR processes in the community.

Rule 3.898 renumbered effective July 1, 2009; adopted as rule 1639 effective March 1, 1994; previously amended and renumbered as rule 3.878 effective January 1, 2007.

Division 9
References

Chapter 1
Reference by Agreement of the Parties Under Code of Civil Procedure Section 638

Rule 3.900.   Purposes of reference

A court must not use the reference procedure under Code of Civil Procedure section 638 to appoint a person to conduct a mediation.

Rule 3.900 adopted effective January 1, 2007.

Advisory Committee Comment

Rule 3.900 is not intended to prohibit a court from appointing a referee to conduct a mandatory settlement conference or, following the conclusion of a reference, from appointing a person who previously served as a referee to conduct a mediation.

Ref.: Cal. Fms Pl. & Pr., Ch. 38, "Reference," Ch. 221, "Dissolution of Marriage: Procedure"; MB Prac. Guide: Cal. Pretrial Proc., §6.07[2][a].

Rule 3.901.   Application for order appointing referee

(a) Stipulation or motion for appointment

A written stipulation or motion for an order appointing a referee under Code of Civil Procedure section 638 must be presented to the judge to whom the case is assigned, or to the presiding judge or law and motion department if the case has not been assigned.

(b) Contents of application

The stipulation or motion for the appointment of a referee under section 638 must:

(1) Clearly state whether the scope of the requested reference includes all issues or is limited to specified issues;

(2) State whether the referee will be privately compensated;

(3) If authorization to use court facilities or court personnel is requested, describe the use requested and state the reasons that this would further the interests of justice;

(4) If the applicant is requesting or the parties have stipulated to the appointment of a particular referee, be accompanied by the proposed referee's certification as required by rule 3.904(a); and

(5) Be accompanied by a proposed order that includes the matters specified in rule 3.902.

Rule 3.901 adopted effective January 1, 2007.

Ref.: Cal. Fms Pl. & Pr., Ch. 38, "Reference," Ch. 221, "Dissolution of Marriage: Procedure," Ch. 372, "Motions and Orders"; MB Prac. Guide: Cal. Pretrial Proc., §§25.03, 25.05[1], [2][a]–[e].

Rule 3.902.   Order appointing referee

An order appointing a referee under Code of Civil Procedure section 638 must be filed with the clerk or entered in the minutes and must specify:

(1) The name, business address, and telephone number of the referee and, if he or she is a member of the State Bar, the referee's State Bar number;

(2) Whether the scope of the reference covers all issues or is limited to specified issues;

(3) Whether the referee will be privately compensated;

(4) Whether the use of court facilities and court personnel is authorized; and

(5) The name and telephone number of a person to contact to arrange for attendance at any proceeding that would be open to the public if held in a courthouse.

Rule 3.902 adopted effective January 1, 2007.

Ref.: Cal. Fms Pl. & Pr., Ch. 38, "Reference," Ch. 221, "Dissolution of Marriage: Procedure"; MB Prac. Guide: Cal. Pretrial Proc., §§25.03, 25.05[1], [2][a]–[e], 25.25.

Rule 3.903.   Selection and qualifications of referee

The court must appoint the referee or referees as provided in the Code of Civil Procedure section 640. If the proposed referee is a former judicial officer, he or she must be an active or an inactive member of the State Bar.

Rule 3.903 adopted effective January 1, 2007.

Ref.: Cal. Fms Pl. & Pr., Ch. 38, "Reference"; MB Prac. Guide: Cal. Pretrial Proc., §25.05[2][a].

Rule 3.904.   Certification and disclosure by referee

(a) Certification by referee

Before a referee begins to serve:

(1) The referee must certify in writing that he or she consents to serve as provided in the order of appointment and is aware of and will comply with applicable provisions of canon 6 of the Code of Judicial Ethics and with the California Rules of Court; and

(2) The referee's certification must be filed with the court.

(Subd (a) adopted effective January 1, 2007.)

(b) Disclosure by referee

In addition to any other disclosure required by law, no later than five days before the deadline for parties to file a motion for disqualification of the referee under Code of Civil Procedure section 170.6 or, if the referee is not aware of his or her appointment or of a matter subject to disclosure at that time, as soon as practicable thereafter, a referee must disclose to the parties:

(1) Any matter subject to disclosure under either canon 6D(5)(a) or 6D(5)(b) of the Code of Judicial Ethics; and

(2) Any significant personal or professional relationship the referee has or has had with a party, attorney, or law firm in the current case, including the number and nature of any other proceedings in the past 24 months in which the referee has been privately compensated by a party, attorney, law firm, or insurance company in the current case for any services. The disclosure must include privately compensated service as an attorney, expert witness, or consultant or as a judge, referee, arbitrator, mediator, settlement facilitator, or other alternative dispute resolution neutral.

(Subd (b) adopted effective January 1, 2007.)

Rule 3.904 adopted effective January 1, 2007.

Ref.: Cal. Fms Pl. & Pr., Ch. 38, "Reference"; MB Prac. Guide: Cal. Pretrial Proc., §§25.03, 25.05[1], [4], 25.09[1][a], [b], [2], 25.26.

Rule 3.905.   Objections to the appointment

A stipulation or an agreement for an order appointing a referee does not constitute a waiver of grounds for objection to the appointment of a particular person as referee under Code of Civil Procedure section 641. Any objection to the appointment of a person as a referee must be made with reasonable diligence and in writing. The objection must be served on all parties and the referee and filed with the court. The objection must be heard by the judge to whom the case is assigned or by the presiding judge or law and motion judge if the case has not been assigned.

Rule 3.905 adopted effective January 1, 2007.

Ref.: Cal. Fms Pl. & Pr., Ch. 38, "Reference," Ch. 221, "Dissolution of Marriage: Procedure"; MB Prac. Guide: Cal. Pretrial Proc., §§25.04[1][a], 25.14, 25.15[1], [2][d], 25.17[1][a], [b], [3][a].

Rule 3.906.   Motion to withdraw stipulation

(a) Good cause requirement

A motion to withdraw a stipulation for the appointment of a referee must be supported by a declaration of facts establishing good cause for permitting the party to withdraw the stipulation. The following do not constitute good cause for withdrawing a stipulation:

(1) A declaration that a ruling is based on an error of fact or law.

(2) The issuance of an order for an appropriate hearing site under rule 3.910.

(Subd (a) adopted effective January 1, 2007.)

(b) Service, filing and hearing of motion

Notice of the motion must be served on all parties and the referee and filed with the court. The motion must be heard by the judge to whom the case is assigned or by the presiding judge or law and motion judge. If the motion is granted, the case must be transferred to the trial court docket.

(Subd (b) adopted effective January 1, 2007.)
Rule 3.906 adopted effective January 1, 2007.

Ref.: Cal. Fms Pl. & Pr., Ch. 38, "Reference," Ch. 221, "Dissolution of Marriage: Procedure"; MB Prac. Guide: Cal. Pretrial Proc., §§25.08[1][c], 25.14, 25.15[1], [2][b], 25.16[1], 25.28.

Rule 3.907.   Motion or application to seal records

A motion or application to seal records in a case pending before a referee must be served on all parties, the referee, and any person or organization that has made their intention to attend the hearing known and be filed with the court. The motion or application must be heard by the judge to whom the case is assigned or by the presiding judge or law and motion judge. Rules 2.550 and 2.551 apply to the motion or application to seal the records.

Rule 3.907 adopted effective January 1, 2007.

Ref.: Cal. Fms Pl. & Pr., Ch. 38, "Reference"; MB Prac. Guide: Cal. Pretrial Proc., §§25.03, 25.05[3].

Rule 3.908.   Motion for leave to file complaint for intervention

A motion for leave to file a complaint for intervention in a case pending before a referee must be served on all parties and the referee and filed with the court. The motion must be heard by the judge to whom the case is assigned or by the presiding judge or law and motion judge if the case has not been assigned. If intervention is allowed, the case must be returned to the trial court docket unless all parties stipulate in the manner prescribed in rule 3.901 to proceed before the referee.

Rule 3.908 adopted effective January 1, 2007.

Ref.: Cal. Fms Pl. & Pr., Ch. 38, "Reference"; MB Prac. Guide: Cal. Pretrial Proc., §§25.15[2][a], 25.16[2], 31.07[2].

Rule 3.909.   Proceedings before privately compensated referees

(a) Use of court facilities and court personnel

A party who has elected to use the services of a privately compensated referee is deemed to have elected to proceed outside the courthouse. Court facilities and court personnel may not be used in proceedings pending before a privately compensated referee, except on a finding by the presiding judge that their use would further the interests of justice.

(Subd (a) adopted effective January 1, 2007.)

(b) Posting of notice in courthouse

For all matters pending before privately compensated referees, the clerk must post a notice in the courthouse identifying the case name and number and the name and telephone number of a person to contact to arrange for attendance at any proceeding that would be open to the public if held in a courthouse.

(Subd (b) adopted effective January 1, 2007.)
Rule 3.909 adopted effective January 1, 2007.

Ref.: Cal. Fms Pl. & Pr., Ch. 38, "Reference," Ch. 221, "Dissolution of Marriage: Procedure"; MB Prac. Guide: Cal. Pretrial Proc., §25.08[1][a], [b].

Rule 3.910.   Request and order for appropriate and accessible hearing site

The court may, on the request of any person or on the court's own motion, order that a case pending before a referee must be heard at a site easily accessible to the public and appropriate for seating those who have notified the court of their intention to attend hearings. A request for hearings at an accessible and appropriate site must state the reasons for the request, be served on all parties and the referee, and be filed with the court. The order may require that notice of trial or of other proceedings be given to the requesting person directly.

Rule 3.910 adopted effective January 1, 2007.

Ref.: Cal. Fms Pl. & Pr., Ch. 38, "Reference"; MB Prac. Guide: Cal. Pretrial Proc., §25.08[1][c].

Chapter 2
Court-Ordered Reference Under Code of Civil Procedure Section 639

Rule 3.920.   Purposes and conditions for appointment of referee

(a) Purposes prescribed by statute

A court may order the appointment of a referee under Code of Civil Procedure section 639 only for the purposes specified in that section.

(Subd (a) adopted effective January 1, 2007.)

(b) No references for mediation

A court must not use the reference procedure under Code of Civil Procedure section 639 to appoint a person to conduct a mediation.

(Subd (b) adopted effective January 1, 2007.)

(c) Conditions for appointment of discovery referee

A discovery referee must not be appointed under Code of Civil Procedure section 639(a)(5) unless the exceptional circumstances of the particular case require the appointment.

(Subd (c) adopted effective January 1, 2007.)

Rule 3.920 adopted effective January 1, 2007.

Advisory Committee Comment

Rule 3.920(b) is not intended to prohibit a court from appointing a referee to conduct a mandatory settlement conference in a complex case or, following the conclusion of a reference, from appointing a person who previously served as a referee to conduct a mediation.

Ref.: Cal. Fms Pl. & Pr., Ch. 38, "Reference," Ch. 221, "Dissolution of Marriage: Procedure"; MB Prac. Guide: Cal. Pretrial Proc., §§6.07[2][a], 25.04[2], 25.06[2].

Rule 3.921. Motion for appointment of a referee

(a) Filing and contents

A motion by a party for the appointment of a referee under Code of Civil Procedure section 639 must be served and filed. The motion must specify the matter or matters to be included in the requested reference. If the applicant is requesting the appointment of a particular referee, the motion must be accompanied by the proposed referee's certification as required by rule 3.924(a).

(Subd (a) adopted effective January 1, 2007.)

(b) Hearing

The motion must be heard by the judge to whom the case is assigned, or by the presiding judge or law and motion judge if the case has not been assigned.

(Subd (b) adopted effective January 1, 2007.)

Rule 3.921 adopted effective January 1, 2007.

Ref.: Cal. Fms Pl. & Pr., Ch. 38, "Reference," Ch. 221, "Dissolution of Marriage: Procedure"; MB Prac. Guide: Cal. Pretrial Proc., §§25.03, 25.06[3], [4][e].

Rule 3.922. Form and contents of order appointing referee

(a) Written order required

An order appointing a referee under Code of Civil Procedure section 639, on the motion of a party or on the court's own motion, must be in writing and must address the matters set forth in (b) through (h).

(Subd (a) adopted effective January 1, 2007.)

(b) Referee information

The order must state the name, business address, and telephone number of the referee and, if he or she is a member of the State Bar, the referee's State Bar number.

(Subd (b) adopted effective January 1, 2007.)

(c) Basis for reference

The order must specify whether the referee is appointed under paragraph (1), (2), (3), (4), or (5) of subdivision (a) of section 639 and:

(1) If the referee is appointed under section 639(a)(1)–(a)(4), the order must state the reason the referee is being appointed.

(2) If the referee is appointed under section 639(a)(5) to hear and determine discovery motions and disputes relevant to discovery, the order must state the exceptional circumstances of the particular case that require the reference.

(Subd (c) adopted effective January 1, 2007.)

(d) Subject matter and scope of reference

(1) The order must specify the subject matter or matters included in the reference.

(2) If the referee is appointed under section 639(a)(5) to hear and determine discovery motions and disputes relevant to discovery, the order must state whether the discovery referee is appointed for all purposes or only for limited purposes.

(Subd (d) adopted effective January 1, 2007.)

(e) Authority of discovery referee

If the referee is appointed under section 639(a)(5) to hear and determine discovery motions and disputes relevant to discovery, the order must state that the referee is authorized to set the date, time, and place for all hearings determined by the referee to be necessary; direct the issuance of subpoenas; preside over hearings; take evidence; and rule on objections, motions, and other requests made during the course of the hearing.

(Subd (e) adopted effective January 1, 2007.)

(f) Referee fees; apportionment

If the referee will be appointed at a cost to the parties, the order must:

(1) Specify the maximum hourly rate the referee may charge and, if any party so requests, the maximum number of hours for which the referee may charge;

(2) Include a finding that either:

(A) No party has established an economic inability to pay a pro rata share of the referee's fee; or

(B) One or more parties has established an economic inability to pay a pro rata share of the referee's fees and another party has agreed voluntarily to pay that additional share of the referee's fees.

(3) When the issue of economic hardship is raised before the referee begins performing services, the court must determine a fair and reasonable apportionment of reference costs. The court may modify its apportionment order and may consider a recommendation by the referee as a factor in determining any modification.

(Subd (f) adopted effective January 1, 2007.)

(g) Use of court facilities and court personnel

The order must specify the extent, if any, to which court facilities and court personnel may be used in connection with the reference.

(Subd (g) adopted effective January 1, 2007.)

(h) Contact to arrange attendance at proceedings before referee

The order must state the name and telephone number of a person to contact to arrange for attendance at any proceeding before the referee.

(Subd (h) adopted effective January 1, 2007.)

Rule 3.922 adopted effective January 1, 2007.

Ref.: Cal. Fms Pl. & Pr., Ch. 38, "Reference," Ch. 221, "Dissolution of Marriage: Procedure"; MB Prac. Guide: Cal. Pretrial Proc., §§25.03, 25.06[4][a]–[d], [f]–[k], 25.10[3], 25.25.

Rule 3.923.   Selection and qualification of referee

The court must appoint the referee or referees as provided in Code of Civil Procedure section 640. If the referee is a former California judicial officer, he or she must be an active or inactive member of the State Bar.

Rule 3.923 adopted effective January 1, 2007.

Ref.: Cal. Fms Pl. & Pr., Ch. 38, "Reference," Ch. 221, "Dissolution of Marriage: Procedure"; MB Prac. Guide: Cal. Pretrial Proc., §25.06[4][d].

Rule 3.924.   Certification and disclosure by referee

(a) Certification by referee

Before a referee begins to serve:

(1) The referee must certify in writing that he or she consents to serve as provided in the order of appointment and is aware of and will comply with applicable provisions of canon 6 of the Code of Judicial Ethics and with the California Rules of Court; and

(2) The referee's certification must be filed with the court.

(Subd (a) adopted effective January 1, 2007.)

(b) Disclosure by referee

In addition to any other disclosure required by law, no later than five days before the deadline for parties to file a motion for disqualification of the referee under Code of Civil Procedure section 170.6 or, if the referee is not aware of his or her appointment or of a matter subject to disclosure at that time, as soon as practicable thereafter, a referee must disclose to the parties:

(1) Any matter subject to disclosure under subdivisions (D)(5)(a) and (D)(5)(b) of canon 6 of the Code of Judicial Ethics; and

(2) Any significant personal or professional relationship the referee has or has had with a party, attorney, or law firm in the current case, including the number and nature of any other proceedings in the past 24 months in which the referee has been privately compensated by a party, attorney, law firm, or insurance company in the current case for any services. The disclosure must include privately compensated service as an attorney, expert witness, or consultant or as a judge, referee, arbitrator, mediator, settlement facilitator, or other alternative dispute resolution neutral.

(Subd (b) amended effective January 1, 2008; adopted effective January 1, 2007.)

Rule 3.924 amended effective January 1, 2008; adopted effective January 1, 2007.

Ref.: Cal. Fms Pl. & Pr., Ch. 38, "Reference," Ch. 221, "Dissolution of Marriage: Procedure"; MB Prac. Guide: Cal. Pretrial Proc., §§25.03, 25.06[5], 25.09[1][a], [b], [2], 25.26.

Rule 3.925.   Objection to reference

The filing of a motion for an order appointing a referee does not constitute a waiver of grounds for objection to the appointment of a particular person as referee under Code of Civil Procedure section 641, or objection to the rate or apportionment of compensation of the referee. Any objection to the appointment of a particular person as a referee must be made with reasonable diligence and in writing. The objection must be heard by the judge to whom the case is assigned, or by the presiding judge or the law and motion judge.

Rule 3.925 adopted effective January 1, 2007.

Ref.: Cal. Fms Pl. & Pr., Ch. 38, "Reference," Ch. 221, "Dissolution of Marriage: Procedure"; MB Prac. Guide: Cal. Pretrial Proc., §§25.14, 25.15[1], [2][d], 25.17[1][a], [c], [3][a].

Rule 3.926.   Use of court facilities

A reference ordered under Code of Civil Procedure section 639 entitles the parties to the use of court facilities and court personnel to the extent provided in the order of reference. The proceedings may be held in a private facility, but, if so, the private facility must be open to the public upon request of any person.

Rule 3.926 adopted effective January 1, 2007.

Ref.: Cal. Fms Pl. & Pr., Ch. 38, "Reference," Ch. 221, "Dissolution of Marriage: Procedure"; MB Prac. Guide: Cal. Pretrial Proc., §25.08[2][a], [b].

Rule 3.927.   Circumstances required for appointment of discovery referee

A discovery referee must not be appointed under Code of Civil Procedure section 639(a)(5) unless the exceptional circumstances of the particular case require the appointment.

Rule 3.927 adopted effective January 1, 2007.

Division 10
Discovery

Chap. 1.   Format of Discovery. Rule 3.1000.
Chap. 2.   Conduct of Discovery. Rule 3.1010.

Chapter 1
Format of Discovery

Rule 3.1000.   Format of supplemental and further discovery

(a) Supplemental interrogatories and responses, etc.

In each set of supplemental interrogatories, supplemental responses to interrogatories, amended answers to interrogatories, and further responses to interrogatories, inspection demands, and admission requests, the following must appear in the first paragraph immediately below the title of the case:

(1) The identity of the propounding, demanding, or requesting party;

(2) The identity of the responding party;

(3) The set number being propounded or responded to; and

(4) The nature of the paper.

(Subd (a) amended effective January 1, 2007; previously amended effective January 1, 1986, and July 1, 1987.)

(b) Identification of responses

Each supplemental or further response and each amended answer must be identified by the same number or letter and be in the same sequence as the corresponding interrogatory, inspection demand, or admission request, but the text of the interrogatory, demand, or request need not be repeated.

(Subd (b) amended effective January 1, 2007; previously amended effective January 1, 1986, and July 1, 1987.)

Rule 3.1000 amended and renumbered effective January 1, 2007; adopted as rule 331 effective January 1, 1984; previously amended effective January 1, 1986, and January 1, 1987.

Ref.: Cal. Fms Pl. & Pr., Ch. 85, "Automobiles: Discovery," Ch. 108, "Captions and Introductions," Ch. 190, "Discovery: Scope, Regulation, and Timing," Ch. 193, "Discovery: Depositions," Ch. 194, "Discovery: Interrogatories," Ch. 195, "Discovery: Inspection of Tangible Evidence," Ch. 196, "Discovery: Requests for Admissions," Ch. 197, "Discovery: Physical and Mental Examinations," Ch. 198, "Discovery: Exchange of Expert Witness Information," Ch. 333, "Landlord and Tenant: Eviction Actions."

Chapter 2
Conduct of Discovery

Rule 3.1010. Oral depositions by telephone, videoconference, or other remote electronic means

(a) Taking depositions

Any party may take an oral deposition by telephone, videoconference, or other remote electronic means, provided:

(1) Notice is served with the notice of deposition or the subpoena;

(2) That party makes all arrangements for any other party to participate in the deposition in an equivalent manner. However, each party so appearing must pay all expenses incurred by it or properly allocated to it;

(3) Any party may be personally present at the deposition without giving prior notice.

(b) Appearing and participating in depositions

Any party may appear and participate in an oral deposition by telephone, videoconference, or other remote electronic means, provided:

(1) Written notice of such appearance is served by personal delivery or fax at least three court days before the deposition;

(2) The party so appearing makes all arrangements and pays all expenses incurred for the appearance.

(Subd (b) amended effective January 1, 2007.)

(c) Party deponent's appearance

A party deponent must appear at his or her deposition in person and be in the presence of the deposition officer.

(d) Nonparty deponent's appearance

A nonparty deponent may appear at his or her deposition by telephone, videoconference, or other remote electronic means with court approval upon a finding of good cause and no prejudice to any party. The deponent must be sworn in the presence of the deposition officer or by any other means stipulated to by the parties or ordered by the court. Any party may be personally present at the deposition.

(e) Court orders

On motion by any person, the court in a specific action may make such other orders as it deems appropriate.

(Subd (e) amended effective January 1, 2007.)

Rule 3.1010 amended and renumbered effective January 1, 2007; adopted as rule 333 effective January 1, 2003.

Chapter 3
Discovery Motions
[Repealed]

Chapter 3 repealed effective January 1, 2009.

Rule 3.1020. Format of discovery motions [Renumbered]

Rule 3.1020 renumbered to rule 3.1345 effective January 1, 2009; adopted as rule 335 effective January 1, 1984; previously amended effective July 1, 1987, January 1, 1992, January 1, 1997, and July 1, 2001; previously amended and renumbered effective January 1, 2007.

Rule 3.1025. Service of motion papers on nonparty deponent [Renumbered]

Rule 3.1025 renumbered to rule 3.1346 effective January 1, 2009; adopted as rule 337 effective January 1, 1984; previously amended effective July 1, 1987; previously amended and renumbered effective January 1, 2007.

Rule 3.1030. Sanctions for failure to provide discovery [Renumbered]

Rule 3.1030 renumbered to rule 3.1348 effective January 1, 2009; adopted as rule 341 effective July 1, 2001; previously renumbered effective January 1, 2007.

Division 11
Law and Motion

Chap. 1. General Provisions. Rules 3.1100–3.1109.
Chap. 2. Format of Motion Papers. Rules 3.1110–3.1116.
Chap. 3. Provisional and Injunctive Relief. Rules 3.1130–3.1184.
Chap. 4. Ex Parte Applications. Rules 3.1200–3.1207.
Chap. 5. Noticed Motions. Rules 3.1300–3.1312.
Chap. 6. Particular Motions. Rules 3.1320–3.1362.
Chap. 7. Other Civil Petitions. Rule 3.1370.

Chapter 1
General Provisions

Rule 3.1100. Application
Rule 3.1103. Definitions and construction
Rule 3.1109. Notice of determination of submitted matters

Rule 3.1100. Application

The rules in this division apply to proceedings in civil law and motion, as defined in rule 3.1103, and to discovery proceedings in family law and probate.

Rule 3.1100 amended and renumbered effective January 1, 2007; adopted as rule 301 effective January 1, 1984; previously amended effective July 1, 1984, July 1, 1997, and January 1, 2002.

Ref.: Cal. Fms Pl. & Pr., Ch. 3, "Abatement of Actions," Ch. 4, "Abortion and Birth Control Methods," Ch. 12E, "Adoptions: Attack on Decree," Ch. 21, "Amended and Supplemental Pleadings," Ch. 38, "Reference," Ch. 56, "Architects," Ch. 76, "Attorney Professional Liability," Ch. 85, "Automobiles: Discovery," Ch. 108, "Captions and Introductions," Ch. 123, "Complaints and Cross Complaints," Ch. 174, "Costs and Attorney's Fees," Ch. 206, "Demurrers and Motions for Judgment on the Pleadings," Ch. 209, "Dentists," Ch. 221, "Dissolution of Marriage: Procedure," Ch. 254, "Executions and Enforcement of Judgments," Ch. 258, "Executions and Enforcement of Judgments," Ch. 276, "Garnishment," Ch. 300, "Indemnity and Contribution," Ch. 317, "Judges," Ch. 321, "Judicial Notice," Ch. 324, "Jurisdiction: Subject Matter Jurisdiction," Ch. 358, "Mandate and Prohibition," Ch. 371, "Motions After Trial," Ch. 372, "Motions and Orders," Ch. 374, "Motions to Reconsider and Renewed Motions," Ch. 375, "Motions to Strike: Pleadings," Ch. 376, "Motions to Strike: Anti-SLAPP," Ch. 417, "Points and Authorities," Ch. 425, "Pretrial Proceedings," Ch. 444, "Probate: Will Contests," Ch. 454, "Probate: Claims Against the Estate," Ch. 473C, "Prehearing Procedures in Agency Adjudications," Ch. 474C, "Procedures in Reviewing Agency Decisions," Ch. 486, "Receivers," Ch. 489, "Relief From Judgments and Orders," Ch. 492, "Review (Certiorari), Writ of," Ch. 518, "Service of Summons and Papers," Ch. 524, "Shortening and Extension of Time," Ch. 551, "Trial," Ch. 573, "Vexatious Litigants"; MB Prac. Guide: Cal. Debt Collection & Enforcement of Judgments, §§8.61, 15.12, 15.15, 20.36; MB Prac. Guide: Cal. Pretrial Proc., §§8.41[1], [2], 11.03, 11.16[4], 11.17[2], 11.59, 26.39, 26.43[5][b], 26.60, 26.63[3], 26.82, 36.67[4][a], [b], 36.72[2][c]; MB Prac. Guide: Cal. Trial & Post-Trial Civ. Proc., §§29.15[2], [5], 29.32[1][b], [c].

Rule 3.1103.   Definitions and construction

(a) Law and motion defined

"Law and motion" includes any proceedings:

(1) On application before trial for an order, except for causes arising under the Welfare and Institutions Code, the Probate Code, the Family Code, or Code of Civil Procedure sections 527.6, 527.7, and 527.8; or

(2) On application for an order regarding the enforcement of judgment, attachment of property, appointment of a receiver, obtaining or setting aside a judgment by default, writs of review, mandate and prohibition, a petition to compel arbitration, and enforcement of an award by arbitration.

(Subd (a) amended effective July 1, 1997.)

(b) Application of rules on extending or shortening time

Rules 1.10(c) and 2.20 on extending or shortening time apply to proceedings under this division.

(Subd (b) amended effective January 1, 2007.)

(c) Application to demurrers

Unless the context or subject matter otherwise requires, the rules in this division apply to demurrers.

(Subd (c) amended effective January 1, 2007.)

Rule 3.1103 amended and renumbered effective January 1, 2007; adopted as rule 303 effective January 1, 1984; previously amended effective July 1, 1984.

Ref.: Cal. Fms Pl. & Pr., Ch. 3, "Abatement of Actions," Ch. 4, "Abortion and Birth Control Methods," Ch. 12E, "Adoptions: Attack on Decree," Ch. 53, "Appeal: Remittitur and Costs on Appeal," Ch. 56, "Architects," Ch. 61, "Associations and Clubs," Ch. 62, "Attachment," Ch. 108, "Captions and Introductions,"

Ch. 124, "Condominiums and Other Common Interest Developments," Ch. 125, "Consolidation, Severance, and Coordination of Actions," Ch. 135, "Contempt," Ch. 136, "Continuances," Ch. 161, "Corporations: Alter Ego Liability," Ch. 165, "Corporations: Corporate Records and Reports," Ch. 166, "Corporations: Shareholders' Meetings and Voting," Ch. 168, "Corporations: Derivative Actions," Ch. 169, "Corporations: Reorganizations," Ch. 170, "Corporations: Dissolution and Winding Up," Ch. 174, "Costs and Attorney's Fees," Ch. 181, "Death and Survival Actions," Ch. 199, "Discovery: Preservation of Evidence," Ch. 200, "Discovery: Review of Discovery Orders," Ch. 206, "Demurrers and Motions for Judgment on the Pleadings," Ch. 221, "Dissolution of Marriage: Procedure," Ch. 254, "Executions and Enforcement of Judgments," Ch. 258, "Executions and Enforcement of Judgments," Ch. 276, "Garnishment," Ch. 290D, "Guardianship and Conservatorship: Actions Against Guardians, Conservators, and Sureties," Ch. 300, "Indemnity and Contribution," Ch. 302, "Initiative, Referendum, and Recall," Ch. 317, "Judges," Ch. 321, "Judicial Notice," Ch. 323, "Jurisdiction: Personal Jurisdiction, Inconvenient Forum, and Appearances," Ch. 324, "Jurisdiction: Subject Matter Jurisdiction," Ch. 346, "Limited Liability Companies," Ch. 357, "Malicious Prosecution and Abuse of Process," Ch. 358, "Mandate and Prohibition," Ch. 361, "Mechanics' Liens," Ch. 371, "Motions After Trial," Ch. 372, "Motions and Orders," Ch. 375, "Motions to Strike: Pleadings," Ch. 376, "Motions to Strike: Anti-SLAPP," Ch. 386, "Newspapers," Ch. 404, "Partnerships: Actions Between Limited Partners and Partnerships," Ch. 417, "Points and Authorities," Ch. 444, "Probate: Will Contests," Ch. 454, "Probate: Claims Against the Estate," Ch. 460, "Products Liability," Ch. 462, "Public Accountants," Ch. 464, "Public Entities and Officers: California Tort Claims Act," Ch. 471B, "Licensing by Public Agencies," Ch. 474C, "Procedures in Reviewing Agency Decisions," Ch. 486, "Receivers," Ch. 489, "Relief From Judgments and Orders," Ch. 491, "Res Judicata," Ch. 492, "Review (Certiorari), Writ of," Ch. 518, "Service of Summons and Papers," Ch. 524, "Shortening and Extension of Time," Ch. 529, "Statement of Decision," Ch. 551, "Trial," Ch. 577, "Workers' Compensation"; MB Prac. Guide: Cal. Debt Collection & Enforcement of Judgments, §§7.21[3], 8.61, 15.08, 15.12, 15.13, 15.15, 20.33, 20.36, 23.34; MB Prac. Guide: Cal. Pretrial Proc., §§1.08, 1.10, 9.11, 9.30, 11.03, 11.16[4], 11.17[2], 12.10, 13.09, 26.01, 26.43[5][b], 36.67[4][a], [b], 36.72[2][c]; MB Prac. Guide: Cal. Trial & Post-Trial Civ. Proc., §§29.15[2], [5], 29.32[1][c].

Rule 3.1109.   Notice of determination of submitted matters

(a) Notice by clerk

When the court rules on a motion or makes an order or renders a judgment in a matter it has taken under submission, the clerk must immediately notify the parties of the ruling, order, or judgment. The notification, which must specifically identify the matter ruled on, may be given by mailing the parties a copy of the ruling, order, or judgment, and it constitutes service of notice only if the clerk is required to give notice under Code of Civil Procedure section 664.5.

(Subd (a) amended and lettered effective January 1, 2007; adopted as part of untitled subd effective January 1, 1984.)

(b) Notice in a case involving more than two parties

In a case involving more than two parties, a clerk's notification made under this rule, or any notice of a ruling or order served by a party, must name the moving party, and the party against whom relief was requested, and specifically identify the particular motion or other matter ruled upon.

(Subd (b) amended and lettered effective January 1, 2007; adopted as part of untitled subd effective January 1, 1984.)

(c) Time not extended by failure of clerk to give notice

The failure of the clerk to give the notice required by this rule does not extend the time provided by law for performing any act except as provided in rules 8.104(a) or 8.824(a).

(Subd (c) adopted effective January 1, 2007.)

Rule 3.1109 amended and renumbered effective January 1, 2007; adopted as rule 309 effective January 1, 1984.

Ref.: Cal. Fms Pl. & Pr., Ch. 206, "Demurrers and Motions for Judgment on the Pleadings," Ch. 372, "Motions and Orders," Ch. 551, "Trial," Ch. 555, "Trust Deeds and Real Property Mortgages"; MB Prac. Guide: Cal. Pretrial Proc., §§11.29[4], 11.59, 26.60, 26.62[3], 26.79.

Chapter 2
Format of Motion Papers

Rule 3.1110. General format
Rule 3.1112. Motions—and other pleadings
Rule 3.1113. Memorandum
Rule 3.1114. Applications, motions, and petitions not requiring a memorandum
Rule 3.1115. Declarations
Rule 3.1116. Deposition testimony as an exhibit

Rule 3.1110.   General format

(a) Notice of motion

A notice of motion must state in the opening paragraph the nature of the order being sought and the grounds for issuance of the order.

(Subd (a) amended effective January 1, 2007.)

(b) Date of hearing and other information

The first page of each paper must specify immediately below the number of the case:

(1) The date, time, and location, if ascertainable, of any scheduled hearing and the name of the hearing judge, if ascertainable;

(2) The nature or title of any attached document other than an exhibit;

(3) The date of filing of the action; and

(4) The trial date, if set.

(Subd (b) amended effective January 1, 2007; previously amended effective July 1, 1997.)

(c) Pagination of documents

Documents bound together must be consecutively paginated.

(Subd (c) amended and lettered effective January 1, 2007; adopted as part of subd (b) effective January 1, 1984.)

(d) Reference to previously filed papers

Any paper previously filed must be referred to by date of execution and title.

(Subd (d) amended and relettered effective January 1, 2007; adopted as subd (c) effective January 1, 1984.)

(e) Binding

All pages of each document and exhibit must be attached together at the top by a method that permits pages to be easily turned and the entire content of each page to be read.

(Subd (e) amended and relettered effective January 1, 2007; adopted as subd (d) effective July 1, 1997.)

(f) Format of exhibits

Each exhibit must be separated by a hard 8½ x 11 sheet with hard paper or plastic tabs extending below the bottom of the page, bearing the exhibit designation. An index to exhibits must be provided. Pages from a single deposition and associated exhibits must be designated as a single exhibit.

(Subd (f) amended and relettered effective January 1, 2007; adopted as subd (e) effective July 1, 1997.)

(g) Translation of exhibits

Exhibits written in a foreign language must be accompanied by an English translation, certified under oath by a qualified interpreter.

(Subd (g) amended and lettered effective January 1, 2007; adopted as part of subd (e) effective July 1, 1997.)

Rule 3.1110 amended and renumbered effective January 1, 2007; adopted as rule 311 effective January 1, 1984; previously amended effective July 1, 1997.

Ref.: Cal. Fms Pl. & Pr., Ch. 3, "Abatement of Actions," Ch. 12E, "Adoptions: Attack on Decree," Ch. 108, "Captions and Introductions," Ch. 125, "Consolidation, Severance, and Coordination of Actions," Ch. 165, "Corporations: Corporate Records and Reports," Ch. 166, "Corporations: Shareholders' Meetings and Voting," Ch. 168, "Corporations: Derivative Actions," Ch. 169, "Corporations: Reorganizations," Ch. 170, "Corporations: Dissolution and Winding Up," Ch. 206, "Demurrers and Motions for Judgment on the Pleadings," Ch. 212, "Dismissal," Ch. 300, "Indemnity and Contribution," Ch. 346, "Limited Liability Companies," Ch. 372, "Motions and Orders," Ch. 406, "Partnerships: Dissolution," Ch. 417, "Points and Authorities," Ch. 460, "Products Liability," Ch. 471B, "Licensing by Public Agencies," Ch. 474, "Availability of Judicial Review of Agency Decisions," Ch. 474C, "Procedures in Reviewing Agency Decisions," Ch. 486, "Receivers," Ch. 492, "Review (Certiorari), Writ of," Ch. 537, "Summary Judgment"; MB Prac. Guide: Cal. Pretrial Proc., §§11.03, 11.15[3], 26.01, 26.43[1], [5][b], [e], 26.65, 26.66, 36.67[4][a]; MB Prac. Guide: Cal. Trial & Post-Trial Civ. Proc., §§14.03, 14.11[1], 29.15[1], [5], 29.32[1][c].

Rule 3.1112.   Motions—and other pleadings

(a) Motions required papers

Unless otherwise provided by the rules in this division, the papers filed in support of a motion must consist of at least the following:

(1) A notice of hearing on the motion;

(2) The motion itself; and

(3) A memorandum in support of the motion or demurrer.

(Subd (a) amended effective January 1, 2007.)

(b) Other papers

Other papers may be filed in support of a motion, including declarations, exhibits, appendices, and other documents or pleadings.

(Subd (b) adopted effective January 1, 2007.)

(c) Form of motion papers

The papers filed under (a) and (b) may either be filed as separate documents or combined in one or more documents if the party filing a combined pleading specifies these items separately in the caption of the combined pleading.

(Subd (c) amended and lettered effective January 1, 2007 adopted as part of subd (a) effective July 1, 1997.)

(d) Motion—required elements

A motion must:

(1) Identify the party or parties bringing the motion;

(2) Name the parties to whom it is addressed;

(3) Briefly state the basis for the motion and the relief sought; and

(4) If a pleading is challenged, state the specific portion challenged.

(Subd (d) amended and relettered effective January 1, 2007; adopted as subd (b) effective July 1, 1997.)

(e) Additional requirements for motions

In addition to the requirements of this rule, a motion [1] **relating** to the subjects specified in chapter 6 of this division must comply with any additional requirements in that chapter.

(Subd (e) amended effective July 1, 2008; previously amended effective January 1, 2007.)

Rule 3.1112(e).   2008 Deletes. [1] elating

(f) Motion in limine

Notwithstanding (a), a motion in limine filed before or during trial need not be accompanied by a notice of hearing. The timing and place of the filing and service of the motion are at the discretion of the trial judge.

(Subd (f) adopted effective January 1, 2007.)

Rule 3.1112 amended effective July 1, 2008; adopted as rule 312 effective July 1, 1997; previously amended and renumbered effective January 1, 2007.

Ref.: Cal. Fms Pl. & Pr., Ch. 125, "Consolidation, Severance, and Coordination of Actions," Ch. 206, "Demurrers and Motions for Judgment on the Pleadings," Ch. 264, "Fax Filing and Service of Papers," Ch. 300, "Indemnity and Contribution," Ch. 321, "Judicial Notice," Ch. 345A, "Limited Civil Cases," Ch. 357, "Malicious Prosecution and Abuse of Process," Ch. 372, "Motions and Orders," Ch. 375, "Motions to Strike: Pleadings," Ch. 417, "Points and Authorities," Ch. 486, "Receivers"; MB Prac. Guide: Cal. Pretrial Proc., §§11.03, 11.13[4], 11.15[1], [3], 11.16[1], 11.20, 26.01, 26.03, 26.05[3], 26.39, 26.41, 26.42, 26.43[2], [5][b], 29.13[1], 36.72[2][c]; MB Prac. Guide: Cal. Trial & Post-Trial Civ. Proc., §§4.20[1], [2], 4.24[1], 4.25[2], 4.26[1][a], [2][a], 14.29, 20.03, 29.15[1], [2].

Rule 3.1113.   Memorandum

(a) Memorandum in support of motion

A party filing a motion, except for a motion listed in rule 3.1114, must serve and file a supporting memorandum. The court may construe the absence of a memorandum as an admission that the motion or special demurrer is not meritorious and cause for its denial and, in the case of a demurrer, as a waiver of all grounds not supported.

(Subd (a) amended effective January 1, 2007; previously amended effective January 1, 2004.)

(b) Contents of memorandum

The memorandum must contain a statement of facts, a concise statement of the law, evidence and arguments relied on, and a discussion of the statutes, cases, and textbooks cited in support of the position advanced.

(Subd (b) amended effective January 1, 2004.)

(c) Case citation format

A case citation must include the official report volume and page number and year of decision. The court must not require any other form of citation.

(Subd (c) amended effective January 1, 2007; previously amended effective July 1, 1984, January 1, 1992, and January 1, 2004.)

(d) Length of memorandum

Except in a summary judgment or summary adjudication motion, no opening or responding memorandum may exceed 15 pages. In a summary judgment or summary adjudication motion, no opening or responding memorandum may exceed 20 pages. No reply or closing memorandum may exceed 10 pages. The page limit does not include exhibits, declarations, attachments, the table of contents, the table of authorities, or the proof of service.

(Subd (d) amended effective January 1, 2004; adopted as part of a longer subd (d); previously amended effective July 1, 1984 and January 1, 1992.)

(e) Application to file longer memorandum

A party may apply to the court ex parte but with written notice of the application to the other parties, at least 24 hours before the memorandum is due, for permission to file a longer memorandum. The application must state reasons why the argument cannot be made within the stated limit.

(Subd (e) amended and relettered effective January 1, 2004; adopted as part of subd (d).)

(f) Format of longer memorandum

A memorandum that exceeds 10 pages must include a table of contents and a table of authorities. A memorandum that exceeds 15 pages must also include an opening summary of argument.

(Subd (f) amended and lettered effective January 1, 2007; adopted as part of subd (d); subd (d) previously amended and relettered as subd (e) effective January 1, 2004.)

(g) Effect of filing an oversized memorandum

A memorandum that exceeds the page limits of these rules must be filed and considered in the same manner as a late-filed paper.

(Subd (g) amended and lettered effective January 1, 2007; adopted as part of subd (d); previously amended and relettered as subd (e) effective January 1, 2004.)

(h) Pagination of memorandum

Notwithstanding any other rule, a memorandum that includes a table of contents and a table of authorities must be paginated as follows:

(1) The caption page or pages must not be numbered;

(2) The pages of the tables must be numbered consecutively using lower-case roman numerals starting on the first page of the tables; and

(3) The pages of the text must be numbered consecutively using Arabic numerals starting on the first page of the text.

(Subd (h) amended and relettered effective January 1, 2007; previously amended and relettered as subd (f) effective January 1, 2004; adopted as subd (e) effective July 1, 2000.)

(i) Copies of non-California authorities

If any authority other than California cases, statutes, constitutional provisions, or state or local rules is cited, a copy of the authority must be lodged with the papers that cite the authority and tabbed as required by rule 3.1110(f). If a California case is cited before the time it is published in the advance sheets of the Official Reports, a copy of that case must also be lodged and tabbed as required by rule 3.1110(f).

(Subd (i) repealed and relettered effective January 1, 2008; adopted as part of subd (e) effective January 1, 1992; previously amended effective July 1, 1997; previously relettered as part of subd (f) effective July 1, 2000; previously amended and relettered

as subd (h) effective January 1, 2004, and as subd (j) effective January 1, 2007.)

(j) Attachments

To the extent practicable, all supporting memorandums and declarations must be attached to the notice of motion.

(Subd (j) relettered effective January 1, 2008; adopted as subd (f) effective July 1, 1997; previously relettered as subd (g) effective July 1, 2000; previously amended and relettered as subd (i) effective January 1, 2004, and as subd (k) effective January 1, 2007.)

(k) Exhibit references

All references to exhibits or declarations in supporting or opposing papers must reference the number or letter of the exhibit, the specific page, and, if applicable, the paragraph or line number.

(Subd (k) relettered effective January 1, 2008; adopted as subd (g) effective July 1, 1997; previously relettered as subd (h) effective July 1, 2000, and as subd (l) effective January 1, 2007; previously amended and relettered as subd (j) effective January 1, 2004.)

(l) Requests for judicial notice

Any request for judicial notice must be made in a separate document listing the specific items for which notice is requested and must comply with rule 3.1306(c).

(Subd (l) relettered effective January 1, 2008; adopted as subd (h) effective July 1, 1997; relettered as subd (i) effective July 1, 2000; previously amended effective January 1, 2003; previously amended and relettered as subd (k) effective January 1, 2004, and as subd (m) effective January 1, 2007.)

(m) Proposed orders or judgments

If a proposed order or judgment is submitted, it must be lodged and served with the moving papers but must not be attached to them.

(Subd (m) relettered effective January 1, 2008; adopted as subd (i) effective July 1, 1997; previously relettered as subd (j) effective July 1, 2000, and as subd (n) effective January 1, 2007; previously amended and relettered as subd (l) effective January 1, 2004.)

Rule 3.1113 amended effective January 1, 2008; adopted as rule 313 effective January 1, 1984; previously amended effective July 1, 1984, January 1, 1992, July 1, 1997, July 1, 2000, January 1, 2003, and January 1, 2004; previously amended and renumbered effective January 1, 2007.

Advisory Committee Comment

See also rule 1.200 concerning the format of citations.

Ref.: Cal. Fms Pl. & Pr., Ch. 2, "Procedural Guide for Civil Actions," Ch. 3, "Abatement of Actions," Ch. 4, "Abortion and Birth Control Methods," Ch. 12E, "Adoptions: Attack on Decree," Ch. 13, "Adverse Possession," Ch. 21, "Amended and Supplemental Pleadings," Ch. 24, "Animals: Liens," Ch. 32, "Contractual Arbitration: Agreements and Compelling Arbitration," Ch. 35, "Arbitration and Conciliation of International Commercial Disputes," Ch. 36, "Judicial Arbitration," Ch. 38, "Reference," Ch. 50, "Appeal: Briefs," Ch. 53, "Appeal: Remittitur and Costs on Appeal," Ch. 58, "Assault and Battery," Ch. 61, "Associations and Clubs," Ch. 62, "Attachment," Ch. 71, "Attorney Discipline," Ch. 72, "Attorney Practice and Ethics," Ch. 76, "Attorney Professional Liability," Ch. 85, "Automobiles: Discovery," Ch. 90, "Automobiles: Vehicle Leasing Act," Ch. 110, "Churches and Religious Organizations," Ch. 119, "Claim and Delivery," Ch. 120, "Class Actions," Ch. 121, "Common Counts," Ch. 123, "Complaints and Cross Complaints," Ch. 124, "Condominiums and Other Common Interest Developments," Ch. 125, "Consolidation, Severance, and Coordination of Actions," Ch. 126, "Conspiracy," Ch. 135, "Continuances," Ch. 136, "Continuances," Ch. 140, "Contracts," Ch. 160, "Corporations: Capacity,"

Ch. 161, "Corporations: Alter Ego Liability," Ch. 165, "Corporations: Corporate Records and Reports," Ch. 166, "Corporations: Shareholders' Meetings and Voting," Ch. 167, "Corporations: Directors and Management," Ch. 168, "Corporations: Derivative Actions," Ch. 169, "Corporations: Reorganizations," Ch. 170, "Corporations: Dissolution and Winding Up," Ch. 174, "Costs and Attorney's Fees," Ch. 177, "Damages," Ch. 181, "Death and Survival Actions," Ch. 190, "Discovery: Scope, Regulation, and Timing," Ch. 192, "Discovery: Sanctions for Discovery Misuse," Ch. 193, "Discovery: Depositions," Ch. 194, "Discovery: Interrogatories," Ch. 195, "Discovery: Inspection of Tangible Evidence," Ch. 196, "Discovery: Requests for Admissions," Ch. 197, "Discovery: Physical and Mental Examinations," Ch. 198, "Discovery: Exchange of Expert Witness Information," Ch. 199, "Discovery: Preservation of Evidence," Ch. 200, "Discovery: Review of Discovery Orders," Ch. 205, "Defaults and Default Judgments," Ch. 206, "Demurrers and Motions for Judgment on the Pleadings," Ch. 211, "Deposit in Court," Ch. 212, "Dismissal," Ch. 221, "Dissolution of Marriage: Procedure," Ch. 240, "Easements," Ch. 247, "Eminent Domain and Inverse Condemnation," Ch. 248, "Employer's Liability for Employee's Torts," Ch. 253, "Escrows," Ch. 254, "Executions and Enforcement of Judgments," Ch. 258, "Family Law Enforcement: General Enforcement Principles and Remedies," Ch. 264, "Fax Filing and Service of Papers," Ch. 276, "Garnishment," Ch. 283, "Guardianship and Conservatorship: Bonds," Ch. 290D, "Guardianship and Conservatorship: Actions Against Guardians, Conservators, and Sureties," Ch. 294, "Homesteads," Ch. 300, "Indemnity and Contribution," Ch. 303, "Injunctions," Ch. 314, "Interpleader," Ch. 317, "Judges," Ch. 318, "Judgments," Ch. 321, "Judicial Notice," Ch. 322, "Juries and Jury Selection," Ch. 323, "Jurisdiction: Personal Jurisdiction, Inconvenient Forum, and Appearances," Ch. 324, "Jurisdiction: Subject Matter Jurisdiction," Ch. 326A, "Jury Verdicts," Ch. 329, "Juvenile Courts: Delinquency Proceedings," Ch. 333, "Landlord and Tenant: Eviction Actions," Ch. 334, "Landlord and Tenant: Claims for Damages," Ch. 340, "Libel and Slander," Ch. 345, "Limitation of Actions," Ch. 345A, "Limited Civil Cases," Ch. 346, "Limited Liability Companies," Ch. 348, "Lis Pendens," Ch. 357, "Malicious Prosecution and Abuse of Process," Ch. 358, "Mandate and Prohibition," Ch. 361, "Mechanics' Liens," Ch. 367, "Minors: Disaffirmation of Judgments," Ch. 371, "Motions After Trial," Ch. 372, "Motions and Orders," Ch. 374, "Motions to Reconsider and Renewed Motions," Ch. 375, "Motions to Strike: Pleadings," Ch. 376, "Motions to Strike: Anti-SLAPP," Ch. 380, "Negligence," Ch. 386, "Newspapers," Ch. 388, "Nonprofit Corporations," Ch. 395, "Parties," Ch. 397, "Partition," Ch. 402, "Partnerships: Actions Between General Partners or Partnership and Third Parties," Ch. 404, "Partnerships: Actions Between Limited Partners and Partnerships," Ch. 414, "Physicians: Licensing and Discipline," Ch. 415, "Physicians: Medical Malpractice," Ch. 417, "Points and Authorities," Ch. 420, "Prayers," Ch. 444, "Probate: Will Contests," Ch. 454, "Probate: Claims Against the Estate," Ch. 460, "Products Liability," Ch. 462, "Public Accountants," Ch. 464, "Public Entities and Officers: California Tort Claims Act," Ch. 467, "Public Entities and Officers: Enforcement of Judgments Against Public Entities," Ch. 486, "Receivers," Ch. 471B, "Licensing by Public Agencies," Ch. 473C, "Prehearing Procedures in Agency Adjudications," Ch. 474C, "Procedures in Reviewing Agency Decisions," Ch. 482, "Quieting Title," Ch. 486, "Receivers," Ch. 489, "Relief From Judgments and Orders," Ch. 491, "Res Judicata," Ch. 492, "Review (Certiorari), Writ of," Ch. 501, "Sales: Retail Installment Sales," Ch. 503, "Sales: Secured Transactions," Ch. 510, "Sanctions," Ch. 518, "Service of Summons and Papers," Ch. 520, "Settlement and Release," Ch. 524, "Shortening and Extension of Time," Ch. 526, "Small Claims," Ch. 529, "Statement of Decision," Ch. 533, "Stipulations," Ch. 535, "Subpoena," Ch. 537, "Summary Judgment," Ch. 538, "Suretyship, Bonds, and Undertakings," Ch. 551, "Trial," Ch. 555, "Trust Deeds and Real Property Mortgages," Ch. 560,

"Trusts: Express, Public, Charitable, and Totten Trusts," Ch. 565, "Unfair Competition," Ch. 571, "Venue," Ch. 572, "Verification," Ch. 573, "Vexatious Litigants," Ch. 575, "Waters"; Cal. Class Actions Prac. & Proc., §§20.03[3], 21.02[2], 21.04[2], 22.04; MB Prac. Guide: Cal. Pretrial Proc., §§4.38, 8.41[1], [2], 11.03, 11.16[2], [3][b], 11.24, 11.38[1], 12.09[1], 20.20, 20.22[3][a], 20.23[5], 20.24[3], 21.13[4], 21.29[4], 26.01, 26.05[3], 26.12, 26.17[1], 26.29[4], 26.39, 26.43[5][a]–[e], 26.60, 26.62[4], 26.63[3], 26.66, 26.67, 26.71, 26.72, 26.76, 26.82, 29.03, 29.13[2], 33.15, 33.16[2][a], [b], 33.27[1][b], 34.08[1][c], 36.36[4], 36.67[4][b], 36.72[2][c], 38.03, 38.15[4][b], 38.17, 38.19, 38.25[2], 38.27[2], 38.33[2]; MB Prac. Guide: Cal. Trial & Post-Trial Civ. Proc., §§2.03[1], 2.07[3], 2.11[1], 2.30[1], 2.35[1], 4.20[1], [2], 4.25[2], 12.25, 14.03, 14.11[3], 14.30.

Rule 3.1114. Applications, motions, and petitions not requiring a memorandum

(a) Memorandum not required

Civil motions, applications, and petitions filed on Judicial Council forms that do not require a memorandum include the following:

(1) Application for appointment of guardian ad litem in a civil case;

(2) Application for an order extending time to serve pleading;

(3) Motion to be relieved as counsel;

(4) Motion filed in small claims case;

(5) Petition for change of name or gender;

(6) Petition for declaration of emancipation of minor;

(7) Petition for injunction prohibiting harassment;

(8) Petition for protective order to prevent elder or dependent adult abuse;

(9) Petition of employer for injunction prohibiting workplace violence;

(10) Petition for order prohibiting abuse (transitional housing);

(11) Petition to approve compromise of claim of a minor or a person with a disability; and

(12) Petition for withdrawal of funds from blocked account.

(Subd (a) amended effective January 1, 2007.)

(b) Submission of a memorandum

Notwithstanding (a), if it would further the interests of justice, a party may submit, or the court may order the submission of, a memorandum in support of any motion, application, or petition. The memorandum must comply with rule 3.1113.

(Subd (b) amended effective January 1, 2007.)

Rule 3.1114 amended and renumbered effective January 1, 2007; adopted as rule 314 effective January 1, 2004.

Ref.: Cal. Fms Pl. & Pr., Ch. 165, "Corporations: Corporate Records and Reports," Ch. 166, "Corporations: Shareholders' Meetings and Voting," Ch. 240, "Easements," Ch. 253, "Escrows," Ch. 291, "Guardians Ad Litem," Ch. 302, "Initiative, Referendum, and Recall," Ch. 348, "Lis Pendens," Ch. 372, "Motions and Orders," Ch. 397, "Partition," Ch. 417, "Points and Authorities," Ch. 460, "Products Liability," Ch. 482, "Quieting Title," Ch. 524, "Shortening and Extension of Time"; MB Prac. Guide: Cal. Pretrial Proc., §§3.30[3][b], 5.24[2], 26.29[4], 26.43[5][a], 27.21[2].

Rule 3.1115. Declarations

The caption of a declaration must state the name of the declarant and must specifically identify the motion or other proceeding that it supports or opposes.

Rule 3.1115 amended and renumbered effective January 1, 2007; adopted as rule 315 effective January 1, 1984.

Ref.: Cal. Fms Pl. & Pr., Ch. 121, "Common Counts," Ch. 125, "Consolidation, Severance, and Coordination of Actions," Ch. 168, "Corporations: Derivative Actions," Ch. 170, "Corporations: Dissolution and Winding Up," Ch. 212, "Dismissal," Ch. 322, "Juries and Jury Selection," Ch. 324, "Jurisdiction: Subject Matter Jurisdiction," Ch. 372, "Motions and Orders," Ch. 417, "Points and Authorities," Ch. 489, "Relief From Judgments and Orders"; MB Prac. Guide: Cal. Pretrial Proc., §§26.66, 36.67[4][b]; MB Prac. Guide: Cal. Trial & Post-Trial Civ. Proc., §§4.20[1], [2], 4.25[2], 29.15[2].

Rule 3.1116. Deposition testimony as an exhibit

(a) Title page

The first page of any deposition used as an exhibit must state the name of the deponent and the date of the deposition.

(Subd (a) amended effective January 1, 2007.)

(b) Deposition pages

Other than the title page, the exhibit must contain only the relevant pages of the transcript. The original page number of any deposition page must be clearly visible.

(Subd (b) amended effective January 1, 2007.)

(c) Highlighting of testimony

The relevant portion of any testimony in the deposition must be marked in a manner that calls attention to the testimony.

(Subd (c) amended effective January 1, 2007.)

Rule 3.1116 amended and renumbered effective January 1, 2007; adopted as rule 316 effective January 1, 1992.

Ref.: Cal. Fms Pl. & Pr., Ch. 193, "Discovery: Depositions," Ch. 537, "Summary Judgment"; MB Prac. Guide: Cal. Pretrial Proc., §§38.03, 38.15[3]; MB Prac. Guide: Cal. Trial & Post-Trial Civ. Proc., §4.25[2].

Chapter 3
Provisional and Injunctive Relief

Art. 1.   General Provisions. Rule 3.1130.
Art. 2.   Writs. Rules 3.1140, 3.1142.
Art. 3.   Injunctions. Rules 3.1150–3.1153.
Art. 4.   Receiverships. Rules 3.1175–3.1184.

Article 1
General Provisions

Rule 3.1130. Bonds and undertakings

(a) Prerequisites to acceptance of corporate sureties

A corporation must not be accepted or approved as surety on a bond or undertaking unless the following conditions are met:

(1) The Insurance Commissioner has certified the corporation as being admitted to do business in the state as a surety insurer;

(2) There is filed in the office of the clerk a copy, duly certified by the proper authority, of the transcript or record of appointment entitling or authorizing the person or persons purporting to execute the bond or undertaking for and in behalf of the corporation to act in the premises; and

(3) The bond or undertaking has been executed under penalty of perjury as provided in Code of Civil Procedure section 995.630, or the fact of execution of the bond or undertaking by the officer or agent of the corporation purporting to become surety has been duly acknowledged before an officer of this state authorized to take and certify acknowledgements.

(Subd (a) amended effective January 1, 2007.)

(b) Certain persons not eligible to act as sureties

An officer of the court or member of the State Bar may not act as a surety.

(Subd (b) amended effective January 1, 2007.)

(c) Withdrawal of bonds and undertakings

An original bond or undertaking may be withdrawn from the files and delivered to the party by whom it was filed on order of the court only if all parties interested in the obligation so stipulate, or upon a showing that the purpose for which it was filed has been abandoned without any liability having been incurred.

Rule 3.1130 amended and renumbered effective January 1, 2007; adopted as rule 381 effective January 1, 1984.

Ref.: Cal. Fms Pl. & Pr., Ch. 62, "Attachment," Ch. 199, "Discovery: Preservation of Evidence," Ch. 283, "Guardianship and Conservatorship: Bonds," Ch. 303, "Injunctions," Ch. 372, "Motions and Orders," Ch. 446, "Probate: Bonds—Increase and Decrease During Administration," Ch. 538, "Suretyship, Bonds, and Undertakings"; MB Prac. Guide: Cal. Pretrial Proc., §§18.11[5][a], [6][a], 35.15E[5].

Article 2
Writs

Rule 3.1140. Lodging of record in administrative mandate cases

Rule 3.1142. Stay of driving license suspension

Rule 3.1140. Lodging of record in administrative mandate cases

The party intending to use a part of the administrative record in a case brought under Code of Civil Procedure section 1094.5 must lodge that part of the record at least five days before the hearing.

Rule 3.1140 amended and renumbered effective January 1, 2007; adopted as rule 347 effective January 1, 1984.

Ref.: Cal. Fms Pl. & Pr., Ch. 372, "Motions and Orders," Ch. 474C, "Procedures in Reviewing Agency Decisions."

Rule 3.1142. Stay of driving license suspension

A request for a stay of a suspension of a driving license must be accompanied by a copy of the petitioner's driving record from the Department of Motor Vehicles.

Rule 3.1142 amended and renumbered effective January 1, 2007; adopted as rule 355 effective January 1, 1984.

Ref.: Cal. Fms Pl. & Pr., Ch. 92, "Automobiles: Drivers' Licenses."

Article 3
Injunctions

Rule 3.1150. Preliminary injunctions and bonds

Rule 3.1151. Requirements for injunction in certain cases

Rule 3.1152. Civil harassment and workplace violence

Rule 3.1153. Minors may appear without counsel to seek specified restraining orders

Rule 3.1150. Preliminary injunctions and bonds

(a) Manner of application and service

A party requesting a preliminary injunction may give notice of the request to the opposing or responding party either by serving a noticed motion under Code of Civil Procedure section 1005 or by obtaining and serving an order to show cause (OSC). An OSC must be used when a temporary restraining order (TRO) is sought, or if the party against whom the preliminary injunction is sought has not appeared in the action. If the responding party has not appeared, the OSC must be served in the same manner as a summons and complaint.

(Subd (a) amended effective January 1, 2007; adopted effective July 1, 1997; previously amended effective July 1, 1999.)

(b) Filing of complaint or obtaining of court file

If the action is initiated the same day a TRO or an OSC is sought, the complaint must be filed first. The moving party must provide a file-stamped copy of the complaint to the judge who will hear the application. If an application for a TRO or an OSC is made in an existing case, the moving party must request that the court file be made available to the judge hearing the application.

(Subd (b) amended effective January 1, 2007; adopted effective July 1, 1997; previously amended effective July 1, 1999.)

(c) Form of OSC and TRO

The OSC and TRO must be stated separately, with the OSC stated first. The restraining language sought in an OSC and a TRO must be separately stated in the OSC and the TRO and may not be incorporated by reference. The OSC must describe the injunction to be sought at the hearing. The TRO must describe the activities to be enjoined pending the hearing. A proposed OSC must contain blank spaces for the time and manner of service on responding parties, the date on which the proof of service must be delivered to the court hearing the OSC, a briefing schedule, and, if applicable, the expiration date of the TRO.

(Subd (c) amended effective January 1, 2007; adopted effective July 1, 1997; previously amended effective July 1, 1999.)

(d) Personal attendance

The moving party or counsel for the moving party must be personally present when the request for a TRO is made.

(Subd (d) amended effective January 1, 2007; adopted as subd (e) effective July 1, 1997; amended as [Proof of service] effective July 1, 1999; previously relettered effective July 1, 1999.)

(e) Previous applications

An application for a TRO or an OSC must state whether there has been any previous application for similar relief and, if so, the result of the application.

(Subd (e) amended effective January 1, 2007; adopted as subd (f) effective July 1, 1997; previously amended and relettered effective July 1, 1999.)

(f) Undertaking

Notwithstanding rule 3.1312, whenever an application for a preliminary injunction is granted, a proposed order must be presented to the judge for signature, with an undertaking in the amount ordered, within one court day after the granting of the application or within the time ordered. Unless otherwise ordered, any restraining order previously granted remains in effect during the time allowed for presentation for signature of the order of injunction and undertaking. If the proposed order and the undertaking required are not presented within the time allowed, the TRO may be vacated without notice. All bonds and undertakings must comply with rule 3.1130.

(Subd (f) amended effective January 1, 2007; previously amended and relettered effective July 1, 1997.)

(g) Ex parte temporary restraining orders

Applications for ex parte temporary restraining orders are governed by the ex parte rules in chapter 4 of this division.

(Subd (g) amended effective January 1, 2007; adopted effective July 1, 1999.)

Rule 3.1150 amended and renumbered effective January 1, 2007; adopted as rule 359 effective January 1, 1984; previously amended effective July 1, 1997, and July 1, 1999.

Ref.: Cal. Fms Pl. & Pr., Ch. 221, "Dissolution of Marriage: Procedure," Ch. 240, "Easements," Ch. 293, "Harassment and Domestic Violence," Ch. 303, "Injunctions," Ch. 372, "Motions and Orders," Ch. 393, "Oil and Gas," Ch. 406, "Partnerships: Dissolution," Ch. 528, "Specific Performance"; MB Prac. Guide: Cal. Debt Collection & Enforcement of Judgments, §§8.24, 8.31, 8.54; MB Prac. Guide: Cal. Pretrial Proc., §§1.02, 18.03, 18.10[3][a]–[c], [4][a], [b], 18.11[3][a], [b], [4][a], [b], [5][a], [c], 26.43[5][b].

Rule 3.1151. Requirements for injunction in certain cases

A petition for an injunction to limit picketing, restrain real property encroachments, or protect easements must depict by drawings, plot plans, photographs, or other appropriate means, or must describe in detail the premises involved, including, if applicable, the length and width of the frontage on a street or alley, the width of sidewalks, and the number, size, and location of entrances.

Rule 3.1151 amended and renumbered effective January 1, 2007; adopted as rule 361 effective January 1, 1984.

Ref.: Cal. Fms Pl. & Pr., Ch. 240, "Easements," Ch. 303, "Injunctions," Ch. 393, "Oil and Gas."

Rule 3.1152. Civil harassment and workplace violence

(a) Scheduling of hearing

On the filing of a petition for an injunction under Code of Civil Procedure section 527.6 or 527.8, a hearing must be set in accordance with the requirements of subdivision (d) of section 527.6 or subdivision (f) of section 527.8.

(Subd (a) amended effective January 1, 2007; previously amended effective July 1, 1995.)

(b) Temporary restraining order

A temporary restraining order may be granted in accordance with the provisions of Code of Civil Procedure section 527.6(c) or 527.8(e), but unless otherwise ordered no memorandum is required.

(Subd (b) amended effective January 1, 2007; previously amended effective July 1, 1995, and January 1, 2002.)

(c) Service of petition and orders

The petition and order to show cause, and any temporary restraining order, must be personally served on the defendant. Service must be made in the manner provided by law for personal service of summons in civil actions.

(Subd (c) amended effective January 1, 2007; previously amended effective January 1, 1993.)

(d) Response by defendant

A response by defendant must be filed and delivered to plaintiff or plaintiff's attorney no later than 48 hours before the hearing.

(Subd (d) amended effective January 1, 2007.)

Rule 3.1152 amended and renumbered effective January 1, 2007; adopted as rule 363 effective January 1, 1984; previously amended effective January 1, 1993, July 1, 1995, January 1, 2000, and January 1, 2002.

Ref.: Cal. Fms Pl. & Pr., Ch. 293, "Harassment and Domestic Violence," Ch. 303, "Injunctions"; MB Prac. Guide: Cal. Pretrial Proc., §18.10[3][a].

Rule 3.1153. Minors may appear without counsel to seek specified restraining orders

A minor, accompanied by a duly appointed and acting guardian ad litem, may be permitted to appear in court without counsel for the limited purpose of obtaining or opposing:

(1) An injunction or temporary restraining order or both to prohibit harassment under Code of Civil Procedure section 527.6;

(2) An injunction or temporary restraining order or both against violence or a credible threat of violence in the workplace under Code of Civil Procedure section 527.8;

(3) A protective order under Family Code section 6200 et seq.; or

(4) A protective order under Family Code sections 7710 and 7720.

In making the determination concerning allowing appearance without counsel, the court should consider whether the minor and the guardian have divergent interests.

Rule 3.1153 amended and renumbered effective January 1, 2007; adopted as rule 364 effective July 1, 1995.

Ref.: Cal. Fms Pl. & Pr., Ch. 293, "Harassment and Domestic Violence," Ch. 412, "Paternity."

Article 4
Receiverships

Rule 3.1175. Ex parte application for appointment of receiver
Rule 3.1176. Confirmation of ex parte appointment of receiver
Rule 3.1177. Nomination of receivers
Rule 3.1178. Amount of undertakings
Rule 3.1179. The receiver
Rule 3.1180. Employment of attorney
Rule 3.1181. Receiver's inventory
Rule 3.1182. Monthly reports
Rule 3.1183. Interim fees and objections
Rule 3.1184. Receiver's final account and report

Rule 3.1175. Ex parte application for appointment of receiver

(a) Application

In addition to any other matters supporting an application for the ex parte appointment of a receiver, the applicant must show in detail by verified complaint or declaration:

(1) The nature of the emergency and the reasons irreparable injury would be suffered by the applicant during the time necessary for a hearing on notice;

Rules of Court

(2) The names, addresses, and telephone numbers of the persons in actual possession of the property for which a receiver is requested, or of the president, manager, or principal agent of any corporation in possession of the property;

(3) The use being made of the property by the persons in possession; and

(4) If the property is a part of the plant, equipment, or stock in trade of any business, the nature and approximate size or extent of the business and facts sufficient to show whether the taking of the property by a receiver would stop or seriously interfere with the operation of the business.

If any of the matters listed above are unknown to the applicant and cannot be ascertained by the exercise of due diligence, the applicant's declaration or verified complaint must fully state the matters unknown and the efforts made to acquire the information.

(Subd (a) amended effective January 1, 2007; previously amended effective January 1, 2002.)

Rule 3.1175 amended and renumbered effective January 1, 2007; adopted as rule 349 effective January 1, 1984; previously amended and renumbered as rule 1900 effective January 1, 2002.

Ref.: Cal. Fms Pl. & Pr., Ch. 258, "Family Law Enforcement: General Enforcement Principles and Remedies," Ch. 334, "Landlord and Tenant: Claims for Damages," Ch. 372, "Motions and Orders," Ch. 387, "Nonmarital Cohabitation," Ch. 406, "Partnerships: Dissolution," Ch. 486, "Receivers," Ch. 504, "Sales: Consumers Legal Remedies Act," Ch. 555, "Trust Deeds and Real Property Mortgages"; MB Prac. Guide: Cal. Debt Collection & Enforcement of Judgments, §§8.54, 8.61, 8.62[2][a], [3][a], 8.83, 8.84, 20.34, 20.36.

Rule 3.1176. Confirmation of ex parte appointment of receiver

(a) Order to show cause

Whenever a receiver is appointed without notice, the matter must be made returnable upon an order to show cause why the appointment should not be confirmed. The order to show cause must be made returnable on the earliest date that the business of the court will admit, but not later than 15 days or, if good cause appears to the court, 22 days from the date the order is issued.

(Subd (a) amended effective January 1, 2002.)

(b) Service of complaint, order to show cause, declarations, and memorandum

The applicant must serve on each of the adverse parties:

(1) A copy of the complaint if not previously served;

(2) The order to show cause stating the date, time, and place of the hearing;

(3) Any declarations supporting the application; and

(4) A memorandum supporting the application.

Service must be made as soon as reasonably practical, but no later than 5 days after the date on which the order to show cause is issued, unless the court orders another time for service.

(Subd (b) amended effective January 1, 2007; previously amended effective January 1, 2002.)

(c) Failure to proceed or serve adverse party

When the matter first comes on for hearing, the party that obtained the appointment must be ready to proceed. If that party is not ready to proceed or has failed to exercise diligence to effect service upon the adverse parties as provided in (b), the court may discharge the receiver.

(Subd (c) amended effective January 1, 2007; previously amended effective January 1, 2002.)

(d) Continuance

The adverse parties are entitled to one continuance to enable them to oppose the confirmation. If a continuance is granted under this subdivision, the order to show cause remains in effect until the date of the continued hearing.

(Subd (d) amended effective January 1, 2002.)

Rule 3.1176 amended and renumbered effective January 1, 2007; adopted as rule 351 effective January 1, 1984; previously amended and renumbered as rule 1901 effective January 1, 2002.

Ref.: Cal. Fms Pl. & Pr., Ch. 258, "Family Law Enforcement: General Enforcement Principles and Remedies," Ch. 372, "Motions and Orders," Ch. 395, "Parties," Ch. 486, "Receivers," Ch. 555, "Trust Deeds and Real Property Mortgages"; MB Prac. Guide: Cal. Pretrial Proc., §26.63[3].

Rule 3.1177. Nomination of receivers

At the hearing of an application for appointment of a receiver on notice or at the hearing for confirmation of an ex parte appointment, each party appearing may, at the time of the hearing, suggest in writing one or more persons for appointment or substitution as receiver, stating the reasons. A party's suggestion is without prejudice to its objection to the appointment or confirmation of a receiver.

Rule 3.1177 renumbered effective January 1, 2007; adopted as rule 353 effective January 1, 1984; previously amended and renumbered as rule 1902 effective January 1, 2002.

Ref.: Cal. Fms Pl. & Pr., Ch. 258, "Family Law Enforcement: General Enforcement Principles and Remedies," Ch. 486, "Receivers," Ch. 555, "Trust Deeds and Real Property Mortgages."

Rule 3.1178. Amount of undertakings

At the hearing of an application for appointment of a receiver on notice or ex parte, the applicant must, and other parties may, propose and state the reasons for the specific amounts of the undertakings required from (1) the applicant by Code of Civil Procedure section 529, (2) the applicant by Code of Civil Procedure section 566(b), and (3) the receiver by Code of Civil Procedure section 567(b), for any injunction that is ordered in or with the order appointing a receiver.

Rule 3.1178 amended and renumbered effective January 1, 2007; adopted as rule 1902.5 effective January 1, 2004.

Ref.: Cal. Fms Pl. & Pr., Ch. 486, "Receivers"; MB Prac. Guide: Cal. Debt Collection & Enforcement of Judgments, §§8.54, 8.61, 8.62[2][d].

Rule 3.1179. The receiver

(a) Agent of the court

The receiver is the agent of the court and not of any party, and as such:

(1) Is neutral;

(2) Acts for the benefit of all who may have an interest in the receivership property; and

(3) Holds assets for the court and not for the plaintiff or the defendant.

(b) Prohibited contracts, agreements, arrangements, and understandings

The party seeking the appointment of the receiver may not, directly or indirectly, require any contract, agreement, arrangement, or understanding with any receiver whom it intends to nominate or recommend to the court, and the receiver may not enter into any such contract, arrangement, agreement, or understanding concerning:

(1) The role of the receiver with respect to the property following a trustee's sale or termination of a receivership, without specific court permission;

(2) How the receiver will administer the receivership or how much the receiver will charge for services or pay for services to appropriate or approved third parties hired to provide services;

(3) Who the receiver will hire, or seek approval to hire, to perform necessary services; or

(4) What capital expenditures will be made on the property.

Rule 3.1179 renumbered effective January 1, 2007; adopted as rule 1903 effective January 1, 2002.

Ref.: Cal. Fms Pl. & Pr., Ch. 258, "Family Law Enforcement: General Enforcement Principles and Remedies," Ch. 486, "Receivers," Ch. 555, "Trust Deeds and Real Property Mortgages"; MB Prac. Guide: Cal. Debt Collection & Enforcement of Judgments, §8.58.

Rule 3.1180.   Employment of attorney

A receiver must not employ an attorney without the approval of the court. The application for approval to employ an attorney must be in writing and must state:

(1) The necessity for the employment;

(2) The name of the attorney whom the receiver proposes to employ; and

(3) That the attorney is not the attorney for, associated with, nor employed by an attorney for any party.

Rule 3.1180 amended and renumbered effective January 1, 2007; adopted as rule 1904 effective January 1, 2002.

Ref.: Cal. Fms Pl. & Pr., Ch. 486, "Receivers," Ch. 555, "Trust Deeds and Real Property Mortgages."

Rule 3.1181.   Receiver's inventory

(a) Filing of inventory

A receiver must, within 30 days after appointment, or within such other time as the court may order, file an inventory containing a complete and detailed list of all property of which the receiver has taken possession by virtue of the appointment.

(Subd (a) lettered effective January 1, 2007; adopted as part of untitled subd effective January 1, 2002.)

(b) Supplemental inventory

The receiver must promptly file a supplementary inventory of all subsequently obtained property.

(Subd (b) lettered effective January 1, 2007; adopted as part of untitled subd effective January 1, 2002.)

Rule 3.1181 amended and renumbered effective January 1, 2007; adopted as rule 1905 effective January 1, 2002.

Ref.: Cal. Fms Pl. & Pr., Ch. 486, "Receivers," Ch. 555, "Trust Deeds and Real Property Mortgages."

Rule 3.1182.   Monthly reports

(a) Content of reports

The receiver must provide monthly reports to the parties and, if requested, to nonparty client lien holders. These reports must include:

(1) A narrative report of events;

(2) A financial report; and

(3) A statement of all fees paid to the receiver, employees, and professionals showing:

(A) Itemized services;

(B) A breakdown of the services by 1/10 hour increments;

(C) If the fees are hourly, the hourly fees; and

(D) If the fees are on another basis, that basis.

(Subd (a) amended effective January 1, 2007.)

(b) Reports not to be filed

The monthly reports are not to be filed with the court unless the court so orders.

Rule 3.1182 amended effective January 1, 2007; adopted as rule 1906 effective January 1, 2002; previously renumbered effective January 1, 2007.

Ref.: Cal. Fms Pl. & Pr., Ch. 486, "Receivers," Ch. 555, "Trust Deeds and Real Property Mortgages."

Rule 3.1183.   Interim fees and objections

(a) Interim fees

Interim fees are subject to final review and approval by the court. The court retains jurisdiction to award a greater or lesser amount as the full, fair, and final value of the services received.

(b) Objections to interim accounts and reports

Unless good cause is shown, objections to a receiver's interim report and accounting must be made within 10 days of notice of the report and accounting, must be specific, and must be delivered to the receiver and all parties entitled to service of the interim report and accounting.

Rule 3.1183 renumbered effective January 1, 2007; adopted as rule 1907 effective January 1, 2002.

Ref.: Cal. Fms Pl. & Pr., Ch. 486, "Receivers," Ch. 555, "Trust Deeds and Real Property Mortgages."

Rule 3.1184.   Receiver's final account and report

(a) Motion or stipulation

A receiver must present by noticed motion or stipulation of all parties:

(1) A final account and report;

(2) A request for the discharge; and

(3) A request for exoneration of the receiver's surety.

(Subd (a) amended and relettered effective January 1, 2004; adopted as part of unlettered subd effective January 1, 2002.)

(b) No memorandum required

No memorandum needs to be submitted in support of the motion or stipulation served and filed under (a) unless the court so orders.

(Subd (b) adopted effective January 1, 2004.)

(c) Notice

Notice of the motion or of the stipulation must be given to every person or entity known to the receiver to have a substantial, unsatisfied claim that will be affected by the order or stipulation, whether or not the person or entity is a party to the action or has appeared in it.

(Subd (c) adopted effective January 1, 2004.)

(d) Claim for compensation for receiver or attorney

If any allowance of compensation for the receiver or for an attorney employed by the receiver is claimed in an account, it must state in detail what services have been performed by the receiver or the attorney and whether previous allowances have been made to the receiver or attorney and the amounts.

(Subd (d) amended and relettered effective January 1, 2007; adopted as part of unlettered subd effective January 1, 2002; amended and lettered effective January 1, 2004.)

Rule 3.1184 amended and renumbered effective January 1, 2007; adopted as rule 1908 effective January 1, 2002; previously amended effective January 1, 2004.

Ref.: Cal. Fms Pl. & Pr., Ch. 486, "Receivers," Ch. 555, "Trust Deeds and Real Property Mortgages"; MB Prac. Guide: Cal. Debt Collection & Enforcement of Judgments, §§20.36, 20.63.

Chapter 4
Ex Parte Applications

Rule 3.1200. Application
Rule 3.1201. Required documents
Rule 3.1202. Contents of application
Rule 3.1203. Time of notice to other parties
Rule 3.1204. Contents of notice and declaration regarding notice
Rule 3.1205. Filing and presentation of the ex parte application
Rule 3.1206. Service of papers
Rule 3.1207. Personal appearance requirements

Rule 3.1200. Application

The rules in this chapter govern ex parte applications and orders in civil cases, unless otherwise provided by a statute or a rule. These rules may be referred to as "the ex parte rules."

Rule 3.1200 adopted effective January 1, 2007.

Ref.: Cal. Fms Pl. & Pr., Ch. 23, "Animals: Civil Liability," Ch. 136, "Continuances," Ch. 254, "Executions and Enforcement of Judgments," Ch. 291, "Guardians Ad Litem," Ch. 303, "Injunctions," Ch. 372, "Motions and Orders," Ch. 417, "Points and Authorities," Ch. 425, "Pretrial Proceedings," Ch. 524, "Shortening and Extension of Time"; MB Prac. Guide: Cal. Debt Collection & Enforcement of Judgments, §8.54; MB Prac. Guide: Cal. Pretrial Proc., §§18.03, 18.27, 26.01 26.03, 26.09[3], 26.23, 26.24, 26.29[5], 26.37, 26.43[5][b], 26.75, 26.76, 27.08, 27.11[3], 27.14, 27.21[2], 27.40, 27.47A, 29.21[2], 30.03, 30.09[4][b], [5][a], 30.20, 31.07[2], 31.20, 34.03[3].

Rule 3.1201. Required documents

A request for ex parte relief must be in writing and must include all of the following:

(1) An application containing the case caption and stating the relief requested;

(2) A declaration in support of the application making the factual showing required under rule 3.1202(c);

(3) A declaration based on personal knowledge of the notice given under rule 3.1204;

(4) A memorandum; and

(5) A proposed order.

Rule 3.1201 adopted effective January 1, 2007.

Ref.: Cal. Fms Pl. & Pr., Ch. 1, "New Developments," Ch. 24, "Animals: Liens," Ch. 193, "Discovery: Depositions," Ch. 194, "Discovery: Interrogatories," Ch. 254, "Executions and Enforcement of Judgments," Ch. 372, "Motions and Orders," Ch. 406, "Partnerships: Dissolution," Ch. 417, "Points and Authorities," Ch. 524, "Shortening and Extension of Time"; MB Prac. Guide:

Cal. Debt Collection & Enforcement of Judgments, §§1.44, 1.53[7][a], 4.13, 4.21, 8.24, 8.54, 8.62[2][a], [3][b], 8.83; MB Prac. Guide: Cal. Pretrial Proc., §§18.03, 18.10[3][a], [b], 26.03, 26.05[2], 26.29[1], [4], [6], 27.11[3], 27.21[2], 30.09[4][b].

Rule 3.1202. Contents of application
(a) Identification of attorney or party

An ex parte application must state the name, address, and telephone number of any attorney known to the applicant to be an attorney for any party or, if no such attorney is known, the name, address, and telephone number of the party if known to the applicant.

(b) Disclosure of previous applications

If an ex parte application has been refused in whole or in part, any subsequent application of the same character or for the same relief, although made upon an alleged different state of facts, must include a full disclosure of all previous applications and of the court's actions.

(c) Affirmative factual showing required

An applicant must make an affirmative factual showing in a declaration containing competent testimony based on personal knowledge of irreparable harm, immediate danger, or any other statutory basis for granting relief ex parte.

(Subd (c) amended effective January 1, 2007.)

Rule 3.1202 amended effective January 1, 2007; adopted effective January 1, 2007.

Ref.: Cal. Fms Pl. & Pr., Ch. 193, "Discovery: Depositions," Ch. 244, "Elevators and Escalators," Ch. 254, "Executions and Enforcement of Judgments," Ch. 365, "Minors: Contract Actions," Ch. 372, "Motions and Orders," Ch. 406, "Partnerships: Dissolution," Ch. 417, "Points and Authorities," Ch. 486, "Receivers," Ch. 524, "Shortening and Extension of Time"; MB Prac. Guide: Cal. Pretrial Proc., §§26.05[2], 26.23, 26.25, 26.29[1], [3], 26.35, 26.38, 27.11[1], [3], 27.21[1], [2], 30.09[4][a], [b].

Rule 3.1203. Time of notice to other parties
(a) Time of notice

A party seeking an ex parte order must notify all parties no later than 10:00 a.m. the court day before the ex parte appearance, absent a showing of exceptional circumstances that justify a shorter time for notice.

(Subd (a) amended effective January 1, 2008; adopted effective January 1, 2007.)

(b) Time of notice in unlawful detainer proceedings

A party seeking an ex parte order in an unlawful detainer proceeding may provide shorter notice than required under (a) provided that the notice given is reasonable.

(Subd (b) adopted effective January 1, 2007.)

Rule 3.1203 amended effective January 1, 2008; adopted effective January 1, 2007.

Ref.: Cal. Fms Pl. & Pr., Ch. 62, "Attachment," Ch. 119, "Claim and Delivery," Ch. 193, "Discovery: Depositions," Ch. 240, "Easements," Ch. 244, "Elevators and Escalators," Ch. 254, "Executions and Enforcement of Judgments," Ch. 302, "Initiative, Referendum, and Recall," Ch. 365, "Minors: Contract Actions," Ch. 372, "Motions and Orders," Ch. 397, "Partition," Ch. 406, "Partnerships: Dissolution," Ch. 418, "Pollution and Environmental Matters," Ch. 486, "Receivers," Ch. 524, "Shortening and Extension of Time"; MB Prac. Guide: Cal. Debt Collection & Enforcement of Judgments, §§1.44, 1.53[7][a], 4.21, 8.62[2][b]; MB Prac. Guide: Cal. Pretrial Proc., §§18.10[3][b], 18.27, 26.03, 26.09[3], 26.23, 26.26, 26.30[1], 26.35, 27.11[3], 27.21[2], 30.09[4][b].

Rule 3.1204.   Contents of notice and declaration regarding notice

(a) Contents of notice

When notice of an ex parte application is given, the person giving notice must:

(1) State with specificity the nature of the relief to be requested and the date, time, and place for the presentation of the application; and

(2) Attempt to determine whether the opposing party will appear to oppose the application.

(Subd (a) adopted effective January 1, 2007.)

(b) Declaration regarding notice

An ex parte application must be accompanied by a declaration regarding notice stating:

(1) The notice given, including the date, time, manner, and name of the party informed, the relief sought, any response, and whether opposition is expected and that, within the applicable time under rule 3.1203, the applicant informed the opposing party where and when the application would be made;

(2) That the applicant in good faith attempted to inform the opposing party but was unable to do so, specifying the efforts made to inform the opposing party; or

(3) That, for reasons specified, the applicant should not be required to inform the opposing party.

(Subd (b) adopted effective January 1, 2007.)

(c) Explanation for shorter notice

If notice was provided later than 10:00 a.m. the court day before the ex parte appearance, the declaration regarding notice must explain:

(1) The exceptional circumstances that justify the shorter notice; or

(2) In unlawful detainer proceedings, why the notice given is reasonable.

(Subd (c) adopted effective January 1, 2007.)
Rule 3.1204 adopted effective January 1, 2007.

Ref.: Cal. Fms Pl. & Pr., Ch. 23, "Animals: Civil Liability," Ch. 24, "Animals: Liens," Ch. 62, "Attachment," Ch. 116, "Civil Rights: Discrimination in Business Establishments," Ch. 117, "Civil Rights: Housing Discrimination," Ch. 119, "Claim and Delivery," Ch. 124, "Condominiums and Other Common Interest Developments," Ch. 136, "Continuances," Ch. 193, "Discovery: Depositions," Ch. 194, "Discovery: Interrogatories," Ch. 206, "Demurrers and Motions for Judgment on the Pleadings," Ch. 240, "Easements," Ch. 242, "Election Campaigns," Ch. 244, "Elevators and Escalators," Ch. 254, "Executions and Enforcement of Judgments," Ch. 302, "Initiative, Referendum, and Recall," Ch. 303, "Injunctions," Ch. 358, "Mandate and Prohibition," Ch. 365, "Minors: Contract Actions," Ch. 369, "Mobilehomes and Mobilehome Parks," Ch. 372, "Motions and Orders," Ch. 374, "Motions to Reconsider and Renewed Motions," Ch. 395, "Parties," Ch. 397, "Partition," Ch. 406, "Partnerships: Dissolution," Ch. 417, "Points and Authorities," Ch. 486, "Receivers," Ch. 492, "Review (Certiorari), Writ of," Ch. 524, "Shortening and Extension of Time," Ch. 549, "Trademarks and Trade Names," Ch. 555, "Trust Deeds and Real Property Mortgages," Ch. 575, "Waters"; MB Prac. Guide: Cal. Debt Collection & Enforcement of Judgments, §§1.44, 1.53[7][a], 4.21, 8.54, 8.62[2][b], [3][b]; MB Prac. Guide: Cal. Pretrial Proc., §§18.10[3][b], 26.23, 26.26, 26.27, 26.29[2], 27.11[3], 27.21[2], 30.09[4][a], [b], 31.20.

Rule 3.1205.   Filing and presentation of the ex parte application

Notwithstanding the failure of an applicant to comply with the requirements of rule 3.1203, the clerk must not reject an ex parte application for filing and must promptly present the application to the appropriate judicial officer for consideration.

Rule 3.1205 adopted effective January 1, 2007.

Ref.: Cal. Fms Pl. & Pr., Ch. 193, "Discovery: Depositions," Ch. 240, "Easements," Ch. 302, "Initiative, Referendum, and Recall," Ch. 372, "Motions and Orders," Ch. 397, "Partition," Ch. 406, "Partnerships: Dissolution"; MB Prac. Guide: Cal. Pretrial Proc., §§18.27, 26.30[1].

Rule 3.1206.   Service of papers

Parties appearing at the ex parte hearing must serve the ex parte application or any written opposition on all other appearing parties at the first reasonable opportunity. Absent exceptional circumstances, no hearing may be conducted unless such service has been made.

Rule 3.1206 adopted effective January 1, 2007.

Ref.: Cal. Fms Pl. & Pr., Ch. 193, "Discovery: Depositions," Ch. 254, "Executions and Enforcement of Judgments," Ch. 372, "Motions and Orders," Ch. 406, "Partnerships: Dissolution"; MB Prac. Guide: Cal. Pretrial Proc., §§26.23, 26.26, 26.30[2], 26.32.

Rule 3.1207.   Personal appearance requirements

An ex parte application will be considered without a personal appearance of the applicant in the following cases only:

(1) Applications to file a memorandum in excess of the applicable page limit;

(2) Applications for extensions of time to serve pleadings;

(3) Setting of hearing dates on alternative writs and orders to show cause; and

(4) Stipulations by the parties for an order.

Rule 3.1207 amended effective January 1, 2008; adopted effective January 1, 2007.

Ref.: Cal. Fms Pl. & Pr., Ch. 193, "Discovery: Depositions," Ch. 303, "Injunctions," Ch. 372, "Motions and Orders," Ch. 406, "Partnerships: Dissolution," Ch. 417, "Points and Authorities," Ch. 486, "Receivers"; MB Prac. Guide: Cal. Pretrial Proc., §§26.23, 26.31, 27.11[4], 27.21[5].

Chapter 5
Noticed Motions

Rule 3.1300. Time for filing and service of motion papers
Rule 3.1302. Place and manner of filing
Rule 3.1304. Time of hearing
Rule 3.1306. Evidence at hearing
Rule 3.1308. Tentative rulings
Rule 3.1310. Reporting of proceedings on motions
Rule 3.1312. Preparation of order

Rule 3.1300.   Time for filing and service of motion papers

(a) In general

Unless otherwise ordered or specifically provided by law, all moving and supporting papers must be served and filed in accordance with Code of Civil Procedure section 1005.

(Subd (a) amended effective January 1, 2007; previously amended effective January 1, 2000.)

(b) Order shortening time

The court, on its own motion or on application for an order shortening time supported by a declaration showing good cause, may prescribe shorter times for the filing and service of papers than the times specified in Code of Civil Procedure section 1005.

(Subd (b) adopted effective January 1, 2000.)

(c) Time for filing proof of service

Proof of service of the moving papers must be filed no later than five court days before the time appointed for the hearing.

(Subd (c) amended effective January 1, 2007; adopted as subd (b) effective January 1, 1984; previously relettered effective January 1, 2000.)

(d) Filing of late papers

No paper may be rejected for filing on the ground that it was untimely submitted for filing. If the court, in its discretion, refuses to consider a late filed paper, the minutes or order must so indicate.

(Subd (d) amended effective January 1, 2007; adopted as subd (c) effective January 1, 1992; previously amended and relettered effective January 1, 2000.)

(e) Computation of time

A paper submitted before the close of the clerk's office to the public on the day the paper is due is deemed timely filed.

(Subd (e) relettered effective January 1, 2000; adopted as subd (d) effective January 1, 1992.)

Rule 3.1300 amended and renumbered effective January 1, 2007; adopted as rule 317 effective January 1, 1984; previously amended effective January 1, 1992, and January 1, 2000.

Ref.: Cal. Fms Pl. & Pr., Ch. 2, "Procedural Guide for Civil Actions," Ch. 38, "Reference," Ch. 62, "Attachment," Ch. 119, "Claim and Delivery," Ch. 190, "Discovery: Scope, Regulation, and Timing," Ch. 193, "Discovery: Depositions," Ch. 194, "Discovery: Interrogatories," Ch. 195, "Discovery: Inspection of Tangible Evidence," Ch. 196, "Discovery: Requests for Admissions," Ch. 206, "Demurrers and Motions for Judgment on the Pleadings," Ch. 212, "Dismissal," Ch. 221, "Dissolution of Marriage: Procedure," Ch. 254, "Executions and Enforcement of Judgments," Ch. 258, "Family Law Enforcement: General Enforcement Principles and Remedies," Ch. 323, "Jurisdiction: Personal Jurisdiction, Inconvenient Forum, and Appearances," Ch. 324, "Jurisdiction: Subject Matter Jurisdiction," Ch. 371, "Motions After Trial," Ch. 372, "Motions and Orders," Ch. 375, "Motions to Strike: Pleadings," Ch. 376, "Motions to Strike: Anti-SLAPP," Ch. 412, "Paternity," Ch. 417, "Points and Authorities," Ch. 457, "Probate: Instructions to Personal Representative," Ch. 464, "Public Entities and Officers: California Tort Claims Act," Ch. 486, "Receivers," Ch. 489, "Relief From Judgments and Orders," Ch. 518, "Service of Summons and Papers," Ch. 524, "Shortening and Extension of Time," Ch. 529, "Statement of Decision," Ch. 537, "Summary Judgment"; MB Prac. Guide: Cal. Debt Collection & Enforcement of Judgments, §§10.08, 10.39, 10.43; MB Prac. Guide: Cal. Pretrial Proc., §§1.08, 1.10, 9.03, 9.11, 9.12, 9.16, 9.21, 9.23, 9.30, 9.31, 9.35, 9.38, 9.46, 12.03, 12.06[2][a]–[c], [e], 12.10, 12.11, 12.17, 12.19, 13.05[3], 13.09, 13.11, 13.16, 13.20, 26.01, 26.05[3], 26.34, 26.39, 26.44[1], [3], [4], 26.46, 27.11[2], 27.35[4][g], 36.67[4][a], 36.72[2][d], 38.03, 38.13[2][a], [b]; MB Prac. Guide: Cal. Trial & Post-Trial Civ. Proc., §§4.07[4], 4.17[5], 4.19[1][a], [f], [2][b], [3], 24.09[1], [2], 27.09, 27.13, 29.15[5], 29.32[1][c].

Rule 3.1302.   Place and manner of filing

(a) Papers filed in clerk's office

Unless otherwise provided by local rule, all papers relating to a law and motion proceeding must be filed in the clerk's office.

(Subd (a) amended effective January 1, 2007.)

(b) Requirements for lodged material

Material lodged with the clerk must be accompanied by an addressed envelope with sufficient postage for mailing the material. After determination of the matter, the clerk may mail the material to the party lodging it.

(Subd (b) amended effective January 1, 2007.)

Rule 3.1302 amended and renumbered effective January 1, 2007; adopted as rule 319 effective January 1, 1984.

Ref.: Cal. Fms Pl. & Pr., Ch. 206, "Demurrers and Motions for Judgment on the Pleadings," Ch. 258, "Family Law Enforcement: General Enforcement Principles and Remedies," Ch. 323, "Jurisdiction: Personal Jurisdiction, Inconvenient Forum, and Appearances," Ch. 324, "Jurisdiction: Subject Matter Jurisdiction," Ch. 372, "Motions and Orders," Ch. 375, "Motions to Strike: Pleadings," Ch. 376, "Motions to Strike: Anti-SLAPP," Ch. 537, "Summary Judgment"; MB Prac. Guide: Cal. Debt Collection & Enforcement of Judgments, §§10.08, 10.39, 10.43.

Rule 3.1304.   Time of hearing

(a) General schedule

The clerk must post a general schedule showing the days and departments for holding each type of law and motion hearing.

(Subd (a) amended effective January 1, 2003.)

(b) Duty to notify if matter not to be heard

The moving party must immediately notify the court if a matter will not be heard on the scheduled date.

(Subd (b) amended effective January 1, 2003.)

(c) Notice of nonappearance

A party may give notice that he or she will not appear at a law and motion hearing and submit the matter without an appearance unless the court orders otherwise. The court must rule on the motion as if the party had appeared.

(Subd (c) amended effective January 1, 2003; previously amended effective January 1, 1992.)

(d) Action if no party appears

If a party fails to appear at a law and motion hearing without having given notice under (c), the court may take the matter off calendar, to be reset only upon motion, or may rule on the matter.

(Subd (d) amended effective January 1, 2003; previously amended and relettered effective January 1, 1992.)

Rule 3.1304 amended and renumbered effective January 1, 2007; adopted as rule 321 effective January 1, 1984; previously amended effective January 1, 1992, and January 1, 2003.

Ref.: Cal. Fms Pl. & Pr., Ch. 38, "Reference," Ch. 206, "Demurrers and Motions for Judgment on the Pleadings," Ch. 212, "Dismissal," Ch. 372, "Motions and Orders," Ch. 537, "Summary Judgment"; MB Prac. Guide: Cal. Debt Collection & Enforcement of Judgments, §§8.61, 20.36; MB Prac. Guide: Cal. Pretrial Proc., §§9.03, 9.14, 9.23, 9.33, 26.01, 26.39, 26.43[7], 26.46, 26.51, 26.56, 26.59[1]–[3], 26.70.

Rule 3.1306.   Evidence at hearing

(a) Restrictions on oral testimony

Evidence received at a law and motion hearing must be by declaration or request for judicial notice without testimony or cross-examination, unless the court orders otherwise for good cause shown.

(Subd (a) amended effective January 1, 2007; previously amended effective January 1, 2003.)

(b) Request to present oral testimony

A party seeking permission to introduce oral evidence, except for oral evidence in rebuttal to oral evidence presented by the other party, must file, no later than three court days before the hearing, a written statement stating the nature and extent of the evidence proposed to be introduced and a reasonable time estimate for the hearing. When the statement is filed less than five court days before the hearing, the filing party must serve a copy on the other parties in a manner to assure delivery to the other parties no later than two days before the hearing.

(Subd (b) amended and relettered effective January 1, 2003; adopted as part of subd (a) effective January 1, 1984.)

(c) Judicial notice

A party requesting judicial notice of material under Evidence Code sections 452 or 453 must provide the court and each party with a copy of the material. If the material is part of a file in the court in which the matter is being heard, the party must:

(1) Specify in writing the part of the court file sought to be judicially noticed; and

(2) Make arrangements with the clerk to have the file in the courtroom at the time of the hearing.

(Subd (c) amended effective January 1, 2007; adopted as subd (b) effective January 1, 1984; previously amended and relettered effective January 1, 2003.)

Rule 3.1306 amended and renumbered effective January 1, 2007; adopted as rule 323 effective January 1, 1984; previously amended effective January 1, 2003.

Ref.: Cal. Fms Pl. & Pr., Ch. 90, "Automobiles: Vehicle Leasing Act," Ch. 120, "Class Actions," Ch. 125, "Consolidation, Severance, and Coordination of Actions," Ch. 126, "Conspiracy," Ch. 206, "Demurrers and Motions for Judgment on the Pleadings," Ch. 212, "Dismissal," Ch. 258, "Family Law Enforcement: General Enforcement Principles and Remedies," Ch. 321, "Judicial Notice," Ch. 323, "Jurisdiction: Personal Jurisdiction, Inconvenient Forum, and Appearances," Ch. 324, "Jurisdiction: Subject Matter Jurisdiction," Ch. 345A, "Limited Civil Cases," Ch. 372, "Motions and Orders," Ch. 417, "Points and Authorities," Ch. 451, "Probate: Inventory and Appraisal," Ch. 486, "Receivers," Ch. 489, "Relief From Judgments and Orders," Ch. 501, "Sales: Retail Installment Sales," Ch. 503, "Sales: Secured Transactions," Ch. 524, "Shortening and Extension of Time," Ch. 537, "Summary Judgment"; Cal. Class Actions Prac. & Proc., §§20.03[3], 22.04; MB Prac. Guide: Cal. Debt Collection & Enforcement of Judgments, §§8.61, 20.36; MB Prac. Guide: Cal. Pretrial Proc., §§9.11, 9.21, 9.30, 9.38, 11.03, 11.16[3][a]–[c], 11.24, 13.09, 21.30[1], 26.01, 26.12, 26.14–26.16, 26.17[2], 26.39, 26.43[3], [4], [9], 26.56, 26.59[3], 26.60, 26.63[3], 26.66, 26.68, 26.71 26.74, 33.15, 33.16[2][c], 33.27[1][c], 36.67[4][b], 38.03, 38.15[4][b], 38.19, 38.37[2]; MB Prac. Guide: Cal. Trial & Post-Trial Civ. Proc., §29.15[2].

Rule 3.1308.   Tentative rulings

(a) Tentative ruling procedures

A trial court that offers a tentative ruling procedure in civil law and motion matters must follow one of the following procedures:

(1) *Notice of intent to appear required*

The court must make its tentative ruling available by telephone and also, at the option of the court, by any other method designated by the court, by no later than 3:00 p.m. the court day before the scheduled hearing. If the court

desires oral argument, the tentative ruling must so direct. The tentative ruling may also note any issues on which the court wishes the parties to provide further argument. If the court has not directed argument, oral argument must be permitted only if a party notifies all other parties and the court by 4:00 p.m. on the court day before the hearing of the party's intention to appear. A party must notify all other parties by telephone or in person. The court must accept notice by telephone and, at its discretion, may also designate alternative methods by which a party may notify the court of the party's intention to appear. The tentative ruling will become the ruling of the court if the court has not directed oral argument by its tentative ruling and notice of intent to appear has not been given.

(2) *No notice of intent to appear required*

The court must make its tentative ruling available by telephone and also, at the option of the court, by any other method designated by the court, by a specified time before the hearing. The tentative ruling may note any issues on which the court wishes the parties to provide further argument at the hearing. This procedure must not require the parties to give notice of intent to appear, and the tentative ruling will not automatically become the ruling of the court if such notice is not given. The tentative ruling, or such other ruling as the court may render, will not become the final ruling of the court until the hearing.

(Subd (a) amended effective January 1, 2007; previously amended effective July 1, 2000.)

(b) No other procedures permitted

Other than following one of the tentative ruling procedures authorized in (a), courts must not issue tentative rulings except:

(1) By posting a calendar note containing tentative rulings on the day of the hearing; or

(2) By announcing the tentative ruling at the time of oral argument.

(Subd (b) amended effective January 1, 2007; previously repealed and adopted effective July 1, 2000.)

(c) Notice of procedure

A court that follows one of the procedures described in (a) must so state in its local rules. The local rule must specify the telephone number for obtaining the tentative rulings and the time by which the rulings will be available.

(Subd (c) amended effective January 1, 2007; previously amended effective July 1, 2000.)

(d) Uniform procedure within court or branch

If a court or a branch of a court adopts a tentative ruling procedure, that procedure must be used by all judges in the court or branch who issue tentative rulings.

(Subd (d) amended and lettered effective January 1, 2007; adopted as part of subd (c) effective July 1, 1992.)

(e) Tentative rulings not required

This rule does not require any judge to issue tentative rulings.

(Subd (e) amended and lettered effective January 1, 2007; adopted as part of subd (c) effective July 1, 1992.)

Rule 3.1308 amended and renumbered effective January 1, 2007; adopted as rule 324 effective July 1, 1992; previously amended effective July 1, 2000.

Ref.: Cal. Fms Pl. & Pr., Ch. 38, "Reference," Ch. 206, "Demurrers and Motions for Judgment on the Pleadings," Ch. 212, "Dismissal," Ch. 372, "Motions and Orders," Ch. 537,

"Summary Judgment"; MB Prac. Guide: Cal. Pretrial Proc., §§11.26, 11.27[1], 26.52, 26.54, 26.55.

Rule 3.1310.   Reporting of proceedings on motions

A court that does not regularly provide for reporting or electronic recording of hearings on motions must so state in its local rules. The rules must also provide a procedure by which a party may obtain a reporter or a recording of the proceedings in order to provide an official verbatim transcript.

Rule 3.1310 amended and renumbered effective January 1, 2007; adopted as rule 324.5 effective January 1, 1992.

Ref.: Cal. Fms Pl. & Pr., Ch. 537, "Summary Judgment."

Rule 3.1312.   Preparation of order

(a) Prevailing party to prepare

Unless the parties waive notice or the court orders otherwise, the party prevailing on any motion must, within five days of the ruling, mail or deliver a proposed order to the other party for approval as conforming to the court's order. Within five days after the mailing or delivery, the other party must notify the prevailing party as to whether or not the proposed order is so approved. The opposing party must state any reasons for disapproval. Failure to notify the prevailing party within the time required shall be deemed an approval. Code of Civil Procedure section 1013, relating to service of papers by mail, does not apply to this rule.

(Subd (a) amended effective January 1, 2007; previously amended effective July 1, 2000.)

(b) Submission of proposed order to court

The prevailing party must, upon expiration of the five-day period provided for approval, promptly transmit the proposed order to the court together with a summary of any responses of the other parties or a statement that no responses were received.

(Subd (b) amended effective January 1, 2007; previously amended effective July 1, 2000.)

(c) Failure of prevailing party to prepare form

If the prevailing party fails to prepare and submit a proposed order as required by (a) and (b) above, any other party may do so.

(Subd (c) amended effective July 1, 2000.)

(d) Motion unopposed

This rule does not apply if the motion was unopposed and a proposed order was submitted with the moving papers, unless otherwise ordered by the court.

(Subd (d) amended effective January 1, 2007; adopted effective July 1, 2000.)

Rule 3.1312 amended and renumbered effective January 1, 2007; adopted as rule 391 effective July 1, 1992; previously amended effective July 1, 2000.

Ref.: Cal. Fms Pl. & Pr., Ch. 42, "Appeal: Notice of Appeal," Ch. 212, "Dismissal," Ch. 303, "Injunctions," Ch. 372, "Motions and Orders," Ch. 395, "Parties," Ch. 537, "Summary Judgment"; MB Prac. Guide: Cal. Pretrial Proc., §§26.62[4], 38.03, 38.19.

Chapter 6
Particular Motions

Art. 1.   Pleading and Venue Motions. Rules 3.1320–3.1327.

Art. 2.   Procedural Motions. Rules 3.1330–3.1335.
Art. 3.   Motions to Dismiss. Rules 3.1340, 3.1342.
Art. 4.   Discovery Motions. Rules 3.1345–3.1348.
Art. 5.   Summary Judgment Motions. Rules 3.1350–3.1354.
Art. 6.   Miscellaneous Motions. Rules 3.1360, 3.1362.

Article 1
Pleading and Venue Motions

Rule 3.1320. Demurrers
Rule 3.1322. Motions to strike
Rule 3.1324. Amended pleadings and amendments to pleadings
Rule 3.1326. Motions for change of venue
Rule 3.1327. Motions to quash or to stay action in summary proceeding involving possession of real property

Rule 3.1320.   Demurrers

(a) Grounds separately stated

Each ground of demurrer must be in a separate paragraph and must state whether it applies to the entire complaint, cross-complaint, or answer, or to specified causes of action or defenses.

(Subd (a) amended effective January 1, 2007.)

(b) Demurrer not directed to all causes of action

A demurrer to a cause of action may be filed without answering other causes of action.

(Subd (b) adopted effective January 1, 2007.)

(c) Notice of hearing

A party filing a demurrer must serve and file therewith a notice of hearing that must specify a hearing date in accordance with the provisions of Code of Civil Procedure section 1005.

(Subd (c) amended and relettered effective January 1, 2007; adopted as subd (b) effective January 1, 1984; previously amended effective July 1, 2000.)

(d) Date of hearing

Demurrers must be set for hearing not more than 35 days following the filing of the demurrer or on the first date available to the court thereafter. For good cause shown, the court may order the hearing held on an earlier or later day on notice prescribed by the court.

(Subd (d) amended and lettered effective January 1, 2007; adopted as part of subd (b) effective January 1, 1984.)

(e) Caption

A demurrer must state, on the first page immediately below the number of the case, the name of the party filing the demurrer and the name of the party whose pleading is the subject of the demurrer.

(Subd (e) amended and relettered effective January 1, 2007; adopted as subd (c) effective January 1, 1984.)

(f) Failure to appear at hearing

When a demurrer is regularly called for hearing and one of the parties does not appear, the demurrer must be disposed of on the merits at the request of the party appearing unless for good cause the hearing is continued. Failure to appear in support of a special demurrer may be construed by the court as an admission that the demurrer is not meritorious and as a waiver of all grounds thereof. If neither party appears, the demurrer may be disposed of on its merits or dropped from the calendar, to be restored on notice or on terms as the court may deem proper, or the hearing may be continued to such time as the court orders.

(Subd (f) amended and relettered effective January 1, 2007; adopted as subd (d) effective January 1, 1984.)

(g) Leave to answer or amend

Following a ruling on a demurrer, unless otherwise ordered, leave to answer or amend within 10 days is deemed granted, except for actions in forcible entry, forcible detainer, or unlawful detainer in which case 5 calendar days is deemed granted.

(Subd (g) amended and relettered effective January 1, 2007; adopted as subd (e) effective January 1, 1984.)

(h) Ex parte application to dismiss following failure to amend

A motion to dismiss the entire action and for entry of judgment after expiration of the time to amend following the sustaining of a demurrer may be made by ex parte application to the court under Code of Civil Procedure section 581(f)(2).

(Subd (h) amended and relettered effective January 1, 2007; adopted as subd (f) effective January 1, 1984; previously amended effective July 1, 1995.)

(i) Motion to strike late-filed amended pleading

If an amended pleading is filed after the time allowed, an order striking the amended pleading must be obtained by noticed motion **under** Code of Civil Procedure section 1010.

(Subd (i) amended effective January 1, 2009; adopted as part of subd (f) effective January 1, 1984; previously amended effective July 1, 1995; previously amended and lettered effective January 1, 2007.)

(j) Time for motion to strike, demur, or otherwise plead after demurrer

Unless otherwise ordered, defendant has 10 days to move to strike, demur, or otherwise plead to the complaint or the remaining causes of action following:

(1) The overruling of the demurrer;

(2) The amendment of the complaint or the expiration of the time to amend if the demurrer was sustained with leave to amend; or

(3) The sustaining of the demurrer if the demurrer was sustained without leave to amend.

(Subd (j) amended and relettered effective January 1, 2007; adopted as subd (g) adopted effective July 1, 1984.)

Rule 3.1320 amended effective January 1, 2009; adopted as rule 325 effective January 1, 1984; previously amended effective July 1, 1984, July 1, 1995, and July 1, 2000; previously amended and renumbered effective January 1, 2007.

Ref.: Cal. Fms Pl. & Pr., Ch. 1, "New Developments," Ch. 2, "Procedural Guide for Civil Actions," Ch. 3, "Abatement of Actions," Ch. 13, "Adverse Possession," Ch. 21, "Amended and Supplemental Pleadings," Ch. 26, "Answers," Ch. 58, "Assault and Battery," Ch. 61, "Associations and Clubs," Ch. 76, "Attorney Professional Liability," Ch. 90, "Automobiles: Vehicle Leasing Act," Ch. 124, "Condominiums and Other Common Interest Developments," Ch. 126, "Conspiracy," Ch. 140, "Contracts," Ch. 161, "Corporations: Alter Ego Liability," Ch. 165, "Corporations: Corporate Records and Reports," Ch. 181, "Death and Survival Actions," Ch. 206, "Demurrers and Motions for Judgment on the Pleadings," Ch. 248, "Employer's Liability for Employee's Torts," Ch. 290D, "Guardianship and Conservatorship: Actions Against Guardians, Conservators, and Sureties," Ch. 303, "Injunctions," Ch. 324, "Jurisdiction: Subject Matter Jurisdiction," Ch. 334, "Landlord and Tenant: Claims for Damages," Ch. 340, "Libel and Slander," Ch. 345, "Limitation of Actions," Ch. 358, "Mandate and Prohibition," Ch. 361, "Mechanics' Liens," Ch. 395, "Parties," Ch. 425, "Pretrial Proceedings," Ch. 444, "Probate: Will Contests," Ch. 464, "Public Entities and Officers: California Tort Claims Act," Ch. 471B, "Licensing by Public Agencies," Ch. 474C, "Procedures in Reviewing Agency Decisions," Ch. 491, "Res Judicata," Ch. 492, "Review (Certiorari), Writ of," Ch. 518, "Service of Summons and Papers," Ch. 560, "Trusts: Express, Public, Charitable, and Totten Trusts"; MB Prac. Guide: Cal. Pretrial Proc., §§1.04, 4.38, 8.38, 8.41[1], 11.03, 11.12[3], 11.15[3], 11.16[1], 11.17[3], 11.26, 11.27[3][a]–[c], 11.29[1][a], [2][c], 11.60, 11.61, 14.03, 14.09[4], 18.32, 34.03[1], 34.10[1].

Rule 3.1322.   Motions to strike

(a) Contents of notice

A notice of motion to strike a portion of a pleading must quote in full the portions sought to be stricken except where the motion is to strike an entire paragraph, cause of action, count, or defense. Specifications in a notice must be numbered consecutively.

(Subd (a) amended and lettered effective January 1, 2007; adopted as part of untitled subd effective January 1, 1984.)

(b) Timing

A notice of motion to strike must be given within the time allowed to plead, and if a demurrer is interposed, concurrently therewith, and must be noticed for hearing and heard at the same time as the demurrer.

(Subd (b) amended and lettered effective January 1, 2007; adopted as part of untitled subd effective January 1, 1984.)

Rule 3.1322 amended and renumbered effective January 1, 2007; adopted as rule 329 effective January 1, 1984.

Ref.: Cal. Fms Pl. & Pr., Ch. 2, "Procedural Guide for Civil Actions," Ch. 206, "Demurrers and Motions for Judgment on the Pleadings," Ch. 372, "Motions and Orders," Ch. 375, "Motions to Strike: Pleadings," Ch. 425, "Pretrial Proceedings"; MB Prac. Guide: Cal. Pretrial Proc., §§11.03, 11.17[2], 12.03, 12.06[1], 12.07, 12.09[1], [2], 12.15.

Rule 3.1324.   Amended pleadings and amendments to pleadings

(a) Contents of motion

A motion to amend a pleading before trial must:

(1) Include a copy of the proposed amendment or amended pleading, which must be serially numbered to differentiate it from previous pleadings or amendments;

(2) State what allegations in the previous pleading are proposed to be deleted, if any, and where, by page, paragraph, and line number, the deleted allegations are located; and

(3) State what allegations are proposed to be added to the previous pleading, if any, and where, by page, paragraph, and line number, the additional allegations are located.

(Subd (a) amended effective January 1, 2002.)

(b) Supporting declaration

A separate declaration must accompany the motion and must specify:

(1) The effect of the amendment;

(2) Why the amendment is necessary and proper;

(3) When the facts giving rise to the amended allegations were discovered; and

(4) The reasons why the request for amendment was not made earlier.

(Subd (b) adopted effective January 1, 2002.)

(c) Form of amendment

The court may deem a motion to file an amendment to a pleading to be a motion to file an amended pleading and require the filing of the entire previous pleading with the approved amendments incorporated into it.

(Subd (c) adopted effective January 1, 2002.)

(d) Requirements for amendment to a pleading

An amendment to a pleading must not be made by alterations on the face of a pleading except by permission of the court. All alterations must be initialed by the court or the clerk.

(Subd (d) amended and relettered effective January 1, 2002; adopted as subd (b) effective January 1, 1984.)

Rule 3.1324 renumbered effective January 1, 2007; adopted as rule 327 effective January 1, 1984; previously amended effective January 1, 2002.

Ref.: Cal. Fms Pl. & Pr., Ch. 2, "Procedural Guide for Civil Actions," Ch. 21, "Amended and Supplemental Pleadings," Ch. 110, "Churches and Religious Organizations," Ch. 123, "Complaints and Cross Complaints," Ch. 206, "Demurrers and Motions for Judgment on the Pleadings," Ch. 388, "Nonprofit Corporations," Ch. 415, "Physicians: Medical Malpractice"; MB Prac. Guide: Cal. Pretrial Proc., §§34.06, 34.08[1][c].

Rule 3.1326.   Motions for change of venue

Following denial of a motion to transfer under Code of Civil Procedure section 396b, unless otherwise ordered, 30 calendar days are deemed granted defendant to move to strike, demur, or otherwise plead if the defendant has not previously filed a response. If a motion to transfer is granted, 30 calendar days are deemed granted from the date the receiving court mails notice of receipt of the case and its new case number.

Rule 3.1326 amended and renumbered effective January 1, 2007; adopted as rule 326 effective January 1, 1984; previously amended effective July 1, 1984.

Ref.: Cal. Fms Pl. & Pr., Ch. 2, "Procedural Guide for Civil Actions," Ch. 206, "Demurrers and Motions for Judgment on the Pleadings," Ch. 372, "Motions and Orders"; MB Prac. Guide: Cal. Pretrial Proc., §§1.04, 11.03, 11.12[4].

Rule 3.1327.   Motions to quash or to stay action in summary proceeding involving possession of real property

(a) Notice

In an unlawful detainer action or other action brought under chapter 4 of title 3 of part 3 of the Code of Civil Procedure (commencing with section 1159), notice of a motion to quash service of summons on the ground of lack of jurisdiction or to stay or dismiss the action on the ground of inconvenient forum must be given in compliance with Code of Civil Procedure sections 1013 and 1167.4.

(Subd (a) adopted effective January 1, 2009.)

(b) Opposition and reply at hearing

Any opposition to the motion and any reply to an opposition may be made orally at the time of hearing or in writing as set forth in (c).

(Subd (b) adopted effective January 1, 2009.)

(c) Written opposition in advance of hearing

If a party seeks to have a written opposition considered in advance of the hearing, the written opposition must be filed and served on or before the court day before the hearing. Service must be by personal delivery, facsimile transmission, express mail, or other means consistent with Code of Civil Procedure sections 1010, 1011, 1012, and 1013, and reasonably calculated to ensure delivery to the other party or parties no later than the close of business on the court day before the hearing. The court, in its discretion, may consider written opposition filed later.

(Subd (c) adopted effective January 1, 2009.)

Rule 3.1327 adopted effective January 1, 2009.

Article 2
Procedural Motions

Rule 3.1330. Motion concerning arbitration
Rule 3.1332. Motion or application for continuance of trial
Rule 3.1335. Motion or application to advance, specially set, or reset trial date

Rule 3.1330.   Motion concerning arbitration

A petition to compel arbitration or to stay proceedings pursuant to Code of Civil Procedure sections 1281.2 and 1281.4 must state, in addition to other required allegations, the provisions of the written agreement and the paragraph that provides for arbitration. The provisions must be stated verbatim or a copy must be attached to the petition and incorporated by reference.

Rule 3.1330 amended and renumbered effective January 1, 2007; adopted as rule 371 effective January 1, 1984.

Ref.: Cal. Fms Pl. & Pr., Ch. 32, "Contractual Arbitration: Agreements and Compelling Arbitration," Ch. 372, "Motions and Orders"; MB Prac. Guide: Cal. Pretrial Proc., §§6.15[2][a], 6.22[2].

Rule 3.1332.   Motion or application for continuance of trial

(a) Trial dates are firm

To ensure the prompt disposition of civil cases, the dates assigned for a trial are firm. All parties and their counsel must regard the date set for trial as certain.

(Subd (a) repealed and adopted effective January 1, 2004; amended effective January 1, 1995.)

(b) Motion or application

A party seeking a continuance of the date set for trial, whether contested or uncontested or stipulated to by the parties, must make the request for a continuance by a noticed motion or an ex parte application under the rules in chapter 4 of this division, with supporting declarations. The party must make the motion or application as soon as reasonably practical once the necessity for the continuance is discovered.

(Subd (b) amended effective January 1, 2007; previously amended effective January 1, 1995.)

(c) Grounds for continuance

Although continuances of trials are disfavored, each request for a continuance must be considered on its own merits. The court may grant a continuance only on an affirmative showing of good cause requiring the continuance. Circumstances that may indicate good cause include:

(1) The unavailability of an essential lay or expert witness because of death, illness, or other excusable circumstances;

(2) The unavailability of a party because of death, illness, or other excusable circumstances;

(3) The unavailability of trial counsel because of death, illness, or other excusable circumstances;

(4) The substitution of trial counsel, but only where there is an affirmative showing that the substitution is required in the interests of justice;

(5) The addition of a new party if:

(A) The new party has not had a reasonable opportunity to conduct discovery and prepare for trial; or

(B) The other parties have not had a reasonable opportunity to conduct discovery and prepare for trial in regard to the new party's involvement in the case;

(6) A party's excused inability to obtain essential testimony, documents, or other material evidence despite diligent efforts; or

(7) A significant, unanticipated change in the status of the case as a result of which the case is not ready for trial.

(Subd (c) amended effective January 1, 2007; adopted effective January 1, 2004.)

(d) Other factors to be considered

In ruling on a motion or application for continuance, the court must consider all the facts and circumstances that are relevant to the determination. These may include:

(1) The proximity of the trial date;

(2) Whether there was any previous continuance, extension of time, or delay of trial due to any party;

(3) The length of the continuance requested;

(4) The availability of alternative means to address the problem that gave rise to the motion or application for a continuance;

(5) The prejudice that parties or witnesses will suffer as a result of the continuance;

(6) If the case is entitled to a preferential trial setting, the reasons for that status and whether the need for a continuance outweighs the need to avoid delay;

(7) The court's calendar and the impact of granting a continuance on other pending trials;

(8) Whether trial counsel is engaged in another trial;

(9) Whether all parties have stipulated to a continuance;

(10) Whether the interests of justice are best served by a continuance, by the trial of the matter, or by imposing conditions on the continuance; and

(11) Any other fact or circumstance relevant to the fair determination of the motion or application.

(Subd (d) adopted effective January 1, 2004.)

Rule 3.1332 amended and renumbered effective January 1, 2007; adopted as rule 375 effective January 1, 1984; previously amended effective January 1, 1985, January 1, 1995, and January 1, 2004.

Ref.: Cal. Fms Pl. & Pr., Ch. 2, "Procedural Guide for Civil Actions," Ch. 136, "Continuances," Ch. 160, "Corporations: Capacity," Ch. 221, "Dissolution of Marriage: Procedure," Ch. 372, "Motions and Orders," Ch. 373, "Motions In Limine," Ch. 425, "Pretrial Proceedings," Ch. 551, "Trial"; MB Prac. Guide: Cal. Pretrial Proc., §§23.27, 30.01–30.03, 30.05, 30.06, 30.07[1]–[3], 30.08[1][a], [2][a], [b], [3][a], [5][a], [c], [9]–[11], 30.09[2][a], [3][a]–[c], [4][a], [5][a], 30.12, 30.13, 30.14[1], [2], 30.20, 30.21, 30.25, 30.27; MB Prac. Guide: Cal. Trial & Post-Trial Civ. Proc., §§1.43, 4.19[5][a], 4.26[1][b], 11.16, 11.18.

Rule 3.1335. Motion or application to advance, specially set, or reset trial date

(a) Noticed motion or application required

A party seeking to advance, specially set, or reset a case for trial must make this request by noticed motion or ex parte application under the rules in chapter 4 of this division.

(Subd (a) amended effective January 1, 2007.)

(b) Grounds for motion or application

The request may be granted only upon an affirmative showing by the moving party of good cause based on a declaration served and filed with the motion or application.

Rule 3.1335 amended and renumbered effective January 1, 2007; adopted as rule 375.1 effective January 1, 2004.

Ref.: Cal. Fms Pl. & Pr., Ch. 2, "Procedural Guide for Civil Actions," Ch. 212, "Dismissal," Ch. 221, "Dissolution of Marriage: Procedure," Ch. 372, "Motions and Orders," Ch. 397, "Partition," Ch. 425, "Pretrial Proceedings," Ch. 551, "Trial"; MB Prac. Guide: Cal. Pretrial Proc., §§23.26[1], [2], 23.36, 23.68, 23.69, 30.04[1][b]; MB Prac. Guide: Cal. Trial & Post-Trial Civ. Proc., §4.19[5][a].

Article 3
Motions to Dismiss

Rule 3.1340. Motion for discretionary dismissal after two years for delay in prosecution
Rule 3.1342. Motion to dismiss for delay in prosecution

Rule 3.1340. Motion for discretionary dismissal after two years for delay in prosecution

(a) Discretionary dismissal two years after filing

The court on its own motion or on motion of the defendant may dismiss an action under Code of Civil Procedure sections 583.410–583.430 for delay in prosecution if the action has not been brought to trial or conditionally settled within two years after the action was commenced against the defendant.

(Subd (a) amended effective January 1, 2007.)

(b) Notice of court's intention to dismiss

If the court intends to dismiss an action on its own motion, the clerk must set a hearing on the dismissal and mail notice to all parties at least 20 days before the hearing date.

(Subd (b) amended and lettered effective January 1, 2007; adopted as part of subd (a) effective January 1, 1990.)

(c) Definition of "conditionally settled"

"Conditionally settled" means:

(1) A settlement agreement conditions dismissal on the satisfactory completion of specified terms that are not to be fully performed within two years after the filing of the case; and

(2) Notice of the settlement is filed with the court as provided in rule 3.1385.

(Subd (c) amended and lettered effective January 1, 2007; adopted as part of subd (a) effective January 1, 1990.)

Rule 3.1340 amended and renumbered effective January 1, 2007; adopted as rule 372 effective January 1, 1990.

Ref.: Cal. Fms Pl. & Pr., Ch. 2, "Procedural Guide for Civil Actions," Ch. 36, "Judicial Arbitration," Ch. 136, "Continuances," Ch. 212, "Dismissal"; MB Prac. Guide: Cal. Pretrial Proc., §§1.09, 30.04[1][c], 40.19[1], 40.20, 40.28.

Rule 3.1342.   Motion to dismiss for delay in prosecution

(a) Notice of motion

A party seeking dismissal of a case **under** Code of Civil Procedure sections 583.410–583.430 must serve and file a notice of motion at least 45 days before the date set for hearing of the motion. The party may, with the memorandum, serve and file a declaration stating facts in support of the motion. The filing of the notice of motion must not preclude the opposing party from further prosecution of the case to bring it to trial.

(Subd (a) amended effective January 1, 2009; previously amended effective January 1, 1986, and January 1, 2007.)

(b) Written opposition

Within 15 days after service of the notice of motion, the opposing party may serve and file a written opposition. The failure of the opposing party to serve and file a written opposition may be construed by the court as an admission that the motion is meritorious, and the court may grant the motion without a hearing on the merits.

(Subd (b) amended effective January 1, 2007.)

(c) Response to opposition

Within 15 days after service of the written opposition, if any, the moving party may serve and file a response.

(Subd (c) amended effective January 1, 2007.)

(d) Reply

Within five days after service of the response, if any, the opposing party may serve and file a reply.

(e) Relevant matters

In ruling on the motion, the court must consider all matters relevant to a proper determination of the motion, including:

(1) The court's file in the case and the declarations and supporting data submitted by the parties and, where applicable, the availability of the moving party and other essential parties for service of process;

(2) The diligence in seeking to effect service of process;

(3) The extent to which the parties engaged in any settlement negotiations or discussions;

(4) The diligence of the parties in pursuing discovery or other pretrial proceedings, including any extraordinary relief sought by either party;

(5) The nature and complexity of the case;

(6) The law applicable to the case, including the pendency of other litigation under a common set of facts or determinative of the legal or factual issues in the case;

(7) The nature of any extensions of time or other delay attributable to either party;

(8) The condition of the court's calendar and the availability of an earlier trial date if the matter was ready for trial;

(9) Whether the interests of justice are best served by dismissal or trial of the case; and

(10) Any other fact or circumstance relevant to a fair determination of the issue.

The court must be guided by the policies set forth in Code of Civil Procedure section 583.130.

(Subd (e) amended effective January 1, 2007; previously amended effective January 1, 1986.)

(f) Court action

The court may grant or deny the motion or, where the facts warrant, the court may continue or defer its ruling on the matter pending performance by either party of any conditions relating to trial or dismissal of the case that may be required by the court to effectuate substantial justice.

Rule 3.1342 amended effective January 1, 2009; adopted as rule 373 effective January 1, 1984; previously amended effective January 1, 1986; previously amended and renumbered effective January 1, 2007.

Ref.: Cal. Fms Pl. & Pr., Ch. 2, "Procedural Guide for Civil Actions," Ch. 212, "Dismissal," Ch. 372, "Motions and Orders," Ch. 425, "Pretrial Proceedings"; MB Prac. Guide: Cal. Pretrial Proc., §§1.09, 8.39[2][b], 9.42[2][b]–[f], 23.36, 26.44[1], 27.04[1] 40.03[1], 40.19[1], [2], 40.23–40.25, 40.27, 40.30–40.33, 40.35; MB Prac. Guide: Cal. Trial & Post-Trial Civ. Proc., §4.19[5][a].

Article 4
Discovery Motions

Title 3, Civil Rules—Division 11, Law and Motion—Chapter 6, Particular Motions—Article 4, Discovery Motions adopted effective January 1, 2009.

Rule 3.1345. Format of discovery motions
Rule 3.1346. Service of motion papers on nonparty deponent
Rule 3.1347. Discovery motions in summary proceeding involving possession of real property
Rule 3.1348. Sanctions for failure to provide discovery

Rule 3.1345.   Format of discovery motions

(a) Separate statement required

Any motion involving the content of a discovery request or the responses to such a request must be accompanied by a separate statement. The motions that require a separate statement include a motion:

(1) To compel further responses to requests for admission;

(2) To compel further responses to interrogatories;

(3) To compel further responses to a demand for inspection of documents or tangible things;

(4) To compel answers at a deposition;

(5) To compel or to quash the production of documents or tangible things at a deposition;

(6) For medical examination over objection; and

(7) For issue or evidentiary sanctions.

(Subd (a) amended effective January 1, 2007; previously amended effective July 1, 1987, January 1, 1992, January 1, 1997, and July 1, 2001.)

(b) Separate statement not required

A separate statement is not required when no response has been provided to the request for discovery.

(Subd (b) adopted effective July 1, 2001.)

(c) Contents of separate statement

A separate statement is a separate document filed and served with the discovery motion that provides all the information necessary to understand each discovery request and all the responses to it that are at issue. The separate statement must be full and complete so that no person is required to review any other document in order to determine the full request and the full response.

Material must not be incorporated into the separate statement by reference. The separate statement must include—for each discovery request (e.g., each interrogatory, request for admission, deposition question, or inspection demand) to which a further response, answer, or production is requested—the following:

(1) The text of the request, interrogatory, question, or inspection demand;

(2) The text of each response, answer, or objection, and any further responses or answers;

(3) A statement of the factual and legal reasons for compelling further responses, answers, or production as to each matter in dispute;

(4) If necessary, the text of all definitions, instructions, and other matters required to understand each discovery request and the responses to it;

(5) If the response to a particular discovery request is dependent on the response given to another discovery request, or if the reasons a further response to a particular discovery request is deemed necessary are based on the response to some other discovery request, the other request and the response to it must be set forth; and

(6) If the pleadings, other documents in the file, or other items of discovery are relevant to the motion, the party relying on them must summarize each relevant document.

(Subd (c) amended effective January 1, 2007; previously repealed and adopted effective July 1, 2001.)

(d) Identification of interrogatories, demands, or requests

A motion concerning interrogatories, inspection demands, or admission requests must identify the interrogatories, demands, or requests by set and number.

(Subd (d) amended effective January 1, 2007; adopted as subd (b) effective January 1, 1984; previously amended effective July 1, 1987; previously relettered effective July 1, 2001.)

Rule 3.1345 renumbered effective January 1, 2009; adopted as rule 335 effective January 1, 1984; previously amended effective July 1, 1987, January 1, 1992, January 1, 1997, and July 1, 2001; previously amended and renumbered as rule 3.1020 effective January 1, 2007.

Ref.: Cal. Fms Pl. & Pr., Ch. 190, "Discovery: Scope, Regulation, and Timing," Ch. 192, "Discovery: Sanctions for Discovery Misuse," Ch. 193, "Discovery: Depositions," Ch. 194, "Discovery: Interrogatories," Ch. 195, "Discovery: Inspection of Tangible Evidence," Ch. 196, "Discovery: Requests for Admissions," Ch. 197, "Discovery: Physical and Mental Examinations," Ch. 198, "Discovery: Exchange of Expert Witness Information."

Rule 3.1346. Service of motion papers on nonparty deponent

A written notice and all moving papers supporting a motion to compel an answer to a deposition question or to compel production of a document or tangible thing from a nonparty deponent must be personally served on the nonparty deponent unless the nonparty deponent agrees to accept service by mail at an address specified on the deposition record.

Rule 3.1346 renumbered effective January 1, 2009; adopted as rule 337 effective January 1, 1984; previously amended effective July 1, 1987; previously amended and renumbered as rule 3.1025 effective January 1, 2007.

Ref.: Cal. Fms Pl. & Pr., Ch. 190, "Discovery: Scope, Regulation, and Timing," Ch. 193, "Discovery: Depositions," Ch.

194, "Discovery: Interrogatories," Ch. 195, "Discovery: Inspection of Tangible Evidence," Ch. 196, "Discovery: Requests for Admissions," Ch. 197, "Discovery: Physical and Mental Examinations," Ch. 198, "Discovery: Exchange of Expert Witness Information."

Rule 3.1347. Discovery motions in summary proceeding involving possession of real property

(a) Notice

In an unlawful detainer action or other action brought under chapter 4 of title 3 of part 3 of the Code of Civil Procedure (commencing with section 1159), notice of a discovery motion must be given in compliance with Code of Civil Procedure sections 1013 and 1170.8.

(Subd (a) adopted effective January 1, 2009.)

(b) Opposition and reply at hearing

Any opposition to the motion and any reply to an opposition may be made orally at the time of hearing or in writing as set forth in (c).

(Subd (b) adopted effective January 1, 2009.)

(c) Written opposition in advance of hearing

If a party seeks to have a written opposition considered in advance of the hearing, the written opposition must be served and filed on or before the court day before the hearing. Service must be by personal delivery, facsimile transmission, express mail, or other means consistent with Code of Civil Procedure sections 1010, 1011, 1012, and 1013, and reasonably calculated to ensure delivery to the other party or parties no later than the close of business on the court day before the hearing. The court, in its discretion, may consider written opposition filed later.

(Subd (c) adopted effective January 1, 2009.)

Rule 3.1347 adopted effective January 1, 2009.

Rule 3.1348. Sanctions for failure to provide discovery

(a) Sanctions despite no opposition

The court may award sanctions under the Discovery Act in favor of a party who files a motion to compel discovery, even though no opposition to the motion was filed, or opposition to the motion was withdrawn, or the requested discovery was provided to the moving party after the motion was filed.

(b) Failure to oppose not an admission

The failure to file a written opposition or to appear at a hearing or the voluntary provision of discovery shall not be deemed an admission that the motion was proper or that sanctions should be awarded.

Rule 3.1348 renumbered effective January 1, 2009; adopted as rule 341 effective July 1, 2001; previously renumbered as rule 3.1030 effective January 1, 2007.

Ref.: Cal. Fms Pl. & Pr., Ch. 190, "Discovery: Scope, Regulation, and Timing," Ch. 192, "Discovery: Sanctions for Discovery Misuse," Ch. 193, "Discovery: Depositions," Ch. 194, "Discovery: Interrogatories," Ch. 195, "Discovery: Inspection of Tangible Evidence," Ch. 196, "Discovery: Requests for Admissions," Ch. 197, "Discovery: Physical and Mental Examinations," Ch. 198, "Discovery: Exchange of Expert Witness Information."

Article 5
Summary Judgment Motions

Title 3, Civil Rules—Division 11, Law and Motion—Chapter 6, Particular Motions—Article 5, Summary Judgment Motions re-

numbered effective January 1, 2009; adopted as article 4 effective January 1, 2007.

Rule 3.1350. Motion for summary judgment or summary adjudication

Rule 3.1351. Motions for summary judgment in summary proceeding involving possession of real property

Rule 3.1352. Objections to evidence

Rule 3.1354. Written objections to evidence

Rule 3.1350. Motion for summary judgment or summary adjudication

(a) Motion

As used in this rule, "motion" refers to either a motion for summary judgment or a motion for summary adjudication.

(b) Motion for summary adjudication

If made in the alternative, a motion for summary adjudication may make reference to and depend on the same evidence submitted in support of the summary judgment motion. If summary adjudication is sought, whether separately or as an alternative to the motion for summary judgment, the specific cause of action, affirmative defense, claims for damages, or issues of duty must be stated specifically in the notice of motion and be repeated, verbatim, in the separate statement of undisputed material facts.

(Subd (b) amended effective January 1, 2007; previously amended effective January 1, 2002.)

(c) Documents in support of motion

Except as provided in Code of Civil Procedure section 437c(r) and rule 3.1351, the motion must contain and be supported by the following documents:

(1) Notice of motion by *[moving party]* for summary judgment or summary adjudication or both;

(2) Separate statement of undisputed material facts in support of *[moving party's]* motion for summary judgment or summary adjudication or both;

(3) Memorandum in support of *[moving party's]* motion for summary judgment or summary adjudication or both;

(4) Evidence in support of *[moving party's]* motion for summary judgment or summary adjudication or both; and

(5) Request for judicial notice in support of *[moving party's]* motion for summary judgment or summary adjudication or both (if appropriate).

(Subd (c) amended effective January 1, 2009; previously amended effective January 1, 2002, and January 1, 2007.)

(d) Separate statement in support of motion

The Separate Statement of Undisputed Material Facts in support of a motion must separately identify each cause of action, claim, issue of duty, or affirmative defense, and each supporting material fact claimed to be without dispute with respect to the cause of action, claim, issue of duty, or affirmative defense. In a two-column format, the statement must state in numerical sequence the undisputed material facts in the first column followed by the evidence that establishes those undisputed facts in that same column. Citation to the evidence in support of each material fact must include reference to the exhibit, title, page, and line numbers.

(Subd (d) amended effective January 1, 2008; previously amended effective January 1, 2002, and January 1, 2007.)

(e) Documents in opposition to motion

Except as provided in Code of Civil Procedure section 437c(r) and rule 3.1351, the opposition to a motion must consist of the following documents, separately stapled and titled as shown:

(1) *[Opposing party's]* memorandum in opposition to *[moving party's]* motion for summary judgment or summary adjudication or both;

(2) *[Opposing party's]* separate statement of undisputed material facts in opposition to *[moving party's]* motion for summary judgment or summary adjudication or both;

(3) *[Opposing party's]* evidence in opposition to *[moving party's]* motion for summary judgment or summary adjudication or both (if appropriate); and

(4) *[Opposing party's]* request for judicial notice in opposition to *[moving party's]* motion for summary judgment or summary adjudication or both (if appropriate).

(Subd (e) amended effective January 1, 2009; previously amended effective January 1, 2002, and January 1, 2007.)

(f) Opposition to motion; content of separate statement

Each material fact claimed by the moving party to be undisputed must be set out verbatim on the left side of the page, below which must be set out the evidence said by the moving party to establish that fact, complete with the moving party's references to exhibits. On the right side of the page, directly opposite the recitation of the moving party's statement of material facts and supporting evidence, the response must unequivocally state whether that fact is "disputed" or "undisputed." An opposing party who contends that a fact is disputed must state, on the right side of the page directly opposite the fact in dispute, the nature of the dispute and describe the evidence that supports the position that the fact is controverted. That evidence must be supported by citation to exhibit, title, page, and line numbers in the evidence submitted.

(Subd (f) amended effective January 1, 2002.)

(g) Documentary evidence

If evidence in support of or in opposition to a motion exceeds 25 pages, the evidence must be separately bound and must include a table of contents.

(Subd (g) amended effective January 1, 2007; previously amended effective January 1, 2002.)

(h) Format for separate statements

Supporting and opposing separate statements in a motion for summary judgment must follow this format:

Supporting statement:

Moving Party's Undisputed Material Facts and Supporting Evidence:

Opposing Party's Response and Supporting Evidence:

1. Plaintiff and defendant entered into a written contract for the sale of widgets. Jackson declaration, 2:17–21; contract, Ex. A to Jackson declaration.

2. No widgets were ever received. Jackson declaration, 3:7–21.

Opposing statement:

Moving Party's Undisputed Material Facts and Alleged Supporting Evidence:

1. Plaintiff and defendant entered into a written contract for the sale of widgets. Jackson declaration, 2:17–21; contract, Ex. A to Jackson declaration.

2. No widgets were ever received. Jackson declaration, 3:7–21.

Supporting and opposing separate statements in a motion for summary adjudication must follow this format:

Supporting statement:

Opposing Party's Response and Evidence:

Undisputed.

Disputed. The widgets were received in New Zealand on August 31, 2001. Baygi declaration, 7:2–5.

ISSUE 1—THE FIRST CAUSE OF ACTION FOR NEGLIGENCE IS BARRED BECAUSE PLAINTIFF EXPRESSLY ASSUMED THE RISK OF INJURY

Moving Party's Undisputed Material Facts and Supporting Evidence:

1. Plaintiff was injured while mountain climbing on a trip with Any Company USA. Plaintiff's deposition, 12:3–4.

2. Before leaving on the mountain climbing trip, plaintiff signed a [1] waiver of liability **for acts of negligence**. Smith declaration, 5:4–5; waiver of liability, Ex. A to Smith declaration.

Opposing statement:

Opposing Party's Response and Supporting Evidence:

ISSUE 1—THE FIRST CAUSE OF ACTION FOR NEGLIGENCE IS BARRED BECAUSE PLAINTIFF EXPRESSLY ASSUMED THE RISK OF INJURY

Moving Party's Undisputed Material Facts and Alleged Supporting Evidence:

1. Plaintiff was injured while mountain climbing on a trip with Any Company USA. Plaintiff's deposition, 12:3–4.

2. Before leaving on the mountain climbing trip, plaintiff signed a waiver of liability for acts of negligence. Smith declaration, 5:4–5; waiver of liability, Ex. A to Smith declaration.

Opposing Party's Response and Evidence:

Undisputed.

Disputed. Plaintiff did not sign the waiver of liability; the signature on the waiver is forged. Jones declaration, 3:6–7.

(Subd (h) amended effective July 1, 2008; previously amended effective January 1, 1999, January 1, 2002, and January 1, 2008.)

Rule 3.1350(h).   2008 Deletes. [1] complete

(i) Request for electronic version of separate statement

On request, a party must within three days provide to any other party or the court an electronic version of its separate statement. The electronic version may be provided in any form on which the parties agree. If the parties are unable to agree on the form, the responding party must provide to the requesting party the electronic version of the separate statement that it used to prepare the document filed with the court. Under this subdivision, a party is not required to create an electronic version or any new version of any document for the purpose of transmission to the requesting party.

(Subd (i) amended effective January 1, 2007; adopted effective January 1, 2002.)

Rule 3.1350 amended effective January 1, 2009; adopted as rule 342 effective July 1, 1997; previously amended effective January 1, 1999, January 1, 2002, January 1, 2008, and July 1, 2008; previously amended and renumbered effective January 1, 2007.

Ref.: Cal. Fms Pl. & Pr., Ch. 1, "New Developments," Ch. 321, "Judicial Notice," Ch. 417, "Points and Authorities," Ch. 537, "Summary Judgment"; MB Prac. Guide: Cal. Debt Collection & Enforcement of Judgments, §7.18[4]; MB Prac. Guide: Cal. Pretrial Proc., §§26.01, 26.43[5][b], 26.71–26.74, 38.03, 38.14, 38.15[5], 38.16[1], 38.17, 38.19, 38.23[7], 38.24[2], 38.25[2], 38.58, 38.60, 38.61, 38.66, 38.68, 38.69.

Rule 3.1351.   Motions for summary judgment in summary proceeding involving possession of real property

(a) Notice

In an unlawful detainer action or other action brought under chapter 4 of title 3 of part 3 of the Code of Civil Procedure (commencing with section 1159), notice of a motion for summary judgment must be given in compliance with Code of Civil Procedure sections 1013 and 1170.7.

(Subd (a) adopted effective January 1, 2009.)

(b) Opposition and reply at hearing

Any opposition to the motion and any reply to an opposition may be made orally at the time of hearing or in writing as set forth in (c).

(Subd (b) adopted effective January 1, 2009.)

(c) Written opposition in advance of hearing

If a party seeks to have a written opposition considered in advance of the hearing, the written opposition must be filed and served on or before the court day before the hearing. Service must be by personal delivery, facsimile transmission, express mail, or other means consistent with Code of Civil Procedure sections 1010, 1011, 1012, and 1013, and reasonably calculated to ensure delivery to the other party or parties no later than the close of business on the court day before the hearing. The court, in its discretion, may consider written opposition filed later.

(Subd (c) adopted effective January 1, 2009.)

Rule 3.1351 adopted effective January 1, 2009.

Rule 3.1352.   Objections to evidence

A party desiring to make objections to evidence in the papers on a motion for summary judgment must either:

(1) Submit objections in writing under rule 3.1354; or

(2) Make arrangements for a court reporter to be present at the hearing.

Rule 3.1352 amended and renumbered effective January 1, 2007; adopted as rule 343 effective January 1, 1984; previously amended effective January 1, 2002.

Ref.: Cal. Fms Pl. & Pr., Ch. 376, "Motions to Strike: Anti-SLAPP," Ch. 537, "Summary Judgment"; MB Prac. Guide: Cal. Pretrial Proc., §§38.19, 38.26[3][a], 38.35, 38.37[1][b].

Rule 3.1354.   Written objections to evidence

(a) Time for filing and service of objections

Unless otherwise excused by the court on a showing of good cause, all written objections to evidence in support of or in opposition to a motion for summary judgment or summary adjudication must be served and filed at the same time as the objecting party's opposition or reply papers are served and filed.

(Subd (a) repealed, amended, and relettered effective January 1, 2007; adopted as untitled subd effective January 1, 1984; previously amended and lettered subd (b) effective January 1, 2007.)

(b) Format of objections

All written objections to evidence must be served and filed separately from the other papers in support of or in opposition to the motion. Objections on specific evidence may be referenced by the objection number in the right column of a separate statement in opposition or reply to a motion, but the objections must not be restated or reargued in the separate statement. Each written objection must be numbered consecutively and must:

(1) Identify the name of the document in which the specific material objected to is located;

(2) State the exhibit, title, page, and line number of the material objected to;

(3) Quote or set forth the objectionable statement or material; and

(4) State the grounds for each objection to that statement or material.

Written objections to evidence must follow one of the following two formats:

(First Format):

Objections to Jackson Declaration

Objection Number 1

"Johnson told me that no widgets were ever received." (Jackson declaration, page 3, lines 7–8.)

Grounds for Objection 1: Hearsay (Evid. Code, § 1200); lack of personal knowledge (Evid. Code, § 702(a)).

Objection Number 2

"A lot of people find widgets to be very useful." (Jackson declaration, page 17, line 5.)

Grounds for Objection 2: Irrelevant (Evid. Code, §§ 210, 350–351).

(Second Format):

Objections to Jackson Declaration

Material Objected to:

1. Jackson declaration, page 3, lines 7–8: "Johnson told me that no widgets were ever received."

2. Jackson declaration, page 17, line 5: "A lot of people find widgets to be very useful."

Grounds for Objection:

Hearsay (Evid. Code, § 1200); lack of personal knowledge (Evid. Code, § 702(a)).

Irrelevant (Evid. Code, §§ 210, 350–351).

(Subd (b) adopted effective January 1, 2007.)

(c) Proposed order

A party submitting written objections to evidence must submit with the objections a proposed order. The proposed order must include places for the court to indicate whether it has sustained or overruled each objection. It must also include a place for the signature of the judge. The proposed order must be in one of the following two formats:

(First Format):

Objections to Jackson Declaration

Objection Number 1

"Johnson told me that no widgets were ever received." (Jackson declaration, page 3, lines 7–8.)

Grounds for Objection 1: Hearsay (Evid. Code, § 1200); lack of personal knowledge (Evid. Code, § 702(a)).

Court's Ruling on Objection 1:   Sustained: _____

Overruled: _____

Objection Number 2

"A lot of people find widgets to be very useful." (Jackson declaration, page 17, line 5.)

Grounds for Objection 2: Irrelevant (Evid. Code, §§ 210, 350–351).

Court's Ruling on Objection 2:   Sustained: _____

Overruled: _____

(Second Format):

Objections to Jackson Declaration

Material Objected to:	Grounds for Objection:	Ruling on the Objection:
1. Jackson declaration, page 3, lines 7–8: "Johnson told me that no widgets were ever received."	Hearsay (Evid. Code, § 1200); lack of personal knowledge (Evid. Code, § 702(a)).	Sustained: _____ Overruled: _____
2. Jackson declaration, page 17, line 5: "A lot of people find widgets to be very useful."	Irrelevant (Evid. Code, §§ 210, 350–351).	Sustained: _____ Overruled: _____

Date: _____

Judge

(Subd (c) adopted effective January 1, 2007.)
Rule 3.1354 amended effective January 1, 2007; adopted as rule 345 effective January 1, 1984; previously amended effective January 1, 2002; previously amended and renumbered effective January 1, 2007.

Ref.: Cal. Fms Pl. & Pr., Ch. 1, "New Developments," Ch. 372, "Motions and Orders," Ch. 376, "Motions to Strike: Anti-SLAPP," Ch. 537, "Summary Judgment"; MB Prac. Guide: Cal. Pretrial Proc., §§38.19, 38.24[2], 38.26[3][b], [c], 38.29, 38.32[1], 38.33A, 38.35, 38.37[1][b], 38.69A.

Article 6
Miscellaneous Motions

Title 3, Civil Rules—Division 11, Law and Motion—Chapter 6, Particular Motions—Article 6, Miscellaneous Motions renum-

bered effective January 1, 2009; adopted as article 5 effective January 1, 2007.

Rule 3.1360. Motion to grant lien on cause of action
Rule 3.1362. Motion to be relieved as counsel

Rule 3.1360. Motion to grant lien on cause of action

A motion that a lien be granted on a cause of action, right to relief, or judgment must be accompanied by an authenticated record of the judgment on which the judgment creditor relies and a declaration as to the identity of the party involved and the amount due.

Rule 3.1360 amended and renumbered effective January 1, 2007; adopted as rule 369 effective January 1, 1984.

Ref.: Cal. Fms Pl. & Pr., Ch. 318, "Judgments," Ch. 372, "Motions and Orders."

Rule 3.1362. Motion to be relieved as counsel

(a) Notice

A notice of motion and motion to be relieved as counsel under Code of Civil Procedure section 284(2) must be directed to the client and must be made on the *Notice of Motion and Motion to Be Relieved as Counsel—Civil* (form MC-051).

(Subd (a) amended effective January 1, 2007; previously amended effective July 1, 2000.)

(b) Memorandum

Notwithstanding any other rule of court, no memorandum is required to be filed or served with a motion to be relieved as counsel.

(Subd (b) amended effective January 1, 2007; adopted effective July 1, 2000.)

(c) Declaration

The motion to be relieved as counsel must be accompanied by a declaration on the *Declaration in Support of Attorney's Motion to Be Relieved as Counsel—Civil* (form MC-052). The declaration must state in general terms and without compromising the confidentiality of the attorney-client relationship why a motion under Code of Civil Procedure section 284(2) is brought instead of filing a consent under Code of Civil Procedure section 284(1).

(Subd (c) amended effective January 1, 2007; adopted as subd (b) effective July 1, 1984; previously relettered and amended effective July 1, 2000.)

(d) Service

The notice of motion and motion [1], the declaration, **and the proposed order** must be served on the client and on all other parties who have appeared in the case. The notice may be by personal service or mail. If the notice is served on the client by mail under Code of Civil Procedure section 1013, it must be accompanied by a declaration stating facts showing that either:

(1) The service address is the current residence or business address of the client; or

(2) The service address is the last known residence or business address of the client and the attorney has been unable to locate a more current address after making reasonable efforts to do so within 30 days before the filing of the motion to be relieved.

As used in this rule, "current" means that the address was confirmed within 30 days before the filing of the

motion to be relieved. Merely demonstrating that the notice was sent to the client's last known address and was not returned is not, by itself, sufficient to demonstrate that the address is current. If the service is by mail, Code of Civil Procedure section 1011(b) applies.

(Subd (d) amended effective January 1, 2009; adopted as subd (c) effective July 1, 1984; previously amended effective July 1, 1991, January 1, 1996, and January 1, 2007; previously relettered and amended effective July 1, 2000.)

Rule 3.1362(d).   2008 Deletes. [1] and

(e) Order

The proposed order relieving counsel must be prepared on the *Order Granting Attorney's Motion to Be Relieved as Counsel—Civil* (form MC-053) and must be lodged with the court [1] with the moving papers. The order must specify all hearing dates scheduled in the action or proceeding, including the date of trial, if known. If no hearing date is presently scheduled, the court may set one and specify the date in the order. After the order is signed, a copy of the signed order must be served on the client and on all parties that have appeared in the case. The court may delay the effective date of the order relieving counsel until proof of service of a copy of the signed order on the client has been filed with the court.

(Subd (e) amended effective January 1, 2009; adopted as subd (d) effective July 1, 1984; previously amended effective January 1, 1996, and January 1, 2007; previously amended and relettered effective July 1, 2000.)

Rule 3.1362(e).   2008 Deletes. [1] and served on the client

Rule 3.1362 amended effective January 1, 2009; adopted as rule 376 effective July 1, 1984; previously amended effective July 1, 1991, January 1, 1996, and July 1, 2000; previously amended and renumbered effective January 1, 2007.

Ref.: Cal. Fms Pl. & Pr., Ch. 72, "Attorney Practice and Ethics," Ch. 372, "Motions and Orders"; MB Prac. Guide: Cal. Pretrial Proc., §§3.27[1], 3.30[3][a]–[e], 3.43–3.45, 3.47; W. Cal. Sum., 11 "Husband and Wife" §74.

Chapter 7
Other Civil Petitions

Rule 3.1370. Emancipation of minors

A petition for declaration of the emancipation of a minor must comply with rule 5.605.

Rule 3.1370 amended and renumbered effective January 1, 2007; adopted as rule 270 effective July 1, 1994.

Ref.: Cal. Fms Pl. & Pr., Ch. 245, "Emancipation of Minors"; W. Cal. Sum., 10 "Parent and Child" §§303, 304.

Division 12
Settlement

Rule 3.1380. Mandatory settlement conferences
Rule 3.1382. Good faith settlement and dismissal
Rule 3.1384. Petition for approval of the compromise of a claim of a minor or a person with a disability; order for deposit of funds; and petition for withdrawal
Rule 3.1385. Duty to notify court and others of settlement of entire case

Rule 3.1380. Mandatory settlement conferences

(a) Setting conferences

On the court's own motion or at the request of any party, the court may set one or more mandatory settlement conferences.

(Subd (a) amended effective January 1, 2008; previously amended effective January 1, 1995, and July 1, 2002.)

(b) Persons attending

Trial counsel, parties, and persons with full authority to settle the case must personally attend the conference, unless excused by the court for good cause. If any consent to settle is required for any reason, the party with that consensual authority must be personally present at the conference.

(Subd (b) amended and relettered effective July 1, 2002; adopted as subd (c) effective January 1, 1985; previously amended effective January 1, 1995.)

(c) Settlement conference statement

No later than five court days before the initial date set for the settlement conference, each party must submit to the court and serve on each party a mandatory settlement conference statement containing:

(1) A good faith settlement demand;

(2) An itemization of economic and noneconomic damages by each plaintiff;

(3) A good faith offer of settlement by each defendant; and

(4) A statement identifying and discussing in detail all facts and law pertinent to the issues of liability and damages involved in the case as to that party.

The settlement conference statement must comply with any additional requirement imposed by local rule.

(Subd (c) amended effective January 1, 2008; adopted as subd (d) effective January 1, 1985; previously amended effective January 1, 1995 and January 1, 2007; previously amended and relettered effective July 1, 2002.)

(d) Restrictions on appointments

A court must not:

(1) Appoint a person to conduct a settlement conference under this rule at the same time as that person is serving as a mediator in the same action; or

(2) Appoint a person to conduct a mediation under this rule.

(Subd (d) adopted effective January 1, 2008.)

Rule 3.1380 amended effective January 1, 2008; adopted as rule 222 effective January 1, 1985; previously amended effective January 1, 1995, July 1, 2001, and July 1, 2002; previously amended and renumbered effective January 1, 2007.

Advisory Committee Comment

Subdivision (d). This provision is not intended to discourage settlement conferences or mediations. However, problems have arisen in several cases, such as *Jeld-Wen v. Superior Court of San Diego County* (2007) 146 Cal.App.4th 536, when distinctions between different ADR processes have been blurred. To prevent confusion about the confidentiality of the proceedings, it is important to clearly distinguish between settlement conferences held under this rule and mediations. The special confidentiality requirements for mediations established by Evidence Code sections 1115–1128 expressly do not apply to settlement conferences under this rule. This provision is not intended to prohibit a court from appointing a person who has previously served as a mediator in a case to conduct a settlement conference in that case following the conclusion of the mediation.

Ref.: Cal. Fms Pl. & Pr., Ch. 1, "New Developments," Ch. 2, "Procedural Guide for Civil Actions," Ch. 31, "Mediation," Ch. 37, "Judicially Mandated Civil Action Mediation," Ch. 191,

"Discovery: Privileges and Other Discovery Limitations," Ch. 220, "Dissolution of Marriage: Master Procedural Guide," Ch. 221, "Dissolution of Marriage: Procedure," Ch. 425, "Pretrial Proceedings," Ch. 510, "Sanctions"; MB Prac. Guide: Cal. Pretrial Proc., §§23.10[2], 23.14, 23.16, 23.17[1]–[3], 23.59, 24.56[4][b], 23.63; MB Prac. Guide: Cal. Trial & Post-Trial Civ. Proc., §4.07[2]; W. Cal. Sum., 5 "Torts" §168.

Rule 3.1382. Good faith settlement and dismissal

A motion or application for determination of good faith settlement may include a request to dismiss a pleading or a portion of a pleading. The notice of motion or application for determination of good faith settlement must list each party and pleading or portion of pleading affected by the settlement and the date on which the affected pleading was filed.

Rule 3.1382 amended and renumbered effective January 1, 2007; adopted as rule 330 effective July 1, 1999.

Ref.: Cal. Fms Pl. & Pr., Ch. 300, "Indemnity and Contribution"; MB Prac. Guide: Cal. Pretrial Proc., §§37.28[1], 37.31[1][a], [2][a], 37.43.

Rule 3.1384. Petition for approval of the compromise of a claim of a minor or a person with a disability; order for deposit of funds; and petition for withdrawal

(a) Petition for approval of the compromise of a claim

A petition for court approval of a compromise or covenant not to sue under Code of Civil Procedure section 372 must comply with rules 7.950, 7.951, and 7.952.

(b) Order for the deposit of funds and petition for withdrawal

An order for the deposit of funds of a minor or a person with a disability, and a petition for the withdrawal of such funds, must comply with rules 7.953 and 7.954.

(Subd (b) amended effective January 1, 2007.)

Rule 3.1384 amended and renumbered effective January 1, 2007; adopted as rule 378 effective January 1, 2002.

Ref.: Cal. Fms Pl. & Pr., Ch. 364, "Minors: Claims and Property of Minors," Ch. 372, "Motions and Orders."

Rule 3.1385. Duty to notify court and others of settlement of entire case

(a) Notice of settlement

(1) Court and other persons to be notified

If an entire case is settled or otherwise disposed of, each plaintiff or other party seeking affirmative relief must immediately file written notice of the settlement or other disposition with the court and serve the notice on all parties and any arbitrator or other court-connected alternative dispute resolution (ADR) neutral involved in the case. Each plaintiff or other party seeking affirmative relief must also immediately give oral notice to all of the above if a hearing, conference, or trial is scheduled to take place within 10 days.

(2) Compensation for failure to provide notice

If the plaintiff or other party seeking affirmative relief does not notify an arbitrator or other court-connected ADR neutral involved in the case of a settlement at least 2 days before the scheduled hearing or session with that arbitrator or neutral, the court may order the party to compensate the arbitrator or other neutral for the scheduled hearing time. The amount of compensation ordered by the court must not exceed the maximum amount of compensation the arbitrator would be entitled to receive for service as an arbitrator under Code of Civil Procedure section 1141.18(b) or that the neutral would have been entitled to receive for service as a neutral at the scheduled hearing or session.

(Subd (a) amended effective January 1, 2007; previously amended effective January 1, 1989, July 1, 2001, July 1, 2002, January 1, 2004, and January 1, 2006.)

(b) Dismissal of case

Except as provided in (c) **or (d)**, each plaintiff or other party seeking affirmative relief must serve and file a request for dismissal of the entire case within 45 days after the date of settlement of the case. If the plaintiff or other party required to serve and file the request for dismissal does not do so, the court must dismiss the entire case 45 days after it receives notice of settlement unless good cause is shown why the case should not be dismissed.

(Subd (b) amended effective January 1, 2009; adopted effective January 1, 1989; previously amended effective July 1, 2002, January 1, 2004, and January 1, 2006.)

(c) Conditional settlement

If the settlement agreement conditions dismissal on the satisfactory completion of specified terms that are not to be performed within 45 days of the settlement, the notice of conditional settlement served and filed by each plaintiff or other party seeking affirmative relief must specify the date by which the dismissal is to be filed. If the plaintiff or other party required to serve and file a request for dismissal within 45 days after the dismissal date specified in the notice does not do so, the court must dismiss the entire case unless good cause is shown why the case should not be dismissed.

(Subd (c) amended effective January 1, 2006; adopted effective January 1, 1989; previously amended effective July 1, 2002, and January 1, 2004.)

(d) Compromise of claims of a minor or disabled person

If the settlement of the case involves the compromise of the claim of a minor or person with a disability, the court must not hold an order to show cause hearing under (b) before the court has held a hearing to approve the settlement, provided the parties have filed appropriate papers to seek court approval of the settlement.

(Subd (d) adopted effective January 1, 2009.)

(e) Request for additional time to complete settlement

If a party who has served and filed a notice of settlement under (a) determines that the case cannot be dismissed within the prescribed 45 days, that party must serve and file a notice and a supporting declaration advising the court of that party's inability to dismiss the case within the prescribed time, showing good cause for its inability to do so, and proposing an alternative date for dismissal. The notice and a supporting declaration must be served and filed at least 5 court days before the time for requesting dismissal has elapsed. If good cause is shown, the court must continue the matter to allow additional time to complete the settlement. The court may take such other actions as may be appropriate for the proper management and disposition of the case.

(Subd (e) adopted effective January 1, 2009.)

Rule 3.1385 amended effective January 1, 2009; adopted as rule 225 effective January 1, 1985; previously amended effective January 1, 1989, January 1, 1992, July 1, 2001, July 1, 2002, January 1, 2004, and January 1, 2006; previously amended and renumbered effective January 1, 2007.

Ref.: Cal. Fms Pl. & Pr., Ch. 2, "Procedural Guide for Civil Actions," Ch. 31, "Mediation," Ch. 36, "Judicial Arbitration," Ch. 212, "Dismissal," Ch. 425, "Pretrial Proceedings," Ch. 520, "Settlement and Release"; MB Prac. Guide: Cal. Pretrial Proc., §§23.04[2], 23.16, 23.17[4], 24.08[1], 24.11, 24.17, 37.18, 37.26, 37.27[1]–[3], 37.65, 40.20.

Division 13
Dismissal of Actions

Rule 3.1390. Service and filing of notice of entry of dismissal

A party that requests dismissal of an action must serve on all parties and file notice of entry of the dismissal.

Rule 3.1390 amended and renumbered effective January 1, 2007; adopted as rule 383 effective January 1, 1984.

Ref.: Cal. Fms Pl. & Pr., Ch. 212, "Dismissal," Ch. 221, "Dissolution of Marriage: Procedure," Ch. 372, "Motions and Orders"; MB Prac. Guide: Cal. Pretrial Proc., §§39.09, 39.19; MB Prac. Guide: Cal. Trial & Post-Trial Civ. Proc., §§12.27, 12.29, 12.43, 12.44.

Division 14
Pretrial
[Reserved]

Division 15
Trial

Chap. 1. General Provisions [Reserved].
Chap. 2. Consolidation or Bifurcation of Cases for Trial [Reserved].
Chap. 3. Nonjury Trials [Reserved].
Chap. 4. Jury Trials. Rule 3.1540.
Chap. 5. Testimony and Evidence [Reserved].
Chap. 6. Expert Witness Testimony [Reserved].
Chap. 7. Jury Instructions. Rule 3.1560.
Chap. 8. Special Verdicts. Rule 3.1580.
Chap. 9. Statement of Decision. Rules 3.1590, 3.1591.

Chapter 1
General Provisions
[Reserved]

Chapter 2
Consolidation or Bifurcation of Cases for Trial
[Reserved]

Chapter 3
Nonjury Trials
[Reserved]

Chapter 4
Jury Trials

Rule 3.1540.   Examination of prospective jurors in civil cases

(a) Application

This rule applies to all civil jury trials.

(Subd (a) amended and lettered effective January 1, 2007; adopted as part of untitled subd effective January 1, 1949.)

(b) Examination of jurors by the trial judge

To select a fair and impartial jury, the trial judge must examine the prospective jurors orally, or by written questionnaire, or by both methods. In examining prospective jurors in civil cases, the judge should consider the policies and recommendations in Standard 3.25 of the Standards of Judicial Administration. The judge may use the *Juror Questionnaire for Civil Cases* (form MC-001).

(Subd (b) amended and lettered effective January 1, 2007; adopted as part of untitled subd effective January 1, 1949.)

(c) Additional questions and examination by counsel

On completion of the initial examination, the trial judge must permit counsel for each party that so requests to submit additional questions that the judge will put to the jurors. On request of counsel, the trial judge must permit counsel to supplement the judge's examination by oral and direct questioning of any of the prospective jurors. The scope of the additional questions or supplemental examination must be within reasonable limits prescribed by the trial judge in the judge's sound discretion.

(Subd (c) amended and lettered effective January 1, 2007; adopted as part of untitled subd effective January 1, 1949.)

(d) Examination of juror outside the judge's presence

The court may, upon stipulation by counsel for all parties appearing in the action, permit counsel to examine the prospective jurors outside a judge's presence.

(Subd (d) amended and lettered effective January 1, 2007; adopted as part of untitled subd effective January 1, 1949.) Rule 3.1540 amended and renumbered effective January 1, 2007; adopted as rule 228 effective January 1, 1949; previously amended effective January 1, 1972, January 1, 1974, January 1, 1975, January 1, 1988, January 1, 1990, June 6, 1990, and July 1, 1993.

Ref.: Cal. Fms Pl. & Pr., Ch. 322, "Juries and Jury Selection," Ch. 551, "Trial"; MB Prac. Guide: Cal. Trial & Post-Trial Civ. Proc., §§6.02, 6.06, 6.08[1], [3], [5], [6], 6.09[2], 6.11[1], [2], 6.12, 6.34.

Chapter 5
Testimony and Evidence
[Reserved]

Chapter 6
Expert Witness Testimony
[Reserved]

Chapter 7
Jury Instructions

Rule 3.1560.   Application

The rules on jury instructions in chapter 4 of division 8 of title 2 of these rules apply to civil cases.

Rule 3.1560 adopted effective January 1, 2007.

Chapter 8
Special Verdicts

Rule 3.1580.   Request for special findings by jury

Whenever a party desires special findings by a jury, the party must, before argument, unless otherwise ordered, present to the judge in writing the issues or questions of fact on which the findings are requested, in proper form for submission to the jury, and serve copies on all other parties.

Rule 3.1580 amended and renumbered effective January 1, 2007; adopted as rule 230 effective January 1, 1949.

Ref.: Cal. Fms Pl. & Pr., Ch. 326, "Jury Instructions," Ch. 326A, "Jury Verdicts," Ch. 551, "Trial"; MB Prac. Guide: Cal. Trial & Post-Trial Civ. Proc., §§17.03, 18.10[4], [5][a], [b], 18.11, 18.17, 18.20[1], [2][b], [c], 18.21.

Chapter 9
Statement of Decision

Rule 3.1590. Announcement of tentative decision, statement of decision, and judgment

Rule 3.1591. Statement of decision, judgment, and motion for new trial following bifurcated trial

Rule 3.1590.   Announcement of tentative decision, statement of decision, and judgment

(a) Announcement and service of tentative decision

On the trial of a question of fact by the court, the court must announce its tentative decision by an oral statement, entered in the minutes, or by a written statement filed with the clerk. Unless the announcement is made in open court in the presence of all parties who appeared at the trial, the clerk must immediately mail to all parties that appeared at the trial a copy of the minute entry or written tentative decision.

(Subd (a) amended effective January 1, 2007; previously amended effective January 1, 1969, July 1, 1973, January 1, 1982, and January 1, 1983.)

(b) Tentative decision not binding

The tentative decision does not constitute a judgment and is not binding on the court. If the court subsequently modifies or changes its announced tentative decision, the clerk must mail a copy of the modification or change to all parties that appeared at the trial.

(Subd (b) amended effective January 1, 2007; adopted as part of subd (a) effective January 1, 1949; previously amended and lettered effective January 1, 2007.)

(c) Provisions in tentative decision

The court in its tentative decision may (1) state whether a statement of decision, if requested, will be prepared by the court or by a designated party, and (2) direct that the tentative decision will be the statement of decision unless within 10 days either party specifies controverted issues or makes proposals not covered in the tentative decision.

(Subd (c) amended and lettered effective January 1, 2007; adopted as part of subd (a) effective January 1, 1949.)

(d) Proposals following request for statement of decision (Code Civ. Proc., § 632)

Any proposals as to the content of the statement of decision must be made within 10 days of the date of request for a statement of decision.

(Subd (d) amended and relettered effective January 1, 2007; adopted as subd (b) effective January 1, 1949; previously amended effective January 1, 1969, and January 1, 1982.)

(e) Preparation and service of proposed statement of decision and judgment

If a statement of decision is requested, the court must, within 15 days after the expiration of the time for proposals as to the content of the statement of decision, prepare and mail a proposed statement of decision and a proposed judgment to all parties that appeared at the trial, unless the court has designated a party to prepare the statement as provided by subdivision (c) or has, within 5 days after the request, notified a party to prepare the statement. A party who has been designated or notified to prepare the statement must within 15 days after the expiration of the time for filing proposals as to the content of the statement, or within 15 days after notice, whichever is later, prepare, serve, and submit to the court a proposed statement of decision and a proposed judgment. If the proposed statement of decision and judgment are not served and submitted within that time, any other party who appeared at the trial may: (1) prepare, serve, and submit to the court a proposed statement of decision and judgment, or (2) serve on all other parties and file a notice of motion for an order that a statement of decision be deemed waived.

(Subd (e) amended and relettered effective January 1, 2007; adopted as subd (c) effective January 1, 1949; previously amended effective January 1, 1969, July 1, 1973, and January 1, 1982.)

(f) Objections to proposed statement of decision

Any party affected by the judgment may, within 15 days after the proposed statement of decision and judgment have been served, serve and file objections to the proposed statement of decision or judgment.

(Subd (f) relettered effective January 1, 2007; adopted as subd (d) effective January 1, 1949; previously amended effective January 1, 1969, and January 1, 1982.)

(g) Preparation and filing of written judgment when statement of decision not requested

If a statement of decision is not requested or has been waived and a written judgment is required, the court must prepare and mail a proposed judgment to all parties who appeared at the trial within 10 days after expiration of the time for requesting a statement of decision or time of waiver. The court may notify a party to prepare, serve, and submit the proposed judgment to the court within 10 days. Any party affected by the judgment may, within 10 days after service of the proposed judgment, serve and file objections thereto.

(Subd (g) amended and relettered effective January 1, 2007; previously amended effective January 1, 1969; previously amended and relettered as subd (e) effective January 1, 1982.)

(h) Signature and filing of judgment

The court must, within 10 days after expiration of the time for filing objections to the proposed judgment or, if a hearing is held, within 10 days after the hearing, sign and file its judgment. The judgment so filed constitutes the decision on which judgment is to be entered under Code of Civil Procedure section 664.

(Subd (h) amended and lettered effective January 1, 2007; adopted as part of subd (e) effective January 1, 1949.)

(i) Hearing

The court may order a hearing on proposals or objections to a proposed statement of decision or the proposed judgment if a statement of decision is not required.

(Subd (i) lettered effective January 1, 2007; adopted as subd (f) effective January 1, 1982.)

(j) Extension of time; relief from noncompliance

The court may, by written order, extend any of the times prescribed by this rule and at any time before the entry of judgment may, for good cause shown and on such terms as may be just, excuse a noncompliance with the time limits prescribed for doing any act required by this rule.

(Subd (j) amended and relettered effective January 1, 2007; previously amended effective January 1, 1969, and July 1, 1973; previously amended and relettered as subd (g) effective January 1, 1982.)

(k) Not applicable to trial within one day

This rule does not apply if the trial was completed within one day.

(Subd (k) amended and relettered effective January 1, 2007; adopted as subd (h) effective January 1, 1983.)

Rule 3.1590 amended effective January 1, 2007; adopted as rule 232 effective January 1, 1949; previously amended effective January 1, 1969, July 1, 1973, January 1, 1982, and January 1, 1983; previously amended and renumbered effective January 1, 2007.

Ref.: Cal. Fms Pl. & Pr., Ch. 2, "Procedural Guide for Civil Actions," Ch. 3, "Abatement of Actions," Ch. 12B, "Adoptions: Unmarried Minors," Ch. 38, "Reference," Ch. 174, "Costs and Attorney's Fees," Ch. 205, "Defaults and Default Judgments," Ch. 220, "Dissolution of Marriage: Master Procedural Guide," Ch. 221, "Dissolution of Marriage: Procedure," Ch. 224, "Dissolution of Marriage: Child Support," Ch. 280, "Guardianship and Conservatorship: Appointment of Guardians," Ch. 281, "Guardianship and Conservatorship: Appointment of Conservators," Ch. 314, "Interpleader," Ch. 318, "Judgments," Ch. 323, "Jurisdiction: Personal Jurisdiction, Inconvenient Forum, and Appearances," Ch. 356, "Lost Papers," Ch. 358, "Mandate and Prohibition," Ch. 386, "Newspapers," Ch. 395, "Parties," Ch. 397, "Partition," Ch. 474C, "Procedures in Reviewing Agency Decisions," Ch. 482, "Quieting Title," Ch. 492, "Review (Certiorari), Writ of," Ch. 529, "Statement of Decision," Ch. 537, "Summary Judgment," Ch. 551, "Trial"; MB Prac. Guide: Cal. Debt Collection & Enforcement of Judgments, §§7.38, 7.40; MB Prac. Guide: Cal. Pretrial Proc., §36.36[4]; MB Prac. Guide: Cal. Trial & Post-Trial Civ. Proc., §§5.04, 5.24, 5.25, 5.27[2], 5.28, 5.33, 5.36[2], 5.37, 5.38[1][a]–[e], [2], 19.33, 26.15, 26.16, 26.17[1], [2], 26.18[2], [3][a], [b], [6]–[8], 26.19[1][b], [2], [3], 26.35–26.39; W. Cal. Sum., 11 "Community Property" §241, 11 "Husband and Wife" §107.

Rule 3.1591. Statement of decision, judgment, and motion for new trial following bifurcated trial

(a) Separate trial of an issue

When a factual issue raised by the pleadings is tried by the court separately and before the trial of other issues, the judge conducting the separate trial must announce the tentative decision on the issue so tried and must, when requested under Code of Civil Procedure section 632, issue a statement of decision as prescribed in rule 3.1590; but the court must not prepare any proposed judgment until the other issues are tried, except when an interlocutory judgment or a separate judgment may otherwise be properly entered at that time.

(Subd (a) amended and lettered effective January 1, 2007; adopted as part of untitled subd effective January 1, 1975.)

(b) Trial of issues by a different judge

If the other issues are tried by a different judge or judges, each judge must perform all acts required by rule 3.1590 as to the issues tried by that judge and the judge trying the final issue must prepare the proposed judgment.

(Subd (b) amended and lettered effective January 1, 2007; adopted as part of untitled subd effective January 1, 1975.)

(c) Trial of subsequent issues before issuance of statement of decision

A judge may proceed with the trial of subsequent issues before the issuance of a statement of decision on previously tried issues. Any motion for a new trial following a bifurcated trial must be made after all the issues are tried and, if the issues were tried by different judges, each judge must hear and determine the motion as to the issues tried by that judge.

(Subd (c) amended and lettered effective January 1, 2007; adopted as part of untitled subd effective January 1, 1975.)

Rule 3.1591 amended and renumbered effective January 1, 2007; adopted as rule 232.5 effective January 1, 1975; previously amended effective January 1, 1982, and January 1, 1985.

Ref.: Cal. Fms Pl. & Pr., Ch. 221, "Dissolution of Marriage: Procedure," Ch. 371, "Motions After Trial," Ch. 529, "Statement of Decision," Ch. 551, "Trial"; MB Prac. Guide: Cal. Trial & Post-Trial Civ. Proc., §§5.04, 21.08, 26.17[1], 26.18[1], [3][a]; W. Cal. Sum., 11 "Husband and Wife" §§106, 107.

Division 16
Post-trial

Rule 3.1600. Notice of intention to move for new trial
Rule 3.1602. Hearing of motion to vacate judgment

Rule 3.1600.   Notice of intention to move for new trial

(a) Time for service of memorandum

Within 10 days after filing notice of intention to move for a new trial in a civil case, the moving party must serve and file a memorandum in support of the motion, and within 10 days thereafter any adverse party may serve and file a memorandum in reply.

(Subd (a) amended and lettered effective January 1, 2007; adopted as part of untitled subd effective January 1, 1949.)

(b) Effect of failure to serve memorandum

If the moving party fails to serve and file a memorandum within the time prescribed in (a), the court may deny the motion for a new trial without a hearing on the merits.

(Subd (b) amended and lettered effective January 1, 2007; adopted as part of untitled subd effective January 1, 1949.)

Rule 3.1600 amended and renumbered effective January 1, 2007; adopted as rule 203 effective January 1, 1949; previously amended effective April 1, 1962, January 1, 1971, January 1, 1984, and January 1, 1987; previously amended and renumbered as rule 236.5 effective January 1, 2003.

Ref.: Cal. Fms Pl. & Pr., Ch. 2, "Procedural Guide for Civil Actions," Ch. 38, "Reference," Ch. 166, "Corporations: Shareholders' Meetings and Voting," Ch. 177, "Damages," Ch. 371, "Motions After Trial," Ch. 372, "Motions and Orders," Ch. 417, "Points and Authorities"; MB Prac. Guide: Cal. Trial & Post-Trial Civ. Proc., §§21.03, 21.07[2], 21.13, 21.15[1], 21.16.

Rule 3.1602.   Hearing of motion to vacate judgment

A motion to vacate judgment under Code of Civil Procedure section 663 must be heard and determined by the judge who presided at the trial; provided, however, that in case of the inability or death of such judge or if at the time noticed for the hearing thereon he is absent from the county where the trial was had, the motion may be heard and determined by another judge of the same court.

Rule 3.1602 amended and renumbered effective January 1, 2007; adopted as rule 236 effective January 1, 1949.

Ref.: Cal. Fms Pl. & Pr., Ch. 221, "Dissolution of Marriage: Procedure," Ch. 371, "Motions After Trial," Ch. 372, "Motions and Orders"; MB Prac. Guide: Cal. Trial & Post-Trial Civ. Proc., §27.08[3].

Division 17
Attorney's Fees and Costs

Rule 3.1700. Prejudgment costs
Rule 3.1702. Claiming attorney's fees

Rule 3.1700.   Prejudgment costs

(a) Claiming costs

(1) Trial costs

A prevailing party who claims costs must serve and file a memorandum of costs within 15 days after the date of mailing of the notice of entry of judgment or dismissal by the clerk under Code of Civil Procedure section 664.5 or the date of service of written notice of entry of judgment or dismissal, or within 180 days after entry of judgment, whichever is first. The memorandum of costs must be verified by a statement of the party, attorney, or agent that to the best of his or her knowledge the items of cost are correct and were necessarily incurred in the case.

(2) Costs on default

A party seeking a default judgment who claims costs must request costs on the *Request for Entry of Default (Application to Enter Default)* (form CIV-100) at the time of applying for the judgment.

(Subd (a) amended effective July 1, 2007; previously amended effective January 1, 2007.)

(b) Contesting costs

(1) Striking and taxing costs

Any notice of motion to strike or to tax costs must be served and filed 15 days after service of the cost memorandum. If the cost memorandum was served by mail, the period is extended as provided in Code of Civil Procedure section 1013.

Rules of Court

(2) *Form of motion*

Unless objection is made to the entire cost memorandum, the motion to strike or tax costs must refer to each item objected to by the same number and appear in the same order as the corresponding cost item claimed on the memorandum of costs and must state why the item is objectionable.

(3) *Extensions of time*

The party claiming costs and the party contesting costs may agree to extend the time for serving and filing the cost memorandum and a motion to strike or tax costs. This agreement must be confirmed in writing, specify the extended date for service, and be filed with the clerk. In the absence of an agreement, the court may extend the times for serving and filing the cost memorandum or the notice of motion to strike or tax costs for a period not to exceed 30 days.

(4) *Entry of costs*

After the time has passed for a motion to strike or tax costs or for determination of that motion, the clerk must immediately enter the costs on the judgment.

(Subd (b) amended effective January 1, 2007.)

Rule 3.1700 amended effective July 1, 2007; adopted as rule 870 effective January 1, 1987; previously amended and renumbered effective January 1, 2007.

Ref.: Cal. Fms Pl. & Pr., Ch. 36, "Judicial Arbitration," Ch. 53, "Appeal: Remittitur and Costs on Appeal," Ch. 87A, "Automobiles: Post Trial," Ch. 174, "Costs and Attorney's Fees," Ch. 205, "Defaults and Default Judgments," Ch. 212, "Dismissal," Ch. 241, "Ejectment," Ch. 254, "Executions and Enforcement of Judgments," Ch. 276, "Garnishment," Ch. 318, "Judgments," Ch. 345A, "Limited Civil Cases," Ch. 358, "Mandate and Prohibition," Ch. 372, "Motions and Orders," Ch. 417, "Points and Authorities," Ch. 474C, "Procedures in Reviewing Agency Decisions," Ch. 492, "Review (Certiorari), Writ of," Ch. 520, "Settlement and Release"; MB Prac. Guide: Cal. Debt Collection & Enforcement of Judgments, §16.07[5]; MB Prac. Guide: Cal. Pretrial Proc., §§24.30[2], 36.34, 39.13, 40.03[1]; MB Prac. Guide: Cal. Trial & Post-Trial Civ. Proc., §§24.02–24.04, 24.32, 24.36, 24.37, 24.41[3], [4], 24.48–24.52, 25A.20[3], 25A.33[2], 29.14[1][a].

Rule 3.1702.   Claiming attorney's fees

(a) Application

Except as otherwise provided by statute, this rule applies in civil cases to claims for statutory attorney's fees and claims for attorney's fees provided for in a contract. Subdivisions (b) and (c) apply when the court determines entitlement to the fees, the amount of the fees, or both, whether the court makes that determination because the statute or contract refers to "reasonable" fees, because it requires a determination of the prevailing party, or for other reasons.

(Subd (a) amended effective January 1, 2007.)

(b) Attorney's fees before trial court judgment

(1) *Time for motion*

A notice of motion to claim attorney's fees for services up to and including the rendition of judgment in the trial court—including attorney's fees on an appeal before the rendition of judgment in the trial court—must be served and filed within the time for filing a notice of appeal under rules 8.104 and 8.108.

(2) *Stipulation for extension of time*

The parties may, by stipulation filed before the expiration of the time allowed under (b)(1), extend the time for filing a motion for attorney's fees:

(A) Until 60 days after the expiration of the time for filing a notice of appeal; or

(B) If a notice of appeal is filed, until the time within which a memorandum of costs must be served and filed under rule [1] **8.278(c)**.

(Subd (b) amended effective January 1, 2009; previously amended effective January 1, 1999, January 1, 2006, and January 1, 2007.)

Rule 3.1702(b).   2008 Deletes. [1] 8.276(d)

(c) Attorney's fees on appeal

(1) *Time for motion*

A notice of motion to claim attorney's fees on appeal—other than the attorney's fees on appeal claimed under (b)—under a statute or contract requiring the court to determine entitlement to the fees, the amount of the fees, or both, must be served and filed within the time for serving and filing the memorandum of costs under rule [1] **8.278(c)(1)**.

(2) *Stipulation for extension of time*

The parties may by stipulation filed before the expiration of the time allowed under (c)(1) extend the time for filing the motion up to an additional 60 days.

(Subd (c) amended effective July 1, 2008; previously amended effective January 1, 1999, January 1, 2006, and January 1, 2007.)

Rule 3.1702(c).   2008 Deletes. [1] 8.276(d)

(d) Extensions

For good cause, the trial judge may extend the time for filing a motion for attorney's fees in the absence of a stipulation or for a longer period than allowed by stipulation.

(Subd (d) amended effective January 1, 2007; adopted effective January 1, 1999.)

(e) Attorney's fees fixed by formula

If a party is entitled to statutory or contractual attorney's fees that are fixed without the necessity of a court determination, the fees must be claimed in the memorandum of costs.

(Subd (e) amended effective January 1, 2007; adopted as subd (d) effective January 1, 1994; previously relettered effective January 1, 1999.)

Rule 3.1702 amended effective January 1, 2009; adopted as rule 870.2 effective January 1, 1994; previously amended and renumbered effective January 1, 2007; previously amended effective January 1, 1999, January 1, 2006, and July 1, 2008.

Ref.: Cal. Fms Pl. & Pr., Ch. 1, "New Developments," Ch. 40, "Appeal: An Overview," Ch. 53, "Appeal: Remittitur and Costs on Appeal," Ch. 54, "Appeal: California Supreme Court Review," Ch. 174, "Costs and Attorney's Fees," Ch. 290F, "Guardianship and Conservatorship: Compensation of Guardian or Conservator," Ch. 345, "Limitation of Actions," Ch. 376, "Motions to Strike: Anti-SLAPP," Ch. 442, "Probate: Initiating Probate Administration," Ch. 458D, "Probate: Accounts, Final Distribution, and Compensation," Ch. 470C, "Public Records Act," Ch. 560, "Trusts: Express, Public, Charitable, and Totten Trusts"; MB Prac. Guide: Cal. Pretrial Proc., §39.13; MB Prac. Guide: Cal. Trial & Post-Trial Civ. Proc., §§25A.02, 25A.07[2], [7], 25A.12[1], 25A.15, 25A.16, 25A.18[6], 25A.19, 25A.20[1], [2], [4]–[6], 25A.33[1]–[3], 29.14[1][a]; W. Cal. Sum., 11 "Husband and Wife" §10, 13 "Trusts" §60.

Division 18
Judgments

Rule 3.1800. Default judgments
Rule 3.1802. Inclusion of interest in judgment
Rule 3.1804. Periodic payment of judgments against public entities
Rule 3.1806. Notation on written instrument of rendition of judgment

Rule 3.1800. Default judgments

(a) Documents to be submitted

A party seeking a default judgment on declarations must use mandatory *Request for Entry of Default (Application to Enter Default)* (form CIV-100). In an unlawful detainer case, a party may, in addition, use optional *Declaration for Default Judgment by Court* (form UD-116) when seeking a court judgment based on declarations. The following must be included in the documents filed with the clerk:

(1) Except in unlawful detainer cases, a brief summary of the case identifying the parties and the nature of plaintiff's claim;

(2) Declarations or other admissible evidence in support of the judgment requested;

(3) Interest computations as necessary;

(4) A memorandum of costs and disbursements;

(5) A declaration of nonmilitary status for each defendant against whom judgment is sought;

(6) A proposed form of judgment;

(7) A dismissal of all parties against whom judgment is not sought or an application for separate judgment against specified parties under Code of Civil Procedure section 579, supported by a showing of grounds for each judgment;

(8) Exhibits as necessary; and

(9) A request for attorney fees if allowed by statute or by the agreement of the parties.

(Subd (a) amended effective July 1, 2007; previously amended effective January 1, 2005, and January 1, 2007.)

(b) Fee schedule

A court may by local rule establish a schedule of attorney's fees to be used by that court in determining the reasonable amount of attorney's fees to be allowed in the case of a default judgment.

(Subd (b) amended effective January 1, 2007.)

Rule 3.1800 amended effective July 1, 2007; adopted as rule 388 effective July 1, 2000; previously amended effective January 1, 2005; previously amended and renumbered effective January 1, 2007.

Ref.: Cal. Fms Pl. & Pr., Ch. 205, "Defaults and Default Judgments"; MB Prac. Guide: Cal. Pretrial Proc., §§36.11, 36.30, 36.31, 36.36[2], [4], 36.54, 36.59[2], 36.75.

Rule 3.1802. Inclusion of interest in judgment

The clerk must include in the judgment any interest awarded by the court and the interest accrued since the entry of the verdict.

Rule 3.1802 amended and renumbered effective January 1, 2007; adopted as rule 875 effective January 1, 1987.

Ref.: Cal. Fms Pl. & Pr., Ch. 174, "Costs and Attorney's Fees," Ch. 177, "Damages," Ch. 318, "Judgments," Ch. 333, "Landlord and Tenant: Eviction Actions," Ch. 420, "Prayers"; MB Prac. Guide: Cal. Trial & Post-Trial Civ. Proc., §§19.09, 19.10, 26.18[5][d].

Rule 3.1804. Periodic payment of judgments against public entities

(a) Notice of election or hearing

A public entity electing to pay a judgment against it by periodic payments under Government Code section 984 must serve and file a notice of election stipulating to the terms of such payments, or a notice of hearing on such terms, by the earlier of:

(1) 30 days after the clerk sends, or a party serves, notice of entry of judgment; or

(2) 60 days after entry of judgment.

(b) Time for hearing

Notwithstanding any contrary local rule or practice, a hearing under (a) must be held within 30 days after service of the notice. The court must make an order for periodic payments at the hearing.

(Subd (b) amended effective January 1, 2007.)

Rule 3.1804 amended and renumbered effective January 1, 2007; adopted as rule 389 effective January 1, 2002.

Rule 3.1806. Notation on written instrument of rendition of judgment

In all cases in which judgment is rendered upon a written obligation to pay money, the clerk must, at the time of entry of judgment, unless otherwise ordered, note over the clerk's official signature and across the face of the writing the fact of rendition of judgment with the date of the judgment and the title of the court and the case.

Rule 3.1806 amended and renumbered effective January 1, 2007; adopted as rule 234 effective January 1, 1949.

Ref.: Cal. Fms Pl. & Pr., Ch. 205, "Defaults and Default Judgments," Ch. 318, "Judgments"; MB Prac. Guide: Cal. Pretrial Proc., §§36.30, 36.36[3].

Division 19
Postjudgment and Enforcement of Judgments

Rule 3.1900. Notice of renewal of judgment

A copy of the application for renewal of judgment must be attached to the notice of renewal of judgment required by Code of Civil Procedure section 683.160.

Rule 3.1900 amended and renumbered effective January 1, 2007; adopted as rule 986 effective July 1, 1983.

Ref.: Cal. Fms Pl. & Pr., Ch. 318, "Judgments"; MB Prac. Guide: Cal. Debt Collection & Enforcement of Judgments, §§13.03[1], 13.10[1].

Division 20
Unlawful Detainers

Rule 3.2000. Unlawful detainer—supplemental costs

(a) Time for filing supplemental cost memorandum

In unlawful detainer proceedings, the plaintiff who has complied with Code of Civil Procedure section 1034.5 may, no later than 10 days after being advised by the sheriff or marshal of the exact amount necessarily used and expended to effect the eviction, file a supplemental cost memorandum claiming the additional costs and specifying the items paid and the amount.

(Subd (a) amended and lettered effective January 1, 2007; adopted as part of untitled subd effective January 1, 1987.)

(b) Motion to tax costs

The defendant may move to tax those costs within 10 days after service of the supplemental cost memorandum.

(Subd (b) amended and lettered effective January 1, 2007; adopted as part of untitled subd effective January 1, 1987.)

(c) Entry of judgment for costs and enforcement

After costs have been fixed by the court, or on failure of the defendant to file a timely notice of motion to tax costs, the clerk must immediately enter judgment for the costs. The judgment may be enforced in the same manner as a money judgment.

(Subd (c) amended and lettered effective January 1, 2007; adopted as part of untitled subd effective January 1, 1987.)

Rule 3.2000 amended and renumbered effective January 1, 2007; adopted as part of rule 870.4 effective January 1, 1987.

Ref.: Cal. Fms Pl. & Pr., Ch. 174, "Costs and Attorney's Fees"; MB Prac. Guide: Cal. Trial & Post-Trial Civ. Proc., §§24.16, 24.41[1].

Division 21
Rules for Small Claims Actions

Chap. 1.   Trial Rules. Rules 3.2100–3.2110.
Chap. 2.   Small Claims Advisors. Rule 3.2120.

Chapter 1
Trial Rules

Rule 3.2100. Compliance with fictitious business name laws
Rule 3.2102. Substituted service
Rule 3.2104. Defendant's claim
Rule 3.2106. Venue challenge
Rule 3.2107. Request for court order
Rule 3.2108. Form of judgment
Rule 3.2110. Role of clerk in assisting small claims litigants

Rule 3.2100.   Compliance with fictitious business name laws

(a) Filing of declaration of compliance

A claimant who is required to file a declaration of compliance with the fictitious business name laws under Code of Civil Procedure section 116.430 must file the declaration in each case filed.

(Subd (a) amended and lettered effective January 1, 2007; adopted as untitled subd effective January 1, 1986.)

(b) Available methods

The clerk must make the declaration of compliance available to the claimant in any one of the following ways:

(1) The declaration of compliance may be placed on a separate form approved by the Judicial Council;

(2) The approved Judicial Council form may be placed on the reverse of the Plaintiff's Statement to the Clerk or on the back of any Judicial Council small claims form with only one side; or

(3) The precise language of the declaration of compliance that appears on the approved Judicial Council form may be incorporated into the Plaintiff's Statement to the Clerk.

(Subd (b) amended and lettered effective January 1, 2007; adopted as part of untitled subd effective January 1, 1986.)

Rule 3.2100 amended and renumbered effective January 1, 2007; adopted as rule 1701 effective January 1, 1986; previously amended effective July 1, 1991.

Ref.: Cal. Fms Pl. & Pr., Ch. 510, "Sanctions," Ch. 526, "Small Claims"; MB Prac. Guide: Cal. Pretrial Proc., §35.07[1][a].

Rule 3.2102.   Substituted service

If substituted service is authorized by Code of Civil Procedure section 116.340 or other provisions of law, no due diligence is required in a small claims court action.

Rule 3.2102 renumbered effective January 1, 2007; adopted as rule 1702 effective July 1, 1991.

Ref.: Cal. Fms Pl. & Pr., Ch. 526, "Small Claims."

Rule 3.2104.   Defendant's claim

A defendant may file a claim against the plaintiff even if the claim does not relate to the same subject or event as the plaintiff's claim, so long as the claim is within the jurisdictional limit of the small claims court.

Rule 3.2104 renumbered effective January 1, 2007; adopted as rule 1703 effective July 1, 1991.

Ref.: Cal. Fms Pl. & Pr., Ch. 526, "Small Claims."

Rule 3.2106.   Venue challenge

A defendant may challenge venue by writing to the court. The defendant is not required to personally appear at the hearing on the venue challenge. If the court denies the challenge and the defendant is not present, the hearing must be continued to another appropriate date. The parties must be given notice of the venue determination and hearing date.

Rule 3.2106 amended and renumbered effective January 1, 2007; adopted as rule 1704 effective July 1, 1991.

Ref.: Cal. Fms Pl. & Pr., Ch. 526, "Small Claims."

Rule 3.2107.   Request for court order

(a) Request before trial

If a party files a written request for a court order before the hearing on the claim, the requesting party must mail or personally deliver a copy to all other parties in the case. The other parties must be given an opportunity to answer or respond to the request before or at the hearing. This subdivision does not apply to a request to postpone the hearing date if the plaintiff's claim has not been served.

(Subd (a) adopted effective January 1, 2007.)

(b) Request after trial

If a party files a written request for a court order after notice of entry of judgment, the clerk must mail a copy of the request to all other parties in the action. A party has 10 calendar days from the date on which the clerk mailed the request to file a response before the court makes an order. The court may schedule a hearing on the request, except that if the request is to vacate the judgment for lack of appearance by the plaintiff, the court must hold a hearing.

The court may give notice of any scheduled hearing with notice of the request, but the hearing must be scheduled at least 11 calendar days after the clerk has mailed the request.

(Subd (b) adopted effective January 1, 2007.)
Rule 3.2107 adopted effective January 1, 2007.

Rule 3.2108.   Form of judgment

The court may give judgment for damages, equitable relief, or both, and may make other orders as the court deems just and equitable for the resolution of the dispute. If specific property is referred to in the judgment, whether it be personal or real, tangible or intangible, the property must be identified with sufficient detail to permit efficient implementation or enforcement of the judgment.

Rule 3.2108 amended and renumbered effective January 1, 2007; adopted as rule 1705 effective July 1, 1991.

Ref.: Cal. Fms Pl. & Pr., Ch. 526, "Small Claims."

Rule 3.2110.   Role of clerk in assisting small claims litigants

(a) Provision of forms and pamphlets

The clerk must provide forms and pamphlets from the Judicial Council.

(Subd (a) amended and lettered effective January 1, 2007; adopted as part of untitled subd effective July 1, 1991.)

(b) Provision of Department of Consumer Affairs materials

The clerk must provide materials from the Department of Consumer Affairs when available.

(Subd (b) amended and lettered effective January 1, 2007; adopted as part of untitled subd effective July 1, 1991.)

(c) Information about small claims advisory service

The clerk must inform litigants of the small claims advisory service.

(Subd (c) amended and lettered effective January 1, 2007; adopted as part of untitled subd effective July 1, 1991.)

(d) Answering questions

The clerk may answer questions relative to filing and service of the claim, designation of the parties, scheduling of hearings, and similar matters.

(Subd (d) amended and lettered effective January 1, 2007; adopted as part of untitled subd effective July 1, 1991.)

Rule 3.2110 amended and renumbered effective January 1, 2007; adopted as rule 1706 effective July 1, 1991.

Ref.: Cal. Fms Pl. & Pr., Ch. 526, "Small Claims."

Chapter 2
Small Claims Advisors

Rule 3.2120.   Advisor assistance

(a) Notice to parties

The clerk must inform the parties, orally or in writing, about:

(1) The availability of advisors to assist small claims litigants at no additional charge as provided in Code of Civil Procedure sections 116.260 and 116.940; and

(2) The provisions of Government Code section 818.9.

(Subd (a) amended effective January 1, 2007; previously amended effective July 1, 1991.)

(b) Training

All small claims advisors must receive training sufficient to ensure competence in the areas of:

(1) Small claims court practice and procedure;

(2) Alternative dispute resolution programs;

(3) Consumer sales;

(4) Vehicular sales, leasing, and repairs;

(5) Credit and financing transactions;

(6) Professional and occupational licensing;

(7) Landlord-tenant law; and

(8) Contract, warranty, tort, and negotiable instruments law.

It is the intent of this rule that the county must provide this training.

(Subd (b) amended effective January 1, 2007; previously adopted effective January 1, 1986; previously repealed and adopted effective July 1, 1991.)

(c) Qualifications

In addition to the training required in subdivision (b), each county may establish additional qualifications for small claims advisors.

(Subd (c) adopted effective July 1, 1991.)

(d) Conflict of interest

A small claims advisor must disclose any known direct or indirect relationship the advisor may have with any party or witness in the action. An advisor must not disclose information obtained in the course of the advisor's duties or use the information for financial or other advantage.

(Subd (d) amended effective January 1, 2007; adopted as subd (c) effective January 1, 1986; previously relettered effective July 1, 1991.)

Rule 3.2120 amended and renumbered effective January 1, 2007; adopted as rule 1725 effective January 1, 1986; previously amended effective July 1, 1991.

Ref.: Cal. Fms Pl. & Pr., Ch. 526, "Small Claims."

TITLE 4
Criminal Rules

Division 1. General Provisions. Rules 4.1–4.3.
Division 2. Pretrial. Rules 4.100–4.155.
Division 3. Trials. Rules 4.200–4.210.
Division 4. Sentencing. Rules 4.300–4.330.
Division 5. Sentencing—Determinate Sentencing Law. Rules 4.401–4.480.
Division 6. Postconviction and Writs. Rules 4.510–4.552.
Division 7. Miscellaneous. Rule 4.601.

Division 1
General Provisions

Rule 4.1. Title
Rule 4.2. Application
Rule 4.3. Reference to Penal Code

Rule 4.1. Title

The rules in this title may be referred to as the Criminal Rules.

Rule 4.1 adopted effective January 1, 2007.

Rule 4.2. Application

The Criminal Rules apply to all criminal cases in the superior courts unless otherwise provided by a statute or rule in the California Rules of Court.

Rule 4.2 adopted effective January 1, 2007.

Rule 4.3. Reference to Penal Code

All statutory references are to the Penal Code unless stated otherwise.

Rule 4.3 adopted effective January 1, 2007.

Division 2
Pretrial

Chap. 1. Pretrial Proceedings. Rules 4.100–4.130.
Chap. 2. Change of Venue. Rules 4.150–4.155.

Chapter 1
Pretrial Proceedings

Rule 4.100. Arraignments
Rule 4.101. Bail in criminal cases
Rule 4.102. Uniform bail and penalty schedules—traffic, boating, fish and game, forestry, public utilities, parks and recreation, business licensing
Rule 4.103. Notice to appear forms
Rule 4.104. Procedures and eligibility criteria for attending traffic violator school
Rule 4.110. Time limits for criminal proceedings on information or indictment
Rule 4.111. Pretrial motions in criminal cases
Rule 4.112. Readiness conference

Rule 4.113. Motions and grounds for continuance of criminal case set for trial
Rule 4.114. Certification under Penal Code section 859a
Rule 4.115. Criminal case assignment
Rule 4.116. Certification to juvenile court
Rule 4.117. Qualifications for appointed trial counsel in capital cases
Rule 4.130. Mental competency proceedings

Rule 4.100. Arraignments

At the arraignment on the information or indictment, unless otherwise ordered for good cause, and on a plea of not guilty, including a plea of not guilty by reason of insanity;

(1) The court must set dates for:

(A) Trial, giving priority to a case entitled to it under law; and

(B) Filing and service of motions and responses and hearing thereon;

(2) A plea of not guilty must be entered if a defendant represented by counsel fails to plead or demur; and

(3) An attorney may not appear specially.

Rule 4.100 amended effective January 1, 2007; adopted as rule 227.4 effective January 1, 1985; previously amended effective June 6, 1990; previously renumbered and amended effective January 1, 2001.

Advisory Committee Comment

Cross reference: Penal Code section 987.1.

Rule 4.101. Bail in criminal cases

The fact that a defendant in a criminal case has or has not asked for a jury trial must not be taken into consideration in fixing the amount of bail and, once set, bail may not be increased or reduced by reason of such fact.

Rule 4.101 amended effective January 1, 2007; adopted as rule 801 effective July 1, 1964; previously renumbered effective January 1, 2001.

Rule 4.102. Uniform bail and penalty schedules—traffic, boating, fish and game, forestry, public utilities, parks and recreation, business licensing

The Judicial Council of California has established the policy of promulgating uniform bail and penalty schedules for certain offenses in order to achieve a standard of uniformity in the handling of these offenses.

In general, bail is used to ensure the presence of the defendant before the court. Under Vehicle Code sections

40512 and 13103, bail may also be forfeited and forfeiture may be ordered without the necessity of any further court proceedings and be treated as a conviction for specified Vehicle Code offenses. A penalty in the form of a monetary sum is a fine imposed as all or a portion of a sentence imposed.

To achieve substantial uniformity of bail and penalties throughout the state in traffic, boating, fish and game, forestry, public utilities, parks and recreation, and business licensing cases, the trial court judges, in performing their duty under Penal Code section 1269b to annually revise and adopt a schedule of bail and penalties for all misdemeanor and infraction offenses except Vehicle Code infractions, must give consideration to the Uniform Bail and Penalty Schedules approved by the Judicial Council. The Uniform Bail and Penalty Schedule for infraction violations of the Vehicle Code will be established by the Judicial Council in accordance with Vehicle Code section 40310. Judges must give consideration to requiring additional bail for aggravating or enhancing factors.

After a court adopts a countywide bail and penalty schedule, under Penal Code section 1269b, the court must, as soon as practicable, mail a copy of the schedule to the Judicial Council with a report stating how the revised schedule differs from the council's uniform traffic bail and penalty schedule, uniform boating bail and penalty schedule, uniform fish and game bail and penalty schedule, uniform forestry bail and penalty schedule, uniform public utilities bail and penalty schedule, uniform parks and recreation bail and penalty schedule, or uniform business licensing bail and penalty schedule.

The purpose of this uniform bail and penalty schedule is to:

(1) Show the standard amount for bail, which for Vehicle Code offenses may also be the amount used for a bail forfeiture instead of further proceedings; and

(2) Serve as a guideline for the imposition of a fine as all or a portion of the penalty for a first conviction of a listed offense where a fine is used as all or a portion of the penalty for such offense. The amounts shown for the misdemeanors on the boating, fish and game, forestry, public utilities, parks and recreation, and business licensing bail and penalty schedules have been set with this dual purpose in mind.

Unless otherwise shown, the maximum penalties for the listed offenses are six months in the county jail or a fine of $1,000, or both. The penalty amounts are intended to be used to provide standard fine amounts for a first offense conviction of a violation shown where a fine is used as all or a portion of the sentence imposed.

Note:

Courts may obtain copies of the Uniform Bail and Penalty Schedules by contacting:

Office of the General Counsel
Administrative Office of the Courts
455 Golden Gate Avenue
San Francisco, CA 94102-3688
(415) 865-7611
Fax (415) 865-4317
www.courtinfo.ca.gov/reference

Rule 4.102 amended effective January 1, 2007; adopted as rule 850 effective January 1, 1965; previously amended effective

January 1, 1970, January 1, 1971, July 1, 1972, January 1, 1973, January 1, 1974, July 1, 1975, July 1, 1979, July 1, 1980, July 1, 1981, January 1, 1983, July 1, 1984, July 1, 1986, January 1, 1989, January 1, 1990, January 1, 1993, January 1, 1995, January 1, 1997, and July 1, 2004; previously renumbered and amended effective January 1, 2001.

Rule 4.103. Notice to appear forms

(a) Traffic offenses

A notice to appear that is issued for any violation of the Vehicle Code other than a felony or for a violation of an ordinance of a city or county relating to traffic offenses must be prepared and filed with the court on Automated Traffic Enforcement System Notice to Appear (form TR-115) or Traffic/Nontraffic Notice to Appear (form TR-130), and must comply with the requirements in the current version of the Judicial Council's instructions, Notice to Appear and Related Forms (form TR-INST).

(Subd (a) amended effective January 1, 2007.)

(b) Nontraffic offenses

A notice to appear issued for a nontraffic infraction or misdemeanor offense that is prepared on Nontraffic Notice to Appear (form TR-120) or Traffic/Nontraffic Notice to Appear (form TR-130), and that complies with the requirements in the current version of the Judicial Council's instructions, Notice to Appear and Related Forms (form TR-INST), may be filed with the court and serve as a complaint as provided in Penal Code section 853.9.

(Subd (b) amended effective January 1, 2007.)

(c) Corrections

Corrections to citations previously issued on Continuation of Notice to Appear (form TR-106), Continuation of Citation (form TR-108), Automated Traffic Enforcement System Notice to Appear (form TR-115), Nontraffic Notice to Appear (form TR-120), or Traffic/Nontraffic Notice to Appear (form TR-130) must be made on a Notice of Correction and Proof of Service (form TR-100).

(Subd (c) amended effective January 1, 2007.)

Rule 4.103 amended effective January 1, 2007; adopted effective January 1, 2004.

Rule 4.104. Procedures and eligibility criteria for attending traffic violator school

(a) Purpose

The purpose of this rule is to establish uniform statewide procedures and criteria for eligibility to attend traffic violator school.

(Subd (a) amended effective January 1, 2003; previously amended effective July 1, 2001.)

(b) Authority of a court clerk to grant pretrial diversion

(1) Eligible offenses

Except as provided in (2), a court clerk is authorized to grant a request to attend traffic violator school when a defendant with a valid driver's license requests to attend an 8-hour traffic violator school as pretrial diversion under Vehicle Code sections 41501(a) and 42005 for any infraction under divisions 11 and 12 (rules of the road and equipment violations) of the Vehicle Code if the violation is reportable to the Department of Motor Vehicles.

(2) Ineligible offenses

A court clerk is not authorized to grant a request to attend traffic violator school for a misdemeanor or any of the following infractions:

(A) A violation that carries a negligent operator point count of more than one point under Vehicle Code section 12810 or one and one-half points or more under Vehicle Code section 12810.5(b)(2);

(B) A violation that occurs within 18 months after the date of a previous violation and the defendant either attended or elected to attend a traffic violator school for the previous violation (Veh. Code, § 1808.7);

(C) A violation of Vehicle Code section 22406.5 (tank vehicles);

(D) A violation related to alcohol use or possession or drug use or possession;

(E) A violation on which the defendant failed to appear under Vehicle Code section 40508(a) unless the failure-to-appear charge has been adjudicated and any fine imposed has been paid;

(F) A violation on which the defendant has failed to appear under Penal Code section 1214.1 unless the civil monetary assessment has been paid;

(G) A speeding violation in which the speed alleged is more than 25 miles over a speed limit as stated in Chapter 7 (commencing with section 22348) of Division 11 of the Vehicle Code;

(H) A violation that occurs in a commercial vehicle as defined in Vehicle Code section 15210(b); and

(I) A violation by a defendant having a class A, class B, or commercial class C driver's license.

(Subd (b) amended effective January 1, 2007; previously amended effective January 1, 2003, September 20, 2005, and January 1, 2007.)

(c) Judicial discretion

(1) A judicial officer may in his or her discretion order attendance at a traffic violator school in an individual case for diversion under Vehicle Code section 41501(a) or 42005(b); sentencing under Vehicle Code section 42005(a); or any other purpose permitted by law. A violation by a defendant having a class A, class B, or commercial class C driver's license or that occurs in a commercial vehicle, as defined in Vehicle Code section 15210(b), is not eligible for diversion under Vehicle Code sections 41501 or 42005.

(2) If a violation occurs within 18 months of a previous violation that was dismissed under Vehicle Code section 41501(a), a judicial officer may order a continuance and dismissal in consideration for completion of a program at a licensed school for traffic violators as specified in Vehicle Code section 41501(a). The program must consist of at least 12 hours of instruction as specified in section 41501(a). Under Vehicle Code section 1808.7, a dismissal for completion of the 12-hour program under this subdivision is not confidential.

(3) A defendant who is otherwise eligible for traffic violator school is not made ineligible by entering a plea other than guilty or by exercising his or her right to trial. A traffic violator school request must be considered based on the individual circumstances of the specific case. The court is not required to state on the record a reason for granting or denying a traffic violator school request.

(Subd (c) amended effective January 1, 2007; amended and relettered as part of subd (b) effective January 1, 2003; previously amended effective January 1, 1998, September 20, 2005, and January 1, 2007.)

Rule 4.104 amended effective January 1, 2007; adopted as rule 851 effective January 1, 1997; previously amended effective January 1, 1998, July 1, 2001, January 1, 2003, and September 20, 2005; previously amended and renumbered effective January 1, 2007.

Advisory Committee Comment

Subdivision (c)(3). Rule 4.104(c)(3) reflects court rulings in cases where defendants wished to plead not guilty and have the court order attendance of traffic violator school if found guilty after trial. A court has discretion to grant or not grant traffic violator school. (*People v. Schindler* (1993) 20 Cal.App.4th 431, 433; *People v. Levinson* (1984) 155 Cal.App.3d Supp. 13, 21.) However, the court may not arbitrarily refuse to consider a request for traffic violator school because a defendant pleads not guilty. (*Schindler,* supra, at p. 433; *People v. Wozniak* (1987) 197 Cal.App.3d Supp. 43, 44; *People v. Enochs* (1976) 62 Cal.App.3d Supp. 42, 44.) If a judicial officer believes that a defendant's circumstances indicate that a defendant would benefit from attending school, such attendance should be authorized and should not be affected by the order in which the plea, explanation, and request for traffic violator school are presented. (*Enochs,* supra, at p. 44.) A court is not required to state its reasons for granting or denying traffic violator school following a defendant's conviction for a traffic violation. (*Schindler,* supra, at p. 433.)

Rule 4.110. Time limits for criminal proceedings on information or indictment

Time limits for criminal proceedings on information or indictment are as follows:

(1) The information must be filed within 15 days after a person has been held to answer for a public offense;

(2) The arraignment of a defendant must be held on the date the information is filed or as soon thereafter as the court directs; and

(3) A plea or notice of intent to demur on behalf of a party represented by counsel at the arraignment must be entered or made no later than seven days after the initial arraignment, unless the court lengthens time for good cause.

Rule 4.110 amended effective January 1, 2007; adopted as rule 227.3 effective January 1, 1985; previously amended effective June 6, 1990; previously renumbered and amended effective January 1, 2001.

Rule 4.111. Pretrial motions in criminal cases

(a) Time for filing papers and proof of service

Unless otherwise ordered or specifically provided by law, all pretrial motions, accompanied by a memorandum, must be served and filed at least 10 calendar days, all papers opposing the motion at least 5 calendar days, and all reply papers at least 2 court days before the time appointed for hearing. Proof of service of the moving papers must be filed no later than 5 calendar days before the time appointed for hearing.

(Subd (a) amended effective January 1, 2007.)

(b) Failure to serve and file timely points and authorities

The court may consider the failure without good cause of the moving party to serve and file a memorandum within the time permitted as an admission that the motion is without merit.

(Subd (b) amended effective January 1, 2007.)

Rule 4.111 amended effective January 1, 2007; adopted as rule 227.5 effective January 1, 1985; previously renumbered effective January 1, 2001.

Rule 4.112. Readiness conference

(a) Date and appearances

The court may hold a readiness conference in felony cases within 1 to 14 days before the date set for trial. At the readiness conference:

(1) All trial counsel must appear and be prepared to discuss the case and determine whether the case can be disposed of without trial;

(2) The prosecuting attorney must have authority to dispose of the case; and

(3) The defendant must be present in court.

(Subd (a) amended effective January 1, 2007; adopted as rule 227.6 effective January 1, 1985; previously amended and relettered effective January 1, 2001; previously amended effective January 1, 2005.)

(b) Motions

Except for good cause, the court should hear and decide any pretrial motion in a criminal case before or at the readiness conference.

(Subd (b) adopted effective January 1, 2001.)

Rule 4.112 amended effective January 1, 2007; subd (a) adopted as rule 227.6 effective January 1, 1985; subd (b) adopted as section 10.1 of the Standards of Judicial Administration effective January 1, 1985; previously amended and renumbered effective January 1, 2001; previously amended effective January 1, 2005.

Rule 4.113. Motions and grounds for continuance of criminal case set for trial

Motions to continue the trial of a criminal case are disfavored and will be denied unless the moving party, under Penal Code section 1050, presents affirmative proof in open court that the ends of justice require a continuance.

Rule 4.113 amended effective January 1, 2007; adopted as rule 227.7 effective January 1, 1985 previously renumbered effective January 1, 2001.

Rule 4.114. Certification under Penal Code section 859a

When a plea of guilty or no contest is entered under Penal Code section 859a, the magistrate must:

(1) Set a date for imposing sentence; and

(2) Refer the case to the probation officer for action as provided in Penal Code sections 1191 and 1203.

Rule 4.114 amended effective January 1, 2007; adopted as rule 227.9 effective January 1, 1985; previously amended and renumbered effective January 1, 2001.

Ref.: Cal. Fms Pl. & Pr., Ch. 317, "Judges."

Rule 4.115. Criminal case assignment

(a) Master calendar departments

To ensure that the court's policy on continuances is firm and uniformly applied, that pretrial proceedings and trial assignments are handled consistently, and that cases are tried on a date certain, each court not operating on a direct calendaring system must assign all criminal matters to one or more master calendar departments. The presiding judge of a master calendar department must conduct or supervise the conduct of all arraignments and pretrial hearings and conferences and assign to a trial department any case requiring a trial or dispositional hearing.

(Subd (a) lettered effective January 1, 2008; adopted as unlettered subd effective January 1, 1985.)

(b) Trial calendaring and continuances

Any request for a continuance, including a request to trail the trial date, must comply with rule 4.113 and the requirement in section 1050 to show good cause to continue a hearing in a criminal proceeding. Active management of trial calendars is necessary to minimize the number of statutory dismissals. Accordingly, courts should avoid calendaring or trailing criminal cases for trial to the last day permitted for trial under section 1382. Courts must implement calendar management procedures, in accordance with local conditions and needs, to ensure that criminal cases are assigned to trial departments before the last day permitted for trial under section 1382.

(Subd (b) adopted effective January 1, 2008.)

Rule 4.115 amended effective January 1, 2008; adopted as section 10 of the Standards of Judicial Administration effective January 1, 1985; amended and renumbered effective January 1, 2001; previously amended effective January 1, 2007.

Advisory Committee Comment

Subdivision (b) clarifies that the "good cause" showing for a continuance under section 1050 applies in all criminal cases, whether or not the case is in the 10-day grace period provided for in section 1382. The Trial Court Presiding Judges Advisory Committee and Criminal Law Advisory Committee observe that the "good cause" requirement for a continuance is separate and distinct from the "good cause" requirement to avoid dismissals under section 1382. There is case law stating that the prosecution is not required to show good cause to avoid a dismissal under section 1382 during the 10-day grace period because a case may not be dismissed for delay during that 10-day period. (See, e.g., *Bryant v. Superior Court* (1986) 186 Cal.App.3d 483, 488.) Yet, both the plain language of section 1050 and case law show that there must be good cause for a continuance under section 1050 during the 10-day grace period. (See, e.g., section 1050 and *People v. Henderson* (2004) 115 Cal.App.4th 922, 939–940.) Thus, a court may not dismiss a case during the 10-day grace period under section 1382, but the committees believe that the court must deny a request for a continuance during the 10-day grace period that does not comply with the good cause requirement under section 1050.

The decision in *Henderson* states that when the prosecutor seeks a continuance but fails to show good cause under section 1050, the trial court "must nevertheless postpone the hearing to another date within the statutory period." (115 Cal.App.4th at p. 940.) That conclusion, however, may be contrary to the plain language of section 1050, which requires a court to deny a continuance if the moving party fails to show good cause. The conclusion also appears to be dicta, as it was not a contested issue on appeal. Given this uncertainty, the rule is silent as to the remedy for failure to show good cause for a requested continuance during the 10-day grace period. The committees note that the remedies under section 1050.5 are available and, but for the *Henderson* dicta, a court would appear to be allowed to deny the continuance request and commence the trial on the scheduled trial date.

Rule 4.116. Certification to juvenile court

(a) Application

This rule applies to all cases not filed in juvenile court in which the person charged by an accusatory pleading appears to be under the age of 18, except (1) when the child has been found not a fit and proper subject to be dealt with under the juvenile court law or (2) when the prosecution was initiated as a criminal case under Welfare and Institutions Code section 602(b) or 707(d).

(Subd (a) amended effective January 1, 2007; adopted effective January 1, 2001.)

(b) Procedure to determine whether certification is appropriate

If an accusatory pleading is pending, and it is suggested or it appears to the court that the person charged was under the age of 18 on the date the offense is alleged to have been committed, the court must immediately suspend proceedings and conduct a hearing to determine the true age of the person charged. The burden of proof of establishing the age of the accused person is on the moving party. If, after examination, the court is satisfied by a preponderance of the evidence that the person was under the age of 18 on the date the alleged offense was committed, the court must immediately certify the matter to the juvenile court and state on the certification order:

(1) The crime with which the person named is charged;

(2) That the person was under the age of 18 on the date of the alleged offense;

(3) The date of birth of the person;

(4) The date of suspension of criminal proceedings; and

(5) The date and time of certification to juvenile court.

(Subd (b) amended effective January 1, 2007; adopted as untitled subd effective January 1, 1991; previously amended and lettered effective January 1, 2001.)

(c) Procedure on certification

If the court determines that certification to the juvenile court is appropriate under (b), copies of the certification, the accusatory pleading, and any police reports must immediately be transmitted to the clerk of the juvenile court. On receipt of the documents, the clerk of the juvenile court must immediately notify the probation officer, who must immediately investigate the matter to determine whether to commence proceedings in juvenile court.

(Subd (c) amended effective January 1, 2007; adopted as untitled subd effective January 1, 1991; previously amended and lettered effective January 1, 2001.)

(d) Procedure if child is in custody

If the person is under the age of 18 and is in custody, the person must immediately be transported to the juvenile detention facility.

(Subd (d) amended effective January 1, 2007; adopted as untitled subd effective January 1, 1991; previously amended and lettered effective January 1, 2001.)

Rule 4.116 amended effective January 1, 2007; adopted as rule 241.2 effective January 1, 1991; previously amended July 1, 1991; previously amended and renumbered effective January 1, 2001.

Ref.: Cal. Fms Pl. & Pr., Ch. 329, "Juvenile Courts: Delinquency Proceedings."

Rule 4.117. Qualifications for appointed trial counsel in capital cases

(a) Purpose

This rule defines minimum qualifications for attorneys appointed to represent persons charged with capital offenses in the superior courts. These minimum qualifications are designed to promote adequate representation in death penalty cases and to avoid unnecessary delay and expense by assisting the trial court in appointing qualified counsel. Nothing in this rule is intended to be used as a standard by which to measure whether the defendant received effective assistance of counsel.

(b) General qualifications

In cases in which the death penalty is sought, the court must assign qualified trial counsel to represent the defendant. The attorney may be appointed only if the court, after reviewing the attorney's background, experience, and training, determines that the attorney has demonstrated the skill, knowledge, and proficiency to diligently and competently represent the defendant. An attorney is not entitled to appointment simply because he or she meets the minimum qualifications.

(c) Designation of counsel

(1) If the court appoints more than one attorney, one must be designated lead counsel and meet the qualifications stated in (d) or (f), and at least one other must be designated associate counsel and meet the qualifications stated in (e) or (f).

(2) If the court appoints only one attorney, that attorney must meet the qualifications stated in (d) or (f).

(Subd (c) amended effective January 1, 2007.)

(d) Qualifications of lead counsel

To be eligible to serve as lead counsel, an attorney must:

(1) Be an active member of the State Bar of California;

(2) Be an active trial practitioner with at least 10 years' litigation experience in the field of criminal law;

(3) Have prior experience as lead counsel in either:

(A) At least 10 serious or violent felony jury trials, including at least 2 murder cases, tried to argument, verdict, or final judgment; or

(B) At least 5 serious or violent felony jury trials, including at least 3 murder cases, tried to argument, verdict, or final judgment;

(4) Be familiar with the practices and procedures of the California criminal courts;

(5) Be familiar with and experienced in the use of expert witnesses and evidence, including psychiatric and forensic evidence;

(6) Have completed within two years before appointment at least 15 hours of capital case defense training approved for Minimum Continuing Legal Education credit by the State Bar of California; and

(7) Have demonstrated the necessary proficiency, diligence, and quality of representation appropriate to capital cases.

(Subd (d) amended effective January 1, 2007.)

(e) Qualifications of associate counsel

To be eligible to serve as associate counsel, an attorney must:

(1) Be an active member of the State Bar of California;

(2) Be an active trial practitioner with at least three years' litigation experience in the field of criminal law;

(3) Have prior experience as:

(A) Lead counsel in at least 10 felony jury trials tried to verdict, including 3 serious or violent felony jury trials tried to argument, verdict, or final judgment; or

(B) Lead or associate counsel in at least 5 serious or violent felony jury trials, including at least 1 murder case, tried to argument, verdict, or final judgment;

(4) Be familiar with the practices and procedures of the California criminal courts;

(5) Be familiar with and experienced in the use of expert witnesses and evidence, including psychiatric and forensic evidence;

(6) Have completed within two years before appointment at least 15 hours of capital case defense training approved for Minimum Continuing Legal Education credit by the State Bar of California; and

(7) Have demonstrated the necessary proficiency, diligence, and quality of representation appropriate to capital cases.

(Subd (e) amended effective January 1, 2007.)

(f) Alternative qualifications

The court may appoint an attorney even if he or she does not meet all of the qualifications stated in (d) or (e) if the attorney demonstrates the ability to provide competent representation to the defendant. If the court appoints counsel under this subdivision, it must state on the record the basis for finding counsel qualified. In making this determination, the court must consider whether the attorney meets the following qualifications:

(1) The attorney is an active member of the State Bar of California or admitted to practice *pro hac vice* under rule 9.40;

(2) The attorney has demonstrated the necessary proficiency, diligence, and quality of representation appropriate to capital cases;

(3) The attorney has had extensive criminal or civil trial experience;

(4) Although not meeting the qualifications stated in (d) or (e), the attorney has had experience in death penalty trials other than as lead or associate counsel;

(5) The attorney is familiar with the practices and procedures of the California criminal courts;

(6) The attorney is familiar with and experienced in the use of expert witnesses and evidence, including psychiatric and forensic evidence;

(7) The attorney has had specialized training in the defense of persons accused of capital crimes, such as experience in a death penalty resource center;

(8) The attorney has ongoing consultation support from experienced death penalty counsel;

(9) The attorney has completed within the past two years before appointment at least 15 hours of capital case defense training approved for Minimum Continuing Legal Education credit by the State Bar of California; and

(10) The attorney has been certified by the State Bar of California's Board of Legal Specialization as a criminal law specialist.

(Subd (f) amended effective January 1, 2007.)

(g) Public defender appointments

When the court appoints the Public Defender under Penal Code section 987.2, the Public Defender should assign an attorney from that office or agency as lead counsel who meets the qualifications described in (d) or assign an attorney that he or she determines would qualify under (f). If associate counsel is designated, the Public Defender should assign an attorney from that office or agency who meets the qualifications described in (e) or assign an attorney he or she determines would qualify under (f).

(Subd (g) amended effective January 1, 2007.)

(h) Standby or advisory counsel

When the court appoints standby or advisory counsel to assist a self-represented defendant, the attorney must qualify under (d) or (f).

(Subd (h) amended effective January 1, 2007.)

(i) Order appointing counsel

When the court appoints counsel to a capital case, the court must complete *Order Appointing Counsel in Capital Case* (form CR-190), and counsel must complete *Declaration of Counsel for Appointment in Capital Case* (form CR-191).

(Subd (i) amended effective January 1, 2007; adopted effective January 1, 2004.)

Rule 4.117 amended effective January 1, 2007; adopted effective January 1, 2003; previously amended effective January 1, 2004.

Rule 4.130. Mental competency proceedings

(a) Application

This rule applies to proceedings in the superior court under Penal Code section 1367 et seq. to determine the mental competency of a criminal defendant.

(Subd (a) adopted effective January 1, 2007.)

(b) Initiation of mental competency proceedings

(1) The court must initiate mental competency proceedings if the judge has a reasonable doubt, based on substantial evidence, about the defendant's competence to stand trial.

(2) The opinion of counsel, without a statement of specific reasons supporting that opinion, does not constitute substantial evidence. The court may allow defense counsel to present his or her opinion regarding the defendant's mental competency in camera if the court finds there is reason to believe that attorney-client privileged information will be inappropriately revealed if the hearing is conducted in open court.

(3) In a felony case, if the judge initiates mental competency proceedings prior to the preliminary examination, counsel for the defendant may request a preliminary examination as provided in Penal Code section 1368.1(a).

(Subd (b) adopted effective January 1, 2007.)

(c) Effect of initiating mental competency proceedings

(1) If mental competency proceedings are initiated, criminal proceedings are suspended and may not be reinstated until a trial on the competency of the defendant has been concluded and the defendant either:

(A) Is found mentally competent; or

(B) Has his or her competency restored under Penal Code section 1372.

(2) In misdemeanor cases, speedy trial requirements are tolled during the suspension of criminal proceedings for mental competency evaluation and trial. If criminal proceedings are later reinstated and time is not waived, the trial must be commenced within 30 days after the reinstatement of the criminal proceedings, as provided by Penal Code section 1382(a)(3).

(3) In felony cases, speedy trial requirements are tolled during the suspension of criminal proceedings for mental competency evaluation and trial. If criminal proceedings are reinstated, unless time is waived, time periods to

commence the preliminary examination or trial are as follows:

(A) If criminal proceedings were suspended before the preliminary hearing had been conducted, the preliminary hearing must be commenced within 10 days of the reinstatement of the criminal proceedings, as provided in Penal Code section 859b.

(B) If criminal proceedings were suspended after the preliminary hearing had been conducted, the trial must be commenced within 60 days of the reinstatement of the criminal proceedings, as provided in Penal Code section 1382(a)(2).

(Subd (c) adopted effective January 1, 2007.)

(d) Examination of defendant after initiation of mental competency proceedings

(1) On initiation of mental competency proceedings, the court must inquire whether the defendant, or defendant's counsel, seeks a finding of mental incompetence.

(A) If the defense informs the court that the defendant is seeking a finding of mental incompetence, the court must appoint at least one expert to examine the defendant.

(B) If the defense informs the court that the defendant is not seeking a finding of mental incompetence, the court must appoint two experts to examine the defendant. The defense and the prosecution may each name one expert from the court's list of approved experts.

(2) Any court-appointed experts must examine the defendant and advise the court on the defendant's competency to stand trial. Experts' reports are to be submitted to the court, counsel for the defendant, and the prosecution.

(3) Statements made by the defendant during the examination to experts appointed under this rule, and products of any such statements, may not be used in a trial on the issue of the defendant's guilt or in a sanity trial should defendant enter a plea of not guilty by reason of insanity.

(Subd (d) adopted effective January 1, 2007.)

(e) Trial on mental competency

(1) Regardless of the conclusions or findings of the court-appointed expert, the court must conduct a trial on the mental competency of the defendant if the court has initiated mental competency proceedings under (b).

(2) At the trial, the defendant is presumed to be mentally competent, and it is the burden of the party contending that the defendant is not mentally competent to prove the defendant's mental incompetence by a preponderance of the evidence.

(3) In addition to the testimony of the experts appointed by the court under (d), either party may call additional experts or other relevant witnesses.

(4) After the presentation of the evidence and closing argument, the trier of fact is to determine whether the defendant is mentally competent or mentally incompetent.

(A) If the matter is tried by a jury, the verdict must be unanimous.

(B) If the parties have waived the right to a jury trial, the court's findings must be made in writing or placed orally in the record.

(Subd (e) adopted effective January 1, 2007.)

(f) Posttrial procedure

(1) If the defendant is found mentally competent, the court must reinstate the criminal proceedings.

(2) If the defendant is found to be mentally incompetent, the criminal proceedings remain suspended and the court must follow the procedures stated in Penal Code section 1370 et seq.

(Subd (f) adopted effective January 1, 2007.)
Rule 4.130 adopted effective January 1, 2007.

Advisory Committee Comment

The case law interpreting Penal Code section 1367 et seq. established a procedure for judges to follow in cases where there is a concern whether the defendant is legally competent to stand trial, but the concern does not necessarily rise to the level of a reasonable doubt based on substantial evidence. Before finding a reasonable doubt as to the defendant's competency to stand trial and initiating competency proceedings under Penal Code section 1368 et seq., the court may appoint an expert to assist the court in determining whether such a reasonable doubt exists. As noted in *People v. Visciotti* (1992) 2 Cal.4th 1, 34–36, the court may appoint an expert when it is concerned about the mental competency of the defendant, but the concern does not rise to the level of a reasonable doubt, based on substantial evidence, required by Penal Code section 1367 et seq. Should the results of this examination present substantial evidence of mental incompetency, the court must initiate competency proceedings under (b).

Once mental competency proceedings under Penal Code section 1367 et seq. have been initiated, the court is to appoint at least one expert to examine the defendant under (d). Under no circumstances is the court obligated to appoint more than two experts. (Pen. Code, § 1369(a).) The costs of the experts appointed under (d) are to be paid for by the court as the expert examinations and reports are for the benefit or use of the court in determining whether the defendant is mentally incompetent. (See Cal. Rules of Court, rule 10.810, function 10.)

Subdivision (d)(3), which provides that the defendant's statements made during the examination cannot be used in a trial on the defendant's guilt or a sanity trial in a not guilty by reason of sanity trial, is based on the California Supreme Court holdings in *People v. Arcega* (1982) 32 Cal.3d 504 and *People v. Weaver* (2001) 26 Cal.4th 876.

Although the court is not obligated to appoint additional experts, counsel may nonetheless retain their own experts to testify at a trial on the defendant's competency. (See *People v. Mayes* (1988) 202 Cal.App.4th 908, 917–918.) These experts are not for the benefit or use of the court, and their costs are not to be paid by the court. (See Cal. Rules of Court, rule 10.810, function 10.)

The expert reports, unless sealed under rule 2.550, are publicly accessible court documents.

Both the prosecution and the defense have the right to a jury trial. (See *People v. Superior Court (McPeters)* (1995) 169 Cal.App.3d 796.) Defense counsel may waive this right, even over the objection of the defendant. (*People v. Masterson* (1994) 8 Cal.4th 965, 970.)

Either defense counsel or the prosecution (or both) may argue that the defendant is not competent to stand trial. (*People v. Stanley* (1995) 10 Cal.4th 764, 804 [defense counsel may advocate that defendant is not competent to stand trial and may present evidence of defendant's mental incompetency regardless of defendant's desire to be found competent].) If the defense declines to present evidence of the defendant's mental incompetency, the prosecution may do so. (Pen. Code, § 1369(b)(2).) If the prosecution elects to present evidence of the defendant's mental incompetency, it is the prosecution's burden to prove the incompetency by a preponderance of the evidence. (*People v. Mixon* (1990) 225 Cal.App.3d 1471, 1484, fn. 12.)

Should both parties decline to present evidence of defendant's mental incompetency, the court may do so. In those cases, the court is not to instruct the jury that a party has the burden of proof. "Rather, the proper approach would be to instruct the jury on the legal standard they are to apply to the evidence before them without allocating the burden of proof to one party or the other." (*People v. Sherik* (1991) 229 Cal.App.3d 444, 459–460.)

Chapter 2
Change of Venue

Rule 4.150. Change of venue: application and general provisions
Rule 4.151. Motion for change of venue
Rule 4.152. Selection of court and trial judge
Rule 4.153. Order on change of venue
Rule 4.154. Proceedings in the receiving court
Rule 4.155. Guidelines for reimbursement of costs in change of venue cases—criminal cases

Rule 4.150.   Change of venue: application and general provisions

(a) Application

Rules 4.150 to 4.155 govern the change of venue in criminal cases under Penal Code section 1033.

(Subd (a) adopted effective January 1, 2006.)

(b) General provisions

When a change of venue has been ordered, the case remains a case of the transferring court. Except on good cause to the contrary, the court must follow the provisions below:

(1) Proceedings before trial must be heard in the transferring court.

(2) Proceedings that are not to be heard by the trial judge must be heard in the transferring court.

(3) Postverdict proceedings, including sentencing, if any, must be heard in the transferring court.

(Subd (b) amended effective January 1, 2007; adopted effective January 1, 2006.)

(c) Appellate review

Review by the Court of Appeal, either by an original proceeding or by appeal, must be heard in the appellate district in which the transferring court is located.

(Subd (c) adopted effective January 1, 2006.)

Rule 4.150 amended effective January 1, 2007; adopted as rule 840 effective March 4, 1972; previously amended and renumbered effective January 1, 2001; previously amended effective January 1, 2006.

Advisory Committee Comment

Subdivision (b)(1). This subdivision is based on Penal Code section 1033(a), which provides that all proceedings before trial are to be heard in the transferring court, except when a particular proceeding must be heard by the trial judge.

Subdivision (b)(2). This subdivision addresses motions heard by a judge other than the trial judge, such as requests for funds under Penal Code section 987.9 or a challenge or disqualification under Code of Civil Procedure section 170 et seq.

Subdivision (b)(3). Reflecting the local community interest in the case, (b)(3) clarifies that after trial the case is to return to the transferring court for any posttrial proceedings. There may be situations where the local interest is outweighed, warranting the receiving court to conduct posttrial hearings. Such hearings may include motions for new trial where juror testimony is necessary and the convenience to the jurors outweighs the desire to conduct the hearings in the transferring court.

Subdivision (c). This subdivision ensures that posttrial appeals and writs are heard in the same appellate district as any writs that may have been heard before or during trial.

Rule 4.151.   Motion for change of venue

(a) Motion procedure

A motion for change of venue in a criminal case under Penal Code section 1033 must be supported by a declaration stating the facts supporting the application. Except for good cause shown, the motion must be filed at least 10 days before the date set for trial, with a copy served on the adverse party at least 10 days before the hearing. At the hearing counterdeclarations may be filed.

(Subd (a) amended effective January 1, 2007; adopted effective January 1, 2006; formerly part of an unlettered subd.)

(b) Policy considerations in ruling on motion

Before ordering a change of venue in a criminal case, the transferring court should consider impaneling a jury that would give the defendant a fair and impartial trial.

(Subd (b) adopted effective January 1, 2006.)

Rule 4.151 amended effective January 1, 2008; adopted as rule 841 effective March 4, 1972; previously amended and renumbered effective January 1, 2001; previously amended effective January 1, 2006, and January 1, 2007.

Advisory Committee Comment

Rule 4.151(b) is not intended to imply that the court should attempt to impanel a jury in every case before granting a change of venue.

Rule 4.152.   Selection of court and trial judge

When a judge grants a motion for change of venue, he or she must inform the presiding judge of the transferring court. The presiding judge, or his or her designee, must:

(1) Notify the Administrative Director of the Courts of the change of venue. After receiving the transferring court's notification, the Administrative Director, in order to expedite judicial business and equalize the work of the judges, must advise the transferring court which courts would not be unduly burdened by the trial of the case.

(2) Select the judge to try the case, as follows:

(A) The presiding judge, or his or her designee, must select a judge from the transferring court, unless he or she concludes that the transferring court does not have adequate judicial resources to try the case.

(B) If the presiding judge, or his or her designee, concludes that the transferring court does not have adequate judicial resources to try the case, he or she must request that the Chief Justice of California determine whether to assign a judge to the transferring court. If the Chief Justice determines not to assign a judge to the transferring court, the presiding judge, or his or her designee, must select a judge from the transferring court to try the case.

Rule 4.152 amended effective January 1, 2006; adopted as rule 842 effective March 4, 1972; previously amended and renumbered effective January 1, 2001.

Rule 4.153.   Order on change of venue

After receiving the list of courts from the Administrative Director of the Courts, the presiding judge, or his or her designee, must:

(1) Determine the court in which the case is to be tried. In making that determination, the court must consider,

under Penal Code section 1036.7, whether to move the jury rather than to move the pending action. In so doing, the court should give particular consideration to the convenience of the jurors.

(2) Transmit to the receiving court a certified copy of the order of transfer and any pleadings, documents, or other papers or exhibits necessary for trying the case.

(3) Enter the order for change of venue in the minutes of the transferring court. The order must include the determinations in (1).

Rule 4.153 amended effective January 1, 2006; adopted as rule 843 effective March 4, 1972; previously amended and renumbered effective January 1, 2001.

Advisory Committee Comment

Rules 4.152 and 4.153 recognize that, although the determination of whether to grant a motion for change of venue is judicial in nature, the selection of the receiving court and the decision whether the case should be tried by a judge of the transferring court are more administrative in nature. Thus, the rules provide that the presiding judge of the transferring court is to make the latter decisions. He or she may delegate those decisions to the trial judge, the supervising judge of the criminal division, or any other judge the presiding judge deems appropriate. If, under the particular facts of the case, the latter decisions are both judicial and administrative, those decisions may be more properly made by the judge who heard the motion for change of venue.

Rule 4.154.   Proceedings in the receiving court

The receiving court must conduct the trial as if the case had been commenced in the receiving court. If it is necessary to have any of the original pleadings or other papers before the receiving court, the transferring court must transmit such papers or pleadings. If, during the trial, any original papers or pleadings are submitted to the receiving court, the receiving court is to file the original. After sentencing, all original papers and pleadings are to be retained by the transferring court.

Rule 4.154 amended effective January 1, 2006; adopted as rule 844 effective March 4, 1972; previously amended and renumbered effective January 1, 2001.

Rule 4.155.   Guidelines for reimbursement of costs in change of venue cases—criminal cases

(a) General

Consistent with Penal Code section 1037(c), the court in which an action originated must reimburse the court receiving a case after an order for change of venue for any ordinary expenditure and any extraordinary but reasonable-and-necessary expenditure that would not have been incurred by the receiving court but for the change of venue.

(Subd (a) amended effective January 1, 2006; previously amended effective January 1, 2001.)

(b) Reimbursable ordinary expenditures—court related

Court-related reimbursable ordinary expenses include:

(1) For prospective jurors on the panel from which the jury is selected and for the trial jurors and alternates seated:

(A) Normal juror per diem and mileage at the rates of the receiving court. The cost of the juror should only be charged to a change of venue case if the juror was not used in any other case on the day that juror was excused from the change of venue case.

(B) If jurors are sequestered, actual lodging, meals, mileage, and parking expenses up to state Board of Control limits.

(C) If jurors are transported to a different courthouse or county, actual mileage and parking expenses.

(2) For court reporters:

(A) The cost of pro tem reporters, even if not used on the change of venue trial, but not the salaries of regular official reporters who would have been paid in any event. The rate of compensation for pro tem reporters should be that of the receiving court.

(B) The cost of transcripts requested during trial and for any new trial or appeal, using the folio rate of the receiving court.

(C) The cost of additional reporters necessary to allow production of a daily or expedited transcript.

(3) For assigned judges: The assigned judge's per diem, travel, and other expenses, up to state Board of Control limits, if the judge is assigned to the receiving court because of the change of venue case, regardless of whether the assigned judge is hearing the change of venue case.

(4) For interpreters and translators:

(A) The cost of the services of interpreters and translators, not on the court staff, if those services are required under Evidence Code sections 750 through 754. Using the receiving court's fee schedule, this cost should be paid whether the services are used in a change of venue trial or to cover staff interpreters and translators assigned to the change of venue trial.

(B) Interpreters' and translators' actual mileage, per diem, and lodging expenses, if any, that were incurred in connection with the trial, up to state Board of Control limits.

(5) For maintenance of evidence: The cost of handling, storing, or maintaining evidence beyond the expenses normally incurred by the receiving court.

(6) For services and supplies: The cost of services and supplies incurred only because of the change of venue trial, for example, copying and printing charges (such as for juror questionnaires), long-distance telephone calls, and postage. A pro rata share of the costs of routine services and supplies should not be reimbursable.

(7) For court or county employees:

(A) Overtime expenditures and compensatory time for staff incurred because of the change of venue case.

(B) Salaries and benefit costs of extra help or temporary help incurred either because of the change of venue case or to replace staff assigned to the change of venue case.

(Subd (b) amended effective January 1, 2007; previously amended effective January 1, 1998, and January 1, 2006.)

(c) Reimbursable ordinary expenses—defendant related

Defendant-related reimbursable ordinary expenses include the actual costs incurred for guarding, keeping, and transporting the defendant, including:

(1) Expenses related to health care: Costs incurred by or on behalf of the defendant such as doctors, hospital

expenses, medicines, therapists, and counseling for diagnosis, evaluation, and treatment.

(2) Cost of food and special clothing for an in-custody defendant.

(3) Transportation: Nonroutine expenses, such as transporting an in-custody defendant from the transferring court to the receiving court. Routine transportation expenses if defendant is transported by usual means used for other receiving court prisoners should not be reimbursable.

(Subd (c) amended effective January 1, 2006.)

(d) Reimbursable ordinary expenditures—defense expenses

Reimbursable ordinary expenses related to providing defense for the defendant include:

(1) Matters covered by Penal Code section 987.9 as determined by the transferring court or by a judge designated under that section.

(2) Payment of other defense costs in accordance with policies of the court in which the action originated, unless good cause to the contrary is shown to the trial court.

(3) Unless Penal Code section 987.9 applies, the receiving court may, in its sound discretion, approve all trial-related expenses including:

(A) Attorney fees for defense counsel and, if any, co-counsel and actual travel-related expenses, up to state Board of Control limits, for staying in the county of the receiving court during trial and hearings.

(B) Paralegal and extraordinary secretarial or office expenditures of defense counsel.

(C) Expert witness costs and expenses.

(D) The cost of experts assisting in preparation before trial or during trial, for example, persons preparing demonstrative evidence.

(E) Investigator expenses.

(F) Defense witness expenses, including reasonable-and-necessary witness fees and travel expenses.

(Subd (d) amended effective January 1, 2006; previously amended effective January 1, 1998.)

(e) Extraordinary but reasonable-and-necessary expenses

Except in emergencies or unless it is impracticable to do so, a receiving court should give notice before incurring any extraordinary expenditures to the transferring court, in accordance with Penal Code section 1037(d). Extraordinary but reasonable-and-necessary expenditures include:

(1) Security-related expenditures: The cost of extra security precautions taken because of the risk of escape or suicide or threats of, or the potential for, violence during the trial. These precautions might include, for example, extra bailiffs or correctional officers, special transportation to the courthouse for trial, television monitoring, and security checks of those entering the courtroom.

(2) Facility remodeling or modification: Alterations to buildings or courtrooms to accommodate the change of venue case.

(3) Renting or leasing of space or equipment: Renting or leasing of space for courtrooms, offices, and other facilities, or equipment to accommodate the change of venue case.

(Subd (e) amended effective January 1, 2006; previously amended effective January 1, 1998.)

(f) Nonreimbursable expenses

Nonreimbursable expenses include:

(1) Normal operating expenses including the overhead of the receiving court, for example:

(A) Salary and benefits of existing court staff that would have been paid even if there were no change of venue case.

(B) The cost of operating the jail, for example, detention staff costs, normal inmate clothing, utility costs, overhead costs, and jail construction costs. These expenditures would have been incurred whether or not the case was transferred to the receiving court. It is, therefore, inappropriate to seek reimbursement from the transferring court.

(2) Equipment that is purchased and then kept by the receiving court and that can be used for other purposes or cases.

(Subd (f) amended effective January 1, 2006.)

(g) Miscellaneous

(1) Documentation of costs: No expense should be submitted for reimbursement without supporting documentation, such as a claim, invoice, bill, statement, or time sheet. In unusual circumstances, a declaration under penalty of perjury may be necessary. The declaration should describe the cost and state that it was incurred because of the change of venue case. Any required court order or approval of costs also should be sent to the transferring court.

(2) Timing of reimbursement: Unless both courts agree to other terms, reimbursement of all expenses that are not questioned by the transferring court should be made within 60 days of receipt of the claim for reimbursement. Payment of disputed amounts should be made within 60 days of the resolution of the dispute.

(Subd (g) amended effective January 1, 2007; previously amended effective January 1, 2006.)

Rule 4.155 amended effective January 1, 2007; adopted as section 4.2 of the Standards of Judicial Administration effective July 1, 1989; amended and renumbered as rule 4.162 effective January 1, 2001; previously amended effective January 1, 1998, and January 1, 2006.

Division 3
Trials

Rule 4.200. Pre-voir dire conference in criminal cases
Rule 4.201. Voir dire in criminal cases
Rule 4.210. Traffic court—trial by written declaration

Rule 4.200. Pre-voir dire conference in criminal cases

(a) The conference

Before jury selection begins in criminal cases, the court must conduct a conference with counsel to determine:

(1) A brief outline of the nature of the case, including a summary of the criminal charges;

(2) The names of persons counsel intend to call as witnesses at trial;

(3) The People's theory of culpability and the defendant's theories;

(4) The procedures for deciding requests for excuse for hardship and challenges for cause;

(5) The areas of inquiry and specific questions to be asked by the court and by counsel and any time limits on counsel's examination;

(6) The schedule for the trial and the predicted length of the trial;

(7) The number of alternate jurors to be selected and the procedure for selecting them; and

(8) The procedure for making *Wheeler/Batson* objections.

The judge must, if requested, excuse the defendant from then disclosing any defense theory.

(Subd (a) amended effective January 1, 2007; previously amended effective January 1, 2006.)

(b) Written questions

The court may require counsel to submit in writing, and before the conference, all questions that counsel requests the court to ask of prospective jurors. This rule applies to questions to be asked either orally or by written questionnaire. The *Juror Questionnaire for Criminal Cases* (form MC-002) may be used.

(Subd (b) amended effective January 1, 2006.)

Rule 4.200 amended effective January 1, 2007; adopted as rule 228.1 effective June 6, 1990; previously amended and renumbered effective January 1, 2001; previously amended effective January 1, 2006.

Advisory Committee Comment

This rule is to be used in conjunction with standard 4.30.

Rule 4.201. Voir dire in criminal cases

To select a fair and impartial jury, the judge must conduct an initial examination of the prospective jurors orally, or by written questionnaire, or by both methods. The *Juror Questionnaire for Criminal Cases* (form MC-002) may be used. After completion of the initial examination, the court must permit counsel to conduct supplemental questioning as provided in Code of Civil Procedure section 223.

Rule 4.201 amended effective January 1, 2008; adopted as rule 228.2 effective June 6, 1990; previously amended and renumbered effective January 1, 2001; previously amended effective January 1, 2006.

Advisory Committee Comment

Although Code of Civil Procedure section 223 creates a preference for nonsequestered voir dire (*People v. Roldan* (2005) 35 Cal.4th 646, 691), a judge may conduct sequestered voir dire on questions concerning media reports of the case and on any other issue deemed advisable. (See, e.g., Cal. Stds. Jud. Admin., std. 4.30(a)(3).) To determine whether such issues are present, a judge may consider factors including the charges, the nature of the evidence that is anticipated to be presented, and any other relevant factors. To that end, a judge should always inform jurors of the possibility of sequestered voir dire if the voir dire is likely to elicit answers that the juror may believe are sensitive in nature. It should also be noted that when written questionnaires are used, jurors must be advised of the right to request a hearing in chambers on sensitive questions rather than answering them on the questionnaire. (*Copley Press Inc. v. Superior Court* (1991) 228 Cal.App.3d 77, 87.)

Rule 4.210. Traffic court—trial by written declaration

(a) Applicability

This rule establishes the minimum procedural requirements for trials by written declaration under Vehicle Code section 40902. The procedures established by this rule must be followed in all trials by written declaration under that section.

(Subd (a) amended effective January 1, 2007.)

(b) Procedure

(1) *Definition of due date*

As used in this subdivision, "due date" means the last date on which the defendant's appearance is timely.

(2) *Extending due date*

If the clerk receives the defendant's written request for a trial by written declaration by the appearance date indicated on the *Notice to Appear,* the clerk must, within 15 calendar days after receiving the defendant's written request, extend the appearance date 25 calendar days and must give or mail notice to the defendant of the extended due date on the *Request for Trial by Written Declaration* (form TR-205) with a copy of the *Instructions to Defendant* (form TR-200) and any other required forms.

(3) *Election*

The defendant must file a *Request for Trial by Written Declaration* (form TR-205) with the clerk by the appearance date indicated on the *Notice to Appear* or the extended due date as provided in (2). The *Request for Trial by Written Declaration* (form TR-205) must be filed in addition to the defendant's written request for a trial by written declaration, unless the defendant's request was made on the election form.

(4) *Bail*

The defendant must deposit bail with the clerk by the appearance date indicated on the *Notice to Appear* or the extended due date as provided in (2).

(5) *Instructions to arresting officer*

If the clerk receives the defendant's *Request for Trial by Written Declaration* (form TR-205) and bail by the due date, the clerk must deliver or mail to the arresting officer's agency *Notice and Instructions to Arresting Officer* (form TR-210) and *Officer's Declaration* (form TR-235) with a copy of the *Notice to Appear* and a specified return date for receiving the officer's declaration. After receipt of the officer's declaration, or at the close of the officer's return date if no officer's declaration is filed, the clerk must submit the case file with all declarations and other evidence received to the court for decision.

(6) *Court decision*

After the court decides the case and returns the file and decision, the clerk must immediately deliver or mail the *Decision and Notice of Decision* (form TR-215) to the defendant and the arresting agency.

(7) *Trial de novo*

If the defendant files a *Request for New Trial (Trial de Novo)* (form TR-220) within 20 calendar days after the date of delivery or mailing of the *Decision and Notice of Decision* (form TR-215), the clerk must set a trial date within 45 calendar days of receipt of the defendant's written request for a new trial. The clerk must deliver or mail to the defendant and to the arresting officer's agency the *Order and Notice to Defendant of New Trial (Trial de Novo)* (form TR-225). If the defendant's request is not timely received, no new trial may be held and the case must be closed.

(8) *Case and time standard*

The clerk must deliver or mail the *Decision and Notice of Decision* (form TR-215) within 90 calendar days after the due date. Acts for which no specific time is stated in this rule must be performed promptly so that the *Decision and Notice of Decision* can be timely delivered or mailed by the clerk. Failure of the clerk or the court to comply with any time limit does not void or invalidate the decision of the court, unless prejudice to the defendant is shown.

(Subd (b) amended effective January 1, 2007; previously amended effective January 1, 2000, and July 1, 2000.)

(c) Due dates and time limits

Due dates and time limits must be as stated in this rule, unless changed or extended by the court. The court may extend any date, but the court need not state the reasons for granting or denying an extension on the record or in the minutes.

(Subd (c) amended effective January 1, 2007.)

(d) Ineligible defendants

If the defendant requests a trial by written declaration and the clerk or the court determines that the defendant is not eligible for a trial by written declaration, the clerk must extend the due date 25 calendar days and notify the defendant by mail of the determination and due date.

(Subd (d) amended effective January 1, 2007.)

(e) Noncompliance

If the defendant does not comply with this rule (including submitting the required bail amount, signing and filing all required forms, and complying with all time limits and due dates), the court may deny a trial by written declaration and may proceed as otherwise provided by statute and court rules.

(Subd (e) amended effective January 1, 2007.)

(f) Evidence

Testimony and other relevant evidence may be introduced in the form of a *Notice to Appear* issued under Vehicle Code section 40500; a business record or receipt; a sworn declaration of the arresting officer; and, on behalf of the defendant, a sworn declaration of the defendant.

(Subd (f) amended effective January 1, 2007.)

(g) Fines, assessments, or penalties

The statute and the rules do not prevent or preclude the court from imposing on a defendant who is found guilty any lawful fine, assessment, or other penalty, and the court is not limited to imposing money penalties in the bail amount, unless the bail amount is the maximum and the only lawful penalty.

(Subd (g) amended effective January 1, 2007.)

(h) Additional forms and procedures

The clerk may approve and prescribe forms, time limits, and procedures that are not in conflict with or not inconsistent with the statute or this rule.

(i) Forms

The following forms are to be used to implement the procedures under this rule:

(1) *Instructions to Defendant* (form TR-200)

(2) *Request for Trial by Written Declaration* (form TR-205)

(3) *Notice and Instructions to Arresting Officer* (form TR-210)

(4) *Officer's Declaration* (form TR-235)

(5) *Decision and Notice of Decision* (form TR-215)

(6) *Request for New Trial (Trial de Novo)* (form TR-220)

(7) *Order and Notice to Defendant of New Trial (Trial de Novo)* (form TR-225)

(Subd (i) amended effective January 1, 2007; previously amended effective January 1, 2000.)

(j) Local forms

A court may adopt additional forms as may be required to implement this rule and the court's local procedures not inconsistent with this rule.

(Subd (j) amended effective January 1, 2007.)

Rule 4.210 amended and renumbered effective January 1, 2007; adopted as rule 828 effective January 1, 1999; previously amended effective January 1, 2000, and July 1, 2000.

Division 4
Sentencing

Rule 4.300. Commitments to nonpenal institutions
Rule 4.305. Notification of appeal rights in felony cases
Rule 4.306. Notification of appeal rights in misdemeanor and infraction cases
Rule 4.310. Determination of presentence custody time credit
Rule 4.315. Setting date for execution of death sentence
Rule 4.320. Records of criminal convictions (Gov. Code, §§ 69844.5, 71280.5)
Rule 4.325. Ignition interlock installation orders: "interest of justice" exceptions
Rule 4.330. Misdemeanor hate crimes

Rule 4.300. Commitments to nonpenal institutions

When a defendant is convicted of a crime for which sentence could be imposed under Penal Code section 1170 and the court orders that he or she be committed to the California Department of Corrections and Rehabilitation, Division of Juvenile Justice under Welfare and Institutions Code section 1731.5, the order of commitment must specify the term of imprisonment to which the defendant would have been sentenced. The term is determined as provided by Penal Code sections 1170 and 1170.1 and these rules, as though a sentence of imprisonment were to be imposed.

Rule 4.300 amended effective January 1, 2007; adopted as rule 453 effective July 1, 1977; previously amended and renumbered effective January 1, 2001; previously amended effective July 28, 1977, and January 1, 2006.

Advisory Committee Comment

Commitments to the California Department of Corrections and Rehabilitation, Division of Juvenile Justice (formerly Youth Authority) cannot exceed the maximum possible incarceration in an adult institution for the same crime. *People v. Olivas* (1976) 17 Cal.3d 236.

Under the indeterminate sentencing law, the receiving institution knew, as a matter of law from the record of the conviction, the maximum potential period of imprisonment for the crime of which the defendant was convicted.

Under the Uniform Determinate Sentencing Act, the court's discretion as to length of term leaves doubt as to the maximum term when only the record of convictions is present.

Rule 4.305.   Notification of appeal rights in felony cases

After imposing sentence or making an order deemed to be a final judgment in a criminal case on conviction after trial, or after imposing sentence following a revocation of probation, except where the revocation is after the defendant's admission of violation of probation, the court must advise the defendant of his or her right to appeal, of the necessary steps and time for taking an appeal, and of the right of an indigent defendant to have counsel appointed by the reviewing court. A reporter's transcript of the proceedings required by this rule must be forthwith prepared and certified by the reporter and filed with the clerk.

Rule 4.305 amended effective January 1, 2007; adopted as rule 250 effective January 1, 1972; previously amended effective July 1, 1972, and January 1, 1977; previously amended and renumbered as rule 470 effective January 1, 1991; previously renumbered effective January 1, 2001.

Ref.: W. Cal. Sum., 10 "Parent and Child" §914.

Rule 4.306.   Notification of appeal rights in misdemeanor and infraction cases

After imposing sentence or making an order deemed to be a final judgment in a misdemeanor case on conviction after trial or following a revocation of probation, the court must orally or in writing advise a defendant not represented by counsel of the right to appeal, the time for filing a notice of appeal, and the right of an indigent defendant to have counsel appointed on appeal. This rule does not apply to infractions or when a revocation of probation is ordered after the defendant's admission of a violation of probation.

Rule 4.306 amended effective January 1, 2007; adopted as rule 535 effective July 1, 1981; previously renumbered effective January 1, 2001.

Rule 4.310.   Determination of presentence custody time credit

At the time of sentencing, the court must cause to be recorded on the judgment or commitment the total time in custody to be credited on the sentence under Penal Code sections 2900.5, 2933.1(c), and 2933.2(c). On referral of the defendant to the probation officer for an investigation and report under Penal Code section 1203(b) or 1203(g), or on setting a date for sentencing in the absence of a referral, the court must direct the sheriff, probation officer, or other appropriate person to report to the court and notify the defendant or defense counsel and prosecuting attorney within a reasonable time before the date set for sentencing as to the number of days that defendant has been in custody and for which he or she may be entitled to credit. Any challenges to the report must be heard at the time of sentencing.

Rule 4.310 amended effective January 1, 2007; adopted as rule 252 effective January 1, 1977; previously amended and renumbered as rule 472 effective January 1, 1991; previously amended and renumbered effective January 1, 2001; previously amended effective July 1, 2004.

Rule 4.315.   Setting date for execution of death sentence

(a) Open session of court; notice required

A date for execution of a judgment of death under Penal Code section 1193 or 1227 must be set at a public session of the court at which the defendant and the People may be represented.

At least 10 days before the session of court at which the date will be set, the court must mail notice of the time and place of the proceeding by first-class mail, postage prepaid, to the Attorney General, the district attorney, the defendant at the prison address, the defendant's counsel or, if none is known, counsel who most recently represented the defendant on appeal or in postappeal legal proceedings, and the executive director of the California Appellate Project in San Francisco. The clerk must file a certificate of mailing copies of the notice. The court may not hold the proceeding or set an execution date unless the record contains a clerk's certificate showing that the notices required by this subdivision were timely mailed.

Unless otherwise provided by statute, the defendant does not have a right to be present in person.

(Subd (a) amended effective January 1, 2007; previously amended effective July 1, 1990.)

(b) Selection of date; notice

If, at the announced session of court, the court sets a date for execution of the judgment of death, the court must mail certified copies of the order setting the date to the warden of the state prison and to the Governor, as required by statute; and must also, within five days of the making of the order, mail by first-class mail, postage prepaid, certified copies of the order setting the date to each of the persons required to be given notice by (a). The clerk must file a certificate of mailing copies of the order.

(Subd (b) amended effective January 1, 2007.)

Rule 4.315 amended effective January 1, 2007; adopted as rule 490 effective July 1, 1989; previously amended effective July 1, 1990; previously renumbered effective January 1, 2001.

Rule 4.320.   Records of criminal convictions (Gov. Code, §§ 69844.5, 71280.5)

(a) Information to be submitted

In addition to the information that the Department of Justice requires from courts under Penal Code section 13151, each trial court must also report, electronically or manually, the following information, in the form and manner specified by the Department of Justice:

(1) Whether the defendant was represented by counsel or waived the right to counsel; and

(2) In the case of a guilty or nolo contendere plea, whether:

(A) The defendant was advised of and understood the charges;

(B) The defendant was advised of, understood, and waived the right to a jury trial, the right to confront witnesses, and the privilege against self-incrimination; and

(C) The court found the plea was voluntary and intelligently made.

For purposes of this rule, a change of plea form signed by the defendant, defense counsel if the defendant was represented by counsel, and the judge, and filed with the court is a sufficient basis for the clerk or deputy clerk to report that the requirements of (2) have been met.

(Subd (a) amended effective January 1, 2007; previously amended effective January 1, 2001.)

(b) Certification required

The reporting clerk or a deputy clerk must certify that the report submitted to the Department of Justice under Penal Code section 13151 and this rule is a correct abstract of the information contained in the court's records in the case.

(Subd (b) amended effective January 1, 2007.)

Rule 4.320 amended effective January 1, 2007; adopted as rule 895 effective July 1, 1998; previously amended and renumbered effective January 1, 2001.

Rule 4.325. Ignition interlock installation orders: "interest of justice" exceptions

If the court finds that the interest of justice requires an exception to the Vehicle Code sections 14601(e), 14601.1(d), 14601.4(c), or 14601.5(g) requirements for installation of an ignition interlock device under Vehicle Code section 23575, the reasons for the finding must be stated on the record.

Rule 4.325 amended and renumbered effective January 1, 2001; adopted as rule 530 effective January 1, 1995.

Rule 4.330. Misdemeanor hate crimes

(a) Application

This rule applies to misdemeanor cases where the defendant is convicted of either (1) a substantive hate crime under section 422.6 or (2) a misdemeanor violation and the facts of the crime constitute a hate crime under section 422.55.

(Subd (a) adopted effective January 1, 2007.)

(b) Sentencing consideration

In sentencing a defendant under (a), the court must consider the goals for hate crime sentencing stated in rule 4.427(e).

(Subd (b) adopted effective January 1, 2007.)

Rule 4.330 adopted effective January 1, 2007.

Division 5
Sentencing—Determinate Sentencing Law

Rule 4.401. Authority
Rule 4.403. Application
Rule 4.405. Definitions
Rule 4.406. Reasons
Rule 4.408. Criteria not exclusive; sequence not significant
Rule 4.409. Consideration of criteria
Rule 4.410. General objectives in sentencing
Rule 4.411. Presentence investigations and reports
Rule 4.411.5. Probation officer's presentence investigation report
Rule 4.412. Reasons—agreement to punishment as an adequate reason and as abandonment of certain claims
Rule 4.413. Probation eligibility when probation is limited
Rule 4.414. Criteria affecting probation
Rule 4.420. Selection of term of imprisonment
Rule 4.421. Circumstances in aggravation
Rule 4.423. Circumstances in mitigation
Rule 4.424. Consideration of applicability of section 654
Rule 4.425. Criteria affecting concurrent or consecutive sentences
Rule 4.426. Violent sex crimes

Rule 4.427. Hate crimes
Rule 4.428. Criteria affecting imposition of enhancements
Rule 4.431. Proceedings at sentencing to be reported
Rule 4.433. Matters to be considered at time set for sentencing
Rule 4.435. Sentencing on revocation of probation
Rule 4.437. Statements in aggravation and mitigation
Rule 4.447. Limitations on enhancements
Rule 4.451. Sentence consecutive to indeterminate term or to term in other jurisdiction
Rule 4.452. Determinate sentence consecutive to prior determinate sentence
Rule 4.453. Commitments to nonpenal institutions
Rule 4.470. Notification of appeal rights in felony cases
Rule 4.472. Determination of presentence custody time credit
Rule 4.480. Judge's statement under section 1203.01

Rule 4.401. Authority

The rules in this division are adopted under Penal Code section 1170.3 and under the authority granted to the Judicial Council by the Constitution, article VI, section 6, to adopt rules for court administration, practice, and procedure.

Rule 4.401 amended effective January 1, 2007; adopted as rule 401 effective July 1, 1977; previously renumbered effective January 1, 2001.

Rule 4.403. Application

These rules apply only to criminal cases in which the defendant is convicted of one or more offenses punishable as a felony by a determinate sentence imposed under Penal Code part 2, title 7, chapter 4.5 (commencing with section 1170).

Rule 4.403 amended effective January 1, 2007; adopted as rule 403 effective July 1, 1977; previously amended and renumbered effective January 1, 2001; previously amended effective July 1, 2003.

Advisory Committee Comment

The sentencing rules do not apply to offenses carrying a life term or other indeterminate sentences for which sentence is imposed under section 1168(b).

The operative portions of section 1170 deal exclusively with prison sentences; and the mandate to the Judicial Council in section 1170.3 is limited to criteria affecting the length of prison sentences and the grant or denial of probation. Criteria dealing with jail sentences, fines, or jail time and fines as conditions of probation, would substantially exceed the mandate of the legislation.

Rule 4.405. Definitions

As used in this division, unless the context otherwise requires:

(1) "These rules" means the rules in this division.

(2) "Base term" is the determinate prison term selected from among the three possible terms prescribed by statute or the determinate prison term prescribed by law if a range of three possible terms is not prescribed.

(3) "Enhancement" means an additional term of imprisonment added to the base term.

(4) "Aggravation" or "circumstances in aggravation" means factors that the court may consider in its broad discretion in imposing one of the three authorized prison terms referred to in section 1170(b).

(5) "Mitigation" or "circumstances in mitigation" means factors that the court may consider in its broad discretion

in imposing one of the three authorized prison terms referred to in section 1170(b) or factors that may justify the court in striking the additional punishment for an enhancement when the court has discretion to do so.

(6) "Sentence choice" means the selection of any disposition of the case that does not amount to a dismissal, acquittal, or grant of a new trial.

(7) "Section" means a section of the Penal Code.

(8) "Imprisonment" means confinement in a state prison.

(9) "Charged" means charged in the indictment or information.

(10) "Found" means admitted by the defendant or found to be true by the trier of fact upon trial.

Rule 4.405 amended effective January 1, 2008; adopted as rule 405 effective July 1, 1977; previously renumbered effective January 1, 2001; previously amended effective July 28, 1977, January 1, 1991, July 1, 2003, January 1, 2007, and May 23, 2007.

Advisory Committee Comment

"Base term" is the term of imprisonment selected under section 1170(b) from the three possible terms. (See section 1170(a)(3); *People v. Scott* (1994) 9 Cal.4th 331, 349.) Following the United States Supreme Court decision in *Cunningham v. California* (2007) 549 U.S. __ [127 S.Ct. 856.], the Legislature amended the determinate sentencing law. (See Sen. Bill 40; Stats. 2007, ch. 3.) To comply with those changes, these rules were also amended. In light of those amendments, for clarity, the phrase "base term" in (4) and (5) was replaced with "one of the three authorized prison terms." It is an open question whether the definitions in (4) and (5) apply to enhancements for which the statute provides for three possible terms. The Legislature in SB 40 amended section 1170(b) but did not modify sections 1170.1(d), 12022.2(a), 12022.3(b), or any other section providing for an enhancement with three possible terms. The latter sections provide that "the court shall impose the middle term unless there are circumstances in aggravation or mitigation." (See, e.g., section 1170.1(d).) It is possible, although there are no cases addressing the point, that this enhancement triad with the presumptive imposition of the middle term runs afoul of *Cunningham*. Because of this open question, rule 4.428(b) was deleted.

"Enhancement." The facts giving rise to an enhancement, the requirements for pleading and proving those facts, and the court's authority to strike the additional term are prescribed by statutes. See, for example, sections 667.5 (prior prison terms), 12022 (being armed with a firearm or using a deadly weapon), 12022.5 (using a firearm), 12022.6 (excessive taking or damage), 12022.7 (great bodily injury), 1170.1(e) (pleading and proof), and 1385(c) (authority to strike the additional punishment). Note: A consecutive sentence is not an enhancement. (See section 1170.1(a); *People v. Tassell* (1984) 36 Cal.3d 77, 90 [overruled on other grounds in *People v. Ewoldt* (1994) 7 Cal.4th 380, 401].)

"Sentence choice." Section 1170(c) requires the judge to state reasons for the sentence choice. This general requirement is discussed in rule 4.406.

"Imprisonment" is distinguished from confinement in other types of facilities.

"Charged" and "found." Statutes require that the facts giving rise to all enhancements be charged and found. See section 1170.1(e).

Rule 4.406. Reasons

(a) How given

If the sentencing judge is required to give reasons for a sentence choice, the judge must state in simple language the primary factor or factors that support the exercise of discretion or, if applicable, state that the judge has no discretion. The statement need not be in the language of these rules. It must be delivered orally on the record.

(Subd (a) amended effective January 1, 2007.)

(b) When reasons required

Sentence choices that generally require a statement of a reason include:

(1) Granting probation;

(2) Imposing a prison sentence and thereby denying probation;

(3) Declining to commit to the Department of Corrections and Rehabilitation, Division of Juvenile Justice an eligible juvenile found amenable for treatment;

(4) Selecting one of the three authorized prison terms referred to in section 1170(b) for either an offense or an enhancement;

(5) Imposing consecutive sentences;

(6) Imposing full consecutive sentences under section 667.6(c) rather than consecutive terms under section 1170.1(a), when the court has that choice;

(7) Striking the punishment for an enhancement;

(8) Waiving a restitution fine;

(9) Not committing an eligible defendant to the California Rehabilitation Center; and

(10) Striking an enhancement or prior conviction allegation under section 1385(a).

(Subd (b) amended effective May 23, 2007; previously amended effective January 1, 2001, July 1, 2003, January 1, 2006, and January 1, 2007.)

Rule 4.406 amended effective May 23, 2007; adopted as rule 406 effective January 1, 1991; previously amended and renumbered effective January 1, 2001; previously amended effective July 1, 2003, January 1, 2006, and January 1, 2007.

Advisory Committee Comment

This rule is not intended to expand the statutory requirements for giving reasons, and is not an independent interpretation of the statutory requirements.

Rule 4.407. [Repealed 2007]

Rule 4.407 repealed effective January 1, 2007; adopted as rule 407 effective July 1, 1977; previously amended effective January 1, 1991; previously renumbered effective January 1, 2001. The repealed rule related to rules of construction.

Rule 4.408. Criteria not exclusive; sequence not significant

(a) The enumeration in these rules of some criteria for the making of discretionary sentencing decisions does not prohibit the application of additional criteria reasonably related to the decision being made. Any such additional criteria must be stated on the record by the sentencing judge.

(Subd (a) amended effective January 1, 2007.)

(b) The order in which criteria are listed does not indicate their relative weight or importance.

Rule 4.408 amended effective January 1, 2007; adopted as rule 408 effective July 1, 1977; previously renumbered effective January 1, 2001.

Advisory Committee Comment

Enumerations of criteria in these rules are not exclusive. The variety of circumstances presented in felony cases is so great that no listing of criteria could claim to be all-inclusive. (Cf., Evid. Code, § 351.)

The relative significance of various criteria will vary from case to case. This, like the question of applicability of various criteria, will be decided by the sentencing judge.

Rule 4.409. Consideration of criteria

Relevant criteria enumerated in these rules must be considered by the sentencing judge, and will be deemed to have been considered unless the record affirmatively reflects otherwise.

Rule 4.409 amended effective January 1, 2007; adopted as rule 409 effective July 1, 1977; previously renumbered effective January 1, 2001.

Advisory Committee Comment

Relevant criteria are those applicable to the facts in the record of the case; not all criteria will be relevant to each case. The judge's duty is similar to the duty to consider the probation officer's report. Section 1203.

In deeming the sentencing judge to have considered relevant criteria, the rule applies the presumption of Evidence Code section 664 that official duty has been regularly performed. See *People v. Moran* (1970) 1 Cal.3d 755 (trial court presumed to have considered referring eligible defendant to California Youth Authority in absence of any showing to the contrary, citing Evidence Code section 664).

Rule 4.410. General objectives in sentencing

(a) General objectives of sentencing include:

(1) Protecting society;

(2) Punishing the defendant;

(3) Encouraging the defendant to lead a law-abiding life in the future and deterring him or her from future offenses;

(4) Deterring others from criminal conduct by demonstrating its consequences;

(5) Preventing the defendant from committing new crimes by isolating him or her for the period of incarceration;

(6) Securing restitution for the victims of crime; and

(7) Achieving uniformity in sentencing.

(Subd (a) amended effective January 1, 2007; previously amended effective July 1, 2003.)

(b) Because in some instances these objectives may suggest inconsistent dispositions, the sentencing judge must consider which objectives are of primary importance in the particular case. The sentencing judge should be guided by statutory statements of policy, the criteria in these rules, and the facts and circumstances of the case.

(Subd (b) lettered effective July 1, 2003; adopted as part of unlettered subd effective July 1, 1977; former subd (b) amended and relettered as part of subd (a) effective July 1, 2003.)

Rule 4.410 amended effective January 1, 2007; adopted as rule 410 effective July 1, 1977; previously renumbered effective January 1, 2001; previously amended effective July 1, 2003.

Advisory Committee Comment

Statutory expressions of policy include:

Welfare and Institutions Code section 1820 et seq., which provides partnership funding for county juvenile ranches, camps, or forestry camps.

Section 1203(b)(3), which requires that eligible defendants be considered for probation and authorizes probation if circumstances in mitigation are found or justice would be served.

Section 1170(a)(1), which expresses the policies of uniformity, proportionality of prison terms to the seriousness of the offense, and the use of imprisonment as punishment.

Other statutory provisions that prohibit the grant of probation in particular cases.

Rule 4.411. Presentence investigations and reports

(a) Eligible defendant

If the defendant is eligible for probation, the court must refer the matter to the probation officer for a presentence investigation and report. Waivers of the presentence report should not be accepted except in unusual circumstances.

(Subd (a) amended effective January 1, 2007.)

(b) Ineligible defendant

Even if the defendant is not eligible for probation, the court should refer the matter to the probation officer for a presentence investigation and report.

(c) Supplemental reports

The court must order a supplemental probation officer's report in preparation for sentencing proceedings that occur a significant period of time after the original report was prepared.

(Subd (c) amended effective January 1, 2007.)

(d) Purpose of presentence investigation report

Probation officers' reports are used by judges in determining the appropriate length of a prison sentence and by the Department of Corrections and Rehabilitation, Division of Adult Operations in deciding on the type of facility and program in which to place a defendant, and are also used in deciding whether probation is appropriate. Section 1203c requires a probation officer's report on every person sentenced to prison; ordering the report before sentencing in probation-ineligible cases will help ensure a well-prepared report.

(Subd (d) amended effective January 1, 2007; previously amended effective January 1, 2006.)

Rule 4.411 amended effective January 1, 2007; adopted as rule 418 effective July 1, 1977; previously amended and renumbered as rule 411 effective January 1, 1991; previously renumbered effective January 1, 2001; previously amended effective January 1, 2006.

Advisory Committee Comment

Section 1203 requires a presentence report in every felony case in which the defendant is eligible for probation. Because such a probation investigation and report are valuable to the judge and to the jail and prison authorities, waivers of the report and requests for immediate sentencing are discouraged, even when the defendant and counsel have agreed to a prison sentence.

Notwithstanding a defendant's statutory ineligibility for probation, a presentence investigation and report should be ordered to assist the court in deciding the appropriate sentence and to facilitate compliance with section 1203c.

This rule does not prohibit pre-conviction, pre-plea reports as authorized by section 1203.7.

Subdivision (c) is based on case law that generally requires a supplemental report if the defendant is to be resentenced a significant time after the original sentencing, as, for example, after a remand by an appellate court, or after the apprehension of a defendant who failed to appear at sentencing. The rule is not intended to expand on the requirements of those cases.

The rule does not require a new investigation and report if a recent report is available and can be incorporated by reference and there is no indication of changed circumstances. This is particularly true if a report is needed only for the Department of Corrections and Rehabilitation because the defendant has waived a report and agreed to a prison sentence. If a full report was prepared in another case in the same or another jurisdiction within the preceeding six months, during which time the defendant was in custody, and that report is available to the Department of Corrections and Rehabilitation, it is unlikely that a new investigation is needed.

Rule 4.411.5.   Probation officer's presentence investigation report

(a) Contents

A probation officer's presentence investigation report in a felony case must include at least the following:

(1) A face sheet showing at least:

(A) The defendant's name and other identifying data;

(B) The case number;

(C) The crime of which the defendant was convicted;

(D) The date of commission of the crime, the date of conviction, and any other dates relevant to sentencing;

(E) The defendant's custody status; and

(F) The terms of any agreement on which a plea of guilty was based.

(2) The facts and circumstances of the crime and the defendant's arrest, including information concerning any co-defendants and the status or disposition of their cases. The source of all such information must be stated.

(3) A summary of the defendant's record of prior criminal conduct, including convictions as an adult and sustained petitions in juvenile delinquency proceedings. Records of an arrest or charge not leading to a conviction or the sustaining of a petition may not be included unless supported by facts concerning the arrest or charge.

(4) Any statement made by the defendant to the probation officer, or a summary thereof, including the defendant's account of the circumstances of the crime.

(5) Information concerning the victim of the crime, including:

(A) The victim's statement or a summary thereof, if available;

(B) The amount of the victim's loss, and whether or not it is covered by insurance; and

(C) Any information required by law.

(6) Any relevant facts concerning the defendant's social history, including those categories enumerated in section 1203.10, organized under appropriate subheadings, including, whenever applicable, "Family," "Education," "Employment and income," "Military," "Medical/psychological," "Record of substance abuse or lack thereof," and any other relevant subheadings.

(7) Collateral information, including written statements from:

(A) Official sources such as defense and prosecuting attorneys, police (subsequent to any police reports used to summarize the crime), probation and parole officers who have had prior experience with the defendant, and correctional personnel who observed the defendant's behavior during any period of presentence incarceration; and

(B) Interested persons, including family members and others who have written letters concerning the defendant.

(8) An evaluation of factors relating to disposition. This section must include:

(A) A reasoned discussion of the defendant's suitability and eligibility for probation, and, if probation is recommended, a proposed plan including recommendation for the conditions of probation and any special need for supervision;

(B) If a prison sentence is recommended or is likely to be imposed, a reasoned discussion of aggravating and mitigating factors affecting the sentence length; and

(C) A discussion of the defendant's ability to make restitution, pay any fine or penalty that may be recommended, or satisfy any special conditions of probation that are proposed.

Discussions of factors affecting suitability for probation and affecting the sentence length must refer to any sentencing rule directly relevant to the facts of the case, but no rule may be cited without a reasoned discussion of its relevance and relative importance.

(9) The probation officer's recommendation. When requested by the sentencing judge or by standing instructions to the probation department, the report must include recommendations concerning the length of any prison term that may be imposed, including the base term, the imposition of concurrent or consecutive sentences, and the imposition or striking of the additional terms for enhancements charged and found.

(10) Detailed information on presentence time spent by the defendant in custody, including the beginning and ending dates of the period or periods of custody; the existence of any other sentences imposed on the defendant during the period of custody; the amount of good behavior, work, or participation credit to which the defendant is entitled; and whether the sheriff or other officer holding custody, the prosecution, or the defense wishes that a hearing be held for the purposes of denying good behavior, work, or participation credit.

(11) A statement of mandatory and recommended restitution, restitution fines, other fines, and costs to be assessed against the defendant, including chargeable probation services and attorney fees under section 987.8 when appropriate, findings concerning the defendant's ability to pay, and a recommendation whether any restitution order should become a judgment under section 1203(j) if unpaid.

(Subd (a) amended effective January 1, 2007; previously amended effective January 1, 1991, and July 1, 2003.)

(b) Format

The report must be on paper 8-½ by 11 inches in size and must follow the sequence set out in (a) to the extent possible.

(Subd (b) amended effective January 1, 2007; previously amended effective January 1, 1991.)

(c) Sources

The source of all information must be stated. Any person who has furnished information included in the report must be identified by name or official capacity unless a reason is given for not disclosing the person's identity.

(Subd (c) amended effective January 1, 2007; previously amended effective January 1, 1991.)

Rule 4.411.5 amended effective January 1, 2007; adopted as rule 419 effective July 1, 1981; previously amended and renumbered as rule 411.5 effective January 1, 1991; previously renumbered effective January 1, 2001; previously amended effective July 1, 2003.

Rule 4.412. Reasons—agreement to punishment as an adequate reason and as abandonment of certain claims

(a) Defendant's agreement as reason

It is an adequate reason for a sentence or other disposition that the defendant, personally and by counsel, has expressed agreement that it be imposed and the prosecuting attorney has not expressed an objection to it. The agreement and lack of objection must be recited on the record. This section does not authorize a sentence that is not otherwise authorized by law.

(Subd (a) amended effective January 1, 2007; previously amended effective January 1, 2001.)

(b) Agreement to sentence abandons section 654 claim

By agreeing to a specified prison term personally and by counsel, a defendant who is sentenced to that term or a shorter one abandons any claim that a component of the sentence violates section 654's prohibition of double punishment, unless that claim is asserted at the time the agreement is recited on the record.

(Subd (b) amended effective January 1, 2007.)

Rule 4.412 amended effective January 1, 2007; adopted as rule 412 effective January 1, 1991; previously amended and renumbered effective January 1, 2001.

Advisory Committee Comment

Subdivision (a). This subdivision is intended to relieve the court of an obligation to give reasons if the sentence or other disposition is one that the defendant has accepted and to which the prosecutor expresses no objection. The judge may choose to give reasons for the sentence even though not obligated to do so.

Judges should also be aware that there may be statutory limitations on "plea bargaining" or on the entry of a guilty plea on the condition that no more than a particular sentence will be imposed. At the time this comment was drafted, such limitations appeared, for example, in sections 1192.5 and 1192.7.

Subdivision (b). This subdivision is based on the fact that a defendant who, with the advice of counsel, expresses agreement to a specified prison term normally is acknowledging that the term is appropriate for his or her total course of conduct. This subdivision applies to both determinate and indeterminate terms.

Rule 4.413. Probation eligibility when probation is limited

(a) Consideration of eligibility

The court must determine whether the defendant is eligible for probation.

(Subd (a) amended effective January 1, 2007.)

(b) Probation in unusual cases

If the defendant comes under a statutory provision prohibiting probation "except in unusual cases where the interests of justice would best be served," or a substantially equivalent provision, the court should apply the criteria in (c) to evaluate whether the statutory limitation on probation is overcome; and if it is, the court should then apply the criteria in rule 4.414 to decide whether to grant probation.

(Subd (b) amended effective January 1, 2007; previously amended effective July 1, 2003.)

(c) Facts showing unusual case

The following facts may indicate the existence of an unusual case in which probation may be granted if otherwise appropriate:

(1) *Facts relating to basis for limitation on probation*

A fact or circumstance indicating that the basis for the statutory limitation on probation, although technically present, is not fully applicable to the case, including:

(A) The fact or circumstance giving rise to the limitation on probation is, in this case, substantially less serious than the circumstances typically present in other cases involving the same probation limitation, and the defendant has no recent record of committing similar crimes or crimes of violence; and

(B) The current offense is less serious than a prior felony conviction that is the cause of the limitation on probation, and the defendant has been free from incarceration and serious violation of the law for a substantial time before the current offense.

(2) *Facts limiting defendant's culpability*

A fact or circumstance not amounting to a defense, but reducing the defendant's culpability for the offense, including:

(A) The defendant participated in the crime under circumstances of great provocation, coercion, or duress not amounting to a defense, and the defendant has no recent record of committing crimes of violence;

(B) The crime was committed because of a mental condition not amounting to a defense, and there is a high likelihood that the defendant would respond favorably to mental health care and treatment that would be required as a condition of probation; and

(C) The defendant is youthful or aged, and has no significant record of prior criminal offenses.

(Subd (c) amended effective January 1, 2007.)

Rule 4.413 amended effective January 1, 2007; adopted as rule 413 effective January 1, 1991; previously renumbered effective January 1, 2001; previously amended effective July 1, 2003.

Rule 4.414. Criteria affecting probation

Criteria affecting the decision to grant or deny probation include facts relating to the crime and facts relating to the defendant.

(a) Facts relating to the crime

Facts relating to the crime include:

(1) The nature, seriousness, and circumstances of the crime as compared to other instances of the same crime;

(2) Whether the defendant was armed with or used a weapon;

(3) The vulnerability of the victim;

(4) Whether the defendant inflicted physical or emotional injury;

(5) The degree of monetary loss to the victim;

(6) Whether the defendant was an active or a passive participant;

(7) Whether the crime was committed because of an unusual circumstance, such as great provocation, which is unlikely to recur;

(8) Whether the manner in which the crime was carried out demonstrated criminal sophistication or professionalism on the part of the defendant; and

(9) Whether the defendant took advantage of a position of trust or confidence to commit the crime.

(Subd (a) amended effective January 1, 2007; previously amended effective January 1, 1991.)

(b) Facts relating to the defendant

Facts relating to the defendant include:

(1) Prior record of criminal conduct, whether as an adult or a juvenile, including the recency and frequency of prior crimes; and whether the prior record indicates a pattern of regular or increasingly serious criminal conduct;

(2) Prior performance on probation or parole and present probation or parole status;

(3) Willingness to comply with the terms of probation;

(4) Ability to comply with reasonable terms of probation as indicated by the defendant's age, education, health, mental faculties, history of alcohol or other substance abuse, family background and ties, employment and military service history, and other relevant factors;

(5) The likely effect of imprisonment on the defendant and his or her dependents;

(6) The adverse collateral consequences on the defendant's life resulting from the felony conviction;

(7) Whether the defendant is remorseful; and

(8) The likelihood that if not imprisoned the defendant will be a danger to others.

(Subd (b) amended effective January 1, 2007; previously amended effective January 1, 1991, and July 1, 2003.)

Rule 4.414 amended effective January 1, 2007; adopted as rule 414 effective July 1, 1977; previously amended effective January 1, 1991; previously renumbered effective January 1, 2001; previously amended effective July 1, 2003.

Advisory Committee Comment

The sentencing judge's discretion to grant probation is unaffected by the Uniform Determinate Sentencing Act (§ 1170(a)(3)).

The decision whether to grant probation is normally based on an overall evaluation of the likelihood that the defendant will live successfully in the general community. Each criterion points to evidence that the likelihood of success is great or small. A single criterion will rarely be determinative; in most cases, the sentencing judge will have to balance favorable and unfavorable facts.

Under criteria (b)(3) and (b)(4), it is appropriate to consider the defendant's expressions of willingness to comply and his or her apparent sincerity, and whether the defendant's home and work environment and primary associates will be supportive of the defendant's efforts to comply with the terms of probation, among other factors.

Rule 4.420. Selection of term of imprisonment

(a) When a sentence of imprisonment is imposed, or the execution of a sentence of imprisonment is ordered suspended, the sentencing judge must select the upper, middle, or lower term on each count for which the defendant has been convicted, as provided in section 1170(b) and these rules.

(Subd (a) amended effective May 23, 2007; previously amended effective July 28, 1977, January 1, 1991, and January 1, 2007.)

(b) In exercising his or her discretion in selecting one of the three authorized prison terms referred to in section 1170(b), the sentencing judge may consider circumstances in aggravation or mitigation, and any other factor reasonably related to the sentencing decision. The relevant circumstances may be obtained from the case record, the probation officer's report, other reports and statements

properly received, statements in aggravation or mitigation, and any [1] evidence introduced at the sentencing hearing.

(Subd (b) amended effective January 1, 2008; previously amended effective July 28, 1977, January 1, 1991, January 1, 2007, and May 23, 2007.)

Rule 4.420(b). 2008 Deletes. [1] further

(c) To comply with section 1170(b), a fact charged and found as an enhancement may be used as a reason for imposing the upper term only if the court has discretion to strike the punishment for the enhancement and does so. The use of a fact of an enhancement to impose the upper term of imprisonment is an adequate reason for striking the additional term of imprisonment, regardless of the effect on the total term.

(Subd (c) adopted effective January 1, 1991.)

(d) A fact that is an element of the crime **upon which punishment is being imposed** may not be used to impose a greater term.

(Subd (d) amended effective January 1, 2008; adopted effective January 1, 1991; previously amended effective January 1, 2007, and May 23, 2007.)

(e) The reasons for selecting one of the three authorized prison terms referred to in section 1170(b) must be stated orally on the record.

(Subd (e) amended effective May 23, 2007; previously amended and relettered effective January 1, 1991; previously amended effective July 28, 1977, and January 1, 2007.)

Rule 4.420 amended effective January 1, 2008; adopted as rule 439 effective July 1, 1977; previously amended and renumbered as rule 420 effective January 1, 1991; previously renumbered effective January 1, 2001; previously amended effective July 28, 1977, January 1, 2007, and May 23, 2007.

Advisory Committee Comment

The determinate sentencing law authorizes the court to select any of the three possible prison terms even though neither party has requested a particular term by formal motion or informal argument. Section 1170(b) vests the court with discretion to impose any of the three authorized prison terms and requires that the court state on the record the reasons for imposing that term.

It is not clear whether the reasons stated by the judge for selecting a particular term qualify as "facts" for the purposes of the rule prohibition on dual use of facts. Until the issue is clarified, judges should avoid the use of reasons that may constitute an impermissible dual use of facts. For example, the court is not permitted to use a reason to impose a greater term if that reason also is either (1) the same as an enhancement that will be imposed, or (2) an element of the crime. The court should not use the same reason to impose a consecutive sentence as to impose an upper term of imprisonment. (*People v. Avalos* (1984) 37 Cal.3d 216, 233.) It is not improper to use the same reason to deny probation and to impose the upper term. (*People v. Bowen* (1992) 11 Cal.App.4th 102, 106.)

The rule makes it clear that a fact charged and found as an enhancement may, in the alternative, be used as a factor in aggravation.

People v. Riolo (1983) 33 Cal.3d 223, 227 (and note 5 on 227) held that section 1170.1(a) does not require the judgment to state the base term (upper, middle, or lower) and enhancements, computed independently, on counts that are subject to automatic reduction under the one-third formula of section 1170.1(a).

Even when sentencing is under section 1170.1, however, it is essential to determine the base term and specific enhancements for each count independently, in order to know which is the principal term count. The principal term count must be determined before any calculation is made using the one-third formula for subordinate terms.

In addition, the base term (upper, middle, or lower) for each count must be determined to arrive at an informed decision whether to make terms consecutive or concurrent; and the base term for each count must be stated in the judgment when sentences are concurrent or are fully consecutive (i.e., not subject to the one-third rule of section 1170.1(a)).

Rule 4.421. Circumstances in aggravation

Circumstances in aggravation include factors relating to the crime and factors relating to the defendant.

(a) Factors relating to the crime

Factors relating to the crime, whether or not charged or chargeable as enhancements include that:

(1) The crime involved great violence, great bodily harm, threat of great bodily harm, or other acts disclosing a high degree of cruelty, viciousness, or callousness;

(2) The defendant was armed with or used a weapon at the time of the commission of the crime;

(3) The victim was particularly vulnerable;

(4) The defendant induced others to participate in the commission of the crime or occupied a position of leadership or dominance of other participants in its commission;

(5) The defendant induced a minor to commit or assist in the commission of the crime;

(6) The defendant threatened witnesses, unlawfully prevented or dissuaded witnesses from testifying, suborned perjury, or in any other way illegally interfered with the judicial process;

(7) The defendant was convicted of other crimes for which consecutive sentences could have been imposed but for which concurrent sentences are being imposed;

(8) The manner in which the crime was carried out indicates planning, sophistication, or professionalism;

(9) The crime involved an attempted or actual taking or damage of great monetary value;

(10) The crime involved a large quantity of contraband; and

(11) The defendant took advantage of a position of trust or confidence to commit the offense.

(12) The crime constitutes a hate crime under section 422.55 and:

(A) No hate crime enhancements under section 422.75 are imposed; and

(B) The crime is not subject to sentencing under section 1170.8.

(Subd (a) amended effective May 23, 2007; previously amended effective January 1, 1991, and January 1, 2007.)

(b) Factors relating to the defendant

Factors relating to the defendant include that:

(1) The defendant has engaged in violent conduct that indicates a serious danger to society;

(2) The defendant's prior convictions as an adult or sustained petitions in juvenile delinquency proceedings are numerous or of increasing seriousness;

(3) The defendant has served a prior prison term;

(4) The defendant was on probation or parole when the crime was committed; and

(5) The defendant's prior performance on probation or parole was unsatisfactory.

(Subd (b) amended effective May 23, 2007; previously amended effective January 1, 1991, and January 1, 2007.)

(c) Other factors

Any other factors statutorily declared to be circumstances in aggravation.

(Subd (c) amended effective May 23, 2007; adopted effective January 1, 1991; previously amended effective January 1, 2007.) Rule 4.421 amended effective May 23, 2007; adopted as rule 421 effective July 1, 1977; previously renumbered effective January 1, 2001; previously amended effective January 1, 1991, and January 1, 2007.

Advisory Committee Comment

Circumstances in aggravation may justify imposition of the upper of three possible prison terms. (Section 1170(b).)

The list of circumstances in aggravation includes some facts that, if charged and found, may be used to enhance the sentence. The rule does not deal with the dual use of the facts; the statutory prohibition against dual use is included, in part, in rule 4.420.

Conversely, such facts as infliction of bodily harm, being armed with or using a weapon, and a taking or loss of great value may be circumstances in aggravation even if not meeting the statutory definitions for enhancements.

Facts concerning the defendant's prior record and personal history may be considered. By providing that the defendant's prior record and simultaneous convictions of other offenses may not be used both for enhancement and in aggravation, section 1170(b) indicates that these and other facts extrinsic to the commission of the crime may be considered in aggravation in appropriate cases. This resolves whatever ambiguity may arise from the phrase "circumstances in aggravation ... of the crime." The phrase "circumstances in aggravation or mitigation of the crime" necessarily alludes to extrinsic facts.

Refusal to consider the personal characteristics of the defendant in imposing sentence would also raise serious constitutional questions. The California Supreme Court has held that sentencing decisions must take into account "the nature of the offense and/or the offender, with particular regard to the degree of danger both present to society." *In re Rodriguez* (1975) 14 Cal.3d 639, 654, quoting *In re Lynch* (1972) 8 Cal.3d 410, 425. In *In re Rodriguez* the court released petitioner from further incarceration because "[I]t appears that neither the circumstances of his offense *nor his personal characteristics* establish a danger to society sufficient to justify such a prolonged period of imprisonment." (*Id.* at 655.) (Footnote omitted, emphasis added.) "For the determination of sentences, justice generally requires ... that there be taken into account the circumstances of the offense together with the character and propensities of the offender." (*Pennsylvania v. Ashe* (1937) 302 U.S. 51, 55, quoted with approval in *Gregg v. Georgia* (1976) 428 U.S. 153, 189.)

The scope of "circumstances in aggravation or mitigation" under section 1170(b) is, therefore, coextensive with the scope of inquiry under the similar phrase in section 1203.

The 1990 amendments to this rule and the comment included the deletion of most section numbers. These changes recognize changing statutory section numbers and the fact that there are numerous additional code sections related to the rule, including numerous statutory enhancements enacted since the rule was originally adopted.

Former subdivision (a)(4), concerning multiple victims, was deleted to avoid confusion; cases in which that possible circumstance in aggravation was relied on were frequently reversed on appeal because there was only a single victim in a particular count. Old age or youth of the victim may be circumstances in aggravation; see section 1170.85(b). Other statutory circumstances in aggravation are listed, for example, in sections 1170.7, 1170.71, 1170.75, 1170.8, and 1170.85.

Ref.: Cal. Fms Pl. & Pr., Ch. 329, "Juvenile Courts: Delinquency Proceedings."

Rule 4.423. Circumstances in mitigation

Circumstances in mitigation include factors relating to the crime and factors relating to the defendant.

(a) Factors relating to the crime

Factors relating to the crime include that:

(1) The defendant was a passive participant or played a minor role in the crime;

(2) The victim was an initiator of, willing participant in, or aggressor or provoker of the incident;

(3) The crime was committed because of an unusual circumstance, such as great provocation, that is unlikely to recur;

(4) The defendant participated in the crime under circumstances of coercion or duress, or the criminal conduct was partially excusable for some other reason not amounting to a defense;

(5) The defendant, with no apparent predisposition to do so, was induced by others to participate in the crime;

(6) The defendant exercised caution to avoid harm to persons or damage to property, or the amounts of money or property taken were deliberately small, or no harm was done or threatened against the victim;

(7) The defendant believed that he or she had a claim or right to the property taken, or for other reasons mistakenly believed that the conduct was legal;

(8) The defendant was motivated by a desire to provide necessities for his or her family or self; and

(9) The defendant suffered from repeated or continuous physical, sexual, or psychological abuse inflicted by the victim of the crime, and the victim of the crime, who inflicted the abuse, was the defendant's spouse, intimate cohabitant, or parent of the defendant's child; and the abuse does not amount to a defense.

(Subd (a) amended effective May 23, 2007; previously amended effective January 1, 1991, July 1, 1993, and January 1, 2007.)

(b) Factors relating to the defendant

Factors relating to the defendant include that:

(1) The defendant has no prior record, or has an insignificant record of criminal conduct, considering the recency and frequency of prior crimes;

(2) The defendant was suffering from a mental or physical condition that significantly reduced culpability for the crime;

(3) The defendant voluntarily acknowledged wrongdoing before arrest or at an early stage of the criminal process;

(4) The defendant is ineligible for probation and but for that ineligibility would have been granted probation;

(5) The defendant made restitution to the victim; and

(6) The defendant's prior performance on probation or parole was satisfactory.

(Subd (b) amended effective May 23, 2007; previously amended effective January 1, 1991, and January 1, 2007.)

Rule 4.423 amended effective May 23, 2007; adopted as rule 423 effective July 1, 1977; previously renumbered effective January 1, 2001; previously amended effective January 1, 1991, July 1, 1993, and January 1, 2007.

Advisory Committee Comment

See comment to rule 4.421.

This rule applies both to mitigation for purposes of motions under section 1170(b) and to circumstances in mitigation justifying the court in striking the additional punishment provided for an enhancement.

Some listed circumstances can never apply to certain enhancements; for example, "the amounts taken were deliberately small" can never apply to an excessive taking under section 12022.6, and "no harm was done" can never apply to infliction of great bodily injury under section 12022.7. In any case, only the facts present may be considered for their possible effect in mitigation.

See also rule 4.409; only relevant criteria need be considered.

Since only the fact of restitution is considered relevant to mitigation, no reference to the defendant's financial ability is needed. The omission of a comparable factor from rule 4.421 as a circumstance in aggravation is deliberate.

Rule 4.424. Consideration of applicability of section 654

Before determining whether to impose either concurrent or consecutive sentences on all counts on which the defendant was convicted, the court must determine whether the proscription in section 654 against multiple punishments for the same act or omission requires a stay of imposition of sentence on some of the counts.

Rule 4.424 amended effective January 1, 2007; adopted as rule 424 effective January 1, 1991; previously renumbered effective January 1, 2001.

Rule 4.425. Criteria affecting concurrent or consecutive sentences

Criteria affecting the decision to impose consecutive rather than concurrent sentences include:

(a) Criteria relating to crimes

Facts relating to the crimes, including whether or not:

(1) The crimes and their objectives were predominantly independent of each other;

(2) The crimes involved separate acts of violence or threats of violence; or

(3) The crimes were committed at different times or separate places, rather than being committed so closely in time and place as to indicate a single period of aberrant behavior.

(Subd (a) amended effective January 1, 2007; previously amended effective January 1, 1991.)

(b) Other criteria and limitations

Any circumstances in aggravation or mitigation may be considered in deciding whether to impose consecutive rather than concurrent sentences, except:

(1) A fact used to impose the upper term;

(2) A fact used to otherwise enhance the defendant's prison sentence; and

(3) A fact that is an element of the crime may not be used to impose consecutive sentences.

(Subd (b) amended effective January 1, 2007; previously amended effective January 1, 1991.)

Rule 4.425 amended effective January 1, 2007; adopted as rule 425 effective July 1, 1977; previously amended effective January 1, 1991; previously renumbered effective January 1, 2001.

Advisory Committee Comment

The sentencing judge should be aware that there are some cases in which the law mandates consecutive sentences.

Rule 4.426. Violent sex crimes

(a) Multiple violent sex crimes

When a defendant has been convicted of multiple violent sex offenses as defined in section 667.6, the sentencing judge must determine whether the crimes involved separate victims or the same victim on separate occasions.

(1) *Different victims*

If the crimes were committed against different victims, a full, separate, and consecutive term must be imposed for a violent sex crime as to each victim, under section 667.6(d).

(2) *Same victim, separate occasions*

If the crimes were committed against a single victim, the sentencing judge must determine whether the crimes were committed on separate occasions. In determining whether there were separate occasions, the sentencing judge must consider whether, between the commission of one sex crime and another, the defendant had a reasonable opportunity to reflect on his or her actions and nevertheless resumed sexually assaultive behavior. A full, separate, and consecutive term must be imposed for each violent sex offense committed on a separate occasion under section 667.6(d).

(Subd (a) amended effective January 1, 2007.)

(b) Same victim, same occasion; other crimes

If the defendant has been convicted of multiple crimes, including at least one violent sex crime, as defined in section 667.6, or if there have been multiple violent sex crimes against a single victim on the same occasion and the sentencing court has decided to impose consecutive sentences, the sentencing judge must then determine whether to impose a full, separate, and consecutive sentence under section 667.6(c) for the violent sex crime or crimes instead of including the violent sex crimes in the computation of the principal and subordinate terms under section 1170.1(a). A decision to impose a fully consecutive sentence under section 667.6(c) is an additional sentence choice that requires a statement of reasons separate from those given for consecutive sentences, but which may repeat the same reasons. The sentencing judge is to be guided by the criteria listed in rule 4.425, which incorporates rules 4.421 and 4.423, as well as any other reasonably related criteria as provided in rule 4.408.

(Subd (b) amended effective January 1, 2007; previously amended effective July 1, 2003.)

Rule 4.426 amended effective January 1, 2007; adopted as rule 426 effective January 1, 1991; previously renumbered effective January 1, 2001; previously amended effective July 1, 2003.

Advisory Committee Comment

Section 667.6(d) requires a full, separate, and consecutive term for each of the enumerated violent sex crimes that involve separate victims, or the same victim on separate occasions. Therefore, if there were separate victims or the court found that there were separate occasions, no other reasons are required.

If there have been multiple convictions involving at least one of the enumerated violent sex crimes, the court may impose a full, separate, and consecutive term for each violent sex crime under section 667.6(c). (See *People v. Coleman* (1989) 48 Cal.3d 112, 161.) A fully consecutive sentence under section 667.6(c) is a sentence choice, which requires a statement of reasons. The court may not use the same fact to impose a sentence under section 667.6(c) that was used to impose an upper term. (See rule 4.425(b).) If the court selects the upper term, imposes consecutive sentences, and uses section 667.6(c), the record must reflect three sentencing choices with three separate statements of reasons, but the same reason may be used for sentencing under section 667.6(c) and to impose consecutive sentences. (See *People v. Belmontes* (1983) 34 Cal.3d 335, 347-349.)

Rule 4.427. Hate crimes

(a) Application

This rule is intended to assist judges in sentencing in felony hate crime cases. It applies to:

(1) Felony sentencing under section 422.7;

(2) Convictions of felonies with a hate crime enhancement under section 422.75; and

(3) Convictions of felonies that qualify as hate crimes under section 422.55.

(Subd (a) adopted effective January 1, 2007.)

(b) Felony sentencing under section 422.7

If one of the three factors listed in section 422.7 is pled and proved, a misdemeanor conviction that constitutes a hate crime under section 422.55 may be sentenced as a felony. The punishment is imprisonment in state prison as provided by section 422.7.

(Subd (b) adopted effective January 1, 2007.)

(c) Hate crime enhancement

If a hate crime enhancement is pled and proved, the punishment for a felony conviction must be enhanced under section 422.75 unless the conviction is sentenced as a felony under section 422.7.

(1) The following enhancements apply:

(A) An enhancement of a term in state prison as provided in section 422.75(a). Personal use of a firearm in the commission of the offense is an aggravating factor that must be considered in determining the enhancement term.

(B) An additional enhancement of one year in state prison for each prior felony conviction that constitutes a hate crime as defined in section 422.55.

(2) The court may strike enhancements under (c) if it finds mitigating circumstances under rule 4.423 and states those mitigating circumstances on the record.

(3) The punishment for any enhancement under (c) is in addition to any other punishment provided by law.

(Subd (c) adopted effective January 1, 2007.)

(d) Hate crime as aggravating factor

If the defendant is convicted of a felony, and the facts of the crime constitute a hate crime under section 422.55, that fact must be considered a circumstance in aggravation in determining the appropriate punishment under rule 4.421 unless:

(1) The court imposed a hate crime enhancement under section 422.75; or

(2) The defendant has been convicted of an offense subject to sentencing under section 1170.8.

(Subd (d) adopted effective January 1, 2007.)

(e) Hate crime sentencing goals

When sentencing a defendant under this rule, the judge must consider the principal goals for hate crime sentencing.

(1) The principal goals for hate crime sentencing, as stated in section 422.86, are:

(A) Punishment for the hate crime committed;

(B) Crime and violence prevention, including prevention of recidivism and prevention of crimes and violence in prisons and jails; and

(C) Restorative justice for the immediate victims of the hate crimes and for the classes of persons terrorized by the hate crimes.

(2) Crime and violence prevention considerations should include educational or other appropriate programs available in the community, jail, prison, and juvenile detention facilities. The programs should address sensitivity or similar training or counseling intended to reduce violent and antisocial behavior based on one or more of the following actual or perceived characteristics of the victim:

(A) Disability;

(B) Gender;

(C) Nationality;

(D) Race or ethnicity;

(E) Religion;

(F) Sexual orientation; or

(G) Association with a person or group with one or more of these actual or perceived characteristics.

(3) Restorative justice considerations should include community service and other programs focused on hate crime prevention or diversity sensitivity. Additionally, the court should consider ordering payment or other compensation to programs that provide services to violent crime victims and reimbursement to the victim for reasonable costs of counseling and other reasonable expenses that the court finds are a direct result of the defendant's actions.

(Subd (e) adopted effective January 1, 2007.)

Rule 4.427 adopted effective January 1, 2007.

Advisory Committee Comment

Multiple enhancements for prior convictions under subdivision (c)(1)(B) may be imposed if the prior convictions have been brought and tried separately. (Pen. Code, § 422.75(d)).

Rule 4.428. Criteria affecting imposition of enhancements

[1]

No reason need be given for imposing a term for an enhancement that was charged and found true.

If the judge has statutory discretion to strike the additional term for an enhancement in the furtherance of justice under section 1385(c) or based on circumstances in mitigation, the court may consider and apply any of the circumstances in mitigation enumerated in these rules or, under rule 4.408, any other reasonable circumstances in mitigation or in the furtherance of justice.

The judge should not strike the allegation of the enhancement.

Rule 4.428 amended effective January 1, 2008; adopted as rule 428 effective January 1, 1991; previously renumbered effective January 1, 2001; previously amended effective January 1, 1998, July 1, 2003, January 1, 2007, and May 23, 2007.

Rule 4.428. 2008 Deletes. [1] Imposing or not imposing enhancement

Rule 4.431. Proceedings at sentencing to be reported

All proceedings at the time of sentencing must be reported.

Rule 4.431 amended effective January 1, 2007; adopted as rule 431 effective July 1, 1977; previously renumbered effective January 1, 2001.

Advisory Committee Comment

Reporters' transcripts of the sentencing proceedings are required on appeal (rule 8.420), and when the defendant is sentenced to prison (section 1203.01).

Ref.: Cal. Fms Pl. & Pr., Ch. 72, "Attorney Practice and Ethics."

Rule 4.433. Matters to be considered at time set for sentencing

(a) In every case, at the time set for sentencing under section 1191, the sentencing judge must hold a hearing at which the judge must:

(1) Hear and determine any matters raised by the defendant under section 1201; and

(2) Determine whether a defendant who is eligible for probation should be granted or denied probation, unless consideration of probation is expressly waived by the defendant personally and by counsel.

(Subd (a) amended effective January 1, 2007.)

(b) If the imposition of a sentence is to be suspended during a period of probation after a conviction by trial, the trial judge must identify **and state** circumstances that would justify imposition of one of the three authorized prison terms referred to in section 1170(b) if probation is later revoked [1]**. The circumstances identified and stated by the judge must be** based on evidence admitted at the trial **or other circumstances properly considered under rule 4.420(b).**

(Subd (b) amended effective January 1, 2008; previously amended effective July 28, 1977, January 1, 2007, and May 23, 2007.)

Rule 4.433(b). 2008 Deletes. [1] ,

(c) If a sentence of imprisonment is to be imposed, or if the execution of a sentence of imprisonment is to be suspended during a period of probation, the sentencing judge must:

(1) Determine, under section 1170(b), whether to impose one of the three authorized prison terms referred to in section 1170(b) and state on the record the reasons for imposing that term.

(2) Determine whether any additional term of imprisonment provided for an enhancement charged and found will be stricken;

(3) Determine whether the sentences will be consecutive or concurrent if the defendant has been convicted of multiple crimes;

(4) Determine any issues raised by statutory prohibitions on the dual use of facts and statutory limitations on enhancements, as required in rules 4.420(c) and 4.447; and

(5) Pronounce the court's judgment and sentence, stating the terms thereof and giving reasons for those matters for which reasons are required by law.

(Subd (c) amended effective May 23, 2007; previously amended effective July 28, 1977, July 1, 2003, and January 1, 2007.)

(d) All these matters must be heard and determined at a single hearing unless the sentencing judge otherwise orders in the interests of justice.

(Subd (d) amended effective January 1, 2007.)

(e) When a sentence of imprisonment is imposed under (c) or under rule 4.435, the sentencing judge must inform the defendant, under section 1170(c), of the parole period provided by section 3000 to be served after expiration of the sentence in addition to any period of incarceration for parole violation.

(Subd (e) amended effective January 1, 2007; previously amended effective July 28, 1977, January 1, 1979, and July 1, 2003.)

Rule 4.433 amended effective January 1, 2008; adopted as rule 433 effective July 1, 1977; previously renumbered effective January 1, 2001; previously amended effective July 28, 1977, January 1, 1979, July 1, 2003, January 1, 2007, and May 23, 2007.

Advisory Committee Comment

This rule summarizes the questions that the court is required to consider at the time of sentencing, in their logical order.

Subdivision (a)(2) makes it clear that probation should be considered in every case, without the necessity of any application, unless the defendant is statutorily ineligible for probation.

Under subdivision (b), when imposition of sentence is to be suspended, the sentencing judge is not to make any determinations as to possible length of a prison term on violation of probation (section 1170(b)). If there was a trial, however, the judge must state on the record the circumstances that would justify imposition of one of the three authorized prison terms based on the trial evidence.

Subdivision (d) makes it clear that all sentencing matters should be disposed of at a single hearing unless strong reasons exist for a continuance.

Rule 4.435. Sentencing on revocation of probation

(a) When the defendant violates the terms of probation or is otherwise subject to revocation of probation, the sentencing judge may make any disposition of the case authorized by statute.

(Subd (a) amended effective January 1, 1991.)

(b) On revocation and termination of probation under section 1203.2, when the sentencing judge determines that the defendant will be committed to prison:

(1) If the imposition of sentence was previously suspended, the judge must impose judgment and sentence after considering any findings previously made and hearing and determining the matters enumerated in rule 4.433(c).

The length of the sentence must be based on circumstances existing at the time probation was granted, and subsequent events may not be considered in selecting the base term or in deciding whether to strike the additional punishment for enhancements charged and found.

(2) If the execution of sentence was previously suspended, the judge must order that the judgment previously pronounced be in full force and effect and that the defendant be committed to the custody of the Secretary of the Department of Corrections and Rehabilitation for the term prescribed in that judgment.

(Subd (b) amended effective January 1, 2007; previously amended effective July 1, 2003, and January 1, 2006.)

Rule 4.435 amended effective January 1, 2007; adopted as rule 435 effective July 1, 1977; previously renumbered effective January 1, 2001; previously amended effective January 1, 1991, July 1, 2003, and January 1, 2006.

Advisory Committee Comment

Subdivision (a) makes it clear that there is no change in the court's power, on finding cause to revoke and terminate probation under section 1203.2(a), to continue the defendant on probation.

The restriction of subdivision (b)(1) is based on *In re Rodriguez* (1975) 14 Cal.3d 639, 652: "[T]he primary term must reflect the circumstances existing at the time of the offense."

A judge imposing a prison sentence on revocation of probation will have the power granted by section 1170(d) to recall the commitment on his or her own motion within 120 days after the date of commitment, and the power under section 1203.2(e) to set aside the revocation of probation, for good cause, within 30 days after the court has notice that execution of the sentence has commenced.

Consideration of conduct occurring after the granting of probation should be distinguished from consideration of preprobation conduct that is discovered after the granting of an order of probation and before sentencing following a revocation and termination of probation. If the preprobation conduct affects or nullifies a determination made at the time probation was granted, the preprobation conduct may properly be considered at sentencing following revocation and termination of probation. (See *People v. Griffith* (1984) 153 Cal.App.3d 796, 801.)

Rule 4.437. Statements in aggravation and mitigation

(a) Time for filing and service

Statements in aggravation and mitigation referred to in section 1170(b) must be filed and served at least four days before the time set for sentencing under section 1191 or the time set for pronouncing judgment on revocation of probation under section 1203.2(c) if imposition of sentence was previously suspended.

(Subd (a) amended effective January 1, 2007.)

(b) Combined statement

A party seeking consideration of circumstances in aggravation or mitigation may file and serve a statement under section 1170(b) and this rule.

(Subd (b) amended effective January 1, 2007.)

(c) Contents of statement

A statement in aggravation or mitigation must include:

(1) A summary of evidence that the party relies on as circumstances justifying the imposition of a particular term; and

(2) Notice of intention to dispute facts or offer evidence in aggravation or mitigation at the sentencing hearing. The statement must generally describe the evidence to be offered, including a description of any documents and the names and expected substance of the testimony of any witnesses. No evidence in aggravation or mitigation may be introduced at the sentencing hearing unless it was described in the statement, or unless its admission is permitted by the sentencing judge in the interests of justice.

(Subd (c) amended effective May 23, 2007; previously amended effective January 1, 2007.)

(d) Support required for assertions of fact

Assertions of fact in a statement in aggravation or mitigation must be disregarded unless they are supported by the record in the case, the probation officer's report or other reports properly filed in the case, or other competent evidence.

(Subd (d) amended effective January 1, 2007.)

(e) Disputed facts

In the event the parties dispute the facts on which the conviction rested, the court must conduct a presentence hearing and make appropriate corrections, additions, or deletions in the presentence probation report or order a revised report.

(Subd (e) amended effective January 1, 2007; adopted effective January 1, 1991.)

Rule 4.437 amended effective January 1, 2008; adopted as rule 437 effective July 1, 1977; previously renumbered effective January 1, 2001; previously amended effective July 28, 1977, January 1, 1991, January 1, 2007, and May 23, 2007.

Advisory Committee Comment

Section 1170(b) states in part:

"At least four days prior to the time set for imposition of judgment, either party or the victim, or the family of the victim if the victim is deceased, may submit a statement in aggravation or mitigation to dispute facts in the record or the probation officer's report, or to present additional facts."

This provision means that the statement is a document giving notice of intention to dispute evidence in the record or the probation officer's report, or to present additional facts.

The statement itself cannot be the medium for presenting new evidence, or for rebutting competent evidence already presented, because the statement is a unilateral presentation by one party or counsel that will not necessarily have any indicia of reliability. To allow its factual assertions to be considered in the absence of corroborating evidence would, therefore, constitute a denial of due process of law in violation of the United States (14th Amend.) and California (art. I, § 7) Constitutions.

"[I]t is now clear that the sentencing process, as well as the trial itself, must satisfy the requirements of the Due Process Clause. Even though the defendant has no substantive right to a particular sentence within the range authorized by statute, the sentencing is a critical stage of the criminal proceeding at which he is entitled to the effective assistance of counsel …. The defendant has a legitimate interest in the character of the procedure which leads to the imposition of sentence …." *Gardner v. Florida* (1977) 430 U.S. 349, 358.

The use of probation officers' reports is permissible because the officers are trained objective investigators. *Williams v. New York* (1949) 337 U.S. 241. Compare sections 1203 and 1204. *People v. Peterson* (1973) 9 Cal.3d 717, 727, expressly approved the holding of *United States v. Weston* (9th Cir. 1971) 448 F.2d 626 that due process is offended by sentencing on the basis of unsubstantiated allegations that were denied by the defendant. Cf., *In re Hancock* (1977) 67 Cal.App.3d 943, 949.

The requirement that the statement include notice of intention to rely on new evidence will enhance fairness to both sides by avoiding surprise and helping to ensure that the time limit on pronouncing sentence is met.

Rule 4.447.   Limitations on enhancements

No finding of an enhancement may be stricken or dismissed because imposition of the term either is prohibited by law or exceeds limitations on the imposition of multiple enhancements. The sentencing judge must impose sentence for the aggregate term of imprisonment computed without reference to those prohibitions and limitations, and must thereupon stay execution of so much of the term as is prohibited or exceeds the applicable limit. The stay will become permanent on the defendant's service of the portion of the sentence not stayed.

Rule 4.447 amended effective January 1, 2007; adopted as rule 447 effective July 1, 1977; previously amended and renumbered

effective January 1, 2001; previously amended effective July 28, 1977, January 1, 1991, and July 1, 2003.

Advisory Committee Comment

Statutory restrictions may prohibit or limit the imposition of an enhancement in certain situations. (See, for example, sections 186.22(b)(1), 667(a)(2), 667.61(f), 1170.1(f) and (g), 12022.53(e)(2) and (f), and Vehicle Code section 23558.)

Present practice of staying execution is followed to avoid violating a statutory prohibition or exceeding a statutory limitation, while preserving the possibility of imposition of the stayed portion should a reversal on appeal reduce the unstayed portion of the sentence. See *People v. Niles* (1964) 227 Cal.App.2d 749, 756.

Only the portion of a sentence or component thereof that exceeds a limitation is prohibited, and this rule provides a procedure for that situation. This rule applies to both determinate and indeterminate terms.

Rule 4.451.   Sentence consecutive to indeterminate term or to term in other jurisdiction

(a) When a defendant is sentenced under section 1170 and the sentence is to run consecutively to a sentence imposed under section 1168(b) in the same or another proceeding, the judgment must specify the determinate term imposed under section 1170 computed without reference to the indeterminate sentence, must order that the determinate term be served consecutively to the sentence under section 1168(b), and must identify the proceedings in which the indeterminate sentence was imposed. The term under section 1168(b), and the date of its completion or parole date, and the sequence in which the sentences are deemed served, will be determined by correctional authorities as provided by law.

(Subd (a) amended effective January 1, 2007; previously amended effective January 1, 1979, and July 1, 2003.)

(b) When a defendant is sentenced under section 1170 and the sentence is to run consecutively to a sentence imposed by a court of the United States or of another state or territory, the judgment must specify the determinate term imposed under section 1170 computed without reference to the sentence imposed by the other jurisdiction, must order that the determinate term be served commencing on the completion of the sentence imposed by the other jurisdiction, and must identify the other jurisdiction and the proceedings in which the other sentence was imposed.

(Subd (b) amended effective January 1, 2007.)

Rule 4.451 amended effective January 1, 2007; adopted as rule 451 effective July 1, 1977; previously renumbered effective January 1, 2001; previously amended effective January 1, 1979, and July 1, 2003.

Advisory Committee Comment

The provisions of section 1170.1(a), which use a one-third formula to calculate subordinate consecutive terms, can logically be applied only when all the sentences are imposed under section 1170. Indeterminate sentences are imposed under section 1168(b). Since the duration of the indeterminate term cannot be known to the court, subdivision (a) states the only feasible mode of sentencing. (See *People v. Felix* (2000) 22 Cal.4th 651, 654-657; *People v. McGahuey* (1981) 121 Cal.App.3d 524, 530-532.)

On the authority to sentence consecutively to the sentence of another jurisdiction and the effect of such a sentence, see *In re Helpman* (1968) 267 Cal.App.2d 307 and cases cited at note 3, *id.*

at 310. The mode of sentencing required by subdivision (b) is necessary to avoid the illogical conclusion that the total of the consecutive sentences will depend on whether the other jurisdiction or California is the first to pronounce judgment.

Rule 4.452. Determinate sentence consecutive to prior determinate sentence

If a determinate sentence is imposed under section 1170.1(a) consecutive to one or more determinate sentences imposed previously in the same court or in other courts, the court in the current case must pronounce a single aggregate term, as defined in section 1170.1(a), stating the result of combining the previous and current sentences. In those situations:

(1) The sentences on all determinately sentenced counts in all of the cases on which a sentence was or is being imposed must be combined as though they were all counts in the current case.

(2) The judge in the current case must make a new determination of which count, in the combined cases, represents the principal term, as defined in section 1170.1(a).

(3) Discretionary decisions of the judges in the previous cases may not be changed by the judge in the current case. Such decisions include the decision to impose one of the three authorized prison terms referred to in section 1170(b), making counts in prior cases concurrent with or consecutive to each other, or the decision that circumstances in mitigation or in the furtherance of justice justified striking the punishment for an enhancement.

Rule 4.452 amended effective May 23, 2007; adopted as rule 452 effective January 1, 1991; previously renumbered effective January 1, 2001; previously amended effective July 1, 2003, and January 1, 2007.

Advisory Committee Comment

The restrictions of subdivision (3) do not apply to circumstances where a previously imposed base term is made a consecutive term on resentencing. If the judge selects a consecutive sentence structure, and since there can be only one principal term in the final aggregate sentence, if a previously imposed full base term becomes a subordinate consecutive term, the new consecutive term normally will become one-third the middle term by operation of law (section 1170.1(a)).

Rule 4.453. Commitments to nonpenal institutions

When a defendant is convicted of a crime for which sentence could be imposed under Penal Code section 1170 and the court orders that he or she be committed to the California Department of Corrections and Rehabilitation, Division of Juvenile Justice under Welfare and Institutions Code section 1731.5, the order of commitment must specify the term of imprisonment to which the defendant would have been sentenced. The term is determined as provided by Penal Code sections 1170 and 1170.1 and these rules, as though a sentence of imprisonment were to be imposed.

Rule 4.453 amended effective January 1, 2007; adopted as rule 453 effective July 1, 1977; previously amended and renumbered effective January 1, 2001; previously amended effective July 28, 1977, and January 1, 2006.

Advisory Committee Comment

Commitments to the Department of Corrections and Rehabilitation, Division of Juvenile Justice (formerly Youth Authority)

cannot exceed the maximum possible incarceration in an adult institution for the same crime. (See *People v. Olivas* (1976) 17 Cal.3d 236.)

Under the indeterminate sentencing law, the receiving institution knew, as a matter of law from the record of the conviction, the maximum potential period of imprisonment for the crime of which the defendant was convicted.

Under the Uniform Determinate Sentencing Act, the court's discretion as to length of term leaves doubt as to the maximum term when only the record of convictions is present.

Rule 4.470. Notification of appeal rights in felony cases

After imposing sentence or making an order deemed to be a final judgment in a criminal case on conviction after trial, or after imposing sentence following a revocation of probation, except where the revocation is after the defendant's admission of violation of probation, the court must advise the defendant of his or her right to appeal, of the necessary steps and time for taking an appeal, and of the right of an indigent defendant to have counsel appointed by the reviewing court. A reporter's transcript of the proceedings required by this rule must be forthwith prepared and certified by the reporter and filed with the clerk.

Rule 4.470 amended effective January 1, 2007; adopted as rule 250 effective January 1, 1972; previously amended effective July 1, 1972, and January 1, 1977; previously amended and renumbered as rule 470 effective January 1, 1991; previously renumbered effective January 1, 2001.

Rule 4.472. Determination of presentence custody time credit

At the time of sentencing, the court must cause to be recorded on the judgment or commitment the total time in custody to be credited on the sentence under sections 2900.5, 2933.1(c), and 2933.2(c). On referral of the defendant to the probation officer for an investigation and report under section 1203(b) or 1203(g), or on setting a date for sentencing in the absence of a referral, the court must direct the sheriff, probation officer, or other appropriate person to report to the court and notify the defendant or defense counsel and prosecuting attorney within a reasonable time before the date set for sentencing as to the number of days that defendant has been in custody and for which he or she may be entitled to credit. Any challenges to the report must be heard at the time of sentencing.

Rule 4.472 amended effective January 1, 2007; adopted as rule 252 effective January 1, 1977; previously amended and renumbered as rule 472 effective January 1, 1991; previously amended and renumbered effective January 1, 2001; previously amended effective July 1, 2003.

Rule 4.480. Judge's statement under section 1203.01

A sentencing judge's statement of his or her views under section 1203.01 respecting a person sentenced to the Department of Corrections and Rehabilitation, Division of Adult Operations is required only in the event that no probation report is filed. Even though it is not required, however, a statement should be submitted by the judge in any case in which he or she believes that the correctional handling and the determination of term and parole should be influenced by information not contained in other court records.

The purpose of a section 1203.01 statement is to provide assistance to the Department of Corrections and Rehabilitation, Division of Adult Operations in its programming and institutional assignment and to the Board of Parole Hearings with reference to term fixing and parole release of persons sentenced indeterminately, and parole waiver of persons sentenced determinately. It may amplify any reasons for the sentence that may bear on a possible suggestion by the Secretary of the Department of Corrections and Rehabilitation or the Board of Parole Hearings that the sentence and commitment be recalled and the defendant be resentenced. To be of maximum assistance to these agencies, a judge's statements should contain individualized comments concerning the convicted offender, any special circumstances that led to a prison sentence rather than local incarceration, and any other significant information that might not readily be available in any of the accompanying official records and reports.

If a section 1203.01 statement is prepared, it should be submitted no later than two weeks after sentencing so that it may be included in the official Department of Corrections and Rehabilitation, Division of Adult Operations case summary that is prepared during the time the offender is being processed at the Reception-Guidance Center of the Department of Corrections and Rehabilitation, Division of Adult Operations.

Rule 4.480 amended effective January 1, 2007; adopted as section 12 of the Standards of Judicial Administration effective January 1, 1973; previously amended and renumbered effective January 1, 2001; previously amended effective July 1, 1978, July 1, 2003, and January 1, 2006.

Division 6
Postconviction and Writs

Chap. 1.   Postconviction. Rule 4.510.
Chap. 2.   Habeas Corpus. Rules 4.550–4.552.

Chapter 1
Postconviction

Rule 4.510.   Reverse remand

(a) Minor prosecuted under Welfare and Institutions Code section 602(b) or 707(d) and convicted of offense listed in Welfare and Institutions Code section 602(b) or 707(d) (Penal Code, § 1170.17)

If the prosecuting attorney lawfully initiated the prosecution as a criminal case under Welfare and Institutions Code section 602(b) or 707(d), and the minor is convicted of a criminal offense listed in those sections, the minor must be sentenced as an adult.

(Subd (a) amended effective January 1, 2007.)

(b) Minor convicted of an offense not listed in Welfare and Institutions Code section 602(b) or 707(d) (Penal Code, § 1170.17)

(1) If the prosecuting attorney lawfully initiated the prosecution as a criminal case and the minor is convicted of an offense not listed in Welfare and Institutions Code section 602(b) or 707(d), but one that would have raised

the presumption of unfitness under juvenile court law, the minor may move the court to conduct a postconviction fitness hearing.

(A) On the motion by the minor, the court must order the probation department to prepare a report as required in rule 5.768.

(B) The court may conduct a fitness hearing or remand the matter to the juvenile court for a determination of fitness.

(C) The minor may receive a disposition hearing under the juvenile court law only if he or she is found to be fit under rule 5.772. However, if the court and parties agree, the minor may be sentenced in adult court.

(D) If the minor is found unfit, the minor must be sentenced as an adult, unless all parties, including the court, agree that the disposition be conducted under juvenile court law.

(2) If the minor is convicted of an offense not listed in Welfare and Institutions Code section 602(b) or 707(d), but one for which the minor would have been presumed fit under the juvenile court law, the minor must have a disposition hearing under juvenile court law, and consistent with the provisions of Penal Code section 1170.19, either in the trial court or on remand to the juvenile court.

(A) If the prosecuting attorney objects to the treatment of the minor as within the juvenile court law and moves for a fitness hearing to be conducted, the court must order the probation department to prepare a report as required by rule 5.768.

(B) The court may conduct a fitness hearing or remand the matter to the juvenile court for a determination of fitness.

(C) If found to be fit under rule 5.770, the minor will be subject to a disposition hearing under juvenile court law and Penal Code section 1170.19.

(D) If the minor is found unfit, the minor must be sentenced as an adult, unless all parties, including the court, agree that the disposition be conducted under juvenile court law.

(3) If the minor is convicted of an offense that would not have permitted a fitness determination, the court must remand the matter to juvenile court for disposition, unless the minor requests sentencing in adult court and all parties, including the court, agree.

(4) Fitness hearings held under this rule must be conducted as provided in title 5, division 3, chapter 14, article 2.

(Subd (b) amended effective January 1, 2007.)

Rule 4.510 amended effective January 1, 2007; adopted effective January 1, 2001.

Chapter 2
Habeas Corpus

Rule 4.550. Habeas corpus application and definitions
Rule 4.551. Habeas corpus proceedings
Rule 4.552. Habeas corpus jurisdiction

Rule 4.550.   Habeas corpus application and definitions

(a) Application

This chapter applies to habeas corpus proceedings in the superior court under Penal Code section 1473 et seq. or any other provision of law authorizing relief from unlawful confinement or unlawful conditions of confinement.

(Subd (a) amended effective January 1, 2007.)

(b) Definitions

In this chapter, the following definitions apply:

(1) A "petition for writ of habeas corpus" is the petitioner's initial filing that commences a proceeding.

(2) An "order to show cause" is an order directing the respondent to file a return. The order to show cause is issued if the petitioner has made a prima facie showing that he or she is entitled to relief; it does not grant the relief requested. An order to show cause may also be referred to as "granting the writ."

(3) The "return" is the respondent's statement of reasons that the court should not grant the relief requested by the petitioner.

(4) The "denial" is the petitioner's pleading in response to the return. The denial may be also referred to as the "traverse."

(5) An "evidentiary hearing" is a hearing held by the trial court to resolve contested factual issues.

(6) An "order on writ of habeas corpus" is the court's order granting or denying the relief sought by the petitioner.

(Subd (b) amended effective January 1, 2007.)

Rule 4.550 amended effective January 1, 2007; adopted effective January 1, 2002.

Ref.: Cal. Fms Pl. & Pr., Ch. 292, "Habeas Corpus," Ch. 304, "Insane and Other Incompetent Persons."

Rule 4.551. Habeas corpus proceedings

(a) Petition; form and court ruling

(1) Except as provided in (2), the petition must be on the *Petition for Writ of Habeas Corpus* (form MC-275) [1].

(2) For good cause, a court may also accept for filing a petition that does not comply with (a)(1). A petition submitted by an attorney need not be on the Judicial Council form. However, a petition that is not on the Judicial Council form must comply with Penal Code section 1474 and must contain the pertinent information specified in the *Petition for Writ of Habeas Corpus* (form MC-275), including the information required regarding other petitions, motions, or applications filed in any court with respect to the conviction, commitment, or issue.

(3) (A) On filing, the clerk of the court must immediately deliver the petition to the presiding judge or his or her designee. The court must rule on a petition for writ of habeas corpus within 60 days after the petition is filed.

(B) If the court fails to rule on the petition within 60 days of its filing, the petitioner may file a notice and request for ruling.

(i) The petitioner's notice and request for ruling must include a declaration stating the date the petition was filed and the date of the notice and request for ruling, and indicating that the petitioner has not received a ruling on the petition. A copy of the original petition must be attached to the notice and request for ruling.

(ii) If the presiding judge or his or her designee determines that the notice is complete and the court has

failed to rule, the presiding judge or his or her designee must assign the petition to a judge and calendar the matter for a decision without appearances within 30 days of the filing of the notice and request for ruling. If the judge assigned by the presiding judge rules on the petition before the date the petition is calendared for decision, the matter may be taken off calendar.

(4) For the purposes of (a)(3), the court rules on the petition by:

(A) Issuing an order to show cause under (c);

(B) Denying the petition for writ of habeas corpus; or

(C) Requesting an informal response to the petition for writ of habeas corpus under (b).

(5) The court must issue an order to show cause or deny the petition within 45 days after receipt of an informal response requested under (b).

(Subd (a) amended effective January 1, 2009; previously amended effective January 1, 2002, January 1, 2004, and January 1, 2007.)

Rule 4.551(a). 2008 Deletes. [1] , and must be served as required in Penal Code section 1475

(b) Informal response

(1) Before passing on the petition, the court may request an informal response from:

(A) The respondent or real party in interest; or

(B) The custodian of any record pertaining to the petitioner's case, directing the custodian to produce the record or a certified copy to be filed with the clerk of the court.

(2) A copy of the request must be sent to the petitioner. The informal response, if any, must be served on the petitioner by the party of whom the request is made. The informal response must be in writing and must be served and filed within 15 days. If any informal response is filed, the court must notify the petitioner that he or she may reply to the informal response within 15 days from the date of service of the response on the petitioner. If the informal response consists of records or copies of records, a copy of every record and document furnished to the court must be furnished to the petitioner.

(3) After receiving an informal response, the court may not deny the petition until the petitioner has filed a timely reply to the informal response or the 15-day period provided for a reply under (b)(2) has expired.

(Subd (b) amended effective January 1, 2007; adopted effective January 1, 2002.)

(c) Order to show cause

(1) The court must issue an order to show cause if the petitioner has made a prima facie showing that he or she is entitled to relief. In doing so, the court takes petitioner's factual allegations as true and makes a preliminary assessment regarding whether the petitioner would be entitled to relief if his or her factual allegations were proved. If so, the court must issue an order to show cause.

(2) On issuing an order to show cause, the court must appoint counsel for any unrepresented petitioner who desires but cannot afford counsel.

(3) An order to show cause is a determination that the petitioner has made a showing that he or she may be entitled to relief. It does not grant the relief sought in the petition.

(Subd (c) amended effective January 1, 2007; adopted effective January 1, 2002.)

(d) Return

If an order to show cause is issued as provided in (c), the respondent may, within 30 days thereafter, file a return. Any material allegation of the petition not controverted by the return is deemed admitted for purposes of the proceeding. The return must comply with Penal Code section 1480 and must be served on the petitioner.

(Subd (d) amended effective January 1, 2007; repealed and adopted effective January 1, 2002; previously amended effective January 1, 2004.)

(e) Denial

Within 30 days after service and filing of a return, the petitioner may file a denial. Any material allegation of the return not denied is deemed admitted for purposes of the proceeding. Any denial must comply with Penal Code section 1484 and must be served on the respondent.

(Subd (e) amended and relettered effective January 1, 2002; adopted as subd (b) effective January 1, 1982.)

(f) Evidentiary hearing; when required

Within 30 days after the filing of any denial or, if none is filed, after the expiration of the time for filing a denial, the court must either grant or deny the relief sought by the petition or order an evidentiary hearing. An evidentiary hearing is required if, after considering the verified petition, the return, any denial, any affidavits or declarations under penalty of perjury, and matters of which judicial notice may be taken, the court finds there is a reasonable likelihood that the petitioner may be entitled to relief and the petitioner's entitlement to relief depends on the resolution of an issue of fact. The petitioner must be produced at the evidentiary hearing unless the court, for good cause, directs otherwise.

(Subd (f) amended and relettered effective January 1, 2002; adopted as subd (c) effective January 1, 1982.)

(g) Reasons for denial of petition

Any order denying a petition for writ of habeas corpus must contain a brief statement of the reasons for the denial. An order only declaring the petition to be "denied" is insufficient.

(Subd (g) amended and relettered effective January 1, 2002; adopted as subd (e) effective January 1, 1982.)

(h) Extending or shortening time

On motion of any party or on the court's own motion, for good cause stated in the order, the court may shorten or extend the time for doing any act under this rule. A copy of the order must be mailed to each party.

(Subd (h) amended and relettered effective January 1, 2002; adopted as subd (f) effective January 1, 1982.)

Rule 4.551 amended effective January 1, 2009; adopted as rule 260 effective January 1, 1982; previously renumbered as rule 4.500 effective January 1, 2001; previously amended and renumbered effective January 1, 2002; previously amended effective January 1, 2004, and January 1, 2007.

Advisory Committee Comment

The court must appoint counsel on the issuance of an order to show cause. (*In re Clark* (1993) 5 Cal.4th 750, 780 and *People v. Shipman* (1965) 62 Cal.2d 226, 231-232.) The Court of Appeal has held that under Penal Code section 987.2, counties bear the expense of appointed counsel in a habeas corpus proceeding challenging the underlying conviction. (*Charlton v. Superior Court* (1979) 93 Cal.App.3d 858, 862.) Penal Code section 987.2 authorizes appointment of the public defender, or private counsel if there is no public defender available, for indigents in criminal proceedings.

Ref.: Cal. Fms Pl. & Pr., Ch. 292, "Habeas Corpus," Ch. 304, "Insane and Other Incompetent Persons."

Rule 4.552. Habeas corpus jurisdiction

(a) Proper court to hear petition

Except as stated in (b) and (c), the petition must be heard and resolved in the court in which it is filed.

(Subd (a) amended effective January 1, 2007; previously amended effective January 1, 2006.)

(b) Transfer of petition—discretionary

(1) The superior court in which the petition is filed must determine, based on the allegations of the petition, whether the matter should be heard by it or in the superior court of another county.

(2) If the superior court in which the petition is filed determines that the matter may be more properly heard by the superior court of another county, it may nonetheless retain jurisdiction in the matter or, without first determining whether a prima facie case for relief exists, order the matter transferred to the other county. Transfer may be ordered in the following circumstances:

(A) If the petition challenges the terms of a judgment, the matter may be transferred to the county in which judgment was rendered.

(B) If the petition challenges the conditions of an inmate's confinement, it may be transferred to the county in which the petitioner is confined. A change in the institution of confinement that effects a change in the conditions of confinement may constitute good cause to deny the petition.

(3) The transferring court must specify in the order of transfer the reason for the transfer.

(4) If the receiving court determines that the reason for transfer is inapplicable, the receiving court must, within 30 days of receipt of the case, order the case returned to the transferring court. The transferring court must retain and resolve the matter as provided by these rules.

(Subd (b) amended effective January 1, 2006.)

(c) Transfer of petition—mandatory

If the petition challenges the denial of parole or the petitioner's suitability for parole and is filed in a superior court other than the court that rendered the underlying judgment, the court in which the petition is filed must transfer the petition to the superior court in which the underlying judgment was rendered. The court must transfer the case before determining whether the petition states a prima facie case for relief and specify in the order of transfer the reason for the transfer.

(Subd (c) adopted effective January 1, 2006.)

(d) Single judge must decide petition

A petition for writ of habeas corpus filed in the superior court must be decided by a single judge; it must not be considered by the appellate division of the superior court.

(Subd (d) relettered effective January 1, 2006; adopted as subd (c) effective January 1, 2002.)

Rule 4.552 amended effective January 1, 2007; adopted effective January 1, 2002; previously amended effective January 1, 2006.

Advisory Committee Comment

Subdivision (c). This subdivision is based on the California Supreme Court decision in *In re Roberts* (2005) 36 Cal.4th 575, which provides that petitions for writ of habeas corpus challenging denial or suitability for parole are to be adjudicated in the court that rendered the underlying judgment.

Ref.: Cal. Fms Pl. & Pr., Ch. 292, "Habeas Corpus."

Division 7
Miscellaneous

Rule 4.601.   Judicial determination of factual innocence form

(a) Form to be confidential

Any *Certificate of Identity Theft: Judicial Finding of Factual Innocence* (form CR-150) that is filed with the court is confidential. The clerk's office must maintain these forms in a manner that will protect and preserve their confidentiality.

(Subd (a) amended effective January 1, 2007.)

(b) Access to the form

Notwithstanding (a), the court, the identity theft victim, the prosecution, and law enforcement agencies may have access to the *Certificate of Identity Theft: Judicial Finding of Factual Innocence* (form CR-150). The court may allow access to any other person on a showing of good cause.

(Subd (b) amended effective January 1, 2007.)

Rule 4.601 amended effective January 1, 2007; adopted effective January 1, 2002.

TITLE 5
Family and Juvenile Rules

Title. Rule 5.1.

Division 1.   Family Rules. Rules 5.5–5.375.

Division 2.   Rules Applicable in Family and Juvenile Proceedings. Rules 5.400–5.487.

Division 3.   Juvenile Rules. Rules 5.500–5.830.

Rule 5.1.   Title

The rules in this title may be referred to as the Family and Juvenile Rules.

Rule 5.1 adopted effective January 1, 2007.

Ref.: Cal. Fms Pl. & Pr., Ch. 44, "Appeal: Preparing and Filing the Record."

Division 1
Family Rules

Chap. 1.   General Provisions. Rules 5.5–5.71.

Chap. 2.   Procedural Rules. Rules 5.100–5.140.

Chap. 3.   Joinder of Parties. Rules 5.150–5.162.

Chap. 4.   Bifurcation and Appeals. Rules 5.175, 5.180.

Chap. 5.   Child Custody. Rules 5.210–5.242.

Chap. 6.   Certification of Statewide Uniform Guideline Support Calculators. Rule 5.275.

Chap. 7.   Rules for Title IV-D Support Actions. Rules 5.300–5.375.

Chapter 1
General Provisions

Rule 5.5. Division title

Rule 5.10. Definitions and use of terms

Rule 5.15. Extensions of time

Rule 5.20. Application of rules

Rule 5.21. General law applicable

Rule 5.22. Other proceedings

Rule 5.25. Status of family law and domestic violence forms

Rule 5.26. Use of forms in nonfamily law proceedings

Rule 5.27. Use of interstate forms

Rule 5.28. Domestic partnerships

Rule 5.35. Minimum standards for the Office of the Family Law Facilitator

Rule 5.70. Nondisclosure of attorney assistance in preparation of court documents

Rule 5.71. Application to be relieved as counsel on completion of limited scope representation

Rule 5.5.   Division title

The rules in this division may be referred to as the Family Rules.

Rule 5.5 adopted effective January 1, 2007.

Ref.: W. Cal. Sum., 11 "Husband and Wife" §§11, 82.

Rule 5.10.   Definitions and use of terms

As used in this division, unless the context or subject matter otherwise requires, the following definitions apply:

(1) "Family Code" means that code enacted by chapter 162 of the Statutes of 1992 and any subsequent amendments to that code.

(2) "Proceeding" means a proceeding under the Family Code for dissolution of marriage, nullity of marriage, legal separation, custody and support of minor children, or actions under the Domestic Violence Prevention Act, the Uniform Parentage Act, the Uniform Child Custody Jurisdiction and Enforcement Act, or the Uniform Interstate Family Support Act; local child support agency actions under the Family Code; and contempt proceedings relating to family law or local child support agency actions.

(3) "Property" includes assets and obligations.

(4) "Best interest of the child" is described in Family Code section 3011.

Rule 5.10 amended effective January 1, 2008; adopted as rule 1201 effective January 1, 1970; previously amended effective January 1, 1994, January 1, 1999, and January 1, 2007; previously amended and renumbered effective January 1, 2003.

Ref.: Cal. Fms Pl. & Pr., Ch. 21, "Amended and Supplemental Pleadings," Ch. 220, "Dissolution of Marriage: Master Procedural Guide," Ch. 221, "Dissolution of Marriage: Procedure," Ch. 223, "Dissolution of Marriage: Child Custody," Ch. 258, "Family Law Enforcement: General Enforcement Principles and Remedies"; W. Cal. Sum., 11 "Husband and Wife" §§11, 82, 144.

Rule 5.15.   Extensions of time

The time within which any act is permitted or required to be done by a party under these rules may be extended by the court upon such terms as may be just.

Rule 5.15 renumbered effective January 1, 2003; adopted as rule 1203 effective January 1, 1970.

Ref.: Cal. Fms Pl. & Pr., Ch. 25, "Annulment (Nullity) of Marriage and Related Spousal Rights," Ch. 221, "Dissolution of Marriage: Procedure," Ch. 524, "Shortening and Extension of Time."

Rule 5.20.   Application of rules

The rules in this division apply to every action and proceeding as to which the Family Code applies and, unless these rules elsewhere explicitly make them applicable, do not apply to any other action or proceeding.

Rule 5.20 amended effective January 1, 2007; adopted as rule 1205 effective January 1, 1970; previously amended effective January 1, 1979, January 1, 1994, and January 1, 1999; previously amended and renumbered effective January 1, 2003.

Ref.: Cal. Fms Pl. & Pr., Ch. 220, "Dissolution of Marriage: Master Procedural Guide," Ch. 221, "Dissolution of Marriage: Procedure."

Rule 5.21.   General law applicable

Except as otherwise provided in these rules, all provisions of law applicable to civil actions generally apply to a proceeding under the Family Code if they would otherwise apply to such proceeding without reference to this rule. To the extent that these rules conflict with provisions in other statutes or rules, these rules prevail.

Rule 5.21 amended and renumbered effective January 1, 2003; adopted as rule 1206 effective January 1, 1970; previously amended effective January 1, 1994.

Ref.: Cal. Fms Pl. & Pr., Ch. 25, "Annulment (Nullity) of Marriage and Related Spousal Rights," Ch. 220, "Dissolution of Marriage: Master Procedural Guide," Ch. 221, "Dissolution of Marriage: Procedure," Ch. 225, "Dissolution of Marriage: Spousal Support," Ch. 226, "Dissolution of Marriage: Attorney's Fees," Ch. 258, "Family Law Enforcement: General Enforcement Principles and Remedies," Ch. 259, "Family Law Enforcement: Special Remedies for Support Enforcement"; W. Cal. Sum., 11 "Community Property" §241, 11 "Husband and Wife" §§5, 11, 67, 99.

Rule 5.22.   Other proceedings

In any action under the Family Code but not otherwise subject to these rules by virtue of rule 5.10(2), all provisions of law applicable to civil actions generally apply. Such an action must be commenced by filing an appropriate petition, and the respondent must file an appropriate response within 30 days after service of the summons and a copy of the petition.

Rule 5.22 amended effective January 1, 2007; adopted as rule 1207 effective January 1, 1970; previously amended effective January 1, 1994; previously amended and renumbered effective January 1, 2003.

Ref.: Cal. Fms Pl. & Pr., Ch. 25, "Annulment (Nullity) of Marriage and Related Spousal Rights," Ch. 122, "Community Property," Ch. 220, "Dissolution of Marriage: Master Procedural Guide," Ch. 221, "Dissolution of Marriage: Procedure," Ch. 224, "Dissolution of Marriage: Child Support," Ch. 359, "Marriage"; W. Cal. Sum., 11 "Husband and Wife" §11.

Rule 5.25.   Status of family law and domestic violence forms

All forms adopted or approved by the Judicial Council for use in any proceeding under the Family Code, including any form in the FL, ADOPT, DV, and FJ series, are adopted as rules of court under the authority of Family Code section 211; article VI, section 6 of the California Constitution; and other applicable law.

Rule 5.25 amended and renumbered effective January 1, 2003; adopted as rule 1278 effective January 1, 2001.

Ref.: W. Cal. Sum., 11 "Husband and Wife" §12.

Rule 5.26.   Use of forms in nonfamily law proceedings

The forms specified by this division may be used, at the option of the party, in any proceeding involving a financial obligation growing out of the relationship of parent and child or husband and wife, to the extent they are appropriate to that proceeding.

Rule 5.26 amended and renumbered effective January 1, 2003; adopted as rule 1275 effective July 1, 1985.

Ref.: W. Cal. Sum., 11 "Husband and Wife" §12.

Rule 5.27.   Use of interstate forms

Notwithstanding any other provision of these rules, all Uniform Interstate Family Support Act forms approved by either the National Conference of Commissioners on Uniform State Laws or the U.S. Department of Health and Human Services are adopted for use in family law and other support actions in California.

Rule 5.27 renumbered effective January 1, 2003; adopted as rule 1276 effective July 1, 1988; amended effective January 1, 1998.

Ref.: Cal. Fms Pl. & Pr., Ch. 260, "Family Law Enforcement: Foreign Judgments"; W. Cal. Sum., 11 "Husband and Wife" §12.

Rule 5.28.   Domestic partnerships

(a) Procedures for obtaining a dissolution, a legal separation, or an annulment of a domestic partnership

(1) *Petition—Domestic Partnership (Family Law)* (form FL-103) must be filed to commence an action for dissolution, legal separation, or annulment of a domestic partnership. *Response—Domestic Partnership (Family Law)* (form FL-123) must be filed in response to this petition.

(2) All other forms and procedures used for the dissolution, legal separation, or annulment of a domestic partnership are the same as those used for the dissolution, legal separation, or annulment of a marriage, except that parties who qualify for a "Notice of Termination of Domestic Partnership" under Family Code section 299 must follow that procedure rather than file a summary dissolution proceeding with the superior court.

(Subd (a) amended effective January 1, 2007.)

(b) Terminology for rules and forms

For the purposes of family law rules and forms, the terms "spouse," "husband," and "wife" encompass "domestic partner." The terms "father" and "mother" encompass "parent." The terms "marriage" and "marital status" encompass "domestic partnership" and "domestic partnership status," respectively.

Rule 5.28 amended effective January 1, 2007; adopted effective January 1, 2005.

Ref.: Cal. Fms Pl. & Pr., Ch. 221, "Dissolution of Marriage: Procedure"; W. Cal. Sum., 11 "Husband and Wife" §§25, 34.

Rule 5.30.   Judicial education for family court judicial officers [Renumbered]

Rule 5.30 renumbered as rule 10.463 effective January 1, 2008.

Rule 5.35.   Minimum standards for the Office of the Family Law Facilitator

(a) Authority

These standards are adopted under Family Code section 10010.

(Subd (a) amended effective January 1, 2003.)

(b) Family law facilitator qualifications

The Office of the Family Law Facilitator must be headed by at least one attorney, who is an active member of the State Bar of California, known as the family law facilitator. Each family law facilitator must possess the following qualifications:

(1) A minimum of five years experience in the practice of law, which must include substantial family law practice including litigation and/or mediation;

(2) Knowledge of family law procedures;

(3) Knowledge of the child support establishment and enforcement process under Title IV-D of the federal Social Security Act (42 U.S.C. § 651 et seq.);

(4) Knowledge of child support law and the operation of the uniform state child support guideline; and

(5) Basic understanding of law and psychological issues related to domestic violence.

(Subd (b) amended effective January 1, 2003.)

(c) Substituted experience

Courts may substitute additional experience, skills, or background appropriate to their community for the qualifications listed above.

(d) Desirable experience

Additional desirable experience for a family law facilitator may include experience in working with low-income, semiliterate, self-represented, or non-English-speaking litigants.

(Subd (d) amended effective January 1, 2007.)

(e) Service provision

Services may be provided by other paid and volunteer members of the Office of the Family Law Facilitator under the supervision of the family law facilitator.

(f) Protocol required

Each court must develop a written protocol to provide services when a facilitator deems himself or herself disqualified or biased.

(g) Grievance procedure

Each court must develop a written protocol for a grievance procedure for processing and responding to any complaints against a family law facilitator.

(Subd (g) adopted effective January 1, 2003.)

(h) Training requirements

Each family law facilitator should attend at least one training per year for family law facilitators provided by the Judicial Council.

(Subd (h) relettered effective January 1, 2003; adopted as subd (g) effective January 1, 2000.)

Rule 5.35 amended effective January 1, 2007; adopted as rule 1208 effective January 1, 2000; previously amended and renumbered effective January 1, 2003.

Ref.: W. Cal. Sum., 10 "Parent and Child" §383.

Rule 5.70. Nondisclosure of attorney assistance in preparation of court documents

(a) Nondisclosure

In a family law proceeding, an attorney who contracts with a client to draft or assist in drafting legal documents, but not to make an appearance in the case, is not required to disclose within the text of the document that he or she was involved in preparing the documents.

(b) Attorney's fees

If a litigant seeks a court order for attorney's fees incurred as a result of document preparation, the litigant must disclose to the court information required for a proper determination of attorney's fees—including the name of the attorney who assisted in the preparation of the documents, the time involved or other basis for billing, the tasks performed, and the amount billed.

(Subd (b) amended effective January 1, 2007.)

(c) Applicability

This rule does not apply to an attorney who has made a general appearance or has contracted with his or her client to make an appearance on any issue that is the subject of the pleadings.

Rule 5.70 amended effective January 1, 2007; adopted as rule 5.170 effective July 1, 2003; previously renumbered effective January 1, 2004.

Ref.: Cal. Fms Pl. & Pr., Ch. 221, "Dissolution of Marriage: Procedure"; W. Cal. Sum., 11 "Husband and Wife" §74.

Rule 5.71. Application to be relieved as counsel on completion of limited scope representation

(a) Applicability of this rule

Notwithstanding rule 3.1362, an attorney who has completed the tasks specified in the *Notice of Limited Scope Representation* (form FL-950) may use the procedure in this rule to request that the attorney be relieved as counsel in cases in which the attorney has appeared before the court as attorney of record and the client has not signed a *Substitution of Attorney—Civil* (form MC-050).

(Subd (a) amended effective July 1, 2007.)

(b) Notice

An application to be relieved as counsel on completion of limited scope representation under Code of Civil Procedure section 284(2) must be directed to the client and made on the *Application to Be Relieved as Counsel Upon Completion of Limited Scope Representation* (form FL-955).

(Subd (b) amended effective January 1, 2007.)

(c) Service

The application must be filed with the court and served on the client and on all other parties and counsel who are of record in the case. The client must also be served with *Objection to Application to Be Relieved as Counsel Upon Completion of Limited Scope Representation* (form FL-956).

(Subd (c) amended effective January 1, 2007.)

(d) No objection

If no objection is filed within 15 days from the date that the *Application to Be Relieved as Counsel Upon Completion of Limited Scope Representation* (form FL-955) is served upon the client, the attorney making the application must file an updated form FL-955 indicating the lack of objection, along with a proposed *Order on Application to Be Relieved as Counsel Upon Completion of Limited Scope Representation* (form FL-958). The clerk will then forward the file with the proposed order for judicial signature.

(e) Objection

If an objection is filed within 15 days, the clerk must set a hearing date on the *Objection to Application to Be Relieved as Counsel Upon Completion of Limited Scope Representation* (form FL-956). The hearing must be scheduled no later than 25 days from the date the objection is filed. The clerk must send the notice of the hearing to the parties and counsel.

(f) Service of the order

After the order is signed, a copy of the signed order must be served by the attorney who has filed the *Application to Be Relieved as Counsel Upon Completion of Limited Scope Representation* (form FL-955) on the client and on all parties who have appeared in the case. The court may delay the effective date of the order relieving counsel until proof of service of a copy of the signed order on the client has been filed with the court.

Rule 5.71 amended effective July 1, 2007; adopted as rule 5.171 effective July 1, 2003; previously renumbered effective January 1, 2004; previously amended effective January 1, 2007.

Ref.: Cal. Fms Pl. & Pr., Ch. 221, "Dissolution of Marriage: Procedure"; W. Cal. Sum., 11 "Husband and Wife" §74.

Chapter 2
Procedural Rules

Rule 5.100.   Designation of parties

In proceedings filed under the Family Code, except for local child support agency actions, the party initiating the proceeding is the petitioner, and the other party is the respondent. In local child support agency actions, the responding party is the defendant and the parent who is not the defendant is referred to as the "Other Parent." Every other proceeding must be prosecuted and defended in the names of the real parties in interest.

Rule 5.100 amended and renumbered effective January 1, 2003; adopted as rule 1210 effective January 1, 1970; previously amended effective January 1, 1999.

Ref.: Cal. Fms Pl. & Pr., Ch. 221, "Dissolution of Marriage: Procedure"; W. Cal. Sum., 11 "Husband and Wife" §76.

Rule 5.102.   Parties to proceeding

(a) Except as provided in (c) or in rules 5.150 through 5.160, the only persons permitted to be parties to a proceeding for dissolution, legal separation, or nullity of marriage are the husband and wife.

(Subd (a) amended effective January 1, 2005; previously amended effective January 1, 1977, January 1, 1999, and January 1, 2003.)

(b) Except as provided in (c) or in rules 5.150 through 5.160, the only persons permitted to be parties to a proceeding for dissolution, legal separation, or nullity of domestic partnership are the domestic partners.

(Subd (b) adopted effective January 1, 2005.)

(c) In a nullity proceeding commenced by a person specified in Family Code section 2211, other than a proceeding commenced by or on behalf of the husband or wife in a marriage or one of the domestic partners in a domestic partnership, the person initiating the proceeding

is a party and the caption on all papers must be suitably modified to reflect that fact.

(Subd (c) amended and relettered effective January 1, 2005; adopted as subd (b) effective January 1, 1970; previously amended effective January 1, 1994, and January 1, 2003.)

Rule 5.102 amended effective January 1, 2005; adopted as rule 1211 effective January 1, 1970; previously amended effective January 1, 1977, January 1, 1994, and January 1, 1999; amended and renumbered effective January 1, 2003.

Ref.: Cal. Fms Pl. & Pr., Ch. 221, "Dissolution of Marriage: Procedure"; W. Cal. Sum., 11 "Husband and Wife" §76.

Rule 5.104.   Other causes of action

Neither party to the proceeding may assert against the other party or any other person any cause of action or claim for relief other than for the relief provided in these rules, Family Code sections 17400, 17402, and 17404, or other sections of the Family Code.

Rule 5.104 amended and renumbered effective January 1, 2003; adopted as rule 1212 effective January 1, 1970; previously amended effective January 1, 1994, and January 1, 1999.

Ref.: Cal. Fms Pl. & Pr., Ch. 221, "Dissolution of Marriage: Procedure," Ch. 387, "Nonmarital Cohabitation"; W. Cal. Sum., 11 "Husband and Wife" §82.

Rule 5.106.   Injunctive relief and reservation of jurisdiction

(a) Upon application as set out in rule 5.118, the court may grant injunctive or other relief against or for the following persons to protect the rights of either or both parties to the proceeding under the Family Code:

(1) A person who has or claims an interest in the controversy;

(2) A person who but for rule 5.102 would be a necessary party to a complete adjudication of the controversy; or

(3) A person who is acting as a trustee, agent, custodian, or similar fiduciary with respect to any property subject to disposition by the court in the proceeding, or other matter subject to the jurisdiction of the court in the proceeding.

(Subd (a) amended and relettered effective January 1, 2003.)

(b) If the court is unable to resolve the issue in the proceeding under the Family Code, the court may reserve jurisdiction over the particular issue until such time as the rights of such person and the parties to the proceeding under the Family Code have been adjudicated in a separate action or proceeding.

(Subd (b) amended effective January 1, 2007; previously amended and relettered effective January 1, 2003.)

Rule 5.106 amended effective January 1, 2007; adopted as rule 1213 effective January 1, 1970; previously amended effective January 1, 1994; amended and renumbered effective January 1, 2003.

Ref.: Cal. Fms Pl. & Pr., Ch. 221, "Dissolution of Marriage: Procedure," Ch. 222, "Dissolution of Marriage: Property Division and Valuation," Ch. 258, "Family Law Enforcement: General Enforcement Principles and Remedies."

Rule 5.108.   Pleadings

(a) The forms of pleading and the rules by which the sufficiency of pleadings is to be determined are solely those prescribed in these rules. Demurrers must not be used.

(Subd (a) amended effective January 1, 2003.)

(b) Amendments to pleadings, amended pleadings, and supplemental pleadings may be served and filed in conformity with the provisions of law applicable to such matters in civil actions generally, but the petitioner is not required to file a reply if the respondent has filed a response. If both parties have filed initial pleadings (petition and response), there may be no default entered on an amended pleading of either party.

(Subd (b) amended effective January 1, 2007; adopted as subd (d) effective January 1, 1970; previously amended and relettered effective January 1, 2003.)

Rule 5.108 amended effective January 1, 2007; adopted as rule 1215 effective January 1, 1970; previously amended effective January 1, 1999; amended and renumbered effective January 1, 2003.

Ref.: Cal. Fms Pl. & Pr., Ch. 21, "Amended and Supplemental Pleadings," Ch. 25, "Annulment (Nullity) of Marriage and Related Spousal Rights," Ch. 206, "Demurrers and Motions for Judgment on the Pleadings," Ch. 221, "Dissolution of Marriage: Procedure," Ch. 222, "Dissolution of Marriage: Property Division and Valuation," Ch. 412, "Paternity"; MB Prac. Guide: Cal. Pretrial Proc., §11.07[3][c]; W. Cal. Sum., 11 "Husband and Wife" §§82, 84.

Rule 5.110. Summons; restraining order

(a) Issuing the summons; form

Except for support proceedings initiated by a local child support agency, the procedure for issuance of summons in the proceeding is that applicable to civil actions generally. The clerk must not return the original summons, but must maintain it in the file.

(Subd (a) amended effective January 1, 2003; previously amended effective January 1, 1999, and January 1, 2001.)

(b) Standard family law restraining order; handling by clerk

Notwithstanding Family Code section 233, a summons (form FL-110 or FL-210) with the standard family law restraining orders must be issued and filed in the same manner as a summons in a civil action and must be served and enforced in the manner prescribed for any other restraining order. If service is by publication, the publication need not include the restraining orders.

(Subd (b) amended effective January 1, 2007; adopted as subd (c) effective July 1, 1990; previously amended effective January 1, 1994, and January 1, 1999; previously amended and relettered effective January 1, 2003.)

(c) Individual restraining order

On application of a party and as provided in the Family Code, a court may issue any individual restraining order that appears to be reasonable or necessary, including those restraining orders included in the standard family law restraining orders. Individual orders supersede the standard family law restraining orders on the Family Law and Uniform Parentage Act summons.

(Subd (c) amended and relettered effective January 1, 2003; adopted as subd (d) effective July 1, 1990; previously amended effective January 1, 1994, and January 1, 1999.)

Rule 5.110 amended effective January 1, 2007; adopted as rule 1216 effective January 1, 1970; previously amended effective July 1, 1990, January 1, 1994, January 1, 1999, and January 1, 2001; previously amended and renumbered effective January 1, 2003.

Ref.: Cal. Fms Pl. & Pr., Ch. 25, "Annulment (Nullity) of Marriage and Related Spousal Rights," Ch. 221, "Dissolution of Marriage: Procedure," Ch. 222, "Dissolution of Marriage: Property Division and Valuation," Ch. 259, "Family Law Enforcement: Special Remedies for Support Enforcement"; W. Cal. Sum., 11 "Husband and Wife" §75.

Rule 5.112. Continuing jurisdiction

The court has jurisdiction of the parties and control of all subsequent proceedings from the time of service of the summons and a copy of the petition. A general appearance of the respondent is equivalent to personal service within this state of the summons and a copy of the petition upon him or her.

Rule 5.112 amended and renumbered effective January 1, 2003; adopted as rule 1217 effective January 1, 1970.

Ref.: Cal. Fms Pl. & Pr., Ch. 221, "Dissolution of Marriage: Procedure."

Rule 5.114. Alternative relief

A party seeking alternative relief must so indicate in the petition or response.

Rule 5.114 amended and renumbered effective January 1, 2003; adopted as rule 1221 effective January 1, 1970.

Ref.: Cal. Fms Pl. & Pr., Ch. 25, "Annulment (Nullity) of Marriage and Related Spousal Rights," Ch. 220, "Dissolution of Marriage: Master Procedural Guide," Ch. 221, "Dissolution of Marriage: Procedure"; W. Cal. Sum., 11 "Husband and Wife" §§83, 84.

Rule 5.116. Stipulation for judgment

(a) A stipulation for judgment (which must be attached to form FL-180 or form FL-250) may be submitted to the court for signature at the time of the hearing on the merits and must contain the exact terms of any judgment proposed to be entered in the case. At the end, immediately above the space reserved for the judge's signature, the stipulation for judgment must contain the following:

The foregoing is agreed to by

_____   _____
(Petitioner)   (Respondent)

_____   _____
(Attorney for Petitioner)   (Attorney for Respondent)

(Subd (a) amended and lettered effective January 1, 2003.)

(b) A stipulation for judgment must include disposition of all matters subject to the court's jurisdiction for which a party seeks adjudication or an explicit reservation of jurisdiction over any matter not proposed for disposition at that time. A stipulation for judgment constitutes a written agreement between the parties as to all matters covered by the stipulation.

(Subd (b) amended and lettered effective January 1, 2003.)

Rule 5.116 amended and renumbered effective January 1, 2003; adopted as rule 1223 effective January 1, 1970; previously amended effective January 1, 1972.

Ref.: Cal. Fms Pl. & Pr., Ch. 221, "Dissolution of Marriage: Procedure," Ch. 222, "Dissolution of Marriage: Property Division and Valuation"; W. Cal. Sum., 11 "Husband and Wife" §112.

Rule 5.118. Application for court order

(a) No memorandum of points and authorities need be filed with an application for a court order unless required by the court on a case-by-case basis.

(Subd (a) amended effective January 1, 2003; previously amended effective January 1, 1972, January 1, 1980, and January 1, 1999.)

(b) A completed *Income and Expense Declaration* (form FL-150) or *Financial Statement (Simplified)* (form FL-155), *Property Declaration* (form FL-160), and *Application for Order and Supporting Declaration* (form FL-310) must be attached to an application for an injunctive or other order when relevant to the relief requested.

(Subd (b) amended effective January 1, 2007; adopted effective January 1, 1972; previously amended effective July 1, 1977, January 1, 1980, January 1, 1999, and January 1, 2003.)

(c) A copy of the *Application for Order and Supporting Declaration* with all attachments and a blank copy of the *Responsive Declaration* (form FL-320) must be served on the person against whom relief is requested. The original application and order must be retained in the court file.

(Subd (c) amended effective January 1, 2007; adopted as part of subd (b) effective January 1, 1972; previously amended and relettered effective January 1, 2003.)

(d) If relief is sought by an *Order to Show Cause*, a copy of the order endorsed by the clerk must be served.

(Subd (d) adopted effective January 1, 2003.)

(e) Blank copies of the *Income and Expense Declaration* or *Financial Statement (Simplified)* and the *Property Declaration* must be served when completed declarations are among the papers required to be served.

(Subd (e) amended and lettered effective January 1, 2003; adopted as part of subd (b) effective January 1, 1972.)

(f) The court may grant or deny the relief solely on the basis of the application and responses and any accompanying memorandum of points and authorities.

(Subd (f) adopted effective January 1, 2004.)

Rule 5.118 amended effective January 1, 2007; adopted as rule 1225 effective January 1, 1970; previously amended effective January 1, 1972, July 1, 1977, January 1, 1980, January 1, 1999, and January 1, 2004; previously amended and renumbered effective January 1, 2003.

Ref.: Cal. Fms Pl. & Pr., Ch. 221, "Dissolution of Marriage: Procedure," Ch. 222, "Dissolution of Marriage: Property Division and Valuation," Ch. 258, "Family Law Enforcement: General Enforcement Principles and Remedies," Ch. 259, "Family Law Enforcement: Special Remedies for Support Enforcement"; W. Cal. Sum., 11 "Husband and Wife" §§87, 197, 199, 200, 202, 207, 289, 11 "Community Property" §233.

Rule 5.120. Appearance

(a) Except as provided in Code of Civil Procedure section 418.10, a respondent or defendant is deemed to have appeared in a proceeding when he or she files:

(1) A response or answer;

(2) A notice of motion to strike, under section 435 of the Code of Civil Procedure;

(3) A notice of motion to transfer the proceeding under section 395 of the Code of Civil Procedure; or

(4) A written notice of his or her appearance.

(Subd (a) amended effective January 1, 2006; amended and lettered effective January 1, 2003.)

(b) After appearance, the respondent or defendant or his or her attorney is entitled to notice of all subsequent proceedings of which notice is required to be given by these rules or in civil actions generally.

(Subd (b) amended and lettered effective January 1, 2003.)

(c) Where a respondent or defendant has not appeared, notice of subsequent proceedings need not be given to the respondent or defendant except as provided in these rules.

(Subd (c) amended and lettered effective January 1, 2003.)

Rule 5.120 amended effective January 1, 2006; adopted as rule 1236 effective January 1, 1970; previously amended and renumbered effective January 1, 2003; previously amended effective January 1, 1972, January 1, 1999, and January 1, 2004.

Ref.: Cal. Fms Pl. & Pr., Ch. 220, "Dissolution of Marriage: Master Procedural Guide," Ch. 221, "Dissolution of Marriage: Procedure," Ch. 225, "Dissolution of Marriage: Spousal Support," Ch. 258, "Family Law Enforcement: General Enforcement Principles and Remedies," Ch. 259, "Family Law Enforcement: Special Remedies for Support Enforcement," Ch. 323, "Jurisdiction: Personal Jurisdiction, Inconvenient Forum, and Appearances."

Rule 5.121. Motion to quash proceeding or responsive relief

(a) Within the time permitted to file a response, the respondent may move to quash the proceeding, in whole or in part, for any of the following reasons:

(1) Lack of legal capacity to sue;

(2) Prior judgment or another action pending between the same parties for the same cause;

(3) Failure to meet the residence requirement of Family Code section 2320; or

(4) Statute of limitations in Family Code section 2211.

(Subd (a) amended effective January 1, 2006.)

(b) The motion to quash must be served in compliance with Code of Civil Procedure section 1005(b). If the respondent files a notice of motion to quash, no default may be entered, and the time to file a response will be extended until 15 days after service of the court's order.

(Subd (b) amended effective January 1, 2006.)

(c) Within 15 days after the filing of the response, the petitioner may move to quash, in whole or in part, any request for affirmative relief in the response for the grounds set forth in (a).

(d) The parties are deemed to have waived the grounds set forth in (a) if they do not file a motion to quash within the time frame set forth.

(e) When a motion to quash is granted, the court may grant leave to amend the petition or response and set a date for filing the amended pleadings. The court may also dismiss the action without leave to amend. The action may also be dismissed if the motion has been sustained with leave to amend and the amendment is not made within the time permitted by the court.

Rule 5.121 amended effective January 1, 2006; adopted effective January 1, 2004.

Ref.: Cal. Fms Pl. & Pr., Ch. 220, "Dissolution of Marriage: Master Procedural Guide," Ch. 221, "Dissolution of Marriage: Procedure."

Rule 5.122. Default

(a) Upon proper application of the petitioner, the clerk must enter the respondent's default if the respondent or defendant fails within the time permitted to:

(1) Make an appearance as stated in rule 5.120;

(2) File a notice of motion to quash service of summons under section 418.10 of the Code of Civil Procedure; or

(3) File a petition for writ of mandate under section 418.10 of the Code of Civil Procedure.

(Subd (a) amended effective January 1, 2007; previously amended and lettered effective January 1, 2003.)

(b) The petitioner may apply to the court for the relief sought in the petition at the time default is entered. The court must require proof to be made of the facts stated in the petition and may enter its judgment accordingly. The court may permit the use of a completed *Income and Expense Declaration* (form FL-155) or *Financial Statement (Simplified)* (form FL-155) and *Property Declaration* (form FL-160) as to all or any part of the proof required or permitted to be offered on any issue as to which they are relevant.

(Subd (b) amended and lettered effective January 1, 2003.)

Rule 5.122 amended effective January 1, 2007; adopted as rule 1237 effective January 1, 1970; previously amended effective January 1, 1972, and January 1, 1980; previously amended and renumbered effective January 1, 2003.

Ref.: Cal. Fms Pl. & Pr., Ch. 221, "Dissolution of Marriage: Procedure"; W. Cal. Sum., 11 "Husband and Wife" §§101, 102.

Rule 5.124.   Request for default

(a) No default may be entered in any proceeding unless a request has been completed in full on a *Request to Enter Default* (form FL-165) and filed by the petitioner. However, an *Income and Expense Declaration* (form FL-150) or *Financial Statement (Simplified)* (form FL-155) are not required if the petition contains no demand for support, costs, or attorney's fees. A *Property Declaration* (form FL-160) is not required if the petition contains no demand for property.

(Subd (a) amended and lettered effective January 1, 2003.)

(b) For the purpose of completing the declaration of mailing, unless service was by publication and the address of respondent is unknown, it is not sufficient to state that the address of the party to whom notice is given is unknown or unavailable.

(Subd (b) lettered effective January 1, 2003.)

Rule 5.124 amended and renumbered effective January 1, 2003; adopted as rule 1240 effective January 1, 1970; previously amended effective January 1, 1979, and January 1, 1980.

Ref.: Cal. Fms Pl. & Pr., Ch. 221, "Dissolution of Marriage: Procedure"; W. Cal. Sum., 11 "Husband and Wife" §§87, 101.

Rule 5.126.   Alternate date of valuation

(a) Notice of motion

An *Application for Separate Trial* (form FL-315) must be used to provide the notice required by Family Code section 2552(b).

(Subd (a) amended effective July 1, 2003; previously amended effective January 1, 2003.)

(b) Declaration accompanying notice

Form FL-315 must be accompanied by a declaration stating the following:

(1) The proposed alternate valuation date;

(2) Whether the proposed alternate valuation date applies to all or only a portion of the assets and, if the motion is directed to only a portion of the assets, the declaration must separately identify each such asset; and

(3) The reasons supporting the alternate valuation date.

(Subd (b) amended effective July 1, 2003; previously amended effective January 1, 2003.)

Rule 5.126 amended effective July 1, 2003; adopted as rule 1242.5 effective July 1, 1995; previously amended and renumbered effective January 1, 2003.

Ref.: Cal. Fms Pl. & Pr., Ch. 222, "Dissolution of Marriage: Property Division and Valuation"; W. Cal. Sum., 11 "Community Property" §193.

Rule 5.128.   Financial declaration

(a) A current *Income and Expense Declaration* (form FL-150) or a current *Financial Statement (Simplified)* (form FL-155), when such form is appropriate, and a current *Property Declaration* (form FL-160) must be served and filed by any party appearing at any hearing at which the court is to determine an issue as to which such declarations would be relevant. "Current" is defined as being completed within the past three months providing no facts have changed. Those forms must be sufficiently completed to allow determination of the issue.

(Subd (a) amended and lettered effective January 1, 2003.)

(b) When a party is represented by counsel and attorney's fees are requested by either party, the section on the *Income and Expense Declaration* pertaining to the amount in savings, credit union, certificates of deposit, and money market accounts must be fully completed, as well as the section pertaining to the amount of attorney's fees incurred, currently owed, and the source of money used to pay such fees.

(Subd (b) amended and lettered effective January 1, 2003.)

(c) A *Financial Statement (Simplified)* is not appropriate for use in proceedings to determine or modify spousal support or to determine attorney's fees.

(Subd (c) lettered effective January 1, 2003.)

Rule 5.128 amended and renumbered effective January 1, 2003; adopted as rule 1243 effective January 1, 1970; previously amended effective January 1, 1972, January 1, 1980, July 1, 1985, and January 1, 1999.

Ref.: Cal. Fms Pl. & Pr., Ch. 25, "Annulment (Nullity) of Marriage and Related Spousal Rights," Ch. 220, "Dissolution of Marriage: Master Procedural Guide," Ch. 221, "Dissolution of Marriage: Procedure," Ch. 225, "Dissolution of Marriage: Spousal Support," Ch. 258, "Family Law Enforcement: General Enforcement Principles and Remedies," Ch. 259, "Family Law Enforcement: Special Remedies for Support Enforcement"; W. Cal. Sum., 11 "Community Property" §233, 11 "Husband and Wife" §§199, 207.

Rule 5.130.   Summary dissolution

(a) Declaration of disclosure

For the purposes of a proceeding for summary dissolution under chapter 5 (beginning with section 2400) of part 3 of division 6 of the Family Code, attachment to the petition of completed worksheet pages listing separate and community property and obligations as well as an *Income and Expense Declaration* (form FL-150) or *Financial Statement (Simplified)* (form FL-155) constitutes compliance with the disclosure requirements of chapter 9 (beginning with section 2100) of part 1 of division 6 of the Family Code.

(Subd (a) amended and relettered effective January 1, 2003; adopted as subd (b) effective January 1, 1993; previously amended effective January 1, 1994.)

(b) Fee for filing

The fee for filing a *Joint Petition for Summary Dissolution of Marriage* (form FL-800) is the same as that charged for filing a *Petition—Marriage* (form FL-100). No additional fee may be charged for the filing of any form prescribed for use in a summary dissolution proceeding, except as required by Government Code section 26859.

(Subd (b) amended effective January 1, 2007; adopted as subd (b) effective January 1, 1979; previously relettered as subd (c) effective January 1, 1993; previously amended and relettered effective January 1, 2003.)

Rule 5.130 amended effective January 1, 2007; adopted as rule 1271 effective January 1, 1979; previously amended effective January 1, 1993, and January 1, 1994; previously amended and renumbered effective January 1, 2003.

Ref.: W. Cal. Sum., 11 "Community Property" §234, 11 "Husband and Wife" §126.

Rule 5.134.   Notice of entry of judgment

(a) Notwithstanding Code of Civil Procedure section 664.5, the clerk must give notice of entry of judgment, using *Notice of Entry of Judgment* (form FL-190), to the attorney for each party or to the party if self-represented, of the following:

(1) A judgment of legal separation;

(2) A judgment of dissolution;

(3) A judgment of nullity;

(4) A judgment establishing parental relationship (on form FL-190); or

(5) A judgment regarding custody or support.

(Subd (a) amended effective January 1, 2007; previously amended and lettered effective January 1, 2003; previously amended effective January 1, 2007.)

(b) This rule applies to local child support agency proceedings except that the notice of entry of judgment must be on *Notice of Entry of Judgment and Proof of Service by Mail* (form FL-635).

(Subd (b) amended effective January 1, 2007; previously amended and lettered effective January 1, 2003.)

Rule 5.134 amended effective January 1, 2007; adopted as rule 1247 effective January 1, 1970; previously amended effective January 1, 1972, January 1, 1982, and January 1, 1999; previously amended and renumbered effective January 1, 2003; previously amended effective January 1, 2007.

Ref.: Cal. Fms Pl. & Pr., Ch. 221, "Dissolution of Marriage: Procedure"; W. Cal. Sum., 11 "Husband and Wife" §110.

Rule 5.136.   Completion of notice of entry of judgment

(a) Required attachments

Every person who submits a judgment for signature by the court must submit:

(1) Stamped envelopes addressed to the parties; and

(2) An original and at least two additional copies of the *Notice of Entry of Judgment* (form FL-190).

(Subd (a) amended and lettered effective January 1, 2003.)

(b) Fully completed

Form FL-190 must be fully completed except for the designation of the date entered, the date of mailing, and signatures. It must specify in the certificate of mailing the place where notices have been given to the other party.

(Subd (b) amended and lettered effective January 1, 2003.)

(c) Address of respondent or defendant

If there has been no appearance by the other party, the address stated in the affidavit of mailing in part 3 of the *Request to Enter Default* (form FL-165) must be the party's last known address and must be used for mailing form FL-190 to that party. In support proceedings initiated by the local child support agency, an envelope addressed to the child support agency need not be submitted. If service was by publication and the address of respondent or defendant is unknown, those facts must be stated in place of the required address.

(Subd (c) amended effective January 1, 2007; previously amended and lettered effective January 1, 2003.)

(d) Consequences of failure to comply

Failure to complete the form or to submit the envelopes is cause for refusal to sign the judgment until compliance with the requirements of this rule.

(Subd (d) amended and lettered effective January 1, 2003.)

(e) Application to local child support agencies

This rule applies to local child support agency proceedings filed under the Family Code except that:

(1) The local child support agency must use form *Notice of Entry of Judgment and Proof of Service by Mail* (form FL-635);

(2) The local child support agency may specify in the certificate of mailing that the address where the *Notice of Entry of Judgment* (form FL-190) was mailed is on file with the local child support agency; and

(3) An envelope addressed to the local child support agency need not be submitted.

(Subd (e) amended effective January 1, 2007; previously amended and lettered effective January 1, 2003.)

Rule 5.136 amended effective January 1, 2007; adopted as rule 1248 effective January 1, 1970; previously amended effective January 1, 1972, January 1, 1980, July 1, 1982, and January 1, 1999; previously amended and renumbered effective January 1, 2003.

Ref.: Cal. Fms Pl. & Pr., Ch. 25, "Annulment (Nullity) of Marriage and Related Spousal Rights," Ch. 221, "Dissolution of Marriage: Procedure"; W. Cal. Sum., 11 "Husband and Wife" §110.

Rule 5.140.   Implied procedures

In the exercise of the court's jurisdiction under the Family Code, if the course of proceeding is not specifically indicated by statute or these rules, any suitable process or mode of proceeding may be adopted by the court that is consistent with the spirit of the Family Code and these rules.

Rule 5.140 amended and renumbered effective January 1, 2003; adopted as rule 1249 effective January 1, 1970; previously amended effective January 1, 1994.

Ref.: Cal. Fms Pl. & Pr., Ch. 220, "Dissolution of Marriage: Master Procedural Guide," Ch. 221, "Dissolution of Marriage: Procedure."

Chapter 3
Joinder of Parties

Rule 5.150. Joinder of persons claiming interest

Notwithstanding any other rule in this division, a person who claims or controls an interest subject to disposition in the proceeding may be joined as a party to the proceeding only as provided in this chapter. Except as otherwise provided in this chapter, all provisions of law relating to joinder of parties in civil actions generally apply to the joinder of a person as a party to the proceeding.

Rule 5.150 renumbered effective January 1, 2003; adopted as rule 1250 effective November 23, 1970; amended effective January 1, 1978.

Ref.: Cal. Fms Pl. & Pr., Ch. 221, "Dissolution of Marriage: Procedure," Ch. 222, "Dissolution of Marriage: Property Division and Valuation"; W. Cal. Sum., 11 "Community Property" §239, 11 "Husband and Wife" §78.

Rule 5.152. "Claimant" defined

As used in this chapter, "claimant" means a person joined or sought or seeking to be joined as a party to the proceeding.

Rule 5.152 renumbered effective January 1, 2003; adopted as rule 1251 effective November 23, 1970; amended effective January 1, 1972.

Ref.: Cal. Fms Pl. & Pr., Ch. 221, "Dissolution of Marriage: Procedure."

Rule 5.154. Persons who may seek joinder

(a) The petitioner or the respondent may apply to the court for an order joining a person as a party to the proceeding who has or claims custody or physical control of any of the minor children subject to the action, or visitation rights with respect to such children, or who has in his or her possession or control or claims to own any property subject to the jurisdiction of the court in the proceeding.

(Subd (a) amended effective January 1, 2006; previously amended effective January 1, 2003.)

(b) A person who has or claims custody or physical control of any of the minor children subject to the action, or visitation rights with respect to such children, may apply to the court for an order joining himself or herself as a party to the proceeding.

(Subd (b) amended effective January 1, 2007; previously amended effective January 1, 2003, and January 1, 2006.)

(c) A person served with an order temporarily restraining the use of property that is in his or her possession or control or that he or she claims to own, or affecting the custody of minor children subject to the action, or visitation rights with respect to such children, may apply to the court for an order joining himself or herself as a party to the proceeding.

(Subd (c) amended effective January 1, 2006; previously amended effective January 1, 2003.)

Rule 5.154 amended effective January 1, 2007; adopted as rule 1252 effective November 23, 1970; amended and renumbered effective January 1, 2003; previously amended effective July 1, 1975, and January 1, 2006.

Ref.: Cal. Fms Pl. & Pr., Ch. 220, "Dissolution of Marriage: Master Procedural Guide," Ch. 221, "Dissolution of Marriage: Procedure," Ch. 222, "Dissolution of Marriage: Property Division and Valuation," Ch. 223, "Dissolution of Marriage: Child Cus-

tody," Ch. 280, "Guardianship and Conservatorship: Appointment of Guardians," Ch. 394, "Parent and Child"; W. Cal. Sum., 10 "Parent and Child" §268, 11 "Community Property" §239, 11 "Husband and Wife" §78.

Rule 5.156. Form of joinder application

(a) All applications for joinder other than for an employee pension benefit plan must be made by serving and filing form a *Notice of Motion and Declaration for Joinder* (form FL-371). The hearing date must be less than 30 days from the date of filing the notice. The completed form must state with particularity the claimant's interest in the proceeding and the relief sought by the applicant, and it must be accompanied by an appropriate pleading setting forth the claim as if it were asserted in a separate action or proceeding.

(Subd (a) amended effective January 1, 2007; previously amended effective January 1, 1972, January 1, 1978, January 1, 1979, January 1, 1994, January 1, 2001, and January 1, 2003.)

(b) A blank copy of *Responsive Declaration to Motion for Joinder and Consent Order for Joinder* (form FL-373) must be served with the *Notice of Motion* and accompanying pleading.

(Subd (b) amended effective January 1, 2007; adopted effective January 1, 1972; previously amended effective January 1, 1978, January 1, 1979, July 1, 1985, January 1, 2001, and effective January 1, 2003.)

Rule 5.156 amended effective January 1, 2007; adopted as rule 1253 effective November 23, 1970; previously amended effective January 1, 1972, January 1, 1978, January 1, 1979, July 1, 1985, January 1, 1994, and January 1, 2001; previously amended and renumbered effective January 1, 2003.

Ref.: Cal. Fms Pl. & Pr., Ch. 221, "Dissolution of Marriage: Procedure," Ch. 222, "Dissolution of Marriage: Property Division and Valuation"; W. Cal. Sum., 11 "Husband and Wife" §87.

Rule 5.158. Determination on joinder

(a) Mandatory joinder

The court must order joined as a party to the proceeding any person the court discovers has physical custody or claims custody or visitation rights with respect to any minor child of the marriage.

(Subd (a) amended effective January 1, 2003.)

(b) Permissive joinder

The court may order that a person be joined as a party to the proceeding if the court finds that it would be appropriate to determine the particular issue in the proceeding and that the person to be joined as a party is either indispensable to a determination of that issue or necessary to the enforcement of any judgment rendered on that issue.

In determining whether it is appropriate to determine the particular issue in the proceeding, the court must consider its effect upon the proceeding, including:

(1) Whether the determination of that issue will unduly delay the disposition of the proceeding;

(2) Whether other parties would need to be joined to render an effective judgment between the parties;

(3) Whether the determination of that issue will confuse other issues in the proceeding; and

(4) Whether the joinder of a party to determine the particular issue will complicate, delay, or otherwise interfere with the effective disposition of the proceeding.

(Subd (b) amended and lettered effective January 1, 2003; adopted as part of subd (a) effective November 23, 1970.)

(c) Procedure upon joinder

If the court orders that a person be joined as a party to the proceeding under subdivision (a) of rule 5.154, the court must direct that a summons be issued on *Summons (Joinder)* (form FL-375) and that the claimant be served with a copy of *Notice of Motion and Declaration for Joinder* (form FL-371), the pleading attached thereto, the order of joinder, and the summons. The claimant has 30 days after service within which to file an appropriate response.

(Subd (c) amended effective January 1, 2007; adopted as subd (b) effective November 23, 1970; previously amended and relettered effective January 1, 2003; previously amended effective July 1, 2003.)

Rule 5.158 amended effective January 1, 2007; adopted as rule 1254 effective November 23, 1970; previously amended and renumbered effective January 1, 2003; previously amended effective July 1, 1997, and July 1, 2003.

Ref.: Cal. Fms Pl. & Pr., Ch. 220, "Dissolution of Marriage: Master Procedural Guide," Ch. 221, "Dissolution of Marriage: Procedure," Ch. 222, "Dissolution of Marriage: Property Division and Valuation"; W. Cal. Sum., 10 "Parent and Child" §268, 11 "Husband and Wife" §78.

Rule 5.160.   Pleading rules applicable

Except as otherwise provided in this chapter or by the court in which the proceeding is pending, the law applicable to civil actions generally governs all pleadings, motions, and other matters pertaining to that portion of the proceeding as to which a claimant has been joined as a party to the proceeding in the same manner as if a separate action or proceeding not subject to these rules had been filed.

Rule 5.160 amended and renumbered effective January 1, 2003; adopted as rule 1255 effective November 23, 1970.

Ref.: Cal. Fms Pl. & Pr., Ch. 221, "Dissolution of Marriage: Procedure"; W. Cal. Sum., 11 "Husband and Wife" §82.

Rule 5.162.   Joinder of employee pension benefit plan

(a) Every request for joinder of employee pension benefit plan and order and every pleading on joinder must be submitted on *Request for Joinder of Employee Benefit Plan and Order* (form FL-372) and *Pleading on Joinder— Employee Benefit Plan* (form FL-370).

(Subd (a) amended effective January 1, 2007; previously amended and lettered effective January 1, 2003.)

(b) Every summons issued on the joinder of employee pension benefit plan must be on *Summons (Joinder)* (form FL-375).

(Subd (b) amended effective January 1, 2007; previously amended and lettered effective January 1, 2003.)

(c) Every notice of appearance of employee pension benefit plan and responsive pleading file under Family Code section 2063(b) must be given on *Notice of Appearance and Response of Employee Benefit Plan* (form FL-374).

(Subd (c) amended effective January 1, 2007; previously amended and lettered effective January 1, 2003.)

Rule 5.162 amended effective January 1, 2007; adopted as rule 1256 effective January 1, 1979; previously amended effective January 1, 1994; previously amended and renumbered effective January 1, 2003.

Ref.: Cal. Fms Pl. & Pr., Ch. 220, "Dissolution of Marriage: Master Procedural Guide," Ch. 221, "Dissolution of Marriage: Procedure," Ch. 222, "Dissolution of Marriage: Property Division and Valuation"; W. Cal. Sum., 11 "Husband and Wife" §79.

Chapter 4
Bifurcation and Appeals

Rule 5.175. Bifurcation of issues
Rule 5.180. Interlocutory appeals

Rule 5.175.   Bifurcation of issues

(a) Bifurcation of issues

On noticed motion of a party, the stipulation of the parties, or its own motion, the court may bifurcate one or more issues to be tried separately before other issues are tried. The motion must be heard not later than the trial-setting conference.

(Subd (a) amended effective January 1, 2003; previously amended effective January 1, 1994.)

(b) Notice by clerk

The clerk must mail copies of the order deciding the bifurcated issue and any statement of decision under rule 232.5 to the parties within 10 days of their filing and must file a certificate of mailing.

(Subd (b) amended and lettered effective January 1, 2003; adopted as part of subd (a) effective July 1, 1989; previously amended effective January 1, 1994.)

(c) When to bifurcate

The court may try separately one or more issues before trial of the other issues if resolution of the bifurcated issue is likely to simplify the determination of the other issues. Issues that may be appropriate to try separately in advance include:

(1) Validity of a postnuptial or premarital agreement;

(2) Date of separation;

(3) Date to use for valuation of assets;

(4) Whether property is separate or community;

(5) How to apportion increase in value of a business; or

(6) Existence or value of business or professional goodwill.

(Subd (c) amended and relettered effective January 1, 2003; adopted as subd (b) effective July 1, 1989.)

Rule 5.175 amended and renumbered effective January 1, 2003; adopted as rule 1269 effective July 1, 1989; previously amended effective January 1, 1994.

Ref.: Cal. Fms Pl. & Pr., Ch. 220, "Dissolution of Marriage: Master Procedural Guide," Ch. 221, "Dissolution of Marriage: Procedure," Ch. 222, "Dissolution of Marriage: Property Division and Valuation"; W. Cal. Sum., 11 "Husband and Wife" §106.

Rule 5.180.   Interlocutory appeals

(a) Applicability

This rule does not apply to appeals from the court's termination of marital status as a separate issue, or to appeals from other orders that are separately appealable.

(Subd (a) amended effective January 1, 2003; previously amended effective January 1, 1994.)

(b) Certificate of probable cause for appeal

(1) The order deciding the bifurcated issue may include an order certifying that there is probable cause for immediate appellate review of the issue.

(2) If it was not in the order, within 10 days after the clerk mails the order deciding the bifurcated issue, a party may notice a motion asking the court to certify that there is probable cause for immediate appellate review of the order. The motion must be heard within 30 days after the order deciding the bifurcated issue is mailed.

(3) The clerk must promptly mail notice of the decision on the motion to the parties. If the motion is not determined within 40 days after mailing of the order on the bifurcated issue, it is deemed granted on the grounds stated in the motion.

(Subd (b) amended effective January 1, 2003; previously amended effective January 1, 2002.)

(c) Content and effect of certificate

(1) A certificate of probable cause must state, in general terms, the reason immediate appellate review is desirable, such as a statement that final resolution of the issue:

(A) Is likely to lead to settlement of the entire case;

(B) Will simplify remaining issues;

(C) Will conserve the courts' resources; or

(D) Will benefit the well-being of a child of the marriage or the parties.

(2) If a certificate is granted, trial of the remaining issues may be stayed. If trial of the remaining issues is stayed, unless otherwise ordered by the trial court on noticed motion, further discovery must be stayed while the certification is pending. These stays terminate upon the expiration of time for filing a motion to appeal if none is filed, or upon the Court of Appeal denying all motions to appeal, or upon the Court of Appeal decision becoming final.

(Subd (c) amended effective January 1, 2003; previously amended effective January 1, 2002.)

(d) Motion to appeal

(1) If the certificate is granted, a party may, within 15 days after the mailing of the notice of the order granting it, serve and file in the Court of Appeal a motion to appeal the decision on the bifurcated issue. On ex parte application served and filed within 15 days, the Court of Appeal or the trial court may extend the time for filing the motion to appeal by not more than an additional 20 days.

(2) The motion must contain:

(A) A brief statement of the facts necessary to an understanding of the issue;

(B) A statement of the issue; and

(C) A statement of why, in the context of the case, an immediate appeal is desirable.

(3) The motion must include or have attached:

(A) A copy of the decision of the trial court on the bifurcated issue;

(B) Any statement of decision;

(C) The certification of the appeal; and

(D) A sufficient partial record to enable the Court of Appeal to determine whether to grant the motion.

(4) A summary of evidence and oral proceedings, if relevant, supported by a declaration of counsel may be used when a transcript is not available.

(5) The motion must be accompanied by the filing fee for an appeal under rule 8.100(c) and Government Code sections 68926 and 68926.1.

(6) A copy of the motion must be served on the trial court.

(Subd (d) amended effective January 1, 2007; previously amended effective January 1, 2002, and January 1, 2003.)

(e) Proceedings to determine motion

(1) Within 10 days after service of the motion, an adverse party may serve and file an opposition to it.

(2) The motion to appeal and any opposition will be submitted without oral argument, unless otherwise ordered.

(3) The motion to appeal is deemed granted unless it is denied within 30 days from the date of filing the opposition or the last document requested by the court, whichever is later.

(4) Denial of a motion to appeal is final forthwith and is not subject to rehearing. A party aggrieved by the denial of the motion may petition for review by the Supreme Court.

(Subd (e) amended effective January 1, 2007; previously amended effective January 1, 2002, and January 1, 2003.)

(f) Proceedings if motion to appeal is granted

(1) If the motion to appeal is granted, the moving party is deemed an appellant, and the rules governing other civil appeals apply except as provided in this rule.

(2) The partial record filed with the motion will be considered the record for the appeal unless, within 10 days from the date notice of the grant of the motion is mailed, a party notifies the Court of Appeal of additional portions of the record that are needed for a full consideration of the appeal.

(3) If a party notifies the court of the need for an additional record, the additional material must be secured from the trial court by augmentation under rule 8.155, unless it appears to the Court of Appeal that some of the material is not needed.

(4) Briefs must be filed under a schedule set for the matter by the Court of Appeal.

(Subd (f) amended effective January 1, 2007; previously amended effective January 1, 2002, and January 1, 2003.)

(g) Review by writ or appeal

The trial court's denial of a certification motion under (b) does not preclude review of the decision on the bifurcated issue by extraordinary writ.

(Subd (g) amended effective January 1, 2003; previously amended effective January 1, 2002.)

(h) Review by appeal

None of the following precludes review of the decision on the bifurcated issue upon appeal of the final judgment:

(1) A party's failure to move for certification under (b) for immediate appeal;

(2) The trial court's denial of a certification motion under (b) for immediate appeal;

(3) A party's failure to move to appeal under (d); and

(4) The Court of Appeals denial of a motion to appeal under (d).

Rule 5.180 amended effective January 1, 2007; adopted as rule 1269.5 effective July 1, 1989; previously amended effective January 1, 1994, and January 1, 2002; amended and renumbered effective January 1, 2003.

Ref.: Cal. Fms Pl. & Pr., Ch. 220, "Dissolution of Marriage: Master Procedural Guide"; W. Cal. Sum., 11 "Husband and Wife" §123.

Chapter 5
Child Custody

Rule 5.210. Court-connected child custody mediation

(a) Authority

This rule of court is adopted under article VI, section 6 of the California Constitution and Family Code sections 211, 3160, and 3162(a).

(b) Purpose

This rule sets forth standards of practice and administration for court-connected child custody mediation services that are consistent with the requirements of Family Code section 3161.

(c) Definitions

(1) "Best interest of the child" is defined in Family Code section 3011.

(2) "Parenting plan" is a plan describing how parents or other appropriate parties will share and divide their decision making and caretaking responsibilities to protect the health, safety, welfare, and best interest of each child who is a subject of the proceedings.

(d) Responsibility for mediation services

(1) Each court must ensure that:

(A) Mediators are impartial, competent, and uphold the standards of practice contained in this rule of court.

(B) Mediation services and case management procedures implement state law and allow sufficient time for parties to receive orientation, participate fully in mediation, and develop a comprehensive parenting plan without unduly compromising each party's right to due process and a timely resolution of the issues.

(C) Mediation services demonstrate accountability by:

(i) Providing for acceptance of and response to complaints about a mediator's performance;

(ii) Participating in statewide data collection efforts; and

(iii) Disclosing the use of interns to provide mediation services.

(D) The mediation program uses a detailed intake process that screens for, and informs the mediator about, any restraining orders or safety-related issues affecting any party or child named in the proceedings to allow compliance with relevant law or court rules before mediation begins.

(E) Whenever possible, mediation is available from bilingual mediators or other interpreter services that meet the requirements of Evidence Code sections 754(f) and 755(a) and section 18 of the California Standards of Judicial Administration.

(F) Mediation services protect, in accordance with existing law, party confidentiality in:

(i) Storage and disposal of records and any personal information accumulated during the mediation process;

(ii) Interagency coordination or cooperation regarding a particular family or case; and

(iii) Management of child abuse reports and related documents.

(G) Mediation services provide a written description of limitations on the confidentiality of the process.

(H) Within one year of the adoption of this rule, the court adopts a local court rule regarding ex parte communications.

(2) Each court-connected mediator must:

(A) Maintain an overriding concern to integrate the child's best interest within the family context;

(B) Inform the parties and any counsel for a minor child if the mediator will make a recommendation to the court as provided under Family Code section 3184; and

(C) Use reasonable efforts and consider safety issues to:

(i) Facilitate the family's transition and reduce acrimony by helping the parties improve their communication skills, focus on the child's needs and areas of stability, identify the family's strengths, and locate counseling or other services;

(ii) Develop a comprehensive parenting agreement that addresses each child's current and future developmental needs; and

(iii) Control for potential power imbalances between the parties during mediation.

(Subd (d) amended effective January 1, 2007; previously amended effective January 1, 2002, and January 1, 2003.)

(e) Mediation process

All court-connected mediation processes must be conducted in accordance with state law and include:

(1) Review of the intake form and court file, if available, before the start of mediation;

(2) Oral or written orientation or parent education that facilitates the parties' informed and self-determined decision making about:

(A) The types of disputed issues generally discussed in mediation and the range of possible outcomes from the mediation process;

(B) The mediation process, including the mediator's role; the circumstances that may lead the mediator to make a particular recommendation to the court; limitations on the confidentiality of the process; and access to information communicated by the parties or included in the mediation file;

(C) How to make best use of information drawn from current research and professional experience to facilitate the mediation process, parties' communication, and co-parenting relationship; and

(D) How to address each child's current and future developmental needs;

191   FAMILY & JUVENILE RULES   Rule 5.210

Rules of Court

(3) Interviews with children at the mediator's discretion and consistent with Family Code section 3180(a). The mediator may interview the child alone or together with other interested parties, including stepparents, siblings, new or step-siblings, or other family members significant to the child. If interviewing a child, the mediator must:

(A) Inform the child in an age-appropriate way of the mediator's obligation to disclose suspected child abuse and neglect and the local policies concerning disclosure of the child's statements to the court; and

(B) With parental consent, coordinate interview and information exchange among agency or private professionals to reduce the number of interviews a child might experience;

(4) Assistance to the parties, without undue influence or personal bias, in developing a parenting plan that protects the health, safety, welfare, and best interest of the child and that optimizes the child's relationship with each party by including, as appropriate, provisions for supervised visitation in high-risk cases; designations for legal and physical custody; a description of each party's authority to make decisions that affect the child; language that minimizes legal, mental health, or other jargon; and a detailed schedule of the time a child is to spend with each party, including vacations, holidays, and special occasions, and times when the child's contact with a party may be interrupted;

(5) Extension of time to allow the parties to gather additional information if the mediator determines that such information will help the discussion proceed in a fair and orderly manner or facilitate an agreement;

(6) Suspension or discontinuance of mediation if allegations of child abuse or neglect are made until a designated agency performs an investigation and reports a case determination to the mediator;

(7) Termination of mediation if the mediator believes that he or she is unable to achieve a balanced discussion between the parties;

(8) Conclusion of mediation with:

(A) A written parenting plan summarizing the parties' agreement or mediator's recommendation that is given to counsel or the parties before the recommendation is presented to the court; and

(B) A written or oral description of any subsequent case management or court procedures for resolving one or more outstanding custody or visitation issues, including instructions for obtaining temporary orders;

(9) Return to mediation to resolve future custody or visitation disputes.

(Subd (e) amended effective January 1, 2007; previously amended effective January 1, 2003.)

(f) Training, continuing education, and experience requirements for mediator, mediation supervisor, and family court services director

As specified in Family Code sections 1815 and 1816:

(1) All mediators, mediation supervisors, and family court service directors must:

(A) Complete a minimum of 40 hours of custody and visitation mediation training within the first six months of initial employment as a court-connected mediator;

(B) Annually complete 8 hours of related continuing education programs, conferences, and workshops. This

requirement is in addition to the annual 4-hour domestic violence update training described in rule 5.215; and

(C) Participate in performance supervision and peer review.

(2) Each mediation supervisor and family court services director must complete at least 24 hours of additional training each calendar year. This requirement may be satisfied in part by the domestic violence training required by Family Code section 1816.

(Subd (f) amended effective January 1, 2005; previously amended effective January 1, 2003.)

(g) Education and training providers

Only education and training acquired from eligible providers meet the requirements of this rule. "Eligible providers" includes the Administrative Office of the Courts and may include educational institutions, professional associations, professional continuing education groups, public or private for-profit or not-for-profit groups, and court-connected groups.

(1) Eligible providers must:

(A) Ensure that the training instructors or consultants delivering the education and training programs either meet the requirements of this rule or are experts in the subject matter;

(B) Monitor and evaluate the quality of courses, curricula, training, instructors, and consultants;

(C) Emphasize the importance of focusing child custody mediations on the health, safety, welfare, and best interest of the child;

(D) Develop a procedure to verify that participants complete the education and training program; and

(E) Distribute a certificate of completion to each person who has completed the training. The certificate must document the number of hours of training offered, the number of hours the person completed, the dates of the training, and the name of the training provider.

(2) Effective July 1, 2005, all education and training programs must be approved by the Administrative Office of the Courts.

(Subd (g) adopted effective January 1, 2005.)

(h) Ethics

Mediation must be conducted in an atmosphere that encourages trust in the process and a perception of fairness. To that end, mediators must:

(1) Meet the practice and ethical standards of the Code of Ethics for the Court Employees of California and of related law;

(2) Maintain objectivity, provide and gather balanced information for both parties, and control for bias;

(3) Protect the confidentiality of the parties and the child in making any collateral contacts and not release information about the case to any individual except as authorized by the court or statute;

(4) Not offer any recommendations about a party unless that party has been evaluated directly or in consultation with another qualified neutral professional;

(5) Consider the health, safety, welfare, and best interest of the child in all phases of the process, including interviews with parents, extended family members, counsel for the child, and other interested parties or collateral contacts;

(6) Strive to maintain the confidential relationship between the child who is the subject of an evaluation and his or her treating psychotherapist;

(7) Operate within the limits of his or her training and experience and disclose any limitations or bias that would affect his or her ability to conduct the mediation;

(8) Not require children to state a custodial preference;

(9) Not disclose any recommendations to the parties, their attorneys, or the attorney for the child before having gathered the information necessary to support the conclusion;

(10) Disclose to the court, parties, attorneys for the parties, and attorney for the child conflicts of interest or dual relationships and not accept any appointment except by court order or the parties' stipulation;

(11) Be sensitive to the parties' socioeconomic status, gender, race, ethnicity, cultural values, religion, family structures, and developmental characteristics; and

(12) Disclose any actual or potential conflicts of interest. In the event of a conflict of interest, the mediator must suspend mediation and meet and confer in an effort to resolve the conflict of interest to the satisfaction of all parties or according to local court rules. The court may order mediation to continue with another mediator or offer the parties alternatives. The mediator cannot continue unless the parties agree in writing to continue mediation despite the disclosed conflict of interest.

(Subd (h) amended effective January 1, 2007; adopted as subd (g) effective July 1, 2001; previously amended effective January 1, 2003; previously relettered effective January 1, 2005.)

Rule 5.210 amended effective January 1, 2007; adopted as rule 1257.1 effective July 1, 2001; amended and renumbered effective January 1, 2003; previously amended effective January 1, 2003, and January 1, 2005.

Ref.: Cal. Fms Pl. & Pr., Ch. 223, "Dissolution of Marriage: Child Custody"; W. Cal. Sum., 10 "Parent and Child" §278.

Rule 5.215. Domestic violence protocol for Family Court Services

(a) Authority

This rule of court is adopted under Family Code sections 211, 1850(a), and 3170(b).

(Subd (a) amended effective January 1, 2007.)

(b) Purpose

This rule sets forth the protocol for Family Court Services' handling of domestic violence cases consistent with the requirement of Family Code section 3170(b).

(c) Definitions

(1) "Domestic violence" is used as defined in Family Code sections 6203 and 6211.

(2) "Protective order" is used as defined in Family Code section 6215, "Emergency protective order"; Family Code section 6218, "Protective order"; and Penal Code section 136.2 (orders by court). "Domestic violence restraining order" is synonymous with "protective order."

(3) "Mediation" refers to proceedings described in Family Code section 3161.

(4) "Evaluation" and "investigation" are synonymous terms.

(5) "Family Court Services" refers to court-connected child custody services and child custody mediation made

available by superior courts under Family Code section 3160.

(6) "Family Court Services staff" refers to contract and employee mediators, evaluators, investigators, and counselors who provide services on behalf of Family Court Services.

(7) "Differential domestic violence assessment" is a process used to assess the nature of any domestic violence issues in the family so that Family Court Services may provide services in such a way as to protect any victim of domestic violence from intimidation, provide services for perpetrators, and correct for power imbalances created by past and prospective violence.

(Subd (c) amended effective January 1, 2003.)

(d) Family Court Services: Description and duties

(1) *Local protocols*

Family Court Services must handle domestic violence cases in accordance with pertinent state laws and all applicable rules of court and must develop local protocols in accordance with this rule.

(2) *Family Court Services duties relative to domestic violence cases*

Family Court Services is a court-connected service that must:

(A) Identify cases in Family Court Services that involve domestic violence, and code Family Court Services files to identify such cases;

(B) Make reasonable efforts to ensure the safety of victims, children, and other parties when they are participating in services provided by Family Court Services;

(C) Make appropriate referrals; and

(D) Conduct a differential domestic violence assessment in domestic violence cases and offer appropriate services as available, such as child custody evaluation, parent education, parent orientation, supervised visitation, child custody mediation, relevant education programs for children, and other services as determined by each superior court.

(3) *No negotiation of violence*

Family Court Services staff must not negotiate with the parties about using violence with each other, whether either party should or should not obtain or dismiss a restraining order, or whether either party should cooperate with criminal prosecution.

(4) *Domestic violence restraining orders*

Notwithstanding the above, to the extent permitted under Family Code section 3183(c), in appropriate cases, Family Court Services staff may recommend that restraining orders be issued, pending determination of the controversy, to protect the well-being of the child involved in the controversy.

(5) *Providing information*

Family Court Services staff must provide information to families accessing their services about the effects of domestic violence on adults and children. Family Court Services programs, including but not limited to orientation programs, must provide information and materials that describe Family Court Services policy and procedures with respect to domestic violence. Where possible, the videotapes provided should be closed-captioned.

(6) *Separate sessions*

In a Family Court Services case in which there has been a history of domestic violence between the parties or in which a protective order as defined in Family Code section 6218 is in effect, at the request of the party who is alleging domestic violence in a written declaration under penalty of perjury or who is protected by the order, the Family Court Services mediator, counselor, evaluator, or investigator must meet with the parties separately and at separate times. When appropriate, arrangements for separate sessions must protect the confidentiality of each party's times of arrival, departure, and meeting with Family Court Services. Family Court Services must provide information to the parties regarding their options for separate sessions under Family Code sections 3113 and 3181. If domestic violence is discovered after mediation or evaluation has begun, the Family Court Services staff member assigned to the case must confer with the parties separately regarding safety-related issues and the option of continuing in separate sessions at separate times. Family Court Services staff, including support staff, must not respond to a party's request for separate sessions as though it were evidence of his or her lack of cooperation with the Family Court Services process.

(7) Referrals

Family Court Services staff, where applicable, must refer family members to appropriate services. Such services may include but are not limited to programs for perpetrators, counseling and education for children, parent education, services for victims, and legal resources, such as family law facilitators.

(8) Community resources

Family Court Services should maintain a liaison with community-based services offering domestic violence prevention assistance and support so that referrals can be made based on an understanding of available services and service providers.

(Subd (d) amended effective January 1, 2003.)

(e) Intake

(1) Court responsibility

Each court must ensure that Family Court Services programs use a detailed intake process that screens for, and informs staff about, any restraining orders, dependency petitions under Welfare and Institutions Code section 300, and other safety-related issues affecting any party or child named in the proceedings.

(2) Intake form

Any intake form that an agency charged with providing family court services requires the parties to complete before the commencement of mediation or evaluation must state that, if a party alleging domestic violence in a written declaration under penalty of perjury or a party protected by a protective order so requests, the Family Court Services staff must meet with the parties separately and at separate times.

(3) Review of intake form and case file

All Family Court Services procedures must be conducted in accordance with state law and must include review of intake forms and court files, when available, by appropriate staff.

(f) Screening

(1) Identification of domestic violence

Screening for a history of domestic violence incidents must be done throughout the Family Court Services process. As early in the case as possible, Family Court Services staff should make every effort to identify cases in which incidents of domestic violence are present. The means by which Family Court Services elicits screening information may be determined by each program. Screening techniques may include but are not limited to questionnaires, telephone interviews, standardized screening devices, and face-to-face interviews.

(2) Procedures for identification

Procedures for identifying domestic violence may include, but are not limited to: (a) determination of an existing emergency protective order or domestic violence restraining order concerning the parties or minor; (b) review of court papers and declarations; (c) telephone interviews; (d) use of an intake form; (e) orientation; (f) information from attorneys, shelters, hospital reports, Child Protective Services, police reports, and criminal background checks; and (g) other collateral sources. Questions specific to incidents of domestic violence should request the following information: date of the parties' separation, frequency of domestic violence, most recent as well as past incidents of domestic violence, concerns about future domestic violence, identities of children and other individuals present at domestic violence incidents or otherwise exposed to the domestic violence, and severity of domestic violence.

(3) Context for screening

In domestic violence cases in which neither party has requested separate sessions at separate times, Family Court Services staff must confer with the parties separately and privately to determine whether joint or separate sessions are appropriate.

(g) Safety issues

(1) Developing a safety plan

When domestic violence is identified or alleged in a case, Family Court Services staff must consult with the party alleging domestic violence away from the presence of the party against whom such allegations are made and discuss the existence of or need for a safety plan. Safety planning may include but is not limited to discussion of safe housing, workplace safety, safety for other family members and children, access to financial resources, and information about local domestic violence agencies.

(2) Safety procedures

Each Family Court Services office should develop safety procedures for handling domestic violence cases.

(3) Confidential addresses

Where appropriate, Family Court Services staff must make reasonable efforts to keep residential addresses, work addresses, and contact information—including but not limited to telephone numbers and e-mail addresses—confidential in all cases and on all Family Court Services documents.

(Subd (g) amended effective January 1, 2007.)

(h) Support persons

(1) Support person

Family Court Services staff must advise the party protected by a protective order of the right to have a support person attend any mediation orientation or mediation sessions, including separate mediation sessions, under Family Code section 6303.

(2) *Excluding support person*

A Family Court Services staff person may exclude a domestic violence support person from a mediation session if the support person participates in the mediation session or acts as an advocate or the presence of a particular support person disrupts the process of mediation. The presence of the support person does not waive the confidentiality of the process, and the support person is bound by the confidentiality of the process.

(Subd (h) amended effective January 1, 2003.)

(i) Accessibility of services

To effectively address domestic violence cases, the court must make reasonable efforts to ensure the availability of safe and accessible services that include, but are not limited to:

(1) *Language accessibility*

Whenever possible, Family Court Services programs should be conducted in the languages of all participants, including those who are deaf. When the participants use only a language other than spoken English and the Family Court Services staff person does not speak their language, an interpreter—certified whenever possible—should be assigned to interpret at the session. A minor child of the parties must not be used as an interpreter. An adult family member may act as an interpreter only when appropriate interpreters are not available. When a family member is acting as an interpreter, Family Court Services staff should attempt to establish, away from the presence of the potential interpreter and the other party, whether the person alleging domestic violence is comfortable with having that family member interpret for the parties.

(2) *Facilities design*

To minimize contact between the parties and promote safety in domestic violence cases, courts must give consideration to the design of facilities. Such considerations must include but are not limited to the following: separate and secure waiting areas, separate conference rooms for parent education and mediation, signs providing directions to Family Court Services, and secure parking for users of Family Court Services.

(j) Training and education

(1) *Training, continuing education, and experience requirements for Family Court Services staff*

All Family Court Services staff must participate in programs of continuing instruction in issues related to domestic violence, including child abuse, as may be arranged for and provided to them, under Family Code section 1816(a).

(2) *Advanced domestic violence training*

Family Court Services staff must complete 16 hours of advanced domestic violence training within the first 12 months of employment and 4 hours of domestic violence update training each year thereafter. The content of the 16 hours of advanced domestic violence training and 4 hours of domestic violence update training must be the same as that required for court-appointed child custody investigators and evaluators as stated in rule 5.230. Those staff members employed by Family Court Services on January 1, 2002, who have not already fulfilled the requirements of

rule 5.230 must participate in the 16-hour training within one year of the rule's effective date.

(3) *Support staff*

Family Court Services programs should, where possible, enable support staff, including but not limited to clerical staff, to participate in training on domestic violence and in handling domestic violence cases appropriately.

(Subd (j) amended effective January 1, 2003.)
Rule 5.215 amended effective January 1, 2007; adopted as rule 1257.2 effective January 1, 2002; previously amended and renumbered effective January 1, 2003.

Ref.: Cal. Fms Pl. & Pr., Ch. 221, "Dissolution of Marriage: Procedure," Ch. 293, "Harassment and Domestic Violence"; W. Cal. Sum., 11 "Husband and Wife" §§10A, 370.

Rule 5.220. Court-ordered child custody evaluations

(a) Authority

This rule of court is adopted under Family Code sections 211 and 3117.

(Subd (a) amended effective January 1, 2007.)

(b) Purpose

Courts order child custody evaluations, investigations, and assessments to assist them in determining the health, safety, welfare, and best interest of children with regard to disputed custody and visitation issues. This rule governs both court-connected and private child custody evaluators appointed under Family Code section 3111, Evidence Code section 730, or Code of Civil Procedure section 2032.

(Subd (b) amended effective January 1, 2003.)

(c) Definitions

For purposes of this rule:

(1) A "child custody evaluator" is a court-appointed investigator as defined in Family Code section 3110.

(2) The "best interest of the child" is as defined in Family Code section 3011.

(3) A "child custody evaluation" is an expert investigation and analysis of the health, safety, welfare, and best interest of children with regard to disputed custody and visitation issues.

(4) A "full evaluation, investigation, or assessment" is a comprehensive examination of the health, safety, welfare, and best interest of the child.

(5) A "partial evaluation, investigation, or assessment" is an examination of the health, safety, welfare, and best interest of the child that is limited by court order in either time or scope.

(6) "Evaluation," "investigation," and "assessment" are synonymous.

(Subd (c) amended effective January 1, 2003.)

(d) Responsibility for evaluation services

(1) Each court must:

(A) Adopt a local rule by January 1, 2000, to:

(i) Implement this rule of court;

(ii) Determine whether a peremptory challenge to a court-appointed evaluator is allowed and when the challenge must be exercised. The rules must specify whether a family court services staff member, other county employee, a mental health professional, or all of them may be challenged;

(iii) Allow evaluators to petition the court to withdraw from a case;

(iv) Provide for acceptance of and response to complaints about an evaluator's performance; and

(v) Address ex parte communications.

(B) Give the evaluator, before the evaluation begins, a copy of the court order that specifies:

(i) The appointment of the evaluator under Evidence Code section 730, Family Code section 3110, or Code of Civil Procedure 2032; and

(ii) The purpose and scope of the evaluation.

(C) Require child custody evaluators to adhere to the requirements of this rule.

(D) Determine and allocate between the parties any fees or costs of the evaluation.

(2) The child custody evaluator must:

(A) Consider the health, safety, welfare, and best interest of the child within the scope and purpose of the evaluation as defined by the court order;

(B) Strive to minimize the potential for psychological trauma to children during the evaluation process; and

(C) Include in the initial meeting with each child an age-appropriate explanation of the evaluation process, including limitations on the confidentiality of the process.

(Subd (d) amended effective January 1, 2007; previously amended effective January 1, 2003.)

(e) Scope of evaluations

All evaluations must include:

(1) A written explanation of the process that clearly describes the:

(A) Purpose of the evaluation;

(B) Procedures used and the time required to gather and assess information and, if psychological tests will be used, the role of the results in confirming or questioning other information or previous conclusions;

(C) Scope and distribution of the evaluation report;

(D) Limitations on the confidentiality of the process; and

(E) Cost and payment responsibility for the evaluation.

(2) Data collection and analysis that are consistent with the requirements of Family Code section 3118; that allow the evaluator to observe and consider each party in comparable ways and to substantiate (from multiple sources when possible) interpretations and conclusions regarding each child's developmental needs; the quality of attachment to each parent and that parent's social environment; and reactions to the separation, divorce, or parental conflict. This process may include:

(A) Reviewing pertinent documents related to custody, including local police records;

(B) Observing parent-child interaction (unless contraindicated to protect the best interest of the child);

(C) Interviewing parents conjointly, individually, or both conjointly and individually (unless contraindicated in cases involving domestic violence), to assess:

(i) Capacity for setting age-appropriate limits and for understanding and responding to the child's needs;

(ii) History of involvement in caring for the child;

(iii) Methods for working toward resolution of the child custody conflict;

(iv) History of child abuse, domestic violence, substance abuse, and psychiatric illness; and

(v) Psychological and social functioning;

(D) Conducting age-appropriate interviews and observation with the children, both parents, stepparents, step- and half-siblings conjointly, separately, or both conjointly and separately, unless contraindicated to protect the best interest of the child;

(E) Collecting relevant corroborating information or documents as permitted by law; and

(F) Consulting with other experts to develop information that is beyond the evaluator's scope of practice or area of expertise.

(3) A written or oral presentation of findings that is consistent with Family Code section 3111, Family Code section 3118, or Evidence Code section 730. In any presentation of findings, the evaluator must:

(A) Summarize the data-gathering procedures, information sources, and time spent, and present all relevant information, including information that does not support the conclusions reached;

(B) Describe any limitations in the evaluation that result from unobtainable information, failure of a party to cooperate, or the circumstances of particular interviews;

(C) Only make a custody or visitation recommendation for a party who has been evaluated. This requirement does not preclude the evaluator from making an interim recommendation that is in the best interest of the child; and

(D) Provide clear, detailed recommendations that are consistent with the health, safety, welfare, and best interest of the child if making any recommendations to the court regarding a parenting plan.

(Subd (e) amended effective January 1, 2007; previously amended effective January 1, 2003, and July 1, 2003.)

(f) Cooperation with professionals in another jurisdiction

When one party resides in another jurisdiction, the custody evaluator may rely on another qualified neutral professional for assistance in gathering information. In order to ensure a thorough and comparably reliable out-of-jurisdiction evaluation, the evaluator must:

(1) Make a written request that includes, as appropriate:

(A) A copy of all relevant court orders;

(B) An outline of issues to be explored;

(C) A list of the individuals who must or may be contacted;

(D) A description of the necessary structure and setting for interviews;

(E) A statement as to whether a home visit is required;

(F) A request for relevant documents such as police records, school reports, or other document review; and

(G) A request that a written report be returned only to the evaluator and that no copies of the report be distributed to parties or attorneys;

(2) Provide instructions that limit the out-of-jurisdiction report to factual matters and behavioral observations rather than recommendations regarding the overall custody plan; and

(3) Attach and discuss the report provided by the professional in another jurisdiction in the evaluator's final report.

(Subd (f) amended effective January 1, 2003.)

(g) Requirements for evaluator qualifications, training, continuing education, and experience

All child custody evaluators must meet the qualifications, training, and continuing education requirements specified in Family Code sections 1815, 1816, and 3111, and rules 5.225 and 5.230.

(Subd (g) amended effective January 1, 2004; previously amended effective July 1, 1999, and January 1, 2003.)

(h) Ethics

In performing an evaluation, the child custody evaluator must:

(1) Maintain objectivity, provide and gather balanced information for both parties, and control for bias;

(2) Protect the confidentiality of the parties and children in collateral contacts and not release information about the case to any individual except as authorized by the court or statute;

(3) Not offer any recommendations about a party unless that party has been evaluated directly or in consultation with another qualified neutral professional;

(4) Consider the health, safety, welfare, and best interest of the child in all phases of the process, including interviews with parents, extended family members, counsel for the child, and other interested parties or collateral contacts;

(5) Strive to maintain the confidential relationship between the child who is the subject of an evaluation and his or her treating psychotherapist;

(6) Operate within the limits of the evaluator's training and experience and disclose any limitations or bias that would affect the evaluator's ability to conduct the evaluation;

(7) Not pressure children to state a custodial preference;

(8) Inform the parties of the evaluator's reporting requirements, including, but not limited to, suspected child abuse and neglect and threats to harm one's self or another person;

(9) Not disclose any recommendations to the parties, their attorneys, or the attorney for the child before having gathered the information necessary to support the conclusion;

(10) Disclose to the court, parties, attorney for a party, and attorney for the child conflicts of interest or dual relationships; and not accept any appointment except by court order or the parties' stipulation; and

(11) Be sensitive to the socioeconomic status, gender, race, ethnicity, cultural values, religion, family structures, and developmental characteristics of the parties.

(Subd (h) amended effective January 1, 2007; previously amended effective January 1, 2003.)

(i) Cost-effective procedures for cross-examination of evaluators

Each local court must develop procedures for expeditious and cost-effective cross-examination of evaluators, including, but not limited to, consideration of the following:

(1) Videoconferences;

(2) Telephone conferences;

(3) Audio or video examination; and

(4) Scheduling of appearances.

(Subd (i) amended effective January 1, 2003.)

Rule 5.220 amended effective January 1, 2007; adopted as rule 1257.3 effective January 1, 1999; previously amended effective July 1, 1999, July 1, 2003, and January 1, 2004; amended and renumbered effective January 1, 2003.

Ref.: Cal. Fms Pl. & Pr., Ch. 221, "Dissolution of Marriage: Procedure," Ch. 223, "Dissolution of Marriage: Child Custody"; W. Cal. Sum., 10 "Parent and Child" §§253, 275.

Rule 5.225. Appointment requirements for child custody evaluators

(a) Purpose

This rule provides the licensing, education and training, and experience requirements for child custody evaluators who are appointed to conduct full or partial child custody evaluations under Family Code sections 3111 and 3118, Evidence Code section 730, or chapter 15 (commencing with section 2032.010) of title 4 of part 4 of the Code of Civil Procedure. This rule is adopted as mandated by Family Code section 3110.5.

(Subd (a) amended and relettered effective January 1, 2007; adopted as subd (b).)

(b) Definitions

For purposes of this rule:

(1) A "child custody evaluator" is a court-appointed investigator as defined in Family Code section 3110.

(2) A "child custody evaluation" is an investigation and analysis of the health, safety, welfare, and best interest of a child with regard to disputed custody and visitation issues conducted under Family Code sections 3111 and 3118, Evidence Code section 730, or Code of Civil Procedure section 2032.010 et seq.

(3) A "full evaluation, investigation, or assessment" is a child custody evaluation that is a comprehensive examination of the health, safety, welfare, and best interest of the child.

(4) A "partial evaluation, investigation, or assessment" is a child custody evaluation that is limited by the court in terms of its scope.

(5) The terms "evaluation," "investigation," and "assessment" are synonymous.

(6) "Best interest of the child" is described in Family Code section 3011.

(7) A "court-connected evaluator" is a superior court employee or a person under contract with a superior court who conducts child custody evaluations.

(Subd (b) amended and relettered effective January 1, 2007; adopted as subd (c).)

(c) Licensing requirements

A person appointed as a child custody evaluator meets the licensing criteria established by Family Code section 3110.5(c)(1)–(5), if:

(1) The person is licensed as a:

(A) Physician and is either a board certified psychiatrist or has completed a residency in psychiatry;

(B) Psychologist;

(C) Marriage and family therapist; or

(D) Clinical social worker.

(2) A person may be appointed as an evaluator even if he or she does not have a license as described in (c)(1) if:

(A) The court certifies that the person is a court-connected evaluator who meets all the qualifications specified in (i); or

(B) The court finds that all the following criteria have been met:

(i) There are no licensed or certified evaluators who are willing and available, within a reasonable period of time, to perform child custody evaluations;

(ii) The parties stipulate to the person; and

(iii) The court approves the person.

(Subd (c) adopted effective January 1, 2007.)

(d) Education and training requirements

Before appointment, a child custody evaluator must complete 40 hours of education and training, which must include all the following topics:

(1) The psychological and developmental needs of children, especially as those needs relate to decisions about child custody and visitation;

(2) Family dynamics, including, but not limited to, parent-child relationships, blended families, and extended family relationships;

(3) The effects of separation, divorce, domestic violence, child sexual abuse, child physical or emotional abuse or neglect, substance abuse, and interparental conflict on the psychological and developmental needs of children and adults;

(4) The assessment of child sexual abuse issues required by Family Code section 3118; local procedures for handling child sexual abuse cases; the effect that court procedures may have on the evaluation process when there are allegations of child sexual abuse; and the areas of training required by Family Code section 3110.5(b)(2)(A)–(F), as listed below:

(A) Children's patterns of hiding and disclosing sexual abuse in a family setting;

(B) The effects of sexual abuse on children;

(C) The nature and extent of sexual abuse;

(D) The social and family dynamics of child sexual abuse;

(E) Techniques for identifying and assisting families affected by child sexual abuse; and

(F) Legal rights, protections, and remedies available to victims of child sexual abuse;

(5) The significance of culture and religion in the lives of the parties;

(6) Safety issues that may arise during the evaluation process and their potential effects on all participants in the evaluation;

(7) When and how to interview or assess adults, infants, and children; gather information from collateral sources; collect and assess relevant data; and recognize the limits of data sources' reliability and validity;

(8) The importance of addressing issues such as general mental health, medication use, and learning or physical disabilities;

(9) The importance of staying current with relevant literature and research;

(10) How to apply comparable interview, assessment, and testing procedures that meet generally accepted clinical, forensic, scientific, diagnostic, or medical standards to all parties;

(11) When to consult with or involve additional experts or other appropriate persons;

(12) How to inform each adult party of the purpose, nature, and method of the evaluation;

(13) How to assess parenting capacity and construct effective parenting plans;

(14) Ethical requirements associated with the child custody evaluator's professional license and rule 5.220;

(15) The legal context within which child custody and visitation issues are decided and additional legal and ethical standards to consider when serving as a child custody evaluator;

(16) The importance of understanding relevant distinctions among the roles of evaluator, mediator, and therapist;

(17) How to write reports and recommendations, where appropriate;

(18) Mandatory reporting requirements and limitations on confidentiality;

(19) How to prepare for and give court testimony;

(20) How to maintain professional neutrality and objectivity when conducting child custody evaluations; and

(21) The importance of assessing the health, safety, welfare, and best interest of the child or children involved in the proceedings.

(Subd (d) repealed, amended, and relettered effective January 1, 2007; adopted as subd (e); previously amended effective January 1, 2005.)

(e) Additional training requirements

In addition to the requirements described in this rule, before appointment, child custody evaluators must comply with the basic and advanced domestic violence training requirements described in rule 5.230.

(Subd (e) adopted effective January 1, 2007.)

(f) Authorized education and training

The education and training described in (d) must be completed:

(1) After January 1, 2000;

(2) Through an eligible provider under this rule; and

(3) By either:

(A) Attending and participating in an approved course; or

(B) Serving as an instructor in an approved course. Each course taught may be counted only once. Instructors may claim and receive credit for only actual classroom time.

(Subd (f) adopted effective January 1, 2007.)

(g) Experience requirements

To satisfy the experience requirements of this rule, persons appointed as child custody evaluators must have participated in the completion of at least four partial or full court-appointed child custody evaluations within the preceding three years, as described below. Each of the four child custody evaluations must have resulted in a written or an oral report.

(1) The child custody evaluator participates in the completion of the child custody evaluations if the evaluator:

(A) Independently conducted and completed the child custody evaluation; or

(B) Materially assisted another child custody evaluator who meets all the following criteria:

(i) Licensing or certification requirements in (c);

(ii) Education and training requirements in (d);

(iii) Basic and advanced domestic violence training in (e);

(iv) Experience requirements in (g)(1)(A) or (g)(2); and

(v) Continuing education and training requirements in (h).

(2) For purposes of appointment:

(A) An evaluator is deemed to be in compliance with the experience requirements of this rule until December 31, 2009, if he or she:

(i) Completed or supervised three court-appointed partial or full child custody evaluations, including a written or an oral report between January 1, 2000, and July 1, 2003; or

(ii) Conducted six child custody evaluations in consultation with another professional who met the experience requirements of the rule.

(B) Effective January 1, 2010, an evaluator who is deemed to be in compliance with the experience requirements described in (A) must participate in the completion of at least four partial or full court-appointed child custody evaluations in the preceding three years as described in (g)(1) to remain in compliance with the experience requirements of this rule.

(3) The court may appoint an individual to conduct the child custody evaluation who does not meet the experience requirements described in (1), if the court finds that all the following criteria have been met:

(A) There are no evaluators who meet the experience requirements of this rule who are willing and available, within a reasonable period of time, to perform child custody evaluations;

(B) The parties stipulate to the person; and

(C) The court approves the person.

(4) Those who supervise court-connected evaluators:

(A) Meet the experience requirements of this rule by conducting or materially assisting in the completion of at least four partial or full court-connected child custody evaluations in the preceding three years; or

(B) If employed as of January 1, 2007, are deemed to comply with the experience requirements of this rule until December 31, 2009. Effective January 1, 2010, these persons meet the experience requirements by conducting or materially assisting in the completion of at least four partial or full court-connected child custody evaluations in the preceding three years.

(Subd (g) amended and relettered effective January 1, 2007; adopted as subd (f).)

(h) Continuing education and training requirements

After completing the education and training requirements described in (d) and (e), persons appointed as child custody evaluators must annually complete the:

(1) Domestic violence update training described in rule 5.230; and

(2) Eight hours of update training covering the subjects described in (d).

(Subd (h) amended effective January 1, 2007; adopted as subd (g) effective January 1, 2002; previously amended and relettered effective January 1, 2005.)

(i) Court-connected evaluators

A court-connected evaluator who does not meet the education and training requirements in (d) may conduct child custody evaluations if, before appointment, he or she:

(1) Completed at least 20 of the 40 hours of education and training required by (d);

(2) Completes the remaining hours of education and training required by (d) within 12 months of conducting his or her first evaluation as a court-connected child custody evaluator;

(3) Complied with the basic and advanced domestic violence training requirements under Family Code sections 1816 and 3110.5 and rule 5.230;

(4) Complies with the experience requirements in (g); and

(5) Is supervised by a court-connected child custody evaluator who meets the requirements of this rule.

(Subd (i) amended effective January 1, 2007; adopted as subd (h) effective January 1, 2002; previously relettered effective January 1, 2005.)

(j) Responsibility of the courts

Each court:

(1) Must develop local court rules that:

(A) Provide for acceptance of and response to complaints about an evaluator's performance; and

(B) Establish a process for informing the public about how to find qualified evaluators in that jurisdiction;

(2) Must use an *Order Appointing Child Custody Evaluator* (form FL-327) to appoint a private child custody evaluator or a court-connected evaluation service. Form FL-327 may be supplemented with local court forms;

(3) Must provide the Judicial Council with a copy of any local court forms used to implement this rule;

(4) As feasible and appropriate, may confer with education and training providers to develop and deliver curricula of comparable quality and relevance to child custody evaluations for both court-connected and private child custody evaluators; and

(5) Must use form *Declaration of Court-Connected Child Custody Evaluator Regarding Qualifications* (form FL-325) to certify that court-connected evaluators have met all the qualifications for court-connected evaluators under this rule for a given year. Form FL-325 may be supplemented with local court rules or forms.

(Subd (j) repealed, amended, and relettered effective January 1, 2007; adopted as subd (l); previously amended and relettered as subd (k) effective January 1, 2005.)

(k) Child custody evaluator

A person appointed as a child custody evaluator must:

(1) Submit to the court a declaration indicating compliance with all applicable education, training, and experience requirements:

(A) Court-connected child custody evaluators practicing as of January 1 of a given year must submit a *Declaration of Court-Connected Child Custody Evaluator Regarding Qualifications* (form FL-325) to the court executive officer or his or her designee by January 30 of that year. Court-connected evaluators beginning practice after January 1 must file form FL-325 before any work on the first child custody evaluation has begun and by January 30 of every year thereafter; and

(B) Private child custody evaluators must complete a *Declaration of Private Child Custody Evaluator Regarding Qualifications* (form FL-326) and file it with the clerk's office no later than 10 days after notification of each appointment and before any work on each child custody evaluation has begun;

(2) At the beginning of the child custody evaluation, inform each adult party of the purpose, nature, and method of the evaluation, and provide information about the evaluator's education, experience, and training;

(3) Use interview, assessment, and testing procedures that are consistent with generally accepted clinical, forensic, scientific, diagnostic, or medical standards;

(4) Have a license in good standing if licensed at the time of appointment, except as described in (c)(2) and Family Code section 3110.5(d);

(5) Be knowledgeable about relevant resources and service providers; and

(6) Before undertaking the evaluation or at the first practical moment, inform the court, counsel, and parties of possible or actual multiple roles or conflicts of interest.

(Subd (k) amended and relettered effective January 1, 2007; adopted as subd (m); previously amended and relettered as subd (l) effective January 1, 2005.)

(*l*) Use of interns

Court-connected and court-appointed child custody evaluators may use interns to assist with the child custody evaluation, if:

(1) The evaluator:

(A) Before or at the time of appointment, fully discloses to the parties and attorneys the nature and extent of the intern's participation in the evaluation;

(B) Obtains the written agreement of the parties and attorneys as to the nature and extent of the intern's participation in the evaluation after disclosure;

(C) Ensures that the extent, kind, and quality of work performed by the intern being supervised is consistent with the intern's training and experience;

(D) Is physically present when the intern interacts with the parties, children, or other collateral persons in the evaluation; and

(E) Ensures compliance with all laws and regulations governing the professional practice of the supervising evaluator and the intern.

(2) The interns:

(A) Are enrolled in a master's or doctorate program or have obtained a graduate degree qualifying for licensure or certification as a clinical social worker, marriage and family therapist, psychiatrist, or psychologist;

(B) Are currently completing or have completed the coursework necessary to qualify for their degree in the subjects of child abuse assessment and spousal or partner abuse assessment; and

(C) Comply with the applicable laws related to the practice of their profession in California when interns are:

(i) Accruing supervised professional experience as defined in the California Code of Regulations; and

(ii) Providing professional services for a child custody evaluator that fall within the lawful scope of practice as a licensed professional.

(Subd (l) adopted effective January 1, 2007.)

(m) Education and training providers

"Eligible providers" includes the Administrative Office of the Courts and may include educational institutions, professional associations, professional continuing education groups, public or private for-profit or not-for-profit groups, and court-connected groups. Eligible providers must:

(1) Ensure that the training instructors or consultants delivering the training and education programs either meet the requirements of this rule or are experts in the subject matter;

(2) Monitor and evaluate the quality of courses, curricula, training, instructors, and consultants;

(3) Emphasize the importance of focusing child custody evaluations on the health, safety, welfare, and best interest of the child;

(4) Develop a procedure to verify that participants complete the education and training program;

(5) Distribute a certificate of completion to each person who has completed the training. The certificate must document the number of hours of training offered, the number of hours the person completed, the dates of the training, and the name of the training provider; and

(6) Meet the approval requirements described in (n).

(Subd (m) amended effective January 1, 2007; adopted as subd (n) effective January 1, 2002; previously amended and relettered effective January 1, 2005.)

(n) Program approval required

All education and training programs must be approved by the Administrative Office of the Courts. Education and training courses that were taken between January 1, 2000, and July 1, 2003, may be applied toward the requirements of this rule if they addressed the subjects listed in (d) and either were certified or approved for continuing education credit by a professional provider group or were offered as part of a related postgraduate degree or licensing program.

(Subd (n) amended effective January 1, 2007; adopted as subd (o) effective January 1, 2002; previously amended and relettered effective January 1, 2005.)

Rule 5.225 amended effective January 1, 2007; adopted as rule 1257.4 effective January 1, 2002; renumbered effective January 1, 2003; previously amended effective January 1, 2005.

Ref.: W. Cal. Sum., 10 "Parent and Child" §275.

Rule 5.230. Domestic violence training standards for court-appointed child custody investigators and evaluators

(a) Authority

This rule of court is adopted under Family Code sections 211 and 3111(d) and (e).

(Subd (a) amended effective January 1, 2007.)

(b) Purpose

Consistent with Family Code sections 3020 and 3111, the purposes of this rule are to require domestic violence training for all court-appointed persons who evaluate or investigate child custody matters and to ensure that this training reflects current research and consensus about best practices for conducting child custody evaluations by prescribing standards that training in domestic violence must meet. Effective January 1, 1998, no person may be a court-appointed investigator under Family Code section

3111(d) or Evidence Code section 730 unless the person has completed domestic violence training described here and in Family Code section 1816.

(Subd (b) amended effective January 1, 2003.)

(c) Definitions

For purposes of this rule, "court-appointed investigator" is considered to be synonymous with "court-appointed evaluator" as defined in Family Code section 3110.

(d) Mandatory training

Persons appointed as child custody investigators under Family Code section 3110 or Evidence Code section 730, and persons who are professional staff or trainees in a child custody or visitation evaluation or investigation, must complete basic training in domestic violence issues as described in Family Code section 1816 and, in addition:

(1) *Advanced training*

Sixteen hours of advanced training must be completed within a 12-month period. The training must include the following:

(A) Twelve hours of instruction, as approved by the Administrative Office of the Courts, in:

(i) The appropriate structuring of the child custody evaluation process, including, but not limited to, maximizing safety for clients, evaluators, and court personnel; maintaining objectivity; providing and gathering balanced information from both parties and controlling for bias; providing for separate sessions at separate times (as specified in Family Code section 3113); and considering the impact of the evaluation report and recommendations with particular attention to the dynamics of domestic violence;

(ii) The relevant sections of local, state, and federal law or rules;

(iii) The range, availability, and applicability of domestic violence resources available to victims, including, but not limited to, battered women's shelters, specialized counseling, drug and alcohol counseling, legal advocacy, job training, parenting classes, battered immigrant victims, and welfare exceptions for domestic violence victims;

(iv) The range, availability, and applicability of domestic violence intervention available to perpetrators, including, but not limited to, arrest, incarceration, probation, applicable Penal Code sections (including Penal Code section 1203.097, which describes certified treatment programs for batterers), drug and alcohol counseling, legal advocacy, job training, and parenting classes; and

(v) The unique issues in family and psychological assessment in domestic violence cases, including the following concepts:

a. The effects of exposure to domestic violence and psychological trauma on children; the relationship between child physical abuse, child sexual abuse, and domestic violence; the differential family dynamics related to parent-child attachments in families with domestic violence; intergenerational transmission of familial violence; and manifestations of post-traumatic stress disorders in children;

b. The nature and extent of domestic violence, and the relationship of gender, class, race, culture, and sexual orientation to domestic violence;

c. Current legal, psychosocial, public policy, and mental health research related to the dynamics of family violence, the impact of victimization, the psychology of perpetration, and the dynamics of power and control in battering relationships;

d. The assessment of family history based on the type, severity, and frequency of violence;

e. The impact on parenting abilities of being a victim or perpetrator of domestic violence;

f. The uses and limitations of psychological testing and psychiatric diagnosis in assessing parenting abilities in domestic violence cases;

g. The influence of alcohol and drug use and abuse on the incidence of domestic violence;

h. Understanding the dynamics of high-conflict relationships and abuser/victim relationships;

i. The importance of, and procedures for, obtaining collateral information from probation departments, children's protective services, police incident reports, restraining order pleadings, medical records, schools, and other relevant sources;

j. Accepted methods for structuring safe and enforceable child custody and parenting plans that assure the health, safety, welfare, and best interest of the child, and safeguards for the parties; and

k. The importance of discouraging participants in child custody matters from blaming victims of domestic violence for the violence and from minimizing allegations of domestic violence, child abuse, or abuse against any family member.

(B) Four hours of community resource networking intended to acquaint the evaluator with domestic violence resources in the geographical communities where the families being evaluated may reside.

(2) *Annual update training*

Four hours of update training are required each year after the year in which the advanced training is completed. These four hours must consist of instruction focused on, but not limited to, an update of changes or modifications in local court practices, case law, and state and federal legislation related to domestic violence, and an update of current social science research and theory, particularly in regard to the impact on children of exposure to domestic violence.

(Subd (d) amended effective January 1, 2005; previously amended effective January 1, 2002, January 1, 2003, and January 1, 2004.)

(e) Education and training providers

Only education and training acquired from eligible providers meets the requirements of this rule. "Eligible providers" includes the Administrative Office of the Courts and may include educational institutions, professional associations, professional continuing education groups, public or private for-profit or not-for-profit groups, and court-connected groups.

(1) Eligible providers must:

(A) Ensure that the training instructors or consultants delivering the education and training programs either meet the requirements of this rule or are experts in the subject matter;

(B) Monitor and evaluate the quality of courses, curricula, training, instructors, and consultants;

(C) Emphasize the importance of focusing child custody evaluations on the health, safety, welfare, and best interest of the child;

(D) Develop a procedure to verify that participants complete the education and training program; and

(E) Distribute a certificate of completion to each person who has completed the training. The certificate must document the number of hours of training offered, the number of hours the person completed, the dates of the training, and the name of the training provider.

(2) Effective July 1, 2005, all education and training programs must be approved by the Administrative Office of the Courts.

(Subd (e) amended effective January 1, 2005.)

(f) Local court rules

Each local court may adopt rules regarding the procedures by which child custody evaluators who have completed the training in domestic violence as mandated by this rule will notify the local court. In the absence of such a local rule of court, child custody evaluators must attach copies of their certificates of completion of the initial 12 hours of advanced instruction and of the most recent annual 4-hour update training in domestic violence to each child custody evaluation report.

(Subd (f) relettered effective January 1, 2005; adopted as subd (g) effective January 1, 1999; amended effective January 1, 2003, and January 1, 2004.)

(g) Previous training accepted

Persons attending training programs offered after January 1, 1996, that meet all of the requirements set forth in subdivision (d)(1)(A) of this rule are deemed to have met the minimum standards set forth in subdivision (d)(1)(A) of this rule, but they must still meet the minimum standards listed in subdivisions (d)(1)(B) and (d)(2) of this rule.

(Subd (g) amended effective January 1, 2007; adopted as subd (h) effective January 1, 1999; relettered effective January 1, 2005.)

Rule 5.230 amended effective January 1, 2007; adopted as rule 1257.7 effective January 1, 1999; amended and renumbered effective January 1, 2003; previously amended effective January 1, 2003, January 1, 2004, and January 1, 2005.

Ref.: Cal. Fms Pl. & Pr., Ch. 223, "Dissolution of Marriage: Child Custody"; W. Cal. Sum., 10 "Parent and Child" §275, 11 "Husband and Wife" §370.

Rule 5.235. Ex parte communication in child custody proceedings

(a) Purpose

Generally, ex parte communication is prohibited in legal proceedings. In child custody proceedings, Family Code section 216 recognizes specific circumstances in which ex parte communication is permitted between court-connected or court-appointed child custody mediators or evaluators and the attorney for any party, the court-appointed counsel for a child, or the court. This rule of court establishes mandatory statewide standards of practice relating to when, and between whom, ex parte communication is permitted in child custody proceedings. This rule applies to all court-ordered child custody mediations or evaluations. As in Family Code section 216, this rule of court does not restrict communications between a court-connected or court-appointed child custody media-

tor or evaluator and a party in a child custody proceeding who is self-represented or represented by counsel.

(b) Definitions

For purposes of this rule,

(1) "Communication" includes any verbal statement made in person, by telephone, by voicemail, or by videoconferencing; any written statement, illustration, photograph, or other tangible item, contained in a letter, document, e-mail, or fax; or other equivalent means, either directly or through third parties.

(2) "Ex parte communication" is a direct or indirect communication on the substance of a pending case without the knowledge, presence, or consent of all parties involved in the matter.

(3) A "court-connected mediator or evaluator" is a superior court employee or a person under contract with a superior court who conducts child custody evaluations or mediations.

(4) A "court-appointed mediator or evaluator" is a professional in private practice appointed by the court to conduct a child custody evaluation or mediation.

(c) Ex parte communication prohibited

In any child custody proceeding under the Family Code, ex parte communication is prohibited between court-connected or court-appointed mediators or evaluators and the attorney for any party, a court-appointed counsel for a child, or the court, except as provided by this rule.

(d) Exception for parties' stipulation

The parties may enter into a stipulation either in open court or in writing to allow ex parte communication between a court-connected or court-appointed mediator or evaluator and:

(1) The attorney for any party; or

(2) The court.

(e) Ex parte communication permitted

In any proceeding under the Family Code, ex parte communication is permitted between a court-connected or court-appointed mediator or evaluator and (1) the attorney for any party, (2) the court-appointed counsel for a child, or (3) the court, only if:

(1) The communication is necessary to schedule an appointment;

(2) The communication is necessary to investigate or disclose an actual or potential conflict of interest or dual relationship as required under rule 5.210(h)(10) and (h)(12);

(3) The court-appointed counsel for a child is interviewing a mediator as provided by Family Code section 3151(c)(5);

(4) The court expressly authorizes ex parte communication between the mediator or evaluator and court-appointed counsel for a child in circumstances other than described in (3); or

(5) The mediator or evaluator is informing the court of the belief that a restraining order is necessary to prevent an imminent risk to the physical safety of the child or party.

(Subd (e) amended effective January 1, 2007.)

(f) Exception for mandated duties and responsibilities

This rule does not prohibit ex parte communication for the purpose of fulfilling the duties and responsibilities that:

(1) A mediator or evaluator may have as a mandated reporter of suspected child abuse;

(2) A mediator or evaluator may have to warn of threatened violent behavior against a reasonably identifiable victim or victims;

(3) A mediator or evaluator may have to address a case involving allegations of domestic violence under Family Code sections 3113, 3181, and 3192 and rule 5.215; and

(4) The court may have to investigate complaints.

(Subd (f) amended effective January 1, 2007.)

Rule 5.235 amended effective January 1, 2007; adopted effective July 1, 2006.

Ref.: W. Cal. Sum., 10 "Parent and Child" §§275, 278, 11 "Husband and Wife" §10A.

Rule 5.240. Appointment of counsel to represent a child in family law proceedings

(a) Appointment considerations

In considering appointing counsel under Family Code section 3150, the court should take into account the following factors, including whether:

(1) The issues of child custody and visitation are highly contested or protracted;

(2) The child is subjected to stress as a result of the dispute that might be alleviated by the intervention of counsel representing the child;

(3) Counsel representing the child would be likely to provide the court with relevant information not otherwise readily available or likely to be presented;

(4) The dispute involves allegations of physical, emotional, or sexual abuse or neglect of the child.

(5) It appears that one or both parents are incapable of providing a stable, safe, and secure environment;

(6) Counsel is available for appointment who is knowledgeable about the issues being raised regarding the child in the proceeding;

(7) The best interest of the child appears to require independent representation; and

(8) If there are two or more children, any child would require separate counsel to avoid a conflict of interest.

(Subd (a) adopted effective January 1, 2008.)

(b) Request for appointment of counsel

The court may appoint counsel to represent the best interest of a child in a family law proceeding on the court's own motion or if requested to do so by:

(1) A party;

(2) The attorney for a party;

(3) The child, or any relative of the child;

(4) A mediator under Family Code section 3184;

(5) A professional person making a custody recommendation under Family Code sections 3111 and 3118, Evidence Code section 730, or Code of Civil Procedure section 2032.010 et seq.;

(6) A county counsel, district attorney, city attorney, or city prosecutor authorized to prosecute child abuse and neglect or child abduction cases under state law; or

(7) A court-appointed guardian ad litem or special advocate;

(8) Any other person who the court deems appropriate.

(Subd (b) adopted effective January 1, 2008.)

(c) Orders appointing counsel for a child

The court must issue written orders when appointing and terminating counsel for a child.

(1) The appointment orders must specify the:

(A) Appointed counsel's name, address, and telephone number;

(B) Name of the child for whom counsel is appointed; and

(C) Child's date of birth.

(2) The appointment orders may include the:

(A) Child's address, if appropriate;

(B) Issues to be addressed in the case;

(C) Tasks related to the case that would benefit from the services of counsel for the child;

(D) Responsibilities and rights of the child's counsel;

(E) Counsel's rate or amount of compensation;

(F) Allocation of fees payable by each party or the court;

(G) Source of funds and manner of reimbursement for costs and attorney's fees;

(H) Allocation of payment of attorney's fees to one party subject to reimbursement by the other party;

(I) Terms and amount of any progress or installment payments; and

(J) Ability of the court to reserve jurisdiction to retroactively modify the order on fees and payment.

(3) Courts may use *Order Appointing Counsel for a Child* (form FL-323) or may supplement form FL-323 with local forms developed under rule 10.613.

(Subd (c) adopted effective January 1, 2008.)

(d) Panel of counsel eligible for appointment

(1) Each court may create and maintain a list or panel of counsel meeting the minimum qualifications of this rule for appointment.

(2) If a list or panel of counsel is maintained, a court may appoint counsel not on the list or panel in special circumstances, taking into consideration factors including language, culture, and the special needs of a child in the following areas:

(A) Child abuse;

(B) Domestic violence;

(C) Drug abuse of a parent or the child;

(D) Mental health issues of a parent or the child;

(E) Particular medical issues of the child; and

(F) Educational issues.

(3) If the court maintains a panel of counsel eligible for appointment and the court appoints counsel who is not on the panel, the court must state the reason for not appointing a panel counsel in writing or on the record.

(Subd (d) adopted effective January 1, 2008.)

(e) Complaint procedures

By January 1, 2010, each court must develop local court rules in accordance with rule 10.613 that provide for acceptance and response to complaints about the performance of the court-appointed counsel for a child.

(Subd (e) adopted effective January 1, 2008.)

(f) Termination of appointment

On entering an appearance on behalf of a child, counsel must continue to represent that child until:

(1) The conclusion of the proceeding for which counsel was appointed;

(2) Relieved by the court;

(3) Substituted by the court with other counsel;

(4) Removed on the court's own motion or request of counsel or parties for good cause shown; or

(5) The child reaches the age of majority or is emancipated.

(Subd (f) adopted effective January 1, 2008.)

Rule 5.240 adopted effective January 1, 2008.

Ref.: Cal. Fms Pl. & Pr., Ch. 223, "Dissolution of Marriage: Child Custody."

Rule 5.241. Compensation of counsel appointed to represent a child in a family law proceeding

(a) Determination of counsel's compensation

The court must determine the reasonable sum for compensation and expenses for counsel appointed to represent the child in a family law proceeding, and the ability of the parties to pay all or a portion of counsel's compensation and expenses.

(1) The court must set the compensation for the child's counsel:

(A) At the time of appointment;

(B) At the time the court determines the parties' ability to pay; or

(C) Within a reasonable time after appointment.

(2) No later than 30 days after counsel is relieved as attorney of record, the court may make a redetermination of counsel's compensation:

(A) On the court's own motion;

(B) At the request of a party or a party's counsel; or

(C) At the request of counsel for the child.

(Subd (a) adopted effective January 1, 2008.)

(b) Determination of ability to pay

The court must determine the respective financial ability of the parties to pay all or a portion of counsel's compensation.

(1) Before determining the parties' ability to pay:

(A) The court should consider factors such as the parties' income and assets reasonably available at the time of the determination, and eligibility for or existence of a fee waiver under Government Code section 68511.3; and

(B) The parties must have on file a current *Income and Expense Declaration* (form FL-150) or *Financial Statement (Simplified)* (form FL-155).

(2) The court should determine the parties' ability to pay:

(A) At the time counsel is appointed;

(B) Within 30 days after appointment; or

(C) At the next subsequent hearing.

(3) No later than 30 days after counsel is relieved as attorney of record, the court may redetermine the parties' ability to pay:

(A) On the court's own motion; or

(B) At the request of counsel or the parties.

(Subd (b) adopted effective January 1, 2008.)

(c) Payment to counsel

(1) If the court determines that the parties have the ability to pay all or a portion of the fees, the court must order that the parties pay in any manner the court determines to be reasonable and compatible with the parties' financial ability, including progress or installment payments.

(2) The court may use its own funds to pay counsel for a child and seek reimbursement from the parties.

(3) The court must inform the parties that the failure to pay fees to the appointed counsel or to the court may result in the attorney or the court initiating legal action against them to collect the money.

(Subd (c) adopted effective January 1, 2008.)

(d) Parties' inability to pay

If the court finds that the parties are unable to pay all or a portion of the cost of the child's counsel, the court must pay the portion the parties are unable to pay.

(Subd (d) adopted effective January 1, 2008.)

Rule 5.241 adopted effective January 1, 2008.

Ref.: Cal. Fms Pl. & Pr., Ch. 223, "Dissolution of Marriage: Child Custody."

Rule 5.242. Qualifications, rights, and responsibilities of counsel appointed to represent a child in family law proceedings

(a) Purpose

This rule governs counsel appointed to represent the best interest of the child in a custody or visitation proceeding under Family Code section 3150.

(Subd (a) adopted effective January 1, 2008.)

(b) General appointment requirements

To be eligible for appointment as counsel for a child, counsel must:

(1) Be an active member in good standing of the State Bar of California;

(2) Have professional liability insurance or demonstrate to the court that he or she is adequately self-insured; and

(3) Meet the education, training, and experience requirements of this rule.

(Subd (b) adopted effective January 1, 2008.)

(c) Education and training requirements

Effective January 1, 2009, before being appointed as counsel for a child in a family law proceeding, counsel must have completed at least 12 hours of applicable education and training which must include all the following subjects:

(1) Statutes, rules of court, and case law relating to child custody and visitation litigation;

(2) Representation of a child in custody and visitation proceedings;

(3) Special issues in representing a child, including the following:

(A) Various stages of child development;

(B) Communicating with a child at various developmental stages and presenting the child's view;

(C) Recognizing, evaluating and understanding evidence of child abuse and neglect, family violence and substance abuse, cultural and ethnic diversity, and gender-specific issues;

(D) The effects of domestic violence and child abuse and neglect on children; and

(E) How to work effectively with multidisciplinary experts.

(Subd (c) adopted effective January 1, 2008.)

(d) Annual education and training requirements

Effective January 1, 2010, to remain eligible for appointment as counsel for a child, counsel must complete during each calendar year a minimum of eight hours of applicable education and training in the subjects listed in (c).

(Subd (d) adopted effective January 1, 2008.)

(e) Applicable education and training

(1) Education and training that addresses the subjects listed in (c) may be applied toward the requirements of this rule if completed through:

(A) A professional continuing education group;

(B) An educational institution;

(C) A professional association;

(D) A court-connected group; or

(E) A public or private for-profit or not-for-profit group.

(2) A maximum of two of the hours may be by self-study under the supervision of an education provider that provides evidence of completion.

(3) Counsel may complete education and training courses that satisfy the requirements of this rule offered by the education providers in (1) by means of video presentations or other delivery means at remote locations. Such courses are not self-study within the meaning of this rule.

(4) Counsel who serve as an instructor in an education and training course that satisfies the requirements of this rule may receive 1.5 hours of course participation credit for each hour of course instruction. All other counsel may claim credit for actual time he or she attended the education and training course.

(Subd (e) adopted effective January 1, 2008.)

(f) Experience requirements

(1) Persons appointed as counsel for a child in a family law proceeding must have represented a party or a child in at least six proceedings involving child custody within the preceding five years as follows:

(A) At least two of the six proceedings must have involved contested child custody and visitation issues in family law; and

(B) Child custody proceedings in dependency or guardianship cases can count for no more than three of the six required for appointment.

(2) Courts may develop local rules that impose additional experience requirements for persons appointed as counsel for a child in a family law proceeding.

(Subd (f) adopted effective January 1, 2008.)

(g) Alternative experience requirements

Counsel who does not meet the initial experience requirements in (f) may be appointed to represent a child in a family law proceeding if he or she meets one of the following alternative experience requirements. Counsel must:

(1) Be employed by a legal services organization, a governmental agency, or a private law firm that has been approved by the presiding or supervising judge of the local family court as qualified to represent a child in family law proceedings and be directly supervised by an attorney in an organization, an agency, or a private law firm who meets the initial experience requirements in (f);

(2) Be an attorney working in consultation with an attorney approved by the presiding or supervising judge of the local family court as qualified to represent a child in family law proceedings; or

(3) Demonstrate substantial equivalent experience as determined by local court rule or procedure.

(Subd (g) adopted effective January 1, 2008.)

(h) Compliance with appointment requirements

A person appointed as counsel for a child must:

(1) File a declaration with the court indicating compliance with the requirements of this rule no later than 10 days after being appointed and before beginning work on the case. Counsel may complete the *Declaration of Counsel for a Child Regarding Qualifications* (form FL-322) or other local court forms for this purpose; and

(2) Notify the court within five days of any disciplinary action taken by the State Bar of California, stating the basis of the complaint, result, and notice of any reproval, probation, or suspension.

(Subd (h) adopted effective January 1, 2008.)

(i) Rights of counsel for a child

Counsel has rights relating to the representation of a child's best interest under Family Code sections 3111, 3151, 3151.5, 3153, and Welfare and Institutions Code section 827, which include the right to:

(1) Reasonable access to the child;

(2) Seek affirmative relief on behalf of the child;

(3) Notice to any proceeding, and all phases of that proceeding, including a request for examination affecting the child;

(4) Take any action that is available to a party to the proceeding, including filing pleadings, making evidentiary objections, and presenting evidence;

(5) Be heard in the proceeding, which may include presenting motions and orders to show cause and participating in settlement conferences and trials, seeking writs, appeals, and arbitrations;

(6) Access the child's medical, dental, mental health, and other health-care records, and school and educational records;

(7) Inspect juvenile case files subject to the provisions of Welfare and Institutions Code section 827;

(8) Interview school personnel, caretakers, health-care providers, mental health professionals, and others who have assessed the child or provided care to the child; however, the release of this information to counsel does not constitute a waiver of the confidentiality of the reports, files, and any disclosed communications;

(9) Interview mediators, subject to the provisions of Family Code sections 3177 and 3182;

(10) Receive reasonable advance notice of and the right to refuse any physical or psychological examination or evaluation, for purposes of the proceeding, that has not been ordered by the court;

(11) Assert or waive any privilege on behalf of the child;

(12) Seek independent psychological or physical examination or evaluation of the child for purposes of the proceeding on approval by the court;

(13) Receive child custody evaluation reports;

(14) Not be called as a witness in the proceedings;

(15) Request the court to authorize release of relevant reports or files, concerning the child represented by the counsel, of the relevant local child protective services agency; and

(16) Receive reasonable compensation and expenses for representing the child, the amount of which will be determined by the court.

(Subd (i) adopted effective January 1, 2008.)

(j) Responsibilities of counsel for a child

Counsel is charged with the representation of the best interest of the child. The role of the child's counsel is to gather facts that bear on the best interest of the child and present those facts to the court, including the child's wishes when counsel deems it appropriate for consideration by the court under Family Code section 3042. Counsel's duties, unless under the circumstances it is inappropriate to exercise the duties, include those under Family Code section 3151:

(1) Interviewing the child;

(2) Reviewing the court files and all accessible relevant records available to both parties;

(3) Making any further investigations that counsel considers necessary to ascertain the facts relevant to the custody or visitation hearings;

(4) Participating in the proceeding to the degree necessary to adequately represent the child, including introducing and examining counsel's own witnesses and presenting arguments to the court concerning the child's welfare; and

(5) Preparing, at the court's request, a written statement of issues and contentions setting forth the facts that bear on the best interest of the child.

(Subd (j) adopted effective January 1, 2008.)

(k) Other considerations

Counsel is not required to assume the responsibilities of a social worker, probation officer, child custody evaluator, or mediator and is not expected to provide nonlegal services to the child. Subject to the terms of the court's order of appointment, counsel for a child may take the following actions to implement his or her statutory duties in representing a child in a family law proceeding:

(1) Interview or observe the child as appropriate to the age and circumstances of the child. In doing so, counsel should consider all possible interview or observation environments and select a location most conducive to both conducting a meaningful interview of the child and investigating the issues relevant to the case at that time.

(2) In a manner and to the extent consistent with the child's age, level of maturity, and ability to understand, and consistent with the order of appointment for the case:

(A) Explain to the child at their first meeting counsel's role and the nature of the attorney-client relationship (including confidentiality issues); and

(B) Advise the child on a continuing basis of possible courses of action and of the risks and benefits of each course of action.

(3) Actively participate in the representation of the child at any hearings that affect custody and visitation of the child and attend and participate in any other hearings relevant to the child. In doing so, counsel may, as appropriate:

(A) Take positions relevant to the child on legal issues before the court;

(B) Seek and advocate for services for the child;

(C) Prepare for any hearings or trials;

(D) Work to settle contested issues and to define trial issues;

(E) Prepare witnesses, including the child if the child is to testify;

(F) Introduce and examine witnesses on behalf of the child;

(G) Cross-examine other witnesses;

(H) Make appropriate evidentiary objections;

(I) Review court files and other pertinent records;

(J) Prepare motions to advance the child's interest, including motions to quash subpoenas for the child and other protective orders;

(K) Present arguments to advance the child's interest;

(L) Prepare trial briefs and other documents if appropriate; and

(M) Request appointment of separate appellate counsel.

(4) Conduct thorough, continuing, and independent investigations and discovery to protect the child's interest, which may include:

(A) Obtaining necessary authorizations for the release of information.

(B) Reviewing the child's social services, mental health, drug and alcohol, medical, law enforcement, education, and other records relevant to the case;

(C) Reviewing the court files of the child and his or her siblings, case-related records of the social service agency, and case-related records of other service providers;

(D) Contacting attorneys for the parties and nonlawyer guardians ad litem, Court Appointed Special Advocates (CASAs), and other service professionals, to the extent permitted by local rule, for background information;

(E) Contacting and meeting with the child's parents, legal guardians, or caretakers, with permission of their attorneys;

(F) Interviewing witnesses and individuals involved with the child, including school personnel, child welfare caseworkers, foster parents and other caretakers, neighbors, relatives, coaches, clergy, mental health professionals, physicians, law enforcement officers, and other potential witnesses;

(G) Reviewing relevant photographs, video- or audiotapes, and other evidence;

(H) Documenting the results of these investigations;

(I) Monitoring compliance with court orders as appropriate, including the provision for and effectiveness of any court-ordered services;

(J) Promoting the timely progression of the case through the judicial system;

(K) Investigating the interests of the child beyond the scope of the proceeding and reporting to the court other interests of the child that may need to be protected by the institution of other administrative or judicial proceedings; however, counsel is not responsible for instituting those proceedings or representing the child in them unless expressly appointed by the court for that purpose; and

(L) After learning of other existing administrative or judicial proceedings involving the child, communicating and cooperating with others to the extent necessary and appropriate to protect the child's interest.

(5) Taking all other steps to represent the child adequately as appropriate to the case, including becoming knowledgeable in other areas affecting minors including:

(A) The Indian Child Welfare Act;

(B) Information about local experts who can provide evaluation, consultation, and testimony; and

(C) Delinquency, dependency, probate, family law, and other proceedings.

(Subd (k) adopted effective January 1, 2008.)
Rule 5.242 adopted effective January 1, 2008.

Ref.: Cal. Fms Pl. & Pr., Ch. 223, "Dissolution of Marriage: Child Custody."

Chapter 6
Certification of Statewide Uniform Guideline Support Calculators

Title 5, Family and Juvenile rules—Division 1, Family Rules—Chapter 6, Certification of Statewide Uniform Guideline Support Calculators amended effective January 1, 2009.

Rule 5.275. Standards for computer software to assist in determining support

(a) Authority

This rule is adopted under Family Code section 3830.

(Subd (a) amended effective January 1, 2007; previously amended effective January 1, 2003.)

(b) Standards

The standards for computer software to assist in determining the appropriate amount of child or spousal support are:

(1) The software must accurately compute the net disposable income of each parent as follows:

(A) Permit entry of the "gross income" of each parent as defined by Family Code section 4058;

(B) Either accurately compute the state and federal income tax liability under Family Code section 4059(a) or permit the entry of a figure for this amount; this figure, in the default state of the program, must not include the tax consequences of any spousal support to be ordered;

(C) Ensure that any deduction for contributions to the Federal Insurance Contributions Act or as otherwise permitted by Family Code section 4059(b) does not exceed the allowable amount;

(D) Permit the entry of deductions authorized by Family Code sections 4059(c) through (f); and

(E) Permit the entry of deductions authorized by Family Code section 4059(g) (hardship) while ensuring that any deduction subject to the limitation in Family Code section 4071(b) does not exceed that limitation.

(2) Using examples provided by the Judicial Council, the software must calculate a child support amount, using its default settings, that is accurate to within 1 percent of the correct amount. In making this determination, the Judicial Council must calculate the correct amount of support for each example and must then calculate the amount for each example using the software program.

Each person seeking certification of software must supply a copy of the software to the Judicial Council. If the software does not operate on a standard Windows 95 or later compatible or Macintosh computer, the person seeking certification of the software must make available to the Judicial Council any hardware required to use the software. The Judicial Council may delegate the responsibility for the calculation and determinations required by this rule.

(3) The software must contain, either on the screen or in written form, a glossary defining each term used on the computer screen or in printed hard copy produced by the software.

(4) The software must contain, either on the screen or in written form, instructions for the entry of each figure that is required for computation of child support using the default setting of the software. These instructions must include but not be limited to the following:

(A) The gross income of each party as provided for by Family Code section 4058;

(B) The deductions from gross income of each party as provided for by Family Code section 4059 and subdivision (b)(1) of this rule;

(C) The additional items of child support provided for in Family Code section 4062; and

(D) The following factors rebutting the presumptive guideline amount: Family Code section 4057(b)(2) (deferred sale of residence) and 4057(b)(3) (income of subsequent partner).

(5) In making an allocation of the additional items of child support under subdivision (b)(4)(C) of this rule, the software must, as its default setting, allocate the expenses one-half to each parent. The software must also provide, in an easily selected option, the alternative allocation of the expenses as provided for by Family Code section 4061(b).

(6) The software or a license to use the software must be available to persons without restriction based on profession or occupation.

(7) The sale or donation of software or a license to use the software to a court or a judicial officer must include a license, without additional charge, to the court or judicial officer to permit an additional copy of the software to be installed on a computer to be made available by the court or judicial officer to members of the public.

(Subd (b) amended effective January 1, 2007; previously amended effective January 1, 2003.)

(c) Expiration of certification

Any certification provided by the Judicial Council under Family Code section 3830 and this rule must expire one year from the date of its issuance unless another expiration date is set forth in the certification. The Judicial Council may provide for earlier expiration of a certification if (1) the provisions involving the calculation of tax consequences change or (2) other provisions involving the calculation of support change.

(Subd (c) amended effective January 1, 2003.)

(d) Statement of certified public accountant

If the software computes the state and federal income tax liability as provided in subdivision (b)(1)(B) of this rule, the application for certification, whether for original certification or for renewal, must be accompanied by a statement from a certified public accountant that

(1) The accountant is familiar with the operation of the software;

(2) The accountant has carefully examined, in a variety of situations, the operation of the software in regard to the computation of tax liability;

(3) In the opinion of the accountant the software accurately calculates the estimated actual state and federal income tax liability consistent with Internal Revenue Service and Franchise Tax Board procedures;

(4) In the opinion of the accountant the software accurately calculates the deductions under the Federal Insurance Contributions Act (FICA), including the amount for social security and for Medicare, and the deductions for California State Disability Insurance and properly annualizes these amounts; and

(5) States which calendar year the statement includes and must clearly indicate any limitations on the statement. The Judicial Council may request a new statement as often as it determines necessary to ensure accuracy of the tax computation.

(Subd (d) amended effective January 1, 2003.)

(e) Renewal of certification

At least three months prior to the expiration of a certification, a person may apply for renewal of the certification. The renewal must include a statement of any changes made to the software since the last application for certification. Upon request, the Judicial Council will keep the information concerning changes confidential.

(Subd (e) amended effective January 1, 2003.)

(f) Modifications to the software

The certification issued by the Judicial Council under Family Code section 3830 and this rule imposes a duty upon the person applying for the certification to promptly notify the Judicial Council of all changes made to the software during the period of certification. Upon request, the Judicial Council will keep the information concerning changes confidential. The Judicial Council may, after receipt of information concerning changes, require that the software be recertified under this rule.

(Subd (f) amended effective January 1, 2003.)

(g) Definitions

As used in this rule:

(1) "Default settings" refers to the status in which the software first starts when it is installed on a computer system. The software may permit the default settings to be changed by the user, either on a temporary or a permanent basis, if (1) the user is permitted to change the settings back to the default without reinstalling the software, (2) the computer screen prominently indicates whether the software is set to the default settings, and (3) any printout from the software prominently indicates whether the software is set to the default settings.

(2) "Contains" means, with reference to software, that the material is either displayed by the program code itself or is found in written documents supplied with the software.

(Subd (g) amended effective January 1, 2003.)

(h) Explanation of discrepancies

Before the Judicial Council denies a certificate because of failure to comply with the standards in paragraph (b)(1) or (b)(2) of this rule, the Judicial Council may request the person seeking certification to explain the differences in results.

(i) Application

An application for certification must be on a form supplied by the Judicial Council and must be accompanied by an application fee of $250.

(Subd (i) amended effective January 1, 2003.)

(j) Acceptability in the courts

(1) In all actions for child or family support brought by or otherwise involving the local child support agency under title IV-D of the Social Security Act, the Department of Child Support Services' California Guideline Child Support Calculator software program must be used by:

(A) Parties and attorneys to present support calculations to the court; and

(B) The court to prepare support calculations.

(2) In all [1] **non-title IV-D proceedings, the court may use and** must permit parties or attorneys to use any software certified by the Judicial Council under this rule.

(Subd (j) amended effective January 1, 2009; adopted as subd (k) effective January 1, 2000; previously relettered effective January 1, 2003.)

Rule 5.275(j).   2008 Deletes. [1] courts

Rule 5.275 amended effective January 1, 2009; adopted as rule 1258 effective December 1, 1993; previously amended effective January 1, 2000, and January 1, 2007; previously amended and renumbered effective January 1, 2003.

Ref.: Cal. Fms Pl. & Pr., Ch. 221, "Dissolution of Marriage: Procedure," Ch. 224, "Dissolution of Marriage: Child Support," Ch. 225, "Dissolution of Marriage: Spousal Support"; W. Cal. Sum., 10 "Parent and Child" §394, 11 "Husband and Wife" §192.

Chapter 7
Rules for Title IV-D Support Actions

Rule 5.375. Procedure for a support obligor to file a motion regarding mistaken identity

Rule 5.300.   Purpose, authority, and definitions

(a) Purpose

The rules in this chapter are adopted to provide practice and procedure for support actions under title IV-D of the Social Security Act and under California statutory provisions concerning these actions.

(Subd (a) amended effective January 1, 2007.)

(b) Authority

These rules are adopted under Family Code sections 211, 3680(b), 4251(a), 4252(b), 10010, 17404, 17432, and 17400.

(Subd (b) amended effective January 1, 2007; previously amended effective January 1, 2003.)

(c) Definitions

As used in these rules, unless the context requires otherwise, "title IV-D support action" refers to an action for child or family support that is brought by or otherwise involves the local child support agency under title IV-D of the Social Security Act.

(Subd (c) amended effective January 1, 2007; previously amended effective January 1, 2003.)

Rule 5.300 amended effective January 1, 2007; adopted as rule 1280 effective January 1, 1977; previously amended and renumbered effective January 1, 2003.

Ref.: W. Cal. Sum., 11 "Husband and Wife" §316.

Rule 5.305.   Hearing of matters by a judge under Family Code sections 4251(a) and 4252(b)(7)

(a) Exceptional circumstances

The exceptional circumstances under which a judge may hear a title IV-D support action include:

(1) The failure of the judge to hear the action would result in significant prejudice or delay to a party including added cost or loss of work time;

(2) Transferring the matter to a commissioner would result in undue consumption of court time;

(3) Physical impossibility or difficulty due to the commissioner being geographically separate from the judge presently hearing the matter;

(4) The absence of the commissioner from the county due to illness, disability, death, or vacation; and

(5) The absence of the commissioner from the county due to service in another county and the difficulty of travel to the county in which the matter is pending.

(Subd (a) amended effective January 1, 2007; previously amended effective January 1, 2003.)

(b) Duty of judge hearing matter

A judge hearing a title IV-D support action under this rule and Family Code sections 4251(a) and 4252(b)(7) must make an interim order and refer the matter to the commissioner for further proceedings.

(Subd (b) amended effective January 1, 2007; previously amended effective January 1, 2003.)

(c) Discretion of the court

Notwithstanding (a) and (b) of this rule, a judge may, in the interests of justice, transfer a case to a commissioner for hearing.

(Subd (c) amended effective January 1, 2007.)

Rule 5.305 amended effective January 1, 2007; adopted as rule 1280.1 effective July 1, 1997; previously amended and renumbered effective January 1, 2003.

Ref.: Cal. Fms Pl. & Pr., Ch. 259, "Family Law Enforcement: Special Remedies for Support Enforcement"; W. Cal. Sum., 11 "Husband and Wife" §327.

Rule 5.310.   Use of existing family law forms

When an existing family law form is required or appropriate for use in a title IV-D support action, the form may be used notwithstanding the absence of a notation for the other parent as a party under Family Code section 17404. The caption of the form must be modified by the person filing it by adding the words "Other parent:" and the name of the other parent to the form.

Rule 5.310 amended effective January 1, 2007; adopted as rule 1280.2 effective July 1, 1997; previously amended and renumbered effective January 1, 2003.

Ref.: Cal. Fms Pl. & Pr., Ch. 221, "Dissolution of Marriage: Procedure"; W. Cal. Sum., 11 "Husband and Wife" §316.

Rule 5.311.   Implementation of new and revised governmental forms by local child support agencies

(a) General extended implementation

A local child support agency providing services as required by Family Code section 17400 must implement any new or revised form approved or adopted by the Judicial Council for support actions under title IV-D of the Social Security Act, and under California statutory provisions concerning these actions, within six months of the effective date of the form. During that six-month period, the local child support agency may properly use and file the immediately prior version of the form.

(Subd (a) amended effective January 1, 2007.)

(b) Judgment regarding parental obligations

When the local child support agency files a proposed judgment or proposed supplemental judgment in any action using *Judgment Regarding Parental Obligations (Governmental)* (form FL-630), a final judgment or supplemental judgment may be filed on:

(1) The same version of the form that was used with the initial action or that was filed as an amended proposed judgment; or

(2) The most current version of the form, unless there have been amendments to the form that result in substantial changes from the filed version. If the most current version of the form has been substantially changed from the filed version, then the filed version must be used for the final judgment. A substantial change is one that would change the relief granted in a final judgment from that noticed in a proposed or amended proposed judgment.

(Subd (b) amended effective January 1, 2007.)

Rule 5.311 amended effective January 1, 2007; adopted effective January 1, 2004.

Ref.: W. Cal. Sum., 11 "Husband and Wife" §316.

Rule 5.315.   Memorandum of points and authorities

Notwithstanding any other rule, including rule 313, a notice of motion in a title IV-D support action must not be required to contain points and authorities if the notice of motion uses a form adopted or approved by the Judicial Council. The absence of points and authorities under these circumstances may not be construed by the court as an admission that the motion is not meritorious and cause for its denial.

Rule 5.315 amended effective January 1, 2007; adopted as rule 1280.3 effective July 1, 1997; previously amended and renumbered effective January 1, 2003.

Ref.: W. Cal. Sum., 11 "Husband and Wife" §316.

Rule 5.320.   Attorney of record in support actions under title IV-D of the Social Security Act

The attorney of record on behalf of a local child support agency appearing in any action under title IV-D of the Social Security Act is the director of the local child support agency, or if the director of that agency is not an attorney, the senior attorney of that agency or an attorney designated by the director for that purpose. Notwithstanding any other rule, including but not limited to rule 2.100-2.119, the name, address, and telephone number of the county child support agency and the name of the attorney of record are sufficient for any papers filed by the child support agency. The name of the deputy or assistant district attorney or attorney of the child support agency, who is not attorney of record, and the State Bar number of the attorney of record or any of his or her assistants are not required.

Rule 5.320 amended effective January 1, 2007; adopted as rule 1280.4 effective July 1, 1997; previously amended effective January 1, 2001; previously amended and renumbered effective January 1, 2003.

Ref.: Cal. Fms Pl. & Pr., Ch. 259, "Family Law Enforcement: Special Remedies for Support Enforcement"; W. Cal. Sum., 11 "Husband and Wife" §318.

Rule 5.324.   Telephone appearance in title IV-D hearings and conferences

(a) Purpose

This rule is intended to improve the administration of the high volume of title IV-D child support hearings and conferences. Participation by both parents is needed for fair and accurate child support orders. The opportunity to appear by telephone fosters parental participation.

(b) Definition

"Telephone appearance," as used in this rule, includes any appearance by telephonic, audiovisual, videoconferencing, digital, or other electronic means.

(c) Permissibility of telephone appearances

Upon request, the court, in its discretion, may permit a telephone appearance in any hearing or conference related to an action for child support when the local child support agency is providing services under title IV-D of the Social Security Act.

(d) Exceptions

A telephone appearance is not permitted for any of the following except as permitted by Family Code section 4930:

(1) Contested trials, contempt hearings, orders of examination, and any matters in which the party or witness has been subpoenaed to appear in person; and

(2) Any hearing or conference for which the court, in its discretion on a case-by-case basis, decides that a personal appearance would materially assist in a determination of the proceeding or in resolution of the case.

(Subd (d) amended effective January 1, 2008.)

(e) Request for telephone appearance

(1) A party, an attorney, a witness, a parent who has not been joined to the action, or a representative of a local child support agency or government agency may request permission of the court to appear and testify by telephone. The local child support agency may request a telephone appearance on behalf of a party, a parent, or a witness when the local child support agency is appearing in the title IV-D support action, as defined by rule 5.300(c). The court may also, on its own motion, allow a telephone appearance.

(2) A party, an attorney, a witness, a parent who has not been joined to the action, or a representative of a local child support agency or government agency who wishes to appear by telephone at a hearing must file a request with the court clerk at least 12 court days before the hearing. A local child support agency that files the request for telephone appearance on behalf of a party, a parent, or a witness must file the request with the court clerk at least 12 court days before the hearing. This request must be served on the other parties, the local child support agency, and attorneys, if any. Service must be by personal delivery, fax, express mail, or other means reasonably calculated to ensure delivery by the close of the next court day.

(3) The mandatory *Request for Telephone Appearance (Governmental)* (form FL-679) must be filed to request a telephone appearance.

(Subd (e) amended effective January 1, 2008.)

(f) Opposition to telephone appearance

Any opposition to a request to appear by telephone must be made by declaration under penalty of perjury under the laws of the State of California. It must be filed with the court clerk and served at least eight court days before the court hearing. Service on the person or agency requesting the telephone appearance; all parties, including the other parent, a parent who has not been joined to the action, the local child support agency; and attorneys, if any, must be accomplished using one of the methods listed in (e)(2).

(Subd (f) amended effective January 1, 2007.)

(g) Shortening time

The court may shorten the time to file, submit, serve, respond, or comply with any of the procedures specified in this rule.

(h) Notice by court

At least five court days before the hearing, the court must notify the person or agency requesting the telephone appearance, the parties, and attorneys, if any, of its decision. The court may direct the court clerk, the court-approved vendor, the local child support agency, a party, or an attorney to provide the notification. This notice may be given in person or by telephone, fax, express mail, e-mail, or other means reasonably calculated to ensure notification no later than five court days before the hearing date.

(Subd (h) amended effective January 1, 2007.)

(i) Need for personal appearance

If, at any time during the hearing, the court determines that a personal appearance is necessary, the court may continue the matter and require a personal appearance.

(j) Vendors, procedure, audibility, reporting, and information

Subdivisions [1] **(i) through (m)** of rule 3.670 apply to telephone appearances under this rule.

(Subd (j) amended effective July 1, 2008; previously amended effective January 1, 2007.)

Rule 5.324(j). 2008 Deletes. [1] (f) through (j)

(k) Technical equipment

Courts that lack the technical equipment to implement telephone appearances are exempt from the rule.

Rule 5.324 amended effective July 1, 2008; adopted effective July 1, 2005; previously amended effective January 1, 2007, and January 1, 2008.

Ref.: Cal. Fms Pl. & Pr., Ch. 259, "Family Law Enforcement: Special Remedies for Support Enforcement"; W. Cal. Sum., 11 "Husband and Wife" §327.

Rule 5.325. Procedures for clerk's handling of combined summons and complaint

(a) Purpose

This rule provides guidance to court clerks in processing and filing the *Summons and Complaint or Supplemental Complaint Regarding Parental Obligations (Governmental)* (form FL-600) for actions under Family Code section 17400 or 17404.

(Subd (a) amended effective January 1, 2007; previously amended effective January 1, 2003.)

(b) Filing of complaint and issuance of summons

The clerk must accept the *Summons and Complaint or Supplemental Complaint Regarding Parental Obligations (Governmental)* (form FL-600) for filing under Code of Civil Procedure section 411.10. The clerk must issue the original summons in accordance with Code of Civil Procedure section 412.20 by filing the original form FL-600 and affixing the seal of the court. The original form FL-600 must be retained in the court's file.

(Subd (b) amended effective January 1, 2003.)

(c) Issuance of copies of combined summons and complaint

Upon issuance of the original summons, the clerk must conform copies of the filed form FL-600 to reflect that the complaint has been filed and the summons has been issued. A copy of form FL-600 so conformed must be served on the defendant in accordance with Code of Civil Procedure section 415.10 et seq.

(Subd (c) amended effective January 1, 2003.)

(d) Proof of service of summons

Proof of service of the *Summons and Complaint or Supplemental Complaint Regarding Parental Obligations (Governmental)* (form FL-600) must be on the form prescribed by rule 2.150 or any other proof of service form that meets the requirements of Code of Civil Procedure section 417.10.

(Subd (d) amended effective January 1, 2007; previously amended effective January 1, 2003.)

(e) Filing of proposed judgment and amended proposed judgment

The proposed judgment must be an attachment to the *Summons and Complaint or Supplemental Complaint*

Regarding Parental Obligations (Governmental) (form FL-600) and must not be file-endorsed separately. An amended proposed judgment submitted for filing must be attached to the *Declaration for Amended Proposed Judgment* (form FL-616), as required by Family Code section 17430(c), and a proof of service by mail, if appropriate. Upon filing, the *Declaration for Amended Proposed Judgment* may be file-endorsed. The amended proposed judgment must not be file-endorsed.

(Subd (e) amended effective January 1, 2007; previously amended effective January 1, 2003.)

Rule 5.325 amended effective January 1, 2007; adopted as rule 1280.5 effective July 1, 1998; previously amended and renumbered effective January 1, 2003.

Ref.: Cal. Fms Pl. & Pr., Ch. 259, "Family Law Enforcement: Special Remedies for Support Enforcement"; W. Cal. Sum., 11 "Husband and Wife" §324.

Rule 5.330. Procedures for child support case registry form

(a) Purpose

This rule provides guidance to court clerks in processing the *Child Support Case Registry Form* (form FL-191).

(Subd (a) amended effective January 1, 2007; previously amended effective January 1, 2003.)

(b) Application

This rule applies to any action or proceeding in which there is an order for child support or family support except for cases in which the local child support agency provides support enforcement services under Family Code section 17400. This rule does not apply to cases in which the local child support agency provides support enforcement services under Family Code section 17400.

(Subd (b) amended effective January 1, 2003.)

(c) Requirement that form be filed

The court must require that a *Child Support Case Registry Form* (form FL-191), completed by one of the parties, be filed each time an initial court order for child support or family support or a modification of a court order for child support or family support is filed with the court. A party attempting to file an initial judgment or order for child support or family support or a modification of an order for child or family support without a completed *Child Support Case Registry Form* (form FL-191) must be given a blank form to complete. The form must be accepted if legibly handwritten in ink or typed. No filing fees may be charged for filing the form.

(Subd (c) amended effective January 1, 2007; previously amended effective January 1, 2003.)

(d) Distribution of the form

Copies of the *Child Support Case Registry Form* (form FL-191) must be made available by the clerk's office and the family law facilitator's office to the parties without cost. A blank copy of the *Child Support Case Registry Form* (form FL-191) must be sent with the notice of entry of judgment to the party who did not submit the judgment or order.

(Subd (d) amended effective January 1, 2003.)

(e) Items on form that must be completed

A form must be considered complete if items 1b, 1c, 2, 5, and 6 are completed. Either item 3 or item 4 must also be completed as appropriate. If the form is submitted with the judgment or order for court approval, the clerk must complete item 1a once the judgment or order has been signed by the judicial officer and filed.

(Subd (e) amended effective January 1, 2003.)

(f) Clerk handling of form

The completed *Child Support Case Registry Form* (form FL-191) must not be stored in the court's file. It should be date and time stamped when received and stored in an area to which the public does not have access. At least once per month all forms received must be mailed to the California Department of Social Services.

(Subd (f) amended effective January 1, 2003.)

(g) Storage of confidential information

Provided that all information is kept confidential, the court may keep either a copy of the form or the information provided on the form in an electronic format.

Rule 5.330 amended effective January 1, 2007; adopted as rule 1280.6 effective July 1, 1999; previously amended and renumbered effective January 1, 2003.

Ref.: Cal. Fms Pl. & Pr., Ch. 224, "Dissolution of Marriage: Child Support"; W. Cal. Sum., 10 "Parent and Child" §§384, 427.

Rule 5.335. Procedures for hearings on interstate income withholding orders

(a) Purpose

This rule provides a procedure for a hearing under Family Code section 4945 in response to an income withholding order.

(Subd (a) amended effective January 1, 2003.)

(b) Filing of request for hearing

A support obligor may contest the validity or enforcement of an income withholding order by filing a completed request for hearing. A copy of the income withholding order must be attached.

(c) Filing fee

The court must not require a filing fee to file the request for hearing under this rule.

(Subd (c) amended effective January 1, 2003.)

(d) Creation of court file

Upon receipt of the completed request for hearing and a copy of the income withholding order, the clerk must assign a case number and schedule a court date. The court date must be no earlier than 30 days from the date of filing and no later than 45 days from the date of filing.

(Subd (d) amended effective January 1, 2003.)

(e) Notice of hearing

The support obligor must provide the clerk with envelopes addressed to the obligor, the support enforcement agency that sent the income withholding order, and the obligor's employer. The support obligor must also provide an envelope addressed to the person or agency designated to receive the support payments if that person or agency is different than the support enforcement agency that sent the income withholding order. The support obligor must provide sufficient postage to mail each envelope provided. Upon scheduling the hearing, the clerk must mail a copy of the request for hearing in each envelope provided by the support obligor.

(Subd (e) amended effective January 1, 2007; previously amended effective January 1, 2003.)

(f) Use of court file in subsequent proceedings

Any subsequent proceedings filed in the same court that involve the same parties and are filed under the Uniform Interstate Family Support Act (UIFSA) must use the file number created under this rule.

(Subd (f) amended effective January 1, 2007; previously amended effective January 1, 2003.)

(g) Definitions

As used in this rule:

(1) An "income withholding order" is the *Order/Notice to Withhold Income for Child Support* (form FL-195) issued by a child support enforcement agency in another state; and

(2) A "request for hearing" is the *Request for Hearing Regarding Wage and Earnings Assignment (Family Law—Governmental—UIFSA)* (form FL-450).

(Subd (g) amended effective January 1, 2007; previously amended effective January 1, 2003.)

Rule 5.335 amended effective January 1, 2007; adopted as rule 1280.7 effective July 1, 1999; previously amended and renumbered effective January 1, 2003.

Ref.: Cal. Fms Pl. & Pr., Ch. 260, "Family Law Enforcement: Foreign Judgments."

Rule 5.340. Judicial education for child support commissioners

Every commissioner whose principal judicial assignment is to hear child support matters must attend the following judicial education programs:

(1) *Basic child support law education*

Within six months of beginning an assignment as a child support commissioner, the judicial officer must attend a basic educational program on California child support law and procedure designed primarily for judicial officers. The training program must include instruction on both state and federal laws concerning child support. A judicial officer who has completed the basic educational program need not attend the basic educational program again.

(2) *Continuing education*

The judicial officer must attend an update on new developments in child support law and procedure at least once each calendar year.

(3) *Other child support education*

To the extent that judicial time and resources are available, the judicial officer is encouraged to attend additional educational programs on child support and other related family law issues.

(4) *Other judicial education*

The requirements of this rule are in addition to and not in lieu of the requirements of rule 10.501(e).

Rule 5.340 amended effective January 1, 2007; adopted as rule 1280.8 effective July 1, 1999; previously amended and renumbered effective January 1, 2003.

Ref.: Cal. Fms Pl. & Pr., Ch. 317, "Judges"; W. Cal. Sum., 11 "Husband and Wife" §327.

Rule 5.350. Procedures for hearings to set aside voluntary declarations of paternity when no previous action has been filed

(a) Purpose

This rule provides a procedure for a hearing to set aside a voluntary declaration of paternity under Family Code section 7575(c).

(b) Filing of request for hearing

A person who has signed a voluntary declaration of paternity, or a local child support agency, may ask that the declaration be set aside by filing a completed *Request for Hearing and Application to Set Aside Voluntary Declaration of Paternity* (form FL-280).

(Subd (b) amended effective January 1, 2006; previously amended effective January 1, 2003.)

(c) Creation of court file

On receipt of the completed request for hearing, the clerk must assign a case number and schedule a court date. The court date must be no earlier than 31 days after the date of filing and no later than 45 days after the date of filing.

(Subd (c) amended effective January 1, 2007; previously amended effective January 1, 2003.)

(d) Notice of hearing

The person who is asking that the voluntary declaration of paternity be set aside must serve, either by personal service or by mail, the request for hearing and a blank *Responsive Declaration to Application to Set Aside Voluntary Declaration of Paternity* (form FL-285) on the other person who signed the voluntary declaration of paternity. If the local child support agency is providing services in the case, the person requesting the set-aside must also serve a copy of the request for hearing on the agency.

(Subd (d) amended effective January 1, 2003.)

(e) Order after hearing

The decision of the court must be written on the *Order After Hearing on Motion to Set Aside Voluntary Declaration of Paternity* (form FL-290). If the voluntary declaration of paternity is set aside, the clerk must mail a copy of the order to the Department of Child Support Services in order that the voluntary declaration of paternity be purged from the records.

(Subd (e) amended effective January 1, 2003.)

(f) Use of court file in subsequent proceedings

Pleadings in any subsequent proceedings, including but not limited to proceedings under the Uniform Parentage Act, that involve the parties and child named in the voluntary declaration of paternity must be filed in the court file that was initiated by the filing of the *Request for Hearing and Application to Set Aside Voluntary Declaration of Paternity* (form FL-280).

(Subd (f) amended effective January 1, 2003.)

Rule 5.350 amended effective January 1, 2007; adopted as rule 1280.10 effective July 1, 2000; previously amended and renumbered effective January 1, 2003; previously amended effective January 1, 2006.

Ref.: Cal. Fms Pl. & Pr., Ch. 412, "Paternity"; W. Cal. Sum., 10 "Parent and Child" §34, 11 "Husband and Wife" §320.

Rule 5.355. Minimum standards of training for court clerk staff whose assignment includes title IV-D child support cases

Any court clerk whose assignment includes title IV-D child support cases must participate in a minimum of six hours of continuing education annually in federal and state laws concerning child support and related issues.

Rule 5.355 amended effective January 1, 2007; adopted as rule 1280.11 effective July 1, 2000; previously amended and renumbered effective January 1, 2003.

Rule 5.360. Appearance by local child support agency

When a local child support agency is providing services as required by Family Code section 17400, that agency may appear in any action or proceeding that it did not initiate by giving written notice to all parties, on *Notice Regarding Payment of Support* (form FL-632), that it is providing services in that action or proceeding under title IV-D of the Social Security Act. The agency must file the original of the notice in the action or proceeding with proof of service by mail on the parties. On service and filing of the notice, the court must not require the local child support agency to file any other notice or pleading before that agency appears in the action or proceeding.

Rule 5.360 amended effective January 1, 2007; adopted as rule 1280.12 effective January 1, 2001; previously amended and renumbered effective January 1, 2003.

Ref.: Cal. Fms Pl. & Pr., Ch. 259, "Family Law Enforcement: Special Remedies for Support Enforcement"; W. Cal. Sum., 11 "Husband and Wife" §317.

Rule 5.365. Procedure for consolidation of child support orders

(a) When an order of consolidation of actions has been made under section 1048(a) of the Code of Civil Procedure in cases in which a local child support agency is appearing under section 17400 of the Family Code, or when a motion to consolidate or combine two or more child support orders has been made under section 17408 of the Family Code, the cases in which those orders were entered must be consolidated as follows:

(1) *Priority of consolidation*

The order consolidating cases that contain child support orders must designate the primary court file into which the support orders must be consolidated and must also designate the court files that are subordinate. Absent an order upon showing of good cause, the cases or child support orders must be consolidated into a single court file according to the following priority, including those cases or orders initiated or obtained by a local child support agency under division 17 of the Family Code that are consolidated under either section 1048(a) of the Code of Civil Procedure or section 17408 of the Family Code:

(A) If one of the cases or child support orders to be consolidated is in an action for nullity, dissolution, or legal separation brought under division 6 of the Family Code, all cases and orders so consolidated must be consolidated into that action, which must be the primary file.

(B) If none of the cases or child support orders to be consolidated is in an action for nullity, dissolution, or legal separation, but one of the child support orders to be consolidated has been issued in an action under the Uniform Parentage Act (Fam. Code, div. 12, pt. 3), all orders so consolidated must be consolidated into that action, which must be the primary file.

(C) If none of the cases or child support orders to be consolidated is in an action for nullity, dissolution, or legal separation or in an action under the Uniform Parentage Act, but one of the child support orders to be consolidated has been issued in an action commenced by a *Petition for Custody and Support of Minor Children* (form FL-260), all orders so consolidated must be consolidated into that action, which must be the primary file.

(D) If none of the cases or child support orders to be consolidated is in an action for nullity, dissolution, or legal separation or in an action under the Uniform Parentage Act, the case or cases with the higher number or numbers must be consolidated into the case with the lowest number, which must be the primary file. Child support orders in cases brought under the Domestic Violence Protection Act (Fam. Code, div. 10, pt. 4) or any similar law may be consolidated under this rule. However, a domestic violence case must not be designated as the primary file.

(2) *Notice of consolidation*

Upon issuance of the consolidation order, the local child support agency must prepare and file in each subordinate case a *Notice of Consolidation* (form FL-920), indicating that the support orders in those actions are consolidated into the primary file. The notice must state the date of the consolidation, the primary file number, and the case number of each of the cases so consolidated. If the local child support agency was not a participant in the proceeding in which the consolidation was ordered, the court must designate the party to prepare and file the notice.

(Subd (a) amended effective January 1, 2007; previously amended effective January 1, 2003.)

(b) Subsequent filings in consolidated cases

Notwithstanding any other rule, including but not limited to rule 367, upon consolidation of cases with child support orders, all filings in those cases, whether dealing with child support or not, must occur in the primary court action and must be filed under that case, caption, and number only. All further orders must be issued only in the primary action, and no further orders may be issued in a subordinate court file. All enforcement and modification of support orders in consolidated cases must occur in the primary court action regardless of in which action the order was originally issued.

(Subd (b) amended effective January 1, 2007; previously amended effective January 1, 2003.)

Rule 5.365 amended effective January 1, 2007; adopted as rule 1285.13 effective January 1, 2001; previously amended and renumbered effective January 1, 2003.

Ref.: Cal. Fms Pl. & Pr., Ch. 221, "Dissolution of Marriage: Procedure"; W. Cal. Sum., 11 "Husband and Wife" §325.

Rule 5.370.   Party designation in interstate and intrastate cases

When a support action that has been initiated in another county or another state is filed, transferred, or registered in a superior court of this state under the Uniform Interstate Family Support Act (Fam. Code, div. 9, pt. 5, ch. 6, commencing with § 4900), the intercounty support enforcement provisions of the Family Code (div. 9, pt. 5, ch. 8, art. 9, commencing with § 5600), or any similar law, the party designations in the caption of the action in the responding court must be as follows:

(1) *New actions initiated under the Uniform Interstate Family Support Act*

The party designation in the superior court of this state, responding to new actions initiated under the Uniform Interstate Family Support Act (Fam. Code, div. 9, pt. 5, ch. 6, commencing with § 4900), must be the party designation that appears on the first page of *the Uniform Support Petition* (form FL-500/OMB 0970-0085) in the action.

(2) *Registered orders under the Uniform Interstate Family Support Act or state law*

The party designation in all support actions registered for enforcement or modification must be the one that appears in the original (earliest) order being registered.

Rule 5.370 amended effective January 1, 2007; adopted as rule 1285.14 effective January 1, 2001; previously amended and renumbered effective January 1, 2003.

Rule 5.375.   Procedure for a support obligor to file a motion regarding mistaken identity

(a) Purpose

This rule applies to a support obligor who claims that support enforcement actions have erroneously been taken against him or her by the local child support agency because of a mistake in the support obligor's identity. This rule sets forth the procedure for filing a motion in superior court to establish the mistaken identity under Family Code section 17530 after the support obligor has filed a claim of mistaken identity with the local child support agency and the claim has been denied.

(Subd (a) amended effective January 1, 2003.)

(b) Procedure for filing motion in superior court

The support obligor's motion in superior court to establish mistaken identity must be filed on *Notice of Motion* (form FL-301), with appropriate attachments. The support obligor must also file as exhibits to the notice of motion a copy of the claim of mistaken identity that he or she filed with the local child support agency and a copy of the local child support agency's denial of the claim.

(Subd (b) amended effective January 1, 2007; previously amended effective January 1, 2003.)

Rule 5.375 amended effective January 1, 2007; adopted as rule 1280.15 effective January 1, 2001; previously amended and renumbered effective January 1, 2003.

Ref.: W. Cal. Sum., 11 "Husband and Wife" §331.

Division 2
Rules Applicable in Family and Juvenile Proceedings

Chapter 1
Contact and Coordination

Chapter 1 adopted effective January 1, 2008.

Rule 5.400.   Contact after adoption agreement

(a) Applicability of rule (Fam. Code, §§ 8714, 8714.5, 8714.7; Welf. & Inst. Code, §§ 358.1, 366.26)

This rule applies to any adoption of a child. The adoption petition must be filed under Family Code sections 8714 and 8714.5. If the child is a dependent of the juvenile court, the adoption petition may be filed in that juvenile court and the clerk must open a confidential adoption file for the child, and this file must be separate and apart from the dependency file, with an adoption case number different from the dependency case number. For the purposes of this rule, a "relative" is defined as follows:

(1) An adult related to the child or the child's sibling or half-sibling by blood or affinity, including a relative whose status is preceded by the word "step," "great," "great-great," or "grand"; or

(2) The spouse or domestic partner of any of the persons described in (1) even if the marriage or domestic partnership was terminated by dissolution or the death of the spouse related to the child.

(Subd (a) amended effective January 1, 2007.)

(b) Contact after adoption agreement (Fam. Code, § 8714.7)

An adoptive parent or parents, a birth relative or relatives, including a birth parent or parents of a child who is the subject of an adoption petition, and the child may enter into a written agreement permitting postadoption contact between the child and birth relatives. No prospective adoptive parent or birth relative may be required by court order to enter into a contact after adoption agreement.

(Subd (b) amended effective July 1, 2003; previously amended effective July 1, 2001, and January 1, 2003.)

(c) Court approval; time of decree (Fam. Code, § 8714.7)

If, at the time the adoption petition is granted, the court finds that the agreement is in the best interest of the child, the court may enter the decree of adoption and grant postadoption contact as reflected in the approved agreement.

(Subd (c) amended effective January 1, 2003.)

(d) Terms of agreement (Fam. Code, § 8714.7)

The terms of the agreement are limited to the following, although they need not include all permitted terms:

(1) Provisions for visitation between the child and a birth parent or parents;

(2) Provisions for visitation between the child and other identified birth relatives, including siblings or half-siblings of the child;

(3) Provisions for contact between the child and a birth parent or parents;

(4) Provisions for contact between the child and other identified birth relatives, including siblings or half-siblings of the child;

(5) Provisions for contact between the adoptive parent or parents and a birth parent or parents;

(6) Provisions for contact between the adoptive parent or parents and other identified birth relatives, including siblings or half-siblings of the child;

(7) Provisions for the sharing of information about the child with a birth parent or parents;

(8) Provisions for the sharing of information about the child with other identified birth relatives, including siblings or half-siblings of the child; and

(9) The terms of any contact after adoption agreement entered into under a petition filed under Family Code section 8714 must be limited to the sharing of information about the child unless the child has an existing relationship with the birth relative.

(Subd (d) amended effective January 1, 2007; previously amended effective July 1, 2001, January 1, 2003, and July 1, 2003.)

(e) Child a party (Fam. Code, § 8714.7)

The child who is the subject of the adoption petition is a party to the agreement whether or not specified as such.

(1) Written consent by a child 12 years of age or older to the terms of the agreement is required for enforcement of the agreement, unless the court finds by a preponderance of the evidence that the agreement is in the best interest of the child and waives the requirement of the child's written consent.

(2) If the child has been found by a juvenile court to be described by section 300 of the Welfare and Institutions Code, an attorney must be appointed to represent the child for purposes of participation in and consent to any contact after adoption agreement, regardless of the age of the child. If the child has been represented by an attorney in the dependency proceedings, that attorney must be appointed for the additional responsibilities of this rule. The attorney is required to represent the child only until the adoption is decreed and dependency terminated.

(Subd (e) amended effective July 1, 2003; previously amended effective July 1, 2001, and January 1, 2003.)

(f) Form and provisions of the agreement (Fam. Code, § 8714.7)

The agreement must be prepared and submitted on *Contact After Adoption Agreement* (form ADOPT-310) with appropriate attachments.

(Subd (f) amended effective January 1, 2007; previously amended effective July 1, 2001, and January 1, 2003.)

(g) Report to the court (Fam. Code, § 8715)

The department or agency participating as a party or joining in the petition for adoption must submit a report to the court. The report must include a criminal record check and descriptions of all social service referrals. If a contact after adoption agreement has been submitted, the report must include a summary of the agreement and a recommendation as to whether it is in the best interest of the child.

(Subd (g) amended effective July 1, 2003; previously amended effective July 1, 2001, and January 1, 2003.)

(h) Enforcement of the agreement (Fam. Code, § 8714.7)

The court that grants the petition for adoption and approves the contact after adoption agreement must retain jurisdiction over the agreement.

(1) Any petition for enforcement of an agreement must be filed on *Request to: Enforce, Change, End Contact After Adoption Agreement* (form ADOPT-315). The form must not be accepted for filing unless completed in full, with documentary evidence attached of participation in, or attempts to participate in, mediation or other dispute resolution.

(2) The court may make its determination on the petition without testimony or an evidentiary hearing and may rely solely on documentary evidence or offers of

proof. The court may order compliance with the agreement only if:

(A) There is sufficient evidence of good-faith attempts to resolve the issues through mediation or other dispute resolution; and

(B) The court finds enforcement is in the best interest of the child.

(3) The court must not order investigation or evaluation of the issues raised in the petition unless the court finds by clear and convincing evidence that:

(A) The best interest of the child may be protected or advanced only by such inquiry; and

(B) The inquiry will not disturb the stability of the child's home to the child's detriment.

(4) Monetary damages must not be ordered.

(Subd (h) amended effective January 1, 2007; previously amended effective July 1, 2001, January 1, 2003, and July 1, 2003.)

(i) Modification or termination of agreement (Fam. Code, § 8714.7)

The agreement may be modified or terminated by the court. Any petition for modification or termination of an agreement must be filed on *Request to: Enforce, Change, End Contact After Adoption Agreement* (form ADOPT-315). The form must not be accepted for filing unless completed in full, with documentary evidence attached of participation in, or attempts to participate in, mediation or other appropriate dispute resolution.

(1) The agreement may be terminated or modified only if:

(A) All parties, including the child of 12 years or older, have signed the petition or have indicated on the *Answer to Request to: Enforce, Change, End Contact After Adoption Agreement* (form ADOPT-320) their consent or have executed a modified agreement filed with the petition; or

(B) The court finds all of the following:

(i) The termination or modification is necessary to serve the best interest of the child;

(ii) There has been a substantial change of circumstances since the original agreement was approved; and

(iii) The petitioner has participated in, or has attempted to participate in, mediation or appropriate dispute resolution.

(2) The court may make its determination without testimony or evidentiary hearing and may rely solely on documentary evidence or offers of proof.

(3) The court may order modification or termination without a hearing if all parties, including the child of 12 years or older, have signed the petition or have indicated on the *Answer to Request to: Enforce, Change, End Contact After Adoption Agreement* (form ADOPT-320) their consent or have executed a modified agreement filed with the petition.

(Subd (i) amended effective January 1, 2007; previously amended effective July 1, 2001, January 1, 2003, and July 1, 2003.)

(j) Costs and fees (Fam. Code, § 8714.7)

The fee for filing a *Request to: Enforce, Change, End Contact After Adoption Agreement* (form ADOPT-315) must not exceed the fee assessed for the filing of an adoption petition. Costs and fees for mediation or other appropriate dispute resolution must be assumed by each

party, with the exception of the child. All costs and fees of litigation, including any court-ordered investigation or evaluation, must be charged to the petitioner unless the court finds that a party other than the child has failed, without good cause, to comply with the approved agreement; all costs and fees must then be charged to that party.

(Subd (j) amended effective January 1, 2007; previously amended effective July 1, 2001, January 1, 2003, and July 1, 2003.)

(k) Adoption final (Fam. Code, § 8714.7)

Once a decree of adoption has been entered, the court may not set aside the decree, rescind any relinquishment, modify or set aside any order terminating parental rights, or modify or set aside any other orders related to the granting of the adoption petition, due to the failure of any party to comply with the terms of a postadoption contact agreement or any subsequent modifications to it.

Rule 5.400 amended effective January 1, 2007; adopted as rule 1180 effective July 1, 1998; previously amended and renumbered effective January 1, 2003; previously amended effective July 1, 2001, and July 1, 2003.

Ref.: Cal. Fms Pl. & Pr., Ch. 12B, "Adoptions: Unmarried Minors"; W. Cal. Sum., 10 "Parent and Child" §104.

Rule 5.410. Request for sibling contact information under Family Code section 9205

(a) Applicability of rule

This rule applies to all persons wishing to exchange contact information with their adopted siblings and all adopted persons wishing to have contact with their siblings, regardless of whether the adoption occurred in juvenile or family court.

(Subd (a) adopted effective January 1, 2008.)

(b) Definitions

As used in this rule:

(1) "Adoptee" means any person adopted under California law.

(2) "Department" means the California Department of Social Services (CDSS).

(3) "Licensed adoption agency" means an agency licensed by the department to provide adoption services and includes a licensed county adoption agency and a licensed private adoption agency under Family Code sections 8521, 8530, and 8533.

(4) "Confidential intermediary" means either the department or a licensed adoption agency that provided adoption services for either sibling.

(5) "Alternate confidential intermediary" means a named entity or person designated by the court in place of a licensed adoption agency when the court finds that the agency would experience economic hardship by serving as confidential intermediary.

(6) "Sibling" means a biological sibling, half-sibling, or stepsibling of the adoptee.

(7) "Waiver" means *Waiver of Rights to Confidentiality for Siblings*, department form AD 904A (used for adoptees or siblings over the age of 18 years) or AD 904B (used for adoptees or siblings under the age of 18).

(8) "Consent" means the consent contained within the Department form AD 904B. It is the approval of the filing of a waiver by a person under the age of 18 years obtained from an adoptive parent, a legal parent, a legal guardian,

or a dependency court when a child is currently a dependent of the court.

(9) "Petition" means Judicial Council form *Request for Appointment of Confidential Intermediary* (form ADOPT-330).

(10) "Order" means Judicial Council form *Order for Appointment of Confidential Intermediary* (form ADOPT-331).

(Subd (b) adopted effective January 1, 2008.)

(c) Waiver submitted by person under the age of 18 years under Family Code section 9205(f)

(1) *Adoptee or sibling waiver*

Each adoptee or sibling under the age of 18 years may submit a waiver to the department or the licensed adoption agency, provided that a consent is also completed.

(2) *Court consent*

If the sibling is currently under the jurisdiction of the juvenile court and his or her parent or legal guardian is unable or unavailable to sign the consent, the court may sign it.

(Subd (c) adopted effective January 1, 2008.)

(d) No waiver on file—sibling requesting contact under Family Code section 9205(g)

If, after contacting the department or licensed adoption agency, the sibling who is seeking contact learns that no waiver is on file for the other sibling, the sibling seeking contact should use the following procedure to ask the court that finalized the adoption of either sibling to designate a confidential intermediary to help locate the other sibling:

(1) *Sibling's request*

(A) A sibling requesting contact under Family Code section 9205 must file a petition and submit a blank order to the court that finalized the adoption of either sibling.

(B) If the sibling requesting contact is under the age of 18 years, the petition must be filed through the sibling's duly appointed guardian ad litem under Code of Civil Procedure section 373 or through the sibling's attorney.

(2) *Appointment of a confidential intermediary*

(A) The court must grant the petition unless the court finds that it would be detrimental to the adoptee or sibling with whom contact is sought. The court may consider any and all relevant information in making this determination, including, but not limited to, a review of the court file.

(B) The court will appoint the department or licensed adoption agency that provided adoption services for either sibling as the confidential intermediary.

(C) If the court finds that the licensed adoption agency that conducted the adoptee's adoption is unable to serve as the intermediary, owing to economic hardship, the court may appoint any one of the following who agrees to serve as an alternate confidential intermediary:

(i) A CASA volunteer or CASA program staff member;

(ii) A court-connected mediator;

(iii) An adoption service provider as defined in Family Code section 8502(a);

(iv) An attorney; or

(v) Another California licensed adoption agency or the California Department of Social Services' Adoptions Support Bureau when no other individuals are available.

(D) When an alternate confidential intermediary is appointed, the licensed adoption agency must provide to the court all records related to the adoptee or sibling for inspection by the alternate confidential intermediary.

(3) *Role of the confidential intermediary*

(A) The confidential intermediary must:

(i) Have access to all records of the adoptee or the sibling, including the court adoption file and adoption agency or CDSS files of either sibling;

(ii) Make all reasonable efforts to locate the adoptee, the sibling, or the adoptive or birth parent;

(iii) Attempt to obtain the consent of the adoptee, the sibling, or the adoptive or birth parent; and

(iv) Notify any located adoptee, sibling, or adoptive or birth parent that consent is optional, not required by law, and does not affect the status of the adoption.

(B) The confidential intermediary must not make any further attempts to obtain consent if the individual denies the request for consent.

(C) The confidential intermediary must use information found in the records of the adoptee or the sibling for authorized purposes only and must not disclose any information obtained in this procedure unless specifically authorized.

(4) *Adopted sibling seeking contact with a sibling who is a dependent child*

An adoptee seeking contact with his or her sibling who is a dependent child must follow the procedure set forth under Welfare and Institutions Code section 388(b) to seek contact with the sibling.

(Subd (d) adopted effective January 1, 2008.)

Rule 5.410 adopted effective January 1, 2008.

Ref.: Cal. Fms Pl. & Pr., Ch. 12D, "Adoptions: Amendment and Inspection of Records."

Rule 5.450. Court communication protocol for domestic violence and child custody orders

(a) Definitions

For purposes of this rule:

(1) "Criminal court protective order" means any court order issued under California Penal Code section 136.2 arising from a complaint, an information, or an indictment in which the victim or witness and the defendant have a relationship as defined in Family Code section 6211.

(2) "Court" means all departments and divisions of the superior court of a single county.

(3) "Cases involving child custody and visitation" include family, juvenile, probate, and guardianship proceedings.

(Subd (a) amended effective January 1, 2007.)

(b) Purpose

(1) This rule is intended to:

(A) Encourage courts to share information about the existence and terms of criminal court protective orders and other orders regarding child custody and visitation that involve the defendant and the victim or witness named in the criminal court protective orders.

(B) Encourage courts hearing cases involving child custody and visitation to take every action practicable to ensure that they are aware of the existence of any criminal court protective orders involving the parties to the action currently before them.

(C) Encourage criminal courts to take every action practicable to ensure that they are aware of the existence of any child custody or visitation court orders involving the defendant in the action currently before them.

(D) Permit appropriate visitation between a criminal defendant and his or her children under civil court orders, but at the same time provide for the safety of the victim or witness by ensuring that a criminal court protective order is not violated.

(E) Protect the rights of all parties and enhance the ability of law enforcement to enforce orders.

(F) Encourage courts to establish regional communication systems with courts in neighboring counties regarding the existence of and terms of criminal court protective orders.

(2) This rule is not intended to change the procedures, provided in Family Code section 6380, for the electronic entry of domestic violence restraining orders into the Domestic Violence Restraining Order System.

(Subd (b) amended effective January 1, 2007.)

(c) Local rule required

Every superior court must, by January 1, 2004, adopt local rules containing, at a minimum, the following elements:

(1) *Court communication*

A procedure for communication among courts issuing criminal court protective orders and courts issuing orders involving child custody and visitation, regarding the existence and terms of criminal protective orders and child custody and visitation orders, including:

(A) A procedure requiring courts issuing any orders involving child custody or visitation to make reasonable efforts to determine whether there exists a criminal court protective order that involves any party to the action; and

(B) A procedure requiring courts issuing criminal court protective orders to make reasonable efforts to determine whether there exist any child custody or visitation orders that involve any party to the action.

(2) *Modification*

A procedure by which the court that has issued a criminal court protective order may, after consultation with a court that has issued a subsequent child custody or visitation order, modify the criminal court protective order to allow or restrict contact between the person restrained by the order and his or her children.

(3) *Penal Code section 136.2*

The requirements of Penal Code section 136.2(f)(1) and (2).

(Subd (c) amended effective January 1, 2007; previously amended effective January 1, 2005.)

Rule 5.450 amended and renumbered effective January 1, 2007; adopted as rule 5.500 effective January 1, 2003; previously amended effective January 1, 2005.

Ref.: W. Cal. Sum., 10 "Parent and Child" §720.

Rule 5.475. Custody and visitation orders following termination of a juvenile court proceeding or probate court guardianship proceeding (Fam. Code, § 3105; Welf. & Inst. Code, § 362.4; Prob. Code, § 1602)

(a) Custody and visitation order from other court divisions

A juvenile court or probate court may transmit a custody or visitation order to a family court for inclusion in a pending family law proceeding or to open a new family law case file, after termination of a juvenile court proceeding or a probate guardianship proceeding under rules 5.700 and 7.1008.

(1) *Procedure for filing custody or visitation orders from juvenile or probate court*

(A) The custody or visitation order of a juvenile court or the visitation order of a former guardian must be filed in any pending nullity, dissolution, paternity, or other family law proceeding, or in any probate guardianship proceeding which affects custody or visitation of the child.

(B) If no dependency, family law, or probate guardianship proceeding affecting custody or visitation of the child is pending, the order may be used as the sole basis to open a file and assign a family law case number.

(C) The clerk must immediately file the custody or visitation order, without a filing fee, in the file of any family law proceeding affecting the custody and visitation of the child.

(2) *Endorsed filed copy—clerk's certificate of mailing*

Within 15 court days after receiving the order, the clerk must send, by first-class mail, an endorsed filed copy of the order showing the receiving court case number to:

(A) The persons whose names and addresses are listed on the order; and

(B) The court that issued the order, with a completed clerk's certificate of mailing, for inclusion in the sending court's file.

(Subd (a) amended effective January 1, 2007.)

(b) Modification of former guardian visitation orders—custodial parent

When a parent of the child has custody of the child following termination of a probate guardianship, proceedings for modification of the probate court visitation order, including an order denying visitation, must be determined in a proceeding under the Family Code.

(Subd (b) amended effective January 1, 2007.)

(c) Independent action for former guardian visitation

(1) If the court terminated a guardianship under the Probate Code and did not issue a visitation order, the former guardian may maintain an independent action for visitation if a dependency proceeding is not pending. The former guardian may bring the action without the necessity of a separate joinder action.

(2) If the child has at least one living parent and has no guardian, visitation must be determined in a proceeding

under the Family Code. If the child does not have at least one living parent, visitation must be determined in a guardianship proceeding, which may be initiated for that purpose.

(3) *Declaration Under Uniform Child Custody Jurisdiction and Enforcement Act (UCCJEA)* (form FL-105/GC-120) must be filed with a petition or motion for visitation by a former guardian.

(Subd (c) amended effective January 1, 2007.)

Rule 5.475 amended effective January 1, 2008; adopted effective January 1, 2006; previously amended effective January 1, 2007.

Ref.: Cal. Fms Pl. & Pr., Ch. 223, "Dissolution of Marriage: Child Custody"; W. Cal. Sum., 10 "Parent and Child" §370, 14 "Wills and Probate" §930.

Chapter 2
Indian Child Welfare Act

Chapter 2 adopted effective January 1, 2008.

Rule 5.480. Application (Fam. Code, §§ 170, 177, 3041; Prob. Code, § 1459.5; Welf. & Inst. Code, §§ 224, 224.1)

Rule 5.481. Inquiry and notice (Fam. Code, §§ 177(a), 180; Prob. Code, §§ 1459.5(b), 1460.2; Welf. & Inst. Code, §§ 224.2, 224.3)

Rule 5.482. Proceedings after notice (Fam. Code, §§ 177(a), 180(d), (e); Prob. Code, §§ 1459.5(b), 1460.2(d), (e); Welf. & Inst. Code, §§ 224.2(c), (d); 25 U.S.C. § 1916(b))

Rule 5.483. Transfer of case (Fam. Code, § 177(a); Prob. Code, § 1459.5(b); Welf. & Inst. Code, § 305.5; Guidelines for State Courts; Indian Child Custody Proceedings, 44 Fed.Reg. 67584 (Nov. 26, 1979) Bureau of Indian Affairs Guideline C)

Rule 5.484. Placement of an Indian child (Fam. Code, § 177(a); Prob. Code, § 1459.5(b); Welf. & Inst. Code, §§ 361, 361.31, 361.7(c))

Rule 5.485. Termination of parental rights (Fam. Code, § 7892.5; Welf. & Inst. Code, §§ 361.7, 366.26(c)(2)(B))

Rule 5.486. Petition to invalidate orders (Fam. Code, § 175(e); Prob. Code, § 1459(e); Welf. & Inst. Code, § 224(e))

Rule 5.487. Adoption record keeping (Fam. Code, § 9208)

Rule 5.480.   Application (Fam. Code, §§ 170, 177, 3041; Prob. Code, § 1459.5; Welf. & Inst. Code, §§ 224, 224.1)

This chapter addressing the Indian Child Welfare Act (25 United States Code section 1901 et seq.) as codified in various sections of the California Family, Probate, and Welfare and Institutions Codes, applies to all proceedings involving Indian children that may result in an involuntary foster care placement; guardianship or conservatorship placement; custody placement under Family Code section 3041; declaration freeing a child from the custody and control of one or both parents; termination of parental rights; or adoptive placement, including:

(1) Proceedings under Welfare and Institutions Code section 300 et seq., and sections 601 and 602 et seq. in which the child is at risk of entering foster care or is in foster care, including detention hearings, jurisdiction hearings, disposition hearings, review hearings, hearings under section 366.26, and subsequent hearings affecting the status of the Indian child;

(2) Proceedings under Family Code section 3041;

(3) Proceedings under the Family Code resulting in adoption or termination of parental rights; and

(4) Proceedings listed in Probate Code section 1459.5 and rule 7.1015.

This chapter does not apply to voluntary foster care and guardianship placements where the child can be returned to the parent or Indian custodian on demand.

Rule 5.480 adopted effective January 1, 2008.

Ref.: Cal. Fms Pl. & Pr., Ch. 12B, "Adoptions: Unmarried Minors."

Rule 5.481.   Inquiry and notice (Fam. Code, §§ 177(a), 180; Prob. Code, §§ 1459.5(b), 1460.2; Welf. & Inst. Code, §§ 224.2, 224.3)

(a) **Inquiry (Fam. Code, § 177(a); Prob. Code, § 1459.5(b); Welf. & Inst. Code, § 224.3)**

The court, court-connected investigator, and party seeking a foster-care placement, guardianship, conservatorship, custody placement under Family Code section 3041, declaration freeing a child from the custody or control of one or both parents, termination of parental rights, or adoption have an affirmative and continuing duty to inquire whether a child is or may be an Indian child in all proceedings identified in rule 5.480. The court, court-connected investigator, and party include the county welfare department, probation department, licensed adoption agency, adoption service provider, investigator, petitioner, appointed guardian or conservator of the person, and appointed fiduciary.

(1) The party seeking a foster-care placement, guardianship, conservatorship, custody placement under Family Code section 3041, declaration freeing a child from the custody or control of one or both parents, termination of parental rights, or adoption must ask the child, if the child is old enough, and the parents, Indian custodian, or legal guardians whether the child is or may be an Indian child and must complete the *Indian Child Inquiry Attachment* (form ICWA-010(A)) and attach it to the petition unless the party is filing a subsequent petition, and there is no new information.

(2) At the first appearance by a parent, Indian custodian, or guardian in any dependency case; or in juvenile wardship proceedings in which the child is at risk of entering foster care or is in foster care; or at the initiation of any guardianship, conservatorship, proceeding for custody under Family Code section 3041, proceeding to terminate parental rights proceeding to declare a child free of the custody and control of one or both parents, or adoption proceeding; the court must order the parent, Indian custodian, or guardian if available, to complete *Parental Notification of Indian Status* (form ICWA-020).

(3) If the parent, Indian custodian, or guardian does not appear at the first hearing, or is unavailable at the initiation of a proceeding, the court must order the person or entity that has the inquiry duty under this rule to use reasonable diligence to find and inform the parent, Indian custodian, or guardian that the court has ordered the parent, Indian custodian, or guardian to complete *Parental Notification of Indian Status* (form ICWA-020).

(4) If the social worker, probation officer, licensed adoption agency, adoption service provider, investigator, or petitioner knows or has reason to know that an Indian child is or may be involved, that person or entity must make further inquiry as soon as practicable by:

(A) Interviewing the parents, Indian custodian, and "extended family members" as defined in 25 United States Code sections 1901 and 1903(2), to gather the information listed in Welfare and Institutions Code section 224.2(a)(5), Family Code section 180(b)(5), or Probate Code section 1460.2(b)(5), which is required to complete the *Notice of Child Custody Proceeding for Indian Child* (form ICWA-030);

(B) Contacting the Bureau of Indian Affairs and the California Department of Social Services for assistance in identifying the names and contact information of the tribes in which the child may be a member or eligible for membership; and

(C) Contacting the tribes and any other person that reasonably can be expected to have information regarding the child's membership status or eligibility.

(5) The circumstances that may provide reason to know the child is an Indian child include the following:

(A) The child or a person having an interest in the child, including an Indian tribe, an Indian organization, an officer of the court, a public or private agency, or a member of the child's extended family, informs or otherwise provides information suggesting that the child is an Indian child to the court, the county welfare agency, the probation department, the licensed adoption agency or adoption service provider, the investigator, the petitioner, or any appointed guardian or conservator;

(B) The residence or domicile of the child, the child's parents, or an Indian custodian is or was in a predominantly Indian community; or

(C) The child or the child's family has received services or benefits from a tribe or services that are available to Indians from tribes or the federal government, such as the U.S. Department of Health and Human Services, Indian Health Service, or Tribal Temporary Assistance to Needy Families benefits.

(Subd (a) adopted effective January 1, 2008.)

(b) Notice (Fam. Code, § 180; Prob. Code, § 1460.2; Welf. & Inst. Code, § 224.2)

(1) If it is known or there is reason to know that an Indian child is involved in a proceeding listed in rule 5.480, except for a wardship proceeding under Welfare and Institutions Code sections 601 and 602 et seq., the social worker, petitioner, or in probate guardianship and conservatorship proceedings, if the petitioner is unrepresented, the court must send *Notice of Child Custody Proceeding for Indian Child* (form ICWA-030) to the parent or legal guardian and Indian custodian of an Indian child, and the Indian child's tribe, in the manner specified in Welfare and Institutions Code section 224.2, Family Law Code section 180, and Probate Code section 1460.2.

(2) If it is known or there is reason to know that an Indian child is involved in a wardship proceeding under Welfare and Institutions Code sections 601 and 602 et seq., and the probation officer has assessed that it is probable the child will be entering foster care, or if the child is already in foster care, the probation officer must send *Notice of Child Custody Proceeding for Indian Child* (form ICWA-030) to the parent or legal guardian, Indian custodian, if any, and the child's tribe, in accordance with Welfare and Institutions Code section 727.4(a)(2).

(3) The circumstances that may provide reason to know the child is an Indian child include the circumstances specified in (a)(5).

(4) Notice to an Indian child's tribe must be sent to the tribal chairperson unless the tribe has designated another agent for service.

(Subd (b) adopted effective January 1, 2008.)
Rule 5.481 adopted effective January 1, 2008.

Ref.: Cal. Fms Pl. & Pr., Ch. 12B, "Adoptions: Unmarried Minors," Ch. 328, "Juvenile Courts: Dependency Proceedings."

Rule 5.482. Proceedings after notice (Fam. Code, §§ 177(a), 180(d), (e); Prob. Code, §§ 1459.5(b), 1460.2(d), (e); Welf. & Inst. Code, §§ 224.2(c), (d); 25 U.S.C. § 1916(b))

(a) Timing of Proceedings (Fam. Code, § 180(d), (e); Prob. Code, § 1460.2(d), (e); Welf. & Inst. Code, § 224.2(c), (d))

(1) If it is known or there is reason to know that a child is an Indian child, the court hearing must not proceed until at least 10 days after the parent, Indian custodian, the tribe, or the Bureau of Indian Affairs have received notice, except as stated in sections (a)(2) and (3).

(2) The detention hearing in dependency cases and in delinquency cases in which the probation officer has assessed that the child is in foster care or it is probable the child will be entering foster care may proceed without delay, provided that:

(A) Notice of the detention hearing must be given as soon as possible after the filing of the petition initiating the proceeding; and

(B) Proof of notice must be filed with the court within 10 days after the filing of the petition.

(3) The parent, Indian custodian, or tribe must be granted a continuance, if requested, of up to 20 days to prepare for the proceeding, except for specified hearings in the following circumstances:

(A) The detention hearing in dependency cases and in delinquency cases in which the probation officer has assessed that the child is in foster care or it is probable the child will be entering foster;

(B) The jurisdiction hearing in a delinquency case in which the court finds the continuance would not conform to speedy trial considerations under Welfare and Institutions Code section 657; and

(C) The disposition hearing in a delinquency case in which the court finds good cause to deny the continuance under Welfare and Institutions Code section 682. A good cause reason includes when probation is recommending the release of a detained child to his or her parent or to a less restrictive placement. The court must follow the placement preferences under rule 5.484 when holding the disposition hearing.

(Subd (a) adopted effective January 1, 2008.)

(b) Proof of notice (Fam. Code, § 180(d); Prob. Code, § 1460.2(d); Welf. & Inst. Code, § 224.2(c))

Proof of notice filed with the court must include *Notice of Child Custody Proceeding for Indian Child* (form ICWA-030), return receipts, and any responses received from the Bureau of Indian Affairs and tribes.

(Subd (b) adopted effective January 1, 2008.)

(c) When there is information or a response from a tribe that requires additional steps

If after notice has been provided as required by federal and state law a tribe responds indicating that the child is eligible for membership if certain steps are followed, the court must proceed as if the child is an Indian child and direct the appropriate individual or agency to provide active efforts under rule 5.484(c) to secure tribal membership for the child.

(Subd (c) adopted effective January 1, 2008.)

(d) When there is no information or response from a tribe (Fam. Code, § 177(a); Prob. Code, § 1459.5(b); Welf. & Inst., Code § 224.3(e)(3))

(1) If after notice has been provided as required by federal and state law and neither the tribe nor the Bureau of Indian Affairs has provided a determinative response within 60 days after receiving that notice, then the court may determine that the Indian Child Welfare Act does not apply to the proceedings, provided that the court must reverse its determination of the inapplicability of the act and must apply it prospectively if a tribe or the Bureau of Indian Affairs subsequently confirms that the child is an Indian child.

(2) If at any time, based on the petition or other information, the court knows or has reason to know the child is an Indian child, the court must proceed as if the child were an Indian child.

(3) The court is not required to delay proceedings until a response to notice is received.

(Subd (d) adopted effective January 1, 2008.)

(e) Intervention (Fam. Code, § 177(a); Prob. Code, § 1459.5(b); Welf. & Inst. Code, § 224.4)

The Indian child's tribe and Indian custodian may intervene, orally or in writing, at any point in the proceedings and may, but are not required to, file with the court the *Notice of Designation of Tribal Representative and Notice of Intervention in a Court Proceeding Involving an Indian Child* (form ICWA-040) to give notice of their intent to intervene.

(Subd (e) adopted effective January 1, 2008.)

(f) Posthearing actions (25 U.S.C. § 1916(b))

Whenever an Indian child is removed from a guardian, conservator, other custodian, foster home, or institution for placement with a different guardian, conservator, custodian, foster home, institution, or preadoptive or adoptive home, the placement must comply with the placement preferences and standards specified in Welfare and Institutions Code section 361.31.

(Subd (f) adopted effective January 1, 2008.)

(g) Consultation with tribe

Any person or court involved in the placement of an Indian child must use the services of the Indian child's tribe, whenever available through the tribe, in seeking to secure placement within the order of placement preference specified in rule 5.484.

(Subd (g) adopted effective January 1, 2008.)

Rule 5.482 adopted effective January 1, 2008.

Ref.: Cal. Fms Pl. & Pr., Ch. 12B, "Adoptions: Unmarried Minors," Ch. 328, "Juvenile Courts: Dependency Proceedings."

Rule 5.483. Transfer of case (Fam. Code, § 177(a); Prob. Code, § 1459.5(b); Welf. & Inst. Code, § 305.5; Guidelines for State Courts; Indian Child Custody Proceedings, 44 Fed.Reg. 67584 (Nov. 26, 1979) Bureau of Indian Affairs Guideline C)

(a) Mandatory transfer of case to tribal court with exclusive jurisdiction

The court must order transfer of a case to the tribal court of the child's tribe if:

(1) The Indian child is a ward of the tribal court; or

(2) The Indian child is domiciled or resides within a reservation of an Indian tribe that has exclusive jurisdiction over Indian child custody proceedings under section 1911 or 1918 of title 25 of the United States Code.

(Subd (a) adopted effective January 1, 2008.)

(b) Presumptive transfer of case to tribal court with concurrent state and tribal jurisdiction

Unless the court finds good cause under subdivision (d), the court must order transfer of a case to the tribal court of the child's tribe if the parent, the Indian custodian, or the child's tribe requests.

(Subd (b) adopted effective January 1, 2008.)

(c) Documentation of request to transfer a case to tribal court

The parent, the Indian custodian, or the child's tribe may request transfer of the case, either orally or in writing or by filing *Notice of Petition and Petition to Transfer Case Involving an Indian Child to Tribal Jurisdiction* (form ICWA-050).

If the request is made orally, the court must document the request and make it part of the record.

(Subd (c) adopted effective January 1, 2008.)

(d) Cause to deny a request to transfer to tribal court with concurrent state and tribal jurisdiction under subdivision (b)

(1) One or more of the following circumstances constitutes mandatory good cause to deny a request to transfer:

(A) One or both of the child's parents objects to the transfer in open court or in an admissible writing for the record;

(B) The child's tribe does not have a "tribal court" or any other administrative body as defined in section 1903 of the Indian Child Welfare Act: "a court with jurisdiction over child custody proceedings and which is either a Court of Indian Offenses, a court established and operated under the code or custom of an Indian tribe, or any other administrative body of a tribe which is vested with authority over child custody proceedings;" or

(C) The tribal court of the child's tribe declines the transfer.

(2) One or more of the following circumstances may constitute discretionary good cause to deny a request to transfer:

(A) The evidence necessary to decide the case cannot be presented in the tribal court without undue hardship to the parties or the witnesses, and the tribal court is unable to mitigate the hardship by making arrangements to receive and consider the evidence or testimony by use of remote communication, by hearing the evidence or testimony at a location convenient to the parties or witnesses, or by use of other means permitted in the tribal court's rules of evidence or discovery;

(B) The proceeding was at an advanced stage when the request to transfer was received and the petitioner did not make the request within a reasonable time after receiving notice of the proceeding, provided the notice complied with statutory requirements. Waiting until reunification efforts have failed and reunification services have been terminated before filing a request to transfer may not, by itself, be considered an unreasonable delay;

(C) The Indian child is over 12 years of age and objects to the transfer; or

(D) The parents of a child over five years of age are not available and the child has had little or no contact with his or her tribe or members of the child's tribe.

(3) If it appears that there is good cause to deny a transfer, the court must hold an evidentiary hearing on the transfer and make its findings on the record.

(Subd (d) adopted effective January 1, 2008.)

(e) Evidentiary considerations under subdivision (b)

The court may not consider socioeconomic conditions and the perceived adequacy of tribal social services, tribal probation, or the tribal judicial systems in its determination that good cause exists to deny a request to transfer to tribal court with concurrent state and tribal jurisdiction.

(Subd (e) adopted effective January 1, 2008.)

(f) Evidentiary burdens under subdivision (b)

(1) The burden of establishing good cause to deny a request to transfer is on the party opposing the transfer.

(2) If the court believes, or any party asserts, that good cause to deny the request exists, the reasons for that belief or assertion must be stated in writing, in advance of the hearing, and made available to all parties who are requesting the transfer, and the petitioner must have the opportunity to provide information or evidence in rebuttal of the belief or assertion.

(Subd (f) adopted effective January 1, 2008.)

(g) Order on request to transfer

The court must issue its final order on the *Order on Petition to Transfer Case Involving an Indian Child to Tribal Jurisdiction* (form ICWA-060).

(Subd (g) adopted effective January 1, 2008.)

(h) Proceeding after transfer

When, under Welfare and Institutions Code section 305.5, Family Code section 177(a), or Probate Code section 1459.5(b), the court transfers any proceeding listed in rule 5.480, the court must proceed as follows:

(1) Dismiss the proceeding or terminate jurisdiction if the court has received proof that the tribal court has accepted the transfer of jurisdiction;

(2) Make an order transferring the physical custody of the child to a designated representative of the tribal court (not necessarily the same "designated representative" identified in the *Notice of Designation of Tribal Represen-*

tative and Notice of Intervention in a Court Proceeding Involving an Indian Child (form ICWA-040)); and

(3) Include in the *Order on Petition to Transfer Case Involving an Indian Child to Tribal Jurisdiction* (form ICWA-060) all contact information for the designated tribal court representative.

(Subd (h) adopted effective January 1, 2008.)
Rule 5.483 adopted effective January 1, 2008.

Ref.: Cal. Fms Pl. & Pr., Ch. 12B, "Adoptions: Unmarried Minors."

Rule 5.484. Placement of an Indian child (Fam. Code, § 177(a); Prob. Code, § 1459.5(b); Welf. & Inst. Code, §§ 361, 361.31, 361.7(c))

(a) Evidentiary burdens (Fam. Code, § 177(a); Prob. Code, § 1459.5(b); Welf. & Inst. Code, §§ 361, 361.31, 361.7(c))

In any child custody proceeding listed in rule 5.480, the court may not order placement of an Indian child unless it finds by clear and convincing evidence that continued custody with the parent or Indian custodian is likely to cause the Indian child serious emotional or physical damage and it considers evidence regarding prevailing social and cultural standards of the child's tribe, including that tribe's family organization and child-rearing practices.

(1) Testimony by a "qualified expert witness," as defined in Welfare and Institutions Code section 224.6, Family Code section 177(a), and Probate Code section 1459.5(b), is required before a court orders a child placed in foster care or terminates parental rights.

(2) Stipulation by the parent, Indian custodian, or tribe, or failure to object, may waive the requirement of producing evidence of the likelihood of serious damage only if the court is satisfied that the person or tribe has been fully advised of the requirements of the Indian Child Welfare Act and has knowingly, intelligently, and voluntarily waived them. Any such stipulation must be agreed to in writing.

(3) Failure to meet non-Indian family and child-rearing community standards, or the existence of other behavior or conditions that meet the removal standards of Welfare and Institutions Code section 361, will not support an order for placement absent the finding that continued custody with the parent or Indian custodian is likely to cause serious emotional or physical damage.

(Subd (a) adopted effective January 1, 2008.)

(b) Standards and preferences in placement of an Indian child (Fam. Code, § 177(a); Prob. Code, § 1459(b); Welf. & Inst. Code, § 361.31)

(1) Unless the court finds good cause to the contrary, all placements of Indian children in any proceeding listed in rule 5.480 must follow the specified placement preferences in Family Code section 177(a), Probate Code section 1459(b), and Welfare and Institutions Code section 361.31.

(2) The court may deviate from the preference order only for good cause, which may include the following considerations:

(A) The requests of the parent or Indian custodian;

(B) The requests of the Indian child, when of sufficient age;

(C) The extraordinary physical or emotional needs of the Indian child as established by a qualified expert witness; or

(D) The unavailability of suitable families based on a documented diligent effort to identify families meeting the preference criteria.

(3) The burden of establishing good cause for the court to deviate from the preference order is on the party requesting that the preference order not be followed.

(4) The tribe, by resolution, may establish a different preference order, which must be followed if it provides for the least restrictive setting.

(5) The preferences and wishes of the Indian child, when of sufficient age, and the parent must be considered, and weight given to a consenting parent's request for anonymity.

(6) When no preferred placement is available, active efforts must be made and documented to place the child with a family committed to enabling the child to have visitation with "extended family members," as defined in rule 5.481(a)(4)(A), and participation in the cultural and ceremonial events of the child's tribe.

(Subd (b) adopted effective January 1, 2008.)

(c) Active efforts (Fam. Code, § 177(a); Prob. Code, § 1459.5(b); Welf. & Inst. Code, § 361.7)

In addition to any other required findings to place an Indian child with someone other than a parent or Indian custodian, or to terminate parental rights, the court must find that active efforts have been made, in any proceeding listed in rule 5.480, to provide remedial services and rehabilitative programs designed to prevent the breakup of the Indian family, and must find that these efforts were unsuccessful.

(1) The court must consider whether active efforts were made in a manner consistent with the prevailing social and cultural conditions and way of life of the Indian child's tribe.

(2) Efforts to provide services must include pursuit of any steps necessary to secure tribal membership for a child if the child is eligible for membership in a given tribe, as well as attempts to use the available resources of extended family members, the tribe, tribal and other Indian social service agencies, and individual Indian caregivers.

(Subd (c) adopted effective January 1, 2008.)
Rule 5.484 adopted effective January 1, 2008.

Ref.: Cal. Fms Pl. & Pr., Ch. 12B, "Adoptions: Unmarried Minors," Ch. 328, "Juvenile Courts: Dependency Proceedings."

Rule 5.485.   Termination of parental rights (Fam. Code, § 7892.5; Welf. & Inst. Code, §§ 361.7, 366.26(c)(2)(B))

(a) Evidentiary burdens

The court may only terminate parental rights to an Indian child or declare an Indian child free of the custody and control of one or both parents if at the hearing terminating parental rights or declaring the child free of the custody and control of one or both parents, the court:

(1) Finds by clear and convincing evidence that active efforts to provide remedial services and rehabilitative programs designed to prevent the breakup of the Indian family were made; and

(2) Makes a determination, supported by evidence beyond a reasonable doubt, including testimony of one or more "qualified expert witnesses" as defined in Welfare and Institutions Code section 224.6 and Family Code section 177(a), that the continued custody of the child by the parent is likely to result in serious emotional or physical damage to the child.

(Subd (a) adopted effective January 1, 2008.)

(b) When parental rights may not be terminated

The court may not terminate parental rights to an Indian child or declare a child free from the custody and control of one or both parents if the court finds a compelling reason for determining that termination of parental rights would not be in the child's best interest. Such a reason may include:

(1) Termination of parental rights would substantially interfere with the child's connection to his or her tribal community or the child's tribal membership rights; or

(2) The child's tribe has identified guardianship, long-term foster care with a fit and willing relative, or another planned permanent living arrangement for the child.

(Subd (b) adopted effective January 1, 2008.)
Rule 5.485 adopted effective January 1, 2008.

Ref.: Cal. Fms Pl. & Pr., Ch. 12B, "Adoptions: Unmarried Minors."

Rule 5.486.   Petition to invalidate orders (Fam. Code, § 175(e); Prob. Code, § 1459(e); Welf. & Inst. Code, § 224(e))

(a) Who may petition

Any Indian child who is the subject of any action for foster-care placement, guardianship placement, or termination of parental rights; any parent or Indian custodian from whose custody such child was removed; and the Indian child's tribe may petition the court to invalidate the action on a showing that the action violated the Indian Child Welfare Act.

(Subd (a) adopted effective January 1, 2008.)

(b) Court of competent jurisdiction

If the Indian child is a dependent child or ward of the juvenile court or the subject of a pending petition, the juvenile court is a court of competent jurisdiction with the authority to hear the request to invalidate the foster placement or termination of parental rights.

(Subd (b) adopted effective January 1, 2008.)

(c) Request to return custody of the Indian child

If a final decree of adoption is vacated or set aside, or if the adoptive parents voluntarily consent to the termination of their parental rights, a biological parent or prior Indian custodian may request a return of custody of the Indian child.

(1) The court must reinstate jurisdiction.

(2) In a juvenile case, the juvenile court must hold a new disposition hearing in accordance with 25 United States Code section 1901 et seq. where the court may consider all placement options as stated in Welfare and Institutions Code sections 361.31(b), (c), (d), and (h).

(3) The court may consider placement with a biological parent or prior Indian custodian if the biological parent or prior Indian custodian can show that placement with him or her is not detrimental to the child and that the placement is in the best interests of the child.

(4) The hearing on the request to return custody of an Indian child must be conducted in accordance with statutory requirements and the relevant sections of this rule.

(Subd (c) adopted effective January 1, 2008.)
Rule 5.486 adopted effective January 1, 2008.

Ref.: Cal. Fms Pl. & Pr., Ch. 12B, "Adoptions: Unmarried Minors."

Rule 5.487.   Adoption record keeping (Fam. Code, § 9208)

(a) Copies of adoption decree and other information to the Secretary of the Interior

After granting a decree of adoption of an Indian child, the court must provide the Secretary of the Interior with a copy of the decree and the following information:

(1) The name and tribal affiliation of the Indian child;

(2) The names and addresses of the biological parents;

(3) The names and addresses of the adoptive parents; and

(4) The agency maintaining files and records regarding the adoptive placement.

(Subd (a) adopted effective January 1, 2008.)

(b) Affidavit of confidentiality to the Bureau of Indian Affairs

If a biological parent has executed an affidavit requesting that his or her identity remain confidential, the court must provide the affidavit to the Bureau of Indian Affairs, which must ensure the confidentiality of the information.

(Subd (b) adopted effective January 1, 2008.)
Rule 5.487 adopted effective January 1, 2008.

Advisory Committee Comment

This chapter was adopted, effective January 1, 2008, as the result of the passage of Senate Bill 678 (Ducheny; Stats. 2006, ch. 838), which codified the federal Indian Child Welfare Act into California's Family, Probate, and Welfare and Institutions Codes affecting all proceedings listed in rule 5.480. Rule 5.664, which applied the Indian Child Welfare Act but was limited in its effect to juvenile proceedings, was repealed effective January 1, 2008, and was replaced by this chapter.

As of January 1, 2008, only the Washoe Tribe of Nevada and California is authorized under the Indian Child Welfare Act to exercise exclusive jurisdiction as discussed in rule 5.483.

Ref.: Cal. Fms Pl. & Pr., Ch. 12B, "Adoptions: Unmarried Minors."

Division 3
Juvenile Rules

Chapter 1
Preliminary Provisions—Title and Definitions

Rule 5.500.   Division title

The rules in this division may be referred to as the Juvenile Rules.

Rule 5.500 adopted effective January 1, 2007.

Ref.: Cal. Fms Pl. & Pr., Ch. 328, "Juvenile Courts: Dependency Proceedings"; W. Cal. Sum., 10 "Parent and Child" §§286, 444, 14 "Wills and Probate" §916.

Rule 5.501.   Preliminary provisions

(a) Application of rules (§§ 200–945)

The rules in this division solely apply to every action and proceeding to which the juvenile court law (Welf. & Inst. Code, div. 2, pt. 1, ch. 2, § 200 et seq.) applies, unless they are explicitly made applicable in any other action or proceeding. The rules in this division do not apply to an action or proceeding heard by a traffic hearing officer, nor to a rehearing or appeal from a denial of a rehearing following an order by a traffic hearing officer.

(Subd (a) amended effective January 1, 2007.)

(b) Authority for and purpose of rules (Cal. Const., art. VI, §§ 6, 265)

The Judicial Council adopted the rules in this division under its constitutional and statutory authority to adopt rules for court administration, practice, and procedure that are not inconsistent with statute. These rules implement the purposes of the juvenile court law by promoting uniformity in practice and procedure and by providing guidance to judicial officers, attorneys, social workers, probation officers, and others participating in the juvenile court.

(Subd (b) amended effective January 1, 2007.)

(c) Rules of construction

Unless the context otherwise requires, these preliminary provisions and the following rules of construction govern the construction of these rules:

(1) Insofar as these rules are substantially the same as existing statutory provisions relating to the same subject matter, these rules must be construed as restatements of those statutes; and

(2) Insofar as these rules may add to existing statutory provisions relating to the same subject matter, these rules

must be construed so as to implement the purposes of the juvenile court law.

(Subd (c) amended effective January 1, 2007.)

(d) Severability clause

If a rule or a subdivision of a rule in this division is invalid, all valid parts that are severable from the invalid part remain in effect. If a rule or a subdivision of a rule in this division is invalid in one or more of its applications, the rule or subdivision remains in effect in all valid applications that are severable from the invalid applications.

Rule 5.501 amended and renumbered effective January 1, 2007; adopted as rule 1400 effective January 1, 1990.

Ref.: Cal. Fms Pl. & Pr., Ch. 280, "Guardianship and Conservatorship: Appointment of Guardians," Ch. 327, "Juvenile Courts: Jurisdiction and General Procedures"; W. Cal. Sum., 10 "Parent and Child" §§443, 444.

Rule 5.502.   Definitions and use of terms

Definitions (§§ 202(e), 319, 361, 361.5(a)(3), 366(a)(1)(B), 628.1, 636, 726, 727.3(c)(2), 727.4(d); 20 U.S.C. § 1415)

As used in these rules, unless the context or subject matter otherwise requires:

(1) "Affinity" means the connection existing between one spouse or domestic partner and the blood or adoptive relatives of the other spouse or domestic partner.

(2) "At risk of entering foster care" means that conditions within a child's family may require that the child be removed from the custody of a parent or guardian and placed in foster care unless or until those conditions are resolved.

(3) "CASA" means Court Appointed Special Advocate as defined in rule 5.655.

(4) "Child Abuse Prevention and Treatment Act (CAPTA) guardian ad litem for a child subject to a juvenile dependency petition" is defined in rule 5.662.

(5) "Child" means a person under the age of 18 years.

(6) "Clerk" means the clerk of the juvenile court.

(7) "Court" means the juvenile court and includes any judicial officer of the juvenile court.

(8) "Court-ordered services" or "court-ordered treatment program" means child welfare services or services provided by an appropriate agency ordered at a disposition hearing at which the child is declared a dependent child of the court, and any hearing thereafter, for the purpose of maintaining or reunifying a child with a parent or guardian.

(9) "Date the child entered foster care" means:

(A) In dependency, the date on which the court sustained the petition filed under section 300 or 60 days after the "initial removal" of the child as defined below, whichever is earlier; or

(B) In delinquency, the date 60 days after the date on which the child was initially removed from the home, unless one of the following exceptions applies:

(i) If the child is detained pending foster care placement and remains detained for more than 60 days, then the "date the child entered foster care" means the date the court declares the child a ward and orders the child placed in foster care under the supervision of the probation officer;

(ii) If, before the child is placed in foster care, the child is committed to a ranch, camp, school, or other institution pending placement, and remains in that facility for more than 60 days, then the "date the child entered foster care" is the date the child is physically placed in foster care; or

(iii) If, at the time the wardship petition was filed, the child was a dependent of the juvenile court and in out-of-home placement, then the "date the child entered foster care" is the date defined in (A).

(10) "De facto parent" means a person who has been found by the court to have assumed, on a day-to-day basis, the role of parent, fulfilling both the child's physical and psychological needs for care and affection, and who has assumed that role for a substantial period.

(11) "Detained" means any removal of the child from the person or persons legally entitled to the child's physical custody, or any release of the child on home supervision under section 628.1 or 636.

(12) "Domestic partner" means two adults who have chosen to share one another's lives in an intimate and committed relationship of mutual caring as described in Family Code section 297.

(13) "Educational representative" means the responsible adult who holds the educational rights for a child when the parent's or guardian's educational rights have been limited by the court. The educational representative acts as the child's spokesperson, educational decision maker, and parent in regard to all educational matters, including those defined in sections 319, 361, and 726; Education Code section 56055; Government Code section 7579.5; and title 20 (commencing with section 1400) of the United States Code and part 300 (commencing with section 300.1) of title 34 of the Code of Federal Regulations. The educational representative holds educational and privacy rights as the child's parent as defined in title 20 United States Code section 1232g and 34 Code of Federal Regulations section 99.3.

(14) "Foster care" means residential care provided in any of the settings described in section 11402.

(15) "Foster parent" includes a relative with whom the child is placed.

(16) "Guardian" means legal guardian of the child.

(17) "Hearing" means a noticed proceeding with findings and orders that are made on a case-by-case basis, heard by either of the following:

(A) A judicial officer, in a courtroom, in which the proceedings are recorded by a court reporter; or

(B) An administrative panel, provided that the hearing meets the conditions described in section 366.3(d) and (e) for dependents and section 727.4(d)(7)(B) for delinquents.

(18) "Initial removal" means the date on which the child, who is the subject of a petition filed under section 300 or 600, was taken into custody by the social worker or a peace officer, or was deemed to have been taken into custody under section 309(b) or 628(c), if removal results in the filing of the petition before the court.

(19) "Member of the household," for purposes of section 300 proceedings, means any person continually or frequently found in the same household as the child.

(20) "Notice" means a paper to be filed with the court accompanied by proof of service on each party required to be served in the manner prescribed by these rules. If a

notice or other paper is required to be given to or served on a party, the notice or service must be given to or made on the party's attorney of record, if any.

(21) "Notify" means to inform, either orally or in writing.

(22) "Petitioner," in section 300 proceedings, means the county welfare department; "petitioner," in section 601 and 602 proceedings, means the probation officer or prosecuting attorney.

(23) "Preadoptive parent" means a licensed foster parent who has been approved to adopt a child by the California State Department of Social Services, when it is acting as an adoption agency, or by a licensed adoption agency.

(24) "Probation officer," in section 300 proceedings, includes a social worker in the county agency responsible for the administration of child welfare.

(25) "Punishment" means the imposition of sanctions, as defined in section 202(e), on a child declared a ward of the court after a petition under section 602 is sustained. A court order to place a child in foster care must not be used as punishment.

(26) "Reasonable efforts" or "reasonable services" means those efforts made or services offered or provided by the county welfare agency or probation department to prevent or eliminate the need for removing the child, or to resolve the issues that led to the child's removal in order for the child to be returned home, or to finalize the permanent placement of the child.

(27) "Relative" means an adult who is related to the child by blood, adoption, or affinity within the fifth degree of kinship, including stepparents, stepsiblings, and all relatives whose status is preceded by the prefix "great," "great-great," or "grand," or the spouse or domestic partner of any of these persons even if the marriage was terminated by death or dissolution.

(28) "Removal" means a court order that takes away the care, custody, and control of a dependent child or ward from the child's parent or guardian, and places the care, custody, and control of the child with the court, under the supervision of the agency responsible for the administration of child welfare or the county probation department.

(29) "Section" means a section of the Welfare and Institutions Code unless stated otherwise.

(30) "Sibling group" means two or more children related to each other by blood, adoption, or affinity through a common legal or biological parent.

(31) "Social study," in section 300, 601, or 602 proceedings, means any written report provided to the court and all parties and counsel by the social worker or probation officer in any matter involving the custody, status, or welfare of a child in a dependency or wardship proceeding.

(32) "Social worker," in section 300 proceedings, means an employee of the county child welfare agency and includes a probation officer performing the child welfare duties.

(33) "Subdivision" means a subdivision of the rule in which the term appears.

Rule 5.502 amended effective January 1, 2008; adopted as rule 1401 effective January 1, 1990; previously amended effective July 1, 1992, July 1, 1997, January 1, 1998, January 1, 1999, January 1, 2001, July 1, 2002, and January 1, 2003; previously amended and renumbered effective January 1, 2007.

Ref.: Cal. Fms Pl. & Pr., Ch. 327, "Juvenile Courts: Jurisdiction and General Procedures," Ch. 328, "Juvenile Courts: Dependency Proceedings"; W. Cal. Sum., 10 "Parent and Child" §§444, 582, 587, 763.

Rule 5.504.　Judicial Council forms

(a) Explanation of Judicial Council legal forms

Rules 1.30–1.37 and 2.131–2.134 apply to Judicial Council legal forms, including forms applicable to the juvenile court.

(Subd (a) amended effective January 1, 2007; repealed and adopted effective January 1, 2001.)

(b) Electronically produced forms

The forms applicable to juvenile court may be produced entirely by computer, word-processor printer, or similar process, or may be produced by the California State Department of Social Services Child Welfare Systems Case Management System.

(Subd (b) amended effective July 1, 2006; adopted as subd (c) effective July 1, 1991; amended and relettered effective January 1, 2001; previously amended effective January 1, 1993, January 1, 1998, and January 1, 2006.)

(c) Implementation of new and revised mandatory forms

To help implement mandatory Judicial Council juvenile forms:

(1) New and revised mandatory forms produced by computer, word-processor printer, or similar process must be implemented within one year of the effective date of the form. During that one-year period the court may authorize the use of a legally accurate alternative form, including any existing local form or the immediate prior version of the Judicial Council form.

(2) Until January 1, 2012, a court may produce court orders in any form or format as long as:

(A) The document is substantively identical to the mandatory Judicial Council form it is modifying;

(B) Any electronically generated form is identical in both language and legally mandated elements, including all notices and advisements, to the mandatory Judicial Council form it is modifying;

(C) The order is an otherwise legally sufficient court order, as provided in rule 1.31(g), concerning orders not on Judicial Council mandatory forms; and

(D) The court sends written notice of its election to change the form or format of the mandatory form to the Family and Juvenile Law Advisory Committee and submits additional informational reports as requested by the committee.

(Subd (c) amended effective January 1, 2007; adopted effective January 1, 2006.)

Rule 5.504 amended effective January 1, 2007; adopted as rule 1402 effective January 1, 1991; previously amended effective July 1, 1991, January 1, 1992, July 1, 1992, January 1, 1993, January 1, 1994, January 1, 1998, January 1, 2001, January 1, 2006, July 1, 2006; and renumbered effective January 1, 2007.

Ref.: Cal. Fms Pl. & Pr., Ch. 327, "Juvenile Courts: Jurisdiction and General Procedures," Ch. 328, "Juvenile Courts: Dependency Proceedings," Ch. 329, "Juvenile Courts: Delinquency Proceedings"; W. Cal. Sum., 10 "Parent and Child" §§444, 445.

Rule 5.505. Juvenile dependency court performance measures

(a) Purpose

The juvenile dependency court performance measures and related procedures set forth in this rule are intended to:

(1) Protect abused and neglected children by assisting courts in promoting children's placement in safe and permanent homes, enhancing their well-being and that of their families, and ensuring that all participants receive timely and fair treatment;

(2) Assist trial courts in meeting the mandated timelines for dependency hearings, securing due process for all litigants, and, in collaboration with the child welfare agency, improving safety, permanency, and well-being outcomes for children and families under the jurisdiction of the juvenile dependency court; and

(3) Assist courts in making well-informed resource allocation decisions.

(Subd (a) adopted effective January 1, 2009.)

(b) Performance measures

Detailed definitions of the performance measures and descriptions of the methods for producing the performance measures in accordance with (c)(2) and (3) are contained in the Judicial Council–approved *Implementation Guide to Juvenile Dependency Court Performance Measures.*

The juvenile dependency court performance measures are:

(1) Hearing timeliness:

(A) Percentage of children for whom the initial hearing is completed within the statutory time frame following the filing of the initial petition;

(B) Percentage of children for whom the jurisdictional hearing is completed within the statutory time frame following the initial hearing;

(C) Percentage of children for whom the disposition hearing is completed within the statutory time frame following the finding of jurisdiction;

(D) Percentage of children for whom a 3-month or other interim review hearing is held;

(E) Percentage of children for whom the 6-month review hearing is completed within 6 months of the date the child entered foster care;

(F) Percentage of children for whom the 12-month permanency hearing is completed within 12 months of the date the child entered foster care;

(G) Percentage of children for whom the 18-month review hearing is completed within 18 months of the date of original protective custody;

(H) Percentage of children for whom the first section 366.26 hearing is completed within 120 days of the termination of reunification services;

(I) Percentage of children whose postpermanency hearing is completed within 6 months of the section 366.26 hearing or the last postpermanency hearing;

(J) Percentage of children in long-term foster care whose subsequent section 366.26 hearing is completed within 12 months of the previous section 366.26 hearing;

(K) Percentage of children whose adoption is finalized within 180 days after termination of parental rights;

(L) Median time from disposition or section 366.26 hearing to order establishing guardianship;

(M) Percentage of children for whom the first and subsequent postpermanency review hearings are completed within the statutory time frame;

(N) Percentage of hearings delayed by reasons for delay and hearing type;

(O) Median time from filing of original petition to implementation of a permanent plan by permanent plan type; and

(P) Median time from filing of original petition to termination of jurisdiction by reason for termination of jurisdiction.

(2) Court procedures and due process:

(A) Percentage of cases in which all hearings are heard by one judicial officer;

(B) Percentage of cases in which all parties and other statutorily entitled individuals are served with a copy of the original petition;

(C) Percentage of hearings in which notice is given to all statutorily entitled parties and individuals within the statutory time frame;

(D) Percentage of hearings in which child or parents are present if statutorily entitled to be present;

(E) Percentage of hearings in which a judicial inquiry is made when a child 10 years of age or older is not present at hearing;

(F) Percentage of hearings in which other statutorily entitled individuals who are involved in the case (e.g., CASA volunteers, caregivers, de facto parents, others) are present;

(G) Percentage of cases in which legal counsel for parents, children, and the child welfare agency are present at every hearing;

(H) Point at which children and parents are assigned legal counsel;

(I) Percentage of cases in which legal counsel for children or parents changes;

(J) Percentage of cases in which no reunification services are ordered and reasons;

(K) Percentage of cases for which youth have input into their case plans; and

(L) Cases in compliance with the requirements of the Indian Child Welfare Act (ICWA).

(3) Child safety in the child welfare system:

(A) Percentage of children who are not victims of another substantiated maltreatment allegation within 6 and 12 months after the maltreatment incident that led to the filing of the initial petition; and

(B) For all children served in foster care during the year, percentage of children who were not victims of substantiated maltreatment by a foster parent or facility staff member.

(4) Child permanency:

(A) Percentage of children reunified in less than 12 months;

(B) Percentage of children who were reunified but reentered foster care within 12 months;

(C) Percentage of children who were discharged from foster care to a finalized adoption within 24 months;

(D) Percentage of children in foster care who were freed for adoption;

(E) Percentage of children in long-term foster care who were discharged to a permanent home before their 18th birthdays;

(F) Of children discharged to emancipation or aging out of foster care, percentage who were in foster care 3 years or longer;

(G) Percentage of children with multiple foster-care placements;

(5) Child and family well-being:

(A) Percentage of children 14 years of age or older with current transitional independent living plans;

(B) Percentage of children for whom a section 391 termination of jurisdiction hearing was held;

(C) Percentage of section 391 termination of jurisdiction hearings that did not result in termination of jurisdiction and reasons jurisdiction did not terminate;

(D) Percentage of youth present at section 391 termination of jurisdiction hearing with judicial confirmation of receipt of all services and documents mandated by section 391(b)(1–5);

(E) Percentage of children placed with all siblings who are also under court jurisdiction, as appropriate;

(F) Percentage of children placed with at least one but not all siblings who are also under court jurisdiction, as appropriate;

(G) For children who have siblings under court jurisdiction but are not placed with all of them, percentage of cases in which sibling visitation is not ordered and reasons;

(H) Percentage of cases in which visitation is not ordered for parents and reasons;

(I) Number of visitation orders for adults other than parents and siblings, (e.g., grandparents, other relatives, extended family members, others) as appropriate;

(J) Number of cases in which the court has requested relative-finding efforts from the child welfare agency;

(K) Percentage of children placed with relatives;

(L) For children 10 years of age or older and in foster care for at least 6 months, percentage for whom the court has inquired whether the social worker has identified persons important to the child; and

(M) For children 10 years of age or older in foster care for at least 6 months, percentage for whom the court has made orders to enable the child to maintain relationships with persons important to that child.

(Subd (b) adopted effective January 1, 2009.)

(c) Data collection

(1) California's Court Case Management System (CCMS) family and juvenile law module must be capable of collecting the data described in the *Implementation Guide to Juvenile Dependency Court Performance Measures* in order to calculate the performance measures and to produce performance measure reports.

(2) Before implementation of the CCMS family and juvenile law module, each local court must collect and submit to the AOC the subset of juvenile dependency data described in (b) and further delineated in the *Implementation Guide to Juvenile Dependency Court Performance Measures* that it is reasonably capable of collecting and submitting with its existing court case management system and resources.

(3) On implementation of the CCMS family and juvenile law module in a local court, and as the necessary data elements become electronically available, the local court must collect and submit to the AOC the juvenile dependency data described in (b) and further delineated in the *Implementation Guide to Juvenile Dependency Court Performance Measures*. For the purposes of this subdivision, "implementation of the CCMS family and juvenile law module" in a local court means that the CCMS family and juvenile law module has been deployed in that court, is functioning, and has the ability to capture the required data elements and that local court staff has been trained to use the system.

(Subd (c) adopted effective January 1, 2009.)

(d) Use of data and development of measures before CCMS implementation

Before CCMS implementation, the AOC must:

(1) Establish a program to assist the local courts in collecting, preparing, analyzing, and reporting the data required by this rule;

(2) Establish a procedure to assist the local courts in submitting the required data to the AOC;

(3) Use the data submitted under (c)(2) to test and refine the detailed definitions of the performance measures and descriptions of the methods for producing the performance measures described in the *Implementation Guide to Juvenile Dependency Court Performance Measures*;

(4) Consult with local courts about the accuracy of the data submitted under (c)(2). After such consultation, use data to generate aggregate data reports on performance measures, consistent with section 16543, while not disclosing identifying information about children, parents, judicial officers, and other individuals in the dependency system; and

(5) Assist the courts in using the data to achieve improved outcomes for children and families in the dependency system, make systemic improvements, and improve resource allocation decisions.

(Subd (d) adopted effective January 1, 2009.)

(e) Use of data after CCMS implementation

On implementation of CCMS, the AOC must:

(1) Use the data submitted under (c)(3) to conduct ongoing testing, refining, and updating of the information in the *Implementation Guide to Juvenile Dependency Court Performance Measures*;

(2) Use the data submitted under (c)(3) to generate aggregate data reports on performance measures, consistent with section 16543, while not disclosing identifying information about children, parents, judicial officers, and other individuals in the dependency system;

(3) Upon the request of any local court, extract data from the system and prepare county-level reports to meet data reporting requirements; and

(4) Assist the courts in using the data to achieve improved outcomes for children and families in the dependency system, make systemic improvements, and improve resource allocation decisions.

(Subd (e) adopted effective January 1, 2009.)

Rule 5.505 adopted effective January 1, 2009.

Advisory Committee Comment

The juvenile dependency court performance measures and related procedures set forth in this rule fulfill the requirements of the Child Welfare Leadership and Accountability Act of 2006 (Welf. & Inst. Code, §§ 16540–16545).

Consistent with section 16545, the Child Welfare Council and the secretary of the California Health and Human Services Agency were consulted in adopting these performance measures. The appropriate court technology groups have also been consulted.

The *Implementation Guide to Juvenile Dependency Court Performance Measures* is a companion publication to this rule, approved by the Judicial Council.

It is anticipated that the Judicial Council will update the *Implementation Guide to Juvenile Dependency Court Performance Measures*, as appropriate, to stay current with Court Case Management System (CCMS) requirements, local court needs, and the most recent versions of the relevant state and federal child welfare measures. Proposed updates other than those that are purely technical will be circulated for public comment prior to publication.

Chapter 2
Commencement of Juvenile Court Proceedings

Rule 5.510. Proper court; determination of child's residence; exclusive jurisdiction
Rule 5.512. Joint assessment procedure
Rule 5.514. Intake; guidelines
Rule 5.516. Factors to consider
Rule 5.518. Court-connected child protection/dependency mediation
Rule 5.520. Filing the petition; application for petition
Rule 5.522. Fax filing
Rule 5.524. Form of petition; notice of hearing
Rule 5.526. Citation to appear; warrants of arrest; subpoenas

Rule 5.510. Proper court; determination of child's residence; exclusive jurisdiction

(a) Proper court (§§ 327, 651)

The proper court in which to commence proceedings to declare a child a dependent or ward of the court is the juvenile court in the county:

(1) In which the child resides;

(2) In which the child is found; or

(3) In which the acts take place or the circumstances exist that are alleged to bring the child within the provisions of section 300 or 601 or 602.

(Subd (a) amended effective January 1, 2007.)

(b) Determination of residence—general rule (§ 17.1)

Unless otherwise provided in the juvenile court law or in these rules, the residence of a child must be determined under section 17.1.

(c) Exclusive jurisdiction (§§ 304, 316.2, 726.4)

(1) Once a petition has been filed under section 300, the juvenile court has exclusive jurisdiction of the following:

(A) All issues regarding custody and visitation of the child; and

(B) All issues and actions regarding paternity of the child under rule 5.635 and Family Code section 7630 or 7631.

(2) Once a petition has been filed under section 601 or 602, the juvenile court has exclusive jurisdiction to hear an action filed under Family Code section 7630 or 7631.

(Subd (c) amended effective January 1, 2007; adopted effective January 1, 1999.)

Rule 5.510 amended and renumbered effective January 1, 2007; adopted as rule 1403 effective January 1, 1991; previously amended effective January 1, 1999.

Ref.: Cal. Fms Pl. & Pr., Ch. 327, "Juvenile Courts: Jurisdiction and General Procedures"; W. Cal. Sum., 10 "Parent and Child" §§369, 444, 456, 520, 886.

Rule 5.512. Joint assessment procedure

(a) Joint assessment requirement (§ 241.1)

Whenever a child appears to come within the description of section 300 and either section 601 or section 602, the responsible child welfare and probation departments must conduct a joint assessment to determine which status will serve the best interest of the child and the protection of society.

(1) The assessment must be completed as soon as possible after the child comes to the attention of either department.

(2) Whenever possible, the determination of status must be made before any petition concerning the child is filed.

(3) The assessment report need not be prepared before the petition is filed but must be provided to the court for the hearing as stated in (e).

(4) If a petition has been filed, on the request of the child, parent, guardian, or counsel, or on the court's own motion, the court may set a hearing for a determination under section 241.1 and order that the joint assessment report be made available as required in (f).

(Subd (a) amended effective January 1, 2007.)

(b) Proceedings in same county

If the petition alleging jurisdiction is filed in a county in which the child is already a dependent or ward, the child welfare and probation departments in that county must assess the child under a jointly developed written protocol and prepare a joint assessment report to be filed in that county.

(Subd (b) amended effective January 1, 2007.)

(c) Proceedings in different counties

If the petition alleging jurisdiction is filed in one county and the child is already a dependent or ward in another county, a joint assessment must be conducted by the responsible departments of each county. If the departments cannot agree on which will prepare the joint assessment report, then the department in the county where the petition is to be filed must prepare the joint assessment report.

(1) The joint assessment report must contain the recommendations and reasoning of both the child welfare and the probation departments.

(2) The report must be filed at least 5 calendar days before the hearing on the joint assessment in the county where the second petition alleging jurisdictional facts under sections 300, 601, or 602 has been filed.

(Subd (c) amended effective January 1, 2007.)

(d) Joint assessment report

The joint assessment report must contain the joint recommendation of the probation and child welfare departments if they agree on the status that will serve the best interest of the child and the protection of society, or the separate recommendation of each department if they do not agree. The report must also include:

(1) A description of the nature of the referral;

(2) The age of the child;

(3) The history of any physical, sexual, or emotional abuse of the child;

(4) The prior record of the child's parents for abuse of this or any other child;

(5) The prior record of the child for out-of-control or delinquent behavior;

(6) The parents' cooperation with the child's school;

(7) The child's functioning at school;

(8) The nature of the child's home environment;

(9) The history of involvement of any agencies or professionals with the child and his or her family;

(10) Any services or community agencies that are available to assist the child and his or her family;

(11) A statement by any counsel currently representing the child; and

(12) A statement by any CASA volunteer currently appointed for the child.

(Subd (d) amended effective January 1, 2007.)

(e) Hearing on joint assessment

If the child is detained, the hearing on the joint assessment report must occur as soon as possible after or concurrent with the detention hearing, but no later than 15 court days after the order of detention and before the jurisdictional hearing. If the child is not detained, the hearing on the joint assessment must occur before the jurisdictional hearing and within 30 days of the date of the petition. The juvenile court must conduct the hearing and determine which type of jurisdiction over the child best meets the child's unique circumstances.

(Subd (e) amended effective January 1, 2007.)

(f) Notice and participation

At least 5 calendar days before the hearing, notice of the hearing and copies of the joint assessment report must be provided to the child, the child's parent or guardian, all attorneys of record, any CASA volunteer, and any other juvenile court having jurisdiction over the child. The notice must be directed to the judicial officer or department that will conduct the hearing.

(Subd (f) amended effective January 1, 2007.)

(g) Conduct of hearing

All parties and their attorneys must have an opportunity to be heard at the hearing. The court must make a determination regarding the appropriate status of the child and state its reasons on the record or in a written order.

(h) Notice of decision after hearing

Within 5 calendar days after the hearing, the clerk of the juvenile court must transmit the court's findings and orders to any other juvenile court with current jurisdiction over the child.

(i) Local protocols

On or before January 1, 2004, the probation and child welfare departments of each county must adopt a written protocol for the preparation of joint assessment reports, including procedures for resolution of disagreements between the probation and child welfare departments, and submit a copy to the Judicial Council.

Rule 5.512 amended and renumbered effective January 1, 2007; adopted as rule 1403.5 effective January 1, 2003.

Ref.: Cal. Fms Pl. & Pr., Ch. 327, "Juvenile Courts: Jurisdiction and General Procedures"; W. Cal. Sum., 10 "Parent and Child" §§444, 450, 959.

Rule 5.514. Intake; guidelines

(a) Role of juvenile court

It is the duty of the presiding judge of the juvenile court to initiate meetings and cooperate with the probation department, welfare department, prosecuting attorney, law enforcement, and other persons and agencies performing an intake function. The goal of the intake meetings is to establish and maintain a fair and efficient intake program designed to promote swift and objective evaluation of the circumstances of any referral and to pursue an appropriate course of action.

(Subd (a) amended effective January 1, 2007.)

(b) Purpose of intake program

The intake program must be designed to:

(1) Provide for settlement at intake of:

(A) Matters over which the juvenile court has no jurisdiction;

(B) Matters in which there is insufficient evidence to support a petition; and

(C) Matters that are suitable for referral to a nonjudicial agency or program available in the community;

(2) Provide for a program of informal supervision of the child under sections 301 and 654; and

(3) Provide for the commencement of proceedings in the juvenile court only when necessary for the welfare of the child or protection of the public.

(Subd (b) amended effective January 1, 2007; previously amended effective January 1, 1995.)

(c) Investigation at intake (§§ 309, 652.5)

The probation officer or the social worker must conduct an investigation and determine whether:

(1) The matter should be settled at intake by:

(A) Taking no action;

(B) Counseling the child and any others involved in the matter; or

(C) Referring the child, the child's family, and any others involved to other agencies and programs in the community for the purpose of receiving services to prevent or eliminate the need for removal;

(2) A program of informal supervision should be undertaken for not more than six months under section 301 or 654; or

(3) A petition should be filed under section 300 or 601, or the prosecuting attorney should be requested to file a petition under section 602.

(Subd (c) amended effective January 1, 2007; previously amended effective January 1, 1994, January 1, 1995, and January 1, 2001.)

(d) Mandatory referrals to the prosecuting attorney (§ 653.5)

Notwithstanding (c), the probation officer must refer to the prosecuting attorney, within 48 hours, all affidavits requesting that a petition be filed under section 602 if it appears to the probation officer that:

(1) The child, regardless of age:

(A) Is alleged to have committed an offense listed in section 707(b);

(B) Has been referred for the sale or possession for sale of a controlled substance under chapter 2 of division 10 of the Health and Safety Code;

(C) Has been referred for a violation of Health and Safety Code section 11350 or 11377 at a school, or for a violation of Penal Code sections 245.5, 626.9, or 626.10;

(D) Has been referred for a violation of Penal Code section 186.22;

(E) Has previously been placed on informal supervision under section 654; or

(F) Has been referred for an alleged offense in which restitution to the victim exceeds $1,000;

(2) The child was 16 years of age or older on the date of the alleged offense and the referral is for a felony offense; or

(3) The child was under 16 years of age on the date of the alleged offense and the referral is not the first referral for a felony offense.

Except for the offenses listed in (1)(C), the provisions of this subdivision do not apply to narcotics and drug offenses listed in Penal Code section 1000.

(Subd (d) amended effective January 1, 2007; previously amended effective January 1, 1994, and January 1, 1995.)

(e) Informal supervision (§§ 301, 654)

(1) If the child is placed on a program of informal supervision for not more than six months under section 301, the social worker may file a petition at any time during the six-month period. If the objectives of a service plan under section 301 have not been achieved within six months, the social worker may extend the period up to an additional six months, with the consent of the parent or guardian.

(2) If a child is placed on a program of informal supervision for not more than six months under section 654, the probation officer may file a petition under section 601, or request that the prosecuting attorney file a petition under section 602, at any time during the six-month period, or within 90 days thereafter. If a child on informal supervision under section 654 has not participated in the specific programs within 60 days, the probation officer must immediately file a petition under section 601, or request that the prosecuting attorney file one under section 602, unless the probation officer determines that the interests of the child and the community can be adequately protected by continuing under section 654.

(Subd (e) amended effective January 1, 2007; previously amended effective January 1, 1995.)

Rule 5.514 amended and renumbered effective January 1, 2007; adopted as rule 1404 effective January 1, 1991; previously amended effective January 1, 1994, January 1, 1995, and January 1, 2001.

Ref.: Cal. Fms Pl. & Pr., Ch. 328, "Juvenile Courts: Dependency Proceedings," Ch. 329, "Juvenile Courts: Delinquency Proceedings"; W. Cal. Sum., 10 "Parent and Child" §§444, 560, 561, 563, 765–767.

Rule 5.516.　Factors to consider

(a) Settlement at intake (§ 653.5)

In determining whether a matter not described in rule 5.514(d) should be settled at intake, the social worker or probation officer must consider:

(1) Whether there is sufficient evidence of a condition or conduct to bring the child within the jurisdiction of the court;

(2) If the alleged condition or conduct is not considered serious, whether the child has previously presented significant problems in the home, school, or community;

(3) Whether the matter appears to have arisen from a temporary problem within the family that has been or can be resolved;

(4) Whether any agency or other resource in the community is available to offer services to the child and the child's family to prevent or eliminate the need to remove the child from the child's home;

(5) The attitudes of the child, the parent or guardian, and any affected persons;

(6) The age, maturity, and capabilities of the child;

(7) The dependency or delinquency history, if any, of the child;

(8) The recommendation, if any, of the referring party or agency; and

(9) Any other circumstances that indicate that settling the matter at intake would be consistent with the welfare of the child and the protection of the public.

(Subd (a) amended effective January 1, 2007; previously amended effective January 1, 2001.)

(b) Informal supervision

In determining whether to undertake a program of informal supervision of a child not described by rule 5.514(d), the social worker or probation officer must consider:

(1) If the condition or conduct is not considered serious, whether the child has had a problem in the home, school, or community that indicates that some supervision would be desirable;

(2) Whether the child and the parent or guardian seem able to resolve the matter with the assistance of the social worker or probation officer and without formal court action;

(3) Whether further observation or evaluation by the social worker or probation officer is needed before a decision can be reached;

(4) The attitudes of the child and the parent or guardian;

(5) The age, maturity, and capabilities of the child;

(6) The dependency or delinquency history, if any, of the child;

(7) The recommendation, if any, of the referring party or agency;

(8) The attitudes of affected persons; and

(9) Any other circumstances that indicate that a program of informal supervision would be consistent with the welfare of the child and the protection of the public.

(Subd (b) amended effective January 1, 2007.)

(c) Filing of petition

In determining whether to file a petition under section 300 or 601 or to request the prosecuting attorney to file a petition under section 602, the social worker or probation officer must consider:

(1) Whether any of the statutory criteria listed in rules 5.770 and 5.772 relating to the fitness of the child are present;

(2) Whether the alleged conduct would be a felony;

(3) Whether the alleged conduct involved physical harm or the threat of physical harm to person or property;

(4) If the alleged condition or conduct is not serious, whether the child has had serious problems in the home, school, or community that indicate that formal court action is desirable;

(5) If the alleged condition or conduct is not serious, whether the child is already a ward or dependent of the court;

(6) Whether the alleged condition or conduct involves a threat to the physical or emotional health of the child;

(7) Whether a chronic, serious family problem exists after other efforts to resolve the problem have been made;

(8) Whether the alleged condition or conduct is in dispute and, if proven, whether court-ordered disposition appears desirable;

(9) The attitudes of the child and the parent or guardian;

(10) The age, maturity, and capabilities of the child;

(11) Whether the child is on probation or parole;

(12) The recommendation, if any, of the referring party or agency;

(13) The attitudes of affected persons;

(14) Whether any other referrals or petitions are pending; and

(15) Any other circumstances that indicate that the filing of a petition is necessary to promote the welfare of the child or to protect the public.

(Subd (c) amended effective January 1, 2007.)

(d) Certification to juvenile court

Copies of the certification, the accusatory pleading, any police reports, and the order of a superior court, certifying that the accused person was under the age of 18 on the date of the alleged offense, must immediately be delivered to the clerk of the juvenile court.

(1) On receipt of the documents, the clerk must immediately notify the probation officer, who must immediately investigate the matter to determine whether to commence proceedings in juvenile court.

(2) If the child is under the age of 18 and is in custody, the child must immediately be transported to the juvenile detention facility.

(Subd (d) amended effective January 1, 2007.)

Rule 5.516 amended effective January 1, 2007; adopted as rule 1405 effective January 1, 1991; previously amended effective January 1, 2001.

Ref.: Cal. Fms Pl. & Pr., Ch. 328, "Juvenile Courts: Dependency Proceedings," Ch. 329, "Juvenile Courts: Delinquency Proceedings"; W. Cal. Sum., 10 "Parent and Child" §§444, 560, 563, 564, 589, 765, 769, 772.

Rule 5.518. Court-connected child protection/dependency mediation

(a) Purpose (§ 350)

This rule establishes mandatory standards of practice and administration for court-connected dependency mediation services in accordance with section 350. This rule is intended to ensure fairness, accountability, and a high quality of service to children and families and to improve the safety, confidentiality, and consistency of dependency mediation programs statewide.

(Subd (a) amended effective January 1, 2007.)

(b) Definitions

(1) "Dependency mediation" is a confidential process conducted by specially trained, neutral third-party mediators who have no decision-making power. Dependency mediation provides a nonadversarial setting in which a mediator assists the parties in reaching a fully informed and mutually acceptable resolution that focuses on the child's safety and best interest and the safety of all family members. Dependency mediation is concerned with any and all issues related to child protection.

(2) "Safety and best interest of the child" refers to the child's physical, psychological, and emotional well-being. Determining the safety and best interest of the child includes consideration of all of the following:

(A) The preservation and strengthening of the family and family relationships whenever appropriate and possible;

(B) The manner in which the child may be protected from the risk of future abuse or neglect;

(C) The child's need for safety, stability, and permanency;

(D) The ongoing need of the child to cope with the issues that caused his or her involvement in the juvenile dependency system;

(E) The child's need for continuity of care and the effect that removal and subsequent placements have had, or may have, on the child; and

(F) The child's education, which includes the child's participation, progress, need for assistance, cognitive development and, if applicable, early childhood education and care, the need for special education and related services, and the extent to which the child has or has had limited English proficiency (LEP).

(3) "Safety of family members" refers to the physical, psychological, and emotional well-being of all family members, with consideration of the following:

(A) The role of domestic violence in creating a perceived or actual threat for the victim; and

(B) The ongoing need of family members to feel safe from physical, emotional, and psychological abuse.

(4) "Differential domestic violence assessment" is a process used to assess the nature of any domestic violence issues in the family so that the mediator may conduct the mediation in such a way as to protect any victim of domestic violence from intimidation and to correct for power imbalances created by past violence and the fear of prospective violence.

(5) "Protocols" refer to any local set of rules, policies, and procedures developed and implemented by juvenile dependency mediation programs. All protocols must be developed in accordance with pertinent state laws, California Rules of Court, and local court rules.

(Subd (b) amended effective January 1, 2008; previously amended effective January 1, 2007.)

(c) Responsibility for mediation services

(1) Each court that has a dependency mediation program must ensure that:

(A) Dependency mediators are impartial, are competent, and uphold the standards established by this rule;

(B) Dependency mediators maintain an appropriate focus on issues related to the child's safety and best interest and the safety of all family members;

(C) Dependency mediators provide a forum for all interested persons to develop a plan focused on the best interest of the child, emphasizing family preservation and strengthening and the child's need for permanency;

(D) Dependency mediation services and case management procedures are consistent with applicable state law without compromising each party's right to due process and a timely resolution of the issues;

(E) Dependency mediation services demonstrate accountability by:

(i) Providing for the processing of complaints about a mediator's performance; and

(ii) Participating in any statewide and national data-collection efforts;

(F) The dependency mediation program uses an intake process that screens for and informs the mediator about any restraining orders, domestic violence, or safety-related issues affecting the child or any other party named in the proceedings;

(G) Whenever possible, dependency mediation is conducted in the shared language of the participants. When the participants speak different languages, interpreters, court-certified when possible, should be assigned to translate at the mediation session; and

(H) Dependency mediation services preserve, in accordance with pertinent law, party confidentiality, whether written or oral, by the:

(i) Storage and disposal of records and any personal information accumulated by the mediation program; and

(ii) Management of any new child abuse reports and related documents.

(2) Each dependency mediator must:

(A) Attempt to assist the mediation participants in reaching a settlement of the issues consistent with preserving the safety and best interest of the child, first and foremost, and the safety of all family members and participants;

(B) Discourage participants from blaming the victim and from denying or minimizing allegations of child abuse or violence against any family member;

(C) Be conscious of the values of preserving and strengthening the family as well as the child's need for permanency;

(D) Not make any recommendations or reports of any kind to the court, except for the terms of any agreement reached by the parties;

(E) Treat all mediation participants in a manner that preserves their dignity and self-respect;

(F) Promote a safe and balanced environment for all participants to express and advocate for their positions and interests;

(G) Identify and disclose potential grounds on which a mediator's impartiality might reasonably be challenged through a procedure that allows for the selection of another mediator within a reasonable time. If a dependency mediation program has only one mediator and the parties are unable to resolve the conflict, the mediator must inform the court;

(H) Identify and immediately disclose to the participants any reasonable concern regarding the mediator's continuing capacity to be impartial, so they can decide whether the mediator should withdraw or continue;

(I) Promote the participants' understanding of the status of the case in relation to the ongoing court process, what the case plan requires of them, and the terms of any agreement reached during the mediation; and

(J) Conduct an appropriate review to evaluate the viability of any agreement reached, including the identification of any provision that depends on the action or behavior of any individual who did not participate in creating the agreement.

(Subd (c) amended effective January 1, 2007.)

(d) Mediation process

The dependency mediation process must be conducted in accordance with pertinent state laws, applicable rules of court, and local protocols. All local protocols must include the following:

(1) The process by which cases are sent to mediation, including:

(A) Who may request mediation;

(B) Who decides which cases are to be sent to mediation;

(C) Whether mediation is voluntary or mandatory;

(D) How mediation appointments are scheduled; and

(E) The consequences, if any, to a party who fails to participate in the mediation process.

(2) A policy on who participates in the mediation, according to the following guidelines:

(A) When at all possible, dependency mediation should include the direct and active participation of the parties, including but not limited to the child, the parents or legal guardian, a representative of the child protective agency, and, at some stage, their respective attorneys.

(B) The child has a right to participate in the dependency mediation process accompanied by his or her attorney. If the child makes an informed choice not to participate, then the child's attorney may participate. If the child is unable to make an informed choice, then the child's attorney may participate.

(C) Any attorney who has not participated in the mediation must have an opportunity to review and agree to any proposal before it is submitted to the court for approval.

(D) As appropriate, other family members and any guardian ad litem, CASA volunteer, or other involved person or professional may participate in the mediation.

(E) A mediation participant who has been a victim of violence allegedly perpetrated by another mediation participant has the right to be accompanied by a support person. Unless otherwise invited or ordered to participate under the protocols developed by the court, a support person may not actively participate in the mediation except to be present as a source of emotional support for the alleged victim.

(3) A method by which the mediator may review relevant case information before the mediation.

(4) A protocol for providing mediation in cases in which domestic violence or violence perpetrated by any other mediation participant has, or allegedly has, occurred. This protocol must include specialized procedures designed to protect victims of domestic violence from intimidation by perpetrators. The protocol must also appropriately address all family violence issues by encouraging the incorporation of appropriate safety and treat-

ment interventions in any settlement. The protocol must require:

(A) A review of case-related information before commencing the mediation;

(B) The performance of a differential domestic violence assessment to determine the nature of the violence, for the purposes of:

(i) Assessing the ability of the victim to fully and safely participate and to reach a noncoerced settlement;

(ii) Clarifying the history and dynamics of the domestic violence issue in order to determine the most appropriate manner in which the mediation can proceed; and

(iii) Assisting the parties, attorneys, and other participants in formulating an agreement following a discussion of appropriate safeguards for the safety of the child and family members; and

(C) A mediation structure designed to meet the need of the victim of violence for safety and for full and noncoerced participation in the process, which structure must include:

(i) An option for the victim to attend the mediation session without the alleged perpetrator being present; and

(ii) Permission for the victim to have a support person present during the mediation process, whether he or she elects to be seen separately from or together with the alleged perpetrator.

(5) An oral or written orientation that facilitates participants' safe, productive, and informed participation and decision making by educating them about:

(A) The mediation process, the typical participants, the range of disputes that may be discussed, and the typical outcomes of mediation;

(B) The importance of keeping confidential all communications, negotiations, or settlement discussions by and between the participants in the course of mediation;

(C) The mediator's role and any limitations on the confidentiality of the process; and

(D) The right of a participant who has been a victim of violence allegedly perpetrated by another mediation participant to be accompanied by a support person and to have sessions with the mediators separate from the alleged perpetrator.

(6) Protocols related to the inclusion of children in the mediation, including a requirement that the mediator explain in an age-appropriate way the mediation process to a participating child. The following information must be explained to the child:

(A) How the child may participate in the mediation;

(B) What occurs during the mediation process;

(C) The role of the mediator;

(D) What the child may realistically expect from the mediation, and the limits on his or her ability to affect the outcome;

(E) Any limitations on the confidentiality of the process;

(F) The child's right to be accompanied, throughout the mediation, by his or her attorney and other support persons; and

(G) The child's right to leave the mediation session if his or her emotional or physical well-being is threatened.

(7) Policy and procedures for scheduling follow-up mediation sessions.

(8) A procedure for suspending or terminating the process if the mediator determines that mediation cannot be conducted in a safe or an appropriately balanced manner or if any party is unable to participate in an informed manner for any reason, including fear or intimidation.

(9) A procedure for ensuring that each participant clearly understands any agreement reached during the mediation, and a procedure for presenting the agreement to the court for its approval. This procedure must include the requirement that all parties and the attorneys who participate in the agreement review and approve it and indicate their agreement in writing before its submission to the court.

(Subd (d) amended effective January 1, 2007; previously amended effective January 1, 2005.)

(e) Education, experience, and training requirements for dependency mediators

Dependency mediators must meet the following minimum qualifications:

(1) Possession of one or more of the following:

(A) A master's or doctoral degree in psychology, social work, marriage and family therapy, conflict resolution, or another behavioral science substantially related to family relationships, family violence, child development, or conflict resolution from an accredited college or university; or

(B) A juris doctorate or bachelor of laws degree;

(2) At least two years of experience as an attorney, a referee, a judicial officer, a mediator, or a child welfare worker in juvenile dependency court, or at least three years of experience in mediation or counseling, preferably in a setting related to juvenile dependency or domestic relations; and

(3) Completion of at least 40 hours of initial dependency mediation training before or within 12 months of beginning practice as a dependency mediator. Currently practicing dependency mediators must complete the required 40 hours of initial training by January 1, 2006. The training must cover the following subject areas as they relate to the practice of dependency mediation:

(A) Multiparty, multi-issue, multiagency, and high-conflict cases, including:

(i) The roles and participation of parents, other family members, children, attorneys, guardians ad litem, children's caregivers, the child welfare agency staff, CASA volunteers, law enforcement, mediators, the court, and other involved professionals and interested participants in the mediation process;

(ii) The impact that the mediation process can have on a child's well-being, and when and how to involve the child in the process;

(iii) The methods to help parties collaboratively resolve disputes and jointly develop plans that consider the needs and best interest of the child;

(iv) The disclosure, recantation, and denial of child abuse and neglect;

(v) Adult mental health issues; and

(vi) The requirements of the laws incorporated in rule 5.651(a)(3) and strategies for appropriately addressing the individual needs of persons with disabilities;

(B) Physical and sexual abuse, exploitation, emotional abuse, endangerment, and neglect of children, and the impacts on children, including safety and treatment issues related to child abuse, neglect, and family violence;

(C) Family violence, its relevance to child abuse and neglect, and its effects on children and adult victims, including safety and treatment issues related to child abuse, neglect, and family violence;

(D) Substance abuse and its impact on children;

(E) Child development and its relevance to child abuse, neglect, and child custody and visitation arrangements;

(F) Juvenile dependency and child welfare systems, including dependency law;

(G) Interfamilial relationships and the psychological needs of children, including, but not limited to:

(i) The effect of removal or nonremoval of children from their homes and family members; and

(ii) The effect of terminating parental rights;

(H) The effect of poverty on parenting and familial relationships;

(I) Awareness of differing cultural values, including cross-generational cultural issues and local demographics;

(J) An overview of the special needs of dependent children, including their educational, medical, psychosocial, and mental health needs; and

(K) Available community resources and services for dealing with domestic and family violence, substance abuse, and housing, educational, medical, and mental health needs for families in the juvenile dependency system.

(Subd (e) amended effective January 1, 2008; previously amended effective January 1, 2005, and January 1, 2007.)

(f) Substitution for education or experience

The court, on a case-by-case basis, may approve substitution of experience for the education, or education for the experience, required by (e)(1) and (e)(2).

(Subd (f) amended effective January 1, 2007.)

(g) Continuing education requirements for mediators

In addition to the 40 hours of training required by (e)(3), all dependency mediators, mediation supervisors, program coordinators and directors, volunteers, interns, and paraprofessionals must participate in at least 12 hours per year of continuing instruction designed to enhance dependency mediation practice, skills, and techniques, including at least 4 hours specifically related to the issue of family violence.

(Subd (g) amended effective January 1, 2007.)

(h) Volunteers, interns, or paraprofessionals

Dependency mediation programs may use volunteers, interns, or paraprofessionals as mediators, but only if they are supervised by a professional mediator who is qualified to act as a professional dependency mediator as described in (e). They must meet the training and continuing education requirements in (e)(3) and (g) unless they co-mediate with another professional who meets the requirements of this rule. They are exempt from meeting the education and experience requirements in (e)(1) and (e)(2).

(Subd (h) amended effective January 1, 2007.)

(i) Education and training providers

Only education and training acquired from eligible providers meet the requirements of this rule. "Eligible providers" includes the Administrative Office of the Courts and may include educational institutions, professional associations, professional continuing education groups, public or private for-profit or not-for-profit groups, and court-connected groups.

(1) Eligible providers must:

(A) Ensure that the training instructors or consultants delivering the education and training programs either meet the requirements of this rule or are experts in the subject matter;

(B) Monitor and evaluate the quality of courses, curricula, training, instructors, and consultants;

(C) Emphasize the importance of focusing dependency mediations on the health, safety, welfare, and best interest of the child;

(D) Develop a procedure to verify that participants complete the education and training program; and

(E) Distribute a certificate of completion to each person who has completed the training. The certificate must document the number of hours of training offered, the number of hours the person completed, the dates of the training, and the name of the training provider.

(2) Effective July 1, 2005, all education and training programs must be approved by the Administrative Office of the Courts.

(Subd (i) amended effective January 1, 2007; adopted effective January 1, 2005.)

(j) Ethics/standards of conduct

Mediators must:

(1) Meet the standards of the applicable code of ethics for court employees.

(2) Maintain objectivity, provide information to and gather information from all parties, and be aware of and control their own biases.

(3) Protect the confidentiality of all parties, including the child. Mediators must not release information or make any recommendations about the case to the court or to any individual except as required by statute (for example, the requirement to make mandatory child abuse reports or reports to authorities regarding threats of harm or violence). Any limitations to confidentiality must be clearly explained to all mediation participants before any substantive issues are discussed in the mediation session.

(4) Maintain the confidential relationship between any family member or the child and his or her treating counselor, including the confidentiality of any psychological evaluations.

(5) Decline to provide legal advice.

(6) Consider the health, safety, welfare, and best interest of the child and the safety of all parties and other participants in all phases of the process and encourage the formulation of settlements that preserve these values.

(7) Operate within the limits of their training and experience and disclose any limitations or bias that would affect their ability to conduct the mediation.

(8) Not require the child to state a preference for placement.

(9) Disclose to the court, to any participant, and to the participant's attorney any conflicts of interest or dual relationships, and not accept any referral except by court

order or the parties' stipulation. In the event of a conflict of interest, the mediator must suspend mediation and meet and confer in an effort to resolve the conflict of interest either to the satisfaction of all parties or according to local court rules. The court may order mediation to continue with another mediator or offer the parties an alternative method of resolving the issues in dispute.

(10) Not knowingly assist the parties in reaching an agreement that would be unenforceable for a reason such as fraud, duress, illegality, overreaching, absence of bargaining ability, or unconscionability.

(11) Protect the integrity of the mediation process by terminating the mediation when a party or participant has no genuine interest in resolving the dispute and is abusing the process.

(12) Terminate any session in which an issue of coercion, inability to participate, lack of intention to resolve the issues at hand, or physical or emotional abuse during the mediation session is involved.

(Subd (j) amended effective January 1, 2007; adopted as subd (i) effective January 1, 2004; previously relettered effective January 1, 2005.)

Rule 5.518 amended effective January 1, 2008; adopted as rule 1405.5 effective January 1, 2004; previously amended effective January 1, 2005; previously amended and renumbered effective January 1, 2007.

Ref.: W. Cal. Sum., 10 "Parent and Child" §§444, 589.

Rule 5.520. Filing the petition; application for petition

(a) Discretion to file (§§ 325, 650)

Except as provided in sections 331, 364, 604, 653.5, 654, and 655, the social worker or probation officer has the sole discretion to determine whether to file a petition under section 300 and 601. The prosecuting attorney has the sole discretion to file a petition under section 602.

(Subd (a) amended effective January 1, 2007.)

(b) Filing the petition (§§ 325, 650)

A proceeding in juvenile court to declare a child a dependent or a ward of the court is commenced by the filing of a petition.

(1) In proceedings under section 300, the social worker must file the petition;

(2) In proceedings under section 601, the probation officer must file the petition; and

(3) In proceedings under section 602, the prosecuting attorney must file the petition. The prosecuting attorney may refer the matter back to the probation officer for appropriate action.

(Subd (b) amended effective January 1, 2007.)

(c) Application for petition (§§ 329, 331, 653, 653.5, 655)

Any person may apply to the social worker or probation officer to commence proceedings. The application must be in the form of an affidavit alleging facts showing the child is described in sections 300, 601, or 602. The social worker or probation officer must proceed under sections 329, 653, or 653.5. The applicant may seek review of a decision not to file a petition by proceeding under section 331 or 655.

(Subd (c) amended effective January 1, 2007.)

Rule 5.520 amended and renumbered effective January 1, 2007; adopted as rule 1406 effective January 1, 1991.

Ref.: Cal. Fms Pl. & Pr., Ch. 327, "Juvenile Courts: Jurisdiction and General Procedures," Ch. 329, "Juvenile Courts: Delinquency Proceedings"; W. Cal. Sum., 10 "Parent and Child" §§444, 561, 562, 564, 766, 772.

Rule 5.522. Fax filing

(a) Applicability

(1) This rule applies to juvenile court proceedings in courts that permit fax filing by local rule or other written instruction.

(2) As used in this rule, "facsimile transmission" or "fax transmission," "facsimile machine" or "fax machine," "facsimile filing" or "fax filing," and "fax" are defined in rule 2.301.

(Subd (a) amended effective January 1, 2007.)

(b) Juvenile court documents that may be filed by fax

The following documents may be filed in juvenile court by the use of a fax machine: petitions filed under sections 300, 601, 602, 342, 387, 388, 777, and 778. Other documents may be filed by the use of a fax machine if permitted by the local rule or other written instruction specified in (a).

(Subd (b) amended and relettered effective January 1, 2007; adopted as subd (c) effective January 1, 1999.)

(c) Persons and agencies that may file by fax

Only the following persons and agencies may file documents stated in (b): any named party to the proceeding; any attorney of record in the proceeding; the county welfare department; the probation department; the office of the district attorney; the office of the county counsel; a CASA volunteer appointed in the case.

(Subd (c) amended and relettered effective January 1, 2007; adopted as subd (d) effective January 1, 1999.)

(d) Procedures for fax filing

A party or agency described in (c) may file by fax directly to any juvenile court that has provided for fax filing by local rule or other written instruction. The local rule or written instruction must provide the fax telephone number or numbers for filings and the business hours during which fax filings will be accepted.

(Subd (d) amended and relettered effective January 1, 2007; adopted as subd (e) effective January 1, 1999.)

(e) Mandatory cover sheet

A fax filing must be accompanied by *Fax Filing Cover Sheet* (form JV-520). The cover sheet must be the first page transferred. The court is not required to retain or file a copy of the cover sheet.

(Subd (e) amended and relettered effective January 1, 2007; adopted as subd (f) effective January 1, 1999.)

(f) Signatures

Notwithstanding any provision of law to the contrary, a signature produced by fax transmission is an original signature.

(Subd (f) relettered effective January 1, 2007; adopted as subd (g) effective January 1, 1999.)

(g) Confidentiality requirements

In order to secure the confidentiality of the documents subject to filing by fax, the following procedures are required:

(1) In each clerk's office designated to receive such documents, a separate fax machine must be provided and dedicated solely to the receipt of the documents described in (b);

(2) The telephone number to be used for these filings must be made available only to those persons and agencies described in (c); and

(3) Any document received for fax filing must be filed or submitted to the court immediately on receipt and must not be placed or stored where anyone not entitled to access may examine it.

(Subd (g) amended and relettered effective January 1, 2007; adopted as subd (h) effective January 1, 1999.)

Rule 5.522 amended and renumbered effective January 1, 2007; adopted as rule 1406.5 effective January 1, 1999.

Ref.: Cal. Fms Pl. & Pr., Ch. 264, "Fax Filing and Service of Papers," Ch. 327, "Juvenile Courts: Jurisdiction and General Procedures," Ch. 328, "Juvenile Courts: Dependency Proceedings"; MB Prac. Guide: Cal. Pretrial Proc., §27.34[5][a]; W. Cal. Sum., 10 "Parent and Child" §§444, 564, 657, 663, 771, 908, 910.

Rule 5.524.   Form of petition; notice of hearing

(a) Form of petition—dependency (§§ 332, 333)

The petition to declare a child a dependent of the court must be verified and may be dismissed without prejudice if not verified. The petition must contain the information stated in section 332.

(Subd (a) amended effective January 1, 2007; previously amended effective January 1, 1995, and January 1, 2006.)

(b) Form of petition—delinquency (§§ 656, 656.1, 656.5, 661)

The petition to declare a child a ward of the court must be verified and may be dismissed without prejudice if not verified. The petition must contain the information stated in sections 656, 656.1, 656.5, 661, and, if applicable, the intent to aggregate other offenses under section 726.

(Subd (b) amended effective January 1, 2007; adopted effective January 1, 2006.)

(c) Use of forms

Dependency petitions must be filed on a Judicial Council form. The filing party must use *Juvenile Dependency Petition (Version One)* (form JV-100) with the *Additional Children Attachment (Juvenile Dependency Petition)* (form JV-101) when appropriate, or *Juvenile Dependency Petition (Version Two)* (form JV-110) as prescribed by local rule or practice. Rules 1.31 and 1.32 govern the use of mandatory and optional forms, respectively.

(Subd (c) amended effective January 1, 2007; adopted as subd (b) effective January 1, 1991; previously amended and relettered effective January 1, 2006.)

(d) Amending the petition (§§ 348, 678)

Chapter 8 of title 6 of part 2 of the Code of Civil Procedure, beginning at section 469, applies to variances and amendments of petitions and proceedings in the juvenile court.

(Subd (d) amended and relettered effective January 1, 2006; adopted as subd (c) effective January 1, 1991.)

(e) Notice of hearing—dependency (§§ 290.1, 290.2, 297, 338)

When the petition is filed, the probation officer or social worker must serve a notice of hearing under section 290.1, with a copy of the petition attached. On filing of the

petition, the clerk must issue and serve notice as prescribed in section 290.2, along with a copy of the petition. CASA volunteers are entitled to the same notice as stated in section 290.1 and 290.2.

(Subd (e) amended effective January 1, 2007; adopted as subd (d) effective January 1, 1991; previously amended and relettered effective January 1, 2006.)

(f) Notice of hearing—delinquency (§§ 630, 630.1, 658, 659, 660)

(1) Immediately after the filing of a petition to detain a child, the probation officer or the prosecuting attorney must issue and serve notice as prescribed in section 630.

(2) When a petition is filed, the clerk must issue and serve a notice of hearing in accordance with sections 658, 659, and 660 with a copy of the petition attached.

(3) After reasonable notification by minor's counsel or his or her parent or guardian, the clerk must provide notice to the minor's attorney as stated in section 630.1.

(Subd (f) amended effective January 1, 2007; adopted effective January 1, 2006.)

(g) Waiver of service (§§ 290.2, 660)

A person may waive service of notice by a voluntary appearance noted in the minutes of the court, or by a written waiver of service filed with the clerk.

(Subd (g) amended and relettered effective January 1, 2006; adopted as subd (h) effective January 1, 1991.)

(h) Oral notice (§§ 290.1, 630)

Notice required by sections 290.1 and 630 may be given orally. The social worker or probation officer must file a declaration stating that oral notice was given and to whom.

(Subd (h) amended effective January 1, 2007; adopted as subd (j) effective January 1, 1991; previously amended and relettered effective January 1, 2006.)

Rule 5.524 amended and renumbered effective January 1, 2007; adopted as rule 1407 effective January 1, 1991; previously amended effective January 1, 1992, January 1, 1995, January 1, 2001, and January 1, 2006.

Ref.: Cal. Fms Pl. & Pr., Ch. 327, "Juvenile Courts: Jurisdiction and General Procedures," Ch. 328, "Juvenile Courts: Dependency Proceedings," Ch. 329, "Juvenile Courts: Delinquency Proceedings"; W. Cal. Sum., 10 "Parent and Child" §§444, 564–566, 600, 656, 664, 668, 773, 774, 776, 778, 820, 908, 910, 911.

Rule 5.526.   Citation to appear; warrants of arrest; subpoenas

(a) Citation to appear (§§ 338, 661)

In addition to the notice required under rule 5.524, the court may issue a citation directing a parent or guardian to appear at a hearing.

(1) The citation must state that the parent or guardian may be required to participate in a counseling program, and the citation may direct the child's present caregiver to bring the child to court.

(2) The citation must be personally served at least 24 hours before the time stated for the appearance.

(Subd (a) amended effective January 1, 2007; previously amended effective January 1, 2006.)

(b) Warrant of arrest (§§ 339, 662)

The court may order a warrant of arrest to issue against the parent, guardian, or present custodian of the child if:

(1) The citation cannot be served;

(2) The person served does not obey it; or

(3) The court finds that a citation will probably be ineffective.

(c) Protective custody or warrant of arrest for child (§§ 340, 663)

The court may order a protective custody warrant or a warrant of arrest for a child if the court finds that:

(1) The conduct and behavior of the child may endanger the health, person, welfare, or property of the child or others; or

(2) The home environment of the child may endanger the health, person, welfare, or property of the child.

(d) Subpoenas (§§ 341, 664)

On the court's own motion or at the request of the petitioner, child, parent, guardian, or present caregiver, the clerk must issue subpoenas requiring attendance and testimony of witnesses and the production of papers at a hearing. If a witness appears in response to a subpoena, the court may order the payment of witness fees as a county charge in the amount and manner prescribed by statute.

(Subd (d) amended effective January 1, 2006.)

Rule 5.526 amended and renumbered effective January 1, 2007; adopted as rule 1408 effective January 1, 1991; previously amended effective January 1, 2006.

Ref.: Cal. Fms Pl. & Pr., Ch. 327, "Juvenile Courts: Jurisdiction and General Procedures," Ch. 329, "Juvenile Courts: Delinquency Proceedings"; W. Cal. Sum., 10 "Parent and Child" §§444, 566, 779–781.

Chapter 3
General Conduct of Juvenile Court Proceedings

Rule 5.530. Persons present
Rule 5.532. Court reporter; transcripts
Rule 5.534. General provisions—all proceedings
Rule 5.536. General provisions—proceedings held before referees
Rule 5.538. Conduct of proceedings held before a referee not acting as a temporary judge
Rule 5.540. Orders of referees not acting as temporary judges
Rule 5.542. Rehearing of proceedings before referees
Rule 5.544. Prehearing motions (§ 700.1)
Rule 5.546. Prehearing discovery
Rule 5.548. Granting immunity to witnesses
Rule 5.550. Continuances
Rule 5.552. Confidentiality of records (§§ 827, 828)
Rule 5.553. Juvenile case file of a deceased child

Rule 5.530. Persons present

(a) Separate session; restriction on persons present (§§ 345, 675)

All juvenile court proceedings must be heard at a special or separate session of the court, and no other matter may be heard at that session. No person on trial, awaiting trial, or accused of a crime, other than a parent, de facto parent, guardian, or relative of the child, may be present at the hearing, except while testifying as a witness.

(Subd (a) amended effective January 1, 2005.)

(b) Persons present (§§ 280, 290.1, 290.2, 332, 347, 349, 353, 656, 658, 677, 679, 681, 700; 25 U.S.C. §§ 1911, 1931–1934)

The following persons are entitled to be present:

(1) The child;

(2) All parents, de facto parents, Indian custodians, and guardians of the child or, if no parent or guardian resides within the state or, if their places of residence are not known;

(A) Any adult relatives residing within the county or, if none;

(B) Any adult relatives residing nearest the court;

(3) Counsel representing the child or the parent, de facto parent, guardian, adult relative, or Indian custodian or the tribe of an Indian child;

(4) The probation officer or social worker;

(5) The prosecuting attorney, as provided in (c) and (d);

(6) Any CASA volunteer;

(7) A representative of the Indian child's tribe;

(8) The court clerk;

(9) The official court reporter, as provided in rule 5.532;

(10) At the court's discretion, a bailiff; and

(11) Any other persons entitled to notice of the hearing under sections 290.1 and 290.2.

(Subd (b) amended effective January 1, 2007; previously amended effective January 1, 1995, January 1, 1997, and January 1, 2005.)

(c) Presence of prosecuting attorney—section 601–602 proceedings (§ 681)

In proceedings brought under section 602, the prosecuting attorney must appear on behalf of the people of the State of California. In proceedings brought under section 601, the prosecuting attorney may appear to assist in ascertaining and presenting the evidence if:

(1) The child is represented by counsel; and

(2) The court consents to or requests the prosecuting attorney's presence, or the probation officer requests and the court consents to the prosecuting attorney's presence.

(Subd (c) amended effective January 1, 2007.)

(d) Presence of petitioner's attorney—section 300 proceedings (§ 317)

In proceedings brought under section 300, the county counsel or district attorney must appear and represent the petitioner if the parent or guardian is represented by counsel and the juvenile court requests the attorney's presence.

(Subd (d) amended effective January 1, 2007.)

(e) Others who may be admitted (§§ 346, 676, 676.5)

Except as provided below, the public must not be admitted to a juvenile court hearing. The court may admit those whom the court deems to have a direct and legitimate interest in the case or in the work of the court.

(1) If requested by a parent or guardian in a hearing under section 300, and consented to or requested by the child, the court may permit others to be present.

(2) In a hearing under section 602:

(A) If requested by the child and a parent or guardian who is present, the court may admit others.

(B) Up to two family members of a prosecuting witness may attend to support the witness, as authorized by Penal Code section 868.5.

(C) Except as provided in section 676(b), members of the public must be admitted to hearings concerning allegations of the offenses stated in section 676(a).

(D) A victim of an offense alleged to have been committed by the child who is the subject of the petition, and up to two support persons chosen by the victim, are entitled to attend any hearing regarding the offense.

(E) Any persons, including the child, may move to exclude a victim or a support person and must demonstrate a substantial probability that overriding interests will be prejudiced by the presence of the individual sought to be excluded. On such motion, the court must consider reasonable alternatives to the exclusion and must make findings as required under section 676.5.

(Subd (e) amended effective January 1, 2007; previously amended effective January 1, 2001.)

Rule 5.530 amended and renumbered effective January 1, 2007; adopted as rule 1410 effective January 1, 1990; previously amended effective January 1, 1995, January 1, 1997, January 1, 2001, and January 1, 2005.

Ref.: Cal. Fms Pl. & Pr., Ch. 327, "Juvenile Courts: Jurisdiction and General Procedures," Ch. 328, "Juvenile Courts: Dependency Proceedings," Ch. 329, "Juvenile Courts: Delinquency Proceedings"; W. Cal. Sum., 10 "Parent and Child" §§288C, 444, 567, 586–588, 592, 593, 782, 808–811, 815.

Rule 5.532.   Court reporter; transcripts

(a) Hearing before judge (§§ 347, 677)

If the hearing is before a judge or a referee acting as a temporary judge by stipulation, an official court reporter or other authorized reporting procedure must record all proceedings.

(Subd (a) amended effective January 1, 2007.)

(b) Hearing before referee (§§ 347, 677)

If the hearing is before a referee not acting as a temporary judge, the judge may direct an official court reporter or other authorized reporting procedure to record all proceedings.

(c) Preparation of transcript (§§ 347, 677)

If directed by the judge or if requested by a party or the attorney for a party, the official court reporter or other authorized transcriber must prepare a transcript of the proceedings within such reasonable time after the hearing as the judge designates and must certify that the proceedings have been correctly reported and transcribed. If directed by the judge, the official court reporter or authorized transcriber must file the transcript with the clerk of the court.

(Subd (c) amended effective January 1, 2007.)

Rule 5.532 amended and renumbered effective January 1, 2007; adopted as rule 1411 effective January 1, 1990.

Ref.: Cal. Fms Pl. & Pr., Ch. 327, "Juvenile Courts: Jurisdiction and General Procedures"; W. Cal. Sum., 10 "Parent and Child" §§444, 591, 814.

Rule 5.534.   General provisions—all proceedings

(a) Control of proceedings (§§ 350, 680)

The court must control all proceedings with a view to quickly and effectively ascertaining the jurisdictional facts and all information relevant to the present condition and welfare of the child.

(Subd (a) amended effective January 1, 2007; previously amended effective July 1, 2002.)

(b) Conduct of proceedings (§§ 350, 680)

Unless there is a contested issue of fact or law, the proceedings must be conducted in a nonadversarial atmosphere.

(Subd (b) amended effective July 1, 2002.)

(c) Testimony of child in chambers (§ 350)

In a hearing under section 300 et seq., a child may testify in chambers and outside the presence of the child's parent or guardian if the parent or guardian is represented by counsel who is present, subject to the right of the parent or guardian to have the court reporter read back the child's testimony, and if the court determines, based on the petitioner's report or other offers of proof or other evidence, that any of the following circumstances exist:

(1) Testimony in chambers is necessary to ensure truthful testimony;

(2) The child is likely to be intimidated by a formal courtroom setting; or

(3) The child is afraid to testify in front of the parent or guardian.

(Subd (c) amended effective January 1, 2007.)

(d) Burden of proof (§§ 350, 701.1)

(1) Meeting the burden of proof:

(A) In any hearing under section 300 in which the county welfare agency has the burden of proof, after completion of the agency's case, and the presentation of evidence by the child, the court may, on motion of any party or on the court's own motion, order whatever action the law requires if the court, based on all the evidence then before it, finds that the burden of proof is not met.

(B) In any hearing under section 601 or 602, after the completion of the petitioner's case, the court may, on the motion of any party, or on the court's own motion, order whatever action the law requires if the burden of proof is not met.

(2) If the motion is denied, the child in a section 300 or section 601 or section 602 hearing, or the parent or guardian in a section 300 hearing, may offer evidence.

(Subd (d) amended effective January 1, 2007; previously amended effective July 1, 1995.)

(e) De facto parents

On a sufficient showing the court may recognize the child's present or previous custodians as de facto parents and grant standing to participate as parties in disposition hearings and any hearing thereafter at which the status of the dependent child is at issue. The de facto parent may:

(1) Be present at the hearing;

(2) Be represented by retained counsel or, at the discretion of the court, by appointed counsel; and

(3) Present evidence.

(Subd (e) amended effective January 1, 2007.)

(f) Relatives

On a sufficient showing the court may permit relatives of the child to:

(1) Be present at the hearing; and

(2) Address the court.

(Subd (f) amended effective January 1, 2007.)

(g) Right to counsel (§§ 317, 633, 634, 700)

At each hearing the court must advise an self represented child, parent, or guardian of the right to be represented by counsel and, if applicable, of the right to have counsel appointed, subject to a claim by the court or the county for reimbursement as provided by law.

(Subd (g) amended effective January 1, 2007; previously amended effective July 1, 2002.)

(h) Appointment of counsel (§§ 317, 633, 634, 700)

(1) In cases petitioned under section 300:

(A) The court must appoint counsel for the child unless the court finds that the child would not benefit from the appointment and makes the findings required by rule 5.660(b); and

(B) The court must appoint counsel for any parent or guardian unable to afford counsel if the child is placed in out-of-home care or the recommendation of the petitioner is for out-of-home care, unless the court finds the parent or guardian has knowingly and intelligently waived the right to counsel.

(2) In cases petitioned under section 601 or section 602:

(A) The court must appoint counsel for any child who appears without counsel, unless the child knowingly and intelligently waives the right to counsel. If the court determines that the parent or guardian can afford counsel but has not retained counsel for the child, the court must appoint counsel for the child and order the parent or guardian to reimburse the county;

(B) The court may appoint counsel for a parent or guardian who desires but cannot afford counsel; and

(C) If the parent has retained counsel for the child and a conflict arises, the court must take steps to ensure that the child's interests are protected.

(Subd (h) amended effective January 1, 2007; previously amended effective July 1, 2002.)

(i) Tribal representatives (25 U.S.C. §§ 1911, 1931–1934)

The tribe of an Indian child is entitled to intervene as a party at any stage of a dependency proceeding concerning the Indian child.

(1) The tribe may appear by counsel or by a representative of the tribe designated by the tribe to intervene on its behalf. When the tribe appears as a party by a representative of the tribe, the name of the representative and a statement of authorization for that individual or agency to appear as the tribe must be submitted to the court in the form of a tribal resolution or other document evidencing an official act of the tribe.

(2) If the tribe of the Indian child does not intervene as a party, the court may permit an individual affiliated with the tribe or, if requested by the tribe, a representative of a program operated by another tribe or Indian organization to:

(A) Be present at the hearing;

(B) Address the court;

(C) Receive notice of hearings;

(D) Examine all court documents relating to the dependency case;

(E) Submit written reports and recommendations to the court; and

(F) Perform other duties and responsibilities as requested or approved by the court.

(Subd (i) amended effective January 1, 2007; adopted effective January 1, 1997; previously amended effective July 1, 2002.)

(j) Appointment of educational representative (§§ 319, 361, 366, 366.27, 726; Gov. Code, § 7579.5)

If the court limits the right of a parent or guardian to make educational decisions for the child, the court must immediately proceed under rule 5.650(b) to appoint an educational representative for the child.

(Subd (j) adopted effective January 1, 2008.)

(k) Advisement of hearing rights (§§ 301, 311, 341, 630, 702.5, 827)

(1) The court must advise the child, parent, and guardian in section 300 cases, and the child in section 601 or section 602 cases, of the following rights:

(A) Any right to assert the privilege against self-incrimination;

(B) The right to confront and cross-examine the persons who prepared reports or documents submitted to the court by the petitioner and the witnesses called to testify at the hearing;

(C) The right to use the process of the court to bring in witnesses; and

(D) The right to present evidence to the court.

(2) The child, parent, guardian, and their attorneys have:

(A) The right to receive probation officer or social worker reports; and

(B) The right to inspect the documents used by the preparer of the report.

(3) Unless prohibited by court order, the child, parent, guardian, and their attorneys also have the right to receive all documents filed with the court.

(Subd (k) relettered effective January 1, 2008; adopted as subd (i) effective January 1, 1991; previously relettered as subd (j) effective January 1, 1997; previously amended effective July 1, 2002, and January 1, 2007.)

(l) Notice

At each hearing under section 300 et seq., the court must determine whether notice has been given as required by law and must make an appropriate finding noted in the minutes.

(Subd (l) relettered effective January 1, 2008; adopted as subd (j) effective January 1, 1991; previously relettered as subd (k) effective January 1, 1997; previously amended effective July 1, 2002, and January 1, 2007.)

(m) Address of parent or guardian—notice (§ 316.1)

At the first appearance by a parent or guardian in proceedings under section 300 et seq., the court must order each parent or guardian to provide a mailing address.

(1) The court must advise that the mailing address provided will be used by the court, the clerk, and the social services agency for the purposes of notice of hearings and the mailing of all documents related to the proceedings.

(2) The court must advise that until and unless the parent or guardian, or the attorney of record for the parent or guardian, submits written notification of a change of mailing address, the address provided will be used, and notice requirements will be satisfied by appropriate service at that address.

(3) *Notification of Mailing Address* (form JV-140) is the preferred method of informing the court and the social services agency of the mailing address of the parent or guardian and change of mailing address.

(A) The form must be delivered to the parent or guardian, or both, with the petition.

(B) The form must be available in the courtroom, in the office of the clerk, and in the offices of the social services agency.

(C) The form must be printed and made available in both English and Spanish.

(Subd (m) relettered effective January 1, 2008; adopted as subd (k) effective January 1, 1994; previously relettered as subd (l) effective January 1, 1997; previously amended effective July 1, 2002, and January 1, 2007.)

(n) Caregiver notice and right to be heard (§§ 290.1–297, 366.21)

For cases filed under section 300 et seq.:

(1) For any child who has been removed from the home, the court must ensure that notice of statutory review hearings, permanency hearings, and section 366.26 hearings has been provided to the current caregiver of the child, including foster parents, preadoptive parents, relative caregivers, and nonrelative extended family members. Notice of dispositional hearings also must be provided to these individuals when the dispositional hearing is serving as a permanency hearing under section 361.5(f).

(2) The current caregiver has the right to be heard in each proceeding listed in paragraph (1), including the right to submit information about the child to the court before the hearing. Written information about the child may be submitted to the court using the *Caregiver Information Form* (form JV-290) or in the form of a letter to the court.

(3) At least 10 calendar days before each hearing listed in paragraph (1), the social worker must provide to the current caregiver:

(A) A summary of his or her recommendations for disposition, and any recommendations for change in custody or status;

(B) *Caregiver Information Form* (form JV-290); and

(C) *Instruction Sheet for Caregiver Information Form* (form JV-290-INFO).

(4) If the caregiver chooses to provide written information to the court using form JV-290 or by letter, the caregiver must follow the procedures set forth below. The court may waive any element of this process for good cause.

(A) If filing in person, the caregiver must bring the original document and 8 copies to the court clerk's office for filing no later than five calendar days before the hearing.

(B) If filing by mail, the caregiver must mail the original document and 8 copies to the court clerk's office for filing no later than seven calendar days before the hearing.

(5) When form JV-290 or a caregiver letter is received by mail the court clerk must immediately file it.

(6) When form JV-290 or a caregiver letter is filed, the court clerk must provide the social worker, all unrepresented parties and all attorneys with a copy of the completed form or letter immediately upon receipt. The clerk also must complete, file, and distribute *Proof of Service—Juvenile* (form JV-510). The clerk may use any technology designed to speed the distribution process, including drop boxes in the courthouse, email or fax to distribute the JV-290 form or letter and proof of service form.

(Subd (n) relettered effective January 1, 2008; adopted as subd (m) effective October 1, 2007.)

(o) Periodic reports

The court may require the petitioner or any other agency to submit reports concerning a child subject to the jurisdiction of the court.

(Subd (o) relettered effective January 1, 2008; adopted as subd (k) effective January 1, 1991; previously relettered as subd (l) effective January 1, 1994, as subd (m) effective January 1, 1997, and as subd (n) effective October 1, 2007.)

(p) Presence of child (§ 349)

If the child is 10 years of age or older and he or she is not present at the hearing, the court must determine whether the child was properly notified of his or her right to attend the hearing and ask why the child is not present at the hearing.

(Subd (p) relettered effective January 1, 2008; adopted as subd (n) effective January 1, 2005; previously relettered subd (o) effective October 1, 2007.)

Rule 5.534 amended effective January 1, 2008; previously amended and renumbered effective January 1, 2007; adopted as rule 1412 effective January 1, 1991; previously amended effective January 1, 1994, July 1, 1995, January 1, 1997, January 1, 2000, July 1, 2002, January 1, 2005, and October 1, 2007.

Advisory Committee Comment

Because the intent of subdivision (m) is to expand access to the courts for caregivers of children in out-of-home care, the rule should be liberally construed. To promote caregiver participation and input, judicial officers are encouraged to permit caregivers to verbally address the court when caregivers would like to share information about the child. In addition, court clerks should allow filings by caregivers even if the caregiver has not strictly adhered to the requirements in the rule regarding number of copies and filing deadlines.

Ref.: Cal. Fms Pl. & Pr., Ch. 327, "Juvenile Courts: Jurisdiction and General Procedures," Ch. 328, "Juvenile Courts: Dependency Proceedings," Ch. 329, "Juvenile Courts: Delinquency Proceedings"; W. Cal. Sum., 10 "Parent and Child" §§288C, 444, 533, 567, 570, 571, 576, 578, 579, 582, 588, 589, 596, 602, 613, 666, 782, 787, 788, 803, 810, 813, 823, 825, 864, 878.

Rule 5.536. General provisions—proceedings held before referees

(a) Referees—appointment; powers (Cal. Const., art. VI, § 22)

One or more referees may be appointed under section 247 to perform subordinate judicial duties assigned by the presiding judge of the juvenile court.

(Subd (a) amended effective January 1, 2007.)

(b) Referee as temporary judge (Cal. Const., art. VI, § 21)

If the referee is an attorney admitted to practice in this state, the parties may stipulate under rule 2.816 that the referee is acting as a temporary judge with the same powers as a judge of the juvenile court. An official court reporter or other authorized reporting procedure must record all proceedings.

(Subd (b) amended effective January 1, 2007.)

Rule 5.536 amended and renumbered effective January 1, 2007; adopted as rule 1415 effective January 1, 1990.

Ref.: Cal. Fms Pl. & Pr., Ch. 327, "Juvenile Courts: Jurisdiction and General Procedures"; W. Cal. Sum., 10 "Parent and Child" §§444, 465, 466, 814.

Rule 5.538. Conduct of proceedings held before a referee not acting as a temporary judge

(a) General conduct (§§ 248, 347, 677)

Proceedings heard by a referee not acting as a temporary judge must be conducted in the same manner as proceedings heard by a judge, except:

(1) An official court reporter or other authorized reporting procedure must record the proceedings if directed by the court; and

(2) The referee must inform the child and parent or guardian of the right to seek review by a juvenile court judge.

(Subd (a) amended effective January 1, 2007.)

(b) Furnishing and serving findings and order; explanation of right to review (§ 248)

After each hearing before a referee, the referee must make findings and enter an order as provided elsewhere in these rules. In each case the referee must cause all of the following to be done promptly:

(1) Furnish a copy of the findings and order to the presiding judge of the juvenile court.

(2) Furnish to the child (if the child is 14 or more years of age or, if younger, as requested) a copy of the findings and order, with a written explanation of the right to seek review of the order by a juvenile court judge.

(3) Serve the parent and guardian, and counsel for the child, parent, and guardian, a copy of the findings and order, with a written explanation of the right to seek review of the order by a juvenile court judge. Service must be by mail to the last known address and is deemed complete at the time of mailing.

(Subd (b) amended effective January 1, 2007.)
Rule 5.538 amended and renumbered effective January 1, 2007; adopted as rule 1416 effective January 1, 1990.

Ref.: Cal. Fms Pl. & Pr., Ch. 327, "Juvenile Courts: Jurisdiction and General Procedures," Ch. 328, "Juvenile Courts: Dependency Proceedings"; W. Cal. Sum., 10 "Parent and Child" §§444, 468–470, 693, 712.

Rule 5.540. Orders of referees not acting as temporary judges

(a) Effective date of order (§ 250)

Except as provided in (b) and subject to the right of review provided for in rule 5.542, all orders of a referee become effective immediately and continue in effect unless vacated or modified on rehearing by order of a juvenile court judge.

(Subd (a) amended effective January 1, 2007.)

(b) Orders requiring express approval of judge (§§ 249, 251)

The following orders made by a referee do not become effective unless expressly approved by a juvenile court judge within two court days:

(1) Any order removing a child from the physical custody of the person legally entitled to custody; or

(2) Any order the presiding judge of the juvenile court requires to be expressly approved.

(Subd (b) amended effective January 1, 2007.)

(c) Finality date of order

An order of a referee becomes final 10 calendar days after service of a copy of the order and findings under rule 5.538, if an application for rehearing has not been made within that time or if the judge of the juvenile court has not within the 10 days ordered a rehearing on the judge's own motion under rule 5.542.

(Subd (c) amended effective January 1, 2007.)
Rule 5.540 amended and renumbered effective January 1, 2007; adopted as rule 1417 effective January 1, 1990.

Ref.: Cal. Fms Pl. & Pr., Ch. 327, "Juvenile Courts: Jurisdiction and General Procedures," Ch. 328, "Juvenile Courts: Dependency Proceedings," Ch. 329, "Juvenile Courts: Delinquency Proceedings"; W. Cal. Sum., 10 "Parent and Child" §§444, 469, 470, 472, 693, 712, 720, 725.

Rule 5.542. Rehearing of proceedings before referees

(a) Application for rehearing (§ 252)

An application for a rehearing of a proceeding before a referee not acting as a temporary judge may be made by the child, parent, or guardian at any time before the expiration of 10 calendar days after service of a copy of the order and findings. The application may be directed to all, or any specified part of, the order or findings and must contain a brief statement of the factual or legal reasons for requesting the rehearing.

(Subd (a) amended effective January 1, 2007.)

(b) If no formal record (§ 252)

A rehearing must be granted if proceedings before the referee were not recorded by an official court reporter or other authorized reporting procedure.

(Subd (b) amended effective January 1, 2007.)

(c) Hearing with court reporter (§ 252)

If the proceedings before the referee have been recorded by an official court reporter or other authorized reporting procedure, the judge of the juvenile court may, after reading the transcript of the proceedings, grant or deny the application for rehearing. If the application is not denied within 20 calendar days following the date of receipt of the application, or within 45 calendar days if the court for good cause extends the time, the application must be deemed granted.

(Subd (c) amended effective January 1, 2007.)

(d) Rehearing on motion of judge (§ 253)

Notwithstanding (a), at any time within 20 court days after a hearing before a referee, the judge, on the judge's own motion, may order a rehearing.

(Subd (d) amended effective January 1, 2007.)

(e) Hearing de novo (§ 254)

Rehearings of matters heard before a referee must be conducted de novo before a judge of the juvenile court. A rehearing of a detention hearing must be held within two court days after the rehearing is granted. A rehearing of other matters heard before a referee must be held within 10 court days after the rehearing is granted.

(Subd (e) amended effective January 1, 2007.)

(f) Advisement of appeal rights—rule 5.590

If the judge of the juvenile court denies an application for rehearing directed in whole or in part to issues arising during a contested jurisdiction hearing, the judge must advise, either orally or in writing, the child and the parent or guardian of all of the following:

(1) The right of the child, parent, or guardian to appeal from the court's judgment;

(2) The necessary steps and time for taking an appeal;

(3) The right of an indigent appellant to have counsel appointed by the reviewing court; and

(4) The right of an indigent appellant to be provided a free copy of the transcript.

(Subd (f) amended effective January 1, 2007.)

Rule 5.542 amended and renumbered effective January 1, 2007; adopted as rule 1418 effective January 1, 1991.

Ref.: Cal. Fms Pl. & Pr., Ch. 327, "Juvenile Courts: Jurisdiction and General Procedures"; W. Cal. Sum., 10 "Parent and Child" §§444, 471–475, 693, 712, 850.

Rule 5.544. Prehearing motions (§ 700.1)

Unless otherwise ordered or specifically provided by law, prehearing motions and accompanying points and authorities must, absent a waiver, be served on the child and opposing counsel and filed with the court:

(1) At least 5 judicial days before the date the jurisdiction hearing is set to begin if the child is detained or the motion is one to suppress evidence obtained as a result of an unlawful search and seizure; or

(2) At least 10 judicial days before the date the jurisdiction hearing is set to begin if the child is not detained and the motion is other than one to suppress evidence obtained as a result of an unlawful search and seizure.

Prehearing motions must be specific, noting the grounds, and supported by points and authorities.

Rule 5.544 amended and renumbered effective January 1, 2007; adopted as rule 1419 effective January 1, 1991.

Ref.: Cal. Fms Pl. & Pr., Ch. 329, "Juvenile Courts: Delinquency Proceedings"; W. Cal. Sum., 10 "Parent and Child" §444.

Rule 5.546. Prehearing discovery

(a) General purpose

This rule must be liberally construed in favor of informal disclosures, subject to the right of a party to show privilege or other good cause not to disclose specific material or information.

(Subd (a) amended effective January 1, 2007.)

(b) Duty to disclose police reports

After filing the petition, petitioner must promptly deliver to or make accessible for inspection and copying by the child and the parent or guardian, or their counsel, copies of the police, arrest, and crime reports relating to the pending matter. Privileged information may be omitted if notice of the omission is given simultaneously.

(Subd (b) amended effective January 1, 2007.)

(c) Affirmative duty to disclose

Petitioner must disclose any evidence or information within petitioner's possession or control favorable to the child, parent, or guardian.

(Subd (c) amended effective January 1, 2007.)

(d) Material and information to be disclosed on request

Except as provided in (g) and (h), petitioner must, after timely request, disclose to the child and parent or guardian, or their counsel, the following material and information within the petitioner's possession or control:

(1) Probation reports prepared in connection with the pending matter relating to the child, parent, or guardian;

(2) Records of statements, admissions, or conversations by the child, parent, or guardian;

(3) Records of statements, admissions, or conversations by any alleged coparticipant;

(4) Names and addresses of witnesses interviewed by an investigating authority in connection with the pending matter;

(5) Records of statements or conversations of witnesses or other persons interviewed by an investigating authority in connection with the pending matter;

(6) Reports or statements of experts made regarding the pending matter, including results of physical or mental examinations and results of scientific tests, experiments, or comparisons;

(7) Photographs or physical evidence relating to the pending matter; and

(8) Records of prior felony convictions of the witnesses each party intends to call.

(Subd (d) amended effective January 1, 2007.)

(e) Disclosure in section 300 proceedings

Except as provided in (g) and (h), the parent or guardian must, after timely request, disclose to petitioner relevant material and information within the parent's or guardian's possession or control. If counsel represents the parent or guardian, a disclosure request must be made through counsel.

(Subd (e) amended effective January 1, 2007.)

(f) Motion for prehearing discovery

If a party refuses to disclose information or permit inspection of materials, the requesting party or counsel may move the court for an order requiring timely disclosure of the information or materials. The motion must specifically and clearly designate the items sought, state the relevancy of the items, and state that a timely request has been made for the items and that the other party has refused to provide them. Each court may by local rule establish the manner and time within which a motion under this subdivision must be made.

(Subd (f) amended effective January 1, 2007.)

(g) Limits on duty to disclose—protective orders

On a showing of privilege or other good cause, the court may make orders restricting disclosures. All material and information to which a party is entitled must be disclosed in time to permit counsel to make beneficial use of them.

(h) Limits on duty to disclose—excision

When some parts of the materials are discoverable under (d) and (e) and other parts are not discoverable, the nondiscoverable material may be excised and need not be disclosed if the requesting party or counsel has been notified that the privileged material has been excised. Material ordered excised must be sealed and preserved in the records of the court for review on appeal.

(Subd (h) amended effective January 1, 2007.)

(i) Conditions of discovery

An order of the court granting discovery under this rule may specify the time, place, and manner of making the discovery and inspection and may prescribe terms and conditions. Discovery must be completed in a timely manner to avoid the delay or continuance of a scheduled hearing.

(Subd (i) amended effective January 1, 2007.)

Rules of Court

(j) Failure to comply; sanctions

If at any time during the course of the proceedings the court learns that a person has failed to comply with this rule or with an order issued under this rule, the court may order the person to permit the discovery or inspection of materials not previously disclosed, grant a continuance, prohibit a party from introducing in evidence the material not disclosed, dismiss the proceedings, or enter any other order the court deems just under the circumstances.

(Subd (j) amended effective January 1, 2007.)

(k) Continuing duty to disclose

If subsequent to compliance with these rules or with court orders a party discovers additional material or information subject to disclosure, the party must promptly notify the child and parent or guardian, or their counsel, of the existence of the additional matter.

(Subd (k) amended effective January 1, 2007.)

Rule 5.546 amended and renumbered effective January 1, 2007; adopted as rule 1420 effective January 1, 1990.

Ref.: Cal. Fms Pl. & Pr., Ch. 327, "Juvenile Courts: Jurisdiction and General Procedures," Ch. 328, "Juvenile Courts: Dependency Proceedings," Ch. 329, "Juvenile Courts: Delinquency Proceedings"; W. Cal. Sum., 10 "Parent and Child" §§444, 612, 860, 861–863.

Rule 5.548. Granting immunity to witnesses

(a) Privilege against self-incrimination

If a person is called as a witness and it appears to the court that the testimony or other evidence being sought may tend to incriminate the witness, the court must advise the witness of the privilege against self-incrimination and of the possible consequences of testifying. The court must also inform the witness of the right to representation by counsel and, if indigent, of the right to have counsel appointed.

(Subd (a) amended effective January 1, 2007.)

(b) Authority of judge to grant immunity

If a witness refuses to answer a question or to produce evidence based on a claim of the privilege against self-incrimination, a judge may grant immunity to the witness under (c) or (d) and order the question answered or the evidence produced.

(Subd (b) amended effective January 1, 2007.)

(c) Request for immunity—section 602 proceedings

In proceedings under section 602, the prosecuting attorney may make a written or oral request on the record that the court order a witness to answer a question or produce evidence. The court must then proceed under Penal Code section 1324.

(1) After complying with an order to answer a question or produce evidence and if, but for those Penal Code sections or this rule, the witness would have been privileged to withhold the answer given or the evidence produced, no testimony or other information compelled under the order or information directly or indirectly derived from the testimony or other information may be used against the witness in any criminal case, including any juvenile court proceeding under section 602.

(2) The prosecuting attorney may request an order granting the witness use or transactional immunity.

(Subd (c) amended effective January 1, 2007; previously amended effective January 1, 1998.)

(d) Request for immunity—section 300 or 601 proceedings

In proceedings under section 300 or 601, the prosecuting attorney or petitioner may make a written or oral request on the record that the judge order a witness to answer a question or produce evidence. They may also make the request jointly.

(1) If the request is not made jointly, the other party must be given the opportunity to show why immunity is not to be granted and the judge may grant or deny the request as deemed appropriate.

(2) If jointly made, the judge must grant the request unless the judge finds that to do so would be clearly contrary to the public interest. The terms of a grant of immunity must be stated in the record.

(3) After complying with the order and if, but for this rule, the witness would have been privileged to withhold the answer given or the evidence produced, any answer given, evidence produced, or information derived there from must not be used against the witness in a juvenile court or criminal proceeding.

(Subd (d) amended effective January 1, 2007.)

(e) No immunity from perjury or contempt

Notwithstanding (c) or (d), a witness may be subject to proceedings under the juvenile court law or to criminal prosecution for perjury, false swearing, or contempt committed in answering or failing to answer or in producing or failing to produce evidence in accordance with the order.

(Subd (e) amended effective January 1, 2007.)

Rule 5.548 amended and renumbered effective January 1, 2007; adopted as rule 1421 effective January 1, 1990; previously amended effective January 1, 1998.

Ref.: Cal. Fms Pl. & Pr., Ch. 328, "Juvenile Courts: Dependency Proceedings," Ch. 329, "Juvenile Courts: Delinquency Proceedings"; W. Cal. Sum., 10 "Parent and Child" §§444, 621, 879–881.

Rule 5.550. Continuances

(a) Cases petitioned under section 300 (§§ 316.2, 352, 354)

(1) The court must not continue a hearing beyond the time set by statute unless the court determines the continuance is not contrary to the interest of the child. In considering the child's interest, the court must give substantial weight to a child's needs for stability and prompt resolution of custody status, and the damage of prolonged temporary placements.

(2) Continuances may be granted only on a showing of good cause, and only for the time shown to be necessary. Stipulation between counsel of parties, convenience of parties, and pending criminal or family law matters are not in and of themselves good cause.

(3) If a child has been removed from the custody of a parent or guardian, the court must not grant a continuance that would cause the disposition hearing under section 361 to be completed more than 60 days after the detention hearing unless the court finds exceptional circumstances. In no event may the disposition hearing be continued more than six months after the detention hearing.

(4) In order to obtain a continuance, written notice with supporting documents must be filed and served on all parties at least two court days before the date set for

hearing, unless the court finds good cause for hearing an oral motion.

(5) The court must state in its order the facts requiring any continuance that is granted.

(6) Failure of an alleged father to return a certified mail receipt of notice as described in rule 5.667 does not, in and of itself, constitute good cause to continue a hearing.

(Subd (a) amended effective January 1, 2007; previously amended effective January 1, 1999, and July 1, 2002.)

(b) Cases petitioned under section 601 or 602 (§ 682)

(1) A continuance may be granted only on a showing of good cause and only for the time shown to be necessary. Stipulation between counsel or parties and convenience of parties are not in and of themselves good cause.

(2) In order to obtain a continuance, written notice with supporting documents must be filed and served on all parties at least two court days before the date set for the hearing, unless the court finds good cause for failure to comply with these requirements.

(3) The court must state in its order the facts requiring any continuance that is granted.

(4) If the child is represented by counsel, failure of counsel or the child to object to an order continuing a hearing beyond the time limit is deemed a consent to the continuance.

(Subd (b) amended effective January 1, 2007; previously amended effective July 1, 2002.)

(c) Continuances of detention hearings (§§ 319, 322, 635, 636, 638)

(1) On the motion of the child, parent, or guardian, the court must continue the detention hearing for one court day or for a reasonable period to permit the moving party to prepare any relevant evidence on the issue of detention. Unless otherwise ordered by the court, the child must remain in custody pending the continued hearing.

(2) At the initial detention hearing, if the court continues the hearing under (c)(1) or for any other reason, or sets the matter for rehearing, the court must either find that the continuance of the child in the parent's or guardian's home is contrary to the child's welfare or order the child released to the custody of the parent or guardian. The court may enter this finding on a temporary basis, without prejudice to any party, and reevaluate the finding at the time of the continued detention hearing.

(Subd (c) amended effective January 1, 2007; adopted effective January 1, 1998; previously amended effective July 1, 2002.)

Rule 5.550 amended and renumbered effective January 1, 2007; adopted effective January 1, 1991; previously amended effective January 1, 1998, January 1, 1999, and July 1, 2002.

Ref.: Cal. Fms Pl. & Pr., Ch. 328, "Juvenile Courts: Dependency Proceedings," Ch. 329, "Juvenile Courts: Delinquency Proceedings"; W. Cal. Sum., 10 "Parent and Child" §§444, 594, 595, 601.

Rule 5.552.   Confidentiality of records (§§ 827, 828)

(a) Definitions

For the purposes of this rule, "juvenile case file" includes:

(1) All documents filed in a juvenile court case;

(2) Reports to the court by probation officers, social workers of child welfare services programs, and CASA volunteers;

(3) Documents made available to probation officers, social workers of child welfare services programs, and CASA volunteers in preparation of reports to the court;

(4) Documents relating to a child concerning whom a petition has been filed in juvenile court that are maintained in the office files of probation officers, social workers of child welfare services programs, and CASA volunteers;

(5) Transcripts, records, or reports relating to matters prepared or released by the court, probation department, or child welfare services program; and

(6) Documents, video or audio tapes, photographs, and exhibits admitted into evidence at juvenile court hearings.

(Subd (a) amended effective January 1, 2007; previously amended effective January 1, 2001.)

(b) General provisions

(1) [1] The following individuals and entities may inspect, receive, and copy the juvenile case file without an order of the juvenile court:

(A) Court personnel;

(B) The district attorney, a city attorney, or a city prosecutor authorized to prosecute criminal or juvenile cases under the law;

(C) The child who is the subject of the proceeding;

(D) The child's parents;

(E) The child's guardians;

(F) The attorneys for the parties, including any trial court or appellate attorney representing a party in the juvenile proceeding or related appellate proceeding;

(G) Judges, referees, other hearing officers, probation officers, and law enforcement officers who are actively participating in criminal or juvenile proceedings involving the child;

(H) The county counsel, city attorney, or any other attorney representing the petitioning agency in a dependency action;

(I) Members of child protective agencies as defined in Penal Code section 11165.9; and

(J) The California Department of Social Services in order to carry out its duty to oversee and monitor county child welfare agencies, children in foster care or receiving foster-care assistance, and out-of-state placements.

(2) The following individuals and entities may inspect the juvenile case file without a court order and may receive a copy of the juvenile case file pursuant to a court order:

(A) All persons and entities listed in Welfare and Institutions Code sections 827 and 828 who are not listed in (b)(1) above; and

(B) An Indian child's tribal representative if the tribe has intervened in the child's case.

(3) Authorization for any other person **or entity** to inspect, obtain, or copy juvenile [2] **case files** may be ordered only by the juvenile court presiding judge or a judicial officer of the juvenile court.

[3] **(4) Juvenile case files** may not be obtained or inspected by civil or criminal subpoena.

[4] **(5)** When a petition is sustained for any offense listed in section 676, the charging petition, the minutes of the proceeding, and the orders of adjudication and dispo-

sition that are contained in the [5] **juvenile case** file must be available for public inspection, unless the court has prohibited disclosure of those records under that section.

(Subd (b) amended effective January 1, 2009; previously amended effective January 1, 2004, and January 1, 2007.)

Rule 5.552(b). 2008 Deletes. [1] Only those persons specified in sections 827 and 828 may inspect, but may not copy, juvenile court records without authorization from the court. (A) Counsel who are entitled to inspect juvenile court records include any trial court or appellate attorney representing a party in the juvenile court proceeding. (B) **[2]** court records **[3]** (C) The child, the child's attorney, the child's parents and their attorneys, the child's social worker, the county counsel, and a child's identified Indian tribe, can obtain a copy of a juvenile case file document that was previously disseminated during the proceedings, while the case is pending. (D) Juvenile court records **[4]** (E) In determining whether to authorize inspection or release of juvenile court records, in whole or in part, the court must balance the interests of the child and other parties to the juvenile court proceedings, the interests of the petitioner, and the interests of the public. (F) The court may permit disclosure of, discovery of, or access to juvenile court records or proceedings only insofar as is necessary, and only if there is a reasonable likelihood that the records in question will disclose information or evidence of substantial relevance to the pending litigation, investigation, or prosecution. (G) The court may issue protective orders to accompany authorized disclosure, discovery, or access. (2) **[5]** court

(c) Petition

With the exception of those persons permitted to inspect juvenile court records without court authorization under sections 827 and 828, every person or agency seeking to inspect or obtain juvenile court records must petition the court for authorization using *Petition for Disclosure of Juvenile Court Records* (form JV-570).

(1) The specific records sought must be identified based on knowledge, information, and belief that such records exist and are relevant to the purpose for which they are being sought.

(2) Petitioner must describe in detail the reasons the records are being sought and their relevancy to the proceeding or purpose for which petitioner wishes to inspect or obtain the records.

(Subd (c) amended effective January 1, 2007; previously amended effective July 1, 1997.)

(d) Notice of petition for disclosure

At least [1] **10** days before the petition is submitted to the court, **the** petitioner must personally or by first-class mail serve [2] *Request for Disclosure of Juvenile Case File* **(form JV-570)**, *Notice of Request for Disclosure of Juvenile Case File* **(form JV-571), and a blank copy of** *Objection to Release of Juvenile Case File* **(form JV-572)** on the **following:**

(A) The county counsel, **city attorney, or any other attorney representing the petitioning agency in a dependency action if the child's petition was filed under section 300;**

(B) The district attorney **if the child's petition was filed under section 601 or 602**;

(C) The child;

(D) The attorney of record for the child who remains a ward or dependent of the court; [3]

(E) The parents of the child [4] **if:**

(i) The child is under 18 years of age; or [5]

(ii) The child's petition was filed under section 300;

(F) The guardians of the child if:

(i) The child is under 18 years of age; or

(ii) The child's petition was filed under section 300;

(G) The probation department or child welfare [6] **agency**, or both, if applicable;

(H) The Indian child's tribe; and

(I) The child's CASA volunteer.

(2) The petitioner must complete *Proof of Service— Request for Disclosure* **(form JV-569) and file it with the court.**

(3) If the petitioner does not know the identity or address of any of the parties in (d)(1) above, the clerk must:

(A) Serve personally or by first-class mail to the last known address a copy of *Request for Disclosure of Juvenile Case File* **(form JV-570),** *Notice of Request for Disclosure of Juvenile Case File* **(form JV-571), and a blank copy of** *Objection to Release of Juvenile Case File* **(form JV-572); and**

(B) Complete *Proof of Service—Request for Disclosure* **(form JV-569) and file it with the court.**

(4) For good cause, the court may, on the motion of the person seeking the order or on its own motion, shorten the time for service of the petition for disclosure.

(Subd (d) amended effective January 1, 2009; previously amended effective January 1, 2007.)

Rule 5.552(d). 2008 Deletes. [1] five **[2]** , or attempt to serve, a copy of the petition **[3]** parent or guardian **[4]** who **[5]** if a dependency petition (§ 300 et seq.) was filed regarding the child; and **[6]** services program

(e) Procedure

(1) The court must review the petition and [1], if petitioner does not show good cause, deny it summarily [2].

(2) If petitioner shows good cause, the court may set a hearing. The clerk must notice [3] the hearing **to the persons and entities listed in (d)(1) above**.

(3) Whether or not the court holds a hearing, if [4] the court determines that there may be information or documents in the records sought to which **the** petitioner may be entitled, [5] the juvenile court judicial officer must **conduct an in camera review of the juvenile case file and any objections and** assume that all legal claims of privilege are asserted.

(4) In determining whether to authorize inspection or release of juvenile case files, in whole or in part, the court must balance the interests of the child and other parties to the juvenile court proceedings, the interests of the petitioner, and the interests of the public.

(5) If the court grants the petition, the court must find that the need for discovery outweighs the policy considerations favoring confidentiality of juvenile case files. The confidentiality of juvenile case files is intended to protect the privacy rights of the child.

(6) The court may permit disclosure of juvenile case files only insofar as is necessary, and only if petitioner shows by a preponderance of the evidence that the records requested are necessary and have substantial relevance to the legitimate need of the petitioner.

(7) If, after in-camera review **and review of any objections,** the court determines that all or a portion of the [6] **juvenile case file** may be disclosed, the court must make appropriate orders, specifying the information to be disclosed and the procedure for providing access to it.

(8) The court may issue protective orders to accompany authorized disclosure, discovery, or access.

(Subd (e) amended effective January 1, 2009; previously amended effective January 1, 2007.)

Rule 5.552(e). 2008 Deletes. [1] grant or [2] , or [3] all parties of [4] at the hearing [5] review of records must be in camera and [6] records

(f) Reports of law enforcement agencies (§ 828)

Except for records sealed under section 389 or 781, or Penal Code section 1203.45, information gathered and retained by a law enforcement agency regarding the taking of a child into custody may be disclosed without court authorization to another law enforcement agency, including a school district police or security department, or to any person or agency that has a legitimate need for the information for the purposes of official disposition of a case.

(1) If the law enforcement agency retaining the report is notified under section 1155 that the child has escaped from a secure detention facility, the agency must release the name of the child and any descriptive information on specific request by any agency or individual whose attempts to apprehend the child will be assisted by the information requested.

(2) In the absence of a specific request, the law enforcement agency retaining the report may release information about a child reported to have escaped from a secure detention facility if the agency determines that the information is necessary to assist in the apprehension of the child or the protection of members of the public from substantial physical harm.

(3) Under section 828, all others seeking to inspect or obtain such reports must petition the juvenile court for authorization, using *Petition to Obtain Report of Law Enforcement Agency* (form JV-575).

(Subd (f) repealed and relettered effective January 1, 2009; adopted as subd (f) effective January 1, 1994; previously relettered as subd (g) effective January 1, 2001; previously amended effective January 1, 2007.)

(g) School notification

When a child enrolled in a public school is found to have committed one of the offenses described in section 827(b)(2), the court must provide written notice of the offense and the disposition to the superintendent of the school district within seven days. The superintendent must disseminate information to the principal of the school the child attends, and the principal may disseminate information to any teacher or administrator for the purposes of the rehabilitation of the child or the protection of other students and staff.

(Subd (g) relettered effective January 1, 2009; adopted as subd (g) effective July 1, 1995; previously relettered effective as subd (h) effective January 1, 2001; previously amended effective January 1, 2007.)

(h) Other applicable statutes

Under no circumstances must this rule or any section of it be interpreted to permit access to or release of records protected under any other federal or state law, including

Penal Code section 11165 et seq., except as provided in those statutes, or to limit access to or release of records permitted under any other federal or state statute, including Government Code section 13968.

(Subd (h) relettered effective January 1, 2009; adopted as subd (f) effective July 1, 1992; previously relettered as subd (g) effective January 1, 1994, and as subd (i) effective January 1, 2001; previously amended and relettered as subd (h) effective July 1, 1995; previously amended effective January 1, 2007.)

Rule 5.552 amended effective January 1, 2009; adopted as rule 1423 effective July 1, 1992; previously amended effective January 1, 1994, July 1, 1995, July 1, 1997, January 1, 2001, and January 1, 2004; previously amended and renumbered effective January 1, 2007.

Ref.: Cal. Fms Pl. & Pr., Ch. 327, "Juvenile Courts: Jurisdiction and General Procedures," Ch. 328, "Juvenile Courts: Dependency Proceedings," Ch. 329, "Juvenile Courts: Delinquency Proceedings"; W. Cal. Sum., 10 "Parent and Child" §§444, 492, 493, 498, 500.

Rule 5.553. Juvenile case file of a deceased child

When the juvenile case file of a deceased child is sought, the court must proceed as follows:

(1) Under section 827(a)(2) if the request is made by a member of the public; or

(2) Under section 16502.5 if the request is made by a county board of supervisors.

Rule 5.553 adopted effective January 1, 2009.

Chapter 4
Subsequent Petitions and Modifications

Rule 5.560. General provisions
Rule 5.565. Hearing on subsequent and supplemental petitions (§§ 342, 364, 386, 387)
Rule 5.570. Request to change court order
Rule 5.575. Joinder
Rule 5.580. Hearing on violation of probation (§ 777)

Rule 5.560. General provisions

(a) General authority of the court (§ 385)

Subject to the procedural requirements prescribed by this chapter, an order made by the court may at any time be changed, modified, or set aside.

(Subd (a) amended effective January 1, 2001.)

(b) Subsequent petitions (§§ 297, 342, 360(b), 364)

All procedures and hearings required for an original petition are required for a subsequent petition. Petitioner must file a subsequent petition if:

(1) A child has previously been found to be a person described by section 300 and the petitioner alleges new facts or circumstances, other than those sustained in the original petition, sufficient to again describe the child as a person under section 300 based on these new facts or circumstances;

(2) At or after the disposition hearing the court has ordered that a parent or guardian retain custody of the dependent child and the petitioner receives information providing reasonable cause to believe the child is now, or once again, described by section 300(a), (d), or (e); or

(3) The family is unwilling or unable to cooperate with services previously ordered under section 301.

(Subd (b) amended effective July 1, 2007; previously amended effective January 1, 2001, January 1, 2006, and January 1, 2007.)

(c) Supplemental petition (§§ 297, 387)

A supplemental petition must be used if petitioner concludes that a previous disposition has not been effective in the protection of a child declared a dependent under section 300 and seeks a more restrictive level of physical custody. For purposes of this chapter, a more restrictive level of custody, in ascending order, is

(1) Placement in the home of the person entitled to legal custody;

(2) Placement in the home of a noncustodial parent;

(3) Placement in the home of a relative or friend;

(4) Placement in a foster home; or

(5) Commitment to a private institution.

(Subd (c) amended effective January 1, 2007; previously amended effective January 1, 2001, and January 1, 2006.)

(d) Petition for modification hearing (§§ 297, 388, 778)

A petition for modification hearing must be used if there is a change of circumstances or new evidence that may require the court to:

(1) Change, modify, or set aside an order previously made; or

(2) Terminate the jurisdiction of the court over the child.

(Subd (d) amended effective January 1, 2007; adopted as subd (e) effective January 1, 1991; previously amended and relettered effective January 1, 2001; previously amended effective January 1, 2006.)

(e) Filing of petition (§§ 297, 388, 778)

A petition for modification hearing may be filed by:

(1) The probation officer, the parent, the guardian, the child, the attorney for the child, or any other person having an interest in a child who is a ward if the requested modification is not for a more restrictive level of custody;

(2) The social worker, regarding a child who is a dependent, if the requested modification is not for a more restrictive level of custody; or

(3) The parent, the guardian, the child, the attorney for the child, or any other person having an interest in a child who is a dependent.

(Subd (e) amended effective January 1, 2007; adopted as subd (f) effective January 1, 1991; previously amended and relettered effective January 1, 2001; previously amended effective January 1, 2006.)

(f) Clerical errors

Clerical errors in judgments, orders, or other parts of the record may be corrected by the court at any time on the court's own motion or on motion of any party and may be entered nunc pro tunc.

(Subd (f) relettered effective January 1, 2001; adopted as subd (g) effective January 1, 1991.)

Rule 5.560 amended effective July 1, 2007; adopted as rule 1430 effective January 1, 1991; previously amended and renumbered effective January 1, 2007; previously amended effective January 1, 2001, and January 1, 2006.

Ref.: Cal. Fms Pl. & Pr., Ch. 328, "Juvenile Courts: Dependency Proceedings," Ch. 329, "Juvenile Courts: Delinquency Proceedings"; W. Cal. Sum., 10 "Parent and Child" §§444, 654, 655, 662, 668, 905, 910.

Rule 5.565. Hearing on subsequent and supplemental petitions (§§ 342, 364, 386, 387)

(a) Contents of subsequent and supplemental petitions (§§ 342, 364, 387)

A subsequent petition and a supplemental petition must be verified and, to the extent known to the petitioner, contain the information required in an original petition as described in rule 5.524. A supplemental petition must also contain a concise statement of facts sufficient to support the conclusion that the previous disposition has not been effective in the protection of the child or, in the case of a dependent child placed with a relative, that the placement is not appropriate in view of the criteria in section 361.3.

(Subd (a) amended effective January 1, 2007; repealed and adopted effective January 1, 1990; previously amended effective January 1, 1992, January 1, 1999, January 1, 2001, and January 1, 2006.)

(b) Setting the hearing (§§ 334, 342, 364, 386, 387)

When a subsequent or supplemental petition is filed, the clerk must immediately set it for hearing within 30 days of the filing date. The hearing must begin within the time limits prescribed for jurisdiction hearings on original petitions under rule 5.670.

(Subd (b) amended effective January 1, 2007; adopted as subd (c) effective January 1, 1990; previously amended and relettered effective January 1, 2001; previously amended effective January 1, 1992, July 1, 1995, and January 1, 2006.)

(c) Notice of hearing (§§ 290.1, 290.2, 292, 297)

For petitions filed under sections 342 or 387, notice must be provided in accordance with sections 290.1, 290.2, and 291. Notice for petitions filed under section 364 must be provided as stated in section 292.

(Subd (c) adopted effective January 1, 2006.)

(d) Initial hearing (§ 387)

Chapter 13, article 1 of these rules applies to the case of a child who is the subject of a supplemental or subsequent petition.

(Subd (d) amended effective January 1, 2007; adopted as subd (d) effective January 1, 1990; amended and relettered as subd (c) effective January 1, 2001; previously amended and relettered effective January 1, 2006.)

(e) Requirement for bifurcated hearing

The hearing on a subsequent or supplemental petition must be conducted as follows:

(1) The procedures relating to jurisdiction hearings prescribed in chapter 13, article 2 apply to the determination of the allegations of a subsequent or supplemental petition. At the conclusion of the hearing on a subsequent petition the court must make a finding that the allegations of the petition are or are not true. At the conclusion of the hearing on a supplemental petition the court must make findings that:

(A) The factual allegations are or are not true; and

(B) The allegation that the previous disposition has not been effective is or is not true.

(2) The procedures relating to disposition hearings prescribed in chapter 13, article 3 apply to the determination of disposition on a subsequent or supplemental petition. If the court finds under a subsequent petition that the child is described by section 300(a), (d), or (e), the court must remove the child from the physical custody of the parent or guardian, if removal was not ordered under the previous disposition.

(Subd (e) amended effective January 1, 2007; adopted as subd (e) effective January 1, 1990; previously amended and relettered as subd (d) effective January 1, 2001; previously relettered effective January 1, 2006.)

(f) Supplemental petition (§ 387)—permanency planning

If a dependent child was returned to the custody of a parent or guardian at the 12-month review or the 18-month review or at an interim review between 12 and 18 months and a 387 petition is sustained and the child removed once again, the court must set a hearing under section 366.26 unless the court finds there is a substantial probability of return within the next 6 months or, if more than 12 months had expired at the time of the prior return, within whatever time remains before the expiration of the maximum 18-month period.

(Subd (f) amended effective January 1, 2007; adopted as subd (f) effective January 1, 1990; relettered as subd (e) effective January 1, 2001; previously amended and relettered effective January 1, 2006.)

Rule 5.565 amended and renumbered effective January 1, 2007; adopted as rule 1431 effective January 1, 1990; previously amended effective January 1, 1992, July 1, 1995, January 1, 1999, July 1, 1999, January 1, 2001, and January 1, 2006.)

Ref.: Cal. Fms Pl. & Pr., Ch. 328, "Juvenile Courts: Dependency Proceedings," Ch. 329, "Juvenile Courts: Delinquency Proceedings"; W. Cal. Sum., 10 "Parent and Child" §§444, 463, 655–658, 661, 668.

Rule 5.570.   Request to change court order

(a) Contents of petition (§§ 388, 778)

A petition for modification must be liberally construed in favor of its sufficiency. The petition must be verified and, to the extent known to the petitioner, must contain the following:

(1) The name of the court to which the petition is addressed;

(2) The title and action number of the original proceeding;

(3) The name and age of the child;

(4) The address of the child, unless confidential under [1] **(c)**;

(5) The name and residence address of the parent or guardian or an adult relative of the child, if appropriate [2] **to receive notice following the procedures found in Welfare and Institutions Code sections 291 and 297(c)**;

(6) The date and general nature of the order sought to be modified;

(7) A concise statement of any change of circumstance or new evidence that requires changing the order;

(8) A concise statement of the proposed change of the order;

(9) A statement of the petitioner's relationship or interest in the child, if the application is made by a person other than the child; and

(10) A statement whether or not all parties agree to the proposed change.

(Subd (a) amended effective January 1, 2009; previously amended effective July 1, 2002, and January 1, 2007.)

Rule 5.570(a).   2008 Deletes. [1] (b) [2] under circumstances described in rule 5.524.

(b) 388 petition

A petition under Welfare and Institutions Code section 388 must be made on form *Request to Change Court Order* (form JV-180).

(Subd (b) adopted effective January 1, 2007.)

(c) Confidentiality

The addresses and telephone numbers of the person requesting to change the court order, the child, and the child's caregiver may be kept confidential by filing form *Confidential Information (Request to Change Court Order)* (form JV-182) with form JV-180. Form JV-182 must be kept in the court file under seal, and only the court, the agency, and the child's attorney may have access to this information.

(Subd (c) adopted effective January 1, 2007.)

(d) Denial of hearing

If the petition fails to state a change of circumstance or new evidence that may require a change of order or termination of jurisdiction, or that the requested modification would promote the best interest of the child, the court may deny the application ex parte.

(Subd (d) amended and relettered effective January 1, 2007; adopted as subd (b).)

(e) Grounds for grant of petition (§§ 388, 778)

If the petition states a change of circumstance or new evidence and it appears that the best interest of the child may be promoted by the proposed change of order or termination of jurisdiction, the court may grant the petition after following the procedures in (f) and (g).

(Subd (e) amended and relettered effective January 1, 2007; adopted as subd (c).)

(f) Hearing on petition

If all parties stipulate to the requested modification, the court may order modification without a hearing. If it appears to the court that the requested modification will be contested or if the court desires to receive further evidence on the issue, the court must order that a hearing on the petition for modification be held within 30 calendar days after the petition is filed.

(Subd (f) relettered effective January 1, 2007; adopted as subd (d) previously amended effective July 1, 2002.)

(g) Notice of petition and hearing (§§ 388, 778)

The clerk must cause notice of the hearing to be given to the persons and in the same manner prescribed by rule 5.524. The present custodian of a dependent child and the tribe of a dependent Indian child must be similarly notified.

(Subd (g) amended and relettered effective January 1, 2007; repealed and adopted as subd (e); previously amended effective January 1, 1992, July 1, 1995, July 1, 2000, and July 1, 2002.)

(h) Conduct of hearing (§ 388)

(1) The petitioner requesting the modification under section 388 has the burden of proof. If the request is for the removal of the child from the child's home, the petitioner must show by clear and convincing evidence that the grounds for removal in section 361(c) exist. If the request is for removal to a more restrictive level of placement, the petitioner must show by clear and convincing evidence that the change is necessary to protect the physical or emotional well-being of the child. All other requests require a preponderance of the evidence to show that the child's welfare requires such a modification.

(2) The hearing must be conducted as a disposition hearing under rules 5.690 and 5.695 if:

(A) The request is for removal from the home of the parent or guardian or to a more restrictive level of placement; or

(B) There is a due process right to confront and cross-examine witnesses.

Otherwise, proof may be by declaration and other documentary evidence, or by testimony, or both, at the discretion of the court.

(Subd (h) amended and relettered effective January 1, 2007; adopted as subd (f); previously amended effective July 1, 2000, July 1, 2002, and January 1, 2003.)

(i) Conduct of hearing (§ 778)

The petitioner requesting the modification under section 778 has the burden of proving by a preponderance of the evidence that the ward's welfare requires the modification. Proof may be by declaration and other documentary evidence, or by testimony, or both, at the discretion of the court.

(Subd (i) amended and relettered effective January 1, 2007; adopted as subd (g); previously amended effective July 1, 2002.) Rule 5.570 amended effective January 1, 2009; adopted as rule 1432 effective January 1, 1991; previously amended effective January 1, 1992, July 1, 1995, July 1, 2000, July 1, 2002, and January 1, 2003; previously amended and renumbered effective January 1, 2007.

Ref.: Cal. Fms Pl. & Pr., Ch. 328, "Juvenile Courts: Dependency Proceedings," Ch. 329, "Juvenile Courts: Delinquency Proceedings"; W. Cal. Sum., 10 "Parent and Child" §§444, 458, 463, 663, 664, 666, 693B, 698, 910, 911.

Rule 5.575. Joinder

(a) Basis for joinder (§§ 362, 727)

After a child has been adjudged a dependent child or a ward of the court, the court may join in the court proceedings any government agency or private service provider (as defined in § 362(e)) that the court determines has failed to meet a legal obligation to provide services to the child.

(Subd (a) amended effective January 1, 2007.)

(b) Notice

On application by a party, counsel, or CASA volunteer, or on the court's own motion, the court may set a hearing and require notice to the agency or provider subject to joinder.

(1) Notice to the agency or provider must be given on *Notice of Hearing on Joinder—Juvenile* (form JV-540). The notice must state the allegations of the agency's or provider's failure to meet a legal obligation, as well as any questions the court wants the agency or provider to address.

(2) The hearing must be set to occur within 30 calendar days of the signing of the notice by the court.

(3) The clerk of the juvenile court must cause the notice to be served on the agency or provider and the persons prescribed by sections 291 and 658 either personally or by first-class mail within 5 days after the signing of the notice.

(4) The court may request, by using section 8 of form JV-540, that agency representatives before the hearing and that the agency submit a written response to the court. Any such response must be filed at least 5 court days before the hearing.

(Subd (b) amended effective January 1, 2007; previously amended effective January 1, 2006.)

(c) Conduct of hearing

The hearing must be conducted under rule 5.570(f) or (g). The court may not impose duties on a government agency or private service provider beyond those required by statute.

(Subd (c) amended effective January 1, 2007.)
Rule 5.575 amended and renumbered effective January 1, 2007; adopted as rule 1434 effective January 1, 2002; previously amended effective January 1, 2006.

Ref.: W. Cal. Sum., 10 "Parent and Child" §§444, 624, 892.

Rule 5.580. Hearing on violation of probation (§ 777)

(a) Notice of hearing (§§ 656, 658, 660)

Notice of a hearing to be held under section 777 must be issued and served as provided in sections 658, 660, and 777 and prepared:

(1) By the probation officer if the child has been declared a ward under section 601; or

(2) By the probation officer or the district attorney if the child is a ward or is on probation under section 602, and the alleged violation of probation is not a crime.

(Subd (a) amended effective January 1, 2007; adopted effective January 1, 2001; previously amended effective January 1, 2006.)

(b) Motion to dismiss

If the probation officer files the notice of hearing, before jeopardy attaches the prosecuting attorney may move the court to dismiss the notice and request that the matter be referred to the probation officer for appropriate action under section 777(a)(3).

(Subd (b) adopted effective January 1, 2001.)

(c) Detention hearing

If the child has been brought into custody, the procedures described in rules 5.524 and 5.752 through 5.764 must be followed.

(Subd (c) amended effective January 1, 2007; adopted as subd (d) effective January 1, 2001; amended and relettered effective January 1, 2006.)

(d) Report of probation officer

Before every hearing the probation officer must prepare a report on those matters relevant to a determination of whether the child has violated a condition of probation. The report must be furnished to all parties at least 48 hours, excluding noncourt days, before the beginning of the hearing unless the child is represented by counsel and waives the right to service of the report.

(Subd (d) amended and relettered effective January 1, 2006; adopted as subd (b) effective January 1, 1990; amended and relettered as subd (e) effective January 1, 2001.)

(e) Evidence considered

The court must consider the report prepared by the probation officer and other relevant and material evidence offered by the parties to the proceeding.

(1) The court may admit and consider reliable hearsay evidence as defined by section 777(c).

(2) The probation officer or prosecuting attorney must prove the alleged violation by a preponderance of the evidence.

(Subd (e) amended and relettered effective January 1, 2006; adopted as subd (e) effective January 1, 1990; amended and relettered as subd (f) effective January 1, 2001.)

Rule 5.580 amended and renumbered effective January 1, 2007; adopted as rule 1433 effective January 1, 1990; previously amended effective January 1, 1992, January 1, 2001, and January 1, 2006.

Ref.: Cal. Fms Pl. & Pr., Ch. 329, "Juvenile Courts: Delinquency Proceedings"; W. Cal. Sum., 10 "Parent and Child" §§444, 908, 909.

Chapter 5
Appeals and Writs

Rule 5.585. Review by appeal
Rule 5.590. Notification of appeal rights in juvenile cases
Rule 5.595. Review by extraordinary writ—section 300 proceedings
Rule 5.600. Writ petition after orders setting hearing under section 366.26; appeal

Rule 5.585.   Review by appeal

(a) Right to appeal—section 601–602 proceedings

In proceedings under section 601 or 602, the child may appeal from any judgment, order, or decree specified in section 800 and is entitled to court-appointed counsel. If the court determines that the parent or guardian can afford counsel but has not retained counsel for the child, the court must appoint counsel for the child at the expense of the parent or guardian.

(Subd (a) amended effective January 1, 2007; previously amended effective July 1, 1999.)

(b) Right to appeal—section 300 proceedings

In proceedings under section 300, the petitioner, child, and the parent or guardian each has the right to appeal from any judgment, order, or decree specified in section 395. Any judgment, order, or decree setting a hearing under section 366.26 may be reviewed on appeal following the order at the section 366.26 hearing only if the procedures in rules 8.450, 8.452, and 5.600 have been followed. All appellants are entitled to representation by counsel and the reviewing court may appoint counsel to represent an indigent child, parent, or guardian.

(Subd (b) amended effective January 1, 2007; repealed and adopted effective January 1, 1990; previously amended effective January 1, 1993, January 1, 1994, January 1, 1995, and July 1, 1999.)

(c) Stay of execution of order or judgment (§§ 395, 800)

The court must not stay an order or judgment pending an appeal unless suitable provision is made for the maintenance, care, and custody of the child.

(Subd (c) amended effective January 1, 2007.)

(d) Advisement of appeal rights—rule 5.590

If at a contested hearing on an issue of fact or law the court finds that the child is described by section 300, 601, or 602 or sustains a supplemental or subsequent petition, the court after making its disposition order must advise, orally or in writing, the child, if of sufficient age, and, if present, the parent or guardian of:

(1) The right of the child, parent, and guardian to appeal from the court order;

(2) The necessary steps and time for taking an appeal;

(3) The right of an indigent appellant to have counsel appointed by the reviewing court; and

(4) The right of an indigent appellant to be provided with a free copy of the transcript.

(Subd (d) amended effective January 1, 2007.)

(e) Notice of trial rights; section 366.26

When the court orders a hearing under section 366.26, the court must advise orally all parties present, and by first class mail for parties not present, that if the party wishes to preserve any right to review on appeal of the order setting the hearing under section 366.26, the party is required to seek an extraordinary writ by filing a *Notice of Intent to File Writ Petition and Request for Record (California Rules of Court, Rule 8.450)* (form JV-820) or other notice of intent to file a writ petition and request for record and a *Petition for Extraordinary Writ (California Rules of Court, Rules 8.452, 8.456)* (form JV-825) or other petition for extraordinary writ.

(1) Within 24 hours of the hearing, notice by first class mail must be provided by the clerk of the court to the last known address of any party who is not present when the court orders the hearing under section 366.26.

(2) Copies of *Petition for Extraordinary Writ (California Rules of Court, Rules 8.452, 8.456)* (form JV-825) and *Notice of Intent to File Writ Petition and Request for Record (California Rules of Court, Rule 8.450)* (form JV-820) must be available in the courtroom and must accompany all mailed notices informing the parties of their rights.

(Subd (e) amended effective January 1, 2007; adopted effective January 1, 1995.)

(f) Time for filing notice of appeal

Notice of appeal must be filed within 60 days after the making of an appealable order or, if the matter was heard by a referee who was not sitting as a temporary judge, within 60 days after the order becomes final under rule 5.540(c). Notice of appeal may be filed on *Notice of Appeal—Juvenile (California Rules of Court, Rule 8.400)* (form JV-800).

(Subd (f) amended effective January 1, 2007; adopted as subd (e) effective January 1, 1992; previously amended effective January 1, 1993; previously relettered effective January 1, 1995.)

(g) Procedure

Procedures for appeals from juvenile court are in title 8, division 1, chapter 5.

(Subd (g) amended effective January 1, 2007; repealed and adopted as subd (e) effective January 1, 1990; previously relettered as subd (f) effective January 1, 1992; previously relettered effective January 1, 1995.)

Rule 5.585 amended and renumbered effective January 1, 2007; adopted as rule 1435 effective January 1, 1990; previously amended effective January 1, 1992, January 1, 1993, January 1, 1994, January 1, 1995, and July 1, 1999.

Ref.: Cal. Fms Pl. & Pr., Ch. 328, "Juvenile Courts: Dependency Proceedings," Ch. 329, "Juvenile Courts: Delinquency Proceedings"; W. Cal. Sum., 10 "Parent and Child" §§444, 692, 695, 700, 708, 709, 712, 713, 717, 782, 913–915, 919.

Rule 5.590.   Notification of appeal rights in juvenile cases

In juvenile court proceedings in which the child is found to be a person described by section 300, 601, or 602 after a contested issue of fact or law, the juvenile court, after making its order at the conclusion of the dispositional hearing or an order changing or modifying a previous disposition at the conclusion of a hearing on a supplemental petition, will advise, either orally or in writing, the child and, if present, the child's parent, guardian, or adult relative of any right to appeal from such order, of the necessary steps and time for taking an appeal, and of the right of an indigent person to have counsel appointed by the reviewing court.

Rule 5.590 amended and renumbered effective January 1, 2007; adopted as rule 251 effective July 1, 1973; previously amended effective July 1, 1978.

Ref.: Cal. Fms Pl. & Pr., Ch. 328, "Juvenile Courts: Dependency Proceedings," Ch. 329, "Juvenile Courts: Delinquency Proceedings"; W. Cal. Sum., 10 "Parent and Child" §§444, 700, 914.

Rule 5.595. Review by extraordinary writ— section 300 proceedings

If review by petition for extraordinary writ is sought regarding judgments, orders, or decrees other than those described in rules 8.450, 8.452, 8.454, 8.456, and 5.600, a *Petition for Extraordinary Writ (California Rules of Court, Rules 8.452, 8.456)* (form JV-825) may be used.

Rule 5.595 amended and renumbered effective January 1, 2007; adopted as rule 1436 effective January 1, 1993; previously amended effective January 1, 1994, January 1, 1995, and January 1, 2006.

Ref.: Cal. Fms Pl. & Pr., Ch. 328, "Juvenile Courts: Dependency Proceedings"; W. Cal. Sum., 10 "Parent and Child" §§444, 716, 920.

Rule 5.600. Writ petition after orders setting hearing under section 366.26; appeal

(a) Writ petition process

Rules 8.450 and 8.452 describe how a party including the petitioner, child, and parent or guardian must proceed if seeking appellate court review of findings and orders of the juvenile court made at a hearing at which the court orders that a hearing under section 366.26 be held.

(Subd (a) amended effective January 1, 2007; previously amended effective January 1, 2006.)

(b) Notice of trial rights; section 366.26

When the court orders a hearing under section 366.26, the court must advise orally all parties present, and by first-class mail for parties not present, that if the party wishes to preserve any right to review on appeal of the order setting the hearing under section 366.26, the party is required to seek an extraordinary writ by filing a *Notice of Intent to File Writ Petition and Request for Record, (California Rules of Court, Rule 8.450)* (form JV-820) or other notice of intent to file a writ petition and request for record and a *Petition for Extraordinary Writ (California Rules of Court, Rules 8.452, 8.456)* (form JV-825) or other petition for extraordinary writ.

(1) Within 24 hours of the hearing, notice by first-class mail must be provided by the clerk of the court to the last known address of any party who is not present when the court orders the hearing under section 366.26.

(2) Copies of *Petition for Extraordinary Writ (California Rules of Court, Rules 8.452, 8.456)* (form JV-825) and *Notice of Intent to File Writ Petition and Request for Record (California Rules of Court, Rule 8.450)* (form JV-820) must be available in the courtroom and must

accompany all mailed notices informing the parties of their rights.

(Subd (b) amended and relettered effective January 1, 2007; adopted as subd (d) effective January 1, 1995.)

(c) Time for filing the notice of intent to file writ petition and request for record

To permit determination of the writ petition before the scheduled date for the hearing under section 366.26 on the selection of the permanent plan, a notice of intent to file a writ petition and request for record must be filed with the clerk of the juvenile court within 7 days of the date of the order setting a hearing under section 366.26. The period for filing a notice of intent to file a writ petition and request for record will be extended 5 days if the party received notice of the order setting the hearing under section 366.26 only by mail. A *Notice of Intent to File Writ Petition and Request for Record (California Rules of Court, Rule 8.450)* (form JV-820) may be used.

(Subd (c) amended and relettered effective January 1, 2007; adopted as subd (e) effective January 1, 1995; previously amended effective July 1, 1995, January 1, 1996, and January 1, 2006.)

(d) Contents of the notice of intent to file writ petition

The notice of intent to file a writ petition must include, if known, all dates of the hearing that resulted in the order setting the hearing under section 366.26.

(Subd (d) amended and relettered effective January 1, 2007; adopted as subd (f) effective January 1, 2006.)

(e) Notice and service

The clerk must serve a copy of the notice of intent to file a writ petition on each person listed in section 294, the child's CASA volunteer, the child's present caregiver, and any de facto parent. The clerk must also serve, by first-class mail or fax, on the clerk of the reviewing court, a copy of the notice of intent to file a writ petition and a proof of service list. On receipt of the notice of intent to file a writ petition, the clerk of the reviewing court must lodge the notice, which gives the reviewing court jurisdiction of the writ proceedings.

(Subd (e) amended and relettered effective January 1, 2007; adopted as subd (g) effective January 1, 2006.)

(f) Record

Immediately on the filing of the notice of intent to file a writ petition and request for record, the clerk of the juvenile court must assemble the record:

(1) Notifying each court reporter by telephone and in writing to prepare a reporter's transcript of each session of the hearing and to deliver the transcript to the clerk no more than 12 days after the notice of intent to file a writ petition and request for record is filed; and

(2) Preparing the clerk's transcript under rule [1] **8.450(g).**

The record must include all reports and minute orders contained in the juvenile court file, a reporter's transcript of all sessions of the hearing at which the order setting a hearing under section 366.26 was made, and any additional evidence or documents considered by the court at that hearing.

Immediately on completion of the transcript, the clerk must certify the record as correct, and deliver it by the most expeditious means to the reviewing court, and transmit copies to the petitioner and parties or counsel of record, by any method as fast as the express mail service of the United States Postal Service. On receipt of the transcript and record, the clerk of the reviewing court must notify all parties that the record has been filed and indicate the date on which the 10-day period for filing the writ petition will expire.

(Subd (f) amended effective January 1, 2009; adopted as subd (f) effective January 1, 1995; previously amended effective January 1, 1996; previously amended and relettered as subd (h) effective January 1, 2006, and as subd (f) effective January 1, 2007.)

Rule 5.600(f).   2008 Deletes. [1] 8.616(a)

(g) Petitioner; trial counsel

Trial counsel for the petitioning party or, in the absence of trial counsel, the party, is responsible for filing the petition for extraordinary writ. Trial counsel is encouraged to seek assistance from, or consult with, attorneys experienced in writ procedures.

(Subd (g) amended and relettered effective January 1, 2007; adopted as subd (g) effective January 1, 1995; previously relettered as subd (i) effective January 1, 2006.)

(h) Petition for extraordinary writ; form JV-825

The petition for extraordinary writ may be filed on a *Petition for Extraordinary Writ (California Rules of Court, Rules 8.452, 8.456)* (form JV-825) or other petition for extraordinary writ. Petitions for extraordinary writ submitted on a *Petition for Extraordinary Writ (California Rules of Court, Rules 8.452, 8.456)* (form JV-825) must be accepted for filing by the appellate court. All petitions must be liberally construed in favor of their sufficiency.

(Subd (h) amended and relettered effective January 1, 2007; adopted as subd (j) effective January 1, 1995; previously amended and relettered as subd (j) effective January 1, 2006.)

(i) Time for filing petition

The petition for extraordinary writ must be served and filed within 10 days after filing any record in the reviewing court.

(Subd (i) relettered effective January 1, 2007; adopted as subd (i) effective January 1, 1995; previously amended and relettered as subd (k) effective January 1, 2006.)

(j) Contents of petition for writ; service

The petition for extraordinary writ must summarize the factual basis for the petition. Petitioner need not repeat facts as they appear in any attached or submitted record, provided, however, that references to specific portions of the record, their significance to the grounds alleged, and disputed aspects of the record will assist the reviewing court and must be noted. Petitioner must attach a memorandum in support of the petition.

(Subd (j) amended and relettered effective January 1, 2007; adopted as subd (j) effective January 1, 1995; previously amended and relettered as subd (l) effective January 1, 2006.)

Rule 5.600 amended effective January 1, 2009; adopted as rule 1436.5 effective January 1, 1995; previously amended effective July 1, 1995, January 1, 1996, and July 1, 2006; previously amended and renumbered effective January 1, 2007.

Ref.: Cal. Fms Pl. & Pr., Ch. 328, "Juvenile Courts: Dependency Proceedings"; W. Cal. Sum., 10 "Parent and Child" §§444, 716, 717, 720–722, 920.

Chapter 6
Emancipation

Rule 5.605.   Emancipation of minors

(a) Petition

A petition for declaration of emancipation of a minor must be submitted on *Petition for Declaration of Emancipation of Minor, Order Prescribing Notice, Declaration of Emancipation, and Order Denying Petition* (form MC-300). Only the minor may petition the court for emancipation, and the petition may be filed in the county in which the minor can provide a verifiable residence address. The petitioner must complete and attach to the petition *Emancipation of Minor—Income and Expense Declaration* (form MC-306).

(Subd (a) amended effective January 1, 2007.)

(b) Dependents and wards of the juvenile court

Petitions to emancipate a child who is a dependent or ward of the juvenile court must be filed and heard in juvenile court.

(Subd (b) amended effective January 1, 2007; previously amended effective January 1, 1995.)

(c) Court

The petition to emancipate a minor other than a dependent or ward of the juvenile court must be filed and will be heard in juvenile court or other superior court department so designated by local rule or by order of the presiding judge.

(Subd (c) amended effective January 1, 2007.)

(d) Filing fee

Unless waived, the petitioner must pay the filing fee as specified. The ability or inability to pay the filing fee is not in and of itself evidence of the financial responsibility of the minor as required for emancipation.

(Subd (d) amended effective January 1, 2007.)

(e) Declaration of emancipation without hearing

If the court finds that all notice and consent requirements have been met or waived, and that emancipation is not contrary to the best interest of the petitioner, the court may grant the petition without a hearing. The presiding judge of the superior court must develop a protocol for the screening, evaluation, or investigation of petitions.

(Subd (e) amended effective January 1, 2007.)

(f) Time limits

The clerk of the court in which the petition is filed must immediately provide or direct the petitioner to provide the petition to the court. Within 30 days from the filing of the petition, the court must (1) grant the petition, (2) deny the petition, or (3) set a hearing on the petition to be conducted within 30 days thereafter. The clerk must immediately provide the petitioner with an endorsed-filed copy of the court's order.

(Subd (f) amended effective January 1, 2007.)

(g) Notice

If the court orders the matter set for hearing, the clerk must notify the district attorney of the time and date of the hearing, which must be within 30 days of the order prescribing notice and setting for hearing. The petitioner is responsible for notifying all other persons to whom the court requires notice.

(Subd (g) amended effective January 1, 2007.)

Rule 5.605 amended and renumbered effective January 1, 2007; adopted as rule 1437 effective July 1, 1994; previously amended effective January 1, 1995.

Ref.: W. Cal. Sum., 10 "Parent and Child" §§303, 304, 444.

Chapter 7
Intercounty Transfers

Rule 5.610. Transfer-out hearing
Rule 5.612. Transfer-in hearing
Rule 5.614. Courtesy supervision (§§ 380, 755)
Rule 5.616. Interstate Compact on the Placement of Children

Rule 5.610.   Transfer-out hearing

(a) Determination of residence—special rule on intercounty transfers (§§ 375, 750)

(1) For purposes of rules 5.610 and 5.612, the residence of the child is the residence of the person who has the legal right to physical custody of the child according to prior court order, including:

(A) A juvenile court order under section 361.2; and

(B) An order appointing a guardian of the person of the child.

(2) If there is no order determining custody, both parents are deemed to have physical custody.

(3) The juvenile court may make a finding of paternity under rule 5.635. If there is no finding of paternity, the mother is deemed to have physical custody.

(4) For the purposes of transfer of wardship, residence of a ward may be with the person with whom the child resides with approval of the court.

(Subd (a) amended effective January 1, 2007; previously amended effective January 1, 2004.)

(b) Verification of residence

The residence of the person entitled to physical custody may be verified by that person in court or by declaration of a social worker or probation officer in the transferring or receiving county.

(Subd (b) amended effective January 1, 2007; previously amended effective January 1, 2004.)

(c) Transfer to county of child's residence (§§ 375, 750)

(1) After making its jurisdictional finding, the court may order the case transferred to the juvenile court of the child's residence if:

(A) The petition was filed in a county other than that of the child's residence; or

(B) The child's residence was changed to another county after the petition was filed.

(2) If the court decides to transfer a delinquency case, the court must order the transfer before beginning the disposition hearing without adjudging the child to be a ward.

(3) If the court decides to transfer a dependency case, the court may order the transfer before or after the disposition hearing.

(Subd (c) amended effective January 1, 2007; previously amended effective January 1, 2004.)

(d) Transfer on subsequent change in child's residence (§§ 375, 750)

If, after the child has been placed under a program of supervision, the residence is changed to another county, the court may, on an application for modification under rule 5.570, transfer the case to the juvenile court of the other county.

(Subd (d) amended effective January 1, 2007; previously amended effective January 1, 2004.)

(e) Conduct of hearing

After the court determines the identity and residence of the child's custodian, the court must consider whether transfer of the case would be in the child's best interest. The court may not transfer the case unless it determines that the transfer will protect or further the child's best interest.

(Subd (e) amended effective January 1, 2007; repealed and adopted effective January 1, 1990; previously amended effective January 1, 1993, and January 1, 2004.)

(f) Order of transfer (§§ 377, 752)

The order of transfer must be entered on *Juvenile Court Transfer Orders* (form JV-550), which must include all required information and findings.

(Subd (f) amended effective January 1, 2007; repealed and adopted effective January 1, 1990; previously amended effective January 1, 1993, and January 1, 2004.)

(g) Modification of form JV-550

Juvenile Court Transfer Orders (form JV-550) may be modified as follows:

(1) Notwithstanding the mandatory use of form JV-550, the form may be modified for use by a formalized regional collaboration of courts to facilitate the efficient processing of transfer cases among those courts if the modification has been approved by the Judicial Council of California, Administrative Office of the Courts.

(2) The mandatory form must be used by a regional collaboration when transferring a case to a court outside the collaboration or when accepting a transfer from a court outside the collaboration.

(Subd (g) adopted effective January 1, 2007.)

(h) Transport of child and transmittal of documents (§§ 377, 752)

(1) If the child is ordered transported in custody to the receiving county, the child must be delivered to the receiving county within 7 court days, and the clerk of the court of the transferring county must prepare a certified copy of the complete case file so that it may be transported with the child to the court of the receiving county.

(2) If the child is not ordered transported in custody, the clerk of the transferring court must transmit to the clerk of the court of the receiving county within 10 court days a certified copy of the complete case file.

(3) A certified copy of the complete case file is deemed an original.

(Subd (h) amended and relettered effective January 1, 2007; repealed and adopted as subd (g) effective, January 1, 1990; previously amended effective January 1, 1992, January 1, 1993, July 1, 1999, and January 1, 2004.)

(i) Appeal of transfer order (§§ 379, 754)

The order of transfer may be appealed by the transferring or receiving county and notice of appeal must be filed in the transferring county, under rule 8.400. Notwithstanding the filing of a notice of appeal, the receiving county must assume jurisdiction of the case on receipt and filing of the order of transfer.

(Subd (i) amended and relettered effective January 1, 2007; repealed and adopted as subd (h) effective January 1, 1990; previously amended effective January 1, 1992, and January 1, 2004.)

Rule 5.610 amended and renumbered effective January 1, 2007; adopted as rule 1425 effective January 1, 1990; previously amended effective January 1, 1992, January 1, 1993, July 1, 1999, and January 1, 2004.

Advisory Committee Comment

Juvenile court judicial officers throughout the state have expressed concern that in determining whether or not to transfer a juvenile court case, the best interest of the subject child is being overlooked or at least outweighed by a desire to shift the financial burdens of case management and foster care. The advisory committee has clarified rule 5.610 in order to stress that in considering an intercounty transfer, as in all matters relating to children within its jurisdiction, the court has a mandate to act in the best interest of the subject children.

Juvenile Court Transfer Orders (form JV-550) was adopted for mandatory use commencing January 1, 1992. Although the finding regarding the best interest of the child was noted on the original form, the language has been emphasized on the amended form.

Ref.: Cal. Fms Pl. & Pr., Ch. 327, "Juvenile Courts: Jurisdiction and General Procedures," Ch. 328, "Juvenile Courts: Dependency Proceedings," Ch. 329, "Juvenile Courts: Delinquency Proceedings"; W. Cal. Sum., 10 "Parent and Child" §§444, 456–463, 598, 819.

Rule 5.612.   Transfer-in hearing

(a) Procedure on transfer (§§ 378, 753)

(1) On receipt and filing of a certified copy of a transfer order, the receiving court must accept jurisdiction of the case. The receiving court may not reject the case. The clerk of the receiving court must immediately place the transferred case on the court calendar for a transfer-in hearing:

(A) Within 2 court days after the transfer-out order and documents are received if the child has been transported in custody and remains detained; or

(B) Within 10 court days after the transfer-out order and documents are received if the child is not detained in custody.

(2) No requests for additional time for the transfer-in hearing may be approved. The clerk must immediately cause notice to be given to the child and the parent or guardian, orally or in writing, of the time and place of the transfer-in hearing. The receiving court must notify the transferring court on receipt and filing of the certified copies of the transfer order and complete case file.

(Subd (a) amended effective January 1, 2007; repealed and adopted effective January 1, 1990; previously amended effective January 1, 1992, July 1, 1999, and January 1, 2004.)

(b) Conduct of hearing

At the transfer-in hearing, the court must:

(1) Advise the child and the parent or guardian of the purpose and scope of the hearing;

(2) Provide for the appointment of counsel if appropriate; and

(3) If the child was transferred to the county in custody, determine whether the child must be further detained under rule 5.667.

(Subd (b) amended effective January 1, 2007; previously amended effective January 1, 2004.)

(c) Subsequent proceedings

The proceedings in the receiving court must commence at the same phase as when the case was transferred. The court may continue the hearing for an investigation and report to a date not to exceed 10 court days if the child is

in custody or 15 court days if the child is not detained in custody.

(Subd (c) amended effective January 1, 2004; previously amended effective July 1, 1999.)

(d) Limitation on more restrictive custody (§§ 387, 777)

If a disposition order has already been made in the transferring county, a more restrictive level of physical custody may not be ordered in the receiving county, except after a hearing on a supplemental petition under rule 5.565.

(Subd (d) amended effective January 1, 2007; previously amended effective January 1, 2004.)

(e) Setting six-month review (§ 366)

When an order of transfer is received and filed relating to a child who has been declared a dependent, the court must set a date for a six-month review within six months of the disposition or the most recent review hearing.

(Subd (e) amended effective January 1, 2004.)

(f) Change of circumstances or additional facts (§§ 388, 778)

If the receiving court believes that a change of circumstances or additional facts indicate that the child does not reside in the receiving county, a transfer-out hearing must be held under rules 5.610 and 5.570. The court may direct the department of social services or the probation department to seek a modification of orders under section 388 or 778 and under rule 5.570.

(Subd (f) amended effective January 1, 2007; adopted effective January 1, 1992; previously amended effective July 1, 1999, and January 1, 2004.)

Rule 5.612 amended and renumbered effective January 1, 2007; adopted as rule 1426 effective January 1, 1990; previously amended effective January 1, 1992, July 1, 1999, and January 1, 2004.

Ref.: Cal. Fms Pl. & Pr., Ch. 327, "Juvenile Courts: Jurisdiction and General Procedures"; W. Cal. Sum., 10 "Parent and Child" §§444, 457, 459, 461, 463.

Rule 5.614.   Courtesy supervision (§§ 380, 755)

The court may authorize a child placed on probation, a ward, or a dependent child to live in another county and to be placed under the supervision of the other county's county welfare agency or probation department with the consent of the agency or department. The court in the county ordering placement retains jurisdiction over the child.

Rule 5.614 amended and renumbered effective January 1, 2007; adopted as rule 1427 effective January 1, 1990.

Ref.: W. Cal. Sum., 10 "Parent and Child" §§444, 464.

Rule 5.616.   Interstate Compact on the Placement of Children

(a) Applicability of rule (Fam. Code, § 7900 et seq.)

This rule implements the purposes and provisions of the Interstate Compact on the Placement of Children. California juvenile courts must apply this rule when placing children who are dependents or wards of the juvenile court and for whom placement is indicated in any other state, the District of Columbia, or the U.S. Virgin Islands.

(1) The rule applies to the placement in California of children who are dependents or wards of the juvenile court in any of the above-named jurisdictions.

Rules of Court

(2) This rule also applies to priority placements as described below in (b)(2).

(3) This rule does not apply to placements made under the Interstate Compact on Juveniles (§ 1300 et seq.).

(Subd (a) amended effective January 1, 2007.)

(b) Definitions

(1) "Placement" is defined in article II(d) of the compact. It includes placements with a stepparent, a grandparent, an adult brother or sister, an adult aunt or uncle, a nonagency guardian of the child, a placement recipient who is not related to the child, a residential institution, a group home, or a treatment facility.

(A) A court directing or making an award of custody to a parent of the child is not a placement within the meaning of this rule, unless the sending court retains dependency jurisdiction over the child or the order or award requests or provides for supervision or other services or places some other condition or restriction on the conduct of the parent.

(B) Except in cases in which a child is placed with a parent and jurisdiction has been terminated or in cases in which dependency is maintained only to provide services to or impose conditions on the noncustodial parent remaining in the sending jurisdiction, the following situations constitute a placement and the compact must be applied:

(i) An order causing a child to be sent or brought to another party in a compact jurisdiction without a specific date of return to the sending jurisdiction; or

(ii) An order causing a child to be sent or brought to another party in a compact jurisdiction with a return date more than 30 days from the start of the visit or beyond the ending date of a school vacation period.

(2) "Priority placement" means a placement or placement request made by a court with specific findings of one or more of the following circumstances:

(A) The proposed placement recipient is a relative belonging to a class of persons who, under article VIII(a) of the compact, could receive the child from another person belonging to such a class, without complying with the compact, if the child is not under the jurisdiction of the court, and if:

(i) The child is under two years of age;

(ii) The child is in an emergency shelter; or

(iii) The court finds that the child has spent a substantial period of time in the home of the proposed placement recipient.

(B) The receiving compact administrator has been in possession of a properly completed interstate compact placement request form and supporting documentation for over 30 business days, but the sending agency has not received a notice under article III(d) of the compact determining whether or not the child may be placed.

(Subd (b) amended effective January 1, 2007.)

(c) Compact requirements (Fam. Code, § 7901)

Whenever the juvenile court makes a placement in another jurisdiction included in the compact or reviews a placement plan, the court must adhere to the provisions and regulations of the compact.

(Subd (c) amended effective January 1, 2007.)

(d) Notice of intention; authorization (Fam. Code, § 7901)

A sending jurisdiction must provide to the designated receiving jurisdiction written notice of intention to place the child, using an interstate compact placement request form.

(1) The representative of the receiving jurisdiction may request and receive additional information as the representative deems necessary.

(2) The child must not be placed until the receiving jurisdiction has determined that the placement is not contrary to the interest of the child and has so notified the sending jurisdiction in writing.

(Subd (d) amended effective January 1, 2007.)

(e) Placement of delinquent children in institutional care

A child declared a ward of the court under section 602 may be placed in an institution in another jurisdiction under the compact only when:

(1) Before the placement, the court has held a hearing at which the child, parent, and guardian have had an opportunity to be heard;

(2) The court has found that equivalent facilities for the child are not available in the sending jurisdiction; and

(3) Institutional care in the other jurisdiction is in the best interest of the child and will not produce undue hardship for the child.

(Subd (e) amended effective January 1, 2007.)

(f) Priority placement

A court in a sending jurisdiction may designate placement as a priority placement and use expedited procedures as described in regulation 7 of the compact.

(1) The court may designate a priority placement on express findings that:

(A) The compact administrator of the receiving jurisdiction has had possession of a properly completed interstate compact placement request form and supporting documents for over 30 business days, and the sending jurisdiction agency has not received a notice indicating whether or not placement in the receiving jurisdiction is contrary to the interest of the child; or

(B) The proposed placement recipient is a parent, stepparent, grandparent, adult sibling, adult uncle or aunt, or guardian of the child; and

(i) The child is under two years of age;

(ii) The child is in an emergency shelter; or

(iii) The court finds that the child has spent a substantial period of time in the home of the proposed placement recipient.

(2) On findings of the court under (f)(1) that a proposed priority placement is necessary, the court must proceed as follows:

(A) The findings must be noted in a written order using *Interstate Compact on the Placement of Children Findings and Orders* (form JV-567), which must include the name, address, telephone number, and fax number of the court and the judicial officer.

(B) The order must be transmitted to the sending agency of the court's jurisdiction within 2 business days.

(C) The sending agency must be ordered to transmit to the compact administrator of the sending jurisdiction within 3 business days the following:

(i) A copy of the completed *Interstate Compact on the Placement of Children Findings and Orders* (form JV-567); and

(ii) A completed interstate compact placement request form and supporting documentation as noted on that form.

(D) Within 2 business days the compact administrator of the sending jurisdiction must transmit by overnight mail the documents described in (C) to the compact administrator of the receiving jurisdiction with a notice that the request is entitled to priority placement.

(3) The compact administrator of the receiving jurisdiction must determine immediately, and no later than 20 business days after receipt, whether or not the placement is acceptable and must transmit the completed interstate compact placement request form by fax to the compact administrator of the sending jurisdiction.

(4) If the compact administrator of the receiving jurisdiction fails to comply with (f)(3) within the required time limit, the sending court may inform an appropriate court in the receiving jurisdiction that the compact administrator in that jurisdiction has not complied with the compact; provide the receiving jurisdiction court with relevant documents, including *Findings and Request for Assistance Under Interstate Compact on the Placement of Children (ICPC)* (form JV-565); and request assistance.

(5) The receiving jurisdiction court that receives notification may render appropriate assistance and may issue orders to secure compliance with the compact and regulations.

(6) The time limits for a single case may be modified by written agreement between the sending court, the sending agency, and the compact administrators of the sending and receiving jurisdictions.

(7) To fulfill its obligations under the compact, a jurisdiction, its local agencies, and the court are required to process interstate cases as quickly as intrastate cases and to devote equal efforts to interstate and intrastate hardship cases.

(A) If in doing so, a receiving jurisdiction's compact administrator finds that extraordinary circumstances make compliance within the time requirements impossible, strict compliance may be excused.

(B) The receiving jurisdiction compact administrator must immediately notify the sending jurisdiction compact administrator by fax of the inability to comply and must designate a date on or before which there will be compliance.

(C) The notice must contain a full identification and explanation of the extraordinary circumstances that are delaying compliance.

(Subd (f) amended effective January 1, 2007.)

(g) Ongoing jurisdiction

If a child is placed in another jurisdiction under the terms of the compact, the sending court must not terminate its jurisdiction until the child is adopted, reaches majority, or is emancipated, or the dependency is terminated with the concurrence of the receiving state authority.

(Subd (g) amended effective January 1, 2007.)

Rule 5.616 amended and renumbered effective January 1, 2007; adopted as rule 1428 effective January 1, 1999.

Ref.: Cal. Fms Pl. & Pr., Ch. 12B, "Adoptions: Unmarried Minors," Ch. 328, "Juvenile Courts: Dependency Proceedings"; W. Cal. Sum., 10 "Parent and Child" §§80, 444.

Chapter 8
Restraining Orders, Custody Orders, and Guardianships General Court Authority

Rule 5.620. Orders after filing under section 300
Rule 5.625. Orders after filing of petition under section 601 or 602
Rule 5.630. Restraining orders

Rule 5.620.   Orders after filing under section 300

(a) Exclusive jurisdiction (§ 304)

Once a petition has been filed in juvenile court alleging that a child is described by a subsection of section 300, and until the petition is dismissed or dependency is terminated, the juvenile court has sole and exclusive jurisdiction over matters relating to the custody of the child and visitation with the child.

(b) Restraining orders (§ 213.5)

After a petition has been filed under section 300, and until the petition is dismissed or dependency is terminated, the court may issue restraining orders as provided in rule 5.630. The restraining orders must be prepared on *Restraining Order—Juvenile (CLETS)* (form JV-250).

(Subd (b) amended effective January 1, 2007.)

(c) Custody and visitation (§ 361.2)

If the court sustains a petition and finds that the child is described by section 300, it may enter findings and orders as described in rule 5.695(a)(7)(A) and (B). These findings and orders may be entered at the disposition hearing under rule 5.700, or at any subsequent review hearing under rule 5.710(g) or 5.715(d)(2) or rule 5.720(b)(1)(B), or on the granting of a motion under section 388 for custody and visitation orders.

(Subd (c) amended effective January 1, 2007.)

(d) Appointment of a legal guardian of the person (§§ 360, 366.26)

If the court finds that the child is described by section 300, it may appoint a legal guardian at the disposition hearing as described in rule 5.695(b), or at the hearing under section 366.26 as described in rule 5.735. The juvenile court maintains jurisdiction over the guardianship, and petitions to terminate or modify such guardianships must be heard in juvenile court under rule 5.740(c).

(Subd (d) amended effective January 1, 2007.)

(e) Termination or modification of previously established guardianships (§ 728)

At any time after the filing of a petition under section 300 and until the petition is dismissed or dependency is terminated, the court may terminate or modify a guardianship of the person previously established by the juvenile court or the probate court. If the social worker recommends to the court, by filing *Juvenile Dependency Petition (Version One)* (form JV-100) and *Request to Change Court Order* (form JV-180), that an existing guardianship be modified or terminated, the court must order the appropriate county agency to file the recommended motion.

(1) The hearing on the motion may be held simultaneously with any regularly scheduled hearing regarding

the child. Notice requirements under Probate Code section 1511 apply.

(2) If the court terminates or modifies a previously established probate guardianship, the court must provide notice of the order to the probate court that made the original appointment. The clerk of the probate court must file the notice in the probate file and send a copy of the notice to all parties of record identified in that file.

(Subd (e) amended effective January 1, 2007.)

Rule 5.620 amended and renumbered effective January 1, 2007; adopted as rule 1429.1 effective January 1, 2000.

Ref.: Cal. Fms Pl. & Pr., Ch. 328, "Juvenile Courts: Dependency Proceedings"; W. Cal. Sum., 10 "Parent and Child" §§369, 444, 453, 520, 627, 628, 695.

Rule 5.625. Orders after filing of petition under section 601 or 602

(a) Restraining orders (§ 213.5)

After a petition has been filed under section 601 or 602, and until the petition is dismissed or wardship is terminated, the court may issue restraining orders as provided in rule 5.630. The restraining orders must be prepared on *Restraining Order—Juvenile (CLETS—JUV)* (form JV-250).

(Subd (a) amended effective January 1, 2007; previously amended effective January 1, 2003.)

(b) Appointment of a legal guardian of the person (§ 728)

At any time during wardship of a person under 18 years, the court may appoint a guardian, or may terminate or modify a previously established guardianship, in accordance with the requirements in rule 5.815.

(Subd (b) amended and relettered effective January 1, 2007; adopted as subd (c) effective January 1, 2000; previously amended effective January 1, 2003.)

Rule 5.625 amended and renumbered effective January 1, 2007; adopted as rule 1429.3 effective January 1, 2000; previously amended effective January 1, 2003.

Ref.: W. Cal. Sum., 10 "Parent and Child" §§444, 453, 892.

Rule 5.630. Restraining orders

(a) Court's authority (§ 213.5)

After a petition has been filed under section 300, 601, or 602, and until the petition is dismissed or dependency or wardship is terminated, or the ward is no longer on probation, the court may issue restraining orders as provided in section 213.5.

(b) Application (§§ 213.5, 304)

Application for restraining orders may be made orally at any scheduled hearing regarding the child who is the subject of a petition under section 300, 601, or 602, or may be made by written application, or may be made on the court's own motion. The written application must be submitted on *Application and Affidavit for Restraining Order—Juvenile* (form JV-245).

(Subd (b) amended effective January 1, 2007; previously amended effective January 1, 2003, and January 1, 2004.)

(c) Protected children (§ 213.5(a) and (b))

Restraining orders may be issued to protect any of the following children:

(1) A child who is the subject of the dependency petition or who is declared a dependent;

(2) Another child in the household of the child named in (1); and

(3) A child who is the subject of a delinquency petition or who is declared a ward.

(Subd (c) adopted effective January 1, 2003.)

(d) Other protected persons (§ 213.5(a))

The court may also issue orders protecting any parent, legal guardian, or current caregiver of the child listed in (c)(1), whether or not that child resides with that parent, legal guardian, or current caregiver.

(Subd (d) amended effective January 1, 2007; adopted effective January 1, 2003.)

(e) Available orders and restrained persons (§ 213.5(a), (b), and (d)–(f))

The court may issue, either ex parte or after notice and hearing, restraining orders that:

(1) Enjoin any person from molesting, attacking, striking, sexually assaulting, stalking, or battering any of the persons listed in (c) or (d);

(2) Exclude any person from the dwelling of the person who has care, custody, and control of the child named in (c)(1) or (3). This order may be issued for the time and on the conditions that the court determines, regardless of which party holds legal or equitable title or is the lessee of the residence or dwelling, on a showing that:

(A) The party who will stay in the dwelling has a right under color of law to possession of the premises;

(B) The party to be excluded has assaulted or threatened to assault the other party or any other person under the care, custody, and control of the other party, or any minor child of the parties or of the other party; and

(C) Physical or emotional harm would otherwise result to the other party, to any person under the care, custody, and control of the other party, or to any minor child of the parties or of the other party;

(3) Enjoin any person from behavior, including contacting, threatening, or disturbing the peace of the persons named in (c) or (d), as necessary to effectuate orders under (e)(1) or (2); and

(4) Enjoin any delinquent child or any child for whom a section 601 or 602 petition has been filed from contacting, threatening, stalking, or disturbing the peace of any person:

(A) Whom the court finds to be at risk from the conduct of the child; or

(B) With whom association would be detrimental to the child.

(Subd (e) amended effective January 1, 2007; adopted effective January 1, 2003.)

(f) Ex parte applications—procedure (§ 213.5(a)–(c) and (f))

The application may be submitted ex parte, and the court may grant the petition and issue a temporary order. The matter may be heard simultaneously with any scheduled hearing regarding the child who is the subject of the section 300, 601, or 602 petition. Notice of the ex parte proceeding is required as stated under rule 3.1204.

(1) In determining whether or not to issue the temporary restraining order ex parte, the court must consider all documents submitted with the application and may review the contents of the juvenile court file regarding the child.

(2) The temporary restraining order must be prepared on *Restraining Order—Juvenile (CLETS—JUV)* (form JV-250) and must state on its face the date of expiration of the order.

(Subd (f) amended effective January 1, 2007; adopted as subd (c) effective January 1, 2000; previously amended and relettered effective January 1, 2003.)

(g) Order to show cause and reissuance (§ 213.5(c))

When a temporary restraining order is granted without notice, the matter must be made returnable on an order to show cause why the order should not be granted, no later than 15 days or, on a showing of good cause, 20 days from the date the temporary restraining order is granted.

(1) On the motion of the person seeking the restraining order or on its own motion, the court may shorten the time for service of the order to show cause on the person to be restrained.

(2) The court may, on its own motion or the filing of an affidavit by the person seeking the restraining order, find that the person to be restrained could not be served within the time required by the law and reissue an order previously issued and dissolved by the court for failure to serve the person to be restrained. The reissued order must state on its face the date of expiration of the order. *Application and Order for Reissuance of Order to Show Cause* (form FL-306/JV-251) must be used for this purpose.

(Subd (g) amended effective January 1, 2007; adopted effective January 1, 2003; previously amended effective January 1, 2004.)

(h) Hearing on application for restraining order (§ 213.5(d) and (f))

The court may issue, after notice and hearing, any of the orders in (e). The restraining order must remain in effect for a period of time determined by the court, but in any case not more than three years.

(1) The matter may be heard simultaneously with any scheduled hearing regarding the child who is the subject of the section 300, 601, or 602 petition.

(2) Proof may be by the application and any attachments, additional declarations or documentary evidence, the contents of the juvenile court file, testimony, or any combination of these.

(3) The order after hearing must be prepared on *Restraining Order—Juvenile (CLETS—JUV)* (form JV-250) and must state on its face the date of expiration of the order.

(Subd (h) amended effective January 1, 2007; adopted as subd (d) effective January 1, 2000; previously amended and relettered effective January 1, 2003.)

(i) Criminal records search (§ 213.5(k) and Stats. 2001, ch. 572, § 7)

(1) Except as provided in (3), before any hearing on the issuance of a restraining order the court must ensure that a criminal records search is or has been conducted as described in Family Code section 6306(a). Before deciding whether to issue a restraining order, the court must consider the information obtained from the search.

(2) If the results of the search indicate that an outstanding warrant exists against the subject of the search, or that the subject of the search is currently on parole or probation, the court must proceed under section 213.5(k)(3).

(3) The requirements of (1) and (2) must be implemented in those courts identified by the Judicial Council

as having resources currently available for these purposes. All other courts must implement the requirements to the extent that funds are appropriated for this purpose in the annual Budget Act.

(Subd (i) amended effective January 1, 2007; adopted effective January 1, 2003.)

(j) Termination or extension of restraining order (§ 213.5(d))

(1) The restraining order may be terminated by the court before the expiration date listed on its face.

(2) The restraining order may be extended beyond the expiration date listed on its face by mutual consent of all parties to the order, or by further order of the court on motion of any party to the order.

(Subd (j) adopted effective January 1, 2003.)

(k) Violation (§ 213.5(h))

Any willful and knowing violation of any order, temporary order, or order after hearing granted under section 213.5 is a misdemeanor, punishable under Penal Code section 273.65.

(Subd (k) amended effective January 1, 2007; adopted effective January 1, 2003.)

(l) Restraining orders issued by other courts (§ 304)

If a restraining order has been issued by the juvenile court under section 213.5, no court other than a criminal court may issue any order contrary to the juvenile court's restraining order.

(Subd (l) amended effective January 1, 2007; adopted effective January 1, 2003.)

Rule 5.630 amended and renumbered effective January 1, 2007; adopted as rule 1429.5 effective January 1, 2000; previously amended effective January 1, 2003, and January 1, 2004.

Ref.: Cal. Fms Pl. & Pr., Ch. 328, "Juvenile Courts: Dependency Proceedings"; W. Cal. Sum., 10 "Parent and Child" §§444, 453, 834.

Chapter 9
Parentage

Rule 5.635. Parentage

(a) Authority to declare; duty to inquire (§§ 316.2, 726.4)

The juvenile court has a duty to inquire about and, if not otherwise determined, to attempt to determine the parentage of each child who is the subject of a petition filed under section 300, 601, or 602. The court may establish and enter a judgment of parentage. Once a petition has been filed to declare a child a dependent or ward, and until the petition is dismissed or dependency or wardship is terminated, the juvenile court with jurisdiction of the action has exclusive jurisdiction to hear an action filed under Family Code section 7630 or 7631.

(Subd (a) amended effective January 1, 2007; previously amended effective January 1, 2001, and January 1, 2006.)

(b) Parentage inquiry (§§ 316.2, 726.4)

At the initial hearing on a petition filed under section 300, 601, or 602, and at hearings thereafter until or unless parentage has been established, the court must inquire of the child's parents present at the hearing and of any other appropriate person present as to the identity and address of any and all presumed or alleged parents of the child. Questions, at the discretion of the court, may include the following and others that may provide information regarding parentage:

(1) Has there been a judgment of parentage?

(2) Was the mother married or did she have a registered domestic partner at or after the time of conception?

(3) Did the mother believe she was married or believe she had a registered domestic partner at or after the time of conception?

(4) Was the mother cohabiting with another adult at the time of conception?

(5) Has the mother received support payments or promises of support for the child or for herself during her pregnancy or after the birth of the child?

(6) Has a man formally or informally acknowledged paternity, including the execution and filing of a voluntary declaration of paternity under Family Code section 7570 et seq., and agreed to have his name placed on the child's birth certificate?

(7) Have genetic tests been administered, and, if so, what were the results?

(8) Has the child been raised jointly with another adult or in any other co-parenting arrangement?

(Subd (b) amended effective January 1, 2007; adopted effective January 1, 2001; previously amended effective January 1, 2006.)

(c) Voluntary declaration

If a voluntary declaration as described in Family Code section 7570 et seq. has been executed and filed with the California Department of Social Services, the declaration establishes the paternity of a child and has the same force and effect as a judgment of paternity by a court. A man is presumed to be the father of the child under Family Code section 7611 if the voluntary declaration has been properly executed and filed.

(Subd (c) amended effective January 1, 2007; adopted effective January 1, 2001; previously amended effective January 1, 2006, and July 1, 2006.)

(d) Issue raised; inquiry

If, at any proceeding regarding the child, the issue of parentage is addressed by the court:

(1) The court must ask the parent or the person alleging parentage, and others present, whether any parentage finding has been made, and, if so, what court made it, or whether a voluntary declaration has been executed and filed under the Family Code;

(2) The court must direct the court clerk to prepare and transmit *Parentage Inquiry—Juvenile* (form JV-500) to the local child support agency requesting an inquiry regarding whether or not parentage has been established through any superior court order or judgment or through the execution and filing of a voluntary declaration under the Family Code;

(3) The office of child support enforcement must prepare and return the completed *Parentage Inquiry—Juvenile* (form JV-500) within 25 judicial days, with certified copies of such order or judgment or proof of the filing of a voluntary declaration attached; and

(4) The juvenile court must take judicial notice of the prior determination of parentage.

(Subd (d) amended effective January 1, 2007; adopted as subd (b) effective July 1, 1995; previously amended and relettered effective January 1, 2001; previously amended effective January 1, 2006.)

(e) No prior determination

If the local child support agency states, or if the court determines through statements of the parties or other evidence, that there has been no prior determination of parentage of the child, the juvenile court must take appropriate steps to make such a determination.

(1) The alleged father and his counsel must complete and submit *Statement Regarding Paternity (Juvenile Dependency)* (form JV-505). Form JV-505 must be made available in the courtroom.

(2) To determine parentage, the juvenile court may order the child and any alleged parents to submit to genetic tests and proceed under Family Code section 7550 et seq.

(3) The court may make its determination of parentage or nonparentage based on the testimony, declarations, or statements of the alleged parents. The court must advise any alleged parent indicating a wish to be declared the parent of the child that if parentage is declared, the declared parent will have responsibility for the financial support of the child, and, if the child receives welfare benefits, the declared parent may be subject to an action to obtain support payments.

(Subd (e) amended effective January 1, 2007; adopted as subd (c) effective July 1, 1995; previously amended and relettered effective January 1, 2001; previously amended effective January 1, 2006.)

(f) Notice to office of child support enforcement

If the court establishes parentage of the child, the court must sign and then direct the clerk to transmit *Parentage–Finding and Judgment* (form JV-501) to the local child support agency.

(Subd (f) amended effective January 1, 2007; adopted as subd (d) effective July 1, 1995; previously amended and relettered effective January 1, 2001; previously amended effective January 1, 2006.)

(g) Dependency and delinquency; notice to alleged parents

If, after inquiry by the court or through other information obtained by the county welfare department or probation department, one or more persons are identified as alleged parents of a child for whom a petition under section 300, 601, or 602 has been filed, the clerk must provide to each named alleged parent, at the last known address, by certified mail, return receipt requested, a copy of the petition, notice of the next scheduled hearing, and *Statement Regarding Parentage (Juvenile)* (form JV-505) unless:

(1) The petition has been dismissed;

(2) Dependency or wardship has been terminated;

(3) The parent has previously filed a form JV-505 denying parentage and waiving further notice; or

(4) The parent has relinquished custody of the child to the county welfare department.

(Subd (g) amended effective January 1, 2007; adopted as subd (e) effective July 1, 1995; previously amended and relettered effective January 1, 2001; previously amended effective January 1, 2006.)

(h) Dependency and delinquency; alleged parents (§§ 316.2, 726.4)

If a person appears at a hearing in dependency matter or at a hearing under section 601 or 602 and requests a judgment of parentage on form JV-505, the court must determine:

(1) Whether that person is the biological parent of the child; and

(2) Whether that person is the presumed parent of the child, if that finding is requested.

(Subd (h) amended effective January 1, 2007; adopted as subd (f) effective January 1, 1999; previously amended and relettered effective January 1, 2001; previously amended effective January 1, 2006.)

Rule 5.635 amended effective January 1, 2007; adopted as rule 1413 effective July 1, 1995; previously amended effective January 1, 1999, January 1, 2001, January 1, 2006, and July 1, 2006.

Ref.: Cal. Fms Pl. & Pr., Ch. 327, "Juvenile Courts: Jurisdiction and General Procedures," Ch. 328, "Juvenile Courts: Dependency Proceedings"; W. Cal. Sum., 10 "Parent and Child" §§46, 444, 583, 603, 622, 882, 886.

Chapter 10
Medication, Mental Health, and Education

Rule 5.640. Psychotropic medications
Rule 5.645. Mental health or condition of child; court procedures
Rule 5.650. Appointment of educational representative
Rule 5.651. Educational rights of children before the juvenile court
Rule 5.652. Access to pupil records for truancy purposes

Rule 5.640.   Psychotropic medications

(a) Definition (§§ 369.5(d), 739.5(d))

For the purposes of this rule, "psychotropic medication" means those medications prescribed to affect the central nervous system to treat psychiatric disorders or illnesses. They may include, but are not limited to, anxiolytic agents, antidepressants, mood stabilizers, antipsychotic medications, anti-Parkinson agents, hypnotics, medications for dementia, and psychostimulants.

(Subd (a) amended effective January 1, 2009; previously amended effective January 1, 2007.)

(b) Authorization to administer (§§ 369.5, 739.5)

(1) Once a child is declared a dependent child of the court and is removed from the custody of the parents or guardian, only a juvenile court judicial officer is authorized to make orders regarding the administration of psychotropic medication to the child.

(2) Once a child is declared a ward of the court, removed from the custody of the parents or guardian, and placed into foster care, as defined in Welfare and Institutions Code section 727.4, only a juvenile court judicial officer is authorized to make orders regarding the administration of psychotropic medication to the child.

(Subd (b) amended effective January 1, 2009.)

(c) Procedure to obtain authorization

(1) *Application Regarding Psychotropic Medication* (form JV-220), *Prescribing Physician's Statement—Attachment* (form JV-220(A)), *Proof of Notice: Application Regarding Psychotropic Medication* (form JV-221), *Opposition to Application Regarding Psychotropic Medication* (form JV-222), and *Order Regarding Application*

for Psychotropic Medication (form JV-223) must be used to obtain authorization to administer psychotropic medication to a dependent **child** of the court **who is removed from the custody of the parents or guardian, or to a ward of the court who is removed from the custody of the parents or guardian and placed into foster care**.

(2) Additional information may be provided to the court through the use of local forms that are consistent with this rule.

(3) Local county practice and local rules of court determine the procedures for completing and filing the forms and for the provision of notice, except as otherwise provided in this rule.

(4) An application must be completed and presented to the court, using *Application Regarding Psychotropic Medication* (form JV-220) and *Prescribing Physician's Statement—Attachment* (form JV-220(A)). The court must approve, deny, or set the matter for a hearing within seven court days of the receipt of the completed application.

(5) *Application Regarding Psychotropic Medication* (form JV-220) may be completed by the prescribing physician, medical office staff, child welfare services staff, probation officer, or the child's caregiver. The physician prescribing the administration of psychotropic medication for the [1] child must complete and sign *Prescribing Physician's Statement—Attachment* (form JV-220(A)).

(6) *Prescribing Physician's Statement—Attachment* (form JV-220(A)) must include all of the following:

(A) The diagnosis of the child's condition that the physician asserts can be treated through the administration of the medication;

(B) The specific medication recommended, with the recommended maximum daily dosage and length of time this course of treatment will continue;

(C) The anticipated benefits to the child of the use of the medication;

(D) A description of possible side effects of the medication;

(E) A list of any other medications, prescription or otherwise, that the child is currently taking, and a description of any effect these medications may produce in combination with the psychotropic medication;

(F) A description of any other therapeutic services related to the child's mental health status; and

(G) A statement that the child has been informed in an age-appropriate manner of the recommended course of treatment, the basis for it, and its possible results. The child's response must be included.

(7) Notice must be provided as follows:

(A) Notice to the parents or legal guardians and their attorneys of record must include:

(i) A statement that a physician is asking to treat the child's emotional or behavioral problems by beginning or continuing the administration of psychotropic medication to the child and the name of the psychotropic medication;

(ii) A statement that an *Application Regarding Psychotropic Medication* (form JV-220) and a *Prescribing Physician's Statement—Attachment* (form JV-220(A)) are pending before the court;

(iii) A copy of *Information About Psychotropic Medication Forms* (form JV-219-INFO) or information on how to obtain a copy of the form; and

(iv) A blank copy of *Opposition to Application Regarding Psychotropic Medication* (form JV-222) or information on how to obtain a copy of the form.

(B) Notice to the child's current caregiver and Court Appointed Special Advocate, if one has been appointed, must include only:

(i) A statement that a physician is asking to treat the child's emotional or behavioral problems by beginning or continuing the administration of psychotropic medication to the child and the name of the psychotropic medication; and

(ii) A statement that an *Application Regarding Psychotropic Medication* (form JV-220) and a *Prescribing Physician's Statement—Attachment* (form JV-220(A)) are pending before the court;

(C) Notice to the child's attorney of record and any Child Abuse Prevention and Treatment Act guardian ad litem for the child must include:

(i) A completed copy of the *Application Regarding Psychotropic Medication* (form JV-220);

(ii) A completed copy of the *Prescribing Physician's Statement—Attachment* (form JV-220(A));

(iii) A copy of *Information About Psychotropic Medication Forms* (form JV-219-INFO) or information on how to obtain a copy of the form; and

(iv) A blank copy of *Opposition to Application Regarding Psychiatric Medication* (form JV-222) or information on how to obtain a copy of the form.

(D) Proof of notice of the application regarding psychotropic medication must be filed with the court using *Proof of Notice: Application Regarding Psychotropic Medication* (form JV-221).

(8) A parent or guardian, his or her attorney of record, a child's attorney of record, or a child's Child Abuse Prevention and Treatment Act guardian ad litem appointed under rule 5.662 of the California Rules of Court who is opposed to the administration of the proposed psychotropic medication must file a completed *Opposition to Application Regarding Psychotropic Medication* (form JV-222) within two court days of receiving notice of the pending application for psychotropic medication.

(9) The court may grant the application without a hearing or may set the matter for hearing at the court's discretion. If the court sets the matter for a hearing, the clerk of the court must provide notice of the date, time, and location of the hearing to the parents or legal guardians, their attorneys of record, the **dependent** child if 12 years of age or older, **a ward of the juvenile court of any age,** the child's attorney of record, the child's current caregiver, the child's social worker, the social worker's attorney of record, the child's Child Abuse Prevention and Treatment Act guardian ad litem, and the child's Court Appointed Special Advocate, if any, at least two court days before the hearing. Notice must be provided to the child's probation officer and the district attorney, if the child is a [2] **ward of the juvenile court**.

(Subd (c) amended effective January 1, 2009; previously amended effective January 1, 2007, and January 1, 2008.)

Rule 5.640(c). 2008 Deletes. [1] dependent [2] delinquent child

(d) Conduct of hearing

At the hearing on the application, the procedures described in rule 5.570 must be followed. The court may deny, grant, or modify the application for authorization and may set a date for review of the child's progress and condition.

(Subd (d) amended effective January 1, 2007.)

(e) Delegation of authority (§ 369.5)

After consideration of an application and attachments and a review of the case file, the court may order that the parent be authorized to approve or deny the administration of psychotropic medication. The order must be based on the following findings, which must be included in the order: (1) the parent poses no danger to the child, and (2) the parent has the capacity to understand the request and the information provided and to authorize the administration of psychotropic medication to the child, consistent with the best interest of the child.

(Subd (e) amended effective January 1, 2008.)

(f) Continued treatment

If the court grants the request or modifies and then grants the request, the order for authorization is effective until terminated or modified by court order or until 180 days from the order, whichever is earlier. If a progress review is set, it may be by an appearance hearing or a report to the court and parties and attorneys, at the discretion of the court.

(g) Emergency treatment

(1) Psychotropic medications may be administered without court authorization in an emergency situation. An emergency situation occurs when:

(A) A physician finds that the child requires psychotropic medication to treat a psychiatric disorder or illness; and

(B) The purpose of the medication is:

(i) To protect the life of the child or others, or

(ii) To prevent serious harm to the child or others, or

(iii) To treat current or imminent substantial suffering; and

(C) It is impractical to obtain authorization from the court before administering the psychotropic medication to the child.

(2) Court authorization must be sought as soon as practical but in no case more than two court days after the emergency administration of the psychotropic medication.

(Subd (g) amended effective January 1, 2008; previously amended effective January 1, 2007.)

(h) Section 601–602 wardships; local rules

A local rule of court may be adopted providing that authorization for the administration of such medication to a child declared a ward of the court under sections 601 and 602 and removed from the custody of the parent or guardian **for placement in a facility that is not considered a foster-care placement** may be similarly restricted to the juvenile court. If the local court adopts such a local rule, then the procedures under this rule apply; any reference to social worker also applies to probation officer.

(Subd (h) amended effective January 1, 2009; adopted as subd (i) effective January 1, 2001; previously amended effective January 1, 2007; previously relettered effective January 1, 2008.)
Rule 5.640 amended effective January 1, 2009; adopted as rule 1432.5 effective January 1, 2001; previously amended effective January 1, 2003, and January 1, 2008; previously amended and renumbered effective January 1, 2007.

Ref.: Cal. Fms Pl. & Pr., Ch. 328, "Juvenile Courts: Dependency Proceedings"; W. Cal. Sum., 10 "Parent and Child" §§444, 629.

Rule 5.645.   Mental health or condition of child; court procedures

(a) Doubt concerning the mental health of a child (§§ 357, 705, 6550, 6551)

Whenever the court believes that the child who is the subject of a petition filed under section 300, 601, or 602 is mentally disabled or may be mentally ill, the court may stay the proceedings and order the child taken to a facility designated by the court and approved by the State Department of Mental Health as a facility for 72-hour treatment and evaluation. The professional in charge of the facility must submit a written evaluation of the child to the court.

(Subd (a) amended effective January 1, 2007.)

(b) Findings regarding a mental disorder (§ 6551)

Article 1 of chapter 2 of part 1 of division 5 (commencing with section 5150) applies.

(1) If the professional reports that the child is not in need of intensive treatment, the child must be returned to the juvenile court on or before the expiration of the 72-hour period, and the court must proceed with the case under section 300, 601, or 602.

(2) If the professional in charge of the facility finds that the child is in need of intensive treatment for a mental disorder, the child may be certified for not more than 14 days of involuntary intensive treatment according to the conditions of sections 5250(c) and 5260(b). The stay of the juvenile court proceedings must remain in effect during this time.

(A) During or at the end of the 14 days of involuntary intensive treatment, a certification may be sought for additional treatment under sections commencing with 5270.10 or for the initiation of proceedings to have a conservator appointed for the child under sections commencing with 5350. The juvenile court may retain jurisdiction over the child during proceedings under sections 5270.10 et seq. and 5350 et seq.

(B) For a child subject to a petition under section 602, if the child is found to be gravely disabled under sections 5300 et seq., a conservator is appointed under those sections, and the professional in charge of the child's treatment or of the treatment facility determines that proceedings under section 602 would be detrimental to the child, the juvenile court must suspend jurisdiction while the conservatorship remains in effect. The suspension of jurisdiction may end when the conservatorship is terminated, and the original 602 matter may be calendared for further proceedings.

(Subd (b) amended effective January 1, 2007.)

(c) Findings regarding mental retardation (§ 6551)

Article [1] 1 of chapter 2 of part 1 of division 5 (commencing with section 5150) applies.

(1) If the professional finds that the child is mentally retarded and recommends commitment to a state hospital, the court may direct the filing in the appropriate court of a petition for commitment of a child as a mentally retarded person to the State Department of Developmental Services for placement in a state hospital.

(2) If the professional finds that the child is not mentally retarded, the child must be returned to the juvenile court on or before the expiration of the 72-hour period, and the court must proceed with the case under section 300, 601, or 602.

(3) The jurisdiction of the juvenile court must be suspended while the child is subject to the jurisdiction of the appropriate court under a petition for commitment of a mentally retarded person, or under remand for 90 days for intensive treatment or commitment ordered by that court.

(Subd (c) amended effective January 1, 2009; previously amended effective January 1, 2007.)

Rule 5.645(c).   2008 Deletes. [1] I

(d) Doubt as to capacity to cooperate with counsel (§§ 601, 602; Pen. Code, § 1367)

If the court finds that there is reason to doubt that a child who is the subject of a petition filed under section 601 or 602 is capable of understanding the proceedings or of cooperating with the child's attorney, the court must stay the proceedings and conduct a hearing regarding the child's competence.

(1) The court may appoint an expert to examine the child to evaluate the child's capacity to understand the proceedings and to cooperate with the attorney.

(2) If the court finds that the child is not capable of understanding the proceedings or of cooperating with the attorney, the court must proceed under section 6550 and (a)–(c) of this rule.

(3) If the court finds that the child is capable of understanding the proceedings and of cooperating with the attorney, the court must proceed with the case.

(Subd (d) amended effective January 1, 2007.)

Rule 5.645 amended effective January 1, 2009; adopted as rule 1498 effective January 1, 1999; previously amended and renumbered effective January 1, 2007.

Ref.: Cal. Fms Pl. & Pr., Ch. 329, "Juvenile Courts: Delinquency Proceedings"; W. Cal. Sum., 10 "Parent and Child" §§444, 567.

Rule 5.650.   Appointment of educational representative

(a) Parent's or guardian's educational rights limited (§§ 319, 361, 366, 366.27, 726; 20 U.S.C. § 1415; 34 C.F.R. §§ 300.519, 300.300)

The court may limit a parent's or guardian's right to make educational decisions for a child who is declared a dependent or ward of the court under section 300, 601, or 602, but the limitations may not exceed those necessary to protect the child. Before disposition, the court may temporarily limit a parent's or guardian's right to make educational decisions under section 319(g). The court may limit a parent's or guardian's educational rights regardless of whether the child is, or may be eligible for, special education and related services.

(1) If the court temporarily limits the parent's or guardian's right to make educational decisions under section 319(g), the court must reconsider the need, if any, to limit educational rights at the disposition hearing.

(2) The child's initial evaluation for special education services need not be postponed to await parental or guardian consent or appointment of an educational representative if one or more of the following circumstances are met:

(A) The court has limited or temporarily limited the educational rights of the parent or guardian, and consent for an initial assessment has been given by an individual appointed by the court to represent the child;

(B) The local education agency cannot discover the whereabouts of the parent or guardian; or

(C) The parent's rights have been terminated or the guardianship has been set aside.

(3) If the court determines that the child is in need of any assessments, evaluations, or services, including special education, mental health, and other related services, the court must direct an appropriate person to take the necessary steps to request those assessments, evaluations, or services.

(Subd (a) amended effective January 1, 2008; previously amended effective January 1, 2004, and January 1, 2007.)

(b) Appointment of educational representative (§§ 319, 361, 366, 366.27, 726; 20 U.S.C. § 1415; 34 C.F.R. § 300.519)

The court must use *Findings and Orders Limiting Right to Make Educational Decisions for the Child, Appointing Educational Representative, and Determining Child's Educational Needs* (form JV-535) when it limits the rights of a parent or guardian to make educational decisions for the child. In its order, the court must document that one of the following actions in (1) or (2) has been taken, or, in the alternative, that a finding under (3) has been made:

(1) The court has appointed an educational representative for the child;

(2) The court has ordered a permanent plan for the child, and the court finds that the foster parent, relative caregiver, or nonrelative extended family member may exercise educational rights as provided in Education Code section 56055 and rule 5.502(13) and is not prohibited from exercising educational rights by section 361 or 726 or by 34 Code of Federal Regulations section 300.519 or 303.19; or

(3) The court cannot identify a responsible adult to serve as the child's educational representative; and

(A) The child is or may be eligible for special education and related services, and the court is referring the child to the responsible local educational agency for appointment of a surrogate parent under section 361 or 726, title 20 United States Code section 1415, and rules 5.502 and 5.650; or

(B) The child is not eligible for special education and related services, there is no foster parent to exercise the authority granted by section 56055 of the Education Code, and the court will, with the input of any interested person, make educational decisions for the child.

(Subd (b) amended effective January 1, 2008; adopted effective January 1, 2004; previously amended effective January 1, 2007.)

(c) Limits on appointment (§§ 361, 726; Ed. Code, § 56055; Gov. Code, § 7579.5(i)–(j); 34 C.F.R. §§ 300.519, 303.19)

(1) The court should consider appointing a responsible adult relative, nonrelative extended family member, foster parent, family friend, mentor, or CASA volunteer as the educational representative if one is available and willing to serve.

(2) The court may not appoint any individual as the educational representative if that person is excluded under, or would have a conflict of interest as defined by section 361(a) or 726(b); Education Code section 56055; Govern-ment Code section 7579.5(i)–(j); title 20 United States Code section 1415(b)(2); or 34 Code of Federal Regulations section 300.519 or 303.19.

(Subd (c) amended effective January 1, 2008; adopted effective January 1, 2004; previously amended effective January 1, 2007.)

(d) Referral to local educational agency to appoint a surrogate parent for a child who is or may be eligible for special education and related services (§§ 361, 726; Gov. Code, § 7579.5; 20 U.S.C. § 1415)

(1) If the court has limited a parent's or guardian's right to make educational decisions for a child but cannot identify an educational representative for the child and the child is or may be eligible for special education and related services or already has an individualized education program, the court must use form JV-535 to refer the child to the responsible local educational agency for prompt appointment of a surrogate parent under Government Code section 7579.5.

(2) If the court refers a child to the local educational agency for appointment of a surrogate parent, the court must order that *Local Educational Agency Response to JV-535—Appointment of Surrogate Parent* (form JV-536) be served by first-class mail on the local educational agency along with form JV-535, no later than seven calendar days after the date of the order.

(3) The court must direct the local education agency that when the local education agency receives form JV-535, requesting prompt appointment of a surrogate parent, the local education agency must make reasonable efforts to assign a surrogate parent within 30 calendar days after the court's referral.

(A) Whenever the local educational agency appoints a surrogate parent for a dependent or ward under Government Code section 7579.5(a)(1), it must notify the court on form JV-536 within seven calendar days of the appointment and must send copies of the notice to the social worker or probation officer identified on the form.

(B) If the local education agency does not appoint a surrogate parent within 30 days of receipt of the form, within the next seven calendar days it must notify the court on form JV-536 of the following:

(i) Its inability to appoint a surrogate parent; and

(ii) Its continuing reasonable efforts to assign a surrogate parent.

(4) Whenever the surrogate parent resigns or the local educational agency terminates the appointment of a surrogate parent for a dependent or ward under Government Code section 7579.5(h) or replaces the surrogate parent for any other reason, it must notify the court and the child's attorney on form JV-536 within seven calendar days of the resignation, termination, or replacement. The child's attorney may request a hearing for appointment of a new educational representative by filing *Request for Hearing Regarding Child's Education* (form JV-539) and must provide notice of the hearing as provided in (g)(2). The court on its own motion may direct the clerk to set a hearing.

(Subd (d) amended effective January 1, 2008; adopted as subd (b) effective July 1, 2002; previously amended and relettered effective January 1, 2004; previously amended effective January 1, 2007.)

(e) Transfer of parent's or guardian's educational rights to educational representative

When an educational representative is appointed, the educational rights of the parent or guardian—including the right to notice of educational meetings and activities, participation in educational meetings and activities, and decisionmaking authority regarding the child's education, including the authority under title 20 United States Code sections 1232g and 1401(23), 34 Code of Federal Regulations section 300.30, and Education Code section 56028—are transferred to the educational representative.

(1) When returning a child to a parent or guardian, the court must consider the child's educational needs. The parent's or guardian's educational rights are reinstated when the court returns custody to the parent or guardian unless the court finds that the parent is not able to act in the child's best interest regarding education.

(2) If the court appoints a guardian for the child under rule 5.735 or 5.815, all of the parent's or guardian's educational rights transfer to the newly appointed guardian unless the court determines that the guardian is not able to act in the child's best interest regarding education.

(Subd (e) amended effective January 1, 2008; adopted effective January 1, 2004; previously amended effective January 1, 2007.)

(f) Authority and responsibilities of educational representative (§§ 319, 360, 361, 635, 706.5, 726; Ed. Code, § 56055; Gov. Code, 7579.5; 34 C.F.R. § 300.519)

(1) The educational representative is responsible for representing the child in the identification, evaluation, and educational placement of the child and with the provision of the child's free, appropriate public education. This includes representing the child in all matters relating to the child's education including:

(A) The stability of the child's school placement;

(B) Placement in the least restrictive educational program appropriate to the child's individual needs;

(C) The child's access to academic resources, services, and extracurricular and enrichment activities;

(D) The child's access to educational supports necessary to meet state academic achievement standards;

(E) School disciplinary matters; and

(F) Other aspects of the provision of a free, appropriate public education.

(2) The educational representative has the following additional responsibilities:

(A) Meeting with the child at least once and as often as necessary to make educational decisions that are in the best interest of the child;

(B) Being culturally sensitive to the child;

(C) Complying with federal and state confidentiality laws including section 827 and Government Code section 7579.1(f);

(D) Participating in, and making decisions regarding, all matters affecting the child's educational needs in a manner consistent with the child's best interest; and

(E) Having knowledge and skills that ensure adequate representation of the child.

(3) The educational representative acts as the parent or guardian in all educational matters regarding the child and has a right to the following:

(A) To the rights afforded the parent or guardian under the Family Education Rights and Privacy Act, title 20 United States Code section 1232g;

(B) To the rights of a parent relating to school discipline issues, meetings, and proceedings;

(C) To represent a child with exceptional needs in matters relating to identification and assessment of those needs, instructional planning and development, educational placement, reviewing and revising the individualized education program, and other aspects of the provision of a free, appropriate public education;

(D) To attend the child's individualized education program and other educational meetings, to consult with persons involved in the child's education, and to sign any consents to education-related services and plans; and

(E) Notwithstanding any other provision of law, to consent to the child's individualized education program, nonemergency medical services, mental health treatment services, and occupational or physical therapy services provided under chapter 26.5 of title 1 of the Government Code.

(Subd (f) adopted effective January 1, 2008.)

(g) Educational representative's term of service (§§ 361, 726; Gov. Code § 7579.5)

(1) The educational representative must make educational decisions for the child until:

(A) The court restores the right of the parent or guardian to make educational decisions for the child;

(B) The child reaches 18 years of age, unless the child chooses not to make his or her own educational decisions or is deemed incompetent by the court;

(C) The court appoints another educational representative for the child under this rule;

(D) The court appoints a successor guardian or conservator; or

(E) The court finds that the foster parent, relative caregiver, or nonrelative extended family member may make educational decisions for the child under Education Code section 56055(a) because:

(i) The child is placed in a planned permanent living arrangement under section 366.21(g)(3), 366.22, 366.26, 727.3(b)(5), or 727.3(b)(6);

(ii) The court has limited the parent's or guardian's educational rights; and

(iii) The foster parent, relative caregiver, or nonrelative extended family member is not otherwise excluded from making education decisions by the court, by section 361 or 726, or by 34 Code of Federal Regulations section 300.519 or 303.19.

(2) If the educational representative resigns from the appointment, he or she must provide notice to the court and to the child's attorney and may use *Educational Representative or Surrogate Parent Information* (form JV-537) to provide this notice. Once notice is received, the child's attorney may request a hearing for appointment of a new educational representative by filing form JV-539 and must provide notice of the hearing to the following: the parents or guardians, unless otherwise indicated on the most recent form JV-535; the social worker; the probation officer; the Court Appointed Special Advocate (CASA) volunteer; and all other persons required to be given notice under section 293. The hearing must be set within 14 days of receipt of the request for hearing. The court on its own motion may direct the clerk to set a hearing.

(Subd (g) adopted effective January 1, 2008.)

(h) Service of order

The clerk will provide a copy of the completed form JV-535 and any received form JV-536 or JV-537 to the child if 10 years or older, the child's attorney, the social worker and the probation officer, the foster youth liaison, as defined in Education Code section 48853.5, and the educational representative at the end of the proceeding or no later than seven calendar days after the date of the order. The clerk will make the form available to the parents or guardians, unless otherwise indicated on the form; the CASA volunteer; and, if requested, all other persons provided notice under section 293. Whoever is directed by the court on form JV-535 must provide a copy of the form to the local education agency.

(Subd (h) adopted effective January 1, 2008.)

(i) Education and training of educational representative

If the educational representative asks for assistance in obtaining education and training in the laws incorporated in rule 5.651(a), the court must direct the clerk, social worker, or probation officer to inform the educational representative of all available resources, including resources available through the California Department of Education and the local education agency.

(Subd (i) adopted effective January 1, 2008.)

(j) Notice and participation in juvenile court hearings

(1) The educational representative must receive notice of all juvenile court hearings regarding or affecting the child's education. This includes the notice and participation provided in rule 5.530 for all regularly scheduled juvenile hearings, rule 5.512 for joint assessment hearings, and rule 5.575 for joinder proceedings.

(2) The educational representative may use form JV-537 to explain the child's educational needs. The court may allow the educational representative to be present for the purposes of participating in the portions of the juvenile court hearing that concern the child's education, including school placement, and of responding to questions or issues raised by the form. The court may allow the educational representative to participate in any mediation as provided in rule 5.518.

(Subd (j) adopted effective January 1, 2008.)

Rule 5.650 amended effective January 1, 2008; adopted as rule 1499 effective July 1, 2002; previously amended effective January 1, 2004; previously amended and renumbered effective January 1, 2007.

Advisory Committee Comment

Under the Individuals With Disabilities Education Act (IDEA), the court may appoint a surrogate parent for a child to represent the child in all matters relating to the identification, evaluation, and educational placement of the child and to the provision of the child's free, appropriate public education. (20 U.S.C. § 1415(b)(2); 34 C.F.R. § 300.519.) Under Welfare and Institutions Code sections 361 and 726, the court may appoint a responsible adult as an educational representative to represent the child's educational needs when the parent's educational rights have been limited. When the court appoints an educational representative, that person is responsible for representing all the child's educational needs, including any special education and related services needs. When making this appointment, the court and all court participants are encouraged to look to all persons in the child's life, including relatives, nonrelated extended family members, and

those persons with whom the child has an important relationship, to represent the child's educational needs.

If the court cannot find anyone to appoint as the child's educational representative and special education needs are not indicated, sections 361 and 726 state that the court can make education decisions for the child with the input of interested persons. However, if the court cannot find someone to appoint as educational representative and special education is indicated, the court must refer the matter to the local education agency (LEA) for appointment of a surrogate parent. Sections 361 and 726 do not permit the court to make educational decisions for a child in these cases. The surrogate parent assigned by the LEA acts as a parent for the purpose of making educational decisions on behalf of the child. (Gov. Code, § 7579.5(c); Ed. Code, § 56028; 34 C.F.R. § 300.30(b)(2); see 20 U.S.C. §§ 1401(9), 1414(d).)

Ref.: Cal. Fms Pl. & Pr., Ch. 328, "Juvenile Courts: Dependency Proceedings"; W. Cal. Sum., 10 "Parent and Child" §§444, 629, 676, 893.

Rule 5.651. Educational rights of children before the juvenile court

(a) Applicability (§§ 213.5, 319, 358, 358.1, 364, 366.21, 366.22, 366.23, 366.26, 366.28, 366.3, 727.2, 11404.1; Gov. Code, § 7579.1; 20 U.S.C. § 1400 et seq.; 29 U.S.C. § 794; 42 U.S.C. § 12101 et seq.)

This rule has the following applicability and incorporates the rights established by the following laws:

(1) The rule applies to all children for whom petitions have been filed under section 300, 601, or 602;

(2) The rule applies to every hearing before the court affecting or related to the child's education, including detention, jurisdiction, disposition, and all regularly scheduled review hearings; and

(3) The rule incorporates the rights established by the following laws: the Individuals With Disabilities Education Act (20 U.S.C. § 1400 et seq.), the Americans With Disabilities Act (42 U.S.C. § 12101 et seq.), section 504 of the Rehabilitation Act of 1973 (29 U.S.C. § 701 et seq.), and the education rights of foster children as provided in Assembly Bill 490 (Stats. 2003, ch. 862) and Assembly Bill 1858 (Stats. 2004, ch. 914).

(Subd (a) adopted effective January 1, 2008.)

(b) Conduct of hearings related to, or that may affect, a child's education

(1) To the extent the information is available, at the initial or detention hearing the court must consider:

(A) Who holds educational rights;

(B) If the child was enrolled in, and is attending, the child's school of origin as defined in Education code section 48853.5(e);

(C) If the child is no longer attending the school of origin, whether;

(i) In accordance with the child's best interest, the educational liaison, as defined in Education Code section 48853.5(b), in consultation with, and with the agreement of, the child and the parent or guardian or other educational representative, recommends that the child's right to attend the school of origin be waived;

(ii) Prior to making any recommendation to move a foster child from his or her school of origin, the educational liaison provided the child and the person holding the right to make educational decisions for the child with a written explanation stating the basis for the recommendation and how this recommendation serves the foster child's best interest as provided in Education Code section 48853.5(d)(3);

(iii) Without obtaining a waiver, the child was not afforded his or her right to attend his or her school of origin under Education Code section 48853.5(d)(1); and

(iv) The child was immediately enrolled in the new school as provided in Education Code section 48853.5(d)(4).

(D) Whether the parent's or guardian's educational rights should be temporarily limited; and

(E) Taking into account other statutory considerations regarding placement, whether the out-of-home placement:

(i) Is the environment best suited to meet the unique needs of children with disabilities and to serve the child's best interest if he or she has a disability; and

(ii) Promotes educational stability through proximity to the child's school.

(2) At the disposition hearing and at all subsequent hearings provided for in (a), the juvenile court must address and determine the child's general and special education needs, identify a plan for meeting those needs, and provide a clear, written statement using *Findings and Orders Limiting Right to Make Educational Decisions for the Child, Appointing Educational Representative, and Determining Child's Educational Needs* (form JV-535), specifying the person who holds the educational rights for the child. The court's findings and orders must address the following:

(A) Whether the child's educational, physical, mental health, and developmental needs are being met;

(B) Any services, assessments, or evaluations, including those for special education and related services, that the child may need;

(C) Who is directed to take the necessary steps for the child to begin receiving any necessary assessments, evaluations, or services;

(D) If the child's educational placement changed during the reporting period, whether

(i) The child's educational records, including any evaluations of a child with a disability, were transferred to the new educational placement within two business days of the request for the child's enrollment in the new educational placement; and

(ii) The child is enrolled in and attending school; and

(E) Whether the parent's or guardian's educational rights should be limited;

(i) If the court finds the parent's or guardian's educational rights should not be limited, the court must direct the parent to his or her rights and responsibilities in regard to the child's education as provided in rule 5.650(e) and (f); or

(ii) If the court finds the parent's or guardian's educational rights should be limited, the court must determine who will hold the child's educational rights. The court must explain to the parent or guardian why the court is limiting his or her educational rights and must direct the parent or guardian to the rights and responsibilities of the education representative as provided in rule 5.650(e) and (f).

(Subd (b) adopted effective January 1, 2008.)

(c) Reports for hearings related to, or that may affect, a child's education

This subdivision applies at all hearings, including disposition and joint assessment hearings. The court must ensure that, to the extent the information was available, the social worker and the probation officer provided the following information in the report for the hearing:

(1) The child's age, behavior, educational and developmental achievement, and any discrepancies in achievement in education and in cognitive, physical, and emotional development;

(2) Identification of the child's educational, physical, mental health, or developmental needs;

(3) Whether the child is participating in developmentally appropriate extracurricular and social activities;

(4) Whether the child is attending a comprehensive, regular, public or private school;

(5) Whether the child may have physical, mental, or learning-related disabilities or other special education needs and is in need of or is already receiving special education and related services as provided by the laws incorporated in rule 5.651(a)(3);

(6) If the child is 0 to 3 years old, whether the child may be eligible for or is already receiving services available under the California Early Intervention Services Act (Gov. Code, § 95000 et seq.), and whether those services are appropriate;

(7) If the child is between 3 and 5 years and is or may be eligible for special education services, whether the child is receiving the early educational opportunities provided by Education Code section 56001;

(8) Whether the child is receiving appropriate services through a current individualized education program;

(9) Whether the child is or may be eligible for regional center services or is already receiving regional center services. Copies of the current individual family plan as defined in section 1436 under title 20 of the United States Code and the current life quality assessments as defined in Welfare and Institutions Code section 4570 should be attached to the report;

(10) Whether the parent's or guardian's educational rights have been or should be limited;

(11) If the social worker or probation officer recommends limiting the parent's or guardian's right to make educational decisions, the reasons those rights should be limited and the actions that the parent or guardian may take to restore those rights if they are limited;

(12) If the parent's or guardian's educational rights have been limited, who holds the child's educational rights;

(13) Recommendations and case plan goals to meet the child's identified educational, physical, mental health, and developmental needs;

(14) Whether any orders to direct an appropriate person to take the necessary steps for the child to begin receiving assessments, evaluations, or services, including those for special education and related services, are requested; and

(15) In the case of joint assessments, a separate statement by each of the two departments regarding whether the respective social worker and probation officer believe that the child may have a disability and whether the child is in need of special education and related services or requires evaluation as required by title 20 United States

Code section 1412(a)(3), Education Code section 56425, or section 504 of the Rehabilitation Act of 1973.

(Subd (c) adopted effective January 1, 2008.)

(d) Continuances or stay of jurisdiction

If any continuance provided for in rules 5.686 and 5.782 or stay of jurisdiction provided for in rule 5.645 is granted, the child must continue to receive all services or accommodations required by the laws incorporated in rule 5.651(a)(3).

(Subd (d) adopted effective January 1, 2008.)

(e) Change of placement affecting the child's right to attend the school of origin

This subdivision applies to all changes of placement including the initial placement and all subsequent changes of placement.

(1) At any hearing that relates to or may affect the child's education and that follows a removal of the child from the school of origin the court must find that:

(A) The social worker or probation officer notified the court, the child's attorney, and the educational representative or surrogate parent that the proposed placement or change of placement would result in a removal of the child from the child's school of origin. The court must find that the notice was provided within 24 hours, excluding nonjudicial days, of the social worker's or probation officer's determination that the proposed change of placement would result in removal of the child from the school of origin.

(B) If the child had a disability and an active individualized education program prior to removal, the social worker or probation officer, at least 10 days before the change of placement, notified in writing the local educational agency that provided a special education program for the child prior to removal and the receiving special education local plan area, as defined in Government Code section 7579.1, of the impending change of placement.

(2) After receipt of the notice in (1):

(A) The child's attorney must, as appropriate, discuss the proposed move from the school of origin with the child and the person who holds educational rights. The child's attorney may request a hearing by filing *Request for Hearing Regarding Child's Education* (form JV-539). If requesting a hearing, the child's attorney must:

(i) File form JV-539 no later than two court days after receipt of the notice in (1); and

(ii) Provide notice of the court date, which will be no later than seven calendar days after the form was filed, to the parents or guardians, unless otherwise indicated on form JV-535; the social worker; the probation officer; the educational representative or surrogate parent; the foster youth liaison, as defined in Education Code section 48853.5; the Court Appointed Special Advocate (CASA) volunteer; and all other persons required by section 293.

(B) The person who holds educational rights may request a hearing by filing form JV-539 no later than two court days after receipt of the notice in (1). After receipt of the form, the clerk must notify the persons in (e)(2)(A)(ii) of the hearing date.

(C) The court on its own motion may direct the clerk to set a hearing.

(3) If removal from the school of origin is disputed, the child must be allowed to remain in the school of origin

pending this hearing and pending any disagreement between the child, parent, guardian, or educational representative and the school district.

(4) If the court, the child's attorney, or the person who holds educational rights requests a hearing, at the hearing the court must find that the social worker or probation officer provided a report no later than two court days after form JV-539 was filed and that the report included the information required by (b)(1)(C)(i) and (ii) and:

(A) Whether the foster child has been allowed to continue his or her education in the school of origin for the duration of the academic school year;

(B) Whether a dispute exists regarding the request of a foster child to remain in the school of origin and whether the foster child has been afforded the right to remain in the school of origin pending resolution of the dispute;

(C) Information addressing whether the information sharing and other requirements in section 16501.1(c)(2) and Education Code section 49069.5 have been followed;

(D) Information addressing how the proposed change serves the best interest of the child;

(E) The responses to the proposed change of placement from the child if over 10 years old, the child's attorney, the parent or guardian, the foster youth liaison, as defined in Education Code section 48853.5, and the child's CASA volunteer, specifying whether each person agrees or disagrees with the proposed change and, if any person disagrees, stating why;

(F) A statement from the person holding educational rights regarding whether the proposed change of placement is in the child's best interest and what efforts have been made to keep the child in the school of origin; and

(G) A statement from the social worker or probation officer confirming that the child has not been segregated in a separate school, or in a separate program within a school, based on the child's status as a child in foster care.

(Subd (e) adopted effective January 1, 2008.)

(f) Court review of proposed change of placement affecting the child's right to attend the school of origin

(1) At the hearing set under (e)(2), the court must:

(A) Determine whether the proposed placement meets the requirements of this rule and Education Code sections 48853.5 and 49069.5 and whether the proposed plan is based on the best interest of the child;

(B) Determine what actions are necessary to ensure the child's educational and disability rights; and

(C) Make the necessary findings and orders to enforce these rights, which may include an order to set a hearing under section 362 to join the necessary agencies regarding provision of services, including the provision of transportation services, so that the child may remain in his or her school of origin.

(2) When considering whether it is in the child's best interest to remain in the school of origin, the court must consider the following:

(A) Whether the parent, guardian, or other educational representative believes that remaining in the school of origin is in the child's best interest;

(B) How the proposed change of placement will affect the stability of the child's school placement and the child's access to academic resources, services, and extracurricular and enrichment activities;

(C) Whether the proposed school placement would allow the child to be placed in the least restrictive educational program; and

(D) Whether the child has the educational supports necessary, including those for special education and related services, to meet state academic achievement standards.

(3) The court may make its findings and orders on *Findings and Orders Regarding Transfer From School of Origin* (form JV-538).

(Subd (f) adopted effective January 1, 2008.)

Rule 5.651 adopted effective January 1, 2008.

Advisory Committee Comment

This rule incorporates the requirement of, and rights established by, Assembly Bill 490 (Steinberg; Stats. 2003, ch. 862), Assembly Bill 1858 (Steinberg; Stats. 2004, ch. 914), the Individuals With Disabilities Education Act (IDEA), the Americans With Disabilities Act (ADA), and section 504 of the Rehabilitation Act of 1973. This rule does not limit these requirements or rights. To the extent necessary, this rule establishes procedures to make these laws meaningful to children in foster care.

With the passage of Assembly Bill 490, a child in, or at risk of entering, foster care has a statutory right to a meaningful opportunity to meet the state's academic achievement standards to which all students are held. To afford the child this right, the juvenile court, advocates, placing agencies, care providers, and educators must work together to maintain stable school placements and ensure that the child is placed in the least restrictive educational programs and has access to the academic resources, services, and extracurricular and enrichment activities that are available to other students. This rule, sections 362 and 727, and rule 5.575 provide procedures for ensuring that the child's educational needs are met.

Congress has found that improving the educational performance of children with disabilities is an essential prerequisite to ensuring their equality of opportunity, full participation in education, and economic self-sufficiency. Children in foster care are disproportionately represented in the population of children with disabilities and inherently face systemic challenges to attaining self-sufficiency. Children in foster care have rights arising out of the IDEA, the ADA, and section 504 of the Rehabilitation Act of 1973. To comply with federal requirements regarding the identification of children with disabilities and the provision of services to those children who qualify, the court, parent or guardian, placing agency, attorneys, CASA volunteer, local education agencies, and educational representatives must affirmatively address the child's educational needs. The court must continually inquire about the education of the child and the progress being made to enforce any rights the child has under these laws.

Rule 5.652.　Access to pupil records for truancy purposes

(a) Conditions of access (Ed. Code, § 49076)

Education Code section 49076 authorizes a school district to permit access to pupil records, including accurate copies, to any judicial officer or probation officer without consent of the pupil's parent or guardian and without a court order for the purposes of:

(1) Conducting a truancy mediation program for the pupil; or

(2) Presenting evidence in a truancy proceeding under section 681(b).

(Subd (a) amended effective January 1, 2007.)

(b) Written certification

The judicial officer or probation officer may request pupil records but must certify in writing that the requested information will be used only for purposes of truancy mediation or a truancy petition. A judicial officer or probation officer must complete and file *Certified Request for Pupil Records—Truancy* (form JV-530) and serve it with *Local Educational Agency Response to JV-530* (form JV-531), by first-class mail to the local educational agency.

(Subd (b) amended effective January 1, 2007.)

(c) Local educational agency response

Form JV-531 must be completed by the local educational agency and returned to the requesting judicial officer or probation officer within 15 calendar days of receipt of the request with copies of any responsive pupil records attached. After receipt the judicial officer or probation officer must file form JV-531 and the attached pupil records in the truancy proceedings.

(1) The school district must inform by telephone or other means, or provide written notification to, the child's parent or guardian within 24 hours of the release of the information.

(2) If a parent's or guardian's educational rights have been terminated, the school must notify the child's surrogate parent, relative, or other individual responsible for the child's education.

(Subd (c) amended effective January 1, 2007.)

Rule 5.652 amended and renumbered effective January 1, 2007; adopted as rule 1499.5 effective July 1, 2002.

Ref.: W. Cal. Sum., 10 "Parent and Child" §§444, 730.

Chapter 11
Advocates for Parties

Rule 5.655.　Program requirements for Court Appointed Special Advocate programs

(a) General provisions

A Court Appointed Special Advocate (CASA) program must comply with this rule to be eligible to receive Judicial Council funding. The Judicial Council may consider compliance with the guidelines delineated in the *CASA Program Policies and Procedures Manual* when determining eligibility for and amount of program funding.

(Subd (a) adopted effective January 1, 2005.)

(b) Definitions

(1) A CASA program is the local child advocate program that adheres to this rule; has been designated by the local presiding juvenile court judge to recruit, screen, select, train, supervise, and support lay volunteers for appointment by the court to help define the best interest of children in juvenile court dependency and wardship pro-

ceedings; and has completed one development grant year and one "start-up" year.

(2) The Judicial Council's Administrative Office of the Courts (AOC) may create a *CASA Program Policies and Procedures Manual* containing recommended program policies and procedures. If the AOC creates a manual, it will be developed in collaboration with the California CASA Association and California CASA program directors. The protocols will address program and fiscal management, and the recruitment, screening, selection, training, and supervision of lay volunteers.

(3) A CASA volunteer is a person who has been recruited, screened, selected, and trained, who is being supervised and supported by a local CASA program, and who has been appointed by the juvenile court as a sworn officer of the court to help define the best interest of a child or children in juvenile court dependency and wardship proceedings.

(4) A "dependency proceeding" is a legal action brought on behalf of an allegedly abused, neglected, or abandoned child under section 300 et seq. The action is designed to protect children, preserve and reunify families, and find permanent homes for children who cannot be returned to their parents. Dependency proceedings include actions to appoint a legal guardian, terminate parental rights, and facilitate adoptions for dependent children of the juvenile court.

(5) A "wardship proceeding" is a legal action involving a child under the age of 18 years who is alleged to be:

(A) A person described under section 601 (who is beyond parental control or habitually disobedient or truant); or

(B) A person described under section 602 (who has violated any state or federal law or any city or county ordinance).

(Subd (b) amended effective January 1, 2007; adopted as subd (a) effective July 1, 1994; previously amended and relettered effective January 1, 2005.)

(c) Recruiting, screening, and selecting CASA volunteers

(1) A CASA program must adopt and adhere to a written plan for the recruitment of potential CASA volunteers. The program staff, in its recruitment effort, must address the demographics of the jurisdiction by making all reasonable efforts to ensure that individuals representing all racial, ethnic, linguistic, and economic sectors of the community are recruited and made available for appointment as CASA volunteers.

(2) A CASA program must adopt and adhere to the following minimum written procedures for screening potential CASA volunteers under section 102(e):

(A) A written application that generates minimum identifying data; information regarding the applicant's education, training, and experience; minimum age requirements; and current and past employment.

(B) Notice to the applicant that a formal security check will be made, including inquiries through appropriate law enforcement agencies, regarding any criminal record, driving record, or other record of conduct that would disqualify the applicant from service as a CASA volunteer. The security check must include fingerprinting. Refusal to consent to a formal security check is grounds for rejecting an applicant.

(C) A minimum of three completed references regarding the character, competence, and reliability of the applicant and his or her suitability for assuming the role of a CASA volunteer.

(D) A personal interview or interviews by a person or persons approved by the presiding juvenile court judge or designee, to probe the essential areas of concern with respect to the qualities of an effective CASA volunteer. A written, confidential record of the interview and the interviewer's assessments and observations must be made and retained in the advocate's file.

(3) If a CASA program allows its volunteers to transport children, the program must ensure that each volunteer transporting children:

(A) Possesses a valid and current driver's license;

(B) Possesses personal automobile insurance that meets the minimum state personal automobile insurance requirements;

(C) Obtains permission from the child's guardian or custodial agency; and

(D) Provides the CASA program with a Department of Motor Vehicles driving record report annually.

(4) A CASA program must adopt a written preliminary procedure for selecting CASA candidates to enter the CASA training program. The selection procedure must state that any applicant found to have been convicted of or to have current charges pending for a felony or misdemeanor involving a sex offense, child abuse, or child neglect must not be accepted as a CASA volunteer. This policy must be stated on the volunteer application form.

(Subd (c) amended effective January 1, 2007; adopted as subd (b) effective July 1, 1994; previously amended effective January 1, 1995; previously amended and relettered effective January 1, 2005.)

(d) Initial training of CASA volunteers (§ 102(d))

A CASA program must adopt and adhere to a written plan for the initial training of CASA volunteers.

(1) The initial training curriculum must include at least 30 hours of formal instruction. This curriculum must include mandatory training topics as listed in section 102(d). The curriculum may also include additional appropriate topics.

(2) The final selection process is contingent on the successful completion of the initial training program, as determined by the presiding judge of the juvenile court or designee.

(Subd (d) amended effective January 1, 2007; adopted as subd (c) effective July 1, 1994; previously amended effective January 1, 1995; previously amended and relettered effective January 1, 2005.)

(e) Oath

At the completion of training, and before assignment to any child's case, the CASA volunteer must take a court-administered oath describing the duties and responsibilities of the advocate under section 103(f). The CASA volunteer must also sign a written affirmation of that oath. The signed affirmation must be retained in the volunteer's file.

(Subd (e) amended effective January 1, 2007; adopted as subd (d) effective July 1, 1994; previously amended and relettered effective January 1, 2005.)

(f) Duties and responsibilities

CASA volunteers serve at the discretion of the court having jurisdiction over the proceeding in which the volunteer has been appointed. A CASA volunteer is an officer of the court and is bound by all court rules under section 103(e). A CASA program must develop and adopt a written description of duties and responsibilities, consistent with local court rules.

(Subd (f) amended effective January 1, 2007; adopted as subd (e) effective July 1, 1994; previously amended effective January 1, 1995; previously amended and relettered effective January 1, 2005.)

(g) Prohibited activities

A CASA program must develop and adopt a written description of activities that are prohibited for CASA volunteers. The specified prohibited activities must include:

(1) Taking a child to the CASA volunteer's home;

(2) Giving legal advice or therapeutic counseling;

(3) Giving money or expensive gifts to the child or family;

(4) Being related to any parties involved in a case or being employed in a position and/or agency that might result in a conflict of interest; and

(5) Any other activities prohibited by the local juvenile court.

(Subd (g) adopted effective January 1, 2005.)

(h) The appointment of CASA volunteers

The CASA program director must develop, with the approval of the presiding juvenile court judge, a written procedure for the selection of cases and the appointment of CASA volunteers for children in juvenile court proceedings.

(Subd (h) amended and relettered effective January 1, 2005; adopted as subd (f) effective July 1, 1994; previously amended effective January 1, 1995.)

(i) Oversight, support, and supervision of CASA volunteers

A CASA program must adopt and adhere to a written plan, approved by the presiding juvenile court judge, for the oversight, support, and supervision of CASA volunteers in the performance of their duties. The plan must:

(1) Include a grievance procedure that covers grievances by any person against a volunteer or CASA program staff and grievances by a volunteer against a CASA program or program staff. The grievance procedure must:

(A) Be incorporated into a document that contains a description of the roles and responsibilities of CASA volunteers. This document must be provided:

(i) When a copy of the court order that appointed the CASA volunteer is provided to any adult involved with the child's case, including but not limited to, teachers, foster parents, therapists, and health-care workers; and

(ii) To any person, including a volunteer, who has a grievance against a volunteer or a CASA program employee.

(B) Include a provision that documentation of any grievance filed by or against a volunteer must be retained in the volunteer's personnel file.

(2) Include a provision for the ongoing training and continuing education of CASA volunteers. Ongoing training opportunities must be provided at least monthly under section 103(a). CASA volunteers must participate in a minimum of 12 hours of continuing education in each year of service.

(Subd (i) amended effective January 1, 2007; adopted as subd (g) effective July 1, 1994; previously amended effective January 1, 1995; previously amended and relettered effective January 1, 2005.)

(j) Removal, resignation, and termination of a CASA volunteer

The CASA program must adopt a written plan for the removal, resignation, or involuntary termination of a CASA volunteer, including the following provisions:

(1) A volunteer may resign or be removed from an individual case at any time by the order of the juvenile court presiding judge or designee.

(2) A volunteer may be involuntarily terminated from the program by the program director.

(3) The volunteer has the right to appeal termination by the program director under the program's grievance procedure.

(Subd (j) amended effective January 1, 2007; adopted as subd (h) effective July 1, 1994; previously amended effective January 1, 1995; previously amended and relettered effective January 1, 2005.)

(k) CASA program administration and management

A CASA program must adopt and adhere to a written plan for program governance and evaluation that includes the following as applicable:

(1) Articles of incorporation, bylaws, and a board of directors. Any CASA program that functions under the auspices of a public agency or private entity must specify in its plan a clear administrative relationship with the parent organization and clearly delineated delegations of authority and accountability. No CASA program may function under the auspices of a probation department or department of social services. CASA programs may receive funds from probation departments, local child welfare agencies, and the California Department of Social Services if:

(A) The CASA program and the contributing agency develop a memorandum of understanding (MOU) or contract stating that the funds will be used only for general operating expenses as determined by the receiving CASA program, and the contributing agency will not oversee or monitor the funds;

(B) A procedure resolving any conflict between the CASA program and contributing agency is implemented so that conflict between the two agencies does not affect funding or the CASA program's ability to retain an independent evaluation separate from that of the contributing agency's; and

(C) Any MOU or contract between a CASA program and the contributing agency is submitted to and approved by AOC staff.

(2) A clear statement of the purpose or mission of the CASA program and express goals and objectives to further that purpose. Where the CASA program is not an independent nonprofit organization, but instead functions under the auspices of a public agency or a private entity, an active advisory council must be established. The advisory council for CASA programs functioning under the auspices of a public agency or a private entity will not function as the governing body of the CASA program. The

board of directors for the private entity or the public agency management will function as the governing body for the CASA program, with guidance from the advisory council.

(3) A procedure for the recruitment, selection, hiring, and evaluation of an executive director for the CASA program.

(4) An administrative manual containing personnel policies, record-keeping practices, and data collection practices.

(5) Local juvenile court rules developed in consultation with the presiding judge of the juvenile court or a designee, as specified in section 100. One local rule must specify when CASA reports are to be submitted to the court, who is entitled to receive a copy of the report, and who will copy and distribute the report. This rule must also specify that the CASA court report must be distributed to the persons entitled to receive it at least two court days before the hearing for which the report was prepared.

(Subd (k) amended effective January 1, 2007; adopted as subd (i) effective July 1, 1994; previously amended effective January 1, 1995, and January 1, 2000; previously amended and relettered effective January 1, 2005.)

(*l*) Finance, facility, and risk management

(1) A CASA program must adopt a written plan for fiscal control. The fiscal plan must include an annual audit, conducted by a qualified professional, that is consistent with generally accepted accounting principles and the audit protocols in the program's contract with the Administrative Office of the Courts.

(2) The fiscal plan must include a written budget with projections that guide the management of financial resources and a strategy for obtaining necessary funding for program operations.

(3) When the program has accounting oversight, it must adhere to written operational procedures in regard to accounting control.

(4) The CASA program's board of directors must set policies for and exercise control over fundraising activities carried out by its employees and volunteers.

(5) The CASA program must have the following insurance coverage for its staff and volunteers:

(A) General liability insurance with limits of liability of not less than $1 million ($1,000,000) for each person per occurrence/aggregate for bodily injury and not less than $1 million ($1,000,000) per occurrence/aggregate for property damage;

(B) Nonowned automobile liability insurance and hired vehicle coverage with limits of liability of not less than $1 million ($1,000,000) combined single limit per occurrence and in the aggregate;

(C) Automobile liability insurance meeting the minimum state automobile liability insurance requirements, if the program owns a vehicle; and

(D) Workers' compensation insurance with a minimum limit of $500,000.

(6) The CASA program must require staff, volunteers, and members of the governing body, when applicable, to immediately notify the CASA program of any criminal charges against themselves.

(7) The nonprofit CASA program must plan for the disposition of property and confidential records in the event of its dissolution.

(Subd (l) adopted effective January 1, 2005.)

(m) Confidentiality

The presiding juvenile court judge and the CASA program director must adopt a written plan governing confidentiality of case information, case records, and personnel records. The written plan must include the following provisions:

(1) All information concerning children and families in the juvenile court process is confidential. Volunteers must not give case information to anyone other than the court, the parties and their attorneys, and CASA staff.

(2) CASA volunteers are required by law (Pen. Code, § 11166 et seq.) to report any reasonable suspicion that a child is a victim of child abuse or serious neglect as described by Penal Code section 273.

(3) The child's original case file must be maintained in the CASA office by a custodian of records and must remain there. Copies of documents needed by a volunteer must be restricted to those actually needed to conduct necessary business outside of the office. No one may have access to the child's original case file except on the approval of the CASA program director or presiding judge of the juvenile court. Controls must be in place to ensure that records can be located at any time. The office must establish a written procedure for the maintenance of case files.

(4) The volunteer's personnel file is confidential. No one may have access to the personnel file except the volunteer, the CASA program director or a designee, or the presiding judge of the juvenile court.

(Subd (m) amended effective January 1, 2007; adopted as subd (j) effective July 1, 1994; previously amended effective January 1, 1995; previously amended and relettered effective January 1, 2005.)

Rule 5.655 amended and renumbered effective January 1, 2007; adopted as rule 1424 effective July 1, 1994; previously amended effective January 1, 1995, January 1, 2000, January 1, 2001, and January 1, 2005.

Advisory Committee Comment

These 1995 guidelines implement the requirements of section 100, which establishes a grant program administered by the Judicial Council to establish or expand CASA programs to assist children involved in juvenile dependency proceedings, including guardianships, adoptions, and actions to terminate parental rights to custody and control.

CASA programs provide substantial benefits to children appearing in dependency proceedings and to the juvenile court having responsibility for these children. Child advocates improve the quality of judicial decision making by providing information to the court concerning the child. Advocates help identify needed services for the children they are assisting and provide a consistent friend and support person for children throughout the long and complex dependency process.

The CASA concept was first implemented in Seattle in 1977. As of 1994, there were more than 30,000 volunteers working in more than 525 CASA programs in nearly every state. The programs recruit, screen, select, train, and supervise lay volunteers to become effective advocates in the juvenile court.

Currently, numerous jurisdictions in California use some variation of the CASA concept. These programs have developed over the past several years under the supervision of local juvenile courts under sections 356.5 and 358. Each program is unique and was designed to respond to the specific needs of the local jurisdiction and community it serves.

These guidelines provide a framework for ensuring the excellence of California CASA programs and volunteers. They are intended to be consistent with the guidelines established by the National CASA Association and to conform with the requirements of California law and procedure. The California CASA Association has assisted in developing these guidelines, which are meant to give the local bench, bar, child welfare professionals, children's advocates, and other interested citizens full rein to adapt the CASA concept to the special needs and circumstances of local communities.

Central to the intent of these guidelines is the effort to provide a vehicle for the presiding judge of the local juvenile court to exercise fully informed and effective oversight of the local CASA program and CASA volunteers. These guidelines are also intended to help CASA programs and juvenile courts develop local court rules. Nothing in these guidelines should limit or restrict the local juvenile court from developing and supporting multiple branches of a CASA program within the community to enable a county to offer comprehensive volunteer advocacy programs for children.

Ref.: Cal. Fms Pl. & Pr., Ch. 328, "Juvenile Courts: Dependency Proceedings"; W. Cal. Sum., 10 "Parent and Child" §§3, 444, 572.

Rule 5.660.   Attorneys for parties (§§ 317, 317.6, 16010.6, 366.26)

(a) Local rules

On or before January 1, 2002, the superior court of each county must amend its local rules regarding the representation of parties in dependency proceedings.

(1) The local rules must be amended after consultation by the court with representatives of the State Bar of California; local offices of the county counsel, district attorney, public defender, and other attorneys appointed to represent parties in these proceedings; county welfare departments; child advocates; current or recent foster youth; and others selected by the court in accordance with standard 5.40(c) of the Standards of Judicial Administration.

(2) The amended rules must address the following as needed:

(A) Representation of children in accordance with other sections of this rule;

(B) Timelines and procedures for settlements, mediation, discovery, protocols, and other issues related to contested matters;

(C) Procedures for the screening, training, and appointment of attorneys representing parties, with particular attention to the training requirements for attorneys representing children;

(D) Establishment of minimum standards of experience, training, and education of attorneys representing parties, including additional training and education in the areas of substance abuse and domestic violence as required;

(E) Establishment of procedures to determine appropriate caseloads for attorneys representing children;

(F) Procedures for reviewing and resolving complaints by parties regarding the performance of attorneys;

(G) Procedures for informing the court of interests of the dependent child requiring further investigation, intervention, or litigation; and

(H) Procedures for appointment of a Child Abuse Prevention and Treatment Act (CAPTA) guardian ad litem, who may be an attorney or a CASA volunteer, in cases in which a prosecution is initiated under the Penal Code arising from neglect or abuse of the child.

(3) Appropriate local forms may be used.

(Subd (a) amended effective January 1, 2007; previously amended effective July 1, 2001, and January 1, 2003.)

(b) Attorneys for children

The court must appoint counsel for a child who is the subject of a petition under section 300 and is unrepresented by counsel, unless the court finds that the child would not benefit from the appointment of counsel.

(1) In order to find that a child would not benefit from the appointment of counsel, the court must find all of the following:

(A) The child understands the nature of the proceedings;

(B) The child is able to communicate and advocate effectively with the court, other counsel, other parties, including social workers, and other professionals involved in the case; and

(C) Under the circumstances of the case, the child would not gain any benefit by being represented by counsel.

(2) If the court finds that the child would not benefit from representation by counsel, the court must make a finding on the record as to each of the criteria in (1) and state the reasons for each finding.

(3) If the court finds that the child would not benefit from representation by counsel, the court must appoint a CASA volunteer for the child, to serve as the CAPTA guardian ad litem, as required in section 326.5.

(Subd (b) amended effective January 1, 2007; adopted effective July 1, 2001; previously amended effective January 1, 2003.)

(c) Conflict of interest guidelines for attorneys representing siblings

(1) *Appointment*

(A) The court may appoint a single attorney to represent a group of siblings involved in the same dependency proceeding.

(B) An attorney must decline to represent one or more siblings in a dependency proceeding, and the court must appoint a separate attorney to represent the sibling or siblings, if, at the outset of the proceedings:

(i) An actual conflict of interest exists among those siblings; or

(ii) Circumstances specific to the case present a reasonable likelihood that an actual conflict of interest will arise among those siblings.

(C) The following circumstances, standing alone, do not necessarily demonstrate an actual conflict of interest or a reasonable likelihood that an actual conflict of interest will arise:

(i) The siblings are of different ages;

(ii) The siblings have different parents;

(iii) There is a purely theoretical or abstract conflict of interest among the siblings;

(iv) Some of the siblings appear more likely than others to be adoptable; or

(v) The siblings may have different permanent plans.

(2) *Withdrawal from appointment or continued representation*

(A) An attorney representing a group of siblings has an ongoing duty to evaluate the interests of each sibling and assess whether there is an actual conflict of interest.

(B) The following circumstances, standing alone, do not necessarily demonstrate an actual conflict of interest:

(i) The siblings are of different ages;

(ii) The siblings have different parents;

(iii) There is a purely theoretical or abstract conflict of interest among the siblings;

(iv) Some of the siblings are more likely to be adopted than others;

(v) The siblings have different permanent plans;

(vi) The siblings express conflicting desires or objectives, but the issues involved are not material to the case; or

(vii) The siblings give different or contradictory accounts of the events, but the issues involved are not material to the case.

(C) It is not necessary for an attorney to withdraw from representing some or all of the siblings if there is merely a reasonable likelihood that an actual conflict of interest will develop.

(D) If an attorney believes that an actual conflict of interest existed at appointment or developed during representation, the attorney must take any action necessary to ensure that the siblings' interests are not prejudiced, including:

(i) Notifying the juvenile court of the existence of an actual conflict of interest among some or all of the siblings; and

(ii) Requesting to withdraw from representation of some or all of the siblings.

(E) If the court determines that an actual conflict of interest exists, the court must relieve an attorney from representation of some or all of the siblings.

(F) After an actual conflict of interest arises, the attorney may continue to represent one or more siblings whose interests do not conflict only if:

(i) The attorney has successfully withdrawn from the representation of all siblings whose interests conflict with those of the sibling or siblings the attorney continues to represent;

(ii) The attorney has exchanged no confidential information with any sibling whose interest conflicts with those of the sibling or siblings the attorney continues to represent; and

(iii) Continued representation of one or more siblings would not otherwise prejudice the other sibling or siblings.

(Subd (c) amended effective January 1, 2007; adopted effective January 1, 2006.)

(d) Competent counsel

Every party in a dependency proceeding who is represented by an attorney is entitled to competent counsel.

(1) *Definition*

"Competent counsel" means an attorney who is a member in good standing of the State Bar of California, who has participated in training in the law of juvenile dependency, and who demonstrates adequate forensic skills, knowledge and comprehension of the statutory scheme, the purposes and goals of dependency proceedings, the specific statutes, rules of court, and cases relevant

to such proceedings, and procedures for filing petitions for extraordinary writs.

(2) *Evidence of competency*

The court may require evidence of the competency of any attorney appointed to represent a party in a dependency proceeding.

(3) *Experience and education*

Only those attorneys who have completed a minimum of eight hours of training or education in the area of juvenile dependency, or who have sufficient recent experience in dependency proceedings in which the attorney has demonstrated competency, may be appointed to represent parties. In addition to a summary of dependency law and related statutes and cases, training and education for attorneys must include information on child development, child abuse and neglect, substance abuse, domestic violence, family reunification and preservation, and reasonable efforts. Within every three years attorneys must complete at least eight hours of continuing education related to dependency proceedings.

(4) *Standards of representation*

Attorneys or their agents are expected to meet regularly with clients, including clients who are children, regardless of the age of the child or the child's ability to communicate verbally, to contact social workers and other professionals associated with the client's case, to work with other counsel and the court to resolve disputed aspects of a case without contested hearing, and to adhere to the mandated timelines. The attorney for the child must have sufficient contact with the child to establish and maintain an adequate and professional attorney-client relationship. The attorney for the child is not required to assume the responsibilities of a social worker and is not expected to perform services for the child that are unrelated to the child's legal representation.

(5) *Attorney contact information*

The attorney for a child for whom a dependency petition has been filed must provide his or her contact information to the child's caregiver no later than 10 days after receipt of the name, address, and telephone number of the child's caregiver. If the child is 10 years of age or older, the attorney must also provide his or her contact information to the child for whom a dependency petition has been filed no later than 10 days after receipt of the caregiver's contact information. The attorney may give contact information to a child for whom a dependency petition has been filed who is under 10 years of age.

(6) *Caseloads for children's attorneys*

The attorney for a child must have a caseload that allows the attorney to perform the duties required by section 317(e) and this rule, and to otherwise adequately counsel and represent the child. To enhance the quality of representation afforded to children, attorneys appointed under this rule must not maintain a maximum full-time caseload that is greater than that which allows them to meet the requirements stated in (3), (4), and (5).

(Subd (d) amended effective January 1, 2007; adopted as subd (b) effective January 1, 1996; amended and relettered as subd (c) effective July 1, 2001; previously amended effective July 1, 1999, and January 1, 2005; previously relettered effective January 1, 2006.)

(e) Client complaints

The court must establish a process for the review and resolution of complaints or questions by a party regarding the performance of an appointed attorney. Each party must be informed of the procedure for lodging the complaint. If it is determined that an appointed attorney has acted improperly or contrary to the rules or policies of the court, the court must take appropriate action.

(Subd (e) relettered effective January 1, 2006; adopted as subd (c) effective January 1, 1996; previously amended and relettered as subd (d) effective July 1, 2001.)

(f) CASA volunteer as CAPTA guardian ad litem (§ 326.5)

If the court makes the findings as outlined in (b) and does not appoint an attorney to represent the child, the court must appoint a CASA volunteer as the CAPTA guardian ad litem of the child.

(1) The required training of CASA volunteers is stated in rule 5.655.

(2) The caseload of a CASA volunteer acting as a CAPTA guardian ad litem must be limited to 10 cases. A case may include siblings, absent a conflict.

(3) CASA volunteers must not assume the responsibilities of attorneys for children.

(4) The appointment of an attorney to represent the child does not prevent the appointment of a CASA volunteer for that child, and courts are encouraged to appoint both an attorney and a CASA volunteer for the child in as many cases as possible.

(Subd (f) amended effective January 1, 2007; adopted as subd (e) effective July 1, 2001; previously amended effective January 1, 2003; previously relettered effective January 1, 2006.)

(g) Interests of the child

At any time following the filing of a petition under section 300 and until juvenile court jurisdiction is terminated, any interested person may advise the court of information regarding an interest or right of the child to be protected or pursued in other judicial or administrative forums.

(1) *Juvenile Dependency Petition (Version One)* (form JV-100) and *Request to Change Court Order* (form JV-180) may be used.

(2) If the attorney for the child, or a CASA volunteer acting as a CAPTA guardian ad litem, learns of any such interest or right, the attorney or CASA volunteer must notify the court immediately and seek instructions from the court as to any appropriate procedures to follow.

(3) If the court determines that further action on behalf of the child is required to protect or pursue any interests or rights, the court must appoint an attorney for the child, if the child is not already represented by counsel, and do one or all of the following:

(A) Refer the matter to the appropriate agency for further investigation and require a report to the court within a reasonable time;

(B) Authorize and direct the child's attorney to initiate and pursue appropriate action;

(C) Appoint a guardian ad litem for the child. The guardian may be the CASA volunteer already appointed as a CAPTA guardian ad litem or a person who will act only if required to initiate appropriate action; or

(D) Take any other action to protect or pursue the interests and rights of the child.

(Subd (g) amended effective January 1, 2007; adopted as subd (d) effective January 1, 1996; previously amended and relettered as subd (f) effective July 1, 2001; amended effective January 1, 2003; previously relettered effective January 1, 2006.)

Rule 5.660 amended and renumbered effective January 1, 2007; adopted as rule 1438 effective January 1, 1996; previously amended effectively July 1, 1999, July 1, 2001, January 1, 2003, January 1, 2005, and January 1, 2006.

Advisory Committee Comment

The court should initially appoint a single attorney to represent all siblings in a dependency matter unless there is an actual conflict of interest or a reasonable likelihood that an actual conflict of interest will arise. (*In re Celine R.* (2003) 31 Cal.4th 45, 58.) After the initial appointment, the court should relieve an attorney from representation of multiple siblings only if an actual conflict of interest arises. (*Ibid.*) Attorneys have a duty to use their best judgment in analyzing whether, under the particular facts of the case, it is necessary to decline appointment or request withdrawal from appointment due to a purported conflict of interest.

Nothing in this rule is intended to expend the permissible scope of any judicial inquiry into an attorney's reasons for declining to represent one or more siblings or requesting to withdraw from representation of one or more siblings, due to an actual or reasonably likely conflict of interest. (See Cal. Bar Rules, Prof. Conduct R 3-310, Subd (C).) While the court has the duty and authority to inquire as to the general nature of an asserted conflict of interest, it cannot require an attorney to disclose any privileged communication, even if such information forms the basis of the alleged conflict. (*In re James S.* (1991) 227 Cal.App.3d 930, 934; *Aceves v. Superior Court* (1996) 51 Cal.App.4th 584, 592–593.)

Ref.: Cal. Fms Pl. & Pr., Ch. 72, "Attorney Practice and Ethics," Ch. 328, "Juvenile Courts: Dependency Proceedings"; W. Cal. Sum., 10 "Parent and Child" §§444, 569, 571–573, 574A, 580.

Rule 5.661. Representation of the child on appeal

(a) Definition

For purposes of this rule, "guardian ad litem" means a person designated as the child's Child Abuse Prevention and Treatment Act (CAPTA) guardian ad litem as defined in rule 5.662.

(Subd (a) adopted effective July 1, 2007.)

(b) Child as appellant

A notice of appeal on behalf of the child must be filed by the child's trial counsel, guardian ad litem, or the child if the child is seeking appellate relief from the trial court's judgment or order.

(Subd (b) adopted effective July 1, 2007.)

(c) Recommendation from child's trial counsel or guardian ad litem

(1) In any juvenile dependency proceeding in which a party other than the child files a notice of appeal, if the child's trial counsel or guardian ad litem concludes that, for purposes of the appeal, the child's best interests cannot be protected without the appointment of separate counsel on appeal, the child's trial counsel or guardian ad litem must file a recommendation in the Court of Appeal requesting appointment of separate counsel.

(2) A child's trial counsel or guardian ad litem who recommends appointment of appellate counsel for a child who is not an appellant must follow the procedures outlined in (d)–(g).

(Subd (c) adopted effective July 1, 2007.)

(d) Time for trial counsel or guardian ad litem to file the recommendation with the Court of Appeal

A recommendation from the child's trial counsel or guardian ad litem may be filed at any time after a notice of appeal has been filed, but absent good cause, must be filed in the Court of Appeal no later than 20 calendar days after the filing of the last appellant's opening brief.

(Subd (d) adopted effective July 1, 2007.)

(e) Service of recommendation

Child's trial counsel or guardian ad litem must serve a copy of the recommendation filed in the Court of Appeal on the district appellate project.

(Subd (e) adopted effective July 1, 2007.)

(f) Factors to be considered

The following are factors to be considered by a child's trial counsel or guardian ad litem in making a recommendation to the Court of Appeal:

(1) An actual or potential conflict exists between the interests of the child and the interests of any respondent;

(2) The child did not have an attorney serving as his or her guardian ad litem in the trial court;

(3) The child is of a sufficient age or development such that he or she is able to understand the nature of the proceedings and,

(A) The child expresses a desire to participate in the appeal, or

(B) The child's wishes differ from his or her trial counsel's position;

(4) The child took a legal position in the trial court adverse to that of one of his or her siblings, and an issue has been raised in an appellant's opening brief regarding the siblings' adverse positions;

(5) The appeal involves a legal issue regarding a determination of parentage, the child's inheritance rights, educational rights, privileges identified in division 8 of the Evidence Code, consent to treatment, or tribal membership;

(6) Postjudgment evidence completely undermines the legal underpinnings of the juvenile court's judgment under review, and all parties recognize this and express a willingness to stipulate to reversal of the juvenile court's judgment;

(7) The child's trial counsel or guardian ad litem, after reviewing the appellate briefs, believes that the legal arguments contained in the respondents' briefs do not adequately represent or protect the best interests of the child; and

(8) The existence of any other factors relevant to the child's best interests.

(Subd (f) adopted effective July 1, 2007.)

(g) Form of recommendation

The child's trial counsel, the guardian ad litem, or the child may use *Recommendation for Appointment of Appellate Attorney for Child* (form JV-810). Any recommendation for an appellate attorney for the child must state a factual basis for the recommendation, include the information provided on form JV-810, and be signed under penalty of perjury.

(Subd (g) adopted effective July 1, 2007.)
Rule 5.661 adopted effective July 1, 2007.

Advisory Committee Comment

Generally, separate counsel for a nonappealing child will not be appointed for the purpose of introducing postjudgment evidence. See California Code Civ. Proc., § 909; *In re Zeth S.* (2003) 31 Cal.4th 396; *In re Josiah Z.* (2005) 36 Cal.4th 664. For further discussion, see *In re Mary C.* (1995) 41 Cal.App.4th 71.

Ref.: Cal. Fms Pl. & Pr., Ch. 328, "Juvenile Courts: Dependency Proceedings"; W. Cal. Sum., 10 "Parent and Child" §444.

Rule 5.662. Child Abuse Prevention and Treatment Act (CAPTA) guardian ad litem for a child subject to a juvenile dependency petition

(a) Authority

This rule is adopted under section 326.5.

(Subd (a) amended effective January 1, 2007.)

(b) Applicability

The definition of the role and responsibilities of a CAPTA guardian ad litem in this rule applies exclusively to juvenile dependency proceedings and is distinct from the definitions of guardian ad litem in all other juvenile, civil, and criminal proceedings. No limitation period for bringing an action based on an injury to the child commences running solely by reason of the appointment of a CAPTA guardian ad litem under section 326.5 and this rule.

(Subd (b) amended effective January 1, 2007.)

(c) Appointment

A CAPTA guardian ad litem must be appointed for every child who is the subject of a juvenile dependency petition under section 300. An attorney appointed under rule 5.660 will serve as the child's CAPTA guardian ad litem under section 326.5. If the court finds that the child would not benefit from the appointment of counsel, the court must appoint a CASA volunteer to serve as the child's CAPTA guardian ad litem. The court must identify on the record the person appointed as the child's CAPTA guardian ad litem.

(Subd (c) amended effective January 1, 2007.)

(d) General duties and responsibilities

The general duties and responsibilities of a CAPTA guardian ad litem are:

(1) To obtain firsthand a clear understanding of the situation and needs of the child; and

(2) To make recommendations to the court concerning the best interest of the child as appropriate under (e) and (f).

(e) Attorney as guardian ad litem

The specific duties and responsibilities of the child's court-appointed attorney who is appointed to serve as the child's CAPTA guardian ad litem are stated in section 317(e) and rule 5.660.

(Subd (e) amended effective January 1, 2007.)

(f) CASA volunteer as CAPTA guardian ad litem

The specific duties and responsibilities of the child's CASA volunteer who is appointed to serve as the child's CAPTA guardian ad litem are stated in section 102(c) and rule 5.655.

(Subd (f) amended effective January 1, 2007.)
Rule 5.662 amended and renumbered effective January 1, 2007; adopted as rule 1448 effective January 1, 2003.

Ref.: Cal. Fms Pl. & Pr., Ch. 328, "Juvenile Courts: Dependency Proceedings"; W. Cal. Sum., 10 "Parent and Child" §§444, 572, 708, 709.

Rule 5.663. Responsibilities of children's counsel in delinquency proceedings (§§ 202, 265, 633, 634, 634.6, 679, 700)

(a) Purpose

This rule is designed to ensure public safety and the protection of the child's best interest at every stage of the delinquency proceedings by clarifying the role of the child's counsel in delinquency proceedings. This rule is not intended to affect any substantive duty imposed on counsel by existing civil standards or professional discipline standards.

(b) Responsibilities of counsel

A child's counsel is charged in general with defending the child against the allegations in all petitions filed in delinquency proceedings and with advocating, within the framework of the delinquency proceedings, that the child receive care, treatment, and guidance consistent with his or her best interest.

(c) Right to representation

A child is entitled to have the child's interests represented by counsel at every stage of the proceedings, including postdispositional hearings. Counsel must continue to represent the child unless relieved by the court on the substitution of other counsel or for cause.

(Subd (c) amended effective January 1, 2007.)

(d) Limits to responsibilities

A child's counsel is not required:

(1) To assume the responsibilities of a probation officer, social worker, parent, or guardian;

(2) To provide nonlegal services to the child; or

(3) To represent the child in any proceedings outside of the delinquency proceedings.

(Subd (d) amended effective January 1, 2007.)

Rule 5.663 amended and renumbered effective January 1, 2007; adopted as rule 1479 effective July 1, 2004.

Ref.: Cal. Fms Pl. & Pr., Ch. 329, "Juvenile Courts: Delinquency Proceedings"; W. Cal. Sum., 10 "Parent and Child" §444.

Chapter 12
Indian Child Welfare Act
[Repealed]

Rule 5.664. Indian Child Welfare Act (25 U.S.C. § 1901 et seq.) [Repealed]

Rule 5.664 repealed effective January 1, 2008; adopted as rule 1439 effective January 1, 1995; amended and renumbered effective January 1, 2007; previously amended effective January 1, 1997, January 1, 1999, January 1, 2001, January 1, 2005, and February 23, 2007.

Another Chapter 12 follows.

Chapter 12
Cases Petitioned Under
Section 300

Chapter 12 renumbered effective January 1, 2008; Adopted as Chapter 7 effective July, 1989; previously renumbered as Chapter

8 effective July 1, 1994, and as Chapter 9 effective January 1, 2000; previously renumbered and amended as Chapter 13 effective January 1, 2007.

Art. 1.   Initial Hearing. Rules 5.667–5.680.
Art. 2.   Jurisdiction. Rules 5.682–5.688.
Art. 3.   Disposition. Rules 5.690–5.705.
Art. 4.   Reviews, Permanent Planning. Rules 5.710–5.740.

Article 1
Initial Hearing

Rule 5.667. Service and notice
Rule 5.668. Commencement of hearing—explanation of proceedings (§§ 316, 316.2)
Rule 5.670. Initial hearing; detention hearings; time limit on custody; setting jurisdiction hearing; visitation
Rule 5.672. Continuances
Rule 5.674. Conduct of hearing; admission, no contest, submission
Rule 5.676. Requirements for detention
Rule 5.678. Findings in support of detention; factors to consider; reasonable efforts; detention alternatives
Rule 5.680. Detention rehearings; prima facie hearings

Rule 5.667. Service and notice

(a) In court order of notice (§ 296)

The court may order the child, or any parent or guardian or Indian custodian of the child who is present in court, to appear again before the court, social worker, probation officer, or county financial officer at a specified time and place as stated in the order.

(Subd (a) amended effective January 1, 2007; previously amended effective January 1, 2006.)

(b) Language of notice

If it appears that the parent or guardian does not read English, the social worker must provide notice in the language believed to be spoken by the parent or guardian.

(Subd (b) amended effective January 1, 2006.)

Rule 5.667 amended and renumbered effective January 1, 2007; repealed and adopted as rule 1440 effective January 1, 1998; previously amended effective January 1, 2006.

Ref.: Cal. Fms Pl. & Pr., Ch. 328, "Juvenile Courts: Dependency Proceedings"; W. Cal. Sum., 10 "Parent and Child" §§444, 463, 589, 598, 600, 668, 706.

Rule 5.668. Commencement of hearing—explanation of proceedings (§§ 316, 316.2)

(a) Commencement of hearing

At the beginning of the initial hearing on the petition, whether the child is detained or not detained, the court must give advisement as required by rule 5.534 and must inform each parent and guardian present, and the child, if present:

(1) Of the contents of the petition;

(2) Of the nature of, and possible consequences of, juvenile court proceedings;

(3) If the child has been taken into custody, of the reasons for the initial detention and the purpose and scope of the detention hearing; and

(4) If the petition is sustained and the child is declared a dependent of the court and removed from the custody of

the parent or guardian, the court-ordered reunification services must be considered to have been offered or provided on the date the petition is sustained or 60 days after the child's initial removal, whichever is earlier. The time for services must not exceed 12 months for a child aged three or over at the time of the initial removal and must not exceed 6 months for a child who was under the age of three at the time of the initial removal if the parent or guardian fails to participate regularly and make substantive progress in any court-ordered treatment program.

(Subd (a) amended effective January 1, 2007; adopted as subd (a) effective January 1, 1999; previously amended effective January 1, 2001.)

(b) Paternity inquiry

The court must also inquire of the child's mother and of any other appropriate person present as to the identity and address of any and all presumed and alleged fathers of the child. Questions, at the discretion of the court, may include:

(1) Has there been a judgment of paternity?

(2) Was the mother married, or did she believe she was married, at or any time after the time of conception?

(3) Was the mother cohabiting with a man at the time of conception?

(4) Has the mother received support payments or promises of support for the child or for the mother during her pregnancy?

(5) Has a man formally or informally acknowledged paternity, including the execution of a voluntary declaration of paternity under Family Code section 7571?

(6) Have paternity tests been administered and, if so, what were the results?

(Subd (b) amended effective January 1, 2007; adopted effective January 1, 1999.)

(c) Health and education information (§ 16010)

The court must order each parent and guardian present either to complete *Your Child's Health and Education* (form JV-225) or to provide the information necessary for the social worker or probation officer, court staff, or representative of the local child welfare agency to complete the form. The social worker or probation officer assigned to the dependency matter must provide the child's attorney with a copy of the completed form. Before each periodic status review hearing, the social worker or probation officer must obtain and include in the reports prepared for the hearing all information necessary to maintain the accuracy of form JV-225.

(Subd (c) amended effective January 1, 2008; adopted effective January 1, 2002; previously amended effective January 1, 2007.) Rule 5.668 amended effective January 1, 2008; repealed and adopted as rule 1441 effective January 1, 1998; previously amended effective January 1, 1999, January 1, 2001, and January 1, 2002; previously amended and renumbered effective January 1, 2007.)

Ref.: Cal. Fms Pl. & Pr., Ch. 328, "Juvenile Courts: Dependency Proceedings"; W. Cal. Sum., 10 "Parent and Child" §§444, 567, 602, 603.

Rule 5.670. Initial hearing; detention hearings; time limit on custody; setting jurisdiction hearing; visitation

(a) Child not detained; filing petition, setting hearing

If the social worker does not take the child into custody but determines that a petition concerning the child should be filed, the social worker must file a petition with the clerk of the juvenile court as soon as possible. The clerk must set an initial hearing on the petition within 15 court days.

(Subd (a) amended effective January 1, 2007.)

(b) Time limit on custody, filing petition, setting hearing (§§ 311, 313)

If the social worker takes the child into custody, the social worker must immediately file a petition with the clerk of the juvenile court, and the clerk must immediately set the matter for hearing on the detention hearing calendar. A child who is detained must be released within 48 hours, excluding noncourt days, unless a petition has been filed.

(Subd (b) amended effective January 1, 2007.)

(c) Detention—child in medical facility (§ 309(b))

For purposes of these rules, a child is deemed taken into custody and delivered to the social worker if the child is under medical care and cannot immediately be moved and there is reasonable cause to believe the child is described by section 300.

(Subd (c) amended effective January 1, 2007.)

(d) Detention hearing—time of (§ 315)

Unless the child has been released sooner, the matter concerning a child who is taken into custody must be brought before the juvenile court for a detention hearing as soon as possible, but in any event before the end of the next court day after a petition has been filed. At the detention hearing, the court must determine whether the child is to continue to be detained in custody. If the detention hearing is not commenced within that time, the child must be immediately released from custody.

(Subd (d) amended effective January 1, 2007.)

(e) Detention hearing—warrant cases, transfers in, changes in placement

Notwithstanding (c), and unless the child has been released sooner, a detention hearing must be held as soon as possible, but no later than 48 hours, excluding noncourt days, after the child arrives at a facility within the county if:

(1) The child was taken into custody in another county and transported in custody to the requesting county under a protective custody warrant issued by the juvenile court;

(2) The child was taken into custody in the county in which a protective custody warrant was issued by the juvenile court; or

(3) The matter was transferred from the juvenile court of another county under rule 5.610 and the child was ordered transported in custody.

At the hearing the court must determine whether the child is to continue to be detained in custody. If the hearing is not commenced within that time, the child must be immediately released from custody.

(Subd (e) amended effective January 1, 2007.)

(f) Setting jurisdiction hearing (§ 334)

If the child is not detained, the court must set a jurisdiction hearing to be held within 30 days of the date the petition is filed. If the court orders the child to be detained, the court must set a jurisdiction hearing within 15 court days of the order of detention.

(Subd (f) amended effective January 1, 2007.)

(g) Visitation

The court must consider the issue of visitation between the child and other persons, including siblings, determine if contact pending the jurisdiction hearing would be beneficial or detrimental to the child, and make appropriate orders.

(Subd (g) amended effective January 1, 2007.)

Rule 5.670 amended and renumbered effective January 1, 2007; repealed and adopted as rule 1442 effective January 1, 1998.

Ref.: Cal. Fms Pl. & Pr., Ch. 328, "Juvenile Courts: Dependency Proceedings"; W. Cal. Sum., 10 "Parent and Child" §§444, 598, 600, 607, 609.

Rule 5.672.   Continuances

(a) Detention hearing; right to one-day continuance; custody pending continued hearing (§§ 319, 322)

On motion of the child, parent, or guardian, the court must continue the detention hearing for one court day. Unless otherwise ordered by the court, the child must remain detained pending completion of the detention hearing or a rehearing. The court must either find that continuance in the home of the parent or guardian is contrary to the child's welfare or order the child released to the custody of the parent or guardian. The court may enter this finding on a temporary basis, without prejudice to any party, and reevaluate the finding at the time of the continued detention hearing.

(Subd (a) amended effective January 1, 2007; previously amended effective July 1, 2002.)

(b) Initial hearing; child not detained

If the child is not detained, motions for continuances of the initial hearing must be made and ruled on under rule 5.550.

(Subd (b) amended effective January 1, 2007; previously amended effective July 1, 2002.)

Rule 5.672 amended and renumbered effective January 1, 2007; repealed and adopted as rule 1443 effective January 1, 1998; previously amended effective July 1, 2002.

Ref.: Cal. Fms Pl. & Pr., Ch. 328, "Juvenile Courts: Dependency Proceedings"; W. Cal. Sum., 10 "Parent and Child" §§444, 598, 601.

Rule 5.674.   Conduct of hearing; admission, no contest, submission

(a) Admission, no contest, submission

(1) At the initial hearing, whether or not the child is detained, the parent or guardian may admit the allegations of the petition, plead no contest, or submit the jurisdictional determination to the court based on the information provided to the court and waive further jurisdictional hearing.

(2) If the court accepts an admission, a plea of no contest, or a submission from each parent and guardian with standing to participate as a party, the court must then proceed according to rules 5.682 and 5.686.

(Subd (a) amended effective January 1, 2007; previously amended effective July 1, 2002.)

(b) Detention hearing; general conduct (§ 319; 42 U.S.C., § 600 et seq.)

The court must read, consider, and reference any reports submitted by the social worker and any relevant evidence submitted by any party or counsel. All detention findings and orders must be made on the record and appear in the written orders of the court.

(Subd (b) amended effective January 1, 2007; adopted effective July 1, 2002.)

(c) Detention hearing; examination by court (§ 319)

Subject to (d), the court must examine the child's parent, guardian, or other person having knowledge relevant to the issue of detention and must receive any relevant evidence that the petitioner, the child, a parent, a guardian, or counsel for a party wishes to present.

(Subd (c) amended effective January 1, 2007; adopted as subd (b) effective January 1, 1998; previously amended and relettered effective July 1, 2002.)

(d) Detention hearing; rights of child, parent, or guardian (§§ 311, 319)

At the detention hearing, the child, the parent, and the guardian have the right to assert the privilege against self-incrimination and the right to confront and cross-examine:

(1) The preparer of a police report, probation or social worker report, or other document submitted to the court; and

(2) Any person examined by the court under (c). If the child, parent, or guardian asserts the right to cross-examine preparers of documents submitted for court consideration, the court may not consider any such report or document unless the preparer is made available for cross-examination.

(Subd (d) amended effective January 1, 2007; adopted as subd (c) effective January 1, 1998; previously amended and relettered effective July 1, 2002.)

Rule 5.674 amended and renumbered effective January 1, 2007; repealed and adopted as rule 1444 effective January 1, 1998; previously amended effective July 1, 2002.

Ref.: Cal. Fms Pl. & Pr., Ch. 328, "Juvenile Courts: Dependency Proceedings"; W. Cal. Sum., 10 "Parent and Child" §§444, 567, 576, 578, 604, 605, 607.

Rule 5.676.   Requirements for detention

(a) Requirements for detention (§ 319)

No child may be ordered detained by the court unless the court finds that:

(1) A prima facie showing has been made that the child is described by section 300;

(2) Continuance in the home of the parent or guardian is contrary to the child's welfare; and

(3) One or more of the grounds for detention in rule 5.678 is found.

(Subd (a) amended effective January 1, 2007; previously amended effective July 1, 2002.)

(b) Evidence required at detention hearing

In making the findings required to support an order of detention, the court may rely solely on written police reports, probation or social worker reports, or other documents.

The reports relied on must include:

(1) A statement of the reasons the child was removed from the parent's custody;

(2) A description of the services that have been provided, including those under section 306, and of any available services or safety plans that would prevent or eliminate the need for the child to remain in custody;

(3) Identification of the need, if any, for the child to remain in custody; and

(4) If continued detention is recommended, information about any parent or guardian of the child with whom the child was not residing at the time the child was taken into custody or about any relative with whom the child may be detained.

(Subd (b) amended effective January 1, 2007; previously amended effective July 1, 2002.)

Rule 5.676 amended and renumbered effective January 1, 2007; repealed and adopted as rule 1445 effective January 1, 1998; previously amended effective July 1, 2002.

Ref.: Cal. Fms Pl. & Pr., Ch. 328, "Juvenile Courts: Dependency Proceedings"; W. Cal. Sum., 10 "Parent and Child" §§444, 604.

Rule 5.678.   Findings in support of detention; factors to consider; reasonable efforts; detention alternatives

(a) Findings in support of detention (§ 319; 42 U.S.C., § 600 et seq.)

The court must order the child released from custody unless the court finds that:

(1) A prima facie showing has been made that the child is described by section 300;

(2) Continuance in the home of the parent or guardian is contrary to the child's welfare; and

(3) Any of the following grounds exist:

(A) There is a substantial danger to the physical health of the child or the child is suffering severe emotional damage, and there are no reasonable means to protect the child's physical or emotional health without removing the child from the parent's or guardian's physical custody;

(B) The child is a dependent of the juvenile court who has left a placement;

(C) The parent, guardian, or responsible relative is likely to flee the jurisdiction of the court with the child; or

(D) The child is unwilling to return home and the petitioner alleges that a person residing in the home has physically or sexually abused the child.

(Subd (a) amended effective January 1, 2007; previously amended effective July 1, 2002.)

(b) Factors to consider

In determining whether to release or detain the child under (a), the court must consider whether the child can be returned home if the court orders services to be provided, including services under section 306.

(Subd (b) amended effective January 1, 2007; previously amended effective July 1, 2002.)

(c) Findings of the court—reasonable efforts (§ 319; 42 U.S.C., § 600 et seq.)

(1) Whether the child is released or detained at the hearing, the court must determine whether reasonable efforts have been made to prevent or eliminate the need for removal and must make one of the following findings:

(A) Reasonable efforts have been made; or

(B) Reasonable efforts have not been made.

(2) The court must not order the child detained unless the court, after inquiry regarding available services, finds that there are no reasonable services that would prevent or eliminate the need to detain the child or that would permit the child to return home.

(3) If the court orders the child detained, the court must:

(A) Determine if there are services that would permit the child to return home pending the next hearing and state the factual bases for the decision to detain the child;

(B) Specify why the initial removal was necessary; and

(C) If appropriate, order services to be provided as soon as possible to reunify the child and the child's family.

(Subd (c) amended effective January 1, 2007; adopted as subd (d) effective January 1, 1998; previously amended and relettered effective July 1, 2002.)

(d) Order of the court (§ 319, 42 U.S.C., § 600 et seq.)

If the court orders the child detained, the court must order that temporary care and custody of the child be vested with the county welfare department pending disposition or further order of the court.

(Subd (d) adopted effective July 1, 2002.)

(e) Detention alternatives (§ 319)

The court may order the child detained in the approved home of a relative, an emergency shelter, another suitable licensed home or facility, a place exempt from licensure if specifically designated by the court, or the approved home of a nonrelative extended family member as defined in section 362.7.

(1) In determining the suitability of detention with a relative or a nonrelative extended family member, the court must consider the recommendations of the social worker based on the approval of the home of the relative or nonrelative extended family member, including the results of checks of criminal records and any prior reports of alleged child abuse.

(2) The court must order any parent and guardian present to disclose the names, residences (if known), and any identifying information of any maternal or paternal relatives of the child.

(Subd (e) amended effective January 1, 2007; adopted effective January 1, 1999; previously amended effective July 1, 2002.)

Rule 5.678 amended and renumbered effective January 1, 2007; repealed and adopted as rule 1446 effective January 1, 1998; previously amended effective January 1, 1999, and July 1, 2002.

Ref.: Cal. Fms Pl. & Pr., Ch. 328, "Juvenile Courts: Dependency Proceedings"; W. Cal. Sum., 10 "Parent and Child" §§444, 599, 607.

Rule 5.680.   Detention rehearings; prima facie hearings

(a) No parent or guardian present and not noticed (§ 321)

If the court orders the child detained at the detention hearing and no parent or guardian is present and no parent or guardian has received actual notice of the detention hearing, a parent or guardian may file an affidavit alleging the failure of notice and requesting a detention rehearing. The clerk must set the rehearing for a time within 24 hours of the filing of the affidavit, excluding noncourt days. At the rehearing the court must proceed under rules 5.670–5.678.

(Subd (a) amended effective January 1, 2007.)

(b) Parent or guardian noticed, not present (§ 321)

If the court determines that the parent or guardian received adequate notice of the detention hearing, and the parent or guardian fails to appear at the hearing, the request of the parent or guardian for a detention rehearing must be denied absent a finding that the failure to appear at the hearing was due to good cause.

(Subd (b) amended effective January 1, 2007.)

(c) Parent or guardian present; preparers available (§ 321)

If a parent or guardian has received notice of the detention hearing, is present at the hearing, and the preparers of any reports or other documents relied on by the court in its order detaining the child are present in court or otherwise available for cross-examination, the request for a detention rehearing must be denied.

(Subd (c) amended effective January 1, 2007.)

(d) Hearing for further evidence; prima facie case (§ 321)

If the court orders the child detained, and the child, a parent, a guardian, or counsel requests that evidence of the prima facie case be presented, the court must set a prima facie hearing for a time within 3 court days to consider evidence of the prima facie case or set the matter for jurisdiction hearing within 10 court days. If at the hearing petitioner fails to establish the prima facie case, the child must be released from custody.

(Subd (d) amended effective January 1, 2007.)

Rule 5.680 amended and renumbered effective January 1, 2007; repealed and adopted as rule 1447 effective January 1, 1998.

Ref.: Cal. Fms Pl. & Pr., Ch. 328, "Juvenile Courts: Dependency Proceedings"; W. Cal. Sum., 10 "Parent and Child" §§444, 606.

Article 2
Jurisdiction

Rule 5.682. Commencement of jurisdiction hearing— advisement of trial rights; admission, no contest, submission

Rule 5.684. Contested hearing on petition

Rule 5.686. Continuance pending disposition hearing

Rule 5.688. Failure to cooperate with services (§ 360(b))

Rule 5.682. Commencement of jurisdiction hearing—advisement of trial rights; admission, no contest, submission

(a) Petition read and explained (§ 353)

At the beginning of the jurisdiction hearing, the petition must be read to those present. On request of the child or the parent, guardian, or adult relative, the court must explain the meaning and contents of the petition and the nature of the hearing, its procedures, and the possible consequences.

(Subd (a) amended effective January 1, 2005.)

(b) Rights explained (§§ 341, 353, 361.1)

After giving the advisement required by rule 5.534, the court must advise the parent or guardian of the following rights:

(1) The right to a hearing by the court on the issues raised by the petition;

(2) The right to assert any privilege against self-incrimination;

(3) The right to confront and to cross-examine all witnesses called to testify;

(4) The right to use the process of the court to compel attendance of witnesses on behalf of the parent or guardian; and

(5) The right, if the child has been removed, to have the child returned to the parent or guardian within two working days after a finding by the court that the child does not come within the jurisdiction of the juvenile court under section 300, unless the parent or guardian and the child welfare agency agree that the child will be released on a later date.

(Subd (b) amended effective January 1, 2007; previously amended effective January 1, 2005.)

(c) Admission of allegations; prerequisites to acceptance

The court must then inquire whether the parent or guardian intends to admit or deny the allegations of the petition. If the parent or guardian neither admits nor denies the allegations, the court must state on the record that the parent or guardian does not admit the allegations. If the parent or guardian wishes to admit the allegations, the court must first find and state on the record that it is satisfied that the parent or guardian understands the nature of the allegations and the direct consequences of the admission, and understands and waives the rights in (b).

(Subd (c) amended effective January 1, 2007.)

(d) Parent or guardian must admit

An admission by the parent or guardian must be made personally by the parent or guardian.

(Subd (d) amended effective January 1, 2007.)

(e) Admission, no contest, submission

The parent or guardian may elect to admit the allegations of the petition, plead no contest, or submit the jurisdictional determination to the court based on the information provided to the court and waive further jurisdictional hearing. *Waiver of Rights—Juvenile Dependency* (form JV-190) may be completed by the parent or guardian and counsel and submitted to the court.

(Subd (e) amended effective January 1, 2007.)

(f) Findings of court (§ 356)

After admission, plea of no contest, or submission, the court must make the following findings noted in the order of the court:

(1) Notice has been given as required by law;

(2) The birthdate and county of residence of the child;

(3) The parent or guardian has knowingly and intelligently waived the right to a trial on the issues by the court, the right to assert the privilege against self-incrimination, and the right to confront and to cross-examine adverse witnesses and to use the process of the court to compel attendance of witnesses on the parent or guardian's behalf;

(4) The parent or guardian understands the nature of the conduct alleged in the petition and the possible consequences of an admission, plea of no contest, or submission;

(5) The admission, plea of no contest, or submission by the parent or guardian is freely and voluntarily made;

(6) There is a factual basis for the parent or guardian's admission;

(7) Those allegations of the petition as admitted are true as alleged; and

(8) The child is described under one or more specific subdivisions of section 300.

(Subd (f) amended effective January 1, 2007.)

(g) Disposition

After accepting an admission, plea of no contest, or submission, the court must proceed to a disposition hearing under rules 5.686 and 5.690.

(Subd (g) amended effective January 1, 2007.)

Rule 5.682 amended and renumbered effective January 1, 2007; adopted as rule 1449 effective January 1, 1991; previously amended effective January 1, 2005.

Ref.: Cal. Fms Pl. & Pr., Ch. 328, "Juvenile Courts: Dependency Proceedings"; W. Cal. Sum., 10 "Parent and Child" §§4, 444, 567, 576, 578, 604, 613, 614.

Rule 5.684. Contested hearing on petition

(a) Contested jurisdiction hearing (§ 355)

If the parent or guardian denies the allegations of the petition, the court must hold a contested hearing and determine whether the allegations in the petition are true.

(Subd (a) amended effective January 1, 2007.)

(b) Admissibility of evidence—general (§§ 355, 355.1)

Except as provided in section 355.1 and (c), (d), and (e), the admission and exclusion of evidence must be in accordance with the Evidence Code as it applies to civil cases.

(Subd (b) amended effective January 1, 2007; previously amended effective July 1, 1997.)

(c) Reports

A social study, with hearsay evidence contained in it, is admissible and is sufficient to support a finding that the child is described by section 300.

(1) The social study must be provided to all parties and their counsel by the county welfare department within a reasonable time before the hearing.

(2) The preparer of the report must be made available for cross-examination on the request of any party. The preparer may be on telephone standby if the preparer can be present in court within a reasonable time.

(Subd (c) amended effective January 1, 2007; previously amended effective July 1, 1997.)

(d) Hearsay in the report (§ 355)

If a party makes an objection with reasonable specificity to particular hearsay in the report and provides petitioner a reasonable period to meet the objection, that evidence must not be sufficient in and of itself to support a jurisdictional finding, unless:

(1) The hearsay is admissible under any statutory or judicial hearsay exception;

(2) The hearsay declarant is a child under 12 years of age who is the subject of the petition, unless the objecting party establishes that the statement was produced by fraud, deceit, or undue influence and is therefore unreliable;

(3) The hearsay declarant is a peace officer, a health practitioner, a social worker, or a teacher and the statement would be admissible if the declarant were testifying in court; or

(4) The hearsay declarant is available for cross-examination.

(Subd (d) amended effective January 1, 2007; previously amended effective July 1, 1997.)

(e) Inapplicable privileges (Evid. Code, §§ 972, 986)

The privilege not to testify or to be called as a witness against a spouse or domestic partner, and the confidential marital communication privilege, does not apply to dependency proceedings.

(Subd (e) amended effective January 1, 2007; previously amended effective July 1, 1997.)

(f) Findings of court—allegations true (§ 356)

If the court determines by a preponderance of the evidence that the allegations of the petition are true, the court must make findings on each of the following, noted in the minutes:

(1) Notice has been given as required by law;

(2) The birthdate and county of residence of the child;

(3) The allegations of the petition are true; and

(4) The child is described under one or more specific subdivisions of section 300.

(Subd (f) amended effective January 1, 2007.)

(g) Disposition (§ 356)

After making the findings in (f), the court must proceed to a disposition hearing under rules 5.686 and 5.690.

(Subd (g) amended effective January 1, 2007; previously amended effective July 1, 1997.)

(h) Findings of court—allegations not proved (§§ 356, 361.1)

If the court determines that the allegations of the petition have not been proved by a preponderance of the evidence, the court must dismiss the petition and terminate any detention orders relating to the petition. The court must order that the child be returned to the physical custody of the parent or guardian immediately but, in any event, not more than two working days following the date of that finding, unless the parent or guardian and the agency with custody of the child agree to a later date for the child's release. The court must make the following findings, noted in the order of the court:

(1) Notice has been given as required by law;

(2) The birthdate and county of residence of the child; and

(3) The allegations of the petition are not proved.

(Subd (h) amended effective January 1, 2007; previously amended effective July 1, 1997, and January 1, 2005.)

Rule 5.684 amended and renumbered effective January 1, 2007; adopted as rule 1450 effective January 1, 1991; previously amended effective July 1, 1997, and January 1, 2005.

Ref.: Cal. Fms Pl. & Pr., Ch. 328, "Juvenile Courts: Dependency Proceedings"; W. Cal. Sum., 10 "Parent and Child" §§444, 615, 617, 618, 620, 622.

Rule 5.686. Continuance pending disposition hearing

(a) Continuance pending disposition hearing (§ 358)

Except as provided in (b), the court may continue the disposition hearing to a date not to exceed 10 court days if the child is detained or, if the child is not detained, to a date not to exceed 30 calendar days from the date of the finding under section 356. The court may for good cause continue the hearing for an additional 15 calendar days if the child is not detained.

(Subd (a) amended effective January 1, 2007.)

(b) Continuance if nonreunification is requested

If petitioner alleges that section 361.5(b) is applicable, the court must continue the proceedings not more than 30 calendar days. The court must order the petitioner to notify each parent or guardian of the contents of section 361.5(b) and must inform each parent that if reunification is not ordered at the disposition hearing, a section 366.26 implementation hearing will be held and parental rights may be terminated.

(Subd (b) amended effective January 1, 2007.)

(c) Detention pending continued hearing (§ 358)

The court in its discretion may order release or detention of the child during the continuance.

Rule 5.686 amended and renumbered effective January 1, 2007; adopted as rule 1451 effective January 1, 1990.

Ref.: Cal. Fms Pl. & Pr., Ch. 328, "Juvenile Courts: Dependency Proceedings"; W. Cal. Sum., 10 "Parent and Child" §§444, 604, 614, 622, 623.

Rule 5.688.   Failure to cooperate with services (§ 360(b))

(a) Petition

If the court has ordered services under section 360(b), and within the time period consistent with section 301 the family is unable or unwilling to cooperate with the services provided, a petition may be filed as provided in section 360(c).

(Subd (a) amended effective July 1, 2000.)

(b) Order

At the hearing on the petition the court must dismiss the petition or order a new disposition hearing to be conducted under rule 5.690.

(Subd (b) amended effective January 1, 2007.)

Rule 5.688 amended and renumbered effective January 1, 2007; adopted as rule 1452 effective January 1, 1990; previously amended effective July 1, 2000.

Ref.: Cal. Fms Pl. & Pr., Ch. 328, "Juvenile Courts: Dependency Proceedings"; W. Cal. Sum., 10 "Parent and Child" §§444, 627.

Article 3
Disposition

Rule 5.690. General conduct of disposition hearing
Rule 5.695. Orders of the court
Rule 5.700. Order determining custody (§§ 304, 361.2, 362.4)
Rule 5.705. Setting a hearing under section 366.26

Rule 5.690.   General conduct of disposition hearing

(a) Social study (§§ 280, 358, 358.1, 360)

The petitioner must prepare a social study of the child, including all matters relevant to disposition, and a recommendation for disposition.

(1) The petitioner must comply with the following when preparing the social study:

(A) If petitioner recommends that the court appoint a legal guardian, petitioner must prepare an assessment under section 360(a), to be included in the social study report prepared for disposition or in a separate document.

(B) If petitioner recommends removal of the child from the home, the social study must include:

(i) A discussion of the reasonable efforts made to prevent or eliminate removal and a recommended plan for reuniting the child with the family, including a plan for visitation;

(ii) A plan for achieving legal permanence for the child if efforts to reunify fail; and

(iii) A statement that each parent has been advised of the option to participate in adoption planning and to voluntarily relinquish the child if an adoption agency is willing to accept the relinquishment, and the parent's response.

(C) If petitioner alleges that section 361.5(b) applies, the social study must state why reunification services should not be provided.

(D) All other relevant requirements of sections 358 and 358.1.

(2) The petitioner must submit the social study and copies of it to the clerk at least 48 hours before the disposition hearing is set to begin, and the clerk must make the copies available to the parties and attorneys. A continuance within statutory time limits must be granted on the request of a party who has not been furnished a copy of the social study in accordance with this rule.

(Subd (a) amended effective January 1, 2007; previously amended effective July 1, 1995, and January 1, 2000.)

(b) Evidence considered (§§ 358, 360)

The court must receive in evidence and consider the social study, a guardianship assessment, the report of any CASA volunteer, the case plan, and any relevant evidence offered by petitioner, the child, or the parent or guardian. The court may require production of other relevant evidence on its own motion. In the order of disposition, the court must state that the social study and the study or evaluation by the CASA volunteer, if any, have been read and considered by the court.

(Subd (b) amended effective January 1, 2007; previously amended effective July 1, 1995.)

(c) Case plan (§ 16501.1)

Whenever child welfare services are provided, the social worker must prepare a case plan.

(1) A written case plan [1] **must** be completed and filed with the court by the date of disposition or within 60 calendar days of initial removal or of the in-person response required under section 16501(f) if the child has not been removed from his or her home, whichever occurs first.

(2) The court must consider the case plan and must find as follows:

(A) The social worker solicited and integrated into the case plan the input of the child, the child's family, the child's identified Indian tribe, and other interested parties; or

(B) The social worker did not solicit and integrate into the case plan the input of the child, the child's family, the child's identified Indian tribe, and other interested parties. If the court finds that the social worker did not solicit and integrate into the case plan the input of the child, the child's family, the child's identified Indian tribe, and other interested parties, the court must order that the social worker solicit and integrate into the case plan the input of the child, the child's family, the child's identified Indian tribe, and other interested parties, unless the court finds that each of these participants was unable, unavailable, or unwilling to participate.

(3) For a child 12 years of age or older and in a permanent placement, the court must consider the case plan and must find as follows:

(A) The child was given the opportunity to review the case plan, sign it, and receive a copy; or

(B) The child was not given the opportunity to review the case plan, sign it, and receive a copy. If the court makes such a finding, the court must order the agency to give the child the opportunity to review the case plan, sign it, and receive a copy.

(Subd (c) amended effective January 1, 2009; adopted effective January 1, 2007.)

Rule 5.690(c). 2008 Deletes. [1] much

Rule 5.690 amended effective January 1, 2009; adopted as rule 1455 effective January 1, 1991; previously amended effective July 1, 1995, and January 1, 2000; previously amended and renumbered effective January 1, 2007.

Ref.: Cal. Fms Pl. & Pr., Ch. 328, "Juvenile Courts: Dependency Proceedings"; W. Cal. Sum., 10 "Parent and Child" §§334, 444, 614, 622, 624–626, 664.

Rule 5.695. Orders of the court

(a) Orders of the court (§§ 245.5, 358, 360, 361, 361.2, 390)

At the disposition hearing, the court may:

(1) Dismiss the petition with specific reasons stated in the minutes;

(2) Place the child under a program of supervision as provided in section 301 and order that services be provided;

(3) Appoint a legal guardian for the child;

(4) Declare dependency and appoint a legal guardian for the child;

(5) Declare dependency, permit the child to remain at home, and order that services be provided;

(6) Declare dependency, permit the child to remain at home, limit the control to be exercised by the parent or guardian, and order that services be provided; or

(7) Declare dependency, remove physical custody from the parent or guardian, and

(A) After stating on the record or in writing the factual basis for the order, order custody to the noncustodial parent, terminate jurisdiction, and direct that *Custody Order—Juvenile—Final Judgment* (form JV-200) be prepared and filed under rule 5.700;

(B) After stating on the record or in writing the factual basis for the order, order custody to the noncustodial parent with services to one or both parents; or

(C) Make a placement order and consider granting specific visitation rights to the child's grandparents.

(Subd (a) amended effective January 1, 2007; previously amended effective July 1, 1995.)

(b) Appointment of a legal guardian (§ 360)

(1) At the disposition hearing, the court may appoint a legal guardian for the child if:

(A) The parent has advised the court that the parent does not wish to receive family maintenance services or family reunification services;

(B) The parent has executed and submitted *Waiver of Reunification Services (Juvenile Dependency)* (form JV-195);

(C) The court finds that the parent, and the child if of sufficient age and comprehension, knowingly and voluntarily waive their rights to reunification services and agree to the appointment of the legal guardian; and

(D) The court finds that the appointment of the legal guardian is in the best interest of the child.

(2) If the court appoints a legal guardian, it must:

(A) State on the record or in the minutes that it has read and considered the assessment;

(B) State on the record or in the minutes its findings and the factual bases for them;

(C) Advise the parent that no reunification services will be offered or provided;

(D) Make any appropriate orders regarding visitation between the child and the parent or other relative, including any sibling; and

(E) Order the clerk to issue letters of guardianship, which are not subject to the confidential protections of juvenile court documents as described in section 827.

(3) The court may appoint a legal guardian without declaring the child a dependent of the court. If dependency is declared, a six-month review hearing must be set.

(Subd (b) amended effective January 1, 2007; adopted effective July 1, 1995; previously amended effective July 1, 1999, and July 1, 2002.)

(c) Limitations on parental control (§§ 245.5, 319, 361, 362; Gov. Code, § 7579.5)

(1) If a child is declared a dependent, the court may clearly and specifically limit the control over the child by a parent or guardian.

(2) If the court orders that a parent or guardian retain physical custody of the child subject to court-ordered supervision, the parent or guardian must be ordered to participate in child welfare services or services provided by an appropriate agency designated by the court.

(3) The court must consider whether it is necessary to limit the right of the parent or guardian to make educational decisions for the child. If the court limits the right, it must follow the procedures stated in rule 5.650.

(Subd (c) amended effective January 1, 2008; adopted as subd (b) effective January 1, 1991; relettered effective July 1, 1995; previously amended effective July 1, 2002, January 1, 2004, and January 1, 2007.)

(d) Removal of custody—required findings (§ 361)

The court may not order a dependent removed from the physical custody of a parent or guardian with whom the child resided at the time the petition was filed, unless the court finds by clear and convincing evidence any of the following:

(1) There is a substantial danger to the physical health, safety, protection, or physical or emotional well-being of the child, or will be if the child is returned home, and there is no reasonable alternative means to protect that child;

(2) The parent or guardian is unwilling to have physical custody of the child and has been notified that if the child remains out of the parent's or guardian's physical custody for the period specified in section 366.26, the child may be declared permanently free of his or her custody and control;

(3) The child is suffering severe emotional damage, as indicated by extreme anxiety, depression, withdrawal, or untoward aggressive behavior toward self or others, and no reasonable alternative means to protect the child's emotional health exists;

(4) The child has been sexually abused by a parent or guardian or member of the household or other person

known to his or her parent and there is no reasonable alternative means to protect the child or the child does not wish to return to the parent or guardian; or

(5) The child has been left without any provisions for his or her support and there is no parent or guardian available to maintain or provide for the care, custody, and control of the child.

(Subd (d) amended effective January 1, 2007; adopted as subd (c) effective January 1, 1991; relettered effective July 1, 1995; previously amended effective July 1, 1997, July 1, 1999, and July 1, 2002.)

(e) Reasonable efforts finding

The court must consider whether reasonable efforts to prevent or eliminate the need for removal have been made and make one of the following findings:

(1) Reasonable efforts have been made; or

(2) Reasonable efforts have not been made.

(Subd (e) amended effective January 1, 2006; adopted as subd (d) effective January 1, 1991; relettered effective July 1, 1995; amended effective July 1, 2002.)

(f) Provision of reunification services (§ 361.5)

(1) Except as provided in (5), if a child is removed from the custody of a parent or guardian, the court must order the county welfare department to provide child welfare services to the child and the child's mother and statutorily presumed father, or the child's legal guardian, to facilitate reunification of the family within 12 months of the date the child entered foster care if the child was three years or older at the time of the initial removal, or within 6 months of the date the child entered foster care if the child was under three at the time of initial removal. The court must inform the parent or guardian of a child who was under three when initially removed that failure to participate regularly and make substantive progress in court-ordered treatment programs may result in the termination of reunification efforts after 6 months from the date the child entered foster care.

(2) If a child is a member of a sibling group removed from parental custody at the same time, and one of the sibling group was under three at the time of the initial removal, reunification services for one or all members of the sibling group may be limited to 6 months from the date the child entered foster care. The court must inform the parent or guardian of a child who is a member of such a sibling group that failure to participate regularly and make substantive progress in court-ordered treatment programs may result in termination of reunification efforts for one or more members of the sibling group.

(3) On a finding and declaration of paternity by the juvenile court or proof of a prior declaration of paternity by any court of competent jurisdiction, the juvenile court may order services for the child and the biological father, if the court determines that such services will benefit the child.

(4) If a child is removed from the custody of a parent or guardian, and reunification services are ordered, the court must order visitation between the child and the parent or guardian for whom services are ordered. Visits are to be as frequent as possible, consistent with the well-being of the child.

(5) Reunification services must not be provided when the parent has voluntarily relinquished the child and the relinquishment has been filed with the State Department of Social Services, or if the court has appointed a guardian under section 360. Reunification services need not be provided to a mother, statutorily presumed father, or guardian if the court finds, by clear and convincing evidence, any of the following:

(A) The whereabouts of the parent or guardian are unknown. This finding must be supported by a declaration or by proof that a reasonably diligent search has failed to locate the parent. Posting or publishing notice is not required.

(B) The parent or guardian is suffering from a mental disability described in chapter 2 (commencing with section 7820) of part 4 of division 12 of the Family Code that renders the parent incapable of using those services.

(C) The child had been previously declared a dependent under any subdivision of section 300 as a result of physical or sexual abuse; following that adjudication the child had been removed from the custody of the parent or guardian under section 361; the child has been returned to the custody of the parent or guardian from whom the child had been taken originally; and the child is being removed under section 361 because of additional physical or sexual abuse.

(D) The parent or guardian of the child has caused the death of another child through abuse or neglect.

(E) The child was brought within the jurisdiction of the court under (e) of section 300 because of the conduct of that parent or guardian.

(F) The child is a dependent as a result of the determination that the child, a sibling, or a half-sibling suffered severe sexual abuse, as defined in section 361.5(b)(6), by the parent or guardian or that the parent or guardian inflicted severe physical harm, as defined in section 361.5(b)(6), on the child, a sibling, or a half-sibling, and the court finds that attempts to reunify would not benefit the child. The court must specify on the record the basis for the finding that the child suffered severe sexual abuse or the infliction of severe physical harm.

(G) The parent or guardian is not receiving reunification services for a sibling or half-sibling of the child, for reasons under (C), (E), or (F).

(H) The child was conceived as a result of the parent having committed an offense listed in Penal Code section 288 or 288.5, or by an act described by either section but committed outside California.

(I) The court has found that the child is described by (g) of section 300, that the child was willfully abandoned by the parent or guardian, and that the abandonment constituted serious danger to the child as defined in section 361.5(b)(9).

(J) The court has terminated reunification services for a sibling or half-sibling of the child because the parent failed to reunify with the sibling or half-sibling, and the parent or guardian has not made a reasonable effort to treat the problems that led to the removal of the sibling or half-sibling from that parent or guardian.

(K) The parental rights of a parent over any sibling or half-sibling of the child have been terminated, and the parent has not subsequently made a reasonable effort to treat the problem that led to the removal of the sibling or half-sibling.

(L) The parent or guardian has been convicted of a violent felony as defined in Penal Code section 667.5(c).

(M) The parent or guardian has a history of extensive, abusive, and chronic use of alcohol or other drugs and has not sought or participated in treatment during the three years immediately prior to the filing of the petition under section 300, or has failed, on at least two prior occasions, to comply with an available and accessible treatment program described in the case plan required by section 358.1, and the removal of the child is based in whole or in part on the risk to the child presented by the use of alcohol or other drugs.

(N) The parent or guardian, who must be represented by counsel, has advised the court through the execution and submission of *Waiver of Reunification Services (Juvenile Dependency)* (form JV-195) that that parent or guardian does not wish to receive family maintenance or reunification services and does not wish the child returned or placed in the custody of that parent or guardian. The court may accept the waiver only on a finding on the record that the parent or guardian has knowingly and intelligently waived the right to services.

(O) On at least one occasion, the parent or guardian has abducted the child or a sibling or half-sibling from placement and has refused to disclose the abducted child's whereabouts or has refused to return custody of the abducted child to the placement or to the social worker.

(6) In deciding whether to order reunification in any case in which petitioner alleges that section 361.5(b) applies, the court must consider the report prepared by petitioner, which must discuss the factors contained in section 361.5(c).

(7) If the petitioner alleges that section 361.5(c) applies, the report prepared for disposition must address the issue of reunification services. At the disposition hearing, the court must consider the factors stated in section 361.5.

(8) If the court finds under (5)(A) that the whereabouts of the parent or guardian are unknown and that a diligent search has failed to locate the parent or guardian, the court may not order reunification services and must set the matter for a 6-month review hearing. If the parent or guardian is located prior to the 6-month review and requests reunification services, the welfare department must seek a modification of the disposition orders. The time limits for reunification services must be calculated from the date of the initial removal, and not from the date the parent is located or services are ordered.

(9) If the court finds that allegations under (5)(B) are proved, the court must nevertheless order reunification services unless evidence by mental health professionals establishes by clear and convincing evidence that the parent is unlikely to be able to care for the child within the next 12 months.

(10) If the court finds that the allegations under (5)(C), (D), (F), (G), (H), (I), (J), (K), (L), (M), (N), or (O) have been proved, the court may not order reunification services unless the party seeking the order for services proves by clear and convincing evidence that reunification is in the best interest of the child. If (5)(F) is found to apply, the court must consider the factors in section 361.5(h) in determining whether the child will benefit from services and must specify on the record the factual findings on which it based its determination that the child will not benefit.

(11) If the court finds that the allegations under (5)(E) have been proved, the court may not order reunification services unless it finds, based on consideration of factors in section 361.5(b) and (c), that services are likely to prevent reabuse or continued neglect or that failure to attempt reunification will be detrimental to the child.

(12) If the mother, statutorily presumed father, or guardian is institutionalized or incarcerated, the court must order reunification services unless it finds by clear and convincing evidence that the services would be detrimental to the child, with consideration of the factors in section 361.5(e). The court may order reunification services with an institutionalized or incarcerated biological father whose paternity has been declared by the juvenile court or another court of competent jurisdiction, if the court determines that such services would benefit the child, with consideration of the factors in section 361.5(e).

(13) If, with the exception of (5)(A), the court orders no reunification services for every parent otherwise eligible for such services under (f)(1) and (2), the court must conduct a hearing under section 366.26 within 120 days.

(14) A judgment, order, or decree setting a hearing under section 366.26 is not an immediately appealable order. Review may be sought only by filing *Petition for Extraordinary Writ (California Rules of Court, Rules 8.452, 8.456)* (form JV-825) or other petition for extraordinary writ. If a party wishes to preserve any right to review on appeal of the findings and orders made under this rule, the party must seek an extraordinary writ under rules 8.450, 8.452, and 5.600.

(15) A judgment, order, or decree setting a hearing under section 366.26 may be reviewed on appeal following the order of the 366.26 hearing only if the following have occurred:

(A) An extraordinary writ was sought by the timely filing of *Petition for Extraordinary Writ (California Rules of Court, Rules 8.452, 8.456)* (form JV-825) or other petition for extraordinary writ; and

(B) The petition for extraordinary writ was summarily denied or otherwise not decided on the merits.

(16) Review on appeal of the order setting a hearing under section 366.26 is limited to issues raised in a previous petition for extraordinary writ that were supported by an adequate record.

(17) Failure to file a petition for extraordinary writ review within the period specified by rules 8.450, 8.452, and 5.600 to substantively address the issues challenged, or to support the challenge by an adequate record, precludes subsequent review on appeal of the findings and orders made under this rule.

(18) When the court orders a hearing under section 366.26, the court must advise orally all parties present, and by first-class mail for parties not present, that if the party wishes to preserve any right to review on appeal of the order setting the hearing under section 366.26, the party must seek an extraordinary writ by filing a *Notice of Intent to File Writ Petition and Request for Record (California Rules of Court, Rule 8.450)* (form JV-820) or other notice of intent to file a writ petition and request for record and a *Petition for Extraordinary Writ (California Rules of Court, Rules 8.452, 8.456)* (form JV-825) or other petition for extraordinary writ.

(A) Within 24 hours of the hearing, notice by first-class mail must be provided by the clerk of the court to the last known address of any party who is not present when the court orders the hearing under section 366.26.

(B) Copies of *Petition for Extraordinary Writ (California Rules of Court, Rules 8.452, 8.456)* (form JV-825) and *Notice of Intent to File Writ Petition and Request for Record (California Rules of Court, Rule 8.450)* (form JV-820) must be available in the courtroom and must accompany all mailed notices informing the parties of their rights.

(Subd (f) amended effective January 1, 2007; adopted as subd (e) effective January 1, 1991; relettered effective July 1, 1995; previously amended effective January 1, 1993, July 1, 1993, January 1, 1994, January 1, 1995, January 1, 1996, July 1, 1997, January 1, 1999, July 1, 1999, January 1, 2001, July 1, 2001, and July 1, 2002.)

(g) Information regarding termination of parent-child relationship (§§ 361, 361.5)

If a child is removed from the physical custody of the parent or guardian under either section 361 or 361.5, the court must:

(1) State the facts on which the decision is based; and

(2) Notify the parents that their parental rights may be terminated if custody is not returned within 6 or 12 months of the specific date the child is determined to have entered foster care, whichever time limit is applicable.

(Subd (g) amended effective July 1, 2002; adopted as subd (f) effective January 1, 1991; relettered effective July 1, 1995; previously amended effective January 1, 2001.)

(h) Setting 6-month review (§§ 361.5, 366)

Review of the status of every dependent child must be performed within 6 months after the date of the original disposition order, and no later than 6 months after the date the child is determined to have entered foster care; the review must be scheduled on the appearance calendar. The court must advise the dependent child of the child's right to petition for modifications of court orders as required in section 353.1.

(Subd (h) amended effective January 1, 2007; adopted as subd (g) effective January 1, 1991; relettered effective July 1, 1995; previously amended effective January 1, 1995, January 1, 2001, and July 1, 2002.)

(i) Fifteen-day reviews (§ 367)

If a child is detained pending the execution of the disposition order, the court must review the case at least every 15 calendar days to determine whether the delay is reasonable. During each review the court must inquire about the action taken by the probation or welfare department to carry out the court's order, the reasons for the delay, and the effect of the delay on the child.

(Subd (i) amended effective January 1, 2007; adopted as subd (h) effective January 1, 1991; relettered effective July 1, 1995; previously amended effective July 1, 2002.)

(j) Setting a hearing under section 366.26

At the disposition hearing, the court may not set a hearing under section 366.26 to consider termination of the rights of only one parent unless that parent is the only surviving parent, or the rights of the other parent have been terminated by a California court of competent jurisdiction or by a court of competent jurisdiction of another state under the statutes of that state, or the other parent has relinquished custody of the child to the county welfare department.

(Subd (j) amended effective July 1, 2002; adopted effective July 1, 1997.)

Rule 5.695 amended effective January 1, 2008; adopted as rule 1456 effective January 1, 1991; previously amended effective January 1, 1993, July 1, 1993, January 1, 1994, January 1, 1995, July 1, 1995, January 1, 1996, January 1, 1997, July 1, 1997, January 1, 1999, July 1, 1999, January 1, 2001, July 1, 2001, July 1, 2002, January 1, 2004, and January 1, 2006; previously amended and renumbered effective January 1, 2007.

Ref.: Cal. Fms Pl. & Pr., Ch. 328, "Juvenile Courts: Dependency Proceedings"; W. Cal. Sum., 10 "Parent and Child" §§334, 444, 627–631, 633, 637, 641, 642, 644, 646–652, 664, 673, 695, 717.

Rule 5.700. Order determining custody (§§ 304, 361.2, 362.4)

(a) Order determining custody—termination of jurisdiction

If the juvenile court orders custody to a parent and terminates jurisdiction, the court may make orders for visitation with the other parent. The court may also issue orders to either parent enjoining any action specified in Family Code section 2045.

(1) *Modification of existing custody orders—new case filings*

The order of the juvenile court must be filed in an existing nullity, dissolution, legal guardianship, or paternity proceeding. If no custody proceeding is filed or pending, the order may be used as the sole basis to open a file.

(2) *Preparation and transmission of order*

The order must be prepared on *Custody Order—Juvenile—Final Judgment* (form JV-200). The court may direct the parent, parent's attorney, county counsel, or the clerk to:

(A) Prepare the order for the court's signature; and

(B) Transmit the order within 10 calendar days after the order is signed to the superior court of the county where a custody proceeding has already been commenced or, if none, to the superior court of the county in which the parent who has been given custody resides.

(3) *Procedures for filing order—receiving court*

After receipt of the juvenile court custody order, the superior court clerk of the receiving county must immediately file the juvenile court order in the existing proceeding or immediately open a file, without a filing fee, and assign a case number.

(4) *Endorsed filed copy—clerk's certificate of mailing*

Within 15 court days after receiving the order, the clerk of the receiving court must send by first-class mail an endorsed filed copy of the order showing the case number of the receiving court to (1) the persons whose names and addresses are listed on the order, and (2) the originating juvenile court, with a completed clerk's certificate of mailing, for inclusion in the child's file.

(Subd (a) amended effective January 1, 2007.)

(b) Order determining custody—continuation of jurisdiction

If the court orders custody to a parent subject to the continuing jurisdiction of the court, with services to one or both parents, the court may direct the order be prepared and filed in the same manner as described in (a).

(Subd (b) amended effective January 1, 2007.)

Rule 5.700 amended and renumbered effective January 1, 2007; adopted as rule 1457 effective January 1, 1990; previously amended effective January 1, 1994, and January 1, 2001.

Ref.: Cal. Fms Pl. & Pr., Ch. 328, "Juvenile Courts: Dependency Proceedings"; W. Cal. Sum., 10 "Parent and Child" §§370, 444, 627, 637, 653, 676, 678, 679.

Rule 5.705. Setting a hearing under section 366.26

At a disposition hearing, a review hearing, or at any other hearing regarding a dependent child, the court must not set a hearing under section 366.26 to consider termination of the rights of only one parent unless that parent is the only surviving parent, or the rights of the other parent have been terminated by a California court of competent jurisdiction or by a court of competent jurisdiction of another state under the statutes of that state, or the other parent has relinquished custody of the child to the county welfare department.

Rule 5.705 amended and renumbered effective January 1, 2007; adopted as rule 1459 effective July 1, 1990; previously amended effective January 1, 1994, and July 1, 1997.

Ref.: W. Cal. Sum., 10 "Parent and Child" §§444, 689.

Article 4
Reviews, Permanent Planning

Rule 5.710. Six-month review hearing
Rule 5.715. Twelve-month review hearing
Rule 5.720. Eighteen-month review hearing
Rule 5.725. Selection of permanent plan (§§ 366.26, 727.31)
Rule 5.726. Prospective adoptive parent designation (§ 366.26(n))
Rule 5.727. Proposed removal (§ 366.26(n))
Rule 5.728. Emergency removal (§ 366.26(n))
Rule 5.730. Adoption
Rule 5.735. Legal guardianship
Rule 5.740. Hearings subsequent to a permanent plan (§§ 366.26, 366.3, 391)

Rule 5.710. Six-month review hearing

(a) Requirement for 6-month review (§§ 364, 366)

The case of a dependent child of the court must be set for review hearing as follows:

(1) If the child was removed from the custody of the parent or guardian under section 361 or 361.5, the review hearing must be held within 6 months after the date the child entered foster care, as defined in rule 5.502; or

(2) If the child remains in the custody of the parent or guardian, the review hearing must be held within 6 months after the date of the declaration of dependency and every 6 months thereafter as long as the child remains a dependent.

(Subd (a) amended effective January 1, 2007; previously amended effective January 1, 2001, and July 1, 2002.)

(b) Notice of hearing; service; contents (§§ 293, 366.21)

Not earlier than 30 nor less than 15 calendar days before the hearing date, the petitioner or the clerk must serve written notice, on *Notice of Review Hearing* (form JV-280), on all persons required to receive notice under section 293 and to any CASA volunteer. The notice must contain the information stated in section 293. The notice of hearing must be served by personal service or by first-class mail or certified mail addressed to the last known address of the person to be notified.

(Subd (b) amended effective January 1, 2007; repealed and adopted effective January 1, 1990; previously amended effective January 1, 1992, January 1, 1999, July 1, 1999, July 1, 2002, and January 1, 2006.)

(c) Report (§§ 366.1, 366.21)

Before the hearing, petitioner must investigate and file a report describing the services offered the family and progress made and, if relevant, the prognosis for return of the child to the parent or guardian.

(1) The report must contain:

(A) Recommendations for court orders and the reasons for those recommendations;

(B) A description of the efforts made to achieve legal permanence for the child if reunification efforts fail; and

(C) A factual discussion of each item listed in sections 366.1 and 366.21(c).

(2) At least 10 calendar days before the hearing, the petitioner must file the report and provide copies to the parent or guardian and his or her counsel, to counsel for the child, and to any CASA volunteer. The petitioner must provide a summary of the recommendations to any foster parents, relative caregivers, or certified foster parents who have been approved for adoption.

(Subd (c) amended effective January 1, 2007; previously amended effective January 1, 2000, July 1, 2002, January 1, 2005, and January 1, 2006.)

(d) Reports

The court must consider the report prepared by petitioner, the report of any CASA volunteer, the case plan submitted for this hearing, and any report submitted by the child's caregiver under section 366.21(d).

(Subd (d) amended effective January 1, 2007; adopted effective January 1, 1992; previously amended effective July 1, 2002, and January 1, 2005.)

(e) Determinations—burden of proof (§§ 366, 366.1, 366.21, 364)

(1) If the child has remained in the custody of the parent or guardian, the court must terminate its dependency jurisdiction unless the court finds that petitioner has established by a preponderance of the evidence that existing conditions would justify initial assumption of jurisdiction under section 300 or that such conditions are likely to exist if supervision is withdrawn. If dependency jurisdiction is continued, the court must order continued services and set a review hearing within 6 months.

(2) If the child has been removed from the custody of the parent or guardian, the court must order the child returned unless the court finds that petitioner has established by a preponderance of the evidence that return would create a substantial risk of detriment to the child. If the child has been removed from the custody of the parent or guardian, the court must consider whether reasonable services have been provided or offered. If the child is returned, the court may order the termination of dependency jurisdiction or order continued dependency services and set a review hearing within 6 months.

(A) The court must find that:

(i) Reasonable services have been offered or provided; or

(ii) Reasonable services have not been offered or provided.

(B) The following factors are not sufficient to support a finding that reasonable services have not been offered or provided:

(i) The child has been placed in a preadoptive home or with a family that is eligible to adopt the child;

(ii) The case plan includes services to achieve legal permanence for the child if reunification cannot be accomplished; or

(iii) Services to achieve legal permanence for the child if reunification efforts fail are being provided concurrently with reunification services.

(C) The court must enter additional findings as required by section 366(a)(1) and (2).

(3) Failure of the parent or guardian to regularly participate and make substantive progress in any court-ordered treatment program is prima facie evidence that continued supervision is necessary or that return would be detrimental.

(4) If the child has been placed out of state, the court must consider whether the placement continues to be the most appropriate placement for the child and in the child's best interest.

(5) The court must consider whether it is necessary to limit the right of the parent or guardian to make educational decisions for the child. If the court limits this right, it must appoint a responsible adult as the educational representative under rule 5.650 to make educational decisions for the child.

(6) The court must consider the case plan submitted for this hearing and must find as follows:

(A) The child was actively involved in the development of his or her own case plan and plan for permanent placement as age and developmentally appropriate; or

(B) The child was not actively involved in the development of his or her own case plan and plan for permanent placement. If the court makes such a finding, the court must order the agency to actively involve the child in the development of his or her own case plan and plan for permanent placement, unless the court finds that the child is unable, unavailable, or unwilling to participate; and

(C) Each parent was actively involved in the development of the case plan and plan for permanent placement; or

(D) Each parent was not actively involved in the development of the case plan and plan for permanent placement. If the court makes such a finding, the court must order the agency to actively involve each parent in the development of the case plan and plan for permanent placement, unless the court finds that each parent is unable, unavailable, or unwilling to participate.

(7) For a child 12 years of age or older and in a permanent placement, the court must consider the case plan submitted for this hearing and must find as follows:

(A) The child was given the opportunity to review the case plan, sign it, and receive a copy; or

(B) The child was not given the opportunity to review the case plan, sign it, and receive a copy. If the court makes such a finding, the court must order the agency to give the child the opportunity to review the case plan, sign it, and receive a copy.

(Subd (e) amended effective January 1, 2007; repealed and adopted as subd (d) effective January 1, 1990; relettered effective January 1, 1992; previously amended effective January 1, 1999, July 1, 1999, January 1, 2001, July 1, 2002, January 1, 2004, and January 1, 2005.)

(f) Conduct of hearing (§ 366.21)

If the court does not return custody of the child:

(1) The court may set a hearing under section 366.26 within 120 days if:

(A) The child was removed under section 300(g) and the court finds by clear and convincing evidence that the parent's whereabouts are still unknown;

(B) The court finds by clear and convincing evidence that the parent has not had contact with the child for 6 months;

(C) The court finds by clear and convincing evidence that the parent has been convicted of a felony indicating parental unfitness;

(D) The parent is deceased; or

(E) The child was under the age of three when initially removed and the court finds by clear and convincing evidence that the parent has failed to participate regularly and make substantive progress in any court-ordered treatment plan, unless the court finds a substantial probability that the child may be returned within 6 months or within 12 months of the date the child entered foster care, whichever is sooner, or that reasonable services have not been offered or provided.

In order to find a substantial probability of return within the applicable time period, the court must find all of the following:

(i) The parent or guardian has consistently and regularly contacted and visited the child;

(ii) The parent or guardian has made significant progress in resolving the problems that led to the removal of the child; and

(iii) The parent or guardian has demonstrated the capacity and ability to complete the objectives of the treatment plan and to provide for the child's safety, protection, physical and emotional health, and special needs.

(2) If the court orders a hearing under section 366.26:

(A) The court must direct that an assessment under section 366.21(i) be prepared;

(B) The court must order the termination of reunification services to the parent or legal guardian;

(C) The court must continue to permit the parent or legal guardian to visit the child, unless it finds that visitation would be detrimental to the child; and

(D) If the child is 10 years of age or older and is placed in out-of-home placement for six months or longer, the court:

(i) Must determine whether the agency has identified individuals, in addition to the child's siblings, who are important to the child and will maintain caring, permanent relationships with the child, consistent with the child's best interest;

(ii) Must determine whether the agency has made reasonable efforts to nurture and maintain the child's relationships with those individuals, consistent with he child's best interest; and

(iii) May make any appropriate order to ensure that those relationships are maintained.

(3) A judgment or an order setting a hearing under section 366.26 is not immediately appealable. Review may be sought only by filing *Petition for Extraordinary Writ (California Rules of Court, Rules 8.452, 8.456)* (form JV-825) or other petition for extraordinary writ. If a party wishes to preserve any right to review on appeal of the findings and orders made under this rule, the party must seek an extraordinary writ under rules 8.450, 8.452, and 5.600.

(4) A judgment, order, or decree setting a hearing under section 366.26 may be reviewed on appeal following the order of the 366.26 hearing only if the following have occurred:

(A) An extraordinary writ was sought by the timely filing of *Petition for Extraordinary Writ (California Rules of Court, Rules 8.452, 8.456)* (form JV-825) or other petition for extraordinary writ; and

(B) The petition for extraordinary writ was summarily denied or otherwise not decided on the merits.

(5) Review on appeal of the order setting a hearing under section 366.26 is limited to issues raised in a previous petition for extraordinary writ that were supported by an adequate record.

(6) Failure to file a petition for extraordinary writ review within the period specified by rules 8.450, 8.452, and 5.600, to substantively address the issues challenged, or to support the challenge by an adequate record, precludes subsequent review on appeal of the findings and orders made under this rule.

(7) When the court orders a hearing under section 366.26, the court must advise all parties that, to preserve any right to review on appeal of the order setting the hearing, the party must seek an extraordinary writ by filing:

(A) A notice of the party's intent to file a writ petition and a request for the record, which may be submitted on *Notice of Intent to File Writ Petition and Request for Record (California Rules of Court, Rule 8.450)* (form JV-820); and

(B) A petition for an extraordinary writ, which may be submitted on *Petition for Extraordinary Writ (California Rules of Court, Rules 8.452, 8.456)* (form JV-825).

(8) Within 24 hours of the review hearing, the clerk of the court must provide notice by first-class mail to the last known address of any party who is not present when the court orders the hearing under section 366.26. This notice must include the advisement required by (f)(7).

(9) Copies of *Petition for Extraordinary Writ (California Rules of Court, Rules 8.452, 8.456)* (form JV-825) and *Notice of Intent to File Writ Petition and Request for Record (California Rules of Court, Rule 8.450)* (form JV-820) must be available in the courtroom and must accompany all mailed notices informing the parties of their rights.

(10) If the court orders a hearing under section 366.26, the court must order that notice of the hearing under section 366.26 must not be provided to any of the following:

(A) A parent, presumed parent, or alleged parent who has relinquished the child for adoption and whose relin-quishment has been accepted and filed with notice under Family Code section 8700; or

(B) An alleged parent who has denied parentage and has completed section 1 of *Statement Regarding Parent-age (Juvenile)* (form JV-505).

(11) If the child is not returned and the court does not set a section 366.26 hearing, then the court must order that any reunification services previously ordered will continue to be offered to the parent or guardian, and the court may modify those services as appropriate. The court must set a date for the next review hearing no later than 12 months from the date the child entered foster care.

(Subd (f) amended effective January 1, 2007; repealed and adopted as subd (e) effective January 1, 1990; previously amended and relettered effective January 1, 1992; previously amended effective January 1, 1993, January 1, 1995, July 1, 1997, January 1, 1999, July 1, 1999, January 1, 2000, January 1, 2001, July 1, 2002, January 1, 2004, January 1, 2005, and January 1, 2006.)

(g) Siblings (§ 366.21)

In determining whether to set a hearing under section 366.26 for one or more members of a sibling group, the court may terminate or continue services for any or all members of the group, based on the following consider-ations and for reasons specified on the record:

(1) Whether the siblings were removed as a group;

(2) The closeness and strength of the sibling bond;

(3) The ages of the siblings;

(4) The appropriateness of maintaining the sibling group together;

(5) The detriment to the child if sibling ties are not maintained;

(6) The likelihood of finding a permanent home for the group;

(7) Whether the group is placed together in a preadoptive home, if there is a concurrent plan for permanency for all siblings in the same home;

(8) The wishes of each child; and

(9) The best interest of each member of the sibling group.

(Subd (g) adopted effective July 1, 2002.)

(h) Noncustodial parents

If the court has previously placed or at this hearing places the child with a noncustodial parent, the court may:

(1) Continue supervision and reunification services;

(2) After stating on the record or in writing the factual basis for the order, order custody to the noncustodial parent, continue supervision, and order family mainte-nance services; or

(3) After stating on the record or in writing the factual basis for the order, order custody to the noncustodial parent, terminate jurisdiction, and direct that *Custody Order—Juvenile—Final Judgment* (form JV-200) be pre-pared and filed under rule 5.700.

(Subd (h) amended effective January 1, 2007; repealed and adopted as subd (f) effective January 1, 1990; previously relet-tered as subd (g) effective January 1, 1992; previously amended effective July 1, 1995; relettered effective July 1, 2002.)

(i) Setting a hearing under section 366.26

At the 6-month review hearing, the court may not set a hearing under section 366.26 to consider termination of the rights of only one parent unless:

(1) That parent is the only surviving parent;

(2) The rights of the other parent have been terminated by a California court of competent jurisdiction or by a court of competent jurisdiction of another state under the statutes of that state; or

(3) The other parent has relinquished custody of the child to the county welfare department.

(Subd (i) amended effective January 1, 2007; adopted as subd (h) effective July 1, 1997; previously amended and relettered effective July 1, 2002.)

Rule 5.710 amended and renumbered effective January 1, 2007; adopted as rule 1460 effective January 1, 1990; previously amended effective January 1, 1992, January 1, 1993, January 1, 1995, July 1, 1995, July 1, 1997, January 1, 1999, July 1, 1999, January 1, 2000, January 1, 2001, July 1, 2002, January 1, 2004, January 1, 2005, and January 1, 2006.

Ref.: Cal. Fms Pl. & Pr., Ch. 328, "Juvenile Courts: Dependency Proceedings"; W. Cal. Sum., 10 "Parent and Child" §§444, 669–677, 681, 682, 701, 717.

Rule 5.715. Twelve-month review hearing

(a) Requirement for 12-month review; setting of hearing; notice (§§ 293, 366.21)

The case of any dependent child whom the court has removed from the custody of the parent or guardian must be set for review hearing within 12 months of the date the child entered foster care, as defined in rule 5.502, and no later than 18 months from the date of the initial removal. Notice of the hearing must be given as provided in section 293.

(Subd (a) amended effective January 1, 2007; previously amended effective January 1, 2001, January 1, 2004, and January 1, 2006.)

(b) Reports (§§ 366.1, 366.21)

Before the hearing the petitioner must prepare a report describing services offered to the family and progress made.

(1) The report must include:

(A) Recommendations for court orders and the reasons for those recommendations;

(B) A description of the efforts made to achieve legal permanence for the child if reunification efforts fail; and

(C) A factual discussion of each item listed in sections 366.1 and 366.21(c).

(2) At least 10 calendar days before the hearing, the petitioner must file the report, provide copies to the parent or guardian and his or her counsel, to counsel for the child, and to any CASA volunteer. The petitioner must provide a summary of the recommendations to any foster parents, relative caregivers, or certified foster parents who have been approved for adoption.

(Subd (b) amended effective January 1, 2007; adopted as subd (c) effective January 1, 2000; relettered effective January 1, 2001; previously amended effective January 1, 2004, January 1, 2005, and January 1, 2006.)

(c) Conduct of hearing

At the hearing, the court must state on the record that the court has read and considered the report of petitioner, the report of any CASA volunteer, the case plan submitted for this hearing, any report submitted by the child's caregiver under section 366.21(d), and any other evidence, and must proceed as follows:

(1) The court must order the child returned to the parent or guardian unless the court finds the petitioner has established, by a preponderance of the evidence, that return would create a substantial risk of detriment to the child. Failure of the parent or guardian to regularly participate and make substantive progress in a court-ordered treatment program is prima facie evidence that return would be detrimental.

(2) If the court has previously placed or at this hearing places the child with a noncustodial parent, the court may:

(A) Continue supervision and reunification services;

(B) After stating on the record or in writing the factual basis for the order, order custody to that parent, continue supervision, and order family maintenance services; or

(C) After stating on the record or in writing the factual basis for the order, order custody to the noncustodial parent, terminate jurisdiction, and direct that *Custody Order—Juvenile—Final Judgment* (form JV-200) be prepared and filed under rule 5.700.

(3) If the court does not order return of the child, the court must specify the factual basis for its finding of risk of detriment to the child. The court must order a permanent plan unless the court determines that there is a substantial probability of return within 18 months of the removal of the child. In order to find a substantial probability of return within the 18-month period, the court must find all of the following:

(A) The parent or guardian has consistently and regularly contacted and visited the child;

(B) The parent or guardian has made significant progress in resolving the problems that led to the removal of the child; and

(C) The parent or guardian has demonstrated the capacity and ability to complete the objectives of the treatment plan and to provide for the child's safety, protection, physical and emotional health, and special needs.

(4) If the child is not returned to the custody of the parent or guardian, the court must consider whether reasonable services have been provided or offered. The court must find that:

(A) Reasonable services have been offered or provided; or

(B) Reasonable services have not been offered or provided.

(5) The following factors are not sufficient to support a finding that reasonable services have not been offered or provided:

(A) The child has been placed in a preadoptive home or with a family that is eligible to adopt the child;

(B) The case plan includes services to achieve legal permanence for the child if reunification cannot be accomplished; or

(C) Services to achieve legal permanence for the child if reunification efforts fail are being provided concurrently with reunification services.

(6) The court must consider whether it is necessary to limit the right of the parent or guardian to make educational decisions for the child. If the court limits this right, it must appoint a responsible adult as the educational representative under rule 5.650 to make educational decisions for the child.

(7) The court must consider the case plan and must find as follows:

(A) The child was actively involved in the development of his or her own case plan and plan for permanent placement as age and developmentally appropriate; or

(B) The child was not actively involved in the development of his or her own case plan and plan for permanent placement as age and developmentally appropriate. If the court makes such a finding, the court must order the agency to involve the child in the development of his or her own case plan and plan for permanent placement, unless the court finds that the child is unable, unavailable, or unwilling to participate; and

(C) Each parent was actively involved in the development of the case plan and plan for permanent placement; or

(D) Each parent was not actively involved in the development of the case plan and plan for permanent placement. If the court makes such a finding, the court must order the agency to actively involve each parent in the development of the case plan and plan for permanent placement, unless the court finds that each parent is unable, unavailable, or unwilling to participate.

(8) For a child 12 years of age or older and in a permanent placement, the court must consider the case plan submitted for this hearing and must find as follows:

(A) The child was given the opportunity to review the case plan, sign it, and receive a copy; or

(B) The child was not given the opportunity to review the case plan, sign it, and receive a copy. If the court makes such a finding, the court must order the agency to give the child the opportunity to review the case plan, sign it, and receive a copy.

(Subd (c) amended effective January 1, 2007; repealed and adopted as subd (c)(2) effective January 1, 1990; previously amended and relettered as subd (c) effective July 1, 1999, as subd (d) effective January 1, 2002, and as subd (c) effective January 1, 2001; previously amended effective January 1, 1992, January 1, 1993, January 1, 1995, July 1, 1995, July 1, 1997, January 1, 1999, January 1, 2004, and January 1, 2005.)

(d) Determinations and orders

The court must proceed as follows:

(1) Continue the case for review hearing to a date not later than 18 months from the date of the initial removal if the court finds that there is a substantial probability of return within that time or that reasonable services have not been offered or provided. If the court continues the case for an 18-month review hearing, the court must inform the parent or guardian that if the child cannot be returned home by the next hearing, a proceeding under section 366.26 may be instituted; or

(2) Order that the child remain in foster care if it finds by clear and convincing evidence already presented that a section 366.26 hearing is not in the best interest of the child because the child is not a proper subject for adoption and has no one willing to accept legal guardianship.

(A) If the court orders that the child remain in foster care, it must identify the foster care setting by name and identify a specific permanency goal for the child. The court may order that the name and address of the foster home remain confidential.

(B) If the child is 10 years of age or older and is placed in out-of-home placement for six months or longer, the court:

(i) Must determine whether the agency has identified individuals, in addition to the child's siblings, who are important to the child and will maintain caring, permanent relationships with the child, consistent with the child's best interest;

(ii) Must determine whether the agency has made reasonable efforts to nurture and maintain the child's relationships with those individuals, consistent with the child's best interest; and

(iii) May make any appropriate order to ensure that those relationships are maintained; or

(3) If the court does not find that there is a substantial probability of return within 18 months of the initial removal, and finds that reasonable services have been offered or provided to the parent or guardian, the court must order a hearing under section 366.26 within 120 days.

(A) If the court orders a hearing under section 366.26, the court must also order termination of reunification services. Visitation must continue unless the court finds it would be detrimental to the child. The court must enter any other appropriate orders to enable the child to maintain relationships with other individuals who are important to the child, consistent with the child's best interest.

(B) If the court orders a hearing under section 366.26, the court must direct that an assessment be prepared as stated in section 366.21(i).

(C) A judgment or an order setting a hearing under section 366.26 is not immediately appealable. Review may be sought only by filing *Petition for Extraordinary Writ (California Rules of Court, Rules 8.452, 8.456)* (form JV-825) or other petition for extraordinary writ. If a party wishes to preserve any right to review on appeal of the findings and orders made under this rule, the party must seek an extraordinary writ under rules 8.450, 8.452, and 5.600.

(D) A judgment, order, or decree setting a hearing under section 366.26 may be reviewed on appeal following the order of the section 366.26 hearing only if the following have occurred:

(i) An extraordinary writ was sought by the timely filing of *Petition for Extraordinary Writ (California Rules of Court, Rules 8.452, 8.456)* (form JV-825) or other petition for extraordinary writ; and

(ii) The petition for extraordinary writ was summarily denied or otherwise not decided on the merits.

(E) Review on appeal of the order setting a hearing under section 366.26 is limited to issues raised in a previous petition for extraordinary writ that were supported by an adequate record.

(F) Failure to file a petition for extraordinary writ review within the period specified by rules 8.450, 8.452, and 5.600, to substantively address the issues challenged, or to support the challenge by an adequate record, precludes subsequent review on appeal of the findings and orders made under this rule.

(G) When the court orders a hearing under section 366.26, the court must advise all parties that, to preserve any right to review on appeal of the order setting the hearing, the party must seek an extraordinary writ by filing:

(i) A notice of intent to file a writ petition and a request for the record, which may be submitted on *Notice of Intent to File Writ Petition and Request for Record (California Rules of Court, Rule 8.450)* (form JV-820); and

(ii) A petition for an extraordinary writ, which may be submitted on *Petition for Extraordinary Writ (California Rules of Court, Rules 8.452, 8.456)* (form JV-825).

(H) Within 24 hours of the review hearing, the clerk of the court must provide notice by first-class mail to the last known address of any party who is not present when the court orders the hearing under section 366.26. This notice must include the advisement required by (d)(3)(G).

(I) Copies of *Petition for Extraordinary Writ (California Rules of Court, Rules 8.452, 8.456)* (form JV-825) and *Notice of Intent to File Writ Petition and Request for Record (California Rules of Court, Rule 8.450)* (form JV-820) must be available in the courtroom and must accompany all mailed notices informing the parties of their trial rights.

(J) If the court orders a hearing under section 366.26, the court must order that notice of the hearing under section 366.26 must not be provided to any of the following:

(i) A parent, presumed parent, or alleged parent who has relinquished the child for adoption and the relinquishment has been accepted and filed with notice under Family Code section 8700; or

(ii) An alleged parent who has denied parentage and has completed section 1 of *Statement Regarding Parentage (Juvenile)* (form JV-505).

(Subd (d) amended effective January 1, 2007; repealed and adopted as subd (c)(3) effective January 1, 1990; previously amended and relettered as subd (d) effective July 1, 1999, as subd (e) effective January 1, 2000, and as subd (d) effective January 1, 2001; previously amended effective January 1, 1992, January 1, 1993, January 1, 1995, July 1, 1995, July 1, 1997, January 1, 1999, January 1, 2004, January 1, 2005, and January 1, 2006.)

(e) Setting a hearing under section 366.26

At the 12-month review hearing, the court may not set a hearing under section 366.26 to consider termination of the rights of only one parent unless:

(1) That parent is the only surviving parent;

(2) The rights of the other parent have been terminated by a California court of competent jurisdiction or by a court of competent jurisdiction of another state under the statutes of that state; or

(3) The other parent has relinquished custody of the child to the county welfare department.

(Subd (e) amended effective January 1, 2004; adopted as subd (d) effective July 1, 1997; relettered as subd (e) effective July 1, 1999, as subd (f) effective January 1, 2000, and as subd (e) January 1, 2001.)

Rule 5.715 amended and renumbered effective January 1, 2007; adopted as rule 1461 effective January 1, 1990; previously amended effective January 1, 1992, January 1, 1993, January 1, 1994, January 1, 1995, July 1, 1995, July 1, 1997, January 1, 1999, July 1, 1999, January 1, 2000, January 1, 2001, January 1, 2004, January 1, 2005, and January 1, 2006.

Ref.: Cal. Fms Pl. & Pr., Ch. 328, "Juvenile Courts: Dependency Proceedings"; W. Cal. Sum., 10 "Parent and Child" §§444, 637, 669, 674, 675, 678, 681, 682, 701, 717.

Rule 5.720.   Eighteen-month review hearing

(a) Setting for hearing; notice (§§ 293, 366.22)

If a child was not returned at the 6- or 12-month review hearing, a permanency review hearing must be held no later than 18 months from the date of the initial removal. Notice of the hearing must be given as provided in section 293.

(Subd (a) amended effective January 1, 2007; adopted as subd (b)(1) effective January 1, 1990; repealed and adopted as subd (a) effective July 1, 1999; previously amended effective January 1, 1992, January 1, 1993, January 1, 1994, January 1, 2001, January 1, 2005, and January 1, 2006.)

(b) Reports (§§ 366.1, 366.21)

Before the hearing the petitioner must prepare a report describing services offered to the family and progress made.

(1) The report must include:

(A) Recommendations for court orders and the reasons for those recommendations;

(B) A description of the efforts made to achieve legal permanence for the child if reunification efforts fail; and

(C) A factual discussion of each item listed in sections 366.1 and 366.21(c).

(2) At least 10 calendar days before the hearing, the petitioner must file the report and provide copies to the parent or guardian and his or her counsel, to counsel for the child, and to any CASA volunteer. The petitioner must provide a summary of the recommendations to any foster parents, relative caregivers, or certified foster parents who have been approved for adoption.

(Subd (b) amended effective January 1, 2007; adopted effective January 1, 2005; previously amended effective January 1, 2006.)

(c) Conduct of hearing (§ 366.22)

At the hearing the court must state on the record that the court has read and considered the report of petitioner, the report of any CASA volunteer, the case plan submitted for this hearing, any report submitted by the child's caregiver under section 366.21(d), and any other evidence, and must proceed as follows:

(1) The court must order the child returned to the parent or guardian unless the court finds the petitioner has established, by a preponderance of the evidence, that return would create a substantial risk of detriment to the child. Failure of the parent or guardian to regularly participate in a court-ordered treatment program is prima facie evidence that continued supervision is necessary or that return would be detrimental.

(2) If the court has previously placed or at this hearing places the child with a noncustodial parent, the court may:

(A) Continue supervision;

(B) After stating on the record or in writing the factual basis for the order, order custody to that parent, continue supervision, and order family maintenance services; or

(C) After stating on the record or in writing the factual basis for the order, order custody to the noncustodial parent, terminate jurisdiction, and direct that *Custody Order—Juvenile—Final Judgment* (form JV-200) be prepared and filed under rule 5.700.

(3) If the court does not order return, the court must specify the factual basis for its finding of risk of detriment, terminate reunification services, and:

(A) Order that the child remain in foster care, if it finds by clear and convincing evidence already presented that a section 366.26 hearing is not in the best interest of the child because the child is not a proper subject for adoption and has no one willing to accept legal guardianship. If the court orders that the child remain in foster care, it must identify the foster care setting by name and identify a specific permanency goal for the child. The court may order that the name and address of the foster home remain confidential. If the child is 10 years of age or older and is placed in out-of-home placement for six months or longer, the court:

(i) Must determine whether the agency has identified individuals, in addition to the child's siblings, who are important to the child and will maintain caring, permanent relationships with the child, consistent with the child's best interest;

(ii) Must determine whether the agency has made reasonable efforts to nurture and maintan the child's relationships with those individuals, consistent with the child's best interest; and

(iii) May make any appropriate order to ensure that those relationships are maintained; or

(B) Order a hearing under section 366.26 within 120 days.

(4) Visitation must continue unless the court finds it would be detrimental to the child. The court may enter any other appropriate orders to enable the child to maintain relationships with other individuals who are important to the child, consistent with the child's best interest.

(5) The court must consider whether reasonable services have been provided. Evidence that the child has been placed with a relative or foster family who is eligible to adopt or that the child has been placed in a preadoptive home is insufficient alone to support a finding that reasonable services have not been offered or provided. The court must find that:

(A) Reasonable services were offered or provided; or

(B) Reasonable services were not offered or provided.

(6) The court must consider the case plan submitted for this hearing and must find as follows:

(A) The child was actively involved in the development of his or her own case plan and plan for permanent placement as age and developmentally appropriate; or

(B) The child was not actively involved in the development of his or her own case plan and plan for permanent placement as age and developmentally appropriate. If the court makes such a finding, the court must order the agency to involve the child in the development of his or her own case plan and plan for permanent placement, unless the court finds that the child is unable, unavailable, or unwilling to participate; and

(C) Each parent was actively involved in the development of the case plan and plan for permanent placement; or

(D) Each parent was not actively involved in the development of the case plan and plan for permanent placement. If the court makes such a finding, the court must order the agency to actively involve each parent in the development of the case plan and plan for permanent placement, unless the court finds that each parent is unable, unavailable, or unwilling to participate.

(7) For a child 12 years of age or older and in a permanent placement, the court must consider the case plan and must find as follows:

(A) The child was given the opportunity to review the case plan, sign it, and receive a copy; or

(B) The child was not given the opportunity to review the case plan, sign it, and receive a copy. If the court makes such a finding, the court must order the agency to give the child the opportunity to review the case plan, sign it, and receive a copy, unless the court finds that the child is unable, unavailable, or unwilling to participate.

(8) If the court orders a hearing under section 366.26, the court must terminate reunification services and direct that an assessment be prepared as stated in section 366.22(b). Visitation must continue unless the court finds it would be detrimental to the child. The court must enter any other appropriate orders to enable the child to maintain relationships with other individuals who are important to the child, consistent with the child's best interest.

(9) A judgment or an order setting a hearing under section 366.26 is not immediately appealable. Review may be sought only by filing *Petition for Extraordinary Writ (California Rules of Court, Rules 8.452, 8.456)* (form JV-825) or other petition for extraordinary writ. If a party wishes to preserve any right to review on appeal of the findings and orders made under this rule, the party is required to seek an extraordinary writ under rules 8.450, 8.452, and 5.600.

(10) A judgment, order, or decree setting a hearing under section 366.26 may be reviewed on appeal following the order of the 366.26 hearing only if the following have occurred:

(A) An extraordinary writ was sought by the timely filing of *Petition for Extraordinary Writ (California Rules of Court, Rules 8.452, 8.456)* (form JV-825) or other petition for extraordinary writ; and

(B) The petition for extraordinary writ was summarily denied or otherwise not decided on the merits.

(11) Review on appeal of the order setting a hearing under section 366.26 is limited to issues raised in a previous petition for extraordinary writ that were supported by an adequate record.

(12) Failure to file a petition for extraordinary writ review within the period specified by rules 8.450, 8.452, and 5.600, to substantively address the issues challenged, or to support the challenge by an adequate record precludes subsequent review on appeal of the findings and orders made under this rule.

(13) When the court orders a hearing under section 366.26, the court must advise orally all parties that to preserve any right to review on appeal of the order setting the hearing, the party is required to seek an extraordinary writ by filing:

(A) A notice of the party's intent to file writ petition and request for the record, which may be submitted on *Notice of Intent to File Writ Petition and Request for Record (California Rules of Court, Rule 8.450)* (form JV-820); and

(B) A petition for an extraordinary writ, which may be submitted on *Petition for Extraordinary Writ (California Rules of Court, Rules 8.452, 8.456)* (form JV-825).

(14) Within 24 hours of the review hearing, the clerk of the court must provide notice by first-class mail to the last known address of any party who is not present when

the court orders the hearing under section 366.26. The notice must include the advisement required by (c)(13).

(15) Copies of *Petition for Extraordinary Writ (California Rules of Court, Rules 8.452, 8.456)* (form JV-825) and *Notice of Intent to File Writ Petition and Request for Record (California Rules of Court, Rule 8.450)* (form JV-820) must be available in the courtroom and must accompany all mailed notices informing the parties of their rights.

(16) If the court orders a hearing under section 366.26, the court must order that notice of the hearing under section 366.26 must not be provided to any of the following:

(A) A parent, presumed parent, or alleged parent who has relinquished the child for adoption and whose relinquishment has been accepted and filed with notice under Family Code section 8700; or

(B) An alleged parent who has denied parentage and has completed section 1 of *Statement Regarding Parentage (Juvenile)* (form JV-505).

(Subd (c) amended effective July 1, 2007; repealed and adopted as subd (b) effective January 1, 1990; previously amended and relettered effective January 1, 2005; previously amended effective July 1, 1991, January 1, 1992, January 1, 1993, January 1, 1995, July 1, 1995, January 1, 1999, July 1, 1999, January 1, 2006, July 1, 2006, and January 1, 2007.)

(d) Setting a hearing under section 366.26

At the 18-month review hearing, the court must not set a hearing under section 366.26 to consider termination of the rights of only one parent unless:

(1) That parent is the only surviving parent;

(2) The rights of the other parent have been terminated by a California court of competent jurisdiction or by a court of competent jurisdiction of another state under the statutes of that state; or

(3) The other parent has relinquished custody of the child to the county welfare department.

(Subd (d) amended effective January 1, 2007; adopted as subd (c) effective July 1, 1997; previously amended and relettered effective January 1, 2005.)

Rule 5.720 amended effective July 1, 2007; repealed and adopted as rule 1462 effective January 1, 1990; previously amended and renumbered effective January 1, 2007; previously amended effective July 1, 1991, January 1, 1992, January 1, 1993, January 1, 1994, January 1, 1995, July 1, 1995, July 1, 1997, January 1, 1999, July 1, 1999, January 1, 2001, January 1, 2005, January 1, 2006, and July 1, 2006.

Ref.: Cal. Fms Pl. & Pr., Ch. 328, "Juvenile Courts: Dependency Proceedings"; W. Cal. Sum., 10 "Parent and Child" §§444, 669, 674, 675, 679, 681, 682, 701, 717.

Rule 5.725.   Selection of permanent plan (§§ 366.26, 727.31)

(a) Application of rule

This rule applies to children who have been declared dependents **or wards of the juvenile court**.

(1) [1] Only section 366.26 and division 12, part 3, chapter 5 (commencing with section 7660) of the Family Code or Family Code sections 8604, 8605, 8606, and 8700 apply for the termination of parental rights. Part 4 (commencing with section 7800) of division 12 of the Family Code [2] does not apply.

(2) The court may not terminate the rights of only one parent under section 366.26 unless that parent is the only surviving parent; or unless the rights of the other parent have been terminated under [3] division 12, part 3, chapter 5 (commencing with section 7660), or **division 12,** part 4 (commencing with section 7800) [4] of the Family Code, or Family Code [5] **sections** 8604, 8605, or 8606; or unless the other parent has relinquished custody of the child to the welfare department.

(3) Only section 366.26 applies for establishing legal guardianship.

(4) For termination of the parental rights of an Indian child, the procedures in this rule and in rule 5.485 must be followed.

(Subd (a) amended effective January 1, 2009; previously amended effective January 1, 1994, July 1, 2002, and January 1, 2007.)

Rule 5.725(a).   2008 Deletes. [1] For those dependents, [2] , or former Civil Code section 232, [3] former Civil Code section 224, 224m, 232, or 7017, or [4] of division 12 [5] section

(b) Notice of hearing (§ 294)

In addition to the requirements stated in section 294, notice must be given to any CASA volunteer, the child's present caregiver, and any de facto parent on *Notice of Hearing on Selection of a Permanent Plan* (form JV-300).

(Subd (b) amended effective January 1, 2007; previously amended effective January 1, 1992, July 1, 1992, July 1, 1995, July 1, 2002, January 1, 2005, and January 1, 2006.)

(c) Report

Before the hearing, petitioner must prepare an assessment under section 366.21(i). At least 10 calendar days before the hearing, the petitioner must file the assessment, provide copies to each parent or guardian and all counsel of record, and provide a summary of the recommendations to the present custodians of the child, to any CASA volunteer, and to the tribe of an Indian child.

(Subd (c) amended effective January 1, 2007; adopted effective January 1, 1992; previously amended effective July 1, 1995, and July 1, 2002.)

(d) Presence of child

The child must be present in court if the child or the child's attorney so request or the court so orders. If the child is 10 years of age or older and is not present at the hearing, the court must determine whether the child was properly notified of his or her right to attend the hearing and ask why the child is not present.

(Subd (d) amended effective January 1, 2006; adopted effective January 1, 2005.)

(e) Conduct of hearing

At the hearing, the court must state on the record that the court has read and considered the report of petitioner, the report of any CASA volunteer, the case plan submitted for this hearing, any report submitted by the child's caregiver under section 366.21(d), and any other evidence, and must proceed as follows:

(1) Order parental rights terminated and the child placed for adoption if the court determines, by clear and convincing evidence, that it is likely the child will be adopted, unless:

(A) At each and every hearing at which the court was required to consider reasonable efforts or services, the court has found that reasonable efforts were not made or that reasonable services were not offered or provided; or

(B) **The child is living with a relative who is unable or unwilling to adopt the child because of circumstances that do not include an unwillingness to accept legal or financial responsibility for the child, but who is willing and capable of providing the child with a stable and permanent environment through legal guardianship, and removal from the home of the relative would be detrimental to the emotional well-being of the child. For an Indian child, "relative" includes an "extended family member," as defined in the federal Indian Child Welfare Act (25 U.S.C. §1903(2)); or**

(C) The court finds a compelling reason to determine that termination would be detrimental to the child because of the existence of one of the following circumstances:

(i) The parents or guardians have maintained regular visitation and contact with the child and the child would benefit from continuing the relationship;

(ii) A child 12 years of age or older objects to termination of parental rights;

(iii) The child is placed in a residential treatment facility and adoption is unlikely or undesirable while the child remains in that placement, and continuation of parental rights will not prevent the finding of an adoptive home if the parents cannot resume custody when residential care is no longer needed;

(iv) The child is living with a [1] foster parent **or Indian custodian** who is unable or unwilling to adopt the child because of exceptional circumstances, but who is willing and capable of providing the child with a stable and permanent home, and removal from the home of the [2] foster parent **or Indian custodian** would be detrimental to the **emotional** well-being of the child. This exception does not apply to (1) a child under 6 or (2) a child who has a sibling under 6 who is also a dependent and with whom the child should be placed permanently; or

(v) There would be a substantial interference with the child's relationship with a sibling, taking into consideration the nature and extent of the relationship. To make this determination, the court may consider whether the child was raised in the same home as the sibling, whether the child and the sibling shared common experiences or have close and strong bonds, and whether ongoing contact with the sibling is in the child's best interest. For purposes of this subdivision, determination of the child's best interest may include a comparison of the child's long-term emotional interest with the benefit of legal permanence in an adoptive home.

(2) The court must not fail to find that the child is likely to be adopted based on the fact that the child is not yet placed in a preadoptive home or with a relative or foster family willing to adopt the child.

(3) The party claiming that termination of parental rights would be detrimental to the child must have the burden of proving the detriment.

(4) If the court finds termination of parental rights to be detrimental to the child for reasons stated in (1)(B), the court must state the reasons in writing or on the record.

(5) If termination of parental rights would not be detrimental to the child, but the child is difficult to place for adoption because the child (1) is a member of a sibling group that should stay together; (2) has a diagnosed medical, physical, or mental handicap; or (3) is 7 years of age or older and no prospective adoptive parent is identified or available, the court may, without terminating parental rights, identify adoption as a permanent placement goal and order the public agency responsible for seeking adoptive parents to make efforts to locate an appropriate adoptive family for a period not to exceed 180 days. During the 180-day period, in order to identify potential adoptive parents, the agency responsible for seeking adoptive parents for each child must, to the extent possible, ask each child who is 10 years of age or older and who is placed in out-of-home placement for six months or longer to identify any individuals who are important to the child. The agency may ask any other child to provide that information, as appropriate. After that period the court must hold another hearing and proceed according to (1) or (6).

(6) If the court finds that (1)(A) or (1)(B) applies, the court must appoint the present custodian or other appropriate person to become the child's legal guardian or must order the child to remain in foster care.

(A) If the court orders that the child remain in foster care, it must identify the foster care setting by name and identify a specific permanency goal for the child. The court may order that the name and address of the foster home remain confidential.

(B) Legal guardianship must be given preference over foster care when it is in the interest of the child and a suitable guardian can be found.

(C) A child who is 10 years of age or older who is placed in out-of-home placement for six months or longer must be asked to identify any adults who are important to him or her in order for the agency to investigate and the court to determine whether any of those adults would be appropriate to serve as legal guardians. Other children may be asked for this information, as age and developmentally appropriate.

(D) If the court finds that removal of the child from the home of a foster parent or relative who is not willing to become a legal guardian for the child would be seriously detrimental to the emotional well-being of the child, then the child must not be removed. The foster parent or relative must be willing to provide, and capable of providing, a stable and permanent home for the child and must have substantial psychological ties with the child.

(E) The court must make an order for visitation with each parent or guardian unless the court finds by a preponderance of the evidence that the visitation would be detrimental to the child.

(7) The court must consider the case plan submitted for this hearing and must find as follows:

(A) The child was actively involved in the development of his or her own case plan and plan for permanent placement as age and developmentally appropriate, including being asked for a statement regarding his or her permanent placement plan, and the case plan contains the social worker's assessment of those stated wishes; or

(B) The child was not actively involved in the development of his or her own case plan and plan for permanent placement, including being asked for a statement regarding his or her permanent placement plan and the case plan does not contain the social worker's assessment of those stated wishes. If the court makes such a finding, the court must order the agency to actively involve the child in the development of his or her own case plan and plan for permanent placement, including asking the child for a statement regarding his or her permanent plan, unless the court finds that the child is unable, unavailable, or unwilling to participate. If the court finds that the case plan does not contain the social worker's assessment of the child's stated wishes, the court must order the agency to submit the assessment to the court.

(8) For a child 12 years of age or older and in a permanent placement, the court must consider the case plan and must find as follows:

(A) The child was given the opportunity to review the case plan, sign it, and receive a copy; or

(B) The child was not given the opportunity to review the case plan, sign it, and receive a copy. If the court makes such a finding, the court must order the agency to give the child the opportunity to review the case plan, sign it, and receive a copy.

(9) If no adult is available to become legal guardian, and no suitable foster home is available, the court may order the care, custody, and control of the child transferred to a licensed foster family agency, subject to further orders of the court.

(Subd (e) amended effective January 1, 2009; repealed and adopted as subd (c) effective January 1, 1991; previously amended and relettered as subd (d) effective January 1, 1992, and as subd (e) effective January 1, 2005; previously amended effective July 1, 1994, January 1, 1999, July 1, 1999, July 1, 2002, January 1, 2006, and January 1, 2007.)

Rule 5.725(e). 2008 Deletes. [1] relative or [2] relative or

(f) Procedures—termination of parental rights

(1) The court may not terminate parental rights if a review of the prior findings and orders reveals that at each and every prior hearing at which the court was required to consider reasonable efforts or services the court found that reasonable efforts had not been made or that reasonable services had not been offered or provided. If at any prior hearing the court found that reasonable efforts had been made or that reasonable services had been offered or provided, the court may terminate parental rights.

(2) An order of the court terminating parental rights under section 366.26 is conclusive and binding on the child, the parent, and all other persons who have been served under the provisions of section 294. The order may not be set aside or modified by the court, except as provided in rules 5.538, 5.540, and 5.542 with regard to orders by a referee.

(3) If the court declares the child free from custody and control of the parents, the court must at the same time order the child referred to a licensed county adoption agency for adoptive placement. A petition for adoption of the child may be filed and heard in the juvenile court, but may not be granted until the appellate rights of the natural parents have been exhausted.

(Subd (f) amended effective January 1, 2007; adopted as subd (d) effective January 1, 1991; relettered as subd (e) effective January 1, 1992, and as subd (f) effective January 1, 2005; previously amended effective July 1, 1992, January 1, 1995, July 1, 2002, and January 1, 2006.)

(g) Procedures—legal guardianship

The proceedings for appointment of a legal guardian for a dependent child of the juvenile court must be in the juvenile court as provided in rule 5.735.

(Subd (g) amended effective January 1, 2007; repealed and adopted as subd (e) effective January 1, 1991; relettered as subd (f) effective January 1, 1992 and as subd (g) effective January 1, 2005; previously amended effective July 1, 1997, and July 1, 2002.)

(h) Purpose of termination of parental rights

The purpose of termination of parental rights is to free the dependent child for adoption. Therefore, the court must not terminate the rights of only one parent unless that parent is the only surviving parent, or the rights of the other parent have been terminated by a California court of competent jurisdiction or by a court of competent jurisdiction of another state under the statutes of that state, or the other parent has relinquished custody of the child to the county welfare department. The rights of the mother, any presumed father, any alleged father, and any unknown father or fathers must be terminated in order to free the child for adoption.

(Subd (h) amended and relettered effective January 1, 2005; adopted as subd (g) effective July 1, 1997; previously amended effective July 1, 2002.)

(i) Advisement of appeal rights

The court must advise all parties of their appeal rights as provided in rule 5.585 and section 366.26(*l*).

(Subd (i) amended effective January 1, 2007; repealed and adopted as subd (f) effective January 1, 1991; previously relettered as subd (g) effective January 1, 1992; amended and relettered as subd (h) effective July 1, 1997; relettered as subd (i) effective January 1, 2005; previously amended effective July 1, 2002, and January 1, 2006.)

Rule 5.725 amended effective January 1, 2009; repealed and adopted as rule 1463 effective January 1, 1991; previously amended effective January 1, 1992, July 1, 1992, January 1, 1994, July 1, 1994, January 1, 1995, July 1, 1995, July 1, 1997, January 1, 1999, July 1, 1999, July 1, 2002, January 1, 2005, and January 1, 2006; previously amended and renumbered effective January 1, 2007.

Ref.: Cal. Fms Pl. & Pr., Ch. 328, "Juvenile Courts: Dependency Proceedings"; W. Cal. Sum., 10 "Parent and Child" §§444, 680–682, 685–690, 692, 693, 695.

Rule 5.726. Prospective adoptive parent designation (§ 366.26(n))

(a) Request procedure

A dependent child's caregiver may be designated as a prospective adoptive parent. The court may make the designation on its own motion or on a request by a caregiver, the child, a social worker, or the attorney for any of these parties.

(1) A request for designation as a prospective adoptive parent may be made at a hearing where parental rights are terminated or thereafter, whether or not the child's removal from the home is at issue.

(2) A request may be made orally.

(3) If a request for prospective adoptive parent designation is made in writing, it must be made on *Request for Prospective Adoptive Parent Designation* (form JV-321).

(4) The address and telephone number of the caregiver and the child may be kept confidential by filing *Confidential Information—Prospective Adoptive Parent* (form JV-322), with form JV-321. Form JV-322 must be kept in the court file under seal, and only the court, the child's attorney, the agency, and the child's CASA volunteer may have access to this information.

(Subd (a) amended effective January 1, 2008; previously amended effective January 1, 2007.)

(b) Criteria for designation as prospective adoptive parent

A caregiver must meet the following criteria to be designated as a prospective adoptive parent:

(1) The child has lived with the caregiver for at least six months;

(2) The caregiver currently expresses a commitment to adopt the child; and

(3) The caregiver has taken at least one step to facilitate the adoption process. Steps to facilitate the adoption process include:

(A) Applying for an adoption home study;

(B) Cooperating with an adoption home study;

(C) Being designated by the court or the licensed adoption agency as the adoptive family;

(D) Requesting de facto parent status;

(E) Signing an adoptive placement agreement;

(F) Discussing a postadoption contact agreement with the social worker, child's attorney, child's CASA volunteer, adoption agency, or court;

(G) Working to overcome any impediments that have been identified by the California Department of Social Services and the licensed adoption agency; and

(H) Attending any of the classes required of prospective adoptive parents.

(Subd (b) amended effective January 1, 2007.)

(c) Hearing on request for prospective adoptive parent designation

The court must evaluate whether the caregiver meets the criteria in (b).

(1) The petitioner must show on the request that the caregiver meets the criteria in (b).

(2) If the court finds that the petitioner does not show that the caregiver meets the criteria in (b), the court may deny the request without a hearing.

(3) If the court finds that the petitioner has shown that the current caregiver meets the criteria in (b), the court must set a hearing as set forth in (4) below.

(4) If it appears to the court that the request for designation as a prospective adoptive parent will be contested, or if the court wants to receive further evidence on the request, the court must set a hearing.

(A) If the request for designation is made at the same time as an objection to removal, the court must set a hearing as follows:

(i) The hearing must be set as soon as possible and not later than five court days after the objection is filed with the court.

(ii) If the court for good cause is unable to set the matter for hearing five court days after the petition is filed, the court must set the matter for hearing as soon as possible.

(iii) The matter may be set for hearing more than five court days after the objection is filed if this delay is necessary to allow participation by the child's identified Indian tribe or the child's Indian custodian.

(B) If the request for designation is made before a request for removal is filed or before an emergency removal has occurred, the court must order that the

hearing be set at a time within 30 calendar days after the filing of the request for designation.

(5) If all parties stipulate to the request for designation of the caregiver as a prospective adoptive parent, the court may order the designation without a hearing.

(Subd (c) amended effective January 1, 2007.)

(d) Notice of designation hearing

After the court has ordered a hearing on a request for prospective adoptive parent designation, notice of the hearing must be as described below.

(1) The following participants must be noticed:

(A) The adoption agency;

(B) The current caregiver,

(C) The child's attorney;

(D) The child, if the child is 10 years of age or older;

(E) The child's identified Indian tribe if any;

(F) The child's Indian custodian if any; and

(G) The child's CASA program if any.

(2) If the request for designation was made at the same time as a request for hearing on a proposed or emergency removal, notice of the designation hearing must be provided with notice of the proposed removal hearing, as stated in rule 5.727.

(3) If the request for designation was made before a request for removal was filed or before an emergency removal occurred, notice must be as follows:

(A) Service of the notice must be either by first-class mail sent at least 15 calendar days before the hearing date to the last known address of the person to be noticed, or by personal service on the person at least 10 calendar days before the hearing.

(B) *Prospective Adoptive Parent Designation Order* (form JV-327) must be used to provide notice of a hearing on the request for prospective adoptive parent designation.

(C) The clerk must provide notice of the hearing to the participants listed in (1) above, if the court, caregiver, or child requested the hearing.

(D) The child's attorney must provide notice of the hearing to the participants listed in (1) above, if the child's attorney requested the hearing.

(E) *Proof of Notice* (form JV-326) must be filed with the court before the hearing on the request for prospective adoptive parent designation.

(Subd (d) amended effective January 1, 2008; previously amended effective January 1, 2007.)

(e) Termination of designation

If the prospective adoptive parent no longer meets the criteria in rule 5.726(b), a request to vacate the order designating the caregiver as a prospective adoptive parent may be filed under section 388 and rule 5.570.

(Subd (e) amended effective January 1, 2007.)

(f) Confidentiality

If the telephone or address of the caregiver or the child is confidential, all forms must be kept in the court file under seal. Only the court, the child's attorney, the agency, and the child's CASA volunteer may have access to this information.

Rule 5.726 amended effective January 1, 2008; adopted as rule 1463.1 effective July 1, 2006; previously amended and renumbered effective January 1, 2007.

Ref.: Cal. Fms Pl. & Pr., Ch. 328, "Juvenile Courts: Dependency Proceedings"; W. Cal. Sum., 10 "Parent and Child" §§444, 693A, 693B.

Rule 5.727. Proposed removal (§ 366.26(n))

(a) Application of rule

This rule applies, after termination of parental rights, to the removal by the Department of Social Services (DSS) or a licensed adoption agency of a dependent child from a prospective adoptive parent under rule 5.726(b) or from a caregiver who may meet the criteria for designation as a prospective adoptive parent under rule 5.726(b). This rule does not apply if the caregiver requests the child's removal.

(Subd (a) amended effective January 1, 2007.)

(b) Participants to be served with notice

Before removing a child from the home of a prospective adoptive parent under rule 5.726(b) or from the home of a caregiver who may meet the criteria of a prospective adoptive parent under rule 5.726(b), and as soon as possible after a decision is made to remove the child, the agency must notify the following participants of the proposed removal:

(1) The court;

(2) The current caregiver, if that caregiver either is a designated prospective adoptive parent or, on the date of service of the notice, meets the criteria in rule 5.726(b);

(3) The child's attorney;

(4) The child, if the child is 10 years of age or older;

(5) The child's identified Indian tribe if any;

(6) The child's Indian custodian if any; and

(7) The child's CASA program if any.

(Subd (b) amended effective January 1, 2007.)

(c) Form of notice

DSS or the agency must provide notice on *Notice of Intent to Remove Child* (form JV-323). A blank copy of *Objection to Removal* (form JV-325) and *Request for Prospective Adoptive Parent Designation* (form JV-321) must also be provided.

(Subd (c) amended effective January 1, 2008; previously amended effective January 1, 2007.)

(d) Service of notice

DSS or the agency must serve notice of its intent to remove a child as follows:

(1) DSS or the agency must serve notice either by first-class mail, sent to the last known address of the person to be noticed, or by personal service.

(2) If service is by first-class mail, service is completed and time to respond is extended by five calendar days.

(3) Notice to the child's identified Indian tribe and Indian custodian must be given under rule 5.664.

(4) Proof of service of the notice on *Proof of Notice* (form JV-326) must be filed with the court.

(Subd (d) amended effective January 1, 2008; previously amended effective January 1, 2007.)

(e) Objection to proposed removal

Each participant who receives notice under (b) may object to the proposed removal of the child and may request a hearing.

(1) A request for hearing on the proposed removal must be made on *Objection to Removal* (form JV-325).

(2) A request for hearing on the proposed removal must be made within five court or seven calendar days from date of notification, whichever is longer. If service is by mail, time to respond is extended by five calendar days.

(3) The court must order a hearing as follows:

(A) The hearing must be set as soon as possible and not later than five court days after the objection is filed with the court.

(B) If the court for good cause is unable to set the matter for hearing five court days after the petition is filed, the court must set the matter for hearing as soon as possible.

(C) The matter may be set for hearing more than five court days after the objection is filed if this delay is necessary to allow participation by the child's identified Indian tribe or the child's Indian custodian.

(Subd (e) amended effective January 1, 2008; previously amended effective January 1, 2007.)

(f) Notice of hearing on proposed removal

After the court has ordered a hearing on a proposed removal, notice of the hearing must be as follows:

(1) The clerk must provide notice of the hearing to the agency and the participants listed in (b) above, if the court, caregiver, or child requested the hearing.

(2) The child's attorney must provide notice of the hearing to the agency and the participants listed in (b) above, if the child's attorney requested the hearing.

(3) Notice must be either by personal service or by telephone. Notice by personal service must include a copy of the forms *Notice of Intent to Remove Child* (form JV-323) and *Objection to Removal* (form JV-325). Telephone notice must include the reasons for and against the removal, as indicated on forms JV-323 and JV-325.

(4) Proof of notice on *Proof of Notice* (form JV-326) must be filed with the court before the hearing on the proposed removal.

(Subd (f) amended effective January 1, 2008; previously amended effective January 1, 2007.)

(g) Burden of proof

At a hearing on an intent to remove the child, the agency intending to remove the child must prove by a preponderance of the evidence that the proposed removal is in the best interest of the child.

(h) Confidentiality

If the telephone or address of the caregiver or the child is confidential, all forms must be kept in the court file under seal. Only the court, the child's attorney, the agency, and the child's CASA volunteer may have access to this information.

(i) Appeal

If the court order made after a hearing on an intent to remove a child is appealed, the appeal must be made under rules 8.454 and 8.456.

(Subd (i) amended effective January 1, 2007.)

Rule 5.727 amended effective January 1, 2008; adopted as rule 1463.3 effective July 1, 2006; previously amended and renumbered effective January 1, 2007.

Ref.: Cal. Fms Pl. & Pr., Ch. 328, "Juvenile Courts: Dependency Proceedings"; W. Cal. Sum., 10 "Parent and Child" §§444, 693A, 693C.

Rule 5.728. Emergency removal (§ 366.26(n))

(a) Application of rule

This rule applies, after termination of parental rights, to the removal by the Department of Social Services (DSS) or a licensed adoption agency of a dependent child from a prospective adoptive parent under rule 5.726(b) or from a caregiver who may meet the criteria for designation as a prospective adoptive parent under rule 5.726(b) when the DSS or the licensed adoption agency has determined a removal must occur immediately due to a risk of physical or emotional harm. This rule does not apply if the child's removal is carried out at the request of the caregiver.

(Subd (a) amended effective January 1, 2007.)

(b) Participants to be noticed

After removing a child from the home of a prospective adoptive parent under rule 5.726(b), or from the home of a caregiver who may meet the criteria of a prospective adoptive parent under rule 5.726(b), because of immediate risk of physical or emotional harm, the agency must notify the following participants of the emergency removal:

(1) The court;

(2) The current caregiver, if that caregiver either is a designated prospective adoptive parent or, on the date of service of the notice, meets the criteria in rule 5.726(b);

(3) The child's attorney;

(4) The child if the child is 10 years of age or older;

(5) The child's identified Indian tribe if any;

(6) The child's Indian custodian if any; and

(7) The child's CASA program if any.

(Subd (b) amended effective January 1, 2007.)

(c) Form of notice

Notice of Emergency Removal (form JV-324) must be used to provide notice of an emergency removal, as described below.

(1) The agency must provide notice of the emergency removal as soon as possible but no later than two court days after the removal.

(2) Notice must be either by telephone or by personal service of the form.

(3) Telephone notice must include the reasons for removal as indicated on the form, and notice of the right to object to the removal.

(4) Whenever possible, the agency, at the time of the removal, must give a blank copy of the form to the caregiver and, if the child is 10 years of age or older, the child.

(5) Notice to the court must be by filing of the form with the court. The proof of notice included on the form must be completed when the form is filed with the court.

(Subd (c) amended effective January 1, 2008; previously amended effective January 1, 2007.)

(d) Objection to emergency removal

Each participant who receives notice under (b) may object to the removal of the child and may request a hearing.

(1) A request for hearing on the emergency removal must be made on *Objection to Removal* (form JV-325).

(2) The court must order a hearing as follows:

(A) The hearing must be set as soon as possible and not later than five court days after the objection is filed with the court.

(B) If the court for good cause is unable to set the matter for hearing within five court days after the petition is filed, the court must set the matter for hearing as soon as possible.

(C) The matter may be set for hearing more than five court days after the objection is filed if this delay is

necessary to allow participation by the child's identified Indian tribe or the child's Indian custodian.

(Subd (d) amended effective January 1, 2008; previously amended effective January 1, 2007.)

(e) Notice of emergency removal hearing

After the court has ordered a hearing on an emergency removal, notice of the hearing must be as follows:

(1) Notice must be either by personal service or by telephone. Notice by personal service must include a copy of *Notice of Emergency Removal* (form JV-324). Telephone notice must include the reasons for and against the removal, as indicated on forms JV-324 and JV-325.

(2) The clerk must provide notice of the hearing to the agency and the participants listed in (b) above, if the court, the caregiver, or the child requested the hearing.

(3) The child's attorney must provide notice of the hearing to the agency and the participants listed in (b) above, if the child's attorney requested the hearing.

(4) Proof of notice on *Proof of Notice* (form JV-326) must be filed with the court before the hearing on the emergency removal.

(Subd (e) amended effective January 1, 2008; previously amended effective January 1, 2007.)

(f) Burden of proof

At a hearing on an emergency removal, the agency that removed the child must prove by a preponderance of the evidence that the removal is in the best interest of the child.

(g) Confidentiality

If the telephone or address of the caregiver or the child is confidential, all forms must be kept in the court file under seal. Only the court, the child's attorney, the agency, and the child's CASA volunteer and program may have access to this information.

Rule 5.728 amended effective January 1, 2008; adopted as rule 1463.5 effective July 1, 2006; previously amended and renumbered effective January 1, 2007.

Ref.: Cal. Fms Pl. & Pr., Ch. 328, "Juvenile Courts: Dependency Proceedings"; W. Cal. Sum., 10 "Parent and Child" §§444, 693A, 693D.

Rule 5.730.   Adoption

(a) Procedures—adoption

(1) The petition for the adoption of a dependent child who has been freed for adoption may be filed in the juvenile court with jurisdiction over the dependency.

(2) All adoption petitions must be completed on *Adoption Request* (form ADOPT-200) and must be verified. In addition, the petitioner must complete *Adoption Agreement* (form ADOPT-210) and *Adoption Order* (form ADOPT-215).

(3) A petitioner seeking to adopt an Indian child must also complete *Adoption of Indian Child* (form ADOPT-220). If applicable, *Parent of Indian Child Agrees to End Parental Rights* (form ADOPT-225) may be filed.

(4) The clerk must open a confidential adoption file for each child and this file must be separate and apart from the dependency file, with an adoption case number different from the dependency case number.

(Subd (a) amended effective January 1, 2007; previously amended effective January 1, 1996, January 1, 1999, and January 1, 2004.)

(b) Notice

The clerk of the court must give notice of the adoption hearing to:

(1) Any attorney of record for the child;

(2) Any CASA volunteer;

(3) The child welfare agency;

(4) The tribe of an Indian child; and

(5) The California Department of Social Services. The notice to the California Department of Social Services must include a copy of the completed *Adoption Request* (form ADOPT-200) and a copy of any adoptive placement agreement or agency joinder filed in the case.

(Subd (b) amended effective January 1, 2007; previously amended effective January 1, 2004.)

(c) Hearing

If the petition for adoption is filed in the juvenile court, the proceeding for adoption must be heard in juvenile court once appellate rights have been exhausted. Each petitioner and the child must be present at the hearing. The hearing may be heard by a referee if the referee is acting as a temporary judge.

(Subd (c) amended effective January 1, 2007; previously amended effective January 1, 1999, and January 1, 2004.)

(d) Record

The record must reflect that the court has read and considered the assessment prepared for the hearing held under section 366.26 and as required by section 366.22(b), the report of any CASA volunteer, and any other reports or documents admitted into evidence.

(Subd (d) amended effective January 1, 2007; previously amended effective January 1, 2004.)

(e) Assessment

The preparer of the assessment may be called and examined by any party to the adoption proceeding.

(f) Consent

At the hearing, each adoptive parent and the child, if 12 years of age or older, must execute *Adoption Agreement* (form ADOPT-210) in the presence of and with the acknowledgment of the court.

(Subd (f) amended effective January 1, 2007; previously amended effective January 1, 1999, and January 1, 2004.)

(g) Dismissal of jurisdiction

If the petition for adoption is granted, the juvenile court must dismiss the dependency, terminate jurisdiction over the child, and vacate any previously set review hearing dates. A completed *Termination of Dependency (Juvenile)* (form JV-364) must be filed in the child's juvenile dependency file.

(Subd (g) amended January 1, 2007; previously amended effective January 1, 1999, and January 1, 2004.)

Rule 5.730 amended and renumbered effective January 1, 2007; adopted as rule 1464 effective July 1, 1995; previously amended January 1, 1996, January 1, 1999, and January 1, 2004.

Ref.: Cal. Fms Pl. & Pr., Ch. 328, "Juvenile Courts: Dependency Proceedings"; W. Cal. Sum., 10 "Parent and Child" §§118, 444, 694.

Rule 5.735. Legal guardianship

(a) Proceedings in juvenile court (§ 366.26(d))

The proceedings for the appointment of a legal guardian for a dependent child must be in the juvenile court. The request for appointment of a guardian must be included in the social study report prepared by the county welfare department or in the assessment prepared for the hearing under section 366.26. Neither a separate petition nor a separate hearing is required.

(Subd (a) amended effective January 1, 2007; previously amended effective July 1, 1997, July 1, 1999, and January 1, 2006.)

(b) Notice; hearing

Notice for the guardianship hearing must be given under section 294, and the hearing must proceed under section 366.26.

(Subd (b) amended effective January 1, 2006; previously amended effective July 1, 1999.)

(c) Conduct of hearing

(1) Before appointing a guardian, the court must read and consider the social study report specified in section 366.26 and note its consideration in the minutes of the court.

(2) The preparer of the social study report may be called in and examined by any party to the proceedings.

(Subd (c) amended effective January 1, 2006; previously amended effective July 1, 1999.)

(d) Findings and orders

(1) If the court finds that legal guardianship is the appropriate permanent plan, the court must appoint the guardian and order the clerk to issue letters of guardianship, which will not be subject to the confidentiality protections of juvenile court documents as described in section 827.

(2) The court may issue orders regarding visitation of the child by a parent or other relative.

(3) On appointment of a guardian under section 366.26, the court may terminate dependency.

(Subd (d) amended effective January 1, 2006; previously amended effective July 1, 1999.)

(e) Notification of appeal rights

The court must advise all parties of their appeal rights as provided in rule 5.585.

(Subd (e) amended effective January 1, 2007; previously amended effective January 1, 2006.)

Rule 5.735 amended and renumbered effective January 1, 2007; adopted as rule 1464 effective January 1, 1991; renumbered as rule 1465 effective July 1, 1995; previously amended effective July 1, 1999, and January 1, 2006.

Ref.: Cal. Fms Pl. & Pr., Ch. 328, "Juvenile Courts: Dependency Proceedings"; W. Cal. Sum., 10 "Parent and Child" §§444, 695.

Rule 5.740. Hearings subsequent to a permanent plan (§§ 366.26, 366.3, 391)

(a) Review hearings—adoption and guardianship

Following an order for termination of parental rights or a plan for the establishment of a guardianship under section 366.26, the court must retain jurisdiction and conduct review hearings at least every 6 months to ensure the expeditious completion of the adoption or guardianship.

(1) At the review hearing, the court must consider the report of the petitioner, as required by section 366.3(f), the report of any CASA volunteer, the case plan submitted for this hearing, and any report submitted by the child's caregiver under section 366.21(d); inquire about the progress

being made to provide a permanent home for the child; consider the safety of the child; and enter findings as required by section 366.3(e).

(2) When adoption is granted, the court must terminate its jurisdiction.

(3) When legal guardianship is granted, the court may continue dependency jurisdiction if it is in the best interest of the child, or the court may terminate dependency jurisdiction and retain jurisdiction over the child as a ward of the guardianship.

(4) Notice of the hearing must be given as provided in section 295.

(Subd (a) amended effective January 1, 2007; repealed and adopted effective January 1, 1991; previously amended effective January 1, 1992, January 1, 1993, July 1, 1999, January 1, 2005, and January 1, 2006.)

(b) Review hearings—foster care

Following the establishment of a plan other than those provided for in (a), review hearings must be conducted at least every 6 months by the court or by a local administrative review panel.

(1) At the review hearing, the court or administrative review panel must consider the report of the petitioner, the report of any CASA volunteer, the case plan submitted for this hearing, and any report submitted by the child's caregiver under section 366.21(d); inquire about the progress being made to provide a permanent home for the child; consider the safety of the child; and enter findings regarding each item listed in section 366.3(e).

(2) The court or administrative review panel must consider the case plan submitted for this hearing and must find as follows:

(A) The child was actively involved in the development of his or her own case plan and plan for permanent placement as age and developmentally appropriate; or

(B) The child was not actively involved in the development of his or her own case plan and plan for permanent placement as age and developmentally appropriate. If the court or administrative review panel makes such a finding, the court must order the agency to actively involve the child in the development of his or her own case plan and plan for permanent placement, unless the court finds that the child is unable, unavailable, or unwilling to participate.

(3) For a child 12 years of age or older and in a permanent placement, the court must consider the case plan and must find as follows:

(A) The child was given the opportunity to review the case plan, sign it, and receive a copy; or

(B) The child was not given the opportunity to review the case plan, sign it, and receive a copy. If the court makes such a finding, the court must order the agency to give the child the opportunity to review the case plan, sign it, and receive a copy.

(4) No less frequently than once every 12 months, the court must conduct a review of the previously ordered permanent plan to consider whether the plan continues to be appropriate for the child. The review of the permanent plan may be combined with the 6-month review.

(5) If circumstances have changed since the permanent plan was ordered, the court may order a new permanent plan under section 366.26 at any subsequent hearing, or any party may seek a new permanent plan by a motion filed under rule 5.570.

(6) Notice of the hearing must be given as provided in section 295.

(7) The court must continue the child in foster care unless the parents prove, by a preponderance of the evidence, that further efforts at reunification are the best alternative for the child. In those cases, the court may order reunification services for a period not to exceed 6 months.

(8) At a review held 12 months after an original or subsequent order for the child to remain in foster care, the court must consider all permanency planning options, including whether the child should be returned to a parent or guardian, placed for adoption, or appointed a legal guardian. If the court orders that the child remain in foster care, it must identify the foster care setting by name and identify a specific permanency goal for the child. The court may order that the name and address of the foster home remain confidential.

(9) At a review held 12 months after an original or subsequent order for the child to remain in foster care, the court must order a hearing under section 366.26 unless the court finds by clear and convincing evidence that there is a compelling reason for determining that a section 366.26 hearing is not in the child's best interest because the child is being returned to the home of the parent, the child is not a proper subject for adoption, or there is no one available to assume guardianship.

(10) If the court makes the findings in (9), the court may order that the child remain in foster care.

(Subd (b) amended effective January 1, 2007; repealed and adopted effective January 1, 1991; previously amended effective January 1, 1992, January 1, 1994, January 1, 1998, January 1, 1999, July 1, 1999, January 1, 2005, and January 1, 2006.)

(c) Hearing on petition to terminate guardianship or modify guardianship orders

A petition to terminate a guardianship established by the juvenile court, to appoint a successor guardian, or to modify or supplement orders concerning the guardianship must be filed in juvenile court. The procedures described in rule 5.570 must be followed, and *Request to Change Court Order* (form JV-180) must be used.

(1) Proceedings on a petition to terminate a guardianship established under section 366.26 must be heard in the juvenile court. If dependency was terminated at the time of or subsequent to the appointment of the guardian, and dependency is later declared in another county, proceedings to terminate the guardianship may be held in the juvenile court with current dependency jurisdiction.

(2) Not less than 15 court days before the hearing date, the petitioner must serve notice of the hearing on the department of social services; the guardian; the child, if 10 years or older; parents whose parental rights have not been terminated; the court that established the guardianship, if in another county; and counsel of record for those entitled to notice.

(3) At the hearing on the petition to terminate the guardianship, the court may do one of the following:

(A) Deny the petition to terminate guardianship;

(B) Deny the petition and request the county welfare department to provide services to the guardian and the ward for the purpose of maintaining the guardianship, consistent with section 301; or

(C) Grant the petition to terminate the guardianship.

(4) If the petition is granted and the court continues or resumes dependency, the court must order that a new plan be developed to provide stability and permanency to the child. Unless the court has already scheduled a hearing to review the child's status, the court must conduct a hearing within 60 days. Parents whose parental rights have not been terminated must be notified of the hearing on the new plan. The court may consider further efforts at reunification only if the parent proves, by a preponderance of the evidence, that the efforts would be the best alternative for the child.

(5) If the court terminates a guardianship established in another county, the clerk of the county of current dependency jurisdiction must transmit a certified copy of the order terminating guardianship within 15 days to the court that established the original guardianship.

(Subd (c) amended effective January 1, 2007; previously amended effective January 1, 1993, July 1, 1994, and July 1, 1999.)

(d) Hearings on termination of jurisdiction—child reaching age of majority (§ 391)

Petitioner must file *Termination of Dependency Jurisdiction—Child Attaining Age of Majority (Juvenile)* (form JV-365) with the court at least 10 calendar days before the hearing to terminate dependency jurisdiction based on the child's age and must provide copies to the child, the parents or guardians, any CASA volunteer, and all counsel of record at least 10 calendar days before the hearing.

(Subd (d) amended effective January 1, 2007; adopted effective July 1, 2002; previously amended effective January 1, 2005.)

Rule 5.740 amended and renumbered effective January 1, 2007; adopted as rule 1465 effective January 1, 1991; renumbered as rule 1466 effective July 1, 1995; previously amended effective January 1, 1992, January 1, 1993, January 1, 1994, July 1, 1994, January 1, 1998, January 1, 1999, July 1, 1999, July 1, 2002, January 1, 2005, and January 1, 2006.

Ref.: Cal. Fms Pl. & Pr., Ch. 328, "Juvenile Courts: Dependency Proceedings"; W. Cal. Sum., 10 "Parent and Child" §§444, 521, 628, 695–699.

Chapter 13
Cases Petitioned Under Sections 601 and 602

Chapter 13 renumbered effective January 1, 2008; adopted as Chapter 11 effective July 1, 2002; previously amended and renumbered as Chapter 14, effective January 1, 2007.

Art. 1.   Initial Appearance. Rules 5.752–5.764.
Art. 2.   Fitness Hearings. Rules 5.766–5.772.
Art. 3.   Jurisdiction. Rules 5.774–5.782.
Art. 4.   Disposition. Rules 5.785–5.805.
Art. 5.   Reviews and Sealing. Rules 5.810–5.830.

Article 1
Initial Appearance

Rule 5.752.   Initial hearing; detention hearings; time limit on custody; setting jurisdiction hearing

(a) Child not detained; filing petition, setting hearing

If the child is not taken into custody and the authorized petitioner (district attorney or probation officer) determines that a petition or notice of probation violation concerning the child should be filed, the petition or notice must be filed with the clerk of the juvenile court as soon as possible. The clerk must set an initial hearing on the petition within 15 court days.

(Subd (a) amended effective January 1, 2007.)

(b) Time limit for custody; filing petition (§§ 604, 631, 631.1)

A child must be released from custody within 48 hours, excluding noncourt days, after first being taken into custody unless a petition or notice of probation violation has been filed either within that time or before the time the child was first taken into custody.

(Subd (b) amended effective January 1, 2007.)

(c) Time limit on custody—willful misrepresentation of age (§ 631.1)

If the child willfully misrepresents the child's age to be 18 years or older, and this misrepresentation causes an unavoidable delay in investigation that prevents the filing of a petition or of a criminal complaint within 48 hours, excluding noncourt days, after the child has been taken into custody, the child must be released unless a petition or complaint has been filed within 48 hours, excluding noncourt days, from the time the true age is determined.

(Subd (c) amended effective January 1, 2007.)

(d) Time limit on custody—certification of child detained in custody (§ 604)

A child must be released from custody within 48 hours, excluding noncourt days, after certification to juvenile court under rules 4.116 and 5.516(d) unless a petition has been filed.

(Subd (d) amended effective January 1, 2007.)

(e) Time limit for detention hearing—warrant or nonward charged with nonviolent misdemeanor (§ 632)

A detention hearing must be set and commenced as soon as possible, but no later than 48 hours, excluding noncourt days, after the child has been taken into custody, if:

(1) The child has been taken into custody on a warrant or by the authority of the probation officer; or

(2) The child is not on probation or parole and is alleged to have committed a misdemeanor not involving violence, the threat of violence, or the possession or use of a weapon.

(Subd (e) amended effective January 1, 2007.)

(f) Time limit for detention hearing—felony, violent misdemeanor, or ward (§ 632)

A detention hearing must be set and commenced as soon as possible, but no later than the expiration of the next court day after the petition or notice of probation violation has been filed, if:

(1) The child is alleged to have committed a felony;

(2) The child is alleged to have committed a misdemeanor involving violence, the threat of violence, or the possession or use of a weapon; or

(3) The child is a ward currently on probation or parole.

(Subd (f) amended effective January 1, 2007.)

(g) Time limit for hearing—arrival at detention facility (§ 632)

A detention hearing must be set and commenced as soon as possible, but no later than 48 hours, excluding noncourt days, after the child arrives at a detention facility within the county if:

(1) The child was taken into custody in another county and transported in custody to the requesting county;

(2) The child was ordered transported in custody when transferred by the juvenile court of another county under rule 5.610; or

(3) The child is a ward temporarily placed in a secure facility pending a change of placement.

(Subd (g) amended effective January 1, 2007.)

(h) Time limit for hearing—violation of home supervision (§§ 628.1, 636)

A child taken into custody for a violation of a written condition of home supervision, which the child has promised in writing to obey under section 628.1 or 636, must be brought before the court for a detention hearing as soon as possible, but no later than 48 hours, excluding noncourt days, after the child was taken into custody.

(Subd (h) amended effective January 1, 2007.)

(i) Time limits—remedy for not observing (§§ 632, 641)

If the detention hearing is not commenced within the time limits, the child must be released immediately, or, if the child is a ward under section 602 awaiting a change of placement, the child must be placed in a suitable, nonsecure facility.

(Subd (i) amended effective January 1, 2007.)

Rule 5.752 amended and renumbered effective January 1, 2007; repealed and adopted as rule 1471 effective January 1, 1998.

Ref.: Cal. Fms Pl. & Pr., Ch. 329, "Juvenile Courts: Delinquency Proceedings"; W. Cal. Sum., 10 "Parent and Child" §§444, 764, 819, 820, 908.

Rule 5.754. Commencement of initial hearing—explanation, advisement, admission

(a) Explanation of proceedings (§ 633)

At the beginning of the initial hearing, whether the child is detained or not detained, the court must give the advisement required by rule 5.534 and must inform the child and each parent and each guardian present of the following:

(1) The contents of the petition;

(2) The nature and possible consequences of juvenile court proceedings; and

(3) If the child has been taken into custody, the reasons for the initial detention and the purpose and scope of the initial hearing.

(Subd (a) amended effective January 1, 2007.)

(b) Admission of allegations; no contest plea

If the child wishes to admit the allegations of the petition or enter a no contest plea at the initial hearing, the court may accept the admission or plea of no contest and must proceed according to rule 5.778.

(Subd (b) amended effective January 1, 2007.)

Rule 5.754 amended and renumbered effective January 1, 2007; repealed and adopted as rule 1472 effective January 1, 1998.

Ref.: Cal. Fms Pl. & Pr., Ch. 329, "Juvenile Courts: Delinquency Proceedings"; W. Cal. Sum., 10 "Parent and Child" §§444, 782, 820, 823, 824, 826, 908.

Rule 5.756. Conduct of detention hearing

(a) Right to inspect (§ 827)

The child, the parent, the guardian, and counsel are permitted to inspect and receive copies of police reports, probation reports, and any other documents filed with the court or made available to the probation officer in preparing the probation recommendations.

(Subd (a) amended effective January 1, 2007.)

(b) Examination by court (§ 635)

Subject to the child's privilege against self-incrimination, the court may examine the child, the parent, the guardian, and any other person present who has knowledge or information relevant to the issue of detention and must consider any relevant evidence that the child, the parent, the guardian, or counsel presents.

(Subd (b) amended effective January 1, 2007.)

(c) Evidence required

The court may base its findings and orders solely on written police reports, probation reports, or other documents.

Rule 5.756 amended and renumbered effective January 1, 2007; repealed and adopted as rule 1473 effective January 1, 1998.

Ref.: Cal. Fms Pl. & Pr., Ch. 329, "Juvenile Courts: Delinquency Proceedings"; W. Cal. Sum., 10 "Parent and Child" §§444, 782, 820, 825, 826, 908.

Rule 5.758. Requirements for detention; prima facie case

(a) Requirements for detention (§§ 635, 636)

The court must release the child unless the court finds that:

(1) A prima facie showing has been made that the child is described by section 601 or 602;

(2) Continuance in the home is contrary to the child's welfare; and

(3) One or more of the grounds for detention stated in rule 5.760 exist. However, except as provided in sections 636.2 and 207, no child taken into custody solely on the basis of being a person described in section 601 may be detained in juvenile hall or any other secure facility.

(Subd (a) amended effective January 1, 2007; previously amended effective July 1, 2002.)

(b) Detention in adult facility

A child must not be detained in a jail or lockup used for the confinement of adults, except as provided in section 207.1.

(Subd (b) amended effective July 1, 2002.)

Rule 5.758 amended and renumbered effective January 1, 2007; repealed and adopted as rule 1474 effective January 1, 1998; previously amended effective July 1, 2002.

Ref.: W. Cal. Sum., 10 "Parent and Child" §§444, 751, 755, 820, 827, 908.

Rule 5.760. Detention hearing; report; grounds; determinations; findings; orders; factors to consider for detention; restraining orders

(a) Conduct of detention hearing (§§ 635, 636)

The court must consider the written report of the probation officer and any other evidence and may examine the child, any parent or guardian, or any other person with relevant knowledge of the child.

(Subd (a) adopted effective January 1, 2007.)

(b) Written detention report (§§ 635, 636)

If the probation officer has reason to believe that the child is at risk of entering foster care placement, the probation officer must submit a written report to the court that includes the following:

(1) The reasons the child has been removed;

(2) Any prior referral for abuse or neglect of the child and any prior filing of a petition regarding the child under section 300;

(3) The need, if any, for continued detention;

(4) Available services to facilitate the return of the child;

(5) Whether there are any relatives able and willing to provide effective care and control over the child;

(6) Documentation that continuance in the home is contrary to the child's welfare; and

(7) Documentation that reasonable efforts were made to prevent or eliminate the need for removal of the child from the home and documentation of the nature and results of the services provided.

(Subd (b) amended and relettered effective January 1, 2007; adopted as subd (a) effective January 1, 2001; previously amended effective July 1, 2002.)

(c) Grounds for detention (§§ 625.3, 635, 636)

The child must be released unless the court finds that continuance in the home is contrary to the child's welfare, and one or more of the following grounds for detention exist:

(1) The child has violated an order of the court;

(2) The child has escaped from a commitment of the court;

(3) The child is likely to flee the jurisdiction of the court;

(4) It is a matter of immediate and urgent necessity for the protection of the child; or

(5) It is reasonably necessary for the protection of the person or property of another.

The court may order the child detained in juvenile hall, or in a suitable place designated by the court, or on home supervision under the conditions stated in sections 628.1 and 636.

(Subd (c) amended and relettered effective January 1, 2007; adopted as subd (a) effective January 1, 1998; amended and relettered as subd (b) effective January 1, 2001; previously amended effective July 1, 2002.)

(d) Required determinations before detention

Before detaining the child, the court must determine whether continuance in the home is contrary to the child's welfare and whether there are available services that would prevent the need for further detention. The court must make these determinations on a case-by-case basis and must state the evidence relied on in reaching its decision.

(1) If the court determines that the child can be returned home, through the provision of services, the court must release the child to the parent or guardian and order that the probation department provide the required services.

(2) If the child cannot be returned home, the court must state the facts on which the detention is based.

(Subd (d) amended and relettered effective January 1, 2007; adopted as subd (c) effective July 1, 2002.)

(e) Required findings to support detention (§ 636)

If the court orders the child detained, the court must make the following findings on the record and in the written, signed orders. The court must reference the probation officer's report or other evidence relied on to make its determinations:

(1) Continuance in the home of the parent or guardian is contrary to the child's welfare;

(2) Temporary placement and care is the responsibility of the probation officer pending disposition or further order of the court; and

(3) Reasonable efforts have been made to prevent or eliminate the need for removal of the child, or reasonable efforts were not made.

(Subd (e) amended and relettered effective January 1, 2007; adopted as subd (b) effective January 1, 1998; previously relettered as subd (c) effective January 1, 2001; previously amended and relettered as subd (d) effective July 1, 2002.)

(f) Required orders to support detention (§ 636)

If the court orders the child detained, the court must make the following additional orders:

(1) As soon as possible, the probation officer must provide services that will enable the child's parent or legal guardian to obtain such assistance as may be needed to effectively provide the care and control necessary for the child to return home; and

(2) The child's placement and care must be the responsibility of the probation department pending disposition or further order of the court.

(Subd (f) relettered effective January 1, 2007; adopted as subd (e) effective July 1, 2002.)

(g) Factors—violation of court order

Regarding ground for detention (c)(1), the court must consider:

(1) The specificity of the court order alleged to have been violated;

(2) The nature and circumstances of the alleged violation;

(3) The severity and gravity of the alleged violation;

(4) Whether the alleged violation endangered the child or others;

(5) The prior history of the child as it relates to any failure to obey orders or directives of the court or probation officer;

(6) Whether there are means to ensure the child's presence at any scheduled court hearing without detaining the child;

(7) The underlying conduct or offense that brought the child before the juvenile court; and

(8) The likelihood that if the petition is sustained, the child will be ordered removed from the custody of the parent or guardian at disposition.

(Subd (g) amended and relettered effective January 1, 2007; adopted as subd (c) effective January 1, 1998; previously relettered as subd (d) effective January 1, 2001; previously amended and relettered as subd (f) effective July 1, 2002.)

(h) Factors—escape from commitment

Regarding ground for detention (c)(2), the court must consider whether or not the child:

(1) Was committed to the California Department of Corrections and Rehabilitation, Division of Juvenile Justice; or a county juvenile home, ranch, camp, forestry camp, or juvenile hall; and

(2) Escaped from the facility or the lawful custody of any officer or person in which the child was placed during commitment.

(Subd (h) amended and relettered effective January 1, 2007; adopted as subd (d) effective January 1, 1998; previously relettered as subd (e) effective January 1, 2001; amended and relettered as subd (g) effective July 1, 2002; previously amended effective January 1, 2006.)

(i) Factors—likely to flee

Regarding ground for detention (c)(3), the court must consider whether or not:

(1) The child has previously fled the jurisdiction of the court or failed to appear in court as ordered;

(2) There are means to ensure the child's presence at any scheduled court hearing without detaining the child;

(3) The child promises to appear at any scheduled court hearing;

(4) The child has a prior history of failure to obey orders or directions of the court or the probation officer;

(5) The child is a resident of the county;

(6) The nature and circumstances of the alleged conduct or offense make it appear likely that the child would flee to avoid the jurisdiction of the court;

(7) The child's home situation is so unstable as to make it appear likely that the child would flee to avoid the jurisdiction of the court; and

(8) Absent a danger to the child, the child would be released on modest bail or own recognizance were the child appearing as an adult in adult court.

(Subd (i) amended and relettered effective January 1, 2007; adopted as subd (e) effective January 1, 1998; previously relettered as subd (f) effective January 1, 2001; previously amended and relettered as subd (h) effective July 1, 2002.)

(j) Factors—protection of child

Regarding ground for detention (c)(4), the court must consider whether or not:

(1) There are means to ensure the care and protection of the child until the next scheduled court appearance;

(2) The child is addicted to or is in imminent danger from the use of a controlled substance or alcohol; and

(3) There exist other compelling circumstances that make detention reasonably necessary.

(Subd (j) amended and relettered effective January 1, 2007; adopted as subd (f) effective January 1, 1998; previously relettered as subd (g) effective January 1, 2001; previously amended and relettered as subd (i) effective July 1, 2002.)

(k) Factors—protection of person or property of another

Regarding ground for detention (c)(5), the court must consider whether or not:

(1) The alleged offense involved physical harm to the person or property of another;

(2) The prior history of the child reveals that the child has caused physical harm to the person or property of another or has posed a substantial threat to the person or property of another; and

(3) There exist other compelling circumstances that make detention reasonably necessary.

(Subd (k) amended and relettered effective January 1, 2007; adopted as subd (g) effective January 1, 1998; previously relettered as subd (h) effective January 1, 2001; previously amended and relettered as subd (j) effective July 1, 2002.)

(l) Restraining orders

As a condition of release or detention on home supervision, the court may issue restraining orders as stated in rule 5.630 or orders restraining the child from any or all of the following:

(1) Molesting, attacking, striking, sexually assaulting, or battering, or from any contact whatsoever with an alleged victim or victim's family;

(2) Presence near or in a particular area or building; or

(3) Associating with or contacting in writing, by phone, or in person any adult or child alleged to have been a companion in the alleged offense.

(Subd (l) amended and relettered effective January 1, 2007; adopted as subd (i) effective January 1, 1998; previously relettered as subd (j) effective January 1, 2001; previously amended and relettered as subd (k) effective July 1, 2002.)

Rule 5.760 amended and renumbered effective January 1, 2007; repealed and adopted as rule 1475 effective January 1, 1998; previously amended effective January 1, 2001, July 1, 2002, and January 1, 2006.

Ref.: Cal. Fms Pl. & Pr., Ch. 329, "Juvenile Courts: Delinquency Proceedings"; W. Cal. Sum., 10 "Parent and Child" §§444, 820, 821, 825, 827–834, 908.

Rule 5.762. Detention rehearings

(a) No parent or guardian present and not noticed

If the court orders the child detained at the detention hearing and no parent or guardian is present and no parent or guardian has received actual notice of the detention hearing, a parent or guardian may file an affidavit alleging the failure of notice and requesting a detention rehearing. The clerk must set the rehearing within 24 hours of the filing of the affidavit, excluding noncourt days. At the rehearing, the court must proceed under rules 5.752–5.760.

(Subd (a) amended effective January 1, 2007.)

(b) Parent or guardian noticed; parent or guardian not present (§ 637)

If the court determines that the parent or guardian has received adequate notice of the detention hearing, and the parent or guardian fails to appear at the hearing, a request from the parent or guardian for a detention rehearing must be denied, absent a finding that the failure was due to good cause.

(Subd (b) amended effective January 1, 2007.)

(c) Parent or guardian noticed; preparers available (§ 637)

If a parent or guardian received notice of the detention hearing, and the preparers of any reports or other documents relied on by the court in its order detaining the child are present at court or otherwise available for cross-examination, there is no right to a detention rehearing.

(Subd (c) amended effective January 1, 2007.)

Rule 5.762 amended and renumbered effective January 1, 2007; repealed and adopted as rule 1476 effective January 1, 1998.

Ref.: Cal. Fms Pl. & Pr., Ch. 329, "Juvenile Courts: Delinquency Proceedings"; W. Cal. Sum., 10 "Parent and Child" §§444, 820, 826, 908.

Rule 5.764.   Prima facie hearings

(a) Hearing for further evidence; prima facie case (§ 637)

If the court orders the child detained, and the child or the child's attorney requests that evidence of the prima facie case be presented, the court must set a prima facie hearing for a time within three court days to consider evidence of the prima facie case.

(b) Continuance (§ 637)

If the court determines that a prima facie hearing cannot be held within three court days because of the unavailability of a witness, a reasonable continuance not to exceed five court days may be granted. If at the hearing petitioner fails to establish the prima facie case, the child must be released from custody.

Rule 5.764 adopted effective January 1, 2007.

Ref.: Cal. Fms Pl. & Pr., Ch. 329, "Juvenile Courts: Delinquency Proceedings"; W. Cal. Sum., 10 "Parent and Child" §§444, 826, 908.

Article 2
Fitness Hearings

Rule 5.766. General provisions
Rule 5.768. Report of probation officer
Rule 5.770. Conduct of fitness hearing under section 707(a)(1)
Rule 5.772. Conduct of fitness hearings under sections 707(a)(2) and 707(c)

Rule 5.766.   General provisions

(a) Fitness hearing (§ 707)

A child who is the subject of a petition under section 602(a) and who was 14 years or older at the time of the alleged offense may be considered for prosecution under the general law in a court of criminal jurisdiction. The prosecuting attorney may request a hearing to determine whether the child is a fit and proper subject to be dealt with under the juvenile court law, in one of the following circumstances:

(1) Under section 707(a)(1), the child was 16 years or older at the time of the alleged offense if the offense is not listed in section 707(b).

(2) Under section 707(a)(2), the child was 16 years or older at the time of the alleged felony offense not listed in section 707(b) and has been declared a ward of the court under section 602 on at least one prior occasion and:

(A) The child has previously been found to have committed two or more felony offenses; and

(B) The felony offenses in the previously sustained petitions were committed when the child was 14 years or older.

(3) Under section 707(c), the child was 14 years or older at the time of the alleged offense listed in section 707(b).

(Subd (a) amended effective January 1, 2001; previously amended January 1, 1996.)

(b) Notice (§ 707)

Notice of the fitness hearing must be given at least five judicial days before the fitness hearing.

(Subd (b) amended effective January 1, 2007.)

(c) Time of fitness hearing—rules 5.774, 5.776

The fitness hearing must be held and the court must rule on the issue of fitness before the jurisdiction hearing begins. Absent a continuance, the jurisdiction hearing must begin within the time limits under rule 5.774.

(Subd (c) amended effective January 1, 2007.)

Rule 5.766 amended and renumbered effective January 1, 2007; adopted as rule 1480 effective January 1, 1991; previously amended January 1, 1996, and January 1, 2001.

Ref.: Cal. Fms Pl. & Pr., Ch. 329, "Juvenile Courts: Delinquency Proceedings"; W. Cal. Sum., 10 "Parent and Child" §§444, 840.

Rule 5.768.   Report of probation officer

(a) Contents of report (§ 707)

The probation officer must investigate the issue of fitness and submit to the court a report on the behavioral patterns and social history of the child being considered. The report must include information relevant to the determination of whether or not the child would be amenable to the care, treatment, and training program available through the facilities of the juvenile court, including information regarding all of the criteria listed in rules 5.770 and 5.772. The report may also include information concerning:

(1) The social, family, and legal history of the child;

(2) Any statement the child chooses to make regarding the alleged offense;

(3) Any statement by a parent or guardian;

(4) If the child is or has been under the jurisdiction of the court, a statement by the social worker, probation officer, or Youth Authority parole agent who has supervised the child regarding the relative success or failure of any program of rehabilitation; and

(5) Any other information relevant to the determination of fitness.

(Subd (a) amended effective January 1, 2007.)

(b) Recommendation of probation officer (§§ 281, 707)

The probation officer must make a recommendation to the court as to whether the child is a fit and proper subject to be dealt with under the juvenile court law.

(Subd (b) amended effective January 1, 2007.)

(c) Copies furnished

The probation officer's report on the behavioral patterns and social history of the child must be furnished to the child, the parent or guardian, and all counsel at least 24 hours before commencement of the fitness hearing. A continuance of 24 hours must be granted on the request of any party who has not been furnished the probation officer's report in accordance with this rule.

(Subd (c) amended effective January 1, 2007.)

Rules of Court

Rule 5.768 amended and renumbered effective January 1, 2007; adopted as rule 1481 effective January 1, 1991.

Ref.: Cal. Fms Pl. & Pr., Ch. 329, "Juvenile Courts: Delinquency Proceedings"; W. Cal. Sum., 10 "Parent and Child" §§444, 841.

Rule 5.770. Conduct of fitness hearing under section 707(a)(1)

(a) Burden of proof (§ 707(a)(1))

In a fitness hearing under section 707(a)(1), the burden of proving that the child is unfit is on the petitioner, by a preponderance of the evidence.

(Subd (a) amended effective July 1, 2002; previously amended effective January 1, 1996, and January 1, 2001.)

(b) Criteria to consider (§ 707(a)(1))

Following receipt of the probation officer's report and any other relevant evidence, the court may find that the child is not a fit and proper subject to be dealt with under juvenile court law if the court finds:

(1) The child was 16 years or older at the time of the alleged offense; and

(2) The child would not be amenable to the care, treatment, and training program available through facilities of the juvenile court, based on an evaluation of all of the following criteria:

(A) The degree of criminal sophistication exhibited by the child;

(B) Whether the child can be rehabilitated before the expiration of jurisdiction;

(C) The child's previous delinquent history;

(D) The results of previous attempts by the court to rehabilitate the child; and

(E) The circumstances and gravity of the alleged offense.

(Subd (b) amended effective January 1, 2007; adopted as subd (b) effective January 1, 1991; previously amended and relettered as subd (c) effective January 1, 1996; previously amended and relettered effective January 1, 2001.)

(c) Findings under section 707(a)(1)

The findings must be stated in the order.

(1) *Finding of fitness*

The court may find the child to be fit and state that finding.

(2) *Finding of unfitness*

If the court determines the child is unfit, the court must find that:

(A) The child was 16 years or older at the time of the alleged offense; and

(B) The child would not be amenable to the care, treatment, and training program available through the juvenile court because of one or a combination of more than one of the criteria listed in (b)(2).

(Subd (c) amended effective January 1, 2007; adopted as subd (c) effective January 1, 1991; previously amended and relettered as subd (d) effective January 1, 1996; amended and relettered effective January 1, 2001; previously amended effective July 1, 2002.)

(d) Maintenance of juvenile court jurisdiction

If the court determines that one or more of the criteria listed in (b)(2) apply to the child, the court may nevertheless find that the child is amenable to the care, treatment, and training program available through the juvenile court and may find the child to be a fit and proper subject to be dealt with under juvenile court law.

(Subd (d) amended effective January 1, 2007; adopted as subd (e) effective January 1, 1996; previously amended and relettered effective January 1, 2001.)

(e) Extenuating circumstances

The court may consider extenuating or mitigating circumstances in the evaluation of each relevant criterion.

(Subd (e) relettered effective January 1, 2001; adopted as subd (f) effective January 1, 1996.)

(f) Procedure following findings

(1) If the court finds the child to be fit, the court must proceed to jurisdiction hearing under rule 5.774.

(2) If the court finds the child to be unfit, the court must make orders under section 707.1 relating to bail and to the appropriate facility for the custody of the child, or release on own recognizance pending prosecution. The court must dismiss the petition without prejudice.

(Subd (f) amended effective January 1, 2007; adopted as subd (d) effective January 1, 1991; previously relettered as subd (g) effective January 1, 1996, and as subd (f) effective January 1, 2001; previously amended effective July 1, 2002.)

(g) Continuance to seek review

If the prosecuting attorney informs the court orally or in writing that a review of a finding of fitness will be sought and requests a continuance of the jurisdiction hearing, the court must grant a continuance for not less than two judicial days to allow time within which to obtain a stay of further proceedings from the reviewing judge or appellate court.

(Subd (g) amended effective January 1, 2007; adopted as subd (e) effective January 1, 1991; previously relettered as subd (h) effective January 1, 1996, and as subd (g) effective January 1, 2001; previously amended effective July 1, 2002.)

(h) Subsequent role of judicial officer

Unless the child objects, the judicial officer who has conducted a fitness hearing may participate in any subsequent contested jurisdiction hearing relating to the same offense.

(Subd (h) amended and relettered effective January 1, 2001; adopted as subd (f) effective January 1, 1991; relettered as subd (i) effective January 1, 1996.)

(i) Review of fitness determination

An order that a child is or is not a fit and proper subject to be dealt with under the juvenile court law is not an appealable order. Appellate review of the order is by petition for extraordinary writ. Any petition for review of a judge's order determining the child unfit, or denying an application for rehearing of the referee's determination of unfitness, must be filed no later than 20 days after the child's first arraignment on an accusatory pleading based on the allegations that led to the unfitness determination.

(Subd (i) amended effective July 1, 2002; adopted as subd (g) effective January 1, 1991; previously relettered as subd (j) effective January 1, 1996; amended and relettered effective 1, 2001.)

Rule 5.770 amended and renumbered effective January 1, 2007; adopted as rule 1482 effective January 1, 1991; previously amended effective January 1, 1996, January 1, 2001, and July 1, 2002.

Ref.: Cal. Fms Pl. & Pr., Ch. 329, "Juvenile Courts: Delinquency Proceedings"; W. Cal. Sum., 10 "Parent and Child" §§444, 772, 836, 841, 842, 844, 849–851.

Rule 5.772.   Conduct of fitness hearings under sections 707(a)(2) and 707(c)

(a) Presumption (§§ 707(a)(2), 707(c))

In a fitness hearing under section 707(a)(2) or 707(c), the child is presumed to be unfit, and the burden of rebutting the presumption is on the child, by a preponderance of the evidence.

(Subd (a) amended effective January 1, 2007; previously amended effective January 1, 1996, and January 1, 2001.)

(b) Prima facie showing

On the child's motion, the court must determine whether a prima facie showing has been made that the offense alleged is a felony or is specified in section 707(b).

(Subd (b) amended effective January 1, 2007; previously amended effective January 1, 1996, and January 1, 2001.)

(c) Criteria to consider (§ 707(a)(2))

Following receipt of the probation officer's report and any other relevant evidence, the court must find that the child is not a fit and proper subject to be dealt with under the juvenile court law, unless the court finds:

(1) The child was under 16 years of age at the time of the alleged felony offense;

(2) The child had not been declared a ward at the time of the alleged offense or any time previously;

(3) The child has not previously been found to have committed two or more felony offenses;

(4) The prior felony offenses were committed before the child had reached the age of 14 years; or

(5) The child would be amenable to the care, treatment, and training program available through the juvenile court, based on evaluation of each of the following criteria:

(A) The degree of criminal sophistication exhibited by the child;

(B) Whether the child can be rehabilitated before the expiration of jurisdiction;

(C) The child's previous delinquent history;

(D) The results of previous attempts by the court to rehabilitate the child; and

(E) The circumstances and gravity of the alleged offense.

(Subd (c) amended effective January 1, 2007; previously amended effective January 1, 1996, and January 1, 2001.)

(d) Findings under section 707(c)

Following receipt of the probation officer's report and any other relevant evidence, the court must find that the child is not a fit and proper subject to be dealt with under the juvenile court law, unless the court finds:

(1) The child was under 14 years of age at the time of the offense specified in section 707(b);

(2) The offense alleged is not listed in section 707(b); or

(3) The child would be amenable to the care, treatment, and training program available through the juvenile court, based on evaluation of each of the criteria described in (c)(5).

(Subd (d) amended effective January 1, 2007.)

(e) Extenuating circumstances

The court may consider extenuating or mitigating circumstances in the evaluation of each relevant criterion.

(Subd (e) amended and relettered effective January 1, 2001; adopted as subd (d) effective January 1, 1996.)

(f) Findings (§§ 707(a)(2), 707(c))

The findings must be stated in the order.

(1) *Finding of unfitness (§ 707(a)(2))*

If the child has failed to rebut the presumption of unfitness, the court must find that:

(A) The child has previously been found to have committed two or more offenses listed in section 707(b) and was 14 years of age or older at the time of the felony offenses; and

(B) The child would not be amenable to the care, treatment, and training program available through the juvenile court because of one or a combination of more than one of the criteria in (c)(5).

(2) *Finding of unfitness (§ 707(c))*

If the child has failed to rebut the presumption of unfitness, the court must find that:

(A) The child was 14 years or older at the time of the alleged offense and the offense is listed in section 707(b); and

(B) The child would not be amenable to the care, treatment, and training program available through the juvenile court because of one or a combination of more than one of the criteria in (c)(5).

(3) *Finding of fitness (§§ 707(a)(2), 707(c))*

In order to find the child fit, the court must find that the child would be amenable to the care, treatment, and training program through the juvenile court on each and every criterion in (c)(5), and the court must state that finding of amenability under each and every criterion.

(Subd (f) amended effective January 1, 2007; adopted as subd (d) effective January 1, 1991; previously amended and relettered as subd (e) effective January 1, 1996; previously relettered effective January 1, 2001.)

(g) Procedure following findings

(1) If the court finds the child to be unfit, the court must make orders under section 707.1 relating to bail, and to the appropriate facility for the custody of the child, or release on own recognizance pending prosecution. The court must dismiss the petition without prejudice.

(2) If the court finds the child to be fit, the court must proceed to jurisdiction hearing under rule 5.774.

(Subd (g) amended effective January 1, 2007; adopted as subd (e) effective January 1, 1991; previously relettered as subd (f) effective January 1, 1996, and as subd (g) effective January 1, 2001.)

(h) Continuance to seek review

If the prosecuting attorney informs the court orally or in writing that a review of a finding of fitness will be sought and requests a continuance of the jurisdiction hearing, the [1] **court** must grant a continuance for not less than 2 judicial days to allow time within which to obtain a stay of further proceedings from the reviewing judge or appellate court.

(Subd (h) amended effective January 1, 2009; adopted as subd (f) effective January 1, 1991; previously relettered as subd (g) effective January 1, 1996; previously amended and relettered effective January 1, 2001; previously amended effective January 1, 2007.)

Rule 5.772(h).   2008 Deletes. [1] cour

(i) Subsequent role of judicial officer

Unless the child objects, the judicial officer who has conducted a fitness hearing may participate in any subsequent contested jurisdiction hearing relating to the same offense.

(Subd (i) amended and relettered effective January 1, 2001; adopted as subd (g) effective January 1, 1991; relettered as subd (h) effective January 1, 1996.)

(j) Review of fitness determination

An order that a child is or is not a fit and proper subject to be dealt with under the juvenile court law is not an appealable order. Appellate review of the order is by extraordinary writ. Any petition for review of a judge's order determining the child to be unfit or denying an application for rehearing of the referee's determination of unfitness must be filed no later than 20 days after the child's first arraignment on an accusatory pleading based on the allegations that led to the unfitness determination.

(Subd (j) amended effective January 1, 2007; adopted as subd (h) effective January 1, 1991; previously relettered as subd (i) effective January 1, 1996, and as subd (j) effective January 1, 2001.)

Rule 5.772 amended effective January 1, 2009; adopted as rule 1483 effective January 1, 1991; previously amended effective January 1, 1996, and January 1, 2001; previously amended and renumbered effective January 1, 2007.

Ref.: Cal. Fms Pl. & Pr., Ch. 329, "Juvenile Courts: Delinquency Proceedings"; W. Cal. Sum., 10 "Parent and Child" §§444, 772, 836, 837, 841–845, 849–851.

Article 3
Jurisdiction

Rule 5.774. Setting petition for hearing—detained and nondetained cases; waiver of hearing
Rule 5.776. Grounds for continuance of jurisdiction hearing
Rule 5.778. Commencement of hearing on section 601 or section 602 petition; right to counsel; advisement of trial rights; admission, no contest
Rule 5.780. Contested hearing on section 601 or section 602 petition
Rule 5.782. Continuance pending disposition hearing

Rule 5.774. Setting petition for hearing—detained and nondetained cases; waiver of hearing

(a) Nondetention cases (§ 657)

If the child is not detained, the jurisdiction hearing on the petition must begin within 30 calendar days from the date the petition is filed.

(Subd (a) amended effective January 1, 2007.)

(b) Detention cases (§ 657)

If the child is detained, the jurisdiction hearing on the petition must begin within 15 judicial days from the date of the order of the court directing detention. If the child is released from detention before the jurisdiction hearing, the court may reset the jurisdiction hearing within the time limit in (a).

(Subd (b) amended effective January 1, 2007.)

(c) Tolling of time period

Any period of delay caused by the child's unavailability or failure to appear must not be included in computing the time limits of (a) and (b).

(Subd (c) amended effective January 1, 2007.)

(d) Dismissal

Absent a continuance under rule 5.776, when a jurisdiction hearing is not begun within the time limits of (a)

and (b), the court must order the petition dismissed. This does not bar the filing of another petition based on the same allegations as in the original petition, but the child must not be detained.

(Subd (d) amended effective January 1, 2007.)

(e) Waiver of hearing (§ 657)

At the detention hearing, or at any time thereafter, a child may admit the allegations of the petition or plead no contest and waive further jurisdiction hearing. The court may accept the admission or no contest plea and proceed according to rules 5.778 and 5.782.

(Subd (e) amended effective January 1, 2007.)

Rule 5.774 amended and renumbered effective January 1, 2007; adopted as rule 1485 effective January 1, 1991.

Ref.: Cal. Fms Pl. & Pr., Ch. 329, "Juvenile Courts: Delinquency Proceedings"; W. Cal. Sum., 10 "Parent and Child" §§444, 775, 824, 840, 842, 856–859, 889.

Rule 5.776. Grounds for continuance of jurisdiction hearing

(a) Request for continuance; consent (§ 682)

A continuance may be granted only on a showing of good cause and only for the time shown to be necessary. Stipulation between counsel or parties and convenience of parties are not in and of themselves good cause.

(1) In order to obtain a continuance, written notice with supporting documents must be filed and served on all parties at least two court days before the date set for the hearing, unless the court finds good cause for failure to comply with these requirements. Absent a waiver of time, a child may not be detained beyond the statutory time limits.

(2) The court must state in its order the facts requiring any continuance that is granted.

(3) If the child is represented by counsel and no objection is made to an order setting or continuing the jurisdiction hearing beyond the time limits of rule 5.774, consent must be implied.

(Subd (a) amended effective January 1, 2007.)

(b) Grounds for continuance—mandatory (§ 700)

The court must continue the jurisdiction hearing for:

(1) A reasonable period to permit the child and the parent, guardian, or adult relative to prepare for the hearing; and

(2) No more than seven calendar days:

(A) For appointment of counsel;

(B) To enable counsel to become acquainted with the case; or

(C) To determine whether the parent, guardian, or adult relative can afford counsel.

(Subd (b) amended effective January 1, 2007.)

(c) Grounds for continuance—discretionary (§§ 700.5, 701)

The court may continue the jurisdiction hearing for no more than seven calendar days to enable the petitioner to subpoena witnesses if the child has made an extrajudicial admission and denies it, or has previously indicated to the court or petitioner an intention to admit the allegations of the petition, and at the time set for jurisdiction hearing denies the allegations.

(d) Grounds for continuance—section 654.2 (§§ 654.2, 654.3, 654.4)

In a case petitioned under section 602, the court may, with the consent of the child and the parent or guardian, continue the jurisdiction hearing for six months. If the court grants the continuance, the court must order the child and the parent or guardian to participate in a program of supervision under section 654, and must order the parent or guardian to participate with the child in a program of counseling or education under section 654.

(Subd (d) amended effective January 1, 2007.)

Rule 5.776 amended and renumbered effective January 1, 2007; adopted as rule 1486 effective January 1, 1991.

Ref.: Cal. Fms Pl. & Pr., Ch. 329, "Juvenile Courts: Delinquency Proceedings"; W. Cal. Sum., 10 "Parent and Child" §§444, 787, 817, 857, 859.

Rule 5.778. Commencement of hearing on section 601 or section 602 petition; right to counsel; advisement of trial rights; admission, no contest

(a) Petition read and explained (§ 700)

At the beginning of the jurisdiction hearing, the petition must be read to those present. On request of the child, or the parent, guardian, or adult relative, the court must explain the meaning and contents of the petition, the nature of the hearing, the procedures of the hearing, and possible consequences.

(Subd (a) amended effective January 1, 2007.)

(b) Rights explained (§ 702.5)

After giving the advisement required by rule 5.534, the court must advise those present of each of the following rights of the child:

(1) The right to a hearing by the court on the issues raised by the petition;

(2) The right to assert the privilege against self-incrimination;

(3) The right to confront and to cross-examine any witness called to testify against the child; and

(4) The right to use the process of the court to compel the attendance of witnesses on the child's behalf.

(Subd (b) amended effective January 1, 2007.)

(c) Admission of allegations; prerequisites to acceptance

The court must then inquire whether the child intends to admit or deny the allegations of the petition. If the child neither admits nor denies the allegations, the court must state on the record that the child does not admit the allegations. If the child wishes to admit the allegations, the court must first find and state on the record that it is satisfied that the child understands the nature of the allegations and the direct consequences of the admission, and understands and waives the rights in (b).

(Subd (c) amended effective January 1, 2007.)

(d) Consent of counsel—child must admit

Counsel for the child must consent to the admission, which must be made by the child personally.

(Subd (d) amended effective January 1, 2007.)

(e) No contest

The child may enter a plea of no contest to the allegations, subject to the approval of the court.

(f) Findings of the court (§ 702)

On an admission or plea of no contest, the court must make the following findings noted in the minutes of the court:

(1) Notice has been given as required by law;

(2) The birthdate and county of residence of the child;

(3) The child has knowingly and intelligently waived the right to a hearing on the issues by the court, the right to confront and cross-examine adverse witnesses and to use the process of the court to compel the attendance of witnesses on the child's behalf, and the right to assert the privilege against self-incrimination;

(4) The child understands the nature of the conduct alleged in the petition and the possible consequences of an admission or plea of no contest;

(5) The admission or plea of no contest is freely and voluntarily made;

(6) There is a factual basis for the admission or plea of no contest;

(7) Those allegations of the petition as admitted are true as alleged;

(8) The child is described by section 601 or 602; and

(9) In a section 602 matter, the degree of the offense and whether it would be a misdemeanor or felony had the offense been committed by an adult. If any offense may be found to be either a felony or misdemeanor, the court must consider which description applies and expressly declare on the record that it has made such consideration and must state its determination as to whether the offense is a misdemeanor or a felony. These determinations may be deferred until the disposition hearing.

(Subd (f) amended effective January 1, 2007; previously amended effective January 1, 1998.)

(g) Disposition

After accepting an admission or plea of no contest, the court must proceed to disposition hearing under rules 5.782 and 5.785.

(Subd (g) amended effective January 1, 2007.)

Rule 5.778 amended and renumbered effective January 1, 2007; adopted as rule 1487 effective January 1, 1991; previously amended effective January 1, 1998.

Ref.: Cal. Fms Pl. & Pr., Ch. 329, "Juvenile Courts: Delinquency Proceedings"; W. Cal. Sum., 10 "Parent and Child" §§444, 782, 824, 855, 864–867, 869.

Rule 5.780. Contested hearing on section 601 or section 602 petition

(a) Contested jurisdiction hearing (§ 701)

If the child denies the allegations of the petition, the court must hold a contested hearing to determine whether the allegations in the petition are true.

(Subd (a) amended effective January 1, 2007.)

(b) Admissibility of evidence—general (§ 701)

In a section 601 matter, the admission and exclusion of evidence must be in accordance with the Evidence Code as it applies in civil cases. In a section 602 matter, the admission and exclusion of evidence must be in accordance with the Evidence Code as it applies in criminal cases.

(Subd (b) amended effective January 1, 2007.)

(c) Probation reports

Except as otherwise provided by law, the court must not read or consider any portion of a probation report relating to the contested petition before or during a contested jurisdiction hearing.

(Subd (c) amended effective January 1, 2007.)

(d) Unrepresented children (§ 701)

If the child is not represented by counsel, objections that could have been made to the evidence must be deemed made.

(Subd (d) amended effective January 1, 2007.)

(e) Findings of court—allegations true (§ 702)

If the court determines by a preponderance of the evidence in a section 601 matter, or by proof beyond a reasonable doubt in a section 602 matter, that the allegations of the petition are true, the court must make findings on each of the following, noted in the order:

(1) Notice has been given as required by law;

(2) The birthdate and county of residence of the child;

(3) The allegations of the petition are true;

(4) The child is described by section 601 or 602; and

(5) In a section 602 matter, the degree of the offense and whether it would be a misdemeanor or a felony had the offense been committed by an adult. If any offense may be found to be either a felony or a misdemeanor, the court must consider which description applies and expressly declare on the record that it has made such consideration, and must state its determination as to whether the offense is a misdemeanor or a felony. These determinations may be deferred until the disposition hearing.

(Subd (e) amended effective January 1, 2007; previously amended effective January 1, 1998.)

(f) Disposition

After making the findings in (e), the court must then proceed to disposition hearing under rules 5.782 and 5.785.

(Subd (f) amended effective January 1, 2007.)

(g) Findings of court—allegations not proved (§ 702)

If the court determines that the allegations of the petition have not been proved by a preponderance of the evidence in a 601 matter, or beyond a reasonable doubt in a 602 matter, the court must make findings on each of the following, noted in the order:

(1) Notice has been given as required by law;

(2) The birthdate and county of residence of the child; and

(3) The allegations of the petition have not been proved.

The court must dismiss the petition and terminate detention orders related to this petition.

(Subd (g) amended effective January 1, 2007.)

Rule 5.780 amended and renumbered effective January 1, 2007; adopted as rule 1488 effective January 1, 1991; previously amended effective January 1, 1998.

Ref.: Cal. Fms Pl. & Pr., Ch. 329, "Juvenile Courts: Delinquency Proceedings"; W. Cal. Sum., 10 "Parent and Child" §§444, 870–872, 878, 882, 894, 895.

Rule 5.782. Continuance pending disposition hearing

(a) Continuance pending disposition hearing (§ 702)

If the court finds that the child is described by section 601 or 602, it must proceed to a disposition hearing. The court may continue the disposition hearing up to 10 judicial days if the child is detained. If the child is not detained, the court may continue the disposition hearing up to 30 calendar days from the date of the filing of the petition and up to an additional 15 calendar days for good cause shown.

(Subd (a) amended effective January 1, 2007.)

(b) Detention pending hearing (§ 702)

The court may release or detain the child during the period of the continuance.

(c) Observation and diagnosis (§ 704)

If the child is eligible for commitment to the Youth Authority, the court may continue the disposition hearing up to 90 calendar days and order the child to be placed temporarily at a Youth Authority diagnostic and treatment center for observation and diagnosis. The court must order the Youth Authority to submit a diagnosis and recommendation within 90 days, and the probation officer or any other peace officer designated by the court must place the child in the diagnostic and treatment center and return the child to the court. After return from the diagnostic and treatment center, the child must be brought to court within 2 judicial days. A disposition hearing must be held within 10 judicial days thereafter.

(Subd (c) amended effective January 1, 2007.)

Rule 5.782 amended and renumbered effective January 1, 2007; adopted as rule 1489 effective January 1, 1991.

Ref.: Cal. Fms Pl. & Pr., Ch. 329, "Juvenile Courts: Delinquency Proceedings"; W. Cal. Sum., 10 "Parent and Child" §§444, 824, 883.

Article 4
Disposition

Rule 5.785. General conduct of hearing
Rule 5.790. Orders of the court
Rule 5.795. Required determinations
Rule 5.800. Deferred entry of judgment
Rule 5.805. California Department of Corrections and Rehabilitation, Division of Juvenile Justice, commitments

Rule 5.785. General conduct of hearing

(a) Social study (§§ 280, 702, 706.5)

The probation officer must prepare a social study of the child, which must contain all matters relevant to disposition, including any parole status information, and a recommendation for disposition.

(1) In any case in which the probation officer is recommending placement in foster care or in which the child is already in foster care placement or pending placement under an earlier order, the social study must include a case plan as described in (c).

(2) The probation officer must submit the social study and copies of it to the clerk at least 48 hours before the disposition hearing is set to begin, and the clerk must make the copies available to the parties and attorneys. A continuance of up to 48 hours must be granted on the request of a party who has not been furnished a copy of the social study in accordance with this rule.

(Subd (a) amended effective January 1, 2007; previously amended effective July 1, 2002.)

(b) Evidence considered (§ 706)

The court must receive in evidence and consider the social study and any relevant evidence offered by the petitioner, the child, or the parent or guardian. The court may require production of other relevant evidence on its own motion. In the order of disposition the court must state that the social study has been read and considered by the court.

(Subd (b) amended effective July 1, 2002.)

(c) Case plan (§§ 636.1, 706.6, 16501.1)

When a child is detained and is at risk of entering foster care placement, the probation officer must prepare a case plan.

(1) The plan must be completed and filed with the court by the date of disposition or within 60 calendar days of initial removal, whichever occurs first.

(2) The court must consider the case plan and must find as follows:

(A) The probation officer solicited and integrated into the case plan the input of the child, the child's family, the child's identified Indian tribe, and other interested parties; or

(B) The probation officer did not solicit and integrate into the case plan the input of the child, the child's family, the child's identified Indian tribe, and other interested parties. If the court finds that the probation officer did not solicit and integrate into the case plan the input of the child, the child's family, the child's identified Indian tribe, and other interested parties, the court must order that the probation officer solicit and integrate into the case plan the input of the child, the child's family, the child's identified Indian tribe, and other interested parties, unless the court finds that each of these participants was unable, unavailable, or unwilling to participate.

(3) For a child 12 years of age or older and in a permanent placement, the court must consider the case plan and must find as follows:

(A) The child was given the opportunity to review the case plan, sign it, and receive a copy; or

(B) The child was not give the opportunity to review the case plan, sign it, and receive a copy. If the court makes such a finding, the court must order the probation officer to give the child the opportunity to review the case plan, sign it, and receive a copy, unless the court finds that the child was unable, unavailable, or unwilling to participate.

(4) If the probation officer believes that the child will be able to return home through reasonable efforts by the child, the parents or guardian, and the probation officer, the case plan must include the elements described in section 636.1(b).

(5) If the probation officer believes that foster care placement is the most appropriate disposition for the child, the case plan must include all of the information required by section 706.6.

(Subd (c) amended effective January 1, 2007; adopted effective July 1, 2002.)

Rule 5.785 amended and renumbered effective January 1, 2007; adopted as rule 1492 effective January 1, 1991; previously amended effective July 1, 2002.

Ref.: Cal. Fms Pl. & Pr., Ch. 329, "Juvenile Courts: Delinquency Proceedings"; W. Cal. Sum., 10 "Parent and Child" §§444, 884–887.

Rule 5.790. Orders of the court

(a) Findings and orders of the court (§§ 654, 654.1, 654.2, 654.3, 654.4, 725, 725.5, 782)

At the disposition hearing:

(1) If the court has not previously considered whether any offense is a misdemeanor or felony, the court must do so at this time and state its finding on the record. If the offense may be found to be either a felony or a misdemeanor, the court must consider which description applies and must expressly declare on the record that it has made such consideration and must state its finding as to whether the offense is a misdemeanor or a felony.

(2) The court may then:

(A) Dismiss the petition in the interests of justice and the welfare of the child or, if the child does not need treatment or rehabilitation, with the specific reasons stated in the minutes;

(B) Place the child on probation for no more than six months, without declaring the child a ward; or

(C) Declare the child a ward of the court.

(Subd (a) amended effective January 1, 2007; previously amended effective January 1, 1998, and July 1, 2002.)

(b) Conditions of probation (§§ 725, 726, 727, 729.2, 729.9, 729.10)

(1) If the child is placed on probation, with or without wardship, the court must set reasonable terms and conditions of probation. Unless the court finds and states its reasons on the record that any of the following conditions is inappropriate, the court must:

(A) Require the child to attend school;

(B) Require the parent to participate with the child in a counseling or education program; and

(C) Require the child to be at the child's residence between 10:00 p.m. and 6:00 a.m. unless accompanied by a parent or a guardian or an adult custodian.

(2) If the child is declared a ward, the court may limit the control over the child by a parent or guardian. Orders must clearly specify the limitations.

(Subd (b) amended effective January 1, 2007; previously amended effective July 1, 2002.)

(c) Custody and visitation (§ 726.5)

At any time while the child is a ward of the juvenile court or at the time wardship is terminated, the court may issue an order determining custody of, or visitation with, the child as described in rule 5.700.

(Subd (c) adopted effective January 1, 2007.)

(d) Removal of custody—required findings (§ 726)

The court must not order a ward removed from the physical custody of a parent or guardian unless the court finds:

(1) The parent or guardian has failed or neglected to provide, or is incapable of providing, proper maintenance, training, and education for the child;

(2) The child has been on probation in the custody of the parent or guardian and during that time has failed to reform; or

(3) The welfare of the child requires that physical custody be removed from the parent or guardian.

(Subd (d) amended and relettered effective January 1, 2007; adopted as subd (c) effective January 1, 1991; previously amended effective July 1, 2002.)

(e) Removal of custody—orders regarding reunification services (§ 727.2)

(1) Whenever the court orders the care, custody, and control of the child to be under the supervision of the

probation officer for placement, the court must order the probation department to ensure the provision of reunification services to facilitate the safe return of the child to his or her home or the permanent placement of the child and to address the needs of the child while in foster care.

(2) Reunification services need not be provided to the parent or guardian if the court finds, by clear and convincing evidence, that one or more of the exceptions listed in section 727.2(b) is true.

(Subd (e) amended and relettered effective January 1, 2007; adopted as subd (d) effective July 1, 2002; previously amended effective January 1, 2004.)

(f) Wardship orders (§§ 726, 727, 727.1, 730, 731)

The court may make any reasonable order for the care, supervision, custody, conduct, maintenance, support, and medical treatment of a child declared a ward.

(1) Subject to the provisions of section 727, the court may order the ward to be on probation without the supervision of the probation officer and may impose on the ward reasonable conditions of behavior.

(2) The court may order the care, custody, control, and conduct of the ward to be under the supervision of the probation officer in the home of a parent or guardian.

(3) If the court orders removal of custody under (d), it must authorize the probation officer to place the ward with a person or organization described in section 727. The decision regarding choice of placement must take into account the following factors:

(A) That the setting is safe;

(B) That the setting is the least restrictive or most family-like environment that is appropriate for the child and available;

(C) That the setting is in close proximity to the parent's home; and

(D) That the setting is the environment best suited to meet the child's special needs and best interest.

The selection must consider, in order of priority, placement with relatives, tribal members, and foster family, group care, and residential treatment under Family Code section 7950.

(4) If the child was declared a ward under section 602, the court may order treatment or commitment of the child under section 730 or 731.

(5) The court must consider whether it is necessary to limit the right of the parent or guardian to make educational decisions for the child. If the court limits this right, it must follow the procedures stated in rule 5.650.

(Subd (f) amended effective January 1, 2008; adopted as subd (d) effective January 1, 1991; previously amended and relettered as subd (e) effective July 1, 2002, and as subd (f) effective January 1, 2007; previously amended effective January 1, 2004.)

(g) California Department of Corrections and Rehabilitation, Division of Juvenile Justice

If, at the time of the disposition hearing, the child is a ward of the California Department of Corrections and Rehabilitation, Division of Juvenile Justice (DJJ) under a prior commitment, the court may either recommit or return the child to the DJJ. If the child is returned to the DJJ, the court may:

(1) Recommend that the ward's parole status be revoked;

(2) Recommend that the ward's parole status not be revoked; or

(3) Make no recommendation regarding revocation of parole.

(Subd (g) amended and relettered effective January 1, 2007; adopted as subd (e) effective January 1, 1991; previously amended and relettered as subd (f) effective July 1, 2002; previously amended effective January 1, 2006.)

(h) Fifteen-day reviews (§ 737)

If the child is detained pending the implementation of a disposition order, the court must review the case at least every 15 days as long as the child is detained. The court must inquire about the action taken by the probation officer to carry out the court's order, the reasons for the delay, and the effects of the delay on the child.

(Subd (h) amended and relettered effective January 1, 2007; adopted as subd (f) effective January 1, 1991; previously amended and relettered as subd (g) effective July 1, 2002.)

Rule 5.790 amended effective January 1, 2008; adopted as rule 1493 effective January 1, 1991; previously amended effective January 1, 1998, July 1, 2002, January 1, 2004, and January 1, 2006; previously amended and renumbered effective January 1, 2007.

Ref.: Cal. Fms Pl. & Pr., Ch. 329, "Juvenile Courts: Delinquency Proceedings"; W. Cal. Sum., 10 "Parent and Child" §§444, 886, 889, 890, 892, 893, 897, 904, 942, 955.

Rule 5.795. Required determinations

(a) Felony or misdemeanor (§ 702)

Unless determined previously, the court must find and note in the minutes the degree of the offense committed by the youth, and whether it would be a felony or a misdemeanor had it been committed by an adult. If any offense may be found to be either a felony or a misdemeanor, the court must consider which description applies and expressly declare on the record that it has made such consideration and must state its determination as to whether the offense is a misdemeanor or a felony.

(Subd (a) amended effective January 1, 2007; previously amended effective January 1, 2003.)

(b) Physical confinement (§ 726)

If the youth is declared a ward under section 602 and ordered removed from the physical custody of a parent or guardian, the court must specify and note in the minutes the maximum period of confinement under section 726.

(Subd (b) amended effective January 1, 2007; previously amended effective January 1, 2003.)

Rule 5.795 amended and renumbered effective January 1, 2007; adopted as rule 1494 effective January 1, 1991; previously amended effective January 1, 2001, and January 1, 2003.

Ref.: Cal. Fms Pl. & Pr., Ch. 329, "Juvenile Courts: Delinquency Proceedings"; W. Cal. Sum., 10 "Parent and Child" §§444, 944.

Rule 5.800. Deferred entry of judgment

(a) Eligibility (§ 790)

A child 14 years or older who is the subject of a petition under section 602 alleging violation of at least one felony offense may be considered for a deferred entry of judgment if all of the following apply:

(1) The child is 14 years or older at the time of the hearing on the application for deferred entry of judgment;

(2) The offense alleged is not listed in section 707(b);

(3) The child has not been previously declared a ward of the court based on the commission of a felony offense;

(4) The child has not been previously committed to the California Department of Corrections and Rehabilitation, Division of Juvenile Justice;

(5) If the child is presently or was previously a ward of the court, probation has not been revoked before completion; and

(6) The child meets the eligibility standards stated in Penal Code section 1203.06.

(Subd (a) amended effective January 1, 2006.)

(b) Procedures for consideration (§ 790)

Before filing a petition alleging a felony offense, or as soon as possible after filing, the prosecuting attorney must review the child's file to determine if the requirements of (a) are met. If the prosecuting attorney's review reveals that the requirements of (a) have been met, the prosecuting attorney must file *Determination of Eligibility—Deferred Entry of Judgment—Juvenile* (form JV-750) with the petition.

(1) If the court, the prosecuting attorney, and the child's attorney agree that the child should receive a deferred entry of judgment, the hearing under this rule must proceed on an expedited basis.

(2) If the court, the prosecuting attorney, and the child's attorney do not agree that the child should receive a deferred entry of judgment, the court may examine the record and make an independent determination. If it is determined that the child should not receive a deferred entry of judgment, the case must proceed under chapter 14, articles 1 through 4, of this division.

(Subd (b) amended effective January 1, 2007.)

(c) Citation (§ 792)

The court must issue *Citation and Written Notification for Deferred Entry of Judgment—Juvenile* (form JV-751) to the child's custodial parent, guardian, or foster parent. The form must be personally served on the custodial adult at least 24 hours before the time set for the appearance hearing.

(Subd (c) amended effective January 1, 2007.)

(d) Determination without a hearing; supplemental information (§ 791)

(1) The court may grant a deferred entry of judgment as stated in (2) or (3).

(2) If the child waives the right to a speedy disposition hearing, the court may summarily grant the deferred entry of judgment.

(3) When appropriate, the court may order the probation department to prepare a report with recommendations on the suitability of the child for deferred entry of judgment or set a hearing on the matter, with or without the order to the probation department for a report.

(A) The probation report must address the following:

(i) The child's age, maturity, educational background, family relationships, motivation, any treatment history, and any other relevant factors regarding the benefit the child would derive from education, treatment, and rehabilitation efforts; and

(ii) The programs best suited to assist the child and the child's family.

(B) The probation report must be submitted to the court, the child, the prosecuting attorney, and the child's attorney at least 48 hours, excluding noncourt days, before the hearing.

(Subd (d) amended effective January 1, 2007.)

(e) Written notification of ineligibility (§ 790)

If it is determined that the child is ineligible for deferred entry of judgment, the prosecuting attorney must complete and provide to the court, the child, and the child's attorney *Determination of Eligibility—Deferred Entry of Judgment—Juvenile* (form JV-750).

(Subd (e) amended effective January 1, 2007.)

(f) Conduct of hearing (§§ 791, 794)

At the hearing, the court must consider the declaration of the prosecuting attorney, any report and recommendations from the probation department, and any other relevant material provided by the child or other interested parties.

(1) If the child consents to the deferred entry of judgment, the child must enter an admission as stated in rule 5.778(c) and (d). A no-contest plea must not be accepted.

(2) The child must waive the right to a speedy disposition hearing.

(3) After acceptance of the child's admission, the court must set a date for review of the child's progress and a date by which the probation department must submit to the court, the child, the child's parent or guardian, the child's attorney, and the prosecuting attorney a report on the child's adherence to the conditions set by the court. Although the date set may be any time within the following 36 months, consideration of dismissal of the petition may not occur until at least 12 months have passed since the court granted the deferred entry of judgment.

(4) If the court grants the deferred entry of judgment, the court must order search-and-seizure probation conditions and may order probation conditions regarding the following:

(A) Education;

(B) Treatment;

(C) Testing for alcohol and other drugs, if appropriate;

(D) Curfew; and

(E) Any other conditions consistent with the identified needs of the child and the factors that led to the conduct of the child.

(Subd (f) amended effective January 1, 2007.)

(g) Compliance with conditions; progress review

Twelve months after the court granted the deferred entry of judgment and on receipt of the progress report ordered at the hearing on the deferred entry of judgment, the court may:

(1) Find that the child has complied satisfactorily with the conditions imposed, dismiss the petition, seal the court records in compliance with section 793(c), and vacate the date set for review hearing; or

(2) Confirm the review hearing. At the hearing the court must:

(A) Find that the child has complied satisfactorily with the conditions imposed, dismiss the petition, and seal the court records in compliance with section 793(c); or

(B) Find that the child has not complied satisfactorily with the conditions imposed, lift the deferred entry of judgment, and set a disposition hearing.

(Subd (g) amended effective January 1, 2007.)

(h) Failure to comply with conditions (§ 793)

(1) Before the date of the progress hearing, if the child is found to have committed a misdemeanor offense or more than one misdemeanor offense on a single occasion, the court may schedule a hearing within 15 court days.

(A) At the hearing, the court must follow the procedure stated in rule 5.580(d) and (e) to determine if the deferred entry of judgment should be lifted, with a disposition hearing to be conducted thereafter.

(B) The disposition hearing must be conducted as stated in rules 5.785 through 5.795.

(C) The child's admission of the charges under a deferred entry of judgment must not constitute a finding that a petition has been sustained unless a judgment is entered under section 793(b).

(2) Before the date of the progress hearing, on the court's own motion, or if the court receives a declaration from the probation department or the prosecuting attorney alleging that the child has not complied with the conditions imposed or that the conditions are not benefiting the child, or if the child is found to have committed a felony offense or two or more misdemeanor offenses on separate occasions, the court must schedule a hearing within 10 court days.

(A) At the hearing, the court must follow the procedure stated in rule 5.580(d) and (e) to determine if the deferred entry of judgment should be lifted, with a disposition hearing to be conducted thereafter.

(B) The disposition hearing must be conducted as stated in rules 5.785 through 5.795.

(C) The child's admission of the charges under a deferred entry of judgment must not constitute a finding that a petition has been sustained unless a judgment is entered under section 793(b).

(3) If the child is found to have committed a felony offense or two or more misdemeanor offenses on separate occasions, the court must schedule a disposition hearing within 10 court days. The disposition hearing must be conducted as stated in rules 5.785 through 5.795.

(4) If the judgment previously deferred is imposed and a disposition hearing is scheduled under section 793(a), the juvenile court must report the complete criminal history of the child to the Department of Justice under section 602.5.

(Subd (h) amended effective January 1, 2007.)

Rule 5.800 amended and renumbered effective January 1, 2007; adopted as rule 1495 effective January 1, 2001; previously amended effective January 1, 2006.

Ref.: Cal. Fms Pl. & Pr., Ch. 329, "Juvenile Courts: Delinquency Proceedings"; W. Cal. Sum., 10 "Parent and Child" §§444, 891.

Rule 5.805.   California Department of Corrections and Rehabilitation, Division of Juvenile Justice, commitments

If the court orders the youth committed to the California Department of Corrections and Rehabilitation, Division of Juvenile Justice (DJJ):

(1) The court must complete *Commitment to the California Department of Corrections and Rehabilitation, Division of Juvenile Justice* (form JV-732).

(2) The court must specify whether the offense is one listed in section 707(b).

(3) The court must order the probation department to forward to the DJJ all required medical information, including previously executed medical releases.

(4) If the youth is taking a prescribed psychotropic medication, the DJJ may continue to administer the medication for up to 60 days, provided that a physician examines the youth on arrival at the facility, and the physician recommends that the medication continue.

(5) The court must provide to the DJJ information regarding the youth's educational needs, including the youth's current individualized education program if one exists. To facilitate this process, the court must ensure that the probation officer communicates with appropriate educational staff.

Rule 5.805 amended and renumbered effective January 1, 2007; adopted as rule 1494.5 effective January 1, 2003; previously amended effective January 1, 2006.

Ref.: W. Cal. Sum., 10 "Parent and Child" §§444, 942, 951, 952.

Article 5
Reviews and Sealing

Rule 5.810. Reviews, hearings, and permanency planning
Rule 5.815. Appointment of legal guardians for wards of the juvenile court; modification or termination of guardianship
Rule 5.820. Termination of parental rights for child in foster care for 15 of the last 22 months
Rule 5.825. Freeing wards for adoption
Rule 5.830. Sealing records

Rule 5.810.   Reviews, hearings, and permanency planning

(a) Six-month status review hearings (§§ 727.2, 11404.1)

For any ward removed from the custody of his or her parent or guardian under section 726 and placed in a home under section 727, the court must conduct a status review hearing no less frequently than once every six months from the date the ward entered foster care. The court may consider the hearing at which the initial order for placement is made as the first status review hearing.

(1) *Consideration of reports (§ 727.2(d))*

The court must review and consider the social study report and updated case plan submitted by the probation officer and the report submitted by any CASA volunteer, and any other reports filed with the court under section 727.2(d).

(2) *Return of child if not detrimental (§ 727.2(f))*

At any status review hearing before the first permanency hearing, the court must order the return of the ward to the parent or guardian unless it finds the probation department has established by a preponderance of evidence that return would create a substantial risk of detriment to the safety, protection, or physical or emotional well-being of the ward. The probation department has the burden of establishing that detriment. In making its determination, the court must review and consider all reports submitted to the court and must consider the efforts and progress demonstrated by the child and the family and the extent to which the child availed himself or herself of the services provided.

(3) *Findings and orders (§ 727.2(d))*

The court must consider the safety of the ward and make findings and orders that determine the following:

(A) The continuing necessity for and appropriateness of the placement;

(B) The extent of the probation department's compliance with the case plan in making reasonable efforts to safely return the child to the child's home and to complete whatever steps are necessary to finalize the permanent placement of the child;

(C) Whether it is necessary to limit the right of the parent or guardian to make educational decisions for the child. If the court limits this right, it must appoint a responsible adult as the educational representative. Any limitation on the right of a parent or guardian to make educational decisions for the child must be specified in the court order. The court must follow the procedures stated in rule 5.650;

(D) The extent of progress that has been made by the child and parent or guardian toward alleviating or mitigating the causes necessitating placement in foster care;

(E) The likely date by which the child may return to and be safely maintained in the home or placed for adoption, legal guardianship, or another permanent plan;

(F) In the case of a child who is 16 years of age or older, the court must determine the services needed to assist the child in making the transition from foster care to independent living; and

(G) Whether or not the child was actively involved in the development of his or her own case plan and plan for permanent placement. If the court makes such a finding, the court must order the probation department to actively involve the child in the development of his or her own case plan and plan for permanent placement, unless the court finds that the child is unable, unavailable, or unwilling to participate; and

(H) Each parent was actively involved in the development of the case plan and plan for permanent placement; or

(I) Each parent was not actively involved in the development of the case plan and plan for permanent placement. If the court makes such a finding, the court must order the agency to actively involve each parent in the development of the case plan and plan for permanent placement, unless the court finds that each parent is unable, unavailable, or unwilling to participate.

(4) The determinations required by (a)(3) must be made on a case-by-case basis, and the court must reference, in its written findings, the probation officer's report and any other evidence relied on in reaching its decision.

(Subd (a) amended effective January 1, 2007; previously amended effective January 1, 1998, January 1, 2001, January 1, 2003, and January 1, 2004.)

(b) Permanency planning hearings (§§ 727.2, 727.3, 11404.1)

A permanency planning hearing for any ward who has been removed from the custody of a parent or guardian and not returned at a previous review hearing must be held within 12 months of the date the ward entered foster care

and periodically thereafter, but no less frequently than once every 12 months while the ward remains in placement. However, when no reunification services are offered to the parents or guardians under section 727.2(b), the first permanency planning hearing must occur within 30 days of disposition.

(1) *Consideration of reports (§ 727.3)*

The court must review and consider the social study report and updated case plan submitted by the probation officer and the report submitted by any CASA volunteer, and any other reports filed with the court under section 727.3(a)(2).

(2) *Findings and orders*

At each permanency planning hearing, the court must consider the safety of the ward and make findings and orders regarding the following:

(A) The continuing necessity for and appropriateness of the placement;

(B) The extent of the probation department's compliance with the case plan in making reasonable efforts to safely return the child to the child's home and to complete whatever steps are necessary to finalize the permanent placement of the child;

(C) The extent of progress that has been made by the child and parent or guardian toward alleviating or mitigating the causes necessitating placement in foster care;

(D) The permanent plan for the child, as described in (3);

(E) Whether or not the child was not actively involved in the development of his or her own case plan and plan for permanent placement. If the court finds that the child was not actively involved in the development of his or her own case plan and plan for permanent placement, the court must order the probation officer to actively involve the child in the development of his or her own case plan and plan for permanent placement, unless the court finds that the child is unable, unavailable, or unwilling to participate; and

(F) Each parent was actively involved in the development of the case plan and plan for permanent placement; or

(G) Each parent was not actively involved in the development of the case plan and plan for permanent placement. If the court makes such a finding, the court must order the agency to actively involve each parent in the development of the case plan and plan for permanent placement, unless the court finds that each parent is unable, unavailable, or unwilling to participate.

(3) *Selection of a permanent plan (§ 727.3(b))*

At the first permanency planning hearing, the court must select a permanent plan. At subsequent permanency planning hearings, the court must either make a finding that the current permanent plan is appropriate or select a different permanent plan, including returning the child home, if appropriate. The court must choose from one of the following permanent plans, which are, in order of priority:

(A) A permanent plan that immediately returns the child to the physical custody of the parent or guardian. This plan must be the permanent plan unless no reunification services were offered under section 727.2(b), or unless the court finds that the probation department has established by a preponderance of evidence that return would create a substantial risk of detriment to the safety, protection, or physical or emotional well being of the ward. The probation department has the burden of establishing that detriment. In making its determination, the court must review and consider all reports submitted to the court and must consider the efforts or progress, or both, demonstrated by the child and family and the extent to which the child availed himself or herself of the services provided.

(B) A permanent plan of return of the child to the physical custody of the parent or guardian, after 6 additional months of reunification services. The court may not order this plan unless the court finds that there is a substantial probability that the child will be able to return home within 18 months of the date of initial removal.

(C) A permanent plan of adoption. When this plan is identified, the court must order that a hearing under section 727.31 be held within 120 days.

(D) A permanent plan of legal guardianship. When this plan is ordered, the court must set a hearing under the procedures described in section 728 and rule 5.815.

(E) A permanent plan of placement with a fit and willing relative. When this plan is ordered, the court must specify that the child will be placed with the appropriate relative on a permanent basis.

(F) A permanent plan of placement in a planned permanent living arrangement. The court may order this permanent plan only after considering, and ruling out, each of the other permanent plan options listed above. If, after doing so, the court concludes that a planned permanent living arrangement is the most appropriate permanent plan for the child, it must also enter a finding, by clear and convincing evidence, that there is a compelling reason, as defined in section 727.3(c), for determining that a plan of termination of parental rights and adoption is not in the best interest of the child. When a planned permanent living arrangement is ordered, the court must specify the type of placement. The court must also specify the goal of the placement, which may include, but is not limited to, a goal of the child returning home, emancipation, guardianship, or permanent placement with a relative.

(4) *Involvement of parents or guardians*

If the child has a continuing involvement with his or her parents or legal guardians, they must be involved in the planning for permanent placement. The permanent plan order must include an order regarding the nature and frequency of visitation with the parents or guardians.

(Subd (b) amended effective January 1, 2007; adopted effective January 1, 2001; previously amended effective January 1, 2003.)

(c) Postpermanency status review hearings (§ 727.2)

A postpermanency status review hearing must be conducted for wards in placement annually, 6 months after each permanency planning hearing.

(1) *Consideration of reports (§ 727.2(d))*

The court must review and consider the social study report and updated case plan submitted for this hearing by the probation officer and the report submitted by any CASA volunteer, and any other reports filed with the court under section 727.2(d).

(2) *Findings and orders*

At each postpermanency status review hearing, the court must consider the safety of the ward and make findings and orders regarding the following:

(A) Whether the current permanent plan continues to be appropriate. If not, the court must select a different permanent plan, including returning the child home, if appropriate. The court must not order the permanent plan of returning home after 6 more months of reunification services, as described in (b)(3)(B), unless it has been 18 months or less since the date the child was removed from home;

(B) The continuing necessity for and appropriateness of the placement;

(C) The extent of the probation department's compliance with the case plan in making reasonable efforts to complete whatever steps are necessary to finalize the permanent plan for the child; and

(D) Whether or not the child was actively involved in the development of his or her own case plan and plan for permanent placement. If the court makes such a finding, the court must order the agency to actively involve the child in the development of his or her own case plan and plan for permanent placement, unless the court finds that the child is unable, unavailable, or unwilling to participate.

(Subd (c) amended effective January 1, 2007; adopted effective January 1, 2001; previously amended effective January 1, 2003.)

(d) Notice of hearings; service; contents (§ 727.4)

Not earlier than 30 nor later than 15 calendar days before each hearing date the probation officer must serve written notice on all persons required to receive notice under section 727.4, as well as the child's present caregiver, any CASA volunteer, and the counsel of record. A *Notice of Hearing—Juvenile Delinquency Proceeding* (form JV-625) must be used.

(Subd (d) amended effective January 1, 2007; adopted effective January 1, 2001; previously amended effective January 1, 2003, and January 1, 2006.)

(e) Report (§§ 706.5, 706.6, 727.2(c), 727.3(a)(1), 727.4(b))

Before each hearing described above, the probation officer must investigate and prepare a social study report, including an updated case plan, that must include all of the information required in sections 706.5, 706.6, 727.2, and 727.3.

(1) The report must contain recommendations for court orders and must document the evidentiary basis for those recommendations.

(2) At least 10 calendar days before each hearing, the petitioner must file the report and provide copies of the report to the ward, the parent or guardian, all attorneys of record, and any CASA volunteer.

(Subd (e) amended effective January 1, 2007; adopted as subd (b) effective January 1, 1991; previously amended effective January 1, 1998; previously amended and relettered as subd (e) effective January 1, 2001; previously amended effective January 1, 2003.)

(f) Hearing by administrative panel (§§ 727.2(h), 727.4(d)(7))

The status review hearings described in (a) and (c) may be conducted by an administrative review panel, provided:

(1) The ward, parent or guardian, and all those entitled to notice under section 727.4 may attend;

(2) Proper notice is provided;

(3) The panel has been appointed by the presiding judge of the juvenile court and includes at least one person who is not responsible for the case management of, or

delivery of service to, the ward or the parent or guardian; and

(4) The panel makes findings as required by (a)(3) or (c)(2) above and submits them to the juvenile court for approval and inclusion in the court record.

(Subd (f) amended effective January 1, 2007; adopted effective January 1, 2001; previously amended effective January 1, 2003.) Rule 5.810 amended and renumbered effective January 1, 2007; adopted as rule 1496 effective January 1, 1991; previously amended effective January 1, 1998, January 1, 2001, January 1, 2003, January 1, 2004, and January 1, 2006.

Ref.: Cal. Fms Pl. & Pr., Ch. 329, "Juvenile Courts: Delinquency Proceedings"; W. Cal. Sum., 10 "Parent and Child" §§444, 896, 898.

Rule 5.815. Appointment of legal guardians for wards of the juvenile court; modification or termination of guardianship

(a) Proceedings in juvenile court (§ 728)

Proceedings for the appointment of a legal guardian for a child who is a ward of the juvenile court under section 725(b) may be held in the juvenile court.

(Subd (a) amended effective January 1, 2007.)

(b) Recommendation for guardianship (§ 728(c))

On the recommendation of the probation officer supervising the child, the motion of the attorney representing the child, or the court's own motion and order that a legal guardian should be appointed for the child, the court must set a hearing to consider the establishment of a legal guardianship and must order the probation officer to prepare an assessment that includes:

(1) A review of the existing relationship between the child and the proposed guardian;

(2) A summary of the child's medical, developmental, educational, mental, and emotional status;

(3) A social history of the proposed guardian, including a screening for criminal records and any prior referrals for child abuse or neglect;

(4) An assessment of the ability of the proposed guardian to meet the child's needs and the proposed guardian's understanding of the legal and financial rights and responsibilities of guardianship; and

(5) A statement confirming that the proposed guardian has been provided with a copy of *Guardianship Pamphlet* (form JV-350) or *Guardianship Pamphlet (Spanish)* (form JV-350S).

(Subd (b) amended effective January 1, 2007.)

(c) Forms

The probation officer or child's attorney may use *Juvenile Wardship Petition* (form JV-600) and *Petition to Modify Previous Orders—Change of Circumstances* (form JV-740) to request that a guardianship hearing be set.

(Subd (c) amended effective January 1, 2007.)

(d) Notice (§ 728(c))

The clerk must provide notice of the hearing to the child, the child's parents, and other individuals as required by Probate Code section 1511.

(e) Conduct of hearing

The court must read and consider the assessment prepared by the probation officer and any other evidence. The preparer of the assessment must be available for examination by the court or any party to the proceedings.

(f) Findings and orders

If the court finds that establishment of a legal guardianship is necessary or convenient and consistent with the rehabilitation and protection of the child and with public safety, the court must appoint a legal guardian and order the clerk to issue letters of guardianship *(Letters of Guardianship (Juvenile)* (form JV-330)).

(1) The court may issue orders regarding visitation and contact between the child and a parent or other relative.

(2) After the appointment of a legal guardian, the court may continue juvenile court wardship and supervision or may terminate wardship.

(Subd (f) amended effective January 1, 2007; previously amended effective July 1, 2006.)

(g) Modification or termination of the guardianship, or appointment of a co-guardian or successor guardian

A petition to terminate a guardianship established by the juvenile court, to appoint a co-guardian or successor guardian, or to modify or supplement orders regarding the guardianship must be filed and heard in juvenile court. The procedures described in rule 5.570 must be followed, and *Juvenile Wardship Petition* (form JV-600) and *Petition to Modify Previous Orders—Change of Circumstances* (form JV-740) must be used. The hearing on the motion may be held simultaneously with any regularly scheduled hearing regarding the child.

(Subd (g) amended effective January 1, 2007.)

Rule 5.815 amended and renumbered effective January 1, 2007; adopted as rule 1496.2 effective January 1, 2004; previously amended effective July 1, 2006.

Ref.: W. Cal. Sum., 10 "Parent and Child" §§444, 892.

Rule 5.820. Termination of parental rights for child in foster care for 15 of the last 22 months

(a) Requirement (§§ 727.32(a), 16508.1)

Whenever a child has been declared a ward and has been in any foster care placement for 15 of the most recent 22 months, the probation department must follow the procedures described in section 727.31 to terminate the parental rights of the child's parents. The probation department is not required to follow these procedures if it has documented a compelling reason in the probation file, as defined in section 727.3(c), for determining that termination of parental rights would not be in the child's best interest, or if it has not provided the family with reasonable efforts necessary to achieve reunification.

(1) If the probation department sets a hearing under section 727.31, it must also make efforts to identify an approved family for adoption.

(2) If the probation department has determined that a compelling reason exists, it must document that reason in the case file. The documentation may be a separate document or may be included in another court document, such as the social study prepared for a permanency planning hearing.

(Subd (a) amended effective January 1, 2007.)

(b) Calculating time in foster care (§ 727.32(d))

The following guidelines must be used to determine if the child has been in foster care for 15 of the most recent 22 months:

(1) Determine the date the child entered foster care, as defined in rule 5.502(a)(9). In some cases, this will be the date the child entered foster care as a dependent.

(2) Calculate the total number of months since the date in (1) that the child has spent in foster care. Do not start over if a new petition is filed or for any other reason.

(3) If the child is in foster care for a portion of a month, calculate the total number of days in foster care during that month. Add one month to the total number of months for every 30 days the child is in foster care.

(4) Exclude time during which the child was detained in the home of a parent or guardian; the child was living at home on formal or informal probation, at home on a trial home visit, or at home with no probationary status; the child was a runaway or "absent without leave" (AWOL); or the child was out of home in a non–foster care setting, including juvenile hall; California Department of Corrections and Rehabilitation, Division of Juvenile Justice; a ranch; a camp; a school; or any other locked facility.

(5) Once the total number of months in foster care has been calculated, determine how many of those months occurred within the most recent 22 months. If that number is 15 or more, the requirement in (a) applies.

(6) If the requirement in (a) has been satisfied once, there is no need to take additional action or provide additional documentation after any subsequent 22-month period.

(Subd (b) amended effective January 1, 2007; previously amended effective January 1, 2006.)

Rule 5.820 amended and renumbered effective January 1, 2007; adopted as rule 1496.3 effective January 1, 2003; previously amended effective January 1, 2006.

Ref.: W. Cal. Sum., 10 "Parent and Child" §§444, 899.

Rule 5.825. Freeing wards for adoption

(a) Applicable law (§§ 294, 366.26, 727.2, 727.3, 727.31)

Except as provided in section 727.31, the procedures for termination of parental rights to free children described in that section for adoption are stated in sections 294 and 366.26. Rules 5.725 and 5.730 are applicable to these proceedings.

(Subd (a) amended effective January 1, 2007; previously amended effective January 1, 2006.)

(b) Joint county protocol

In each county, the county probation department and the county child welfare department must jointly develop a protocol for freeing wards for adoption. The protocol should address questions such as:

(1) When and how will wards be referred to the licensed county adoption agency, or State Department of Social Services when it is acting as the adoption agency, for a determination of whether the ward is adoptable, as described by section 727.3(i)(2)?

(2) Once a finding has been made that the permanent plan for the ward must be adoption and the case is set for a section 727.31 hearing, how will the referral be made to the licensed county adoption agency, or to the State Department of Social Services when it is acting as the adoption agency, to prepare an adoption assessment, as required by section 727.3(j)?

(3) Will the probation department continue to have ongoing case management and supervision of the case, pending the termination of parental rights hearing?

(4) Will the probation department or the child welfare department prepare the notices and other legal documents required before a termination of parental rights hearing?

(5) In counties in which different judicial officers hear delinquency and dependency matters, what procedure will be used to ensure that the dependency judge will hear each 727.31 hearing?

(6) Will the probation department or the child welfare department prepare the petition for adoption and other forms needed after the 727.31 hearing to complete the adoption process?

(Subd (b) amended effective January 1, 2007.)

Rule 5.825 amended and renumbered effective January 1, 2007; adopted as rule 1496.5 effective January 1, 2001; previously amended effective January 1, 2006.

Ref.: W. Cal. Sum., 10 "Parent and Child" §§444, 899.

Rule 5.830. Sealing records

(a) Sealing records—former wards (§ 781)

A former ward of the court may apply to petition the court to order juvenile records sealed. Determinations under section 781 must be made by the court in the county in which wardship was last terminated.

(1) *Application—submission*

The application for a petition to seal records must be submitted to the probation department in the county in which wardship was last terminated.

(2) *Investigation*

If the probation officer determines that under section 781 the former ward is eligible to petition for sealing, the probation officer must do all of the following:

(A) Prepare the petition;

(B) Conduct an investigation under section 781;

(C) Prepare a report to the court with a recommendation supporting or opposing the requested sealing; and

(D) Within 90 days from receipt of the application if only the records of the investigating county are to be reviewed, or within 180 days from receipt of the application if records of other counties are to be reviewed:

(i) File the petition;

(ii) Set the matter for a hearing, which may be nonappearance; and

(iii) Notify the prosecuting attorney of the hearing.

(3) The court must review the petition and the report of the probation officer, and the court must grant or deny the petition.

(4) If the petition is granted, the court must order the sealing of all records described in section 781. The order must apply in the county of the court hearing the petition and in all other counties in which there are juvenile records concerning the petitioner.

(Subd (a) amended effective January 1, 2007.)

(b) Sealing—nonwards

For all other persons described in section 781, application may be submitted to the probation department in any county in which there is a juvenile record concerning the petitioner, and the procedures of (a) must be followed.

(Subd (b) amended effective January 1, 2007.)

(c) Destruction of records

All records sealed must be destroyed according to section 781(d).

(Subd (c) amended effective January 1, 2007.)

(d) Distribution of order

The clerk of the issuing court must:

(1) Send a copy of the order to each agency and official listed in the order; and

(2) Send a certified copy of the order to the clerk in each county in which a record is ordered sealed.

(Subd (d) amended effective January 1, 2007.)

(e) Deadline for sealing

Each agency and official notified must immediately seal all records as ordered.

(Subd (e) amended effective January 1, 2007.)

Rule 5.830 amended and renumbered effective January 1, 2007; adopted as rule 1499 effective January 1, 1991; previously renumbered as rule 1497 effective January 1, 1999.

Ref.: Cal. Fms Pl. & Pr., Ch. 329, "Juvenile Courts: Delinquency Proceedings"; W. Cal. Sum., 10 "Parent and Child" §§444, 503.

TITLE 6
[Reserved]

TITLE 7
Probate Rules

Chapter 1
General Provisions

Rule 7.1.   Probate Rules

The rules in this title may be referred to as the Probate Rules.

Rule 7.1 adopted effective January 1, 2007.

Ref.: Cal. Fms Pl. & Pr., Ch. 442, "Probate: Initiating Probate Administration," Ch. 445, "Probate: Independent Administration of Estates," Ch. 510, "Sanctions"; MB Prac. Guide: Cal. Pretrial Proc., §35.07[1][a]; W. Cal. Sum., 13 "Trusts" §226, 14 "Wills and Probate" §§4, 372, 960.

Rule 7.2.   Preliminary provisions
(a) Application of rules

The rules in this title apply to every action and proceeding to which the Probate Code applies and, unless they are elsewhere explicitly made applicable, do not apply to any other action or proceeding.

(Subd (a) amended effective January 1, 2007.)

(b) Purpose of rules

The rules in this title are designed to implement the purposes of the probate law by promoting uniformity in practice and procedure.

(Subd (b) amended effective January 1, 2007.)

(c) Rules of construction

Unless the context otherwise requires, these preliminary provisions and the following rules of construction govern the construction of the rules in this title:

(1) To the extent that the rules in this title are substantially the same as existing statutory provisions relating to the same subject matter, they must be construed as a restatement and a continuation of those statutes; and

(2) To the extent that the rules in this title may add to existing statutory provisions relating to the same subject matter, they must be construed so as to implement the purposes of the probate law.

(Subd (c) amended effective January 1, 2007; previously amended effective January 1, 2003.)

(d) Jurisdiction

The rules in this title are not intended to expand, limit, or restrict the jurisdiction of the court in proceedings under the Probate Code.

(Subd (d) adopted effective January 1, 2003.)

Rule 7.2 amended and renumbered effective January 1, 2007; adopted as rule 7.1 effective January 1, 2000; previously amended effective January 1, 2003.

Ref.: Cal. Fms Pl. & Pr., Ch. 280, "Guardianship and Conservatorship: Appointment of Guardians," Ch. 284, "Guardianship and Conservatorship: Notice," Ch. 442, "Probate: Initiating Probate Administration"; W. Cal. Sum., 14 "Wills and Probate" §§4, 372, 377, 385.

Rule 7.3.   Definitions and use of terms

As used in the rules in this title, unless the context or subject matter otherwise requires:

(1) The definitions in division 1, part 2 of the Probate Code apply.

(2) "Pleading" means a contest, answer, petition, application, objection, response, statement of interest, report, or account filed in proceedings under the Probate Code.

(3) "Amended pleading" means a pleading that completely restates and supersedes the pleading it amends for all purposes.

(4) "Amendment to a pleading" means a pleading that modifies another pleading and alleges facts or requests relief materially different from the facts alleged or the relief requested in the modified pleading. An amendment to a pleading does not restate or supersede the modified pleading but must be read together with that pleading.

(5) "Supplement to a pleading" and "supplement" mean a pleading that modifies another pleading but does

not allege facts or request relief materially different from the facts alleged or the relief requested in the supplemented pleading. A supplement to a pleading may add information to or may correct omissions in the modified pleading.

Rule 7.3 amended and renumbered effective January 1, 2007; adopted as rule 7.2 effective January 1, 2000; previously amended effective January 1, 2002, and January 1, 2003.

Ref.: Cal. Fms Pl. & Pr., Ch. 442, "Probate: Initiating Probate Administration"; W. Cal. Sum., 14 "Wills and Probate" §§4, 372, 377, 385.

Rule 7.4. Waiver of rules in probate proceedings

The court for good cause may waive the application of the rules in this title in an individual case.

Rule 7.4 renumbered effective January 1, 2007; adopted as rule 7.3 effective January 1, 2000; previously amended effective January 1, 2003.

Ref.: Cal. Fms Pl. & Pr., Ch. 442, "Probate: Initiating Probate Administration"; W. Cal. Sum., 14 "Wills and Probate" §§4, 372.

Rule 7.10. Ex parte communications in proceedings under the probate code and certain other proceedings

(a) Definitions

As used in this rule, the following terms have the meanings stated below:

(1) "Fiduciary" has the meaning specified in Probate Code section 39, and includes LPS conservators.

(2) "Person" has the meaning specified in Probate Code section 56.

(3) "Pleading" has the meaning specified in rule 7.3, but also includes petitions and objections or other opposition filed in LPS conservatorships. The term does not include creditors' claims and requests for special notice.

(4) A "party" is a fiduciary appointed in a proceeding under the Probate Code or an LPS conservatorship proceeding, and any other person who has filed a pleading in the proceeding concerning a matter then pending in the court.

(5) A "ward" is a minor subject to a guardianship under Division 4 of the Probate Code, including a proposed ward concerning whom a petition for appointment of a guardian has been filed.

(6) "Ex parte communication" is a communication between any party, attorney, or person in a proceeding under the Probate Code or an LPS conservatorship proceeding and the court outside the presence of all parties and attorneys, including written communications sent to the court without copies having been provided to other interested persons.

(7) "LPS Act" is the Lanterman-Petris-Short Act, part 1 of division 5 of the Welfare and Institutions Code, commencing with section 5000.

(8) "LPS Conservatorship" is a conservatorship proceeding under chapter 3 of the LPS Act, commencing with section 5350 of the Welfare and Institutions Code, for persons gravely disabled as the result of a mental disorder or impairment by chronic alcoholism.

(9) A "conservatee" is a person subject to a conservatorship under division 4 of the Probate Code or chapter 3

of the LPS Act, including a proposed conservatee concerning whom a petition for appointment of a conservator has been filed.

(10) A "matter then pending in the court" in proceedings under the Probate Code or in an LPS conservatorship proceeding refers to a request for relief or opposition in pleadings filed in the proceeding that has not yet been resolved by a decision of the court or an agreement of the parties.

(11) Concerning a proceeding under the Probate Code or an LPS conservatorship proceeding, the term "open proceeding" refers to a proceeding that has been commenced and has not been concluded by the final discharge of all fiduciaries or otherwise terminated as provided by law, whether or not there is a matter then pending in the court in the proceeding at any point in time.

(Subd (a) adopted effective January 1, 2008.)

(b) Ex parte communications by parties and attorneys prohibited

(1) Except under a stipulation of all parties to the contrary, no ex parte communications may be made by a party or an attorney for a party and the court concerning a matter then pending in the court in proceedings under the Probate Code or in an LPS conservatorship proceeding.

(2) Except as provided in (c)(1), the court must treat an ex parte communication to the court described in (1) in the same way that an ex parte communication from a party or attorney for a party must be treated in other civil actions or proceedings or in criminal actions.

(Subd (b) adopted effective January 1, 2008.)

(c) Ex parte communications received and considered

(1) Notwithstanding (b)(2), a judicial officer or court staff may receive an ex parte communication concerning an open proceeding under the Probate Code or an open LPS conservatorship proceeding for the limited purpose of ascertaining whether it is a communication described in (b) or a communication described in (c)(2).

(2) Subject to the requirements of (c)(3), a judicial officer may consider an ex parte communication from a person about a fiduciary's performance of his or her duties and responsibilities or regarding a conservatee or ward in an open proceeding under the Probate Code or an open LPS conservatorship proceeding. The court may decline to take further action on the communication, with or without replying to the person or returning any written communication received from the person. The court may also take appropriate action, consistent with due process and California law, including one or any combination of the following:

(A) Review the court file and take any action that is supported by the record, including ordering a status report or accounting if it appears that a status report or accounting should have been filed by a fiduciary but is delinquent.

(B) Refer the communication to a court investigator for further action, and receive, consider, and respond to any report from the investigator concerning it;

(C) If the communication discloses possible criminal activity, refer the matter to the appropriate law enforcement agency or prosecutor's office;

(D) If the communication discloses conduct that might subject a person or organization to disciplinary action on a license, refer the matter to the appropriate licensing agency;

(E) If the communication discloses possible elder or dependent adult abuse, or child abuse, refer the matter to appropriate state or local governmental agencies, including adult protective or child protective service departments; and

(F) Set a hearing regarding the communication, compel the fiduciary's attendance, and require a response from the fiduciary concerning the issues raised by the communication.

(3) The court must fully disclose communications described in (c)(2) and any response made by the court to the fiduciary and all other parties to any matter then pending in the court, and their attorneys, unless the court finds good cause to dispense with the disclosure if necessary to protect a conservatee or ward from harm. If the court dispenses with disclosure to any party or attorney, it must make written findings in support of its determination of good cause, and preserve the communication received and any response made by the court. The court may place its findings and the preserved communication under seal or otherwise secure their confidentiality.

(Subd (c) adopted effective January 1, 2008.)
Rule 7.10 adopted effective January 1, 2008.

Ref.: Cal. Fms Pl. & Pr., Ch. 280, "Guardianship and Conservatorship: Appointment of Guardians."

Chapter 2
Notices, Publication, and Service

Rule 7.50. Description of pleading in notice of hearing
Rule 7.51. Service of notice of hearing
Rule 7.52. Service of notice when recipient's address unknown
Rule 7.53. Notice of hearing of amended or supplemented pleadings
Rule 7.54. Publication of Notice of Petition to Administer Estate
Rule 7.55. Ex parte application for order

Rule 7.50. Description of pleading in notice of hearing

The notice of hearing on a pleading filed in a proceeding under the Probate Code must state the complete title of the pleading to which the notice relates.

Rule 7.50 adopted effective January 1, 2003.

Ref.: Cal. Fms Pl. & Pr., Ch. 284, "Guardianship and Conservatorship: Notice," Ch. 447, "Probate: Statutory Notice Requirements"; W. Cal. Sum., 14 "Wills and Probate" §§4, 386.

Rule 7.51. Service of notice of hearing

(a) Direct notice required

(1) Except as otherwise permitted in the Probate Code, a notice sent by mail under Probate Code section 1220 must be mailed individually and directly to the person entitled to notice.

(2) A notice mailed to a person in care of another person is insufficient unless the person entitled to notice is an adult and has directed the party giving notice in writing to send the notice in care of the second person.

(3) Notices mailed to more than one person in the same household must be sent separately to each person.

(b) Notice to attorney

If a notice is required or permitted to be given to a person who is represented by an attorney of record in the proceeding, the notice must be sent as required in Probate Code section 1214.

(c) Notice to guardian or conservator

(1) When a guardian or conservator has been appointed for a person entitled to notice, the notice must be sent to the guardian or conservator.

(2) A copy of the notice must also be sent to the ward or conservatee unless:

(A) The court dispenses with such notice; or

(B) Under Probate Code section 1210 in a decedent's estate proceeding, the notice is personally served on a California-resident guardian or conservator of the estate of the ward or conservatee.

(Subd (c) amended effective January 1, 2004.)

(d) Notice to minor

Except as permitted in Probate Code section 1460.1 for guardianships, conservatorships, and certain protective proceedings under division 4 of the Probate Code, notice to a minor must be sent directly to the minor. A separate copy of the notice must be sent to the person or persons having legal custody of the minor, with whom the minor resides.

(e) Notice required in a decedent's estate when a beneficiary has died

(1) *Notice when a beneficiary dies after the decedent*

Notice must be sent to the personal representative of a beneficiary who died after the decedent and survived for a period required by the decedent's will. If no personal representative has been appointed for the postdeceased beneficiary, notice must be sent to his or her beneficiaries or other persons entitled to succeed to his or her interest in the decedent's estate.

(2) *Notice when a beneficiary of the decedent's will dies before the decedent*

When a beneficiary under the will of the decedent died before the decedent or fails to survive the decedent for a period required by the decedent's will, notice must be sent to the persons named in the decedent's will as substitute beneficiaries of the gift to the predeceased beneficiary. If the decedent's will does not make a substitute disposition of that gift, notice must be sent as follows:

(A) If the predeceased beneficiary is a "transferee" under Probate Code section 21110(c), to the issue of the predeceased beneficiary determined under Probate Code section 240 and to the residuary beneficiaries of the decedent or to the decedent's heirs if decedent's will does not provide for distribution of the residue of the estate.

(B) If the predeceased beneficiary is not a "transferee" under Probate Code section 21110(c), to the residuary beneficiaries of the decedent or to the decedent's heirs if decedent's will does not provide for distribution of the residue of the estate.

Rule 7.51 amended effective January 1, 2004; adopted January 1, 2003.

Ref.: Cal. Fms Pl. & Pr., Ch. 284, "Guardianship and Conservatorship: Notice," Ch. 447, "Probate: Statutory Notice Requirements"; W. Cal. Sum., 14 "Wills and Probate" §§4, 388, 390, 392, 910.

Rule 7.52. Service of notice when recipient's address unknown

(a) Declaration of diligent search

Petitioner must file a declaration describing efforts made to locate a person entitled to notice in a proceeding under the Probate Code, but whose address is unknown, before the court will prescribe an alternate form of notice or dispense with notice under (c). The declaration must state the name of the person whose address is unknown, the last known address of the person, the approximate date when the person was last known to reside there, the efforts made to locate the person, and any facts that explain why the person's address cannot be obtained. The declaration must include a description of the attempts to learn of the person's business and residence addresses by:

(1) Inquiry of the relatives, friends, acquaintances, and employers of the person entitled to notice and of the person who is the subject of the proceeding;

(2) Review of appropriate city telephone directories and directory assistance; and

(3) Search of the real and personal property indexes in the recorder's and assessor's offices for the county where the person was last known or believed to reside.

(b) Mailed notice to county seat

Mailing notice to a person at a county seat is not a manner of giving notice reasonably calculated to give actual notice.

(c) The court may prescribe or dispense with notice

If a person entitled to notice cannot be located after diligent search, the court may prescribe the manner of giving notice to that person or may dispense with notice to that person.

Rule 7.52 adopted effective January 1, 2003.

Ref.: Cal. Fms Pl. & Pr., Ch. 284, "Guardianship and Conservatorship: Notice," Ch. 447, "Probate: Statutory Notice Requirements"; W. Cal. Sum., 14 "Wills and Probate" §§4, 391.

Rule 7.53. Notice of hearing of amended or supplemented pleadings

(a) Amended pleading and amendment to a pleading

An amended pleading or an amendment to a pleading requires the same notice of hearing (including publication) as the pleading it amends.

(b) Supplement to a pleading

A supplement to a pleading does not require additional notice of hearing, but a copy of a supplement to a pleading must be served if service of a copy of the pleading was required, unless waived by the court.

Rule 7.53 adopted effective January 1, 2003.

Ref.: Cal. Fms Pl. & Pr., Ch. 284, "Guardianship and Conservatorship: Notice," Ch. 447, "Probate: Statutory Notice Requirements"; W. Cal. Sum., 14 "Wills and Probate" §§4, 377, 385.

Rule 7.54. Publication of Notice of Petition to Administer Estate

Publication and service of a *Notice of Petition to Administer Estate* (form DE-121) under Probate Code

sections 8110–8125 is sufficient notice of any instrument offered for probate that is filed with, and specifically referred to in, the petition for which notice is given. Any other instrument must be presented in an amended petition, and a new notice must be published and served.

Rule 7.54 amended effective January 1, 2007; adopted effective January 1, 2003.

Ref.: Cal. Fms Pl. & Pr., Ch. 442, "Probate: Initiating Probate Administration"; W. Cal. Sum., 14 "Wills and Probate" §§4, 589.

Rule 7.55. Ex parte application for order

(a) Special notice allegation

An ex parte application for an order must allege whether special notice has been requested.

(Subd (a) amended effective January 1, 2007.)

(b) Allegation if special notice requested

If special notice has been requested, the application must identify each person who has requested special notice and must allege that special notice has been given to or waived by each person who has requested it.

(Subd (b) amended effective January 1, 2007.)

(c) Proof of service or waiver of special notice

Proofs of service of special notice or written waivers of special notice must be filed with the application.

(Subd (c) amended effective January 1, 2007.)

Rule 7.55 amended effective January 1, 2007; adopted effective January 1, 2003.

Ref.: Cal. Fms Pl. & Pr., Ch. 447, "Probate: Statutory Notice Requirements"; W. Cal. Sum., 14 "Wills and Probate" §§4, 395.

Chapter 3
Pleadings

Rule 7.101. Use of Judicial Council forms
Rule 7.101.5. Electronic generation of mandatory Judicial Council form orders
Rule 7.102. Titles of pleadings and orders
Rule 7.103. Signature and verification of pleadings
Rule 7.104. Execution and verification of amended pleadings, amendments to pleadings, and supplements to pleadings; use of Judicial Council forms

Rule 7.101. Use of Judicial Council forms

(a) Use of mandatory forms

If a petition, an order, or another document to be submitted to the court is one for which the Judicial Council has adopted a mandatory form, that form must be used. Except as provided in this rule, if the Judicial Council has adopted a mandatory form in more than one alternative version, one of the alternative versions must be used. If that form is inadequate in a particular situation, an addendum may be attached to it.

(Subd (a) amended and lettered effective January 1, 2007; adopted as untitled subd effective January 1, 2001.)

(b) Alternative mandatory forms

The following forms have been adopted by the Judicial Council as alternative mandatory forms for use in probate proceedings:

(1) *Petition for Appointment of Guardian of Minor* (form GC-210) and *Petition for Appointment of Guardian of the Person* (form GC-210(P));

(2) *Petition for Appointment of Temporary Guardian or Conservator* (form GC-110) and *Petition for Appointment of Temporary Guardian of the Person* (form GC-110(P)).

(Subd (b) adopted effective January 1, 2007.)

(c) Use of guardianship petitions

Notwithstanding any other provision of this rule, a party petitioning for appointment of a temporary guardian of the person of a minor may file either form GC-110 or form GC-110(P). A party petitioning for appointment of a general guardian of the person of a minor may file either form GC-210 or form GC-210(P). A party petitioning for appointment of a temporary guardian of the estate or the person and estate of a minor must file form GC-110. A party petitioning for appointment of a general guardian of the estate or the person and estate of a minor must file form GC-210.

(Subd (c) adopted effective January 1, 2007.)

Rule 7.101 amended effective January 1, 2007; adopted effective January 1, 2001; previously amended effective January 1, 2002.

Ref.: Cal. Fms Pl. & Pr., Ch. 280, "Guardianship and Conservatorship: Appointment of Guardians," Ch. 281, "Guardianship and Conservatorship: Appointment of Conservators," Ch. 282, "Guardianship and Conservatorship: Temporary Guardians and Conservators," Ch. 284, "Guardianship and Conservatorship: Notice," Ch. 285, "Guardianship and Conservatorship: Care of Ward or Conservatee," Ch. 286, "Guardianship and Conservatorship: Inventory and Appraisal," Ch. 290A, "Guardianship and Conservatorship: Asset Management and Investment," Ch. 290H, "Guardianship and Conservatorship: Termination of Guardianships and Conservatorships," Ch. 441, "Probate: Disposition Without Administration," Ch. 442, "Probate: Initiating Probate Administration," Ch. 444, "Probate: Will Contests," Ch. 445, "Probate: Independent Administration of Estates," Ch. 447, "Probate: Statutory Notice Requirements," Ch. 451, "Probate: Inventory and Appraisal," Ch. 454, "Probate: Claims Against the Estate," Ch. 455, "Probate: Sale of Estate Property," Ch. 458E, "Probate: Discharge," Ch. 560, "Trusts: Express, Public, Charitable, and Totten Trusts"; W. Cal. Sum., 13 "Trusts" §226, 14 "Wills and Probate" §§4, 373, 915, 919, 975.

Rule 7.101.5. [Repealed January 1, 2012] Electronic generation of mandatory Judicial Council form orders

(a) Applicability

This rule applies to the following mandatory Judicial Council form orders used in proceedings under the Probate Code:

(1) *Order for Probate* (form DE-140);

(2) *Order Prescribing Notice* (form DE-200/GC-022);

(3) *Order Appointing Guardian ad Litem—Probate* (form DE-351/GC-101);

(4) *Order Dispensing With Notice* (form GC-021);

(5) *Order Fixing Residence Outside the State of California* (form GC-090);

(6) *Order Appointing Temporary Guardian or Conservator* (form GC-140);

(7) *Order Appointing Guardian of Minor* (form GC-240);

(8) *Order Terminating Guardianship* (form GC-260);

(9) *Order Appointing Court Investigator* (form GC-330);

(10) *Ex Parte Order Re Completion of Capacity Declaration—HIPAA* (form GC-334);

(11) *Order Appointing Probate Conservator* (form GC-340); and

(12) *Order Authorizing Conservator to Give Consent for Medical Treatment* (form GC-385).

(Subd (a) adopted effective January 1, 2007.)

(b) Definitions

(1) "CCMS" is the California Case Management System, a statewide integrated software application for managing all case types in the superior courts of this state.

(2) "Electronic generation of a court order" is the electronic generation by a court of a Judicial Council form order listed in (a).

(Subd (b) adopted effective January 1, 2007.)

(c) Modification of electronically generated court orders

(1) Any court using CCMS for case management of proceedings under the Probate Code may modify any of the Judicial Council mandatory form orders listed in (a) by generating the order electronically in a way that includes in the order signed by the judicial officer only the party-appearance and other preliminary information, findings, and orders actually selected by the court.

(2) An electronically generated court order under this rule must express the findings and orders selected by the court in substantially the same language as the equivalent findings and orders in the Judicial Council form order, and must provide substantially the same party-appearance and other preliminary information provided in the form order.

(3) An electronically generated court order under this rule must have the same general appearance as the Judicial Council form order, including case name, case number, and court address captions and a footer, except that the order may be longer or shorter than the form order. The order must contain a recitation in the footer that it is an electronically generated court order in lieu of a mandatory Judicial Council form order under this rule.

(4) The orders listed in (a) are mandatory forms for all purposes under rule 1.31, except as provided in this rule. An order listed in (a) prepared and submitted to the court by a party or attorney for a party must be prepared on the mandatory Judicial Council form.

(5) A court that elects to electronically generate court orders under this rule may also use or require the use of the Judicial Council form orders listed in (a) in any individual case or proceeding.

(Subd (c) adopted effective January 1, 2007.)

(d) Notification to advisory committees

Any court electing to electronically generate court orders under this rule must send written notice of its election to do so to the Probate and Mental Health and the Court Technology Advisory Committees and submit additional informational reports as requested by either committee.

(Subd (d) adopted effective January 1, 2007.)

(e) Expiration date

Unless amended or reenacted by Judicial Council action effective after the effective date of this rule, this rule is repealed effective January 1, 2012.

(Subd (e) adopted effective January 1, 2007.)

Rule 7.101.5 adopted effective January 1, 2007.

Ref.: W. Cal. Sum., 14 "Wills and Probate" §§4, 373, 915.

Rule 7.102. Titles of pleadings and orders

The title of each pleading and of each proposed order must clearly and completely identify the nature of the relief sought or granted.

Rule 7.102 amended effective January 1, 2003; adopted effective January 1, 2001; previously amended effective January 1, 2002.

Ref.: Cal. Fms Pl. & Pr., Ch. 560, "Trusts: Express, Public, Charitable, and Totten Trusts"; W. Cal. Sum., 13 "Trusts" §226, 14 "Wills and Probate" §§4, 376.

Rule 7.103. Signature and verification of pleadings

(a) Signature of parties

A pleading must be in writing and must be signed by all persons joining in it.

(b) Verification by parties

All pleadings filed in proceedings under the Probate Code must be verified. If two or more persons join in a pleading, it may be verified by any of them.

(c) Signature and verification by attorney

If a person is absent from the county where his or her attorney's office is located, or for some other cause is unable to sign or verify a pleading, the attorney may sign or verify it, unless the person is, or is seeking to become, a fiduciary appointed in the proceeding.

Rule 7.103 adopted effective January 1, 2003.

Ref.: Cal. Fms Pl. & Pr., Ch. 280, "Guardianship and Conservatorship: Appointment of Guardians," Ch. 281, "Guardianship and Conservatorship: Appointment of Conservators," Ch. 282, "Guardianship and Conservatorship: Temporary Guardians and Conservators," Ch. 290F, "Guardianship and Conservatorship: Compensation of Guardian or Conservator," Ch. 442, "Probate: Initiating Probate Administration"; W. Cal. Sum., 14 "Wills and Probate" §§4, 376.

Rule 7.104. Execution and verification of amended pleadings, amendments to pleadings, and supplements to pleadings; use of Judicial Council forms

(a) Amended pleading and amendment to a pleading

(1) All persons required to sign a pleading must sign an amended pleading. One of the persons required to verify a pleading must verify an amended pleading.

(2) All persons required to sign a pleading must sign an amendment to that pleading. One of the persons required to verify a pleading must verify an amendment to that pleading.

(3) A Judicial Council form must be used for an amended pleading, with the word "Amended" added to its caption, if the form was used for the pleading that is amended. A Judicial Council form must not be used for an amendment to a pleading.

(b) Supplement to a pleading

(1) A supplement to a pleading must be signed and verified by one of the persons who were required to sign and verify the pleading that is supplemented. However, the court may, in the exercise of its discretion, accept for filing and consider a supplement to a pleading signed under penalty of perjury by an attorney for the party offering it, where the information contained in the supplement is particularly within the knowledge of the attorney.

(2) A Judicial Council form must not be used for a supplement to a pleading.

Rule 7.104 adopted effective January 1, 2003.

Ref.: W. Cal. Sum., 14 "Wills and Probate" §§4, 376, 377.

Chapter 4
Appointment of Executors and Administrators

Rule 7.150. Acknowledgment of receipt of statement of duties and liabilities of personal representative

Rule 7.151. Reimbursement of graduated filing fee by successful subsequent petitioner

Rule 7.150. Acknowledgment of receipt of statement of duties and liabilities of personal representative

Before the court issues letters, each personal representative of a decedent's estate (other than a company authorized to conduct a trust business in California) must execute and file an acknowledgment of receipt of *Duties and Liabilities of Personal Representative* (form DE-147).

Rule 7.150 amended effective January 1, 2007; adopted effective January 1, 2000; previously amended effective January 1, 2002.

Ref.: Cal. Fms Pl. & Pr., Ch. 442, "Probate: Initiating Probate Administration"; W. Cal. Sum., 14 "Wills and Probate" §§4, 447.

Rule 7.151. Reimbursement of graduated filing fee by successful subsequent petitioner

(a) Duty to reimburse

In decedents' estates commenced on or after August 18, 2003, **and before January 1, 2008**, a general personal representative appointed on a [1] *Petition for Probate* **(form DE-111)** that was not the first-filed petition for appointment of a general personal representative in the proceeding must reimburse the unsuccessful petitioner on the first-filed petition for a portion of the filing fee paid by the unsuccessful petitioner.

(Subd (a) amended effective March 1, 2008; previously amended effective January 1, 2007.)

Rule 7.151(a).   2008 Deletes. [1] Petition for Probate

(b) Amount of reimbursement

The reimbursement required under this rule is in the amount of:

(1) The filing fee paid by the unsuccessful petitioner in excess of the filing fee that would have been payable on that date for a [1] *Petition for Probate* **filed to commence administration** of an estate valued at less than $250,000, less

(2) The unpaid amount of any costs or sanctions awarded against the unsuccessful petitioner in favor of the party that sought the personal representative's appointment in the proceeding.

(Subd (b) amended effective March 1, 2008; previously amended effective January 1, 2007.)

Rule 7.151(b).   2008 Deletes. [1] Petition for Probate

(c) When reimbursement payable

The personal representative must make the reimbursement payment required under this rule in cash and in full no later than the date the [1] *Inventory and Appraisal*

(form DE-160/GC-040) is due under Probate Code section 8800(b), including additional time allowed by the court under that provision.

(Subd (c) amended effective March 1, 2008.)

Rule 7.151(c).   2008 Deletes. [1] Inventory and Appraisal

(d) Payment from estate funds

The reimbursement payment under this rule is an authorized expense of administration and may be made from estate funds without a prior court order.

(e) Receipt from unsuccessful petitioner

The unsuccessful petitioner must give [1] **a** signed receipt for the reimbursement payment made under this rule.

(Subd (e) amended effective March 1, 2008.)

Rule 7.151(e).   2008 Deletes. [1] its

(f) Personal representative's right to claim refund

A personal representative that is required to but fails to make the reimbursement payment under this rule may not claim a refund of the difference between the estimated filing fee and the corrected filing fee under rule 7.552(c).

(g) Petitioner on dismissed *Petition for Probate*

A petitioner that is eligible to receive a refund of filing fee for a dismissed [1] *Petition for Probate* under rule 7.552(d) is not an unsuccessful petitioner within the meaning of this rule.

(Subd (g) amended effective March 1, 2008; previously amended effective January 1, 2007.)

Rule 7.151(g).   2008 Deletes. [1] Petition for Probate

Rule 7.151 amended effective March 1, 2008; adopted effective January 1, 2004; previously amended effective January 1, 2007.

Ref.: Cal. Fms Pl. & Pr., Ch. 442, "Probate: Initiating Probate Administration"; W. Cal. Sum., 14 "Wills and Probate" §§4, 585.

Chapter 5
Bonding of Personal Representatives, Guardians, Conservators, and Trustees

Rule 7.201. Waiver of bond in will
Rule 7.202. Two or more personal representatives
Rule 7.203. Separate bonds for individuals
Rule 7.204. Duty to apply for order increasing bond
Rule 7.205. Independent power to sell real property
Rule 7.206. Bond upon sale of real property
Rule 7.207. Bonds of conservators and guardians

Rule 7.201.   Waiver of bond in will

(a) Statement of waiver in petition

If the will waives bond, the Petition for Probate must so state.

(Subd (a) amended effective January 1, 2007; previously amended effective January 1, 2001, and January 1, 2002.)

(b) Court's discretion to require bond

The court may require bond if the proposed personal representative resides outside California or for other good cause, even if the will waives bond.

(Subd (b) amended effective January 1, 2001.)

Rule 7.201 amended effective January 1, 2007; adopted effective January 1, 2000; previously amended effective January 1, 2001, and January 1, 2002.

Ref.: Cal. Fms Pl. & Pr., Ch. 442, "Probate: Initiating Probate Administration," Ch. 445, "Probate: Independent Administration of Estates," Ch. 446, "Probate: Bonds—Increase and Decrease During Administration"; W. Cal. Sum., 13 "Trusts" §226, 14 "Wills and Probate" §§4, 450, 960.

Rule 7.202.   Two or more personal representatives

If a will admitted to probate names two or more persons to serve as executors but not all serve and the will does not expressly waive bond if fewer than all of the named persons serve, the court must require each executor to give a bond unless the court waives this requirement under Probate Code section 8481(a)(2).

Rule 7.202 amended effective January 1, 2002; adopted effective January 1, 2000.

Ref.: Cal. Fms Pl. & Pr., Ch. 442, "Probate: Initiating Probate Administration," Ch. 446, "Probate: Bonds—Increase and Decrease During Administration"; W. Cal. Sum., 14 "Wills and Probate" §§4, 448.

Rule 7.203.   Separate bonds for individuals

Because a corporate fiduciary (whether personal representative, guardian, conservator, or trustee) cannot assume responsibility for the acts of an individual cofiduciary, an individual cofiduciary who is required to give a bond must provide a separate bond, except to the extent that the court orders the assets to be held solely by the corporate cofiduciary.

Rule 7.203 amended effective January 1, 2002; adopted effective January 1, 2000.

Ref.: Cal. Fms Pl. & Pr., Ch. 442, "Probate: Initiating Probate Administration," Ch. 446, "Probate: Bonds—Increase and Decrease During Administration"; W. Cal. Sum., 13 "Trusts" §48, 14 "Wills and Probate" §§4, 448, 983.

Rule 7.204.   Duty to apply for order increasing bond

(a) Ex parte application for order

Immediately upon the occurrence of facts making it necessary or appropriate to increase the amount of the bond, the personal representative, or the guardian or conservator of the estate, must make an ex parte application for an order increasing the bond.

(Subd (a) amended effective January 1, 2003; previously amended effective January 1, 2002.)

(b) Attorney's duty

If the personal representative, or the guardian or conservator of the estate, has not already made application under (a), the attorney for the personal representative, or the attorney for the guardian or conservator of the estate, must make the ex parte application immediately upon becoming aware of the need to increase bond.

(Subd (b) amended effective January 1, 2003; previously amended effective January 1, 2002.)

(c) Amount

(1) The application by a personal representative under (a) or by the attorney for a personal representative under (b) must show the value of the estate's personal property and the probable annual gross income of the estate.

(2) The application by a guardian or conservator of the estate under (a) or by the attorney for a guardian or conservator of the estate under (b) must show the value of

the estate's personal property, the probable annual gross income of all of the property of the estate, and the sum of the probable annual gross payments of the public benefits of the ward or conservatee identified in Probate Code section 2320(c)(3).

(3) If the personal representative has full Independent Administration of Estates Act (IAEA) authority or the guardian or conservator of the estate has authority to sell estate real property without court confirmation, the application must also show the amount of the equity in estate real property.

(Subd (c) amended effective January 1, 2003; previously amended effective January 1, 2002.)

Rule 7.204 amended effective January 1, 2002; adopted effective January 1, 2000.

Ref.: Cal. Fms Pl. & Pr., Ch. 283, "Guardianship and Conservatorship: Bonds," Ch. 442, "Probate: Initiating Probate Administration," Ch. 446, "Probate: Bonds—Increase and Decrease During Administration," Ch. 451, "Probate: Inventory and Appraisal"; W. Cal. Sum., 14 "Wills and Probate" §§4, 449, 592, 985, 1033.

Rule 7.205.   Independent power to sell real property

If the personal representative requests or has been granted an independent power to sell or hypothecate real estate or to lease it for a term of more than one year, the personal representative must state in the request to fix the amount of the bond the value of the real property less encumbrances.

Rule 7.205 amended effective January 1, 2002; adopted effective January 1, 2000.

Ref.: Cal. Fms Pl. & Pr., Ch. 442, "Probate: Initiating Probate Administration," Ch. 446, "Probate: Bonds—Increase and Decrease During Administration," Ch. 455, "Probate: Sale of Estate Property"; W. Cal. Sum., 14 "Wills and Probate" §§4, 449.

Rule 7.206.   Bond upon sale of real property

If a bond or additional bond is required in an order confirming sale of real estate, the court must not file the order until the additional bond is filed.

Rule 7.206 amended effective January 1, 2002; adopted effective January 1, 2000.

Ref.: Cal. Fms Pl. & Pr., Ch. 442, "Probate: Initiating Probate Administration," Ch. 446, "Probate: Bonds—Increase and Decrease During Administration," Ch. 455, "Probate: Sale of Estate Property"; W. Cal. Sum., 14 "Wills and Probate" §§4, 449.

Rule 7.207.   Bonds of conservators and guardians

(a) Bond for appointments after December 31, 2007

Except as otherwise provided by statute, every conservator or guardian of the estate appointed after December 31, 2007, must furnish a bond that includes an amount determined under (c) as a reasonable amount for the cost of recovery to collect on the bond under Probate Code section 2320(c)(4).

(Subd (a) adopted effective January 1, 2008.)

(b) Additional bond for appointments before January 1, 2008

Except as otherwise provided by statute, every conservator or guardian of the estate appointed before January 1, 2008, and the conservator's or guardian's attorney, must

after that date apply to increase the bond in the manner described in rule 7.204 to include an additional amount determined under (c), and must, no later than June 30, 2008, furnish the increased amount of bond ordered by the court.

(Subd (b) adopted effective January 1, 2008.)

(c) Amount of bond for the cost of recovery on the bond

The reasonable amount of bond for the cost of recovery to collect on the bond, including attorney's fees and costs, under Probate Code section 2320(c)(4) is:

(1) Ten percent (10%) of the value up to and including $500,000 of the following:

(A) The appraised value of personal property of the estate;

(B) The appraised value, less encumbrances, of real property of the estate that the guardian or conservator has the independent power to sell without approval or confirmation of the court under Probate Code sections 2590 and 2591(d);

(C) The probable annual income from all assets of the estate; and

(D) The probable annual gross payments described in Probate Code section 2320(c)(3); and

(2) Twelve percent (12%) of the value above $500,000 up to and including $1,000,000 of the property, income, and payments described in (1); and

(3) Two percent (2%) of the value above $1,000,000 of the property, income, and payments described in (1).

(Subd (c) adopted effective January 1, 2008.)

Rule 7.207 adopted effective January 1, 2008.

Ref.: Cal. Fms Pl. & Pr., Ch. 283, "Guardianship and Conservatorship: Bonds."

Chapter 6
Independent Administration of Estates

Rule 7.250.   Report of actions taken under the Independent Administration of Estates Act

(a) Report required

In any accounting, report, petition for preliminary distribution, or petition for final distribution, the petitioner must list and describe all actions taken without prior court approval under the Independent Administration of Estates Act (IAEA) if notice of the proposed action was required. The description of the action must include the following:

(1) The nature of the action;

(2) When the action was taken;

(3) A statement of when and to whom notice was given;

(4) Whether notice was waived, and if so, by whom; and

(5) Whether any objections were received.

(Subd (a) amended effective January 1, 2002.)

(b) Actions reported in previous reports

An action taken under the IAEA that was (1) properly listed and described in a prior accounting, report, or petition for distribution, and (2) approved by the court, need not be listed and described in a subsequent account, report, or petition for distribution.

(Subd (b) amended effective January 1, 2007.)

Rule 7.250 amended effective January 1, 2007; adopted effective January 1, 2000; previously amended effective January 1, 2002.

Ref.: Cal. Fms Pl. & Pr., Ch. 442, "Probate: Initiating Probate Administration," Ch. 445, "Probate: Independent Administration of Estates," Ch. 458C, "Probate: Preliminary Distribution and Partial Allowance of Compensation," Ch. 458D, "Probate: Accounts, Final Distribution, and Compensation"; W. Cal. Sum., 14 "Wills and Probate" §§4, 384, 730, 731.

Chapter 7
Spousal or Domestic Partner Property Petitions

Rule 7.301.　Spousal or domestic partner property petition filed with petition for probate

A petition for spousal or domestic partner property determination or confirmation must be filed separately from a petition for probate of will or for letters of administration, even if both petitions are filed at the same time. The two petitions must be filed under the same case number.

Rule 7.301 amended effective January 1, 2007; adopted effective January 1, 2000; previously amended effective January 1, 2002.

Ref.: Cal. Fms Pl. & Pr., Ch. 441, "Probate: Disposition Without Administration"; W. Cal. Sum., 14 "Wills and Probate" §§4, 829.

Chapter 8
Petitions for Instructions
[Reserved]

Chapter 9
Creditors' Claims

Rule 7.401. Personal representative's action on the claim
Rule 7.402. Court's action on the claim
Rule 7.403. Listing all claims in the final report

Rule 7.401.　Personal representative's action on the claim

For each creditor's claim filed with the court, the personal representative (whether or not acting under the Independent Administration of Estates Act (IAEA)) must:

(1) Allow or reject in whole or in part the claim in writing;

(2) Serve a copy of the allowance or rejection on the creditor and the creditor's attorney; and

(3) File a copy of the allowance or rejection with proof of service with the court.

Rule 7.401 amended effective January 1, 2002; adopted effective January 1, 2000.

Ref.: Cal. Fms Pl. & Pr., Ch. 454, "Probate: Claims Against the Estate"; W. Cal. Sum., 14 "Wills and Probate" §§4, 640.

Rule 7.402.　Court's action on the claim

Except as to claims of the personal representative or the attorney, if the personal representative has authority to act under the Independent Administration of Estates Act (IAEA), the court must not act on the personal represen-

tative's allowance or rejection of a creditor's claim unless good cause is shown.

Rule 7.402 amended effective January 1, 2002; adopted effective January 1, 2000.

Ref.: Cal. Fms Pl. & Pr., Ch. 454, "Probate: Claims Against the Estate"; W. Cal. Sum., 14 "Wills and Probate" §§4, 641.

Rule 7.403.　Listing all claims in the final report

For each claim presented, the personal representative must state in the final report or petition for final distribution:

(1) The claimant's name;

(2) The date of filing of the claim;

(3) The nature of the claim;

(4) The amount claimed;

(5) The disposition of the claim; and

(6) If the claim was rejected, the date of service of the rejection and whether or not a lawsuit was filed.

Rule 7.403 amended effective January 1, 2002; adopted effective January 1, 2000.

Ref.: Cal. Fms Pl. & Pr., Ch. 454, "Probate: Claims Against the Estate," Ch. 458D, "Probate: Accounts, Final Distribution, and Compensation"; W. Cal. Sum., 14 "Wills and Probate" §§4, 640, 731.

Chapter 10
Sales of Real and Personal Property

Rule 7.451. Refusal to show property to prospective buyers
Rule 7.452. Petitioner or attorney required at hearing
Rule 7.453. Petition for exclusive listing
Rule 7.454. Ex parte application for order authorizing sale of securities or other personal property

Rule 7.451.　Refusal to show property to prospective buyers

Upon a showing that the fiduciary has denied any bona fide prospective buyer or his or her broker a reasonable opportunity to inspect the property, the court must not confirm the sale but must continue the sale to allow inspection unless good cause is shown for the court to confirm the sale.

Rule 7.451 amended effective January 1, 2002; adopted effective January 1, 2000.

Ref.: Cal. Fms Pl. & Pr., Ch. 455, "Probate: Sale of Estate Property"; W. Cal. Sum., 14 "Wills and Probate" §§4, 689, 695, 1017.

Rule 7.452.　Petitioner or attorney required at hearing

The court must not proceed with the hearing on a petition to confirm a sale of property unless the petitioner's attorney or petitioner, if unrepresented, is present.

Rule 7.452 amended effective January 1, 2002; adopted effective January 1, 2000.

Ref.: Cal. Fms Pl. & Pr., Ch. 455, "Probate: Sale of Estate Property"; W. Cal. Sum., 14 "Wills and Probate" §§4, 689, 695, 1017.

Rule 7.453.　Petition for exclusive listing

A petition for approval of an exclusive listing under Probate Code section 10150(c) must state the following:

(1) A description of the property to be sold;

(2) The name of the broker to be employed;

(3) A summary of the terms of the exclusive listing agreement or include a copy of the listing agreement; and

(4) A detailed statement of the facts supporting the "necessity and the advantage" to the estate of having the exclusive listing.

Rule 7.453 amended effective January 1, 2002; adopted effective January 1, 2000.

Ref.: Cal. Fms Pl. & Pr., Ch. 455, "Probate: Sale of Estate Property"; W. Cal. Sum., 14 "Wills and Probate" §§4, 678.

Rule 7.454. Ex parte application for order authorizing sale of securities or other personal property

An ex parte application for authority to sell or to surrender tangible or intangible personal property must state whether or not the property is specifically devised. If it is specifically devised, the written consent of the specific devisee to the sale or surrender must be filed.

Rule 7.454 adopted effective January 1, 2003.

Ref.: Cal. Fms Pl. & Pr., Ch. 455, "Probate: Sale of Estate Property"; W. Cal. Sum., 14 "Wills and Probate" §§4, 684, 700.

Chapter 11
Inventory and Appraisal

Rule 7.501. Inventory and Appraisal to show sufficiency of bond

(a) Statement required

Every Inventory and Appraisal must contain one of the following statements:

(1) "Bond is waived";

(2) "Bond has been filed in the amount of $ *(specify amount)* and is insufficient"; or

(3) "Bond has been filed in the amount of $ *(specify amount)* and is sufficient."

(Subd (a) amended effective January 1, 2007; previously amended effective January 1, 2002.)

(b) Insufficient bond

If the bond is insufficient, the fiduciary (the personal representative, or the guardian or conservator of the estate), or the attorney for the fiduciary, must immediately make ex parte application as provided in rule 7.204 for an order increasing the amount of the bond.

(Subd (b) amended effective January 1, 2003; previously amended effective January 1, 2002.)

(c) Statement signed by attorney

The statement required by (a) must be signed by the attorney of record for each fiduciary who has an attorney of record and by each fiduciary who does not.

(Subd (c) amended effective January 1, 2003; previously amended effective January 1, 2002.)

Rule 7.501 amended effective January 1, 2007; adopted effective January 1, 2000; previously amended effective January 1, 2002, and January 1, 2003.

Ref.: Cal. Fms Pl. & Pr., Ch. 283, "Guardianship and Conservatorship: Bonds," Ch. 446, "Probate: Bonds—Increase and Decrease During Administration," Ch. 451, "Probate: Inventory and Appraisal"; W. Cal. Sum., 14 "Wills and Probate" §§4, 592, 1033.

Chapter 12
Accounts and Reports of Executors, Administrators, Conservators, and Guardians

Chapter 12 amended effective January 1, 2008.

Rule 7.550. Effect of waiver of account

Rule 7.551. Final accounts or reports in estates with nonresident beneficiaries

Rule 7.552. Graduated filing fee adjustments for estates commenced on or after August 18, 2003, and before January 1, 2008

Rule 7.553. Graduated filing fee statements for decedents' estates commenced on or after January 1, 2008

Rule 7.575. Accounts of conservators and guardians

Rule 7.550. Effect of waiver of account

(a) Waiver of account

Except as provided in (b), if an accounting is waived under Probate Code section 10954, the details of receipts and disbursements need not be listed in the report required under section 10954(c)(1).

(Subd (a) amended effective January 1, 2007; adopted as part of unlettered subdivision effective January 1, 2003; previously amended effective January 1, 2004.)

(b) Information required in report on waiver of account

The report required when an account has been waived must list the information required by law, including information as to:

(1) Creditors' claims;

(2) Sales, purchases, or exchanges of assets;

(3) Changes in the form of assets;

(4) Assets on hand;

(5) Whether the estate is solvent;

(6) Detailed schedules of receipts and gains or losses on sale (where an amount other than the amount of the Inventory and Appraisal is used as a basis for calculating fees or commissions);

(7) Costs of administration (if reimbursement of these costs is requested);

(8) The amount of any fees or commissions paid or to be paid;

(9) The calculation of such fees or commissions as described in rule 7.705; and

(10) For decedent's estate proceedings commenced on or after August 18, 2003, the information required by rule 7.552(a) and (b).

(Subd (b) amended effective January 1, 2007; adopted as part of unlettered subdivision effective January 1, 2003; previously amended effective January 1, 2004.)

Rule 7.550 amended effective January 1, 2007; adopted effective January 1, 2003; previously amended effective January 1, 2004.

Ref.: Cal. Fms Pl. & Pr., Ch. 458D, "Probate: Accounts, Final Distribution, and Compensation"; W. Cal. Sum., 14 "Wills and Probate" §§4, 529, 712.

Rule 7.551. Final accounts or reports in estates with nonresident beneficiaries

(a) Final account

Under Revenue and Taxation Code section 19513 and the regulations of the Franchise Tax Board, the court must not approve a final account in an estate that has a total appraised value greater than $1,000,000 and from which more than $250,000 in the aggregate has been distributed or is distributable to beneficiaries who are not residents of California, until the executor or administrator has filed the Franchise Tax Board's state income tax certificate showing that all state personal income taxes, additions to tax, penalties, and interest imposed on the estate or the decedent have been paid or that payment has been secured.

(b) Final report

If a final account is waived under Probate Code section 10954 in an estate described in (a), the court must not approve the final report required by section 10954(c)(1) until the executor or administrator has filed the Franchise Tax Board's state income tax certificate showing that all state personal income taxes, additions to tax, penalties, and interest imposed on the estate or the decedent have been paid or that payment has been secured.

(c) Expiration date of certificate

If the certificate described in (a) or (b) is issued on the condition that the final account or report must be approved before a date specified in the certificate, the court must not approve the final account or report after that date unless the executor or administrator first files a new or revised certificate.

Rule 7.551 adopted effective January 1, 2004.

Ref.: Cal. Fms Pl. & Pr., Ch. 458D, "Probate: Accounts, Final Distribution, and Compensation"; W. Cal. Sum., 14 "Wills and Probate" §§4, 717.

Rule 7.552. Graduated filing fee adjustments for estates commenced on or after August 18, 2003, and before January 1, 2008

This rule applies to decedents' estate proceedings commenced on or after August 18, 2003, and before January 1, 2008. Rule 7.553 applies to decedents' estate proceedings commenced on or after January 1, 2008.

(a) Separate schedule for graduated fee information

The final account or report filed in every decedent's estate proceeding commenced on or after August 18, 2003, and before January 1, 2008, must include a separate schedule showing the following information:

(1) The name of each petitioner on the first-filed [1] *Petition for Probate* (form DE-111) in the proceeding;

(2) The date the first-filed [2] *Petition for Probate* was filed in the proceeding;

(3) The estimated value of the estate shown in item 3, "estimated value of the estate for filing fee purposes," of the first-filed [3] *Petition for Probate* in the proceeding;

(4) The filing fee paid by or for the petitioner on the first-filed [4] *Petition for Probate* in the proceeding; **and**

(5) The following information from the [5] **inventories** filed in the proceeding:

(A) The date each partial, supplemental, final, or corrected [6] *Inventory and Appraisal* (form DE-160/GC-040) was filed;

(B) The total appraised value of the assets of the estate shown in each filed partial, supplemental, or final [7] *Inventory and Appraisal*;

(C) Changes in the appraised value of the assets of the estate shown in each filed corrected [8] *Inventory and Appraisal*; and

(D) The combined total appraised value of the estate shown in all filed partial, supplemental, final, and corrected [9] **inventories.**

(6) A statement of the amount of filing fee that would have been payable under Government Code section [10] **70650**, as amended effective on the date the first-filed [11] *Petition for Probate* was filed in the proceeding, if the total actual appraised value of the estate had been used as the estimated value for filing fee purposes (the "corrected filing fee");

(7) Calculation of the difference between the estimated filing fee paid under Government Code section [12] **70650** on filing the first [13] *Petition for Probate* in the proceeding (the "estimated filing fee") and the "corrected filing fee," as determined under (6) and subdivision (e) of this rule; and

(8) The following information concerning filing fee reimbursement payments made by a personal representative in the proceeding under rule 7.151:

(A) The amount of each payment;

(B) The date each payment was made; and

(C) The name, address, and telephone number of the payee and of any attorney of record for the payee in the proceeding.

(Subd (a) amended effective March 1, 2008; previously amended effective January 1, 2007.)

Rule 7.552(a). 2008 Deletes. [1] Petition for Probate [2] Petition for Probate [3] Petition for Probate [4] Petition for Probate [5] Inventories and Appraisals [6] Inventory and Appraisal [7] Inventory and Appraisal [8] Inventory and Appraisal [9] Inventories and Appraisals; [10] 26827 [11] Petition for Probate [12] 26827 [13] Petition for Probate

(b) If estimated filing fee less than corrected filing fee

If the estimated filing fee is less than the corrected filing fee, as determined under (a) and (e), the petition filed with the final account or report must allege that the difference between them has been paid to the clerk of the court. A copy of the clerk's receipt for the payment, and, if applicable, a receipt or other evidence satisfactory to the court of payment of the reimbursement required under rule 7.151, must be attached as an exhibit to the account or report.

(c) If estimated filing fee more than corrected filing fee

(1) Subject to the provisions of rule 7.151, if the estimated filing fee is more than the corrected filing fee, as determined under (a) and (e), the personal representative of the decedent's estate is eligible under this subdivision to receive a refund of the difference between them, without interest.

(2) The personal representative must apply to the court for the refund, in accordance with the court's local rules and practices for such payments.

(3) Unless authorized to retain a reserve against closing expenses that expressly is to include the court's refund payment after the personal representative's discharge, the personal representative must not apply for a discharge while an application for refund of filing fee under this subdivision is pending and before the court's refund payment is received.

(d) Refund on voluntarily dismissed *Petition for Probate*

(1) A petitioner that files a [1] *Petition for Probate* on or after August 18, 2003, and voluntarily dismisses the petition at any time within 90 days after it is filed and before an order granting or denying the petition is filed, is eligible under this subdivision to receive a refund, without interest, of all filing fees paid in excess of the filing fees that would have been payable on the original filing date for a [2] *Petition for Probate* of an estate valued at less than $250,000.

(2) The petitioner on a dismissed [3] *Petition for Probate* under (1) must apply to the court for the refund, in accordance with the court's local rules and practices for such payments.

(Subd (d) amended effective March 1, 2008.)

Rule 7.552(d). 2008 Deletes. [1] Petition for Probate **[2]** petition for probate **[3]** Petition for Probate

(e) Additional adjustment in corrected filing fee in insolvent estates

If **the property of the estate is insufficient to pay** the expenses of administration [1] in full, the court may approve a determination of the corrected filing fee [2] that reflects the proportionate reduction of those expenses [3] **under Probate Code section 11420.** The corrected filing fee may not be reduced below the minimum fee required by Government Code section [4] **70650** on the date the estimated fee was paid.

(Subd (e) amended effective March 1, 2008.)

Rule 7.552(e). 2008 Deletes. [1] must be proportionately reduced under Probate Code section 11420 because the property in the estate is insufficient to pay them **[2]** under this rule **[3]** , provided that **[4]** 26827

(f) Sample schedule of graduated fee information

The schedule of graduated fee information required under (a) may be substantially as follows:

SCHEDULE _____
Graduated Filing Fee Information

1. The first-filed [1] *Petition for Probate* in this proceeding was filed on [Date] by [name of each petitioner].

2. The estimated value of the estate for filing fee purposes shown on the first-filed [2] *Petition for Probate* in this proceeding is $_____.

3. The filing fee paid by or for the petitioners on the first-filed [3] *Petition for Probate* in this proceeding was $_____.

4. The following [4] **inventories** have been filed in this proceeding:

Type	Date Filed	Appraised Value
[Partial no. _____]	[09/30/09]	$
[Partial no. _____]		$
Final		$
[Supplemental]		$
[Correcting]		$ (or $)_____
Total appraised value of estate:		$_____

5. Corrected Filing Fee:

Total appraised value of estate:	$
Filing fee as of the date in 1 above, based on total appraised value of estate:	$
Adjustment to reflect proportional reduction of expenses of administration for insolvent estate under Cal. Rules of Court, rule 7.552(e):	($ _____)
Corrected Filing Fee:	$ _____

6. Difference between estimated and corrected filing fee:

Estimated filing fee from 3 above:	$
Corrected filing fee from 5 above:	($ _____)
Difference:	$ (or $) _____

7. Filing fee reimbursements under rule 7.151:

Payee(s)	Date Paid	Amount
[Name, address, and telephone number of each payee and attorney of record in the proceeding]	[10/25/09]	$

(Subd (f) amended effective March 1, 2008; previously amended effective January 1, 2007.)

Rule 7.552(f). 2008 Deletes. [1] Petition for Probate **[2]** Petition for Probate **[3]** Petition for Probate **[4]** Inventories and Appraisals

Rule 7.552 amended effective March 1, 2008; adopted effective January 1, 2004; previously amended effective January 1, 2007.

Ref.: Cal. Fms Pl. & Pr., Ch. 442, "Probate: Initiating Probate Administration," Ch. 458D, "Probate: Accounts, Final Distribution, and Compensation"; W. Cal. Sum., 14 "Wills and Probate" §§4, 383, 585.

Rule 7.553. Graduated filing fee statements for decedents' estates commenced on or after January 1, 2008

This rule applies to decedents' estates commenced on or after January 1, 2008.

(a) Separate schedule for graduated fee information

The final account or report or petition for final distribution filed in every decedent's estate proceeding commenced on or after January 1, 2008, must include a separate schedule showing the following information:

(1) The date the first-filed *Petition for Probate* (form DE-111) was filed in the proceeding; and

(2) The following information from the inventories filed in the proceeding:

(A) The date each partial, supplemental, final, or corrected *Inventory and Appraisal* (form DE-160/GC-040) was filed;

(B) The total appraised value of the assets of the estate shown in each filed partial, supplemental, or final *Inventory and Appraisal*;

(C) Changes in the appraised value of the assets of the estate shown in each filed corrected *Inventory and Appraisal*; and

(D) The combined total appraised value of the estate shown in all filed partial, supplemental, final, and corrected inventories.

(Subd (a) adopted effective March 1, 2008.)

(b) Adjustment in corrected filing fee in insolvent estates

If the property of the estate is insufficient to pay expenses of administration in full, the court may approve a determination of the corrected filing fee under this rule that reflects the proportionate reduction of those expenses under Probate Code section 11420. The corrected filing fee may not be reduced below the minimum fee required by Government Code section 70650 on the date the estate was commenced.

(Subd (b) adopted effective March 1, 2008.)

(c) Sample schedule of filing fee information

The schedule of graduated fee information required under (a) may be substantially as follows:

SCHEDULE _____
Graduated Filing Fee Information

1. The first-filed *Petition for Probate* in this proceeding was filed on [Date] by [name of each petitioner].
2. The following inventories have been filed in this proceeding:

Type	Date Filed	Appraised Value
[Partial no. _____]	[09/30/09]	$
[Partial no. _____]		$
Final		$
[Supplemental]		$
[Correcting]		$ (or $)_____
Total appraised value of estate:		$ _____

3. Graduated Filing Fee:
   Total appraised value of estate: $
   Filing fee as of the date in 1 above, based on total appraised value of estate: $
   Adjustment to reflect proportional reduction of expenses of administration for insolvent estate under Cal. Rules of Court, rule 7.553(b): ($ _____)
   Corrected Filing Fee: $ _____

(Subd (c) adopted effective March 1, 2008.)
Rule 7.553 adopted effective March 1, 2008.

Rule 7.575. Accounts of conservators and guardians

This rule defines standard and simplified accountings filed by conservators and guardians under Probate Code section 2620(a), provides when each type of accounting must or may be filed, and prescribes the use of Judicial Council accounting forms in both types of accountings.

(a) Standard and simplified accountings

A standard accounting lists receipts and disbursements in subject-matter categories, with each receipt and disbursement category subtotaled. A simplified accounting lists receipts and disbursements chronologically, by receipt or payment date, without subject-matter categories.

(Subd (a) adopted effective January 1, 2008.)

(b) Standard accounting authorized or required

A conservator or guardian may file any accounting required or authorized by Probate Code section 2620 as a standard accounting under this rule and must file a standard accounting if:

(1) The estate contains income real property;

(2) The estate contains a whole or partial interest in a trade or business;

(3) The appraised value of the estate is $500,000 or more, exclusive of the conservatee's or ward's personal residence;

(4) Except as provided in (c), Schedule A (receipts) or Schedule C (disbursements) prepared in a simplified accounting format exceeds five pages in length; or

(5) The court directs that a standard accounting be filed.

(Subd (b) adopted effective January 1, 2008.)

(c) Simplified accounting authorized

A conservator or guardian may file a simplified accounting in all cases not listed in (b). If required by this rule to file a standard accounting only because a receipts or disbursements schedule is longer than five pages under (b)(4), a conservator or guardian may file a simplified accounting, except for that schedule, which must be prepared in a standard accounting format.

(Subd (c) adopted effective January 1, 2008.)

(d) Standard and simplified accounting forms

Judicial Council forms designated as GC-400 are standard accounting forms. Forms designated as GC-405 are simplified accounting forms. Forms designated as GC-400/GC-405 are forms for both standard and simplified accountings. Each form is also designated by a suffix following its accounting designator that identifies the form's intended use, based either on the form's schedule letter as shown in the *Summary of Account* (form GC-400(SUM)/GC-405(SUM)) or the form's subject matter.

(Subd (d) adopted effective January 1, 2008.)

(e) Mandatory and optional forms

(1) Judicial Council accounting forms adopted as mandatory forms must be used by standard and simplified accounting filers. Judicial Council accounting forms approved as optional forms may be used by all accounting filers. Judicial Council accounting forms designated as GC-400/GC-405 that are approved as optional forms may be used by standard accounting filers but must be used by simplified accounting filers.

(2) Standard accounting filers electing not to use optional Judicial Council accounting forms must:

(A) State receipts and disbursements in the subject-matter categories specified in the optional Judicial Council forms for receipts and disbursements schedules;

(B) Provide the same information about any asset, property, transaction, receipt, disbursement, or other matter that is required by the applicable Judicial Council accounting form; and

(C) Provide the information in the same general layout as the applicable Judicial Council accounting form, but instructional material contained in the form and material contained or requested in the form's header and footer need not be provided.

(Subd (e) adopted effective January 1, 2008.)

(f) Required information in all accounts

Notwithstanding any other provision of this rule and the Judicial Council accounting forms, all standard and simplified accounting filers must provide all information in their accounting schedules or their *Summary of Account* that is required by Probate Code sections 1060–1063 and must provide all information required by Probate Code section 1064 in the petition for approval of their account or the report accompanying their account.

(Subd (f) adopted effective January 1, 2008.)

Rule 7.575 adopted effective January 1, 2008.

Ref.: Cal. Fms Pl. & Pr., Ch. 1, "New Developments."

Chapter 13
Taxes
[Reserved]

Chapter 14
Preliminary and Final Distributions

Rule 7.650. Decree of distribution establishing testamentary trusts

(a) Determining the trust

Upon distribution, the court must:

(1) Determine whether or not a valid trust has been created by the will;

(2) Determine the terms of the trust; and

(3) Order distribution of the trust property to the trustee.

(Subd (a) amended effective January 1, 2002.)

(b) Terms of the trust

The order for distribution must incorporate the terms of the trust so as to give effect to the conditions existing at the time distribution is ordered. The pertinent provisions must be stated in the present tense and in the third person instead of quoting the will verbatim.

(Subd (b) amended effective January 1, 2002.)

Rule 7.650 amended effective January 1, 2002; adopted effective January 1, 2000.

Ref.: Cal. Fms Pl. & Pr., Ch. 458D, "Probate: Accounts, Final Distribution, and Compensation"; W. Cal. Sum., 14 "Wills and Probate" §§4, 731.

Rule 7.651. Description of property in petition for distribution

(a) Property description

A petition for distribution must list and describe in detail the property to be distributed, in the body of the petition or in an attachment that is incorporated in the petition by reference. If an account is filed with the petition, the description must be included in a schedule in the account.

(b) Specific description requirements

The description under (a) must:

(1) Include the amount of cash on hand;

(2) Indicate whether promissory notes are secured or unsecured, and describe in detail the security interest of any secured notes;

(3) Include the complete legal description, street address (if any), and assessor's parcel number (if any) of real property; and

(4) Include the complete description of each individual security held in "street name" in security brokers' accounts.

Rule 7.651 adopted effective January 1, 2004.

Ref.: Cal. Fms Pl. & Pr., Ch. 458D, "Probate: Accounts, Final Distribution, and Compensation"; W. Cal. Sum., 14 "Wills and Probate" §§4, 731.

Rule 7.652. Allegations in petition for distribution concerning character of property

(a) Required allegations

If the character of property to be distributed may affect the distribution, a petition for distribution must allege:

(1) The character of the property to be distributed, whether separate, community, or quasi-community; and

(2) That the community or quasi-community property to be distributed is either the decedent's one-half interest only, or the entire interest of the decedent and the decedent's spouse.

(b) Compliance with Probate Code section 13502

If any property is to be distributed outright to the surviving spouse, a written election by the surviving spouse that complies with Probate Code section 13502 must have been filed, and the petition must show the filing date of the election.

Rule 7.652 adopted effective January 1, 2004.

Ref.: Cal. Fms Pl. & Pr., Ch. 458D, "Probate: Accounts, Final Distribution, and Compensation"; W. Cal. Sum., 14 "Wills and Probate" §§4, 731.

Chapter 15
Compensation of Personal Representatives and Attorneys

Rule 7.700. Compensation paid in advance
Rule 7.701. Allowance on account of statutory compensation
Rule 7.702. Petition for extraordinary compensation
Rule 7.703. Extraordinary compensation
Rule 7.704. Apportionment of statutory compensation
Rule 7.705. Calculation of statutory compensation
Rule 7.706. Compensation when personal representative is an attorney
Rule 7.707. Application of compensation provisions

Rule 7.700.   Compensation paid in advance

(a) No compensation in advance of court order

The personal representative must neither pay nor receive, and the attorney for the personal representative must not receive, statutory commissions or fees or fees for extraordinary services in advance of an order of the court authorizing their payment.

(b) Surcharge for payment or receipt of advance compensation

In addition to removing the personal representative and imposing any other sanctions authorized by law against the personal representative or the attorney for the personal representative, the court may surcharge the personal representative for payment or receipt of statutory commissions or fees or fees for extraordinary services in advance of an order of the court authorizing their payment. The surcharge may include interest at the legal rate from the date of payment.

Rule 7.700 adopted effective January 1, 2003.

Ref.: Cal. Fms Pl. & Pr., Ch. 290F, "Guardianship and Conservatorship: Compensation of Guardian or Conservator," Ch. 304, "Insane and Other Incompetent Persons," Ch. 458D, "Probate: Accounts, Final Distribution, and Compensation"; W. Cal. Sum., 14 "Wills and Probate" §§4, 451, 541, 1044.

Rule 7.701.   Allowance on account of statutory compensation

The court may authorize an allowance of statutory fees or commissions on account before approval of the final account and the decree of final distribution. Any allowance made before settlement of the final account must be low enough to avoid the possibility of overpayment. The allowance:

(1) Must be based on the estimated amount of statutory compensation payable on the estate determined as of the date of the petition for allowance;

(2) Must be in proportion to the work actually performed; and

(3) Must be based upon a detailed description of the ordinary services performed and remaining to be performed.

Rule 7.701 adopted effective January 1, 2003.

Ref.: Cal. Fms Pl. & Pr., Ch. 458D, "Probate: Accounts, Final Distribution, and Compensation"; W. Cal. Sum., 14 "Wills and Probate" §§4, 541.

Rule 7.702.   Petition for extraordinary compensation

A petition for extraordinary compensation must include, or be accompanied by, a statement of the facts upon which the petition is based. The statement of facts must:

(1) Show the nature and difficulty of the tasks performed;

(2) Show the results achieved;

(3) Show the benefit of the services to the estate;

(4) Specify the amount requested for each category of service performed;

(5) State the hourly rate of each person who performed services and the hours spent by each of them;

(6) Describe the services rendered in sufficient detail to demonstrate the productivity of the time spent; and

(7) State the estimated amount of statutory compensation to be paid by the estate, if the petition is not part of a final account or report.

Rule 7.702 adopted effective January 1, 2003.

Ref.: Cal. Fms Pl. & Pr., Ch. 290F, "Guardianship and Conservatorship: Compensation of Guardian or Conservator," Ch. 304, "Insane and Other Incompetent Persons," Ch. 458D, "Probate: Accounts, Final Distribution, and Compensation"; W. Cal. Sum., 14 "Wills and Probate" §§4, 540, 1044.

Rule 7.703.   Extraordinary compensation

(a) Discretion of the court

An award of extraordinary compensation to the personal representative or to the attorney for the personal representative is within the discretion of the court. The court may consider the amount of statutory compensation when determining compensation for extraordinary services.

(b) Examples of extraordinary services by personal representative

The following is a nonexclusive list of activities for which extraordinary compensation may be awarded to the personal representative:

(1) Selling, leasing, exchanging, financing, or foreclosing real or personal property;

(2) Carrying on decedent's business if necessary to preserve the estate or under court order;

(3) Preparing tax returns; and

(4) Handling audits or litigation connected with tax liabilities of the decedent or of the estate.

(c) Examples of extraordinary services by attorney

The following is a nonexclusive list of activities for which extraordinary compensation may be awarded to the attorney for the personal representative:

(1) Legal services in connection with the sale of property held in the estate;

(2) Services to secure a loan to pay estate debts;

(3) Litigation undertaken to benefit the estate or to protect its interests;

(4) Defense of the personal representative's account;

(5) Defense of a will contested after its admission to probate;

(6) Successful defense of a will contested before its admission to probate;

(7) Successful defense of a personal representative in a removal proceeding;

(8) Extraordinary efforts to locate estate assets;

(9) Litigation in support of attorney's request for extraordinary compensation, where prior compensation awards are not adequate compensation under all the circumstances;

(10) Coordination of ancillary administration; and

(11) Accounting for a deceased, incapacitated, or absconded personal representative under Probate Code section 10953.

(d) Contingency fee agreement for extraordinary legal services

An attorney may agree to perform extraordinary services for a personal representative on a contingent-fee basis on the following conditions:

(1) The agreement must be in writing and must comply with section 6147 of the Business and Professions Code;

(2) The court must approve the agreement in the manner provided in Probate Code section 10811(c), based on findings that the compensation under the agreement is just and reasonable, that the agreement is to the advantage of the estate, and that the agreement is in the best interest of the persons interested in the estate; and

(3) In the absence of an emergency or other unusual circumstances, the personal representative must obtain the court's approval of the contingency fee agreement before services are performed under it.

(Subd (d) amended effective January 1, 2007.)

(e) Use of paralegals in the performance of extraordinary services

Extraordinary legal services may include the services of a paralegal acting under the direction and supervision of an attorney. A request for extraordinary legal fees for a paralegal's services must:

(1) Describe the qualifications of the paralegal (including education, certification, continuing education, and experience);

(2) State the hours spent by the paralegal and the hourly rate requested for the paralegal's services;

(3) Describe the services performed by the paralegal;

(4) State why it was appropriate to use the paralegal's services in the particular case; and

(5) Demonstrate that the total amount requested for the extraordinary services of the attorney and the paralegal does not exceed the amount appropriate if the attorney had performed the services without the paralegal's assistance.

Rule 7.703 amended effective January 1, 2007; adopted effective January 1, 2003.

Ref.: Cal. Fms Pl. & Pr., Ch. 290F, "Guardianship and Conservatorship: Compensation of Guardian or Conservator,"

Ch. 458D, "Probate: Accounts, Final Distribution, and Compensation"; W. Cal. Sum., 14 "Wills and Probate" §§4, 534, 536, 538, 1046.

Rule 7.704. Apportionment of statutory compensation

(a) One statutory commission and fee

There is one statutory commission for ordinary services by the personal representative of the estate and one statutory attorney fee for ordinary legal services to the personal representative, regardless of the number of personal representatives or attorneys performing the services. The court may apportion statutory commissions and fees among multiple, successive, and concurrent personal representatives or attorneys. The apportionment must be based on the agreement of the multiple personal representatives or attorneys or, if there is no agreement, according to the services actually rendered by each of them.

(b) Notice of hearing

If there has been a change of personal representative or a substitution of attorneys for the personal representative, notice of hearing of any interim or final petition seeking or waiving an award of statutory compensation must be given to all prior personal representatives or attorneys unless:

(1) A waiver of notice executed by all prior personal representatives or attorneys is on file or is filed with the petition;

(2) A written, signed agreement on the allocation of statutory commissions or fees between the present personal representative or attorney and all prior personal representatives or attorneys is on file or is included in or filed with the petition; or

(3) The court's file and the petition demonstrate that the commissions or fees of the prior personal representatives or attorneys have been previously provided for and allowed by the court.

Rule 7.704 adopted effective January 1, 2003.

Ref.: Cal. Fms Pl. & Pr., Ch. 458D, "Probate: Accounts, Final Distribution, and Compensation"; W. Cal. Sum., 14 "Wills and Probate" §§4, 532.

Rule 7.705. Calculation of statutory compensation

(a) Account filed

A petition for statutory commissions or attorney fees must state the amount of statutory compensation payable and set forth the estate accounted for and the calculation of statutory compensation. The calculation must be stated in the petition in substantially the following form:

COMMISSION OR FEE BASE

Inventory and Appraisal	$____
Receipts, Excluding Principal	$____
Gains on Sales	$____
Losses on Sales	$(____)
TOTAL COMMISSION OR FEE BASE	$____

COMMISSION OR FEE COMPUTATION

4% on first $100,000   ($___)[1] $___[2]

3% on next $100,000   ($___) $_____
2% on next $800,000   ($___) $_____
1% on next $9,000,000   ($___) $_____
½ of 1% on next $15,000,000 ($___) $_____
Amount requested from the
court for estates above
$25,000,000   ($___) $_____
TOTAL COMMISSION
OR FEE $___[3]

1. Enter in this column the amount of the estate accounted for in each category. The sum of the entries in this column would equal the total commission or fee base.

2. Enter in this column the product of the amount of the estate accounted for in each category multiplied by the percentage for that category.

3. Enter here the sum of the products entered in this column.

(b) Account waived

When an account has been waived, the report must contain the information required by rule 7.550. If the report is accompanied by a request for statutory commissions or fees, the basis for their computation must be included in the petition substantially in the form provided in (a). Notwithstanding the waiver of account, if the petition and report requests statutory commissions or fees based on any amount other than the amount of the Inventory and Appraisal, detailed schedules of receipts and gains and losses on sales must be included.

Rule 7.705 adopted effective January 1, 2003.

Ref.: Cal. Fms Pl. & Pr., Ch. 458D, "Probate: Accounts, Final Distribution, and Compensation"; W. Cal. Sum., 14 "Wills and Probate" §§4, 529, 712.

Rule 7.706. Compensation when personal representative is an attorney

(a) Personal representative's compensation only

Notwithstanding the provisions of the decedent's will, a personal representative who is an attorney may receive the personal representative's compensation but may not receive compensation for legal services as the attorney for the personal representative unless the court approves the right to compensation for legal services in advance and finds the arrangement is to the advantage, benefit, and best interest of the decedent's estate.

(b) Agreement not to participate in compensation

A law firm of which the personal representative is a partner or shareholder may request compensation for legal services in addition to the personal representative's compensation if a written agreement not to participate in each other's compensation, signed by the personal representative and by authorized representatives of the law firm, has been filed in the estate proceeding.

Rule 7.706 adopted effective January 1, 2003.

Ref.: Cal. Fms Pl. & Pr., Ch. 458D, "Probate: Accounts, Final Distribution, and Compensation"; W. Cal. Sum., 14 "Wills and Probate" §§4, 533.

Rule 7.707. Application of compensation provisions

For proceedings commenced after June 30, 1991, the law in effect on the date of the court's order awarding statutory compensation determines the amount of such compensation.

Rule 7.707 adopted effective January 1, 2003.

Ref.: Cal. Fms Pl. & Pr., Ch. 458D, "Probate: Accounts, Final Distribution, and Compensation"; W. Cal. Sum., 14 "Wills and Probate" §4.

Chapter 16
Compensation in All Matters Other Than Decedents' Estates

Rule 7.750. Application of rules to guardianships and conservatorships
Rule 7.751. Petitions for orders allowing compensation for guardians or conservators and their attorneys
Rule 7.752. Court may order accounting before allowing compensation
Rule 7.753. Contingency fee agreements in guardianships and conservatorships
Rule 7.754. Use of paralegals in the performance of legal services for the guardian or conservator
Rule 7.755. Advance payments and periodic payments to guardians, conservators, and to their attorneys on account for future services
Rule 7.756. Compensation of conservators and guardians
Rule 7.776. Compensation of trustees

Rule 7.750. Application of rules to guardianships and conservatorships

The rules in this chapter apply to guardianships and conservatorships under division 4 of the Probate Code (Prob. Code, § 1400 et seq.) and to conservatorships under the Lanterman-Petris-Short Act (Welf. & Inst. Code, §§ 5350–5371). They do not apply to guardianships under chapter 2 of division 2 of the Welfare and Institutions Code (Welf. & Inst. Code, § 200 et seq.). Under Probate Code section 2646, the rules in this chapter applicable to guardianships and conservatorships apply only to compensation payable from the estate of the ward or conservatee or from money or property recovered or collected for the estate of the ward or conservatee.

Rule 7.750 adopted effective January 1, 2003.

Ref.: Cal. Fms Pl. & Pr., Ch. 304, "Insane and Other Incompetent Persons"; W. Cal. Sum., 13 "Trusts" §226, 14 "Wills and Probate" §§4, 960, 1044.

Rule 7.751. Petitions for orders allowing compensation for guardians or conservators and their attorneys

(a) Petition for allowance of compensation for services performed before appointment of guardian or conservator

A petition for allowance of compensation to a guardian or conservator or to the attorney for a guardian or conservator may include a request for compensation for services rendered before an order appointing a guardian or conservator. The petition must show facts demonstrating the necessity for preappointment services.

(Subd (a) amended effective January 1, 2007.)

(b) Required showing in petition for allowance of compensation

All petitions for orders fixing and allowing compensation must comply with the requirements of rule 7.702 concerning petitions for extraordinary compensation in decedents' estates, to the extent applicable to guardianships and conservatorships, except that the best interest of the ward or conservatee is to be considered instead of the interest of beneficiaries of the estate.

Rule 7.751 amended effective January 1, 2007; adopted effective January 1, 2003.

Ref.: Cal. Fms Pl. & Pr., Ch. 290F, "Guardianship and Conservatorship: Compensation of Guardian or Conservator," Ch. 304, "Insane and Other Incompetent Persons"; W. Cal. Sum., 14 "Wills and Probate" §§4, 1044, 1045.

Rule 7.752.   Court may order accounting before allowing compensation

Notwithstanding the time period after which a petition may be filed for an allowance of compensation to a guardian, conservator, or an attorney for a guardian or conservator, the court may order the guardian or conservator to file an accounting before or at the time a petition for an allowance of compensation is filed or heard.

Rule 7.752 adopted effective January 1, 2003.

Ref.: Cal. Fms Pl. & Pr., Ch. 290F, "Guardianship and Conservatorship: Compensation of Guardian or Conservator," Ch. 304, "Insane and Other Incompetent Persons"; W. Cal. Sum., 14 "Wills and Probate" §§4, 1044.

Rule 7.753.   Contingency fee agreements in guardianships and conservatorships

A guardian or conservator of the estate may contract with an attorney for a contingency fee for the attorney's services on behalf of the ward or conservatee, or the estate, in connection with a matter that is of a type customarily the subject of a contingency fee agreement, if the court has authorized the guardian or conservator to do so, or if the agreement has been approved by the court under Probate Code section 2644. The agreement must also satisfy the requirements of rule 7.703(d)(1).

Rule 7.753 adopted effective January 1, 2003.

Ref.: Cal. Fms Pl. & Pr., Ch. 290F, "Guardianship and Conservatorship: Compensation of Guardian or Conservator"; W. Cal. Sum., 14 "Wills and Probate" §§4, 1046.

Rule 7.754.   Use of paralegals in the performance of legal services for the guardian or conservator

An attorney for a guardian or conservator may use the services of a paralegal acting under the direction and supervision of the attorney. A request for an allowance of compensation for the services of a paralegal must satisfy the requirements of rule 7.703(e).

Rule 7.754 adopted effective January 1, 2003.

Ref.: Cal. Fms Pl. & Pr., Ch. 290F, "Guardianship and Conservatorship: Compensation of Guardian or Conservator"; W. Cal. Sum., 14 "Wills and Probate" §§4, 1046.

Rule 7.755.   Advance payments and periodic payments to guardians, conservators, and to their attorneys on account for future services

(a) No advance payments

A guardian or conservator must neither pay nor receive, and the attorney for a guardian or conservator must not receive, any payment from the estate of the ward or conservatee for services rendered in advance of an order

of the court authorizing the payment. If an advance payment is made or received, the court may surcharge the guardian or conservator in the manner provided in rule 7.700(b), in addition to removing the guardian or conservator or imposing any other sanction authorized by law on the guardian or conservator or on the attorney.

(b) Periodic payments to attorneys on account

A guardian or conservator may request the court to authorize periodic payment of attorney fees on account of future services under Probate Code section 2643 on a showing of an ongoing need for legal services.

Rule 7.755 adopted effective January 1, 2003.

Ref.: Cal. Fms Pl. & Pr., Ch. 290F, "Guardianship and Conservatorship: Compensation of Guardian or Conservator," Ch. 304, "Insane and Other Incompetent Persons"; W. Cal. Sum., 14 "Wills and Probate" §§4, 451, 1044, 1047, 1048.

Rule 7.756.   Compensation of trustees [Renumbered]

Rule 7.756 renumbered as rule 7.776 effective January 1, 2008.

Another Rule 7.756 follows.

Rule 7.756.   Compensation of conservators and guardians

(a) Standards for determining just and reasonable compensation

The court may consider the following nonexclusive factors in determining just and reasonable compensation for a conservator from the estate of the conservatee or a guardian from the estate of the ward:

(1) The size and nature of the conservatee's or ward's estate;

(2) The benefit to the conservatee or ward, or his or her estate, of the conservator's or guardian's services;

(3) The necessity for the services performed;

(4) The conservatee's or ward's anticipated future needs and income;

(5) The time spent by the conservator or guardian in the performance of services;

(6) Whether the services performed were routine or required more than ordinary skill or judgment;

(7) Any unusual skill, expertise, or experience brought to the performance of services;

(8) The conservator's or guardian's estimate of the value of the services performed; and

(9) The compensation customarily allowed by the court in the community where the court is located for the management of conservatorships or guardianships of similar size and complexity.

(Subd (a) adopted effective January 1, 2008.)

(b) No single factor determinative

No single factor listed in (a) should be the exclusive basis for the court's determination of just and reasonable compensation.

(Subd (b) adopted effective January 1, 2008.)

(c) No inflexible maximum or minimum compensation or maximum approved hourly rate

This rule is not authority for a court to set an inflexible maximum or minimum compensation or a maximum approved hourly rate for compensation.

(Subd (c) adopted effective January 1, 2008.)

Rule 7.756 adopted effective January 1, 2008.

Ref.: Cal. Fms Pl. & Pr., Ch. 290F, "Guardianship and Conservatorship: Compensation of Guardian or Conservator."

Rule 7.776. Compensation of trustees

In determining or approving compensation of a trustee, the court may consider, among other factors, the following:

(1) The gross income of the trust estate;

(2) The success or failure of the trustee's administration;

(3) Any unusual skill, expertise, or experience brought to the trustee's work;

(4) The fidelity or disloyalty shown by the trustee;

(5) The amount of risk and responsibility assumed by the trustee;

(6) The time spent in the performance of the trustee's duties;

(7) The custom in the community where the court is located regarding compensation authorized by settlors, compensation allowed by the court, or charges of corporate trustees for trusts of similar size and complexity; and

(8) Whether the work performed was routine, or required more than ordinary skill or judgment.

Rule 7.776 renumbered effective January 1, 2008; adopted as rule 7.756 effective January 1, 2003; previously amended effective January 1, 2007.

Ref.: Cal. Fms Pl. & Pr., Ch. 560, "Trusts: Express, Public, Charitable, and Totten Trusts"; W. Cal. Sum., 14 "Wills and Probate" §§4, 55, 226.

Chapter 17
Contested Hearings and Trials

Rule 7.801. Objections and responses

If the court continues a matter to allow a written objection or response to be made, and the responding or objecting party fails to serve and file a timely objection or response, the court may deem the objections or responses waived.

Rule 7.801 adopted effective January 1, 2000.

Ref.: Cal. Fms Pl. & Pr., Ch. 442, "Probate: Initiating Probate Administration," Ch. 444, "Probate: Will Contests," Ch. 454, "Probate: Claims Against the Estate," Ch. 455, "Probate: Sale of Estate Property," Ch. 458, "Probate: Determination of Heirship," Ch. 458A, "Probate: Simultaneous Death," Ch. 458C, "Probate: Preliminary Distribution and Partial Allowance of Compensation," Ch. 458D, "Probate: Accounts, Final Distribution, and Compensation"; W. Cal. Sum., 13 "Trusts" §226, 14 "Wills and Probate" §§4, 378.

Chapter 18
Discovery
[Reserved]

Chapter 19
Trusts

Rule 7.901. Trustee's accounts
Rule 7.902. Beneficiaries to be listed in petitions and accounts

Rule 7.901.   Trustee's accounts

(a) Period covered

A trustee's account must state the period covered by the account.

(Subd (a) amended effective January 1, 2002.)

(b) First account

The first account in a testamentary trust must reconcile the initial assets on hand with the decree of distribution of the estate.

(Subd (b) amended effective January 1, 2002.)

(c) Principal and income

All trustee's accounts in a trust that distributes income to a beneficiary must allocate receipts and disbursements between (1) principal receipts and disbursements, and (2) income receipts and disbursements.

(Subd (c) amended effective January 1, 2002.)

Rule 7.901 amended effective January 1, 2002; adopted effective January 1, 2001.

Ref.: Cal. Fms Pl. & Pr., Ch. 560, "Trusts: Express, Public, Charitable, and Totten Trusts"; W. Cal. Sum., 13 "Trusts" §§88, 226, 14 "Wills and Probate" §4.

Rule 7.902.   Beneficiaries to be listed in petitions and accounts

A petition and account involving a trust must state the names and last known addresses of all vested or contingent beneficiaries, including all persons in being who may or will receive income or corpus of the trust, provided, however, that (1) during the time that the trust is revocable and the person holding the power to revoke the trust is competent, the names and last known addresses of beneficiaries who do not hold the power to revoke do not need to be stated, and (2) the petition or account does not need to state the name and last known address of any beneficiary who need not be given notice under Probate Code section 15804.

Rule 7.902 amended effective January 1, 2007; adopted effective January 1, 2002.

Ref.: Cal. Fms Pl. & Pr., Ch. 560, "Trusts: Express, Public, Charitable, and Totten Trusts"; MB Prac. Guide: Cal. Debt Collection & Enforcement of Judgments, §20.06[2]; W. Cal. Sum., 13 "Trusts" §§88, 226, 14 "Wills and Probate" §4.

Rule 7.903.   Trusts funded by court order

(a) Definitions

(1) "Trust funded by court order" under this rule means and refers to a trust that will receive funds under Probate Code section 2580 et seq. (substituted judgment); section 3100 et seq. (proceedings for particular transactions involving disabled spouses or registered domestic partners); or section 3600 et seq. (settlement of claims or actions or disposition of judgments involving minors or persons with disabilities).

(2) "Continuing jurisdiction of the court" under (b) means and refers to the court's continuing subject matter jurisdiction over trust proceedings under division 9 of the Probate Code (Prob. Code, § 15000 et seq.).

(3) "Court supervision under the Probate Code" under (b) means and refers to the court's authority to require prior court approval or subsequent confirmation of the

actions of the trustee as for the actions of a guardian or conservator of the estate under division 4 of the Probate Code (Prob. Code, § 1400 et seq.).

(b) Continuing jurisdiction and court supervision

The order creating or approving the funding of a trust funded by court order must provide that the trust is subject to the continuing jurisdiction of the court and may provide that the trust is to be subject to court supervision under the Probate Code.

(c) Required provisions in trust instruments

Except as provided in (d), unless the court otherwise orders for good cause shown, trust instruments for trusts funded by court order must:

(1) Not contain "no-contest" provisions;

(2) Prohibit modification or revocation without court approval;

(3) Clearly identify the trustee and any other person with authority to direct the trustee to make disbursements;

(4) Prohibit investments by the trustee other than those permitted under Probate Code section 2574;

(5) Require persons identified in (3) to post bond in the amount required under Probate Code section 2320 et seq.;

(6) Require the trustee to file accounts and reports for court approval in the manner and frequency required by Probate Code sections 1060 et seq. and 2620 et seq.;

(7) Require court approval of changes in trustees and a court order appointing any successor trustee; and

(8) Require compensation of the trustee, the members of any advisory committee, or the attorney for the trustee, to be in just and reasonable amounts that must be fixed and allowed by the court. The instrument may provide for periodic payments of compensation on account, subject to the requirements of Probate Code section 2643 and rule 7.755.

(Subd (c) amended effective January 1, 2007; previously amended effective July 1, 2005.)

(d) Trust instruments for smaller trusts

Unless the court otherwise orders for good cause shown, the requirements of (c)(5)–(8) of this rule do not apply to trust instruments for trusts that will have total assets of $20,000 or less after receipt of the property ordered by the court.

Rule 7.903 amended effective January 1, 2007; adopted effective January 1, 2005; previously amended effective July 1, 2005.

Advisory Committee Comment

Subdivision (a) of this rule defines a court-funded trust as a product of three court proceedings. Two of these—a petition for substituted judgment in a probate conservatorship (Prob. Code, § 2580) and a proceeding for a particular transaction in the property of an impaired spouse or domestic partner without a conservator (Prob. Code, § 3100; Fam. Code, § 297.5)—are regularly heard in the probate department of the court. The third proceeding, an application for an order approving the settlement of a minor's claim or a pending action involving a minor or person with a disability or approving the disposition of the proceeds of a judgment in favor of a minor or person with a disability (Prob. Code, § 3600), may be heard in either a probate or a civil department.

The Judicial Council has adopted standard 7.10 of the Standards of Judicial Administration to address proceedings under Probate Code section 3600 that involve court-funded trusts and are heard in civil departments. The standard makes two recommendations concerning the expertise of judicial officers who hear

these proceedings on trust issues. The recommendations are to develop practices and procedures that (1) provide for determination of the trust issues in these matters by the probate department of the court or by a judicial officer who regularly hears probate proceedings or (2) ensure that judicial officers who hear these matters have experience or receive training in substantive and technical issues involving trusts, including special needs trusts.

Ref.: Cal. Fms Pl. & Pr., Ch. 290C, "Guardianship and Conservatorship: Actions and Disputed Claims," Ch. 364, "Minors: Claims and Property of Minors"; W. Cal. Sum., 14 "Wills and Probate" §§4, 1027, 1062, 1071, 1072.

Chapter 20
Claims of Minors and Persons With Disabilities

Rule 7.950. Petition for approval of the compromise of a claim
Rule 7.951. Disclosure of the attorney's interest in a petition to compromise a claim
Rule 7.952. Attendance at hearing on the petition to compromise a claim
Rule 7.953. Order for the deposit of funds of a minor or a person with a disability
Rule 7.954. Petition for the withdrawal of funds deposited for a minor or a person with a disability
Rule 7.955. Attorney's fees for services to a minor or a person with a disability

Rule 7.950. Petition for approval of the compromise of a claim

A petition for court approval of a compromise or covenant not to sue under the Probate Code or under Code of Civil Procedure section 372 must be verified by the petitioner and must contain a full disclosure of all information that has any bearing upon the reasonableness of the compromise or covenant. The information must include, but is not limited to, the following:

(1) The name, birthdate, age, and sex of the minor or person with a disability;

(2) An account of the facts or events and the circumstances out of which the claim or injury arose, including the time, the place, and the identity of the persons involved;

(3) A description of the nature and extent of the injury giving rise to the claim, with sufficient particularity to inform the court whether the injury is permanent or temporary;

(4) An original or a photocopy of all doctors' reports containing a diagnosis of and prognosis for the injury, and a report of the claimant's present condition;

(5) In all cases in which payment for medical or hospital care or treatment for the claimant is sought, the names of the hospitals, doctors, and other providers furnishing the care, the amounts of the respective charges for the care (whether paid or owing), the amounts paid (whether covered by insurance or not), the amounts of any negotiated reductions of the charges, and the net amount owed to each provider;

(6) The amount of attorney's fees requested and the basis for the fees, with an itemization of the costs sought to be allowed and charged against the settlement;

(7) The gross and net amounts of the settlement;

(8) A description of the manner in which the settlement proceeds will be distributed;

(9) A full disclosure of all amounts, if any, paid or to be paid to other claimants;

(10) A statement of whether the petitioner is a plaintiff in the same action with the minor or claimant with a disability and, if so, whether the pendency or disposition of the petitioner's claim on his or her own behalf has in any way affected the proposed compromise of the claim;

(11) A statement of whether the petitioner is a claimant against the recovery of the minor or claimant with a disability and, if so, whether the pendency or disposition of petitioner's claim on his or her own behalf has in any way affected the proposed compromise of the claim;

(12) If settlement money is to be deposited in an account or accounts subject to withdrawal only upon order of the court, the name and address of the proposed depository;

(13) A statement whether notice of the action or claim has been given under Welfare and Institutions Code section 14124.73; and

(14) If the petition requests an order for payment of money to a special needs trust, a statement of the method by which all statutory liens will be satisfied under Probate Code section 3604.

Rule 7.950 amended effective January 1, 2007; adopted effective January 1, 2002.

Ref.: Cal. Fms Pl. & Pr., Ch. 364, "Minors: Claims and Property of Minors"; W. Cal. Sum., 14 "Wills and Probate" §§4, 506, 1014, 1069.

Rule 7.951.   Disclosure of the attorney's interest in a petition to compromise a claim

If the petitioner has been represented or assisted by an attorney in preparing the petition to compromise the claim or in any other respect with regard to the claim, the petition must disclose the following information:

(1) The name, state bar number, law firm, if any, and business address of the attorney;

(2) Whether the attorney became involved with the petition, directly or indirectly, at the instance of any party against whom the claim is asserted or of any party's insurance carrier;

(3) Whether the attorney represents or is employed by any other party or any insurance carrier involved in the matter;

(4) Whether the attorney has received any attorney's fees or other compensation for services provided in connection with the claim giving rise to the petition or with the preparation of the petition, and, if so, the amounts and the identity of the person who paid the fees or other compensation;

(5) If the attorney has not received any attorney's fees or other compensation for services provided in connection with the claim giving rise to the petition or with the preparation of the petition, whether the attorney expects to receive any fees or other compensation for these services, and, if so, the amounts and the identity of the person who is expected to pay the fees or other compensation; and

(6) The terms of any agreement between the petitioner and the attorney.

Rule 7.951 adopted effective January 1, 2002.

Rule 7.952.   Attendance at hearing on the petition to compromise a claim

(a) Attendance of the petitioner and claimant

The person compromising the claim on behalf of the minor or person with a disability and the minor or person with a disability must attend the hearing on the compromise of the claim unless the court for good cause dispenses with their personal appearance.

(Subd (a) amended effective January 1, 2007.)

(b) Attendance of the physician and other witnesses

At the hearing, the court may require the presence and testimony of witnesses, including the attending or examining physician.

Rule 7.952 amended effective January 1, 2007; adopted effective January 1, 2002.

Ref.: Cal. Fms Pl. & Pr., Ch. 364, "Minors: Claims and Property of Minors"; W. Cal. Sum., 14 "Wills and Probate" §§4, 1014, 1069.

Rule 7.953.   Order for the deposit of funds of a minor or a person with a disability

(a) Acknowledgment of receipt by financial institution

In any case in which the court orders that funds to be received by a minor or a person with a disability must be deposited in a financial institution and not disbursed without further order of the court, the order must include a provision that a certified or filed endorsed copy of the order must be delivered to a manager at the financial institution where the funds are to be deposited, and that a receipt from the financial institution must be promptly filed with the court, acknowledging receipt of both the funds deposited and the order for deposit of funds.

(Subd (a) amended effective January 1, 2007.)

(b) Order permitting the withdrawal of funds by a former minor

If, in the order approving the compromise of a minor's claim, there is a finding that the minor will attain the age of majority on a definite date, the order for deposit may require that the depository permit the withdrawal of funds by the former minor after that date, without further order of the court.

Rule 7.953 amended effective January 1, 2007; adopted effective January 1, 2002.

Ref.: Cal. Fms Pl. & Pr., Ch. 364, "Minors: Claims and Property of Minors"; W. Cal. Sum., 14 "Wills and Probate" §§4, 1004, 1071.

Rule 7.954.   Petition for the withdrawal of funds deposited for a minor or a person with a disability

(a) Verified petition required

A petition for the withdrawal of funds deposited for a minor or a person with a disability must be verified and must include the identity of the depository, a showing of the amounts previously withdrawn, a statement of the balance on deposit at the time of the filing of the petition, and a justification for the withdrawal.

(Subd (a) amended effective January 1, 2007.)

(b) Ex parte or noticed hearing

A petition for the withdrawal of funds may be considered ex parte or set for a hearing at the discretion of the court.

Rule 7.954 amended effective January 1, 2007; adopted effective January 1, 2002.

Ref.: Cal. Fms Pl. & Pr., Ch. 364, "Minors: Claims and Property of Minors"; W. Cal. Sum., 14 "Wills and Probate" §§4, 1004, 1071.

Rule 7.955. Attorney's fees for services to a minor or a person with a disability

In all cases under Code of Civil Procedure section 372 or Probate Code sections 3600–3601, the court must use a reasonable fee standard when approving and allowing the amount of attorney's fees payable from money or property paid or to be paid for the benefit of a minor or a person with a disability. The court may approve and allow attorney fees under a contingency fee agreement made in accordance with law, provided that the amount of fees is reasonable under all the facts and circumstances.

Rule 7.955 amended effective January 1, 2007; adopted effective January 1, 2003.

Advisory Committee Comment

This rule requires the court to approve and allow attorney fees in an amount that is reasonable under all the facts and circumstances, under Probate Code section 3601. The rule is declaratory of existing law concerning attorney's fees under a contingency fee agreement when the fees must be approved by the court. The facts and circumstances that the court may consider are discussed in a large body of decisional law under section 3601 and under other statutes that require the court to determine reasonable attorney's fees. The rule permits, but does not require, the court to allow attorney's fees in an amount specified in a contingency fee agreement. The amount of attorney's fees allowed by the court must meet the reasonableness standard of section 3601 no matter how they are determined. That standard may support the court's allowance of attorney's fees that are higher or lower than fees determined by applying the formulas in some current local rules.

Ref.: W. Cal. Sum., 14 "Wills and Probate" §§4, 1070.

Chapter 21
Guardianships

Rule 7.1001. Guardian screening form

(a) Screening form to be submitted with petition

Each proposed probate guardian, except a public guardian, or a bank or other entity entitled to conduct the business of a trust company, must submit to the court with the petition for appointment of guardian a completed *Confidential Guardian Screening Form* (form GC-212).

(Subd (a) amended effective January 1, 2002.)

(b) Use of form

The information on the *Confidential Guardian Screening Form* is used by the court and by persons or agencies designated by the court to assist the court in determining whether a proposed guardian should be appointed.

(Subd (b) amended effective January 1, 2002.)

(c) Form to be confidential

The *Confidential Guardian Screening Form* and the information contained on the form are confidential. The clerk must maintain these forms in a manner that will protect and preserve their confidentiality.

(Subd (c) amended effective January 1, 2007; previously amended effective January 1, 2002.)

Rule 7.1001 amended effective January 1, 2007; adopted effective January 1, 2001; previously amended effective January 1, 2002.

Ref.: Cal. Fms Pl. & Pr., Ch. 280, "Guardianship and Conservatorship: Appointment of Guardians"; W. Cal. Sum., 14 "Wills and Probate" §§4, 919, 960.

Rule 7.1002. Acknowledgment of receipt of Duties of Guardian

Before the court issues letters, each guardian must execute and file an acknowledgment of receipt of the *Duties of Guardian* (form GC-248).

Rule 7.1002 amended effective January 1, 2007; adopted effective January 1, 2001; previously amended effective January 1, 2002.

Ref.: Cal. Fms Pl. & Pr., Ch. 280, "Guardianship and Conservatorship: Appointment of Guardians"; W. Cal. Sum., 14 "Wills and Probate" §§4, 926, 960.

Rule 7.1003. Confidential guardianship status report form

(a) Due date of status report

Each guardian required by the court to complete, sign, and file the status report authorized by Probate Code section 1513.2 must file the completed and signed report no later than one month after the anniversary of the date of the order appointing him or her as guardian. Co-guardians may sign and file their reports jointly.

(b) Court clerk's duties

The clerk of each court that requires guardians to file the status report authorized by Probate Code section 1513.2 must:

(1) Determine the annual due date for the completed report from each appointed guardian required to file the report;

(2) Fill in the due date for the completed report, in the space provided in the form for that purpose, on each blank

copy of the form that must be mailed to appointed guardians under (3); and

(3) Mail by first class mail to each appointed guardian no later than one month prior to the date the status report is due under (a) a blank copy of *Confidential Guardianship Status Report* (form GC-251) for each child under guardianship under the same case number.

(Subd (b) amended effective January 1, 2007.)

Rule 7.1003 amended effective January 1, 2007; adopted effective January 1, 2004.

Ref.: Cal. Fms Pl. & Pr., Ch. 280, "Guardianship and Conservatorship: Appointment of Guardians"; W. Cal. Sum., 14 "Wills and Probate" §§4, 929, 960.

Rule 7.1004.   Termination of guardianship

(a) Operation of law or court order

A guardianship of the person or estate of a minor may terminate by operation of law or may be terminated by court order where the court determines that it would be in the ward's best interest to terminate the guardianship.

(b) Guardian of the person

Under Probate Code section 1600 a guardianship of the person terminates by operation of law, and the guardian of the person need not file a petition for its termination, when the ward attains majority, dies, is adopted, or is emancipated.

(c) Duty of guardian of estate on termination

A guardian of the estate whose administration is terminated by operation of law or court order must file and obtain the court's approval of a final account or report of the administration.

Rule 7.1004 adopted effective January 1, 2004.

Ref.: Cal. Fms Pl. & Pr., Ch. 280, "Guardianship and Conservatorship: Appointment of Guardians," Ch. 290H, "Guardianship and Conservatorship: Termination of Guardianships and Conservatorships"; W. Cal. Sum., 14 "Wills and Probate" §§930, 960.

Rule 7.1005.   Service of copy of final account or report after resignation or removal of guardian

A resigned or removed guardian of the estate must serve a copy of the guardian's final account or report and the petition for its settlement, with the notice of hearing that must be served on the successor guardian of the estate under Probate Code section 1460(b)(1), unless the court dispenses with such service.

Rule 7.1005 adopted effective January 1, 2004.

Ref.: Cal. Fms Pl. & Pr., Ch. 280, "Guardianship and Conservatorship: Appointment of Guardians," Ch. 290G, "Guardianship and Conservatorship: Removal or Resignation of Guardians and Conservators"; W. Cal. Sum., 14 "Wills and Probate" §§4, 930, 960.

Rule 7.1006.   Service of copy of final account on termination of guardianship

(a) Minor living

In addition to service of notices of hearing required under Probate Code section 1460(b), on termination of the guardianship the guardian of the estate must serve a copy of the guardian's final account and petition for its settle-

ment on the minor, unless the court dispenses with such service.

(b) Personal representative of deceased minor

If the minor is deceased, in addition to service of notices of hearing required under Probate Code section 1460(b), on termination of the guardianship the guardian of the estate must serve a notice of hearing and a copy of the guardian's final account and petition for its settlement on the personal representative of the deceased minor's estate, unless the court dispenses with such service.

(c) Successors in interest to deceased minor

If the minor is deceased and no personal representative of the minor's estate has been appointed or qualified or if the personal representative of the minor's estate is also the guardian, on termination of the guardianship, in addition to the notices of hearing required under Probate Code section 1460(b), the guardian of the estate must serve a notice of hearing and a copy of the guardian's final account and petition for its settlement on the persons entitled to succeed to the deceased minor's estate, unless the court dispenses with such service.

Rule 7.1006 adopted effective January 1, 2004.

Ref.: Cal. Fms Pl. & Pr., Ch. 280, "Guardianship and Conservatorship: Appointment of Guardians," Ch. 290H, "Guardianship and Conservatorship: Termination of Guardianships and Conservatorships"; W. Cal. Sum., 14 "Wills and Probate" §§4, 930, 960.

Rule 7.1007.   Settlement of accounts and release by former minor

(a) Release of guardian of estate by ward after majority

A ward who has attained majority may settle accounts with his or her guardian of the estate and may give a valid release to the guardian if the court determines, at the time of the hearing on the final account, or on the final report and petition for termination on waiver of account, that the release has been obtained fairly and without undue influence. The release is not effective to discharge the guardian until one year after the ward has attained majority.

(b) Appearance of ward

The court may require the personal appearance of the ward at the hearing on the final account or report of the guardian of the estate after termination of the guardianship.

Rule 7.1007 adopted effective January 1, 2004.

Ref.: Cal. Fms Pl. & Pr., Ch. 280, "Guardianship and Conservatorship: Appointment of Guardians," Ch. 290H, "Guardianship and Conservatorship: Termination of Guardianships and Conservatorships"; W. Cal. Sum., 14 "Wills and Probate" §§4, 960, 1039.

Rule 7.1008.   Visitation by former guardian after termination of guardianship

(a) Visitation order at time of termination of guardianship

Subject to the provisions of Welfare and Institutions Code section 304, a guardian may request the court to order visitation with the child under guardianship at the time of termination of the guardianship either in the guardian's petition for termination or in the guardian's objections or other pleading filed in response to the petition of another party for termination. The court may then order visitation if it is in the best interest of the child.

(b) Request for visitation after termination of guardianship

If no order was entered under (a) concerning visitation between the former guardian and the former ward at termination of the guardianship and no dependency proceedings for the child are pending, the former guardian may request the court to order visitation with the former ward after termination of the guardianship as provided in Family Code section 3105, Probate Code section 1602, rule 5.475, and this rule, as follows:

(1) If either parent of the former ward is living, in an independent action for visitation under the Family Code; or

(2) If neither parent of the former ward is living, in a guardianship proceeding under the Probate Code, including a proceeding commenced for that purpose.

(c) Declaration under UCCJEA

A guardian or former guardian requesting visitation under this rule must file a *Declaration Under Uniform Child Custody Jurisdiction and Enforcement Act (UCCJEA)* (form FL-105/GC-120) with his or her request for visitation.

(Subd (c) amended effective January 1, 2007.)

(d) Transmission of visitation order

Following the termination of the guardianship the clerk of the superior court issuing the visitation order concerning the guardian or former guardian and the ward or former ward must promptly transmit an endorsed filed copy of the order to the superior court of the county where a custody proceeding under the Family Code is pending or, if none, to the superior court of the county in which the custodial parent resides. An order transmitted to the court in the county where the custodial parent resides may be sent to the receiving court's Court Operations Manager, Family Division, or similar senior manager or clerk responsible for the operations of the family law departments of the court. If the receiving court has more than one location, the order may be sent to the main or central district of the court.

Rule 7.1008 amended effective January 1, 2007; adopted effective January 1, 2006.

Ref.: Cal. Fms Pl. & Pr., Ch. 290H, "Guardianship and Conservatorship: Termination of Guardianships and Conservatorships"; W. Cal. Sum., 14 "Wills and Probate" §§4, 930, 960.

Rule 7.1009. Standards of conduct for the guardian of the estate

Except as otherwise required by statute, in the exercise of ordinary care and diligence in managing and controlling the estates of the ward, the guardian of the estate is to be guided by the following principles:

(a) Avoidance of actual and apparent conflicts of interest with the ward

The guardian must avoid actual conflicts of interest and, consistent with his or her fiduciary duty to the ward, the appearance of conflicts of interest. The guardian must avoid any personal, business, or professional interest or relationship that is or reasonably could be perceived as being self-serving or adverse to the best interest of the ward. In particular:

(1) Except as appropriate for guardians who are not professional fiduciaries with full disclosure to the court, the guardian should not personally provide medical or legal services to the ward;

(2) The guardian must be independent from all service providers, except when (a) no other guardian or service providers are reasonably available, (b) the exception is in the best interest of the ward, (c) the circumstances are fully disclosed to the court, and (d) prior court approval has been obtained;

(3) The guardian must neither solicit nor accept incentives from service providers; and

(4) The guardian must not engage his or her family members to provide services to the ward for a profit or fee when other alternatives are reasonably available. Where family members do provide such services, their relationship to the guardian must be fully disclosed to the court, the terms of engagement must be in the best interest of the ward compared to the terms available from independent service providers, the services must be competently performed, and the guardian must be able to exercise appropriate control and supervision.

A guardian's employees, including family members, are not service providers and are not providing services to the ward for a profit or fee within the meaning of this rule if their compensation is paid by the guardian and their services are either included in the guardian's petition for allowance of the guardian's compensation or are not paid from the ward's estate.

(Subd (a) adopted effective January 1, 2008.)

(b) Guardianship estate management

In addition to complying with applicable standards of estate management specified in rule 7.1059(b), the guardian of the estate must:

(1) Manage the estate primarily for the ward's long-term benefit if the ward has a parent available who can provide sufficient support;

(2) If it would be in the best interest of the ward and the estate, consider requesting court authority to support the ward from the estate if the ward does not have a parent available who can provide sufficient support.

(Subd (b) adopted effective January 1, 2008.)

Rule 7.1009 adopted effective January 1, 2008.

Advisory Committee Comment

The Probate and Mental Health Advisory Committee consulted with several organizations in the development of rule 7.1009, including the National Guardianship Association, a nationwide voluntary association of professional and family fiduciaries, guardians, and allied professionals. In developing this rule, the Probate and Mental Heath Advisory Committee considered the National Guardianship Association's Standards of Practice. Some of these standards have been incorporated into the rule.

Ref.: Cal. Fms Pl. & Pr., Ch. 285, "Guardianship and Conservatorship: Care of Ward or Conservatee."

Rule 7.1010. Qualifications and continuing education requirements for private professional guardians [Repealed]

Rule 7.1010 repealed effective July 1, 2008; amended effective January 1, 2007; adopted effective January 1, 2006; previously amended effective July 1, 2006.

Rule 7.1011. Taking possession of an asset of the ward at an institution or opening or changing ownership of an account or safe-deposit box in a financial institution

(a) Definitions

As used in this rule, the following terms have the meanings stated below:

(1) An "institution" is an insurance company, insurance broker, insurance agent, investment company, investment bank, securities broker-dealer, investment advisor, financial planner, financial advisor, or any other person who takes, holds, or controls an asset subject to a guardianship that is not a "financial institution" within the meaning of this rule;

(2) A "financial institution" is a bank, trust (except as provided in (d)), savings and loan association, savings bank, industrial bank, or credit union; and

(3) "Taking possession" or "taking control" of an asset held or controlled by an institution includes changing title to the asset, withdrawing all or any portion of the asset, or transferring all or any portion of the asset from the institution.

(Subd (a) adopted effective January 1, 2009.)

(b) Responsibilities of the guardian when taking possession or control of an asset of the ward at an institution

When taking possession or control of an asset held by an institution in the name of the ward, the temporary or general guardian of the estate must provide the following to the institution:

(1) A certified copy of the guardian's *Letters of Temporary Guardianship or Conservatorship* (form GC-150) or *Letters of Guardianship* (form GC-250) containing the Notice to Institutions and Financial Institutions on the second page; and

(2) A blank copy of a *Notice of Taking Possession or Control of an Asset of Minor or Conservatee* (form GC-050).

(Subd (b) adopted effective January 1, 2009.)

(c) Responsibilities of the guardian when opening or changing the name on an account or a safe-deposit box in a financial institution

When opening or changing the name on an account or a safe-deposit box in a financial institution, the temporary or general guardian of the estate must provide the following to the financial institution:

(1) A certified copy of the guardian's *Letters of Temporary Guardianship or Conservatorship* (form GC-150) or *Letters of Guardianship* (form GC-250) containing the Notice to Institutions and Financial Institutions on the second page; and

(2) A blank copy of a *Notice of Opening or Changing a Guardianship or Conservatorship Account or Safe-Deposit Box* (form GC-051).

(Subd (c) adopted effective January 1, 2009.)

(d) Application of this rule to trust arrangements

This rule applies to Totten trust accounts but does not apply to any other trust arrangement described in Probate Code section 82(b).

(Subd (d) adopted effective January 1, 2009.)
Rule 7.1011 adopted effective January 1, 2009.

Rule 7.1012. The good cause exception to notice of the hearing on a petition for appointment of a temporary guardian

(a) Purpose

The purpose of this rule is to establish uniform standards for the good cause exception to the notice of the hearing required on a petition for appointment of a temporary guardian under Probate Code section [1] **2250(e)**.

(Subd (a) amended effective January 1, 2009; adopted effective January 1, 2008.)

Rule 7.1012(a). 2008 Deletes. [1] 2250(c)

(b) Good cause for exceptions to notice limited

Good cause for an exception to the notice required by section [1] **2250(e)** must be based on a showing that the exception is necessary to protect the proposed ward or his or her estate from immediate and substantial harm.

(Subd (b) amended effective January 1, 2009; adopted effective January 1, 2008.)

Rule 7.1012(b). 2008 Deletes. [1] 2250(c)

(c) Court may waive or change the time or manner of giving notice

An exception to the notice requirement of section [1] **2250(e)** may include one or any combination of the following:

(1) Waiving notice to one, more than one, or all persons entitled to notice;

(2) Requiring a different period of notice; and

(3) Changing the required manner of giving notice, including requiring notice by telephone, fax, e-mail, or a combination of these methods, instead of notice by personal delivery to the proposed ward's parents or to a person with a visitation order.

(Subd (c) amended effective January 1, 2009; adopted effective January 1, 2008.)

Rule 7.1012(c). 2008 Deletes. [1] 2250(c)

(d) Good cause exceptions to notice

Good cause for an exception to the notice requirement of section [1] **2250(e)** may include a showing of:

(1) Harm caused by the passage of time. The showing must demonstrate the immediate and substantial harm to the ward or the ward's estate that could occur during the notice period.

(2) Harm that one or more persons entitled to notice might do to the proposed ward, including abduction; or harm to the proposed ward's estate if notice to those persons is given. Such a showing would not support an exception to the requirement to give notice to any other person entitled to notice unless it also demonstrates that notice cannot reasonably be given to the other person without also giving notice to the persons who might cause harm.

(3) The death or incapacity of the proposed ward's custodial parent and the petitioner's status as the custodial parent's nominee.

(4) Medical emergency. The emergency must be immediate and substantial and treatment (1) must be reasonably unavailable unless a temporary guardian is appointed and (2) cannot be deferred for the notice period because of the proposed ward's pain or extreme discomfort or a significant risk of harm.

(5) Financial emergency. The emergency must be immediate and substantial and other means shown likely to

be ineffective to prevent loss or further loss to the proposed ward's estate or loss of support for the proposed ward during the notice period.

(Subd (d) amended effective January 1, 2009; adopted effective January 1, 2008.)

Rule 7.1012(d).   2008 Deletes. [1] 2250(c)

(e) Contents of request for good cause exception to notice

(1) When the temporary guardianship petition is prepared on the *Petition for Appointment of Temporary Guardian* (form GC-110), a request for a good cause exception to the notice requirement of section [1] **2250(e)** must be in writing, separate from the petition for appointment of a temporary guardian, and must include:

[2] **(A)** An application containing the case caption and stating the relief requested;

[3] **(B)** An affirmative factual showing in support of the application in a declaration under penalty of perjury containing competent testimony based on personal knowledge;

[4] **(C)** A declaration under penalty of perjury based on personal knowledge containing the information required for an ex parte application under rule 3.1204(b); [5] **and**

(D) A proposed order.

(2) When the temporary guardianship petition is prepared on the *Petition for Appointment of Temporary Guardian of the Person* (form GC-110(P)), a request for a good cause exception to the notice requirement of section 2250(e) may be included in the petition.

(Subd (e) amended effective January 1, 2009; adopted effective January 1, 2008.)

Rule 7.1012(e).   2008 Deletes. [1] 2250(c) [2] (1) [3] (2) [4] (3) [5] (4) A memorandum; and (5)

Rule 7.1012 amended effective January 1, 2009; adopted effective January 1, 2008.

Ref.: Cal. Fms Pl. & Pr., Ch. 282, "Guardianship and Conservatorship: Temporary Guardians and Conservators."

Rule 7.1013.   Change of ward's residence

(a) Pre-move notice of change of personal residence required

Unless an emergency requires a shorter period of notice, the guardian of the person must mail copies of a notice of an intended change of the ward's personal residence to the persons listed below at least 15 days before the date of the proposed change, and file the original notice with proof of mailing with the court. Copies of the notice must be mailed to:

(1) The ward if he or she is 12 years of age or older;

(2) The attorney of record for the ward;

(3) The ward's parents;

(4) Any person who had legal custody of the ward when the first petition for appointment of a guardian was filed in the proceeding;

(5) A guardian of the ward's estate; and

(6) Any person who was nominated as guardian of the ward under Probate Code sections 1500 or 1501 but was not appointed guardian in the proceeding.

(Subd (a) adopted effective January 1, 2008.)

(b) Ward's personal residence

The "ward's personal residence" under (a) is the ward's residence when the first petition for appointment of a guardian was filed in the proceeding.

(Subd (b) adopted effective January 1, 2008.)

(c) Post-move notice of a change of residence required

The guardian of the person of a minor must file a notice of a change of the ward's residence with the court within 30 days of the date of any change. Unless waived by the court for good cause to prevent harm to the ward, the guardian, the guardian's attorney, or an employee of the guardian's attorney must also mail a copy of the notice to the persons listed below and file a proof of mailing with the original notice. Unless waived, copies of the notice must be mailed to:

(1) The ward's attorney of record;

(2) The ward's parents;

(3) Any person who had legal custody of the ward when the first petition for appointment of a guardian was filed in the proceeding;

(4) A guardian of the ward's estate; and

(5) Any person who was nominated as guardian of the ward under Probate Code sections 1500 or 1501 but was not appointed guardian in the proceeding.

(Subd (c) adopted effective January 1, 2008.)

(d) Ward's residence

The "ward's residence" under (c) is the ward's residence at any time after appointment of a guardian.

(Subd (d) adopted effective January 1, 2008.)

(e) Use of Judicial Council forms GC-079 and GC-080

(1) The *Pre-Move Notice of Proposed Change of Personal Residence of Conservatee or Ward* (form GC-079) must be used for the pre-move notice required under (a) and Probate Code section 2352(e)(3). The guardian, the guardian's attorney, or an employee of the attorney may complete the mailing and sign the proof of mailing on page 2 of the form. If the notice is mailed less than 15 days before the date of the move because an emergency requires a shorter period of notice, the basis for the emergency must be stated in the notice.

(2) The *Post-Move Notice of Change of Residence of Conservatee or Ward* (form GC-080) must be used for the post-move notice required under (c) and Probate Code section 2352(e)(1) and (2). The guardian, the guardian's attorney, or an employee of the attorney may complete the mailing and sign the proof of mailing on page 2 of the form.

(Subd (e) adopted effective January 1, 2008.)

(f) Prior court approval required to establish ward's residence outside California

Notwithstanding any other provision of this rule, prior court approval is required before a ward's residence may be established outside the state of California.

(Subd (f) adopted effective January 1, 2008.)

Rule 7.1013 adopted effective January 1, 2008.

Ref.: Cal. Fms Pl. & Pr., Ch. 285, "Guardianship and Conservatorship: Care of Ward or Conservatee."

Rule 7.1015.   Indian Child Welfare Act in guardianship and certain conservatorship proceedings (Prob. Code, §§ 1459.5, 1460.2)

(a) Definitions

As used in this rule, unless the context or subject matter otherwise requires:

(1) "Act" means the Indian Child Welfare Act (25 United States Code sections 1901–1963).

(2) "Petitioner" means and refers to a petitioner for the appointment of a guardian of the person of a child or a petitioner for the appointment of a conservator of the person of a formerly married minor child.

(Subd (a) adopted effective January 1, 2008.)

(b) Applicability of this rule and rules 5.480 through 5.487

(1) This rule applies to the following proceedings under division 4 of the Probate Code when the proposed ward or conservatee is an Indian child, within the meaning of the act:

(A) A guardianship of the person or the person and estate in which the proposed guardian of the person is not the proposed ward's natural parent or Indian custodian within the meaning of the act;

(B) A conservatorship of the person or the person and estate of a formerly married minor in which the proposed conservator is not a natural parent or Indian custodian of the minor and is seeking physical custody of the proposed conservatee.

(2) Unless the context otherwise requires, rules 5.480 through 5.487 apply to the proceedings listed in (1).

(3) When applied to the proceedings listed in (1), references in rules 5.480 through 5.487 to social workers, probation officers, county probation departments, or county social welfare departments are references to the petitioner or petitioners for the appointment of a guardian or conservator of the person of an Indian child and to an Indian child's appointed temporary or general guardian or conservator of the person.

(4) If the court appoints a temporary or general guardian or conservator of the person of the child involved in a proceeding listed in (1), the duties and responsibilities of a petitioner under this rule are transferred to and become the duties and responsibilities of the appointed guardian or conservator. The petitioner must cooperate with and provide any information the petitioner has concerning the child to the appointed guardian or conservator.

(Subd (b) adopted effective January 1, 2008.)

(c) Notice

If, at any time after the filing of a petition for appointment of a guardian or conservator for a minor child, the court or petitioner knows or has reason to know, within the meaning of Probate Code sections 1449 and 1459.5 and Welfare and Institutions Code section 224.3(b), that an Indian child is involved, the petitioner and the court must notify the child's parents or legal guardian and Indian custodian, and the Indian child's tribe, of the pending proceeding and the right of the tribe to intervene, as follows:

(1) Notice to the Indian child's parents, Indian custodian, and Indian tribe of the commencement of a guardianship or conservatorship must be given by serving copies of the completed *Notice of Child Custody Proceeding for Indian Child* (form ICWA-030), the petition for appointment of a guardian or conservator, and all attachments, by certified or registered mail, fully prepaid with return receipt requested.

(2) The petitioner and his or her attorney, if any, must complete the *Notice* and the petitioner must date and sign the declaration. If there is more than one petitioner, the statements about the child's ancestors and background provided in the *Notice of Child Custody Proceeding for Indian Child* (form ICWA-030) must be based on all information known to each petitioner, and all petitioners must sign the declaration.

(3) When the petitioner is represented by an attorney in the proceeding, the attorney must serve copies of the *Notice of Child Custody Proceeding for Indian Child* (form ICWA-030) in the manner described in (1) and sign the declaration of mailing on the *Notice*.

(4) When the guardianship or conservatorship petitioner or petitioners are not represented by an attorney in the proceeding, the clerk of the court must serve the *Notice* in the manner described in (1) and sign the certificate of mailing on the *Notice*.

(5) The original of all *Notices of Child Custody Proceeding for Indian Child* (form ICWA-030) served under the act, and all return receipts and responses received, must be filed with the court before the hearing.

(6) Notice to an Indian child's tribe must be sent to the tribal chairperson unless the tribe has designated another agent for service.

(7) Notice must be served on all tribes of which the child may be a member or eligible for membership. If there are more tribes or bands to be served than can be listed on the last page of the *Notice*, the additional tribes or bands may be listed on an *Attachment to Notice of Child Custody Proceeding for Indian Child* (form ICWA-030(A)).

(8) Notice under the act must be served whenever there is any reason to know that the child is or may be an Indian child and for every hearing after the first hearing unless and until it is determined that the act does not apply to the proceeding.

(9) If, after a reasonable time following the service of notice under the act—but in no event less than 60 days—no determinative response to the *Notice of Child Custody Proceeding for Indian Child* (form ICWA-030) is received, the court may determine that the act does not apply to the proceeding unless further evidence of its applicability is later received.

(10) If an Indian child's tribe intervenes in the proceeding, service of the *Notice of Child Custody Proceeding for Indian Child* (form ICWA-030) is no longer required and subsequent notices to the tribe may be sent to all parties in the form and in the manner required under the Probate Code and these rules. All other provisions of the act, this rule, and rules 5.480 through 5.487 continue to apply.

(11) Notice under the act must be served in addition to all notices otherwise required for the particular proceeding under the provisions of the Probate Code.

(Subd (c) adopted effective January 1, 2008.)

(d) Duty of inquiry

(1) The court, a court investigator or county officer appointed to conduct an investigation under Probate Code section 1513 or 1826, a petitioner, and an appointed temporary or general guardian or conservator of the person of a minor child each have an affirmative and

continuing duty to inquire whether the child involved in the matters identified in (b)(1) is or may be an Indian child.

(2) Before filing his or her petition, the petitioner must ask the child involved in the proceeding, if the child is old enough, and the parents or any other legal guardian, whether the child is or may be an Indian child, and must complete the *Indian Child Inquiry Attachment* (form ICWA-010(A)) and attach it to his or her petition.

(3) At the first personal appearance by a parent or previously appointed legal guardian at a hearing in a guardianship or conservatorship, the court must if requested by petitioner, or may on its own motion, order the parent or legal guardian to complete a *Parental Notification of Indian Status* (form ICWA-020) and deliver the completed form to the petitioner.

(4) If the parent, Indian custodian, or guardian does not personally appear at a hearing in a proceeding identified in (b)(1), the court may order the petitioner to use reasonable diligence to find and ask the parent, Indian custodian, or legal guardian to complete and deliver to petitioner a *Parental Notification of Indian Status* (form ICWA-020).

(5) If the court or county investigator, petitioner, appointed guardian or conservator, or the attorney for a petitioner or appointed guardian or conservator, knows or has reason to know that an Indian child is involved in the proceeding, he or she must make further inquiry as soon as practicable by:

(A) Interviewing the parents, Indian custodian, and "extended family members" as defined in 25 United States Code section 1903(2), to gather the information listed in Probate Code section 1460.2(b)(5) that is required to complete the *Notice of Child Custody Proceeding for Indian Child* (form ICWA-030);

(B) Contacting the U.S. Department of the Interior, Bureau of Indian Affairs and the California Department of Social Services for assistance in identifying the names and contact information of the tribes of which the child may be a member or eligible for membership; and

(C) Contacting the tribes and any other person who reasonably can be expected to have information regarding the child's tribal membership status or eligibility for membership.

(6) If the court knows or has reason to know that an Indian child is involved in the proceeding, the court may direct any of the persons named in (5) to conduct the inquiry described in that paragraph.

(7) The circumstances that may provide reason to know the child is an Indian child include the following:

(A) The child or person having an interest in the child, including an Indian tribe, an Indian organization, an officer of the court, a public or private agency, or a member of the child's extended family, informs or otherwise provides information suggesting that the child is an Indian child to the court or to any person listed in (5);

(B) The residence or domicile of the child, the child's parents, or an Indian custodian is in a predominantly Indian community; or

(C) The child or the child's family has received services or benefits from a tribe or services that are available to Indians from tribes or the federal government,

such as the U.S. Department of Health and Human Services, Indian Health Service, or Tribal Temporary Assistance to Needy Families benefits.

(Subd (d) adopted effective January 1, 2008.)
Rule 7.1015 adopted effective January 1, 2008.

Ref.: Cal. Fms Pl. & Pr., Ch. 280, "Guardianship and Conservatorship: Appointment of Guardians."

Chapter 22
Conservatorships

Rule 7.1050. Conservator forms
Rule 7.1051. Acknowledgment of receipt of Duties of Conservator
Rule 7.1052. Termination of conservatorship
Rule 7.1053. Service of final account of removed or resigned conservator
Rule 7.1054. Service of final account after termination of conservatorship
Rule 7.1059. Standards of conduct for the conservator of the estate
Rule 7.1061. Taking possession of an asset of the conservatee at an institution or opening or changing ownership of an account or safe-deposit box in a financial institution
Rule 7.1062. The good cause exception to notice of the hearing on a petition for appointment of a temporary conservator
Rule 7.1063. Change of conservatee's residence

Rule 7.1050.　Conservator forms
(a) Forms to be submitted with petition

Each petitioner, unless the petitioner is a bank or other entity entitled to conduct the business of a trust company, must submit to the court with the petition for appointment of conservator a completed *Confidential Supplemental Information* statement (form GC-312). In addition, each proposed conservator, except a bank or other entity entitled to conduct the business of a trust company, or a public guardian, must submit a completed *Confidential Conservator Screening Form* (form GC-314).

(Subd (a) amended effective January 1, 2007; previously amended effective January 1, 2002.)

(b) Use of form

The information on the *Confidential Conservator Screening Form* is used by the court and by persons or agencies designated by the court to assist the court in determining whether a proposed conservator should be appointed.

(Subd (b) amended effective January 1, 2002.)

(c) Forms to be confidential

The *Confidential Conservator Screening Form*, the *Confidential Supplemental Information* statement, and the information contained on these forms are confidential. The clerk must maintain these forms in a manner that will protect and preserve their confidentiality.

(Subd (c) amended effective January 1, 2007; previously amended effective January 1, 2002.)
Rule 7.1050 amended effective January 1, 2007; adopted effective January 1, 2001; previously amended effective January 1, 2002.

Ref.: Cal. Fms Pl. & Pr., Ch. 281, "Guardianship and Conservatorship: Appointment of Conservators"; W. Cal. Sum., 14 "Wills and Probate" §§4, 938, 960.

Rule 7.1051.　Acknowledgment of receipt of Duties of Conservator

Before the court issues letters, each conservator must

execute and file an acknowledgment of receipt of the *Duties of Conservator and Acknowledgment of Receipt of Handbook* (form GC-348).

Rule 7.1051 amended effective January 1, 2002; adopted effective January 1, 2001.

Ref.: Cal. Fms Pl. & Pr., Ch. 281, "Guardianship and Conservatorship: Appointment of Conservators"; W. Cal. Sum., 14 "Wills and Probate" §§4, 947, 960.

Rule 7.1052. Termination of conservatorship

(a) Operation of law or court order

A conservatorship of the person or estate may terminate by operation of law or may be terminated by court order if the court determines that it is no longer required.

(b) Conservator of the person

Under Probate Code section 1860(a), a conservatorship of the person terminates by operation of law when the conservatee dies, and the conservator of the person need not file a petition for its termination.

(c) Duty of conservator of estate on termination

A conservator of the estate whose administration is terminated by operation of law or by court order must file and obtain the court's approval of a final account of the administration.

Rule 7.1052 adopted effective January 1, 2004.

Ref.: Cal. Fms Pl. & Pr., Ch. 290H, "Guardianship and Conservatorship: Termination of Guardianships and Conservatorships"; W. Cal. Sum., 14 "Wills and Probate" §§4, 951, 952, 960.

Rule 7.1053. Service of final account of removed or resigned conservator

A resigned or removed conservator of the estate must serve a copy of the conservator's final account and the petition for its settlement with the notice of hearing that must be served on the successor conservator of the estate under Probate Code section 1460(b)(1), unless the court dispenses with such service.

Rule 7.1053 adopted effective January 1, 2004.

Ref.: Cal. Fms Pl. & Pr., Ch. 290G, "Guardianship and Conservatorship: Removal or Resignation of Guardians and Conservators"; W. Cal. Sum., 14 "Wills and Probate" §§4, 952, 960.

Rule 7.1054. Service of final account after termination of conservatorship

After termination of the conservatorship, the conservator of the estate must serve copies of the conservator's final account and the petition for its settlement with the notices of hearing that must be served on the former conservatee and on the spouse or domestic partner of the former conservatee under Probate Code sections 1460(b)(2) and (3), unless the court dispenses with such service.

Rule 7.1054 adopted effective January 1, 2004.

Ref.: Cal. Fms Pl. & Pr., Ch. 290H, "Guardianship and Conservatorship: Termination of Guardianships and Conservatorships"; W. Cal. Sum., 14 "Wills and Probate" §§4, 952, 960.

Rule 7.1059. Standards of conduct for the conservator of the estate

Except as otherwise required by statute, in the exercise of ordinary care and diligence in managing and controlling the estate of the conservatee, the conservator of the estate is to be guided by the following principles:

(a) Avoidance of actual and apparent conflicts of interest with the conservatee

The conservator must avoid actual conflicts of interest and, consistent with his or her fiduciary duty to the conservatee, the appearance of conflicts of interest. The conservator must avoid any personal, business, or professional interest or relationship that is or reasonably could be perceived as being self-serving or adverse to the best interest of the conservatee. In particular:

(1) Except as appropriate for conservators who are not professional fiduciaries with full disclosure to the court, the conservator should not personally provide housing, medical, or legal services to the conservatee;

(2) The conservator must be independent from all service providers, except when (a) no other conservator or service providers are reasonably available, (b) the exception is in the best interest of the conservatee, (c) the circumstances are fully disclosed to the court, and (d) prior court approval has been obtained;

(3) The conservator must neither solicit nor accept incentives from service providers; and

(4) The conservator must not engage his or her family members to provide services to the conservatee for a profit or fee when other alternatives are reasonably available. Where family members do provide such services, their relationship to the conservator must be fully disclosed to the court, the terms of engagement must be in the best interest of the conservatee compared to the terms available from independent service providers, the services must be competently performed, and the conservator must be able to exercise appropriate control and supervision.

A conservator's employees, including family members, are not service providers and are not providing services to the conservatee for a profit or fee within the meaning of this rule if their compensation is paid by the conservator and their services are either included in the conservator's petition for allowance of the conservator's compensation or are not paid from the conservatee's estate.

(Subd (a) adopted effective January 1, 2008.)

(b) Conservatorship estate management

The conservator of the estate must:

(1) Provide competent management of the conservatee's property, with the care of a prudent person dealing with someone else's property;

(2) Refrain from unreasonably risky investments;

(3) Refrain from making loans or gifts of estate property, except as authorized by the court after full disclosure;

(4) Manage the estate for the benefit of the conservatee;

(5) Subject to the duty of full disclosure to the court and persons entitled under law to receive it, closely guard against unnecessary or inappropriate disclosure of the conservatee's financial information;

(6) Keep the money and property of the estate separate from the conservator's or any other person's money or property, except as may be permitted under statutes authorizing public guardians or public conservators and certain regulated private fiduciaries to maintain common trust funds or similar common investments;

(7) Hold title reflecting the conservatorship in individual securities, mutual funds, securities broker accounts, and accounts with financial institutions;

(8) Keep accurate records of all transactions. Professional fiduciaries must maintain prudent accounting systems and procedures designed to protect against embezzlement and other cash-asset mismanagement;

(9) Undertake as soon as possible after appointment and qualification to locate and safeguard the conservatee's estate planning documents, including wills, living trusts, powers of attorney for health care and finances, life insurance policies, and pension records;

(10) Undertake as soon as possible after appointment and qualification to secure the real and personal property of the estate, insuring it at appropriate levels, and protecting it against damage, destruction, or loss;

(11) Make reasonable efforts to preserve property identified in the conservatee's estate planning documents;

(12) Communicate as necessary and appropriate with the conservator of the person of the conservatee, if any, and with the trustee of any trust of which the conservatee is a beneficiary;

(13) Pursue claims against others on behalf of the estate when it would be in the best interest of the conservatee or the estate to do so. Consider requesting prior court authority to pursue or compromise large or complex claims, particularly those that might require litigation and the assistance of counsel and those that might result in an award of attorneys' fees for the other party against the estate if unsuccessful, and request such approval before entering into a contingent fee agreement with counsel;

(14) Defend against actions or claims against the estate when it would be in the best interest of the conservatee or the estate to do so. Consider requesting court approval or instructions concerning the defense or compromise of litigation against the estate;

(15) Collect all public and insurance benefits for which the conservatee is eligible;

(16) Evaluate the conservatee's ability to manage cash or other assets and take appropriate action, including obtaining prior court approval when necessary or appropriate, to enable the conservatee to do so to the level of his or her ability;

(17) When disposing of the conservatee's tangible personal property, inform the conservatee's family members in advance and give them an opportunity to acquire the property, with approval or confirmation of the court; and

(18) In deciding whether it is in the best interest of the conservatee to dispose of property of the estate, consider the following factors, among others, as appropriate in the circumstances:

(A) The likely benefit or improvement of the conservatee's life that disposing of the property would bring;

(B) The likelihood that the conservatee would need or benefit from the property in the future;

(C) Subject to the factors specified in Probate Code section 2113, the previously expressed or current desires of the conservatee concerning the property;

(D) The provisions of the conservatee's estate plan concerning the property;

(E) The tax consequences of the disposition transaction;

(F) The impact of the disposition transaction on the conservatee's entitlement to public benefits;

(G) The condition of the entire estate;

(H) Alternatives to disposition of the property;

(I) The likelihood that the property will deteriorate or be subject to waste if retained in the estate; and

(J) The benefit versus the cost or liability of maintaining the property in the estate.

(Subd (b) adopted effective January 1, 2008.)

Rule 7.1059 adopted effective January 1, 2008.

Advisory Committee Comment

The Probate and Mental Health Advisory Committee consulted with several organizations in the development of rule 7.1059, including the National Guardianship Association, a nationwide voluntary association of professional and family fiduciaries, guardians, and allied professionals. In developing this rule, the Probate and Mental Heath Advisory Committee considered the National Guardianship Association's Standards of Practice. Some of these standards have been incorporated into the rules.

Rule 7.1060. Qualifications and continuing education requirements for private professional conservators [Repealed]

Rule 7.1060 repealed effective July 1, 2008; amended effective January 1, 2007; adopted effective January 1, 2006.

Rule 7.1061. Taking possession of an asset of the conservatee at an institution or opening or changing ownership of an account or safe-deposit box in a financial institution

(a) Definitions

As used in this rule, the following terms have the meanings stated below:

(1) An "institution" is an insurance company, insurance broker, insurance agent, investment company, investment bank, securities broker-dealer, investment advisor, financial planner, financial advisor, or any other person who takes, holds, or controls an asset subject to a guardianship that is not a "financial institution" within the meaning of this rule;

(2) A "financial institution" is a bank, trust (except as provided in (d)), savings and loan association, savings bank, industrial bank, or credit union; and

(3) "Taking possession" or "taking control" of an asset held or controlled by an institution includes changing title to the asset, withdrawing all or any portion of the asset, or transferring all or any portion of the asset from the institution.

(Subd (a) adopted effective January 1, 2009.)

(b) Responsibilities of the conservator when taking possession or control of an asset of the conservatee at an institution

When taking possession or control of an asset held by an institution in the name of the conservatee, the temporary, general, or limited conservator of the estate must provide the following to the institution:

(1) A certified copy of the conservator's *Letters of Temporary Guardianship or Conservatorship* (form GC-150) or *Letters of Conservatorship* (form GC-350) containing the Notice to Institutions and Financial Institutions on the second page; and

(2) A blank copy of a *Notice of Taking Possession or Control of an Asset of Minor or Conservatee* (form GC-050).

(Subd (b) adopted effective January 1, 2009.)

(c) Responsibilities of the conservator when opening or changing the name on an account or a safe-deposit box at a financial institution

When opening or changing the name on an account or a safe-deposit box in a financial institution, the temporary, general, or limited conservator of the estate must provide the following to the financial institution:

(1) A certified copy of the guardian's *Letters of Temporary Guardianship or Conservatorship* (form GC-150) or *Letters of Conservatorship* (form GC-350) containing the Notice to Institutions and Financial Institutions on the second page; and

(2) A blank copy of a *Notice of Opening or Changing a Guardianship or Conservatorship Account or Safe-Deposit Box* (form GC-051).

(Subd (c) adopted effective January 1, 2009.)

(d) Application of this rule to Totten trust accounts

This rule applies to Totten trust accounts but does not apply to any other trust arrangement described in Probate Code section 82(b).

(Subd (d) adopted effective January 1, 2009.)
Rule 7.1061 adopted effective January 1, 2009.

Rule 7.1062.   The good cause exception to notice of the hearing on a petition for appointment of a temporary conservator

(a) Purpose

The purpose of this rule is to establish uniform standards for the good cause exception to the notice of the hearing required on a petition for appointment of a temporary conservator under Probate Code section [1] **2250(e).**

(Subd (a) amended effective January 1, 2009; adopted effective January 1, 2008.)

Rule 7.1062(a).   2008 Deletes. [1] 2250(c)

(b) Good cause for exceptions to notice limited

Good cause for an exception to the notice required by section [1] **2250(e)** must be based on a showing that the exception is necessary to protect the proposed conservatee or his or her estate from immediate and substantial harm.

(Subd (b) amended effective January 1, 2009; adopted effective January 1, 2008.)

Rule 7.1062(b).   2008 Deletes. [1] 2250(c)

(c) Court may change the time or manner of giving notice

An exception to the notice requirement of section [1] **2250(e)** may include one or any combination of the following:

(1) Waiving notice to one, more than one, or all persons entitled to notice;

(2) Requiring a different period of notice; and

(3) Changing the required manner of giving notice, including requiring notice by telephone, fax, e-mail, or personal delivery, or a combination of these methods, instead of or in addition to notice by mail to the proposed conservatee's spouse or registered domestic partner and relatives.

(Subd (c) amended effective July 1, 2008; adopted effective January 1, 2008.)

Rule 7.1062(c).   2008 Deletes. [1] 2250(c)

(d) Good cause exceptions to notice

Good cause for an exception to the notice requirement of section [1] **2250(e)** may include a showing of:

(1) Harm caused by the passage of time. The showing must demonstrate the immediate and substantial harm to the conservatee or the conservatee's estate that could occur during the notice period.

(2) Harm that one or more persons entitled to notice might do to the proposed conservatee or the proposed conservatee's estate if notice is given. Such a showing would not support an exception to the requirement to give notice to any other person entitled to notice unless it also demonstrates that notice cannot reasonably be given to the other person without also giving notice to the persons who might cause harm.

(3) Medical emergency. The emergency must be immediate and substantial and treatment (1) must be reasonably unavailable unless a temporary conservator is appointed and (2) cannot be deferred for the notice period because of the proposed conservatee's pain or extreme discomfort or a significant risk of harm.

(4) Financial emergency. The emergency must be immediate and substantial and other means shown likely to be ineffective to prevent loss or further loss to the proposed conservatee's estate during the notice period.

(Subd (d) amended effective January 1, 2009; adopted effective January 1, 2008.)

Rule 7.1062(d).   2008 Deletes. [1] 2250(c)

(e) Contents of request for good cause exception to notice

A request for a good cause exception to the notice requirement of section [1] **2250(e)** must be in writing, separate from the petition for appointment of a temporary conservator, and must include:

(1) An application containing the case caption and stating the relief requested;

(2) An affirmative factual showing in support of the application in a declaration under penalty of perjury containing competent testimony based on personal knowledge;

(3) A declaration under penalty of perjury based on personal knowledge containing the information required for an ex parte application under rule 3.1204(b); **and**

(4) [2] A proposed order.

(Subd (e) amended effective January 1, 2009; adopted effective January 1, 2008.)

Rule 7.1062(e).   2008 Deletes. [1] 2250(c) **[2]** A memorandum; and (5)

Rule 7.1062 amended effective January 1, 2009; adopted effective January 1, 2008; previously amended effective July 1, 2008.

Ref.: Cal. Fms Pl. & Pr., Ch. 282, "Guardianship and Conservatorship: Temporary Guardians and Conservators."

Rule 7.1063.   Change of conservatee's residence

(a) Pre-move notice of change of personal residence required

Unless an emergency requires a shorter period of notice, the conservator of the person must mail copies of a notice of an intended change of the conservatee's personal residence to the persons listed below at least 15 days before the date of the proposed change, and file the original notice with proof of mailing with the court. Copies of the notice must be mailed to:

(1) The conservatee;

(2) The conservatee's attorney of record;

(3) The conservatee's spouse or registered domestic partner; and

(4) The conservatee's relatives named in the *Petition for Appointment of Probate Conservator* (form GC-310), including the conservatee's "deemed relatives" under Probate Code section 1821(b)(1)–(4) if the conservatee has no spouse or registered domestic partner and no second-degree relatives.

(Subd (a) adopted effective January 1, 2008.)

(b) Conservatee's personal residence

(1) The "conservatee's personal residence" under (a) is the residence the conservatee understands or believes, or reasonably appears to understand or believe, to be his or her permanent residence on the date the first petition for appointment of a conservator was filed in the proceeding, whether or not the conservatee is living in that residence on that date. A residential care facility, including a board and care, intermediate care, skilled nursing, or secured perimeter facility, may be the conservatee's personal residence under this rule.

(2) If the conservatee cannot form or communicate an understanding or belief concerning his or her permanent residence on the date the first petition for appointment of a conservator was filed in the proceeding, his or her personal residence under this rule is the residence he or she last previously understood or believed, or appeared to understand or believe, to be his or her permanent residence.

(3) For purposes of this rule, the following changes of residence are or are not changes of the conservatee's personal residence, as indicated:

(A) A move from the conservatee's personal residence under this rule to a residential care facility or other residence is a change of the conservatee's personal residence under (a).

(B) A move from a residential care facility or other residence to another residence that is not the conservatee's personal residence under this rule is a change of the conservatee's personal residence under (a).

(C) A move from a residential care facility or other residence to the conservatee's personal residence under this rule is not a change of the conservatee's personal residence under (a).

(Subd (b) adopted effective January 1, 2008.)

(c) Post-move notice of a change of residence required

The conservator of the person must file a notice of a change of the conservatee's residence with the court within 30 days of the date of the change. Unless waived by the court for good cause to prevent harm to the conservatee, the conservator must mail a copy of the notice to the persons named below and file a proof of mailing with the original notice filed with the court. Unless waived, the notice must be mailed to:

(1) The conservatee's attorney of record;

(2) The conservatee's spouse or registered domestic partner; and

(3) The conservatee's relatives named in the *Petition for Appointment of Probate Conservator* (form GC-310), including the conservatee's "deemed relatives" under Probate Code section 1821(b)(1)–(4) if the conservatee has no spouse or registered domestic partner and no second-degree relatives.

(Subd (c) adopted effective January 1, 2008.)

(d) Conservatee's residence

The "conservatee's residence" under (c) is the conservatee's residence at any time after appointment of a conservator.

(Subd (d) adopted effective January 1, 2008.)

(e) Use of Judicial Council forms GC-079 and GC-080

(1) The *Pre-Move Notice of Proposed Change of Personal Residence of Conservatee or Ward* (form GC-079) must be used for the pre-move notice required under (a) and Probate Code section 2352(e)(3). The conservator, the conservator's attorney, or an employee of the attorney may complete the mailing and sign the Proof of Mailing on page 2 of the form. If the notice is mailed less than 15 days before the date of the move because an emergency requires a shorter period of notice, the basis for the emergency must be stated in the notice.

(2) The *Post-Move Notice of Change of Residence of Conservatee or Ward* (form GC-080) must be used for the post-move notice required under (c) and Probate Code section 2352(e)(1) and (2). The conservator, the conservator's attorney, or an employee of the attorney may complete the mailing and sign the Proof of Mailing on page 2 of the form.

(Subd (e) adopted effective January 1, 2008.)

(f) Prior court approval required to establish conservatee's residence outside California

Notwithstanding any other provision of this rule, prior court approval is required before a conservatee's residence may be established outside the state of California.

(Subd (f) adopted effective January 1, 2008.)

Rule 7.1063 adopted effective January 1, 2008.

Ref.: Cal. Fms Pl. & Pr., Ch. 285, "Guardianship and Conservatorship: Care of Ward or Conservatee."

Chapter 23
Court-Appointed Counsel in Probate Proceedings

Chapter 23 adopted effective January 1, 2008.

Rule 7.1101.   Qualifications and continuing education required of counsel appointed by the court in guardianships and conservatorships

(a) Definitions

As used in this rule, the following terms have the meanings stated below:

(1) "Appointed counsel" or "counsel appointed by the court" are legal counsel appointed by the court under Probate Code sections 1470 or 1471, including counsel in private practice and deputy public defenders directly

responsible for the performance of legal services under the court's appointment of a county's public defender.

(2) A "probate guardianship" or "probate conservatorship" is a guardianship or conservatorship proceeding under division 4 of the Probate Code.

(3) "LPS" and "LPS Act" refer to the Lanterman-Petris-Short Act, Welfare and Institutions Code section 5000 et seq.

(4) An "LPS conservatorship" is a conservatorship proceeding for a gravely disabled person under chapter 3 of the LPS Act, Welfare and Institutions Code sections 5350–5371.

(5) A "contested matter" in a probate or LPS conservatorship proceeding is a matter that requires a noticed hearing and in which written objections are filed by any party or made by the conservatee or proposed conservatee orally in open court.

(6) "AOC" is the Administrative Office of the Courts.

(7) "Counsel in private practice" includes attorneys employed by or performing services under contracts with nonprofit organizations.

(Subd (a) amended effective January 1, 2009; adopted effective January 1, 2008.)

(b) Qualifications of appointed counsel in private practice

Except as provided in this rule, each counsel in private practice appointed by the court on or after January 1, 2008, must be an active member of the State Bar of California for at least three years immediately before the date of appointment, with [1] no discipline imposed within the 12 months immediately preceding [2] **any** date of [3] availability for appointment after January 1, 2008; and

(1) *Appointments to represent minors in guardianships*

For an appointment to represent a minor in a guardianship:

(A) Within the five years immediately before the date of first availability for appointment after January 1, 2008, must have represented at least three wards or proposed wards in probate guardianships, three children in juvenile court dependency or delinquency proceedings, or three children in custody proceedings under the Family Code; or

(B) At the time of appointment, must be qualified:

(i) For appointments to represent children in juvenile dependency proceedings under rule 5.660 and the court's local rules governing court-appointed juvenile court dependency counsel; or

(ii) For appointments to represent children in custody proceedings under the Family Code under rule 5.242, including the alternative experience requirements of rule 5.242(g).

(C) Counsel qualified for appointments in guardianships under (B) must satisfy the continuing education requirements of this rule in addition to the education or training requirements of the rules mentioned in (B).

(2) *Appointments to represent conservatees or proposed conservatees*

For an appointment to represent a conservatee or a proposed conservatee, within the five years immediately before the date of first availability for appointment after January 1, 2008, counsel in private practice must have:

(A) Represented at least three conservatees or proposed conservatees in either probate or LPS conservatorships; or

(B) Completed any three of the following five tasks:

(i) Represented petitioners for the appointment of a conservator at commencement of three probate conservatorship proceedings, from initial contact with the petitioner through the hearing and issuance of Letters of Conservatorship;

(ii) Represented a petitioner, a conservatee or a proposed conservatee, or an interested third party in two contested probate or LPS conservatorship matters. A contested matter that qualifies under this item and also qualifies under (i) may be applied toward satisfaction of both items;

(iii) Represented a party for whom the court could appoint legal counsel in a total of three matters described in Probate Code sections 1470, 1471, 1954, 2356.5, 2357, 2620.2, 3140, or 3205;

(iv) Represented fiduciaries in three separate cases for settlement of a court-filed account and report, through filing, hearing, and settlement, in any combination of probate conservatorships or guardianships, decedent's estates, or trust proceedings under division 9 of the Probate Code; or

(v) Prepared five wills or trusts, five durable powers of attorney for health care, and five durable powers of attorney for asset management.

(3) **Except as provided in (e)(2),** private counsel qualified under (1) or (2) must also be covered by professional liability insurance satisfactory to the court in the amount of at least $100,000 per claim and $300,000 per year.

(Subd (b) amended effective January 1, 2009; adopted effective January 1, 2008.)

Rule 7.1101(b). 2008 Deletes. [1] no disciplinary proceedings pending and [2] the [3] first

(c) Qualifications of deputy public defenders performing legal services on court appointments of the public defender

(1) Except as provided in this rule, beginning on January 1, 2008, each county deputy public defender with direct responsibility for the performance of legal services in a particular case on the appointment of the county public defender under Probate Code sections 1470 or 1471 must be an active member of the State Bar of California for at least three years immediately before the date of appointment; and either

(A) Satisfy the experience requirements for private counsel in (b)(1) for appointments in guardianships or (b)(2) for appointments in conservatorships; or

(B) Have a minimum of three years' experience representing minors in juvenile dependency or delinquency proceedings or patients in postcertification judicial proceedings or conservatorships under the LPS Act.

(2) A deputy public defender qualified under (1) must also be covered by professional liability insurance satisfactory to the court in the amount of at least $100,000 per claim and $300,000 per year, or be covered for professional liability at an equivalent level by a self-insurance program for the professional employees of his or her county.

(3) A deputy public defender who is not qualified under this rule may periodically substitute for a qualified deputy public defender with direct responsibility for the

performance of legal services in a particular case. In that event, the county public defender or his or her designee, who may be the qualified supervisor, must certify to the court that the substitute deputy is working under the direct supervision of a deputy public defender who is qualified under this rule.

(Subd (c) adopted effective January 1, 2008.)

(d) Transitional provisions on qualifications

(1) Counsel appointed before January 1, 2008, may continue to represent their clients through March 2008, whether or not they are qualified under (b) or (c). After March 2008, through conclusion of these matters, the court may retain or replace appointed counsel who are not qualified under (b) or (c) or may appoint qualified co-counsel to assist them.

(2) In January, February, and March 2008, the court may appoint counsel in new matters who have not filed the certification of qualifications required under (h) at the time of appointment but must replace counsel appointed under this paragraph who have not filed the certificate before April 1, 2008.

(Subd (d) adopted effective January 1, 2008.)

(e) Exemption for small courts

(1) Except as provided in (2) **and (3)**, the qualifications required under (b) or (c) may be waived by a court with four or fewer authorized judges if it cannot find qualified counsel or for other grounds of hardship.

(2) **A court described in (1) may, without a waiver, appoint counsel in private practice who do not satisfy the insurance requirements of (b)(3) if counsel demonstrate to the court that they are adequately self-insured.**

(3) A court may not waive **or disregard** the [1] self-insurance requirements of [2] (c)(2) **applicable to deputy public defenders**.

[3] **(4)** A court waiving the qualifications required under (b) or (c) must make express written findings showing the circumstances supporting the waiver and disclosing all alternatives considered, including appointment of qualified counsel from adjacent counties and other alternatives not selected.

(Subd (e) amended effective January 1, 2009; adopted effective January 1, 2008.)

Rule 7.1101(e).   2008 Deletes. [1] insurance or [2] (b)(3) or [3] (3)

(f) Continuing education of appointed counsel

Beginning on January 1, 2008, counsel appointed by the court must complete three hours of education each calendar year that qualifies for [1] **Minimum Continuing Legal Education** credit for State Bar–certified specialists in estate planning, trust, and probate law.

(Subd (f) amended effective January 1, 2009; adopted effective January 1, 2008.)

Rule 7.1101(f).   2008 Deletes. [1] mandatory continuing legal education

(g) Additional court-imposed qualifications, education, and other requirements

The qualifications in (b) and (c) and the continuing education requirement in (f) are minimums. A court may establish higher qualification or continuing education requirements, including insurance requirements; require initial education or training; and impose other requirements, including an application by private counsel.

(Subd (g) adopted effective January 1, 2008.)

(h) Initial certification of qualifications; annual post-qualification reports and certifications

(1) Each counsel appointed or eligible for appointment by the court before January 1, 2008, including deputy public defenders, must certify to the court in writing before April 1, 2008, that he or she satisfies the qualifications under (b) or (c) to be eligible for a new appointment on or after that date.

(2) After March 2008, each counsel must certify to the court that he or she is qualified under (b) or (c) before becoming eligible for an appointment under this rule.

(3) **Each counsel appointed or eligible for appointment by the court under this rule must immediately advise the court of the imposition of any State Bar discipline.**

(4) Beginning in 2009, each appointed counsel must certify to the court before the end of March of each year that**:**

(A) His or her history of State Bar discipline and professional liability insurance coverage or, if appointed by a court with four or fewer authorized judges under (e)(2), the adequacy of his or her self-insurance, either has or has not changed since the date of his or her qualification certification or last annual certification; and

(B) He or she has completed the continuing education required for the preceding calendar year.

(5) Annual certifications required under this subdivision showing changes in State Bar disciplinary history, professional liability insurance coverage, or adequacy of self-insurance must include descriptions of the changes.

[1] **(6)** Certifications required under this subdivision must be submitted to the court but are not to be filed or lodged in a case file.

(Subd (h) amended effective January 1, 2009; adopted effective January 1, 2008.)

Rule 7.1101(h).   2008 Deletes. [1] (4)

(i) Reporting

The AOC may require courts to report appointed counsel's qualifications and completion of continuing education required by this rule to ensure compliance with Probate Code section 1456.

(Subd (i) adopted effective January 1, 2008.)

Rule 7.1101 amended effective January 1, 2009; adopted effective January 1, 2008.

Ref.: Cal. Fms Pl. & Pr., Ch. 280, "Guardianship and Conservatorship: Appointment of Guardians," Ch. 281, "Guardianship and Conservatorship: Appointment of Conservators."

TITLE 8
Appellate Rules

Division 1.   Rules Relating to the Supreme Court and Courts of Appeal. Rules 8.1–8.642.

Division 2.   Rules Relating to the Superior Court Appellate Division. Rules 8.800–8.936.

Division 3.   Trial of Small Claims Cases on Appeal. Rules 8.950–8.966.

Division 4.   Transfer of Appellate Division Cases to the Court of Appeal. Rules 8.1000–8.1018.

Division 5.   Publication of Appellate Opinions. Rules 8.1100–8.1125.

Division 1
Rules Relating to the Supreme Court and Courts of Appeal

Chap. 1.   General Provisions. Rules 8.1–8.68.
Chap. 2.   Civil Appeals. Rules 8.100–8.278.
Chap. 3.   Criminal Appeals. Rules 8.300–8.368.
Chap. 4.   Habeas Corpus Appeals and Writs. Rules 8.380–8.388.
Chap. 5.   Juvenile Appeals and Writs. Rules 8.400–8.474.
Chap. 6.   Conservatorship Appeals. Rules 8.480, 8.482.
Chap. 7.   Writs of Mandate, Certiorari, and Prohibition in the Supreme Court and Court of Appeal. Rules 8.485–8.493.
Chap. 8.   Miscellaneous Writs of Review. Rules 8.495–8.499.
Chap. 9.   Proceedings in the Supreme Court. Rules 8.500–8.552.
Chap. 10.   Appeals From Judgments of Death. Rules 8.600–8.642.

Chapter 1
General Provisions

Art. 1.   In General. Rules 8.1–8.23.
Art. 2.   Service, Filing, Form, and Number of Documents. Rules 8.25–8.44.
Art. 3.   Applications and Motions; Extending and Shortening Time. Rules 8.50–8.68.

Article 1
In General

Rule 8.1. Title
Rule 8.4. Application of division
Rule 8.7. Construction
Rule 8.10. Definitions and use of terms
Rule 8.13. Amendments to rules
Rule 8.16. Amendments to statutes
Rule 8.18. Documents violating rules not to be filed
Rule 8.20. California Rules of Court prevail
Rule 8.23. Sanctions to compel compliance

Rule 8.1. Title

The rules in this title may be referred to as the Appellate Rules. All references in this title to "these rules" are to the Appellate Rules.

Rule 8.1 adopted effective January 1, 2007.

Ref.: Cal. Fms Pl. & Pr., Ch. 46, "Appeal: Extending or Shortening Time," Ch. 474C, "Procedures in Reviewing Agency Decisions."

Rule 8.4. Application of division

The rules in this division apply to:

(1) Appeals from the superior courts, except appeals to the appellate divisions of the superior courts;

(2) Original proceedings, motions, applications, and petitions in the Courts of Appeal and the Supreme Court; and

(3) Proceedings for transferring cases within the appellate jurisdiction of the superior court to the Court of Appeal for review, unless rules 8.1000–8.1018 provide otherwise.

Rule 8.4 amended and renumbered effective January 1, 2007; repealed and adopted as rule 53 effective January 1, 2005.

Ref.: Cal. Fms Pl. & Pr., Ch. 44, "Appeal: Preparing and Filing the Record," Ch. 51, "Appeal: Hearing and Decision," Ch. 61, "Associations and Clubs," Ch. 358, "Mandate and Prohibition."

Rule 8.7. Construction

The rules of construction stated in rule 1.5 apply to these rules. In addition, in these rules the headings of divisions, chapters, articles, rules, and subdivisions are substantive.

Rule 8.7 adopted effective January 1, 2007.

Ref.: Cal. Fms Pl. & Pr., Ch. 45, "Appeal: Motion Procedure," Ch. 51, "Appeal: Hearing and Decision."

Rule 8.10. Definitions and use of terms

Unless the context or subject matter requires otherwise, the definitions and use of terms in rule 1.6 apply to these rules. In addition, the following apply:

(1) "Appellant" means the appealing party.

(2) "Respondent" means the adverse party.

(3) "Party" includes any attorney of record for that party.

(4) "Judgment" includes any judgment or order that may be appealed.

(5) "Superior court" means the court from which an appeal is taken.

(6) "Reviewing court" means the Supreme Court or the Court of Appeal to which an appeal is taken, in which an original proceeding is begun, or to which an appeal or original proceeding is transferred.

(7) The word "briefs" includes petitions for rehearing, petitions for review, and answers thereto. It does not

include petitions for extraordinary relief in original proceedings.

Rule 8.10 amended and renumbered effective January 1, 2007; repealed and adopted as rule 40 effective January 1, 2005.

Ref.: Cal. Fms Pl. & Pr., Ch. 40, "Appeal: An Overview," Ch. 42, "Appeal: Notice of Appeal," Ch. 45, "Appeal: Motion Procedure," Ch. 50, "Appeal: Briefs," Ch. 51, "Appeal: Hearing and Decision," Ch. 54, "Appeal: California Supreme Court Review," Ch. 292, "Habeas Corpus."

Rule 8.13. Amendments to rules

Only the Judicial Council may amend these rules, except the rules in division 5, which may be amended only by the Supreme Court. An amendment by the Judicial Council must be published in the advance pamphlets of the Official Reports and takes effect on the date ordered by the Judicial Council.

Rule 8.13 amended and renumbered effective January 1, 2007; repealed and adopted as rule 54 effective January 1, 2005.

Rule 8.16. Amendments to statutes

In these rules, a reference to a statute includes any subsequent amendment to the statute.

Rule 8.16 adopted effective January 1, 2007.

Ref.: Cal. Fms Pl. & Pr., Ch. 45, "Appeal: Motion Procedure."

Rule 8.18. Documents violating rules not to be filed

Except as these rules provide otherwise, the reviewing court clerk must not file any record or other document that does not conform to these rules.

Rule 8.18 amended effective January 1, 2009; repealed and adopted as rule 46 effective January 1, 2005; previously amended and renumbered effective January 1, 2007.

Advisory Committee Comment

The exception in this rule acknowledges that there are different rules that apply to certain non-conforming documents. For example, this rule does not apply to nonconforming or late briefs, which are addressed by rules 8.204(e) and 8.220(a), respectively, or to nonconforming supporting documents accompanying a writ petition under chapter 7, which are addressed by rule 8.486(c)(2).

Ref.: Cal. Fms Pl. & Pr., Ch. 40, "Appeal: An Overview," Ch. 44, "Appeal: Preparing and Filing the Record," Ch. 45, "Appeal: Motion Procedure," Ch. 50, "Appeal: Briefs," Ch. 54, "Appeal: California Supreme Court Review"; W. Cal. Sum., 3 "Agency and Employment" §672.

Rule 8.20. California Rules of Court prevail

A Court of Appeal must accept for filing a record, brief, or other document that complies with the California Rules of Court despite any local rule imposing other requirements.

Rule 8.20 amended and renumbered effective January 1, 2007; repealed and adopted as rule 80 effective January 1, 2005.

Ref.: Cal. Fms Pl. & Pr., Ch. 40, "Appeal: An Overview," Ch. 50, "Appeal: Briefs," Ch. 212, "Dismissal."

Rule 8.23. Sanctions to compel compliance

The failure of a court reporter or clerk to perform any duty imposed by statute or these rules that delays the filing of the appellate record is an unlawful interference with the reviewing court's proceedings. It may be treated as an interference in addition to or instead of any other sanction that may be imposed by law for the same breach of duty. This rule does not limit the reviewing court's power to define and remedy any other interference with its proceedings.

Rule 8.23 renumbered effective January 1, 2007; repealed and adopted as rule 46.5 effective January 1, 2005.

Ref.: Cal. Fms Pl. & Pr., Ch. 40, "Appeal: An Overview," Ch. 44, "Appeal: Preparing and Filing the Record."

Article 2
Service, Filing, Form, and Number of Documents

Rule 8.25. Service and filing
Rule 8.29. Service on nonparty public officer or agency
Rule 8.32. Address and telephone number of record; notice of change
Rule 8.36. Substituting parties; substituting or withdrawing attorneys
Rule 8.40. Form of filed documents
Rule 8.44. Number of copies of filed documents

Rule 8.25. Service and filing

(a) Service

(1) Before filing any document, a party must serve, by any method permitted by the Code of Civil Procedure, one copy of the document on the attorney for each party separately represented, on each unrepresented party, and on any other person or entity when required by statute or rule.

(2) The party must attach to the document presented for filing a proof of service showing service on each person or entity required to be served under (1). The proof must name each party represented by each attorney served.

(Subd (a) amended effective January 1, 2007.)

(b) Filing

(1) A document is deemed filed on the date the clerk receives it.

(2) [1] **Unless otherwise provided by these rules or other law,** a filing is not timely unless the clerk receives the document before the time to file it expires.

(3) A brief, a petition for rehearing, an answer to a petition for rehearing, a petition for review, an answer to a petition for review, or a reply to an answer to a petition for review is timely if the time to file it has not expired on the date of:

(A) Its mailing by priority or express mail as shown on the postmark or the postal receipt; or

(B) Its delivery to a common carrier promising overnight delivery as shown on the carrier's receipt.

(4) The provisions of (3) do not apply to original proceedings.

(Subd (b) amended effective January 1, 2009; previously amended effective January 1, 2007.)

Rule 8.25(b). 2008 Deletes. [1] Except as provided in (3)

Rule 8.25 amended effective January 1, 2009; adopted as rule 40.1 effective January 1, 2005; previously amended and renumbered effective January 1, 2007.

Advisory Committee Comment

Subdivision (a). Subdivision (a)(1) requires service "by any method permitted by the Code of Civil Procedure." The reference is to the several permissible methods of service provided in Code of Civil Procedure sections 1010–1020. *Information Sheet for Proof of Service (Court of Appeal)* (form APP-009-INFO) provides additional information about how to serve documents and how to provide proof of service.

Subdivision (b)(2). In general, to be filed on time, a document must be received by the clerk before the time for filing that document expires. There are, however, some limited exceptions to this general rule. For example, the rules currently provide that if the superior court clerk receives a notice of appeal in a criminal, juvenile, or conservatorship case or notice of intent in a juvenile dependency case by mail from a custodial institution after the deadline for filing the notice has expired but the envelope shows that the notice was mailed or delivered to custodial officials for mailing before the deadline expired, the notice is deemed timely (see rules 8.308(e), 8.400(f), 8.450(e)(5), 8.480(a)). These provisions reflect the "prison-delivery" exception articulated by the California Supreme Court in *In re Jordan* (1992) 4 Cal.4th 116.

Ref.: Cal. Fms Pl. & Pr., Ch. 18, "Alcoholic Beverage Licenses," Ch. 40, "Appeal: An Overview," Ch. 42, "Appeal: Notice of Appeal," Ch. 44, "Appeal: Preparing and Filing the Record," Ch. 45, "Appeal: Motion Procedure," Ch. 46, "Appeal: Extending or Shortening Time," Ch. 48, "Appeal: Abandonment, Dismissal, and Stipulated Reversal," Ch. 50, "Appeal: Briefs," Ch. 52, "Appeal: Rehearing," Ch. 54, "Appeal: California Supreme Court Review," Ch. 135, "Contempt," Ch. 300, "Indemnity and Contribution," Ch. 358, "Mandate and Prohibition," Ch. 492, "Review (Certiorari), Writ of."

Rule 8.29.   Service on nonparty public officer or agency

(a) Proof of service

When a statute or this rule requires a party to serve any document on a nonparty public officer or agency, the party must file proof of such service with the document unless a statute permits service after the document is filed, in which case the proof of service must be filed immediately after the document is served on the public officer or agency.

(Subd (a) relettered effective January 1, 2007; adopted as subd (b) effective January 1, 2004.)

(b) Identification on cover

When a statute or this rule requires a party to serve any document on a nonparty public officer or agency, the cover of the document must contain a statement that identifies the statute or rule requiring service of the document on the public officer or agency in substantially the following form: "Service on [insert name of the officer or agency] required by [insert citation to the statute or rule]."

(Subd (b) relettered effective January 1, 2007; adopted as subd (c) effective January 1, 2004.)

(c) Service on the Attorney General

In addition to any statutory requirements for service of briefs on public officers or agencies, a party must serve its brief or petition on the Attorney General if the brief or petition:

(1) Questions the constitutionality of a state statute; or

(2) Is filed on behalf of the State of California, a county, or an officer whom the Attorney General may lawfully represent in:

(A) A criminal case;

(B) A case in which the state or a state officer in his or her official capacity is a party; or

(C) A case in which a county is a party, unless the county's interest conflicts with that of the state or a state officer in his or her official capacity.

(Subd (c) adopted effective January 1, 2007.)
Rule 8.29 amended and renumbered effective January 1, 2007; adopted as rule 44.5 effective January 1, 2004; previously amended effective July 1, 2004.

Advisory Committee Comment

Rule 8.29 refers to statutes that require a party to serve documents on a nonparty public officer or agency. For a list of examples of such statutory requirements, please see the *Civil Case Information Statement* (form APP-004).

Ref.: Cal. Fms Pl. & Pr., Ch. 46, "Appeal: Extending or Shortening Time," Ch. 50, "Appeal: Briefs," Ch. 200, "Discovery: Review of Discovery Orders."

Rule 8.32.   Address and telephone number of record; notice of change

(a) Address and telephone number of record

In any case pending before the court, the court will use the address and telephone number that an attorney or unrepresented party provides on the first document filed in that case as the address and telephone number of record unless the attorney or unrepresented party files a notice under (b).

(Subd (a) adopted effective January 1, 2007.)

(b) Notice of change

(1) An attorney or unrepresented party whose address or telephone number changes while a case is pending must promptly serve and file a written notice of the change in the **reviewing** court in which the case is pending.

(2) The notice must specify the title and number of the case or cases to which it applies. If an attorney gives the notice, the notice must include the attorney's California State Bar number.

(Subd (b) amended effective July 1, 2008; adopted as subd (a) effective January 1, 2005; previously amended and relettered effective January 1, 2007.)

(c) Matters affected by notice

If the notice under (b) does not identify the case or cases in which the new address or telephone number applies, the clerk may use the new address or telephone number as the person's address and telephone number of record in all pending and concluded cases.

(Subd (c) amended and relettered effective January 1, 2007; adopted as subd (b) effective January 1, 2005.)

(d) Multiple addresses

If an attorney **or an unrepresented party** has more than one [1] **address**, only one [2] address for that attorney **or unrepresented party** may be used in a given case.

(Subd (d) amended effective July 1, 2008; adopted as subd (c) effective January 1, 2005; previously amended and relettered effective January 1, 2007; previously amended effective January 1, 2008.)

Rule 8.32(d).   2008 Deletes. [1] office **[2]** office

Rule 8.32 amended effective July 1, 2008; repealed and adopted as rule 40.5 effective January 1, 2005; previously amended and renumbered effective January 1, 2007; previously amended effective January 1, 2008.

Ref.: Cal. Fms Pl. & Pr., Ch. 40, "Appeal: An Overview," Ch. 45, "Appeal: Motion Procedure," Ch. 54, "Appeal: California Supreme Court Review."

Rule 8.36.   Substituting parties; substituting or withdrawing attorneys

(a) Substituting parties

Substitution of parties in an appeal or original proceeding must be made by serving and filing a motion in the reviewing court. The clerk of that court must notify the superior court of any ruling on the motion.

(b) Substituting attorneys

A party may substitute attorneys by serving and filing in the reviewing court a substitution signed by the party represented and the new attorney. In all appeals and in original proceedings related to a superior court proceeding, the party must also serve the superior court.

(c) Withdrawing attorney

(1) An attorney may request withdrawal by filing a motion to withdraw. Unless the court orders otherwise, the motion need be served only on the party represented and the attorneys directly affected.

(2) The proof of service need not include the address of the party represented. But if the court grants the motion, the withdrawing attorney must promptly provide the court and the opposing party with the party's current or last known address and telephone number.

(3) In all appeals and in original proceedings related to a superior court proceeding, the reviewing court clerk must notify the superior court of any ruling on the motion.

(4) If the motion is filed in any proceeding pending in the Supreme Court after grant of review, the Supreme Court clerk must also notify the Court of Appeal of any ruling on the motion.

Rule 8.36 renumbered effective January 1, 2007; repealed and adopted as rule 48 effective January 1, 2005.

Ref.: Cal. Fms Pl. & Pr., Ch. 40, "Appeal: An Overview," Ch. 45, "Appeal: Motion Procedure," Ch. 72, "Attorney Practice and Ethics"; MB Prac. Guide: Cal. Debt Collection & Enforcement of Judgments, §§14.03, 14.12[2][b], 14.17; MB Prac. Guide: Cal. Pretrial Proc., §§3.29[1], 3.34[4].

Rule 8.40. Form of filed documents

(a) Form

Except as these rules provide otherwise, documents filed in a reviewing court may be either produced on a computer or typewritten and must comply with the relevant provisions of rule 8.204(b).

(Subd (a) amended effective January 1, 2007.)

(b) Cover color

(1) As far as practicable, the covers of briefs and petitions must be in the following colors:

Appellant's opening brief or appendix . . . green
Respondent's brief or appendix . . . . . . yellow
Appellant's reply brief or appendix . . . . . . tan
Joint appendix . . . . white
Amicus curiae brief . . . . gray
Answer to amicus curiae brief . . . . blue
Petition for rehearing . . . . orange
Answer to petition for rehearing . . . . . . blue
Petition for original writ . . . . red
Answer (or opposition) to petition for original writ . . . . red
Reply to answer (or opposition) to petition for original writ . . . . red
Petition for review . . . . white
Answer to petition for review . . . . blue
Reply to answer to petition for review . . . white

Opening brief on the merits . . . . white
Answer brief on the merits . . . . blue
Reply brief on the merits . . . . white

(2) In appeals under rule 8.216, the cover of a combined respondent's brief and appellant's opening brief must be yellow, and the cover of a combined reply brief and respondent's brief must be tan.

(3) A brief or petition not conforming to (1) or (2) must be accepted for filing, but in case of repeated violations by an attorney or party the court may proceed as provided in rule 8.204(e)(2).

(Subd (b) amended and relettered effective January 1, 2007; adopted as subd (c) effective January 1, 2005.)

(c) Cover information

The cover—or first page if there is no cover—of every document filed by an attorney in a reviewing court must comply with rule 8.204(b)(10)(D).

(Subd (c) amended and relettered effective January 1, 2007; adopted as subd (d) effective January 1, 2005.)

Rule 8.40 amended and renumbered effective January 1, 2007; repealed and adopted as rule 44 effective January 1, 2005; previously amended effective January 1, 2006.

Ref.: Cal. Fms Pl. & Pr., Ch. 18, "Alcoholic Beverage Licenses," Ch. 22, "Amicus Curiae," Ch. 40, "Appeal: An Overview," Ch. 43, "Appeal: Stay of Proceedings," Ch. 44, "Appeal: Preparing and Filing the Record," Ch. 45, "Appeal: Motion Procedure," Ch. 48, "Appeal: Abandonment, Dismissal, and Stipulated Reversal," Ch. 50, "Appeal: Briefs," Ch. 51, "Appeal: Hearing and Decision," Ch. 52, "Appeal: Rehearing," Ch. 54, "Appeal: California Supreme Court Review," Ch. 71, "Attorney Discipline," Ch. 243, "Elections," Ch. 292, "Habeas Corpus," Ch. 300, "Indemnity and Contribution," Ch. 317, "Judges," Ch. 358, "Mandate and Prohibition," Ch. 474C, "Procedures in Reviewing Agency Decisions," Ch. 492, "Review (Certiorari), Writ of."

Rule 8.44. Number of copies of filed documents

Except as these rules provide otherwise, the number of copies of every brief, petition, motion, application, or other document that must be filed in a reviewing court is as follows:

(a) Documents filed in the Supreme Court

(1) Except as provided in (4), an original and 13 copies of a petition for review, an answer, a reply, a brief on the merits, an amicus curiae brief, an answer to an amicus curiae brief, a petition for rehearing, or an answer to a petition for rehearing;

(2) Unless the court orders otherwise, an original and 10 copies of a petition for a writ within the court's original jurisdiction, an opposition or other response to the petition, or a reply;

(3) Unless the court orders otherwise, an original and 2 copies of any supporting document accompanying a petition for writ of habeas corpus, an opposition or other response to the petition, or a reply;

(4) An original and 8 copies of a petition for review to exhaust state remedies under rule 8.508, an answer, or a reply, or an amicus curiae letter under rule 8.500(g);

(5) An original and 8 copies of a motion or an opposition or other response to a motion; and

(6) An original and 1 copy of an application, including an application to extend time, or any other document.

(b) Documents filed in a Court of Appeal

(1) An original and 4 copies of a brief, an amicus curiae brief, or an answer to an amicus curiae brief, and, in civil appeals, proof of delivery of 4 copies to the Supreme Court;

(2) An original of a petition for writ of habeas corpus filed under rule 8.380 by a person who is not represented by an attorney and 1 set of any supporting documents;

(3) An original and 4 copies of any other petition, an answer, opposition or other response to a petition, or a reply;

(4) An original and 3 copies of a motion or an opposition or other response to a motion;

(5) Unless the court orders otherwise by local rule or in the specific case, 1 set of any separately bound supporting documents accompanying a document filed under (3) or (4);

(6) An original and 1 copy of an application, other than an application to extend time, or any other document; and

(7) An original and 1 copy of an application to extend time. In addition, 1 copy for each separately represented and unrepresented party must be provided to the court.

Rule 8.44 amended effective January 1, 2007; adopted effective January 1, 2007.)

Advisory Committee Comment

The initial sentence of this rule acknowledges that there are exceptions to this rule's requirements concerning the number of copies; see, for example, rule 8.150, which specifies the number of copies of the record that must be filed.

Ref.: Cal. Fms Pl. & Pr., Ch. 45, "Appeal: Motion Procedure," Ch. 46, "Appeal: Extending or Shortening Time," Ch. 47, "Appeal: Relief From Default," Ch. 48, "Appeal: Abandonment, Dismissal, and Stipulated Reversal," Ch. 49, "Appeal: Sanctions," Ch. 50, "Appeal: Briefs," Ch. 52, "Appeal: Rehearing," Ch. 54, "Appeal: California Supreme Court Review," Ch. 70, "Attorney Admission," Ch. 71, "Attorney Discipline," Ch. 200, "Discovery: Review of Discovery Orders," Ch. 292, "Habeas Corpus," Ch. 358, "Mandate and Prohibition," Ch. 474C, "Procedures in Reviewing Agency Decisions," Ch. 492, "Review (Certiorari), Writ of"; W. Cal. Sum., 10 "Parent and Child" §715.

Article 3
Applications and Motions; Extending and Shortening Time

Rule 8.50. Applications
Rule 8.54. Motions
Rule 8.57. Motions before the record is filed
Rule 8.60. Extending time
Rule 8.63. Policies and factors governing extensions of time
Rule 8.66. Extending time because of public emergency
Rule 8.68. Shortening time

Rule 8.50.   Applications

(a) Service and filing

Except as these rules provide otherwise, parties must serve and file all applications in the reviewing court, including applications to extend the time to file records, briefs, or other documents, and applications to shorten time. For good cause, the Chief Justice or presiding justice may excuse advance service.

(Subd (a) amended effective January 1, 2007.)

(b) Contents

The application must state facts showing good cause—or making an exceptional showing of good cause, when required by these rules—for granting the application and must identify any previous application filed by any party.

(Subd (b) amended effective January 1, 2007.)

(c) Envelopes

An application to a Court of Appeal must be accompanied by addressed, postage-prepaid envelopes for the clerk's use in mailing copies of the order on the application to all parties.

(d) Disposition

Unless the court determines otherwise, the Chief Justice or presiding justice may rule on the application.

Rule 8.50 amended and renumbered effective January 1, 2007; repealed and adopted as rule 43 effective January 1, 2005.

Advisory Committee Comment

Rule 8.50 addresses applications generally. Rules 8.60, 8.63, and 8.68 address applications to extend or shorten time.

Subdivision (b). An exceptional showing of good cause is required in applications in certain juvenile proceedings under rules 8.416, 8.450, 8.452, and 8.454.

Ref.: Cal. Fms Pl. & Pr., Ch. 40, "Appeal: An Overview," Ch. 45, "Appeal: Motion Procedure," Ch. 46, "Appeal: Extending or Shortening Time," Ch. 48, "Appeal: Abandonment, Dismissal, and Stipulated Reversal," Ch. 50, "Appeal: Briefs," Ch. 54, "Appeal: California Supreme Court Review," Ch. 372, "Motions and Orders," Ch. 492, "Review (Certiorari), Writ of," Ch. 524, "Shortening and Extension of Time."

Rule 8.54.   Motions

(a) Motion and opposition

(1) Except as these rules provide otherwise, a party wanting to make a motion in a reviewing court must serve and file a written motion stating the grounds and the relief requested and identifying any documents on which the motion is based.

(2) A motion must be accompanied by a memorandum and, if it is based on matters outside the record, by declarations or other supporting evidence.

(3) Any opposition must be served and filed within 15 days after the motion is filed.

(Subd (a) amended effective January 1, 2007.)

(b) Disposition

(1) The court may rule on a motion at any time after an opposition or other response is filed or the time to oppose has expired.

(2) On a party's request or its own motion, the court may place a motion on calendar for a hearing. The clerk must promptly send each party a notice of the date and time of the hearing.

(c) Failure to oppose motion

A failure to oppose a motion may be deemed a consent to the granting of the motion.

Rule 8.54 amended and renumbered effective January 1, 2007; repealed and adopted as rule 41 effective January 1, 2005.

Advisory Committee Comment

Subdivision (c). Subdivision (c) provides that a "failure to oppose a motion" may be deemed a consent to the granting of the motion. The provision is not intended to indicate a position on the question whether there is an implied right to a hearing to oppose a motion to dismiss an appeal.

Ref.: Cal. Fms Pl. & Pr., Ch. 40, "Appeal: An Overview," Ch. 42, "Appeal: Notice of Appeal," Ch. 44, "Appeal: Preparing and Filing the Record," Ch. 45, "Appeal: Motion Procedure," Ch. 46, "Appeal: Extending or Shortening Time," Ch. 47, "Appeal: Relief From Default," Ch. 48, "Appeal: Abandonment, Dismissal, and Stipulated Reversal," Ch. 49, "Appeal: Sanctions," Ch. 50, "Appeal: Briefs," Ch. 51, "Appeal: Hearing and Decision," Ch. 53, "Appeal: Remittitur and Costs on Appeal," Ch. 54, "Appeal: California Supreme Court Review," Ch. 72, "Attorney Practice and Ethics," Ch. 321, "Judicial Notice," Ch. 372, "Motions and Orders," Ch. 492, "Review (Certiorari), Writ of."

Rule 8.57. Motions before the record is filed

(a) Motion to dismiss appeal

A motion to dismiss an appeal before the record is filed in the reviewing court must be accompanied by a certificate of the superior court clerk, a declaration, or both, stating:

(1) The nature of the action and the relief sought by the complaint and any cross-complaint or complaint in intervention;

(2) The names, addresses, and telephone numbers of all attorneys of record—stating whom each represents—and unrepresented parties;

(3) A description of the judgment or order appealed from, its entry date, and the service date of any written notice of its entry;

(4) The factual basis of any extension of the time to appeal under rule 8.108;

(5) The filing dates of all notices of appeal and the courts in which they were filed;

(6) The filing date of any document necessary to procure the record on appeal; and

(7) The status of the record preparation process, including any order extending time to prepare the record.

(Subd (a) amended effective January 1, 2007.)

(b) Other motions

Any other motion filed before the record is filed in the reviewing court must be accompanied by a declaration or other evidence necessary to advise the court of the facts relevant to the relief requested.

Rule 8.57 amended and renumbered effective January 1, 2007; repealed and adopted as rule 42 effective January 1, 2005.

Ref.: Cal. Fms Pl. & Pr., Ch. 40, "Appeal: An Overview," Ch. 45, "Appeal: Motion Procedure," Ch. 47, "Appeal: Relief From Default," Ch. 48, "Appeal: Abandonment, Dismissal, and Stipulated Reversal," Ch. 372, "Motions and Orders."

Rule 8.60. Extending time

(a) Computing time

The Code of Civil Procedure governs computing and extending the time to do any act required or permitted under these rules.

(b) Extending time

Except as these rules provide otherwise, for good cause—or on an exceptional showing of good cause, when required by these rules—the Chief Justice or presiding justice may extend the time to do any act required or permitted under these rules.

(Subd (b) amended effective January 1, 2007.)

(c) Application for extension

(1) An application to extend time must include a declaration stating facts, not mere conclusions, and must be served on all parties. For good cause, the Chief Justice or presiding justice may excuse advance service.

(2) The application must state:

(A) The due date of the document to be filed;

(B) The length of the extension requested;

(C) Whether any earlier extensions have been granted and, if so, their lengths and whether granted by stipulation or by the court; and

(D) Good cause—or an exceptional showing of good cause, when required by these rules—for granting the extension, consistent with the factors in rule 8.63(b).

(Subd (c) amended and relettered effective January 1, 2007; adopted as subd (d) effective January 1, 2005.)

(d) Relief from default

For good cause, a reviewing court may relieve a party from default for any failure to comply with these rules except the failure to file a timely notice of appeal or a timely statement of reasonable grounds in support of a certificate of probable cause.

(Subd (d) relettered effective January 1, 2007; adopted as subd (e) effective January 1, 2005.)

(e) No extension by superior court

Except as these rules provide otherwise, a superior court may not extend the time to do any act to prepare the appellate record.

(Subd (e) relettered effective January 1, 2007; adopted as subd (f) effective January 1, 2005.)

(f) Notice to party

(1) In a civil case, counsel must deliver to his or her client or clients a copy of any stipulation or application to extend time that counsel files. Counsel must attach evidence of such delivery to the stipulation or application, or certify in the stipulation or application that the copy has been delivered.

(2) In a class action, the copy required under (1) need be delivered to only one represented party.

(3) The evidence or certification of delivery under (1) need not include the address of the party notified.

(Subd (f) amended and relettered effective January 1, 2007; adopted as subd (g) effective January 1, 2005.)

Rule 8.60 amended and renumbered effective January 1, 2007; repealed and adopted as rule 45 effective January 1, 2005.

Advisory Committee Comment

Subdivisions (b) and (c). An exceptional showing of good cause is required in applications in certain juvenile proceedings under rules 8.416, 8.450, 8.452, and 8.454.

Ref.: Cal. Fms Pl. & Pr., Ch. 40, "Appeal: An Overview," Ch. 42, "Appeal: Notice of Appeal," Ch. 44, "Appeal: Preparing and Filing the Record," Ch. 45, "Appeal: Motion Procedure," Ch. 46, "Appeal: Extending or Shortening Time," Ch. 47, "Appeal: Relief From Default," Ch. 48, "Appeal: Abandonment, Dismissal, and Stipulated Reversal," Ch. 50, "Appeal: Briefs," Ch. 52, "Appeal: Rehearing," Ch. 54, "Appeal: California Supreme Court Review," Ch. 524, "Shortening and Extension of Time."

Rule 8.63. Policies and factors governing extensions of time

(a) Policies

(1) The time limits prescribed by these rules should generally be met to ensure expeditious conduct of appellate business and public confidence in the efficient administration of appellate justice.

(2) The effective assistance of counsel to which a party is entitled includes adequate time for counsel to prepare briefs or other documents that fully advance the party's interests. Adequate time also allows the preparation of accurate, clear, concise, and complete submissions that assist the courts.

(3) For a variety of legitimate reasons, counsel may not always be able to prepare briefs or other documents within the time specified in the rules of court. To balance the competing policies stated in (1) and (2), applications to extend time in the reviewing courts must demonstrate good cause—or an exceptional showing of good cause, when required by these rules—under (b). If good cause is shown, the court must extend the time.

(Subd (a) amended effective January 1, 2007.)

(b) Factors considered

In determining good cause—or an exceptional showing of good cause, when required by these rules—the court must consider the following factors when applicable:

(1) The degree of prejudice, if any, to any party from a grant or denial of the extension. A party claiming prejudice must support the claim in detail.

(2) In a civil case, the positions of the client and any opponent with regard to the extension.

(3) The length of the record, including the number of relevant trial exhibits. A party relying on this factor must specify the length of the record. In a civil case, a record containing one volume of clerk's transcript or appendix and two volumes of reporter's transcript is considered an average-length record.

(4) The number and complexity of the issues raised. A party relying on this factor must specify the issues.

(5) Whether there are settlement negotiations and, if so, how far they have progressed and when they might be completed.

(6) Whether the case is entitled to priority.

(7) Whether counsel responsible for preparing the document is new to the case.

(8) Whether other counsel or the client needs additional time to review the document.

(9) Whether counsel responsible for preparing the document has other time-limited commitments that prevent timely filing of the document. Mere conclusory statements that more time is needed because of other pressing business will not suffice. Good cause requires a specific showing of other obligations of counsel that:

(A) Have deadlines that as a practical matter preclude filing the document by the due date without impairing its quality; or

(B) Arise from cases entitled to priority.

(10) Illness of counsel, a personal emergency, or a planned vacation that counsel did not reasonably expect to conflict with the due date and cannot reasonably rearrange.

(11) Any other factor that constitutes good cause in the context of the case.

(Subd (b) amended effective January 1, 2007.)
Rule 8.63 amended and renumbered effective January 1, 2007; repealed and adopted as rule 45.5 effective January 1, 2005.

Advisory Committee Comment

An exceptional showing of good cause is required in applications in certain juvenile proceedings under rules 8.416, 8.450, 8.452, and 8.454.

Ref.: Cal. Fms Pl. & Pr., Ch. 40, "Appeal: An Overview," Ch. 44, "Appeal: Preparing and Filing the Record," Ch. 45, "Appeal: Motion Procedure," Ch. 46, "Appeal: Extending or Shortening Time," Ch. 50, "Appeal: Briefs," Ch. 54, "Appeal: California Supreme Court Review."

Rule 8.66. Extending time because of public emergency

(a) Emergency extensions of time

If made necessary by the occurrence or danger of an earthquake, fire, or other public emergency, or by the destruction of or danger to a building housing a reviewing court, the Chair of the Judicial Council, notwithstanding any other rule in this title, may:

(1) Extend by no more than 14 additional days the time to do any act required or permitted under these rules; or

(2) Authorize specified courts to extend by no more than 30 additional days the time to do any act required or permitted under these rules.

(Subd (a) amended effective January 1, 2007.)

(b) Applicability of order

(1) An order under (a) must specify whether it applies throughout the state, only to specified courts, or only to courts or attorneys in specified geographic areas, or applies in some other manner.

(2) An order of the Chair of the Judicial Council under (a)(2) must specify the length of the authorized extension.

(c) Additional extensions

If made necessary by the nature or extent of the public emergency, the Chair of the Judicial Council may extend or renew an order issued under (a) for an additional period of:

(1) No more than 14 days for an order under (a)(1); or

(2) No more than 30 days for an order under (a)(2).

(Subd (c) amended effective January 1, 2007.)
Rule 8.66 amended and renumbered effective January 1, 2007; repealed and adopted as rule 45.1 effective January 1, 2005.

Advisory Committee Comment

The Chief Justice of California is the Chair of the Judicial Council (see rule 10.2).

Ref.: Cal. Fms Pl. & Pr., Ch. 42, "Appeal: Notice of Appeal," Ch. 46, "Appeal: Extending or Shortening Time," Ch. 524, "Shortening and Extension of Time"; MB Prac. Guide: Cal. Trial & Post-Trial Civ. Proc., §§19.29[1], 25A.20[2]; W. Cal. Sum., 10 "Parent and Child" §712.

Rule 8.68. Shortening time

For good cause and except as these rules provide otherwise, the Chief Justice or presiding justice may shorten the time to do any act required or permitted under these rules.

Rule 8.68 adopted effective January 1, 2007.

Ref.: Cal. Fms Pl. & Pr., Ch. 45, "Appeal: Motion Procedure," Ch. 46, "Appeal: Extending or Shortening Time."

Chapter 2
Civil Appeals

Art. 4.   Hearing and Decision in the Court of Appeal.
Rules 8.240–8.278.

Article 1
Taking the Appeal

Rule 8.100. Filing the appeal
Rule 8.104. Time to appeal
Rule 8.108. Extending the time to appeal
Rule 8.112. Petition for writ of supersedeas
Rule 8.116. Request for writ of supersedeas or temporary stay

Rule 8.100.   Filing the appeal

(a) Notice of appeal

(1) To appeal from a superior court judgment or an appealable order of a superior court, other than in a limited civil case, an appellant must serve and file a notice of appeal in that superior court. The appellant or the appellant's attorney must sign the notice.

(2) The notice of appeal must be liberally construed. The notice is sufficient if it identifies the particular judgment or order being appealed. The notice need not specify the court to which the appeal is taken; the appeal will be treated as taken to the Court of Appeal for the district in which the superior court is located.

(3) Failure to serve the notice of appeal neither prevents its filing nor affects its validity, but the appellant may be required to remedy the failure.

(b) Fee and deposit

(1) Unless otherwise provided by law, the notice of appeal must be accompanied by a $655 filing fee under Government Code sections 68926 and 68926.1(b), an application for a waiver of court fees and costs on appeal under rules 3.50–3.63, or an order granting such an application. The fee should be paid by check or money order payable to "Clerk, Court of Appeal"; if the fee is paid in cash, the clerk must give a receipt.

(2) The appellant must also deposit $100 with the superior court clerk under Government Code section 68926.1, unless otherwise provided by law or the superior court waives the deposit under rules 3.50–3.63.

(3) The clerk must file the notice of appeal even if the appellant does not present the filing fee, the deposit, or an application for, or order granting, a waiver under rules 3.50–3.63.

(Subd (b) amended effective January 1, 2007; previously amended effective August 17, 2003.)

(c) Failure to pay filing fee

(1) The reviewing court clerk must promptly notify the appellant in writing if:

(A) The reviewing court receives a notice of appeal without the filing fee required by (b)(1), a certificate of cash payment under (e)(5), or an application for, or order granting, a fee waiver under rules 3.50–3.63;

(B) A check for the filing fee is dishonored; or

(C) An application for a waiver under rules 3.50–3.63 is denied.

(2) A clerk's notice under (1) must state that the court may dismiss the appeal unless, within 15 days after the notice is sent, the appellant either:

(A) Pays the fee; or

(B) Files an application for a waiver under rules 3.50–3.63 if the appellant has not previously filed such an application.

(3) If the appellant fails to take the action specified in a notice given under (2), the reviewing court may dismiss the appeal, but may vacate the dismissal for good cause.

(Subd (c) amended effective January 1, 2008; previously amended effective January 1, 2007.)

(d) Failure to pay deposit

(1) If the appellant fails to pay the deposit to the superior court required under (b)(2), the superior court clerk must promptly notify the appellant in writing that the reviewing court may dismiss the appeal unless, within 15 days after the notice is sent, the appellant either:

(A) Makes the deposit; or

(B) Files an application in the superior court for a waiver under rules 3.50–3.63 if the appellant has not previously filed such an application.

(2) If the appellant fails to take the action specified in a notice given under (1), the superior court clerk must notify the reviewing court of the default.

(3) If the superior court clerk notifies the reviewing court of a default under (2), the reviewing court may dismiss the appeal, but may vacate the dismissal for good cause.

(Subd (d) adopted effective January 1, 2008.)

(e) Superior court clerk's duties

(1) The superior court clerk must promptly mail a notification of the filing of the notice of appeal to the attorney of record for each party, to any unrepresented party, and to the reviewing court clerk.

(2) The notification must show the date it was mailed and must state the number and title of the case and the date the notice of appeal was filed. If the information is available, the notification must include:

(A) The name, address, telephone number, and California State Bar number of each attorney of record in the case;

(B) The name of the party each attorney represented in the superior court; and

(C) The name, address, and telephone number of any unrepresented party.

(3) A copy of the notice of appeal is sufficient notification under (1) if the required information is on the copy or is added by the superior court clerk.

(4) The mailing of a notification under (1) is a sufficient performance of the clerk's duty despite the death of the party or the discharge, disqualification, suspension, disbarment, or death of the attorney.

(5) With the notification of the appeal, the superior court clerk must send the reviewing court the filing fee or an application for, or order granting, a waiver of that fee. If the fee was paid in cash, the clerk must send the reviewing court a certificate of payment and thereafter a check for the amount of the fee.

(6) Failure to comply with any provision of this subdivision does not affect the validity of the notice of appeal.

(Subd (e) relettered effective January 1, 2008; adopted as subd (d) effective January 1, 2002; previously amended effective January 1, 2007.)

(f) Notice of cross-appeal

As used in this rule, "notice of appeal" includes a notice of cross-appeal and "appellant" includes a respondent filing a notice of cross-appeal.

(Subd (f) relettered effective January 1, 2008; adopted as subd (e) effective January 1, 2002.)

(g) Civil case information statement

(1) On receiving notice of the filing of a notice of appeal under (e)(1), the reviewing court clerk must promptly mail the appellant a copy of the *Civil Case Information Statement* (form APP-004) and a notice that the statement must be filed within 10 days.

(2) Within 10 days after the clerk mails the notice required by (1), the appellant must serve and file in the reviewing court a completed *Civil Case Information Statement*, attaching a copy of the judgment or appealed order that shows the date it was entered.

(3) If the appellant fails to timely file a case information statement under (2), the reviewing court clerk must notify the appellant by mail that the appellant must file the statement within 15 days after the clerk's notice is mailed and that if the appellant fails to comply, the court may either impose monetary sanctions or dismiss the appeal. If the appellant fails to file the statement as specified in the notice, the court may impose the sanctions specified in the notice.

(Subd (g) amended and relettered effective January 1, 2008; adopted as subd (f) effective January 1, 2003; previously amended effective January 1, 2007.)

Rule 8.100 amended effective January 1, 2008; repealed and adopted as rule 1 effective January 1, 2002; previously amended effective January 1, 2003, and August 17, 2003; previously amended and renumbered effective January 1, 2007.

Advisory Committee Comment

Subdivision (a). In subdivision (a)(1), the reference to "judgment" is intended to include part of a judgment. Subdivision (a)(1) includes an explicit reference to "appealable order" to ensure that litigants do not overlook the applicability of this rule to such orders.

Subdivision (b). In the interest of consistency, subdivision (b)(1) recommends a preferred wording—"Clerk, Court of Appeal"—for the name of the payee of checks or money orders for the filing fee. The provision is not mandatory.

Subdivision (e). Under subdivision (e)(2), a notification of the filing of a notice of appeal must show the date that the clerk mailed the document. This provision is intended to establish the date when the 20-day extension of the time to file a cross-appeal under rule 8.108(e) begins to run.

Subdivision (e)(1) requires the clerk to mail a notification of the filing of the notice of appeal to the appellant's attorney or to the appellant if unrepresented. Knowledge of the date of that notification allows the appellant's attorney or the appellant to track the running of the 20-day extension of time to file a cross-appeal under rule 8.108(e).

Ref.: Cal. Fms Pl. & Pr., Ch. 2, "Procedural Guide for Civil Actions," Ch. 12E, "Adoptions: Attack on Decree," Ch. 40, "Appeal: An Overview," Ch. 42, "Appeal: Notice of Appeal," Ch. 44, "Appeal: Preparing and Filing the Record," Ch. 45, "Appeal: Motion Procedure," Ch. 46, "Appeal: Extending or Shortening Time," Ch. 49, "Appeal: Sanctions," Ch. 51, "Appeal: Hearing and Decision," Ch. 250, "Employment Law: Wage and Hour Disputes," Ch. 324, "Jurisdiction: Subject Matter Jurisdiction," Ch. 328, "Juvenile Courts: Dependency Proceedings"; W. Cal. Sum., 11 "Husband and Wife" §123.

Rule 8.104.   Time to appeal
(a) Normal time

Unless a statute or rule 8.108 provides otherwise, a notice of appeal must be filed on or before the earliest of:

(1) 60 days after the superior court clerk mails the party filing the notice of appeal a document entitled "Notice of Entry" of judgment or a file-stamped copy of the judgment, showing the date either was mailed;

(2) 60 days after the party filing the notice of appeal serves or is served by a party with a document entitled "Notice of Entry" of judgment or a file-stamped copy of the judgment, accompanied by proof of service; or

(3) 180 days after entry of judgment.

(Subd (a) amended effective January 1, 2007.)

(b) No extension of time; late notice of appeal

Except as provided in rule 8.66, no court may extend the time to file a notice of appeal. If a notice of appeal is filed late, the reviewing court must dismiss the appeal.

(Subd (b) amended effective January 1, 2007; adopted effective January 1, 2005.)

(c) Periodic payment of judgments against public entities

If a public entity elects, under Government Code section 984 and rule 3.1804, to pay a judgment in periodic payments, subdivision (a) of this rule governs the time to appeal from that judgment but the periods prescribed in (a)(1) and (2) are each 90 days.

(Subd (c) amended effective January 1, 2007; adopted as subd (b) effective January 1, 2002; relettered effective January 1, 2005.)

(d) What constitutes entry

For purposes of this rule:

(1) The entry date of a judgment is the date the judgment is filed under Code of Civil Procedure section 668.5, or the date it is entered in the judgment book.

(2) The entry date of an appealable order that is entered in the minutes is the date it is entered in the permanent minutes. But if the minute order directs that a written order be prepared, the entry date is the date the signed order is filed; a written order prepared under rule 3.1312 or similar local rule is not such an order prepared by direction of a minute order.

(3) The entry date of an appealable order that is not entered in the minutes is the date the signed order is filed.

(4) The entry date of a decree of distribution in a probate proceeding is the date it is entered at length in the judgment book or other permanent court record.

(Subd (d) amended effective January 1, 2007; adopted as subd (c) effective January 1, 2002; relettered effective January 1, 2005.)

(e) Premature notice of appeal

(1) A notice of appeal filed after judgment is rendered but before it is entered is valid and is treated as filed immediately after entry of judgment.

(2) The reviewing court may treat a notice of appeal filed after the superior court has announced its intended ruling, but before it has rendered judgment, as filed immediately after entry of judgment.

(Subd (e) relettered effective January 1, 2005; adopted as subd (d) effective January 1, 2002.)

(f) Appealable order

As used in (a) and (e), "judgment" includes an appealable order if the appeal is from an appealable order.

(Subd (f) amended effective January 1, 2005.)

Rule 8.104 amended and renumbered effective January 1, 2007; repealed and adopted as rule 2 effective January 1, 2002; previously amended effective January 1, 2005.

Advisory Committee Comment

Subdivision (a). Under subdivision (a)(1), a notice of entry of judgment (or a copy of the judgment) must show the date on which the clerk mailed the document. This provision is intended to establish the date that the 60-day period under subdivision (a)(1) begins to run.

Subdivision (a)(2) requires that a notice of entry of judgment (or a copy of the judgment) served by or on a party be accompanied by proof of service. The proof of service establishes the date that the 60-day period under subdivision (a)(2) begins to run. Although the general rule on service (rule 8.25(a)) requires proof of service for all documents served by parties, the requirement is reiterated here because of the serious consequence of a failure to file a timely notice of appeal (see subd. (e)).

Subdivision (b). Subdivision (b) is declarative of the case law, which holds that the reviewing court lacks jurisdiction to excuse a late-filed notice of appeal. (*Hollister Convalescent Hosp., Inc. v. Rico* (1975) 15 Cal.3d 660, 666–674; *Estate of Hanley* (1943) 23 Cal.2d 120, 122–124.)

In criminal cases, the time for filing a notice of appeal is governed by rule 8.408 and by the case law of "constructive filing." (See, e.g., *In re Jordan* (1992) 4 Cal.4th 116; *In re Benoit* (1973) 10 Cal.3d 72.)

Ref.: Cal. Fms Pl. & Pr., Ch. 1, "New Developments," Ch. 2, "Procedural Guide for Civil Actions," Ch. 12E, "Adoptions: Attack on Decree," Ch. 40, "Appeal: An Overview," Ch. 42, "Appeal: Notice of Appeal," Ch. 46, "Appeal: Extending or Shortening Time," Ch. 48, "Appeal: Abandonment, Dismissal, and Stipulated Reversal," Ch. 174, "Costs and Attorney's Fees," Ch. 206, "Demurrers and Motions for Judgment on the Pleadings," Ch. 221, "Dissolution of Marriage: Procedure," Ch. 318, "Judgments," Ch. 358, "Mandate and Prohibition," Ch. 372, "Motions and Orders," Ch. 374, "Motions to Reconsider and Renewed Motions," Ch. 376, "Motions to Strike: Anti-SLAPP," Ch. 386, "Newspapers," Ch. 397, "Partition," Ch. 458D, "Probate: Accounts, Final Distribution, and Compensation," Ch. 474C, "Procedures in Reviewing Agency Decisions," Ch. 492, "Review (Certiorari), Writ of," Ch. 510, "Sanctions," Ch. 524, "Shortening and Extension of Time"; MB Prac. Guide: Cal. Pretrial Proc., §§9.48, 26.62[3], 29.05[3], 29.28[1]; MB Prac. Guide: Cal. Trial & Post-Trial Civ. Proc., §§12.16, 14.18, 14.23[1], 14.24, 14.28, 19.25, 19.29[1], [2][b], 25A.20[2], 26.02, 26.26, 29.03[4][a], [b], 29.09[2], 29.66, 29.69[3][f]; W. Cal. Sum., 11 "Community Property" §243.

Rule 8.108. Extending the time to appeal

(a) Extension of time

This rule operates only to extend the time to appeal otherwise prescribed in rule 8.104(a); it does not shorten the time to appeal. If the normal time to appeal stated in rule 8.104(a) is longer than the time provided in this rule, the time to appeal stated in rule 8.104(a) governs.

(Subd (a) adopted effective January 1, 2008.)

(b) Motion for new trial

If any party serves and files a valid notice of intention to move for a new trial, the time to appeal from the judgment is extended for all parties as follows:

(1) If the motion is denied, until the earliest of:

(A) 30 days after the superior court clerk mails, or a party serves, an order denying the motion or a notice of entry of that order;

(B) 30 days after denial of the motion by operation of law; or

(C) 180 days after entry of judgment.

(2) If any party serves an acceptance of a conditionally ordered additur or remittitur of damages pursuant to a trial court finding of excessive or inadequate damages, until 30 days after the date the party serves the acceptance.

(Subd (b) amended and relettered effective January 1, 2008; adopted as subd (a) effective January 1, 2002.)

(c) Motion to vacate judgment

If, within the time prescribed by rule 8.104 to appeal from the judgment, any party serves and files a valid notice of intention to move—or a valid motion—to vacate the judgment, the time to appeal from the judgment is extended for all parties until the earliest of:

(1) 30 days after the superior court clerk mails, or a party serves, an order denying the motion or a notice of entry of that order;

(2) 90 days after the first notice of intention to move—or motion—is filed; or

(3) 180 days after entry of judgment.

(Subd (c) relettered effective January 1, 2008; adopted as subd (b) effective January 1, 2002; previously amended effective January 1, 2007.)

(d) Motion for judgment notwithstanding the verdict

(1) If any party serves and files a valid motion for judgment notwithstanding the verdict and the motion is denied, the time to appeal from the judgment is extended for all parties until the earliest of:

(A) 30 days after the superior court clerk mails, or a party serves, an order denying the motion or a notice of entry of that order;

(B) 30 days after denial of the motion by operation of law; or

(C) 180 days after entry of judgment.

(2) Unless extended by (e)(2), the time to appeal from an order denying a motion for judgment notwithstanding the verdict is governed by rule 8.104.

(Subd (d) relettered effective January 1, 2008; adopted as subd (c) effective January 1, 2002; previously amended effective January 1, 2007.)

(e) Motion to reconsider appealable order

If any party serves and files a valid motion to reconsider an appealable order under Code of Civil Procedure section 1008, subdivision (a), the time to appeal from that order is extended for all parties until the earliest of:

(1) 30 days after the superior court clerk mails, or a party serves, an order denying the motion or a notice of entry of that order;

(2) 90 days after the first motion to reconsider is filed; or

(3) 180 days after entry of the appealable order.

(Subd (e) relettered effective January 1, 2008; adopted as subd (d) effective January 1, 2002.)

(f) Cross-appeal

(1) If an appellant timely appeals from a judgment or appealable order, the time for any other party to appeal from the same judgment or order is extended until 20 days after the superior court clerk mails notification of the first appeal.

(2) If an appellant timely appeals from an order granting a motion for new trial, an order granting—within 150 days after entry of judgment—a motion to vacate the

judgment, or a judgment notwithstanding the verdict, the time for any other party to appeal from the original judgment or from an order denying a motion for judgment notwithstanding the verdict is extended until 20 days after the clerk mails notification of the first appeal.

(Subd (f) relettered effective January 1, 2008; adopted as subd (e) effective January 1, 2002.)

(g) Showing date of order or notice; proof of service

An order or notice mailed by the clerk under this rule must show the date it was mailed. An order or notice served by a party must be accompanied by proof of service.

(Subd (g) relettered effective January 1, 2008; adopted as subd (f) effective January 1, 2002.)

Rule 8.108 amended effective January 1, 2008; repealed and adopted as rule 3 effective January 1, 2002; previously amended and renumbered effective January 1, 2007.

Advisory Committee Comment

Subdivisions (b)–(e) operate only when a party serves and files a "valid" motion or notice of intent to move for the relief in question. As used in these provisions, the word "valid" means only that the motion or notice complies with all procedural requirements; it does not mean that the motion or notice must also be substantively meritorious. For example, under the rule a timely new trial motion on the ground of excessive damages (Code Civ. Proc., § 657) extends the time to appeal from the judgment even if the trial court ultimately determines the damages were not excessive. Similarly, a timely motion to reconsider (*id.*, § 1008) extends the time to appeal from an appealable order for which reconsideration was sought even if the trial court ultimately determines the motion was not "based upon new or different facts, circumstances, or law," as subdivision (a) of section 1008 requires.

Subdivision (b). Subdivision (b)(1) provides that the denial of a motion for new trial triggers a 30-day extension of the time to appeal from the judgment beginning on the date that the superior court clerk mails, or a party serves, either the order of denial or a notice of entry of that order. This provision is intended to eliminate a trap for litigants and to make the rule consistent with the primary rule on the time to appeal from the judgment (rule 8.104(a)).

Subdivision (c). The Code of Civil Procedure provides two distinct statutory motions to vacate a judgment: (1) a motion to vacate a judgment and enter "another and different judgment" because of judicial error (*id.*, § 663), which requires a notice of intention to move to vacate (*id.*, § 663a); and (2) a motion to vacate a judgment because of mistake, inadvertence, surprise, or neglect, which requires a motion to vacate but not a notice of intention to so move (*id.*, § 473, subd. (b)). The courts also recognize certain nonstatutory motions to vacate a judgment, e.g., when the judgment is void on the face of the record or was obtained by extrinsic fraud. (See 8 Witkin, Cal. Procedure (4th ed. 1997) Attack on Judgment in Trial Court, §§ 222–236, pp. 726–750.) Subdivision (c) is intended to apply to all such motions.

In subdivision (c) the phrase "within the time prescribed by rule 8.104 to appeal from the judgment" is intended to incorporate in full the provisions of rule 8.104(a).

Under subdivision (c)(1), the 30-day extension of the time to appeal from the judgment begins when the superior court clerk mails, or a party serves, the order denying the motion or notice of entry of that order. This provision is discussed further under subdivision (b) of this comment.

Subdivision (d). Subdivision (d)(1) provides an extension of time after an order denying a motion for judgment notwithstand-

ing the verdict regardless of whether the moving party also moved unsuccessfully for a new trial.

Subdivision (d) further specifies the times to appeal when, as often occurs, a motion for judgment notwithstanding the verdict is joined with a motion for new trial and both motions are denied. Under subdivision (b), the appellant has 30 days after notice of the denial of the new trial motion to appeal from the judgment. Subdivision (d) allows the appellant the longer time provided by rule 8.104 to appeal from the order denying the motion for judgment notwithstanding the verdict, subject to that time being further extended in the circumstances covered by subdivision (f)(2).

Under subdivision (d)(1)(A), the 30-day extension of the time to appeal from the judgment begins when the superior court clerk mails, or a party serves, the order denying the motion or notice of entry of that order. This provision is discussed further under subdivision (b) of this comment.

Subdivision (e). The scope of subdivision (e) is specific. It applies to any "appealable order," whether made before or after judgment (see Code Civ. Proc., § 904.1, subd. (a)(2)–(12)), but it extends only the time to appeal "from that order." The subdivision thus takes no position on whether a judgment is subject to a motion to reconsider (see, e.g., *Ramon v. Aerospace Corp.* (1996) 50 Cal.App.4th 1233, 1236–1238 [postjudgment motion to reconsider order granting summary judgment did not extend time to appeal from judgment because trial court had no power to rule on such motion after entry of judgment]), or whether an order denying a motion to reconsider is itself appealable (compare *Santee v. Santa Clara County Office of Education* (1990) 220 Cal.App.3d 702, 710–711 [order appealable if motion based on new facts] with *Rojes v. Riverside General Hospital* (1988) 203 Cal.App.3d 1151, 1160–1161 [order not appealable under any circumstances]). Both these issues are legislative matters.

Subdivision (e) applies only when a "party" makes a valid motion to "reconsider" an appealable order under subdivision (a) of Code of Civil Procedure section 1008; it therefore does not apply when a court reconsiders an order on its own motion (*id.*, subd. (d)) or when a party makes "a subsequent application for the same order" (*id.*, subd. (c)). The statute provides no time limits within which either of the latter events must occur.

Under subdivision (e)(1), the 30-day extension of the time to appeal from the order begins when the superior court clerk mails, or a party serves, the order denying the motion or notice of entry of that order. The purpose of this provision is discussed further under subdivision (b) of this comment.

Among its alternative periods of extension of the time to appeal, subdivision (e) provides in paragraph (2) for a 90-day period beginning on the filing of the motion to reconsider or, if there is more than one such motion, the filing of the first such motion. The provision is consistent with subdivision (c)(2), governing motions to vacate judgment; as in the case of those motions, there is no time limit for a ruling on a motion to reconsider.

Subdivision (f). Consistent with case law, subdivision (f)(1) extends the time to appeal after another party appeals only if the later appeal is taken "from the same order or judgment as the first appeal." (*Commercial & Farmers Nat. Bank v. Edwards* (1979) 91 Cal.App.3d 699, 704.)

The former rule (former rule 3(c), second sentence) provided an extension of time for filing a protective cross-appeal from the judgment when the trial court granted a motion for new trial or a motion to vacate the judgment, but did not provide the same extension when the trial court granted a motion for judgment notwithstanding the verdict. One case declined to infer that the omission was unintentional, but suggested that the Judicial Council might consider amending the rule to fill the gap. (*Lippert v. AVCO Community Developers, Inc.* (1976) 60 Cal.App.3d 775, 778 & fn. 3.) Rule 8.108(e)(2) fills the gap thus identified.

Subdivision (g). Under subdivision (g), an order or notice mailed by the clerk under this rule must show the date on which the clerk mailed the document, analogously to the clerk's "certificate of mailing" currently in use in many superior courts. This provision is intended to establish the date when an extension of the time to appeal begins to run after the clerk mails such an order or notice.

Subdivision (g) also requires that an order or notice served by a party under this rule be accompanied by proof of service. The proof of service establishes the date when an extension of the time to appeal begins to run after the party serves such an order or notice.

Ref.: Cal. Fms Pl. & Pr., Ch. 2, "Procedural Guide for Civil Actions," Ch. 12E, "Adoptions: Attack on Decree," Ch. 40, "Appeal: An Overview," Ch. 42, "Appeal: Notice of Appeal," Ch. 44, "Appeal: Preparing and Filing the Record," Ch. 48, "Appeal: Abandonment, Dismissal, and Stipulated Reversal," Ch. 50, "Appeal: Briefs," Ch. 174, "Costs and Attorney's Fees," Ch. 221, "Dissolution of Marriage: Procedure," Ch. 254, "Executions and Enforcement of Judgments," Ch. 318, "Judgments," Ch. 358, "Mandate and Prohibition," Ch. 371, "Motions After Trial," Ch. 374, "Motions to Reconsider and Renewed Motions," Ch. 474C, "Procedures in Reviewing Agency Decisions," Ch. 489, "Relief From Judgments and Orders," Ch. 524, "Shortening and Extension of Time"; MB Prac. Guide: Cal. Pretrial Proc., §§29.05[2], 29.28[1], [2]; MB Prac. Guide: Cal. Trial & Post-Trial Civ. Proc., §§19.25, 19.29[1], [2][a]–[c], 21.26, 21.30, 25A.20[2], 29.09[2], 29.66, 29.69[3][f]; W. Cal. Sum., 11 "Community Property" §243.

Rule 8.112.   Petition for writ of supersedeas

(a) Petition

(1) A party seeking a stay of the enforcement of a judgment or order pending appeal may serve and file a petition for writ of supersedeas in the reviewing court.

(2) The petition must bear the same title as the appeal and, if known, the appeal's docket number.

(3) The petition must explain the necessity for the writ and include a memorandum.

(4) If the record has not been filed in the reviewing court:

(A) The petition must include a statement of the case sufficient to show that the petitioner will raise substantial issues on appeal, including a fair summary of the material facts, the issues that are likely to be raised on appeal, and any oral statement by the court supporting its rulings related to these issues.

(B) The petitioner must file the following documents with the petition:

(i) The judgment or order, showing its date of entry;

(ii) The notice of appeal, showing its date of filing;

(iii) Any application for a stay filed in the trial court and any opposition to that application; and

(iv) Any other document from the trial court proceeding that is necessary for proper consideration of the petition.

(C) The documents listed in (B) must comply with the following requirements:

(i) They must be bound together at the end of the petition or in a separate volumes not exceeding 300 pages each. The pages must be consecutively numbered;

(ii) They must be index-tabbed by number or letter, and

(iii) They must begin with a table of contents listing each document by its title and its index-tab number or letter.

(5) The petition must be verified.

(Subd (a) amended effective January 1, 2008; previously amended effective January 1, 2007.)

(b) Opposition

(1) Unless otherwise ordered, any opposition must be served and filed within 15 days after the petition is filed.

(2) An opposition must state any material facts not included in the petition and include a memorandum.

(3) The court may not issue a writ of supersedeas until the respondent has had the opportunity to file an opposition.

(Subd (b) amended effective January 1, 2007.)

(c) Temporary stay

(1) The petition may include a request for a temporary stay under rule 8.116 pending the ruling on the petition.

(2) A separately filed request for a temporary stay must be served on the respondent. For good cause, the Chief Justice or presiding justice may excuse advance service.

(Subd (c) amended effective January 1, 2007.)

(d) Issuing the writ

(1) The court may issue the writ on any conditions it deems just.

(2) The court must hold a hearing before it may issue a writ staying an order that awards or changes the custody of a minor.

(3) The court must notify the superior court, under rule [1] **8.489**, of any writ or temporary stay that it issues.

(Subd (d) amended effective January 1, 2009; previously amended effective January 1, 2007, and January 1, 2008.)

Rule 8.112(d).   2008 Deletes. [1] 8.490(k)

Rule 8.112 amended effective January 1, 2009; repealed and adopted as rule 49 effective January 1, 2005; previously amended and renumbered effective January 1, 2007; previously amended effective January 1, 2008.

Ref.: Cal. Fms Pl. & Pr., Ch. 40, "Appeal: An Overview," Ch. 43, "Appeal: Stay of Proceedings," Ch. 220, "Dissolution of Marriage: Master Procedural Guide," Ch. 328, "Juvenile Courts: Dependency Proceedings," Ch. 492, "Review (Certiorari), Writ of"; MB Prac. Guide: Cal. Debt Collection & Enforcement of Judgments, §§15.25, 15.26[3], [4]; W. Cal. Sum., 10 "Parent and Child" §288.

Rule 8.116.   Request for writ of supersedeas or temporary stay

(a) Information on cover

If a petition for original writ, petition for review, or any other document requests a writ of supersedeas or temporary stay from a reviewing court, the cover of the document must:

(1) Prominently display the notice "STAY REQUESTED"; and

(2) Identify the nature and date of the proceeding or act sought to be stayed.

(Subd (a) amended effective January 1, 2007.)

(b) Additional information

The following information must appear either on the cover or at the beginning of the text:

(1) The trial court and department involved; and

(2) The name and telephone number of the trial judge whose order the request seeks to stay.

(Subd (b) amended effective January 1, 2007.)

(c) Sanction

If the document does not comply with (a) and (b), the reviewing court may decline to consider the request for writ of supersedeas or temporary stay.

Rule 8.116 amended and renumbered effective January 1, 2007; repealed and adopted as rule 49.5 effective January 1, 2005.

Ref.: Cal. Fms Pl. & Pr., Ch. 40, "Appeal: An Overview," Ch. 43, "Appeal: Stay of Proceedings," Ch. 135, "Contempt," Ch. 328, "Juvenile Courts: Dependency Proceedings," Ch. 348, "Lis Pendens," Ch. 358, "Mandate and Prohibition," Ch. 492, "Review (Certiorari), Writ of"; MB Prac. Guide: Cal. Debt Collection & Enforcement of Judgments, §§15.25, 15.26[3], 15.27, 15.39.

Article 2
Record on Appeal

Rule 8.120. Record on appeal
Rule 8.121. Notice designating the record on appeal
Rule 8.122. Clerk's transcript
Rule 8.123. Record of administrative proceedings
Rule 8.124. Appendixes
Rule 8.128. Superior court file instead of clerk's transcript
Rule 8.130. Reporter's transcript
Rule 8.134. Agreed statement
Rule 8.137. Settled statement
Rule 8.140. Failure to procure the record
Rule 8.144. Form of the record
Rule 8.147. Record in multiple or later appeals in same case
Rule 8.150. Filing the record
Rule 8.153. Lending the record
Rule 8.155. Augmenting and correcting the record
Rule 8.160. Sealed records
Rule 8.163. Presumption from the record

Rule 8.120.   Clerk's transcript [Renumbered]

Rule 8.120 renumbered as Rule 8.122 effective January 1, 2008.

Another Rule 8.120 follows.

Rule 8.120.   Record on appeal

Except as otherwise provided in this chapter, the record on an appeal in a civil case must contain the records specified in (a) and (b), which constitute the normal record on appeal.

(a) Record of written documents

(1) A record of the written documents from the superior court proceedings in the form of one of the following:

(A) A clerk's transcript under rule 8.122;

(B) An appendix under rule 8.124;

(C) The original superior court file under rule 8.128, if a local rule of the reviewing court permits this form of the record;

(D) An agreed statement under rule 8.134(a)(2); or

(E) A settled statement under rule 8.137.

(2) If an appellant intends to raise any issue that requires consideration of the record of an administrative proceeding that was admitted in evidence, refused, or lodged in the superior court, the record on appeal must include that administrative record, transmitted under rule 8.123.

(Subd (a) adopted effective January 1, 2008.)

(b) Record of the oral proceedings

If an appellant intends to raise any issue that requires consideration of the oral proceedings in the superior court, the record on appeal must include a record of these oral proceedings in the form of one of the following:

(1) A reporter's transcript under rule 8.130;

(2) An agreed statement under rule 8.134; or

(3) A settled statement under rule 8.137.

(Subd (b) adopted effective January 1, 2008.)

Rule 8.120 adopted effective January 1, 2008.

Ref.: Cal. Fms Pl. & Pr., Ch. 42, "Appeal: Notice of Appeal," Ch. 44, "Appeal: Preparing and Filing the Record," Ch. 326, "Jury Instructions," Ch. 474C, "Procedures in Reviewing Agency Decisions."

Rule 8.121.   Notice designating the record on appeal

(a) Time to file

Within 10 days after filing the notice of appeal, an appellant must serve and file a notice in the superior court designating the record on appeal. The appellant may combine its notice designating the record with its notice of appeal.

(Subd (a) adopted effective January 1, 2008.)

(b) Contents

(1) The notice must:

(A) Specify the date the notice of appeal was filed.

(B) Specify which form of the record of the written documents from the superior court proceedings listed in rule 8.120(a)(1) the appellant elects to use. If the appellant elects to use a clerk's transcript, the notice must also designate the documents to be included in the clerk's transcript as required under rule 8.122(b)(1).

(C) Specify whether the appellant elects to proceed with or without a record of the oral proceedings in the trial court. If the appellant elects to proceed with a record of the oral proceedings in the trial court, the notice must specify which form of the record listed in rule 8.120(b) the appellant elects to use. If the appellant elects to use a reporter's transcript, the notice must designate the proceedings to be included in the transcript as required under rule 8.130.

(2) If an appellant intends to raise any issue that requires consideration of the record of an administrative proceeding that was admitted in evidence, refused, or lodged in the superior court, the notice must also request that this administrative record be transmitted to the reviewing court under rule 8.123.

(Subd (b) adopted effective January 1, 2008.)

(c) Copy to the reviewing court

The clerk must promptly send the reviewing court a copy of any notice filed under this rule.

(Subd (c) adopted effective January 1, 2008.)

Rule 8.121 adopted effective January 1, 2008.

Advisory Committee Comment

The Judicial Council has adopted an optional form—*Appellant's Notice Designating Record on Appeal* (form APP-003)—that can be used to provide the notice required by this rule.

This rule makes the filing of a notice designating the record an "act required to procure the record" within the meaning of rule 8.140(a). Under that rule, a failure to file such a notice triggers the clerk's duty to issue a 15-day notice of default and thereby allows the appellant to cure the default in superior court.

Ref.: Cal. Fms Pl. & Pr., Ch. 40, "Appeal: An Overview," Ch. 42, "Appeal: Notice of Appeal," Ch. 44, "Appeal: Preparing and Filing the Record."

Rule 8.122.   Clerk's transcript

(a) Designation

(1) A notice designating documents to be included in a clerk's transcript must identify each designated document by its title and filing date or, if the filing date is not available, the date it was signed. The notice may specify portions of designated documents that are not to be included in the transcript. For minute orders or instructions, it is sufficient to collectively designate all minute orders or all minute orders entered between specified dates, or all written jury instructions given, refused, or withdrawn.

(2) Within 10 days after the appellant serves its notice designating a clerk's transcript, the respondent may serve and file a notice in superior court designating any additional documents the respondent wants included in the transcript.

(3) Except as provided in (b)(4), all exhibits admitted in evidence, refused, or lodged are deemed part of the record, but a party wanting a copy of an exhibit included in the transcript must specify that exhibit by number or letter in its notice of designation. If the superior court has returned a designated exhibit to a party, the party in possession of the exhibit must promptly deliver it to the superior court clerk on receipt of the designation.

(Subd (a) amended effective January 1, 2008; previously amended effective January 1, 2005, and January 1, 2007.)

(b) Contents of transcript

(1) The transcript must contain:

(A) The notice of appeal;

(B) Any judgment appealed from and any notice of its entry;

(C) Any order appealed from and any notice of its entry;

(D) Any notice of intention to move for a new trial, or motion to vacate the judgment, for judgment notwithstanding the verdict, or for reconsideration of an appealed order, with supporting and opposing memoranda and attachments, and any order on such motion and any notice of its entry;

(E) Any notices or stipulations to prepare clerk's or reporter's transcripts or to proceed by agreed or settled statement; and

(F) The register of actions, if any.

(2) Each document listed in (1)(A), (B), (C), and (D) must show the date necessary to determine the timeliness of the appeal under rule 8.104 or 8.108.

(3) Except as provided in (4), if designated by any party, the transcript must also contain:

(A) Any other document filed or lodged in the case in superior court;

(B) Any exhibit admitted in evidence, refused, or lodged; and

(C) Any jury instruction that any party submitted in writing and the cover page required by rule 2.1055(b)(2)

indicating the party requesting it, and any written jury instructions given by the court.

(4) Unless the reviewing court orders or the parties stipulate otherwise:

(A) The clerk must not copy or transmit to the reviewing court the original of a deposition.

(B) The clerk must not include in the transcript the record of an administrative proceeding that was admitted in evidence, refused, or lodged in the trial court. Any such administrative record must be transmitted to the reviewing court as specified in rule 8.123.

(Subd (b) amended effective January 1, 2008; previously amended effective January 1, 2007.)

(c) Deposit for cost of transcript

(1) Within 30 days after the respondent files a designation under (a)(2) or the time for filing it expires, whichever first occurs, the superior court clerk must send:

(A) To the appellant, notice of the estimated cost to prepare an original and one copy of the clerk's transcript; and

(B) To each party other than the appellant, notice of the estimated cost to prepare a copy of the clerk's transcript for that party's use.

(2) A notice under (1) must show the date it was sent.

(3) Within 10 days after the clerk sends a notice under (1), the appellant and any party wanting to purchase a copy of the clerk's transcript must deposit the estimated cost with the clerk, unless otherwise provided by law or the party submits an application for, or an order granting, a waiver of the cost under rules 3.50–3.63.

(Subd (c) amended effective January 1, 2008; previously amended effective January 1, 2007.)

(d) Preparation of transcript

(1) Within 30 days after the appellant deposits the estimated cost of the transcript or the court files an order waiving that cost, the clerk must:

(A) Prepare an original and one copy of the transcript, and certify the original; and

(B) Prepare additional copies for which the parties have made deposits.

(2) If the appeal is abandoned or dismissed before the clerk has completed preparation of the transcript, the clerk must refund any portion of the deposit under (c) exceeding the preparation cost actually incurred.

(Subd (d) amended effective January 1, 2007; previously amended effective January 1, 2003.)

Rule 8.122 amended and renumbered effective January 1, 2008; repealed and adopted as rule 5 effective January 1, 2002; previously amended effective January 1, 2003, and January 1, 2005; previously amended and renumbered as rule 8.120 effective January 1, 2007.

Advisory Committee Comment

Subdivision (a). Subdivision (a)(1) allows a party designating documents for inclusion in the clerk's transcript to specify *portions* of such documents that are not to be included, e.g., because they are duplicates of other designated documents or are not necessary for proper consideration of the issues raised in the appeal. The notice of designation should identify any portion to be omitted by means of a descriptive reference, e.g., by specific page or exhibit numbers. This provision is intended to simplify and therefore expedite the preparation of the clerk's transcript, to reduce its cost to the parties, and to relieve the courts of the burden of reviewing a record containing redundant, irrelevant, or immaterial documents.

Subdivision (b). Subdivision (b)(1)(F) requires the clerk's transcript to include the register of actions, if any. This provision is intended to assist the reviewing court in determining the accuracy of the clerk's transcript.

Subdivision (c). Under subdivision (c)(2), a clerk who sends a notice under subdivision (c)(1) must include a certificate stating the date on which the clerk sent it. This provision is intended to establish the date when the 10-day period for depositing the cost of the clerk's transcript under this rule begins to run.

Ref.: Cal. Fms Pl. & Pr., Ch. 40, "Appeal: An Overview," Ch. 42, "Appeal: Notice of Appeal," Ch. 44, "Appeal: Preparing and Filing the Record."

Rule 8.123.   Record of administrative proceedings

(a) Application
This rule applies if the record of an administrative proceeding was admitted in evidence, refused, or lodged in the superior court.

(Subd (a) adopted effective January 1, 2008.)

(b) Designation
(1) An appellant's notice designating the record on appeal under rule 8.121 that requests a record of an administrative proceeding be transmitted to the reviewing court must identify the administrative record by the title and date or dates of the administrative proceedings.

(2) If an appellant does not request that an administrative record admitted in evidence, refused, or lodged in the superior court be transmitted to the reviewing court, the respondent, within 10 days after the appellant serves its notice designating the record on appeal, may serve and file in the superior court a notice requesting that this administrative record be transmitted to the reviewing court.

(Subd (b) adopted effective January 1, 2008.)

(c) Administrative records returned to parties
If the superior court has returned a designated administrative record to a party, the party in possession of the administrative record must deliver it to the superior court clerk within 15 days after the notice designating the record on appeal is served.

(Subd (c) adopted effective January 1, 2008.)

(d) Transmittal to the reviewing court
If any administrative record is designated by a party, the superior court clerk must transmit the original administrative record with any clerk's or reporter's transcript sent to the reviewing court under rule 8.150. If the appellant has elected under rule 8.121 to use neither a clerk's transcript nor a reporter's transcript, the superior court clerk must transmit any administrative record designated by a party to the reviewing court no later than 45 days after the respondent files a designation under (b)(2) or the time for filing it expires, whichever first occurs.

(Subd (d) adopted effective January 1, 2008.)

(e) Return by reviewing court
On request, the reviewing court may return an administrative record to the superior court. When the remittitur issues, the reviewing court must return any administrative record to the superior court.

(Subd (e) adopted effective January 1, 2008.)
Rule 8.123 adopted effective January 1, 2008.

Rule 8.124.   Appendixes

(a) Notice of election
(1) If in the notice designating the record on appeal under rule 8.121, the appellant elects to use an appendix under this rule, or if, within 10 days after the notice of appeal is filed, the respondent serves and files a notice in the superior court electing to use an appendix under this rule, this rule governs unless the superior court orders otherwise on a motion served and filed within 10 days after the notice of election is served.

(2) When a party files a notice electing to use an appendix under this rule, the superior court clerk must promptly send a copy of the register of actions, if any, to the attorney of record for each party and to any unrepresented party.

(3) The parties may prepare separate appendixes, but are encouraged to stipulate to a joint appendix.

(Subd (a) amended effective January 1, 2008; previously amended effective January 1, 2005, and January 1, 2007.)

(b) Contents of appendix
(1) A joint appendix or an appellant's appendix must contain:

(A) All items required by rule 8.122(b)(1), showing the dates required by rule 8.122(b)(2);

(B) Any item listed in rule 8.122(b)(3) that is necessary for proper consideration of the issues, including, for an appellant's appendix, any item that the appellant should reasonably assume the respondent will rely on;

(C) The notice of election; and

(D) For a joint appendix, the stipulation designating its contents.

(2) An appendix must not:

(A) Contain documents or portions of documents filed in superior court that are unnecessary for proper consideration of the issues.

(B) Contain transcripts of oral proceedings that may be designated under rule 8.130.

(C) Contain the record of an administrative proceeding that was admitted in evidence, refused, or lodged in the trial court. Any such administrative record must be transmitted to the reviewing court as specified in rule 8.123.

(D) Incorporate any document by reference except the record on appeal in another case pending in the reviewing court or the record in a prior appeal in the same case.

(3) All exhibits admitted in evidence, refused, or lodged are deemed part of the record, whether or not the appendix contains copies of them.

(4) A respondent's appendix may contain any document that could have been included in the appellant's appendix or a joint appendix.

(5) An appellant's reply appendix may contain any document that could have been included in the respondent's appendix.

(Subd (b) amended effective January 1, 2008; previously amended effective January 1, 2007.)

(c) Exhibit held by other party
If a party preparing an appendix wants it to contain a copy of an exhibit in the possession of another party:

(1) The party must first ask the party possessing the exhibit to provide a copy or lend it for copying. All parties should reasonably cooperate with such requests.

(2) If the attempt under (1) is unsuccessful, the party may serve and file in the reviewing court a notice specifying the exhibit's trial court designation and requesting the party possessing the exhibit to deliver it to the requesting party or, if the possessing party prefers, to the reviewing court. The possessing party must comply with the request within 10 days after the notice was served.

(3) If the party possessing the exhibit sends it to the requesting party, that party must copy and return it to the possessing party within 10 days after receiving it.

(4) If the party possessing the exhibit sends it to the reviewing court, that party must:

(A) Accompany the exhibit with a copy of the notice served by the requesting party; and

(B) Immediately notify the requesting party that it has sent the exhibit to the reviewing court.

(5) On request, the reviewing court may return an exhibit to the party that sent it. When the remittitur issues, the reviewing court must return all exhibits to the party that sent them.

(Subd (c) amended effective January 1, 2007; adopted effective January 1, 2005.)

(d) Form of appendix

(1) An appendix must comply with the requirements of rule 8.144(a)–(c) for a clerk's transcript.

(2) In addition to the information required on the cover of a brief by rule 8.204(b)(10), the cover of an appendix must prominently display the title "Joint Appendix" or "Appellant's Appendix" or "Respondent's Appendix" or "Appellant's Reply Appendix."

(3) An appendix must not be bound with a brief.

(Subd (d) amended effective January 1, 2007; adopted as subd (c) effective January 1, 2002; relettered effective January 1, 2005.)

(e) Service and filing

(1) A party preparing an appendix must:

(A) Serve the appendix on each party, unless otherwise agreed by the parties or ordered by the reviewing court; and

(B) File the appendix in the reviewing court.

(2) A joint appendix or an appellant's appendix must be served and filed with the appellant's opening brief.

(3) A respondent's appendix, if any, must be served and filed with the respondent's brief.

(4) An appellant's reply appendix, if any, must be served and filed with the appellant's reply brief.

(Subd (e) amended effective January 1, 2007; adopted as subd (d) effective January 1, 2002; relettered effective January 1, 2005.)

(f) Cost of appendix

(1) Each party must pay for its own appendix.

(2) The cost of a joint appendix must be paid:

(A) By the appellant;

(B) If there is more than one appellant, by the appellants equally; or

(C) As the parties may agree.

(Subd (f) amended effective January 1, 2007; adopted as subd (e) effective January 1, 2002; relettered effective January 1, 2005.)

(g) Inaccurate or noncomplying appendix

Filing an appendix constitutes a representation that the appendix consists of accurate copies of documents in the superior court file. The reviewing court may impose monetary or other sanctions for filing an appendix that contains inaccurate copies or otherwise violates this rule.

(Subd (g) adopted as subd (f) effective January 1, 2002; relettered effective January 1, 2005.)

Rule 8.124 amended effective January 1, 2008; repealed and adopted as rule 5.1 effective January 1, 2002; previously amended effective January 1, 2005; previously amended and renumbered effective January 1, 2007.

Advisory Committee Comment

Subdivision (a). Under this provision either party may elect to have the appeal proceed by way of an appendix. A respondent's timely election to use an appendix will govern unless the superior court orders otherwise. This election procedure differs from all other appellate rules governing designation of a record on appeal. In those rules, the appellant's designation, or the stipulation of the parties, determines the type of record on appeal.

Subdivision (a)(2) is intended to assist appellate counsel in preparing an appendix by providing them with the list of pleadings and other filings found in the register of actions or "docket sheet" in those counties that maintain such registers. (See Gov. Code, § 69845.) The provision is derived from rule 10-1 of the United States Circuit Rules (9th Cir.).

Subdivision (b). Under subdivision (b)(1)(A), a joint appendix or an appellant's appendix must contain any register of actions that the clerk sent to the parties under subdivision (a)(2). This provision is intended to assist the reviewing court in determining the accuracy of the appendix. The provision is derived from rule 30-1.3(a)(ii) of the United States Circuit Rules (9th Cir.).

In support of or opposition to pleadings or motions, the parties may have filed a number of lengthy documents in the proceedings in superior court, including, for example, declarations, memorandums, trial briefs, documentary exhibits (e.g., insurance policies, contracts, deeds), and photocopies of judicial opinions or other publications. Subdivision (b)(2)(A) prohibits the inclusion of such documents in an appendix when they are not necessary for proper consideration of the issues raised in the appeal. Even if a document is otherwise includable in an appendix, the rule prohibits the inclusion of any substantial *portion* of the document that is not necessary for proper consideration of the issues raised in the appeal. The prohibition is intended to simplify and therefore expedite the preparation of the appendix, to reduce its cost to the parties, and to relieve the courts of the burden of reviewing a record containing redundant, irrelevant, or immaterial documents. The provision is adapted from rule 30-1.4 of the United States Circuit Rules (9th Cir.).

Subdivision (b)(2)(B) prohibits the inclusion in an appendix of transcripts of oral proceedings that may be made part of a reporter's transcript. (Compare rule 8.130(e)(3) [the reporter must not copy into the reporter's transcript any document includable in the clerk's transcript under rule 8.122].) The prohibition is intended to prevent a party filing an appendix from evading the requirements and safeguards imposed by rule 8.130 on the process of designating and preparing a reporter's transcript, or the requirements imposed by rule 8.144(d) on the use of daily or other transcripts instead of a reporter's transcript (i.e., renumbered pages, required indexes). In addition, if an appellant were to include in its appendix a transcript of less than all the proceedings, the respondent would not learn of any need to designate additional proceedings (under rule 8.130(a)(3)) until the appellant had served its appendix with its brief, when it would be too late to designate them. Note also that a party may file a certified transcript of designated proceedings instead of a deposit for the reporter's fee (rule 8.130(b)(3)).

Subdivision (d). In current practice, served copies of filed documents often bear no clerk's date stamp and are not conformed by the parties serving them. Consistently with this practice, subdivision (d) does not require such documents to be conformed. The provision thereby relieves the parties of the burden of obtaining conformed copies at the cost of considerable time and expense and expedites the preparation of the appendix and the processing of the appeal. It is to be noted, however, that under subdivision (b)(1)(A) each document necessary to determine the timeliness of the appeal must show the date required under rule 8.104 or 8.108. Note also that subdivision (g) of rule 8.124 provides that a party filing an appendix represents under penalty of sanctions that its copies of documents are accurate.

Subdivision (e). Subdivision (e)(2) requires a joint appendix to be filed with the appellant's opening brief. The provision is intended to improve the briefing process by enabling the appellant's opening brief to include citations to the record. To provide for the case in which a respondent concludes in light of the appellant's opening brief that the joint appendix should have included additional documents, subdivision (b)(4) permits such a respondent to present in an appendix filed with its respondent's brief (see subd. (e)(3)) any document that could have been included in the joint appendix.

Under subdivision (e)(2)–(4) an appendix is required to be filed "with" the associated brief. This provision is intended to clarify that an extension of a briefing period ipso facto extends the filing period of an appendix associated with the brief.

Subdivision (g). Under subdivision (g), sanctions do not depend on the degree of culpability of the filing party—i.e., on whether the party's conduct was willful or negligent—but on the nature of the inaccuracies and the importance of the documents they affect.

Ref.: Cal. Fms Pl. & Pr., Ch. 40, "Appeal: An Overview," Ch. 42, "Appeal: Notice of Appeal," Ch. 44, "Appeal: Preparing and Filing the Record," Ch. 50, "Appeal: Briefs," Ch. 474C, "Procedures in Reviewing Agency Decisions."

Rule 8.128.   Superior court file instead of clerk's transcript

(a) Stipulation; time to file

(1) If a local rule of the reviewing court permits, the parties may stipulate to use the original superior court file instead of a clerk's transcript under rule 8.122. This rule and any supplemental provisions of the local rule then govern unless the superior court orders otherwise after notice to the parties.

(2) Parties intending to proceed under this rule must file their stipulation in superior court with the appellant's notice designating the record on appeal under rule 8.121. The parties must serve the reviewing court with a copy of the stipulation.

(Subd (a) amended effective January 1, 2008; previously amended effective January 1, 2007.)

(b) Cost estimate; preparation of file; transmittal

(1) Within 10 days after a stipulation under (a) is filed, the superior court clerk must mail the appellant an estimate of the cost to prepare the file, including the cost of sending the index under (3). The appellant must deposit the cost within 10 days after the clerk mails the estimate.

(2) Within 10 days after the appellant deposits the cost, the superior court clerk must put the superior court file in chronological order, number the pages, and attach a chronological index and a list of all attorneys of record, the parties they represent, and any unrepresented parties.

(3) The clerk must send copies of the index to all attorneys of record and any unrepresented parties for their use in paginating their copies of the file to conform to the index.

(4) The clerk must send the prepared file to the reviewing court with the reporter's transcript. If the appellant elected to proceed without a reporter's transcript, the clerk must immediately send the prepared file to the reviewing court.

Rule 8.128 amended effective January 1, 2008; repealed and adopted as rule 5.2 effective January 1, 2002; previously amended and renumbered effective January 1, 2007.

Ref.: Cal. Fms Pl. & Pr., Ch. 40, "Appeal: An Overview," Ch. 42, "Appeal: Notice of Appeal," Ch. 44, "Appeal: Preparing and Filing the Record."

Rule 8.130.   Reporter's transcript

(a) Notice

(1) If in the notice designating the record on appeal under rule 8.121, the appellant elects to use a reporter's transcript, in that notice the appellant must specify the date of each proceeding to be included in the transcript, and may specify portions of designated proceedings that are not to be included.

(2) If the appellant designates less than all the testimony, the notice must state the points to be raised on appeal; the appeal is then limited to those points unless, on motion, the reviewing court permits otherwise.

(3) If the appellant serves and files a notice designating a reporter's transcript, the respondent may, within 10 days after such service, serve and file a notice in superior court designating any additional proceedings the respondent wants included in the transcript.

(4) If the appellant elects to proceed without a reporter's transcript, the respondent cannot require that a reporter's transcript be prepared. But the reviewing court, on its own or the respondent's motion, may order the record augmented under rule 8.155 to prevent a miscarriage of justice. Unless the court orders otherwise, the appellant is responsible for the cost of any reporter's transcript the court may order under this subdivision.

(5) Any notice of designation must be served on each known reporter of the designated proceedings.

(Subd (a) amended effective January 1, 2008; previously amended effective January 1, 2005, and January 1, 2007.)

(b) Deposit or substitute for cost of transcript

(1) With its notice of designation, a party must deposit with the superior court clerk the approximate cost of transcribing the proceedings it designates, using either:

(A) The reporter's written estimate; or

(B) An amount calculated at $325 per fraction of the day's proceedings that did not exceed three hours, or $650 per day or fraction that exceeded three hours.

(2) If the reporter believes the deposit is inadequate, within 15 days after the clerk mails the notice under (d)(2) the reporter may file with the clerk and mail to the designating party an estimate of the transcript's total cost, showing the additional deposit required. The party must deposit the additional sum within 10 days after the reporter mails the estimate.

(3) Instead of a deposit, the party may substitute the reporter's written waiver of a deposit, a copy of a Transcript Reimbursement Fund application filed under (c)(1), or a certified transcript of the designated proceedings. A reporter may waive the deposit for—and a party may submit a certified transcript of—a part of the desig-

nated proceedings, but such a waiver or transcript replaces the deposit for only that part.

(Subd (b) amended effective January 1, 2007.)

(c) Transcript Reimbursement Fund application

(1) With its notice of designation, a party may serve and file a copy of its application to the Court Reporters Board for payment or reimbursement from the Transcript Reimbursement Fund under Business and Professions Code section 8030.2 et seq.

(2) If the Court Reporters Board approves the application for payment or reimbursement, the reporter's time to prepare the transcript under (f)(1) begins when the reporter receives notice of the approval.

(3) If the Court Reporters Board denies the application for payment or reimbursement, the party's time to deposit the reporter's fee or substitute under (b), or to file an agreed or settled statement under rule 8.134 or 8.137, is extended until 30 days after the board mails notice of the denial.

(Subd (c) amended effective January 1, 2007.)

(d) Superior court clerk's duties

(1) If a party designates proceedings to be included in a reporter's transcript and has presented the fee deposit or a substitute under (b)(3), the clerk must promptly mail the reporter notice of the designation and of the deposit or substitute. The notice must show the date it was mailed.

(2) If a party does not present the deposit or a substitute with its notice of designation, the clerk must file the notice and promptly issue a notice of default under rule 8.140.

(3) The clerk must promptly notify the reporter if a check for a deposit is dishonored or an appeal is abandoned or is dismissed before the reporter has filed the transcript.

(Subd (d) amended effective January 1, 2008; previously amended effective January 1, 2007.)

(e) Contents of transcript

(1) The reporter must transcribe all designated proceedings for which a certified transcript has not been substituted under (b)(3), and must note in the transcript where any proceedings were omitted and the nature of those proceedings. The reporter must also note where any exhibit was marked for identification and where it was admitted or refused, identifying such exhibits by number or letter.

(2) If a party designates a portion of a witness's testimony to be transcribed, the reporter must transcribe the witness's entire testimony unless the parties stipulate otherwise.

(3) The reporter must not copy any document includable in the clerk's transcript under rule 8.122.

(Subd (e) amended effective January 1, 2008; previously amended effective January 1, 2007.)

(f) Filing the transcript; copies; payment

(1) Within 30 days after notice is received under (c)(2) or mailed under [1] **(d)(1)**, the reporter must prepare and certify an original of the transcript and file it in superior court. The reporter must also file one copy of the original transcript, or more than one copy if multiple appellants equally share the cost of preparing the record (see rule 8.147(a)(2)). Only the reviewing court can extend the time to prepare the reporter's transcript (see rule 8.60).

(2) When the transcript is completed, the reporter must bill each designating party at the statutory rate and send a copy of the bill to the superior court clerk. The clerk must pay the reporter from that party's deposited funds and refund any excess deposit or notify the party of any additional funds needed. In a multiple reporter case, the clerk must pay each reporter who certifies under penalty of perjury that his or her transcript portion is completed.

(3) If the appeal is abandoned or is dismissed before the reporter has filed the transcript, the reporter must inform the superior court clerk of the cost of the portion of the transcript that the reporter has completed. The clerk must pay that amount to the reporter from the appellant's deposited funds and refund any excess deposit.

(4) On request, and unless the superior court orders otherwise, the reporter must provide any party with a copy of the reporter's transcript in computer-readable format. Each computer-readable copy must comply with the format, labeling, content, and numbering requirements of Code of Civil Procedure section 271(b).

(Subd (f) amended effective July 1, 2008; previously amended effective January 1, 2007.)

Rule 8.130(f). 2008 Deletes. [1] (d)(2)

(g) Agreed or settled statement when proceedings cannot be transcribed

(1) If any portion of the designated proceedings cannot be transcribed, the superior court clerk must so notify the designating party by mail; the notice must show the date it was mailed. The party may then substitute an agreed or settled statement for that portion of the designated proceedings by complying with either (A) or (B):

(A) Within 10 days after the notice is mailed, the party may file in superior court, under rule 8.134, an agreed statement or a stipulation that the parties are attempting to agree on a statement. If the party files a stipulation, within 30 days thereafter the party must file the agreed statement, move to use a settled statement under rule 8.137, or proceed without such a statement; or

(B) Within 10 days after the notice is mailed, the party may move in superior court to use a settled statement. If the court grants the motion, the statement must be served, filed, and settled as rule 8.137 provides, but the order granting the motion must fix the times for doing so.

(2) If the agreed or settled statement contains all the oral proceedings, it will substitute for the reporter's transcript; if it contains a portion of the proceedings, it will be incorporated into that transcript.

(3) This remedy supplements any other available remedies.

(Subd (g) amended effective January 1, 2007.)

Rule 8.130 amended effective July 1, 2008; repealed and adopted as rule 4 effective January 1, 2002; previously amended effective January 1, 2005, and January 1, 2008; previously amended and renumbered effective January 1, 2007.

Advisory Committee Comment

Under rule 8.121 an appellant may serve and file a notice *designating* a reporter's transcript and the notice must identify the proceedings to be *included*. The wording recognizes that under rule 8.130(b)(3) the appellant, instead of depositing the reporter's cost to transcribe the proceedings, may substitute certified transcripts of proceedings that have already been transcribed (e.g., daily transcripts) and hence need only be designated for inclusion in the transcript.

Subdivision (a). Subdivision (a)(1) requires that every notice designating a reporter's transcript identify which proceedings are to be included, and that it do so by specifying the date or dates on which those proceedings took place; if the appellant does not want a portion of the proceedings on a given date to be included, the notice should identify that portion by means of a descriptive reference (e.g., "August 3, 2004, but not the proceedings on defendant's motion to tax costs").

As used in subdivision (a)(1), the phrase "oral proceedings" includes all instructions that the court gives, whether or not submitted in writing, and any instructions that counsel orally propose but the court refuses; all such instructions are included in the reporter's transcript if designated under this rule. All instructions that counsel submit in writing, whether or not given to the jury, are lodged with the superior court clerk and are included in the clerk's transcript if designated under rule 8.122.

Under subdivision (a), portions of depositions read in open court but not reported, or not read but lodged with the superior court clerk, are included in the clerk's transcript if designated under rule 8.122.

Subdivision (b). To eliminate any ambiguity, subdivision (b)(3) recognizes, first, that a party may substitute a waiver or a certified transcript for part of the designated proceedings and, second, that in such event the waiver or transcript replaces the deposit for only that part.

Subdivision (c). Under subdivision (c), an application to the Court Reporters Board for payment or reimbursement of the cost of the reporter's transcript from the Transcript Reimbursement Fund (Bus. & Prof. Code, §8030.8) is a permissible substitute for the required deposit of the reporter's fee (subd. (b)(3)) and thereby prevents issuance of a notice of default (subd. (d)(4)).

Business and Professions Code sections 8030.6 and 8030.8 use the term "reimbursement" to mean not only a true reimbursement, i.e., repaying a party who has previously paid the reporter out of the party's own funds (see id., §8030.8, subd. (d)), but also a direct payment to a reporter who has not been previously paid by the party (see id., §8030.6, subds. (b) and (d)). Subdivision (f) recognizes this special dual meaning by consistently using the compound phrase "payment or reimbursement."

Subdivision (d). Under subdivision (d)(1), the clerk's notice to the reporter must show the date on which the clerk mailed the notice. This provision is intended to establish the date when the period for preparing the reporter's transcript under subdivision (f)(1) begins to run.

Subdivision (e). Subdivision (e)(3) is not intended to relieve the reporter of the duty to report all oral proceedings, including the reading of instructions or other documents.

Subdivision (f). Subdivision (f)(1) requires the reporter to prepare and file additional copies of the record "if multiple appellants equally share the cost of preparing the record ...." The reason for the requirement is explained in the comment to rule 8.147(a)(2).

Implementing statutory provisions (e.g., Code Civ. Proc., §269, subd. (c); Gov. Code, § 69954), subdivision (f)(4) requires the reporter to provide a party, on request, with a copy of the reporter's transcript in computer-readable format. But in recognition of the fact that in some instances the reporter may be unable to provide a copy in that format, the subdivision also authorizes the reporter to apply to the superior court for relief from this requirement.

Ref.: Cal. Fms Pl. & Pr., Ch. 40, "Appeal: An Overview," Ch. 42, "Appeal: Notice of Appeal," Ch. 44, "Appeal: Preparing and Filing the Record," Ch. 326, "Jury Instructions," Ch. 492, "Review (Certiorari), Writ of," Ch. 474C, "Procedures in Reviewing Agency Decisions," Ch. 533, "Stipulations."

Rule 8.134.   Agreed statement
(a) Contents of statement

(1) The record on appeal may consist wholly or partly of an agreed statement. The statement must explain the nature of the action, the basis of the reviewing court's jurisdiction, and how the superior court decided the points to be raised on appeal. The statement should recite only those facts needed to decide the appeal and must be signed by the parties.

(2) If the agreed statement replaces a clerk's transcript, the statement must be accompanied by copies of all items required by rule 8.122(b)(1), showing the dates required by rule 8.122(b)(2).

(3) The statement may be accompanied by copies of any document includable in the clerk's transcript under rule 8.122(b)(3) and (4).

(Subd (a) amended effective January 1, 2008; previously amended effective January 1, 2007.)

(b) Time to file; extension of time

(1) An appellant intending to proceed under this rule must file either an agreed statement or a stipulation that the parties are attempting to agree on a statement in superior court with its notice designating the record on appeal under rule 8.121.

(2) If the appellant files the stipulation and the parties can agree on the statement, the appellant must file the statement within 40 days after filing the notice of appeal.

(3) If the appellant files the stipulation and the parties cannot agree on the statement, the appellant must file a new notice designating the record on appeal under rule 8.121 within 50 days after filing the notice of appeal.

(Subd (b) amended effective January 1, 2008; previously amended effective January 1, 2007.)
Rule 8.134 amended effective January 1, 2008; repealed and adopted as rule 6 effective January 1, 2002; previously amended and renumbered effective January 1, 2007.

Advisory Committee Comment
Subdivision (b). Subdivision (b)(1) requires the appellant to file, with the appellant's notice designating the record under rule 8.121, either an agreed statement or a stipulation that the parties are attempting to agree on a statement. The provision is intended to prevent issuance of a notice of default while the parties are preparing an agreed statement.

Ref.: Cal. Fms Pl. & Pr., Ch. 44, "Appeal: Preparing and Filing the Record," Ch. 474C, "Procedures in Reviewing Agency Decisions," Ch. 524, "Shortening and Extension of Time."

Rule 8.137.   Settled statement
(a) Motion to use settled statement

(1) An appellant intending to proceed under this rule must serve and file in superior court with its notice designating the record on appeal under rule 8.121 a motion to use a settled statement instead of a reporter's transcript or both reporter's and clerk's transcripts.

(2) The motion must be supported by a showing that:

(A) A substantial cost saving will result and the statement can be settled without significantly burdening opposing parties or the court;

(B) The designated oral proceedings were not reported or cannot be transcribed; or

(C) The appellant is unable to pay for a reporter's transcript and funds are not available from the Transcript Reimbursement Fund (see rule 8.130(c)). A party proceeding in forma pauperis is deemed unable to pay for a transcript.

(3) If the court denies the motion, the appellant must file a new notice designating the record on appeal under rule 8.121 within 10 days after the superior court clerk mails, or a party serves, the order of denial.

(Subd (a) amended effective January 1, 2008; previously amended effective January 1, 2007.)

(b) Time to file; contents of statement

(1) Within 30 days after the superior court clerk mails, or a party serves, an order granting a motion to use a settled statement, the appellant must serve and file in superior court a condensed narrative of the oral proceedings that the appellant believes necessary for the appeal. Subject to the court's approval in settling the statement, the appellant may present some or all of the evidence by question and answer.

(2) If the condensed narrative describes less than all the testimony, the appellant must state the points to be raised on appeal; the appeal is then limited to those points unless, on motion, the reviewing court permits otherwise.

(3) An appellant intending to use a settled statement instead of both reporter's and clerk's transcripts must accompany the condensed narrative with copies of all items required by rule 8.122(b)(1), showing the dates required by rule 8.122(b)(2).

(4) Within 20 days after the appellant serves the condensed narrative, the respondent may serve and file proposed amendments.

(5) The proposed statement and proposed amendments may be accompanied by copies of any document includable in the clerk's transcript under rule 8.122(b)(3) and (4).

(Subd (b) amended effective January 1, 2008; previously amended effective January 1, 2007.)

(c) Settlement, preparation, and certification

(1) The clerk must set a date for a settlement hearing by the trial judge that is no later than 10 days after the respondent files proposed amendments or the time to do so expires, whichever is earlier, and must give the parties at least five days' notice of the hearing date.

(2) At the hearing, the judge must settle the statement and fix the times within which the appellant must prepare, serve, and file it.

(3) If the respondent does not object to the prepared statement within five days after it is filed, it will be deemed properly prepared and the clerk must present it to the judge for certification.

(4) The parties' stipulation that the statement as originally served or as prepared is correct is equivalent to the judge's certification.

Rule 8.137 amended effective January 1, 2008; repealed and adopted as rule 7 effective January 1, 2002; previously amended and renumbered effective January 1, 2007.

Advisory Committee Comment

Subdivision (b). This rule requires the appellant to file only one copy of the settled statement, i.e., for the use of the reviewing court. Because all parties participate in preparing the settled statement, it may be assumed that each will retain a copy for its own use.

Ref.: Cal. Fms Pl. & Pr., Ch. 44, "Appeal: Preparing and Filing the Record," Ch. 474C, "Procedures in Reviewing Agency Decisions."

Rule 8.140.   Failure to procure the record

(a) Notice of default

If a party fails to timely do an act required to procure the record, the superior court clerk must promptly notify the party by mail that it must do the act specified in the notice within 15 days after the notice is mailed, and that if it fails to comply, the reviewing court may impose one of the following sanctions:

(1) If the defaulting party is the appellant, the court may dismiss the appeal; or

(2) If the defaulting party is the respondent, the court may proceed with the appeal on the record designated by the appellant.

(Subd (a) amended effective January 1, 2008; previously amended effective January 1, 2007.)

(b) Sanctions

If a party fails to take the action specified in a notice given under (a), the superior court clerk must promptly notify the reviewing court of the default, and the reviewing court may impose one of the following sanctions:

(1) If the defaulting party is the appellant, the reviewing court may dismiss the appeal, but may vacate the dismissal for good cause; or

(2) If the defaulting party is the respondent, the reviewing court may order the appeal to proceed on the record designated by the appellant, but the respondent may obtain relief from default under rule 8.60(d).

(Subd (b) amended effective January 1, 2008; previously amended effective January 1, 2007.)

(c) Motion for sanctions

If the superior court clerk fails to give a notice required by (a), a party may serve and file a motion for sanctions under (b) in the reviewing court, but the motion must be denied if the defaulting party cures the default within 15 days after the motion is served.

Rule 8.140 amended effective January 1, 2008; adopted as rule 8 effective January 1, 2002; previously amended and renumbered effective January 1, 2007.

Advisory Committee Comment

Subdivision (a). In subdivision (a), the reference to a failure to "timely" do a required act is intended to include any valid extension of that time.

Ref.: Cal. Fms Pl. & Pr., Ch. 44, "Appeal: Preparing and Filing the Record," Ch. 48, "Appeal: Abandonment, Dismissal, and Stipulated Reversal."

Rule 8.144.   Form of the record

(a) Paper and format

(1) In the clerk's and reporter's transcripts:

(A) The paper must be white or unbleached, recycled, 8½ by 11 inches, and of at least 20-pound weight;

(B) The text must be reproduced as legibly as printed matter;

(C) The contents must be arranged chronologically;

(D) The pages must be consecutively numbered, except as provided in (e);

(E) The margin must be at least 1¼ inches on the bound edge of the page.

(2) In the clerk's transcript only one side of the paper may be used; in the reporter's transcript both sides may be used, but the margins must then be 1¼ inches on each edge.

(3) In the reporter's transcript the lines on each page must be consecutively numbered, and must be double-

spaced or one-and-a-half-spaced; double-spaced means three lines to a vertical inch.

(Subd (a) amended effective January 1, 2007.)

(b) Indexes

At the beginning of the first volume of each:

(1) The clerk's transcript must contain alphabetical and chronological indexes listing each document and the volume and page where it first appears;

(2) The reporter's transcript must contain alphabetical and chronological indexes listing the volume and page where each witness's direct, cross, and any other examination, begins; and

(3) The reporter's transcript must contain an index listing the volume and page where any exhibit is marked for identification and where it is admitted or refused. The index must identify each exhibit by number or letter and a brief description of the exhibit.

(Subd (b) amended effective January 1, 2008; previously amended effective January 1, 2007.)

(c) Binding and cover

(1) Clerk's and reporter's transcripts must be bound on the left margin in volumes of no more than 300 sheets.

(2) Each volume's cover, preferably of recycled stock, must state the title and trial court number of the case, the names of the trial court and each participating trial judge, the names and addresses of appellate counsel for each party, the volume number, and the inclusive page numbers of that volume.

(3) In addition to the information required by (2), the cover of each volume of the reporter's transcript must state the dates of the proceedings reported in that volume.

(d) Daily transcripts

Daily or other certified transcripts may be used for all or part of the reporter's transcript, but the pages must be renumbered consecutively and the required indexes and covers must be added.

(e) Pagination in multiple reporter cases

(1) In a multiple reporter case, each reporter must estimate the number of pages in each segment reported and inform the designated primary reporter of the estimate. The primary reporter must then assign beginning and ending page numbers for each segment.

(2) If a segment exceeds the assigned number of pages, the reporter must number the additional pages with the ending page number, a hyphen, and a new number, starting with 1 and continuing consecutively.

(3) If a segment has fewer than the assigned number of pages, the reporter must add a hyphen to the last page number used, followed by the segment's assigned ending page number, and state in parentheses "(next page number is _____)."

(f) Agreed or settled statements

Agreed or settled statements must conform with this rule insofar as practicable.

Rule 8.144 amended effective January 1, 2008; repealed and adopted as rule 9 effective January 1, 2002; previously amended and renumbered effective January 1, 2007.

Ref.: Cal. Fms Pl. & Pr., Ch. 44, "Appeal: Preparing and Filing the Record," Ch. 45, "Appeal: Motion Procedure," Ch. 345A, "Limited Civil Cases," Ch. 492, "Review (Certiorari), Writ of"; W. Cal. Sum., 10 "Parent and Child" §713.

Rule 8.147. Record in multiple or later appeals in same case

(a) Multiple appeals

(1) If more than one appeal is taken from the same judgment or a related order, only one record need be prepared, which must be filed within the time allowed for filing the record in the latest appeal.

(2) If there is more than one separately represented appellant, they must equally share the cost of preparing the record, unless otherwise agreed by the appellants or ordered by the superior court. Appellants equally sharing the cost are each entitled to a copy of the record.

(b) Later appeal

In an appeal under rule 8.122 or 8.130:

(1) A party wanting to incorporate by reference parts of a record in a prior appeal in the same case must specify those parts in its designation of the record, with page numbers if available.

(2) A party wanting any incorporated parts of a prior record to be copied into the later record must serve and file a notice specifying those parts and must deposit the estimated copying cost within 10 days after the clerk mails notice of that cost.

(Subd (b) amended effective January 1, 2008; previously amended effective January 1, 2007.)

Rule 8.147 amended effective January 1, 2008; repealed and adopted as rule 10 effective January 1, 2002; previously amended and renumbered effective January 1, 2007.

Advisory Committee Comment

Subdivision (a). Subdivision (a)(1) provides broadly for a single record whenever there are multiple appeals "from the same judgment or a related order." Multiple appeals from the *same judgment* include all cases in which opposing parties, or multiple parties on the same side of the case, appeal from the judgment. Multiple appeals from a judgment *and a related order* include all cases in which one party appeals from the judgment and another party appeals from any appealable order arising from or related to the judgment, i.e., not only orders contemplated by rule 8.108 (e.g., denying a motion for judgment notwithstanding the verdict) but also, for example, posttrial orders granting or denying attorney fees. The purpose is to encourage, when practicable, the preparation of a single record for all appeals taken in the same case. In specifying that "only one *record* need be prepared," of course, the rule does not depart from the basic requirement that an *original* and at least one *copy* of the record be prepared.

The second sentence of subdivision (a)(2) applies when multiple appellants equally share the cost of preparing the record and that cost includes the cost of a copy for each appellant. An appellant wanting the reporter to prepare an additional copy of the record—i.e., additional to the copy required by rule 8.130(f)(1)—must make a timely deposit adequate to cover the cost of that copy.

Ref.: Cal. Fms Pl. & Pr., Ch. 42, "Appeal: Notice of Appeal," Ch. 44, "Appeal: Preparing and Filing the Record," Ch. 45, "Appeal: Motion Procedure."

Rule 8.150. Filing the record

(a) Superior court clerk's duties

When the record is complete, the superior court clerk must promptly send the original to the reviewing court and the copy to the appellant.

(Subd (a) amended effective January 1, 2007.)

(b) Reviewing court clerk's duties

On receiving the record, the reviewing court clerk must promptly file the original and mail notice of the filing date to the parties.

(Subd (b) amended and lettered effective January 1, 2007; adopted as part of subd (a) effective January 1, 2002.)

Rule 8.150 amended and renumbered effective January 1, 2007; repealed and adopted as rule 11 effective January 1, 2002.

Ref.: Cal. Fms Pl. & Pr., Ch. 44, "Appeal: Preparing and Filing the Record," Ch. 50, "Appeal: Briefs."

Rule 8.153.   Lending the record

(a) Request

Within 20 days after the record is filed in the reviewing court, a party that has not purchased its own copy of the record may request another party, in writing, to lend it that party's copy of the record. The other party must then lend its copy of the record when it serves its brief.

(b) Time to return

The borrowing party must return the copy of the record when it serves its brief or the time to file its brief has expired.

(c) Cost

The borrowing party must bear the cost of sending the copy of the record to and from the borrowing party.

Rule 8.153 adopted effective January 1, 2007.

Ref.: Cal. Fms Pl. & Pr., Ch. 44, "Appeal: Preparing and Filing the Record."

Rule 8.155.   Augmenting and correcting the record

(a) Augmentation

(1) At any time, on motion of a party or its own motion, the reviewing court may order the record augmented to include:

(A) Any document filed or lodged in the case in superior court; or

(B) A certified transcript—or agreed or settled statement—of oral proceedings not designated under rule 8.130. Unless the court orders otherwise, the appellant is responsible for the cost of any additional transcript the court may order under this subdivision.

(2) A party must attach to its motion a copy, if available, of any document or transcript that it wants added to the record. The pages of the attachments must be consecutively numbered, beginning with the number one. If the reviewing court grants the motion it may augment the record with the copy.

(3) If the party cannot attach a copy of the matter to be added, the party must identify it as required under rules 8.122 and 8.130.

(Subd (a) amended effective January 1, 2008; previously amended effective January 1, 2007.)

(b) Omissions

(1) If a clerk or reporter omits a required or designated portion of the record, a party may serve and file a notice in superior court specifying the omitted portion and requesting that it be prepared, certified, and sent to the reviewing court. The party must serve a copy of the notice on the reviewing court.

(2) The clerk or reporter must comply with a notice under (1) within 10 days after it is filed. If the clerk or reporter fails to comply, the party may serve and file a motion to augment under (a), attaching a copy of the notice.

(c) Corrections

(1) On motion of a party, on stipulation, or on its own motion, the reviewing court may order the correction or certification of any part of the record.

(2) The reviewing court may order the superior court to settle disputes about omissions or errors in the record.

(d) Notice

The reviewing court clerk must send all parties notice of the receipt and filing of any matter under this rule.

Rule 8.155 amended effective January 1, 2008; repealed and adopted as rule 12 effective January 1, 2002; previously amended and renumbered effective January 1, 2007.

Advisory Committee Comment

Subdivision (a). Subdivision (a)(1) makes it clear that a party may apply for—and the reviewing court may order—augmentation of the record at any time. Whether the motion is made within a reasonable time and is not for the purpose of delay, however, are among the factors the reviewing court may consider in ruling on such a motion.

Ref.: Cal. Fms Pl. & Pr., Ch. 40, "Appeal: An Overview," Ch. 41, "Appeal: Review Standards and Appellate Rules of Law," Ch. 44, "Appeal: Preparing and Filing the Record," Ch. 45, "Appeal: Motion Procedure"; W. Cal. Sum., 10 "Parent and Child" §§713, 721, 725, 11 "Husband and Wife" §123.

Rule 8.160.   Sealed records

(a) Application

This rule applies to sealed records and records proposed to be sealed on appeal and in original proceedings, but does not apply to records required to be kept confidential by law.

(Subd (a) amended effective January 1, 2007; previously amended effective January 1, 2006.)

(b) Definitions

(1) "Record" means all or part of a document, paper, exhibit, transcript, or other thing filed or lodged with the court.

(2) A "sealed" record is a record closed to public inspection by court order.

(3) A "lodged" record is a record temporarily deposited with the court but not filed.

(c) Record sealed by the trial court

If a record sealed by the trial court is part of the record on appeal:

(1) The sealed record must be filed under seal in the reviewing court and remain sealed unless that court orders otherwise under (f).

(2) The record on appeal must include:

(A) The motion or application to seal;

(B) All documents filed in the trial court supporting or opposing the motion or application; and

(C) The order sealing the record.

(3) The reviewing court may examine the sealed record.

(Subd (c) amended effective January 1, 2007; previously amended effective January 1, 2004.)

(d) Record not sealed by the trial court

A record filed or lodged publicly in the trial court and not ordered sealed by that court must not be filed under seal in the reviewing court.

(e) Record not filed in the trial court; motion or application to file under seal

(1) A record not filed in the trial court may be filed under seal in the reviewing court only by order of that court; it must not be filed under seal solely by stipulation or agreement of the parties.

(2) To obtain an order under (1), a party must serve and file a motion or application in the reviewing court, accompanied by a declaration containing facts sufficient to justify the sealing. At the same time, the party must lodge the record under (3), unless good cause is shown not to lodge it.

(3) To lodge a record, the party must put the record in an envelope or other appropriate container, seal it, and attach a cover sheet that complies with rule 8.40(c) and labels the contents as "CONDITIONALLY UNDER SEAL."

(4) If necessary to prevent disclosure, any motion or application, any opposition, and any supporting documents must be filed in a public redacted version and lodged in a complete version conditionally under seal. Unless the court orders otherwise, any party that already possesses copies of the records to be placed under seal must be served with a complete, unredacted version of all papers as well as a redacted version.

(5) On receiving a lodged record, the clerk must note the date of receipt on the cover sheet and retain but not file the record. The record must remain conditionally under seal pending determination of the motion or application.

(6) The court may order a record filed under seal only if it makes the findings required by rule 2.550(d)–(e).

(7) If the court denies the motion or application, the clerk must not place the lodged record in the case file but must return it to the submitting party unless that party notifies the clerk in writing within 10 days after the order denying the motion or application that the record is to be filed.

(8) An order sealing the record must direct the sealing of only those documents and pages or, if reasonably practical, portions of those documents and pages, that contain the material that needs to be placed under seal. All other portions of each document or page must be included in the public file.

(9) Unless the sealing order provides otherwise, it prohibits the parties from disclosing the contents of any materials that have been sealed in any subsequently filed records or papers.

(Subd (e) amended effective January 1, 2007; previously amended effective July 1, 2002, and January 1, 2004.)

(f) Unsealing a record in the reviewing court

(1) A sealed record must not be unsealed except on order of the reviewing court.

(2) Any person or entity may serve and file a motion, application, or petition in the reviewing court to unseal a record. If necessary to preserve confidentiality, the motion, application, or petition; any opposition; and any supporting documents must be filed in both a public redacted version and a sealed complete version.

(3) If the reviewing court proposes to order a record unsealed on its own motion, the court must mail notice to the parties. Any party may serve and file an opposition within 10 days after the notice is mailed or as the court

specifies. Any other party may file a response within 5 days after an opposition is filed.

(4) In determining whether to unseal a record, the court must consider the matters addressed in rule 2.550(c)–(e).

(5) The order unsealing a record must state whether the record is unsealed entirely or in part. If the order unseals only part of the record or unseals the record only as to certain persons, the order must specify the particular records that are unsealed, the particular persons who may have access to the record, or both.

(6) If, in addition to the records in the sealed envelope or container, a court has previously ordered the sealing order, the register of actions, or any other court records relating to the case to be sealed, the unsealing order must state whether these additional records are unsealed.

(Subd (f) amended effective January 1, 2007; previously amended effective January 1, 2004.)

(g) Disclosure of nonpublic material in public records prohibited

A record filed publicly in the reviewing court must not disclose material contained in a record that is sealed, lodged conditionally under seal, or otherwise subject to a pending motion to file under seal.

(Subd (g) amended effective January 1, 2007.)

Rule 8.160 amended and renumbered effective January 1, 2007; repealed and adopted as rule 12.5 effective January 1, 2002; previously amended effective July 1, 2002, January 1, 2004, and January 1, 2006.

Advisory Committee Comment

This rule and rules 2.550–2.551 for the trial courts provide a standard and procedures for courts to use when a request is made to seal a record. The standard is based on *NBC Subsidiary (KNBC-TV), Inc. v. Superior Court* (1999) 20 Cal.4th 1178. The sealed records rules apply to civil and criminal cases. They recognize the First Amendment right of access to documents used at trial or as a basis of adjudication. The rules do not apply to records that courts must keep confidential by law. Examples of confidential records to which public access is restricted by law are records of the family conciliation court (Fam. Code, § 1818, subd. (b)) and in forma pauperis applications (Cal. Rules of Court, rule 3.60). Except as otherwise expressly provided in rule 8.160, motions in a reviewing court relating to the sealing or unsealing of a record must follow rule 8.54.

Ref.: Cal. Fms Pl. & Pr., Ch. 44, "Appeal: Preparing and Filing the Record," Ch. 45, "Appeal: Motion Procedure," Ch. 50, "Appeal: Briefs," Ch. 358, "Mandate and Prohibition," Ch. 492, "Review (Certiorari), Writ of."

Rule 8.163. Presumption from the record

The reviewing court will presume that the record in an appeal includes all matters material to deciding the issues raised. If the appeal proceeds without a reporter's transcript, this presumption applies only if the claimed error appears on the face of the record.

Rule 8.163 amended and renumbered effective January 1, 2007; repealed and adopted as rule 52 effective January 1, 2005.

Advisory Committee Comment

The intent of rule 8.163 is explained in the case law. (See, e.g., *Dumas v. Stark* (1961) 56 Cal.2d 673, 674.)

Ref.: Cal. Fms Pl. & Pr., Ch. 40, "Appeal: An Overview," Ch. 41, "Appeal: Review Standards and Appellate Rules of Law," Ch. 44, "Appeal: Preparing and Filing the Record," Ch. 50, "Appeal: Briefs."

Article 3
Briefs in the Court of Appeal

Rule 8.200. Briefs by parties and amici curiae
Rule 8.204. Contents and form of briefs
Rule 8.208. Certificate of Interested Entities or Persons
Rule 8.212. Service and filing of briefs
Rule 8.216. Appeals in which a party is both appellant and respondent
Rule 8.220. Failure to file a brief
Rule 8.224. Transmitting exhibits

Rule 8.200.   Briefs by parties and amici curiae

(a) Parties' briefs

(1) Each appellant must serve and file an appellant's opening brief.

(2) Each respondent must serve and file a respondent's brief.

(3) Each appellant may serve and file a reply brief.

(4) No other brief may be filed except with the permission of the presiding justice, unless it qualifies under (b) or (c)(6).

(5) Instead of filing a brief, or as part of its brief, a party may join in or adopt by reference all or part of a brief in the same or a related appeal.

(Subd (a) amended effective January 1, 2003.)

(b) Supplemental briefs after remand or transfer from Supreme Court

(1) Within 15 days after finality of a Supreme Court decision remanding or order transferring a cause to a Court of Appeal for further proceedings, any party may serve and file a supplemental opening brief in the Court of Appeal. Within 15 days after such a brief is filed, any opposing party may serve and file a supplemental responding brief.

(2) Supplemental briefs must be limited to matters arising after the previous Court of Appeal decision in the cause, unless the presiding justice permits briefing on other matters.

(3) Supplemental briefs may not be filed if the previous decision of the Court of Appeal was a denial of a petition for a writ within its original jurisdiction without issuance of an alternative writ or order to show cause.

(Subd (b) adopted effective January 1, 2003.)

(c) Amicus curiae briefs

(1) Within 14 days after the last appellant's reply brief is filed or could have been filed under rule 8.212, whichever is earlier, any person or entity may serve and file an application for permission of the presiding justice to file an amicus curiae brief. For good cause, the presiding justice may allow later filing.

(2) The application must state the applicant's interest and explain how the proposed amicus curiae brief will assist the court in deciding the matter.

(3) The application must also identify:

(A) Any party or any counsel for a party in the pending appeal who:

(i) Authored the proposed amicus brief in whole or in part; or

(ii) Made a monetary contribution intended to fund the preparation or submission of the brief; and

(B) Every person or entity who made a monetary contribution intended to fund the preparation or submission of the brief, other than the amicus curiae, its members, or its counsel in the pending appeal.

(4) The proposed brief must be served and must accompany the application, and may be combined with it.

[1] (5) The covers of the application and proposed brief must identify the party the applicant supports, if any.

[2] (6) If the court grants the application, any party may file an answer within the time the court specifies. The answer must be served on all parties and the amicus curiae.

[3] (7) The Attorney General may file an amicus curiae brief without the presiding justice's permission, unless the brief is submitted on behalf of another state officer or agency. The Attorney General must serve and file the brief within 14 days after the last appellant's reply brief is filed or could have been filed under rule 8.212, whichever is earlier, and must provide the information required by (2) and comply with [4] (5). Any party may serve and file an answer within 14 days after the brief is filed.

(Subd (c) amended effective January 1, 2009; adopted as subd (b) effective January 1, 2002; previously relettered effective January 1, 2003; previously amended effective January 1, 2007, and January 1, 2008.)

Rule 8.200(c).   2008 Deletes. [1] (4) [2] (5) [3] (6) [4] (4)
Rule 8.200 amended effective January 1, 2009; repealed and adopted as rule 13 effective January 1, 2002; previously amended and renumbered effective January 1, 2007; previously amended effective January 1, 2003, and January 1, 2008.

Advisory Committee Comment

Subdivision (b). After the Supreme Court remands or transfers a cause to the Court of Appeal for further proceedings (i.e., under rules 8.528(c)–(e) or 10.1000(a)(1)(B)), the parties are permitted to file supplemental briefs. The first 15-day briefing period begins on the day of *finality* (under rule 8.532) of the Supreme Court decision remanding or order transferring the cause to the Court of Appeal. The rule specifies that "any party" may file a supplemental opening brief, and if such a brief is filed, "any opposing party" may file a supplemental responding brief. In this context the phrase "any party" is intended to mean any *or all* parties. Such a decision or order of transfer to the Court of Appeal thus triggers, first, a 15-day period in which any or all parties may file supplemental opening briefs and, second—if any party files such a brief—an additional 15-day period in which any opposing party may file a supplemental responding brief.

Subdivision (c)(1). The time within which a reply brief "could have been filed under rule 8.212" includes any authorized extension of the deadline specified in rule 8.212.

Ref.: Cal. Fms Pl. & Pr., Ch. 22, "Amicus Curiae," Ch. 40, "Appeal: An Overview," Ch. 45, "Appeal: Motion Procedure," Ch. 50, "Appeal: Briefs," Ch. 54, "Appeal: California Supreme Court Review."

Rule 8.204.   Contents and form of briefs

(a) Contents

(1) Each brief must:

(A) Begin with a table of contents and a table of authorities separately listing cases, constitutions, statutes, court rules, and other authorities cited;

(B) State each point under a separate heading or subheading summarizing the point, and support each point by argument and, if possible, by citation of authority; and

(C) Support any reference to a matter in the record by a citation to the volume and page number of the record where the matter appears. If any part of the record is submitted in an electronic format, citations to that part must identify, with the same specificity required for the printed record, the place in the record where the matter appears.

(2) An appellant's opening brief must:

(A) State the nature of the action, the relief sought in the trial court, and the judgment or order appealed from;

(B) State that the judgment appealed from is final, or explain why the order appealed from is appealable; and

(C) Provide a summary of the significant facts limited to matters in the record.

(Subd (a) amended effective January 1, 2006.)

(b) Form

(1) A brief may be reproduced by any process that produces a clear, black image of letter quality. The paper must be white or unbleached, recycled, 8½ by 11 inches, and of at least 20-pound weight.

(2) Any conventional typeface may be used. The typeface may be either proportionally spaced or monospaced.

(3) The type style must be roman; but for emphasis, italics or boldface may be used or the text may be underscored. Case names must be italicized or underscored. Headings may be in uppercase letters.

(4) Except as provided in (11), the type size, including footnotes, must not be smaller than 13-point, and both sides of the paper may be used.

(5) The lines of text must be unnumbered and at least one-and-a-half-spaced. Headings and footnotes may be single-spaced. Quotations may be block-indented and single-spaced. Single-spaced means six lines to a vertical inch.

(6) The margins must be at least 1½ inches on the left and right and 1 inch on the top and bottom.

(7) The pages must be consecutively numbered. The tables and the body of the brief may have different numbering systems.

(8) The brief must be bound on the left margin. If the brief is stapled, the bound edge and staples must be covered with tape.

(9) The brief need not be signed.

(10) The cover, preferably of recycled stock, must be in the color prescribed by rule 8.40(b) and must state:

(A) The title of the brief;

(B) The title, trial court number, and Court of Appeal number of the case;

(C) The names of the trial court and each participating trial judge;

(D) The name, address, telephone number, and California State Bar number of each attorney filing or joining in the brief, but the cover need not state the bar number of any supervisor of the attorney responsible for the brief; and

(E) The name of the party that each attorney on the brief represents.

(11) If the brief is produced on a typewriter:

(A) A typewritten original and carbon copies may be filed only with the presiding justice's permission, which will ordinarily be given only to unrepresented parties proceeding in forma pauperis. All other typewritten briefs must be filed as photocopies.

(B) Both sides of the paper may be used if a photocopy is filed; only one side may be used if a typewritten original and carbon copies are filed.

(C) The type size, including footnotes, must not be smaller than standard pica, 10 characters per inch. Unrepresented incarcerated litigants may use elite type, 12 characters per inch, if they lack access to a typewriter with larger characters.

(Subd (b) amended effective January 1, 2007; previously amended effective January 1, 2004, July 1, 2004, and January 1, 2006.)

(c) Length

(1) A brief produced on a computer must not exceed 14,000 words, including footnotes. Such a brief must include a certificate by appellate counsel or an unrepresented party stating the number of words in the brief. The person certifying may rely on the word count of the computer program used to prepare the brief.

(2) A brief produced on a typewriter must not exceed 50 pages.

(3) The tables, a certificate under (1), and any attachment under (d) are excluded from the limits stated in (1) or (2).

(4) A combined brief in an appeal governed by rule 8.216 must not exceed double the limits stated in (1) or (2).

(5) On application, the presiding justice may permit a longer brief for good cause.

(Subd (c) amended effective January 1, 2007.)

(d) Attachments to briefs

A party filing a brief may attach copies of exhibits or other materials in the appellate record or copies of relevant local, state, or federal regulations or rules, out-of-state statutes, or other similar citable materials that are not readily accessible. These attachments must not exceed a combined total of 10 pages, but on application the presiding justice may permit additional pages of attachments for good cause. A copy of an opinion required to be attached to the brief under rule 8.1115(c) does not count toward this 10-page limit.

(Subd (d) amended effective January 1, 2007.)

(e) Noncomplying briefs

If a brief does not comply with this rule:

(1) The reviewing court clerk may decline to file it, but must mark it "received but not filed" and return it to the party; or

(2) If the brief is filed, the reviewing court may, on its own or a party's motion, with or without notice:

(A) Order the brief returned for corrections and refiling within a specified time;

(B) Strike the brief with leave to file a new brief within a specified time; or

(C) Disregard the noncompliance.

(Subd (e) amended effective January 1, 2006.)

Rule 8.204 amended effective January 1, 2008; repealed and adopted as rule 14 effective January 1, 2002; previously amended effective January 1, 2004, July 1, 2004, and January 1, 2006; previously amended and renumbered effective January 1, 2007.

Advisory Committee Comment

Subdivision (b). The first sentence of subdivision (b)(1) confirms that any method of reproduction is acceptable provided it results in a clear black image of letter quality. The provision is derived from subdivision (a)(1) of rule 32 of the Federal Rules of Appellate Procedure (28 U.S.C.) (FRAP 32).

Paragraphs (2), (3), and (4) of subdivision (b) state requirements of *typeface*, *type style*, and *type size* (see also subd. (b)(11)(C)). The first two terms are defined in *The Chicago Manual of Style* (15th ed., 2003) p. 839. Note that computer programs often refer to typeface as "font."

Subdivision (b)(2) allows the use of any conventional typeface—e.g., Times New Roman, Courier, Arial, Helvetica, etc.—and permits the typeface to be either proportionally spaced or monospaced.

Subdivision (b)(3) requires the type style to be roman, but permits the use of italics, boldface, or underscoring for emphasis; it also requires case names to be italicized or underscored. These provisions are derived from FRAP 32(a)(6).

Subdivision (b)(5) allows headings to be single-spaced; it is derived from FRAP 32(a)(4). The provision also permits quotations of any length to be block-indented and single-spaced at the discretion of the brief writer.

See also rule 1.200 concerning the format of citations. Brief writers are encouraged to follow the citation form of the *California Style Manual* (4th ed., 2000).

Subdivision (c). Subdivision (c) governs the maximum permissible length of a brief. It is derived from the federal procedure of measuring the length of a brief produced on a computer by the number of words in the brief. (FRAP 32(a)(7).) Subdivision (c)(1), like FRAP 32(a)(7)(B)(i), imposes a limit of 14,000 words if the brief is produced on a computer. Subdivision (c)(1) implements this provision by requiring the writer of a brief produced on a computer to include a certificate stating the number of words in the brief, but allows the writer to rely on the word count of the computer program used to prepare the brief. This requirement, too, is adapted from the federal rule. (FRAP 32(a)(7)(C).) For purposes of this rule, a "brief produced on a computer" includes a commercially printed brief.

Subdivision (c)(5) clarifies that a party seeking permission to exceed the page or word limits stated in subdivision (c)(1) and (2) must proceed by application under rule 8.50 rather than by motion under rule 8.54, and must show good cause.

Subdivision (d). Subdivision (d) permits a party filing a brief to attach copies of exhibits or other materials, provided they are part of the record on appeal and do not exceed a total of 10 pages. If the brief writer attaches, under rule 8.1115(c), a copy of an unpublished opinion or an opinion available only in computerized form, that opinion does not count toward the 10-page limit stated in rule 8.204(d).

Subdivision (e). Subdivision (e) states the consequences of submitting briefs that do not comply with this rule: (e)(1) recognizes the power of the reviewing court clerk to decline to file such a brief, and (e)(2) recognizes steps the reviewing court may take to obtain a brief that does comply with the rule. Subdivision (e)(2) does not purport to limit the inherent power of the reviewing court to fashion other sanctions for such noncompliance.

Ref.: Cal. Fms Pl. & Pr., Ch. 3, "Abatement of Actions," Ch. 18, "Alcoholic Beverage Licenses," Ch. 22, "Amicus Curiae," Ch. 40, "Appeal: An Overview," Ch. 41, "Appeal: Review Standards and Appellate Rules of Law," Ch. 43, "Appeal: Stay of Proceedings," Ch. 44, "Appeal: Preparing and Filing the Record," Ch. 45, "Appeal: Motion Procedure," Ch. 50, "Appeal: Briefs," Ch. 52, "Appeal: Rehearing," Ch. 54, "Appeal: California Supreme Court Review," Ch. 292, "Habeas Corpus," Ch. 300, "Indemnity and Contribution," Ch. 317, "Judges," Ch. 345A,

"Limited Civil Cases," Ch. 358, "Mandate and Prohibition," Ch. 372, "Motions and Orders," Ch. 474C, "Procedures in Reviewing Agency Decisions," Ch. 492, "Review (Certiorari), Writ of," Ch. 577, "Workers' Compensation"; MB Prac. Guide: Cal. Pretrial Proc., §26.02.

Rule 8.208. Certificate of Interested Entities or Persons

(a) Purpose and intent

The California Code of Judicial Ethics states the circumstances under which an appellate justice must disqualify himself or herself from a proceeding. The purpose of this rule is to provide justices of the Courts of Appeal with additional information to help them determine whether to disqualify themselves from a proceeding.

(b) Application

This rule applies in appeals in civil cases other than family, juvenile, guardianship, and conservatorship cases.

(Subd (b) adopted effective January 1, 2008.)

(c) Definitions

For purposes of this rule:

(1) "Certificate" means a Certificate of Interested Entities or Persons signed by appellate counsel or an unrepresented party.

(2) "Entity" means a corporation, a partnership, a firm, or any other association, but does not include a governmental entity or its agencies or a natural person.

(Subd (c) relettered effective January 1, 2008; adopted as subd (b) effective July 1, 2006.)

(d) Serving and filing a certificate

(1) Except as otherwise provided in this rule, if a party files a motion, an application, or an opposition to such motion or application in the Court of Appeal before filing its principal brief, the party must serve and file its certificate at the time it files the first such motion, application, or opposition and must include a copy of this certificate in the party's principal brief. If no motion, application, or opposition to such motion or application is filed before the parties file their principal briefs, each party must include its certificate in its principal brief. The certificate must appear after the cover and before the tables.

(2) If the identity of any party **or any entity or person subject to disclosure under this rule** has not been publicly disclosed in the proceedings **and a party wants to keep that identity confidential**, the party may serve and file an application for permission to file its certificate under seal separately from its principal brief, motion, application, or opposition. **If the application is granted, the party must file the certificate under seal and without service within 10 days of the court's order granting the application.**

[1] (3) If a party fails to file a certificate as required under (1), the clerk must notify the party by mail that the party must file the certificate within 15 days after the clerk's notice is mailed and that if the party fails to comply, the court may impose one of the following sanctions:

(A) If the party is the appellant, the court may strike the document or dismiss the appeal; or

(B) If the party is the respondent, the court may strike the document or decide the appeal on the record, the opening brief, and any oral argument by the appellant.

[2] **(4)** If the party fails to file the certificate as specified in the notice under (2), the court may impose the sanctions specified in the notice.

(Subd (d) amended effective January 1, 2009; adopted as subd (c) effective July 1, 2006; previously amended and relettered effective January 1, 2008.)

Rule 8.208(d).   2008 Deletes. [1] (2) **[2]** (3)

(e) Contents of certificate

(1) If an entity is a party, that party's certificate must list any other entity or person that the party knows has an ownership interest of 10 percent or more in the party.

(2) If a party knows of any [1] person or entity, **other than the parties themselves,** that has a financial or other interest in the outcome of the proceeding that the party reasonably believes the justices should consider in determining whether to disqualify themselves under canon 3E of the Code of Judicial Ethics, the party's certificate must list that entity or person and identify the nature of the interest of the person or entity. For purposes of this subdivision:

(A) A mutual or common investment fund's ownership of securities or bonds issued by an entity does not constitute a financial interest in that entity.

(B) An interest in the outcome of the proceeding does not arise solely because the entity or person is in the same industry, field of business, or regulatory category as a party and the case might establish a precedent that would affect that industry, field of business, or regulatory category.

(C) A party's insurer does not have a financial interest in the outcome of the proceeding solely on the basis of its status as insurer for that party.

(3) If the party knows of no entity or person that must be listed under (1) or (2), the party must so state in the certificate.

(Subd (e) amended effective January 1, 2009; adopted as subd (d) effective July 1, 2006; previously amended effective January 1, 2007; previously relettered effective January 1, 2008.)

Rule 8.208(e).   2008 Deletes. [1] other

(f) Supplemental information

A party that learns of changed or additional information that must be disclosed under (e) must promptly serve and file a supplemental certificate in the reviewing court.

(Subd (f) amended and relettered effective January 1, 2008; adopted as subd (e) effective July 1, 2006.)
Rule 8.208 amended effective January 1, 2009; adopted as rule 14.5 effective July 1, 2006; previously amended and renumbered effective January 1, 2007; previously amended effective January 1, 2008.

Advisory Committee Comment

The Judicial Council has adopted an optional form, *Certificate of Interested Entities or Persons* (form APP-008), that can be used to file the certificate required by this rule.

Subdivision (e). This subdivision requires a party to list on its certificate entities or persons that the party *knows* have specified interests. This subdivision does not impose a duty on a party to gather information not already known by that party.

Ref.: Cal. Fms Pl. & Pr., Ch. 1, "New Developments," Ch. 18, "Alcoholic Beverage Licenses," Ch. 50, "Appeal: Briefs," Ch. 120, "Class Actions," Ch. 135, "Contempt," Ch. 200, "Discovery: Review of Discovery Orders," Ch. 328, "Juvenile Courts: Dependency Proceedings," Ch. 358, "Mandate and Prohibition," Ch.

480, "Public Utilities," Ch. 492, "Review (Certiorari), Writ of," Ch. 577, "Workers' Compensation."

Rule 8.212.   Service and filing of briefs

(a) Time to file

(1) An appellant must serve and file its opening brief within:

(A) 30 days after the record—or the reporter's transcript, after a rule 8.124 election—is filed in the reviewing court; or

(B) 70 days after the filing of a rule 8.124 election, if the appeal proceeds without a reporter's transcript.

(2) A respondent must serve and file its brief within 30 days after the appellant files its opening brief.

(3) An appellant must serve and file its reply brief, if any, within 20 days after the respondent files its brief.

(Subd (a) amended effective January 1, 2007.)

(b) Extensions of time

(1) The parties may extend each period under (a) by up to 60 days by filing one or more stipulations in the reviewing court before the brief is due. Stipulations must be signed by and served on all parties. The original signature of at least one party must appear on the stipulation filed in the reviewing court; the signatures of the other parties may be in the form of fax copies of the signed signature page of the stipulation.

(2) A stipulation under (1) is effective on filing. The reviewing court may not shorten a stipulated extension.

(3) Before the brief is due, a party may apply to the presiding justice for an extension of each period under (a), or under rule 8.200(c)(5) or (6), on a showing that there is good cause and that:

(A) The applicant was unable to obtain—or it would have been futile to seek—the extension by stipulation; or

(B) The parties have stipulated to the maximum extension permitted under (1) and the applicant seeks a further extension.

(4) A party need not apply for an extension or relief from default if it can file its brief within the time prescribed by rule 8.220. The clerk must file a brief submitted within that time if it otherwise complies with these rules.

(Subd (b) amended effective January 1, 2007; previously amended effective January 1, 2003, and July 1, 2005.)

(c) Service

(1) One copy of each brief must be served on the superior court clerk for delivery to the trial judge.

(2) One electronic copy or four paper copies of each brief must be served on the Supreme Court as provided in either (A) or (B).

(A) One copy of each brief may be served on the Supreme Court electronically by sending the copy to the Supreme Court's electronic notification address.

(i) The copy must be a single computer file in text-searchable Portable Document Format (PDF), and it must exactly duplicate the appearance of the paper copy, including the order and pagination of all of the brief's components. By electronically serving the copy, the filer certifies that the copy complies with these requirements and that all reasonable steps have been taken to ensure that the copy does not contain computer code, including viruses, that might be harmful to the court's electronic filing system and to other users of that system.

(ii) If the Court of Appeal has ordered the brief sealed, the party serving the brief must include as the first page in the PDF document a cover sheet that contains the information required by rule 8.204(b)(10) and labels the contents as "CONDITIONALLY UNDER SEAL." The Court of Appeal clerk must promptly notify the Supreme Court of any court order unsealing the brief. In the absence of such notice, the Supreme Court clerk must keep all copies of the brief under seal.

(B) Instead of serving an electronic copy, four paper copies of each brief may be served on the Supreme Court. If the Court of Appeal has ordered the brief sealed, the party serving the brief must place all four copies of the brief in a sealed envelope and attach a cover sheet that contains the information required by rule 8.204(b)(10) and labels the contents as "CONDITIONALLY UNDER SEAL." The Court of Appeal clerk must promptly notify the Supreme Court of any court order unsealing the brief. In the absence of such notice the Supreme Court clerk must keep all copies of the brief under seal.

(3) One copy of each brief must be served on a public officer or agency when required by rule 8.29.

(Subd (c) amended effective January 1, 2008; previously amended effective January 1, 2004, January 1, 2005, and January 1, 2007.)

Rule 8.212 amended effective January 1, 2008; repealed and adopted as rule 15 effective January 1, 2002; previously amended effective January 1, 2003, January 1, 2004, January 1, 2005, and July 1, 2005; previously amended and renumbered effective January 1, 2007.

Advisory Committee Comment

Subdivision (b). In criminal cases, stipulated extensions of time to file briefs are prohibited by rule. (See rule 8.360(c)(4).)

Subdivision (b)(2) clarifies that a party seeking an extension of time from the presiding justice must proceed by application under rule 8.50 rather than by motion under rule 8.54.

Subdivision (c). "Electronic notification address" is defined in rule 2.250. The Supreme Court's electronic filing address can be found on the California Courts Web site at *www.courtinfo.ca.gov/courts/supreme*.

In subdivision (c)(3) the word "brief" means only (1) an appellant's opening brief, (2) a respondent's brief, (3) an appellant's reply brief, (4) a petition for rehearing, (5) an answer thereto, or (6) an amicus curiae brief. It follows that no other documents or papers filed in the Court of Appeal, whatever their nature, should be served on the Supreme Court. Further, only briefs filed in the Court of Appeal "in a civil appeal" must be served on the Supreme Court. It follows that no briefs filed in the Court of Appeal in criminal appeals or in original proceedings should be served on the Supreme Court.

Ref.: Cal. Fms Pl. & Pr., Ch. 18, "Alcoholic Beverage Licenses," Ch. 22, "Amicus Curiae," Ch. 40, "Appeal: An Overview," Ch. 44, "Appeal: Preparing and Filing the Record," Ch. 46, "Appeal: Extending or Shortening Time," Ch. 47, "Appeal: Relief From Default," Ch. 48, "Appeal: Abandonment, Dismissal, and Stipulated Reversal," Ch. 50, "Appeal: Briefs," Ch. 51, "Appeal: Hearing and Decision," Ch. 52, "Appeal: Rehearing," Ch. 54, "Appeal: California Supreme Court Review," Ch. 243, "Elections."

Rule 8.216. Appeals in which a party is both appellant and respondent

(a) Briefing sequence and time to file briefs

In an appeal in which any party is both an appellant and a respondent:

(1) The parties must jointly—or separately if unable to agree—submit a proposed briefing sequence to the reviewing court within 20 days after the second notice of appeal is filed.

(2) After receiving the proposal, the reviewing court must order a briefing sequence and prescribe briefing periods consistent with rule 8.212(a).

(3) Extensions of time are governed by rule 8.212(b).

(Subd (a) amended effective January 1, 2007.)

(b) Contents of briefs

(1) A party that is both an appellant and a respondent must combine its respondent's brief with its appellant's opening brief or its reply brief, if any, whichever is appropriate under the briefing sequence that the reviewing court orders.

(2) A combined brief must address **the points raised in** each appeal separately **but may include a single summary of the significant facts**.

(3) A party must confine a reply brief, or the reply portion of a combined brief, to points raised in its appeal.

(Subd (b) amended effective January 1, 2009; previously amended effective January 1, 2007.)

Rule 8.216 amended effective January 1, 2009; repealed and adopted as rule 16 effective January 1, 2002; previously amended and renumbered effective January 1, 2007.

Advisory Committee Comment

Rule 8.216 applies, first, to all cases in which opposing parties both appeal from the judgment. In addition, it applies to all cases in which one party appeals from the judgment and another party appeals from any appealable order arising from or related to the judgment, i.e., not only orders contemplated by rule 8.108 (denying a motion for judgment notwithstanding the verdict) but also, for example, posttrial orders granting or denying attorney fees. The purpose of the rule is to provide, in all such appeals, a single unified procedure for resolving uncertainties as to the order in which the parties must file their briefs.

As used in this rule, "appellant" includes cross-appellant and "respondent" includes cross-respondent. (Compare rule 8.100(e).)

Subdivision (a). Subdivision (a) implements the above-stated purpose by providing a procedure for determining both the briefing *sequence*—i.e., the order in which the parties must file their briefs—and the briefing *periods*—i.e., the periods of time (e.g., 30 days or 70 days, etc.) within which the briefs must be filed. Subdivision (a)(1) places the burden on the parties in the first instance to propose a briefing sequence, jointly if possible but separately if not. The purpose of this requirement is to assist the reviewing court by giving it the benefit of the parties' views on what is the most efficient briefing sequence in the circumstances of the case. Subdivision (a)(2) then prescribes the role of the reviewing court: after considering the parties' proposal, the court will decide on the briefing sequence, prescribe the briefing periods, and notify the parties of both. The reviewing court, of course, may thereafter modify its order just as it may do in a single-appeal case. Extensions of time are governed by rule 8.212(b).

Subdivision (b). The purpose of subdivision (b)(2) is to ensure that in its reply brief a party addresses only issues germane to its own appeal. For example, a cross-appellant may not use its *cross-appellant's* reply brief to answer points raised in the *appellant's* reply brief.

Ref.: Cal. Fms Pl. & Pr., Ch. 40, "Appeal: An Overview," Ch. 46, "Appeal: Extending or Shortening Time," Ch. 50, "Appeal: Briefs," Ch. 524, "Shortening and Extension of Time."

Rule 8.220. Failure to file a brief

(a) Notice to file

If a party fails to timely file an appellant's opening brief or a respondent's brief, the reviewing court clerk must promptly notify the party by mail that the brief must be filed within 15 days after the notice is mailed and that if the party fails to comply, the court may impose one of the following sanctions:

(1) If the brief is an appellant's opening brief, the court may dismiss the appeal;

(2) If the brief is a respondent's brief, the court may decide the appeal on the record, the opening brief, and any oral argument by the appellant.

(Subd (a) amended effective January 1, 2008; previously amended effective January 1, 2007.)

(b) Combined brief

A party that is both an appellant and a respondent under rule 8.216 may file its combined respondent's brief and appellant's reply brief within the period specified in the notice under (a).

(Subd (b) amended effective January 1, 2007.)

(c) Sanction

If a party fails to file the brief as specified in a notice under (a), the court may impose the sanction specified in the notice.

(Subd (c) amended effective January 1, 2008.)

(d) Extension of time

Within the period specified in the notice under (a), a party may apply to the presiding justice for an extension of that period for good cause. If the extension is granted and the brief is not filed within the extended period, the court may impose the sanction under (c) without further notice.

Rule 8.220 amended effective January 1, 2008; repealed and adopted as rule 17 effective January 1, 2002; previously amended and renumbered effective January 1, 2007.

Advisory Committee Comment

Subdivision (a). Subdivision (a) applies to all appellant's opening briefs and respondent's briefs, but does not apply to reply briefs.

A brief is "timely" under subdivision (a) if it is filed within the normal rule time prescribed for that brief or any extension of that time.

A party that fails to timely file a required brief need not make a formal motion to permit a late filing (e.g., under rule 8.60(d)); it is sufficient to file the brief within the 15-day grace period specified in the notice under subdivision (a).

Subdivision (d). Subdivision (d) clarifies that a party seeking an extension of time from the presiding justice must proceed by application under rule 8.50 rather than by motion under rule 8.54. In conformity with current practice, the subdivision also clarifies that if a brief is not filed within an extension granted by the court, the court may impose sanctions without further notice.

Ref.: Cal. Fms Pl. & Pr., Ch. 44, "Appeal: Preparing and Filing the Record," Ch. 47, "Appeal: Relief From Default," Ch. 48, "Appeal: Abandonment, Dismissal, and Stipulated Reversal," Ch. 50, "Appeal: Briefs," Ch. 51, "Appeal: Hearing and Decision"; W. Cal. Sum., 10 "Parent and Child" §715.

Rule 8.224. Transmitting exhibits

(a) Notice of designation

(1) Within 10 days after the last respondent's brief is filed or could be filed under rule 8.220, a party wanting the reviewing court to consider any original exhibits that were admitted in evidence, refused, or lodged but that were not copied in the clerk's transcript under rule 8.122 or the appendix under rule 8.124 must serve and file a notice in superior court designating such exhibits.

(2) Within 10 days after a notice under (1) is served, any other party wanting the reviewing court to consider additional exhibits must serve and file a notice in superior court designating such exhibits.

(3) A party filing a notice under (1) or (2) must serve a copy on the reviewing court.

(Subd (a) amended effective January 1, 2008; previously amended effective January 1, 2007.)

(b) Transmittal

Unless the reviewing court orders otherwise, within 20 days after the first notice under (a) is filed:

(1) The superior court clerk must put any designated exhibits in the clerk's possession into numerical or alphabetical order and send them to the reviewing court with two copies of a list of the exhibits sent. If the reviewing court clerk finds the list correct, the clerk must sign and return one copy to the superior court clerk.

(2) Any party in possession of designated exhibits returned by the superior court must put them into numerical or alphabetical order and send them to the reviewing court with two copies of a list of the exhibits sent. If the reviewing court clerk finds the list correct, the clerk must sign and return one copy to the party.

(c) Application for later transmittal

After the periods specified in (a) have expired, a party may apply to the reviewing court for permission to send an exhibit to that court.

(d) Request and return by reviewing court

At any time the reviewing court may direct the superior court or a party to send it an exhibit. On request, the reviewing court may return an exhibit to the superior court or to the party that sent it. When the remittitur issues, the reviewing court must return all exhibits to the superior court or to the party that sent them.

Rule 8.224 amended effective January 1, 2008; repealed and adopted as rule 18 effective January 1, 2002; previously amended and renumbered effective January 1, 2007.

Advisory Committee Comment

Subdivision (b). Subdivision (b)(2) provides a procedure by which parties send designated exhibits directly to the reviewing court in cases in which the superior court has returned the exhibits to the parties under Code of Civil Procedure section 1952 or other provision. (See also rule 8.122(a)(3).)

Subdivision (c). Subdivision (c) addresses the case in which a party's need to designate a certain exhibit does not arise until after the period specified in subdivision (a) has expired—for example, when the appellant makes a point in its reply brief that the respondent reasonably believes justifies the reviewing court's consideration of an exhibit it had not previously designated. In that event, the subdivision authorizes the party to apply to the reviewing court for permission to send the exhibit on a showing of good cause.

Ref.: Cal. Fms Pl. & Pr., Ch. 40, "Appeal: An Overview," Ch. 44, "Appeal: Preparing and Filing the Record"; W. Cal. Sum., 10 "Parent and Child" §713.

Article 4
Hearing and Decision in the Court of Appeal

Rule 8.240. Calendar preference
Rule 8.244. Settlement, abandonment, voluntary dismissal, and compromise
Rule 8.248. Prehearing conference
Rule 8.252. Judicial notice; findings and evidence on appeal
Rule 8.256. Oral argument and submission of the cause
Rule 8.260. Opinions [Reserved]
Rule 8.264. Filing, finality, and modification of decision
Rule 8.268. Rehearing
Rule 8.272. Remittitur
Rule 8.276. Sanctions
Rule 8.278. Costs on appeal

Rule 8.240. Calendar preference

A party seeking calendar preference must promptly serve and file a motion for preference in the reviewing court. As used in this rule, "calendar preference" means an expedited appeal schedule, which may include expedited briefing and preference in setting the date of oral argument.

Rule 8.240 amended and renumbered effective January 1, 2007; repealed and adopted as rule 19 effective January 1, 2003.

Advisory Committee Comment

Rule 8.240 requires a party claiming preference to file a motion for preference in the reviewing court. The motion requirement relieves the reviewing court of the burden of searching the record to determine if preference should be ordered. The requirement is not intended to bar the court from ordering preference without a motion when the ground is apparent on the face of the appeal, e.g., in appeals from judgments of dependency (Welf. & Inst. Code, §395).

The rule is broad in scope: it includes motions for preference on the grounds (1) that a statute provides for preference in the reviewing court (e.g., Code Civ. Proc., §§44 [probate proceedings, contested elections, libel by public official], 45 [judgment freeing minor from parental custody]); (2) that the reviewing court should exercise its discretion to grant preference when a statute provides for trial preference (e.g., *id.,* §§35 [certain election matters], 36 [party over 70 and in poor health; party with terminal illness; minor in wrongful death action]; see *Warren v. Schecter* (1997) 57 Cal.App.4th 1189, 1198–1199); and (3) that the reviewing court should exercise its discretion to grant preference on a nonstatutory ground (e.g., economic hardship).

Because valid grounds for preference could arise after the filing of the reply brief, e.g., a diagnosis of terminal illness, the rule requires the motion to be filed "promptly," i.e., as soon as the ground for preference arises.

Ref.: Cal. Fms Pl. & Pr., Ch. 40, "Appeal: An Overview," Ch. 45, "Appeal: Motion Procedure," Ch. 50, "Appeal: Briefs," Ch. 51, "Appeal: Hearing and Decision."

Rule 8.244. Settlement, abandonment, voluntary dismissal, and compromise

(a) Notice of settlement

(1) If a civil case settles after a notice of appeal has been filed either as a whole or as to any party, the appellant who has settled must immediately serve and file a notice of settlement in the Court of Appeal. If the parties have designated a clerk's or a reporter's transcript and the record has not been filed in the Court of Appeal, the appellant must also immediately serve a copy of the notice on the superior court clerk.

(2) If the case settles after the appellant receives a notice setting oral argument or a prehearing conference, the appellant must also immediately notify the Court of Appeal of the settlement by telephone or other expeditious method.

(3) Within 45 days after filing a notice of settlement—unless the court has ordered a longer time period on a showing of good cause—the appellant who filed the notice of settlement must file either an abandonment under (b), if the record has not yet been filed in the Court of Appeal, or a request to dismiss under (c), if the record has already been filed in the Court of Appeal.

(4) If the appellant does not file an abandonment, a request to dismiss, or a letter stating good cause why the appeal should not be dismissed within the time period specified under (3), the court may dismiss the appeal as to that appellant and order each side to bear its own costs on appeal.

(5) This subdivision does not apply to settlements requiring findings to be made by the Court of Appeal under Code of Civil Procedure section 128(a)(8).

(Subd (a) amended effective January 1, 2007; previously amended effective January 1, 2006.)

(b) Abandonment

(1) Before the record is filed in the Court of Appeal, the appellant may serve and file in superior court an abandonment of the appeal or a stipulation to abandon the appeal. The filing effects a dismissal of the appeal and restores the superior court's jurisdiction.

(2) The superior court clerk must promptly notify the Court of Appeal and the parties of the abandonment or stipulation.

(c) Request to dismiss

(1) After the record is filed in the Court of Appeal, the appellant may serve and file in that court a request or a stipulation to dismiss the appeal.

(2) On receipt of a request or stipulation to dismiss, the court may dismiss the appeal and direct immediate issuance of the remittitur.

(d) Approval of compromise

If a guardian or conservator seeks approval of a proposed compromise of a pending appeal, the Court of Appeal may, before ruling on the compromise, direct the trial court to determine whether the compromise is in the minor's or the conservatee's best interests and to report its findings.

Rule 8.244 amended and renumbered effective January 1, 2007; repealed and adopted as rule 20 effective January 1, 2003; previously amended effective January 1, 2006.

Ref.: Cal. Fms Pl. & Pr., Ch. 40, "Appeal: An Overview," Ch. 42, "Appeal: Notice of Appeal," Ch. 44, "Appeal: Preparing and Filing the Record," Ch. 45, "Appeal: Motion Procedure," Ch. 48, "Appeal: Abandonment, Dismissal, and Stipulated Reversal," Ch. 50, "Appeal: Briefs," Ch. 51, "Appeal: Hearing and Decision," Ch. 520, "Settlement and Release," Ch. 533, "Stipulations"; MB Prac. Guide: Cal. Pretrial Proc., §37.51; W. Cal. Sum., 10 "Parent and Child" §709.

Rule 8.248. Prehearing conference

(a) Statement and conference

After the notice of appeal is filed in a civil case, the presiding justice may:

(1) Order one or more parties to serve and file a concise statement describing the nature of the case and the issues presented; and

(2) Order all necessary persons to attend a conference to consider a narrowing of the issues, settlement, and other relevant matters.

(Subd (a) amended effective January 1, 2007.)

(b) Agreement

An agreement reached in a conference must be signed by the parties and filed. Unless the Court of Appeal orders otherwise, the agreement governs the appeal.

(c) Proceedings after conference

(1) Unless allowed by a filed agreement, no matter recited in a statement under (a)(1) or discussed in a conference under (a)(2) may be considered in any subsequent proceeding in the appeal other than in another conference.

(2) Neither the presiding officer nor any court personnel present at a conference may participate in or influence the determination of the appeal.

(d) Time to file brief

The time to file a party's brief under rule 8.212(a) is tolled from the date the Court of Appeal mails notice of the conference until the date it mails notice that the conference is concluded.

(Subd (d) amended effective January 1, 2007.)
Rule 8.248 amended and renumbered effective January 1, 2007; repealed and adopted as rule 21 effective January 1, 2003.

Advisory Committee Comment

Subdivision (a). Subdivision (a)(1) requires each party to *serve* any statement it files. (Cf. rule 3.1380(c) [pretrial settlement conference statement must be served on each party].) The service requirement is not intended to prohibit the presiding justice from ordering the parties to submit additional, confidential material in appropriate cases.

Subdivision (d). If a prehearing conference is ordered before the due date of the appellant's opening brief, the time to file the brief is not *extended* but *tolled*, in order to avoid unwarranted lengthening of the briefing process. For example, if the conference is ordered 15 days after the start of the normal 30-day briefing period, the rule simply *suspends* the running of that period; when the period resumes, the party will not receive an automatic extension of a full 30 days but rather the remaining 15 days of the original briefing period, unless the period is otherwise extended.

Under subdivision (d) the tolling period continues "until the date [the Court of Appeal] mails notice that the conference is *concluded*" (italics added). This provision is intended to accommodate the possibility that the conference may not conclude on the date it begins.

Whether or not the conference concludes on the date it begins, subdivision (d) requires the Court of Appeal clerk to mail the parties a notice that the conference is concluded. This provision is intended to facilitate the calculation of the new briefing due dates.

Ref.: Cal. Fms Pl. & Pr., Ch. 50, "Appeal: Briefs," Ch. 51, "Appeal: Hearing and Decision," Ch. 71, "Attorney Discipline," Ch. 533, "Stipulations."

Rule 8.252.   Judicial notice; findings and evidence on appeal

(a) Judicial notice

(1) To obtain judicial notice by a reviewing court under Evidence Code section 459, a party must serve and file a separate motion with a proposed order.

(2) **The motion must state:**

(A) Why the matter to be noticed is relevant to the appeal;

(B) Whether the matter to be noticed was presented to the trial court and, if so, whether judicial notice was taken by that court; and

(C) Whether the matter to be noticed relates to proceedings occurring after the order or judgment that is the subject of the appeal.

(3) If the matter to be noticed is not in the record, the party must serve and file a copy with the motion or explain why it is not practicable to do so.

(Subd (a) amended effective January 1, 2009.)

(b) Findings on appeal

A party may move that the reviewing court make findings under Code of Civil Procedure section 909. The motion must include proposed findings.

(c) Evidence on appeal

(1) A party may move that the reviewing court take evidence.

(2) An order granting the motion must:

(A) State the issues on which evidence will be taken;

(B) Specify whether the court, a justice, or a special master or referee will take the evidence; and

(C) Give notice of the time and place for taking the evidence.

(3) For documentary evidence, a party may offer the original, a certified copy, or a photocopy. The court may admit the document in evidence without a hearing.

(Subd (c) amended effective January 1, 2007.)
Rule 8.252 amended effective January 1, 2009; repealed and adopted as rule 22 effective January 1, 2003; previously amended and renumbered effective January 1, 2007.

Advisory Committee Comment

Subdivisions (b) and (c). Although appellate courts are authorized to take evidence and make findings of fact on appeal by Code of Civil Procedure section 909 and this rule, this authority should be exercised sparingly. (See *In re Zeth S.* (2003) 31 Cal.4th 396.)

Ref.: Cal. Fms Pl. & Pr., Ch. 40, "Appeal: An Overview," Ch. 44, "Appeal: Preparing and Filing the Record," Ch. 45, "Appeal: Motion Procedure," Ch. 50, "Appeal: Briefs," Ch. 51, "Appeal: Hearing and Decision," Ch. 321, "Judicial Notice," Ch. 529, "Statement of Decision."

Rule 8.256.   Oral argument and submission of the cause

(a) Frequency and location of argument

(1) Each Court of Appeal and division must hold a session at least once each quarter.

(2) A Court of Appeal may hold sessions at places in its district other than the court's permanent location.

(3) Subject to approval by the Chair of the Judicial Council, a Court of Appeal may hold a session in another district to hear a cause transferred to it from that district.

(b) Notice of argument

The Court of Appeal clerk must send a notice of the time and place of oral argument to all parties at least 20 days before the argument date. The presiding justice may shorten the notice period for good cause; in that event, the clerk must immediately notify the parties by telephone or other expeditious method.

(c) Conduct of argument

Unless the court provides otherwise by local rule or order:

(1) The appellant, petitioner, or moving party has the right to open and close. If there are two or more such parties, the court must set the sequence of argument.

(2) Each side is allowed 30 minutes for argument. If multiple parties are represented by separate counsel, or if an amicus curiae—on written request—is granted permission to argue, the court may apportion or expand the time.

(3) Only one counsel may argue for each separately represented party.

(d) When the cause is submitted

(1) A cause is submitted when the court has heard oral argument or approved its waiver and the time has expired to file all briefs and papers, including any supplemental brief permitted by the court.

(2) If the Supreme Court transfers a cause to the Court of Appeal and supplemental briefs may be filed under rule 8.200(b), the cause is submitted when the last such brief is or could be timely filed. The Court of Appeal may order the cause submitted at an earlier time if the parties so stipulate.

(Subd (d) amended effective January 1, 2007.)

(e) Vacating submission

(1) Except as provided in (2), the court may vacate submission only by an order stating its reasons and setting a timetable for resubmission.

(2) If a cause is submitted under (d)(2), an order setting oral argument vacates submission and the cause is resubmitted when the court has heard oral argument or approved its waiver.

(Subd (e) amended effective January 1, 2007.)

Rule 8.256 amended and renumbered effective January 1, 2007; repealed and adopted as rule 23 effective January 1, 2003.

Ref.: Cal. Fms Pl. & Pr., Ch. 40, "Appeal: An Overview," Ch. 48, "Appeal: Abandonment, Dismissal, and Stipulated Reversal," Ch. 51, "Appeal: Hearing and Decision," Ch. 54, "Appeal: California Supreme Court Review," Ch. 71, "Attorney Discipline."

Rule 8.260.   Opinions [Reserved]
Rule 8.260 adopted effective January 1, 2007.

Rule 8.264.   Filing, finality, and modification of decision

(a) Filing the decision

(1) The Court of Appeal clerk must promptly file all opinions and orders of the court and promptly send copies showing the filing date to the parties and, when relevant, to the lower court or tribunal.

(2) A decision by opinion must identify the participating justices, including the author of the majority opinion and of any concurring or dissenting opinion, or the justices participating in a "by the court" opinion.

(b) Finality of decision

(1) Except as otherwise provided in this rule, a Court of Appeal decision **in a civil appeal**, including an order dismissing an appeal involuntarily, is final in that court 30 days after filing.

(2) The following Court of Appeal decisions are final in that court on filing:

(A) [1] The denial of a petition for writ of supersedeas; **and**

[2] **(B)** The dismissal of an appeal on request or stipulation.

(3) [3] If a Court of Appeal certifies its opinion for publication or partial publication after filing its decision and before its decision becomes final in that court, the finality period runs from the filing date of the order for publication.

(Subd (b) amended effective January 1, 2009; previously amended effective January 1, 2007.)

Rule 8.264(b).   2008 Deletes. [1] The denial of a petition for a writ within the court's original jurisdiction without issuance of an alternative writ or order to show cause; (B) **[2]** (C) The denial of an application for bail or to reduce bail pending appeal; (D) The denial of a transfer of a case within the appellate jurisdiction of the superior court; and (E) **[3]** If necessary to prevent mootness or frustration of the relief granted or to otherwise promote the interests of justice, a Court of Appeal may order early finality in that court of a decision granting a petition for a writ within its original jurisdiction or denying such a petition after issuing an alternative writ or order to show cause. The decision may provide for finality in that court on filing or within a stated period of less than 30 days. (4) A Court of Appeal decision denying a petition for writ of habeas corpus without issuing an order to show cause is final in that court on the same day that its decision in a related appeal is final if the two decisions are filed on the same day. If the Court of Appeal orders rehearing of the decision in the appeal, its decision denying the petition for writ of habeas corpus is final when its decision on rehearing is final. (5)

(c) Modification of decision

(1) A reviewing court may modify a decision until the decision is final in that court. If the clerk's office is closed on the date of finality, the court may modify the decision on the next day the clerk's office is open.

(2) An order modifying an opinion must state whether it changes the appellate judgment. A modification that does not change the appellate judgment does not extend the finality date of the decision. If a modification changes the appellate judgment, the finality period runs from the filing date of the modification order.

(d) Consent to increase or decrease in amount of judgment

If a Court of Appeal decision conditions the affirmance of a money judgment on a party's consent to an increase or decrease in the amount, the judgment is reversed unless, before the decision is final under (b), the party serves and files two copies of a consent in the Court of Appeal. If a consent is filed, the finality period runs from the filing date of the consent. The clerk must send one file-stamped copy of the consent to the superior court with the remittitur.

Rule 8.264 amended effective January 1, 2009; repealed and adopted as rule 24 effective January 1, 2003; previously amended and renumbered effective January 1, 2007.

Advisory Committee Comment

Subdivision (b). As used in subdivision (b)(1), "decision" includes all interlocutory orders of the Court of Appeal. (See Advisory Committee Comment to rule 8.500(a) and (e).) This provision addresses the finality of decisions in civil appeals and, through a cross-reference in rule 8.470, in juvenile appeals. See rule 8.366 for provisions addressing the finality of decisions in proceedings under chapter 3, relating to criminal appeals; rule 8.387 for provisions addressing finality of decisions under chapter 4, relating to habeas corpus proceedings; and rule 8.490 for provisions addressing the finality of decisions in proceedings under chapter 7, relating to writs of mandate, certiorari, and prohibition.

Subdivision (b)(3) provides that a postfiling decision of the Court of Appeal to publish its opinion in whole under rule 8.1105(c) or in part under rule 8.1100(a) restarts the 30-day finality period. This provision is based on rule 40-2 of the United States Circuit Rules (9th Cir.). It is intended to allow parties sufficient time to petition the Court of Appeal for rehearing and/or the Supreme Court for review—and to allow potential amici curiae sufficient time to express their views—when the Court of Appeal changes the publication status of an opinion. The rule thus recognizes that the publication status of an opinion may affect a party's decision whether to file a petition for rehearing and/or a petition for review.

Ref.: Cal. Fms Pl. & Pr., Ch. 40, "Appeal: An Overview," Ch. 41, "Appeal: Review Standards and Appellate Rules of Law," Ch. 48, "Appeal: Abandonment, Dismissal, and Stipulated Reversal," Ch. 51, "Appeal: Hearing and Decision," Ch. 52, "Appeal: Rehearing," Ch. 53, "Appeal: Remittitur and Costs on Appeal," Ch. 54, "Appeal: California Supreme Court Review," Ch. 71, "Attorney Discipline," Ch. 324, "Jurisdiction: Subject Matter Jurisdiction," Ch. 358, "Mandate and Prohibition," Ch. 417, "Points and Authorities," Ch. 492, "Review (Certiorari), Writ of," Ch. 524, "Shortening and Extension of Time"; MB Prac. Guide: Cal. Pretrial Proc., §10.04[3]; W. Cal. Sum., 2 "Workers' Compensation" §440.

Rule 8.268. Rehearing

(a) Power to order rehearing

(1) On petition of a party or on its own motion, a reviewing court may order rehearing of any decision that is not final in that court on filing.

(2) An order for rehearing must be filed before the decision is final. If the clerk's office is closed on the date of finality, the court may file the order on the next day the clerk's office is open.

(b) Petition and answer

(1) A party may serve and file a petition for rehearing within 15 days after:

(A) The filing of the decision;

(B) A publication order restarting the finality period under rule [1] **8.264(b)(3)**, if the party has not already filed a petition for rehearing;

(C) A modification order changing the appellate judgment under rule 8.264(c)(2); or

(D) The filing of a consent under rule 8.264(d).

(2) A party must not file an answer to a petition for rehearing unless the court requests an answer. The clerk must promptly send to the parties copies of any order requesting an answer and immediately notify the parties by telephone or another expeditious method. Any answer must be served and filed within 8 days after the order is filed unless the court orders otherwise. A petition for rehearing normally will not be granted unless the court has requested an answer.

(3) The petition and answer must comply with the relevant provisions of rule 8.204.

(4) Before the decision is final and for good cause, the presiding justice may relieve a party from a failure to file a timely petition or answer.

(Subd (b) amended effective January 1, 2009; previously amended effective January 1, 2004, and January 1, 2007.)

Rule 8.268(b). 2008 Deletes. [1] 8.264(b)(5)

(c) No extension of time

The time for granting or denying a petition for rehearing in the Court of Appeal may not be extended. If the court does not rule on the petition before the decision is final, the petition is deemed denied.

(d) Effect of granting rehearing

An order granting a rehearing vacates the decision and any opinion filed in the case and sets the cause at large in the Court of Appeal.

Rule 8.268 amended effective January 1, 2009; repealed and adopted as rule 25 effective January 1, 2003; previously amended effective January 1, 2004; previously amended and renumbered effective January 1, 2007.

Ref.: Cal. Fms Pl. & Pr., Ch. 40, "Appeal: An Overview," Ch. 46, "Appeal: Extending or Shortening Time," Ch. 47, "Appeal: Relief From Default," Ch. 50, "Appeal: Briefs," Ch. 52, "Appeal: Rehearing," Ch. 53, "Appeal: Remittitur and Costs on Appeal," Ch. 54, "Appeal: California Supreme Court Review," Ch. 71, "Attorney Discipline," Ch. 358, "Mandate and Prohibition," Ch. 492, "Review (Certiorari), Writ of"; MB Prac. Guide: Cal. Pretrial Proc., §10.04[3]; W. Cal. Sum., 2 "Workers' Compensation" §440.

Rule 8.272. Remittitur

(a) Issuance of remittitur

A Court of Appeal must issue a remittitur after a decision in an appeal.

(Subd (a) amended effective January 1, 2008; previously amended effective January 1, 2007.)

(b) Clerk's duties

(1) If a Court of Appeal decision is not reviewed by the Supreme Court:

(A) The Court of Appeal clerk must issue a remittitur immediately after the Supreme Court denies review, or the period for granting review expires, or the court dismisses review under rule 8.528(b); and

(B) The clerk must send the lower court or tribunal the Court of Appeal remittitur and a file-stamped copy of the opinion or order.

(2) After Supreme Court review of a Court of Appeal decision:

(A) On receiving the Supreme Court remittitur, the Court of Appeal clerk must issue a remittitur immediately if there will be no further proceedings in the Court of Appeal; and

(B) The clerk must send the lower court or tribunal the Court of Appeal remittitur, a copy of the Supreme Court remittitur, and a file-stamped copy of the Supreme Court opinion or order.

(Subd (b) amended effective January 1, 2007.)

(c) Immediate issuance, stay, and recall

(1) A Court of Appeal may direct immediate issuance of a remittitur only on the parties' stipulation or on dismissal of the appeal under rule 8.244(c)(2).

(2) On a party's or its own motion or on stipulation, and for good cause, the court may stay a remittitur's issuance for a reasonable period or order its recall.

(3) An order recalling a remittitur issued after a decision by opinion does not supersede the opinion or affect its publication status.

(Subd (c) amended effective January 1, 2007.)

(d) Notice

(1) The remittitur is deemed issued when the clerk enters it in the record. The clerk must immediately send the parties notice of issuance of the remittitur, showing the date of entry.

(2) If, without requiring further proceedings in the trial court, the decision changes the length of a state prison sentence, applicable credits, or the maximum permissible confinement to the Department of Corrections and Rehabilitation, Division of Juvenile Justice, the clerk must send a copy of the remittitur and opinion or order to either the Department of Corrections and Rehabilitation or the Division of Juvenile Justice.

(Subd (d) amended effective January 1, 2007.)

Rule 8.272 amended effective January 1, 2009; repealed and adopted as rule 26 effective January 1, 2003; previously amended effective January 1, 2007, and January 1, 2008.

Advisory Committee Comment

See rule 8.386 for provisions addressing remittitur in habeas corpus proceedings and rule 8.490 for provisions addressing remittitur in other writ proceedings.

Ref.: Cal. Fms Pl. & Pr., Ch. 40, "Appeal: An Overview," Ch. 44, "Appeal: Preparing and Filing the Record," Ch. 45, "Appeal: Motion Procedure," Ch. 48, "Appeal: Abandonment, Dismissal, and Stipulated Reversal," Ch. 51, "Appeal: Hearing and Decision," Ch. 53, "Appeal: Remittitur and Costs on Appeal," Ch. 54, "Appeal: California Supreme Court Review," Ch. 317, "Judges," Ch. 492, "Review (Certiorari), Writ of."

Rule 8.276. Sanctions

(a) Grounds for sanctions

On motion of a party or its own motion, a Court of Appeal may impose sanctions, including the award or denial of costs under rule 8.278, on a party or an attorney for:

(1) Taking a frivolous appeal or appealing solely to cause delay;

(2) Including in the record any matter not reasonably material to the appeal's determination;

(3) Filing a frivolous motion; or

(4) Committing any other unreasonable violation of these rules.

(Subd (a) amended and relettered effective January 1, 2008; adopted as subd (e) effective January 1, 2003; previously amended effective January 1, 2007.)

(b) Motions for sanctions

(1) A party's motion under (a) must include a declaration supporting the amount of any monetary sanction sought and must be served and filed before any order dismissing the appeal but no later than 10 days after the appellant's reply brief is due.

(2) If a party files a motion for sanctions with a motion to dismiss the appeal and the motion to dismiss is not granted, the party may file a new motion for sanctions within 10 days after the appellant's reply brief is due.

(Subd (b) amended and lettered effective January 1, 2008; adopted as part of subd (e) effective January 1, 2003; previously amended effective January 1, 2007.)

(c) Notice

The court must give notice in writing if it is considering imposing sanctions.

(Subd (c) amended and lettered effective January 1, 2008; adopted as part of subd (e) effective January 1, 2003; previously amended effective January 1, 2007.)

(d) Opposition

Within 10 days after the court sends such notice, a party or attorney may serve and file an opposition, but failure to do so will not be deemed consent. An opposition may not be filed unless the court sends such notice.

(Subd (d) amended and lettered effective January 1, 2008; adopted as part of subd (e) effective January 1, 2003; previously amended effective January 1, 2007.)

(e) Oral argument

Unless otherwise ordered, oral argument on the issue of sanctions must be combined with oral argument on the merits of the appeal.

(Subd (e) amended and lettered effective January 1, 2008; adopted as part of subd (e) effective January 1, 2003; previously amended effective January 1, 2007.)

Rule 8.276 amended effective January 1, 2008; repealed and adopted as rule 27 effective January 1, 2003; previously amended and renumbered effective January 1, 2007.

Ref.: Cal. Fms Pl. & Pr., Ch. 40, "Appeal: An Overview," Ch. 44, "Appeal: Preparing and Filing the Record," Ch. 45, "Appeal: Motion Procedure," Ch. 48, "Appeal: Abandonment, Dismissal, and Stipulated Reversal," Ch. 49, "Appeal: Sanctions," Ch. 50, "Appeal: Briefs," Ch. 51, "Appeal: Hearing and Decision," Ch. 52, "Appeal: Rehearing," Ch. 53, "Appeal: Remittitur and Costs on Appeal," Ch. 54, "Appeal: California Supreme Court Review," Ch. 174, "Costs and Attorney's Fees," Ch. 226, "Dissolution of Marriage: Attorney's Fees," Ch. 345A, "Limited Civil Cases," Ch. 510, "Sanctions," Ch. 526, "Small Claims"; MB Prac. Guide: Cal. Trial & Post-Trial Civ. Proc., §§25A.20[3], 25A.25, 25A.33[2], 29.69[3][f]; W. Cal. Sum., 14 "Wills and Probate" §400.

Rule 8.278. Costs on appeal

(a) Award of costs

(1) Except as provided in this rule, the party prevailing in the Court of Appeal in a civil case other than a juvenile case is entitled to costs on appeal.

(2) The prevailing party is the respondent if the Court of Appeal affirms the judgment without modification or dismisses the appeal. The prevailing party is the appellant if the court reverses the judgment in its entirety.

(3) If the Court of Appeal reverses the judgment in part or modifies it, or if there is more than one notice of appeal, the opinion must specify the award or denial of costs.

(4) In probate cases, the prevailing party must be awarded costs unless the Court of Appeal orders otherwise, but the superior court must decide who will pay the award.

(5) In the interests of justice, the Court of Appeal may also award or deny costs as it deems proper.

(Subd (a) adopted effective January 1, 2008.)

(b) Judgment for costs

(1) The Court of Appeal clerk must enter on the record, and insert in the remittitur, a judgment awarding costs to the prevailing party under (a)(2) or as directed by the court under (a)(3), (a)(4), or (a)(5).

(2) If the clerk fails to enter judgment for costs, the court may recall the remittitur for correction on its own motion, or on a party's motion made not later than 30 days after the remittitur issues.

(Subd (b) adopted effective January 1, 2008.)

(c) Procedure for claiming or opposing costs

(1) Within 40 days after the clerk sends notice of issuance of the remittitur, a party claiming costs awarded by a reviewing court must serve and file in the superior court a verified memorandum of costs under rule 3.1700.

(2) A party may serve and file a motion in the superior court to strike or tax costs claimed under (1) in the manner required by rule 3.1700.

(3) An award of costs is enforceable as a money judgment.

(Subd (c) adopted effective January 1, 2008.)

(d) Recoverable costs

(1) A party may recover only the following costs, if reasonable:

(A) Filing fees;

(B) The amount the party paid for any portion of the record, whether an original or a copy or both. The cost to copy parts of a prior record under rule 8.147(b)(2) is not recoverable unless the Court of Appeal ordered the copying;

(C) The cost to produce additional evidence on appeal;

(D) The costs to notarize, serve, mail, and file the record, briefs, and other papers;

(E) The cost to print and reproduce any brief, including any petition for rehearing or review, answer, or reply; and

(F) The cost to procure a surety bond, including the premium and the cost to obtain a letter of credit as collateral, unless the trial court determines the bond was unnecessary.

(2) Unless the court orders otherwise, an award of costs neither includes attorney's fees on appeal nor precludes a party from seeking them under rule 3.1702.

(Subd (d) adopted effective January 1, 2008.)

Rule 8.278 amended effective January 1, 2009; adopted effective January 1, 2008.

Advisory Committee Comment

This rule is not intended to expand the categories of appeals subject to the award of costs. See rule 8.493 for provisions addressing costs in writ proceedings.

Subdivision (c). Subdivision (c)(2) provides the procedure for a party to move in the trial court to strike or tax costs that another party has claimed under subdivision (c)(1). It is not intended that the trial court's authority to strike or tax unreasonable costs be limited by any failure of the moving party to move for sanctions in the Court of Appeal under rule 8.276; a party may seek to strike or tax costs on the ground that an opponent included unnecessary materials in the record even if the party did not move the Court of Appeal to sanction the opponent under that rule.

Subdivision (d). Subdivision (d)(1)(B) is intended to refer not only to a normal record prepared by the clerk and the reporter under rules 8.122 and 8.130 but also, for example, to an appendix prepared by a party under rule 8.124 and to a superior court file to which the parties stipulate under rule 8.128.

Ref.: Cal. Fms Pl. & Pr., Ch. 40, "Appeal: An Overview," Ch. 43, "Appeal: Stay of Proceedings," Ch. 49, "Appeal: Sanctions," Ch. 51, "Appeal: Hearing and Decision," Ch. 53, "Appeal: Remittitur and Costs on Appeal," Ch. 54, "Appeal: California Supreme Court Review," Ch. 174, "Costs and Attorney's Fees," Ch. 358, "Mandate and Prohibition," Ch. 492, "Review (Certiorari), Writ of."

Chapter 3
Criminal Appeals

Art. 1. Taking the Appeal. Rules 8.300–8.316.
Art. 2. Record on Appeal. Rules 8.320–8.346.
Art. 3. Briefs, Hearing, and Decision. Rules 8.360–8.368.

Article 1
Taking the Appeal

Rule 8.300. Appointment of appellate counsel by the Court of Appeal
Rule 8.304. Filing the appeal; certificate of probable cause
Rule 8.308. Time to appeal
Rule 8.312. Stay of execution and release on appeal
Rule 8.316. Abandoning the appeal

Rule 8.300. Appointment of appellate counsel by the Court of Appeal

(a) Procedures

(1) Each Court of Appeal must adopt procedures for appointing appellate counsel for indigents not represented by the State Public Defender in all cases in which indigents are entitled to appointed counsel.

(2) The procedures must require each attorney seeking appointment to complete a questionnaire showing the attorney's California State Bar number, date of admission, qualifications, and experience.

(b) List of qualified attorneys

(1) The Court of Appeal must evaluate the attorney's qualifications for appointment and, if the attorney is qualified, place the attorney's name on a list to receive appointments in appropriate cases.

(2) Each court's appointments must be based on criteria approved by the Judicial Council or its designated oversight committee.

(Subd (b) amended effective January 1, 2007.)

(c) Demands of the case

In matching counsel with the demands of the case, the Court of Appeal should consider:

(1) The length of the sentence;

(2) The complexity or novelty of the issues;

(3) The length of the trial and of the reporter's transcript; and

(4) Any questions concerning the competence of trial counsel.

(Subd (c) amended effective January 1, 2007.)

(d) Evaluation

The court must review and evaluate the performance of each appointed counsel to determine whether counsel's name should remain on the list at the same level, be placed on a different level, or be deleted from the list.

(e) Contracts to perform administrative functions

(1) The court may contract with an administrator having substantial experience in handling appellate court appointments to perform any of the duties prescribed by this rule.

(2) The court must provide the administrator with the information needed to fulfill the administrator's duties.

Rule 8.300 amended and renumbered effective January 1, 2007; repealed and adopted as rule 76.5 effective January 1, 2005.

Advisory Committee Comment

Subdivision (b). The "designated oversight committee" referred to in subdivision (b)(2) is currently the Appellate Indigent Defense Oversight Advisory Committee. The criteria approved by this committee can be found on the judicial branch's public website at www.courtinfo.ca.gov.

Rule 8.304. Filing the appeal; certificate of probable cause

(a) Notice of appeal

(1) To appeal from a judgment or an appealable order of the superior court in a felony case—other than a judgment imposing a sentence of death—the defendant or the People must file a notice of appeal in that superior court. To appeal after a plea of guilty or nolo contendere or after an admission of probation violation, the defendant must also comply with (b).

(2) As used in (1), "felony case" means any criminal action in which a felony is charged, regardless of the outcome. A felony is "charged" when an information or indictment accusing the defendant of a felony is filed or a complaint accusing the defendant of a felony is certified to the superior court under Penal Code section 859a. A felony case includes an action in which the defendant is charged with:

(A) A felony and a misdemeanor or infraction, but is convicted of only the misdemeanor or infraction;

(B) A felony, but is convicted of only a lesser offense; or

(C) An offense filed as a felony but punishable as either a felony or a misdemeanor, and the offense is thereafter deemed a misdemeanor under Penal Code section 17(b).

(3) If the defendant appeals, the defendant or the defendant's attorney must sign the notice of appeal. If the People appeal, the attorney for the People must sign the notice.

(4) The notice of appeal must be liberally construed. Except as provided in (b), the notice is sufficient if it identifies the particular judgment or order being appealed. The notice need not specify the court to which the appeal is taken; the appeal will be treated as taken to the Court of Appeal for the district in which the superior court is located.

(Subd (a) amended effective January 1, 2007.)

(b) Appeal after plea of guilty or nolo contendere or after admission of probation violation

(1) Except as provided in (4), to appeal from a superior court judgment after a plea of guilty or nolo contendere or after an admission of probation violation, the defendant must file in that superior court—with the notice of appeal required by (a)—the statement required by Penal Code section 1237.5 for issuance of a certificate of probable cause.

(2) Within 20 days after the defendant files a statement under (1), the superior court must sign and file either a certificate of probable cause or an order denying the certificate.

(3) If the defendant does not file the statement required by (1) or if the superior court denies a certificate of probable cause, the superior court clerk must mark the notice of appeal "Inoperative," notify the defendant, and send a copy of the marked notice of appeal to the district appellate project.

(4) The defendant need not comply with (1) if the notice of appeal states that the appeal is based on:

(A) The denial of a motion to suppress evidence under Penal Code section 1538.5; or

(B) Grounds that arose after entry of the plea and do not affect the plea's validity.

(5) If the defendant's notice of appeal contains a statement under (4), the reviewing court will not consider any issue affecting the validity of the plea unless the defendant also complies with (1).

(Subd (b) amended effective July 1, 2007; previously amended effective January 1, 2007.)

(c) Notification of the appeal

(1) When a notice of appeal is filed, the superior court clerk must promptly mail a notification of the filing to the attorney of record for each party, to any unrepresented defendant, to the reviewing court clerk, to each court reporter, and to any primary reporter or reporting supervisor. If the defendant also files a statement under (b)(1), the clerk must not mail the notification unless the superior court files a certificate under (b)(2).

(2) The notification must show the date it was mailed, the number and title of the case, and the dates the notice of appeal and any certificate under (b)(2) were filed. If the information is available, the notification must also include:

(A) The name, address, telephone number, and California State Bar number of each attorney of record in the case;

(B) The name of the party each attorney represented in the superior court; and

(C) The name, address, and telephone number of any unrepresented defendant.

(3) The notification to the reviewing court clerk must also include a copy of the notice of appeal, any certificate filed under (b), and the sequential list of reporters made under rule 2.950.

(4) A copy of the notice of appeal is sufficient notification under (1) if the required information is on the copy or is added by the superior court clerk.

(5) The mailing of a notification under (1) is a sufficient performance of the clerk's duty despite the discharge, disqualification, suspension, disbarment, or death of the attorney.

(6) Failure to comply with any provision of this subdivision does not affect the validity of the notice of appeal.

(Subd (c) amended effective January 1, 2007.)

Rule 8.304 amended effective July 1, 2007; repealed and adopted as rule 30 effective January 1, 2004; previously amended and renumbered effective January 1, 2007.

Advisory Committee Comment

Subdivision (a). Penal Code section 1235(b) provides that an appeal from a judgment or appealable order in a "felony case" is taken to the Court of Appeal, and Penal Code section 691(f) defines "felony case" to mean "a criminal action in which a felony is charged. . . ." Rule 8.304(a)(2) makes it clear that a "felony case" is an action in which a felony is charged *regardless of the outcome of the action.* Thus the question whether to file a notice of appeal under this rule or under the rules governing appeals to the appellate division of the superior court (rule 8.700 et seq.) is answered simply by examining the accusatory pleading: if that document charged the defendant with at least one count of felony (as defined in Penal Code, section 17(a)), the Court of Appeal has appellate jurisdiction and the appeal must be taken under this rule *even if the prosecution did not result in a punishment of imprisonment in a state prison.*

It is settled case law that an appeal is taken to the Court of Appeal not only when the defendant is charged with and convicted of a felony, but also when the defendant is charged with both a felony and a misdemeanor (Pen. Code, § 691(f)) but is convicted of only the misdemeanor (e.g., *People v. Brown* (1970) 10 Cal.App.3d 169); when the defendant is charged with a felony but is convicted of only a lesser offense (Pen. Code, § 1159; e.g., *People v. Spreckels* (1954) 125 Cal.App.2d 507); and when the defendant is charged with an offense filed as a felony but punishable as either a felony or a misdemeanor, and the offense is thereafter deemed a misdemeanor under Penal Code section 17(b) (e.g., *People v. Douglas* (1999) 20 Cal.4th 85; *People v. Clark* (1971) 17 Cal.App.3d 890).

Trial court unification did not change this rule: after as before unification, "Appeals in felony cases lie to the [C]ourt of [A]ppeal, regardless of whether the appeal is from the superior court, the municipal court, or the action of a magistrate. *Cf.* Cal. Const. art. VI, § 11(a) [except in death penalty cases, Courts of Appeal have appellate jurisdiction when superior courts have original jurisdiction 'in causes of a type within the appellate jurisdiction of the [C]ourts of [A]ppeal on June 30, 1995. . . .']." ("Recommendation on Trial Court Unification" (July 1998) 28 *Cal. Law Revision Com. Rep.* 455–56.)

Subdivision (b). Under (b)(1), the defendant is required to file both a notice of appeal and the statement required by Penal Code section 1237.5(a) for issuance of a certificate of probable cause. Requiring a notice of appeal in all cases simplifies the rule, permits compliance with the signature requirement of rule 8.304(a)(3), ensures that the defendant's intent to appeal will not be misunderstood, and makes the provision consistent with the rule in civil appeals and with current practice as exemplified in the Judicial Council form governing criminal appeals.

Because of the drastic consequences of failure to file the statement required for issuance of a certificate of probable cause in an appeal after a plea of guilty or nolo contendere or after an admission of probation violation, (b)(5) alerts appellants to a relevant rule of case law, i.e., that although such an appeal may be maintained without a certificate of probable cause if the notice of appeal states the appeal is based on the denial of a motion to suppress evidence or on grounds arising after entry of the plea and not affecting its validity (rule 8.304(b)(4)), no *issue* challenging the validity of the plea is cognizable on that appeal without a certificate of probable cause. (*People v. Mendez* (1999) 19 Cal.4th 1084, 1104.)

Rule 8.308.   Time to appeal

(a) Normal time

Except as provided in (b) or as otherwise provided by law, a notice of appeal and any statement required by Penal Code section 1237.5 must be filed within 60 days after the rendition of the judgment or the making of the order being appealed. Except as provided in rule 8.66, no court may extend the time to file a notice of appeal.

(Subd (a) amended effective July 1, 2007; previously amended effective January 1, 2005, and January 1, 2007.)

(b) Cross-appeal

If the defendant or the People timely appeals from a judgment or appealable order, the time for any other party to appeal from the same judgment or order is either the time specified in (a) or 30 days after the superior court clerk mails notification of the first appeal, whichever is later.

(Subd (b) amended effective January 1, 2008; adopted effective January 1, 2007.)

(c) Premature notice of appeal

A notice of appeal filed before the judgment is rendered or the order is made is premature, but the reviewing court may treat the notice as filed immediately after the rendition of judgment or the making of the order.

(Subd (c) relettered effective January 1, 2007; adopted as subd (b) effective January 1, 2004.)

(d) Late notice of appeal

The superior court clerk must mark a late notice of appeal "Received [date] but not filed," notify the party that the notice was not filed because it was late, and send a copy of the marked notice of appeal to the district appellate project.

(Subd (d) relettered effective January 1, 2007; adopted as subd (c) effective January 1, 2004.)

(e) Receipt by mail from custodial institution

If the superior court clerk receives a notice of appeal by mail from a custodial institution after the period specified in (a) has expired but the envelope shows that the notice was mailed or delivered to custodial officials for mailing within the period specified in (a), the notice is deemed timely. The clerk must retain in the case file the envelope in which the notice was received.

(Subd (e) relettered effective January 1, 2007; adopted as subd (d) effective January 1, 2004.)

Rule 8.308 amended effective January 1, 2008; adopted as rule 30.1 effective January 1, 2004; previously amended and renumbered effective January 1, 2007; previously amended effective January 1, 2005, and July 1, 2007.

Advisory Committee Comment

Subdivision (c). The subdivision requires the clerk to send a copy of a late notice of appeal, marked with the date it was received but not filed, to the appellate project for the district; that entity is charged with the duty, among others, of dealing with indigent criminal appeals that suffer from procedural defect, but it can do so efficiently only if it is promptly notified of such cases.

Subdivision (d). The subdivision is not intended to limit a defendant's appeal rights under the case law of constructive filing. (See, e.g., *In re Jordan* (1992) 4 Cal.4th 116; *In re Benoit* (1973) 10 Cal.3d 72.)

Ref.: Cal. Fms Pl. & Pr., Ch. 42, "Appeal: Notice of Appeal," Ch. 46, "Appeal: Extending or Shortening Time," Ch. 524, "Shortening and Extension of Time."

Rule 8.312.   Stay of execution and release on appeal

(a) Application

Pending appeal, the defendant may apply to the reviewing court:

(1) For a stay of execution after a judgment of conviction or an order granting probation; or

(2) For bail, to reduce bail, or for release on other conditions.

(Subd (a) amended effective January 1, 2007.)

(b) Showing

The application must include a showing that the defendant sought relief in the superior court and that the court unjustifiably denied the application.

(c) Service

The application must be served on the district attorney and on the Attorney General.

(d) Interim relief

Pending its ruling on the application, the reviewing court may grant the relief requested. The reviewing court must notify the superior court under rule [1] **8.489** of any stay that it grants.

(Subd (d) amended effective January 1, 2009; previously amended effective January 1, 2007.)

Rule 8.312(d).   2008 Deletes. [1] 8.490(k)

Rule 8.312 amended effective January 1, 2009; adopted as rule 30.2 effective January 1, 2004; previously amended and renumbered effective January 1, 2007.

Advisory Committee Comment

Subdivision (a). The remedy of an application for bail under (a)(2) is separate from but consistent with the statutory remedy of a petition for habeas corpus under Penal Code section 1490. (*In re Brumback* (1956) 46 Cal.2d 810, 815, fn. 3.)

An order of the Court of Appeal denying bail or reduction of bail, or for release on other conditions, is final on filing. (See rule 8.366(b)(2)(A).)

Subdivision (d). The first sentence of (d) recognizes the case law holding that a reviewing court may grant bail or reduce bail, or release the defendant on other conditions, pending its ruling on an application for that relief. (See, e.g., *In re Fishman* (1952) 109 Cal.App.2d 632, 633; *In re Keddy* (1951) 105 Cal.App.2d 215, 217.) The second sentence of the subdivision requires the reviewing court to notify the superior court under rule 8.489 when it grants either (1) a stay to preserve the status quo pending its ruling on a stay application or (2) the stay requested by that application.

Rule 8.316.   Abandoning the appeal

(a) How to abandon

An appellant may abandon the appeal at any time by filing an abandonment of the appeal signed by the appellant or the appellant's attorney of record.

(b) Where to file; effect of filing

(1) If the record has not been filed in the reviewing court, the appellant must file the abandonment in the superior court. The filing effects a dismissal of the appeal and restores the superior court's jurisdiction.

(2) If the record has been filed in the reviewing court, the appellant must file the abandonment in that court. The reviewing court may dismiss the appeal and direct immediate issuance of the remittitur.

(c) Clerk's duties

(1) The clerk of the court in which the appellant files the abandonment must immediately notify the adverse party of the filing or of the order of dismissal. If the defendant abandons the appeal, the clerk must notify both the district attorney and the Attorney General.

(2) If the appellant files the abandonment in the superior court, the clerk must immediately notify the reviewing court.

(3) The clerk must immediately notify the reporter if the appeal is abandoned before the reporter has filed the transcript.

Rule 8.316 renumbered effective January 1, 2007; adopted as rule 30.3 effective January 1, 2004.

Ref.: Cal. Fms Pl. & Pr., Ch. 36, "Judicial Arbitration"; W. Cal. Sum., 10 "Parent and Child" §709.

Article 2
Record on Appeal

Rule 8.320. Normal record; exhibits
Rule 8.324. Application in superior court for addition to normal record
Rule 8.328. Confidential records
Rule 8.332. Juror-identifying information
Rule 8.336. Preparing, certifying, and sending the record
Rule 8.340. Augmenting or correcting the record in the Court of Appeal
Rule 8.344. Agreed statement
Rule 8.346. Settled statement

Rule 8.320.   Normal record; exhibits

(a) Contents

If the defendant appeals from a judgment of conviction, or if the People appeal from an order granting a new trial, the record must contain a clerk's transcript and a reporter's transcript, which together constitute the normal record.

(b) Clerk's transcript

The clerk's transcript must contain:

(1) The accusatory pleading and any amendment;

(2) Any demurrer or other plea;

(3) All court minutes;

(4) All jury instructions that any party submitted in writing and the cover page required by rule 2.1055(b)(2) indicating the party requesting each instruction, and any written jury instructions given by the court;

(5) Any written communication between the court and the jury or any individual juror;

(6) Any verdict;

(7) Any written opinion of the court;

(8) The judgment or order appealed from and any abstract of judgment or commitment;

(9) Any motion for new trial, with supporting and opposing memoranda and attachments;

(10) The notice of appeal and any certificate of probable cause filed under rule 8.304(b);

(11) Any transcript of a sound or sound-and-video recording furnished to the jury or tendered to the court under rule 2.1040;

(12) Any application for additional record and any order on the application;

(13) And, if the appellant is the defendant:

(A) Any written defense motion denied in whole or in part, with supporting and opposing memoranda and attachments;

(B) If related to a motion under (A), any search warrant and return and the reporter's transcript of any preliminary examination or grand jury hearing;

(C) Any document admitted in evidence to prove a prior juvenile adjudication, criminal conviction, or prison term. If a record was closed to public inspection in the trial court because it is required to be kept confidential by law, it must remain closed to public inspection in the reviewing court unless that court orders otherwise; and

(D) The probation officer's report.

(Subd (b) amended effective January 1, 2008; previously amended effective January 1, 2005, and January 1, 2007.)

(c) Reporter's transcript

The reporter's transcript must contain:

(1) The oral proceedings on the entry of any plea other than a not guilty plea;

(2) The oral proceedings on any motion in limine;

(3) The oral proceedings at trial, but excluding the voir dire examination of jurors and any opening statement;

(4) All instructions given orally;

(5) Any oral communication between the court and the jury or any individual juror;

(6) Any oral opinion of the court;

(7) The oral proceedings on any motion for new trial;

(8) The oral proceedings at sentencing, granting or denying of probation, or other dispositional hearing;

(9) And, if the appellant is the defendant:

(A) The oral proceedings on any defense motion denied in whole or in part except motions for disqualification of a judge and motions under Penal Code section 995;

(B) The closing arguments; and

(C) Any comment on the evidence by the court to the jury.

(Subd (c) amended effective January 1, 2007.)

(d) Limited normal record in certain appeals

If the People appeal from a judgment on a demurrer to the accusatory pleading, or if the defendant or the People appeal from an appealable order other than a ruling on a motion for new trial, the normal record is composed of a reporter's transcript of any oral proceedings incident to the judgment or order being appealed and a clerk's transcript containing:

(1) The accusatory pleading and any amendment;

(2) Any demurrer or other plea;

(3) Any written motion or notice of motion granted or denied by the order appealed from, with supporting and opposing memoranda and attachments;

(4) The judgment or order appealed from and any abstract of judgment or commitment;

(5) Any court minutes relating to the judgment or order appealed from; and

(6) The notice of appeal.

(Subd (d) amended effective January 1, 2007.)

(e) Exhibits

Exhibits admitted in evidence, refused, or lodged are deemed part of the record, but may be transmitted to the reviewing court only as provided in rule 8.224.

(Subd (e) amended effective January 1, 2007.)

(f) Stipulation for partial transcript

If counsel for the defendant and the People stipulate in writing before the record is certified that any part of the record is not required for proper determination of the appeal, that part must not be prepared or sent to the reviewing court.

(g) Form of record

The clerk's and reporter's transcripts must comply with rule 8.144.

(Subd (g) amended effective January 1, 2007.)

Rule 8.320 amended effective January 1, 2008; repealed and adopted as rule 31 effective January 1, 2004; previously amended effective January 1, 2005; previously amended and renumbered effective January 1, 2007.

Ref.: Cal. Fms Pl. & Pr., Ch. 533, "Stipulations."

Rule 8.324. Application in superior court for addition to normal record

(a) Appeal by the People

The People, as appellant, may apply to the superior court for inclusion in the record of any item that would be part of the normal record in a defendant's appeal.

(b) Application by either party

Either the People or the defendant may apply to the superior court for inclusion in the record of any of the following items:

(1) In the clerk's transcript: any written defense motion granted in whole or in part or any written motion by the People, with supporting and opposing memoranda and attachments;

(2) In the reporter's transcript:

(A) The voir dire examination of jurors;

(B) Any opening statement; and

(C) The oral proceedings on motions other than those listed in rule 8.320(c).

(Subd (b) amended effective January 1, 2007.)

(c) Application

(1) An application for additional record must describe the material to be included and explain how it may be useful in the appeal.

(2) The application must be filed in the superior court with the notice of appeal or as soon thereafter as possible, and will be treated as denied if it is filed after the record is sent to the reviewing court.

(3) The clerk must immediately present the application to the trial judge.

(d) Order

(1) Within five days after the application is filed, the judge must order that the record include as much of the additional material as the judge finds proper to fully present the points raised by the applicant. Denial of the application does not preclude a motion in the reviewing court for augmentation under rule 8.155.

(2) If the judge does not rule on the application within the time prescribed by (1), the requested material—other than exhibits—must be included in the clerk's transcript or the reporter's transcript without a court order.

(3) The clerk must immediately notify the reporter if additions to the reporter's transcript are required under (1) or (2).

(Subd (d) amended effective January 1, 2007.)

Rule 8.324 amended and renumbered effective January 1, 2007; adopted as rule 31.1 effective January 1, 2004.

Rule 8.328. Confidential records

(a) Application

This rule applies to records required to be kept confidential by law but does not apply to records sealed under rules 2.550–2.551 or records proposed to be sealed under rule 8.160.

(Subd (a) adopted effective January 1, 2007.)

(b) *Marsden* hearing

(1) The reporter's transcript of any hearing held under *People v. Marsden* (1970) 2 Cal.3d 118 must be kept confidential. The chronological index to the reporter's transcript must include the *Marsden* hearing but list it as "CONFIDENTIAL" or the equivalent.

Rules of Court

(2) The superior court clerk must send the original and one copy of the confidential transcript to the reviewing court with the record.

(3) The superior court clerk must send one copy of the confidential transcript to the defendant's appellate counsel or, if the defendant is not yet represented by appellate counsel, to the appellate project for the district.

(4) If the defendant raises a *Marsden* issue in the opening brief, the defendant must serve and file with the brief a notice stating whether the confidential transcript contains any confidential material not relevant to the issues on appeal. If the defendant states that the transcript contains confidential material not relevant to the issues on appeal, the notice must identify the page and line numbers of the transcript containing this irrelevant material.

(5) If the defendant serves and files a notice under (4), stating that the transcript contains confidential material not relevant to the issues on appeal, the People may move to obtain a copy of any relevant portion of the confidential transcript. If the defendant serves and files a notice under (4), stating that no such irrelevant material is contained in the transcript, the reviewing court clerk must send a copy of the confidential transcript to the People.

(6) If the defendant raises a *Marsden* issue in the opening brief but does not serve and file a notice under (4), on written application the People may request a copy of the confidential transcript. Within 10 days after the application is filed, the defendant may serve and file opposition to this application on the basis that the transcript contains confidential material not relevant to the issues on appeal. Any such opposition must identify the page and line numbers of the transcript containing this irrelevant material. If the defendant does not timely serve and file opposition to the application, the reviewing court clerk must send a copy of the confidential transcript to the People.

(Subd (b) amended and relettered effective January 1, 2007; adopted as subd (a) effective January 1, 2004.)

(c) Other in-camera proceedings and confidential records

(1) Any party may apply to the superior court for an order that the record include:

(A) A confidential, separately paginated reporter's transcript of any in-camera proceeding at which a party was not allowed to be represented; and

(B) Any item that the trial court withheld from a party on the ground that it was confidential.

(2) The application and any ruling under (1) must comply with rule 8.324.

(3) If the court grants an application for a reporter's transcript of any in-camera proceeding, it may order the reporter who attended the in-camera proceeding to personally prepare the transcript. The chronological index to the reporter's transcript must include the proceeding but list it as "CONFIDENTIAL—MAY NOT BE EXAMINED WITHOUT COURT ORDER" or the equivalent.

(4) The superior court clerk must send the transcript of the in-camera proceeding or the confidential item to the reviewing court in a sealed envelope labeled "CONFIDENTIAL—MAY NOT BE EXAMINED WITHOUT COURT ORDER." The reviewing court clerk must file the envelope and store it separately from the remainder of the record.

(5) The superior court clerk must prepare an index of any material sent to the reviewing court under (4), except confidential material relating to a request for funds under Penal Code section 987.9(b), showing the date and the names of all parties present at each proceeding, but not disclosing the substance of the sealed matter, and send the index:

(A) To the People; and

(B) To the defendant's appellate counsel or, if the defendant is not yet represented by appellate counsel, to the appellate project for the district.

(6) Unless the reviewing court orders otherwise, confidential material sent to the reviewing court under (4) may be examined only by a reviewing court justice personally; but parties and their attorneys who had access to the material in the trial court may also examine it.

(Subd (c) amended and relettered effective January 1, 2007; adopted as subd (b) effective January 1, 2004; previously amended effective January 1, 2005.)

(d) Omissions

If at any time the superior court clerk or the reporter learns that the record omits material that any rule requires to be included and that this rule requires to be kept confidential:

(1) The clerk and the reporter must comply with rule 8.340(b); and

(2) The clerk must comply with the provisions of this rule requiring that the record be kept confidential and prescribing which party's counsel, if any, must receive a copy of sealed material.

(Subd (d) amended and relettered effective January 1, 2007; adopted as subd (c) effective January 1, 2004.)

Rule 8.328 amended and renumbered effective January 1, 2007; adopted as rule 31.2 effective January 1, 2004; previously amended effective January 1, 2005.

Advisory Committee Comment

Subdivision (c). Subdivision (c)(5) requires the clerk to prepare and send to the parties an index of any confidential materials sent to the reviewing court, showing the date and the names of all parties present. The purpose of this provision is to assist the parties in making—and the court in adjudicating—motions to unseal portions of the record. To protect confidentiality until a record is unsealed, however, the index must endeavor to identify the sealed matter without disclosing its substance.

Rule 8.332. Juror-identifying information

(a) Application

A clerk's transcript, a reporter's transcript, or any other document in the record that contains juror-identifying information must comply with this rule.

(Subd (a) amended effective January 1, 2007.)

(b) Juror names, addresses, and telephone numbers

(1) The name of each trial juror or alternate sworn to hear the case must be replaced with an identifying number wherever it appears in any document. The superior court clerk must prepare and keep under seal in the case file a table correlating the jurors' names with their identifying numbers. The clerk and the reporter must use the table in preparing all transcripts or other documents.

(2) The addresses and telephone numbers of trial jurors and alternates sworn to hear the case must be deleted from all documents.

(c) Potential jurors

Information identifying potential jurors called but not sworn as trial jurors or alternates must not be sealed unless otherwise ordered under Code of Civil Procedure section 237(a)(1).

Rule 8.332 amended and renumbered effective January 1, 2007; adopted as rule 31.3 effective January 1, 2004.

Advisory Committee Comment

Rule 8.332 implements Code of Civil Procedure section 237.

Rule 8.336. Preparing, certifying, and sending the record

(a) Immediate preparation when appeal is likely

(1) The reporter and the clerk must begin preparing the record immediately after a verdict or finding of guilt of a felony is announced following a trial on the merits, unless the judge determines that an appeal is unlikely under (2).

(2) In determining the likelihood of an appeal, the judge must consider the facts of the case and the fact that an appeal is likely if the defendant has been convicted of a crime for which probation is prohibited or is prohibited except in unusual cases, or if the trial involved a contested question of law important to the outcome.

(3) A determination under (2) is an administrative decision intended to further the efficient operation of the court and not intended to affect any substantive or procedural right of the defendant or the People. The determination cannot be cited to prove or disprove any legal or factual issue in the case and is not reviewable by appeal or writ.

(b) Appeal after plea of guilty or nolo contendere or after admission of probation violation

In an appeal under rule 8.304(b)(1), the time to prepare, certify, and file the record begins when the court files a certificate of probable cause under rule 8.304(b)(2).

(Subd (b) amended effective January 1, 2007.)

(c) Clerk's transcript

(1) Except as provided in (a) or (b), the clerk must begin preparing the clerk's transcript immediately after the notice of appeal is filed.

(2) Within 20 days after the notice of appeal is filed, the clerk must complete preparation of an original and two copies of the clerk's transcript, one for defendant's counsel and one for the Attorney General or the district attorney, whichever is the counsel for the People on appeal.

(3) On request, the clerk must prepare an extra copy for the district attorney or the Attorney General, whichever is not counsel for the People on appeal.

(4) If there is more than one appealing defendant, the clerk must prepare an extra copy for each additional appealing defendant represented by separate counsel.

(5) The clerk must certify as correct the original and all copies of the clerk's transcript.

(Subd (c) amended effective January 1, 2007.)

(d) Reporter's transcript

(1) Except as provided in (a) or (b), the reporter must begin preparing the reporter's transcript immediately on being notified by the clerk under rule 8.304(c)(1) that the notice of appeal has been filed.

(2) The reporter must prepare an original and the same number of copies of the reporter's transcript as (c) requires of the clerk's transcript, and must certify each as correct.

(3) The reporter must deliver the original and all copies to the superior court clerk as soon as they are certified, but no later than 20 days after the notice of appeal is filed.

(4) Any portion of the transcript transcribed during trial must not be retyped unless necessary to correct errors, but must be repaginated and bound with any portion of the transcript not previously transcribed. Any additional copies needed must not be retyped but must be prepared by photocopying or an equivalent process.

(5) In a multireporter case, the clerk must accept any completed portion of the transcript from the primary reporter one week after the time prescribed by (3) even if other portions are uncompleted. The clerk must promptly pay each reporter who certifies that all portions of the transcript assigned to that reporter are completed.

(Subd (d) amended effective January 1, 2007.)

(e) Extension of time

(1) The superior court may not extend the time for preparing the record.

(2) The reviewing court may order one or more extensions of time for preparing the record, not exceeding a total of 60 days, on receipt of:

(A) An affidavit showing good cause; and

(B) In the case of a reporter's transcript, certification by the superior court presiding judge, or a court administrator designated by the presiding judge, that an extension is reasonable and necessary in light of the workload of all reporters in the court.

(Subd (e) amended effective January 1, 2007.)

(f) Sending the transcripts

(1) When the clerk and reporter's transcripts are certified as correct, the clerk must promptly send:

(A) The original transcripts to the reviewing court, noting the sending date on each original;

(B) One copy of each transcript to appellate counsel for each defendant represented by separate counsel and to the Attorney General or the district attorney, whichever is counsel for the People on appeal; and

(C) One copy of each transcript to the district attorney or Attorney General if requested under (c)(3).

(2) If the defendant is not represented by appellate counsel when the transcripts are certified as correct, the clerk must send that defendant's counsel's copy of the transcripts to the district appellate project.

(Subd (f) amended effective January 1, 2007.)

(g) Probation officer's report

The probation officer's report included in the clerk's transcript under rule 8.320(b) must appear in all copies of the appellate record. The reviewing court's copy of the report must be placed in a sealed envelope marked "CONFIDENTIAL—MAY NOT BE EXAMINED WITHOUT COURT ORDER—PROBATION OFFICER REPORT."

(Subd (g) amended effective January 1, 2007.)

(h) Supervision of preparation of record

Each Court of Appeal clerk, under the supervision of the administrative presiding justice or the presiding justice, must take all appropriate steps to ensure that superior court clerks and reporters promptly perform their duties under this rule. This provision does not affect the superior courts' responsibility for the prompt preparation of appellate records.

Rule 8.336 amended and renumbered effective January 1, 2007; repealed and adopted as rule 32 effective January 1, 2004.

Advisory Committee Comment

Subdivision (a). Subdivision (a) implements Code of Civil Procedure section 269(b).

Rule 8.340. Augmenting or correcting the record in the Court of Appeal

(a) Subsequent trial court orders

(1) If, after the record is certified, the trial court amends or recalls the judgment or makes any other order in the case, including an order affecting the sentence or probation, the clerk must promptly certify and send a copy of the amended abstract of judgment or other order—as an augmentation of the record—to:

(A) The reviewing court, the probation officer, the defendant;

(B) The defendant's appellate counsel for each defendant represented by separate counsel, and the Attorney General or the district attorney, whichever is counsel for the People on appeal; and

(C) The district attorney or Attorney General, whichever is not counsel for the People on appeal, if he or she requested a copy of the clerk's transcript under 8.336(c)(3).

(2) If there is any additional document or transcript related to the amended judgment or new order that any rule or order requires be included in the record, the clerk must send this document or transcript with the amended abstract of judgment or other order. The clerk must promptly copy and certify any such document, and the reporter must promptly prepare and certify any such transcript.

(Subd (a) amended effective January 1, 2007.)

(b) Omissions

(1) If, after the record is certified, the superior court clerk or the reporter learns that the record omits a document or transcript that any rule or order requires to be included, the clerk must promptly copy and certify the document or the reporter must promptly prepare and certify the transcript. Without the need for a court order, the clerk must promptly send the document or transcript—as an augmentation of the record—to all those who are listed under (a)(1).

(Subd (b) amended effective January 1, 2007.)

(c) Augmentation or correction by the reviewing court

At any time, on motion of a party or on its own motion, the reviewing court may order the record augmented or corrected as provided in rule 8.155. The clerk must send any document or transcript added to the record to all those who are listed under (a)(1).

(Subd (c) amended and relettered effective January 1, 2007; adopted as subd (d) effective January 1, 2004.)

(d) Defendant not yet represented

If the defendant is not represented by appellate counsel when the record is augmented or corrected, the clerk must send that defendant's counsel's copy of the augmentations or corrections to the district appellate project.

(Subd (d) adopted effective January 1, 2007.)

Rule 8.340 amended and renumbered effective January 1, 2007; adopted as rule 32.1 effective January 1, 2004.

Advisory Committee Comment

Subdivision (b). The words "or order" in the first sentence of (b) are intended to refer to any court order to include additional material in the record, e.g., an order of the superior court under rule 8.324(d)(1).

Ref.: W. Cal. Sum., 10 "Parent and Child" §713.

Rule 8.344. Agreed statement

If the parties present the appeal on an agreed statement, they must comply with the relevant provisions of rule 8.134, but the appellant must file an original and three copies of the statement in superior court within 25 days after filing the notice of appeal.

Rule 8.344 amended and renumbered effective January 1, 2007; adopted as rule 32.2 effective January 1, 2004.

Ref.: W. Cal. Sum., 10 "Parent and Child" §713.

Rule 8.346. Settled statement

(a) Application

As soon as a party learns that any portion of the oral proceedings cannot be transcribed, the party may serve and file in superior court an application for permission to prepare a settled statement. The application must explain why the oral proceedings cannot be transcribed.

(b) Order and proposed statement

The judge must rule on the application within five days after it is filed. If the judge grants the application, the parties must comply with the relevant provisions of rule 8.137, but the applicant must deliver a proposed statement to the judge for settlement within 30 days after it is ordered, unless the reviewing court extends the time.

(Subd (b) amended effective January 1, 2007.)

(c) Serving and filing the settled statement

The applicant must prepare, serve, and file in superior court an original and three copies of the settled statement.

Rule 8.346 amended and renumbered effective January 1, 2007; adopted as rule 32.3 effective January 1, 2004.

Ref.: W. Cal. Sum., 10 "Parent and Child" §713.

Article 3
Briefs, Hearing, and Decision

Rule 8.360. Briefs by parties and amici curiae

(a) Contents and form

Except as provided in this rule, briefs in criminal appeals must comply as nearly as possible with rules 8.200 and 8.204.

(Subd (a) amended effective January 1, 2007.)

(b) Length

(1) A brief produced on a computer must not exceed 25,500 words, including footnotes. Such a brief must include a certificate by appellate counsel or an unrepresented defendant stating the number of words in the brief;

the person certifying may rely on the word count of the computer program used to prepare the brief.

(2) A typewritten brief must not exceed 75 pages.

(3) The tables, a certificate under (1), and any attachment permitted under rule 8.204(d) are excluded from the limits stated in (1) or (2).

(4) A combined brief in an appeal governed by (e) must not exceed double the limit stated in (1) or (2).

(5) On application, the presiding justice may permit a longer brief for good cause.

(Subd (b) amended effective January 1, 2007.)

(c) Time to file

(1) The appellant's opening brief must be served and filed within 40 days after the record is filed in the reviewing court.

(2) The respondent's brief must be served and filed within 30 days after the appellant's opening brief is filed.

(3) The appellant must serve and file a reply brief, if any, within 20 days after the respondent files its brief.

(4) The time to serve and file a brief may not be extended by stipulation, but only by order of the presiding justice under rule 8.60.

(5) If a party fails to timely file an appellant's opening brief or a respondent's brief, the reviewing court clerk must promptly notify the party by mail that the brief must be filed within 30 days after the notice is mailed, and that failure to comply may result in one of the following sanctions:

(A) If the brief is an appellant's opening brief:

(i) If the appellant is the People, the court will dismiss the appeal;

(ii) If the appellant is the defendant and is represented by appointed counsel on appeal, the court will relieve that appointed counsel and appoint new counsel;

(iii) If the appellant is the defendant and is not represented by appointed counsel, the court will dismiss the appeal; or

(B) If the brief is a respondent's brief, the court will decide the appeal on the record, the opening brief, and any oral argument by the appellant.

(6) If a party fails to comply with a notice under (5), the court may impose the sanction specified in the notice.

(Subd (c) amended effective January 1, 2007.)

(d) Service

(1) Defendant's appellate counsel must serve each brief for the defendant on the People and the district attorney, and must send a copy of each to the defendant personally unless the defendant requests otherwise.

(2) The proof of service under (1) must state that a copy of the defendant's brief was sent to the defendant, or counsel must file a signed statement that the defendant requested in writing that no copy be sent.

(3) For each appealing defendant, the People must serve two copies of their briefs on the defendant's appellate counsel and one copy on the district appellate project.

(4) A copy of each brief must be served on the superior court clerk for delivery to the trial judge.

(e) When a defendant and the People appeal

When both a defendant and the People appeal, the defendant must file the first opening brief unless the

reviewing court orders otherwise, and rule 8.216(b) governs the contents of the briefs.

(Subd (e) amended effective January 1, 2007.)

(f) Amicus curiae briefs

Amicus curiae briefs may be filed as provided in rule 8.200(c).

(Subd (f) amended effective January 1, 2007.)

Rule 8.360 amended and renumbered effective January 1, 2007; repealed and adopted as rule 33 effective January 1, 2004.

Advisory Committee Comment

Subdivision (b). Subdivision (b)(1) states the maximum permissible length of a brief produced on a computer in terms of word count rather than page count. This provision tracks a provision in rule 8.204(c) governing Court of Appeal briefs and is explained in the comment to that provision. The word count assumes a brief using one-and-one-half spaced lines of text, as permitted by rule 8.204(b)(5).

The maximum permissible length of briefs in death penalty appeals is prescribed in rule 8.630.

Ref.: W. Cal. Sum., 10 "Parent and Child" §715.

Rule 8.361.   Certificate of interested entities or persons

In criminal cases in which an entity is a defendant, that defendant must comply with the requirements of rule 8.208 concerning serving and filing a certificate of interested entities or persons.

Rule 8.361 adopted effective January 1, 2009.

Advisory Committee Comment

Under rule 8.208(c), for purposes of certificates of interested entities or persons, an "entity" means a corporation, a partnership, a firm, or any other association but does not include a governmental entity or its agencies or a natural person.

Rule 8.366.   Hearing and decision in the Court of Appeal

(a) General application of rules 8.252–8.272

Except as provided in this rule, rules [1] **8.252–8.272** govern the hearing and decision in the Court of Appeal of an appeal in a criminal case.

(Subd (a) amended and lettered effective January 1, 2009; adopted as unlettered subd effective January 1, 2004.)

Rule 8.366(a).   2008 Deletes. [1] 8.252 through 8.272

(b) Finality

(1) Except as otherwise provided in this rule, a Court of Appeal decision in a proceeding under this chapter, including an order dismissing an appeal involuntarily, is final in that court 30 days after filing.

(2) The following Court of Appeal decisions are final in that court on filing:

(A) The denial of an application for bail or to reduce bail pending appeal; and

(B) The dismissal of an appeal on request or stipulation.

(3) If a Court of Appeal certifies its opinion for publication or partial publication after filing its decision and before its decision becomes final in that court, the finality period runs from the filing date of the order for publication.

(4) If an order modifying an opinion changes the appellate judgment, the finality period runs from the filing date of the modification order.

(Subd (b) adopted effective January 1, 2009.)

(c) Sanctions

Except for (a)(1), rule 8.276 [1] applies in criminal appeals.

(Subd (c) amended and lettered effective January 1, 2009; adopted as unlettered subd effective January 1, 2004.)

Rule 8.366(c). 2008 Deletes. [1] also

Rule 8.366 amended effective January 1, 2009; adopted as rule 33.1 effective January 1, 2004; previously amended and renumbered effective January 1, 2007; previously amended effective January 1, 2008.

Advisory Committee Comment

Subdivision (b). As used in subdivision (b)(1), "decision" includes all interlocutory orders of the Court of Appeal. (See Advisory Committee Comment to rule 8.500(a) and (e).) This provision addresses the finality of decisions in criminal appeals. See rule 8.264(b) for provisions addressing the finality of decisions in proceedings under chapter 2, relating to civil appeals, and rule 8.490 for provisions addressing the finality of proceedings under chapter 7, relating to writs of mandate, certiorari, and prohibition.

Rule 8.368. Hearing and decision in the Supreme Court

Rules 8.500 through 8.552 govern the hearing and decision in the Supreme Court of an appeal in a criminal case.

Rule 8.368 amended and renumbered effective January 1, 2007; adopted as rule 33.2 effective January 1, 2004.

Chapter 4
Habeas Corpus Appeals and Writs

Rule 8.380. Petition for writ of habeas corpus filed by petitioner not represented by an attorney
Rule 8.384. Petition for writ of habeas corpus filed by an attorney for a party
Rule 8.385. Proceedings after the petition is filed
Rule 8.386. Proceedings if the return is ordered to be filed in the reviewing court
Rule 8.387. Decision in habeas corpus proceedings
Rule 8.388. Appeal from order granting relief by writ of habeas corpus

Rule 8.380. Petition for writ of habeas corpus filed by petitioner not represented by an attorney

(a) Required Judicial Council form

[1] A person who is not represented by an attorney and who petitions a reviewing court for writ of habeas corpus seeking release from, or modification of the conditions of, custody of a person confined in a state or local penal institution, hospital, narcotics treatment facility, or other institution must file the petition on *Petition for Writ of Habeas Corpus* (form MC-275). For good cause the court may permit the filing of a petition that is not on that form.

(Subd (a) amended effective January 1, 2009; previously amended effective January 1, 2006, and January 1, 2007.)

Rule 8.380(a). 2008 Deletes. [1] (1)

(b) Form and content

[1] A petition filed under [2] **(a)** need not comply with the provisions of rules 8.40, 8.204, or [3] **8.486** that

prescribe the form and content of a petition and require the petition to be accompanied by a memorandum.

(Subd (b) repealed, amended and lettered effective January 1, 2009; adopted as part of subd (a) effective January 1, 2005.)

Rule 8.380(b). 2008 Deletes. [1] (2) **[2]** (1) **[3]** 8.490

(c) Number of copies

[1] In the Court of Appeal, the petitioner must file the original of the petition under [2] **(a)** and one set of any supporting documents. In the Supreme Court, the petitioner must file an original and 10 copies of the petition and an original and 2 copies of any supporting document accompanying the petition unless the court orders otherwise.

(Subd (c) repealed, amended and lettered effective January 1, 2009; adopted as part of subd (a) effective January 1, 2005.)

Rule 8.380(c). 2008 Deletes. [1] (3) **[2]** (1)

(d) Petition filed in an inappropriate court [Repealed]

(Subd (d) repealed effective January 1, 2009; adopted as subd (e) effective January 1, 2005; previously amended and relettered effective January 1, 2006; previously amended effective January 1, 2007.)

Rule 8.380 amended effective January 1, 2009; repealed and adopted as rule 60 effective January 1, 2005; previously amended effective January 1, 2006; previously amended and renumbered effective January 1, 2007.

Ref.: Cal. Fms Pl. & Pr., Ch. 1, "New Developments," Ch. 59, "Assemblies, Meetings, and Demonstrations," Ch. 292, "Habeas Corpus," Ch. 304, "Insane and Other Incompetent Persons," Ch. 328, "Juvenile Courts: Dependency Proceedings."

Rule 8.384. Petition for writ of habeas corpus filed by an attorney for a party

(a) Form and content of petition and memorandum

(1) A petition for habeas corpus filed by an attorney need not be filed on *Petition for Writ of Habeas Corpus* (form MC-275), but must contain the information requested in that form. **All petitions filed by attorneys, whether or not on form MC-275, must be either typewritten or produced on a computer,** and must comply with **this rule and** rules [1] **8.40(b)–(c)** relating **to document covers and 8.204(a)(1)(A) relating to tables of contents and authorities. A petition that is not on form MC-275 must also comply with the remainder of rule 8.204(a) and 8.204(b).**

(2) Any memorandum accompanying the petition must comply with rule 8.204(a)–(b). **Except in habeas corpus proceedings related to sentences of death, any memorandum must also comply with the length limits in rule 8.204(c).**

(3) [2] The petition and any memorandum must support any reference to a matter in the supporting documents by a citation to its index tab and page.

(Subd (a) repealed, amended and lettered effective January 1, 2009; adopted as part of subd (b) effective January 1, 2006.)

Rule 8.384(a). 2008 Deletes. [1] 8.40(c)–(d), 8.204(a)–(b), and 8.490(b)(6) **[2]** The petition must be accompanied by a copy of any petition—excluding exhibits—pertaining to the same judgment and petitioner that was previously filed in any lower state court or any federal court. If such documents have previously been filed in the Supreme Court, the petition need only so state. (4) If the petition asserts a claim that was the subject of an evidentiary hearing, the petition must be accompanied by a certified transcript of that hearing. (5) Any supporting documents accompanying the petition must comply with rule 8.490(d). (6)

2008 Note: Subdivision (a) was repealed, being now derived from former subdivisions (b)(1), (2) and (6).

(b) Supporting documents

[1] **(1)** The petition must be accompanied by a copy of any petition—excluding exhibits—pertaining to the same judgment and petitioner that was previously filed in any [2] state court or any federal court. If such documents have previously been filed **in the same Court of Appeal where the petition is filed or** in the Supreme Court [3] **and** the petition [4] **so states and identifies the documents by case name and number, copies of these documents need not be included in the supporting documents.**

(2) If the petition asserts a claim that was the subject of an evidentiary hearing, the petition must be accompanied by a certified transcript of that hearing.

[5] **(3) Rule 8.486(c)(1) and (2) govern the form of** any supporting documents accompanying the petition [6].

(Subd (b) amended effective January 1, 2009; previously amended effective January 1, 2007.)

Rule 8.384(b).   2008 Deletes. [1] (3) [2] lower [3] , [4] need only so state. (4) [5] (5) [6] must comply with rule 8.490(d)

2008 Note: Subdivision (b) was amended, now comprised of former subdivisions (b)(3)–(5).

(c) Number of copies

[1] If the petition is filed in the Supreme Court, the attorney must file the number of copies of the petition and supporting documents required by rule 8.44(a). If the petition is filed in the Court of Appeal, the attorney must file the number of copies of the petition **and supporting documents** required by rule 8.44(b).

(Subd (c) amended and lettered effective January 1, 2009; adopted as part of subd (b) effective January 1, 2006.)

Rule 8.384(c).   2008 Deletes. [1] (7)

2008 Note: Subdivision (c) was adopted, being derived from former subdivision (b)(7).

(d) Noncomplying petitions

[1] The clerk must file an attorney's petition not complying with [2] **(a)–(c)** if it otherwise complies with the rules of court, but the court may notify the attorney that it may strike the petition or impose a lesser sanction if the petition is not brought into compliance within a stated reasonable time of not less than five days.

(Subd (d) amended and lettered effective January 1, 2009; adopted as part of subd (b) effective January 1, 2006.)

Rule 8.384(d).   2008 Deletes. [1] (8) [2] (1)–(7)

2008 Note: Subdivision (d) was adopted, being derived from former subdivision (b)(8).

Rule 8.384 amended effective January 1, 2009; adopted as rule 60.5 effective January 1, 2006; previously amended and renumbered effective January 1, 2007.

Ref.: Cal. Fms Pl. & Pr., Ch. 1, "New Developments," Ch. 59, "Assemblies, Meetings, and Demonstrations," Ch. 292, "Habeas Corpus," Ch. 304, "Insane and Other Incompetent Persons," Ch. 328, "Juvenile Courts: Dependency Proceedings."

Rule 8.385.   Proceedings after the petition is filed

(a) Record

Before ruling on the petition, the court may order the custodian of any relevant record to produce the record or a certified copy to be filed with the court.

(Subd (a) adopted effective January 1, 2009.)

(b) Informal response

(1) Before ruling on the petition, the court may request an informal written response from the respondent, the real party in interest, or an interested person. The court must send a copy of any request to the petitioner.

(2) The response must be served and filed within 15 days or as the court specifies.

(3) If a response is filed, the court must notify the petitioner that a reply may be served and filed within 15 days or as the court specifies. The court may not deny the petition until that time has expired.

(Subd (b) adopted effective January 1, 2009.)

(c) Petition filed in an inappropriate court

(1) A Court of Appeal may deny without prejudice a petition for writ of habeas corpus that is based primarily on facts occurring outside the court's appellate district, including petitions that question:

(A) The validity of judgments or orders of trial courts located outside the district; or

(B) The conditions of confinement or the conduct of correctional officials outside the district.

(2) A Court of Appeal must deny without prejudice a petition for writ of habeas corpus that challenges the denial of parole or the petitioner's suitability for parole if the issue was not first adjudicated by the trial court that rendered the underlying judgment.

(3) If the court denies a petition solely under (1), the order must state the basis of the denial and must identify the appropriate court in which to file the petition.

(Subd (c) adopted effective January 1, 2009.)

(d) Order to show cause

If the petitioner has made the required prima facie showing that he or she is entitled to relief, the court must issue an order to show cause. An order to show cause does not grant the relief sought in the petition.

(Subd (d) adopted effective January 1, 2009.)

(e) Return to the superior court

The reviewing court may order the respondent to file a return in the superior court. The order vests jurisdiction over the cause in the superior court, which must proceed under rule 4.551.

(Subd (e) adopted effective January 1, 2009.)

(f) Return to the reviewing court

If the return is ordered to be filed in the Supreme Court or the Court of Appeal, rule 8.386 applies and the court in which the return is ordered filed must appoint counsel for any unrepresented petitioner who desires but cannot afford counsel.

(Subd (f) adopted effective January 1, 2009.)
Rule 8.385 adopted effective January 1, 2009.

Advisory Committee Comment

Subdivision (c). Except for subdivision (c)(2), rule 8.385(c) restates former section 6.5 of the Standards of Judicial Administration. Subdivision (c)(2) is based on the California Supreme Court decision in *In re Roberts* (2005) 36 Cal.4th 575, which provides that petitions for writ of habeas corpus challenging denial or suitability for parole are first to be adjudicated in the trial court that rendered the underlying judgment.

Subdivision (d). Case law establishes the specificity of the factual allegations and support for these allegations required in a petition for a writ of habeas corpus (see, e.g., *People v. Duvall*

(1995) 9 Cal.4th 464, 474–475, and *Ex parte Swain* (1949) 34 Cal.2d 300, 303–304). A court evaluating whether a petition meeting these requirements makes a prima facie showing asks whether, assuming the petition's factual allegations are true, the petitioner would be entitled to relief (*People v. Duvall*, supra).

Issuing an order to show cause is just one of the actions a court might take on a petition for a writ of habeas corpus. Examples of other actions that a court might take include denying the petition summarily, requesting an informal response from the respondent under (b), or denying the petition without prejudice under (c) because it is filed in an inappropriate court.

Rule 8.386.   Remittitur in habeas corpus proceedings [Renumbered]

Rule 8.386 amended and renumbered to rule 8.387 effective January 1, 2009; adopted effective January 1, 2008.

Another rule 8.386 follows.

Rule 8.386.   Proceedings if the return is ordered to be filed in the reviewing court

(a) Application

This rule applies if the Supreme Court orders the return to be filed in the Supreme Court or the Court of Appeal or if the Court of Appeal orders the return to be filed in the Court of Appeal.

(Subd (a) adopted effective January 1, 2009.)

(b) Serving and filing return

(1) Unless the court orders otherwise, any return must be served and filed within 30 days after the court issues the order to show cause.

(2) If the return is filed in the Supreme Court, the attorney must file the number of copies of the return and any supporting documents required by rule 8.44(a). If the return is filed in the Court of Appeal, the attorney must file the number of copies of the return and any supporting documents required by rule 8.44(b). Two copies of the return and any supporting documents must be served on the petitioner's counsel, and if the return is to the Court of Appeal and the petitioner is not represented by privately retained counsel, one copy must be served on the district appellate project.

(Subd (b) adopted effective January 1, 2009.)

(c) Form and content of return

(1) The return must be either typewritten or produced on a computer and must comply with Penal Code section 1480 and rules 8.40(b)–(c) and 8.204(a)–(b). Except in habeas corpus proceedings related to sentences of death, any return must also comply with the length limits in rule 8.204(c).

(2) Rule 8.486(c)(1) and (2) govern the form of any supporting documents accompanying the return. The return must support any reference to a matter in the supporting documents by a citation to its index tab and page.

(3) Any material allegation of the petition not controverted by the return is deemed admitted for purposes of the proceeding.

(Subd (c) adopted effective January 1, 2009.)

(d) Traverse

(1) Unless the court orders otherwise, within 30 days after the respondent files a return, the petitioner may serve and file a traverse.

(2) Any traverse must be either typewritten or produced on a computer and must comply with Penal Code section 1484 and rules 8.40(b)–(c) and 8.204(a)–(b). Except in habeas corpus proceedings related to sentences of death, any traverse must also comply with the length limits in rule 8.204(c).

(3) Any material allegation of the return not denied in the traverse is deemed admitted for purposes of the proceeding.

(4) If the return is filed in the Supreme Court, the attorney must file the number of copies of the traverse required by rule 8.44(a). If the return is filed in the Court of Appeal, the attorney must file the number of copies of the traverse required by rule 8.44(b).

(Subd (d) adopted effective January 1, 2009.)

(e) Judicial notice

Rule 8.252(a) governs judicial notice in the reviewing court.

(Subd (e) adopted effective January 1, 2009.)

(f) Evidentiary hearing ordered by the reviewing court

(1) An evidentiary hearing is required if, after considering the verified petition, the return, any traverse, any affidavits or declarations under penalty of perjury, and matters of which judicial notice may be taken, the court finds there is a reasonable likelihood that the petitioner may be entitled to relief and the petitioner's entitlement to relief depends on the resolution of an issue of fact.

(2) The court may appoint a referee to conduct the hearing and make recommended findings of fact.

(Subd (f) adopted effective January 1, 2009.)

(g) Oral argument and submission of the cause

Unless the court orders otherwise:

(1) Rule 8.256 governs oral argument and submission of the cause in the Court of Appeal.

(2) Rule 8.524 governs oral argument and submission of the cause in the Supreme Court.

(Subd (g) adopted effective January 1, 2009.)
Rule 8.386 adopted effective January 1, 2009.

Rule 8.387.   Decision in habeas corpus proceedings

(a) Filing the decision

(1) Rule 8.264(a) governs the filing of the decision in the Court of Appeal.

(2) Rule 8.532(a) governs the filing of the decision in the Supreme Court.

(Subd (a) adopted effective January 1, 2009.)

(b) Finality of decision in the Court of Appeal

(1) *General finality period*

Except as otherwise provided in this rule, a Court of Appeal decision in a habeas corpus proceeding is final in that court 30 days after filing.

(2) *Denial of a petition for writ of habeas corpus without issuance of an order to show cause*

(A) Except as provided in (B), a Court of Appeal decision denying a petition for writ of habeas corpus without issuance of an order to show cause is final in the Court of Appeal upon filing.

(B) A Court of Appeal decision denying a petition for writ of habeas corpus without issuing an order to show cause is final in that court on the same day that its decision in a related appeal is final if the two decisions are filed on the same day. If the Court of Appeal orders rehearing of the decision in the appeal, its decision denying the petition for writ of habeas corpus is final when its decision on rehearing is final.

(3) *Decision in a habeas corpus proceeding after issuance of an order to show cause*

(A) If necessary to prevent mootness or frustration of the relief granted or to otherwise promote the interests of justice, a Court of Appeal may order early finality in that court of a decision in a habeas corpus proceeding after issuing an order to show cause. The decision may provide for finality in that court on filing or within a stated period of less than 30 days.

(B) If a Court of Appeal certifies its opinion for publication or partial publication after filing its decision and before its decision becomes final in that court, the finality period runs from the filing date of the order for publication.

(Subd (b) adopted effective January 1, 2009.)

(c) Finality of decision in the Supreme Court

Rule 8.532(b) governs finality of a decision in the Supreme Court.

(Subd (c) adopted effective January 1, 2009.)

(d) Modification of decision

(1) A reviewing court may modify a decision until the decision is final in that court. If the clerk's office is closed on the date of finality, the court may modify the decision on the next day the clerk's office is open.

(2) An order modifying an opinion must state whether it changes the appellate judgment. A modification that does not change the appellate judgment does not extend the finality date of the decision. If a modification changes the appellate judgment, the finality period runs from the filing date of the modification order.

(Subd (d) adopted effective January 1, 2009.)

(e) Rehearing

(1) Rule 8.268 governs rehearing in the Court of Appeal.

(2) Rule 8.536 governs rehearing in the Supreme Court.

(Subd (e) adopted effective January 1, 2009.)

(f) Remittitur

A Court of Appeal must issue a remittitur in a habeas corpus proceeding under this chapter except when the court denies the petition without issuing an order to show cause **or orders the return filed in the superior court**. Rule 8.272(b)–(d) governs issuance of a remittitur **by a Court of Appeal** in habeas corpus proceedings.

(Subd (f) amended and lettered effective January 1, 2009; adopted as unlettered subd effective January 1, 2008.)

Rule 8.387 amended and renumbered effective January 1, 2009; adopted as rule 8.386 effective January 1, 2008.

Advisory Committee Comment

A party may seek review of a Court of Appeal decision in a habeas corpus proceeding by way of a petition for review in the Supreme Court under rule 8.500.

Rule 8.388. Appeal from order granting relief by writ of habeas corpus

(a) Application

Except as otherwise provided in this rule, rules 8.304–8.368 and 8.508 govern appeals under Penal Code section 1506 or 1507 from orders granting all or part of the relief sought in a petition for writ of habeas corpus.

(Subd (a) amended effective January 1, 2007.)

(b) Contents of record

In an appeal under this rule, the record must contain:

(1) The petition, the return, and the traverse;

(2) The order to show cause;

(3) All court minutes;

(4) All documents and exhibits submitted to the court;

(5) The reporter's transcript of any oral proceedings;

(6) Any written opinion of the court;

(7) The order appealed from; and

(8) The notice of appeal.

(Subd (b) amended effective January 1, 2007.)

Rule 8.388 amended and renumbered effective January 1, 2007; repealed and adopted as rule 39.2 effective January 1, 2005.

Ref.: Cal. Fms Pl. & Pr., Ch. 292, "Habeas Corpus."

Chapter 5
Juvenile Appeals and Writs

Art. 1. Appeals. Rules 8.400–8.416.
Art. 2. Writs. Rules 8.450–8.456.
Art. 3. Hearing and Decision. Rules 8.470–8.474.

Article 1
Appeals

Rule 8.400. Appeals in juvenile cases generally
Rule 8.404. Record on appeal
Rule 8.406. Record in multiple appeals in the same case
Rule 8.408. Preparing, sending, augmenting, and correcting the record
Rule 8.412. Briefs by parties and amici curiae
Rule 8.416. Appeals from all terminations of parental rights; dependency appeals in Orange, Imperial, and San Diego Counties

Rule 8.400. Appeals in juvenile cases generally

(a) Application

Rules 8.400–8.474 govern:

(1) Appeals from judgments or appealable orders in:

(A) Dependency and delinquency cases under the Welfare and Institutions Code; and

(B) Actions to free a child from parental custody and control under Family Code section 7800 et seq.; and

(2) Writ petitions under Welfare and Institutions Code sections 366.26 and 366.28.

(Subd (a) amended effective January 1, 2007.)

(b) Confidentiality

(1) Except as provided in (3), the record on appeal and documents filed by the parties may be inspected only by reviewing court and appellate project personnel, the parties or their attorneys, and other persons the court may designate.

(2) To protect anonymity, a party must be referred to by first name and last initial in all filed documents and court orders and opinions; but if the first name is unusual

or other circumstances would defeat the objective of anonymity, the party's initials may be used.

(3) Filed documents that protect anonymity as required by (2) may be inspected by any person or entity that is considering filing an amicus curiae brief.

(4) The court may limit or prohibit public admittance to oral argument.

(c) Notice of appeal

(1) To appeal from a judgment or appealable order under these rules, the appellant must file a notice of appeal in the superior court. The appellant or the appellant's attorney must sign the notice.

(2) The notice of appeal must be liberally construed, and is sufficient if it identifies the particular judgment or order being appealed. The notice need not specify the court to which the appeal is taken; the appeal will be treated as taken to the Court of Appeal for the district in which the superior court is located.

(d) Time to appeal

(1) Except as provided in (2) and (3), a notice of appeal must be filed within 60 days after the rendition of the judgment or the making of the order being appealed. Except as provided in rule 8.66, no court may extend the time to file a notice of appeal.

(2) In matters heard by a referee not acting as a temporary judge, a notice of appeal must be filed within 60 days after the referee's order becomes final under rule 5.540(c).

(3) When an application for rehearing of an order of a referee not acting as a temporary judge is denied under rule 5.542, a notice of appeal from the referee's order must be filed within 60 days after that order is served under rule 5.538(b)(3) or 30 days after entry of the order denying rehearing, whichever is later.

(Subd (d) amended effective January 1, 2008; previously amended effective January 1, 2007.)

(e) Cross-appeal

If an appellant timely appeals from a judgment or appealable order, the time for any other party to appeal from the same judgment or order is either the time specified in (d) or 20 days after the superior court clerk mails notification of the first appeal, whichever is later.

(Subd (e) amended and relettered effective January 1, 2008; adopted as part of subd (d) effective January 1, 2005; previously amended effective January 1, 2007.)

(f) Receipt by mail from custodial institution

If the superior court clerk receives a notice of appeal by mail from a custodial institution after the period specified in (d) has expired but the envelope shows that the notice was mailed or delivered to custodial officials for mailing within the period specified in (d), the notice is deemed timely. The clerk must retain in the case file the envelope in which the notice was received.

(Subd (f) relettered effective January 1, 2008; adopted as subd (e) effective January 1, 2006.)

(g) Premature or late notice of appeal

(1) A notice of appeal is premature if filed before the judgment is rendered or the order is made, but the reviewing court may treat the notice as filed immediately after the rendition of judgment or the making of the order.

(2) The superior court clerk must mark a late notice of appeal "Received [date] but not filed," notify the party that the notice was not filed because it was late, and send a copy of the marked notice of appeal to the district appellate project.

(Subd (g) relettered effective January 1, 2008; adopted as subd (e) effective January 1, 2005; previously relettered as subd (f) effective January 1, 2006.)

(h) Superior court clerk's duties

(1) When a notice of appeal is filed, the superior court clerk must immediately:

(A) Mail a notification of the filing to each party— including the minor—other than the appellant, to all attorneys of record, and to the reviewing court clerk; and

(B) Notify the reporter by telephone and in writing to prepare a reporter's transcript and deliver it to the clerk within 20 days after the notice of appeal is filed.

(2) The clerk must immediately mail a notification of the filing to any de facto parent, any Court Appointed Special Advocate (CASA) volunteer, and any Indian tribe that has appeared in the proceedings.

(3) The notification must show the name of the appellant, the date it was mailed, the number and title of the case, and the date the notice of appeal was filed. If the information is available, the notification must also include:

(A) The name, address, telephone number, and California State Bar number of each attorney of record in the case;

(B) The name of the party that each attorney represented in the superior court; and

(C) The name, address, and telephone number of any unrepresented party.

(4) The notification to the reviewing court clerk must also include a copy of the notice of appeal and any sequential list of reporters made under rule 2.950.

(5) A copy of the notice of appeal is sufficient notification if the required information is on the copy or is added by the superior court clerk.

(6) The mailing of a notification is a sufficient performance of the clerk's duty despite the discharge, disqualification, suspension, disbarment, or death of the attorney.

(7) Failure to comply with any provision of this subdivision does not affect the validity of the notice of appeal.

(Subd (h) relettered effective January 1, 2008; adopted as subd (f) effective January 1, 2005; previously relettered effective January 1, 2006; previously amended effective January 1, 2007.)
Rule 8.400 amended effective January 1, 2008; adopted as rule 37 effective January 1, 2005; previously amended effective January 1, 2006; previously amended and renumbered effective January 1, 2007.

Ref.: Cal. Fms Pl. & Pr., Ch. 328, "Juvenile Courts: Dependency Proceedings," Ch. 329, "Juvenile Courts: Delinquency Proceedings"; W. Cal. Sum., 10 "Parent and Child" §§355, 709, 712, 716, 918.

Rule 8.404. Record on appeal

(a) Normal record: clerk's transcript

The clerk's transcript must contain:

(1) The petition;

(2) Any notice of hearing;

(3) All court minutes;

(4) Any report or other document submitted to the court;

(5) The jurisdictional and dispositional findings and orders;

(6) The judgment or order appealed from;

(7) Any application for rehearing;

(8) The notice of appeal and any order pursuant to the notice;

(9) Any transcript of a sound or sound-and-video recording tendered to the court under rule 2.1040;

(10) Any application for additional record and any order on the application; and

(11) Any opinion or dispositive order of a reviewing court in the same case.

(Subd (a) amended effective January 1, 2007.)

(b) Normal record: reporter's transcript

The reporter's transcript must contain:

(1) Except as provided in (2), the oral proceedings at any hearing that resulted in the order or judgment being appealed;

(2) In appeals from dispositional orders, the oral proceedings at hearings on

(A) Jurisdiction and disposition; and

(B) Any motion by the appellant that was denied in whole or in part; and

(3) Any oral opinion of the court.

(Subd (b) amended effective January 1, 2007.)

(c) Application in superior court for addition to normal record

(1) Any party or tribe may apply to the superior court for inclusion in the record of any of the following items:

(A) In the clerk's transcript: any written motion or notice of motion by any party, with supporting and opposing memoranda and attachments, and any written opinion of the court; and

(B) In the reporter's transcript: any oral proceedings.

(2) An application for additional record must describe the material to be included and explain how it may be useful in the appeal.

(3) The application must be filed in the superior court with the notice of appeal or as soon thereafter as possible, and will be treated as denied if it is filed after the record is sent to the reviewing court.

(4) The clerk must immediately present the application to the trial judge.

(5) Within five days after the application if filed, the judge must order that the record include as much of the additional material as the judge finds proper to fully present the points raised by the applicant. Denial of the application does not preclude a motion in the reviewing court for augmentation under rule 8.155.

(6) If the judge does not rule on the application within the time prescribed by (5), the requested material–other than exhibits–must be included in the clerk's transcript or the reporter's transcript without a court order.

(7) The clerk must immediately notify the reporter if additions to the reporter's transcript are required under (5) or (6).

(Subd (c) amended effective January 1, 2007.)

(d) Agreed or settled statement

To proceed by agreed or settled statement, the parties must comply with rule 8.344 or 8.346, as applicable.

(Subd (d) amended effective January 1, 2007.)

(e) Form of record

Except in cases governed by rule 8.416(b), the clerk's and reporter's transcripts must comply with rule 8.144.

(Subd (e) amended effective January 1, 2007.)

(f) Transmitting exhibits

Exhibits that were admitted in evidence, refused, or lodged may be transmitted to the reviewing court as provided in rule 8.224.

(Subd (f) amended effective January 1, 2007.)

Rule 8.404 amended and renumbered effective January 1, 2007; adopted as rule 37.1 effective January 1, 2005.

Advisory Committee Comment

Subdivision (b). Subdivision (b)(1) provides that only the reporter's transcript of a hearing that resulted in the order being appealed must be included in the normal record. This provision is intended to achieve consistent record requirements in all juvenile appeals and to reduce the delays and expense caused by transcribing proceedings not necessary to the appeal.

Subdivision (b)(2)(A) recognizes that findings made in a jurisdictional hearing are not separately appealable and can be challenged only in an appeal from the ensuing dispositional order. The rule therefore specifically provides that a reporter's transcript of jurisdictional proceedings must be included in the normal record on appeal from a dispositional order.

Subdivision (b)(2)(B) specifies that the oral proceedings on any motion by the appellant that was denied in whole or in part must be included in the normal record on appeal from a disposition order. Rulings on such motions usually have some impact on either the jurisdictional findings or the subsequent disposition order. Routine inclusion of these proceedings in the record will promote expeditious resolution of juvenile appeals.

Ref.: Cal. Fms Pl. & Pr., Ch. 328, "Juvenile Courts: Dependency Proceedings," Ch. 577, "Workers' Compensation"; W. Cal. Sum., 10 "Parent and Child" §§713, 716, 721, 725, 919.

Rule 8.406.   Record in multiple appeals in the same case

If more than one appeal is taken from the same judgment or related order, only one appellate record need be prepared, which must be filed within the time allowed for filing the record in the latest appeal.

Rule 8.406 adopted effective January 1, 2007.

Ref.: Cal. Fms Pl. & Pr., Ch. 44, "Appeal: Preparing and Filing the Record"; W. Cal. Sum., 10 "Parent and Child" §§713, 716.

Rule 8.408.   Preparing, sending, augmenting, and correcting the record

(a) Application

Except as provided in (b), this rule does not apply to cases under rule 8.416.

(Subd (a) amended effective January 1, 2007.)

(b) Preparing and certifying the transcripts

Within 20 days after the notice of appeal is filed:

(1) The clerk must prepare and certify as correct an original of the clerk's transcript and sufficient copies to comply with (d); and

(2) The reporter must prepare, certify as correct, and deliver to the clerk an original of the reporter's transcript and the same number of copies as (1) requires of the clerk's transcript.

(Subd (b) amended effective January 1, 2007.)

(c) Extension of time

(1) The superior court may not extend the time to prepare the record.

(2) The reviewing court may order one or more extensions of time, not exceeding a total of 60 days, on receipt of:

(A) A declaration showing good cause; and

(B) In the case of a reporter's transcript, certification by the superior court presiding judge, or a court administrator designated by the presiding judge, that an extension is reasonable and necessary in light of the workload of all reporters in the court.

(Subd (c) amended effective January 1, 2007.)

(d) Sending the record

(1) When the transcripts are certified as correct, the superior court clerk must immediately send:

(A) The original transcripts to the reviewing court, noting the sending date on each original; and

(B) One copy of each transcript to the appellate counsel for the appellant, the respondent, and the minor.

(2) If appellate counsel has not yet been retained or appointed when the transcripts are certified as correct, the clerk must send that counsel's copy of the transcripts to the district appellate project.

(3) The clerk must not send a copy of the transcripts to the Attorney General or the district attorney unless that office represents a party.

(Subd (d) amended effective January 1, 2007.)

(e) Augmenting and correcting the record in the reviewing court

(1) Rule 8.340(a)–(b) governs augmentation of the record without court order.

(2) On request of a party or on its own motion, the reviewing court may order the record augmented or corrected as provided in rule 8.155(a) and (c).

(Subd (e) amended effective January 1, 2007.)

Rule 8.408 amended and renumbered effective January 1, 2007; adopted as rule 37.2 effective January 1, 2005.

Advisory Committee Comment

Subdivision (a). Subdivision (a) calls litigants' attention to the fact that a different rule (rule 8.416) governs *sending, augmenting, and correcting* the record in appeals from judgments or orders terminating parental rights and in dependency appeals in certain counties. Rule 8.408(b) governs *preparing and certifying* the record in those appeals. (See rule 8.416(a)(2) ["In all respects not provided for in this rule, rules 8.400–8.412 apply."].)

Ref.: Cal. Fms Pl. & Pr., Ch. 328, "Juvenile Courts: Dependency Proceedings"; W. Cal. Sum., 10 "Parent and Child" §§713, 714, 716, 919.

Rule 8.412. Briefs by parties and amici curiae

(a) Contents, form, and length

Rule 8.360(a)–(b) governs the contents, form, and length of briefs.

(Subd (a) amended effective January 1, 2007.)

(b) Time to file

(1) Except in cases governed by rule 8.416(e), the appellant must serve and file the appellant's opening brief within 40 days after the record is filed in the reviewing court.

(2) The respondent must serve and file the respondent's brief within 30 days after the appellant's opening brief is filed.

(3) The appellant must serve and file any reply brief within 20 days after the respondent's brief is filed.

(4) In dependency cases in which the child is not an appellant but has appellate counsel, the child must serve and file any brief within 10 days after the respondent's brief is filed.

(5) Rule 8.220 applies if a party fails to timely file an appellant's opening brief or a respondent's brief, but the period specified in the notice required by that rule must be 30 days.

(Subd (b) amended effective January 1, 2007.)

(c) Extensions of time

The superior court may not order any extensions of time to file briefs. Except in cases governed by rule 8.416(f), the reviewing court may order extensions of time for good cause.

(Subd (c) amended effective January 1, 2007.)

(d) Failure to file a brief

(1) Except in dependency appeals in Orange, Imperial, and San Diego Counties, and in appeals from the termination of parental rights, if a party fails to timely file an appellant's opening brief or a respondent's brief the reviewing court clerk must promptly notify the party's counsel, or if not represented, the party, by mail that the brief must be filed within 30 days after the notice is mailed, and that failure to comply may result in one of the following sanctions:

(A) If the brief is an appellant's opening brief:

(i) If the appellant is the county, the court will dismiss the appeal;

(ii) If the appellant is other than the county and is represented by appointed counsel on appeal, the court will relieve that appointed counsel and appoint new counsel;

(iii) If the appellant is other than the county and is not represented by appointed counsel, the court will dismiss the appeal.

(B) If the brief is a respondent's brief, the court will decide the appeal on the record, the opening brief, and any oral argument by the appellant.

(2) If a party fails to comply with a notice under (1), the court may impose the sanction specified in the notice.

(3) Within the period specified in the notice under (1), a party may apply to the presiding justice for an extension of that period for good cause. If an extension is granted beyond the 30-day period and the brief is not filed within the extended period, the court may impose the sanction under (2) without further notice.

(Subd (d) adopted effective January 1, 2007.)

(e) Additional service requirements

(1) A copy of each brief must be served on the superior court clerk for delivery to the superior court judge.

(2) A copy of each brief must be served on the child's trial counsel, or, if the child is not represented by trial counsel, on the child's guardian ad litem appointed under rule 5.662.

(3) If the Court of Appeal has appointed counsel for any party:

(A) The county child welfare department and the People must serve two copies of their briefs on that counsel; and

(B) Each party must serve a copy of its brief on the district appellate project.

(4) In delinquency cases the parties must serve copies of their briefs on the Attorney General and the district attorney. In all other cases the parties must not serve copies of their briefs on the Attorney General or the district attorney unless that office represents a party.

(5) The parties must not serve copies of their briefs on the Supreme Court under rule 8.44(b)(1).

(Subd (e) amended effective July 1, 2007; adopted as subd (d) effective January 1, 2005; previously amended and relettered effective January 1, 2007.)

Rule 8.412 amended effective July 1, 2007; adopted as rule 37.3 effective January 1, 2005; previously amended and renumbered effective January 1, 2007.

Advisory Committee Comment

Subdivision (b). Subdivision (b)(1) calls litigants' attention to the fact that a different rule (rule 8.416(e)) governs the time to file an appellant's opening brief in appeals from judgments or orders terminating parental rights and in dependency appeals in certain counties.

Subdivision (c). Subdivision (c) calls litigants' attention to the fact that a different rule (rule 8.416(f)) governs the showing required for extensions of time to file briefs in appeals from judgments or orders terminating parental rights and in dependency appeals in certain counties.

Ref.: Cal. Fms Pl. & Pr., Ch. 328, "Juvenile Courts: Dependency Proceedings"; W. Cal. Sum., 10 "Parent and Child" §§711, 715, 716.

Rule 8.416. Appeals from all terminations of parental rights; dependency appeals in Orange, Imperial, and San Diego Counties

(a) Application

(1) This rule governs:

(A) Appeals from judgments or appealable orders of all superior courts terminating parental rights under Welfare and Institutions Code section 366.26 or freeing a child from parental custody and control under Family Code section 7800 et seq.; and

(B) Appeals from judgments or appealable orders of the Superior Courts of Orange, Imperial, and San Diego Counties in all juvenile dependency cases.

(2) In all respects not provided for in this rule, rules 8.400–8.412 apply.

(Subd (a) amended effective January 1, 2007.)

(b) Cover of record

(1) In appeals under (a)(1)(A), the cover of the record must prominently display the title "Appeal From [Judgment or Order] Terminating Parental Rights Under [Welfare and Institutions Code Section 366.26 or Family Code Section 7800 et seq.]," whichever is appropriate.

(2) In appeals from judgments or appealable orders of the Superior Courts of Orange, Imperial, and San Diego Counties, the cover of the record must prominently display the title "Appeal From [Judgment or Order] Under [Welfare and Institutions Code Section 300 et seq. or Family Code Section 7800 et seq.]," whichever is appropriate.

(c) Sending the record

(1) When the clerk's and reporter's transcripts are certified as correct, the clerk must immediately send:

(A) The original transcripts to the reviewing court by the most expeditious method, noting the sending date on each original; and

(B) One copy of each transcript to the attorneys of record for the appellant, the respondent, and the minor, and to the district appellate project, by any method as fast as United States Postal Service express mail.

(2) If appellate counsel has not yet been retained or appointed when the transcripts are certified as correct, the clerk must send that counsel's copies of the transcripts to the district appellate project.

(Subd (c) amended effective January 1, 2007.)

(d) Augmenting or correcting the record in the reviewing court

(1) Except as provided in (2) and (3), rule 8.155 governs any augmentation or correction of the record.

(2) An appellant must serve and file any request for augmentation or correction within 15 days after receiving the record. A respondent must serve and file any such request within 15 days after the appellant's opening brief is filed.

(3) The clerk and the reporter must prepare any supplemental transcripts within 20 days, giving them the highest priority.

(4) The clerk must certify and send any supplemental transcripts as required by (c).

(Subd (d) amended effective January 1, 2007.)

(e) Time to file appellant's opening brief

To permit determination of the appeal within 250 days after the notice of appeal is filed, the appellant must serve and file the appellant's opening brief within 30 days after the record is filed in the reviewing court.

(f) Extensions of time

The superior court may not order any extensions of time to prepare the record or to file briefs; the reviewing court may order extensions of time, but must require an exceptional showing of good cause.

(g) Failure to file a brief

Rule 8.412 applies if a party fails to timely file an appellant's opening brief or a respondent's brief, but the period specified in the notice required by that rule must be 15 days.

(Subd (g) adopted effective January 1, 2007.)

(h) Oral argument and submission of the cause

(1) Unless the reviewing court orders otherwise, counsel must serve and file any request for oral argument no later than 15 days after the appellant's reply brief is filed or due to be filed. Failure to file a timely request will be deemed a waiver.

(2) The court must hear oral argument within 60 days after the appellant's last reply brief is filed or due to be filed, unless the court extends the time for good cause or counsel waive argument.

(3) If counsel waive argument, the cause is deemed submitted no later than 60 days after the appellant's reply brief is filed or due to be filed.

(Subd (h) relettered effective January 1, 2007; adopted as subd (g) effective January 1, 2005.)

Rule 8.416 amended and renumbered effective January 1, 2007; adopted as rule 37.4 effective January 1, 2005.

Advisory Committee Comment

Subdivision (g). Effective January 1, 2007, revised rule 8.416 incorporates a new subdivision (g) to address a failure to timely file a brief in all termination of parental rights cases and in dependency appeals in Orange, Imperial, and San Diego Counties. Under the new subdivision, appellants would not have the full 30-day grace period given in rule 8.412(d) in which to file a late brief, but instead would have the standard 15-day grace period that is given in civil cases. The intent of this revision is to balance the need to determine the appeal within 250 days with the need to protect appellants' rights in this most serious of appeals.

Subdivision (h). Subdivision (h)(1) recognizes certain reviewing courts' practice of requiring counsel to file any request for oral argument within a time period other than 15 days after the appellant's reply brief is filed or due to be filed. The reviewing court is still expected to determine the appeal "within 250 days after the notice of appeal is filed." (*Id.*, Subd 8.416(e).)

Ref.: Cal. Fms Pl. & Pr., Ch. 328, "Juvenile Courts: Dependency Proceedings"; W. Cal. Sum., 10 "Parent and Child" §§711, 713, 715, 716.

Article 2
Writs

Rule 8.450. Notice of intent to file writ petition to review order setting hearing under Welfare and Institutions Code section 366.26
Rule 8.452. Writ petition to review order setting hearing under Welfare and Institutions Code section 366.26 and rule 5.600
Rule 8.454. Notice of intent to file writ petition under Welfare and Institutions Code section 366.28 to review order designating specific placement of a dependent child after termination of parental rights
Rule 8.456. Writ petition under Welfare and Institutions Code section 366.28 to review order designating or denying specific placement of a dependent child after termination of parental rights

Rule 8.450. Notice of intent to file writ petition to review order setting hearing under Welfare and Institutions Code section 366.26

(a) Application

Rules 8.450–8.452 and 5.600 govern writ petitions to review orders setting a hearing under Welfare and Institutions Code section 366.26. [1] **Rules 8.485–8.493 do** not apply to petitions governed by these rules.

(Subd (a) amended effective January 1, 2009; previously amended effective January 1, 2006, July 1, 2006, and January 1, 2007.)

Rule 8.450(a). 2008 Deletes. [1] Rule 8.490 does

(b) Purpose

Rules 8.450–8.452 are intended to encourage and assist the reviewing courts to determine on their merits all writ petitions filed under these rules within the 120-day period for holding a hearing under Welfare and Institutions Code section 366.26.

(Subd (b) amended effective January 1, 2007.)

(c) Who may file

The petitioner's trial counsel, or, in the absence of trial counsel, the party, is responsible for filing any notice of intent and writ petition under rules 8.450–8.452. Trial counsel is encouraged to seek assistance from or consult with attorneys experienced in writ procedure.

(Subd (c) amended effective January 1, 2008; previously amended effective January 1, 2007.)

(d) Extensions of time

The superior court may not extend any time period prescribed by rules 8.450–8.452. The reviewing court may extend any time period, but must require an exceptional showing of good cause.

(Subd (d) amended effective January 1, 2007.)

(e) Notice of intent

(1) A party seeking writ review under rules 8.450–8.452 must file a notice of intent to file a writ petition and a request for the record.

(2) The notice must include all known dates of the hearing that resulted in the order under review.

(3) The notice must be signed by the party intending to file the petition or, if filed on behalf of a child, by the attorney of record for the child. The reviewing court may waive this requirement for good cause on the basis of a declaration by the attorney of record explaining why the party could not sign the notice.

(4) The date of the order setting the hearing is the date on which the court states the order on the record orally, or issues an order in writing, whichever occurs first. The notice of intent must be filed according to the following timeline requirements:

(A) If the party was present at the hearing when the court ordered a hearing under Welfare and Institutions Code section 366.26, the notice of intent must be filed within 7 days after the date of the order setting the hearing.

(B) If the party was notified of the order setting the hearing only by mail, the notice of intent must be filed within 12 days after the date the clerk mailed the notification.

(C) If the party was notified of the order setting the hearing by mail, and the notice was mailed to an address outside California but within the United States, the notice of intent must be filed within 17 days after the date the clerk mailed the notification.

(D) If the party was notified of the order setting the hearing by mail, and the notice was mailed to an address outside the United States, the notice of intent must be filed within 27 days after the date the clerk mailed the notification.

(E) If the order was made by a referee not acting as a temporary judge, the party has an additional 10 days to file the notice of intent as provided in rule 5.540(c).

(5) If the superior court clerk receives a notice of intent by mail from a party in a custodial institution after the time specified in (4) has expired but the envelope containing the notice of intent shows that it was mailed or delivered to custodial officials for mailing within the time specified in (4), the notice is deemed timely. The clerk must retain in the case file the envelope in which the notice was received.

(Subd (e) amended effective January 1, 2007.)

(f) Sending the notice of intent

(1) When the notice of intent is filed, the superior court clerk must immediately mail a copy of the notice to:

(A) Each counsel of record;

(B) Each party, including the child, if the child is 10 years of age or older; the mother; the father; the presumed and alleged parents; the dependent child's present caregiver; any legal guardian; and any person who has been declared a de facto parent and given standing to participate in the juvenile court proceedings;

(C) The probation officer or social worker;

(D) Any Court Appointed Special Advocate (CASA) volunteer;

(E) The grandparents of the child, if their address is known and if the parents' whereabouts are unknown; and

(F) The Indian custodian and tribe of the child or the Bureau of Indian Affairs if the identify or location of the parent or Indian custodian and the tribe cannot be determined.

(2) The clerk must promptly send a copy of the notice of intent and a proof of service list to the reviewing court, by first-class mail or fax. If the party was notified of the order setting the hearing only by mail, the clerk must include the date that the notification was mailed.

(Subd (f) amended effective January 1, 2007; previously amended effective January 1, 2006, and July 1, 2006.)

(g) Preparing the record

When the notice of intent is filed, the superior court clerk must:

(1) Immediately notify the reporter by telephone and in writing to prepare a reporter's transcript of the oral proceedings at each session of the hearing that resulted in the order under review and deliver the transcript to the clerk within 12 calendar days after the notice of intent is filed; and

(2) Within 20 days after the notice of intent is filed, prepare a clerk's transcript that includes the notice of intent, proof of service, and all items listed in rule 8.404(a).

(Subd (g) amended effective January 1, 2008; previously amended effective January 1, 2006, and January 1, 2007.)

(h) Sending the record

When the transcripts are certified as correct, the superior court clerk must immediately send:

(1) The original transcripts to the reviewing court by the most expeditious method, noting the sending date on each original, and

(2) One copy of each transcript to each counsel of record and any unrepresented party by any means as fast as United States Postal Service express mail.

(Subd (h) amended effective January 1, 2007.)

(i) Reviewing court clerk's duties

(1) The reviewing court clerk must immediately lodge the notice of intent. When the notice is lodged, the reviewing court has jurisdiction of the writ proceedings.

(2) When the record is filed in the reviewing court, that court's clerk must immediately notify the parties, stating the date on which the 10-day period for filing the writ petition under rule 8.452(c)(1) will expire.

(Subd (i) amended effective January 1, 2007.)

Rule 8.450 amended effective January 1, 2009; adopted as rule 38 effective January 1, 2005; previously amended and renumbered effective January 1, 2007; previously amended effective January 1, 2006, July 1, 2006, and January 1, 2008.

Advisory Committee Comment

Subdivision (d). The case law generally recognizes that the reviewing courts may grant extensions of time under these rules for exceptional good cause. (See, e.g., *Jonathan M. v. Superior Court* (1995) 39 Cal.App.4th 1826, and *In re Cathina W.* (1998) 68 Cal.App.4th 716 [recognizing that a late notice of intent may be filed on a showing of exceptional circumstances not under the petitioner's control].)

Ref.: Cal. Fms Pl. & Pr., Ch. 328, "Juvenile Courts: Dependency Proceedings"; W. Cal. Sum., 10 "Parent and Child" §§705, 709, 716, 717, 720–722, 920.

Rule 8.452.   Writ petition to review order setting hearing under Welfare and Institutions Code section 366.26 and rule 5.600

(a) Petition

(1) The petition must include:

(A) The identities of the parties;

(B) The date on which the superior court made the order setting the hearing;

(C) The date on which the hearing is scheduled to be held;

(D) A summary of the grounds of the petition; and

(E) The relief requested.

(2) The petition must be liberally construed.

(3) The petition must be accompanied by a memorandum.

(Subd (a) amended effective January 1, 2007.)

(b) Contents of the memorandum

(1) The memorandum must provide a summary of the significant facts, limited to matters in the record.

(2) The memorandum must state each point under a separate heading or subheading summarizing the point and support each point by argument and citation of authority.

(3) The memorandum must support any reference to a matter in the record by a citation to the record. The memorandum should explain the significance of any cited portion of the record and note any disputed aspects of the record.

(Subd (b) amended effective January 1, 2007.)

(c) Time to file petition and response

(1) The petition must be served and filed within 10 days after the record is filed in the reviewing court.

(2) Any response must be served and filed:

(A) Within 10 days—or, if the petition was served by mail, within 15 days—after the petition is filed; or

(B) Within 10 days after a respondent receives a request from the reviewing court for a response, unless the court specifies a shorter time.

(Subd (c) amended effective January 1, 2007.)

(d) Sending the writ

Petitioner must send the writ to all parties entitled to receive notice under Welfare and Institutions Code section 294, the child's Court Appointed Special Advocate (CASA) volunteer, the child's present caregiver, and any de facto parent given standing to participate in the juvenile court proceedings.

(Subd (d) adopted effective January 1, 2006.)

(e) Order to show cause or alternative writ

If the court intends to determine the petition on the merits, it must issue an order to show cause or alternative writ.

(Subd (e) relettered effective January 1, 2006; adopted as subd (d) effective January 1, 2005.)

(f) Augmenting or correcting the record in the reviewing court

(1) Except as provided in (2) and (3), rule 8.155 governs any augmentation or correction of the record.

(2) The petitioner must serve and file any request for augmentation or correction within 5 days—or, if the record exceeds 300 pages, within 7 days; or, if the record exceeds 600 pages, within 10 days—after receiving the record. A respondent must serve and file any such request

within 5 days after the petition is filed or an order to show cause has issued, whichever is later.

(3) An order augmenting or correcting the record may grant no more than 15 days for compliance. The clerk and the reporter must give the order the highest priority.

(4) The clerk must certify and send any supplemental transcripts as required by rule 8.450(h). If the augmentation or correction is ordered, the time to file any petition or response is extended by the number of additional days granted to augment or correct the record.

(Subd (f) amended effective January 1, 2007; adopted as subd (e) effective January 1, 2005; previously relettered effective January 1, 2006.)

(g) Stay

The reviewing court may stay the hearing set under Welfare and Institutions Code section 366.26, but must require an exceptional showing of good cause.

(Subd (g) relettered effective January 1, 2006; adopted as subd (f) effective January 1, 2005.)

(h) Oral argument

(1) The reviewing court must hear oral argument within 30 days after the response is filed or due to be filed, unless the court extends the time for good cause or counsel waive argument.

(2) If argument is waived, the cause is deemed submitted not later than 30 days after the response is filed or due to be filed.

(Subd (h) relettered effective January 1, 2006; adopted as subd (g) effective January 1, 2005.)

(i) Decision

(1) Absent exceptional circumstances, the reviewing court must decide the petition on the merits by written opinion.

(2) The reviewing court clerk must promptly notify the parties of any decision and must promptly send a certified copy of any writ or order to the court named as respondent.

(3) If the writ or order stays or prohibits proceedings set to occur within 7 days or requires action within 7 days—or in any other urgent situation—the reviewing court clerk must make a reasonable effort to notify the clerk of the respondent court by telephone. The clerk of the respondent court must then notify the judge or officer most directly concerned.

(4) The reviewing court clerk need not give telephonic notice of the summary denial of a writ, unless a stay previously issued will be dissolved.

(Subd (i) amended effective January 1, 2007; adopted as subd (h) effective January 1, 2005; relettered as subd (i) effective January 1, 2006.)

Rule 8.452 amended and renumbered effective January 1, 2007; adopted as rule 38.1 effective January 1, 2005; previously amended effective January 1, 2006.

Advisory Committee Comment

Subdivision (e). Subdivision (e) tracks the second sentence of former rule 39.1B(*l*). (But see *Maribel M. v. Superior Court* (1998) 61 Cal.App.4th 1469, 1471–1476.)

Subdivision (i). Subdivision (i)(1) tracks former rule 39.1B(o). (But see *Maribel M. v. Superior Court* (1998) 61 Cal.App.4th 1469, 1471–1476.)

Ref.: Cal. Fms Pl. & Pr., Ch. 328, "Juvenile Courts: Dependency Proceedings"; W. Cal. Sum., 10 "Parent and Child" §§705, 716, 717, 720, 722, 723, 727, 920.

Rule 8.454. Notice of intent to file writ petition under Welfare and Institutions Code section 366.28 to review order designating specific placement of a dependent child after termination of parental rights

(a) Application

Rules 8.454–8.456 govern writ petitions to review placement orders following termination of parental rights entered on or after January 1, 2005. "Posttermination placement order" as used in this rule and rule 8.456 refers to orders following termination of parental rights. [1] **Rules 8.485–8.493 do** not apply to petitions governed by these rules.

(Subd (a) amended effective January 1, 2009; previously amended effective January 1, 2007.)

Rule 8.454(a). 2008 Deletes. [1] Rule 8.490 does

(b) Purpose

The purpose of this rule is to facilitate and implement Welfare and Institutions Code section 366.28. Delays caused by appeals from court orders designating the specific placement of a dependent child after parental rights have been terminated may cause a substantial detriment to the child.

(c) Who may file

The petitioner's trial counsel, or, in the absence of trial counsel, the party, is responsible for filing any notice of intent and writ petition under rules 8.454–8.456. Trial counsel is encouraged to seek assistance from, or consult with, attorneys experienced in writ procedure.

(Subd (c) amended effective January 1, 2008; previously amended effective January 1, 2007.)

(d) Extensions of time

The superior court may not extend any time period prescribed by rules 8.454–8.456. The reviewing court may extend any time period, but must require an exceptional showing of good cause.

(Subd (d) amended effective January 1, 2007.)

(e) Notice of intent

(1) A party seeking writ review under rules 8.454–8.456 must file a notice of intent to file a writ petition and a request for the record.

(2) The notice must include all known dates of the hearing that resulted in the order under review.

(3) The notice must be signed by the party intending to file the petition or, if filed on behalf of the child, by the attorney of record for the child. The reviewing court may waive this requirement for good cause on the basis of a declaration by the attorney of record explaining why the party could not sign the notice.

(4) The notice must be served and filed within 7 days after the date of the posttermination placement order or, if the order was made by a referee not acting as a temporary judge, within 7 days after the referee's order becomes final under rule 5.540(c). The date of the posttermination placement order is the date on which the court states the order on the record orally or in writing, whichever first occurs.

(5) If the party was notified of the posttermination placement order only by mail, the notice of intent must be filed within 12 days after the date that the clerk mailed the notification.

(Subd (e) amended effective January 1, 2007.)

(f) Premature or late notice of intent to file writ petition

(1) A notice of intent to file a writ petition under Welfare and Institutions Code section 366.28 is premature if filed before a date for a postdetermination placement order has been made. The reviewing court may treat the notice as filed immediately after the postdetermination order has been made.

(2) The superior court clerk must mark a late notice of intent to file a writ petition under section 366.28 "Received [date] but not filed," notify the party that the notice was not filed because it was late, and send a copy of the marked notice to the party's counsel of record, if applicable.

(Subd (f) amended effective January 1, 2007; adopted effective January 1, 2006.)

(g) Sending the notice of intent

(1) When the notice of intent is filed, the superior court clerk must immediately mail a copy of the notice to:

(A) Each counsel of record;

(B) Each relevant party, including the child, if the child is 10 years of age or older, the child's present caregiver, any legal guardian, and any person who has been declared a de facto parent and given standing to participate in the juvenile court proceedings;

(C) The probation officer or social worker;

(D) The child's Court Appointed Special Advocate (CASA) volunteer; and

(E) The tribe of an Indian child and the Indian custodian.

(2) The clerk must promptly send a copy of the notice and a proof of service list to the reviewing court, by first-class mail or fax. If the party was notified of the posttermination placement order only by mail, the clerk must include the date that the notification was mailed.

(Subd (g) amended effective January 1, 2007; adopted as subd (f) effective January 1, 2005; relettered effective January 1, 2006.)

(h) Preparing the record

When the notice of intent is filed, the superior court clerk must:

(1) Immediately notify the reporter by telephone and in writing to prepare a reporter's transcript of the oral proceedings at each session of the hearing that resulted in the order under review and to deliver the transcript to the clerk within 12 calendar days after the notice of intent is filed; and

(2) Within 20 days after the notice of intent is filed, prepare a clerk's transcript that includes the notice of intent, proof of service, and all items listed in rule 8.404(a).

(Subd (h) amended effective January 1, 2008; adopted as subd (g) effective January 1, 2005; previously amended and relettered effective January 1, 2006; previously amended effective July 1, 2006, and January 1, 2007.)

(i) Sending the record

When the transcripts are certified as correct, the superior court clerk must immediately send:

(1) The original transcripts to the reviewing court by the most expeditious method, noting the sending date on each original; and

(2) One copy of each transcript to each counsel of record and any unrepresented party and unrepresented custodian of the dependent child by any means as fast as United States Postal Service express mail.

(Subd (i) amended effective January 1, 2007; adopted as subd (h) effective January 1, 2005; relettered effective January 1, 2006.)

(j) Reviewing court clerk's duties

(1) The reviewing court clerk must promptly lodge the notice of intent. When the notice is lodged, the reviewing court has jurisdiction over the writ proceedings.

(2) When the record is filed in the reviewing court, that court's clerk must immediately notify the parties, stating the date on which the 10-day period for filing the writ petition under rule 8.456(c)(1) will expire.

(Subd (j) amended effective January 1, 2007; adopted as subd (i) effective January 1, 2005; relettered effective January 1, 2006.)

Rule 8.454 amended effective January 1, 2009; adopted as rule 38.2 effective January 1, 2005; previously amended and renumbered effective January 1, 2007; previously amended effective January 1, 2006, July 1, 2006, and January 1, 2008.

Ref.: Cal. Fms Pl. & Pr., Ch. 328, "Juvenile Courts: Dependency Proceedings"; W. Cal. Sum., 10 "Parent and Child" §§693C, 704, 716, 724–726, 920.

Rule 8.456. Writ petition under Welfare and Institutions Code section 366.28 to review order designating or denying specific placement of a dependent child after termination of parental rights

(a) Petition

(1) The petition must include:

(A) The identities of the parties;

(B) The date on which the superior court made the posttermination placement order;

(C) A summary of the grounds of the petition; and

(D) The relief requested.

(2) The petition must be liberally construed.

(3) The petition must be accompanied by a memorandum.

(Subd (a) amended effective January 1, 2007.)

(b) Contents of memorandum

(1) The memorandum must provide a summary of the significant facts, limited to matters in the record.

(2) The memorandum must state each point under a separate heading or subheading summarizing the point and support each point by argument and citation of authority.

(3) The memorandum must support any reference to a matter in the record by a citation to the record. The memorandum should explain the significance of any cited portion of the record and note any disputed aspects of the record.

(Subd (b) amended effective January 1, 2007.)

(c) Time to file petition and response

(1) The petition must be served and filed within 10 days after the record is filed in the reviewing court. The petitioner must give notice to all parties entitled to receive notice under rule 8.454.

(2) Any response must be served and filed:

(A) Within 10 days—or, if the petition was served by mail, within 15 days—after the petition is filed; or

(B) Within 10 days after a respondent receives a request from the reviewing court for a response, unless the court specifies a shorter time.

(Subd (c) amended effective January 1, 2007; previously amended effective January 1, 2006.)

(d) Sending the writ

Petitioner must send the writ to all parties entitled to receive notice under Welfare and Institutions Code section 294, any Court Appointed Special Advocate (CASA) volunteer, the child's present caregiver, the child's prospective adoptive parties, and any de facto parent given standing to participate in the juvenile court proceedings.

(Subd (d) adopted effective January 1, 2006.)

(e) Order to show cause or alternative writ

If the court intends to determine the petition on the merits, it must issue an order to show cause or alternative writ.

(Subd (e) relettered effective January 1, 2006; adopted as subd (d) effective January 1, 2005.)

(f) Augmenting or correcting the record in the reviewing court

(1) Except as provided in (2) and (3), rule 8.155 governs augmentation or correction of the record.

(2) The petitioner must serve and file any request for augmentation or correction within 5 days—or, if the record exceeds 300 pages, within 7 days; or, if the record exceeds 600 pages, within 10 days—after receiving the record. A respondent must serve and file any such request within 5 days after the petition is filed or an order to show cause has issued, whichever is later.

(3) An order augmenting or correcting the record may grant no more than 15 days for compliance. The clerk and the reporter must give the order the highest priority.

(4) The clerk must certify and send any supplemental transcripts as required by rule 8.454(i). If the augmentation or correction is ordered, the time to file any petition or response is extended by the number of additional days granted to augment or correct the record.

(Subd (f) amended effective January 1, 2007; adopted as subd (e) effective January 1, 2005; previously relettered effective January 1, 2006.)

(g) Stay

A request by petitioner for a stay of the posttermination placement order will not be granted unless the writ petition shows that implementation of the superior court's placement order pending the reviewing court's decision is likely to cause detriment to the child if the order is ultimately reversed.

(Subd (g) amended effective February 24, 2006; adopted as subd (f) effective January 1, 2005; previously relettered effective January 1, 2006.)

(h) Oral argument

(1) The reviewing court must hear oral argument within 30 days after the response is filed or due to be filed, unless the court extends the time for good cause or counsel waive argument.

(2) If argument is waived, the cause is deemed submitted not later than 30 days after the response is filed or due to be filed.

(Subd (h) relettered effective January 1, 2006; adopted as subd (g) effective January 1, 2005.)

(i) Decision

(1) Absent exceptional circumstances, the reviewing court must review the petition and decide it on the merits by written opinion.

(2) The reviewing court clerk must promptly notify the parties of any decision and must promptly send a certified copy of any writ or order to the court named as respondent.

(3) If the writ or order stays or requires action within 7 days—or in any other urgent situation—the reviewing court clerk must make a reasonable effort to notify the clerk of the respondent court by telephone. The clerk of the respondent court must then notify the judge or officer most directly concerned.

(4) The reviewing court clerk need not give telephonic notice of the summary denial of a writ, unless a stay previously issued and will be dissolved.

(Subd (i) amended effective January 1, 2007; adopted as subd (h) effective January 1, 2005; relettered effective January 1, 2006.)

(j) Right to appeal other orders

This section does not affect the right of a parent, a legal guardian, or the child to appeal any order that is otherwise appealable and that is issued at a hearing held under Welfare and Institutions Code section 366.26.

(Subd (j) amended effective January 1, 2007; adopted as subd (i) effective January 1, 2005; previously relettered effective January 1, 2006.)

Rule 8.456 amended and renumbered effective January 1, 2007; adopted as rule 38.3 effective January 1, 2005; previously amended effective January 1, 2006, and February 24, 2006.

Ref.: Cal. Fms Pl. & Pr., Ch. 328, "Juvenile Courts: Dependency Proceedings"; W. Cal. Sum., 10 "Parent and Child" §§704, 716, 717, 722, 723, 725–727, 920.

Article 3
Hearing and Decision

Rule 8.470. Hearing and decision in the Court of Appeal
Rule 8.472. Hearing and decision in the Supreme Court
Rule 8.474. Procedures and data

Rule 8.470.   Hearing and decision in the Court of Appeal

Except as provided in rules 8.400–8.456, rules 8.252–8.272 govern hearing and decision in the Court of Appeal in juvenile cases.

Rule 8.470 amended and renumbered effective January 1, 2007; adopted as rule 38.4 effective January 1, 2005; previously amended effective July 1, 2005.

Ref.: Cal. Fms Pl. & Pr., Ch. 328, "Juvenile Courts: Dependency Proceedings"; W. Cal. Sum., 10 "Parent and Child" §§709, 716.

Rule 8.472.   Hearing and decision in the Supreme Court

Rules 8.500–8.552 govern hearing and decision in the Supreme Court in juvenile cases.

Rule 8.472 amended and renumbered effective January 1, 2007; adopted as rule 38.5 effective January 1, 2005; previously amended effective July 1, 2005.

Ref.: Cal. Fms Pl. & Pr., Ch. 328, "Juvenile Courts: Dependency Proceedings."

Rule 8.474. Procedures and data

(a) Procedures

The judges and clerks of the superior courts and the reviewing courts must adopt procedures to identify the records and expedite the processing of all appeals and writs in juvenile cases.

(b) Data

The clerks of the superior courts and the reviewing courts must the provide data required to assist the Judicial Council in evaluating the effectiveness of the rules governing appeals and writs in juvenile cases.

Rule 8.474 renumbered effective January 1, 2007; adopted as rule 38.6 effective January 1, 2005.

Ref.: Cal. Fms Pl. & Pr., Ch. 328, "Juvenile Courts: Dependency Proceedings"; W. Cal. Sum., 10 "Parent and Child" §§355, 709, 716.

Chapter 6
Conservatorship Appeals

Rule 8.480. Appeal from order establishing conservatorship
Rule 8.482. Appeal from judgment authorizing conservator to consent to sterilization of conservatee

Rule 8.480. Appeal from order establishing conservatorship

(a) Application

Except as otherwise provided in this rule, rules 8.304–8.368 and 8.508 govern appeals from orders establishing conservatorships under Welfare and Institutions Code section 5350 et seq.

(Subd (a) amended effective January 1, 2007.)

(b) Clerk's transcript

The clerk's transcript must contain:

(1) The petition;

(2) Any demurrer or other plea;

(3) Any written motion with supporting and opposing memoranda and attachments;

(4) Any filed medical or social worker reports;

(5) All court minutes;

(6) All instructions submitted in writing, each noting the party requesting it;

(7) Any verdict;

(8) Any written opinion of the court;

(9) The judgment or order appealed from;

(10) The notice of appeal; and

(11) Any application for additional record and any order on the application.

(Subd (b) amended effective January 1, 2007.)

(c) Reporter's transcript

The reporter's transcript must contain all oral proceedings, excluding the voir dire examination of jurors and any opening statement.

(d) Sending the record

The clerk must not send a copy of the record to the Attorney General or the district attorney unless that office represents a party.

(e) Briefs

The parties must not serve copies of their briefs:

(1) On the Attorney General or the district attorney, unless that office represents a party; or

(2) On the Supreme Court under rule 8.44(b)(1).

(Subd (e) amended effective January 1, 2007.)

Rule 8.480 amended and renumbered effective January 1, 2007; repealed and adopted as rule 39 effective January 1, 2005.

Ref.: Cal. Fms Pl. & Pr., Ch. 12A, "Adoptions: Termination of Parental Rights"; W. Cal. Sum., 10 "Parent and Child" §460.

Rule 8.482. Appeal from judgment authorizing conservator to consent to sterilization of conservatee

(a) Application

Except as otherwise provided in this rule, rules 8.304–8.368 and 8.508 govern appeals from judgments authorizing a conservator to consent to the sterilization of a developmentally disabled adult conservatee.

(Subd (a) amended effective January 1, 2007.)

(b) When appeal is taken automatically

An appeal from a judgment authorizing a conservator to consent to the sterilization of a developmentally disabled adult conservatee is taken automatically, without any action by the conservatee, when the judgment is rendered.

(c) Superior court clerk's duties

After entering the judgment, the clerk must immediately:

(1) Begin preparing a clerk's transcript and notify the reporter to prepare a reporter's transcript; and

(2) Mail certified copies of the judgment to the Court of Appeal and the Attorney General.

(Subd (c) amended effective January 1, 2007.)

(d) Clerk's transcript

The clerk's transcript must contain:

(1) The petition and notice of hearing;

(2) All court minutes;

(3) Any application, motion, or notice of motion, with supporting and opposing memoranda and attachments;

(4) Any report or other document submitted to the court;

(5) Any transcript of a proceeding pertaining to the case;

(6) The statement of decision; and

(7) The judgment or order appealed from.

(Subd (d) amended effective January 1, 2007.)

(e) Reporter's transcript

The reporter's transcript must contain all oral proceedings, including:

(1) All proceedings at the hearing on the petition, with opening statements and closing arguments;

(2) All proceedings on motions;

(3) Any comments on the evidence by the court; and

(4) Any oral opinion or oral statement of decision.

(Subd (e) amended effective January 1, 2007.)

(f) Preparing and sending transcripts

(1) The clerk and the reporter must prepare and send an original and two copies of each of the transcripts as provided in rule 8.336.

(2) Probate Code section 1963 governs the cost of preparing the record on appeal.

(Subd (f) amended effective January 1, 2007.)

(g) Confidential material

(1) Written reports of physicians, psychologists, and clinical social workers, and any other matter marked confidential by the court, may be inspected only by court personnel, the parties and their counsel, the district appellate project, and other persons designated by the court.

(2) Material under (1) must be sent to the reviewing court in a sealed envelope marked "CONFIDENTIAL— MAY NOT BE EXAMINED WITHOUT COURT ORDER."

(h) Trial counsel's continuing representation

To expedite preparation and certification of the record, the conservatee's trial counsel must continue to represent the conservatee until appellate counsel is retained or appointed.

(i) Appointment of appellate counsel

If appellate counsel has not been retained for the conservatee, the reviewing court must appoint such counsel.

Rule 8.482 amended and renumbered effective January 1, 2007; repealed and adopted as rule 39.1 effective January 1, 2005.

Ref.: Cal. Fms Pl. & Pr., Ch. 12A, "Adoptions: Termination of Parental Rights"; W. Cal. Sum., 10 "Parent and Child" §357, 14 "Wills and Probate" §1059.

Chapter 7
Writs of Mandate, Certiorari, and Prohibition in the Supreme Court and Court of Appeal

Title 8, Appellate Rules—Division 1, Rules Relating to the Supreme Court and Courts of Appeal—Chapter 7, Writs of Mandate, Certiorari, and Prohibition in the Supreme Court and Court of Appeal adopted effective January 1, 2009.

Rule 8.485.   Application

(a) Writ proceedings governed

Except as provided in (b), the rules in this chapter govern petitions to the Supreme Court and Court of Appeal for writs of mandate, certiorari, or prohibition, or other writs within the original jurisdiction of these courts. In all respects not provided for in these rules, rule 8.204 governs the form and content of documents in the proceedings governed by this chapter.

(Subd (a) adopted effective January 1, 2009.)

(b) Writ proceedings not governed

These rules do not apply to petitions for writs of mandate, certiorari, or prohibition in the appellate division of the superior court under rules 8.930–8.936, petitions for writs of supersedeas under rule 8.116, petitions for writs of habeas corpus except as provided in rule 8.384, or petitions for writs of review under rules 8.495–8.498.

(Subd (b) adopted effective January 1, 2009.)
Rule 8.485 adopted effective January 1, 2009.

Rule 8.486.   Petitions

(a) Contents of petition

(1) If the petition could have been filed first in a lower court, it must explain why the reviewing court should issue the writ as an original matter.

(2) If the petition names as respondent a judge, court, board, or other officer acting in a public capacity, it must disclose the name of any real party in interest.

(3) If the petition seeks review of trial court proceedings that are also the subject of a pending appeal, the notice "Related Appeal Pending" must appear on the cover of the petition and the first paragraph of the petition must state:

(A) The appeal's title, trial court docket number, and any reviewing court docket number; and

(B) If the petition is filed under Penal Code section 1238.5, the date the notice of appeal was filed.

(4) The petition must be verified.

(5) The petition must be accompanied by a memorandum, which need not repeat facts alleged in the petition.

(6) Rule 8.204(c) governs the length of the petition and memorandum, but the tables, the certificate, the verification, and any supporting documents are excluded from the limits stated in rule 8.204(c)(1) and (2).

(7) If the petition requests a temporary stay, it must comply with [1] **the following or the reviewing court may decline to consider the request for a temporary stay:**

(A) The petition must explain the urgency.

(B) The cover of the petition must prominently display the notice "STAY REQUESTED" and identify the nature and date of the proceeding or act sought to be stayed.

(C) The trial court and department involved and the name and telephone number of the trial judge whose order the request seeks to stay must appear either on the cover or at the beginning of the text.

(Subd (a) repealed, amended and relettered effective January 1, 2009; adopted as subd (b) effective January 1, 2005; previously amended effective January 1, 2006, and January 1, 2007.)

Rule 8.486(a).   2008 Deletes. [1] rule 8.116 and

(b) Contents of supporting documents

(1) A petition that seeks review of a trial court ruling must be accompanied by an adequate record, including copies of:

(A) The ruling from which the petition seeks relief;

(B) All documents and exhibits submitted to the trial court supporting and opposing the petitioner's position;

(C) Any other documents or portions of documents submitted to the trial court that are necessary for a complete understanding of the case and the ruling under review; and

(D) A reporter's transcript of the oral proceedings that resulted in the ruling under review.

(2) **In exigent circumstances, the petition may be filed without the documents required by (1)(A)–(C) if**

counsel or, **if the petitioner is unrepresented, the petitioner files a declaration that explains the urgency and the circumstances making the documents unavailable and fairly summarizes their substance.**

(3) If a transcript under (1)(D) is unavailable, the record must include a declaration by counsel **or, if the petitioner is unrepresented, the petitioner**:

(A) Explaining why the transcript is unavailable and fairly summarizing the proceedings, including [1] **the petitioner's** arguments and any statement by the court supporting its ruling. **This declaration may omit a full summary of the proceedings if part of the relief sought is an order to prepare a transcript for use by an indigent criminal defendant in support of the petition and if the declaration demonstrates the petitioner's need for and entitlement to the transcript**; or

(B) Stating that the transcript has been ordered, the date it was ordered, and the date it is expected to be filed, which must be a date before any action requested of the reviewing court other than issuance of a temporary stay supported by other parts of the record.

[2] **(4)** If the petitioner does not submit the required record or explanations or does not present facts sufficient to excuse the failure to submit them, the court may summarily deny a stay request, the petition, or both.

(Subd (b) amended and relettered effective January 1, 2009; adopted as subd (c) effective January 1, 2005; previously amended effective January 1, 2006, July 1, 2006, and January 1, 2007.)

Rule 8.486(b).   2008 Deletes. [1] counsel's [2] (3) A declaration under (2) may omit a full summary of the proceedings if part of the relief sought is an order to prepare a transcript for use by an indigent criminal defendant in support of the petition and if the declaration demonstrates the petitioner's need for and entitlement to the transcript. (4) In exigent circumstances, the petition may be filed without the documents required by (1)(A)–(C) if counsel files a declaration that explains the urgency and the circumstances making the documents unavailable and fairly summarizes their substance. (5)

(c) Form of supporting documents

(1) Documents submitted under [1] **(b)** must comply with the following requirements:

(A) They must be bound together at the end of the petition or in separate volumes not exceeding 300 pages each. The pages must be consecutively numbered.

(B) They must be index-tabbed by number or letter.

(C) They must begin with a table of contents listing each document by its title and its index-tab number or letter. If a document has attachments, the table of contents must give the title of each attachment and a brief description of its contents.

(2) The clerk must file any supporting documents not complying with (1), but the court may notify the petitioner that it may strike or summarily deny the petition if the documents are not brought into compliance within a stated reasonable time of not less than 5 days.

(3) Rule 8.44(a) governs the number of copies of supporting documents to be filed in the Supreme Court. Rule 8.44(b) governs the number of supporting documents to be filed in the Court of Appeal.

(Subd (c) amended and relettered effective January 1, 2009; adopted as subd (d) effective January 1, 2005; previously amended effective January 1, 2006, and January 1, 2007.)

Rule 8.486(c).   2008 Deletes. [1] (c)

(d) Sealed records

Rule 8.160 applies if a party seeks to lodge or file a sealed record or to unseal a record.

(Subd (d) relettered effective January 1, 2009; adopted as subd (e) effective January 1, 2005; previously amended effective January 1, 2007.)

(e) Service

(1) If the respondent is the superior court or a judge of that court, the petition and one set of supporting documents must be served on any named real party in interest, but only the petition must be served on the respondent.

(2) If the respondent is not the superior court or a judge of that court, both the petition and one set of supporting documents must be served on the respondent and on any named real party in interest.

(3) In addition to complying with the requirements of rule 8.25, the proof of service must give the telephone number of each attorney served.

(4) The petition must be served on a public officer or agency when required by statute or rule 8.29.

(5) The clerk must file the petition even if its proof of service is defective, but if the petitioner fails to file a corrected proof of service within 5 days after the clerk gives notice of the defect the court may strike the petition or impose a lesser sanction.

(6) The court may allow the petition to be filed without proof of service.

(Subd (e) relettered effective January 1, 2009; adopted as subd (f) effective January 1, 2005; previously amended effective January 1, 2007.)

(f) Service [Relettered]

(Subd (f) relettered to subd (e) effective January 1, 2009; adopted effective January 1, 2005; previously amended effective January 1, 2007.)

(g) Preliminary opposition [Repealed]

(Subd (g) repealed effective January 1, 2009; amended effective January 1, 2007.)

(h) Return or opposition; reply [Repealed]

(Subd (h) repealed effective January 1, 2009.)

(i) Certificate of Interested Entities or Persons [Repealed]

(Subd (i) repealed effective January 1, 2009; adopted effective July 1, 2006; previously amended effective January 1, 2007 and January 1, 2008.)

(j) Attorney General's amicus curiae brief [Repealed]

(Subd (j) repealed effective January 1, 2009; adopted as subd (i) effective January 1, 2005; relettered effective July 1, 2006; previously amended effective January 1, 2007.)

(k) Notice to trial court [Repealed]

(Subd (k) repealed effective January 1, 2009; adopted as subd (j) effective January 1, 2005; relettered effective July 1, 2006, previously amended effective January 1, 2007.)

(l) Responsive pleading under Code of Civil Procedure section 418.10 [Repealed]

(Subd (l) repealed effective January 1, 2009; adopted as subd (k) effective January 1, 2005; previously relettered effective July 1, 2006.)

(m) Costs [Repealed]

(Subd (m) repealed effective January 1, 2009; adopted as subd (l) effective January 1, 2005; previously amended effective July 1, 2005; relettered effective July 1, 2006; previously amended effective January 1, 2007 and January 1, 2008.)

Rules of Court

(n) Sanctions [Repealed]

(Subd (n) repealed effective January 1, 2009; adopted effective January 1, 2008.)

Rule 8.486 amended and renumbered effective January 1, 2009; repealed and adopted as rule 56 effective January 1, 2005; previously amended and renumbered as rule 8.490 effective January 1, 2007; previously amended effective July 1, 2005, January 1, 2006, July 1, 2006, and January 1, 2008.

Advisory Committee Comment

Subdivision (a). Because of the importance of the point, rule 8.486(a)(6) explicitly states that the provisions of rule 8.204(c)—and hence the word-count limits imposed by that rule—apply to a petition for original writ.

Subdivision (e). Rule 8.25, which generally governs service and filing in reviewing courts, also applies to the original proceedings covered by this rule.

Ref.: Cal. Fms Pl. & Pr., Ch. 2, "Procedural Guide for Civil Actions," Ch. 3, "Abatement of Actions," Ch. 4, "Abortion and Birth Control Methods," Ch. 18, "Alcoholic Beverage Licenses," Ch. 61, "Associations and Clubs," Ch. 71, "Attorney Discipline," Ch. 92, "Automobiles: Drivers' Licenses," Ch. 110, "Churches and Religious Organizations," Ch. 120, "Class Actions," Ch. 135, "Contempt," Ch. 200, "Discovery: Review of Discovery Orders," Ch. 212, "Dismissal," Ch. 220, "Dissolution of Marriage: Master Procedural Guide," Ch. 243, "Elections," Ch. 292, "Habeas Corpus," Ch. 300, "Indemnity and Contribution," Ch. 317, "Judges," Ch. 323, "Jurisdiction: Personal Jurisdiction, Inconvenient Forum, and Appearances," Ch. 328, "Juvenile Courts: Dependency Proceedings," Ch. 348, "Lis Pendens," Ch. 358, "Mandate and Prohibition," Ch. 462, "Public Accountants," Ch. 470C, "Public Records Act," Ch. 474, "Availability of Judicial Review of Agency Decisions," Ch. 474C, "Procedures in Reviewing Agency Decisions," Ch. 492, "Review (Certiorari), Writ of," Ch. 577, "Workers' Compensation"; Cal. Class Actions Prac. & Proc., §§20.03[9], 21.07[2][b], [d][iii]; MB Prac. Guide: Cal. Pretrial Proc., §§9.50[2][c], 21.22, 21.23[1A], 33.20[4]; W. Cal. Sum., 10 "Parent and Child" §§717, 724.

Rule 8.487. Opposition and Attorney General amicus briefs

(a) Preliminary opposition

(1) Within 10 days after the petition is filed, the respondent or any real party in interest, separately or jointly, may serve and file a preliminary opposition.

(2) A preliminary opposition must contain a memorandum and a statement of any material fact not included in the petition.

(3) Within 10 days after a preliminary opposition is filed, the petitioner may serve and file a reply.

(4) Without requesting preliminary opposition or waiting for a reply, the court may grant or deny a request for temporary stay, deny the petition, issue an alternative writ or order to show cause, or notify the parties that it is considering issuing a peremptory writ in the first instance.

(Subd (a) adopted effective January 1, 2009.)

(b) Return or opposition; reply

(1) If the court issues an alternative writ or order to show cause, the respondent or any real party in interest, separately or jointly, may serve and file a return by demurrer, verified answer, or both. If the court notifies the parties that it is considering issuing a peremptory writ in the first instance, the respondent or any real party in interest may serve and file an opposition.

(2) Unless the court orders otherwise, the return or opposition must be served and filed within 30 days after

the court issues the alternative writ or order to show cause or notifies the parties that it is considering issuing a peremptory writ in the first instance.

(3) Unless the court orders otherwise, the petitioner may serve and file a reply within 15 days after the return or opposition is filed.

(4) If the return is by demurrer alone and the demurrer is not sustained, the court may issue the peremptory writ without granting leave to answer.

(Subd (b) adopted effective January 1, 2009.)

(c) Attorney General's amicus curiae brief

(1) If the court issues an alternative writ or order to show cause, the Attorney General may file an amicus curiae brief without the permission of the Chief Justice or presiding justice, unless the brief is submitted on behalf of another state officer or agency.

(2) The Attorney General must serve and file the brief within 14 days after the return is filed or, if no return is filed, within 14 days after the date it was due.

(3) The brief must provide the information required by rule 8.200(c)(2) and comply with rule 8.200(c)(4).

(4) Any party may serve and file an answer within 14 days after the brief is filed.

(Subd (c) adopted effective January 1, 2009.)

Rule 8.487 adopted effective January 1, 2009.

Advisory Committee Comment

Subdivision (a). Consistent with practice, rule 8.487 draws a distinction between a "preliminary opposition," which the respondent or a real party in interest may file before the court takes any action on the petition ((a)(1)), and a more formal "opposition," which the respondent or a real party in interest may file if the court notifies the parties that it is considering issuing a peremptory writ in the first instance ((b)(1)).

Subdivision (a)(1) allows the respondent or any real party in interest to serve and file a preliminary opposition within 10 days after the petition is filed. The reviewing court retains the power to act in any case without obtaining preliminary opposition ((a)(4)).

Subdivision (a)(3) allows a petitioner to serve and file a reply within 10 days after a preliminary opposition is filed. To permit prompt action in urgent cases, however, the provision recognizes that the reviewing court may act on the petition without waiting for a reply.

Subdivision (a)(4) recognizes that the reviewing court may "grant or deny a request for temporary stay" without requesting preliminary opposition or waiting for a reply.

The several references in rule 8.487 to the power of the court to issue a peremptory writ in the first instance after notifying the parties that it is considering doing so ((a)–(b)) implement the rule of *Palma v. U.S. Industrial Fasteners, Inc.* (1984) 36 Cal.3d 171.

Subdivision (b). Subdivision (b)(2) requires that the return or opposition be served and filed within 30 days after the court issues the alternative writ or order to show cause or notifies the parties that it is considering issuing a peremptory writ in the first instance. To permit prompt action in urgent cases, however, the provision recognizes that the reviewing court may order otherwise.

Subdivision (b)(3) formalizes the common practice of permitting petitioners to file replies to returns and specifies that such a reply must be served and filed within 15 days after the return is filed. To permit prompt action in urgent cases, however, the provision recognizes that the reviewing court may order otherwise.

Rule 8.488. Certificate of Interested Entities or Persons

(a) Application

This rule applies in writ proceedings in criminal cases in which an entity is the defendant and in civil cases other than family, juvenile, guardianship, and conservatorship cases.

(Subd (a) adopted effective January 1, 2009.)

(b) Compliance with rule 8.208

Each party in a civil case and any entity that is a defendant in a criminal case must comply with the requirements of rule 8.208 concerning serving and filing a certificate of interested entities or persons.

(Subd (b) adopted effective January 1, 2009.)

(c) Placement of certificates

(1) The petitioner's certificate must be included in the petition.

(2) The certificates of the respondent and real party in interest must be included in their preliminary opposition or, if no such opposition is filed, in their return, if any.

(3) The certificate must appear after the cover and before the tables.

(4) If the identity of any party has not been publicly disclosed in the proceedings, the party may file an application for permission to file its certificate under seal separately from the petition, preliminary opposition, or return.

(Subd (c) adopted effective January 1, 2009.)

(d) Failure to file a certificate

(1) If a party fails to file a certificate as required under (b) and (c), the clerk must notify the party by mail that the party must file the certificate within 10 days after the clerk's notice is mailed and that if the party fails to comply, the court may impose one of the following sanctions:

(A) If the party is the petitioner, the court may strike the petition; or

(B) If the party is the respondent or the real party in interest, the court may strike that party's document.

(2) If the party fails to file the certificate as specified in the notice under (1), the court may impose the sanctions specified in the notice.

(Subd (d) adopted effective January 1, 2009.)

Rule 8.488 adopted effective January 1, 2009.

Advisory Committee Comment

The Judicial Council has adopted an optional form, *Certificate of Interested Entities or Persons* (form APP-008), that can be used to file the certificate required by this provision.

Subdivision (a). Under rule 8.208(c), for purposes of certificates of interested entities or persons, an "entity" means a corporation, a partnership, a firm, or any other association, but does not include a governmental entity or its agencies or a natural person.

Rule 8.489. Notice to trial court

(a) Notice if writ issues

If a writ or order issues directed to any judge, court, board, or other officer, the reviewing court clerk must promptly send a certified copy of the writ or order to the person or entity to whom it is addressed.

(Subd (a) adopted effective January 1, 2009.)

(b) Notice by telephone

(1) If the writ or order stays or prohibits proceedings set to occur within 7 days or requires action within 7 days—or in any other urgent situation—the reviewing court clerk must make a reasonable effort to notify the clerk of the respondent court by telephone. The clerk of the respondent court must then notify the judge or officer most directly concerned.

(2) The clerk need not give telephonic notice of the summary denial of a writ, whether or not a stay previously issued.

(Subd (b) adopted effective January 1, 2009.)

Rule 8.489 adopted effective January 1, 2009.

Rule 8.490. Petitions for writ of mandate, certiorari, or prohibition [Renumbered]

Rule 8.490 renumbered to rule 8.486 effective January 1, 2009; repealed and adopted as rule 56 effective January 1, 2005; previously amended effective July 1, 2005, January 1, 2006, July 1, 2006 and January 1, 2008; previously amended and renumbered effective January 1, 2007.

Another rule 8.490 follows.

Rule 8.490. Filing, finality, and modification of decisions; remittitur

(a) Filing and modification of decisions

Rule 8.264(a) and (c) govern the filing and modification of decisions in writ proceedings.

(Subd (a) adopted effective January 1, 2009.)

(b) Finality of decision

(1) The denial of a petition for a writ within the court's original jurisdiction without issuance of an alternative writ or order to show cause is final in that court when filed.

(2) Except as otherwise provided in this rule, a decision in a writ proceeding is final 30 days after the decision is filed.

(3) If necessary to prevent mootness or frustration of the relief granted or to otherwise promote the interests of justice, the court may order early finality in that court of a decision granting a petition for a writ within its original jurisdiction or denying such a petition after issuing an alternative writ or order to show cause. The decision may provide for finality in that court on filing or within a stated period of less than 30 days.

(4) If a Court of Appeal certifies its opinion for publication or partial publication after filing its decision and before its decision becomes final in that court, the finality period runs from the filing date of the order for publication.

(5) If an order modifying an opinion changes the appellate judgment, the finality period runs from the filing date of the modification order.

(Subd (b) adopted effective January 1, 2009.)

(c) Remittitur

A Court of Appeal must issue a remittitur in a writ proceeding under this chapter except when the court denies the petition without issuing an alternative writ or order to show cause. Rule 8.272(b)–(d) governs issuance of a remittitur by a Court of Appeal in writ proceedings under this chapter.

(Subd (c) adopted effective January 1, 2009.)

Rule 8.490 adopted effective January 1, 2009.

Advisory Committee Comment

Subdivision (b). This provision addresses the finality of decisions in proceedings relating to writs of mandate, certiorari, and prohibition. See rule 8.264(b) for provisions addressing the finality of decisions in proceedings under chapter 2, relating to civil appeals, and rule 8.366 for provisions addressing the finality of decisions in proceedings under chapter 3, relating to criminal appeals.

Ref.: Cal. Class Actions Prac. & Proc., §§20.03[9], 21.07[2][b], [d][iii].

Rule 8.491. Responsive pleading under Code of Civil Procedure section 418.10

If the Court of Appeal denies a petition for writ of mandate brought under Code of Civil Procedure section 418.10(c) and the Supreme Court denies review of the Court of Appeal's decision, the time to file a responsive pleading in the trial court is extended until 10 days after the Supreme Court files its order denying review.

Rule 8.491 adopted effective January 1, 2009.

Rule 8.492. Sanctions

(a) Grounds for sanctions

On motion of a party or its own motion, a Court of Appeal may impose sanctions, including the award or denial of costs under rule 8.493, on a party or an attorney for:

(1) Filing a frivolous petition or filing a petition solely to cause delay; or

(2) Committing any other unreasonable violation of these rules.

(Subd (a) adopted effective January 1, 2009.)

(b) Notice

The court must give notice in writing if it is considering imposing sanctions.

(Subd (b) adopted effective January 1, 2009.)

(c) Opposition

Within 10 days after the court sends such notice, a party or attorney may serve and file an opposition, but failure to do so will not be deemed consent. An opposition may not be filed unless the court sends such notice.

(Subd (c) adopted effective January 1, 2009.)

(d) Oral argument

Unless otherwise ordered, oral argument on the issue of sanctions must be combined with any oral argument on the merits of the petition.

(Subd (d) adopted effective January 1, 2009.)
Rule 8.492 adopted effective January 1, 2009.

Rule 8.493. Costs

(a) Award of costs

(1) Except in a criminal or juvenile or other proceeding in which a party is entitled to court-appointed counsel:

(A) Unless otherwise ordered by the court under (B), the prevailing party in an original proceeding is entitled to costs if the court resolves the proceeding by written opinion after issuing an alternative writ, an order to show cause, or a peremptory writ in the first instance.

(B) In the interests of justice, the court may also award or deny costs as it deems proper in the proceedings listed in (A) and in other circumstances.

(2) The opinion or order resolving the proceeding must specify the award or denial of costs.

(Subd (a) adopted effective January 1, 2009.)

(b) Procedures for recovering costs

Rule 8.278(b)–(d) governs the procedure for recovering costs under this rule.

(Subd (b) adopted effective January 1, 2009.)
Rule 8.493 adopted effective January 1, 2009.

Rule 8.494. Review of Workers' Compensation Appeals Board cases [Renumbered]

Rule 8.494 renumbered to rule 8.495 effective January 1, 2009; repealed and adopted as rule 57 effective January 1, 2005; previously amended effective July 1, 2006; previously amended and renumbered effective January 1, 2007.

Chapter 8
Miscellaneous Writs of Review

Title 8, Appellate Rules—Division 1, Rules Relating to the Supreme Court and Courts of Appeal—Chapter 8, Miscellaneous Writs of Review amended and renumbered effective January 1, 2009; adopted as chapter 7 effective January 1, 2007.

Rule 8.495. Review of Workers' Compensation Appeals Board cases

(a) Petition

(1) A petition to review an order, award, or decision of the Workers' Compensation Appeals Board must include:

(A) The order, award, or decision to be reviewed; and

(B) The workers' compensation judge's minutes of hearing and summary of evidence, findings and opinion on decision, and report and recommendation on the petition for reconsideration.

(2) If the petition claims that the board's ruling is not supported by substantial evidence, it must fairly state and attach copies of all the relevant material evidence.

(3) The petition must be accompanied by proof of service of two copies of the petition on the Secretary of the Workers' Compensation Appeals Board in San Francisco and one copy on each party who appeared in the action and whose interest is adverse to the petitioner. Service on the board's local district office is not required.

(Subd (a) amended effective January 1, 2007.)

(b) Answer and reply

(1) Within 25 days after the petition is filed, the board or any real party in interest may serve and file an answer and any relevant exhibits not included in the petition.

(2) Within 15 days after an answer is filed, the petitioner may serve and file a reply.

(c) Certificate of Interested Entities or Persons

(1) Each party other than the board must comply with the requirements of rule 8.208 concerning serving and filing a Certificate of Interested Entities or Persons.

(2) The petitioner's certificate must be included in the petition and the real party in interest's certificate must be

included in the answer. The certificate must appear after the cover and before the tables.

(3) If a party fails to file a certificate as required under (1) and (2), the clerk must notify the party by mail that the party must file the certificate within 10 days after the clerk's notice is mailed and that failure to comply will result in one of the following sanctions:

(A) If the party is the petitioner, the court will strike the petition; or

(B) If the party is the real party in interest, the court will strike the document.

(4) If the party fails to comply with the notice under (3), the court may impose the sanctions specified in the notice.

(Subd (c) amended effective January 1, 2007; adopted effective July 1, 2006.)

Rule 8.495 renumbered effective January 1, 2009; repealed and adopted as rule 57 effective January 1, 2005; previously amended effective July 1, 2006; previously amended and renumbered as rule 8.494 effective January 1, 2007.

Advisory Committee Comment

Subdivision (a). Subdivision (a)(3) specifies that the petition must be served on the Secretary of the Workers' Compensation Appeals Board in San Francisco. Neither the petition nor a courtesy copy should be served on the local district office of the board.

Subdivision (b). To clarify that a respondent may rely on exhibits filed with the petition without duplicating them in the answer, (b)(1) specifies that exhibits filed with an answer must be limited to exhibits "not included in the petition."

Ref.: Cal. Fms Pl. & Pr., Ch. 1, "New Developments," Ch. 577, "Workers' Compensation"; W. Cal. Sum., 2 "Workers' Compensation" §§424, 438.

Rule 8.496.   Review of Public Utilities Commission cases

(a) Petition

(1) A petition to review an order or decision of the Public Utilities Commission must be verified and must be served on the executive director and general counsel of the commission and any real parties in interest.

(2) A real party in interest is one who was a party of record to the proceeding and took a position adverse to the petitioner.

(b) Answer and reply

(1) Within 35 days after the petition is filed, the commission or any real party in interest may serve and file an answer.

(2) Within 25 days after an answer is filed, the petitioner may serve and file a reply.

(c) Certificate of Interested Entities or Persons

(1) Each party other than the commission must comply with the requirements of rule 8.208 concerning serving and filing a Certificate of Interested Entities or Persons.

(2) The petitioner's certificate must be included in the petition and the real party in interest's certificate must be included in the answer. The certificate must appear after the cover and before the tables.

(3) If a party fails to file a certificate as required under (1) and (2), the clerk must notify the party by mail that the party must file the certificate within 10 days after the

clerk's notice is mailed and that failure to comply will result in one of the following sanctions:

(A) If the party is the petitioner, the court will strike the petition; or

(B) If the party is the real party in interest, the court will strike the document.

(4) If the party fails to comply with the notice under (3), the court may impose the sanctions specified in the notice.

(Subd (c) amended effective January 1, 2007; adopted effective July 1, 2006.)

Rule 8.496 amended and renumbered effective January 1, 2007; repealed and adopted as rule 58 effective January 1, 2005; previously amended effective July 1, 2006.

Ref.: Cal. Fms Pl. & Pr., Ch. 54, "Appeal: California Supreme Court Review," Ch. 480, "Public Utilities."

Rule 8.498.   Review of Agricultural Labor Relations Board and Public Employment Relations Board cases

(a) Petition

(1) A petition to review an order or decision of the Agricultural Labor Relations Board or the Public Employment Relations Board must be filed in the Court of Appeal and served on the executive secretary of the Agricultural Labor Relations Board or the general counsel of the Public Employment Relations Board in Sacramento and on any real parties in interest.

(2) A real party in interest is a party of record to the proceeding.

(3) The petition must be verified.

(b) Record

Within the time permitted by statute, the board must file the certified record of the proceedings and simultaneously file and serve on all parties an index to that record.

(c) Briefs

(1) The petitioner must serve and file its brief within 35 days after the index is filed.

(2) Within 35 days after the petitioner's brief is filed, the board must—and any real party in interest may—serve and file a respondent's brief.

(3) Within 25 days after the respondent's brief is filed, the petitioner may serve and file a reply brief.

(d) Certificate of Interested Entities or Persons

(1) Each party other than the board must comply with the requirements of rule 8.208 concerning serving and filing a Certificate of Interested Entities or Persons.

(2) The petitioner's certificate must be included in the petition and the real party in interest's certificate must be included in the answer. The certificate must appear after the cover and before the tables.

(3) If a party fails to file a certificate as required under (1) and (2), the clerk must notify the party by mail that the party must file the certificate within 10 days after the clerk's notice is mailed and that failure to comply will result in one of the following sanctions:

(A) If the party is the petitioner, the court will strike the petition; or

(B) If the party is the real party in interest, the court will strike the document.

(4) If the party fails to comply with the notice under (3), the court may impose the sanctions specified in the notice.

(Subd (d) amended effective January 1, 2007; adopted effective July 1, 2006.)

Rule 8.498 amended and renumbered effective January 1, 2007; repealed and adopted as rule 59 effective January 1, 2005; previously amended effective July 1, 2006.

Ref.: Cal. Fms Pl. & Pr., Ch. 474B, "Standards in Reviewing Agency Decisions"; W. Cal. Sum., 3 "Agency and Employment" §672.

Rule 8.499.   Remittitur

A Court of Appeal must issue a remittitur in a writ proceeding under this chapter except when the court denies the petition without issuing an alternative writ or order to show cause. Rule 8.272(b)–(d) governs issuance of a remittitur in writ proceedings under this chapter.

Rule 8.499 adopted effective January 1, 2008.

Chapter 9
Proceedings in the Supreme Court

Title 8, Appellate Rules—Division 1, Rules Relating to the Supreme Court and Courts of Appeal—Chapter 9, Proceedings in the Supreme Court renumbered effective January 1, 2009; adopted as chapter 8 effective January 1, 2007.

Rule 8.500. Petition for review
Rule 8.504. Form and contents of petition, answer, and reply
Rule 8.508. Petition for review to exhaust state remedies
Rule 8.512. Ordering review
Rule 8.516. Issues on review
Rule 8.520. Briefs by parties and amici curiae; judicial notice
Rule 8.524. Oral argument and submission of the cause
Rule 8.528. Disposition
Rule 8.532. Filing, finality, and modification of decision
Rule 8.536. Rehearing
Rule 8.540. Remittitur
Rule 8.544. Costs and sanctions
Rule 8.548. Decision on request of a court of another jurisdiction
Rule 8.552. Transfer for decision

Rule 8.500.   Petition for review

(a) Right to file a petition, answer, or reply

(1) A party may file a petition in the Supreme Court for review of any decision of the Court of Appeal, including any interlocutory order, except the denial of a transfer of a case within the appellate jurisdiction of the superior court.

(2) A party may file an answer responding to the issues raised in the petition. In the answer, the party may ask the court to address additional issues if it grants review.

(3) The petitioner may file a reply to the answer.

(Subd (a) amended effective January 1, 2004.)

(b) Grounds for review

The Supreme Court may order review of a Court of Appeal decision:

(1) When necessary to secure uniformity of decision or to settle an important question of law;

(2) When the Court of Appeal lacked jurisdiction;

(3) When the Court of Appeal decision lacked the concurrence of sufficient qualified justices; or

(4) For the purpose of transferring the matter to the Court of Appeal for such proceedings as the Supreme Court may order.

(Subd (b) amended effective January 1, 2007.)

(c) Limits of review

(1) As a policy matter, on petition for review the Supreme Court normally will not consider an issue that the petitioner failed to timely raise in the Court of Appeal.

(2) A party may petition for review without petitioning for rehearing in the Court of Appeal, but as a policy matter the Supreme Court normally will accept the Court of Appeal opinion's statement of the issues and facts unless the party has called the Court of Appeal's attention to any alleged omission or misstatement of an issue or fact in a petition for rehearing.

(d) Petitions in nonconsolidated proceedings

If the Court of Appeal decides an appeal and denies a related petition for writ of habeas corpus without issuing an order to show cause and without formally consolidating the two proceedings, a party seeking review of both decisions must file a separate petition for review in each proceeding.

(e) Time to serve and file

(1) A petition for review must be served and filed within 10 days after the Court of Appeal decision is final in that court [1]. For purposes of this rule, the date of finality is not extended if it falls on a day on which the clerk's office is closed.

(2) The time to file a petition for review may not be extended, but the Chief Justice may relieve a party from a failure to file a timely petition for review if the time for the court to order review on its own motion has not expired.

(3) If a petition for review is presented for filing before the Court of Appeal decision is final in that court, the Supreme Court clerk must accept it and file it on the day after finality.

(4) Any answer to the petition must be served and filed within 20 days after the petition is filed.

(5) Any reply to the answer must be served and filed within 10 days after the answer is filed.

(Subd (e) amended effective January 1, 2009; previously amended effective January 1, 2007.)

Rule 8.500(e).   2008 Deletes. [1] under rule 8.264

(f) Additional requirements

(1) The petition must also be served on the superior court clerk and the Court of Appeal clerk.

(2) A copy of each brief must be served on a public officer or agency when required by statute or by rule 8.29.

(3) The Supreme Court clerk must file the petition even if its proof of service is defective, but if the petitioner fails to file a corrected proof of service within 5 days after the clerk gives notice of the defect the court may strike the petition or impose a lesser sanction.

(Subd (f) amended effective January 1, 2007; previously amended effective January 1, 2004.)

(g) Amicus curiae letters

(1) Any person or entity wanting to support or oppose a petition for review or for an original writ must serve on all parties and send to the Supreme Court an amicus curiae letter rather than a brief.

(2) The letter must describe the interest of the amicus curiae. Any matter attached to the letter or incorporated by reference must comply with rule 8.504(e).

(3) Receipt of the letter does not constitute leave to file an amicus curiae brief on the merits under rule 8.520(f).

(Subd (g) amended effective January 1, 2007; previously amended effective July 1, 2004.)

Rule 8.500 amended effective January 1, 2009; repealed and adopted as rule 28 effective January 1, 2003; previously amended effective January 1, 2004, and July 1, 2004; previously amended and renumbered effective January 1, 2007.

Advisory Committee Comment

Subdivision (a). Subdivision (a)(1) makes it clear that any interlocutory order of the Court of Appeal—such as an order denying an application to appoint counsel, to augment the record, or to allow oral argument—is a "decision" that may be challenged by petition for review.

Subdivision (e). Subdivision (e)(1) provides that a petition for review must be served and filed within 10 days after the Court of Appeal decision is *final in that court.* Finality in the Court of Appeal is generally governed by rules 8.264(b) (civil appeals), 8.366(b) (criminal appeals), 8.387(b) (habeas corpus proceedings), and 8.480 (proceedings for writs of mandate, certiorari, and prohibition). These rules declare the general rule that a Court of Appeal decision is final in that court 30 days after filing. They then carve out specific exceptions—decisions that they declare to be final immediately on filing (see rules 8.264(b)(2), 8.366(b)(2), and 8.490(b)(1)). The plain implication is that all other Court of Appeal orders—specifically, interlocutory orders that may be the subject of a petition for review—are *not* final on filing. This implication is confirmed by current practice, in which parties may be allowed to apply for—and the Courts of Appeal may grant—reconsideration of such interlocutory orders; reconsideration, of course, would be impermissible if the orders were in fact final on filing.

Contrary to paragraph (2) of subdivision (e), paragraphs (4) and (5) do not prohibit extending the time to file an answer or reply; because the subdivision thus expressly forbids an extension of time only with respect to the petition for review, by clear negative implication it permits an application to extend the time to file an answer or reply under rule 8.50.

Subdivision (f). The general requirements relating to service of documents in the appellate courts are established by rule 8.25. Subdivision (f)(1) requires that the petition (but not an answer or reply) be served on the Court of Appeal clerk. To assist litigants, (f)(1) also states explicitly what is impliedly required by rule 8.212(c), i.e., that the petition must also be served on the superior court clerk (for delivery to the trial judge).

Ref.: Cal. Fms Pl. & Pr., Ch. 22, "Amicus Curiae," Ch. 40, "Appeal: An Overview," Ch. 41, "Appeal: Review Standards and Appellate Rules of Law," Ch. 46, "Appeal: Extending or Shortening Time," Ch. 47, "Appeal: Relief From Default," Ch. 50, "Appeal: Briefs," Ch. 51, "Appeal: Hearing and Decision," Ch. 52, "Appeal: Rehearing," Ch. 54, "Appeal: California Supreme Court Review," Ch. 324, "Jurisdiction: Subject Matter Jurisdiction," Ch. 345A, "Limited Civil Cases," Ch. 358, "Mandate and Prohibition," Ch. 492, "Review (Certiorari), Writ of"; W. Cal. Sum., 2 "Workers' Compensation" §440.

Rule 8.504.   Form and contents of petition, answer, and reply

(a) In general

Except as provided in this rule, a petition for review, answer, and reply must comply with the relevant provisions of rule 8.204.

(Subd (a) amended effective January 1, 2007.)

(b) Contents of a petition

(1) The body of the petition must begin with a concise, nonargumentative statement of the issues presented for review, framing them in terms of the facts of the case but without unnecessary detail.

(2) The petition must explain how the case presents a ground for review under rule 8.500(b).

(3) If a petition for rehearing could have been filed in the Court of Appeal, the petition for review must state whether it was filed and, if so, how the court ruled.

(4) If the petition seeks review of a Court of Appeal opinion, a copy of the opinion showing its filing date and a copy of any order modifying the opinion or directing its publication must be bound at the back of the original petition and each copy filed in the Supreme Court.

(5) **If the petition seeks review of a Court of Appeal order, a copy of the order showing the date it was entered must be bound at the back of the original petition and each copy filed in the Supreme Court.**

(6) The title of the case and designation of the parties on the cover of the petition must be identical to the title and designation in the Court of Appeal opinion or order that is the subject of the petition.

[1] **(7)** Rule 8.508 governs the form and content of a petition for review filed by the defendant in a criminal case for the sole purpose of exhausting state remedies before seeking federal habeas corpus review.

(Subd (b) amended effective January 1, 2009; previously amended effective January 1, 2004, and January 1, 2007.)

Rule 8.504(b).   2008 Deletes. [1] (6)

(c) Contents of an answer

An answer that raises additional issues for review must contain a concise, nonargumentative statement of those issues, framing them in terms of the facts of the case but without unnecessary detail.

(d) Length

(1) If produced on a computer, a petition or answer must not exceed 8,400 words, including footnotes, and a reply must not exceed 4,200 words, including footnotes. Each petition, answer, or reply must include a certificate by appellate counsel or an unrepresented party stating the number of words in the document. The person certifying may rely on the word count of the computer program used to prepare the document.

(2) If typewritten, a petition or answer must not exceed 30 pages and a reply must not exceed 15 pages.

(3) The tables, the Court of Appeal opinion, a certificate under (1), and any attachment under (e)(1) are excluded from the limits stated in (1) and (2).

(4) On application and for good cause, the Chief Justice may permit a longer petition, answer, reply, or attachment.

(Subd (d) amended effective January 1, 2007; adopted as subd (e) effective January 1, 2003; previously relettered effective January 1, 2004.)

(e) Attachments and incorporation by reference

(1) No attachments are permitted except:

(A) An opinion or order [1] **required to be attached under (b)(4) or (5);**

(B) Exhibits or orders of a trial court or Court of Appeal that the party considers unusually significant;

(C) Copies of relevant local, state, or federal regulations or rules, out-of-state statutes, or other similar citable materials that are not readily accessible; and

(D) An opinion required to be attached under rule 8.1115(c).

(2) The attachments under [2] **(1)(B)–(C)** must not exceed a combined total of 10 pages.

(3) No incorporation by reference is permitted except a reference to a petition, an answer, or a reply filed by another party in the same case or filed in a case that raises the same or similar issues and in which a petition for review is pending or has been granted.

(Subd (e) amended effective January 1, 2009; adopted as subd (f) effective January 1, 2003; previously relettered effective January 1, 2004; previously amended effective January 1, 2007.)

Rule 8.504(e). 2008 Deletes. [1] from which the party seeks relief [2] (1)(A)–(C)

Rule 8.504 amended effective January 1, 2009; adopted as rule 28.1 effective January 1, 2003; previously amended effective January 1, 2004; previously amended and renumbered effective January 1, 2007.

Advisory Committee Comment

Subdivision (d). Subdivision (d) states in terms of word counts rather than page counts the maximum permissible lengths of a petition for review, answer, or reply produced on a computer. This provision tracks a provision in rule 8.204(c) governing Court of Appeal briefs and is explained in the advisory committee comment to that provision.

Ref.: Cal. Fms Pl. & Pr., Ch. 22, "Amicus Curiae," Ch. 54, "Appeal: California Supreme Court Review," Ch. 317, "Judges," Ch. 524, "Shortening and Extension of Time."

Rule 8.508. Petition for review to exhaust state remedies

(a) Purpose

After decision by the Court of Appeal in a criminal case, a defendant may file an abbreviated petition for review in the Supreme Court for the sole purpose of exhausting state remedies before presenting a claim for federal habeas corpus relief.

(b) Form and contents

(1) The words "Petition for Review to Exhaust State Remedies" must appear prominently on the cover of the petition.

(2) Except as provided in (3), the petition must comply with rule 8.504.

(3) The petition need not comply with rule 8.504(b)(1)–(2) but must include:

(A) A statement that the case presents no grounds for review under rule 8.500(b) and the petition is filed solely to exhaust state remedies for federal habeas corpus purposes;

(B) A brief statement of the underlying proceedings, including the nature of the conviction and the punishment imposed; and

(C) A brief statement of the factual and legal bases of the claim.

(Subd (b) amended effective January 1, 2007.)

(c) Service

The petition must be served on the Court of Appeal clerk but need not be served on the superior court clerk.

Rule 8.508 amended and renumbered effective January 1, 2007; adopted as rule 33.3 effective January 1, 2004.

Advisory Committee Comment

Subdivision (b). Although a petition under this rule must state that "the case presents no grounds for review under rule 8.500(b)" (see (b)(3)(A)), this does not mean the Supreme Court cannot

order review if it determines the case warrants review. The list of grounds for granting review in rule 8.500(b) is not intended to be exclusive, and from time to time the Supreme Court has exercised its discretion to order review in a case that does not present one of the listed grounds. (Compare U.S. Supreme Court Rule 10 [the listed grounds for granting certiorari, "although neither controlling nor fully measuring the Court's discretion, indicate the character of the reasons the Court considers"].)

Subdivision (b)(3)(C) requires the petition to include a statement of the factual and legal bases of the claim. This showing is required by federal law: "for purposes of exhausting state remedies, a claim for relief [in state court] … must include reference to a specific federal constitutional guarantee, as well as a statement of the facts that entitle the petitioner to relief." (*Gray v. Netherland* (1996) 518 U.S. 152, 162–163, citing *Picard v. Connor* (1971) 404 U.S. 270.) The federal courts will decide whether a petition filed in compliance with this rule satisfies federal exhaustion requirements, and practitioners should consult federal law to determine whether the petition's statement of the factual and legal bases for the claim is sufficient for that purpose.

Rule 8.512. Ordering review

(a) Transmittal of record

On receiving a copy of a petition for review or on request of the Supreme Court, whichever is earlier, the Court of Appeal clerk must promptly send the record to the Supreme Court. If the petition is denied, the Supreme Court clerk must promptly return the record to the Court of Appeal.

(b) Determination of petition

(1) The court may order review within 60 days after the last petition for review is filed. Before the 60-day period or any extension expires, the court may order one or more extensions to a date not later than 90 days after the last petition is filed.

(2) If the court does not rule on the petition within the time allowed by (1), the petition is deemed denied.

(Subd (b) amended effective January 1, 2004.)

(c) Review on the court's own motion

(1) If no petition for review is filed, the Supreme Court may, on its own motion, order review of a Court of Appeal decision within 30 days after the decision is final in that court. Before the 30-day period or any extension expires, the Supreme Court may order one or more extensions to a date not later than 90 days after the decision is final in the Court of Appeal. If any such period ends on a day on which the clerk's office is closed, the court may order review on its own motion on the next day the clerk's office is open.

(2) If a petition for review is filed, the Supreme Court may deny the petition but order review on its own motion within the periods prescribed in (b)(1).

(Subd (c) amended and relettered effective January 1, 2004; adopted as subd (d) effective January 1, 2003.)

(d) Order; grant and hold

(1) An order granting review must be signed by at least four justices; an order denying review may be signed by the Chief Justice alone.

(2) On or after granting review, the court may order action in the matter deferred until the court disposes of another matter or pending further order of the court.

(Subd (d) adopted effective January 1, 2004.)

Rule 8.512 renumbered effective January 1, 2007; adopted as rule 28.2 effective January 1, 2003; previously amended effective January 1, 2004.

Advisory Committee Comment

Subdivision (b). The Supreme Court deems the 60-day period within which it may grant review to begin on the filing date of the last petition for review that either (1) is timely in the sense that it is filed within the rule time for such petitions (i.e., 10 days after finality of the Court of Appeal decision) or (2) is treated as timely—although presented for filing after expiration of the rule time—in the sense that it is filed with permission of the Chief Justice on a showing of good cause for relief from default. In each circumstance it is the filing of the petition that triggers the 60-day period.

Ref.: Cal. Fms Pl. & Pr., Ch. 40, "Appeal: An Overview," Ch. 46, "Appeal: Extending or Shortening Time," Ch. 54, "Appeal: California Supreme Court Review," Ch. 524, "Shortening and Extension of Time."

Rule 8.516.   Issues on review

(a) Issues to be briefed and argued

(1) On or after ordering review, the Supreme Court may specify the issues to be briefed and argued. Unless the court orders otherwise, the parties must limit their briefs and arguments to those issues and any issues fairly included in them.

(2) Notwithstanding an order specifying issues under (1), the court may, on reasonable notice, order oral argument on fewer or additional issues or on the entire cause.

(b) Issues to be decided

(1) The Supreme Court may decide any issues that are raised or fairly included in the petition or answer.

(2) The court may decide an issue that is neither raised nor fairly included in the petition or answer if the case presents the issue and the court has given the parties reasonable notice and opportunity to brief and argue it.

(3) The court need not decide every issue the parties raise or the court specifies.

Rule 8.516 renumbered effective January 1, 2007; repealed and adopted as rule 29 effective January 1, 2003.

Ref.: Cal. Fms Pl. & Pr., Ch. 40, "Appeal: An Overview," Ch. 54, "Appeal: California Supreme Court Review," Ch. 324, "Jurisdiction: Subject Matter Jurisdiction."

Rule 8.520.   Briefs by parties and amici curiae; judicial notice

(a) Parties' briefs; time to file

(1) Within 30 days after the Supreme Court files the order of review, the petitioner must serve and file in that court either an opening brief on the merits or the brief it filed in the Court of Appeal.

(2) Within 30 days after the petitioner files its brief or the time to do so expires, the opposing party must serve and file either an answer brief on the merits or the brief it filed in the Court of Appeal.

(3) The petitioner may file a reply brief on the merits or the reply brief it filed in the Court of Appeal. A reply brief must be served and filed within 20 days after the opposing party files its brief.

(4) A party filing a brief it filed in the Court of Appeal must attach to the cover a notice of its intent to rely on the brief in the Supreme Court.

(5) The time to serve and file a brief may not be extended by stipulation but only by order of the Chief Justice under rule 8.60.

(6) The court may designate which party is deemed the petitioner or otherwise direct the sequence in which the parties must file their briefs.

(Subd (a) amended effective January 1, 2007.)

(b) Form and content

(1) Briefs filed under this rule must comply with the relevant provisions of rule 8.204.

(2) The body of the petitioner's brief on the merits must begin by quoting either:

(A) Any order specifying the issues to be briefed; or, if none,

(B) The statement of issues in the petition for review and, if any, in the answer.

(3) Unless the court orders otherwise, briefs on the merits must be limited to the issues stated in (2) and any issues fairly included in them.

(Subd (b) amended effective January 1, 2007.)

(c) Length

(1) If produced on a computer, [1] **an opening or answering** brief on the merits must not exceed 14,000 words, including footnotes, and a reply brief on the merits must not exceed [2] **8,400** words, including footnotes. Each brief must include a certificate by appellate counsel or an unrepresented party stating the number of words in the brief. The person certifying may rely on the word count of the computer program used to prepare the brief.

(2) If typewritten, [3] **an opening or answering** brief on the merits must not exceed 50 pages and a reply brief **on the merits** must not exceed [4] **30** pages.

(3) The tables, a certificate under (1), any attachment under (h), and any quotation of issues required by (b)(2) are excluded from the limits stated in (1) and (2).

(4) On application and for good cause, the Chief Justice may permit a longer brief.

(Subd (c) amended effective January 1, 2009; previously amended effective January 1, 2007.)

Rule 8.520(c).   2008 Deletes. [1] a **[2]** 4,200 **[3]** a **[4]** 15

(d) Supplemental briefs

(1) A party may file a supplemental brief limited to new authorities, new legislation, or other matters that were not available in time to be included in the party's brief on the merits.

(2) A supplemental brief must not exceed 2,800 words, including footnotes, if produced on a computer or 10 pages if typewritten, and must be served and filed no later than 10 days before oral argument.

(Subd (d) amended effective January 1, 2007.)

(e) Briefs on the court's request

The court may request additional briefs on any or all issues, whether or not the parties have filed briefs on the merits.

(f) Amicus curiae briefs

(1) After the court orders review, any person or entity may serve and file an application for permission of the Chief Justice to file an amicus curiae brief.

(2) The application must be filed no later than 30 days after all briefs that the parties may file under this rule—other than supplemental briefs—have been filed or were required to be filed. For good cause, the Chief Justice may allow later filing.

(3) The application must state the applicant's interest and explain how the proposed amicus curiae brief will assist the court in deciding the matter.

(4) **The application must also identify:**

(A) **Any party or any counsel for a party in the pending appeal who:**

(i) **Authored the proposed amicus brief in whole or in part; or**

(ii) **Made a monetary contribution intended to fund the preparation or submission of the brief; and**

(B) **Every person or entity who made a monetary contribution intended to fund the preparation or submission of the brief, other than the amicus curiae, its members, or its counsel in the pending appeal.**

(5) The proposed brief must be served. It must accompany the application and may be combined with it.

[1] **(6)** The covers of the application and proposed brief must identify the party the applicant supports, if any.

[2] **(7)** If the court grants the application, any party may file an answer within 20 days after the amicus curiae brief is filed. It must be served on all parties and the amicus curiae.

[3] **(8)** The Attorney General may file an amicus curiae brief without the Chief Justice's permission unless the brief is submitted on behalf of another state officer or agency. The Attorney General must serve and file the brief within the time specified in (2) and must provide the information required by (3) and comply with [4] **(6)**. Any answer must comply with [5] **(7)**.

(Subd (f) amended effective January 1, 2009; previously amended effective January 1, 2008.)

Rule 8.520(f). 2008 Deletes. [1] (5) [2] (6) [3] (7) [4] (5) [5] (6)

(g) **Judicial notice**

To obtain judicial notice by the Supreme Court under Evidence Code section 459, a party must comply with rule 8.252(a).

(Subd (g) amended effective January 1, 2007.)

(h) **Attachments**

A party filing a brief may attach copies of relevant local, state, or federal regulations or rules, out-of-state statutes, or other similar citable materials that are not readily accessible. These attachments must not exceed a combined total of 10 pages. A copy of an opinion required to be attached to the brief under rule 8.1115(c) does not count toward this 10-page limit.

(Subd (h) adopted effective January 1, 2007.)

Rule 8.520 amended effective January 1, 2009; adopted as rule 29.1 effective January 1, 2003; previously amended and renumbered effective January 1, 2007; previously amended effective January 1, 2008.

Advisory Committee Comment

Subdivisions (c) and (d). Subdivisions (c) and (d) state in terms of word count rather than page count the maximum permissible lengths of Supreme Court briefs produced on a computer. This provision tracks an identical provision in rule 8.204(c) governing Court of Appeal briefs and is explained in the advisory committee comment to that provision.

Ref.: Cal. Fms Pl. & Pr., Ch. 22, "Amicus Curiae," Ch. 40, "Appeal: An Overview," Ch. 50, "Appeal: Briefs," Ch. 54, "Appeal: California Supreme Court Review."

Rule 8.524. Oral argument and submission of the cause

(a) **Application**

This rule governs oral argument in the Supreme Court unless the court provides otherwise in its Internal Operating Practices and Procedures or by order.

(b) **Place of argument**

The Supreme Court holds regular sessions in San Francisco, Los Angeles, and Sacramento on a schedule fixed by the court, and may hold special sessions elsewhere.

(c) **Notice of argument**

The Supreme Court clerk must send notice of the time and place of oral argument to all parties at least 20 days before the argument date. The Chief Justice may shorten the notice period for good cause; in that event, the clerk must immediately notify the parties by telephone or other expeditious method.

(d) **Sequence of argument**

The petitioner for Supreme Court relief has the right to open and close. If there are two or more petitioners—or none—the court must set the sequence of argument.

(e) **Time for argument**

Each side is allowed 30 minutes for argument.

(f) **Number of counsel**

(1) Only one counsel on each side may argue—regardless of the number of parties on the side—unless the court orders otherwise on request.

(2) Requests to divide oral argument among multiple counsel must be filed within 10 days after the date of the order setting the case for argument.

(3) Multiple counsel must not divide their argument into segments of less than 10 minutes per person, except that one counsel for the opening side—or more, if authorized by the Chief Justice on request—may reserve any portion of that counsel's time for rebuttal.

(g) **Argument by amicus curiae**

An amicus curiae is not entitled to argument time but may ask a party for permission to use a portion or all of the party's time, subject to the 10-minute minimum prescribed in (f)(3). If permission is granted, counsel must file a request under (f)(2).

(h) **Submission of the cause**

(1) A cause is submitted when the court has heard oral argument or approved its waiver and the time has expired to file all briefs and papers, including any supplemental brief permitted by the court.

(2) The court may vacate submission only by an order stating the court's reasons and setting a timetable for resubmission.

Rule 8.524 renumbered effective January 1, 2007; repealed and adopted as rule 29.2 effective January 1, 2003.

Advisory Committee Comment

Subdivision (d). In subdivision (d), "The petitioner for Supreme Court relief" can be a petitioner for review, a petitioner for transfer (rule 8.552), a petitioner in an original proceeding in the Supreme Court, or a party designated as petitioner in a proceeding on request of a court of another jurisdiction (rule 8.548(b)(1)).

The number of petitioners is "none" when the court grants review on its own motion or transfers a cause to itself on its own motion.

Subdivision (e). The time allowed for argument in death penalty appeals is prescribed in rule 8.638.

Subdivision (f). The number of counsel allowed to argue on each side in death penalty appeals is prescribed in rule 8.638.

Ref.: Cal. Fms Pl. & Pr., Ch. 51, "Appeal: Hearing and Decision," Ch. 54, "Appeal: California Supreme Court Review."

Rule 8.528. Disposition

(a) Normal disposition

After review, the Supreme Court normally will affirm, reverse, or modify the judgment of the Court of Appeal, but may order another disposition.

(b) Dismissal of review

(1) The Supreme Court may dismiss review. The Supreme Court clerk must promptly send an order dismissing review to all parties and the Court of Appeal.

(2) When the Court of Appeal receives an order dismissing review, the decision of that court is final and its clerk must promptly issue a remittitur or take other appropriate action.

(3) After an order dismissing review, the Court of Appeal opinion remains unpublished unless the Supreme Court orders otherwise.

(c) Remand for decision on remaining issues

If it decides fewer than all the issues presented by the case, the Supreme Court may remand the cause to a Court of Appeal for decision on any remaining issues.

(d) Transfer without decision

After ordering review, the Supreme Court may transfer the cause to a Court of Appeal without decision but with instructions to conduct such proceedings as the Supreme Court orders.

(e) Retransfer without decision

After transferring to itself, before decision, a cause pending in the Court of Appeal, the Supreme Court may retransfer the cause to a Court of Appeal without decision.

(f) Court of Appeal briefs after remand or transfer

Any supplemental briefing in the Court of Appeal after remand or transfer from the Supreme Court is governed by rule 8.200(b).

(Subd (f) amended effective January 1, 2007.)

Rule 8.528 amended and renumbered effective January 1, 2007; repealed and adopted as rule 29.3 effective January 1, 2003.

Advisory Committee Comment

Subdivision (a). Subdivision (a) serves two purposes. First, it declares that the Supreme Court's normal disposition of a cause after completing its review is to affirm, reverse, or modify *the judgment of the Court of Appeal.* Second, the subdivision recognizes that, when necessary, the Supreme Court may order "another disposition" appropriate to the circumstances. Subdivisions (b)–(e) provide examples of such "other dispositions," but the list is not intended to be exclusive.

As used in subdivision (a), "the judgment of the Court of Appeal" includes a decision of that court denying a petition for original writ without issuing an alternative writ or order to show cause. The Supreme Court's method of disposition after reviewing such a decision, however, has evolved. In earlier cases the Supreme Court itself denied or granted the requested writ, in effect treating the matter as if it were an original proceeding in the Supreme Court. (E.g., *City of San Jose v. Superior Court* (1993) 5 Cal.4th 47, 58 ["The alternative writ of mandate is discharged and the petition for a peremptory writ of mandate is denied."].) By contrast, current Supreme Court practice is to affirm or reverse the judgment of the Court of Appeal summarily denying the writ petition. (E.g., *People v. Superior Court (Laff)* (2001) 25 Cal.4th 703, 742–743 ["The judgment of the Court of Appeal is reversed with directions to vacate its order denying the petition, and to

issue a writ of mandate...."]; *State Comp. Ins. Fund v. Superior Court* (2001) 24 Cal.4th 930, 944 ["The judgment of the Court of Appeal summarily denying the petition for writ of mandate is affirmed and the order to show cause ... is discharged."].) As the cited cases illustrate, if the Supreme Court affirms such a judgment it will normally discharge any alternative writ or order to show cause it issued when granting review; if the court reverses the judgment it will normally include a direction to the Court of Appeal, e.g., to issue the requested writ or to reconsider the petition.

Subdivision (b). An earlier version of this rule purported to limit Supreme Court *dismissals of review* to cases in which the court had "improvidently" granted review. In practice, however, the court may dismiss review for a variety of other reasons. For example, after the court decides a "lead" case, its current practice is to dismiss review in any pending companion case (i.e., a "grant and hold" matter under rule 8.512(c)) that appears correctly decided in light of the lead case and presents no additional issue requiring resolution by the Supreme Court or the Court of Appeal. The Supreme Court may also dismiss review when a supervening event renders the case moot for any reason, e.g., when the parties reach a settlement, when a party seeking personal relief dies, or when the court orders review to construe a statute that is then repealed before the court can act. Reflecting this practice, the Supreme Court now dismisses review—even in the rare case in which the grant of review was arguably "improvident"—by an order that says simply that "review is dismissed."

An order of review ipso facto transfers jurisdiction of the cause to the Supreme Court. By the same token, an order dismissing review ipso facto retransfers jurisdiction to the Court of Appeal. The Court of Appeal has no discretion to exercise after the Supreme Court dismisses review: the Supreme Court clerk must promptly send the dismissal order to the Court of Appeal; when the Court of Appeal clerk files that order, the Court of Appeal decision immediately becomes final.

If the decision of the Court of Appeal made final by (b)(2) requires issuance of a remittitur under rule 8.272(a), the clerk must issue the remittitur; if the decision does not require issuance of a remittitur—e.g., if the decision is an interlocutory order (see rule 8.500(a)(1))—the clerk must take whatever action is appropriate in the circumstances.

Subdivision (d). Subdivision (d) is intended to apply primarily to two types of cases: (1) those in which the court granted review "for the purpose of transferring the matter to the Court of Appeal for such proceedings as the Supreme Court may order" (rule 8.500(b)(4)) and (2) those in which the court, after deciding a "lead case," determines that a companion "grant and hold" case (rule 8.512(c)) should be reconsidered by the Court of Appeal in light of the lead case or presents an additional issue or issues that require resolution by the Court of Appeal.

Subdivision (e). Subdivision (e) is intended to apply to cases in which the Supreme Court, after *transferring* to itself before decision a cause pending in the Court of Appeal, *retransfers* the matter to that court without decision and with or without instructions.

Ref.: Cal. Fms Pl. & Pr., Ch. 52, "Appeal: Rehearing," Ch. 54, "Appeal: California Supreme Court Review," Ch. 324, "Jurisdiction: Subject Matter Jurisdiction."

Rule 8.532. Filing, finality, and modification of decision

(a) Filing the decision

The Supreme Court clerk must promptly file all opinions and orders issued by the court and promptly send copies showing the filing date to the parties and, when relevant, to the lower court or tribunal.

(b) Finality of decision

(1) Except as provided in (2), a Supreme Court decision is final 30 days after filing unless:

(A) The court orders a shorter period; or

(B) Before the 30-day period or any extension expires the court orders one or more extensions, not to exceed a total of 60 additional days.

(2) The following Supreme Court decisions are final on filing:

(A) The denial of a petition for review of a Court of Appeal decision;

(B) A disposition ordered under rule 8.528(b), (d), or (e);

(C) The denial of a petition for a writ within the court's original jurisdiction without issuance of an alternative writ or order to show cause; and

(D) The denial of a petition for writ of supersedeas.

(Subd (b) amended effective January 1, 2007.)

(c) Modification of decision

The Supreme Court may modify a decision as provided in rule 8.264(c).

(Subd (c) amended effective January 1, 2007.)

Rule 8.532 amended and renumbered effective January 1, 2007; repealed and adopted as rule 29.4 effective January 1, 2003.

Advisory Committee Comment

Subdivision (b). Subdivision (b)(2)(A) recognizes the general rule that the denial of a petition for review of a Court of Appeal decision is final on filing. Subdivision (b)(2)(B)–(D) recognizes several additional types of Supreme Court decisions that are final on filing. Thus (b)(2)(B) recognizes that a dismissal, a transfer, and a retransfer under (b), (d), and (e), respectively, of rule 8.528 are decisions final on filing. A remand under rule 8.528(c) is not a decision final on filing because it is not a separately filed order; rather, as part of its appellate judgment at the end of its opinion in such cases the Supreme Court simply orders the cause remanded to the Court of Appeal for disposition of the remaining issues in the appeal.

Subdivision (b)(2)(C) recognizes that an order denying a petition for a writ within the court's original jurisdiction without issuance of an alternative writ or order to show cause is final on filing. The provision reflects the settled Supreme Court practice, since at least 1989, of declining to file petitions for rehearing in such matters. (See, e.g., *In re Hayes* (S004421) Minutes, Cal. Supreme Ct., July 28, 1989 ["The motion to vacate this court's order of May 18, 1989 [denying a petition for habeas corpus without opinion] is denied. Because the California Rules of Court do not authorize the filing of a petition for rehearing of such an order, the alternate request to consider the matter as a petition for rehearing is denied."].)

Subdivision (b)(2)(D) recognizes that an order denying a petition for writ of supersedeas is final on filing.

Ref.: Cal. Fms Pl. & Pr., Ch. 51, "Appeal: Hearing and Decision," Ch. 52, "Appeal: Rehearing," Ch. 54, "Appeal: California Supreme Court Review," Ch. 358, "Mandate and Prohibition."

Rule 8.536. Rehearing

(a) Power to order rehearing

The Supreme Court may order rehearing as provided in rule 8.268(a).

(Subd (a) amended effective January 1, 2007.)

(b) Petition and answer

A petition for rehearing and any answer must comply with rule 8.268(b)(1) and (3). Any answer to the petition must be served and filed within eight days after the petition is filed. Before the Supreme Court decision is final and for good cause, the Chief Justice may relieve a party from a failure to file a timely petition or answer.

(Subd (b) amended effective January 1, 2007; previously amended effective January 1, 2004.)

(c) Extension of time

The time for granting or denying a petition for rehearing in the Supreme Court may be extended under rule 8.532(b)(1)(B). If the court does not rule on the petition before the decision is final, the petition is deemed denied.

(Subd (c) amended effective January 1, 2007.)

(d) Determination of petition

An order granting a rehearing must be signed by at least four justices; an order denying rehearing may be signed by the Chief Justice alone.

(e) Effect of granting rehearing

An order granting a rehearing vacates the decision and any opinion filed in the case and sets the cause at large in the Supreme Court.

Rule 8.536 amended and renumbered effective January 1, 2007; repealed and adopted as rule 29.5 effective January 1, 2003; previously amended effective January 1, 2004.

Ref.: Cal. Fms Pl. & Pr., Ch. 40, "Appeal: An Overview," Ch. 46, "Appeal: Extending or Shortening Time," Ch. 52, "Appeal: Rehearing," Ch. 54, "Appeal: California Supreme Court Review," Ch. 358, "Mandate and Prohibition."

Rule 8.540. Remittitur

(a) Proceedings requiring issuance of remittitur

The Supreme Court must issue a remittitur after a decision in:

(1) A review of a Court of Appeal decision; or

(2) An appeal from a judgment of death or in a cause transferred to the court under rule 8.552.

(Subd (a) amended effective January 1, 2007.)

(b) Clerk's duties

(1) The clerk must issue a remittitur when a decision of the court is final. The remittitur is deemed issued when the clerk enters it in the record.

(2) After review of a Court of Appeal decision, the Supreme Court clerk must address the remittitur to the Court of Appeal and send that court two copies of the remittitur and two file-stamped copies of the Supreme Court opinion or order.

(3) After a decision in an appeal from a judgment of death or in a cause transferred to the court under rule 8.552, the clerk must send the remittitur and a file-stamped copy of the Supreme Court opinion or order to the lower court or tribunal.

(4) The clerk must comply with the requirements of rule 8.272(d).

(Subd (b) amended effective January 1, 2007.)

(c) Immediate issuance, stay, and recall

(1) The Supreme Court may direct immediate issuance of a remittitur on the parties' stipulation or for good cause.

(2) On a party's or its own motion and for good cause, the court may stay a remittitur's issuance for a reasonable period or order its recall.

(3) An order recalling a remittitur issued after a decision by opinion does not supersede the opinion or affect its publication status.

Rule 8.540 amended and renumbered effective January 1, 2007; repealed and adopted as rule 29.6 effective January 1, 2003.

Ref.: Cal. Fms Pl. & Pr., Ch. 12A, "Adoptions: Termination of Parental Rights," Ch. 40, "Appeal: An Overview," Ch. 53, "Appeal: Remittitur and Costs on Appeal," Ch. 54, "Appeal: California Supreme Court Review."

Rule 8.544. Costs and sanctions

In a civil case, the Supreme Court may direct the Court of Appeal to award costs, if any; or may order the parties to bear their own costs; or may make any other award of costs the Supreme Court deems proper. The Supreme Court may impose sanctions on a party or an attorney under rule [1] **8.276** for committing any unreasonable violation of these rules.

Rule 8.544 amended effective July 1, 2008; adopted as rule 29.7 effective January 1, 2003; previously amended and renumbered effective January 1, 2007.

Rule 8.544. 2008 Deletes. [1] 8.276(e)

Advisory Committee Comment

If the Supreme Court makes an award of costs, the party claiming such costs must proceed under rule 8.278(c).

Ref.: Cal. Fms Pl. & Pr., Ch. 51, "Appeal: Hearing and Decision," Ch. 54, "Appeal: California Supreme Court Review."

Rule 8.548. Decision on request of a court of another jurisdiction

(a) Request for decision

On request of the United States Supreme Court, a United States Court of Appeals, or the court of last resort of any state, territory, or commonwealth, the Supreme Court may decide a question of California law if:

(1) The decision could determine the outcome of a matter pending in the requesting court; and

(2) There is no controlling precedent.

(Subd (a) amended effective January 1, 2007.)

(b) Form and contents of request

The request must take the form of an order of the requesting court containing:

(1) The title and number of the case, the names and addresses of counsel and any unrepresented party, and a designation of the party to be deemed the petitioner if the request is granted;

(2) The question to be decided, with a statement that the requesting court will accept the decision;

(3) A statement of the relevant facts prepared by the requesting court or by the parties and approved by the court; and

(4) An explanation of how the request satisfies the requirements of (a).

(Subd (b) amended effective January 1, 2007.)

(c) Supporting materials

Copies of all relevant briefs must accompany the request. At any time, the Supreme Court may ask the requesting court to furnish additional record materials, including transcripts and exhibits.

(d) Serving and filing the request

The requesting court clerk must file an original and 10 copies of the request in the Supreme Court with a certificate of service on the parties.

(e) Letters in support or opposition

(1) Within 20 days after the request is filed, any party or other person or entity wanting to support or oppose the request must send a letter to the Supreme Court, with service on the parties and on the requesting court.

(2) Within 10 days after service of a letter under (1), any party may send a reply letter to the Supreme Court, with service on the other parties and the requesting court.

(3) A letter or reply asking the court to restate the question under (f)(5) must propose new wording.

(f) Proceedings in the Supreme Court

(1) In exercising its discretion to grant or deny the request, the Supreme Court may consider whether resolution of the question is necessary to secure uniformity of decision or to settle an important question of law, and any other factor the court deems appropriate.

(2) An order granting the request must be signed by at least four justices; an order denying the request may be signed by the Chief Justice alone.

(3) If the court grants the request, the rules on review and decision in the Supreme Court govern further proceedings in that court.

(4) If, after granting the request, the court determines that a decision on the question may require an interpretation of the California Constitution or a decision on the validity or meaning of a California law affecting the public interest, the court must direct the clerk to send to the Attorney General—unless the Attorney General represents a party to the litigation—a copy of the request and the order granting it.

(5) At any time, the Supreme Court may restate the question or ask the requesting court to clarify the question.

(6) After filing the opinion, the clerk must promptly send file-stamped copies to the requesting court and the parties and must notify that court and the parties when the decision is final.

(7) Supreme Court decisions pursuant to this rule are published in the Official Reports and have the same precedential effect as the court's other decisions.

(Subd (f) amended effective January 1, 2007.)

Rule 8.548 amended and renumbered effective January 1, 2007; adopted as rule 29.8 effective January 1, 2003.

Ref.: Cal. Fms Pl. & Pr., Ch. 22, "Amicus Curiae," Ch. 54, "Appeal: California Supreme Court Review," Ch. 324, "Jurisdiction: Subject Matter Jurisdiction"; W. Cal. Sum., 1 "Contracts" §210, 2 "Insurance" §269, 13 "Equity" §88.

Rule 8.552. Transfer for decision

(a) Time of transfer

On a party's petition or its own motion, the Supreme Court may transfer to itself, for decision, a cause pending in a Court of Appeal.

(b) When a cause is pending

For purposes of this rule, a cause within the appellate jurisdiction of the superior court is not pending in the Court of Appeal until that court orders it transferred under rule 8.1002. Any cause pending in the Court of Appeal remains pending until the decision of the Court of Appeal is final in that court [1].

(Subd (b) amended effective January 1, 2009; previously amended effective January 1, 2007.)

Rule 8.552(b). 2008 Deletes. [1] under rule 8.264

(c) Grounds

The Supreme Court will not order transfer under this rule unless the cause presents an issue of great public importance that the Supreme Court must promptly resolve.

(d) Petition and answer

A party seeking transfer under this rule must promptly serve and file in the Supreme Court a petition explaining how the cause satisfies the requirements of (c). Within 20 days after the petition is filed, any party may serve and file an answer. The petition and any answer must conform to the relevant provisions of rule 8.504.

(Subd (d) amended effective January 1, 2007.)

(e) Order

Transfer under this rule requires a Supreme Court order signed by at least four justices; an order denying transfer may be signed by the Chief Justice alone.

Rule 8.552 amended effective January 1, 2009; repealed and adopted as rule 29.9 effective January 1, 2003; previously amended and renumbered effective January 1, 2007.

Advisory Committee Comment

Rule 8.552 applies only to causes that the Supreme Court transfers to itself for the purpose of reaching a decision on the merits. The rule implements a portion of article VI, section 12(a) of the Constitution. As used in article VI, section 12(a) and the rule, the term "cause" is broadly construed to include " 'all cases, matters, and proceedings of every description' " adjudicated by the Courts of Appeal and the Supreme Court. (*In re Rose* (2000) 22 Cal.4th 430, 540, quoting *In re Wells* (1917) 174 Cal. 467, 471.)

Subdivision (b). For provisions addressing the finality of Court of Appeal decisions, see rules 8.264(b) (civil appeals), 8.366(b) (criminal appeals), 8.490 (proceedings for writs of mandate, certiorari, and prohibition), and 8.1018(a) (transfer of appellate division cases).

Ref.: Cal. Fms Pl. & Pr., Ch. 40, "Appeal: An Overview," Ch. 54, "Appeal: California Supreme Court Review."

Chapter 10
Appeals From Judgments of Death

Title 8, Appellate Rules—Division 1, Rules Relating to the Supreme Court and Courts of Appeal—Chapter 10, Appeals From Judgments of Death amended and renumbered effective January 1, 2009; adopted as chapter 9 effective January 1, 2007.

Art. 1. General Provisions. Rules 8.600, 8.605.
Art. 2. Record on Appeal. Rules 8.610–8.625.
Art. 3. Briefs, Hearing, and Decision. Rules 8.630–8.642.

Article 1
General Provisions

Rule 8.600. In general
Rule 8.605. Qualifications of counsel in death penalty appeals and habeas corpus proceedings

Rule 8.600. In general

(a) Automatic appeal to Supreme Court

If a judgment imposes a sentence of death, an appeal by the defendant is automatically taken to the Supreme Court.

(b) Copies of judgment

When a judgment of death is rendered, the superior court clerk must immediately send certified copies of the commitment to the Supreme Court, the Attorney General, the Governor, and the California Appellate Project in San Francisco.

(c) Extensions of time

When a rule in this part authorizes a trial court to grant an extension of a specified time period, the court must consider the relevant policies and factors stated in rule 8.63.

(Subd (c) amended effective January 1, 2007.)

(d) Supervising preparation of record

The Supreme Court clerk, under the supervision of the Chief Justice, must take all appropriate steps to ensure that superior court clerks and reporters promptly perform their duties under the rules in this part. This provision does not affect the superior courts' responsibility for the prompt preparation of appellate records in capital cases.

(e) Definitions

For purposes of this part:

(1) The delivery date of a transcript sent by mail is the mailing date plus five days; and

(2) "Trial counsel" means both the defendant's trial counsel and the prosecuting attorney.

(Subd (e) amended effective January 1, 2007.)

Rule 8.600 amended and renumbered effective January 1, 2007; repealed and adopted as rule 34 effective January 1, 2004.

Ref.: MB Prac. Guide: Cal. Pretrial Proc., §10.04[2].

Rule 8.605. Qualifications of counsel in death penalty appeals and habeas corpus proceedings

(a) Purpose

This rule defines the minimum qualifications for attorneys appointed by the Supreme Court in death penalty appeals and habeas corpus proceedings related to sentences of death. An attorney is not entitled to appointment simply because the attorney meets these minimum qualifications.

(b) General qualifications

The Supreme Court may appoint an attorney only if it has determined, after reviewing the attorney's experience, writing samples, references, and evaluations under (d) through (f), that the attorney has demonstrated the commitment, knowledge, and skills necessary to competently represent the defendant. An appointed attorney must be willing to cooperate with an assisting counsel or entity that the court may designate.

(c) Definitions

As used in this rule:

(1) "Appointed counsel" or "appointed attorney" means an attorney appointed to represent a person in a death penalty appeal or death penalty–related habeas corpus proceedings in the Supreme Court. Appointed counsel may be either lead counsel or associate counsel.

(2) "Lead counsel" means an appointed attorney or an attorney in the Office of the State Public Defender, the Habeas Corpus Resource Center, or the California Appellate Project in San Francisco who is responsible for the overall conduct of the case and for supervising the work of associate and supervised counsel. If two or more attorneys are appointed to represent a defendant jointly in a death penalty appeal, in death penalty–related habeas corpus proceedings, or in both classes of proceedings together, one such attorney will be designated as lead counsel.

(3) "Associate counsel" means an appointed attorney who does not have the primary responsibility for the case but nevertheless has casewide responsibility to perform the duties for which that attorney was appointed, whether they are appellate, habeas corpus, or appellate and habeas corpus duties. Associate counsel must meet the same minimum qualifications as lead counsel.

(4) "Supervised counsel" means an attorney who works under the immediate supervision and direction of lead or associate counsel but is not appointed by the Supreme Court. Supervised counsel must be an active member of the State Bar of California.

(5) "Assisting counsel or entity" means an attorney or entity designated by the Supreme Court to provide appointed counsel with consultation and resource assistance. Entities that may be designated include the Office of the State Public Defender, the Habeas Corpus Resource Center, and the California Appellate Project in San Francisco.

(d) Qualifications for appointed appellate counsel

An attorney appointed as lead or associate counsel in a death penalty appeal must have at least the following qualifications and experience:

(1) Active practice of law in California for at least four years.

(2) Either:

(A) Service as counsel of record for a defendant in seven completed felony appeals, including one murder case; or

(B) Service as counsel of record for a defendant in five completed felony appeals and as supervised counsel for a defendant in two death penalty appeals in which the opening brief has been filed. Service as supervised counsel in a death penalty appeal will apply toward this qualification only if lead or associate counsel in that appeal attests that the supervised attorney performed substantial work on the case and recommends the attorney for appointment.

(3) Familiarity with Supreme Court practices and procedures, including those related to death penalty appeals.

(4) Within three years before appointment, completion of at least nine hours of Supreme Court–approved appellate criminal defense training, continuing education, or course of study, at least six hours of which involve death penalty appeals. If the Supreme Court has previously appointed counsel to represent a defendant in a death penalty appeal or a related habeas corpus proceeding, and counsel has provided active representation within three years before the request for a new appointment, the court, after reviewing counsel's previous work, may find that such representation constitutes compliance with this requirement.

(5) Proficiency in issue identification, research, analysis, writing, and advocacy, taking into consideration all of the following:

(A) Two writing samples—ordinarily appellate briefs—written by the attorney and presenting an analysis of complex legal issues;

(B) If the attorney has previously been appointed in a death penalty appeal or death penalty–related habeas corpus proceeding, the evaluation of the assisting counsel or entity in that proceeding;

(C) Recommendations from two attorneys familiar with the attorney's qualifications and performance; and

(D) If the attorney is on a panel of attorneys eligible for appointments to represent indigents in the Court of Appeal, the evaluation of the administrator responsible for those appointments.

(Subd (d) amended effective January 1, 2007.)

(e) Qualifications for appointed habeas corpus counsel

An attorney appointed as lead or associate counsel to represent a person in death penalty–related habeas corpus proceedings must have at least the following qualifications and experience:

(1) Active practice of law in California for at least four years.

(2) Either:

(A) Service as counsel of record for a defendant in five completed felony appeals or writ proceedings, including one murder case, and service as counsel of record for a defendant in three jury trials or three habeas corpus proceedings involving serious felonies; or

(B) Service as counsel of record for a defendant in five completed felony appeals or writ proceedings and service as supervised counsel in two death penalty–related habeas corpus proceedings in which the petition has been filed. Service as supervised counsel in a death penalty–related habeas corpus proceeding will apply toward this qualification only if lead or associate counsel in that proceeding attests that the attorney performed substantial work on the case and recommends the attorney for appointment.

(3) Familiarity with the practices and procedures of the California Supreme Court and the federal courts in death penalty–related habeas corpus proceedings.

(4) Within three years before appointment, completion of at least nine hours of Supreme Court–approved appellate criminal defense or habeas corpus defense training, continuing education, or course of study, at least six hours of which address death penalty habeas corpus proceedings. If the Supreme Court has previously appointed counsel to represent a defendant in a death penalty appeal or a related habeas corpus proceeding, and counsel has provided active representation within three years before the request for a new appointment, the court, after reviewing counsel's previous work, may find that such representation constitutes compliance with this requirement.

(5) Proficiency in issue identification, research, analysis, writing, investigation, and advocacy, taking into consideration all of the following:

(A) Three writing samples—ordinarily two appellate briefs and one habeas corpus petition—written by the attorney and presenting an analysis of complex legal issues;

(B) If the attorney has previously been appointed in a death penalty appeal or death penalty–related habeas corpus proceeding, the evaluation of the assisting counsel or entity in that proceeding;

(C) Recommendations from two attorneys familiar with the attorney's qualifications and performance; and

(D) If the attorney is on a panel of attorneys eligible for appointments to represent indigent appellants in the Court of Appeal, the evaluation of the administrator responsible for those appointments.

(Subd (e) amended effective January 1, 2007.)

(f) Alternative qualifications

The Supreme Court may appoint an attorney who does not meet the requirements of (d)(1) and (2) or (e)(1) and (2) if the attorney has the qualifications described in (d)(3)–(5) or (e)(3)–(5) and:

(1) The court finds that the attorney has extensive experience in another jurisdiction or a different type of practice (such as civil trials or appeals, academic work, or work for a court or prosecutor) for at least four years, providing the attorney with experience in complex cases substantially equivalent to that of an attorney qualified under (d) or (e).

(2) Ongoing consultation is available to the attorney from an assisting counsel or entity designated by the court.

(3) Within two years before appointment, the attorney has completed at least 18 hours of Supreme Court–approved appellate criminal defense or habeas corpus defense training, continuing education, or course of study, at least nine hours of which involve death penalty appellate or habeas corpus proceedings. The Supreme Court will determine in each case whether the training, education, or course of study completed by a particular attorney satisfies the requirements of this subdivision in light of the attorney's individual background and experience. If the Supreme Court has previously appointed counsel to represent a defendant in a death penalty appeal or a related habeas corpus proceeding, and counsel has provided active representation within three years before the request for a new appointment, the court, after reviewing counsel's previous work, may find that such representation constitutes compliance with this requirement.

(g) Attorneys without trial experience

If an evidentiary hearing is ordered in a death penalty–related habeas corpus proceeding and an attorney appointed under either (e) or (f) to represent a defendant in that proceeding lacks experience in conducting trials or evidentiary hearings, the attorney must associate an attorney who has such experience.

(h) Use of supervised counsel

An attorney who does not meet the qualifications described in (d), (e), or (f) may assist lead or associate counsel, but must work under the immediate supervision and direction of lead or associate counsel.

(i) Appellate and habeas corpus appointment

(1) An attorney appointed to represent a defendant in both a death penalty appeal and death penalty–related habeas corpus proceedings must meet the minimum qualifications of both (d) and (e) or of (f).

(2) Notwithstanding (1), two attorneys together may be eligible for appointment to represent a defendant jointly in both a death penalty appeal and death penalty–related habeas corpus proceedings if the Supreme Court finds that their qualifications in the aggregate satisfy the provisions of both (d) and (e) or of (f).

(j) Designated entities as appointed counsel

(1) Notwithstanding any other provision of this rule, the State Public Defender is qualified to serve as appointed counsel in death penalty appeals, the Habeas Corpus Resource Center is qualified to serve as appointed counsel in death penalty–related habeas corpus proceedings, and the California Appellate Project in San Francisco is qualified to serve as appointed counsel in both classes of proceedings.

(2) When serving as appointed counsel in a death penalty appeal, the State Public Defender or the California Appellate Project in San Francisco must not assign any attorney as lead counsel unless it finds the attorney qualified under (d)(1)–(5) or the Supreme Court finds the attorney qualified under (f).

(3) When serving as appointed counsel in a death penalty–related habeas corpus proceeding, the Habeas Corpus Resource Center or the California Appellate Project in San Francisco must not assign any attorney as lead counsel unless it finds the attorney qualified under (e)(1)–(5) or the Supreme Court finds the attorney qualified under (f).

(k) Attorney appointed by federal court

Notwithstanding any other provision of this rule, the Supreme Court may appoint an attorney who is under appointment by a federal court in a death penalty–related habeas corpus proceeding for the purpose of exhausting state remedies in the Supreme Court and for all subsequent state proceedings in that case, if the Supreme Court finds that attorney has the commitment, proficiency, and knowledge necessary to represent the defendant competently in state proceedings.

Rule 8.605 amended and renumbered effective January 1, 2007; repealed and adopted as rule 76.6 effective January 1, 2005.

Advisory Committee Comment

Subdivision (c). The definition of "associate counsel" in (c)(3) is intended to make it clear that although appointed lead counsel has overall and supervisory responsibility in a capital case, appointed associate counsel also has casewide responsibility to perform the duties for which he or she was appointed, whether they are appellate duties, habeas corpus duties, or appellate *and* habeas corpus duties.

Article 2
Record on Appeal

Rule 8.610. Contents and form of the record
Rule 8.613. Preparing and certifying the record of preliminary proceedings
Rule 8.616. Preparing the trial record
Rule 8.619. Certifying the trial record for completeness
Rule 8.622. Certifying the trial record for accuracy
Rule 8.625. Certifying the record in pre-1997 trials

Rule 8.610.   Contents and form of the record

(a) Contents of the record

(1) The record must include a clerk's transcript containing:

(A) The accusatory pleading and any amendment;

(B) Any demurrer or other plea;

(C) All court minutes;

(D) All instructions submitted in writing, each one indicating the party requesting it;

(E) Any written communication between the court and the jury or any individual juror;

(F) Any verdict;

(G) Any written opinion of the court;

(H) The judgment or order appealed from and any abstract of judgment or commitment;

(I) Any motion for new trial, with supporting and opposing memoranda and attachments;

(J) Any transcript of a sound or sound-and-video recording furnished to the jury or tendered to the court under rule 2.1040;

(K) Any application for additional record and any order on the application;

(L) Any written defense motion or any written motion by the People, with supporting and opposing memoranda and attachments;

(M) If related to a motion under (L), any search warrant and return and the reporter's transcript of any preliminary examination or grand jury hearing;

(N) Any document admitted in evidence to prove a prior juvenile adjudication, criminal conviction, or prison term;

(O) The probation officer's report; and

(P) Any other document filed or lodged in the case, including each juror questionnaire, whether or not the juror was selected.

(2) The record must include a reporter's transcript containing:

(A) The oral proceedings on the entry of any plea other than a not guilty plea;

(B) The oral proceedings on any motion in limine;

(C) The voir dire examination of jurors;

(D) Any opening statement;

(E) The oral proceedings at trial;

(F) All instructions given orally;

(G) Any oral communication between the court and the jury or any individual juror;

(H) Any oral opinion of the court;

(I) The oral proceedings on any motion for new trial;

(J) The oral proceedings at sentencing, granting or denying of probation, or other dispositional hearing;

(K) The oral proceedings on any motion under Penal Code section 1538.5 denied in whole or in part;

(L) The closing arguments;

(M) Any comment on the evidence by the court to the jury;

(N) The oral proceedings on motions in addition to those listed above; and

(O) Any other oral proceedings in the case, including any proceedings that did not result in a verdict or sentence of death because the court ordered a mistrial or a new trial.

(3) All exhibits admitted in evidence, refused, or lodged are deemed part of the record, but may be transmitted to the reviewing court only as provided in rule 8.634.

(4) The superior court or the Supreme Court may order that the record include additional material.

(Subd (a) amended effective January 1, 2007.)

(b) Confidential records

(1) All documents filed or lodged confidentially under Penal Code section 987.9 or 987.2 must be sealed. Documents filed or lodged under Penal Code section 987.9 must be bound separately from documents filed under Penal Code section 987.2. Unless otherwise ordered, copies must be provided only to the Supreme Court and to counsel for the defendant to whom the documents relate.

(2) All reporter's transcripts of in camera proceedings must be sealed. Unless otherwise ordered, copies must be

provided only to the Supreme Court and to counsel for parties present at the proceedings.

(3) Records sealed under this rule must comply with rule 8.328.

(Subd (b) amended effective January 1, 2007.)

(c) Juror-identifying information

Any document in the record containing juror-identifying information must be edited in compliance with rule 8.332. Unedited copies of all such documents and a copy of the table required by the rule, under seal and bound together, must be included in the record sent to the Supreme Court.

(Subd (c) amended effective January 1, 2007.)

(d) Form of record

The clerk's transcript and the reporter's transcript must comply with rule 8.144, but the indexes for the clerk's transcript must separately list all sealed documents in that transcript, and the indexes for the reporter's transcript must separately list all sealed reporter's transcripts with the date and the names of all parties present. The indexes must not list any confidential material relating to a request for funds under Penal Code section 987.9 or disclose the substance of any sealed matter.

(Subd (d) amended effective January 1, 2007; previously amended effective January 1, 2005.)

Rule 8.610 amended and renumbered effective January 1, 2007; adopted as rule 34.1 effective January 1, 2004; previously amended effective January 1, 2005.

Advisory Committee Comment

Subdivision (a). Subdivision (a) restates Penal Code section 190.7(a).

Subdivision (b). Under the third sentence of (b)(1), copies of sealed documents must be given only to the Supreme Court and to the defendant concerned "[u]nless otherwise ordered." The qualification recognizes the statutory right of the Attorney General to request, under certain circumstances, copies of documents filed confidentially under Penal Code section 987.9(d). To facilitate compliance with such requests, the second sentence of rule 8.610(b)(1) requires such documents to be bound separately from documents filed confidentially under Penal Code section 987.2.

Subdivision (d). Subdivision (d) requires that the master indexes of the clerk and reporter's transcripts separately list all documents and transcripts each contains that were filed in sealed form under subdivision (b). The purpose of this provision is to assist the parties in making—and the court in adjudicating—motions to unseal portions of the record. To protect confidentiality until a record is unsealed, however, each index must endeavor to identify the sealed matter it lists without disclosing its substance.

Rule 8.613. Preparing and certifying the record of preliminary proceedings

(a) Definitions

For purposes of this rule:

(1) The "preliminary proceedings" are all proceedings held before and including the filing of the information or indictment, whether in open court or otherwise, and include the preliminary examination or grand jury proceeding;

(2) The "record of the preliminary proceedings" is the court file and the reporter's transcript of the preliminary proceedings;

(3) The "responsible judge" is the judge assigned to try the case or, if none is assigned, the presiding superior court judge or designee of the presiding judge; and

(4) The "designated judge" is the judge designated by the presiding judge to supervise preparation of the record of preliminary proceedings.

(Subd (a) amended effective January 1, 2007.)

(b) Notice of intent to seek death penalty

In any case in which the death penalty may be imposed:

(1) If the prosecution notifies the responsible judge that it intends to seek the death penalty, the judge must notify the presiding judge and the clerk. The clerk must promptly enter the information in the court file.

(2) If the prosecution does not give notice under (1)—and does not give notice to the contrary—the clerk must notify the responsible judge 60 days before the first date set for trial that the prosecution is presumed to seek the death penalty. The judge must notify the presiding judge, and the clerk must promptly enter the information in the court file.

(c) Assignment of judge designated to supervise preparation of record of preliminary proceedings

(1) Within five days after receiving notice under (b), the presiding judge must designate a judge to supervise preparation of the record of the preliminary proceedings.

(2) If there was a preliminary examination, the designated judge must be the judge who conducted it.

(d) Notice to prepare transcript

Within five days after receiving notice under (b)(1) or notifying the judge under (b)(2), the clerk must notify each reporter who reported a preliminary proceeding to prepare a transcript of the proceeding. If there is more than one reporter, the designated judge may assign a reporter or another designee to perform the functions of the primary reporter.

(e) Reporter's duties

(1) The reporter must prepare an original and five copies of the reporter's transcript and two additional copies for each codefendant against whom the death penalty is sought. The transcript must include the preliminary examination or grand jury proceeding unless a transcript of that examination or proceeding has already been filed in superior court for inclusion in the clerk's transcript.

(2) The reporter must certify the original and all copies of the reporter's transcript as correct.

(3) Within 20 days after receiving the notice to prepare the reporter's transcript, the reporter must deliver the original and all copies of the transcript to the clerk.

(f) Review by counsel

(1) Within five days after the reporter delivers the transcript, the clerk must deliver the original to the designated judge and one copy to each trial counsel. If a different attorney represented the defendant or the People in the preliminary proceedings, both attorneys must perform the tasks required by (2).

(2) Each trial counsel must promptly:

(A) Review the reporter's transcript for errors or omissions;

(B) Review the docket sheets and minute orders to determine whether all preliminary proceedings have been transcribed;

(C) Consult with opposing counsel to determine whether any other proceedings or discussions should have been transcribed; and

(D) Review the court file to determine whether it is complete.

(Subd (f) amended effective January 1, 2007.)

(g) Declaration and request for corrections or additions

(1) Within 30 days after the clerk delivers the transcript, each trial counsel must serve and file a declaration stating that counsel or another person under counsel's supervision has performed the tasks required by (f), and must serve and file either:

(A) A request for corrections or additions to the reporter's transcript or court file; or

(B) A statement that counsel does not request any corrections or additions.

(2) If a different attorney represented the defendant in the preliminary proceedings, that attorney must also file the declaration required by (1).

(3) A request for additions to the reporter's transcript must state the nature and date of the proceedings and, if known, the identity of the reporter who reported them.

(4) If any counsel fails to timely file a declaration under (1), the designated judge must not certify the record and must set the matter for hearing, require a showing of good cause why counsel has not complied, and fix a date for compliance.

(Subd (g) amended effective January 1, 2007.)

(h) Corrections or additions to the record of preliminary proceedings

If any counsel files a request for corrections or additions:

(1) Within 15 days after the last request is filed, the designated judge must hold a hearing and order any necessary corrections or additions.

(2) If any portion of the proceedings cannot be transcribed, the judge may order preparation of a settled statement under rule 8.346.

(3) Within 20 days after the hearing under (1), the original reporter's transcript and court file must be corrected or augmented to reflect all corrections or additions ordered. The clerk must promptly send copies of the corrected or additional pages to trial counsel.

(4) The judge may order any further proceedings to correct or complete the record of the preliminary proceedings.

(5) When the judge is satisfied that all corrections and additions ordered have been made and copies of all corrected or additional pages have been sent to the parties, the judge must certify the record of the preliminary proceedings as complete and accurate.

(6) The record of the preliminary proceedings must be certified as complete and accurate within 120 days after the presiding judge orders preparation of the record.

(Subd (h) amended effective January 1, 2007.)

(i) Computer-readable copies

(1) When the record of the preliminary proceedings is certified as complete and accurate, the clerk must promptly notify the reporter to prepare five computer-readable copies of the transcript and two additional computer-readable copies for each codefendant against whom the death penalty is sought.

(2) Each computer-readable copy must comply with the format, labeling, content, and numbering requirements

of Code of Civil Procedure section 271(b) and any additional requirements prescribed by the Supreme Court, and must be further labeled to show the date it was made.

(3) A computer-readable copy of a sealed transcript must be placed on a separate disk and clearly labeled as confidential.

(4) The reporter is to be compensated for computer-readable copies as provided in Government Code section 69954(b).

(5) Within 20 days after the clerk notifies the reporter under (1), the reporter must deliver the computer-readable copies to the clerk.

(Subd (i) amended effective January 1, 2007.)

(j) Delivery to the superior court

Within five days after the reporter delivers the computer-readable copies, the clerk must deliver to the responsible judge, for inclusion in the record:

(1) The certified original reporter's transcript of the preliminary proceedings and the copies that have not been distributed to counsel, including the computer-readable copies; and

(2) The complete court file of the preliminary proceedings or a certified copy of that file.

(Subd (j) amended effective January 1, 2007.)

(k) Extension of time

(1) Except as provided in (2), the designated judge may extend for good cause any of the periods specified in this rule.

(2) The period specified in (h)(6) may be extended only as follows:

(A) The designated judge may request an extension of the period by presenting a declaration to the responsible judge explaining why the time limit cannot be met; and

(B) The responsible judge may order an extension not exceeding 90 additional days; in an exceptional case the judge may order an extension exceeding 90 days, but must state on the record the specific reason for the greater extension.

(Subd (k) amended effective January 1, 2007.)

(*l*) Notice that the death penalty is no longer sought

After the presiding judge has ordered preparation of the pretrial record, if the death penalty is no longer sought, the clerk must promptly notify the reporter that this rule does not apply.

(Subd (l) amended effective January 1, 2007.)
Rule 8.613 amended and renumbered effective January 1, 2007; adopted as rule 34.2 effective January 1, 2004.

Advisory Committee Comment

Rule 8.613 implements Penal Code section 190.9(a). Rules 8.613–8.622 govern the process of preparing and certifying the record in any appeal from a judgment of death imposed after a trial that began on or after January 1, 1997; specifically, rule 8.613 provides for the record of the preliminary proceedings in such an appeal. Rule 8.625 governs the process of certifying the record in any appeal from a judgment of death imposed after a trial that began before January 1, 1997.

Subdivision (f). As used in subdivision (f)—as in all rules in this chapter—trial counsel "means both the defendant's trial counsel and the prosecuting attorney." (Rule 8.600(e)(2).)

Subdivision (i). Subdivision (i)(4) restates a provision of former rule 35(b), second paragraph, as it was in effect on December 31, 2003.

Rule 8.616.   Preparing the trial record

(a) Clerk's duties

(1) The clerk must promptly—and no later than five days after the judgment of death is rendered—notify the reporter to prepare the reporter's transcript.

(2) The clerk must prepare an original and eight copies of the clerk's transcript and two additional copies for each codefendant sentenced to death.

(3) The clerk must certify the original and all copies of the clerk's transcript as correct.

(b) Reporter's duties

(1) The reporter must prepare an original and five copies of the reporter's transcript and two additional copies for each codefendant sentenced to death.

(2) Any portion of the transcript transcribed during trial must not be retyped unless necessary to correct errors, but must be repaginated and bound with any portion of the transcript not previously transcribed. Any additional copies needed must not be retyped but must be prepared by photocopying or an equivalent process.

(3) The reporter must certify the original and all copies of the reporter's transcript as correct and deliver them to the clerk.

(c) Sending the record to trial counsel

Within 30 days after the judgment of death is rendered, the clerk must deliver one copy of the clerk's and reporter's transcripts to each trial counsel, retaining the original transcripts and the remaining copies. If counsel does not receive the transcripts within that period, counsel must promptly notify the superior court.

(d) Extension of time

(1) On request of the clerk or a reporter and for good cause, the superior court may extend the period prescribed in (c) for no more than 30 days. For any further extension the clerk or reporter must file a request in the Supreme Court, showing good cause.

(2) A request under (1) must be supported by a declaration explaining why the extension is necessary. The court may presume good cause if the clerk's and reporter's transcripts combined will likely exceed 10,000 pages.

(3) If the superior court orders an extension under (1), the order must specify the reason justifying the extension. The clerk must promptly send a copy of the order to the Supreme Court.

Rule 8.616 renumbered effective January 1, 2007; repealed and adopted as rule 35 effective January 1, 2004.

Advisory Committee Comment

Rule 8.616 implements Penal Code section 190.8(b).

Ref.: W. Cal. Sum., 10 "Parent and Child" §721.

Rule 8.619.   Certifying the trial record for completeness

(a) Review by counsel during trial

During trial, counsel must call the court's attention to any errors or omissions they may find in the transcripts. The court must periodically ask counsel for lists of any such errors or omissions and may hold hearings to verify them.

(b) Review by counsel after trial

When the clerk delivers the clerk's and reporter's transcripts to trial counsel, each counsel must promptly:

(1) Review the docket sheets and minute orders to determine whether the reporter's transcript is complete;

(2) Consult with opposing counsel to determine whether any other proceedings or discussions should have been transcribed; and

(3) Review the court file to determine whether the clerk's transcript is complete.

(Subd (b) amended effective January 1, 2007.)

(c) Declaration and request for additions or corrections

(1) Within 30 days after the clerk delivers the transcripts, each trial counsel must serve and file a declaration stating that counsel or another person under counsel's supervision has performed the tasks required by (b), and must serve and file either:

(A) A request to include additional materials in the record or to correct errors that have come to counsel's attention; or

(B) A statement that counsel does not request any additions or corrections.

(2) A request for additions to the reporter's transcript must state the nature and date of the proceedings and, if known, the identity of the reporter who reported them.

(3) If any counsel fails to timely file a declaration under (1), the judge must not certify the record and must set the matter for hearing, require a showing of good cause why counsel has not complied, and fix a date for compliance.

(Subd (c) amended effective January 1, 2007.)

(d) Completion of the record

If any counsel files a request for additions or corrections:

(1) The clerk must promptly deliver the original transcripts to the judge who presided at the trial.

(2) Within 15 days after the last request is filed, the judge must hold a hearing and order any necessary additions or corrections. The order must require that any additions or corrections be made within 10 days of its date.

(3) The clerk must promptly—and in any event within five days—notify the reporter of an order under (2). If any portion of the proceedings cannot be transcribed, the judge may order preparation of a settled statement under rule 8.346.

(4) The original transcripts must be augmented or corrected to reflect all additions or corrections ordered. The clerk must promptly send copies of the additional or corrected pages to trial counsel.

(5) Within five days after the augmented or corrected transcripts are filed, the judge must set another hearing to determine whether the record has been completed or corrected as ordered. The judge may order further proceedings to complete or correct the record.

(6) When the judge is satisfied that all additions or corrections ordered have been made and copies of all additional or corrected pages have been sent to trial counsel, the judge must certify the record as complete and redeliver the original transcripts to the clerk.

(7) The judge must certify the record as complete within 90 days after the judgment of death is rendered.

(Subd (d) amended effective January 1, 2007.)

(e) Computer-readable copies

(1) When the record is certified as complete, the clerk must promptly notify the reporter to prepare five computer-readable copies of the transcript and two additional computer-readable copies for each codefendant sentenced to death.

(2) Each computer-readable copy must comply with the format, labeling, content, and numbering requirements of Code of Civil Procedure section 271(b) and any additional requirements prescribed by the Supreme Court, and must be further labeled to show the date it was made.

(3) A computer-readable copy of a sealed transcript must be placed on a separate disk and clearly labeled as confidential.

(4) The reporter is to be compensated for computer-readable copies as provided in Government Code section 69954(b).

(5) Within 10 days after the clerk notifies the reporter under (1), the reporter must deliver the computer-readable copies to the clerk.

(f) Extension of time

(1) The court may extend for good cause any of the periods specified in this rule.

(2) An application to extend the 30-day period to review the record under (c) must be served and filed within that period. If the clerk's and reporter's transcripts combined exceed 10,000 pages, the court may grant an additional three days for each 1,000 pages over 10,000.

(3) If the court orders an extension of time, the order must specify the justification for the extension. The clerk must promptly send a copy of the order to the Supreme Court.

(g) Sending the certified record

When the record is certified as complete, the clerk must promptly send:

(1) To each defendant's appellate counsel and each defendant's habeas corpus counsel: one paper copy of the entire record and one computer-readable copy of the reporter's transcript. If either counsel has not been retained or appointed, the clerk must keep that counsel's copies until counsel is retained or appointed.

(2) To the Attorney General, the Habeas Corpus Resource Center, and the California Appellate Project in San Francisco: one paper copy of the clerk's transcript and one computer-readable copy of the reporter's transcript.

(h) Notice of delivery

When the clerk sends the record to the defendant's appellate counsel, the clerk must serve a notice of delivery on the Supreme Court clerk.

Rule 8.619 amended and renumbered effective January 1, 2007; adopted as rule 35.1 effective January 1, 2004.

Advisory Committee Comment

Rule 8.619 implements Penal Code section 190.8(c)–(e).

Subdivision (e)(4) restates a provision of former rule 35(b), second paragraph, as it was in effect on December 31, 2003.

Rule 8.622. Certifying the trial record for accuracy

(a) Request for corrections or additions

(1) Within 90 days after the clerk delivers the record to defendant's appellate counsel, any party may serve and file a request for corrections or additions.

(2) A request for additions to the reporter's transcript must state the nature and date of the proceedings and, if known, the identity of the reporter who reported them.

(b) Correction of the record

(1) If any counsel files a request for corrections or additions, the procedures and time limits of rule 8.619(d)(1)–(5) must be followed.

(2) When the judge is satisfied that all corrections or additions ordered have been made, the judge must certify the record as accurate and redeliver the record to the clerk.

(3) The judge must certify the record as accurate within 120 days after it is delivered to appellate counsel.

(Subd (b) amended effective January 1, 2007.)

(c) Computer-readable copies

(1) When the record is certified as accurate, the clerk must promptly notify the reporter to prepare six computer-readable copies of the reporter's transcript and two additional computer-readable copies for each codefendant sentenced to death.

(2) In preparing the computer-readable copies, the procedures and time limits of rule 8.619(e)(2)–(5) must be followed.

(Subd (c) amended effective January 1, 2007.)

(d) Extension of time

(1) The court may extend for good cause any of the periods specified in this rule.

(2) An application to extend the 90-day period to request corrections or additions under (a) must be served and filed within that period. If the clerk's and reporter's transcripts combined exceed 10,000 pages, the court may grant an additional 15 days for each 1,000 pages over 10,000.

(3) If the court orders an extension of time, the order must specify the justification for the extension. The clerk must promptly send a copy of the order to the Supreme Court.

(4) If the court orders an extension of time, the court may conduct a status conference or require the counsel who requested the extension to file a status report on counsel's progress in reviewing the record.

(e) Sending the certified record

When the record is certified as accurate, the clerk must promptly send:

(1) To the Supreme Court: the corrected original record, including the judge's certificate of accuracy, and a computer-readable copy of the reporter's transcript.

(2) To each defendant's appellate counsel, each defendant's habeas corpus counsel, the Attorney General, the Habeas Corpus Resource Center, and the California Appellate Project in San Francisco: a copy of the order certifying the record and a computer-readable copy of the reporter's transcript.

(3) To the Governor: the copies of the transcripts required by Penal Code section 1218, with copies of any corrected or augmented pages inserted.

Rule 8.622 amended and renumbered effective January 1, 2007; adopted as rule 35.2 effective January 1, 2004.

Advisory Committee Comment

Rule 8.622 implements Penal Code section 190.8(g).

Rule 8.625. Certifying the record in pre-1997 trials

(a) Application

This rule governs the process of certifying the record in any appeal from a judgment of death imposed after a trial that began before January 1, 1997.

(b) Sending the transcripts to counsel for review

(1) When the clerk and the reporter certify that their respective transcripts are correct, the clerk must promptly send a copy of each transcript to each defendant's trial counsel, to the Attorney General, to the district attorney, to the California Appellate Project in San Francisco, and to the Habeas Corpus Resource Center, noting the sending date on the originals.

(2) The copies of the reporter's transcript sent to the California Appellate Project and the Habeas Corpus Resource Center must be computer-readable copies complying with the format, labeling, content, and numbering requirements of Code of Civil Procedure section 271(b) and any additional requirements prescribed by the Supreme Court, and must be further labeled to show the date they were made.

(3) When the clerk is notified of the appointment or retention of each defendant's appellate counsel, the clerk must promptly send that counsel copies of the clerk's transcript and the reporter's transcript, noting the sending date on the originals. The clerk must notify the Supreme Court, the Attorney General, and each defendant's appellate counsel in writing of the date the transcripts were sent to appellate counsel.

(c) Correcting, augmenting, and certifying the record

(1) Within 90 days after the clerk delivers the transcripts to each defendant's appellate counsel, any party may serve and file a request for correction or augmentation of the record. Any request for extension of time must be served and filed in the Supreme Court no later than five days before the 90-day period expires.

(2) If no party files a timely request for correction or augmentation, the clerk must certify on the original transcripts that no party objected to the accuracy or completeness of the record within the time allowed by law.

(3) Within 10 days after any party files a timely request for correction or augmentation, the clerk must deliver the request and the transcripts to the trial judge.

(4) Within 60 days after receiving a request and transcripts under (3), the judge must order the reporter, clerk, or party to make any necessary corrections or do any act necessary to complete the record, fixing the time for performance. If any portion of the oral proceedings cannot be transcribed, the judge may order preparation of a settled statement under rule 8.346.

(5) The clerk must promptly send a copy of any order under (4) to the parties and to the Supreme Court, but any request for extension of time to comply with the order must be addressed to the trial judge.

(6) The original transcripts must be corrected or augmented to reflect all corrections or augmentations ordered. The clerk must promptly send copies of all corrected or augmented pages to the parties.

(7) The judge must allow the parties a reasonable time to review the corrections or augmentations. If no party objects to the corrections or augmentations as prepared,

the judge must certify that the record is complete and accurate. If any party objects, the judge must resolve the objections before certifying the record.

(8) If the record is not certified within 90 days after the clerk sends the transcripts to appellate counsel under (b)(2), the judge must monitor preparation of the record to expedite certification and report the status of the record monthly to the Supreme Court.

(Subd (c) amended effective January 1, 2007.)

(d) Sending the certified record

When the clerk certifies that no party objected to the record or the judge certifies that the record is complete and accurate, the clerk must promptly send:

(1) To the Supreme Court: the original record, including the original certification by the trial judge.

(2) To each defendant's appellate counsel, the Attorney General, and the California Appellate Project in San Francisco: a copy of the order certifying the record.

(3) To the Governor: the copies of the transcripts required by Penal Code section 1218, with copies of any corrected or augmented pages inserted.

(e) Subsequent trial court orders; omissions

(1) If, after the record is certified, the trial court amends or recalls the judgment or makes any other order in the case, including an order affecting the sentence, the clerk must promptly certify and send a copy of the amended abstract of judgment or other order—as an augmentation of the record—to the persons and entities listed in (d).

(2) If, after the record is certified, the superior court clerk or the reporter learns that the record omits a document or transcript that any rule or court order requires to be included, the clerk must promptly copy and certify the document or the reporter must promptly prepare and certify the transcript. Without the need for further court order, the clerk must send the document or transcript—as an augmentation of the record—to the persons and entities listed in (d).

Rule 8.625 amended and renumbered effective January 1, 2007; adopted as rule 35.3 effective January 1, 2004.

Article 3
Briefs, Hearing, and Decision

Rule 8.630. Briefs by parties and amici curiae
Rule 8.631. Applications to file overlength briefs in appeals from a judgment of death
Rule 8.634. Transmitting exhibits; augmenting the record in the Supreme Court
Rule 8.638. Oral argument and submission of the cause
Rule 8.642. Filing, finality, and modification of decision; rehearing; remittitur

Rule 8.630. Briefs by parties and amici curiae

(a) Contents and form

Except as provided in this rule, briefs in appeals from judgments of death must comply as nearly as possible with rules 8.200 and 8.204.

(Subd (a) amended effective January 1, 2007.)

(b) Length

(1) A brief produced on a computer must not exceed the following limits, including footnotes:

(A) Appellant's opening brief: 102,000 words.

(B) Respondent's brief: 102,000 words. If the Chief Justice permits the appellant to file an opening brief that exceeds the limit set in (1)(A) or (3)(A), respondent's brief may not exceed the length of appellant's opening brief approved by the Chief Justice.

(C) Reply brief: 47,600 words.

(D) Petition for rehearing and answer: 23,800 words each.

(2) A brief under (1) must include a certificate by appellate counsel stating the number of words in the brief; counsel may rely on the word count of the computer program used to prepare the brief.

(3) A typewritten brief must not exceed the following limits:

(A) Appellant's opening brief: 300 pages.

(B) Respondent's brief: 300 pages. If the Chief Justice permits the appellant to file an opening brief that exceeds the limit set in (1)(A) or (3)(A), respondent's brief may not exceed the length of appellant's opening brief approved by the Chief Justice.

(C) Reply brief: 140 pages.

(D) Petition for rehearing and answer: 70 pages each.

(4) The tables, a certificate under (2), and any attachment permitted under rule 8.204(d) are excluded from the limits stated in (1) and (3).

(5) On application, the Chief Justice may permit a longer brief for good cause. An application in any case in which the certified record is filed in the California Supreme Court on or after January 1, 2008, must comply with rule 8.631.

(Subd (b) amended effective January 1, 2008; previously amended effective January 1, 2007.)

(c) Time to file

(1) Except as provided in (2), the times to file briefs in an appeal from a judgment of death are as follows:

(A) The appellant's opening brief must be served and filed within 210 days after the record is certified as complete or the superior court clerk delivers the completed record to the defendant's appellate counsel, whichever is later. The Supreme Court clerk must promptly notify the defendant's appellate counsel and the Attorney General of the due date for the appellant's opening brief.

(B) The respondent's brief must be served and filed within 120 days after the appellant's opening brief is filed. The Supreme Court clerk must promptly notify the defendant's appellate counsel and the Attorney General of the due date for the respondent's brief.

(C) If the clerk's and reporter's transcripts combined exceed 10,000 pages, the time limits stated in (A) and (B) are extended by 15 days for each 1,000 pages of combined transcript over 10,000 pages.

(D) The appellant must serve and file a reply brief, if any, within 60 days after the respondent files its brief.

(2) In any appeal from a judgment of death imposed after a trial that began before January 1, 1997, the time to file briefs is governed by rule 8.360(c).

(3) The Chief Justice may extend the time to serve and file a brief for good cause.

(Subd (c) amended effective January 1, 2007.)

(d) Supplemental briefs

Supplemental briefs may be filed as provided in rule 8.520(d).

(Subd (d) amended effective January 1, 2007.)

(e) Amicus curiae briefs

Amicus curiae briefs may be filed as provided in rule 8.520(f).

(Subd (e) amended effective January 1, 2007.)

(f) Briefs on the court's request

The court may request additional briefs on any or all issues.

(g) Service

(1) The Supreme Court Policy on Service of Process by Counsel for Defendant governs service of the defendant's briefs.

(2) The Attorney General must serve two copies of the respondent's brief on each defendant's appellate counsel and, for each defendant sentenced to death, one copy on the California Appellate Project in San Francisco.

(3) A copy of each brief must be served on the superior court clerk for delivery to the trial judge.

(h) Judicial notice

To obtain judicial notice by the Supreme Court under Evidence Code section 459, a party must comply with rule 8.252(a).

(Subd (h) amended effective January 1, 2007.)

Rule 8.630 amended effective January 1, 2008; repealed and adopted as rule 36 effective January 1, 2004; previously amended and renumbered effective January 1, 2007.

Advisory Committee Comment

Subdivision (b). Subdivision (b)(1) states the maximum permissible lengths of briefs produced on a computer in terms of word count rather than page count. This provision tracks a provision in rule 8.204(c) governing Court of Appeal briefs and is explained in the comment to that provision. Each word count assumes a brief using one-and-one-half spaced lines of text, as permitted by rule 8.204(b)(5).

Subdivision (g). Subdivision (g)(1) is a cross-reference to Policy 4 of the Supreme Court Policies Regarding Cases Arising From Judgments of Death.

Rule 8.631. Applications to file overlength briefs in appeals from a judgment of death

(a) Cases in which this rule applies

This rule applies in appeals from a judgment of death in which the certified record is filed in the California Supreme Court on or after January 1, 2008.

(Subd (a) adopted effective January 1, 2008.)

(b) Policies

(1) The brief limits set by rule 8.630 are substantially higher than for other appellate briefs in recognition of the number, significance, and complexity of the issues generally presented in appeals from judgments of death and are designed to be sufficient to allow counsel to prepare adequate briefs in the majority of such appeals.

(2) In a small proportion of such appeals, counsel may not be able to prepare adequate briefs within the limits set by rule 8.630. In those cases, necessary additional briefing will be permitted.

(3) A party may not file a brief that exceeds the limit set by rule 8.630 unless the court finds that good cause has been shown in an application filed within the time limits set in (d).

(Subd (b) adopted effective January 1, 2008.)

(c) Factors considered

The court will consider the following factors in determining whether good cause exists to grant an application to file a brief that exceeds the limit set by rule 8.630:

(1) The unusual length of the record. A party relying on this factor must specify the length of each of the following components of the record:

(A) The reporter's transcript;

(B) The clerk's transcript; and

(C) The portion of the clerk's transcript that is made up of juror questionnaires.

(2) The number of codefendants in the case and whether they were tried separately from the appellant;

(3) The number of homicide victims in the case and whether the homicides occurred in more than one incident;

(4) The number of other crimes in the case and whether they occurred in more than one incident;

(5) The number of rulings by the trial court on unusual, factually intensive, or legally complex motions that the party may assert are erroneous and prejudicial. A party relying on this factor must briefly describe the nature of these motions;

(6) The number of rulings on objections by the trial court that the party may assert are erroneous and prejudicial;

(7) The number and nature of unusual, factually intensive, or legally complex hearings held in the trial court that the party may assert raise issues on appeal; and

(8) Any other factor that is likely to contribute to an unusually high number of issues or unusually complex issues on appeal. A party relying on this factor must briefly specify those issues.

(Subd (c) adopted effective January 1, 2008.)

(d) Time to file and contents of application

(1) An application to file a brief that exceeds the limits set by rule 8.630 must be served and filed as follows:

(A) For an appellant's opening brief or respondent's brief:

(i) If counsel has not filed an application requesting an extension of time to file the brief, no later than 45 days before the brief is due.

(ii) If counsel has filed an application requesting an extension of time to file the brief, within the time specified by the court in its order regarding the extension of time.

(B) For an appellant's reply brief:

(i) If counsel has not filed an application requesting an extension of time to file the brief, no later than 30 days before the brief is due.

(ii) If counsel has filed an application requesting an extension of time to file the brief, within the time specified by the court in its order regarding the extension of time.

(2) After the time specified in (1), an application to file a brief that exceeds the applicable limit may be filed only under the following circumstances:

(A) New authority substantially affects the issues presented in the case and cannot be adequately addressed without exceeding the applicable limit. Such an application must be filed within 30 days of finality of the new authority; or

(B) Replacement counsel has been appointed to represent the appellant and has determined that it is necessary to file a brief that exceeds the applicable limit. Such an application must be filed within the time specified by the court in its order setting the deadline for replacement counsel to file the appellant's brief.

(3) The application must:

(A) State the number of additional words or typewritten pages requested.

(B) State good cause for granting the additional words or pages requested, consistent with the factors in (c). The number of additional words or pages requested must be commensurate with the good cause shown. The application must explain why the factors identified demonstrate good cause in the particular case. The application must not state mere conclusions or make legal arguments regarding the merits of the issues on appeal.

(C) Not exceed 5,100 words if produced on a computer or 15 pages if typewritten.

(Subd (d) adopted effective January 1, 2008.)

Rule 8.631 adopted effective January 1, 2008.

Advisory Committee Comment

Subdivision (a). In all cases in which a judgment of death was imposed after a trial that began after January 1, 1997, the record filed with the Supreme Court will be the record that has been certified for accuracy under rule 8.622. In cases in which a judgment of death was imposed after a trial that began before January 1, 1997, the record filed with the Supreme Court will be the certified record under rule 8.625.

Subdivision (c)(1)(A). As in guideline 8 of the Supreme Court's Guidelines for Fixed Fee Appointments, juror questionnaires generally will not be taken into account in considering whether the length of the record is unusual unless these questionnaires are relevant to an issue on appeal. A record of 10,000 pages or less, excluding juror questionnaires, is not considered a record of unusual length; 70 percent of the records in capital appeals filed between 2001 and 2004 were 10,000 pages or less, excluding juror questionnaires.

Subdivision (c)(1)(E). Examples of unusual, factually intensive, or legally complex motions include motions to change venue, admit scientific evidence, or determine competency.

Subdivisions (c)(1)(E)–(I). Because an application must be filed before briefing is completed, the issues identified in the application will be those that the party anticipates *may* be raised on appeal. If the party does not ultimately raise all of these issues on appeal, the party is expected to have reduced the length of the brief accordingly.

Subdivision (c)(1)(I). Examples of unusual, factually intensive, or legally complex hearings include jury composition proceedings and hearings to determine the defendant's competency or sanity, whether the defendant is mentally retarded, and whether the defendant may represent himself or herself.

Subdivision (d)(1)(A)(ii). To allow the deadline for an application to file an overlength brief to be appropriately tied to the deadline for filing that brief, if counsel requests an extension of time to file a brief, the court will specify in its order regarding the request to extend the time to file the brief, when any application to file an overlength brief is due. Although the order will specify the deadline by which an application must be filed, counsel are encouraged to file such applications sooner, if possible.

Subdivision (d)(3). These requirements apply to applications filed under either (d)(1) or (d)(2).

Rule 8.634. Transmitting exhibits; augmenting the record in the Supreme Court

(a) Application

Except as provided in (b), rule 8.224 governs the transmission of exhibits to the Supreme Court.

(Subd (a) amended effective January 1, 2007; previously amended effective January 1, 2004.)

(b) Time to file notice of designation

No party may file a notice designating exhibits under rule 8.224(a) until the Supreme Court clerk notifies the parties of the time and place of oral argument.

(Subd (b) amended effective January 1, 2007.)

(c) Augmenting the record in the Supreme Court

At any time, on motion of a party or on its own motion, the Supreme Court may order the record augmented or corrected as provided in rule 8.155.

(Subd (c) amended effective January 1, 2007; adopted effective January 1, 2004.)

Rule 8.634 amended and renumbered effective January 1, 2007; adopted as rule 36.1 effective January 1, 2003; previously amended effective January 1, 2004.

Rule 8.638. Oral argument and submission of the cause

(a) Application

Except as provided in (b), rule 8.524 governs oral argument and submission of the cause in the Supreme Court unless the court provides otherwise in its Internal Operating Practices and Procedures or by order.

(Subd (a) amended effective January 1, 2007; previously amended effective January 1, 2004.)

(b) Procedure

(1) The appellant has the right to open and close.

(2) Each side is allowed 45 minutes for argument.

(3) Two counsel may argue on each side if, within 10 days after the date of the order setting the case for argument, they notify the court that the case requires it.

(Subd (b) amended effective January 1, 2004.)

Rule 8.638 amended and renumbered effective January 1, 2007; adopted as rule 36.2 effective January 1, 2003; previously amended effective January 1, 2004.

Rule 8.642. Filing, finality, and modification of decision; rehearing; remittitur

Rules 8.532 through 8.540 govern the filing, finality, and modification of decision, rehearing, and issuance of remittitur by the Supreme Court in an appeal from a judgment of death.

Rule 8.642 amended and renumbered effective January 1, 2007; adopted as rule 36.3 effective January 1, 2004.

Division 2
Rules on Appeal to the Superior Court
[Repealed]

Division 2 repealed effective January 1, 2009.

2008 Note: Disposition Tables appear on pages lix–lxviii.

Chapter 1
Appellate Division Rules
[Repealed]

Rule 8.700.   Appellate rules [Repealed]

Rule 8.700 repealed effective January 1, 2009; adopted as rule 100 effective June 3, 1998; previously renumbered effective January 1, 2007.

Rule 8.701.   Appellate division assignments [Repealed]

Rule 8.701 repealed effective January 1, 2009; adopted as rule 100.5 effective June 3, 1998; previously amended and renumbered effective January 1, 2007.

Rule 8.702.   Sessions [Repealed]

Rule 8.702 repealed effective January 1, 2009; adopted as rule 101; previously renumbered effective January 1, 2007.

Rule 8.703.   Powers of presiding judge [Repealed]

Rule 8.703 repealed effective January 1, 2009; adopted as rule 102; previously amended effective July 1, 1972, January 1, 1977, and July 1, 1996; previously renumbered effective January 1, 2007.

Rule 8.704.   Calendars and notice of hearing [Repealed]

Rule 8.704 repealed effective January 1, 2009; adopted as rule 103; previously renumbered effective January 1, 2007.

Rule 8.705.   Motions [Repealed]

Rule 8.705 repealed effective January 1, 2009; adopted as rule 104; previously renumbered effective January 1, 2007.

Rule 8.706.   Briefs and records [Repealed]

Rule 8.706 repealed effective January 1, 2009; adopted as rule 105; previously amended effective January 1, 1967, July 1, 1969, July 1, 1971, July 1, 1972, January 1, 1976, July 1, 1976, July 1, 1977, July 1, 1980, July 1, 1996, July 1, 1997, July 1, 1999, and July 1, 2000; previously amended and renumbered effective January 1, 2007.

Rule 8.707.   Decisions [Repealed]

Rule 8.707 repealed effective January 1, 2009; repealed and adopted as rule 106 effective January 1, 2003; previously renumbered effective January 1, 2007.

Rule 8.708.   Finality, modification, and rehearing [Repealed]

Rule 8.708 repealed effective January 1, 2009; repealed and adopted as rule 107 effective January 1, 2003; previously amended and renumbered effective January 1, 2007.

Rule 8.709.   Consent to modification [Repealed]

Rule 8.709 repealed effective January 1, 2009; adopted as rule 108; previously amended effective July 1, 1980; previously amended and renumbered effective January 1, 2007.

Chapter 2
Appeals to the Appellate Division in Limited Civil Cases
[Repealed]

Rule 8.750.   Filing notice of appeal [Repealed]

Rule 8.750 repealed effective January 1, 2009; adopted as rule 121; previously amended effective July 1, 1964, January 1, 1977, and January 1, 1980; previously renumbered effective January 1, 2007.

Rule 8.751.   Time of filing notice of appeal [Repealed]

Rule 8.751 repealed effective January 1, 2009; adopted as rule 122; previously amended effective January 5, 1953, July 1, 1964, September 17, 1965, July 1, 1978, January 1, 1982, September 22, 1982, and January 1, 1991; previously amended and renumbered effective January 1, 2007.

Rule 8.752.   Extension of time and cross-appeal [Repealed]

Rule 8.752 repealed effective January 1, 2009; adopted as rule 123; previously amended effective January 5, 1953, January 2, 1962, July 1, 1964, September 17, 1965, January 1, 1971, and January 1, 1976; previously amended and renumbered effective January 1, 2007.

Rule 8.753.   Reporter's transcript [Repealed]

Rule 8.753 repealed effective January 1, 2009; adopted as rule 124; previously amended effective January 5, 1953, July 21, 1964, and January 1, 1992; previously amended and renumbered effective January 1, 2007.

Rule 8.754.   Clerk's transcript and original papers [Repealed]

Rule 8.754 repealed effective January 1, 2009; adopted as rule 125; previously amended effective January 1, 1953, January 5, 1953, July 1, 1964, July 1, 1968, and July 1, 1971; previously amended and renumbered effective January 1, 2007.

Rule 8.755.   Agreed statement [Repealed]

Rule 8.755 repealed effective January 1, 2009; adopted as rule 126; previously amended effective January 5, 1953, and July 1, 1964; previously amended and renumbered effective January 1, 2007.

Rule 8.756.   Settled statement [Repealed]

Rule 8.756 repealed effective January 1, 2009; adopted as rule 127; previously renumbered effective January 1, 2007.

Rule 8.757.   Correction and certification of record [Repealed]

Rule 8.757 repealed effective January 1, 2009; adopted as rule 128; previously amended effective January 5, 1953; previously renumbered effective January 1, 2007.

Rule 8.758.   Form of record [Repealed]

Rule 8.758 repealed effective January 1, 2009; adopted as rule 129; previously amended effective January 5, 1953, January 1, 1968, July 1, 1969, and July 1, 1971; previously amended and renumbered effective January 1, 2007.

Rule 8.759.   Transmission and filing of record [Repealed]

Rule 8.759 repealed effective January 1, 2009; adopted as rule 130; previously amended effective July 1, 1964, July 1, 1970, January 1, 1977, and January 1, 1980; previously renumbered effective January 1, 2007.

Rule 8.760.   Record on cross-appeal [Repealed]

Rule 8.760 repealed effective January 1, 2009; adopted as rule 131; previously amended effective January 5, 1953, and July 1, 1964; previously amended and renumbered effective January 1, 2007.

Rule 8.761.   Augmentation and correction of record [Repealed]

Rule 8.761 repealed effective January 1, 2009; adopted as rule 132; previously amended effective January 5, 1953, and July 1, 1964; previously renumbered effective January 1, 2007.

Rule 8.762.   Abandonment and dismissal [Repealed]

Rule 8.762 repealed effective January 1, 2009; adopted as rule 133; previously amended effective January 6, 1947, January 5, 1953, and July 1, 1964; previously renumbered effective January 1, 2007.

Rule 8.763.   Hearing [Repealed]

Rule 8.763 repealed effective January 1, 2009; adopted as rule 134 effective January 5, 1953; previously amended effective July 1, 1964, and January 1, 1977; previously amended and renumbered effective January 1, 2007.

Rule 8.764.   Costs on appeal [Repealed]

Rule 8.764 repealed effective January 1, 2009; adopted as rule 135; previously amended effective July 1, 1964, January 1, 1987, July 1, 1991, and July 1, 2000; previously amended and renumbered effective January 1, 2007.

Rule 8.765.   Definitions [Repealed]

Rule 8.765 repealed effective January 1, 2009; adopted as rule 136; previously amended effective January 5, 1953, July 1, 1964, and January 1, 1977; previously amended and renumbered effective January 1, 2007.

Rule 8.766.   Applications on routine matters [Repealed]

Rule 8.766 repealed effective January 1, 2009; adopted as rule 137; previously amended effective January 1, 1974, January 1, 1975, and July 1, 1996; previously amended and renumbered effective January 1, 2007.

Rule 8.767.   Extension and shortening of time [Repealed]

Rule 8.767 repealed effective January 1, 2009; adopted as rule 138; previously amended effective July 1, 1964, January 1, 1974, and January 1, 1977; previously amended and renumbered effective January 1, 2007.

Rule 8.768.   Substitution of parties and attorneys [Repealed]

Rule 8.768 repealed effective January 1, 2009; adopted as rule 139; previously amended effective July 1, 1964, and January 1, 1977; previously renumbered effective January 1, 2007.

Rule 8.769.   Writ of supersedeas [Repealed]

Rule 8.769 repealed effective January 1, 2009; adopted as rule 140; previously amended effective January 1, 1984; previously amended and renumbered effective January 1, 2007.

Rule 8.770.   Substitute judge where trial judge unavailable [Repealed]

Rule 8.770 repealed effective January 1, 2009; adopted as rule 141; previously renumbered effective January 1, 2007.

Rule 8.771.   Presumption where record not complete [Repealed]

Rule 8.771 repealed effective January 1, 2009; adopted as rule 142; previously amended effective January 5, 1953; previously renumbered effective January 1, 2007.

Rule 8.772.   Scope and construction [Repealed]

Rule 8.772 repealed effective January 1, 2009; adopted as rule 143; previously amended effective July 1, 1964, and January 1, 1977; previously renumbered effective January 1, 2007.

Rule 8.773.   Remittitur [Repealed]

Rule 8.773 repealed effective January 1, 2009; adopted as rule 144; previously amended effective July 1, 1964, and January 1, 1977; previously renumbered effective January 1, 2007.

Chapter 3
Appeals to the Appellate Division in Criminal Cases
[Repealed]

Rule 8.780.   Applicability to felonies, misdemeanors, infractions [Repealed]

Rule 8.780 repealed effective January 1, 2009; adopted as rule 180 effective January 1, 1994; previously amended and renumbered effective January 1, 2007.

Rule 8.781.   Definitions [Repealed]

Rule 8.781 repealed effective January 1, 2009; adopted as rule 181 effective January 1, 1983; previously amended and renumbered effective January 1, 2007.

Rule 8.782.   Notice of appeal [Repealed]

Rule 8.782 repealed effective January 1, 2009; adopted as rule 182; previously amended September 15, 1961, July 1, 1964, November 13, 1968, January 1, 1972, and January 1, 1982; previously renumbered effective January 1, 2007.

Rule 8.783.   Record on appeal [Repealed]

Rule 8.783 repealed effective January 1, 2009; adopted as rule 183; previously amended effective January 6, 1947, and July 1, 1971; previously amended and renumbered effective January 1, 2007.

Rule 8.784.   Statement or transcript [Repealed]

Rule 8.784 repealed effective January 1, 2009; adopted as rule 184; previously amended effective July 31, 1938, January 6, 1947, and July 1, 1980; previously amended and renumbered effective January 1, 2007.

Rule 8.785.   Amendments to statement or transcript [Repealed]

Rule 8.785 repealed effective January 1, 2009; adopted as rule

185; previously amended effective January 1, 1973, and July 1, 1980; previously renumbered effective January 1, 2007.

Rule 8.786.   Counsel on appeal [Repealed]

Rule 8.786 repealed effective January 1, 2009; adopted as rule 185.5 effective January 1, 1994; previously renumbered effective January 1, 2007.

Rule 8.787.   Extensions of time and relief from default [Repealed]

Rule 8.787 repealed effective January 1, 2009; adopted as rule 186; previously amended effective January 6, 1947, and July 1, 1971; previously amended and renumbered effective January 1, 2007.

Rule 8.788.   Settlement of statement or transcript [Repealed]

Rule 8.788 repealed effective January 1, 2009; adopted as rule 187; previously amended effective July 1, 1989; previously renumbered effective January 1, 2007.

Rule 8.789.   Experimental rule on use of recordings to facilitate settlement of statements [Repealed]

Rule 8.789 repealed effective January 1, 2009; adopted as rule 187.5 effective January 1, 1983; previously amended effective January 1, 2003; previously amended and renumbered effective January 1, 2007.

Rule 8.790.   Abandonment of appeal [Repealed]

Rule 8.790 repealed effective January 1, 2009; adopted as rule 188; previously amended effective January 6, 1947; previously renumbered effective January 1, 2007.

Rule 8.791.   Additions to record [Repealed]

Rule 8.791 repealed effective January 1, 2009; adopted as rule 189; previously renumbered effective January 1, 2007.

Rule 8.792.   Hearings and dismissals [Repealed]

Rule 8.792 repealed effective January 1, 2009; adopted as rule 190; previously effective January 1, 1977; previously renumbered effective January 1, 2007.

Rule 8.793.   Remittiturs [Repealed]

Rule 8.793 repealed effective January 1, 2009; adopted as rule 191; previously amended effective January 2, 1962, and July 1, 1964; previously renumbered effective January 1, 2007.

Another Division 2 follows.

Division 2
Rules Relating to the Superior Court Appellate Division

Division 2 adopted effective January 1, 2009.

Advisory Committee Comment

Division 2. The rules relating to the superior court appellate division begin with Chapter 1, which contains general rules applicable to appeals in all three types of cases within the jurisdiction of the appellate division—limited civil, misdemeanor,

and infraction. Because the procedures relating to taking appeals and preparing the record in limited civil, misdemeanor, and infraction appeals differ, there are separate chapters addressing these topics: Chapter 2 addresses taking appeals and record preparation in limited civil cases, and Chapter 3 addresses taking appeals and record preparation in misdemeanor cases. Because the procedures for briefing and rendering decisions are generally the same in limited civil and misdemeanor appeals, Chapter 4 addresses these procedures in appeals of both types of cases. To make the distinct procedures for appeals in infraction proceedings easier to find and understand, these procedures are located in a separate chapter—Chapter 5. Chapter 6 addresses writ proceedings in the appellate division.

2008 Note: Disposition Tables appear on pages lix–lxviii.

Chap. 1.   General Rules Applicable to Appellate Division Proceedings. Rules 8.800–8.817.
Chap. 2.   Appeals and Records in Limited Civil Cases. Rules 8.820–8.843.
Chap. 3.   Appeals and Records in Misdemeanor Cases. Rules 8.850–8.873.
Chap. 4.   Briefs, Hearing, and Decision in Limited Civil and Misdemeanor Appeals. Rules 8.880–8.891.
Chap. 5.   Appeals in Infraction Cases. Rules 8.900–8.929.
Chap. 6.   Writ Proceedings. Rules 8.930–8.936.

Chapter 1
General Rules Applicable to Appellate Division Proceedings

Chapter 1 adopted effective January 1, 2009.

Rule 8.800. Application of division
Rule 8.802. Construction
Rule 8.804. Definitions
Rule 8.805. Amendments to rules and statutes
Rule 8.806. Applications
Rule 8.808. Motions
Rule 8.810. Extending time
Rule 8.811. Policies and factors governing extensions of time
Rule 8.812. Relief from default
Rule 8.813. Shortening time
Rule 8.814. Substituting parties; substituting or withdrawing attorneys
Rule 8.816. Address and telephone number of record; notice of change
Rule 8.817. Service and filing

Rule 8.800.   Application of division

The rules in this division apply to:

(1) Appeals in the appellate division of the superior court; and

(2) Writ proceedings, motions, applications, and petitions in the appellate division of the superior court.

Rule 8.800 adopted effective January 1, 2009.

Rule 8.802.   Construction

(a) Construction

The rules in this division must be construed to ensure that the proceedings they govern will be justly and speedily determined.

(Subd (a) adopted effective January 1, 2009.)

(b) Terminology

As used in this division:

(1) "Must" is mandatory;

(2) "May" is permissive;

(3) "May not" means is not permitted to;

(4) "Will" expresses a future contingency or predicts action by a court or person in the ordinary course of events, but does not signify a mandatory duty; and

(5) "Should" expresses a preference or a nonbinding recommendation.

(Subd (b) adopted effective January 1, 2009.)

(c) Construction of additional terms

In the rules:

(1) Each tense (past, present, or future) includes the others;

(2) Each gender (masculine, feminine, or neuter) includes the others;

(3) Each number (singular or plural) includes the other; and

(4) The headings of divisions, chapters, articles, rules, and subdivisions are substantive.

(Subd (c) adopted effective January 1, 2009.)
Rule 8.802 adopted effective January 1, 2009.

Rule 8.804. Definitions

As used in this division, unless the context or subject matter otherwise requires:

(1) "Action" includes special proceeding.

(2) "Case" includes action or proceeding.

(3) "Civil case" means a case prosecuted by one party against another for the declaration, enforcement, or protection of a right or the redress or prevention of a wrong. Civil cases include all cases except criminal cases.

(4) "Unlimited civil cases" and "limited civil cases" are defined in Code of Civil Procedure section 85 et seq.

(5) "Criminal case" means a proceeding by which a party charged with a public offense is accused and brought to trial and punishment.

(6) "Rule" means a rule of the California Rules of Court.

(7) "Local rule" means every rule, regulation, order, policy, form, or standard of general application adopted by a court to govern practice and procedure in that court or by a judge of the court to govern practice or procedure in that judge's courtroom.

(8) "Presiding judge" includes the acting presiding judge or the judge designated by the presiding judge.

(9) "Judge" includes, as applicable, a judge of the superior court, a commissioner, or a temporary judge.

(10) "Person" includes a corporation or other legal entity as well as a natural person.

(11) "Appellant" means the appealing party.

(12) "Respondent" means the adverse party.

(13) "Party" is a person appearing in an action. Parties include both self-represented persons and persons represented by an attorney of record. "Party," "applicant," "petitioner," or any other designation of a party includes the party's attorney of record.

(14) "Attorney" means a member of the State Bar of California.

(15) "Counsel" means an attorney.

(16) "Prosecuting attorney" means the city attorney, county counsel, or district attorney prosecuting an infraction or misdemeanor case.

(17) "Complaint" includes a citation.

(18) "Service" means service in the manner prescribed by a statute or rule.

(19) "Declaration" includes "affidavit."

(20) "Recycled" as applied to paper means "recycled printing and writing paper" as defined by Public Contract Code section 12209.

(21) "Trial court" means the superior court from which an appeal is taken.

(22) "Reviewing court" means the appellate division of the superior court.

(23) "Judgment" includes any judgment or order that may be appealed.

Rule 8.804 adopted effective January 1, 2009.

Advisory Committee Comment

Item (18). See rule 1.21 for general requirements relating to service, including proof of service.

Rule 8.805. Amendments to rules and statutes

(a) Amendments to rules

Only the Judicial Council may amend these rules, except the rules in division 5, which may be amended only by the Supreme Court. An amendment by the Judicial Council must be published in the advance pamphlets of the Official Reports and takes effect on the date ordered by the Judicial Council.

(Subd (a) adopted effective January 1, 2009.)

(b) Amendments to statutes

In these rules, a reference to a statute includes any subsequent amendment to the statute.

(Subd (b) adopted effective January 1, 2009.)
Rule 8.805 adopted effective January 1, 2009.

Rule 8.806. Applications

(a) Service and filing

Except as these rules provide otherwise, parties must serve and file all applications, including applications to extend time to file records, briefs, or other documents and applications to shorten time. Applications to extend the time to prepare the record on appeal may be filed in either the trial court or the appellate division. All other applications must be filed in the appellate division. For good cause, the presiding judge of the court where the application was filed, or his or her designee, may excuse advance service.

(Subd (a) adopted effective January 1, 2009.)

(b) Contents

The application must:

(1) State facts showing good cause to grant the application; and

(2) Identify any previous applications relating to the same subject filed by any party in the same appeal or writ proceeding.

(Subd (b) adopted effective January 1, 2009.)

(c) Envelopes

An application must be accompanied by addressed, postage-prepaid envelopes for the clerk's use in mailing copies of the order on the application to all parties.

(Subd (c) adopted effective January 1, 2009.)

(d) Disposition

Unless the court determines otherwise, the presiding judge of the court in which the application was filed, or his or her designee, may rule on the application.

(Subd (d) adopted effective January 1, 2009.)
Rule 8.806 adopted effective January 1, 2009.

Advisory Committee Comment

Subdivision (a). See rule 1.21 for the meaning of "serve and file," including the requirements for proof of service.

Subdivisions (a) and (d). These provisions permit the presiding judge to designate another judge, such as the trial judge, to handle applications.

Rule 8.808. Motions

(a) Motion and opposition

(1) Except as these rules provide otherwise, to make a motion in the appellate division a party must serve and file a written motion, stating the grounds and the relief requested and identifying any documents on which it is based.

(2) A motion must be accompanied by a memorandum and, if it is based on matters outside the record, by declarations or other supporting evidence.

(3) Any opposition to the motion must be served and filed within 15 days after the motion is filed.

(Subd (a) adopted effective January 1, 2009.)

(b) Disposition

(1) The court may rule on a motion at any time after an opposition or other response is filed or the time to oppose has expired.

(2) On a party's request or its own motion, the appellate division may place a motion on calendar for a hearing. The clerk must promptly send each party a notice of the date and time of the hearing.

(Subd (b) adopted effective January 1, 2009.)
Rule 8.808 adopted effective January 1, 2009.

Advisory Committee Comment

Subdivision (a)(1). See rule 1.21 for the meaning of "serve and file," including the requirements for proof of service.

Subdivision (b). Although a party may request a hearing on a motion, a hearing will be held only if the court determines that one is needed.

Rule 8.810. Extending time

(a) Computing time

The Code of Civil Procedure governs computing and extending the time to do any act required or permitted under these rules.

(Subd (a) adopted effective January 1, 2009.)

(b) Extension by trial court

(1) For good cause and except as these rules provide otherwise, the presiding judge of the trial court, or his or her designee, may extend the time to do any act to prepare the record on appeal.

(2) The trial court may not extend the time to do an act if that time—including any valid extension—has expired.

(3) Notwithstanding anything in these rules to the contrary, the trial court may grant an initial extension to any party to do any act to prepare the record on appeal on an ex parte basis.

(Subd (b) adopted effective January 1, 2009.)

(c) Extension by appellate division

For good cause and except as these rules provide otherwise, the presiding judge of the appellate division, or his or her designee, may extend the time to do any act required or permitted under these rules, except the time to file a notice of appeal.

(Subd (c) adopted effective January 1, 2009.)

(d) Application for extension

(1) An application to extend time must include a declaration stating facts, not mere conclusions, and must be served on all parties. For good cause, the presiding judge of the appellate division, or his or her designee, may excuse advance service.

(2) The application must state:

(A) The due date of the document to be filed;

(B) The length of the extension requested;

(C) Whether any earlier extensions have been granted and, if so, their lengths; and

(D) Good cause for granting the extension, consistent with the policies and factors stated in rule 8.811.

(Subd (d) adopted effective January 1, 2009.)

(e) Notice to party

(1) In a civil case, counsel must deliver to his or her client or clients a copy of any stipulation or application to extend time that counsel files. Counsel must attach evidence of such delivery to the stipulation or application or certify in the stipulation or application that the copy has been delivered.

(2) The evidence or certification of delivery under (1) need not include the address of the party notified.

(Subd (e) adopted effective January 1, 2009.)
Rule 8.810 adopted effective January 1, 2009.

Advisory Committee Comment

Subdivision (b)(1). This provision permits the presiding judge to designate another judge, such as the trial judge, to handle applications to extend time.

Rule 8.811. Policies and factors governing extensions of time

(a) Policies

(1) The time limits prescribed by these rules should generally be met to ensure expeditious conduct of appellate business and public confidence in the efficient administration of appellate justice.

(2) The effective assistance of counsel to which a party is entitled includes adequate time for counsel to prepare briefs or other documents that fully advance the party's interests. Adequate time also allows the preparation of accurate, clear, concise, and complete submissions that assist the courts.

(3) For a variety of legitimate reasons, counsel or self-represented litigants may not always be able to prepare briefs or other documents within the time specified in the rules of court. To balance the competing policies stated in (1) and (2), applications to extend time in the appellate division must demonstrate good cause under (b). If good cause is shown, the court must extend the time.

(Subd (a) adopted effective January 1, 2009.)

(b) Factors considered

In determining good cause, the court must consider the following factors when applicable:

(1) The degree of prejudice, if any, to any party from a grant or denial of the extension. A party claiming prejudice must support the claim in detail.

(2) In a civil case, the positions of the client and any opponent with regard to the extension.

(3) The length of the record, including the number of relevant trial exhibits. A party relying on this factor must specify the length of the record.

(4) The number and complexity of the issues raised. A party relying on this factor must specify the issues.

(5) Whether there are settlement negotiations and, if so, how far they have progressed and when they might be completed.

(6) Whether the case is entitled to priority.

(7) Whether counsel responsible for preparing the document is new to the case.

(8) Whether other counsel or the client needs additional time to review the document.

(9) Whether counsel or a self-represented party responsible for preparing the document has other time-limited commitments that prevent timely filing of the document. Mere conclusory statements that more time is needed because of other pressing business will not suffice. Good cause requires a specific showing of other obligations of counsel or a self-represented party that:

(A) Have deadlines that as a practical matter preclude filing the document by the due date without impairing its quality; or

(B) Arise from cases entitled to priority.

(10) Illness of counsel or a self-represented party, a personal emergency, or a planned vacation that counsel or a self-represented party did not reasonably expect to conflict with the due date and cannot reasonably rearrange.

(11) Any other factor that constitutes good cause in the context of the case.

(Subd (b) adopted effective January 1, 2009.)
Rule 8.811 adopted effective January 1, 2009.

Rule 8.812. Relief from default

For good cause, the presiding judge of the appellate division, or his or her designee, may relieve a party from a default for any failure to comply with these rules, except the failure to file a timely notice of appeal.
Rule 8.812 adopted effective January 1, 2009.

Rule 8.813. Shortening time

For good cause and except as these rules provide otherwise, the presiding judge of the appellate division, or his or her designee, may shorten the time to do any act required or permitted under these rules.
Rule 8.813 adopted effective January 1, 2009.

Rule 8.814. Substituting parties; substituting or withdrawing attorneys

(a) Substituting parties

Substitution of parties in an appeal or original proceeding must be made by serving and filing a motion in the appellate division. The clerk of the appellate division must notify the trial court of any ruling on the motion.

(Subd (a) adopted effective January 1, 2009.)

(b) Substituting attorneys

A party may substitute attorneys by serving and filing in the appellate division a stipulation signed by the party represented and the new attorney.

(Subd (b) adopted effective January 1, 2009.)

(c) Withdrawing attorney

(1) An attorney may request withdrawal by filing a motion to withdraw. Unless the court orders otherwise, the motion need be served only on the party represented and the attorneys directly affected.

(2) The proof of service need not include the address of the party represented. But if the court grants the motion, the withdrawing attorney must promptly provide the court and the opposing party with the party's current or last known address and telephone number.

(3) In all appeals and in original proceedings related to a trial court proceeding, the appellate division clerk must notify the trial court of any ruling on the motion.

(Subd (c) adopted effective January 1, 2009.)
Rule 8.814 adopted effective January 1, 2009.

Rule 8.816. Address and telephone number of record; notice of change

(a) Address and telephone number of record

In any case pending before the appellate division, the appellate division will use the address and telephone number that an attorney or unrepresented party provides on the first document filed in that case as the address and telephone number of record unless the attorney or unrepresented party files a notice under (b).

(Subd (a) adopted effective January 1, 2009.)

(b) Notice of change

(1) An attorney or unrepresented party whose address or telephone number changes while a case is pending must promptly serve and file a written notice of the change in the appellate division in which the case is pending.

(2) The notice must specify the title and number of the case or cases to which it applies. If an attorney gives the notice, the notice must include the attorney's California State Bar number.

(Subd (b) adopted effective January 1, 2009.)

(c) Matters affected by notice

If the notice under (b) does not identify the case or cases in which the new address or telephone number applies, the clerk may use the new address or telephone number as the person's address and telephone number of record in all pending and concluded cases.

(Subd (c) adopted effective January 1, 2009.)

(d) Multiple addresses

If an attorney or unrepresented party has more than one address, only one address may be used in a given case.

(Subd (d) adopted effective January 1, 2009.)
Rule 8.816 adopted effective January 1, 2009.

Rule 8.817. Service and filing

(a) Service

(1) Before filing any document, a party must serve, by any method permitted by the Code of Civil Procedure, one copy of the document on the attorney for each party separately represented, on each unrepresented party, and

on any other person or entity when required by statute or rule.

(2) The party must attach to the document presented for filing a proof of service showing service on each person or entity required to be served under (1). The proof must name each party represented by each attorney served.

(Subd (a) adopted effective January 1, 2009.)

(b) Filing

(1) A document is deemed filed on the date the clerk receives it.

(2) Unless otherwise provided by these rules or other law, a filing is not timely unless the clerk receives the document before the time to file it expires.

(3) A brief, a petition for rehearing, or an answer to a petition for rehearing is timely if the time to file it has not expired on the date of:

(A) Its mailing by priority or express mail as shown on the postmark or the postal receipt; or

(B) Its delivery to a common carrier promising overnight delivery as shown on the carrier's receipt.

(4) The provisions of (3) do not apply to original proceedings.

(Subd (b) adopted effective January 1, 2009.)
Rule 8.817 adopted effective January 1, 2009.

Advisory Committee Comment

Subdivision (a). Subdivision (a)(1) requires service "by any method permitted by the Code of Civil Procedure." The reference is to the several permissible methods of service provided in Code of Civil Procedure sections 1010–1020. *What Is Proof of Service?* (form APP-109-INFO) provides additional information about how to serve documents and how to provide proof of service.

Subdivision (b)(2). In general, to be filed on time, a document must be received by the clerk before the time for filing that document expires. There are, however, some limited exceptions to this general rule. For example, rule 8.853(e) provides that in a misdemeanor appeal, if the superior court clerk receives a notice of appeal by mail from a custodial institution after the deadline for filing the notice has expired but the envelope shows that the notice was mailed or delivered to custodial officials for mailing before the deadline expired, the notice is deemed timely. This provision reflects the "prison-delivery" exception articulated by the California Supreme Court in *In re Jordan* (1992) 4 Cal.4th 116.

Chapter 2
Appeals and Records in Limited Civil Cases

Chapter 2 adopted effective January 1, 2009.

Art. 1. Taking Civil Appeals. Rules 8.820–8.825.
Art. 2. Record in Civil Appeals. Rules 8.830–8.843.

Article 1
Taking Civil Appeals

Article 1 adopted effective January 1, 2009.

Rule 8.820. Application of chapter
Rule 8.821. Notice of appeal
Rule 8.822. Time to appeal
Rule 8.823. Extending the time to appeal
Rule 8.824. Writ of supersedeas

Rule 8.825. Abandonment, voluntary dismissal, and compromise

Rule 8.820. Application of chapter

The rules in this chapter apply to appeals in limited civil cases, except small claims cases.
Rule 8.820 adopted effective January 1, 2009.

Advisory Committee Comment

Chapters 1 and 4 of this division also apply in appeals in limited civil cases.

Rule 8.821. Notice of appeal

(a) Notice of appeal

(1) To appeal from a judgment or appealable order in a limited civil case, except a small claims case, an appellant must serve and file a notice of appeal in the superior court that issued the judgment or order being appealed. The appellant or the appellant's attorney must sign the notice.

(2) The notice of appeal must be liberally construed and is sufficient if it identifies the particular limited civil case judgment or order being appealed.

(3) Failure to serve the notice of appeal neither prevents its filing nor affects its validity, but the appellant may be required to remedy the failure.

(Subd (a) adopted effective January 1, 2009.)

(b) Filing fee

(1) Unless otherwise provided by law, the notice of appeal must be accompanied by the filing fee required under Government Code section 70621, an application for a waiver of court fees and costs on appeal under rules 3.50–3.63, or an order granting such an application. The filing fee is nonrefundable.

(2) The clerk must file the notice of appeal even if the appellant does not present the filing fee or an application for, or order granting, a waiver under rules 3.50–3.63.

(Subd (b) adopted effective January 1, 2009.)

(c) Failure to pay filing fee

(1) The clerk must promptly notify the appellant in writing if:

(A) The court receives a notice of appeal without the filing fee required by (b) or an application for, or order granting, a fee waiver under rules 3.50–3.63;

(B) A check for the filing fee is dishonored; or

(C) An application for a waiver under rules 3.50–3.63 is denied.

(2) A clerk's notice under (1) must state that the court may dismiss the appeal unless, within 15 days after the notice is sent, the appellant either:

(A) Pays the fee; or

(B) Files an application for a waiver under rules 3.50–3.63 if the appellant has not previously filed such an application.

(3) If the appellant fails to take the action specified in the notice given under (2), the appellate division may dismiss the appeal, but may vacate the dismissal for good cause.

(Subd (c) adopted effective January 1, 2009.)

(d) Notification of the appeal

(1) When the notice of appeal is filed, the trial court clerk must promptly mail a notification of the filing of the

notice of appeal to the attorney of record for each party and to any unrepresented party. The clerk must also mail or deliver this notification to the appellate division clerk.

(2) The notification must show the date it was mailed and must state the number and title of the case and the date the notice of appeal was filed.

(3) A copy of the notice of appeal is sufficient notification under (1) if the required information is on the copy or is added by the trial court clerk.

(4) The mailing of a notification under (1) is a sufficient performance of the clerk's duty despite the death of the party or the discharge, disqualification, suspension, disbarment, or death of the attorney.

(5) Failure to comply with any provision of this subdivision does not affect the validity of the notice of appeal.

(Subd (d) adopted effective January 1, 2009.)

(e) Notice of cross-appeal

As used in this rule, "notice of appeal" includes a notice of cross-appeal and "appellant" includes a respondent filing a notice of cross-appeal.

(Subd (e) adopted effective January 1, 2009.)
Rule 8.821 adopted effective January 1, 2009.

Advisory Committee Comment

Subdivision (a). *Notice of Appeal/Cross-Appeal (Limited Civil Case)* (form APP-102) may be used to file the notice of appeal required under this rule. This form is available at any courthouse or county law library or online at *www.courtinfo.ca.gov/forms*.

Subdivision (b). The filing fee required under Government Code section 70621 is $180 if the amount claimed in the case is $10,000 or less and $300 if the amount claimed in the case is more than $10,000.

Rule 8.822.   Time to appeal
(a) Normal time

Unless a statute or rule 8.823 provides otherwise, a notice of appeal must be filed on or before the earliest of:

(1) 30 days after the trial court clerk mails the party filing the notice of appeal a document entitled "Notice of Entry" of judgment or a file-stamped copy of the judgment, showing the date either was mailed;

(2) 30 days after the party filing the notice of appeal serves or is served by a party with a document entitled "Notice of Entry" of judgment or a file-stamped copy of the judgment, accompanied by proof of service; or

(3) 90 days after the entry of judgment.

(Subd (a) adopted effective January 1, 2009.)

(b) What constitutes entry

For purposes of this rule:

(1) The entry date of a judgment is the date the judgment is filed under Code of Civil Procedure section 668.5 or the date it is entered in the judgment book.

(2) The date of entry of an appealable order that is entered in the minutes is the date it is entered in the permanent minutes. But if the minute order directs that a written order be prepared, the entry date is the date the signed order is filed; a written order prepared under rule 3.1312 or similar local rule is not such an order prepared by direction of a minute order.

(3) The entry date of an order that is not entered in the minutes is the date the signed order is filed.

(Subd (b) adopted effective January 1, 2009.)

(c) Premature notice of appeal

(1) A notice of appeal filed after judgment is rendered but before it is entered is valid and is treated as filed immediately after entry of judgment.

(2) The appellate division may treat a notice of appeal filed after the trial court has announced its intended ruling, but before it has rendered judgment, as filed immediately after entry of judgment.

(Subd (c) adopted effective January 1, 2009.)

(d) Late notice of appeal

If a notice of appeal is filed late, the appellate division must dismiss the appeal.

(Subd (d) adopted effective January 1, 2009.)
Rule 8.822 adopted effective January 1, 2009.

Advisory Committee Comment

Under rule 8.804(23), the term "judgment" includes any order that may be appealed.

Rule 8.823.   Extending the time to appeal
(a) Extension of time

This rule operates only to increase the time to appeal otherwise prescribed in rule 8.822(a); it does not shorten the time to appeal. If the normal time to appeal stated in rule 8.822(a) would be longer than the time provided in this rule, the time to appeal stated in rule 8.822(a) governs.

(Subd (a) adopted effective January 1, 2009.)

(b) Motion for a new trial

If any party serves and files a valid notice of intention to move for a new trial, the time to appeal from the judgment is extended for all parties as follows:

(1) If the motion is denied, until the earliest of:

(A) 15 days after the trial court clerk mails, or a party serves, an order denying the motion or a notice of entry of that order;

(B) 15 days after denial of the motion by operation of law; or

(C) 90 days after entry of judgment; or

(2) If any party serves an acceptance of a conditionally ordered additur or remittitur of damages under a trial court finding of excessive or inadequate damages, until 15 days after the date the party serves the acceptance.

(Subd (b) adopted effective January 1, 2009.)

(c) Motion to vacate judgment

If, within the time prescribed by rule 8.822 to appeal from the judgment, any party serves and files a valid notice of intention to move to vacate the judgment or a valid motion to vacate the judgment, the time to appeal from the judgment is extended for all parties until the earliest of:

(1) 15 days after the trial court clerk mails, or a party serves, an order denying the motion or a notice of entry of that order;

(2) 45 days after the first notice of intention to move or motion is filed; or

(3) 90 days after entry of judgment.

(Subd (c) adopted effective January 1, 2009.)

(d) Motion for judgment notwithstanding the verdict

(1) If any party serves and files a valid motion for judgment notwithstanding the verdict and the motion is

denied, the time to appeal from the judgment is extended for all parties until the earliest of:

(A) 15 days after the trial court clerk mails, or a party serves, an order denying the motion or a notice of entry of that order;

(B) 15 days after denial of the motion by operation of law; or

(C) 90 days after entry of judgment.

(2) Unless extended by (e)(2), the time to appeal from an order denying a motion for judgment notwithstanding the verdict is governed by rule 8.822.

(Subd (d) adopted effective January 1, 2009.)

(e) Motion to reconsider appealable order

If any party serves and files a valid motion to reconsider an appealable order under Code of Civil Procedure section 1008(a), the time to appeal from that order is extended for all parties until the earliest of:

(1) 15 days after the superior court clerk mails, or a party serves, an order denying the motion or a notice of entry of that order;

(2) 45 days after the first motion to reconsider is filed; or

(3) 90 days after entry of the appealable order.

(Subd (e) adopted effective January 1, 2009.)

(f) Cross-appeal

(1) If an appellant timely appeals from a judgment or appealable order, the time for any other party to appeal from the same judgment or order is extended until 10 days after the trial court clerk mails notification of the first appeal.

(2) If an appellant timely appeals from an order granting a motion for a new trial, an order granting—within 75 days after entry of judgment—a motion to vacate the judgment, or a judgment notwithstanding the verdict, the time for any other party to appeal from the original judgment or from an order denying a motion for judgment notwithstanding the verdict is extended until 10 days after the clerk mails notification of the first appeal.

(Subd (f) adopted effective January 1, 2009.)

(g) Showing date of order or notice; proof of service

An order or notice mailed by the clerk under this rule must show the date it was mailed. An order or notice served by a party must be accompanied by proof of service.

(Subd (g) adopted effective January 1, 2009.)
Rule 8.823 adopted effective January 1, 2009.

Rule 8.824.   Writ of supersedeas

(a) Petition

(1) A party seeking a stay of the enforcement of a judgment or order pending appeal may serve and file a petition for writ of supersedeas in the appellate division.

(2) The petition must bear the same title as the appeal.

(3) The petition must explain the necessity for the writ and include a memorandum.

(4) If the record has not been filed in the reviewing court:

(A) The petition must include a statement of the case sufficient to show that the petitioner will raise substantial issues on appeal, including a fair summary of the material facts, the issues that are likely to be raised on appeal, and

any oral statement by the court supporting its rulings related to these issues.

(B) The petitioner must file the following documents with the petition:

(i) The judgment or order, showing its date of entry;

(ii) The notice of appeal, showing its date of filing;

(iii) Any application for a stay filed in the trial court and any opposition to that application; and

(iv) Any other document from the trial court proceeding that is necessary for proper consideration of the petition.

(C) The documents listed in (B) must comply with the following requirements:

(i) They must be bound together at the end of the petition or in separate volumes not exceeding 300 pages each. The pages must be consecutively numbered;

(ii) They must be index-tabbed by number or letter; and

(iii) They must begin with a table of contents listing each document by its title and its index-tab number or letter.

(5) The petition must be verified.

(Subd (a) adopted effective January 1, 2009.)

(b) Opposition

(1) Unless otherwise ordered, any opposition must be served and filed within 15 days after the petition is filed.

(2) An opposition must state any material facts not included in the petition and include a memorandum.

(3) The court may not issue a writ of supersedeas until the respondent has had the opportunity to file an opposition.

(Subd (b) adopted effective January 1, 2009.)

(c) Temporary stay

(1) The petition may include a request for a temporary stay pending the ruling on the petition.

(2) A separately filed request for a temporary stay must be served on the respondent. For good cause, the presiding judge may excuse advance service.

(Subd (c) adopted effective January 1, 2009.)

(d) Issuing the writ

(1) The court may issue the writ on any conditions it deems just.

(2) The court must notify the trial court, under rule 8.904, of any writ or stay that it issues.

(Subd (d) adopted effective January 1, 2009.)
Rule 8.824 adopted effective January 1, 2009.

Rule 8.825.   Abandonment, voluntary dismissal, and compromise

(a) Notice of settlement

(1) If a civil case settles after a notice of appeal has been filed, either as a whole or as to any party, the appellant who has settled must immediately serve and file a notice of settlement in the appellate division. If the parties have designated a clerk's or a reporter's transcript and the record has not been filed in the appellate division, the appellant must also immediately serve a copy of the notice on the trial court clerk.

(2) If the case settles after the appellant receives a notice setting oral argument, the appellant must also

immediately notify the appellate division of the settlement by telephone or other expeditious method.

(3) Within 45 days after filing a notice of settlement—unless the court has ordered a longer time period on a showing of good cause—the appellant who filed the notice of settlement must file an abandonment under (b).

(4) If the appellant does not file an abandonment or a letter stating good cause why the appeal should not be dismissed within the time period specified under (3), the court may dismiss the appeal as to that appellant and order each side to bear its own costs on appeal.

(5) Subdivision (a) does not apply to settlements requiring findings to be made by the Court of Appeal under Code of Civil Procedure section 128(a)(8).

(Subd (a) adopted effective January 1, 2009.)

(b) Abandonment

(1) The appellant may serve and file an abandonment of the appeal or a stipulation to abandon the appeal in the appellate division.

(2) If the record has not been filed in the appellate division, the filing of an abandonment effects a dismissal of the appeal and restores the trial court's jurisdiction. If the record has been filed in the appellate division, the appellate division may dismiss the appeal and direct immediate issuance of the remittitur.

(3) The clerk must promptly notify the adverse party of an abandonment. If the record has not been filed in the appellate division, the clerk must also immediately notify the trial court.

(4) If the appeal is abandoned before the clerk has completed preparation of the transcript, the clerk must refund any portion of a deposit exceeding the preparation cost actually incurred.

(5) If the appeal is abandoned before the reporter has filed the transcript, the reporter must inform the trial court clerk of the cost of the portion of the transcript that the reporter has completed. The clerk must pay that amount to the reporter from the appellant's deposited funds and refund any excess deposit.

(Subd (b) adopted effective January 1, 2009.)

(c) Approval of compromise

If a guardian or conservator seeks approval of a proposed compromise of a pending appeal, the appellate division may, before ruling on the compromise, direct the trial court to determine whether the compromise is in the minor's or the conservatee's best interest and to report its findings.

(Subd (c) adopted effective January 1, 2009.)
Rule 8.825 adopted effective January 1, 2009.

Advisory Committee Comment

Abandonment of Appeal (Limited Civil Case) (form APP-106) may be used to file an abandonment under this rule. This form is available at any courthouse or county law library or online at *www.courtinfo.ca.gov/forms.*

Article 2
Record in Civil Appeals

Article 2 adopted effective January 1, 2009.

Rule 8.830. Record on appeal
Rule 8.831. Notice designating the record on appeal
Rule 8.832. Clerk's transcript

Rule 8.830. Record on appeal

(a) Normal record

Except as otherwise provided in this chapter, the record on an appeal to the appellate division in a civil case must contain the following, which constitute the normal record on appeal:

(1) A record of the written documents from the trial court proceedings in the form of one of the following:

(A) A clerk's transcript under rule 8.832;

(B) If the court has a local rule for the appellate division electing to use this form of the record, the original trial court file under rule 8.833; or

(C) An agreed statement under rule 8.836.

(2) If an appellant wants to raise any issue that requires consideration of the oral proceedings in the trial court, the record on appeal must include a record of these oral proceedings in the form of one of the following:

(A) A reporter's transcript under rule 8.834 or a transcript prepared from an official electronic recording under rule 8.835;

(B) If the court has a local rule for the appellate division permitting this form of the record, an official electronic recording of the proceedings under rule 8.835;

(C) An agreed statement under rule 8.836; or

(D) A statement on appeal under rule 8.837.

(Subd (a) adopted effective January 1, 2009.)

(b) Presumption from the record

The appellate division will presume that the record in an appeal includes all matters material to deciding the issues raised. If the appeal proceeds without a reporter's transcript, this presumption applies only if the claimed error appears on the face of the record.

(Subd (b) adopted effective January 1, 2009.)
Rule 8.830 adopted effective January 1, 2009.

Advisory Committee Comment

Subdivision (a). The options of using the original trial court file instead of a clerk's transcript under (1)(B) or an electronic recording itself, rather than a transcript, under (2)(B) are available only if the court has local rules for the appellate division authorizing these options.

Rule 8.831. Notice designating the record on appeal

(a) Time to file

Within 10 days after filing the notice of appeal, an appellant must serve and file a notice in the trial court designating the record on appeal. The appellant may combine its notice designating the record with its notice of appeal.

(Subd (a) adopted effective January 1, 2009.)

(b) Contents

The notice must specify:

(1) The date the notice of appeal was filed;

(2) Which form of the record of the written documents from the trial court proceedings listed in rule 8.830(a)(1) the appellant elects to use. If the appellant elects to use a clerk's transcript, the notice must also:

(A) Provide the filing date of each document that is required to be included in the clerk's transcript under 8.832(a)(1) or, if the filing date is not available, the date it was signed; and

(B) Designate, as provided under 8.832(b), any documents in addition to those required under 8.832(a)(1) that the appellant wants included in the clerk's transcript;

(3) Whether the appellant elects to proceed with or without a record of the oral proceedings in the trial court;

(4) If the appellant elects to proceed with a record of the oral proceedings in the trial court, the notice must specify which form of the record listed in rule 8.830(a)(2) the appellant elects to use;

(5) If the appellant elects to use a reporter's transcript, the notice must designate the proceedings to be included in the transcript as required under rule 8.834;

(6) If the appellant elects to use an official electronic recording, the appellant must attach a copy of the stipulation required under rule 8.835(c); and

(7) If the appellant elects to use an agreed statement, the appellant must attach to the notice either the agreed statement or stipulation as required under rule 8.836(c)(1).

(Subd (b) adopted effective January 1, 2009.)

Rule 8.831 adopted effective January 1, 2009.

Advisory Committee Comment

Notice Designating Record on Appeal (Limited Civil Case) (form APP-103) may be used to file the designation required under this rule. This form is available at any courthouse or county law library or online at *www.courtinfo.ca.gov/forms*. To assist parties in making appropriate choices, courts are encouraged to include information about whether the proceedings were recorded by a court reporter or officially electronically recorded in any information that the court provides to parties concerning their appellate rights.

If the appellant designates a clerk's transcript or reporter's transcript under this rule, the respondent will have an opportunity to designate additional documents to be included in the clerk's transcript under rule 8.832(b)(2) or additional proceedings to be included in the reporter's transcript under rule 8.834(a)(3).

Rule 8.832.   Clerk's transcript

(a) Contents of clerk's transcript

(1) The clerk's transcript must contain:

(A) The notice of appeal;

(B) Any judgment appealed from and any notice of its entry;

(C) Any order appealed from and any notice of its entry;

(D) Any notice of intention to move for a new trial, or motion to vacate the judgment, for judgment notwithstanding the verdict, or for reconsideration of an appealed order, with supporting and opposing memoranda and attachments, and any order on such motion and any notice of its entry;

(E) The notice designating the record on appeal; and

(F) The register of actions, if any.

(2) Each document listed in (1)(A), (B), (C), and (D) must show the date necessary to determine the timeliness of the appeal under rule 8.822 or 8.823.

(3) If designated by any party, the clerk's transcript must also contain:

(A) Any other document filed or lodged in the case in the trial court;

(B) Any exhibit admitted in evidence, refused, or lodged; and

(C) Any jury instructions that any party submitted in writing, the cover page required by rule 2.1055(b)(2), and any written jury instructions given by the court.

(Subd (a) adopted effective January 1, 2009.)

(b) Notice of designation

(1) Within 10 days after the appellant serves a notice under rule 8.831 indicating that the appellant elects to use a clerk's transcript, the respondent may serve and file a notice in the trial court designating any additional documents the respondent wants included in the clerk's transcript.

(2) A notice designating documents to be included in a clerk's transcript must identify each designated document by its title and filing date or, if the filing date is not available, the date it was signed. A notice designating documents in addition to those listed in (a)(1) may specify portions of designated documents that are not to be included in the clerk's transcript. For minute orders or jury instructions, it is sufficient to collectively designate all minute orders or all minute orders entered between specified dates, or all written instructions given, refused, or withdrawn.

(3) All exhibits admitted in evidence, refused, or lodged are deemed part of the record, but a party wanting an exhibit included in the transcript must specify that exhibit by number or letter in its designation. If the trial court has returned a designated exhibit to a party, the party in possession of the exhibit must promptly deliver it to the trial court clerk.

(Subd (b) adopted effective January 1, 2009.)

(c) Deposit for cost of clerk's transcript

(1) Within 30 days after the respondent files a designation under (b)(1) or the time to file it expires, whichever first occurs, the trial court clerk must send:

(A) To the appellant, notice of the estimated cost to prepare an original and one copy of the clerk's transcript; and

(B) To each party other than the appellant, notice of the estimated cost to prepare a copy of the clerk's transcript for that party's use.

(2) A notice under (1) must show the date it was sent.

(3) Within 10 days after the clerk sends a notice under (1), the appellant and any party wanting to purchase a copy of the clerk's transcript must deposit the estimated cost with the clerk, unless otherwise provided by law or the party submits an application for, or an order granting, a waiver of the cost under rules 3.50–3.63.

(Subd (c) adopted effective January 1, 2009.)

(d) Preparing the clerk's transcript

(1) Within 30 days after the appellant deposits the estimated cost of the transcript or the court files an order waiving that cost, the clerk must:

(A) Prepare an original and one copy of the clerk's transcript and certify the original; and

(B) Prepare any additional copies for which the parties have made deposits.

(2) If the appeal is abandoned or dismissed before the clerk has completed preparation of the transcript, the clerk must refund any portion of the deposit under (c)(3) exceeding the preparation cost actually incurred.

(Subd (d) adopted effective January 1, 2009.)
Rule 8.832 adopted effective January 1, 2009.

Rule 8.833. Trial court file instead of clerk's transcript

(a) Application

If the court has a local rule for the appellate division electing to use this form of the record, the original trial court file may be used instead of a clerk's transcript. This rule and any supplemental provisions of the local rule then govern unless the trial court orders otherwise after notice to the parties.

(Subd (a) adopted effective January 1, 2009.)

(b) Cost estimate; preparation of file; transmittal

(1) Within 10 days after the appellant serves a notice under rule 8.831 indicating that the appellant elects to use a clerk's transcript, the trial court clerk may mail the appellant a notice indicating that the appellate division for that court has elected by local court rule to use the original trial court file instead of a clerk's transcript and providing the appellant with an estimate of the cost to prepare the file, including the cost of sending the index under (4).

(2) Within 10 days after the clerk mails the estimate under (1), the appellant must deposit the estimated cost with the clerk, unless otherwise provided by law or the party submits an application for, or an order granting, a waiver of the cost under rules 3.50–3.63.

(3) Within 10 days after the appellant deposits the cost or the court files an order waiving that cost, the trial court clerk must put the trial court file in chronological order, number the pages, and attach a chronological index and a list of all attorneys of record, the parties they represent, and any unrepresented parties.

(4) The clerk must send copies of the index to all attorneys of record and any unrepresented parties for their use in paginating their copies of the file to conform to the index.

(5) If the appellant elected to proceed with a reporter's transcript, the clerk must send the prepared file to the appellate division with the reporter's transcript. If the appellant elected to proceed without a reporter's transcript, the clerk must immediately send the prepared file to the appellate division.

(Subd (b) adopted effective January 1, 2009.)
Rule 8.833 adopted effective January 1, 2009.

Rule 8.834. Reporter's transcript

(a) Notice

(1) A notice designating a reporter's transcript under rule 8.831 must specify the date of each proceeding to be included in the transcript and may specify portions of the designated proceedings that are not to be included.

(2) If the appellant designates less than all the testimony, the notice must state the points to be raised on the

appeal; the appeal is then limited to those points unless, on motion, the appellate division permits otherwise.

(3) If the appellant serves and files a notice under 8.831 designating a reporter's transcript, the respondent may, within 10 days after such service, serve and file a notice in the trial court designating any additional proceedings the respondent wants included in the reporter's transcript.

(4) The clerk must promptly mail a copy of each notice to the reporter. The copy must show the date it was mailed.

(Subd (a) adopted effective January 1, 2009.)

(b) Deposit or waiver

(1) Within 10 days after the clerk mails a notice under (a)(4), the reporter must file the estimate with the clerk—or notify the clerk in writing of the date that he or she notified the appellant directly—of the estimated cost of preparing the reporter's transcript.

(2) Within 10 days after the clerk notifies the appellant of the estimated cost of preparing the reporter's transcript or within 10 days after the reporter notifies the appellant directly—the appellant must deposit with the clerk an amount equal to the estimated cost or file with the clerk a waiver of the deposit signed by the reporter. The clerk must then promptly notify the reporter to prepare the transcript.

(Subd (b) adopted effective January 1, 2009.)

(c) Contents of reporter's transcript

(1) The reporter must transcribe all designated proceedings and must note in the transcript where any proceedings were omitted and the nature of those proceedings. The reporter must also note where any exhibit was marked for identification and where it was admitted or refused, identifying such exhibits by number or letter.

(2) The reporter must not transcribe the voir dire examination of jurors, any opening statement, or the proceedings on a motion for new trial, unless they are designated.

(3) If a party designates a portion of a witness's testimony to be transcribed, the reporter must transcribe the witness's entire testimony unless the parties stipulate otherwise.

(4) The reporter must not copy any document includable in the clerk's transcript under rule 8.832.

(Subd (c) adopted effective January 1, 2009.)

(d) Filing the reporter's transcript; copies; payment

(1) Within 20 days after the clerk notifies the reporter to prepare the transcript under (b)(2)—or the reporter receives the fees from the appellant—the reporter must prepare and certify an original of the reporter's transcript and file it in the trial court. The reporter must also file one copy of the original transcript or more than one copy if multiple appellants equally share the cost of preparing the record.

(2) When the transcript is completed, the reporter must bill each designating party at the statutory rate and send a copy of the bill to the clerk. The clerk must pay the reporter from that party's deposited funds and refund any excess deposit or notify the party of any additional funds needed. In a multiple reporter case, the clerk must pay each reporter who certifies under penalty of perjury that his or her transcript portion is completed.

(3) If the appeal is abandoned or is dismissed before the reporter has filed the transcript, the reporter must inform the clerk of the cost of the portion of the transcript that the reporter has completed. The clerk must pay that amount to the reporter from the appellant's deposited funds and refund any excess deposit.

(Subd (d) adopted effective January 1, 2009.)

(e) Notice when proceedings cannot be transcribed

(1) If any portion of the designated proceedings were not reported or cannot be transcribed, the trial court clerk must so notify the designating party by mail; the notice must show the date it was mailed.

(2) Within 10 days after the notice under (1) is mailed, the designating party must notify the court whether the party elects to proceed with or without a record of the oral proceedings that were not reported or cannot be transcribed. If the party elects to proceed with a record of these oral proceedings, the notice must specify which form of the record listed in rule 8.830(a)(2) other than a reporter's transcript the party elects to use. The party must comply with the requirements applicable to the form of the record elected.

(3) This remedy supplements any other available remedies.

(Subd (e) adopted effective January 1, 2009.)

Rule 8.834 adopted effective January 1, 2009.

Rule 8.835.   Record when trial proceedings were officially electronically recorded

(a) Application

This rule applies only if:

(1) The trial court proceedings were officially recorded electronically under Government Code section 69957; and

(2) The electronic recording was prepared in compliance with applicable rules regarding electronic recording of court proceedings.

(Subd (a) adopted effective January 1, 2009.)

(b) Transcripts from official electronic recording

Written transcripts of official electronic recordings may be prepared under rule 2.952. A transcript prepared and certified as provided in that rule is prima facie a true and complete record of the oral proceedings it purports to cover and satisfies any requirement in these rules or in any statute for a reporter's transcript of oral proceedings.

(Subd (b) adopted effective January 1, 2009.)

(c) Use of official recording as record of oral proceedings

If the court has a local rule for the appellate division permitting this, on stipulation of the parties or on order of the trial court under rule 8.837(d), the original of an official electronic recording of the trial court proceedings, or a copy made by the court, may be transmitted as the record of these oral proceedings without being transcribed. Such an official electronic recording satisfies any requirement in these rules or in any statute for a reporter's transcript of these proceedings.

(Subd (c) adopted effective January 1, 2009.)

(d) Notice when proceedings were not officially electronically recorded or cannot be transcribed

(1) If the appellant elects under rule 8.831 to use a transcript prepared from an official electronic recording or the recording itself, the trial court clerk must notify the appellant by mail if any portion of the designated proceedings was not officially electronically recorded or cannot be transcribed. The notice must show the date it was mailed.

(2) Within 10 days after the notice under (1) is mailed, the appellant must notify the court whether the appellant elects to proceed with or without a record of the oral proceedings that were not recorded or cannot be transcribed. If the party elects to proceed with a record of these oral proceedings, the notice must specify which form of the record listed in rule 8.830(a)(2) other than an electronic recording the appellant elects to use. The appellant must comply with the requirements applicable to the form of the record elected.

(Subd (d) adopted effective January 1, 2009.)

Rule 8.835 adopted effective January 1, 2009.

Rule 8.836.   Agreed statement

(a) What is an agreed statement

An agreed statement is a summary of the trial court proceedings that is agreed to by the parties. If the parties have prepared an agreed statement or stipulated to prepare one, the appellant can elect under rule 8.831 to use an agreed statement as the record of the documents filed in the trial court, replacing the clerk's transcript, and as the record of the oral proceedings in the trial court, replacing the reporter's transcript.

(Subd (a) adopted effective January 1, 2009.)

(b) Contents of an agreed statement

(1) The agreed statement must explain the nature of the action, the basis of the appellate division's jurisdiction, and the rulings of the trial court relating to the points to be raised on appeal. The statement should recite only those facts that a party considers relevant to decide the appeal and must be signed by the parties.

(2) If the agreed statement replaces a clerk's transcript, the statement must be accompanied by copies of all items required by rule 8.832(a)(1), showing the dates required by rule 8.832(a)(2).

(3) The statement may be accompanied by copies of any document includable in the clerk's transcript under rule 8.832(a)(3).

(Subd (b) adopted effective January 1, 2009.)

(c) Time to file; extension of time

(1) If an appellant indicates on its notice designating the record under rule 8.831 that it elects to use an agreed statement under this rule, the appellant must file with the notice designating the record either the agreed statement or a stipulation that the parties are attempting to agree on a statement.

(2) If the appellant files a stipulation under (1), within 30 days after filing the notice of designation under rule 8.831, the appellant must either:

(A) File the statement if the parties were able to agree on the statement; or

(B) File both a notice stating that the parties were not able to agree on the statement and a new notice designating the record under rule 8.831. In the new notice designating the record, the appellant may not elect to use an agreed statement.

(Subd (c) adopted effective January 1, 2009.)

Rule 8.836 adopted effective January 1, 2009.

Rule 8.837.   Statement on appeal

(a) Description

A statement on appeal is a summary of the trial court proceedings that is approved by the trial court. An appellant can elect under rule 8.831 to use a statement on appeal as the record of the oral proceedings in the trial court, replacing the reporter's transcript.

(Subd (a) adopted effective January 1, 2009.)

(b) Preparing the proposed statement

(1) If the appellant elects in its notice designating the record under rule 8.831 to use a statement on appeal, the appellant must serve and file a proposed statement within 20 days after filing the notice under rule 8.831. If the appellant does not file a proposed statement within this time, the trial court clerk must promptly notify the appellant by mail that it must file the proposed statement within 15 days after the notice is mailed and that failure to comply will result in the appeal being dismissed.

(2) Appellants who are not represented by an attorney must file their proposed statement on *Statement on Appeal (Limited Civil Case)* (form APP-104). For good cause, the court may permit the filing of a statement that is not on form APP-104.

(Subd (b) adopted effective January 1, 2009.)

(c) Contents of the proposed statement

The proposed statement must contain:

(1) A condensed narrative of the oral proceedings that the appellant believes necessary for the appeal and a summary of the trial court's holding and judgment. Subject to the court's approval, the appellant may present some or all of the evidence by question and answer.

(2) A statement of the points the appellant is raising on appeal. If the condensed narrative under (A) covers only a portion of the oral proceedings, then the appeal is limited to the points identified in the statement unless, on motion, the appellate division permits otherwise.

(A) The statement must specify the intended grounds of appeal by clearly stating each point to be raised but need not identify each particular ruling or matter to be challenged.

(B) The statement must include as much of the evidence or proceeding as necessary to support the stated grounds. Any evidence or portion of a proceeding not included will be presumed to support the judgment or order appealed from.

(C) If one of the grounds of appeal is insufficiency of the evidence, the statement must specify how it is insufficient.

(D) If one of the grounds of appeal challenges the giving, refusal, or modification of a jury instruction, the statement must include any instructions submitted orally and identify the party that requested the instruction and any modification.

(Subd (c) adopted effective January 1, 2009.)

(d) Review of the appellant's proposed statement

(1) Within 10 days after the appellant files the proposed statement, the respondent may serve and file proposed amendments to that statement.

(2) No later than 10 days after the respondent files proposed amendments or the time to do so expires, a party may request a hearing to review and correct the proposed statement. No hearing will be held unless ordered by the trial court judge, and the judge will not ordinarily order a hearing unless there is a factual dispute about a material aspect of the trial court proceedings.

(3) If a hearing is ordered, the court must promptly set the hearing date and provide the parties with at least 5 days' written notice of the hearing date.

(4) Except as provided in (6), if no hearing is ordered, no later than 10 days after the time for requesting a hearing expires, the trial court judge must review the proposed statement and any proposed amendments and make any corrections or modifications to the statement necessary to ensure that it is an accurate summary of the trial court proceedings. If a hearing is ordered, the trial court judge must make any corrections or modifications to the statement within 10 days after the hearing.

(5) The trial court judge must not eliminate the appellant's specification of grounds of appeal from the proposed statement.

(6) If the trial court proceedings were reported by a court reporter or officially electronically recorded under Government Code section 69957 and the trial court judge determines that it would save court time and resources, instead of correcting a proposed statement on appeal:

(A) If the court has a local rule for the appellate division permitting the use of an official electronic recording as the record of the oral proceedings, the trial court judge may order that the original of an official electronic recording of the trial court proceedings, or a copy made by the court, be transmitted as the record of these oral proceedings without being transcribed. The court will pay for any copy of the official electronic recording ordered under this subdivision; or

(B) Unless the court has a local rule providing otherwise, the trial court judge may order that a transcript be prepared as the record of the oral proceedings. The court will pay for any transcript ordered under this subdivision.

(Subd (d) adopted effective January 1, 2009.)

(e) Review of the corrected statement

(1) If the trial court judge makes any corrections or modifications to the proposed statement under (d), the clerk must send copies of the corrected or modified statement to the parties.

(2) Within 10 days after the statement is sent to the parties, any party may serve and file proposed modifications or objections to the statement.

(Subd (e) adopted effective January 1, 2009.)

(f) Certification of the statement on appeal

(1) If the trial court judge does not make any corrections or modifications to the proposed statement under (d)(4) and does not order either the use of an official electronic recording or the preparation of a transcript in lieu of correcting the proposed statement under (d)(6), the judge must promptly certify the statement.

(2) If the trial court judge corrects or modifies an appellant's proposed statement under (d), within five days after the time for filing proposed modifications or objections has expired, the judge must review any proposed modifications or objections to the statement filed by the parties, make any corrections or modifications to the statement necessary to ensure that it is an accurate summary of the trial court proceedings, and certify the statement.

(Subd (f) adopted effective January 1, 2009.)
Rule 8.837 adopted effective January 1, 2009.

Advisory Committee Comment

Subdivision (b). *Proposed Statement on Appeal (Limited Civil Case)* (form APP-104) is available at any courthouse or county law library or online at *www.courtinfo.ca.gov/forms.*

Subdivision (d). Under rule 8.804, the term "judge" includes a commissioner or a temporary judge.

Rule 8.838.   Form of the record

(a) Paper and format

Except as otherwise provided in this rule, clerk's and reporter's transcripts must comply with the paper and format requirements of rule 8.144(a).

(Subd (a) adopted effective January 1, 2009.)

(b) Indexes

At the beginning of the first volume of each:

(1) The clerk's transcript must contain alphabetical and chronological indexes listing each document and the volume and page where it first appears;

(2) The reporter's transcript must contain alphabetical and chronological indexes listing the volume and page where each witness's direct, cross, and any other examination, begins; and

(3) The reporter's transcript must contain an index listing the volume and page where any exhibit is marked for identification and where it is admitted or refused.

(Subd (b) adopted effective January 1, 2009.)

(c) Binding and cover

(1) Clerk's and reporter's transcripts must be bound on the left margin in volumes of no more than 300 sheets, except that transcripts may be bound at the top if required by a local rule of the appellate division.

(2) Each volume's cover, preferably of recycled stock, must state the title and trial court number of the case, the names of the trial court and each participating trial judge, the names and addresses of appellate counsel for each party, the volume number, and the inclusive page numbers of that volume.

(3) In addition to the information required by (2), the cover of each volume of the reporter's transcript must state the dates of the proceedings reported in that volume.

(Subd (c) adopted effective January 1, 2009.)
Rule 8.838 adopted effective January 1, 2009.

Rule 8.839.   Record in multiple appeals

(a) Single record

If more than one appeal is taken from the same judgment or a related order, only one record need be prepared, which must be filed within the time allowed for filing the record in the latest appeal.

(Subd (a) adopted effective January 1, 2009.)

(b) Cost

If there is more than one separately represented appellant, they must equally share the cost of preparing the record, unless otherwise agreed by the appellants or ordered by the trial court. Appellants equally sharing the cost are each entitled to a copy of the record.

(Subd (b) adopted effective January 1, 2009.)
Rule 8.839 adopted effective January 1, 2009.

Rule 8.840.   Filing the record

When the record is complete, the trial court clerk must promptly send the original to the appellate division and send to the appellant and respondent copies of any certified statement on appeal and any copies of transcripts or official electronic recordings that they have purchased. The appellate division clerk must promptly file the original and mail notice of the filing date to the parties.

Rule 8.840 adopted effective January 1, 2009.

Rule 8.841.   Augmenting and correcting the record in the appellate division

(a) Augmentation

(1) At any time, on motion of a party or its own motion, the appellate division may order the record augmented to include:

(A) Any document filed or lodged in the case in the trial court; or

(B) A certified transcript—or agreed statement or a statement on appeal—of oral proceedings not designated under rule 8.831.

(2) A party must attach to its motion a copy, if available, of any document or transcript that it wants added to the record. The pages of the attachments must be consecutively numbered, beginning with the number 1. If the appellate division grants the motion, it may augment the record with the copy.

(3) If the party cannot attach a copy of the matter to be added, the party must identify it as required under rules 8.831.

(Subd (a) adopted effective January 1, 2009.)

(b) Correction

(1) On agreement of the parties, motion of a party, or on its own motion, the appellate division may order the correction or certification of any part of the record.

(2) The appellate division may order the trial court to settle disputes about omissions or errors in the record or to make corrections pursuant to stipulation filed by the parties in that court.

(Subd (b) adopted effective January 1, 2009.)

(c) Omissions

(1) If a clerk or reporter omits a required or designated portion of the record, a party may serve and file a notice in the trial court specifying the omitted portion and requesting that it be prepared, certified, and sent to the appellate division. The party must serve a copy of the notice on the appellate division.

(2) The clerk or reporter must comply with a notice under (1) within 10 days after it is filed. If the clerk or reporter fails to comply, the party may serve and file a motion to augment under (a), attaching a copy of the notice.

(Subd (c) adopted effective January 1, 2009.)

(d) Notice

The appellate division clerk must send all parties notice of the receipt and filing of any matter under this rule.

(Subd (d) adopted effective January 1, 2009.)
Rule 8.841 adopted effective January 1, 2009.

Rule 8.842.   Failure to procure the record

(a) Notice of default

If a party fails to do any act required to procure the record, the trial court clerk must promptly notify that party by mail that it must do the act specified in the notice within 15 days after the notice is mailed and that, if it fails to comply, the reviewing court may impose the following sanctions:

(1) If the defaulting party is the appellant, the court may dismiss the appeal; or

(2) If the defaulting party is the respondent, the court may proceed with the appeal on the record designated by the appellant.

(Subd (a) adopted effective January 1, 2009.)

(b) Sanctions

If the party fails to take the action specified in a notice given under (a), the trial court clerk must promptly notify the appellate division of the default, and the appellate division may impose one of the following sanctions:

(1) If the defaulting party is the appellant, the reviewing court may dismiss the appeal but may vacate the dismissal for good cause; or

(2) If the defaulting party is the respondent, the reviewing court may order the appeal to proceed on the record designated by the appellant, but the respondent may obtain relief from default under rule 8.60(d).

(Subd (b) adopted effective January 1, 2009.)
Rule 8.842 adopted effective January 1, 2009.

Rule 8.843.　Transmitting exhibits

(a) Notice of designation

(1) If a party wants the appellate division to consider any original exhibits that were admitted in evidence, refused, or lodged but that were not copied in the clerk's transcript under rule 8.832 or included in the original file under rule 8.833, within 10 days after the last respondent's brief is filed or could be filed under rule 8.882 the party must serve and file a notice in the trial court designating such exhibits.

(2) Within 10 days after a notice under (1) is served, any other party wanting the appellate division to consider additional exhibits must serve and file a notice in the trial court designating such exhibits.

(3) A party filing a notice under (1) or (2) must serve a copy on the appellate division.

(Subd (a) adopted effective January 1, 2009.)

(b) Application for later transmittal

After the periods specified in (a) have expired, a party may apply to the appellate division for permission to send an exhibit to that court.

(Subd (b) adopted effective January 1, 2009.)

(c) Request by appellate division

At any time the appellate division may direct the trial court or a party to send it an exhibit.

(Subd (c) adopted effective January 1, 2009.)

(d) Transmittal

Unless the appellate division orders otherwise, within 20 days after notice under (a) is filed or after the appellate division directs that an exhibit be sent:

(1) The trial court clerk must put any designated exhibits in the clerk's possession into numerical or alphabetical order and send them to the appellate division with two copies of a list of the exhibits sent. If the appellate

division clerk finds the list correct, the clerk must sign and return one copy to the trial court clerk.

(2) Any party in possession of designated exhibits returned by the trial court must put them into numerical or alphabetical order and send them to the appellate division with two copies of a list of the exhibits sent. If the appellate division clerk finds the list correct, the clerk must sign and return one copy to the party.

(Subd (d) adopted effective January 1, 2009.)

(e) Return by appellate division

On request, the appellate division may return an exhibit to the trial court or to the party that sent it. When the remittitur issues, the appellate division must return all exhibits to the trial court or to the party that sent them.

(Subd (e) adopted effective January 1, 2009.)
Rule 8.843 adopted effective January 1, 2009.

Chapter 3
Appeals and Records in Misdemeanor Cases

Chapter 3 adopted effective January 1, 2009.

Art. 1.　Taking Appeals in Misdemeanor Cases. Rules 8.850–8.855.

Art. 2.　Record in Misdemeanor Appeals. Rules 8.860–8.873.

Article 1
Taking Appeals in Misdemeanor Cases

Article 1 adopted effective January 1, 2009.

Rule 8.850. Application of chapter
Rule 8.851. Appointment of appellate counsel
Rule 8.852. Notice of appeal
Rule 8.853. Time to appeal
Rule 8.854. Stay of execution and release on appeal
Rule 8.855. Abandoning the appeal

Rule 8.850.　Application of chapter

The rules in this chapter apply only to appeals in misdemeanor cases. In postconviction appeals, misdemeanor cases are cases in which the defendant was convicted of a misdemeanor and was not charged with any felony. In preconviction appeals, misdemeanor cases are cases in which the defendant was charged with a misdemeanor but was not charged with any felony. A felony is "charged" when an information or indictment accusing the defendant of a felony is filed or a complaint accusing the defendant of a felony is certified to the superior court under Penal Code section 859a.

Rule 8.850 adopted effective January 1, 2009.

Advisory Committee Comment

Chapters 1 and 4 of this division also apply in appeals from misdemeanor cases. The rules that apply in appeals in felony cases are located in chapter 3 of division 1 of this title.

Penal Code section 1466 provides that an appeal in a "misdemeanor or infraction case" is to the appellate division of the superior court, and Penal Code section 1235(b), in turn, provides that an appeal in a "felony case" is to the Court of Appeal. Penal Code section 691(g) defines "misdemeanor or infraction case" to mean "a criminal action in which a misdemeanor or infraction is charged *and does not include a criminal action in which a felony is charged* in conjunction with a misdemeanor or infraction" (emphasis added), and section 691(f) defines "felony case" to mean "a criminal action in which a felony is charged *and includes a criminal action in which a misdemeanor or infraction is charged in conjunction with a felony*" (emphasis added).

As rule 8.304 from the rules on felony appeals provides, the following types of cases are felony cases, not misdemeanor cases: (1) an action in which the defendant is charged with a felony and a misdemeanor, but is convicted of only the misdemeanor; (2) an action in which the defendant is charged with felony, but is convicted of only a lesser offense; or (3) an action in which the defendant is charged with an offense filed as a felony but punishable as either a felony or a misdemeanor, and the offense is thereafter deemed a misdemeanor under Penal Code section 17(b). Rule 8.304 makes it clear that a "felony case" is an action in which a felony is charged *regardless of the outcome of the action.* Thus the question of which rules apply—these rules governing appeals in misdemeanor cases or the rules governing appeals in felony cases—is answered simply by examining the accusatory pleading: if that document charged the defendant with at least one count of felony (as defined in Penal Code, section 17(a)), the Court of Appeal has appellate jurisdiction and the appeal must be taken under the rules on felony appeals *even if the prosecution did not result in a punishment of imprisonment in a state prison.*

It is settled case law that an appeal is taken to the Court of Appeal not only when the defendant is charged with and convicted of a felony, but also when the defendant is charged with both a felony and a misdemeanor (Pen. Code, § 691(f)) but is convicted of only the misdemeanor (e.g., *People v. Brown* (1970) 10 Cal.App.3d 169); when the defendant is charged with a felony but is convicted of only a lesser offense (Pen. Code, § 1159; e.g., *People v. Spreckels* (1954) 125 Cal.App.2d 507); and when the defendant is charged with an offense filed as a felony but punishable as either a felony or a misdemeanor, and the offense is thereafter deemed a misdemeanor under Penal Code section 17(b) (e.g., *People v. Douglas* (1999) 20 Cal.4th 85; *People v. Clark* (1971) 17 Cal.App.3d 890).

Trial court unification did not change this rule: after as before unification, "Appeals in felony cases lie to the [C]ourt of [A]ppeal, regardless of whether the appeal is from the superior court, the municipal court, or the action of a magistrate. *Cf.* Cal. Const. art. VI, § 11(a) [except in death penalty cases, Courts of Appeal have appellate jurisdiction when superior courts have original jurisdiction 'in causes of a type within the appellate jurisdiction of the [C]ourts of [A]ppeal on June 30, 1995....'']." ("Recommendation on Trial Court Unification" (July 1998) 28 *Cal. Law Revision Com. Rep.* 455–56.)

Rule 8.851.   Appointment of appellate counsel

(a) Standards for appointment

(1) On application, the appellate division must appoint appellate counsel for a defendant convicted of a misdemeanor who:

(A) Is subject to incarceration or a fine of more than $500 (including penalty and other assessments), or who is likely to suffer significant adverse collateral consequences as a result of the conviction; and

(B) Was represented by appointed counsel in the trial court or establishes indigency.

(2) On application, the appellate division may appoint counsel for any other indigent defendant convicted of a misdemeanor.

(3) A defendant is subject to incarceration or a fine if the incarceration or fine is in a sentence, is a condition of probation, or may be ordered if the defendant violates probation.

(Subd (a) adopted effective January 1, 2009.)

(b) Application; duties of trial counsel and clerk

(1) If defense trial counsel has reason to believe that the client is indigent and will file an appeal, counsel must prepare and file in the trial court an application to the appellate division for appointment of counsel.

(2) If the defendant was represented by appointed counsel in the trial court, the application must include trial counsel's declaration to that effect. If the defendant was not represented by appointed counsel in the trial court, the application must include a declaration of indigency in the form required by the Judicial Council.

(3) When the trial court receives an application, the clerk must promptly send it to the appellate division. A defendant may, however, apply directly to the appellate division for appointment of counsel at any time after filing the notice of appeal.

(Subd (b) adopted effective January 1, 2009.)

(c) Defendant found able to pay in trial court

(1) If a defendant was represented by appointed counsel in the trial court and was found able to pay all or part of the cost of counsel in proceedings under Penal Code section 987.8 or 987.81, the findings in those proceedings must be included in the record or, if the findings were made after the record is sent to the appellate division, must be sent as an augmentation of the record.

(2) In cases under (1), the appellate division may determine the defendant's ability to pay all or part of the cost of counsel on appeal, and if it finds the defendant able, may order the defendant to pay all or part of that cost.

(Subd (c) adopted effective January 1, 2009.)

Rule 8.851 adopted effective January 1, 2009.

Advisory Committee Comment

Request for Court-Appointed Lawyer in Misdemeanor Appeal (form CR-133) may be used to request that appellate counsel be appointed in a misdemeanor case. If the appellant was not represented by the public defender or other appointed counsel in the trial court, the appellant must use *Defendant's Financial Statement on Eligibility for Appointment of Counsel and Reimbursement and Record on Appeal at Public Expense* (form MC-210) to show indigency. These forms are available at any courthouse or county law library or online at *www.courtinfo.ca.gov/forms.*

Rule 8.852.   Notice of appeal

(a) Notice of appeal

(1) To appeal from a judgment or an appealable order of the trial court in a misdemeanor case, the defendant or the People must file a notice of appeal in the trial court. The notice must specify the judgment or order—or part of it—being appealed.

(2) If the defendant appeals, the defendant or the defendant's attorney must sign the notice of appeal. If the People appeal, the attorney for the People must sign the notice.

(3) The notice of appeal must be liberally construed in favor of its sufficiency.

(Subd (a) adopted effective January 1, 2009.)

(b) Notification of the appeal

(1) When a notice of appeal is filed, the trial court clerk must promptly mail a notification of the filing to the attorney of record for each party and to any unrepresented defendant. The clerk must also mail or deliver this notification to the appellate division clerk.

(2) The notification must show the date it was mailed or delivered, the number and title of the case, the date the notice of appeal was filed, and whether the defendant was represented by appointed counsel.

(3) The notification to the appellate division clerk must also include a copy of the notice of appeal.

(4) A copy of the notice of appeal is sufficient notification under (1) if the required information is on the copy or is added by the trial court clerk.

(5) The mailing of a notification under (1) is a sufficient performance of the clerk's duty despite the discharge, disqualification, suspension, disbarment, or death of the attorney.

(6) Failure to comply with any provision of this subdivision does not affect the validity of the notice of appeal.

(Subd (b) adopted effective January 1, 2009.)
Rule 8.852 adopted effective January 1, 2009.

Advisory Committee Comment

Notice of Appeal (Misdemeanor) (form CR-132) may be used to file the notice of appeal required under this rule. This form is available at any courthouse or county law library or online at *www.courtinfo.ca.gov/forms.*

Subdivision (a). The only orders that a defendant can appeal in a misdemeanor case are (1) orders granting or denying a motion to suppress evidence (Penal Code section 1538.5(j)); and (2) orders made after the final judgment that affects the substantial rights of the defendant (Penal Code section 1466).

Rule 8.853. Time to appeal

(a) Normal time

A notice of appeal must be filed within 30 days after the rendition of the judgment or the making of the order being appealed. If the defendant is committed before final judgment for insanity or narcotics addiction, the notice of appeal must be filed within 30 days after the commitment.

(Subd (a) adopted effective January 1, 2009.)

(b) Cross-appeal

If the defendant or the People timely appeal from a judgment or appealable order, the time for any other party to appeal from the same judgment or order is either the time specified in (a) or 15 days after the trial court clerk mails notification of the first appeal, whichever is later.

(Subd (b) adopted effective January 1, 2009.)

(c) Premature notice of appeal

A notice of appeal filed before the judgment is rendered or the order is made is premature, but the appellate division may treat the notice as filed immediately after the rendition of the judgment or the making of the order.

(Subd (c) adopted effective January 1, 2009.)

(d) Late notice of appeal

The trial court clerk must mark a late notice of appeal "Received [date] but not filed" and notify the party that the notice was not filed because it was late.

(Subd (d) adopted effective January 1, 2009.)

(e) Receipt by mail from custodial institution

If the trial court clerk receives a notice of appeal by mail from a custodial institution after the period specified in (a) has expired but the envelope shows that the notice was mailed or delivered to custodial officials for mailing within the period specified in (a), the notice is deemed timely. The clerk must retain in the case file the envelope in which the notice was received.

(Subd (e) adopted effective January 1, 2009.)
Rule 8.853 adopted effective January 1, 2009.

Rule 8.854. Stay of execution and release on appeal

(a) Application

Pending appeal, the defendant may apply to the appellate division:

(1) For a stay of execution after a judgment of conviction or an order granting probation; or

(2) For bail for release from custody, to reduce bail for release from custody, or for release on other conditions.

(Subd (a) adopted effective January 1, 2009.)

(b) Showing

The application must include a showing that the defendant sought relief in the trial court and that the court unjustifiably denied the application.

(Subd (b) adopted effective January 1, 2009.)

(c) Service

The application must be served on the prosecuting attorney.

(Subd (c) adopted effective January 1, 2009.)

(d) Interim relief

Pending its ruling on the application, the appellate division may grant the relief requested. The appellate division must notify the trial court of any stay that it grants.

(Subd (d) adopted effective January 1, 2009.)
Rule 8.854 adopted effective January 1, 2009.

Advisory Committee Comment

Subdivision (c). As defined in rule 8.804, the "prosecuting attorney" may be the city attorney, county counsel, district attorney, or state Attorney General, depending on what government agency filed the criminal charges.

Rule 8.855. Abandoning the appeal

(a) How to abandon

An appellant may abandon the appeal at any time by filing an abandonment of the appeal signed by the appellant or the appellant's attorney of record.

(Subd (a) adopted effective January 1, 2009.)

(b) Where to file; effect of filing

(1) The appellant must file the abandonment in the appellate division.

(2) If the record has not been filed in the appellate division, the filing of an abandonment effects a dismissal of the appeal and restores the trial court's jurisdiction.

(3) If the record has been filed in the appellate division, the appellate division may dismiss the appeal and direct immediate issuance of the remittitur.

(Subd (b) adopted effective January 1, 2009.)

(c) Clerk's duties

(1) The appellate division clerk must immediately notify the adverse party of the filing or of the order of dismissal.

(2) If the record has not been filed in the appellate division, the clerk must immediately notify the trial court.

(3) If a reporter's transcript has been requested, the clerk must immediately notify the reporter if the appeal is abandoned before the reporter has filed the transcript.

(Subd (c) adopted effective January 1, 2009.)

Rule 8.855 adopted effective January 1, 2009.

Advisory Committee Comment

Abandonment of Appeal (Misdemeanor) (form CR-137) may be used to file an abandonment under this rule. This form is available at any courthouse or county law library or online at *www.courtinfo.ca.gov/forms.*

Article 2
Record in Misdemeanor Appeals

Article 2 adopted effective January 1, 2009.

Rule 8.860. Normal record on appeal
Rule 8.861. Contents of clerk's transcript
Rule 8.862. Preparation of clerk's transcript
Rule 8.863. Trial court file instead of clerk's transcript
Rule 8.864. Record of oral proceedings
Rule 8.865. Contents of reporter's transcript
Rule 8.866. Preparation of reporter's transcript
Rule 8.867. Limited normal record in certain appeals
Rule 8.868. Record when trial proceedings were officially electronically recorded
Rule 8.869. Statement on appeal
Rule 8.870. Exhibits
Rule 8.871. Juror-identifying information
Rule 8.872. Sending and filing the record in the appellate division
Rule 8.873. Augmenting or correcting the record in the appellate division

Rule 8.860. Normal record on appeal

(a) Contents

Except as otherwise provided in this chapter, the record on an appeal to a superior court appellate division in a misdemeanor criminal case must contain the following, which constitute the normal record on appeal:

(1) A record of the written documents from the trial court proceedings in the form of one of the following:

(A) A clerk's transcript under rule 8.861 or 8.867; or

(B) If the court has a local rule for the appellate division electing to use this form of the record, the original trial court file under rule 8.863.

(2) If an appellant wants to raise any issue that requires consideration of the oral proceedings in the trial court, the record on appeal must include a record of the oral proceedings in the form of one of the following:

(A) A reporter's transcript under rules 8.865–8.867 or a transcript prepared from an official electronic recording under rule 8.868;

(B) If the court has a local rule for the appellate division permitting this form of the record, an official electronic recording of the proceedings under rule 8.868; or

(C) A statement on appeal under rule 8.869.

(Subd (a) adopted effective January 1, 2009.)

(b) Stipulation for limited record

If, before the record is certified, the appellant or counsel for the appellant and the People stipulate in writing that any part of the record is not required for proper determination of the appeal and file that stipulation in the trial court, that part of the record must not be prepared or sent to the appellate division.

(Subd (b) adopted effective January 1, 2009.)

Rule 8.860 adopted effective January 1, 2009.

Rule 8.861. Contents of clerk's transcript

Except in appeals covered by rule 8.867 or when the parties have filed a stipulation under rule 8.860(b) that any of these items is not required for proper determination of the appeal, the clerk's transcript must contain:

(1) The complaint, including any notice to appear, and any amendment;

(2) Any demurrer or other plea;

(3) All court minutes;

(4) Any jury instructions that any party submitted in writing, the cover page required by rule 2.1055(b)(2), and any written jury instructions given by the court;

(5) Any written communication between the court and the jury or any individual juror;

(6) Any verdict;

(7) Any written findings or opinion of the court;

(8) The judgment or order appealed from;

(9) Any motion or notice of motion for new trial, in arrest of judgment, or to dismiss the action, with supporting and opposing memoranda and attachments;

(10) Any transcript of a sound or sound-and-video recording furnished to the jury or tendered to the court under rule 2.1040; and

(11) The notice of appeal; and

(12) If the appellant is the defendant:

(A) Any written defense motion denied in whole or in part, with supporting and opposing memoranda and attachments;

(B) If related to a motion under (A), any search warrant and return;

(C) Any document admitted in evidence to prove a prior juvenile adjudication, criminal conviction, or prison term. If a record was closed to public inspection in the trial court because it is required to be kept confidential by law, it must remain closed to public inspection in the appellate division unless that court orders otherwise; and

(D) The probation officer's report.

Rule 8.861 adopted effective January 1, 2009.

Rule 8.862. Preparation of clerk's transcript

(a) When preparation begins

Unless the original court file will be used in place of a clerk's transcript under rule 8.863, the clerk must begin preparing the clerk's transcript immediately after the notice of appeal is filed.

(Subd (a) adopted effective January 1, 2009.)

(b) Format of transcript

The clerk's transcript must comply with rule 8.144.

(Subd (b) adopted effective January 1, 2009.)

(c) When preparation must be completed

Within 20 days after the notice of appeal is filed, the clerk must complete preparation of an original clerk's transcript for the appellate division, one copy for the appellant, and one copy for the prosecuting attorney. If there is more than one appellant, the clerk must prepare an extra copy for each additional appellant who is represented by separate counsel or self-represented.

(Subd (c) adopted effective January 1, 2009.)

(d) Certification

The clerk must certify as correct the original and all copies of the clerk's transcript.

(Subd (d) adopted effective January 1, 2009.)
Rule 8.862 adopted effective January 1, 2009.

Advisory Committee Comment

Rule 8.872 addresses when the clerk's transcript is sent to the appellate division in misdemeanor appeals.

Rule 8.863. Trial court file instead of clerk's transcript

(a) Application

If the court has a local rule for the appellate division electing to use this form of the record, the original trial court file may be used instead of a clerk's transcript. This rule and any supplemental provisions of the local rule then govern unless the trial court orders otherwise after notice to the parties.

(Subd (a) adopted effective January 1, 2009.)

(b) When original file must be prepared

Within 20 days after the filing of the notice of appeal, the trial court clerk must put the trial court file in chronological order, number the pages, and attach a chronological index and a list of all attorneys of record, the parties they represent, and any unrepresented parties.

(Subd (b) adopted effective January 1, 2009.)

(c) Copies

The clerk must send a copy of the index to the appellant and the prosecuting attorney for use in paginating their copies of the file to conform to the index. If there is more than one appellant, the clerk must prepare an extra copy of the index for each additional appellant who is represented by separate counsel or self-represented.

(Subd (c) adopted effective January 1, 2009.)
Rule 8.863 adopted effective January 1, 2009.

Advisory Committee Comment

Rule 8.872 addresses when the original file is sent to the appellate division in misdemeanor appeals.

Rule 8.864. Record of oral proceedings

(a) Appellant's election

The appellant must notify the trial court whether he or she elects to proceed with or without a record of the oral proceedings in the trial court. If the appellant elects to proceed with a record of the oral proceedings in the trial court, the notice must specify which form of the record of the oral proceedings in the trial court the appellant elects to use:

(1) A reporter's transcript under rules 8.865–8.867 or a transcript prepared from an official electronic recording of the proceedings under rule 8.868(b). If the appellant elects to use a reporter's transcript, the clerk must promptly mail a copy of appellant's notice making this election and the notice of appeal to each court reporter;

(2) An official electronic recording of the proceedings under rule 8.868(c). If the appellant elects to use the official electronic recording itself, rather than a transcript

prepared from that recording, the appellant must attach a copy of the stipulation required under rule 8.868(c); or

(3) A statement on appeal under rule 8.869.

(Subd (a) adopted effective January 1, 2009.)

(b) Time for filing election

The notice of election required under (a) must be filed no later than the following:

(1) If no application for appointment of counsel is filed, 20 days after the notice of appeal is filed; or

(2) If an application for appointment of counsel is filed before the period under (A) expires, either 10 days after the court appoints counsel to represent the defendant on appeal or denies the application for appointment of counsel or 20 days after the notice of appeal is filed, whichever is later.

(Subd (b) adopted effective January 1, 2009.)

(c) Statement on appeal when proceedings cannot be transcribed or were not recorded

(1) If the appellant elects under (a) to use a reporter's transcript or a transcript prepared from an official electronic recording or the recording itself, the trial court clerk must notify the appellant within 10 days after the appellant files this election if any portion of the oral proceedings listed in rule 8.865 was not reported or officially recorded electronically or cannot be transcribed. The notice must indicate that the appellant may use a statement on appeal as the record of the portion of the proceedings that was not recorded or cannot be transcribed.

(2) Within 15 days after this notice is mailed by the clerk, the appellant must file a notice with the court stating whether the appellant elects to use a statement on appeal as the record of the portion of the proceedings that was not recorded or cannot be transcribed.

(Subd (c) adopted effective January 1, 2009.)
Rule 8.864 adopted effective January 1, 2009.

Advisory Committee Comment

Notice Regarding Record of Oral Proceedings (Misdemeanor) (form CR-134) may be used to file the election required under this rule. This form is available at any courthouse or county law library or online at *www.courtinfo.ca.gov/forms.* To assist parties in making an appropriate election, courts are encouraged to include information about whether the proceedings were recorded by a court reporter or officially electronically recorded in any information that the court provides to parties concerning their appellate rights.

Rule 8.865. Contents of reporter's transcript

Except in appeals covered by rule 8.867 or when the parties have filed a stipulation under rule 8.860(b) or the trial court has ordered that any of these items is not required for proper determination of the appeal, the reporter's transcript must contain:

(1) The oral proceedings on the entry of any plea other than a not guilty plea;

(2) The oral proceedings on any motion in limine;

(3) The oral proceedings at trial, but excluding the voir dire examination of jurors and any opening statement;

(4) Any jury instructions given orally;

(5) Any oral communication between the court and the jury or any individual juror;

(6) Any oral opinion of the court;

(7) The oral proceedings on any motion for new trial;

(8) The oral proceedings at sentencing, granting or denying probation, or other dispositional hearing;

(9) If the appellant is the defendant, the reporter's transcript must also contain:

(A) The oral proceedings on any defense motion denied in whole or in part except motions for disqualification of a judge;

(B) Any closing arguments; and

(C) Any comment on the evidence by the court to the jury.

Rule 8.865 adopted effective January 1, 2009.

Rule 8.866.   Preparation of reporter's transcript

(a) When preparation begins

(1) Unless the court has a local rule providing otherwise, the reporter must immediately begin preparing the reporter's transcript if the notice sent to the reporter by the clerk under rule 8.864(a)(1) indicates either:

(A) That the defendant was represented by appointed counsel at trial; or

(B) That the appellant is the People.

(2) If the notice sent to the reporter by the clerk under rule 8.864(a)(1) indicates that the appellant is the defendant and that the defendant was not represented by appointed counsel at trial:

(A) Within 10 days after the date the clerk mailed the notice under rule 8.864(a)(1), the reporter must file with the clerk the estimated cost of preparing the reporter's transcript; and

(B) The clerk must promptly notify the appellant and his or her counsel of the estimated cost of preparing the reporter's transcript. The notification must show the date it was mailed.

(C) Within 10 days after the date the clerk mailed the notice under (B), the appellant must do one of the following:

(i) Deposit with the clerk an amount equal to the estimated cost of preparing the transcript;

(ii) File a declaration of indigency supported by evidence in the form required by the Judicial Council; or

(iii) Notify the clerk that he or she will be using a statement on appeal instead of a reporter's transcript.

(D) The clerk must promptly notify the reporter to begin preparing the transcript when:

(i) The clerk receives the required deposit under (C)(i); or

(ii) The trial court determines that the defendant is indigent and orders that the defendant receive the transcript without cost.

(Subd (a) adopted effective January 1, 2009.)

(b) Format of transcript

The reporter's transcript must comply with rule 8.144.

(Subd (b) adopted effective January 1, 2009.)

(c) Copies and certification

The reporter must prepare an original and the same number of copies of the reporter's transcript as rule 8.862 requires of the clerk's transcript and must certify each as correct.

(Subd (c) adopted effective January 1, 2009.)

(d) When preparation must be completed

The reporter must deliver the original and all copies to the trial court clerk as soon as they are certified but no later than 20 days after the reporter is required to begin preparing the transcript under (a).

(Subd (d) adopted effective January 1, 2009.)

(e) Multi-reporter cases

In a multi-reporter case, the clerk must accept any completed portion of the transcript from the primary reporter one week after the time prescribed by (d) even if other portions are uncompleted. The clerk must promptly pay each reporter who certifies that all portions of the transcript assigned to that reporter are completed.

(Subd (e) adopted effective January 1, 2009.)

Rule 8.866 adopted effective January 1, 2009.

Advisory Committee Comment

Subdivision (a). If the appellant was not represented by the public defender or other appointed counsel in the trial court, the appellant must use *Defendant's Financial Statement on Eligibility for Appointment of Counsel and Reimbursement and Record on Appeal at Public Expense* (form MC-210) to show indigency. This form is available at any courthouse or county law library or online at *www.courtinfo.ca.gov/forms.*

Rule 8.867.   Limited normal record in certain appeals

If the People appeal from a judgment on a demurrer to the complaint, including any notice to appear, or if the defendant or the People appeal from an appealable order other than a ruling on a motion for new trial, the normal record is composed of:

(1) *Record of the documents filed in the trial court*

A clerk's transcript or original trial court file containing:

(A) The complaint, including any notice to appear, and any amendment;

(B) Any demurrer or other plea;

(C) Any motion or notice of motion granted or denied by the order appealed from, with supporting and opposing memoranda and attachments;

(D) The judgment or order appealed from and any abstract of judgment or commitment;

(E) Any court minutes relating to the judgment or order appealed from; and

(F) The notice of appeal.

(2) *Record of the oral proceedings in the trial court*

If an appellant wants to raise any issue which requires consideration of the oral proceedings in the trial court, a reporter's transcript, transcript prepared under rule 8.866 or a settled statement under rule 8.869 summarizing any oral proceedings incident to the judgment or order being appealed.

Rule 8.867 adopted effective January 1, 2009.

Rule 8.868.   Record when trial proceedings were officially electronically recorded

(a) Application

This rule applies only if:

(1) The trial court proceedings were officially recorded electronically under Government Code section 69957; and

(2) The electronic recording was prepared in compliance with applicable rules regarding electronic recording of court proceedings.

(b) Transcripts from official electronic recording

Written transcripts of an official electronic recording may be prepared under rule 2.952. A transcript prepared and certified as provided in that rule is prima facie a true and complete record of the oral proceedings it purports to cover, and satisfies any requirement in these rules or in any statute for a reporter's transcript of oral proceedings.

(Subd (b) adopted effective January 1, 2009.)

(c) Use of official recording as record of oral proceedings

If the court has a local rule for the appellate division permitting this, on stipulation of the parties or on order of the trial court under rule 8.869(d)(5), the original of an official electronic recording of the trial court proceedings, or a copy made by the court, may be transmitted as the record of these oral proceedings without being transcribed. Such an electronic recording satisfies any requirement in these rules or in any statute for a reporter's transcript of these proceedings.

(Subd (c) adopted effective January 1, 2009.)

(d) When preparation begins

(1) If the appellant files an election under rule 8.864 to use a transcript of an official electronic recording or a copy of the official electronic recording as the record of the oral proceedings, unless the trial court has a local rule providing otherwise, preparation of a transcript or a copy of the recording must begin immediately if either:

(A) The defendant was represented by appointed counsel at trial; or

(B) The appellant is the People.

(2) If the appellant is the defendant and the defendant was not represented by appointed counsel at trial:

(A) Within 10 days after the date the defendant files the election under rule 8.864(a)(1), the clerk must notify the appellant and his or her counsel of the estimated cost of preparing the transcript or the copy of the recording.

The notification must show the date it was mailed.

(B) Within 10 days after the date the clerk mailed the notice under (A), the appellant must do one of the following:

(i) Deposit with the clerk an amount equal to the estimated cost of preparing the transcript or the copy of the recording;

(ii) File a declaration of indigency supported by evidence in the form required by the Judicial Council; or

(iii) Notify the clerk that he or she will be using a statement on appeal instead of a transcript or copy of the recording.

(C) Preparation of the transcript must begin when:

(i) The clerk receives the required deposit under (B)(i); or

(ii) The trial court determines that the defendant is indigent and orders that the defendant receive the transcript or the copy of the recording without cost.

(Subd (d) adopted effective January 1, 2009.)

Rule 8.868 adopted effective January 1, 2009.

Advisory Committee Comment

Subdivision (d). If the appellant was not represented by the public defender or other appointed counsel in the trial court, the appellant must use *Defendant's Financial Statement on Eligibility*

for Appointment of Counsel and Reimbursement and Record on Appeal at Public Expense (form MC-210) to show indigency. This form is available at any courthouse or county law library or online at *www.courtinfo.ca.gov/forms.*

Rule 8.869. Statement on appeal

(a) Description

A statement on appeal is a summary of the trial court proceedings that is approved by the trial court. An appellant can elect under rule 8.864 to use a statement on appeal as the record of the oral proceedings in the trial court, replacing the reporter's transcript.

(Subd (a) adopted effective January 1, 2009.)

(b) Preparing the proposed statement

(1) If the appellant elects under rule 8.864 to use a statement on appeal, the appellant must prepare, serve, and file a proposed statement within 20 days after filing the record preparation election.

(2) Appellants who are not represented by an attorney must file their proposed statement on *Proposed Statement on Appeal (Misdemeanor)* (form CR-135). For good cause, the court may permit the filing of a statement that is not on form CR-135.

(3) If the appellant does not file a proposed statement within the time specified in (1), the trial court clerk must promptly notify the appellant by mail that the proposed statement must be filed within 15 days after the notice is mailed and that failure to comply will result in the appeal being dismissed.

(Subd (b) adopted effective January 1, 2009.)

(c) Contents of the proposed statement on appeal

A proposed statement prepared by the appellant must contain:

(1) A condensed narrative of the oral proceedings that the appellant believes necessary for the appeal and a summary of the trial court's holding and the sentence imposed on the appellant. Subject to the court's approval, the appellant may present some or all of the evidence by question and answer; and

(2) A statement of the points the appellant is raising on appeal. The appeal is then limited to those points unless the appellate division determines that the record permits the full consideration of another point.

(A) The statement must specify the intended grounds of appeal by clearly stating each point to be raised but need not identify each particular ruling or matter to be challenged.

(B) The statement must include as much of the evidence or proceeding as necessary to support the stated grounds. Any evidence or portion of a proceeding not included will be presumed to support the judgment or order appealed from.

(C) If one of the grounds of appeal is insufficiency of the evidence, the statement must specify how it is insufficient.

(D) If one of the grounds of appeal challenges the giving, refusal, or modification of a jury instruction, the statement must include any instructions submitted orally and identify the party that requested the instruction and any modification.

(Subd (c) adopted effective January 1, 2009.)

(d) Review of the appellant's proposed statement

(1) Within 10 days after the appellant files the proposed statement, the respondent may serve and file proposed amendments to that statement.

(2) No later than 10 days after either the respondent files proposed amendments or the time to do so expires, a party may request a hearing to review and correct the proposed statement. No hearing will be held unless ordered by the trial court judge, and the judge will not ordinarily order a hearing unless there is a factual dispute about a material aspect of the trial court proceedings.

(3) If a hearing is ordered, the court must promptly set the hearing date and provide the parties with at least 5 days' written notice.

(4) Except as provided in (6), if no hearing is ordered, no later than 10 days after the time for requesting a hearing expires, the trial court judge must review the proposed statement and any proposed amendments and make any corrections or modifications to the statement necessary to ensure that it is an accurate summary of the trial court proceedings. If a hearing is ordered, the trial court judge must make any corrections or modifications to the statement within 10 days after the hearing.

(5) The trial court judge must not eliminate the appellant's specification of grounds of appeal from the proposed statement.

(6) If the trial court proceedings were reported by a court reporter or officially recorded electronically under Government Code section 69957 and the trial court judge determines that it would save court time and resources, instead of correcting a proposed statement on appeal:

(A) If the court has a local rule for the appellate division permitting the use of an official electronic recording as the record of the oral proceedings, the trial court judge may order that the original of an official electronic recording of the trial court proceedings, or a copy made by the court, be transmitted as the record of these oral proceedings without being transcribed. The court will pay for any copy of the official electronic recording ordered under this subdivision; or

(B) Unless the court has a local rule providing otherwise, the trial court judge may order that a transcript be prepared as the record of the oral proceedings. The court will pay for any transcript ordered under this subdivision.

(Subd (d) adopted effective January 1, 2009.)

(e) Review of the corrected statement

(1) If the trial court judge makes any corrections or modifications to the statement under (d), the clerk must send copies of the corrected or modified statement to the parties.

(2) Within 10 days after the statement is sent to the parties, any party may serve and file proposed modifications or objections to the statement.

(Subd (e) adopted effective January 1, 2009.)

(f) Certification of the statement on appeal

(1) If the trial court judge does not make any corrections or modifications to the proposed statement under (d)(4) and does not order either the use of an official electronic recording or preparation of a transcript in lieu of correcting the proposed statement under (d)(6), the judge must promptly certify the statement.

(2) If the trial court judge corrects or modifies an appellant's proposed statement under (d), within five days

after the time for filing proposed modifications or objections under (e) has expired, the judge must review any proposed modifications or objections to the statement filed by the parties, make any corrections or modifications to the statement necessary to ensure that it is an accurate summary of the trial court proceedings, and certify the statement.

(Subd (f) adopted effective January 1, 2009.)

(g) Extensions of time

For good cause, the trial court may grant an extension of not more than 15 days to do any act required or permitted under this rule.

(Subd (g) adopted effective January 1, 2009.)
Rule 8.869 adopted effective January 1, 2009.

Advisory Committee Comment

Rules 8.806, 8.810, and 8.812 address applications for extensions of time and relief from default.

Subdivision (b). *Proposed Statement on Appeal (Misdemeanor)* (form CR-135) is available at any courthouse or county law library or online at *www.courtinfo.ca.gov/forms.*

Subdivision (d). Under rule 8.804, the term "judge" includes a commissioner or a temporary judge.

Rule 8.870.　Exhibits

(a) Exhibits deemed part of record

Exhibits admitted in evidence, refused, or lodged are deemed part of the record, but may be transmitted to the appellate division only as provided in this rule.

(Subd (a) adopted effective January 1, 2009.)

(b) Notice of designation

(1) Within 10 days after the last respondent's brief is filed or could be filed under rule 8.882, if the appellant wants the appellate division to consider any original exhibits that were admitted in evidence, refused, or lodged, the appellant must serve and file a notice in the trial court designating such exhibits.

(2) Within 10 days after a notice under (1) is served, any other party wanting the appellate division to consider additional exhibits must serve and file a notice in trial court designating such exhibits.

(3) A party filing a notice under (1) or (2) must serve a copy on the appellate division.

(Subd (b) adopted effective January 1, 2009.)

(c) Request by appellate division

At any time, the appellate division may direct the trial court or a party to send it an exhibit.

(Subd (c) adopted effective January 1, 2009.)

(d) Transmittal

Unless the appellate division orders otherwise, within 20 days after the first notice under (b) is filed or after the appellate division directs that an exhibit be sent:

(1) The trial court clerk must put any designated exhibits in the clerk's possession into numerical or alphabetical order and send them to the appellate division with two copies of a list of the exhibits. If the appellate division clerk finds the list correct, the clerk must sign and return one copy to the trial court clerk.

(2) Any party in possession of designated exhibits returned by the trial court must put them into numerical or alphabetical order and send them to the appellate division with two copies of a list of the exhibits sent. If the

appellate division clerk finds the list correct, the clerk must sign and return one copy to the party.

(Subd (d) adopted effective January 1, 2009.)

(e) Return by appellate division

On request, the appellate division may return an exhibit to the trial court or to the party that sent it. When the remittitur issues, the appellate division must return all exhibits to the trial court or to the party that sent them.

(Subd (e) adopted effective January 1, 2009.)

Rule 8.870 adopted effective January 1, 2009.

Rule 8.871.   Juror-identifying information

(a) Applicability

In a criminal case, a clerk's transcript, a reporter's transcript, or any other document in the record that contains juror-identifying information must comply with this rule.

(Subd (a) adopted effective January 1, 2009.)

(b) Juror names, addresses, and telephone numbers

(1) The name of each trial juror or alternate sworn to hear the case must be replaced with an identifying number wherever it appears in any document. The trial court clerk must prepare and keep under seal in the case file a table correlating the jurors' names with their identifying numbers. The clerk and the reporter must use the table in preparing all transcripts or other documents.

(2) The addresses and telephone numbers of trial jurors and alternates sworn to hear the case must be deleted from all documents.

(Subd (b) adopted effective January 1, 2009.)

(c) Potential jurors

Information identifying potential jurors called but not sworn as trial jurors or alternates must not be sealed unless otherwise ordered under Code of Civil Procedure section 237(a)(1).

(Subd (c) adopted effective January 1, 2009.)

Rule 8.871 adopted effective January 1, 2009.

Advisory Committee Comment

This rule implements Code of Civil Procedure section 237.

Rule 8.872.   Sending and filing the record in the appellate division

(a) When the record is complete

(1) If the appellant elected under rule 8.864 to proceed without a record of the oral proceedings in the trial court, the record is complete when the clerk's transcript is certified as correct or, if the original trial court file will be used instead of the clerk's transcript, when that original file is ready for transmission as provided under rule 8.863(b).

(2) If the appellant elected under rule 8.864 to proceed with a record of the oral proceedings in the trial court, the record is complete when the clerk's transcript is certified as correct or the original file is ready for transmission as provided in (1) and:

(A) If the appellant elected to use a reporter's transcript, the certified reporter's transcript is delivered to the court under rule 8.866;

(B) If the appellant elected to use a transcript prepared from an official electronic recording, the transcript has been prepared under rule 8.868;

(C) If the parties stipulated to the use of an official electronic recording of the proceedings, the electronic recording has been prepared under rule 8.868; or

(D) If the appellant elected to use a statement on appeal, the statement on appeal has been certified by the trial court or a transcript or an official electronic recording has been prepared under rule 8.869(d)(6).

(Subd (a) adopted effective January 1, 2009.)

(b) Sending the record

When the record is complete, the clerk must promptly send:

(1) The original record to the appellate division;

(2) One copy of the clerk's transcript or index to the original court file and one copy of any record of the oral proceedings to each appellant who is represented by separate counsel or is self-represented; and

(3) One copy of the clerk's transcript or index to the original court file and one copy of any record of the oral proceedings to the respondent.

(Subd (b) adopted effective January 1, 2009.)

(c) Filing the record

On receipt, the appellate division clerk must promptly file the original record and mail notice of the filing date to the parties.

(Subd (c) adopted effective January 1, 2009.)

Rule 8.872 adopted effective January 1, 2009.

Rule 8.873.   Augmenting or correcting the record in the appellate division

(a) Subsequent trial court orders

If, after the record is certified, the trial court amends or recalls the judgment or makes any other order in the case, including an order affecting the sentence or probation, the clerk must promptly certify and send a copy of the amended abstract of judgment or other order as an augmentation of the record to all those who received the record under rule 8.872(b). If there is any additional document or transcript related to the amended judgment or new order that any rule or order requires be included in the record, the clerk must send these documents or transcripts with the amended abstract of judgment or other order. The clerk must promptly copy and certify any such document and the reporter must promptly prepare and certify any such transcript.

(Subd (a) adopted effective January 1, 2009.)

(b) Omissions

If, after the record is certified, the trial court clerk or the reporter learns that the record omits a document or transcript that any rule or order requires to be included, the clerk must promptly copy and certify the document or the reporter must promptly prepare and certify the transcript. Without the need for a court order, the clerk must promptly send the document or transcript as an augmentation of the record to all those who received the record under rule 8.872(b).

(Subd (b) adopted effective January 1, 2009.)

(c) Augmentation or correction by the appellate division

At any time, on motion of a party or on its own motion, the appellate division may order the record augmented or corrected as provided in rule 8.841.

(Subd (c) adopted effective January 1, 2009.)
Rule 8.873 adopted effective January 1, 2009.

Chapter 4
Briefs, Hearing, and Decision in Limited Civil and Misdemeanor Appeals

Chapter 4 adopted effective January 1, 2009.

Rule 8.880. Application
Rule 8.881. Notice of briefing schedule
Rule 8.882. Briefs by parties and amici curiae
Rule 8.883. Contents and form of briefs
Rule 8.884. Appeals in which a party is both appellant and respondent
Rule 8.885. Oral argument
Rule 8.886. Submission of the cause
Rule 8.887. Decisions
Rule 8.888. Finality and modification of decision
Rule 8.889. Rehearing
Rule 8.890. Remittitur
Rule 8.891. Costs and sanctions in civil appeals

Rule 8.880.   Application

Except as otherwise provided, the rules in this chapter apply to both civil and misdemeanor appeals in the appellate division.
Rule 8.880 adopted effective January 1, 2009.

Rule 8.881.   Notice of briefing schedule

When the record is filed, the clerk of the appellate division must promptly mail a notice to each appellate counsel or unrepresented party giving the dates the briefs are due.
Rule 8.881 adopted effective January 1, 2009.

Rule 8.882.   Briefs by parties and amici curiae

(a) Briefs by parties

(1) The appellant must serve and file an appellant's opening brief within 30 days after the record is filed in the appellate division.

(2) Any respondent's brief must be served and filed within 30 days after the appellant files its opening brief.

(3) Any appellant's reply brief must be served and filed within 20 days after the respondent files its brief.

(4) No other brief may be filed except with the permission of the presiding judge.

(5) Instead of filing a brief, or as part of its brief, a party may join in a brief or adopt by reference all or part of a brief in the same or a related appeal.

(Subd (a) adopted effective January 1, 2009.)

(b) Extensions of time

(1) In a civil case, the parties may extend each period under (a) by up to 30 days by filing one or more stipulations in the appellate division before the brief is due. Stipulations must be signed by and served on all parties. The original signature of at least one party must appear on the stipulation filed in the appellate division; the signatures of the other parties may be in the form of fax copies of the signed signature page of the stipulation.

(2) A stipulation under (1) is effective on filing. The appellate division may not shorten such a stipulated extension.

(Subd (b) adopted effective January 1, 2009.)

(c) Failure to file a brief

(1) If a party in a civil appeal fails to timely file an appellant's opening brief or a respondent's brief, the appellate division clerk must promptly notify the party by mail that the brief must be filed within 15 days after the notice is mailed and that if the party fails to comply, the court may impose one of the following sanctions:

(A) If the brief is an appellant's opening brief, the court may dismiss the appeal; or

(B) If the brief is a respondent's brief, the court may decide the appeal on the record, the appellant's opening brief, and any oral argument by the appellant.

(2) If the appellant in a misdemeanor appeal fails to timely file an opening brief, the appellate division clerk must promptly notify the appellant by mail that the brief must be filed within 30 days after the notice is mailed and that if the appellant fails to comply, the court may impose one of the following sanctions:

(A) If the appellant is the defendant and is represented by appointed counsel on appeal, the court may relieve that appointed counsel and appoint new counsel; or

(B) In all other cases, the court may dismiss the appeal.

(3) If the respondent in a misdemeanor appeal is the defendant and the respondent fails to timely file a brief, the appellate division clerk must promptly notify the respondent by mail that the brief must be filed within 30 days after the notice is mailed and that if the respondent fails to comply, the court will decide the appeal on the record, the appellant's opening brief, and any oral argument by the appellant.

(4) If a party fails to comply with a notice under (1), (2), or (3), the court may impose the sanction specified in the notice.

(Subd (c) relettered effective January 1, 2009; adopted as subd (b) effective January 1, 2009.)

(d) Amicus curiae briefs

(1) Within 14 days after the appellant's reply brief is filed or was required to be filed, whichever is earlier, any person or entity may serve and file an application for permission of the presiding judge to file an amicus curiae brief. For good cause, the presiding judge may allow later filing.

(2) The application must state the applicant's interest and explain how the proposed amicus curiae brief will assist the court in deciding the matter.

(3) **The application must also identify:**

(A) **Any party or any counsel for a party in the pending appeal who:**

(i) **Authored the proposed amicus brief in whole or in part; or**

(ii) **Made a monetary contribution intended to fund the preparation or submission of the brief; and**

(B) **Every person or entity who made a monetary contribution intended to fund the preparation or submission of the brief, other than the amicus curiae, its members, or its counsel in the pending appeal.**

(4) The proposed brief must be served and must accompany the application and may be combined with it.

[1] (5) The Attorney General may file an amicus curiae brief without the presiding judge's permission, unless the brief is submitted on behalf of another state officer or agency; but the presiding judge may prescribe reasonable conditions for filing and answering the brief.

(Subd (d) amended and relettered effective January 1, 2009; adopted as subd (c) effective January 1, 2009.)

Rule 8.882(d).   2008 Deletes. [1] (4)

(e) Service and filing

(1) Copies of each brief must be served as required by rule 8.25.

(2) Unless the **[1] court** provides otherwise by local rule or order in the specific case, only the original brief, with proof of service, must be filed in the appellate division.

(3) A copy of each brief must be served on the trial court clerk for delivery to the judge who tried the case.

(4) A copy of each brief must be served on a public officer or agency when required by rule 8.29.

(Subd (e) amended and relettered effective January 1, 2009; adopted as subd (d) effective January 1, 2009.)

Rule 8.882(e).   2008 Deletes. [1] appellate division
Rule 8.882 amended effective January 1, 2009; adopted effective January 1, 2009.

Rule 8.883.   Contents and form of briefs

(a) Contents

(1) Each brief must:

(A) State each point under a separate heading or subheading summarizing the point and support each point by argument and, if possible, by citation of authority; and

(B) Support any reference to a matter in the record by a citation to the volume and page number of the record where the matter appears.

(2) An appellant's opening brief must:

(A) State the nature of the action, the relief sought in the trial court, and the judgment or order appealed from;

(B) State that the judgment appealed from is final or explain why the order appealed from is appealable; and

(C) Provide a summary of the significant facts limited to matters in the record.

(Subd (a) adopted effective January 1, 2009.)

(b) Length

(1) A brief produced on a computer must not exceed 6,800 words, including footnotes. Such a brief must include a certificate by appellate counsel or an unrepresented party stating the number of words in the brief. The person certifying may rely on the word count of the computer program used to prepare the brief.

(2) A brief produced on a typewriter must not exceed 20 pages.

(3) The certificate under (1) and any attachment under (d) are excluded from the limits stated in (1) or (2).

(4) On application, the presiding judge may permit a longer brief for good cause. A lengthy record or numerous or complex issues on appeal will ordinarily constitute good cause. If the court grants an application to file a longer brief, it may order that the brief include a table of contents and a table of authorities.

(Subd (b) adopted effective January 1, 2009.)

(c) Form

(1) A brief may be reproduced by any process that produces a clear, black image of letter quality. The paper must be white or unbleached, recycled, 8½ by 11 inches, and of at least 20-pound weight. Both sides of the paper may be used if the brief is not bound at the top.

(2) Any conventional typeface may be used. The typeface may be either proportionally spaced or monospaced.

(3) The type style must be roman; but for emphasis, italics or boldface may be used or the text may be underscored. Case names must be italicized or underscored. Headings may be in uppercase letters.

(4) Except as provided in (10), the type size, including footnotes, must not be smaller than 13-point.

(5) The lines of text must be at least one-and-a-half-spaced. Headings and footnotes may be single-spaced. Quotations may be block-indented and single-spaced. Single-spaced means six lines to a vertical inch.

(6) The margins must be at least 1½ inches on the left and right and 1 inch on the top and bottom.

(7) The pages must be consecutively numbered.

(8) The brief must be bound on the left margin, except that briefs may be bound at the top if required by a local rule of the appellate division. If the brief is stapled, the bound edge and staples must be covered with tape.

(9) The brief need not be signed.

(10) If the brief is produced on a typewriter:

(A) A typewritten original and carbon copies may be filed only with the presiding justice's permission, which will ordinarily be given only to unrepresented parties proceeding in forma pauperis. All other typewritten briefs must be filed as photocopies.

(B) Both sides of the paper may be used if a photocopy is filed; only one side may be used if a typewritten original and carbon copies are filed.

(C) The type size, including footnotes, must not be smaller than standard pica, 10 characters per inch. Unrepresented incarcerated litigants may use elite type, 12 characters per inch, if they lack access to a typewriter with larger characters.

(Subd (c) adopted effective January 1, 2009.)

(d) Noncomplying briefs

If a brief does not comply with this rule:

(1) The reviewing court clerk may decline to file it, but must mark it "received but not filed" and return it to the party; or

(2) If the brief is filed, the presiding judge may with or without notice:

(A) Order the brief returned for corrections and refiling within a specified time;

(B) Strike the brief with leave to file a new brief within a specified time; or

(C) Disregard the noncompliance.

(Subd (d) adopted effective January 1, 2009.)
Rule 8.883 adopted effective January 1, 2009.

Rule 8.884.   Appeals in which a party is both appellant and respondent

(a) Briefing sequence and time to file briefs

In an appeal in which any party is both an appellant and a respondent:

(1) The parties must jointly—or separately if unable to agree—submit a proposed briefing sequence to the appellate division within 20 days after the second notice of appeal is filed.

(2) After receiving the proposal, the appellate division must order a briefing sequence and prescribe briefing periods consistent with rule 8.882(a).

(Subd (a) adopted effective January 1, 2009.)

(b) Contents of briefs

(1) A party that is both an appellant and a respondent must combine its respondent's brief with its appellant's opening brief or its reply brief, if any, whichever is appropriate under the briefing sequence that the appellate division orders under (a).

(2) A party must confine a reply brief to points raised in its own appeal.

(3) A combined brief must address **the points raised in** each appeal separately **but may include a single summary of the significant facts**.

(Subd (b) amended effective January 1, 2009; adopted effective January 1, 2009.)

Rule 8.884 amended effective January 1, 2009; adopted effective January 1, 2009.

Rule 8.885. Oral argument

(a) Calendaring and sessions

Unless otherwise ordered, all appeals in which the last reply brief was filed or the time for filing this brief expired 45 or more days before the date of a regular appellate division session must be placed on the calendar for that session by the appellate division clerk. By order of the presiding judge or the division, any appeal may be placed on the calendar for oral argument at any session.

(Subd (a) adopted effective January 1, 2009.)

(b) Notice of argument

As soon as all parties' briefs are filed or the time for filing these briefs has expired, the appellate division clerk must send a notice of the time and place of oral argument to all parties. The notice must be sent at least 20 days before the date for oral argument. The presiding judge may shorten the notice period for good cause; in that event, the clerk must immediately notify the parties by telephone or other expeditious method.

(Subd (b) adopted effective January 1, 2009.)

(c) Waiver of argument

Parties may waive oral argument.

(Subd (c) adopted effective January 1, 2009.)

(d) Conduct of argument

Unless the court provides otherwise:

(1) The appellant, petitioner, or moving party has the right to open and close. If there are two or more such parties, the court must set the sequence of argument.

(2) Each side is allowed 10 minutes for argument. If multiple parties are represented by separate counsel, or if an amicus curiae—on written request—is granted permission to argue, the court may apportion or expand the time.

(3) Only one counsel may argue for each separately represented party.

(Subd (d) adopted effective January 1, 2009.)

Rule 8.885 adopted effective January 1, 2009.

Advisory Committee Comment

Subdivision (a). Under rule 10.1108, the appellate division must hold a session at least once each quarter, unless no matters are set for oral argument that quarter, but may choose to hold sessions more frequently.

Rule 8.886. Submission of the cause

(a) When the cause is submitted

A cause is submitted when the court has heard oral argument or approved its waiver and the time has expired to file all briefs and papers, including any supplemental brief permitted by the court. The appellate division may order the cause submitted at an earlier time if the parties so stipulate.

(Subd (a) adopted effective January 1, 2009.)

(b) Vacating submission

The court may vacate submission only by an order stating its reasons and setting a timetable for resubmission.

(Subd (b) adopted effective January 1, 2009.)

Rule 8.886 adopted effective January 1, 2009.

Rule 8.887. Decisions

(a) Written opinions

Appellate division judges are not required to prepare a written opinion in any case but may do so when they deem it advisable or in the public interest. A decision by opinion must identify the participating judges, including the author of the majority opinion and of any concurring or dissenting opinion, or the judges participating in a "by the court" opinion.

(Subd (a) adopted effective January 1, 2009.)

(b) Filing the decision

The appellate division clerk must promptly file all opinions and orders of the court and promptly send copies showing the filing date to the parties and, when relevant, to the trial court.

(Subd (b) adopted effective January 1, 2009.)

(c) Opinions certified for publication

(1) Opinions certified for publication must comply to the extent practicable with the *California Style Manual*.

(2) When the decision is final as to the appellate division in a case in which the opinion is certified for publication, the clerk must immediately send:

(A) To the Reporter of Decisions: two paper copies and one electronic copy in a format approved by the Reporter.

(B) To the Courts of Appeal for the district: one copy bearing the notation "To be published in the Official Reports." The Courts of Appeal clerk must promptly file that copy or make a docket entry showing its receipt.

(Subd (c) adopted effective January 1, 2009.)

Rule 8.887 adopted effective January 1, 2009.

Rule 8.888. Finality and modification of decision

(a) Finality of decision

(1) Except as otherwise provided in this rule, an appellate division decision, including an order dismissing an appeal involuntarily, is final 30 days after the decision is filed.

(2) If the appellate division certifies a written opinion for publication or partial publication after its decision is filed and before its decision becomes final in that court, the finality period runs from the filing date of the order for publication.

(3) The following appellate division decisions are final in that court when filed:

(A) The denial of a petition for writ of supersedeas;

(B) The denial of an application for bail or to reduce bail pending appeal; and

(C) The dismissal of an appeal on request or stipulation.

(Subd (a) adopted effective January 1, 2009.)

(b) Modification of judgment

(1) The appellate division may modify its decision until the decision is final in that court. If the clerk's office is closed on the date of finality, the court may modify the decision on the next day the clerk's office is open.

(2) An order modifying a decision must state whether it changes the appellate judgment. A modification that does not change the appellate judgment does not extend the finality date of the decision. If a modification changes the appellate judgment, the finality period runs from the filing date of the modification order.

(Subd (b) adopted effective January 1, 2009.)

(c) Consent to increase or decrease in amount of judgment

If an appellate division decision conditions the affirmance of a money judgment on a party's consent to an increase or decrease in the amount, the judgment is reversed unless, before the decision is final under (a), the party serves and files two copies of a consent in the appellate division. If a consent is filed, the finality period runs from the filing date of the consent. The clerk must send one file-stamped copy of the consent to the trial court with the remittitur.

(Subd (c) adopted effective January 1, 2009.)
Rule 8.888 adopted effective January 1, 2009.

Rule 8.889. Rehearing

(a) Power to order rehearing

(1) On petition of a party or on its own motion, the appellate division may order rehearing of any decision that is not final in that court on filing.

(2) An order for rehearing must be filed before the decision is final. If the clerk's office is closed on the date of finality, the court may file the order on the next day the clerk's office is open.

(Subd (a) adopted effective January 1, 2009.)

(b) Petition and answer

(1) A party may serve and file a petition for rehearing within 15 days after:

(A) The decision is filed;

(B) A publication order restarting the finality period under rule 8.888(a)(2), if the party has not already filed a petition for rehearing;

(C) A modification order changing the appellate judgment under rule 8.888(b); or

(D) The filing of a consent under rule 8.888(c).

(2) A party must not file an answer to a petition for rehearing unless the court requests an answer. The clerk must promptly send to the parties copies of any order requesting an answer and immediately notify the parties by telephone or another expeditious method. Any answer must be served and filed within 8 days after the order is filed unless the court orders otherwise. A petition for rehearing normally will not be granted unless the court has requested an answer.

(3) The petition and answer must comply with the relevant provisions of rule 8.883.

(4) Before the decision is final and for good cause, the presiding judge may relieve a party from a failure to file a timely petition or answer.

(Subd (b) adopted effective January 1, 2009.)

(c) No extensions of time

The time for granting or denying a petition for rehearing in the appellate division may not be extended. If the court does not rule on the petition before the decision is final, the petition is deemed denied.

(Subd (c) adopted effective January 1, 2009.)

(d) Effect of granting rehearing

An order granting a rehearing vacates the decision and any opinion filed in the case. If the appellate division orders rehearing, it may place the case on calendar for further argument or submit it for decision.

(Subd (d) adopted effective January 1, 2009.)
Rule 8.889 adopted effective January 1, 2009.

Rule 8.890. Remittitur

(a) Proceedings requiring issuance of remittitur

An appellate division must issue a remittitur after a decision in an appeal.

(Subd (a) adopted effective January 1, 2009.)

(b) Clerk's duties

(1) If an appellate division case is not transferred to the Court of Appeal under rule 8.1000 et seq., the appellate division clerk must:

(A) Issue a remittitur immediately after the Court of Appeal denies transfer, or the period for granting transfer under rule 8.1008(c) expires;

(B) Send the remittitur to the trial court with a file-stamped copy of the opinion or order; and

(C) Return to the trial court with the remittitur all original records, exhibits, and documents sent to the appellate division in connection with the appeal, except any certification for transfer under rule 8.1005, the transcripts or statement on appeal, briefs, and the notice of appeal.

(2) If an appellate division case is transferred to a Court of Appeal under rule 8.1000 et seq., on receiving the Court of Appeal remittitur, the appellate division clerk must issue a remittitur and return documents to the trial court as provided in rule 8.1018.

(Subd (b) adopted effective January 1, 2009.)

(c) Immediate issuance, stay, and recall

(1) The appellate division may direct immediate issuance of a remittitur only on the parties' stipulation or on dismissal of the appeal on the request or stipulation of the parties under rule 8.825(c)(2).

(2) On a party's or its own motion or on stipulation, and for good cause, the court may stay a remittitur's issuance for a reasonable period or order its recall.

(3) An order recalling a remittitur issued after a decision by opinion does not supersede the opinion or affect its publication status.

(Subd (c) adopted effective January 1, 2009.)

(d) Notice

The remittitur is deemed issued when the clerk enters it in the record. The clerk must immediately send the parties notice of issuance of the remittitur, showing the date of entry.

(Subd (d) adopted effective January 1, 2009.)

Rule 8.890 adopted effective January 1, 2009.

Rule 8.891.   Costs and sanctions in civil appeals

(a) Right to costs

(1) Except as provided in this rule, the prevailing party in a civil appeal is entitled to costs on appeal.

(2) The prevailing party is the respondent if the appellate division affirms the judgment without modification or dismisses the appeal. The prevailing party is the appellant if the appellate division reverses the judgment in its entirety.

(3) If the appellate division reverses the judgment in part or modifies it, or if there is more than one notice of appeal, the appellate division must specify the award or denial of costs in its decision.

(4) In the interests of justice, the appellate division may also award or deny costs as it deems proper.

(Subd (a) adopted effective January 1, 2009.)

(b) Judgment for costs

(1) The appellate division clerk must enter on the record and insert in the remittitur judgment awarding costs to the prevailing party under (a).

(2) If the clerk fails to enter judgment for costs, the appellate division may recall the remittitur for correction on its own motion or on a party's motion made not later than 30 days after the remittitur issues.

(Subd (b) adopted effective January 1, 2009.)

(c) Procedure for claiming or opposing costs

(1) Within 30 days after the clerk sends notice of issuance of the remittitur, a party claiming costs awarded by the appellate division must serve and file in the trial court a verified memorandum of costs under rule 3.1702(a)(1).

(2) A party may serve and file a motion in the trial court to strike or tax costs claimed under (1) in the manner required by rule 3.1700.

(3) An award of costs is enforceable as a money judgment.

(Subd (c) adopted effective January 1, 2009.)

(d) Recoverable costs

(1) A party may recover only the costs of the following, if reasonable:

(A) Filing fees;

(B) The amount the party paid for any portion of the record, whether an original or a copy or both, subject to reduction by the appellate division under subdivision (e);

(C) The cost to produce additional evidence on appeal;

(D) The costs to notarize, serve, mail, and file the record, briefs, and other papers;

(E) The cost to print and reproduce any brief, including any petition for rehearing or review, answer, or reply; and

(F) The cost to procure a surety bond, including the premium and the cost to obtain a letter of credit as collateral, unless the trial court determines the bond was unnecessary.

(2) Unless the court orders otherwise, an award of costs neither includes attorney's fees on appeal nor precludes a party from seeking them under rule 3.1702.

(Subd (d) adopted effective January 1, 2009.)

(e) Sanctions

(1) On motion of a party or its own motion, the appellate division may impose sanctions, including the award or denial of costs, on a party or an attorney for:

(A) Taking a frivolous appeal or appealing solely to cause delay; or

(B) Committing any unreasonable violation of these rules.

(2) A party's motion under (1) must include a declaration supporting the amount of any monetary sanction sought and must be served and filed before any order dismissing the appeal but no later than 10 days after the appellant's reply brief is due. If a party files a motion for sanctions with a motion to dismiss the appeal and the motion to dismiss is not granted, the party may file a new motion for sanctions within 10 days after the appellant's reply brief is due.

(3) The court must give notice in writing if it is considering imposing sanctions. Within 10 days after the court sends such notice, a party or attorney may serve and file an opposition, but failure to do so will not be deemed consent. An opposition may not be filed unless the court sends such notice.

(4) Unless otherwise ordered, oral argument on the issue of sanctions must be combined with oral argument on the merits of the appeal.

(Subd (e) adopted effective January 1, 2009.)

Rule 8.891 adopted effective January 1, 2009.

Chapter 5
Appeals in Infraction Cases

Chapter 5 adopted effective January 1, 2009.

Article 1
Taking Appeals in Infraction Cases

Article 1 adopted effective January 1, 2009.

Rule 8.900.   Application [Renumbered]

Rule 8.900 renumbered to rule 8.950 effective January 1, 2009;

adopted as rule 151 effective July 1, 1964; previously amended effective January 1, 1977, and January 1, 2005; previously amended and renumbered effective January 1, 2007.

Another rule 8.900 follows.

Rule 8.900. Application of chapter

The rules in this chapter apply only to appeals in infraction cases. An infraction case is a case in which the defendant was convicted only of an infraction and was not charged with any felony. A felony is "charged" when an information or indictment accusing the defendant of a felony is filed or a complaint accusing the defendant of a felony is certified to the superior court under Penal Code section 859a.

Rule 8.900 adopted effective January 1, 2009.

Advisory Committee Comment

Chapter 1 of this division also applies in appeals from infraction cases. Chapters 3 and 4 of this division apply to appeals in misdemeanor cases. The rules that apply in appeals in felony cases are located in chapter 3 of division 1 of this title.

Penal Code section 1466 provides that an appeal in a "misdemeanor or infraction case" is to the appellate division of the superior court, and Penal Code section 1235(b), in turn, provides that an appeal in a "felony case" is to the Court of Appeal. Penal Code section 691(g) defines "misdemeanor or infraction case" to mean "a criminal action in which a misdemeanor or infraction is charged *and does not include a criminal action in which a felony is charged* in conjunction with a misdemeanor or infraction" (emphasis added), and section 691(f) defines "felony case" to mean "a criminal action in which a felony is charged *and includes a criminal action in which a misdemeanor or infraction is charged in conjunction with a felony*" (emphasis added).

As rule 8.304 from the rules on felony appeals makes clear, a "felony case" is an action in which a felony is charged *regardless of the outcome of the action.* Thus the question of which rules apply—these appellate division rules or the rules governing appeals in felony cases—is answered simply by examining the accusatory pleading: if that document charged the defendant with at least one count of felony (as defined in Penal Code, section 17(a)), the Court of Appeal has appellate jurisdiction and the appeal must be taken under the rules on felony appeals *even if the prosecution did not result in a punishment of imprisonment in a state prison.*

It is settled case law that an appeal is taken to the Court of Appeal not only when the defendant is charged with and convicted of a felony, but also when the defendant is charged with both a felony and a misdemeanor (Pen. Code, § 691(f)) but is convicted of only the misdemeanor (e.g., *People v. Brown* (1970) 10 Cal.App.3d 169); when the defendant is charged with a felony but is convicted of only a lesser offense (Pen. Code, § 1159; e.g., *People v. Spreckels* (1954) 125 Cal.App.2d 507); and when the defendant is charged with an offense filed as a felony but punishable as either a felony or a misdemeanor, and the offense is thereafter deemed a misdemeanor under Penal Code section 17(b) (e.g., *People v. Douglas* (1999) 20 Cal.4th 85; *People v. Clark* (1971) 17 Cal.App.3d 890).

Trial court unification did not change this rule: after as before unification, "Appeals in felony cases lie to the [C]ourt of [A]ppeal, regardless of whether the appeal is from the superior court, the municipal court, or the action of a magistrate. *Cf.* Cal. Const. art. VI, § 11(a) [except in death penalty cases, Courts of Appeal have appellate jurisdiction when superior courts have original jurisdiction 'in causes of a type within the appellate jurisdiction of the [C]ourts of [A]ppeal on June 30, 1995....'].'' ("Recommendation on Trial Court Unification" (July 1998) 28 *Cal. Law Revision Com. Rep.* 455–56.)

Rule 8.901. Notice of appeal

(a) Notice of appeal

(1) To appeal from a judgment or an appealable order in an infraction case, the defendant or the People must file a notice of appeal in the trial court that issued the judgment or order being appealed. The notice must specify the judgment or order—or part of it—being appealed.

(2) If the defendant appeals, the defendant or the defendant's attorney must sign the notice of appeal. If the People appeal, the attorney for the People must sign the notice.

(3) The notice of appeal must be liberally construed in favor of its sufficiency.

(Subd (a) adopted effective January 1, 2009.)

(b) Notification of the appeal

(1) When a notice of appeal is filed, the trial court clerk must promptly mail a notification of the filing to the attorney of record for each party and to any unrepresented defendant. The clerk must also mail or deliver this notification to the appellate division clerk.

(2) The notification must show the date it was mailed or delivered, the number and title of the case, and the date the notice of appeal was filed.

(3) The notification to the appellate division clerk must also include a copy of the notice of appeal.

(4) A copy of the notice of appeal is sufficient notification under (1) if the required information is on the copy or is added by the trial court clerk.

(5) The mailing of a notification under (1) is a sufficient performance of the clerk's duty despite the discharge, disqualification, suspension, disbarment, or death of the attorney.

(6) Failure to comply with any provision of this subdivision does not affect the validity of the notice of appeal.

(Subd (b) adopted effective January 1, 2009.)
Rule 8.901 adopted effective January 1, 2009.

Advisory Committee Comment

Notice of Appeal and Record of Oral Proceedings (Infraction) (form CR-142) may be used to file the notice of appeal required under this rule. This form is available at any courthouse or county law library or online at *www.courtinfo.ca.gov/forms.*

Rule 8.902. Definitions [Renumbered]

Rule 8.902 renumbered to rule 8.952 effective January 1, 2009; adopted as rule 158 effective July 1, 1964; previously amended and renumbered as rule 156 effective July 1, 1991; previously amended effective January 1, 2005; previously amended and renumbered effective January 1, 2007.

Another rule 8.902 follows.

Rule 8.902. Time to appeal

(a) Normal time

A notice of appeal must be filed within 30 days after the rendition of the judgment or the making of the order being appealed. If the defendant is committed before final judgment for insanity or narcotics addiction, the notice of appeal must be filed within 30 days after the commitment.

(Subd (a) adopted effective January 1, 2009.)

(b) Cross-appeal

If the defendant or the People timely appeals from a judgment or appealable order, the time for any other party to appeal from the same judgment or order is either the time specified in (a) or 30 days after the trial court clerk mails notification of the first appeal, whichever is later.

(Subd (b) adopted effective January 1, 2009.)

(c) Premature notice of appeal

A notice of appeal filed before the judgment is rendered or the order is made is premature, but the appellate division may treat the notice as filed immediately after the rendition of the judgment or the making of the order.

(Subd (c) adopted effective January 1, 2009.)

(d) Late notice of appeal

The trial court clerk must mark a late notice of appeal "Received [date] but not filed" and notify the party that the notice was not filed because it was late.

(Subd (d) adopted effective January 1, 2009.)

(e) Receipt by mail from custodial institution

If the trial court clerk receives a notice of appeal by mail from a custodial institution after the period specified in (a) has expired but the envelope shows that the notice was mailed or delivered to custodial officials for mailing within the period specified in (a), the notice is deemed timely. The clerk must retain in the case file the envelope in which the notice was received.

(Subd (e) adopted effective January 1, 2009.)
Rule 8.902 adopted effective January 1, 2009.

Rule 8.903. Stay of execution on appeal

(a) Application

Pending appeal, the defendant may apply to the appellate division for a stay of execution after a judgment of conviction.

(Subd (a) adopted effective January 1, 2009.)

(b) Showing

The application must include a showing that the defendant sought relief in the trial court and that the court unjustifiably denied the application.

(Subd (b) adopted effective January 1, 2009.)

(c) Service

The application must be served on the prosecuting attorney.

(Subd (c) adopted effective January 1, 2009.)

(d) Interim relief

Pending its ruling on the application, the appellate division may grant the relief requested. The appellate division must notify the trial court of any stay that it grants.

(Subd (d) adopted effective January 1, 2009.)
Rule 8.903 adopted effective January 1, 2009.

Advisory Committee Comment

Subdivision (c). Under rule 8.804, the prosecuting attorney means the city attorney, county counsel, or district attorney prosecuting the infraction.

Rule 8.904. Filing the appeal [Renumbered]

Rule 8.904 renumbered to rule 8.954 effective January 1, 2009; adopted as rule 152 effective July 1, 1964; previously amended effective July 1, 1973, January 1, 1977, January 1, 1979, January 1, 1984, July 1, 1991, and January 1, 2005; previously amended and renumbered effective January 1, 2007.

Another rule 8.904 follows.

Rule 8.904. Abandoning the appeal

(a) How to abandon

An appellant may abandon the appeal at any time by filing an abandonment of the appeal signed by the appellant or the appellant's attorney of record.

(Subd (a) adopted effective January 1, 2009.)

(b) Where to file; effect of filing

(1) The appellant must file the abandonment in the appellate division.

(2) If the record has not been filed in the appellate division, the filing of an abandonment effects a dismissal of the appeal and restores the trial court's jurisdiction.

(3) If the record has been filed in the appellate division, the appellate division may dismiss the appeal and direct immediate issuance of the remittitur.

(Subd (b) adopted effective January 1, 2009.)

(c) Clerk's duties

(1) The appellate division clerk must immediately notify the adverse party of the filing or of the order of dismissal.

(2) If the record has not been filed in the appellate division, the clerk must immediately notify the trial court.

(3) If a reporter's transcript has been requested, the clerk must immediately notify the reporter if the appeal is abandoned before the reporter has filed the transcript.

(Subd (c) adopted effective January 1, 2009.)
Rule 8.904 adopted effective January 1, 2009.

Advisory Committee Comment

Abandonment of Appeal (Infraction) (form CR-145) may be used to file an abandonment under this rule. This form is available at any courthouse or county law library or online at *www.courtinfo.ca.gov/forms.*

Rule 8.907. Record on appeal [Renumbered]

Rule 8.907 renumbered to rule 8.957 effective January 1, 2009; adopted as rule 153 effective July 1, 1964; previously amended effective July 1, 1972, July 1, 1973, January 1, 1977, and January 1, 2005; previously amended and renumbered effective January 1, 2007.

Article 2
Record in Infraction Appeals

Article 2 adopted effective January 1, 2009.

Rule 8.910. Normal record on appeal
Rule 8.911. Prosecuting attorney's notice regarding the record
Rule 8.912. Contents of clerk's transcript
Rule 8.913. Preparation of clerk's transcript
Rule 8.914. Trial court file instead of clerk's transcript
Rule 8.915. Record of oral proceedings
Rule 8.916. Statement on appeal
Rule 8.917. Record when trial proceedings were officially electronically recorded
Rule 8.918. Contents of reporter's transcript
Rule 8.919. Preparation of reporter's transcript
Rule 8.920. Limited normal record in certain appeals
Rule 8.921. Exhibits
Rule 8.922. Sending and filing the record in the appellate division
Rule 8.923. Augmenting or correcting the record in the appellate division

Rule 8.910. Continuances [Renumbered]

Rule 8.910 renumbered to rule 8.960 effective January 1, 2009; adopted as rule 154 effective July 1, 1964; previously amended effective January 1, 1977, July 1, 1991, and January 1, 2005; previously renumbered effective January 1, 2007.

Another rule 8.910 follows.

Rule 8.910. Normal record on appeal

(a) Contents

Except as otherwise provided in this chapter, the record on an appeal to a superior court appellate division in an infraction criminal case must contain the following, which constitute the normal record on appeal:

(1) A record of the written documents from the trial court proceedings in the form of one of the following:

(A) A clerk's transcript under rule 8.912 or 8.920; or

(B) If the court has a local rule for the appellate division electing to use this form of the record, the original trial court file under rule 8.914.

(2) If an appellant wants to raise any issue that requires consideration of the oral proceedings in the trial court, the record on appeal must include a record of the oral proceedings in the form of one of the following:

(A) A statement on appeal under rule 8.916;

(B) If the court has a local rule for the appellate division permitting this form of the record, an official electronic recording of the proceedings under rule 8.917; or

(C) A reporter's transcript under rules 8.918–8.920 or a transcript prepared from an official electronic recording under rule 8.917.

(Subd (a) adopted effective January 1, 2009.)

(b) Stipulation for limited record

If before the record is certified, the appellant, or counsel for the appellant, and the People stipulate in writing that any part of the record is not required for proper determination of the appeal and file the stipulation in the trial court, that part of the record must not be prepared or sent to the appellate division.

(Subd (b) adopted effective January 1, 2009.)
Rule 8.910 adopted effective January 1, 2009.

Rule 8.911. Prosecuting attorney's notice regarding the record

If the prosecuting attorney does not want to receive a copy of the record on appeal, within 10 days after the notification of the appeal under rule 8.901(b) is mailed to the prosecuting attorney, the prosecuting attorney must serve and file a notice indicating that he or she does not want to receive the record.

Rule 8.911 adopted effective January 1, 2009.

Rule 8.912. Contents of clerk's transcript

Except in appeals covered by rule 8.920 or when the parties have filed a stipulation under rule 8.910(b) that any of these items is not required for proper determination of the appeal, the clerk's transcript must contain:

(1) The complaint, including any notice to appear, and any amendment;

(2) Any demurrer or other plea;

(3) All court minutes;

(4) Any written findings or opinion of the court;

(5) The judgment or order appealed from;

(6) Any motion or notice of motion for new trial, in arrest of judgment, or to dismiss the action, with supporting and opposing memoranda and attachments;

(7) Any transcript of a sound or sound-and-video recording tendered to the court under rule 2.1040;

(8) The notice of appeal; and

(9) If the appellant is the defendant:

(A) Any written defense motion denied in whole or in part, with supporting and opposing memoranda and attachments; and

(B) If related to a motion under (A), any search warrant and return.

Rule 8.912 adopted effective January 1, 2009.

Rule 8.913. Abandonment, dismissal, and judgment for failure to bring to trial [Renumbered]

Rule 8.913 renumbered to rule 8.963 effective January 1, 2009; adopted as rule 157 effective July 1, 1964; amended and renumbered as rule 155 effective July 1, 1991; previously amended effective January 1, 1972, July 1, 1972, and January 1, 2005; previously amended and renumbered effective January 1, 2007.

Another rule 8.913 follows.

Rule 8.913. Preparation of clerk's transcript

(a) When preparation begins

Unless the original court file will be used in place of a clerk's transcript under rule 8.914, the clerk must begin preparing the clerk's transcript immediately after the notice of appeal is filed.

(Subd (a) adopted effective January 1, 2009.)

(b) Format of transcript

The clerk's transcript must comply with rule 8.144.

(Subd (b) adopted effective January 1, 2009.)

(c) When preparation must be completed

Within 20 days after the notice of appeal is filed, the clerk must complete preparation of an original clerk's transcript for the appellate division and one copy for the appellant. If there is more than one appellant, the clerk must prepare an extra copy for each additional appellant who is represented by separate counsel or self-represented. If the defendant is the appellant, a copy must also be prepared for the prosecuting attorney unless the prosecuting attorney has notified the court under rule 8.911 that he or she does not want to receive the record. If the People are the appellant, a copy must also be prepared for the respondent.

(Subd (c) adopted effective January 1, 2009.)

(d) Certification

The clerk must certify as correct the original and all copies of the clerk's transcript.

(Subd (d) adopted effective January 1, 2009.)
Rule 8.913 adopted effective January 1, 2009.

Advisory Committee Comment

Rule 8.922 addresses when the clerk's transcript is sent to the appellate division in infraction appeals.

Rule 8.914. Trial court file instead of clerk's transcript

(a) Application

If the court has a local rule for the appellate division electing to use this form of the record, the original trial court file may be used instead of a clerk's transcript. This rule and any supplemental provisions of the local rule then govern unless the trial court orders otherwise after notice to the parties.

(Subd (a) adopted effective January 1, 2009.)

(b) When original file must be prepared

Within 20 days after the filing of the notice of appeal, the trial court clerk must put the trial court file in chronological order, number the pages, and attach a chronological index and a list of all attorneys of record, the parties they represent, and any unrepresented parties.

(Subd (b) adopted effective January 1, 2009.)

(c) Copies

The clerk must send a copy of the index to the appellant for use in paginating his or her copy of the file to conform to the index. If there is more than one appellant, the clerk must prepare an extra copy of the index for each additional appellant who is represented by separate counsel or self-represented. If the defendant is the appellant, a copy must also be prepared for the prosecuting attorney unless the prosecuting attorney has notified the court under rule 8.911 that he or she does not want to receive the record. If the People are the appellant, a copy must also be prepared for the respondent.

(Subd (c) adopted effective January 1, 2009.)
Rule 8.914 adopted effective January 1, 2009.

Advisory Committee Comment

Rule 8.922 addresses when the original file is sent to the appellate division in infraction appeals.

Rule 8.915.   Record of oral proceedings

(a) Appellant's election

The appellant must notify the trial court whether he or she elects to proceed with or without a record of the oral proceedings in the trial court. If the appellant elects to proceed with a record of the oral proceedings in the trial court, the notice must specify which form of the record of the oral proceedings in the trial court the appellant elects to use:

(1) A statement on appeal under rule 8.916;

(2) If the court has a local rule for the appellate division permitting this, an official electronic recording of the proceedings under rule 8.917(c). The appellant must attach to the notice a copy of the stipulation required under rule 8.917(c); or

(3) A reporter's transcript under rules 8.918–8.920 or a transcript prepared from an official electronic recording of the proceedings under rule 8.917(b). If the appellant elects to use a reporter's transcript, the clerk must promptly mail a copy of appellant's notice making this election and the notice of appeal to each court reporter.

(Subd (a) adopted effective January 1, 2009.)

(b) Time for filing election

The notice of election required under (a) must be filed with the notice of appeal.

(Subd (b) adopted effective January 1, 2009.)

(c) Statement on appeal when proceedings cannot be transcribed or were not recorded

(1) If the appellant elects under (a) to use a reporter's transcript or a transcript prepared from an official elec-

tronic recording or the recording itself, the trial court clerk must notify the appellant within 10 days after the appellant files this election if any portion of the oral proceedings listed in rule 8.918 was not reported or officially recorded electronically or cannot be transcribed. The notice must indicate that the appellant may use a statement on appeal as the record of the portion of the proceedings that was not recorded or cannot be transcribed.

(2) Within 15 days after this notice is mailed by the clerk, the appellant must serve and file a notice with the court stating whether the appellant elects to use a statement on appeal as the record of the portion of the proceedings that was not recorded or cannot be transcribed.

(Subd (c) adopted effective January 1, 2009.)
Rule 8.915 adopted effective January 1, 2009.

Advisory Committee Comment

Notice of Appeal and Record of Oral Proceedings (Infraction) (form CR-142) may be used to file the election required under this rule. This form is available at any courthouse or county law library or online at *www.courtinfo.ca.gov/forms*. To assist appellants in making an appropriate election, courts are encouraged to include information about whether the proceedings were recorded by a court reporter or officially electronically recorded in any information that the court provides to parties concerning their appellate rights.

Rule 8.916.   Examination of witnesses [Renumbered]

Rule 8.916 renumbered to rule 8.966 effective January 1, 2009; adopted as rule 157 effective July 1, 1999; previously amended and renumbered effective January 1, 2007.

Another rule 8.916 follows.

Rule 8.916.   Statement on appeal

(a) Description

A statement on appeal is a summary of the trial court proceedings that is approved by the trial court.

(Subd (a) adopted effective January 1, 2009.)

(b) Preparing the proposed statement

(1) If the appellant elects under rule 8.915 to use a statement on appeal, the appellant must prepare and file a proposed statement within 20 days after filing the record preparation election. If the defendant is the appellant and the prosecuting attorney appeared in the case, the defendant must serve a copy of the proposed statement on the prosecuting attorney. If the People are the appellant, the prosecuting attorney must serve a copy of the proposed statement on the respondent.

(2) Appellants who are not represented by an attorney must file their proposed statements on *Proposed Statement on Appeal (Infraction)* (form CR-143). For good cause, the court may permit the filing of a statement that is not on form CR-143.

(3) If the appellant does not file a proposed statement within the time specified in (1), the trial court clerk must promptly notify the appellant by mail that the proposed statement must be filed within 15 days after the notice is mailed and that failure to comply will result in the appeal being dismissed.

(Subd (b) adopted effective January 1, 2009.)

(c) Contents of the proposed statement on appeal

A proposed statement prepared by the appellant must contain:

(1) A condensed narrative of the oral proceedings that the appellant believes necessary for the appeal and a summary of the trial court's holding and the sentence imposed on the appellant. Subject to the court's approval, the appellant may present some or all of the evidence by question and answer; and

(2) A statement of the points the appellant is raising on appeal. The appeal is then limited to those points unless the appellate division determines that the record permits the full consideration of another point.

(A) The statement must specify the intended grounds of appeal by clearly stating each point to be raised but need not identify each particular ruling or matter to be challenged.

(B) The statement must include as much of the evidence or proceeding as necessary to support the stated grounds. Any evidence or portion of a proceeding not included will be presumed to support the judgment or order appealed from.

(C) If one of the grounds of appeal is insufficiency of the evidence, the statement must specify how it is insufficient.

(Subd (c) adopted effective January 1, 2009.)

(d) Review of the appellant's proposed statement

(1) Within 10 days after the appellant files the proposed statement, the respondent may serve and file proposed amendments to that statement.

(2) No later than 10 days after the respondent files proposed amendments or the time to do so expires, a party may request a hearing to review and correct the proposed statement. No hearing will be held unless ordered by the trial court judge, and the judge will not ordinarily order a hearing unless there is a factual dispute about a material aspect of the trial court proceedings.

(3) If a hearing is ordered, the court must promptly set the hearing date and provide the parties with at least 5 days' written notice of the hearing date.

(4) Except as provided in (6), if no hearing is ordered, no later than 10 days after the time for requesting a hearing expires, the trial court judge must review the proposed statement and any proposed amendments and make any corrections or modifications to the statement necessary to ensure that it is an accurate summary of the trial court proceedings. If a hearing is ordered, the trial court judge must make any corrections or modifications to the statement within 10 days after the hearing.

(5) The trial court judge must not eliminate the appellant's specification of grounds of appeal from the proposed statement.

(6) If the trial court proceedings were reported by a court reporter or officially recorded electronically under Government Code section 69957 and the trial court judge determines that it would save court time and resources, instead of correcting a proposed statement on appeal:

(A) If the court has a local rule for the appellate division permitting the use of an official electronic recording as the record of the oral proceedings, the trial court judge may order that the original of an official electronic recording of the trial court proceedings, or a copy made by the court, be transmitted as the record of these oral

proceedings without being transcribed. The court will pay for any copy of the official electronic recording ordered under this subdivision; or

(B) Unless the court has a local rule providing otherwise, the trial court judge may order that a transcript be prepared as the record of the oral proceedings. The court will pay for any transcript ordered under this subdivision.

(Subd (d) adopted effective January 1, 2009.)

(e) Review of the corrected statement

(1) If the trial court judge makes any corrections or modifications to the statement under (d), the clerk must send copies of the corrected or modified statement to the parties. If the prosecuting attorney did not appear at the trial, the clerk will not send a copy of the statement to the prosecuting attorney.

(2) Within 10 days after the statement is sent to the parties, any party may serve and file proposed modifications or objections to the statement.

(Subd (e) adopted effective January 1, 2009.)

(f) Certification of the statement on appeal

(1) If the trial court judge does not make any corrections or modifications to the proposed statement under (d)(4) and does not direct the preparation of a transcript in lieu of correcting the proposed statement under (d)(6), the judge must promptly certify the statement.

(2) If the trial court judge corrects or modifies an appellant's proposed statement under (d), within five days after the time for filing proposed modifications or objections under (e) has expired, the judge must review any proposed modifications or objections to the statement filed by the parties, make any corrections or modifications to the statement necessary to ensure that it is an accurate summary of the trial court proceedings, and certify the statement.

(Subd (f) adopted effective January 1, 2009.)

(g) Extensions of time

For good cause, the trial court may grant an extension of not more than 15 days to do any act required or permitted under this rule.

(Subd (g) adopted effective January 1, 2009.)
Rule 8.916 adopted effective January 1, 2009.

Advisory Committee Comment

Rules 8.806, 8.810, and 8.812 address applications for extensions of time and relief from default.

Subdivision (b). *Proposed Statement on Appeal (Infraction)* (form CR-143) is available at any courthouse or county law library or online at *www.courtinfo.ca.gov/forms.*

Subdivision (d). Under rule 8.804, the term "judge" includes a commissioner or a temporary judge.

Rule 8.917.   Record when trial proceedings were officially electronically recorded

(a) Application

This rule applies only if:

(1) The trial court proceedings were officially recorded electronically under Government Code section 69957; and

(2) The electronic recording was prepared in compliance with applicable rules regarding electronic recording of court proceedings.

(Subd (a) adopted effective January 1, 2009.)

(b) Transcripts from official electronic recording

Written transcripts of official electronic recordings may be prepared under rule 2.952. A transcript prepared and certified as provided in that rule is prima facie a true and complete record of the oral proceedings it purports to cover, and satisfies any requirement in these rules or in any statute for a reporter's transcript of oral proceedings.

(Subd (b) adopted effective January 1, 2009.)

(c) Use of official recording as record of oral proceedings

If the court has a local rule for the appellate division permitting this, on stipulation of the parties or on order of the trial court under rule 8.916(b), the original of an official electronic recording of the trial court proceedings, or a copy made by the court, may be transmitted as the record of these oral proceedings without being transcribed. This official electronic recording satisfies any requirement in these rules or in any statute for a reporter's transcript of these proceedings.

(Subd (c) adopted effective January 1, 2009.)

(d) When preparation begins

(1) If the appellant is the People, preparation of a transcript or a copy of the recording must begin immediately after the appellant files an election under rule 8.915(a) to use a transcript of an official electronic recording or a copy of the official electronic recording as the record of the oral proceedings.

(2) If the appellant is the defendant:

(A) Within 10 days after the date the appellant files the election under rule 8.915(a), the clerk must notify the appellant and his or her counsel of the estimated cost of preparing the transcript or the copy of the recording. The notification must show the date it was mailed.

(B) Within 10 days after the date the clerk mailed the notice under (A), the appellant must do one of the following:

(i) Deposit with the clerk an amount equal to the estimated cost of preparing the transcript or the copy of the recording;

(ii) File a declaration of indigency supported by evidence in the form required by the Judicial Council; or

(iii) Notify the clerk that he or she will be using a statement on appeal instead of a transcript or copy of the recording.

(C) Preparation of the transcript must begin when:

(i) The clerk receives the required deposit under (B)(i); or

(ii) The trial court determines that the defendant is indigent and orders that the defendant receive the transcript or the copy of the recording without cost.

(Subd (d) adopted effective January 1, 2009.)

Rule 8.917 adopted effective January 1, 2009.

Advisory Committee Comment

Subdivision (d). The appellant must use *Defendant's Financial Statement on Eligibility for Appointment of Counsel and Reimbursement and Record on Appeal at Public Expense* (form MC-210) to show indigency. This form is available at any courthouse or county law library or online at *www.courtinfo.ca.gov/ forms.*

Rule 8.918.   Contents of reporter's transcript

Except in appeals covered by rule 8.920 or when the parties have filed a stipulation under rule 8.910(b) or the trial court has ordered that any of these items is not required for proper determination of the appeal, the reporter's transcript must contain:

(1) The oral proceedings on the entry of any plea other than a not guilty plea;

(2) The oral proceedings on any motion in limine;

(3) The oral proceedings at trial, but excluding any opening statement;

(4) Any oral opinion of the court;

(5) The oral proceedings on any motion for new trial;

(6) The oral proceedings at sentencing or other dispositional hearing;

(7) If the appellant is the defendant, the reporter's transcript must also contain:

(A) The oral proceedings on any defense motion denied in whole or in part except motions for disqualification of a judge; and

(B) The closing arguments.

Rule 8.918 adopted effective January 1, 2009.

Rule 8.919.   Preparation of reporter's transcript

(a) When preparation begins

(1) The reporter must immediately begin preparing the reporter's transcript if the notice sent to the reporter by the clerk under rule 8.915(a)(3) indicates that the appellant is the People.

(2) If the notice sent to the reporter by the clerk under rule 8.915(a)(3) indicates that the appellant is the defendant:

(A) Within 10 days after the date the clerk mailed the notice under rule 8.915(a)(3), the reporter must file with the clerk the estimated cost of preparing the reporter's transcript; and

(B) The clerk must promptly notify the appellant and his or her counsel of the estimated cost of preparing the reporter's transcript. The notification must show the date it was mailed.

(C) Within 10 days after the date the clerk mailed the notice under (B), the appellant must do one of the following:

(i) Deposit with the clerk an amount equal to the estimated cost of preparing the transcript;

(ii) File a declaration of indigency supported by evidence in the form required by the Judicial Council; or

(iii) Notify the clerk that he or she will be using a statement on appeal instead of a reporter's transcript.

(D) The clerk must promptly notify the reporter to begin preparing the transcript when:

(i) The clerk receives the required deposit under (C)(i); or

(ii) The trial court determines that the defendant is indigent and orders that the defendant receive the transcript without cost.

(Subd (a) adopted effective January 1, 2009.)

(b) Format of transcript

The reporter's transcript must comply with rule 8.144.

(Subd (b) adopted effective January 1, 2009.)

(c) Copies and certification

The reporter must prepare an original and the same number of copies of the reporter's transcript as rule

8.913(c) requires of the clerk's transcript and must certify each as correct.

(Subd (c) adopted effective January 1, 2009.)

(d) When preparation must be completed

The reporter must deliver the original and all copies to the trial court clerk as soon as they are certified but no later than 20 days after the reporter is required to begin preparing the transcript under (a).

(Subd (d) adopted effective January 1, 2009.)

(e) Multi-reporter cases

In a multi-reporter case, the clerk must accept any completed portion of the transcript from the primary reporter one week after the time prescribed by (d) even if other portions are uncompleted. The clerk must promptly pay each reporter who certifies that all portions of the transcript assigned to that reporter are completed.

(Subd (e) adopted effective January 1, 2009.)

Rule 8.919 adopted effective January 1, 2009.

Advisory Committee Comment

Subdivision (a). The appellant must use *Defendant's Financial Statement on Eligibility for Appointment of Counsel and Reimbursement and Record on Appeal at Public Expense* (form MC-210) to show indigency. This form is available at any courthouse or county law library or online at *www.courtinfo.ca.gov/forms.*

Rule 8.920.   Limited normal record in certain appeals

If the People appeal from a judgment on a demurrer to the complaint, including any notice to appear, or if the defendant or the People appeal from an appealable order other than a ruling on a motion for new trial, the normal record is composed of:

(1) *Record of the documents filed in the trial court*

A clerk's transcript or original trial court file containing:

(A) The complaint, including any notice to appear, and any amendment;

(B) Any demurrer or other plea;

(C) Any motion or notice of motion granted or denied by the order appealed from, with supporting and opposing memoranda and attachments;

(D) The judgment or order appealed from and any abstract of judgment;

(E) Any court minutes relating to the judgment or order appealed from; and

(F) The notice of appeal.

(2) *Record of the oral proceedings in the trial court*

If an appellant wants to raise any issue that requires consideration of the oral proceedings in the trial court, a reporter's transcript, transcript prepared under rule 8.918, or a settled statement under rule 8.915 summarizing any oral proceedings incident to the judgment or order being appealed.

Rule 8.920 adopted effective January 1, 2009.

Rule 8.921.   Exhibits

(a) Exhibits deemed part of record

Exhibits admitted in evidence, refused, or lodged are deemed part of the record but may be transmitted to the appellate division only as provided in this rule.

(Subd (a) adopted effective January 1, 2009.)

(b) Notice of designation

(1) Within 10 days after the last respondent's brief is filed or could be filed under rule 8.927, if the appellant wants the appellate division to consider any original exhibits that were admitted in evidence, refused, or lodged, the appellant must serve and file a notice in the trial court designating such exhibits.

(2) Within 10 days after a notice under (1) is served, any other party wanting the appellate division to consider additional exhibits must serve and file a notice in trial court designating such exhibits.

(3) A party filing a notice under (1) or (2) must serve a copy on the appellate division.

(Subd (b) adopted effective January 1, 2009.)

(c) Request by appellate division

At any time the appellate division may direct the trial court or a party to send it an exhibit.

(Subd (c) adopted effective January 1, 2009.)

(d) Transmittal

Unless the appellate division orders otherwise, within 20 days after notice under (b) is filed or after the appellate division directs that an exhibit be sent:

(1) The trial court clerk must put any designated exhibits in the clerk's possession into numerical or alphabetical order and send them to the appellate division with two copies of a list of the exhibits sent. If the appellate division clerk finds the list correct, the clerk must sign and return one copy to the trial court clerk.

(2) Any party in possession of designated exhibits returned by the trial court must put them into numerical or alphabetical order and send them to the appellate division with two copies of a list of the exhibits sent. If the appellate division clerk finds the list correct, the clerk must sign and return one copy to the party.

(Subd (d) adopted effective January 1, 2009.)

(e) Return by appellate division

On request, the appellate division may return an exhibit to the trial court or to the party that sent it. When the remittitur issues, the appellate division must return all exhibits to the trial court or to the party that sent them.

(Subd (e) adopted effective January 1, 2009.)

Rule 8.921 adopted effective January 1, 2009.

Rule 8.922.   Sending and filing the record in the appellate division

(a) When the record is complete

(1) If the appellant elected under rule 8.915 to proceed without a record of the oral proceedings in the trial court, the record is complete when the clerk's transcript is certified as correct or, if the original trial court file will be used instead of the clerk's transcript, when that original file is ready for transmission as provided under rule 8.914(b).

(2) If the appellant elected under rule 8.915 to proceed with a record of the oral proceedings in the trial court, the record is complete when the clerk's transcript is certified as correct or the original file is ready for transmission as provided in (1) and:

(A) If the appellant elected to use a reporter's transcript, the certified reporter's transcript is delivered to the court under rule 8.919;

(B) If the appellant elected to use a transcript prepared from an official electronic recording, the transcript has been prepared under rule 8.917;

(C) If the parties stipulated to the use of an official electronic recording of the proceedings, the electronic recording has been prepared under rule 8.917; or

(D) If the appellant elected to use a statement on appeal, the statement on appeal has been certified by the trial court or a transcript or copy of an official electronic recording has been prepared under rule 8.916(d)(6).

(Subd (a) adopted effective January 1, 2009.)

(b) Sending the record

When the record is complete, the clerk must promptly send:

(1) The original record to the appellate division;

(2) One copy of the clerk's transcript or index to the original court file and one copy of any record of the oral proceedings to each appellant who is represented by separate counsel or is self-represented;

(3) If the defendant is the appellant, one copy of the clerk's transcript or index to the original court file and one copy of any record of the oral proceedings to the prosecuting attorney unless the prosecuting attorney has notified the court under rule 8.911 that he or she does not want to receive the record; and

(4) If the People are the appellant, a copy of the clerk's transcript or index to the original court file and one copy of any record of the oral proceedings to the respondent.

(Subd (b) adopted effective January 1, 2009.)

(c) Filing the record

On receipt, the appellate division clerk must promptly file the original record and mail notice of the filing date to the parties.

(Subd (c) adopted effective January 1, 2009.)

Rule 8.922 adopted effective January 1, 2009.

Rule 8.923.   Augmenting or correcting the record in the appellate division

(a) Subsequent trial court orders

If, after the record is certified, the trial court amends or recalls the judgment or makes any other order in the case, including an order affecting the sentence or probation, the clerk must promptly certify and send a copy of the amended abstract of judgment or other order as an augmentation of the record to all those who received the record under rule 8.872(b). If there is any additional document or transcript related to the amended judgment or new order that any rule or order requires be included in the record, the clerk must send these documents or transcripts with the amended abstract of judgment or other order. The clerk must promptly copy and certify any such document and the reporter must promptly prepare and certify any such transcript.

(Subd (a) adopted effective January 1, 2009.)

(b) Omissions

If, after the record is certified, the trial court clerk or the reporter learns that the record omits a document or transcript that any rule or order requires to be included, the clerk must promptly copy and certify the document or the reporter must promptly prepare and certify the transcript. Without the need for a court order, the clerk must promptly send the document or transcript as an augmen-

tation of the record to all those who received the record under rule 8.922(b).

(Subd (b) adopted effective January 1, 2009.)

(c) Augmentation or correction by the appellate division

At any time, on motion of a party or on its own motion, the appellate division may order the record augmented or corrected as provided in rule 8.841.

(Subd (c) adopted effective January 1, 2009.)

Rule 8.923 adopted effective January 1, 2009.

Article 3
Briefs, Hearing, and Decision in Infraction Appeals

Article 3 adopted effective January 1, 2009.

Rule 8.925. General application of chapter 4
Rule 8.926. Notice of briefing schedule
Rule 8.927. Briefs
Rule 8.928. Contents and form of briefs
Rule 8.929. Oral argument

Rule 8.925.   General application of chapter 4

Except as provided in this article, rules 8.880–8.890 govern briefs, hearing, and decision in the appellate division in infraction cases.

Rule 8.925 adopted effective January 1, 2009.

Rule 8.926.   Notice of briefing schedule

When the record is filed, the clerk of the appellate division must promptly mail, to each appellate counsel or unrepresented party, a notice giving the dates the briefs are due.

Rule 8.926 adopted effective January 1, 2009.

Rule 8.927.   Briefs

(a) Time to file briefs

(1) The appellant must serve and file an appellant's opening brief within 30 days after the record is filed in the appellate division.

(2) Any respondent's brief must be served and filed within 30 days after the appellant files its opening brief.

(3) Any appellant's reply brief must be served and filed within 20 days after the respondent files its brief.

(4) No other brief may be filed except with the permission of the presiding judge.

(5) Instead of filing a brief, or as part of its brief, a party may join in a brief or adopt by reference all or part of a brief in the same or a related appeal.

(Subd (a) adopted effective January 1, 2009.)

(b) Failure to file a brief

(1) If the appellant fails to timely file an opening brief, the appellate division clerk must promptly notify the appellant by mail that the brief must be filed within 20 days after the notice is mailed and that if the appellant fails to comply, the court may dismiss the appeal.

(2) If the respondent is the defendant and the respondent fails to timely file a brief, the appellate division clerk must promptly notify the respondent by mail that the brief must be filed within 20 days after the notice is mailed and that if the respondent fails to comply, the court will decide

the appeal on the record, the appellant's opening brief, and any oral argument by the appellant.

(3) If a party fails to comply with a notice under (1) or (2), the court may impose the sanction specified in the notice.

(Subd (b) adopted effective January 1, 2009.)

(c) Service and filing

(1) Copies of each brief must be served as required by rule 8.25.

(2) Unless the appellate division provides otherwise by local rule or order in the specific case, only the original brief, with proof of service, must be filed in the appellate division.

(3) A copy of each brief must be served on the trial court clerk for delivery to the judge who tried the case.

(4) A copy of each brief must be served on a public officer or agency when required by rule 8.29.

(Subd (c) adopted effective January 1, 2009.)
Rule 8.927 adopted effective January 1, 2009.

Rule 8.928.   Contents and form of briefs

(a) Contents

(1) Each brief must:

(A) State each point under a separate heading or subheading summarizing the point and support each point by argument and, if possible, by citation of authority; and

(B) Support any reference to a matter in the record by a citation to the volume and page number of the record where the matter appears.

(2) An appellant's opening brief must:

(A) State the nature of the action, the relief sought in the trial court, and the judgment or order appealed from;

(B) State that the judgment appealed from is final or explain why the order appealed from is appealable; and

(C) Provide a summary of the significant facts limited to matters in the record.

(Subd (a) adopted effective January 1, 2009.)

(b) Length

(1) A brief produced on a computer must not exceed 5,100 words, including footnotes. Such a brief must include a certificate by appellate counsel or an unrepresented party stating the number of words in the brief. The person certifying may rely on the word count of the computer program used to prepare the brief.

(2) A brief produced on a typewriter must not exceed 15 pages.

(3) The certificate under (1) and any attachment under (d) are excluded from the limits stated in (1) or (2).

(4) On application, the presiding judge may permit a longer brief for good cause. A lengthy record or numerous or complex issues on appeal will ordinarily constitute good cause.

(Subd (b) adopted effective January 1, 2009.)

(c) Form

(1) A brief may be reproduced by any process that produces a clear, black image of letter quality. The paper must be white or unbleached, recycled, 8½ by 11 inches, and of at least 20-pound weight. Both sides of the paper may be used if the brief is not bound at the top.

(2) Any conventional typeface may be used. The typeface may be either proportionally spaced or monospaced.

(3) The type style must be roman; but for emphasis, italics or boldface may be used or the text may be underscored. Case names must be italicized or underscored. Headings may be in uppercase letters.

(4) Except as provided in (10), the type size, including footnotes, must not be smaller than 13-point.

(5) The lines of text must be unnumbered and at least one-and-a-half-spaced. Headings and footnotes may be single-spaced. Quotations may be block-indented and single-spaced. Single-spaced means six lines to a vertical inch.

(6) The margins must be at least 1½ inches on the left and right and 1 inch on the top and bottom.

(7) The pages must be consecutively numbered.

(8) The brief must be bound on the left margin, except that briefs may be bound at the top if required by a local rule of the appellate division. If the brief is stapled, the bound edge and staples must be covered with tape.

(9) The brief need not be signed.

(10) If the brief is produced on a typewriter:

(A) A typewritten original and carbon copies may be filed only with the presiding justice's permission, which will ordinarily be given only to unrepresented parties proceeding in forma pauperis. All other typewritten briefs must be filed as photocopies.

(B) Both sides of the paper may be used if a photocopy is filed; only one side may be used if a typewritten original and carbon copies are filed.

(C) The type size, including footnotes, must not be smaller than standard pica, 10 characters per inch. Unrepresented incarcerated litigants may use elite type, 12 characters per inch, if they lack access to a typewriter with larger characters.

(Subd (c) adopted effective January 1, 2009.)

(d) Noncomplying briefs

If a brief does not comply with this rule:

(1) The reviewing court clerk may decline to file it, but must mark it "received but not filed" and return it to the party; or

(2) If the brief is filed, the presiding judge may with or without notice:

(A) Order the brief returned for corrections and refiling within a specified time;

(B) Strike the brief with leave to file a new brief within a specified time; or

(C) Disregard the noncompliance.

(Subd (d) adopted effective January 1, 2009.)
Rule 8.928 adopted effective January 1, 2009.

Rule 8.929.   Oral argument

(a) Calendaring and sessions

Unless otherwise ordered, all appeals in which the last reply brief was filed or the time for filing this brief expired 45 or more days before the date of a regular appellate division session must be placed on the calendar for that session by the appellate division clerk. By order of the presiding judge or the appellate division, any appeal may be placed on the calendar for oral argument at any session.

(Subd (a) adopted effective January 1, 2009.)

(b) Notice of argument

As soon as all parties' briefs are filed or the time for filing these briefs has expired, the appellate division clerk must send a notice of the time and place of oral argument to all parties. The notice must be sent at least 20 days before the date for oral argument. The presiding judge may shorten the notice period for good cause; in that event, the clerk must immediately notify the parties by telephone or other expeditious method.

(Subd (b) adopted effective January 1, 2009.)

(c) Waiver of argument

Parties may waive oral argument.

(Subd (c) adopted effective January 1, 2009.)

(d) Conduct of argument

Unless the court provides otherwise:

(1) The appellant, petitioner, or moving party has the right to open and close. If there are two or more such parties, the court must set the sequence of argument.

(2) Each side is allowed 5 minutes for argument. If multiple parties are represented by separate counsel, or if an amicus curiae—on written request—is granted permission to argue, the court may apportion or expand the time.

(3) Only one counsel may argue for each separately represented party.

(Subd (d) adopted effective January 1, 2009.)
Rule 8.929 adopted effective January 1, 2009.

Advisory Committee Comment

Subdivision (a). Under rule 10.1108, the appellate division must hold a session at least once each quarter, unless no matters are set for oral argument that quarter, but may choose to hold sessions more frequently.

Chapter 6
Writ Proceedings

Chapter 6 adopted effective January 1, 2009.

Rule 8.930. Application
Rule 8.931. Petitions filed by persons not represented by an attorney
Rule 8.932. Petitions filed by an attorney for a party
Rule 8.933. Opposition
Rule 8.934. Notice to trial court
Rule 8.935. Finality and remittitur
Rule 8.936. Costs

Rule 8.930. Application

(a) Writ proceedings governed

Except as provided in (b), the rules in this chapter govern proceedings in the appellate division for writs of mandate, certiorari, or prohibition, or other writs within the original jurisdiction of the appellate division. In all respects not provided for in this chapter, rule 8.883, regarding the form and content of briefs, applies.

(Subd (a) adopted effective January 1, 2009.)

(b) Writ proceedings not governed

The rules in this chapter do not apply to petitions for writs of supersedeas under rule 8.824 or writs not within the original jurisdiction of the appellate division.

(Subd (b) adopted effective January 1, 2009.)
Rule 8.930 adopted effective January 1, 2009.

Advisory Committee Comment

Information on Writ Proceedings in Misdemeanor, Infraction, and Limited Civil Cases (form APP-150-INFO) provides additional information about proceedings for writs in the appellate

division of the superior court. This form at is available at any courthouse or county law library or online at *www.courtinfo.ca.gov/forms.*

Subdivision (b). The superior courts, not the appellate divisions, have original jurisdiction in habeas corpus proceedings (see Cal. Const., art. VI, § 10). Habeas corpus proceedings in the superior courts are governed by rules 4.550 et seq.

Rule 8.931. Petitions filed by persons not represented by an attorney

(a) Petitions

A person who is not represented by an attorney and who petitions the appellate division for a writ under this chapter must file the petition on *Petition for Writ (Misdemeanor, Infraction, or Limited Civil Case)* (form APP-151). For good cause the court may permit an unrepresented party to file a petition that is not on form APP-151.

(Subd (a) adopted effective January 1, 2009.)

(b) Contents of supporting documents

(1) The petition must be accompanied by an adequate record, including copies of:

(A) The ruling from which the petition seeks relief;

(B) All documents and exhibits submitted to the trial court supporting and opposing the petitioner's position;

(C) Any other documents or portions of documents submitted to the trial court that are necessary for a complete understanding of the case and the ruling under review; and

(D) A reporter's transcript or electronic recording of the oral proceedings that resulted in the ruling under review.

(2) In extraordinary circumstances, the petition may be filed without the documents required by (1)(A)–(C) if the petitioner files a declaration that explains the urgency and the circumstances making the documents unavailable and fairly summarizes their substance.

(3) If a transcript or electronic recording under (1)(D) is unavailable, the record must include a declaration by [1] the petitioner:

(A) Explaining why the transcript or electronic recording is unavailable and fairly summarizing the proceedings, including the petitioner's arguments and any statement by the court supporting its ruling. **This declaration may omit a full summary of the proceedings if part of the relief sought is an order to prepare a transcript for use by an indigent criminal defendant in support of the petition and if the declaration demonstrates the petitioner's need for and entitlement to the transcript**; or

(B) Stating that the transcript or electronic recording has been ordered, the date it was ordered, and the date it is expected to be filed, which must be a date before any action requested of the appellate division other than issuance of a temporary stay supported by other parts of the record.

[2] **(4)** If the petitioner does not submit the required record or explanations or does not present facts sufficient to excuse the failure to submit them, the court may summarily deny a stay request, the petition, or both.

(Subd (b) amended effective January 1, 2009; adopted effective January 1, 2009.)

Rule 8.931(b).   2008 Deletes. [1] counsel or, if the petitioner is unrepresented, by [2] (3) A declaration under (2) may omit a full summary of the proceedings if part of the relief sought is an order to prepare a transcript for use by an indigent criminal defendant in support of the petition and if the declaration demonstrates the petitioner's need for and entitlement to the transcript. (4) In extraordinary circumstances, the petition may be filed without the documents required by (1)(A)–(C) if counsel or, if the petitioner is unrepresented, the petitioner files a declaration that explains the urgency and the circumstances making the documents unavailable and fairly summarizes their substance. (5)

(c) Form of supporting documents

(1) Documents submitted under (b) must comply with the following requirements:

(A) They must be bound together at the end of the petition or in separate volumes not exceeding 300 pages each. The pages must be consecutively numbered.

(B) They must be index-tabbed by number or letter.

(C) They must begin with a table of contents listing each document by its title and its index-tab number or letter. If a document has attachments, the table of contents must give the title of each attachment and a brief description of its contents.

(2) The clerk must file any supporting documents not complying with (1), but the court may notify the petitioner that it may strike or summarily deny the petition if the documents are not brought into compliance within a stated reasonable time of not less than five days.

(3) Unless the court orders otherwise by local rule or in the specific case, only one set of any separately bound supporting documents needs to be filed in support of a petition, answer, opposition, or reply.

(Subd (c) adopted effective January 1, 2009.)

(d) Service

(1) The petition and one set of supporting documents must be served on any named real party in interest, but only the petition must be served on the respondent.

(2) The proof of service must give the telephone number of each attorney or unrepresented party served.

(3) The petition must be served on a public officer or agency when required by statute or rule 8.29.

(4) The clerk must file the petition even if its proof of service is defective, but if the petitioner fails to file a corrected proof of service within five days after the clerk gives notice of the defect the court may strike the petition or impose a lesser sanction.

(5) The court may allow the petition to be filed without proof of service.

(Subd (d) adopted effective January 1, 2009.)
Rule 8.931 amended effective January 1, 2009; adopted effective January 1, 2009.

Advisory Committee Comment

Subdivision (a). *Petition for Writ (Misdemeanor, Infraction, or Limited Civil Case)* (form APP-151) is available at any courthouse or county law library or online at *www.courtinfo.ca.gov/ forms.*

Subdivision (d). Rule 8.25, which generally governs service and filing in appellate divisions, also applies to the original proceedings covered by this rule.

Rule 8.932. Petitions filed by an attorney for a party

(a) General application of rule 8.931

Except as provided in this rule, rule 8.931 applies to any petition for an extraordinary writ filed by an attorney.

(Subd (a) adopted effective January 1, 2009.)

(b) Form and content of petition

(1) A petition for an extraordinary writ filed by an attorney may, but is not required to be, filed on *Petition for Writ (Misdemeanor, Infraction, or Limited Civil Case)* (form APP-151).

(2) The petition must disclose the name of any real party in interest.

(3) If the petition seeks review of trial court proceedings that are also the subject of a pending appeal, the notice "Related Appeal Pending" must appear on the cover of the petition, and the first paragraph of the petition must state the appeal's title and any appellate division docket number.

(4) The petition must be verified.

(5) The petition must be accompanied by a memorandum, which need not repeat facts alleged in the petition.

(6) Rule 8.883(b) governs the length of the petition and memorandum, but the verification and any supporting documents are excluded from the limits stated in rule 8.883(b)(1) and (2).

(7) If the petition requests a temporary stay, it must explain the urgency.

(Subd (b) adopted effective January 1, 2009.)
Rule 8.932 adopted effective January 1, 2009.

Rule 8.933. Opposition

(a) Preliminary opposition

(1) Within 10 days after the petition is filed, the respondent or any real party in interest, separately or jointly, may serve and file a preliminary opposition.

(2) An opposition must contain a memorandum and a statement of any material fact not included in the petition.

(3) Within 10 days after an opposition is filed, the petitioner may serve and file a reply.

(4) Without requesting opposition or waiting for a reply, the court may grant or deny a request for temporary stay, deny the petition, issue an alternative writ or order to show cause, or notify the parties that it is considering issuing a peremptory writ in the first instance.

(Subd (a) adopted effective January 1, 2009.)

(b) Return or opposition; reply

(1) If the court issues an alternative writ or order to show cause, the respondent or any real party in interest, separately or jointly, may serve and file a return by demurrer, verified answer, or both. If the court notifies the parties that it is considering issuing a peremptory writ in the first instance, the respondent or any real party in interest may serve and file an opposition.

(2) Unless the court orders otherwise, the return or opposition must be served and filed within 30 days after the court issues the alternative writ or order to show cause or notifies the parties that it is considering issuing a peremptory writ in the first instance.

(3) Unless the court orders otherwise, the petitioner may serve and file a reply within 15 days after the return or opposition is filed.

(4) If the return is by demurrer alone and the demurrer is not sustained, the court may issue the peremptory writ without granting leave to answer.

(Subd (b) adopted effective January 1, 2009.)

Rule 8.933 adopted effective January 1, 2009.

Rule 8.934.   Notice to trial court
(a) Notice if writ issues
If a writ or order issues directed to any judge, court, or other officer, the appellate division clerk must promptly send a certified copy of the writ or order to the person or entity to whom it is directed.

(Subd (a) adopted effective January 1, 2009.)

(b) Notice by telephone
(1) If the writ or order stays or prohibits proceedings set to occur within seven days or requires action within seven days—or in any other urgent situation—the appellate division clerk must make a reasonable effort to notify the clerk of the respondent court by telephone. The clerk of the respondent court must then notify the judge or officer most directly concerned.

(2) The clerk need not give notice by telephone of the summary denial of a writ, whether or not a stay previously issued.

(Subd (b) adopted effective January 1, 2009.)
Rule 8.934 adopted effective January 1, 2009.

Rule 8.935.   Finality and remittitur
(a) Finality of decision
(1) Except as otherwise provided in this rule, an appellate division decision in a writ proceeding is final 30 days after the decision is filed.

(2) The denial of a petition for a writ within the appellate division's original jurisdiction without issuance of an alternative writ or order to show cause is final in that court when filed.

(3) If necessary to prevent mootness or frustration of the relief granted or to otherwise promote the interests of justice, an appellate division may order early finality in that court of a decision granting a petition for a writ within its original jurisdiction or denying such a petition after issuing an alternative writ or order to show cause. The decision may provide for finality in that court on filing or within a stated period of less than 30 days.

(Subd (a) adopted effective January 1, 2009.)

(b) Remittitur
The appellate division must issue a remittitur after a decision in a writ proceeding, except when the court denies a writ petition without issuing an alternative writ or order to show cause. Rule 8.890 governs issuance of a remittitur in these proceedings.

(Subd (b) adopted effective January 1, 2009.)
Rule 8.935 adopted effective January 1, 2009.

Rule 8.936.   Costs
(a) Entitlement to costs
Except in a criminal proceeding or other proceeding in which a party is entitled to court-appointed counsel, the prevailing party in an original proceeding is entitled to costs if the court resolves the proceeding after issuing an alternative writ, an order to show cause, or a peremptory writ in the first instance.

(Subd (a) adopted effective January 1, 2009.)

(b) Award of costs
(1) In the interests of justice, the court may award or deny costs as it deems proper.

(2) The opinion or order resolving the proceeding must specify the award or denial of costs.

(3) Rule 8.891(b)–(d) governs the procedure for recovering costs under this rule.

(Subd (b) adopted effective January 1, 2009.)
Rule 8.936 adopted effective January 1, 2009.

Division 3
Trial of Small Claims Cases on Appeal

Rule 8.950. Application
Rule 8.952. Definitions
Rule 8.954. Filing the appeal
Rule 8.957. Record on appeal
Rule 8.960. Continuances
Rule 8.963. Abandonment, dismissal, and judgment for failure to bring to trial
Rule 8.966. Examination of witnesses

Rule 8.950.   Application
The rules in this division supplement article 7 of the Small Claims Act, Code of Civil Procedure sections 116.710 et seq., providing for new trials of small claims cases on appeal, and must be read in conjunction with those statutes.

Rule 8.950 renumbered effective January 1, 2009; adopted as rule 151 effective July 1, 1964; previously amended effective January 1, 1977, and January 1, 2005; previously amended and renumbered as rule 8.900 effective January 1, 2007.

Ref.: Cal. Fms Pl. & Pr., Ch. 526, "Small Claims."

Rule 8.952.   Definitions
The definitions in rule 1.6 apply to these rules unless the context or subject matter requires otherwise. In addition, the following definitions apply to these rules:

(1) "Small claims court" means the trial court from which the appeal is taken.

(2) "Appeal" means a new trial before a different judge on all claims, whether or not appealed.

(3) "Appellant" means the party appealing; "respondent" means the adverse party. "Plaintiff" and "defendant" refer to the parties as they were designated in the small claims court.

Rule 8.952 renumbered effective January 1, 2009; adopted as rule 158 effective July 1, 1964; previously amended and renumbered as rule 156 effective July 1, 1991; previously amended effective January 1, 2005; previously amended and renumbered as rule 8.902 effective January 1, 2007.

Rule 8.954.   Filing the appeal
(a) Notice of appeal
To appeal from a judgment in a small claims case, an appellant must file a notice of appeal in the small claims court. The appellant or the appellant's attorney must sign the notice. The notice is sufficient if it states in substance that the appellant appeals from a specified judgment or, in the case of a defaulting defendant, from the denial of a motion to vacate the judgment. A notice of appeal must be liberally construed.

(Subd (a) amended effective January 1, 2007; previously amended effective July 1, 1973, January 1, 1977, January 1, 1979, January 1, 1984, July 1, 1991, and January 1, 2005.)

(b) Notification by clerk

(1) The clerk of the small claims court must promptly mail a notification of the filing of the notice of appeal to each other party at the party's last known address.

(2) The notification must state the number and title of the case and the date the notice of appeal was filed. If a party dies before the clerk mails the notification, the mailing is a sufficient performance of the clerk's duty.

(3) A failure of the clerk to give notice of the judgment or notification of the filing of the notice of appeal does not extend the time for filing the notice of appeal or affect the validity of the appeal.

(Subd (b) amended effective January 1, 2007; previously amended and relettered effective January 1, 1977; previously amended effective July 1, 1991, and January 1, 2005.)

(c) Premature notice of appeal

A notice of appeal filed after judgment is rendered but before it is entered is valid and is treated as filed immediately after entry. A notice of appeal filed after the judge has announced an intended ruling but before judgment is rendered may, in the discretion of the reviewing court be treated as filed immediately after entry of the judgment.

(Subd (c) amended effective January 1, 2007; adopted as subd (d) effective July 1, 1964; relettered effective January 1, 1977; previously amended effective July 1, 1991, and January 1, 2005.) Rule 8.954 renumbered effective January 1, 2009; adopted as rule 152 effective July 1, 1964; previously amended effective July 1, 1973, January 1, 1977, January 1, 1979, January 1, 1984, July 1, 1991, and January 1, 2005; previously amended and renumbered as rule 8.904 effective January 1, 2007.

Ref.: Cal. Fms Pl. & Pr., Ch. 526, "Small Claims."

Rule 8.957.   Record on appeal

Within five days after the filing of the notice of appeal and the payment of any fees required by law, the clerk of the small claims court must transmit the file and all related papers, including the notice of appeal, to the clerk of the court assigned to hear the appeal.

Rule 8.957 renumbered effective January 1, 2009; adopted as rule 153 effective July 1, 1964; previously amended effective July 1, 1972, July 1, 1973, January 1, 1977, and January 1, 2005; previously amended and renumbered as rule 8.907 effective January 1, 2007.

Ref.: Cal. Fms Pl. & Pr., Ch. 526, "Small Claims."

Rule 8.960.   Continuances

For good cause, the court assigned to hear the appeal may continue the trial. A request for a continuance may be presented by one party or by stipulation. The court may grant a continuance not to exceed 30 days, but in a case of extreme hardship the court may grant a continuance exceeding 30 days.

Rule 8.960 renumbered effective January 1, 2009; adopted as rule 154 effective July 1, 1964; previously amended effective January 1, 1977, July 1, 1991, and January 1, 2005; previously renumbered as rule 8.910 effective January 1, 2007.

Ref.: Cal. Fms Pl. & Pr., Ch. 526, "Small Claims."

Rule 8.963.   Abandonment, dismissal, and judgment for failure to bring to trial

(a) Before the record is filed

Before the record has been transmitted to the court assigned to hear the appeal, the appellant may file in the small claims court an abandonment of the appeal or a stipulation to abandon the appeal. Either filing operates to dismiss the appeal and return the case to the small claims court.

(Subd (a) amended effective January 1, 2007; previously amended effective July 1, 1972, January 1, 1977, and January 1, 2005.)

(b) After the record is filed

After the record has been transmitted to the court assigned to hear the appeal, the court may dismiss the appeal on the appellant's written request or the parties' stipulation filed in that court.

(Subd (b) amended effective January 1, 2007; previously amended effective January 1, 2005.)

(c) Dismissal or judgment by the court

(1) The court must dismiss the appeal if the case is not brought to trial within one year after the date of filing the appeal. If a new trial is ordered, the court must dismiss the appeal if the case is not brought to trial within one year after the entry date of the new trial order.

(2) Notwithstanding (1), the court must not order dismissal or enter judgment if there was in effect a written stipulation extending the time for trial or on a showing that the appellant exercised reasonable diligence to bring the case to trial.

(3) Notwithstanding (1) and (2), the court must dismiss the appeal if the case is not brought to trial within three years after either the notice of appeal is filed or the most recent new trial order is entered in the court assigned to hear the appeal.

(Subd (c) amended effective January 1, 2007; previously amended effective January 1, 1977, July 1, 1991, and January 1, 2005.)

(d) Notification by clerk

If an appellant files an abandonment, the clerk of the court in which it is filed must immediately notify the adverse party of the filing. The clerk of the court assigned to hear the appeal must immediately notify the parties of any order of dismissal or any judgment for defendant made by the court under (c).

(Subd (d) amended effective January 1, 2007; previously amended effective January 1, 2005.)

(e) Return of papers

If an appeal is dismissed, the clerk of the court assigned to hear the appeal must promptly transmit to the small claims court a copy of the dismissal order and all original papers and exhibits sent to the court assigned to hear the appeal. The small claims court must then proceed with the case as if no appeal had been taken.

(Subd (e) amended effective January 1, 2007; previously amended effective January 1, 2005.)

(f) Approval of compromise

If a guardian or conservator seeks approval of a proposed compromise of a pending appeal in which a new trial has been ordered, the court assigned to hear the appeal may, before ruling on the compromise, hear and determine whether the proposed compromise is for the best interest of the ward or conservatee.

(Subd (f) amended effective January 1, 2007; previously amended effective January 1, 2005.)

Rule 8.963 renumbered effective January 1, 2009; adopted as rule 157 effective July 1, 1964; amended and renumbered as rule 155 effective July 1, 1991; previously amended effective January 1, 1972, July 1, 1972, and January 1, 2005; previously amended and renumbered as rule 8.913 effective January 1, 2007.

Ref.: Cal. Fms Pl. & Pr., Ch. 526, "Small Claims."

Rule 8.966. Examination of witnesses

The court may allow parties or attorneys representing parties to the appeal to conduct direct and cross-examination, subject to the court's discretion to control the manner, mode, and duration of examination in keeping with informality and the circumstances.

Rule 8.966 renumbered effective January 1, 2009; adopted as rule 157 effective July 1, 1999; previously amended and renumbered as rule 8.916 effective January 1, 2007.

Ref.: Cal. Fms Pl. & Pr., Ch. 526, "Small Claims."

Division 4
Transfer of Appellate Division Cases to the Court of Appeal

Rule 8.1000. Application
Rule 8.1002. Transfer authority
Rule 8.1005. Certification
Rule 8.1008. Transfer
Rule 8.1010. Record on transfer
Rule 8.1012. Briefs
Rule 8.1014. Proceedings in the appellate division after certification
Rule 8.1016. Disposition of transferred case
Rule 8.1018. Finality and remittitur

Rule 8.1000.   Application

Rules 8.1000–8.1018 apply to proceedings for transferring cases within the appellate jurisdiction of the superior court—other than appeals in small claims cases—to the Court of Appeal for review. Unless the context requires otherwise, the term "case" as used in these rules means cases within that jurisdiction.

Rule 8.1000 amended and renumbered effective January 1, 2007; repealed and adopted as rule 61 effective January 1, 2003.

Ref.: MB Prac. Guide: Cal. Pretrial Proc., §10.04[3].

Rule 8.1002.   Transfer authority

A Court of Appeal may order a case transferred to it for hearing and decision if the appellate division certifies under rule 8.1005—or the Court of Appeal determines under rule 8.1008—that transfer is necessary to secure uniformity of decision or to settle an important question of law.

Rule 8.1002 amended and renumbered effective January 1, 2007; repealed and adopted as rule 62 effective January 1, 2003.

Ref.: Cal. Fms Pl. & Pr., Ch. 324, "Jurisdiction: Subject Matter Jurisdiction," Ch. 345A, "Limited Civil Cases."

Rule 8.1005.   Certification

(a) Authority to certify

(1) The appellate division may certify a case for transfer to the Court of Appeal on its own motion or on a party's application.

(2) A case may be certified by a majority of the appellate division judges to whom the case has been assigned or who decided the appeal or, if the case has not yet been assigned, by any two appellate division judges. If an assigned or deciding judge is unable to act on the certification, a judge designated or assigned to the appellate division by the chair of the Judicial Council may act in that judge's place.

(Subd (a) amended effective January 1, 2007.)

(b) Application for certification

(1) A party may serve and file an application for certification at any time after the record on appeal is filed in the appellate division and within 15 days after judgment is pronounced or a modification order changing the appellate judgment is filed. The party may include the application in a petition for rehearing.

(2) The application must explain why transfer is necessary to secure uniformity of decision or to settle an important question of law.

(3) Within five days after the application is filed, any other party may serve and file an opposition.

(4) No hearing will be held on the application. Failure to certify the case is deemed a denial of the application.

(c) Finality of appellate division judgments

An appellate division judgment is final in that court as provided in rule 8.708.

(Subd (c) amended effective January 1, 2007.)

(d) Time to certify

A case may be certified at any time after the record on appeal is filed in the appellate division and before the appellate division judgment is final in that court.

(e) Contents of certification

A certification must:

(1) Briefly describe any conflict of decision—citing the decisions creating the conflict—or important question of law to be settled; and

(2) State whether there was a judgment on appeal and, if so, its date and disposition.

(Subd (e) amended effective January 1, 2007.)

(f) Superior court clerk's duties

(1) If the appellate division orders certification, the clerk must promptly send a copy of the order to the Court of Appeal clerk, the parties, and, in a criminal case, the Attorney General.

(2) If the appellate division denies an application by order, the clerk must promptly send a copy to the parties.

Rule 8.1005 amended and renumbered effective January 1, 2007; repealed and adopted as rule 63 effective January 1, 2003.

Ref.: Cal. Fms Pl. & Pr., Ch. 42, "Appeal: Notice of Appeal," Ch. 46, "Appeal: Extending or Shortening Time," Ch. 324, "Jurisdiction: Subject Matter Jurisdiction," Ch. 345A, "Limited Civil Cases," Ch. 524, "Shortening and Extension of Time"; MB Prac. Guide: Cal. Pretrial Proc., §10.04[3].

Rule 8.1008.   Transfer

(a) Authority to transfer on Court of Appeal's own motion or a party's petition

The Court of Appeal may order transfer of a case on the court's own motion or on a party's petition to transfer.

(b) Petition to transfer

(1) If the appellate division denies an application for certification and does not certify its opinion for publication, a party may serve and file in the Court of Appeal a petition to transfer the case to that court.

(2) The petition must be served and filed within 15 days after the appellate division judgment is final in that court and must show delivery of a copy to the appellate division.

(3) The petition must explain why transfer is necessary to secure uniformity of opinion or to settle an important question of law.

(4) A party must not file an answer to a petition for transfer unless the court requests an answer. The clerk must promptly send to the parties copies of any order requesting an answer and immediately notify the parties by telephone or another expeditious method. Any answer must be served and filed within 10 days after the order is filed unless the court orders otherwise. A petition for transfer normally will not be granted unless the court has requested an answer.

(5) The petition and any answer must comply as nearly as possible with rule 8.504.

(Subd (b) amended effective January 1, 2008; previously amended effective July 1, 2003, and January 1, 2007.)

(c) Time to transfer

(1) The Court of Appeal may order transfer:

(A) After certification or on its own motion, within 20 days after the record on transfer is filed in the Court of Appeal; or

(B) On petition to transfer, within 20 days after the petition is filed.

(2) Within either period specified in (1), the Court of Appeal may order an extension not exceeding 20 days.

(3) If the Court of Appeal does not timely order transfer, transfer is deemed denied.

(Subd (c) amended effective January 1, 2007.)

(d) Letter supporting or opposing transfer

(1) Except when a party files a petition to transfer under (b), any party may send the Court of Appeal a letter supporting or opposing transfer within 10 days after a record on transfer is filed in that court. The letter must be served on all other parties.

(2) The letter must be double-spaced and must not exceed 1,400 words if produced on a computer or five pages if typewritten.

(e) Limitation of issues

(1) On or after ordering transfer, the Court of Appeal may specify the issues to be briefed and argued. Unless the court orders otherwise, the parties must limit their briefs and arguments to those issues and any issues fairly included in those issues.

(2) Notwithstanding an order specifying issues under (1), the court may, on reasonable notice, order oral argument on fewer or additional issues or on the entire case.

(f) Court of Appeal clerk's duties

(1) When a transfer order is filed, the clerk must promptly send a copy to the superior court clerk, the parties, and, in a criminal case, the Attorney General.

(2) With the copy of the transfer order sent to the parties and the Attorney General, the clerk must send notice of the time to serve and file any briefs ordered under rule 8.1012 and, if specified by the Court of Appeal, the issues to be briefed and argued.

(3) If the court denies transfer after certification or petition, the clerk must return the record on transfer and any exhibits to the superior court clerk and promptly send notice of the denial to the parties and, in a criminal case, the Attorney General.

(4) Failure to send any order or notice under this subdivision does not affect the jurisdiction of the Court of Appeal.

(Subd (f) amended effective January 1, 2007.)

Rule 8.1008 amended effective January 1, 2008; repealed and adopted as rule 64 effective January 1, 2003; previously amended effective July 1, 2003; previously amended and renumbered effective January 1, 2007.

Ref.: Cal. Fms Pl. & Pr., Ch. 46, "Appeal: Extending or Shortening Time," Ch. 54, "Appeal: California Supreme Court Review," Ch. 345A, "Limited Civil Cases"; MB Prac. Guide: Cal. Pretrial Proc., §10.04[3].

Rule 8.1010. Record on transfer

(a) Contents

The record on transfer must contain:

(1) The original record on appeal prepared under rules 8.753–8.761 in a limited civil case or under rules 8.783–8.785 in a criminal case;

(2) Any briefs filed in the appellate division; and

(3) Any order or opinion of the appellate division.

(Subd (a) amended effective January 1, 2007.)

(b) Clerks' duties

(1) The superior court clerk must promptly send the record on transfer to the Court of Appeal and notify the parties that the record was sent when:

(A) The appellate division certifies a case;

(B) The superior court clerk sends a copy of an appellate division opinion certified for publication to the Court of Appeal under rule 8.707;

(C) The superior court clerk receives a copy of a petition to transfer; or

(D) The superior court receives a request from the Court of Appeal for the record on transfer.

(2) The Court of Appeal clerk must promptly notify the parties when the record on transfer is filed.

(Subd (b) amended effective January 1, 2007.)

Rule 8.1010 amended and renumbered effective January 1, 2007; repealed and adopted as rule 65 effective January 1, 2003.

Ref.: Cal. Fms Pl. & Pr., Ch. 345A, "Limited Civil Cases."

Rule 8.1012. Briefs

(a) Who may file

(1) After transfer, the parties may file briefs in the Court of Appeal only if ordered on a party's application or the court's own motion. The court must prescribe the briefing sequence in any briefing order.

(2) Instead of filing a brief, or as part of its brief, a party may join in or adopt by reference all or part of a brief in the same or a related case.

(b) Time to file

(1) The opening brief must be served and filed within 20 days after entry of the briefing order.

(2) The responding brief must be served and filed within 20 days after the opening brief is filed.

(3) Any reply brief must be served and filed within 10 days after the responding brief is filed.

(c) Additional service requirements

(1) Any brief of a defendant in a criminal case must be served on the prosecuting attorney and the Attorney General.

(2) Every brief must show delivery of a copy to the appellate division from which the case was transferred.

(d) Form

No brief may exceed 5,600 words if produced on a computer or 20 pages if typewritten. In all other respects briefs must comply with rule 8.204.

(Subd (d) amended effective January 1, 2007.)

Rule 8.1012 amended and renumbered effective January 1, 2007; repealed and adopted as rule 66 effective January 1, 2003.

Ref.: Cal. Fms Pl. & Pr., Ch. 345A, "Limited Civil Cases."

Rule 8.1014.   Proceedings in the appellate division after certification

When the appellate division certifies a case or the Court of Appeal orders transfer, further action by the appellate division is limited to preparing and sending the record until termination of the proceedings in the Court of Appeal.

Rule 8.1014 renumbered effective January 1, 2007; repealed and adopted as rule 67 effective January 1, 2003.

Ref.: Cal. Fms Pl. & Pr., Ch. 345A, "Limited Civil Cases."

Rule 8.1016.   Disposition of transferred case

(a) Decision on limited issues

The Court of Appeal may decide fewer than all the issues raised and may retransfer the case to the appellate division for decision on any remaining issues.

(b) Retransfer without decision

(1) The Court of Appeal may vacate a transfer order without decision and retransfer the case to the appellate division with or without directions to conduct further proceedings.

(2) If the appellate division pronounced judgment before transfer and the Court of Appeal directs no further proceedings, the judgment is final when the appellate division receives the order vacating transfer, and its clerk must promptly issue a remittitur.

(Subd (b) amended effective January 1, 2007.)

Rule 8.1016 amended and renumbered effective January 1, 2007; repealed and adopted as rule 68 effective January 1, 2003.

Ref.: Cal. Fms Pl. & Pr., Ch. 324, "Jurisdiction: Subject Matter Jurisdiction."

Rule 8.1018.   Finality and remittitur

(a) Finality

The denial of a transfer of a case from the appellate division of the superior court is final immediately.

(Subd (a) adopted effective January 1, 2009.)

(b) Court of Appeal remittitur

The Court of Appeal clerk must promptly issue a remittitur when a decision of the court is final. The clerk must address the remittitur to the appellate division and send that court two copies of the remittitur and two

file-stamped copies of the Court of Appeal opinion or order.

(Subd (b) relettered effective January 1, 2009; adopted as subd (a) effective January 1, 2003.)

(c) Appellate division remittitur

On receiving the Court of Appeal remittitur, the appellate division clerk must promptly issue a remittitur if there will be no further proceedings in that court.

(Subd (c) relettered effective January 1, 2009; adopted as subd (b) effective January 1, 2003.)

(d) Documents to be returned

Each reviewing court clerk must return all original records, documents, and exhibits with the remittitur but need not return any certification, transcripts on appeal, briefs, or notice of appeal.

(Subd (d) relettered effective January 1, 2009; adopted as subd (c) effective January 1, 2003.)

Rule 8.1018 amended effective January 1, 2009; repealed and adopted as rule 69 effective January 1, 2003; previously renumbered effective January 1, 2007.

Advisory Committee Comment

Subdivision (a). The finality of Court of Appeal decisions in appeals is generally addressed in rules 8.264 (civil appeals) and 8.366 (criminal appeals).

Ref.: Cal. Fms Pl. & Pr., Ch. 345A, "Limited Civil Cases"; MB Prac. Guide: Cal. Pretrial Proc., §10.04[3].

Division 5
Publication of Appellate Opinions

Rule 8.1100. Authority
Rule 8.1105. Publication of appellate opinions
Rule 8.1110. Partial publication
Rule 8.1115. Citation of opinions
Rule 8.1120. Requesting publication of unpublished opinions
Rule 8.1125. Requesting depublication of published opinions

Rule 8.1100.   Authority

The rules governing the publication of appellate opinions are adopted by the Supreme Court under section 14 of article VI of the California Constitution and published in the California Rules of Court at the direction of the Judicial Council.

Rule 8.1100 adopted effective January 1, 2007.

Rule 8.1105.   Publication of appellate opinions

(a) Supreme Court

All opinions of the Supreme Court are published in the Official Reports.

(b) Courts of Appeal and appellate divisions

Except as provided in [1] **(e)**, an opinion of a Court of Appeal or a superior court appellate division is published in the Official Reports if a majority of the rendering court certifies the opinion for publication before the decision is final in that court.

(Subd (b) amended effective July 23, 2008; adopted effective April 1, 2007.)

Rule 8.1105(b).   2008 Deletes. [1] (d)

(c) Standards for certification

An opinion of a Court of Appeal or a superior court appellate division — whether it affirms or reverses a trial court order or judgment — should be certified for publication in the Official Reports if the opinion:

(1) Establishes a new rule of law;

(2) Applies an existing rule of law to a set of facts significantly different from those stated in published opinions;

(3) Modifies, explains, or criticizes with reasons given, an existing rule of law;

(4) Advances a new interpretation, clarification, criticism, or construction of a provision of a constitution, statute, ordinance, or court rule;

(5) Addresses or creates an apparent conflict in the law;

(6) Involves a legal issue of continuing public interest;

(7) Makes a significant contribution to legal literature by reviewing either the development of a common law rule or the legislative or judicial history of a provision of a constitution, statute, or other written law;

(8) Invokes a previously overlooked rule of law, or reaffirms a principle of law not applied in a recently reported decision; or

(9) Is accompanied by a separate opinion concurring or dissenting on a legal issue, and publication of the majority and separate opinions would make a significant contribution to the development of the law.

(Subd (c) amended effective April 1, 2007; previously amended effective January 1, 2007.)

(d) Factors not to be considered

Factors such as the workload of the court, or the potential embarrassment of a litigant, lawyer, judge, or other person should not affect the determination of whether to publish an opinion.

(Subd (d) adopted effective April 1, 2007.)

(e) Changes in publication status

(1) Unless otherwise ordered under (2), an opinion is no longer considered published if the Supreme Court grants review or the rendering court grants rehearing.

(2) The Supreme Court may order that an opinion certified for publication is not to be published or that an opinion not certified is to be published. The Supreme Court may also order publication of an opinion, in whole or in part, at any time after granting review.

(Subd (e) relettered effective April 1, 2007; adopted as subd (d) effective January 1, 2005.)

(f) Editing

(1) Computer versions of all opinions of the Supreme Court and Courts of Appeal must be provided to the Reporter of Decisions on the day of filing. Opinions of superior court appellate divisions certified for publication must be provided as prescribed in rule 8.707.

(2) The Reporter of Decisions must edit opinions for publication as directed by the Supreme Court. The Reporter of Decisions must submit edited opinions to the courts for examination, correction, and approval before finalization for the Official Reports.

(Subd (f) relettered effective April 1, 2007; adopted as subd (e) effective January 1, 2005; previously amended effective January 1, 2007.)

Rule 8.1105 amended effective July 23, 2008; repealed and adopted as rule 976 effective January 1, 2005; previously
amended and renumbered effective January 1, 2007; previously amended effective April 1, 2007.

Ref.: Cal. Fms Pl. & Pr., Ch. 40, "Appeal: An Overview," Ch. 41, "Appeal: Review Standards and Appellate Rules of Law," Ch. 48, "Appeal: Abandonment, Dismissal, and Stipulated Reversal," Ch. 54, "Appeal: California Supreme Court Review," Ch. 362, "Mental Suffering and Emotional Distress," Ch. 417, "Points and Authorities."

Rule 8.1110. Partial publication

(a) Order for partial publication

A majority of the rendering court may certify for publication any part of an opinion meeting a standard for publication under rule 8.1105.

(Subd (a) amended effective January 1, 2007.)

(b) Opinion contents

The published part of the opinion must specify the part or parts not certified for publication. All material, factual and legal, including the disposition, that aids in the application or interpretation of the published part must be published.

(c) Construction

For purposes of rules 8.1105, 8.1115, and 8.1120, the published part of the opinion is treated as a published opinion and the unpublished part as an unpublished opinion.

(Subd (c) amended effective January 1, 2007.)

Rule 8.1110 amended and renumbered effective January 1, 2007; repealed and adopted as rule 976.1 effective January 1, 2005.

Ref.: Cal. Fms Pl. & Pr., Ch. 41, "Appeal: Review Standards and Appellate Rules of Law," Ch. 417, "Points and Authorities."

Rule 8.1115. Citation of opinions

(a) Unpublished opinion

Except as provided in (b), an opinion of a California Court of Appeal or superior court appellate division that is not certified for publication or ordered published must not be cited or relied on by a court or a party in any other action.

(b) Exceptions

An unpublished opinion may be cited or relied on:

(1) When the opinion is relevant under the doctrines of law of the case, res judicata, or collateral estoppel; or

(2) When the opinion is relevant to a criminal or disciplinary action because it states reasons for a decision affecting the same defendant or respondent in another such action.

(Subd (b) amended effective January 1, 2007.)

(c) Citation procedure

A copy of an opinion citable under (b) or of a cited opinion of any court that is available only in a computer-based source of decisional law must be furnished to the court and all parties by attaching it to the document in which it is cited or, if the citation will be made orally, by letter within a reasonable time in advance of citation.

(d) When a published opinion may be cited

A published California opinion may be cited or relied on as soon as it is certified for publication or ordered published.

Rule 8.1115 amended and renumbered effective January 1, 2007; repealed and adopted as rule 977 effective January 1, 2005.

Advisory Committee Comment

A footnote to a previous version of this rule stated that a citation to an opinion ordered published by the Supreme Court after grant of review should include a reference to the grant of review and to any subsequent Supreme Court action in the case. This footnote has been deleted because it was not part of the rule itself and the event it describes rarely occurs in practice.

Ref.: Cal. Fms Pl. & Pr., Ch. 40, "Appeal: An Overview," Ch. 41, "Appeal: Review Standards and Appellate Rules of Law," Ch. 45, "Appeal: Motion Procedure," Ch. 50, "Appeal: Briefs," Ch. 54, "Appeal: California Supreme Court Review," Ch. 321, "Judicial Notice," Ch. 358, "Mandate and Prohibition," Ch. 362, "Mental Suffering and Emotional Distress," Ch. 417, "Points and Authorities"; Cal. Class Actions Prac. & Proc., §15.02.

Rule 8.1120. Requesting publication of unpublished opinions

(a) Request

(1) Any person may request that an unpublished opinion be ordered published.

(2) The request must be made by a letter to the court that rendered the opinion, concisely stating the person's interest and the reason why the opinion meets a standard for publication.

(3) The request must be delivered to the rendering court within 20 days after the opinion is filed.

(4) The request must be served on all parties.

(b) Action by rendering court

(1) If the rendering court does not or cannot grant the request before the decision is final in that court, it must forward the request to the Supreme Court with a copy of its opinion, its recommendation for disposition, and a brief statement of its reasons. The rendering court must forward these materials within 15 days after the decision is final in that court.

(2) The rendering court must also send a copy of its recommendation and reasons to all parties and any person who requested publication.

(c) Action by Supreme Court

The Supreme Court may order the opinion published or deny the request. The court must send notice of its action to the rendering court, all parties, and any person who requested publication.

(d) Effect of Supreme Court order to publish

A Supreme Court order to publish is not an expression of the court's opinion of the correctness of the result of the decision or of any law stated in the opinion.

Rule 8.1120 renumbered effective January 1, 2007; repealed and adopted as rule 978 effective January 1, 2005.

Advisory Committee Comment

Subdivision (a). This rule previously required generally that a publication request be made "promptly," but in practice the term proved so vague that requests were often made after the Court of Appeal had lost jurisdiction. To assist persons intending to request publication and to give the Court of Appeal adequate time to act, this rule was revised to specify that the request must be made within 20 days after the opinion is filed. The change is substantive.

Subdivision (b). This rule previously did not specify the time within which the Court of Appeal was required to forward to the Supreme Court a publication request that it had not or could not have granted. In practice, however, it was not uncommon for the court to forward such a request after the Supreme Court had

denied a petition for review in the same case or, if there was no such petition, had lost jurisdiction to grant review on its own motion. To assist the Supreme Court in timely processing publication requests, therefore, this rule was revised to require the Court of Appeal to forward the request within 15 days after the decision is final in that court. The change is substantive.

Ref.: Cal. Fms Pl. & Pr., Ch. 40, "Appeal: An Overview," Ch. 41, "Appeal: Review Standards and Appellate Rules of Law," Ch. 45, "Appeal: Motion Procedure," Ch. 51, "Appeal: Hearing and Decision," Ch. 54, "Appeal: California Supreme Court Review," Ch. 417, "Points and Authorities."

Rule 8.1125. Requesting depublication of published opinions

(a) Request

(1) Any person may request the Supreme Court to order that an opinion certified for publication not be published.

(2) The request must not be made as part of a petition for review, but by a separate letter to the Supreme Court not exceeding 10 pages.

(3) The request must concisely state the person's interest and the reason why the opinion should not be published.

(4) The request must be delivered to the Supreme Court within 30 days after the decision is final in the Court of Appeal.

(5) The request must be served on the rendering court and all parties.

(b) Response

(1) Within 10 days after the Supreme Court receives a request under (a), the rendering court or any person may submit a response supporting or opposing the request. A response submitted by anyone other than the rendering court must state the person's interest.

(2) A response must not exceed 10 pages and must be served on the rendering court, all parties, and any person who requested depublication.

(c) Action by Supreme Court

(1) The Supreme Court may order the opinion depublished or deny the request. It must send notice of its action to the rendering court, all parties, and any person who requested depublication.

(2) The Supreme Court may order an opinion depublished on its own motion, notifying the rendering court of its action.

(d) Effect of Supreme Court order to depublish

A Supreme Court order to depublish is not an expression of the court's opinion of the correctness of the result of the decision or of any law stated in the opinion.

Rule 8.1125 renumbered effective January 1, 2007; repealed and adopted as rule 979 effective January 1, 2005.

Advisory Committee Comment

Subdivision (a). This subdivision previously required depublication requests to be made "by letter to the Supreme Court," but in practice many were incorporated in petitions for review. To clarify and emphasize the requirement, the subdivision was revised specifically to state that the request "must not be made as part of a petition for review, but by a separate letter to the Supreme Court not exceeding 10 pages." The change is not substantive.

Ref.: Cal. Fms Pl. & Pr., Ch. 40, "Appeal: An Overview," Ch. 41, "Appeal: Review Standards and Appellate Rules of Law," Ch.

45, "Appeal: Motion Procedure," Ch. 51, "Appeal: Hearing and Decision," Ch. 54, "Appeal: California Supreme Court Review," Ch. 417, "Points and Authorities."

TITLE 9
Rules On Law Practice, Attorneys, And Judges

Division 1. General Provisions. Rules 9.1, 9.2.

Division 2. Attorney Admission and Disciplinary Proceedings and Review of State Bar Proceedings. Rules 9.5–9.31.

Division 3. Legal Specialists. Rule 9.35.

Division 4. Appearances and Practice by Individuals Who Are Not Members of the State Bar of California. Rules 9.40–9.48.

Division 5. Censure, Removal, Retirement, or Private Admonishment of Judges. Rules 9.60, 9.61.

Division 1
General Provisions

Rule 9.1. Title
Rule 9.2. Source

Rule 9.1. Title
The rules in this title may be referred to as the Rules on Law Practice, Attorneys, and Judges.
Rule 9.1 adopted effective January 1, 2007.

Rule 9.2. Source
The rules in this title were adopted by the Supreme Court under its inherent authority over the admission and discipline of attorneys and under subdivisions (d) and (f) of section 18 of article VI of the Constitution of the State of California.
Rule 9.2 adopted effective January 1, 2007.

Division 2
Attorney Admission and Disciplinary Proceedings and Review of State Bar Proceedings

Chap. 1. General Provisions. Rules 9.5, 9.6.
Chap. 2. Attorney Disciplinary Proceedings. Rules 9.10–9.23.
Chap. 3. Legal Education. Rules 9.30, 9.31.

Chapter 1
General Provisions

Rule 9.5. Definitions
Rule 9.6. Roll of attorneys admitted to practice

Rule 9.5. Definitions
As used in this division, unless the context otherwise requires:
(1) "Member" means a member of the State Bar of California.

(2) "State Bar Court" means the Hearing Department or the Review Department established under Business and Professions Code sections 6079.1 and 6086.65.

(3) "Review Department" means the Review Department of the State Bar Court established under Business and Professions Code section 6086.65.

(4) "General Counsel" means the general counsel of the State Bar of California.

(5) "Chief Trial Counsel" means the chief trial counsel of the State Bar of California appointed under Business and Professions Code section 6079.5.
Rule 9.5 amended and renumbered effective January 1, 2007; adopted as rule 950 effective December 1, 1990.

Rule 9.6. Roll of attorneys admitted to practice
(a) State Bar to maintain the roll of attorneys
The State Bar must maintain, as part of the official membership records of the State Bar, the Roll of Attorneys of all persons admitted to practice in this state. Such records must include the information specified in Business and Professions Code section 6002.1 and 6064 and other information as directed by the Supreme Court.
(Subd (a) lettered effective June 1, 2007; adopted as unlettered subdivision effective May 1, 1996; previously amended effective January 1, 2007.)

(b) Annual State Bar recommendation for one-time expungement of suspension for nonpayment of membership fees
The State Bar is authorized to transmit to the Supreme Court on an annual basis the names of those members who meet all of the following criteria, along with a recommendation that their public record of suspension for nonpayment of membership fees be expunged:

(1) The member has not on any previous occasion obtained an expungement under the terms of this rule;

(2) The suspension was for 90 days or less;

(3) The suspension ended at least seven years before the date of the submission of member's name to the Supreme Court;

(4) The member has no other record of suspension or involuntary inactive enrollment for discipline or otherwise.
(Subd (b) adopted effective June 1, 2007.)

(c) Records to be maintained by State Bar
Upon order of the Supreme Court of expungement of a member's record under (b) of this rule, the State Bar will

remove or delete the record of such suspension from the member's record. Notwithstanding any other provision of this rule, the State Bar must maintain such internal records as are necessary to apply the terms of (b) of this rule and to report to the Commission on Judicial Nominees Evaluation or appropriate governmental entities involved in judicial elections the member's eligibility for a judgeship under the California Constitution, article VI, section 15.

(Subd (c) adopted effective June 1, 2007.)

(d) Duty of disclosure by member

Expungement of a member's suspension under (b) of this rule will not relieve the member of his or her duty to disclose the suspension for purpose of determining the member's eligibility for a judgeship under the California Constitution, article VI, section 15. For all other purposes the suspension expunged under (b) of this rule is deemed not to have occurred and the member may answer accordingly any question relating to his or her membership record.

(Subd (d) adopted effective June 1, 2007.)

(e) Authorization for the Board of Governors of the State Bar to adopt rules and regulations

The Board of Governors of the State Bar is authorized to adopt such rules and regulations as it deems necessary and appropriate in order to comply with this rule.

(Subd (e) adopted effective June 1, 2007.)

(f) Inherent power of Supreme Court

Nothing in this rule may be construed as affecting the power of the Supreme Court to exercise its inherent power to direct the State Bar to expunge its records.

(Subd (f) adopted effective June 1, 2007.)

Rule 9.6 amended effective June 1, 2007; adopted as rule 950.5 by the Supreme Court effective May 1, 1996; previously amended and renumbered effective January 1, 2007.

Chapter 2
Attorney Disciplinary Proceedings

Rule 9.10.   Authority of the State Bar Court

(a) Conviction proceedings

The State Bar Court exercises statutory powers under Business and Professions Code sections 6101 and 6102 with respect to the discipline of attorneys convicted of crimes. (See Bus. & Prof. Code section 6087.) For purposes of this rule, a judgment of conviction is deemed final when the availability of appeal has been exhausted and the time for filing a petition for certiorari in the United States Supreme Court on direct review of the judgment of conviction has elapsed and no petition has been filed, or if filed the petition has been denied or the judgment of conviction has been affirmed. The State Bar Court must impose or recommend discipline in conviction matters as in other disciplinary proceedings. The power conferred upon the State Bar Court by this rule includes the power to place attorneys on interim suspension under subdivisions (a) and (b) of section 6102, and the power to vacate, delay the effective date of, and temporarily stay the effect of such orders.

(Subd (a) amended effective January 1, 2007.)

(b) Professional responsibility examination

The State Bar Court may:

(1) Extend the time within which a member of the State Bar must take and pass a professional responsibility examination;

(2) Suspend a member for failing to take and pass such examination; and

(3) Vacate a member's suspension for failing to take and pass such examination.

(Subd (b) amended effective January 1, 2007.)

(c) Probation

The State Bar Court for good cause, may:

(1) Approve stipulations between the member and the Chief Trial Counsel for modification of the terms of a member's probation; and

(2) Make corrections and minor modifications to the terms of a member's disciplinary probation.

The order of the State Bar Court must be filed promptly with the Clerk of the Supreme Court.

(Subd (c) amended effective January 1, 2007.)

(d) Rule 9.20 compliance

The State Bar Court for good cause, may extend the time within which a member must comply with the provisions of rule 9.20 of the California Rules of Court.

(Subd (d) amended effective January 1, 2007.)

(e) Commencement of suspension

The State Bar Court for good cause, may delay temporarily the effective date of, or temporarily stay the effect of, an order for a member's disciplinary suspension from practice.

(Subd (e) amended effective January 1, 2007.)

(f) Readmission and reinstatement

Applications for readmission or reinstatement must, in the first instance, be filed and heard by the State Bar Court. Applicants for readmission or reinstatement must:

(1) Pass a professional responsibility examination;

(2) Establish their rehabilitation and present moral qualifications for readmission; and

(3) Establish present ability and learning in the general law. The State Bar may require applicants who fail to make the affirmative showing of sufficient present learning in the general law to demonstrate such learning by passing

one of the General Examinations required of applicants for admission.

(Subd (f) amended effective January 1, 2007.)

(g) Inherent power of Supreme Court

Nothing in these rules may be construed as affecting the power of the Supreme Court to exercise its inherent jurisdiction over the lawyer discipline and admissions system.

(Subd (g) amended effective January 1, 2007.)

Rule 9.10 amended and renumbered effective January 1, 2007; adopted as rule 951 effective December 1, 1990; previously amended by the Supreme Court effective April 1, 1996.

Ref.: Cal. Fms Pl. & Pr., Ch. 71, "Attorney Discipline."

Rule 9.11.   State Bar Court judges

(a) Applicant Evaluation and Nomination Committee

(1) **In order to ensure that individuals appointed by the Supreme Court or by the executive or legislative branches have been evaluated objectively,** the Supreme Court has established an **independent** Applicant Evaluation and Nomination Committee to solicit, receive, screen, and evaluate all applications for appointment or reappointment to any appointive position of judge of the State Bar Court (hearing judge, presiding judge, and review department judge). **The role of the committee is to determine whether appointees possess not only the statutorily enumerated qualifications, but also any qualifications that may be required by the Supreme Court to assist in the exercise of its ultimate authority over the discipline and admission of attorneys (See *Obrien v. Jones* (2000) 23 Cal.4th 40; *In re Attorney Discipline* (1998) 19 Cal.4th 582; Cal. Const., art VI, sec. 9).**

(2) The committee serves at the pleasure of the Supreme Court. It [1] **shall consist** of seven members appointed by the court of whom four must be members of the State Bar in good standing, two must be retired or active judicial officers, and one must be a public member who has never been a member of the State Bar or admitted to practice before any court in the United States. Two members of the committee must be present members of the Board of Governors of the State Bar (neither of whom may be from the Board's Discipline Committee).

(3) The committee must adopt, and implement upon approval by the Supreme Court, procedures for:

(A) Timely notice to potential applicants of vacancies;

(B) Receipt of applications for appointments to those positions from both incumbents and other qualified persons;

(C) Solicitation and receipt of public comment;

(D) Evaluation and rating of applicants; and

(E) Transmittal of the materials specified in (b) of this rule to the Supreme Court and, as applicable, other appointing authorities.

The procedures adopted by the committee must include provisions to ensure confidentiality comparable to those followed by the Judicial Nominees Evaluation Commission established under Government Code section 12011.5.

(4) The Board of Governors of the State Bar, in consultation with the Supreme Court if necessary, must provide facilities and support staff needed by the committee to carry out its obligations under this rule.

(Subd (a) amended effective January 1, 2009; previously amended effective February 15, 1995, July 1, 2000, and January 1, 2007.)

Rule 9.11(a).   2008 Deletes. [1] consists

(b) Evaluations

(1) The committee must evaluate the qualifications of and rate all applicants for positions appointed by the Supreme Court and must submit to the Supreme Court the nominations of at least three qualified candidates for each vacancy. **Candidates shall be rated as "not recommended," "recommended," and "highly recommended." A rating of "not recommended" relates only to the position under consideration and does not indicate any lack of ability or expertise of the applicant generally.** The committee must report in confidence to the Supreme Court its evaluation [1]**, rating and recommendation for applicants** for appointment and the reasons [2] **therefore**, including a succinct summary of their qualifications, at a time to be designated by the Supreme Court. The report must include written comments received by the committee, which must be transmitted to the Supreme Court together with the nominations.

(2) The committee must evaluate the qualifications of and rate all applicants for positions appointed by the Governor, the Senate Committee on Rules, or the Speaker of the Assembly, and must submit in confidence to the Supreme Court and, as applicable, to other appointing authorities, all applications for such positions together with the committee's evaluation [3]**, rating and recommendation for** these applicants, including any written comments received by the committee, at a time to be designated by the Supreme Court.

(3) In determining the qualifications of an applicant for appointment or reappointment the committee must consider, among other appropriate factors, the following: industry, legal and judicial experience (including prior service as a judge of the State Bar Court), judicial temperament, honesty, objectivity, community respect, integrity, and ability. **The committee must consider legal work experience broadly, including, but not limited to, litigation and non-litigation experience, legal work for a business or nonprofit entity, experience as a law professor or other academic position, legal work in any of the three branches of government, and legal work in dispute resolution,**

The committee shall consider whether an applicant has demonstrated the ability to write cogently and to analyze legal provisions and principles. Among the issues the committee may also consider are 1) the applicant's demonstrated capacity to work independently and to set and meet performance goals, 2) the applicant's knowledge and experience relevant to issues that give rise to the majority of State Bar Court proceedings, including professional ethics and fiduciary obligations, 3) knowledge of practice and demeanor in the courtroom, and (4) whether the applicant has been in practice for 10 or more years. The committee shall accord weight to all experience that has provided the applicant with legal experience and exposure during which the individual has demonstrated the underlying skills necessary to serve as an effective State Bar Court judge. The committee shall apply the same criteria to candidates seeking appointment from

all of the appointing authorities. Any evaluation or rating of an applicant and any recommendation for appointment or reappointment by the committee must be made in conformity with Business and Professions Code section 6079.1(b) and in light of the factors specified in Government Code section 12011.5 (d), and those specified in this paragraph.

(4) Upon transmittal of its report to the Supreme Court, the committee must notify any incumbent who has applied for reappointment by the Supreme Court if he or she is or is not among the applicants recommended for appointment to the new term by the committee. The applicable appointing authority must notify as soon as possible an incumbent who has applied for reappointment but is not selected.

(Subd (b) amended effective January 1, 2009; adopted effective February 15, 1995; previously amended effective July 1, 2000 and January 1, 2007.)

Rule 9.11(b). 2008 Deletes. [1] and rating of applicants recommended [2] therefor [3] and rating of

(c) Appointments

Only applicants [1] **who are rated as recommended or highly recommended** by the committee or by the Supreme Court may be appointed. At the request of the Governor, the Senate Committee on Rules, or the Speaker of the Assembly, the Supreme Court will reconsider a finding by the committee that a particular applicant is not [2] **recommended**. The Supreme Court may make such orders as to the appointment of applicants as it deems appropriate, including extending the term of incumbent judges pending such order or providing for staggered terms.

(Subd (c) amended effective January 1, 2009; adopted effective February 15, 1995; previously amended effective July 1, 2000 and January 1, 2007.)

Rule 9.11(c). 2008 Deletes. [1] found to be qualified [2] qualified

(d) Discipline for misconduct or disability

A judge of the State Bar Court is subject to discipline or retirement on the same grounds as a judge of a court of this state. Complaints concerning the conduct of a judge of the State Bar Court must be addressed to the Executive Director–Chief Counsel of the Commission on Judicial Performance, who is the Supreme Court's investigator for the purpose of evaluating those complaints, conducting any necessary further investigation, and determining whether formal proceedings should be instituted. If there is reasonable cause to institute formal proceedings, the investigator must notify the Supreme Court of that fact and must serve as or appoint the examiner and make other appointments and arrangements necessary for the hearing. The Supreme Court will then appoint one or more active or retired judges of superior courts or Courts of Appeal as its special master or masters to hear the complaint and the results of the investigation, and to report to the Supreme Court on the resulting findings, conclusions, and recommendations as to discipline. The procedures of the Commission on Judicial Performance must be followed by the investigator and special masters, to the extent feasible. The procedures in the Supreme Court after a discipline recommendation is filed will, to the extent feasible, be the same as the procedures followed when a determination of the Commission on Judicial Performance is filed.

(Subd (d) amended effective January 1, 2007; adopted as subd (b) effective December 1, 1990; relettered effective February 15, 1995; previously amended effective July 1, 2000.)

Rule 9.11 amended effective January 1, 2009; adopted as rule 961 effective December 1, 1990; previously amended February 15, 1995, and July 1, 2000; previously amended and renumbered effective January 1, 2007.

Ref.: Cal. Fms Pl. & Pr., Ch. 71, "Attorney Discipline."

Rule 9.12.   Standard of review for State Bar Court Review Department

In reviewing the decisions, orders, or rulings of a hearing judge under rule 301 of the Rules of Procedure of the State Bar of California or such other rule as may be adopted governing the review of any decisions, orders, or rulings by a hearing judge that fully disposes of an entire proceeding, the Review Department of the State Bar Court must independently review the record and may adopt findings, conclusions, and a decision or recommendation different from those of the hearing judge.

Rule 9.12 amended and renumbered effective January 1, 2007; adopted as rule 951.5 by the Supreme Court effective February 23, 2000.

Rule 9.13.   Review of State Bar Court decisions

(a) Review of recommendation of disbarment or suspension

A petition to the Supreme Court by a member to review a decision of the State Bar Court recommending his or her disbarment or suspension from practice must be filed within 60 days after a certified copy of the decision complained of is filed with the Clerk of the Supreme Court. The State Bar may serve and file an answer to the petition within 15 days of service of the petition. Within 5 days after service of the answer, the petitioner may serve and file a reply. If review is ordered by the Supreme Court, the State Bar must serve and file a supplemental brief within 45 days after the order is filed. Within 15 days of service of the supplemental brief, the petitioner may serve and file a reply brief.

(Subd (a) amended effective January 1, 2007; previously relettered and amended effective October 1, 1973; previously amended effective July 1, 1968, and December 1, 1990.)

(b) Review of State Bar recommendation to set aside stay of suspension or modify probation

A petition to the Supreme Court by a member to review a recommendation of the State Bar Court that a stay of an order of suspension be set aside or that the duration or conditions of probation be modified on account of a violation of probation must be filed within 15 days after a certified copy of the recommendation complained of is filed with the Clerk of the Supreme Court. Within 15 days after service of the petition, the State Bar may serve and file an answer. Within 5 days after service of the answer, the petitioner may serve and file a reply.

(Subd (b) amended effective January 1, 2007; adopted effective October 1, 1973; previously amended effective December 1, 1990.)

(c) Review of interim decisions

A petition to the Supreme Court by a member to review a decision of the State Bar Court regarding interim suspension, the exercise of powers delegated by rule

9.10(b)–(e), or another interlocutory matter must be filed within 15 days after written notice of the adverse decision of the State Bar Court is mailed by the State Bar to the petitioner and to his or her counsel of record, if any, at their respective addresses under section 6002.1. Within 15 days after service of the petition, the State Bar may serve and file an answer. Within 5 days after service of the answer, the petitioner may serve and file a reply.

(Subd (c) amended effective January 1, 2007; adopted effective December 1, 1990.)

(d) Review of other decisions

A petition to the Supreme Court to review any other decision of the State Bar Court or action of the Board of Governors of the State Bar, or of any board or committee appointed by it and authorized to make a determination under the provisions of the State Bar Act, or of the chief executive officer of the State Bar or the designee of the chief executive officer authorized to make a determination under article 10 of the State Bar Act or these rules of court, must be filed within 60 days after written notice of the action complained of is mailed to the petitioner and to his or her counsel of record, if any, at their respective addresses under section 6002.1. Within 15 days after service of the petition, the State Bar may serve and file an answer and brief. Within 5 days after service of the answer and brief, the petitioner may serve and file a reply. If review is ordered by the Supreme Court, the State Bar, within 45 days after filing of the order, may serve and file a supplemental brief. Within 15 days after service of the supplemental brief, the petitioner may file a reply brief.

(Subd (d) amended effective January 1, 2007; previously amended effective July 1, 1968, May 1, 1986, and April 2, 1987; previously relettered and amended effective October 1, 1973, and December 1, 1990.)

(e) Contents of petition

(1) A petition to the Supreme Court filed under (a) and (b) of this rule must be verified, must specify the grounds relied upon, must show that review within the State Bar Court has been exhausted, must address why review is appropriate under one or more of the grounds specified in rule 9.16, and must have attached a copy of the State Bar Court decision from which relief is sought.

(2) When review is sought under (c) and (d) of this rule, the petition must also be accompanied by a record adequate to permit review of the ruling, including:

(A) Legible copies of all documents and exhibits submitted to the State Bar Court supporting and opposing petitioner's position;

(B) Legible copies of all other documents submitted to the State Bar Court that are necessary for a complete understanding of the case and the ruling; and

(C) A transcript of the proceedings in the State Bar Court leading to the decision or, if a transcript is unavailable, a declaration by counsel explaining why a transcript is unavailable and fairly summarizing the proceedings, including arguments by counsel and the basis of the State Bar Court's decision, if stated; or a declaration by counsel stating that the transcript has been ordered, the date it was ordered, and the date it is expected to be filed, which must be a date before any action is requested from the Supreme Court other than issuance of a stay supported by other parts of the record.

(3) A petitioner who requests an immediate stay must explain in the petition the reasons for the urgency and set forth all relevant time constraints.

(4) If a petitioner does not submit the required record, the court may summarily deny the stay request, the petition, or both.

(Subd (e) amended effective January 1, 2007; previously repealed and adopted by the Supreme Court effective December 1, 1990, and February 1, 1991; previously repealed and adopted effective March 15, 1991.)

(f) Service

All petitions, briefs, reply briefs, and other pleadings filed by a petitioner under this rule must be accompanied by proof of service of three copies on the General Counsel of the State Bar at the San Francisco office of the State Bar, and of one copy on the Clerk of the State Bar Court at the Los Angeles office of the State Bar Court. The State Bar must serve the member at his or her address under Business and Professions Code section 6002.1, and his or her counsel of record, if any.

(Subd (f) amended effective January 1, 2007; adopted by the Supreme Court effective December 1, 1990; previously amended by the Supreme Court effective February 1, 1991; previously amended effective March 15, 1991.)

Rule 9.13 amended and renumbered effective January 1, 2007; adopted as rule 59 by the Supreme Court effective April 20, 1943, and by the Judicial Council effective July 1, 1943; previously amended and renumbered as rule 952 effective October 1, 1973; previously amended effective July 1, 1976, May 1, 1986, April 2, 1987, December 1, 1990, February 1, 1991, and March 15, 1991.

Ref.: Cal. Fms Pl. & Pr., Ch. 70, "Attorney Admission," Ch. 71, "Attorney Discipline," Ch. 324, "Jurisdiction: Subject Matter Jurisdiction," Ch. 471B, "Licensing by Public Agencies," Ch. 474C, "Procedures in Reviewing Agency Decisions"; MB Prac. Guide: Cal. Pretrial Proc., §10.04[2].

Rule 9.14. Petitions for review by the Chief Trial Counsel

(a) Time for filing

The Chief Trial Counsel may petition for review of recommendations and decisions of the State Bar Court as follows:

(1) From recommendations that a member be suspended, within 60 days of the date the recommendation is filed with the Supreme Court.

(2) From recommendations that the duration or conditions of probation be modified, or a reinstatement application be granted, within 15 days of the date the recommendation is filed with the Supreme Court.

(3) From decisions not to place an eligible member on interim suspension, or vacating interim suspension, or a denial of a petition brought under section 6007(c), within 15 days of notice under the rules adopted by the State Bar.

(4) From decisions dismissing disciplinary proceedings or recommending approval, within 60 days of notice under the rules adopted by the State Bar.

(Subd (a) amended effective January 1, 2007; adopted effective March 15, 1991; previously adopted by the Supreme Court effective December 10, 1990.)

(b) Procedures

Proceedings under this rule with regard to briefing, service of process, and applicable time periods therefor must correspond to proceedings brought under rule 9.13, except that the rights and duties of the member and the State Bar under that rule are reversed.

(Subd (b) amended and relettered effective January 1, 2007; adopted as part of subd (d) effective March 15, 1991; previously adopted by the Supreme Court effective December 10, 1991.) Rule 9.14 amended and renumbered effective January 1, 2007; adopted as rule 952.5 effective March 15, 1991.

Ref.: Cal. Fms Pl. & Pr., Ch. 71, "Attorney Discipline."

Rule 9.15.   Petitions for review by the Committee of Bar Examiners; grounds for review; confidentiality

(a) Petition for review by the Committee of Bar Examiners

The Committee of Bar Examiners may petition for review of the decision of the Review Department of the State Bar Court in moral character proceedings. All petitions under this rule must be filed with the Clerk of the Supreme Court within 60 days after the State Bar Court decision is filed and served on the General Counsel of the State Bar at the San Francisco office of the State Bar. The applicant may file and serve an answer within 15 days of service of the petition. Within 5 days after service of the answer the Committee of Bar Examiners may serve and file a reply. If review is ordered by the Supreme Court, within 45 days after filing of the order, the applicant may file a supplemental brief. Within 15 days after service of the supplemental brief, the petitioner may serve and file a reply brief.

(Subd (a) amended effective January 1, 2007.)

(b) Contents of petition

A petition to the Supreme Court filed under this rule must show that review within the State Bar Court has been exhausted, must address why review is appropriate under one or more of the grounds specified in rule 9.16, and must have attached a copy of the State Bar Court decision for which review is sought.

(Subd (b) amended effective January 1, 2007.)

(c) Service

All petitions, briefs, reply briefs, and other pleadings filed by the Committee of Bar Examiners must include a proof of service by mail to the applicant's last address provided to the State Bar or the applicant's attorney of record, if any. Filings by the applicant must include a proof of service of three copies on the General Counsel of the State Bar at the San Francisco office of the State Bar and one copy on the Clerk of the State Bar Court at the Los Angeles office of the State Bar Court.

(Subd (c) amended effective January 1, 2007; previously amended effective April 20, 1998.)

(d) Confidentiality

All filings under this rule are confidential unless: (1) the applicant waives confidentiality in writing; or (2) the Supreme Court grants review. Once the Supreme Court grants review, filings under this rule are open to the public; however, if good cause exists, the Supreme Court may order portions of the record or the identity of witnesses or other third parties to the proceedings to remain confidential.

(Subd (d) amended effective January 1, 2007; adopted effective April 20, 1998.)

Rule 9.15 amended and renumbered effective January 1, 2007; adopted as rule 952.6 by the Supreme Court effective July 1,

1993, and by the Judicial Council May 6, 1998; previously amended by the Supreme Court effective April 20, 1998.

Ref.: Cal. Fms Pl. & Pr., Ch. 70, "Attorney Admission."

Rule 9.16.   Grounds for review of State Bar Court decisions in the Supreme Court

(a) Grounds

The Supreme Court will order review of a decision of the State Bar Court recommending disbarment or suspension from practice when it appears:

(1) Necessary to settle important questions of law;

(2) The State Bar Court has acted without or in excess of jurisdiction;

(3) Petitioner did not receive a fair hearing;

(4) The decision is not supported by the weight of the evidence; or

(5) The recommended discipline is not appropriate in light of the record as a whole.

(Subd (a) amended effective January 1, 2007; adopted by the Supreme Court effective February 1, 1991.)

(b) Denial of review

Denial of review of a decision of the State Bar Court is a final judicial determination on the merits and the recommendation of the State Bar Court will be filed as an order of the Supreme Court.

(Subd (b) amended effective January 1, 2007; adopted by the Supreme Court effective February 1, 1991.)

Rule 9.16 amended and renumbered effective January 1, 2007; adopted as rule 954 effective February 1, 1991.

Ref.: Cal. Fms Pl. & Pr., Ch. 71, "Attorney Discipline," Ch. 72, "Attorney Practice and Ethics."

Rule 9.17.   Remand with instructions

At any time before the final disposition of a decision of the State Bar Court filed under Business and Professions Code section 6081, the Supreme Court may remand the matter to the State Bar Court with instructions to conduct such further proceedings as the Supreme Court deems necessary.

Rule 9.17 amended and renumbered effective January 1, 2007; adopted as rule 953.5 effective February 1, 1991.

Ref.: Cal. Fms Pl. & Pr., Ch. 71, "Attorney Discipline."

Rule 9.18.   Effective date of disciplinary orders and decisions

(a) Effective date of Supreme Court orders

Unless otherwise ordered, all orders of the Supreme Court imposing discipline or opinions deciding causes involving the State Bar become final 30 days after filing. The Supreme Court may grant a rehearing at any time before the decision or order becomes final. Petitions for rehearing may be filed within 15 days of the date the decision or order was filed. Unless otherwise ordered, when petitions for review under rules 9.13(c) and 9.14(a)(3) are acted upon summarily, the orders of the Supreme Court are final forthwith and do not have law-of-the-case effect in subsequent proceedings in the Supreme Court.

(Subd (a) amended effective January 1, 2007; adopted effective March 15, 1991; previously adopted by the Supreme Court effective December 1, 1990.)

(b) Effect of State Bar Court orders when no review sought

Unless otherwise ordered, if no petition for review is filed within the time allowed by rule 9.13 (a), (b), and (d), or rule 9.14 (a)(1) and (2), as to a recommendation of the State Bar Court for the disbarment, suspension, or reinstatement of a member, the vacation of a stay, or modification of the duration or conditions of a probation, the recommendation of the State Bar Court will be filed as an order of the Supreme Court following the expiration of the time for filing a timely petition. The Clerk of the Supreme Court will mail notice of this effect to the member and his or her attorney of record, if any, at their respective addresses under Business and Professions Code section 6002.1 and to the State Bar.

(Subd (b) amended effective January 1, 2007; adopted effective March 15, 1991; previously adopted by the Supreme Court effective December 1, 1990.)

(c) Effect of State Bar Court orders in moral character proceedings when no review sought

Unless otherwise ordered, if no petition for review is filed within the time allowed by rule 9.15(a), as to a recommendation of the State Bar Court in moral character proceedings, the recommendation of the State Bar Court will be filed as an order of the Supreme Court following the expiration of the time for filing a timely petition. The Clerk of the Supreme Court will mail notice of this effect to the applicant's last address provided to the State Bar or to the applicant's attorney of record, if any, and to the State Bar.

(Subd (c) amended effective January 1, 2007.)

Rule 9.18 amended and renumbered effective January 1, 2007; adopted as rule 953 effective March 15, 1991; previously amended effective February 1, 1996.

Ref.: Cal. Fms Pl. & Pr., Ch. 70, "Attorney Admission," Ch. 71, "Attorney Discipline," Ch. 72, "Attorney Practice and Ethics."

Rule 9.19.   Conditions attached to reprovals

(a) Attachment of conditions to reprovals

The State Bar may attach conditions, effective for a reasonable time, to a public or private reproval administered upon a member of the State Bar. Conditions so attached must be based on a finding by the State Bar that protection of the public and the interests of the member will be served thereby. The State Bar when administering the reproval must give notice to the member that failure to comply with the conditions may be punishable.

(Subd (a) amended effective January 1, 2007.)

(b) Sanctions for failure to comply

A member's failure to comply with conditions attached to a public or private reproval may be cause for a separate proceeding for willful breach of rule 9-101 of the Rules of Professional Conduct.

(Subd (b) amended effective January 1, 2007.)

Rule 9.19 amended and renumbered effective January 1, 2007; adopted as rule 956 effective November 18, 1983.

Ref.: Cal. Fms Pl. & Pr., Ch. 71, "Attorney Discipline."

Rule 9.20.   Duties of disbarred, resigned, or suspended attorneys

(a) Disbarment, suspension, and resignation orders

The Supreme Court may include in an order disbarring or suspending a member of the State Bar, or accepting his or her resignation, a direction that the member must, within such time limits as the Supreme Court may prescribe:

(1) Notify all clients being represented in pending matters and any co-counsel of his or her disbarment, suspension, or resignation and his or her consequent disqualification to act as an attorney after the effective date of the disbarment, suspension, or resignation, and, in the absence of co-counsel, also notify the clients to seek legal advice elsewhere, calling attention to any urgency in seeking the substitution of another attorney or attorneys;

(2) Deliver to all clients being represented in pending matters any papers or other property to which the clients are entitled, or notify the clients and any co-counsel of a suitable time and place where the papers and other property may be obtained, calling attention to any urgency for obtaining the papers or other property;

(3) Refund any part of fees paid that have not been earned; and

(4) Notify opposing counsel in pending litigation or, in the absence of counsel, the adverse parties of the disbarment, suspension, or resignation and consequent disqualification to act as an attorney after the effective date of the disbarment, suspension, or resignation, and file a copy of the notice with the court, agency, or tribunal before which the litigation is pending for inclusion in the respective file or files.

(Subd (a) amended effective January 1, 2007; previously amended effective December 1, 1990.)

(b) Notices to clients, co-counsel, opposing counsel, and adverse parties

All notices required by an order of the Supreme Court or the State Bar Court under this rule must be given by registered or certified mail, return receipt requested, and must contain an address where communications may be directed to the disbarred, suspended, or resigned member.

(Subd (b) amended effective January 1, 2007; previously amended effective December 1, 1990.)

(c) Filing proof of compliance

Within such time as the order may prescribe after the effective date of the member's disbarment, suspension, or resignation, the member must file with the Clerk of the State Bar Court an affidavit showing that he or she has fully complied with those provisions of the order entered under this rule. The affidavit must also specify an address where communications may be directed to the disbarred, suspended, or resigned member.

(Subd (c) amended effective January 1, 2007; previously amended effective December 1, 1990.)

(d) Sanctions for failure to comply

A disbarred or resigned member's willful failure to comply with the provisions of this rule is a ground for denying his or her application for reinstatement or readmission. A suspended member's willful failure to comply with the provisions of this rule is a cause for disbarment or suspension and for revocation of any pending probation. Additionally, such failure may be punished as a contempt or a crime.

(Subd (d) amended effective January 1, 2007; previously relettered and amended effective December 1, 1990.)

Rule 9.20 amended and renumbered effective January 1, 2007; adopted as rule 955 effective April 4, 1973; previously amended effective December 1, 1990.

Ref.: Cal. Fms Pl. & Pr., Ch. 70, "Attorney Admission," Ch. 71, "Attorney Discipline," Ch. 72, "Attorney Practice and Ethics."

Rule 9.21. Resignations of members of the State Bar with disciplinary charges pending

(a) General provisions

A member of the State Bar against whom disciplinary charges are pending may tender a written resignation from membership in the State Bar and relinquishment of the right to practice law. The written resignation must be signed and dated by the member at the time it is tendered and must be tendered to the Office of the Clerk, State Bar Court, 1149 South Hill Street, Los Angeles, California 90015. The resignation must be substantially in the form specified in (b) of this rule. In submitting a resignation under this rule, a member of the State Bar agrees to be transferred to inactive membership in the State Bar effective on the filing of the resignation by the State Bar. Within 30 days after filing of the resignation, the member must perform the acts specified in rule 9.20(a)(1)–(4) and (b) and within 40 days after filing of the resignation, the member must file with the Office of the Clerk, State Bar Court, at the above address, the proof of compliance specified in rule 9.20(c). No resignation is effective unless and until it is accepted by the Supreme Court after consideration and recommendation by the Board of Governors of the State Bar.

(Subd (a) amended effective January 1, 2007.)

(b) Form of resignation

The member's written resignation must be in substantially the following form:

"I, *[name of member]*, against whom charges are pending, hereby resign as a member of the State Bar of California and relinquish all right to practice law in the State of California. I agree that, in the event that this resignation is accepted and I later file a petition for reinstatement, the State Bar will consider in connection therewith all disciplinary matters and proceedings against me at the time this resignation is accepted, in addition to other appropriate matters. I further agree that, on the filing of this resignation by the Office of the Clerk, State Bar Court, I will be transferred to inactive membership of the State Bar. On such transfer, I acknowledge that I will be ineligible to practice law or to advertise or hold myself out as practicing or as entitled to practice law. I further agree that, within 30 days of the filing of the resignation by the Office of the Clerk, State Bar Court, I will perform the acts specified in rule 9.20(a)–(b) of the California Rules of Court, and within 40 days of the date of filing of this resignation by the Office of the Clerk, State Bar Court, I will notify that office as specified in rule 9.20(c) of the California Rules of Court."

(Subd (b) amended effective January 1, 2007.)

(c) Consideration of resignation by State Bar Board of Governors and Supreme Court

When the Office of the Clerk of the State Bar Court receives a member's resignation tendered in conformity with this rule, it must promptly file the resignation. The Board of Governors of the State Bar must thereafter consider the member's resignation and recommend to the Supreme Court whether the resignation should be accepted and, if so, whether testimony should be preserved.

The Office of the Clerk of the State Bar Court must transmit to the Clerk of the Supreme Court, three certified copies of the Board's recommendation together with the member's resignation, when, by the terms of the Board's recommendation, the resignation should be transmitted to the Supreme Court.

(Subd (c) amended effective January 1, 2007.)

(d) Grounds for rejection of resignation by the Supreme Court

The Supreme Court will make such orders concerning the member's resignation as it deems appropriate. The Supreme Court may decline to accept the resignation based on a report by the Board of Governors that:

(1) Preservation of necessary testimony is not complete;

(2) After transfer to inactive status, the member has practiced law or has advertised or held himself or herself out as entitled to practice law;

(3) The member has failed to perform the acts specified by rule 9.20(a)–(b);

(4) The member has failed to provide proof of compliance as specified in rule 9.20(c);

(5) The Supreme Court has filed an order of disbarment as to the member; or

(6) On such other evidence as may show that acceptance of the resignation of the member will reasonably be inconsistent with the need to protect the public, the courts, or the legal profession.

(Subd (d) amended and relettered effective January 1, 2007; adopted as part of subd (c) effective December 14, 1984.)

Rule 9.21 amended and renumbered effective January 1, 2007; adopted as rule 960 by the Supreme Court effective December 14, 1984.

Ref.: Cal. Fms Pl. & Pr., Ch. 71, "Attorney Discipline."

Rule 9.22. Suspension of members of the State Bar for failure to comply with judgment or order for child or family support

(a) Annual State Bar recommendation for suspension of delinquent members

Under Family Code section 17520, the State Bar is authorized to transmit to the Supreme Court on an annual basis the names of those members listed by the State Department of Social Services as delinquent in their payments of court-ordered child or family support with a recommendation for their suspension from the practice of law.

(Subd (a) amended effective January 1, 2007.)

(b) Condition for reinstatement of suspended members

A member suspended under this rule may be reinstated only after receipt by the Supreme Court of notification from the State Bar that the member's name has been removed from the State Department of Social Services list.

(Subd (b) amended and lettered effective January 1, 2007; adopted as part of subd (a) effective January 31, 1993.)

(c) Additional recommendation for suspension by the State Bar

Under Family Code section 17520(*l*), the State Bar is further authorized to promptly transmit to the Supreme Court with a recommendation for their suspension from the practice of law the names of those members previously listed by the State Department of Social Services as delinquent in their payments of court-ordered child or family support, who obtained releases under Family Code section 17520(h), and who have subsequently been identified by the Department of Social Services as again being delinquent.

(Subd (c) amended and lettered effective January 1, 2007; adopted as part of subd (a) effective January 31, 1993.)

(d) Authorization for the Board of Governors of the State Bar to adopt rules and regulations

The Board of Governors of the State Bar is authorized to adopt such rules and regulations as it deems necessary and appropriate in order to comply with this rule. The rules and regulations of the State Bar must contain procedures governing the notification, suspension, and reinstatement of members of the State Bar in a manner not inconsistent with Family Code section 17520.

(Subd (d) amended and relettered effective January 1, 2007; adopted as subd (b) effective January 31, 1993.)

Rule 9.22 amended and renumbered effective January 1, 2007; adopted as rule 962 effective January 31, 1993; previously amended by the Supreme Court effective April 1, 1996.

Ref.: Cal. Fms Pl. & Pr., Ch. 71, "Attorney Discipline," Ch. 259, "Family Law Enforcement: Special Remedies for Support Enforcement"; W. Cal. Sum., 11 "Husband and Wife" §338.

Rule 9.23.   Enforcement as money judgment disciplinary orders directing the payment of costs and disciplinary orders requiring reimbursement of the Client Security Fund

(a) Authority to obtain money judgment

Under Business and Professions Code section 6086.10(a) the State Bar is authorized to enforce as a money judgment any disciplinary order assessing costs. Under Business and Professions Code section 6140.5(d) the State Bar is authorized to enforce as a money judgment any disciplinary order requiring reimbursement of the State Bar Client Security Fund.

(Subd (a) adopted by the Supreme Court effective April 1, 2007.)

(b) Duty of clerk of the superior court

The State Bar may file a certified copy of a final disciplinary order assessing costs or requiring reimbursement of the Client Security Fund, along with a certified copy of the certificate of costs and any record of Client Security Fund payments and costs, with the clerk of the superior court of any county. The clerk must immediately enter judgment in conformity with the order.

(Subd (b) adopted by the Supreme Court effective April 1, 2007.)

(c) Compromise of judgment

Motions for the compromise of any judgment entered under this rule must, in the first instance, be filed and heard by the State Bar Court.

(Subd (c) adopted by the Supreme Court effective April 1, 2007.)

(d) Power of the Supreme Court

Nothing in this rule may be construed as affecting the power of the Supreme Court to alter the amounts owed.

(Subd (d) adopted by the Supreme Court effective April 1, 2007.)

Rule 9.23 adopted by the Supreme Court effective April 1, 2007.

Chapter 3
Legal Education

Rule 9.30. Law school study in schools other than those accredited by the examining committee
Rule 9.31. Minimum continuing legal education

Rule 9.30.   Law school study in schools other than those accredited by the examining committee

(a) Receipt of credit

A person who seeks to be certified to the Supreme Court for admission in and licensed to practice law under section 6060(e)(2) of the Business and Professions Code may receive credit for:

(1) Study in a law school in the United States other than one accredited by the examining committee established by the Board of Governors of the State Bar under Business and Professions Code section 6046 only if the law school satisfies the requirements of (b) or (c) of this rule; or

(2) Instruction in law from a correspondence school only if the correspondence school requires 864 hours of preparation and study per year for four years and satisfies the requirements of (d) of this rule; or

(3) Study in a law school outside the United States other than one accredited by the examining committee established by the Board of Governors of the State Bar under Business and Professions Code section 6046 only if the examining committee is satisfied that the academic program of such law school is substantially equivalent to that of a law school qualified under (b) of this rule.

(Subd (a) amended effective January 1, 2007; previously amended effective April 2, 1984.)

(b) Requirements for unaccredited law schools in state

A law school in this state that is not accredited by the examining committee must:

(1) Be authorized to confer professional degrees by the laws of this state;

(2) Maintain a regular course of instruction in law, with a specified curriculum and regularly scheduled class sessions;

(3) Require classroom attendance of its students for a minimum of 270 hours a year for at least four years, and further require regular attendance of each student at not less than 80 percent of the regularly scheduled class hours in each course in which such student was enrolled and maintain attendance records adequate to determine each student's compliance with these requirements;

(4) Maintain, in a fixed location, physical facilities capable of accommodating the classes scheduled for that location;

(5) Have an adequate faculty of instructors in law. The faculty will prima facie be deemed adequate if at least 80 percent of the instruction in each academic period is by persons who possess one or more of the following qualifications:

(A) Admission to the general practice of the law in any jurisdiction in the United States;

(B) Judge of a United States court or a court of record in any jurisdiction in the United States; or

(C) Graduation from a law school accredited by the examining committee.

(6) Own and maintain a library consisting of not less than the following sets of books, all of which must be current and complete:

(A) The published reports of the decisions of California courts, with advance sheets and citator;

(B) A digest or encyclopedia of California law;

(C) An annotated set of the California codes; and

(D) A current, standard text or treatise for each course or subject in the curriculum of the school for which such a text or treatise is available.

(7) Establish and maintain standards for academic achievement, advancement in good standing and graduation, and provide for periodic testing of all students to determine the quality of their performance in relation to such standards; and

(8) Register with the examining committee, and maintain such records (available for inspection by the examining committee) and file with the examining committee such reports, notices, and certifications as may be required by the rules of the examining committee.

(Subd (b) amended effective January 1, 2007; previously amended effective April 2, 1984.)

(c) Requirements for unaccredited law schools outside the state

A law school in the United States that is outside the state of California and is not accredited by the examining committee must:

(1) Be authorized to confer professional degrees by the law of the state in which it is located;

(2) Comply with (b)(2), (3), (4), (5), (7), and (8) of this rule; and

(3) Own and maintain a library that is comparable in content to that specified in (b)(6) of this rule.

(Subd (c) amended effective January 1, 2007; previously amended effective April 2, 1984.)

(d) Registration and reports

A correspondence law school must register with the examining committee and file such reports, notices, and certifications as may be required by the rules of the examining committee concerning any person whose mailing address is in the state of California or whose application to, contract with, or correspondence with or from the law school indicates that the instruction by correspondence is for the purpose or with the intent of qualifying that person for admission to practice law in California.

(Subd (d) amended effective January 1, 2007.)

(e) Inspections

The examining committee may make such inspection of law schools not accredited by the committee or correspondence schools as may be necessary or proper to give effect to the provisions of Business and Professions Code section 6060, this rule, and the rules of the examining committee.

(Subd (e) amended effective January 1, 2007.)

(f) Application

This rule does not apply to any person who, on the effective date of the rule, had commenced the study of law in a manner authorized by Business and Professions Code section 6060(e) and registered as a law student before January 1, 1976 (as provided in Business and Professions

Code section 6060(d) and otherwise satisfies the requirements of Business and Professions Code section 6060(e), provided that after January 1, 1976, credit will be given such person for any study in an unaccredited law school or by correspondence only if the school complies with the requirements of (b)(8) or (d) of this rule, whichever is applicable, and permits inspection under (e) of this rule.

(Subd (f) amended effective January 1, 2007.)

Rule 9.30 amended and renumbered effective January 1, 2007; adopted as rule 957 by the Supreme Court effective October 8, 1975; previously amended effective April 2, 1984.

Rule 9.31. Minimum continuing legal education

(a) Statutory authorization

This rule is adopted under Business and Professions Code section 6070.

(Subd (a) amended effective January 1, 2007.)

(b) State Bar minimum continuing legal education program

The State Bar must establish and administer a minimum continuing legal education program under rules adopted by the Board of Governors of the State Bar. These rules may provide for carryforward of excess credit hours, staggering of the education requirement for implementation purposes, and retroactive credit for legal education.

(Subd (b) amended effective January 1, 2007; previously amended effective September 27, 2000.)

(c) Minimum continuing legal education requirements

Each active member of the State Bar (1) not exempt under Business and Professions Code section 6070, (2) not a full-time employee of the United States Government, its departments, agencies, and public corporations, acting within the scope of his or her employment, and (3) not otherwise exempt under rules adopted by the Board of Governors of the State Bar, must, within 36-month periods designated by the State Bar, complete at least 25 hours of legal education approved by the State Bar or offered by a State Bar-approved provider. Four of those hours must address legal ethics. Members may be required to complete legal education in other specified areas within the 25-hour requirement under rules adopted by the State Bar. Each active member must report his or her compliance to the State Bar under rules adopted by the Board of Governors of the State Bar.

(Subd (c) amended effective January 1, 2007; previously amended effective September 27, 2000.)

(d) Failure to comply with program

A member of the State Bar who fails to satisfy the requirements of the State Bar's minimum continuing legal education program must be enrolled as an inactive member of the State Bar under rules adopted by the Board of Governors of the State Bar.

(Subd (d) amended effective January 1, 2007.)

(e) Fees and penalties

The State Bar has the authority to set and collect appropriate fees and penalties.

(Subd (e) amended effective January 1, 2007.)

Rule 9.31 amended and renumbered effective January 1, 2007; adopted as rule 958 effective December 6, 1990; previously amended effective December 25, 1992; previously amended by the Supreme Court effective September 27, 2000.

Division 3
Legal Specialists

Rule 9.35.   Certified legal specialists

(a) Definition

A "certified specialist" is a California attorney who holds a current certificate as a specialist issued by the State Bar of California Board of Legal Specialization or any other entity approved by the State Bar to designate specialists.

(b) State Bar Legal Specialization Program

The State Bar must establish and administer a program for certifying legal specialists and may establish a program for certifying entities that certify legal specialists under rules adopted by the Board of Governors of the State Bar.

(Subd (b) amended effective January 1, 2007.)

(c) Authority to practice law

No attorney may be required to obtain certification as a certified specialist as a prerequisite to practicing law in this state. Any attorney, alone or in association with any other attorney, has the right to practice in any field of law in this state and to act as counsel in every type of case, even though he or she is not certified as a specialist.

(Subd (c) amended effective January 1, 2007.)

(d) Failure to comply with program

A certified specialist who fails to comply with the requirements of the Legal Specialization Program of the State Bar will have her or his certification suspended or revoked under rules adopted by the Board of Governors of the State Bar.

(Subd (d) amended effective January 1, 2007.)

(e) Fee and penalty

The State Bar has the authority to set and collect appropriate fees and penalties for this program.

(Subd (e) amended effective January 1, 2007.)

(f) Inherent power of Supreme Court

Nothing in these rules may be construed as affecting the power of the Supreme Court to exercise its inherent jurisdiction over the practice of law in California.

(Subd (f) amended effective January 1, 2007.)

Rule 9.35 amended and renumbered effective January 1, 2007; adopted as rule 983.5 effective January 1, 1996.

Division 4
Appearances and Practice by Individuals Who Are Not Members of the State Bar of California

Rule 9.40. Counsel *pro hac vice*
Rule 9.41. Appearances by military counsel
Rule 9.42. Certified law students
Rule 9.43. Out-of-state attorney arbitration counsel
Rule 9.44. Registered foreign legal consultant
Rule 9.45. Registered legal services attorneys
Rule 9.46. Registered in-house counsel
Rule 9.47. Attorneys practicing law temporarily in California as part of litigation
Rule 9.48. Nonlitigating attorneys temporarily in California to provide legal services

Rule 9.40.   Counsel *pro hac vice*

(a) Eligibility

A person who is not a member of the State Bar of California but who is a member in good standing of and eligible to practice before the bar of any United States court or the highest court in any state, territory, or insular possession of the United States, and who has been retained to appear in a particular cause pending in a court of this state, may in the discretion of such court be permitted upon written application to appear as counsel *pro hac vice*, provided that an active member of the State Bar of California is associated as attorney of record. No person is eligible to appear as counsel *pro hac vice* under this rule if the person is:

(1) A resident of the State of California;

(2) Regularly employed in the State of California; or

(3) Regularly engaged in substantial business, professional, or other activities in the State of California.

(Subd (a) amended effective January 1, 2007.)

(b) Repeated appearances as a cause for denial

Absent special circumstances, repeated appearances by any person under this rule is a cause for denial of an application.

(Subd (b) lettered effective January 1, 2007; adopted as part of subd (a) effective September 13, 1972.)

(c) Application

(1) *Application in superior court*

A person desiring to appear as counsel *pro hac vice* in a superior court must file with the court a verified application together with proof of service by mail in accordance with Code of Civil Procedure section 1013a of a copy of the application and of the notice of hearing of the application on all parties who have appeared in the cause and on the State Bar of California at its San Francisco office. The notice of hearing must be given at the time prescribed in Code of Civil Procedure section 1005 unless the court has prescribed a shorter period.

(2) *Application in Supreme Court or Court of Appeal*

An application to appear as counsel *pro hac vice* in the Supreme Court or a Court of Appeal must be made as provided in rule 8.54, with proof of service on all parties who have appeared in the cause and on the State Bar of California at its San Francisco office.

(Subd (c) amended and relettered effective January 1, 2007; adopted as part of subd (b) effective September 13, 1972; subd (b) previously amended effective October 3, 1973, September 3, 1986, January 17, 1991, and March 15, 1991.)

(d) Contents of application

The application must state:

(1) The applicant's residence and office address;

(2) The courts to which the applicant has been admitted to practice and the dates of admission;

(3) That the applicant is a member in good standing in those courts;

(4) That the applicant is not currently suspended or disbarred in any court;

(5) The title of court and cause in which the applicant has filed an application to appear as counsel *pro hac vice*

in this state in the preceding two years, the date of each application, and whether or not it was granted; and

(6) The name, address, and telephone number of the active member of the State Bar of California who is attorney of record.

(Subd (d) amended and lettered effective January 1, 2007; adopted as part of subd (b) effective September 13, 1972; subd (b) previously amended effective October 3, 1973, September 3, 1986, January 17, 1991, and March 15, 1991.)

(e) Fee for application

An applicant for permission to appear as counsel *pro hac vice* under this rule must pay a reasonable fee not exceeding $50 to the State Bar of California with the copy of the application and the notice of hearing that is served on the State Bar. The Board of Governors of the State Bar of California will fix the amount of the fee:

(1) To defray the expenses of administering the provisions of this rule that are applicable to the State Bar and the incidental consequences resulting from such provisions; and

(2) Partially to defray the expenses of administering the Board's other responsibilities to enforce the provisions of the State Bar Act relating to the competent delivery of legal services and the incidental consequences resulting therefrom.

(Subd (e) amended and relettered effective January 1, 2007; adopted as subd (c) effective September 3, 1986.)

(f) Counsel *pro hac vice* subject to jurisdiction of courts and State Bar

A person permitted to appear as counsel *pro hac vice* under this rule is subject to the jurisdiction of the courts of this state with respect to the law of this state governing the conduct of attorneys to the same extent as a member of the State Bar of California. The counsel *pro hac vice* must familiarize himself or herself and comply with the standards of professional conduct required of members of the State Bar of California and will be subject to the disciplinary jurisdiction of the State Bar with respect to any of his or her acts occurring in the course of such appearance. Article 5, chapter 4, division III of the Business and Professions Code and the Rules of Procedure of the State Bar govern in any investigation or proceeding conducted by the State Bar under this rule.

(Subd (f) amended and relettered effective January 1, 2007; previously relettered as subd (d) effective September 3, 1986.)

(g) Supreme Court and Court of Appeal not precluded from permitting argument in a particular case

This rule does not preclude the Supreme Court or a Court of Appeal from permitting argument in a particular case from a person who is not a member of the State Bar, but who is licensed to practice in another jurisdiction and who possesses special expertise in the particular field affected by the proceeding.

(Subd (g) amended and relettered effective January 1, 2007; previously relettered as subd (e) effective September 3, 1986.) Rule 9.40 amended and renumbered effective January 1, 2007; adopted as rule 983 by the Supreme Court effective September 13, 1972; previously amended effective October 3, 1973, September 3, 1986, January 17, 1991, and March 15, 1991.

Ref.: Cal. Fms Pl. & Pr., Ch. 40, "Appeal: An Overview," Ch. 45, "Appeal: Motion Procedure," Ch. 54, "Appeal: California Supreme Court Review," Ch. 70, "Attorney Admission," Ch. 72, "Attorney Practice and Ethics," Ch. 551, "Trial"; MB Prac. Guide: Cal. Pretrial Proc., §7.07[1].

Rule 9.41. Appearances by military counsel

(a) Permission to appear

A judge advocate (as that term is defined at 10 United States Code section 801(13)) who is not a member of the State Bar of California but who is a member in good standing of and eligible to practice before the bar of any United States court or of the highest court in any state, territory, or insular possession of the United States may, in the discretion of a court of this state, be permitted to appear in that court to represent a person in the military service in a particular cause pending before that court, under the Servicemembers Civil Relief Act, 50 United States Code Appendix section 501 et seq., if:

(1) The judge advocate has been made available by the cognizant Judge Advocate General (as that term is defined at 10 United States Code section 801(1)) or a duly designated representative; and

(2) The court finds that retaining civilian counsel likely would cause substantial hardship for the person in military service or that person's family; and

(3) The court appoints a judge advocate as attorney to represent the person in military service under the Servicemembers Civil Relief Act.

Under no circumstances is the determination of availability of a judge advocate to be made by any court within this state, or reviewed by any court of this state. In determining the likelihood of substantial hardship as a result of the retention of civilian counsel, the court may take judicial notice of the prevailing pay scales for persons in the military service.

(Subd (a) amended effective January 1, 2007.)

(b) Notice to parties

The clerk of the court considering appointment of a judge advocate under this rule must provide written notice of that fact to all parties who have appeared in the cause. A copy of the notice, together with proof of service by mail in accordance with Code of Civil Procedure section 1013a, must be filed by the clerk of the court. Any party who has appeared in the matter may file a written objection to the appointment within 10 days of the date on which notice was given unless the court has prescribed a shorter period. If the court determines to hold a hearing in relation to the appointment, notice of the hearing must be given at least 10 days before the date designated for the hearing unless the court has prescribed a shorter period.

(Subd (b) amended effective January 1, 2007.)

(c) Appearing judge advocate subject to court and State Bar jurisdiction

A judge advocate permitted to appear under this rule is subject to the jurisdiction of the courts of this state with respect to the law of this state governing the conduct of attorneys to the same extent as a member of the State Bar of California. The judge advocate must become familiar with and comply with the standards of professional conduct required of members of the State Bar of California and is subject to the disciplinary jurisdiction of the State Bar of California. Division 3, chapter 4, article 5 of the Business and Professions Code and the Rules of Procedure of the State Bar of California govern any investigation or proceeding conducted by the State Bar under this rule.

(Subd (c) amended effective January 1, 2007.)

(d) Appearing judge advocate subject to rights and obligations of State Bar members concerning professional privileges

A judge advocate permitted to appear under this rule is subject to the rights and obligations with respect to attorney-client privilege, work-product privilege, and other professional privileges to the same extent as a member of the State Bar of California.

(Subd (d) amended effective January 1, 2007.)

Rule 9.41 amended and renumbered effective January 1, 2007; adopted as rule 983.1 by the Supreme Court effective February 19, 1992; adopted by the Judicial Council effective February 21, 1992.

Ref.: Cal. Fms Pl. & Pr., Ch. 72, "Attorney Practice and Ethics."

Rule 9.42.   Certified law students

(a) Definitions

(1) A "certified law student" is a law student who has a currently effective certificate of registration as a certified law student from the State Bar.

(2) A "supervising attorney" is a member of the State Bar who agrees to supervise a certified law student under rules established by the State Bar and whose name appears on the application for certification.

(Subd (a) amended effective January 1, 2007.)

(b) State Bar Certified Law Student Program

The State Bar must establish and administer a program for registering law students under rules adopted by the Board of Governors of the State Bar.

(Subd (b) amended effective January 1, 2007.)

(c) Eligibility for certification

To be eligible to become a certified law student, an applicant must:

(1) Have successfully completed one full year of studies (minimum of 270 hours) at a law school accredited by the American Bar Association or the State Bar of California, or both, or have passed the first year law students' examination;

(2) Have been accepted into, and be enrolled in, the second, third, or fourth year of law school in good academic standing or have graduated from law school, subject to the time period limitations specified in the rules adopted by the Board of Governors of the State Bar; and

(3) Have either successfully completed or be currently enrolled in and attending academic courses in evidence and civil procedure.

(d) Permitted activities

Subject to all applicable rules, regulations, and statutes, a certified law student may:

(1) Negotiate for and on behalf of the client subject to final approval thereof by the supervising attorney or give legal advice to the client, provided that the certified law student:

(A) Obtains the approval of the supervising attorney to engage in the activities;

(B) Obtains the approval of the supervising attorney regarding the legal advice to be given or plan of negotiation to be undertaken by the certified law student; and

(C) Performs the activities under the general supervision of the supervising attorney;

(2) Appear on behalf of the client in depositions, provided that the certified law student:

(A) Obtains the approval of the supervising attorney to engage in the activity;

(B) Performs the activity under the direct and immediate supervision and in the personal presence of the supervising attorney (or, exclusively in the case of government agencies, any deputy, assistant, or other staff attorney authorized and designated by the supervising attorney); and

(C) Obtains a signed consent form from the client on whose behalf the certified law student acts (or, exclusively in the case of government agencies, from the chief counsel or prosecuting attorney) approving the performance of such acts by such certified law student or generally by any certified law student;

(3) Appear on behalf of the client in any public trial, hearing, arbitration, or proceeding, or before any arbitrator, court, public agency, referee, magistrate, commissioner, or hearing officer, to the extent approved by such arbitrator, court, public agency, referee, magistrate, commissioner, or hearing officer, provided that the certified law student:

(A) Obtains the approval of the supervising attorney to engage in the activity;

(B) Performs the activity under the direct and immediate supervision and in the personal presence of the supervising attorney (or, exclusively in the case of government agencies, any deputy, assistant, or other staff attorney authorized and designated by the supervising attorney);

(C) Obtains a signed consent form from the client on whose behalf the certified law student acts (or, exclusively in the case of government agencies, from the chief counsel or prosecuting attorney) approving the performance of such acts by such certified law student or generally by any certified law student; and

(D) As a condition to such appearance, either presents a copy of the consent form to the arbitrator, court, public agency, referee, magistrate, commissioner, or hearing officer, or files a copy of the consent form in the court case file; and

(4) Appear on behalf of a government agency in the prosecution of criminal actions classified as infractions or other such minor criminal offenses with a maximum penalty or a fine equal to the maximum fine for infractions in California, including any public trial:

(A) Subject to approval by the court, commissioner, referee, hearing officer, or magistrate presiding at such public trial; and

(B) Without the personal appearance of the supervising attorney or any deputy, assistant, or other staff attorney authorized and designated by the supervising attorney, but only if the supervising attorney or the designated attorney has approved in writing the performance of such acts by the certified law student and is immediately available to attend the proceeding.

(Subd (d) amended effective January 1, 2007.)

(e) Failure to comply with program

A certified law student who fails to comply with the requirements of the State Bar Certified Law Student Program must have his or her certification withdrawn under rules adopted by the Board of Governors of the State Bar.

(Subd (e) amended effective January 1, 2007.)

(f) Fee and penalty

The State Bar has the authority to set and collect appropriate fees and penalties for this program.

(Subd (f) amended effective January 1, 2007.)

(g) Inherent power of Supreme Court

Nothing in these rules may be construed as affecting the power of the Supreme Court to exercise its inherent jurisdiction over the practice of law in California.

(Subd (g) amended effective January 1, 2007.)

Rule 9.42 amended and renumbered effective January 1, 2007; adopted as rule 983.2 by the Supreme Court effective December 29, 1993.

Rule 9.43. Out-of-state attorney arbitration counsel

(a) Definition

An "out-of-state attorney arbitration counsel" is an attorney who is:

(1) Not a member of the State Bar of California but who is a member in good standing of and eligible to practice before the bar of any United States court or the highest court in any state, territory, or insular possession of the United States, and who has been retained to appear in the course of, or in connection with, an arbitration proceeding in this state;

(2) Has served a certificate in accordance with the requirements of Code of Civil Procedure section 1282.4 on the arbitrator, the arbitrators, or the arbitral forum, the State Bar of California, and all other parties and counsel in the arbitration whose addresses are known to the attorney; and

(3) Whose appearance has been approved by the arbitrator, the arbitrators, or the arbitral forum.

(Subd (a) amended effective January 1, 2007.)

(b) State Bar Out-of-State Attorney Arbitration Counsel Program

The State Bar of California must establish and administer a program to implement the State Bar of California's responsibilities under Code of Civil Procedure section 1282.4. The State Bar of California's program may be operative only as long as the applicable provisions of Code of Civil Procedure section 1282.4 remain in effect.

(Subd (b) amended effective January 1, 2007.)

(c) Eligibility to appear as an out-of-state attorney arbitration counsel

To be eligible to appear as an out-of-state attorney arbitration counsel, an attorney must comply with all of the applicable provisions of Code of Civil Procedure section 1282.4 and the requirements of this rule and the related rules and regulations adopted by the State Bar of California.

(Subd (c) amended effective January 1, 2007.)

(d) Discipline

An out-of-state attorney arbitration counsel who files a certificate containing false information or who otherwise fails to comply with the standards of professional conduct required of members of the State Bar of California is subject to the disciplinary jurisdiction of the State Bar

with respect to any of his or her acts occurring in the course of the arbitration.

(Subd (d) amended effective January 1, 2007.)

(e) Disqualification

Failure to timely file and serve a certificate or, absent special circumstances, appearances in multiple separate arbitration matters are grounds for disqualification from serving in the arbitration in which the certificate was filed.

(Subd (e) amended effective January 1, 2007.)

(f) Fee

Out-of-state attorney arbitration counsel must pay a reasonable fee not exceeding $50 to the State Bar of California with the copy of the certificate that is served on the State Bar.

(Subd (f) amended effective January 1, 2007.)

(g) Inherent power of Supreme Court

Nothing in these rules may be construed as affecting the power of the Supreme Court to exercise its inherent jurisdiction over the practice of law in California.

(Subd (g) amended effective January 1, 2007.)

Rule 9.43 amended and renumbered effective January 1, 2007; adopted as rule 983.4 by the Supreme Court effective July 1, 1999.

Ref.: Cal. Fms Pl. & Pr., Ch. 33, "Contractual Arbitration: Appointment of Arbitrator and Conduct of Proceeding," Ch. 72, "Attorney Practice and Ethics."

Rule 9.44. Registered foreign legal consultant

(a) Definition

A "registered foreign legal consultant" is a person who:

(1) Is admitted to practice and is in good standing as an attorney or counselor-at-law or the equivalent in a foreign country; and

(2) Has a currently effective certificate of registration as a registered foreign legal consultant from the State Bar.

(Subd (a) amended effective January 1, 2007.)

(b) State Bar Registered Foreign Legal Consultant Program

The State Bar must establish and administer a program for registering foreign attorneys or counselors-at-law or the equivalent under rules adopted by the Board of Governors of the State Bar.

(Subd (b) amended effective January 1, 2007.)

(c) Eligibility for certification

To be eligible to become a registered foreign legal consultant, an applicant must:

(1) Present satisfactory proof that the applicant has been admitted to practice and has been in good standing as an attorney or counselor-at-law or the equivalent in a foreign country for at least four of the six years immediately preceding the application and, while so admitted, has actually practiced the law of that country;

(2) Present satisfactory proof that the applicant possesses the good moral character requisite for a person to be licensed as a member of the State Bar of California;

(3) Agree to comply with the provisions of the rules adopted by the Board of Governors of the State Bar relating to security for claims against a foreign legal consultant by his or her clients;

(4) Agree to comply with the provisions of the rules adopted by the Board of Governors of the State Bar

relating to maintaining an address of record for State Bar purposes;

(5) Agree to notify the State Bar of any change in his or her status in any jurisdiction where he or she is admitted to practice or of any discipline with respect to such admission;

(6) Agree to be subject to the jurisdiction of the courts of this state with respect to the laws of the State of California governing the conduct of attorneys, to the same extent as a member of the State Bar of California;

(7) Agree to become familiar with and comply with the standards of professional conduct required of members of the State Bar of California;

(8) Agree to be subject to the disciplinary jurisdiction of the State Bar of California;

(9) Agree to be subject to the rights and obligations with respect to attorney client privilege, work-product privilege, and other professional privileges, to the same extent as attorneys admitted to practice law in California; and

(10) Agree to comply with the laws of the State of California, the rules and regulations of the State Bar of California, and these rules.

(Subd (c) amended effective January 1, 2007.)

(d) Authority to practice law

Subject to all applicable rules, regulations, and statutes, a registered foreign legal consultant may render legal services in California, except that he or she may not:

(1) Appear for a person other than himself or herself as attorney in any court, or before any magistrate or other judicial officer, in this state or prepare pleadings or any other papers or issue subpoenas in any action or proceeding brought in any court or before any judicial officer;

(2) Prepare any deed, mortgage, assignment, discharge, lease, or any other instrument affecting title to real estate located in the United States;

(3) Prepare any will or trust instrument affecting the disposition on death of any property located in the United States and owned by a resident or any instrument relating to the administration of a decedent's estate in the United States;

(4) Prepare any instrument in respect of the marital relations, rights, or duties of a resident of the United States, or the custody or care of the children of a resident; or

(5) Otherwise render professional legal advice on the law of the State of California, any other state of the United States, the District of Columbia, the United States, or of any jurisdiction other than the jurisdiction named in satisfying the requirements of (c) of this rule, whether rendered incident to preparation of legal instruments or otherwise.

(Subd (d) amended effective January 1, 2007.)

(e) Failure to comply with program

A registered foreign legal consultant who fails to comply with the requirements of the State Bar Registered Foreign Legal Consultant Program will have her or his certification suspended or revoked under rules adopted by the Board of Governors of the State Bar.

(Subd (e) amended effective January 1, 2007.)

(f) Fee and penalty

The State Bar has the authority to set and collect appropriate fees and penalties for this program.

(Subd (f) amended effective January 1, 2007.)

(g) Inherent power of Supreme Court

Nothing in these rules may be construed as affecting the power of the Supreme Court to exercise its inherent jurisdiction over the practice of law in California.

(Subd (g) amended effective January 1, 2007.)

Rule 9.44 amended and renumbered effective January 1, 2007; adopted as rule 988 effective December 1, 1993.

Rule 9.45.   Registered legal services attorneys

(a) Definitions

The following definitions apply in this rule:

(1) "Qualifying legal services provider" means either of the following, provided that the qualifying legal services provider follows quality-control procedures approved by the State Bar of California:

(A) A nonprofit entity incorporated and operated exclusively in California that as its primary purpose and function provides legal services without charge in civil matters to indigent persons, especially underserved client groups, such as the elderly, persons with disabilities, juveniles, and non-English-speaking persons; or

(B) A program operated exclusively in California by a nonprofit law school approved by the American Bar Association or accredited by the State Bar of California that has operated for at least two years at a cost of at least $20,000 per year as an identifiable law school unit with a primary purpose and function of providing legal services without charge to indigent persons.

(2) "Active member in good standing of the bar of a United States state, jurisdiction, possession, territory, or dependency" means an attorney who:

(A) Is a member in good standing of the entity governing the practice of law in each jurisdiction in which the member is licensed to practice law;

(B) Remains an active member in good standing of the entity governing the practice of law in at least one United States state, jurisdiction, possession, territory, or dependency other than California while practicing law as a registered legal services attorney in California; and

(C) Has not been disbarred, has not resigned with charges pending, or is not suspended from practicing law in any other jurisdiction.

(Subd (a) relettered effective January 1, 2007; adopted as subd (j) effective November 15, 2004.)

(b) Scope of practice

Subject to all applicable rules, regulations, and statutes, an attorney practicing law under this rule may practice law in California only while working, with or without pay, at a qualifying legal services provider, as defined in this rule, and, at that institution and only on behalf of its clients, may engage, under supervision, in all forms of legal practice that are permissible for a member of the State Bar of California.

(Subd (b) amended and relettered effective January 1, 2007; adopted as subd (a) effective November 15, 2004.)

(c) Requirements

For an attorney to practice law under this rule, the attorney must:

(1) Be an active member in good standing of the bar of a United States state, jurisdiction, possession, territory, or dependency;

(2) Register with the State Bar of California and file an Application for Determination of Moral Character;

(3) Meet all of the requirements for admission to the State Bar of California, except that the attorney:

(A) Need not take the California bar examination or the Multistate Professional Responsibility Examination; and

(B) May practice law while awaiting the result of his or her Application for Determination of Moral Character;

(4) Comply with the rules adopted by the Board of Governors relating to the State Bar Registered Legal Services Attorney Program;

(5) Practice law exclusively for a single qualifying legal services provider, except that, if so qualified, an attorney may, while practicing under this rule, simultaneously practice law as registered in-house counsel;

(6) Practice law under the supervision of an attorney who is employed by the qualifying legal services provider and who is a member in good standing of the State Bar of California;

(7) Abide by all of the laws and rules that govern members of the State Bar of California, including the Minimum Continuing Legal Education (MCLE) requirements;

(8) Satisfy in his or her first year of practice under this rule all of the MCLE requirements, including ethics education, that members of the State Bar of California must complete every three years; and

(9) Not have taken and failed the California bar examination within five years immediately preceding application to register under this rule.

(Subd (c) relettered effective January 1, 2007; adopted as subd (b) effective November 15, 2004.)

(d) Application

To qualify to practice law as a registered legal services attorney, the attorney must:

(1) Register as an attorney applicant and file an Application for Determination of Moral Character with the Committee of Bar Examiners;

(2) Submit to the State Bar of California a declaration signed by the attorney agreeing that he or she will be subject to the disciplinary authority of the Supreme Court of California and the State Bar of California and attesting that he or she will not practice law in California other than under supervision at a qualifying legal services provider during the time he or she practices law as a registered legal services attorney in California, except that, if so qualified, the attorney may, while practicing under this rule, simultaneously practice law as registered in-house counsel; and

(3) Submit to the State Bar of California a declaration signed by a qualifying supervisor on behalf of the qualifying legal services provider in California attesting that the applicant will work, with or without pay, as an attorney for the organization; that the applicant will be supervised as specified in this rule; and that the qualifying legal services provider and the supervising attorney assume professional responsibility for any work performed by the applicant under this rule.

(Subd (d) relettered effective January 1, 2007; adopted as subd (c) effective November 15, 2004.)

(e) Duration of practice

An attorney may practice for no more than a total of three years under this rule.

(Subd (e) relettered effective January 1, 2007; adopted as subd (d) effective November 15, 2004.)

(f) Application and registration fees

The State Bar of California may set appropriate application fees and initial and annual registration fees to be paid by registered legal services attorneys.

(Subd (f) amended and relettered effective January 1, 2007; adopted as subd (e) effective November 15, 2004.)

(g) State Bar Registered Legal Services Attorney Program

The State Bar may establish and administer a program for registering California legal services attorneys under rules adopted by the Board of Governors of the State Bar.

(Subd (g) relettered effective January 1, 2007; adopted as subd (f) effective November 15, 2004.)

(h) Supervision

To meet the requirements of this rule, an attorney supervising a registered legal services attorney:

(1) Must be an active member in good standing of the State Bar of California;

(2) Must have actively practiced law in California and been a member in good standing of the State Bar of California for at least the two years immediately preceding the time of supervision;

(3) Must have practiced law as a full-time occupation for at least four years;

(4) Must not supervise more than two registered legal services attorneys concurrently;

(5) Must assume professional responsibility for any work that the registered legal services attorney performs under the supervising attorney's supervision;

(6) Must assist, counsel, and provide direct supervision of the registered legal services attorney in the activities authorized by this rule and review such activities with the supervised attorney, to the extent required for the protection of the client;

(7) Must read, approve, and personally sign any pleadings, briefs, or other similar documents prepared by the registered legal services attorney before their filing, and must read and approve any documents prepared by the registered legal services attorney for execution by any person who is not a member of the State Bar of California before their submission for execution; and

(8) May, in his or her absence, designate another attorney meeting the requirements of (1) through (7) to provide the supervision required under this rule.

(Subd (h) relettered effective January 1, 2007; adopted as subd (g) effective November 15, 2004.)

(i) Inherent power of Supreme Court

Nothing in this rule may be construed as affecting the power of the Supreme Court of California to exercise its inherent jurisdiction over the practice of law in California.

(Subd (i) amended and relettered effective January 1, 2007; adopted as subd (h) effective November 15, 2004.)

(j) Effect of rule on multijurisdictional practice

Nothing in this rule limits the scope of activities permissible under existing law by attorneys who are not members of the State Bar of California.

(Subd (j) relettered effective January 1, 2007; adopted as subd (i) effective November 15, 2004.)

Rule 9.45 amended and renumbered effective January 1, 2007; adopted as rule 964 by the Supreme Court effective November 15, 2004.

Ref.: Cal. Fms Pl. & Pr., Ch. 70, "Attorney Admission."

Rule 9.46.   Registered in-house counsel

(a) Definitions

The following definitions apply to terms used in this rule:

(1) "Qualifying institution" means a corporation, a partnership, an association, or other legal entity, including its subsidiaries and organizational affiliates. Neither a governmental entity nor an entity that provides legal services to others can be a qualifying institution for purposes of this rule. A qualifying institution must:

(A) Employ at least 10 employees full time in California; or

(B) Employ in California an attorney who is an active member in good standing of the State Bar of California.

(2) "Active member in good standing of the bar of a United States state, jurisdiction, possession, territory, or dependency" means an attorney who meets all of the following criteria:

(A) Is a member in good standing of the entity governing the practice of law in each jurisdiction in which the member is licensed to practice law;

(B) Remains an active member in good standing of the entity governing the practice of law in at least one United States state, jurisdiction, possession, territory, or dependency, other than California, while practicing law as registered in-house counsel in California; and

(C) Has not been disbarred, has not resigned with charges pending, or is not suspended from practicing law in any other jurisdiction.

(Subd (a) relettered effective January 1, 2007; adopted as subd (j) effective November 15, 2004.)

(b) Scope of practice

Subject to all applicable rules, regulations, and statutes, an attorney practicing law under this rule is:

(1) Permitted to provide legal services in California only to the qualifying institution that employs him or her;

(2) Not permitted to make court appearances in California state courts or to engage in any other activities for which *pro hac vice* admission is required if they are performed in California by an attorney who is not a member of the State Bar of California; and

(3) Not permitted to provide personal or individual representation to any customers, shareholders, owners, partners, officers, employees, servants, or agents of the qualifying institution.

(Subd (b) amended and relettered effective January 1, 2007; adopted as subd (a) effective November 15, 2004.)

(c) Requirements

For an attorney to practice law under this rule, the attorney must:

(1) Be an active member in good standing of the bar of a United States state, jurisdiction, possession, territory, or dependency;

(2) Register with the State Bar of California and file an Application for Determination of Moral Character;

(3) Meet all of the requirements for admission to the State Bar of California, except that the attorney:

(A) Need not take the California bar examination or the Multistate Professional Responsibility Examination; and

(B) May practice law while awaiting the result of his or her Application for Determination of Moral Character;

(4) Comply with the rules adopted by the Board of Governors relating to the State Bar Registered In-House Counsel Program;

(5) Practice law exclusively for a single qualifying institution, except that, while practicing under this rule, the attorney may, if so qualified, simultaneously practice law as a registered legal services attorney;

(6) Abide by all of the laws and rules that govern members of the State Bar of California, including the Minimum Continuing Legal Education (MCLE) requirements;

(7) Satisfy in his or her first year of practice under this rule all of the MCLE requirements, including ethics education, that members of the State Bar of California must complete every three years and, thereafter, satisfy the MCLE requirements applicable to all members of the State Bar; and

(8) Reside in California.

(Subd (c) relettered effective January 1, 2007; adopted as subd (b) effective November 15, 2004.)

(d) Application

To qualify to practice law as registered in-house counsel, an attorney must:

(1) Register as an attorney applicant and file an Application for Determination of Moral Character with the Committee of Bar Examiners;

(2) Submit to the State Bar of California a declaration signed by the attorney agreeing that he or she will be subject to the disciplinary authority of the Supreme Court of California and the State Bar of California and attesting that he or she will not practice law in California other than on behalf of the qualifying institution during the time he or she is registered in-house counsel in California, except that if so qualified, the attorney may, while practicing under this rule, simultaneously practice law as a registered legal services attorney; and

(3) Submit to the State Bar of California a declaration signed by an officer, a director, or a general counsel of the applicant's employer, on behalf of the applicant's employer, attesting that the applicant is employed as an attorney for the employer, that the nature of the employment conforms to the requirements of this rule, that the employer will notify the State Bar of California within 30 days of the cessation of the applicant's employment in California, and that the person signing the declaration believes, to the best of his or her knowledge after reasonable inquiry, that the applicant qualifies for registration under this rule and is an individual of good moral character.

(Subd (d) relettered effective January 1, 2007; adopted as subd (c) effective November 15, 2004.)

(e) Duration of practice

A registered in-house counsel must renew his or her registration annually. There is no limitation on the number of years in-house counsel may register under this rule.

Registered in-house counsel may practice law under this rule only for as long as he or she remains employed by the same qualifying institution that provided the declaration in support of his or her application. If an attorney practicing law as registered in-house counsel leaves the employment of his or her employer or changes employers, he or she must notify the State Bar of California within 30 days. If an attorney wishes to practice law under this rule for a new employer, he or she must first register as in-house counsel for that employer.

(Subd (e) amended and relettered effective January 1, 2007; adopted as subd (d) effective November 15, 2004.)

(f) Eligibility

An application to register under this rule may not be denied because:

(1) The attorney applicant has practiced law in California as in-house counsel before the effective date of this rule.

(2) The attorney applicant is practicing law as in-house counsel at or after the effective date of this rule, provided that the attorney applies under this rule within six months of its effective date.

(Subd (f) amended and relettered effective January 1, 2007; adopted as subd (e) effective November 15, 2004.)

(g) Application and registration fees

The State Bar of California may set appropriate application fees and initial and annual registration fees to be paid by registered in-house counsel.

(Subd (g) amended and relettered effective January 1, 2007; adopted as subd (f) effective November 15, 2004.)

(h) State Bar Registered In-House Counsel Program

The State Bar must establish and administer a program for registering California in-house counsel under rules adopted by the Board of Governors.

(Subd (h) amended and relettered effective January 1, 2007; adopted as subd (g) effective November 15, 2004.)

(i) Inherent power of Supreme Court

Nothing in this rule may be construed as affecting the power of the Supreme Court of California to exercise its inherent jurisdiction over the practice of law in California.

(Subd (i) amended and relettered effective January 1, 2007; adopted as subd (h) effective November 15, 2004.)

(j) Effect of rule on multijurisdictional practice

Nothing in this rule limits the scope of activities permissible under existing law by attorneys who are not members of the State Bar of California.

(Subd (j) relettered effective January 1, 2007; adopted as subd (i) effective November 15, 2004.)

Rule 9.46 amended and renumbered effective January 1, 2007; adopted as rule 965 by the Supreme Court effective November 15, 2004.

Ref.: Cal. Fms Pl. & Pr., Ch. 70, "Attorney Admission."

Rule 9.47. Attorneys practicing law temporarily in California as part of litigation

(a) Definitions

The following definitions apply to the terms used in this rule:

(1) "A formal legal proceeding" means litigation, arbitration, mediation, or a legal action before an administrative decision-maker.

(2) "Authorized to appear" means the attorney is permitted to appear in the proceeding by the rules of the jurisdiction in which the formal legal proceeding is taking place or will be taking place.

(3) "Active member in good standing of the bar of a United States state, jurisdiction, possession, territory, or dependency" means an attorney who meets all of the following criteria:

(A) Is a member in good standing of the entity governing the practice of law in each jurisdiction in which the member is licensed to practice law;

(B) Remains an active member in good standing of the entity governing the practice of law in at least one United States state, jurisdiction, possession, territory, or dependency while practicing law under this rule; and

(C) Has not been disbarred, has not resigned with charges pending, or is not suspended from practicing law in any other jurisdiction.

(Subd (a) relettered effective January 1, 2007; adopted as subd (g) effective November 15, 2004.)

(b) Requirements

For an attorney to practice law under this rule, the attorney must:

(1) Maintain an office in a United States jurisdiction other than California and in which the attorney is licensed to practice law;

(2) Already be retained by a client in the matter for which the attorney is providing legal services in California, except that the attorney may provide legal advice to a potential client, at the potential client's request, to assist the client in deciding whether to retain the attorney;

(3) Indicate on any Web site or other advertisement that is accessible in California either that the attorney is not a member of the State Bar of California or that the attorney is admitted to practice law only in the states listed; and

(4) Be an active member in good standing of the bar of a United States state, jurisdiction, possession, territory, or dependency.

(Subd (b) relettered effective January 1, 2007; adopted as subd (a) effective November 15, 2004.)

(c) Permissible activities

An attorney meeting the requirements of this rule, who complies with all applicable rules, regulations, and statutes, is not engaging in the unauthorized practice of law in California if the attorney's services are part of:

(1) A formal legal proceeding that is pending in another jurisdiction and in which the attorney is authorized to appear;

(2) A formal legal proceeding that is anticipated but is not yet pending in California and in which the attorney reasonably expects to be authorized to appear;

(3) A formal legal proceeding that is anticipated but is not yet pending in another jurisdiction and in which the attorney reasonably expects to be authorized to appear; or

(4) A formal legal proceeding that is anticipated or pending and in which the attorney's supervisor is authorized to appear or reasonably expects to be authorized to appear.

The attorney whose anticipated authorization to appear in a formal legal proceeding serves as the basis for practice under this rule must seek that authorization promptly after it becomes possible to do so. Failure to seek that authorization promptly, or denial of that authorization, ends eligibility to practice under this rule.

(Subd (c) relettered effective January 1, 2007; adopted as subd (b) effective November 15, 2004.)

(d) Restrictions

To qualify to practice law in California under this rule, an attorney must not:

(1) Hold out to the public or otherwise represent that he or she is admitted to practice law in California;

(2) Establish or maintain a resident office or other systematic or continuous presence in California for the practice of law;

(3) Be a resident of California;

(4) Be regularly employed in California;

(5) Regularly engage in substantial business or professional activities in California; or

(6) Have been disbarred, have resigned with charges pending, or be suspended from practicing law in any other jurisdiction.

(Subd (d) relettered effective January 1, 2007; adopted as subd (c) effective November 15, 2004.)

(e) Conditions

By practicing law in California under this rule, an attorney agrees that he or she is providing legal services in California subject to:

(1) The jurisdiction of the State Bar of California;

(2) The jurisdiction of the courts of this state to the same extent as is a member of the State Bar of California; and

(3) The laws of the State of California relating to the practice of law, the State Bar Rules of Professional Conduct, the rules and regulations of the State Bar of California, and these rules.

(Subd (e) relettered effective January 1, 2007; adopted as subd (d) effective November 15, 2004.)

(f) Inherent power of Supreme Court

Nothing in this rule may be construed as affecting the power of the Supreme Court of California to exercise its inherent jurisdiction over the practice of law in California.

(Subd (f) amended and relettered effective January 1, 2007; adopted as subd (e) effective November 15, 2004.)

(g) Effect of rule on multijurisdictional practice

Nothing in this rule limits the scope of activities permissible under existing law by attorneys who are not members of the State Bar of California.

(Subd (g) relettered effective January 1, 2007; adopted as subd (f) effective November 15, 2004.)

Rule 9.47 amended and renumbered effective January 1, 2007; adopted as rule 966 by the Supreme Court effective November 15, 2004.

Rule 9.48. Nonlitigating attorneys temporarily in California to provide legal services

(a) Definitions

The following definitions apply to terms used in this rule:

(1) "A transaction or other nonlitigation matter" includes any legal matter other than litigation, arbitration, mediation, or a legal action before an administrative decision-maker.

(2) "Active member in good standing of the bar of a United States state, jurisdiction, possession, territory, or dependency" means an attorney who meets all of the following criteria:

(A) Is a member in good standing of the entity governing the practice of law in each jurisdiction in which the member is licensed to practice law;

(B) Remains an active member in good standing of the entity governing the practice of law in at least one United States state, jurisdiction, possession, territory, or dependency other than California while practicing law under this rule; and

(C) Has not been disbarred, has not resigned with charges pending, or is not suspended from practicing law in any other jurisdiction.

(Subd (a) relettered effective January 1, 2007; adopted as subd (h) effective November 15, 2004.)

(b) Requirements

For an attorney to practice law under this rule, the attorney must:

(1) Maintain an office in a United States jurisdiction other than California and in which the attorney is licensed to practice law;

(2) Already be retained by a client in the matter for which the attorney is providing legal services in California, except that the attorney may provide legal advice to a potential client, at the potential client's request, to assist the client in deciding whether to retain the attorney;

(3) Indicate on any Web site or other advertisement that is accessible in California either that the attorney is not a member of the State Bar of California or that the attorney is admitted to practice law only in the states listed; and

(4) Be an active member in good standing of the bar of a United States state, jurisdiction, possession, territory, or dependency.

(Subd (b) relettered effective January 1, 2007; adopted as subd (a) effective November 15, 2004.)

(c) Permissible activities

An attorney who meets the requirements of this rule and who complies with all applicable rules, regulations, and statutes is not engaging in the unauthorized practice of law in California if the attorney:

(1) Provides legal assistance or legal advice in California to a client concerning a transaction or other nonlitigation matter, a material aspect of which is taking place in a jurisdiction other than California and in which the attorney is licensed to provide legal services;

(2) Provides legal assistance or legal advice in California on an issue of federal law or of the law of a jurisdiction other than California to attorneys licensed to practice law in California; or

(3) Is an employee of a client and provides legal assistance or legal advice in California to the client or to the client's subsidiaries or organizational affiliates.

(Subd (c) relettered effective January 1, 2007; adopted as subd (b) effective November 15, 2004.)

(d) Restrictions

To qualify to practice law in California under this rule, an attorney must not:

(1) Hold out to the public or otherwise represent that he or she is admitted to practice law in California;

(2) Establish or maintain a resident office or other systematic or continuous presence in California for the practice of law;

(3) Be a resident of California;

(4) Be regularly employed in California;

(5) Regularly engage in substantial business or professional activities in California; or

(6) Have been disbarred, have resigned with charges pending, or be suspended from practicing law in any other jurisdiction.

(Subd (d) amended and relettered effective January 1, 2007; adopted as subd (c) effective November 15, 2004.)

(e) Conditions

By practicing law in California under this rule, an attorney agrees that he or she is providing legal services in California subject to:

(1) The jurisdiction of the State Bar of California;

(2) The jurisdiction of the courts of this state to the same extent as is a member of the State Bar of California; and

(3) The laws of the State of California relating to the practice of law, the State Bar Rules of Professional Conduct, the rules and regulations of the State Bar of California, and these rules.

(Subd (e) amended and relettered effective January 1, 2007; adopted as subd (d) effective November 15, 2004.)

(f) Scope of practice

An attorney is permitted by this rule to provide legal assistance or legal services concerning only a transaction or other nonlitigation matter.

(Subd (f) relettered effective January 1, 2007; adopted as subd (e) effective November 15, 2004.)

(g) Inherent power of Supreme Court

Nothing in this rule may be construed as affecting the power of the Supreme Court of California to exercise its inherent jurisdiction over the practice of law in California.

(Subd (g) amended and relettered effective January 1, 2007; adopted as subd (f) effective November 15, 2004.)

(h) Effect of rule on multijurisdictional practice

Nothing in this rule limits the scope of activities permissible under existing law by attorneys who are not members of the State Bar of California.

(Subd (h) relettered effective January 1, 2007; adopted as subd (g) effective November 15, 2004.)

Rule 9.48 amended and renumbered effective January 1, 2007; adopted as rule 967 by the Supreme Court effective November 15, 2004.

Division 5
Censure, Removal, Retirement, or Private Admonishment of Judges

Rule 9.60. Review of determinations by the Commission on Judicial Performance

(a) Time for petition for review to Supreme Court

A petition to the Supreme Court by a judge or former judge to review a determination by the Commission on Judicial Performance to retire, remove, censure, admonish, or disqualify the judge or former judge must be served and filed within 60 days after:

(1) The Commission, under its rules, notifies the judge or former judge that its determination has been filed or entered in its records; or

(2) The determination becomes final as to the Commission under its rules, whichever event is later.

(Subd (a) amended effective January 1, 2007.)

(b) Time for answer to petition for review and reply

Within 45 days after service of the petition, the Commission may serve and file an answer. Within 20 days after service of the answer, the judge or former judge may serve and file a reply. Each petition, answer, or reply submitted for filing must be accompanied by proof of service, including service on the Commission of three copies of any petition or reply filed by a judge or former judge. Extensions of time to file the petition, answer, or reply are disfavored and will be granted only upon a specific and affirmative showing of good cause. Good cause does not include ordinary press of business.

(Subd (b) lettered effective January 1, 2007; adopted as part of subd (a) effective December 1, 1996.)

(c) Contents and form

The petition, answer, and reply must address both the appropriateness of review and the merits of the Commission's determination, and they will serve as briefs on the merits in the event review is granted. Except as provided in these rules, the form of the petition, answer, and reply must, insofar as practicable, conform to rule 8.504 except that the lengths of the petition, answer, and reply must conform to the limits specified in rule 8.204(c). Each copy of the petition must contain:

(1) A copy of the Commission's determination;

(2) A copy of the notice of filing or entry of the determination in the records of the Commission;

(3) A copy of any findings of fact and conclusions of law; and

(4) A cover that bears the conspicuous notation "PETITION FOR REVIEW OF DETERMINATION BY COMMISSION ON JUDICIAL PERFORMANCE (RULE 9.60)" or words of like effect.

(Subd (c) amended and relettered effective January 1, 2007; adopted as subd (b) effective December 1, 1996.)

(d) Transmission of the record

Promptly upon the service and filing of the petition, the Commission must transmit to the Clerk of the Supreme Court the original record, including a transcript of the testimony, briefs, and all original papers and exhibits on file in the proceeding.

(Subd (d) amended and relettered effective January 1, 2007; adopted as subd (c) effective December 1, 1996.)

(e) Applicable rules on review

In the event review is granted, the rules adopted by the Judicial Council governing appeals from the superior court in civil cases, other than rule 8.272 relating to costs, apply to proceedings in the Supreme Court for review of a determination of the Commission except where express provision is made to the contrary or where such application would otherwise be clearly impracticable or inappropriate.

(Subd (e) amended and relettered effective January 1, 2007; adopted as subd (d) effective December 1, 1996.)

Rule 9.60 amended and renumbered effective January 1, 2007; adopted as rule 935 effective December 1, 1996.

Ref.: Cal. Fms Pl. & Pr., Ch. 317, "Judges."

Rule 9.61. Proceedings involving public or private admonishment, censure, removal, or retirement of a judge of the Supreme Court

(a) Selection of appellate tribunal

Immediately on the filing of a petition to review a determination by the Commission on Judicial Performance to retire, remove, censure, admonish, or disqualify a justice of the Supreme Court, the Clerk of the Supreme Court must select, by lot, seven Court of Appeal justices who must elect one of their number presiding justice and

perform the duties of the tribunal created under article VI, section 18(f) of the Constitution. This selection must be made upon notice to the Commission, the justice, and the counsel of record in a proceeding open to the public. No court of appeal justice who has served as a master or a member of the Commission in the particular proceeding or is otherwise disqualified may serve on the tribunal.

(Subd (a) amended effective January 1, 2007; previously amended effective December 1, 1996.)

(b) Clerk of Supreme Court as clerk of tribunal

The Clerk of the Supreme Court serves as the clerk of the tribunal.

(Subd (b) amended effective January 1, 2007.)

Rule 9.61 amended and renumbered effective January 1, 2007; adopted as rule 921 effective November 13, 1976; previously amended and renumbered as rule 936 effective December 1, 1996.

Ref.: Cal. Fms Pl. & Pr., Ch. 317, "Judges."

TITLE 10
Judicial Administration Rules

Division 1.   Judicial Council. Rules 10.1–10.81.
Division 2.   Administration of the Judicial Branch. Rules 10.101–10.491.
Division 3.   Judicial Administration Rules Applicable to All Courts. Rules 10.502–10.505.
Division 4.   Trial Court Administration. Rules 10.601–10.960.
Division 5.   Appellate Court Administration. Rules 10.1000–10.1108.

Division 1
Judicial Council

Chap. 1.   The Judicial Council and Internal Committees. Rules 10.1–10.22.
Chap. 2.   Judicial Council Advisory Committees and Task Forces. Rules 10.30–10.70.
Chap. 3.   Administrative Office of the Courts. Rules 10.80, 10.81.

Chapter 1
The Judicial Council and Internal Committees

Rule 10.1. Authority, duties, and goals of the Judicial Council
Rule 10.2. Judicial Council membership and terms
Rule 10.3. Nonvoting members
Rule 10.4. Nominations and appointments to the Judicial Council
Rule 10.5. Notice and agenda of council meetings
Rule 10.6. Judicial Council meetings
Rule 10.10. Judicial Council internal committees
Rule 10.11. Executive and Planning Committee
Rule 10.12. Policy Coordination and Liaison Committee
Rule 10.13. Rules and Projects Committee
Rule 10.14. Litigation Management Committee
Rule 10.20. Proposals for new or amended rules, standards, or forms; rule-making process in general
Rule 10.21. Proposals from members of the public for changes to rules, standards, or forms
Rule 10.22. Rule-making procedures

Rule 10.1.   Authority, duties, and goals of the Judicial Council

(a) The Judicial Council

(1) The Judicial Council is a state entity established by the California Constitution and chaired by the Chief Justice of California. The purpose of the Judicial Council is to set the direction and provide leadership for improving the quality of justice and advancing its consistent, independent, impartial, and accessible administration on behalf of the public and the court system as a whole.

(2) The council establishes policies and sets priorities for the judicial branch of government. The council may seek advice and recommendations from committees, task forces, and the public.

(Subd (a) amended effective January 1, 2007.)

(b) Constitutional duties

Article VI, section 6 of the California Constitution requires the council to improve the administration of justice by doing the following:

(1) Surveying judicial business;

(2) Making recommendations to the courts;

(3) Making annual recommendations to the Governor and the Legislature;

(4) Adopting rules for court administration and rules of practice and procedure that are not inconsistent with statute; and

(5) Performing other functions prescribed by statute.

(c) Goals

The council develops policies to achieve the following goals:

(1) The improvement of access, fairness, and diversity in the judicial branch;

(2) The institutional independence of the judiciary as a separate branch of government with the resources necessary for its support and the independence and impartiality of judicial decision making;

(3) The modernization and improvement of judicial administration practices;

(4) Fair and responsive judicial service to the public in all courts; and

(5) The promotion of the goals of the Judicial Council through judicial branch education and professional development.

(Subd (c) amended effective January 1, 2007.)

(d) Long-range strategic plan

The council adopts and publishes a statement of goals and long-term strategies to meet those goals. This publication is referred to as the "Long-Range Strategic Plan."

(Subd (d) amended effective January 1, 2007.)

(e) The Administrative Office of the Courts

The Administrative Office of the Courts supports the council in performing its functions. The Administrative Director is the Secretary of the Judicial Council.

(Subd (e) amended effective January 1, 2007.)

Rule 10.1 amended and renumbered effective January 1, 2007; adopted as rule 6.1 effective January 1, 1999.

Ref.: Cal. Fms Pl. & Pr., Ch. 317, "Judges."

Rule 10.2.   Judicial Council membership and terms

(a) Constitutional provision on membership and terms

Under article VI, section 6 of the California Constitution, the Judicial Council consists of the Chief Justice and one other justice of the Supreme Court, 3 justices of Courts of Appeal, 10 judges of superior courts, 2 nonvoting court administrators, and such other nonvoting members as determined by the voting membership of the council, each appointed by the Chief Justice to three-year terms; 4 members of the State Bar appointed by its governing body to three-year terms; and 1 member of each house of the Legislature appointed as provided by the house.

Council membership terminates if a member ceases to hold the position that qualified the member for appointment. A vacancy is filled by the appointing power for the remainder of the term.

(Subd (a) amended effective January 1, 2007.)

(b) Chair

The Chief Justice of California is the Chair of the Judicial Council. A reference to the Chair of the Judicial Council in the statutes or rules of this state means the Chief Justice of California. The Chair may designate a vice-chair to act in the Chair's absence.

(c) Role of members

Council members do not represent a specific constituency but shall act in the best interests of the public and the entire court system.

(d) Terms

Council members are appointed to terms beginning September 15 and ending September 14. Terms for judge members are staggered. To the extent feasible, the State Bar and the Legislature should create staggered terms for their appointees.

(e) Restrictions on advisory committee membership

Unless the Chief Justice waives this provision, neither council members nor nonvoting advisory council members may concurrently serve on a council advisory committee. This provision does not apply to the following advisory committees:

(1) Administrative Presiding Justices;

(2) Trial Court Presiding Judges; and

(3) Court Executives.

(Subd (e) amended effective January 1, 2007.)

Rule 10.2 amended and renumbered effective January 1, 2007; adopted as rule 6.2 effective January 1, 1999.

Ref.: Cal. Fms Pl. & Pr., Ch. 317, "Judges."

Rule 10.3.   Nonvoting members

(a) Appointment

The Chief Justice appoints nonvoting advisory council members as specified in article VI, section 6 of the California Constitution or as approved by the Judicial Council.

(b) Voting

A nonvoting council member may make or second motions at a council meeting but may not vote. A nonvoting member may vote on an internal committee matter as specified in rule 10.10(d).

(Subd (b) amended effective January 1, 2007.)

Rule 10.3 amended and renumbered effective January 1, 2007; adopted as rule 6.3 effective January 1, 1999.

Rule 10.4.   Nominations and appointments to the Judicial Council

(a) Nomination procedures

The Executive and Planning Committee assists the Chief Justice in selecting council members by submitting a list of nominees for each position. The committee uses the following procedures:

(1) The committee publicizes vacancies and solicits nominations. Nominations for advisory member positions are solicited from the Court Executives Advisory Committee, the Appellate Court Clerks Association, the California Court Commissioners Association, and other related bodies. The selected nominees should represent diverse backgrounds, experiences, and geographic locations.

(2) The committee submits a list of at least three nominees to the Chief Justice for each vacant position, except for the Supreme Court associate justice position. The committee gives added consideration to persons who have served on advisory committees or task forces.

(3) If the Chief Justice is a member of the Executive and Planning Committee, the Chief Justice does not participate in discussions relating to nominations.

(Subd (a) amended effective January 1, 2007.)

(b) Appointing order

The Chief Justice makes appointments to the council by order.

Rule 10.4 amended and renumbered effective January 1, 2007; adopted as rule 6.4 effective January 1, 1999.

Rule 10.5.   Notice and agenda of council meetings

(a) Generally

The Judicial Council meets at the call of the Chief Justice no fewer than four times a year.

(Subd (a) amended effective January 1, 2004.)

(b) Meeting schedule

The Administrative Office of the Courts must publish a regular annual schedule that states the planned date, purpose, and location of each meeting. Additional meetings may be scheduled as necessary.

(Subd (b) amended effective January 1, 2007; previously amended effective January 1, 2004.)

(c) Notice of business meetings

"Business meetings" are council meetings at which a majority of voting members are present to discuss and decide matters within the council's jurisdiction. The Administrative Office of the Courts must give public notice of the date, location, and agenda of each business meeting at least seven days before the meeting. The notice must state whether the meeting is open or closed. If the meeting is partly closed, the notice must indicate which agenda items are closed. A meeting may be conducted without notice in case of an emergency requiring prompt action.

(Subd (c) amended effective January 1, 2004.)

(d) Budget meetings

A "budget meeting" is that portion of any business meeting at which trial court budgets are to be discussed. The Administrative Office of the Courts must provide notice of a budget meeting in the same manner as any other business meeting. Budget meetings normally are scheduled as follows:

(1) A budget priority meeting, normally in February of each year, at which the Judicial Council adopts budget priorities for the trial courts for the budget year that begins July 1 of the next calendar year.

(2) A meeting at which the proposed budget is approved, normally in August of each year, at which the Judicial Council takes action on the following:

(A) Staff recommendations on trial court budget change requests for the next fiscal year;

(B) A total baseline budget for each trial court for the next fiscal year; and

(C) Any proposed changes in funding for a trial court.

(3) A budget allocation meeting, normally at the first council meeting after the state's budget is enacted, at which the Judicial Council approves the final budget allocations for each trial court, including approved budget adjustments.

(4) Other meetings following substantive changes to the trial court portion of the proposed State Budget made by the Governor in the proposed Governor's budget or by a committee or house of the Legislature, at which the Judicial Council will take appropriate action, if any.

(Subd (d) adopted effective January 1, 2004.)

(e) Form of notice

The notice and agenda for council meetings must be posted at the Administrative Office of the Courts and on the California Courts Web site (*www.courtinfo.ca.gov*). In addition, the notice and agenda for budget meetings must be provided to designated employee representatives who have submitted a written request to the Administrative Office of the Courts (attention Secretariat).

(Subd (e) amended effective January 1, 2007; adopted as subd (d) effective January 1, 1999; previously amended and relettered effective January 1, 2004.)

(f) Contents of agenda

The agenda must contain a brief description of each item to be considered at the council meeting. All items are classified as discussion items, consent items, or informational items.

(1) *Consent items deemed approved*

All consent items are deemed approved without further action at the adjournment of each council meeting.

(2) *Moving consent items to discussion agenda*

A consent item must be moved to the discussion agenda if a council member so requests by giving 48 hours' advance notice to the Executive and Planning Committee, or if the Chief Justice moves the item to the discussion agenda.

(Subd (f) amended and relettered effective January 1, 2004; adopted as subd (e) effective January 1, 1999.)

(g) Meeting materials

(1) *General materials*

General meeting materials must be distributed to council members at least three business days before the date of the meeting, except in extraordinary circumstances. The Administrative Director may make copies of materials available to the media or attendees in advance of a business meeting and may specify that the materials are provided on agreement by the recipient that they will be kept confidential until the council has discussed or acted on specified items. The council may charge a fee to cover the costs of replicating and mailing these materials to members of the public.

(2) *Budget materials*

(A) *When available*

Materials involving trial court budgets must be made available at least five business days before the meeting if they have been distributed by that time to the members of the council. All other materials involving trial court budgets must be made available at the same time as the information is distributed to the council.

(B) *Distribution*

Materials must be made available by posting on the California Courts Web site and by distribution to designated employee representatives who have submitted a written request to the Administrative Office of the Courts (attention Secretariat).

(C) *Contents at the budget approval meeting*

Materials involving trial court budget proposals presented at the budget approval meeting must include proposed statewide requests for funding, existing trial court baseline budgets, adjustments proposed for any trial court baseline budget, and any court-specific budget change requests.

(Subd (g) amended effective January 1, 2007; adopted as subd (f) effective January 1, 1999; previously amended and relettered effective January 1, 2004.)

(h) Circulating orders

Between business meetings, the council may act by circulating order on urgent matters if the Chief Justice or the Administrative Director approves. Prior public notice of a proposed circulating order is not required. Each circulating order adopted by the council must be included on the agenda for the next business meeting as an information item.

(Subd (h) amended and relettered effective January 1, 2004; adopted as subd (g) effective January 1, 1999.)

Rule 10.5 amended and renumbered effective January 1, 2007; adopted as rule 6.5 effective January 1, 1999; previously amended effective January 1, 2004.

Rule 10.6.   Judicial Council meetings

(a) Open meeting policy

Business meetings are open to the public unless they are closed under (b). Other meetings, such as orientation, planning, and educational meetings, may be made open to the public at the discretion of the Chief Justice. The Chief Justice may seek a recommendation from the Executive and Planning Committee on whether all or part of any meeting should be open or closed. Any discussion or decision of the full council at a business meeting regarding a trial court budget allocation must take place in an open meeting of the council, except for an executive session as provided in (b).

(Subd (a) amended effective January 1, 2007; previously amended effective January 1, 2004.)

(b) Closed sessions

The Chief Justice may close all or part of a business meeting because of the nature of the meeting or of matters to be discussed. The following matters will ordinarily be discussed in closed session:

(1) A personnel matter or a discussion of the character, competence, or physical or mental health of an individual;

(2) Claims or litigation in which the Judicial Council has an interest;

(3) Contract, labor, or legislative negotiations;

(4) The purchase, sale, or lease of real property;

(5) Security plans or procedures;

(6) Allegations of criminal or professional misconduct; and

(7) Discussions protected by the attorney-client privilege.

(c) Conduct at meeting

Members of the public who attend open meetings must remain orderly. The Chief Justice may order the removal of any disorderly persons.

(Subd (c) amended effective January 1, 2004.)

(d) Requests to speak—general

The Executive and Planning Committee, in its discretion, may allow a member of the public to speak at a business meeting. Unless the Chief Justice waives this requirement, any member of the public who wishes to speak at a business meeting must submit a request of no more than two pages to the chair of the Executive and Planning Committee by delivering it to the Administrative Office of the Courts at least four business days before the meeting.

(1) *Contents of the request*

The request must include the following:

(A) A description of the agenda item to be addressed;

(B) A specific recitation of the proposed statement with an explanation of its relevance to the agenda item and the reasons it would be of benefit to the council in its deliberations;

(C) The name, residence, and occupation of the person asking to speak and, if applicable, the name, address, and purpose of the agency or organization that the speaker represents;

(D) If available, telephone and fax numbers and e-mail address of the person asking to speak and, if applicable and available, the telephone, fax numbers, and e-mail address of the agency or organization that the speaker represents;

(E) The words "Request to Speak at Judicial Council Meeting" displayed prominently in letters at least one-quarter-inch high on the envelope containing the request; and

(F) A copy of any written materials the speaker proposes to distribute at the meeting.

(2) *Notice of decision*

The Executive and Planning Committee must respond to the request at least two business days before the meeting. The committee may grant the request in part or whole, request additional information, circulate any written materials, or take other action it deems appropriate.

(Subd (d) amended effective January 1, 2007; previously amended effective January 1, 2004.)

(e) Presentation of information on trial court budget matters

(1) *Presentation of written information*

Any designated employee representative has a right to provide written information on trial court budget allocations to the council.

(2) *Oral presentation*

Any designated employee representative who wishes to make an oral presentation to the Judicial Council must make a written request to the Administrative Office of the Courts (attention Secretariat) no later than 24 hours before

the meeting unless the issue has arisen within the last five business days before the meeting, in which case the written request may be made on the day of the meeting.

(3) *Limit on number and time*

The Chief Justice or his or her designee may limit the number and time of speakers in order to avoid cumulative discussion.

(Subd (e) amended effective January 1, 2007; adopted effective January 1, 2004.)

(f) Video recording, photographing, and broadcasting at meeting

The Chief Justice may permit video recording, photographing, or broadcasting of a meeting. Any such video recording, photographing, or broadcasting is subject to regulations that ensure the meeting's security and dignity. A request to record, photograph, or broadcast a council meeting must be received by the Chief Justice at least two business days before the meeting.

(Subd (f) relettered effective January 1, 2004; adopted as subd (e) effective January 1, 1999.)

(g) Minutes as official records

The Secretary of the Judicial Council must prepare written minutes of each council meeting for approval at the next council meeting. When approved by the council, the minutes constitute the official record of the meeting.

(Subd (g) amended and relettered effective January 1, 2004; adopted as subd (f) effective January 1, 1999.)

Rule 10.6 amended and renumbered effective January 1, 2007; adopted as rule 6.6 effective January 1, 1999; previously amended effective January 1, 2004.

Rule 10.10.   Judicial Council internal committees

(a) Membership and appointment

The Chief Justice appoints each council member and advisory council member to one or more internal committees for a one-year term.

(Subd (a) amended effective January 1, 2007.)

(b) Committee chairs

The Chief Justice may chair any internal committee or may appoint a committee member as chair or vice-chair.

(c) Meetings

Each internal committee meets as often as necessary to perform its responsibilities. The Administrative Director of the Courts may attend and participate in the meetings of each internal committee. Internal committee meetings are closed to the public but may be opened at the committee chair's discretion.

(d) Voting

An advisory council member may vote on any internal committee matter unless the committee is taking final action on behalf of the council.

(e) Council review

The council may overrule or modify an action taken by an internal committee.

(f) Reporting to the council

As often as necessary, each internal committee must report to the council on the committee's activities.

(Subd (f) amended effective January 1, 2007.)

Rule 10.10 amended and renumbered effective January 1, 2007; adopted as rule 6.10 effective January 1, 1999.

Rule 10.11. Executive and Planning Committee

(a) Coordinating council meetings

The Executive and Planning Committee coordinates the annual schedule and establishes agendas for council meetings. The committee determines:

(1) Whether each item submitted should be placed on the council's agenda and is presented in a form that gives the council the information it needs to make a well-informed decision; and

(2) Whether each item should be on the consent, discussion, or information agenda; how much time is to be allotted for discussion; what presenters should be invited to speak; and, when appropriate, which specific issues should be discussed.

(Subd (a) amended effective January 1, 2007; previously amended effective January 1, 2002.)

(b) Internal operating procedures

The committee develops and administers the internal operating procedures of the council.

(Subd (b) amended effective January 1, 2002.)

(c) Nominations

The committee coordinates nominations for the Chief Justice's appointments to the council, advisory committees, and task forces.

(Subd (c) amended effective January 1, 2007; previously amended effective January 1, 2002.)

(d) Actions on behalf of the council

Between council meetings the committee may take action on behalf of the council except for:

(1) Adopting rules of court, standards of judicial administration, or council forms;

(2) Making statutory appointments; and

(3) Taking actions that are delegated to other internal committees.

(e) Planning

The committee oversees the development and implementation of the council's long-range strategic plan by:

(1) Recommending responses to forces and trends that are likely to affect the judiciary's operations and resources;

(2) Planning and conducting the council's annual strategic planning meeting and related efforts; and

(3) Collaborating with the Administrative Director of the Courts regarding proposed judicial branch budgets, proposed allocation schedules, and related budgetary issues.

(Subd (e) amended effective January 1, 2005; previously amended effective January 1, 2002.)

(f) Budget

The committee must ensure that proposed judicial branch budgets and related budgetary issues are brought to the Judicial Council in a timely manner and in a format that permits the council to establish funding priorities in the context of the council's annual program objectives, statewide policies, and long-range strategic plan. The Administrative Director of the Courts assists the Executive and Planning Committee in carrying out this function, as directed by the Executive and Planning Committee and as otherwise provided in these rules.

(Subd (f) amended effective January 1, 2005; previously amended effective January 1, 2002.)

(g) Oversight of advisory committees and task forces

The committee provides guidance and direction to advisory committees and task forces, as specified in rules 10.30, 10.34, and 10.70.

(Subd (g) amended effective January 1, 2007; adopted effective September 1, 2003.)

Rule 10.11 amended and renumbered effective January 1, 2007; adopted as rule 6.11 effective January 1, 1999; previously amended effective January 1, 2002, September 1, 2003, and January 1, 2005.

Rule 10.12. Policy Coordination and Liaison Committee

(a) Relations with other entities

The Policy Coordination and Liaison Committee acts as the council's liaison with other governmental entities, the bar, the media, the judiciary, and the public.

(Subd (a) amended effective September 1, 2003.)

(b) Legislative activities

With the assistance of the Office of Governmental Affairs, the committee performs the following functions regarding proposed legislation:

(1) Taking a position on behalf of the council on pending legislative bills, provided that the position is consistent with the council's established policies and precedents;

(2) Making recommendations to the council on proposals for council-sponsored legislation. The committee annually proposes a legislative agenda to the Judicial Council after evaluating input from advisory committees, staff, and courts; and

(3) Representing the council's position before the Legislature and other bodies or agencies.

(Subd (b) amended effective September 1, 2003.)

(c) Coordination

The committee develops an annual plan for communication and interaction with the judiciary, other branches and levels of government, components of the justice system, the bar, the media, and the public.

(Subd (c) amended effective September 1, 2003.)

(d) Advisory committees

The committee may direct any advisory committee to provide it with analysis or recommendations on any pending or proposed legislation, and reviews all recommendations from advisory committees regarding pending or proposed legislation.

(Subd (d) amended effective January 1, 2007; adopted effective September 1, 2003.)

Rule 10.12 amended and renumbered effective January 1, 2007; adopted as rule 6.12 effective January 1, 1999; previously amended effective September 1, 2003.

Rule 10.13. Rules and Projects Committee

(a) Oversight of advisory committees and task forces

The Rules and Projects Committee provides guidance and direction to advisory committees and task forces, as specified in rules 10.30, 10.34, and 10.70.

(Subd (a) amended effective January 1, 2007; previously amended effective September 1, 2003.)

(b) Recommendations

The committee recommends to the Executive and Planning Committee whether each proposal for new or amended rules, standards, or forms should be on the council's consent or discussion agenda and how much time should be allocated for discussion. It also recommends to the council whether such a proposal should be approved and, when appropriate, identifies issues for discussion. If the committee recommends against approval, it must state the reasons for doing so.

(Subd (b) amended effective January 1, 2007; previously amended effective September 1, 2003.)

(c) Rules, standards, and forms

The committee must establish and maintain a rule-making process that is understandable and accessible to the public. It assists the council in making informed decisions about rules of court administration, practice, and procedure by:

(1) Identifying the need for new rules, standards, and forms;

(2) Reviewing proposals for rules, standards, and forms and circulating them for public comment in accordance with the committee's procedures and guidelines;

(3) Establishing and publishing procedures that solicit and consider relevant input from the public for each proposal for the adoption of rules, standards, and forms;

(4) Providing guidelines for the style and format of rules and ensuring that each proposal presented to the council is consistent with the guidelines;

(5) Ensuring that proposals for new or amended rules, standards, and forms do not conflict with statutes or other rules;

(6) Recommending whether the council should approve, modify, or reject each proposal; and

(7) Initiating circulating orders to allow the council to adopt rules, standards, and forms between council meetings if necessary.

(Subd (c) amended effective January 1, 2007; previously amended effective September 1, 2003.)

(d) Jury instructions

The committee must establish and maintain a process for obtaining public comment on the jury instructions approved by the Judicial Council, and must assist the council in making informed decisions about jury instructions by making recommendations to the council on whether to approve proposed new or modified instructions submitted by the advisory committees on jury instructions.

(Subd (d) amended effective January 1, 2007; adopted effective September 1, 2003.)

Rule 10.13 amended and renumbered effective January 1, 2007; adopted as rule 6.13 effective January 1, 1999; previously amended effective September 1, 2003.

Rule 10.14. Litigation Management Committee

(a) Litigation oversight

The Litigation Management Committee must oversee litigation and claims against trial court judges, appellate court justices, the Judicial Council, the Administrative Office of the Courts, the trial and appellate courts, and the employees of those bodies that seek recovery of $50,000 or more or raise important policy issues by:

(1) Reviewing and approving any proposed settlement, stipulated judgment, or offer of judgment; and

(2) Consulting with the Administrative Director or

General Counsel, on request, regarding important strategy issues.

(Subd (a) amended effective January 1, 2007; previously amended effective January 1, 2003.)

(b) Recommendations

The committee must make recommendations to the Judicial Council for policies governing the management of litigation involving the courts.

(c) Strategic decisions

On presentation by the Office of the General Counsel of the written objection described in rule 10.202(d), the committee must resolve the objection.

(Subd (c) amended effective January 1, 2007; previously adopted effective January 1, 2003.)

Rule 10.14 amended and renumbered effective January 1, 2007; adopted as rule 6.14 effective January 1, 2001; previously amended effective January 1, 2003.

Rule 10.15. Interim Court Facilities Panel [Repealed]

Rule 10.15 repealed by its own provision effective June 30, 2007; adopted as rule 6.15 effective June 23, 2004; previously amended and renumbered effective January 1, 2007.

Rule 10.20. Proposals for new or amended rules, standards, or forms; rule-making process in general

(a) Council meetings to consider proposals

The Judicial Council meets twice a year, generally in April and October, to consider proposals for the adoption, amendment, or repeal of California Rules of Court, California Standards of Judicial Administration, and Judicial Council forms.

(b) Proposals

The council will consider proposals that are submitted to it by an internal committee, an advisory committee, a task force, or the Administrative Office of the Courts, in accordance with rule 10.22 and any policies and procedures established by the Rules and Projects Committee.

(Subd (b) amended effective January 1, 2007; repealed and adopted effective January 1, 2002.)

(c) Statewide uniformity

The council will establish uniform statewide practices and procedures where appropriate to achieve equal access to justice throughout California.

(Subd (c) relettered effective January 1, 2002; adopted as subd (g) effective January 1, 1999.)

Rule 10.20 amended and renumbered effective January 1, 2007; adopted as rule 6.20 effective January 1, 1999; previously amended effective January 1, 2002.

Rule 10.21. Proposals from members of the public for changes to rules, standards, or forms

(a) Application

This rule applies to proposals for changes to rules, standards, or forms by a member of the public (any person or organization other than a Judicial Council internal committee, advisory committee, or task force, or the Administrative Office of the Courts).

(b) Submission and content of proposals

Proposals must be submitted in writing to: Judicial Council of California, Attention: General Counsel. Proposals should include:

(1) The text of the proposed rule, standard, form, or amendment;

(2) A description of the problem to be addressed;

(3) The proposed solution and alternative solutions;

(4) Any likely implementation problems;

(5) Any need for urgent consideration;

(6) Known proponents and opponents;

(7) Any known fiscal impact; and

(8) If known, any previous action by the council or an advisory committee on the proposal.

(c) Advisory committee's review of proposal

The General Counsel must refer each proposal from a member of the public to an appropriate advisory committee for consideration and recommendation, or, if no appropriate advisory committee exists, to the Rules and Projects Committee. An Administrative Office of the Courts staff member may independently review the proposal and present an analysis and a recommendation to the committee. The committee may take one of the following actions:

(1) Accept the proposal, either as submitted or modified, and proceed under rule 10.22;

(2) Request further information or analysis; or

(3) Reject the proposal.

(Subd (c) amended effective January 1, 2007.)

Rule 10.21 amended and renumbered effective January 1, 2007; adopted as rule 6.21 effective January 1, 2002.

Rule 10.22. Rule-making procedures

(a) Who may make proposals

A Judicial Council internal committee, advisory committee, task force, or the Administrative Office of the Courts may recommend that the council adopt, amend, or repeal a rule or standard or adopt, approve, revise, or revoke a form.

(Subd (a) amended effective January 1, 2007.)

(b) Legal and advisory committee review

The internal committee, advisory committee, task force, or Administrative Office of the Courts (the proponent) must first submit its proposal to the Office of the General Counsel for legal and drafting review. If the proponent is not an advisory committee, and an appropriate advisory committee exists, the proponent must also submit the proposal to that advisory committee for review.

(Subd (b) amended effective January 1, 2007.)

(c) Recommendation to Rules and Projects Committee

After the proposal has been reviewed by the Office of the General Counsel and any appropriate advisory committee, the proponent must submit the proposal to the Rules and Projects Committee with a recommendation that it be (1) circulated for public comment or (2) submitted to the council for approval without public comment.

(d) Review by Rules and Projects Committee

The Rules and Projects Committee must review the recommendation and may take one of the following actions:

(1) Circulate the proposal for public comment;

(2) If the proposal presents a nonsubstantive technical change or correction or a minor substantive change that is unlikely to create controversy, recommend that the council adopt it without circulating it for comment;

(3) Postpone circulation for comment and either request further information or analysis by the proponent or refer the matter to another council internal or advisory committee, the full council, or the Chief Justice; or

(4) Reject the proposal if it is contrary to statute, conflicts with other rules or standards, or is contrary to established council policy.

(Subd (d) amended effective January 1, 2007.)

(e) Review of comments

After a proposal is circulated, the proponent must review the comments and decide whether to reject the proposal or to recommend that the council adopt it, with or without modifications.

(f) Submission to council

If, after reviewing the comments, the proponent recommends that the council adopt the proposal, the matter will be placed on the council's agenda. The Rules and Projects Committee must review the recommendation and submit its own recommendation to the council. The council may adopt, modify, or reject the proposal.

(g) Compelling circumstances

The procedures established in this rule must be followed unless the Rules and Projects Committee finds that compelling circumstances necessitate a different procedure. The committee's finding and a summary of the procedure used must be presented to the council with any recommendation to the council made under this subdivision.

Rule 10.22 amended and renumbered effective January 1, 2007; adopted as rule 6.22 effective January 1, 2002.

Chapter 2
Judicial Council Advisory Committees and Task Forces

Rule 10.59. Advisory Committee on Criminal Jury Instructions
Rule 10.70. Task forces

Rule 10.30. Judicial Council advisory committees

(a) Creation

In addition to the advisory committees established by the rules in this division, the Chief Justice may create additional advisory committees by order.

(b) Functions

Working under the council's direction, advisory committees assist the council by using their collective experience, opinions, and wisdom to provide advice, options, and recommendations to the council on topics affecting the administration of justice.

(Subd (b) amended effective September 1, 2003.)

(c) Committee charges

Each advisory committee's general charge is stated in the rules in this division. Each advisory committee is overseen by either the Executive and Planning Committee or the Rules and Projects Committee, as designated by the Chief Justice. The designated internal committee may give an annual charge to each advisory committee that specifies the work product the council expects during the year. The advisory committee may pursue matters in addition to those specified in its annual charge, as long as the matters are consistent with the committee's general charge and the committee operates within the limits of the resources available to the committee and within any other limitations specified by the council, the designated internal committee, or the Administrative Director of the Courts.

(Subd (c) amended effective January 1, 2007; adopted effective January 1, 2003; previously amended effective September 1, 2003.)

(d) Staff

Advisory committees are assisted by the staff of the Administrative Office of the Courts. The duties of staff members include drafting committee work plans, managing the committee's budget and resources, coordinating committee activities, providing legal and policy analysis to the committee, organizing and drafting reports, selecting and supervising consultants, providing technical assistance, and presenting the committee's recommendations to the Judicial Council. Staff may provide independent legal or policy analysis of issues that is different from the committee's position.

(Subd (d) amended effective September 1, 2003.)

(e) Subcommittees

An advisory committee may form subcommittees, composed entirely of committee members, to carry out the committee's duties, subject to available resources.

(f) Preference for using advisory committees

Unless substantial reasons dictate otherwise, new projects requiring committee involvement must be assigned to existing advisory committees.

(Subd (f) amended effective September 1, 2003.)

Rule 10.30 amended and renumbered effective January 1, 2007; adopted as rule 6.30 effective January 1, 1999; previously amended effective September 1, 2003.

Rule 10.31. Advisory committee membership and terms

(a) Membership

The categories of membership of each advisory committee are specified in the rules in this chapter. Each advisory committee consists of between 12 and 18 members, unless a different number is specified by the Chief Justice or required by these rules. Advisory committee members do not represent a specific constituency but must act in the best interests of the public and the entire court system.

(Subd (a) amended effective September 1, 2003.)

(b) Terms

The Chief Justice appoints advisory committee members to three-year terms unless another term is specified in these rules. Terms are staggered so that an approximately equal number of each committee's members changes annually. The Chief Justice also may appoint judicial officers who have served less than two years on the bench to one-year terms.

(Subd (b) amended effective January 1, 2007; previously amended effective November 1, 2004.)

(c) Chair and vice-chair

The Chief Justice appoints an advisory committee member to be a committee chair or vice-chair for a one-year term except for the chair and vice-chair of the Court Executives Advisory Committee, who may be appointed to two-year terms.

(Subd (c) amended effective January 1, 2007; previously amended effective September 1, 2000, and January 1, 2004.)

(d) Advisory members

On the request of the advisory committee, the Chief Justice may designate an advisory member to assist an advisory committee or a subcommittee. Advisory members may participate in discussions and make or second motions but cannot vote.

(Subd (d) amended effective January 1, 2007.)

(e) Termination of membership

Committee membership terminates if a member leaves the position that qualified the member for the advisory committee unless the Chief Justice determines that the individual may complete the current term.

(f) Vacancies

Vacancies are filled as they occur according to the nomination procedures described in rule 10.32.

(Subd (f) amended effective January 1, 2007.)

(g) Retired judges

A judge's retirement does not cause a vacancy on the committee if the judge is eligible for assignment. A retired judge who is eligible for assignment may hold a committee position based on his or her last judicial position.

Rule 10.31 amended and renumbered effective January 1, 2007; adopted as rule 6.31 effective January 1, 1999; previously amended effective September 1, 2000, September 1, 2003, January 1, 2004, and November 1, 2004.

Rule 10.32. Nominations and appointments to advisory committees

(a) Nomination procedures

The Executive and Planning Committee assists the Chief Justice in selecting advisory committee members by submitting a list of nominees for each position. Unless otherwise specified in the rule applicable to a particular advisory committee, the nomination procedures are as follows:

(1) The Executive and Planning Committee must publicize vacancies and solicit nominations. If any group is designated to submit nominations for a position, the Executive and Planning Committee will request that the group submit at least three nominations for each advisory committee vacancy.

(2) The Executive and Planning Committee must submit at least three nominees for each advisory committee vacancy to the Chief Justice. The nominees should represent diverse backgrounds and experiences as well as geographic locations throughout California.

(Subd (a) amended effective September 1, 2003.)

(b) Court executive or administrator members

A court executive or administrator member may be a county clerk, a court administrator, or an executive officer if the member also serves as the clerk of the court.

(c) Judicial administrator member

A judicial administrator member may be any person experienced in court administration and is not required to be currently employed by a court.

(d) Judicial officer

A judicial officer member may be a judge of the superior court or a court commissioner or referee.

(Subd (d) amended effective September 1, 2003.)

(e) Appointing order

The Chief Justice appoints advisory committee members by order.

(Subd (e) amended effective September 1, 2003.)

Rule 10.32 amended and renumbered effective January 1, 2007; adopted as rule 6.32 effective January 1, 1999; previously amended effective September 1, 2003.

Rule 10.33. Advisory committee meetings

Each advisory committee may meet as often as its chair deems necessary, within available resources. Meetings may be in person or by teleconference.

Rule 10.33 renumbered effective January 1, 2007; adopted as rule 6.33 effective January 1, 1999; previously amended effective September 1, 2003.

Rule 10.34. Duties and responsibilities of advisory committees

(a) In general

Advisory committees make recommendations and offer options to the Judicial Council for improving the administration of justice within their designated areas of focus by doing the following:

(1) Identifying issues and concerns affecting court administration and recommending appropriate solutions to the council;

(2) Proposing necessary changes to rules, standards, and forms on the following schedule:

(A) As needed for selected provisions in response to legislative and case law changes as well as to proposals from committee members and others; and

(B) At least every 10 years for all provisions within the committee's area of focus;

(3) Reviewing pending legislation and making recommendations to the Policy Coordination and Liaison Committee on whether to support or oppose it;

(4) Recommending new legislation to the council;

(5) Recommending to the council pilot projects to evaluate new procedures or practices;

(6) Acting on assignments referred by the council or an internal committee; and

(7) Making other appropriate recommendations to the council.

(Subd (a) amended effective September 1, 2003.)

(b) Work plan

Each committee must submit an annual proposed work plan that is reviewed by the internal committee with oversight responsibility, as designated by the Chief Justice. This subdivision does not apply to the Administrative Presiding Justices Advisory Committee.

(Subd (b) amended effective January 1, 2007; previously amended effective January 1, 2002, and September 1, 2003.)

(c) Contents of work plan

The work plan must contain the following items:

(1) A prioritized list and description of all current committee projects and activities and estimated dates of completion;

(2) A list of existing rules, standards, and forms that the committee will review and recommend for amendment, reorganization, or repeal;

(3) Proposals for new projects that the committee wishes to undertake; and

(4) Estimated cost and staff needed to complete each project or activity.

(Subd (c) amended effective September 1, 2003.)

(d) Review of work plans

The internal committee that is responsible for oversight of the advisory committee reviews the proposed work plan and provides the advisory committee with an annual charge to ensure that its activities are consistent with the council's goals and priorities. The annual charge may:

(1) Approve or disapprove the work plan in whole or in part;

(2) Direct the committee to pursue specific projects on the work plan;

(3) Add or delete specific projects; and

(4) Reassign priorities.

An advisory committee may pursue matters in addition to those specified in its annual charge as long as the matters are consistent with the advisory committee's general charge, its approved work plan, and the council's long-range strategic plan. The additional matters must also be within the committee's authorized budget and available resources, as specified by the council or the Administrative Director of the Courts.

(Subd (d) amended effective January 1, 2007; previously amended effective September 1, 2003.)

(e) Reporting to internal committee

Each advisory committee must periodically report to the internal committee with oversight responsibility on its continuing work and must provide analysis of issues and make recommendations as requested by the internal committee.

(Subd (e) amended effective January 1, 2007; previously amended effective September 1, 2003.)

(f) Review of need for advisory committees

Every five years each advisory committee must report in writing to the internal committee with oversight responsibility about whether the advisory committee should continue to exist and whether it should maintain its current structure. The internal committee may make a recommendation to the council.

(Subd (f) amended effective September 1, 2003.)

Rule 10.34 amended and renumbered effective January 1, 2007; adopted as rule 6.34 effective January 1, 1999; previously amended effective January 1, 2002, and September 1, 2003.

Rule 10.40. Appellate Advisory Committee

(a) Area of focus

The committee makes recommendations to the council for improving the administration of justice in appellate proceedings.

(Subd (a) amended effective January 1, 2007; previously amended effective January 1, 2002.)

(b) Additional duty

In addition to the duties described in rule 10.34 the committee makes proposals on training for justices and appellate support staff to the Governing Committee of the Center for Judicial Education and Research.

(Subd (b) amended effective January 1, 2007; previously amended effective January 1, 2002.)

(c) Membership

The committee must include at least one member from each of the following categories:

(1) Supreme Court justice;

(2) Court of Appeal justice;

(3) Trial court judicial officer with experience in the appellate division;

(4) Supreme Court clerk administrator;

(5) Appellate court administrator;

(6) Trial court judicial administrator;

(7) Civil appellate lawyer;

(8) Criminal defense appellate lawyer;

(9) State Public Defender; and

(10) Appellate lawyer of the Attorney General's Office.

(Subd (c) amended effective January 1, 2007; previously amended effective January 1, 2002.)

Rule 10.40 amended and renumbered effective January 1, 2007; adopted as rule 6.40 effective January 1, 1999; previously amended effective January 1, 2002.

Rule 10.41. Civil and Small Claims Advisory Committee

(a) Area of focus

The committee makes recommendations to the council for improving the administration of justice in civil and small claims proceedings.

(Subd (a) amended effective January 1, 2007.)

(b) Membership

The committee must include at least one member from each of the following categories:

(1) Appellate court justice;

(2) Trial court judicial officer;

(3) Judicial administrator;

(4) Lawyer whose primary area of practice is civil law;

(5) Legal secretary; and

(6) Person knowledgeable about small claims law and procedure.

(Subd (b) amended effective January 1, 2007.)

Rule 10.41 amended and renumbered effective January 1, 2007; adopted as rule 6.41 effective January 1, 1999.

Rule 10.42. Criminal Law Advisory Committee

(a) Area of focus

The committee makes recommendations to the council for improving the administration of justice in criminal proceedings.

(Subd (a) amended effective January 1, 2007.)

(b) Membership

The committee must include at least one member from each of the following categories:

(1) Appellate court justice;

(2) Trial court judicial officer;

(3) Judicial administrator;

(4) Prosecutor; and

(5) Criminal defense lawyer.

(Subd (b) amended effective January 1, 2007.)

Rule 10.42 amended and renumbered effective January 1, 2007; adopted as rule 6.42 effective January 1, 1999.

Rule 10.43. Family and Juvenile Law Advisory Committee

(a) Area of focus

The committee makes recommendations to the council for improving the administration of justice in all cases involving marriage, family, or children.

(Subd (a) amended effective January 1, 2007.)

(b) Membership

The committee must include at least one member from each of the following categories:

(1) Appellate court justice;

(2) Trial court judicial officer;

(3) Judicial administrator;

(4) Child custody mediator;

(5) Lawyer whose primary practice area is family law;

(6) Lawyer from a public or private defender's office whose primary practice area is juvenile law;

(7) Chief probation officer;

(8) Child welfare director;

(9) Court Appointed Special Advocate (CASA) director;

(10) County counsel assigned to juvenile dependency cases;

(11) Domestic violence prevention advocate;

(12) District attorney assigned to juvenile delinquency cases;

(13) Lawyer from the California Department of Child Support Services or a local child support agency; and

(14) Public-interest children's rights lawyer.

(Subd (b) amended effective January 1, 2007; previously amended effective July 1, 2005.)

Rule 10.43 amended and renumbered effective January 1, 2007; adopted as rule 6.43 effective January 1, 1999; previously amended effective July 1, 2005.

Ref.: W. Cal. Sum., 10 "Parent and Child" §441.

Rule 10.44.   Probate and Mental Health Advisory Committee

(a) Area of focus

The committee makes recommendations to the council for improving the administration of justice in proceedings involving:

(1) Decedents' estates, trusts, conservatorships, guardianships, and other probate matters; and

(2) Mental health and developmental disabilities issues.

(Subd (a) amended effective January 1, 2007.)

(b) Additional duty

The committee must coordinate activities and work with the Family and Juvenile Law Advisory Committee in areas of common concern and interest.

(Subd (b) amended effective January 1, 2007.)

(c) Membership

The committee must include at least one member from each of the following categories:

(1) Judicial officer with experience in probate;

(2) Lawyer whose primary practice involves decedents' estates, trusts, guardianships, conservatorships, or elder abuse law;

(3) Lawyer or examiner who works for the court on probate or mental health matters;

(4) Investigator who works for the court to investigate probate guardianships or conservatorships;

(5) Person knowledgeable in mental health or developmental disability law;

(6) Person knowledgeable in private management of probate matters in a fiduciary capacity; and

(7) County counsel, public guardian, or other similar public officer familiar with guardianship and conservatorship issues.

(Subd (c) amended effective January 1, 2008; previously amended effective January 1, 2007.)

Rule 10.44 amended effective January 1, 2008; adopted as rule 6.44 effective July 1, 2000; previously amended and renumbered effective January 1, 2007.

Rule 10.45.   Trial Court Budget Working Group

The Administrative Director of the Courts must appoint annually a Trial Court Budget Working Group to advise the director on trial court budget issues. The working group must include trial court judicial officers and trial court executive officers reflecting the diversity of state trial courts, including location, size, and adequacy of funding. The working group may also include others selected by the Administrative Director of the Courts.

Rule 10.45 renumbered effective January 1, 2007; repealed and adopted as rule 6.45 effective January 1, 2005.

Rule 10.46.   Trial Court Presiding Judges Advisory Committee

(a) Area of focus

The committee contributes to the statewide administration of justice by monitoring areas of significance to the justice system and making recommendations to the Judicial Council on policy issues affecting the trial courts.

(Subd (a) amended effective January 1, 2007; previously amended effective September 1, 2000, and April 18, 2003.)

(b) Additional duties

In addition to the duties specified in rule 10.34, the committee may:

(1) Recommend methods and policies within its area of focus to improve trial court presiding judges' access to and participation in council decision making, increase communication between the council and the trial courts, and provide for training programs for judicial and court support staff;

(2) Respond and provide input to the Judicial Council, appropriate advisory committees, or the Administrative Office of the Courts on pending policy proposals and offer new recommendations on policy initiatives in the areas of legislation, rules, forms, standards, studies, and recommendations concerning court administration; and

(3) Provide for liaison between the trial courts and the Judicial Council, its advisory committees, task forces, and working groups, and the Administrative Office of the Courts.

(Subd (b) amended effective January 1, 2007; previously amended effective September 1, 2000, and April 18, 2003.)

(c) Membership

The committee consists of the presiding judge of each superior court.

(Subd (c) amended effective January 1, 2007; previously amended effective September 1, 2000, and April 18, 2003.)

(d) Executive Committee

The advisory committee may establish an Executive Committee that, in addition to other powers provided by the advisory committee, may act on behalf of the full advisory committee between its meetings.

(Subd (d) amended effective April 18, 2003; adopted effective September 1, 2000.)

(e) Subcommittee membership

The committee has standing subcommittees on rules and legislation. The chair may create other subcommittees as he or she deems appropriate. The chair must strive for representation of courts of all sizes on subcommittees.

(Subd (e) repealed and adopted effective April 18, 2003.)

(f) Chair

The advisory committee must annually submit to the Chief Justice three nominations for the chair of the advisory committee. The Chief Justice will select a chair from among the names suggested. The chair of the advisory committee serves as chair of any Executive Committee established under (d) and as an advisory member of the Judicial Council.

(Subd (f) amended effective January 1, 2007; adopted as subd (d) effective January 1, 1999; previously amended and relettered effective September 1, 2000; previously amended effective April 18, 2003.)

Rule 10.46 amended and renumbered effective January 1, 2007; adopted as rule 6.46 effective January 1, 1999; previously amended effective September 1, 2000, and April 18, 2003.

Rule 10.48.   Court Executives Advisory Committee

(a) Area of focus

The committee makes recommendations to the council on policy issues affecting the trial courts.

(Subd (a) amended effective January 1, 2004.)

(b) Additional duties

In addition to the duties specified in rule 10.34, the committee must:

(1) Recommend methods and policies to improve trial court administrators' access to and participation in council decision making;

(2) Review and comment on legislation, rules, forms, standards, studies, and recommendations concerning court administration proposed to the council;

(3) Review and make proposals concerning the Judicial Branch Statistical Information System or other large-scope data collection efforts;

(4) Suggest methods and policies to increase communication between the council and the trial courts;

(5) Serve as the Executive Committee for the Conference of Court Executives, as described in rule 10.49; and

(6) Meet periodically with the Administrative Office of the Courts' directors to enhance branch communications.

(Subd (b) amended effective January 1, 2007; previously amended effective January 1, 2004.)

(c) Consultation with the Conference of Court Executives

To assist it in formulating proposals and recommendations to the council, the committee may seek the advice of the Conference of Court Executives.

(Subd (c) amended effective January 1, 2007.)

(d) Membership

The committee consists of the following members:

(1) Nine executive officers from trial courts that have 48 or more judges;

(2) Four executive officers from trial courts that have 16 to 47 judges;

(3) Two executive officers from trial courts that have 6 to 15 judges;

(4) Two executive officers from trial courts that have 2 to 5 judges;

(5) One member from the six clerk/administrators of the Courts of Appeal selected from three nominations made by the Appellate Court Clerks Association; and

(6) One at-large member appointed from the trial courts by the committee chair to a one-year term.

(Subd (d) amended effective January 1, 2007; previously amended effective January 1, 2004.)

(e) Nominations

The Conference of Court Executives must submit to the Court Executives Advisory Committee nominations for each vacancy on the committee. The Court Executives Advisory Committee will recommend three nominees for each committee vacancy from the nominations received and submit its recommendations to the Executive and Planning Committee of the Judicial Council. The list of nominees must enable the Chief Justice to appoint a committee that reflects a variety of experience, expertise, and types (e.g., urban, suburban, and rural) that is geographically balanced. Membership on this committee does not preclude appointment to any other advisory committee or task force.

(Subd (e) amended effective January 1, 2007; previously amended effective January 1, 2004.)

(f) Chair and vice-chair

The Chief Justice may appoint the chair and vice-chair of the committee for up to a two-year term from the current membership of the Court Executives Advisory Committee.

(Subd (f) amended effective January 1, 2008; previously amended effective January 1, 2004, and January 1, 2007.)

Rule 10.48 amended effective January 1, 2008; adopted as rule 6.48 effective January 1, 1999; previously amended effective January 1, 2004; previously amended and renumbered effective January 1, 2007.

Rule 10.49.   Conference of Court Executives

(a) Function

The functions of the Conference of Court Executives are to:

(1) Increase the opportunities for court executive officers to participate in the Judicial Council decision-making process; and

(2) Provide a forum for the education of court executives.

(b) Duties

The Conference of Court Executives must:

(1) Provide information and advice, when requested, to the Court Executives Advisory Committee; and

(2) Conduct educational sessions for its members on matters related to court management, such as legislation, training, information management, judicial branch policy issues, professional development, best practices, and current issues facing the trial courts.

(Subd (b) amended effective January 1, 2004.)

(c) Membership

All court executive officers and clerk/administrators of the Courts of Appeal are members of the Conference of Court Executives. A court executive who is unable to participate in a meeting may designate his or her deputy to vote in his or her place.

(Subd (c) amended effective January 1, 2007; previously amended effective January 1, 2004.)

(d) Chair and vice-chair

The chair and vice-chair of the Court Executives Advisory Committee are the chair and vice-chair of the conference.

(Subd (d) amended effective January 1, 2004.)

(e) Executive Committee

The conference's Executive Committee is the Court Executives Advisory Committee. The Executive Committee must:

(1) Establish the schedule and agenda for meetings; and

(2) As necessary, appoint subcommittees consisting of principal and associate members of the conference.

(Subd (e) amended effective January 1, 2004.)

(f) Nominations subcommittee

The Court Executives Advisory Committee must submit to the Executive and Planning Committee of the Judicial Council nominations for members of the committee, the advisory members of the Judicial Council who are court executives, and members of other advisory committees who are court executives or judicial administrators.

(Subd (f) amended effective January 1, 2004.)

(g) Meetings

The conference must meet during at least two statewide meetings a year. One meeting must be held at the annual California Judicial Administration Conference. The conference must also meet at least two times a year by region for court administration updates, focused discussions, and educational opportunities.

(Subd (g) amended effective January 1, 2004.)

(h) Reimbursement for meetings

Reimbursement for meeting travel per diem expenses for conference members will be subject to availability of funds.

(Subd (h) adopted effective January 1, 2004.)

Rule 10.49 amended and renumbered effective January 1, 2007; adopted as rule 6.49 effective January 1, 1999; previously amended effective January 1, 2004.

Rule 10.50. Governing Committee of the Center for Judicial Education and Research

(a) Establishment and purpose

In 1973, the Judicial Council of California and the California Judges Association created the Center for Judicial Education and Research (CJER), which subsequently became the Education Division of the Administrative Office of the Courts. The Governing Committee of CJER was made an advisory committee to the council in 1993 through the adoption of former rule 1029. In 2001, the rule that specifies the CJER Governing Committee's duties was made consistent with the rules pertaining to other Judicial Council advisory committees, but it continues to acknowledge the historic participation of the California Judges Association.

(Subd (a) amended effective January 1, 2007; adopted effective December 18, 2001.)

(b) Area of focus

The committee makes recommendations to the council for improving the administration of justice through comprehensive and quality education and training for judicial officers and other judicial branch personnel.

(Subd (b) relettered and amended effective December 18, 2001; adopted as subd (a).)

(c) Additional duties

In addition to the duties described in rule 10.34, the committee must:

(1) Recommend rules, standards, policies, and procedures for judicial branch education;

(2) Recommend a strategic long-range plan for judicial branch education;

(3) Evaluate the effectiveness of judicial branch education, the quality of participation, the efficiency of delivery, and the impact on service to the public;

(4) Review and comment on proposals from other advisory committees and task forces that include education and training of judicial officers or court staff in order to ensure coordination, consistency, and collaboration in educational services;

(5) Establish educational priorities for implementation of curricula, programs, publications, and delivery systems;

(6) Identify the need for and appoint education committees to implement the priorities, long-range plan, and programs and products of judicial branch education; create and adopt procedures for their operation; and review and approve their projects and products;

(7) Identify and foster collaborative opportunities with courts to promote and ensure the availability of training at the local court level;

(8) Identify, analyze, and implement systems to enhance the delivery of education and training statewide; and

(9) Identify and foster collaborative opportunities with internal and external partners to maximize the resources dedicated to education and training.

(Subd (c) amended effective January 1, 2007; adopted as subd (b) effective January 1, 1999; previously relettered and amended effective December 18, 2001.)

(d) Membership

The committee consists of at least the following members:

(1) Eight sitting judicial officers, including at least one appellate court justice;

(2) Three judicial administrators;

(3) The Administrative Director of the Courts as an advisory member;

(4) The president of the California Judges Association or his or her designee as an advisory member; and

(5) Other advisory members as the Chief Justice may appoint.

(Subd (d) relettered and amended effective December 18, 2001; adopted as subd (c).)

(e) Nominations

Nominations for vacant positions on the Governing Committee will be solicited under the procedures described in rule 10.32. The president of the California Judges Association may submit nominations to the Executive and Planning Committee.

(Subd (e) amended effective January 1, 2007; previously amended effective December 18, 2001.)

(f) Chair and vice-chair

The Chief Justice appoints the chair and vice-chair. The committee may make recommendations to the Chief Justice for these two positions.

(Subd (f) amended effective December 18, 2001.)

Rule 10.50 amended and renumbered effective January 1, 2007; adopted as rule 6.50 effective January 1, 1999; previously amended effective December 18, 2001.

Rule 10.51. Court Interpreters Advisory Panel

(a) Area of focus

To assist the council in performing its duties under Government Code sections 68560 through 68566 and to promote access to spoken-language interpreters and interpreters for deaf and hearing-impaired persons, the advisory panel is charged with making recommendations to the council on:

(1) Interpreter use and need for interpreters in court proceedings; and

(2) Certification, registration, renewal of certification and registration, testing, recruiting, training, continuing education, and professional conduct of interpreters.

(Subd (a) amended effective October 1, 2004.)

(b) Additional duty

The advisory panel is charged with reviewing and making recommendations to the council on the findings of the study of language and interpreter use and need for interpreters in court proceedings that is conducted by the

Administrative Office of the Courts every five years under Government Code section 68563.

(Subd (b) amended effective October 1, 2004.)

(c) Membership

The advisory panel consists of 11 members. A majority of the members must be court interpreters. The advisory panel must include the specified numbers of members from the following categories:

(1) Four certified or registered court interpreters working as employees in trial courts, one from each of the four regions established by Government Code section 71807. For purposes of the appointment of members under this rule, the Superior Court of California, County of Ventura, is considered part of Region 1 as specified in section 71807, and the Superior Court of California, County of Solano, is considered part of Region 2 as specified in section 71807;

(2) Two interpreters certified or registered in a language other than Spanish, each working either in a trial court as an independent contractor or in an educational institution;

(3) One appellate court justice;

(4) Two trial court judges; and

(5) Two court administrators, including at least one trial court executive officer.

(Subd (c) amended effective October 1, 2004; previously amended effective July 1, 1999.)

(d) Advisors

The Chief Justice may also appoint nonmember advisors to assist the advisory panel.

(Subd (d) adopted effective October 1, 2004.)

Rule 10.51 renumbered effective January 1, 2007; adopted as rule 6.51 effective January 1, 1999; previously amended effective July 1, 1999, and October 1, 2004.

Rule 10.52.   Administrative Presiding Justices Advisory Committee

(a) Area of focus

The committee makes recommendations to the council on policy issues affecting the administration and operation of the Courts of Appeal.

(Subd (a) amended effective January 1, 2007.)

(b) Additional duties

In addition to the duties described in rule 10.34, the committee must:

(1) Establish administrative policies that promote the quality of justice by advancing the efficient functioning of the appellate courts;

(2) Advise the council of the appellate courts' resource requirements and solicit the council's support in meeting budget, administrative, and staffing requirements;

(3) Make proposals on training for justices and appellate support staff to the Governing Committee of the Center for Judicial Education and Research; and

(4) Comment on and make recommendations to the council about appellate court operations, including:

(A) Initiatives to be pursued by the council or the Administrative Office of the Courts; and

(B) The council's goals and strategies.

(Subd (b) amended effective January 1, 2007.)

(c) Membership

The committee consists of:

(1) The Chief Justice as chair; and

(2) The administrative presiding justices of the Courts of Appeal designated under rule 10.1004.

(Subd (c) amended effective January 1, 2007.)

(d) Funding

Each year, the committee must recommend budget change proposals to be submitted to the Chief Justice for legislative funding to operate the appellate courts. These proposals must be consistent with the budget management guidelines of the Finance Division of the Administrative Office of the Courts.

(Subd (d) amended effective January 1, 2007.)

(e) Allocations

The committee allocates resources among the appellate courts and approves budget management guidelines based on the actual allocation made by the Chief Justice.

(Subd (e) amended effective January 1, 2007.)

(f) Administrative Director of the Courts

The Administrative Director must meet regularly with the committee and must notify and, when appropriate, consult with the committee about appellate court personnel matters.

(Subd (f) amended effective January 1, 2007.)

Rule 10.52 amended and renumbered effective January 1, 2007; adopted as rule 6.52 effective January 1, 1999.

Rule 10.53.   Court Technology Advisory Committee

(a) Area of focus

The committee makes recommendations to the council for improving the administration of justice through the use of technology and for fostering cooperative endeavors to resolve common technological issues with other stakeholders in the justice system.

(Subd (a) amended effective January 1, 2007.)

(b) Additional duties

In addition to the duties described in rule 10.34, the committee must:

(1) Recommend standards to ensure compatibility in information and communication technologies in the judicial branch;

(2) Review and comment on requests for the funding of judicial branch technology projects to ensure compatibility with goals established by the council and standards promulgated by the committee;

(3) Review and recommend legislation, rules, or policies to balance the interests of privacy, access, and security in relation to court technology;

(4) Make proposals for technology education and training in the judicial branch;

(5) Assist courts in acquiring and developing useful technologies; and

(6) Maintain a long-range plan.

(Subd (b) amended effective January 1, 2007.)

(c) Membership

The committee must include at least one member from each of the following categories:

(1) Appellate justice;

(2) Trial court judicial officer;

(3) Trial court judicial administrator;

(4) Appellate court judicial administrator;

(5) Member of the Senate;

(6) Member of the Assembly;

(7) Representative of the executive branch; and

(8) Lawyer.

(Subd (c) amended effective January 1, 2007.)

(d) Member selection

The two legislative members are appointed by the respective houses. The executive member is appointed by the Governor. The lawyer member is appointed by the State Bar.

(e) Chair

The Chief Justice appoints a judicial officer or justice member to serve as chair.

Rule 10.53 amended and renumbered effective January 1, 2007; adopted as rule 6.53 effective January 1, 1999.

Rule 10.54. Traffic Advisory Committee

(a) Area of focus

The committee makes recommendations to the council for improving the administration of justice in the area of traffic procedure, practice, and case management and in other areas as stated in the fish and game, boating, forestry, public utilities, parks and recreation, and business licensing bail schedules.

(Subd (a) amended effective January 1, 2007.)

(b) Membership

The committee must include at least one member from each of the following categories:

(1) Trial court judicial officer;

(2) Judicial administrator;

(3) Juvenile traffic hearing officer;

(4) Representative from the California Highway Patrol;

(5) Representative from the Department of Motor Vehicles;

(6) Representative from the Office of Traffic Safety; and

(7) Criminal defense lawyer.

(Subd (b) amended effective January 1, 2007.)

Rule 10.54 amended and renumbered January 1, 2007; adopted as rule 6.54 effective January 1, 1999.

Rule 10.55. Access and Fairness Advisory Committee

(a) Area of focus

The committee makes recommendations for improving access to the judicial system and fairness in the state courts.

(Subd (a) amended effective January 1, 2007.)

(b) Additional duties

In addition to the duties described in rule 10.34, the committee must recommend to the Center for Judicial Education and Research proposals for the education and training of judicial officers and court staff.

(Subd (b) amended effective January 1, 2007.)

(c) Membership

The committee must include at least one member from each of the following categories:

(1) Appellate justice;

(2) Trial court judicial officer;

(3) Lawyer with expertise or interest in disability issues;

(4) Other lawyer;

(5) Judicial administrator; and

(6) Public member.

(Subd (c) amended effective January 1, 2007.)

Rule 10.55 amended and renumbered January 1, 2007; adopted as rule 6.55 effective January 1, 1999.

Rule 10.56. Collaborative Justice Courts Advisory Committee

(a) Area of focus

The committee makes recommendations to the Judicial Council on criteria for identifying and evaluating collaborative justice courts and for improving the processing of cases in these courts, which include drug courts, domestic violence courts, youth courts, and other collaborative justice courts. Those recommendations include "best practices" guidelines and methods for collecting data to evaluate the long-term effectiveness of collaborative justice courts.

(Subd (a) amended effective January 1, 2007.)

(b) Additional duties

In addition to the duties described in rule 10.34, the committee must:

(1) Assess and measure the success and effectiveness of local collaborative justice courts;

(2) Identify and disseminate to trial courts locally generated best practices;

(3) Recommend minimum judicial education standards and educational activities to support those standards to the Governing Committee of the Center for Judicial Education and Research;

(4) Advise the council of potential funding sources;

(5) Make recommendations regarding grant funding programs that are administered by the Administrative Office of the Courts for drug courts and other treatment courts; and

(6) Recommend appropriate outreach activities needed to support collaborative justice courts.

(Subd (b) amended effective January 1, 2007.)

(c) Membership

The committee must include the following:

(1) At least five judicial officers. Nominations for these appointments must be made in accordance with rule 10.32. The list of nominees should enable the Chair of the Judicial Council to appoint a committee that reflects a variety of court experience (e.g., criminal, juvenile, family, general civil), expertise, and court sizes and types (e.g., urban, suburban, and rural; and small, medium, and large).

(2) At least one member from each of the following categories:

(A) Judicial administrator;

(B) District attorney;

(C) Criminal defense attorney;

(D) Law enforcement (police/sheriff);

(E) Treatment provider or rehabilitation provider;

(F) Probation officer;

(G) Court-treatment coordinator;

(H) Treatment court graduate; and

(I) Public member.

(Subd (c) amended effective January 1, 2007.)

Rule 10.56 amended and renumbered effective January 1, 2007; adopted as rule 6.56 effective January 1, 2000; previously amended effective January 1, 2002.

Rule 10.57.   Judicial Service Advisory Committee

(a) Area of focus

The committee makes recommendations for improving judicial service, retention, and compensation.

(Subd (a) amended effective January 1, 2007.)

(b) Additional duties

In addition to the duties described in rule 10.34, the committee must identify and evaluate best current national and local practices and develop or recommend necessary training related to the following issues:

(1) A "cafeteria plan" of benefits; wellness subsidies; professional development allowances; personal leave; and supplemental life, disability, or liability insurance;

(2) Health-care benefits, including services and programs;

(3) Compensation and retirement, including recommendations for 401(k) and other deferred compensation programs and the most appropriate mechanism for setting judicial salaries;

(4) Resources and programs for quality of judicial life, particularly those dealing with health, stress, and relationships;

(5) Mentorship programs; and

(6) Special needs and programs for new and retired judges.

(Subd (b) amended effective January 1, 2007.)

(c) Membership

The committee must include at least one member from each of the following categories:

(1) Appellate court justice;

(2) Retired jurist;

(3) Superior court judge from a court with 15 or more judges;

(4) Superior court judge from a court with 5 to 14 judges;

(5) Superior court judge from a court with 4 or fewer judges;

(6) Superior court executive officer from a court with 15 or more judges;

(7) Superior court executive officer from a court with 14 or fewer judges;

(8) Member of the Administrative Presiding Justices Advisory Committee; and

(9) Member of the Trial Court Presiding Judges Advisory Committee.

(Subd (c) amended effective January 1, 2007.)

Rule 10.57 amended and renumbered effective January 1, 2007; adopted as rule 6.57 effective January 1, 2003.

Rule 10.58.   Advisory Committee on Civil Jury Instructions

(a) Area of focus

The committee regularly reviews case law and statutes affecting jury instructions and makes recommendations to the Judicial Council for updating, amending, and adding topics to the council's civil jury instructions.

(Subd (a) amended effective January 1, 2007.)

(b) Membership

The committee must include at least one member from each of the following categories, and a majority of the members must be judges:

(1) Appellate court justice;

(2) Trial court judge;

(3) Lawyer whose primary area of practice is civil law; and

(4) Law professor whose primary area of expertise is civil law.

Rule 10.58 amended and renumbered effective January 1, 2007; adopted as rule 6.58 effective September 1, 2003.

Rule 10.59.   Advisory Committee on Criminal Jury Instructions

(a) Area of focus

The committee regularly reviews case law and statutes affecting jury instructions and makes recommendations to the Judicial Council for updating, amending, and adding topics to the council's criminal jury instructions.

(b) Membership

The committee must include at least one member from each of the following categories, and a majority of the members must be judges:

(1) Appellate court justice;

(2) Trial court judge;

(3) Lawyer whose primary area of practice is criminal defense;

(4) Deputy district attorney or other attorney who represents the People of the State of California in criminal matters; and

(5) Law professor whose primary area of expertise is criminal law.

Rule 10.59 renumbered effective January 1, 2007; adopted as rule 6.59 effective July 1, 2005.

Rule 10.70.   Task forces

The Chief Justice, the Administrative Director of the Courts, or the council may establish task forces to work on specific projects that cannot be addressed by existing advisory committees. Each task force may be required to report to one of the internal committees, as designated in its charge. The Administrative Office of the Courts maintains a list of current task forces.

Rule 10.70 renumbered effective January 1, 2007; adopted as rule 6.70 effective January 1, 1999; previously amended effective September 1, 2003.

Rule 10.71.   Court Facilities Transitional Task Force [Repealed]

Rule 10.71 repealed by its own provision effective June 30, 2007; adopted as rule 6.60 effective June 23, 2004; previously amended and renumbered effective January 1, 2007.

Chapter 3
Administrative Office of the Courts

Rule 10.80. Administrative Director of the Courts
Rule 10.81. Administrative Office of the Courts

Rule 10.80. Administrative Director of the Courts

The Administrative Director of the Courts, appointed by the Judicial Council under article VI, section 6 of the Constitution, performs those functions prescribed by the Constitution and laws of the state, or delegated to the director by the Judicial Council or its chair.

Rule 10.80 amended and renumbered effective January 1, 2007; adopted as rule 6.80 effective January 1, 1999.

Ref.: Cal. Fms Pl. & Pr., Ch. 317, "Judges."

Rule 10.81. Administrative Office of the Courts

(a) Establishment

The Administrative Director of the Courts, under the supervision of the Chair of the Judicial Council, employs, organizes, and directs a staff, known as the Administrative Office of the Courts.

(Subd (a) amended effective January 1, 2007.)

(b) Duties

The Administrative Office of the Courts assists the council and its chair in carrying out their duties under the Constitution and laws of the state.

(Subd (b) amended effective January 1, 2007.)

(c) Reporting

The Administrative Office of the Courts must annually submit to the Judicial Council a management report that describes its current activities and internal operations.

(Subd (c) amended effective January 1, 2007.)

Rule 10.81 amended and renumbered effective January 1, 2007; adopted as rule 6.81 effective January 1, 1999.

Ref.: Cal. Fms Pl. & Pr., Ch. 317, "Judges."

Division 2
Administration of the Judicial Branch

Chapter 1
Budget and Fiscal Management

Rule 10.101. Role of the Judicial Council and Administrative Office of the Courts
Rule 10.102. Acceptance of gifts
Rule 10.103. Limitation on intrabranch contracting
Rule 10.104. Limitation on contracting with former employees
Rule 10.105. Allocation of new fee, fine, and forfeiture revenue
Rule 10.106. Judicial branch travel expense reimbursement policy

Rule 10.101. Role of the Judicial Council and Administrative Office of the Courts

(a) Purpose

This rule specifies the responsibilities of the Judicial Council, the Chief Justice, the Administrative Director of the Courts, and the Administrative Office of the Courts with respect to the judiciary's budget.

(Subd (a) amended effective January 1, 2007; previously amended effective January 1, 2005.)

(b) Duties of the Judicial Council

The Judicial Council must:

(1) Establish responsible fiscal priorities that best enable the judiciary to achieve its goals;

(2) Develop the budget of the judiciary based on the priorities established and the needs of the courts;

(3) Communicate and advocate the budget of the judiciary to the Governor and the Legislature;

(4) Allocate funds in a manner that ensures equal access to justice for all citizens of the state, ensures the ability of the courts to carry out their functions effectively, promotes implementation of statewide policies as established by statute and the Judicial Council, and promotes implementation of efficiencies and cost-saving measures;

(5) Resolve appeals on budget and allocation issues; and

(6) Ensure that the budget of the judiciary remains within the limits of the appropriation set by the Legislature.

(Subd (b) amended effective January 1, 2007.)

(c) Authority of the Chief Justice and Administrative Director of the Courts

(1) The Chief Justice and the Administrative Director of the Courts may take the following actions, on behalf of the Judicial Council, with regard to any of the Judicial Council's recommended budgets for the Supreme Court, the Courts of Appeal, the trial courts, the Judicial Council, and the Habeas Corpus Resource Center:

(A) Make technical changes; and

(B) Make changes during negotiations with the legislative and executive branches consistent with the goals and priorities adopted by the Judicial Council. The Chief Justice and the Administrative Director of the Courts must advise the council of the results of the negotiations.

(2) The Chief Justice and the Administrative Director of the Courts, on behalf of the Judicial Council, may

allocate funding appropriated in the annual State Budget to the Supreme Court, the Courts of Appeal, the Judicial Council, and the Habeas Corpus Resource Center.

(3) After the end of each fiscal year, the Administrative Director of the Courts must report to the Judicial Council on the actual expenditures from the budgets for the Supreme Court, the Courts of Appeal, the trial courts, the Judicial Council, and the Habeas Corpus Resource Center.

(Subd (c) adopted effective January 1, 2005.)

(d) Duties of the Administrative Director of the Courts

The Administrative Director of the Courts implements the directives of the Judicial Council and must:

(1) Develop policies and procedures for the creation and implementation of a yearly budget for the judiciary;

(2) Present the judiciary's budget in negotiations with the Governor and the Legislature; and

(3) Allocate to the trial courts, on behalf of the Judicial Council, a portion of the prior fiscal year baseline allocation for the trial courts following approval of the State Budget and before the allocation of state trial court funding by the Judicial Council. The portion of the prior fiscal year baseline allocation that may be so allocated is limited to the amount estimated to be necessary for the operation of the courts pending action by the Judicial Council, and may not exceed 25 percent of the prior fiscal year baseline allocation for each trial court.

(Subd (d) amended effective January 1, 2007; adopted as subd (c) effective July 1, 1998; previously amended effective January 1, 2001; previously relettered effective January 1, 2005.)

(e) Duties of the Director of the Finance Division

The Director of the Finance Division of the Administrative Office of the Courts, under the direction of the Administrative Director of the Courts, administers the budget policies and procedures developed by the Administrative Director of the Courts and approved by the Judicial Council. The Director of the Finance Division must:

(1) Develop and administer a budget preparation process for the judiciary, and ensure the submission of a final budget recommendation for the judiciary to the Department of Finance by November 1 of each year;

(2) Develop, in consultation with the State Controller's Office and the Department of Finance, a manual of procedures for the budget request process, revenues, expenditures, allocations, and payments;

(3) Monitor all revenues and expenditures for the judiciary;

(4) Develop recommendations for fiscal priorities and the allocation and reallocation of funds; and

(5) Assist all courts and the Administrative Director of the Courts in preparing and managing budgets.

(Subd (e) amended effective January 1, 2007; adopted as subd (d) effective July 1, 1998; previously relettered effective January 1, 2005.)

Rule 10.101 amended and renumbered effective January 1, 2007; adopted as rule 2301 effective July 1, 1998; renumbered as rule 6.101 effective January 1, 1999; previously amended effective January 1, 2001, and January 1, 2005.

Ref.: Cal. Fms Pl. & Pr., Ch. 317, "Judges."

Rule 10.102.   Acceptance of gifts

(a) Administrative Director of the Courts' authority to accept gifts

The Administrative Director of the Courts may accept on behalf of any entity listed in (b) any gift of real or personal property if the gift and any terms and conditions are found to be in the best interest of the state. Any applicable standards used by the Director of Finance under Government Code section 11005.1 may be considered in accepting gifts.

(Subd (a) amended effective January 1, 2007; adopted as unlettered subd; previously amended and lettered effective January 1, 2004.)

(b) Delegation of authority

The Administrative Director may delegate the authority to accept gifts to the following, under any guidelines established by the Administrative Office of the Courts:

(1) The executive officer of a superior court, for gifts to the superior court;

(2) The clerk/administrator of a Court of Appeal, for gifts to a Court of Appeal;

(3) The clerk of the Supreme Court, for gifts to the Supreme Court; and

(4) The Director of the Finance Division of the Administrative Office of the Courts, for gifts to the Judicial Council and the Administrative Office of the Courts.

(Subd (b) amended effective January 1, 2007; previously adopted effective January 1, 2004.)

Rule 10.102 amended and renumbered effective January 1, 2007; adopted as rule 989.7 effective September 13, 1991; previously amended and renumbered as rule 6.102 effective January 1, 2004.

Rule 10.103.   Limitation on intrabranch contracting

(a) Definitions

For purposes of this rule, "judicial branch entity" includes a trial court, a Court of Appeal, the Supreme Court, and the Administrative Office of the Courts.

(b) Application

This rule is not applicable to:

(1) Part-time commissioners, with respect to services as a commissioner;

(2) Part-time court interpreters who are not subject to the cross-assignment system under Government Code section 71810, with respect to interpreter services provided to a court; and

(3) Court reporters, with respect to reporter services provided to a court.

(Subd (b) amended effective January 1, 2007.)

(c) Intrabranch limitations

An employee of a judicial branch entity must not:

(1) Engage in any employment, enterprise, or other activity from which he or she receives compensation or in which he or she has a financial interest and that is sponsored or funded by any judicial branch entity through or by a contract for goods or services for which compensation is paid, unless the activity is required as a condition of his or her regular judicial branch employment; or

(2) Contract with any judicial branch entity, on his or her own behalf, to provide goods or services for which compensation is paid.

(Subd (c) amended effective January 1, 2007.)

(d) Multiple employment

This rule does not prohibit any person from being employed by more than one judicial branch entity.

525   JUDICIAL ADMINISTRATION RULES   Rule 10.106

Rules of Court

Rule 10.103 amended and renumbered effective January 1, 2007; adopted as rule 6.103 effective January 1, 2004.

Rule 10.104. Limitation on contracting with former employees

(a) Trial and appellate court contracts with former employees

A trial or appellate court may not enter into a contract for goods or services for which compensation is paid with a person previously employed by that court or by the Administrative Office of the Courts:

(1) For a period of 12 months following the date of the former employee's retirement, dismissal, or separation from service, if he or she was employed in a policymaking position in the same general subject area as the proposed contract within the 12-month period before his or her retirement, dismissal, or separation; or

(2) For a period of 24 months following the date of the former employee's retirement, dismissal, or separation from service, if he or she engaged in any of the negotiations, transactions, planning, arrangements, or any part of the decision-making process relevant to the contract while employed in any capacity by the court or the Administrative Office of the Courts.

(b) Administrative Office of the Courts contracts with former employees

The Administrative Office of the Courts may not enter into a contract for goods or services for which compensation is paid with a person previously employed by it:

(1) For a period of 12 months following the date of the former employee's retirement, dismissal, or separation from service, if he or she was employed in a policymaking position at the Administrative Office of the Courts in the same general subject area as the proposed contract within the 12-month period before his or her retirement, dismissal, or separation; or

(2) For a period of 24 months following the date of the former employee's retirement, dismissal, or separation from service, if he or she engaged in any of the negotiations, transactions, planning, arrangements, or any part of the decision-making process relevant to the contract while employed in any capacity by the Administrative Office of the Courts.

(Subd (b) amended effective January 1, 2007.)

(c) Policymaking position

"Policymaking position" includes:

(1) In a trial court, the court's executive officer and any other position designated by the court as a policymaking position;

(2) In an appellate court, the clerk/administrator and any other position designated by the court as a policymaking position; and

(3) In the Administrative Office of the Courts, the Administrative Director of the Courts, the Chief Deputy Director, any director, and any other position designated by the Administrative Director as a policymaking position.

(d) Scope

This rule does not prohibit any court or the Administrative Office of the Courts from (1) employing any person or (2) contracting with any former judge or justice.

Rule 10.104 amended and renumbered effective January 1, 2007; adopted as rule 6.104 effective January 1, 2004.

Rule 10.105. Allocation of new fee, fine, and forfeiture revenue

(a) Allocation

The Judicial Council must annually allocate 80 percent of the amount of fee, fine, and forfeiture revenue deposited in the Trial Court Improvement Fund under Government Code section 77205(a) that exceeds the amount of fee, fine, and forfeiture revenue deposited in the Trial Court Improvement Fund in fiscal year 2002–2003 to one or more of the following:

(1) To the trial courts in the counties from which the increased amount is attributable;

(2) To other trial courts to support trial court operations; or

(3) For retention in the Trial Court Improvement Fund.

(Subd (a) amended effective January 1, 2007.)

(b) Methodology

The Administrative Office of the Courts must recommend a methodology for the allocation and must recommend an allocation based on this methodology. On approval of a methodology by the Judicial Council, the Administrative Office of the Courts must issue a Finance Memo stating the methodology adopted by the Judicial Council.

(Subd (b) amended effective January 1, 2007.)

Rule 10.105 amended and renumbered effective January 1, 2007; adopted as rule 6.105 effective December 10, 2004.

Rule 10.106. Judicial branch travel expense reimbursement policy

(a) Adoption

The Judicial Council must adopt a fiscally responsible judicial branch travel expense reimbursement policy, under Government Code section 68506.5, that provides appropriate accountability for the use of public resources. Before adopting the initial policy, the Judicial Council must receive comments from the courts, court employee organizations, and other interested groups.

(Subd (a) adopted effective July 1, 2008.)

(b) Applicability

The judicial branch travel expense reimbursement policy applies to official state business travel by:

(1) Judicial officers and judicial officers sitting by assignment;

(2) Officers, employees, retired annuitants, and members of the Supreme Court, the Courts of Appeal, superior courts, the Judicial Council, the Administrative Office of the Courts, the Habeas Corpus Resource Center, and the Commission on Judicial Performance; and

(3) Members of task forces, working groups, commissions, or similar bodies appointed by the Chief Justice, the Judicial Council, or the Administrative Director of the Courts.

(Subd (b) adopted effective July 1, 2008.)

(c) Amendments

The Judicial Council delegates to the Administrative Director of the Courts, under article VI, section 6(c) of the California Constitution and other applicable law, the authority to make technical changes and clarifications to the judicial branch travel expense reimbursement policy. The changes and clarifications must be fiscally responsible, provide for appropriate accountability, and be in general compliance with the policy initially adopted by the Judicial Council.

(Subd (c) adopted effective July 1, 2008.)

Rule 10.106 adopted effective July 1, 2008.

Chapter 2
Court Security

Rule 10.170. Working Group on Court Security

Rule 10.171. Working Group on Court Security Fiscal Guidelines

Rule 10.172. Court security plans

Rule 10.173. Court security committees

Rule 10.170.   Working Group on Court Security

(a) Purpose

The Judicial Council has established the Working Group on Court Security. The purpose of the working group is to recommend uniform standards and guidelines that may be used by the Judicial Council and any sheriff or marshal for the implementation of trial court security services. The Working Group on Court Security must also consult with the Administrative Office of the Courts' Office of Court Construction and Management regarding security considerations for court facilities. The Judicial Council, after receiving recommendations from the Working Group on Court Security, may adopt rules, standards, guidelines, and policy directions for the trial courts in order to achieve efficiencies that will reduce security operating costs and constrain growth in those costs.

(Subd (a) amended effective January 1, 2007.)

(b) Composition

The group is composed as follows:

(1) Eight representatives from the judicial branch of government selected by the Chief Justice;

(2) Two representatives of the counties selected by the California State Association of Counties;

(3) Three representatives of the county sheriffs selected by the California State Sheriffs' Association;

(4) One representative of labor selected by the California Coalition of Law Enforcement Associations; and

(5) One representative selected by the Peace Officers Research Association of California.

(c) Chair

The Chief Justice may appoint an appellate court justice to serve as nonvoting chair.

(Subd (c) amended effective January 1, 2007.)

(d) Initial terms

(1) The initial terms of the members of the working group are as follows:

(A) Four years for three representatives of the judicial branch, one representative of the counties, one representative of the county sheriffs, one representative of the California Coalition of Law Enforcement Associations, and one representative of the Peace Officers Research Association of California.

(B) Three years for three representatives of the judicial branch, one representative of the counties, and one representative of the county sheriffs.

(C) Two years for two representatives of the judicial branch and one representative of the county sheriffs.

(2) The appointing authority may designate which members are appointed to two-, three-, and four-year terms.

(Subd (d) amended effective January 1, 2007.)

(e) Terms

After the initial terms of members of the working group as provided in (d), the terms of members are three years. The appointing authority may fill any vacancy occurring for the remainder of the term.

(Subd (e) amended effective January 1, 2007.)

Rule 10.170 amended and renumbered effective January 1, 2007; adopted as rule 6.170 effective October 15, 2003.

Rule 10.171.   Working Group on Court Security Fiscal Guidelines

(a) Purpose

The Judicial Council has established the Working Group on Court Security Fiscal Guidelines. The purpose of the working group is to consider whether modifications are necessary and appropriate to the template that determines security costs, under Government Code section 69927(a)(1) ("template review"), and to recommend changes to the limit for allowable costs, as stated in Government Code section 69927(a)(5) ("allowable costs review"). Template review may involve, among other items, that part of the template affecting law enforcement or security personnel in courtrooms or court detention facilities ("personnel template review").

(Subd (a) amended effective January 1, 2007; previously amended effective March 1, 2003, and October 15, 2003.)

(b) Composition

(1) *Composition for allowable costs review and template review, except personnel template review*

In performing allowable costs review and template review, except personnel template review, the group is composed as follows:

(A) Six representatives from the judicial branch from the Working Group on Court Security established in rule 10.170, as selected by the Administrative Director of the Courts;

(B) The two representatives of the counties from the Working Group on Court Security established in rule 10.170; and

(C) The three representatives of the county sheriffs from the Working Group on Court Security established in rule 10.170.

(2) *Composition for personnel template review*

In performing personnel template review, the group is composed as follows:

(A) The six representatives from the judicial branch of government selected by the Administrative Director of the Courts, under (b)(1)(A);

(B) The two representatives of the counties under (b)(1)(B);

(C) Two of the three representatives of the county sheriffs under (b)(1)(C) as determined by the California State Sheriffs' Association; and

(D) Two representatives of labor selected by the California Coalition of Law Enforcement Associations.

(Subd (b) amended effective January 1, 2007; previously repealed and adopted effective March 1, 2003; previously amended effective October 15, 2003.)

(c) Chair

The Administrative Director of the Courts may designate one of the judicial branch members to be chair of the working group.

(d) Terms

(1) The initial and subsequent terms of the members of the Working Group on Court Security Fiscal Guidelines who are members because they are members of the working group established in rule 10.170 expire when their terms on that working group expire. The terms of any other members of the Working Group on Court Security Fiscal Guidelines are three years.

(2) The appointing authority may fill any vacancy occurring for the remainder of the term.

(Subd (d) amended effective January 1, 2007; previously amended effective October 15, 2003.)

Rule 10.171 amended and renumbered effective January 1, 2007; adopted as rule 6.170 effective January 1, 2003; adopted as rule 6.171 effective October 15, 2003.

Rule 10.172. Court security plans

(a) Responsibility

The presiding judge and the sheriff or marshal are responsible for developing an annual or multiyear comprehensive, countywide court security plan.

(Subd (a) adopted effective January 1, 2009.)

(b) Scope of security plan

(1) Each court security plan must, at a minimum, address the following general security subject areas:

(A) Composition and role of court security committees;

(B) Composition and role of executive team;

(C) Incident command system;

(D) Self-assessments and audits of court security;

(E) Mail handling security;

(F) Identification cards and access control;

(G) Courthouse landscaping security plan;

(H) Parking plan security;

(I) Interior and exterior lighting plan security;

(J) Intrusion and panic alarm systems;

(K) Fire detection and equipment;

(L) Emergency and auxiliary power;

(M) Use of private security contractors;

(N) Use of court attendants and employees;

(O) Administrative/clerk's office security;

(P) Jury personnel and jury room security;

(Q) Security for public demonstrations;

(R) Vital records storage security;

(S) Evacuation planning;

(T) Security for after-hours operations;

(U) Custodial services;

(V) Computer and data security;

(W) Workplace violence prevention; and

(X) Public access to court proceedings.

(2) Each court security plan must, at a minimum, address the following law enforcement subject areas:

(A) Security personnel and staffing;

(B) Perimeter and entry screening;

(C) Prisoner and inmate transport;

(D) Holding cells;

(E) Interior and public waiting area security;

(F) Courtroom security;

(G) Jury trial procedures;

(H) High-profile and high-risk trial security;

(I) Judicial protection;

(J) Incident reporting and recording;

(K) Security personnel training;

(L) Courthouse security communication;

(M) Hostage, escape, lockdown, and active shooter procedures;

(N) Firearms policies and procedures; and

(O) Restraint of defendants.

(3) Each court security plan should address additional security issues as needed.

(Subd (b) adopted effective January 1, 2009.)

(c) Court security assessment and assessment report

At least once every two years, the presiding judge and the sheriff or marshal are responsible for conducting an assessment of security with respect to all court operations. The assessment must include a comprehensive review of the court's physical security profile and security protocols and procedures. The assessment should identify security weaknesses, resource deficiencies, compliance with the court security plan, and any need for changes to the court security plan. The assessment must be summarized in a written assessment report.

(Subd (c) adopted effective January 1, 2009.)

(d) Submission of court security plan to the Administrative Office of the Courts

On or before November 1, 2009, each superior court must submit a court security plan to the Administrative Office of the Courts (AOC). On or before February 1, 2011, and each succeeding February 1, each superior court must report to the AOC whether it has made any changes to the court security plan and, if so, identify each change made and provide copies of the current court security plan and current assessment report. In preparing any submission, a court may request technical assistance from the AOC.

(Subd (d) adopted effective January 1, 2009.)

(e) Plan review process

The AOC will evaluate for completeness submissions identified in (d). Annually, the submissions and evaluations will be provided to the Working Group on Court Security. Any submissions determined by the working group to be incomplete or deficient must be returned to the submitting court for correction and completion. No later than July 1 of each year, the working group must submit to the Judicial Council a summary of the submissions for the Judicial Council's report to the Legislature.

(Subd (e) adopted effective January 1, 2009.)

(f) Delegation

The presiding judge may delegate any of the specific duties listed in this rule to another judge or, if the duty does not require the exercise of judicial authority, to the court executive officer or other court employee. The presiding judge remains responsible for all duties listed in this rule even if he or she has delegated particular tasks to someone else.

(Subd (f) adopted effective January 1, 2009.)

Rule 10.172 adopted effective January 1, 2009.

Advisory Committee Comment

This rule is adopted to comply with the mandate in Government Code section 69925, which requires the Judicial Council to provide for the areas to be addressed in a court security plan and to establish a process for the review of such plans. The Working Group on Court Security is authorized by Government Code section 69927 and established by rule 10.170 for the purpose of studying and making recommendation to the Judicial Council regarding court security matters. For the assistance of the courts and sheriffs in preparing and submitting their court security plans, the Working Group on Court Security has prepared *Court Security Plan Guidelines* with respect to each of the subject areas identified in subsections (b)(1) and (b)(2). The courts and sheriffs may obtain copies of the *Court Security Plan Guidelines* from the Administrative Office of the Courts' Emergency Response and Security unit.

Rule 10.173.   Court security committees

(a) Establishment

Each superior court must establish a standing court security committee.

(Subd (a) adopted effective January 1, 2009.)

(b) Role of the court security committee

The court security committee and any subcommittees advise the presiding judge and sheriff or marshal on the preparation of court security plans and on the formulation and implementation of all other policies and procedures related to security for court operations and security for facilities where the court conducts its operations. The presiding judge and sheriff or marshal may delegate to a court security committee or subcommittee the responsibility for conducting the court security assessment and preparing the assessment report.

(Subd (b) adopted effective January 1, 2009.)

(c) Members

(1) The court security committee must be chaired by the presiding judge or a judge designated by the presiding judge.

(2) In addition to the chair, each court security committee must include at least one representative designated by the sheriff or marshal and either the court executive officer or other court administrator as designated by the presiding judge.

(3) The chair may appoint additional members as appropriate. Additional members may include representatives from other government agencies, including:

(A) The facilities management office of the government entity, or entities, that hold title to or are responsible for the facilities where the court conducts its operations;

(B) Local fire protection agencies;

(C) Agencies that occupy portions of a court facility; and

(D) Agencies other than the sheriff that manage local corrections or state prison facilities.

(Subd (c) adopted effective January 1, 2009.)

(d) Facility contact person

In those courts having more than one court facility, the chair of the court security committee must designate for each facility a single contact person to coordinate activities in the event of an emergency and to collaborate with the court security committee, at its request.

(Subd (d) adopted effective January 1, 2009.)

(e) Subcommittees

The chair of the court security committee may form subcommittees if appropriate, including a subcommittee for each court facility. The chair must determine the composition of each subcommittee based on the individual court's circumstances.

(Subd (e) adopted effective January 1, 2009.)

Rule 10.173 adopted effective January 1, 2009.

Chapter 3
Court Facilities

Rule 10.180.   Court facilities standards

(a) Development of standards

The Administrative Office of the Courts is responsible for developing and maintaining standards for the alteration, remodeling, renovation, and expansion of existing court facilities and for the construction of new court facilities.

(Subd (a) amended effective April 21, 2006.)

(b) Adoption by the Judicial Council

The standards developed by the Administrative Office of the Courts must be submitted to the Judicial Council for review and adoption as the standards to be used for court facilities in the state. Nonsubstantive changes to the standards may be made by the Administrative Office of the Courts; substantive changes must be submitted to the Judicial Council for review and adoption.

(Subd (b) amended effective April 21, 2006.)

(c) Use of standards

The Judicial Council, the Administrative Office of the Courts, affected courts, and advisory groups on court facilities issues created under these rules must use the standards adopted under (b) in reviewing or recommending proposed alteration, remodeling, renovation, or expansion of an existing court facility or new construction. Courts and advisory groups must report deviations from the standards to the Administrative Office of the Courts through a process established for that purpose.

(Subd (c) amended effective April 21, 2006; previously amended effective June 23, 2004.)

Rule 10.180 renumbered effective January 1, 2007; adopted as rule 6.150 effective July 1, 2002; previously amended effective June 23, 2004, and April 21, 2006.

Rule 10.181.   Court facilities policies, procedures, and standards

(a) Responsibilities of the Administrative Office of the Courts

The Administrative Office of the Courts, after consultation with the Court Facilities Transitional Task Force, must prepare and present to the Judicial Council recommendations for policies, procedures, and standards concerning the operation, maintenance, alteration, remodeling, renovation, expansion, acquisition, space programming, design, and construction of appellate and trial court facilities under Government Code sections 69204(c) and 70391(e).

(Subd (a) lettered and amended effective January 1, 2007; adopted as part of unlettered subd.)

(b) Consultations with the affected court and with local governmental and community interests

The policies, procedures, and standards must ensure that decisions are made in consultation with the affected court, when appropriate, and that decisions concerning acquisition, design, and construction of court facilities are made in consultation with local governmental and community interests, when appropriate.

(Subd (b) lettered and amended effective January 1, 2007; adopted as part of unlettered subd.)

Rule 10.181 amended and renumbered effective January 1, 2007; adopted as rule 6.180 effective June 23, 2004; previously amended effective April 21, 2006.

Rule 10.182. Operation and maintenance of court facilities

(a) Intent

The intent of this rule is to allocate responsibility and decision making for the operation and maintenance of court facilities among the courts and the Administrative Office of the Courts.

(b) Responsibilities of the Administrative Office of the Courts

(1) In addition to those matters expressly authorized by statute, the Administrative Office of the Courts is responsible for:

(A) Taking action on the operation of court facilities, including the day-to-day operation of a building and maintenance of a facility. The Administrative Office of the Courts must, in cooperation with the court, perform its responsibilities concerning operation of the court facility to effectively and efficiently support the day-to-day operation of the court system and services of the court. These actions include maintaining proper heating, ventilation, and air conditioning levels; providing functional electrical, fire safety, vertical transportation, mechanical, and plumbing systems through preventive maintenance and responsive repairs; and maintaining structural, nonstructural, security, and telecommunications infrastructures.

(B) Preparing and submitting budget allocation proposals to the Judicial Council, as part of the yearly judicial branch budget development cycle, specifying the amounts to be spent for the operation of court facilities as provided in (A).

(C) Developing policies, procedures, and guidelines concerning court facilities for submission to the Judicial Council.

(2) The Administrative Office of the Courts must consult with affected courts concerning the annual operations and maintenance needs assessment, development of annual priorities, and fiscal planning for the operational and maintenance needs of court facilities.

(3) The Administrative Office of the Courts may, when appropriate, delegate its responsibilities for ongoing operation and management to the court for some or all of the existing court facilities used by that court. Any delegation of responsibility must ensure that:

(A) The management of court facilities is consistent with the statewide goals and policies of the judicial branch;

(B) Access to all court facilities in California is promoted;

(C) Facilities decisions are made with consideration of operational costs and enhance economical, efficient, and effective court operations; and

(D) Courts have adequate and sufficient facilities and appropriate resources to undertake these delegated tasks.

(4) The Administrative Office of the Courts must, whenever feasible, seek review and recommendations from the Court Facilities Transitional Task Force before recommending action on appellate and trial court facilities issues to the Judicial Council.

(Subd (b) amended effective January 1, 2007.)

(c) Responsibilities of the courts

(1) The affected courts must consult with the Administrative Office of the Courts concerning the annual operations and maintenance needs assessment, development of annual priorities, and fiscal planning for the operational and maintenance needs of court facilities, including contingency planning for unforeseen facility maintenance needs.

(2) Each court to which responsibility is delegated under (b)(3) must report to the Administrative Office of the Courts quarterly or more often, as provided in the delegation. The report must include the activities and expenditures related to the delegation that are specified for reporting in the delegation. Each court must also account to the Administrative Office of the Courts for all expenditures related to the delegation. The Administrative Office of the Courts may conduct an internal audit of any receipts and expenditures.

(Subd (c) amended effective January 1, 2007.)

Rule 10.182 amended and renumbered effective January 1, 2007; adopted as rule 6.181 effective June 23, 2004.

Rule 10.183. Decision making on transfer of responsibility for trial court facilities

(a) Intent

The intent of this rule is to allocate among the Judicial Council, the trial courts, and the Administrative Office of the Courts, responsibility and decision making for the transfer of responsibility for trial court facilities from the counties to the Judicial Council.

(b) Definitions

As used in this rule, the following terms have the same meaning as provided by Government Code section 70301:

(1) "Court facilities";

(2) "Maintenance";

(3) "Responsibility for facilities"; and

(4) "Shared use."

(Subd (b) amended effective January 1, 2007.)

(c) Responsibilities of the Judicial Council and the Executive and Planning Committee

The Judicial Council must determine the following issues concerning transfer of responsibility of court facilities, except in the case of a need for urgent action between meetings of the council, in which case the Executive and Planning Committee is authorized to act under rule 10.11(d).

(1) Rejection of transfer of responsibility for a building under Government Code section 70326; and

(2) A decision to dispose of a surplus court facility under Government Code section 70391(c).

(Subd (c) amended effective January 1, 2007.)

(d) Responsibilities of the Administrative Office of the Courts

The Administrative Office of the Courts is responsible for the following matters related to transfer of responsibility for court facilities, in addition to matters expressly authorized by statute:

(1) Keeping the courts informed and involved, as appropriate, in the negotiations with the counties for transfer of responsibility for court facilities;

(2) Except as provided in (c)(1), approving an agreement transferring responsibility for a court facility to the state;

(3) Administering a shared-use court facility, including:

(A) Making a decision to displace a minority county tenant under Government Code section 70344(b);

(B) Seeking a change in the amount of court space under Government Code section 70342; and

(C) Responding to a county seeking a change in the amount of county space under Government Code section 70342; and

(4) Auditing the collection of fees by trial courts under Government Code section 70391(d)(1) and the money in local courthouse construction funds under Government Code section 70391(d)(2).

(Subd (d) amended effective January 1, 2007.)

(e) Appeal of county facilities payment amount

The Administrative Director of the Courts must obtain the approval of the Executive and Planning Committee before pursuing correction of a county facilities payment amount under Government Code section 70367. This provision does not preclude the Administrative Director of the Courts from submitting a declaration as required by Government Code section 70367(a). The Administrative Director of the Courts must report to the Executive and Planning Committee any decision not to appeal a county facilities payment amount.

Rule 10.183 amended and renumbered effective January 1, 2007; adopted as rule 6.182 effective June 23, 2004.

Rule 10.184.   Acquisition, space programming, construction, and design of court facilities

(a) Intent

The intent of this rule is to allocate responsibility and decision making for acquisition, space programming, construction, and design of court facilities among the courts and the Administrative Office of the Courts.

(b) Responsibilities of the Administrative Office of the Courts

(1) In addition to those matters expressly provided by statute, the Administrative Office of the Courts is responsible for the acquisition, space programming, construction, and design of a court facility, consistent with the facilities policies and procedures adopted by the Judicial Council and the California Rules of Court.

(2) The Administrative Office of the Courts must prepare and submit to the Judicial Council separate annual capital outlay proposals for the appellate courts and the trial courts, as part of the yearly judicial branch budget development cycle, specifying the amounts to be spent for these purposes. The capital outlay proposal for the trial courts must specify the money that is proposed to be spent from the State Court Facilities Construction Fund and from other sources. The annual capital outlay proposals must be consistent with the Five-Year Capital Infrastructure Plan or must recommend appropriate changes in the Five-Year Capital Infrastructure Plan. The Administrative Office of the Courts must, whenever feasible, seek review and recommendations from the Court Facilities Transitional Task Force before recommending action to the Judicial Council on these issues.

(3) The Administrative Office of the Courts must consult with the affected courts concerning the annual capital needs of the courts.

(Subd (b) amended effective January 1, 2007.)

(c) Responsibilities of the courts

(1) Affected courts must consult with the Administrative Office of the Courts concerning the courts' annual capital needs.

(2) An affected court must work with the advisory group that is established for any court construction or major renovation project.

(d) Advisory group for construction projects

The Administrative Office of the Courts, in consultation with the leadership of the affected court, must establish and work with an advisory group for each court construction or major renovation project. The advisory group consists of court judicial officers, other court personnel, and others affected by the court facility. The advisory group must work with the Administrative Office of the Courts on issues involved in the construction or renovation, from the selection of a space programmer and architect through occupancy of the facility.

Rule 10.184 amended and renumbered effective January 1, 2007; adopted as rule 6.183 effective June 23, 2004.

Chapter 4
Management of Claims and Litigation

Rule 10.201. Claim and litigation procedure
Rule 10.202. Claims and litigation management
Rule 10.203. Contractual indemnification

Rule 10.201.   Claim and litigation procedure

(a) Definitions

As used in this chapter:

(1) "Judicial branch entity" is as defined in Government Code section 900.3;

(2) "Judge" means a judge or justice of a judicial branch entity;

(3) "Office of the General Counsel" means the Office of the General Counsel of the Administrative Office of the Courts; and

(4) "Litigation Management Committee" means the Litigation Management Committee of the Judicial Council.

(Subd (a) amended effective January 1, 2007.)

(b) Procedure for action on claims

To carry out the Judicial Council's responsibility under Government Code section 912.7 to act on a claim, claim amendment, or application for leave to present a late claim against a judicial branch entity or a judge, the Office of the General Counsel, under the direction of the Administrative Director of the Courts, must:

(1) On receipt of a claim, claim amendment, or application for leave to present a late claim forwarded by a judicial branch entity, promptly consult with a representative of that entity about the merits of the claim, claim amendment, or application for leave to present a late claim;

(2) Grant or deny an application for leave to present a late claim under Government Code section 911.6(b);

(3) If determined by the Office of the General Counsel to be appropriate, refer a claim or claim amendment for further investigation to a claims adjuster or other investigator under contract with the Administrative Office of the Courts;

(4) Reject a claim if it is not a proper charge against the judicial branch entity or judge;

(5) Allow a claim in the amount justly due as determined by the Office of the General Counsel if it is a proper charge against the judicial branch entity and the amount is less than $50,000; and

(6) Make recommendations to the Litigation Management Committee regarding proposed settlements of claims requiring payments of $50,000 or more.

(Subd (b) amended effective January 1, 2007.)

(c) Allowance and payment of claims

The following may allow and authorize payment of any claim arising out of the activities of a judicial branch entity or judge:

(1) The Office of the General Counsel, under the direction of the Administrative Director of the Courts, if the payment is less than $50,000; or

(2) The Litigation Management Committee, for any claim.

(d) Settlement of lawsuits and payment of judgments

The following may settle lawsuits, after consultation with the affected entity and any judge or employee being defended by the Judicial Council, and authorize payment of judgments arising out of the activities of a judicial branch entity or judge:

(1) The Office of the General Counsel, under the direction of the Administrative Director of the Courts, if the payment is less than $50,000 and the lawsuit does not raise important policy issues; or

(2) The Litigation Management Committee, for any settlement or judgment.

Rule 10.201 amended and renumbered effective January 1, 2007; adopted as rule 6.201 effective January 1, 2003.

Ref.: W. Cal. Sum., 5 "Torts" §233.

Rule 10.202. Claims and litigation management

(a) Intent

The intent of this rule is to:

(1) Ensure that the trial and appellate courts are provided with timely, quality legal assistance; and

(2) Promote the cost-effective, prompt, and fair resolution of actions, proceedings, and claims that affect the trial and appellate courts and involve justices of the Courts of Appeal or the Supreme Court, trial court judges, subordinate judicial officers, court executive officers or administrators, or employees of the trial and appellate courts.

(Subd (a) amended effective January 1, 2007; previously amended effective January 1, 2003.)

(b) Duties of the Office of the General Counsel

To carry out the duty of the Judicial Council to provide for the representation, defense, and indemnification of justices of the Courts of Appeal or the Supreme Court, judges, subordinate judicial officers, court executive officers and administrators, and trial and appellate court employees under part 1 (commencing with section 810) to part 7 (commencing with section 995), inclusive, of the Government Code, the Office of the General Counsel under the direction of the Administrative Director of the Courts and the General Counsel, must:

(1) Develop, manage, and administer a litigation management program for investigating and resolving all claims and lawsuits affecting the trial and appellate courts;

(2) Provide legal assistance to the trial or appellate court, and to any justice, judge, subordinate judicial officer, court executive officer or administrator, and trial or appellate court employee who is named as a defendant or responsible party, subject to the defense and indemnification provisions of part 1 (commencing with section 810) to part 7 (commencing with section 995), inclusive, of the Government Code, on receipt of notice of a claim or lawsuit affecting the trial or appellate court or of a dispute that is likely to result in a claim or lawsuit;

(3) Select and direct any counsel retained to represent any trial or appellate court, justice, judge, subordinate judicial officer, court executive officer or administrator, and trial or appellate court employee being provided legal representation under (2), after consultation with the trial or appellate court and any such individual defendant;

(4) Make settlement decisions in all claims and lawsuits other than those identified in (5), after consultation with the affected trial or appellate court, and any justice, judge, subordinate judicial officer, court executive officer or administrator, and trial or appellate court employee being provided legal representation under (2);

(5) Make recommendations to the Litigation Management Committee regarding proposed settlements of claims or lawsuits requiring payments of $50,000 or more or raising important policy issues;

(6) Develop and implement risk avoidance programs for the trial and appellate courts;

(7) Provide an annual report to the Litigation Management Committee concerning the litigation management program; and

(8) Provide an annual report to each trial and appellate court concerning claims and lawsuits filed against that trial or appellate court.

(Subd (b) amended effective January 1, 2007; previously amended effective July 1, 2002, and January 1, 2003.)

(c) Duties of trial and appellate courts

The trial and appellate courts must:

(1) Notify the Office of the General Counsel promptly on receipt of notice of a dispute that is likely to result in a claim or lawsuit, or of a claim or lawsuit filed, against the court, a justice, a judge or subordinate judicial officer, a court executive officer or administrator, or a court employee, and forward the claim and lawsuit to the Office of the General Counsel for handling; and

(2) Consult with the Office of the General Counsel regarding strategic and settlement decisions in claims and lawsuits.

(Subd (c) amended effective January 1, 2007; previously amended effective July 1, 2002, and January 1, 2003.)

(d) Disagreements about major strategic decisions

Following consultation with the Office of the General Counsel, a presiding judge or administrative presiding justice may object to a proposed decision of the Office of the General Counsel about major strategic decisions, such as retention of counsel and proposed settlements, by presenting to the Office of the General Counsel a written statement of the objection. The Office of the General Counsel must present the written objection to the Litigation Management Committee, which will resolve the objection.

(Subd (d) amended effective January 1, 2007; previously adopted effective January 1, 2003.)

Rule 10.202 amended and renumbered effective January 1, 2007; adopted as rule 6.800 effective January 1, 2001; previously amended effective July 1, 2002; previously renumbered as rule 6.202 effective January 1, 2003.

Ref.: W. Cal. Sum., 5 "Torts" §233.

Rule 10.203. Contractual indemnification

(a) Intent

The intent of this rule is to facilitate the use of contractual indemnities that allocate legal risk and liability to parties that contract with a superior court or Court of Appeal, the Supreme Court, the Judicial Council, or the Administrative Office of the Courts (a "judicial branch entity" as defined in Gov. Code, § 900.3).

(b) Defense and indemnification provisions

Notwithstanding rule 10.14, 10.201, or 10.202, a judicial branch entity may enter into a contract that requires the contractor or the contractor's insurer to indemnify, defend, and hold harmless the entity and its officers, agents, and employees against claims, demands, liability, damages, attorney fees, costs, expenses, or losses arising from the performance of the contract. Upon receipt of notice of a claim or lawsuit that may be subject to contractual indemnities, the judicial branch entity must notify the Office of the General Counsel, which will manage the claim or lawsuit to obtain the benefits of the contractual indemnities to the extent consistent with the interests of the public and the judicial branch.

(Subd (b) amended effective January 1, 2007.)

Rule 10.203 amended and renumbered effective January 1, 2007; adopted as rule 6.203 effective October 15, 2003.

Chapter 5
Ethics Training

Rule 10.301. Ethics training for Judicial Council members and judicial branch employees

(a) Authority

This rule is adopted under Government Code section 11146 et seq. and article VI, section 6 of the California Constitution.

(Subd (a) amended effective January 1, 2007.)

(b) Definitions

For purposes of this rule, "judicial branch employee" includes an employee of a trial or appellate court or the Administrative Office of the Courts, but does not include court commissioners or referees.

(c) Judicial Council members and judicial branch employees

(1) The Administrative Office of the Courts must provide an ethics orientation course for Judicial Council members and for judicial branch employees who are required to file a statement of economic interests.

(2) Judicial Council members must take the orientation course within six months of appointment. If a member is appointed to a subsequent term, he or she must take the course within six months of the reappointment.

(3) Judicial branch employees who are required to file a statement of economic interests must take the orientation course as follows:

(A) For employees who have taken the orientation course before the effective date of this rule, at least once during each consecutive two calendar years after the date of the last attendance.

(B) For new employees, within six months of becoming an employee and at least once during each consecutive two calendar years thereafter.

(C) For all other employees, within six months of the effective date of this rule and at least once during each consecutive two calendar years thereafter.

Rule 10.301 amended and renumbered effective January 1, 2007; adopted as rule 6.301 effective January 1, 2004.

Chapter 6
Management of Human Resources

Rule 10.350. Workers' compensation program

(a) Intent

The intent of this rule is to:

(1) Establish procedures for the Administrative Office of the Courts' workers' compensation program for the trial courts; and

(2) Ensure that the trial courts' workers' compensation coverage complies with applicable law and is cost-efficient.

(Subd (a) amended effective January 1, 2007.)

(b) Duties of the Administrative Office of the Courts

To carry out the duty of the Judicial Council to establish a workers' compensation program for the trial courts, the Administrative Office of the Courts, through its Human Resources Division, must:

(1) Maintain a contract with a vendor to provide courts, on a voluntary basis, with a cost-efficient workers' compensation coverage program;

(2) Monitor the performance of the vendor with which it contracts to provide such services;

(3) Timely notify the trial courts concerning the terms of the workers' compensation coverage program;

(4) Timely inform the trial courts about the legal requirements with which a workers' compensation program must comply;

(5) Make personnel available by telephone to consult with trial courts regarding the cost and benefits of the plan being offered by the Administrative Office of the Courts; and

(6) Review and approve or disapprove any other workers' compensation programs identified by a trial court for consideration as a vendor to provide workers' compensation benefits to its employees.

(Subd (b) amended effective January 1, 2007.)

(c) Duties of the trial courts

(1) Each trial court that elects to participate in the program made available through the Administrative Office of the Courts must:

(A) Timely notify the Human Resources Division of its decision to participate in the workers' compensation program being offered through the Administrative Office of the Courts;

(B) Timely complete and return necessary paperwork to the Human Resources Division; and

(C) Timely pay all costs associated with the program.

(2) Each trial court that elects not to participate in the workers' compensation program available through the Administrative Office of the Courts must:

(A) Independently identify a workers' compensation benefits provider that fulfills all legal responsibilities to offer such benefits in California in a cost-efficient manner;

(B) Timely submit to the Human Resources Division for its approval the information necessary to evaluate the workers' compensation program identified by the trial court to provide benefits for its employees; and

(C) Maintain a contract with a workers' compensation benefits provider that fulfills all legal responsibilities to offer such benefits in California in a cost-efficient manner.

(Subd (c) amended effective January 1, 2007.)
Rule 10.350 amended and renumbered effective January 1, 2007; adopted as rule 6.302 effective January 1, 2005.

Chapter 7
Court Technology, Information, and Automation

Rule 10.400. Judicial Branch Statistical Information System (JBSIS)

(a) Purpose of rule

Consistent with article VI, section 6 of the California Constitution and Government Code section 68505, the Judicial Branch Statistical Information System (JBSIS) is established by the Judicial Council to provide accurate, consistent, and timely information for the judicial branch, the Legislature, and other state agencies that require information from the courts to fulfill their mandates.

(Subd (a) amended effective January 1, 2007.)

(b) Reporting required

Each trial court must collect and report to the Judicial Council information according to its capability and level of automation as prescribed by the *JBSIS Manual* adopted by the Judicial Council.

(Subd (b) amended effective January 1, 2007.)

(c) Automated JBSIS collection and reporting

By July 1, 1998, each trial court must develop a plan for meeting reporting requirements prescribed by the *JBSIS Manual*. By January 1, 2001, subject to adequate funding being made available, each trial court must develop, upgrade, replace, or procure automated case management systems needed to meet or exceed JBSIS data collection and reporting requirements prescribed by the *JBSIS Manual*.

(Subd (c) amended effective January 1, 2007; previously amended effective January 1, 2000.)
Rule 10.400 amended and renumbered effective January 1, 2007; adopted as rule 996 effective January 1, 1998; previously amended effective January 1, 2000.

Chapter 8
Minimum Education Requirements, Expectations, and Recommendations

Rule 10.451. Judicial branch education

(a) Purpose

Judicial branch education for all justices, judges, subordinate judicial officers, and court personnel is essential to enhance the fair, effective, and efficient administration of justice. Participation in education activities is part of the official duties of judicial officers and court personnel. Judicial branch education is acknowledged as a vital component in achieving the goals of the Judicial Council's Long-Range Strategic Plan, which include access, fairness, and diversity; branch independence and accountability; modernization of management and administration; and quality of justice and service to the public. The responsibility for planning, conducting, and overseeing judicial branch education properly resides in the judicial branch.

(Subd (a) adopted effective January 1, 2007.)

(b) Education objectives

Justices, judges, subordinate judicial officers, court personnel, education committees, and others who plan and deliver education will endeavor to achieve the following objectives:

(1) To provide justices, judges, subordinate judicial officers, and court personnel with the knowledge, skills, and abilities required to perform their responsibilities competently, fairly, and efficiently;

(2) To ensure that education, including opportunities for orientation, continuing education, and professional development, is available to all justices, judges, subordinate judicial officers, and court personnel;

(3) To assist justices, judges, subordinate judicial officers, and court personnel in preserving the integrity and impartiality of the judicial system through their efforts to ensure that all members of the public have equal access to the courts and equal ability to participate in court proceedings and are treated in a fair and just manner;

(4) To promote the adherence of justices, judges, subordinate judicial officers, and court personnel to the highest ideals of personal and official conduct, as set forth in the California Code of Judicial Ethics and the Code of Ethics for the Court Employees of California;

(5) To improve the administration of justice, reduce court delay, and promote fair and efficient management of court proceedings;

(6) To promote standardized court practices and procedures; and

(7) To implement the recommendations adopted by the Judicial Council in the California Standards of Judicial Administration.

(Subd (b) adopted effective January 1, 2007.)
Rule 10.451 adopted effective January 1, 2007.

Ref.: W. Cal. Sum., 10 "Parent and Child" §447.

Rule 10.452. Minimum education requirements, expectations, and recommendations

(a) Purpose

Justices, judges, and subordinate judicial officers are entrusted by the public with the impartial and knowledgeable handling of proceedings that affect the freedom, livelihood, and happiness of the people involved. Court personnel assist justices, judges, and subordinate judicial officers in carrying out their responsibilities and must provide accurate and timely services to the public. Each justice, judge, and subordinate judicial officer and each court staff member is responsible for maintaining and improving his or her professional competence. To assist

them in enhancing their professional competence, the judicial branch will develop and maintain a comprehensive and high-quality education program, including minimum education requirements, expectations, and recommendations, to provide educational opportunities for all justices, judges, subordinate judicial officers, and court personnel.

(Subd (a) amended effective January 1, 2008; adopted effective January 1, 2007.)

(b) Goals

The minimum education requirements, expectations, and recommendations set forth in rules 10.461–10.479 are intended to achieve two complementary goals:

(1) To ensure that both individuals who are new to the bench or the court and those who are experienced on the bench or court but are beginning a new assignment or role obtain education on the tasks, skills, abilities, and knowledge necessary to be successful in the new roles; and

(2) To establish broad parameters, based on time, for continuing education for individuals who are experienced both on the bench or court and in their assignments or roles, while preserving the ability of the individual, working with the individual who oversees his or her work, to determine the appropriate content and provider.

(Subd (b) amended effective January 1, 2008; adopted effective January 1, 2007.)

(c) Relationship of minimum education requirements and expectations to education recommendations

The education requirements and expectations set forth in rules 10.461–10.462 and 10.471–10.474 are minimums. Justices, judges, and subordinate judicial officers should participate in more judicial education than is required and expected, related to each individual's responsibilities and particular judicial assignment or assignments and in accordance with the judicial education recommendations set forth in rule 10.469. Additional education requirements related to the specific responsibility of hearing family law matters are set forth in rule 10.463. Clerk/administrators, court executive officers, and other court personnel should participate in more education than is required, related to each individual's responsibilities and in accordance with the education recommendations set forth in rule 10.479.

(Subd (c) amended effective January 1, 2008; adopted effective January 1, 2007.)

(d) Responsibilities of Chief Justice and administrative presiding justices

The Chief Justice and each administrative presiding justice:

(1) Must grant sufficient leave to Supreme Court and Court of Appeal justices, the clerk/administrator, and the managing attorney to enable them to complete the minimum education requirements stated in rules 10.461, 10.471, and 10.472, respectively;

(2) To the extent compatible with the efficient administration of justice, must grant to all justices, the clerk/administrator, and the managing attorney sufficient leave to participate in education programs consistent with the education recommendations stated in rules 10.469 and 10.479. After a justice has completed any new justice education required under rule 10.461 or after a justice has completed the first year on the bench, the Chief Justice or the administrative presiding justice should grant each justice at least eight court days per calendar year to

participate in continuing education relating to the justice's responsibilities;

(3) In addition to the educational leave required under (d)(1)–(2), should grant leave to a justice, clerk/administrator, or managing attorney to serve on education committees and as a faculty member at education programs when the individual's services have been requested for these purposes by the Administrative Office of the Courts, the California Judges Association, or the court. If a court's calendar would not be adversely affected, the court should grant additional leave for a justice, the clerk/administrator, or the managing attorney to serve on an educational committee or as a faculty member for judicial branch education;

(4) Should establish an education plan for his or her court to facilitate the involvement of justices, the clerk/administrator, and the managing attorney as both participants and faculty in judicial education activities;

(5) Must ensure that justices, the clerk/administrator, and the managing attorney are reimbursed by their court in accordance with the travel policies issued by the Administrative Office of the Courts for travel expenses incurred in attending in-state education programs as a participant, except to the extent that: (i) certain expenses are covered by the Administrative Office of the Courts; or (ii) the education provider or sponsor of the program pays the expenses. Provisions for these expenses must be part of every court's budget. The Chief Justice or the administrative presiding justice may approve reimbursement of travel expenses incurred by justices, the clerk/administrator, and the managing attorney in attending out-of-state education programs as a participant; and

(6) Must retain the records and cumulative histories of participation provided by justices. These records and cumulative histories are subject to periodic audit by the Administrative Office of the Courts. The Chief Justice and the administrative presiding justice must report the data from the records and cumulative histories on an aggregate basis to the Judicial Council, on a form provided by the Judicial Council, within six months after the end of each three-year period.

(Subd (d) amended effective January 1, 2008; adopted effective January 1, 2007.)

(e) Responsibilities of presiding judges

Each presiding judge:

(1) Must grant sufficient leave to all judges and subordinate judicial officers and to the court executive officer to enable them to complete the minimum education requirements and expectations stated in rules 10.462 and 10.473, respectively;

(2) To the extent compatible with the efficient administration of justice, must grant to all judges and subordinate judicial officers and to the court executive officer sufficient leave to participate in education programs consistent with the education recommendations stated in rules 10.469 and 10.479. After a judge or subordinate judicial officer has completed the new judge education required under rule 10.462, the presiding judge should grant each judge and subordinate judicial officer at least eight court days per calendar year to participate in continuing education relating to the judge or subordinate judicial officer's responsibilities or current or future court assignment;

(3) In addition to the educational leave required or authorized under rule 10.603 or (e)(1)–(2), should grant leave to a judge or subordinate judicial officer or the executive officer to serve on education committees and as a faculty member at education programs when the judicial officer's or executive officer's services have been requested for these purposes by the Judicial Council, the California Judges Association, or the court. If a court's calendar would not be adversely affected, the presiding judge should grant additional leave for a judge or subordinate judicial officer or executive officer to serve on an educational committee or as a faculty member for judicial branch education;

(4) Should establish an education plan for his or her court to facilitate the involvement of judges, subordinate judicial officers, and the executive officer as both participants and faculty in education activities and should consult with each judge, each subordinate judicial officer, and the executive officer regarding their education needs and requirements related to their current and future assignments;

(5) Should use his or her assignment powers to enable all judges and subordinate judicial officers, particularly those assigned to specific calendar courts, to participate in educational activities;

(6) Must ensure that judges, subordinate judicial officers, and the court executive officer are reimbursed by their court in accordance with the Trial Court Financial Policies and Procedures Manual for travel expenses incurred in attending in-state education programs as a participant, except to the extent that: (i) certain expenses are covered by the Administrative Office of the Courts; or (ii) the education provider or sponsor of the program pays the expenses. Provisions for these expenses must be part of every court's budget. The presiding judge may approve reimbursement of travel expenses incurred by judges, subordinate judicial officers, and the court executive officer in attending out-of-state education programs as a participant; and

(7) Must retain the records and cumulative histories of participation provided by judges. These records and cumulative histories are subject to periodic audit by the Administrative Office of the Courts (AOC). The presiding judge must report the data from the records and cumulative histories on an aggregate basis to the Judicial Council, on a form provided by the Judicial Council, within six months after the end of each three-year period.

(Subd (e) amended effective January 1, 2008; adopted effective January 1, 2007.)

(f) Responsibilities of Supreme Court and Court of Appeal justices, clerk/administrators, managing attorneys, and supervisors

Each court's justices, clerk/administrator, managing attorney, and supervisors:

(1) Must grant sufficient leave to all court personnel to enable them to complete the minimum education requirements stated in rule 10.472;

(2) To the extent compatible with the efficient administration of justice, must grant to all court personnel sufficient leave to participate in education programs consistent with the education recommendations stated in rule 10.479;

(3) Should allow and encourage court personnel, in addition to participating as students in educational activities, to serve on court personnel education committees and as faculty at court personnel education programs when an employee's services have been requested for these purposes by the Administrative Office of the Courts or the court; and

(4) Should establish an education plan for their court to facilitate the involvement of court personnel as both participants and faculty in educational activities, and should consult with each court staff member regarding his or her education needs and requirements and professional development.

(5) Must ensure that supervisors and other court personnel are reimbursed by their court in accordance with the travel policies issued by the Administrative Office of the Courts for travel expenses incurred in attending in-state education programs as a participant, except to the extent that: (i) certain expenses are covered by the Administrative Office of the Courts; or (ii) the education provider or sponsor of the program pays the expenses. Provisions for these expenses must be part of every court's budget. The clerk/administrator or the managing attorney may approve reimbursement of travel expenses incurred by supervisors and other court personnel in attending out-of-state education programs as a participant.

(Subd (f) adopted effective January 1, 2008.)

(g) Responsibilities of trial court executive officers, managers, and supervisors

Each trial court's executive officer, managers, and supervisors:

(1) Must grant sufficient leave to all court personnel to enable them to complete the minimum education requirements stated in rule 10.474;

(2) To the extent compatible with the efficient administration of justice, must grant to all court personnel sufficient leave to participate in education programs consistent with the education recommendations stated in rule 10.479;

(3) Should allow and encourage court personnel, in addition to participating as students in education activities, to serve on court personnel education committees and as faculty at court personnel education programs when an employee's services have been requested for these purposes by the Judicial Council or the court;

(4) Should establish an education plan for their court to facilitate the involvement of court personnel as both participants and faculty in educational activities, and should consult with each court staff member regarding his or her education needs and requirements and professional development; and

(5) Must ensure that managers, supervisors, and other court personnel are reimbursed by their court in accordance with the Trial Court Financial Policies and Procedures Manual for travel expenses incurred in attending in-state education programs as a participant, except to the extent that: (i) certain expenses are covered by the Administrative Office of the Courts; or (ii) the education provider or sponsor of the program pays the expenses. Provisions for these expenses must be part of every court's budget. The court executive officer may approve reimbursement of travel expenses incurred by managers, supervisors, and other court personnel in attending out-of-state education programs as a participant.

(Subd (g) amended and relettered effective January 1, 2008; adopted as subd (f) effective January 1, 2007.)

Rule 10.452 amended effective January 1, 2008; adopted effective January 1, 2007.

Ref.: Cal. Fms Pl. & Pr., Ch. 1, "New Developments," Ch. 317, "Judges."

Rule 10.461. Minimum education requirements for Supreme Court and Court of Appeal justices

(a) Applicability

All California Court of Appeal justices must complete the minimum judicial education requirements for new justices under (b), and all Supreme Court and Court of Appeal justices must complete minimum continuing education requirements as outlined under (c). All justices should participate in more judicial education than is required, related to each individual's responsibilities and in accordance with the judicial education recommendations set forth in rule 10.469.

(Subd (a) adopted effective January 1, 2008.)

(b) Content-based requirement

Each new Court of Appeal justice, within two years of confirmation of appointment, must attend a new appellate judge orientation program sponsored by a national provider of appellate orientation programs or by the Administrative Office of the Courts' Education Division/Center for Judicial Education and Research.

(Subd (b) amended and lettered effective January 1, 2008; adopted as unlettered subd effective January 1, 2007.)

(c) Hours-based continuing education

(1) Each justice must complete 30 hours of continuing judicial education every three years, beginning on the dates outlined:

(A) A new Supreme Court justice enters the three-year continuing education period on January 1 of the year following confirmation of appointment, and a new Court of Appeal justice enters the three-year continuing education period on January 1 of the year following completion of the required new justice education; continuing education requirements are prorated based on the number of years remaining in the three-year period.

(B) For all other justices, the first continuing education period begins January 1, 2008.

(C) The first continuing education period for Supreme Court and Court of Appeal justices is for two years from January 1, 2008, through December 31, 2009, rather than three years. The continuing education requirements and limitations in (c) are consequently prorated for this two-year period. The first three-year period then begins January 1, 2010.

(2) The following education applies toward the required 30 hours of continuing judicial education:

(A) Any education offered by a provider listed in rule 10.481(a) and any other education, including education taken to satisfy a statutory or other education requirement, approved by the Chief Justice or the administrative presiding justice as meeting the criteria listed in rule 10.481(b).

(B) Each hour of participation in traditional (face-to-face) education, distance education such as broadcast and videoconference courses, online coursework, and self-directed study counts toward the continuing education requirement on an hour-for-hour basis. The hours applied for participation in online coursework and self-directed study are limited to a combined total of 7 hours in each three-year period; this limit is prorated for individuals who enter the three-year period after it has begun.

(C) A justice who serves as faculty for a California court-based audience (i.e., justices, judges, subordinate judicial officers, temporary judges, or court personnel) may apply the following hours of faculty service: 3 hours for each hour of presentation the first time a given course is presented and 2 hours for each hour of presentation each subsequent time that course is presented. The hours applied for faculty service are limited to 15 in each three-year period; this limit is prorated for individuals who enter the three-year period after it has begun.

(Subd (c) adopted effective January 1, 2008.)

(d) Extension of time

(1) For good cause, the Chief Justice or the administrative presiding justice may grant a one-year extension of time to complete the continuing education requirement in (c).

(2) If the Chief Justice or the administrative presiding justice grants a request for an extension of time, the justice, in consultation with the Chief Justice or the administrative presiding justice, should also pursue interim means of obtaining relevant educational content.

(3) An extension of time to complete the hours-based continuing education requirement does not affect what is required in the next three-year period.

(Subd (d) adopted effective January 1, 2008.)

(e) Records and summaries of participation for justices

Each justice is responsible for:

(1) Tracking his or her own participation in education and keeping a record of participation [1] for three years after each course or activity that is applied toward the requirements, **on a form provided by the Chief Justice for the Supreme Court or by the administrative presiding justice for each appellate district of the Court of Appeal. The form must include the information regarding a justice's participation in education that is needed by the Chief Justice or the administrative presiding justice to complete the aggregate form required by rule 10.452(d)(6)**;

(2) At the end of each year, giving the Chief Justice or the administrative presiding justice a copy of his or her record of participation in education for that year, on [2] **the** form provided by the [3] **Chief Justice or the administrative presiding justice**; and

(3) At the end of each three-year period, giving the Chief Justice or the administrative presiding justice a copy of his or her record of participation in education for that year and a cumulative history of participation for that three-year period, on [4] **the** form provided by the [5] **Chief Justice or the administrative presiding justice**.

(Subd (e) amended effective August 15, 2008; adopted effective January 1, 2008.)

Rule 10.461(e). 2008 Deletes. [1] , on a form provided by the Judicial Council, **[2]** a **[3]** Judicial Council **[4]** a **[5]** Judicial Council

Rule 10.461 amended effective August 15, 2008; adopted effective January 1, 2007; previously amended effective January 1, 2008.

Advisory Committee Comment

The requirements formerly contained in subdivision (e)(2) of rule 970, which has been repealed, are carried forward without change in rule 10.461(b).

The Administrative Office of the Courts (AOC) has developed both a manual format and an automated format of the individual justice's recording and reporting form referenced in rule 10.461(e) that gathers all the information needed by the Chief Justice or the administrative presiding justice to complete the aggregate report to the Judicial Council required under rule 10.452(d)(6). The Chief Justice or the administrative presiding justice may determine which form should be used in his or her court and may provide the manual or automated format of the AOC-developed form (available from the AOC's Education Division/Center for Judicial Education and Research) or may provide another appropriate form that has been developed by his or her court or by another court that gathers all the information needed by the Chief Justice or the administrative presiding justice to complete the aggregate report to the Judicial Council.

Ref.: Cal. Fms Pl. & Pr., Ch. 317, "Judges."

Rule 10.462. Minimum education requirements and expectations for trial court judges and subordinate judicial officers

(a) Applicability

All California trial court judges must complete the minimum judicial education requirements for new judges under (c)(1) and are expected to participate in continuing education as outlined under (d). All subordinate judicial officers must complete the minimum education requirements for new subordinate judicial officers under (c)(1) and for continuing education as outlined under (d). All trial court judges and subordinate judicial officers who hear family law matters must complete additional education requirements set forth in rule 10.463. All trial court judges and subordinate judicial officers should participate in more judicial education than is required and expected, related to each individual's responsibilities and particular judicial assignment or assignments and in accordance with the judicial education recommendations set forth in rule 10.469.

(Subd (a) amended effective January 1, 2008; adopted effective January 1, 2007.)

(b) Definitions

Unless the context or subject matter otherwise requires, "subordinate judicial officers" as used in this rule means subordinate judicial officers as defined in rule 10.701.

(Subd (b) adopted effective January 1, 2007.)

(c) Content-based requirements

(1) Each new trial court judge and subordinate judicial officer must complete the "new judge education" provided by the Administrative Office of the Courts' Education Division/Center for Judicial Education and Research (CJER) as follows:

(A) The New Judge Orientation Program within six months of taking the oath as a judge or subordinate judicial officer. For purposes of the New Judge Orientation Program, a judge or subordinate judicial officer is considered "new" only once, and any judge or subordinate **judicial** officer who has completed the New Judge Orientation Program, as required under this rule or under former rule 970, is not required to complete the program again. A judge or subordinate **judicial** officer who was appointed, elected, or hired before rule 970 was adopted on January 1, 1996, is not required to complete the program.

(B) An orientation course in his or her primary assignment (civil, criminal, family, juvenile delinquency or dependency, probate, or traffic) within one year of taking the oath as a judge or subordinate judicial officer; and

(C) The B. E. Witkin Judicial College of California within two years of taking the oath as a judge or subordinate judicial officer.

(2) Each new supervising judge is expected to complete the following education:

(A) For a judge who has administrative responsibility, CJER's Supervising Judges Overview course within one year of beginning the supervising judge role, preferably before beginning the role;

(B) For a judge who has calendar management responsibility, a calendar management overview course, provided either by the local court or by CJER, within one year of beginning the supervising judge role, preferably before beginning the role;

(C) For a judge who has both administrative and calendar management responsibility, both overview courses within one year of beginning the role.

(3) Each new presiding judge is expected to complete CJER's Presiding Judges Orientation and Court Management Program within one year of beginning the presiding judge role, preferably before beginning the role.

(4) Each judge is expected to and each subordinate judicial officer must, if beginning a new primary assignment (unless he or she is returning to an assignment after less than two years in another assignment), complete a course on the new primary assignment, provided by CJER, the California Judges Association (CJA), or the local court, within six months of beginning the new assignment. CJER is responsible for identifying content for these courses and will share the identified content with CJA and the local courts.

(Subd (c) amended effective July 1, 2008; adopted effective January 1, 2007; previously amended effective January 1, 2008.)

(d) Hours-based continuing education

(1) Each judge is expected to and each subordinate judicial officer must complete 30 hours of continuing judicial education every three years, beginning on the dates outlined:

(A) A new judge or new subordinate judicial officer enters the three-year continuing education period on January 1 of the year following completion of the required new judge education; continuing education expectations for judges and requirements for subordinate judicial officers are prorated based on the number of years remaining in the three-year period.

(B) For all other judges and subordinate judicial officers, the first three-year period begins on January 1, 2007.

(2) The following education applies toward the expected or required 30 hours of continuing judicial education:

(A) The content-based courses under (c)(2), (3), and (4) for a new supervising judge, a new presiding judge, and a judge or subordinate judicial officer beginning a new primary assignment; and

(B) Any other education offered by a provider listed in rule 10.481(a) and any other education, including education taken to satisfy a statutory or other education requirement, approved by the presiding judge as meeting the criteria listed in rule 10.481(b).

(3) Each hour of participation in traditional (face-to-face) education, distance education such as broadcast and videoconference courses, online coursework, and self-directed study counts toward the continuing education expectation or requirement on an hour-for-hour basis. The hours applied for participation in online coursework and self-directed study are limited to a combined total of 7 hours in each three-year period; this limit is prorated for individuals who enter the three-year period after it has begun.

(4) A judge or subordinate judicial officer who serves as faculty for a California court-based audience (i.e., justices, judges, subordinate judicial officers, temporary judges, or court personnel) may apply the following hours of faculty service: 3 hours for each hour of presentation the first time a given course is presented and 2 hours for each hour of presentation each subsequent time that course is presented. The hours applied for faculty service are limited to 15 in each three-year period; this limit is prorated for individuals who enter the three-year period after it has begun.

(5) The presiding judge may require subordinate judicial officers to participate in specific courses or participate in education in a specific subject matter area as part of their continuing education.

(Subd (d) amended effective January 1, 2008; adopted effective January 1, 2007.)

(e) Extension of time

(1) For good cause, a presiding judge may grant an extension of time to complete the education expectations or requirements in (c)(2)–(4) and the continuing education expectation or requirement in (d) as follows:

(A) A time extension to complete the content-based expectations or requirements in (c)(2)–(4) is limited to the original time period provided for completion—that is, one year, one year, or six months, respectively.

(B) A time extension to complete the hours-based continuing education expectation or requirement in (d) is limited to one year.

(2) If the presiding judge grants a request for an extension of time, the judge or subordinate judicial officer, in consultation with the presiding judge, should also pursue interim means of obtaining relevant educational content.

(3) An extension of time to complete the hours-based continuing education expectation or requirement does not affect what is expected or required in the next three-year period.

(Subd (e) adopted effective January 1, 2007.)

(f) Records and cumulative histories of participation for judges

Each judge is responsible for:

(1) Tracking his or her own participation in education and keeping a record of participation [1] for three years after each course or activity that is applied toward the requirements and expectations, **on a form provided by the presiding judge. The form must include the infor-**

mation regarding a judge's participation in education that is needed by the presiding judge to complete the aggregate form required by rule 10.452(e)(7);

(2) At the end of each year, giving the presiding judge a copy of his or her record of participation in education for that year, on [2] **the** form provided by the [3] **presiding judge**; and

(3) At the end of each three-year period, giving the presiding judge a copy of his or her record of participation in education for that year and a cumulative history of participation for that three-year period, on [4] **the** form provided by the [5] **presiding judge**.

(Subd (f) amended effective August 15, 2008; adopted effective January 1, 2007; previously amended effective January 1, 2008.)

Rule 10.462(f). 2008 Deletes. [1], on a form provided by the Judicial Council, [2] a [3] Judicial Council [4] a [5] Judicial Council

(g) Records of participation for subordinate judicial officers

(1) Each court is responsible for tracking participation in education and for tracking completion of minimum education requirements for its subordinate judicial officers.

(2) Each subordinate judicial officer must keep records of his or her own participation for three years after each course or activity that is applied toward the requirements.

(Subd (g) adopted effective January 1, 2007.)

Rule 10.462 amended effective August 15, 2008; adopted effective January 1, 2007; previously amended effective January 1, 2008 and July 1, 2008.

Advisory Committee Comment

The minimum judicial education requirements in rule 10.462 do not apply to retired judges seeking to sit on regular court assignment in the Assigned Judges Program. Retired judges who seek to serve in the Assigned Judges Program must comply with the Chief Justice's Standards and Guidelines for Judges Who Serve on Assignment, which includes education requirements.

The Administrative Office of the Courts (AOC) has developed both a manual format and an automated format of the individual judge's recording and reporting form referenced in rule 10.462(f) that gathers all the information needed by the presiding judge to complete the aggregate report to the Judicial Council required under rule 10.452(e)(7). The presiding judge may determine which form should be used in his or her court and may provide the manual or automated format of the AOC-developed form (available from the AOC's Education Division/Center for Judicial Education and Research) or may provide another appropriate form that has been developed by his or her court or by another court that gathers all the information needed by the presiding judge to complete the aggregate report to the Judicial Council.

Rule 10.463. Trial court executive officers [Renumbered]

Rule 10.463 renumbered as rule 10.473 effective January 1, 2008.

Another Rule 10.463 follows.

Rule 10.463. Education requirements for family court judges and subordinate judicial officers

Each judge or subordinate judicial officer whose primary assignment is to hear family law matters or who is the sole judge hearing family law matters must complete the following education:

(a) Basic family law education

Within six months of beginning a family law assignment, or within one year of beginning a family law assignment in courts with five or fewer judges, the judge or subordinate judicial officer must complete a basic educational program on California family law and procedure designed primarily for judicial officers. A judge or subordinate judicial officer who has completed the basic educational program need not complete the basic educational program again. All other judicial officers who hear family law matters, including retired judges who sit on court assignment, must complete appropriate family law educational programs.

(Subd (a) amended effective January 1, 2008; adopted as (1) effective January 1, 1992; previously amended and lettered effective January 1, 2003.)

(b) Continuing family law education

The judge or subordinate judicial officer must complete a periodic update on new developments in California family law and procedure.

(Subd (b) amended effective January 1, 2008; adopted as (2) effective January 1, 1992; previously amended and lettered effective January 1, 2003.)

(c) Other family law education

To the extent that judicial time and resources are available, the judge or subordinate judicial officer must complete additional educational programs on other aspects of family law including interdisciplinary subjects relating to the family.

(Subd (c) amended effective January 1, 2008; adopted as (3) effective January 1, 1992; previously amended and lettered effective January 1, 2003.)

Rule 10.463 amended and renumbered effective January 1, 2008; adopted as rule 1200 effective January 1, 1992; previously amended and renumbered as rule 5.30 effective January 1, 2003.

Ref.: Cal. Fms Pl. & Pr., Ch. 317, "Judges."

Rule 10.464. Trial court managers, supervisors, and personnel [Renumbered]

Rule 10.464 renumbered as rule 10.474 effective January 1, 2008.

Rule 10.468. Content-based and hours-based education for superior court judges and subordinate judicial officers regularly assigned to hear probate proceedings

(a) Definitions

As used in this rule, the following terms have the meanings stated below:

(1) "Judge" means a judge of the superior court.

(2) "Subordinate judicial officer" has the meaning specified in rule 10.701(a).

(3) "Judicial officer" means a judge or a subordinate judicial officer.

(4) "Probate proceedings" are decedents' estates, guardianships and conservatorships under division 4 of the Probate Code, trust proceedings under division 9 of the Probate Code, and other matters governed by provisions of that code and the rules in title 7 of the California Rules of Court.

(5) A judicial officer "regularly assigned to hear probate proceedings" is a judicial officer who is:

(A) Assigned to a dedicated probate department where probate proceedings are customarily heard on a full-time basis;

(B) Responsible for hearing most of the probate proceedings filed in a court that does not have a dedicated probate department; or

(C) Responsible for hearing probate proceedings on a regular basis in a department in a branch or other location remote from the main or central courthouse, whether or not he or she also hears other kinds of matters in that department and whether or not there is a dedicated probate department in the main or central courthouse; or

(D) Designated by the presiding judge of a court with four or fewer authorized judges.

(6) "AOC" is the Administrative Office of the Courts.

(7) "CJER" is the AOC Education Division/Center for Judicial Education and Research.

(8) "CJA" is the California Judges Association.

(Subd (a) adopted effective January 1, 2008.)

(b) Content-based requirements

(1) Each judicial officer beginning a regular assignment to hear probate proceedings after the effective date of this rule—unless he or she is returning to this assignment after less than two years in another assignment—must complete, as soon as possible but not to exceed six months from the assignment's commencement date, 6 hours of education on probate guardianships and conservatorships, including court-supervised fiduciary accounting.

(2) The education required in (1) is in addition to the New Judge Orientation program for new judicial officers and the B. E. Witkin Judicial College required under rule 10.462(c)(1)(A) and (C) and may be applied toward satisfaction of the 30 hours of continuing education expected of judges and required of subordinate judicial officers under rule 10.462(d).

(3) The education required in (1) must be provided by CJER, CJA, or the judicial officer's court. CJER is responsible for identifying content for this education and will share the identified content with CJA and the courts.

(4) The education required in (1) may be by traditional (face to face) or distance-learning means, such as broadcasts, videoconferences, or online coursework, but may not be by self-study.

(Subd (b) adopted effective January 1, 2008.)

(c) Hours-based continuing education

(1) In a court with five or more authorized judges, each judicial officer regularly assigned to hear probate proceedings must complete 18 hours of continuing education every three years, with a minimum of six hours required in the first year, on probate guardianships and conservatorships, including court-supervised fiduciary accounting. The three-year period begins on January 1 of the year following the judicial officer's completion of the education required in (b)(1) or, if he or she is exempt from that education, on January 1 of the year the assignment commenced after the effective date of this rule.

(2) In a court with four or fewer authorized judges, each judicial officer regularly assigned to hear probate proceedings must complete nine hours of continuing education every three years, with a minimum of three hours per year, on probate guardianships and conservatorships, including court-supervised fiduciary accounting. The three-year period begins on January 1 of the year following the judicial officer's completion of the education required in (b)(1) or, if he or she is exempt from that education, on January 1 of the year the assignment commenced after the effective date of this rule.

(3) The first continuing education period for judicial officers who were regularly assigned to hear probate proceedings before the effective date of this rule and who continue in the assignment after that date is two years, from January 1, 2008, through December 31, 2009, rather than three years. The continuing education requirements in (1) are prorated for the first continuing education under this paragraph. The first full three-year period of continuing education for judicial officers under this paragraph begins on January 1, 2010.

(4) The number of hours of education required in (1) or (2) may be reduced proportionately for judicial officers whose regular assignment to hear probate proceedings is for a period of less than three years.

(5) The education required in (1) or (2) may be applied toward satisfaction of the 30 hours of continuing education expected of judges or required of subordinate judicial officers under rule 10.462(d).

(6) A judicial officer may fulfill the education requirement in (1) or (2) through AOC-sponsored education, a provider listed in rule 10.481(a), or a provider approved by the judicial officer's presiding judge as meeting the education criteria specified in rule 10.481(b).

(7) The education required in (1) or (2) may be by traditional (face-to-face) or distance-learning means, such as broadcasts, videoconferences, or online coursework but may not be by self-study.

(8) A judicial officer who serves as faculty for a California court-based audience, as defined in rule 10.462(d)(4), for education required in (1) or (2) may be credited with three hours of participation for each hour of presentation the first time a course is given and two hours for each hour of presentation each subsequent time the course is given.

(Subd (c) adopted effective January 1, 2008.)

(d) Extension of time

The provisions of rule 10.462(e) concerning extensions of time apply to the content-based and hours-based education required under (b) and (c) of this rule.

(Subd (d) adopted effective January 1, 2008.)

(e) Record keeping and reporting

(1) The provisions of rule 10.462(f) and (g) concerning, respectively, tracking participation, record keeping, and summarizing participation by judges and tracking participation by subordinate judicial officers, apply to the education required under this rule.

(2) Presiding judges' records of judicial officer participation in the education required by this rule are subject to audit by the AOC under rule 10.462. The AOC may require courts to report participation by judicial officers in the education required by this rule to ensure compliance with Probate Code section 1456.

(Subd (e) adopted effective January 1, 2008.)

Rule 10.468 adopted effective January 1, 2008.

Rule 10.469. Judicial education recommendations for justices, judges, and subordinate judicial officers

(a) Judicial education recommendations generally

Each justice, judge, and subordinate judicial officer, as part of his or her continuing judicial education, should regularly participate in educational activities related to his or her responsibilities and particular judicial assignment or assignments. Minimum education requirements and expectations related to judicial responsibilities and assignments are set forth in rules 10.461–10.462. Additional education requirements related to the specific responsibility of hearing family law matters are set forth in rule 10.463. The following recommendations illustrate for some specific responsibilities and assignments how justices, judges, and subordinate judicial officers should participate in more judicial education than is required and expected.

(Subd (a) adopted effective January 1, 2008.)

(b) Jury trial assignment

Each judge or subordinate judicial officer assigned to jury trials should regularly use Center for Judicial Education and Research (CJER) educational materials or other appropriate materials and should regularly complete CJER or other appropriate educational programs devoted to the conduct of jury voir dire and the treatment of jurors.

(Subd (b) adopted effective January 1, 2008.)

(c) Hearing of juvenile dependency matters

Each judge or subordinate judicial officer who hears juvenile dependency matters, including retired judges who sit on court assignment, should regularly use appropriate educational materials and should annually complete appropriate education programs on juvenile dependency law and procedure, consistent with the requirements in Welfare and Institutions Code section 304.7.

(Subd (c) adopted effective January 1, 2008.)

(d) Capital case assignment

Each judge assigned to hear a capital case should complete before the commencement of the trial a comprehensive education program on California law and procedure relevant to capital cases provided by CJER. A judge with a subsequent assignment to a capital case should complete a periodic update course within two years before the commencement of the trial. The periodic update may be provided through actual classroom instruction or through video, audio, or other media as determined by CJER.

(Subd (d) adopted effective January 1, 2008.)

(e) Fairness and access education

In order to achieve the objective of assisting judicial officers in preserving the integrity and impartiality of the judicial system through the prevention of bias, each justice, judge, and subordinate judicial officer should regularly participate in education on fairness and access. The education should include the following subjects: race and ethnicity, gender, sexual orientation, persons with disabilities, and sexual harassment.

(Subd (e) adopted effective January 1, 2008.)
Rule 10.469 adopted effective January 1, 2008.

Ref.: Cal. Fms Pl. & Pr., Ch. 317, "Judges."

Rule 10.471. Approved providers; approved course criteria [Renumbered]

Rule 10.471 renumbered as rule 10.481 effective January 1, 2008.

Another Rule 10.471 follows.

Rule 10.471. Minimum education requirements for Supreme Court and Court of Appeal clerk/administrators

(a) Applicability

All California Supreme Court and Court of Appeal clerk/administrators must complete these minimum education requirements. All clerk/administrators should participate in more education than is required, related to each individual's responsibilities and in accordance with the education recommendations set forth in rule 10.479.

(Subd (a) adopted effective January 1, 2008.)

(b) Hours-based requirement

(1) Each clerk/administrator must complete 30 hours of continuing education every three years beginning on the following date:

(A) For a new clerk/administrator, the first three-year period begins on January 1 of the year following his or her hire.

(B) For all other clerk/administrators, the first three-year period begins on January 1, 2008.

(2) The following education applies toward the required 30 hours of continuing education:

(A) Any education offered by a provider listed in rule 10.481(a) and any other education, including education taken to satisfy a statutory or other education requirement, approved by the Chief Justice or the administrative presiding justice as meeting the criteria listed in rule 10.481(b).

(B) Each hour of participation in traditional (face-to-face) education, distance education such as broadcast and videoconference courses, online coursework, and self-directed study counts toward the requirement on an hour-for-hour basis. The hours applied for participation in online coursework and self-directed study are limited to a combined total of 7 hours in each three-year period.

(C) A clerk/administrator who serves as faculty for a California court-based audience (i.e., justices, judges, subordinate judicial officers, temporary judges, or court personnel) may apply the following hours of faculty service: 3 hours for each hour of presentation the first time a given course is presented and 2 hours for each hour of presentation each subsequent time that course is presented. The hours applied for faculty service are limited to 15 in each three-year period.

(Subd (b) adopted effective January 1, 2008.)

(c) Extension of time

(1) For good cause, the Chief Justice or the administrative presiding justice may grant a one-year extension of time to complete the education requirements in (b).

(2) If the Chief Justice or the administrative presiding justice grants a request for an extension of time, the clerk/administrator, in consultation with the Chief Justice or the administrative presiding justice, must also pursue interim means of obtaining relevant educational content.

(3) An extension of time to complete the hours-based requirement does not affect the timing of the clerk/administrator's next three-year period.

(Subd (c) adopted effective January 1, 2008.)

(d) Record of participation; statement of completion

Each clerk/administrator is responsible for:

(1) Tracking his or her own participation in education and keeping a record of participation for three years after each course or activity that is applied toward the requirements;

(2) At the end of each year, giving the Chief Justice or the administrative presiding justice a copy of his or her record of participation in education for that year; and

(3) At the end of each three-year period, giving the Chief Justice or the administrative presiding justice a signed statement of completion for that three-year period.

(Subd (d) adopted effective January 1, 2008.)
Rule 10.471 adopted effective January 1, 2008.

Rule 10.472. Minimum education requirements for Supreme Court and Court of Appeal managing attorneys, supervisors, and other personnel

(a) Applicability

All California Supreme Court and Court of Appeal managing attorneys, supervisors, and other personnel must complete these minimum education requirements. All managing attorneys, supervisors, and other personnel should participate in more education than is required related to each individual's responsibilities and in accordance with the education recommendations set forth in rule 10.479.

(Subd (a) adopted effective January 1, 2008.)

(b) Content-based requirements

(1) Each new managing attorney or supervisor must complete orientation courses within six months of becoming a managing attorney or supervisor, unless the individual's supervisor determines that the new managing attorney or supervisor has already completed these orientation courses or courses covering equivalent content. The courses must include orientation about:

(A) The judicial branch of California;

(B) The local court; and

(C) Basic management and supervision.

(2) Each new court employee who is not a managing attorney or supervisor must complete orientation courses within six months of becoming a court employee, unless the employee's supervisor determines that the new court employee has already completed these orientation courses or courses covering equivalent content. The courses must include orientation about:

(A) The judicial branch of California;

(B) The local court;

(C) Basic employee issues, such as sexual harassment and safety; and

(D) The employee's specific job.

(3) The clerk/administrator, the managing attorney, or the employee's supervisor may determine the appropriate content, delivery mechanism, and length of orientation based on the needs and role of each individual employee.

(Subd (b) adopted effective January 1, 2008.)

(c) Hours-based requirements

(1) Each managing attorney, supervisor, or appellate judicial attorney must complete 12 hours of continuing education every two years.

(2) Each court employee who is not a managing attorney, supervisor, or appellate judicial attorney must complete 8 hours of continuing education every two years, with the exception of employees who do not provide court administrative or operational services. Those employees are not subject to the continuing education hours-based requirement but must complete any education or training required by law and any other education required by the clerk/administrator.

(3) The first two-year period for all managing attorneys, supervisors, and other personnel begins on January 1, 2008. The orientation education required for new managing attorneys, supervisors, and other personnel under (b) does not apply toward the required hours of continuing education because it must be completed before they enter the two-year period. Each new managing attorney, supervisor, or employee enters the two-year continuing education period on the first day of the quarter following his or her completion of the orientation education required under (b); the quarters begin on January 1, April 1, July 1, and October 1. Each managing attorney, supervisor, or employee who enters the two-year continuing education period after it has begun must complete a prorated number of continuing education hours for that two-year period, based on the number of quarters remaining in it.

(4) Any education offered by a provider listed in rule 10.481(a) and any other education, including education taken to satisfy a statutory, rules-based, or other education requirement, that is approved by the clerk/administrator, the managing attorney, or the employee's supervisor as meeting the criteria listed in rule 10.481(b) applies toward the orientation education required under (b) and the continuing education required under (c)(1) and (2).

(5) Each hour of participation in traditional (face-to-face) education, distance education such as broadcast and videoconference courses, and online coursework counts toward the requirement on an hour-for-hour basis. The hours applied for participation in online coursework are limited to a total of 4 hours for managers, supervisors, and appellate judicial attorneys and to a total of 3 hours for other personnel in each two-year period; these limits are prorated for individuals who enter the two-year period after it has begun. Self-directed study is encouraged for professional development but does not apply toward the required hours.

(6) A managing attorney, supervisor, or other employee who serves as faculty for a California court-based audience (i.e., justices, judges, subordinate judicial officers, temporary judges, or court personnel) may apply the following hours of faculty service: 3 hours for each hour of presentation the first time a given course is presented and 2 hours for each hour of presentation each subsequent time that the course is presented. The hours applied for faculty service are limited to 6 hours for managers, supervisors, and appellate judicial attorneys and to 4 hours for other personnel in each two-year period; these limits are prorated for individuals who enter the two-year period after it has begun.

(7) The clerk/administrator, the managing attorney, or the employee's supervisor may require supervisors and other court personnel to participate in specific courses or to participate in education in a specific subject matter area as part of their continuing education.

(Subd (c) adopted effective January 1, 2008.)

(d) Extension of time

(1) For good cause, a justice (for that justice's chambers staff), the managing attorney, the clerk/administrator, or a supervisor, if delegated by the clerk/administrator, or the employee's supervisor may grant a six-month extension of time to complete the education requirements in this rule.

(2) If the justice, managing attorney, clerk/administrator, or supervisor grants a request for an extension of time, the managing attorney, supervisor, or employee who made the request, in consultation with the justice, managing attorney, clerk/administrator, or supervisor, must also pursue interim means of obtaining relevant educational content.

(3) An extension of time to complete the hours-based requirement does not affect the timing of the next two-year period.

(Subd (d) adopted effective January 1, 2008.)

(e) Records of participation

(1) Each court is responsible for tracking participation in education and for tracking completion of minimum education requirements for its managing attorneys, supervisors, and other personnel.

(2) Each managing attorney, supervisor, and employee must keep records of his or her own participation for two years after each course or activity that is applied toward the requirements.

(Subd (e) adopted effective January 1, 2008.)
Rule 10.472 adopted effective January 1, 2008.

Rule 10.473. Minimum education requirements for trial court executive officers

(a) Applicability

All California trial court executive officers must complete these minimum education requirements. All executive officers should participate in more education than is required, related to each individual's responsibilities, and in accordance with the education recommendations set forth in rule 10.479.

(Subd (a) amended effective January 1, 2008; adopted effective January 1, 2007.)

(b) Content-based requirement

(1) Each new executive officer must complete the Presiding Judges Orientation and Court Management Program provided by the Administrative Office of the Courts' Education Division/Center for Judicial Education and Research (CJER) within one year of becoming an executive officer and should participate in additional education during the first year.

(2) Each executive officer should participate in CJER's Presiding Judges Orientation and Court Management Program each time a new presiding judge from his or her court participates in the course and each time the executive officer becomes the executive officer in a different court.

(Subd (b) adopted effective January 1, 2007.)

(c) Hours-based requirement

(1) Each executive officer must complete 30 hours of continuing education every three years beginning on the following date:

(A) For a new executive officer, the first three-year period begins on January 1 of the year following completion of the required education for new executive officers.

(B) For all other executive officers, the first three-year period begins on January 1, 2007.

(2) The following education applies toward the required 30 hours of continuing education:

(A) Any education offered by a provider listed in rule 10.481(a) and any other education, including education taken to satisfy a statutory or other education requirement, approved by the presiding judge as meeting the criteria listed in rule 10.481(b).

(B) Each hour of participation in traditional (face-to-face) education, distance education such as broadcast and videoconference courses, online coursework, and self-directed study counts toward the requirement on an hour-for-hour basis. The hours applied for participation in online coursework and self-directed study are limited to a combined total of 7 hours in each three-year period.

(C) An executive officer who serves as faculty for a California court-based audience (i.e., justices, judges, subordinate judicial officers, temporary judges, or court personnel) may apply the following hours of faculty service: 3 hours for each hour of presentation the first time a given course is presented and 2 hours for each hour of presentation each subsequent time that course is presented. The hours applied for faculty service are limited to 15 in each three-year period.

(Subd (c) amended effective January 1, 2008; adopted effective January 1, 2007.)

(d) Extension of time

(1) For good cause, a presiding judge may grant a one-year extension of time to complete the education requirements in (b) and (c).

(2) If the presiding judge grants a request for an extension of time, the executive officer, in consultation with the presiding judge, must also pursue interim means of obtaining relevant educational content.

(3) An extension of time to complete the hours-based requirement does not affect the timing of the executive officer's next three-year period.

(Subd (d) adopted effective January 1, 2007.)

(e) Record of participation; statement of completion

Each executive officer is responsible for:

(1) Tracking his or her own participation in education and keeping a record of participation for three years after each course or activity that is applied toward the requirements;

(2) At the end of each year, giving the presiding judge a copy of his or her record of participation in education for that year; and

(3) At the end of each three-year period, giving the presiding judge a signed statement of completion for that three-year period.

(Subd (e) amended effective January 1, 2008; adopted effective January 1, 2007.)

Rule 10.473 amended and renumbered effective January 1, 2008; adopted as rule 10.463 effective January 1, 2007.

Rule 10.474. Trial court managers, supervisors, and other personnel

(a) Applicability

All California trial court managers, supervisors, and other personnel must complete these minimum education requirements. All managers, supervisors, and other personnel should participate in more education than is required, related to each individual's responsibilities and in accordance with the education recommendations set forth in rule 10.479.

(Subd (a) amended effective January 1, 2008; adopted effective January 1, 2007.)

(b) Content-based requirements

(1) Each new manager or supervisor must complete orientation courses within six months of becoming a manager or supervisor, unless the court's executive officer determines that the new manager or supervisor has already completed these orientation courses or courses covering equivalent content. The courses must include orientation about:

(A) The judicial branch of California;

(B) The local court; and

(C) Basic management and supervision.

(2) Each new court employee who is not a manager or supervisor must complete orientation courses within six months of becoming a court employee, unless the employee's supervisor determines that the new court employee has already completed these orientation courses or courses covering equivalent content. The courses must include orientation about:

(A) The judicial branch of California;

(B) The local court; and

(C) Basic employee issues, such as sexual harassment and safety; and

(D) The employee's specific job.

(3) The court executive officer may determine the appropriate content, delivery mechanism, and length of orientation based on the needs and role of each individual employee.

(Subd (b) amended effective January 1, 2008; adopted effective January 1, 2007.)

(c) Hours-based requirements

(1) Each court manager or supervisor must complete 12 hours of continuing education every two years.

(2) Each court employee who is not a manager or supervisor must complete 8 hours of continuing education every two years, with the exception of employees who do not provide court administrative or operational services. Those employees are not subject to the continuing education hours-based requirement but must complete any education or training required by law and any other education required by the court executive officer.

(3) The first two-year period for all court managers, supervisors, and other personnel begins on January 1, 2007. The orientation education required for new managers, supervisors, and other personnel under (b) does not apply toward the required hours of continuing education because it must be completed before they enter the two-year period. Each new manager, supervisor, or employee enters the two-year continuing education period on the first day of the quarter following his or her completion of the orientation education required under (b); the quarters begin on January 1, April 1, July 1, and October 1. Each manager, supervisor, or employee who enters the two-year continuing education period after it has begun must complete a prorated number of continuing education hours for that two-year period, based on the number of quarters remaining in it.

(4) Any education offered by a provider listed in rule 10.481(a) and any other education, including education taken to satisfy a statutory, rules-based, or other education requirement, that is approved by the executive officer or the employee's supervisor as meeting the criteria listed in rule 10.481(b) applies toward the orientation education required under (b) and the continuing education required under (c)(1) and (2).

(5) Each hour of participation in traditional (face-to-face) education, distance education such as broadcast and videoconference courses, and online coursework counts toward the requirement on an hour-for-hour basis. The hours applied for participation in online coursework are limited to a total of 4 hours for managers and supervisors and to a total of 3 hours for other personnel in each two-year period; these limits are prorated for individuals who enter the two-year period after it has begun. Self-directed study is encouraged for professional development but does not apply toward the required hours.

(6) A manager, supervisor, or employee who serves as faculty for a California court-based audience (i.e., justices, judges, subordinate judicial officers, temporary judges, or court personnel) may apply the following hours of faculty service: 3 hours for each hour of presentation the first time a given course is presented and 2 hours for each hour of presentation each subsequent time that the course is presented. The hours applied for faculty service are limited to 6 hours for managers and supervisors and to 4 hours for other personnel in each two-year period; these limits are prorated for individuals who enter the two-year period after it has begun.

(7) The court executive officer may require managers, supervisors and other court personnel to participate in specific courses or to participate in education in a specific subject matter area as part of their continuing education.

(Subd (c) amended effective January 1, 2008; adopted effective January 1, 2007.)

(d) Extension of time

(1) For good cause, the executive officer or a supervisor, if delegated by the executive officer, may grant a six-month extension of time to complete the education requirements in this rule.

(2) If the executive officer or supervisor grants a request for an extension of time, the manager, supervisor, or employee who made the request, in consultation with the executive officer or supervisor, must also pursue interim means of obtaining relevant educational content.

(3) An extension of time to complete the hours-based requirement does not affect the timing of the next two-year period.

(Subd (d) adopted effective January 1, 2007.)

(e) Records of participation

(1) Each court is responsible for tracking participation in education and for tracking completion of minimum

education requirements for its managers, supervisors, and other personnel.

(2) Each manager, supervisor, and employee must keep records of his or her own participation for two years after each course or activity that is applied toward the requirements.

(Subd (e) adopted effective January 1, 2007.)

Rule 10.474 amended and renumbered effective January 1, 2008; adopted as rule 10.464 effective January 1, 2007.

Rule 10.478. Content-based and hours-based education for court investigators, probate attorneys, and probate examiners

(a) Definitions

As used in this rule, the following terms have the meanings specified below, unless the context or subject matter otherwise require:

(1) A "court investigator" is a person described in Probate Code section 1454(a) employed by or under contract with a court to provide the investigative services for the court required or authorized by law in guardianships, conservatorships, and other protective proceedings under division 4 of the Probate Code;

(2) A "probate attorney" is an active member of the State Bar of California who is employed by a court to perform the functions of a probate examiner and also to provide legal analysis, recommendations, advice, and other services to the court pertaining to probate proceedings;

(3) A "probate examiner" is a person employed by a court to review filings in probate proceedings in order to assist the court and the parties to get the filed matters properly ready for consideration by the court in accordance with the requirements of the Probate Code, the rules in title 7 of the California Rules of Court, and the court's local rules;

(4) "Probate proceedings" are decedents' estates, guardianships and conservatorships under division 4 of the Probate Code, trust proceedings under division 9 of the Probate Code, and other matters governed by provisions of that code and the rules in title 7 of the California Rules of Court;

(5) "AOC" is the Administrative Office of the Courts;

(6) "CJER" is the AOC Education Division/Center for Judicial Education and Research.

(Subd (a) adopted effective January 1, 2008.)

(b) Content-based requirements for court investigators

(1) Each court investigator must complete 18 hours of education within one year of his or her start date after the effective date of this rule. The education must include the following general topics:

(A) Court process and legal proceedings;

(B) Child abuse and neglect and the effect of domestic violence on children (guardianship investigators); elder and dependent adult abuse, including undue influence and other forms of financial abuse (conservatorship investigators);

(C) Medical issues;

(D) Access to and use of criminal-record information, confidentiality, ethics, conflicts of interest;

(E) Accessing and evaluating community resources for children and mentally impaired elderly or developmentally disabled adults; and

(F) Interviewing children and persons with mental function or communication deficits.

(2) A court investigator may fulfill the education requirement in (1) through AOC-sponsored education, a provider listed in rule 10.481(a), or a provider approved by the court executive officer or the court investigator's supervisor as meeting the education criteria specified in rule 10.481(b).

(3) The education required in (1) may be applied to the specific-job portion of the orientation course required for all new court employees under rule 10.474(b)(2)(D) and the continuing education required for all nonmanagerial or non-supervisory court employees under rule 10.474(c)(2).

(4) The education required in (1) may be by traditional (face-to-face) or distance-learning means, such as broadcasts, videoconferences, or online coursework, but may not be by self-study.

(Subd (b) adopted effective January 1, 2008.)

(c) Content-based education for probate attorneys

(1) Each probate attorney must complete 18 hours of education within six months of his or her start date after January 1, 2008, in probate-related topics, including guardianships, conservatorships, and court-supervised fiduciary accounting.

(2) A probate attorney may fulfill the education requirement in (1) through AOC-sponsored education, a provider listed in rule 10.481(a), or a provider approved by the court executive officer or the probate attorney's supervisor as meeting the education criteria specified in rule 10.481(b).

(3) The education required in (1) may be applied to the specific-job portion of the orientation course required for all new court employees under rule 10.474(b)(2)(D) and the continuing education required for all nonmanagerial or non-supervisory court employees under rule 10.474(c)(2).

(4) The education required in (1) may be by traditional (face-to-face) or distance-learning means, such as broadcasts, videoconferences, or online coursework, but may not be by self-study.

(Subd (c) adopted effective January 1, 2008.)

(d) Content-based education for probate examiners

(1) Each probate examiner must complete 30 hours of education within one year of his or her start date after January 1, 2008, in probate-related topics, of which 18 hours must be in guardianships and conservatorships, including court-appointed fiduciary accounting.

(2) A probate examiner may fulfill the education requirement in (1) through AOC-sponsored education, a provider listed in rule 10.481(a), or a provider approved by the court executive officer or the probate examiner's supervisor as meeting the education criteria specified in rule 10.481(b).

(3) The education required in (1) may be applied to the specific-job portion of the orientation course required for all new court employees under rule 10.474(b)(2)(D) and the continuing education required for all nonmanagerial or non-supervisory court employees under rule 10.474(c)(2).

(4) The education required in (1) may be by traditional (face-to-face) or distance-learning means, such as broad-

casts, videoconferences, or online coursework, but may not be by self-study.

(Subd (d) adopted effective January 1, 2008.)

(e) Hours-based education for court investigators

(1) Each court investigator must complete 12 hours of continuing education on some or all of the general topics listed in (b)(1) each calendar year. For court investigators employed by or performing services under contract with the court before the effective date of this rule, the first calendar year the education is required begins on January 1, 2008. For court investigators who begin their employment or performance of services under contract with the court after the effective date of this rule, the first year this education is required begins on January 1 of the year immediately following completion of the education required in (b).

(2) A court investigator may fulfill the education requirement in (1) through AOC-sponsored education, a provider listed in rule 10.481(a), or a provider approved by the court executive officer or the court investigator's supervisor as meeting the education criteria specified in rule 10.481(b).

(3) The education required in (1) may be applied to the continuing education required for all nonmanagerial or nonsupervisory court employees under rule 10.474(c)(2).

(4) The education required in (1) may be by traditional (face-to-face) or distance-learning means, such as broadcasts, videoconferences, or online coursework, but may not be by self-study.

(Subd (e) adopted effective January 1, 2008.)

(f) Hours-based education for probate attorneys

(1) Each probate attorney must complete 12 hours of continuing education each calendar year in probate-related subjects, of which six hours per year must be in guardianships and conservatorships, including court-supervised fiduciary accounting. For probate attorneys employed by or performing services under contract with the court before the effective date of this rule, the first calendar year the education is required begins on January 1, 2008. For probate attorneys who begin their employment with the court after the effective date of this rule, the first year this education is required begins on January 1 of the year immediately following completion of the education required in (c).

(2) A probate attorney may fulfill the education requirement in (1) through AOC-sponsored education, a provider listed in rule 10.481(a), or a provider approved by the court executive officer or the probate attorney's supervisor as meeting the education criteria specified in rule 10.481(b).

(3) The education required in (1) may be applied to the continuing education required for all nonmanagerial or nonsupervisory court employees under rule 10.474(c)(2).

(4) The education required in (1) may be by traditional (face-to-face) or distance-learning means, such as broadcasts, videoconferences, or online coursework, but may not be by self-study.

(Subd (f) adopted effective January 1, 2008.)

(g) Hours-based education for probate examiners

(1) Each probate examiner must complete 12 hours of continuing education each calendar year in probate-related subjects, of which six hours per year must be in

guardianships and conservatorships, including court-appointed fiduciary accounting. For probate examiners employed by the court before the effective date of this rule, the first calendar year the education is required begins on January 1, 2008. For probate examiners who begin their employment with the court after the effective date of this rule, the first year this education is required begins on January 1 of the year immediately following completion of the education required in (d).

(2) A probate examiner may fulfill the education requirement in (1) through AOC-sponsored education, a provider listed in rule 10.481(a), or a provider approved by the court executive officer or the probate examiner's supervisor as meeting the education criteria specified in rule 10.481(b).

(3) The education required in (1) may be applied to the continuing education required for all nonmanagerial or nonsupervisory court employees under rule 10.474(c)(2).

(4) The education required in (1) may be by traditional (face-to-face) or distance-learning means, such as broadcasts, videoconferences, or online coursework, but may not be by self-study.

(Subd (g) adopted effective January 1, 2008.)

(h) Extension of time

The provisions of rule 10.474(d) concerning extensions of time apply to the content-based and hours-based education required under this rule.

(Subd (h) adopted effective January 1, 2008.)

(i) Record keeping and reporting

(1) The provisions of rule 10.474(e) concerning the responsibilities of courts and participating court employees to keep records and track the completion of educational requirements apply to the education required under this rule.

(2) The AOC may require courts to report participation by court investigators, probate attorneys, and probate examiners in the education required by this rule as necessary to ensure compliance with Probate Code section 1456.

(Subd (i) adopted effective January 1, 2008.)

Rule 10.478 adopted effective January 1, 2008.

Rule 10.479.   Education recommendations for appellate and trial court personnel

(a) Education recommendations generally

Each appellate and trial court executive or administrative officer, manager, supervisor, and other employee, as part of his or her continuing education, should regularly participate in educational activities related to his or her responsibilities. Minimum education requirements for court personnel are set forth in rules 10.471–10.474. The following recommendations illustrate for some specific responsibilities how executive and administrative officers, managers, supervisors, and other personnel should participate in more education than is required.

(Subd (a) adopted effective January 1, 2008.)

(b) Education on treatment of jurors

The presiding judge of each trial court should ensure that all court executives and all court employees who interact with jurors are properly trained in the appropriate treatment of jurors. Court executives and jury staff employees should regularly use CJER educational materials or other appropriate materials and should regularly participate in CJER programs or other appropriate programs devoted to the treatment of jurors.

(Subd (b) adopted effective January 1, 2008.)

(c) Fairness and access education

In order to achieve the objective of assisting court employees in preserving the integrity and impartiality of the judicial system through the prevention of bias, all court personnel should regularly participate in education on fairness and access. The education should include instruction on race and ethnicity, gender, sexual orientation, persons with disabilities, and sexual harassment.

(Subd (c) adopted effective January 1, 2008.)

(d) Education on quality service to court users

Employees should regularly participate in education covering appropriate skills and conduct for working with court customers offered locally or by the Judicial Council through CJER.

(Subd (d) adopted effective January 1, 2008.)
Rule 10.479 adopted effective January 1, 2008.

Ref.: Cal. Fms Pl. & Pr., Ch. 317, "Judges."

Rule 10.481. Approved providers; approved course criteria

(a) Approved providers

Any education program offered by any of the following providers that is relevant to the work of the courts or enhances the individual participant's ability to perform his or her job may be applied toward the education requirements and expectations stated in rules 10.461–10.479, except for the requirements stated in rules 10.461(b), [1] **10.462(c)**, and 10.473(b), for which specific providers are required:

(1) California Administrative Office of the Courts;

(2) California Judges Association;

(3) Supreme Court of California;

(4) California Courts of Appeal;

(5) Superior Courts of California;

(6) State Bar of California;

(7) National Judicial College;

(8) National Center for State Courts;

(9) National Council of Juvenile and Family Court Judges;

(10) National Association of Women Judges;

(11) American Bar Association;

(12) National Association for Court Management;

(13) American Judges Association;

(14) American Academy of Judicial Education;

(15) Dwight D. Opperman Institute of Judicial Administration;

(16) National Institute of Justice;

(17) Law schools accredited by the American Bar Association;

(18) Accredited colleges and universities;

(19) Continuing Education of the Bar—California;

(20) Local California bar associations;

(21) California Court Association;

(22) Superior Court Clerks' Association of the State of California;

(23) Council of Chief Judges of Courts of Appeal;

(24) Roscoe Pound Institute, Annual Forum for State Appellate Court Judges;

(25) National Conference of Appellate Court Clerks;

(26) AEI-Brookings Joint Center;

(27) The Rutter Group; [2]

(28) American Board of Trial Advocates**; and**

(29) California Association of Superior Court Investigators.

(Subd (a) amended effective January 1, 2008; adopted effective January 1, 2007; previously amended effective January 1, 2008.)

Rule 10.481(a). 2008 Deletes. [1] 10.462(b) **[2]** and

(b) Approved education criteria

Education is not limited to the approved providers listed in (a). Any education from a provider not listed in (a) that is approved by the Chief Justice, the administrative presiding justice, or the presiding judge as meeting the criteria listed below may be applied toward the continuing education expectations and requirements for justices, judges, and subordinate judicial officers or requirements for clerk/administrators or court executive officers. Similarly, any education from a provider not listed in (a) that is approved by the clerk/administrator, the court executive officer**,** or the employee's supervisor as meeting the criteria listed below may be applied toward the orientation or continuing education requirements for managers, supervisors, and other employees **or the content-based or continuing education for probate court investigators, probate attorneys, and probate examiners in rule 10.478**.

(1) The education must meet the following three criteria:

(A) The subject matter is relevant to the work of the courts or the judicial branch;

(B) The education is at least one hour in length; and

(C) Anticipated learning outcomes (how new knowledge, skills, or abilities will be applied, demonstrated, or used) are identified prior to the education work.

(2) The education must also meet at least two of the following five criteria:

(A) The learning environment is educationally sound (e.g., distractions are limited and the physical location is conducive to learning the subject matter);

(B) The participant receives or has access to all the reference tools and other materials and resources (such as handouts) that are required for learning and applying the content (such as job aids or scripts);

(C) The participant has an opportunity to practice using or applying the new information or skill (through direct experience, role-play, or case studies/hypothetical situations) as part of the learning experience;

(D) The participant has the opportunity to interact with knowledgeable faculty or other experts in the topical area to pose questions or clarify understanding;

(E) An assessment tool or activity (such as the development of an action plan to apply the newly gained knowledge or skill) enables the participant to determine whether the skills, abilities, or knowledge gained through the education can be used in the future in his or her work.

(Subd (b) amended effective January 1, 2008; adopted effective January 1, 2007; previously amended January 1, 2008.)
Rule 10.481 amended effective January 1, 2008; adopted as rule 10.471 effective January 1, 2007; previously amended and renumbered effective January 1, 2008.

Rule 10.491. Minimum education requirements for Administrative Office of the Courts executives, managers, supervisors, and other employees

(a) Applicability

All Administrative Office of the Courts (AOC) executives, managers, supervisors, and other employees must complete these minimum education requirements.

(Subd (a) adopted effective January 1, 2008.)

(b) Content-based requirements

(1) Each new manager or supervisor must complete the AOC's New Manager/Supervisor Orientation within six months of being hired or assigned as a manager or supervisor.

(2) Each new employee, including each new manager or supervisor, must complete the AOC's New Employee Orientation within six months of being hired and should complete it as soon as possible after being hired.

(3) The Administrative Director of the Courts may require new managers, supervisors, and other employees to complete specific AOC compliance courses in addition to the required orientation courses.

(Subd (b) adopted effective January 1, 2008.)

(c) Hours-based requirements

(1) Each executive must complete 30 hours of continuing education every two years.

(2) Each manager or supervisor must complete 18 hours of continuing education every two years.

(3) Each employee who is not an executive, manager, or supervisor must complete 12 hours of continuing education every two years.

(4) The first two-year period begins on January 1, 2008. The orientation courses and the compliance courses required for new managers, supervisors, and other employees under (b) do not apply toward the required hours of continuing education. Each new executive enters the two-year continuing education period on the first day of the quarter following his or her appointment, and each new manager, supervisor, and employee enters the two-year continuing education period on the first day of the quarter following his or her completion of the orientation courses and the compliance courses required under (b); the quarters begin on January 1, April 1, July 1, and October 1. Each executive, manager, supervisor, or employee who enters the two-year continuing education period after it has begun must complete a prorated number of continuing education hours for that two-year period, based on the number of quarters remaining in it.

(5) Any education offered by a provider listed in rule 10.481(a) and any other education, including education taken to satisfy a statutory, rules-based, or other education requirement, that is approved by the employee's supervisor as meeting the criteria listed in rule 10.481(b) applies toward the continuing education required under (c)(1)–(3).

(6) Each hour of participation in traditional (face-to-face) education, distance education such as broadcast and videoconference courses, and online coursework counts toward the requirement on an hour-for-hour basis. The hours applied for participation in online coursework and self-directed study are limited to a total of 10 hours for executives, 6 hours for managers and supervisors, and 4 hours for other employees in each two-year period; these

limits are prorated for individuals who enter the two-year period after it has begun.

(7) An executive, manager, supervisor, or employee who serves as faculty teaching courses at the AOC or on behalf of the AOC at another location may apply the following hours of faculty service: 3 hours for each hour of presentation the first time a given course is presented and 2 hours for each hour of presentation each subsequent time that the course is presented. The hours applied for faculty service are limited to 15 hours for executives, 9 hours for managers and supervisors, and 6 hours for other personnel in each two-year period; these limits are prorated for individuals who enter the two-year continuing education period after it has begun.

(8) The Administrative Director of the Courts may require executives, managers, supervisors, and other employees to complete specific AOC compliance courses as part of the continuing education requirements.

(Subd (c) adopted effective January 1, 2008.)

(d) Extension of time

(1) For good cause, the Administrative Director of the Courts or an executive, manager, or supervisor, if delegated by the Administrative Director, may grant a six-month extension of time to complete the education requirements in this rule.

(2) If the Administrative Director, or an executive, manager, or supervisor, grants a request for an extension of time, the individual who made the request, in consultation with the Administrative Director or the individual's supervisor, must also pursue interim means of obtaining relevant educational content.

(3) An extension of time to complete the hours-based requirement does not affect the timing of the next two-year period.

(Subd (d) adopted effective January 1, 2008.)

(e) Records of participation

(1) An employee's completion of any course listed in the Human Resources Education Management System (HREMS) is automatically tracked in HREMS.

(2) An employee's completion of specified online training is automatically tracked in HREMS.

(3) Each employee is responsible for tracking completion of any training that is not automatically tracked in HREMS. After completion of the training, the employee must enter it in the employee's individual record in HREMS.

(Subd (e) adopted effective January 1, 2008.)

(f) Responsibilities of Administrative Director of the Courts and of AOC executives, managers, and supervisors

The Administrative Director of the Courts and each AOC executive, manager, and supervisor:

(1) Must grant sufficient time to all employees to enable them to complete the minimum education requirements stated in (b)–(c);

(2) Should allow and encourage employees, in addition to participating as students in education activities, to serve on employee education committees and as faculty at judicial branch education programs when an employee's services have been requested for these purposes; and

(3) Should establish an education plan for their employees to facilitate their involvement as both participants

and faculty in educational activities, and should consult with each employee regarding his or her education needs and requirements and professional development.

(4) Must ensure that executives, managers, supervisors, and other employees are reimbursed by the AOC in accordance with the travel policies issued by the Administrative Office of the Courts for travel expenses incurred in attending in-state education programs as a participant in order to complete the minimum education requirements in (b)–(c). Provisions for these expenses must be part of the AOC's budget. The Administrative Director of the Courts may approve reimbursement of travel expenses incurred by executives, managers, supervisors, and other [1] **employees** in attending out-of-state education programs as participants.

(Subd (f) amended effective July 1, 2008; adopted effective January 1, 2008.)

Rule 10.491(f). 2008 Deletes. [1] court personnel
Rule 10.491 amended effective July 1, 2008; adopted effective January 1, 2008.

Division 3
Judicial Administration Rules Applicable to All Courts

Rule 10.502. Judicial sabbatical pilot program
Rule 10.503. Use of recycled paper by all courts
Rule 10.504. Smoking prohibited in all courts
Rule 10.505. Judicial robes

Rule 10.501. Judicial education [Repealed]
Rule 10.501 repealed effective January 1, 2007; adopted as rule 970 effective January 1, 1996. The repealed rule related to judicial education.

Rule 10.502. Judicial sabbatical pilot program
(a) Objective
Sabbatical leave is a privilege available to jurists by statute. The objective of sabbatical leave is to facilitate study, teaching, research, or another activity that will benefit the administration of justice and enhance judges' performance of their duties.

(b) Eligibility
(1) A judge or justice is eligible to apply for a paid sabbatical under Government Code section 77213 if:

(A) He or she has served for at least seven years as a California judicial officer, including service as a subordinate judicial officer;

(B) He or she has not taken a sabbatical within seven years of the date of the proposed sabbatical; and

(C) He or she agrees to continue to serve as a judicial officer for at least three years after the sabbatical.

(2) Any judge is eligible to apply for an unpaid sabbatical under Government Code section 68554.

(c) Application
(1) An eligible judge may apply for a sabbatical by submitting a sabbatical proposal to the Administrative Director of the Courts with a copy to the presiding judge or justice.

(2) The sabbatical proposal must include:

(A) The judge's certification that he or she meets the eligibility requirements established in (b);

(B) The beginning and ending dates of the proposed sabbatical;

(C) A description of the sabbatical project, including an explanation of how the sabbatical will benefit the administration of justice and the judge's performance of his or her duties; and

(D) A statement from the presiding judge or justice of the affected court, indicating approval or disapproval of the sabbatical request and the reasons for such approval or disapproval, forwarded to the Judicial Sabbatical Review Committee with a copy to the judge.

(Subd (c) amended effective January 1, 2007.)

(d) Judicial Sabbatical Review Committee
A Judicial Sabbatical Review Committee will be appointed to make recommendations to the Judicial Council regarding sabbatical requests.

(1) *Membership*
The committee must include at least one member from each of the following groups:

(A) Administrative Presiding Justices Advisory Committee;

(B) Trial Court Presiding Judges Advisory Committee;

(C) Court Executives Advisory Committee;

(D) Governing Committee of the Center for Judicial Education and Research;

(E) Judicial Service Advisory Committee; and

(F) California Judges Association (liaison).

(2) *Staffing*
The committee will be staffed by the Human Resources Division of the Administrative Office of the Courts and may elect its chair and vice-chair.

(Subd (d) amended effective January 1, 2007.)

(e) Evaluation
(1) The Administrative Director of the Courts must forward all sabbatical requests that comply with (c) to the Judicial Sabbatical Review Committee.

(2) The Judicial Sabbatical Review Committee must recommend granting or denying the sabbatical request after it considers the following factors:

(A) Whether the sabbatical will benefit the administration of justice in California and the judge's performance of his or her duties; and

(B) Whether the sabbatical leave will be detrimental to the affected court.

(3) The Judicial Sabbatical Review Committee may recommend an unpaid sabbatical if there is insufficient funding for a paid sabbatical.

(f) Length
(1) A paid sabbatical taken under Government Code section 77213 may not exceed 120 calendar days. A judge may be allowed to add unpaid sabbatical time onto the end of a paid sabbatical if the purpose of the unpaid sabbatical is substantially similar to the work of the paid sabbatical.

(2) An unpaid sabbatical taken under Government Code section 68554 may not exceed one year.

(g) Ethics and compensation
A judge on sabbatical leave is subject to the California Code of Judicial Ethics and, while on a paid sabbatical, must not accept compensation for activities performed

during that sabbatical leave but may receive reimbursement for the expenses provided in canon 4H(2) of the Code of Judicial Ethics.

(h) Judge's report

On completion of a sabbatical leave, the judge must report in writing to the Judicial Council on how the leave benefited the administration of justice in California and on its effect on his or her official duties as a judicial officer.

(Subd (h) amended effective January 1, 2007.)

(i) Retirement and benefits

(1) A judge on a paid sabbatical leave under Government Code section 77213 continues to receive all the benefits of office and accrues service credit toward retirement.

(2) A judge on unpaid sabbatical leave under Government Code section 68554 receives no compensation, and the period of absence does not count as service toward retirement. The leave does not affect the term of office.

(j) Judicial assignment replacement

Funds must be made available from the Judicial Administration Efficiency and Modernization Fund to allocate additional assigned judges to those courts whose judges' requests for paid sabbaticals are approved.

Rule 10.502 amended and renumbered effective January 1, 2007; adopted as rule 6.151 effective January 1, 2003.

Ref.: Cal. Fms Pl. & Pr., Ch. 317, "Judges."

Rule 10.503.   Use of recycled paper by all courts

All courts must use recycled paper for all purposes except for uses for which recycled paper is not practically available.

Rule 10.503 amended and renumbered effective January 1, 2007; adopted as rule 989.1 effective January 1, 1994.

Ref.: Cal. Fms Pl. & Pr., Ch. 317, "Judges."

Rule 10.504.   Smoking prohibited in all courts

(a) Definition

"Court facilities" means courthouses and all areas of multipurpose buildings used for court operations.

(b) Smoking prohibited

Smoking is prohibited in all court facilities.

(Subd (b) amended effective January 1, 2007.)

(c) Signs

Conspicuous no-smoking signs must be placed in all court facilities.

(Subd (c) amended effective January 1, 2007.)

Rule 10.504 amended and renumbered effective January 1, 2007; adopted as rule 989.5 effective July 1, 1991.

Ref.: Cal. Fms Pl. & Pr., Ch. 317, "Judges."

Rule 10.505.   Judicial robes

(a) Color and length

The judicial robe required by Government Code section 68110 must be black, must extend in front and back from the collar and shoulders to below the knees, and must have sleeves to the wrists.

(Subd (a) amended and lettered effective January 1, 2007; adopted as subd (e) effective September 24, 1959; relettered as subd (d) effective July 1, 1963; amended as an unlettered subd effective January 1, 2003.)

(b) Style

The judicial robe must conform to the style customarily worn in courts in the United States.

(Subd (b) amended and lettered effective January 1, 2007; adopted as subd (e) effective September 24, 1959; relettered as subd (d) effective July 1, 1963; amended as an unlettered subd effective January 1, 2003.)

Rule 10.505 amended and renumbered effective January 1, 2007; adopted as rule 249 effective January 1, 1949; previously amended effective September 24, 1959, and July 1, 1963; amended and renumbered as rule 299 effective January 1, 2003.

Ref.: Cal. Fms Pl. & Pr., Ch. 317, "Judges."

Division 4
Trial Court Administration

Chap. 1.   General Rules on Trial Court Management. Rules 10.601–10.630.
Chap. 2.   Trial Court Management of Human Resources. Rules 10.650–10.670.
Chap. 3.   Subordinate Judicial Officers. Rules 10.700–10.703.
Chap. 4.   Referees [Reserved].
Chap. 5.   Temporary Judges. Rules 10.740–10.746.
Chap. 6.   Court Interpreters. Rules 10.761, 10.762.
Chap. 7.   Qualifications of Court Investigators, Probate Attorneys, and Probate Examiners. Rules 10.776, 10.777.
Chap. 8.   Alternative Dispute Resolution Programs. Rules 10.780–10.783.
Chap. 9.   Trial Court Budget and Fiscal Management. Rules 10.800–10.830.
Chap. 10.   Trial Court Records Management. Rules 10.851–10.856.
Chap. 11.   Trial Court Automation. Rule 10.870.
Chap. 12.   Trial Court Management of Civil Cases. Rules 10.900–10.910.
Chap. 13.   Trial Court Management of Criminal Cases. Rules 10.950–10.953.
Chap. 14.   Management of Self-Help Centers. Rule 10.960.

Chapter 1
General Rules on Trial Court Management

Rule 10.601. Superior court management
Rule 10.602. Selection and term of presiding judge
Rule 10.603. Authority and duties of presiding judge
Rule 10.605. Executive committee
Rule 10.608. Duties of all judges
Rule 10.610. Duties of court executive officer
Rule 10.611. Nondiscrimination in court appointments
Rule 10.612. Use of gender-neutral language
Rule 10.613. Local court rules—adopting, filing, distributing, and maintaining
Rule 10.614. Local court forms
Rule 10.620. Public access to administrative decisions of trial courts
Rule 10.625. Certain demographic data relating to regular grand jurors
Rule 10.630. Reporting of reciprocal assignment orders

Rule 10.601.   Superior court management

(a) Purpose

The rules in this division establish a system of trial court management that:

(1) Promotes equal access to the courts;

(2) Establishes decentralized management of trial court resources; and

(3) Enables the trial courts to operate in an efficient, effective, and accountable manner in serving the people of California.

(Subd (a) amended effective January 1, 2007.)

(b) Goals

The rules in this division are intended to ensure the authority and responsibility of the superior courts to do the following, consistent with statutes, rules of court, and standards of judicial administration:

(1) Manage their day-to-day operations with sufficient flexibility to meet the needs of those served by the courts;

(2) Establish the means of selecting presiding judges, assistant presiding judges, executive officers or court administrators, clerks of court, and jury commissioners;

(3) Manage their personnel systems, including the adoption of personnel policies;

(4) Manage their budget and fiscal operations, including allocating funding and moving funding between functions or line items;

(5) Provide input to the Judicial Council, the Trial Court Budget Working Group, and the Administrative Office of the Courts on the trial court budget process; and

(6) Develop and implement processes and procedures to improve court operations and responsiveness to the public.

(Subd (b) amended effective January 1, 2007; previously amended effective January 1, 2002.)

(c) Decentralized management

"Decentralized management" as used in the rules in this division refers to the administration of the trial courts on a countywide basis, unless an alternative structure has been approved by the Judicial Council, consistent with applicable statutes, rules, and standards of judicial administration.

(Subd (c) amended effective January 1, 2007.)

Rule 10.601 amended and renumbered effective January 1, 2007; adopted as rule 2501 effective July 1, 1998; renumbered as rule 6.601 effective January 1, 1999; previously amended effective January 1, 2002.

Ref.: Cal. Fms Pl. & Pr., Ch. 317, "Judges."

Rule 10.602. Selection and term of presiding judge

(a) Selection

(1) *Courts with three or more judges*

Each court that has three or more judges must select a presiding judge. Selection of the presiding judge may be by secret ballot. The court should establish an internal local rule or policy for the selection of the presiding judge and assistant presiding judge, if any.

(2) *Two-judge courts*

In a court having two judges, the selection of the presiding judge must conform to Government Code section 69508.5. If selection cannot be agreed on and neither judge has at least four years of experience, the senior judge must hold the office of presiding judge until both judges have at least four years of experience.

(Subd (a) amended effective January 1, 2007; previously amended effective January 1, 2005.)

(b) Requisite experience and waiver

A presiding judge must have at least four years of experience as a judge, unless this requirement is waived by a majority vote of the judges of the court. Nomination and selection of a presiding judge should take into consideration the judge's:

(1) Management and administrative ability;

(2) Interest in serving in the position;

(3) Experience and familiarity with a variety of trial court assignments;

(4) Ability to motivate and educate other judicial officers and court personnel;

(5) Ability to evaluate the strengths of the court's bench officers and make assignments based on those strengths as well as the best interests of the public and the court; and

(6) Other appropriate factors.

(Subd (b) amended effective January 1, 2007; previously amended effective January 1, 2005.)

(c) Term

A presiding judge in a court with two judges must be elected for a term of not less than one year. A presiding judge in a court with three or more judges must be elected for an initial term of not less than two years. The presiding judge may be elected for additional terms. The court may change the duration of the initial or additional term by local rule or policy so long as the initial term is not less than the duration specified in this rule. A presiding judge may be removed by a majority vote of the judges of the court.

(Subd (c) amended effective January 1, 2007; previously amended effective January 1, 2005.)

(d) Assistant presiding judge and acting presiding judge

(1) The court may elect an assistant presiding judge.

(2) If the court's internal local rule or policy does not provide for the designation of an acting presiding judge to serve if the presiding judge is absent or unable to act, the presiding judge must designate one.

(3) The court should provide the assistant presiding judge with training to foster an orderly succession to the office of presiding judge.

(Subd (d) amended effective January 1, 2007; previously amended effective January 1, 2005.)

(e) Caseload adjustment

To the extent possible, the judicial caseload should be adjusted to provide the presiding judge with sufficient time and resources to devote to the management and administrative duties of the office.

Rule 10.602 amended and renumbered effective January 1, 2007; adopted as rule 6.602 effective January 1, 2001; previously amended effective January 1, 2005.

Advisory Committee Comment

The internal local rule described in this rule relates only to the internal management of the court, and as such is exempt from the requirements in rule 10.613. (See rule 10.613(j).)

Ref.: Cal. Fms Pl. & Pr., Ch. 317, "Judges."

Rule 10.603. Authority and duties of presiding judge

(a) General responsibilities

The presiding judge is responsible, with the assistance of the court executive officer, for leading the court, establishing policies, and allocating resources in a manner that promotes access to justice for all members of the public, provides a forum for the fair and expeditious resolution of disputes, maximizes the use of judicial and other resources, increases efficiency in court operations, and enhances service to the public. The presiding judge is responsible for:

(1) Ensuring the effective management and administration of the court, consistent with any rules, policies, strategic plan, or budget adopted by the Judicial Council or the court;

(2) Ensuring that the duties of all judges specified under rule 10.608 are timely and orderly performed; and

(3) Ensuring that the court has adopted written policies and procedures allowing the presiding judge to perform efficiently the administrative duties of that office.

(Subd (a) amended effective January 1, 2007.)

(b) Authority

(1) The presiding judge is authorized to:

(A) Assign judges to departments and designate supervising judges for divisions, districts, or branch courts;

(B) Apportion the business of the court, including assigning and reassigning cases to departments;

(C) Call meetings of the judges;

(D) Appoint standing and special committees of judges;

(E) Act as the spokesperson for the court;

(F) Authorize and direct expenditures from the court's Trial Court Operations Fund; and

(G) Perform all acts necessary to accomplish the duties specified by the rules of court.

(2) No local rule or policy may limit the authority of the presiding judge as granted in the rules of court.

(Subd (b) amended effective January 1, 2007.)

(c) Duties

(1) *Assignments*

The presiding judge has ultimate authority to make judicial assignments. The presiding judge must:

(A) Designate a judge to preside in each department, including a master calendar judge when appropriate, and designate a presiding judge of the juvenile division and a supervising judge for each division, district, or branch court. In making judicial assignments, the presiding judge must take into account the following:

(i) The needs of the public and the court, as they relate to the efficient and effective management of the court's calendar;

(ii) The knowledge and abilities demanded by the assignment;

(iii) The judge's judicial and nonjudicial experience, including specialized training or education;

(iv) The judge's interests;

(v) The need for continuity in the assignment;

(vi) The desirability of exposing the judge to a particular type of assignment; and

(vii) Other appropriate factors. Judicial assignments must not be based solely or primarily on seniority;

(B) Assign to a master calendar judge any of the duties that may more appropriately be performed by that department;

(C) Supervise the court's calendar, apportion the business of the court among the several departments of the court as equally as possible, and publish for general distribution copies of a current calendar specifying the judicial assignments of the judges and the times and places assigned for hearings;

(D) Reassign cases between departments as convenience or necessity requires; and

(E) Designate a judge to act if by law or the rules of court a matter is required to be presented to or heard by a particular judge and that judge is absent, deceased, or unable to act.

(2) *Judicial schedules*

(A) The presiding judge must adopt a process for scheduling judges' vacations and absences from court for attendance at schools, conferences, workshops, and community outreach activities, and must prepare a plan for these vacations and absences from court.

(B) The plan should take into account the principles contained in standards 10.11–10.13 (on judicial education) and standard 10.5 (on community activities) of the Standards of Judicial Administration.

(C) The presiding judge must review requests from judges for time absent from court and may approve any request that is consistent with the plan and with the orderly operation of the court.

(D) The presiding judge must allow each judge to take two days of personal leave per year. Personal leave may be taken at any time that is approved by the presiding judge.

(E) The presiding judge must allow the following number of days of vacation for each judge annually:

(i) 24 days for judges with less than 7 years of service as a California judge;

(ii) 27 days for judges with at least 7 but less than 14 years of service as a California judge; and

(iii) 30 days for judges with 14 or more years of service as a California judge.

(F) The presiding judge may authorize a judge to take more time off than is specified in (c)(2)(E) as justified by extraordinary circumstances, if the circumstances are documented and the authorization is in writing.

(G) The presiding judge, in his or her discretion, may allow a judge to take additional vacation days equal to the number of vacation days that the judge did not use in the previous year, up to a maximum of 30 such days. A court may, by local rule, establish a lower maximum number of such days. This paragraph applies only to vacation days accrued after January 1, 2001. It does not affect any unused vacation days that a judge may have accrued before January 1, 2001, which are governed by local court policy, nor does it create any right to compensation for unused vacation days.

(H) The court must, by local rule, define a day of vacation. Absence from court to attend an authorized education program, conference, or workshop for judges, or to participate in Judicial Council or other authorized committees or community outreach activities, is not vacation time if attendance is in accordance with the plan and has the prior approval of the presiding judge. Absence from court due to illness is not vacation time. This rule does not limit the time a judge may be absent from court when unable to work because of illness.

(I) To ensure compliance with the plan, the presiding judge must establish a system to monitor judges' absences from court and maintain records of those absences.

(3) *Submitted cases*

The presiding judge must supervise and monitor the number of causes under submission before the judges of the court and ensure that no cause under submission remains undecided and pending for longer than 90 days. As an aid in accomplishing this goal, the presiding judge must:

(A) Require each judge to report to the presiding judge all causes under submission for more than 30 days and, with respect to each cause, designate whether it has been under submission for 30 through 60 days, 61 through 90 days, or over 90 days;

(B) Compile a list of all causes under submission before judges of the court, designated as the submitted list, which must include the name of each judge, a list of causes under submission before that judge, and the length of time each cause has been under submission;

(C) Circulate monthly a complete copy of the submitted list to each judge of the court;

(D) Contact and alert each judge who has a cause under submission for over 30 days and discuss ways to ensure that the cause is timely decided;

(E) Consider providing assistance to a judge who has a cause under submission for over 60 days; and

(F) Consider requesting the services of the Administrative Office of the Courts to review the court's calendar management procedures and make recommendations whenever either of the following conditions exists in the court for the most recent three months:

(i) More than 90 civil active cases are pending for each judicial position; or

(ii) More than 10 percent of the cases on the civil active list have been pending for one year or more.

(4) *Oversight of judicial officers*

The presiding judge must:

(A) *Judges*

Notify the Commission on Judicial Performance of:

(i) A judge's substantial failure to perform judicial duties, including any habitual neglect of duty, persistent refusal to carry out assignments as assigned by the presiding judge, or persistent refusal to carry out the directives of the presiding judge as authorized by the rules of court; or

(ii) Any absences caused by disability totaling more than 90 court days in a 12-month period, excluding absences authorized under (c)(2);

(B) *Notice*

Give the judge a copy of the notice to the commission under (A) if appropriate. If a copy is not given to the judge, the presiding judge must inform the commission of the reasons why so notifying the judge was deemed inappropriate;

(C) *Commissioners*

Prepare and submit to the judges for consideration and adoption procedures for receiving, inquiring into, and resolving complaints lodged against court commissioners and referees, consistent with rule 10.703;

(D) *Temporary judges*

Be responsible for the recruitment, training, supervision, approval, and performance of temporary judges as provided in rules 2.810–2.819 and rules 10.740–10.746; and

(E) *Assigned judges*

For each assigned retired judge:

(i) Complete a confidential evaluation form;

(ii) Submit the form annually to the Administrative Director of the Courts;

(iii) Direct complaints against the assigned judge to the Chief Justice, by forwarding them to the attention of the Administrative Director of the Courts, and provide requested information in writing to the Administrative Director of the Courts in a timely manner; and

(iv) Assist the Administrative Director in the process of investigating, evaluating, and making recommendations to the Chief Justice regarding complaints against retired judges who serve on assignment.

(5) *Personnel*

The presiding judge must provide general direction to and supervision of the court executive officer, or, if the court has no executive officer, perform the duties of the court executive regarding personnel as specified in rule 10.610(c)(1).

(6) *Budget and fiscal management*

The presiding judge must:

(A) Establish a process for consulting with the judges of the court on budget requests, expenditure plans, and other budget or fiscal matters that the presiding judge deems appropriate;

(B) Establish responsible budget priorities and submit budget requests that will best enable the court to achieve its goals; and

(C) Approve procurements, contracts, expenditures, and the allocation of funds in a manner that promotes the implementation of state and local budget priorities and that ensures equal access to justice and the ability of the court to carry out its functions effectively. In a court with an executive officer, the presiding judge may delegate these duties to the court executive officer, but the presiding judge must ensure that the court executive officer performs such delegated duties consistent with the court's established budget.

(7) *Meetings and committees*

The presiding judge must establish a process for consulting with the judges of the court and may call meetings of the judges as needed. The presiding judge may appoint standing and special committees of judges as needed to assist in the proper performance of the duties and functions of the court.

(8) *Liaison*

The presiding judge must:

(A) Provide for liaison between the court and the Judicial Council, the Administrative Office of the Courts, and other governmental and civic agencies;

(B) Meet with or designate a judge or judges to meet with any committee of the bench, bar, news media, or community to review problems and to promote understanding of the administration of justice, when appropriate; and

(C) Support and encourage the judges to actively engage in community outreach to increase public understanding of and involvement with the justice system and to obtain appropriate community input regarding the administration of justice, consistent with the California Code of Judicial Ethics and standard 10.5 of the Standards of Judicial Administration.

(9) *Planning*

The presiding judge must:

(A) Prepare, with the assistance of appropriate court committees and appropriate input from the community, a long-range strategic plan that is consistent with the plan and policies of the Judicial Council, for adoption in accordance with procedures established by local rules or policies; and

(B) Ensure that the court regularly and actively examines access issues, including any physical, language, or economic barriers that impede the fair administration of justice.

(10) *Appellate records*

The presiding judge is responsible for ensuring the timely preparation of records on appeal.

(A) The presiding judge ordinarily should delegate the following duties to the executive officer:

(i) Maintaining records of outstanding transcripts to be completed by each court reporter;

(ii) Reassigning court reporters as necessary to facilitate prompt completion of transcripts; and

(iii) Reviewing court reporters' requests for extensions of time to complete transcripts in appeals of criminal cases.

(B) After reasonable notice and hearing, the presiding judge must declare any reporter of the court who is delinquent in completing a transcript on appeal not competent to act as a reporter in court, under Government Code section 69944.

(11) *Local rules*

The presiding judge must prepare, with the assistance of appropriate court committees, proposed local rules to expedite and facilitate court business in accordance with Government Code section 68071 and rules 2.100, 3.20, and 10.613.

(Subd (c) amended effective January 1, 2007; previously amended effective January 1, 2001, January 1, 2002, January 1, 2006, and July 1, 2006.)

(d) Delegation

The presiding judge may delegate any of the specific duties listed in this rule to another judge or, if the duty does not require the exercise of judicial authority, to the court executive officer. The presiding judge remains responsible for all duties listed in this rule even if he or she has delegated particular tasks to someone else.

(Subd (d) amended effective January 1, 2007.)

Rule 10.603 amended and renumbered effective January 1, 2007; adopted as rule 6.603 effective January 1, 2001; previously amended effective January 1, 2002, January 1, 2006, and July 1, 2006.

Ref.: Cal. Fms Pl. & Pr., Ch. 317, "Judges," Ch. 551, "Trial."

Rule 10.605. Executive committee

In accordance with the internal policies of the court, an executive committee may be established by the court to advise the presiding judge or to establish policies and procedures for the internal management of the court. An executive committee may be appointed by the presiding judge to advise the presiding judge.

Rule 10.605 renumbered effective January 1, 2007; adopted rule 6.605 effective January 1, 2001.

Ref.: Cal. Fms Pl. & Pr., Ch. 317, "Judges."

Rule 10.608. Duties of all judges

Each judge must:

(1) Hear all assigned matters unless:

(A) He or she is disqualified; or

(B) He or she has stated in writing the reasons for refusing to hear a cause assigned for trial, and the presiding judge, supervising judge, or master calendar judge has concurred;

(2) Immediately notify the master calendar judge or the presiding judge on the completion or continuation of a trial or any other matter assigned for hearing;

(3) Request approval of the presiding judge for any intended absence of one-half day or more, within a reasonable time before the intended absence;

(4) Follow the court's personnel plan in dealing with employees; and

(5) Follow directives of the presiding judge in matters of court management and administration, as authorized by the rules of court and the local rules and internal policies of the court.

Rule 10.608 amended and renumbered effective January 1, 2007; adopted as rule 6.608 effective January 1, 2001; previously amended effective January 1, 2006.

Ref.: Cal. Fms Pl. & Pr., Ch. 317, "Judges," Ch. 551, "Trial."

Rule 10.610. Duties of court executive officer

(a) Selection

A court may employ an executive officer selected in accordance with procedures adopted by the court.

(b) General responsibilities

Acting under the direction of the presiding judge, the court executive officer is responsible for overseeing the management and administration of the nonjudicial operations of the court and allocating resources in a manner that promotes access to justice for all members of the public, provides a forum for the fair and expeditious resolution of disputes, maximizes the use of judicial and other resources, increases efficiency in court operations, and enhances service to the public.

(Subd (b) amended effective January 1, 2007.)

(c) Duties

Under the direction of the presiding judge and consistent with the law and rules of court, the court executive officer must perform the following duties, where they are not inconsistent with the authorized duties of the clerk of the court:

(1) *Personnel*

Provide general direction to and supervision of the employees of the court, and draft for court approval and administer a personnel plan for court employees that complies with rule 10.670. The court executive officer has the authority, consistent with the personnel plan, to hire, discipline, and terminate nonjudicial employees of the court.

(2) *Budget*

Make recommendations to the presiding judge on budget priorities; prepare and implement court budgets, including accounting, payroll, and financial controls; and employ sound budget and fiscal management practices and procedures to ensure that annual expenditures are within the court's budget.

(3) *Contracts*

Negotiate contracts on behalf of the court, in accordance with established contracting procedures and all applicable laws.

(4) *Calendar management*

Supervise and employ efficient calendar and case flow management systems, including analyzing and evaluating pending caseloads and recommending effective calendar management techniques.

(5) *Technology*

Analyze, evaluate, and implement technological and automated systems to assist the court.

(6) *Jury management*

Manage the jury system in the most efficient and effective way.

(7) *Facilities*

Plan physical space needs, and purchase and manage equipment and supplies.

(8) *Records*

Create and manage uniform record-keeping systems, collecting data on pending and completed judicial business and the internal operation of the court, as required by the court and the Judicial Council.

(9) *Recommendations*

Identify problems, recommending procedural and administrative changes to the court.

(10) *Public relations*

Provide a clearinghouse for news releases and other publications for the media and public.

(11) *Liaison*

Act as liaison to other governmental agencies.

(12) *Committees*

Provide staff for judicial committees.

(13) *Other*

Perform other duties as the presiding judge directs.

(Subd (c) amended effective January 1, 2007.)

Rule 10.610 amended and renumbered effective January 1, 2007; adopted as rule 6.610 effective January 1, 2001.

Ref.: Cal. Fms Pl. & Pr., Ch. 317, "Judges."

Rule 10.611. Nondiscrimination in court appointments

Each court should select attorneys, arbitrators, mediators, referees, masters, receivers, and other persons appointed by the court on the basis of merit. No court may discriminate in such selection on the basis of gender, race, ethnicity, disability, sexual orientation, or age.

Rule 10.611 amended and renumbered effective January 1, 2007; adopted as rule 989.2 effective January 1, 1999.

Ref.: Cal. Fms Pl. & Pr., Ch. 317, "Judges."

Rule 10.612. Use of gender-neutral language

Each court must use gender-neutral language in all new local rules, forms, and documents and must review and

revise those now in use to ensure that they are written in gender-neutral language.

Rule 10.612 adopted effective January 1, 2007.

Ref.: Cal. Fms Pl. & Pr., Ch. 317, "Judges."

Rule 10.613. Local court rules—adopting, filing, distributing, and maintaining

(a) Definitions

As used in this rule:

(1) "Court" means a trial court; and

(2) "Local rule" means every rule, regulation, order, policy, form, or standard of general application adopted by a court to govern practice or procedure in that court or by a judge of the court to govern practice or procedure in that judge's courtroom.

(Subd (a) amended and relettered effective July 1, 1999; adopted as subd (b) and repealed effective July 1, 1991.)

(b) Local inspection and copying of rules

Each court must make its local rules available for inspection and copying in every location of the court that generally accepts filing of papers. The court may impose a reasonable charge for copying the rules and may impose a reasonable page limit on copying. The rules must be accompanied by a notice indicating where a full set of the rules may be purchased or otherwise obtained.

(Subd (b) amended effective January 1, 2003; adopted as subd (c) effective July 1, 1991; previously relettered effective July 1, 1999.)

(c) Publication of rules

(1) Each court executive officer must be the official publisher of the court's local rules unless the court, by a majority vote of the judges, appoints another public agency or a private company.

(2) The official publisher must have the local rules reproduced and make copies available for distribution to attorneys and litigants.

(3) The court must adopt rules in sufficient time to permit reproduction of the rules by the official publisher before the effective date of the changes.

(4) The official publisher may charge a reasonable fee.

(5) Within 30 days of selecting an official publisher or changing an official publisher, each court must notify the Judicial Council of the name, address, and telephone number of the official publisher. Within 30 days of a change in the cost of the rules, each court must notify the Judicial Council of the charge for the local rules. This information will be published annually by the Judicial Council.

(Subd (c) amended effective January 1, 2003; adopted as subd (d) effective July 1, 1991; amended and relettered effective July 1, 1999.)

(d) Filing rules with the Judicial Council

(1) [1] **Forty-five** days before the effective date of January 1 or July 1, each court must file with the Judicial Council an electronic copy of rules and amendments to rules adopted by the court in a format authorized by the Judicial Council.

(2) The filing must be accompanied by a certificate from the presiding judge or court executive officer stating that:

(A) The court has complied with the applicable provisions of this rule;

(B) The court does or does not post local rules on the court's Web site; and

(C) The court does or does not provide assistance to members of the public in accessing the Internet or the court has delegated to and obtained the written consent of the county law librarian to provide public assistance under (e).

(3) Rules that do not comply with this rule will not be accepted for filing by the Judicial Council.

(Subd (d) amended effective January 1, 2009; adopted as subd (e) effective July 1, 1991; amended and relettered effective July 1, 1999; previously amended effective January 1, 2003, and January 1, 2007.)

Rule 10.613(d).   2008 Deletes. [1] Thirty

(e) Deposit and maintenance of rules statewide for public inspection

(1) The Judicial Council must publish a list of courts that have filed rules and amendments to rules with the Judicial Council. The Judicial Council must deposit a paper copy of each rule and amendment in the office of the executive officer of each superior court that does not provide assistance to members of the public in accessing the Internet or has not obtained agreement from the county law librarian to provide assistance under this subdivision.

(2) The executive officer must make a complete current set of local rules and amendments available for public examination either in paper copy or through the Internet with public assistance. In a county maintaining an organized county law library, if the executive officer is satisfied that the rules and amendments will be maintained as required by this paragraph, the executive officer, with the approval of the superior court and the written consent of the county law librarian, may delegate the authority to the county law librarian to either receive and maintain paper copies of the rules and amendments, or make the rules and amendments available through the Internet with assistance to members of the public.

(3) On or before January 1 of each year, the executive officer of each court must notify the Judicial Council of the street address and room number of the place where the rules are maintained under this subdivision.

(Subd (e) amended effective January 1, 2007; adopted as subd (f) effective July 1, 1991; amended and relettered effective July 1, 1999; previously amended effective January 1, 2003.)

(f) Format of rules

(1) *Paper and electronic copies*

Paper copies may be typewritten or printed or produced by other process of duplication at the option of the court. Electronic rules must be prepared in a format authorized by the Judicial Council. All copies must be clear and legible.

(2) *Format of paper copies*

Paper copies must conform, as far as is practicable, to the requirements of chapter 1 of division 2 of title 2, except that both sides of the paper may be used, lines need not be numbered and may be single spaced, and the pages must not be permanently bound across the top but may be bound at the left side. ("Permanently bound" does not include binding with staples.) The left margin on the front and the right margin on the reverse must be at least one inch. The name of the court must be at the top of each page. The effective date of each rule and amended rule must be stated in parentheses following the text of the rule.

(3) *New pages and filing instructions*

New pages must be issued for added, repealed, or amended rules, with a list of currently effective rules and the date of adoption or of the latest amendment to each rule. Filing instructions must accompany each set of replacement pages.

(4) *Table of contents*

The rules must have a table of contents. The rules must list all local forms and indicate whether their use is mandatory or optional. If the total length of the court rules exceeds five pages, the rules must have an alphabetical subject matter index at the end of the rules. All courts must use any subject matter index the Judicial Council may have specified.

(Subd (f) amended effective January 1, 2007; adopted as subd (g) effective July 1, 1991; amended and relettered effective July 1, 1999; previously amended effective January 1, 2003.)

(g) Comment period for proposed rules

(1) *Timing*

Except for rules specifying the time of hearing and similar calendaring matters, the court must distribute each proposed rule for comment at least 45 days before it is adopted.

(2) *Organizations*

A proposed rule must be distributed for comment to the following organizations in each county located within a 100-mile radius of the county seat of the county in which the court is located:

(A) Civil rules to the county bar association in each county, the nearest office of the State Attorney General, and the county counsel in each county;

(B) Criminal rules to the county bar association in each county, the nearest office of the State Attorney General, the district attorney in each county, and the public defender in each county; and

(C) On request, any bar organization, newspaper, or other interested party.

(3) *Methods*

A court may distribute a proposed rule for comment by either of the following methods:

(A) Distributing a copy of the proposal to every organization listed in (g)(2); or

(B) Posting the proposal on the court's Web site and distributing to every organization listed in (g)(2) a notice that the proposed rule has been posted for comment and that a hard copy of the proposal is available on request.

(Subd (g) amended effective January 1, 2007; adopted as subd (h) effective July 1, 1991; relettered effective July 1, 1999; previously amended effective January 1, 2003.)

(h) Periodic review

Each court must periodically review its local rules and repeal rules that have become outdated, unnecessary, or inconsistent with statewide rules or statutes.

(Subd (h) amended effective January 1, 2007; adopted as subd (g) effective July 1, 1991; relettered effective July 1, 1999; previously amended effective January 1, 2003.)

(i) Alternative effective date

A court may adopt a rule to take effect on a date other than as provided by Government Code section 68071 if:

(1) The presiding judge submits to the Judicial Council the proposed rule and a statement of reasons constituting good cause for making the rule effective on the stated date;

(2) The Chair of the Judicial Council authorizes the rule to take effect on the date proposed; and

(3) The rule is made available for inspection as provided in (b) on or before the effective date.

(Subd (i) amended effective January 1, 2007; adopted as subd (j) effective January 1, 1993; relettered effective July 1, 1999; previously amended effective July 1, 2001.)

(j) Limitation

Except for (i), this rule does not apply to local rules that relate only to the internal management of the court.

(Subd (j) amended effective January 1, 2007; adopted effective July 1, 1999; previously amended effective July 1, 2001.)

Rule 10.613 amended effective January 1, 2009; adopted as rule 981 effective July 1, 1991; previously amended effective January 1, 1993, July 1, 1999, July 1, 2001, and January 1, 2003; previously amended and renumbered effective January 1, 2007.

Ref.: Cal. Fms Pl. & Pr., Ch. 220, "Dissolution of Marriage: Master Procedural Guide," Ch. 317, "Judges," Ch. 425, "Pretrial Proceedings," Ch. 551, "Trial."

Rule 10.614. Local court forms

Local forms must comply with the following:

(1) Each form must be on paper measuring no more than 8½ by 11 inches and no less than 8½ by 5 inches.

(2) The court must make copies of its forms available in the clerk's office. A court may, as an alternative, make its forms available in a booklet from which photocopies of the forms may be made. The court may charge for either copies of forms or the booklet of forms.

(3) The court must assign to each form a unique designator consisting of numbers or letters, or both. The designator must be positioned on the form in the same manner as the designator on a Judicial Council form.

(4) The effective date of each form must be placed on the form in the same manner as the effective date on a Judicial Council form, and each form must state whether it is a "Mandatory Form" or an "Optional Form" in the lower left corner of the first page.

(5) Each court must make available a current list of forms adopted or approved by that court. The list must include, for each form, its name, number, effective date, and whether the form is mandatory or optional. There must be two versions of the list, one organized by form number and one organized by form name. The court must modify its lists whenever it adopts, approves, revises, or repeals any form.

(6) Each form must be designed so that no typing is required on it within 1 inch of the top or within ½ inch of the bottom.

(7) All forms and copies of forms made available by, or presented for filing to, the court must be reproduced on recycled paper as defined in rule 2.102(2).

(8) All forms presented for filing must be firmly bound at the top and must contain two prepunched, normal-sized holes centered 2½ inches apart and ⅝ inch from the top of the form.

(9) If a form is longer than one page, the form may be filed on sheets printed on only one side even if the original form has two printed sides to a sheet. If a form is filed on a sheet printed on two sides, the reverse side must be rotated 180 degrees (printed head to foot).

Rule 10.614 amended and renumbered effective January 1, 2007; adopted as rule 201.3 effective January 1, 2003.

Ref.: Cal. Fms Pl. & Pr., Ch. 317, "Judges."

Rule 10.620. Public access to administrative decisions of trial courts

(a) Interpretation

The provisions of this rule concern public access to administrative decisions by trial courts as provided in this rule. This rule does not modify existing law regarding public access to the judicial deliberative process and does not apply to the adjudicative functions of the trial courts or the assignment of judges.

(b) Budget priorities

The Administrative Office of the Courts may request, on 30 court days' notice, recommendations from the trial courts concerning judicial branch budget priorities. The notice must state that if a trial court is to make recommendations, the trial court must also give notice, as provided in (g), that interested members of the public may send input to the Administrative Office of the Courts.

(Subd (b) amended effective January 1, 2007; previously amended effective January 1, 2005.)

(c) Budget requests

Before making recommendations, if any, to the Judicial Council on items to be included in the judicial branch budget that is submitted annually to the Governor and the Legislature, a trial court must seek input from the public, as provided in (e), on what should be included in the recommendations.

(Subd (c) amended effective January 1, 2007.)

(d) Other decisions requiring public input

Each trial court must seek input from the public, as provided in (e), before making the following decisions:

(1) A request for permission from the Administrative Office of the Courts to reallocate budget funds from one program component to another in an amount greater than $400,000 or 10 percent of the total trial court budget, whichever is greater.

(2) The execution of a contract without competitive bidding in an amount greater than $400,000 or 10 percent of the total trial court budget, whichever is greater. This subdivision does not apply to a contract entered into between a court and a county that is provided for by statute.

(3) The planned, permanent closure of any court location for an entire day or for more than one-third of the hours the court location was previously open for either court sessions or filing of papers. As used in this subdivision, planned closure does not include closure of a location on a temporary basis for reasons including holidays, illness, or other unforeseen lack of personnel, or public safety.

(4) The cessation of any of the following services at a court location:

(A) The Family Law Facilitator; or

(B) The Family Law Information Center.

(Subd (d) amended effective January 1, 2007.)

(e) Manner of seeking public input

When a trial court is required to seek public input under this rule, it must provide public notice of the request at least 15 court days before the date on which the decision is to be made or the action is to be taken. Notice must be given as provided in (g). Any interested person or entity who wishes to comment must send the comment to the court in writing or electronically unless the court requires that all public comment be sent either by e-mail or through a response system on the court's Web site. For good cause, in the event an urgent action is required, a trial court may take immediate action if it (1) gives notice of the action as provided in (f), (2) states the reasons for urgency, and (3) gives any public input received to the person or entity making the decision.

(Subd (e) amended effective January 1, 2007.)

(f) Information about other trial court administrative matters

A trial court must provide notice, not later than 15 court days after the event, of the following:

(1) Receipt of the annual allocation of the trial court budget from the Judicial Council after enactment of the Budget Act.

(2) The awarding of a grant to the trial court that exceeds the greater of $400,000 or 10 percent of the total trial court budget.

(3) The solicitation of proposals or the execution of a contract that exceeds the greater of $400,000 or 10 percent of the trial court budget.

(4) A significant permanent increase in the number of hours that a court location is open during any day for either court sessions or filing of papers. As used in this paragraph, a significant increase does not include an emergency or one-time need to increase hours.

(5) A significant permanent decrease in the number of hours that a court location is open during any day for either court sessions or filing of papers, except those governed by (d)(3). As used in this paragraph, a significant decrease does not include a decrease in response to an emergency need to close a location on a temporary basis for reasons including illness or other unforeseen lack of personnel or public safety.

(6) The action taken on any item for which input from the public was required under (d). The notice must show the person or persons who made the decision and a summary of the written and e-mail input received.

(Subd (f) amended effective January 1, 2007.)

(g) Notice

When notice is required to be given by this rule, it must be given in the following ways:

(1) Posted on the trial court's Web site, if any.

(2) Sent to any of the following persons or entities— subject to the requirements of (h)—who have requested in writing or by electronic mail to the court executive officer to receive such notice:

(A) A newspaper, radio station, and television station in the county;

(B) The president of a local or specialty bar association in the county;

(C) Representatives of a trial court employees organization;

(D) The district attorney, public defender, and county counsel;

(E) The county administrative officer; and

(F) If the court is sending notice electronically using the provisions of (h), any other person or entity that submits an electronic mail address to which the notice will be sent.

(3) Posted at all locations of the court that accept papers for filing.

(Subd (g) amended effective January 1, 2007.)

(h) Electronic notice

A trial court may require a person or entity that is otherwise entitled to receive notice under (g)(2) to submit an electronic mail address to which the notice will be sent.

(Subd (h) amended effective January 1, 2007.)

(i) Materials

When a trial court is required to seek public input under (b), (c), or (d), it must also provide for public viewing at one or more locations in the county of any written factual materials that have been specifically gathered or prepared for the review at the time of making the decision of the person or entity making the decision. This subdivision does not require the disclosure of materials that are otherwise exempt from disclosure or would be exempt from disclosure under the state Public Records Act (beginning with Government Code section 6250). The materials must be mailed or otherwise be made available not less than five court days before the decision is to be made except if the request is made within the five court days before the decision is to be made, the materials must be mailed or otherwise be made available the next court day after the request is made. A court must either (1) provide copies to a person or entity that requests copies of these materials in writing or by electronic mail to the executive officer of the court or other person designated by the executive office in the notice, if the requesting person or entity pays all mailing and copying costs as determined by any mailing and copy cost recovery policies established by the trial court, or (2) make all materials available electronically either on its Web site or by e-mail. This subdivision does not require the trial court to prepare reports. A person seeking documents may request the court to hold the material for pickup by that person instead of mailing.

(Subd (i) amended effective January 1, 2007.)

(j) Other requirements

This rule does not affect any other obligations of the trial court including any obligation to meet and confer with designated employee representatives. This rule does not change the procedures a court must otherwise follow in entering into a contract or change the types of matters for which a court may contract.

(Subd (j) amended effective January 1, 2007.)

(k) Enforcement

This rule may be enforced under Code of Civil Procedure section 1085.

Rule 10.620 amended and renumbered effective January 1, 2007; adopted as rule 6.620 effective January 1, 2004; previously amended effective January 1, 2005.

Ref.: Cal. Fms Pl. & Pr., Ch. 317, "Judges."

Rule 10.625. Certain demographic data relating to regular grand jurors

(a) Definitions

The following definitions apply under this rule:

(1) "Regular grand jury" means a body of citizens of a county selected by the court to investigate matters of civil concern in the county, whether or not that body has jurisdiction to return indictments.

(2) "Race or ethnicity" reflects the concept of race used by the United States Census Bureau and reflects self-identification by people according to the race or races with which they most closely identify. These categories are sociopolitical constructs and should not be interpreted as being scientific or anthropological in nature. The categories include both racial and national-origin groups.

(3) "Prospective regular grand juror" means those citizens who (a) respond in person to the jury summonses or questionnaires from the court for the purposes of grand jury service and are eligible to serve as regular grand jurors, or (b) either submit applications, are recruited, or are nominated by judicial officers and are eligible to serve as regular grand jurors.

(4) "Eligible to serve" means that the prospective regular grand juror meets each of the criteria set forth in Penal Code section 893(a) and is not disqualified by any factor set forth in section 893(b).

(Subd (a) adopted effective January 1, 2007.)

(b) Jury commissioner duties and responsibilities

(1) The jury commissioner or designee must create a method to capture the following data from prospective regular grand jurors:

(A) Age range, specifically:

(i) 18–25

(ii) 26–34

(iii) 35–44

(iv) 45–54

(v) 55–64

(vi) 65–74

(vii) 75 and over

(B) Gender; and

(C) Race or ethnicity from the following categories (candidates may select more than one category):

(i) American Indian or Alaska Native

(ii) Asian

(iii) Black or African American

(iv) Hispanic/Latino

(v) Native Hawaiian or other Pacific Islander

(vi) White

(vii) Other race or ethnicity (please state: _____)

(viii) Decline to answer

(2) Develop and maintain a database containing the following information regarding prospective regular grand jurors, the candidates who are ultimately selected by the court to serve as grand jurors, and any carry-over grand jurors: name, age range, occupation, gender, race or ethnicity, and the year(s) served on the regular grand jury. The database should indicate how the juror initially became a candidate (by random draw, application, or nomination).

(Subd (b) adopted effective January 1, 2007.)

(c) Annual summary

(1) The court must develop and maintain an annual summary of the information in the database maintained under (b)(2). The summary must not include the names of the candidates and must be made available to the public.

(Subd (c) adopted effective January 1, 2007.)
Rule 10.625 adopted effective January 1, 2007.

Advisory Committee Comment

This rule is intended to facilitate the courts' continued efforts to achieve the goals stated in standard 10.50 [formerly section 17] of the Standards of Judicial Administration, which encourages courts to employ various methods of soliciting prospective candidates to serve on regular grand juries that reflect a representative cross-section of the community they serve. Those methods include obtaining recommendations for grand jurors who encompass a cross-section of the county's population base, solicited from a broad representation of community-based organizations, civic leaders, and superior court judges, referees, and commissioners subdivision (b)(2)); having the court consider carry-over grand jury selections under Penal Code section 901(b) to ensure broad-based representation (Subd (c)); and encouraging judges who nominate persons for grand jury service under Penal Code section 903.4 to select candidates from the list returned by the jury commissioner or otherwise employing a nomination procedure to ensure broad-based representation from the community.

This rule is also intended to assist the courts in establishing a formal mechanism whereby they can monitor the extent to which they achieve the goal of seating representative regular grand juries through a process comparable to that stated in Penal Code section 904.6(e), which requires that persons selected for the "criminal grand jury shall be selected at random from a source or sources reasonably representative of a cross section of the population which is eligible for jury service in the county."

Rule 10.630. Reporting of reciprocal assignment orders

A "reciprocal assignment order" is an order issued by the Chief Justice that permits judges in courts of different counties to serve in each other's courts. A court must report to the Administrative Office of the Courts, on a monthly basis, each assignment of a judge from another county to its court under a reciprocal assignment order.
Rule 10.630 amended and renumbered effective January 1, 2007; adopted as rule 813 effective July 1, 1990.

Ref.: Cal. Fms Pl. & Pr., Ch. 317, "Judges."

Chapter 2
Trial Court Management of Human Resources

Art. 1.   Trial Court Employee Labor Relations. Rules 10.650–10.660.

Art. 2.   Other Human Resources Rules. Rule 10.670.

Article 1
Trial Court Employee Labor Relations

Rule 10.650. Court Employee Labor Relations Rules
Rule 10.651. Purpose
Rule 10.652. Definitions
Rule 10.653. Right and obligation to meet and confer
Rule 10.654. Scope of representation
Rule 10.655. Governing court employee labor relations
Rule 10.656. Transition provisions
Rule 10.657. Construction
Rule 10.658. Interpretation
Rule 10.659. Other provisions
Rule 10.660. Enforcement of agreements—petitions (Gov. Code, §§ 71639.5, 71825.2)

Rule 10.650.   Court Employee Labor Relations Rules

Rules 10.651–10.659 in this chapter are referred to as the Court Employee Labor Relations Rules.

Rule 10.650 adopted effective January 1, 2007.

Ref.: Cal. Fms Pl. & Pr., Ch. 317, "Judges."

Rule 10.651.   Purpose

The purpose of the Court Employee Labor Relations Rules is to extend to trial court employees the right, and to require trial courts, to meet and confer in good faith over matters that the court, as opposed to the county, has authority to determine that are within the scope of representation, consistent with the procedures stated in this division.

The adoption of the Court Employee Labor Relations Rules is not intended to require changes in existing representation units, memoranda of agreements, statutes, or court rules relating to trial court employees, except as they would otherwise normally occur as provided for in this division.

Rule 10.651 amended and renumbered effective January 1, 2007; adopted as rule 2201 effective January 1, 1998, the effective date of Stats. 1997, ch. 850.

Ref.: Cal. Fms Pl. & Pr., Ch. 317, "Judges."

Rule 10.652.   Definitions

As used in the Court Employee Labor Relations Rules:

(1) "Court" means a superior court.

(2) "Court employee" means any employee of a court, except those employees whose job classification confers safety retirement status.

(3) "Meet and confer in good faith" means that a court or such representatives as it may designate, and representatives of recognized employee organizations, have the mutual obligation personally to meet and confer promptly on request by either party and to continue for a reasonable period of time in order to exchange freely information, opinions, and proposals, and to endeavor to reach agreement on matters within the scope of representation. The process should include adequate time for the resolution of impasses where specific procedures for such resolution are contained in this division or a local rule, regulation, or ordinance, or when such procedures are used by mutual consent.

(4) "Recognized employee organization" means an employee organization that has been formally acknowledged by the county to represent court employees under the provisions of Government Code sections 3500–3510 or by the court under its rules or policies.

Rule 10.652 amended and renumbered effective January 1, 2007; adopted as rule 2202 effective January 1, 1998, the effective date of Stats. 1997, ch. 850.

Rule 10.653.   Right and obligation to meet and confer

(a) Recognized employee organization

A recognized employee organization has the right to represent its court employee members in their employment relations with a court as to matters covered by the Court Employee Labor Relations Rules. Nothing in these rules prohibits any court employee from appearing in his or her own behalf regarding employment relations with a court.

(Subd (a) amended effective January 1, 2007.)

(b) Representatives of a court

Representatives of a court must meet and confer in good faith regarding matters within the scope of representation, as defined in the Court Employee Labor Relations Rules, with representatives of a recognized employee organization, and must consider fully such presentations as are made by the recognized employee organization on behalf of its members before arriving at a determination of policy or course of action. In meeting this obligation a court must also comply with the procedures and provisions stated in Government Code sections 3504.5, 3505.1, 3505.2, and 3505.3 applicable to a public agency.

(Subd (b) amended effective January 1, 2007.)

(c) Joint negotiations and designations

In fulfilling the provisions of (b), the court and the county must consult with each other, may negotiate jointly, and each may designate the other in writing as its agent on any matters within the scope of representation.

(Subd (c) amended effective January 1, 2007.)

(d) Intimidation

A court or a recognized employee organization must not interfere with, intimidate, restrain, coerce, or discriminate against court employees because of their exercise of any rights they may have under the Court Employee Labor Relations Rules or Government Code sections 3500–3510.

(Subd (d) amended effective January 1, 2007.)

Rule 10.653 amended and renumbered effective January 1, 2007; adopted as rule 2203 effective January 1, 1998, the effective date of Stats. 1997, ch. 850.

Ref.: Cal. Fms Pl. & Pr., Ch. 317, "Judges."

Rule 10.654.   Scope of representation

(a) Matters included in the scope of representation

For purposes of the Court Employee Labor Relations Rules, the scope of representation includes all matters within the court's authority to determine relating to employment conditions and employer-employee relations, including, but not limited to, wages, hours, and terms and other conditions of employment, except, however, that the scope of representation does not include consideration of the merits, necessity, or organization of any service or activity provided by law or executive order.

(Subd (a) amended effective January 1, 2007.)

(b) Matters outside the scope of representation

In view of the unique and special responsibilities of the courts in the administration of justice, decisions regarding the following matters are not included within the scope of representation:

(1) The merits and administration of the court system;

(2) Coordination, consolidation, and merger of trial courts and support staff;

(3) Automation, including but not limited to fax filing, electronic recording, and implementation of information systems;

(4) Design, construction, and location of court facilities;

(5) Delivery of court services; and

(6) Hours of operation of the courts and court system.

(Subd (b) amended effective January 1, 2007.)

(c) Impact

Impact from such matters as in (b) must be included within the scope of representation as those matters affect wages, hours, terms, and conditions of employment of court employees, to the extent such matters are within the court's authority to determine.

(Subd (c) amended effective January 1, 2007.)

(d) Assignments and transfers

The superior court continues to have the right to determine assignments and transfers of court employees, provided that the process, procedures, and criteria for assignments and transfers are included within the scope of representation.

(Subd (d) amended effective January 1, 2007.)

Rule 10.654 amended and renumbered effective January 1, 2007; adopted as rule 2204 effective January 1, 1998, the effective date of Stats. 1997, ch. 850.

Rule 10.655. Governing court employee labor relations

(a) County rules and procedures

As they relate to court employees in their relations with the court, matters described in Government Code section 3507(a) through (d) are governed by any rules and administrative procedures and provisions adopted by the county under section 3507 that may apply to county employees generally, with the right of review by the appropriate Court of Appeal.

(Subd (a) amended effective January 1, 2007.)

(b) Court rules and policies

A court may adopt reasonable rules and policies after consultation in good faith with representatives of a recognized employee organization or organizations for the administration of employer-employee relations under this rule as to matters described in Government Code section 3507(e)–(i). The court and county jointly will establish procedures to determine the appropriateness of any bargaining unit of court employees. The court must consult with the county about any rules and policies that the court may adopt under this section. If the court does not adopt rules by January 1, 1998, the court is bound by existing county rules until the court adopts rules.

(Subd (b) amended effective January 1, 2007.)

Rule 10.655 amended and renumbered effective January 1, 2007; adopted as rule 2205 effective January 1, 1998, the effective date of Stats. 1997, ch. 850.

Ref.: W. Cal. Sum., 3 "Agency and Employment" §585.

Rule 10.656. Transition provisions

(a) Court employee organization

On the effective date of the Court Employee Labor Relations Rules, the court must recognize the employee organization that represented its court employees at the time of adoption. The court and the recognized employee organization are bound by the terms of any memorandum of understanding or agreement to which the court is a party that is in effect as of the date of adoption of the Court Employee Labor Relations Rules for its duration, or until it expires or, before then, is replaced by a subsequent memorandum of understanding.

(Subd (a) amended effective January 1, 2007.)

(b) Court personnel rules and policies

A court's local rules governing court employees and a court's personnel rules, policies, and practices in effect at the time of the adoption of the Court Employee Labor

Relations Rules, to the extent they are not contrary to or inconsistent with the obligations and duties provided for in these rules, continue in effect until changed by the court. Before changing any rule, policy, or practice that affects any matter within the scope of representation as stated in these rules, the court must meet and confer in good faith with the recognized employee organization as provided for in these rules.

(Subd (b) amended effective January 1, 2007.)

(c) County employee representation units

Nothing contained in these rules is intended to preclude court employees from continuing to be included in representation units that contain county employees.

(Subd (c) amended effective January 1, 2007.)

Rule 10.656 amended and renumbered effective January 1, 2007; adopted as rule 2206 effective January 1, 1998, the effective date of Stats. 1997, ch. 850.

Rule 10.657. Construction

The enactment of the Court Employee Labor Relations Rules is not to be construed as making the provisions of Labor Code section 923 applicable to court employees.

Rule 10.657 amended and renumbered effective January 1, 2007; adopted as rule 2207 effective January 1, 1998, the effective date of Stats. 1997, ch. 850.

Rule 10.658. Interpretation

Where the language of the Court Employee Labor Relations Rules is the same or substantially the same as that contained in Government Code sections 3500 to 3510, it must be interpreted and applied in accordance with judicial interpretations of the same language.

Rule 10.658 amended and renumbered effective January 1, 2007; adopted as rule 2208 effective January 1, 1998, the effective date of Stats. 1997, ch. 850.

Rule 10.659. Other provisions

(a) Mediation

If, after a reasonable period of time, representatives of the court and the recognized employee organization fail to reach agreement, the court and the recognized employee organization or recognized employee organizations together may agree on the appointment of a mediator mutually agreeable to the parties. Costs of mediation are to be divided one-half to the court and one-half to the recognized employee organization or recognized employee organizations.

(Subd (a) amended effective January 1, 2007.)

(b) Submission for dispute resolution

In the absence of local procedures and provisions for resolving disputes on the appropriateness of a unit of representation, on the request of any of the parties, the dispute must be submitted to the Division of Conciliation of the Department of Industrial Relations for mediation or for recommendation for resolving the dispute.

(Subd (b) amended effective January 1, 2007.)

(c) Dues deduction

Nothing in the Court Employee Labor Relations Rules affects the right of a court employee to authorize a dues deduction from his or her salary or wages under Government Code sections 1157.1, 1157.2, 1157.3, 1157.4, 1157.5, or 1157.7.

(Subd (c) amended effective January 1, 2007.)

(d) Applicability of Government Code section 3502.5

The procedures and provisions stated in Government Code section 3502.5 are applicable to court employees.

(Subd (d) amended effective January 1, 2007.)

Rule 10.659 amended and renumbered effective January 1, 2007; adopted as rule 2209 effective January 1, 1998, the effective date of Stats. 1997, ch. 850.

Rule 10.660. Enforcement of agreements—petitions (Gov. Code, §§ 71639.5, 71825.2)

(a) Application

This rule applies to petitions filed under Government Code sections [1] **71639.5 and 71825.2.**

(Subd (a) amended effective October 24, 2008; previously amended effective December 10, 2004, and January 1, 2007.)

Rule 10.660(a). 2008 Deletes. [1] 71639.5(a) and 71825.2(a)

(b) Assignment of Court of Appeal justice to hear the petition

(1) The petition must state the following on the first page, below the case number, in the statement of the character of the proceeding (see rule 2.111(6)): "Petition filed under Government Code sections 71639.5 and 71825.2—Assignment of Court of Appeal justice required."

(2) When the petition is filed, the clerk of the court must immediately request of the Judicial Assignments Unit of the Administrative Office of the Courts the assignment of a hearing judge from the panel established under (e).

(3) The judge assigned to hear the petition in the superior court must be a justice from a Court of Appeal for a district other than the district for that superior court.

(Subd (b) amended effective January 1, 2007; previously amended effective December 10, 2004.)

(c) Superior court hearing

(1) The superior court must hear and decide the petition on an expedited basis and must give the petition priority over other matters to the extent permitted by law and the rules of court.

(2) The petition must be heard by a judge assigned by the Chief Justice from the panel of hearing judges established under (e).

(Subd (c) amended effective January 1, 2007.)

(d) Appeal

An appeal of the superior court decision must be heard and decided on an expedited basis in the Court of Appeal for the district in which the petition was heard and must be given priority over other matters to the extent permitted by law and the rules of court. The notice of appeal must state the following on the first page, below the case number, in the statement of the character of the proceeding (see rule 2.111(6)): "Notice of Appeal on Petition filed under Government Code sections 71639.5 and 71825.2—Expedited Processing Requested."

(Subd (d) amended effective January 1, 2007; previously amended effective December 10, 2004.)

(e) Panel of hearing judges

The panel of judges who may hear the petitions in the superior court must consist of Court of Appeal justices selected by the Chief Justice as follows:

(1) The panel must include at least one justice from each district of the Court of Appeal.

(2) Each justice assigned to hear a petition under (c)(2) must have received training on hearing the petitions as specified by the Chief Justice.

Rule 10.660 amended effective October 24, 2008; adopted as rule 2211 effective January 1, 2001; previously amended effective December 10, 2004; previously amended and renumbered effective January 1, 2007.

Article 2
Other Human Resources Rules

Rule 10.670. Trial court personnel plans

(a) Purpose

This rule establishes the authority and responsibility of the superior courts, on a countywide basis, to create and implement a system of personnel management designed to achieve lawful, uniform, and fair employment practices and procedures.

(Subd (a) amended effective January 1, 2007.)

(b) Countywide personnel plans

The superior court of each county must establish a single personnel plan on a countywide basis, consistent with applicable statutes, rules, and standards of judicial administration.

(Subd (b) amended effective January 1, 2007.)

(c) Provisions of a personnel plan

The personnel plan must ensure that treatment of employees complies with current law. The personnel plan should address the following issues:

(1) A salary-setting procedure;

(2) Regular review of job classifications and titles;

(3) An equal employment opportunity policy applying to all employees in accordance with applicable state and federal law;

(4) Recruitment, selection, and promotion policies;

(5) A sexual harassment prevention policy;

(6) A reasonable accommodation policy;

(7) Grievance or complaint procedures covering, but not limited to, sexual harassment, discrimination, and denial of reasonable accommodation;

(8) An employee benefits plan that includes health benefits, retirement benefits, workers' compensation benefits, disability leave, and paid and unpaid leave in compliance with state and federal law;

(9) Timekeeping and payroll policies and procedures that comply with applicable state and federal law;

(10) A records management policy, including confidentiality and retention of personnel records;

(11) Job-related training and continuing education programs for all personnel concerning at least the following:

(A) Sexual harassment awareness;

(B) Discrimination and bias; and

(C) Safety;

(12) A policy statement on professional behavior requiring that all employees conduct themselves in a professional manner at all times and refrain from offensive conduct or comments that reflect bias or harassment;

(13) A policy regarding conflicts of interest and incompatible activities;

(14) Procedures for discipline and discharge; and

(15) A labor policy consistent with rules 10.653–10.659.

(Subd (c) amended effective January 1, 2007.)

(d) Optional provisions

A personnel plan may contain additional provisions, including the following:

(1) Criteria and schedules for performance evaluations for all levels of employees;

(2) Job-related training and continuing education programs for all personnel as appropriate, with provisions for both paid and unpaid educational leave concerning:

(A) Career development, including basic and managerial skills; and

(B) Equal employment opportunity concepts and recruitment methods.

(3) An employee benefit plan that may include:

(A) Flex-time, part-time, job-sharing, and other alternative work schedules;

(B) Cafeteria options to use pretax dollars for dependent care and medical care and for sick leave for the care of dependents;

(C) An employee assistance program; and

(D) A deferred compensation plan.

(Subd (d) amended effective January 1, 2007.)

(e) Submission of personnel plans

The superior court of each county must submit to the Judicial Council a personnel plan in compliance with these provisions by March 1, 1999. The superior court of each county must submit to the Judicial Council any changes to this plan by March 1 of every following year. If requested by a superior court, the Administrative Office of the Courts must review the court's personnel plan and provide the court with technical assistance in preparing the plan.

(Subd (e) amended effective January 1, 2007.)

Rule 10.670 amended and renumbered effective January 1, 2007; adopted as rule 2520 effective July 1, 1998; previously renumbered as rule 6.650 effective January 1, 1999.

Ref.: Cal. Fms Pl. & Pr., Ch. 317, "Judges."

Chapter 3
Subordinate Judicial Officers

Rule 10.700. Role of subordinate judicial officers
Rule 10.701. Qualifications and education of subordinate judicial officers
Rule 10.702. Subordinate judicial officers: practice of law
Rule 10.703. Complaints against subordinate judicial officers

Rule 10.700. Role of subordinate judicial officers

(a) Application

This rule applies to all subordinate judicial officers except those acting as child support commissioners under Family Code section 4251.

(b) Role of subordinate judicial officers

The primary role of subordinate judicial officers is to perform subordinate judicial duties. However, a presiding judge may assign a subordinate judicial officer to sit as a temporary judge where lawful, if the presiding judge

determines that, because of a shortage of judges, it is necessary for the effective administration of justice.

Rule 10.700 renumbered effective January 1, 2007; adopted as rule 6.609 effective July 1, 2002.

Ref.: Cal. Fms Pl. & Pr., Ch. 317, "Judges."

Rule 10.701. Qualifications and education of subordinate judicial officers

(a) Definition

For purposes of this rule, "subordinate judicial officer" means a person appointed by a court to perform subordinate judicial duties as authorized by article VI, section 22 of the California Constitution, including a commissioner, a referee, and a hearing officer.

(Subd (a) amended effective January 1, 2007.)

(b) Qualifications

Except as provided in (d), a person is ineligible to be a subordinate judicial officer unless the person is a member of the State Bar and:

(1) Has been admitted to practice law in California for at least 10 years or, on a finding of good cause by the presiding judge, for at least 5 years; or

(2) Is serving as a subordinate judicial officer in a trial court as of January 1, 2003.

(Subd (b) amended effective January 1, 2007.)

(c) Education

A subordinate judicial officer must comply with the education requirements of any position to which he or she is assigned, even if it is not his or her principal assignment. Such requirements include the following, as applicable: rules 5.30, 5.340, and 10.501 of the California Rules of Court, and Welfare and Institutions Code section 304.7.

(Subd (c) amended effective January 1, 2007.)

(d) Juvenile referees and hearing officers

A person appointed as a juvenile referee or as a hearing officer under Welfare and Institutions Code sections [1] 255 or 5256.1 must meet the qualification requirements established by those sections. Such a person is ineligible to exercise the powers and perform the duties of another type of subordinate judicial officer unless he or she meets the qualifications established in (b).

(Subd (d) amended effective July 1, 2008; previously amended effective January 1, 2007.)

Rule 10.701(d). 2008 Deletes. [1] 247, 255,

Rule 10.701 amended effective July 1, 2008; adopted as rule 6.660 effective January 1, 2003; previously amended and renumbered effective January 1, 2007.

Ref.: Cal. Fms Pl. & Pr., Ch. 317, "Judges."

Rule 10.702. Subordinate judicial officers: practice of law

A subordinate judicial officer may practice law only to the extent permitted by the Code of Judicial Ethics.

Rule 10.702 renumbered effective January 1, 2007; adopted as rule 6.665 effective January 1, 2003.

Ref.: Cal. Fms Pl. & Pr., Ch. 317, "Judges."

Rule 10.703. Complaints against subordinate judicial officers

(a) Intent

The procedures in this rule for processing complaints against subordinate judicial officers do not:

(1) Create a contract of employment;

(2) Change the existing employee-employer relationship between the subordinate judicial officer and the court; or

(3) Change the status of a subordinate judicial officer from an employee terminable at will to an employee terminable only for cause.

(Subd (a) amended effective January 1, 2007.)

(b) Definitions

Unless the context requires otherwise, the following definitions apply to this rule:

(1) "Subordinate judicial officer" means an attorney employed by a court to serve as a commissioner or referee, whether the attorney is acting as a commissioner, referee, or temporary judge. The term does not include any other attorney acting as a temporary judge.

(2) "Presiding judge" includes the person or group the presiding judge designates to perform any duty required by this rule to be performed by a presiding judge.

(3) "Commission" means the Commission on Judicial Performance. The commission exercises discretionary jurisdiction over the discipline of subordinate judicial officers under article VI, section 18.1 of the California Constitution.

(c) Application

(1) A court that employs a subordinate judicial officer must use the procedures in this rule for processing complaints against the subordinate judicial officer if the complaint alleges conduct that if alleged against a judge would be within the jurisdiction of the commission under article VI, section 18 of the California Constitution.

(2) If a complaint against a subordinate judicial officer does not allege conduct that would be within the jurisdiction of the commission, the court must process the complaint following local procedures adopted under rule 10.603(c)(4)(C). The local process may include any procedures from this rule for the court's adjudication of the complaint other than the provisions for referring the matter to the commission under (g) or giving notice of commission review under (*l*)(2)(B).

(3) A court may adopt additional policies and procedures for the adjudication of complaints against subordinate judicial officers not inconsistent with this rule.

(Subd (c) amended effective January 1, 2007; previously amended effective July 1, 2002.)

(d) Promptness required

The presiding judge must ensure that the court processes each complaint promptly. To the extent reasonably possible, the court must complete action on each complaint within 90 days after the complaint is submitted.

(Subd (d) amended effective January 1, 2007.)

(e) Confidentiality

(1) All proceedings by a presiding judge under this rule must be conducted in a manner that is as confidential as is reasonably possible consistent with the need to conduct a thorough and complete investigation and the need for proper administration of the court.

(2) This rule does not prohibit access by the commission to any information relevant to the investigation of a complaint against a subordinate judicial officer.

(Subd (e) amended effective January 1, 2007.)

(f) Written complaints to presiding judge

(1) A complaint about the conduct of a subordinate judicial officer must be in writing and be submitted to the presiding judge.

(2) Persons who are unable to file a written complaint because of a disability may present an oral complaint, which the presiding judge must commit to writing.

(3) The presiding judge must give written notice of receipt of the complaint to the complainant.

(Subd (f) amended effective January 1, 2007.)

(g) Initial review of the complaint

(1) The presiding judge must review each complaint and determine if the complaint:

(A) May be closed after initial review;

(B) Needs preliminary investigation; or

(C) Requires formal investigation.

(2) A presiding judge may request that the commission investigate and adjudicate the complaint if a local conflict of interest or disqualification prevents the court from acting on the complaint.

(3) In exceptional circumstances a presiding judge may request the commission to investigate a complaint on behalf of the court and provide the results of the investigation to the court for action.

(4) The court must maintain a file on every complaint received, containing the following:

(A) The complaint;

(B) The response of the subordinate judicial officer, if any;

(C) All evidence and reports produced by the investigation of the complaint, if any; and

(D) The final action taken on the complaint.

(Subd (g) amended effective January 1, 2007.)

(h) Closing a complaint after initial review

(1) After a preliminary review the presiding judge may close without further action any complaint that:

(A) Relates to the permissible exercise of judicial or administrative discretion by the subordinate judicial officer; or

(B) Does not allege conduct that if alleged against a judge would be within the jurisdiction of the commission under article VI, section 18 of the California Constitution.

(2) The presiding judge must notify the complainant in writing of the decision to close the investigation on the complaint. The notice must include the information required under (*l*).

(3) The presiding judge must advise the subordinate judicial officer in writing of the disposition.

(Subd (h) amended effective January 1, 2007.)

(i) Complaints requiring preliminary investigation

(1) If after an initial review of the complaint the presiding judge finds a basis for further inquiry, the presiding judge must conduct a preliminary investigation appropriate to the nature of the complaint.

(2) The investigation may include interviews of witnesses and a review of court records.

(3) The presiding judge may give the subordinate judicial officer a copy of the complaint or a summary of its allegations and allow him or her an opportunity to respond. The presiding judge must give the subordinate

judicial officer a copy of the complaint or a summary of its allegations and allow the subordinate judicial officer an opportunity to respond before the presiding judge takes appropriate informal action as described in (i)(4)(B).

(4) After completing the preliminary investigation, the presiding judge must:

(A) Terminate the investigation and close action on the complaint if the presiding judge finds the complaint lacks merit; or

(B) Terminate the investigation and close action on the complaint by taking appropriate informal action, which may include a reprimand or warning to the subordinate judicial officer, if the presiding judge finds a basis for taking informal action; or

(C) Proceed with a formal investigation under (j) if the presiding judge finds a basis for proceeding further.

(5) If the presiding judge terminates the investigation and closes action on the complaint, the presiding judge must:

(A) Notify the complainant in writing of the decision to close the investigation on the complaint. The notice must include the information required under (l); and

(B) Advise the subordinate judicial officer in writing of the disposition.

(Subd (i) amended effective January 1, 2007; previously amended effective January 1, 2006.)

(j) Complaints requiring formal investigation

(1) If after a preliminary investigation the presiding judge finds a basis for proceeding with the investigation, the presiding judge must conduct a formal investigation appropriate to the nature of the complaint.

(A) The investigation may include interviews of witnesses and a review of court records.

(B) As soon as practicable, the presiding judge must give the subordinate judicial officer a copy of the complaint or a summary of its allegations and allow the subordinate judicial officer an opportunity to respond.

(2) Within 10 days after the completion of the investigation or as soon thereafter as is reasonably possible, the presiding judge must give the subordinate judicial officer the following in writing:

(A) Notice of the intended final action on the complaint; and

(B) The facts and other information forming the basis for the proposed action and the source of the facts and information, sufficient to allow a meaningful response to the allegations.

(3) Final action on the complaint may include:

(A) A finding that no further action need be taken on the complaint;

(B) An oral or written warning to the subordinate judicial officer;

(C) A private written reprimand to the subordinate judicial officer;

(D) A public written reprimand to the subordinate judicial officer;

(E) Suspension of the subordinate judicial officer;

(F) Termination of the subordinate judicial officer; and

(G) Any other action the court may deem appropriate.

(4) The notice of the intended final action on the complaint in (j)(2)(A) must include the following advice:

(A) The subordinate judicial officer may request an opportunity to respond within 10 days after service of the notice; and

(B) If the subordinate judicial officer does not request an opportunity to respond within 10 days after service of the notice, the proposed action will become final.

(5) If the subordinate judicial officer requests an opportunity to respond, the presiding judge should allow the subordinate judicial officer an opportunity to respond to the notice of the intended final action, either orally or in writing as specified by the presiding judge, in accordance with local rules.

(6) Within 10 days after the subordinate judicial officer has responded, the presiding judge must give the subordinate judicial officer and the complainant written notice of the final action taken on the complaint. The notice to the complainant must include the information required under (l).

(7) If the subordinate judicial officer does not request or has not been given an opportunity to respond, the presiding judge must promptly give written notice of the final action to the complainant. The notice must include the information required under (l).

(Subd (j) amended effective January 1, 2007.)

(k) Report to the Commission on Judicial Performance

(1) If after a formal investigation under (j) the complaint results in the written reprimand, suspension, or removal of the subordinate judicial officer for conduct that if alleged against a judge would be within the jurisdiction of the commission under article VI, section 18 of the California Constitution, the presiding judge must promptly forward to the commission a copy of the portions of the court file on the complaint that reasonably reflect the basis of the action taken by the court, including the complaint and the subordinate judicial officer's response.

(2) If the subordinate judicial officer resigns while an investigation is pending, the presiding judge must within 15 days of the resignation, or as soon thereafter as is reasonably possible, forward to the commission the entire court file on any pending complaint.

(3) On request by the commission, the presiding judge must forward to the commission any requested information about a complaint against a subordinate judicial officer.

(Subd (k) amended effective January 1, 2007.)

(l) Notice of final court action

(1) When the court has completed its action on a complaint, the presiding judge must promptly notify the complainant and the subordinate judicial officer of the final court action.

(2) The notice to the complainant of the final court action must:

(A) Provide a general description of the action taken by the court consistent with any law limiting the disclosure of confidential employee information; and

(B) Include the following statement:

If you are dissatisfied with the court's action on your complaint, you have the right to request the Commission on Judicial Performance to review this matter under its discretionary jurisdiction to oversee the discipline of subordinate judicial officers. No further action will be taken on your complaint unless the commission receives your written request within 30 days after the date this notice was mailed. The commission's address is:

Commission on Judicial Performance

455 Golden Gate Avenue, Suite 14400

San Francisco, California 94102-3660

(Subd (1) amended effective January 1, 2007; previously amended effective April 29, 1999.)

Rule 10.703 amended and renumbered effective January 1, 2007; adopted as rule 6.655 effective November 20, 1998; previously amended effective April 29, 1999, July 1, 2002, and January 1, 2006.

Ref.: Cal. Fms Pl. & Pr., Ch. 317, "Judges."

Chapter 4
Referees
[Reserved]

Chapter 5
Temporary Judges

Rule 10.740. Responsibilities of the trial courts for temporary judge programs

Rule 10.741. Duties and authority of the presiding judge

Rule 10.742. Use of attorneys as court-appointed temporary judges

Rule 10.743. Administrator of temporary judges program

Rule 10.744. Application procedures to serve as a court-appointed temporary judge

Rule 10.745. Performance

Rule 10.746. Complaints

Rule 10.740.   Responsibilities of the trial courts for temporary judge programs

Each trial court that uses temporary judges must develop, institute, and operate—by itself or in collaboration with another court or courts—a program to recruit, select, train, and evaluate attorneys qualified to serve as temporary judges.

Rule 10.740 amended and renumbered effective January 1, 2007; adopted as rule 6.740 effective July 1, 2006.

Ref.: Cal. Fms Pl. & Pr., Ch. 317, "Judges."

Rule 10.741.   Duties and authority of the presiding judge

(a)   General duties

The presiding judge is responsible for the recruitment, selection, training, appointment, supervision, assignment, performance, and evaluation of court-appointed temporary judges. In carrying out these responsibilities, the presiding judge is assisted by the Temporary Judge Administrator as provided in rule 10.743.

(Subd (a) amended effective January 1, 2007.)

(b)   Authority to remove or discontinue

The presiding judge has the discretion to remove a court-appointed temporary judge or to discontinue using an attorney as a court-appointed temporary judge at any time.

Rule 10.741 amended and renumbered effective January 1, 2007; adopted as rule 6.741 effective July 1, 2006.

Rule 10.742.   Use of attorneys as court-appointed temporary judges

(a)   Responsibility of the presiding judge

The presiding judge of the trial court is responsible for determining whether that court needs to use attorneys as temporary judges and, if so, the specific purposes for which attorneys are to be appointed as temporary judges.

(b)   Conditions for the use of court-appointed temporary judges

The presiding judge may appoint an attorney as a court-appointed temporary judge only if all the following circumstances apply:

(1) The appointment of an attorney to serve as a temporary judge is necessary to fill a judicial need in that court;

(2) The attorney serving as a temporary judge has been approved by the court where the attorney will serve under rule 2.810 et seq.;

(3) The appointment of the attorney as a temporary judge does not result in any conflict of interest; and

(4) There is no appearance of impropriety resulting from the appointment of the attorney to serve as a temporary judge.

(Subd (b) amended effective January 1, 2007.)

(c)   Record and report of uses

Each trial court that uses attorneys as temporary judges must record and report to the Administrative Office of the Courts on a quarterly basis information concerning its use of them. The report must state:

(1) The number of attorneys used as temporary judges by that court each month;

(2) The number and types of cases, and the amount of time, on which the temporary judges were used each month; and

(3) Whether any of the appointments of temporary judges were made under the exception in rule 2.810(d) and, if so, the number of and reasons for these appointments.

(Subd (c) amended effective January 1, 2007.)

Rule 10.742 amended and renumbered effective January 1, 2007; adopted as rule 6.742 effective July 1, 2006.

Advisory Committee Comment

Subdivisions (a)–(b). These subdivisions provide that the presiding judge in each court is responsible for determining whether court-appointed temporary judges need to be used in that court, and these subdivisions furnish the criteria for determining when their use is proper. Under (b)(1), the use and appointment of court-appointed temporary judges must be based on judicial needs. Under (b)(3), an attorney serving as a temporary judge would have a conflict of interest if the disqualifying factors in the Code of Judicial Ethics exist. Under (b)(4), the test for the appearance of impropriety is whether a person aware of the facts might entertain a doubt that the judge would be able to act with integrity, impartiality, and competence. In addition to the disqualifying factors listed in the Code of Judicial Ethics, an appearance of impropriety would be generated if any of the limitations in family law, unlawful detainer, and other cases identified in the Code of Judicial Ethics are present.

Subdivision (c). Regular recording and reporting of information concerning each court's use of temporary judges assists the courts in monitoring and managing their use of temporary judges. This information is also important for establishing the need for additional judicial positions.

Rule 10.743. Administrator of temporary judges program

(a) Administrator

The presiding judge who appoints attorneys as temporary judges must designate a clerk, executive officer, or other court employee knowledgeable about temporary judges to serve as the Temporary Judge Administrator in that court.

(b) Duties of administrator

Under the supervision of the presiding judge, the Temporary Judge Administrator is responsible for the management of the temporary judges program in the court. The administrator's duties include:

(1) Receiving and processing applications from attorneys to serve as temporary judges with the court;

(2) Verifying the information on the applications;

(3) Assisting the presiding judge in the recruitment and selection of attorneys to serve as temporary judges;

(4) Administering the court's program for the education and training of temporary judges;

(5) Maintaining records of attendance and completion of required courses by all attorneys serving as temporary judges in the court;

(6) Determining that attorneys have satisfied all the conditions required to be appointed as a temporary judge in that court, including continuing education requirements;

(7) Maintaining a list of attorneys currently appointed and qualified to serve as temporary judges in the court;

(8) Managing support services for temporary judges, such as providing mentoring programs and reference materials;

(9) Receiving and processing complaints and other information concerning the performance of attorneys serving as temporary judges;

(10) Assisting the presiding judge in identifying judicial needs that require the use of temporary judges and in addressing these needs; and

(11) Maintaining records, gathering statistics, and preparing and transmitting quarterly reports on the court's use of temporary judges as required under rule 10.742(c).

(Subd (b) amended effective January 1, 2007.)

Rule 10.743 amended and renumbered effective January 1, 2007; adopted as rule 6.743 effective July 1, 2006.

Advisory Committee Comment

The goal of this rule is to ensure the effective and efficient administration of the courts' use of temporary judges. The rule should be applied flexibly. In courts with large temporary judge programs, the court may want to designate a full-time administrator, and some of the administrator's duties may be delegated to other individuals. On the other hand, in courts that use only a few temporary judges, the Temporary Judge Administrator position may consume only part of the administrator's time and be combined with other duties. Also, courts that use only a small number of temporary judges may work with other courts, or may cooperate on a regional basis, to perform the functions and duties prescribed under this rule.

Ref.: Cal. Fms Pl. & Pr., Ch. 317, "Judges."

Rule 10.744. Application procedures to serve as a court-appointed temporary judge

(a) Application

Every attorney who applies for appointment as a temporary judge in a trial court must complete an application to serve as a temporary judge.

(b) Information required

The attorney must provide all applicable information requested on the application. This information must include:

(1) The attorney's name and contact information as required by the court;

(2) The attorney's State Bar number;

(3) The date of the attorney's admission to the State Bar of California and the dates of his or her admissions to practice in any other state;

(4) Length of membership in the State Bar of California and of practice in any other state;

(5) Whether the attorney is in good standing with the State Bar of California and in good standing as an attorney in any other state where the attorney has been admitted to practice;

(6) Whether the attorney has ever been disciplined, or is the subject of a pending disciplinary proceeding, by the State Bar of California or by any other state bar association or court of record; and, if so, an explanation of the circumstances;

(7) The areas of specialization for which the attorney has been certified in California or in any other state;

(8) The attorney's major area or areas of practice;

(9) Whether the attorney holds himself or herself out publicly as representing exclusively one side in any of the areas of litigation in which the attorney practices;

(10) Whether the attorney represents one side in more than 90 percent of all cases in any areas of litigation in which the attorney specializes or concentrates his or her practice;

(11) The location or locations in which the attorney principally practices;

(12) How often the attorney appears in the court where he or she is applying to serve as a temporary judge;

(13) A list of the attorney's previous service as a temporary judge in the court where the attorney is applying and in any other court;

(14) Whether the attorney has ever been removed as a temporary judge by any court;

(15) The types of cases on which the attorney is willing to serve as a temporary judge;

(16) Whether the attorney has ever been convicted of a felony or misdemeanor, or is a defendant in any pending felony or misdemeanor proceeding, and, if so, a statement about the conviction or pending proceeding;

(17) Whether the attorney has been a party in any legal proceeding and, if so, a brief description of the proceedings;

(18) Information concerning any circumstances or conditions that would adversely affect or limit the attorney's ability to serve as a temporary judge;

(19) Any facts concerning the attorney's background that may reflect positively or negatively on the attorney or that should be disclosed to the court; and

(20) Such additional information as the court may require.

(c) Continuing duty to disclose

An attorney appointed by a court to serve as a temporary judge has a continuing duty to disclose to the court any material changes in facts or circumstances that affect his or her ability to serve as a temporary judge. The attorney must disclose the changes to the court before the next time the attorney is assigned to serve as a temporary judge.

(d) Review of application

The presiding judge, assisted by the Temporary Judge Administrator, must review all applications and determine whether each applicant is qualified, has satisfied the requirements of rule 2.812, and should be appointed as a temporary judge. The presiding judge may delegate this task to another judge or a committee of judges, assisted by the Temporary Judge Administrator. In appointing attorneys as temporary judges, the presiding judge may go beyond the minimum qualifications and standards required under the California Rules of Court. The decision whether to appoint, use, retrain, remove, or discontinue using any particular attorney as a temporary judge is at the sole discretion of the presiding judge.

(Subd (d) amended effective January 1, 2007.)

Rule 10.744 amended and renumbered effective January 1, 2007; adopted as rule 6.744 effective July 1, 2006.

Ref.: Cal. Fms Pl. & Pr., Ch. 317, "Judges," Ch. 526, "Small Claims."

Rule 10.745. Performance

(a) Review required

The court must review on a regular basis the performance of temporary judges appointed by that court.

(b) Monitoring performance

In monitoring and reviewing the performance of court-appointed temporary judges, the court may use direct observation, audiotaping of hearings, reports by court staff, comments from mentor judges, and such other means as may be helpful.

Rule 10.745 renumbered effective January 1, 2007; adopted as rule 6.745 effective July 1, 2006.

Rule 10.746. Complaints

Each court must have procedures for receiving, investigating, and resolving complaints against court-appointed temporary judges.

Rule 10.746 renumbered effective January 1, 2007; adopted as rule 6.746 effective July 1, 2006.

Chapter 6
Court Interpreters

Rule 10.761. Regional Court Interpreter Employment Relations Committees

(a) Creation

Government Code sections 71807–71809 establish four Regional Court Interpreter Employment Relations Committees. Each committee has the authority, for spoken language court interpreters within its region as defined under Government Code section 71807(a), to:

(1) Set the terms and conditions of employment for court interpreters, subject to meet and confer in good faith, as authorized by Government Code section 71808;

(2) Adopt reasonable rules and regulations for the administration of employer-employee relations with recognized employee organizations, as authorized by Government Code section 71823(a); and

(3) Act as the representative of the superior courts within the region in bargaining with a recognized employee organization as authorized by Government Code section 71809.

(b) Membership

(1) Each Regional Court Interpreter Employment Committee consists of one representative from each superior court that has at least one interpreter employed as a court interpreter as defined by Government Code section 71806 and not excluded by section 71828(d).

(2) The following regions are established by Government Code section 71807:

(A) Region 1: Los Angeles, Santa Barbara, and San Luis Obispo Counties.

(B) Region 2: Counties of the First and Sixth Appellate Districts, except Solano County.

(C) Region 3: Counties of the Third and Fifth Appellate Districts.

(D) Region 4: Counties of the Fourth Appellate District.

(3) The court executive officer of each superior court may appoint the court's representative, under rule 10.610, which authorizes the court executive officer, acting under the direction of the presiding judge, to oversee the management and administration of the nonjudicial operations of the court.

(4) Each Regional Court Interpreter Employment Relations Committee may appoint a chief negotiator to bargain with recognized employee organizations. The chief negotiator may be staff of the Administrative Office of the Courts.

(5) Any superior court that is not entitled to appoint a representative under this rule, including the superior courts of Ventura and Solano Counties, may appoint an advisory member to the committee for its region.

(Subd (b) amended effective January 1, 2007; previously amended effective January 1, 2006.)

(c) Rules of procedure

Each Regional Court Interpreter Employment Relations Committee may adopt its own rules of procedure, including the procedure for selecting its chair, advisory members, and chief negotiator.

(d) Voting

(1) Each representative of a superior court has a number of votes equal to the number of court interpreter employees in that trial court as defined by Government Code section 71806 and not excluded by section 71828(d).

(2) On July 1, 2004, and annually thereafter each Regional Court Interpreter Employment Relations Committee must recalculate the number of votes of each representative of a superior court to equal the number of court interpreter employees in that court.

(Subd (d) amended effective January 1, 2006.)

(e) Administrative Office of the Courts

The staff of the Administrative Office of the Courts will assist each Regional Court Interpreter Employment Relations Committee in performing its functions.

Rule 10.761 amended and renumbered effective January 1, 2007; adopted as rule 6.661 effective March 1, 2003; previously amended effective January 1, 2006.

Ref.: Cal. Fms Pl. & Pr., Ch. 317, "Judges."

Rule 10.762. Cross-assignments for court interpreter employees

(a) Purpose

This rule implements a process for cross-assignment of a court interpreter employed by a superior court under Government Code section 71810(b).

(Subd (a) amended effective January 1, 2007.)

(b) Definitions

As used in this rule:

(1) "Home court" means the superior court in which the court interpreter is an employee. An employee's home court includes all locations of a superior court within a county.

(2) "Away court" means the superior court to which the court interpreter is temporarily cross-assigned.

(3) "Cross-assignment" means any assignment to perform spoken language interpretation for a superior court other than the interpreter's home court.

(4) "Regional court interpreter coordinator" means an employee of the Administrative Office of the Courts whose duty it is to locate, assign, and schedule available court interpreter employees for courts within and across regions, which are described under Government Code section 71807(a).

(5) "Local court interpreter coordinator" means an employee of a superior court whose duty it is to locate, assign, and schedule available court interpreter employees for his or her court.

(Subd (b) amended effective January 1, 2007.)

(c) Procedure for cross-assignments

(1) Under Government Code section 71804.5(b) a court interpreter employed by a superior court is not permitted to be an employee of more than one superior court. A court interpreter employed by a superior court may not contract with another court, but may accept appointments to provide services to more than one court through cross-assignments.

(2) A superior court may attempt to fill an interpreting assignment with the employee of another court before hiring an independent contract court interpreter.

(3) If a superior court wants to fill an interpreting assignment with the employee of another court, the court must notify the regional court interpreter coordinator to locate an employee of a court within or across regions.

(4) Each local court interpreter coordinator must provide the schedule of each court interpreter employee available for cross-assignment to the regional court interpreter coordinator.

(5) A superior court may adopt additional internal procedures for cross-assigning a court interpreter employee that are not inconsistent with Government Code section 71810 and this rule.

(6) A Regional Court Interpreter Employment Relations Committee may approve alternative procedures for cross-assigning a court interpreter employee that permit the interpreter to directly arrange cross-assignments with an "away" court, provided that the procedures require notice to the regional coordinator.

(Subd (c) amended effective January 1, 2007.)

(d) Payment for cross-assignments

The home court must issue payment to the court interpreter for all cross-assignments, including per diem compensation and mileage reimbursement. The Administrative Office of the Courts will administer funding to the home court for payments associated with cross-assignments.

(Subd (d) amended effective January 1, 2007.)

(e) Duties of a court interpreter on cross-assignment

A court interpreter who accepts a cross-assignment is responsible for following the personnel rules of the home court while performing services for the away court.

(f) Superior courts of Ventura and Solano Counties

The superior courts of Ventura and Solano Counties may participate in the procedure for cross-assignments as follows:

(1) The Superior Court of Ventura County may accept or provide interpreters on cross-assignment under the procedures established in Region 1, as defined by Government Code section 71807.

(2) The Superior Court of Solano County may accept or provide interpreters on cross-assignment under the procedures established in Region 2, as defined by Government Code section 71807.

(Subd (f) amended effective January 1, 2007.)

Rule 10.762 amended and renumbered effective January 1, 2007; adopted as rule 6.662 effective March 1, 2003.

Ref.: Cal. Fms Pl. & Pr., Ch. 317, "Judges."

Chapter 7
Qualifications of Court Investigators, Probate Attorneys, and Probate Examiners

Chapter 7 adopted effective January 1, 2008.

Rule 10.776. Definitions
Rule 10.777. Qualifications of court investigators, probate attorneys, and probate examiners

Rule 10.776. Definitions

As used in the rules in this chapter, the following terms have the meanings stated below:

(1) A "court investigator" is a person described in Probate Code section 1454(a) employed by or under contract with a court to provide the investigative services for the court required or authorized by law in guardianships, conservatorships, and other protective proceedings under division 4 of the Probate Code;

(2) A "probate examiner" is a person employed by a court to review filings in probate proceedings in order to assist the court and the parties to get the filed matters ready for consideration by the court in accordance with the

requirements of the Probate Code, title 7 of the California Rules of Court, and the court's local rules;

(3) A "probate attorney" is an active member of the State Bar of California who is employed by a court to perform the functions of a probate examiner and also to provide legal analysis, recommendations, advice, and other services to the court pertaining to probate proceedings;

(4) "Probate proceedings" are decedents' estates, guardianships and conservatorships under division 4 of the Probate Code, trust proceedings under division 9 of the Probate Code, and other matters governed by provisions of that code and the rules in title 7 of the California Rules of Court;

(5) An "accredited educational institution" is a college or university, including a community or junior college, accredited by a regional accrediting organization recognized by the Council for Higher Education Accreditation; and

(6) "AOC" is the Administrative Office of the Courts.
Rule 10.776 adopted effective January 1, 2008.

Rule 10.777.   Qualifications of court investigators, probate attorneys, and probate examiners

(a) Qualifications of court investigators

Except as otherwise provided in this rule, a person who begins employment with a court or enters into a contract to perform services with a court as a court investigator on or after January 1, 2008, must:

(1) Have a bachelor of arts or bachelor of science degree in a science, a social science, a behavioral science, liberal arts, or nursing from an accredited educational institution; and

(2) Have a minimum of two years' employment experience performing casework or investigations in a legal, financial, law enforcement, or social services setting.
(Subd (a) adopted effective January 1, 2008.)

(b) Qualifications of probate attorneys

Except as otherwise provided in this rule, a person who begins employment with a court as a probate attorney on or after January 1, 2008, must:

(1) Be an active member of the State Bar of California for:

(A) A minimum of five years; or

(B) A minimum of two years, plus a minimum of five years' current or former active membership in the equivalent organization of another state or eligibility to practice in the highest court of another state or in a court of the United States; and

(2) Have a minimum of two years' total experience, before or after admission as an active member of the State Bar of California, in one or more of the following positions:

(A) Court-employed staff attorney;

(B) Intern, court probate department (minimum six-month period);

(C) Court-employed probate examiner or court-employed or court-contracted court investigator;

(D) Attorney in a probate-related public or private legal practice;

(E) Deputy public guardian or conservator;

(F) Child protective services or adult protective services worker or juvenile probation officer; or

(G) Private professional fiduciary appointed by a court or employee of a private professional fiduciary or bank or trust company appointed by a court, with significant fiduciary responsibilities, including responsibility for court accountings.
(Subd (b) adopted effective January 1, 2008.)

(c) Qualifications of probate examiners

Except as otherwise provided in this rule, a person who begins employment with a court as a probate examiner on or after January 1, 2008, must have:

(1) A bachelor of arts or bachelor of science degree from an accredited educational institution and a minimum of two years' employment experience with one or more of the following employers:

(A) A court;

(B) A public or private law office; or

(C) A public administrator, public guardian, public conservator, or private professional fiduciary; or

(2) A paralegal certificate or an Associate of Arts degree from an accredited educational institution and a minimum of a total of four years' employment experience with one or more of the employers listed in (1); or

(3) A juris doctor degree from an educational institution approved by the American Bar Association or accredited by the Committee of Bar Examiners of the State Bar of California and a minimum of six months' employment experience with an employer listed in (1).
(Subd (c) adopted effective January 1, 2008.)

(d) Additional court-imposed qualifications and requirements

The qualifications in (a), (b), and (c) are minimums. A court may establish higher qualification standards for any position covered by this rule and may require applicants to comply with its customary hiring or personal-service contracting practices, including written applications, personal references, personal interviews, or entrance examinations.
(Subd (d) adopted effective January 1, 2008.)

(e) Exemption for smaller courts

The qualifications required under this rule may be waived by a court with eight or fewer authorized judges if it cannot find suitable qualified candidates for the positions covered by this rule or for other grounds of hardship. A court electing to waive a qualification under this subdivision must make express written findings showing the circumstances supporting the waiver and disclosing all alternatives considered, including those not selected.
(Subd (e) adopted effective January 1, 2008.)

(f) Record keeping and reporting

The AOC may require courts to report on the qualifications of the court investigators, probate attorneys, or probate examiners hired or under contract under this rule, and on waivers made under (e), as necessary to ensure compliance with Probate Code section 1456.
(Subd (f) adopted effective January 1, 2008.)

Rule 10.777 adopted effective January 1, 2008.

Chapter 8
Alternative Dispute Resolution Programs

Chapter 8 renumbered effective January 1, 2008; adopted as Chapter 7 effective January 1, 2007.

Rule 10.780. Administration of alternative dispute resolution (ADR) programs
Rule 10.781. Court-related ADR neutrals
Rule 10.782. ADR program information
Rule 10.783. ADR program administration

Rule 10.780. Administration of alternative dispute resolution (ADR) programs

The rules in this chapter concern alternative dispute resolution (ADR) programs administered by the trial courts. General provisions concerning ADR are located in title 3, division 8.

Rule 10.780 amended effective January 1, 2008; adopted effective January 1, 2007.

Ref.: Cal. Fms Pl. & Pr., Ch. 317, "Judges."

Rule 10.781. [Effective Until July 1, 2009] Court-related ADR neutrals

(a) Lists of neutrals

If a court makes available to litigants a list of ADR neutrals, the list must contain, at a minimum, the following information concerning each neutral listed:

(1) The types of ADR services available from the neutral;

(2) The neutral's résumé, including ADR training and experience; and

(3) The fees charged by the neutral for each type of service.

(Subd (a) amended effective January 1, 2007.)

(b) Requirements to be on lists

In order to be included on a court list of ADR neutrals, an ADR neutral must sign a statement or certificate agreeing to:

(1) Comply with all applicable ethics requirements and rules of court; and

(2) Serve as an ADR neutral on a pro bono or modest-means basis in at least one case per year, not to exceed eight hours, if requested by the court. The court must establish the eligibility requirements for litigants to receive, and the application process for them to request, ADR services on a pro bono or modest-means basis.

(Subd (b) amended effective January 1, 2007.)

Rule 10.781 amended and renumbered effective January 1, 2007; adopted as rule 1580.1 effective January 1, 2001.

Ref.: Cal. Fms Pl. & Pr., Ch. 33, "Contractual Arbitration: Appointment of Arbitrator and Conduct of Proceeding," Ch. 317, "Judges."

Rule 10.781. [Effective July 1, 2009] Court-related ADR neutrals

(a) Lists of neutrals

If a court makes available to litigants a list of ADR neutrals, the list must contain, at a minimum, the following information concerning each neutral listed:

(1) The types of ADR services available from the neutral;

(2) The neutral's résumé, including ADR training and experience; and

(3) The fees charged by the neutral for each type of service.

(Subd (a) amended effective January 1, 2007.)

(b) Requirements to be on lists

In order to be included on a court list of ADR neutrals, an ADR neutral must sign a statement or certificate agreeing to:

(1) Comply with all applicable ethics requirements and rules of court; and

(2) Serve as an ADR neutral on a pro bono or modest-means basis in at least one case per year, not to exceed eight hours, if requested by the court. The court must establish the eligibility requirements for litigants to receive, and the application process for them to request, ADR services on a pro bono or modest-means basis.

(Subd (b) amended effective January 1, 2007.)

(c) Privilege to serve as a court-program neutral

Inclusion on a court list of ADR neutrals and eligibility to be recommended, appointed, or compensated by the court to serve as a neutral are privileges that are revocable and confer no vested right on the neutral.

(Subd (c) adopted effective July 1, 2009.)

Rule 10.781 amended effective July 1, 2009; adopted as rule 1580.1 effective January 1, 2001; previously amended and renumbered effective January 1, 2007.

Advisory Committee Comment

Subdivision (c). A court has absolute discretion to determine who may be included on a court list of ADR neutrals or is eligible to be recommended, selected, appointed, or compensated by the court to serve as a neutral (except as otherwise expressly provided by statute or rule of court).

Ref.: Cal. Fms Pl. & Pr., Ch. 33, "Contractual Arbitration: Appointment of Arbitrator and Conduct of Proceeding," Ch. 317, "Judges."

Rule 10.782. ADR program information

(a) Report to Judicial Council

Each court must report information on its ADR programs to the Judicial Council, as requested by the Administrative Office of the Courts.

(Subd (a) amended effective January 1, 2007.)

(b) Parties and ADR neutrals to supply information

Subject to applicable limitations, including the confidentiality requirements in Evidence Code section 1115 et seq., courts must require parties and ADR neutrals, as appropriate, to supply pertinent information for the reports required under (a).

(Subd (b) amended effective January 1, 2007.)

Rule 10.782 amended and renumbered effective January 1, 2007; adopted as rule 1580.2 effective January 1, 2001.

Ref.: Cal. Fms Pl. & Pr., Ch. 317, "Judges."

Rule 10.783. ADR program administration

(a) ADR program administrator

The presiding judge in each trial court must designate the clerk or executive officer, or another court employee who is knowledgeable about ADR processes, to serve as

ADR program administrator. The duties of the ADR program administrator must include:

(1) Developing informational material concerning the court's ADR programs;

(2) Educating attorneys and litigants about the court's ADR programs;

(3) Supervising the development and maintenance of any panels of ADR neutrals maintained by the court; and

(4) Gathering statistical and other evaluative information concerning the court's ADR programs.

(Subd (a) amended effective January 1, 2007; previously amended effective January 1, 2004.)

(b) ADR committee

(1) *Membership in courts with 18 or more authorized judges*

In each superior court that has 18 or more authorized judges, there must be an ADR committee. The members of the ADR committee must include, insofar as is practicable:

(A) The presiding judge or a judge designated by the presiding judge;

(B) One or more other judges designated by the presiding judge;

(C) The ADR program administrator;

(D) Two or more active members of the State Bar chosen by the presiding judge as representatives of those attorneys who regularly represent parties in general civil cases before the court, including an equal number of attorneys who represent plaintiffs and who represent defendants in these cases;

(E) One or more members of the court's panel of arbitrators chosen by the presiding judge; and

(F) If the court makes available to litigants a list of any ADR neutrals other than arbitrators, one or more neutrals chosen by the presiding judge from that list.

(2) *Additional members*

The ADR committee may include additional members selected by the presiding judge.

(3) *ADR committee in other courts*

Any other court may by rule establish an ADR committee as provided in (b)(1). Otherwise, the presiding judge or a judge designated by the presiding judge must perform the functions and have the powers of an ADR committee as provided in these rules.

(4) *Term of membership*

ADR committee membership is for a two-year term. The members of the ADR committee may be reappointed and may be removed by the presiding judge.

(5) *Responsibilities of ADR committee*

The ADR committee is responsible for overseeing the court's alternative dispute resolution programs for general civil cases, including those responsibilities relating to the court's judicial arbitration program specified in rule 3.813(b).

(Subd (b) amended effective January 1, 2007; previously adopted effective January 1, 2004.)

Rule 10.783 amended and renumbered effective January 1, 2007; adopted as rule 1580.3 effective January 1, 2001; previously amended effective January 1, 2004.

Ref.: Cal. Fms Pl. & Pr., Ch. 317, "Judges."

Chapter 9
Trial Court Budget and Fiscal Management

Chapter 9 renumbered effective January 1, 2008; adopted as Chapter 3 effective July 1, 1998; previously renumbered as Chapter 8 effective January 1, 2007.

Rule 10.800.   Superior court budgeting

(a) Purpose

This rule provides for local authority and accountability for development of budget requests and management of court operations within the authorized funding level. Superior courts must manage their budgets in a manner that is responsive to local needs, ensures equal access to justice, is consistent with Judicial Council policy and legislative direction, and does not exceed the total allocated budget.

(Subd (a) amended effective January 1, 2007; previously amended effective January 1, 2002.)

(b) Development of budget requests

Each superior court must prepare and submit to the Administrative Office of the Courts a budget according to the schedule and procedures established by the Judicial Council.

(Subd (b) amended effective January 1, 2007; previously amended effective January 1, 2002.)

(c) Allocation of funding

(1) The funding allocation to each superior court is based on the amounts incorporated for that court in budget change proposals that have been funded through the Budget Act, except as otherwise ordered by the Judicial Council. The superior court of each county may distribute and periodically redistribute its annual allocation between programs, locations, and line items as needed, within the parameters of the *Trial Court Financial Policies and Procedures Manual* and consistent with council policy direction, to promote accessible justice and the effective, efficient, and accountable operation of the courts. The Judicial Council may make additional allocations as it deems appropriate.

(2) Each superior court is accountable for achieving the expected outcomes of the programs funded for that year. If a court is unable to do so, it must report the reasons to the Judicial Council.

(Subd (c) amended effective January 1, 2007; previously amended effective January 1, 2002.)

Rule 10.800 amended and renumbered effective January 1, 2007; adopted as rule 2530 effective July 1, 1998; renumbered as rule 6.700 effective January 1, 1999; previously amended effective January 1, 2002.

Ref.: Cal. Fms Pl. & Pr., Ch. 317, "Judges."

Rule 10.801. Superior court budget procedures

(a) Adoption of budget procedures by the Administrative Office of the Courts

The Administrative Office of the Courts must adopt superior court budget procedures to be included in the *Trial Court Financial Policies and Procedures Manual,* the annual Baseline Budget Development Package, and the annual *Budget Change Request Package.* These procedures include the following:

(1) Procedures permitting the superior courts to comment on the proposed budget procedures;

(2) Procedures for budget development, submission, and appeal;

(3) Procedures for budget implementation, including expenditure and revenue reporting;

(4) Reasonable time frames to comply with requirements or changes in the budget procedures;

(5) Procedures to ensure the reporting to the Judicial Council of relevant information on the implementation of programs funded;

(6) Procedures for providing timely management information to the Judicial Council on the baseline budget, revenues, and expenditures.

(7) An annual budget development and implementation calendar;

(8) Procedures for a superior court to follow if it projects that its budget will be exhausted before the end of the fiscal year, preventing the court from meeting its financial obligations or continuing operations; and

(9) Procedures governing the transfer of funds between individual programs and operations of expenditure.

(Subd (a) amended effective January 1, 2007; previously amended effective January 1, 2002.)

(b) Technical assistance

The Administrative Office of the Courts, on request, provides technical assistance and ongoing training in budget development and implementation to the superior courts.

(Subd (b) amended effective January 1, 2007; previously amended effective January 1, 2002.)

Rule 10.801 amended and renumbered effective January 1, 2007; adopted as rule 2531 effective July 1, 1998; renumbered as rule 6.701 effective January 1, 1999; previously amended effective January 1, 2002.

Ref.: Cal. Fms Pl. & Pr., Ch. 317, "Judges."

Rule 10.802. Maintenance of and public access to budget and management information

(a) Maintenance of information by the superior court

Each superior court must maintain for a period of three years from the close of the fiscal year to which the following relate:

(1) Official documents of the superior court pertaining to the approved superior court budget allocation adopted by the Judicial Council and actual final year-end superior court revenue and expenditure reports as required in budget procedures issued by the Administrative Office of the Courts to be maintained or reported to the council, including budget allocation, revenue, and expenditure reports;

(2) Records or other factual management information on matters that are within the scope of representation as defined in Government Code section 71634 unless distribution is otherwise precluded by law; and

(3) Records or other factual management information on other matters referred to in Government Code section 71634 unless distribution is otherwise precluded by law.

(Subd (a) amended effective January 1, 2007; previously amended effective January 1, 2004.)

(b) Maintenance of information by the Administrative Office of the Courts

The Administrative Office of the Courts must maintain for a period of three years from the close of the fiscal year to which the following relate:

(1) Official approved budget allocations for each superior court;

(2) Actual final year-end superior court revenue and expenditure reports required by budget procedures issued by the Administrative Office of the Courts to be maintained or reported to the council that are received from the courts including budget revenues and expenditures for each superior court;

(3) Budget priorities as adopted by the council; and

(4) Documents concerning superior court budgets considered or adopted by the council at council business meetings on court budgets.

(Subd (b) amended effective January 1, 2007; previously amended effective January 1, 2004.)

(c) Legislative priorities or mandates

The information maintained under (a) and (b) must indicate, to the extent known, the legislative requirements the funding is intended to address, if any, and any itemization of the funding allocation by purpose, program or function, and item of expense.

(Subd (c) amended effective January 1, 2004.)

(d) Public access

(1) Each superior court must, on written request, make available to the requesting person those documents required to be maintained under (a).

(2) The Administrative Office of the Courts must, on written request, make available to the requesting person those documents required to be maintained under (b).

(Subd (d) amended effective January 1, 2007; previously amended effective January 1, 2004.)

(e) Time for response

Information requested under this rule must be made available within 10 business days of receipt of the written request for information relating to the current or immediate previous fiscal year. Information relating to other fiscal years must be made available within 20 business days of receipt of the written request for information. If the information requested is not within the scope of this rule, the Administrative Office of the Courts or the superior court must so inform the requesting party within 10 business days of receipt of the written request.

(Subd (e) amended effective January 1, 2007; previously amended effective January 1, 2004.)

(f) Costs

The Administrative Office of the Courts and the superior court may charge a reasonable fee to cover any cost of copying any document provided under this rule. The amount of the fee must not exceed the direct cost of duplication. A recognized employee organization and a superior court may provide for a different amount in their memorandum of understanding.

(Subd (f) amended effective January 1, 2007; previously amended effective January 1, 2004.)

(g) Preparation of reports not required

This rule does not require the Judicial Council, the Administrative Office of the Courts, or any superior court to prepare any budgetary, revenue, or expense report or documentation that is not otherwise expressly required to be prepared by this rule or any other provision of law or rule of court.

(Subd (g) amended effective January 1, 2007; previously amended effective January 1, 2004.)

(h) Effect on other rules

This rule is not intended to repeal, amend, or modify the application of any rule adopted by the council before the effective date of this rule. To the extent that any other rule is contrary to the provisions of this rule, this rule applies.

(Subd (h) amended effective January 1, 2007; adopted as subd (i) effective January 1, 2001; previously amended and relettered effective January 1, 2004.)

(i) Public Records Act

The information required to be provided by (a) and (b) of this rule must be interpreted consistently with the requirement that the same information be provided under the Public Records Act (beginning with Government Code section 6250), and the terms have the same meaning as under that act. This rule does not require the disclosure of information that would not be subject to disclosure under that act.

(Subd (i) amended effective January 1, 2007; adopted as subd (j) effective January 1, 2001; previously amended and relettered effective January 1, 2004.)

(j) Internal memoranda

Nothing in this rule requires disclosure of internal memoranda unless otherwise required by law.

(Subd (j) amended and relettered effective January 1, 2004; adopted as subd (k) effective January 1, 2001.)

(k) Rights of exclusive bargaining agent

Nothing in this rule is intended to restrict the rights to disclosure of information otherwise granted by law to a recognized employee organization.

(Subd (k) amended and relettered effective January 1, 2004; adopted as subd (l) effective January 1, 2001.)

(l) Informational sessions

The Administrative Office of the Courts will provide informational sessions and materials on superior court budgets for the general public and designated employee representatives. The information will include the following areas, among others:

(1) Description and timing of the budget development process, including decisions made at each phase of the cycle, and how budget priorities are determined;

(2) Availability of budget information, including the type of information available, when it is available, and how it can be obtained; and

(3) The authority of a superior court to reallocate funds between budget program components.

(Subd (l) amended effective January 1, 2007; adopted effective January 1, 2004.)

Rule 10.802 amended and renumbered effective January 1, 2007; adopted as rule 6.702 effective January 1, 2001; previously amended effective July 1, 2001, July 1, 2002, and January 1, 2004.

Ref.: Cal. Fms Pl. & Pr., Ch. 317, "Judges."

Rule 10.803. Information access disputes—writ petitions (Gov. Code, § 71675)

(a) Availability

This rule applies to petitions filed under Government Code section 71675(b).

(Subd (a) amended effective January 1, 2007.)

(b) Assignment of Court of Appeal justice to hear the petition

(1) The petition must state the following on the first page, below the case number, in the statement of the character of the proceeding (see rule 2.111(6)):

"Writ petition filed under Government Code section 71675—Assignment of Court of Appeal justice required."

(2) When the petition is filed, the clerk of the court must immediately request of the Judicial Assignments Unit of the Administrative Office of the Courts the assignment of a hearing judge from the panel established under (e).

(3) The judge assigned to hear the petition in the superior court must be a justice from a Court of Appeal for a district other than the district for that superior court.

(Subd (b) amended effective January 1, 2007.)

(c) Superior court hearing

(1) The superior court must hear and decide the petition on an expedited basis and must give the petition priority over other matters to the extent permitted by law and the rules of court.

(2) The petition must be heard by a judge assigned by the Chief Justice from the panel of hearing judges established under (e).

(Subd (c) amended effective January 1, 2007.)

(d) Appeal

An appeal of the superior court decision must be heard and decided on an expedited basis in the Court of Appeal for the district in which the petition was heard and must be given priority over other matters to the extent permitted by law and the rules of court. The notice of appeal must state the following on the first page, below the case number, in the statement of the character of the proceeding (see rule 2.111(6)):

"Notice of Appeal on Writ Petition filed under Government Code section 71675—Expedited Processing Requested."

(Subd (d) amended effective January 1, 2007.)

(e) Panel of hearing judges

The panel of judges who may hear the petitions in the superior court must consist of Court of Appeal justices selected by the Chief Justice as follows:

(1) The panel must include at least one justice from each district of the Court of Appeal.

(2) Each justice assigned to hear a petition under (c)(2) must have received training on hearing the petitions as specified by the Chief Justice.

Rule 10.803 amended and renumbered effective January 1, 2007; adopted as rule 6.710 effective October 15, 2004.

Ref.: Cal. Fms Pl. & Pr., Ch. 317, "Judges."

Rule 10.804. Superior court financial policies and procedures

(a) Adoption of financial policies and procedures by the Administrative Office of the Courts

The Administrative Office of the Courts must prepare and adopt a financial policies and procedures manual for the superior courts (the *"Trial Court Financial Policies and Procedures Manual"*), consistent with the rules of court and policies adopted by the Judicial Council. The manual must include accounting standards for superior courts and policies and procedures for procurement and contracting by superior courts. These policies and procedures must not modify superior courts' existing authority to procure, contract for, or use goods or services or the requirement that a court have authorized funding available in order to procure or contract for any good or service.

(Subd (a) amended effective January 1, 2007.)

(b) Comment period for financial policies and procedures

Before issuing or amending the *Trial Court Financial Policies and Procedures Manual*, the Administrative Office of the Courts must make it available for comment from the superior courts and from the Department of Finance and the State Controller's Office for 30 days.

(Subd (b) amended effective January 1, 2007.)

(c) Date of adherence to financial policies and procedures

Superior courts must adhere to the requirements contained in the *Trial Court Financial Policies and Procedures Manual*, except as otherwise provided in the manual. Superior courts must not be required to adhere to any amendment to the manual sooner than 60 days after the amendment is adopted.

(Subd (c) amended effective January 1, 2007.)

Rule 10.804 amended and renumbered effective January 1, 2007; adopted as rule 6.707 effective January 1, 2001.

Ref.: Cal. Fms Pl. & Pr., Ch. 317, "Judges."

Rule 10.805. Notice of change in court-county relationship

If, under Government Code section 77212, the county gives notice to the superior court that the county will no longer provide a specific county service or the court gives notice to the county that the court will no longer use a specific county service, the court must, within 10 days of receiving or giving such notice, provide a copy of this notice to the Finance Division of the Administrative Office of the Courts.

Rule 10.805 amended and renumbered effective January 1, 2007; adopted as rule 6.705 effective January 1, 2000.

Ref.: Cal. Fms Pl. & Pr., Ch. 317, "Judges."

Rule 10.810. Court operations

(a) Definition

Except as provided in subdivision (b) and subject to the requirements of subdivisions (c) and (d), "court operations" as defined in Government Code section 77003 includes the following costs:

(1) *(judicial salaries and benefits)* salaries, benefits, and public agency retirement contributions for superior and municipal court judges and for subordinate judicial officers;

(2) *(nonjudicial salaries and benefits)* salaries, benefits, and public agency retirement contributions for superior and municipal court staff whether permanent, temporary, full- or part-time, contract or per diem, including but not limited to all municipal court staff positions specifically prescribed by statute and county clerk positions directly supporting the superior courts;

(3) salaries and benefits for those sheriff, marshal, and constable employees as the court deems necessary for court operations in superior and municipal courts and the supervisors of those sheriff, marshal, and constable employees who directly supervise the court security function;

(4) court-appointed counsel in juvenile dependency proceedings, and counsel appointed by the court to represent a minor as specified in Government Code section 77003;

(5) *(services and supplies)* operating expenses in support of judicial officers and court operations;

(6) *(collective bargaining)* collective bargaining with respect to court employees; and

(7) *(indirect costs)* a share of county general services as defined in subdivision (d), Function 11, and used by the superior and municipal courts.

(Subd (a) amended effective July 1, 1995; previously amended effective January 1, 1989, July 1, 1990, and July 1, 1991.)

(b) Exclusions

Excluded from the definition of "court operations" are the following:

(1) law library operations conducted by a trust pursuant to statute;

(2) courthouse construction and site acquisition, including space rental (for other than court records storage), alterations/remodeling, or relocating court facilities;

(3) district attorney services;

(4) probation services;

(5) indigent criminal and juvenile delinquency defense;

(6) civil and criminal grand jury expenses and operations (except for selection);

(7) pretrial release services;

(8) equipment and supplies for use by official reporters of the courts to prepare transcripts as specified by statute; and

(9) county costs as provided in subdivision (d) as unallowable.

(Subd (b) amended effective July 1, 1995; adopted effective July 1, 1988 as subd (c); previously amended effective January 1, 1989, and July 1, 1990.)

(c) Budget appropriations

Costs for court operations specified in subdivision (a) shall be appropriated in county budgets for superior and municipal courts, including contract services with county agencies or private providers except for the following:

(1) salaries, benefits, services, and supplies for sheriff, marshal, and constable employees as the court deems necessary for court operations in superior and municipal courts;

(2) salaries, benefits, services, and supplies for county clerk activities directly supporting the superior court; and

(3) costs for court-appointed counsel specified in Government Code section 77003.

Except as provided in this subdivision, costs not appropriated in the budgets of the courts are unallowable.

(Subd (c) amended effective July 1, 1995; adopted as subd (d) effective July 1, 1990.)

(d) Functional budget categories

Trial court budgets and financial reports shall identify all allowable court operations in the following eleven (11) functional budget categories. Costs for salary, wages, and benefits of court employees are to be shown in the appropriate functions provided the individual staff member works at least 25 percent time in that function. Individual staff members whose time spent in a function is less than 25 percent are reported in Function 10, All Other Court Operations. The functions and their respective costs are as follows:

Function 1. Judicial Officers
Costs reported in this function are
  Salaries and state benefits of
    Judges
      Full- or part-time court commissioners
      Full- or part-time court referees
  Assigned judges' in-county travel expenses

Costs not reported in this function include
  County benefits of judicial officers (Function 10)
  Juvenile traffic hearing officers (Function 10)
  Mental health hearing officers (Function 10)
  Pro tem hearing officers (Function 10)
  Commissioner and referee positions specifically excluded by statute from state trial court funding (unallowable)
  Related data processing (Function 9)
  Any other related services, supplies, and equipment (Function 10)

Function 2. Jury Services
Costs reported in this function are
  Juror expenses of per diem fees and mileage
  Meals and lodging for sequestered jurors
  Salaries, wages, and benefits of jury commissioner and jury services staff (including selection of grand jury)
  Contractual jury services
  Jury-related office expenses (other than information technology)
  Jury-related communications, including "on call" services

Costs not reported in this function include
  Juror parking (unallowable)
  Civil and criminal grand jury costs (unallowable)
  Jury-related information systems (Function 9)

Function 3. Verbatim Reporting
Costs reported in this function are
  Salaries, wages, and benefits of court reporters who are court employees
  Salaries, wages, and benefits of electronic monitors and support staff
  Salaries, wages, and benefits of verbatim reporting coordinators and clerical support staff
  Contractual court reporters and monitors
  Transcripts for use by appellate or trial courts, or as otherwise required by law
  Related office expenses and equipment (purchased, leased, or rented) used to record court proceedings, except as specified in Government Code § 68073, e.g.,
    notepaper, pens, and pencils
    ER equipment and supplies

Costs not reported in this function include
  Office expenses and equipment for use by reporters to prepare transcripts (unallowable)
  Expenses specified in Government Code § 69073 (unallowable)
  Space use charges for court reporters (unallowable)

Function 4. Court Interpreters
Costs reported in this function are
  Salaries, wages, and benefits of courtroom interpreters and interpreter coordinators
  Per diem and contractual courtroom interpreters, including contractual transportation and travel allowances

Costs not reported in this function include
  Related data processing (Function 9)
  Any other related services, supplies, and equipment (Function 10)

Function 5. Collections Enhancement
Collections performed in the enforcement of court orders for fees, fines, forfeitures, restitutions, penalties, and assessments (beginning with the establishment of the accounts receivable record)

Costs reported in this function are
  Salaries, wages, and benefits of collection employees of the court, e.g.,
      financial hearing officers
      evaluation officers
      collection staff
  Contract collections costs
  County charges for collection services provided to the court by county agencies
  Related services, supplies, and equipment (except data processing, Function 9)

Costs not reported in this function include
  Staff whose principal involvement is in collecting "forthwith" payments, e.g.,
      counter clerks (Function 10)
      cashiers (Function 10)

Function 6. Dispute Resolution Programs
Costs reported in this function are
  Arbitrators' fees in mandatory judicial arbitration programs
  Salaries, wages, and benefits of court staff providing child custody and visitation mediation and related investigation services, e.g.,
      Director of Family Court Services
      mediators
      conciliators
      investigators
      clerical support staff
  Contract mediators providing child custody and visitation mediation services
  Salaries, wages, benefits, fees, and contract costs for other arbitration and mediation programs (programs not mandated by statute), e.g.,
      arbitration administrators
      clerical support staff
      arbitrators' fees and expenses

Costs not reported in this function include
  Related data processing (Function 9)
  Any other related services, supplies, and equipment (Function 10)

Function 7. Court-Appointed Counsel (Noncriminal)
Costs reported in this function are
  Expenses for court-appointed counsel as specified in Government Code § 77003

Function 8. Court Security
Court security services as deemed necessary by the court. Includes only the duties of
(a) courtroom bailiff,
(b) perimeter security (i.e., outside the courtroom but inside the court facility), and
(c) at least .25 FTE dedicated supervisors of these activities.

Costs reported in this function are
  Salary, wages, and benefits (including overtime) of sheriff, marshal, and constable employees who perform the court's security, i.e.,
      bailiffs
      weapons-screening personnel
  Salary, wages, and benefits (including overtime) of court staff performing court security, e.g.,
      court attendants

Contractual security services

Salary, wages, and benefits of supervisors of sheriff, marshal, and constable employees whose duties are greater than .25 FTE dedicated to this function

Sheriff, marshal, and constable employee training

Purchase of security equipment

Maintenance of security equipment

Costs not reported in this function include

Other sheriff, marshal, or constable employees (unallowable)

Court attendant training (Function 10)

Overhead costs attributable to the operation of the sheriff and marshal offices (unallowable)

Costs associated with the transportation and housing of detainees from the jail to the courthouse (unallowable)

Service of process in civil cases (unallowable)

Services and supplies, including data processing, not specified above as allowable

Supervisors of bailiffs and perimeter security personnel of the sheriff, marshal, or constable office who supervise these duties less than .25 FTE time (unallowable)

Function 9. Information Technology

Costs reported in this function are

Salaries, wages, and benefits of court employees who plan, implement, and maintain court data processing and information technologies, e.g.,

    programmers

    analysts

Contract and consulting services associated with court information/data processing needs and systems

County Information Systems/Data Processing Department charges made to court for court systems, e.g.,

    jury-related systems

    court and case management, including courts' share of a criminal justice information system

    accounts receivable/collections systems

Related services, supplies, and equipment, e.g.,

    software purchases and leases

    maintenance of automation equipment

    training associated with data processing systems' development

Costs not reported in this function include

Information technology services not provided directly to the courts (i.e., services used by other budget units)

Data processing for county general services, e.g., payroll, accounts payable (Function 11)

Function 10. All Other Court Operations

Costs reported in this function are

Salaries, wages, and benefits (including any pay differentials and overtime) of court staff

    (a) not reported in Functions 2-9, or

    (b) whose time cannot be allocated to Functions 2-9 in increments of at least 25 percent time (.25 FTE);

Judicial benefits, county-paid

Allowable costs not reported in Functions 2-9.

(Nonjudicial staff) Cost items may include, for example,

    juvenile traffic hearing officer

    mental health hearing officer

    court-appointed hearing officer (pro tem)

    executive officer

    court administrator

    clerk of the court

    administrative assistant

    personnel staff

    legal research personnel; staff attorney; planning and research staff

    secretary

    courtroom clerk

    clerical support staff

    calendar clerk

    deputy clerk

    accountant

    cashier

    counter clerk

    microfilming staff

    management analyst

    probate conservatorship and guardianship investigators

    probate examiner

    training staff employed by the court

Personnel costs not reported in this function:
　　Any of the above not employed by the court
(Services and supplies) Cost items may include, for example,
　　office supplies
　　printing
　　postage
　　communications
　　publications and legal notices, by the court
　　miscellaneous departmental expenses
　　books, publications, training fees, and materials for court personnel (judicial and nonjudicial)
　　travel and transportation (judicial and nonjudicial)
　　professional dues
　　memberships and subscriptions
　　statutory multidistrict judges' association expenses
　　research, planning, and program coordination expenses
　　small claims advisor program costs
　　court-appointed expert witness fees (for the court's needs)
　　court-ordered forensic evaluations and other professional services (for the court's own use)
　　pro tem judges' expenses
　　micrographics expenses
　　public information services
　　vehicle use, including automobile insurance
　　equipment (leased, rented, or purchased) and furnishings, including interior painting, replacement/maintenance of flooring, and furniture repair
　　maintenance of office equipment
　　janitorial services
　　legal services for allowable court operations (County Counsel and contractual)
　　fidelity and faithful performance insurance (bonding and personal liability insurance on judges and court employees)
　　insurance on cash money and securities (hold-up and burglary)
　　general liability/comprehensive insurance for other than faulty maintenance or design of facility (e.g., "slip and fall," other injury, theft and damage of court equipment, slander, discrimination)
　　risk management services related to allowable insurance
　　space rental for court records
　　county records retention/destruction services
　　county messenger/mail service
　　court audits mandated under Government Code § 71383
Service and supply costs not reported in this function include
　　Civic association dues (unallowable)
　　Facility damages insurance (unallowable)
　　County central service department charges not appropriated in the court budget (unallowable)

Function 11. County General Services ("Indirect Costs")

General county services are defined as all eligible accounting, payroll, budgeting, personnel, purchasing, and county administrator costs rendered in support of court operations. Costs for included services are allowable to the extent the service is provided to the court. The following costs, regardless of how characterized by the county or by which county department they are performed, are reported in this function only and are subject to the statutory maximum for indirect costs as specified in Government Code § 77003. To the extent costs are allowable under this rule, a county's approved Cost Plan may be used to determine the specific cost although the cost categories, or functions, may differ.

Cost items within the meaning of rule 10.810(a)(7) and the county departments often performing the service may include, for example,
　　County Administrator
　　　　budget development and administration
　　　　interdepartmental budget unit administration and operations
　　　　personnel (labor) relations and administration
　　Auditor-Controller
　　　　payroll
　　　　financial audits
　　　　warrant processing
　　　　fixed asset accounting
　　　　departmental accounting for courts, e.g., fines, fees, forfeitures, restitutions, penalties, and assessments; accounting for the Trial Court Special Revenue Fund
　　　　accounts payable
　　　　grant accounting
　　　　management reporting
　　　　banking

Personnel
  recruitment and examination of applicants
  maintenance and certification of eligible lists
  position classification
  salary surveys
  leave accounting
  employment physicals
  handling of appeals
Treasurer/Tax Collector
  warrant processing
  bank reconciliation
  retirement system administration
  receiving, safeguarding, investing, and disbursing court funds
Purchasing Agent
  process departmental requisitions
  issue and analyze bids
  make contracts and agreements for the purchase or rental of personal property
  store surplus property and facilitate public auctions
Unallowable costs
  Unallowable court-related costs are those
    (a) in support of county operations,
    (b) expressly prohibited by statute,
    (c) facility-related, or
    (d) exceptions of the nature referenced in Functions 1-11.

Unallowable cost items, including any related data processing costs, are not reported in Functions 1-11 and may include, for example,

Communications
  central communication control and maintenance for county emergency and general government radio equipment
Central Collections
  processing accounts receivable for county departments (not courts)
County Administrator
  legislative analysis and activities
  preparation and operation of general directives and operating procedures
  responses to questions from the Board, outside agencies, and the public executive functions: Board of Supervisors
  county advisory councils
Treasurer/Tax Collector
  property tax determination, collection, etc.
General Services
  rental and utilities support
  coordinate county's emergency services
Property Management
  negotiations for the acquisition, sale, or lease of property, except for space rented for storage of court records
  making appraisals
  negotiating utility relocations
  assisting County Counsel in condemnation actions
  preparing deeds, leases, licenses, easements
  collecting rents
  building lease management services (except for storage of court records)
Facility-related
  construction services
  right-of-way and easement services
  purchase of land and buildings
  construction
  depreciation of buildings/use allowance
  space rental/building rent (except for storage of court records)
  building maintenance and repairs (except interior painting and to replace/repair flooring)
  purchase, installation, and maintenance of H/V/A/C equipment
  maintenance and repair of utilities
  utility use charges (e.g., heat, light, water)
  elevator purchase and maintenance
  alterations/remodeling
  landscaping and grounds maintenance services
  exterior lighting and security
  insurance on building damages (e.g., fire, earthquake, flood, boiler and machinery)
  grounds' liability insurance
  parking lot or facility maintenance
  juror parking

(Subd (d) amended effective January 1, 2007; previously amended and relettered effective July 1, 1995.)

Rule 10.810 amended and renumbered effective January 1, 2007; adopted as rule 810 effective July 1, 1988; previously amended effective July 1, 1989, July 1, 1990, July 1, 1991, and July 1, 1995.

Advisory Committee Comment

Rule 10.810 is identical to former rule 810, except for the rule number. All references in statutes or rules to rule 810 apply to this rule.

Ref.: Cal. Fms Pl. & Pr., Ch. 317, "Judges."

Rule 10.811.   Reimbursement of costs associated with homicide trials

(a) Intent

This rule permits courts that meet certain criteria to request reimbursement of extraordinary costs of homicide trials.

(Subd (a) amended effective January 1, 2007.)

(b) Criteria

A court that requests reimbursement of extraordinary costs of a homicide trial must meet all the following criteria:

(1) Be located in a county with a population of 300,000 or less;

(2) Have incurred extraordinary costs of a homicide trial; and

(3) Demonstrate an actual need for reimbursement.

(c) Submission

A request for reimbursement must be submitted by the court's presiding judge or executive officer to the Administrative Office of the Courts. All requests for reimbursement must comply with guidelines approved by the Judicial Council and include a completed *Request for Reimbursement of Extraordinary Homicide Trial Costs* form.

Rule 10.811 amended and renumbered effective January 1, 2007; adopted as rule 6.711 effective January 1, 2005.

Ref.: Cal. Fms Pl. & Pr., Ch. 317, "Judges."

Rule 10.815.   Fees to be set by the court

(a) Authority

Under Government Code section 70631, a superior court may charge a reasonable fee for a service or product not to exceed the costs of providing the service or product, if the Judicial Council approves the fee.

(b) Approved fees

The Judicial Council authorizes courts to charge a reasonable fee not to exceed costs for the following products and services unless courts are prohibited by law from charging a fee for, or providing, the product or service:

(1) Forms;

(2) Packages of forms;

(3) Information materials;

(4) Publications, including books, pamphlets, and local rules;

(5) Compact discs;

(6) DVDs;

(7) Audiotapes;

(8) Videotapes;

(9) Microfiches;

(10) Envelopes;

(11) Postage;

(12) Shipping;

(13) Off-site retrieval of documents;

(14) Direct fax filing under rule 2.304 (fee per page);

(15) Returning filed-stamped copies of documents by fax to persons who request that a faxed copy be sent to them;

(16) Training programs for attorneys who serve as court-appointed temporary judges, including the materials and food provided to the participants; and

(17) Other training programs or events, including materials and food provided to the participants.

(Subd (b) amended effective January 1, 2007; previously amended effective July 1, 2006.)

(c) Guidelines for determining costs

The fee charged for any product or service listed in (b) may not exceed the court's cost in providing the product or service. In determining the costs of a product or service, the court must:

(1) Identify the specific product or service; and

(2) Prepare an analysis of the direct and indirect costs on which the fee is based.

(d) Reasonableness

In deciding what specific fee or fees, if any, to charge for a product or service under (b), the court must determine that the fee charged is reasonable considering relevant factors such as the benefits to the court and the public from providing the product or service and the effects of charging the fee on public access to the court.

(e) Reporting requirement

Each court that charges a fee under this rule must provide the Administrative Office of the Courts with a description of the fee, how the amount of the fee was determined, and how the fee is applied.

(f) Public notice

The court must notify the public of any fee that it charges under this rule by providing information concerning the fee in a conspicuous place such as the court's fee schedule.

(g) Procedure for adoption of fee

If a court proposes to change any fee authorized under (b) that it is already charging or to charge any new fee authorized under (b), the court must follow the procedures for adopting or amending a local rule under rule 10.613 of the California Rules of Court.

(Subd (g) amended effective January 1, 2007; previously amended effective July 1, 2006.)

Rule 10.815 amended and renumbered effective January 1, 2007; adopted as rule 6.712 effective January 1, 2006; previously amended effective July 1, 2006.

Ref.: Cal. Fms Pl. & Pr., Ch. 317, "Judges."

Rule 10.820.   Acceptance of credit cards by the superior courts

(a) Delegation of authority to Administrative Director of the Courts

The Administrative Director of the Courts is authorized, under rule 10.80, to approve on behalf of the Judicial Council requests from the superior courts to accept credit cards for the payment of court fees or to impose a charge for the use of credit cards. The authority is given to the Judicial Council by Government Code section 6159.

(Subd (a) amended effective January 1, 2007.)

(b) Standards for use of credit cards

The Administrative Director of the Courts is authorized to approve requests under (a) for acceptance of credit cards if all of the following are true:

(1) The court (A) imposes a fee for the use of the credit card, or (B) demonstrates that the cost of acceptance of credit cards is not greater than the cost of acceptance of other means of payment of fees, or (C) demonstrates that it can absorb the cost of the acceptance of the credit card;

(2) The court has obtained a credit card acceptance contract that is competitive with other possible contracts the court could obtain; and

(3) The court provides alternative means for a person to pay court fees.

(Subd (b) amended effective January 1, 2007.)

(c) Standards for charge for the use of credit cards

The Administrative Director of the Courts is authorized to approve requests under (a) for the imposition of a charge for the use of credit cards if both of the following are true:

(1) The proposed fee is not greater than the cost for acceptance of a credit card; and

(2) The proposed fee would not result in an undue hardship on people wishing to use credit cards for payment of fees.

(Subd (c) amended effective January 1, 2007.)

(d) Referral to Judicial Council

The Administrative Director of the Courts may refer any request under (a) to the Judicial Council for its action.

(Subd (d) amended effective January 1, 2007.)

(e) Existing approvals ratified

The approval of any board of supervisors for **any** superior court to accept credit cards or charge a fee for the use of credit cards that was effective as of December 31, 1999, is ratified by the council as of January 1, 2000.

(Subd (e) amended effective January 1, 2009; previously amended effective January 1, 2007.)

Rule 10.820 amended effective January 1, 2009; adopted as rule 6.703 effective January 1, 2000; previously amended and renumbered effective January 1, 2007.

Ref.: Cal. Fms Pl. & Pr., Ch. 317, "Judges," Ch. 518, "Service of Summons and Papers."

Rule 10.821. Acceptance of checks and other negotiable paper

(a) Conditions for acceptance

A personal check, bank cashier's check, money order, or traveler's check tendered in payment of any fee, fine, or bail deposit under Government Code section 71386 or Vehicle Code section 40510 or 40521 must be accepted by the court:

(1) If the personal check is drawn on a banking institution located in California by a person furnishing satisfactory proof of residence in California, is payable to the court without a second party endorsement, and is in an amount not exceeding the amount of the payment and is not postdated or staledated, unless the person drawing the

check is known to have previously tendered worthless checks; or

(2) If the bank cashier's check or money order is drawn on a banking institution located in the United States and is in an amount not exceeding the amount of the payment; or

(3) If the person presenting the traveler's check shows satisfactory identification.

(Subd (a) amended effective January 1, 2007.)

(b) Requiring satisfactory proof of good credit

Except for checks tendered under the conditions specified in Vehicle Code section 40521(a), a court may require that a person drawing a personal check furnish satisfactory proof of good credit by showing a valid recognized credit card or by any other reasonable means.

(Subd (b) amended effective January 1, 2007.)

(c) Written policy for acceptance or rejection

A court may accept or reject any check or money order not meeting the requirements of this rule, under a written policy adopted by the court under Government Code section 71386(a).

(Subd (c) amended effective January 1, 2007.)

Rule 10.821 amended and renumbered effective January 1, 2007; adopted as rule 805 effective July 1, 1981.

Ref.: Cal. Fms Pl. & Pr., Ch. 317, "Judges."

Rule 10.830. Disposal of surplus court personal property

(a) Disposal of surplus property

Except as provided in (b), a superior court may:

(1) Sell, at fair market value, any personal property of the court that is no longer needed for court use;

(2) Trade or exchange any surplus personal property of the court, according to such terms and conditions as are agreed on, for personal property of another court, the state, a county, a city, a federal agency, a community redevelopment agency, a housing authority, a community development commission, a surplus property authority, a school district, or any irrigation, flood control, county board of education, or other special district, if the property to be acquired by the court is needed for court use;

(3) Donate, sell at less than fair market value, or otherwise transfer to another court, the state, a county, a city, a federal agency, a community redevelopment agency, a housing authority, a community development commission, a surplus property authority, a school district, or any irrigation, flood control, county board of education, or other special district, according to such terms and conditions as are agreed on, any personal property of the court that is no longer needed for court use; and

(4) Dispose of any personal property of the court that is no longer needed for court use, and that has negligible or no economic value, in any manner the court deems appropriate.

(Subd (a) amended effective January 1, 2007.)

(b) Exception for disposal of technology equipment acquired on or after July 1, 2000

A superior court that wishes to dispose of surplus technology equipment to which the court acquired title on or after July 1, 2000 must provide a written description of such technology equipment to the Administrative Director of the Courts. If, within 60 days of receipt of the description, the Administrative Director determines that another court of record of the State of California is in need of the surplus technology equipment, the court holding title to the equipment must donate it to the court determined to be in need. If the Administrative Director determines that no other court needs the equipment or makes no determination within 60 days of receiving the written description of it, the court holding title to the equipment may dispose of it as provided in (a), (c), and (d). The Administrative Director must provide to the courts a definition of the term "technology equipment" as used in this rule and must provide 30 days' notice of any amendment to the definition.

(Subd (b) amended effective January 1, 2007.)

(c) Notice of disposal

Unless the property to be transferred under this rule is valued at $500 or less or the entity to which the property is to be transferred is another court of record of the State of California, the transferring superior court must, at least one week before the transfer, place a notice of its intended action:

(1) In three public places; or

(2) On the court's Web site; or

(3) In a newspaper of general circulation published in the county.

(Subd (c) amended effective January 1, 2007.)

(d) Proceeds of disposal

Any proceeds of a sale or other transfer under this rule must be deposited in the superior court's operations fund.

(Subd (d) amended effective January 1, 2007.)

Rule 10.830 amended and renumbered effective January 1, 2007; adopted as rule 6.709 effective January 1, 2001.

Ref.: Cal. Fms Pl. & Pr., Ch. 317, "Judges."

Chapter 10
Trial Court Records Management

Chapter 10 renumbered effective January 1, 2008; adopted as Chapter 4 effective January 1, 2001; previously amended and renumbered as Chapter 9 effective January 1, 2007.

Rule 10.851. Court indexes—automated maintenance
Rule 10.855. Superior court records sampling program
Rule 10.856. Notice of superior court records destruction

Rule 10.851.   Court indexes—automated maintenance

(a) Authorized media

The clerk of each trial court may create, maintain, update, and make accessible the indexes required by law by photographic, microphotographic, photocopy, mechanical, magnetic, or electronic means. The clerk must make provision for preserving the information on a medium that will ensure its permanence and protect it from loss or damage arising from electronic failure or mechanical defect.

(Subd (a) amended effective January 1, 2007; adopted as unlettered subd; previously relettered and amended effective January 1, 2001.)

(b) Alphabetic index

A single alphabetic index may be maintained so long as the plaintiff-defendant distinction is retained.

(Subd (b) adopted effective January 1, 2001.)

(c) Public access

The indexes maintained under automated procedures must be accessible for public examination and use.

(Subd (c) amended effective January 1, 2007; adopted as part of unlettered subd; previously lettered and amended effective January 1, 2001.)

Rule 10.851 amended and renumbered effective January 1, 2007; adopted as rule 1010 effective January 1, 1975; renumbered as rule 999 effective January 1, 2003; amended and renumbered as rule 6.751 effective January 1, 2001.

Ref.: Cal. Fms Pl. & Pr., Ch. 317, "Judges."

Rule 10.855.   Superior court records sampling program

(a) Purpose

This rule establishes a program to preserve in perpetuity for study by historians and other researchers all superior court records filed before 1911 and a sample of superior court records filed after December 31, 1910, to document the progress and development of the judicial system, and to preserve evidence of significant events and social trends. This rule is not intended to restrict a court from preserving more records than the minimum required.

(Subd (a) amended effective January 1, 2007.)

(b) Scope

"Records" of the superior court, as used in this rule, does not include records of limited civil, small claims, misdemeanor, or infraction cases.

(Subd (b) adopted effective January 1, 2001.)

(c) Comprehensive records

Each superior court must preserve forever comprehensive court records as follows:

(1) All records filed before 1911;

(2) If practicable, all records filed after 1910 and before 1950;

(3) All case indexes;

(4) All judgment books if the court maintains judgment records separate from the case files;

(5) All minute books if the court maintains minutes separate from the case files; and

(6) All registers of action if the court maintains them.

(Subd (c) amended effective January 1, 2007; adopted as subd (b) effective July 1, 1992; previously amended and relettered effective January 1, 2001.)

(d) Sample records

If a superior court destroys court records without preserving them in a medium described in (h), the court must preserve forever a sample of each year's court records as provided by this rule of all cases, including sealed, expunged, and other confidential records to the extent permitted by law.

(Subd (d) amended effective January 1, 2007; adopted as subd (c) effective July 1, 1992; relettered effective January 1, 2001.)

(e) Court record defined

The "court record" under this rule consists of the following:

(1) All papers and documents in the case folder; but if no case folder is created by the court, all papers and documents that would have been in the case folder if one had been created; and

(2) The case folder, unless all information on the case folder is in papers and documents preserved in a medium described in (h); and

(3) If available, corresponding depositions, paper exhibits, daily transcripts, and tapes of electronically recorded proceedings.

(Subd (e) amended effective January 1, 2007; adopted as subd (d) effective July 1, 1992; previously amended and relettered effective January 1, 2001.)

(f) Sampling technique

Three courts assigned in rotation by the Judicial Council must preserve 100 percent of their court records for a calendar year ("longitudinal sample"). All other courts must preserve a systematic sample of 10 percent or more of each year's court records and a 2 percent subjective sample of the court records scheduled to be destroyed, as follows:

(1) The "systematic sample" must be selected as follows after grouping all cases scheduled to be destroyed by filing year:

(A) If the cases scheduled to be destroyed for a filing year number more than 1,000 cases, the sample must consist of all cases in which the last digit of the case number (0–9) coincides with the last digit of the year in which the case was filed.

(B) If the cases scheduled to be destroyed for a filing year number from 100 to 1,000, the sample must consist of cases selected by (1) dividing the number of cases filed by 100, rounding fractions down to the next lower number, and (2) counting the cases and preserving each case with a position number in the files or other record that corresponds with the number computed (for example, 670 cases ÷ 100 = 6.7; select every sixth case).

(C) If fewer than 100 cases of a filing year are scheduled to be destroyed, all of the cases must be preserved.

(D) If the records to be destroyed are old, unnumbered cases, the sample must consist of cases identified by counting the cases (0–9) and preserving each case with a position number in the file or other record that corresponds with the number determined under (A) or (B), unless fewer than 100 cases are to be destroyed.

(2) The "subjective sample" must consist of at least 2 percent of all cases scheduled to be destroyed, but not fewer than the court records of 20 cases, and must include (1) all cases accepted for review by the California Supreme Court, (2) "fat files" or the thickest perceived case files, and (3) cases deemed by the court to be of local, national, or international significance. These cases must be identified by stamp or mark to distinguish them from the systematic sample. The Judicial Council will provide each court with a list of cases accepted for review by the California Supreme Court each year.

(Subd (f) amended effective January 1, 2007; adopted as subd (e) effective July 1, 1992; repealed, amended, and relettered effective January 1, 2001.)

(g) Augmented sample; designated advisory consultant

(1) The Judicial Council may designate a consultant to review, under the guidance of a qualified historian or archivist, court records scheduled for destruction and determine if the court's systematic sample should be augmented to improve representation of the variety of cases filed.

(2) The court should give the designated consultant 60 days' notice of intent to destroy any court records that it does not plan to retain for the sample.

(3) The designated consultant's role is advisory to the court. If the consultant determines that the systematic sample does not represent the variety of cases filed in a sample year, the court should select a random sample of cases to augment the systematic sample.

(4) Final selection of the court records to augment the sample is to be made by the clerk of the superior court.

(Subd (g) amended effective January 1, 2007.)

(h) Preservation medium

(1) Comprehensive court records under (c) filed before 1911 must be preserved in their original paper form unless the paper is not available.

(2) If practicable, courts should preserve paper records filed after January 1, 1911, because they are preferred by historians and researchers. Courts may, however, reproduce such paper records on microfilm or other electronic or micrographic media, if the records are maintained and reproduced in accordance with archival standards recommended by the American National Standards Institute or the Association for Information and Image Management and the condition of the paper records permits reproduction without damage to the originals. [NOTE: As of the effective date of this rule, optical disk storage is not recognized as an archival medium, although it may become so with advances in the technology.]

(Subd (h) amended effective January 1, 2007; previously amended effective January 1, 2001.)

(i) Storage

Until statewide or regional archival facilities are established, each court is responsible for maintaining its comprehensive and sample court records in a secure and safe environment consistent with the archival significance of the records. The court may deposit the court records in a suitable California archival facility such as a university, college, library, historical society, museum, archive, or research institution whether publicly supported or privately endowed. The court must ensure that the records are kept and preserved according to commonly recognized archival principles and practices of preservation.

(Subd (i) amended effective January 1, 2007.)

(j) Access

The court must ensure the following:

(1) The comprehensive and sample court records are made reasonably available to all members of the public.

(2) Sealed and confidential records are made available to the public only as provided by law.

(3) If the records are preserved in a medium other than paper, equipment is provided to permit public viewing of the records.

(4) Reasonable provision is made for duplicating the records at cost.

(Subd (j) amended effective January 1, 2007.)

(k) Choosing an archival facility

If a local archival facility is maintaining the court records, the court may continue to use that facility's services if it meets the storage and access requirements under (i) and (j). If the court solicits archival facilities interested in maintaining the comprehensive and sample court records, the court must follow the procedures specified under rule 10.856, except that the comprehensive and sample court records must not be destroyed. Courts may enter into agreements for long-term deposit of records subject to the storage and access provisions of this rule.

(Subd (k) amended effective January 1, 2007; previously amended effective January 1, 1994, and January 1, 2001.)

(*l*) Reporting requirement

Each superior court must submit semiannually to the Judicial Council a *Report to the Judicial Council: Superior Court Records Destroyed, Preserved, and Transferred* (form 982.8A), including the following information:

(1) A list by year of filing of the court records destroyed;

(2) A list by year of filing and location of the court records of the comprehensive and sample court records preserved; and

(3) A list by year of filing and location of the court records transferred to entities under rule 10.856.

(Subd (l) amended effective January 1, 2007; previously amended effective January 1, 1994, January 1, 1995, and January 1, 2001.)

Rule 10.855 amended and renumbered effective January 1, 2007; adopted as rule 243.5 effective July 1, 1992; previously amended effective January 1, 1994, and January 1, 1995; previously amended and renumbered as rule 6.755 effective January 1, 2001.

Ref.: Cal. Fms Pl. & Pr., Ch. 317, "Judges," Ch. 551, "Trial."

Rule 10.856. Notice of superior court records destruction

(a) Scope

"Records" of the superior court, as used in this rule, do not include records of limited civil, small claims, misdemeanor, or infraction cases.

(Subd (a) adopted effective January 1, 2007.)

(b) Notice

The superior court must give 30 days' written notice of its intent to destroy court records open to public inspection to entities maintained on a master list by the Judicial Council and to any other entities that have informed the court directly that they wish to be notified.

(Subd (b) amended and relettered effective January 1, 2007; adopted as subd (a); previously amended effective January 1, 2001, and July 1, 2001.)

(c) Transfer to requesting entity

Records scheduled for destruction must be permanently transferred to the entity requesting possession of the records on written order of the presiding judge unless the request is denied for good cause shown. The cost of transferring the records must be paid by the requesting party.

(Subd (c) amended and relettered effective January 1, 2007; adopted as subd (b); previously amended effective January 1, 2001.)

(d) Request by two or more entities

If two or more entities request the same records, the presiding judge must order the transfer of those records to the entity that shows the greatest capability of caring for and preserving the records according to commonly recognized archival principles and practices of preservation and access, and that provides the greatest likelihood of making them available for historical or research purposes.

(Subd (d) amended and relettered effective January 1, 2007; adopted as subd (c); previously amended effective January 1, 2001.)

(e) Public access

No entity may receive the records unless the entity agrees to make the records reasonably available to all members of the public. Provision must be made for duplicating the records at cost.

(Subd (e) amended and relettered effective January 1, 2007; adopted as subd (d); previously amended effective January 1, 2001.)

(f) Destruction

If after 30 days no request for transfer of records scheduled for destruction has been received by the court, the clerk may destroy the records not designated for the historical and research program under rule 10.855, under a written order of the presiding judge of the court and in accordance with provisions of the Government Code.

(Subd (f) amended and relettered effective January 1, 2007; adopted as subd (e); previously amended effective January 1, 2001.)

(g) Extension of time

The time for retention of any of the court records specified in the notice may be extended by order of the court on its own motion, or on application of any interested member of the public for good cause shown and on such terms as are just. No fee may be charged for making the application.

(Subd (g) amended and relettered effective January 1, 2007; adopted as subd (f); previously amended effective January 1, 2001.)

(h) Forms

The court must use the following forms to implement the requirements of this rule:

(1) *Notice of Intent to Destroy Superior Court Records; Offer to Transfer Possession* (form 982.8(1)(N) with a form on the reverse titled *Request for Transfer or Extension of Time for Retention of Superior Court Records* (form 982.8(1)(R)), for optional use by the recipient of the notice; and

(2) *Notice of Hearing on Request for Transfer or Extension of Time for Retention of Superior Court Records; Court Order; Release and Receipt of Superior Court Records* (form 982.8(2)(N)).

(Subd (h) amended and relettered effective January 1, 2007; adopted as subd (g); previously amended effective January 1, 2001.)

Rule 10.856 amended and renumbered effective January 1, 2007; adopted as rule 243.6 effective January 1, 1994; previously amended and renumbered rule 6.756 effective January 1, 2001; previously amended effective July 1, 2001.

Ref.: Cal. Fms Pl. & Pr., Ch. 317, "Judges," Ch. 551, "Trial."

Chapter 11
Trial Court Automation

Chapter 11 renumbered effective January 1, 2008; adopted as Chapter 5 effective January 1, 2001; previously amended and renumbered as Chapter 10 effective January 1, 2007.

Rule 10.870. Trial court automation standards

Each superior court that acquires, develops, enhances, or maintains automated accounting or case management systems through funding provided under Government Code section 68090.8 must comply with the standards approved by the Judicial Council. The approved standards are stated in *Judicial Council Trial Court Automation Standards* published by the Administrative Office of the Courts.

Rule 10.870 amended and renumbered effective January 1, 2007; adopted as rule 1011 effective March 1, 1992; renumbered as rule 999.1 effective July 1, 1993.

Ref.: Cal. Fms Pl. & Pr., Ch. 317, "Judges."

Chapter 12
Trial Court Management of Civil Cases

Chapter 12 renumbered effective January 1, 2008; adopted as Chapter 11 effective January 1, 2007.

Rule 10.900. Case management and calendaring system
Rule 10.901. Internal management procedures
Rule 10.910. Assigned cases to be tried or dismissed—notification to presiding judge

Rule 10.900.   Case management and calendaring system

Each superior court must adopt a case management and calendaring system for general civil cases that will advance the goals stated in standard 2.1 of the California Standards of Judicial Administration.

Rule 10.900 amended and renumbered effective January 1, 2007; adopted as rule 204.1 effective July 1, 2002.

Ref.: Cal. Fms Pl. & Pr., Ch. 317, "Judges," Ch. 425, "Pretrial Proceedings"; MB Prac. Guide: Cal. Pretrial Proc., §23.04[1][a].

Rule 10.901.   Internal management procedures

Each court must:

(1) Maintain a calendar and caseflow management system that will ensure that a sufficient number of cases are set for trial, based on the court's experience, so that all departments will be occupied with judicial business;

(2) Adopt for judges and court personnel an internal operations manual of policies and procedures necessary for the efficient operation and management of the court;

(3) Maintain and periodically review for accuracy written local court procedures, policies, and operating practices not contained in local rules for quick, accurate, and complete reference; and

(4) Ensure that calendaring functions are performed as directed by the court and that personnel rendering direct and immediate service to the court are within its administrative control to the maximum extent consistent with the existing organizational structures.

Rule 10.901 amended and renumbered effective January 1, 2007; adopted as rule 208 effective January 1, 1985; previously amended and renumbered as rule 204.2 effective July 1, 2002.

Ref.: Cal. Fms Pl. & Pr., Ch. 317, "Judges."

Rule 10.910.   Assigned cases to be tried or dismissed—notification to presiding judge

(a) Assignment of cases for trial

In a court employing the master calendar, each case transferred to a trial department must be tried, ordered off the calendar, or dismissed unless, for good cause arising after the commencement of the trial, the judge of the trial department continues the case for further hearing or, with the consent of the judge supervising the master calendar, reassigns the case to the judge supervising the master calendar for further disposition.

(Subd (a) amended effective January 1, 2007; adopted as untitled subd effective January 1, 1985; previously amended and lettered effective July 1, 2002.)

(b) Notification to presiding judge

A judge who has finished or continued the trial of a case or any special matter must immediately notify the judge supervising the master calendar. The judge to whose department a cause is assigned for trial or for hearing must accept the assignment unless disqualified or, for other good cause stated to the judge supervising the master calendar, the judge supervising the master calendar determines that in the interest of justice the cause should not be tried or heard before the judge. When the judge has refused a cause and is not disqualified, the judge must state the reasons in writing unless the judge supervising the master calendar has concurred.

(Subd (b) amended and lettered effective July 1, 2002; adopted as untitled subd effective January 1, 1985.)

Rule 10.910 amended and renumbered effective January 1, 2007; adopted as rule 226 effective January 1, 1985; previously amended effective July 1, 2002.

Ref.: Cal. Fms Pl. & Pr., Ch. 136, "Continuances," Ch. 317, "Judges," Ch. 425, "Pretrial Proceedings," Ch. 551, "Trial"; MB Prac. Guide: Cal. Pretrial Proc., §23.11[4].

Chapter 13
Trial Court Management of Criminal Cases

Chapter 13 renumbered effective January 1, 2008; adopted as Chapter 12 effective January 1, 2007.

Rule 10.950. Role of presiding judge, supervising judge, criminal division, and master calendar department in courts having more than three judges
Rule 10.951. Duties of supervising judge of the criminal division
Rule 10.952. Meetings concerning the criminal court system
Rule 10.953. Procedures for disposition of cases before the preliminary hearing

Rule 10.950.   Role of presiding judge, supervising judge, criminal division, and master calendar department in courts having more than three judges

The presiding judge of a court having more than three judges may designate one or more departments primarily to hear criminal cases. Two or more departments so designated must be the criminal division. The presiding judge may designate supervising judges for the criminal division, but retains final authority over all criminal and civil case assignments.

Rule 10.950 amended and renumbered effective January 1, 2007; adopted as rule 227.1 effective January 1, 1985.

Ref.: Cal. Fms Pl. & Pr., Ch. 317, "Judges."

Rule 10.951. Duties of supervising judge of the criminal division

(a) Duties

In addition to any other duties assigned by the presiding judge or imposed by these rules, a supervising judge of the criminal division must assign criminal matters requiring a hearing or cases requiring trial to a trial department.

(Subd (a) amended effective January 1, 2007.)

(b) Arraignments, pretrial motions, and readiness conferences

The presiding judge, supervising judge, or other designated judge must conduct arraignments, hear and determine any pretrial motions, preside over readiness conferences, and, where not inconsistent with law, assist in the disposition of cases without trial.

(Subd (b) amended effective January 1, 2008; previously amended effective January 1, 2007.)

(c) Additional judges

To the extent that the business of the court requires, the presiding judge may designate additional judges under the direction of the supervising judge to perform the duties specified in this rule.

(d) Courts without supervising judge

In a court having no supervising judge, the presiding judge performs the duties of a supervising judge.

(Subd (d) amended effective January 1, 2007.)

Rule 10.951 amended effective January 1, 2008; adopted as rule 227.2 effective January 1, 1985; previously amended and renumbered effective January 1, 2007.

Ref.: Cal. Fms Pl. & Pr., Ch. 317, "Judges."

Rule 10.952. Meetings concerning the criminal court system

The supervising judge or, if none, the presiding judge must designate judges of the court to attend regular meetings to be held with the district attorney, public defender, representatives of the local bar, probation department, court personnel, and other interested persons to identify and eliminate problems in the criminal court system and to discuss other problems of mutual concern.

Rule 10.952 amended and renumbered effective January 1, 2007; adopted as rule 227.8 effective January 1, 1985.

Ref.: Cal. Fms Pl. & Pr., Ch. 317, "Judges."

Rule 10.953. Procedures for disposition of cases before the preliminary hearing

(a) Disposition before preliminary hearing

Superior courts having more than three judges must, in cooperation with the district attorney and defense bar, adopt procedures to facilitate dispositions before the preliminary hearing and at all other stages of the proceedings. The procedures may include:

(1) Early, voluntary, informal discovery, consistent with part 2, title 6, chapter 10 of the Penal Code (commencing with section 1054); and

(2) The use of superior court judges as magistrates to conduct readiness conferences before the preliminary hearing and to assist, where not inconsistent with law, in the early disposition of cases.

(Subd (a) amended effective January 1, 2007; previously amended effective June 6, 1990, and January 1, 1991.)

(b) Case to be disposed of under rule 4.114

Pleas of guilty or no contest resulting from proceedings under (a) must be disposed of as provided in rule 4.114.

(Subd (b) amended effective January 1, 2007; previously amended effective July 1, 2001.)

Rule 10.953 amended and renumbered effective January 1, 2007; adopted as rule 227.10 effective January 1, 1985; previously amended effective June 6, 1990, January 1, 1991, and July 1, 2001.

Ref.: Cal. Fms Pl. & Pr., Ch. 317, "Judges."

Chapter 14
Management of Self-Help Centers

Chapter 14 adopted effective July 1, 2008.

Rule 10.960. Court self-help centers

(a) Scope and application

This rule applies to all court-based self-help centers whether the services provided by the center are managed by the court or by an entity other than the court.

(Subd (a) adopted effective January 1, 2008.)

(b) Purpose and core court function

Providing access to justice for self-represented litigants is a priority for California courts. The services provided by court self-help centers facilitate the timely and cost-effective processing of cases involving self-represented litigants and improve the delivery of justice to the public. Court programs, policies, and procedures designed to assist self-represented litigants and effectively manage cases involving self-represented litigants at all stages must be incorporated and budgeted as core court functions.

(Subd (b) adopted effective January 1, 2008.)

(c) Staffing

Court self-help centers provide assistance to self-represented litigants. A court self-help center must include an attorney and other qualified staff who provide information and education to self-represented litigants about the justice process, and who work within the court to provide for the effective management of cases involving self-represented litigants.

(Subd (c) adopted effective January 1, 2008.)

(d) Neutrality and availability

The information and education provided by court self-help centers must be neutral and unbiased, and services must be available to all sides of a case.

(Subd (d) adopted effective January 1, 2008.)

(e) Guidelines and procedures

The Administrative Office of the Courts, in collaboration with judges, court executives, attorneys, and other parties with demonstrated interest in services to self-represented litigants, must develop and disseminate guidelines and procedures for the operation of court self-help centers to the trial courts by March 1, 2008. The guidelines and procedures must address the following topics:

(1) Location and hours of operation;

(2) Scope of services;

(3) Attorney qualifications;

(4) Other staffing qualifications and supervision requirements;

(5) Language access;

(6) Contracts with entities other than the court that provide self-help services;

(7) Use of technology;

(8) Ethics;

(9) Efficiency of operation; and

(10) Security.

The Administrative Office of the Courts, in collaboration with judges, court executives, attorneys, and other parties with demonstrated interest in services to self-represented litigants, must review and update the guidelines and procedures at least every three years.

(Subd (e) adopted effective January 1, 2008.)

(f) Budget and funding

A court must include in its annual budget funding necessary for operation of its self-help center. In analyzing and making recommendations on the allocation of funding for a court self-help center, the Administrative Office of the Courts will consider the degree to which individual courts have been successful in meeting the guidelines and procedures for the operation of the self-help center.

(Subd (f) adopted effective January 1, 2008.)

Rule 10.960 adopted effective January 1, 2008.

Division 5
Appellate Court
Administration

Chap. 1. Rules Relating to the Supreme Court and Courts of Appeal. Rules 10.1000–10.1030.

Chap. 2. Rules Relating to the Superior Court Appellate Division. Rules 10.1100–10.1108.

Chapter 1
Rules Relating to the Supreme Court and Courts of Appeal

Rule 10.1000. Transfer of causes

(a) Transfer by Supreme Court

(1) The Supreme Court may transfer a cause:

(A) To itself from a Court of Appeal;

(B) From itself to a Court of Appeal;

(C) Between Courts of Appeal; or

(D) Between divisions of a Court of Appeal.

(2) The clerk of the transferee court must promptly send each party a copy of the transfer order with the new case number, if any.

(Subd (a) amended effective January 1, 2007.)

(b) Transfer by a Court of Appeal administrative presiding justice

(1) A Court of Appeal administrative presiding justice may transfer causes between divisions of that court as follows:

(A) If multiple appeals or writ petitions arise from the same trial court action or proceeding, the presiding justice may transfer the later appeals or petitions to the division assigned the first appeal or petition.

(B) If, because of recusals, a division does not have three justices qualified to decide a cause, the presiding justice may transfer it to a division randomly selected by the clerk.

(2) The clerk must promptly notify the parties of the division to which the cause was transferred.

Rule 10.1000 amended and renumbered effective January 1, 2007; adopted as rule 47.1 effective January 1, 2003.

Advisory Committee Comment

Subdivision (a). Subdivision (a)(1) implements article VI, section 12(a) of the Constitution. As used in article VI, section 12(a) and in the rule, the term "cause" is broadly construed to include " 'all cases, matters, and proceedings of every description' " adjudicated by the Courts of Appeal and the Supreme Court. (*In re Rose* (2000) 22 Cal.4th 430, 540, quoting *In re Wells* (1917) 174 Cal. 467, 471.)

Ref.: Cal. Fms Pl. & Pr., Ch. 18, "Alcoholic Beverage Licenses," Ch. 40, "Appeal: An Overview," Ch. 42, "Appeal: Notice of Appeal," Ch. 45, "Appeal: Motion Procedure," Ch. 51, "Appeal: Hearing and Decision," Ch. 54, "Appeal: California Supreme Court Review," Ch. 317, "Judges," Ch. 358, "Mandate and Prohibition," Ch. 480, "Public Utilities," Ch. 492, "Review (Certiorari), Writ of."

Rule 10.1004. Court of Appeal administrative presiding justice

(a) Designation

(1) In a Court of Appeal with more than one division, the Chief Justice may designate a presiding justice to act as administrative presiding justice. The administrative presiding justice serves at the pleasure of the Chief Justice for the period specified in the designation order.

(2) The administrative presiding justice must designate another member of the court to serve as acting administrative presiding justice in the administrative presiding justice's absence. If the administrative presiding justice does not make that designation, the Chief Justice must do so.

(3) In a Court of Appeal with only one division, the presiding justice acts as the administrative presiding justice.

(Subd (a) amended effective January 1, 2007.)

(b) Responsibilities

The administrative presiding justice is responsible for leading the court, establishing policies, promoting access to justice for all members of the public, providing a forum for the fair and expeditious resolution of disputes, and maximizing the use of judicial and other resources.

(c) Duties

The administrative presiding justice must perform any duties delegated by a majority of the justices in the district with the Chief Justice's concurrence. In addition, the administrative presiding justice has responsibility for the following matters:

(1) *Personnel*

The administrative presiding justice has general direction and supervision of the clerk/administrator and all court employees except those assigned to a particular justice or division;

(2) *Unassigned matters*

The administrative presiding justice has the authority of a presiding justice with respect to any matter that has not been assigned to a particular division;

(3) *Judicial Council*

The administrative presiding justice cooperates with the Chief Justice and any officer authorized to act for the Chief Justice in connection with the making of reports and the assignment of judges or retired judges under article VI, section 6 of the California Constitution;

(4) *Transfer of cases*

The administrative presiding justice cooperates with the Chief Justice in expediting judicial business and equalizing the work of judges by recommending, when appropriate, the transfer of cases by the Supreme Court under article VI, section 12 of the California Constitution;

(5) *Administration*

The administrative presiding justice supervises the administration of the court's day-to-day operations, including personnel matters, but must secure the approval of a majority of the justices in the district before implementing any change in court policies;

(6) *Budget*

The administrative presiding justice has sole authority in the district over the budget as allocated by the Chair of the Judicial Council, including budget transfers, execution of purchase orders, obligation of funds, and approval of payments; and

(7) *Facilities*

The administrative presiding justice, except as provided in (d), has sole authority in the district over the operation, maintenance, renovation, expansion, and assignment of all facilities used and occupied by the district.

(Subd (c) amended effective January 1, 2007.)

(d) Geographically separate divisions

Under the general oversight of the administrative presiding justice, the presiding justice of a geographically separate division:

(1) Generally directs and supervises all of the division's court employees not assigned to a particular justice;

(2) Has authority to act on behalf of the division regarding day-to-day operations;

(3) Administers the division budget for day-to-day operations, including expenses for maintenance of facilities and equipment; and

(4) Operates, maintains, and assigns space in all facilities used and occupied by the division.

(Subd (d) amended effective January 1, 2007.)

Rule 10.1004 amended and renumbered effective January 1, 2007; repealed and adopted as rule 75 effective January 1, 2005.

Ref.: Cal. Fms Pl. & Pr., Ch. 317, "Judges."

Rule 10.1008.   Courts of Appeal with more than one division

Appeals and original proceedings filed in a Court of Appeal with more than one division, or transferred to such

a court without designation of a division, may be assigned to divisions in a way that will equalize the distribution of business among them. The Court of Appeal clerk must keep records showing the divisions in which cases and proceedings are pending.

Rule 10.1008 amended and renumbered effective January 1, 2007; repealed and adopted as rule 47 effective January 1, 2005.

Ref.: Cal. Fms Pl. & Pr., Ch. 40, "Appeal: An Overview," Ch. 51, "Appeal: Hearing and Decision," Ch. 317, "Judges."

Rule 10.1012.   Supervising progress of appeals

(a) Duty to ensure prompt filing

The administrative presiding justices of Courts of Appeal with more than one division in the same city and the presiding justices of all other Courts of Appeal are generally responsible for ensuring that all appellate records and briefs are promptly filed. Staff must be provided for that purpose, to the extent that funds are appropriated and available.

(Subd (a) amended effective January 1, 2007.)

(b) Authority

Notwithstanding any other rule, the administrative presiding justices and presiding justices referred to in (a) may:

(1) Grant or deny applications to extend the time to file records, briefs, and other documents, except that a presiding justice may extend the time to file briefs in conjunction with an order to augment the record;

(2) Order the dismissal of an appeal or any other authorized sanction for noncompliance with these rules, if no application to extend time or for relief from default has been filed before the order is entered; and

(3) Grant relief from default or from a sanction other than dismissal imposed for the default.

(Subd (b) amended effective January 1, 2007.)

Rule 10.1012 amended and renumbered effective January 1, 2007; repealed and adopted as rule 77 effective January 1, 2005.

Ref.: Cal. Fms Pl. & Pr., Ch. 317, "Judges."

Rule 10.1016.   Notice of failure to perform judicial duties

(a) Notice

(1) The Chief Justice or presiding justice must notify the Commission on Judicial Performance of a reviewing court justice's:

(A) Substantial failure to perform judicial duties, including any habitual neglect of duty; or

(B) Disability-caused absences totaling more than 90 court days in a 12-month period, excluding absences for authorized vacations and for attending schools, conferences, and judicial workshops.

(2) If the affected justice is a presiding justice, the administrative presiding justice must give the notice.

(Subd (a) amended effective January 1, 2007.)

(b) Copy to justice

The Chief Justice, administrative presiding justice, or presiding justice must give the affected justice a copy of any notice under (a).

Rule 10.1016 amended and renumbered effective January 1, 2007; repealed and adopted as rule 78 effective January 1, 2005.

Ref.: Cal. Fms Pl. & Pr., Ch. 317, "Judges."

Rule 10.1020.   Reviewing court clerk/administrator

(a) Selection

A reviewing court may employ a clerk/administrator selected in accordance with procedures adopted by the court.

(b) Responsibilities

Acting under the general direction and supervision of the administrative presiding justice, the clerk/administrator is responsible for planning, organizing, coordinating, and directing, with full authority and accountability, the management of the clerk's office and all nonjudicial support activities in a manner that promotes access to justice for all members of the public, provides a forum for the fair and expeditious resolution of disputes, and maximizes the use of judicial and other resources.

(c) Duties

Under the direction of the administrative presiding justice, the clerk/administrator has the following duties:

(1) *Personnel*

The clerk/administrator directs and supervises all court employees assigned to the clerk/administrator by the administrative presiding justice and ensures that the court receives a full range of human resources support;

(2) *Budget*

The clerk/administrator develops, administers, and monitors the court budget and develops practices and procedures to ensure that annual expenditures are within the budget;

(3) *Contracts*

The clerk/administrator negotiates contracts on the court's behalf in accord with established contracting procedures and applicable laws;

(4) *Calendar management*

The clerk/administrator employs and supervises efficient calendar and caseflow management, including analyzing and evaluating pending caseloads and recommending effective calendar management techniques;

(5) *Technology*

The clerk/administrator coordinates technological and automated systems activities to assist the court;

(6) *Facilities*

The clerk/administrator coordinates facilities, space planning, court security, and business services support, including the purchase and management of equipment and supplies;

(7) *Records*

The clerk/administrator creates and manages uniform record-keeping systems, collecting data on pending and completed judicial business and the court's internal operation as the court and Judicial Council require;

(8) *Recommendations*

The clerk/administrator identifies problems and recommends policy, procedural, and administrative changes to the court;

(9) *Public relations*

The clerk/administrator represents the court to internal and external customers—including the other branches of government—on issues pertaining to the court;

(10) *Liaison*

The clerk/administrator acts as liaison with other governmental agencies;

(11) *Committees*

The clerk/administrator provides staff for judicial committees;

(12) *Administration*

The clerk/administrator develops and implements administrative and operational programs and policies for the court and the clerk's office; and

(13) *Other*

The clerk/administrator performs other duties as the administrative presiding justice directs.

(Subd (c) amended effective January 1, 2007.)

(d) Geographically separate divisions

Under the general oversight of the clerk/administrator, an assistant clerk/administrator of a geographically separate division has responsibility for the nonjudicial support activities of that division.

Rule 10.1020 amended and renumbered effective January 1, 2007; repealed and adopted as rule 76.1 effective January 1, 2005.

Ref.: Cal. Fms Pl. & Pr., Ch. 317, "Judges."

Rule 10.1024.   Court of Appeal minutes

(a) Purpose

Court of Appeal minutes should record the court's significant public acts and permit the public to follow the major events in the history of cases coming before the court.

(b) Required contents of minutes

The minutes must include:

(1) The filing date of each opinion, showing whether it was ordered published;

(2) Orders granting or denying rehearings or modifying opinions;

(3) Orders affecting an opinion's publication status, if issued after the opinion was filed;

(4) Summaries of all courtroom proceedings, showing at a minimum:

(A) The cases called for argument;

(B) The justices hearing argument;

(C) The name of the attorney arguing for each party; and

(D) Whether the case was submitted at the close of argument or the court requested further briefing;

(5) The date of submission, if other than the date of argument;

(6) Orders vacating submission, including the reason for vacating and the resubmission date;

(7) Orders dismissing appeals for lack of jurisdiction;

(8) Orders consolidating cases;

(9) Orders affecting a judgment or its finality date; and

(10) Orders changing or correcting any of the above.

(Subd (b) amended effective January 1, 2007.)

(c) Optional contents of minutes

At the court's discretion, the minutes may include such other matter as:

(1) Assignments of justices by the Chief Justice;

(2) Reports of the Commission on Judicial Appointments confirming justices; and

(3) Memorials.

(Subd (c) amended effective January 1, 2007.)

Rule 10.1024 amended and renumbered effective January 1, 2007; adopted as rule 71 effective January 1, 2005.

Ref.: Cal. Fms Pl. & Pr., Ch. 317, "Judges."

Rule 10.1028. Preservation and destruction of Court of Appeal records

(a) Form in which records may be preserved

(1) Court of Appeal records may be preserved in any appropriate medium, including paper or an optical, electronic, magnetic, photographic, or microphotographic medium or other technology capable of accurately reproducing the original. The medium used must comply with the minimum standards or guidelines for the preservation and reproduction of the medium adopted by the American National Standards Institute or the Association for Information and Image Management.

(2) If records are preserved in a medium other than paper, the following provisions of Government Code section 68150 apply: subdivisions (b)–(d); (f), excluding subdivision (f)(1); and (g)–(h).

(b) Permanent records

The Court of Appeal clerk must permanently keep the court's minutes and a register of appeals and original proceedings.

(c) Time to keep other records

(1) Except as provided in (2), the clerk may destroy all other records in a case 10 years after the decision becomes final, as ordered by the administrative presiding justice or, in a court with only one division, by the presiding justice.

(2) In a criminal case in which the court affirms a judgment of conviction, the clerk must keep the original reporter's transcript for 20 years after the decision becomes final.

Rule 10.1028 renumbered effective January 1, 2007; adopted as rule 70 effective January 1, 2005.

Ref.: Cal. Fms Pl. & Pr., Ch. 317, "Judges."

Rule 10.1030. Local rules of Courts of Appeal

(a) Publication

(1) A Court of Appeal must submit any local rule it adopts to the Reporter of Decisions for publication in the advance pamphlets of the Official Reports.

(2) As used in this rule, "publication" means printing in the manner in which amendments to the California Rules of Court are printed.

(Subd (a) relettered effective January 1, 2007.)

(b) Effective date

A local rule cannot take effect sooner than 45 days after the publication date of the advance pamphlet in which it is printed.

(Subd (b) relettered effective January 1, 2007.)

Rule 10.1030 amended and renumbered effective January 1, 2007; repealed and adopted as rule 80 effective January 1, 2005.

Ref.: Cal. Fms Pl. & Pr., Ch. 317, "Judges."

Chapter 2
Rules Relating to the Superior Court Appellate Division

Chapter 2 adopted effective January 1, 2009.

Rule 10.1100. Assignments to the appellate division
Rule 10.1104. Presiding judge
Rule 10.1108. Sessions

Rule 10.1100. Assignments to the appellate division

(a) Goal

In making assignments to the appellate division, the Chief Justice will consider the goal of promoting the independence and the quality of the appellate division.

(Subd (a) adopted effective January 1, 2009.)

(b) Factors considered

Factors considered in making the assignments may include:

(1) Length of service as a judge;

(2) Reputation in the judicial community;

(3) Degree of separateness of the appellate division work from the judge's regular assignments; and

(4) Any recommendation of the presiding judge.

(Subd (b) adopted effective January 1, 2009.)

(c) Who may be assigned

Judges assigned may include judges from another county, judges retired from the superior court or a court of higher jurisdiction, or a panel of judges from different superior courts who sit in turn in each of those superior courts.

(Subd (c) adopted effective January 1, 2009.)

(d) Terms of service

In specifying terms of service to the appellate division, the Chief Justice will consider the needs of the court.

(Subd (d) adopted effective January 1, 2009.)

Rule 10.1100 adopted effective January 1, 2009.

Advisory Committee Comment

The Chief Justice is responsible for assigning judges to the appellate division as provided in article VI, section 4 of the California Constitution and by statute.

Rule 10.1104. Presiding judge

(a) Designation of acting presiding judge

(1) The presiding judge of the appellate division must designate another member of the appellate division to serve as acting presiding judge in the absence of the presiding judge. If the presiding judge does not make that designation, the appellate division judge among those present who has the greatest seniority in the appellate division must act as presiding judge. When the judges are of equal seniority in the appellate division, the judge who is also senior in service in the superior court must act as presiding judge.

(2) As used in these rules, "presiding judge" includes acting presiding judge.

(Subd (a) adopted effective January 1, 2009.)

(b) Responsibilities

The presiding judge of the appellate division may convene the appellate division at any time and must supervise the business of the division.

(Subd (b) adopted effective January 1, 2009.)

Rule 10.1104 adopted effective January 1, 2009.

Advisory Committee Comment

Under Code of Civil Procedure section 77(a), the Chief Justice is responsible for designating one of the judges of each appellate division as the presiding judge.

Rule 10.1108. Sessions

The appellate division of each superior court must hold a session at least once each quarter unless there are no matters set for oral argument that quarter. The time and place of any session is determined by the presiding judge of the appellate division.

Rule 10.1108 adopted effective January 1, 2009.

Standards of Judicial Administration

Title 1.   Standards for All Courts [Reserved].
Title 2.   Standards for Proceedings in the Trial Courts. Standards 2.1–2.30.
Title 3.   Standards for Civil Cases. Standards 3.1–3.25.
Title 4.   Standards for Criminal Cases. Standards 4.10–4.42.
Title 5.   Standards for Cases Involving Children and Families. Standards 5.20–5.45.
Title 6.   [Reserved].
Title 7.   Standards for Probate Proceedings. Standard 7.10.
Title 8.   Standards for the Appellate Courts. Standard 8.1.
Title 9.   Standards on Law Practice, Attorneys, and Judges [Reserved].
Title 10. Standards for Judicial Administration. Standards 10.5–10.80.

Title 1
Standards for All Courts
[Reserved]

Title 2
Standards for Proceedings in the Trial Courts

Standard 2.1. Case management and delay reduction—statement of general principles
Standard 2.2. Trial court case disposition time goals
Standard 2.10. Procedures for determining the need for an interpreter and a preappearance interview
Standard 2.11. Interpreted proceedings—instructing participants on procedure
Standard 2.20. Trial management standards
Standard 2.25. Uninterrupted jury selection
Standard 2.30. Judicial comment on verdict or mistrial

Standard 2.1.   Case management and delay reduction—statement of general principles

(a) Elimination of all unnecessary delays

Trial courts should be guided by the general principle that from the commencement of litigation to its resolution, whether by trial or settlement, any elapsed time other than reasonably required for pleadings, discovery, preparation, and court events is unacceptable and should be eliminated.

(Subd (a) amended and lettered effective January 1, 2004; adopted as part of unlettered subdivision effective July 1, 1987.)

(b) Court responsible for the pace of litigation

To enable the just and efficient resolution of cases, the court, not the lawyers or litigants, should control the pace of litigation. A strong judicial commitment is essential to reducing delay and, once achieved, maintaining a current docket.

(Subd (b) amended and lettered effective January 1, 2004; adopted as part of unlettered subdivision effective July 1, 1987.)

(c) Presiding judge's role

The presiding judge of each court should take an active role in advancing the goals of delay reduction and in formulating and implementing local rules and procedures to accomplish the following:

(1) The expeditious and timely resolution of cases, after full and careful consideration consistent with the ends of justice;

(2) The identification and elimination of local rules, forms, practices, and procedures that are obstacles to delay reduction, are inconsistent with statewide case management rules, or prevent the court from effectively managing its cases;

(3) The formulation and implementation of a system of tracking cases from filing to disposition; and

(4) The training of judges and nonjudicial administrative personnel in delay reduction rules and procedures adopted in the local jurisdiction.

(Subd (c) amended and lettered effective January 1, 2004; adopted as part of unlettered subdivision effective July 1, 1987.)
Standard 2.1 amended and renumbered effective January 1, 2007; adopted as sec. 2 effective July 1, 1987; previously amended effective January 1, 1994, and January 1, 2004.

Standard 2.2.   Trial court case disposition time goals

(a) Trial Court Delay Reduction Act

The recommended goals for case disposition time in the trial courts in this standard are adopted under Government Code sections 68603 and 68620.

(Subd (a) amended effective January 1, 2007; adopted effective July 1, 1987; relettered effective January 1, 1989; previously amended effective January 1, 2004.)

(b) Statement of purpose

The recommended time goals are intended to guide the trial courts in applying the policies and principles of standard 2.1. They are administrative, justice-oriented guidelines to be used in the management of the courts. They are intended to improve the administration of justice by encouraging prompt disposition of all matters coming before the courts. The goals apply to all cases filed and are not meant to create deadlines for individual cases. Through its case management practices, a court may achieve or exceed the goals stated in this standard for the overall disposition of cases. The goals should be applied in a fair, practical, and flexible manner. They are not to be used as the basis for sanctions against any court or judge.

(Subd (b) amended effective January 1, 2007; adopted effective July 1, 1987, as (1); relettered effective January 1, 1989; previously amended effective January 1, 2004.)

(c) Definition

The definition of "general civil case" in rule 1.6 applies to this section. It includes both unlimited and limited civil cases.

(Subd (c) amended effective January 1, 2007; adopted effective January 1, 2004.)

(d) Civil cases—processing time goals

The goal of each trial court should be to process general civil cases so that all cases are disposed of within two years of filing.

(Subd (d) amended and relettered effective January 1, 2004; adopted effective July 1, 1987, as (2); previously amended effective July 1, 1988; amended and relettered as subd (c) effective January 1, 1989.)

(e) Civil cases—rate of disposition

Each trial court should dispose of at least as many civil cases as are filed each year and, if necessary to meet the case-processing goal in (d), dispose of more cases than are filed. As the court disposes of inactive cases, it should identify active cases that may require judicial attention.

(Subd (e) amended effective January 1, 2007; adopted effective July 1, 1987, as (3); previously amended effective July 1, 1988; previously amended and relettered as subd (d) effective January 1, 1989, and as subd (e) effective January 1, 2004.)

(f) General civil cases—case disposition time goals

The goal of each trial court should be to manage general civil cases, except those exempt under (g), so that they meet the following case disposition time goals:

(1) *Unlimited civil cases:*

The goal of each trial court should be to manage unlimited civil cases from filing so that:

(A) 75 percent are disposed of within 12 months;

(B) 85 percent are disposed of within 18 months; and

(C) 100 percent are disposed of within 24 months.

(2) *Limited civil cases:*

The goal of each trial court should be to manage limited civil cases from filing so that:

(A) 90 percent are disposed of within 12 months;

(B) 98 percent are disposed of within 18 months; and

(C) 100 percent are disposed of within 24 months.

(3) *Individualized case management*

The goals in (1) and (2) are guidelines for the court's disposition of all unlimited and limited civil cases filed in that court. In managing individual civil cases, the court must consider each case on its merits. To enable the fair and efficient resolution of civil cases, each case should be set for trial as soon as appropriate for that individual case consistent with rule 3.729.

(Subd (f) amended effective January 1, 2007; adopted as subd (g) effective July 1, 1987; relettered as subd (h) effective January 1, 1989; amended effective July 1, 1991; previously amended and relettered as subd (f) effective January 1, 2004.)

(g) Exceptional civil cases

A general civil case that meets the criteria in rules 3.715 and 3.400 and that involves exceptional circumstances or will require continuing review is exempt from the time goals in (d) and (f). Every exceptional case should be monitored to ensure its timely disposition consistent with the exceptional circumstances, with the goal of disposing of the case within three years.

(Subd (g) amended effective January 1, 2007; adopted effective January 1, 2004.)

(h) Small claims cases

The goals for small claims cases are:

(1) 90 percent disposed of within 75 days after filing; and

(2) 100 percent disposed of within 95 days after filing.

(Subd (h) adopted effective January 1, 2004.)

(i) Unlawful detainer cases

The goals for unlawful detainer cases are:

(1) 90 percent disposed of within 30 days after filing; and

(2) 100 percent disposed of within 45 days after filing.

(Subd (i) adopted effective January 1, 2004.)

(j) Felony cases—processing time goals

Except for capital cases, all felony cases disposed of should have a total elapsed processing time of no more than one year from the defendant's first arraignment to disposition.

(Subd (j) amended effective January 1, 2007; adopted effective January 1, 2004.)

(k) Misdemeanor cases

The goals for misdemeanor cases are:

(1) 90 percent disposed of within 30 days after the defendant's first arraignment on the complaint;

(2) 98 percent disposed of within 90 days after the defendant's first arraignment on the complaint; and

(3) 100 percent disposed of within 120 days after the defendant's first arraignment on the complaint.

(Subd (k) adopted effective January 1, 2004.)

(*l*) Felony preliminary examinations

The goal for felony cases at the time of the preliminary examination (excluding murder cases in which the prosecution seeks the death penalty) should be disposition by dismissal, by interim disposition by certified plea of guilty, or by finding of probable cause, so that:

(1) 90 percent of cases are disposed of within 30 days after the defendant's first arraignment on the complaint;

(2) 98 percent of cases are disposed of within 45 days after the defendant's first arraignment on the complaint; and

(3) 100 percent of cases are disposed of within 90 days after the defendant's first arraignment on the complaint.

(Subd (l) adopted effective January 1, 2004.)

(m) Exceptional criminal cases

An exceptional criminal case is not exempt from the time goal in (j), but case progress should be separately reported under the Judicial Branch Statistical Information System (JBSIS) regulations.

(Subd (m) amended effective January 1, 2007; adopted effective January 1, 2004.)

(n) Cases removed from court's control excluded from computation of time

If a case is removed from the court's control, the period of time until the case is restored to court control should be excluded from the case disposition time goals. The matters that remove a case from the court's control for the purposes of this section include:

(1) Civil cases:

(A) The filing of a notice of conditional settlement under rule 3.1385;

(B) An automatic stay resulting from the filing of an action in a federal bankruptcy court;

(C) The removal of the case to federal court;

(D) An order of a federal court or higher state court staying the case;

(E) An order staying the case based on proceedings in a court of equal standing in another jurisdiction;

(F) The pendency of contractual arbitration under Code of Civil Procedure section 1281.4;

(G) The pendency of attorney fee arbitration under Business and Professions Code section 6201;

(H) A stay by the reporting court for active military duty or incarceration; and

(I) For 180 days, the exemption for uninsured motorist cases under rule 3.712(b).

(2) Felony or misdemeanor cases:

(A) Issuance of warrant;

(B) Imposition of a civil assessment under Penal Code section 1214.1;

(C) Pendency of completion of diversion under Penal Code section 1000 et seq.;

(D) Evaluation of mental competence under Penal Code section 1368;

(E) Evaluation as a narcotics addict under Welfare and Institutions Code sections 3050 and 3051;

(F) 90-day diagnostic and treatment program under Penal Code section 1203.3;

(G) 90-day evaluation period for a juvenile under Welfare and Institutions Code section 707.2;

(H) Stay by a higher court or by a federal court for proceedings in another jurisdiction;

(I) Stay by the reporting court for active military duty or incarceration; and

(J) Time granted by the court to secure counsel if the defendant is not represented at the first appearance.

(Subd (n) amended effective January 1, 2007; adopted effective January 1, 2004.)

(o) Problems

A court that finds its ability to comply with these goals impeded by a rule of court or statute should notify the Judicial Council.

(Subd (o) amended effective January 1, 2007; adopted effective January 1, 2004.)

Standard 2.2 amended and renumbered effective January 1, 2007; adopted as sec. 2.1 effective July 1, 1987; previously amended effective January 1, 1988, July 1, 1988, January 1, 1989, January 1, 1990, July 1, 1991, and January 1, 2004.

Standard 2.10.   Procedures for determining the need for an interpreter and a preappearance interview

(a) When an interpreter is needed

An interpreter is needed if, after an examination of a party or witness, the court concludes that:

(1) The party cannot understand and speak English well enough to participate fully in the proceedings and to assist counsel; or

(2) The witness cannot speak English so as to be understood directly by counsel, court, and jury.

(Subd (a) amended effective January 1, 2007.)

(b) When an examination is required

The court should examine a party or witness on the record to determine whether an interpreter is needed if:

(1) A party or counsel requests such an examination; or

(2) It appears to the court that the party or witness may not understand and speak English well enough to participate fully in the proceedings.

(Subd (b) amended effective January 1, 2007.)

(c) Examination of party or witness

To determine if an interpreter is needed, the court should normally include questions on the following:

(1) Identification (for example: name, address, birthdate, age, place of birth);

(2) Active vocabulary in vernacular English (for example: "How did you come to the court today?" "What kind of work do you do?" "Where did you go to school?" "What was the highest grade you completed?" "Describe what you see in the courtroom." "What have you eaten today?"). Questions should be phrased to avoid "yes" or "no" replies;

(3) The court proceedings (for example: the nature of the charge or the type of case before the court, the purpose of the proceedings and function of the court, the rights of a party or criminal defendant, and the responsibilities of a witness).

(Subd (c) amended effective January 1, 2007.)

(d) Record of examination

After the examination, the court should state its conclusion on the record. The file in the case should be clearly marked and data entered electronically when appropriate by court personnel to ensure that an interpreter will be present when needed in any subsequent proceeding.

(Subd (d) amended effective January 1, 2007.)

(e) Good cause for preappearance interview

For good cause, the court should authorize a preappearance interview between the interpreter and the party or witness. Good cause exists if the interpreter needs clarification on any interpreting issues, including: colloquialisms, culturalisms, dialects, idioms, linguistic capabilities and traits, regionalisms, register, slang, speech patterns, or technical terms.

(Subd (e) amended effective January 1, 2007.)

Standard 2.10 amended and renumbered effective January 1, 2007; repealed and adopted as sec. 18 effective January 1, 1999.

Standard 2.11.   Interpreted proceedings— instructing participants on procedure

(a) Instructions to interpreters

The court or the court's designee should give the following instructions to interpreters, either orally or in writing:

(1) Do not discuss the pending proceedings with a party or witness.

(2) Do not disclose communications between counsel and client.

(3) Do not give legal advice to a party or witness. Refer legal questions to the attorney or to the court.

(4) Inform the court if you are unable to interpret a word, expression, special terminology, or dialect, or have doubts about your linguistic expertise or ability to perform adequately in a particular case.

(5) Interpret all words, including slang, vulgarisms, and epithets, to convey the intended meaning.

(6) Use the first person when interpreting statements made in the first person. (For example, a statement or question should not be introduced with the words, "He says ....")

(7) Direct all inquiries or problems to the court and not to the witness or counsel. If necessary, you may request permission to approach the bench with counsel to discuss a problem.

(8) Position yourself near the witness or party without blocking the view of the judge, jury, or counsel.

(9) Inform the court if you become fatigued during the proceedings.

(10) When interpreting for a party at the counsel table, speak loudly enough to be heard by the party or counsel but not so loudly as to interfere with the proceedings.

(11) Interpret everything, including objections.

(12) If the court finds good cause under rule 2.893(e), hold a preappearance interview with the party or witness to become familiar with speech patterns and linguistic traits and to determine what technical or special terms may be used. Counsel may be present at the preappearance interview.

(13) During the preappearance interview with a non-English-speaking witness, give the witness the following instructions on the procedure to be followed when the witness is testifying:

(A) The witness must speak in a loud, clear voice so that the entire court and not just the interpreter can hear.

(B) The witness must direct all responses to the person asking the question, not to the interpreter.

(C) The witness must direct all questions to counsel or to the court and not to the interpreter. The witness may not seek advice from or engage in any discussion with the interpreter.

(14) During the preappearance interview with a non-English-speaking party, give the following instructions on the procedure to be used when the non-English-speaking party is not testifying:

(A) The interpreter will interpret all statements made in open court.

(B) The party must direct any questions to counsel. The interpreter will interpret all questions to counsel and the responses. The party may not seek advice from or engage in discussion with the interpreter.

(Subd (a) amended effective January 1, 2007.)

(b) Instructions to counsel

The court or the court's designee should give the following instructions to counsel, either orally or in writing:

(1) When examining a non-English-speaking witness, direct all questions to the witness and not to the interpreter. (For example, do not say to the interpreter, "Ask him if ....")

(2) If there is a disagreement with the interpretation, direct any objection to the court and not to the interpreter. Ask permission to approach the bench to discuss the problem.

(3) If you have a question regarding the qualifications of the interpreter, you may request permission to conduct

a supplemental examination on the interpreter's qualifications.

Standard 2.11 amended and renumbered effective January 1, 2007; repealed and adopted as sec. 18.1 effective January 1, 1999.

Standard 2.20.   Trial management standards

(a) General principles

The trial judge has the responsibility to manage the trial proceedings. The judge should take appropriate action to ensure that all parties are prepared to proceed, the trial commences as scheduled, all parties have a fair opportunity to present evidence, and the trial proceeds to conclusion without unnecessary interruption. When the trial involves a jury, the trial judge should manage proceedings with particular emphasis on the needs of the jury.

(Subd (a) amended effective January 1, 2007.)

(b) Techniques of trial management

The trial judge should employ the following trial management techniques:

(1) Participate with trial counsel in a trial management conference before trial.

(2) After consultation with counsel, set reasonable time limits.

(3) Arrange the court's docket to start trial as scheduled and inform parties of the number of hours set each day for the trial.

(4) Ensure that once trial has begun, momentum is maintained.

(5) Be receptive to using technology in managing the trial and the presentation of evidence.

(6) Attempt to maintain continuity in days of trial and hours of trial.

(7) Schedule arguments on legal issues at the beginning or end of the day so as not to interrupt the presentation of evidence.

(8) Permit sidebar conferences only when necessary, and keep them as short as possible.

(9) In longer trials, consider scheduling trial days to permit jurors time for personal business.

(Subd (b) amended effective January 1, 2007.)
Standard 2.20 amended and renumbered effective January 1, 2007; adopted as sec 8.9 effective July 1, 1997.

Standard 2.25.   Uninterrupted jury selection

When practical, the trial judge, with the cooperation of the other judges of the court, should schedule court business to allow for jury selection uninterrupted by other court business.

Standard 2.25 amended and renumbered effective January 1, 2007; adopted as sec. 8.6 effective July 1, 1990.

Standard 2.30.   Judicial comment on verdict or mistrial

At the conclusion of a trial, or on declaring a mistrial for failure of a jury to reach a verdict, it is appropriate for the trial judge to thank jurors for their public service, but the judge's comments should not include praise or criticism of the verdict or the failure to reach a verdict.

Standard 2.30 amended and renumbered effective January 1, 2007; adopted as sec. 14 effective January 1, 1976.

Title 3
Standards for Civil Cases

Standard 3.1. Appearance by telephone
Standard 3.10. Complex civil litigation
Standard 3.25. Examination of prospective jurors in civil cases

Standard 3.1.　Appearance by telephone

(a) Recommended criteria for telephone equipment

Each court should have adequate telephone equipment for use in hearings at which counsel may appear by telephone. This equipment should:

(1) Permit each person participating in the hearing, whether in person or by telephone, to hear all other persons;

(2) Handle at least three incoming calls at one time and place those calls into a conference call in a simple and quick manner;

(3) Have a silent (visible) ringer;

(4) Be simple to learn and use;

(5) Be reasonable in cost; and

(6) Have full-duplex, simultaneous bidirectional speaker capability.

(Subd (a) amended effective January 1, 2007.)

(b) Optional features for telephone equipment

It is desirable if the telephone equipment can:

(1) Dial previously stored telephone numbers;

(2) Record conversations;

(3) Be moved easily from location to location; and

(4) Automatically queue incoming calls.

(Subd (b) amended effective January 1, 2007.)

(c) Award of attorney's fees

A court should consider, in awarding attorney's fees under any applicable provision of law, whether an attorney is claiming fees for appearing in person in a proceeding in which that attorney could have appeared by telephone.

(Subd (c) repealed and relettered effective January 1, 2008; adopted as subd (d) effective January 1, 1989; previously amended effective January 1, 2007.)

(d) Local procedures for telephone appearance

Each court should adopt a local rule or uniform local written policy specifying the following:

(1) Whether the court or the attorney initiates the telephone call for a telephone appearance;

(2) Whether the court sets a specified time for a telephone appearance or a time range; and

(3) How the parties are notified, in advance of the hearing, of the time or time range of the telephone appearance. In those courts using a tentative ruling recording system, that notice should be part of the tentative ruling recording.

(Subd (d) relettered effective January 1, 2008; adopted as subd (e) effective January 1, 1989; previously amended effective January 1, 2007.)

Standard 3.1 amended effective January 1, 2008; repealed and adopted as sec. 21 effective January 1, 1989; previously amended effective July 1, 1992, and January 1, 2007.

Standard 3.10.　Complex civil litigation

(a) Judicial management

In complex litigation, judicial management should begin early and be applied continuously and actively, based on knowledge of the circumstances of each case.

(b) All-purpose assignment

Complex litigation should be assigned to one judge for all purposes. If such an assignment is not possible, a single judge should be assigned to hear law and motion matters and discovery matters.

(Subd (b) amended effective January 1, 2007; adopted as subd (d) effective July 1, 1982; previously relettered effective January 1, 2000.)

(c) Selection of judges for complex litigation assignments

In selecting judges for complex litigation assignments, the presiding judge should consider the needs of the court and the judge's ability, interest, training, experience (including experience with complex civil cases), and willingness to participate in educational programs related to the management of complex cases. Commissioners should not be employed in any phase of complex litigation, except under the judge's direct supervision to assist in the management of the case.

(Subd (c) amended and relettered effective January 1, 2000; adopted as subd (e) effective July 1, 1982.)

(d) Establishing time limits

Time limits should be regularly used to expedite major phases of complex litigation. Time limits should be established early, tailored to the circumstances of each case, firmly and fairly maintained, and accompanied by other methods of sound judicial management.

(Subd (d) relettered effective January 1, 2000; adopted as subd (f) effective July 1, 1982.)

(e) Preparation for trial

Litigants in complex litigation cases should be required to minimize evidentiary disputes and to organize efficiently their exhibits and other evidence before trial.

(Subd (e) amended and relettered effective January 1, 2007; adopted as subd (i) effective July 1, 1982; previously relettered as subd (g) effective January 1, 2000.)

(f) Dilatory tactics

Judges involved in complex litigation should be sensitive to dilatory or abusive litigation tactics and should be prepared to invoke disciplinary procedures for violations.

(Subd (f) relettered effective January 1, 2007; adopted as subd (j) effective July 1, 1982; previously relettered as subd (h) effective January 1, 2000.)

(g) Educational programs

Judges should be encouraged to attend educational programs on the management of complex litigation.

(Subd (g) relettered effective January 1, 2007; adopted as subd (k) effective July 1, 1982; previously amended and relettered as subd (i) effective January 1, 2000.)

(h) Staff assignment

Judges assigned to handle complex cases should be given research attorney and administrative staff assistance when possible.

(Subd (h) amended and relettered effective January 1, 2007; adopted as subd (j) effective January 1, 2000.)

Standard 3.10 amended and renumbered effective January 1, 2007; adopted as sec. 19 effective July 1, 1982; previously amended effective January 1, 1995, and January 1, 2000.

Standard 3.25. Examination of prospective jurors in civil cases

(a) In general

(1) *Methods and scope of examination*

The examination of prospective jurors in a civil case may be oral, by written questionnaire, or by both methods, and should include all questions necessary to ensure the selection of a fair and impartial jury. The *Juror Questionnaire for Civil Cases* (form MC-001) may be used. During any supplemental examination conducted by counsel for the parties, the trial judge should permit liberal and probing examination calculated to discover possible bias or prejudice with regard to the circumstances of the particular case.

(2) *Examination by counsel*

When counsel requests to be allowed to conduct a supplemental voir dire examination, the trial judge should permit counsel to conduct such examination without requiring prior submission of the questions to the judge unless a particular counsel has demonstrated unwillingness to avoid the type of examination proscribed in (f). In exercising his or her sound discretion as to the form and subject matter of voir dire questions, the trial judge should consider, among other criteria: (1) any unique or complex elements, legal or factual, in the case, and (2) the individual responses or conduct of jurors that may evince attitudes inconsistent with suitability to serve as a fair and impartial juror in the particular case. Questions regarding personal relationships of jurors should be relevant to the subject matter of the case.

(*Subd (a) amended effective January 1, 2007; adopted effective January 1, 1972; previously amended effective January 1, 1974, July 1, 1993, and January 1, 2004.*)

(b) Pre-voir dire conference

Before the examination the trial judge should, outside the prospective jurors' hearing and with a court reporter present, confer with counsel, at which time specific questions or areas of inquiry may be proposed that the judge in his or her discretion may inquire of the jurors. Thereafter, the judge should advise counsel of the questions or areas to be inquired into during the examination and voir dire procedure. The judge should also obtain from counsel the names of the witnesses whom counsel then plan to call at trial and a brief outline of the nature of the case, including any alleged injuries or damages and, in an eminent domain action, the respective contentions of the parties concerning the value of the property taken and any alleged severance damages and special benefits.

(*Subd (b) amended effective January 1, 2007; adopted effective January 1, 1972; previously amended effective January 1, 1974.*)

(c) Examination of jurors

Except as otherwise provided in (d), the trial judge's examination of prospective jurors should include the following areas of inquiry and any other matters affecting their qualifications to serve as jurors in the case:

(1) *To the entire jury panel after it has been sworn and seated:*

I am now going to question the prospective jurors who are seated in the jury box concerning their qualifications to serve as jurors in this case. All members of this jury panel, however, should pay close attention to my questions, making note of the answers you would give if these questions were put to you personally. If and when any other member of this panel is called to the jury box, the member will be asked to give his or her answers to these questions.

(2) In the trial of this case the parties are entitled to have a fair, unbiased, and unprejudiced jury. If there is any reason why any of you might be biased or prejudiced in any way, you must disclose such reason when you are asked to do so. It is your duty to make this disclosure.

(3) *In lengthy trials:*

This trial will likely take _____ days to complete, but it may take longer. Will any of you find it difficult or impossible to participate for this period of time?

(4) The nature of this case is as follows: (*Describe briefly, including any alleged injuries or damages and, in an eminent domain action, the name of the condemning agency, a description of the property being acquired, and the particular public project or purpose of the condemnation.*)

(5) The parties to this case and their respective attorneys are: (*Specify.*) Have you heard of or been acquainted with any of these parties or their attorneys?

(6) During the trial of this case, the following witnesses may be called to testify on behalf of the parties. These witnesses are: (*Do not identify the party on whose behalf the witnesses might be called.*) Have any of you heard of or been otherwise acquainted with any of the witnesses just named? The parties are not required and might not wish to call all of these witnesses, and they may later find it necessary to call other witnesses.

(7) Have any of you heard of, or have you any knowledge of, the facts or events in this case? Are any of you familiar with the places or property mentioned in this case?

(8) Do any of you believe that a case of this nature should not be brought into court for determination by a jury?

(9) Do any of you have any belief or feeling toward any of the parties, attorneys, or witnesses that might be regarded as a bias or prejudice for or against any of them? Do you have any interest, financial or otherwise, in the outcome of this case?

(10) Have any of you served as a juror or witness involving any of these parties, attorneys, or witnesses?

(11) Have any of you served as a juror in any other case? (If so, was it a civil or criminal case?) You must understand that there is a basic difference between a civil case and a criminal case. In a criminal case a defendant must be found guilty beyond a reasonable doubt; in a civil case such as this, you need only find that the evidence you accept as the basis of your decision is more convincing, and thus has the greater probability of truth, than the contrary evidence.

In the following questions I will be using the terms "family," "close friend," and "anyone with whom you have a significant personal relationship." The term "anyone with whom you have a significant personal relationship" means a domestic partner, life partner, former spouse, or anyone with whom you have an influential or intimate relationship that you would characterize as important.

(12) *If a corporation or "company" is a party:*

(A) Have you or, to your knowledge, has any member of your family, a close friend, or anyone with whom you have a significant personal relationship ever had any connection with, or any dealings with, the _____ corporation (or company)?

(B) Are any of you or them related to any officer, director, or employee of this corporation (or company) to your knowledge?

(C) Do you or they own any stock or other interest in this corporation (or company) to your knowledge?

(D) Have you or they ever done business as a corporation (or company)?

(E) The fact that a corporation (or company) is a party in this case must not affect your deliberations or your verdict. You may not discriminate between corporations (or companies) and natural individuals. Both are persons in the eyes of the law and both are entitled to have a fair and impartial trial based on the same legal standards. Do any of you have any belief or feeling for or against corporations (or companies) that might prevent you from being a completely fair and impartial juror in this case?

(13) Have you or, to your knowledge, has any member of your family, a close friend, or anyone with whom you have a significant personal relationship ever sued anyone, or presented a claim against anyone in connection with a matter similar to this case? (If so, did the matter terminate satisfactorily so far as you were concerned?)

(14) Has anyone ever sued you, or presented a claim against you or, to your knowledge, against any member of your family, a close friend, or anyone with whom you have a significant personal relationship, in connection with a matter similar to this case? (If so, did the matter terminate satisfactorily so far as you were concerned?)

(15) Are you or, to your knowledge, is any member of your family, a close friend, or anyone with whom you have a significant personal relationship presently involved in a lawsuit of any kind?

(16) *When appropriate:*

It may appear that one or more of the parties, witnesses, or attorneys come from a particular national, racial, or religious group (or may have a lifestyle different than your own). Would this in any way affect your judgment or the weight and credibility you would give to their testimony or to their contentions?

(17) Have you or, to your knowledge, has any member of your family, a close friend, or anyone with whom you have a significant personal relationship had any special training in: *(Describe briefly the fields of expertise involved in the case, such as law, medicine, nursing, or any other branch of the healing arts.)*

(18) *In personal injury or wrongful death cases:*

(A) You may be called on in this case to award damages for personal injury, pain, and suffering. Do any of you have any religious or other belief that pain and suffering are not real or any belief that would prevent you from awarding damages for pain and suffering if liability for them is established?

(B) Are there any of you who would not employ a medical doctor?

(C) Have you or, to your knowledge, has any member of your family, a close friend, or anyone with whom you

have a significant personal relationship ever engaged in investigating or otherwise acting on claims for damages?

(D) Have you or they, to your knowledge, ever been in an accident with the result that a claim for personal injuries or for substantial property damage was made by someone involved in that accident, whether or not a lawsuit was filed?

(E) Have you or they, to your knowledge, ever been involved in an accident in which someone died or received serious personal injuries, whether or not a lawsuit was filed?

(F) Are there any of you who do not drive an automobile? (If so, have you ever driven an automobile, and if you have, give your reason for not presently driving.) Does your spouse or anyone with whom you have a significant personal relationship drive an automobile? (If that person does not drive but did so in the past, why did that person stop driving?)

(G) Plaintiff (or cross-complainant) _____ is claiming injuries. *(Describe briefly the general nature of the alleged injuries.)* Do you or, to your knowledge, does any member of your family, a close friend, or anyone with whom you have a significant personal relationship suffer from similar injuries? Have you or they, to your knowledge, suffered from similar injuries in the past? (If so, would that fact affect your point of view in this case to the extent that you might not be able to render a completely fair and impartial verdict?)

(19) It is important that I have your assurance that you will, without reservation, follow my instructions and rulings on the law and will apply that law to this case. To put it somewhat differently, whether you approve or disapprove of the court's rulings or instructions, it is your solemn duty to accept as correct these statements of the law. You may not substitute your own idea of what you think the law ought to be. Will all of you follow the law as given to you by me in this case?

(20) Each of you should now state your:

(A) Name;

(B) Children's ages and the number of children, if any;

(C) Occupation;

(D) Occupational history; and

(E) Present employer;

And for your spouse or anyone with whom you have a significant personal relationship, their:

(F) Names;

(G) Occupations;

(H) Occupational histories; and

(I) Present employers.

Please begin with juror number one.

(21) Do you know of any other reason, or has anything occurred during this question period, that might make you doubtful you would be a completely fair and impartial juror in this case? If there is, it is your duty to disclose the reason at this time.

(Subd (c) amended effective January 1, 2007; adopted effective January 1, 1972; previously amended effective January 1, 1974, and January 1, 2004.)

(d) Examination of jurors in eminent domain cases

In eminent domain cases, the trial judge's examination of prospective jurors should include, in the areas of inquiry in (c)(1) through (c)(12), the following matters, and any other matters affecting their qualifications to serve as jurors in the case:

(1) Have you or, to your knowledge, has any member of your family, a close friend, or anyone with whom you have a significant personal relationship ever had any connection with, or dealings with, the plaintiff agency? Are you or any of them related to any officer or employee of the plaintiff agency?

(2) Have you or, to your knowledge, has any member of your family, a close friend, or anyone with whom you have a significant personal relationship ever been involved in an eminent domain proceeding such as this or are you or they likely to become involved in such a proceeding in the future?

(3) To your knowledge, do you have relatives, close friends, or anyone with whom you have a significant personal relationship who has been or will be affected by the proposed project or a similar public project? (If so, who and how affected?)

(4) Have you or, to your knowledge, has any member of your family, a close friend, or anyone with whom you have a significant personal relationship ever sold property to a public agency having the power of eminent domain?

(5) Are you or, to your knowledge, is any member of your family, a close friend, or anyone with whom you have a significant personal relationship presently involved in a lawsuit of any kind? (If so, does the lawsuit involve a public agency?)

(6) Have you or, to your knowledge, has any member of your family, a close friend, or anyone with whom you have a significant personal relationship ever been involved in a lawsuit involving a public agency?

(7) *When appropriate:*

It may appear that one or more of the parties, witnesses, or attorneys come from a particular national, racial, or religious group (or may have a lifestyle different from your own). Would this in any way affect your judgment or the weight and credibility you would give to their testimony or contentions?

(8) Have you or, to your knowledge, has any member of your family, a close friend, or anyone with whom you have a significant personal relationship had any special training in: *(Describe briefly the fields of expertise involved in the case, such as law, real estate, real estate appraising, engineering, surveying, geology, etc.)*

(9) Have you, has your spouse, or, to your knowledge, has any member of your family, a close friend, or anyone with whom you have a significant personal relationship ever been engaged in any phase of the real estate business including:

(A) Acting as a real estate agent, broker, or salesperson;

(B) Acting as a real estate appraiser;

(C) Dealing in trust deeds;

(D) Buying or selling real property as a business;

(E) Owning or managing income property; or

(F) Engaging in the construction business?

(10) Have you or, to your knowledge, has any member of your family, a close friend, or anyone with whom you have a significant personal relationship ever studied or engaged in: (State type of business, if any, conducted on subject property.)

(11) Have you or, to your knowledge, has any member of your family, a close friend, or anyone with whom you have a significant personal relationship ever been engaged in any work involving the acquisition of private property for public purposes? Or involving the zoning or planning of property?

(12) Under the law of this state, all private property is held subject to the necessary right of eminent domain, which is the right of the state or its authorized agencies to take private property for public use whenever the public interest so requires. The right of eminent domain is exercised through proceedings commonly called a condemnation action. This is a condemnation action.

(13) The Constitution of this state requires that a property owner be paid just compensation for the taking (or damaging) of his or her property for public use. It will be the duty of the jury ultimately selected in this case to determine the just compensation to be paid.

(14) *If no claim of severance damages:*

In order to find the amount of just compensation in this case, the jury will be called on to determine the fair market value of the real property being acquired.

(15) *If severance damages are claimed:*

In order to find the amount of just compensation in this case, the jury will be called on to determine the following:

(A) The fair market value of the real property being acquired.

(B) Severance damages, if any, to the defendant's remaining real property; that is, the depreciation in market value by reason of the severance of the part taken, or by the construction of the improvements in the manner proposed by the plaintiff, or both.

(C) *When applicable:* Special benefits, if any, to the defendant's remaining real property. *(The trial judge on request may advise the jury on the concept of special benefits.)*

(16) Just compensation is measured in terms of fair market value as of *(date)*, the date of value in this case.

(17) I will give you more specific instructions on the issues and determinations to be made in this case at the conclusion of all the evidence. However, I will now advise you of the definition of fair market value: *(See CACI 3501.)*

(18) *Private ownership of property:*

(A) Do you have any objection to the concept of private ownership of property?

(B) Do you have any objection to the right of the owner of private property to develop or use that property in whatever lawful way its owner sees fit?

(19) Do you have any objection to the plaintiff acquiring private property for a public use as long as just compensation is paid for the property?

(20) Do you have any objection to the defendant(s) seeking just compensation in these proceedings in the form of the fair market value of the subject property (and the damages that the defendant(s) contend will be caused to the remaining property)?

(21) Do you have any objection to the particular public project involved in this proceeding, previously referred to as the *(name of project)*?

(22) Are you or, to your knowledge, is any member of your family, a close friend, or anyone with whom you have a significant personal relationship a member of any organization that is opposed to such public projects?

(23) Do you have any objection to the concept that just compensation is measured by fair market value as I have defined that term for you earlier?

(24) Do you have any feeling that, because the plaintiff needs the property for public purposes, it should pay anything other than its fair market value?

(25) In these cases, the evidence of value is introduced for the most part by what the courts sometimes refer to as expert testimony. This expert testimony frequently is introduced through appraisers or real estate brokers. Do you have any prejudice against real estate brokers or appraisers, or that type of testimony?

(26) In a condemnation case the property owner produces all of his or her evidence of value first, then the government calls its witnesses. Having this in mind, will you keep your mind open throughout all the case and not determine the matter in your mind until all of the evidence is in?

(27) It is important that I have your assurance that you will, without reservation, follow my instructions and rulings on the law and will apply that law to this case. To put it somewhat differently, whether you approve or disapprove of the court's rulings or instructions, it is your solemn duty to accept as correct these statements of the law. You may not substitute your own idea of what you think the law ought to be. Will all of you follow the law as given to you by me in this case?

(28) Each of you should now state your:

(A) Name;

(B) Children's ages and number of children, if any;

(C) Occupation;

(D) Occupational history; and

(E) Present employer;

And for your spouse or anyone with whom you have a significant personal relationship, their:

(F) Names;

(G) Occupations;

(H) Occupational histories; and

(I) Present employers.

Please begin with juror number one.

(29) Each of you should now state whether you, your spouse, or anyone with whom you have a significant personal relationship owns or has an interest in any real property and, if so, whether its value or use is affected by the public project involved in this case.

We will again start with juror number one.

(30) Do you know of any other reason, or has anything occurred during this question period, that might make you doubtful you would be a completely fair and impartial juror in this case? If there is, it is your duty to disclose the reason at this time.

(Subd (d) amended effective January 1, 2007; adopted effective January 1, 1974; previously amended effective January 1, 1989, and January 1, 2004.)

(e) Subsequent conference and examination

On completion of the initial examination and on request of counsel for any party that the trial judge put additional questions to the jurors, the judge should, outside the jurors' hearing and with a court reporter present, confer with counsel, at which time additional questions or areas of inquiry may be proposed that the judge may inquire of the jurors.

(Subd (e) amended effective January 1, 2007; adopted effective January 1, 1972; previously amended effective January 1, 1974.)

(f) Improper questions

When any counsel examines the prospective jurors, the trial judge should not permit counsel to attempt to precondition the prospective jurors to a particular result or allow counsel to comment on the personal lives and families of the parties or their attorneys. Nor should the trial judge allow counsel to question the jurors concerning the pleadings, the applicable law, the meaning of particular words and phrases, or the comfort of the jurors, except in unusual circumstances, where, in the trial judge's sound discretion, such questions become necessary to insure the selection of a fair and impartial jury.

(Subd (f) amended effective January 1, 2007; adopted effective January 1, 1972; previously amended effective January 1, 1974.) Standard 3.25 amended and renumbered effective January 1, 2007; adopted as sec. 8 effective January 1, 1972; previously amended effective January 1, 1974, January 1, 1989, July 1, 1993, and January 1, 2004.)

Title 4
Standards for Criminal Cases

Standard 4.10. Guidelines for diversion drug court programs

(a) Minimum components

The components specified in this standard should be included as minimum requirements in any pre-plea diversion drug court program developed under Penal Code section 1000.5.

(Subd (a) amended effective January 1, 2007.)

(b) Early entry

Eligible participants should be identified early and enter into a supervision and treatment program promptly.

(1) A declaration of eligibility should be filed by the district attorney no later than the date of the defendant's first appearance in court.

(2) Participants designated as eligible by the district attorney should be ordered by the assigned drug court judge to report for assessment and treatment supervision within five days of the first court appearance.

(c) Treatment services

Participants should be given access to a continuum of treatment and rehabilitative services.

(1) The county drug program administrator should specify and certify appropriate drug treatment programs under Penal Code section 1211.

(2) The certified treatment programs should provide a minimum of two levels of treatment services to match

participants to programs according to their needs for treatment, recognizing that some divertees may be at the stage of experimenting with illicit drugs while others may be further along in the addiction's progression.

(3) Each treatment level should be divided into phases in order to provide periodic reviews of treatment progress. Each phase may vary in length. It should be recognized that a participant is expected to progress in treatment but may relapse. Most participants, however, should be able to successfully complete the treatment program within 12 months.

(4) Each pre-plea diversion drug court program should have an assessment component to ensure that participants are initially screened and then periodically assessed by treatment personnel to ensure that appropriate treatment services are provided and to monitor the participants' progress through the phases.

(5) Treatment services should include educational and group outpatient treatment. Individual counseling, however, should be made available in special circumstances if an assessment based on acceptable professional standards indicates that individual counseling is the only appropriate form of treatment. Referrals should be made for educational and vocational counseling if it is determined to be appropriate by the judge.

(Subd (c) amended effective January 1, 2007.)

(d) Monitoring

Abstinence from and use of drugs should be monitored by frequent drug testing.

(1) Alcohol and other drug (AOD) testing is essential and should be mandatory in each pre-plea diversion drug court program to monitor participant compliance.

(2) Testing may be administered randomly or at scheduled intervals, but should occur no less frequently than one time per week during the first 90 days of treatment.

(3) The probation officer and court should be immediately notified when a participant has tested positive, has failed to submit to AOD testing, or has submitted an adulterated sample. In such cases, an interim hearing should be calendared and required as outlined in (e)(4).

(4) Participants should not be considered to have successfully completed the treatment program unless they have consistently had negative test results for a period of four months.

(Subd (d) amended effective January 1, 2007.)

(e) Judicial supervision

There should be early and frequent judicial supervision of each diversion drug court participant.

(1) Each participant should appear in court before a specifically assigned diversion drug court judge within 30 days after the first court appearance. At this time the participant should provide proof of registration, proof of completion of assessment, proof of entry into a specific treatment program, and initial drug test results.

(2) The second drug court appearance should be held no later than 30 days after the first drug court appearance. The third drug court appearance should be held no later than 60 days after the second drug court appearance.

(3) A final drug court appearance should be required no sooner than 12 months from entry into treatment unless continued treatment is found to be appropriate and necessary.

(4) Interim drug court appearances should be required within one week of the following: positive drug test results, failure to test, adulterated test, or failure to appear or participate in treatment.

(5) At each drug court appearance, the judge should receive a report of the participant's progress in treatment and drug test results and should review, monitor, and impose rewards and sanctions based on the participant's progress or lack of progress.

(f) Sanctions and incentives

The drug court responds directly to each participant's compliance or noncompliance with graduated sanctions or incentives.

(1) A clear regimen of incentives and sanctions should be established and implemented at each court hearing.

(2) The suggested range of incentives should be as follows:

(A) Encouragement;

(B) Advancement to next treatment phase;

(C) Reduction in diversion program fees (other than state-mandated fees);

(D) Completion of treatment and required court appearances and shortening of the term of diversion; and

(E) Other incentives the court may deem necessary or appropriate.

(3) The suggested range of sanctions should be as follows:

(A) Demotion to earlier treatment phase;

(B) Increased frequency of testing, supervision, or treatment requirements;

(C) Graduated length of incarceration for violating diversion order to abstain from use of illegal drugs and for nonparticipation in treatment; and

(D) Reinstatement of criminal proceedings.

(4) A participant should be terminated from the pre-plea diversion drug court, and criminal proceedings reinstated, if the drug court judge, after a hearing, makes a final and specific finding and determination at any time during the period of diversion that the participant has:

(A) Not performed satisfactorily in treatment;

(B) Failed to benefit from education, treatment, or rehabilitation;

(C) Been convicted of a misdemeanor that reflects the participant's propensity for violence; or

(D) Engaged in criminal conduct rendering him or her unsuitable for continued treatment.

(Subd (f) amended effective January 1, 2007.)

(g) National standards

In addition to meeting the minimum guidelines provided in this standard, courts are encouraged to look to the nationally accepted guidelines, *Defining Drug Courts: The Key Components,* developed by the National Association of Drug Court Professionals in cooperation with the Department of Justice, for further and detailed guidance in developing an effective diversion drug court program.

(Subd (g) amended effective January 1, 2007.)
Standard 4.10 amended and renumbered effective January 1, 2007; adopted as sec. 36 effective January 1, 1998.

Standard 4.30. Examination of prospective jurors in criminal cases

(a) In general

Rules of Court

(1) This standard applies in all criminal cases.

(2) The examination of prospective jurors in a criminal case should include all questions necessary to insure the selection of a fair and impartial jury.

(3) The court may consider conducting sequestered voir dire on issues that are sensitive to prospective jurors, on questions concerning media reports of the case, and on any other issue that the court deems advisable.

(Subd (a) amended effective January 1, 2007; previously amended effective January 1, 1988, January 1, 1990, June 6, 1990, and January 1, 2006.)

(b) Examination of jurors

The trial judge's examination of prospective jurors in criminal cases should include the areas of inquiry listed below and any other matters affecting their qualifications to serve as jurors in the case. The trial judge may want to use the *Juror Questionnaire for Criminal Cases* (form MC-002) to assist in the examination of prospective jurors. Form MC-002 is an optional form and is not intended to constitute the complete examination of prospective jurors. Form MC-002 is a tool for trial judges to use to make the initial examination of prospective jurors more efficient. If the court chooses to use form MC-002, its use and any supplemental questions submitted by counsel must be discussed at the pre-voir dire conference required by rule 4.200. Excusing jurors based on questionnaire answers alone is generally not advisable.

(1) *Address to entire jury panel:*

Do any of you have any vision, hearing, or medical difficulties that may affect your jury service? *(Response.)*

(2) *In particular, for lengthy trials. Address to entire jury panel:*

This trial will likely take _____ days to complete, but it may take longer. *(State the days and times during the day when the trial will be in session.)*

Will any of you find it difficult or impossible to participate for this period of time? *(After the entire panel has been screened for time hardships, direct the excused jurors to return to the jury assembly room for possible reassignment to other courtrooms for voir dire.)*

(3) *At this point the court may wish to submit any juror questionnaire that has been developed to assist in voir dire. The court should remind panel members that their answers on the questionnaire are given under penalty of perjury. In addition, if a questionnaire is used, the court and counsel may wish to question individual prospective jurors further based on their responses to particular questions, and a procedure for doing so should be established at the pre-voir dire conference. Therefore, it may not be necessary to ask all of the prospective jurors questions 5 through 25 that follow, although the text may assist the court with following up with individual jurors about answers given on the questionnaire.*

To the entire jury panel:

I am now going to question the prospective jurors who are seated in the jury box concerning their qualifications to serve as jurors in this case. All the remaining members of this jury panel, however, should pay close attention to my questions, making note of the answers you would give if these questions were put to you personally. If and when any other member of this panel is called to the jury box, he or she will be asked to answer these questions.

(4) *To the prospective jurors seated in the jury box:*

In the trial of this case each side is entitled to have a fair, unbiased, and unprejudiced jury. If there is any fact or any reason why any of you might be biased or prejudiced in any way, you must disclose such reasons when you are asked to do so. It is your duty to make this disclosure.

(5) *To the prospective jurors seated in the jury box:*

Do any of you know anyone else on this jury panel? *(Response.)*

(6) Ladies and gentlemen of the jury: This is a criminal case entitled The People of the State of California v. _____. The (defendant is)(defendants are) seated _____.

(A) (Mr.)(Ms.)(defendant), please stand and face the prospective jurors in the jury box and in the audience seats. *(Defendant complies.)* Is there any member of the jury panel who is acquainted with the defendant or who may have heard (his)(her) name before today? If your answer is yes, please raise your hand.

(B) The defendant, _____, is represented by (his)(her) attorney, _____, who is seated _____. (Mr.)(Ms.)(defense attorney), would you please stand? Is there any member of the jury panel who knows or who has seen (Mr.)(Ms.) _____ before today?

(C) *(If there is more than one defendant, repeat (a) and (b) for each codefendant.)*

(7) The People are represented by _____, Deputy District Attorney, who is seated _____. (Mr.)(Ms.)(district attorney), would you please stand? Is there any member of the jury panel who knows or who has seen (Mr.)(Ms.) _____ before today?

(8) The defendant is charged by an (information)(indictment) filed by the district attorney with having committed the crime of _____, in violation of section _____ of the _____ Code, it being alleged that on or about _____ in the County of _____, the defendant did *(describe the offense)*. To (this charge)(these charges) the defendant has pleaded not guilty, and the jury will have to decide whether the defendant's guilt has been proved beyond a reasonable doubt. Having heard the charge(s) that (has)(have) been filed against the defendant, is there any member of the jury panel who feels that he or she cannot give this defendant a fair trial because of the nature of the charge(s) against (him)(her)?

(9) Have any of you heard of, or have you any prior knowledge of, the facts or events in this case?

(10) Do any of you have any ethical, religious, political, or other beliefs that would prevent you from serving as a juror in this case?

(11) During the trial of this case, the following persons may be called as witnesses to testify on behalf of the parties or their names may be mentioned in evidence: _____ *(Do not identify the side on whose behalf the witness might be called.)* Have any of you heard of or otherwise been acquainted with any of the witnesses just named? You should note that the parties are not required and might not wish to call all of these witnesses, and they may later find it necessary to call other witnesses.

(12) Do any of you have any financial or personal interest in the outcome of this case?

(13) How many of you have served previously as jurors in a criminal case?

To each person whose hand is raised:

(A) (Mr.)(Ms.)_____(or Juror ID number), you indicated you have been a juror in a criminal case. What were the charges in that case? *(Response.)*

(B) Do you feel you can put aside whatever you heard in that case and decide this case on the evidence to be presented and the law as I will state it to you? *(Response.)*

(14) May I see the hands of those jurors who have served on civil cases, but who have never served on a criminal case? *(Response.)* You must understand that there are substantial differences in the rules applicable to the trial of criminal cases from those applicable to the trial of civil cases. This is particularly true respecting the burden of proof that is placed on the People. In a civil case we say that the plaintiff must prove (his) (her) case by a preponderance of the evidence. In a criminal case, the defendant is presumed to be innocent, and before (he)(she) may be found guilty, the People must prove (his)(her) guilt beyond a reasonable doubt. If the jury has a reasonable doubt, the defendant must be acquitted. Will each of you be able to set aside the instructions that you received in your previous cases and try this case on the instructions given by me in this case?

(15) The fact that the defendant is in court for trial, or that charges have been made against (him)(her), is no evidence whatever of (his)(her) guilt. The jurors are to consider only evidence properly received in the courtroom in determining whether the defendant's guilt has been proved beyond a reasonable doubt. The defendant has entered a plea of "not guilty," which is a complete denial, making it necessary for the People, acting through the district attorney, to prove beyond a reasonable doubt the case against the defendant. If the evidence does not convince you of the truth of the charges beyond a reasonable doubt, the defendant is entitled to a verdict of not guilty.

In the following questions I will be using the terms "relative," "close friend," and "anyone with whom you have a significant personal relationship." The term "anyone with whom you have a significant personal relationship" means a domestic partner, life partner, former spouse, or anyone with whom you have an influential or intimate relationship that you would characterize as important.

(16) Have you or, to your knowledge, has any relative, close friend, or anyone with whom you have a significant personal relationship, ever been the victim of any crime? *(Response.)*

(17) Have you or, to your knowledge, has any relative, close friend, or anyone with whom you have a significant personal relationship, ever had any contact with law enforcement, including being: (a) stopped by the police? (b) accused of misconduct, whether or not it was a crime? (c) investigated as a suspect in a criminal case? (d) charged with a crime? or (e) a criminal defendant? *(Response.)*

(18) Have you or, to your knowledge, has any relative, close friend, or anyone with whom you have a significant personal relationship, had any law enforcement training or experience or been a member of or been employed by any law enforcement agency? By law enforcement agency, I include any police department, sheriff's office, highway patrol, district attorney's office, city attorney's office, attorney general's office, United States attorney's office, FBI, and others. *(If so, elicit the details of the experience or connection.)*

(19) Would you be able to listen to the testimony of a police or other peace officer and measure it the same way you would that of any other witness?

(20) *When appropriate:*

It may appear that one or more of the parties, attorneys, or witnesses come from a particular national, racial, or religious group (or may have a lifestyle different from your own). Would this in any way affect your judgment or the weight and credibility you would give to their testimony?

(21) It is important that I have your assurance that you will follow my instructions and rulings on the law and will apply that law to this case. To put it somewhat differently, whether you approve or disapprove of the court's rulings or instructions, it is your solemn duty to accept as correct these statements of the law. You must accept and follow my instructions even if you disagree with the law. You may not substitute your own idea of what you think the law ought to be. Will all of you follow the law as given to you by me in this case?

(22) Each of you should now state your:

(A) (Name)(or juror ID number);

(B) Children's ages and the number of children, if any;

(C) Occupation;

(D) Occupational history; and

(E) Present employer;

And for your spouse or anyone with whom you have a significant personal relationship, their:

(F) Occupations;

(G) Occupational histories; and

(H) Present employers;

And for your adult children, their:

(I) Occupations;

(J) Occupational histories; and

(K) Present employers.

Please begin with juror number one.

(23) Do you know of any other reason, or has anything occurred during this question period, that might make you doubtful you would be a completely fair and impartial juror in this case or why you should not be on this jury? If there is, it is your duty to disclose the reason at this time.

(24) *After the court conducts the initial examination, Code of Civil Procedure section 223 allows counsel to ask supplemental questions for the purposes of uncovering possible bias or prejudice relevant to challenges for cause. The court may, in the exercise of its discretion, limit the oral and direct questioning of prospective jurors by counsel. The court may specify the maximum amount of time that counsel for each party may question an individual juror, or may specify an aggregate amount of time for each party, which can then be allocated among the prospective jurors by counsel.*

(25) *After the conclusion of counsel questioning, the court asks each side to exercise any challenges for cause.*

(26) *After ruling on challenges for cause, if any, the*

court calls on each side, alternately, to exercise any preemptory challenges.

(27) *If a new prospective juror is seated, the court should ask him or her:*

(A) Have you heard my questions to the other prospective jurors?

(B) Have any of the questions I have asked raised any doubt in your mind as to whether you could be a fair and impartial juror in this case?

(C) Can you think of any other reason why you might not be able to try this case fairly and impartially to both the prosecution and defendant, or why you should not be on this jury?

(D) Give us the personal information requested concerning your occupation, that of your spouse or anyone with whom you have a significant personal relationship, that of your adult children, and your prior jury experience.

(Thereupon, as to each new juror seated, the court must permit counsel to ask supplemental questions, and proceed with challenges as above.)

(Subd (b) amended effective January 1, 2007; adopted as subd (c) effective July 1, 1974; amended and relettered effective June 6, 1990; previously amended effective January 1, 1997, January 1, 2004, and January 1, 2006.)

(c) Improper questions

When any counsel examines the prospective jurors, the trial judge should not permit counsel to attempt to precondition the prospective jurors to a particular result or allow counsel to comment on the personal lives and families of the parties or their attorneys.

(Subd (c) amended effective January 1, 2006; adopted as subd (e) effective July 1, 1974; previously amended and relettered as subd (d) effective June 6, 1990; relettered as subd (c) effective January 1, 1997.)

Standard 4.30 amended and renumbered effective January 1, 2007; adopted as sec. 8.5 July 1, 1974; previously amended effective January 1, 1988, January 1, 1990, June 6, 1990, January 1, 1997, January 1, 2004, and January 1, 2006.)

Standard 4.40.   Traffic infraction procedures

To insure the prompt and efficient disposition of traffic infraction cases, each court should:

(1) Authorize the clerk, within limits set by the court, to grant defendants extensions of time for the posting of bail and payment of fines.

(2) Authorize the clerk or other court official to accept offers of proof of correction or compliance in accordance with the bail schedule without the necessity of a court appearance.

Standard 4.40 amended and renumbered effective January 1, 2007; adopted as sec. 10.5 effective July 1, 1977.

Standard 4.41.   Courtesy notice—traffic procedures

(a) Mailed courtesy notice

Each court should promptly mail a "courtesy notice" to the address shown on the Notice to Appear. The date of mailing should allow for the plea-by-mail option in infraction cases.

(Subd (a) amended and lettered effective January 1, 2007; adopted as part of unlettered subdivision effective January 1, 1987.)

(b) Minimum information in courtesy notice

In addition to information obtained from the Notice to Appear, the courtesy notice should contain at least the following information:

(1) An appearance date, time, and location;

(2) Whether a court appearance is mandatory or optional;

(3) The total bail amount if forfeitable;

(4) The procedure required for remitting bail;

(5) The plea-by-mail option in infraction cases and the number of appearances required where trial is requested;

(6) The consequences of failure to appear; and

(7) A telephone number to call for additional information.

(Subd (b) amended and lettered effective January 1, 2007; adopted as part of unlettered subdivision effective January 1, 1987.)

(c) Additional information in courtesy notice

Courts should provide additional information in the courtesy notice, as appropriate, including the following:

(1) Informal trial, trial by declaration, traffic violators' school, and telephone scheduling options; and

(2) Correction requirements and procedures.

(Subd (c) amended and lettered effective January 1, 2007; adopted as part of unlettered subdivision effective January 1, 1987.)

Standard 4.41 amended and renumbered effective January 1, 2007; adopted as sec. 10.6 effective January 1, 1987.

Standard 4.42.   Traffic infraction trial scheduling

(a) Review of procedures

Courts should adopt and periodically review procedures governing the scheduling of traffic infraction trials that minimize appearance time and costs for defendants, witnesses, and law enforcement officers.

(Subd (a) amended and lettered effective January 1, 2007; adopted as part of unlettered subdivision effective January 1, 1987.)

(b) Meetings

Courts should hold periodic meetings with representatives from local law enforcement agencies, the prosecution and defense bars, and other interested groups as appropriate in an effort to achieve this goal.

(Subd (b) amended and lettered effective January 1, 2007; adopted as part of unlettered subdivision effective January 1, 1987.)

Standard 4.42 amended and renumbered effective January 1, 2007; adopted as sec. 10.7 effective January 1, 1987.

Title 5

Standards for Cases Involving Children and Families

Standard 5.10. Guidelines for determining payment for costs of appointed counsel for children in family court [Repealed]

Standard 5.10 repealed effective January 1, 2008; adopted as sec. 20.6 effective January 1, 1992; previously amended effective January 1, 2005, and July 1, 2005; previously amended and renumbered effective January 1, 2007.

Standard 5.11. Guidelines for appointment of counsel for minors when time with or responsibility for the minor is disputed [Repealed]

Standard 5.11 repealed effective January 1, 2008; adopted as sec. 20.5 effective January 1, 1990; previously amended and renumbered effective January 1, 2007.

Standard 5.20. Uniform standards of practice for providers of supervised visitation

(a) Scope of service

This standard defines the standards of practice, including duties and obligations, for providers of supervised visitation under Family Code section 3200. Unless specified otherwise, the standards of practice are designed to apply to all providers of supervised visitation, whether the provider is a friend, relative, paid independent contractor, employee, intern, or volunteer operating independently or through a supervised visitation center or agency. The goal of these standards of practice is to assure the safety and welfare of the child, adults, and providers of supervised visitation. Once safety is assured, the best interest of the child is the paramount consideration at all stages and particularly in deciding the manner in which supervision is provided. Each court is encouraged to adopt local court rules necessary to implement these standards of practice.

(Subd (a) amended effective January 1, 2007.)

(b) Definition

Family Code section 3200 defines the term "provider" as including any individual or supervised visitation center that monitors visitation. Supervised visitation is contact between a noncustodial party and one or more children in the presence of a neutral third person. These standards of practice and this definition do not apply to supervision of visitation exchanges only, but may be useful in that context.

(Subd (b) amended effective January 1, 2007.)

(c) Qualifications of the provider

Who provides the supervision and the manner in which supervision is provided depends on different factors, including local resources, the financial situation of the parties, and the degree of risk in each case. While the court makes the final decision as to the manner in which supervision is provided and any terms or conditions, the court may consider recommendations by the attorney for the child, the parties and their attorneys, Family Court Services staff, evaluators, therapists, and providers of supervised visitation.

(1) A "nonprofessional provider" is any person who is not paid for providing supervised visitation services. Unless otherwise ordered by the court or stipulated by the parties, the nonprofessional provider should:

(A) Be 21 years of age or older;

(B) Have no conviction for driving under the influence (DUI) within the last 5 years;

(C) Not have been on probation or parole for the last 10 years;

(D) Have no record of a conviction for child molestation, child abuse, or other crimes against a person;

(E) Have proof of automobile insurance if transporting the child;

(F) Have no civil, criminal, or juvenile restraining orders within the last 10 years;

(G) Have no current or past court order in which the provider is the person being supervised;

(H) Not be financially dependent on the person being supervised;

(I) Have no conflict of interest under (g); and

(J) Agree to adhere to and enforce the court order regarding supervised visitation.

(2) A "professional provider" is any person paid for providing supervised visitation services, or an independent contractor, employee, intern, or volunteer operating independently or through a supervised visitation center or agency. The professional provider should:

(A) Be 21 years of age or older;

(B) Have no conviction for driving under the influence (DUI) within the last 5 years;

(C) Not have been on probation or parole for the last 10 years;

(D) Have no record of a conviction for child molestation, child abuse, or other crimes against a person;

(E) Have proof of automobile insurance if transporting the child;

(F) Have no civil, criminal, or juvenile restraining orders within the last 10 years;

(G) Have no current or past court order in which the provider is the person being supervised;

(H) Be able to speak the language of the party being supervised and of the child, or the provider must provide a neutral interpreter over the age of 18 who is able to do so;

(I) Have no conflict of interest under (g); and

(J) Agree to adhere to and enforce the court order regarding supervised visitation.

(3) A "therapeutic provider" is a licensed mental health professional paid for providing supervised visitation services, including a psychiatrist, a psychologist, a clinical social worker, a marriage and family counselor, or an intern working under direct supervision of a qualified licensed mental health professional. A therapeutic provider should meet the qualifications provided in (c)(2). A judicial officer may order therapeutic supervision for cases requiring a clinical setting.

(Subd (c) amended effective January 1, 2007.)

(d) Training for providers

(1) Each court is encouraged to make available to all providers informational materials about the role of a provider, the terms and conditions of supervised visitation, and the legal responsibilities and obligations of a provider under this standard.

(2) In addition, professional and therapeutic providers should receive training that should include the following subjects:

(A) The role of a professional and therapeutic provider;

(B) Child abuse reporting laws;

(C) Record-keeping procedures;

(D) Screening, monitoring, and termination of visitation;

(E) Developmental needs of children;

(F) Legal responsibilities and obligations of a provider;

(G) Cultural sensitivity;

(H) Conflicts of interest;

(I) Confidentiality; and

(J) Issues relating to substance abuse, child abuse, sexual abuse, and domestic violence.

(Subd (d) adopted effective January 1, 2007.)

(e) Safety and security procedures

All providers should make every reasonable effort to assure the safety and welfare of the child and adults during the visitation. Supervised visitation centers should establish a written protocol with the assistance of the local law enforcement agency that describes the emergency assistance and responses that can be expected from the local law enforcement agency. In addition, the professional and therapeutic provider should:

(1) Establish and state in writing minimum security procedures and inform the parties of these procedures before the commencement of supervised visitation;

(2) Conduct comprehensive intake and screening to assess the nature and degree of risk for each case. The procedures for intake should include separate interviews with the parties before the first visit. During the interview, the provider should obtain identifying information and explain the reasons for temporary suspension or termination of a visit under this standard. If the child is of sufficient age and capacity, the provider should include the child in part of the intake or orientation process. Any discussion should be presented to the child in a manner appropriate to the child's developmental stage;

(3) Obtain during the intake process:

(A) Copies of any protective order;

(B) Current court orders;

(C) Any Judicial Council form relating to supervised visitation orders;

(D) A report of any written records of allegations of domestic violence or abuse; and

(E) An account of the child's health needs if the child has a chronic health condition;

(4) Establish written procedures that must be followed in the event a child is abducted during supervised visitation; and

(5) Suspend or terminate supervised visitation if the provider determines that the risk factors present are placing in jeopardy the safety and welfare of the child or provider as enumerated in (j).

(Subd (e) amended and relettered effective January 1, 2007; adopted as subd (d) effective January 1, 1998.)

(f) Ratio of children to provider

The ratio of children to a professional provider should be contingent on:

(1) The degree of risk factors present in each case;

(2) The nature of supervision required in each case;

(3) The number and ages of the children to be supervised during a visit;

(4) The number of people visiting the child during the visit;

(5) The duration and location of the visit; and

(6) The experience of the provider.

(Subd (f) amended and relettered effective January 1, 2007; adopted as subd (e) effective January 1, 1998.)

(g) Conflict of interest

All providers should maintain neutrality by refusing to discuss the merits of the case or agree with or support one party over another. Any discussion between a provider and the parties should be for the purposes of arranging visitation and providing for the safety of the children. In order to avoid a conflict of interest, the provider should not:

(1) Be financially dependent on the person being supervised;

(2) Be an employee of the person being supervised;

(3) Be an employee of or affiliated with any superior court in the county in which the supervision is ordered unless specified in the employment contract; or

(4) Be in an intimate relationship with the person being supervised.

(Subd (g) amended and relettered effective January 1, 2007; adopted as subd (f) effective January 1, 1998.)

(h) Maintenance and disclosure of records

(1) Professional and therapeutic providers should keep a record for each case, including the following:

(A) A written record of each contact and visit, including the date, time, and duration of the contact or visit;

(B) Who attended the visit;

(C) A summary of activities during the visit;

(D) Actions taken by the provider, including any interruptions, terminations of a visit, and reasons for these actions;

(E) An account of critical incidents, including physical or verbal altercations and threats;

(F) Violations of protective or court visitation orders;

(G) Any failure to comply with the terms and conditions of the visitation; and

(H) Any incidence of abuse as required by law.

(2) Case recordings should be limited to facts, observations, and direct statements made by the parties, not personal conclusions, suggestions, or opinions of the provider. All contacts by the provider in person, in writing, or by telephone with either party, the children, the court, attorneys, mental health professionals, and referring agencies should be documented in the case file. All entries should be dated and signed by the person recording the entry.

(3) If ordered by the court or requested by either party or the attorney for either party or the attorney for the child, a report about the supervised visit should be produced. These reports should include facts, observations, and direct statements and not opinions or recommendations regarding future visitation unless ordered by the court. A copy of any report should be sent to all parties, their attorneys, and the attorney for the child.

(4) Any identifying information about the parties and the child, including addresses, telephone numbers, places

of employment, and schools, is confidential, should not be disclosed, and should be deleted from documents before releasing them to any court, attorney, attorney for the child, party, mediator, evaluator, mental health professional, social worker, or referring agency, except as required in reporting suspected child abuse.

(Subd (h) amended and relettered effective January 1, 2007; adopted as subd (g) effective January 1, 1998.)

(i) Confidentiality

Communications between parties and providers of supervised visitation are not protected by any privilege of confidentiality. The psychotherapist-patient privilege does not apply during therapeutic supervision. Professional and therapeutic providers should, whenever possible, maintain confidentiality regarding the case except when:

(1) Ordered by the court;

(2) Subpoenaed to produce records or testify in court;

(3) Requested to provide information about the case by a mediator or evaluator in conjunction with a court-ordered mediation, investigation, or evaluation;

(4) Required to provide information about the case by Child Protective Services; or

(5) Requested to provide information about the case by law enforcement.

(Subd (i) amended and relettered effective January 1, 2007; adopted as subd (h) effective January 1, 1998.)

(j) Delineation of terms and conditions

The provider bears the sole responsibility for enforcement of all the terms and conditions of any supervised visitation. Unless otherwise ordered by the court, the provider should:

(1) Monitor conditions to assure the safety and welfare of the child;

(2) Enforce the frequency and duration of the visits as ordered by the court;

(3) Avoid any attempt to take sides with either party;

(4) Ensure that all contact between the child and the noncustodial party is within the provider's hearing and sight at all times, and that discussions are audible to the provider;

(5) Speak in a language spoken by the child and the noncustodial party;

(6) Allow no derogatory comments about the other parent, his or her family, caretaker, child, or child's siblings;

(7) Allow no discussion of the court case or possible future outcomes;

(8) Allow neither the provider nor the child to be used to gather information about the other party or caretaker or to transmit documents, information, or personal possessions;

(9) Allow no spanking, hitting, or threatening the child;

(10) Allow no visits to occur while the visiting party appears to be under the influence of alcohol or illegal drugs;

(11) Allow no emotional, verbal, physical, or sexual abuse; and

(12) Ensure that the parties follow any additional rules set forth by the provider or the court.

(Subd (j) amended and relettered effective January 1, 2007; adopted as subd (i) effective January 1, 1998.)

(k) Safety considerations for sexual abuse cases

In cases where there are allegations of sexual abuse, in addition to the requirements of (j), the provider should comply with the following terms and conditions, unless otherwise ordered by the court:

(1) Allow no exchanges of gifts, money, or cards;

(2) Allow no photographing, audiotaping, or videotaping of the child;

(3) Allow no physical contact with the child such as lap sitting, hair combing, stroking, hand holding, prolonged hugging, wrestling, tickling, horseplaying, changing diapers, or accompanying the child to the bathroom;

(4) Allow no whispering, passing notes, hand signals, or body signals; and

(5) Allow no supervised visitation in the location where the alleged sexual abuse occurred.

(Subd (k) amended and relettered effective January 1, 2007; adopted as subd (j) effective January 1, 1998.)

(l) Legal responsibilities and obligations of a provider

All providers of supervised visitation should:

(1) Advise the parties before commencement of supervised visitation that no confidential privilege exists;

(2) Report suspected child abuse to the appropriate agency, as provided by law, and inform the parties of the provider's obligation to make such reports;

(3) Implement the terms and conditions under (j); and

(4) Suspend or terminate visitation under (n).

(Subd (l) amended and relettered effective January 1, 2007; adopted as subd (k) effective January 1, 1998.)

(m) Additional legal responsibilities of professional and therapeutic providers

In addition to the legal responsibilities and obligations required in (l), professional and therapeutic providers should:

(1) Prepare a written contract to be signed by the parties before commencement of the supervised visitation. The contract should inform each party of the terms and conditions of supervised visitation;

(2) Review custody and visitation orders relevant to the supervised visitation;

(3) Implement an intake and screening procedure under (e)(2); and

(4) Comply with additional requirements under (o).

(Subd (m) amended and relettered effective January 1, 2007; adopted as subd (l) effective January 1, 1998.)

(n) Temporary suspension or termination of supervised visitation

(1) All providers should make every reasonable effort to provide a safe visit for the child and the noncustodial party.

(2) However, if a provider determines that the rules of the visit have been violated, the child has become acutely distressed, or the safety of the child or the provider is at risk, the visit may be temporarily interrupted, rescheduled at a later date, or terminated.

(3) All interruptions or terminations of visits should be recorded in the case file.

(4) All providers should advise both parties of the reasons for interruption of a visit or termination.

(Subd (n) amended and relettered effective January 1, 2007; adopted as subd (m) effective January 1, 1998.)

(o) Additional requirements for professional and therapeutic providers

Professional and therapeutic providers should state the reasons for temporary suspension or termination of supervised visitation in writing and provide the written statement to both parties, their attorneys, the attorney for the child, and the court.

(Subd (o) amended and relettered effective January 1, 2007; adopted as subd (n) effective January 1, 1998.)

Standard 5.20 amended and renumbered effective January 1, 2007; adopted as sec. 26.2 effective January 1, 1998.

Standard 5.30. Family court matters

(a) Judicial assignments to family court

In a court with a separate family court, the presiding judge of the superior court should assign judges to the family court to serve for a minimum of three years. In selecting judges for family court assignments, the presiding judge should consider, in addition to rule 10.603(c)(1)(A) of the California Rules of Court, the judge's prior experience in family law litigation and mediation, as well as whether the judge prefers to serve in a family law department.

(Subd (a) adopted effective January 1, 2007.)

(b) Case assignment to same department

To the extent possible, family law actions related to the same family should be assigned to the same judicial officer for all purposes, so that all decisions that are made in a case through final judgment are issued by the same judicial officer.

(Subd (b) adopted effective January 1, 2007.)

(c) Importance of family court

The supervising judge in the family court, in consultation with the presiding judge of the superior court, should:

(1) Motivate and educate other judges regarding the significance of family court; and

(2) Work to ensure that sufficient judicial officers, court staff, family law facilitators, child custody mediators and evaluators, interpreters, financial resources, and adequate facilities are assigned to the family court to allow adequate time to hear and decide the matters before it.

(Subd (c) adopted effective January 1, 2007.)

(d) Compensation for court-appointed attorneys

The supervising judge of the family court should ensure that court-appointed attorneys in the family court are compensated at a level equivalent to attorneys appointed by the court in comparable types of cases.

(Subd (d) adopted effective January 1, 2007.)

(e) Training and education

Family court law is a specialized area of the law that requires dedication and study. The supervising judge of the family court has a responsibility to maintain high-quality services in family court. The quality of services provided by judicial officers and court staff depends, in significant part, on appropriate training and education, from the beginning of the family court assignment and on a continuing basis thereafter.

(1) Family court judicial officers, family law facilitators, child custody mediators and evaluators, interpreters, other court staff, and court-appointed attorneys should have sufficient training to perform their jobs competently.

(2) The supervising judge of the family court should promote access to printed, electronic, Internet, and other family law resources.

(Subd (e) adopted effective January 1, 2007.)

(f) Unique role of a family court

Under the direction of the presiding judge of the superior court, the family court, to the extent that it does not interfere with the adjudication process or violate any ethical constraints, is encouraged to:

(1) Provide active leadership within the community in determining the needs of, and obtaining and developing resources and services for children and families who participate in the family law court system;

(2) Investigate and determine the availability of specific prevention, intervention, and treatment services in the community for families who come before the family courts;

(3) Take an active role in helping the court develop rules and procedures that will result in the ordering of appropriate treatment and services for children and families;

(4) Exercise a leadership role in the development and maintenance of services for self-represented and financially disadvantaged litigants;

(5) Take an active part in the formation of a community-wide network to promote and coordinate private- and public-sector efforts to focus attention and resources on the needs of family law litigants;

(6) Educate the community and its institutions, including the media, concerning the role of the family court in meeting the complex needs of families;

(7) Encourage the development of community services and resources to assist families and children in the family court system, including self-help information; supervised visitation; substance abuse and drug prevention, intervention, and treatment; services for families with domestic violence issues; counseling; parenting education; vocational training; mediation; alternative dispute resolution options; and other resources to support families;

(8) Manage cases more efficiently and effectively to avoid conflicting orders;

(9) Take an active role in promoting completion of cases in a timely manner;

(10) Appoint counsel for children in appropriate family law custody cases; and

(11) Ensure that the best interest of children is served throughout the family court process.

(Subd (f) adopted effective January 1, 2007.)

(g) Appointment of attorneys and other persons

A court should follow the guidelines of standard 10.21 of the California Standards of Judicial Administration when appointing attorneys, arbitrators, mediators, referees, masters, receivers, and other persons.

(Subd (g) adopted effective January 1, 2007.)

Standard 5.30 adopted effective January 1, 2007.

Advisory Committee Comment

Standard 5.30. Family court matters include proceedings under the Family Code for dissolution of marriage, nullity of marriage, legal separation, custody and support of minor children; or actions under the Domestic Violence Prevention Act, the Uniform Parentage Act, the Uniform Child Custody Jurisdiction and Enforcement Act, Domestic Partner Registration Act, and the

Uniform Interstate Family Support Act; local child support agency actions under the Family Code; and contempt proceedings relating to family law or local child support agency actions.

Subdivision (a). This subdivision implements the legislative mandate of Family Code section 2330.3(b) requiring the Judicial Council to adopt a standard of judicial administration prescribing a minimum length of a judge's family law assignment. Standard 5.30 sets a standard in family court that is similar to the juvenile court standards stated in standard 5.40, Juvenile Court Matters.

Family law is complex and constantly evolving. The laws concerning child custody, support, domestic violence, and property division are always changing. Not only does the family law judge have to understand family law and procedure but also issues that involve bankruptcy, estate planning, insurance, state and federal tax law, business, immigration, and criminal law, which can frequently arise in the context of a family law case. Because of the complexity and long-range impact of the judicial determinations, the presiding judge should strive to place experienced judges in family law assignments.

Considering the constantly evolving changes in the law, as well as the unique nature of the proceedings in family court, the family court judge should be willing to commit to a minimum tenure of three years. Not only does this tenure afford the judge the opportunity to become well acquainted with the complexity of the family court process, but it also provides continuity to a system that demands it.

Subdivision (b). This subdivision implements the legislative mandate of Family Code section 2330.3(a), which requires that dissolution actions, to the greatest extent possible, be assigned to the same superior court department for all purposes, so that all decisions in a case are made by the same judicial officer. This subdivision expands the Legislature's requirement by including other related family court matters, such as those filed under the Uniform Parentage Act, Domestic Violence Prevention Act, in recognition that the same families may enter the family court through a variety of actions.

The committee recognizes that having the same judicial officer hear all actions involving the same family may not be practical in all cases for reasons that include funding limitations, assignment rotations, illness, vacations, and retirements. In some courts, one judge does not hear all aspects of a family's legal problems because of multiple courthouse locations or specifically designated funding of certain issues (e.g., Title IV-D child support issues). However, the committee agrees with the legislative intent in enacting section 2330.3(a), which was to expedite and simplify the dissolution process, reduce the litigation expenses and costs, and encourage greater judicial supervision of cases involving dissolution of marriage. Family law actions often involve a succession of hearings to resolve the various issues that arise. A single judge's involvement over this period of time allows the judge to be more familiar with the particular actions and issues, which creates judicial efficiencies that expedite their handling. One judge hearing all actions involving a family also helps avoid conflicting orders, alleviates the need to hold multiple hearings on the same issue, improves the court process, promotes consistency, and enhances fairness in family proceedings.

Subdivision (c). The family court is an integral part of the justice system. Decisions made by family law judges can have significant and lasting impacts on the lives of the parties and their children. The work of the family court has a significant impact on the health of families and ultimately on the strength of the community. The parties deserve to have adequate time to present their cases, and the judges should have the resources they need to enable them to make informed decisions. It is only through the constant exertion of pressure to maintain resources and the continuous education of court-related personnel and administrators that the historic trend to give less priority and provide fewer resources to the family court can be changed.

Subdivision (d). Fees paid to court-appointed attorneys who represent children in family court are sometimes less than the fees paid attorneys doing other comparable legal work thereby demeaning the work of the family court and leading many to believe that such work is less important. It may also discourage attorneys from accepting these appointments. Compensation for legal work in the family court should reflect the importance of the work.

Subdivision (e)(2). A significant barrier to having well-trained attorneys and educated self-represented litigants is a lack of current educational materials relating to family court practice. Law libraries, law offices, and court systems traditionally have not devoted adequate resources to purchase such educational materials. With advances in technology, resources can be accessed, shared, developed, or made available through electronic/computer-based, online, and multimedia means, audiotape and videotape, DVD, CD, Web-based audiocasts and videocasts, and other media to supplement print materials.

Subdivision (f). In addition to the traditional role of fairly and efficiently resolving disputes before the court, a family court judge occupies a unique position within California's judiciary. California law empowers the family court judge not only to order relief related to the needs of families under its jurisdiction but also to enforce and review the compliance with such orders. This oversight function includes the obligation to understand and work with those public and private agencies that provide services for families. As such, the family court assignment requires a dramatic shift in emphasis from judging in the traditional sense. Active and public judicial support and encouragement of programs serving children and families in family court poses no conflict with traditional concepts of judicial ethics and is an important function of the family court judge. These efforts enhance the overall administration of justice for families.

Standard 5.40.   Juvenile court matters

(a) Assignments to juvenile court

The presiding judge of the superior court should assign judges to the juvenile court to serve for a minimum of three years. Priority should be given to judges who have expressed an interest in the assignment.

(Subd (a) adopted effective July 1, 1989.)

(b) Importance of juvenile court

The presiding judge of the juvenile court, in consultation with the presiding judge of the superior court, should:

(1) Motivate and educate other judges regarding the significance of juvenile court.

(2) Work to ensure that sufficient judges and staff, facilities, and financial resources are assigned to the juvenile court to allow adequate time to hear and decide the matters before it.

(Subd (b) amended effective January 1, 2007; adopted effective July 1, 1989.)

(c) Standards of representation and compensation

The presiding judge of the juvenile court should:

(1) Encourage attorneys who practice in juvenile court, including all court-appointed and contract attorneys, to continue their practice in juvenile court for substantial periods of time. A substantial period of time is at least two years and preferably from three to five years.

(2) Confer with the county public defender, county district attorney, county counsel, and other public law office leaders and encourage them to raise the status of attorneys working in the juvenile courts as follows: hire attorneys who are interested in serving in the juvenile court for a substantial part of their careers; permit and encourage attorneys, based on interest and ability, to

remain in juvenile court assignments for significant periods of time; and work to ensure that attorneys who have chosen to serve in the juvenile court have the same promotional and salary opportunities as attorneys practicing in other assignments within a law office.

(3) Establish minimum standards of practice to which all court-appointed and public office attorneys will be expected to conform. These standards should delineate the responsibilities of attorneys relative to investigation and evaluation of the case, preparation for and conduct of hearings, and advocacy for their respective clients.

(4) In conjunction with other leaders in the legal community, ensure that attorneys appointed in the juvenile court are compensated in a manner equivalent to attorneys appointed by the court in other types of cases.

(Subd (c) amended effective January 1, 2007; adopted effective July 1, 1992.)

(d) Training and orientation

The presiding judge of the juvenile court should:

(1) Establish relevant prerequisites for court-appointed attorneys and advocates in the juvenile court.

(2) Develop orientation and in-service training programs for judicial officers, attorneys, volunteers, law enforcement personnel, court personnel, and child advocates to ensure that all are adequately trained concerning all issues relating to special education rights and responsibilities, including the right of each child with exceptional needs to receive a free, appropriate public education and the right of each child with educational disabilities to receive accommodations.

(3) Promote the establishment of a library or other resource center in which information about juvenile court practice (including books, periodicals, videotapes, and other training materials) can be collected and made available to all participants in the juvenile system.

(4) Ensure that attorneys who appear in juvenile court have sufficient training to perform their jobs competently, as follows: require that all court-appointed attorneys meet minimum training and continuing legal education standards as a condition of their appointment to juvenile court matters; and encourage the leaders of public law offices that have responsibilities in juvenile court to require their attorneys who appear in juvenile court to have at least the same training and continuing legal education required of court-appointed attorneys.

(Subd (d) amended effective January 1, 2001; adopted effective July 1, 1989; previously amended and relettered effective July 1, 1992.)

(e) Unique role of a juvenile court judge

Judges of the juvenile court, in consultation with the presiding judge of the juvenile court and the presiding judge of the superior court, to the extent that it does not interfere with the adjudication process, are encouraged to:

(1) Provide active leadership within the community in determining the needs of and obtaining and developing resources and services for at-risk children and families. At-risk children include delinquents, dependents, and status offenders.

(2) Investigate and determine the availability of specific prevention, intervention, and treatment services in the community for at-risk children and their families.

(3) Exercise their authority by statute or rule to review, order, and enforce the delivery of specific services and treatment for at-risk children and their families.

(4) Exercise a leadership role in the development and maintenance of permanent programs of interagency cooperation and coordination among the court and the various public agencies that serve at-risk children and their families.

(5) Take an active part in the formation of a communitywide network to promote and unify private and public sector efforts to focus attention and resources for at-risk children and their families.

(6) Maintain close liaison with school authorities and encourage coordination of policies and programs.

(7) Educate the community and its institutions through every available means, including the media, concerning the role of the juvenile court in meeting the complex needs of at-risk children and their families.

(8) Evaluate the criteria established by child protection agencies for initial removal and reunification decisions and communicate the court's expectations of what constitutes "reasonable efforts" to prevent removal or hasten return of the child.

(9) Encourage the development of community services and resources to assist homeless, truant, runaway, and incorrigible children.

(10) Be familiar with all detention facilities, placements, and institutions used by the court.

(11) Act in all instances consistent with the public safety and welfare.

(Subd (e) amended effective January 1, 2007; adopted effective July 1, 1989; previously relettered effective July 1, 1992.)

(f) Appointment of attorneys and other persons

For the appointment of attorneys, arbitrators, mediators, referees, masters, receivers, and other persons, each court should follow rule 10.611 and the guidelines of standard 10.21.

(Subd (f) amended effective January 1, 2007; adopted effective January 1, 1999.)

(g) Educational rights of children in the juvenile court

The juvenile court should be guided by certain general principles:

(1) A significant number of children in the juvenile court process have exceptional needs that, if properly identified and assessed, would qualify such children to receive special education and related services under federal and state education law (a free, appropriate public education) (see Ed. Code, § 56000 et seq. and 20 U.S.C. § 1400 et seq.);

(2) Many children in the juvenile court process have disabilities that, if properly identified and assessed, would qualify such children to receive educational accommodations (see § 504 of the Rehabilitation Act of 1973 [29 U.S.C. § 794; 34 C.F.R. § 104.1 et seq.]);

(3) Unidentified and unremediated exceptional needs and unaccommodated disabilities have been found to correlate strongly with juvenile delinquency, substance abuse, mental health issues, teenage pregnancy, school failure and dropout, and adult unemployment and crime; and

(4) The cost of incarcerating children is substantially greater than the cost of providing special education and related services to exceptional needs children and provid-

ing educational accommodations to children with disabilities.

(Subd (g) adopted effective January 1, 2001.)

(h) Role of the juvenile court

The juvenile court should:

(1) Take responsibility, with the other juvenile court participants at every stage of the child's case, to ensure that the child's educational needs are met, regardless of whether the child is in the custody of a parent or is suitably placed in the custody of the child welfare agency or probation department and regardless of where the child is placed in school. Each child under the jurisdiction of the juvenile court with exceptional needs has the right to receive a free, appropriate public education, specially designed, at no cost to the parents, to meet the child's unique special education needs. (See Ed. Code, § 56031 and 20 U.S.C. § 1401(8).) Each child with disabilities under the jurisdiction of the juvenile court has the right to receive accommodations. (See § 504 of the Rehabilitation Act of 1973 [29 U.S.C. § 794; 34 C.F.R. § 104.1 et seq. (1980)].) The court should also ensure that each parent or guardian receives information and assistance concerning his or her child's educational entitlements as provided by law.

(2) Provide oversight of the social service and probation agencies to ensure that a child's educational rights are investigated, reported, and monitored. The court should work within the statutory framework to accommodate the sharing of information between agencies. A child who comes before the court and is suspected of having exceptional needs or other educational disabilities should be referred in writing for an assessment to the child's school principal or to the school district's special education office. (See Ed. Code, §§ 56320–56329.) The child's parent, teacher, or other service provider may make the required written referral for assessment. (See Ed. Code, § 56029.)

(3) Require that court reports, case plans, assessments, and permanency plans considered by the court address a child's educational entitlements and how those entitlements are being satisfied, and contain information to assist the court in deciding whether the right of the parent or guardian to make educational decisions for the child should be limited by the court under Welfare and Institutions Code section 361(a) or 726(b). Information concerning whether the school district has met its obligation to provide educational services to the child, including special educational services if the child has exceptional needs under Education Code section 56000 et seq., and to provide accommodations if the child has disabilities as defined in section 504 of the Rehabilitation Act of 1973 (29 U.S.C. § 794; 34 C.F.R. § 104.1 et seq. (1980)) should also be included, along with a recommendation for disposition.

(4) Facilitate coordination of services by joining the local educational agency as a party when it appears that an educational agency has failed to fulfill its legal obligations to provide special education and related services or accommodations to a child in the juvenile court who has been identified as having exceptional needs or educational disabilities. (See Welf. & Inst. Code, §§ 362(a), 727(a).)

(5) Make appropriate orders limiting the educational rights of a parent or guardian who cannot be located or identified, or who is unwilling or unable to be an active participant in ensuring that the child's educational needs are met, and appoint a responsible adult as educational representative for such a child or, if a representative cannot be identified and the child may be eligible for special education and related services or already has an individualized education program, use form JV-535 to refer the child to the local educational agency for special education and related services and prompt appointment of a surrogate parent. (Welf. & Inst. Code, §§ 361, 726; Ed. Code, § 56156.)

(6) Ensure that special education, related services, and accommodations to which the child is entitled are provided whenever the child's school placement changes. (See Ed. Code, § 56325.)

(Subd (h) amended effective January 1, 2007; adopted effective January 1, 2001; previously amended effective January 1, 2004.)

Standard 5.40 amended and renumbered effective January 1, 2007; adopted as sec. 24 effective January 1, 1989; previously amended effective July 1, 1992, January 1, 1999; January 1, 2001, and January 1, 2004.

Advisory Committee Comment

Subdivision (a). Considering the constantly evolving changes in the law, as well as the unique nature of the proceedings in juvenile court, the juvenile court judge should be willing to commit to a tenure of three years. Not only does this tenure afford the judge the opportunity to become well acquainted with the total juvenile justice complex, but it also provides continuity to a system that demands it.

Dependency cases under Welfare and Institutions Code section 300 for the most part last 18 months. The juvenile court judge has a responsibility to oversee these cases, and a single judge's involvement over this period of time is important to help ensure positive results. The ultimate goal should be to perfect a system that serves the needs of both recipients and providers. This can only be done over time and with constant application of effective energy.

Subdivision (b)(2). The juvenile court is an integral part of the justice system. It is only through the constant exertion of pressure to maintain resources and the continuous education of court-related personnel and administrators that the historic trend to minimize the juvenile court can be contained.

Subdivision (c)(4). The quality of justice in the juvenile court is in large part dependent on the quality of the attorneys who appear on behalf of the different parties before the court. The presiding judge of the juvenile court plays a significant role in ensuring that a sufficient number of attorneys of high quality are available to the parties appearing in juvenile court.

Juvenile court practice requires attorneys who have both a special interest in and a substantive understanding of the work of the court. Obtaining and retaining qualified attorneys for the juvenile court requires effective recruiting, training, and employment considerations.

The importance of juvenile court work must be stressed to ensure that juvenile court assignments have the same status and career enhancement opportunities as other assignments for public law office attorneys.

The presiding judge of the juvenile court should urge leaders of public law offices serving the juvenile court to assign experienced, interested, and capable attorneys to that court, and to establish hiring and promotional policies that will encourage the development of a division of the office dedicated to working in the juvenile court.

National commentators are in accord with these propositions: "Court-appointed and public attorneys representing children in abuse and neglect cases, as well as judges, should be specially trained or experienced. Juvenile and family courts should not be the 'training ground' for inexperienced attorneys or judges." (Metropolitan Court Judges Committee, National Council of Juvenile and Family Court Judges, *Deprived Children: A Judicial Response—73 Recommendations* (1986) p. 14.)

Fees paid to attorneys appearing in juvenile court are sometimes less than the fees paid attorneys doing other legal work. Such a payment scheme demeans the work of the juvenile court, leading many to believe that such work is less important. It may discourage attorneys from selecting juvenile court practice as a career option. The incarceration of a child in a detention facility or a child's permanent loss of his or her family through a termination of parental rights proceeding is at least as important as any other work in the legal system. Compensation for the legal work in the juvenile court should reflect the importance of this work.

Subdivision (d)(4). Juvenile court law is a specialized area of the law that requires dedication and study. The juvenile court judge has a responsibility to maintain high quality in the practice of law in the juvenile court. The quality of representation in the juvenile court depends in good part on the education of the lawyers who appear there. In order to make certain that all parties receive adequate representation, it is important that attorneys have adequate training before they begin practice in juvenile court and on a continuing basis thereafter. The presiding judge of the juvenile court should mandate such training for all court-appointed attorneys and urge leaders of public law offices to provide at least comparable training for attorneys assigned to juvenile court.

A minimum of six hours of continuing legal education is suggested; more hours are recommended. Education methods can include lectures and tapes that meet the legal education requirements.

In addition to basic legal training in juvenile dependency and delinquency law, evidentiary issues, and effective trial practice techniques, training should also include important related issues, including child development, alternative resources for families, effects and treatment of substance abuse, domestic violence, abuse, neglect, modification and enforcement of all court orders, dependency, delinquency, guardianships, conservatorships, interviewing children, and emancipation. Education may also include observational experience such as site visits to institutions and operations critical to the juvenile court.

A significant barrier to the establishment and maintenance of well-trained attorneys is a lack of educational materials relating to juvenile court practice. Law libraries, law offices, and court systems traditionally do not devote adequate resources to the purchase of such educational materials.

Effective January 1, 1993, guidelines and training material will be available from the Administrative Office of the Courts.

Subdivision (e)(11). A superior court judge assigned to the juvenile court occupies a unique position within California's judiciary. In addition to the traditional role of fairly and efficiently resolving disputes before the court, the juvenile court judge is statutorily required to discharge other duties. California law empowers the juvenile court judge not only to order services for children under its jurisdiction, but also to enforce and review the delivery of those services. This oversight function includes the obligation to understand and work with the public and private agencies, including school systems, that provide services and treatment programs for children and families. As such, the juvenile court assignment requires a dramatic shift in emphasis from judging in the traditional sense.

The legislative directive to juvenile court judges to "improve system performance in a vigorous and ongoing manner" (Welf. & Inst. Code, § 202) poses no conflict with traditional concepts of judicial ethics. Active and public judicial support and encourage-

ment of programs serving children and families at risk are important functions of the juvenile court judge that enhance the overall administration of justice.

The standards in (e) are derived from statutory requirements in the following sections of the Welfare and Institutions Code as well as the supplementary material promulgated by the National Council of Juvenile and Family Court Judges and others: (1) Welfare and Institutions Code, sections 202, 209, 300, 317, 318, 319, 362, 600, 601, 654, 702, 727; (2) California Code of Judicial Conduct, canon 4; (3) Metropolitan Court Judges Committee, National Council of Juvenile and Family Court Judges, *Deprived Children: A Judicial Response—73 Recommendations* (1986), Recommendations 1–7, 14, 35, 40; and (4) National Council of Juvenile and Family Court Judges, Child Welfare League of America, Youth Law Center, and the National Center for Youth Law, *Making Reasonable Efforts: Steps for Keeping Families Together* pp. 43–59.

Standard 5.45. Resource guidelines for child abuse and neglect cases

(a) Guidelines

To improve the fair and efficient administration of child abuse and neglect cases in the California juvenile dependency system, judges and judicial officers assigned to the juvenile court, in consultation with the presiding judge of the juvenile court and the presiding judge of the superior or consolidated court, are encouraged to follow the resource guidelines of the National Council of Juvenile and Family Court Judges, titled "Resource Guidelines: Improving Court Practice in Child Abuse & Neglect Cases." The guidelines are meant to be goals to help courts achieve, among other objectives, the following:

(1) Adherence to statutory timelines;

(2) Effective calendar management;

(3) Effective representation by counsel;

(4) Child-friendly court facilities;

(5) Timely and thorough reports and services to ensure informed judicial decisions, including reasonable efforts findings; and

(6) Minimum time allocations for specified hearings.

(Subd (a) amended effective January 1, 2007.)

(b) Distribution of guidelines

The Administrative Office of the Courts will distribute a copy of the resource guidelines to each juvenile court and will provide individual copies to judicial officers and court administrators on written request.

(Subd (b) amended effective January 1, 2007.)

Standard 5.45 amended and renumbered effective January 1, 2007; adopted as sec. 24.5 effective July 1, 1997.

Advisory Committee Comment

Child abuse and neglect cases impose a special obligation on juvenile court judges to oversee case progress. Case oversight includes monitoring the agency's fulfillment of its responsibilities and parental cooperation with the case plan. Court involvement in child welfare cases occurs simultaneously with agency efforts to assist the family. Federal and state legal mandates assign to the juvenile court a series of interrelated and complex decisions that shape the course of state intervention and determine the future of the child and family.

Unlike almost all other types of cases in the court system, child abuse and neglect cases deal with an ongoing and changing situation. In a child welfare case, the court must focus on agency casework and parental behavior over an extended period of time. In making a decision, the court must take into account the agency's plan to help the family and anticipated changes in parental behavior. At the same time, the court must consider the evolving circumstances and needs of each child.

The purpose of these resource guidelines is to specify the essential elements of properly conducted court hearings. The guidelines describe the requirements of juvenile courts in fulfilling their oversight role under federal and state laws, and they specify the necessary elements of a fair, thorough, and speedy court process in child abuse and neglect cases. The guidelines cover all stages of the court process, from the initial removal hearing to the end of juvenile court involvement. These guidelines assume that the court will remain involved until after the child has been safely returned home, has been placed in another permanent home, or has reached adulthood.

Currently, juvenile courts in California operate under the same juvenile court law and rules, and yet the rules are implemented with considerable variation throughout the state. In part, this is due to the lack of resource guidelines. The adoption of the proposed resource guidelines will help encourage more consistent juvenile court procedures in the state.

The guidelines are meant to be goals, and, as such, some of them may appear out of reach because of fiscal constraints or lack of judicial and staff resources. The Judicial Council Family and Juvenile Law Advisory Committee and staff of the Administrative Office of the Courts are committed to providing technical assistance to each juvenile court to aid in implementing these goals.

Title 6
[Reserved]

Title 7
Standards for Probate Proceedings

Standard 7.10.   Settlements or judgments in certain civil cases involving minors or persons with disabilities

In matters assigned to or pending in civil departments of the court where court approval of trusts that will receive proceeds of settlements or judgments is required under Probate Code section 3600, each court should develop practices and procedures that:

(1) Provide for determination of the trust issues by the probate department of the court or, in a court that does not have a probate department, a judicial officer who regularly hears proceedings under the Probate Code; or

(2) Ensure that judicial officers who hear these matters are experienced or have received training in substantive and technical issues involving trusts (including special needs trusts).

Standard 7.10 amended and renumbered effective January 1, 2007; adopted as sec. 40 effective January 1, 2005.

Title 8
Standards for the Appellate Courts

Standard 8.1.   Memorandum opinions
The Courts of Appeal should dispose of causes that

raise no substantial issues of law or fact by memorandum or other abbreviated form of opinion. Such causes could include:

(1) An appeal that is determined by a controlling statute which is not challenged for unconstitutionality and does not present any substantial question of interpretation or application;

(2) An appeal that is determined by a controlling decision which does not require a reexamination or restatement of its principles or rules; or

(3) An appeal raising factual issues that are determined by the substantial evidence rule.

Standard 8.1 amended and renumbered effective January 1, 2007; adopted as sec. 6 effective July 1, 1970.

Title 9
Standards on Law Practice, Attorneys, and Judges
[Reserved]

Title 10
Standards for Judicial Administration

Standard 10.5. The role of the judiciary in the community
Standard 10.16. Model code of ethics for court employees
Standard 10.17. Trial court performance standards
Standard 10.20. Court's duty to prohibit bias
Standard 10.21. Appointment of attorneys, arbitrators, mediators, referees, masters, receivers, and other persons
Standard 10.24. Children's waiting room
Standard 10.25. Reasonable accommodation for court personnel
Standard 10.31. Master jury list
Standard 10.41. Court sessions at or near state penal institutions
Standard 10.50. Selection of regular grand jury
Standard 10.51. Juror complaints
Standard 10.55. Local program on waste reduction and recycling
Standard 10.70. Implementation and coordination of mediation and other alternative dispute resolution (ADR) programs
Standard 10.71. Alternative dispute resolution (ADR) committees
Standard 10.72. ADR committees and criteria for referring cases to dispute resolution neutrals
Standard 10.80. Court records management standards

Standard 10.5.   The role of the judiciary in the community
(a) **Community outreach an official judicial function**
Judicial participation in community outreach activities should be considered an official judicial function to promote public understanding of and confidence in the administration of justice. This function should be performed in a manner consistent with the California Code of Judicial Ethics.

615   STANDARDS OF JUDICIAL ADMINISTRATION   Standard 10.17

Rules of Court

(Subd (a) lettered effective January 1, 2007; adopted as part of unlettered subdivision effective April 1, 1999.)

(b) Encouraged outreach activities

The judiciary is encouraged to:

(1) Provide active leadership within the community in identifying and resolving issues of access to justice within the court system;

(2) Develop local education programs for the public designed to increase public understanding of the court system;

(3) Create local mechanisms for obtaining information from the public about how the court system may be more responsive to the public's needs;

(4) Serve as guest speakers, during or after normal court hours, to address local civic, educational, business, and charitable groups that have an interest in understanding the court system but do not espouse a particular political agenda with which it would be inappropriate for a judicial officer to be associated; and

(5) Take an active part in the life of the community where the participation of the judiciary will serve to increase public understanding and promote public confidence in the integrity of the court system.

(Subd (b) amended effective January 1, 2007.)

Standard 10.5 amended and renumbered effective January 1, 2007; adopted as sec. 39 effective April 1, 1999.

Standard 10.10.   Judicial branch education [Repealed]

Standard 10.10 repealed effective January 1, 2008; adopted as sec. 25 effective January 1, 1999; previously amended and renumbered effective January 1, 2007.

Standard 10.11.   General judicial education standards [Repealed]

Standard 10.11 repealed effective January 1, 2008; adopted as sec. 25 effective January 1, 1990; previously amended and renumbered as Sec. 25.1 effective January 1, 1999; previously amended and renumbered effective January 1, 2007.

Standard 10.12.   Judicial education for judicial officers in particular judicial assignments [Repealed]

Standard 10.12 repealed effective January 1, 2008; adopted as sec. 25.2 effective January 1, 1999; previously amended and renumbered effective January 1, 2007.

Standard 10.13.   Judicial education curricula provided in particular judicial assignments [Repealed]

Standard 10.13 repealed effective January 1, 2008; repealed and adopted as sec. 25.3 effective January 1, 1999; previously amended and renumbered effective January 1, 2007.

Standard 10.14.   Judicial education for judges hearing capital cases [Repealed]

Standard 10.14 repealed effective January 1, 2008; adopted as sec. 25.4 effective January 1, 2004; previously amended and renumbered effective January 1, 2007.

Standard 10.15.   General court employee education standards [Repealed]

Standard 10.15 repealed effective January 1, 2008; adopted as

sec. 25.6 effective January 1, 1999; previously amended and renumbered effective January 1, 2007.

Standard 10.16.   Model code of ethics for court employees

Each trial and appellate court should adopt a code of ethical behavior for its support staff, and in doing so should consider rule [1] **10.670(c)(12)** of the California Rules of Court, and the model Code of Ethics for the Court Employees of California approved by the Judicial Council on May 17, 1994, and any subsequent revisions. The approved model code is published by the Administrative Office of the Courts.

Standard 10.16 amended effective July 1, 2008; adopted as sec. 35 effective July 1, 1994; previously amended and renumbered effective January 1, 2007.

Standard 10.16.   2008 Deletes. [1] 10.650(c)(12)

Standard 10.17.   Trial court performance standards

(a) Purpose

These standards are intended to be used by trial courts, in cooperation with the Judicial Council, for purposes of internal evaluation, self-assessment, and self-improvement. They are not intended as a basis for cross-court comparisons, nor are they intended as a basis for evaluating the performance of individual judges.

(Subd (a) lettered effective January 1, 2007; adopted as part of unlettered subdivision effective January 25, 1995.)

(b) Standards

The standards for trial court performance are as follows:

(1) *Access to justice*

(A) The court conducts its proceedings and other public business openly.

(B) Court facilities are safe, accessible, and convenient to use.

(C) All who appear before the court are given the opportunity to participate effectively without undue hardship or inconvenience.

(D) Judges and other trial court personnel are courteous and responsive to the public and accord respect to all with whom they come into contact.

(E) The costs of access to the trial court's proceedings and records—whether measured in terms of money, time, or the procedures that must be followed—are reasonable, fair, and affordable.

(2) *Expedition and timeliness*

(A) The trial court establishes and complies with recognized guidelines for timely case processing while, at the same time, keeping current with its incoming caseload.

(B) The trial court disburses funds promptly, provides reports and information according to required schedules, and responds to requests for information and other services on an established schedule that assures their effective use.

(C) The trial court promptly implements changes in law and procedure.

(3) *Equality, fairness, and integrity*

(A) Trial court procedures faithfully adhere to relevant laws, procedural rules, and established policies.

(B) Jury lists are representative of the jurisdiction from which they are drawn.

(C) Trial courts give individual attention to cases, deciding them without undue disparity among like cases and on legally relevant factors.

(D) Decisions of the trial court unambiguously address the issues presented to it and make clear how compliance can be achieved.

(E) The trial court takes appropriate responsibility for the enforcement of its orders.

(F) Records of all relevant court decisions and actions are accurate and properly preserved.

(4) *Independence and accountability*

(A) A trial court maintains its institutional integrity and observes the principle of comity in its governmental relations.

(B) The trial court responsibly seeks, uses, and accounts for its public resources.

(C) The trial court uses fair employment practices.

(D) The trial court informs the community of its programs.

(E) The trial court anticipates new conditions or emergent events and adjusts its operations as necessary.

(5) *Public trust and confidence*

(A) The trial court and the justice it delivers are perceived by the public as accessible.

(B) The public has trust and confidence that the basic trial court functions are conducted expeditiously and fairly and that its decisions have integrity.

(C) The trial court is perceived to be independent, not unduly influenced by other components of government, and accountable.

(Subd (b) lettered effective January 1, 2007; adopted as part of unlettered subdivision effective January 25, 1995.)

Standard 10.17 amended and renumbered effective January 1, 2007; adopted as sec. 30 effective January 25, 1995.

Standard 10.20.   Court's duty to prohibit bias

(a) General

To preserve the integrity and impartiality of the judicial system, each judge should:

(1) *Ensure fairness*

Ensure that courtroom proceedings are conducted in a manner that is fair and impartial to all of the participants.

(2) *Refrain from and prohibit biased conduct*

In all courtroom proceedings, refrain from engaging in conduct and prohibit others from engaging in conduct that exhibits bias, including but not limited to bias based on disability, gender, race, religion, ethnicity, and sexual orientation, whether that bias is directed toward counsel, court personnel, witnesses, parties, jurors, or any other participants.

(3) *Ensure unbiased decisions*

Ensure that all orders, rulings, and decisions are based on the sound exercise of judicial discretion and the balancing of competing rights and interests and are not influenced by stereotypes or biases.

(Subd (a) amended effective January 1, 2007; previously amended effective January 1, 1994, and January 1, 1998.)

(b) Creation of local committees on bias

Each court should establish a local committee with local bar associations to assist in maintaining a courtroom environment free of bias or the appearance of bias. Courts within one or more counties may choose to form a single committee. The local committee should:

(1) Be composed of representative members of the court community, including but not limited to judges, lawyers, court administrators, and representatives and individuals from minority, women's, and gay and lesbian bar associations and from organizations that represent persons with disabilities;

(2) Sponsor or support educational programs designed to eliminate bias within the court and legal communities, including but not limited to bias based on disability, gender, race, religion, ethnicity, and sexual orientation; and

(3) Develop and maintain an informal procedure for receiving complaints relating to bias in the courtroom, including but not limited to bias based on disability, gender, race, religion, ethnicity, and sexual orientation.

(Subd (b) amended effective January 1, 2007; adopted effective January 1, 1994; previously amended effective January 1, 1998.)

(c) Minimum components of a complaint procedure

An informal complaint procedure developed and maintained by a local committee on bias should:

(1) Contain a provision specifying that the intent of the procedure is to educate with the purpose of ameliorating the problem rather than disciplining the person who is the subject of the complaint;

(2) Accommodate local needs and allow for local flexibility;

(3) Apply to all participants in courtroom proceedings;

(4) Apply only to complaints as to which the identity of the complainant is known;

(5) To the extent possible and unless disclosure is required by law, protect the confidentiality of the complainant, the person who is the subject of the complaint, and other interested persons;

(6) Relate to incidents of behavior or conduct occurring in courtroom proceedings;

(7) Apply to incidents of bias whether they relate to race, sex, religion, national origin, disability, age, sexual orientation, or socioeconomic status;

(8) Contain a provision that exempts activities constituting legitimate advocacy when matters of race, sex, religion, national origin, disability, age, sexual orientation, or socioeconomic status are relevant to issues in the courtroom proceeding;

(9) Focus on incidents that do not warrant discipline but that should be corrected;

(10) With respect to those incidents that if substantiated would warrant discipline, advise the complaining party of the appropriate disciplinary authority;

(11) Contain a provision specifying that nothing in the procedure in any way limits the ability of any person to submit a complaint of misconduct to the appropriate disciplinary body; and

(12) To the extent possible and unless disclosure is required by law, prohibit retention of written records of complaints received but permit collection of data on types of complaints or underlying anecdotes that might be useful in educational programs.

(Subd (c) amended effective January 1, 2007; adopted effective January 1, 1994.)

(d) Application of local rules

The existence of the local committee, its purpose, and the features of the informal complaint procedure should be memorialized in the applicable local rules of court.

(Subd (d) amended effective January 1, 2007; adopted effective January 1, 1994.)

Standard 10.20 amended and renumbered effective January 1, 2007; adopted as sec. 1 effective January 1, 1987; previously amended effective January 1, 1994, and January 1, 1998.

Ref.: CACI Nos. 107, 5003 (Matthew Bender).

Standard 10.21. Appointment of attorneys, arbitrators, mediators, referees, masters, receivers, and other persons

(a) Nondiscrimination in appointment lists

In establishing and maintaining lists of qualified attorneys, arbitrators, mediators, referees, masters, receivers, and other persons who are eligible for appointment, courts should ensure equal access for all applicants regardless of gender, race, ethnicity, disability, sexual orientation, or age.

(b) Nondiscrimination in recruitment

Each trial court should conduct a recruitment procedure for the appointment of attorneys, arbitrators, mediators, referees, masters, receivers, and other persons appointed by the court (the "appointment programs") by publicizing the existence of the appointment programs at least once annually through state and local bar associations, including specialty bar associations. This publicity should encourage and provide an opportunity for all eligible individuals, regardless of gender, race, ethnicity, disability, sexual orientation, or age, to seek positions on the rosters of the appointment programs. Each trial court also should use other methods of publicizing the appointment programs that maximize the opportunity for a diverse applicant pool.

(c) Nondiscrimination in application and selection procedure

Each trial court should conduct an application and selection procedure for the appointment programs that ensures that the most qualified applicants for an appointment are selected, regardless of gender, race, ethnicity, disability, sexual orientation, or age.

(Subd (c) amended effective January 1, 2007.)

Standard 10.21 amended and renumbered effective January 1, 2007; adopted as sec. 1.5 effective January 1, 1999.

Standard 10.24. Children's waiting room

Each court should endeavor to provide a children's waiting room located in the courthouse for the use of minors under the age of 16 who are present on court premises as participants or who accompany persons who are participants in court proceedings. The waiting room should be supervised and open during normal court hours. If a court does not have sufficient space in the courthouse for a children's waiting room, the court should create the necessary space when court facilities are reorganized or remodeled or when new facilities are constructed.

Standard 10.24 renumbered effective January 1, 2007; adopted as sec. 1.3 effective January 1, 1987.

Standard 10.25. Reasonable accommodation for court personnel

At least to the extent required by state and federal law, each court should evaluate existing facilities, programs, and services available to employees to ensure that no barriers exist to prevent otherwise-qualified employees with known disabilities from performing their jobs or participating fully in court programs or activities.

Standard 10.25 renumbered effective January 1, 2007; adopted as sec. 1.4 effective January 1, 1998.

Standard 10.31. Master jury list

The jury commissioner should use the National Change of Address System or other comparable means to update jury source lists and create as accurate a master jury list as reasonably practical.

Standard 10.31 amended and renumbered effective January 1, 2007; adopted as sec. 4.6 effective July 1, 1997.

Standard 10.40. Court security [Repealed]

Standard 10.40 repealed effective January 1, 2009; adopted as sec. 7 effective July 1, 1971; previously amended and renumbered effective January 1, 2007.

Standard 10.41. Court sessions at or near state penal institutions

(a) Provision of adequate protection

Facilities used regularly for judicial proceedings should not be located on the grounds of or immediately adjacent to a state penal institution unless the location, design, and setting of the court facility provide adequate protection against the possible adverse influence that the prison facilities and activities might have on the fairness of judicial proceedings.

(Subd (a) amended effective January 1, 2007.)

(b) Factors to be considered

In determining whether adequate protection is provided, the following factors should be considered:

(1) The physical and visual remoteness of the court facility from the facilities and activities of the prison;

(2) The location and appearance of the court facility with respect to the adjacent public areas through which jurors and witnesses would normally travel in going to and from the court;

(3) The accessibility of the facility to the press and the general public; and

(4) Any other factors that might affect the fairness of the judicial proceedings.

(Subd (b) lettered effective January 1, 2007; adopted as part of subd (a) effective July 1, 1975.)

(c) Compelling reasons of safety or court convenience

Unless the location, design, and setting of the facility for conducting court sessions meet the criteria in (a) and (b):

(1) Court sessions should not be conducted in or immediately adjacent to a state penal institution except for compelling reasons of safety or convenience of the court; and

(2) Court sessions should not be conducted at such a location when the trial is by jury or when the testimony of

witnesses who are neither inmates nor employees of the institution will be required.

(Subd (c) amended and relettered effective January 1, 2007; adopted as subd (b) effective July 1, 1975.)

Standard 10.41 amended and renumbered effective January 1, 2007; adopted as sec. 7.5 effective July 1, 1975.

Standard 10.50.   Selection of regular grand jury

(a) Definition

"Regular grand jury" means a body of citizens of a county selected by the court to investigate matters of civil concern in the county, whether or not that body has jurisdiction to return indictments.

(b) Regular grand jury list

The list of qualified candidates prepared by the jury commissioner to be considered for nomination to the regular grand jury should be obtained by one or more of the following methods:

(1) Names of members of the public obtained at random in the same manner as the list of trial jurors. However, the names obtained for nomination to the regular grand jury should be kept separate and distinct from the trial jury list, consistent with Penal Code section 899.

(2) Recommendations for grand jurors that encompass a cross-section of the county's population base, solicited from a broad representation of community-based organizations, civic leaders, and superior court judges, referees, and commissioners.

(3) Applications from interested citizens solicited through the media or a mass mailing.

(Subd (b) amended effective January 1, 2007.)

(c) Carryover grand jurors

The court is encouraged to consider carryover grand jury selections under Penal Code section 901(b) to ensure broad-based representation.

(d) Nomination of grand jurors

Judges who nominate persons for grand jury selection under Penal Code section 903.4 are encouraged to select candidates from the list returned by the jury commissioner or to otherwise employ a nomination procedure that will ensure broad-based representation from the community.

(Subd (d) amended effective January 1, 2007.)

(e) Disfavored nominations

Judges should not nominate to the grand jury a spouse or immediate family member (within the first degree of consanguinity) of any superior court judge, commissioner, or referee; elected official; or department head of any city, county, or governmental entity subject to grand jury scrutiny.

(Subd (e) amended effective January 1, 2007.)

Standard 10.50 amended and renumbered effective January 1, 2007; adopted as sec. 17 effective July 1, 1992.

Standard 10.51.   Juror complaints

Each court should establish a reasonable mechanism for receiving and responding to juror complaints.

Standard 10.51 renumbered effective January 1, 2007; adopted as sec. 4.5 effective July 1, 1997.

Standard 10.55.   Local program on waste reduction and recycling

Each court should adopt a program for waste reduction and recycling or participate in a county program.

Standard 10.55 amended and renumbered effective January 1, 2007; adopted as sec. 17.5 effective January 1, 1991.

Standard 10.70.   Implementation and coordination of mediation and other alternative dispute resolution (ADR) programs

(a) Implementation of mediation programs for civil cases

Superior courts should implement mediation programs for civil cases as part of their core operations.

(Subd (a) adopted effective January 1, 2006.)

(b) Promotion of ADR programs

Superior courts should promote the development, implementation, maintenance, and expansion of successful mediation and other alternative dispute resolution (ADR) programs, through activities that include:

(1) Establishing appropriate criteria for determining which cases should be referred to ADR, and what ADR processes are appropriate for those cases. These criteria should include whether the parties are likely to benefit from the use of the ADR process;

(2) Developing, refining, and using lists of qualified ADR neutrals;

(3) Adopting appropriate criteria for referring cases to qualified ADR neutrals;

(4) Developing ADR information and providing educational programs for parties who are not represented by counsel; and

(5) Providing ADR education for judicial officers.

(Subd (b) amended effective January 1, 2007; adopted as unlettered subdivision effective July 1, 1992; lettered and amended effective January 1, 2006.)

(c) Coordination of ADR programs

Superior courts should coordinate ADR promotional activities and explore joint funding and administration of ADR programs with each other and with professional and community-based organizations.

(Subd (c) adopted effective January 1, 2006.)

Standard 10.70 amended and renumbered effective January 1, 2007; adopted as sec. 32 effective July 1, 1992; previously amended effective January 1, 2006.

Standard 10.71.   Alternative dispute resolution (ADR) committees

Courts that are not required and that do not elect to have an ADR administrative committee as provided in rule 10.783 of the California Rules of Court should form committees of judges, attorneys, alternative dispute resolution (ADR) neutrals, and county ADR administrators, if any, to oversee the court's ADR programs and panels of neutrals for general civil cases.

Standard 10.71 amended and renumbered effective January 1, 2007; adopted as sec. 32.1 effective January 1, 2006.

Standard 10.72.   ADR committees and criteria for referring cases to dispute resolution neutrals

(a) Training, experience, and skills

Courts should evaluate the ADR training, experience, and skills of potential ADR neutrals.

(Subd (a) amended effective January 1, 2006.)

(b) Additional considerations for continuing referrals

After a court has sufficient experience with an ADR neutral, the court should also consider indicators of client satisfaction, settlement rate, continuing ADR education, and adherence to applicable standards of conduct in determining whether to continue referrals to that neutral.

(Subd (b) amended effective January 1, 2006.)

Standard 10.72 amended and renumbered effective January 1, 2007; adopted as sec. 33 effective July 1, 1992; previously amended effective January 1, 2006.

Advisory Committee Comment

Although settlement rate is an important indicator of a neutral's effectiveness, it should be borne in mind that some disputes will not resolve, despite the best efforts of a skilled neutral. Neutrals should not feel pressure to achieve a high settlement rate through resolutions that may not be in the interest of one or more parties.

Accordingly, settlement rate should be used with caution as a criterion for court referral of disputes to neutrals.

Standard 10.80. Court records management standards

Each court should develop records management practices consistent with the standards approved by the Judicial Council. The approved standards are specified in Judicial Council Court Records Management Standards, published by the Administrative Office of the Courts.

Implementation of these standards, which cover creation, use, maintenance, and destruction of records, should lead to more efficient court administration, better protection and preservation of records, and improved public access to records.

Standard 10.80 amended and renumbered effective January 1, 2007; adopted as sec. 34 effective January 1, 1993.

California Code of Judicial Ethics

Effective January 1, 2008, the Code of Judicial Ethics is not part of the California Rules of Court. The Publisher has placed this material in the *Supplement to the California Rules of Court* and can be found on page 669 of this volume.

Ethics Standards for Neutral Arbitrators in Contractual Arbitration

Standard 1.   Purpose, intent, and construction.

(a)   These standards are adopted under the authority of Code of Civil Procedure section 1281.85 and establish the minimum standards of conduct for neutral arbitrators who are subject to these standards. They are intended to guide the conduct of arbitrators, to inform and protect participants in arbitration, and to promote public confidence in the arbitration process.

(b)   For arbitration to be effective there must be broad public confidence in the integrity and fairness of the process. Arbitrators are responsible to the parties, the other participants, and the public for conducting themselves in accordance with these standards so as to merit that confidence.

(c)   These standards are to be construed and applied to further the purpose and intent expressed in subdivisions (a) and (b) and in conformance with all applicable law.

(d)   These standards are not intended to affect any existing civil cause of action or create any new civil cause of action.

Comment to Standard 1

Code of Civil Procedure section 1281.85 provides that, beginning July 1, 2002, a person serving as a neutral arbitrator pursuant to an arbitration agreement shall comply with the ethics standards for arbitrators adopted by the Judicial Council pursuant to that section.

While the grounds for vacating an arbitration award are established by statute, not these standards, an arbitrator's violation of these standards may, under some circumstances, fall within one of those statutory grounds. (See Code Civ. Proc., §1286.2.) A failure to disclose within the time required for disclosure a ground for disqualification of which the arbitrator was then aware is a ground for vacatur of the arbitrator's award. (See Code Civ. Proc., §1286.2(a)(6)(A).) Violations of other obligations under these standards may also constitute grounds for vacating an arbitration award under section 1286.2(a)(3) if "the rights of the party were substantially prejudiced" by the violation.

While vacatur may be an available remedy for violation of these standards, these standards are not intended to affect any civil cause of action that may currently exist nor to create any new

civil cause of action. These standards are also not intended to establish a ceiling on what is considered good practice in arbitration or to discourage efforts to educate arbitrators about best practices.

Standard 2.   Definitions.

As used in these standards:

(a)   **Arbitrator and neutral arbitrator**

(1)   "Arbitrator" and "neutral arbitrator" mean any arbitrator who is subject to these standards and who is to serve impartially, whether selected or appointed:

(A)   Jointly by the parties or by the arbitrators selected by the parties;

(B)   By the court, when the parties or the arbitrators selected by the parties fail to select an arbitrator who was to be selected jointly by them; or

(C)   By a dispute resolution provider organization, under an agreement of the parties.

(2)   Where the context includes events or acts occurring before an appointment is final, "arbitrator" and "neutral arbitrator" include a person who has been served with notice of a proposed nomination or appointment.

(b)   "Applicable law" means constitutional provisions, statutes, decisional law, California Rules of Court, and other statewide rules or regulations that apply to arbitrators who are subject to these standards.

(c)   "Conclusion of the arbitration" means the following:

(1)   When the arbitrator is disqualified or withdraws or the case is settled or dismissed before the arbitrator makes an award, the date on which the arbitrator's appointment is terminated;

(2)   When the arbitrator makes an award and no party makes a timely application to the arbitrator to correct the award, the final date for making an application to the arbitrator for correction; or

(3)   When a party makes a timely application to the arbitrator to correct the award, the date on which the arbitrator serves a corrected award or a denial on each party, or the date on which denial occurs by operation of law.

(d)   "Consumer arbitration" means an arbitration conducted under a predispute arbitration provision contained in a contract that meets the criteria listed in paragraphs (1) through (3) below. "Consumer arbitration" excludes arbitration proceedings conducted under or arising out of public or private sector labor-relations laws, regulations, charter provisions, ordinances, statutes, or agreements.

(1)   The contract is with a consumer party, as defined in these standards;

(2)   The contract was drafted by or on behalf of the nonconsumer party; and

(3)   The consumer party was required to accept the arbitration provision in the contract.

(e)   "Consumer party" is a party to an arbitration agreement who, in the context of that arbitration agreement, is any of the following:

(1) An individual who seeks or acquires, including by lease, any goods or services primarily for personal, family, or household purposes including, but not limited to, financial services, insurance, and other goods and services as defined in section 1761 of the Civil Code;

(2) An individual who is an enrollee, a subscriber, or insured in a health-care service plan within the meaning of section 1345 of the Health and Safety Code or health-care insurance plan within the meaning of section 106 of the Insurance Code;

(3) An individual with a medical malpractice claim that is subject to the arbitration agreement; or

(4) An employee or an applicant for employment in a dispute arising out of or relating to the employee's employment or the applicant's prospective employment that is subject to the arbitration agreement.

(f) "Dispute resolution neutral" means a temporary judge appointed under article VI, section 21 of the California Constitution, a referee appointed under Code of Civil Procedure section 638 or 639, an arbitrator, a neutral evaluator, a special master, a mediator, a settlement officer, or a settlement facilitator.

(g) "Dispute resolution provider organization" and "provider organization" mean any nongovernmental entity that, or individual who, coordinates, administers, or provides the services of two or more dispute resolution neutrals.

(h) "Domestic partner" means a domestic partner as defined in Family Code section 297.

(i) "Financial interest" means a financial interest within the meaning of Code of Civil Procedure section 170.5.

(j) "Gift" means a gift as defined in Code of Civil Procedure section 170.9(*l*).

(k) "Honoraria" means honoraria as defined in Code of Civil Procedure section 170.9(h) and (i).

(*l*) "Lawyer in the arbitration" means the lawyer hired to represent a party in the arbitration.

(m) "Lawyer for a party" means the lawyer hired to represent a party in the arbitration and any lawyer or law firm currently associated in the practice of law with the lawyer hired to represent a party in the arbitration.

(n) "Member of the arbitrator's immediate family" means the arbitrator's spouse or domestic partner and any minor child living in the arbitrator's household.

(o) "Member of the arbitrator's extended family" means the parents, grandparents, great-grandparents, children, grandchildren, great-grandchildren, siblings, uncles, aunts, nephews, and nieces of the arbitrator or the arbitrator's spouse or domestic partner or the spouse of such person.

(p) Party

(1) "Party" means a party to the arbitration agreement:

(A) Who seeks to arbitrate a controversy pursuant to the agreement;

(B) Against whom such arbitration is sought; or

(C) Who is made a party to such arbitration by order of a court or the arbitrator upon such party's application, upon the application of any other party to the arbitration, or upon the arbitrator's own determination.

(2) "Party" includes the representative of a party, unless the context requires a different meaning.

(q) "Party-arbitrator" means an arbitrator selected unilaterally by a party.

(r) "Private practice of law" means private practice of law as defined in Code of Civil Procedure section 170.5.

(s) "Significant personal relationship" includes a close personal friendship.

Comment to Standard 2

Subdivision (a). The definition of "arbitrator" and "neutral arbitrator" in this standard is intended to include all arbitrators who are to serve in a neutral and impartial manner and to exclude unilaterally selected arbitrators.

Subdivisions (*l*) and (m). Arbitrators should take special care to note that there are two different terms used in these standards to refer to lawyers who represent parties in the arbitration. In particular, arbitrators should note that the term "lawyer for a party" includes any lawyer or law firm currently associated in the practice of law with the lawyer hired to represent a party in the arbitration.

Subdivision (p)(2). While this provision generally permits an arbitrator to provide required information or notices to a party's attorney as that party's representative, a party's attorney should not be treated as a "party" for purposes of identifying matters that an arbitrator must disclose under standards 7 or 8, as those standards contain separate, specific requirements concerning the disclosure of relationships with a party's attorney.

Other terms that may be pertinent to these standards are defined in Code of Civil Procedure section 1280.

Standard 3. Application and effective date.

(a) Except as otherwise provided in this standard and standard 8, these standards apply to all persons who are appointed to serve as neutral arbitrators on or after July 1, 2002, in any arbitration under an arbitration agreement, if:

(1) The arbitration agreement is subject to the provisions of title 9 of part III of the Code of Civil Procedure (commencing with section 1280); or

(2) The arbitration hearing is to be conducted in California.

(b) These standards do not apply to:

(1) Party arbitrators, as defined in these standards; or

(2) Any arbitrator serving in:

(A) An international arbitration proceeding subject to the provisions of title 9.3 of part III of the Code of Civil Procedure;

(B) A judicial arbitration proceeding subject to the provisions of chapter 2.5 of title 3 of part III of the Code of Civil Procedure;

(C) An attorney-client fee arbitration proceeding subject to the provisions of article 13 of chapter 4 of division 3 of the Business and Professions Code;

(D) An automobile warranty dispute resolution process certified under California Code of Regulations title 16, division 33.1;

(E) An arbitration of a workers' compensation dispute under Labor Code sections 5270 through 5277;

(F) An arbitration conducted by the Workers' Compensation Appeals Board under Labor Code section 5308;

(G) An arbitration of a complaint filed against a contractor with the Contractors State License Board under

Business and Professions Code sections 7085 through 7085.7; or

(H) An arbitration conducted under or arising out of public or private sector labor-relations laws, regulations, charter provisions, ordinances, statutes, or agreements.

(c) Persons who are serving in arbitrations in which they were appointed to serve as arbitrators before July 1, 2002, are not subject to these standards in those arbitrations. Persons who are serving in arbitrations in which they were appointed to serve as arbitrators before January 1, 2003, are not subject to standard 8 in those arbitrations.

Comment to Standard 3

With the exception of standard 8, these standards apply to all neutral arbitrators appointed on or after July 1, 2002, who meet the criteria of subdivision (a). Arbitration provider organizations, although not themselves subject to these standards, should be aware of them when performing administrative functions that involve arbitrators who are subject to these standards. A provider organization's policies and actions should facilitate, not impede, compliance with the standards by arbitrators who are affiliated with the provider organization.

Standard 4.   Duration of duty.

(a) Except as otherwise provided in these standards, an arbitrator must comply with these ethics standards from acceptance of appointment until the conclusion of the arbitration.

(b) If, after the conclusion of the arbitration, a case is referred back to the arbitrator for reconsideration or rehearing, the arbitrator must comply with these ethics standards from the date the case is referred back to the arbitrator until the arbitration is again concluded.

Standard 5.   General duty.

An arbitrator must act in a manner that upholds the integrity and fairness of the arbitration process. He or she must maintain impartiality toward all participants in the arbitration at all times.

Comment to Standard 5

This standard establishes the overarching ethical duty of arbitrators. The remaining standards should be construed as establishing specific requirements that implement this overarching duty in particular situations.

Maintaining impartiality toward all participants during all stages of the arbitration is central to upholding the integrity and fairness of the arbitration. An arbitrator must perform his or her duties impartially, without bias or prejudice, and must not, in performing these duties, by words or conduct manifest partiality, bias, or prejudice, including but not limited to partiality, bias, or prejudice based upon race, sex, religion, national origin, disability, age, sexual orientation, socioeconomic status, or the fact that a party might select the arbitrator to serve as an arbitrator in additional cases. After accepting appointment, an arbitrator should avoid entering into any relationship or acquiring any interest that might reasonably create the appearance of partiality, bias, or prejudice. An arbitrator does not become partial, biased, or prejudiced simply by having acquired knowledge of the parties, the issues or arguments, or the applicable law.

Standard 6.   Duty to refuse appointment.

Notwithstanding any contrary request, consent, or waiver by the parties, a proposed arbitrator must decline appointment if he or she is not able to be impartial.

Standard 7.   Disclosure.

(a) Intent

This standard is intended to identify the matters that must be disclosed by a person nominated or appointed as an arbitrator. To the extent that this standard addresses matters that are also addressed by statute, it is intended to include those statutory disclosure requirements, not to eliminate, reduce, or otherwise limit them.

(b) General provisions

For purposes of this standard:

(1) *Collective bargaining cases excluded*

The terms "cases" and "any arbitration" do not include collective bargaining cases or arbitrations conducted under or arising out of collective bargaining agreements between employers and employees or between their respective representatives.

(2) *Offers of employment or professional relationship*

If an arbitrator has disclosed to the parties in an arbitration that he or she will entertain offers of employment or of professional relationships from a party or lawyer for a party while the arbitration is pending as required by subdivision (b) of standard 12, the arbitrator is not required to disclose to the parties in that arbitration any such offer from a party or lawyer for a party that he or she subsequently receives or accepts while that arbitration is pending.

(3) *Names of parties in cases*

When making disclosures about other pending or prior cases, in order to preserve confidentiality, it is sufficient to give the name of any party who is not a party to the pending arbitration as "claimant" or "respondent" if the party is an individual and not a business or corporate entity.

(c) Time and manner of disclosure

Within ten calendar days of service of notice of the proposed nomination or appointment, a proposed arbitrator must disclose to all parties in writing all matters listed in subdivisions (d) and (e) of this standard of which the arbitrator is then aware. If an arbitrator subsequently becomes aware of a matter that must be disclosed under either subdivision (d) or (e) of this standard, the arbitrator must disclose that matter to the parties in writing within 10 calendar days after the arbitrator becomes aware of the matter.

(d) Required disclosures

A person who is nominated or appointed as an arbitrator must disclose all matters that could cause a person aware of the facts to reasonably entertain a doubt that the proposed arbitrator would be able to be impartial, including all of the following:

(1) *Family relationships with party*

The arbitrator or a member of the arbitrator's immediate or extended family is a party, a party's spouse or domestic partner, or an officer, director, or trustee of a party.

(2) *Family relationships with lawyer in the arbitration*

The arbitrator, or the spouse, former spouse, domestic partner, child, sibling, or parent of the arbitrator or the arbitrator's spouse or domestic partner is:

(A) A lawyer in the arbitration;

(B)   The spouse or domestic partner of a lawyer in the arbitration; or

(C)   Currently associated in the private practice of law with a lawyer in the arbitration.

(3)   *Significant personal relationship with party or lawyer for a party*

The arbitrator or a member of the arbitrator's immediate family has or has had a significant personal relationship with any party or lawyer for a party.

(4)   *Service as arbitrator for a party or lawyer for party*

(A)   The arbitrator is serving or, within the preceding five years, has served:

(i)   As a neutral arbitrator in another prior or pending noncollective bargaining case involving a party to the current arbitration or a lawyer for a party.

(ii)   As a party-appointed arbitrator in another prior or pending noncollective bargaining case for either a party to the current arbitration or a lawyer for a party.

(iii)   As a neutral arbitrator in another prior or pending noncollective bargaining case in which he or she was selected by a person serving as a party-appointed arbitrator in the current arbitration

(B)   Case information

If the arbitrator is serving or has served in any of the capacities listed under (A), he or she must disclose:

(i)   The names of the parties in each prior or pending case and, where applicable, the name of the attorney representing the party in the current arbitration who is involved in the pending case, who was involved in the prior case, or whose current associate is involved in the pending case or was involved in the prior case.

(ii)   The results of each prior case arbitrated to conclusion, including the date of the arbitration award, identification of the prevailing party, the amount of monetary damages awarded, if any, and the names of the parties' attorneys.

(C)   Summary of case information

If the total number of the cases disclosed under (A) is greater than five, the arbitrator must provide a summary of these cases that states:

(i)   The number of pending cases in which the arbitrator is currently serving in each capacity;

(ii)   The number of prior cases in which the arbitrator previously served in each capacity;

(iii)   The number of prior cases arbitrated to conclusion; and

(iv)   The number of such prior cases in which the party to the current arbitration, the party represented by the lawyer for a party in the current arbitration or the party represented by the party-arbitrator in the current arbitration was the prevailing party.

(5)   *Compensated service as other dispute resolution neutral*

The arbitrator is serving or has served as a dispute resolution neutral other than an arbitrator in another pending or prior noncollective bargaining case involving a party or lawyer for a party and the arbitrator received or expects to receive any form of compensation for serving in this capacity.

(A)   Time frame

For purposes of this paragraph (5), "prior case" means any case in which the arbitrator concluded his or her service as a dispute resolution neutral within two years before the date of the arbitrator's proposed nomination or appointment, but does not include any case in which the arbitrator concluded his or her service before January 1, 2002.

(B)   Case information

If the arbitrator is serving or has served in any of the capacities listed under this paragraph (5), he or she must disclose:

(i)   The names of the parties in each prior or pending case and, where applicable, the name of the attorney in the current arbitration who is involved in the pending case, who was involved in the prior case, or whose current associate is involved in the pending case or was involved in the prior case;

(ii)   The dispute resolution neutral capacity (mediator, referee, etc.) in which the arbitrator is serving or served in the case; and

(iii)   In each such case in which the arbitrator rendered a decision as a temporary judge or referee, the date of the decision, the prevailing party, the amount of monetary damages awarded, if any, and the names of the parties' attorneys.

(C)   Summary of case information

If the total number of cases disclosed under this paragraph (5) is greater than five, the arbitrator must also provide a summary of the cases that states:

(i)   The number of pending cases in which the arbitrator is currently serving in each capacity;

(ii)   The number of prior cases in which the arbitrator previously served in each capacity;

(iii)   The number of prior cases in which the arbitrator rendered a decision as a temporary judge or referee; and

(iv)   The number of such prior cases in which the party to the current arbitration or the party represented by the lawyer for a party in the current arbitration was the prevailing party.

(6)   *Current arrangements for prospective neutral service*

Whether the arbitrator has any current arrangement with a party concerning prospective employment or other compensated service as a dispute resolution neutral or is participating in or, within the last two years, has participated in discussions regarding such prospective employment or service with a party.

(7)   *Attorney-client relationship*

Any attorney-client relationship the arbitrator has or has had with a party or lawyer for a party. Attorney-client relationships include the following:

(A)   An officer, a director, or a trustee of a party is or, within the preceding two years, was a client of the arbitrator in the arbitrator's private practice of law or a client of a lawyer with whom the arbitrator is or was associated in the private practice of law;

(B)   In any other proceeding involving the same issues, the arbitrator gave advice to a party or a lawyer in the arbitration concerning any matter involved in the arbitration; and

(C) The arbitrator served as a lawyer for or as an officer of a public agency which is a party and personally advised or in any way represented the public agency concerning the factual or legal issues in the arbitration.

(8) *Other professional relationships*

Any other professional relationship not already disclosed under paragraphs (2)-(7) that the arbitrator or a member of the arbitrator's immediate family has or has had with a party or lawyer for a party, including the following:

(A) The arbitrator was associated in the private practice of law with a lawyer in the arbitration within the last two years;

(B) The arbitrator or a member of the arbitrator's immediate family is or, within the preceding two years, was an employee of or an expert witness or a consultant for a party; and

(C) The arbitrator or a member of the arbitrator's immediate family is or, within the preceding two years, was an employee of or an expert witness or a consultant for a lawyer in the arbitration.

(9) *Financial interests in party*

The arbitrator or a member of the arbitrator's immediate family has a financial interest in a party.

(10) *Financial interests in subject of arbitration*

The arbitrator or a member of the arbitrator's immediate family has a financial interest in the subject matter of the arbitration.

(11) *Affected interest*

The arbitrator or a member of the arbitrator's immediate family has an interest that could be substantially affected by the outcome of the arbitration.

(12) *Knowledge of disputed facts*

The arbitrator or a member of the arbitrator's immediate or extended family has personal knowledge of disputed evidentiary facts relevant to the arbitration. A person who is likely to be a material witness in the proceeding is deemed to have personal knowledge of disputed evidentiary facts concerning the proceeding.

(13) *Membership in organizations practicing discrimination*

The arbitrator's membership in any organization that practices invidious discrimination on the basis of race, sex, religion, national origin, or sexual orientation. Membership in a religious organization, an official military organization of the United States, or a nonprofit youth organization need not be disclosed unless it would interfere with the arbitrator's proper conduct of the proceeding or would cause a person aware of the fact to reasonably entertain a doubt concerning the arbitrator's ability to act impartially.

(14) Any other matter that:

(A) Might cause a person aware of the facts to reasonably entertain a doubt that the arbitrator would be able to be impartial;

(B) Leads the proposed arbitrator to believe there is a substantial doubt as to his or her capacity to be impartial, including, but not limited to, bias or prejudice toward a party, lawyer, or law firm in the arbitration; or

(C) Otherwise leads the arbitrator to believe that his or her disqualification will further the interests of justice.

(e) Inability to conduct or timely complete proceedings

In addition to the matters that must be disclosed under subdivision (d), an arbitrator must also disclose:

(1) If the arbitrator is not able to properly perceive the evidence or properly conduct the proceedings because of a permanent or temporary physical impairment; and

(2) Any constraints on his or her availability known to the arbitrator that will interfere with his or her ability to commence or complete the arbitration in a timely manner.

(f) Continuing duty

An arbitrator's duty to disclose the matters described in subdivisions (d) and (e) of this standard is a continuing duty, applying from service of the notice of the arbitrator's proposed nomination or appointment until the conclusion of the arbitration proceeding.

Comment to Standard 7

This standard requires arbitrators to disclose to all parties, in writing within 10 days of service of notice of their proposed nomination or appointment, all matters they are aware of at that time that could cause a person aware of the facts to reasonably entertain a doubt that the proposed arbitrator would be able to be impartial and to disclose any additional such matters within 10 days of becoming aware of them.

Timely disclosure to the parties is the primary means of ensuring the impartiality of an arbitrator. It provides the parties with the necessary information to make an informed selection of an arbitrator by disqualifying or ratifying the proposed arbitrator following disclosure. See also standard 12, concerning disclosure and disqualification requirements relating to concurrent and subsequent employment or professional relationships between an arbitrator and a party or attorney in the arbitration. A party may disqualify an arbitrator for failure to comply with statutory disclosure obligations (see Code Civ. Proc., §1281.91(a)). Failure to disclose, within the time required for disclosure, a ground for disqualification of which the arbitrator was then aware is a ground for *vacatur* of the arbitrator's award (see Code Civ. Proc., §1286.2(a)(6)(A)).

The arbitrator's overarching duty under this standard, which mirrors the duty set forth in Code of Civil Procedure section 1281.9, is to inform parties about matters that could cause a person aware of the facts to reasonably entertain a doubt that the proposed arbitrator would be able to be impartial. While the remaining subparagraphs of (d) require the disclosure of specific interests, relationships, or affiliations, these are only examples of common matters that could cause a person aware of the facts to reasonably entertain a doubt that the arbitrator would be able to be impartial. The absence of the particular interests, relationships, or affiliations listed in the subparagraphs does not necessarily mean that there is no matter that could reasonably raise a question about the arbitrator's ability to be impartial and that therefore must be disclosed. An arbitrator must make determinations concerning disclosure on a case-by-case basis, applying the general criteria for disclosure under paragraph (d).

Code of Civil Procedure section 1281.85 specifically requires that the ethical standards adopted by the Judicial Council address the disclosure of interests, relationships, or affiliations that may constitute conflicts of interest, including prior service as an arbitrator or other dispute resolution neutral entity. Section 1281.85 further provides that the standards "shall be consistent with the standards established for arbitrators in the judicial arbitration program and may expand but may not limit the disclosure and disqualification requirements established by this chapter [chapter 2 of title 9 of part III, Code of Civil Procedure, sections 1281–1281.95]."

Code of Civil Procedure section 1281.9 already establishes detailed requirements concerning disclosures by arbitrators, including a specific requirement that arbitrators disclose the existence of any ground specified in Code of Civil Procedure section 170.1 for disqualification of a judge. This standard does not eliminate or otherwise limit those requirements; in large part, it simply consolidates and integrates those existing statutory disclosure requirements by topic area. This standard does, however, expand upon or clarify the existing statutory disclosure requirements in the following ways:

Requiring arbitrators to disclose to the parties any matter about which they become aware after the time for making an initial disclosure has expired, within 10 calendar days after the arbitrator becomes aware of the matter (subdivision (f)).

Expanding required disclosures about the relationships or affiliations of an arbitrator's family members to include those of an arbitrator's domestic partner (subdivisions (d)(1) and (2); see also definitions of immediate and extended family in standard 2).

Requiring arbitrators, in addition to making statutorily required disclosures regarding prior service as an arbitrator for a party or attorney for a party, to disclose prior services both as neutral arbitrator selected by a party arbitrator in the current arbitration and as any other type of dispute resolution neutral for a party or attorney in the arbitration (e.g., temporary judge, mediator, or referee) (subdivisions (d)(4)(C) and (5)).

Requiring the arbitrator to disclose if he or she or a member of his or her immediate family is or was an employee, expert witness, or consultant for a party or a lawyer in the arbitration (subdivisions (d)(8)(A) and (B)).

Requiring the arbitrator to disclose if he or she or a member of his or her immediate family has an interest that could be substantially affected by the outcome of the arbitration (subdivision (d)(11)).

If a disclosure includes information about five or more cases, requiring arbitrators to provide a summary of that information (subdivisions (d)(4) and (5).

Requiring arbitrators to disclose membership in organizations that practice invidious discrimination on the basis of race, sex, religion, national origin, or sexual orientation (subdivision (d)(13)).

Requiring the arbitrator to disclose any constraints on his or her availability known to the arbitrator that will interfere with his or her ability to commence or complete the arbitration in a timely manner (subdivision (d)).

Clarifying that the duty to make disclosures is a continuing obligation, requiring disclosure of matters that were not known at the time of nomination or appointment but that become known afterward (subdivision (e)).

It is good practice for an arbitrator to ask each participant to make an effort to disclose any matters that may affect the arbitrator's ability to be impartial.

Standard 8.   Additional disclosures in consumer arbitrations administered by a provider organization.

(a)   General provisions

(1)   *Reliance on information provided by provider organization*

Except as to the information in (c)(1), an arbitrator may rely on information supplied by the administering provider organization in making the disclosures required by this standard. If the information that must be disclosed is available on the Internet, the arbitrator may comply with the obligation to disclose this information by providing the Internet address at which the information is located and notifying the party that the arbitrator will supply hard copies of this information upon request.

(2)   *Reliance on representation that not a consumer arbitration*

An arbitrator is not required to make the disclosures required by this standard if he or she reasonably believes that the arbitration is not a consumer arbitration based on reasonable reliance on a consumer party's representation that the arbitration is not a consumer arbitration.

(b)   Additional disclosures required

In addition to the disclosures required under standard 7, in a consumer arbitration as defined in standard 2 in which a dispute resolution provider organization is coordinating, administering, or providing the arbitration services, a person who is nominated or appointed as an arbitrator on or after January 1, 2003 must disclose the following within the time and in the same manner as the disclosures required under standard 7(c):

(1)   *Relationships between the provider organization and party or lawyer in arbitration*

Any significant past, present, or currently expected financial or professional relationship or affiliation between the administering dispute resolution provider organization and a party or lawyer in the arbitration. Information that must be disclosed under this standard includes:

(A)   A party, a lawyer in the arbitration, or a law firm with which a lawyer in the arbitration is currently associated is a member of the provider organization.

(B)   Within the preceding two years the provider organization has received a gift, bequest, or favor from a party, a lawyer in the arbitration, or a law firm with which a lawyer in the arbitration is currently associated.

(C)   The provider organization has entered into, or the arbitrator currently expects that the provider organization will enter into, an agreement or relationship with any party or lawyer in the arbitration or a law firm with which a lawyer in the arbitration is currently associated under which the provider organization will administer, coordinate, or provide dispute resolution services in other non-collective bargaining matters or will provide other consulting services for that party, lawyer, or law firm.

(D)   The provider organization is coordinating, administering, or providing dispute resolution services or has coordinated, administered, or provided such services in another pending or prior noncollective bargaining case in which a party or lawyer in the arbitration was a party or a lawyer. For purposes of this paragraph, "prior case" means a case in which the dispute resolution neutral affiliated with the provider organization concluded his or her service within the two years before the date of the arbitrator's proposed nomination or appointment, but does not include any case in which the dispute resolution neutral concluded his or her service before July 1, 2002.

(2)   *Case information*

If the provider organization is acting or has acted in any of the capacities described in paragraph (1)(D), the arbitrator must disclose:

(A)   The names of the parties in each prior or pending case and, where applicable, the name of the attorney in the current arbitration who is involved in the pending case or who was involved in the prior case;

(B)   The type of dispute resolution services (arbitration, mediation, reference, etc.) coordinated, administered, or provided by the provider organization in the case; and

(C)   In each prior case in which a dispute resolution neutral affiliated with the provider organization rendered a decision as an arbitrator, a temporary judge appointed under article VI, §4 of the California Constitution, or a referee appointed under Code of Civil Procedure sections 638 or 639, the date of the decision, the prevailing party, the amount of monetary damages awarded, if any, and the names of the parties' attorneys.

(3)   *Summary of case information*

If the total number of cases disclosed under paragraph (1)(D) is greater than five, the arbitrator must also provide a summary of these cases that states:

(A)   The number of pending cases in which the provider organization is currently providing each type of dispute resolution services;

(B)   The number of prior cases in which the provider organization previously provided each type of dispute resolution services;

(C)   The number of such prior cases in which a neutral affiliated with the provider organization rendered a decision as an arbitrator, a temporary judge, or a referee; and

(D)   The number of prior cases in which the party to the current arbitration or the party represented by the lawyer in the current arbitration was the prevailing party.

(c)   Relationship between provider organization and arbitrator

If a relationship or affiliation is disclosed under paragraph (b), the arbitrator must also provide information about the following:

(1)   Any financial relationship or affiliation the arbitrator has with the provider organization other than receiving referrals of cases, including whether the arbitrator has a financial interest in the provider organization or is an employee of the provider organization;

(2)   The provider organization's process and criteria for recruiting, screening, and training the panel of arbitrators from which the arbitrator in this case is to be selected;

(3)   The provider organization's process for identifying, recommending, and selecting potential arbitrators for specific cases; and

(4)   Any role the provider organization plays in ruling on requests for disqualification of the arbitrator.

(d)   Effective date

The provisions of this standard take effect on January 1, 2003. Persons who are serving in arbitrations in which they were appointed to serve as arbitrators before January 1, 2003, are not subject to this standard in those pending arbitrations.

Comment to Standard 8

This standard only applies in consumer arbitrations in which a dispute resolution provider organization is administering the arbitration. Like standard 7, this standard expands upon the existing statutory disclosure requirements. Code of Civil Procedure section 1281.95 requires arbitrators in certain construction defect arbitrations to make disclosures concerning relationships between their employers or arbitration services and the parties in the arbitration. This standard requires arbitrators in all consumer arbitrations to disclose any financial or professional relationship between the administering provider organization and any party,

attorney, or law firm in the arbitration and, if any such relationship exists, then the arbitrator must also disclose his or her relationship with the dispute resolution provider organization. This standard does not require an arbitrator to disclose if the provider organization has a financial interest in a party or lawyer in the arbitration or if a party or lawyer in the arbitration has a financial interest in the provider organization because provider organizations are prohibited under Code of Civil Procedure section 1281.92 from administering any consumer arbitration where any such relationship exists.

Subdivision (b). Currently expected relationships or affiliations that must be disclosed include all relationships or affiliations that the arbitrator, at the time the disclosure is made, expects will be formed. For example, if the arbitrator knows that the administering provider organization has agreed in concept to enter into a business relationship with a party, but they have not yet signed a written agreement formalizing that relationship, this would be a "currently expected" relationship that the arbitrator would be required to disclose.

Standard 9.   Arbitrators' duty to inform themselves about matters to be disclosed.

(a)   General duty to inform him or herself

A person who is nominated or appointed as an arbitrator must make a reasonable effort to inform himself or herself of matters that must be disclosed under standards 7 and 8.

(b)   Obligation regarding extended family

An arbitrator can fulfill the obligation under this standard to inform himself or herself of relationships or other matters involving his or her extended family and former spouse that are required to be disclosed under standard 7 by:

(1)   Seeking information about these relationships and matters from the members of his or her immediate family and any members of his or her extended family living in his or her household; and

(2)   Declaring in writing that he or she has made the inquiry in (1).

(c)   Obligation regarding relationships with associates of lawyer in the arbitration

An arbitrator can fulfill the obligation under this standard to inform himself or herself of relationships with any lawyer associated in the practice of law with the lawyer in the arbitration that are required to be disclosed under standard 7 by:

(1)   Informing the lawyer in the arbitration, in writing, of all such relationships within the arbitrator's knowledge and asking the lawyer if the lawyer is aware of any other such relationships; and

(2)   Declaring in writing that he or she has made the inquiry in (1) and attaching to this declaration copies of his or her inquiry and any response from the lawyer in the arbitration.

(d)   Obligation regarding service as a neutral other than an arbitrator before July 1, 2002

An arbitrator can fulfill the obligation under this standard to inform himself or herself of his or her service as a dispute resolution neutral other than as an arbitrator in cases that commenced prior to July 1, 2002 by:

(1)   Asking any dispute resolution provider organization that administered those prior services for this information; and

(2) Declaring in writing that he or she has made the inquiry in (1) and attaching to this declaration copies of his or her inquiry and any response from the provider organization.

(e) Obligation regarding relationships with provider organization

An arbitrator can fulfill his or her obligation under this standard to inform himself or herself of the information that is required to be disclosed under standard 8 by:

(1) Asking the dispute resolution provider organization for this information; and

(2) Declaring in writing that he or she has made the inquiry in (1) and attaching to this declaration copies of his or her inquiry and any response from the provider organization.

Comment to Standard 9

This standard expands arbitrators existing duty of reasonable inquiry that applies with respect to financial interests under Code of Civil Procedure section 170.1(a)(3), to require arbitrators to make a reasonable effort to inform themselves about all matters that must be disclosed. This standard also clarifies what constitutes a reasonable effort by an arbitrator to inform himself or herself about specified matters, including relationships or other matters concerning his or her extended family and relationships with attorneys associated in the practice of law with the attorney in the arbitration (such as associates encompassed within the term "lawyer for a party").

Standard 10. Disqualification.

(a) An arbitrator is disqualified if:

(1) The arbitrator fails to comply with his or her obligation to make disclosures and a party serves a notice of disqualification in the manner and within the time specified in Code of Civil Procedure section 1281.91;

(2) The arbitrator complies with his or her obligation to make disclosures within 10 calendar days of service of notice of the proposed nomination or appointment and, based on that disclosure, a party serves a notice of disqualification in the manner and within the time specified in Code of Civil Procedure section 1281.91;

(3) The arbitrator makes a required disclosure more than 10 calendar days after service of notice of the proposed nomination or appointment and, based on that disclosure, a party serves a notice of disqualification in the manner and within the time specified in Code of Civil Procedure section 1281.91; or

(4) A party becomes aware that an arbitrator has made a material omission or material misrepresentation in his or her disclosure and, within 15 days after becoming aware of the omission or misrepresentation and within the time specified in Code of Civil Procedure section 1281.91(c), the party serves a notice of disqualification that clearly describes the material omission or material misrepresentation and how and when the party became aware of this omission or misrepresentation; or

(5) If any ground specified in Code of Civil Procedure section 170.1 exists and the party makes a demand that the arbitrator disqualify himself or herself in the manner and within the time specified in Code of Civil Procedure section 1281.91(d).

(b) For purposes of this standard, "obligation to make disclosure" means an arbitrator's obligation to make

disclosures under standards 7 or 8 or Code of Civil Procedure section 1281.9.

(c) Notwithstanding any contrary request, consent, or waiver by the parties, an arbitrator must disqualify himself or herself if he or she concludes at any time during the arbitration that he or she is not able to conduct the arbitration impartially.

Comment to Standard 10

Code of Civil Procedure section 1281.91 already establishes requirements concerning disqualification of arbitrators. This standard does not eliminate or otherwise limit those requirements or change existing authority or procedures for challenging an arbitrator's failure to disqualify himself or herself. The provisions of subdivisions (a)(1), (2), and (5) restate existing disqualification procedures under section 1281.91; (b) and (d) when an arbitrator makes, or fails to make, initial disclosures or where a section 170.1 ground exists. The provisions of subdivisions (a)(3) and (4) clarify the requirements relating to disqualification based on disclosure made by the arbitrator after appointment or based on the discovery by the party of a material omission or misrepresentation in the arbitrator's disclosure.

Standard 11. Duty to refuse gift, bequest, or favor.

(a) An arbitrator must not, under any circumstances, accept a gift, bequest, favor, or honoraria from a party or any other person or entity whose interests are reasonably likely to come before the arbitrator in the arbitration.

(b) From service of notice of appointment or appointment until two years after the conclusion of the arbitration, an arbitrator must not, under any circumstances, accept a gift, bequest, favor, or honoraria from a party or any other person or entity whose interests have come before the arbitrator in the arbitration.

(c) An arbitrator must discourage members of his or her family residing in his or her household from accepting a gift, bequest, favor, or honoraria that the arbitrator would be prohibited from accepting under subdivisions (a) or (b).

(d) This standard does not prohibit an arbitrator from demanding or receiving a fee for services or expenses.

Comment to Standard 11

Gifts and favors do not include any rebate or discount made available in the regular course of business to members of the public.

Standard 12. Duties and limitations regarding future professional relationships or employment.

(a) Offers as lawyer, expert witness, or consultant

From the time of appointment until the conclusion of the arbitration, an arbitrator must not entertain or accept any offers of employment or new professional relationships as a lawyer, an expert witness, or a consultant from a party or a lawyer for a party in the pending arbitration.

(b) Offers for other employment or professional relationships

In addition to the disclosures required by standards 7 and 8, within ten calendar days of service of notice of the proposed nomination or appointment, a proposed arbitrator must disclose to all parties in writing if, while that arbitration is pending, he or she will entertain offers of employment or new professional relationships in any capacity other than as a lawyer, expert witness, or consultant from a party or a lawyer for a party, including offers to serve as a dispute resolution neutral in another case. A party may disqualify the arbitrator based on this disclosure by serving a notice of disqualification in the manner and within the time specified in Code of Civil Procedure section 1281.91(b).

(c) Acceptance of offers prohibited unless intent disclosed

If an arbitrator fails to make the disclosure required by subdivision (b) of this standard, from the time of appointment until the conclusion of the arbitration the arbitrator must not entertain or accept any such offers of employment or new professional relationships, including offers to serve as a dispute resolution neutral.

(d) Relationships and use of confidential information related to the arbitrated case

An arbitrator must not at any time:

(1) Without the informed written consent of all parties, enter into any professional relationship or accept any professional employment as a lawyer, an expert witness, or a consultant relating to the case arbitrated; or

(2) Without the informed written consent of the party, enter into any professional relationship or accept employment in another matter in which information that he or she has received in confidence from a party by reason of serving as an arbitrator in a case is material.

Standard 13.   Conduct of proceeding.

(a) An arbitrator must conduct the arbitration fairly, promptly, and diligently and in accordance with the applicable law relating to the conduct of arbitration proceedings.

(b) In making the decision, an arbitrator must not be swayed by partisan interests, public clamor, or fear of criticism.

Comment to Standard 13

Subdivision (a). The arbitrator's duty to dispose of matters promptly and diligently must not take precedence over the arbitrator's duty to dispose of matters fairly.

Conducting the arbitration in a procedurally fair manner includes conducting a balanced process in which each party is given an opportunity to participate. When one but not all parties are unrepresented, an arbitrator must ensure that the party appearing without counsel has an adequate opportunity to be heard and involved. Conducting the arbitration promptly and diligently requires expeditious management of all stages of the proceeding and concluding the case as promptly as the circumstances reasonably permit. During an arbitration, an arbitrator may discuss the issues, arguments, and evidence with the parties or their counsel, make interim rulings, and otherwise to control or direct the arbitration. This standard is not intended to restrict these activities.

The arbitrator's duty to uphold the integrity and fairness of the arbitration process includes an obligation to make reasonable efforts to prevent delaying tactics, harassment of any participant, or other abuse of the arbitration process. It is recognized, however, that the arbitrator's reasonable efforts may not successfully control all conduct of the participants.

For the general law relating to the conduct of arbitration proceedings, see chapter 3 of title 9 of part III of the Code of Civil Procedure, sections 1282–1284.2, relating to the conduct of arbitration proceedings. See also Code of Civil Procedure section

1286.2 concerning an arbitrator's unreasonable refusal to grant a continuance as grounds for *vacatur* of the award.

Standard 14.   Ex parte communications.

(a) An arbitrator must not initiate, permit, or consider any ex parte communications or consider other communications made to the arbitrator outside the presence of all of the parties concerning a pending or impending arbitration, except as permitted by this standard, by agreement of the parties, or by applicable law.

(b) An arbitrator may communicate with a party in the absence of other parties about administrative matters, such as setting the time and place of hearings or making other arrangements for the conduct of the proceedings, as long as the arbitrator reasonably believes that the communication will not result in a procedural or tactical advantage for any party. When such a discussion occurs, the arbitrator must promptly inform the other parties of the communication and must give the other parties an opportunity to respond before making any final determination concerning the matter discussed.

(c) An arbitrator may obtain the advice of a disinterested expert on the subject matter of the arbitration if the arbitrator notifies the parties of the person consulted and the substance of the advice and affords the parties a reasonable opportunity to respond.

Comment to Standard 14

See also Code of Civil Procedure sections 1282.2(e) regarding the arbitrator's authority to hear a matter when a party fails to appear and 1282.2(g) regarding the procedures that must be followed if an arbitrator intends to base an award on information not obtained at the hearing.

Standard 15.   Confidentiality.

(a) An arbitrator must not use or disclose information that he or she received in confidence by reason of serving as an arbitrator in a case to gain personal advantage. This duty applies from acceptance of appointment and continues after the conclusion of the arbitration.

(b) An arbitrator must not inform anyone of the award in advance of the time that the award is given to all parties. This standard does not prohibit an arbitrator from providing all parties with a tentative or draft decision for review or from providing an award to an assistant or to the provider organization that is coordinating, administering, or providing the arbitration services in the case for purposes of copying and distributing the award to all parties.

Standard 16.   Compensation.

(a) An arbitrator must not charge any fee for services or expenses that is in any way contingent on the result or outcome of the arbitration.

(b) Before accepting appointment, an arbitrator, a dispute resolution provider organization, or another person or entity acting on the arbitrator's behalf must inform all parties in writing of the terms and conditions of the arbitrator's compensation. This information must include any basis to be used in determining fees and any special fees for cancellation, research and preparation time, or other purposes.

Standard 17. Marketing.

(a) An arbitrator must be truthful and accurate in marketing his or her services and must not make any representation that directly or indirectly implies favoritism or a specific outcome. An arbitrator must ensure that his or her personal marketing activities and any activities carried out on his or her behalf, including any activities of a provider organization with which the arbitrator is affiliated, comply with this requirement.

(b) An arbitrator must not solicit business from a participant in the arbitration while the arbitration is pending.

Comment to Standard 17

Subdivision (b). This provision is not intended to prohibit an arbitrator from accepting another arbitration from a party or attorney in the arbitration while the first matter is pending, as long as the arbitrator complies with the provisions of standard 12 and there was no express solicitation of this business by the arbitrator.

Appendix A
Judicial Council Legal Forms List

Under Government Code section 68511, the Judicial Council may "prescribe" certain forms. Use of prescribed forms is mandatory. Under rule 1.31, each mandatory Judicial Council legal form is identified as mandatory by an asterisk (*) on the list of Judicial Council legal forms published in this appendix. Mandatory forms bear the word "adopted" in the lower left corner of the first page.

Optional forms bear the word "approved" in the lower left corner of the first page. Use of an approved (optional) form is not mandatory, but the form must be accepted by all courts in appropriate cases (rule 1.35(a)).

A local court may not reject any Judicial Council form, optional or mandatory, for any of the reasons listed in rule 1.42.

The forms are available on the California Courts Web site in both a fillable and a PDF format at *www.courtinfo.ca.gov/ forms*.

JUDICIAL COUNCIL FORMS

Form No.	Year	Title	[Rev. January 1, 2009]

ADOPTION

ADOPT-050	1/1/2003	How to Adopt a Child in California
ADOPT-200*	1/1/2007	Adoption Request
ADOPT-210*	7/1/2007	Adoption Agreement
ADOPT-215*	7/1/2007	Adoption Order
ADOPT-220*	1/1/2003	Adoption of Indian Child
ADOPT-225*	1/1/2005	Parent Of Indian Child Agrees To End Parental Rights
ADOPT-226*	1/1/2008	*[Revoked]* Notice of Adoption Proceedings for a Possible Indian Child
ADOPT-230*	1/1/2007	Adoption Expenses
ADOPT-310*	1/1/2003	Contact After Adoption Agreement
ADOPT-315*	1/1/2003	Request to: Enforce, Change, End Contact After Adoption Agreement
ADOPT-320*	1/1/2003	Answer to Request to: Enforce, Change, End Contact After Adoption Agreement
ADOPT-325*	1/1/2003	Judge's Order to: Enforce, Change, End Contact After Adoption Agreement
ADOPT-330*	1/1/2008	Request for Appointment of Confidential Intermediary
ADOPT-331*	1/1/2008	Order for Appointment of Confidential Intermediary

ALTERNATIVE DISPUTE RESOLUTION

ADR-100*	1/1/2003	Statement of Agreement or Nonagreement
ADR-101*	1994	ADR Information Form
ADR-102	1/1/2007	Request for Trial De Novo After Judicial Arbitration
ADR-103	1/1/2004	Petition After Attorney-Client Fee Dispute Arbitration Award
ADR-104	1/1/2004	Rejection of Award and Request for Trial After Attorney-Client Fee Arbitration (Alternative Dispute Resolution)
ADR-105	1/1/2009	Information Regarding Rights After Attorney-Client Fee Arbitration (Alternative Dispute Resolution)
ADR-106	1/1/2004	Petition to Confirm, Correct, or Vacate Contractual Arbitration Award (Alternative Dispute Resolution)
ADR-107	7/1/2009	Attendance Sheet for Court-Program Mediation of Civil Case (Alternative Dispute Resolution)
ADR-109	1/1/2007	Stipulation Or Motion For Order Appointing Referee (Alternative Dispute Resolution)
ADR-110	1/1/2007	Order Appointing Referee (Alternative Dispute Resolution)
ADR-111	1/1/2006	Report of Referee (Alternative Dispute Resolution)

APPELLATE

APP-001	1/1/2007	Information On Appeal Procedures For Unlimited Civil Cases
APP-002	1/1/2007	Notice of Appeal/Cross-Appeal (Unlimited Civil Case)
APP-003	1/1/2008	Appellant's Notice Designating Record on Appeal (Unlimited Civil Case)
APP-004*	7/1/2007	Civil Case Information Statement (Appellate)
APP-005	1/1/2007	Abandonment Of Appeal (Unlimited Civil Case)
APP-006	1/1/2007	Application For Extension Of Time To File Brief (Civil Case)
APP-007	7/1/2007	Request for Dismissal of Appeal (Civil Case)
APP-008	1/1/2009	Certificate of Interested Entities or Persons
APP-009	1/1/2009	Proof of Service (Court of Appeal)
APP-009-INFO	1/1/2009	Information Sheet For Proof of Service (Court of Appeal)
APP-101-INFO	1/1/2009	Information on Appeal Procedures for Limited Civil Cases
APP-102	1/1/2009	Notice of Appeal/Cross-Appeal (Limited Civil Case)
APP-103	1/1/2009	Notice Designating Record on Appeal (Limited Civil Case)
APP-104	1/1/2009	Proposed Statement on Appeal (Limited Civil Case)
APP-105	1/1/2009	Order Concerning Appellant's Proposed Statement on Appeal (Limited Civil Case)
APP-106	1/1/2009	Abandonment of Appeal (Limited Civil Case)
APP-109	1/1/2009	Proof of Service (Appellate Division)

---

* Adopted for mandatory use by all courts.

APP-109-INFO	1/1/2009	What Is Proof of Service?
APP-150-INFO	1/1/2009	Information on Writ Proceedings in Misdemeanor, Infraction, and Limited Civil Cases
APP-151	1/1/2009	Petition for Writ (Misdemeanor, Infraction, or Limited Civil Case)

ATTACHMENT

AT-105	1/1/2000	Application for Attachment, Temporary Protective Order, Etc.
AT-115	1/1/2000	Notice of Application and Hearing for Right to Attach Order and Writs of Attachment
AT-120	1/1/2000	Right to Attach Order After Hearing and Order for Issuance of Writ of Attachment
AT-125	1/1/2000	Ex Parte Right to Attach Order and Order for Issuance of Writ of Attachment (Resident)
AT-130	1/1/2000	Ex Parte Right to Attach Order and Order for Issuance of Writ of Attachment (Nonresident)
AT-135	1/1/2003	Writ of Attachment
AT-138*	7/1/2000	Application and Order for Appearance and Examination *[same as EJ-125]*
AT-140	1/1/2000	Temporary Protective Order
AT-145	1983	Application and Notice of Hearing for Order to Terminate, Modify, or Vacate Temporary Protective Order
AT-150	1983	Order to Terminate, Modify, or Vacate Temporary Protective Order
AT-155	1983	Notice of Opposition to Right to Attach Order and Claim of Exemption
AT-160*	1/1/2006	Undertaking by Personal Sureties (Attachment and Claim and Delivery)
AT-165	1/1/2003	Notice of Attachment
AT-167	1983	Memorandum of Garnishee *[same as EJ-152]*
AT-170	1983	Application to Set Aside Right to Attach Order and Release Attached Property, Etc.
AT-175	1983	Order to Set Aside Attachment, to Substitute Undertaking, Etc.
AT-180	1985	Notice of Lien *[same as EJ-185]*

CASE MANAGEMENT

CM-010*	7/1/2007	Civil Case Cover Sheet
CM-015	7/1/2007	Notice of Related Case
CM-020	1/1/2008	Ex Parte Application for Extension of Time to Serve Pleading and Orders
CM-110*	1/1/2009	Case Management Statement
CM-180*	1/1/2007	Notice of Stay of Proceedings
CM-181*	1/1/2007	Notice of Termination or Modification of Stay
CM-200*	1/1/2007	Notice of Settlement of Entire Case

CIVIL

CIV-010*	1/1/2008	Application and Order for Appointment of Guardian Ad Litem—Civil
CIV-025	1/1/2007	Application and Order for Reissuance of Order to Show Cause and Temporary Restraining Order
CIV-050*	1/1/2007	Statement of Damages (Personal Injury or Wrongful Death)
CIV-090	1/1/2008	Offer to Compromise and Acceptance Under Code of Civil Procedure Section 998
CIV-100*	1/1/2007	Request for Entry of Default (Application to Enter Default)
CIV-110*	1/1/2007	Request for Dismissal
CIV-120*	1/1/2007	Notice of Entry of Dismissal and Proof of Service

CIVIL HARASSMENT

CH-100*	7/1/2007	Request for Orders to Stop Harassment (Civil Harassment)
CH-101*	7/1/2007	*[Revoked]* Request and Order for Free Service of Restraining Order (Sexual Assault or Stalking) *[same as DV-290*]*
CH-101* C	7/1/2007	*[Revoked]* Request and Order for Free Service of Restraining Order (Sexual Assault or Stalking)—Chinese *[same as DV-290* C]*

---

* Adopted for mandatory use by all courts.

CH-101* K	7/1/2007	*[Revoked]* Request and Order for Free Service of Restraining Order (Sexual Assault or Stalking)—Korean *[same as DV-290* K]*
CH-101* S	7/1/2007	*[Revoked]* Request and Order for Free Service of Restraining Order (Sexual Assault or Stalking)—Spanish *[same as DV-290* S]*
CH-101* V	7/1/2007	*[Revoked]* Request and Order for Free Service of Restraining Order (Sexual Assault or Stalking)—Vietnamese *[same as DV-290* V]*
CH-102*	7/1/2007	Confidential CLETS Information (Domestic Violence, Civil Harassment, Elder Abuse) *[same as DV-260* and EA-102*]*
CH-102* C	7/1/2007	Confidential CLETS Information (Domestic Violence, Civil Harassment, Elder Abuse)—Chinese *[same as DV-260* C and EA-102* C]*
CH-102* K	7/1/2007	Confidential CLETS Information (Domestic Violence, Civil Harassment, Elder Abuse)—Korean *[same as DV-260* K and EA-102* K]*
CH-102* S	7/1/2007	Confidential CLETS Information (Domestic Violence, Civil Harassment, Elder Abuse)—Spanish *[same as DV-260* S and EA-102* S]*
CH-102* T	7/1/2007	Confidential CLETS Information (Domestic Violence, Civil Harassment, Elder Abuse)—Tagalog *[same as DV-260* T and EA-102* T]*
CH-102* V	7/1/2007	Confidential CLETS Information (Domestic Violence, Civil Harassment, Elder Abuse)—Vietnamese *[same as DV-260* V and EA-102* V]*
CH-110*	1/1/2005	Answer to Request for Orders to Stop Harassment (Civil Harassment)
CH-120*	7/1/2007	Notice of Hearing and Temporary Restraining Order (CLETS) (Civil Harassment)
CH-125*	1/1/2005	Reissue Temporary Restraining Order (Civil Harassment)
CH-130	1/1/2005	Proof of Personal Service (Civil Harassment)
CH-131	1/1/2005	Proof of Service by Mail (Civil Harassment)
CH-135	1/1/2005	What Is Proof of Service? (Civil Harassment)
CH-140*	7/1/2007	Restraining Order After Hearing to Stop Harassment (CLETS) (Civil Harassment)
CH-145	1/1/2005	Proof of Firearms Turned in or Sold (Civil Harassment)
CH-150	7/1/2007	Can a Civil Harassment Restraining Order Help Me? (Civil Harassment)
CH-151	1/1/2005	How Can I Answer a Request for Orders to Stop Harassment? (Civil Harassment)

COURT RECORDS

REC-001(N)*[1]	1/1/2007	Notice of Intent to Destroy Superior Court Records; Offer to Transfer Possession *(formerly 982.8(1)(N))*
REC-001(R)*	1/1/2007	Request for Transfer or Extension of Time for Retention of Superior Court Records *(formerly 982.8(1)(R))*
REC-002(N)*[2]	1/1/2007	Notice of Hearing on Request for Transfer or Extension of Time for Retention of Superior Court Records; Court Record; Release and Receipt of Records *(formerly 982.8(2)(N))*
REC-002(R)*	1/1/2007	Release and Receipt of Superior Court Records *(formerly 982.8(2)(R))*
REC-003*	1/1/2007	Report to the Judicial Council: Superior Court Records Destroyed, Preserved, and Transferred *(formerly 982.8A)*

CLAIM AND DELIVERY

CD-100*	1/1/2006	Application for Writ of Possession (Claim and Delivery)
CD-110*	1/1/2006	Notice of Application for Writ of Possession and Hearing (Claim and Delivery)
CD-120*	1/1/2006	Order for Writ of Possession (Claim and Delivery)
CD-130*	1/1/2006	Writ of Possession (Claim and Delivery)
CD-140*	1/1/2006	Undertaking By Personal Sureties (Attachment and Claim and Delivery)
CD-160*	1/1/2006	Application and Notice of Application and Hearing for Order to Quash Ex Parte Writ of Possession (Claim and Delivery)
CD-170*	1/1/2006	Order for Release and Redelivery of Property (Claim and Delivery)
CD-180*	1/1/2006	Declaration for Ex Parte Writ of Possession (Claim and Delivery)
CD-190*	1/1/2006	Application for Temporary Restraining Order (Claim and Delivery)

---

* Adopted for mandatory use by all courts.

[1] Form REC-001(R) to be printed on reverse side of form REC-001(N).

[2] Form REC-002(R) to be printed on reverse side of form REC-002(N).

| CD-200* | 1/1/2006 | Temporary Restraining Order (Claim and Delivery) |

CRIMINAL

CR-100*	7/1/2007	Fingerprint Form
CR-101	7/1/2008	Plea Form, With Explanations and Waiver of Rights—Felony
CR-110	1/1/2008	Order for Restitution and Abstract of Judgment [same as JV-790]
CR-112	1/1/2004	Instructions: Order for Restitution and Abstract of Judgment
CR-115*	7/1/2000	Defendant's Statement of Assets
CR-117	1/1/2004	Instructions: Defendant's Statement of Assets
CR-118	1/1/2005	Information Regarding Income Deduction Order (Pen. Code, §1202.42)
CR-119	1/1/2005	Order for Income Deduction (Pen. Code, §1202.42)
CR-120	1/1/2007	Notice of Appeal—Felony (Defendant)
CR-125*	7/1/2007	Order to Attend Court or Provide Documents: Subpoena/Subpoena Duces Tecum (Criminal and Juvenile) [same as JV-525*]
CR-130	1/1/2007	Notice of Appeal—Misdemeanor (Defendant)
CR-131-INFO	1/1/2009	Information on Appeal Procedures for Misdemeanors
CR-132	1/1/2009	Notice of Appeal (Misdemeanor)
CR-133	1/1/2009	Request for Court-Appointed Lawyer in Misdemeanor Appeal
CR-134	1/1/2009	Notice Regarding Record of Oral Proceedings (Misdemeanor)
CR-135	1/1/2009	Proposed Statement on Appeal (Misdemeanor)
CR-136	1/1/2009	Order Concerning Appellant's Proposed Statement on Appeal (Misdemeanor)
CR-137	1/1/2009	Abandonment of Appeal (Misdemeanor)
CR-141-INFO	1/1/2009	Information on Appeal Procedures for Infractions
CR-142	1/1/2009	Notice of Appeal and Record of Oral Proceedings (Infraction)
CR-143	1/1/2009	Proposed Statement on Appeal (Infraction)
CR-144	1/1/2009	Order Concerning Appellant's Proposed Statement on Appeal (Infraction)
CR-145	1/1/2009	Abandonment of Appeal (Infraction)
CR-150*	1/1/2002	Certificate of Identity Theft: Judicial Finding of Factual Innocence
CR-151	1/1/2005	Petition for Certificate of Identity Theft (Pen. Code, §530.6)
CR-160*	1/1/2009	Criminal Protective Order—Domestic Violence (CLETS—CPO) (Penal Code, §§ 136.2, 1203.097(a)(2), 273.5(i), and 646.9(k).)
CR-160* C	7/1/2007	Criminal Protective Order—Domestic Violence (CLETS—CPO) (Penal Code, §§ 136.2 and 1203.097(a)(2))—Chinese
CR-160* K	7/1/2007	Criminal Protective Order—Domestic Violence (CLETS—CPO) (Penal Code, §§ 136.2 and 1203.097(a)(2))—Korean
CR-160* S	7/1/2007	Criminal Protective Order—Domestic Violence (CLETS—CPO) (Penal Code, §§ 136.2 and 1203.097(a)(2))—Spanish
CR-160* T	7/1/2007	Criminal Protective Order—Domestic Violence (CLETS—CPO) (Penal Code, §§ 136.2 and 1203.097(a)(2))—Tagalog
CR-160* V	7/1/2007	Criminal Protective Order—Domestic Violence (CLETS—CPO) (Penal Code, §§ 136.2 and 1203.097(a)(2))—Vietnamese
CR-161*	1/1/2009	Criminal Protective Order—Other Than Domestic Violence (CLETS—CPO) (Penal Code, §§ 136.2 and 646.9(k).)
CR-162*	7/1/2007	Order to Surrender Firearms in Domestic Violence Case (CLETS—CPO) (Penal Code, § 136.2(a)(7)(B))
CR-165*	1/1/2009	Notice of Termination of Protective Order in Criminal Proceeding (CLETS) (Penal Code, §§136.2, 1203.097(a)(2), 273.5(i), and 646.9(k))
CR-168	1/1/2007	Batterer Intervention Program Progress Report
CR-170	1/1/2003	Notification of Decision Whether to Challenge Recommendation (Pen. Code, §2972.1)
CR-175	1/1/2004	Notice and Request for Ruling (Criminal)
CR-180	1/1/2009	Petition for Dismissal (Pen. Code, §§17, 1203.4, 1203.4a)
CR-181	1/1/2009	Order for Dismissal (Pen. Code, §§17, 1203.4, 1203.4a)
CR-185	1/1/2009	Petition for Expungement of DNA Profiles and Samples (Pen. Code, §299) [same as JV-796]
CR-186	1/1/2009	Order for Expungement of DNA Profiles and Samples (Pen. Code, §299) [same as JV-798]
CR-190*	1/1/2004	Order Appointing Counsel in Capital Case
CR-191*	1/1/2007	Declaration Of Counsel For Appointment In Capital Case
CR-200	1/1/2006	Form Interrogatories—Crime Victim Restitution

---

* Adopted for mandatory use by all courts.

DISCOVERY

DISC-001	1/1/2008	Form Interrogatories—General
DISC-002	1/1/2009	Form Interrogatories—Employment Law
DISC-003	1/1/2009	Form Interrogatories—Unlawful Detainer *[same as UD-106]*
DISC-004	1/1/2007	Form Interrogatories—Limited Civil Cases (Economic Litigation)
DISC-010*	1/1/2007	Case Questionnaire—For Limited Civil Cases (Under $25,000)
DISC-015*	1/1/2007	Request For Statement Of Witnesses And Evidence—For Limited Civil Cases (Under $25,000)
DISC-020	1/1/2008	Request for Admission
DISC-030	1/1/2008	Commission to Take Deposition Outside California

DOMESTIC VIOLENCE PREVENTION

DV-100*	7/1/2007	Request for Order (Domestic Violence Prevention)
DV-100* C	7/1/2007	Request for Order (Domestic Violence Prevention)—Chinese
DV-100* K	7/1/2007	Request for Order (Domestic Violence Prevention)—Korean
DV-100* S	7/1/2007	Request for Order (Domestic Violence Prevention)—Spanish
DV-100* V	7/1/2007	Request for Order (Domestic Violence Prevention)—Vietnamese
DV-101	1/1/2003	Description of Abuse (Domestic Violence Prevention)
DV-101 C	1/1/2003	Description of Abuse (Domestic Violence Prevention)—Chinese
DV-101 K	1/1/2003	Description of Abuse (Domestic Violence Prevention)—Korean
DV-101 S	1/1/2003	Description of Abuse (Domestic Violence Prevention)—Spanish
DV-101 V	1/1/2003	Description of Abuse (Domestic Violence Prevention)—Vietnamese
DV-105*	1/1/2004	Child Custody, Visitation, and Support Request (Domestic Violence Prevention)
DV-105* C	1/1/2004	Child Custody, Visitation, and Support Request (Domestic Violence Prevention)—Chinese
DV-105* K	1/1/2004	Child Custody, Visitation, and Support Request (Domestic Violence Prevention)—Korean
DV-105* S	1/1/2004	Child Custody, Visitation, and Support Request (Domestic Violence Prevention)—Spanish
DV-105* V	1/1/2004	Child Custody, Visitation, and Support Request (Domestic Violence Prevention)—Vietnamese
DV-108*	7/1/2003	Request for Order: No Travel with Children (Domestic Violence Prevention)
DV-108* C	7/1/2003	Request for Order: No Travel with Children (Domestic Violence Prevention)—Chinese
DV-108* K	7/1/2003	Request for Order: No Travel with Children (Domestic Violence Prevention)—Korean
DV-108* S	7/1/2003	Request for Order: No Travel with Children (Domestic Violence Prevention—Spanish)
DV-108* V	7/1/2003	Request for Order: No Travel with Children (Domestic Violence Prevention)—Vietnamese
DV-110*	7/1/2007	Temporary Restraining Order and Notice of Hearing (CLETS—TRO) (Domestic Violence Prevention)
DV-110* C	7/1/2007	Temporary Restraining Order and Notice of Hearing (CLETS—TRO) (Domestic Violence Prevention)—Chinese
DV-110* K	7/1/2007	Temporary Restraining Order and Notice of Hearing (CLETS—TRO) (Domestic Violence Prevention)—Korean
DV-110* S	7/1/2007	Temporary Restraining Order and Notice of Hearing (CLETS—TRO) (Domestic Violence Prevention)—Spanish
DV-110* V	7/1/2007	Temporary Restraining Order and Notice of Hearing (CLETS—TRO) (Domestic Violence Prevention)—Vietnamese
DV-120*	7/1/2007	Answer to Temporary Restraining Order (Domestic Violence Prevention)
DV-120* C	7/1/2007	Answer to Temporary Restraining Order (Domestic Violence Prevention)—Chinese
DV-120* K	7/1/2007	Answer to Temporary Restraining Order (Domestic Violence Prevention)—Korean
DV-120* S	7/1/2007	Answer to Temporary Restraining Order (Domestic Violence Prevention)—Spanish

---

* Adopted for mandatory use by all courts.

DV-120* V	7/1/2007	Answer to Temporary Restraining Order (Domestic Violence Prevention)—Vietnamese
DV-125*	7/1/2003	Reissue Temporary Restraining Order (Domestic Violence Prevention)
DV-125* C	7/1/2003	Reissue Temporary Restraining Order (Domestic Violence Prevention)—Chinese
DV-125* K	7/1/2003	Reissue Temporary Restraining Order (Domestic Violence Prevention)—Korean
DV-125* S	7/1/2003	Reissue Temporary Restraining Order (Domestic Violence Prevention)—Spanish
DV-125* V	7/1/2003	Reissue Temporary Restraining Order (Domestic Violence Prevention)—Vietnamese
DV-126-INFO	7/1/2006	How to Reissue a Temporary Restraining Order (Domestic Violence Prevention)
DV-126-INFO-C	7/1/2006	How to Reissue a Temporary Restraining Order (Domestic Violence Prevention)—Chinese
DV-126-INFO-K	7/1/2006	How to Reissue a Temporary Restraining Order (Domestic Violence Prevention)—Korean
DV-126-INFO-S	7/1/2006	How to Reissue a Temporary Restraining Order (Domestic Violence Prevention)—Spanish
DV-126-INFO-V	7/1/2006	How to Reissue a Temporary Restraining Order (Domestic Violence Prevention)—Vietnamese
DV-130*	7/1/2007	Restraining Order After Hearing (CLETS—OAH) (Order of Protection) (Domestic Violence Prevention)
DV-130* C	7/1/2007	Restraining Order After Hearing (CLETS—OAH) (Order of Protection) (Domestic Violence Prevention)—Chinese
DV-130* K	7/1/2007	Restraining Order After Hearing (CLETS—OAH) (Order of Protection) (Domestic Violence Prevention)—Korean
DV-130* S	7/1/2007	Restraining Order After Hearing (CLETS—OAH) (Order of Protection) (Domestic Violence Prevention)—Spanish
DV-130* V	7/1/2007	Restraining Order After Hearing (CLETS—OAH) (Order of Protection) (Domestic Violence Prevention)—Vietnamese
DV-140*	7/1/2003	Child Custody and Visitation Order (Domestic Violence Prevention)
DV-140* C	7/1/2003	Child Custody and Visitation Order (Domestic Violence Prevention)—Chinese
DV-140* K	7/1/2003	Child Custody and Visitation Order (Domestic Violence Prevention)—Korean
DV-140* S	7/1/2003	Child Custody and Visitation Order (Domestic Violence Prevention)—Spanish
DV-140* V	7/1/2003	Child Custody and Visitation Order (Domestic Violence Prevention)—Vietnamese
DV-145*	7/1/2003	Order: No Travel with Children (Domestic Violence Prevention)
DV-145* C	7/1/2003	Order: No Travel with Children (Domestic Violence Prevention)—Chinese
DV-145* K	7/1/2003	Order: No Travel with Children (Domestic Violence Prevention)—Korean
DV-145* S	7/1/2003	Order: No Travel with Children (Domestic Violence Prevention)—Spanish
DV-145* V	7/1/2003	Order: No Travel with Children (Domestic Violence Prevention)—Vietnamese
DV-150*	7/1/2003	Supervised Visitation Order (Domestic Violence Prevention)
DV-150* C	7/1/2003	Supervised Visitation Order (Domestic Violence Prevention)—Chinese
DV-150* K	7/1/2003	Supervised Visitation Order (Domestic Violence Prevention)—Korean
DV-150* S	7/1/2003	Supervised Visitation Order (Domestic Violence Prevention)—Spanish
DV-150* V	7/1/2003	Supervised Visitation Order (Domestic Violence Prevention)—Vietnamese
DV-160	7/1/2008	Child Support Order—Order of Protection (Domestic Violence Prevention)
DV-160 C	7/1/2007	Child Support Order—Order of Protection (Domestic Violence Prevention)—Chinese
DV-160 K	7/1/2007	Child Support Order—Order of Protection (Domestic Violence Prevention)—Korean
DV-160 S	7/1/2007	Child Support Order—Order of Protection (Domestic Violence Prevention)—Spanish
DV-160 V	7/1/2007	Child Support Order—Order of Protection (Domestic Violence Prevention)—Vietnamese
DV-170*	7/1/2006	Other Orders (Domestic Violence Prevention)

---

* Adopted for mandatory use by all courts.

DV-170* C	7/1/2006	Other Orders (Domestic Violence Prevention)—Chinese
DV-170* K	7/1/2006	Other Orders (Domestic Violence Prevention)—Korean
DV-170* S	7/1/2006	Other Orders (Domestic Violence Prevention)—Spanish
DV-170* V	7/1/2006	Other Orders (Domestic Violence Prevention)—Vietnamese
DV-200	1/1/2003	Proof of Service (In Person) (CLETS) (Domestic Violence Prevention)
DV-200 C	1/1/2003	Proof of Service (In Person) (CLETS) (Domestic Violence Prevention)—Chinese
DV-200 K	1/1/2003	Proof of Service (In Person) (CLETS) (Domestic Violence Prevention)—Korean
DV-200 S	1/1/2003	Proof of Service (In Person) (CLETS) (Domestic Violence Prevention)—Spanish
DV-200 V	1/1/2003	Proof of Service (In Person) (CLETS) (Domestic Violence Prevention)—Vietnamese
DV-210-INFO	7/1/2008	What is "Proof of Service"? (Domestic Violence Prevention)
DV-210-INFO C	7/1/2006	What is "Proof of Service"? (Domestic Violence Prevention)—Chinese
DV-210-INFO K	7/1/2006	What is "Proof of Service"? (Domestic Violence Prevention)—Korean
DV-210-INFO S	7/1/2006	What is "Proof of Service"? (Domestic Violence Prevention)—Spanish
DV-210-INFO V	7/1/2006	What is "Proof of Service"? (Domestic Violence Prevention)—Vietnamese
DV-250	7/1/2003	Proof of Service by Mail (CLETS) (Domestic Violence Prevention)
DV-250 C	7/1/2003	Proof of Service by Mail (CLETS) (Domestic Violence Prevention)—Chinese
DV-250 K	7/1/2003	Proof of Service by Mail (CLETS) (Domestic Violence Prevention)—Korean
DV-250 S	7/1/2003	Proof of Service by Mail (CLETS) (Domestic Violence Prevention)—Spanish
DV-250 V	7/1/2003	Proof of Service by Mail (CLETS) (Domestic Violence Prevention)—Vietnamese
DV-260*	7/1/2007	Confidential CLETS Information (Domestic Violence, Civil Harassment, Elder Abuse) *[same as CH-102* and EA-102*]*
DV-260* C	7/1/2007	Confidential CLETS Information (Domestic Violence, Civil Harassment, Elder Abuse)—Chinese *[same as CH-102* C and EA-102* C]*
DV-260* K	7/1/2007	Confidential CLETS Information (Domestic Violence, Civil Harassment, Elder Abuse)—Korean *[same as CH-102* K and EA-102* K]*
DV-260* S	7/1/2007	Confidential CLETS Information (Domestic Violence, Civil Harassment, Elder Abuse)—Spanish *[same as CH-102* S and EA-102* S]*
DV-260* T	7/1/2007	Confidential CLETS Information (Domestic Violence, Civil Harassment, Elder Abuse)—Tagalog *[same as CH-102* T and EA-102* T]*
DV-260* V	7/1/2007	Confidential CLETS Information (Domestic Violence, Civil Harassment, Elder Abuse)—Vietnamese *[same as CH-102* V and EA-102* V]*
DV-290*	7/1/2007	*[Revoked]* Request and Order for Free Service of Restraining Order (Sexual Assault or Stalking) *[same as CH-101*]*
DV-290* C	7/1/2007	*[Revoked]* Request and Order for Free Service of Restraining Order (Sexual Assault or Stalking)—Chinese *[same as CH-101* C]*
DV-290* K	7/1/2007	*[Revoked]* Request and Order for Free Service of Restraining Order (Sexual Assault or Stalking)—Korean *[same as CH-101* K]*
DV-290* S	7/1/2007	*[Revoked]* Request and Order for Free Service of Restraining Order (Sexual Assault or Stalking)—Spanish *[same as CH-101* S]*
DV-290* V	7/1/2007	*[Revoked]* Request and Order for Free Service of Restraining Order (Sexual Assault or Stalking)—Vietnamese *[same as CH-101* V]*
DV-500-INFO	7/1/2008	Can a Domestic Violence Restraining Order Help Me? (Domestic Violence Prevention)
DV-500-INFO-C	7/1/2006	Can a Domestic Violence Restraining Order Help Me? (Domestic Violence Prevention)—Chinese
DV-500-INFO-K	7/1/2006	Can a Domestic Violence Restraining Order Help Me? (Domestic Violence Prevention)—Korean
DV-500-INFO-S	7/1/2006	Can a Domestic Violence Restraining Order Help Me? (Domestic Violence Prevention)—Spanish
DV-500-INFO-V	7/1/2006	Can a Domestic Violence Restraining Order Help Me? (Domestic Violence Prevention)—Vietnamese
DV-505	7/1/2005	Forms You Need for a Temporary Restraining Order (Domestic Violence Prevention)

* Adopted for mandatory use by all courts.

DV-505 C	7/1/2005	Forms You Need for a Temporary Restraining Order (Domestic Violence Prevention)—Chinese
DV-505 K	7/1/2005	Forms You Need for a Temporary Restraining Order (Domestic Violence Prevention)—Korean
DV-505 S	7/1/2005	Forms You Need for a Temporary Restraining Order (Domestic Violence Prevention)—Spanish
DV-505 V	7/1/2005	Forms You Need for a Temporary Restraining Order (Domestic Violence Prevention)—Vietnamese
DV-510-INFO	7/1/2006	I Filled Out the Forms—What Now? (Domestic Violence Prevention)
DV-510-INFO-C	7/1/2006	I Filled Out the Forms—What Now? (Domestic Violence Prevention)—Chinese
DV-510-INFO-K	7/1/2006	I Filled Out the Forms—What Now? (Domestic Violence Prevention)—Korean
DV-510-INFO-S	7/1/2006	I Filled Out the Forms—What Now? (Domestic Violence Prevention)—Spanish
DV-510-INFO-V	7/1/2006	I Filled Out the Forms—What Now? (Domestic Violence Prevention)—Vietnamese
DV-520-INFO	7/1/2007	Get Ready for Your Hearing (For Protected Person) (Domestic Violence Prevention)
DV-520-INFO-C	7/1/2007	Get Ready for Your Hearing (For Protected Person) (Domestic Violence Prevention)—Chinese
DV-520-INFO-K	7/1/2007	Get Ready for Your Hearing (For Protected Person) (Domestic Violence Prevention)—Korean
DV-520-INFO-S	7/1/2007	Get Ready for Your Hearing (For Protected Person) (Domestic Violence Prevention)—Spanish
DV-520-INFO-V	7/1/2007	Get Ready for Your Hearing (For Protected Person) (Domestic Violence Prevention)—Vietnamese
DV-530-INFO	7/1/2006	How to Enforce Your Order (Domestic Violence Prevention)
DV-530-INFO-C	7/1/2006	How to Enforce Your Order (Domestic Violence Prevention)—Chinese
DV-530-INFO-K	7/1/2006	How to Enforce Your Order (Domestic Violence Prevention)—Korean
DV-530-INFO-S	7/1/2006	How to Enforce Your Order (Domestic Violence Prevention)—Spanish
DV-530-INFO-V	7/1/2006	How to Enforce Your Order (Domestic Violence Prevention)—Vietnamese
DV-540-INFO	7/1/2006	Information for the Restrained Person (Domestic Violence Prevention)
DV-540-INFO-C	7/1/2006	Information for the Restrained Person (Domestic Violence Prevention)—Chinese
DV-540-INFO-K	7/1/2006	Information for the Restrained Person (Domestic Violence Prevention)—Korean
DV-540-INFO-S	7/1/2006	Information for the Restrained Person (Domestic Violence Prevention)—Spanish
DV-540-INFO-V	7/1/2006	Information for the Restrained Person (Domestic Violence Prevention)—Vietnamese
DV-550-INFO	7/1/2006	Get Ready for Your Hearing (For Restrained Person) (Domestic Violence Prevention)
DV-550-INFO-C	7/1/2006	Get Ready for Your Hearing (For Restrained Person) (Domestic Violence Prevention)—Chinese
DV-550-INFO-K	7/1/2006	Get Ready for Your Hearing (For Restrained Person) (Domestic Violence Prevention)—Korean
DV-550-INFO-S	7/1/2006	Get Ready for Your Hearing (For Restrained Person) (Domestic Violence Prevention)—Spanish
DV-550-INFO-V	7/1/2006	Get Ready for Your Hearing (For Restrained Person) (Domestic Violence Prevention)—Vietnamese
DV-560	1/1/2003	How Can I Make the Order Permanent? (Domestic Violence Prevention)
DV-560 C	1/1/2003	How Can I Make the Order Permanent? (Domestic Violence Prevention)—Chinese
DV-560 K	1/1/2003	How Can I Make the Order Permanent? (Domestic Violence Prevention)—Korean
DV-560 S	1/1/2003	How Can I Make the Order Permanent? (Domestic Violence Prevention)—Spanish
DV-560 V	1/1/2003	How Can I Make the Order Permanent? (Domestic Violence Prevention)—Vietnamese
DV-570	1/1/2003	Which Financial Form—FL-155 or FL-150? (Domestic Violence Prevention)
DV-570 C	1/1/2003	Which Financial Form—FL-155 or FL-150? (Domestic Violence Prevention)—Chinese

DV-570 K	1/1/2003	Which Financial Form—FL-155 or FL-150? (Domestic Violence Prevention)—Korean
DV-570 S	1/1/2003	Which Financial Form—FL-155 or FL-150? (Domestic Violence Prevention)—Spanish
DV-570 V	1/1/2003	Which Financial Form—FL-155 or FL-150? (Domestic Violence Prevention)—Vietnamese
DV-600	7/1/2003	Register Out-of-State Restraining Order (CLETS) (Domestic Violence Prevention)
DV-600 C	7/1/2003	Register Out-of-State Restraining Order (CLETS) (Domestic Violence Prevention)—Chinese
DV-600 K	7/1/2003	Register Out-of-State Restraining Order (CLETS) (Domestic Violence Prevention)—Korean
DV-600 S	7/1/2003	Register Out-of-State Restraining Order (CLETS) (Domestic Violence Prevention)—Spanish
DV-600 V	7/1/2003	Register Out-of-State Restraining Order (CLETS) (Domestic Violence Prevention)—Vietnamese
DV-700*	1/1/2003	Request to Renew Restraining Order (Domestic Violence Prevention)
DV-700* C	1/1/2003	Request to Renew Restraining Order (Domestic Violence Prevention)—Chinese
DV-700* K	1/1/2003	Request to Renew Restraining Order (Domestic Violence Prevention)—Korean
DV-700* S	1/1/2003	Request to Renew Restraining Order (Domestic Violence Prevention)—Spanish
DV-700* V	1/1/2003	Request to Renew Restraining Order (Domestic Violence Prevention)—Vietnamese
DV-710*	7/1/2003	Notice of Hearing to Renew Restraining Order (CLETS) (Domestic Violence Prevention)
DV-710* C	7/1/2003	Notice of Hearing to Renew Restraining Order (CLETS) (Domestic Violence Prevention)—Chinese
DV-710* K	7/1/2003	Notice of Hearing to Renew Restraining Order (CLETS) (Domestic Violence Prevention)—Korean
DV-710* S	7/1/2003	Notice of Hearing to Renew Restraining Order (CLETS) (Domestic Violence Prevention)—Spanish
DV-710* V	7/1/2003	Notice of Hearing to Renew Restraining Order (CLETS) (Domestic Violence Prevention)—Vietnamese
DV-720-INFO	7/1/2006	How Do I Ask the Court to Renew my Restraining Order? (Domestic Violence)
DV-720-INFO-C	7/1/2006	How Do I Ask the Court to Renew my Restraining Order? (Domestic Violence)—Chinese
DV-720-INFO-K	7/1/2006	How Do I Ask the Court to Renew my Restraining Order? (Domestic Violence)—Korean
DV-720-INFO-S	7/1/2006	How Do I Ask the Court to Renew my Restraining Order? (Domestic Violence)—Spanish
DV-720-INFO-V	7/1/2006	How Do I Ask the Court to Renew my Restraining Order? (Domestic Violence)—Vietnamese
DV-800	1/1/2003	Proof of Firearms Turned In or Sold (Domestic Violence Prevention)
DV-800 C	1/1/2003	Proof of Firearms Turned In or Sold (Domestic Violence Prevention)—Chinese
DV-800 K	1/1/2003	Proof of Firearms Turned In or Sold (Domestic Violence Prevention)—Korean
DV-800 S	1/1/2003	Proof of Firearms Turned In or Sold (Domestic Violence Prevention)—Spanish
DV-800 V	1/1/2003	Proof of Firearms Turned In or Sold (Domestic Violence Prevention)—Vietnamese
DV-810	1/1/2003	What Do I Do With My Gun or Firearm? (Domestic Violence Prevention)
DV-810 C	1/1/2003	What Do I Do With My Gun or Firearm? (Domestic Violence Prevention)—Chinese
DV-810 K	1/1/2003	What Do I Do With My Gun or Firearm? (Domestic Violence Prevention)—Korean
DV-810 S	1/1/2003	What Do I Do With My Gun or Firearm? (Domestic Violence Prevention)—Spanish

* Adopted for mandatory use by all courts.

| DV-810 V | 1/1/2003 | What Do I Do With My Gun or Firearm? (Domestic Violence Prevention)—Vietnamese |

ELDER OR DEPENDENT ADULT ABUSE

EA-100*	7/1/2008	Request for Orders to Stop Elder or Dependent Adult Abuse
EA-102*	7/1/2007	Confidential CLETS Information (Domestic Violence, Civil Harassment, Elder Abuse) *[same as CH-102* and DV-260*]*
EA-102* C	7/1/2007	Confidential CLETS Information (Domestic Violence, Civil Harassment, Elder Abuse)—Chinese *[same as CH-102* C and DV-260* C]*
EA-102* K	7/1/2007	Confidential CLETS Information (Domestic Violence, Civil Harassment, Elder Abuse)—Korean *[same as CH-102* K and DV-260* K]*
EA-102* S	7/1/2007	Confidential CLETS Information (Domestic Violence, Civil Harassment, Elder Abuse)—Spanish *[same as CH-102* S and DV-260* S]*
EA-102* T	7/1/2007	Confidential CLETS Information (Domestic Violence, Civil Harassment, Elder Abuse)—Tagalog *[same as CH-260* T and DV-102* T]*
EA-102* V	7/1/2007	Confidential CLETS Information (Domestic Violence, Civil Harassment, Elder Abuse)—Vietnamese *[same as CH-102* V and DV-260* V]*
EA-110*	1/1/2007	Response to Request for Orders to Stop Elder or Dependent Adult Abuse
EA-120*	7/1/2008	Notice of Hearing and Temporary Restraining Order (CLETS—TEA or TEF)
EA-125*	1/1/2007	Request and Order for Reissuance of Temporary Restraining Order (CLETS—TEA or TEF)
EA-130*	7/1/2008	Order After Hearing Restraining Elder or Dependent Adult Abuse (CLETS—EAR or EAF)
EA-140	1/1/2007	Proof of Personal Service—CLETS
EA-141	1/1/2007	Proof of Service by Mail—CLETS
EA-142-INFO	7/1/2008	What Is "Proof of Service"?
EA-145	1/1/2007	Proof of Firearms Turned In or Sold
EA-150	7/1/2008	*[Revoked]* Instructions on Petition for a Protective Order to Prevent Elder of Dependent Adult Abuse
EA-150-INFO	7/1/2008	Can a Restraining Order To Prevent Elder or Dependent Adult Abuse Help Me? *(formerly EA-150)*
EA-151-INFO	1/1/2007	How Can I Respond to a Request for Orders to Stop Elder or Dependent Adult Abuse?

EMERGENCY PROTECTIVE ORDER

EPO-001*	1/1/2007	Emergency Protective Order (CLETS—EPO) (Domestic Violence, Child Abuse, Elder or Dependent Adult Abuse, or Stalking)
EPO-001* C	1/1/2004	Emergency Protective Order (CLETS) (Domestic Violence, Child Abuse, Elder or Dependent Adult Abuse, or Stalking (Workplace Violence, Civil Harassment))—Chinese
EPO-001* K	1/1/2004	Emergency Protective Order (CLETS) (Domestic Violence, Child Abuse, Elder or Dependent Adult Abuse, or Stalking (Workplace Violence, Civil Harassment))—Korean
EPO-001* S	1/1/2004	Emergency Protective Order (CLETS) (Domestic Violence, Child Abuse, Elder or Dependent Adult Abuse, or Stalking (Workplace Violence, Civil Harassment))—Spanish
EPO-001* V	1/1/2004	Emergency Protective Order (CLETS) (Domestic Violence, Child Abuse, Elder or Dependent Adult Abuse, or Stalking (Workplace Violence, Civil Harassment))—Vietnamese

ENFORCEMENT OF JUDGMENT

EJ-001*	1/1/2008	Abstract of Judgment—Civil and Small Claims
EJ-100	1/1/2005	Acknowledgment of Satisfaction of Judgment
EJ-105	1983	Application for Entry of Judgment on Sister-State Judgment
EJ-110	1983	Notice of Entry of Judgment on Sister-State Judgment
EJ-125*	7/1/2000	Application and Order for Appearance and Examination *[same as AT-138]*
EJ-130	1/1/2006	Writ of Execution
EJ-150	1/1/2002	Notice of Levy—Enforcement of Judgment
EJ-152	1983	Memorandum of Garnishee *[same as AT-167]*

---

* Adopted for mandatory use by all courts.

EJ-155	1/1/2005	Exemptions from the Enforcement of Judgments
EJ-160	1/1/2009	Claim of Exemption (Enforcement of Judgment)
EJ-165*	1/1/2007	Financial Statement (Wage Garnishment—Enforcement of Judgment) [same as WG-007*]
EJ-170	1983	Notice of Opposition to Claim of Exemption
EJ-175	1/1/2007	Notice of Hearing on Claim of Exemption (Wage Garnishment—Enforcement of Judgment) [same as WG-010]
EJ-180	1985	Notice of Hearing on Right to Homestead Exemption
EJ-182	1985	Notice of Rehearing on Right to Homestead Exemption
EJ-185	1985	Notice of Lien [same as AT-180]
EJ-190	1/1/2002	Application for and Renewal of Judgment
EJ-195*	1/1/2007	Notice of Renewal of Judgment

FAMILY LAW
Dissolution, Legal Separation, Annulment

FL-100*	1/1/2005	Petition—Marriage (Family Law)
FL-103*	1/1/2005	Petition—Domestic Partnership (Family Law)
FL-105*	1/1/2009	Declaration Under Uniform Child Custody Jurisdiction and Enforcement Act (UCCJEA) [same as GC-120]
FL-105(A)*	1/1/2009	Attachment to Declaration Under Uniform Child Custody Jurisdiction and Enforcement Act (UCCJEA) [same as GC-120(A)]
FL-110*	1/1/2006	Summons (Family Law)
FL-115	1/1/2005	Proof of Service of Summons (Family Law—Uniform Parentage—Custody and Support)
FL-117	1/1/2005	Notice and Acknowledgment of Receipt (Family Law)
FL-120*	1/1/2005	Response—Marriage (Family Law)
FL-123*	1/1/2005	Response—Domestic Partnership (Family Law)
FL-130	1/1/2006	Appearance, Stipulations, and Waivers (Family Law—Uniform Parentage—Custody and Support)
FL-140*	1/1/2003	Declaration of Disclosure (Family Law)
FL-141*	1/1/2003	Declaration Regarding Service of Declaration of Disclosure (Family Law)
FL-142	1/1/2005	Schedule of Assets and Debts (Family Law)
FL-144	1/1/2007	Stipulation and Waiver of Final Declaration of Disclosure
FL-145	1/1/2006	Form Interrogatories—Family Law
FL-150*	1/1/2007	Income and Expense Declaration
FL-150* S	1/1/2008	Income and Expense Declaration (Spanish)
FL-155	1/1/2004	Financial Statement (Simplified)
FL-160*	1/1/2007	Property Declaration (Family Law)
FL-161*	1/1/2003	Continuation of Property Declaration (Family Law)
FL-165*	1/1/2005	Request to Enter Default (Family Law—Uniform Parentage)
FL-170*	1/1/2007	Declaration For Default Or Uncontested Dissolution or Legal Separation (Family Law)
FL-180*	1/1/2007	Judgment (Family Law)
FL-190*	1/1/2005	Notice of Entry of Judgment (Family Law—Uniform Parentage—Custody and Support)
FL-191*	7/1/2005	Child Support Case Registry Form
FL-191 S	7/1/2005	Child Support Case Registry Form — Spanish
FL-192	7/1/2007	Notice of Rights and Responsibilities (Health-Care Costs and Reimbursement Procedures)
FL-192 S	7/1/2007	Aviso Sobre Derechos y Responsabilidades Procedimientos relativos a costos de salud y devolución de dichos costos
FL-195	7/1/2008	Order/Notice to Withholding Income for Child Support
FL-196	7/1/2008	Instructions to Complete the Order/Notice to Withholding Income for Child Support

FAMILY LAW
Parentage Action

| FL-200 | 1/1/2003 | Petition to Establish Parental Relationships (Uniform Parentage) |
| FL-210* | 1/1/2007 | Summons (Uniform Parentage—Petition for Custody and Support) |

---

* Adopted for mandatory use by all courts.

FL-220	1/1/2006	Response to Petition to Establish Parental Relationship (Uniform Parentage)
FL-230*	1/1/2003	Declaration for Default or Uncontested Judgment (Uniform Parentage—Custody and Support)
FL-235	1/1/2003	Advisement and Waiver of Rights Re: Establishment of Parental Relationship (Uniform Parentage)
FL-240*	1/1/2003	Stipulation for Entry of Judgment Re: Establishment of Parental Relationship (Uniform Parentage)
FL-250*	1/1/2004	Judgment (Uniform Parentage—Custody and Support)
FL-260	1/1/2004	Petition for Custody and Support of Minor Children
FL-270	1/1/2004	Response to Petition for Custody and Support of Minor Children
FL-272*	1/1/2006	Notice of Motion to Set Aside Judgment of Paternity (Family Law—Government)
FL-272 S	1/1/2006	Notice of Motion to Set Aside Judgment of Paternity (Family Law—Government) (Spanish)
FL-273*	1/1/2006	Declaration in Support of Motion to Set Aside Judgment of Paternity (Family Law—Governmental)
FL-273 S	1/1/2006	Declaration in Support of Motion to Set Aside Judgment of Paternity (Family Law—Governmental) (Spanish)
FL-274	1/1/2006	Information Sheet for Completing Notice of Motion to Set Aside Judgment of Paternity (Family Law—Governmental)
FL-274 S	1/1/2006	Information Sheet for Completing Notice of Motion to Set Aside Judgment of Paternity (Family Law—Governmental) (Spanish)
FL-276*	1/1/2006	Response to Notice of Motion to Set Aside Judgment of Paternity (Family Law—Governmental)
FL-276 S	1/1/2006	Response to Notice of Motion to Set Aside Judgment of Paternity (Family Law—Governmental) (Spanish)
FL-278*	1/1/2006	Order After Hearing on Motion to Set Aside Judgment of Paternity (Family Law—Governmental)
FL-278 S	1/1/2006	Order After Hearing on Motion to Set Aside Judgment of Paternity (Family Law—Governmental) (Spanish)
FL-280*	1/1/2006	Request for Hearing and Application to Set Aside Voluntary Declaration of Paternity (Family Law—Governmental)
FL-280 S	1/1/2006	Request for Hearing and Application to Set Aside Voluntary Declaration of Paternity (Family Law—Governmental) (Spanish)
FL-281	1/1/2006	Information Sheet for Completing Request for Hearing and Application to Set Aside Voluntary Declaration of Paternity (Family Law—Governmental)
FL-281 S	1/1/2006	Information Sheet for Completing Request for Hearing and Application to Set Aside Voluntary Declaration of Paternity (Family Law—Governmental) (Spanish)
FL-285*	1/1/2006	Responsive Declaration to Application to Set Aside Voluntary Declaration of Paternity (Family Law—Governmental)
FL-285 S	1/1/2006	Responsive Declaration to Application to Set Aside Voluntary Declaration of Paternity (Family Law—Governmental) (Spanish)
FL-290*	1/1/2006	Order After Hearing on Motion to Set Aside Voluntary Declaration of Paternity (Family Law—Governmental)
FL-290 S	1/1/2006	Order After Hearing on Motion to Set Aside Voluntary Declaration of Paternity (Family Law—Governmental) (Spanish)

FAMILY LAW
Motions and Attachments

FL-300*	1/1/2007	Order To Show Cause
FL-301*	1/1/2007	Notice Of Motion
FL-305*	7/1/2003	Temporary Orders
FL-306*	1/1/2003	Application and Order for Reissuance of Order to Show Cause (Family Law—Governmental—Uniform Parentage—Custody and Support—Juvenile)
FL-310*	1/1/2007	Application for Order and Supporting Declaration
FL-311	7/1/2005	Child Custody and Visitation Application Attachment
FL-312*	7/1/2003	Request for Child Abduction Prevention Orders
FL-314-INFO	7/1/2008	Child Custody Information Sheet
FL-314-INFO C	7/1/2008	Child Custody Information Sheet (Chinese)

---

* Adopted for mandatory use by all courts.

FL-314-INFO K	7/1/2008	Child Custody Information Sheet (Korean)
FL-314-INFO S	7/1/2008	Child Custody Information Sheet (Spanish)
FL-314-INFO V	7/1/2008	Child Custody Information Sheet (Vietnamese)
FL-315*	1/1/2009	Application or Response to Application for Separate Trial (Family Law)
FL-318-INFO	1/1/2009	Retirement Plan Joinder—Information Sheet (Family Law)
FL-320*	1/1/2003	Responsive Declaration to Order to Show Cause or Notice of Motion
FL-322	1/1/2008	Declaration of Counsel for a Child Regarding Qualifications
FL-323	1/1/2008	Order Appointing Counsel for a Child
FL-325*	1/1/2007	Declaration of Court-Connected Child Custody Evaluator Regarding Qualifications
FL-326*	1/1/2007	Declaration of Private Child Custody Evaluator Regarding Qualifications
FL-327*	1/1/2008	Order Appointing Child Custody Evaluator
FL-330	1/1/2003	Proof of Personal Service
FL-335	1/1/2003	Proof of Service by Mail
FL-340*	7/1/2003	Findings and Order After Hearing (Family Law—Custody and Support—Uniform Parentage)
FL-341	7/1/2006	Child Custody and Visitation Order Attachment
FL-341(A)*	1/1/2003	Supervised Visitation Order
FL-341(B)*	1/1/2005	Child Abduction Prevention Order Attachment
FL-341(C)	1/1/2005	Children's Holiday Schedule Attachment
FL-341(D)	1/1/2005	Additional Provisions—Physical Custody Attachment
FL-341(E)	1/1/2005	Joint Legal Custody Attachment
FL-342(A)*	1/1/2008	Non-Guideline Child Support Findings Attachment
FL-342*	7/1/2008	Child Support Information and Order Attachment
FL-343	1/1/2005	Spousal, Partner, or Family Support Order Attachment (Family Law)
FL-344*	1/1/2007	Property Order Attachment To Findings And Order After Hearing (Family Law)
FL-345	1/1/2007	Property Order Attachment To Judgment (Family Law)
FL-347*	1/1/2009	Bifurcation of Status of Marriage or Domestic Partnership—Attachment (Family Law)
FL-348	1/1/2009	Pension Benefits—Attachment to Judgment *(Attach to form FL-180)*
FL-350*	7/1/2008	Stipulation to Establish or Modify Child Support and Order
FL-355	1/1/2004	Stipulation and Order for Custody and/or Visitation of Children
FL-360*	1/1/2007	Request For Hearing And Application To Set Aside Support Order Under Family Code Section 3691
FL-365*	1/1/2003	Responsive Declaration to Application to Set Aside Support Order
FL-367*	1/1/2003	Order After Hearing on Motion to Set Aside Support Order
FL-370*	1/1/2003	Pleading on Joinder—Employees Benefit Plan
FL-371*	1/1/2003	Notice of Motion and Declaration for Joinder
FL-372*	1/1/2003	Request for Joinder of Employee Benefit Plan Order
FL-373*	1/1/2003	Responsive Declaration to Motion for Joinder and Consent Order of Joinder
FL-374*	1/1/2003	Notice of Appearance and Response of Employee Benefit Plan
FL-375*	1/1/2003	Summons (Joinder)
FL-380*	1/1/2003	Application for Expedited Child Support Order
FL-381*	1/1/2003	Response to Application for Expedited Child Support Order and Notice of Hearing
FL-382*	1/1/2003	Expedited Child Support Order
FL-390*	1/1/2003	Notice of Motion and Motion for Simplified Modification of Order for Child, Spousal, or Family Support
FL-391	7/1/2008	Information Sheet—Simplified Way to Change Child, Spousal, or Family Support
FL-392*	1/1/2003	Responsive Declaration to Motion for Simplified Modification of Order for Child, Spousal, or Family Support
FL-393	7/1/2008	Information Sheet—How to Oppose a Request to Change Child, Spousal, or Family Support
FL-395*	1/1/2003	Ex Parte Application for Restoration of Former Name After Entry of Judgment and Order (Family Law)
FL-396*	1/1/2003	Request for Production of an Income and Expense Declaration After Judgment
FL-397*	1/1/2003	Request for Income and Benefit Information From Employer

---

* Adopted for mandatory use by all courts.

| FL-398* | 12/2/2005 | Notice of Activation of Military Service and Deployment and Request to Modify a Support Order |

FAMILY LAW
Enforcement

FL-400*	1/1/2003	Order for Child Support Security Deposit and Evidence of Deposit
FL-401*	1/1/2003	Application for Disbursement and Order for Disbursement From Child Support Security Deposit
FL-410*	1/1/2003	Order to Show Cause and Affidavit for Contempt
FL-411*	1/1/2003	Affidavit of Facts Constituting Contempt (Financial and Injunctive Orders)
FL-412*	1/1/2003	Affidavit of Facts Constituting Contempt (Domestic Violence/Custody and Visitation)
FL-415	7/1/2003	Findings and Order Regarding Contempt (Family Law—Domestic Violence Prevention—Uniform Parentage—Governmental)
FL-420*	1/1/2003	Declaration of Payment History (Family Law—Governmental—Uniform Parentage Act)
FL-421	7/1/2003	Payment History Attachment (Family Law—Governmental—Uniform Parentage Act)
FL-430*	1/1/2003	Ex Parte Application for Earnings Assignment Order
FL-435*	1/1/2005	Earnings Assignment Order for Spousal or Partner Support (Family Law)
FL-440	1/1/2003	Statement for Registration of California Support Order
FL-450*	7/1/2008	Request for Hearing Regarding Earnings Assignment (Family Law—Governmental—UIFSA)
FL-455*	1/1/2003	Stay of Service of Earnings Assignment and Order
FL-460	1/1/2003	Qualified Domestic Relations Order for Support (Earnings Assignment Order for Support)
FL-461	1/1/2003	Attachment to Qualified Domestic Relations Order for Support (Earnings Assignment Order for Support)
FL-470*	1/1/2007	Application And Order For Health Insurance Coverage
FL-475*	1/1/2003	Employer's Health Insurance Return
FL-478*	1/1/2007	Request And Notice Of Hearing Regarding Health Insurance Assignment
FL-478-INFO	1/1/2007	Information Sheet And Instructions For Request And Notice Of Hearing Regarding Health Insurance Assignment
FL-480*	1/1/2003	Abstract of Support Judgment
FL-485*	1/1/2003	Notice of Delinquency
FL-490*	7/1/2003	Application to Determine Arrearages

FAMILY LAW
Interstate Actions

FL-500	1/1/2008	*[Revoked]* Uniform Support Petition
FL-505	1/1/2008	*[Revoked]* Child Support Enforcement Transmittal #1—Initial Request
FL-510*	1/1/2003	Summons (UIFSA)
FL-511*	1/1/2003	Ex Parte Application for Order for Nondisclosure of Address and Order (UIFSA)
FL-515*	1/1/2003	Order to Show Cause (UIFSA)
FL-520*	1/1/2003	Response to Uniform Support Petition (UIFSA)
FL-525	1/1/2008	*[Revoked]* Affidavit in Support of Establishing Paternity
FL-526	1/1/2008	*[Revoked]* General Testimony
FL-530*	7/1/2005	Judgment Regarding Parental Obligations (UIFSA)
FL-556	1/1/2008	*[Revoked]* Registration Statement
FL-557	1/1/2008	*[Revoked]* Child Support Enforcement Transmittal #2—Subsequent Actions
FL-558	1/1/2008	*[Revoked]* Locate Data Sheet
FL-559	1/1/2008	*[Revoked]* Child Support Enforcement Transmittal #3—Request for Assistance/Discovery
FL-560*	1/1/2003	Ex Parte Application for Transfer and Order (UIFSA)
FL-570	1/1/2003	Notice of Registration of Out-of-State Support Order
FL-571	1/1/2008	*[Revoked]* Notice of Determination of Controlling Order

* Adopted for mandatory use by all courts.

FL-575*	7/1/2007	Request for Hearing Regarding Registration of Support Order
FL-580	1/1/2006	Registration of Out-of-State Custody Order
FL-585	1/1/2003	Request for Hearing Regarding Registration of Out-of-State Custody Decree

FAMILY LAW
Governmental Child Support

FL-600*	1/1/2007	Summons and Complaint or Supplemental Complaint Regarding Parental Obligations (Governmental)
FL-605*	1/1/2007	Notice And Acknowledgment Of Receipt (Governmental)
FL-610*	1/1/2003	Answer to Complaint or Supplemental Complaint Regarding Parental Obligations (Governmental)
FL-611	1/1/2003	Information Sheet for Service of Process
FL-615*	1/1/2009	Stipulation for Judgment or Supplemental Judgment Regarding Parental Obligations and Judgment (Governmental)
FL-615 C*	1/1/2009	Stipulation for Judgment or Supplemental Judgment Regarding Parental Obligations and Judgment (Governmental) (Chinese)
FL-615 K*	1/1/2009	Stipulation for Judgment or Supplemental Judgment Regarding Parental Obligations and Judgment (Governmental) (Korean)
FL-615 S*	1/1/2009	Stipulation for Judgment or Supplemental Judgment Regarding Parental Obligations and Judgment (Governmental) (Spanish)
FL-615 T*	1/1/2009	Stipulation for Judgment or Supplemental Judgment Regarding Parental Obligations and Judgment (Governmental) (Tagalog)
FL-615 V*	1/1/2009	Stipulation for Judgment or Supplemental Judgment Regarding Parental Obligations and Judgment (Governmental) (Vietnamese)
FL-616*	1/1/2003	Declaration for Amended Proposed Judgment (Governmental)
FL-618*	1/1/2008	Request for Dismissal (Governmental, UIFSA)
FL-618* S	1/1/2008	Request for Dismissal (Governmental, UIFSA) (Spanish)
FL-620*	1/1/2005	Request to Enter Default Judgment (Governmental)
FL-625*	1/1/2009	Stipulation and Order (Governmental)
FL-625 C*	1/1/2009	Stipulation and Order (Governmental) (Chinese)
FL-625 K*	1/1/2009	Stipulation and Order (Governmental) (Korean)
FL-625 S*	1/1/2009	Stipulation and Order (Governmental) (Spanish)
FL-625 T*	1/1/2009	Stipulation and Order (Governmental) (Tagalog)
FL-625 V*	1/1/2009	Stipulation and Order (Governmental) (Vietnamese)
FL-626	1/1/2009	Stipulation and Order Waiving Unassigned Arrears (Governmental)
FL-626 C	1/1/2009	Stipulation and Order Waiving Unassigned Arrears (Governmental) (Chinese)
FL-626 K	1/1/2009	Stipulation and Order Waiving Unassigned Arrears (Governmental) (Korean)
FL-626 S	1/1/2009	Stipulation and Order Waiving Unassigned Arrears (Governmental) (Spanish)
FL-626 T	1/1/2009	Stipulation and Order Waiving Unassigned Arrears (Governmental) (Tagalog)
FL-626 V	1/1/2009	Stipulation and Order Waiving Unassigned Arrears (Governmental) (Vietnamese)
FL-627*	1/1/2003	Order for Genetic (Parentage) Testing
FL-630*	7/1/2008	Judgment Regarding Parental Obligations (Governmental)
FL-632*	7/1/2008	Notice Regarding Payment of Support (Governmental)
FL-635*	7/1/2004	Notice of Entry of Judgment and Proof of Service by Mail (Governmental)
FL-640*	1/1/2005	Notice and Motion to Cancel (Set Aside) Support Order Based on Presumed Income (Governmental)
FL-643	1/1/2007	Declaration Of Obligor's Income During Judgment Period—Presumed Income Set—Aside Request
FL-645*	1/1/2003	Notice to Local Child Support Agency of Intent to Take Independent Action to Enforce Support Order (Governmental)
FL-646*	1/1/2003	Response of Local Child Support Agency to Notice of Intent to Take Independent Action to Enforce Support Order (Governmental)
FL-650*	1/1/2003	Statement for Registration of California Support Order (Governmental)
FL-651*	1/1/2004	Notice of Registration of California Support Order (Governmental)
FL-660*	1/1/2003	Ex Parte Motion by Local Child Support Agency and Declaration for Joinder of Other Parent (Governmental)

---

* Adopted for mandatory use by all courts.

FL-661	1/1/2003	Notice of Motion and Declaration for Joinder of Other Parent in Governmental Action (Governmental)
FL-662*	7/1/2005	Responsive Declaration to Motion for Joinder of Other Parent—Consent Order of Joinder (Governmental)
FL-663*	1/1/2009	Stipulation and Order for Joinder of Other Parent (Governmental)
FL-663 C*	1/1/2009	Stipulation and Order for Joinder of Other Parent (Governmental) (Chinese)
FL-663 K*	1/1/2009	Stipulation and Order for Joinder of Other Parent (Governmental) (Korean)
FL-663 S*	1/1/2009	Stipulation and Order for Joinder of Other Parent (Governmental) (Spanish)
FL-663 T*	1/1/2009	Stipulation and Order for Joinder of Other Parent (Governmental) (Tagalog)
FL-663 V*	1/1/2009	Stipulation and Order for Joinder of Other Parent (Governmental) (Vietnamese)
FL-665*	7/1/2008	Findings and Recommendation of Commissioner (Governmental)
FL-666*	1/1/2003	Notice of Objection (Governmental)
FL-667*	1/1/2003	Review of Commissioner's Findings of Fact and Recommendation (Governmental)
FL-670*	1/1/2003	Notice of Motion for Judicial Review of License Denial (Governmental)
FL-675*	1/1/2003	Order After Judicial Review of License Denial (Governmental)
FL-676*	1/1/2003	Request for Judicial Determination of Support Arrearages (Governmental)
FL-677*	1/1/2007	Notice Of Opposition And Notice Of Motion On Claim Of Exemption (Governmental)
FL-678*	1/1/2003	Order Determining Claim of Exemption or Third-Party Claim (Governmental)
FL-679*	1/1/2008	Request for Telephone Appearance (Governmental)
FL-679* S	1/1/2008	Request for Telephone Appearance (Governmental) (Spanish)
FL-679-INFO*	1/1/2008	Information Sheet—Request for Telephone Appearance (Governmental)
FL-679-INFO S	1/1/2008	Information Sheet—Request for Telephone Appearance (Governmental) (Spanish)
FL-680*	7/1/2005	Notice of Motion (Governmental)
FL-681	7/1/2005	Clerk Calendar Cover Sheet (For Court Clerk Use Only)
FL-683*	7/1/2005	Order to Show Cause (Governmental)
FL-684*	7/1/2008	Request for Order and Supporting Declaration (Governmental)
FL-685*	1/1/2003	Response to Governmental Notice of Motion or Order to Show Cause (Governmental)
FL-687*	7/1/2008	Order After Hearing (Governmental)
FL-688*	7/1/2005	Short Form Order After Hearing (Governmental)
FL-692*	1/1/2008	Minutes and Order or Judgment (Governmental)
FL-692 S	1/1/2005	Minutes and Order or Judgment (Governmental)—Spanish
FL-693	1/1/2003	Guideline Findings Attachment (Governmental)
FL-694	1/1/2003	Advisement and Waiver of Rights for Stipulation (Governmental)
FL-697*	1/1/2003	Declaration for Default or Uncontested Judgment (Governmental)

FAMILY LAW
Summary Dissolutions

FL-800*	1/1/2008	Joint Petition for Summary Dissolution of Marriage (Family Law—Summary Dissolution)
FL-810*	1/1/2008	Summary Dissolution Information
FL-810* S	1/1/2008	Summary Dissolution Information (Spanish)
FL-820*	1/1/2003	Request for Judgment, Judgment of Dissolution of Marriage, and Notice of Entry of Judgment (Family Law—Summary Dissolution)
FL-830*	1/1/2003	Notice of Revocation of Petition for Summary Dissolution (Family Law—Summary Dissolution)

FAMILY LAW
Miscellaneous

FL-910	1/1/2009	Request of Minor to Marry (Family Law)
FL-915	1/1/2009	Order on Request of Minor to Marry (Family Law)
FL-920	1/1/2003	Notice of Consolidation
FL-935	1/1/2008	Application and Order for Appointment of Guardian Ad Litem of Minor—Family Law

---

* Adopted for mandatory use by all courts.

FL-940	1/1/2003	Office of the Family Law Facilitator Disclosure
FL-940 C	1/1/2003	Office of the Family Law Facilitator Disclosure—Chinese
FL-940 K	1/1/2003	Office of the Family Law Facilitator Disclosure—Korean
FL-940 S	1/1/2003	Office of the Family Law Facilitator Disclosure—Spanish
FL-940 V	1/1/2003	Office of the Family Law Facilitator Disclosure—Vietnamese
FL-945	1/1/2003	Family Law Information Center Disclosure
FL-950*	7/1/2003	Notice of Limited Scope Representation
FL-955	1/1/2007	Application to Be Relieved as Counsel Upon Completion of Limited Scope Representation
FL-956	1/1/2007	Objection to Application to Be Relieved as Counsel Upon Completion of Limited Scope Representation
FL-958	1/1/2007	Order on Application to Be Relieved as Counsel Upon Completion of Limited Scope Representation
FL-960*	1/1/2003	Notice of Withdrawal of Attorney of Record
FL-970*	1/1/2003	Request and Declaration for Final Judgment of Dissolution of Marriage (Family Law)

FEE WAIVER

FW-001-INFO*	2/13/2008	Information Sheet on Waiver of Court Fees and Costs (California Rules of Court, rules 3.50–3.63)
FW-001*	7/1/2007	Application for Waiver of Court Fees and Costs (Fee Waiver)
FW-002*	1/1/2007	Application for Waiver of Additional Court Fees and Costs (formerly 982(a)(20))
FW-003*	1/1/2007	Order on Application for Waiver of Court Fees and Costs (In Forma Pauperis) (formerly 982(a)(18))
FW-004*	1/1/2007	Order On Application For Waiver Of Additional Court Fees And Costs (formerly 982(a)(18.1))
FW-005*	1/1/2007	Notice of Waiver of Court Fees and Costs (formerly 982(a)(19))

IGNITION INTERLOCK

ID-100	7/1/2008	Order to Install Ignition Interlock Device (Ignition Interlock Device)
ID-110	7/1/2005	Ignition Interlock Installation Verification (Ignition Interlock Device)
ID-120	7/1/2005	Ignition Interlock Calibration Verification and Tamper Report (Ignition Interlock Device)
ID-130	1/1/2000	Ignition Interlock Noncompliance Report
ID-140	7/1/2008	Ignition Interlock Removal and Modification to Probation Order (Ignition Interlock Device)
ID-150	7/1/2005	Notice to Employers of Ignition Interlock Restriction (Ignition Interlock Device)

INDIAN CHILD WELFARE ACT

ICWA-005-INFO	1/1/2008	Information Sheet on Indian Child Inquiry Attachment and Notice of Child Custody Proceeding for Indian Child
ICWA-005-INFO S	1/1/2008	Information Sheet on Indian Child Inquiry Attachment and Notice of Child Custody Proceeding for Indian Child (Spanish)
ICWA-010(A)*	1/1/2008	Indian Child Inquiry Attachment
ICWA-010(A)* S	1/1/2008	Indian Child Inquiry Attachment (Spanish)
ICWA-020*	1/1/2008	Parental Notification of Indian Status
ICWA-020* S	1/1/2008	Parental Notification of Indian Status (Spanish)
ICWA-030*	1/1/2008	Notice of Child Custody Proceeding for Indian Child
ICWA-030* S	1/1/2008	Notice of Child Custody Proceeding for Indian Child (Spanish)
ICWA-030(A)	1/1/2008	Attachment to Notice of Child Custody Proceeding for Indian Child (Indian Child Welfare Act)
ICWA-030(A) S	1/1/2008	Attachment to Notice of Child Custody Proceeding for Indian Child (Indian Child Welfare Act) (Spanish)
ICWA-040	1/1/2008	Notice of Designation of Tribal Representative and Notice of Intervention in a Court Proceeding Involving an Indian Child

* Adopted for mandatory use by all courts.

| ICWA-050 | 1/1/2008 | Notice of Petition and Petition to Transfer Case Involving an Indian Child to Tribal Jurisdiction |
| ICWA-060 | 1/1/2008 | Order on Petition to Transfer Case Involving an Indian Child to Tribal Jurisdiction |

INTERPRETER

INT-001*	1/1/2009	Semiannual Report to the Judicial Council on the Use of Noncertified or Nonregistered Interpreters
INT-002(A)*	1/1/2009	Semiannual Report to the Judicial Council on the Use of Nonregistered Interpreters (Attachment to INT-001)
INT-100-INFO*	1/1/2009	Procedures and Guidelines to Appoint a Noncertified or Nonregistered Interpreter in Criminal and Juvenile Delinquency Proceedings
INT-110*	1/1/2009	Qualifications of a Noncertified or Nonregistered Interpreter (Provisional Qualification by Order of Presiding Judge)
INT-120*	1/1/2009	Certification of Unavailability of Certified or Registered Interpreter
INT-200	7/1/2008	Foreign Language Interpreter's Duties—Civil and Small Claims (For Noncertified and Nonregistered Interpreters)

JUVENILE LAW

JV-050	1/1/1999	Information for Parents (Juvenile Dependency)
JV-050 C	1/1/1999	Information for Parents (Juvenile Dependency)—Chinese
JV-050 CM	1/1/1999	Information for Parents (Juvenile Dependency)—Cambodian
JV-050 H	1/1/1999	Information for Parents (Juvenile Dependency)—Hmong
JV-050 K	1/1/1999	Information for Parents (Juvenile Dependency)—Korean
JV-050 R	1/1/1999	Information for Parents (Juvenile Dependency)—Russian
JV-050 S	1/1/1999	Information for Parents (Juvenile Dependency)—Spanish
JV-050 V	1/1/1999	Information for Parents (Juvenile Dependency)—Vietnamese
JV-055	1/1/2001	Juvenile Court—The Dependency Court: How It Works
JV-055 C	1/1/2001	Juvenile Court—The Dependency Court: How It Works—Chinese
JV-055 CM	1/1/2001	Juvenile Court—The Dependency Court: How It Works—Cambodian
JV-055 H	1/1/2001	Juvenile Court—The Dependency Court: How It Works—Hmong
JV-055 K	1/1/2001	Juvenile Court—The Dependency Court: How It Works—Korean
JV-055 R	1/1/2001	Juvenile Court—The Dependency Court: How It Works—Russian
JV-055 S	1/1/2001	Juvenile Court—The Dependency Court: How It Works—Spanish
JV-055 V	1/1/2001	Juvenile Court—The Dependency Court: How It Works—Vietnamese
JV-060	1/1/2006	Juvenile Court—Information for Parents
JV-060 C	1/1/2000	Information for Parents—Chinese
JV-060 CM	1/1/2000	Information for Parents—Cambodian
JV-060 H	1/1/2000	Information for Parents—Hmong
JV-060 K	1/1/2000	Information for Parents—Korean
JV-060 R	1/1/2000	Information for Parents—Russian
JV-060 S	1/1/2006	Juvenile Court—Information for Parents—Spanish
JV-060 V	1/1/2000	Information for Parents—Vietnamese
JV-100*	7/1/2008	Juvenile Dependency Petition (Version One)
JV-100* S	7/1/2008	Juvenile Dependency Petition (Version One) (Spanish)
JV-101*	1/1/2007	Additional Children Attachment (Juvenile Dependency Petition)
JV-101* S	1/1/2007	Additional Children Attachment (Juvenile Dependency Petition)—Spanish
JV-101(A)*	1/1/2008	Additional Children Attachment—Juvenile Dependency Petition
JV-101(A)* S	1/1/2008	Additional Children Attachment—Juvenile Dependency Petition (Spanish)
JV-110*	1/1/2008	Juvenile Dependency Petition (Version Two) (Welfare and Institutions Code, § 300 et seq.)
JV-110* S	1/1/2008	Juvenile Dependency Petition (Version Two) (Welfare and Institutions Code, § 300 et seq.) (Spanish)
JV-120	1/1/2007	Serious Physical Harm (§ 300(a))
JV-120 S	1/1/2007	Serious Physical Harm (§ 300(a))—Spanish
JV-121	1/1/2007	Failure to Protect (§ 300(b))
JV-121 S	1/1/2007	Failure to Protect (§ 300(b))—Spanish
JV-122	1/1/2007	Serious Emotional Damage (§ 300(c))
JV-122 S	1/1/2007	Serious Emotional Damage (§ 300(c))—Spanish

---

* Adopted for mandatory use by all courts.

JV-123*	1/1/2007	Sexual Abuse (§ 300(d))
JV-123* S	1/1/2007	Sexual Abuse (§ 300(d))—Spanish
JV-124	1/1/2007	Severe Physical Abuse (§ 300(e))
JV-124 S	1/1/2007	Severe Physical Abuse (§ 300(e))—Spanish
JV-125	1/1/2007	Caused Another Child's Death Through Abuse or Neglect (§ 300(f))
JV-125 S	1/1/2007	Caused Another Child's Death Through Abuse or Neglect (§ 300(f))— Spanish
JV-126	1/1/2007	No Provision for Support (§ 300(g))
JV-126 S	1/1/2007	No Provision for Support (§ 300(g))—Spanish
JV-127	1/1/2007	Freed for Adoption (§ 300(h))
JV-127 S	1/1/2007	Freed for Adoption (§ 300(h))—Spanish
JV-128	1/1/2007	Cruelty (§ 300(i))
JV-128 S	1/1/2007	Cruelty (§ 300(i))—Spanish
JV-129	1/1/2007	Abuse of Sibling (§ 300(i))
JV-129 S	1/1/2007	Abuse of Sibling (§ 300(i))—Spanish
JV-130*	1/1/2008	*[Revoked]* Parental Notification of Indian Status (Juvenile Court)
JV-135*	1/1/2008	*[Revoked]* Notice of Involuntary Child Custody Proceedings for an Indian Child (Juvenile Court)
JV-140*	1/1/2007	Notification of Mailing Address
JV-140* S	1/1/2007	Notification of Mailing Address—Spanish
JV-150*	1/1/2007	Supplemental Petition for More Restrictive Placement (Attachment) (Welfare and Institutions Code, § 387)
JV-150* S	1/1/2007	Supplemental Petition for More Restrictive Placement (Attachment) (Welfare and Institutions Code, § 387)—Spanish
JV-180*	1/1/2009	Request to Change Court Order
JV-180 S*	1/1/2009	Request to Change Court Order (Spanish)
JV-182*	1/1/2007	Confidential Information (Request to Change Court Order)
JV-183*	1/1/2009	Court Order on Form JV-180, *Request to Change Court Order*
JV-184*	1/1/2009	Order After Hearing on Form JV-180, *Request to Change Court Order*
JV-185	7/1/2006	Child's Information Sheet—Request to Change Court Order (Welf. & Inst. Code, §§ 353.1, 388)
JV-190*	1/1/2007	Waiver of Rights—Juvenile Dependency
JV-190* S	1/1/2007	Waiver of Rights—Juvenile Dependency—Spanish
JV-195*	7/1/1998	Waiver of Reunification Services
JV-195 S	7/1/1998	Waiver of Reunification Services—Spanish
JV-200*	7/1/2007	Custody Order—Juvenile—Final Judgment
JV-200* S	7/1/2007	Custody Order—Juvenile—Final Judgment—Spanish
JV-205*	1/1/2007	Visitation Order—Juvenile
JV-205* S	1/1/2007	Visitation Order—Juvenile—Spanish
JV-210	1/1/2001	Application to Commence Proceedings by Affidavit and Decision by Social Worker (Welf. & Inst. Code, §329)
JV-210 S	1/1/2001	Application to Commence Proceedings by Affidavit and Decision by Social Worker (Welf. & Inst. Code, §329)—Spanish
JV-215	1/1/2001	Application to Review Decision by Social Worker Not to Commence Proceedings (Welf. & Inst. Code, §331)
JV-215 S	1/1/2001	Application to Review Decision by Social Worker Not to Commence Proceedings (Welf. & Inst. Code, §331)—Spanish
JV-219-INFO*	1/1/2009	Information About Psychotropic Medication Forms
JV-219-INFO S*	1/1/2009	Information About Psychotropic Medication Forms (Spanish)
JV-220*	1/1/2008	Application Regarding Psychotropic Medication
JV-220* S	1/1/2008	Application Regarding Psychotropic Medication (Spanish)
JV-220A*	1/1/2008	*[Revoked]* Opposition To Application For Order For Authorization To Administer Psychotropic Medication—Juvenile
JV-220(A)*	1/1/2008	Prescribing Physician's Statement—Attachment
JV-220(A)* S	1/1/2008	Prescribing Physician's Statement—Attachment (Spanish)
JV-221*	1/1/2008	Proof of Notice: Application Regarding Psychotropic Medication
JV-221* S	1/1/2008	Proof of Notice: Application Regarding Psychotropic Medication (Spanish)
JV-222*	1/1/2008	Opposition to Application Regarding Psychotropic Medication
JV-222* S	1/1/2008	Opposition to Application Regarding Psychotropic Medication (Spanish)
JV-223*	1/1/2008	Order Regarding Application for Psychotropic Medication
JV-223* S	1/1/2008	Order Regarding Application for Psychotropic Medication (Spanish)

* Adopted for mandatory use by all courts.

JV-224*	1/1/2007	Order Regarding Eligibility for Special Immigrant Juvenile Status
JV-225*	1/1/2008	Your Child's Health and Education
JV-225* S	1/1/2008	Your Child's Health and Education (Spanish)
JV-245*	1/1/2007	Application and Affidavit for Restraining Order—Juvenile
JV-245* S	1/1/2007	Application and Affidavit for Restraining Order—Juvenile—Spanish
JV-250*	7/1/2006	Restraining Order—Juvenile (CLETS—JUV)
JV-251*	1/1/2003	Application and Order for Reissuance of Order to Show Cause (Family Law—Governmental—Uniform Parentage—Custody and Support—Juvenile)
JV-251 S	1/1/2003	Application and Order for Reissuance of Order to Show Cause (Family Law—Governmental—Uniform Parentage—Custody and Support—Juvenile)—Spanish
JV-252	1/1/2003	Proof of Firearms Turned In or Sold (Domestic Violence Prevention)
JV-252 C	1/1/2003	Proof of Firearms Turned In or Sold (Domestic Violence Prevention)—Chinese
JV-252 K	1/1/2003	Proof of Firearms Turned In or Sold (Domestic Violence Prevention)—Korean
JV-252 S	1/1/2003	Proof of Firearms Turned In or Sold (Domestic Violence Prevention)—Spanish
JV-252 V	1/1/2003	Proof of Firearms Turned In or Sold (Domestic Violence Prevention)—Vietnamese
JV-280*	1/1/2007	Notice of Review Hearing
JV-280* S	1/1/2007	Notice of Review Hearing—Spanish
JV-290	10/1/2007	Caregiver Information Form
JV-290-INFO	10/1/2007	Instruction Sheet for Caregiver Information Form
JV-290 C	10/1/2007	Caregiver Information Form (Chinese)
JV-290-INFO C	10/1/2007	Instruction Sheet for Caregiver Information Form (Chinese)
JV-290 K	10/1/2007	Caregiver Information Form (Korean)
JV-290-INFO K	10/1/2007	Instruction Sheet for Caregiver Information Form (Korean)
JV-290 S	10/1/2007	Caregiver Information Form (Spanish)
JV-290-INFO S	10/1/2007	Instruction Sheet for Caregiver Information Form (Spanish)
JV-290 V	10/1/2007	Caregiver Information Form (Vietnamese)
JV-290-INFO V	10/1/2007	Instruction Sheet for Caregiver Information Form (Vietnamese)
JV-295*	1/1/2007	De Facto Parent Request
JV-295* S	1/1/2007	De Facto Parent Request—Spanish
JV-296*	1/1/2007	De Facto Parent Statement
JV-296* S	1/1/2007	De Facto Parent Statement—Spanish
JV-297*	1/1/2007	De Facto Parent Order
JV-297* S	1/1/2007	De Facto Parent Order—Spanish
JV-298*	1/1/2007	Order Ending De Facto Parent Status
JV-298* S	1/1/2007	Order Ending De Facto Parent Status—Spanish
JV-299	1/1/2007	De Facto Parent Pamphlet
JV-299 C	1/1/2007	De Facto Parent Pamphlet—Chinese
JV-299 K	1/1/2007	De Facto Parent Pamphlet—Korean
JV-299 S	1/1/2007	De Facto Parent Pamphlet—Spanish
JV-299 V	1/1/2007	De Facto Parent Pamphlet—Vietnamese
JV-300*	1/1/2007	Notice of Hearing on Selection of a Permanent Plan
JV-300* S	1/1/2007	Notice of Hearing on Selection of a Permanent Plan—Spanish
JV-305*	1/1/2007	Citation for Publication Under Welfare and Institutions Code Section 294
JV-305* S	1/1/2007	Citation for Publication Under Welfare and Institutions Code Section 294—Spanish
JV-310*	1/1/2007	Proof of Service Under Section 366.26 of the Welfare and Institutions Code
JV-310* S	1/1/2007	Proof of Service Under Section 366.26 of the Welfare and Institutions Code—Spanish
JV-320*	1/1/2009	Orders Under Welfare and Institutions Code Sections 366.26, 727.3, 727.31
JV-320 S*	1/1/2009	Orders Under Welfare and Institutions Code Sections 366.26, 727.3, 727.31 (Spanish)
JV-321*	1/1/2008	Request for Prospective Adoptive Parent Designation
JV-322*	1/1/2007	Confidential Information—Prospective Adoptive Parent
JV-323*	1/1/2008	Notice of Intent to Remove Child
JV-324*	1/1/2008	Notice of Emergency Removal
JV-325*	1/1/2008	*[Revoked]* Proof of Notice of Hearing

---

* Adopted for mandatory use by all courts.

JV-325*	1/1/2008	Objection to Removal
JV-325-INFO	1/1/2008	*[Revoked]* Instructions for Notice of Prospective Adoptive Parent Hearing
JV-326*	1/1/2008	Proof of Notice
JV-326-INFO	1/1/2008	Instructions for Notice of Prospective Adoptive Parent Hearing
JV-327*	1/1/2008	Prospective Adoptive Parent Designation Order
JV-328*	1/1/2008	Prospective Adoptive Parent Order After Hearing
JV-330*	7/1/2006	Letters of Guardianship (Juvenile)
JV-330 S	7/1/1999	Letters of Guardianship (Juvenile)—Spanish *(formerly JV-325)*
JV-350*	1/1/2001	Guardianship Pamphlet
JV-350 C	1/1/2001	Guardianship Pamphlet—Chinese
JV-350 K	1/1/2001	Guardianship Pamphlet—Korean
JV-350 S	1/1/2001	Guardianship Pamphlet—Spanish
JV-350 V	1/1/2001	Guardianship Pamphlet—Vietnamese
JV-364*	1/1/2007	Termination of Dependency
JV-364* S	1/1/2007	Termination of Dependency—Spanish
JV-365*	1/1/2008	Termination of Dependency Jurisdiction—Child Attaining Age of Majority (Juvenile)
JV-365* S	1/1/2008	Termination of Dependency Jurisdiction—Child Attaining Age of Majority (Juvenile) (Spanish)
JV-400	1/1/2007	Visitation Attachment: Parent, Legal Guardian, Indian Custodian, Other Important Person
JV-401	1/1/2007	Visitation Attachment: Sibling
JV-402	1/1/2007	Visitation Attachment: Grandparent
JV-405	1/1/2007	Continuance—Detention Hearing
JV-406	1/1/2007	Continuance—General
JV-410	1/1/2007	Findings and Orders After Detention Hearing (Welf. & Inst. Code, § 319)
JV-412	1/1/2007	Findings and Orders After Jurisdictional Hearing (Welf. & Inst. Code, § 356)
JV-415	1/1/2007	Findings and Orders After Dispositional Hearing (Welf. & Inst. Code, § 361 et seq.)
JV-416	1/1/2007	Dispositional Attachment: Dismissal of Petition With or Without Informal Supervision (Welf. & Inst. Code, § 360(b))
JV-417	1/1/2007	Dispositional Attachment: In-Home Placement With Formal Supervision (Welf. & Inst. Code, § 361)
JV-418	1/1/2007	Dispositional Attachment: Appointment of Guardian (Welf. & Inst. Code, § 360(a))
JV-419	1/1/2007	Guardianship (Juvenile)—Consent and Waiver of Rights
JV-419A	1/1/2007	Guardianship (Juvenile)—Child's Consent and Waiver of Rights
JV-420	1/1/2007	Dispositional Attachment: Removal From Custodial Parent—Placement With Previously Noncustodial Parent (Welf. & Inst. Code, §§ 361, 361.2)
JV-421	1/1/2007	Dispositional Attachment: Removal From Custodial Parent—Placement With Nonparent (Welf. & Inst. Code, §§ 361, 361.2)
JV-425	1/1/2007	Findings and Orders After In-Home Status Review Hearing (Welf. & Inst. Code, § 364)
JV-426	1/1/2007	Findings and Orders After In-Home Status Review Hearing—Child Placed With Previously Noncustodial Parent (Welf. & Inst. Code, §§ 364, 366.21)
JV-430	1/1/2007	Findings and Orders After Six-Month Prepermanency Hearing (Welf. & Inst. Code, § 366.21(e))
JV-431	1/1/2007	Six-Month Prepermanency Attachment: Child Reunified (Welf. & Inst. Code, § 366.21(e))
JV-432	1/1/2007	Six-Month Prepermanency Attachment: Reunification Services Continued (Welf. & Inst. Code, § 366.21(e))
JV-433	1/1/2007	Six-Month Prepermanency Attachment: Reunification Services Terminated (Welf. & Inst. Code, § 366.21(e))
JV-435	1/1/2007	Findings and Orders After 12-Month Permanency Hearing (Welf. & Inst. Code, § 366.21(f))
JV-436	1/1/2007	Twelve-Month Permanency Attachment: Child Reunified (Welf. & Inst. Code, § 366.21(f))
JV-437	1/1/2007	Twelve-Month Permanency Attachment: Reunification Services Continued (Welf. & Inst. Code, § 366.21(f))

---

* Adopted for mandatory use by all courts.

JV-438	1/1/2007	Twelve-Month Permanency Attachment: Reunification Services Terminated (Welf. & Inst. Code, § 366.21(f))
JV-440	1/1/2007	Findings and Orders After Eighteen-Month Permanency Hearing (Welf. & Inst. Code, § 366.22)
JV-441	1/1/2007	Eighteen-Month Permanency Attachment: Child Reunified (Welf. & Inst. Code, § 366.22)
JV-442	1/1/2007	Eighteen-Month Permanency Attachment: Reunification Services Terminated (Welf. & Inst. Code, § 366.22)
JV-445	1/1/2007	Findings and Orders After Postpermanency Hearing—Parental Rights Terminated; Permanent Plan of Adoption (Welf. & Inst. Code, § 366.3(f))
JV-446	7/1/2008	Findings and Orders After Postpermanency Hearing—Permanent Plan Other Than Adoption (Welf. & Inst. Code, § 366.3)
JV-448	1/1/2006	Order Granting Authority to Consent to Medical, Surgical, and Dental Care (Welf. & Inst. Code, § 366.27)
JV-450*	7/1/2006	Order for Prisoner's Appearance at Hearing Affecting Prisoner's Parental Rights and Waiver of Appearance
JV-450 S	1/1/2006	Order for Prisoner's Appearance at Hearing Affecting Prisoner's Parental Rights and Waiver of Appearance (Spanish)
JV-500*	1/1/2007	Parentage Inquiry—Juvenile
JV-500* S	1/1/2007	Parentage Inquiry—Juvenile—Spanish
JV-501*	1/1/2007	Parentage—Findings and Judgment (Juvenile)
JV-501* S	1/1/2007	Parentage—Findings and Judgment (Juvenile)—Spanish
JV-505*	1/1/2008	Statement Regarding Parentage (Juvenile)
JV-505* S	1/1/2008	Statement Regarding Parentage (Juvenile) (Spanish)
JV-510	1/1/2007	Proof of Service—Juvenile
JV-510 S	1/1/2007	Proof of Service—Juvenile—Spanish
JV-520*	1/1/2007	Fax Filing Cover Sheet (Juvenile)
JV-520* S	1/1/2007	Fax Filing Cover Sheet (Juvenile)—Spanish
JV-525*	7/1/2007	Order to Attend Court or Provide Documents: Subpoena/Subpoena Duces Tecum (Criminal and Juvenile) *[same as CR-125*]*
JV-530*	7/1/2002	Certified Request for Pupil Records—Truancy
JV-530 S	7/1/2002	Certified Request for Pupil Records—Truancy—Spanish
JV-531*	7/1/2002	Local Educational Agency Response to JV-530
JV-531 S	7/1/2002	Local Educational Agency Response to JV-530—Spanish
JV-535*	7/1/2008	Findings and Orders Limiting Right to Make Educational Decisions for the Child, Appointing Educational Representative, and Determining Child's Educational Needs
JV-535* S	7/1/2008	Findings and Orders Limiting Right to Make Educational Decisions for the Child, Appointing Educational Representative, and Determining Child's Educational Needs (Spanish)
JV-536*	1/1/2008	Local Educational Agency Response to JV-535—Appointment of Surrogate Parent
JV-536* S	1/1/2008	Local Educational Agency Response to JV-535—Appointment of Surrogate Parent (Spanish)
JV-537	1/1/2008	Educational Representative or Surrogate Parent Information
JV-537 S	1/1/2008	Educational Representative or Surrogate Parent Information (Spanish)
JV-538	1/1/2008	Findings and Orders Regarding Transfer from School of Origin
JV-539	1/1/2008	Request for Hearing Regarding Child's Education
JV-539 S	1/1/2008	Request for Hearing Regarding Child's Education (Spanish)
JV-540*	1/1/2002	Notice of Hearing on Joinder—Juvenile
JV-540 S	1/1/2002	Notice of Hearing on Joinder—Juvenile—Spanish
JV-550*	1/1/2007	Juvenile Court Transfer Orders
JV-550* S	1/1/2007	Juvenile Court Transfer Orders — Spanish
JV-565*	1/1/2007	Findings and Request for Assistance Under Interstate Compact on the Placement of Children (ICPC)
JV-565* S	1/1/2007	Findings and Request for Assistance Under Interstate Compact on the Placement of Children (ICPC)—Spanish
JV-567*	1/1/2007	Interstate Compact on the Placement of Children Findings and Orders
JV-567* S	1/1/2007	Interstate Compact on the Placement of Children Findings and Orders—Spanish
JV-569*	1/1/2009	Proof of Service—Request for Disclosure

---

* Adopted for mandatory use by all courts.

Rules of Court

JV-570*	1/1/2009	Request for Disclosure of Juvenile Case File
JV-570 S*	1/1/2009	Request for Disclosure of Juvenile Case File (Spanish)
JV-571*	1/1/2009	Notice of Request for Disclosure of Juvenile Case File
JV-572*	1/1/2009	Objection to Release of Juvenile Case File
JV-573*	1/1/2009	Order on Request for Disclosure of Juvenile Case File
JV-574*	1/1/2009	Order After Judicial Review
JV-575*	1/1/2007	Petition to Obtain Report of Law Enforcement Agency
JV-575* S	1/1/2007	Petition to Obtain Report of Law Enforcement Agency—Spanish
JV-580*	1/1/2006	Notice to Child and Parent/Guardian RE: Release of Juvenile Police Records and Objection
JV-580 S	1/1/2006	Notice to Child and Parent/Guardian RE: Release of Juvenile Police Records and Objection (Spanish)
JV-590*	1/1/2007	Order to Seal Juvenile Records
JV-590* S	1/1/2007	Order to Seal Juvenile Records—Spanish
JV-600*	1/1/2008	Juvenile Wardship Petition
JV-600* S	1/1/2008	Juvenile Wardship Petition (Spanish)
JV-610	1/1/2007	Child Habitually Disobedient (§ 601(a))
JV-610 S	1/1/2007	Child Habitually Disobedient (§ 601(a))—Spanish
JV-611	1/1/2007	Child Habitually Truant (§ 601(b))
JV-611 S	1/1/2007	Child Habitually Truant (§ 601(b))—Spanish
JV-615*	1/1/2006	Deferred Entry of Judgment Notice of Noncompliance
JV-615* S	1/1/2006	Deferred Entry of Judgment Notice of Noncompliance—Spanish
JV-620*	1/1/2007	Violation of Law By Child
JV-620* S	1/1/2007	Violation of Law By Child—Spanish
JV-622	1/1/2006	Informal Probation Agreement
JV-624	1/1/2007	Terms and Conditions
JV-625*	1/1/2006	Notice of Hearing—Juvenile Delinquency Proceeding
JV-625* S	1/1/2006	Notice of Hearing—Juvenile Delinquency Proceeding (Spanish)
JV-635*	1/1/2006	Promise to Appear—Juvenile Delinquency (Juvenile 14 years or Older)
JV-635* S	1/1/2006	Promise to Appear—Juvenile Delinquency (Juvenile 14 years or Older) (Spanish)
JV-640*	1/1/2006	Juvenile Court Delinquency Proceeding
JV-642*	1/1/2007	Initial Appearance Hearing—Juvenile Delinquency
JV-644*	1/1/2007	Jurisdiction Hearing—Juvenile Delinquency
JV-665*	1/1/2007	Disposition—Juvenile Delinquency
JV-710*	1/1/2007	Juvenile Fitness Hearing Order (Welfare and Institutions Code, § 707)
JV-710* S	1/1/2007	Juvenile Fitness Hearing Order (Welfare and Institutions Code, § 707)—Spanish
JV-720	1/1/2008	*[Revoked]* Supplemental Petition for More Restrictive Placement (Attachment) (Welfare & Institutions Code, § 777(a))
JV-720 S	1/1/2008	*[Revoked]* Supplemental Petition for More Restrictive Placement (Attachment) Welfare and Institutions Code, §777(a)—Spanish
JV-730	1/1/2008	*[Revoked]* Supplemental Petition for Commitment for 30 Days or Less (Attachment) (Welfare & Institutions Code, § 777(b))
JV-730 S	1/1/2008	*[Revoked]* Supplemental Petition for Commitment for 30 Days or Less (Attachment) Welfare and Institutions Code, § 777(b)—Spanish
JV-732*	1/1/2009	Commitment to the California Department of Corrections and Rehabilitation, Division of Juvenile Justice
JV-732 S*	1/1/2009	Commitment to the California Department of Corrections and Rehabilitation, Division of Juvenile Justice (Spanish)
JV-735*	1/1/2007	Notice of Hearing to Modify, Change, or Set Aside Previous Orders (Welf. & Inst. Code, § 777)
JV-735* S	1/1/2007	Notice of Hearing to Modify, Change, or Set Aside Previous Orders (Welf. & Inst. Code, § 777)—Spanish
JV-740*	1/1/2007	Petition to Modify Previous Orders—Change of Circumstances
JV-740* S	1/1/2007	Petition to Modify Previous Orders—Change of Circumstances—Spanish
JV-750*	1/1/2006	Determination of Eligibility—Deferred Entry of Judgment—Juvenile
JV-750* S	1/1/2006	Determination of Eligibility— Deferred Entry of Judgment—Juvenile (Spanish)
JV-751*	1/1/2006	Citation and Written Notification for Deferred Entry of Judgment—Juvenile

---

* Adopted for mandatory use by all courts.

JV-751* S	1/1/2006	Citation and Written Notification for Deferred Entry of Judgment—Juvenile (Spanish)
JV-755*	1/1/2006	Deferred Entry of Judgment—Dismissal and Sealing of Juvenile Records
JV-755* S	1/1/2006	Deferred Entry of Judgment—Dismissal and Sealing of Juvenile Records (Spanish)
JV-760*	1/1/2007	Deferred Entry of Judgment Order
JV-790	1/1/2008	Order for Restitution and Abstract of Judgment [same as CR-110]
JV-790 S	1/1/2004	Order for Restitution and Abstract of Judgment—Spanish
JV-792	1/1/2004	Instructions: Order for Restitution and Abstract of Judgment
JV-792 S	1/1/2004	Instructions: Order for Restitution and Abstract of Judgment—Spanish
JV-794*	1/1/2006	Petition to Terminate Wardship and Order
JV-796	1/1/2009	Petition for Expungement of DNA Profiles and Samples (Pen. Code, §299) [same as CR-185]
JV-798	1/1/2009	Order for Expungement of DNA Profiles and Samples (Pen. Code, §299) [same as CR-186]
JV-800	1/1/2007	Notice of Appeal—Juvenile (California Rules of Court, Rule 8.400)
JV-800 S	1/1/2007	Notice of Appeal—Juvenile (California Rules of Court, Rule 8.400)—Spanish
JV-810	7/1/2007	Recommendation for Appointment of Appellate Attorney for Child (California Rules of Court, Rule 5.661)
JV-820	1/1/2007	Notice of Intent to File Writ Petition and Request for Record to Review Order Setting a Hearing Under Welfare and Institutions Code Section 366.26 (California Rules of Court, Rule 8.450)
JV-820 S	1/1/2007	Notice of Intent to File Writ Petition and Request for Record to Review Order Setting a Hearing Under Welfare and Institutions Code Section 366.26 (California Rules of Court, Rule 8.450)—Spanish
JV-822	1/1/2007	Notice of Intent to File Writ Petition and Request for Record to Review Order Designating or Denying Specific Placement of a Dependent Child After Termination of Parental Rights (California Rules of Court, Rule 8.454)
JV-825	1/1/2007	Petition for Extraordinary Writ (California Rules of Court, Rules 8.452, 8.456)
JV-825 S	1/1/2007	Petition for Extraordinary Writ (California Rules of Court, Rules 8.452, 8.456)—Spanish
JV-826	1/1/2007	Denial of Petition (California Rules of Court, Rules 8.452, 8.456)
JV-826 S	1/1/2007	Denial of Petition (California Rules of Court, Rules 8.452, 8.456)—Spanish
JV-828	1/1/2007	Notice of Action (California Rules of Court, Rule 8.452)
JV-828 S	1/1/2007	Notice of Action (California Rules of Court, Rule 8.452)—Spanish

JUDGMENT

| JUD-100 | 1/1/2002 | Judgment |

MISCELLANEOUS

CP10	1991	Claim of Right to Possession [Unofficial form for use by levying officers in unlawful detainer cases]
CP10.5	1991	Prejudgment Claim of Right to Possession [Unofficial form for service with summons in unlawful detainer cases]
MC-001	1/1/2004	Juror Questionnaire for Civil Cases
MC-002	7/1/2006	Juror Questionnaire for Criminal Cases/Capital Case Supplement
MC-005*	1/1/2007	Facsimile Transmission Cover Sheet (Fax Filing)
MC-010	7/1/1999	Memorandum of Costs (Summary)
MC-011	7/1/1999	Memorandum of Costs (Worksheet)
MC-012*	1/1/2000	Memorandum of Costs After Judgment, Acknowledgment of Credit, and Declaration of Accrued Interest
MC-013*	1/1/2007	Memorandum of Costs on Appeal
MC-020	1987	Additional Page [to be attached to any form]
MC-025	1/1/2007	Attachment to Judicial Council Form
MC-030	1/1/2006	Declaration
MC-031	7/1/2005	Attached Declaration
MC-040	1/1/2007	Notice of Change of Address

---

* Adopted for mandatory use by all courts.

MC-050*	1/1/2009	Substitution of Attorney—Civil (Without Court Order)
MC-051*	1/1/2007	Notice of Motion and Motion to Be Relieved as Counsel—Civil
MC-052*	1/1/2007	Declaration in Support of Attorney's Motion to Be Relieved as Counsel—Civil
MC-053*	1/1/2007	Order Granting Attorney's Motion to Be Relieved as Counsel—Civil
MC-060*	1/1/2007	Confidential Cover Sheet False Claims Action
MC-070	1/1/2007	Juror's Motion To Set Aside Sanctions And Order
MC-095*	1/1/2004	Petition and Declaration Regarding Unresolved Claims and Deposit of Undistributed Surplus Proceeds of Trustee's Sale
MC-100	7/1/1999	Petition for Order Striking and Releasing Lien, etc. (Government Employee)
MC-101	7/1/1999	Order to Show Cause (Government Employee)
MC-120*	1/1/2008	Confidential Reference List of Identifiers
MC-200	1/1/2002	Claim Opposing Forfeiture
MC-201	1/1/2009	Claim Opposing Forfeiture of Vehicle (Vehicle Code, § 14607.6)
MC-202	1995	Petition for Forfeiture of Vehicle and Notice of Hearing
MC-210	1/1/2009	Defendant's Financial Statement on Eligibility for Appointment of Counsel and Reimbursement and Record on Appeal at Public Expense
MC-265	1994	Petition for Writ of Habeas Corpus—LPS Act (Mental Health)
MC-270	1/1/2007	Petition for Writ of Habeas Corpus—Penal Commitment (Mental Health)
MC-275	1/1/2009	Petition for Writ of Habeas Corpus
MC-280	1/1/2005	Order for Commitment (Sexually Violent Predator)
MC-281	1/1/2005	Order for Extended Commitment (Sexually Violent Predator)
MC-300*	1/1/2008	Petition for Declaration of Emancipation of Minor, Order Prescribing Notice, Declaration of Emancipation, and Order Denying Petition
MC-301*	1995	Emancipation Pamphlet
MC-301 C	1995	Emancipation Pamphlet—Chinese
MC-301 K	1995	Emancipation Pamphlet—Korean
MC-301 S	1995	Emancipation Pamphlet—Spanish
MC-301 V	1995	Emancipation Pamphlet—Vietnamese
MC-305*	1994	Notice of Hearing—Emancipation of Minor
MC-306*	1/1/2007	Emancipation of Minor Income and Expense Declaration
MC-310*	1994	Declaration of Emancipation of Minor After Hearing
MC-315	1994	Emancipated Minor's Application to California Department of Motor Vehicles
MC-350*	1/1/2007	Petition to Approve Compromise of Disputed Claim or Pending Action or Disposition of Proceeds of Judgment for Minor or Adult Person With a Disability (Miscellaneous)
MC-351*	1/1/2007	Order Approving Compromise of Disputed Claim or Pending Action or Disposition of Proceeds of Judgment for Minor or Adult Person With a Disability (Miscellaneous)
MC-355*	1/1/2007	Order to Deposit Money into Blocked Account
MC-356*	1/1/2007	Receipt and Acknowledgment of Order for the Deposit of Money Into Blocked Account
MC-357*	1/1/2007	Petition for Withdrawal of Funds from Blocked Account
MC-358*	1/1/2007	Order for Withdrawal of Funds from Blocked Account
MC-360	1/1/2004	Petition to Establish Record of Death
MC-360A	1/1/2004	Declaration in Support of Petition to Establish Record of Death
MC-400	1986	Proof of Enrollment or Completion (Alcohol or Drug Program)
MC-410	1/1/2007	Request for Accommodations by Persons With Disabilities and Response
MC-500*	1/1/2007	Media Request to Photograph, Record, or Broadcast
MC-510*	1/1/2007	Order on Media Request to Permit Coverage
MC-600	1990	Petition to Determine If Dog Is Potentially Dangerous or Vicious (Menacing Dog)
MC-601	1990	Notice of Hearing (Menacing Dog)
MC-602	1990	Order After Hearing (Menacing Dog)
MC-603	1990	Notice of Appeal (Menacing Dog)
MC-700*	1997	Prefiling Order—Vexatious Litigant
MC-701	1/1/2008	Request and Order to File New Litigation by Vexatious Litigant
MC-800	1/1/2002	Court Clerks Office: Signage
MC-950*	1/1/2007	Notice of Limited Scope Representation

---

* Adopted for mandatory use by all courts.

MC-955	1/1/2007	Application to Be Relieved as Attorney on Completion of Limited Scope Representation
MC-956	1/1/2007	Objection to Application to Be Relieved as Attorney on Completion of Limited Scope Representation
MC-958	1/1/2007	Order on Application to Be Relieved as Attorney on Completion of Limited Scope Representation

NAME CHANGE

NC-100*	7/1/2007	Petition for Change of Name (Change of Name)
NC-110*	1/1/2003	Attachment to Petition for Change of Name
NC-110G*	1/1/2001	Supplemental Attachment to Petition for Change of Name (Declaration of Guardian)
NC-120*	7/1/2007	Order to Show Cause for Change of Name (Change of Name)
NC-121*	1/1/2001	Proof of Service of Order to Show Cause
NC-130*	7/1/2007	Decree Changing Name (Change of Name)
NC-130G*	7/1/2007	Decree Changing Name (Change of Name of Minor by Guardian)
NC-200*	7/1/2006	Petition for Change of Name and Gender
NC-210	7/1/2006	Declaration of Physician—Attachment to Petition (Change of Name and Gender/Change of Gender) *[same as NC-310]*
NC-220*	1/1/2003	Order to Show Cause for Change of Name and Gender
NC-230*	1/1/2003	Decree Changing Name and Gender
NC-300	7/1/2006	Petition for Change of Gender and Issuance of New Birth Certificate
NC-310	7/1/2006	Declaration of Physician—Attachment to Petition (Change of Name and Gender/Change of Gender) *[same as NC-210]*
NC-320	7/1/2006	Notice of Hearing on Petition for Change of Gender and Issuance of New Birth Certificate
NC-330	7/1/2006	Order for Change of Gender and Issuance of New Birth Certificate

NOTICE TO APPEAR AND RELATED FORMS

TR-100*	1/1/2004	Notice of Correction and Proof of Service
TR-106	1/1/2004	Continuation of Notice to Appear
TR-108	1/1/2004	Continuation of Citation
TR-115	9/20/2005	Automated Traffic Enforcement System Notice to Appear
TR-120	9/20/2005	Nontraffic Notice to Appear
TR-130	9/20/2005	Traffic/Nontraffic Notice to Appear
TR-INST	9/20/2005	Notice to Appear and Related Forms

PLEADINGS
Contract

PLD-C-001	1/1/2007	Complaint—Contract *(formerly 982.1(20))*
PLD-C-001(1)	1/1/2007	Cause of Action—Breach of Contract *(formerly 982.1(21))*
PLD-C-001(2)	1/1/2009	Cause of Action—Common Counts *(formerly 982.1(22))*
PLD-C-001(3)	1/1/2007	Cause of Action—Fraud *(formerly 982.1(23))*
PLD-C-010	1/1/2007	Answer—Contract *(formerly 982.1(35))*

PLEADINGS
General

| PLD-050* | 1/1/2009 | General Denial *(formerly 982(a)(13))* |

PLEADINGS
Personal Injury

PLD-PI-001	1/1/2007	Complaint—Personal Injury, Property Damage, Wrongful Death *(formerly 982.1(1))*
PLD-PI-001(1)	1/1/2007	Cause of Action—Motor Vehicle *(formerly 982.1(2))*
PLD-PI-001(2)	1/1/2007	Cause of Action—General Negligence *(formerly 982.1(3))*
PLD-PI-001(3)	1/1/2007	Cause of Action—Intentional Tort *(formerly 982.1(4))*

---

* Adopted for mandatory use by all courts.

PLD-PI-001(4)	1/1/2007	Cause of Action—Premises Liability *(formerly 982.1(5))*
PLD-PI-001(5)	1/1/2007	Cause of Action—Products Liability *(formerly 982.1(6))*
PLD-PI-001(6)	1/1/2007	Exemplary Damages Attachment *(formerly 982.1(13))*
PLD-PI-002	1/1/2007	Cross-Complaint—Personal Injury, Property Damage, Wrongful Death *(formerly 982.1(14))*
PLD-PI-003	1/1/2007	Answer—Personal Injury, Property Damage, Wrongful Death *(formerly 982.1(15))*

PLEADINGS
Unlawful Detainer (Landlord/Tenant)

UD-100	7/1/2005	Complaint—Unlawful Detainer
UD-105	1/1/2007	Answer—Unlawful Detainer
UD-106	1/1/2009	Form Interrogatories—Unlawful Detainer *[same as DISC-003]*
UD-110	1/1/2003	Judgment—Unlawful Detainer
UD-110 S	1/1/2003	Judgment—Unlawful Detainer Attachment
UD-115	1/1/2003	Stipulation for Entry of Judgment (Unlawful Detainer)
UD-116	7/1/2003	Declaration for Default Judgment by Court (Unlawful Detainer—Civ. Proc., §585(d))
UD-150*	1/1/2005	Request/Counter-Request To Set Case For Trial—Unlawful Detainer

PROBATE
Decedents Estates

DE-111*	3/1/2008	Petition for Probate (Probate—Decedents Estates)
DE-120(MA)	7/1/2005	Attachment to Notice of Hearing Proof of Service by Mail (Probate—Decedents' Estates and Guardianships and Conservatorships)
DE-120(P)	7/1/2005	Proof of Personal Service of Notice of Hearing—Decedent's Estate or Trust (Probate—Decedents' Estates)
DE-120(PA)	7/1/2005	Attachment to Notice of Hearing Proof of Personal Service (Probate—Decedents' Estates and Guardianships and Conservatorships)
DE-120*	7/1/2005	Notice of Hearing—Decedent's Estate or Trust (Probate—Decedents' Estates)
DE-121(MA)	1/1/2006	Attachment to Notice of Petition to Administer Estate—Proof of Service by Mail (Probate—Decedents' Estates)
DE-121*	1/1/2006	Notice of Petition to Administer Estate (Probate—Decedents' Estates)
DE-122*	1/1/2006	Citation—Probate (Probate—Decedents' Estates and Guardianships and Conservatorships)
DE-125*	1/1/1998	Summons (Probate)
DE-131*	1/1/1998	Proof of Subscribing Witness
DE-135*	1/1/1998	Proof of Holographic Instrument
DE-140*	1/1/1998	Order for Probate
DE-147*	1/1/2002	Duties and Liabilities of Personal Representative
DE-147* S	1/1/2001	Confidential Supplement to Duties and Liabilities of Personal Representative
DE-150*	1/1/1998	Letters
DE-154*	1/1/1998	Request for Special Notice *[same as GC-035]*
DE-157*	1/1/1998	Notice of Administration to Creditors
DE-160*	1/1/2007	Inventory and Appraisal *[same as GC-040]*
DE-161*	1/1/1998	Inventory and Appraisal Attachment *[same as GC-041]*
DE-165*	1/1/1998	Notice of Proposed Action (Objection—Consent)
DE-166*	1/1/1998	Waiver of Notice of Proposed Action
DE-172*	1/1/1998	Creditor's Claim
DE-174*	1/1/2009	Allowance or Rejection of Creditor's Claim (Probate—Decedents' Estates)
DE-200*	1/1/1998	Order Prescribing Notice *[same as GC-022]*
DE-221*	1/1/2005	Spousal or Domestic Partner Property Petition (Probate—Decedents Estates)
DE-226*	1/1/2005	Spousal or Domestic Partner Property Order (Probate—Decedents Estates)
DE-260*	1/1/2006	Report of Sale and Petition for Order Confirming Sale of Real Property (Probate—Decedents' Estates and Guardianships and Conservatorships)
DE-265*	1/1/2006	Order Confirming Sale of Real Property (Probate—Decedents' Estate and Guardianships and Conservatorships)

* Adopted for mandatory use by all courts.

DE-270*	1/1/1998	Ex Parte Petition for Authority to Sell Securities and Order *[same as GC-070]*
DE-275*	1/1/1998	Ex Parte Petition for Approval of Sale of Personal Property and Order *[same as GC-075]*
DE-295*	1/1/2006	Ex Parte Petition for Final Discharge and Order (Probate—Decedents' Estates and Conservatorships and Guardianships)
DE-305*	7/1/2008	Affidavit re Real Property of Small Value (Probate)
DE-310*	1/1/1998	Petition to Determine Succession to Real Property (Estates $100,000 or Less)
DE-315*	1/1/2003	Order Determining Succession to Real Property (Probate)
DE-350*	1/1/2008	Petition for Appointment of Guardian Ad Litem—Probate *[same as GC-100*]*
DE-351*	1/1/2004	Order Appointing Guardian Ad Litem—Probate *[same as GC-101]*

PROBATE
Guardianships and Conservatorships

GC-005*	7/1/2007	Declaration of Private Professional Conservator or Guardian—Qualifications (Probate—Guardianships and Conservatorships)
GC-006*	7/1/2007	Declaration of Private Professional Conservator or Guardian—Continuing Education (Probate—Guardianships and Conservatorships)
GC-010*	1/1/2009	Certification of Attorney Concerning Qualifications for Court Appointment in Conservatorships or Guardianships (Probate—Guardianships and Conservatorships)
GC-011*	1/1/2009	Annual Certification of Court-Appointed Attorney (Probate—Guardianships and Conservatorships)
GC-020(C)	7/1/2005	Clerk's Certificate of Posting Notice of Hearing—Guardianship or Conservatorship (Probate—Guardianships and Conservatorships)
GC-020(MA)	7/1/2005	Attachment to Notice of Hearing Proof of Service by Mail (Probate—Decedents' Estates and Guardianships and Conservatorships)
GC-020(P)	7/1/2005	Proof of Personal Service of Notice of Hearing—Guardianship or Conservatorship (Probate—Guardianships and Conservatorships)
GC-020(PA)	7/1/2005	Attachment to Notice of Hearing Proof of Personal Service (Probate—Decedents' Estates and Guardianships and Conservatorships)
GC-020*	7/1/2005	Notice of Hearing—Guardianship or Conservatorship (Probate—Guardianships and Conservatorships)
GC-021*	1/1/1998	Order Dispensing with Notice
GC-022*	1/1/1998	Order Prescribing Notice *[same as DE-200]*
GC-035*	1/1/1998	Request for Special Notice *[same as DE-154]*
GC-040*	1/1/2007	Inventory and Appraisal *[same as DE-160]*
GC-041*	1/1/1998	Inventory and Appraisal Attachment *[same as DE-161]*
GC-042(MA)	1/1/2008	Attachment to Notice of Filing of Inventory and Appraisal and How to Object to the Inventory or the Appraised Value of Property
GC-042*	1/1/2008	Notice of Filing of Inventory and Appraisal and How to Object to the Inventory or the Appraised Value of Property
GC-045	1/1/2008	Objections to Inventory and Appraisal of Conservator or Guardian
GC-050*	1/1/2009	Notice of Taking Possession or Control of an Asset of Minor or Conservatee (Probate—Guardianships and Conservatorships)
GC-051*	7/1/2005	Notice of Opening or Changing a Guardianship or Conservatorship Account or Safe Deposit Box
GC-060*	1/1/2006	Report of Sale and Petition for Order Confirming Sale of Real Property (Probate—Decedents' Estates and Guardianships and Conservatorships)
GC-065*	1/1/2006	Order Confirming Sale of Real Property (Probate—Decedents' Estates and Guardianships and Conservatorships)
GC-070*	1/1/1998	Ex Parte Petition for Authority to Sell Securities and Order *[same as DE-270]*
GC-075*	1/1/1998	Ex Parte Petition for Approval of Sale of Personal Property and Order *[same as DE-275]*
GC-079(MA)	1/1/2008	Attachment to Pre-Move Notice of Proposed Change of Personal Residence of Conservatee or Ward

---

* Adopted for mandatory use by all courts.

GC-079*	1/1/2008	Pre-Move Notice of Proposed Change of Personal Residence of Conservatee or Ward
GC-080(MA)	1/1/2008	Attachment to Post-Move Notice of Change of Residence of Conservatee or Ward
GC-080*	1/1/2008	Change of Residence Notice
GC-085*	1/1/2000	Petition to Fix Residence Outside the State of California
GC-090*	1/1/2000	Order Fixing Residence Outside the State of California
GC-100*	1/1/2008	Petition for Appointment of Guardian Ad Litem—Probate [same as DE-350*]
GC-101*	1/1/2004	Order Appointing Guardian Ad Litem — Probate [same as DE-351]
GC-110*	7/1/2008	Petition for Appointment of Temporary Guardian
GC-110(P)*	1/1/2009	Petition for Appointment of Temporary Guardian of the Person (Probate—Guardianships and Conservatorships)
GC-111*	7/1/2008	Petition for Appointment of Temporary Conservator
GC-112	1/1/2009	Ex Parte Application for Good Cause Exception to Notice of Hearing on Petition for Appointment of Temporary Conservator (Probate—Guardianships and Conservatorships)
GC-112(A-1)	1/1/2009	Declaration in Support of Ex Parte Application for Good Cause Exception to Notice of Hearing on Petition for Appointment of Temporary Conservator (Probate—Guardianships and Conservatorships)
GC-112(A-2)	1/1/2009	Declaration Continuation Page (Probate—Guardianships and Conservatorships)
GC-115	1/1/2009	Order on Ex Parte Application for Good Cause Exception to Notice of Hearing on Petition for Appointment of Temporary Conservator (Probate—Guardianships and Conservatorships)
GC-120*	1/1/2009	Declaration Under Uniform Child Custody Jurisdiction and Enforcement Act (UCCJEA) [same as FL-105]
GC-120(A)*	1/1/2009	Attachment to Declaration Under Uniform Child Custody Jurisdiction and Enforcement Act (UCCJEA) [same as FL-105(A)]
GC-140*	1/1/2009	Order Appointing Temporary Guardian (Probate—Guardianships and Conservatorships)
GC-141*	1/1/2009	Order Appointing Temporary Conservator (Probate—Guardianships and Conservatorships)
GC-150*	1/1/2009	Letters of Temporary Guardianship or Conservatorship (Probate—Guardianships and Conservatorships)
GC-205*	1/1/2001	Guardianship Pamphlet
GC-205 C	1/1/2001	Guardianship Pamphlet—Chinese
GC-205 K	1/1/2001	Guardianship Pamphlet—Korean
GC-205 S	1/1/2001	Guardianship Pamphlet—Spanish
GC-205 V	1/1/2001	Guardianship Pamphlet—Vietnamese
GC-210*	1/1/2007	Petition for Appointment of Guardian of Minor
GC-210(P)*	1/1/2007	Petition for Appointment of Guardian of the Person
GC-210(CA)*	1/1/2008	Guardianship Petition—Child Information Attachment (Probate—Guardianships and Conservatorships)
GC-211*	1/1/2004	Consent of Proposed Guardian, Nomination of Guardian, and Consent to Appointment of Guardian and Waiver of Notice
GC-212*	1/1/2006	Confidential Guardian Screening Form (Probate—Guardianships and Conservatorships)
GC-240*	1/1/1998	Order Appointing Guardian of Minor
GC-248*	1/1/2001	Duties of Guardian (Probate)
GC-250*	1/1/2009	Letters of Guardianship (Probate—Guardianships and Conservatorships)
GC-251*	7/1/2003	Confidential Guardianship Status Report
GC-255*	1/1/2006	Petition for Termination of Guardianship (Probate—Guardianships and Conservatorships)
GC-260*	1/1/2006	Order Terminating Guardianship (Probate—Guardianships and Conservatorships)
GC-310*	1/1/2006	Petition for Appointment of Probate Conservator (Probate—Guardianships and Conservatorships)
GC-312*	1/1/2001	Confidential Supplemental Information (Probate Conservatorship)
GC-313*	1/1/2003	Attachment Requesting Special Orders Regarding Dementia

* Adopted for mandatory use by all courts.

GC-314*	1/1/2006	Confidential Conservator Screening Form (Probate—Guardianships and Conservatorships)
GC-320*	1/1/2006	Citation for Conservatorship (Probate—Guardianships and Conservatorships)
GC-322*	1/1/2006	Citation—Probate (Probate—Decedents' Estates and Guardianships and Conservatorships)
GC-330*	1/1/1998	Order Appointing Court Investigator
GC-333*	7/1/2005	Ex Parte Application for Order Authorizing Completion of Capacity Declaration—HIPAA (Probate—Guardianships and Conservatorships)
GC-334*	7/1/2005	Ex Parte Order Re Completion of Capacity Declaration—HIPAA (Probate—Guardianships and Conservatorships)
GC-335*	1/1/2004	Capacity Declaration—Conservatorship
GC-335A*	1/1/2004	Dementia Attachment to Capacity Declaration—Conservatorship
GC-340*	7/1/2008	Order Appointing Probate Conservator (Probate—Guardianships and Conservatorships)
GC-341(MA)	1/1/2008	Attachment to Notice of Conservatee's Rights
GC-341*	1/1/2008	Notice of Conservatee's Rights
GC-348*	1/1/2002	Duties of Conservator and Acknowledgment of Receipt of Handbook
GC-350*	1/1/2009	Letters of Conservatorship (Probate—Guardianships and Conservatorships)
GC-380*	1/1/1998	Petition for Exclusive Authority to Give Consent for Medical Treatment
GC-385*	1/1/1998	Order Authorizing Conservator to Give Consent for Medical Treatment
GC-395*	1/1/2006	Ex Parte Petition for Final Discharge and Order (Probate—Decedents' Estates and Conservatorships and Guardianships)
GC-400(A)(1)	1/1/2008	Schedule A, Receipts, Dividends—Standard Account
GC-400(A)(2)	1/1/2008	Schedule A, Receipts, Interest—Standard Account
GC-400(A)(3)	1/1/2008	Schedule A, Receipts, Pensions, Annuities, and Other Regular Periodic Payments—Standard Account
GC-400(A)(4)	1/1/2008	Schedule A, Receipts, Rent—Standard Account
GC-400(A)(5)	1/1/2008	Schedule A, Receipts, Social Security, Veterans' Benefits, Other Public Benefits—Standard Account
GC-400(A)(6)	1/1/2008	Schedule A, Receipts, Other Receipts—Standard Account
GC-400(A)(C)	1/1/2008	Schedule A and C, Receipts and Disbursements Worksheet—Standard Account
GC-400(AP)	1/1/2008	Additional Property Received During Period of Account—Standard and Simplified Accounts [same as GC-405(AP)]
GC-400(B)	1/1/2008	Schedule B, Gains on Sales—Standard and Simplified Accounts [same as GC-405(B)]
GC-400(C)(1)	1/1/2008	Schedule C, Disbursements, Conservatee's Caregiver Expenses—Standard Account
GC-400(C)(2)	1/1/2008	Schedule C, Disbursements, Conservatee's Residential or Long-Term Care Facility Living Expenses—Standard Account
GC-400(C)(3)	1/1/2008	Schedule C, Disbursements, Ward's Education Expenses—Standard Account
GC-400(C)(4)	1/1/2008	Schedule C, Disbursements, Fiduciary and Attorney Fees—Standard Account
GC-400(C)(5)	1/1/2008	Schedule C, Disbursements, General Administration Expenses—Standard Account
GC-400(C)(6)	1/1/2008	Schedule C, Disbursements, Investment Expenses—Standard Account
GC-400(C)(7)	1/1/2008	Schedule C, Disbursements, Living Expenses—Standard Account
GC-400(C)(8)	1/1/2008	Schedule C, Disbursements, Medical Expenses—Standard Account
GC-400(C)(9)	1/1/2008	Schedule C, Disbursements, Property Sale Expenses—Standard Account
GC-400(C)(10)	1/1/2008	Schedule C, Disbursements, Rental Property Expenses—Standard Account
GC-400(C)(11)	1/1/2008	Schedule C, Disbursements, Other Expenses—Standard Account
GC-400(D)	1/1/2008	Schedule D, Losses on Sales—Standard and Simplified Accounts [same as GC-405(D)]
GC-400(DIST)	1/1/2008	Distributions to Conservatee or Ward—Standard and Simplified Accounts [same as GC-405(DIST)]
GC-400(E)(1)	1/1/2008	Cash Assets on Hand at End of Account Period—Standard and Simplified Accounts [same as GC-405(E)(1)]
GC-400(E)(2)	1/1/2008	Non-Cash Assets on Hand at End of Account Period—Standard and Simplified Accounts [same as GC-405(E)(2)]
GC-400(F)	1/1/2008	Schedule F, Changes in Form of Assets—Standard and Simplified Accounts [same as GC-405(F)]

* Adopted for mandatory use by all courts.

GC-400(G)	1/1/2008	Schedule G, Liabilities at End of Account Period—Standard and Simplified Accounts *[same as GC-405(G)]*
GC-400(NI)	1/1/2008	Net Income From a Trade or Business—Standard Account
GC-400(NL)	1/1/2008	Net Loss From a Trade or Business—Standard Account
GC-400(OCH)	1/1/2008	Other Charges—Standard and Simplified Accounts *[same as GC-405(OCH)]*
GC-400(OCR)	1/1/2008	Other Credits—Standard and Simplified Accounts *[same as GC-405(OCR)]*
GC-400(PH)(1)	1/1/2008	Cash Assets on Hand at Beginning of Account Period—Standard and Simplified Accounts *[same as GC-405(PH)(1)]*
GC-400(PH)(2)	1/1/2008	Non-Cash Assets on Hand at Beginning of Account Period—Standard and Simplified Accounts *[same as GC-405(PH)(2)]*
GC-400(SUM)*	1/1/2008	Summary of Account—Standard and Simplified Accounts *[same as GC-405(SUM)*]*
GC-405(A)*	1/1/2008	Schedule A, Receipts—Simplified Account
GC-405(AP)	1/1/2008	Additional Property Received During Period of Account—Standard and Simplified Accounts *[same as GC-400(AP)]*
GC-405(B)	1/1/2008	Schedule B, Gains on Sales—Standard and Simplified Accounts *[same as GC-400(B)]*
GC-405(C)*	1/1/2008	Schedule C, Disbursements—Simplified Account
GC-405(D)	1/1/2008	Schedule D, Losses on Sales—Standard and Simplified Accounts *[same as GC-400(D)]*
GC-405(DIST)	1/1/2008	Distributions to Conservatee or Ward—Standard and Simplified Accounts *[same as GC-400(DIST)]*
GC-405(E)(1)	1/1/2008	Cash Assets on Hand at End of Account Period—Standard and Simplified Accounts *[same as GC-400(E)(1)]*
GC-405(E)(2)	1/1/2008	Non-Cash Assets on Hand at End of Account Period —Standard and Simplified Accounts *[same as GC-400(E)(2)]*
GC-405(F)	1/1/2008	Schedule F, Changes in Form of Assets—Standard and Simplified Accounts *[same as GC-400(F)]*
GC-405(G)	1/1/2008	Schedule G, Liabilities at End of Account Period—Standard and Simplified Accounts *[same as GC-400(G)]*
GC-405(OCH)	1/1/2008	Other Charges—Standard and Simplified Accounts *[same as GC-400(OCH)]*
GC-405(OCR)	1/1/2008	Other Credits—Standard and Simplified Accounts *[same as GC-400(OCR)]*
GC-405(PH)(1)	1/1/2008	Cash Assets on Hand at Beginning of Account Period—Standard and Simplified Accounts *[same as GC-400(PH)(1)]*
GC-405(PH)(2)	1/1/2008	Non-Cash Assets on Hand at Beginning of Account Period—Standard and Simplified Accounts *[same as GC-400(PH)(2)]*
GC-405(SUM)*	1/1/2008	Summary of Account—Standard and Simplified Accounts *[same as GC-400(SUM)*]*
GC-505	7/1/2007	Forms You Need to Ask the Court to Appoint a Guardian of the Person (Probate—Guardianships and Conservatorships)
GC-510	7/1/2007	What is "Proof of Service" in a Guardianship? (Probate—Guardianships and Conservatorships)

PROOF OF SERVICE

POS-010*	1/1/2007	Proof of Service of Summons
POS-015*	1/1/2005	Notice And Acknowledgment Of Receipt—Civil
POS-020	1/1/2005	Proof Of Personal Service—Civil (Proof of Service) / Information Sheet For Proof Of Personal Service—Civil
POS-020(D)	1/1/2005	Attachment to Proof of Personal Service—Civil (Documents Served) (Proof of Service)
POS-020(P)	1/1/2005	Attachment to Proof of Personal Service—Civil (Persons Served) (Proof of Service)
POS-030	1/1/2005	Proof of Service by First-Class Mail—Civil (Proof of Service) / Information Sheet for Proof of Service by First-Class Mail—Civil
POS-030(D)	1/1/2005	Attachment to Proof of Service by First-Class Mail—Civil (Documents Service) (Proof of Service)
POS-030(P)	1/1/2005	Attachment to Proof of Service by First-Class Mail—Civil (Persons Served) (Proof of Service)
POS-040	1/1/2009	Proof of Service—Civil (Proof of Service)

---

* Adopted for mandatory use by all courts.

| POS-040(D) | 1/1/2005 | Attachment to Proof of Service—Civil (Documents Served) (Proof of Service) |
| POS-040(P) | 1/1/2009 | Attachment to Proof of Service—Civil (Persons Served) (Proof of Service) |

RECEIVERSHIP

RC-200	1/1/2007	Ex Parte Order Appointing Receiver and Order to Show Cause and Temporary Restraining Order—Rents, Issues, and Profits (Receivership)
RC-210	1/1/2007	Order Confirming Appointment of Receiver and Preliminary Injunction—Rents, Issues, and Profits (Receivership)
RC-300	1/1/2007	Order to Show Cause and Temporary Restraining Order—Rents, Issues, and Profits (Receivership)
RC-310	1/1/2007	Order Appointing Receiver After Hearing and Preliminary Injunction—Rents, Issues, and Profits (Receivership)

SMALL CLAIMS

SC-100*	1/1/2008	Plaintiff's Claim and ORDER to Go to Small Claims Court
SC-100A*	1/1/2007	Other Plaintiffs or Defendants (Attachment to Plaintiff's Claim and ORDER to Go to Small Claims Court)
SC-101*	7/1/2007	Attorney Fee Dispute (After Arbitration) (Attachment to Plaintiff's Claim and ORDER to Go to Small Claims Court)
SC-103	1/1/2006	Fictitious Business Name (Small Claims)
SC-104	1/1/2009	Proof of Service (Small Claims)
SC-104A	1/1/2006	Proof of Mailing (Substituted Service) (Small Claims)
SC-104B	1/1/2006	What Is "Proof of Service"? (Small Claims)
SC-104C	7/1/2007	How to Serve a Business or Public Entity (Small Claims)
SC-105	1/1/2007	Request for Court Order and Answer
SC-105A	1/1/2007	Order on Request for Court Order
SC-106	1992	Request to Pay Judgment in Installments
SC-107*	1/1/2000	Small Claims Subpoena for Personal Appearance and Production of Documents at Trial or Hearing and Declaration
SC-108	1/1/2007	Request to Correct or Cancel Judgment and Answer
SC-108A	1/1/2007	Order on Request to Correct or Cancel Judgment
SC-109	1/1/2007	Authorization to Appear
SC-110	1/1/2004	Request to Postpone Small Claims Hearing
SC-111	1/1/2004	Order on Request to Postpone Small Claims Hearings
SC-114	1/1/2004	Request to Amend Claim Before Hearing (Small Claims)
SC-120*	7/1/2007	Defendant's Claim and ORDER to Go to Small Claims Court (Small Claims)
SC-120A*	1/1/2007	Other Plaintiffs or Defendants (Attachment to Defendant's Claim and ORDER to Go to Small Claims Court)
SC-130*	7/1/2007	Notice of Entry of Judgment (Small Claims)
SC-132*	1/1/2007	Attorney-Client Fee Dispute (Attachment to Notice of Entry of Judgment)
SC-133*	1/1/2004	Judgment Debtor's Statement of Assets (Small Claims)
SC-134*	1/1/2007	Application and Order to Produce Statement of Assets and to Appear for Examination
SC-135	1/1/2007	Notice of Motion to Vacate Judgment and Declaration
SC-140	1/1/2007	Notice of Appeal (Small Claims)
SC-145*	1/1/2007	Request to Pay Judgment to Court
SC-150*	1/1/2008	Information for the Small Claims Plaintiff

SUBPOENA

SUBP-001*	1/1/2007	Civil Subpoena for Personal Appearance at Trial or Hearing
SUBP-002*	1/1/2009	Civil Subpoena (Duces Tecum) for Personal Appearance and Production of Documents and Things at Trial or Hearing and Declaration
SUBP-010*	1/1/2007	Deposition Subpoena for Production of Business Records
SUBP-015*	1/1/2009	Deposition Subpoena for Personal Appearance
SUBP-020*	1/1/2009	Deposition Subpoena for Personal Appearance and Production of Documents and Things

---

* Adopted for mandatory use by all courts.

SUBP-025*　　1/1/2008　　Notice to Consumer or Employee and Objection

SUMMONS

SUM-100*	1/1/2004	Summons
SUM-110*	1/1/2009	Summons—Cross-Complaint
SUM-120*	1/1/2004	Summons (Joint Debtor)
SUM-130*	1/1/2004	Summons—Unlawful Detainer—Eviction
SUM-140*	1/1/2004	Summons—Storage Lien Enforcement
SUM-145*	1/1/2009	Summons—Enforcement of State Housing Law
SUM-200(A)*	1/1/2007	Additional Parties Attachment (Attachment to Summons) (formerly 982(a)(9)(A))
SUM-300*	1/1/2007	Declaration of Lost Summons After Service (formerly 982(a)(12))

TRAFFIC INFRACTIONS

TR-150	1/1/2007	Instructions on Appeal Procedures for Infractions
TR-155	1/1/2007	Notice of Appeal (Infraction)
TR-160	1/1/2007	Proposed Statement on Appeal (Infraction)
TR-165	1/1/2007	Abandonment of Appeal (Infraction)
TR-200*	1/1/1999	Instructions to Defendant
TR-205*	1/1/1999	Request for Trial by Written Declaration
TR-210*	1/1/1999	Notice and Instructions to Arresting Officer
TR-215*	1/1/1999	Decision and Notice of Decision
TR-220*	1/1/1999	Request for New Trial (Trial de Novo)
TR-225*	1/1/1999	Order and Notice to Defendant of New Trial (Trial de Novo)
TR-235*	1/1/2000	Officer's Declaration
TR-300*	4/1/2008	Agreement to Pay and Forfeit Bail in Installments
TR-310*	4/1/2008	Agreement to Pay Traffic Violator School Fees in Installments

TRANSITIONAL CONDUCT

TH-100*	1992	Petition for Order Prohibiting Abuse or Program Misconduct
TH-110*	1992	Order to Show Cause and Temporary Restraining Order
TH-120*	1992	Participant's Response
TH-130*	1992	Order After Hearing
TH-140*	1992	Proof of Personal Service
TH-190	1992	Restatement of Transitional Housing Misconduct Act
TH-200*	1992	Instructions for Program Operators
TH-210*	1992	Instructions for Participants

WAGE GARNISHMENT

WG-001	1/1/2007	Application for Earnings Withholding Order (Wage Garnishment) (formerly 982.5(1))
WG-002*	7/24/2008	Earnings Withholding Order (Wage Garnishment)
WG-003	7/1/2008	Employee Instructions (Wage Garnishment)
WG-004	1/1/2007	Earnings Withholding Order for Support (Wage Garnishment) (formerly 982.5(3))
WG-005*	7/1/2007	Employer's Return (Wage Garnishment) (formerly 982.5(4))
WG-006	1/1/2009	Claim of Exemption (Wage Garnishment) (formerly 982.5(5))
WG-007*	1/1/2007	Financial Statement (Wage Garnishment—Enforcement of Judgment) [same as EJ-165*]
WG-008*	1/1/2007	Notice of Filing of Claim of Exemption (Wage Garnishment) (formerly 982.5(6))
WG-009	1/1/2007	Notice of Opposition to Claim of Exemption (Wage Garnishment) (formerly 982.5(7))
WG-010	1/1/2007	Notice of Hearing on Claim of Exemption (Wage Garnishment—Enforcement of Judgment) [same as EJ-175]
WG-011	1/1/2007	Order Determining Claim of Exemption (Wage Garnishment) (formerly 982.5(9))

---

* Adopted for mandatory use by all courts.

WG-012	1/1/2007	Notice of Termination or Modification of Earnings Withholding Order (Wage Garnishment) *(formerly 982.5(10))*
WG-020*	1/1/2007	Application for Earnings Withholding Order for Taxes (Wage Garnishment—State Tax Liability) *(formerly 982.5(11))*
WG-021*	1/1/2007	Confidential Supplement to Application for Earnings Withholding Order for Taxes (Wage Garnishment—State Tax Liability) *(formerly 982.5(11S))*
WG-022*	1/1/2007	Earnings Withholding Order for Taxes (Wage Garnishment—State Tax Liability) *(formerly 982.5(12))*
WG-023*	1/1/2007	Notice of Hearing—Earnings Withholding Order for Taxes (Wage Garnishment—State Tax Liability) *(formerly 982.5(13))*
WG-024*	1/1/2007	Temporary Earnings Withholding Order for Taxes (Wage Garnishment—State Tax Liability) *(formerly 982.5(14))*
WG-025*	1/1/2007	Confidential Supplement to Temporary Earnings Withholding Order for Taxes (Wage Garnishment—State Tax Liability) *(formerly 982.5(14S))*
WG-026*	1/1/2007	Claim of Exemption and Financial Declaration (Wage Garnishment—State Tax Liability) *(formerly 982.5(15))*

WORKPLACE VIOLENCE

WV-100*	1/1/2007	Petition of Employer for Injunction Prohibiting Violence or Threats of Violence Against Employee (Workplace Violence)
WV-110*	7/1/2004	Response to Petition of Employer for Injunction Prohibiting Violence or Threats of Violence Against Employee (Workplace Violence)
WV-120*	1/1/2007	Order to Show Cause and Temporary Restraining Order (CLETS) (Workplace Violence)
WV-130	1/1/2005	Proof of Personal Service (Workplace Violence)
WV-131	1/1/2005	Proof of Service by Mail of Completed Response (Workplace Violence)
WV-132	1/1/2005	Proof of Service by Personal Delivery of Completed Response (Workplace Violence)
WV-140*	1/1/2007	Order After Hearing on Petition of Employer for Injunction Prohibiting Violence or Threats of Violence Against Employee (CLETS) (Workplace Violence)
WV-145	7/1/2007	Proof of Sale or Turning In of Firearms
WV-150-INFO*	1/1/2007	Instructions for Petitions to Prohibit Workplace Violence

---

* Adopted for mandatory use by all courts.

Appendix B
Liability Limits of a Parent or Guardian Having Custody and Control of a Minor for the Torts of a Minor
(Civil Code, § 1714.1)

Formula

Pursuant to Civil Code section 1714.1, the joint and several liability limit of a parent or guardian having custody and control of a minor under subdivisions (a) and (b) for each tort of the minor shall be computed and adjusted as follows:

$$\text{Adjusted limit} = \left[\frac{\text{Current CCPI-January 1, 1995, CCPI}}{\text{January 1, 1995, CCPI}} + 1 \right] \times \begin{array}{c} \text{January 1, 1995,} \\ \text{limit} \end{array}$$

Definition

"CCPI" means the California Consumer Price Index, as established by the California Department of Industrial Relations.

January 1, 2007, calculation and adjustment

The joint and several liability of a parent or guardian having custody and control of a minor under Civil Code section 1714.1, subdivision (a) or (b), effective January 1, 2007, shall not exceed $34,700 for each tort. The calculation is as follows:

$$\$34,735 = \left[\frac{210.5 - 151.5}{151.5} + 1 \right] \times 25,000$$

Under section 1714.1, subdivision (c), the adjusted limit is rounded to the nearest hundred dollars.

Appendix B amended effective January 1, 2007; adopted effective January 1, 1997; previously amended January 1, 1999, January 1, 2001, January 1, 2003, and January 1, 2005.

Appendix C
Guidelines for the Operation of Family Law Information Centers and Family Law Facilitator Offices

(1) *Independence and integrity*

An attorney and other staff working in a family law information center or family law facilitator office should, at all times, uphold the independence and integrity of the center or office in conjunction with its role within the court and the legal system.

(2) *Role as representative of the court*

An attorney and other staff working in a family law information center or family law facilitator office should recognize that they are representatives of the court and, as such, should avoid all acts of impropriety and the appearance of impropriety at all times.

(3) *Impartiality and diligence*

An attorney working in a family law information center or family law facilitator office should perform his or her duties impartially and diligently. Impartiality means delivering services to all eligible litigants in a neutral manner. Diligence requires that the attorney provide the litigants with pertinent information to allow them to bring their matter before the court. This may include appropriate referrals to other resources as well as direct information and assistance at the center or office. The attorney should require similar conduct of all personnel.

(4) *Respect and patience*

An attorney working in a family law information center or family law facilitator office should be aware of the social and economic differences that exist among litigants and maintain patience with and respect for the litigants who seek the services of the center or office. The attorney should require similar conduct of all personnel. However, if a litigant becomes unruly or disruptive, the attorney may ask the litigant to leave the center or office.

(5) *Bias and prejudice*

An attorney working in a family law information center or family law facilitator office should assist the litigants who seek assistance without exhibiting bias or prejudice based on race, sex, religion, national origin, disability, age, sexual orientation, socioeconomic status, or other similar factors, and should require similar conduct of all personnel.

(6) *Competent legal information*

An attorney working in a family law information center or family law facilitator office and his or her staff should provide the litigants who seek assistance with procedural and legal information and education so that the litigants will have increased access to the court. Family law information centers and family law facilitator offices are not intended to replace private counsel.

(7) *Full notification of limits of service*

An attorney working in a family law information center or family law facilitator office should ensure that conspicuous notice is given, as set forth in Family Code section 10013, that no attorney-client relationship exists between the center or office, or its staff, and the family law litigant. The notice should include the advice that the absence of an attorney-client relationship means that communications between the party and the family law information center or family law facilitator office are not privileged and that the services may be provided to the other party. Additionally, the family law information center must use *Family Law Information Center Disclosure* (form FL-945) or provide similar notice. The family law facilitator office must use *Office of the Family Law Facilitator Disclosure* (form FL-940) or provide similar notice of the warnings set forth in Family Code section 10015.

(8) *Public comment*

An attorney working in a family law information center or family law facilitator office and his or her staff must at all times comply with Family Code section 10014, and must not make any public comment about the litigants or about any pending or impending matter in the court.

(9) *Gifts or payments*

An attorney working in a family law information center or family law facilitator office and his or her staff should not accept any gifts, favors, bequests, or loans from the litigants whom they assist, since this may give the appearance of impropriety or partiality—except for nominal gifts such as baked goods, as allowed by local rules.

(10) *Communications with bench officer*

An attorney working in a family law information center or family law facilitator office and his or her staff should avoid all ex parte communications with a bench officer, except as provided in accordance with Family Code section 10005. In addition, an attorney should avoid all communications with a bench officer in which he or she offers an opinion on how the bench officer should rule on a pending case. Communications about purely procedural matters or the functioning of the court are allowed and encouraged.

(11) *Communications with represented litigants*

An attorney working in a family law information center or family law facilitator office and his or her staff should not assist a litigant who is represented by an attorney unless the litigant's attorney consents or the court has referred the litigant for assistance.

Advisory Committee Comment

These guidelines are promulgated as directed by former Family Code section 15010(f). They are intended to guide the attorneys providing assistance in family law information centers and family law facilitator offices created by Family Code sections 10000–10015.

These guidelines are not intended to be exclusive. Attorneys who work in the family law information centers and family law facilitator offices are also bound by the State Bar Act, the Rules of Professional Conduct, local and state court employee rules, and relevant opinions of the California courts to the extent that they apply.

The authorities that govern attorney conduct in California apply to all California attorneys regardless of the capacity in which they are acting in a particular matter. (*Libarian v. State Bar* 25 Cal.2d. 314 (1944).) "Permission" not to comply with these authorities may not be given by the State Bar. (*Sheffield v. State Bar* 22 Cal.2d. 627 (1943).)

Thus, California attorneys, regardless of the capacity in which they are performing in a particular matter, must conform their conduct to the governing California authorities. However, because the disciplinary authorities are activity-specific, not all authorities apply in all instances. For example, a transactional attorney who never appears in court is not likely to be at risk of violating the rules that govern court appearances. The transactional attorney is not immune from those rules; the nature of his or her practice simply minimizes the impact of those rules upon the services he or she performs. Thus, although center and facilitator attorneys will not be immune from the governing authorities, certain rules and requirements will apply more directly to the nature of the services being provided than will others.

Just as the Rules of Professional Conduct are activity-specific in general professional practice, so are center and facilitator office attorneys. Although the Rules of Professional Conduct and related authorities will apply generally, and will apply directly when the attorney is representing clients in an attorney-client relationship, they will not directly be invoked when a center or facilitator attorney provides assistance to a nonclient in a court-based program that does not, by definition, represent "clients."

To the extent that the above-mentioned Family Code sections establish by law that there is no attorney-client relationship or privilege for services provided by a family law information center or family law facilitator office, the Rules of Professional Conduct that specifically address the attorney-client relationship and the conduct of that relationship would not be invoked if the attorney were providing services within the scope of those sections. However, the Rules of Professional Conduct would govern attorneys employed by centers or facilitator offices who also continued to maintain a law practice and worked with actual clients in an attorney-client relationship.

Although center and facilitator office attorneys are not exempt from the Rules of Professional Conduct, the employing court may promulgate guidelines for the services provided by a center or facilitator office that are more applicable to the center or office than are some of the Rules of Professional Conduct, however, any such restrictions must still be fully consistent with the Rules of Professional Conduct. The principles set forth in the California

Code of Judicial Ethics are often more applicable to the centers and facilitator offices and are consistent with the Rules of Professional Conduct. Those principles form the basis for the guidelines contained in these standards. The court may enforce these guidelines through its employee disciplinary process for court employees. Following are the areas of the Rules of Professional Conduct where these guidelines provide standards that are more applicable to the role of the family law information center or family law facilitator office as an entity of the court.

Rule 2-100 (Communication With a Represented Party)—see proposed guideline 11 (Communication with represented litigants).

Rule 2-400 (Prohibited Discriminatory Conduct in a Law Practice)—see proposed guideline 5 (Bias and prejudice);

Rule 3-110 (Failing to Act Competently)—see proposed guidelines 3 (Impartiality and diligence) and 6 (Competent legal information);

Rule 3-120 (Sexual Relations With Client)—see proposed guideline 2 (Role as representative of the court);

Rule 3-200 (Prohibited Objectives of Employment)—see proposed guideline 2 (Role as representative of the court);

Rule 3-210 (Advising the Violation of Law)—see proposed guideline 2 (Role as representative of the court);

Rule 3-320 (Relationship With Other Party's Lawyer)—see proposed guideline 2 (Role as representative of the court);

Rule 4-300 (Purchasing Property at a Foreclosure or a Sale Subject to Judicial Review)—see proposed guideline 2 (Role as representative of the court);

Rule 4-400 (Gifts From Client)—see proposed guideline 9 (Gifts or payments);

Rule 5-120 (Trial Publicity)—see proposed guideline 8 (Public comment);

Rule 5-220 (Suppression of Evidence)—see proposed guideline 2 (Role as representative of the court);

Rule 5-300 (Contact With Officials)—see proposed guideline 10 (Communications with bench officers);

Rule 5-310 (Prohibited Contact With Witnesses)—see proposed guideline 2 (Role as representative of the court); and

Rule 5-320 (Contact With Jurors)—see proposed guideline 2 (Role as representative of the court).

SUPPLEMENT TO THE CALIFORNIA RULES OF COURT

California Code of Judicial Ethics.

Internal Operating Practices and Procedures of the California Supreme Court.

Supreme Court Policies Regarding Cases Arising From Judgments of Death. Policy Statements 1-4.

Payment Guidelines for Appointed Counsel Representing Indigent Criminal Appellants in the California Supreme Court.

Guidelines for Fixed Fee Appointments, On Optional Basis, to Automatic Appeals and Related Habeas Corpus Proceedings in the California Supreme Court.

Guidelines for the Commission on Judicial Appointments. Guidelines 1-8.

Local Rules and Internal Operating Practices and Procedures of the Courts of Appeal.

First Appellate District. Rules 1-15; Internal Operating Practices and Procedures.

Second Appellate District. Rules 1-6; Internal Operating Practices and Procedures.

Third Appellate District. Rules 1-4; Internal Operating Practices and Procedures.

Fourth Appellate District. Rules 1-5; Internal Operating Practices and Procedures, Division One; Internal Operating Practices and Procedures, Division Two; Internal Operating Practices and Procedures, Division Three.

Fifth Appellate District. Rules 1-5; Local Court Form; Internal Operating Practices and Procedures.

Sixth Appellate District. Internal Operating Practices and Procedures.

California Code of Judicial Ethics

[Adopted by the Supreme Court pursuant to article VI, section 18(m) of the California Constitution]

[Amended by the Supreme Court of California effective January 1, 2008; previously amended March 4, 1999, December 13, 2000, December 30, 2002, June 18, 2003, December 22, 2003, January 1, 2005, June 1, 2005, July 1, 2006, January 1, 2007]

Preface
Preamble
Terminology
Canon 1. A judge shall uphold the integrity and independence of the judiciary.
Canon 2. A judge shall avoid impropriety and the appearance of impropriety in all of the judge's activities.
Canon 3. A judge shall perform the duties of judicial office impartially and diligently.
Canon 4. A judge shall so conduct the judge's quasi-judicial and extrajudicial activities as to minimize the risk of conflict with judicial obligations.
Canon 5. A judge or judicial candidate shall refrain from inappropriate political activity.
Canon 6. Compliance with the code of judicial ethics.

Preface

Formal standards of judicial conduct have existed for more than 50 years. The original Canons of Judicial Ethics promulgated by the American Bar Association were modified and adopted in 1949 for application in California by the Conference of California Judges (now the California Judges Association).

In 1969, the American Bar Association determined that current needs and problems warranted revision of the Canons. In the revision process, a special American Bar Association committee, headed by former California Chief Justice Roger Traynor, sought and considered the views of the bench and bar and other interested persons. The American Bar Association Code of Judicial Conduct was adopted by the House of Delegates of the American Bar Association August 16, 1972.

Effective January 5, 1975, the California Judges Association adopted a new California Code of Judicial Conduct adapted from the American Bar Association 1972 Model Code. The California code was recast in gender-neutral form in 1986.

In 1990, the American Bar Association Model Code was further revised after a lengthy study. The California Judges Association again reviewed the model code and adopted a revised California Code of Judicial Conduct on October 5, 1992.

Proposition 190 (amending Cal. Const., art. VI, §18(m), effective March 1, 1995) created a new constitutional provision that states, "The Supreme Court shall make rules for the conduct of judges, both on and off the bench, and for judicial candidates* in the conduct of their campaigns. These rules shall be referred to as the Code of Judicial Ethics."

The Supreme Court formally adopted the 1992 Code of Judicial Conduct in March 1995, as a transitional measure pending further review.

The Supreme Court formally adopted the Code of Judicial Ethics effective January 15, 1996.

---

* Terms with an asterisk (*) are defined in the Terminology section.

The Supreme Court formally adopted amendments to the Code of Judicial Ethics, effective April 15, 1996. The *Advisory Committee Commentary* is published by the Supreme Court Advisory Committee on Judicial Ethics.

Preamble

Our legal system is based on the principle that an independent, fair, and competent judiciary will interpret and apply the laws that govern us. The role of the judiciary is central to American concepts of justice and the rule of law. Intrinsic to this code are the precepts that judges, individually and collectively, must respect and honor the judicial office as a public trust and strive to enhance and maintain confidence in our legal system. The judge is an arbiter of facts and law for the resolution of disputes and a highly visible member of government under the rule of law.

The Code of Judicial Ethics ("Code") establishes standards for ethical conduct of judges on and off the bench and for candidates for judicial office. The Code consists of broad declarations called Canons, with subparts, and a Terminology section. Following each Canon is a Commentary section prepared by the Supreme Court Advisory Committee on the Code of Judicial Ethics. The Commentary, by explanation and example, provides guidance as to the purpose and meaning of the Canons. The Commentary does not constitute additional rules and should not be so construed. All members of the judiciary must comply with the Code. Compliance is required to preserve the integrity of the bench and to ensure the confidence of the public.

The Canons should be read together as a whole, and each provision should be construed in context and consistent with every other provision. They are to be applied in conformance with constitutional requirements, statutes, other court rules, and decisional law. Nothing in the Code shall either impair the essential independence of judges in making judicial decisions or provide a separate basis for civil liability or criminal prosecution.

The Code governs the conduct of judges and judicial candidates* and is binding upon them. Whether disciplinary action is appropriate, and the degree of discipline to be imposed, requires a reasoned application of the text and consideration of such factors as the seriousness of the transgression, whether there is a pattern of improper activity, and the effect of the improper activity on others or on the judicial system.

Terminology

Terms explained below are noted with an asterisk (*) in the Canons where they appear. In addition, the Canons in which terms appear are cited after the explanation of each term below.

"Appropriate authority" denotes the authority with responsibility for initiation of the disciplinary process with respect to a violation to be reported. See Commentary to Canon 3D.

"Candidate." A candidate is a person seeking election for or retention of judicial office by election. A person becomes a candidate for judicial office as soon as he or she makes a public announcement of candidacy, declares or files as a candidate with the election authority, or authorizes solicitation or acceptance of contributions or support. The term "candidate" has the same meaning when applied to a judge seeking election to nonjudicial office, unless on leave of absence. See Preamble and Canons 2B(3), the preliminary paragraph of 5, 5A, 5B, 5C, and 6E.

"Court personnel" does not include the lawyers in a proceeding before a judge. See Canons 3B(4), 3B(7)(b), 3B(9), and 3C(2).

"Fiduciary" includes such relationships as executor, administrator, trustee, and guardian. See Canons 4E, 6B, and 6F (*Commentary*).

"Law" denotes court rules as well as statutes, constitutional provisions, and decisional law. See Canons 1 (*Commentary*), 2A, 2C (*Commentary*), 3A, 3B(2), 3B(7), 3E, 4B (*Commentary*), 4C, 4D(6)(a)-(b), 4F, 4H, and 5D.

"Member of the judge's family" denotes a spouse, registered domestic partner, child, grandchild, parent, grandparent, or other relative or person with whom the judge maintains a close familial relationship. See Canons 2B(2), 4D(1) (*Commentary*), 4D(2), 4E, 4G (*Commentary*), and 5A.

"Member of the judge's family residing in the judge's household" denotes a spouse or registered domestic partner and those persons who reside in the judge's household who are relatives of the judge including relatives by marriage, or persons with whom the judge maintains a close familial relationship. See Canons 4D(5) and 4D(6).

"Nonprofit youth organization" is any nonprofit corporation or association, not organized for the private gain of any person, whose purposes are irrevocably dedicated to benefiting and serving the interests of minors and which maintains its nonprofit status in accordance with applicable state and federal tax laws. See Canon 2C.

"Nonpublic information" denotes information that, by law, is not available to the public. Nonpublic information may include but is not limited to information that is sealed by statute or court order, impounded, or communicated in camera; and information offered in grand jury proceedings, presentencing reports, dependency cases, or psychiatric reports. See Canon 3B(11).

"Political organization" denotes a political party, political action committee, or other group, the principal purpose of which is to further the election or appointment of candidates to nonjudicial office. See Canon 5A.

"Registered domestic partner" denotes a person who has registered for domestic partnership pursuant to state law or who is recognized as a domestic partner pursuant to Family Code section 299.2.

"Require." Any Canon prescribing that a judge "require" certain conduct of others means that a judge is to exercise reasonable direction and control over the conduct of those persons subject to the judge's direction and control. See Canons 3B(3), 3B(4), 3B(6), 3B(8) (*Commentary*), 3B(9), and 3C(2).

"Subordinate judicial officer." A subordinate judicial officer is, for the purposes of this Code, a person appointed pursuant to article VI, section 22 of the California Con-

---

* Terms with an asterisk (*) are defined in the Terminology section.

stitution, including, but not limited to, a commissioner, referee, and hearing officer. See Canon 6A.

"Temporary Judge." A temporary judge is an active or inactive member of the bar who, pursuant to article VI, section 21 of the California Constitution, serves or expects to serve as a judge once, sporadically, or regularly on a part-time basis under a separate court appointment for each period of service or for each case heard. See Canons 4C(3)(d)(i), 6A, and 6D.

Canon 1.   A judge shall uphold the integrity and independence of the judiciary.

An independent and honorable judiciary is indispensable to justice in our society. A judge should participate in establishing, maintaining, and enforcing high standards of conduct, and shall personally observe those standards so that the integrity and independence of the judiciary will be preserved. The provisions of this Code are to be construed and applied to further that objective. A judicial decision or administrative act later determined to be incorrect legally is not itself a violation of this Code.

ADVISORY COMMITTEE COMMENTARY

Deference to the judgments and rulings of courts depends upon public confidence in the integrity and independence of judges. The integrity and independence of judges depend in turn upon their acting without fear or favor. Although judges should be independent, they must comply with the law* and the provisions of this Code. Public confidence in the impartiality of the judiciary is maintained by the adherence of each judge to this responsibility. Conversely, violations of this Code diminish public confidence in the judiciary and thereby do injury to the system of government under law.

The basic function of an independent and honorable judiciary is to maintain the utmost integrity in decision making, and this Code should be read and interpreted with that function in mind.

Canon 2.   A judge shall avoid impropriety and the appearance of impropriety in all of the judge's activities.

A.   Promoting Public Confidence

A judge shall respect and comply with the law* and shall act at all times in a manner that promotes public confidence in the integrity and impartiality of the judiciary.

ADVISORY COMMITTEE COMMENTARY

Public confidence in the judiciary is eroded by irresponsible or improper conduct by judges. A judge must avoid all impropriety and appearance of impropriety. A judge must expect to be the subject of constant public scrutiny. A judge must therefore accept restrictions on the judge's conduct that might be viewed as burdensome by other members of the community and should do so freely and willingly.

The prohibition against behaving with impropriety or the appearance of impropriety applies to both the professional and personal conduct of a judge.

The test for the appearance of impropriety is whether a person aware of the facts might reasonably entertain a doubt that the judge would be able to act with integrity, impartiality, and competence.

See also Commentary under Canon 2C.

B.   Use of the Prestige of Judicial Office

(1)   A judge shall not allow family, social, political, or other relationships to influence the judge's judicial conduct or judgment, nor shall a judge convey or permit others to convey the impression that any individual is in a special position to influence the judge.

(2)   A judge shall not lend the prestige of judicial office or use the judicial title in any manner, including any oral or written communication, to advance the pecuniary or personal interests of the judge or others. This Canon does not prohibit the following:

(a)   A judge may testify as a character witness, provided the judge does so only when subpoenaed.

(b)   A judge may, without a subpoena, provide the Commission on Judicial Performance with a written communication containing (i) factual information regarding a matter pending before the commission, or (ii) information related to the character of a judge who has a matter pending before the commission, provided that any such factual or character information is based on personal knowledge. In commission proceedings, a judge shall provide information responsive to a subpoena or when officially requested to do so by the commission.

(c)   A judge may provide factual information in State Bar disciplinary proceedings and shall provide information responsive to a subpoena or when officially requested to do so by the State Bar.

(d)   A judge may respond to judicial selection inquiries, provide recommendations (including a general character reference, relating to the evaluation of persons being considered for a judgeship), and otherwise participate in the process of judicial selection.

(e)   A judge may serve as a reference or provide a letter of recommendation only if based on the judge's personal knowledge of the individual. These written communications may include the judge's title and be written on stationery that uses the judicial title.

(3)   A judge shall not initiate communications with a sentencing judge or a probation or corrections officer, but may provide them with information for the record in response to an official request. A judge may initiate communications with a probation or corrections officer concerning a member of the judge's family,* provided the judge is not identified as a judge in the communication.

ADVISORY COMMITTEE COMMENTARY

A strong judicial branch, based on the prestige which comes from effective and ethical performance, is essential to a system of government in which the judiciary functions independently of the executive and legislative branches. Judges should distinguish between proper and improper use of the prestige of office in all of their activities.

A judge must avoid lending the prestige of judicial office for the advancement of the private interests of the judge or others. For example, a judge must not use the judicial position to gain advantage in a civil suit involving a member of the judge's family;* or use his or her position to gain deferential treatment when stopped by a police officer for a traffic offense.

As to the use of a judge's title to identify a judge's role in the presentation and creation of legal education programs and materials, see Commentary to Canon 4B. In contracts for publication of a judge's writings, a judge should retain control

---

* Terms with an asterisk (*) are defined in the Terminology section.

over the advertising, to the extent feasible, to avoid exploitation of the judge's office. As to the acceptance of awards, see Canon 4D(6)(c) and Commentary.

This Canon does not afford judges a privilege against testifying in response to any official summons.

See also Canons 3D(1) and 3D(2) concerning a judge's obligation to take appropriate corrective action regarding other judges who violate any provision of the Code of Judicial Ethics and attorneys who violate any provision of the Rules of Professional Conduct.

This Canon does not preclude internal discussions among judges regarding the application of substantive or procedural provisions of law to any pending criminal or civil case.

(Canon 2B amended effective January 1, 2008.)

C. Membership in Organizations

A judge shall not hold membership in any organization that practices invidious discrimination on the basis of race, sex, religion, national origin, or sexual orientation.

This Canon does not apply to membership in a religious organization or an official military organization of the United States. So long as membership does not violate Canon 4A, this Canon does not bar membership in a nonprofit youth organization.*

ADVISORY COMMITTEE COMMENTARY

Membership of a judge in an organization that practices invidious discrimination gives rise to a perception that the judge's impartiality is impaired. This Canon exempts membership in religious and military organizations and, subject to Canon 4A, does not bar membership in nonprofit youth organizations. These exemptions are necessary because membership in United States military organizations is subject to current valid military regulations, and religious beliefs are constitutionally protected. Membership in nonprofit youth organizations* is not barred to accommodate individual rights of intimate association and free expression. See also Canon 3E and its Commentary concerning disqualification and disclosure.*

Canon 2C refers to the current practices of the organization. Whether an organization practices invidious discrimination is often a complex question to which judges should be sensitive. The answer cannot be determined from a mere examination of an organization's current membership rolls but rather depends on how the organization selects members and other relevant factors, such as whether the organization is dedicated to the preservation of religious, ethnic, or cultural values of legitimate common interest to its members, or whether it is in fact and effect an intimate, purely private organization whose membership limitations could not be constitutionally prohibited. Absent such factors, an organization is generally said to discriminate invidiously if it arbitrarily excludes from membership on the basis of race, religion, sex, national origin, or sexual orientation persons who would otherwise be admitted to membership.

Although Canon 2C relates only to membership in organizations that invidiously discriminate on the basis of race, sex, religion, national origin, or sexual orientation, a judge's membership in an organization that engages in any discriminatory membership practices prohibited by law also violates Canon 2 and Canon 2A and gives the appearance of impropriety. In addition, it would be a violation of Canon 2 and Canon 2A for a judge to arrange a meeting at a club that the judge knows practices such invidious discrimination or for the judge to use such a club regularly. Moreover, public manifestation by a judge of the judge's knowing approval of invidious discrimination on any basis gives the appearance of impropriety under Canon 2 and*

diminishes public confidence in the integrity and impartiality of the judiciary in violation of Canon 2A.

(Canon 2C amended effective June 18, 2003.)

Canon 3. A judge shall perform the duties of judicial office impartially and diligently.

A. Judicial Duties in General

All of the judicial duties prescribed by law* shall take precedence over all other activities of every judge. In the performance of these duties, the following standards apply.

B. Adjudicative Responsibilities

(1) A judge shall hear and decide all matters assigned to the judge except those in which he or she is disqualified.

ADVISORY COMMITTEE COMMENTARY

Canon 3B(1) is based upon the affirmative obligation contained in the Code of Civil Procedure.

(2) A judge shall be faithful to the law* regardless of partisan interests, public clamor, or fear of criticism, and shall maintain professional competence in the law.*

(3) A judge shall require* order and decorum in proceedings before the judge.

(4) A judge shall be patient, dignified, and courteous to litigants, jurors, witnesses, lawyers, and others with whom the judge deals in an official capacity, and shall require* similar conduct of lawyers and of all court staff and personnel* under the judge's direction and control.

(5) A judge shall perform judicial duties without bias or prejudice. A judge shall not, in the performance of judicial duties, engage in speech, gestures, or other conduct that would reasonably be perceived as (1) bias or prejudice, including but not limited to bias or prejudice based upon race, sex, religion, national origin, disability, age, sexual orientation, or socioeconomic status, or (2) sexual harassment.

(Canon 3B(5) amended effective December 22, 2003.)

(6) A judge shall require* lawyers in proceedings before the judge to refrain from manifesting, by words or conduct, bias or prejudice based upon race, sex, religion, national origin, disability, age, sexual orientation, or socioeconomic status against parties, witnesses, counsel, or others. This Canon does not preclude legitimate advocacy when race, sex, religion, national origin, disability, age, sexual orientation, socioeconomic status or other similar factors are issues in the proceeding.

(7) A judge shall accord to every person who has a legal interest in a proceeding, or that person's lawyer, full right to be heard according to law.* A judge shall not initiate, permit, or consider ex parte communications, or consider other communications made to the judge outside the presence of the parties concerning a pending or impending proceeding, except as follows:

(a) A judge may obtain the advice of a disinterested expert on the law* applicable to a proceeding before the judge if the judge gives notice to the parties of the person consulted and the substance of the advice, and affords the parties reasonable opportunity to respond.

(b) A judge may consult with court personnel* whose function is to aid the judge in carrying out the judge's adjudicative responsibilities or with other judges.

---

* Terms with an asterisk (*) are defined in the Terminology section.

(c)   A judge may, with the consent of the parties, confer separately with the parties and their lawyers in an effort to mediate or settle matters pending before the judge.

(d)   A judge may initiate ex parte communications, where circumstances require, for scheduling, administrative purposes, or emergencies that do not deal with substantive matters provided:

(i)   the judge reasonably believes that no party will gain a procedural or tactical advantage as a result of the ex parte communication, and

(ii)   the judge makes provision promptly to notify all other parties of the substance of the ex parte communication and allows an opportunity to respond.

(e)   A judge may initiate or consider any ex parte communication when expressly authorized by law* to do so.

ADVISORY COMMITTEE COMMENTARY

The proscription against communications concerning a proceeding includes communications from lawyers, law professors, and other persons who are not participants in the proceeding, except to the limited extent permitted by the exceptions noted in Canon 3B(7).

This Canon does not prohibit a judge from initiating or considering an ex parte communication when authorized to do so by stipulation of the parties.

This Canon does not prohibit court staff from communicating scheduling information or carrying out similar administrative functions.

An appropriate and often desirable procedure for a court to obtain the advice of a disinterested expert on legal issues is to invite the expert to file an amicus curiae brief.

A judge must not independently investigate facts in a case and must consider only the evidence presented, unless otherwise authorized by law.* For example, a judge is statutorily authorized to investigate and consult witnesses informally in small claims cases.

(8)   A judge shall dispose of all judicial matters fairly, promptly, and efficiently. A judge shall manage the courtroom in a manner that provides all litigants the opportunity to have their matters fairly adjudicated in accordance with the law.

ADVISORY COMMITTEE COMMENTARY

The obligation of a judge to dispose of matters promptly and efficiently must not take precedence over the judge's obligation to dispose of the matters fairly and with patience. For example, when a litigant is self-represented, a judge has the discretion to take reasonable steps, appropriate under the circumstances and consistent with the law and the canons, to enable the litigant to be heard. A judge should monitor and supervise cases so as to reduce or eliminate dilatory practices, avoidable delays, and unnecessary costs. A judge should encourage and seek to facilitate settlement, but parties should not feel coerced into surrendering the right to have their controversy resolved by the courts.

Prompt disposition of the court's business requires a judge to devote adequate time to judicial duties, to be punctual in attending court and expeditious in determining matters under submission, and to require* that court officials, litigants, and their lawyers cooperate with the judge to that end.

(Canon 3B(8) amended effective January 1, 2008.)

(9)   A judge shall not make any public comment about a pending or impending proceeding in any court, and shall not make any nonpublic comment that might substantially interfere with a fair trial or hearing. The judge shall require* similar abstention on the part of court personnel* subject to the judge's direction and control. This Canon does not prohibit judges from making statements in the course of their official duties or from explaining for public information the procedures of the court, and does not apply to proceedings in which the judge is a litigant in a personal capacity. Other than cases in which the judge has personally participated, this Canon does not prohibit judges from discussing in legal education programs and materials, cases and issues pending in appellate courts. This educational exemption does not apply to cases over which the judge has presided or to comments or discussions that might interfere with a fair hearing of the case.

ADVISORY COMMITTEE COMMENTARY

The requirement that judges abstain from public comment regarding a pending or impending proceeding continues during any appellate process and until final disposition. This Canon does not prohibit a judge from commenting on proceedings in which the judge is a litigant in a personal capacity, but in cases such as a writ of mandamus where the judge is a litigant in an official capacity, the judge must not comment publicly.

(10)   A judge shall not commend or criticize jurors for their verdict other than in a court order or opinion in a proceeding, but may express appreciation to jurors for their service to the judicial system and the community.

ADVISORY COMMITTEE COMMENTARY

Commending or criticizing jurors for their verdict may imply a judicial expectation in future cases and may impair a juror's ability to be fair and impartial in a subsequent case.

(11)   A judge shall not disclose or use, for any purpose unrelated to judicial duties, nonpublic information* acquired in a judicial capacity.

ADVISORY COMMITTEE COMMENTARY

This Canon makes it clear that judges cannot make use of information from affidavits, jury results, or court rulings, before they become public information, in order to gain a personal advantage.

C.   Administrative Responsibilities

(1)   A judge shall diligently discharge the judge's administrative responsibilities without bias or prejudice and maintain professional competence in judicial administration, and shall cooperate with other judges and court officials in the administration of court business.

(2)   A judge shall require* staff and court personnel* under the judge's direction and control to observe appropriate standards of conduct and to refrain from manifesting bias or prejudice based upon race, sex, religion, national origin, disability, age, sexual orientation, or socioeconomic status in the performance of their official duties.

(3)   A judge with supervisory authority for the judicial performance of other judges shall take reasonable measures to ensure the prompt disposition of matters before them and the proper performance of their other judicial responsibilities.

(4)   A judge shall not make unnecessary court appointments. A judge shall exercise the power of appointment impartially and on the basis of merit. A judge shall avoid

---

* Terms with an asterisk (*) are defined in the Terminology section.

nepotism and favoritism. A judge shall not approve compensation of appointees above the reasonable value of services rendered.

ADVISORY COMMITTEE COMMENTARY

Appointees of a judge include assigned counsel, officials such as referees, commissioners, special masters, receivers, and guardians, and personnel such as clerks, secretaries, court reporters, court interpreters, and bailiffs. Consent by the parties to an appointment or an award of compensation does not relieve the judge of the obligation prescribed by Canon 3C(4).

(5) A judge shall perform administrative duties without bias or prejudice. A judge shall not, in the performance of administrative duties, engage in speech, gestures, or other conduct that would reasonably be perceived as (1) bias or prejudice, including but not limited to bias or prejudice based upon race, sex, religion, national origin, disability, age, sexual orientation, or socioeconomic status, or (2) sexual harassment.

(Canon 3C(5) adopted effective December 22, 2003.)

D. Disciplinary Responsibilities

(1) Whenever a judge has reliable information that another judge has violated any provision of the Code of Judicial Ethics, the judge shall take or initiate appropriate corrective action, which may include reporting the violation to the appropriate authority.*

(2) Whenever a judge has personal knowledge that a lawyer has violated any provision of the Rules of Professional Conduct, the judge shall take appropriate corrective action.

(3) A judge shall promptly report in writing to the Commission on Judicial Performance when he or she is charged in court by misdemeanor citation, prosecutorial complaint, information, or indictment, with any crime in the United States as specified below. Crimes that must be reported are: (1) all crimes, other than those that would be considered misdemeanors not involving moral turpitude or infractions under California law; and (2) all misdemeanors involving violence (including assaults), the use or possession of controlled substances, the misuse of prescriptions, or the personal use or furnishing of alcohol. A judge also shall promptly report in writing upon conviction of such crimes.

If the judge is a retired judge serving in the Assigned Judges Program, he or she shall promptly report such information in writing to the Chief Justice rather than to the Commission on Judicial Performance. If the judge is a subordinate judicial officer, he or she shall promptly report such information in writing to both the presiding judge of the court in which the subordinate judicial officer sits and the Commission on Judicial Performance.

ADVISORY COMMITTEE COMMENTARY

Appropriate corrective action could include direct communication with the judge or lawyer who has committed the violation, other direct action if available, or a report of the violation to the presiding judge, appropriate authority, or other agency or body. Judges should note that in addition to the action required by Canon 3D(2), California law imposes additional reporting requirements regarding lawyers.*

(Canon 3D(3) amended effective January 1, 2008; previously amended effective June 19, 1997 and March 4, 1999; adopted effective January 15, 1996.)

E. Disqualification.

(1) A judge shall disqualify himself or herself in any proceeding in which disqualification is required by law.

(2) In all trial court proceedings, a judge shall disclose on the record information that is reasonably relevant to the question of disqualification under Code of Civil Procedure section 170.1, even if the judge believes there is no actual basis for disqualification.

(Canon 3E(2) amended effective January 1, 2008.)

(3) Ownership of a corporate bond issued by a party to a proceeding and having a fair market value exceeding one thousand five hundred dollars is disqualifying. Ownership of government bonds issued by a party to a proceeding is disqualifying only if the outcome of the proceeding could substantially affect the value of the judge's bond. Ownership in a mutual or common investment fund that holds bonds is not a disqualifying financial interest.

ADVISORY COMMITTEE COMMENTARY

The distinction between corporate and government bonds is consistent with the Political Reform Act (see Gov. Code, §82034), which requires disclosure of corporate bonds, but not government bonds. Canon 3E(3) is intended to assist judges in complying with Code of Civil Procedure section 170.1(a)(3) and Canon 3E(5)(d).

(Canon 3E(3) adopted effective December 22, 2003; renumbered effective January 1, 2005.)

(4) An appellate justice shall disqualify himself or herself in any proceeding if for any reason:

(a) the justice believes his or her recusal would further the interest of justice; or

(b) the justice substantially doubts his or her capacity to be impartial; or

(c) the circumstances are such that a reasonable person aware of the facts would doubt the justice's ability to be impartial.

(Canon 3E(4) renumbered effective January 1, 2005.)

(5) Disqualification of an appellate justice is also required in the following instances:

(a) The appellate justice has appeared or otherwise served as a lawyer in the pending matter, or has appeared or served as a lawyer in any other matter involving any of the same parties if that other matter related to the same contested issues of fact and law as the present matter.

(b) Within the last two years, (i) a party to the proceeding, or an officer, director or trustee thereof, either was a client of the justice when the justice was engaged in the private practice of law or was a client of a lawyer with whom the justice was associated in the private practice of law; or (ii) a lawyer in the proceeding was associated with the justice in the private practice of law.

(c) The appellate justice represented a public officer or entity and personally advised or in any way represented such officer or entity concerning the factual or legal issues in the present proceeding in which the public officer or entity now appears.

(d) The appellate justice, or his or her spouse or registered domestic partner, or a minor child residing in the household, has a financial interest or is a fiduciary who has a financial interest in the proceeding, or is a director, advisor, or other active participant in the affairs of a party.

* Terms with an asterisk (*) are defined in the Terminology section.

A financial interest is defined as ownership of more than a 1 percent legal or equitable interest in a party, or a legal or equitable interest in a party of a fair market value exceeding one thousand five hundred dollars. Ownership in a mutual or common investment fund that holds securities does not itself constitute a financial interest; holding office in an educational, religious, charitable, fraternal or civic organization does not confer a financial interest in the organization's securities; and a proprietary interest of a policyholder in a mutual insurance company or mutual savings association or similar interest is not a financial interest unless the outcome of the proceeding could substantially affect the value of the interest. A justice shall make reasonable efforts to keep informed about his or her personal and fiduciary interests and those of his or her spouse or registered domestic partner and of minor children living in the household.

(e)　The justice or his or her spouse or registered domestic partner, or a person within the third degree of relationship to either of them, or the spouse or registered domestic partner thereof, is a party or an officer, director or trustee of a party to the proceeding, or a lawyer or spouse or registered domestic partner of a lawyer in the proceeding is the spouse, registered domestic partner, former spouse, former registered domestic partner, child, sibling, or parent of the justice or of the justice's spouse or registered domestic partner, or such a person is associated in the private practice of law with a lawyer in the proceeding.

(f)　The justice (i) served as the judge before whom the proceeding was tried or heard in the lower court, (ii) has a personal knowledge of disputed evidentiary facts concerning the proceeding, or (iii) has a personal bias or prejudice concerning a party or a party's lawyer.

(g)　A temporary or permanent physical impairment renders the justice unable properly to perceive the evidence or conduct the proceedings.

(h)　The justice has a current arrangement concerning prospective employment or other compensated service as a dispute resolution neutral or is participating in, or, within the last two years has participated in, discussions regarding prospective employment or service as a dispute resolution neutral, or has been engaged in such employment or service, and any of the following applies:

(i)　The arrangement is, or the prior employment or discussion was, with a party to the proceeding;

(ii)　The matter before the justice includes issues relating to the enforcement of either an agreement to submit a dispute to an alternative dispute resolution process or an award or other final decision by a dispute resolution neutral;

(iii)　The justice directs the parties to participate in an alternative dispute resolution process in which the dispute resolution neutral will be an individual or entity with whom the justice has the arrangement, has previously been employed or served, or is discussing or has discussed the employment or service; or

(iv)　The justice will select a dispute resolution neutral or entity to conduct an alternative dispute resolution process in the matter before the justice, and among those available for selection is an individual or entity with whom the justice has the arrangement, with whom the justice has previously been employed or served, or with whom the justice is discussing or has discussed the employment or service.

For purposes of this canon, "participating in discussions" or "has participated in discussions" means that the justice solicited or otherwise indicated an interest in accepting or negotiating possible employment or service as an alternative dispute resolution neutral or responded to an unsolicited statement regarding, or an offer of, such employment or service by expressing an interest in that employment or service, making any inquiry regarding the employment or service, or encouraging the person making the statement or offer to provide additional information about that possible employment or service. If a justice's response to an unsolicited statement regarding, a question about, or offer of, prospective employment or other compensated service as a dispute resolution neutral is limited to responding negatively, declining the offer, or declining to discuss such employment or service, that response does not constitute participating in discussions.

For purposes of this canon, "party" includes the parent, subsidiary, or other legal affiliate of any entity that is a party and is involved in the transaction, contract, or facts that gave rise to the issues subject to the proceeding.

For purposes of this canon, "dispute resolution neutral" means an arbitrator, a mediator, a temporary judge appointed under section 21 of article VI of the California Constitution, a referee appointed under Code of Civil Procedure section 638 or 639, a special master, a neutral evaluator, a settlement officer, or a settlement facilitator.

(i)　The justice's spouse or registered domestic partner or a person within the third degree of relationship to the justice or his or her spouse or registered domestic partner, or the person's spouse or registered domestic partner, was a witness in the proceeding.

ADVISORY COMMITTEE COMMENTARY

Canon 3E(1) sets forth the general duty to disqualify applicable to a judge of any court. Sources for determining when recusal or disqualification is appropriate may include the applicable provisions of the Code of Civil Procedure, other provisions of the Code of Judicial Ethics, the Code of Conduct for United States Judges, the American Bar Association's Model Code of Judicial Conduct, and related case law.

The decision whether to disclose information under Canon 3E(2) is a decision based on the facts of the case before the judge. A judge is required to disclose only information that is related to the grounds for disqualification set forth in Code of Civil Procedure section 170.1.

Canon 3E(4) sets forth the general standards for recusal of an appellate justice. The term "appellate justice" includes justices of both the Courts of Appeal and the Supreme Court. Generally, the provisions concerning disqualification of an appellate justice are intended to assist justices in determining whether recusal is appropriate and to inform the public why recusal may occur.

However, the rule of necessity may override the rule of disqualification. For example, a judge might be required to participate in judicial review of a judicial salary statute, or might be the only judge available in a matter requiring judicial action, such as a hearing on probable cause or a temporary restraining order. In the latter case, the judge must promptly disclose on the record the basis for possible disqualification and use reasonable efforts to transfer the matter to another judge as soon as practicable.

In some instances, membership in certain organizations may have the potential to give an appearance of partiality, although membership in the organization generally may not be barred by Canon 2C, Canon 4, or any other specific canon. A judge holding membership in an organization should disqualify himself or herself whenever doing so would be appropriate in accordance with Canon 3E(1), 3E(4), or 3E(5) or statutory requirements. In addition, in some circumstances, the parties or their lawyers may consider a judge's membership in an organization relevant to the question of disqualification, even if the judge believes there is no actual basis for disqualification. In accordance with this Canon, a judge should disclose to the parties his or her membership in an organization, in any proceeding in which that information is reasonably relevant to the question of disqualification under Code of Civil Procedure section 170.1, even if the judge concludes there is no actual basis for disqualification.

(Canon 3E(5) amended effective January 1, 2008; renumbered effective January 1, 2005; previously amended effective January 1, 2007.)

(Canon 3E amended effective January 1, 2008; adopted effective January 15, 1996; previously amended effective April 15, 1996, June 19, 1997, March 4, 1999, December 13, 2000, June 18, 2003, December 22, 2003, January 1, 2005, and January 1, 2007.)

Ref.: CACI Nos. 107, 5003 (Matthew Bender).

Canon 4.   A judge shall so conduct the judge's quasi-judicial and extrajudicial activities as to minimize the risk of conflict with judicial obligations.

A.   Extrajudicial Activities in General

A judge shall conduct all of the judge's extrajudicial activities so that they do not

(1)   cast reasonable doubt on the judge's capacity to act impartially;

(2)   demean the judicial office; or

(3)   interfere with the proper performance of judicial duties.

ADVISORY COMMITTEE COMMENTARY

Complete separation of a judge from extrajudicial activities is neither possible nor wise; a judge should not become isolated from the community in which the judge lives.

Expressions of bias or prejudice by a judge, even outside the judge's judicial activities, may cast reasonable doubt on the judge's capacity to act impartially as a judge. Expressions which may do so include jokes or other remarks demeaning individuals on the basis of a classification such as their race, sex, religion, sexual orientation, or national origin. See Canon 2C and accompanying Commentary.

B.   Quasi-judicial and Avocational Activities

A judge may speak, write, lecture, teach, and participate in activities concerning legal and nonlegal subject matters, subject to the requirements of this Code.

ADVISORY COMMITTEE COMMENTARY

As a judicial officer and person specially learned in the law,* a judge is in a unique position to contribute to the improvement of the law,* the legal system, and the administration of justice, including revision of substantive and procedural law* and improvement of criminal and juvenile justice. To the extent that time permits, a judge may do so, either independently or through a bar or judicial association or other group dedicated to the improvement of the law.*

It may be necessary to promote legal education programs and materials by identifying authors and speakers by judicial title.

This is permissible, provided such use of the judicial title does not contravene Canons 2A and 2B.

Judges are not precluded by their office from engaging in other social, community, and intellectual endeavors so long as they do not interfere with the obligations under Canons 2C and 4A.

C.   Governmental, Civic, or Charitable Activities

(1)   A judge shall not appear at a public hearing or officially consult with an executive or legislative body or public official except on matters concerning the law,* the legal system, or the administration of justice or in matters involving the judge's private economic or personal interests.

ADVISORY COMMITTEE COMMENTARY

See Canon 2B regarding the obligation to avoid improper influence.

(2)   A judge shall not accept appointment to a governmental committee or commission or other governmental position that is concerned with issues of fact or policy on matters other than the improvement of the law,* the legal system, or the administration of justice. A judge may, however, serve in the military reserve or represent a national, state, or local government on ceremonial occasions or in connection with historical, educational, or cultural activities.

ADVISORY COMMITTEE COMMENTARY

Canon 4C(2) prohibits a judge from accepting any governmental position except one relating to the law,* legal system, or administration of justice as authorized by Canon 4C(3). The appropriateness of accepting extrajudicial assignments must be assessed in light of the demands on judicial resources and the need to protect the courts from involvement in extrajudicial matters that may prove to be controversial. Judges shall not accept governmental appointments that are likely to interfere with the effectiveness and independence of the judiciary, or which constitute a public office within the meaning of the California Constitution, article VI, section 17.

Canon 4C(2) does not govern a judge's service in a nongovernmental position. See Canon 4C(3) permitting service by a judge with organizations devoted to the improvement of the law,* the legal system, or the administration of justice and with educational, religious, charitable, fraternal, or civic organizations not conducted for profit. For example, service on the board of a public educational institution, other than a law school, would be prohibited under Canon 4C(2), but service on the board of a public law school or any private educational institution would generally be permitted under Canon 4C(3).

(3)   Subject to the following limitations and the other requirements of this Code,

(a)   a judge may serve as an officer, director, trustee, or nonlegal advisor of an organization or governmental agency devoted to the improvement of the law,* the legal system, or the administration of justice provided that such position does not constitute a public office within the meaning of the California Constitution, article VI, section 17;

(b)   a judge may serve as an officer, director, trustee, or nonlegal advisor of an educational, religious, charitable, fraternal, or civic organization not conducted for profit;

ADVISORY COMMITTEE COMMENTARY

Canon 4C(3) does not apply to a judge's service in a governmental position unconnected with the improvement of the

---

* Terms with an asterisk (*) are defined in the Terminology section.

Rules of Court

law,* the legal system, or the administration of justice. See Canon 4C(2).

Canon 4C(3) uses the phrase, "Subject to the following limitations and the other requirements of this Code." As an example of the meaning of the phrase, a judge permitted by Canon 4C(3) to serve on the board of a fraternal institution may be prohibited from such service by Canon 2C or 4A if the institution practices invidious discrimination or if service on the board otherwise casts reasonable doubt on the judge's capacity to act impartially as a judge.

Service by a judge on behalf of a civic or charitable organization may be governed by other provisions of Canon 4 in addition to Canon 4C. For example, a judge is prohibited by Canon 4G from serving as a legal advisor to a civic or charitable organization.

Service on the board of a homeowners' association or a neighborhood protective group is proper if it is related to the protection of the judge's own economic interests. See Canons 4D(2) and 4D(4). See Canon 2B regarding the obligation to avoid improper use of the prestige of a judge's office.

(c) a judge shall not serve as an officer, director, trustee, or nonlegal advisor if it is likely that the organization

(i) will be engaged in judicial proceedings that would ordinarily come before the judge, or

(ii) will be engaged frequently in adversary proceedings in the court of which the judge is a member or in any court subject to the appellate jurisdiction of the court of which the judge is a member;

ADVISORY COMMITTEE COMMENTARY

The changing nature of some organizations and of their relationship to the law* makes it necessary for the judge regularly to reexamine the activities of each organization with which the judge is affiliated to determine if it is proper for the judge to continue the affiliation. Some organizations regularly engage in litigation to achieve their goals or fulfill their purposes. Judges should avoid a leadership role in such organizations as it could compromise the appearance of impartiality.

(d) a judge as an officer, director, trustee, or nonlegal advisor, or as a member or otherwise

(i) may assist such an organization in planning fund raising and may participate in the management and investment of the organization's funds, but shall not personally participate in the solicitation of funds or other fund-raising activities, except that a judge may privately solicit funds for such an organization from other judges (excluding court commissioners, referees, retired judges, and temporary judges*);

(ii) may make recommendations to public and private fund-granting organizations on projects and programs concerning the law,* the legal system, or the administration of justice;

(iii) shall not personally participate in membership solicitation if the solicitation might reasonably be perceived as coercive or if the membership solicitation is essentially a fund-raising mechanism, except as permitted in Canon 4C(3)(d)(i);

(iv) shall not permit the use of the prestige of his or her judicial office for fund raising or membership solicitation but may be a speaker, guest of honor, or recipient of an award for public or charitable service provided the

judge does not personally solicit funds and complies with Canon 4A(1), (2), and (3).

ADVISORY COMMITTEE COMMENTARY

A judge may solicit membership or endorse or encourage membership efforts for an organization devoted to the improvement of the law,* the legal system, or the administration of justice, or a nonprofit educational, religious, charitable, fraternal, or civic organization as long as the solicitation cannot reasonably be perceived as coercive and is not essentially a fund-raising mechanism. Solicitation of funds for an organization and solicitation of memberships similarly involve the danger that the person solicited will feel obligated to respond favorably to the solicitor if the solicitor is in a position of influence or control. A judge must not engage in direct, individual solicitation of funds or memberships in person, in writing, or by telephone except in the following cases: (1) a judge may solicit other judges (excluding court commissioners, referees, retired judges, court-appointed arbitrators, and temporary judges*) for funds or memberships; (2) a judge may solicit other persons for membership in the organizations described above if neither those persons nor persons with whom they are affiliated are likely ever to appear before the court on which the judge serves; and (3) a judge who is an officer of such an organization may send a general membership solicitation mailing over the judge's signature.

Use of an organization letterhead for fund raising or membership solicitation does not violate Canon 4C(3)(d), provided the letterhead lists only the judge's name and office or other position in the organization, and designates the judge's judicial title only if other persons whose names appear on the letterhead have comparable designations. In addition, a judge must also make reasonable efforts to ensure that the judge's staff, court officials, and others subject to the judge's direction and control do not solicit funds on the judge's behalf for any purpose, charitable or otherwise.

D. Financial Activities

(1) A judge shall not engage in financial and business dealings that

(a) may reasonably be perceived to exploit the judge's judicial position, or

(b) involve the judge in frequent transactions or continuing business relationships with lawyers or other persons likely to appear before the court on which the judge serves.

ADVISORY COMMITTEE COMMENTARY

The Time for Compliance provision of this Code (Canon 6F) postpones the time for compliance with certain provisions of this Canon in some cases.

A judge must avoid financial and business dealings that involve the judge in frequent transactions or continuing business relationships with persons likely to appear either before the judge personally or before other judges on the judge's court. A judge shall discourage members of the judge's family* from engaging in dealings that would reasonably appear to exploit the judge's judicial position or that involve family members in frequent transactions or continuing business relationships with persons likely to appear before the judge. This rule is necessary to avoid creating an appearance of exploitation of office or favoritism and to minimize the potential for disqualification.

Participation by a judge in financial and business dealings is subject to the general prohibitions in Canon 4A against activities that tend to reflect adversely on impartiality, demean the judicial office, or interfere with the proper performance of judicial duties. Such participation is also subject to the general prohibition in Canon 2 against activities involving impropriety or the appear-

---

* Terms with an asterisk (*) are defined in the Terminology section.

ance of impropriety and the prohibition in Canon 2B against the misuse of the prestige of judicial office.

In addition, a judge must maintain high standards of conduct in all of the judge's activities, as set forth in Canon 1.

(2) A judge may, subject to the requirements of this Code, hold and manage investments of the judge and members of the judge's family,* including real estate, and engage in other remunerative activities. A judge shall not participate in, nor permit the judge's name to be used in connection with, any business venture or commercial advertising that indicates the judge's title or affiliation with the judiciary or otherwise lend the power or prestige of his or her office to promote a business or any commercial venture.

(3) A judge shall not serve as an officer, director, manager, or employee of a business affected with a public interest, including, without limitation, a financial institution, insurance company, or public utility.

ADVISORY COMMITTEE COMMENTARY

Although participation by a judge in business activities might otherwise be permitted by Canon 4D, a judge may be prohibited from participation by other provisions of this Code when, for example, the business entity frequently appears before the judge's court or the participation requires significant time away from judicial duties. Similarly, a judge must avoid participating in any business activity if the judge's participation would involve misuse of the prestige of judicial office. See Canon 2B.

(4) A judge shall manage personal investments and financial activities so as to minimize the necessity for disqualification. As soon as reasonably possible, a judge shall divest himself or herself of investments and other financial interests that would require frequent disqualification.

(5) Under no circumstance shall a judge accept a gift, bequest, or favor if the donor is a party whose interests have come or are reasonably likely to come before the judge. A judge shall discourage members of the judge's family residing in the judge's household* from accepting similar benefits from parties who have come or are reasonably likely to come before the judge.

ADVISORY COMMITTEE COMMENTARY

In addition to the prohibitions set forth in Canon 4D(5) regarding gifts, other laws may be applicable to judges, including, for example, Code of Civil Procedure section 170.9 and the Political Reform Act of 1974 (Gov. Code, §81000 et seq.).

Canon 4D(5) does not apply to contributions to a judge's campaign for judicial office, a matter governed by Canon 5.

Because a gift, bequest, or favor to a member of the judge's family residing in the judge's household* might be viewed as intended to influence the judge, a judge must inform those family members of the relevant ethical constraints upon the judge in this regard and discourage those family members from violating them. A judge cannot, however, reasonably be expected to know or control all of the financial or business activities of all family members residing in the judge's household.*

The application of Canon 4D(5) requires recognition that a judge cannot reasonably be expected to anticipate all persons or interests that may come before the court.

(6) A judge shall not accept and shall discourage members of the judge's family residing in the judge's household* from accepting a gift, bequest, favor, or loan from anyone except as hereinafter provided:

(a) any gift incidental to a public testimonial, books, tapes, and other resource materials supplied by publishers on a complimentary basis for official use, or an invitation to the judge and the judge's spouse or registered domestic partner or guest to attend a bar-related function or an activity devoted to the improvement of the law,* the legal system, or the administration of justice;

(b) advances or reimbursement for the reasonable cost of travel, transportation, lodging, and subsistence which is directly related to participation in any judicial, educational, civic, or governmental program or bar-related function or activity, devoted to the improvement of the law,* the legal system, or the administration of justice;

ADVISORY COMMITTEE COMMENTARY

Acceptance of an invitation to a law-related function is governed by Canon 4D(6)(a); acceptance of an invitation paid for by an individual lawyer or group of lawyers is governed by Canon 4D(6)(d).

(c) a gift, award, or benefit incident to the business, profession, or other separate activity of a spouse or registered domestic partner or other member of the judge's family residing in the judge's household,* including gifts, awards, and benefits for the use of both the spouse or registered domestic partner or other family member and the judge, provided the gift, award, or benefit could not reasonably be perceived as intended to influence the judge in the performance of judicial duties;

(d) ordinary social hospitality;

ADVISORY COMMITTEE COMMENTARY

Although Canon 4D(6)(d) does not preclude ordinary social hospitality between members of the bench and bar, a judge should carefully weigh acceptance of such hospitality to avoid any appearance of bias. See Canon 2B.

(e) a gift for a special occasion from a relative or friend, if the gift is fairly commensurate with the occasion and the relationship;

ADVISORY COMMITTEE COMMENTARY

A gift to a judge, or to a member of the judge's family residing in the judge's household,* that is excessive in value raises questions about the judge's impartiality and the integrity of the judicial office and might require disqualification of the judge where disqualification would not otherwise be required. See, however, Canon 4D(6)(f).

(f) a gift, bequest, favor, or loan from a relative or close personal friend whose appearance or interest in a case would in any event require disqualification under Canon 3E;

(g) a loan in the regular course of business on the same terms generally available to persons who are not judges;

(h) a scholarship or fellowship awarded on the same terms and based on the same criteria applied to other applicants.

(Canon 4D amended effective January 1, 2007.)

E. Fiduciary Activities

(1) A judge shall not serve as executor, administrator, or other personal representative, trustee, guardian, attorney in fact, or other fiduciary,* except for the estate, trust, or person of a member of the judge's family,* and then only if such service will not interfere with the proper performance of judicial duties.

---

* Terms with an asterisk (*) are defined in the Terminology section.

(2)   A judge shall not serve as a fiduciary* if it is likely that the judge as a fiduciary* will be engaged in proceedings that would ordinarily come before the judge, or if the estate, trust, or minor or conservatee becomes engaged in contested proceedings in the court on which the judge serves or one under its appellate jurisdiction.

(3)   The same restrictions on financial activities that apply to a judge personally also apply to the judge while acting in a fiduciary* capacity.

ADVISORY COMMITTEE COMMENTARY

The Time for Compliance provision of this Code (Canon 6F) postpones the time for compliance with certain provisions of this Canon in some cases.

The restrictions imposed by this Canon may conflict with the judge's obligation as a fiduciary. For example, a judge shall resign as trustee if detriment to the trust would result from divestiture of trust holdings the retention of which would place the judge in violation of Canon 4D(4).*

F.   Service as Arbitrator or Mediator

A judge shall not act as an arbitrator or mediator or otherwise perform judicial functions in a private capacity unless expressly authorized by law.*

ADVISORY COMMITTEE COMMENTARY

Canon 4F does not prohibit a judge from participating in arbitration, mediation, or settlement conferences performed as part of his or her judicial duties.

G.   Practice of Law

A judge shall not practice law.

ADVISORY COMMITTEE COMMENTARY

This prohibition refers to the practice of law in a representative capacity and not in a pro se capacity. A judge may act for himself or herself in all legal matters, including matters involving litigation and matters involving appearances before or other dealings with legislative and other governmental bodies. However, in so doing, a judge must not abuse the prestige of office to advance the interests of the judge or member of the judge's family. See Canon 2B.*

This prohibition applies to subordinate judicial officers, magistrates, special masters, and judges of the State Bar Court.

(Canon 4G amended effective January 1, 2005.)

H.   Compensation and Reimbursement

A judge may receive compensation and reimbursement of expenses as provided by law* for the extrajudicial activities permitted by this Code, if the source of such payments does not give the appearance of influencing the judge's performance of judicial duties or otherwise give the appearance of impropriety.

(1)   Compensation shall not exceed a reasonable amount nor shall it exceed what a person who is not a judge would receive for the same activity.

(2)   Expense reimbursement shall be limited to the actual cost of travel, food, lodging, and other costs reasonably incurred by the judge and, where appropriate to the occasion, by the judge's spouse or registered domestic partner or guest. Any payment in excess of such an amount is compensation.

ADVISORY COMMITTEE COMMENTARY

Judges should be aware of the statutory limitations on accepting gifts, including honoraria.

(Canon 4H amended effective January 1, 2007.)

Canon 5.   A judge or judicial candidate* shall refrain from inappropriate political activity.

Judges are entitled to entertain their personal views on political questions. They are not required to surrender their rights or opinions as citizens. They shall, however, avoid political activity that may create the appearance of political bias or impropriety. Judicial independence and impartiality should dictate the conduct of judges and candidates* for judicial office.

A.   Political Organizations

Judges and candidates* for judicial office shall not

(1)   act as leaders or hold any office in a political organization;*

(2)   make speeches for a political organization* or candidate* for nonjudicial office or publicly endorse or publicly oppose a candidate for nonjudicial office; or

(3)   personally solicit funds for a political organization* or nonjudicial candidate;* or make contributions to a political party or political organization* or to a nonjudicial candidate in excess of five hundred dollars in any calendar year per political party or political organization* or candidate,* or in excess of an aggregate of one thousand dollars in any calendar year for all political parties or political organizations* or nonjudicial candidates.*

ADVISORY COMMITTEE COMMENTARY

The term "political activity" should not be construed so narrowly as to prevent private comment.

This provision does not prohibit a judge from signing a petition to qualify a measure for the ballot without the use of the judge's official title.

In judicial elections, judges are neither required to shield themselves from campaign contributions nor are they prohibited from soliciting contributions from anyone including attorneys. Nevertheless, there are necessary limits on judges facing election if the appearance of impropriety is to be avoided. Although it is improper for a judge to receive a gift from an attorney subject to exceptions noted in Canon 4D(6), a judge's campaign may receive attorney contributions.

Although attendance at political gatherings is not prohibited, any such attendance should be restricted so that it would not constitute an express public endorsement of a nonjudicial candidate or a measure not directly affecting the administration of justice otherwise prohibited by this Canon.*

Subject to the monetary limitation herein to political contributions, a judge may purchase tickets for political dinners or other similar dinner functions. Any admission price to such a political dinner or function in excess of the actual cost of the meal shall be considered a political contribution. The prohibition in Canon 5A(3) does not preclude judges from contributing to a campaign fund for distribution among judges who are candidates for reelection or retention, nor does it apply to contributions to any judge or candidate for judicial office.*

Under this Canon, a judge may publicly endorse another judicial candidate. Such endorsements are permitted because judicial officers have a special obligation to uphold the integrity and impartiality of the judiciary and are in a unique position to know the qualifications necessary to serve as a competent judicial officer.*

Although members of the judge's family are not subject to the provisions of this Code, a judge shall not avoid compliance with*

---

* Terms with an asterisk (*) are defined in the Terminology section.

this Code by making contributions through a spouse or registered domestic partner or other family member.

(Canon 5A amended effective January 1, 2007.)

B. Conduct During Judicial Campaigns

A candidate* for election or appointment to judicial office shall not (1) make statements to the electorate or the appointing authority that commit the candidate with respect to cases, controversies, or issues that could come before the courts, or (2) knowingly, or with reckless disregard for the truth, misrepresent the identity, qualifications, present position, or any other fact concerning the candidate or his or her opponent.

ADVISORY COMMITTEE COMMENTARY

This code does not contain the "announce clause" that was the subject of the United States Supreme Court's decision in Republican Party of Minnesota v. White (2002) 536 U.S. 765. That opinion did not address the "commit clause," which is contained in Canon 5B(1). The phrase "appear to commit" has been deleted because, although judicial candidates cannot promise to take a particular position on cases, controversies, or issues prior to taking the bench and presiding over individual cases, the phrase may have been overinclusive.

Canon 5B(2) prohibits making knowing misrepresentations, including false or misleading statements, during an election campaign because doing so would violate Canons 1 and 2A, and may violate other canons.

(Canon 5B amended effective December 22, 2003.)

C. Speaking at Political Gatherings

Candidates* for judicial office may speak to political gatherings only on their own behalf or on behalf of another candidate for judicial office.

D. Measures to Improve the Law

Except as otherwise permitted in this Code, judges shall not engage in any political activity, other than in relation to measures concerning the improvement of the law,* the legal system, or the administration of justice.

Canon 6. Compliance with the Code of Judicial Ethics.

A. Judges

Anyone who is an officer of the state judicial system and who performs judicial functions, including, but not limited to, a subordinate judicial officer, magistrate, court-appointed arbitrator, judge of the State Bar Court, temporary judge, and special master, is a judge within the meaning of this Code. All judges shall comply with this Code except as provided below.

ADVISORY COMMITTEE COMMENTARY

For the purposes of this Canon, if a retired judge is serving in the assigned judges program, the judge is considered to "perform judicial functions." Because retired judges who are privately retained may perform judicial functions, their conduct while performing those functions should be guided by this Code.

(Canon 6A amended effective January 1, 2005.)

B. Retired Judge Serving in the Assigned Judges Program

A retired judge who has filed an application to serve on assignment, meets the eligibility requirements set by the Chief Justice for service, and has received an acknowledgment of participation in the assigned judges program shall comply with all provisions of this Code, except for the following:

4C(2)   Appointment to governmental positions
4E   Fiduciary* activities

(Canon 6B amended effective January 1, 2005.)

C. Retired Judge as Arbitrator or Mediator

A retired judge serving in the assigned judges program is not required to comply with Canon 4F of this Code relating to serving as an arbitrator or mediator, or performing judicial functions in a private capacity, except as otherwise provided in the *Standards and Guidelines for Judges Serving on Assignment* promulgated by the Chief Justice.

ADVISORY COMMITTEE COMMENTARY

In California, article VI, section 6 of the California Constitution provides that a "retired judge who consents may be assigned to any court" by the Chief Justice. Retired judges who are serving in the assigned judges program pursuant to the above provision are bound by Canon 6B, including the requirement of Canon 4G barring the practice of law. Other provisions of California law, and standards and guidelines for eligibility and service set by the Chief Justice, further define the limitations on who may serve on assignment.

D. Temporary Judge*, Referee, or Court-Appointed Arbitrator[1]

A temporary judge, a person serving as a referee pursuant to Code of Civil Procedure section 638 or 639, or a court-appointed arbitrator shall comply only with the following Code provisions:

(1) A temporary judge, referee, or court-appointed arbitrator shall comply with Canons 1 [integrity and independence of the judiciary], 2A [promoting public confidence], 3B(3) [order and decorum] and (4) [patient, dignified, and courteous treatment], 3B(6) [require lawyers to refrain from manifestations of any form of bias or prejudice], 3D(1) [action regarding misconduct by another judge] and (2) [action regarding misconduct by a lawyer], when the temporary judge, referee, or court-appointed arbitrator is actually presiding in a proceeding or communicating with the parties, counsel, or court personnel while serving in the capacity of a temporary judge, referee, or court-appointed arbitrator in the case.

(2) A temporary judge, referee, or court-appointed arbitrator shall, from the time of notice and acceptance of appointment until termination of the appointment:

(a) Comply with Canons 2B(1) [not allow family or other relationships to influence judicial conduct], 3B(1) [hear and decide all matters unless disqualified] and (2) [be faithful to and maintain competence in the law], 3B(5) [perform judicial duties without bias or prejudice], 3B(7) [accord full right to be heard to those entitled; avoid ex parte communications, except as specified] and (8) [dispose of matters fairly and promptly], 3C(1) [discharge administrative responsibilities without bias and with competence and cooperatively], (2) [require staff and personnel to observe standards of conduct and refrain from bias

---

* Terms with an asterisk (*) are defined in the Terminology section.

[1] Reference should be made to relevant commentary to analogous or individual Canons cited or described in this Canon and appearing elsewhere in this Code.

and prejudice] and (4) [make only fair, necessary, and appropriate appointments];

(b) Not personally solicit memberships or donations for religious, fraternal, educational, civic, or charitable organizations from the parties and lawyers appearing before the temporary judge, referee, or court-appointed arbitrator;

(c) Under no circumstance accept a gift, bequest, or favor if the donor is a party, person, or entity whose interests are reasonably likely to come before the temporary judge, referee, or court-appointed arbitrator. A temporary judge, referee, or court-appointed arbitrator shall discourage members of the judge's family residing in the judge's household from accepting benefits from parties who are reasonably likely to come before the temporary judge, referee, or court-appointed arbitrator.

(3) A temporary judge shall, from the time of notice and acceptance of appointment until termination of the appointment, disqualify himself or herself in any proceeding as follows:

(a) A temporary judge—other than a temporary judge solely conducting settlement conferences—is disqualified to serve in a proceeding if any one or more of the following is true:

(i) the temporary judge has personal knowledge (as defined in Code of Civil Procedure section 170.1(a)(1)) of disputed evidentiary facts concerning the proceeding;

(ii) the temporary judge has served as a lawyer (as defined in Code of Civil Procedure section 170.1(a)(2)) in the proceeding;

(iii) the temporary judge, within the past five years, has given legal advice to, or served as a lawyer (as defined in Code of Civil Procedure section 170.1(a)(2), except that this provision requires disqualification if the temporary judge represented a party in the past five years rather than the two-year period specified in section 170.1(a)(2)) for a party in the present proceeding;

(iv) the temporary judge has a financial interest (as defined in Code of Civil Procedure sections 170.1(a)(3) and 170.5) in the subject matter in the proceeding or in a party to the proceeding;

(v) the temporary judge, or the spouse or registered domestic partner of the temporary judge, or a person within the third degree of relationship to either of them, or the spouse or registered domestic partner of such a person is a party to the proceeding or is an officer, director, or trustee of a party;

(vi) a lawyer or a spouse or registered domestic partner of a lawyer in the proceeding is the spouse, former spouse, registered domestic partner, former registered domestic partner, child, sibling, or parent of the temporary judge or the temporary judge's spouse or registered domestic partner, or if such a person is associated in the private practice of law with a lawyer in the proceeding; or

(vii) for any reason:

(A) the temporary judge believes his or her recusal would further the interests of justice;

(B) the temporary judge believes there is a substantial doubt as to his or her capacity to be impartial; or

(C) a person aware of the facts might reasonably entertain a doubt that the temporary judge would be able to be impartial. Bias or prejudice toward an attorney in the proceeding may be grounds for disqualification;

ADVISORY COMMITTEE COMMENTARY

The application of Canon 6D(3)(a)(iii), providing that a temporary judge is disqualified if he or she has given legal advice or served as a lawyer for a party to the proceeding in the past five years, may depend on the type of assignment and the amount of time available to investigate whether the temporary judge has previously represented a party. If time permits, the temporary judge must conduct such an investigation. Thus, if a temporary judge is privately compensated by the parties or is presiding over a particular matter known in advance of the hearing, the temporary judge is presumed to have adequate time to investigate. If, however, a temporary judge is assigned to a high volume calendar, such as traffic or small claims, and has not been provided with the names of the parties prior to the assignment, the temporary judge may rely on his or her memory to determine whether he or she has previously represented a party.

(b) A temporary judge before whom a proceeding was tried or heard is disqualified from participating in any appellate review of that proceeding.

(c) If the temporary judge has a current arrangement concerning prospective employment or other compensated service as a dispute resolution neutral or is participating in, or, within the last two years has participated in, discussions regarding prospective employment or service as a dispute resolution neutral, or has been engaged in such employment or service, and any of the following applies:

(i) The arrangement or current employment is, or the prior employment or discussion was, with a party to the proceeding.

(ii) The temporary judge directs the parties to participate in an alternative dispute resolution process in which the dispute resolution neutral will be an individual or entity with whom the temporary judge has the arrangement, is currently employed or serves, has previously been employed or served, or is discussing or has discussed the employment or service.

(iii) The temporary judge will select a dispute resolution neutral or entity to conduct an alternative dispute resolution process in the matter before the temporary judge, and among those available for selection is an individual or entity with whom the temporary judge has the arrangement, is currently employed or serves, has previously been employed or served, or is discussing or has discussed the employment or service.

For the purposes of canon 6D(3)(c), the definitions of "participating in discussions," "has participated in discussions," "party," and "dispute resolution neutral" are set forth in Code of Civil Procedure section 170.1(a)(8), except that the words "temporary judge" shall be substituted for the word "judge" in such definitions.

(d) A lawyer is disqualified from serving as a temporary judge in a family law or unlawful detainer proceeding if in the same type of proceeding:

(i) the lawyer holds himself or herself out to the public as representing exclusively one side; or

(ii) the lawyer represents one side in 90 percent or more of the cases in which he or she appears.

ADVISORY COMMITTEE COMMENTARY

Under Canon 6D(3)(d), "one side" means a category of persons such as landlords, tenants, or litigants exclusively of one gender.

(4) After a temporary judge who has determined himself or herself to be disqualified from serving under Canon 6D(3)(a)–(d) has disclosed the basis for his or her disqualification on the record, the parties and their lawyers may agree to waive the disqualification and the temporary judge may accept the waiver. The temporary judge shall not seek to induce a waiver and shall avoid any effort to discover which lawyers or parties favored or opposed a waiver.

ADVISORY COMMITTEE COMMENTARY

Provisions addressing waiver of mandatory disqualifications or limitations, late discovery of grounds for disqualification or limitation, notification of the court when a disqualification or limitation applies, and requests for disqualification by the parties are located in rule 2.818 of the California Rules of Court. Rule 2.818 states that the waiver must be in writing, must recite the basis for the disqualification or limitation, and must state that it was knowingly made. It also states that the waiver is effective only when signed by all parties and their attorneys and filed in the record.

(5) A temporary judge, referee, or court-appointed arbitrator shall, from the time of notice and acceptance of appointment until termination of the appointment:

(a) In all proceedings, disclose in writing or on the record information as required by law, or information that is reasonably relevant to the question of disqualification under Canon 6D(3), including personal or professional relationships known to the temporary judge, referee, or court-appointed arbitrator that he or she or his or her law firm has had with a party, lawyer, or law firm in the current proceeding, even though the temporary judge, referee, or court-appointed arbitrator concludes that there is no actual basis for disqualification; and

(b) In all proceedings, disclose in writing or on the record membership of the temporary judge, referee, or court-appointed arbitrator, in any organization that practices invidious discrimination on the basis of race, sex, religion, national origin, or sexual orientation, except for membership in a religious or an official military organization of the United States and membership in a nonprofit youth organization so long as membership does not violate Canon 4A [conduct of extrajudicial activities].

(6) A temporary judge, referee, or court-appointed arbitrator, from the time of notice and acceptance of appointment until the case is no longer pending in any court, shall not make any public comment about a pending or impending proceeding in which the temporary judge, referee, or court-appointed arbitrator has been engaged, and shall not make any nonpublic comment that might substantially interfere with such proceeding. The temporary judge, referee, or court-appointed arbitrator shall require similar abstention on the part of court personnel subject to his or her control. This Canon does not prohibit the following:

(a) Statements made in the course of the official duties of the temporary judge, referee, or court-appointed arbitrator; and

(b) Explanations for public information about the procedures of the court.

(7) From the time of appointment and continuing for two years after the case is no longer pending in any court, a temporary judge, referee, or court-appointed arbitrator shall under no circumstances accept a gift, bequest, or favor from a party, person, or entity whose interests have come before the temporary judge, referee, or court-appointed arbitrator in the matter. The temporary judge, referee, or court-appointed arbitrator shall discourage family members residing in the household of the temporary judge, referee, or court-appointed arbitrator from accepting any benefits from such parties, persons or entities during the time period stated in this subdivision. The demand for or receipt by a temporary judge, referee, or court-appointed arbitrator of a fee for his or her services rendered or to be rendered shall not be a violation of this Canon.

(8) A temporary judge, referee, or court-appointed arbitrator shall, from time of notice and acceptance of appointment and continuing indefinitely after the termination of the appointment:

(a) Comply with Canons 3(B)(11) [no disclosure of nonpublic information acquired in a judicial capacity] (except as required by law);

(b) Not commend or criticize jurors sitting in a proceeding before the temporary judge, referee, or court-appointed arbitrator for their verdict other than in a court order or opinion in such proceeding, but may express appreciation to jurors for their service to the judicial system and the community; and

(c) Not lend the prestige of judicial office to advance his, her, or another person's pecuniary or personal interests and not use his or her judicial title in any written communication intended to advance his, her, or another person's pecuniary or personal interests, except to show his, her, or another person's qualifications.

(9)(a) A temporary judge appointed under rule 2.810 of the California Rules of Court, from the time of appointment and continuing indefinitely after the termination of the appointment, shall not use his or her title or service as a temporary judge as a description of the lawyer's current or former principal profession, vocation, or occupation on a ballot designation for judicial or other elected office, in an advertisement about the lawyer's law firm or business, or on a letterhead, business card, or other document that is distributed to the public identifying the lawyer or the lawyer's law firm.

(b) This Canon does not prohibit a temporary judge appointed under rule 2.810 of the California Rules of Court from using his or her title or service as a temporary judge on an application to serve as a temporary judge, including an application in other courts, on an application for employment or for an appointment to a judicial position, on an individual resume or a descriptive statement submitted in connection with an application for employment or for appointment or election to a judicial position, or in response to a request for information about the public service in which the lawyer has engaged.

(10) A temporary judge, referee, or court-appointed arbitrator shall comply with Canon 6D(2) until the appointment has been terminated formally or until there is no reasonable probability that the temporary judge, referee, or court-appointed arbitrator will further participate in the matter. A rebuttable presumption that the appointment has been formally terminated shall arise if, within one year from the appointment or from the date of the last hearing scheduled in the matter, whichever is later, neither the appointing court nor counsel for any party in the matter

has informed the temporary judge, referee, or court-appointed arbitrator that the appointment remains in effect.

(11) A lawyer who has been a temporary judge, referee, or court-appointed arbitrator in a matter shall not accept any representation relating to the matter without the informed written consent of all parties.

(12) When by reason of serving as a temporary judge, referee, or court-appointed arbitrator in a matter, he or she has received confidential information from a party, the person shall not, without the informed written consent of the party, accept employment in another matter in which the confidential information is material.

ADVISORY COMMITTEE COMMENTARY

Any exceptions to the Canons do not excuse a judicial officer's separate statutory duty to disclose information that may result in the judicial officer's recusal or disqualification.

(Canon 6D amended effective January 1, 2008; adopted effective January 15, 1996; previously amended effective April 15, 1996, March 4, 1999, July 1, 2006, and January 1, 2007.)

E. Judicial Candidate

A candidate* for judicial office shall comply with the provisions of Canon 5.

F. Time for Compliance

A person to whom this Code becomes applicable shall comply immediately with all provisions of this Code except Canons 4D(2) and 4F and shall comply with these Canons as soon as reasonably possible and shall do so in any event within a period of one year.

ADVISORY COMMITTEE COMMENTARY

If serving as a fiduciary* when selected as a judge, a new judge may, notwithstanding the prohibitions in Canon 4F, continue to serve as fiduciary* but only for that period of time necessary to

---

avoid adverse consequences to the beneficiary of the fiduciary relationship and in no event longer than one year. Similarly, if engaged at the time of judicial selection in a business activity, a new judge may, notwithstanding the prohibitions in Canon 4D(2), continue in that activity for a reasonable period but in no event longer than one year.

(Canon 6G repealed effective June 1, 2005; adopted December 30, 2002.)

H. Judges on Leave Running for Other Public Office

A judge who is on leave while running for other public office pursuant to article VI, section 17 of the California Constitution shall comply with all provisions of this Code, except for the following, insofar as the conduct relates to the campaign for public office for which the judge is on leave:

2B(2)—Lending the prestige of judicial office to advance the judge's personal interest

2B(4)—Using the judicial title in written communications intended to advance the judge's personal interest

4C(1)—Appearing at public hearings

5—Engaging in political activity (including soliciting and accepting campaign contributions for the other public office)

ADVISORY COMMITTEE COMMENTARY

These exceptions are applicable only during the time the judge is on leave while running for other public office. All of the provisions of this Code will become applicable at the time a judge resumes his or her position as a judge.

Conduct during elections for judicial office is governed by Canon 5.

(Canon 6H adopted effective January 1, 2005.)

---

* Terms with an asterisk (*) are defined in the Terminology section.

INTERNAL OPERATING PRACTICES AND PROCEDURES OF THE CALIFORNIA SUPREME COURT

(Revised October 22, 2003, November 24, 2003, August 25, 2004, and January 1, 2007)[1]

The following internal operating practices and procedures are observed by the California Supreme Court in the performance of its duties.[2]

I. ACTING CHIEF JUSTICE

An Acting Chief Justice performs the functions of the Chief Justice when the Chief Justice is absent or unable to participate in a matter. The Chief Justice, pursuant to constitutional authority (Cal. Const., art. VI, § 6), selects on a rotational basis an associate justice to serve as Acting Chief Justice.

II. TRANSFER OF CASES

A. All transfers to the Supreme Court of a cause in a Court of Appeal pursuant to article VI, section 12 of the California Constitution are accomplished by order of the Chief Justice made on a vote of four justices assenting thereto.

B. Unless otherwise ordered by the Chief Justice, all applications for writs of mandate and/or prohibition that have not previously been filed with the proper Court of Appeal are transferred to such court.

III. CONFERENCES

A. Unless otherwise directed by the Chief Justice, regular conferences are held each Wednesday, excluding the Wednesday of regular calendar sessions and the first Wednesday of July and August.

B. Special conferences may be called by the Chief Justice whenever deemed necessary or desirable.

C. Four justices constitute a quorum for any regular or special conference.

D. A judge assigned by the Chief Justice to assist the court, or to act in the place of a regular member of the court who is disqualified or otherwise unable to act, may be counted to obtain a quorum for a conference. A regular member of the court, present at a conference, who is not participating in a particular matter is not counted in determining a quorum for that matter.

E. A justice who has ascertained that he or she will not be present at a conference or will not be participating in a particular matter will notify the Chief Justice or the Calendar Coordinator, as specified by sections XII.C and XIII.A. The absent justice may communicate in writing to the Calendar Coordinator his or her votes on some or all of the matters on any given conference, and may be counted to constitute a quorum for each such conference matter on which a vote has been cast.

F. Matters in which time is of the essence may be considered by the court without a formal conference. In such matters, because time is of the essence, an order will be filed as soon as four justices vote for a particular disposition.

IV. CONFERENCE MEMORANDA

A. Unless otherwise directed by the Chief Justice, a conference memorandum is prepared for each petition requiring conference consideration or action.

B. Upon the filing of a petition, motion, or application, the Calendar Coordinator, under the direction of the Chief Justice, assigns it a conference date and refers it to one of the central staffs or a member of the court for preparation of a conference memorandum as follows:

1. Petitions in civil cases, to the civil central staff.

2. Petitions in or derived from criminal cases, other than cases arising from judgments of death, to the criminal central staff.

3. Applications for writs of habeas corpus arising out of criminal proceedings, other than cases arising from judgments of death, to the criminal central staff.

4. Motions in criminal cases arising from judgments of death, to the six associate justices and the Chief Justice, or to the capital central staff.

5. Applications for writs of habeas corpus arising out of

---

[1] These practices and procedures may be amended from time to time, as needed, to facilitate the court's ability to discharge its duties. Amendments are reflected in updated versions of the practices and procedures on the California Courts Web site at <http://www.courtinfo.ca.gov/courts/supreme/iopp.htm>. Section VIII.D was amended October 22, 2003; sections III.E, IX, X, and XII were amended November 24, 2003; sections IV.J and XIII.B were amended August 25, 2004; and, rules references throughout were amended effective January 1, 2007, to reflect the reorganization and renumbering of the California Rules of Court effective on that date.

[2] Various provisions of the California Constitution, codes, and rules of court, as well as numerous provisions of the decisional law, bear on how the court functions. The court's internal operating practices and procedures should be considered in that context.

judgments of death, to the six associate justices and the Chief Justice, or to the capital central staff.

6. Applications to the Supreme Court pursuant to article V, section 8 of the California Constitution for a recommendation regarding the granting of a pardon or commutation to a person twice convicted of a felony, to the criminal central staff.

7. Petitions for review of State Bar proceedings pursuant to rule 9.13 et seq. of the California Rules of Court, to the civil central staff.

8. All other petitions and applications, to the six associate justices and the Chief Justice in rotation so that, at the end of a given period of time, each justice will have been assigned an equal number of petitions. Petitions for rehearing after decision in the Supreme Court are referred to a justice, other than the author, who concurred in the majority opinion.

C. The recommendation set forth in a conference memorandum will generally be one of the following: (1) "Grant," (2) "Grant and Hold," (3) "Grant and Transfer," (4) "Deny," (5) "Submitted," (6) "Denial Submitted," and (7) "Deny and Depublish." The designation "submitted" is used when the author believes the case warrants special discussion. The designation "denial submitted" is used when the author believes the petition should be denied, but nevertheless believes some ground exists that could arguably justify a grant, or an issue is raised that otherwise warrants discussion by the court. The designation "deny and depublish" is used when the author does not believe the decision warrants review, but nevertheless believes the opinion is potentially misleading and should not be relied on as precedent.

D. The author of the conference memorandum assigns it to either the "A" or the "B" list. Cases assigned to the "A" list include all those in which the recommendation is to grant or take affirmative action of some kind, e.g., "grant and transfer" or "deny and depublish," in which a dissenting opinion has been filed in the Court of Appeal, or in which the author believes denial is appropriate, but that the case poses questions that deserve special attention. Cases assigned to the "B" list concern routine matters, or application of settled law.

E. Conference memoranda are delivered by the author to the Calendar Coordinator for reproduction and distribution to the justices no later than the Tuesday of the week before the conference, thus providing ample time for the justices and their staffs to review the petition and the court's internal memoranda.

F. The court's Calendar Coordinator divides the weekly conference agenda into an "A" and "B" list, based on the designation appearing on each conference memorandum.

G. Matters appearing on the "A" list are called and considered at the conference for which they are scheduled. Before or after a vote is taken, any justice may request that a case be put over to a subsequent conference within the jurisdictional time limit for further study, preparation of a supplemental memorandum, or both. The time within which action thereon must be taken will be extended pursuant to rules 8.264 and 8.500 of the California Rules of Court, if necessary.

H. Matters appearing on the "B" list will be denied in accordance with the recommendation of the memoran-

dum, at the conference at which they are scheduled, unless a justice requests that a case be put over to a subsequent conference within the jurisdictional time limit for further study, preparation of a supplemental memorandum, or both.

I. In any case in which the petition, application, or motion is denied, a justice may request that his or her vote be recorded in the court minutes.

J. When a justice is unavailable or disqualified to participate in a vote on a petition for review or other matter and four justices cannot agree on a disposition, the Chief Justice, pursuant to constitutional authority (Cal. Const., art. VI, § 6), assigns in alphabetical order (except as set forth below) a Court of Appeal justice as a pro tempore justice to participate in the vote on the petition or matter. The assigned justice is furnished all pertinent petitions, motions, applications, answers, briefs, memoranda, and other material. A newly-appointed Court of Appeal justice will be assigned as a pro tempore justice of the Supreme Court only after he or she has served on the Court of Appeal for one year. If a Court of Appeal justice is unable to serve on a particular case, the next justice on the alphabetical list will be assigned, and the Court of Appeal justice who was unable to serve will be assigned in the next case in which a pro tempore appointment is required.

K. Either at the time review is granted, or at any time thereafter, the court may specify which of the issues presented should be briefed and argued.

L. Within 15 days after review is granted in a civil case or a criminal case in which a corporate entity is a party, each party must file a "Certification of Interested Entities or Persons" that lists any persons, associations of persons, firms, partnerships, corporations (including parent and subsidiary corporations) or other entities other than the parties themselves known by the party to have either (i) a financial interest in the subject matter of the controversy or in a party to the proceeding; or (ii) any other kind of interest that could be substantially affected by the outcome of the proceeding. This requirement does not apply to any governmental entity or its agencies. The Clerk's Office shall notify all parties including real parties in interest in writing of this requirement at the time the parties are notified of the court's grant of review.

Revised effective January 1, 2007.

V. CALENDAR SESSIONS FOR ORAL ARGUMENT

Regular sessions of the court are held each year, on a day or days as determined by the Chief Justice, in San Francisco, Los Angeles, and Sacramento. Special sessions may be held elsewhere by order of the Chief Justice or by order on a vote of four justices assenting thereto.

Unless otherwise ordered by the Chief Justice, the court convenes at 9:00 a.m.

Unless otherwise ordered, only one counsel may be heard for each side. Counsel wishing to divide the time for oral argument must request permission from the Court not later than ten days after the case has been set for oral argument. In no event shall oral argument be divided into segments of less than ten minutes, except that one counsel for the opening side (unless additional counsel are so authorized) may reserve a portion of his or her allotted time for rebuttal.

VI. CALENDARS AND CALENDAR MEMORANDA

A. The purpose of the calendar memorandum is to present the facts and legal issues, and to propose a resolution of the legal issues.

B. At the request of the justice preparing a calendar memorandum, or on direction of the Chief Justice, or on the affirmative vote of a majority of the court, the Clerk's Office will request counsel for the parties to be prepared to argue and to submit additional briefs on any points that are deemed omitted or inadequately covered by the briefs or in which the court is particularly interested.

C. In assigning cases for the preparation of calendar memoranda, the Chief Justice takes into account the following considerations, but may depart from these considerations for the purpose of equalizing the workload of the justices or expediting the work of the court:

1. The case is assigned to one of the justices who voted for review. If a case involves substantially the same issues as one already assigned for preparation of a calendar memorandum, it may be assigned to the justice who has the similar case. Preference in case assignments may be given to a justice who authored the conference memorandum or supplemental conference memorandum on which the petition was granted, unless other factors, such as equalization of workload, suggest a different assignment.

2. Granted petitions in other matters and State Bar proceedings originally referred to the central staffs are generally assigned to the justices in such a manner as to equalize each justice's allotment of cases.

3. Appeals in cases in which the death penalty has been imposed are assigned in rotation as they are filed.

4. When a rehearing has been granted and a supplemental calendar memorandum is needed, the matter will ordinarily be assigned to the justice who prepared the prior opinion if it appears that he or she can present the views of the majority. Otherwise, the case will be assigned to a justice who is able to do so.

D. The court's general procedures for circulation of calendar memoranda, etc., are as follows:

1. The justice to whom a case is assigned prepares and circulates a calendar memorandum within a prescribed time after the filing of the last brief. When the calendar memorandum circulates, the Calendar Coordinator distributes copies of the briefs to each justice. The record remains with the Calendar Coordinator, to be borrowed as needed by a justice or his or her staff.

2. Within a prescribed time after the calendar memorandum circulates, each justice states his or her preliminary response to the calendar memorandum (i.e., that he or she concurs, concurs with reservations, is doubtful, or does not concur). Each justice also indicates whether he or she intends to write a separate concurring or dissenting calendar memorandum in the case. If it appears from the preliminary responses that a majority of the justices concur in the original calendar memorandum, the Chief Justice places the case on a pre-argument conference (§ VI.D.4, *post*). If it appears from the preliminary responses that a majority of the justices will probably not concur in

the original calendar memorandum or a modified version of that memorandum, the Chief Justice places the matter on a conference for discussion or reassigns the case.

3. Each justice who wishes to write a concurring or dissenting calendar memorandum does so and circulates that memorandum within a prescribed time after the original calendar memorandum circulates. Soon after any concurring or dissenting calendar memorandum circulates, each justice either confirms his or her agreement with the original calendar memorandum or indicates his or her agreement with the concurring or dissenting calendar memorandum. If the original calendar memorandum thereby loses its tentative majority, the Chief Justice places the matter on a conference for discussion or reassigns the case.

4. The Chief Justice convenes a pre-argument conference at least once each month. The purpose of the conference is to identify those cases that appear ready for oral argument. The Chief Justice constructs the calendars from those cases.

The Chief Justice places on the agenda of the conference any case in which all concurring or dissenting calendar memoranda have circulated and the "majority" calendar memorandum has been approved by at least four justices or is likely to be approved by four justices at the conference. The Chief Justice also includes on the agenda any case in which discussion could facilitate resolution of the issues.

VII. SUBMISSION

A. A cause is submitted when the court has heard oral argument or has approved a waiver of argument and the time has passed for filing all briefs and papers, including any supplementary brief permitted by the court.

B. Submission may be vacated only by an order of the Chief Justice stating in detail the reasons therefor. The order shall provide for prompt resubmission of the cause.

VIII. ASSIGNMENTS FOR PREPARATION OF OPINIONS

A. After argument the Chief Justice convenes a conference to determine whether the calendar memorandum continues to represent the views of a majority of the justices. In light of that discussion, the Chief Justice assigns the case for opinion.

B. The Chief Justice assigns the cases for preparation of opinions in the following manner:

1. If a majority of the justices agree with the disposition suggested in the calendar memorandum, ordinarily the case is assigned to the author of that memorandum.

2. If a majority of the justices disagree with the disposition reached in the memorandum, the case is reassigned to one of the majority.

3. When a case is argued on rehearing, it ordinarily remains with the justice who prepared the prior opinion or the supplemental calendar memorandum if it appears that he or she can express the majority view. If he or she does not agree with the majority view, the case is reassigned to a justice who is a member of the majority.

4. In making assignments pursuant to these guidelines, the Chief Justice takes several considerations into account,

including the following: (a) the fair distribution of work among the members of the court; (b) the likelihood that a justice can express the view of the majority of the court in a particular case; (c) the amount of work he or she has done on that case or on the issues involved; and (d) the status of the unfiled cases theretofore assigned to him or her.

C. Every reasonable effort is made by the justices to agree on the substance of opinions, and whenever possible, dissents or special concurrence on minor matters are avoided. When a justice discovers that he or she objects to something in a proposed opinion, he or she will call it to the author's attention. In addition, the objecting justice may prepare and circulate a memorandum setting forth his or her concerns and suggestions for the purpose of giving the author an opportunity to conform to any proposed changes and to remove or meet the objections raised. These practices and filing policies (see § X, post) reflect the court's strong preference for assuring that each opinion author be allowed sufficient time to consider the views of every justice before the opinion is released for filing.

D. Unless otherwise ordered by the Chief Justice, all opinions in State Bar and Commission on Judicial Performance cases and all memorandum opinions are issued "By the Court." All other opinions identify the author and the concurring justices unless a majority of the court conclude that because substantial portions of the opinion have been drafted by a number of justices, or for other compelling reasons, the opinion should be issued "By the Court."

E. The rules of the *California Style Manual* are consulted in the preparation of opinions as well as conference and calendar memoranda.

IX. CIRCULATION OF OPINIONS

Within a prescribed time after submission, the justice to whom the case is assigned circulates the proposed majority opinion. Within a prescribed time after the proposed majority opinion circulates, all concurring or dissenting opinions circulate. If the author of the proposed majority opinion wishes to respond by change or by memorandum to any concurring or dissenting opinion, he or she does so promptly after that opinion circulates. The author of the concurring or dissenting opinion thereafter has a prescribed time in which to respond.

All opinions are cite-checked and proofread before circulating. Only copies of an opinion circulate; the original remains in the Calendar Coordination Office. A justice may indicate his or her concurrence in an opinion (including an opinion authored by the justice) by signing the original that is retained in the Calendar Coordination Office or by transmitting to the Calendar Coordinator, by facsimile, a signed copy of the signature page of the opinion, indicating the justice's concurrence. When possible, it is preferred that a justice indicate his or her concurrence by signing the original that is retained in the Calendar Coordination Office.

X. FILING OF OPINIONS

When the circulation process has been completed, the Calendar Coordination Office shall notify the authoring justice of each proposed opinion that the matter appears ready for filing, and shall inquire whether each authoring justice is releasing his or her opinion for filing. When all opinions have been released for filing, the Calendar Coordination Office shall provide for the duplication of the opinion, and shall notify the Clerk of the Court and the Reporter of Decisions of the scheduled filing date. The Clerk of the Court shall file the opinion on the scheduled date at the San Francisco office of the Supreme Court.

Opinions are completed in time for reproduction and filing on a normal opinion-filing day. Unless good cause to vacate submission appears, the opinions are filed on or before the 90th day after submission. Internal circulation of an opinion after the 80th day following submission may result in the inability of the author of the proposed majority or of another timely circulated opinion to afford the views contained in the late circulated opinion full consideration and response. Such late circulated opinions will not be filed until at least 10 days but in no event more than 20 days after the filing of the majority opinion. At any time before the majority or lead opinion is final, the court may modify or grant rehearing pursuant to the applicable rules of court.

XI. REVIEW OF DETERMINATIONS BY THE COMMISSION ON JUDICIAL PERFORMANCE

A petition for review of a determination by the Commission on Judicial Performance to retire, remove, censure, admonish, or disqualify a judge or former judge under subdivision (d) of section 18 of article VI of the California Constitution must address both the appropriateness of review and the merits of the commission's determination. The commission may file a response, and the petitioner a reply, within prescribed times. The petition is assigned by the Calendar Coordinator, under the direction of the Chief Justice, to the civil central staff. When briefing is complete, the staff prepares a conference memorandum in which the recommendation generally will be either to "Deny" or "Retain for Further Consideration." If a majority of the justices vote to "deny," the petition is denied, and an order to that effect is filed forthwith. If a majority vote to "retain for further consideration," the Chief Justice assigns the case to a justice who voted to retain. This justice then prepares a memorandum on the merits, which will serve as a calendar memorandum if an order granting review subsequently is filed. The court's usual procedures for circulation of calendar memoranda then are followed. Once all concurring and dissenting memoranda have circulated, and it appears there is a majority for a particular disposition, the matter is considered at a conference. If a majority vote to deny review, an order to that effect is filed forthwith. If a majority vote to grant review, an order to that effect is filed, and the case is simultaneously set for oral argument at the soonest possible time under the court's usual scheduling rules. Because of the time limitations in subdivision (d) of section 18 of article VI of the California Constitution, continuance of oral argument rarely will be granted. Following oral argument and submission of the cause, the court's usual rules for preparation and circulation of opinions apply.

XII. Temporary Absence of Justices

A. As soon as a justice knows that he or she will not be attending a conference of the court, he or she will notify the Chief Justice. Any justice who will not be present at conference may communicate his or her votes on any given conference matter as set forth in section III.E. A justice may communicate such votes whether he or she is within or temporarily outside of California. A case may be assigned to a justice for the preparation of a calendar memorandum, under the procedures set forth in section VI, regardless of whether he or she is within or temporarily outside of California at the time the order granting review or issuing a writ or order to show cause is filed.

B. Any justice who is participating in the decision of a case, and who is temporarily outside of California, may communicate his or her concurrence in an opinion (including an opinion authored by that justice) by transmitting to the Calendar Coordinator, by facsimile, a signed copy of the signature page of the opinion, indicating the justice's concurrence, as set forth in section IX. If an opinion is concurred in by four justices, it may be filed as provided above in section X, even though one or more of the concurring justices are temporarily absent from the state and regardless of whether an absent justice is the author of the opinion.

XIII. Disqualification of Justices and Assignment of Retired Justices

A. As soon as a justice discovers that he or she is disqualified in any case or, although not technically disqualified, deems it advisable not to participate, he or she will notify the Calendar Coordinator.

B. When it is known after a case is granted but before argument that a justice for any reason is unable to participate in a matter, the Chief Justice pursuant to constitutional authority (Cal. Const., art. VI, § 6) assigns on an alphabetical rotational basis (under the procedure described ante, section IV.J) a Court of Appeal justice to assist the court in place of the nonparticipating justice. The assigned justice is furnished all pertinent petitions, motions, applications, answers, briefs, memoranda, and other material.

C. If an assigned justice has participated in the decision of a case before this court, that justice will also participate in any further proceedings — including requests for modification, petitions for rehearing, and rehearings — until such time as the decision has become final. This procedure is to be followed unless the original assignment was necessitated by the absence of a regular justice of this court, in which event a regular justice, if able to do so, will participate in lieu of the assigned justice in the consideration of any petition for rehearing and, if rehearing is granted, in any subsequent proceeding.

D. If a justice retires before a case in which he or she has heard oral argument is final, he or she may be assigned to continue to participate in the case. When a permanent replacement justice appointed to fill the vacancy created by the retirement of that justice has taken the oath of office, and the opinion has been filed, any petition for rehearing will be acted on by the permanent replacement justice.

XIV. Applications for Recommendations for Executive Clemency, Habeas Corpus, and Stays

A. An application for a recommendation for executive clemency comes before this court pursuant to article V, section 8, subdivision (a) of the California Constitution and Penal Code section 4851. When such applications are received by the Clerk's Office, they are given a file number, and the fact that they have been filed is a matter of public record. The papers and documents transmitted to the court by the Governor with the application often contain material that the Governor may have the right to withhold from the public. (See Gov. Code, § 6254, subds. (c), (f), & (l); Civ. Code, § 1798.40, subd. (c).) Accordingly, the court treats these files as confidential and does not make them available to the public.

Applications are denied unless four or more justices vote to recommend that clemency be granted. The Chief Justice informs the Governor by letter of the court's recommendation, and a copy of such letter is included in the court's file and considered a matter of public record. Pursuant to the provisions of Penal Code section 4852, the Clerk transmits the record to the office of the Governor if the court's recommendation is favorable to the applicant. Otherwise, the documents remain in the files of the court. (See Pen. Code, § 4852.)

B. When a defendant in a criminal case files a petition for review after denial without opinion by the Court of Appeal of a petition for prohibition or mandate attacking a Penal Code section 995 or section 1538.5 ruling, the matter will be placed on the agenda of a regular conference and will not be accelerated. Absent extraordinary circumstances, no order staying the trial will issue. If the case goes to trial and the matter becomes moot before the regular conference, the memorandum need only so state, and the petition may then be denied as moot without the necessity of considering its merits.

When the Court of Appeal has denied such a writ petition with opinion, a request to stay the trial pending action by the Supreme Court on the petition for review will be granted when necessary to prevent the matter from becoming moot.

C. When a misdemeanor conviction has become final on appeal or a final contempt order has been filed by a trial court and the defendant or contemner files a petition for review following denial of a timely habeas corpus or certiorari petition by a Court of Appeal or files a timely original petition, a stay of execution of the judgment or order will issue pending determination of the petition. The Chief Justice may condition the stay on the filing of a bond or on the continuation of an appeal bond, if any, if he or she deems it appropriate to do so. If the petition appears to lack merit, however, expedited consideration will be given to deny the petition in preference to releasing an incarcerated petitioner.

D. Pending disposition of a petition for writ of habeas corpus to review an order permitting extradition, the Chief Justice may stay extradition on behalf of the court. If the petition appears to lack merit, however, expedited consideration will be given to deny the petition in preference to staying the extradition proceedings.

E. In cases not covered by subdivisions B and C of this section, and when not precluded by subdivision G of this section, the Chief Justice may, in his or her discretion, grant applications for stays of judicial proceedings or orders pending regular conference consideration of the matters involved.

F. Except as provided in subdivisions B through E of this section and except in emergencies, petitions for habeas corpus, applications for stays of judicial proceedings or orders, and applications for stays of execution are to be resolved at the weekly case conference.

G. Stays governed by special provisions of statutes or rules of court will be issued only in compliance with such provisions. (See, e.g., Pub. Util. Code, §§ 1761–1766; Cal. Rules of Court, rule 8.112.)

H. Applications to stay actions by public agencies or private parties pending consideration of petitions for writs of mandate (i.e., *Emeryville*-type stays [see *People ex rel. S. F. Bay etc. Com. v. Town of Emeryville* (1968) 69 Cal.2d 533]) are to be resolved at the weekly case conference.

I. Upon receipt of a proper notice of bankruptcy relating to a pending petition for review in a creditor's action or an action that would diminish the relevant estate, the court will file an order noting the stay of proceedings and suspending the operation of the applicable rule 8.500 time period. (See 11 U.S.C. § 362(a)(1).) Thereafter, the parties will be directed to file quarterly status reports to apprise the court of the current status of the bankruptcy proceedings. Upon receipt of a proper notice terminating the bankruptcy stay, the court shall enter an order terminating the stay of proceedings and indicating that the applicable time period of rule 8.500(a) shall begin running anew from the date of the order.

Revised effective January 1, 2007.

XV. APPOINTMENT OF ATTORNEYS IN CRIMINAL CASES

A. In criminal matters, upon a verified or certified statement of indigency, the court, acting through the Clerk's Office, will appoint an attorney for a party in the following instances:

1. In a pending case in which the petition for review has been granted;

2. In a pending automatic appeal and/or related state habeas corpus/executive clemency proceedings;

3. In an original proceeding in which an alternative writ or an order to show cause has been issued;

4. In capital cases in the following proceedings:

(a) Proceedings for appellate or other postconviction review of state court judgments in the United States Supreme Court, subject however to the power of that court to appoint counsel therein; and

(b) Conduct of sanity hearings when indicated.

B. At or after the time the court appoints appellate counsel to represent an indigent appellant on direct appeal, the court also shall offer to appoint habeas corpus/executive clemency counsel for each indigent capital appellant. Following that offer, the court shall appoint habeas corpus/executive clemency counsel unless the court finds, after a hearing if necessary (held before a referee appointed by the court), that the appellant rejected the offer with full understanding of the legal consequences of the decision.

C. The court's Automatic Appeals Monitor is responsible for recruiting, evaluating, and recommending the appointment of counsel on behalf of indigent appellants in capital appeals and/or related state habeas corpus/executive clemency proceedings.

D. Counsel in automatic appeals and/or related state habeas corpus/executive clemency proceedings are compensated by one of two alternative methods: Under the "time and costs" method, counsel are compensated on an hourly basis and reimbursed for necessary expenses that were reasonably incurred. The court makes partial payments on counsel's fee claims while these claims are pending full review. Under the alternative optional "fixed fee and expenses" method, counsel are paid a fixed amount at regular stages of a case, according to a predetermined assessment of its difficulty.

E. Habeas corpus petitions in capital cases are governed by the timeliness and compensation standards set out in the "Supreme Court Policies Regarding Cases Arising From Judgments of Death." Habeas corpus counsel appointed in capital cases have the duty to investigate factual and legal grounds for the filing of a petition for a writ of habeas corpus, as delineated in those policies.

XVI. COMMUNICATIONS FROM COUNSEL IN PENDING CASES

Whenever a matter is pending before the court, any communication to the court from counsel is to be addressed to the Clerk's Office, with copies to all counsel.

XVII. SUSPENSION OF PROCEDURES

Whenever exceptional or emergency conditions require speedy action, or whenever there is other good cause for special action regarding any matter, the operation of these procedures may be temporarily suspended by affirmative vote of four justices.

The Chief Justice may extend any applicable time limit (except that stated in section X) on written request by a justice stating good cause and the date by which he or she expects to comply.

SUPREME COURT POLICIES REGARDING CASES ARISING FROM JUDGMENTS OF DEATH

(Adopted by the Supreme Court effective June 6, 1989.)

(Amended effective September 28, 1989, September 19, 1990, January 27, 1992, December 21, 1992, July 29, 1993, December 22, 1993, June 20, 1996, January 22, 1997, January 22, 1998, February 4, 1998, August 23, 2001, December 19, 2001, January 16, 2002, July 17, 2002, July 26, 2002, November 20, 2002, November 30, 2005, and January 1, 2008.)

Stays of execution. Policy Statement 1.

Withdrawal of counsel. Policy Statement 2.

Standards governing filing of habeas corpus petitions and compensation of counsel in relation to such petitions. Policy Statement 3.

Service of process by counsel for defendant. Policy Statement 4.

Policy Statement 1.   Stays of execution.

The court will consider a motion for a stay of execution only if such a motion is made in connection with a petition for a writ of habeas corpus filed in this court, or to permit certiorari review by the United States Supreme Court.

Adopted June 6, 1989.

Policy Statement 2.   Withdrawal of counsel.

In the absence of exceptional circumstances—for example, when an appointed counsel becomes mentally or physically incapacitated—the court will consider a motion to withdraw as attorney of record only if appropriate replacement counsel is ready and willing to accept appointment for the balance of the representation for which the withdrawing attorney has been appointed (i.e., appellate representation, habeas corpus/executive clemency representation, or both).

Adopted June 6, 1989; amended effective Jan. 22, 1998.

Policy Statement 3.   Standards governing filing of habeas corpus petitions and compensation of counsel in relation to such petitions.

The Supreme Court promulgates these standards as a means of implementing the following goals with respect to petitions for writs of habeas corpus relating to capital cases: (i) ensuring that potentially meritorious habeas corpus petitions will be presented to and heard by this court in a timely fashion; (ii) providing appointed counsel some certainty of payment for authorized legal work and investigation expenses; and (iii) providing this court with a means to monitor and regulate expenditure of public funds paid to counsel who seek to investigate and file habeas corpus petitions.

For these reasons, effective June 6, 1989, all petitions for writs of habeas corpus arising from judgments of death, whether the appeals therefrom are pending or previously resolved, are governed by these standards:

1. Timeliness standards

1-1. Appellate counsel in a capital case shall take and maintain detailed, understandable and computerized transcript notes and shall compile and maintain a detailed list of potentially meritorious habeas corpus issues that have come to appellate counsel's attention. In addition, if appellate counsel's appointment does not include habeas corpus representation, until separate counsel is appointed for that purpose, appellate counsel shall preserve evidence that comes to the attention of appellate counsel if that evidence appears relevant to a potential habeas corpus investigation. If separate "post-conviction" habeas corpus/ executive clemency counsel (hereafter "habeas corpus" counsel) is appointed, appellate counsel shall deliver to habeas corpus counsel copies of the list of potentially meritorious habeas corpus issues, copies of the transcript notes, and any preserved evidence relevant to a potential habeas corpus investigation, and thereafter shall update the issues list and transcript notes as warranted. Appellate counsel shall consult with and work cooperatively with habeas corpus counsel to facilitate timely investigation, and timely preparation and filing (if warranted) of a habeas corpus petition by habeas corpus counsel.

Habeas corpus counsel in a capital cases shall have a duty to investigate factual and legal grounds for the filing of a petition for a writ of habeas corpus. The duty to investigate is limited to investigating potentially meritorious grounds for relief that come to counsel's attention in the course of reviewing appellate counsel's list of potentially meritorious habeas corpus issues, the transcript notes prepared by appellate counsel, the appellate record, trial counsel's existing case files, and the appellate briefs, and in the course of making reasonable efforts to discuss the case with the defendant, trial counsel and appellate counsel. The duty to investigate does not impose on counsel an obligation to conduct, nor does it authorize the expenditure of public funds for, an unfocused investigation having as its object uncovering all possible factual bases for a collateral attack on the judgment. Instead, counsel has a duty to investigate potential habeas corpus claims only if counsel has become aware of information that might reasonably lead to actual facts supporting a potentially meritorious claim. All petitions for writs of habeas corpus should be filed without substantial delay.

[As amended effective July 29, 1993, and Jan. 22, 1998.]

1-1.1. A petition for a writ of habeas corpus will be presumed to be filed without substantial delay if it is filed within 180 days after the final due date for the filing of appellant's reply brief on the direct appeal or within 36 months after appointment of habeas corpus counsel, whichever is later.

[As amended effective Sept. 19, 1990, Jan. 22, 1998, July 17, 2002, and Nov. 30, 2005.]

1-1.2. A petition filed more than 180 days after the final due date for the filing of appellant's reply brief on the direct appeal, or more than 36 months after appointment of habeas corpus counsel, whichever is later, may establish absence of substantial delay if it alleges with specificity facts showing the petition was filed within a reasonable time after petitioner or counsel (a) knew, or should have known, of facts supporting a claim and (b) became aware, or should have become aware, of the legal basis for the claim.

[As amended effective Sept. 19, 1990, July 29, 1993, Jan. 22, 1998, July 17, 2002, and Nov. 30, 2005.]

Official Note No. 1: The amendments to standards 1-1.1 and 1-1.2, effective July 17, 2002, changing "90 days" to "180 days," shall apply to all petitions for a writ of habeas corpus arising from a judgment of death that were pending before the Supreme Court on July 17, 2002, and to all such petitions filed after that date. *[Note added by Supreme Court order, July 26, 2002.]*

Official Note No. 2: The amendments to standards 1-1.1 and 1-1.2, effective November 30, 2005, changing "24 months" to "36 months," shall apply to all petitions for a writ of habeas corpus arising from a judgment of death that were pending before the Supreme Court on November 30, 2005, and to all such petitions filed after that date. *[Note added by Supreme Court order, Nov. 30, 2005.]*

1-1.3. [Repealed effective Jan. 22, 1998]

1-2. If a petition is filed after substantial delay, the petitioner must demonstrate good cause for the delay. A petitioner may establish good cause by showing particular circumstances sufficient to justify substantial delay.

1-3. Any petition that fails to comply with these requirements may be denied as untimely.

1-4. The court may toll the 180-day period of presumptive timeliness for the filing of a capital-related habeas corpus petition (which begins to run from the final due date to file the appellant's reply brief in the appeal) when it authorizes the appellant to file supplemental briefing. The court will not toll before the 180-day presumptive timeliness period begins to run or after it has finished running.

Ordinarily, the court will toll the 180-day presumptive timeliness period only when the appellant is represented by the same counsel on appeal and also for related habeas corpus/executive clemency proceedings.

If the court determines that it will toll such 180-day presumptive timeliness period, it will so provide in its order authorizing the appellant to file supplemental briefing.

When the court provides for tolling of the 180-day presumptive timeliness period in its order authorizing the appellant to file supplemental briefing, it will determine a reasonable period of time for the appellant to devote to whatever supplemental briefing is authorized, add that period of time to the final due date to file the appellant's reply brief in the appeal, and indicate the new date by which the appellant may file a presumptively timely habeas corpus petition.

Other than under these circumstances, the court will not toll, or otherwise extend, the period in which to file a presumptively timely capital-related habeas corpus petition.

[Standard adopted effective Nov. 20, 2002.]

2. Compensation standards

2-1. This court's appointment of appellate counsel for a person under a sentence of death is for the following: (i) pleadings and proceedings related to preparation and certification of the appellate record; (ii) representation in the direct appeal before the California Supreme Court; (iii) preparation and filing of a petition for a writ of certiorari, or an answer thereto, in the United States Supreme Court and, if certiorari is granted, preparation and filing of a brief or briefs on the merits and preparation and presentation of oral argument; and (iv) representation in the trial court relating to proceedings pursuant to Penal Code section 1193.

This court's appointment of habeas corpus counsel for a person under a sentence of death shall be made simultaneously with appointment of appellate counsel or at the earliest practicable time thereafter. The appointment of habeas corpus counsel is for the following: (i) investigation, and preparation and filing (if warranted), of a habeas corpus petition in the California Supreme Court, including any informal briefing and evidentiary hearing ordered by the court and any petition to exhaust state remedies; (ii) representation in the trial court relating to proceedings pursuant to Penal Code section 1227; and (iii) represen-

tation in executive clemency proceedings before the Governor of California.

Absent prior authorization by this court, this court will not compensate counsel for the filing of any other motion, petition, or pleading in any other California or federal court or court of another state. Counsel who seek compensation for representation in another court should secure appointment by, and compensation from, that court.

[As amended effective Dec. 22, 1993, Jan. 22, 1998, and Feb. 4, 1998.]

2-2. Habeas corpus counsel should expeditiously investigate potentially meritorious bases for filing a petition for a writ of habeas corpus. If the timing of separate appointments permits, this investigation should be done concurrently with appellate counsel's review of the appellate record and briefing on appeal, and in any event, in cooperation with appellate counsel.

[As amended effective Dec. 21, 1992, and Jan. 22, 1998.]

2-2.1. In all cases in which counsel was appointed on or after the October 12, 1997, enactment of Senate Bill No. 513 (Stats. 1997, ch. 869), counsel, without prior authorization of the court, may incur expenses up to a total of $25,000 for habeas corpus investigation, and may submit claims to the court for reimbursement up to that amount. Investigative expenses include travel associated with habeas corpus investigation, and services of law clerks, paralegals, and others serving as habeas corpus investigators. The reasonable cost of photocopying defense counsel's trial files is not considered an investigative expense, and will be separately reimbursed. The court will reimburse counsel for expenses up to $25,000 that were reasonably incurred pursuant to the duty to investigate as described in standard 1-1, but it will not authorize counsel to expend, nor will it reimburse counsel for, habeas corpus investigation expenses exceeding $25,000 before the issuance of an order to show cause. This policy applies to both hourly ("time and costs") and fixed fee appointments.

The policy described in the foregoing paragraph shall also apply to those cases in which counsel was appointed prior to October 12, 1997 (the enactment of Sen. Bill No. 513), and in which, by January 22, 1998, the effective date of the above-described policy, the defendant has not filed a habeas corpus petition in this court and no more than 90 days **[now 180 days]** have passed since the final due date for the filing of the appellant's reply brief on direct appeal.

As to those cases in which, by January 1, 2008 (the effective date of Assem. Bill No. 1248), the defendant has not filed a capital-related habeas corpus petition in this court and the date by which to file a presumptively timely petition has not yet passed, counsel may be reimbursed up to $50,000 for those investigative services and expenses incurred on or after that date. Such investigative funding for expenses incurred after January 1, 2008, also is available in those cases in which a presumptively timely petition has been filed by January 1, 2008, but petitioner's reply to the informal response has not been filed and the time to do so (with any extensions of time) has not passed as of that date.

[As amended effective Jan. 16, 2002, and Jan. 1, 2008; standard adopted effective Jan. 22, 1998.]

2-2.2. In all cases in which counsel was appointed on an hourly basis prior to October 12, 1997, and in which, by January 22, 1998, either a petition for a writ of habeas corpus has been filed in this court, or more than 90 days have passed since the final due date for the filing of the appellant's reply brief on direct appeal, requests by appointed counsel for authorization to incur, and reimbursement of, investigation expenses shall be governed by the following standards (2-2.3 through 2-4.4):

2-2.3. Without prior authorization of the court, counsel may incur expenses up to a total of $3,000 for habeas corpus investigation relating to a death penalty judgment, and may submit claims to the court for reimbursement up to that amount. The court will reimburse counsel for expenses up to $3,000 that were reasonably incurred pursuant to the duty to investigate as described in standard 1-1.

2-2.4. If after incurring $3,000 in investigation expenses (or if $3,000 in reimbursement for investigation funds previously has been granted on behalf of the same defendant/petitioner with regard to the same underlying death penalty judgment), counsel determines it is necessary to incur additional expenses for which he or she plans to seek reimbursement from the court, counsel must seek and obtain prior authorization from the court. As a general rule, the court will *not* reimburse counsel for expenses exceeding $3,000, without prior authorization of the court. Requests by appointed counsel for prior authorization to incur investigation expenses shall be governed by the following standards.

2-3. Counsel shall file with this court a "Confidential request for authorization to incur expenses to investigate potential habeas corpus issues," showing good cause why the request was not filed on or before the date the appellant's opening brief on appeal was filed.

[As amended effective Dec. 21, 1992, and Jan. 22, 1998.]

2-4. The confidential request for authorization to incur expenses shall set out:

2-4.1. The issues to be explored;

2-4.2. Specific facts that suggest there may be an issue of possible merit;

2-4.3. An itemized list of the expenses requested for each issue of the proposed habeas corpus petition; and

2-4.4. (a) An itemized listing of all expenses previously sought from, and/or approved by any court of this state and/or any federal court in connection with any habeas corpus proceeding or investigation concerning the same judgment and petitioner; (b) A statement summarizing the status of any proceeding or investigation in any court of this state and/or any federal court concerning the same judgment and petitioner; and (c) A copy of any related petition previously filed in any trial and/or lower appellate court of this state and/or any federal court concerning the same judgment and petitioner.

[As amended effective Jan. 27, 1992, and Dec. 21, 1992.]

2-5. Counsel generally will not be awarded compensation for fees and expenses relating to matters that are clearly not cognizable in a petition for a writ of habeas corpus.

[As renumbered effective Dec. 21, 1992.]

2-6. When a petition is pending in this court to exhaust claims presented in a federal habeas corpus petition, a request by counsel for investigative funds to bolster or augment claims already presented in the petition normally will be denied absent a showing of strong justification for the request. A request for investigative funds may be granted if the petitioner demonstrates that he or she has timely discovered new and potentially meritorious areas of investigation not previously addressed in the petitioner's federal or state petitions. This has been the internal operating policy of the court since December 16, 1992.

[Standard adopted effective June 20, 1996.]

2-7. Each request for fees relating to a habeas corpus petition must be accompanied by: (a) An itemized listing of all fees previously sought from, and/or approved by any court of this state and/or any federal court in connection with any habeas corpus proceeding or investigation concerning the same judgment and petitioner; (b) A statement summarizing the status of any proceeding or investigation in any court of this state and/or any federal court concerning the same judgment and petitioner; and (c) A copy of any related petition previously filed in any trial and/or lower appellate court of this state and/or any federal court concerning the same judgment and petitioner.

[As renumbered and amended effective Dec. 21, 1992, and as renumbered effective June 20, 1996.]

2-8. In a case in which the court orders an evidentiary hearing, and counsel and the court do not enter into a "fixed fee and expenses agreement" covering the evidentiary hearing (see "Guideline 10" of the "Guidelines for Fixed Fee Appointments, on Optional Basis, to Automatic Appeals and Related Habeas Corpus Proceedings in the California Supreme Court"), requests for reimbursement of necessary and reasonable expenses incurred in preparation for and presentation of the evidentiary hearing shall be governed by the following standards:

2-8.1. Counsel may incur "incidental" expenses (i.e., travel to and from the evidentiary hearing and related hearings before the referee, meals and lodging during the hearing, telephone charges, photocopying, etc.) without prior approval, and the court will reimburse counsel for such itemized, reasonable and necessarily incurred expenses pursuant to the court's "Payment Guidelines for Appointed Counsel Representing Indigent Criminal Appellants in the California Supreme Court," part III ("Necessary Expenses").

2-8.2. Counsel should seek and obtain from this court prior approval for all investigation and witness expenses, including, but not limited to, investigator fees and costs, expert fees and costs, and expert witness fees and costs.

2-8.3. Counsel may submit requests for reimbursement of expenses every 60 days to this court, and will be reimbursed for necessary and reasonable expenses consistently with part III of the "Payment Guidelines," *supra.*

[Standard adopted effective Jan. 22, 1997.]

Policy Statement 4.   Service of process by counsel for defendant.

Consistently with longstanding practice and court policy, except as specified below, counsel for the defendant must serve his or her client, any separate counsel of record in any matter related to the same judgment, counsel of record for every other party, the trial court, the assisting entity or attorney for counsel for the defendant and any separate counsel of record, and trial counsel, with a copy of each motion, request for extension of time, brief, petition or other public document filed in this court or in the trial court on the client's behalf, including any supporting declaration, with attached proof of service. A declaration submitted in support of any motion or request may refer to and incorporate by reference matters set forth in a current "confidential 60-day status report" simultaneously provided only to this court. Counsel also must serve any additional person or entity as requested by this court.

Counsel for the defendant need not serve (1) trial counsel with any matter upon or after the filing in this court of the certified record on appeal; (2) the trial court with any extension-of-time request related to appellate briefing; and (3) the trial court or trial counsel with any matter related to habeas corpus briefing.

If counsel for the defendant elects to serve the defendant personally with the document, counsel may indicate on the proof of service the date by which counsel will so serve the defendant (not to exceed 30 calendar days), and counsel shall thereafter notify the court in writing that the defendant has been served. In the alternative, counsel for the defendant need not serve the defendant with any specific document to be filed if counsel for the defendant attaches to the proof of service for that specific document (1) a declaration by the defendant stating that he or she does not wish to be served with that specific document, and (2) a declaration by counsel for the defendant stating that he or she has described to the defendant the substance and purpose of that specific document.

[Policy amended effective Dec. 19, 2001.]

PAYMENT GUIDELINES FOR APPOINTED COUNSEL REPRESENTING INDIGENT CRIMINAL APPELLANTS IN THE CALIFORNIA SUPREME COURT

(Revised September 19, 1990, and December 22, 1993)

(Amended effective September 1, 1995, January 1, 1997, July 30, 1997, January 22, 1998, February 4, 1998, January 16, 2002, August 25, 2004, October 1, 2005, November 30, 2005, July 1, 2006, October 1, 2007, July 23, 2008, and August 27, 2008)

I. INTRODUCTION

The California Supreme Court determines the compensation of appointed counsel representing indigent criminal appellants. The guidelines set forth below are a general statement of the factors considered by the court in deter-

mining appropriate compensation for the time devoted to indigent criminal appeals (and related habeas corpus representation) and the reasonable and necessary expenses incurred by appointed counsel. In reviewing these guidelines, counsel should bear in mind the following:

A. Although most of the guidelines apply routinely, the application of others, such as the reimbursement of travel expenses or of the cost of expert witnesses and investigators, depends on the circumstances of each case.

B. The rates in the guidelines are subject to periodic change. These include the hourly compensation of appointed counsel, mileage and per diem rates for travel, and rates for the reimbursement of the cost of services by others.

C. For the most current information concerning these matters, and the payment guidelines generally, counsel are encouraged to contact the California Appellate Project (CAP). CAP is the appointed counsel administrator that assists private counsel with automatic appeals. CAP's address and telephone number are as follows:

California Appellate Project
101 Second Street, Suite 600
San Francisco, CA 94105
(415) 495-0500

II. REASONABLE COMPENSATION

A. Compensation rate The compensation rate for members of the State Bar of California who are appointed as counsel in indigent criminal appeals is the same allowable-hour rate appointed counsel received or was eligible to receive in the Court of Appeal, except for automatic appeals and/or related habeas corpus/executive clemency proceedings, for which the rate is [1] **$145** per allowable hour.

B. "Allowable hours" The compensation rate is multiplied by the number of "allowable hours" of appellate work to determine a reasonable sum for compensation. Benchmarks for "allowable hours" in capital cases (i.e., an estimate of the time an attorney experienced in the handling of criminal appeals might devote to the various stages of capital litigation) are set out below, in part II.*I*.3.

C. Recording of hours Appointed counsel should record the number of hours devoted to the following phases of appellate work:

1. Record review
2. Record correction
3. Motions and applications
4. Sixty-day status reports
5. Researching and writing opening brief
6. Researching and writing reply brief
7. Researching and writing supplemental brief(s)
8. Investigating and writing habeas corpus petition
9. Reply to response(s) to habeas corpus petition
10. Evidentiary hearing
11. Oral argument (includes preparation)
12. Post-oral argument representation
13. Rehearing petition or opposition
14. Certiorari petition or opposition (and briefing and

argument in the United States Supreme Court after grant of certiorari; see post, subpart *I*.3.(i))

15. Client communication
16. Travel
17. Other services (specify)

D. Factors considered by the court   The following factors are considered by the court in determining the number of allowable hours:

1. Whether the billed hours are within the benchmarks, or whether there exists good cause to depart from the benchmarks.
2. Length of the record.
3. Complexity and novelty of the legal issues.
4. Quality of work.

E. Exceptional procedural matters   Counsel should provide the court with an explanation of the time spent on exceptional procedural matters, such as repeated applications for augmentation of the record on appeal.

F. Travel time   Travel time will be compensated to the extent that the time could not reasonably be spent working on the case.

G. Circumstances warranting additional compensation   If counsel believes there exist extraordinary circumstances that justify compensation beyond that set out in these guidelines, counsel should bring such factors to the attention of the court at the time a claim for payment of compensation and expenses is presented. Counsel's showing of justification should be commensurate with the extent to which he or she seeks to exceed the benchmarks.

H. Submission of payment requests   Counsel may submit a request for payment of compensation and expenses every 90 days.

I. Special rules for capital cases   The following rules apply to capital cases only:

1. *Delay in certification of record or filing of brief*   If delay in the certification of the record on appeal or in the filing of the appellant's opening brief (AOB) is due to a lack of diligence on the part of appointed counsel, payment of compensation will be deferred until the record is certified or the AOB is filed.
2. *Forms and reports*   Counsel must submit a cumulative hours compensation form and the most recent status report with every request for payment. The cumulative hours compensation form will be provided by the court or may be obtained from CAP. Counsel should retain a copy of each cumulative hours compensation form submitted. These forms will facilitate completion of the data form for automatic appeals, which must accompany the request for final payment for services rendered in this court. Note that although a request for payment may be submitted every 90 days, a current status report must be submitted every 60 days.
3. *"Allowable hours" benchmarks*   The court, after consultation with representatives of a cross-section of the criminal justice bar, has established the following benchmarks for the various stages of capital representation:

(i) APPEAL

Reading the record and producing detailed, understandable and computerized transcript notes:	40 pp./hr.
Record correction:	20–120 hrs.
Client communication:	15–30 hrs.
Appellant's opening brief (AOB):	260–600 hrs.
Appellant's reply brief (ARB):	55–160 hrs.
Oral argument:	40–80 hrs.
Supplemental briefs:	20–80 hrs.
Rehearing petition:	25–75 hrs.
Certiorari petition:	40–75 hrs.
Briefing and argument in the United States Supreme Court after grant of certiorari:	

Counsel shall seek compensation for such services from the United States Supreme Court. Should that court deny compensation for such services, this court will authorize reasonable compensation for such services up to a maximum of $6,000.

(ii) HABEAS CORPUS

a. Investigation and Presentation of Petition

(For cases in which appellate counsel also handles habeas corpus responsibilities):

  Client communication related to habeas corpus investigation: Up to 60 hours, as follows: Up to 30 hrs. in the first year after appointment; and up to 15 hrs. per year thereafter.

Investigate and present habeas corpus petition:	140–400 hrs.

(For cases in which separate appointed counsel handles habeas corpus responsibilities):

  Client communication related to habeas corpus investigation: Up to 70 hours, as follows: Up to 40 hrs. in the first year after appointment; and up to 15 hrs. per year thereafter.

Record review:	50 pp./hr.
Investigate and present habeas corpus petition:	180–500 hrs.

For all cases:

Informal reply:	50–120 hrs.
Traverse:	50–120 hrs.

b. Habeas Corpus Evidentiary Hearing

Preparation:	150–300 hrs.

Evidentiary hearing: 72–144 hrs.
(i.e., 3–6
days)

*Post-hearing litigation
before the referee:*   75–125 hrs.

c. Post-Hearing Briefs in the Supreme Court

*Brief on the merits,
response brief, and
supplemental brief:*   50–150 hrs.

(iii) EXECUTIVE CLEMENCY

*Representation in
executive clemency
proceedings before the
Governor of
California:*   40–80 hrs.

These benchmarks are guidelines for the expected hours in "typical" cases, and are neither ceilings nor floors for fees in any given case. The court will continue to monitor its fee payment data to determine whether adjustment of the benchmarks is warranted in the future. Counsel is advised to review the benchmarks carefully, and to bear the following in mind throughout the course of representation (i.e., at each "stage" of the litigation):

a. *The "lower range" of the benchmarks* A case that has a relatively short record (i.e., 3,000-6,000 pages), and that raises standard (albeit fact-specific) issues already resolved in prior cases, should generally produce hours near or below the "lower range" of the benchmarks. Based on experience, the court expects a substantial percentage of cases to be completed under the lower range of the benchmarks.

Counsel should determine at an early stage of representation whether the case meets the description of a "lower range" case. If counsel has such a case, and submits a fee request substantially exceeding the lower range of the benchmarks for any particular stage of the litigation, he or she must include in each request a detailed explanation of why fees exceeding the lower range of the benchmarks should be awarded. The court will award fees substantially exceeding the appropriate benchmark range only if it is convinced that on the facts of the case, such fees are warranted.

b. *The "upper range" of the benchmarks* Based on experience, the court anticipates a number of cases will produce fee hours at or near the upper range of the benchmarks, and occasionally, over that range. The following important caveats apply in such cases: The upper range of the benchmarks is generally reserved for those cases with relatively long records (i.e., 10,000 or more pages), *and* that raise novel or difficult issues. The mere fact that the record may be long does *not* indicate that "upper range" or "over-benchmark" hours will be appropriate in any or each stage of the litigation.

If a case does not meet the above description of an

"upper range" or "over-benchmark" case, counsel should not expect to receive "upper range" or "over-benchmark" fees. In order to secure such fees in a case not otherwise meeting the above description, counsel must include in the request a detailed explanation of why the fees requested should be awarded. The court will award fees near or exceeding the appropriate benchmark range only if it is convinced that on the facts of the case, such fees are warranted.

4. *Second counsel "override"* In cases in which appointed counsel deems it necessary to associate with second counsel, and the court approves the association, the court may in its discretion, and on a showing of good cause, approve compensation to appointed counsel for hours incurred exceeding the "appeal" through "habeas corpus briefing" benchmarks by 5-15 percent. As a general rule the court will allow the full 15 percent override in cases in which counsel divides the hours fairly evenly for the stage for which fees are sought. If counsel divides the work less evenly, the override will be diminished accordingly. The court will continue to monitor the cases to determine whether the 15 percent ceiling should be increased.

III. NECESSARY EXPENSES

A. Items not qualifying as expenses The hourly fee should cover all overhead related to a case, *including secretarial services, word processing, and the like.* Expenses listed below will be reimbursed to the extent they are itemized, reasonable, and necessarily incurred during the course of the appeal, and otherwise comply with the court's procedures (see below, part III.B). Note that these guidelines apply not only to appointed counsel, but to those persons, including experts and investigators, who assist appointed counsel with the appeal.

B. Prior approval Prior approval is required for extraordinary expenses, such as for out-of-state travel, expert witnesses and investigators. *In capital cases,* expense requests are governed by the court's "Standards Governing Filing of Habeas Corpus Petitions and Compensation of Counsel in Relation to Such Petitions," published in the Official Reports advance sheets, pamphlet No. [2] __ (_____, 2008), rules pages [3] __–__. (See *id.,* std. 2-1 et seq.)

C. Reimbursable expenses In general, when making a request for reimbursement, counsel must itemize *all* expenses, and must provide in the request the original receipts for the following: (i) travel expenses (airfare, car rental, hotel bills, etc.) over $47 per day; (ii) telephone and copying expenses over $50 and $100 per month, respectively (see below); and (iii) all other single transactions that exceed $100. Counsel should keep all receipts in the event documentation is later required.

1. *Photocopying* The cost of photocopying will be reimbursed, at not more than 10 cents per page, whether the copying is done inside or outside counsel's office. If counsel represents that photocopying was billed at 10 cents per page or less, receipts will not be required unless the expenses are in excess of $100 per month.

In addition to investigative expenses as set forth in

the "Supreme Court Policies Regarding Cases Arising From Judgments of Death," Policy 3, standard 2-2.1, counsel appointed to handle habeas corpus/executive clemency representation will be reimbursed the reasonable cost of photocopying defense counsel's trial files, at the rate of not more than 10 cents per page, after filing of the certified record on appeal. Counsel must provide a receipt or invoice showing the number of pages copied, and the cost per page. Reimbursement will not be paid for photocopying of items already contained in the record on appeal, such as daily transcripts or exhibits.

2. *Postage and delivery costs* Expenses for express mail/messenger service will be reimbursed only on a showing that use of express mail/messenger service was necessary and reasonable.

3. *Telephone charges* Receipts will not be required unless the expenses are in excess of $50 per month.

4. *Travel expenses*

a. The court will determine the reasonableness and necessity of travel expenses on a case-by-case basis. Counsel are cautioned that travel expenses are not considered necessary when the purpose of a trip may reasonably be accomplished in another way, such as by telephone or correspondence. Further, counsel should use the least expensive alternative means of travel. For motor vehicles, the mileage rate is the prevailing amount established by the Administrative Office of the Courts.

b. When travel is required by appointed counsel or a person authorized to assist appointed counsel, reasonable and necessary meals and lodging may be claimed, to the extent allowed under State Board of Control rules. Counsel should contact CAP for further information.

c. Some of the lesser known provisions of the Board of Control rules are as follows:

(1) The per diem allowance does not apply for trips of 25 miles or less.

(2) Lunch is not covered unless the travel period is 24 hours or more.

(3) The cost of collision coverage in a contract for a rental car is not covered.

5. *Computerized legal research* The reasonable cost of computerized legal research (as opposed to the costs of installation and monthly access fees), when the use is specifically attributable to the case, will be reimbursed to the extent reasonably and necessarily incurred. Counsel must explain in writing the specific nature of the computer expenses (e.g., Shepard's, Autocite, issue searches, etc.), and must explain why computerized research was more efficient than the same research performed "manually."

6. *Services of law clerks, paralegals, and State Bar members*

a. Counsel shall be reimbursed for the compensation of the following individuals at a rate not to exceed the following:

(1) Law clerks who are not members of the State Bar of California at $40 per allowable hour.

(2) Paralegals at $40 per allowable hour.

(3) Members of the State Bar of California, who are not

appointed to the case, at the rate of $98 per allowable hour.

b. Reimbursement of the compensation for all persons performing legal services, other than appointed counsel, shall be subject to the following conditions:

(1) In submitting a claim for reimbursement, counsel shall describe with specificity the legal services and number of hours of work performed by each other person so the court can evaluate the reasonableness of the services and expenses as part of appointed counsel's overall claim. *It is expected that the hours devoted to legal services by nonappointed counsel, and any "exceptionally high" hours attributed to law clerks and paralegals (i.e., hours exceeding 30 percent of the benchmark hours for appointed counsel for any given stage), will reduce the hours that appointed counsel will devote to those services.*

(2) Appointed counsel shall not delegate to others those functions that require the ability and experience for which counsel was appointed.

(3) Appointed counsel shall supervise and have full responsibility for the services performed by others.

7. *Services of investigators and experts*

a. An investigator or expert shall be compensated at a rate not to exceed the maximum rates listed below. Counsel must establish that use of an expert's services is reasonably necessary under the facts of the case. Counsel seeking to use the services of multiple experts relating to a single or common issue must demonstrate a compelling necessity for such use of multiple experts. In addition, counsel must include in the request for reimbursement a representation that the rate requested

(1) does not exceed the investigator's or expert's customary rates for the services performed, and

(2) does not exceed local prevailing rates for the services performed.

b. The maximum rates are as follows

(1) Investigators, [4] **$55-90** per hour.

(2) Penalty phase consultants, [5] **$60-125** per hour.

(3) Psychiatrists and other medically licensed mental health experts, [6] **$200-350** per hour.

(4) Other forensic experts, [7] **$125-225** per hour.

(5) Psychologists (Ph.D.'s), [8] **$150-275** per hour.

(6) Attorneys serving as experts, [9] **$125-145** per hour. (*Note:* Until an order to show cause is issued, or the People submit an expert declaration in their informal opposition to a habeas corpus petition, the court will not approve payment for attorney "expert opinion" in the form of declarations, etc.)

(7) Any expert listed above testifying at a court proceeding, eight times the hourly rate per day or four times the hourly rate per half day.

c. In exceptional circumstances, when the need for services at a greater rate of compensation is documented and prior authorization is obtained from the Supreme Court, compensation beyond the maximum may be paid.

8. *Proceedings returnable in superior court following order to show cause on alleged mental retardation of condemned inmate*

In proceedings pending in superior court pursuant to an order to show cause issued by the California Supreme Court, and returnable before the superior court, regarding a condemned inmate's alleged mental retardation and resulting ineligibility for the death penalty within the meaning of *Atkins v. Virginia* (2002) 536 U.S. 304 (see also *In re Hawthorne* (2005) 35 Cal.4th 40), the following practices apply to requests by counsel appointed in the California Supreme Court for the reimbursement of investigation services and expenses incurred in superior court for experts, investigators and law clerks/paralegals:

a. The decision whether to authorize funding for any experts, investigators or law clerks/paralegals is to be made by, and is within the discretion of, the superior court in which the proceedings are pending.

b. Appointed counsel may engage experts, investigators and law clerks/paralegals either in the locality where counsel's offices are situated or in the locality where the superior court proceedings are being held, at counsel's option.

c. The California Supreme Court will pay for investigation services and expenses at the rate prevailing where the services are engaged, if otherwise permissible within the maximum hourly rates and other applicable provisions set forth within these payment guidelines.

IV. FEE AND EXPENSE DISALLOWANCES

The court will provide reasons in writing for fee disallowances of $1,000 or more, and expense disallowances of $500 or more.

V. COURT ACTION UPON NONPERFORMANCE OF WORK, AND REIMBURSEMENT OF FEES UPON AUTHORIZED WITHDRAWAL OF APPOINTED COUNSEL

A. Nonperformance of counsel In the rare circumstance in which appointed counsel ceases work on a case and refuses to complete the work with reasonable diligence, the court has had, and will continue to exercise as appropriate, the following nonexclusive options: The court may enforce its legal rights; the court may refer the matter to the State Bar; and finally, the court may institute contempt proceedings to enforce its orders.

B. Authorized withdrawal of counsel In the event that the court permits appointed counsel to withdraw before completion of counsel's duties in a case, the court will, as appropriate under the circumstances, authorize payment to counsel for legal work completed. Alternatively, the court may, as appropriate under the circumstances, order counsel to reimburse the court for fees paid, less a credit for work performed that is determined by the court to be of value to the court.

Adopted Jan. 1, 1991; amended Dec. 22, 1993; Sept. 1, 1995; Jan. 1, 1997; July 30, 1997; Jan. 22, 1998; Feb. 4, 1998; Jan. 16, 2002; Aug. 25, 2004; Oct. 1, 2005; Nov. 30, 2005; July 1, 2006; Oct. 1, 2007; July 23, 2008; Aug. 27, 2008.

Payment Guidelines. 2008 Deletes. [1] $140 [2] 4 (February 7, 2008) [3] 16–23 [4] $55-75 [5] $60-75 [6] $200-275 [7] $125-200 [8] $150-200 [9] $125

GUIDELINES FOR FIXED FEE APPOINTMENTS, ON OPTIONAL BASIS, TO AUTOMATIC APPEALS AND RELATED HABEAS CORPUS PROCEEDINGS IN THE CALIFORNIA SUPREME COURT

(Adopted by the Supreme Court December 14, 1993, effective January 1, 1994)

(Amended effective September 1, 1995, January 1, 1997, January 22, 1997, July 30, 1997, January 22, 1998, February 4, 1998, July 18, 2001, January 16, 2002, March 21, 2002, October 1, 2005, November 30, 2005, July 1, 2006, October 1, 2007, and January 1, 2008)

Introduction

Presently, appointed counsel in automatic appeals are compensated on a "time and costs" basis, under the Payment Guidelines for Appointed Counsel Representing Indigent Criminal Appellants in the California Supreme Court (as revised [Off. Reps. Adv. Pamp. No. [1] **4 (February 7, 2008) Rules pp. 25–35**]) (hereafter Payment Guidelines). Under the Payment Guidelines, appointed counsel must submit a detailed and lengthy cumulative hours compensation form with every request for payment of fees and reimbursement of expenses. Moreover, "allowable hours" benchmarks limit the fees available for each stage of the capital representation; other provisions limit or exclude reimbursement for expenses. Requests for prior approval of extraordinary expenses are governed by the Supreme Court Policies Regarding Cases Arising From Judgments of Death (as revised [Off. Reps. Adv. Pamp. No. [2] **4**, *supra*, Rules pp. [3] **16–24**]).

In an effort to provide appointed counsel in capital cases greater predictability, consistency and control over compensation and expenses, and to reduce administrative burdens on both counsel and the Court, the Court has adopted an optional fixed fee and expenses payment system.

The categories of fixed fees set out below in Guidelines 1, 1.1, and 1.2 establish the compensation and responsibilities of appointed counsel for all services and "incidental expenses" (habeas corpus investigation expenses are separately provided for in Guideline 2):

(1) In cases in which counsel is appointed to represent the defendant both on appeal and in related habeas corpus/executive clemency proceedings, fixed fee compensation is for: (a) the direct appeal, through the filing of a certiorari petition to the United States Supreme Court, or an answer thereto (but not including any briefs or appearances in the United States Supreme Court after grant of certiorari or any briefs or appearances on remand to the California Supreme Court, which work would be compensated under the terms and limitations of the Payment

Guidelines); (b) state habeas corpus investigation, and preparation and filing (if warranted) of a state habeas corpus petition and informal reply, and any subsequent habeas corpus petition, including any petition to exhaust state remedies, in the California Supreme Court (but not including any traverse, habeas corpus evidentiary hearing or post-hearing briefs in the California Supreme Court, which work would be compensated under the terms and limitations of the Payment Guidelines); (c) any trial court proceedings under Penal Code sections 1193 and 1227 to set an execution date; and (d) representation in executive clemency proceedings before the Governor of California. (See Cal. Supreme Ct., Policies Regarding Cases Arising From Judgments of Death, *supra*, Compensation Stds., std. 2-1.)

(2) In cases in which counsel is appointed to represent the defendant on appeal only, fixed fee compensation is for: (a) the direct appeal, through the filing of a certiorari petition to the United States Supreme Court, or an answer thereto (but not including any briefs or appearances in the United States Supreme Court after grant of certiorari or any briefs or appearances on remand to the California Supreme Court, which work would be compensated under the terms and limitations of the Payment Guidelines); and (b) any trial court proceedings under Penal Code section 1193 to set an execution date. (See Cal. Supreme Ct., Policies Regarding Cases Arising From Judgments of Death, *supra*, Compensation Stds., std. 2-1.)

(3) In cases in which counsel is appointed to represent the defendant in habeas corpus/executive clemency proceedings only, fixed fee compensation is for: (a) state habeas corpus investigation, and preparation and filing (if warranted) of a state habeas corpus petition and informal reply, and any subsequent habeas corpus petition, including any petition to exhaust state remedies, in the California Supreme Court (but not including any traverse, habeas corpus evidentiary hearing or post-hearing briefs in the California Supreme Court, which work would be compensated under the terms and limitations of the Payment Guidelines); (b) any trial court proceedings under Penal Code section 1227 to set an execution date; and (c) representation in executive clemency proceedings before the Governor of California. (See Cal. Supreme Ct., Policies Regarding Cases Arising From Judgments of Death, *supra*, Compensation Stds., std. 2-1.)

1. Fixed Fee Categories for Cases in Which Counsel Is Appointed to Handle the Appeal and Related Habeas Corpus/Executive Clemency Proceedings

Category I: [4] **$160,000**

A. An appeal from a judgment based on a guilty plea and penalty phase; or

B. An appeal from a judgment on remand following a reversal limited to penalty.

C. Caveat: An appeal from a judgment on limited remand for a new hearing on the automatic motion to modify the death verdict (Pen. Code, § 190.4, subd. (e)) likely will be valued well below [5] **$160,000**. (See also Guideline 4 [Case Evaluation], *post*.)

Category II: [6] **$231,000**

A. An appeal from a judgment on remand following a reversal limited to the special circumstance finding(s) and penalty; or

B. An appeal otherwise in category I(A) or I(B) that presents a more complex case, in the Court's view, by reason of, but not limited to, one or more of the following factors: The combined record on appeal is 4,000 or more pages; there was more than one homicide victim, and the homicides occurred in more than one incident; there were numerous pretrial and/or penalty phase motions; there were multiple defendants and/or appellants; or

C. An initial appeal or an appeal from a judgment on remand following a reversal of guilt, in which the combined record on appeal is under 6,000 pages.

Category III: [7] **$283,000**

A. An initial appeal or an appeal from a judgment on remand following a reversal of guilt, in which the combined record on appeal is between 6,000 and 12,000 pages; or

B. An appeal otherwise in category II(A) or II(C) that presents a more complex case, in the Court's view, by reason of, but not limited to, one or more of the following factors: The combined record on appeal is 5,000 or more pages; there was more than one homicide victim, and the homicides occurred in more than one incident; there were numerous pretrial and/or penalty phase motions; there were multiple defendants and/or appellants.

Category IV: [8] **$322,000**

A. An initial appeal or an appeal from a judgment on remand following a reversal of guilt, in which the combined record on appeal is 12,000 or more pages; or

B. An appeal otherwise in category III(A) that presents a more complex case, in the Court's view, by reason of, but not limited to, one or more of the following factors: The combined record on appeal is 10,000 or more pages; there was more than one homicide victim, and the homicides occurred in more than one incident; there were numerous pretrial and/or penalty phase motions; there were multiple defendants and/or appellants.

Category V: [9] **$368,000** base fee

Exceptional cases that occur infrequently, involve many victims and incidents, and have a combined record on appeal of 25,000 or more pages. In this category, appointed counsel may present a justification at the outset for a fixed fee higher than the base fee.

1.1. Fixed Fee Categories for Cases in Which Counsel Is Appointed to Handle the Appeal Only

Category I: [10] **$65,000**

A. An appeal from a judgment based on a guilty plea and penalty phase; or

B. An appeal from a judgment on remand following a reversal limited to penalty.

C. Caveat: An appeal from a judgment on limited remand for a new hearing on the automatic motion to modify the death verdict (Pen. Code, § 190.4, subd. (e)) likely will be valued well below [11] **$65,000**. (See also Guideline 4 [Case Evaluation], *post*.)

Category II: [12] **$136,000**

A. An appeal from a judgment on remand following a reversal limited to the special circumstance finding(s) and penalty; or

B. An appeal otherwise in category I(A) or I(B) that presents a more complex case, in the Court's view, by reason of, but not limited to, one or more of the following factors: The combined record on appeal is 4,000 or more pages; there was more than one homicide victim, and the homicides occurred in more than one incident; there were numerous pretrial and/or penalty phase motions; there were multiple defendants and/or appellants; or

C. An initial appeal or an appeal from a judgment on remand following a reversal of guilt, in which the combined record on appeal is under 6,000 pages.

Category III: [13] **$178,000**

A. An initial appeal or an appeal from a judgment on remand following a reversal of guilt, in which the combined record on appeal is between 6,000 and 12,000 pages; or

B. An appeal otherwise in category II(A) or II(C) that presents a more complex case, in the Court's view, by reason of, but not limited to, one or more of the following factors: The combined record on appeal is 5,000 or more pages; there was more than one homicide victim, and the homicides occurred in more than one incident; there were numerous pretrial and/or penalty phase motions; there were multiple defendants and/or appellants.

Category IV: [14] **$219,000**

A. An initial appeal or an appeal from a judgment on remand following a reversal of guilt, in which the combined record on appeal is 12,000 or more pages; or

B. An appeal otherwise in category III(A) that presents a more complex case, in the Court's view, by reason of, but not limited to, one or more of the following factors: The combined record on appeal is 10,000 or more pages; there was more than one homicide victim, and the homicides occurred in more than one incident; there were numerous pretrial and/or penalty phase motions; there were multiple defendants and/or appellants.

Category V: [15] **$263,000** base fee

Exceptional cases that occur infrequently, involve many victims and incidents, and have a combined record on appeal of 25,000 or more pages. In this category, appointed counsel may present a justification at the outset for a fixed fee higher than the base fee.

1.2. Fixed Fee Categories for Cases in Which Counsel Is Appointed to Handle Habeas Corpus/Executive Clemency Proceedings Only

Category I: [16] **$85,000**, plus an additional fixed fee calculated at the rate of [17] **$145** for every 50 pages of transcript in the combined record on appeal.

A. Habeas corpus representation related to a case that would fall within Fixed Fee Guideline 1.1, Categories I or II.

B. Habeas corpus representation related to a case that would fall within Fixed Fee Guideline 1.1, Categories III, IV, or V, but that, for case-specific reasons, is of below-average complexity.

Category II: [18] **$110,000**, plus an additional fixed fee calculated at the rate of [19] **$145** for every 50 pages of transcript in the combined record on appeal.

A. Habeas corpus representation related to a case that would fall within Fixed Fee Guideline 1.1, Categories III, IV, or V.

B. Habeas corpus representation related to a case that would fall within Fixed Fee Guideline 1.1, Categories I or II, but that, for case-specific reasons, nevertheless is of average complexity.

Category III: [20] **$127,000**, plus an additional fixed fee calculated at the rate of [21] **$145** for every 50 pages of transcript in the combined record on appeal, for cases of above-average complexity.

For cases of exceptional complexity, appointed counsel may present a justification at the outset for a fixed fee higher than the [22] $127,000 base fee.

1.3. Factors Affecting Fee Categories

The California Supreme Court considers four factors in determining the fee in fixed fee appointments in capital proceedings: *complexity, difficulty, extraordinary costs,* and *time-intensiveness*. The case-specific issues that influence the applicability of these factors often overlap, but examples of such issues include the following:

- Multiple defendants
- Motion for change of venue
- Joint or separate trials with co-defendants
- Multiple homicides or multiple incidents (including multiple victims in separate incidents)
- Mistrials and re-trial(s)
- Substitution of trial counsel; additional trial proceedings or phases (e.g., grand jury, competency phase, sanity phase)
- Multiple special circumstances
- Prior convictions or unadjudicated criminal conduct admitted at penalty phase
- Prosecution's use of informants
- Extensive litigation of the admissibility of evidence

- Forensic testing, analysis, and evidence (e.g., DNA, hair, fingerprint, blood, ballistics) introduced at trial or necessary for habeas investigation
- Mentally ill, mentally impaired, or mentally retarded capital defendants
- Non-English-speaking or foreign national capital defendant
- Non-English-speaking witnesses
- Minimal guilt and/or penalty phase investigation done for trial
- Investigation requirements in multiple locations and/or out of the state or country
- Extended elapsed time since offenses/trial
- Necessity of expert witnesses
- Necessity of using some fees to cover investigative and incidental expenses
- Length of record
- Number of trial witnesses

1.4. Suggested Format and Contents of Fixed Fee Requests

Counsel may submit requests for consideration of a case for a particular fixed fee category. Lengthy letters are not necessary or encouraged. Letters for the most complex cases should not exceed seven pages. A suggested format that will assist the Court in making a fixed fee determination includes the following elements:

Fixed fee request: An opening paragraph stating the fee category and base fee requested, plus additional amounts sought for transcript length and cases of exceptional complexity.

Short summary of the case: This paragraph should not extensively reiterate the facts of the case or the procedural history.

Discussion of the applicability of the four factors to this particular case: An explanation of why the appointed case is particularly complex, difficult, costly, and/or time-intensive.

2. Incidental and Investigative Expenses

All incidental expenses for the direct appeal and habeas corpus/executive clemency representation are included in the fixed fee. Incidental expenses include photocopying, postage, telephone charges, computerized legal research, travel (other than for habeas corpus investigation) and services of law clerks and paralegals (other than for habeas corpus investigation). In addition to the agreed-upon fixed fee, counsel may also incur up to $25,000 in habeas corpus investigative expenses, without prior Court authorization, subject to the Court's Payment Guidelines, *supra*, part III, subpart C, paragraphs 1-7, inclusive ("Reimbursable expenses"). Investigative expenses include travel associated with habeas corpus investigation, and services of law clerks, paralegals, and others serving as habeas corpus investigators. Counsel will be reimbursed for all such habeas corpus investigative expenses that were reasonably incurred, up to $25,000. The Court will not authorize or reimburse habeas corpus investigative expenses exceeding $25,000 prior to the issuance of an order to show cause.

As to those cases in which, by January 1, 2008 (the effective date of Assem. Bill No. 1248), the defendant has not filed a capital-related habeas corpus petition in this court and the date by which to file a presumptively timely petition has not yet passed, counsel may be reimbursed up to $50,000 for those investigative services and expenses incurred on or after that date. Such investigative funding for expenses incurred after January 1, 2008, also is available in those cases in which a presumptively timely petition has been filed by January 1, 2008, but petitioner's reply to the informal response has not been filed and the time to do so (with any extensions of time) has not passed as of that date. (See also Cal. Supreme Ct., Policies Regarding Cases Arising From Judgments of Death, *supra*, Timeliness Stds., std. 1-1, & Compensation Stds., std. 2-2.1.)

3. Requests for Additional Fees

In extraordinary and unique situations, the Court will entertain requests for additional fees based on exceptional circumstances (e.g., circumstances that were unforeseeable at the time of the appointment of counsel on a fixed fee basis). In such situations, counsel shall have the burden of proof to justify any additional fees.

4. Case Evaluation

There will be agreement on the fixed fee prior to the appointment of counsel. (See also, Guideline 6 [Conversion From Time and Costs Appointment to Fixed Fee], *post*.) Initially, applicant counsel selected to consider an appointment to a specific automatic appeal and/or habeas corpus/executive clemency proceedings will have the option of investigating that case for purposes of proposing a fixed fee pursuant to these alternative guidelines, rather than the traditional time and costs method. At any given time, there will be only one set of applicant counsel investigating a specific automatic appeal and/or habeas corpus/executive clemency proceedings for purposes of a possible appointment. Applicant counsel are encouraged to consult with trial counsel, examine any available transcript "dailies" prepared during the trial or other proceedings, and examine any available materials normally found in the clerk's transcript. Counsel are also encouraged to examine additional materials and information that may be available from the California Appellate Project in San Francisco.

Using these alternative guidelines, applicant counsel opting to be appointed on a fixed fee basis will propose a category and hence a fee for all services and expenses in the case. The Court's concurrence is required for any such appointment.

Discussions with applicant counsel regarding proposals for fixed fee appointments shall be conducted through the Automatic Appeals Monitor.

The fixed fee encompasses counsel's investigative costs in reviewing the case for purposes of considering an appointment. If counsel's proposal for a fixed fee is not accepted by the Court, counsel will not be reimbursed for those investigative costs; however, counsel may request an appointment to that case pursuant to the traditional time and costs method of the Payment Guidelines.

---

5. Progress Payments

Until appointed appellate counsel files the appellant's opening brief or appointed habeas corpus counsel files a petition, a current status report must be filed every 60 days. Other than reimbursement for habeas corpus investigative expenses, documentation and itemization of hours and expenses by appointed counsel are not required under these alternative fixed fee guidelines.

Counsel appointed for both the direct appeal *and* habeas corpus/executive clemency proceedings will receive progress payments after specified stages of representation as follows: (i) one-sixth of the fixed amount shortly after counsel is appointed; (ii) one-sixth after counsel (a) submits to the assisting entity or counsel (e.g., the Habeas Corpus Resource Center, the California Appellate Project, or other assisting counsel) detailed, understandable and computerized transcript notes, a list of potentially meritorious habeas corpus issues, and a draft first request for correction of the record (and, if appropriate, any motion for augmentation and/or settled statement), and (b) files this first request; (iii) one-sixth after certification of the record and filing of the record in this court (one-half of this progress payment will be advanced upon request after the trial court's order disposing of the consolidated motion to augment, correct, and settle the record on appeal); (iv) one-sixth after counsel (a) files a confidential declaration that he or she has made reasonable efforts to consult with defendant and trial counsel about potential habeas corpus issues, (b) submits to the assisting entity or counsel a detailed outline of potential habeas corpus issues to be investigated, and (c) files the appellant's opening brief (one-quarter of this progress payment will be advanced upon request after counsel's submission to the assisting entity or counsel of a complete draft of the statement of the case and statement of the facts portion of the appellant's opening brief; one-quarter after submission of a complete draft of the guilt phase and special circumstance issues portion of the appellant's opening brief; and one-quarter after submission of a complete draft of the penalty phase issues portion of the appellant's opening brief [counsel may request these advances before progress payment (iii) has been paid in full]); (v) one-sixth after counsel (a) submits to the assisting entity or counsel a draft reply brief, (b) files a reply brief, and (c) files a confidential declaration that counsel has substantially completed the habeas corpus investigation (to the extent possible given funding provided therefor), and has submitted for review to the assisting entity or counsel a draft habeas corpus petition with necessary exhibits and declarations (or, in the alternative, that counsel has submitted for review to the assisting entity or counsel a draft declaration indicating that all potential leads have been substantially pursued to the extent possible given funding provided therefor, and that it appears that no habeas corpus petition will be filed) (one-half of this progress payment will be advanced upon request after the following: (a) the Attorney General files the respondent's brief, and (b) counsel files a confidential declaration that counsel has completed approximately one-half of the anticipated habeas corpus investigation, and has submitted to the assisting entity or counsel a detailed outline of the remainder of the planned investigation); (vi) one-sixth,

less $10,000, after counsel files a habeas corpus petition in this court on behalf of counsel's client, and after oral argument and submission of the matter on the direct appeal (except that if counsel files no petition, counsel must instead file a confidential declaration indicating that all potential leads have been pursued to the extent possible given funding provided therefor, and that no habeas corpus petition will be filed, after which counsel will receive no sixth progress payment, except upon a showing that in view of work performed, full or partial payment is warranted); and finally (vii) the sum of $10,000 after completion of representation in executive clemency proceedings before the Governor of California. With each request for payment except for those set forth above in (i), (vi), and (vii), counsel shall provide to the court a statement from the assisting entity or counsel that counsel's submission to the entity or counsel substantially complies with the conditions set forth for payment.

Counsel appointed for the direct appeal only will receive progress payments after specified stages of representation as follows: (i) one-sixth of the fixed amount shortly after counsel is appointed; (ii) one-sixth after counsel (a) submits to the assisting entity or counsel (e.g., the Habeas Corpus Resource Center, the California Appellate Project, or other assisting counsel) detailed, understandable and computerized transcript notes, and a draft first request for correction of the record (and, if appropriate, any motion for augmentation and/or settled statement), and (b) files this first request; (iii) one-sixth after certification of the record and filing of the record in this court (one-half of this progress payment will be advanced upon request after the trial court's order disposing of the consolidated motion to augment, correct, and settle the record on appeal); (iv) one-sixth after counsel files the appellant's opening brief (one-quarter of this progress payment will be advanced upon request after counsel's submission to the assisting entity or counsel of a complete draft of the statement of the case and statement of the facts portion of the appellant's opening brief; one-quarter after submission of a complete draft of the guilt phase and special circumstance issues portion of the appellant's opening brief; and one-quarter after submission of a complete draft of the penalty phase issues portion of the appellant's opening brief [counsel may request these advances before progress payment (iii) has been paid in full]); (v) one-sixth after counsel (a) submits to the assisting entity or counsel a draft of the appellant's reply brief, and (b) files the reply brief; and (vi) one-sixth after oral argument and submission of the matter on the direct appeal. With each request for payment except for those set forth above in (i) and (vi), counsel shall provide to the court a statement from the assisting entity or counsel that counsel's submission to the entity or counsel substantially complies with the conditions set forth for payment.

Counsel whose appointment is limited to habeas corpus/executive clemency proceedings will receive progress payments after specified stages of representation as follows: (i) one-fifth of the fixed amount shortly after counsel is appointed; (ii) one-fifth after counsel files a confidential declaration that counsel has reviewed the record on appeal and the detailed transcript notes and list of potentially meritorious habeas corpus issues provided by appointed counsel on the direct appeal, has made reasonable efforts to consult with defendant, appellate counsel and trial counsel, and has submitted to the assisting entity or counsel (e.g., the Habeas Corpus Resource Center, the California Appellate Project, or other assisting counsel) a detailed outline of potential habeas corpus issues to be investigated; (iii) one-fifth after counsel files a confidential declaration that counsel has completed approximately one-half of the anticipated habeas corpus investigation, and has submitted to the assisting entity or counsel a detailed outline of the remainder of the planned investigation; (iv) one-fifth after counsel files a confidential declaration that counsel has submitted for review to the assisting entity or counsel a draft habeas corpus petition with necessary exhibits and declarations (or, in the alternative, that counsel has submitted for review to the assisting entity or counsel a draft declaration indicating that all potential leads have been pursued to the extent possible given funding provided therefor, and that no habeas corpus petition will be filed) (one-half of this progress payment will be advanced upon request after counsel files a confidential declaration that counsel has completed the habeas corpus investigation to the extent possible given the funding provided therefor); (v) one-fifth, less $10,000, after counsel files a habeas corpus petition in this court on behalf of his or her client (except that if counsel files no petition, counsel must instead file a confidential declaration indicating that all potential leads have been pursued to the extent possible given funding provided therefor, and that no habeas corpus petition will be filed, after which counsel will receive no fifth progress payment, except upon a showing that in view of work performed, full or partial payment is warranted); and finally (vi) $10,000 after completion of representation in executive clemency proceedings before the Governor of California. With each request for payment except for those set forth above in (i), (v), and (vi), counsel shall provide to the court a statement from the assisting entity or counsel that counsel's submission to the entity or counsel substantially complies with the conditions set forth for payment.

Under limited circumstances (e.g., a delay in the certification of the record not due to a lack of diligence on the part of appointed counsel), the court will authorize partial payments before completion of the relevant stage(s) of representation.

In the event the proceedings terminate prior to the completion of all of the stages set forth in the progress payment schedule (as a result, for example, of the death of the defendant), appointed counsel shall memorialize all work completed and the court shall determine and pay an appropriate sum to compensate counsel for work performed prior to the termination of the proceedings.

6. Conversion From Time and Costs Appointment to Fixed Fee

Counsel appointed to an automatic appeal and/or habeas corpus/executive clemency proceedings under the traditional time and costs basis of the Payment Guidelines are encouraged to consider converting their method of compensation pursuant to this optional, fixed fee payment system. Any such conversion must take into account any payments previously made to counsel, and must be approved by the Court. Ordinarily, conversion will not be approved after the filing of the appellant's opening brief, or, in the case of habeas corpus/executive clemency counsel, after six months following counsel's appointment, whichever is later.

Counsel approved by the Court for an appointment to his/her first automatic appeal and/or habeas corpus/executive clemency proceedings should carefully consider an initial appointment under the time and costs basis of the Payment Guidelines. A conversion to a fixed fee appointment pursuant to these alternative guidelines may be more appropriate after such counsel has become familiar with the case.

7. Second Counsel

The Court encourages association with second counsel. Unlike the procedure under the traditional time and costs appointment scheme of the Payment Guidelines, the fixed fees provided by this optional payment system are intended to adequately compensate appointed counsel and any associate counsel. Hence, the Court will not recognize a "second counsel override" in fixed fee cases.

8. Valuation and Length of Record on Appeal

In determining the length of the combined record on appeal as part of the process whereby a case may be valued within a fixed fee category, the Court will take into consideration whether an unusual proportion of the record is comprised of jury voir dire and/or preliminary hearing transcript. When appropriate, the Court may treat the combined record as having a reduced length. Moreover, consistent with this court's historical practice, when determining the appropriate fixed fee category, the Court will not include, in determining the size of the combined record on appeal, the juror questionnaires completed by actual or prospective jurors.

9. Applicability of Supreme Court Policies Regarding Cases Arising From Judgments of Death

The Supreme Court Policies Regarding Cases Arising From Judgments of Death, as amended, apply to all automatic appeals and habeas corpus/executive clemency proceedings in which counsel has opted for a fixed fee pursuant to these alternative guidelines. However, standard 2-2.2 of the Compensation Standards, through standard 2-4.4 of the Compensation Standards (governing authorization to incur, and reimbursement of, habeas corpus investigation expenses), shall not apply to fixed fee cases.

10. Fixed Legal Fees and Expenses For Evidentiary Hearings

In a case in which the Court orders an evidentiary hearing, counsel may elect to enter a fixed legal fee and expenses agreement covering (i) preparation for the evidentiary hearing, (ii) presentation of the evidentiary hearing, (iii) post-hearing litigation before the referee, and (iv) post-hearing briefs and proceedings in this Court.

(1) Fixed Legal Fee and Expense Categories. The Court and counsel for petitioner will agree to fix legal fees and expenses within one of the following categories.

Each agreement shall specify one fixed dollar sum covering *all* legal fees and *all* expenses—"incidental" and investigative—(e.g., photocopying, postage, telephone charges, travel, computerized legal research, services of law clerks and paralegals, services of and witness fees for investigators and experts, and any other witness expenses).

The fixed sum agreement shall also specify separately a dollar amount for the "legal fee component" and the "expenses component" of the fixed sum.

Category A: [23] **$52,500 ($49,000** legal fees; **$3,500** expenses).

A matter presenting a single issue or limited issues expected to require minimal additional investigation, minimal or no services of experts, and to consume 1-2 hearing days.

Category A(1): [24] **$57,500 ($49,000** legal fees; **$8,500** expenses)

A matter otherwise within category A, but which is expected to require significant additional investigation and use of experts.

Category B: [25] **$80,500 ($72,000** legal fees; **$8,500** expenses)

A matter expected to require significant additional investigation and/or significant use of experts, and to consume 3-4 hearing days.

Category B(1): [26] **$86,000 ($72,000** legal fees; $14,000 expenses)

A matter otherwise within category B, but which is expected to require substantial additional investigation and use of experts.

Category C: [27] **$116,000 ($102,000** legal fees; $14,000 expenses)

A matter expected to require substantial additional investigation and/or services of experts, and to consume 5-6 hearing days.

Category C(1): [28] **$123,000 ($102,000** legal fees; $21,000 expenses)

A matter otherwise within category C, but which is expected to require substantial additional investigation and use of experts.

Category D: [29] **$148,000** *base sum* **($124,000** base amount for legal fees; $24,000 base amount for expenses)

A matter that is expected to require substantial additional investigation and services of experts, and to consume 7 or more hearing days. In this category, counsel may present justification at the outset for a fixed sum higher than the base amount.

(2) Requests for Additional Legal Fees. In extraordinary and unique situations, the Court will entertain requests for additional fees based on exceptional circumstances, as set out *ante*, Fixed Fee Appointment Guideline 3.

(3) Case Evaluation. A fixed fee and expenses agreement shall be reached within 60 days after the Court issues its order appointing a referee. Discussions with applicant counsel regarding proposals for such an agreement shall be conducted through the Automatic Appeals Monitor.

(4) Fixed Legal Fee and Expense Payments.

Fixed legal fee payments. Counsel shall be entitled to be paid one-fourth of the *legal fee component* of the amount set out in the fixed legal fee and expenses agreement upon the filing of the Court's order making the fixed legal fee and expenses appointment. Thereafter, counsel will receive, on written request (but without the necessity of providing an itemization of hours), a one-fourth progress payment of the legal fee component after (i) the evidentiary hearing commences, (ii) the post-hearing litigation before the referee is completed, and (iii) the post-hearing briefing in this Court is completed. Under limited circumstances (e.g., substantial delay not due to lack of diligence on the part of counsel), the Court will authorize partial payments before completion of the aforementioned stages.

Expense payments. Every 30 days, counsel may request reimbursement from this Court for all necessary and reasonable expenses, up to the amount set out in the fixed legal fee and expenses agreement. Reimbursement shall be governed by and calculated in accordance with the Court's Payment Guidelines, *supra*, part III ("Necessary Expenses").

11. Court Action Upon Nonperformance of Work, and Reimbursement of Fees Upon Authorized Withdrawal of Appointed Counsel

The provisions of "Guideline V" of the "Payment Guidelines for Appointed Counsel Representing Indigent Criminal Appellants in the California Supreme Court" apply as well to counsel appointed on a "fixed fee" basis.

12. Reimbursement for Photocopying Defense Counsel's Trial Files

In addition to investigative expenses as set forth in the "Supreme Court Policies Regarding Cases Arising From

Judgments of Death," Policy 3, standard 2-2.1, counsel appointed to handle habeas corpus/executive clemency representation will be reimbursed the reasonable cost of photocopying defense counsel's trial files, at the rate of not more than 10 cents per page, after filing of the certified record on appeal. Counsel must provide a receipt or invoice showing the number of pages copied, and the cost per page. Reimbursement will not be paid for photocopying of items already contained in the record on appeal, such as daily transcripts or exhibits.

Adopted Dec. 14, 1993, effective Jan. 1, 1994; amended Sept. 1, 1995; Jan. 1, 1997; Jan. 22, 1997; July 30, 1997; Jan. 22, 1998; Feb. 4, 1998; Jan. 16, 2002; March 21, 2002; Oct. 1, 2005; Nov. 30, 2005; July 1, 2006; Oct. 1, 2007; and Jan. 1, 2008.

Fixed Fee Guidelines.   2008 Deletes. [1] 26 (September 21, 2006) Rules pp. 9–19 **[2]** 26 **[3]** 1–8 **[4]** $153,000 **[5]** $153,000 **[6]** $222,000 **[7]** $272,000 **[8]** $309,000 **[9]** $354,000 **[10]** $62,000 **[11]** $62,000 **[12]** $130,000 **[13]** $171,000 **[14]** $210,000 **[15]** $253,000 **[16]** $81,000 **[17]** $140 **[18]** $105,000 **[19]** $140 **[20]** $121,000 **[21]** $140 **[22]** *$121,000* **[23]** $50,500 ($47,000 **[24]** $55,500 ($47,000 **[25]** $77,500 ($69,000 **[26]** $83,000 ($69,000 **[27]** $112,000 ($98,000 **[28]** $119,000 ($98,000 **[29]** $143,000 *base sum* ($119,000

GUIDELINES FOR THE COMMISSION ON JUDICIAL APPOINTMENTS

(Adopted by the Commission on Judicial Appointments, effective May 18, 1999; amended effective July 1, 2005, March 1, 2006, February 23, 2007, and November 19, 2007.)

Guideline 1.   Definitions; commission headquarters.

(a)   [Definition] "Nomination" and "nominee" also refer to appointments and appointees, as described in article VI, section 16(d), of the California Constitution.
Adopted effective May 18, 1999.

(b)   [Definition] "Court days" refer to days on which the California courts are open for official business. Normally, Mondays through Fridays are counted as court days, except for judicial holidays.
Adopted effective May 18, 1999.

(c)   [Commission headquarters] The headquarters and mailing address of the Commission on Judicial Appointments (commission) are:

Commission on Judicial Appointments
c/o Chief Justice of California
Supreme Court of California
350 McAllister Street

San Francisco, California 94102
Attention: The Secretary to the Commission

The commission's facsimile transmission (fax) number is (415) 865-7181, and its telephone number is (415) 865-7060.

Amended effective February 23, 2007; adopted effective May 18, 1999; previously amended effective March 1, 2006.

Guideline 2.   Commission membership (Cal. Const., art. VI, § 7).

The commission consists of the Chief Justice of California, the Attorney General, and the presiding justice of the Court of Appeal of the affected district or, if there are two or more presiding justices, the one who has presided longest or, for a nomination to the Supreme Court, the presiding justice who has presided longest as a presiding justice on any Court of Appeal.

Amended effective July 1, 2005; adopted effective May 18, 1999.

Guideline 3.   Commission chairperson.

(a)   [Chairperson] The Chief Justice (or Acting Chief Justice) shall serve as chairperson of the commission.
Adopted effective May 18, 1999.

(b)   [Powers] The chairperson shall preside at the confirmation hearing. The chairperson also is authorized to:

(1)   act on behalf of the commission in all matters arising between hearings;

(2)   adopt such internal guidelines and order measures as deemed appropriate to implement these guidelines, or for good cause extend or shorten the time periods set forth in these guidelines;

(3)   set time limits for the testimony of witnesses;

(4)   at the hearing, limit or terminate a witness's testimony for failure to comply with these guidelines;

(5)   exclude any person from the hearing who disrupts the proceedings; and

(6)   make security arrangements for the confirmation hearing.

Amended effective March 1, 2006; adopted effective May 18, 1999; previously amended effective July 1, 2005.

Guideline 4.   Pre-hearing procedures.

(a)   [Scheduling, notice, and location of public hearing] The chairperson shall schedule the confirmation hearing within a reasonable time after the nomination and shall issue a press release announcing the time, place, and subject of the hearing.
Adopted effective May 18, 1999.

(b)   [Commission on Judicial Nominees Evaluation (Gov. Code, § 12011.5)] The chairperson shall request the Commission on Judicial Nominees Evaluation of the State Bar (JNE) to:

(1)   submit to the commission as soon as practicable, but in no event later than the time specified in paragraph (d) of this guideline, its written recommendations to the commission concerning the nominee, and the reasons therefor, and, if specifically requested, all prior JNE recommendations, including the date of evaluation and the court for which the nominee was evaluated; and

(2) designate a representative to testify at the hearing as to the JNE evaluation of the nominee.

Adopted effective May 18, 1999.

(c) [Communications with the commission] All communications regarding a nominee must be made in writing to the commission and/or by testimony at the hearing. Communications regarding a nomination or nominee should be made to the commission as a whole rather than to any commission member individually, and shall be distributed promptly to the members of the commission. Communications may be sent to the commission by United States Mail, overnight delivery, messenger service, or fax, to arrive within the time specified in these guidelines. The commission generally will not formally acknowledge receipt of written presentations concerning a nominee's qualifications. Communications that are received by the commission after the time specified in these guidelines shall be returned to the sender by the secretary to the commission.

Amended effective March 1, 2006; adopted effective May 18, 1999.

(d) [Written presentations and requests to testify; time for submission]

(1) Individuals, including the nominee, who submit a written presentation or request to testify before the commission must identify themselves by name, address, and occupation, and, if applicable, shall identify the name, address, and purpose of any agency or organization for which they are acting in a representative capacity. Telephone numbers and any fax numbers of these individuals and organizations must be included.

(2) Except for the nominee's list of those witnesses whom he or she wishes to testify, as described under paragraph (g), all requests to testify before the commission must be in writing and must specifically state whether the witness will be testifying in support of or in opposition to the nominee, and describe the proposed testimony, its relevance to the nominee's qualifications, and the facts upon which the witness's testimony and opinion will be based. All written presentations or requests to testify must be received by the commission no later than 5:00 p.m. on the fifth court day before the hearing. (For example, if a hearing is to be held on a Monday, the fifth court day before the hearing would be the preceding Monday, unless a judicial holiday falls in between. Each intervening judicial holiday requires an additional court day's notice.)

Amended effective March 1, 2006; adopted effective May 18, 1999; previously amended effective July 1, 2005.

(e) [Permissible testimony] The commission shall review requests to testify and shall permit testimony that is relevant to the nominee's qualifications. Testimony relating to the judicial system generally or to the overall nomination or confirmation process will not be received. Testimony that is unduly cumulative to or repetitive of other testimony may be excluded. A person whose request to testify is denied shall be so informed by the commission as soon as possible before the hearing, by telephone or fax.

Amended effective March 1, 2006; adopted effective May 18, 1999.

(f) [Notice to nominee] The commission promptly shall provide the nominee with a copy of all the written presentations or requests to testify it receives and shall afford the nominee an opportunity to refute, clarify, or

comment, either at the hearing or before the hearing in writing, or both. Similarly, if the commission receives any record, public or private, or any other communication relating to the nominee's qualifications, it promptly shall provide the nominee with a copy thereof, and afford the nominee an opportunity to refute, clarify, or comment on that record or communication (consistent with the provisions of Cal. Const. art. VI, § 18.5). All written responses by the nominee must be received by the commission no later than 5:00 p.m. on the third court day before the hearing.

Adopted effective May 18, 1999.

(g) [Nominee's witness list] The nominee shall present the commission with a list of any witnesses he or she wishes to testify at the hearing. This list must include the information required by paragraph (d)(1) and shall be received by the commission no later than 5:00 p.m. on the third court day before the hearing.

Adopted effective May 18, 1999.

(h) [Release of lists of speakers and communications] No later than 2:00 p.m. on the second court day before the scheduled hearing, the commission shall release to the public the following:

(1) the names of witnesses who will testify at the hearing;

(2) the names of any individuals or organizations that have submitted written communications to the commission;

(3) correspondence and public reports received by the commission concerning the nominee's qualifications, including any reports submitted by JNE pursuant to paragraph (b), and the nominee's Personal Data Questionnaire submitted by the Governor to the commission. The commission, however, shall delete any confidential personal information such as an individual's residential address, or Social Security or driver's license number. The written material released shall be made available for copying at the requesting party's expense.

Amended effective July 1, 2005; adopted effective May 18, 1999.

Guideline 5. Hearing procedures.

(a) [Conference] The commission members may confer before the confirmation hearing to consider procedural issues.

Adopted effective May 18, 1999.

(b) [Absence of commission member] Concurrence of at least two commission members present at the hearing is necessary to confirm a nominee. If the Chief Justice is recused or unavailable, the Acting Chief Justice shall serve as the chairperson. If the presiding justice described in Guideline 2 is recused or unavailable, the presiding justice of the affected district who has presided next longest as presiding justice, or, in districts with a single presiding justice, the acting presiding justice, or for a nomination to the Supreme Court, the presiding justice who has presided next longest as presiding justice on any Court of Appeal, shall serve. (See Cal. Const., art. VI, §§ 2, 3, and 7.) A request that a commission member not participate in proceedings of the commission shall be decided by that member alone. The hearing may proceed if two members of the commission are present.

Amended effective July 1, 2005; adopted effective May 18, 1999.

(c) [Witnesses] Witnesses shall be heard in the following order:

(1) witnesses in support of the nominee;

(2) witnesses in opposition to the nominee;

(3) the JNE representative;

(4) the nominee.

Adopted effective May 18, 1999.

(d) [Exhibits and demonstrative evidence] Witnesses must testify orally and have no right to present exhibits or demonstrative evidence at the hearing.

Adopted effective May 18, 1999.

(e) [Record of hearing] The hearing proceedings shall be recorded by audio or video recorder, court reporter, or any other means appropriate for preserving the testimony. A nominee who wishes to make his or her own arrangements to record the hearing by video recorder or other means shall notify the commission in writing. This notice must be received by the commission no later than 5:00 p.m. on the second court day before the hearing.

Adopted effective May 18, 1999.

(f) [Public attendance and broadcasting] The hearing shall be open to the public and to the media. Any request to broadcast, photograph, or record the hearing requires the approval of the chairperson, upon written application received no later than 5:00 p.m. on the second court day before the hearing. The request, as well as the broadcasting, photographing, and recording, shall comply with the provisions of California Rules of Court, rules 1.150 and 2.954, where applicable.

Amended effective November 19, 2007; adopted effective May 18, 1999; previously amended effective July 1, 2005.

(g) [Announcement of decision] The commission may deliberate privately, but shall announce its decision publicly at the hearing, as well as by subsequent news release. If necessary, the hearing may be continued to a future date for further proceedings.

Adopted effective May 18, 1999.

(h) [Official record] The commission's minutes shall be the official record of the hearing.

Adopted effective May 18, 1999.

Guideline 6. Staff to the commission.

The chairperson of the commission may designate a person to act as secretary to the commission and one or more persons to act as assistant secretaries. The secretary shall maintain custody of the commission's files. The Administrative Office of the Courts, at the chairperson's direction, shall provide additional staff and financial support as necessary to enable the commission to perform its duties.

Adopted effective May 18, 1999.

Guideline 7. Post-hearing procedures.

(a) [Access to the commission's files] Except as otherwise provided in paragraph (b) of this guideline, after the conclusion of any nomination proceedings of the commission subject to these guidelines, a person, agency, or organization, upon written request to the commission's secretary, may obtain access to the public portions of the

commission's files, as defined in guideline 4(h), as well as any transcript of the hearing prepared by a court reporter as a record of those proceedings pursuant to guideline 5(e), for inspection and copying at the requesting party's expense.

(b) [Audio or video recording] Any audio or video recording prepared as a record of the hearing pursuant to guideline 5(e) shall be copyrighted and made available for viewing at a time and location specified by the commission's secretary, but shall not be available for copying by the requesting party unless such copying is authorized by the commission.

Amended effective July 1, 2005; adopted effective May 18, 1999.

Guideline 8. Publication and distribution of these guidelines.

(a) [Official guidelines] These guidelines for the Commission on Judicial Appointments shall be published by the Reporter of Decisions in the advance pamphlets of the California Official Reports and shall be made available on the judicial branch's Web site (at *www.courtinfo.ca.gov/reference/documents/guidelinescja.pdf*) or by calling the Public Information Office of the Administrative Office of the Courts at (415) 865-7740.

Amended effective November 19, 2007; adopted effective May 18, 1999; previously amended effective July 1, 2005.

(b) [News release] Information regarding access to these guidelines shall accompany each news release announcing a commission hearing.

Adopted effective May 18, 1999.

(c) [Copies] A copy of these guidelines shall be sent to the nominee with the notice of the hearing, and to each designated witness.

Adopted effective May 18, 1999.

LOCAL RULES AND INTERNAL OPERATING PRACTICES AND PROCEDURES OF THE COURTS OF APPEAL

First Appellate District. Rules 1-15; Internal Operating Practices and Procedures.

Second Appellate District. Rules 1-6; Internal Operating Practices and Procedures.

Third Appellate District. Rules 1-4; Internal Operating Practices and Procedures.

Fourth Appellate District. Rules 1-5; Internal Operating Practices and Procedures, Division One; Internal Operating Practices and Procedures, Division Two; Internal Operating Practices and Procedures, Division Three.

Fifth Appellate District. Rules 1-5; Local Court Form; Internal Operating Practices and Procedures.

Sixth Appellate District. Internal Operating Practices and Procedures.

FIRST APPELLATE DISTRICT LOCAL RULES

[Adopted effective October 16, 2006]

Rule 1. Criminal and Juvenile Docketing Statements

(a) [Application of Rule] In all criminal appeals, juvenile appeals from proceedings arising under sections 300, 601, or 602 of the Welfare and Institutions Code, and juvenile writ proceedings seeking to review findings and orders setting a hearing under section 366.26 of the Welfare and Institutions Code, the clerk of the superior court must, upon the filing of a notice of appeal or notice of intent, prepare a docketing statement and promptly forward it to the Court of Appeal with the notice of appeal or notice of intent and a copy of the (abstract of) judgment, minutes or order that is under appeal or challenged by writ.

(b) [Forms] The following forms of docketing statements shall be used:

(1) Docketing Statement for Criminal Notice of Appeal

(2) Docketing Statement for Juvenile Notice of Appeal and Juvenile Notice of Intent to File Writ Petition

(c) [Sanctions] The failure of a clerk of a superior court to file a docketing statement as required by this rule may result in the imposition of sanctions under the California Rules of Court.

Rule 1 adopted, effective October 16, 2006.

Rule 2. Mediation in Civil Appeals

(a) [Mediation Program] To aid the expeditious and just resolution of civil appeals, the Court of Appeal for the First District has established a mediation Program ("Program"). Procedures for mediation and operation of the Program shall be promulgated by the First District Mediation Committee ("Committee"). The Program will be directed by a Mediation Program Administrator ("Administrator") acting under Committee procedures and supervision by the Administrative Presiding Justice or a designated Supervising Justice.

(b) [Scope of Mediation Program] Any civil appeal may be placed in the Program if selected by the Administrator or requested in writing by a party. The Adminis-

trator may remove an appeal from the Program and shall record the reasons for removal.

(c) [Mediators] The Committee shall specify the qualifications, training, and process for appointment of mediators in the Program. The Administrator will assign mediators to appeals. Mediation services will be furnished by the court without fee to the parties, provided that a mediation session exceeding 3 hours may be terminated by the mediator unless the parties and the mediator agree upon a fee payable to the mediator for continued services. The Administrator may replace a selected mediator upon written request by a party supported by a showing of good cause or upon request of the mediator.

For a list of Civil Appeals Mediators, see http://www.courtinfo.ca.gov/courts/courtsofappeal/1stDistrict/faq/mediators.pdf.

(d) [Mediation Process]

(1) Within 10 days of the filing of the notice of appeal, the appellant shall file with the Clerk and shall serve on all other parties a completed Case Screening Form. Within 15 days of the filing of the notice of appeal, the other parties shall file with the Clerk and shall serve on all other parties their Case Screening Forms. The Case Screening Forms shall be transmitted by the Clerk to the Administrator and shall not be entered in the court file.

For the court's mediation forms, see http://www.courtinfo.ca.gov/courts/courtsofappeal/1stDistrict/forms.htm#mediation.

(2) The Administrator, within 10 days of receipt of the Case Screening Forms, shall notify the parties when a case is selected for mediation and furnish the name, address and telephone number of the mediator. At the same time, the Administrator shall furnish the mediator copies of the Case Screening Forms.

(3) Selection of a case for mediation will not suspend preparation of the appellate record or briefing, except pursuant to an order granting an application for an extension of time or a stipulation for an extension of time as provided in the California Rules of Court.

(4) The Administrator, within 5 days of selection of the mediator, shall furnish to the parties 3 dates within the next 30 days when the mediator is available for the mediation session.

(5) The parties, within 5 days of receipt of these dates, shall advise the Administrator of their scheduling preferences. The Administrator, after conferring with the mediator, promptly shall select the date and site for the mediation session and shall notify the parties.

(6) The mediator, with the approval of the Administrator, may, for good cause, postpone or continue a mediation session to a date certain.

(7) The mediator may require parties or their counsel to furnish information, documents, records or other items specified by the mediator.

(8) The mediator may at any time communicate with any of the parties or their counsel with or without notice to the other parties or their counsel.

(9) All parties and their counsel of record must attend all mediation sessions in person with full settlement authority. If the party is not an individual, then a party representative with full authority to settle all appeals and cross-appeals must attend all mediation sessions in person,

in addition to counsel. If a party has potential insurance coverage applicable to any of the issues in dispute, a representative of each insurance carrier whose policy may apply must also attend all mediation sessions in person, with full settlement authority. Any exception to this requirement must be approved in writing by the Administrator.

The mediator may invite participation by any additional person or entity if the mediator concludes that such participation would facilitate mediation.

(10) No later than 10 days after completion of mediation, the mediator shall submit to the Administrator a Mediation Attendance Form, listing all participants in the mediation, and a Mediator's Statement, notifying the Administrator of the results of the mediation.

(11) No later than 10 days after completion of mediation, the parties and their counsel shall separately complete and submit to the Administrator evaluations of the mediation and the mediator on a form provided by the Administrator.

(12) The parties and their counsel shall promptly take the steps necessary to implement the agreements reached in mediation. An appellant who has settled must immediately serve and file a notice of settlement in the Court of Appeal and, thereafter, must seek abandonment or dismissal of the appeal as provided in the California Rules of Court.

(e) [Confidentiality] Except as otherwise required by law, information disclosed to the mediator, the parties, counsel, or any other participant in the mediation, or to the Administrator or the Coordinator of the mediation Program, shall be confidential and shall not be disclosed to anyone not participating in the mediation Program.

(f) [Ethical Standards] Mediators shall adhere to the Rules of Conduct for Mediators in Court-Connected Mediation Programs for Civil Cases set forth in the California Rules of Court.

(g) [Appellate Process] Parties and counsel shall comply with all rules applicable to processing appeals while concurrently participating in the mediation Program.

(h) [Sanctions] Monetary sanctions may be imposed by the Administrative Presiding Justice or Supervising Justice for failure to comply with these rules.

Rule 2 adopted, effective October 16, 2006.

Rule 3.   Settlement Conferences in Civil Appeals

(a) [Application of Rule] This rule applies to all appeals in civil cases except appeals from proceedings under sections 601 and 602 of the Welfare and Institutions Code, appeals arising in proceedings involving jurisdiction over an abused or neglected child or to establish or terminate parental rights, and appeals from original proceedings ancillary to a criminal prosecution. This rule is operative in addition to Local Rule 2.

(b) [Request or Order for Settlement Conference]

(1) A settlement conference will be scheduled if requested in writing by counsel for all parties to the appeal. The request may be made at any time prior to the close of briefing and shall be addressed to the Clerk/Administrator. A request by counsel for any party which declares that

counsel for all other parties join in the request is adequate for this purpose.

(2) At any time during the pendency of an appeal, the panel to which the appeal has been assigned may order a settlement conference even though none was requested.

(3) The pendency of settlement proceedings will not suspend preparation of the appellate record or briefing, except pursuant to an order granting an application for an extension of time or a stipulation for an extension of time as provided in the California Rules of Court.

(c) [The Settlement Conference]

(1) A justice selected by the court from outside the division to which the appeal is assigned shall preside over the settlement conference. The Settlement Conference Justice will provide each party with written notice of the date and time of the conference. All subsequent communications regarding the settlement conference shall be directed to the Settlement Conference Justice and shall not be entered in the court file. The Settlement Conference Justice may continue the conference from time to time to allow further opportunity for negotiation and agreement, and may make any order necessary to effectuate the conference.

(2) All parties and their counsel of record must attend all settlement conference sessions in person with full settlement authority. If the party is not an individual, then a party representative with full authority to settle all appeals and cross-appeals must attend all settlement conference sessions in person, in addition to counsel. If a party has potential insurance coverage applicable to any of the issues in dispute, a representative of each insurance carrier whose policy may apply must also attend all settlement conference sessions in person, with full settlement authority. Any exception to this requirement must be approved in writing by the Settlement Conference Justice.

The Settlement Conference Justice may invite participation by any additional person or entity if the Settlement Conference Justice concludes that such participation would facilitate settlement.

(d) [Implementation of Settlement Agreements] The parties and their counsel shall promptly take the steps necessary to implement the agreements reached at the settlement conference. An appellant who has settled must immediately serve and file a notice of settlement in the Court of Appeal and, thereafter, must seek abandonment or dismissal of the appeal as provided in the California Rules of Court.

(e) [Confidentiality] Except as otherwise required by law, information disclosed to the Settlement Conference Justice, the parties, counsel, or any other participant in the settlement conference shall be confidential and shall not be disclosed to anyone not participating in the settlement conference.

(f) [Appellate Process] Parties and counsel shall comply with all rules applicable to processing appeals while concurrently participating in the Settlement Conference Program.

(g) [Sanctions] Monetary sanctions may be imposed by the Administrative Presiding Justice, the Supervising Justice of the Settlement Conference Program, or the Settlement Conference Justice for failure to comply with these rules.

Rule 3 adopted, effective October 16, 2006.

Rule 4. Motions for Stipulated Reversal of Judgment

A motion filed in this court for stipulated reversal of a judgment of a trial court must include a joint declaration of counsel that (1) describes the parties and the factual and legal issues presented at trial; (2) indicates whether the judgment involves important public rights or unfair, illegal or corrupt practices, or torts affecting a significant number of persons, or otherwise affects the public or a significant number of persons not parties to the litigation (if the judgment is against a state licensee, the declaration must also disclose whether it exposes such person to any possible disciplinary proceeding); and (3) discloses whether the judgment sought to be reversed may have collateral estoppel or other effects in potential future litigation and, if so, whether any third parties who might be prejudiced by stipulated reversal of the judgment have received notice of the motion therefor. A copy of the judgment must accompany the motion.

The parties must provide a sufficient showing to support the findings required by Code of Civil Procedure section 128, subdivision (a)(8).

Rule 4 adopted, effective October 16, 2006.

Rule 5. Timely Preparation of Clerk's and Reporter's Transcripts

(a) [Extensions of Time] A request for an extension of time for the preparation of the clerk's or reporter's transcript on appeal will not be granted without an affirmative showing of good cause.

(b) [Defaults] In all cases in which a court reporter is in default, this court will promptly issue an order directing the court reporter to show cause why he or she should not be declared incompetent to act as an official reporter, pursuant to the provisions of section 69944 of the Government Code.

(c) [Sanctions] Sanctions may be imposed under the California Rules of Court for defaults in the preparation of clerk's or reporter's transcripts.

(d) [Forms] A motion for the extension of time to file a transcript shall be in substantially the form of one of the following:

(1) Clerk's Affidavit and Order for Extension of Time to File Transcript on Appeal

(2) Reporter's Affidavit and Order for Extension of Time to File Transcript on Appeal

Rule 5 adopted, effective October 16, 2006.

Rule 6. Contents of Reporter's Transcript in Criminal and Juvenile Delinquency Appeals

In addition to the normal record prescribed by the California Rules of Court, all records in criminal and juvenile delinquency appeals before the Court of Appeal, First Appellate District, are hereby augmented to include reporter's transcripts of the following proceedings:

(a) [*Marsden* Hearings] Any hearing held pursuant to *People v. Marsden* (1970) 2 Cal.3d 118. The original and two copies of the sealed transcript shall accompany the record upon certification and delivery to this court. The court shall provide appellant's counsel with a copy of the transcript. If appellant raises a *Marsden* issue, a copy of the transcript shall then be provided to the Attorney General in the manner prescribed in the California Rules of Court.

(b) [Pretrial Motions] Pretrial motions as follows: (1) motion to suppress identification; (2) motion to suppress statements of defendant (*Miranda v. Arizona* (1966) 384 U.S. 436); (3) motion to permit or preclude impeachment of defendant or witness with prior offenses (*People v. Castro* (1985) 38 Cal.3d 301); (4) motion to determine competence of defendant (Pen. Code, § 1368); (5) motion for severance or joinder; (6) motion for change of venue; (7) motion for discovery of police officer records (*Pitchess v. Superior Court* (1974) 11 Cal.3d 531); (8) motion for self-representation (*Faretta v. California* (1975) 422 U.S. 806); and (9) in limine motions held by the trial judge immediately preceding the trial or impanelment of the jury.

These motions shall be included only when denied in whole or in part, except for a People's motion for joinder or to impeach defendant, which shall be included only if granted in whole or in part.

Motions held in camera or under seal shall be transmitted to this court only, and no sealed copies shall be provided counsel for either party except on application to this court.

(c) [Revocation of Probation—Plea Proceedings] In appeals from revocation of probation: (1) the original sentencing proceeding at which probation was imposed; (2) the proceedings at the time of entry of a guilty plea or nolo contendere plea if the original judgment of conviction is based on such plea; and (3) the proceedings at which probation is revoked and the defendant is sentenced.

Rule 6 adopted, effective October 16, 2006.

Rule 7. Augmentation of Record

(a) [Material Inadvertently Omitted] Counsel should not file a motion to augment the record when items have been inadvertently omitted by the clerk or certified shorthand reporter from the designated (civil) or normal (criminal) record. In such cases, counsel should immediately notify the clerk of the trial court who shall forthwith transmit the omitted item to this court and send a copy to counsel.

(b) [When to File Motion to Augment] Appellant should file requests for augmentation in one motion made within 30 days of the filing of the record or within 30 days after the expiration of the 10-day administrator review period in assisted criminal cases. Respondent should file requests for augmentation in one motion made within 30 days of the filing of appellant's opening brief. Thereafter, motions to augment will only be entertained upon a showing of good cause.

(c) [Clerk's Transcript] A motion to augment the clerk's transcript should be accompanied by that document (or documents) and, if not, must identify the document (or documents) with specificity; such motion and accompanying documents must be simultaneously served on opposing counsel. The requested augmented materials shall have been filed or lodged with the trial court, and the motion shall be accompanied by a declaration shall so stating.

(d) [Reporter's Transcript] A motion to augment the reporter's transcript shall identify the portion of the record with specificity, including the reporter and date of hearing. It shall establish with some certainty how the requested materials may be useful on appeal. Requests for jury voir dire should specify the exact questioning by which counsel of which juror together with the reason justifying the request.

(e) [Good Faith Required] A motion to augment shall be made in good faith and shall not be made for the purpose of delay.

Rule 7 adopted, effective October 16, 2006.

Rule 8. Stipulation for Use of Original Superior Court File

The California Rules of Court authorize the use of the original superior court file in lieu of the clerk's transcript on appeal in those cases where the parties so stipulate. The procedure therein is approved for use by the superior courts within this district in all civil cases in which the trial court retains no continuing jurisdiction. The stipulation shall be in substantially the form of the following: Stipulation for Use of Original Superior Court File in Lieu of Clerk's Transcript.

Rule 8 adopted, effective October 16, 2006.

Rule 9. Judicial Notice Requests

(a) [Form of Request] Any request that the court take judicial notice under Evidence Code section 459 shall be submitted as provided in the California Rules of Court. A motion seeking judicial notice pursuant to Evidence Code section 452 must include a showing of the relevance of the information to be judicially noticed.

(b) [If the Court Defers Ruling] If the motion is filed at the same time as the moving party's brief or if the court, with or without notifying the parties, has deferred ruling on a judicial notice motion, any party may in its brief rely upon the items the moving party sought to have noticed. However, if the court denies the motion it will disregard any such matter or materials not judicially noticed.

Rule 9 adopted, effective October 16, 2006.

Rule 10. Filing by Facsimile

(a) [By the Trial Court] The trial court may transmit the following documents to this court via facsimile: (1) notices of appeal; (2) criminal and juvenile docketing statements; and (3) extension requests for court reporters and the superior court clerk's office.

(b) [By Counsel] Counsel may transmit the following documents to this court via facsimile: (1) civil case information statements; (2) stipulations for extensions of time; (3) changes of address; and (4) requests for oral argument.

Rule 10 adopted, effective October 16, 2006.

Rule 11. Extensions of Time for Filing Briefs

(a) [Procedure] The times for filing briefs in civil, criminal, and juvenile appeals are specified in the California Rules of Court. In civil cases, the parties may, by stipulation, extend the time for filing each brief not more than 60 days. In criminal and juvenile cases, extensions of time by stipulation are not allowed. Extensions of time may be granted by the court only on a showing of good cause.

An application for an extension of time to file a brief is not necessary, either before or after a default notice under the California Rules of Court, if the brief can be filed within the pertinent default period. The clerk shall accept such a brief as timely filed.

(b) [Forms] An application for an extension of time to file a brief shall comply with the requirements of the California Rules of Court and shall be in substantially the form of one of the following:

(1) Application for Extension of Time to File Brief (Civil Case) (Judicial Council Form)

(2) Application for Extension of Time to File Brief (Criminal Case)

(3) Application for Extension of Time to File Brief (Juvenile Case)

(c) [Copies and Preaddressed Envelopes] The applicant shall provide the clerk with additional copies of the application, proposed order, and preaddressed envelopes with prepaid postage for mailing of the court's order to all parties.

Rule 11 adopted, effective October 16, 2006.

Rule 12. Bankruptcy Stays

(a) [Conditions for Giving Notice] Any party to a matter pending before this court who acquires knowledge of a proceeding in bankruptcy which may cause or impose a stay of proceedings in this court must promptly give notice of such bankruptcy proceedings, as set forth below.

(b) [Procedure for Notice] The notice required by subdivision (a) shall be filed with the court and served on all parties and shall include (1) a copy of the most recent order of the bankruptcy court and of any stay order issued by that court and (2) an explanation of whether a stay order or an automatic stay is in effect and why the stay applies to the pending appeal or writ proceeding. Any party disputing the notifying party's documentation or explanation shall promptly serve and file an opposing statement.

(c) [Status Reports] On the first court days of January, April, July, and October, the debtor or other party for whose benefit the stay is taken shall serve and file brief status reports to apprise the court of the current status of the bankruptcy proceedings.

(d) [Notice to Proceed] Any party may, at any time, serve and file notice of any circumstances or orders permitting the appeal or writ proceeding to proceed, including evidence that the bankruptcy stay has been lifted, the bankruptcy proceeding has been dismissed, or the party has obtained relief from the stay.

Rule 12 adopted, effective October 16, 2006.

Rule 13. Argument by Teleconference System

(a) [Teleconference System] The First Appellate District has a telephone conference call system that enables attorneys to present oral arguments by telephone, as an alternative to personal appearance in court. All oral arguments by telephone conference call will be heard by the justices on the bench in the courtroom, which will be open to the public.

(b) [Option of Counsel] In all cases, civil, criminal, and juvenile, in which a party has a right to present oral argument, counsel may elect to present oral argument either by personal appearance in the courtroom or by telephone conference call. The decision whether to present oral argument by telephone or in person is within the sole discretion of counsel and the parties, except that the court may direct counsel to appear in person.

In deciding whether to present oral argument by personal appearance or by telephone, counsel should consider the expense of a personal appearance to the parties and to the state and should determine whether the matters at issue can be satisfactorily argued by telephone conference call without incurring that expense.

(c) [Notice to Other Counsel] Upon receipt of oral argument notice from the court, counsel shall notify the court and all other parties in writing if he or she requests oral argument. If oral argument is requested, counsel shall indicate whether he or she elects to present oral argument in person or by telephone conference call. The notice shall be given within the time allowed for requesting oral argument.

If one counsel elects to argue by telephone and the other elects to appear in person, the counsel who elected to argue by telephone shall have the right to change his or her request and appear in person. The requested change shall be communicated in writing to the divisional deputy clerk and opposing counsel without delay.

(d) [Written Request for Oral Argument] Counsel's request to present oral argument by telephone conference call shall be made in writing and shall contain the following information: (1) the number and title of the case; (2) the name of counsel who will present oral argument; (3) the name of the party counsel is representing; and (4) the telephone number to be used for the conference call.

(e) [Fee to Cover Costs] The cost of the telephone system and service is billed to the court. No fee shall be charged to court-appointed counsel in any criminal, juvenile, or civil case or to the Attorney General or counsel representing the state, a county, a municipality or other government agency. In all other cases, a fee of $20 shall be paid by each party whose counsel requests oral argument by telephone conference call. A check in that amount, payable to the Court of Appeal, shall accompany counsel's request for oral argument. Additionally, telephone conference calls made to counsel outside the geographic boundaries of the First Appellate District will be made collect.

(f) [Notice of Time of Oral Argument] When a party requests oral argument by telephone conference call, the divisional deputy clerk shall notify counsel of the date, the approximate time of oral argument, and may indicate the maximum amount of time the court will allow for argument. The deputy clerk will arrange the conference call when the court calls the case for argument. If counsel fails to be available when the case is called, the court may deem oral argument waived.

(g) [Recording of Oral Argument] The court may record oral arguments presented by telephone conference call. A request for oral argument by telephone will be deemed consent to such recording.

Rule 13 adopted, effective October 16, 2006.

Rule 14.   Circuit Riding Sessions

The court will conduct its hearings in its courtroom in San Francisco, California, except in the following instances:

(a) For the convenience of the litigants and attorneys, sessions may also be held in those cities or communities within the First Appellate District outside San Francisco from which sufficient appeals have been perfected to constitute one full day's calendar.

A session of the court may be held in the interest of justice at an appropriate educational institution within the First Appellate District. The court will not deviate from its normal calendar-scheduling practices in order to accumulate sufficient cases for a full day of hearings in any city or community.

(b) For the convenience of the court and court personnel, court sessions not held in the courtroom in San Francisco will be held only when suitable courtroom facilities are provided. Suitable courtroom facilities require security adequate to ensure the safety of the public and the court.

Rule 14 adopted, effective October 16, 2006.

Rule 15.   Media Coverage of Matters at Oral Argument

Media coverage will be permitted only on written order of the presiding justice of the division hearing argument. The presiding justice in his or her discretion may permit, refuse, limit, or terminate media coverage. Any request for media coverage must be made on the Judicial Council form titled Media Request to Photograph, Broadcast, or Record. The form must be filed at least five court days in advance of the proceedings unless good cause is shown. The court directs the media's attention to the California Rules of Court, which specifically require pooling by media agencies.

Rule 15 adopted, effective October 16, 2006.

INTERNAL OPERATING PRACTICES AND PROCEDURES FIRST APPELLATE DISTRICT

(Adopted effective April 2, 2007)

I. INTRODUCTION

A. Purpose and Scope

The purpose of this document is to inform members of the bar and other interested persons about the organization of the court and its procedures for processing cases. It is not intended to duplicate the California Rules of Court, the Local Rules of the First Appellate District, or the statutes and constitutional provisions governing the processing of cases.

B. General Information

The court's address is:

California Court of Appeal
First Appellate District
350 McAllister Street
San Francisco, CA 94102

The clerk's office is located on the first floor in Room 1185 and is open to the public from 9 a.m. to 5 p.m., Monday through Friday, exclusive of state holidays. Its internet e-mail address is: first.district@jud.ca.gov

The court's telephone numbers are:

(415) 865-7200 (Clerk's Office)
(415) 865-7209 (Clerk's Office Fax)
(415) 865-7300 (Chambers' Receptionist)
(415) 865-7309 (Reception Fax)

The court's website is:
http://www.courtinfo.ca.gov/courts/
courtsofappeal/1stDistrict/

II. ORGANIZATION OF THE COURT

A. Justices and Staff

The First Appellate District is comprised of five divisions, each consisting of a presiding justice and three associate justices. Each division operates as a separate unit for the purpose of hearing and deciding cases.

The presiding justice of each division convenes conferences and presides at hearings (oral arguments) in the division and has overall responsibility for calendaring cases, managing the caseload of the division, and all other divisional administrative matters. If the presiding justice is absent or disqualified or not a member of the three-justice panel assigned to decide a matter, the presiding justice usually designates the senior associate justice of the division to serve as acting presiding justice. The Chief Justice of California has designated one of the court's presiding justices to serve as its administrative presiding justice, as prescribed in the California Rules of Court.

Each of the court's justices employs a judicial assistant and two chambers attorneys. Some of the court's justices also utilize law student externs to assist in their individual chambers. In addition, each division employs a writ attorney and a divisional attorney, who are selected by the justices of the division and supervised by its presiding justice.

B. Clerk/Administrator, Clerk's Office Staff, and Administrative Support Staff

The court's clerk/administrator is selected by the justices of the court and works under the general direction and supervision of the administrative presiding justice. The clerk/administrator is responsible for planning, organizing, coordinating, and directing the management of the clerk's office and its personnel. The clerk/administrator also supervises the court's administrative support staff. The clerk/administrator is responsible for all nonjudicial support activities, including personnel, budget, technology, and facilities.

C. Managing Attorney and Central Staff

The court's managing attorney is selected by the justices of the court and works under the general direction and supervision of the administrative presiding justice. The managing attorney serves as legal advisor to the court, its justices, and the clerk's office on a variety of issues, including personnel and matters of appellate procedure. The managing attorney also supervises the court's central staff attorneys and judicial assistants.

D. Mediation Program Administrator and Support Staff

The court's mediation program administrator is selected by the administrative presiding justice and works under the general direction and supervision of the administrative presiding justice or a designated supervising justice. The mediation program administrator is responsible for the day-to-day administration of the court's mediation program and supervises its support staff.

III. PROCEDURES FOR PROCESSING CASES

A. Assignment of Cases to Divisions

1. *In General.* Appeals are assigned to a division when the clerk's office receives the notices of appeal from the superior court where they were filed. Writ petitions are assigned to a division when they are filed with the clerk's office. Assignments are made in rotation, without regard to subject matter or complexity. Exceptions to the random assignment procedures are made if multiple appeals or writ petitions arise from the same trial court action or proceeding, in which case later appeals or writ petitions are assigned to the same division to which the first appeal or writ petition was assigned.

2. *Transfer of Cases.* If, subsequent to the initial assignment of an appeal or writ petition to a division, it is determined that it arises from the same trial court action or proceeding as a prior appeal or writ petition, the administrative presiding justice may transfer the later appeal or writ petition to the same division to which the first appeal or writ petition was assigned. If multiple appeals or writ petitions arise from different trial court actions or proceedings, but involve the same parties or co-parties and the same or related subject matter, transaction, or incident, the court may request that the Supreme Court transfer later appeals or writ petitions to the same division to which the first appeal or writ petition was assigned.

B. Processing of Appeals

1. *Assignment of Appeals to Panels.* When an appeal is fully briefed, it is ready for assignment to a panel of three justices for decision. The court maintains a computer-generated list of fully briefed civil appeals and a separate list of fully briefed criminal and juvenile appeals. The appeals are listed in the order in which they became fully briefed. Appeals entitled to priority on calendar are assigned first, followed by non-priority appeals in the order in which they became fully briefed. Appeals are assigned to panels in rotation, equalizing the number of cases in which each justice participates. One of the three justices on the panel is designated as the lead justice for each appeal. Appeals are assigned randomly, without regard to subject matter, except that an appeal may be assigned to the same panel to which a related appeal or writ petition was previously assigned.

2. *Draft Opinions.* After an appeal is assigned to a panel, the lead justice prepares a draft opinion. Although the format may vary somewhat from justice to justice or division to division, the draft opinion generally includes the following information: (1) a statement of the pertinent factual and procedural history of the case; (2) an analysis of each issue necessary to resolve the appeal; and (3) a proposed disposition. The primary purpose of the draft opinion is to provide the panel with all of the relevant information it needs to decide the appeal. Upon completion, the lead justice distributes the draft opinion to the other two justices on the panel for their review. The panel may also meet to discuss the case. Conferencing practices vary from division to division.

3. *Oral Argument and Submission of the Cause.* When an appeal is assigned to a panel of three justices for decision, the court initially notifies the parties that oral argument will be deemed waived unless one of the parties requests oral argument within the time designated in the notice. If the parties request oral argument, or if the court otherwise determines that oral argument would be helpful, the clerk's office then notifies the parties of the date, time, and place of the hearing. A continuance of oral argument will be granted only upon written application and a showing of good cause. Counsel may not stipulate to a continuance. At the conclusion of oral argument, the presiding justice or acting presiding justice will declare the matter submitted, unless submission is deferred pending further briefing.

4. *Preparation and Filing of Opinions.* After oral argument or the waiver of oral argument, the lead justice prepares a final draft of the opinion. If the other two justices on the panel concur in the opinion, they sign it and it is delivered to the clerk's office for filing. If an individual justice does not subscribe to all of the reasoning of an opinion, he or she may file a separate opinion. If the lead justice fails to obtain the concurrence of at least one of the other justices on the panel, the case may be reassigned to one of the other panel members for the preparation of an opinion. An opinion is published if a majority of the justices on the panel certifies it for publication.

5. *Rehearings.* When a petition for rehearing is filed, the clerk's office delivers the petition to the justice who authored the court's opinion. After reviewing the petition

and conducting whatever research he or she deems necessary, the authoring justice circulates the petition to the other two justices on the panel with a recommended ruling. Two votes are necessary to grant or deny a petition for rehearing. A petition for rehearing normally will not be granted unless the court has requested an answer. An order granting rehearing vacates the court's original opinion and sets the case for full reconsideration. Generally, the parties have no right to reargue the case; however, the court, in its discretion, may invite either written briefing or oral argument, or both, before resubmitting the matter and filing its new opinion.

C. Processing of Original Proceedings

After a writ petition has been filed, the clerk's office delivers the petition to the writ attorney for the division to which the writ is assigned. Depending upon the nature of the petition and its urgency, the writ attorney may present the petition to a panel of justices shortly after its filing, or may perform extensive research. In appropriate cases, the court may request opposition from the real party or parties in interest. If an opinion is required, the matter is assigned to one of the justices on the writ panel and is thereafter handled much like the court handles an appeal. The specific procedures governing various types of writ petitions are enumerated in the California Rules of Court.

SECOND APPELLATE DISTRICT LOCAL RULES

[Amended effective May 5, 2008]

Rule 1.   Contents of Reporter's and Clerk's Transcripts in Criminal and Juvenile Appeals

In addition to the normal record prescribed by rules 8.320, 8.328, and 8.404 of the California Rules of Court, all records in defendants' criminal appeals and juvenile appeals before the Court of Appeal, Second Appellate District, are hereby augmented under rule 8.155 of the California Rules of Court to include reporter's and clerk's transcripts of the following:

(1) [Jury examination and opening statement]

Except if a conviction was obtained by plea or admission, reporter's transcripts of (a) jury voir dire whenever a motion regarding the composition of the jury or jury panel (for example, a motion under *People* v. *Wheeler* (1978) 22 Cal.3d 258 [148 Cal.Rptr. 890, 583 P.2d 748]) or a motion for a mistrial was made during the jury voir dire and decided in whole or in part adversely to the defendant; and (b) opening statements.

(2) [Sealed and in camera hearings]

Except if a conviction was obtained by plea or admission, oral proceedings of all sealed and in camera hearings resulting in rulings adverse in whole or in part to the appellant. These transcripts shall be listed in the index to the reporter's transcript, and the original and two copies of the sealed transcripts shall be transmitted to this court in sealed envelopes marked "CONFIDENTIAL—MAY NOT BE EXAMINED WITHOUT COURT ORDER." This court shall provide a copy of the sealed transcripts, other than transcripts of a hearing from which the appellant and defense counsel were excluded, to the appellant's counsel on appeal, upon his or her application. If the appellant raises an issue on appeal relating to the sealed transcripts, copies of transcripts shall then be provided to the Attorney General upon their written request. Unless otherwise ordered by this court, the sealed transcripts of a hearing from which the appellant and defense counsel were excluded may be examined only by a justice of this court personally.

(3) [Waivers of constitutional rights]

Reporter's transcripts of oral proceedings at which the appellant's constitutional rights were waived.

(4) [Guilty or nolo contendere pleas]

Proceedings at which the appellant moved to withdraw a guilty or nolo contendere plea, and proceedings at which sentence was imposed.

(5) [Pretrial proceedings]

(a) The following pretrial proceedings: (i) proceeding to determine competence of the appellant (Pen. Code, § 1368); and (ii) motion for self-representation (*Faretta* v. *California* (1975) 422 U.S. 806 [95 S.Ct. 2525, 45 L.Ed.2d 562]).

(b) Except if a conviction was obtained by plea or admission, the following pretrial proceedings which were decided in whole or in part adversely to the appellant: (i) motion to suppress identification; (ii) motion to suppress statements of the appellant; (iii) motion to permit or preclude impeachment of the appellant or a witness with prior offenses (*People* v. *Castro* (1985) 38 Cal.3d 301 [211 Cal.Rptr. 719, 696 P.2d 111]); (iv) motion for severance or joinder; (v) motion for change of venue; (vi) motion for discovery of police officer records (*Pitchess* v. *Superior Court* (1974) 11 Cal.3d 531 [113 Cal.Rptr. 897, 522 P.2d 305]); and (vii) *in limine* motions.

(6) [Revocation of probation]

In appeals from revocation of probation: (a) the original sentencing proceeding at which probation was imposed; (b) the proceedings at the time of entry of a guilty plea or nolo contendere plea if the original judgment of conviction is based on such plea; and (c) the proceedings at which probation is revoked and the appellant is sentenced.

Rule 1 adopted Aug. 1, 1992; amended Mar. 8, 1993; Jan. 1, 2005; Mar. 20, 2006; Jan. 1, 2007.

Rule 2. Augmentation of Record and Correction of Omissions From Record

(a) [Material inadvertently omitted]

Counsel should not file a motion to augment the record when items have been omitted from the designated (civil) or normal (criminal) record on appeal. In those cases

counsel should immediately notify the clerk of the superior court, who shall forthwith comply with rule 8.340(b) of the California Rules of Court.

(Adopted Aug. 1, 1992; amended Jan. 1, 2007.)

(b) [When to file motion to augment]

Appellant should file requests for augmentation in one motion within 40 days of the filing of the record. Respondent should file requests for augmentation in one motion made within 30 days of the filing of appellant's opening brief. Thereafter, motions to augment will not be granted except upon a showing of good cause for the delay.

(Adopted Aug. 1, 1992; amended Jan. 1, 2005; Jan. 1, 2007.)

(c) [Clerk's transcript]

A motion to augment or correct the clerk's transcript shall be accompanied by the documents requested. If the documents are not provided, the motion must identify them with specificity and contain an explanation for their omission. The motion and the accompanying documents must be served simultaneously on opposing counsel. The requested augmented materials shall have been filed or lodged with the trial court and the declaration shall so state.

(Adopted Aug. 1, 1992.)

(d) [Reporter's transcript]

A motion to augment the reporter's transcript shall identify the portion of the record with specificity, including the reporter's name and the date of the hearing. The motion shall establish with some certainty how the requested materials may be useful on appeal.

(Adopted Aug. 1, 1992.)

(e) [Extensions of time]

The time to perform any act required or permitted by the California Rules of Court will not be automatically extended by the filing of or ruling on a motion to augment. If additional time is needed, counsel may request an extension of time in the motion to augment.

(Adopted Aug. 1, 1992.)

(f) [Good faith required]

A motion to augment shall be made in good faith and shall not be made for the purpose of delay.

(Adopted Aug. 1, 1992.)

(g) [Proposed order]

A motion to augment must be accompanied by a proposed order. The form *Order Re: Augmentation* may be used.

(Adopted Aug. 3, 1998.)

(h) [Attachments]

When more than one document or transcript are attached to or submitted with a motion to augment the record pursuant to California Rules of Court, rule 8.155(a)(2), the pages of the documents and transcripts must be consecutively numbered.

(Adopted Sept. 15, 2003; amended Jan. 1, 2007.)

Rule 2 adopted Aug. 1, 1992; amended Aug. 3, 1998; Sept. 15, 2003; Jan. 1, 2005; Jan. 1, 2007.

Rule 3. Designation of the Record in Civil Appeals Under California Rules of Court, Rules 8.130 and 8.120

(a) [Contents of the notice and designation of record]

The notice to prepare a reporter's transcript and the designation of the contents of a clerk's transcript required to be filed with the clerk of the superior court by California Rules of Court, rules 8.130 and 8.120, shall include the following information:

(1) [Reporter's transcript]

The notice to prepare the reporter's transcript shall state for each oral proceeding to be included in the record (1) the date, (2) the department number, (3) the name of the reporter or electronic recording monitor, and (4) the nature of the proceeding.

(2) [Clerk's transcript]

The designation of the contents of the clerk's transcript shall state for each paper or record to be included (1) the title and (2) the date of filing. For each exhibit to be included in the clerk's transcript, the designation shall include (1) the exhibit number, (2) a brief description, and (3) the admission status.

(Adopted May 17, 1996; amended Jan. 1, 2007.)

(b) [Form to designate record]

The form *Designation of the Record on Appeal* may be used to designate the record in civil appeals.

(Adopted May 17, 1996.)

(c) [Sanctions]

Failure to comply with this local rule is a failure to properly designate the record under California Rules of Court, rules 8.130 and 8.120, and may result in the dismissal of the appeal or the imposition of monetary sanctions.

(Adopted May 17, 1996; amended Jan. 1, 2007.)

Rule 3 adopted May 17, 1996; amended Jan. 1, 2007.

Rule 4.   Proposed Orders

Any motion or application filed with this court must be accompanied by a proposed order. Failure to comply with this local rule may result in the denial of the motion or application.

Rule 4 adopted Aug. 3, 1998.

Rule 5.   Requests for Judicial Notice [Repealed]

Rule 5 adopted Apr. 12, 1999; repealed Jan. 1, 2005.

Another Rule 5 follows.

Rule 5.   Extensions of Time for Filing Briefs

File only the original of an application for an extension of time. Do not submit extra copies of the application or self addressed, postage-paid envelopes. The Clerk will send notice of ruling in every case.

Rule 5 adopted effective May 5, 2008.

Rule 6.   Case Information Statement [Repealed]

Rule 6 adopted Aug. 28, 2000, effective Oct. 30, 2000; repealed Mar. 3, 2003.

Another Rule 6 follows.

Rule 6.   Advance Notice of Request for Immediate Relief in Juvenile Dependency Writ Petitions

Before filing a petition for extraordinary writ with a request for immediate relief in a juvenile dependency proceeding, the petitioner must use best efforts to provide notice in person, by telephone, by facsimile or by e-mail to all parties at the earliest possible time and, when practical, at least 24 hours before filing. In addition, before filing such a petition, the petitioner must deliver to all parties in person, by facsimile, or by e-mail a copy of the petition. A declaration of notice and delivery, including the date, time, manner, name of the individual notified, any response of the individual notified, and whether any opposition will be filed, or a declaration stating the reasons why notice or delivery could not be accomplished, must accompany the petition. Noncompliance with this rule will not prevent the court from exercising its discretion in the best interest of the child.

Rule 6 adopted Sept. 15, 2003.

Policy Statement.   Policy Statement for Voluntary Settlement Conference in Civil Appeals [Repealed]

Policy Statement adopted Feb. 16, 1984; repealed April 22, 2002.

INTERNAL OPERATING PRACTICES AND PROCEDURES SECOND APPELLATE DISTRICT

Purpose
Structure
Assignment of Cases
Motions
Mediation/Settlement Procedures
Preparation of Cases
Argument
Determination
Rehearing
Publication
Local Rules of the Second Appellate District
Assigned Justices
Externs

Purpose

The purpose of these procedures is to provide members of the bar and other interested persons with general information concerning the internal organization of the Second Appellate District and its internal procedures for processing cases. The discussion of practices and procedures is necessarily general and the practices and procedures may be altered in particular cases for a variety of reasons.

Structure

The Second District covers four counties and consists of eight separate divisions. Divisions One through Five, Seven and Eight are located at 300 South Spring Street, Los Angeles, California, 90013 and handle all matters arising from Los Angeles County. Division Six is located at 200 East Santa Clara Street, Ventura, California, 93001 and handles all matters arising from Ventura, Santa Barbara, and San Luis Obispo Counties. Each division is a separate unit for the purpose of hearing and deciding cases assigned to it and consists of four justices, one of whom is the Presiding Justice. Presiding Justices are appointed by the Governor. Research attorneys, secretaries, clerks, and externs are assigned to the justices and divisions.

The divisions share a common clerk's office, certain support personnel, and physical facilities. One of the Presiding Justices is appointed Administrative Presiding Justice by the Chief Justice and performs the duties prescribed in rule 76 of the California Rules of Court. The Administrative Presiding Justice serves as chair of the Executive Committee, which is comprised of one justice from each division, usually the Presiding Justice. It is the function of the Executive Committee to recommend to the Administrative Presiding Justice the expenditure of funds and the employment of personnel within the District.

Assignment of Cases

All original proceedings and appeals arising in Ventura, Santa Barbara, and San Luis Obispo Counties are assigned to Division Six. Original proceedings and appeals arising in Los Angeles County are assigned to the divisions in Los Angeles (One through Five, Seven and Eight) on a random pro rata basis. Once a case has been assigned to a division it remains in that division for all further proceedings, unless a request is made to the Supreme Court to transfer the case to another division under article VI, section 12 of the California Constitution and rule 20 of the California Rules of Court. Usually, such a request is made by the clerk, upon direction of the Presiding Justice of the division involved.

When an appeal has been fully briefed and is "ready," it is assigned on a random pro rata basis to a three-justice panel with one of the justices designated the lead justice responsible for preparing a bench memorandum. The matter is also set for oral argument on the next available calendar. Oral argument may be waived by the parties.

Original proceedings which do not seek immediate relief are usually reviewed by a writs attorney assigned to the particular division within one to two weeks. The attorney prepares and distributes a memorandum and copies of the petition, exhibits, and any preliminary opposition to the justices for discussion at periodic writ conferences, usually weekly or bi-weekly, at which the justices will determine how to proceed on the matter. If the original proceeding seeks immediate relief, the writs attorney will review the matter shortly after receiving it and distribute a memorandum and supporting documents to the justices then available to review it at which time a determination will be made. If relief is granted which requires a hearing, it will be scheduled at the earliest available date.

Motions

The Presiding Justice of each division determines the manner in which motions are handled within that division.

Mediation/Settlement Procedures

The Second District participates in a courtwide voluntary mediation program conducted prior to the time the record is required to be filed. Notice is sent by the Superior Court to the appellant upon filing of a notice of appeal and if all parties desire to participate in the program, a form is returned to the superior court triggering the process. The mediation process is presided over by a volunteer attorney who is an appellate/mediation specialist. If the parties do not originally opt to enter the mediation program but later desire to explore mediation or settlement with the help of the court, the clerk's office of the Second District should be contacted. Some divisions also afford parties an opportunity to discuss settlement and the clerk of that division should be contacted.

Preparation of Cases

Each justice maintains a chambers which consists of the justice, a secretary, and research attorneys. For each case to which the justice is assigned the lead, the justice and the research attorneys are responsible for reading the briefs, reviewing the record, and preparing a bench memorandum. Each justice also reviews the briefs for each case on which the justice serves as a panel member, but is not the lead justice. Justices and research attorneys may confer with each other informally from time to time as the cases are being prepared. On occasion, if an issue arises which has not been adequately briefed by the parties, a letter pursuant to Government Code section 68081 will be sent to the parties requesting further briefing or advising the parties to be prepared to address the issue at oral argument.

As they are completed, or shortly before argument, bench memoranda are distributed to the other chambers for review by the panel justices. The cases are usually conferenced among the justices on the panel. Each division differs to some extent on the manner in which the cases are conferenced among the justices.

Argument

Each division generally schedules hearings for two days each month and entertains argument on those matters for which oral argument has not been waived by the parties. Each division differs to some extent on the manner in which calendars are called and the order in which the matters are scheduled for argument. Unless further briefing is allowed, the cases are submitted at close of argument and an opinion is filed within 90 days thereafter. If further briefing is allowed, the date of submission will depend upon the order of the court.

Determination

The bench memorandum is circulated for approval. If the parties have waived oral argument or no change is required after argument, and all justices have approved the bench memorandum, it will form the basis of the opinion to be filed. If oral argument suggests issues which need to be considered or consensus does not exist based upon the bench memorandum, the bench memorandum may be altered or discarded and a new memorandum may be circulated. Concurring and dissenting opinions may also be prepared.

Rehearing

Timely petitions for rehearing are immediately presented to the author of the opinion and to the panel members for review. In many instances rulings denying these petitions are made prior to the time opposition is due, and if the court desires opposition, the clerk will usually be directed to call counsel and request that a response be filed. In some instances a modification may be issued and rehearing otherwise denied. Grant of a petition for rehearing may or may not result in a request for further briefing, and oral argument is at the pleasure of the court.

Publication

If a majority of the panel rendering the decision deems that the opinion, or any part of it, meets the standards for publication contained within rule [1] **8.1105**, subdivision (b), of the California Rules of Court, then the opinion may be published or partially published.

Local Rules of the Second Appellate District

The Second District has adopted a number of local rules. (See Local Rules of the Courts of Appeal.)

Assigned Justices

Upon request, the Chief Justice from time to time assigns judges, retired judges, and retired justices to sit as a justice of the Court of Appeal for a 90-day period. The court utilizes the services of assigned justices to assist with its workload. Assigned justices permit the court to cover judicial vacancies and disqualifications, complete in a timely fashion its determination of complex or jumbo appeals, and maintain its current status.

Externs

The District maintains an unpaid extern program utilizing law students on a part-time or full-time basis in return for law school credit. This is a centralized program with one justice responsible for recruitment and assignment of externs to justices throughout the court. Once assigned to a justice, externs work under the close supervision of that justice and the justice's staff. In recent years, externs have come to the court from Boalt Hall, Georgetown, Hastings, Loyola, McGeorge, Northeastern, Northwestern, NYU, Pepperdine, Southwestern, Tulane, U.C. Davis, UCLA, University of Connecticut, University of Illinois, University of Minnesota, USC, University of San Diego, and Whittier. In addition to the District's centralized extern program, individual justices may accept extern applications.

Amended Jan. 1, 2007; Jan. 1, 2008.

IOPPs. 2008 Deletes. [1] 976

THIRD APPELLATE DISTRICT LOCAL RULES

[As amended effective March 2, 2007; as amended, reorganized, and renumbered effective October 2, 2006; adopted effective January 1, 1977, and previously amended May 1, 1982, December 31, 1982, November 10, 1986, September 4, 1989, and July 6, 1993]

Mediation in civil appeals. Rule 1.

Stipulation for use of original superior court file. Rule 2.
Time for oral argument. Rule 3.
Judicial notice of legislative history materials. Rule 4.
Internal Operating Practices and Procedures.

MISC. ORDER 2008-001

This order supersedes Miscellaneous Order 2006-006 and subsequent Amended Miscellaneous Order 2006-006 effective October 2, 2006, Miscellaneous Order 2006-016, Miscellaneous Order 2007-001, and Miscellaneous Order 2007-009, all relating to the implementation of the Mediation Program adopted by the Court of Appeal, Third Appellate District. (See Ct. App. Third Dist., Local Rules of Ct., rule 1, Mediation in Civil Appeals (*adopted eff. October 2, 2006, and amended eff. March 2, 2007*).)

BY THE COURT:

Upon filing of any civil notice of appeal, the provisions of rules 8.121 and 8.216 of the California Rules of Court requiring designation of the record and payment of estimated costs for preparation of the record or the filing of a proposed briefing sequence are suspended, pending this court's decision to select or not select the civil appeal for mediation. If a civil appeal is selected for mediation, then the suspension of rules 8.121 and 8.216 remains in effect until completion of mediation. If a civil appeal is not selected for mediation, the coordinator of the Mediation Program must concurrently notify the parties, the superior court, and this court, in writing, that suspension of rules 8.121 and 8.216 are terminated. The parties' obligation to comply with the requirements of rules 8.121 or 8.216 commences as if notice of appeal was filed on the date specified in the notification.

If the parties stipulate to placement of a civil appeal in the Mediation Program, then upon the superior court's timely receipt of its copy of that stipulation, the provisions of rules 8.121 and 8.216 requiring designation of the record and payment of the estimated costs of preparation of the record or the filing of a proposed briefing sequence are suspended.

If this court accepts the stipulation and refers the case for mediation, suspension of rules 8.121 and 8.216 remains in effect until completion of mediation. If the case is not referred to mediation, the coordinator of the Mediation Program must concurrently notify the parties, the superior court, and this court, in writing, that suspension of rules 8.121 and 8.216 are terminated. The parties' obligation to comply with the requirements of rules 8.121 or 8.216 commences as if notice of appeal was filed on the date specified in the notification.

If completion of mediation does not result in disposition of the appeal, the coordinator of the Mediation Program must, within 10 days after notice of completion of the mediation, notify the parties, the superior court, and this court, in writing, that suspension of rules 8.121 and 8.216 are terminated. The parties' obligation to comply with the requirements of rules 8.121 or 8.216 commences as if notice of appeal was filed on the date specified in the notification.

Nothing in this order prohibits the superior court from collecting the deposit required by section 68926.1 of the Government Code and by rule 8.100(b)(2) of the California Rules of Court.

Any appeal taken from a judgment or order entered in a conservatorship proceeding is exempt from this court's Appellate Mediation Program. Any appeal taken from a judgment or order entered in an action brought pursuant to Public Resources Code sections 21167, 21168, or 21168.5, to challenge acts, decisions, determinations or findings of a public agency for noncompliance with the California Environmental Quality Act, is also exempt from this court's Mediation Program. Appeals in these cases are not subject to the automatic stay of record designation or preparation otherwise provided in Local Rule 1. However, nothing in this order shall preclude the parties from stipulating to participation in the Mediation Program.

Dated: January 2, 2008

SCOTLAND, P.J.

MISC. ORDER 2007-003

BY THE COURT:

In pending appeals in which an appellant's opening brief was filed prior to the date this order is issued, and in which an opinion has not yet been filed, an application for leave to file a supplemental brief shall not be required before filing of a supplemental brief arguing, based on the decision of the United States Supreme Court in *Cunningham v. California*, (No. 05-6551. January 22, 2007, __ U.S. __; __ S.Ct. __; __ L.Ed.2d __; 2007 WL 135687; 2007 U.S. LEXIS 1324; 2007 DJDAR 965), that imposition of the upper term is unconstitutional. Henceforth, appellants shall not submit for filing any application for leave to file a supplemental brief challenging imposition of the upper term premised on *Cunningham*.

Any supplemental appellant's opening brief submitted pursuant to this order shall be served and filed on or before February 23, 2007. If a supplemental brief is filed pursuant to this order, the time for filing respondent's brief shall be extended by 30 days.

If respondent's brief has already been filed, respondent shall have leave to file a supplemental respondent's brief within 15 days of filing of the supplemental opening brief, and any appellant's supplemental reply brief shall be served and filed within 10 days of filing of the supplemental respondent's brief.

Dated: January 24, 2007

SCOTLAND, P.J.

Rule 1.   Applicability—Settlement Conference Procedures [Repealed]

Rule 1 adopted Jan. 1, 1977; amended May 1, 1982; Dec. 31, 1982; Nov. 10, 1986; Sept. 4, 1989; repealed eff. Oct. 2, 2006.

Another Rule 1 follows.

Rule 1.   Mediation in Civil Appeals

(a) **[Mediation Program]** To enable efficient case management and more expeditious resolution of civil appeals, the Court of Appeal, Third Appellate District, has established a Mediation Program ("Program"). The Program will be administered by a Mediation Program Coordinator ("Coordinator") acting at the direction of a Mediation Committee ("Committee") and under the supervision of the Administrative Presiding Justice or a designated Supervising Associate Justice.

(Adopted eff. October 2, 2006.)

(b) **[Scope of Mediation Program]** A civil appeal will be placed in the Program if selected by the Administrative Presiding Justice, designated Supervising Associate Justice, or the Coordinator. With permission of the Court, a civil appeal not selected for mediation may be placed in the Program by stipulation of the parties. (See subd. (d)(5), *post*.)

(Adopted eff. October 2, 2006.)

(c) **[Mediators]** The Committee must specify the qualifications, training, and process for appointment of mediators in the Program. The Coordinator will assign mediators to appeals selected for the Program. The Coordinator may replace a selected mediator upon written request by a party supported by a showing of good cause or upon request of the mediator. Mediation services will be furnished by the Court without fee to the parties, provided that a mediation session exceeding 4 hours may be terminated by the mediator. The parties and the mediator may agree on a fee payable to the mediator for continued mediation services.

(Adopted eff. October 2, 2006.)

(d) **[Mediation Process]**

(1) Pursuant to Miscellaneous Order 2006-006 [published at www.courtinfo.ca.gov/courts/courtsofappeal/3rdDistrict/; copies available at the clerk's office of the Court of Appeal, Third Appellate District, and the clerk's offices in the superior courts located within the jurisdiction of the Third Appellate District], effective upon filing of any civil notice of appeal, the provisions of rules 8.120, 8.124, 8.128, 8.130, 8.134, and 8.137 of the California Rules of Court requiring designation of the record and payment of estimated costs for preparation of the record are suspended, pending the Court's decision to select or not select the civil appeal for mediation. If a civil appeal is selected for mediation, suspension of rules 8.120, 8.124, 8.128, 8.130, 8.134, and 8.137 must remain in effect until completion of mediation. If a civil appeal is not selected for mediation, the Coordinator must concurrently notify the parties, the superior court, and this Court of Appeal, in writing, that the suspension of rules 8.120, 8.124, 8.128, 8.130, 8.134, and 8.137 is terminated. The parties' obligation to comply with the requirements of rules 8.120, 8.124, 8.128, 8.130, 8.134, and 8.137 commences as if notice of appeal was filed on the date specified in the notification.

(2) On receiving notice of filing of a civil notice of appeal, the Clerk must promptly mail to appellant a Civil Case Information Statement attached to which will be a Civil Appeal Mediation Statement. Within 10 days after the Clerk mails the Statements, appellant must serve and file a completed Civil Case Information Statement, including a completed Civil Appeal Mediation Statement.

(3) On receiving notice of filing of a civil notice of appeal, the Clerk must mail to respondent a Civil Appeal Mediation Statement. Within 10 days after filing of appellant's Civil Case Information Statement, respondent must serve and file a completed Civil Appeal Mediation Statement.

(4) The Coordinator, within 10 days after the Court files respondent's Civil Appeal Mediation Statement, must notify the parties whether the Court has or has not selected

the civil appeal for mediation. If a civil appeal is selected for the Program, the Coordinator must furnish the parties with the name, address, and telephone number of the mediator, and three dates when the mediator is available for the mediation session. At the same time, the Coordinator must furnish the mediator copies of the Civil Appeal Mediation Statements. Within 10 days after receipt of the dates the mediator is available, the parties must advise the Coordinator of their scheduling preferences. The Coordinator, after conferring with the mediator, promptly must select the date and site for the mediation session and must notify the parties by telephone and in writing.

(5) If a civil appeal is not selected for mediation, the parties may stipulate to placement in the Program. The stipulation must be served on the superior court and filed with this Court within 10 days after issuance of notification that the Court did not select the appeal for the Program. Pursuant to Miscellaneous Order 2006-006, upon receipt of the stipulation by the superior court, the provisions of rules 8.120, 8.124, 8.128, 8.130, 8.134, and 8.137 of the California Rules of Court requiring designation of the record and payment of the estimated costs for preparation of the record are suspended. The Court will decide whether to accept the stipulation of the parties and refer the case for mediation. If the case is referred for mediation, suspension of rules 8.120, 8.124, 8.128, 8.130, 8.134, and 8.137 must remain in effect until completion of mediation. If the case is not referred to mediation, the Coordinator must concurrently notify the parties, the superior court, and this Court of Appeal, in writing, that suspension of rules 8.120, 8.124, 8.128, 8.130, 8.134, and 8.137 is terminated. The parties' obligation to comply with the requirements of rules 8.120, 8.124, 8.128, 8.130, 8.134, and 8.137 commences as if notice of appeal was filed on the date specified in the notification.

(6) The mediator, with the approval of the Coordinator, may, for good cause, postpone or continue a mediation session to a date certain.

(7) The mediator may require parties or their counsel to furnish information, documents, records or other items specified by the mediator.

(8) The mediator may at any time communicate with any of the parties or their counsel with or without notice to the other parties or their counsel.

(9) All parties and their counsel of record must attend all mediation sessions in person with full settlement authority. If a party is not an individual, then a party representative with full authority to settle all appeals and cross-appeals must attend all mediation sessions in person, in addition to counsel. If a party has potential insurance coverage applicable to any of the issues in dispute, a representative of each insurance carrier whose policy may apply also must attend all mediation sessions in person, with full settlement authority. Any exception to this requirement must be approved in writing by the mediator. The mediator may invite participation by any additional person or entity if the mediator concludes that such participation would facilitate mediation.

(10) Within 10 days after completion of mediation, the mediator must submit to the Coordinator a Mediation Attendance Form, listing all participants in the mediation, and a Mediator's Statement, notifying the Coordinator of the results of the mediation.

(11) Within 10 days after completion of mediation, the parties and their counsel must separately complete and submit to the Coordinator confidential evaluations of the mediation and the mediator on a form provided by the Coordinator.

(12) Pursuant to Miscellaneous Order 2006-006, if completion of mediation does not result in disposition of the appeal, the Coordinator must, within 10 days after notice of completion of the mediation, notify the parties, the superior court, and this Court of Appeal that suspension of rules 8.120, 8.124, 8.128, 8.130, 8.134, and 8.137 of the California Rules of Court is terminated. The parties' obligation to comply with the requirements of rules 8.120, 8.124, 8.128, 8.130, 8.134, and 8.137 commences as if notice of appeal was filed on the date specified in the notification.

(Adopted eff. October 2, 2006; amended eff. March 2, 2007.)

(e) [Confidentiality] Except as otherwise required by law, information disclosed to the mediator, the parties, counsel, or any other participant in the mediation, or to the Coordinator of the Program, must be confidential and must not be disclosed to anyone not participating in the Program. The parties and the mediator are required to sign a confidentiality agreement in a form designated by the court.

(Adopted eff. October 2, 2006.)

(f) [Ethical Standards] Mediators must adhere to the rules of conduct for mediators in court-connected mediation programs for civil cases, as specified in the California Rules of Court.

(Adopted eff. October 2, 2006.)

(g) [Sanctions] Monetary sanctions may be imposed by the Administrative Presiding Justice or Supervising Associate Justice for failure to comply with these rules.

(Adopted eff. October 2, 2006.)

Rule 1 adopted eff. October 2, 2006; amended eff. March 2, 2007.

Rule 2.   Notification of Counsel [Repealed]

Rule 2 adopted Jan. 1, 1977; amended May 1, 1982; Dec. 31, 1982; Nov. 10, 1986; repealed eff. Oct. 2, 2006.

Another Rule 2 follows.

Rule 2.   Stipulation for Use of Original Superior Court File

Rule 8.128 of the California Rules of Court provides for the use of the original superior court file in lieu of the clerk's transcript on appeal in those civil cases where the parties so stipulate. In accordance with rule 8.128 of the California Rules of Court, the procedure therein is approved for use by the superior courts within this district.

Rule 2 adopted as Rule 22, eff. Sept. 4, 1989; renumbered from rule 22 eff. October 2, 2006; amended eff. March 2, 2007.

Rule 3.   Settlement Conference Statement [Repealed]

Rule 3 adopted Jan. 1, 1977; amended May 1, 1982; Dec. 31, 1982; Nov. 10, 1986; repealed eff. Oct. 2, 2006.

Another Rule 3 follows.

Rule 3.   Time for Oral Argument

Each side is allowed 15 minutes for oral argument. Where there are more than two parties, a "side" consists of all parties whose interests are not adverse. If there are more than two parties represented by separate counsel who request oral argument, or if counsel for amicus curiae requests oral argument, the court may apportion or expand the time according to the respective interests of the parties and of amicus curiae. Any request for additional time for oral argument must be made by written application submitted to the court within 10 calendar days of the date of the order setting oral argument. The application must be served contemporaneously on all other parties and must specify the amount of time requested and the issues to which additional oral argument will be addressed. When an application is granted, the time allotted to the other side or sides will be similarly enlarged. All parties will be advised of the disposition of any such application prior to hearing.

Rule 3 adopted, eff. April 10, 1998; renumbered from rule 23 eff. October 2, 2006.

Rule 4. Sanctions and Excuse for Non-Compliance [Repealed]

Rule 4 adopted Jan. 1, 1977; amended May 1, 1982; Dec. 31, 1982; July 6, 1993; repealed eff. Oct. 2, 2006.

Another Rule 4 follows.

Rule 4. Judicial Notice of Legislative History Materials

A party making a motion to have the Court take judicial notice of legislative history documents must identify each such document as a separate exhibit and must provide legal authority supporting the consideration of each document as cognizable legislative history. (See *Kaufman & Broad Communities, Inc. v. Performance Plastering, Inc.* (2005) 133 Cal.App.4th 26.)

Rule 4 adopted eff. October 2, 2006.

Rule 5. Court-Ordered Conference [Repealed]

Rule 5 adopted Jan. 1, 1977; amended May 1, 1982; Dec. 31, 1982; Nov. 10, 1986; Sept. 4, 1989; repealed eff. Oct. 2, 2006.

Rule 6. Postponement of Briefing [Repealed]

Rule 6 adopted Jan. 1, 1977; amended May 1, 1982; Dec. 31, 1982; Nov. 10, 1986; repealed eff. Oct. 2, 2006.

Rule 7. The Settlement Conference [Repealed]

Rule 7 adopted Jan. 1, 1977; amended May 1, 1982; Dec. 31, 1982; repealed eff. Oct. 2, 2006.

Rule 8. Conference Without Appellate Record [Repealed]

Rule 8 adopted Jan. 1, 1977; amended May 1, 1982; Dec. 31, 1982; Nov. 10, 1986; Sept. 4, 1989; repealed eff. Oct. 2, 2006.

Rule 9. Exclusion From Conference Requirement [Repealed]

Rule 9 amended Nov. 10, 1986; repealed eff. Oct. 2, 2006.

Rule 10. Disqualification of Conference Justice [Repealed]

Rule 10 repealed eff. Oct. 2, 2006.

Rule 21. Tabbing of Exhibits [Repealed]

Rule 21 adopted Jan. 1, 1977; repealed eff. July 6, 1993.

Rule 22. Stipulation for Use of Original Superior Court File [Renumbered]

Rule 22 adopted Sept. 4, 1989; renumbered to rule 2 eff. Oct. 2, 2006.

Rule 23. Time for Oral Argument [Renumbered]

Rule 23 adopted Apr. 10, 1998; renumbered to rule 3 eff. Oct. 2, 2006.

Rule 31. Location of Hearings [Repealed]

Rule 31 repealed eff. Oct. 2, 2006.

INTERNAL OPERATING PRACTICES AND PROCEDURES THIRD APPELLATE DISTRICT

I. INTRODUCTION
II. STRUCTURE OF THE COURT
III. FILINGS
IV. ORGANIZATION AND DUTIES OF STAFF ATTORNEYS
V. WRIT PETITIONS, MOTIONS AND OTHER APPLICATIONS
VI. JUDICIAL ASSIGNMENTS IN APPEALS
VII. PREPARATION OF A DRAFT OPINION
VIII. ORAL ARGUMENT
IX. CALENDAR
X. FILING OF THE COURT'S DECISION; REHEARING
XI. SETTLEMENT CONFERENCES

I. INTRODUCTION

The purpose of this publication is to advise the bar and interested members of the public regarding the internal rules and general operating practices of this court. No attempt is made to restate or amplify the California Rules of Court or constitutional provisions and statutes governing the practices and procedures of a Court of Appeal. This publication supersedes previous statements of the court's internal operating practices and procedures.

II. STRUCTURE OF THE COURT

The Third Appellate District is authorized eleven justices: an administrative presiding justice and ten associate justices.

There are no divisions of this court. The court operates in three-justice panels selected at random on a rotational basis.

The courtroom and judicial offices are located in the Library and Courts Building, 914 Capitol Mall, Sacramento, California 95814. The clerk's office is located in the Library and Courts Building II, 900 N Street, Suite 400, Sacramento, California 95814, and is open for business Monday through Friday, from 8:30 a.m. to 5:00 p.m., except for judicial holidays.

III. FILINGS

All matters are filed with the clerk's office. The clerk processes and files the material, distributing matters to justices and staff if judicial action is required.

Routine motions or applications, such as requests for extensions of time, are referred to the administrative presiding justice. More substantive motions and extraordinary writ petitions are referred to a three-justice panel.

Generally, upon the completion of briefing, appeals are evaluated and designated for handling by the court based on the number and apparent complexity of the issues raised, the subject matter, and the length of the record. In order to expedite certain proceedings, evaluation of an appeal may be done upon the filing of the last respondent's brief.

IV. ORGANIZATION AND DUTIES OF STAFF ATTORNEYS

Each justice is authorized two staff attorneys who work exclusively for the justice. Some of the justices also utilize law student externs who work under their direct supervision.

In addition, the court maintains a central staff consisting of sixteen attorneys: a managing attorney who directs the work of the staff, four writ attorneys, and eleven other central staff attorneys. The central staff attorneys, including the managing attorney, work under the general supervision of the administrative presiding justice and are responsible to the entire court.

The primary responsibility of staff attorneys assigned to an individual justice is the preparation of memoranda for the appeals that are assigned to the justice's chambers. The attorney studies the record and the briefs, analyzes and researches the legal issues, discusses the issues with the justice, and then prepares a legal memorandum with guidance from the justice. The memorandum is prepared for the exclusive use of the court.

The central staff has two main functions. Central staff writ attorneys study and familiarize themselves with each nonroutine motion, writ petition, and other extraordinary application filed with the court. After analyzing and researching the matter, the writ attorney presents the motion, petition, or application to a three-justice panel of the court for its determination. The other central staff attorneys work on appeals that are not assigned directly to chambers. The central staff attorney reads the record and the briefs, researches and analyzes the legal issues, and orally presents the appeal to a three-justice panel selected each week to consider such appeals. The composition of such a panel varies from week to week, with each justice participating approximately the same number of times as the other justices. After the appeal is orally presented to the panel, the central staff attorney prepares a legal memorandum with guidance from the panel. The memorandum is prepared for the exclusive use of the court.

V. WRIT PETITIONS, MOTIONS AND OTHER APPLICATIONS

At the weekly writ conference, usually held on Thursdays, a three-justice panel rules on pending writ petitions, nonroutine motions, and other applications. The writ panel varies from week to week, with each justice participating approximately the same number of times during the year as the other justices.

The writ panel considers the parties' written submissions, and central staff writ attorneys make an oral presentation on each matter. The panel discusses each matter and decides what action to take. Unless it summarily denies a writ petition, the panel will issue an alternative writ, an order to show cause, or a writ of review, or the panel will notify the parties that it is considering issuing a peremptory writ in the first instance. If an alternative writ, an order to show cause, or a writ of review is issued, the matter is assigned to one of the justices on the writ panel and is thereafter handled much like the court does with an appeal (see discussion, *post*).

At times, the court is presented with a writ petition, motion, or application that purportedly requires urgent or immediate action. Such matters are promptly assigned to a central staff writ attorney for review. If immediate action is required, a panel of three justices is assembled to hear the matter.

VI. JUDICIAL ASSIGNMENTS IN APPEALS

Assignments of appeals to individual justices are not governed by fixed rules or set formula. Each appeal is evaluated and assigned a weight to reflect its relative complexity. Effort is made to fairly apportion the caseload so that no justice is assigned a disproportionate number of the more difficult or less difficult appeals, and to balance and diversify the types of cases assigned to each justice. Subject matter is not a basis for assignment of an appeal to a particular justice, except that, where a panel has been assigned to the same case in an earlier appeal, a new appeal in that case often will be assigned to the same panel.

The three-justice panels are selected at random in order to vary their composition so that over a period of time each justice will participate with all other members of the court in the multiple combinations possible.

The initial designation of the author of the opinion in an appeal is done on a random basis at the time the case is assigned to chambers or after a case is presented to a three-justice panel by a central staff attorney. However, where there has been an earlier appeal in a case, the justice who authored the opinion in the earlier appeal often will receive the initial designation as author of the opinion in a subsequent appeal. Each justice is initially designated to author approximately the same number of opinions that will be authored by each of the other justices during the course of the year. Of course, whether the justice initially designated to author an opinion ultimately does so depends upon whether the justice obtains the concurrence of at least one other member of the panel. If the justice fails to do so, one of the other panel members will take over the responsibility of authoring the opinion of the court.

VII. PREPARATION OF A DRAFT OPINION

A legal memorandum prepared by a staff attorney is submitted to the justice initially designated to author the opinion in the appeal. After examining and evaluating the record, the parties' briefs, and the staff attorney memorandum, and after engaging in any necessary independent research and analysis, the justice prepares a draft opinion for the exclusive use of the court. A copy of the draft opinion, the briefs, and the record are then circulated, in order of seniority, to the other two participating justices. Each of the other participating justices indicates his or her tentative concurrence or dissent, or otherwise recommends changes to the draft opinion. All three justices also indicate their tentative positions on whether the ultimate opinion of the court should be certified for publication. The decision to publish the opinion requires approval by a majority of the three-justice panel.

VIII. ORAL ARGUMENT

When the draft opinion is circulated, each justice assigned to the case indicates whether he or she wants the case calendared for oral argument or whether a waiver of oral argument should be solicited by the court. At the request of one justice, the case will be calendared for oral argument.

If the justices agree to solicit a waiver of oral argument, the clerk's office sends the parties a letter indicating that the court is prepared to decide the case without oral argument and that oral argument will be waived unless it is requested by either counsel within ten days. If there is no response from either counsel within that time, the case is submitted for decision upon the record and the briefs.

If either counsel requests oral argument, the case is placed on calendar. Counsel are notified approximately thirty days in advance of the date set for oral argument. With the court's approval, a party may waive its appearance at oral argument requested by another party. Continuances are disfavored and will not be granted in the absence of a showing of unusually compelling circumstances. Oral argument will not be continued by stipulation of parties. The matter is deemed submitted for decision at the conclusion of oral argument or, if supplemental briefing is requested by the court, at the time the last brief is filed.

The panel holds a postargument conference, in most cases on the same day that the case is heard. Often the case is finally decided at this conference, and suggestions may be made to the assigned author concerning the content of the opinion. If there is not agreement at this stage, areas of disagreement may be identified and refined.

An opinion will be filed within ninety days of the date of submission.

IX. CALENDAR

The court sits twelve times a year, once each month. The calendar is usually set to begin on the third Monday or Tuesday of each month and generally lasts for five or six days. Special calendars, although rare, may be held by the court.

Each calendar consists of both civil and criminal appeals and other proceedings ready for decision. The administrative presiding justice is responsible for the final composition of the calendar.

X. FILING OF THE COURT'S DECISION; REHEARING

After oral argument or waiver of oral argument, a final draft opinion is circulated among the participating justices.

A justice may indicate conditional approval if certain changes are made or otherwise forward comments on the draft to the author and the other participating justice. If there are to be separate concurring or dissenting opinions, they are circulated in final draft form among the participating justices. At the same time, the panel makes a final decision on publication.

Before the opinion is put in final form for filing, transcript references and citations are verified again.

When the opinion is signed, it is taken to the clerk's office, where it is filed as a decision and opinion of the court. Counsel of record are mailed copies of the opinion on that same day. Copies also are available in the clerk's office for the news media and interested members of the public.

For sixty days, the Reporter of Decisions posts published opinions of the Court of Appeal, Third Appellate District, at http://www.courtinfo.ca.gov/opinions/

Unpublished opinions of the court are posted for sixty days at http://www.courtinfo.ca.gov/opinions/nonpub.htm

Timely petitions for rehearing are immediately presented to the author of the opinion and the other panel members for review. A decision on the petition is filed after the period for opposition has expired. If the petition lacks merit, it is denied. In some cases, the opinion may be modified and rehearing otherwise denied. The granting of a petition for rehearing may or may not result in a request by the court for additional briefing or oral argument.

XI. SETTLEMENT CONFERENCES

The court has discontinued its settlement conference program until adequate resources are available to operate it efficiently and effectively.

FOURTH APPELLATE DISTRICT LOCAL RULES

[Amended effective January 1, 2007, November 9, 2007]

Requests for an immediate stay or other immediate relief in writ proceedings. Rule 1.
Covers on documents filed with the court. Rule 2.
Stipulation for use of original superior court file. Rule 3.
Civil settlement conference procedures (Division Two only). Rule 4.
Filing by facsimile. Rule 5.
Internal Operating Practices and Procedures Fourth Appellate District, Division One.
Internal Operating Practices and Procedures Fourth Appellate District, Division Two.
Internal Operating Practices and Procedures Fourth Appellate District, Division Three.

Rule 1.   Service of Writ Petitions Requesting Immediate Relief [Repealed]

Rule 1 adopted Sept. 9, 1996; repealed Oct. 29, 2004.

Another Rule 1 follows.

Rule 1.   Requests for an Immediate Stay or Other Immediate Relief in Writ Proceedings

A request that an immediate stay be issued or other immediate relief be granted is to be served on the respondent and each real party in interest by (1) personal delivery or (2) by an expeditious method consented to in advance by the party served. If the respondent or any real party in interest is not served personally or by an expeditious method consented to in advance by the party served, the court will not act on the request for five days, except to deny it summarily, absent a showing of good cause. The document cover must state conspicuously "STAY REQUESTED" or "IMMEDIATE RELIEF REQUESTED" or words of similar effect.

The court may issue a stay or other order necessary to preserve the status quo or the court's jurisdiction without opposition. However, a request for immediate relief, other than a stay or other order necessary to preserve the status quo or the court's jurisdiction, will not be granted unless the court has received an unsolicited opposition or, alternatively, has requested opposition.

Rule 1 adopted, eff. Oct. 29, 2004.

Rule 2.   Covers on Documents Filed With the Court

The court will not accept for filing any document that has a plastic or acetate cover or does not conform strictly to rules 8.144 and 8.204 of the California Rules of Court. *Rule 2 amended, eff. Jan. 1, 2007; adopted, eff. Oct. 2, 1983; and previously amended, eff. Oct. 29, 2004.*

Rule 3.   Petitions for Extraordinary Writs (Division One Only) [Repealed]

Rule 3 adopted Aug. 10, 1982; repealed Oct. 29, 2004.

Another Rule 3 follows.

Rule 3.   Stipulation for Use of Original Superior Court File

Rule 8.128 of the California Rules of Court provides for the use of the original superior court file in lieu of the clerk's transcript on appeal in those civil cases where the parties so stipulate. In accordance with rule 8.128 of the California Rules of Court, the procedure therein is approved for use by the superior courts within this district unless the Court of Appeal orders otherwise in a particular case.

Rule 3 amended, eff. Jan. 1, 2007; former rule 10 adopted, eff. April 26, 1992; and renumbered, eff. Oct. 29, 2004.

Rule 4.   Civil Settlement Conference Procedures (Division Two Only)

(a) [Application of rule] This rule is adopted pursuant to rule 8.248, California Rules of Court, and shall apply to all civil cases except appeals from proceedings under sections 300, 601, and 602 of the Welfare and Institutions Code, appeals from proceedings under sections 221 and 232 of the Civil Code, and appeals from original proceedings ancillary to a criminal prosecution.

(Amended, eff. Jan. 1, 2007; adopted, eff. Oct. 13, 1992; and previously amended, eff. Oct. 29, 2004.)

(b) [Notice of availability of conference] Upon receipt of notice of the filing of a notice of appeal, the clerk of this court shall mail a copy of this rule to counsel for all parties.

(Adopted, eff. Oct. 13, 1992.)

(c) [General settlement conference procedure]

(1) The presiding justice may schedule a settlement conference and order the parties' attendance at any time during the pendency of an appeal.

(2) Written notice of the date and time of the settlement conference will be given by the court.

(3) Immediately upon accepting a case for the settlement conference procedure, all further proceedings, including the filing of briefs, shall be suspended until further order of the court. However, this rule shall not suspend preparation of the appellate record unless a specific order is issued directing suspension of record preparation.

(Adopted, eff. Oct. 13, 1992.)

(d) [Prebriefing settlement conference procedure and sanctions]

(1) A request for a settlement conference to be held prior to completion of briefing shall be served and filed within 30 days from the date of mailing of the notice specified in subdivision (b). Opposition to a request for a settlement conference must be served and filed within 15 days after the request's filing date.

(2) If the court orders a settlement conference prior to the completion of briefing, the parties shall each serve and file an original and one copy of a settlement conference statement at least 15 days before the settlement conference. The parties may file by the same date a joint settlement conference statement in lieu of separate statements. Failure to timely serve and file a settlement conference statement complying with this rule may result in the imposition of sanctions including dismissal of the appeal. Every settlement conference statement shall contain the following:

(A) The trial court name and case title and number;

(B) The name of the judge who rendered the judgment or order appealed and the date of its entry;

(C) The date the notice of appeal was filed;

(D) The names, address, and telephone numbers of counsel for all parties to the appeal;

(E) A brief description of the judgment or order appealed;

(F) A concise statement of the case, including a brief procedural history and all facts material to consideration of the issues presented; and,

(G) The issues expected to be raised in the briefs.

(Amended, eff. Oct. 29, 2004; adopted, eff. Oct. 13, 1992.)

(e) [Postbriefing settlement conference procedure and sanctions] After briefing is completed, the court may request the parties to provide information helpful to the court in deciding whether to order the parties to participate in a settlement conference. The parties shall complete all post-briefing settlement conference questionnaires and respond to all confidential settlement conference inquiries within 15 days of mailing by the clerk of the court. Failure to timely respond to a settlement conference inquiry or questionnaire may result in the imposition of sanctions including dismissal of the appeal.

(Amended, eff. Jan. 1, 2007; adopted, eff. Oct. 13, 1992.)

(f) [Settlement conference and sanctions]

(1) The court shall maintain a list of attorneys who have developed expertise in specified areas of law, are generally respected in the legal community, and are willing to mediate settlement conferences at this court. These attorneys shall be designated as settlement confer-

ence mediators and preside over every settlement conference unless otherwise ordered. A justice or assigned justice may be designated as a settlement conference mediator and preside over a settlement conference if so ordered.

(2) The mediator presiding over a settlement conference may in his or her discretion continue it from time to time to allow for further negotiation.

(3) Counsel for every party to the appeal and their clients shall attend any settlement conference. Failure to attend a settlement conference may result in the imposition of sanctions against any party or counsel, including dismissal.

(4) The settlement conference mediator may invite parties to the action who are not parties to the appeal, or any person who has an interest in the action, to attend the settlement conference if it appears to the mediator that their presence may facilitate settlement of the case. Any party to the appeal may serve and file a written request for the attendance of such a party or person at least 15 days before the settlement conference.

(5) Counsel shall confer with their clients in advance and be thoroughly familiar with the case and prepared to present their contentions in detail.

(6) The presiding justice, a justice designated by the presiding justice, or the settlement conference mediator may excuse a client's personal attendance upon request and a showing that hardship or unusual circumstances make the client's attendance impossible or impractical. If personal attendance is excused, counsel either shall have obtained full authority to agree to a settlement that binds the client or the client shall be available for consultation by telephone.

(7) Where settlement cannot be reached, partial settlement will be sought. Any settlement shall be reduced to writing and signed by counsel. After a complete settlement has been agreed to in writing, the parties shall promptly file a stipulation to dismiss the appeal on the ground that the case has been settled. The stipulation shall specify the allocation of costs on appeal and state whether the remittitur is to issue immediately.

(Amended, eff. Jan. 1, 2007; adopted, eff. Oct. 13, 1992.)

(g) [Disqualification of settlement conference justice]

(1) A justice or assigned justice who participates in a settlement conference that does not result in complete settlement shall not thereafter participate in any way in the consideration or disposition of the case on its merits.

(2) A justice or assigned justice of the court will not be disqualified to participate in the consideration or disposition of a case on its merits because he or she has ruled on a request for a settlement conference, ordered that a settlement conference be held, signed orders granting relief from default for an act required by a party under this rule, extended or shortened any time period specified in this rule, or otherwise signed an order concerning a procedural aspect of the settlement conference process. Only mediating a settlement conference shall disqualify a justice from consideration or disposition of the case on its merits.

(Adopted, eff. Oct. 13, 1992.)

Rule 4 amended, eff. Jan. 1, 2007; adopted, eff. Oct. 13, 1992; and previously amended, eff. Oct. 29, 2004.

Rule 5.   Payment of Filing Fee in Civil Appeals [Repealed]

Rule 5 adopted, eff. Oct. 5, 1984; repealed, eff. Sept. 9, 1996.

Another Rule 5 follows.

Rule 5.   Filing by Facsimile

(a) Counsel may transmit the following documents to the Divisions of the Fourth Appellate District: (1) request for dismissal; (2) substitution/association; (3) change of address; (4) bankruptcy status letter; (5) request for oral argument; (6) certificate of interested entities or persons; (7) Attorney General/County Counsel full concession letters; (8) County Counsel Sade C. letter; (9) civil case information statement (Divisions One and Three only); (10) stipulation or request for extension of time; and (11) service copy pursuant to California Rules of Court, rule 8.340. The filing party is responsible for verifying that documents are acceptable for fax filing. Other documents may be fax-filed only at the request of the court.

(b) The facsimile document must comply with all rules as would be required during traditional filing (i.e. proof of service, etc.). There is no fee for fax filing the documents listed above. The facsimile document must not exceed ten (10) pages in length. Each document must have a Facsimile Transmission Cover Sheet. [A copy of the form follows these rules.] The caption page must contain the phrase "By Facsimile" or "By Fax" immediately below the title of the document.

(c) The document that is filed by facsimile shall have the same legal effect as an original paper document. Signatures on fax-filed documents are considered originals. The parties shall retain original signed documents should disputes arise requiring the court to verify original signatures.

(d) Service between the parties by facsimile is permitted by written agreement between the parties. This agreement should not be filed with the court, but may be requested by the court should a dispute arise regarding agreement to accept fax service.

(e) The court will not use facsimile transmission for service of court orders.

(f) The court will not send conformed copies of fax filings. Copies of any documents in the court file can be made by a copying service. In Divisions One and Three, a public copy machine is available in the clerk's office during public office hours.

(g) The standard confirmation option of a fax machine shall serve as confirmation of the transmittal of a document to the court. If the confirmation returns unsuccessful, the filing party should notify the court for the problem to be addressed. Counsel may verify the filing of the document through the court's web site. If the fax filing is not filed with the court because of error in transmission or clerical error, the party may make a motion to the court for an order filing the document nunc pro tunc.

(h) The court's fax filing machine shall be available 24 hours a day, although filings received after public office hours, on weekends or court holidays, shall be deemed filed on the next court day. The fax filing numbers are: Division One — (619) 645-2495; Division Two — (951) 248-0235; and Division Three — (714) 567-6128.

Rule 5 adopted Nov. 9, 2007.

Court of Appeal
FOURTH APPELLATE DISTRICT
Facsimile Transmission Cover Sheet

DATE: _____

ADDRESSED TO:

NAME: Court of Appeal, Fourth Appellate
          District
FAX #:   Division One - (619) 645-2495
          Division Two - (951) 248-0235
          Division Three - (714) 567-6128

TRANSMITTED FROM:

NAME: _____
FAX #: _____
PHONE #: _____
TO THE COURT: _____

CASE NUMBER: _____

1. Please file the following transmitted documents in the
order listed below:

    Document Name   No. of pages

2. Special handling instructions:

Rule 6. Writ Petitions: Supporting Records and Stay Requests [Repealed]

Rule 6 adopted, eff. May 18, 1987; repealed, eff. Sept. 9, 1996.

Rule 7. Civil Settlement Conference Procedures (Division Three Only) [Repealed]

Rule 7 adopted, eff. Sept. 14, 1989; repealed, eff. Dec. 1, 2003.

Rule 8. Attachments to Briefs (Division One Only) [Repealed]

Rule 8 adopted, eff. April 2, 1990; repealed, eff. Oct. 29, 2004.

Rule 9. Civil Docketing Statement; Form [Repealed]

Rule 9 adopted, eff. Jan. 3, 1997; repealed, eff. March 10, 2003.

Rule 10. Stipulation for Use of Original Superior Court File [Renumbered]

Rule 10 adopted, eff. April 26, 1992; renumbered to rule 3, eff. Oct. 29, 2004.

INTERNAL OPERATING PRACTICES AND PROCEDURES FOURTH APPELLATE DISTRICT, DIVISION ONE

(Revised effective January 1, 2008)

I. INTRODUCTION

II. THE COURT
III. PROFESSIONAL STAFF
IV. CLERK'S OFFICE
V. ORIGINAL PROCEEDINGS
VI. APPEALS
A. Screening and Processing of Cases
B. Central Staff Assisted Appeals
C. Chambers Appeals
VII. ORAL ARGUMENT
VIII. SETTLEMENT CONFERENCES—LITIGANT INITI-
      ATED
IX. SETTLEMENT CONFERENCES—COURT INITI-
      ATED
X. EXTERN PROGRAM
XI. MOTIONS

I. INTRODUCTION

This document describes the internal operating practices and procedures of the Court of Appeal for the Fourth
Appellate District, Division One, for review of appeals
and original proceedings.

II. THE COURT

The Court of Appeal for the Fourth Appellate District
consists of three divisions. Division One, covering cases
arising in San Diego and Imperial Counties, is located in
San Diego with ten justices, one of whom is the Presiding
Justice. (Gov. Code, § 69104.) Divisions Two, covering
cases from Riverside, San Bernardino and Inyo Counties,
and Three, covering cases from Orange County, are
located in Riverside and Santa Ana respectively.

III. PROFESSIONAL STAFF

Each justice has two staff attorneys and one judicial
assistant to assist him or her in the chambers work. In
addition, there is a Central Staff, which consists of a
Managing Appellate Court Attorney, a Supervising Appellate Court Attorney (Supervising Writ Attorney), and staff
attorneys who assist the court in processing petitions for
writs, Central Staff assisted appeals, record review in
criminal cases as mandated by *People v. Wende* (1979) 25
Cal.3d 436, juvenile dependency matters, and motions.
Central staff attorneys are also periodically assigned to
assist the justices in processing chambers assignable cases
as necessary to accommodate the case management needs
of the court. One central staff attorney handles cases in
which bankruptcy has been filed by one of the parties.

Support staff includes a librarian, two systems administrators, a budget analyst, central staff judicial assistants,
and a human resources department.

IV. CLERK'S OFFICE

The Clerk's Office consists of the Clerk Administrator,
who oversees the entire District and is currently located in
Division One, an Assistant Clerk Administrator, a Supervising Deputy Clerk, deputies, an appellate court records
assistant, and a receptionist. Certain deputies are designated "terminal digit deputies" (terminal digit is the last
number in the six-digit appellate case "D" number) and
process all filings on cases assigned to them from the time
the case is assigned a case number until the matter is final

except for the calendaring process. Practitioners should ask to speak with the appropriate terminal digit deputy for information or assistance on a case or the calendaring deputy if the case has been placed on calendar. The court has a security guard physically located in the Clerk's Office. However, the California Highway Patrol oversees and provides the court's overall security needs.

V. ORIGINAL PROCEEDINGS

The Clerk's Office forwards all writ petitions to the Supervising Writ Attorney, who reviews each petition as it comes into the Writ Department to determine its urgency. If it appears an immediate stay or other form of urgent action is required, the writ attorney orally presents the petition to the writ panel, a panel of three justices that rotates on a monthly basis.

Absent unusual urgency, petitions are processed in order of their filing with adjustments for impending hearing or trial dates in particular cases. The writ attorney or central staff attorney assigned to the Writ Department normally reviews the petition without waiting for a response (but may solicit a response if desired), prepares a written memorandum evaluating the petition, and circulates it to the writ panel.

After the memorandum circulates, the panel may alternatively (1) request a response, (2) deny the petition regardless of whether a response has been requested or filed, (3) issue a peremptory writ in the first instance without oral argument, but only when a response has been requested or filed and the parties have been notified by telephone, and then in writing, of the possibility, or (4) issue an alternative writ or order to show cause. It is the court's policy to request an initial response to the petition before issuing an alternative writ or order to show cause. If the panel issues an alternative writ or order to show cause, the real party will be given an opportunity to file a formal response and the cause will be placed on calendar. Generally, the writ attorney who prepared the written memorandum will assist the lead justice in drafting the opinion when the court intends to issue a peremptory writ in the first instance. Otherwise, one of the lead justice's chambers attorneys will assist in drafting the opinion when the court has issued an alternative writ or an order to show cause.

VI. APPEALS

A. Screening and Processing of Cases

In civil cases, a Civil Case Information Statement is filed within 10 days after the clerk mails appellant a notice that the form must be filed. (Cal. Rules of Court, rule [1] **8.100(g)**.) From the information on the Civil Case Information Statement, the court determines whether there is any issue regarding jurisdiction or appealability, whether the case is entitled to priority, and whether there has been a previous writ or appeal in the same or a closely related matter.

When the respondent's brief is filed in a civil or criminal appeal, or the time stated in California Rules of Court, rules 8.220(a) or 8.360(c)(5) has run, the Managing Attorney or designee screens the case and assigns it to one

of two procedural tracks for processing under the supervision of the authoring justice: the "Central Staff Assisted" track or the "Chambers" track.

Juvenile dependency cases are handled separately since they are expedited under California Rules of Court, rule 8.416.

B. Central Staff Assisted Appeals

If the appeal involves issues that can be resolved with little difficulty based upon well-established case law or by statute and there appears to be no likelihood of dispute as to how the law applies to the facts, the case will be assigned to Central Staff to assist in its processing under the supervision of the authoring justice. These cases are done chronologically and assigned randomly to an authoring justice who supervises the preparation of an opinion. If the case is appropriate for central staff assistance, then a central staff attorney assists the authoring justice in preparing the draft opinion. If argument has been waived, the authoring justice initials the draft opinion and circulates it, along with the entire appellate file, to the other justices on the panel in order of seniority. If the other justices approve and initial the proposed opinion, it will be filed. If oral argument has been requested, the proposed opinion is not circulated but instead is included in the justice's calendar book for the month of argument and handled along with all the other argued cases.

Central staff attorneys similarly assist justices randomly assigned to author juvenile dependency appeals.

In *Wende* cases (*People v. Wende, supra,* 25 Cal.3d 436), where appellant's counsel is unable to find any reasonably arguable issues, counsel asks the court to review the entire record for error. After the Attorney General's Office acknowledges the case is a *Wende,* the defendant is given the opportunity to file a brief within 30 days. Once that brief is filed, or the time to file it has expired, the case is processed as any other Central Staff assisted appeal. A central staff attorney reviews the record for error and prepares a proposed opinion, which is delivered to the assigned lead justice and, if approved, circulated to the panel for signature and filing. If the defendant or the staff attorney discovers an issue requiring briefing, however, counsel for both parties are asked to file briefs and, as in any other appeal, may request oral argument. The case will then be argued with all the other cases for that particular monthly calendar.

C. Chambers Appeals

Other appeals are assigned directly to "chambers." The Managing Attorney or designee estimates the amount of time it will take to prepare the case, assigning values between three (relatively little time) through eight (substantial amount of time) in an attempt to equalize the workloads of the individual chambers. Once "weighed", the cases are randomly distributed to the justices unless the court has issued an opinion in a previous appeal or writ in the same or closely related matter, in which case an attempt is made to assign the case to the same authoring justice and possibly the same panel. The assignment calendar is issued approximately two months before oral argument with each justice assigned to author, on average, a core of six cases. Additional juvenile and criminal cases are added to each chambers calendar depending on the needs of the court. Several chambers in a given month may also be assigned additional civil cases to be prepared with the assistance of a specially assigned central staff attorney. The internal procedures for assigning and preparing cases in chambers vary. The draft opinions of cases to be orally argued are placed in a calendar book, generally the first Monday of the month. The justices review all cases in which they are to participate in advance of oral argument and confer on all cases argued immediately after argument.

In cases where oral argument has been waived, a proposed opinion is prepared and circulated in order of seniority to the other justices assigned to the panel for that case. If the other justices concur, the opinion will be filed without delay.

VII. ORAL ARGUMENT

Oral argument is generally held during the second week of the month. Specific cases will be calendared during other times when resolution of the matter is urgent or for other good cause. Argument is limited to no more than 15 minutes per side, unless the time is extended by advance written request and leave of court.

Those matters that are orally argued are generally submitted at the conclusion of counsel's arguments. If argument has been waived, the case will be submitted at the conclusion of the entire argument calendar. Submission of the case triggers the 90-day rule for the filing of the opinion. (Cal. Const., art. VI, § 19.)

VIII. SETTLEMENT CONFERENCES — LITIGANT INITIATED

The general information packet sent to parties at the commencement of the appeal includes guidelines for the settlement program and an appellate settlement request form. The program is voluntary and available at the request of both parties or, should there be more than two parties, at the request of any two opposing parties. The request for a settlement conference may be made as soon as the notice of appeal is filed and settlement proceedings may commence before briefing but, in any event, the request must be received no later than 30 days after the filing of the last brief. The request normally will not interrupt or extend the briefing schedule. The Presiding Justice in selecting the settlement justice will consider the parties' request for a particular settlement justice. Should settlement efforts prove unsuccessful, the settlement justice will be recused on the ensuing appeal. In such instances, all settlement papers are strictly confidential and are kept separate from the appellate record.

IX. SETTLEMENT CONFERENCES — COURT INITIATED

From time to time the court has a court-initiated settlement program which is a joint effort with the superior court to resolve civil appeals without the time delay and additional costs associated with the traditional appellate process. The court selects cases suitable for possible

settlement from a review of the Civil Case Information Statements. The court sends a questionnaire to all counsel in the selected cases to get additional information as to possible issues on appeal. After review, the settlement judge, a superior court judge sitting on assignment, conducts a conference call with all counsel to discuss the case further and to determine whether it would be beneficial to schedule a settlement conference with counsel and the parties. The court attempts to schedule settlement conferences after the record has been filed but before briefing has begun and, if needed, counsel may be asked to provide limited briefing. If settlement appears to be possible, a conference will be set for the earliest mutually convenient time. Additional conferences, if needed, will be set after the first conference. All documents filed for the settlement proceedings will be kept separate from the pending appeal and the settlement judge will not participate in any related panel discussions or decisions. No record is made unless the case settles.

X. EXTERN PROGRAM

The court offers an extern program for select law school students three times a year (Fall, Spring and Summer sessions). Externs are selected by the specific justices with whom they then work for 20-40 hours per week during the session. The Managing Attorney administers the program, which consists of a two-day orientation, a series of substantive and procedural law lectures, and monthly group meetings. If students participate as part of their school's extern/clinic program, they may earn course credit for their efforts.

XI. MOTIONS

Applications in routine matters (see Cal. Rules of Court, rule 8.50) are reviewed by a central staff attorney and presented to the Presiding or Acting Presiding Justice for a ruling. Applications in non-routine matters, such as a motion to dismiss an appeal, are presented to a panel of the court for ruling. Extensions of time are ruled on immediately. Motions in writ proceedings are not held for opposition absent a request by the parties.

(Adopted Sept. 1, 2004; amended Jan. 1, 2005; Jan. 1, 2007; Jan. 1, 2008.)

IOPPs. 2008 Deletes. [1] 8.100(f)

INTERNAL OPERATING PRACTICES AND PROCEDURES
FOURTH APPELLATE DISTRICT, DIVISION TWO

(March 2005 Revision)

SECTION IX. FILING OPINIONS
SECTION X. PRESIDING JUSTICE
SECTION XI. STAFF

SECTION I. INTRODUCTION

To implement the rules governing appellate court procedure, each district and division of the Court of Appeal has developed local customs and practices that may be similar to or different from other districts and divisions. This statement of the internal operating procedures and practices describes the more important customs of this court. The purpose of the statement is to inform the public and the bar of the general manner in which this court conducts its business.

SECTION II. THE COURT

Division Two of the Fourth District is located in Riverside and operates with almost complete autonomy from Division One located in San Diego and Division Three located in Santa Ana. Under the supervision of the Administrative Presiding Justice of the Fourth District, a clerk/administrator plans, organizes, coordinates, and manages the budget, personnel, facilities, and non-judicial activities of the district as a whole. Under the supervision of the Presiding Justice of each division (the Administrative Presiding Justice is also the Presiding Justice of Division One), an assistant clerk administrator is responsible for assisting the clerk/administrator in managing personnel and non-judicial programs within organizational and policy confines of an appellate court. In Divisions Two and Three the assistant clerk/administrator has total responsibility for all administrative activities of the division.

Division Two currently has seven justices including a presiding justice and six associate justices. Division Two handles all appellate matters arising in Inyo, Riverside, and San Bernardino Counties. Division One handles all appellate matters arising in San Diego and Imperial Counties. Division Three handles all appellate matters arising in Orange County. Additionally, cases originating in one division may be transferred to another division by the Administrative Presiding Justice if required because of recusals or decision of an earlier case by a different division. (See Cal. Rules of Court, rule 47.1(b).)

SECTION III. ORIGINAL PROCEEDINGS

Original proceedings are assigned to panels of three justices selected each month by a rotation distinct from the rotation from which panel assignments are made for appeals. Three writ attorneys assist the justices by preparing written summaries. The justices review the summaries and meet informally or formally as necessary to decide the case.

More urgent writ matters, including those requesting immediate stays, are the subject of immediate action by the justices facilitated by oral summaries by writ attorneys. If an alternative writ or order to show cause is issued, the issuing justice normally prepares the tentative opinion (see Section VIII., below) with the assistance of the writ attorney who prepared the summary.

SECTION IV. CIVIL CASE INFORMATION STATEMENT

California Rules of Court, rule 1(f), requires the filing of a civil case information statement in the Court of Appeal with a copy of the judgment or order appealed in all civil appeals within 10 days after the clerk mails the notice to do so and the required form. Under the supervision of the Presiding Justice, a central staff attorney reviews the civil case information statement to determine the appealability of the ruling designated in the notice of appeal, the timeliness of its filing, consolidation with other related appeals, and the apparent appellate case title and parties.

This court uses the civil case information statement to implement this court's policy to honor its jurisdictional limitations. Thus, this court will not construe a nonappealable ruling to include language of judgment or dismissal, or allow the appellant to belatedly obtain an appealable ruling, to "save" an appeal. (See *Shpiller v. Harry C's Redlands* (1993) 13 Cal.App.4th 1177, 1179-1181; *Passavanti v. Williams* (1990) 225 Cal.App.3d 1602, 1608-1610.) This court also uses the civil case information statement to initially screen cases for the court's settlement program. (See Section V., below.)

SECTION V. CIVIL APPELLATE SETTLEMENT PROGRAM

Division Two of the Fourth District began its civil appellate settlement program using volunteer attorney mediators in June 1991, the first program of its kind in California. The program helped dramatically in reducing backlog by freeing justices to work on cases that could not be settled. The program received the 1997 Kleps Award for court administration. Approximately 70 volunteer attorney mediators are now approaching 600 cases settled with the value of these settlements nearing an estimated 400 million dollars. This division has a population-to-justice ratio of 540,000 to 1 (compared to the First District's 280,000 to 1) and includes the fastest growing two-county area in California. The resulting increase in case filings now makes the settlement program more necessary than ever.

Volunteer attorney mediators chosen and scheduled by the Presiding Justice in cooperation with the court's settlement coordinator conduct most of the settlement conferences for civil appeals. On occasion, justices also act as mediators in selected cases. The volunteer mediators are experienced and respected attorneys from Riverside and San Bernardino Counties who are assigned cases for settlement according to their areas of expertise. The Presiding Justice selects cases for settlement based on settlement conference information forms filed by counsel and the availability of an appropriate mediator. Once a case has been selected by the court for settlement proceedings, participation is mandatory.

Settlement conferences may be held either before or after briefing is completed. Postbriefing settlement conferences were the rule when the court was using the program to reduce its backlog in the early and mid-1990's, but since the court has eliminated its backlog, prebriefing conferences are the rule and postbriefing conferences rare and generally discouraged. When cases are selected for a prebriefing settlement conference, generally the court permits a record produced by the superior court to be filed but stays filing of the briefs. Parties file a settlement conference statement within 10 days after notice that the case has been selected. Settlement conferences are held over a period of time before settlement is achieved or determined not to be possible. All documents relating to settlement proceedings are retained in a separate, confidential file for the case, and the proceedings and results are confidential and not revealed to the panel that decides the case if settlement is not achieved. Postbriefing settlement cases that do not settle are given priority over other civil cases. Court of Appeal, Fourth District, Division Two, Local Rules of Court, rule 4 authorizes the program.

SECTION VI. EXTENSIONS TO FILE BRIEFS

Extensions to file briefs are granted or denied based on the factors listed in California Rules of Court, rule 45.5(b). When further extensions on the usual grounds (the existence of other time limited commitments, the size of the record and number and complexity of the issues, and planned vacations) are no longer appropriate, counsel is so notified in an order granting the last extension on the usual grounds. Thereafter, no extensions will be granted except upon other factors listed in rule 45.5(b). If a further extension is obtained on one or more of those grounds, counsel is again notified that no further extensions will be granted on the usual grounds or the grounds stated in the application. A request for an extension on an excluded ground will be denied, and the clerk directed to issue a notice of default in failing to timely file the brief. (Cal. Rules of Court, rule 17(a)(1), (2).)

SECTION VII. CASE ASSIGNMENT

When a case is ready for assignment, the record is checked to see if any justice was involved in trial court proceedings or for other reasons should not be involved in deciding the case. The court under the supervision of the Presiding Justice maintains a confidential recusal list, which is reviewed prior to final case assignment. Cases are divided into five categories: unusually difficult chambers cases, chambers cases, "fast track" dependency cases (Cal. Rules of Court, rule 37.4(a)(1)(A)), dependency writs reviewing orders setting a hearing under Welfare and Institutions Code section 336.26 (Cal. Rules of Court, rules 38-38.1), and central staff cases. The cases are randomly assigned to a justice as author, and those in the categories of the unusually difficult, "fast track" dependency, and rules 38-38.1 writs are assigned by a rotation. Assignments to authors are usually made weekly, except the "fast track" cases and rules 38-38.1 writs are assigned immediately. When the author has prepared the tentative opinion (see Section VIII, below), the case is randomly assigned to a panel.

SECTION VIII. TENTATIVE OPINIONS AND ORAL ARGUMENT

A tentative opinion is the preliminary draft of the court's decision prepared by the author and reviewed by the panel members. The author circulates the tentative opinion with a cover sheet to the other two justices and notes a recommendation for or against oral argument. The two panel justices consider the briefs and record and note on the cover sheet their preliminary responses and evaluation of the need for oral argument.

Depending on the author's and panel justices' evaluation of the need for oral argument, one of two notices regarding oral argument is mailed to counsel with the tentative opinion. The first notice invites participation in oral argument and informs counsel that a notice will be mailed at least 30 days in advance of the date and time of oral argument. The second notice informs counsel that, while "[t]he court is not unalterably bound by the tentative opinion and is willing to amend or discard the tentative opinion if counsel's arguments persuade the court that the tentative opinion is incorrect in any way," *"at present, in this case the court believes that the record and briefs thoroughly present the facts and legal arguments such that the court is prepared to rule as set forth in the tentative opinion without oral argument."* The notice advises the parties that oral argument will be deemed waived unless the clerk of the court receives a request for oral argument on the form attached to the notice on or before 12 days after the date of the notice.

Oral argument is held on the first Tuesday and Wednesday of each month, with slight adjustments occasionally made for holidays. If a party requests oral argument or the justices have decided that oral argument would be helpful, the clerk prepares the calendar and mails it to counsel at least 30 days in advance of the hearing. Two or three weeks before oral argument, the justices discuss the cases set for oral argument at a calendar conference.

SECTION IX. FILING OPINIONS

After oral argument, or waiver of oral argument, authors and panel justices develop the tentative opinions and preliminary responses into the opinions, concurrences, and dissents filed as the final decisions. If oral argument is deemed waived in a case, the opinion is circulated for signature to the other panel members as soon as it is signed by the author. The opinion is filed as soon as it is signed by all members of the panel. The sooner oral argument is waived, the sooner the opinion is filed, so that opinions in waived cases tend to be filed more quickly than cases in which oral argument is held. The additional time required to file opinions in orally argued cases results from the time it takes to schedule oral argument and/or from continuances requested by counsel or required by the absence of one of the panel members.

Argued cases are deemed submitted on the date of oral argument, and the opinions are generally filed within the same month.

SECTION X. PRESIDING JUSTICE

In addition to the regular duties of an associate justice, the Presiding Justice handles the administrative operation of the court including the functions designated in California Rules of Court, rule 77. In so doing, the Presiding Justice performs a number of tasks essential to the functioning of the court. These include without limitation policymaking, personnel, budgeting, oversight of facilities, grounds, furnishings, and equipment, case assignment, calendar preparation, backlog management, decision of all motions and applications until the case is assigned to an author, opinions in all criminal cases in which appellants file briefs under *People v. Wende* (1979) 25 Cal.3d 436, appointments of counsel, supervision of, and selection of cases for, the settlement program, and supervision of the central staff and clerk's office. Staff assist in these tasks when necessary in the Presiding Justice's discretion.

SECTION XI. STAFF

This division currently has 24 attorneys. Fourteen of these positions are chambers attorneys hired by the individual justices. The remaining 10 attorneys form the central staff consisting of one managing (formerly principal) attorney, one senior attorney acting as an assistant managing attorney, three writ attorneys, and five other central staff attorneys who primarily research and draft opinions. All central staff attorneys are under the supervision of the Presiding Justice, who assigns each attorney to a particular justice to research and draft opinions.

The clerk's office includes an assistant clerk/administrator, a number of deputy clerks, and other supporting clerical personnel. A settlement coordinator manages the volunteer attorney mediator settlement conference program. A systems administrator and an assistant maintain the court's computer systems. A librarian organizes and updates a central library, distributes materials to the justices' and attorneys' libraries, assists justices and attorneys with legal research, and prepares a library budget for approval by the Presiding Justice. There are also 10 judicial assistants employed by the court, who facilitate case flow in and out of the chambers and perform secretarial services for the justices and attorneys.

INTERNAL OPERATING PRACTICES AND PROCEDURES FOURTH APPELLATE DISTRICT, DIVISION THREE

(Revised effective January 1, 2008)

SECTION I. INTRODUCTION

This document describes the general internal operating practices and procedures of this court. These practices and procedures supplement the statutes and rules of court that otherwise govern the court's business.

SECTION II. STRUCTURE OF COURT AND ORGANIZATION OF STAFF

Division Three of the Fourth Appellate District is currently authorized eight justices — a presiding justice and seven associate justices. The Chairperson of the Judicial Council periodically assigns pro tem justices to assist the court.

Each justice's staff consists of two or three judicial attorneys and a judicial assistant. The managing appellate court attorney supervises a separate central staff. The managing appellate court attorney and central staff work under the direction and supervision of the presiding justice. They review original proceedings, motions, and extension requests, act as counsel for the clerk's office, and assist in the evaluation of cases. Many of the justices also utilize law student externs who may receive academic credit, without pay, while working at the court.

The assistant clerk/administrator supervises the court's administrative staff under the direction of the presiding justice. The court's administrative staff consists of deputy clerks, librarian, court systems administrators, and office assistants.

SECTION III. PROCEDURES FOR PROCESSING CASES

A. Appeals.

1. When an appeal is fully briefed, the clerk's office sends out a notice to the parties who have appeared to give them an opportunity to request oral argument. (Cal. Rules of Court, rule 8.220(a).) Cases are generally scheduled for oral argument in order of the requests. Statutory priorities are enforced, and parties claiming calendar preference must promptly serve and file a motion for preference. (Cal. Rules of Court, rule 8.240.) Non-oral argument cases are similarly assigned in order based on the date oral argument is waived. Panels, including a justice tentatively designated to author the opinion, are **generally** assigned on a random rotating basis, **subject to the presiding justice's responsibility to ensure that the court's resources are allocated in an effective and efficient manner to fairly and expeditiously resolve disputes, and to promote access to justice for all members of the public. (Cal. Rules of Court, rule 10.603(a).).** [1]

2. A confidential written summary is prepared by the authoring justice and provided to each panel member prior to oral argument. The panel may conference on a case before argument and always conferences after oral argu-

ment is completed. Thereafter, a proposed final opinion circulates among the panel members for comments and/or approval. Proposed opinions for cases in which oral argument has been waived generally circulate among panel members without a formal conference. All cases may routinely be discussed among the justices and staff members informally on an as-needed basis.

3. All requests for continuances of oral argument must be in writing and contain a particularized showing of compelling circumstances. The written request must inform the court of opposing counsel's position regarding any continuance. No request will be forwarded to the presiding justice until the court is made aware of opposing counsel's position. Counsel's stipulation to continue oral argument is not sufficient in the absence of a showing of compelling cause.

4. Any post-briefing citation of additional authorities must be made by letter to the court, without further legal argument, and served upon opposing counsel. The court retains discretion to strike or disregard late-filed or untimely citations of authority as they deprive the court and opposing counsel of sufficient opportunity to prepare for oral argument.

5. The court offers remote video appearances for oral argument on criminal matters, allowing counsel to appear via video from Division One in San Diego.

B. Original Proceedings.

1. The presiding justice assigns on a quarterly basis three justices to serve as the court's writ panel for a three-month period. The writ panel members also rule on motions requiring a three-judge panel.

2. The clerk's office notifies the managing appellate court attorney when an original proceeding is filed. The managing appellate court attorney determines the urgency of the relief sought. The matter is calendared for the weekly writ panel conference if court action is not required before then. Impromptu writ conferences are held when court action is required earlier. The managing appellate court attorney and central staff attorneys prepare written summaries of original proceedings which are provided to the writ panel members before their weekly conference.

C. Motions.

1. The court's practice is to hold motions on appeals (Cal. Rules of Court, rule 8.54) in the clerk's office until (1) an opposition has been served and filed, or (2) the time has passed to serve and file an opposition, whichever is earlier. To expedite the processing of an unopposed motion, the moving party should file a stipulation of nonopposition from other counsel.

2. Motions in writ proceedings are not generally held for opposition absent a request by the parties.

D. Filings by Facsimile, E-mail or Other Electronic Means

The court does not accept filings by facsimile, e-mail or other electronic means unless specifically authorized by court order or court rule. **Local Rule 5 provides for a** **voluntary fax filing pilot project throughout the Fourth Appellate District for specified documents, but not briefs.**

SECTION IV. JUDICIAL SETTLEMENT PROGRAM

A. Purpose and Structure.

1. The court has established a judicial settlement program to mediate appellate disputes, and, where appropriate, to establish briefing schedules, to simplify appellate issues, and to address procedural concerns. The court encourages appellate mediations and settlement conferences, and will make its resources available to parties who attempt in good faith to resolve a dispute on appeal.

2. The judicial settlement program is directed by the presiding justice, who appoints a supervising judicial attorney to administer the program and to conduct settlement conferences. In addition, a senior clerk schedules the settlement conferences and provides an interface between the public and the court.

B. Filings.

All papers pertaining to the judicial settlement program should be filed with the clerk's office at the courthouse, located at 925 No. Spurgeon Street, or mailed to the court at the following address:

California Court of Appeal
Fourth Appellate District, Division Three
P.O. Box 22055
Santa Ana, CA 92702
Attn: Judicial Settlement Program

These papers ordinarily are retained separately from the other documents filed on appeal, and, where appropriate, are confidential and for the purposes of the Judicial Settlement Program only.

C. Location and Telephone.

1. The judicial settlement program is physically housed in the Civic Center Professional Plaza, about one-half mile from the Spurgeon Street courthouse. The street address is:

Civic Center Professional Plaza
500 West Santa Ana Blvd., Room [2] **400**
Santa Ana, CA 92701

2. The telephone number is (714) 564-3600. The fax number is (714) 567-6060. Callers also may use the court's general telephone number: (714) 558-6777.

D. Settlement Conference Information Forms (SCIF's).

1. The presiding justice may order any pending civil appeal to be scheduled for a settlement conference pursuant to the California Rules of Court, rule 8.248. This decision is based upon the court's review of Settlement Conference Information Forms (SCIF), which are prepared by the parties and filed with the court. Preference is

given to any stipulated requests for a settlement conference.

2. Request or stipulation for SCIF orders should be made in writing, directed to the Judicial Settlement Program. Requests may be made in confidence.

E. Settlement Conferences.

1. TIMING. Settlement conferences may be ordered before, during or after briefing. The court generally does not schedule a conference after an appeal has been set for oral argument except for good cause. The court tries to accommodate stipulations for specific day or dates. Parties may ascertain available settlement conference dates by telephoning the settlement conference clerk.

2. SETTLEMENT CONFERENCE OFFICER. The presiding justice appoints the person who conducts the settlement conference. In addition to the supervising attorney who manages the judicial settlement program, the settlement conference officer may be an individual justice, assigned pro tem justice, or other judicial attorney.

3. PERSONAL ATTENDANCE. Unless otherwise specified, all parties and their counsel must attend any settlement conference in person, and must have full settlement authority. Attendance by counsel claiming settlement authority is not sufficient. Any exceptions must be approved in advance by the court.

a. INSTITUTIONAL LITIGANTS. If the party is not an individual, then a party representative with full authority to settle must personally attend all settlement conferences in person, in addition to counsel.

b. INSURANCE. If a party has potential insurance coverage applicable to any of the issues in dispute, a representative of each insurance carrier whose policy may apply also must personally attend all settlement conferences, with full settlement authority.

c. TELEPHONIC APPEARANCES. The court prefers in-person settlement conferences and does not ordinarily grant requests for telephonic appearances. Parties who desire to participate by telephone must promptly serve and file a written request at least five court days before any settlement conference explaining why the attendee's personal presence is impossible or impracticable.

4. ADDITIONAL PARTICIPANTS. The court may order other necessary persons (whether or not a party to the appeal) to personally attend settlement conferences. In addition, the conference officer may invite parties to the action who are not parties to the appeal, or any person or entity having interest in the action, to attend. Any party may serve and file a written request for the attendance of such a party or person at least five court days before any settlement conference. No other person may attend a settlement conference without the permission of the conference officer.

5. SETTLEMENT BRIEFS. If a settlement conference is held before appellate briefing or record preparation, the conference officer may direct that the parties provide settlement conference briefs, or other appropriate documents, to facilitate a meaningful and productive settlement conference.

6. PRE-CONFERENCE PREPARATION. Counsel should confer with their clients in advance of any settlement conference and be thoroughly familiar with the case and prepared to present their contentions in detail. Counsel should review their SCIFs for completeness and accuracy and promptly notify the conference officer of any material changes or omissions at least three court days before the settlement conference.

7. LOCATION. Settlement conferences generally are held at the court's settlement conference facilities. (See IVC, above for address.) Settlement conferences also may be held at the Spurgeon Street courthouse. Participants should carefully check the notice of a settlement conference for the correct location.

8. DURATION. Participants should be prepared to remain for the duration of the day, or until dismissed by the conference officer. No person who has been ordered to appear may leave without permission of the conference officer. At the conclusion of a prehearing conference, the conference officer may continue the conference to another date to allow for further discussions.

9. CONTINUANCES. Parties who seek to continue a settlement conference should attempt to do so by stipulation, with a mutually agreeable alternative date. Any request for continuances should be made in writing, with reasons stated, and served and filed at least five court days before the conference. Continuances are not granted, except for good cause.

10. EX PARTE COMMUNICATIONS. The conference officer may communicate with any of the parties or their counsel with or without notice to the other parties or their counsel.

11. CONFIDENTIALITY. All discussions and information imparted during the settlement conference are confidential, and the conference officer cannot testify about them.

F. "Workout" Conferences.

The presiding justice may order that a prehearing "workout" conference be held for any of the following purposes: (1) to simplify issues on appeal, (2) to establish a briefing schedule, (3) to address procedural questions, issues or outstanding motions or applications, (4) to lay the groundwork for a future settlement conference, (5) to facilitate ongoing settlement discussions, (6) to monitor the progress of a pending settlement or private mediation, or (7) for any other reason or reasons. Unlike settlement conferences, workout conferences are conducted either in person or by telephone. Generally, only counsel, not clients, participate in "workout" conferences.

G. Private Mediations.

The presiding justice entertains stipulated requests to stay of appellate proceedings to allow private mediations. Stay requests shall not exceed 60 days except for good cause. Any such stipulated request shall specify the identity of the mediator, the scheduled day or dates for mediation, and any other pertinent factors.

H. Stays; Tolling.

Appeals are not automatically stayed merely because parties are ordered to prepare a SCIF, or to choose dates for a settlement conference. The tolling provisions for briefs (Cal. Rules of Court, rule 8.248(d)) commence to run only when the court mails notice of a settlement conference for a specific date and time. Record preparation is not automatically stayed without a court order. The court's policy is to conduct settlement conferences as expeditiously as possible, and to issue a rule 8.248(d) notice lifting any stay or tolling order within 90 days from the date of the notice of the settlement conference.

I. Disqualification.

Disqualification of justices is governed by the Canon 3E of the California Code of Judicial Ethics. Justices are not disqualified to hear appeals merely because they rule on settlement conference requests or sign orders pertaining to procedural aspects of the settlement conference process. If appeals do not settle, neither the conference officer nor any other court personnel present at a conference will participate further in the determination of the appeal on the merits. (Cal. Rules of Court, rule 8.248(c)(2).)

J. Sanctions.

The judicial settlement program shall not be employed by any party in bad faith or for purposes of delay. The court may impose sanctions for (1) failure to appear at a prehearing (settlement) conference, (2) failure to participate in good faith in the judicial settlement program, or to cooperate in good faith with the conference officer, or (3) failure to comply with a court order or court rule. Sanctions may include monetary awards, or, in the case of an appellant's failure to comply, dismissal of the appeal.

SECTION V. SETTLEMENT NOTICES & STIPULATIONS

A. Notice of Settlements.

The settling appellants shall immediately serve and file notices of settlement of any pending civil appeal, and telephone the court if the case has been calendared for oral argument. (See Cal. Rules of Court, rule 8.244(a) for other requirements concerning notice of settlements.) Settling appellants also should e-mail or telephone the settlement conference clerk if the appeal has been placed in the judicial settlement program.

B. Stipulated Requests for Dismissal.

Counsel should promptly serve and file stipulated requests for dismissal because of settlements. The stipulation should specify the allocation of costs on appeal and whether the remittitur is to issue immediately. (Cal. Rules of Court, rule 8.244(c).)

C. Stipulated Requests for Reversal. (Code Civ. Proc., §128, subd. (a)(8).)

Stipulated requests for a reversal of the judgment ordinarily are heard by the writ panel, unless the appeal already has been assigned to a panel for decision.

1. GOOD CAUSE. The parties must provide a sufficient showing to satisfy the statutory criteria in Code of Civil Procedure section 128, subdivision (a)(8). A copy of the judgment shall accompany the motion.

2. JOINT DECLARATION. The motion shall include a joint declaration of counsel that (1) describes the parties and the factual and legal issues presented at trial; (2) indicates whether the judgment involves important public rights or unfair, illegal or corrupt practices, or torts affecting a significant number of persons, or otherwise affects the public or a significant number of persons not parties to the litigation (if the judgment is against a state licensee, the declaration must also disclose whether it exposes such person to any possible disciplinary proceeding); (3) discloses whether the judgment sought to be reversed may have collateral estoppel or other effects in potential future litigation and, if so, whether any third parties who might be prejudiced by stipulated reversal of the judgment have received notice of the motion and (4) discloses whether the judgment involves discretionary determinations by the trial court that cannot be reversed by stipulation of the parties alone without independent appellate review (see, e.g., *Garabedian v. Los Angeles Cellular Telephone Co.* (2004) 118 Cal.App.4th 123; *Stewart v. Stewart* (1955) 130 Cal.App.2d 186, 193.)

3. NOTICE TO PARTY. The joint declaration shall include a certification that a copy of the stipulation and joint declaration has been delivered to the client. The certification need not include the address of the party notified. In a class action, the copy required need be delivered to only one represented party.

SECTION VI. ETHICAL SCREENS

The court maintains an ethical screening process for its judicial attorneys, judicial assistants, clerks, externs and other staff members in order to maintain and preserve public confidence in the judicial system. The purpose of this process is to inform the justices at the earliest possible opportunity of any circumstances of an actual or potential conflict of interest involving a court staff member that could give rise to the need for an ethical screen. If applicable, the ethical screen is promptly implemented.

(Amended Apr. 14, 2004; Mar. 1, 2005; Jan. 1, 2007; Jan. 1, 2008.)

IOPPs. 2008 Deletes. [1] The court also offers remote video appearances for oral argument on criminal matters, allowing counsel to appear via video from Division One in San Diego. **[2]** 401

FIFTH APPELLATE DISTRICT LOCAL RULES

[As amended effective August 17, 2007; adopted, effective July 1, 1981; and previously amended February 25, 1983, February 8, 1985, October 2, 1992, November 15, 1993, June 25, 1999, August 25, 2003 and January 1, 2007.]

Internal Operating Practices and Procedures.

Rule 1.   Circuit-Riding Sessions [Repealed]
Rule 1 adopted July 1, 1981; repealed Aug. 25, 2003.

Another Rule 1 follows.

Rule 1.   Augmentation of Record and Correction of Omissions from Record

(a) [Material inadvertently omitted] Counsel should not file a motion to augment the record when items have been omitted from the normal (criminal) record on appeal. In those cases counsel should immediately notify the clerk of the superior court, who shall forthwith comply with rule 8.155(b).

(b) [When to file motion to augment] Appellant should file requests for augmentation in one motion within 40 days of the filing of the record. Respondent should file requests for augmentation in one motion made within 30 days of the filing of appellant's opening brief. Thereafter, motions to augment will not be granted except upon a showing of good cause for the delay.

(c) [Clerk's transcript] A motion to augment or correct the clerk's transcript shall be accompanied either by certified copies of the documents requested, or, if the documents are not provided, the motion must identify them with specificity and contain an explanation for their omission.

(d) [Reporter's transcript] A motion to augment the reporter's transcript shall identify the portion of the record with specificity, including the reporter's name and the date of the hearing. The motion shall establish with some certainty how the requested materials may be useful on appeal.

(e) [Extension of time] The time to perform any act required or permitted by the California Rules of Court will not be automatically extended in civil cases by the filing of or ruling on a motion to augment. If additional time is needed, counsel may request an extension of time in the motion to augment.

(f) [Good faith required] A motion to augment shall be made in good faith and shall not be made for the purpose of delay.

Rule 1 adopted Nov. 15, 1993; renumbered from Rule 2 Aug. 25, 2003; amended Jan. 1, 2007; Aug. 17, 2007.

Rule 2.   Settlement Conferences in Civil Appeals

(a) [Application of rule] This rule shall apply to all appeals in civil cases except to appeals from proceedings under sections 300, 601, and 602 of the Welfare and Institutions Code and sections 7802, 7807, 7808, 7820 to 7829, 7890, 7892 of the Family Code and appeals from original proceedings ancillary to a criminal prosecution.

(Adopted Jan. 28, 1982; amended Feb. 25, 1983; Feb. 8, 1985; renumbered Nov. 15, 1993; amended June 25, 1999; amended and renumbered from Rule 4 Aug. 25, 2003.)

(b) [Notice of availability of conference] Upon filing of the record on appeal, the clerk of this court shall send a copy of this rule and notice of the availability of a settlement conference to counsel for all parties to the appeal.

(Adopted Jan. 28, 1982; amended Feb. 25, 1983; Feb. 8, 1985; renumbered Nov. 15, 1993; renumbered from Rule 4 Aug. 25, 2003.)

(c) [Request for a settlement conference] Upon written request by counsel for all parties, a settlement conference will be scheduled, and written notice of the date and time of the conference will be give by the court. A copy of any request shall be sent to all other parties.

Upon request of any party or upon its own motion, the court may invite parties to the action who are not parties to the appeal if it appears to the court their presence may facilitate settlement of the case.

(Adopted Jan. 28, 1982; amended Feb. 25, 1983; Feb. 8, 1985; renumbered Nov. 15, 1993; renumbered from Rule 4 Aug. 25, 2003; amended Aug. 17, 2007.)

(d) [Settlement conference statement] Not later than ten days before the date set for the settlement conference, each party shall serve upon all other parties to the appeal and shall lodge with the clerk of this court a settlement conference statement. The statement shall contain the following:

(1) Case title and number

(2) Identification of trial court

(3) Date of judgment or order appealed from

(4) Name of judge or judges who made the disposition or dispositions from which appeal is taken

(5) Date notice of appeal filed

(6) Name, address and telephone number of counsel for all parties to the appeal

(7) A brief description of the trial court disposition from which the appeal is taken

(8) A concise statement of the case, including a brief procedural history and all facts material to consideration of the issues presented by the appeal

(9) The issues to be raised in the brief on the appeal or cross-appeal

(Adopted Jan. 28, 1982; amended Feb. 25, 1983; Feb. 8, 1985; Oct. 2, 1992; renumbered Nov. 15, 1993; renumbered from Rule 4 Aug. 25, 2003; amended Aug. 17, 2007.)

(e) [Postponement of briefing] Upon the setting of a settlement conference, further briefing shall be suspended until the settlement conference judge determines that the settlement conference proceedings should be terminated and notice is given that briefing time shall commence.

(Adopted Jan. 28, 1982; amended Feb. 25, 1983; Feb. 8, 1985; renumbered Nov. 15, 1993; renumbered from Rule 4 Aug. 25, 2003.)

(f) [Court-ordered conference] In cases where the parties have not requested a settlement conference, the court may, before or after the record on appeal is filed, order the parties to attend a conference at a specified date and time. Such an order will suspend further briefing in the appeal.

(Adopted Jan. 28, 1982; amended Feb. 25, 1983; Feb. 8, 1985; renumbered Nov. 15, 1993; renumbered from Rule 4 Aug. 25, 2003; amended Aug. 17, 2007.)

(g) [The settlement conference and sanctions] A justice of the court will preside over every settlement conference. The justice presiding over the conference may in his or her discretion continue it from time to time to allow further opportunity for negotiation and agreement.

Counsel for every party to the appeal must attend a scheduled settlement conference. Failure to attend may result in the imposition of sanctions against any party, including dismissal of an appeal or cross-appeal.

Counsel are required to bring their client to the settlement conference except where hardship or other unusual circumstance makes it impossible or impractical to do so. In the rare case where it is impossible to have the client present, with permission of the court, the client shall be available for consultation by telephone.

Counsel shall confer with their clients in advance and be thoroughly familiar with the case and prepared to present their contentions in detail. Where complete settlement cannot be reached, partial settlement will be sought.

(Adopted Jan. 28, 1982; amended Feb. 25, 1983; Feb. 8, 1985; renumbered Nov. 15, 1993; renumbered from Rule 4 Aug. 25, 2003; amended Aug. 17, 2007.)

(h) [Disqualification of settlement conference justice] Any justice who participates in a settlement conference shall not thereafter participate in any way in the consideration or disposition of the appeal on its merits.

(Adopted Jan. 28, 1982; amended Feb. 25, 1983; Feb. 8, 1985; renumbered Nov. 15, 1993; renumbered from Rule 4 Aug. 25, 2003.)

Rule 2 adopted Jan. 28, 1982; amended Feb. 25, 1983; Feb. 8, 1985; Oct. 2, 1992; amended & renumbered to Rule 4 Nov. 15, 1993; amended June 25, 1999; renumbered from Rule 4 Aug. 25, 2003; amended Aug. 17, 2007.

Rule 3. Stipulation for Use of Original Superior Court File [Repealed]

Rule 3 adopted Dec. 29, 1989; repealed Aug. 25, 2003.

Another Rule 3 follows.

Rule 3. Writ Petitions, Supporting Records and Stay Requests

All petitions for extraordinary writs, other than habeas corpus, shall be accompanied by a properly completed face sheet, the *Appellate Court Writ Petition Information Sheet*. This form is available from the clerk of the court.

A petition for an extraordinary writ that seeks review of a trial court ruling shall be accompanied by the following:

(1) a copy of the order or judgment from which relief is sought;

(2) copies of all documents submitted to the trial court supporting and opposing petitioner's position;

(3) a transcript of the proceedings leading to the order or judgment below, or if a transcript is unnecessary or unavailable, a declaration by counsel (i) explaining why a transcript is unnecessary or unavailable and (ii) fairly summarizing the proceedings, including arguments by counsel and the basis of the trial court's decision, if stated.

A petitioner who requests an immediate stay shall explain in the petition the reasons for the urgency and set forth all relevant time constraints.

If a petitioner does not submit the required record and explanations or does not present facts sufficient to excuse the failure to submit them, the court may summarily deny the stay request.

Rule 3 adopted Nov. 15, 1993; amended and renumbered from Rule 5 Aug. 25, 2003.

Rule 4. Settlement Conferences in Civil Appeals [Renumbered]

Rule 4 adopted Jan. 28, 1985; renumbered to Rule 2 Aug. 25, 2003.

Another Rule 4 follows.

Rule 4. The Teleconference Oral Argument Option

The court has a teleconference system that enables attorneys to stay in their office until such time as contacted by the court for oral argument before the court.

Teleconference Procedures

1. Counsel who have requested oral argument will have returned to the court a questionnaire designating the attorney arguing the case and the time requested. If counsel has not specifically designated on the questionnaire a request for personal appearance, the attorney shall be deemed to have consented to teleconference oral argument.

2. The questionnaire requests a current California telephone number for counsel, which the court utilizes unless otherwise notified by counsel. The courtroom clerk will telephone each counsel's office in the sequence the cases are called on the calendar. Counsel are expected to be at the telephone number previously given to the court during the time oral argument has been scheduled and until such time as it has been completed.

Failure to be available to receive the telephone call will be treated in the same manner as a failure to personally appear for scheduled oral argument. Counsel is responsible for notifying the court if the designated telephone number is changed.

3. At the conclusion of the teleconference oral argument, the matter is submitted or the court will issue further directives as necessary.

4. Retained counsel participating in a teleconference call shall receive a nominal billing from the court following oral argument to cover the cost of the teleconference call and the administrative time involved.

5. Any deviation by appointed or retained counsel from these procedures shall not be permitted except by express prior approval of the court.

Rule 4 adopted Nov. 15, 1993; renumbered from Rule 6 Aug. 25, 2003; amended Aug. 17, 2007.

Rule 5. Writ Petitions: Supporting Records and Stay Requests [Renumbered]

Rule 5 adopted Nov. 15, 1993; renumbered to Rule 3 Aug. 25, 2003.

Another Rule 5 follows.

Rule 5. Stipulation for Use of Original Superior Court File

The California Rules of Court authorize the use of the original superior court file in lieu of the clerk's transcript on appeal in those cases where the parties so stipulate. The procedure therein is approved for use by the superior courts within this district in all civil cases in which the trial court retains no continuing jurisdiction. The stipulation shall be in substantially the form of the following: Stipulation for Use of Original Superior Court File in Lieu of Clerk's Transcript.

Rule 5 adopted Oct. 16, 2006.

Rule 6.　The Teleconference Oral Argument Option [Renumbered]

Rule 6 adopted Nov. 15, 1993; renumbered to Rule 4 Aug. 25, 2003.

Local Court Form.　Appellate Court Writ Petition Information Sheet

By order dated November 23, 1982, all petitions for extraordinary writs, other than habeas corpus, shall be accompanied by a properly completed face sheet, the *Appellate Court Writ Petition Information Sheet*. This form is available from the clerk of the court, and also is available on the court Web site.

Local Court Form amended Aug. 25, 2003; amended Aug. 17, 2007.

INTERNAL OPERATING PRACTICES AND PROCEDURES FIFTH APPELLATE DISTRICT

(Adopted August 1993, revised February 2005, January 1, 2007)

I. INTRODUCTION
II. STRUCTURE OF COURT AND ORGANIZATION OF STAFF
III. PRACTICES AFFECTING THE DECISIONAL PROCESS
  A. Regular Appeals
  B. Routine Dispositions
  C. Writs
  D. Motions
  E. Petitions for Rehearing and Applications for Publication
  F. Settlement Conferences in Civil Cases.
IV. TELEPHONIC ORAL ARGUMENT OPTION
V. PRELIMINARY REVIEW OF APPELLANT'S OPENING BRIEF IN CIVIL CASES

I. INTRODUCTION

The purpose of this memorandum is to acquaint the bar and litigants with the general internal operating procedures of this court. It does not duplicate the California Rules of Court nor the statutes that govern the processes of the Courts of Appeal.

II. STRUCTURE OF COURT AND ORGANIZATION OF STAFF

The court is currently authorized ten judges — a presiding justice and nine associate justices.

The court is not divided into divisions and normally operates with three panels. The justices are rotated among the panels each month so that over time each justice will sit an equal number of times with every other justice on the court.

Each justice is authorized two staff attorneys. In addition, the court has a central staff consisting of experienced attorneys who write draft opinions in cases that are screened for routine disposition. The court also employs experienced writ and motion attorneys. The central staff and writ and motion attorneys work under the direction and supervision of the presiding justice.

III. PRACTICES AFFECTING THE DECISIONAL PROCESS

The workload of the court is divided into six principal categories: regular appeals (those not screened for routine disposition treatment); routine disposition appeals; writs; motions; petitions for rehearing and applications for publication; and settlement conferences in civil cases.

A. Regular Appeals.

When the appellant's reply brief has been filed or the time for filing that brief has passed, the case is ready for disposition by written opinion. The cases are placed on the ready list in the order in which they become ready and are set in that order absent a granted motion to advance or a statutory priority. Although the clerk attempts to note those cases that are entitled to statutory priority, counsel is advised to remind the court of any particular case that is entitled to priority.

When placed on the ready list, the managing attorney screens all cases under the supervision of the presiding justice. Those cases subject to routine disposition in accordance with the procedure described below are so designated on the list of ready cases. The balance of the cases are designated as regular appeals.

During the last two weeks of each month the managing attorney under the supervision of the presiding justice prepares a list of the cases to be set on the regular calendar in the third following month. For example, cases to be set in April are selected in the last two weeks of January. In order to equalize the workload among the justices, the managing attorney assigns a weight to all cases according to degree of difficulty. Consistent with the goal of achieving an equal caseload for each justice, and absent a compelling reason to the contrary, the cases are then assigned at random to the individual justices for authorship. The total weight of the cases assigned to each justice is approximately equal. Two other justices from the same panel are assigned to participate in deciding each case. The cases are then calendared for oral argument, and notices of the settings are sent to the attorneys of record. The court does not look with favor upon requests for continuance of the hearing date and will normally refuse to grant a continuance unless a request is received within five days of the time the notice is sent and good cause is shown for the continuance.

If oral argument is requested, counsel may utilize the telephonic oral argument option which is available in this court (Oral argument by telephone option — see Section IV, post.)

When a case is calendared for oral argument, one of the staff attorneys for the justice to whom the case is assigned prepares a memorandum of facts and law in that case. Memoranda in all cases are normally completed during the month following the setting. For example, memoranda for cases calendared for April are completed in February. When completed, the memorandum is distributed to the three justices assigned to decide the case. The authoring justice will normally prepare a proposed opinion in each case to be distributed to the other two justices assigned to that case prior to the pre-argument conference which is held shortly before the date set for oral argument. Each of the justices will have read the briefs, as much of the record as they deem necessary, the case memorandum and the proposed opinion, if any, prior to the pre-argument conference.

Well in advance of oral argument, each case is reviewed by the court to determine if the issues can be narrowed or if the court will accept waiver of oral argument. In the former case, the court may advise counsel by letter of the particular issues upon which the court would like to hear oral argument. In the latter case, the court will advise counsel by letter that it is willing to accept a waiver of oral argument.

As a result of the court's preparation for oral argument, the justices are thoroughly familiar with the facts and issues before oral argument commences. The court normally asks questions of counsel during oral argument in an effort to pinpoint those issues that are particularly troublesome, to clear up any areas of confusion or uncertainty, and to further narrow the issues. Occasionally, supplementary briefing is permitted or requested. Otherwise, cases are submitted for decision at the conclusion of oral argument. (See Cal. Rules of Court, rule 8.256(d).)

After argument, the participating justices hold a post-argument conference. Thereafter, the authoring justice circulates a draft opinion to the other justices on the panel for their concurrence or dissent. In the event a majority of the justices do not eventually concur in the opinion of the justice to whom the case was assigned for authorship, a non-concurring justice prepares the majority opinion.

Discussion as to whether an opinion qualifies for full or partial publication under California Rules of Court, rules 8.1105 or 8.1110, normally occurs at the pre and post-oral argument conferences, though the question remains open until the opinion becomes final.

If oral argument is waived, the case is ordered removed from the calendar and submitted for decision. The opinion may be filed any time thereafter. The decisional process is substantially the same as that outlined above except for the pre-oral argument conference.

B. Routine Dispositions.

A routine disposition is a case on appeal which raises no new or novel questions of law, is not of wide public interest, and can be disposed of by the application of settled principles of law to the facts. The draft opinion is written by an experienced attorney assigned to the central staff or by a justice.

The court is sensitive to the concern that the judicial input into this type of case may be diluted and therefore carefully supervises these cases. First, the presiding justice supervises the initial selection of the case for treatment as a routine disposition. Second, a panel of three justices is selected at random to participate on the case. Third, in each case a lead justice will read the briefs, the record

where indicated, and approve or disapprove the draft opinion in writing. If the lead justice approves the draft opinion either as written or with changes, the two other justices must read and approve the opinion in writing. Fourth, if any justice so requests, a conference will be held among the justices and the author of the draft opinion. If, after a conference, any justice is of the opinion the case is inappropriate for routine disposition treatment, its designation as a regular appeal is restored and the case is processed in accordance with the procedure for regular appeals.

Last, when a draft opinion is approved by the justices, counsel are sent a letter indicating the court is willing to accept waiver of oral argument. Counsel are free to request oral argument and, if requested, the case is then placed on the oral argument calendar. Oral argument is requested in only a small percentage of these cases.

Appointed counsel are advised that the court will consider the extent to which requested oral argument was a reasonable consideration by counsel and the extent to which such argument, if presented, adds to or enhances the arguments presented in the briefs in evaluating compensation claimed for preparation time and travel time. If oral argument is requested, counsel should consider utilizing the telephonic oral argument option, which is available in this court. (See Section IV, post.)

If oral argument is waived or if oral argument is requested, after argument and post-argument conference, the opinion as written or as modified may be filed either as a signed opinion or as an unsigned per curiam opinion. In the latter case, the participating justices' names appear at the bottom of the first page.

C. Writs.

The term "writs" as used here includes the traditional writs (mandamus, prohibition, certiorari, supersedeas, habeas corpus, error coram vobis), also writs of review, petitions in Workers' Compensation Appeals Board cases, Agricultural Labor Relations Board matters, Public Employment Relations Board, Alcoholic Beverage Control Board, and Public Utilities Commission cases.

The court has two writ panels of three justices each, the membership of which is rotated among all the justices from month to month. Writs are assigned to the panels so as to approximately equalize the workload. Writ conferences are held by each panel at least once per week, usually on Thursday mornings.

When a writ petition is filed, copies are distributed to the writ attorneys who, under the supervision of the presiding justice, assign them to the panels. A memorandum is prepared in each case by the writ attorney and delivered to each justice on the assigned panel prior to the writ conference. Emergency writs, usually involving a request for a stay of a proceeding in the trial court, are by necessity considered and disposed of as required by the particular circumstances, the constraints of time involved, and other court business. Other than issuance of a temporary stay order, writs will not be issued prior to the receipt of a response from parties who would be adversely affected or unless such parties inform the court that no response will be filed. A petition for a writ may be denied without a response being filed.

If it appears the matter is one in which relief may be appropriate but a peremptory grant would be inappropriate, an order to show cause or alternative writ is issued and the case may be calendared for oral argument. The case is then handled in accordance with the procedure for regular appeals.

Occasionally, if the issuance of a peremptory writ in the first instance has been prayed, and the facts are clear, and the case has been fully briefed and nothing would be added by oral argument, relief by way of peremptory writ may be granted without the issuance of an order to show cause or alternative writ. In these cases, a short opinion or a written order with reasons stated will be filed. Summary denials are more frequent, in which event, the law of the case doctrine does not apply. (See *Kowis v. Howard* (1992) 3 Cal.4th 888.)

California Rules of Court, rule 8.452 writ petitions taken from orders setting a hearing under Welfare and Institutions Code section 366.26 are handled on the writ calendar. Such cases, generated by the filing of a notice of intent to file a writ petition are distributed to a central staff attorney specializing in juvenile dependency law and rule 8.452 writ practice. The central staff attorney works under the supervision of the presiding justice and assigns such cases to panels on a rotating basis. Once the time passes under rule 8.452 for the filing of a response to such a writ petition, the central staff attorney prepares an Order to Show Cause setting the case for oral argument with the proviso that, in the event the parties do not advise this court of their desire to orally argue the case within seven days' time, the matter will be submitted. Thereafter, the central staff attorney prepares a memorandum, which in most cases addresses the merits of the writ petition, and delivers the memorandum to each justice on the assigned panel prior to the writ conference. The case is then handled in accordance with the procedure for routine dispositions.

Petitions for review of Agricultural Labor Relations Board decisions, of orders and awards of the Workers' Compensation Appeals Board, the Public Employment Relations Board, the Public Utilities Commission, and the Alcoholic Beverage Control Board, and review of decisions of appellate divisions of superior courts pursuant to California Rules of Court, rule 8.1002, are handled on the writ calendar. If a petition for review is granted, or the certification under rule 8.1005 is accepted, the case is set for oral argument after briefing is completed. The case is then disposed of in accordance with the procedure for handling regular appeals.

D. Motions.

Non-routine motions and applications, including applications for bail, are processed in accordance with the procedure for handling writs.

Applications in routine matters (see Cal. Rules of Court, rules 8.50, 8.57), including motions to augment or correct the record, requests for extensions of time, and disciplinary proceedings against attorneys and court reporters for failure to timely file briefs and records, are normally disposed of by the presiding justice with the assistance of a writ attorney.

E. Petitions for Rehearing and Applications for Publication.

Petitions for rehearing and applications for publication are assigned for disposition to the same panel members who participated in the initial opinion.

F. Settlement Conferences in Civil Cases.

Upon stipulation of all parties to a civil case pending in the court or on the presiding justice's own motion, a settlement conference will be calendared and held pursuant to California Rules of Court, rule 8.284. Notice of availability of a settlement conference is sent to counsel at the time the record on appeal is filed. For further details, see local rule 2 on settlement conferences in civil appeals, a copy of which will be furnished upon request.

IV. TELEPHONIC ORAL ARGUMENT OPTION

The court has in place a teleconferencing system that allows up to five attorneys in different offices to present their argument over the telephone in a single case. Attorneys selecting this option remains in their office until the clerk notifies them that their case has been called. The attorneys will then come on the line and are part of a telephone conference call. The system broadcasts the attorney's voice over the courtroom public address system as well as to other counsel appearing by telephone. The justices are convened in open court and speak into microphones which broadcast into court and through the telephone system. Counsel can hear each other and the court. The system allows one or more attorneys to appear in court and argue while other counsel listen and present their argument over the telephone. The argument is tape-recorded just as if all attorneys were present in court.

The teleconferencing option was implemented to accommodate counsel's time and to provide a significant cost savings to clients and the state by eliminating travel time and costs, as well as time spent waiting for a case to be called. Retained counsel selecting the telephonic oral argument receive a nominal billing from the court following the argument to cover the cost of the conference call and administrative time involved.

Details of the practices and procedures related to the telephonic oral argument option are available from the clerk upon request and may be found in the California Rules of Court, Local Rules of the Courts of Appeal.

V. PRELIMINARY REVIEW OF APPELLANT'S OPENING BRIEF IN CIVIL CASES

The court presumes that briefs filed by counsel will comply with applicable standards. (See Cal. Rules of Court, rule 8.204 [Contents and form of briefs]). Unfortunately, many briefs do not. This adds to the court's workload and delays resolution of appeals.

Therefore, in civil appeals in this court:

(1.) After appellant's opening brief is filed, the managing attorney reviews the brief for basic compliance with pertinent rules, statutes, and case law. The review is non-substantive; the court does not engage in advocacy for the parties.

(2.) Should the brief fail to comply with minimum standards, the court may strike or return the brief and give counsel the opportunity to file an adequate brief within a specified time.

(3.) Should a subsequent brief continue to fail minimum standards, the court may dismiss the appeal without further notice. (*In re S.C.* (2006) 138 Cal.App. 4th 396, 406-407.)

The same standards apply to briefs filed by pro se appellants. A party proceeding inpropria persona is treated like any other party and is entitled to the same, but no greater consideration than other litigants and attorneys. A propria persona litigant is held to the same rules of procedure as an attorney. (*First American Title Co. v. Mirzaian* (2003) 108 Cal.App.4th 956, 958, fn. 1.)

(Amended Jan. 1, 2007.)

SIXTH APPELLATE DISTRICT LOCAL RULES

Rule 1.   Location of Court Hearings
[Repealed]
Rule 1 adopted Aug. 16, 1985; repealed Dec. 20, 2006.

INTERNAL OPERATING PRACTICES AND PROCEDURES SIXTH APPELLATE DISTRICT

(Revised effective January 1, 2008)

INTRODUCTION
I. STRUCTURE OF THE COURT AND ORGANIZATION OF STAFF
A. JUSTICES
B. PRESIDING JUSTICE
C. CLERK/ADMINISTRATOR
D. RESEARCH ATTORNEYS
E. LAW LIBRARIAN
F. JUDICIAL ASSISTANTS TO APPELLATE COURT JUSTICES
II. PROCESSING APPEALS
A. In General
B. Preparation and Filing of Opinions
C. Rehearings
D. Original and Discretionary Proceedings
E. Communications with Counsel or Parties
F. Settlement

INTRODUCTION

The purpose of this document is to acquaint the bar and interested members of the public with the general operating practices of the Court of Appeal, Sixth Appellate District.

The internal procedures of the Court of Appeal are largely governed by the California Constitution, statutes, and the appellate rules adopted by the Judicial Council. The Court of Appeal may adopt and publish its own rules that do not conflict with a statute or rule adopted by the Judicial Council.

I. STRUCTURE OF THE COURT AND ORGANIZATION OF STAFF

A. JUSTICES

The court has seven authorized judicial positions, consisting of a presiding justice and six associate justices.

The Chief Justice, as Chairperson of the Judicial Council, may assign a retired justice or judge, or an active trial court judge to serve temporarily on a Court of Appeal. Justices pro tem may be assigned (1) when there is a judicial vacancy, or (2) when a Court of Appeal justice is absent or unable to serve, or is disqualified in a given case, or (3) when the court needs assistance in reducing a backlog of cases.

Justices sit in panels of three that change periodically.

The courtroom and office of the clerk of the court are located in the Comerica Bank building at 333 West Santa Clara Street, Suite 1060, San Jose, California 95113.

B. PRESIDING JUSTICE

The presiding justice convenes conferences and presides at hearings (oral argument) when he or she is a member of the three-justice panel assigned to hear a case. The presiding justice has specific authority under rule 10.1012 of the California Rules of Court to grant or deny applications and to extend time for filing of records and briefs on appeal. The rule also gives the presiding justice limited authority to dismiss an appeal for noncompliance with the Rules of Court and to grant relief from default. The presiding justice also has overall responsibility for the calendaring of cases, the management of the caseload within the district, and the scheduling of oral arguments.

If the presiding justice is absent or disqualified, or not a member of the three-justice panel that is to decide a matter, the presiding justice designates the senior associate justice to serve as acting presiding justice.

C. CLERK/ADMINISTRATOR

The Clerk/Administrator is responsible for maintaining the court's public records and files and for advising litigants, counsel, and the public of the status of matters before the court.

Appointed by the court, the clerk assists in the preparation of the court's calendar, dockets its cases, and supervises other administrative functions required for the court's operation. The clerk is aided by an assistant clerk/administrator, six deputy clerks and a support staff.

D. RESEARCH ATTORNEYS

1. Attorneys Assigned to Justices
Each justice is currently authorized to employ two permanent research attorneys.

Research attorneys employed by or assigned to a justice work primarily on appeals assigned to the justice. The attorney's work involves legal research, examination of the trial court record, conferring with the justices assigned to the case, and preparing written memoranda and draft opinions.

2. Writ Attorneys

The court is currently authorized to employ two writ attorneys who assist the court in reviewing petitions for various writs, such as mandate, prohibition, certiorari or review, habeas corpus, and error coram vobis.

3. Central Staff

In addition to the writ attorneys and research attorneys assigned to justices, the court employs a staff of several senior research attorneys. This staff is known as the "central staff" because it provides research and analysis assistance for the justices of the court. Central staff attorneys are assigned to individual justices by the court and provide the same research and assistance required of the justices' permanent research staff.

4. Externs

The Sixth Appellate District cooperates with law schools in enabling law students to earn academic credits by working one semester, without pay, performing research for individual justices. These law students are selected and supervised by individual justices.

E. LAW LIBRARIAN

The court's law library collection of approximately 25,000 volumes is maintained by a professional Law Librarian. The collection includes the latest technological developments in legal research such as: a wide variety of CD-ROM's on the Local Area Network (LAN); access to various online research services including the Internet; and a selection of microforms, audio tapes and video tapes, in addition to the books. The Law Librarian is also responsible for keeping current on technology and legal trends, which affords the court staff the opportunity to do efficient and effective research on all issues before the court.

F. JUDICIAL ASSISTANTS TO APPELLATE COURT JUSTICES

Each justice is authorized to employ one judicial assistant who is responsible for the timely processing of the justice's opinions, including circulating draft opinions for review by other members of the panel, typing judicial correspondence, cite-checking and shepardizing draft opinions, and delivering opinions to the clerk for filing. The court employs other secretarial support staff as needed.

II. PROCESSING APPEALS

A. In General

When a criminal or civil appeal is fully briefed, it is identified on a computer-generated list indicating the case is ready for analysis and decision. The appeals are considered by the court after they are fully briefed. Decisions may be made and the opinions filed in a different order depending on factors such as the complexity of the litigation and whether oral argument is requested. The California Constitution requires the filing of a written opinion in every appeal.

1. Assignment of Cases

Assignment of cases to individual justices is generally made by rotation from the list of ready cases. The justice assigned to a particular case then has lead or primary responsibility for that case in the course of conference discussions, research and preparation of the opinion.

2. Preliminary Case Conferences

In the course of preparing an opinion, conferences are held at the request of the author or other panel members. In difficult or complex cases, more than one conference may be held. Conferences are generally not held in cases involving routine issues.

3. Oral Argument

When a case is ready for possible argument, the clerk will write and ask the parties whether they desire to exercise their right to appear personally for oral argument or to argue by teleconference. [The Sixth District Court of Appeal Teleconferencing Oral Argument Procedures Manual is available from the clerk's office upon request.] If oral argument is requested, the case is placed on an oral argument calendar.

After the case is scheduled for oral argument, any party or counsel for a party may contact the clerk's office and be informed of the names of the justices assigned to the case.

The order in which cases are to be argued is determined by the presiding justice. Because of the considerable investment of court time and resources necessary to prepare a case for oral argument, continuances are disfavored and will be granted only on a showing of good cause. Oral argument will not be continued by stipulation of counsel absent a showing of good cause. If no appearance is made, the case may be ordered submitted.

The order and the time allotted for counsel to make their presentations are specified in rule 8.256 of the California Rules of Court.

In most instances, the presiding justice will inform counsel at the beginning of each session that the court has reviewed the briefs and is familiar with the facts and issues. The court requests that counsel not merely reiterate the argument contained in his or her brief. Oral argument is generally most helpful and effective when reasonably brief and when counsel focuses on the decisive issues, succinctly clarifies the facts as they relate to a given issue, or clarifies the holding or reasoning of potentially applicable or controlling authority.

The court disfavors the submission of untimely citations of authority as it deprives the court and opposing counsel of sufficient opportunity to prepare for oral argument. The court retains discretion to strike or disregard such citations.

When oral argument has concluded in a given case, the justice presiding will declare the cause submitted, unless submission has been deferred for additional briefing.

4. Post-Oral Argument Conference

A post-oral argument conference is held in which the justices again discuss the case and finally determine the decision to be reached.

B. Preparation and Filing of Opinions

1. Signed Opinions

Unless the two other participating justices disagree with the disposition proposed by the assigned author, the justice assigned will prepare the majority opinion. When a proposed majority opinion has been drafted, it is circulated to the other participating justices. They indicate approval, disapproval, or proposed changes. Differences of opinion as to the language of the opinion or the ultimate disposition of the case may be taken up in conference. The opinion may then be modified in a manner acceptable to the justices. If two justices agree, a written opinion is filed.

2. Concurring or Dissenting Opinions

Where a difference of opinion exists among the justices participating in a case, a justice who agrees with the result reached but not with the reasoning of the majority may write a separate concurring opinion, or may merely indicate concurrence only in the judgment reached by the majority. Likewise, a justice who disagrees with the result reached by the majority may write a dissenting opinion. Each panel member has a full opportunity to consider the views of associates prior to the completion and filing of the opinion.

3. Publication of Opinions

A decision of the court is not published in the official reports unless it is certified for publication by a majority of the participating justices. The criteria for publication and publication requests are set forth in rules 8.1105 and 8.1120, respectively, of the California Rules of Court.

C. Rehearings

The procedure for filing a petition for rehearing is governed by rule 8.268 of the California Rules of Court. When a petition for rehearing is filed, the petition is routed to the justice who authored the opinion with copies to the participating justices. The authoring justice reviews the petition, and then indicates whether he or she votes to grant or deny the petition. The petition, along with any staff memorandum, is then circulated to the other two justices on the panel for their decisions. Two votes are necessary to grant or deny a petition for rehearing.

D. Original and Discretionary Proceedings

Petitions for writ of mandate, prohibition, certiorari, and habeas corpus, statutory review petitions, other miscellaneous applications to the original jurisdiction of the court, and applications for supersedeas or other relief pending appeal under Code of Civil Procedure section 923 or other statutory provisions are normally handled independently of the court's appellate caseload.

In original proceedings the court expects counsel to comply with the provisions of rule 8.490 of the California Rules of Court and all applicable time limitations, to explain any substantial delay in seeking relief in matters to which specific time limits do not apply, and to lodge with the court (and serve on adverse parties) a properly organized and indexed record sufficient to permit informed review. Any request for a stay of proceedings must be clearly labeled as such (Cal. Rules of Court, rule 8.116), and circumstances that require expedited consid-

eration should be clearly identified in the petition or application and noted on its cover. Counsel should advise the clerk of the next trial court date at the time the petition or application is filed.

Parties to statutory writ review proceedings should comply with applicable briefing schedules (for example, Cal. Rules of Court, rules 8.494(b), 8.498(c)). The court will strictly apply those schedules, absent a timely application for exception supported by a showing of good cause.

In habeas corpus matters, the court in appropriate cases will request an informal response and provide for a reply to the response under rule 8.380(c) of the California Rules of Court.

In other original proceedings it is the court's policy not to grant affirmative relief (beyond a temporary stay) without first giving adverse parties an opportunity to submit a memorandum of points and authorities in opposition. Opposition need not be submitted in these matters unless expressly requested by the court. If requested, opposition must be submitted on or before the date stated in the request, unless an extension is obtained before that date.

Original proceedings are referred to the writ attorney for initial review. The writ attorney thereafter communicates with the court concerning the matter. The court will conduct a writ conference and meet specially when necessary. All written submissions by any party, and any written staff memoranda, are distributed to and reviewed by all participating justices.

If affirmative relief is to be granted, the Sixth District will issue an alternative writ of mandate or prohibition, which directs the relief prayed for in the petition or, in the alternative, that the respondent appear and show cause why the relief should not be granted. An order to show cause may be issued without the alternative writ. In limited circumstances, the court may issue a peremptory writ in the first instance without allowing oral argument.

Counsel seeking writ relief should carefully review the "Sixth District Court of Appeal Outline on Original Proceedings and Relief Ancillary to Appeal," which is available on request from the clerk's office or available for download in .pdf or .doc format [1].

E. Communications with Counsel or Parties

Except in oral argument, the justices do not communicate directly with counsel or parties concerning pending cases. Any necessary communications are handled by the clerk.

Attorneys employed by the court do not communicate with counsel or parties concerning pending cases.

F. Settlement

The parties must immediately notify the court of the settlement of any pending case (Cal. Rules of Court, rule 8.244).

Upon the request of all parties to a pending case, the court will schedule and conduct a settlement conference. The conference will be conducted before a justice of the court or an assigned judge. The settlement conference must be attended by the parties unless counsel or another authorized representative in attendance have full authority to settle.

No justice conducting a settlement conference will participate in deciding the case or discuss the case with any justice deciding the case if the case is not settled.

(Amended Jan. 1, 2007; Jan. 1, 2008.)

IOPPs.   2008 Deletes. [1] from the court's website

CALIFORNIA RULES OF PROFESSIONAL CONDUCT

2009 EDITION

Rules of Professional Conduct adopted by the Board of Governors of the State Bar and approved by the Supreme Court operative May 27, 1989.

Rules of Professional Conduct promulgated by the Board of Governors of the State Bar and approved by the Supreme Court with amendments current through November 15, 2008.

Table Showing Changes Promulgated by The State Bar of California
From November 1, 2007 Through November 15, 2008

Rule	Effect	Date
1-110	Amended	July 11, 2008
1-311(a)(2)	Amended	July 11, 2008
1-311 Discussion	Amended	July 11, 2008

Rules of Conduct

CONTENTS

CONTENTS

Table of Contents

CALIFORNIA RULES OF PROFESSIONAL CONDUCT

[References are to Judicial Council of California Civil Jury Instructions (Matthew Bender, Official Publisher).]

CHAPTER 1
PROFESSIONAL INTEGRITY IN GENERAL

Rule 1-100. Rules of Professional Conduct, in General.

(A) Purpose and Function.

The following rules are intended to regulate professional conduct of members of the State Bar through discipline. They have been adopted by the Board of Governors of the State Bar of California and approved by the Supreme Court of California pursuant to Business and Professions Code sections 6076 and 6077 to protect the public and to promote respect and confidence in the legal profession. These rules together with any standards adopted by the Board of Governors pursuant to these rules shall be binding upon all members of the State Bar.

For a willful breach of any of these rules, the Board of Governors has the power to discipline members as provided by law.

The prohibition of certain conduct in these rules is not exclusive. Members are also bound by applicable law including the State Bar Act (Bus. & Prof. Code, §6000 et seq.) and opinions of California courts. Although not binding, opinions of ethics committees in California should be consulted by members for guidance on proper professional conduct. Ethics opinions and rules and standards promulgated by other jurisdictions and bar associations may also be considered.

These rules are not intended to create new civil causes of action. Nothing in these rules shall be deemed to create, augment, diminish, or eliminate any substantive legal duty of lawyers or the non-disciplinary consequences of violating such a duty.

(B) Definitions.

(1) "Law Firm" means:

(a) two or more lawyers whose activities constitute the practice of law, and who share its profits, expenses, and liabilities; or

(b) a law corporation which employs more than one lawyer; or

(c) a division, department, office, or group within a business entity, which includes more than one lawyer who performs legal services for the business entity; or

(d) a publicly funded entity which employs more than one lawyer to perform legal services.

(2) "Member" means a member of the State Bar of California.

(3) "Lawyer" means a member of the State Bar of California or a person who is admitted in good standing of and eligible to practice before the bar of any United States court or the highest court of the District of Columbia or any state, territory, or insular possession of the United States, or is licensed to practice law in, or is admitted in good standing and eligible to practice before the bar of the highest court of, a foreign country or any political subdivision thereof.

(4) "Associate" means an employee or fellow employee who is employed as a lawyer.

(5) "Shareholder" means a shareholder in a professional corporation pursuant to Business and Professions Code section 6160 et seq.

(C) Purpose of Discussions.

Because it is a practical impossibility to convey in black letter form all of the nuances of these disciplinary rules, the comments contained in the Discussions of the rules, while they do not add independent basis for imposing discipline, are intended to provide guidance for interpreting the rules and practicing in compliance with them.

(D) Geographic Scope of Rules.

(1) As to members:

These rules shall govern the activities of members in and outside this state, except as members lawfully practicing outside this state may be specifically required by a jurisdiction in which they are practicing to follow rules of professional conduct different from these rules.

(2) As to lawyers from other jurisdictions who are not members:

These rules shall also govern the activities of lawyers while engaged in the performance of lawyer functions in this state; but nothing contained in these rules shall be deemed to authorize the performance of such functions by such persons in this state except as otherwise permitted by law.

(E) These rules may be cited and referred to as "Rules of Professional Conduct of the State Bar of California."

Discussion:

The Rules of Professional Conduct are intended to establish the standards for members for purposes of discipline. (See *Ames v. State Bar* (1973) 8 Cal.3d 910 [106 Cal.Rptr. 489].) The fact that a member has engaged in conduct that may be contrary to these rules does not automatically give rise to a civil cause of action. (See *Noble v. Sears, Roebuck & Co.* (1973) 33 Cal.App.3d 654 [109 Cal.Rptr. 269]; *Wilhelm v. Pray, Price, Williams & Russell* (1986) 186 Cal.App.3d 1324 [231 Cal.Rptr. 355].) These rules are not intended to supercede existing law relating to members in non-disciplinary contexts. (See, e.g., *Klemm v. Superior Court* (1977) 75 Cal.App.3d 893 [142 Cal.Rptr. 509] (motion for disqualification of counsel due to a conflict of interest); *Academy of California Optometrists, Inc. v. Superior Court* (1975) 51 Cal.App.3d 999 [124 Cal.Rptr. 668] (duty to return client files); *Chronometrics, Inc. v. Sysgen, Inc.* (1980) 110 Cal.App.3d 597 [168 Cal.Rptr. 196] (disqualification of member appropriate remedy for improper communication with adverse party).)

Law firm, as defined by subparagraph (B)(1), is not intended to include an association of lawyers who do not share profits, expenses, and liabilities. The subparagraph is not intended to imply that a law firm may include a person who is not a member in violation of the law governing the unauthorized practice of law.

Adopted Nov. 28, 1988, eff. May 27, 1989; amended eff. Sept. 14, 1992.

Rule 1-110.   Disciplinary Authority of the State Bar.

A member shall comply with conditions attached to public or private reprovals or other discipline administered by the State Bar pursuant to Business and Professions Code sections 6077 and 6078 and rule [1] **9.19**, California Rules of Court.

Adopted Nov. 28, 1988, eff. May 27, 1989; amended by order of the Supreme Court, operative July 11, 2008.

Rule 1.110.   2008 Deletes. [1] 956

Rule 1-120.   Assisting, Soliciting, or Inducing Violations.

A member shall not knowingly assist in, solicit, or induce any violation of these rules or the State Bar Act.

Adopted Nov. 28, 1988, eff. May 27, 1989.

Rule 1-200.   False Statement Regarding Admission to the State Bar.

(A) A member shall not knowingly make a false statement regarding a material fact or knowingly fail to disclose a material fact in connection with an application for admission to the State Bar.

(B) A member shall not further an application for admission to the State Bar of a person whom the member knows to be unqualified in respect to character, education, or other relevant attributes.

(C) This rule shall not prevent a member from serving as counsel of record for an applicant for admission to practice in proceedings related to such admission.

Discussion:

For purposes of rule 1-200 "admission" includes readmission.

Adopted Nov. 28, 1988, eff. May 27, 1989.

Rule 1-300.   Unauthorized Practice of Law.

(A) A member shall not aid any person or entity in the unauthorized practice of law.

(B) A member shall not practice law in a jurisdiction where to do so would be in violation of regulations of the profession in that jurisdiction.

Adopted Nov. 28, 1988, eff. May 27, 1989.

Rule 1-310.   Forming a Partnership With a Non-Lawyer.

A member shall not form a partnership with a person who is not a lawyer if any of the activities of that partnership consist of the practice of law.

Discussion:

Rule 1-310 is not intended to govern members' activities which cannot be considered to constitute the practice of law. It is intended solely to preclude a member from being involved in the practice of law with a person who is not a lawyer.

Adopted Nov. 28, 1988, eff. May 27, 1989; amended eff. Sept. 14, 1992.

Rule 1-311.   Employment of Disbarred, Suspended, Resigned, or Involuntarily Inactive Member.

(A) For purposes of this rule:

(1) "Employ" means to engage the services of another, including employees, agents, independent contractors and consultants, regardless of whether any compensation is paid;

(2) "Involuntarily inactive member" means a member who is ineligible to practice law as a result of action taken pursuant to Business and Professions Code sections 6007, 6203(c), or California Rule of Court [1] **9.31**; and

(3) "Resigned member" means a member who has resigned from the State Bar while disciplinary charges are pending.

(B) A member shall not employ, associate professionally with, or aid a person the member knows or reasonably should know is a disbarred, suspended, resigned, or involuntarily inactive member to perform the following on behalf of the member's client:

(1) Render legal consultation or advice to the client;

(2) Appear on behalf of a client in any hearing or proceeding or before any judicial officer, arbitrator, mediator, court, public agency, referee, magistrate, commissioner, or hearing officer;

(3) Appear as a representative of the client at a deposition or other discovery matter;

(4) Negotiate or transact any matter for or on behalf of the client with third parties;

(5) Receive, disburse or otherwise handle the client's funds; or

(6) Engage in activities which constitute the practice of law.

(C) A member may employ, associate professionally with, or aid a disbarred, suspended, resigned, or involuntarily inactive member to perform research, drafting or clerical activities, including but not limited to:

(1)   Legal work of a preparatory nature, such as legal research, the assemblage of data and other necessary information, drafting of pleadings, briefs, and other similar documents;

(2)   Direct communication with the client or third parties regarding matters such as scheduling, billing, updates, confirmation of receipt or sending of correspondence and messages; or

(3)   Accompanying an active member in attending a deposition or other discovery matter for the limited purpose of providing clerical assistance to the active member who will appear as the representative of the client.

(D)   Prior to or at the time of employing a person the member knows or reasonably should know is a disbarred, suspended, resigned, or involuntarily inactive member, the member shall serve upon the State Bar written notice of the employment, including a full description of such person's current bar status. The written notice shall also list the activities prohibited in paragraph (B) and state that the disbarred, suspended, resigned, or involuntarily inactive member will not perform such activities. The member shall serve similar written notice upon each client on whose specific matter such person will work, prior to or at the time of employing such person to work on the client's specific matter. The member shall obtain proof of service of the client's written notice and shall retain such proof and a true and correct copy of the client's written notice for two years following termination of the member's employment with the client.

(E)   A member may, without client or State Bar notification, employ a disbarred, suspended, resigned, or involuntarily inactive member whose sole function is to perform office physical plant or equipment maintenance, courier or delivery services, catering, reception, typing or transcription, or other similar support activities.

(F)   Upon termination of the disbarred, suspended, resigned, or involuntarily inactive member, the member shall promptly serve upon the State Bar written notice of the termination.

Adopted July 11, 1996, eff. Aug. 1, 1996; amended by order of the Supreme Court, operative July 11, 2008.

Rule 1.311.   2008 Deletes. [1] 958(d)

Discussion:

For discussion of the activities that constitute the practice of law, see *Farnham v. State Bar* (1976) 17 Cal.3d 605 [131 Cal.Rptr. 611]; *Bluestein v. State Bar* (1974) 13 Cal.3d 162 [118 Cal.Rptr. 175]; *Baron v. City of Los Angeles* (1970) 2 Cal.3d 535 [86 Cal.Rptr. 673]; *Crawford v. State Bar* (1960) 54 Cal.2d 659 [7 Cal.Rptr. 746]; *People v. Merchants Protective Corporation* (1922) 189 Cal. 531, 535 [209 P. 363]; *People v. Landlords Professional Services* (1989) 215 Cal.App.3d 1599 [264 Cal.Rptr. 548]; and *People v. Sipper* (1943) 61 Cal.App.2d Supp. 844 [142 P.2d 960].

Paragraph (D) is not intended to prevent or discourage a member from fully discussing with the client the activities that will be performed by the disbarred, suspended, resigned, or involuntarily inactive member on the client's matter. If a member's client is an organization, then the written notice required by paragraph (D) shall be served upon the highest authorized officer, employee, or constituent overseeing the particular engagement. (See rule 3-600.)

Nothing in rule 1-311 shall be deemed to limit or preclude any activity engaged in pursuant to rules [1] **9.40, 9.41, 9.42, and 9.44**

of the California Rules of Court, or any local rule of a federal district court concerning admission pro hac vice.

Adopted July 11, 1996, eff. Aug. 1, 1996; amended by order of the Supreme Court, operative July 11, 2008.

Rule 1-311 Discussion.   2008 Deletes. [1] 983, 983.1, 983.2, and 988

Rule 1-320.   Financial Arrangements With Non-Lawyers.

(A)   Neither a member nor a law firm shall directly or indirectly share legal fees with a person who is not a lawyer, except that:

(1)   An agreement between a member and a law firm, partner, or associate may provide for the payment of money after the member's death to the member's estate or to one or more specified persons over a reasonable period of time; or

(2)   A member or law firm undertaking to complete unfinished legal business of a deceased member may pay to the estate of the deceased member or other person legally entitled thereto that proportion of the total compensation which fairly represents the services rendered by the deceased member; or

(3)   A member or law firm may include non-member employees in a compensation, profit-sharing, or retirement plan even though the plan is based in whole or in part on a profit-sharing arrangement, if such plan does not circumvent these rules or Business and Professions Code section 6000 et seq.; or

(4)   A member may pay a prescribed registration, referral, or participation fee to a lawyer referral service established, sponsored, and operated in accordance with the State Bar of California's Minimum Standards for a Lawyer Referral Service in California.

(B)   A member shall not compensate, give, or promise anything of value to any person or entity for the purpose of recommending or securing employment of the member or the member's law firm by a client, or as a reward for having made a recommendation resulting in employment of the member or the member's law firm by a client. A member's offering of or giving a gift or gratuity to any person or entity having made a recommendation resulting in the employment of the member or the member's law firm shall not of itself violate this rule, provided that the gift or gratuity was not offered or given in consideration of any promise, agreement, or understanding that such a gift or gratuity would be forthcoming or that referrals would be made or encouraged in the future.

(C)   A member shall not compensate, give, or promise anything of value to any representative of the press, radio, television, or other communication medium in anticipation of or in return for publicity of the member, the law firm, or any other member as such in a news item, but the incidental provision of food or beverage shall not of itself violate this rule.

Discussion:

Rule 1-320(C) is not intended to preclude compensation to the communications media in exchange for advertising the member's or law firm's availability for professional employment.

Adopted Nov. 28, 1988, eff. May 27, 1989; amended eff. Sept. 14, 1992.

Rule 1-400. Advertising and Solicitation.

(A) For purposes of this rule, "communication" means any message or offer made by or on behalf of a member concerning the availability for professional employment of a member or a law firm directed to any former, present, or prospective client, including but not limited to the following:

(1) Any use of firm name, trade name, fictitious name, or other professional designation of such member or law firm; or

(2) Any stationery, letterhead, business card, sign, brochure, or other comparable written material describing such member, law firm, or lawyers; or

(3) Any advertisement (regardless of medium) of such member or law firm directed to the general public or any substantial portion thereof; or

(4) Any unsolicited correspondence from a member or law firm directed to any person or entity.

(B) For purposes of this rule, a "solicitation" means any communication:

(1) Concerning the availability for professional employment of a member or a law firm in which a significant motive is pecuniary gain; and

(2) Which is;

(a) delivered in person or by telephone, or

(b) directed by any means to a person known to the sender to be represented by counsel in a matter which is a subject of the communication.

(C) A solicitation shall not be made by or on behalf of a member or law firm to a prospective client with whom the member or law firm has no family or prior professional relationship, unless the solicitation is protected from abridgment by the Constitution of the United States or by the Constitution of the State of California. A solicitation to a former or present client in the discharge of a member's or law firm's professional duties is not prohibited.

(D) A communication or a solicitation (as defined herein) shall not:

(1) Contain any untrue statement; or

(2) Contain any matter, or present or arrange any matter in a manner or format which is false, deceptive, or which tends to confuse, deceive, or mislead the public; or

(3) Omit to state any fact necessary to make the statements made, in the light of circumstances under which they are made, not misleading to the public; or

(4) Fail to indicate clearly, expressly, or by context, that it is a communication or solicitation, as the case may be; or

(5) Be transmitted in any manner which involves intrusion, coercion, duress, compulsion, intimidation, threats, or vexatious or harassing conduct.

(6) State that a member is a "certified specialist" unless the member holds a current certificate as a specialist issued by the Board of Legal Specialization, or any other entity accredited by the State Bar to designate specialists pursuant to standards adopted by the Board of Governors, and states the complete name of the entity which granted certification.

(E) The Board of Governors of the State Bar shall formulate and adopt standards as to communications which will be presumed to violate this rule 1-400. The standards shall only be used as presumptions affecting the burden of proof in disciplinary proceedings involving alleged violations of these rules. "Presumption affecting the burden of proof" means that presumption defined in Evidence Code sections 605 and 606. Such standards formulated and adopted by the Board, as from time to time amended, shall be effective and binding on all members.

(F) A member shall retain for two years a true and correct copy or recording of any communication made by written or electronic media. Upon written request, the member shall make any such copy or recording available to the State Bar, and, if requested, shall provide to the State Bar evidence to support any factual or objective claim contained in the communication.

Standards:

Pursuant to rule 1-400(E) the Board of Governors of the State Bar has adopted the following standards, effective May 27, 1989, unless noted otherwise, as forms of "communication" defined in rule 1-400(A) which are presumed to be in violation of rule 1-400:

(1) A "communication" which contains guarantees, warranties, or predictions regarding the result of the representation.

(2) A "communication" which contains testimonials about or endorsements of a member unless such communication also contains an express disclaimer such as "this testimonial or endorsement does not constitute a guarantee, warranty, or prediction regarding the outcome of your legal matter."

(3) A "communication" which is delivered to a potential client whom the member knows or should reasonably know is in such a physical, emotional, or mental state that he or she would not be expected to exercise reasonable judgment as to the retention of counsel.

(4) A "communication" which is transmitted at the scene of an accident or at or en route to a hospital, emergency care center, or other health care facility.

(5) A "communication," except professional announcements, seeking professional employment for pecuniary gain, which is transmitted by mail or equivalent means which does not bear the word "Advertisement," "Newsletter" or words of similar import in 12 point print on the first page. If such communication, including firm brochures, newsletters, recent legal development advisories, and similar materials, is transmitted in an envelope, the envelope shall bear the word "Advertisement," "Newsletter" or words of similar import on the outside thereof.

(6) A "communication" in the form of a firm name, trade name, fictitious name, or other professional designation which states or implies a relationship between any member in private practice and a government agency or instrumentality or a public or non-profit legal services organization.

(7) A "communication" in the form of a firm name, trade name, fictitious name, or other professional designation which states or implies that a member has a relationship to any other lawyer or a law firm as a partner or associate, or officer or shareholder pursuant to Business and Professions Code sections 6160–6172 unless such relationship in fact exists.

(8) A "communication" which states or implies that a member or law firm is "of counsel" to another lawyer or a law firm unless the former has a relationship with the latter (other than as a partner or associate, or officer or shareholder pursuant to Business and Professions Code sections 6160–6172) which is close, personal, continuous, and regular.

(9) A "communication" in the form of a firm name, trade name, fictitious name, or other professional designation used by a member or law firm in private practice which differs materially

from any other such designation used by such member or law firm at the same time in the same community.

(10) A "communication" which implies that the member or law firm is participating in a lawyer referral service which has been certified by the State Bar of California or as having satisfied the Minimum Standards for Lawyer Referral Services in California, when that is not the case.

(11) [Repealed, effective June 1, 1997.]

(12) A "communication," except professional announcements, in the form of an advertisement primarily directed to seeking professional employment primarily for pecuniary gain transmitted to the general public or any substantial portion thereof by mail or equivalent means or by means of television, radio, newspaper, magazine or other form of commercial mass media which does not state the name of the member responsible for the communication. When the communication is made on behalf of a law firm, the communication shall state the name of at least one member responsible for it.

(13) A "communication" which contains a dramatization unless such communication contains a disclaimer which states "this is a dramatization" or words of similar import.

(14) A "communication" which states or implies "no fee without recovery" unless such communication also expressly discloses whether or not the client will be liable for costs.

(15) A "communication" which states or implies that a member is able to provide legal services in a language other than English unless the member can actually provide legal services in such language or the communication also states in the language of the communication (a) the employment title of the person who speaks such language and (b) that the person is not a member of the State Bar of California, if that is the case.

(16) An unsolicited "communication" transmitted to the general public or any substantial portion thereof primarily directed to seeking professional employment primarily for pecuniary gain which sets forth a specific fee or range of fees for a particular service where, in fact, the member charges a greater fee than advertised in such communication within a period of 90 days following dissemination of such communication, unless such communication expressly specifies a shorter period of time regarding the advertised fee. Where the communication is published in the classified or "yellow pages" section of telephone, business or legal directories or in other media not published more frequently than once a year, the member shall conform to the advertised fee for a period of one year from initial publication, unless such communication expressly specifies a shorter period of time regarding the advertised fee.

Adopted Nov. 28, 1988, eff. May 27, 1989; amended eff. Sept. 14, 1992, Oct. 29, 1992, April 9, 1994, June 1, 1997.

Rule 1-500. Agreements Restricting a Member's Practice.

(A) A member shall not be a party to or participate in offering or making an agreement, whether in connection with the settlement of a lawsuit or otherwise, if the agreement restricts the right of a member to practice law, except that this rule shall not prohibit such an agreement which:

(1) Is a part of an employment, shareholders', or partnership agreement among members provided the restrictive agreement does not survive the termination of the employment, shareholder, or partnership relationship; or

(2) Requires payments to a member upon the member's retirement from the practice of law; or

(3) Is authorized by Business and Professions Code sections 6092.5 subdivision (i), or 6093.

(B) A member shall not be a party to or participate in offering or making an agreement which precludes the reporting of a violation of these rules.

Discussion:

Paragraph (A) makes it clear that the practice, in connection with settlement agreements, of proposing that a member refrain from representing other clients in similar litigation, is prohibited. Neither counsel may demand or suggest such provisions nor may opposing counsel accede or agree to such provisions.

Paragraph (A) permits a restrictive covenant in a law corporation, partnership, or employment agreement. The law corporation shareholder, partner, or associate may agree not to have a separate practice during the existence of the relationship; however, upon termination of the relationship (whether voluntary or involuntary), the member is free to practice law without any contractual restriction except in the case of retirement from the active practice of law.

Adopted Nov. 28, 1988, eff. May 27, 1989; amended eff. Sept. 14, 1992.

Rule 1-600. Legal Service Programs.

(A) A member shall not participate in a nongovernmental program, activity, or organization furnishing, recommending, or paying for legal services, which allows any third person or organization to interfere with the member's independence of professional judgment, or with the client-lawyer relationship, or allows unlicensed persons to practice law, or allows any third person or organization to receive directly or indirectly any part of the consideration paid to the member except as permitted by these rules, or otherwise violates the State Bar Act or these rules.

(B) The Board of Governors of the State Bar shall formulate and adopt Minimum Standards for Lawyer Referral Services, which, as from time to time amended, shall be binding on members.

Discussion:

The participation of a member in a lawyer referral service established, sponsored, supervised, and operated in conformity with the Minimum Standards for a Lawyer Referral Service in California is encouraged and is not, of itself, a violation of these rules.

Rule 1-600 is not intended to override any contractual agreement or relationship between insurers and insureds regarding the provision of legal services.

Rule 1-600 is not intended to apply to the activities of a public agency responsible for providing legal services to a government or to the public.

For purposes of paragraph (A), "a nongovernmental program, activity, or organization" includes, but is not limited to group, prepaid, and voluntary legal service programs, activities, or organizations.

Adopted Nov. 28, 1988, eff. May 27, 1989.

Rule 1-700. Member as Candidate for Judicial Office.

(A) A member who is a candidate for judicial office in California shall comply with Canon 5 of the Code of Judicial Ethics.

(B) For purposes of this rule, "candidate for judicial office" means a member seeking judicial office by election. The determination of when a member is a candidate for judicial office is defined in the terminology section of the California Code of Judicial Ethics. A member's duty to comply with paragraph (A) shall end when the member announces withdrawal of the member's candidacy or when the results of the election are final, whichever occurs first.

Discussion:

Nothing in rule 1-700 shall be deemed to limit the applicability of any other rule or law.

Adopted November 21, 1997.

Rule 1-710. Member as Temporary Judge, Referee, or Court-Appointed Arbitrator.

A member who is serving as a temporary judge, referee, or court-appointed arbitrator, and is subject under the Code of Judicial Ethics to Canon 6D, shall comply with the terms of that canon.

Discussion:

This rule is intended to permit the State Bar to discipline members who violate applicable portions of the Code of Judicial Ethics while acting in a judicial capacity pursuant to an order or appointment by a court.

Nothing in rule 1-710 shall be deemed to limit the applicability of any other rule or law.

Adopted March 18, 1999.

CHAPTER 2
RELATIONSHIP AMONG MEMBERS

Communication with a represented party. Rule 2-100.
Financial arrangements among lawyers. Rule 2-200.
Sale or purchase of a law practice of a member, living or deceased. Rule 2-300.
Prohibited discriminatory conduct in a law practice. Rule 2-400.

Rule 2-100. Communication With a Represented Party.

(A) While representing a client, a member shall not communicate directly or indirectly about the subject of the representation with a party the member knows to be represented by another lawyer in the matter, unless the member has the consent of the other lawyer.

(B) For purposes of this rule, a "party" includes:

(1) An officer, director, or managing agent of a corporation or association, and a partner or managing agent of a partnership; or

(2) An association member or an employee of an association, corporation, or partnership, if the subject of the communication is any act or omission of such person in connection with the matter which may be binding upon or imputed to the organization for purposes of civil or criminal liability or whose statement may constitute an admission on the part of the organization.

(C) This rule shall not prohibit:

(1) Communications with a public officer, board, committee, or body; or

(2) Communications initiated by a party seeking advice or representation from an independent lawyer of the party's choice; or

(3) Communications otherwise authorized by law.

Discussion:

Rule 2-100 is intended to control communications between a member and persons the member knows to be represented by counsel unless a statutory scheme or case law will override the rule. There are a number of express statutory schemes which authorize communications between a member and person who would otherwise be subject to this rule. These statutes protect a variety of other rights such as the right of employees to organize and to engage in collective bargaining, employee health and safety, or equal employment opportunity. Other applicable law also includes the authority of government prosecutors and investigators to conduct criminal investigations, as limited by the relevant decisional law.

Rule 2-100 is not intended to prevent the parties themselves from communicating with respect to the subject matter of the representation, and nothing in the rule prevents a member from advising the client that such communication can be made. Moreover, the rule does not prohibit a member who is also a party to a legal matter from directly or indirectly communicating on his or her own behalf with a represented party. Such a member has independent rights as a party which should not be abrogated because of his or her professional status. To prevent any possible abuse in such situations, the counsel for the opposing party may advise that party (1) about the risks and benefits of communications with a lawyer-party, and (2) not to accept or engage in communications with the lawyer-party.

Rule 2-100 also addresses the situation in which member A is contacted by an opposing party who is represented and, because of dissatisfaction with that party's counsel, seeks A's independent advice. Since A is employed by the opposition, the member cannot give independent advice.

As used in paragraph (A), "the subject of the representation," "matter," and "party" are not limited to a litigation context.

Paragraph (B) is intended to apply only to persons employed at the time of the communication. (See *Triple A Machine Shop, Inc. v. State of California* (1989) 213 Cal.App.3d 131 [261 Cal.Rptr. 493].)

Subparagraph (C)(2) is intended to permit a member to communicate with a party seeking to hire new counsel or to obtain a second opinion. A member contacted by such a party continues to be bound by other Rules of Professional Conduct. (See, e.g., rules 1-400 and 3-310.)

Adopted Nov. 28, 1988, eff. May 27, 1989; amended eff. Sept. 14, 1992.

Rule 2-200. Financial Arrangements Among Lawyers.

(A) A member shall not divide a fee for legal services with a lawyer who is not a partner of, associate of, or shareholder with the member unless:

(1) The client has consented in writing thereto after a full disclosure has been made in writing that a division of fees will be made and the terms of such division; and

(2) The total fee charged by all lawyers is not increased solely by reason of the provision for division of fees and is not unconscionable as that term is defined in rule 4-200.

(B) Except as permitted in paragraph (A) of this rule or rule 2-300, a member shall not compensate, give, or promise anything of value to any lawyer for the purpose of recommending or securing employment of the member or the member's law firm by a client, or as a reward for having made a recommendation resulting in employment of the member or the member's law firm by a client. A member's offering of or giving a gift or gratuity to any lawyer who has made a recommendation resulting in the employment of the member or the member's law firm shall not of itself violate this rule, provided that the gift or gratuity was not offered in consideration of any promise, agreement, or understanding that such a gift or gratuity would be forthcoming or that referrals would be made or encouraged in the future.

Adopted Nov. 28, 1988, eff. May 27, 1989.

Rule 2-300. Sale or Purchase of a Law Practice of a Member, Living or Deceased.

All or substantially all of the law practice of a member, living or deceased, including goodwill, may be sold to another member or law firm subject to all the following conditions:

(A) Fees charged to clients shall not be increased solely by reason of such sale.

(B) If the sale contemplates the transfer of responsibility for work not yet completed or responsibility for client files or information protected by Business and Professions Code section 6068, subdivision (e), then;

(1) if the seller is deceased, or has a conservator or other person acting in a representative capacity, and no member has been appointed to act for the seller pursuant to Business and Professions Code section 6180.5, then prior to the transfer;

(a) the purchaser shall cause a written notice to be given to the client stating that the interest in the law practice is being transferred to the purchaser; that the client has the right to retain other counsel; that the client may take possession of any client papers and property, as required by rule 3-700(D); and that if no response is received to the notification within 90 days of the sending of such notice, or in the event the client's rights would be prejudiced by a failure to act during that time, the purchaser may act on behalf of the client until otherwise notified by the client. Such notice shall comply with the requirements as set forth in rule 1-400(D) and any provisions relating to attorney-client fee arrangements, and

(b) the purchaser shall obtain the written consent of the client provided that such consent shall be presumed until otherwise notified by the client if no response is received to the notification specified in subparagraph (a) within 90 days of the date of the sending of such notification to the client's last address as shown on the records of the seller, or the client's rights would be prejudiced by a failure to act during such 90-day period.

(2) in all other circumstances, not less than 90 days prior to the transfer;

(a) the seller, or the member appointed to act for the seller pursuant to Business and Professions Code section 6180.5, shall cause a written notice to be given to the client stating that the interest in the law practice is being transferred to the purchaser; that the client has the right to retain other counsel; that the client may take possession of any client papers and property, as required by rule 3-700(D); and that if no response is received to the notification within 90 days of the sending of such notice, the purchaser may act on behalf of the client until otherwise notified by

the client. Such notice shall comply with the requirements as set forth in rule 1-400(D) and any provisions relating to attorney-client fee arrangements, and

(b) the seller, or the member appointed to act for the seller pursuant to Business and Professions Code section 6180.5, shall obtain the written consent of the client prior to the transfer provided that such consent shall be presumed until otherwise notified by the client if no response is received to the notification specified in subparagraph (a) within 90 days of the date of the sending of such notification to the client's last address as shown on the records of the seller.

(C) If substitution is required by the rules of a tribunal in which a matter is pending, all steps necessary to substitute a member shall be taken.

(D) All activity of a purchaser or potential purchaser under this rule shall be subject to compliance with rules 3-300 and 3-310 where applicable.

(E) Confidential information shall not be disclosed to a non-member in connection with a sale under this rule.

(F) Admission to or retirement from a law partnership or law corporation, retirement plans and similar arrangements, or sale of tangible assets of a law practice shall not be deemed a sale or purchase under this rule.

Discussion:

Paragraph (A) is intended to prohibit the purchaser from charging the former clients of the seller a higher fee than the purchaser is charging his or her existing clients.

"All or substantially all of the law practice of a member" means, for purposes of rule 2-300, that, for example, a member may retain one or two clients who have such a longstanding personal and professional relationship with the member that transfer of those clients' files is not feasible. Conversely, rule 2-300 is not intended to authorize the sale of a law practice in a piecemeal fashion except as may be required by subparagraph (B)(1)(a) or paragraph (D).

Transfer of individual client matters, where permitted, is governed by rule 2-200. Payment of a fee to a non-lawyer broker for arranging the sale or purchase of a law practice is governed by rule 1-320.

Adopted Nov. 28, 1988, eff. May 27, 1989; amended eff. Sept. 14, 1992.

Rule 2-400. Prohibited Discriminatory Conduct in a Law Practice.

(A) For purposes of this rule:

(1) "law practice" includes sole practices, law partnerships, law corporations, corporate and governmental legal departments, and other entities which employ members to practice law;

(2) "knowingly permit" means a failure to advocate corrective action where the member knows of a discriminatory policy or practice which results in the unlawful discrimination prohibited in paragraph (B); and

(3) "unlawfully" and "unlawful" shall be determined by reference to applicable state or federal statutes or decisions making unlawful discrimination in employment and in offering goods and services to the public.

(B) In the management or operation of a law practice, a member shall not unlawfully discriminate or knowingly permit unlawful discrimination on the basis of race, national origin, sex, sexual orientation, religion, age or disability in:

(1) hiring, promoting, discharging, or otherwise determining the conditions of employment of any person; or

(2) accepting or terminating representation of any client.

(C) No disciplinary investigation or proceeding may be initiated by the State Bar against a member under this rule unless and until a tribunal of competent jurisdiction, other than a disciplinary tribunal, shall have first adjudicated a complaint of alleged discrimination and found that unlawful conduct occurred. Upon such adjudication, the tribunal finding or verdict shall then be admissible evidence of the occurrence or non-occurrence of the alleged discrimination in any disciplinary proceeding initiated under this rule. In order for discipline to be imposed under this rule, however, the finding of unlawfulness must be upheld and final after appeal, the time for filing an appeal must have expired, or the appeal must have been dismissed.

Discussion:

In order for discriminatory conduct to be actionable under this rule, it must first be found to be unlawful by an appropriate civil administrative or judicial tribunal under applicable state or federal law. Until there is a finding of civil unlawfulness, there is no basis for disciplinary action under this rule.

A complaint of misconduct based on this rule may be filed with the State Bar following a finding of unlawfulness in the first instance even though that finding is thereafter appealed.

A disciplinary investigation or proceeding for conduct coming within this rule may be initiated and maintained, however, if such conduct warrants discipline under California Business and Professions Code sections 6106 and 6068, the California Supreme Court's inherent authority to impose discipline, or other disciplinary standard.

Adopted eff. March 1, 1994; amended Jan. 1, 2007.

CHAPTER 3
PROFESSIONAL RELATIONSHIP WITH CLIENTS

Confidential information of a client. Rule 3-100.
Failing to act competently. Rule 3-110.
Sexual relations with client. Rule 3-120.
Prohibited objectives of employment. Rule 3-200.
Advising the violation of law. Rule 3-210.
Avoiding interests adverse to a client. Rule 3-300.
Avoiding the representation of adverse interests. Rule 3-310.
Relationship with other party's lawyer. Rule 3-320.
Limiting liability to client. Rule 3-400.
Communication. Rule 3-500.
Communication of settlement offer. Rule 3-510.
Organization as client. Rule 3-600.
Termination of employment. Rule 3-700.

Rule 3-100. Confidential Information of a Client.

(A) A member shall not reveal information protected from disclosure by Business and Professions Code section 6068, subdivision (e)(1) without the informed consent of the client, or as provided in paragraph (B) of this rule.

(B) A member may, but is not required to, reveal confidential information relating to the representation of a client to the extent that the member reasonably believes the disclosure is necessary to prevent a criminal act that

the member reasonably believes is likely to result in death of, or substantial bodily harm to, an individual.

(C) Before revealing confidential information to prevent a criminal act as provided in paragraph (B), a member shall, if reasonable under the circumstances:

(1) make a good faith effort to persuade the client: (i) not to commit or to continue the criminal act or (ii) to pursue a course of conduct that will prevent the threatened death or substantial bodily harm; or do both (i) and (ii); and

(2) inform the client, at an appropriate time, of the member's ability or decision to reveal information as provided in paragraph (B).

(D) In revealing confidential information as provided in paragraph (B), the member's disclosure must be no more than is necessary to prevent the criminal act, given the information known to the member at the time of the disclosure.

(E) A member who does not reveal information permitted by paragraph (B) does not violate this rule.

Discussion:

[1] *Duty of confidentiality.* Paragraph (A) relates to a member's obligations under Business and Professions Code section 6068, subdivision (e)(1), which provides it is a duty of a member: "To maintain inviolate the confidence, and at every peril to himself or herself to preserve the secrets, of his or her client." A member's duty to preserve the confidentiality of client information involves public policies of paramount importance. (*In Re Jordan* (1974) 12 Cal.3d 575, 580 [116 Cal.Rptr. 371].) Preserving the confidentiality of client information contributes to the trust that is the hallmark of the client-lawyer relationship. The client is thereby encouraged to seek legal assistance and to communicate fully and frankly with the lawyer even as to embarrassing or legally damaging subject matter. The lawyer needs this information to represent the client effectively and, if necessary, to advise the client to refrain from wrongful conduct. Almost without exception, clients come to lawyers in order to determine their rights and what is, in the complex of laws and regulations, deemed to be legal and correct. Based upon experience, lawyers know that almost all clients follow the advice given, and the law is upheld. Paragraph (A) thus recognizes a fundamental principle in the client-lawyer relationship, that, in the absence of the client's informed consent, a member must not reveal information relating to the representation. (See, e.g., *Commercial Standard Title Co. v. Superior Court* (1979) 92 Cal.App.3d 934, 945 [155 Cal.Rptr. 393].)

[2] *Client-lawyer confidentiality encompasses the attorney-client privilege, the work-product doctrine and ethical standards of confidentiality.* The principle of client-lawyer confidentiality applies to information relating to the representation, whatever its source, and encompasses matters communicated in confidence by the client, and therefore protected by the attorney-client privilege, matters protected by the work product doctrine, and matters protected under other ethical standards of confidentiality, all as established in law, rule and policy. (*See In the Matter of Johnson* (Rev. Dept. 2000) 4 Cal. State Bar Ct. Rptr. 179; *Goldstein v. Lees* (1975) 46 Cal.3d 614, 621 [120 Cal.Rptr. 253].) The attorney-client privilege and work-product doctrine apply in judicial and other proceedings in which a member may be called as a witness or be otherwise compelled to produce evidence concerning a client. A member's ethical duty of confidentiality is not so limited in its scope of protection for the client-lawyer relationship of trust and prevents a member from revealing the client's confidential information even when not confronted with such compulsion. Thus, a member may not reveal such information except with the consent of the client or as authorized or required by the State Bar Act, these rules, or other law.

[3] *Narrow exception to duty of confidentiality under this Rule.* Notwithstanding the important public policies promoted by lawyers adhering to the core duty of confidentiality, the overriding value of life permits disclosures otherwise prohibited under Business & Professions Code section 6068(e), subdivision (1). Paragraph (B), which restates Business and Professions Code section 6068, subdivision (e)(2), identifies a narrow confidentiality exception, absent the client's informed consent, when a member reasonably believes that disclosure is necessary to prevent a criminal act that the member reasonably believes is likely to result in the death of, or substantial bodily harm to an individual. Evidence Code section 956.5, which relates to the evidentiary attorney-client privilege, sets forth a similar express exception. Although a member is not permitted to reveal confidential information concerning a client's past, completed criminal acts, the policy favoring the preservation of human life that underlies this exception to the duty of confidentiality and the evidentiary privilege permits disclosure to prevent a future or ongoing criminal act.

[4] *Member not subject to discipline for revealing confidential information as permitted under this Rule.* Rule 3-100, which restates Business and Professions Code section 6068, subdivision (e)(2), reflects a balancing between the interests of preserving client confidentiality and of preventing a criminal act that a member reasonably believes is likely to result in death or substantial bodily harm to an individual. A member who reveals information as permitted under this rule is not subject to discipline.

[5] *No duty to reveal confidential information.* Neither Business and Professions Code section 6068, subdivision (e)(2) nor this rule imposes an affirmative obligation on a member to reveal information in order to prevent harm. (See rule 1-100(A).) A member may decide not to reveal confidential information. Whether a member chooses to reveal confidential information as permitted under this rule is a matter for the individual member to decide, based on all the facts and circumstances, such as those discussed in paragraph [6] of this discussion.

[6] *Deciding to reveal confidential information as permitted under paragraph (B).* Disclosure permitted under paragraph (B) is ordinarily a last resort, when no other available action is reasonably likely to prevent the criminal act. Prior to revealing information as permitted under paragraph (B), the member must, if reasonable under the circumstances, make a good faith effort to persuade the client to take steps to avoid the criminal act or threatened harm. Among the factors to be considered in determining whether to disclose confidential information are the following:

(1) the amount of time that the member has to make a decision about disclosure;

(2) whether the client or a third party has made similar threats before and whether they have ever acted or attempted to act upon them;

(3) whether the member believes the member's efforts to persuade the client or a third person not to engage in the criminal conduct have or have not been successful;

(4) the extent of adverse effect to the client's rights under the Fifth, Sixth and Fourteenth Amendments of the United States Constitution and analogous rights and privacy rights under Article 1 of the Constitution of the State of California that may result from disclosure contemplated by the member;

(5) the extent of other adverse effects to the client that may result from disclosure contemplated by the member; and

(6) the nature and extent of information that must be disclosed to prevent the criminal act or threatened harm.

A member may also consider whether the prospective harm to the victim or victims is imminent in deciding whether to disclose the confidential information. However, the imminence of the harm is not a prerequisite to disclosure and a member may disclose the information without waiting until immediately before the harm is likely to occur.

[7] *Counseling client or third person not to commit a criminal act reasonably likely to result in death of substantial bodily harm.* Subparagraph (C)(1) provides that before a member may reveal confidential information, the member must, if reasonable under the circumstances, make a good faith effort to persuade the client not to commit or to continue the criminal act, or to persuade the client to otherwise pursue a course of conduct that will prevent the threatened death or substantial bodily harm, or if necessary, do both. The interests protected by such counseling is the client's interest in limiting disclosure of confidential information and in taking responsible action to deal with situations attributable to the client. If a client, whether in response to the member's counseling or otherwise, takes corrective action — such as by ceasing the criminal act before harm is caused — the option for permissive disclosure by the member would cease as the threat posed by the criminal act would no longer be present. When the actor is a nonclient or when the act is deliberate or malicious, the member who contemplates making adverse disclosure of confidential information may reasonably conclude that the compelling interests of the member or others in their own personal safety preclude personal contact with the actor. Before counseling an actor who is a nonclient, the member should, if reasonable under the circumstances, first advise the client of the member's intended course of action. If a client or another person has already acted but the intended harm has not yet occurred, the member should consider, if reasonable under the circumstances, efforts to persuade the client or third person to warn the victim or consider other appropriate action to prevent the harm. Even when the member has concluded that paragraph (B) does not permit the member to reveal confidential information, the member nevertheless is permitted to counsel the client as to why it may be in the client's best interest to consent to the attorney's disclosure of that information.

[8] *Disclosure of confidential information must be no more than is reasonably necessary to prevent the criminal act.* Under paragraph (D), disclosure of confidential information, when made, must be no more extensive than the member reasonably believes necessary to prevent the criminal act. Disclosure should allow access to the confidential information to only those persons who the member reasonably believes can act to prevent the harm. Under some circumstances, a member may determine that the best course to pursue is to make an anonymous disclosure to the potential victim or relevant law-enforcement authorities. What particular measures are reasonable depends on the circumstances known to the member. Relevant circumstances include the time available, whether the victim might be unaware of the threat, the member's prior course of dealings with the client, and the extent of the adverse effect on the client that may result from the disclosure contemplated by the member.

[9] *Informing client of member's ability or decision to reveal confidential information under subparagraph (C)(2).* A member is required to keep a client reasonably informed about significant developments regarding the employment or representation. Rule 3-500; Business and Professions Code, section 6068, subdivision (m). Paragraph (C)(2), however, recognizes that under certain circumstances, informing a client of the member's ability or decision to reveal confidential information under paragraph (B) would likely increase the risk of death or substantial bodily harm, not only to the originally-intended victims of the criminal act, but also to the client or members of the client's family, or to the member or the member's family or associates. Therefore, paragraph (C)(2) requires a member to inform the client of the member's ability or decision to reveal confidential information as provided in paragraph (B) only if it is reasonable to do so under the circumstances. Paragraph (C)(2) further recognizes that the appropriate time for the member to inform the client may vary depending upon the circumstances. (See paragraph [10] of this

discussion.) Among the factors to be considered in determining an appropriate time, if any, to inform a client are:

(1) whether the client is an experienced user of legal services;

(2) the frequency of the member's contact with the client;

(3) the nature and length of the professional relationship with the client;

(4) whether the member and client have discussed the member's duty of confidentiality or any exceptions to that duty;

(5) the likelihood that the client's matter will involve information within paragraph (B);

(6) the member's belief, if applicable, that so informing the client is likely to increase the likelihood that a criminal act likely to result in the death of, or substantial bodily harm to, an individual; and

(7) the member's belief, if applicable, that good faith efforts to persuade a client not to act on a threat have failed.

[10] *Avoiding a chilling effect on the lawyer-client relationship.* The foregoing flexible approach to the member's informing a client of his or her ability or decision to reveal confidential information recognizes the concern that informing a client about limits on confidentiality may have a chilling effect on client communication. (See Discussion paragraph [1].) To avoid that chilling effect, one member may choose to inform the client of the member's ability to reveal information as early as the outset of the representation, while another member may choose to inform a client only at a point when that client has imparted information that may fall under paragraph (B), or even choose not to inform a client until such time as the member attempts to counsel the client as contemplated in Discussion paragraph [7]. In each situation, the member will have discharged properly the requirement under subparagraph (C)(2), and will not be subject to discipline.

[11] *Informing client that disclosure has been made; termination of the lawyer-client relationship.* When a member has revealed confidential information under paragraph (B), in all but extraordinary cases the relationship between member and client will have deteriorated so as to make the member's representation of the client impossible. Therefore, the member is required to seek to withdraw from the representation (see rule 3-700(B)), unless the member is able to obtain the client's informed consent to the member's continued representation. The member must inform the client of the fact of the member's disclosure unless the member has a compelling interest in not informing the client, such as to protect the member, the member's family or a third person from the risk of death or substantial bodily harm.

[12] *Other consequences of the member's disclosure.* Depending upon the circumstances of a member's disclosure of confidential information, there may be other important issues that a member must address. For example, if a member will be called as a witness in the client's matter, then rule 5-210 should be considered. Similarly, the member should consider his or her duties of loyalty and competency (rule 3-110).

[13] *Other exceptions to confidentiality under California law.* Rule 3-100 is not intended to augment, diminish, or preclude reliance upon, any other exceptions to the duty to preserve the confidentiality of client information recognized under California law.

Adopted June 23, 2004, eff. July 1, 2004.

Rule 3-110. Failing to Act Competently.

(A) A member shall not intentionally, recklessly, or repeatedly fail to perform legal services with competence.

(B) For purposes of this rule, "competence" in any legal service shall mean to apply the 1) diligence, 2) learning and skill, and 3) mental, emotional, and physical ability reasonably necessary for the performance of such service.

(C) If a member does not have sufficient learning and skill when the legal service is undertaken, the member may nonetheless perform such services competently by 1) associating with or, where appropriate, professionally consulting another lawyer reasonably believed to be competent, or 2) by acquiring sufficient learning and skill before performance is required.

Discussion:

The duties set forth in rule 3-110 include the duty to supervise the work of subordinate attorney and non-attorney employees or agents. (See, e.g., *Waysman v. State Bar* (1986) 41 Cal.3d 452; *Trousil v. State Bar* (1985) 38 Cal.3d 337, 342 [211 Cal.Rptr. 525]; *Palomo v. State Bar* (1984) 36 Cal.3d 785 [205 Cal.Rptr. 834]; *Crane v. State Bar* (1981) 30 Cal.3d 117, 122; *Black v. State Bar* (1972) 7 Cal.3d 676, 692 [103 Cal.Rptr. 288; 499 P.2d 968]; *Vaughn v. State Bar* (1972) 6 Cal.3d 847, 857–858 [100 Cal.Rptr. 713; 494 P.2d 1257]; *Moore v. State Bar* (1964) 62 Cal.2d 74, 81 [41 Cal.Rptr. 161; 396 P.2d 577].)

In an emergency a lawyer may give advice or assistance in a matter in which the lawyer does not have the skill ordinarily required where referral to or consultation with another lawyer would be impractical. Even in an emergency, however, assistance should be limited to that reasonably necessary in the circumstances.

Adopted Nov. 28, 1988, eff. May 27, 1989; amended eff. Sept. 14, 1992.

Ref.: CACI Nos. 600, 604 (Matthew Bender).

Rule 3-120. Sexual Relations With Client.

(A) For purposes of this rule, "sexual relations" means sexual intercourse or the touching of an intimate part of another person for the purpose of sexual arousal, gratification, or abuse.

(B) A member shall not:

(1) Require or demand sexual relations with a client incident to or as a condition of any professional representation; or

(2) Employ coercion, intimidation, or undue influence in entering into sexual relations with a client; or

(3) Continue representation of a client with whom the member has sexual relations if such sexual relations cause the member to perform legal services incompetently in violation of rule 3-110.

(C) Paragraph (B) shall not apply to sexual relations between members and their spouses or to ongoing consensual sexual relationships which predate the initiation of the lawyer-client relationship.

(D) Where a lawyer in a firm has sexual relations with a client but does not participate in the representation of that client, the lawyers in the firm shall not be subject to discipline under this rule solely because of the occurrence of such sexual relations.

Discussion:

Rule 3-120 is intended to prohibit sexual exploitation by a lawyer in the course of a professional representation. Often, based upon the nature of the underlying representation, a client exhibits great emotional vulnerability and dependence upon the advice and guidance of counsel. Attorneys owe the utmost duty of good faith and fidelity to clients. (See, e.g., *Greenbaum v. State Bar* (1976) 15 Cal.3d 893, 903 [126 Cal.Rptr. 785]; *Alkow v. State Bar* (1971) 3 Cal.3d 924, 935 [92 Cal.Rptr. 278]; *Cutler v. State Bar*

(1969) 71 Cal.2d 241, 251 [78 Cal.Rptr. 172]; *Clancy v. State Bar* (1969) 71 Cal.2d 140, 146 [77 Cal.Rptr. 657].) The relationship between an attorney and client is a fiduciary relationship of the very highest character and all dealings between an attorney and client that are beneficial to the attorney will be closely scrutinized with the utmost strictness for unfairness. (See, e.g., *Giovanazzi v. State Bar* (1980) 28 Cal.3d 465, 472 [169 Cal.Rptr. 581]; *Benson v. State Bar* (1975) 13 Cal.3d 581, 586 [119 Cal.Rptr. 297]; *Lee v. State Bar* (1970) 2 Cal.3d 927, 939 [88 Cal.Rptr. 361]; *Clancy v. State Bar* (1969) 71 Cal.2d 140, 146 [77 Cal.Rptr. 657].) Where attorneys exercise undue influence over clients or take unfair advantage of clients, discipline is appropriate. (See, e.g., *Magee v. State Bar* (1962) 58 Cal.2d 423 [24 Cal.Rptr. 839]; *Lantz v. State Bar* (1931) 212 Cal. 213 [298 P. 497].) In all client matters, a member is advised to keep clients' interests paramount in the course of the member's representation.

For purposes of this rule, if the client is an organization, any individual overseeing the representation shall be deemed to be the client. (See rule 3-600.)

Although paragraph (C) excludes representation of certain clients from the scope of rule 3-120, such exclusion is not intended to preclude the applicability of other Rules of Professional Conduct, including rule 3-110.

Adopted eff. Sept. 14, 1992.

Rule 3-200. Prohibited Objectives of Employment.

A member shall not seek, accept, or continue employment if the member knows or should know that the objective of such employment is:

(A)   To bring an action, conduct a defense, assert a position in litigation, or take an appeal, without probable cause and for the purpose of harassing or maliciously injuring any person; or

(B)   To present a claim or defense in litigation that is not warranted under existing law, unless it can be supported by a good faith argument for an extension, modification, or reversal of such existing law.

Adopted Nov. 28, 1988, eff. May 27, 1989.

Rule 3-210. Advising the Violation of Law.

A member shall not advise the violation of any law, rule, or ruling of a tribunal unless the member believes in good faith that such law, rule, or ruling is invalid. A member may take appropriate steps in good faith to test the validity of any law, rule, or ruling of a tribunal.

Discussion:

Rule 3-210 is intended to apply not only to the prospective conduct of a client but also to the interaction between the member and client and to the specific legal service sought by the client from the member. An example of the former is the handling of physical evidence of a crime in the possession of the client and offered to the member. (See *People v. Meredith* (1981) 29 Cal.3d 682 [175 Cal.Rptr. 612].) An example of the latter is a request that the member negotiate the return of stolen property in exchange for the owner's agreement not to report the theft to the police or prosecutorial authorities. (See *People v. Pic'l* (1982) 31 Cal.3d 731 [183 Cal.Rptr. 685].)

Adopted Nov. 28, 1988, eff. May 27, 1989.

Rule 3-300. Avoiding Interests Adverse to a Client.

A member shall not enter into a business transaction with a client; or knowingly acquire an ownership, posses-

sory, security, or other pecuniary interest adverse to a client, unless each of the following requirements has been satisfied:

(A)   The transaction or acquisition and its terms are fair and reasonable to the client and are fully disclosed and transmitted in writing to the client in a manner which should reasonably have been understood by the client; and

(B)   The client is advised in writing that the client may seek the advice of an independent lawyer of the client's choice and is given a reasonable opportunity to seek that advice; and

(C)   The client thereafter consents in writing to the terms of the transaction or the terms of the acquisition.

Discussion:

Rule 3-300 is not intended to apply to the agreement by which the member is retained by the client, unless the agreement confers on the member an ownership, possessory, security, or other pecuniary interest adverse to the client. Such an agreement is governed, in part, by rule 4-200.

Rule 3-300 is not intended to apply where the member and client each make an investment on terms offered to the general public or a significant portion thereof. For example, rule 3-300 is not intended to apply where A, a member, invests in a limited partnership syndicated by a third party. B, A's client, makes the same investment. Although A and B are each investing in the same business, A did not enter into the transaction "with" B for the purposes of the rule.

Rule 3-300 is intended to apply where the member wishes to obtain an interest in client's property in order to secure the amount of the member's past due or future fees.

Adopted Nov. 28, 1988, eff. May 27, 1989; amended eff. Sept. 14, 1992.

Rule 3-310. Avoiding the Representation of Adverse Interests.

(A)   For purposes of this rule:

(1)   "Disclosure" means informing the client or former client of the relevant circumstances and of the actual and reasonably foreseeable adverse consequences to the client or former client;

(2)   "Informed written consent" means the client's or former client's written agreement to the representation following written disclosure;

(3)   "Written" means any writing as defined in Evidence Code section 250.

(B)   A member shall not accept or continue representation of a client without providing written disclosure to the client where:

(1)   The member has a legal, business, financial, professional, or personal relationship with a party or witness in the same matter; or

(2)   The member knows or reasonably should know that:

(a)   the member previously had a legal, business, financial, professional, or personal relationship with a party or witness in the same matter; and

(b)   the previous relationship would substantially affect the member's representation; or

(3)   The member has or had a legal, business, financial, professional, or personal relationship with another person or entity the member knows or reasonably should

know would be affected substantially by resolution of the matter; or

(4) The member has or had a legal, business, financial, or professional interest in the subject matter of the representation.

(C) A member shall not, without the informed written consent of each client:

(1) Accept representation of more than one client in a matter in which the interests of the clients potentially conflict; or

(2) Accept or continue representation of more than one client in a matter in which the interests of the clients actually conflict; or

(3) Represent a client in a matter and at the same time in a separate matter accept as a client a person or entity whose interest in the first matter is adverse to the client in the first matter.

(D) A member who represents two or more clients shall not enter into an aggregate settlement of the claims of or against the clients without the informed written consent of each client.

(E) A member shall not, without the informed written consent of the client or former client, accept employment adverse to the client or former client where, by reason of the representation of the client or former client, the member has obtained confidential information material to the employment.

(F) A member shall not accept compensation for representing a client from one other than the client unless:

(1) There is no interference with the member's independence of professional judgment or with the client-lawyer relationship; and

(2) Information relating to representation of the client is protected as required by Business and Professions Code section 6068, subdivision (e); and

(3) The member obtains the client's informed written consent, provided that no disclosure or consent is required if:

(a) such nondisclosure is otherwise authorized by law; or

(b) the member is rendering legal services on behalf of any public agency which provides legal services to other public agencies or the public.

Discussion:

Rule 3-310 is not intended to prohibit a member from representing parties having antagonistic positions on the same legal question that has arisen in different cases, unless representation of either client would be adversely affected.

Other rules and laws may preclude making adequate disclosure under this rule. If such disclosure is precluded, informed written consent is likewise precluded. (See, e.g., Business and Professions Code section 6068, subdivision (e).)

Paragraph (B) is not intended to apply to the relationship of a member to another party's lawyer. Such relationships are governed by rule 3-320.

Paragraph (B) is not intended to require either the disclosure of the new engagement to a former client or the consent of the former client to the new engagement. However, both disclosure and consent are required if paragraph (E) applies.

While paragraph (B) deals with the issues of adequate disclosure to the present client or clients of the member's present or past relationships to other parties or witnesses or present interest in the subject matter of the representation, paragraph (E) is intended to protect the confidences of another present or former client. These two paragraphs are to apply as complementary provisions.

Paragraph (B) is intended to apply only to a member's own relationships or interests, unless the member knows that a partner or associate in the same firm as the member has or had a relationship with another party or witness or has or had an interest in the subject matter of the representation.

Subparagraphs (C)(1) and (C)(2) are intended to apply to all types of legal employment, including the concurrent representation of multiple parties in litigation or in a single transaction or in some other common enterprise or legal relationship. Examples of the latter include the formation of a partnership for several partners or a corporation for several shareholders, the preparation of an ante-nuptial agreement, or joint or reciprocal wills for a husband and wife, or the resolution of an "uncontested" marital dissolution. In such situations, for the sake of convenience or economy, the parties may well prefer to employ a single counsel, but a member must disclose the potential adverse aspects of such multiple representation (e.g., Evid. Code, §962) and must obtain the informed written consent of the clients thereto pursuant to subparagraph (C)(1). Moreover, if the potential adversity should become actual, the member must obtain the further informed written consent of the clients pursuant to subparagraph (C)(2).

Subparagraph (C)(3) is intended to apply to representations of clients in both litigation and transactional matters.

In *State Farm Mutual Automobile Insurance Company v. Federal Insurance Company* (1999) 72 Cal.App.4th 1422 [86 Cal.Rptr.2d 20], the court held that subparagraph (C)(3) was violated when a member, retained by an insurer to defend one suit, and while that suit was still pending, filed a direct action against the same insurer in an unrelated action without securing the insurer's consent. Notwithstanding *State Farm*, subparagraph (C)(3) is not intended to apply with respect to the relationship between an insurer and a member when, in each matter, the insurer's interest is only as an indemnity provider and not as a direct party to the action.

There are some matters in which the conflicts are such that written consent may not suffice for non-disciplinary purposes. (See *Woods v. Superior Court* (1983) 149 Cal.App.3d 931 [197 Cal.Rptr. 185]; *Klemm v. Superior Court* (1977) 75 Cal.App.3d 893 [142 Cal.Rptr. 509]; *Ishmael v. Millington* (1966) 241 Cal.App.2d 520 [50 Cal.Rptr. 592].)

Paragraph (D) is not intended to apply to class action settlements subject to court approval.

Paragraph (F) is not intended to abrogate existing relationships between insurers and insureds whereby the insurer has the contractual right to unilaterally select counsel for the insured, where there is no conflict of interest. (See *San Diego Navy Federal Credit Union v. Cumis Insurance Society* (1984) 162 Cal.App.3d 358 [208 Cal.Rptr. 494].)

Adopted Nov. 28, 1988, eff. May 27, 1989; amended eff. Sept. 14, 1992, Mar. 3, 2003.

Rule 3-320. Relationship With Other Party's Lawyer.

A member shall not represent a client in a matter in which another party's lawyer is a spouse, parent, child, or sibling of the member, lives with the member, is a client of the member, or has an intimate personal relationship with the member, unless the member informs the client in writing of the relationship.

Discussion:

Rule 3-320 is not intended to apply to circumstances in which a member fails to advise the client of a relationship with another lawyer who is merely a partner or associate in the same law firm as the adverse party's counsel, and who has no direct involvement in the matter.

Adopted Nov. 28, 1988, eff. May 27, 1989; amended eff. Sept. 14, 1992.

Rule 3-400.   Limiting Liability to Client.

A member shall not:

(A)   Contract with a client prospectively limiting the member's liability to the client for the member's professional malpractice; or

(B)   Settle a claim or potential claim for the member's liability to the client for the member's professional malpractice, unless the client is informed in writing that the client may seek the advice of an independent lawyer of the client's choice regarding the settlement and is given a reasonable opportunity to seek that advice.

Discussion:

Rule 3-400 is not intended to apply to customary qualifications and limitations in legal opinions and memoranda, nor is it intended to prevent a member from reasonably limiting the scope of the member's employment or representation.

Adopted Nov. 28, 1988, eff. May 27, 1989; amended eff. Sept. 14, 1992.

Rule 3-500.   Communication.

A member shall keep a client reasonably informed about significant developments relating to the employment or representation, including promptly complying with reasonable requests for information and copies of significant documents when necessary to keep the client so informed.

Discussion:

Rule 3-500 is not intended to change a member's duties to his or her clients. It is intended to make clear that, while a client must be informed of significant developments in the matter, a member will not be disciplined for failing to communicate insignificant or irrelevant information. (See Bus. & Prof. Code, §6068, subd. (m).)

A member may contract with the client in their employment agreement that the client assumes responsibility for the cost of copying significant documents. This rule is not intended to prohibit a claim for the recovery of the member's expense in any subsequent legal proceeding.

Rule 3-500 is not intended to create, augment, diminish, or eliminate any application of the work product rule. The obligation of the member to provide work product to the client shall be governed by relevant statutory and decisional law. Additionally, this rule is not intended to apply to any document or correspondence that is subject to a protective order or non-disclosure agreement, or to override applicable statutory or decisional law requiring that certain information not be provided to criminal defendants who are clients of the member.

Adopted Nov. 28, 1988, eff. May 27, 1989; amended eff. June 5, 1997.

Rule 3-510.   Communication of Settlement Offer.

(A)   A member shall promptly communicate to the member's client:

(1)   All terms and conditions of any offer made to the client in a criminal matter; and

(2)   All amounts, terms, and conditions of any written offer of settlement made to the client in all other matters.

(B)   As used in this rule, "client" includes a person who possesses the authority to accept an offer of settlement or plea, or, in a class action, all the named representatives of the class.

Discussion:

Rule 3-510 is intended to require that counsel in a criminal matter convey all offers, whether written or oral, to the client, as give and take negotiations are less common in criminal matters, and, even were they to occur, such negotiations should require the participation of the accused.

Any oral offers of settlement made to the client in a civil matter should also be communicated if they are "significant" for the purposes of rule 3-500.

Adopted Nov. 28, 1988, eff. May 27, 1989.

Rule 3-600.   Organization as Client.

(A)   In representing an organization, a member shall conform his or her representation to the concept that the client is the organization itself, acting through its highest authorized officer, employee, body, or constituent overseeing the particular engagement.

(B)   If a member acting on behalf of an organization knows that an actual or apparent agent of the organization acts or intends or refuses to act in a manner that is or may be a violation of law reasonably imputable to the organization, or in a manner which is likely to result in substantial injury to the organization, the member shall not violate his or her duty of protecting all confidential information as provided in Business and Professions Code section 6068, subdivision (e). Subject to Business and Professions Code section 6068, subdivision (e), the member may take such actions as appear to the member to be in the best lawful interest of the organization. Such actions may include among others:

(1)   Urging reconsideration of the matter while explaining its likely consequences to the organization; or

(2)   Referring the matter to the next higher authority in the organization, including, if warranted by the seriousness of the matter, referral to the highest internal authority that can act on behalf of the organization.

(C)   If, despite the member's actions in accordance with paragraph (B), the highest authority that can act on behalf of the organization insists upon action or a refusal to act that is a violation of law and is likely to result in substantial injury to the organization, the member's response is limited to the member's right, and, where appropriate, duty to resign in accordance with rule 3-700.

(D)   In dealing with an organization's directors, officers, employees, members, shareholders, or other constituents, a member shall explain the identity of the client for whom the member acts, whenever it is or becomes apparent that the organization's interests are or may become adverse to those of the constituent(s) with whom the member is dealing. The member shall not mislead such a constituent into believing that the constituent may communicate confidential information to the member in a way that will not be used in the organization's interest if that is or becomes adverse to the constituent.

(E)   A member representing an organization may also represent any of its directors, officers, employees, members, shareholders, or other constituents, subject to the provisions of rule 3-310. If the organization's consent to the dual representation is required by rule 3-310, the consent shall be given by an appropriate constituent of the organization other than the individual or constituent who is to be represented, or by the shareholder(s) or organization members.

Discussion:

Rule 3-600 is not intended to enmesh members in the intricacies of the entity and aggregate theories of partnership.

Rule 3-600 is not intended to prohibit members from representing both an organization and other parties connected with it, as for instance (as simply one example) in establishing employee benefit packages for closely held corporations or professional partnerships.

Rule 3-600 is not intended to create or to validate artificial distinctions between entities and their officers, employees, or members, nor is it the purpose of the rule to deny the existence or importance of such formal distinctions. In dealing with a close corporation or small association, members commonly perform professional engagements for both the organization and its major constituents. When a change in control occurs or is threatened, members are faced with complex decisions involving personal and institutional relationships and loyalties and have frequently had difficulty in perceiving their correct duty. (See *People ex rel. Deukmejian v. Brown* (1981) 29 Cal.3d 150 [172 Cal.Rptr. 478]; *Goldstein v. Lees* (1975) 46 Cal.App.3d 614 [120 Cal.Rptr. 253]; *Woods v. Superior Court* (1983) 149 Cal.App.3d 931 [197 Cal.Rptr. 185]; *In re Banks* (1978) 283 Ore. 459 [584 P.2d 284]; 1 A.L.R.4th 1105.) In resolving such multiple relationships, members must rely on case law.

Adopted Nov. 28, 1988, eff. May 27, 1989.

Rule 3-700.   Termination of Employment.

(A)   In General.

(1)   If permission for termination of employment is required by the rules of a tribunal, a member shall not withdraw from employment in a proceeding before that tribunal without its permission.

(2)   A member shall not withdraw from employment until the member has taken reasonable steps to avoid reasonably foreseeable prejudice to the rights of the client, including giving due notice to the client, allowing time for employment of other counsel, complying with rule 3-700(D), and complying with applicable laws and rules.

(B)   Mandatory Withdrawal.

A member representing a client before a tribunal shall withdraw from employment with the permission of the tribunal, if required by its rules, and a member representing a client in other matters shall withdraw from employment, if:

(1)   The member knows or should know that the client is bringing an action, conducting a defense, asserting a position in litigation, or taking an appeal, without probable cause and for the purpose of harassing or maliciously injuring any person; or

(2)   The member knows or should know that continued employment will result in violation of these rules or of the State Bar Act; or

(3)   The member's mental or physical condition renders it unreasonably difficult to carry out the employment effectively.

(C)   Permissive Withdrawal.

If rule 3-700(B) is not applicable, a member may not request permission to withdraw in matters pending before a tribunal, and may not withdraw in other matters, unless such request or such withdrawal is because:

(1)   The client

(a)   insists upon presenting a claim or defense that is not warranted under existing law and cannot be supported by good faith argument for an extension, modification, or reversal of existing law, or

(b)   seeks to pursue an illegal course of conduct, or

(c)   insists that the member pursue a course of conduct that is illegal or that is prohibited under these rules or the State Bar Act, or

(d)   by other conduct renders it unreasonably difficult for the member to carry out the employment effectively, or

(e)   insists, in a matter not pending before a tribunal, that the member engage in conduct that is contrary to the judgment and advice of the member but not prohibited under these rules or the State Bar Act, or

(f)   breaches an agreement or obligation to the member as to expenses or fees.

(2)   The continued employment is likely to result in a violation of these rules or of the State Bar Act; or

(3)   The inability to work with co-counsel indicates that the best interests of the client likely will be served by withdrawal; or

(4)   The member's mental or physical condition renders it difficult for the member to carry out the employment effectively; or

(5)   The client knowingly and freely assents to termination of the employment; or

(6)   The member believes in good faith, in a proceeding pending before a tribunal, that the tribunal will find the existence of other good cause for withdrawal.

(D)   Papers, Property, and Fees.

A member whose employment has terminated shall:

(1)   Subject to any protective order or non-disclosure agreement, promptly release to the client, at the request of the client, all the client papers and property. "Client papers and property" includes correspondence, pleadings, deposition transcripts, exhibits, physical evidence, expert's reports, and other items reasonably necessary to the client's representation, whether the client has paid for them or not; and

(2)   Promptly refund any part of a fee paid in advance that has not been earned. This provision is not applicable to a true retainer fee which is paid solely for the purpose of ensuring the availability of the member for the matter.

Discussion:

Subparagraph (A)(2) provides that "a member shall not withdraw from employment until the member has taken reasonable steps to avoid reasonably foreseeable prejudice to the rights of the clients." What such steps would include, of course, will vary according to the circumstances. Absent special circumstances, "reasonable steps" do not include providing additional services to the client once the successor counsel has been employed and rule 3-700(D) has been satisfied.

Paragraph (D) makes clear the member's duties in the recurring situation in which new counsel seeks to obtain client files from a member discharged by the client. It codifies existing case law. (See *Academy of California Optometrists v. Superior Court* (1975) 51 Cal.App.3d 999 [124 Cal.Rptr. 668]; *Weiss v. Marcus*

(1975) 51 Cal.App.3d 590 [124 Cal.Rptr. 297].) Paragraph (D) also requires that the member "promptly" return unearned fees paid in advance. If a client disputes the amount to be returned, the member shall comply with rule 4-100(A)(2).

Paragraph (D) is not intended to prohibit a member from making, at the member's own expense, and retaining copies of papers released to the client, nor to prohibit a claim for the recovery of the member's expense in any subsequent legal proceeding.

Adopted Nov. 28, 1988, eff. May 27, 1989.

CHAPTER 4
FINANCIAL RELATIONSHIP WITH CLIENTS

Preserving identity of funds and property of a client. Rule 4-100.
Fees for legal services. Rule 4-200.
Payment of personal or business expenses incurred by or for a client. Rule 4-210.
Purchasing property at a foreclosure or a sale subject to judicial review. Rule 4-300.
Gifts from client. Rule 4-400.

Rule 4-100. Preserving Identity of Funds and Property of a Client.

(A) All funds received or held for the benefit of clients by a member or law firm, including advances for costs and expenses, shall be deposited in one or more identifiable bank accounts labeled "Trust Account," "Client's Funds Account" or words of similar import, maintained in the State of California, or, with written consent of the client, in any other jurisdiction where there is a substantial relationship between the client or the client's business and the other jurisdiction. No funds belonging to the member or the law firm shall be deposited therein or otherwise commingled therewith except as follows:

(1) Funds reasonably sufficient to pay bank charges.

(2) In the case of funds belonging in part to a client and in part presently or potentially to the member or the law firm, the portion belonging to the member or law firm must be withdrawn at the earliest reasonable time after the member's interest in that portion becomes fixed. However, when the right of the member or law firm to receive a portion of trust funds is disputed by the client, the disputed portion shall not be withdrawn until the dispute is finally resolved.

(B) A member shall:

(1) Promptly notify a client of the receipt of the client's funds, securities, or other properties.

(2) Identify and label securities and properties of a client promptly upon receipt and place them in a safe deposit box or other place of safekeeping as soon as practicable.

(3) Maintain complete records of all funds, securities, and other properties of a client coming into the possession of the member or law firm and render appropriate accounts to the client regarding them; preserve such records for a period of no less than five years after final appropriate distribution of such funds or properties; and comply with any order for an audit of such records issued pursuant to the Rules of Procedure of the State Bar.

(4) Promptly pay or deliver, as requested by the client, any funds, securities, or other properties in the

possession of the member which the client is entitled to receive.

(C) The Board of Governors of the State Bar shall have the authority to formulate and adopt standards as to what "records" shall be maintained by members and law firms in accordance with subparagraph (B)(3). The standards formulated and adopted by the Board, as from time to time amended, shall be effective and binding on all members.

Standards:

Pursuant to rule 4-100(C) the Board of Governors of the State Bar adopted the following standards, effective January 1, 1993, as to what "records" shall be maintained by members and law firms in accordance with subparagraph (B)(3).

(1) A member shall, from the date of receipt of client funds through the period ending five years from the date of appropriate disbursement of such funds, maintain:

(a) a written ledger for each client on whose behalf funds are held that sets forth:

(i) the name of such client,

(ii) the date, amount and source of all funds received on behalf of such client,

(iii) the date, amount, payee and purpose of each disbursement made on behalf of such client, and

(iv) the current balance for such client;

(b) a written journal for each bank account that sets forth:

(i) the name of such account,

(ii) the date, amount and client affected by each debit and credit, and

(iii) the current balance in such account;

(c) all bank statements and canceled checks for each bank account; and

(d) each monthly reconciliation (balancing) of (a), (b), and (c).

(2) A member shall, from the date of receipt of all securities and other properties held for the benefit of client through the period ending five years from the date of appropriate disbursement of such securities and other properties, maintain a written journal that specifies:

(a) each item of security and property held;

(b) the person on whose behalf the security or property is held;

(c) the date of receipt of the security or property;

(d) the date of distribution of the security or property; and

(e) person to whom the security or property was distributed.

Adopted Nov. 28, 1988, eff. May 27, 1989; amended eff. Jan. 1, 1993.

Rule 4-200. Fees for Legal Services.

(A) A member shall not enter into an agreement for, charge, or collect an illegal or unconscionable fee.

(B) Unconscionability of a fee shall be determined on the basis of all the facts and circumstances existing at the time the agreement is entered into except where the parties contemplate that the fee will be affected by later events. Among the factors to be considered, where appropriate, in determining the conscionability of a fee are the following:

(1) The amount of the fee in proportion to the value of the services performed.

(2) The relative sophistication of the member and the client.

(3) The novelty and difficulty of the questions involved and the skill requisite to perform the legal service properly.

(4) The likelihood, if apparent to the client, that the acceptance of the particular employment will preclude other employment by the member.

(5) The amount involved and the results obtained.

(6) The time limitations imposed by the client or by the circumstances.

(7) The nature and length of the professional relationship with the client.

(8) The experience, reputation, and ability of the member or members performing the services.

(9) Whether the fee is fixed or contingent.

(10) The time and labor required.

(11) The informed consent of the client to the fee.

Adopted Nov. 28, 1988, eff. May 27, 1989; amended eff. Sept. 14, 1992.

Rule 4-210. Payment of Personal or Business Expenses Incurred by or for a Client.

(A) A member shall not directly or indirectly pay or agree to pay, guarantee, represent, or sanction a representation that the member or member's law firm will pay the personal or business expenses of a prospective or existing client, except that this rule shall not prohibit a member:

(1) With the consent of the client, from paying or agreeing to pay such expenses to third persons from funds collected or to be collected for the client as a result of the representation; or

(2) After employment, from lending money to the client upon the client's promise in writing to repay such loan; or

(3) From advancing the costs of prosecuting or defending a claim or action or otherwise protecting or promoting the client's interests, the repayment of which may be contingent on the outcome of the matter. Such costs within the meaning of this subparagraph (3) shall be limited to all reasonable expenses of litigation or reasonable expenses in preparation for litigation or in providing any legal services to the client.

(B) Nothing in rule 4-210 shall be deemed to limit rules 3-300, 3-310, and 4-300.

Adopted Nov. 28, 1988, eff. May 27, 1989; amended eff. Sept. 14, 1992.

Rule 4-300. Purchasing Property at a Foreclosure or a Sale Subject to Judicial Review.

(A) A member shall not directly or indirectly purchase property at a probate, foreclosure, receiver's, trustee's, or judicial sale in an action or proceeding in which such member or any lawyer affiliated by reason of personal, business, or professional relationship with that member or with that member's law firm is acting as a lawyer for a party or as executor, receiver, trustee, administrator, guardian, or conservator.

(B) A member shall not represent the seller at a probate, foreclosure, receiver, trustee, or judicial sale in an action or proceeding in which the purchaser is a spouse or relative of the member or of another lawyer in the

member's law firm or is an employee of the member or the member's law firm.

Adopted Nov. 28, 1988, eff. May 27, 1989; amended eff. Sept. 14, 1992.

Rule 4-400. Gifts From Client.

A member shall not induce a client to make a substantial gift, including a testamentary gift, to the member or to the member's parent, child, sibling, or spouse, except where the client is related to the member.

Discussion:

A member may accept a gift from a member's client, subject to general standards of fairness and absence of undue influence. The member who participates in the preparation of an instrument memorializing a gift which is otherwise permissible ought not to be subject to professional discipline. On the other hand, where impermissible influence occurred, discipline is appropriate. (See *Magee v. State Bar* (1962) 58 Cal.2d 423 [24 Cal.Rptr. 839].)

Adopted Nov. 28, 1988, eff. May 27, 1989.

CHAPTER 5
ADVOCACY AND REPRESENTATION

Threatening criminal, administrative, or disciplinary charges. Rule 5-100.
Performing the duty of member in government service. Rule 5-110.
Trial publicity. Rule 5-120.
Trial conduct. Rule 5-200.
Member as witness. Rule 5-210.
Suppression of evidence. Rule 5-220.
Contact with officials. Rule 5-300.
Prohibited contact with witnesses. Rule 5-310.
Contact with jurors. Rule 5-320.

Rule 5-100. Threatening Criminal, Administrative, or Disciplinary Charges.

(A) A member shall not threaten to present criminal, administrative, or disciplinary charges to obtain an advantage in a civil dispute.

(B) As used in paragraph (A) of this rule, the term "administrative charges" means the filing or lodging of a complaint with a federal, state, or local governmental entity which may order or recommend the loss or suspension of a license, or may impose or recommend the imposition of a fine, pecuniary sanction, or other sanction of a quasi-criminal nature but does not include filing charges with an administrative entity required by law as a condition precedent to maintaining a civil action.

(C) As used in paragraph (A) of this rule, the term "civil dispute" means a controversy or potential controversy over the rights and duties of two or more parties under civil law, whether or not an action has been commenced, and includes an administrative proceeding of a quasi-civil nature pending before a federal, state, or local governmental entity.

Discussion:

Rule 5-100 is not intended to apply to a member's threatening to initiate contempt proceedings against a party for a failure to comply with a court order.

Paragraph (B) is intended to exempt the threat of filing an administrative charge which is a prerequisite to filing a civil complaint on the same transaction or occurrence.

For purposes of paragraph (C), the definition of "civil dispute" makes clear that the rule is applicable prior to the formal filing of a civil action.

Adopted Nov. 28, 1988, eff. May 27, 1989.

Rule 5-110. Performing the Duty of Member in Government Service.

A member in government service shall not institute or cause to be instituted criminal charges when the member knows or should know that the charges are not supported by probable cause. If, after the institution of criminal charges, the member in government service having responsibility for prosecuting the charges becomes aware that those charges are not supported by probable cause, the member shall promptly so advise the court in which the criminal matter is pending.

Adopted Nov. 28, 1988, eff. May 27, 1989.

Rule 5-120. Trial Publicity.

(A) A member who is participating or has participated in the investigation or litigation of a matter shall not make an extrajudicial statement that a reasonable person would expect to be disseminated by means of public communication if the member knows or reasonably should know that it will have a substantial likelihood of materially prejudicing an adjudicative proceeding in the matter.

(B) Notwithstanding paragraph (A), a member may state:

(1) the claim, offense or defense involved and, except when prohibited by law, the identity of the persons involved;

(2) the information contained in a public record;

(3) that an investigation of the matter is in progress;

(4) the scheduling or result of any step in litigation;

(5) a request for assistance in obtaining evidence and information necessary thereto;

(6) a warning of danger concerning the behavior of a person involved, when there is reason to believe that there exists the likelihood of substantial harm to an individual or the public interest; and

(7) in a criminal case, in addition to subparagraphs (1) through (6):

(a) the identity, residence, occupation, and family status of the accused;

(b) if the accused has not been apprehended, the information necessary to aid in apprehension of that person;

(c) the fact, time, and place of arrest; and

(d) the identity of investigating and arresting officers or agencies and the length of the investigation.

(C) Notwithstanding paragraph (A), a member may make a statement that a reasonable member would believe is required to protect a client from the substantial undue prejudicial effect of recent publicity not initiated by the member or the member's client. A statement made pursuant to this paragraph shall be limited to such information as is necessary to mitigate the recent adverse publicity.

Discussion:

Rule 5-120 is intended to apply equally to prosecutors and criminal defense counsel.

Whether an extrajudicial statement violates rule 5-120 depends on many factors, including: (1) whether the extrajudicial statement presents information clearly inadmissible as evidence in the matter for the purpose of proving or disproving a material fact in issue; (2) whether the extrajudicial statement presents information the member knows is false, deceptive, or the use of which would violate Business and Professions Code section 6068(d); (3) whether the extrajudicial statement violates a lawful "gag" order, or protective order, statute, rule of court, or special rule of confidentiality (for example, in juvenile, domestic, mental disability, and certain criminal proceedings); and (4) the timing of the statement.

Paragraph (A) is intended to apply to statements made by or on behalf of the member.

Subparagraph (B)(6) is not intended to create, augment, diminish, or eliminate any application of the lawyer-client privilege or of Business and Professions Code section 6068(e) regarding the member's duty to maintain client confidence and secrets.

Adopted eff. Oct. 1, 1995.

Rule 5-200. Trial Conduct.

In presenting a matter to a tribunal, a member:

(A) Shall employ, for the purpose of maintaining the causes confided to the member such means only as are consistent with truth;

(B) Shall not seek to mislead the judge, judicial officer, or jury by an artifice or false statement of fact or law;

(C) Shall not intentionally misquote to a tribunal the language of a book, statute, or decision;

(D) Shall not, knowing its invalidity, cite as authority a decision that has been overruled or a statute that has been repealed or declared unconstitutional; and

(E) Shall not assert personal knowledge of the facts at issue, except when testifying as a witness.

Adopted Nov. 28, 1988, eff. May 27, 1989.

Rule 5-210. Member as Witness.

A member shall not act as an advocate before a jury which will hear testimony from the member unless:

(A) The testimony relates to an uncontested matter; or

(B) The testimony relates to the nature and value of legal services rendered in the case; or

(C) The member has the informed written consent of the client. If the member represents the People or a governmental entity, the consent shall be obtained from the head of the office or a designee of the head of the office by which the member is employed and shall be consistent with principles of recusal.

Discussion:

Rule 5-210 is intended to apply to situations in which the member knows or should know that he or she ought to be called as a witness in litigation in which there is a jury. This rule is not intended to encompass situations in which the member is representing the client in an adversarial proceeding and is testifying before a judge. In non-adversarial proceedings, as where the member testifies on behalf of the client in a hearing before a legislative body, rule 5-210 is not applicable.

Rule 5-210 is not intended to apply to circumstances in which a lawyer in an advocate's firm will be a witness.

Adopted Nov. 28, 1988, eff. May 27, 1989; amended eff. Sept. 14, 1992.

Rules of Conduct

Rule 5-220. Suppression of Evidence.

A member shall not suppress any evidence that the member or the member's client has a legal obligation to reveal or to produce.

Adopted Nov. 28, 1988, eff. May 27, 1989.

Rule 5-300. Contact With Officials.

(A)   A member shall not directly or indirectly give or lend anything of value to a judge, official, or employee of a tribunal unless the personal or family relationship between the member and the judge, official, or employee is such that gifts are customarily given and exchanged. Nothing contained in this rule shall prohibit a member from contributing to the campaign fund of a judge running for election or confirmation pursuant to applicable law pertaining to such contributions.

(B)   A member shall not directly or indirectly communicate with or argue to a judge or judicial officer upon the merits of a contested matter pending before such judge or judicial officer, except:

(1)   In open court; or

(2)   With the consent of all other counsel in such matter; or

(3)   In the presence of all other counsel in such matter; or

(4)   In writing with a copy thereof furnished to such other counsel; or

(5)   In ex parte matters.

(C)   As used in this rule, "judge" and "judicial officer" shall include law clerks, research attorneys, or other court personnel who participate in the decision-making process.

Adopted Nov. 28, 1988, eff. May 27, 1989; amended eff. Sept. 14, 1992.

Rule 5-310. Prohibited Contact With Witnesses.

A member shall not:

(A)   Advise or directly or indirectly cause a person to secrete himself or herself or to leave the jurisdiction of a tribunal for the purpose of making that person unavailable as a witness therein.

(B)   Directly or indirectly pay, offer to pay, or acquiesce in the payment of compensation to a witness contingent upon the content of the witness's testimony or the outcome of the case.

Except where prohibited by law, a member may advance, guarantee, or acquiesce in the payment of:

(1)   Expenses reasonably incurred by a witness in attending or testifying.

(2)   Reasonable compensation to a witness for loss of time in attending or testifying.

(3)   A reasonable fee for the professional services of an expert witness.

Adopted Nov. 28, 1988, eff. May 27, 1989.

Rule 5-320. Contact With Jurors.

(A)   A member connected with a case shall not communicate directly or indirectly with anyone the member knows to be a member of the venire from which the jury will be selected for trial of that case.

(B)   During trial a member connected with the case shall not communicate directly or indirectly with any juror.

(C)   During trial a member who is not connected with the case shall not communicate directly or indirectly concerning the case with anyone the member knows is a juror in the case.

(D)   After discharge of the jury from further consideration of a case a member shall not ask questions of or make comments to a member of that jury that are intended to harass or embarrass the juror or to influence the juror's actions in future jury service.

(E)   A member shall not directly or indirectly conduct an out of court investigation of a person who is either a member of the venire or a juror in a manner likely to influence the state of mind of such person in connection with present or future jury service.

(F)   All restrictions imposed by this rule also apply to communications with, or investigations of, members of the family of a person who is either a member of the venire or a juror.

(G)   A member shall reveal promptly to the court improper conduct by a person who is either a member of a venire or a juror, or by another toward a person who is either a member of a venire or a juror or a member of his or her family, of which the member has knowledge.

(H)   This rule does not prohibit a member from communicating with persons who are members of a venire or jurors as a part of the official proceedings.

(I)   For purposes of this rule, "juror" means any empaneled, discharged, or excused juror.

Adopted Nov. 28, 1988, eff. May 27, 1989; amended eff. Sept. 14, 1992; eff. Jan. 1, 2007.

RULES AND POLICY DECLARATIONS OF THE COMMISSION ON JUDICIAL PERFORMANCE

2009 EDITION

The Rules of the Commission on Judicial Performance were adopted at the commission's October 22-23, 1996 meeting. The rules are effective December 1, 1996, and supersede Rules 901–922 of the Rules of Court.

The Policy Declarations of the Commission on Judicial Performance were approved by the commission on May 28, 1997.

The Rules and Policy Declarations of the Commission on Judicial Performance promulgated and adopted by the commission with amendments from November 1, 2007 through November 15, 2008.

The Rules of the Commission on Judicial Performance were last amended October 17, 2007. The Policy Declarations of the Commission on Judicial Performance were last amended October 22, 2008.

PREFACE

From 1961 to 1994, the Judicial Council was responsible for promulgating rules of procedure for the Commission on Judicial Performance. The Judicial Council adopted rules 901-922 of the Rules of Court as rules for the censure, removal, retirement or private admonishment of judges.

Since its early history, the commission has deliberated on and recorded in its minutes its resolutions regarding significant policy issues. These resolutions address areas not detailed in its governing provisions (California Constitution, Rules of Court, and Government Code) including internal organization and management, staff functions, and implementation of the rules and statutes regarding formal proceedings and disability matters. In 1984, the commission collected the statements of existing policy in a single, amendable document entitled Policy Declarations of the Commission on Judicial Performance.

Proposition 190, approved by California voters in the November 1994 general election, took effect March 1, 1995. One of the most significant changes implemented by Proposition 190 was a change in authority for promulgating rules regarding commission procedures and confidentiality. The commission now has the authority to promulgate its own rules.

In April 1995, the commission adopted rules 901-922 of the Rules of Court as interim rules pending a comprehensive review of the rules. The commission also adopted Policy Declarations 1.1 through 4.4, amended rule 917 to require a vote of six members of the commission, and adopted transitional Rules 1, 2 and 3. The commission adopted two new rules, Rules 120 and 127, as interim rules in May 1996.

At its October 22-23, 1996 meeting, the commission adopted the Rules of the Commission on Judicial Performance. The commission Rules took effect December 1, 1996 and replaced rules 901-918 and 922 of the Rules of Court and transitional Rules 1, 2 and 3. Rules 919, 920 and 921 concern Supreme Court review of commission determinations and were not reviewed by the commission.

The Policy Declarations of the Commission on Judicial Performance were approved by the commission on May 28, 1997.

Table Showing Changes Promulgated by the Commission on Judicial Performance
From November 1, 2007 Through November 15, 2008

Policy Declaration	Effect	Date
1.14	Adopted	May 22, 2008
Div. VI Preface	Amended	Dec. 13, 2007
6.3	Amended	Dec. 13, 2007
Div. VII	Adopted	Oct. 22, 2008
7.1	Adopted	Oct. 22, 2008

Rules of Jud Perf

RULES OF THE COMMISSION ON JUDICIAL PERFORMANCE

Rule 101. Interested Party.

Judges who are members of the commission or of the Supreme Court may not participate as such in any commission proceedings involving themselves.

Adopted Oct. 24, 1996, effective Dec. 1, 1996.

Rule 102. Confidentiality and Disclosure.

(a) **(Scope of rule)** Except as provided in this rule, all papers filed with and proceedings before the commis-

sion shall be confidential. Nothing in this rule prohibits the respondent judge or anyone other than a commission member or member of commission staff from making statements regarding the judge's conduct underlying a complaint or proceeding.

(b) **(Disclosure after institution of formal proceedings)** When the commission institutes formal proceedings, the following shall not be confidential:

(1) The notice of formal proceedings and all subsequent papers filed with the commission and the special masters, all stipulations entered, all findings of fact and conclusions of law made by the special masters and by the commission, and all determinations of removal, censure and public admonishment made by the commission;

(2) The formal hearing before the special masters and the appearance before the commission.

(c) **(Explanatory statements)** The commission may issue explanatory statements under article VI, section 18(k) of the California Constitution.

(d) **(Submission of proposed statement of clarification and correction regarding commission proceedings by judge)** Notwithstanding rule 102(a), if public reports concerning a commission proceeding result in substantial unfairness to the judge involved in the proceeding, including unfairness resulting from reports which are false or materially misleading or inaccurate, the involved judge may submit a proposed statement of clarification and correction to the commission and request its issuance. The commission shall either issue the requested statement, advise the judge in writing that it declines to issue the requested statement, or issue a modified statement.

(e) **(Disclosure to complainant)** Upon completion of an investigation or proceeding, the commission shall disclose to the person complaining against the judge that the commission (1) has found no basis for action against the judge or determined not to proceed further in this matter, (2) has taken an appropriate corrective action, the nature of which shall not be disclosed, or (3) has publicly admonished, censured, removed, or retired the judge, or has found the person unfit to serve as a subordinate judicial officer. Where a matter is referred to the commission by a presiding judge or other public official in his or her official capacity, disclosure under this subdivision concerning that matter shall be made to the individual serving in that office at the time the matter is concluded. The name of the judge shall not be used in any written communication to the complainant, unless formal proceedings have been instituted or unless the complainant is a presiding judge or other public official in his or her official capacity. Written communications in which the judge's name is not used shall include the date of the complaint as a cross-reference.

(f) (Public safety) When the commission receives information concerning a threat to the safety of any person or persons, information concerning such a threat may be provided to the person threatened, to persons or organizations responsible for the safety of the person threatened, and to law enforcement and/or any appropriate prosecutorial agency.

(g) (Disclosure of information to prosecuting authorities) The commission may release to prosecuting authorities at any time information which reveals possible criminal conduct by the judge or former judge or by any other individual or entity.

(h) (Disclosure of records to public entity upon request or consent of judge) If a judge or former judge requests or consents to release of commission records to a public entity, the commission may release that judge's records.

(i) (Disclosure of records of disciplinary action to appointing authorities) The commission shall, upon request, provide to the Governor of any State of the Union, the President of the United States, or the Commission on Judicial Appointments the text of any private admonishment or advisory letter issued after March 1, 1995 or any other disciplinary action together with any information that the commission deems necessary to a full understanding of the commission's action, with respect to any applicant under consideration for any judicial appointment, provided that:

(1) The request is in writing; and

(2) Any information released to the appointing authority is simultaneously provided to the applicant.

All information disclosed to appointing authorities under this subdivision remains privileged and confidential. Private admonishments and advisory letters issued before March 1, 1995 shall only be disclosed under this section with the judge's written consent.

(j) (Disclosure of information regarding pending proceedings to appointing authorities) The commission may, upon request, in the interest of justice or to maintain public confidence in the administration of justice, provide to the Governor of any State of the Union, the President of the United States, the Commission on Judicial Appointments, or any other state or federal authorities responsible for judicial appointments information concerning any pending investigation or proceeding with respect to any applicant under consideration for any judicial appointment, provided that:

(1) The request is in writing; and

(2) Any information released to the appointing authority is simultaneously provided to the applicant.

If a disclosure about a pending matter is made and that matter subsequently is closed by the commission without discipline being imposed, disclosure of the latter fact shall be made promptly to the appointing authority and the judge.

All information disclosed to appointing authorities under this subdivision remains privileged and confidential.

(k) (Disclosure of information to regulatory agencies upon retirement or resignation) If a judge retires or resigns from office or if a subordinate judicial officer retires, resigns or is terminated from employment after a complaint is filed with the commission, or if a complaint is filed with the commission after the retirement, resignation or termination, the commission may, in the interest of justice or to maintain public confidence in the administration of justice, release information concerning the complaint, investigation and proceedings to the State Bar or to other regulatory agencies, provided that the commission has commenced a preliminary investigation or other proceeding and the judge or subordinate judicial officer has had an opportunity to respond to the commission's inquiry or preliminary investigation letter.

(l) (Disclosure of information about subordinate judicial officers to presiding judges) The commission may release to a presiding judge or his or her designee information concerning a complaint, investigation or disposition involving a subordinate judicial officer, including the name of the subordinate judicial officer, consistent with the commission's jurisdiction under article VI, section 18.1 of the California Constitution.

(m) (Disclosure of information regarding disciplinary action and pending proceedings to the Chief Justice) With respect to any judge who is under consideration for judicial assignment following retirement or resignation, or is sitting on assignment, the commission may, upon the request of the Chief Justice of California and with the consent of that judge, in the interest of justice or to maintain public confidence in the administration of justice, provide the Chief Justice information concerning any record of disciplinary action or any pending investigation or proceeding with respect to that judge, provided that:

(1) The request and consent are in writing;

(2) If the disclosure involves a pending investigation or proceeding, the judge has had an opportunity to respond to the pending investigation or proceeding; and

(3) Any information released to the Chief Justice is simultaneously provided to the judge seeking assignment.

If the disclosure involves disciplinary action, the commission may include any information the commission deems necessary to a full understanding of its action.

If a disclosure about a pending matter is made and that matter subsequently is closed by the commission without discipline being imposed, disclosure of the latter fact shall be made promptly to the Chief Justice and the judge.

All information disclosed to the Chief Justice under this subdivision remains privileged and confidential.

(n) (Disclosure of information to presiding judges about possible lack of capacity or other inability to perform) The commission may release to a presiding judge or his or her designee information concerning an investigation involving possible lack of capacity or other inability to perform judicial duties on the part of a judge of that court, except that no confidential medical information concerning the judge may be released.

Adopted Oct. 24, 1996, effective Dec. 1, 1996; amended Oct. 8, 1998; Feb. 11, 1999; Jan. 29, 2003; Aug. 26, 2004; Oct. 25, 2005; May 23, 2007.

Rule 103. Protection From Liability for Statements.

The making of statements to the commission, the filing of papers with or the giving of testimony before the commission, or before the masters appointed by the

Supreme Court pursuant to rule 121, shall not give rise to civil liability for the person engaged in such acts. This privilege extends to any motions or petitions filed in the Supreme Court, as well as papers filed in connection therewith. No other publication of such statements, papers or proceedings shall be so privileged.

Adopted Oct. 24, 1996, effective Dec. 1, 1996.

Rule 104. Duty to Cooperate; Response by Respondent Judge.

(a) A respondent judge shall cooperate with the commission in all proceedings in accordance with Government Code section 68725. The judge's cooperation or lack of cooperation may be considered by the commission in determining the appropriate disciplinary sanction or disposition as well as further proceedings to be taken by the commission but may not be considered in making evidentiary determinations.

(b) A respondent judge shall, within the time limits set forth in rules 110(a) and 111(a), respond to the merits of a staff inquiry letter or preliminary investigation letter.

(c) A respondent judge shall, within the time limits set forth in rule 119(b), file an answer to a notice of formal proceedings which comports with the requirements set forth in rule 119(c).

(d) A respondent judge shall file all other responses and documents required in commission proceedings within such reasonable time as the commission may prescribe, and shall comply with all other requirements of commission proceedings, including the discovery requirements set forth in rule 122.

(e) In accordance with California Evidence Code section 913, no inference shall be drawn as to any matter in issue or to the credibility of the judge based on a refusal to respond as required by this rule or to respond to a question at a hearing under rule 123 when such refusal is based on the exercise of the privilege against self-incrimination or of any other Evidence Code privilege or of any other privilege recognized by law.

Adopted Oct. 24, 1996, effective Dec. 1, 1996; amended Oct. 25, 2005.

Rule 105. Medical Examination.

A judge shall, upon a finding of good cause by seven members of the commission and within such reasonable time as the commission may prescribe, submit to a medical examination ordered by the commission. The examination must be limited to the conditions stated in the finding of good cause. No examination by a specialist in psychiatry may be required without the consent of the judge.

Adopted Oct. 24, 1996, effective Dec. 1, 1996.

Rule 106. Judge's Representation by Counsel.

A judge may be represented by counsel in all commission proceedings. The written communications of counsel shall be deemed to be the written communications of the judge. Counsel has the authority to bind the judge as to all matters except a stipulation as to discipline.

Any paper filed with the commission and any written statement made to the commission or to its staff must be signed by the judge or the judge's counsel. A stipulation as to discipline must be signed by the judge. The signing of any document or statement warrants that the signer has personal knowledge of the matter contained in the document or statement or has investigated the matter and has a good faith belief in the accuracy of the representations contained in the document or statement.

This rule applies to the filing of responses to staff inquiry letters and preliminary investigation letters under rules 110 and 111, to the filing of answers in formal proceedings under rule 119, and to all other filings with the commission and the masters and all other correspondence with the commission.

Adopted Oct. 24, 1996, effective Dec. 1, 1996.

Rule 107. Notice Requirements.

(a) **(Notices of staff inquiry, preliminary investigation, intended private admonishment, and intended public admonishment)** All notices of a staff inquiry, preliminary investigation, or intended private admonishment or public admonishment shall be sent to a judge at chambers or at his or her residence unless otherwise requested, and a copy thereof shall be mailed to counsel of record. If a judge does not occupy chambers and his or her place of residence is unknown, the notice shall be sent to the judge's last known address. If the notice relates to a staff inquiry, the notice shall be given by first-class mail. If the notice relates to a preliminary investigation or intended private admonishment or public admonishment, the notice shall be given by prepaid (1) certified mail return receipt requested, or (2) overnight mail delivery with a proof of delivery service, or (3) personal service with proof of service. If the judge's last known address is outside of the United States, service shall be made by recorded delivery. Envelopes containing such notices shall be marked "personal and confidential"; the inscription "Commission on Judicial Performance" shall not be used on the envelopes. In the event of service by certified or recorded mail, service is complete at the time of mailing.

(b) **(Service of notice of formal proceedings, other notices and correspondence in connection with formal proceedings)** After institution of formal proceedings, the service of the notice of formal proceedings shall be made as set forth in rule 118, and the giving of notice or sending of other correspondence in connection with the formal proceedings shall be accomplished as set forth in rule 126.

Adopted Oct. 24, 1996, effective Dec. 1, 1996; amended Oct. 25, 2005.

Rule 108. Extensions of Time.

(a) **(Extensions for response to staff inquiry letters)** A judge may, upon submission of a written request for extension to the chairperson prior to the expiration of time for filing a response to a staff inquiry letter under rule 110, obtain a 30-day extension of time for filing the response to the staff inquiry letter.

(b) **(Extensions for response to preliminary investigation letter and for answer to notice of formal proceedings)** Upon a showing of good cause submitted by the judge, the chairperson may extend the time for filing a response to a preliminary investigation letter under rule 111 or for filing an answer to a notice of formal proceedings.

(c) (Extension of time for commencing hearing before the special masters) In order to maintain public confidence in the integrity of the judiciary and protect the welfare of the public, all hearings before the special masters shall be heard at the earliest possible time after the issuance under rule 118 of the notice of formal proceedings. In accordance with this policy, extensions of time for commencing a hearing before the special masters are disfavored. The chairperson of the commission or the presiding master may extend the time for commencing a hearing before the special masters upon a showing of good cause, supported by declaration detailing specific facts showing that a continuance is necessary. Good cause does not include the ordinary press of business.

(d) (Extension of time for filing report of the masters) The chairperson may, upon request of the masters, extend the time for the filing of the report of the masters under rule 129.

(e) (Other extensions of time) Any other or further extension of time may be granted by the chairperson only upon a showing of good cause.

(f) (Alternative authority) The chairperson may delegate his or her authority under this rule to another member, and the commission may designate any member to act instead of the chairperson.

Adopted Oct. 24, 1996, effective Dec. 1, 1996; amended Oct. 8, 1998; Jan. 26, 2000; Oct. 25, 2005; interim amendment Jan. 31, 2007; amended May 23, 2007.

Rule 109. Commencement of Commission Action.

(a) (Receipt of written statement) Upon receiving a written statement alleging facts indicating that a judge is guilty of willful misconduct in office, persistent failure or inability to perform the duties of office, habitual intemperance in the use of intoxicants or drugs, or conduct prejudicial to the administration of justice that brings the judicial office into disrepute, or that the judge has a disability that seriously interferes with the performance of the duties of office and is or is likely to become permanent, or that the judge has engaged in an improper action or a dereliction of duty, the commission may:

(1) In an appropriate case, determine that the statement is obviously unfounded or frivolous and dismiss the proceeding;

(2) If the statement is not obviously unfounded or frivolous, make a staff inquiry to determine whether sufficient facts exist to warrant a preliminary investigation; or

(3) If sufficient facts are determined in the course of a staff inquiry or otherwise, make a preliminary investigation to determine whether formal proceedings should be instituted and a hearing held.

(b) (Staff inquiry or preliminary investigation on commission's own motion) The commission may make a staff inquiry or preliminary investigation on the basis of information received by the commission not contained in a written report indicating that a judge is guilty of willful misconduct in office, persistent failure or inability to perform the duties of office, habitual intemperance in the

use of intoxicants or drugs, or conduct prejudicial to the administration of justice that brings the judicial office into disrepute, or that the judge has a disability that seriously interferes with the performance of the duties of office and is or is likely to become permanent, or that the judge has engaged in an improper action or a dereliction of duty.

(c) (Staff inquiry or preliminary investigation of subordinate judicial officers) The commission may make a staff inquiry or a preliminary investigation of a subordinate judicial officer whenever:

(1) The commission receives from a complainant a written request within 30 days after the date of mailing of notice to the complainant by the local court of the disposition of a complaint against a subordinate judicial officer, and the commission concludes that the local court may have abused its discretion in its disposition of such complaint;

(2) The commission receives from a local court a request that the commission investigate or adjudicate a complaint against a subordinate judicial officer;

(3) The commission receives from a local court information that a complaint resulted in the written reprimand, suspension, or removal of the subordinate judicial officer; or

(4) The commission receives from a local court information that a subordinate judicial officer resigned while an investigation was pending and before a final decision was made by the local court.

Subsection (c) applies only to complaints about a subordinate judicial officer received in the local court on or after June 3, 1998; subdivision (1) of subsection (c) applies only in cases in which the complainant was apprised by the local court of the 30-day time limit for seeking review by the commission.

(d) (Notification of disposition at the judge's request) Upon request from a judge who is the subject of a complaint before the commission, the commission shall notify the judge in writing of the disposition of the complaint if:

(1) The judge's request to the commission specifically describes the underlying incident giving rise to the complaint;

(2) The pendency of the complaint has become generally known to the public; or

(3) The judge has received written notice of the complaint from someone who is not associated with the commission.

Adopted Oct. 24, 1996, effective Dec. 1, 1996; amended Oct. 8, 1998; Feb. 11, 1999; Jan. 29, 2003; Oct. 25, 2005.

Rule 110. Staff Inquiry; Advisory Letter After Staff Inquiry.

(a) (Notice prior to issuance of advisory letter) If the commission makes a staff inquiry, the judge shall be notified of the inquiry and the nature of the charge, before the commission issues an advisory letter. The respondent judge so notified shall be afforded a reasonable opportunity in the course of the inquiry to present such matters as the judge may choose. A reasonable time for a judge to respond to an inquiry letter shall be 20 days from the date the letter was mailed to the judge unless the time is extended pursuant to rule 108.

(b) **(Termination of staff inquiry)** If the staff inquiry does not disclose sufficient cause to warrant issuance of a confidential advisory letter or further proceedings, the commission shall terminate the staff inquiry and notify the judge in writing of such action if the judge was notified of the staff inquiry pursuant to subdivision (a).

(c) **(Advisory letter)** At any time after notice of a staff inquiry and a reasonable opportunity to respond has been given to the judge, the commission may determine that the judge's conduct does not constitute a basis for further proceedings and issue a confidential advisory letter to the judge.

Adopted Oct. 24, 1996, effective Dec. 1, 1996.

Rule 111. Preliminary Investigation.

(a) **(Notice)** If the commission commences a preliminary investigation, the judge shall be notified of the investigation and the nature of the charge, and shall be afforded a reasonable opportunity in the course of the preliminary investigation to present such matters as the judge may choose. A reasonable time for a judge to respond to a preliminary investigation letter shall be 20 days from the date the letter was mailed to the judge unless the time is extended pursuant to rule 108.

(b) **(Termination of investigation)** If the preliminary investigation does not disclose sufficient cause to warrant further proceedings, the commission shall terminate the investigation and notify the judge in writing.

(c) **(Advisory letter)** At any time after notice of a preliminary investigation and a reasonable opportunity to respond has been given to the judge, the commission may determine that the judge's conduct does not constitute a basis for further proceedings and may terminate the investigation by issuing a confidential advisory letter to the judge.

Adopted Oct. 24, 1996, effective Dec. 1, 1996.

Rule 111.5. Correction of Advisory Letter.

A judge who receives an advisory letter under either rule 110(c) or rule 111(c) may, within 30 days of the mailing thereof, apply to the commission for correction of an error of fact or law or both. The application shall be determined by the commission without an appearance by the judge before the commission unless the commission determines otherwise.

Adopted Oct. 25, 2005.

Rule 112. Monitoring.

The commission may defer termination of a preliminary investigation for a period not to exceed two years for observation and review of a judge's conduct. The judge shall be advised in writing of the type of behavior for which the judge is being monitored. (Such disclosure shall not limit the commission's consideration of misconduct involving other types of behavior which may be observed or reported during the period of monitoring.)

Adopted Oct. 24, 1996, effective Dec. 1, 1996.

Rule 113. Notice of Intended Private Admonishment.

If after a preliminary investigation the commission determines that there is good cause for a private admon-

ishment, the commission may issue a notice of intended private admonishment to the judge by certified mail. The notice shall include a statement of facts found by the commission and the reasons for the proposed admonishment. The notice shall also contain an advisement as to the judge's options under rule 114. The notice may cite any discipline that was imposed on the judge prior to issuance of the notice.

Adopted Oct. 24, 1996, effective Dec. 1, 1996; amended Feb. 11, 1999; May 23, 2007.

Rule 114. Private Admonishment Procedure.

A judge who receives a notice of intended private admonishment pursuant to rule 113 has the following options:

(a) **(Acceptance of private admonishment)** The judge may choose not to contest the intended private admonishment. If the judge does not contest the intended private admonishment within 30 days after the mailing of a notice of intended private admonishment, the admonishment becomes effective.

(b) **(Appearance before commission)** The judge may, within 30 days of the mailing of a notice of intended private admonishment, file with the commission written objections to the intended private admonishment, waive the right to formal proceedings under rule 118 and to review by the Supreme Court, and demand an appearance before the commission to contest the intended private admonishment.

After the time set for the appearance before the commission, the commission may:

(1) Close the matter without disciplinary action;

(2) Close the matter with a confidential advisory letter; or

(3) Issue a private admonishment.

If the commission determines to issue discipline, it may in its final decision modify the notice in response to the judge's written objections and any oral presentation.

(c) **(Formal proceedings)** The judge may, within 30 days of the mailing of a notice of intended private admonishment, file with the commission a demand for formal proceedings pursuant to rule 118.

Adopted Oct. 24, 1996, effective Dec. 1, 1996; amended Jan. 29, 2003; Oct. 25, 2005; Jan. 31, 2007.

Rule 115. Notice of Intended Public Admonishment.

If the commission determines following a preliminary investigation that there is good cause for public discipline, the commission may issue a notice of intended public admonishment to the judge by certified mail. The notice shall include a statement of facts found by the commission and the reasons for the proposed admonishment. The notice shall also contain an advisement as to the judge's options under rule 116. The notice may cite any discipline that was imposed on the judge prior to issuance of the notice.

Adopted Oct. 24, 1996, effective Dec. 1, 1996; amended Feb. 11, 1999; May 23, 2007.

Rule 116. Public Admonishment Procedure.

A judge who receives a notice of intended public

Rules of Jud Perf

admonishment pursuant to rule 115 has the following options:

(a) **(Acceptance of public admonishment)** The judge may choose not to contest the intended public admonishment. If the judge does not contest the intended public admonishment within 30 days after the mailing of a notice of intended public admonishment, the admonishment becomes effective.

(b) **(Appearance before commission)** The judge may, within 30 days of the mailing of a notice of intended public admonishment, file with the commission written objections to the intended public admonishment, waive the right to formal proceedings under rule 118 and to review by the Supreme Court, and demand an appearance before the commission to contest the intended public admonishment.

After the time set for the appearance before the commission, the commission may:

(1) Close the matter without disciplinary action;

(2) Close the matter with a confidential advisory letter;

(3) Issue a private admonishment; or

(4) Issue a public admonishment.

If the commission determines to issue discipline, it may in its final decision modify the notice in response to the judge's written objections and any oral presentation.

(c) **(Formal proceedings)** The judge may, within 30 days of the mailing of a notice of intended public admonishment, file with the commission a demand for formal proceedings pursuant to rule 118.

Adopted Oct. 24, 1996, effective Dec. 1, 1996; amended Jan. 29, 2003; Oct. 25, 2005.

Rule 116.5.　Negotiated Settlement During Preliminary Investigation.

At any time during a preliminary investigation or an admonishment proceeding under rules 113-116, the commission may designate trial counsel or another attorney authorized by the commission to negotiate with the judge a resolution of any matter at issue. A proposed resolution shall be jointly submitted to the commission, which may accept it, reject it or return it to the judge and examiner to consider modifications to it. No agreement between the judge and legal staff is binding unless approved by the commission. A settlement proposal rejected by the commission cannot be used against the judge in any proceedings. After formal proceedings are instituted, settlement negotiations are governed by rule 127.

Adopted May 23, 2007.

Rule 117.　Use and Retention of Commission Records.

(a) **(Use of records outside the limitation period)** Commission records of complaints against a judge shall not be used for any purpose if the complaints (1) relate to actions occurring more than six years prior to the commencement of the judge's current term and (2) did not result in issuance of an advisory letter, public or private admonishment, censure, or removal of the judge.

(b) **(Records disposition program)** The commission shall adopt a records disposition program designed to

dispose of those records which cannot be used for any purpose under this rule or which are no longer necessary for the performance of its duties.

Adopted Oct. 24, 1996, effective Dec. 1, 1996.

Rule 118.　Notice of Formal Proceedings.

(a) **(Issuance of notice)** After the preliminary investigation has been completed, if the commission concludes that formal proceedings should be instituted, the commission shall without delay issue a written notice to the judge advising the judge of the institution of formal proceedings to inquire into the charges against the judge. Such proceedings shall be entitled:

"BEFORE THE COMMISSION ON JUDICIAL PERFORMANCE Inquiry Concerning Judge ＿＿＿＿＿＿, No.＿＿＿＿＿."

(b) **(Content of notice)** The notice shall specify in ordinary and concise language the charges against the judge and the alleged facts upon which such charges are based, and shall advise the judge of the duty to file a written answer to the charges within 20 days after service of the notice upon the judge.

(c) **(Service of notice)** After a notice of formal proceedings is signed by the chairperson of the commission, the chairperson's designee or other member designated by the commission, the notice shall be served by personal service of a copy thereof on the judge, unless the judge personally or through counsel waives personal service and consents to service by mail. If there is no consent to service by mail and it appears to the chairperson of the commission upon affidavit that, after reasonable effort for a period of 10 days, personal service could not be had, service may be made upon the judge by mailing, by prepaid certified mail, copies of the notice addressed to the judge at the judge's chambers and last known residence. In the event of service by certified mail, service is complete at the time of mailing.

(d) **(Public announcement)** Not less than five days after service of the notice of formal proceedings as set forth above, the commission shall issue a public announcement advising that formal proceedings have been instituted, and shall make public the notice of formal proceedings. The public announcement shall set forth the date the judge's answer to the notice of formal proceedings is due, and shall indicate that the answer to the notice of formal proceedings will be made public.

Adopted Oct. 24, 1996, effective Dec. 1, 1996; amended Feb. 11, 1999; Oct. 25, 2005; Oct. 17, 2007.

Rule 119.　Answer.

(a) **(Pleadings and motions)** The notice of formal proceedings and answer shall constitute the pleadings. No further pleadings shall be filed and no motion or demurrer shall be filed against any of the pleadings.

(b) **(Filing of answer)** Within 20 days after service of the notice of formal proceedings the judge shall serve, in accordance with rule 119.5, and file with the commission an answer, which shall be verified and shall conform in style to subdivision (b) of rule 8.204 of the California Rules of Court. The chairperson, the chairperson's designee or other member designated by the commission may grant an extension of time only upon timely written request establishing good cause for an extension of time.

(c) (Content of answer) The answer shall be as complete and straightforward as the information reasonably available to the respondent judge permits. The answer shall (1) admit each allegation which is true, (2) deny each allegation which is untrue, and (3) specify each allegation as to the truth of which the judge lacks sufficient information or knowledge. If a respondent judge gives lack of information or knowledge as a reason for a failure to admit or deny any allegation, the respondent judge shall state in the answer that a reasonable inquiry concerning the matter in the particular allegation has been made, and that the information known or readily obtainable is insufficient to enable the respondent judge to admit or deny the matter.

Adopted Oct. 24, 1996, effective Dec. 1, 1996; amended Jan. 26, 2000; Jan. 29, 2003; Jan. 31, 2007.

Rule 119.5. Filing With the Commission During Formal Proceedings.

After institution of formal proceedings, all briefs and other papers to be filed with the commission shall be delivered to commission staff at the commission office during regular business hours and shall be accompanied by a proof of service of the document upon the other party or parties, and upon the special masters if they have been appointed in the matter. This includes documents submitted in conjunction with a hearing before the special masters, other than exhibits to be admitted at the hearing. Exhibits admitted at a hearing before the masters shall be transmitted to the commission office pursuant to rule 125.5. A document is filed with the commission when the original is stamped or otherwise marked "filed" with the date. The commission's agent for purposes of filing documents after institution of formal proceedings is the Legal Advisor to Commissioners or the Legal Advisor's designee. A filing may be evidenced by a conformed copy of the cover page of each document submitted for filing.

Adopted Feb. 11, 1999; amended Oct. 25, 2005; interim amendment Jan. 31, 2007; amended May 23, 2007.

Rule 120. Disqualification.

(a) (Disqualification upon determination to remove, retire or bar from assignments) If the commission determines that a judge should be removed or retired from office, the commission will, in its order of removal or retirement, also order pursuant to article VI, section 18(b) of the California Constitution that the judge be disqualified from acting as a judge, without loss of salary, until the commission's determination becomes final or until any decision by the Supreme Court on any petition for review becomes final. If the commission determines to censure and bar a former judge from receiving assignments, the commission will, in its order of censure, also order that the judge be barred from receiving assignments until the commission's determination becomes final or until any decision by the Supreme Court on any petition for review becomes final.

(b) (Disqualification upon notice of formal proceedings) Before the commission has reached a determination regarding removal or retirement of a judge, the commission may temporarily disqualify a judge with-

out loss of salary upon notice of formal proceedings pursuant to article VI, section 18(b) of the California Constitution if the commission determines that the continued service of the judge is causing immediate, irreparable, and continuing public harm.

If good cause for disqualification is apparent, the commission may issue a notice of intention to temporarily disqualify the judge along with a notice of formal proceedings. Subsequent to the filing of a notice of formal proceedings, the examiner may file with the commission a motion to temporarily disqualify the judge. The commission's notice of intention to disqualify or the examiner's motion to disqualify shall be by personal service or service upon the judge's counsel. If such service cannot be effectuated, service shall be by prepaid certified mail upon the judge at his or her chambers and last known residence. If service is by mail, the notice shall be accompanied by an affidavit or certificate of mailing and an affidavit shall be filed regarding the inability to effectuate personal service or service upon counsel.

The judge shall have an opportunity to respond in writing within 10 days of receipt of the commission's notice of intention to disqualify or the examiner's motion to disqualify, or within 15 days after the mailing of the notice, whichever occurs first. The time for filing a response shall not be subject to extension under rule 108. The judge's response may include points and authorities in support of any legal arguments, and may include verified statements, other testimony, medical or other expert reports and any other evidence in opposition to the facts on which the commission's notice of intention to disqualify or the examiner's motion to disqualify is based. Upon the filing of a response or expiration of time for filing a response, the commission may issue an order of temporary disqualification.

(c) (Accelerated disposition of charges) In cases in which a judge is temporarily disqualified under rule 120(b) the disposition of the charges in the notice of formal proceedings shall be accelerated and the formal proceedings shall proceed without appreciable delay. In such cases, the commission may reduce the number of days provided in rules 122, 129, and 130 for the filing of papers in connection with the formal proceedings.

(d) (Duration of temporary disqualification) An order for temporary disqualification of a judge under subdivision (b) of this rule shall remain in effect until further order of the commission or until the pending formal proceedings have been concluded by the commission.

Adopted Oct. 24, 1996, effective Dec. 1, 1996; amended Oct. 8, 1998; Feb. 11, 1999.

Rule 120.5. Suspension; Termination of Suspension; Removal of Suspended Judge.

(a) (Felony) When the commission receives proof that a judge has pled guilty or no contest to, or has been found guilty of, a felony under California or federal law, the commission shall promptly issue an order suspending the judge from office without salary.

(b) (Crime punishable as a felony or that involves moral turpitude) When the commission receives proof that a judge has pled guilty or no contest to, or has been found guilty of, a crime that is not a felony under California or federal law but is punishable as a felony under that law or involves moral turpitude under that law, the commission shall promptly issue a notice of intention to suspend the judge without salary in accordance with subdivision (e) of this rule.

(c) (Reversal of conviction) If a judge is suspended by reason of article VI, section 18, subdivision (c) of the California Constitution, and the commission receives proof that the conviction has been reversed, the commission shall promptly issue a notice of intention to terminate the suspension in accordance with subdivision (e) of this rule.

(d) (Finality of conviction) If a judge is suspended by reason of article VI, section 18, subdivision (c) of the California Constitution, and the commission receives proof that the conviction is final, the commission shall promptly issue a notice of intention to remove the judge from office in accordance with subdivision (e) of this rule.

(e) (Notice) Any notice issued pursuant to this rule shall be in accordance with the following:

(1) The notice shall be given to the judge or judge's counsel and to the examiner or other attorney designated by the commission to receive notice in the matter.

(2) The notice shall be by personal service or service upon the judge's counsel. If such service cannot be effectuated, service shall be by prepaid certified mail upon the judge at his or her chambers and last known residence. If service is by mail, the notice shall be accompanied by an affidavit or certificate of mailing and an affidavit shall be filed regarding the inability to effectuate personal service or service upon counsel. If the service is by certified mail, service is complete at the time of mailing.

(3) The judge shall have an opportunity to respond in writing within 10 days of receipt by the judge of a notice of intended suspension under subdivision (b) or a notice of intended removal under subdivision (d), or within 15 days after the mailing of the notice, whichever occurs first. Within five days after receipt of the judge's response, or within 20 days of the mailing of the notice if no response is filed, whichever occurs first, the examiner or other attorney designated by the commission may present points and authorities respecting the notice and in reply to any response. The commission may request additional briefing. Extensions of time under this subdivision are disfavored and will be granted only upon a specific and affirmative showing of good cause. Good cause does not include ordinary press of business.

(4) The examiner or other attorney designated by the commission shall have an opportunity to respond in writing within 10 days of receipt of a notice of intended termination of suspension under subdivision (c). Within five days after receipt of the response of the examiner or other attorney designated by the commission, or within 15 days of the mailing of the notice if no response is filed, whichever occurs first, the judge may present points and authorities respecting the notice and in reply to any response. The commission may request additional briefing. Extensions of time under this subdivision are disfavored and will be granted only upon a specific and affirmative showing of good cause. Good cause does not include ordinary press of business.

(5) Upon receipt of the points and authorities or reply or the expiration of the time for the filing thereof, whichever occurs first, or upon receipt of any additional briefs as may be requested by the commission, the commission shall promptly issue its order if it concludes that the relevant standards specified in article VI, section 18, subdivision (c) of the California Constitution have been met.

Adopted Oct. 25, 2005; amended Jan. 31, 2007.

Rule 121. Setting for Hearing Before Commission or Masters.

(a) (Time for setting for hearing) On filing or on expiration of the time for filing an answer, the commission shall set the matter for hearing.

(b) (Appointment of special masters or master) Unless the commission determines to hold the hearing before itself, the commission may request the Supreme Court to appoint three special masters to hear and take evidence in the matter, and to report to the commission. On a vote of seven members of the commission and with the consent of the judge involved, the commission may request the Supreme Court to appoint one special master in place of three special masters. Consent of the judge shall be defined as (1) written agreement by the judge or counsel of record, or (2) failure to object in writing within 30 days of notice of the commission's intention to request the appointment of one special master.

(c) (Requirements for special masters) Special masters shall be judges. When there are three special masters, not more than two of them may be retired judges from courts of record.

(d) (Notice to respondent judge of appointment of special masters and examiner) Upon appointment of special masters or a single special master by the Supreme Court and appointment of an examiner by the commission, the respondent judge shall be given notice of the orders appointing the masters and the examiner, and the examiner shall be given notice of the order appointing the special masters.

(e) (Notice of hearing) The commission shall set a time and place for hearing before itself or before the masters and shall give notice by mail confirming the date and place of the hearing to the judge and the examiner at least 20 days before the hearing.

Adopted Oct. 24, 1996, effective Dec. 1, 1996.

Rule 122. Discovery Procedures.

(a) (Exclusive procedures) The procedures in this rule shall constitute the exclusive procedures for discovery. Discovery may be obtained only after a written notice of formal proceedings is issued.

(b) (Applicability to both parties) The examiner and the judge are each entitled to discovery from the other in accordance with these procedures.

(c) (Initial discovery provided by trial counsel) At the time of service of the notice of formal proceedings, the judge shall be provided copies of all documents and other information specified in rule 122(e) which is not privileged and is in the possession of the commission. Such information shall be made available at the commission offices. Alternatively, if a judge requests that the materials be sent to a specific address, the commission shall provide the judge with copies of said documents and information at that address.

(d) (Discovery requests) Discovery requests may be made in writing at any time after the filing of the notice of formal proceedings. All requests for discovery must be made in writing to the opposing side within 30 days after service of the answer to the written notice of formal proceedings or within 30 days after service of the written notice of formal proceedings if no answer has yet been filed, or within 15 days after service of any amendment to the notice.

(e) (Inspection and copying) The following items may be inspected or copied by the side requesting discovery:

(1) The names, and if known, the business addresses and business telephone numbers of persons the opposing side then intends to call as witnesses at the hearing;

(2) The names, and if known, the business addresses and business telephone numbers of those persons who may be able to provide substantial material information favorable to the judge. Substantial material information favorable to the judge is evidence bearing directly on the truth of the charges relevant to the credibility of a witness intended to be called;

(3) All statements about the subject matter of the proceedings, including any impeaching evidence, made by any witness then intended to be called by either side;

(4) All statements about the subject matter of the proceedings made by a person named or described in the notice, or amendment to the notice, other than the judge when it is claimed that an act or omission of the judge as to the person described is a basis for the formal proceeding;

(5) All investigative reports made by or on behalf of the commission, the examiner, or the judge, about the subject matter of the proceeding;

(6) All writings, including reports of mental, physical, and blood examinations, then intended to be offered in evidence by the opposing side;

(7) All physical items of evidence then intended to be offered in evidence;

(8) All writings or physical items of evidence which would be admissible in evidence at the hearing.

(f) (Compliance with request) If either side receives a written request for discovery in accordance with these procedures, the side receiving the request shall have a continuing duty to provide discovery of items listed in the request until proceedings before the masters are concluded. When a written request for discovery is made in accordance with these rules, discovery shall be provided within a reasonable time after any discoverable items become known to the side obligated to provide discovery.

(g) (Depositions) After the filing of the notice of formal proceedings, depositions shall be allowed as provided in this subdivision. The party requesting the deposition shall bear all costs for service of process, reporter, transcripts and facility usage, and in the case of a videotaped deposition to perpetuate testimony under subpart (1), all direct costs incurred in videotaping the deposition.

(1) (Depositions to perpetuate testimony) The commission or the special masters shall order the taking of the deposition of any person upon a showing by the side requesting the deposition that the proposed deponent is a material witness who is unable or cannot be compelled to attend the hearing. If a deposition is ordered, the procedures stated in Government Code section 68753 shall be followed. Depositions to perpetuate testimony may be videotaped.

(2) (Discovery depositions) In addition to depositions to perpetuate testimony provided for under subpart (1) of this subdivision, discovery depositions are permitted as provided in this subpart (2). Discovery depositions may not be videotaped.

a. The judge shall have the right to take depositions of up to four material witnesses, and the examiner shall have the right to take depositions of the judge and up to three other material witnesses. Depositions of commission members or staff are not permitted. Bench officers, other than the respondent judge, and court staff shall be afforded counsel for the deposition, upon request, by the Administrative Office of the Courts.

b. If the examiner and judge stipulate in writing that a deposition may be taken as a matter of right under subpart (a), the commission shall issue a subpoena for such deposition. If the examiner and judge are unable to agree that a witness is material, or unable to agree concerning the manner, time and place of a deposition, the party seeking the deposition may file a request for deposition subpoena with the commission. Objections shall be filed within five days of filing the request. The commission may place restrictions or conditions on the manner, time and place of any deposition.

c. Each deposition upon oral examination is limited to one day of seven hours. Any objection during a deposition upon oral examination must be stated concisely and in a non-argumentative and non-suggestive manner. A person may instruct a deponent not to answer only when necessary to preserve a privilege, to enforce a limitation directed by the commission, or to present a motion to the commission that the deposition is being conducted in bad faith or in such manner unreasonably to annoy, embarrass or oppress the deponent or party.

d. Depositions shall be completed 30 days prior to the hearing, unless a cut-off time otherwise is set by the commission or by stipulation of the examiner and the judge.

e. Any motion under this subpart (2) shall be presented to the commission. The commission may designate the chairperson or the chairperson's designee to perform all or any part of its duties under this subdivision. If special masters have been appointed pursuant to rule 121, subdivision (b), the chairperson may designate one or more of them to perform all or any part of the commission's duties under this subpart.

The provisions of subpart (2) of subsection (g) of rule 122 shall take effect January 1, 2008, and shall be operative until December 31, 2010, unless after review, they are reenacted by the commission.

(h) (Failure to comply with discovery request) If any party fails to comply with a discovery request as authorized by these procedures, the items withheld shall be suppressed or, if the items have been admitted into evidence, shall be stricken from the record. If testimony is elicited during direct examination and the side eliciting the testimony withheld any statement of the testifying witness in violation of these discovery procedures, the testimony shall be ordered stricken from the record. Upon a showing of good cause for failure to comply with a discovery request, the commission, master, or masters may admit the items withheld or direct examination testimony of a witness whose statement was withheld upon condition that the side against whom the evidence is sought to be admitted is granted a reasonable continuance to prepare against the evidence, or may order the items or testimony suppressed or stricken from the record. The commission may, upon review of any hearing, order any evidence stricken from the record for violation of a valid discovery request if the evidence could have been ordered stricken by the masters for violation of a valid discovery request.

   (i)   (Applicable privileges)   Nothing in these procedures shall authorize the discovery of any writing or thing which is privileged from disclosure by law or is otherwise protected or made confidential as the work product of the attorney, including memoranda by commission staff and examiners. Statements of any witness interviewed by the examiner, by any investigators for either side, by the judge, or by the judge's attorney shall not be protected as work product.

   (j)   (Definition of statement)   For purposes of these procedures, "statement" shall mean either (1) a written statement prepared by or at the direction of the declarant or signed by the declarant, or (2) an oral statement of the declarant which has been recorded stenographically, mechanically, or electronically, or which has been videotaped, transcribed, or summarized in writing.

   (k)   (Return of discovery, continued confidentiality of discovery)   Upon the completion or termination of commission proceedings, the respondent judge shall return to the commission all materials provided to the judge under this rule that have not become part of the public record. All items provided in discovery pursuant to this rule remain confidential under rule 102 until and unless those items become part of the public record.

   (*l*)   (Protective orders)   The commission or the masters may, upon application supported by a showing of good cause, issue protective orders to the extent necessary to maintain in effect such privileges and other protections as are otherwise provided by law.

   Adopted Oct. 24, 1996, effective Dec. 1, 1996; amended Jan. 29, 2003; Oct. 17, 2007.

Rule 123.   Hearing.

   (a)   (Hearing without answer or appearance by judge)   At the time and place set for hearing, the commission, or the masters when the hearing is before masters, shall proceed with the hearing whether or not the judge has filed an answer or appears at the hearing. The examiner shall present the case in support of the charges in the notice of formal proceedings.

   (b)   (Consideration of failure to answer, appear, or respond to questions)   The failure of the judge to answer the charges or to appear at the hearing shall not,

standing alone, be taken as evidence of the truth of the facts alleged to constitute grounds for censure, removal, retirement or public or private admonishment. In accordance with California Evidence Code section 413, in reviewing the evidence and facts in the case against the judge, the commission and the masters may consider the judge's failure to explain or deny evidence or facts in the case or any willful suppression of evidence if that is the case, unless the failure or suppression is due to the judge's exercise of any legally recognized privilege. A lack of cooperation by the judge may be considered by the commission under rule 104.

   (c)   (Reporting of hearing)   A verbatim record shall be made of the proceedings at the hearing.

   (d)   (Number of commission members at hearing)   When the hearing is before the commission, not fewer than six members shall be present when the evidence is produced.

   Adopted Oct. 24, 1996, effective Dec. 1, 1996; amended Oct. 25, 2005.

Rule 124.   Media at Hearing.

   All applications for film or electronic coverage of hearings in formal proceedings are to be submitted to the commission a reasonable time prior to the commencement of the hearing. The commission shall promptly inform the respondent judge of any requests for film or electronic coverage of the hearing. Applications for film or electronic coverage of the hearing are to be decided by the chairperson of the commission or the chairperson's designee after conferring with the masters or presiding master, if masters have been appointed.

   Adopted Oct. 24, 1996, effective Dec. 1, 1996.

Rule 125.   Evidence.

   (a)   (Applicable law and agreed statement)   The California Evidence Code shall be applicable to all hearings before the commission or masters. Oral evidence shall be taken only on oath or affirmation. The examiner or the judge may propose to the other party an agreed statement in place of all or a part of the testimony. An agreed statement shall not foreclose argument to the commission or masters.

   (b)   (Prior disciplinary action)   Any prior disciplinary action may be received in evidence to prove that conduct is persistent or habitual or to determine what action should be taken regarding discipline. Prior disciplinary action includes any disciplinary action which is in effect before the conclusion of a commission proceeding, including review by the Supreme Court.

   Adopted Oct. 24, 1996, effective Dec. 1, 1996.

Rule 125.5.   Exhibits at Hearing.

   Original exhibits admitted at a hearing before the special masters shall be transmitted by the masters to the commission office at the completion of the evidentiary portion of the hearing, unless the masters determine that there is reason to retain the original exhibit or exhibits to assist in the preparation of their report to the commission. Any original exhibits retained by the masters shall be transmitted to the commission at or before the time the report of the masters is submitted to the commission.

Adopted as interim rule Jan. 31, 2007; adopted May 23, 2007.

Rule 126. Procedural Rights of Judge in Formal Proceedings.

(a) (Enumeration of rights, subpoenas) When formal proceedings have been instituted, a judge shall have the right and reasonable opportunity to defend against the charges by the introduction of evidence, to be represented by counsel, and to examine and cross-examine witnesses. The judge shall also have the right to the issuance of subpoenas for attendance of witnesses to testify or produce books, papers, and other evidentiary matter. Subpoenas are to be issued by the chairperson of the commission, the chairperson's designee, or the special masters. Subpoenas addressed to the commission or its staff may only be obtained from the special masters upon a showing of good cause with notice to the commission.

(b) (Transcripts) When a transcript of the testimony has been prepared at the expense of the commission, a copy thereof shall, upon request, be available for use by the judge and his counsel in connection with the proceedings at the judge's expense, or the judge may arrange to procure a copy from the reporter at the judge's expense. The judge shall have the right, without any order or approval, to have all or any portion of the testimony in the proceedings transcribed at the judge's expense.

(c) (Manner of service) Subject to rule 118(c), concerning service of a notice of formal proceedings, all notices and correspondence in connection with formal proceedings shall be sent to the judge's chambers, unless otherwise requested, and a copy thereof shall be mailed to counsel of record.

(d) (Appointment of conservator) If the judge is adjudged insane or incompetent, or if it appears to the commission at any time during the proceedings that the judge is not competent to act for himself or herself, the commission may petition a court of competent jurisdiction for the appointment of a conservator unless the judge has a conservator who will represent the judge. If a conservator is or has been appointed for a judge, the conservator may claim and exercise any right and privilege and make any defense for the judge with the same force and effect as if claimed, exercised, or made by the judge, if competent, and whenever these rules provide for serving, giving notice or sending any matter to the judge, such notice or matter shall be served, given, or sent to the conservator.

Adopted Oct. 24, 1996, effective Dec. 1, 1996; amended Jan. 31, 2007; May 23, 2007.

Rule 127. Discipline by Consent.

(a) (Negotiations) Either respondent or the examiner may initiate negotiations on discipline by consent. Both the examiner and respondent must agree to any proposed disposition before submission to the commission. No agreement between the examiner and respondent is binding until approved by the commission.

(b) (Submission to commission) At any time after the initiation of formal charges and before final disposition, the respondent may agree with the examiner that the respondent shall admit to any or all of the charges in exchange for a stated sanction. The agreement shall be submitted to the commission, which shall accept or reject the agreement.

(c) (Rejection of agreement) If the stated sanction is rejected by the commission, the admission shall be withdrawn and cannot be used against the respondent in any proceedings.

(d) (Affidavit of consent) A respondent who consents to a stated sanction shall personally execute an affidavit stating that:

(1)   The respondent consents to the sanction;

(2)   The consent is freely and voluntarily rendered;

(3)   The respondent admits the truth of the charges as alleged; and

(4)   The respondent waives review by the Supreme Court.

Adopted Oct. 24, 1996, effective Dec. 1, 1996.

Rule 128. Amendments to Notice or Answer; Dismissals.

(a) (Amendments) The masters, at any time prior to the conclusion of the hearing, or the commission, at any time prior to its determination, may allow or require amendments to the notice of formal proceedings and may allow amendments to the answer. The notice may be amended to conform to proof or to set forth additional facts, whether occurring before or after the commencement of the hearing. In case such an amendment is made, the judge shall be given reasonable time both to answer the amendment and to prepare and present his or her defense against the matters charged thereby.

(b) (Dismissals by examiner) At any time after the filing of formal charges and before final disposition, where exigent circumstances prevent consideration by the full commission, the examiner, with the concurrence of the director/chief counsel and the chairperson, may dismiss any charge from the notice of formal proceedings, if it appears that the available evidence is insufficient to sustain the charge or that dismissal is otherwise in the interest of justice, and such dismissal is not tantamount to dismissal of the proceedings as a whole.

Adopted Oct. 24, 1996, effective Dec. 1, 1996.

Rule 129. Report of Masters.

(a) (Transcript) Upon the completion of a hearing before the masters, a transcript of the hearing shall be promptly prepared and submitted to the Legal Advisor who shall promptly mail a copy to each of the special masters, the examiner and the respondent judge.

(b) (Submission of proposed findings of fact and conclusions of law) Within 30 days after mailing of the hearing transcript, the examiner and the respondent judge shall submit to the masters proposed findings of fact and conclusions of law, with citations to the transcript and exhibits, unless the masters waive the submission of such proposed findings and conclusions. Submission to the masters shall occur by a delivery method that results in actual receipt by them of the documents on or before the specified due date for submission.

(c) (Preparation of report of masters) Within 60 days after mailing of the hearing transcript or within 30 days after submission of the parties' proposed findings of fact and conclusions of law, whichever occurs later, the masters shall submit a report to the commission. Prior to the submission of their report, the masters may require such additional briefing and argument by the examiner and the respondent judge as the masters may desire.

(d) (Content of report of masters) The report of the masters shall contain findings of fact and conclusions of law, along with an analysis of the evidence and reasons for the findings and conclusions, but shall not contain a recommendation as to discipline.

(e) (Copy of report to judge and examiner) Upon receiving the report of the masters, the commission shall promptly mail a copy to the judge and the examiner.

Adopted Oct. 24, 1996, effective Dec. 1, 1996; amended Jan. 29, 2003; Oct. 25, 2005.

Rule 130.   Briefs to the Commission.

(a) (Filing of opening briefs) Within 15 days after the date of mailing of the copy of the masters' report to the judge as reflected on the proof of service by mail, the examiner or the judge may file with the commission opening briefs which may consist of objections to the report of the special masters and points and authorities concerning the issues in the matter, including the issue of sanctions. Objections to the masters' report and all factual statements shall be specific and shall be supported by reference to the book and page number of the record. Briefs shall conform in style to subdivision (b) of rule 8.204 of the California Rules of Court, shall follow the length limitations set forth in subdivision (c) of rule 8.204 of the California Rules of Court, and, when filed by the examiner, a copy shall be sent by first-class mail to the judge.

(b) (Response to briefs) Within 10 days after the filing of opening briefs, the examiner or the judge may file with the commission a response.

(c) (Reply to response) Within five days after the filing of a response, the examiner or the judge may file a reply to the response.

Adopted Oct. 24, 1996, effective Dec. 1, 1996; amended Jan. 29, 2003; Jan. 31, 2007.

Rule 131.   Participation by Non-Parties.

Briefs of amicus curiae will be considered by the commission if they present legal issues or represent perspectives not otherwise presented or represented by the parties. An amicus curiae brief may not be used to present inadmissible or non-admitted evidentiary materials to the commission.

A brief of an amicus curiae may be filed only if accompanied by the written consent of all parties, or upon a motion demonstrating to the chairperson of the commission or the chairperson's designee that the filing of the brief would be helpful to the commission in the resolution of the pending matter. When consent to the filing of a brief of an amicus curiae is refused by a party to the case, a motion for leave to file the brief, accompanied by the proposed brief, may be presented to the chairperson or the chairperson's designee. The motion shall concisely state the nature of the applicant's interest and set forth facts or questions of law that have not been, or reasons for believing that they will not be, presented by the parties and

their relevancy to the disposition of the case. The motion may be in letter form but may not exceed four pages. The commission shall forward copies of any such motion and proposed brief to both the examiner and the judge.

The cover of the amicus brief must identify the party supported, and the brief shall not exceed 50 pages in length. Evidentiary references shall include citation to the record before the commission.

An amicus brief shall be submitted or filed within the time limits prescribed for the party that the brief supports. No reply briefs or briefs of an amicus curiae in support of reconsideration shall be received.

Any brief of an amicus curiae that fails to comply with this rule will not be considered by the commission.

Adopted Oct. 24, 1996, effective Dec. 1, 1996.

Rule 132.   Appearance Before Commission.

Upon receipt of the masters' report and any objections, the commission shall give the judge and the examiner an opportunity to be heard orally before the commission, and written notice of the time and place of such hearing shall be mailed to the judge, at least 10 days prior thereto.

Adopted Oct. 24, 1996, effective Dec. 1, 1996.

Rule 133.   Hearing Additional Evidence.

(a) The commission may order a hearing for the taking of additional evidence at any time while the matter is pending before it. The order shall set the time and place of hearing and shall indicate the matters on which the evidence is to be taken. A copy of such order shall be sent by mail to the judge at least 10 days prior to the date of hearing.

(b) In any case in which masters have been appointed, the hearing of additional evidence may be before such masters or before the commission, and the proceedings therein shall be in conformance with the provisions of rules 121 to 130, inclusive.

Adopted Oct. 24, 1996, effective Dec. 1, 1996; amended Jan. 29, 2003.

Rule 134.   Commission Vote.

The commission may privately or publicly admonish, censure, remove or retire a judge, or find a person unfit to serve as a subordinate judicial officer. The affirmative vote of six members of the commission who have considered the record and report of the masters and who were present at any oral hearing as provided in rule 132 or, when the hearing was before the commission without masters, of six members of the commission who have considered the record, and at least four of whom were present when the evidence was produced, is required for a private or public admonishment, censure, removal or retirement of a judge, or a finding that a person is unfit to serve as a subordinate judicial officer, or for dismissal of the proceedings.

Adopted Oct. 24, 1996, effective Dec. 1, 1996; amended Oct. 8, 1998; Feb. 11, 1999; Jan. 29, 2003.

Rule 134.5.   Rule of Necessity.

A commission member shall not be subject to disqualification based on an actual or potential conflict of interest if his or her disqualification would prevent the existence of a quorum. This rule does not apply if a quorum can be convened with members who are not actually present. The basis of the commission member's actual or potential conflict and the reason the member's participation was necessary shall be recorded in the minutes and included in any resulting discipline.

Adopted May 23, 2007.

Rule 135.　Record of Commission Proceedings.

The commission shall maintain records of all actions taken by the commission concerning a judge. Notice of any disciplinary determination and notice of any disqualification under article VI, section 18(b) of the California Constitution shall be mailed to the judge. In all formal proceedings, the commission shall prepare a transcript of the testimony and of all proceedings and shall make written findings of fact and conclusions of law.

Adopted Oct. 24, 1996, effective Dec. 1, 1996.

Rule 136.　Finality.

A commission determination to impose discipline upon a judge following formal proceedings under rule 118 shall become final 30 days after the date of the order regarding the disciplinary determination.

Adopted Oct. 24, 1996, effective Dec. 1, 1996.

Rule 137.　Retroactivity.

Those cases in which formal proceedings have been instituted on or before February 28, 1995 will be governed by the provisions of article VI, section 18 of the California Constitution which are operative and in effect as of February 28, 1995. Those cases in which formal proceedings are instituted on or after March 1, 1995 will be governed by the provisions of article VI, section 18 of the California Constitution operative as of March 1, 1995.

Adopted Oct. 24, 1996, effective Dec. 1, 1996.

Rule 138.　Definitions.

In these rules, unless the context or subject matter otherwise requires:

(a)　"Commission" means the Commission on Judicial Performance.

(b)　"Judge" means a judge of any court of this state or a retired judge who has elected to serve on senior judge status or former judge as provided in California Constitution, article VI, section 18(d). For purposes of these rules, "judge" also means a court commissioner or referee, included as subordinate judicial officers in the commission's jurisdiction under California Constitution, article VI, section 18.1.

(c)　"Chairperson" includes the acting chairperson.

(d)　"Masters" means the special master or special masters appointed by the Supreme Court upon request of the commission.

(e)　"Presiding master" means the master so designated by the Supreme Court or, if no designation is made, the judge selected by the panel.

(f)　"Examiner" means the counsel designated by the commission to gather and present evidence before the masters or commission with respect to the charges against a judge.

(g)　"Shall" is mandatory and "may" is permissive.

(h)　"Mail" and "mailed" include ordinary mail and personal delivery.

(i)　"Filing" means delivering to commission staff at the commission office during regular business hours. A filing may be evidenced by a conformed copy of the cover page of each document submitted for filing. To be filed, a document must be accompanied by a proof of service of the document upon the other party or parties.

Adopted Oct. 24, 1996, effective Dec. 1, 1996; amended Oct. 8, 1998; Feb. 11, 1999.

POLICY DECLARATIONS OF THE COMMISSION ON JUDICIAL PERFORMANCE

PREAMBLE

In consideration of the need for both uniformity and continuity of procedure and equitable, expeditious resolution of recurrent and detailed issues of procedure, the commission has authorized the formulation of the following policy declarations detailing commission policies, procedures and practices. These policy declarations are to reflect internal procedural detail neither duplicative of nor inconsistent with constitutional mandate or statutes or Commission Rules. These policy declarations are based upon concepts of utility, experience, and fair hearing of matters before the commission.

Rules referred to in the policy declarations are Commission Rules.

TITLE

These policy declarations shall be known and may be cited as the Policy Declarations of the Commission on Judicial Performance.

DIVISION I
COMPLAINTS AND INVESTIGATIONS

Policy Declaration 1.1.   Anonymous Complaints.

Staff will evaluate anonymous complaints for merit; if a complaint is deemed sufficiently meritorious, it will be placed on the oversight agenda for consideration by the commission as to whether or not it should be docketed.

Approved May 28, 1997.

Policy Declaration 1.2.   Staff Inquiries.

The staff inquiry is one of the commission's two levels of investigation. A staff inquiry may, but need not, precede a preliminary investigation. The purpose of a staff inquiry is to determine whether sufficient facts exist to warrant a preliminary investigation.

At the conclusion of a staff inquiry the commission may take any of the following actions:

(1) Close the matter;

(2) Authorize a preliminary investigation; or

(3) Issue an advisory letter.

A judge must receive an inquiry letter and be afforded an opportunity to respond before an advisory letter may issue.

Approved May 28, 1997.

Policy Declaration 1.3.   Staff Inquiry Letters.

An inquiry letter includes specification of the allegations and may include: the date of the conduct; the location(s) where the conduct occurred; if applicable, the name(s) of the case(s) or identification of the court proceeding(s) in relation to which the conduct occurred. If the inquiry concerns statements made by or to the judge, the letter may also include the text or summaries of the comments.

The purpose of the inquiry letter is to afford the judge an opportunity to provide such matters as the judge may choose, including information about the factual aspects of the allegations and other relevant comment.

Approved May 28, 1997.

Policy Declaration 1.4.   Preliminary Investigations.

The preliminary investigation is the second of the commission's two levels of investigation. A preliminary investigation may follow a staff inquiry or may be instituted without a staff inquiry having been conducted. Where the allegations, if true, would warrant consideration of commission action greater than issuance of an advisory letter or when the use of investigation subpoenas and more formal investigative procedures are contemplated, the commission may commence with a preliminary investigation. The purpose of a preliminary investigation is to determine whether formal proceedings should be instituted and a hearing held.

At the conclusion of a preliminary investigation, or at the conclusion of a period of monitoring under rule 112, the commission may take any of the following actions:

(1) Close the matter;

(2) Issue an advisory letter;

(3) Issue a notice of intended private admonishment or notice of intended public admonishment; or

(4) Institute formal proceedings.

A judge must receive an inquiry letter and be afforded an opportunity to respond before an advisory letter may issue. A judge must receive a preliminary investigation letter and be afforded an opportunity to respond before a notice of intended private admonishment or notice of intended public admonishment may issue or formal proceedings may be instituted.

Approved May 28, 1997.

Policy Declaration 1.5.   Preliminary Investigation Letters.

A preliminary investigation letter provides the judge notice of the investigation and the nature of the charge under review and may include: the date of the conduct; the location(s) where the conduct occurred; if applicable, the name of the case(s) or identification of the court proceeding(s) in relation to which the conduct occurred. If the investigation concerns statements made by or to the judge, the letter may also include the text or summaries of the comments.

The purpose of the preliminary investigation letter is to afford the judge an opportunity to provide such matters as the judge may choose including information about the factual aspects of the allegations and other relevant comment.

Approved May 28, 1997.

Policy Declaration 1.6.   Authorization for Staff Inquiries and Preliminary Investigations Between Meetings.

In instances where a matter comes to the attention of the commission between meetings, which on its face appears to warrant a staff inquiry or a preliminary investigation and there has already been direct communication with the subject judge or other exigent circumstances exist, an effort should be made, whenever possible, to poll all of the commission members for authorization of a staff inquiry or preliminary investigation. If, in the discretion of the chairperson or acting chairperson, polling all of the members is not feasible, the chairperson or acting chairperson may authorize the staff inquiry or preliminary investigation. When a staff inquiry or preliminary investigation is authorized without a poll of the members, the members shall be promptly notified of the action taken.

Approved May 28, 1997.

Policy Declaration 1.7.   Staff Inquiry and Preliminary Investigation Letters Not Authorized or Determined Not to Be Warranted.

At the time a staff inquiry or preliminary investigation is authorized by the commission, the authorization may or may not include writing the judge a letter, in addition to other investigation. If information acquired during the inquiry or preliminary investigation establishes that there is no basis for further proceedings, the inquiry or preliminary investigation may be closed without the judge being contacted. An inquiry or preliminary investigation letter authorized by the commission need not be sent if information obtained by staff before the letter is sent shows that the letter may not be warranted.

Approved May 28, 1997.

Policy Declaration 1.8.   Cases Removed From Active Calendar.

The commission may defer its consideration of a pending matter and direct that the staff inquiry or preliminary investigation be removed from the commission's active calendar. Circumstances which may warrant deferral in the commission's consideration of a matter include: when the case from which the complaint arose is still pending before the judge; when an appeal or ancillary proceeding is pending in which factual issues or claims relevant to the complaint are to be resolved; when criminal or other proceedings involving the judge are pending.

When a matter is removed from the commission's active calendar, it shall be placed on the commission agenda periodically as required by the circumstances, at intervals not to exceed six (6) months, and subject to active consideration at the discretion of the commission.

Approved May 28, 1997.

Policy Declaration 1.9.   Admonishments to Persons Giving Interviews and Statements.

In the course of a staff inquiry or preliminary investigation, persons questioned or interviewed to ascertain the validity of allegations shall be admonished that the inquiry or investigation is confidential under the California Constitution and Commission Rules. When it appears that there may be use of the elicited information in connection with possible testimony or discovery, the person providing the information shall be so advised.

Approved May 28, 1997.

Policy Declaration 1.10. Consent, Preservation of Witness Interviews and Statements.

Consent to mechanical recording may be obtained from interviewees. Statements and interviews may be transcribed and preserved, and may be submitted to interviewees for signature and verification.

Approved May 28, 1997.

Policy Declaration 1.11. Independent Record of Witness Statements.

Where a witness statement or interview is not transcribed or recorded, it is not to be conveyed, commented upon or otherwise communicated to the commission by commission staff unless an independent memorialization of the statement has been prepared by staff (a writing other than a case memorandum or report from staff to the commission).

Approved May 28, 1997.

Policy Declaration 1.12. Investigation Subpoenas.

Commission investigation subpoenas may issue upon application to the commission chairperson, vice-chairperson or the designee of either, stating the name, address and title, if any, of the person from whom information is sought, and whether or not a statement under oath is to be taken.

Approved May 28, 1997.

Policy Declaration 1.13. Witness Statements Under Oath.

When the statement of a witness is taken under oath pursuant to Government Code section 68750, the witness may be given an opportunity to review and make corrections to the transcript of the witness's testimony at the office of the court reporter before whom the statement was taken. A copy of the statement shall not otherwise be furnished to the witness unless formal proceedings are instituted in the matter in which the testimony was given and the witness's statement is discoverable under rule 122.

Approved June 25, 1998.

Policy Declaration 1.14. Submission of Character Letters.

(1) Written communications submitted during staff inquiry or preliminary investigation

During a staff inquiry or preliminary investigation, written communications containing information related to the character of a judge who has a matter pending before the commission may be submitted to the commission. Such written communications must be delivered to the commission office, and shall not be delivered to individual commission members.

In determining the weight to be given to written character references, the commission may consider, but is not limited to, the following list of factors:

(1) The length of time the author of the written communication has known the judge, and the nature and extent of the author's contact with the judge;

(2) Whether the character reference is submitted in the form of a declaration signed under penalty of perjury; and

(3) Whether the information provided by a person other than a judge or subordinate judicial officer is based on personal knowledge.

Pursuant to canon 2B, character references submitted by judges or subordinate judicial officers must be based on personal knowledge.

(2) Written communications submitted after the initiation of formal proceedings

After the initiation of formal proceedings, written communications related to the character of the respondent judge may only be submitted by stipulation of the parties at the hearing held pursuant to rule 123 or rule 133. After the completion of the evidentiary hearing pursuant to rule 123 or 133, such communications shall not be accepted by the commission.

Approved May 22, 2008.

DIVISION II
APPEARANCES AND FORMAL PROCEEDINGS

Policy Declaration 2.1. Opposition to Proposed Private and Proposed Public Admonishments; Statement of Objections and Appearance.

An appearance before the commission to contest the imposition of a proposed private admonishment under rule 114, or to contest the imposition of a proposed public admonishment under rule 116, means an opportunity for a judge to informally contest the imposition of an admonishment in argument before the commission based on the proceedings which resulted in the issuance of a notice of intended admonishment and the judge's statement of objections.

A judge's demand for an appearance after notice of intended private admonishment under rule 114, or notice of intended public admonishment under rule 116, may include a written statement of the judge's objections, both legal and factual, to the commission's proposed findings. The judge's statement may include points and authorities in support of any legal arguments and verified statements in opposition to the commission's factual findings. The appearance before the commission will be scheduled after receipt of the judge's demand for appearance and statement of objections. The commission may request further briefing.

At the appearance before the commission, the judge may appear with or without counsel. The appearance is not

Rules of Jud Perf

an evidentiary hearing and there is no testimony by witnesses. Argument shall be limited to oral presentation not to exceed twenty (20) minutes by the judge and twenty (20) minutes by trial counsel or other attorney designated by the commission to present argument in support of the admonishment.

Approved May 28, 1997.

Policy Declaration 2.2.   Date of Hearing.

Absent unusual circumstances, the evidentiary hearing on the charges set forth in a notice of formal proceedings shall be set to commence two to four months following the issuance under rule 118 of the notice of formal proceedings.

Approved May 28, 1997; amended Aug. 26, 2004.

Policy Declaration 2.3.   Prehearing Proceedings.

The commission or the special masters may require prehearing status statements, briefs or conferences (either by telephone or in person), or require any other appropriate prehearing proceeding. The purpose of such prehearing proceedings is to provide the commission or the special masters with pertinent information for prehearing and to ensure that the hearing proceeds efficiently. The masters may issue appropriate prehearing orders and may determine whether any such order needs be in writing.

Approved May 28, 1997; amended Aug. 26, 2004.

Policy Declaration 2.4.   Agreed Statement and Discipline by Consent.

An agreed statement under rule 125(a) may be offered by the respondent judge and the examiner in place of all or part of the evidence after institution of formal proceedings. An agreement between the respondent judge and the examiner for discipline by consent under rule 127 may be submitted to the commission after institution of formal proceedings. The examiner is responsible for handling negotiations with the respondent judge or respondent judge's counsel concerning agreed statements and agreements for discipline by consent.

Approved May 28, 1997.

Policy Declaration 2.5.   Order Barring Assignments to Former Judges.

If the commission determines to bar a former judge from receiving an assignment, appointment to or reference of work from any California state court, pursuant to article VI, section 18(d) of the California Constitution, the order barring the judge from receiving assignments will be included in the commission's order of censure.

Notice of an order barring a former judge from receiving assignments shall be given to the Chief Justice and to the Administrative Office of the Courts for distribution to the presiding judges of the state courts.

Approved June 25, 1998.

Policy Declaration 2.6.   Modification of Decision Following Formal Proceedings.

At any time before a commission determination to impose discipline upon a judge following formal proceed-

ings becomes final under rule 136, the commission may modify the order regarding the disciplinary determination to eliminate any erroneous statement of fact or law in the order.

Adopted June 29, 2005.

DIVISION III
COMMISSION ADMINISTRATION

Setting regular and special meetings. Policy Declaration 3.1.
Organizational meeting; election of chairperson and vice-chairperson. Policy Declaration 3.2.
Preparation of annual report. Policy Declaration 3.3.
Availability of commission rules and policy declarations. Policy Declaration 3.4.
Review of commission rules, proposed changes. Policy Declaration 3.5.
Policy declarations. Policy Declaration 3.6.
Staff authorization for announcements between meetings. Policy Declaration 3.7.
Announcement at conclusion of previously-announced investigation. Policy Declaration 3.7.5.
Duties of trial counsel. Policy Declaration 3.8.
Legal advisor to commissioners. Policy Declaration 3.9.
Records disposition policy. Policy Declaration 3.10.
Biennial adjustment of gift limitation amount. Policy Declaration 3.11.
Extensions of time. Policy Declaration 3.12.

Policy Declaration 3.1.   Setting Regular and Special Meetings.

(1) Before the end of each calendar year, staff will propose a choice of dates for each meeting for the next calendar year. At its March organizational meeting, the commission will approve the meeting dates for the remainder of the year.

(2) A special meeting shall be called (a) upon not less than five (5) days notice by the chairperson or acting chairperson, or (b) upon notice of request of not less than four (4) members.

Approved May 28, 1997.

Policy Declaration 3.2.   Organizational Meeting; Election of Chairperson and Vice-Chairperson.

At its March meeting each year, the commission shall organize itself for the conduct of business for the ensuing year and shall select a chairperson and vice-chairperson.

Approved May 28, 1997.

Policy Declaration 3.3.   Preparation of Annual Report.

At the end of each calendar year, staff will prepare a draft annual report for circulation to the commission or such members as the commission delegates for review of the draft report. After the draft report is reviewed and suggestions made, staff will revise the draft report in accordance therewith and will submit the report in final form to the chairperson for approval for publication within the first quarter of the calendar year.

Approved May 28, 1997; amended Feb. 11, 1999.

Policy Declaration 3.4.   Availability of Commission Rules and Policy Declarations.

The rules and policy declarations of the commission will be published by the commission and distributed to the public upon request. The commission's rules and policy declarations are also to be published, to the extent possible, in legal publications including the California Official Reports Advance Sheets and other legal publications and on-line services.

Approved May 28, 1997; amended Feb. 11, 1999.

Policy Declaration 3.5.   Review of Commission Rules, Proposed Changes.

Every two years, in even-numbered years, the commission shall review its rules and any proposed enactments, amendments or repeals. Comments regarding proposed changes to the rules which are received by the commission other than during its biennial rules review may be considered by the commission and either deferred to the next review of the rules or acted upon as may be appropriate.

Approved May 28, 1997; amended Feb. 4, 2004.

Policy Declaration 3.6.   Policy Declarations.

When there is commission approval for staff to draft a policy declaration, any proposed enactment, amendment or repeal shall be submitted to each commission member at least ten (10) days immediately preceding the meeting at which a vote thereon is taken. The commission may have the proposed enactment, amendment or repeal reviewed by the rules committee prior to a vote by the commission.

Approved May 28, 1997.

Policy Declaration 3.7.   Staff Authorization for Announcements Between Meetings.

When the director believes an announcement pursuant to California Constitution, article VI, section 18(k) or pursuant to rule 102(c) is appropriate between meetings in a particular proceeding, the director shall so advise the chairperson or acting chairperson. An effort should be made, whenever possible, to poll all of the members for authorization of the announcement. If, in the discretion of the chairperson or acting chairperson, polling all of the members is not feasible, the chairperson or acting chairperson may authorize the announcement. When an announcement is authorized without a poll of the members, the members shall be promptly notified of the action taken.

Approved May 28, 1997.

Policy Declaration 3.7.5.   Announcement at Conclusion of Previously-Announced Investigation.

When the commission has issued a public statement announcing or confirming that a matter is under investigation pursuant to article VI, section 18(k) or pursuant to rule 102(c), at the conclusion of the investigation, the commission shall issue a public statement indicating that the previously-announced investigation has been completed. If the matter has been concluded by the commission, the announcement shall so state. If the commission has instituted formal proceedings, the announcement shall so state, and the announcement may include an explanation of formal proceedings.

Approved Feb. 11, 1999.

Policy Declaration 3.8.   Duties of Trial Counsel.

Trial counsel shall serve as examiner in formal proceedings instituted by the commission and shall represent the commission in litigation before the California Supreme Court and other courts when directed to do so by the commission. Trial counsel shall serve under the direction of the commission's director-chief counsel.

Approved May 28, 1997.

Policy Declaration 3.9.   Legal Advisor to Commissioners.

The commission has established the position of Legal Advisor to Commissioners and shall designate an attorney to serve in that capacity. The Legal Advisor reports directly to the commission and shall assist the commission in its adjudicatory function, including in its consideration and adjudication of matters in which formal proceedings have been instituted and matters in which judges contest intended private admonishments or intended public admonishments.

The Legal Advisor shall not participate in the investigation of complaints or prosecution of charges against judges. If the Legal Advisor previously participated in an investigation or adversarial proceeding in another capacity as an attorney for the commission, he or she shall not assist the commission in its deliberations or adjudication of that matter absent a written waiver by the judge.

The Legal Advisor shall present to the commission proposals for disposition of matters in which formal proceedings have been instituted which have been jointly offered by trial counsel and the judge or judge's counsel. After institution of formal proceedings, the Legal Advisor shall be responsible for requesting the appointment of special masters by the Supreme Court and shall serve as the commission's liaison to special masters appointed in formal proceedings.

The Legal Advisor shall perform such additional duties as may be assigned by the commission that do not require or cause the Legal Advisor to participate in the commission's investigatory or prosecutorial functions.

Approved May 28, 1997; amended Aug. 26, 2004.

Policy Declaration 3.10.   Records Disposition Policy.

At the beginning of each calendar year, the commission shall destroy all files which did not result in an advisory letter, public or private admonishment, public reproval, censure, removal or involuntary retirement, resignation or retirement with proceedings pending, or finding that a person was unfit to serve as a subordinate judicial officer as follows:

(1) Files involving complaints against municipal or superior court judges dated or docketed by the commission in the thirteenth year prior to the new calendar year; and

(2) Files involving complaints against appellate or Supreme Court justices dated or docketed by the commission in the nineteenth year prior to the new calendar year; and

(3) Files involving complaints against subordinate judicial officers dated or docketed by the commission in the thirteenth year prior to the new calendar year.

Approved May 28, 1997; amended Feb. 11, 1999.

Policy Declaration 3.11. Biennial Adjustment of Gift Limitation Amount.

(1) Code of Civil Procedure section 170.9(a) limits to $250 the total value of gifts that an individual judge may accept from any single source in any calendar year. Section 170.9(d) requires that the commission adjust that amount biennially to reflect changes in the Consumer Price Index, rounded to the nearest $10. Since section 170.9(d) took effect January 1, 1995, an adjustment must be made in subsequent odd-numbered years (commencing in 1997).

(2) The adjusted gift limitation amount shall apply as of January 1 of the year in which the adjustment is announced and shall remain in effect until January 1 of the next odd-numbered year.

(3) The adjusted gift limitation amount shall be calculated by the commission as follows:

(a) The base dollar amount ($250) shall be increased or decreased by the percentage change in the annual average California Consumer Price Index (CCPI) for all urban consumers from the base year (1994) to the end of the calendar year immediately preceding the year of adjustment.

(b) Formula: The base dollar amount ($250) is multiplied by a fraction whose numerator is the annual average CCPI for the even-numbered year preceding the year of adjustment and whose denominator is the 1994 annual average CCPI (151.5). The resulting dollar amount is rounded to the nearest $10, unless that amounts ends in the numeral five with no cents, in which case it is not rounded in either direction.

Approved May 28, 1997.

Policy Declaration 3.12. Extensions of Time.

Unnecessary delay in commission proceedings is incompatible with the commission's mandate to protect the public and the judiciary in general. Accordingly, extensions of time are disfavored.

Approved Aug. 26, 2004.

DIVISION IV
DISCLOSURE OF INFORMATION

Policy Declaration 4.1. Public Safety.

The disclosure of information concerning a threat to public safety under rule 102(f) may be made by the chairperson, the director or the designee of either.

Approved May 28, 1997.

Policy Declaration 4.2. Disclosure of Information to Prosecuting Authorities.

When, in the course of evaluating complaints or conducting investigations, commission staff acquires information revealing possible criminal conduct by a judge, former judge or by any other individual or entity, such information shall be brought to the attention of the commission at the earliest possible opportunity for consideration of a referral of the information to prosecuting authorities. Such a referral requires a vote of a majority of the commission members.

Approved May 28, 1997.

Policy Declaration 4.3. Disclosure of Disciplinary Records to Public Entity Upon Request/With Consent of Judge.

When a judge requests or consents to the release of commission records of disciplinary action under rule 102(h), the judge's request must be made in writing to the commission office. If the judge is consenting to a request by a public entity for records of disciplinary action, the judge's written consent and a copy of the entity's request must be received by the commission office. Copies of any information released to the public entity shall be provided simultaneously to the judge requesting or consenting to the release of records.

Approved May 28, 1997.

Policy Declaration 4.4. Disclosure of Records of Disciplinary Action to Appointing Authorities.

Requests by an appointing authority for records of disciplinary action pursuant to California Constitution, article VI, section 18.5 or rule 102(i) must be made in writing to the commission office. Copies of any information provided to the appointing authority shall be provided simultaneously to the applicant judge.

Approved May 28, 1997.

Policy Declaration 4.5. Disclosure of Information Regarding Pending Proceedings to Appointing Authorities.

Requests by an appointing authority for information regarding pending investigations or proceedings pursuant to rule 102(j) must be made in writing to the commission office. Copies of any information provided to the appointing authority shall be provided simultaneously to the applicant judge.

Approved May 28, 1997.

Policy Declaration 4.5.5.   Limitation on Disclosure to Appointing Authorities— Complaints Not Yet Reviewed by the Commission.

When responding to a request for information regarding pending investigations from appointing authorities (rule 102(j)), the Director-Chief Counsel shall state that the commission's discretionary authority to release information concerning pending investigations does not encompass comment on any complaint that may have been received by the commission and has not yet been reviewed by the commission to determine whether or not to authorize an investigation or whether any such complaint exists.

Approved Mar. 13, 2002.

Policy Declaration 4.6.   Disclosure of Information to Public Entities Upon Retirement or Resignation.

The release of information to a public entity following a judge's retirement or resignation, pursuant to rule 102(k), requires a vote of a majority of the commission members. The commission may, in its discretion, notify the judge that such disclosure is being made. Copies of any information being disclosed to the public entity may, in the commission's discretion, be made available to the judge who has retired or resigned.

Approved May 28, 1997; amended Jan. 29, 2003.

DIVISION V
DISABILITY RETIREMENT APPLICATIONS

Policy Declaration 5.1.   Disability Applications: Confidentiality.

The commission shall treat as confidential any information which is presented to the commission by a judge for retirement purposes, except as follows:

(1)   The fact and date that an application has been filed and has been approved or rejected or remains pending may be revealed.

(2)   If the Judges' Retirement System (JRS) submits a written request for information concerning a particular disability retirement application pursuant to Government Code section 75080(d), the commission shall provide to JRS any information that the commission deems necessary to a full understanding of the commission's action, in furtherance of the statutory scheme embodied in articles 3 and 4 of the Judges' Retirement Law. The commission shall furnish the judge in question with a copy of any documents provided to JRS. All information released under this section shall remain confidential and privileged.

Approved May 28, 1997; amended June 21, 2000; Aug. 26, 2004.

Policy Declaration 5.2.   Disability Applications: Medical Consultants.

The commission may arrange with the University of California Medical Centers and/or other qualified medical practitioners for medical consultants to provide independent medical examinations for disability retirement applicants, to assist the commission as necessary in evaluating disability retirement applications under Government Code section 75060, making findings under Policy Declaration 5.4(4) in order to facilitate implementation of Government Code section 75080(d), and/or reevaluating the medical status of a judge retired on disability under Government Code section 75060.6.

Approved May 28, 1997; amended June 21, 2000.

Policy Declaration 5.3.   Reexamination of Judges Retired for Disability.

When approving a request for disability retirement, the commission shall decide on a case-by-case basis whether and when the judge shall be required to be reexamined pursuant to Government Code section 75060.6. Notwithstanding such decision, a judge retired for disability may be required to undergo reexamination pursuant to Government Code section 75060.6.

Approved May 28, 1997.

Policy Declaration 5.4.   Procedure in Disability Retirement Matters.

(1)   An application for disability retirement must include: a consent to disability retirement, executed by the judge, and a medical certificate of disability, executed under penalty of perjury by a licensed physician. To complete the application, the commission ordinarily will require a medical report prepared by that physician in support of certification, which shall include a statement specifying the nature of the judicial duties that cannot be efficiently discharged due to the judge's disability, and all pertinent medical documentation.

(2)   When a judge submits an application for disability retirement, the commission will advise the judge if the certifying physician's report or other medical documentation supporting the application is inadequate, and will give the judge thirty (30) days to supply more complete data.

(3)   Following receipt of a complete application, the commission may request review of medical reports and documents by independent consultants and/or medical examiners. One or more independent medical examinations and/or additional medical information may be requested within one hundred twenty (120) days of the first commission meeting after receipt of complete medical records. This time may be extended for good cause. If an independent medical examination is conducted, the commission will provide a copy of the examiner's report to the judge. If the examiner concludes that the judge suffers from a disability that precludes the efficient discharge of

judicial duties and is permanent or likely to become so, the examiner's report shall include a statement specifying the nature of the judicial duties that cannot be efficiently discharged due to the disability.

(4)   Within sixty (60) days of the first commission meeting after receipt of all reports by consultants and medical examiners, the commission will: approve the application, or tentatively deny it, or extend its time to act on the application for good cause, "good cause" to include circumstances in which the judge's condition cannot yet be deemed permanent or likely to become so, within the meaning of Government Code section 75060. If the commission extends its time to act, notice of such extension shall be provided to the judge. If the commission approves the application, the commission may prepare a statement of findings specifying the nature of the judicial duties that cannot be efficiently discharged due to the disability.

(5)   If the commission tentatively denies the application, the commission will within thirty (30) days issue a tentative decision setting forth the reasons for the denial. The tentative decision will be provided to the judge upon issuance.

(6)   A tentative denial becomes final thirty (30) days after issuance unless, within thirty (30) days of the tentative denial, the judge files a request to present additional evidence. Within thirty (30) days of the first commission meeting after such filing, the commission will appoint a special master authorized to take evidence, obtain additional medical information, and take any other steps the special master deems necessary to resolve the matter.

(7)   Within one hundred eighty (180) days after the appointment of a special master, the master will refer the matter back to the commission with a report containing proposed findings.

(8)   Within ninety (90) days of the first commission meeting following such referral, the commission will make a decision either approving the application and referring it to the Chief Justice or denying the application and advising the Chief Justice.

Approved May 28, 1997; amended June 21, 2000.

Policy Declaration 5.5.   Disability Applications: Burden of Proof.

Unless Government Code section 75062, 75063 or 75064 applies, a judge seeking disability retirement must establish by a preponderance of the evidence that the judge is unable to discharge efficiently the duties of judicial office by reason of mental or physical disability that is or is likely to become permanent.

Approved May 28, 1997.

Policy Declaration 5.6.   Procedure in Restoration to Capacity Matters.

(1)   An application for restoration to capacity must be in writing, executed by the judge, and be accompanied by one or more medical reports sufficient to establish that the judge is no longer mentally or physically incapacitated and is capable of discharging efficiently the duties of judicial office.

(2)   When a judge submits an application for restoration to capacity, the commission will advise the judge if the certifying physician's report or other medical documentation supporting the application is inadequate, and will give the judge thirty (30) days to supply more complete data.

(3)   Following receipt of a complete application, the commission may request review of medical reports and documents by independent consultants and/or medical examiners. One or more independent medical examinations may be requested within one hundred twenty (120) days of the first commission meeting after receipt of complete medical records. This time may be extended for good cause. If an independent medical examination is conducted, the commission will provide a copy of the examiner's report to the judge.

(4)   Within sixty (60) days of the first commission meeting after receipt of all reports by consultants and medical examiners, the commission will either approve the application or tentatively deny it.

(5)   If the commission tentatively denies the application, the commission will within thirty (30) days issue a tentative decision setting forth the reasons for the denial. The tentative decision will be provided to the judge upon issuance.

(6)   A tentative denial becomes final thirty (30) days after issuance unless, within thirty (30) days of the tentative denial, the judge files a request to present additional evidence. Within thirty (30) days of the first commission meeting after such filing, the commission will appoint a special master authorized to take evidence, obtain additional medical information, and take any other steps the special master deems necessary to resolve the matter.

(7)   Within one hundred eighty (180) days after the appointment of a special master, the master will refer the matter back to the commission with a report containing proposed findings.

(8)   Within ninety (90) days of the first commission meeting following such referral, the commission will make a decision either approving the application for restoration to capacity or denying it.

Approved May 28, 1997.

DIVISION VI
CODE OF ETHICS FOR COMMISSION MEMBERS

Recusal. Policy Declaration 6.1.
Confidentiality. Policy Declaration 6.2.
Ex parte contacts. Policy Declaration 6.3.
Judicial election activities. Policy Declaration 6.4.
Impropriety and appearance of impropriety. Policy Declaration 6.5.

Preface

As the agency charged with enforcing standards of judicial conduct in order to maintain the integrity and independence of the judiciary, the California Commission on Judicial Performance (commission) recognizes the importance of observing high standards of ethical conduct in the performance of its responsibilities. The Code of Ethics (Code) set forth in these policy declarations describes ethical standards expected of a commission member. The Code does not confer any substantive or procedural due process rights **other than those provided by law**, or create a separate basis for civil liability or criminal prosecution.

For purposes of this Code, the judge who is the subject of a complaint, an investigation, or formal proceedings before the commission shall be referred to as the "subject judge."

Adopted Jan. 31, 2007; amended Dec. 13, 2007.

Policy Declaration 6.1.   Recusal.

(1)   A commission member shall recuse himself or herself if:

(a)   The member does not think he or she is able to act fairly and impartially in a matter;

(b)   The member or an immediate family member is the subject of the investigation;

(c)   The member served as a lawyer in any proceedings that are the subject of the investigation;

(d)   The member has a case pending before the subject judge either as a litigant or in the member's capacity as a lawyer;

(e)   A lawyer with whom the member practices is involved in the complaint;

(f)   The member has a bias or prejudice for or against the subject judge; or

(g)   A reasonable person aware of the facts would entertain a substantial doubt that the member would be able to be impartial.

(2)   If a member determines to recuse himself or herself:

(a)   The member shall recuse himself or herself promptly;

(b)   The recused member may, but is not required to, state the reason(s) for his or her recusal;

(c)   The recused member shall leave the room, not comment further or otherwise participate in the commission's consideration of the matter from which the member is recused; and

(d)   The recused member shall not receive further written materials on the matter from which the member is recused.

Adopted Jan. 31, 2007.

Policy Declaration 6.2.   Confidentiality.

(1)   Confidentiality shall be maintained with regard to all new, pending, and closed matters pursuant to rule 102 and other applicable legal requirements.

(2)   Members shall ensure that all confidential documents are secured. When the members are notified in writing (e.g., through the meeting minutes) that documents in selected matters may be discarded, members who choose to discard such documents shall ensure that they are destroyed. Members who choose to retain such documents shall ensure that they are secured.

(3)   A member shall not use or disclose, for any purpose unrelated to commission duties, non-public or confidential information acquired in his or her capacity as a commission member.

Adopted Jan. 31, 2007.

Policy Declaration 6.3.   Ex Parte Contacts.

(1)   **A member shall not initiate, permit, or consider ex parte communications regarding a matter pending or impending before the commission, other than authorized communications with other commission members and staff.**

(2)   If a member is contacted about a new or pending matter by a subject judge, a judge's attorney [1] or other agent, or a subject judge's family or friends, the member shall not discuss the matter, but may refer the person to the Director-Chief Counsel.

[2] **(3)**   If a member is contacted by a complainant, witness, or potential witness about a new, pending, or closed matter, the member shall not discuss the matter, but may refer the person to the Director-Chief Counsel. Correspondence from complainants about commission business shall be referred to the Director-Chief Counsel for acknowledgement and disposition.

(4)   After the initiation of formal proceedings, commission members shall not initiate communications with or receive communications from the Director-Chief Counsel, investigative staff, or trial counsel concerning the matter except as provided by commission rules or stipulation of all parties in the proceeding.

Adopted Jan. 31, 2007; amended Dec. 13, 2007.

PD 6.3.   2008 Deletes. [1] , [2] (2)

Policy Declaration 6.4.   Judicial Election Activities.

(1)   A member of the commission shall not publicly support or oppose a candidate for election to judicial office while a member of the commission. For purposes of this guideline, both incumbent judges and attorneys seeking election to a judicial position are considered candidates for judicial office.

(2)   A member of the commission shall not personally contribute funds directly to any candidate for election to judicial office while a member of the commission. If a commission member is a member of a partnership or professional corporation that contributes funds to candidates for judicial office, the commission member should not participate in such contribution decisions. If a commission member is assessed a portion of any contribution made to a candidate for judicial office by the member's firm, the commission member's recusal from matters involving the judge may be appropriate under some circumstances. In assessing whether to recuse, relevant factors include: whether the amount of money assessed from the commission member is de minimis (less than $10), whether the commission member's name is included in the firm name, the number of other partners in the member's firm, and the total number of judges in the county in which the judicial candidate was elected.

(3)   A member of the commission who is also a member of the board of an organization which is involved in judicial election activities should exercise caution over his or her participation in such activities. A member of the

commission should not participate in the organization's endorsements of or opposition to specific judicial candidates. Ideally, any publication of the organization's endorsement of or opposition to specific judicial candidates would state that the commission member on the board of the organization had not participated in the endorsement or opposition. In some instances, depending on the size of the organization, its purpose and its activities, the commission member should consider resigning from the organization's board if an appearance of conflict of interest or other impropriety cannot otherwise be avoided.

Adopted Jan. 31, 2007.

Policy Declaration 6.5. Impropriety and Appearance of Impropriety.

(1) A member shall not lend the prestige of his or her commission office to advance his or her private interests or the interests of others; nor shall the member convey or permit others to convey the impression that they are in a special position to influence the commission.

(2) A member shall not be swayed by partisan interests, public clamor, or fear of criticism with respect to the conduct of commission business.

(3) In conducting commission business, a member shall refrain from manifesting by word or action bias or prejudice based on race, sex, religion, national origin, disability, age, sexual orientation or socio-economic status against parties, witnesses, counsel, or others.

Adopted Jan. 31, 2007.

DIVISION VII
DISCIPLINE

Policy Declaration 7.1. Non-Exclusive Factors Relevant to Sanctions.

The following non-exclusive factors may be relevant in considering the appropriate discipline to be ordered. Because each case is considered on its own facts, the applicability and weight given to any factor is within the discretion of the commission.

(1) Characteristics of Misconduct.

(a) The number of acts of misconduct.

(b) The nature and seriousness of the misconduct.

(c) Whether the misconduct occurred in the judge's official capacity or in the judge's private life.

(d) Whether the misconduct involved dishonesty or lack of integrity.

(e) Whether the misconduct was intentional, premeditated, negligent, or spontaneous.

(f) The nature and extent to which the misconduct has been injurious to other persons.

(g) Whether the judge was motivated by a desire to satisfy a personal or venal interest, vindictiveness, or an interest in justice, or compassion.

(h) Whether the misconduct undermines the integrity of the judiciary, respect for the judiciary or the administration of justice.

(i) Whether the misconduct involves unequal application of justice on the basis of such considerations as race, ethnicity or national origin, gender, sexual orientation, or religion.

(2) Service and Demeanor of the Judge.

(a) Whether the judge has acknowledged the acts occurred and has shown an appreciation of the impropriety of his or her acts.

(b) Whether the judge cooperated fully and honestly in the commission proceedings.

(c) Whether the judge has evidenced an effort to change or modify the conduct.

(d) The judge's length of service in a judicial capacity.

(e) Whether there has been prior disciplinary action concerning the judge.

(f) Whether there are exceptional personal circumstances that warrant consideration.

(g) The judge's reputation for administering his or her judicial duties in a fair, impartial, and dignified manner and for making positive contributions to the court or community.

Approved Oct. 22, 2008.

INDEX

CIVIL CODE

CODE OF CIVIL PROCEDURE

EVIDENCE CODE

FAMILY CODE

PROBATE CODE

RULES OF COURT

RULES OF PROFESSIONAL CONDUCT

RULES OF COMMISSION ON JUDICIAL PERFORMANCE

GOVERNMENT CODE [ADMINISTRATIVE PROCEDURE ACT,

GOVERNMENT CLAIMS ACT & MISCELLANEOUS FEE PROVISIONS]

ABBREVIATIONS

CC .... Civil Code

CCP .... Code of Civil Procedure

Ev .... Evidence Code

Fam .... Family Code

Gov .... Government Code

Pro .... Probate Code

JudPerR .... Rules of Commission on Judicial Performance

JudPerPolicy .... Policy Declarations of the Commission on Judicial Performance

ProfC .... Rules of Professional Conduct

CRC .... Rules of Court

CRCAppx .... Rules of Court Appendix

CRCSupp .... Rules of Court Supplement

CRC ArbEthicsStand .... Rules of Court Ethics Standards for Neutral Arbitrators in Contractual Arbitration

CRC JudAdminStand .... Rules of Court Standards of Judicial Administration

CRCSupp JudEthicsCanon .... Code of Judicial Ethics

INDEX
TO THE
CIVIL, CIVIL PROCEDURE,
EVIDENCE, FAMILY, PROBATE CODES,
RULES OF COURT, RULES OF PROFESSIONAL CONDUCT,
RULES OF COMMISSION ON JUDICIAL PERFORMANCE,
GOVERNMENT CODE [ADMINISTRATIVE PROCEDURE ACT,
GOVERNMENT CLAIMS ACT & MISCELLANEOUS FEE PROVISIONS]

Abbreviations used in references are listed in Table of Abbreviations on facing page.

A

ABANDONMENT
Adoption proceedings for abandoned child **Fam 7822, 8606, 8607**
Animals **CC 1834.5**
Appellate rules
   Superior court appeals (See **APPELLATE RULES, SUPERIOR COURT APPEALS**)
   Supreme court and courts of appeal
      Dismissal (See **APPELLATE RULES, SUPREME COURT AND COURTS OF APPEAL**)
Children (See **PARENT AND CHILD**)
Decedent's estate, abandonment of personal property of (See **ADMINISTRATION OF ESTATES**)
Easements (See **EASEMENTS**)
Eminent domain proceedings **CCP 1268.510**
Escheat after (See **ESCHEAT**)
Floating homes (See **FLOATING HOMES**)
Homestead property, abandonment of **CCP 704.980, 704.990**
Husband and wife privileges waived in proceedings for **Ev 972, 985**
Infants (See **PARENT AND CHILD**)
Landlord and tenant
   Abandoned personal property, disposition of
      Commercial real property **CC 1993 to 1993.09**
Landlord disposing tenant's property **CCP 1174**
Leased premises abandoned by lessee **CC 1951 to 1951.7, CCP 415.47**
Mineral rights (See **MINERALS AND MINERAL RIGHTS**)
Minor children (See **PARENT AND CHILD**)
Mobilehome, sale of **CC 798.61**
Money orders **CCP 1511, 1513, 1542, 1581**
Parents (See **PARENT AND CHILD**)
Retirement funds (See **RETIREMENT**)
Statute of limitation, effect of **CCP 1476**
Tenant's abandoned property after termination of tenancy, disposition of **CC 1980 to 1991**
Traveler's checks **CCP 1511, 1513, 1542, 1581**
Unclaimed property (See **UNCLAIMED PROPERTY**)

ABATEMENT
Bequests, abatement of (See **ADMINISTRATION OF ESTATES**)
Cause of action, abatement of
   Disability of party during pending action or proceeding, effect of **CCP 375**
   Transfer of interests, effect of **CCP 368.5**
Nuisances, abatement of (See **NUISANCES**)

ABATEMENT—Cont.
Well drilled for oil or gas, limitation of actions to enjoin, abate or for damages on account of trespass by means of **CCP 349¾**

ABBREVIATIONS
Use in legal papers **CCP 186**

ABDUCTION (See **KIDNAPPING AND CHILD ABDUCTION**)

ABETTING (See **AIDING AND ABETTING**)

ABORTIONS
Commercial blockage tort affecting medical care facilities **CC 3427 to 3427.4**
Genetic defects, failure of parent to abort on discovery of **CC 43.6**
Minor, consent required for abortion by **Fam 6925**
Parental consent **Fam 6925**

ABROGATION
Enactment of code, effect on existing statutes of **CCP 18**

ABSENCE
Adjournment for absence of judge **CCP 139**
Annulment of marriage after first spouse found to be alive **Fam 2210**
Claims against decedents' estates, deposit of funds for absent claimants with **Pro 11428**
Conservatees (See **CONSERVATORS**)
Cotrustee, absence as grounds for incapacity of **Pro 15622**
Defendant absent from state, tolling statutes of limitation against **CCP 351**
Judge's absence, adjournment on **CCP 139**
Judicial arbitration proceedings, absence of party to **CRC 3.821**
Military (See **MILITARY**)
Missing persons (See **MISSING PERSONS**)
Personal representatives of decedents' estates (See **EXECUTORS AND ADMINISTRATORS**)
Unknown persons (See **UNKNOWN PERSONS**)
Witness **Ev 240**

ABSOLUTE FEE (See **FEE SIMPLE**)

ABSOLUTE OWNERSHIP
Definition **CC 678, 679**

ABSTRACT OF JUDGMENT
Generally **CCP 674**

1

Index

Index

Index

ADMINISTRATIVE ADJUDICATION—Cont.
Judicial review—Cont.
    First Amendment rights, expedited procedures for review
        of permit or entitlement decision implicating **CCP
        1094.8**
    Local agency decision, procedural requirements for review
        of **CCP 1094.6**
    Procedure for obtaining **CCP 1094.5, 1094.6, Gov 11523**
    Reconsideration of agency decision, effect of failure to seek
        Gov 11523
Language assistance
    Generally **Gov 11435.20**
    Alternate interpreter **Gov 11435.55**
    Certified interpreters **Gov 11435.30 to 11435.50**
    Confidentiality **Gov 11435.65**
    Costs and fees
        Interpreter examination and certification renewal
           Gov 11435.45
        Payment of interpreters **Gov 11435.25**
    Deaf or hard-of-hearing party **Gov 11435.10**
    Defined **Gov 11435.05**
    Notice of right to **Gov 11435.60**
    Removal of name from certified interpreter list **Gov
        11435.50**
    State agencies providing **Gov 11435.15**
Legislature
    Applicability of adjudicative provisions **Gov 11410.20**
    Suspension or adoption of procedures to avoid loss of
        federal funds, Governor's report of **Gov 11415.30**
Licenses and privileges
    Accusations against holder of (See subhead: **Accusations**)
    Decisions (See subhead: **Decisions**)
    Discovery (See subhead: **Discovery**)
    Filing requirements for proceedings involving (See sub-
        head: **Filing requirements**)
    Hearings involving (See subhead: **Hearings**)
    Informal hearings, availability of **Gov 11445.20**
    Medical disciplinary proceedings (See subhead: **Health
        care professionals disciplinary proceedings**)
    Regulatory agencies subject to formal hearing provisions
        Gov 11501
    Reinstatement of license or reduction of penalty, petition for
        Gov 11522
    Response to accusations (See subhead: **Response to accu-
        sation**)
    Settlement, timing of **Gov 11415.60**
    Statement of issues
        Generally **Gov 11504**
        Procedural requirements for accusations, applicability
           of **Gov 11504, 11504.5**
Local agency
    Applicability of provisions to **Gov 11410.30**
    Judicial review, procedure for obtaining **CCP 1094.6**
Mail and mailing
    Notice of defense, mailing of **Gov 11505**
    Service by (See subhead: **Service of papers**)
    Voting by agency members **Gov 11526**
Mandate, writ of (See subhead: **Judicial review**)
Mediation (See subhead: **Alternative dispute resolution**)
Medical disciplinary proceedings (See subhead: **Health care
    professionals disciplinary proceedings**)
Medical examination, language assistance provided for (See
    subhead: **Language assistance**)
Mistake or clerical error in decision, correction of **Gov 11518.5**
New proceeding after nonbinding arbitration **Gov 11420.10**
Nonbinding arbitration (See subhead: **Alternative dispute reso-
    lution**)
Notice
    Accusation amended after submission for decision **Gov
        11516**

ADMINISTRATIVE ADJUDICATION—Cont.
Notice—Cont.
    Affidavits as evidence, notice to introduce **Gov 11514**
    Conversion of proceeding **Gov 11470.40**
    Declaratory decision, application for **Gov 11465.30**
    Defense, notice of (See subhead: **Response to accusation**)
    Emergency decision **Gov 11460.40, 11460.50**
    Hearings (See subhead: **Hearings**)
    Language assistance, right to **Gov 11435.60**
    Official notice of matters as evidence **Gov 11515**
    Reduction of penalty, notice to Attorney General of petition
        for **Gov 11522**
    Subpoenas, written notice in lieu of **Gov 11450.50**
Notice of defense (See subhead: **Response to accusation**)
Oaths
    Authority to administer oath **Gov 11528**
    Refusal to take oath as grounds for contempt **Gov
        11455.10**
Office of Administrative Hearings (See **ADMINISTRATIVE
    PROCEDURE ACT**)
Official notice of matters as evidence, agency taking **Gov
    11515**
Orders
    Contempt (See subhead: **Contempt sanction**)
    Deposition, order to appear for **Gov 11511**
    Judicial review of (See subhead: **Judicial review**)
    Prehearing orders **Gov 11511.5**
Penalties
    Agency's authority to reduce penalty proposed by ALJ
        Gov 11517
    Limitation on **Gov 11425.50**
    Reduction, petition for **Gov 11522**
Pending proceedings, communications regarding **Gov
    11430.10 to 11430.80**
Petitions
    License reinstatement, petition for **Gov 11522**
    Penalty reduction, petition for **Gov 11522**
    Reconsideration of agency decision, petition for **Gov
        11521**
    Writ of mandate (See subhead: **Judicial review**)
Physician disciplinary proceedings (See subhead: **Health care
    professionals disciplinary proceedings**)
Place of hearing **Gov 11508**
Podiatric Medicine Board disciplinary proceedings, generally
    (See subhead: **Health care professionals disciplinary pro-
    ceedings**)
Postponement **Gov 11505**
Precedent decisions **Gov 11425.60**
Prehearing conferences
    Generally **Gov 11511.5**
    Public meeting requirement, exception to **Gov 11425.20**
Presiding officers
    Bad faith or frivolous tactics, authority to award expenses
        for **Gov 11455.30**
    Conversion of proceedings (See subhead: **Conversion of
        proceedings**)
    Cross-examination in informal hearings, actions concerning
        use of **Gov 11445.50**
    Disqualification
        Generally **Gov 11425.40**
        Prohibited communications, receipt of **Gov
           11430.60**
    Eligibility **Gov 11425.30**
    Ethics, Administrative Adjudication Code of **Gov 11475
        to 11475.70**
    Exclusion of evidence, authority for **Gov 11513**
    Informal hearings, regulation of **Gov 11445.40**
    Judicial review, generally (See subhead: **Judicial Review**)
    Prohibited communications **Gov 11430.10 to 11430.80**
    Subpoena powers **Gov 11450.20, 11450.30**

Index

ADMINISTRATIVE ADJUDICATION—Cont.
Prevailing law **Gov 11415.20**
Privileged communications, generally (See **PRIVILEGED COMMUNICATIONS**)
Probation **Gov 11519**
Prohibited communications **Gov 11430.10 to 11430.80**
Quash subpoena, motion to **Gov 11450.30**
Quasi-public entity, applicability of administrative adjudication provisions to **Gov 11410.60**
Reconsideration of decision
    Generally **Gov 11521**
    Judicial review, effect of failure to request agency reconsideration on **Gov 11523**
Record of proceedings
    Converted proceeding, use of original record in **Gov 11470.30**
    Decision based on **Gov 11517**
    Emergency decision **Gov 11460.70**
    Formal hearing **Gov 11512**
    Judicial review, preparation of record for **CCP 1094.5, 1094.6, Gov 11523**
    Public record **Gov 11517**
Regulatory agencies subject to formal hearing provisions **Gov 11501**
Reinstatement of license, petition for **Gov 11522**
Request for hearing by respondent **Gov 11505**
Response to accusation
    Generally **Gov 11506**
    Amended or supplemental accusation, response to **Gov 11507**
    Failure to file notice of defense, effect of **Gov 11520**
    Objection to **Gov 11506**
    Request for hearing **Gov 11505, 11506**
Restitution **Gov 11519**
Sanctions
    Bad faith or frivolous action causing delay, award of expenses for **Gov 11455.30**
    Contempt sanction (See subhead: **Contempt sanction**)
    Settlement including **Gov 11415.60**
Service of papers
    Accusations, service of **Gov 11505**
    Corrected decision **Gov 11518.5**
    Decision **Gov 11518**
    Discovery, motion or petition to compel **Gov 11507.7**
    Mail, service by
        Generally **Gov 11440.20**
        Subpoenas **Gov 11450.20**
    Manner of **Gov 11440.20**
    Statement of issues, service of **Gov 11504**
    Subpoenas **Gov 11450.20**
    Written notice in lieu of subpoena **Gov 11450.50**
Settlement
    Conference **Gov 11511.7**
    Decision by **Gov 11415.60**
    License, timing of settlement of proceeding involving **Gov 11415.60**
    Public hearing requirement, applicability of **Gov 11425.20**
    Sanctions included in **Gov 11415.60**
Sexual harassment, assault or battery, evidence in proceedings alleging **Gov 11440.40**
Statements
    Factual basis for decision **Gov 11425.50**
    License or privilege action, statement of issues in (See subhead: **Licenses and privileges**)
    Respondent, statement to **Gov 11505**
Stay of execution
    Generally **Gov 11519**
    Pending judicial review **CCP 1094.5**

ADMINISTRATIVE ADJUDICATION—Cont.
Subpoenas
    Applicability of procedures **Gov 11450.05**
    Issuance of **Gov 11450.10, 11450.20**
    Mileage and fees of witness **Gov 11450.40**
    Objection to **Gov 11450.30**
    Presiding officers, subpoena powers of **Gov 11450.20, 11450.30**
    Quash, motion to **Gov 11450.30**
    Satisfaction of subpoena duces tecum **Gov 11450.10**
    Service of **Gov 11450.20**
    Written notice in lieu of **Gov 11450.50**
Supplemental accusations, filing of **Gov 11507**
Sympathy expressed to accident victim or family
    Evidentiary effect **Gov 11440.45**
Telephone, television or electronic means
    Hearings, generally **Gov 11425.20, 11440.30**
    Prehearing conference conducted by **Gov 11511.5**
    Settlement conference conducted by **Gov 11511.7**
Television (See subhead: **Telephone, television or electronic means**)
Temporary decision (See subhead: **Emergency decisions**)
Time
    Filing requirements (See subhead: **Filing requirements**)
    Hearing **Gov 11508**
Translators (See subhead: **Language assistance**)
Vacate decision, motion to **Gov 11520**
Verification
    Accusations, verification of **Gov 11503**
    Statement of issues, verification of **Gov 11504**
Voting by agency members
    Adjudicatory proceedings, voting on decisions in **Gov 11517**
    Mail, voting by **Gov 11526**
Waiver of rights, generally **Gov 11415.40**
Witnesses
    Deposition of **Gov 11511**
    Examination
        Generally **Gov 11513**
        Affiants, cross-examination of **Gov 11514**
    Exchange of witness lists at prehearing conference **Gov 11511.5**
    Mileage and fees **Gov 11450.40**
    Oaths (See subhead: **Oaths**)
Writ of mandate (See subhead: **Judicial review**)
Written decision **Gov 11425.50**

ADMINISTRATIVE CODE (See **ADMINISTRATIVE PROCEDURE ACT**)

ADMINISTRATIVE LAW
Generally (See **ADMINISTRATIVE PROCEDURE ACT**)
Adjudicative proceedings (See **ADMINISTRATIVE ADJUDICATION**)

ADMINISTRATIVE OFFICE OF THE COURTS (See **JUDICIAL COUNCIL**)

ADMINISTRATIVE PRESIDING JUSTICE
Appellate rules, supreme court and courts of appeal (See **APPELLATE RULES, SUPREME COURT AND COURTS OF APPEAL**)
Superior courts
    Presiding judge (See **SUPERIOR COURTS**)

ADMINISTRATIVE PROCEDURE ACT
Adjudicative proceedings (See **ADMINISTRATIVE ADJUDICATION**)
Administrative Code (See subhead: **Code of Regulations**)
Administrative Code Supplement (See subhead: **Regulatory Code Supplement**)

Index

Index

Index

Index

Index

Index

Index

Index

Index

Index

Index

Index

Index

Index

Index

Index

Index

ATTACHMENT—Cont.

Discovery rights of plaintiff allowed under attachment order CCP 485.230

Districts   CCP 481.200

Duty of levying officer   CCP 488.020

Dwelling attachment of personalty used as   CCP 488.415

Earnings (See subhead: **Salaries and wages**)

Endorsement of instrument for payment   CCP 488.710

Entry of judgment in pending action, consent of plaintiff for CCP 491.440

Equipment
   Generally   CCP 487.010
   Defined   CCP 481.100
   Going business   CCP 488.375

Excessive amount of property interest, effect of   CCP 482.120, 488.720

Excessive levy   CCP 482.120

Exemption
   Generally   CCP 485.010, 487.020
   Affidavits supporting claims of   CCP 484.050, 484.070, 484.350
   Art dealers holding money for payment of artists   CC 986
   Bonuses   CCP 487.020
   Compensation   CCP 487.020
   Denial of claim   CCP 484.530
   Homesteads   CCP 487.025
   Notice of opposition to claims of   CCP 484.070, 484.360
   Original writs, claims in   CCP 484.050, 484.070
   Pending action, defendant's application for exemption from lien in   CCP 491.470
   Points and authorities supporting claims of   CCP 484.070, 484.350, 484.360
   Procedure for   CCP 482.100, 487.030
   Salaries   CCP 486.060, 487.020
   Subordinate judicial duty, contested claim as   CCP 482.060
   Time for claiming   CCP 485.610
   Wrongful attachments   CCP 490.010

Ex parte procedure
   Additional writs in   CCP 485.510 to 485.540
   Affidavits supporting applications for   CCP 484.510, 485.210
   Application for   CCP 484.510, 484.520, 485.210
   Exemptions   CCP 482.100, 484.530
   Findings   CCP 484.520, 485.220, 485.540
   Injury as grounds for issuing writ   CCP 485.010
   Protective orders, effect of ex parte application on   CCP 486.100
   Quash, motion to   CCP 485.240
   Release, motion for   CCP 485.240
   Setting aside, motion for   CCP 485.240

Extension of lien   CCP 488.510

Farm products, timber or minerals
   Generally   CCP 481.110, 487.010
   Going business, attachment of farm products of   CCP 488.395, 488.405
   Levy procedure   CCP 488.325
   Protective orders (See subhead: **Protective orders**)
   Transfer of property   CCP 486.050

Fees (See subhead: **Costs and fees**)

Filing, plaintiff requesting secrecy of   CCP 482.050

Final money judgments   CCP 488.480

Financial institutions
   Defined   CCP 481.113
   Deposits with (See subhead: **Deposits**)

Findings
   Generally   CCP 484.090, 484.100
   Additional writs   CCP 484.370, 485.540
   Amount attaching   CCP 492.090
   Ex parte procedure   CCP 484.520, 485.220

ATTACHMENT—Cont.

Findings—Cont.
   Foreign corporations, grounds for issuance of writ   CCP 492.030
   Other states, grounds for issuance of writ   CCP 492.030
   Protective orders   CCP 486.020

Foreign attachment (See subhead: **Other states**)

Forms
   Judicial council legal forms   CRCAppx A

Furniture, use determining wrongful attachment   CCP 490.010

Garnishment (See **GARNISHMENT**)

General intangibles
   Generally   CCP 488.470
   Defined   CCP 481.115

Going business
   Equipment, attachment of   CCP 488.375
   Farm products, attachment of   CCP 488.395
   Inventory, attachment of   CCP 488.395, 488.405
   Vehicle, attachment of   CCP 488.385

Hearings
   Continuance of   CCP 484.080
   Findings   CCP 484.090, 484.100, 484.370, 484.520
   Notices on   CCP 484.040, 484.050, 484.340, 1005
   Original writs   CCP 484.040
   Service of notice of application and hearing for writ, time for   CCP 1005
   Time   CCP 482.100

Homesteads, right to attach   CCP 487.025

Household purposes, claim based on sale, services or loan for CCP 483.010

Injunctive relief, effect on   CCP 482.020

Insolvency (See subhead: **Bankruptcy**)

Instructions
   Conforming with instructions, liability of levying officer for CCP 488.140
   Name and address of plaintiff in   CCP 488.040
   Writing, requirement for   CCP 488.030

Instruments
   Generally   CCP 488.440
   Defined   CCP 481.117
   Endorsement and presentation of instrument for payment CCP 488.710
   Negotiable instruments   CCP 487.010, 488.445

Intervention by plaintiff in pending action   CCP 491.430

Inventory
   Generally   CCP 481.120, 487.010
   Going business, attaching inventory of   CCP 488.395, 488.405
   Return of writ including   CCP 488.130
   Transfer of property   CCP 486.050

Issuance of writ
   Notice of opposition against right to attach orders, filing of CCP 484.060, 484.070

Joinder of defendant   CCP 491.320

Judicial and subordinate judicial duties   CCP 482.060

Judicial Council forms and rules, generally   CCP 482.030

Jurisdiction for third party examination   CCP 491.150

Jury trial on creditor's suit   CCP 491.350

Law and motion rules, applicability   CRC 3.1103

Levy
   By registered process server   CCP 488.080
   Exemption (See subhead: **Exemption**)
   General provisions   CCP 488.010 to 488.140
   Liens (See subhead: **Liens**)
   Methods of levy   CCP 488.300 to 488.485
   Temporary protective order (See subhead: **Protective orders**)
   Third persons, duties and liabilities after levy   CCP 488.600 to 488.620

Index

ATTORNEYS—Cont.

Decedents' estates—Cont.

Probate attorneys —Cont.

Qualifications   **CRC 10.776, 10.777**

Delaying tactics, assessment against attorney of expenses and attorney fees incurred as result of (See **SANCTIONS**)

Deliberation and verdict, post-trial discussions with jurors regarding   **CCP 206**

Dependent children

Guardian ad litem

Child abuse and treatment act (CAPTA) guardians ad litem   **CRC 5.662**

Depositions

Subpoenas

Issuance by attorney of record   **CCP 2020.210**

Deposit of estate-planning documents with attorney (See **TRUSTS; WILLS**)

Disability of attorney, appointment of practice administrator in event of   **Pro 2468, 17200**

Disability of plaintiff tolling statute of limitation for legal malpractice actions   **CCP 340.6**

Discipline

Attorney discipline generally (See **ATTORNEY DISCIPLINE**)

Rules of professional conduct generally (See subhead: **Rules of professional conduct**)

Discovery (See **DISCOVERY**)

Discrimination

Court appointment   **CRC 10.611, CRC JudAdminStand 10.21**

Discriminatory conduct in law practice, prohibition on   **ProfC 2-400**

Dismissal, consent of or notice to attorney of   **CCP 581**

Disqualification of judges (See **JUDGES, DISQUALIFICATION OF**)

Electronic court records

Access by attorneys and parties   **CRC 2.501**

Emancipation of children (See **EMANCIPATION OF MINORS**)

Enforcement of judgments (See **ENFORCEMENT OF JUDGMENTS**)

Executors and administrators (See **EXECUTORS AND ADMINISTRATORS**)

Ex parte proceedings

Identification of attorney or party   **CRC 3.1202**

Extension of time

Court's assumption of jurisdiction over practice   **CCP 353.1**

Legislature, time extension for attorneys attending   **CCP 1054.1**

Family law facilitators, minimum standards for   **CRC 5.35**

Family law proceedings

Appointment by court

Applicable guidelines for appointment   **CRC JudAdminStand 5.30**

Compensation of court-appointed attorneys   **CRC JudAdminStand 5.30**

Limited basis representation

Nondisclosure of attorney assistance in document preparation   **CRC 5.70**

Relief as counsel, application   **CRC 5.71**

Service of papers on attorney of record   **Fam 215**

Title IV-D support enforcement

Attorney of record in support actions   **CRC 5.320**

Fax transmissions, attorney-client privilege for   **Ev 952**

Fees (See **ATTORNEY'S FEES**)

Foreign legal consultants   **CRC 9.44**

Freedom from parental custody and control, appointment of counsel in proceedings for   **Fam 7860 to 7864**

ATTORNEYS—Cont.

Frivolous actions, assessment against attorney of expenses and attorney fees incurred as result of (See **SANCTIONS**)

Gifts

Inducing client to make substantial gift to attorney, prohibition against   **ProfC 4-400**

Judge or judicial officer, prohibition against gifts to   **ProfC 5-300**

Referrals, gift or gratuity for   **ProfC 1-320, 2-200**

Guardianship (See **GUARDIAN AND WARD**)

Habeas corpus

Petitions filed by attorneys   **CRC 8.384**

Harassment, bringing action or asserting position in litigation for purpose of   **ProfC 3-200**

Health care provider's negligence, noncompliance with notice requirement for commencement of action for   **CCP 365**

Indigent persons (See **INDIGENT PERSONS**)

In-house counsel

Registered in-house counsel   **CRC 9.46**

Inspection of records by (See **INSPECTION**)

Insurance (See **INSURANCE**)

International wills, authorized persons re   **Pro 6388, 6389**

Judge advocate, appearance in state court   **CRC 9.41**

Judges

Practice of law   **CRCSupp JudEthicsCanons 3, 4**

Temporary judges

Appointment of attorney as temporary judge   **CRC 2.810, 2.812**

Judges' right to representation in proceedings for censure, removal or admonishment   **JudPerR 106, 126**

Judicial arbitration proceedings   **CRC 3.821**

Jurisdiction over practice

Extension of limitations period on   **CCP 353.1**

Relief from judgment or other proceedings   **CCP 473.1**

Juvenile rules

Appeals

Representation of child on appeal   **CRC 5.661**

Delinquency proceedings

Responsibilities of children's counsel in delinquency proceedings   **CRC 5.663**

Law and motion rules

Relieving counsel, motion for order   **CRC 3.1362**

Law practice

Agreements restricting member's practice   **ProfC 1-500**

In-house counsel

Registered in-house counsel   **CRC 9.46**

Partnership with non-lawyer   **ProfC 1-310**

Registered legal services attorney   **CRC 9.45**

Rules governing law practice, attorneys and judges   **CRC 9.1 to 9.61**

Attorney discipline   **CRC 9.10 to 9.22**

Authority for rules   **CRC 9.2**

Contents of rules   **CRC 1.4**

Continuing legal education   **CRC 9.31**

Definitions   **CRC 9.5**

Legal specialists, certification   **CRC 9.35**

Non-bar members, appearances and practice by   **CRC 9.40 to 9.48**

Title of rules   **CRC 9.1**

Unaccredited law schools, study in   **CRC 9.30**

Law schools not accredited, study in   **CRC 9.30**

Law students (See **LAW STUDENTS**)

Lawyer referral service, immunity from liability for referrals by   **CC 43.95**

Legal service programs

Participation in   **ProfC 1-600**

Registered legal services attorneys   **CRC 9.45**

Legislature

Extension of time for attorneys attending   **CCP 1054.1**

Index

AWARDS

Attorneys' fees (See **ATTORNEY'S FEES**)

International commercial arbitration awards (See **INTERNATIONAL COMMERCIAL ARBITRATION AND CONCILIATION**)

Judicial arbitration awards (See **JUDICIAL ARBITRATION**)

Non-judicial arbitration awards (See **ARBITRATION**)

B

BABYSITTING AND BABYSITTERS (See **CHILD CARE**)

BACKGROUND

Expert witnesses **Ev 802**

BAD CHECKS (See **CHECKS**)

BAD FAITH

Award of expenses and attorney's fees incurred as result of bad-faith actions or tactics (See **SANCTIONS**)

Landlord, bad faith retention of deposits by **CC 1950.7**

Small claims court judgment, award of attorney's fees on appeal from **CCP 116.790**

Summary judgment motion support or opposition presented in bad faith **CCP 437c**

BAGGAGE

Bus, liability for loss by operator of **CC 2205**

Common carriers liens for fares **CC 2191**

Delivery requirements **CC 2183**

Foreclosure of deposit liens **CC 1857**

Free carriage of **CC 2180, 2181**

Higher value declaration **CC 2177, 2205**

Hotel, apartment, lodging or hospital, limitation of action for recovery or conversion of personal property left at **CCP 341a**

Hotel keeper's lien on **CC 1861**

Lien for rent **CC 1861, 1861a**

Limitation on liability

    Carrier's liability **CC 2178, 2182**

    Innkeeper's liability **CC 1859**

Notice of valuable goods **CC 2177**

Place for carrying **CC 2183**

Tagging requirements **CC 2205**

BAIL

Amount of bail

    Jury trial, request for as affecting amount **CRC 4.101**

    Schedules **CRC 4.102**

Appeal, bail pending **CRC 8.312**

    Finality of court of appeals ruling on bail **CRC 8.366**

Boating violations

    Bail schedule **CRC 4.102**

Business licensing violations, bail schedule **CRC 4.102**

Check, payment by means of **CRC 10.821**

Contempt proceedings **CCP 1213, 1215, 1216**

Fish and game violations, bail schedule **CRC 4.102**

Forestry violations, bail schedule **CRC 4.102**

Jury trial request, effect of **CRC 4.101**

Parks and recreation violations, bail schedule **CRC 4.102**

Payment **CRC 10.821**

Public utilities violations, bail schedule **CRC 4.102**

Reduction of bail

    Pending appeal **CRC 8.312**

Schedules **CRC 4.102**

Uniform Bail and Penalty Schedules **CRC 4.102**

BAILIFFS

Appointment **CRCSupp JudEthicsCanon 3**

Juvenile court proceedings **CRC 5.530**

BAILMENT

Automobiles (See **AUTOMOBILES**)

Death of party to **CC 1934**

Default on obligations by lessor **CC 1957**

Delivery of property under **CC 1955**

Demand for return of property loaned **CC 1894**

Deposits (See **DEPOSITS**)

Enforcement of judgments (See **ENFORCEMENT OF JUDGMENTS**)

Expenses and upkeep **CC 1956, 2078**

Fitness requirement of property held under **CC 1955**

Gratuitous bailee **CC 1505, 2078**

Hiring contracts **CC 1925 to 1935**

Indemnity requirements **CC 1893, 1894**

Loss from early termination of **CC 1894, 1935**

Negligence **CC 1888, 1928, 2078**

Notice of expenditures **CC 1957**

Offer of contract **CC 1503**

Place for redelivery of property held under **CC 1896, 1958**

Possession, transfer of **CC 1925**

Quiet enjoyment, right of **CC 1955**

Repairs **CC 1889, 1929**

Return of bailed property **CC 1958**

Termination of agreement **CC 1894 to 1896, 1931 to 1934**

Use, bailment for **CC 1884 to 1896**

Vessels held under charter-party agreement **CC 1959**

BALLOON PAYMENTS (See **TRUST DEEDS AND MORTGAGES**)

BALLOT MEASURES

Precedence to cases involving certification of **CCP 35**

BANK DRAFTS (See **CHECKS**)

BANKING (See **BANKS AND BANKING**)

BANKRUPTCY (See also **INSOLVENCY**)

Assignment for benefit of creditors (See **ASSIGNMENT FOR BENEFIT OF CREDITORS**)

Attachment (See **ATTACHMENT**)

Child support obligations discharged in **Fam 4013**

Credit reporting (See **CREDIT REPORTING**)

Debt collectors, effect on **CC 1788.14**

Enforcement of judgments (See **ENFORCEMENT OF JUDGMENTS**)

1st Appellate District local rule, duty of party to inform court of pending bankruptcy proceedings pursuant to **CRCSupp 1st AppDist**

Fraudulent transfers (See **FRAUDULENT TRANSFERS**)

Gift certificates

    Issuer's duty to honor **CC 1749.6**

Homestead exemption, applicability of **CCP 703.140**

    Amount of exemption, determination **CCP 703.150**

Investigative agencies, restrictions on information of **CC 1785.18**

Judicial notice of general orders and forms in **Ev 451**

Landlord, priority of deposits by tenant to **CC 1950.7**

Liens, effect on **CCP 493.030 to 493.050**

Property settlement agreements, discharge of obligations in **Fam 3592**

Small claims court, trustee in bankruptcy filing in **CCP 116.420**

BANKS AND BANKING

Administrators of decedents' estates (See **EXECUTORS AND ADMINISTRATORS**)

Armenian genocide victims, claims against banks

    Limitation of actions **CCP 354.45**

Attachment (See **ATTACHMENT**)

Index

Index

CHILD SUPPORT—Cont.

Enforcement—Cont.

Parent Locator Service and Central Registry   **Fam 17506**

Penalties (See subhead: **Penalties**)

Period of enforceability for possession or sale of property   **Fam 291, 4502**

Private child support collectors   **Fam 5610 to 5616**

Relief from support judgments or orders   **Fam 2120 to 2129, 3690 to 3693, 17432**

Renewal requirements, judgments exempt from   **CCP 683.310, Fam 291, 4502**

Retirement benefits of judgment debtor   **CCP 704.110, 704.114, 704.115, Fam 17528**

Satisfaction of money judgment for child support, priorities for crediting money received in   **CCP 695.221**

Self-help materials   **Fam 291**

Social security payments   **Fam 4504, 17516**

Tax refund owed judgment debtor, claim against   **CCP 708.730, 708.740, 708.780**

Unemployment compensation benefits, enforcement against   **CCP 704.120, Fam 17518**

Workers' compensation benefits, enforcement against   **CCP 704.160, Fam 17510**

Enforcement of judgments

Levy and execution

Application for writ of execution, priority   **CCP 699.510**

Equal responsibility of parents for   **Fam 4001**

Escrow relating to support judgment lien, demand statement needed to close   **CCP 697.360**

Evasion of obligation

Knowingly assisting obligor   **CC 1714.4**

Conduct constituting   **CC 1714.41**

Evidence

Admissibility of income and benefit information provided by employer in proceeding to modify or terminate support   **Ev 1567**

Deposit of money to secure future payments   **Fam 4562**

Execution writ to enforce support order   **Fam 5100 to 5104**

Ex parte restraining orders   **Fam 4610, 4620**

Expedited support order   **Fam 3620 to 3634**

Expenses

Added to amount of support   **Fam 4061 to 4063**

County, expenses and fees charged to   **Fam 4203**

Declaration (See subhead: **Income and expense declaration**)

Travel expenses for visitation   **Fam 4061, 4062**

Family home, rental value of   **Fam 4057**

Family law facilitators for unrepresented parties   **Fam 10000 to 10015**

Family law information centers for unrepresented low-income litigants   **Fam 15000 to 15012**

Family law rules (See **FAMILY RULES**)

Family support defined   **Fam 92**

Federal law, compliance with   **Fam 4553**

Fees

Title IV-D child support agency involved   **Gov 70672**

Financial hardship (See subhead: **Hardship**)

Financial institution match system

Delinquency

Collection of delinquency   **Fam 17453**

Findings on support at request of party   **Fam 4005**

Foreign country judgments   **CCP 1715**

Formulas for award calculation (See subhead: **Statewide uniform guidelines**)

Garnishment (See **GARNISHMENT**)

Government support enforcement services   **CRC 5.300 to 5.375, Fam 4002, 4200 to 4205, 4351**

Abduction records, disclosure of   **Fam 17514**

Abstract of judgment, recordation of   **Fam 4506.1**

CHILD SUPPORT—Cont.

Government support enforcement services —Cont.

Actions under Social Security Act Title IV-D   **CRC 5.320**

Address of obligor, requirements on receipt of   **Fam 17401**

Agreement, judgment based on   **Fam 17416**

Answers to complaints in actions brought by local support agencies   **Fam 17400, 17404**

Appeals by Attorney General   **Fam 17407**

Appearance in actions   **CRC 5.360**

Attorney-client relationship, disclaimer of   **Fam 17406**

Attorney of record for actions under Social Security Act Title IV-D   **CRC 5.320**

Attorneys' fees award against governmental agency   **Fam 273**

Child Support Collections Recovery Fund   **Fam 17402.5**

Child Support Services Advance fund   **Fam 17703**

Civil procedure for enforcement actions, generally   **Fam 17400, 17404**

Commissioners (See subhead: **Court commissioners**)

Complaints

Local support agencies, complaints against by custodial and noncustodial parents   **Fam 17800 to 17804**

Local support agencies, complaints and answers in actions brought by   **CRC 5.325, Fam 17400, 17404, 17428**

Compromise of arrears program   **Fam 17560**

Confidentiality of records   **Fam 17212, 17514**

Consolidation of support orders   **Fam 17408**

County assessments

Compliance by county with standards, assessment   **Fam 17702**

Data collection and reporting by local support agencies   **Fam 17600**

Debt compromise of obligor parent's liabilities for public assistance   **Fam 17550, 17552**

Deduction of support payment from aid received by obligee, first $50 as exempt from requirement for   **Fam 17504**

Default judgment in enforcement action   **Fam 17430, 17433**

Definitions   **Fam 17000**

Delinquency notice   **Fam 17525**

Departmental regulations to be promulgated for case referrals to local child support agencies   **Fam 17552**

Department of Child Support Services (See subhead: **Department of Child Support Services**)

Designation of local child support agency as assigned payee   **Fam 3030, 3752, 4200 to 4205, 17000**

State disbursement unit as payee   **Fam 4200, 4201, 4204**

Disabled obligor, modification of child support enforcement order for   **Fam 17400.5**

Earnings assignment for support, enforcement of   **CCP 704.114, Fam 5212, 5244 to 5247, 17420**

Earnings withholding order for support, enforcement by local child support agency of   **CCP 706.030, Fam 17509**

Effective date of support order in proposed judgment   **Fam 17400.5**

Electronic fund transfers for employer payment of withholding   **Fam 17309.5**

Electronic signatures

Substitution for original signatures   **Fam 17400**

Employment and training services for noncustodial parents, administration of   **Fam 17211**

Erroneous enforcement action, remediation of   **Fam 17433, 17530**

Expedited modification of support order   **Fam 17441**

Index

Index

Index

CODICIL
Generally (See **WILLS**)
Will defined to include **CCP 17**

COERCION
Mitigating circumstances **CRC 4.423**
Privileged matter disclosed **Ev 919**

COHABITATION
Battered cohabitant, sentencing **CRC 4.423**
Domestic violence protective orders **Fam 2045 to 2049, 7710 to 7730**
Denial of petition for ex parte order, reasons to be provided **Fam 6320.5**
Fraudulent promise, action for damages for **CC 43.4**
Presumption concerning child of marriage **Fam 7540, 7541, 7611**
Spousal support affected by supported spouse cohabiting with opposite sex **Fam 4323**

COLLABORATIVE JUSTICE COURTS
Judicial council advisory committee **CRC 10.56**

COLLABORATIVE LAW PROCESS
Family law matters **Fam 2013**

COLLATERAL ATTACK
Letters of administration, limitation on attack on orders granting **Pro 8007**

COLLATERAL ESTOPPEL
Citation of unpublished opinions **CRC 8.1115**
Economic litigation provision **CCP 99**

COLLATERAL KINDRED
Claims of **Pro 6402, 6402.5**

COLLATERAL SOURCE RULE **CC 3333.1**

COLLECTION
Attachment (See **ATTACHMENT**)
Enforcement of judgment (See **ENFORCEMENT OF JUDGMENTS**)

COLLECTION AGENCIES
Generally **CC 1788 to 1788.32, 2021**
Identity theft
Debt collector's duties upon notice from victim of identity theft **CC 1788.18**
Mortgage or deed of trust, notice by agent for collection under promissory note secured by **CC 2924.3**
Notice
Consumer collection notice **CC 1812.700 to 1812.702**
Scope of duties of collection agent **CC 2021**
Sexual harassment, civil action for
Construction or application of provisions in issue, solicitor general notified **CC 51.1**

COLLECTION CASE MANAGEMENT **CRC 3.740, 3.741**

COLLECTIVE BARGAINING BY PUBLIC EMPLOYEES
PERB decisions, review by Court of Appeal **CRC 8.498**

COLLEGES (See **UNIVERSITIES AND COLLEGES**)

COMMENCEMENT OF ACTIONS
Filing complaint **CCP 411.10**
Filing fees **CCP 411.20**
Underpayment **CCP 411.21**
Governmental agencies, presentation of claims as prerequisite to commencement of actions against **CCP 313**

COMMENCEMENT OF ACTIONS—Cont.
Health care provider's professional negligence, notice of intention to commence action based on **CCP 364**
Objection to jurisdiction **CCP 418.10, 418.11**
Pleadings, generally (See **PLEADINGS**)
Quieting title **CCP 761.010**
Service of process (See **PROCESS AND SERVICE OF PROCESS**)
Summons (See **PROCESS AND SERVICE OF PROCESS**)
Survival of actions (See **SURVIVAL OF ACTIONS**)
Time for commencing actions (See **STATUTES OF LIMITATION**)

COMMENT OF COUNSEL (See **ARGUMENT AND COMMENT OF COUNSEL**)

COMMERCIAL CREDIT REPORTING (See **CREDIT REPORTING**)

COMMERCIAL FISHING
Fines and penalties
Bail schedule **CRC 4.102**

COMMERCIAL REAL PROPERTY LEASES (See **LEASES**)

COMMINGLING
Sales contracts **CC 1497**

COMMISSION (See **COMPENSATION; FEES; SALARIES AND WAGES**)

COMMISSIONERS
Acknowledgment of instruments **CC 1182, 1183**
Bond executed by **CCP 571**
Court commissioners (See **COURT COMMISSIONERS**)
Innkeeper's liens, writ of possession on **CC 1861.28**
Jury commissioner (See **JURY COMMISSIONER**)
Public utilities (See **PUBLIC UTILITIES COMMISSION**)
Service of process on **CCP 416.50**

COMMISSION MERCHANTS (See **FACTORS AND COMMISSION MERCHANTS**)

COMMISSION ON JUDICIAL PERFORMANCE (See **JUDGES**)

COMMITTEES
Judicial council
Advisory committees and task forces **CRC 10.30 to 10.70**
Medical review committees not subject to discovery proceedings **Ev 1157, 1157.5**
Peer review committees (See **PEER REVIEW COMMITTEES**)
Professional committee's proceeding against staff member, action for damages from **CC 43.7, 43.8**
State Bar Court judges, Applicant Evaluation and Nomination Committee **CRC 9.11**

COMMON ACCIDENT CAUSING DEATH (See **SIMULTANEOUS DEATH**)

COMMON AREAS
Common interest developments (See **COMMON INTEREST DEVELOPMENTS**)
Condominiums **CC 1358, 1359**
Mobilehome parks **CC 798.24**

COMMON CARRIERS
Aircraft (See **AIRCRAFT AND AVIATION**)
Apportionment of freightage **CC 2140, 2141**

Index

Index

COMPETENT REPRESENTATION
Attorney's duty to perform legal services with competence **ProfC 3-110**

COMPETITION, UNFAIR (See **UNFAIR COMPETITION**)

COMPLAINTS
Amendment
    Amendment as of course   **CCP 472**
    Answers   **CCP 471.5**
    Cross-complaints (See **CROSS-COMPLAINTS**)
    Filing fee   **Gov 70614**
        Amendment of complaint or other subsequent pleadings, effect on filing fee   **Gov 70613.5**
    Health care providers, amended pleadings for punitive damages against   **CCP 425.13**
    Service on defendant   **CCP 471.5**
    True name of defendant designated as unknown   **CCP 474**
Art, infringement   **CCP 429.30**
Attorney conspiring with client, complaint or pleading alleging **CC 1714.10**
Authors, infringement   **CCP 429.30**
Books, infringement   **CCP 429.30**
Case cover sheets   **CRC 3.220**
Certificate of merit (See **CERTIFICATE OF MERIT**)
Child support enforcement services, complaints in actions brought by government   **Fam 17400, 17404, 17428**
Compulsory joinder, complaint stating names of persons subject to   **CCP 389**
Construction-related accessibility claims
    Advisory to defendant building owner, tenant, etc to be included by attorney with complaint or demand for money   **CC 55.3**
Contents of   **CCP 425.10**
Cover sheet requirement   **CRC 3.220**
Criminal complaints (See **INDICTMENT, INFORMATION AND COMPLAINT**)
Cross-complaints (See **CROSS-COMPLAINTS**)
Default judgments (See **DEFAULT JUDGMENTS**)
Defined   **CCP 426.10**
Demurrers to (See **DEMURRERS**)
Description of property   **CCP 455**
Destroyed land records relief law proceedings   **CCP 751.04**
Earthquakes, boundary reestablishment after   **CCP 751.53**
Economic litigation provisions for limited civil cases   **CCP 92**
Eminent domain proceedings   **CCP 1250.110**
Filing
    Amended complaint
        Effect of amended complaint or other subsequent pleading on filing fee   **Gov 70613.5**
        Fee for filing   **Gov 26826.01**
    Check for filing fees
        Returned unpaid   **CCP 411.20**
        Underpayment   **CCP 411.21**
    Children's waiting room in courthouse, surcharge to fund **Gov 70640**
    Cover sheet requirement   **CRC 3.220**
    Cross-complaint, fee for filing   **Gov 26826.01**
    Initial filing fees   **Gov 70611, 70613**
        Permissible additional fees   **Gov 70603**
    Riverside County
        Courthouse seismic repair costs, additional filing fees authorized to defray   **Gov 70622**
    TRO or OSC sought   **CRC 3.1150**
Forcible entry and detainer proceedings   **CCP 1166, 1166a, 1167.3, 1173**
Grounds for objection to   **CCP 430.10**
Health care providers, amended pleading for punitive damages against   **CCP 425.13**
Indictment (See **INDICTMENT, INFORMATION AND COMPLAINT**)

COMPLAINTS—Cont.
Initial filing fees   **Gov 70611, 70613**
    Permissible additional fees   **Gov 70603**
Injunction granted at any time prior to judgment on   **CCP 527**
Interplead and litigate claims, complaint to compel conflicting claimants to   **CCP 386**
Intervention, complaint in   **CCP 387**
Judgment on the pleadings, motion for   **CCP 438**
Judicial Council to develop and approve official forms   **CCP 425.12**
Libel and slander (See **LIBEL AND SLANDER**)
Literary property, infringement   **CCP 429.30**
Medical personnel, complaints from public concerning   **CC 43.96**
Motion for supplemental complaints   **CCP 464**
Music, infringement   **CCP 429.30**
Names of parties in title of   **CCP 422.40**
Objections to allegations in   **CCP 430.10, 430.30**
Paintings, infringement   **CCP 429.30**
Parties, names of   **CCP 422.40**
Partition (See **PARTITION**)
Permissible pleadings   **CCP 422.10**
Permissive joinder of causes of action   **CCP 427.10**
Personal injuries   **CCP 425.10 to 425.12**
Process and service of process
    Time for service   **CRC 3.110**
Public improvement assessment, action to determine adverse interests in real property arising out of   **CCP 801.2, 801.3**
Quieting title action   **CCP 761.010, 761.020**
Quo warranto proceedings   **CCP 804**
Real property, description of   **CCP 455**
Sculpture rights, infringement   **CCP 429.30**
Service of complaints (See **PROCESS AND SERVICE OF PROCESS**)
Strike, motion to (See **MOTION TO STRIKE**)
Subordinate judicial officers, complaints against   **CRC 10.703**
Supplemental complaints   **CCP 464**
True name of defendant designated as unknown, amendments to add   **CCP 474**
Unknown persons as defendants   **CCP 474**
Unlawful detainer (See **UNLAWFUL DETAINER**)
Venue, affidavit or complaint stating facts indicating   **CCP 396a**
Voided filing
    Check for filing fees returned unpaid   **CCP 411.20**
    Underpayment of filing fee   **CCP 411.21**
Wrongful death actions   **CCP 425.10 to 425.12**

COMPLEX LITIGATION
Case management   **CRC 3.750, 3.751**
Coordination of complex actions   **CRC 3.501 to 3.550**
    Add-on cases
        Determining whether to coordinate add-ons   **CRC 3.544**
        Identification of potential add-ons   **CRC 3.531**
        Petition for coordination when cases already coordinated   **CRC 3.532**
    Administrative office of courts
        General administration of coordinated actions   **CRC 3.550**
    Ancillary proceedings, court for   **CRC 3.545**
    Appeals   **CRC 3.505**
    Applicable provisions in coordination proceedings   **CRC 3.504**
        Procedural rules   **CRC 3.510 to 3.515**
    Attorneys
        Coordination attorneys   **CRC 3.550**
    Case number   **CRC 3.550**
    Contents of petition   **CRC 3.521**
    Coordination attorneys   **CRC 3.550**

Index

COMPUTERS—Cont.

Entry of judgment in judgment book, alternatives to **CCP 668.5**

Evidence

Electronic transactions, admissibility of evidence of records and signatures related to **CC 1633.13**

Judicial notice of computer-generated records relating to criminal conviction **Ev 452.5**

Printed representations, presumption of accuracy of (See subhead: **Presumption of accuracy of printed representations**)

Information technology provided directly to courts, costs reported as **CRC 10.810**

Judicial notice of computer-generated records relating to criminal conviction **Ev 452.5**

Point-of-sale systems **CC 7100 to 7106**

Presumption of accuracy of printed representations

Computer information or computer program, generally **Ev 1552**

Images stored on digital medium **Ev 1553**

Pro per court documents, interactive computer system authorized to prepare standardized **CCP 1062.20**

Schools, terms for leasing or selling equipment to **CC 998**

Secondary evidence (See subhead: **Presumption of accuracy of printed representations**)

Standardized information, system authorized to provide **CCP 1062.20**

Support payments, use of software to determine **CRC 5.275, Fam 3830**

Transcripts in computer-readable form, duty to supply **CCP 271**

Trial court automation **CRC 10.870**

Year 2000 Problem (See **YEAR 2000 PROBLEM**)

CONCEALMENT

Adoption proceedings, concealment of child **Fam 8713, 8803**

Attorney's performance of professional services, concealment tolling statute of limitation for actions arising out of **CCP 340.6**

Dissolution of marriage proceedings, concealment of property in **Fam 2040 to 2045**

Executors and administrators (See **EXECUTORS AND ADMINISTRATORS**)

Family law proceedings, temporary restraining orders in **Fam 2040 to 2045**

Health care providers, intentional concealment tolling statute of limitation for actions against **CCP 340.5**

Witnesses **ProfC 5-310**

CONCESSIONAIRES

Disclosure of personal information by law enforcement agencies to city or county agencies screening prospective concessionaires **CC 1798.24a**

CONCILIATION COURTS   Fam 1800 to 1802

Child custody **Fam 1841, 3089**

Citation to act **Fam 1800**

Confidentiality of hearings, conferences, and papers **Fam 1818**

Coordination of mediation and conciliation services **Fam 1850 to 1852**

Costs

Court operations, salaries and benefits of court personnel included as costs of **CRC 10.810**

Petition, filing fees for **Fam 1835**

Counselors of conciliation

Appointment of **Fam 1814 to 1816**

Continuing education programs **Fam 1816**

Powers and duties of **Fam 1814**

Qualification of **Fam 1815**

Salaries and benefits as costs of court operations **CRC 10.810**

CONCILIATION COURTS—Cont.

Counties agreeing to joint conciliation court services **Fam 1820**

Custody of child proceedings **Fam 1841, 3089**

Destruction of records **Fam 1819**

Domestic violence, jurisdiction in cases of **Fam 1834**

Experts, assistance of **Fam 1838**

Fees for filing petition **Fam 1835**

Functional budget categories **CRC 10.810**

Hearings

Confidentiality of **Fam 1818**

Informality of **Fam 1838**

Notice of **Fam 1836**

Time and place of **Fam 1837**

Informal hearings **Fam 1838**

Joint conciliation court services **Fam 1820**

Joint custody of children **Fam 3089**

Judges **Fam 1811 to 1813**

Judicial council, duties of **Fam 1850 to 1852**

Jurisdiction

Generally **Fam 1810, 1830**

Domestic violence cases **Fam 1834**

Mediators **Fam 1816, 3160, 3164**

Medical specialists, assistance of **Fam 1838**

Minor child, transfer of proceedings involving **Fam 1841**

Notice of hearings **Fam 1836**

Orders **Fam 1839**

Pastors, assistance of **Fam 1838**

Pendency of other proceeding affecting **Fam 1840**

Petitions

Generally **Fam 1831**

Caption **Fam 1832**

Contents of **Fam 1833**

Filing fee **Fam 1835**

Preparation of **Fam 1834**

Place of hearings **Fam 1837**

Probation officers **Fam 1817**

Purpose of act **Fam 1801**

Reconciliation agreements **Fam 1839**

Recycled paper, court's use of **CRC 10.503**

Secretary, appointment of **Fam 1814**

Sessions, number of **Fam 1811**

Stay on filing petition for dissolution of marriage **Fam 1840**

Substitute judges **Fam 1813**

Summary dissolution of marriage, brochure on **Fam 2406**

Support orders **Fam 1839**

Time of hearings **Fam 1837**

Transfer of proceedings **Fam 1812, 1841, 1842**

CONCILIATION OF INTERNATIONAL COMMERCIAL DISPUTES (See **INTERNATIONAL COMMERCIAL ARBITRATION AND CONCILIATION**)

CONCLUSIONS OF LAW

Statement of decision in lieu of **CCP 632**

CONCURRENT JURISDICTION (See **JURISDICTION**)

CONDEMNATION (See **EMINENT DOMAIN**)

CONDITIONAL ESTATES

Conditions precedent (See **CONDITIONS PRECEDENT**)

Conditions subsequent (See **CONDITIONS SUBSEQUENT**)

Fee, limitations on **CC 764**

Marriage restraints **CC 710**

Possibility of reverter **CC 1045**

Time of enjoyment **CC 707**

CONDITIONAL SALES (See also **CHATTEL MORTGAGES; SECURED TRANSACTIONS**)

Administration of decedents' estates, sale of personal property of **Pro 10257, 10258**

Automobiles (See **AUTOMOBILES**)

CONDITIONAL SALES—Cont.
Household goods and personal property as collateral, use of
 CC 1799.100
Religious materials as security interest CC 1799.97
Residential property, disclosures required for sale of CC
 2956 to 2967
Unlawful detainer, holding over after sale pursuant to default
 provisions as act constituting CCP 1161a

CONDITION OF SENTENCE
Attorney reprovals CRC 9.19
Juveniles CRC 5.790

CONDITIONS PRECEDENT
Generally CC 708
Contracts, pleadings alleging facts as to CCP 457
Offer CC 1498
Pleadings alleging performance of CCP 457, 459
Specific performance in absence of performing CC 3392
Vesting of title CC 1110
Wrongful act CC 709

CONDITIONS SUBSEQUENT
Generally CC 708
Reconveyance requirement CC 1109
Transfer of property for breach of CC 1046

**CONDOMINIUMS (See COMMON INTEREST DEVELOP-
 MENTS)**

CONDUCT
Admissibility of evidence to prove Ev 1100 to 1106
Family law proceedings, award of attorney's fees and costs as
 sanctions based on conduct of party or attorney Fam 271
Misleading conduct or statement of party, evidentiary effect of
 Ev 623

CONDUITS
Public liability for injury caused by condition of Gov 831.8,
 831.9

CONFERENCES
Pretrial conferences (See PRETRIAL CONFERENCES)

CONFESSION OF JUDGMENTS
Automobile sales contract, prohibited provision in CC 2983.7
Cases in which applicable CCP 1132
Contingent liability, entry for purpose of securing person against
 CCP 1132, 1133
Costs CCP 1134
Debts due, judgment by confession for CCP 1132
Fees for filing CCP 1134
 Superior court fees, specified services Gov 70626
Statement confessing judgment
 Contents and execution CCP 1133
 Filing and endorsement CCP 1134
 Judgment roll, part of CCP 1134

CONFESSIONS
Generally Ev 1220 to 1228
Admissibility of Ev 402

CONFIDENTIAL MATTERS
Acceptance of employment adverse to client or former client by
 attorney having confidential information material to employ-
 ment ProfC 3-310
Adoption records (See ADOPTION)
Attorneys
 Confidential information of client
 Duties of attorney ProfC 3-100
Automobile reacquisition by manufacturer or distributor, restric-
 tions on confidentiality agreements concerning terms of CC
 1793.26

CONFIDENTIAL MATTERS—Cont.
Change of name
 Financial institutions, change of name information for
 conservatorship and guardianship assets as filed by Pro
 2891, 2893
 Witness Protection Program or domestic violence address
 confidentiality program CCP 1277
Child support enforcement agency records Fam 17212, 17514
Conciliation Court hearings, conferences, and papers Fam
 1818
Custody of children, mediation proceedings Fam 3177
Driver's licenses
 Encoded information use CC 1798.90.1
Fax filing of court documents and papers (See FAX FILING
 AND SERVICE)
Indian child welfare act involuntary placements
 Adoption
 Affidavit of confidentiality to bureau of Indian affairs
 CRC 5.487
International commercial conciliation proceedings, confidential-
 ity of statements made in CCP 1297.371
International wills Pro 6389
Judges, proceedings against JudPerR 102
Judicial performance, commission on
 Ethics code for commission members
 Confidentiality of proceedings JudPerPolicy 6.2
Juvenile court records (See JUVENILE COURTS)
Marriages, confidential (See MARRIAGE,,subhead: Confi-
 dential marriages)
Mediation (See MEDIATION)
Medical information CC 56.101, 56.104, 56 to 56.37
 Employer release CC 56.21
 Marketing
 Defined CC 56.05
 Disclosure of information for use in marketing CC
 56.10
 Pharmaceutical company requiring disclosure as condition
 of receiving pharmaceuticals CC 56.102
Privacy protection (See INFORMATION PRACTICES ACT)
Privileged communications (See PRIVILEGED COMMUNI-
 CATIONS)
Rent control provisions, confidentiality of tenant information
 disclosed for purposes of establishing compliance with CC
 1947.7
Social security numbers
 Annulment, dissolution of marriage or legal separation
 Confidentiality of persons involved Fam 2024.5
 Prohibiting posting or display to general public of CC
 1798.85
Uniform Parentage Act (See UNIFORM PARENTAGE ACT)

CONFIRMATION
Arbitration awards (See ARBITRATION)
Decedent's property, sale of (See ADMINISTRATION OF
 ESTATES)
Receivers, sale by CCP 568.5
Small estates without administration (See SMALL ESTATES
 WITHOUT ADMINISTRATION)

CONFLICTING TESTIMONY (See WITNESSES)

CONFLICT OF INTERESTS
Administrators Pro 9880
Adoption proceedings, attorney representing both parties in
 independent adoption Fam 8800
Appellate rules, supreme court and courts of appeal
 Briefs
 Certificates of interested entities or persons CRC
 8.208, 8.361, 8.488
Arbitration and arbitrators
 Ethical standards for neutral arbitrators CRC ArbEthic-
 sStand 1 to CRC ArbEthicsStand 17

Index

Index

Index

CONSUMER CREDIT CONTRACTS—Cont.
Household goods, security interests in   CC 1799.100
Investment property pledged as collateral on consumer credit contract, restrictions concerning   CC 1799.103
Marital relationships, effect on   CC 1799.98
Notice requirement
    Action or enforcement prohibited against person entitled to notice but not given notice   CC 1799.95
    Contents of   CC 1799.91
    Federal notice requirement
        Actions against person subject to   CC 1799.99
        Applicability of   CC 1799.96
    Federal notice requirement, applicability of   CC 1799.96
    Placement or inclusion of notice within sales agreement   CC 1799.92
    Rights and obligations of parties, effect on   CC 1799.94
Personal property, security interests in   CC 1799.100
Religious books and materials, validity of security interests in   CC 1799.97
Signatures required   CC 1799.93
Suretyship transactions, effect on   CC 1799.98
Waiver of protections   CC 1799.104

CONSUMER DEBT COLLECTION
Notice for consumer collections   CC 1812.700 to 1812.702
    Change of notice   CC 1812.701
    Third party debt collector notice to debtor   CC 1812.700
    Violations of provisions   CC 1812.702
Waiver of protections   CC 1788.33

CONSUMER GOODS AND SERVICES
Venue in actions founded on obligations for   CCP 395, 396a

CONSUMER PROTECTION
Generally   CC 1750 to 1756
Actions authorized   CC 1780 to 1784
Aged persons, remedies for   CC 1780, 3345
Arbitration and arbitrators
    Disclosures by and disqualification of arbitrators   CCP 1281.9 to 1281.95
Autographed sports memorabilia, dealer's sale of   CC 1739.7
Class actions   CC 1752, 1781
Commencement of action   CC 1780
Conditional sales (See **CONDITIONAL SALES**)
Consumer Contract Awareness Act (See **CONSUMER AWARENESS CONTRACT ACT**)
Credit cards (See **CREDIT CARDS**)
Credit contracts (See **CONDITIONAL SALES**)
Credit reports (See **CREDIT REPORTING**)
Credit services organizations (See **CREDIT SERVICES ORGANIATIONS**)
Damages
    Generally   CC 1780
    Warranties, recovery on   CC 1794, 1794.1
Deceptive practices   CC 1770
Definitions   CC 1761
Delivery of goods purchased under retail sales contract within 4-hour period   CC 1722
Demand for correction or repair as prerequisite to action for damages by consumer   CC 1782
Disabled persons, remedies for   CC 1780, 3345
Discount buying services contracts   CC 1812.100 to 1812.129
Electronic commercial services (See **ELECTRONIC COMMERCIAL SERVICES**)
Garnishment regulated by Consumer Credit Protection Act   CCP 706.151
Gift certificates, prohibition against expiration dates on   CC 1749.5
    Bankruptcy of issuer, duty to honor   CC 1749.6
    Waiver of protections
        Void   CC 1749.51
Grey market goods sales (See **GREY MARKET GOODS**)

CONSUMER PROTECTION—Cont.
Home Equity Loan Disclosure Act   CC 2970 to 2971
Home solicitation sales contracts (See **HOME SOLICITATION SALES CONTRACTS**)
Injunctive relief   CC 1782
Installment sales regulated (See **RETAIL INSTALLMENT SALES**)
Layaway plans   CC 1749 to 1749.4
Leased consumer goods, warranties for   CC 1791, 1795.4
Married women, discrimination against   CC 1812.30, 1812.31
Products liability (See **PRODUCTS LIABILITY**)
Repair and replacement
    Demand for correction or repair as prerequisite to action for damages by consumer   CC 1782
    Presence of consumer required during repair or service, 4-hour time period for commencement of contracted repairs when   CC 1722
    Warranty, goods under   CC 1793.2, 1793.3, 1793.6
Retail installment sales (See **RETAIL INSTALLMENT SALES**)
Return of goods under warranty   CC 1793.2
Seller assisted marketing plans   CC 1812.200 to 1812.221
Senior citizens, remedies for   CC 1780, 3345
Small claims court judges, bench book availability   CCP 116.930
Small claims courts
    Selection of forum outside of state
        Contracts for personal, family or household purposes   CCP 116.225
Subpoena of consumer's records   CCP 1985.3, 1985.4
Unsolicited goods   CC 1584.5, 1584.6
Venue of consumer actions   CC 1780
Warranties (See **WARRANTIES**)

CONSUMER REPRESENTATIVES
Small claims advisory committee, composition of   CCP 116.950

CONSUMER WARRANTY PROTECTION
Electronic online warranty
    Disclosures   CC 1793.1
Product registration card
    Disclosures   CC 1793.1

CONTAGIOUS DISEASES
Libel and slander   CC 46
Medical information disclosures by providers
    Prevention or controlling of diseases, injuries, etc   CC 56.10
Minor's treatment of   Fam 6926

CONTAINERS
Fair packaging and labeling
    Attorney general, civil actions to enforce provisions
        Fees and costs for attorney general   CCP 1021.8

CONTEMPT
Acts and omissions constituting   CCP 1209
Administrative adjudication (See **ADMINISTRATIVE ADJUDICATION**)
Affidavit in indirect contempt proceeding   CCP 1211, 1211.5
Arrest   CCP 1212, 1214, 1220
Attachments, failing to transfer possession   CCP 482.080
Attorney fees and costs, contemnor ordered to pay   CCP 1218
Attorneys, stay of contempt orders against   CCP 128, 1209
Bail   CCP 1213, 1215, 1216
Breach of peace during trial   CCP 1209
Child support proceedings (See **CHILD SUPPORT**)
Clerks of court   CCP 1209
Community service imposed on contemner   CCP 1218
Concealment of assets by estate representative   Pro 8870, 8873

Index

Index

Index

Index

Index

Index

Index

Index

CUSTOMER RECORDS

Computerized personal information owned or licensed by businesses

Release to unauthorized persons by breach in security system

Disclosures to persons affected **CC 1798.82, 1798.84**

Contracts

Security procedures to protect personal information

Third party users of records to be contractually obligated to provide security procedures **CC 1798.81.5**

Definitions **CC 1798.80**

Destruction of customer's records containing personal information, requirement for **CC 1798.81**

Disclosure of personal information of customer **CC 1798.83**

Remedies of customer **CC 1798.84**

Remedies available to customer injured by failure to destroy customer records containing personal information **CC 1798.82, 1798.84**

Security procedures to protect personal information **CC 1798.81.5**

Social security numbers, prohibiting posting or display to general public of **CC 1798.85**

Financial institutions, continued use **CC 1786.60**

Waiver of protections **CC 1798.86**

Waiver of protections **CC 1798.84**

CUSTOMS COURT

Judicial notice of rules of **Ev 451**

CY PRES DOCTRINE

Institutional funds management

Restrictions in gift instruments

Release **Pro 18506**

Rule against perpetuities, effect on **Pro 21220**

D

DAIRIES AND DAIRY PRODUCTS

Attachments proceedings **CCP 481.110**

Claim and delivery **CCP 511.040**

Nuisance, dairy operations as **CC 3482.5, 3482.6**

DALKON SHIELD

Limitations statute extension for claims resulting from use of **CCP 340.7**

DAMAGES

Accounting companies, disclosure of information by **CC 1799.2**

Additur of damages

Consent to on appeal **CRC 8.264**

Administrators of decedents' estates

Generally (See **ADMINISTRATION OF ESTATES**)

Executors and administrators, liability of (See **EXECUTORS AND ADMINISTRATORS**)

Adoption facilitators

Enforcement of provisions **Fam 8638**

Adverse possession **CCP 740, 741**

Advertising, unauthorized use of name or likeness in **CC 3344, 3344.1**

Advisers on investments, liability of **CC 3372**

Agent's authority, breach of warranty of **CC 3318**

Alcoholic beverages

Commercial motor vehicle employer for vehicle accident caused by intoxicated employee **CC 3333.7**

Social host's liability after serving **CC 1714**

Aliens

Civil rights enforcement, irrelevance of immigration status **CC 3339**

DAMAGES—Cont.

Alternative judgment in replevin **CCP 667**

Animals

Cruelty to **CC 3340**

Dogs (See **DOGS**)

Artists, seller of art withholding payment to **CC 986**

Art works, destruction or defacement of **CC 987**

Attachment (See **ATTACHMENT**)

Attorneys' professional societies, liability of **CC 43.7, 43.95**

Automobile lease violations (See **AUTOMOBILES**)

Bad checks, liability for making **CC 1719**

Buyer's loss, determination of **CC 3354**

Cable television companies (See **CABLE TELEVISION COMPANIES**)

Campaign advertising (See **CANDIDATES FOR OFFICE**)

Certainty of **CC 3301**

Child support, assisting obligor in avoiding payment **CC 1714.4, 1714.41**

Chiropractor (See **MALPRACTICE**)

Civil rights actions **CC 52, 52.1, 54.3**

Construction or application of provisions in issue, solicitor general notified **CC 51.1, 55.2**

Gender violence **CC 52.4**

Claim and delivery **CCP 627**

Claims against public entities and employees (See **CLAIMS AGAINST PUBLIC ENTITIES AND EMPLOYEES**)

Commencement of action, injury sustained after **CC 3283**

Commercial blockage tort affecting health care facility, damages for **CC 3427.2**

Common carriers, breach of contract by **CC 3315 to 3317**

Common interest developments (See **COMMON INTEREST DEVELOPMENTS**)

Community property (See **COMMUNITY PROPERTY**)

Conservation easement, impairment of **CC 815.7**

Construction defects, actions for **CC 943**

Measure of damages **CC 944**

Construction, intentional destruction of property under **CC 1721**

Construction-related accessibility claims

Statutory damages

Liability **CC 55.56**

Consumer protection actions (See **CONSUMER PROTECTION**)

Contracts

Conveyance **CC 3306**

Interest rate for breach of contract **CC 3288**

Rescission of **CC 1692**

Sales contracts (See subhead: **Sales contracts**)

Contribution among joint defendants (See **CONTRIBUTION**)

Conversion **CC 3336 to 3338**

Conveyances

Contract to convey land, breach of **CC 3306**

Right to convey land, breach of covenant of **CC 3304**

Conviction (See subhead: **Criminal acts**)

Costs of suit, recovery of (See **COSTS**)

Credit card holder, damages against vendor for eliciting personal information concerning **CC 1747.08**

Credit card violations, recovery for **CC 1747.50 to 1747.80**

Credit denial, failure to state reasons for **CC 1787.2**

Credit reporting (See **CREDIT REPORTING**)

Credit services organizations, action against **CC 1789.21**

Criminal acts

Attorney's fees in action against felons for damages, award of **CCP 1021.4**

Homicide, liability for exemplary damages for **CC 3294**

Sexual battery, exemplary damages for **CC 1708.5**

Victim sued by felon for injuries arising from crime on which felony conviction based, exemplary damages for **CCP 128.5, 128.6, 128.7**

Cruelty to animals **CC 3340**

DECEDENTS' ESTATES—Cont.

Probate examiners
  Education requirements   **CRC 10.478**
  Qualifications   **CRC 10.776, 10.777**
Probate rules generally   **CRC 7.1 to 7.1101**
Securities (See **CORPORATE SHARES AND SHAREHOLDERS**)
Severance of matters associated with proceedings and actions under Probate Code   **Pro 801**
Small estates (See **SMALL ESTATES**)
Surviving domestic partners
  Health insurance
    Survivors of firefighters and peace officers, continuance   **Pro 13600**
    Intestate share   **Pro 6401**
Surviving spouses
  Health insurance
    Survivors of firefighters and peace officers, continuance   **Pro 13600**
Taxation, generally (See **ESTATE TAX**)
Tax liens and other federal liens, filing of notice of   **CCP 2101**
Testate succession (See **WILLS**)
Trusts (See **TRUSTS**)
Uniform Parentage Act
  Vacation or setting aside of judgment
    Payments made in good faith by estate, trustees, insurers, etc., based on paternity judgment   **Fam 7649.5**
Waivers
  Accounting
    Effect   **CRC 7.550**

DECEIT (See FRAUD)

DECENCY (See INDECENCY AND OBSCENITY)

DECEPTIVE PRACTICES   CC 1770

DECISIONS

Generally (See **JUDGMENTS**)
Administrative agencies
  Adjudicative proceeding (See **ADMINISTRATIVE ADJUDICATION**)
  Office of Administrative Law (See **ADMINISTRATIVE PROCEDURE ACT**)
Findings of fact (See **FINDINGS**)
Statement of decision (See **STATEMENT OF DECISION**)

DECLARATION AGAINST INTEREST (See ADMISSIONS)

DECLARATIONS

Child support, income and expense declaration (See **CHILD SUPPORT**)
Common interest developments (See **COMMON INTEREST DEVELOPMENTS**)
Defined   **CCP 116.130**
Dissolution of marriage (See **DISSOLUTION OF MARRIAGE**)
Economic litigation provision for use of declaration in lieu of direct testimony   **CCP 98**
Emancipation of minors (See **EMANCIPATION OF MINORS**)
Homesteads (See **HOMESTEADS**)
Identity of judgment debtor, declaration under penalty of perjury executed by judgment creditor as to   **CCP 680.135**
Judicial officer's power to take and certify   **CCP 179**
Legal separation, assets and liabilities disclosure required for   **Fam 2100 to 2113**
Mortgages, satisfaction of   **CC 2941.7**
Oath defined to include declaration   **CCP 17**
Part offered in evidence   **Ev 356**

DECLARATIONS—Cont.

Paternity declarations   **Fam 20102, 20103**
Penalty of perjury, declaration of written instrument executed under   **CCP 2015.5**
Property   **Fam 2330.5**
Property declarations defined   **Fam 115**
Small claims court (See **SMALL CLAIMS COURTS**)
Survival of actions, execution of supporting declaration in (See **SURVIVAL OF ACTIONS**)
Trust deeds, satisfaction of   **CC 2941.7**
Written instrument executed under penalty of perjury, declaration of   **CCP 2015.5**

DECLARATORY JUDGMENTS

Administrative law
  Action for declaratory relief (See **ADMINISTRATIVE PROCEDURE ACT**)
  Adjudication proceeding, declaratory decision in (See **ADMINISTRATIVE ADJUDICATION**)
Contracts, determining rights under   **CCP 1060**
Cross-complaint provisions, applicability of   **CCP 426.60**
Cumulative remedies   **CCP 1062**
Deeds, determining rights under   **CCP 1060**
Health care providers, insurer of   **CCP 1062.5**
Identity theft, declaratory relief in actions involving   **CC 1798.93**
Income tax liability of nonresident   **CCP 1060.5**
Limited civil cases, unavailability of declaratory relief in   **CCP 580**
Necessary relief   **CCP 1061**
Parks, purpose in taking for   **CCP 1240.700**
Precedence over other matters   **CCP 1062.3**
Professional liability insurer's liability   **CCP 1062.5**
Rivers, determining natural flow of   **CCP 1060**
State agency proceedings (See subhead: **Administrative law**)
Will probate
  Construction of writing   **CCP 1060**
  No contest clauses, declaratory relief   **Pro 21320 to 21322**

DECREES (See JUDGMENTS)

DEDICATION

Decedent's estate, property of   **Pro 9900, 9901**
Prescriptive use   **CC 813, 1007**
Public land, private property used as   **CC 1009**
Quieting title action, effect on   **CCP 771.010, 771.020**
Title held under   **CC 670**
Trust property   **Pro 16230**

DEEDS (See also COVENANTS AND CONDITIONS)

Acknowledgments
  Superior court fees, specified services   **Gov 70626**
Administrators of decedents' estates (See **EXECUTORS AND ADMINISTRATORS**)
Adverse possession by person claiming title founded on written instrument   **CCP 322, 323**
Advertising for sale, restrictions on   **CC 712**
Boundary determination   **CCP 2077**
Conclusive against grantor   **CC 1107**
Conflicting clauses   **CC 1070**
Consolidation of   **CC 1093**
Construction of   **CC 1066 to 1070, CCP 2077**
Copies, admissibility of   **Ev 1600 to 1605**
Declaratory judgments determining rights under   **CCP 1060**
Delivery   **CC 1054 to 1056, 1059, 1627**
Description   **CCP 2077**
Executors of decedents' estates (See **EXECUTORS AND ADMINISTRATORS**)
Fee-simple title presumed   **CC 1105**
Form for transfer   **CC 1092**
Hearsay rule affecting admissibility of statements in   **Ev 1330**

Index

Index

Index

Index

Index

DE NOVO PROCEEDING
Administrative adjudication, de novo proceeding after nonbinding arbitration in   **Gov 11420.10**
Trial (See **NEW TRIAL**)

DENTAL CARE
Caregiver authorization and affidavit for dental treatment of minors   **Fam 6550, 6552**
Emancipated minor's consent   **Fam 7050**
Minors, care of (See **MINORS**)
Noncustodial parent's access to child's dental records   **Fam 3025**

DENTAL HYGIENISTS
Discovery, review committee records exempt from   **Ev 1157**
Liability of review committees   **CC 43.7, 43.8**

DENTISTS
Bond required to secure costs in action against   **CCP 1029.6**
Confidentiality of records   **CC 56.101, 56 to 56.37**
Discovery, dental committee records subject to   **Ev 1156, 1157**
Inspection of records by attorneys   **CCP 1985.7, Ev 1158**
Insurance underwriting committee, liability of dentist member of   **CC 43.7, 43.8**
Malpractice (See **MALPRACTICE**)
Noncustodial parent's right to dental records   **Fam 3025**
Peer review committees, liability of   **CC 43.7, 43.8**
Professional committees, liability of   **CC 43.7, 43.8**
Rescission of dental plan or services   **CC 1689.3**
Review committees, liability of   **CC 43.7, 43.8**
Sexual harassment, civil action for
    Construction or application of provisions in issue, solicitor general notified   **CC 51.1**

DEPARTMENT OF CHILD SUPPORT SERVICES (See **CHILD SUPPORT**)

DEPARTMENT OF CONSUMER AFFAIRS
Small claims court administration   **CCP 116.920, 116.930, 116.950**

DEPARTMENT OF CORRECTIONS
Exemption for funds of incarcerated judgment debtors   **CCP 704.090**
Small claims court (See **SMALL CLAIMS COURTS**)

DEPARTMENT OF MOTOR VEHICLES (See **MOTOR VEHICLES DEPARTMENT**)

DEPARTMENT OF TRANSPORTATION
Claims against public entities and employees (See **CLAIMS AGAINST PUBLIC ENTITIES AND EMPLOYEES**)

DEPARTMENT OF WATER RESOURCES
Actions arising out of work of   **Gov 956**

DEPENDENT ADULTS
Discovery
    Elder abuse and dependent adult civil protection act   **CCP 2017.310, 2017.320**
Forms
    Judicial council legal forms   **CRCAppx A**

DEPENDENT CHILDREN
Adoption proceedings   **CRC 5.730**
Advice of hearing rights   **CRC 5.534, 5.682**
Appeals   **CRC 5.585**
    Advisement of rights   **CRC 5.585, 5.590**
    Dependency judgments   **CRC 5.585**
    Notice of appeal, time for filing   **CRC 5.585**
    Precedence for appeal of order freeing dependent child of court from parental custody and control   **CCP 45**

DEPENDENT CHILDREN—Cont.
Appeals —Cont.
    Representation of child on appeal   **CRC 5.661**
    Stay of judgment or order   **CRC 5.585**
    Transfer of case between counties   **CRC 5.610**
Arrest warrant against custodial parent or guardian   **CRC 5.526**
Assessments
    Joint assessment procedure   **CRC 5.512**
Burden of proof   **CRC 5.534**
Caregivers
    Notice of proceedings to current caregivers   **CRC 5.534**
Child advocate
    Court-appointed Special Advocate (CASA) program   **CRC 5.655**
    Notice of proceedings   **CRC 5.524, 5.710**
Child welfare services
    Case plan for child welfare services   **CRC 5.690**
Child welfare services case plan, parents' failure to cooperate in   **Ev 1228.1**
Citation to appear in addition to notice   **CRC 5.526**
Commencement of hearing   **CRC 5.668**
Competence of child to cooperate with counsel   **CRC 5.645**
Continuances
    Detention hearings   **CRC 5.672**
    Disposition hearing pending   **CRC 5.686**
    Educational rights of children before juvenile court   **CRC 5.651**
    Initial hearings   **CRC 5.672**
    Jurisdictional hearings   **CRC 5.550, 5.686**
Control by parents or guardians, limitation by court   **CRC 5.695**
Counseling
    Family reunification services, order for   **CRC 5.695**
    Notice of requirement   **CRC 5.526**
Court Appointed Special Advocate (CASA)
    Appointment of as guardian ad litem   **CRC 5.660**
Court orders
    Disposition hearings   **CRC 5.695**
Cross-examination
    Right of   **CRC 5.674**
Custody of
    Order determining custody   **CRC 5.475**
    Stay of judgment affecting custody   **CCP 917.7**
Deceased child
    Juvenile case file of deceased child, release   **CRC 5.553**
De facto parents
    Defined   **CRC 5.502**
    Standing to participate in proceedings   **CRC 5.534**
Definitions   **CRC 5.502**
Delinquent children
    Placement under interstate compact   **CRC 5.616**
Dependent child of court proceedings
    Admission of petition allegations at initial hearing   **CRC 5.674**
    Appeals   **CRC 5.585**
        Certain counties   **CRC 8.416**
        Extraordinary writ review as prerequisite to appeal   **CRC 5.600**
        Marsden hearing and other in-camera proceedings, record   **CRC 8.328**
        Right to appeal, notification   **CRC 5.590**
        Supreme court and courts of appeal   **CRC 8.400 to 8.474**
    Appearance by minor without guardian ad litem   **CCP 372**
    Application to probation officer or social worker to commence   **CRC 5.520**
    Attendance at proceedings   **CRC 5.530**
        Presence of child   **CRC 5.534**
    Attorneys
        Appointment   **CRC 5.534, 5.660**
        CASA programs   **CRC 5.655**

Index

Index

Index

Index

DISCOVERY—Cont.

Withdrawal of legal service agency attorney for indigent client, effect on time limitations of **CCP 285.3**

Work product doctrine

Attorney work product generally **CCP 2018.010 to 2018.080**

Writings

Defined **CCP 2016.020**

DISCOVERY ABUSES, SANCTIONS FOR

Abuse of discovery procedure **CCP 2023.010**

Failure to confer **CCP 2023.010, 2023.020**

Failure to provide discovery **CRC 3.1348**

Juvenile court proceedings **CRC 5.546**

Mental examinations, discovery procedure for

Failure to produce another for examination **CCP 2032.420**

Failure to submit **CCP 2032.410**

Protective orders, unsuccessfully making or opposing motion for **CCP 2032.510**

Reports of examination **CCP 2032.650**

Misuse of discovery process **CCP 2023.010, 2023.030**

Physical examinations, discovery procedure for

Failure to produce another for examination **CCP 2032.420**

Failure to submit **CCP 2032.410**

Plaintiffs, personal injury cases **CCP 2032.240, 2032.250**

Protective orders, unsuccessfully making or opposing motion for **CCP 2032.510**

Reports of examination **CCP 2032.620, 2032.650**

Protective orders

Unsuccessfully making or opposing motion for protective order **CCP 2017.020**

Request for sanctions **CCP 2023.040**

Sexual conduct of plaintiff

Unsuccessfully making or opposing motions **CCP 2017.220**

DISCRETION OF COURT

Amendment of pleadings, generally **CCP 473**

Demurrer sustained, discretion to grant leave to amend pleadings where **CCP 472a**

Mandamus proceedings determining abuse of discretion **CCP 1094.5**

Motion to strike granted, discretion to grant leave to amend pleadings where **CCP 472a**

New trial, abusing discretion as grounds for **CCP 657**

Separate trial of issues **CCP 598**

Voir dire examination of prospective jurors **CCP 222.5, 223**

DISCRIMINATION

Adoption, prohibited discrimination in placement for **Fam 8708**

Aliens

Enforcement of employment law not dependent on immigration status **CC 3339**

Attorney general

Civil rights violation, bringing action for

Fees and costs for attorney general **CCP 1021.8**

Attorney's fees **CC 52, 52.1, 54.3**

Construction or application of provisions in issue, solicitor general notified **CC 51.1, 55.2**

Business transactions, prohibition against discrimination in **CC 51.5**

Construction or application of provisions in issue, solicitor general notified **CC 51.1**

Civil penalties **CC 52, 52.1**

Construction or application of civil rights provisions in issue, solicitor general notified **CC 51.1**

Court appointments, prohibition against discriminatory **CRC 10.611, CRC JudAdminStand 10.21**

DISCRIMINATION—Cont.

Court performance standards **CRC JudAdminStand 10.17**

Covenants based on race **CC 53, 782, 782.5**

Credit cards (See **CREDIT CARDS**)

Credit transactions by women **CC 1812.30 to 1812.35**

Damages for discriminatory acts **CC 52, 52.1, 54.3**

Construction or application of civil rights provisions in issue, solicitor general notified **CC 51.1**

Gender violence **CC 52.4**

Measure of damages

Immigration status not to affect **CC 3339**

Dealerships, granting of **CC 80 to 86**

Disabled persons

Construction or application of provisions in issue, solicitor general notified **CC 55.2**

Dogs

Law enforcement officers or firefighters assigned to canine unit serving outside jurisdiction

Prohibition on discrimination in lodging, eating, or transportation due to dog **CC 54.25**

Equality of accommodations in business establishments

Construction or application of provisions in issue

Solicitor general notified **CC 51.1**

Foster care placement **Fam 7950**

Franchises, granting of **CC 51.8**

Gender violence

Actions for damages **CC 52.4**

Housing

Age discrimination in housing **CC 51.2**

Deed restrictions, applicability of prohibitions on restrictions to housing for elderly **CC 782, 782.5**

Covenants based on race **CC 53, 782, 782.5**

Disabled persons' equal access to housing accommodations **CC 54, 54.1, 54.3, 54.4, 55**

Construction or application of provisions in issue, solicitor general notified **CC 55.2**

Senior citizen housing, requirements for (See **SENIOR CITIZENS**)

Unruh Civil Rights Act **CC 51**

Construction or application of provisions in issue, solicitor general notified **CC 51.1**

Immigration status

Enforcement of employment law not dependent on immigration status **CC 3339**

Independent civil actions

Construction or application of civil rights provisions in issue, solicitor general notified **CC 51.1**

Injunctive relief, availability of **CC 52.1**

Construction or application of civil rights provisions in issue, solicitor general notified **CC 51.1**

Interference with exercise of rights

Construction or application of civil rights provisions in issue, solicitor general notified **CC 51.1**

Intimidation

Thread of violence

Construction or application of provisions in issue, solicitor general notified **CC 51.1**

Judges, membership in discriminatory organizations **CRC-Supp JudEthicsCanon 2**

Judicial administration standards

Appointments by court, nondiscrimination in **CRC JudAdminStand 10.21**

Duty of court to prevent bias **CRC JudAdminStand 10.20**

Jurisdiction for civil rights actions **CC 52.2**

Law practice, prohibited discriminatory conduct in **ProfC 2-400**

Marital status **CC 51**

Mobilehome park, club membership in **CC 798.20**

Penal damages for **CC 52**

Index

Index

Index

Index

EFFECTIVE DATES
Code of Civil Procedure   **CCP 2**

EGRESS (See **ACCESS**)

ELDER ABUSE (See **SENIOR CITIZENS**)

ELDERLY PERSONS (See **SENIOR CITIZENS**)

ELECTION OF RIGHTS OR REMEDIES
Judicial arbitration, election for (See **JUDICIAL ARBITRA-TION**)
Small claims court advisory services, election with respect to **CCP 116.940**

ELECTION OF SURVIVING SPOUSE
Small estates without administration (See **SMALL ESTATES WITHOUT ADMINISTRATION**)
Will, election to take against (See **WILLS**)

ELECTIONS AND ELECTIONS PROCEEDINGS
Campaign funds
    Judges, contributions by   **CRCSupp JudEthicsCanon 5**
Campaigns
    Judges, political activities by   **CRCSupp JudEthicsCanon 5**
Candidates for office (See **CANDIDATES FOR OFFICE**)
Conservatee's right to vote   **Pro 1865, 1910**
Judicial elections
    Code of judicial ethics
       Leave, applicability of code to judge on leave to pursue election to other office   **CRCSupp JudEthicsCanon 6**
       Ethical obligations of candidates   **CRCSupp JudEthicsCanon 6**
       Judicial performance, commission on
          Ethics code for commission members   **JudPerPolicy 6.4**
       Political activities by judges   **CRCSupp JudEthicsCanon 5**
Mobilehomes
    Signs, placement of
       Political campaign signs   **CC 798.51, 799.10**
Political vote, evidentiary privilege to refuse disclosure of   **Ev 1050**
Precedence
    Certification of ballot measures, cases involving   **CCP 35**
    Certification of candidates, cases involving   **CCP 35**
    Contested elections cases   **CCP 35, 44**
    Courts of appeal and Supreme Court, hearings in   **CCP 44**
    Libel or slander action by candidate   **CCP 44, 460.7**
    Voter registration, cases involving   **CCP 35**
Registration of voters
    Action to compel registration
       Fees, clerk not to charge   **Gov 70633**
Sale of political items   **CC 1739 to 1739.4**
Service of process   **CCP 416.80**
Shortening of time to respond to complaint in action for libel alleged to have occurred during election campaign   **CCP 460.7**
Unauthorized signatures in campaign advertisements, action for damages for   **CC 3344.5**
U.SCongress, members of (See **CONGRESS**)

ELECTIVE OFFICE
Preference in courts of appeal and Supreme Court in hearing actions for libel or slander by person holding elective office or by candidate   **CCP 44**
Shortening of time to respond to complaint in action for libel alleged to have occurred during election campaign   **CCP 460.7**

ELECTRIC APPLIANCES (See **APPLIANCES**)

ELECTRICITY AND ELECTRIC COMPANIES
Cancellation of utility, cable, etc, services on behalf of deceased person
       In-person cancellation not to be required   **Pro 217**
Credit cards
    Surcharge on credit card transaction, prohibition against
       Exception for electrical, gas or water corporation **CC 1748.1**
Debit cards
    Surcharge on debit card transaction, prohibition against
       Exception for electrical, gas or water corporation **CC 1748.1**
Diversion or tampering with electrical utility services, action for **CC 1882 to 1882.6**
Home energy ratings, duty of seller or broker to disclose information regarding   **CC 2079.10**
Inspection warrants to determine violations   **CCP 1822.50**
Landlord and tenant (See **LANDLORD AND TENANT**)
Repairs or service during specified time period where subscriber's presence required, liability for failure to provide   **CC 1722**
Small business action, costs in   **CCP 1028.5**
Unclaimed deposits and payments (See **UNCLAIMED DEPOSITS AND PAYMENTS**)

ELECTRONIC COMMERCIAL SERVICES
Generally   **CC 1789**
Applicability of Electronic Commerce Act   **CC 1789.7, 1789.8**
Citation   **CC 1789.1**
Definitions   **CC 1789.2**
Disclosure requirements   **CC 1789.3**
Liability of provider   **CC 1789.6**
Penalties for violation of Electronic Commerce Act   **CC 1789.5**
Waiver of protections   **CC 1789.9**

ELECTRONIC COURT RECORDS
Access   **CRC 2.501**
    Calendars   **CRC 2.507**
    Fees for electronic access   **CRC 2.506**
    Indexes   **CRC 2.507**
    Notice to persons accessing records   **CRC 2.504**
    Public access   **CRC 2.503**
       Criminal cases, remote electronic access in individual criminal cases   **CRC 2.503**
    Registers of actions   **CRC 2.507**
Applicability of provisions   **CRC 2.501**
Bulk distribution   **CRC 2.503**
Calendars
    Electronic access   **CRC 2.507**
Conditions on use   **CRC 2.504**
Contracts with vendors to provide public access   **CRC 2.505**
Court calendars
    Electronic access   **CRC 2.507**
Criminal cases
    Remote electronic access in individual criminal cases **CRC 2.503**
Definitions   **CRC 2.502**
    Bulk distribution   **CRC 2.503**
    Feasible   **CRC 2.503**
Fees for electronic access   **CRC 2.506**
Indexes
    Electronic access   **CRC 2.507**
Limitations and conditions of use   **CRC 2.504**
Notice to persons accessing records   **CRC 2.504**
Off-site access   **CRC 2.503**
Privacy policy
    Posting   **CRC 2.504**
Public access   **CRC 2.503**
    Criminal cases
       Remote electronic access in individual criminal cases **CRC 2.503**

Index

EMANCIPATION OF MINORS—Cont.
Welfare benefits, effect of declaration on **Fam 7111**
Wills, capacity to make **Fam 7050**

EMBARRASSMENT
Court orders to prevent **CCP 379.5**

EMBEZZLEMENT (See also **THEFT**)
Accrual of cause of action **CCP 338**
Decedents' estates, embezzled property from **Pro 8870 to 8873**
Discount buying organization officer **CC 1812.106**
Public employees (See **PUBLIC OFFICERS AND EMPLOYEES**)

EMBLEMENTS
Severable **CC 660**

EMERGENCIES (See also **NATURAL CATASTROPHES**)
Administrative adjudicative proceedings under emergency decision procedure **Gov 11460.10 to 11460.80**
Appellate courts, special time rule **CRC 8.66**
Cardiopulmonary resuscitation, immunity from liability for emergency care through **CC 1714.2, 1714.21**
Defibrillator, immunity from liability for emergency care using **CC 1714.21**
Deposit of goods during time of **CC 1815**
Disclosure of medical information during **CC 56.10**
Domestic violence, emergency protective orders (See **DOMESTIC VIOLENCE**)
Eminent domain for emergency projects **CCP 1245.230**
Home solicitation contract provisions, emergency services excepted from **CC 1689.13**
Hospital lien for emergency treatment **CC 3045.1 to 3045.6**
Injured emergency personnel, liability to **CC 1714.9**
Juvenile court proceedings
  Adoption of child
    Prospective adoptive parents, emergency removal from **CRC 5.728**
Landlord entering because of **CC 1954**
Opioid antagonist for drug overdose
  Immunity **CC 1714.22**
Psychotropic medications, administering to minors **CRC 5.640**
Resuscitative measures, requests regarding **Pro 4780 to 4786**
  Health care providers **Pro 4781**
Statutory violations in complying with governor's orders under **CC 1714.6**
Traffic control signal controlled by emergency vehicle, public entity liability for operation of **Gov 830.9**

EMERGENCY PROTECTIVE ORDERS (See **PROTECTIVE ORDERS**)

EMINENT DOMAIN
Generally **CCP 1230.020 to 1230.060, Ev 810 to 822**
Abandonment of proceedings **CCP 1268.510**
Acquisition (See subhead: **Taking**)
Agreement specifying manner of payment of compensation **CCP 1263.015**
Alternative dispute resolution, postponement of eminent domain proceedings for **CCP 1250.430**
Apportionment of taxes (See subhead: **Taxes**)
Appraisals
  Fee payment for **CCP 1235.140**
  Offer to purchase under threat of eminent domain
    Independent appraisal following offer **CCP 1263.025**
    Valuation data, appraisal report used for **CCP 1258.260**
Arbitration
  Compensation for taking, arbitration of controversies as to **CCP 1273.010 to 1273.050**

EMINENT DOMAIN—Cont.
Arbitration—Cont.
  Referral of eminent domain proceedings to arbitrator **CCP 1250.420**
Award (See subhead: **Compensation**)
Benefits derived **Ev 812**
Citation of statutes **CCP 1230.010**
Comparable property as basis for opinion evidence **Ev 816**
Compensation
  Generally **CCP 1263.010, 1263.020**
  Agreement specifying manner of payment of **CCP 1263.015**
  Appraisal following offer to purchase under threat of eminent domain **CCP 1263.025**
  Arbitration of controversies as to compensation for taking **CCP 1273.010 to 1273.050**
  Crops **CCP 1263.250**
  Date of valuation **CCP 1263.110 to 1263.150**
  Deposit in court (See subhead: **Deposit in court**)
  Evidence affecting **CCP 1260.210**
  Fair market value **CCP 1263.310 to 1263.330**
  Final judgments, payment of **CCP 1268.010 to 1268.030**
  Final offer and demand for **CCP 1250.410**
  Future interests **CCP 1265.410, 1265.420**
  Goodwill for business, compensation of **CCP 1263.510 to 1263.530**
    Leaseback agreements **CCP 1263.510, 1263.615**
  Interest on money judgment **CCP 1263.015, 1268.310 to 1268.360**
  Leaseback agreements, when required **CCP 1263.615**
  Liens, impairment of security for **CCP 1265.210 to 1265.240**
  Measure of **CCP 1263.310 to 1263.330**
  Other interests, compensation for **CCP 1265.010**
  Possession after judgment **CCP 1268.210 to 1268.240**
  Probable amount of compensation, deposit of **CCP 1255.010 to 1255.080**
  Remainder property (See subhead: **Remainder property**)
  Separation of assessments **CCP 1260.220, 1260.230**
  Severance, damages for **CCP 1240.150**
  Valuation data, exchange of **CCP 1258.210 to 1258.300**
  Withdrawal of deposit for **CCP 1255.210 to 1255.280, 1268.110 to 1268.170**
Complaints in proceedings for **CCP 1250.110**
Corporate officers giving evidence on value **Ev 813**
Costs
  Definition of **CCP 1235.140**
  Inverse condemnation proceedings **CCP 1036**
  Litigation expenses, payment of **CCP 1250.410, 1268.610, 1268.620**
  Payment of **CCP 1268.710, 1268.720**
Crops, compensation for **CCP 1263.250**
Cross complaints in proceedings for **CCP 426.70**
Damages (See subhead: **Compensation**)
Date of valuation **CCP 1263.110 to 1263.150**
Default judgments in proceedings for **CCP 1250.125**
Defendants in action for **CCP 1250.220 to 1250.240**
Definitions **CCP 1235.110 to 1235.210**
Demurrers **CCP 1250.350 to 1250.370**
Deposit in court
  After entry of judgment **CCP 1268.110 to 1268.170**
  Before entry of judgment **CCP 1255.010 to 1255.080**
Discovery
  Generally **CCP 1258.010 to 1258.030**
  Expert testimony (See subhead: **Expert testimony**)
  Time for completion of discovery **CCP 2024.040**
Dismissal
  Mandamus petition **CCP 1245.255**
  Taxes unpaid, effect on **CCP 1268.420**
Easements (See **EASEMENTS**)
Electric utility property (See subhead: **Public utilities**)

Index

Index

Index

Index

Index

Index

FACT OF DEATH—Cont.
Recording evidence of   **Ev 1281 to 1283, Pro 210 to 212**

FACTORIES (See **MANUFACTURERS**)

FACTORS AND COMMISSION MERCHANTS
Agency relationship of   **CC 2367 to 2369**
Consignment of property to   **CC 2027**
Defined   **CC 2026, 2367**
Lien for services by   **CC 3053**
Sale of property by   **CC 2027 to 2030, 2368**
Unclaimed property, sale of   **CC 2081.5, 2081.6**

FACTS
Disqualification of judges, personal knowledge of evidentiary facts as grounds for   **CCP 170.1**
Questions of fact (See **QUESTIONS OF LAW OR FACT**)

FAILURE OF CONSIDERATION
Rescission of contract because of   **CC 1689**

FAIR DEALERSHIP LAW   **CC 80 to 86**

FAIR DEBT COLLECTION PRACTICES   **CC 1788 to 1788.33** (See **CONSUMER DEBT COLLECTION**)

FAIRS AND EXPOSITIONS
Guide dogs permitted in   **CC 54.2, 54.3**
     Construction or application of provisions in issue, solicitor general notified   **CC 55.2**

FALLER
Lien of   **CC 3065 to 3065c**

FALSE ARREST
Domestic violence protective orders, immunity for officers enforcing   **Fam 6383**
Liability of law enforcement officer for   **Gov 820.4**

FALSE CLAIMS
Case management of false claims act cases   **CRC 2.573**
Filing records under seal   **CRC 2.570 to 2.573**
     Access to sealed records   **CRC 2.570**
     Applicability   **CRC 2.570**
     Case management   **CRC 2.573**
     Confidentiality of records filed under act   **CRC 2.570**
     Custody of sealed records   **CRC 2.571**
     Definitions   **CRC 2.570**
     Extension of time, motions for   **CRC 2.572**
     Papers, filing under seal   **CRC 2.571**
     Procedures for filing records under seal   **CRC 2.571**
     Unsealing records   **CRC 2.573**

FALSE IMPRISONMENT
Domestic violence protective orders, immunity for officers enforcing   **Fam 6383**
Heir's false imprisonment of elderly or dependent decedent, effect on inheritance rights of   **Pro 259**
Liability of law enforcement officer for   **Gov 820.4**
Limitation of actions   **CCP 340**

FALSE PERSONATION
Debt collectors   **CC 1788.13**

FALSE PRETENSES
Personal information from public records, wrongfully obtaining   **CC 1798.56**

FAMILY
Allowance (See **FAMILY ALLOWANCE**)
Conservatorships for support of family (See **CONSERVATORS**)
Counseling (See **MARRIAGE AND FAMILY COUNSELORS**)

FAMILY—Cont.
Debt collectors communicating with   **CC 1788.12**
Domestic violence (See **DOMESTIC VIOLENCE**)
Dwelling
     Generally (See **DWELLING HOUSES**)
     Family home (See **FAMILY HOME**)
History (See **FAMILY HISTORY**)
Home (See **FAMILY HOME**)
Judges' actions on behalf of family members, Code of Judicial Ethics provisions concerning   **CRCSupp JudEthicsCanon 2**
Medical information disclosures to family members   **CC 56.1007**
Mobilehome park rates based on number in   **CC 798.35**
Parent-child relationship (See **PARENT AND CHILD**)
Warranties for goods sold for   **CC 1790 to 1795.8**

FAMILY ALLOWANCE
Generally   **Pro 6540 to 6545**
Appeals   **Pro 3103, 6545**
Continuation of administration to pay allowance   **Pro 12203**
Defined   **Pro 38**
Dissolution of marriage proceedings   **Fam 2337**
Expenses of administration, payments charged as   **Pro 6544**
Independent administration, payment under   **Pro 10535**
Modification of   **Pro 6541, 6543**
Other income, effect of   **Pro 6540**
Petition for   **Pro 6541**
Physical disability as basis for receiving   **Pro 6540**
Priority of family allowance payments for purposes of estate distribution   **Pro 11420, 11421**
Quick sale of estate assets to provide for   **Pro 10252, 10259**
Sale of personalty to provide for   **Pro 10252, 10259**

FAMILY CODE
Amendments and additions to   **Fam 4, 7**
Citation of code   **Fam 1**
Construction of code   **Fam 3, 6, 9 to 12**
Continuation of existing law   **Fam 2**
Definitions   **Fam 50 to 155**
Headings, effect of   **Fam 5**
Operative date of   **Fam 4**
Repeal of provisions   **Fam 4**
Restatement of existing law   **Fam 2**
Severability of provisions   **Fam 13**
Tense, construction of   **Fam 9**
Uniform act, construction of provisions drawn from   **Fam 3**

FAMILY CONCILIATION COURT LAW (See **CONCILIATION COURTS**)

FAMILY HISTORY
Generally   **Ev 1310**
Bible entries   **Ev 1312**
Church records concerning   **Ev 1315**
Community reputation concerning   **Ev 1314**
Crypts   **Ev 1312**
Friends, statements by   **Ev 1311**
Heirlooms   **Ev 1312**
Neighbor's testimony concerning   **Ev 1314**
Relative's statements   **Ev 1311**
Reputation among family members   **Ev 1313**
Tombstones   **Ev 1312**
Urns   **Ev 1312**

FAMILY HOME
Child support proceedings, rental value of family home for purposes of   **Fam 4057**
Deferred sale of family home, request of custodial parent for   **Fam 3800 to 3810**
Excluding party from dwelling   **Fam 6321, 6340**
Service of process at home of person being served   **CCP 415.20**

Index

Index

Index

FINGERPRINTING—Cont.

Microphotographed files, records, photographs, etc., in custody of criminal justice agency

    Reproductions, admissibility   **Ev 1550.1**

FIREARMS AND OTHER WEAPONS

Aggravation, circumstances in   **CRC 4.421**

Ammunition

    Nuisance abatement

        Unlawful weapons or ammunition purpose   **CC 3485**

Assault weapons

    Nuisance abatement

        Unlawful weapons or ammunition purpose   **CC 3485**

Domestic violence protective order, prohibition on firearm ownership or possession by person subject to   **Fam 6389**

Harassment, injunction or order prohibiting

    Address or location of complaining party or family, prohibition on enjoined party from obtaining   **CCP 527.10**

    Firearm purchases or possession while order in effect   **CCP 527.6**

    Relinquishing and disposition of firearms   **CCP 527.9**

Nuisance abatement

    Weapons or ammunition unlawfully on real property   **CC 3485**

Parental liability for minors discharging   **CC 1714.3**

School grounds, threats to commit violence using firearm or deadly weapon on   **CC 48.8**

Sentence and punishment

    Aggravation, circumstances in   **CRC 4.421**

Serial numbers of   **CC 1710.1**

Shooting range exemption from liability for noise pollution   **CC 3482.1**

Workplace violence or threats of violence, injunctions or orders against

    Address or location of complaining party or family, prohibition on enjoined party from obtaining   **CCP 527.10**

    Firearm possession or purchase by person subject to   **CCP 527.8**

    Proof of sale or turning in of firearm

        Judicial council legal forms   **CRCAppx A**

    Relinquishing and disposition of firearms   **CCP 527.9**

FIRE DEPARTMENTS

Firefighters (See **FIREFIGHTERS**)

FIREFIGHTERS

Arbitration procedure under collective bargaining agreement (See **ARBITRATION, subhead: Firefighters and law enforcement officers**)

Contempt orders, stay of execution of   **CCP 128**

Dogs

    Assignment of firefighter to canine unit outside jurisdiction

        Discrimination in lodging, eating, or transportation due to dog   **CC 54.25**

Injuries willfully inflicted on firemen, responsibility for   **CC 1714.9**

Liability for costs of firefighting

    Attorney general, civil actions to enforce provisions

        Fees and costs for attorney general   **CCP 1021.8**

Public liability for injuries resulting from fire protection activities   **Gov 850 to 850.8**

Resuscitative measures, requests regarding   **Pro 4780 to 4786**

    Health care providers   **Pro 4781**

Volunteer firefighters

    Donations of fire protection apparatus to volunteer departments

        Immunity from liability of donators   **CC 1714.11**

Witnesses, firefighters subpoenaed as   **Gov 68097.1, 68907.2**

FIREFIGHTERS—Cont.

Work-related death, health care benefits for survivors

    Continuity for survivors   **Pro 13600**

FIRE MARSHAL

State agencies, approval of fire safety regulations adopted by   **Gov 11359**

FIREMEN (See FIREFIGHTERS)

FIRES

Appellate court procedures, emergency rule applicable to   **CRC 8.66**

Business records destroyed by   **CCP 1953.10 to 1953.13**

Common interest developments

    Roofs

        Fire retardant roof coverings   **CC 1353.7**

Construction defects, actions for

    Fire protection issues

        Actionable defects   **CC 896**

Court record destroyed by   **CCP 1953 to 1953.06**

Destroyed land records relief law   **CCP 751.01 to 751.28**

Inspection warrants   **CCP 1822.50**

Maps destroyed by   **CCP 1953.10 to 1953.13**

New trial, destroying bill of exceptions as grounds for   **CCP 663.1**

Nunc pro tunc filing where public records lost or destroyed   **CCP 1046a**

Public liability for injuries resulting from fire protection activities   **Gov 850 to 850.8**

Repairs, fire destroying property left for   **CC 1858.2**

Sale of realty, hazard disclosure requirements for   **CC 1103 to 1103.14**

State agencies, adoption of fire safety regulations by   **Gov 11359**

Will revoked by burning   **Pro 6120, 6121**

FIRST AID

Personal injury liability of governmental agency for   **CC 1714.5**

FIRST AMENDMENT RIGHTS

Judicial review of permit or entitlement decision implicating First Amendment rights, expedited procedures for   **CCP 1094.8**

Motion to strike causes of action with chilling effect on person's exercise of   **CCP 425.16, 425.17**

    SLAPPback actions   **CCP 425.18**

FIRST DAY

Computation of time in which act provided by law is to be done   **CCP 12**

FISH AND FISHING

Easement rights   **CC 801, 802**

Fish and wildlife laws

    Attorney general, civil actions to enforce provisions

        Fees and costs for attorney general   **CCP 1021.8**

Owner's liability for recreational land   **CC 846**

Statute of limitation in action commenced under Section 1603.1 or 5650.1 of Fish and Game Code   **CCP 338**

Warrant for inspection of location where aquaculture is stored or held   **CCP 1822.58**

FISH AND GAME DEPARTMENT

Eminent domain taking by   **CCP 1245.210**

FISH AND GAME MANAGEMENT

Bail and penalty schedules for violations   **CRC 4.102**

FITNESS

Assistive devices, implied warranty of fitness   **CC 1793.02**

Consumer goods, implied warranty of fitness of   **CC 1791.1**

Index

FORMS—Cont.

Legal separation

    Judicial council legal forms   **CRCAppx A**

Letters of administration   **Pro 8405**

Liens (See **LIENS**)

Local court forms   **CRC 10.614**

Marriage license   **Fam 355**

Mechanics lien, preliminary notice   **CC 3097.1**

Medical malpractice arbitration clauses   **CCP 1295**

Merchandise offered for consumers, order forms for   **CC 1584.5, 1584.6**

Mortgages (See **TRUST DEEDS AND MORTGAGES**)

Name change

    Judicial council legal forms   **CRCAppx A**

Notarial acts by officers in armed services   **CC 1183.5**

Notice to appear forms

    Judicial council legal forms   **CRCAppx A**

Oaths (See **OATHS**)

Partition action, affidavit stating death of party to   **CCP 872.530**

Paternity

    Judicial council legal forms   **CRCAppx A**

Pleadings

    Judicial council legal forms   **CRCAppx A**

Power of attorney (See **POWER OF ATTORNEY**)

Probate

    Judicial council legal forms   **CRCAppx A**

        Electronic generation of mandatory judicial council form orders   **CRC 7.101.5**

Process (See **PROCESS AND SERVICE OF PROCESS**)

Protective orders

    Emergency protective orders

        Judicial council legal forms   **CRCAppx A**

Receipt of summons, acknowledgment of   **CCP 415.30**

Receivers and receiverships

    Judicial council legal forms   **CRCAppx A**

Requests for admissions

    Form requests for admissions

        List of judicial council legal forms   **CRCAppx A**

Salaries (See **SALARIES AND WAGES**)

Service of process (See **PROCESS AND SERVICE OF PROCESS**)

Small claims actions, approval or adoption of claim form for   **CCP 116.320**

Statutory references on forms   **CRC 1.40**

Subpoenaed witness notified to call attorney   **CCP 1985.2**

Summary dissolution of marriage (See **SUMMARY DISSOLUTION OF MARRIAGE**)

Summons (See **PROCESS AND SERVICE OF PROCESS**)

Superior courts (See **SUPERIOR COURTS**)

Surety bonds   **CCP 995.330**

Termination of parental rights

    Judicial council legal forms   **CRCAppx A**

Traffic violations, trial by written declaration   **CRC 4.210**

    List of judicial council legal forms   **CRCAppx A**

Trial, notice of   **CCP 594**

Trust deeds (See **TRUST DEEDS AND MORTGAGES**)

Uniform Interstate Family Support Act   **CRC 5.27**

Uniform Transfers to Minors Act, transfer under   **Pro 3909**

Unlawful detainer (See **UNLAWFUL DETAINER**)

Wages (See **SALARIES AND WAGES**)

Will, California statutory   **Pro 6240 to 6243**

Workplace violence

    Judicial council legal forms   **CRCAppx A**

FORMS, MOLDS AND DIES

Ownership of   **CC 1140**

FOR SALE, LEASE, OR EXCHANGE SIGNS

Mobilehome condominiums, restrictions on   **CC 799.1.5**

Real property, sale of   **CC 712, 713**

FORUM NON CONVENIENS (See **INCONVENIENT FORUM**)

FOSTER CARE HOMES

Adoption by foster parents (See **ADOPTION**)

Alienation of affection, cause of action against foster parent for   **CC 43.56**

Definitions

    At risk of entering foster care   **CRC 5.502**

    Date child entered foster care   **CRC 5.502**

    Foster care   **CRC 5.502**

Dependent child, placement in

    At risk of entering foster care defined   **CRC 5.502**

Discrimination in placement decision   **Fam 7950**

Education

    Change in placement affecting school of origin   **CRC 5.651**

    Educational rights of children before juvenile court   **CRC 5.651**

Freedom from parental custody (See **FREEDOM FROM PARENTAL CUSTODY AND CONTROL**)

Home study of prospective parents

    Interstate situations   **Fam 7901.1, 7906.5**

Indian children

    Involuntary placements

        Indian Child Welfare Act, rules governing   **CRC 5.480 to 5.487** (See **INDIAN CHILD WELFARE ACT INVOLUNTARY PLACEMENTS**)

Interstate Compact on Placement of Children   **CRC 5.616, Fam 7900 to 7912**

    Children covered by compact   **Fam 7907.5**

    Home environment study request from another state   **Fam 7901.1**

        Interstate situations   **Fam 7906.5**

Intestate succession provisions, establishing parent-child relationship under   **Pro 6454**

Minor's right to make statement regarding placement   **Fam 7952**

Relative, preference for placement with   **Fam 7950**

Short term placement, statutory criteria inapplicable to   **Fam 7951**

Termination of parental rights

    Child in foster care for 15 of last 22 months   **CRC 5.820**

FOUNDRIES

Lien of proprietor of   **CC 3051**

FOUR YEARS (See **STATUTES OF LIMITATION**)

FOWL (See **POULTRY**)

FRANCHISES

Discrimination by   **CC 51.8**

Eminent domain (See **EMINENT DOMAIN**)

Enforcement of judgments (See **ENFORCEMENT OF JUDGMENTS**)

Seller assisted marketing plans   **CC 1812.201**

Usurpation of franchise   **CCP 802 to 811**

FRANCHISE TAX BOARD

Social security numbers

    Public posting or display

        Implementation of provisions   **CC 1798.85**

FRATERNAL ORGANIZATIONS

Charitable aid exempt for purposes of enforcement of judgments   **CCP 704.170**

Judge's office in organization not a financial interest for purposes of disqualification   **CCP 170.5**

FRAUD

Accrual of cause of action   **CCP 338**

Administrator (See **EXECUTORS AND ADMINISTRATORS**)

Index

Index

GIFT CERTIFICATES—Cont.
Ownership of value   **CC 1749.6**
Prepaid calling cards
    Applicability of provisions   **CC 1749.45**

GIFTS
Ademption   **Pro 21131 to 21139**
Arbitrators
    Ethics standards
        Refusal of gifts   **CRC ArbEthicsStand 11**
Attorney in fact, authority of   **Pro 4264**
Community property (See **COMMUNITY PROPERTY**)
Death, gifts in view of (See **DEATH**)
Definition   **CC 1146**
Delivery   **CC 1147**
Dispositions under will (See **WILL CONSTRUCTION**)
Exoneration   **Pro 21131 to 21139**
Inducing client to make substantial gift to attorney, prohibition against   **ProfC 4-400**
Judges
    Gifts to judges or relatives   **CRCSupp JudEthicsCanon 5**
    Limitations on acceptance of gifts by   **CCP 170.9, ProfC 5-300**
Judicial council
    Administrative director of the courts
        Gifts, acceptance   **CRC 10.102**
Marital deduction gifts (See **MARITAL DEDUCTION GIFTS**)
Marriage refusal, recovery of gifts after   **CC 1590**
Mediation
    Standards of conduct for mediators
        Compensation and gifts   **CRC 3.859**
Minors (See **UNIFORM TRANSFERS TO MINORS ACT**)
Quieting title action, admissibility of evidence in   **CCP 764.020**
Referrals, gift or gratuity for   **ProfC 1-320, 2-200**
Revocation   **CC 1148**
Stock (See **CORPORATE SHARES AND SHAREHOLDERS**)
Uniform prudent management of institutional funds act   **Pro 18501 to 18510** (See **INSTITUTIONAL FUNDS MANAGEMENT**)
Uniform Transfers to Minors Act (See **UNIFORM TRANSFERS TO MINORS ACT**)
Unsolicited goods   **CC 1584.5, 1584.6**

GLASSWARE
Common carrier's liability for   **CC 2200**

GOATS
Dogs injuring   **CC 3341**

GOING BUSINESS (See **BUSINESS**)

GOING FORWARD, BURDEN OF (See **BURDEN OF GOING FORWARD**)

GOLD
Common carrier's liability for transporting   **CC 2200**

GOOD CAUSE
Attorney or law firm appointed to represent indigent client without compensation   **CCP 285.4**
Defined   **CCP 116.130**

GOOD FAITH
Agreed case   **CCP 1138**
Attorney's fee award in actions not filed in good faith   **CCP 1021.7**
Bona fide purchasers (See **BONA FIDE PURCHASERS**)
Contracts, performance in good faith   **CC 1493**
Decedents' estates, payment of claims of   **Pro 11005**
Improver of property of another (See **GOOD FAITH IMPROVER**)

GOOD FAITH—Cont.
Landlord, bad faith retention of deposits by   **CC 1950.7**
Marital deduction gift provisions, election in good faith by fiduciary regarding   **Pro 21526**
Minor's disaffirmance of contract   **Fam 6713**
Performance of contract   **CC 1493**
Public entities (See **PUBLIC ENTITIES**)
Settlement entered into by plaintiff and joint tortfeasor, contest of good faith of   **CCP 877.6**
Settlements in good faith (See **SETTLEMENT AND COMPROMISE**)
Small estates without administration, good faith purchaser of real property subject to   **Pro 13203**
Spouse called as adverse witness   **Ev 971**
Temporary restraining order, good faith attempt to notify party of   **CCP 527**
Trusts (See **TRUSTS**)
Unpleaded cause, permission to assert   **CCP 426.50**
Will probate proceedings, complying in good faith with notice requirements for   **Pro 8122**
Writ of execution, property incorrectly levied upon under   **CCP 699.090**

GOOD FAITH IMPROVER
Amount in controversy, action for relief treated as unlimited civil case regardless of   **CCP 871.3**
Authority to adjust rights, equities and interests   **CCP 871.5**
Burden to establish relief   **CCP 871.3**
Defined   **CCP 871.1**
Encroachment on adjoining land   **CCP 871.6**
Public entity or use, nonapplicability to   **CCP 871.7**
Removal of improvements as alternative remedy   **CCP 871.4**
Setoff
    Alternative remedy   **CCP 871.4**
    Withholding property, value of improvements set off against damages for   **CCP 741**
Statutes of limitation   **CCP 340**

GOODWILL
Ownership of   **CC 655**
Value   **CCP 1263.510 to 1263.530**

GOVERNMENTAL ENTITIES (See **PUBLIC ENTITIES**)

GOVERNMENT TORT CLAIMS (See **CLAIMS AGAINST PUBLIC ENTITIES AND EMPLOYEES**)

GOVERNOR
Administrative Procedure Act (See **ADMINISTRATIVE PROCEDURE ACT**)
Commissioners appointed by Governor acknowledging instruments   **CC 1182, 1183**
Small claims advisory committee, appointments to   **CCP 116.950**
White Cane Safety Day, proclamation of   **CC 54.5**

GRAFFITI
Admissibility as evidence   **Ev 1410.5**

GRAIN
Barley (See **BARLEY**)
Bins   **CC 1880 to 1881.2**
Oats (See **OATS**)
Storage in bulk after sale of   **CC 1880 to 1881.2**

GRAIN ELEVATORS
Storage regulated   **CC 1880 to 1881.2**

GRANDCHILDREN
Administrator, priority for serving as   **Pro 8461**
Support of grandchild   **Fam 3930**

Index

Index

Index

HEALTH STUDIO SERVICES CONTRACTS

Anabolic steroid warning, mandatory contract provision regarding   **CC 1812.97 (Title 2.55 version of section)**

Assignments of   **CC 1812.88**

Cancellation of   **CC 1812.85, 1812.89**

Commencement of performance   **CC 1812.85**

Consideration requirements   **CC 1812.86**

Copy of contract, health studio customer receiving   **CC 1812.82**

Damages   **CC 1812.94**

Death of buyer, effect of   **CC 1812.89**

Defined   **CC 1812.81**

Disability of buyer, effect of   **CC 1812.89**

Duration of   **CC 1812.84**

Fraud, effect of   **CC 1812.92**

Money received prior to opening

     Trust account to hold money   **CC 1812.96**

Month-to-month contracts   **CC 1812.98**

Multiple contracts, effect of overlapping   **CC 1812.83**

New facilities

     Money received prior to opening

         Trust account to hold money   **CC 1812.96**

Noncompliance with act, effect of   **CC 1812.91**

Notes to third parties for health studio fees, execution of   **CC 1812.87, 1812.88**

Pre-opening contracts

     Money held in trust   **CC 1812.96**

Public policy   **CC 1812.80**

Refunds   **CC 1812.85, 1812.89**

Remedies, availability of   **CC 1812.90**

Severability clause of act   **CC 1812.95**

Waiver by buyer, effect of   **CC 1812.93**

Writing requirement   **CC 1812.82**

HEARING IMPAIRED PERSONS (See DEAF AND HEARING-IMPAIRED PERSONS)

HEARINGS

Administration of decedents' estates

     Generally (See **ADMINISTRATION OF ESTATES**)

     Executors and administrators (See **EXECUTORS AND ADMINISTRATORS**)

     Independent administration   **Pro 10451**

Administrative hearings

     Adjudicative proceedings (See **ADMINISTRATIVE ADJUDICATION**)

     Rules and regulations (See **ADMINISTRATIVE PROCEDURE ACT**)

Adoption, authorization for, permanency planning hearing   **CRC 5.710 to 5.740**

Appellate review in civil cases

     Prehearing conferences   **CRC 8.248**

     Rehearings   **CRC 8.268**

         Supreme court   **CRC 8.536**

Appellate rules, supreme court and courts of appeal (See **APPELLATE RULES, SUPREME COURT AND COURTS OF APPEAL**)

Arbitration

     Generally (See **ARBITRATION**)

     Administrative adjudication proceedings (See **ADMINISTRATIVE ADJUDICATION**)

     International commercial arbitration (See **INTERNATIONAL COMMERCIAL ARBITRATION AND CONCILIATION**)

     Judicial arbitration (See **JUDICIAL ARBITRATION**)

Arraignments in superior court   **CRC 4.100**

Attachment (See **ATTACHMENT**)

Attorney discipline

     Testimony by judges   **CRCSupp JudEthicsCanon 2**

Chain of title, hearing on identity of party in   **CCP 770.060, 770.070**

HEARINGS—Cont.

Change of names   **CCP 1278**

Child support (See **CHILD SUPPORT**)

Claim and delivery (See **CLAIM AND DELIVERY**)

Conciliation courts (See **CONCILIATION COURTS**)

Confession of judgments   **CCP 1138**

Conservators (See **CONSERVATORS**)

Coordination of actions

     Add-on cases   **CRC 3.544**

         Evidence   **CRC 3.514**

         Notice of hearing on petition   **CRC 3.527**

         Separate hearing on specified issues   **CRC 3.528**

Demurrers, notice of hearing   **CRC 3.1320**

Disclaimer of estate interest   **Pro 277**

Domestic violence protective order   **Fam 6340 to 6345**

Emancipation of children (See **EMANCIPATION OF MINORS**)

Eminent domain (See **EMINENT DOMAIN**)

Enforcement of judgments (See **ENFORCEMENT OF JUDGMENTS**)

Executors of decedents' estates (See **EXECUTORS AND ADMINISTRATORS**)

Fact of death, hearing regarding establishment of   **Pro 203**

Family law rules (See **FAMILY RULES**)

Financial institutions commissioner, superior court hearings on sale of properties of savings and loan association whose business, properties and assets are in possession of   **CCP 73c, 73d**

Garnishment (See **GARNISHMENT**)

Guardianship (See **GUARDIAN AND WARD**)

Habeas corpus   **CRC 4.551**

Heirship determination proceedings   **Pro 11704**

Homesteads (See **HOMESTEADS**)

Independent administration of estate   **Pro 10451**

Indigent parents, adult child's petition to be relieved of obligation to support   **Fam 4412, 4414**

Innkeeper's liens, writ of possession on   **CC 1861.6, 1861.8**

International commercial arbitration and conciliation (See **INTERNATIONAL COMMERCIAL ARBITRATION AND CONCILIATION**)

Investment of funds of decedents estate   **Pro 9732**

Judges (See **JUDGES**)

Judicial arbitration (See **JUDICIAL ARBITRATION**)

Judicial notice

     Habeas corpus petition hearings   **CRC 4.551**

     Law and motion hearings   **CRC 3.1306**

Law and motion rules   **CRC 3.1304, 3.1306**

     Date, time and location of hearing, papers to specify   **CRC 3.1110**

     Demurrers   **CRC 3.1320**

     Evidence at hearing   **CRC 3.1306**

     Failure to appear, effect of   **CRC 3.1304**

     Injunctions   **CRC 3.1152**

     Telephone appearance at law and motion hearings   **CCP 367.5, CRC 3.670**

     Time for hearing   **CRC 3.1304**

Leases of city property, public hearings on   **CC 719**

Livestock service liens, sale under   **CC 3080.03 to 3080.22**

Mandamus   **CCP 1094, 1094.5, 1094.6**

Mechanic's lien, release from   **CC 3154**

Mine co-owners failing to pay taxes   **CCP 854**

Missing persons (See **MISSING PERSONS**)

New trial motions   **CCP 660, 663.2**

Office of Administrative Hearings (See **ADMINISTRATIVE PROCEDURE ACT**)

Partition (See **PARTITION**)

Power of attorney, notice of time and place of hearing on petitions involving   **Pro 4544**

Pretrial conferences (See **PRETRIAL CONFERENCES**)

Rehearings (See **REHEARINGS**)

Index

Index

Index

INSURANCE—Cont.

Application

Denials based on information from investigative consumer reporting agencies or other sources

Information as to reports given rejected applicant CC 1786.40

Arbitration of liability coverage disputes

Agreements to arbitrate **CCP 1784**

Amount in controversy **CCP 1777**

Court-ordered mediation or arbitration, relief from obligation to participate in **CCP 1780**

Definitions **CCP 1776**

Presumption of insurer's good faith **CCP 1778, 1779**

Removal from arbitration **CCP 1779**

Requests for arbitration **CCP 1777**

Tolling of limitations periods and suspension of case-management requirements **CCP 1780**

Armenian genocide victims, jurisdiction and limitation period for actions against insurers by **CCP 354.4**

Attorneys

Independent counsel, insurance defense cases requiring representation of insured by **CC 2860**

Liability of attorney as member of insurance underwriting committee **CC 43.7**

Automobile insurance (See **AUTOMOBILE INSURANCE**)

Child support (See **CHILD SUPPORT**)

Claims against decedent's estate (See **CLAIMS AGAINST ESTATES**)

Collateral source rule **CC 3333.1**

Common interest developments (See **COMMON INTEREST DEVELOPMENTS**)

Complex litigation defined **CRC 3.400**

Conflict of interests in insurance defense cases requiring representation of insured by independent counsel **CC 2860**

Conservators

Assets of ward

Taking possession or control, responsibilities of guardian **CRC 7.1061**

Credit disability insurance (See **CREDIT DISABILITY INSURANCE**)

Credit reports (See **CREDIT REPORTING**)

Discovery of insurance coverage

Scope of discovery **CCP 2017.210**

Dissolution of insurer, disposition of unclaimed property following **CCP 1517**

Dissolution of marriage proceedings (See **DISSOLUTION OF MARRIAGE**)

Emancipated minors, contracts by **Fam 7051**

Exemptions from liability, pleadings for **CCP 431.50**

Guardianships

Assets of ward

Taking possession or control, responsibilities of guardian **CRC 7.1011**

Hazard insurance coverage imposed by lender, limitations on **CC 2955.5**

Health, accident, and disability insurance (See **HEALTH, ACCIDENT, AND DISABILITY INSURANCE**)

Holocaust victims, jurisdiction and limitation period for actions against insurers by **CCP 354.5**

Hospital lien notice transmitted to **CC 3045.3**

Independent counsel, conflict of interests in insurance defense cases requiring representation by **CC 2860**

Investigative consumer reporting agencies (See **INVESTIGATIVE CONSUMER REPORTING AGENCIES**)

Judgment debtor, assignment of right to payment due **CCP 708.510 to 708.560**

Life insurance (See **LIFE INSURANCE**)

Mediation

Civil action mediation

Insurers, circumstances requiring attendance **CRC 3.874**

INSURANCE—Cont.

Medical information, release of **CC 56.15, 56.27**

Mortgages (See **TRUST DEEDS AND MORTGAGES**)

Northridge earthquake of 1994, revival of cause of action for damages arising out of **CCP 340.9**

Pleadings for liability exemption **CCP 431.50**

Power of attorney (See **POWER OF ATTORNEY**)

Premiums

Increase based on information from investigative consumer reporting agencies or other sources

Information as to reports given to policy holder **CC 1786.40**

Professional liability insurance (See **PHYSICIANS AND SURGEONS**)

Proposition 103 rebate, disposition of unclaimed **CCP 1523**

Public entities, insurance considerations in claims against **Gov 989 to 991.2**

Punitive damages award against insurer, special notice of **CC 3296**

Real property sales contract, insurance payments received under **CC 2985.4**

Rebate under Proposition 103, disposition of unclaimed **CCP 1523**

Repairs, protecting property left for **CC 1858 to 1858.3**

Rescission of policy

Generally **CC 1689**

Statute of limitation for rescission based on misrepresentation **CCP 337**

Retail installment sales (See **RETAIL INSTALLMENT SALES**)

Small claims court, appearance of insurers in (See **SMALL CLAIMS COURTS**)

Third-party cause of action for unfair claims settlement practices by liability insurers **CC 2870, 2871**

Trust deeds (See **TRUST DEEDS AND MORTGAGES**)

Trusts (See **TRUSTS**)

Unclaimed deposits and payments

Demutualization

Property distributable as part of demutualization **CCP 1515.5**

Underwriting committees' liability for evaluations pursuant to **CC 43.7, 43.8**

Unfair claims settlement practices by liability insurers, third-party cause of action for **CC 2870, 2871**

Uniform parentage act

Vacation or setting aside of judgment

Payments made in good faith by estate, trustees, insurers, etc., based on paternity judgment **Fam 7649.5**

Volunteer health professionals, insurance for **Gov 990.9**

Workers' compensation (See **WORKERS' COMPENSATION**)

INTENT

Contracts, construction of **CC 1636, 1637, 1648 to 1650**

Fraud, class of persons, intended for **CC 1711**

Fraudulent transfers

Actual intent to hinder, delay or defraud creditors **CC 3439.04**

Effect on **CC 3439.07**

Infants (See **MINORS**)

Ordinary consequences from voluntary acts, presumption of intent for **Ev 665**

Pleadings, objection to **CCP 430.10, 430.20**

Presumption of unlawful intent arising from doing unlawful act **Ev 668**

Trusts, creation of **Pro 15201**

Waters, intent for appropriation of **CC 1415**

Wills (See **WILLS**)

INTERCOUNTRY ADOPTION OF CHILDREN (See **ADOPTION**)

INTERESTED PERSONS
Process shown to   **CCP 262.2**

INTEREST IN OUTCOME
Challenge of juror for implied bias   **CCP 229**

INTEREST ON INVESTMENTS
Interpleader deposits   **CCP 386.1**

INTEREST ON MONEY
Adjustable rate mortgages (See **TRUST DEEDS AND MORT-GAGES**)
Administration of decedents' estates
    Generally (See **ADMINISTRATION OF ESTATES**)
    Claims against decedents' estates (See **CLAIMS AGAINST ESTATES**)
Annual interest rates
    Credit card holders' right to request annual report concerning finance charges   **CC 1748.5**
    Presumptions   **CC 1916**
Annuities, accrual of interest on   **Pro 12004**
Child support judgment or support order   **CCP 695.211**
Contracts
    Award for breach of   **CC 3288**
    Rate of interest   **CC 1916.12-1**
Damages (See **DAMAGES**)
Decedents' estates (See subhead: **Administration of decedents' estates**)
Deposit in lieu of surety bond where no proceedings pending, payment of interest on   **CCP 995.740**
Earnings withholding order, interest included in   **CCP 706.028**
Eminent domain compensation award acquiring   **CCP 1263.015, 1268.310 to 1268.360**
Employee Retirement Income Security Act (See **ERISA**)
Enforcement of judgments (See **ENFORCEMENT OF JUDG-MENTS**)
Housing loans by public entities, assumption of   **CC 711.5**
Impound accounts   **CC 2954.8**
Income of property   **CC 748**
International commercial arbitration award, interest on   **CCP 1297.317**
Inverse condemnation, computation of interest award in action for   **CCP 1268.311**
Judgments
    Enforcement of judgments (See **ENFORCEMENT OF JUDGMENTS**)
    Inclusion in interest in   **CRC 3.1802**
Legacies by will, interest on (See **WILLS**)
Legal rate of interest   **CC 1916.12-1**
Offer to perform as terminating   **CC 1504**
Partition referees contracts providing for   **CCP 873.150**
Permanently escheated property   **CCP 1320**
Political items, illegal sale of   **CC 1739.4**
Precomputed interest   **CC 1799.5**
    Waiver of protections   **CC 1799.6**
Prejudgment interest, award of   **CC 3291**
Presumption of loan on interest   **CC 1914 to 1916.5**
Public entity defendant, interest on liquidated claim against   **Gov 926.10**
Public entity loans for purchase or rehabilitation of realty   **CC 711.5**
Public retirement system loans, exemption from usury laws for   **CC 1916.2**
Real estate brokers, interest on loans by   **CC 1916.1**
Shared appreciation loans (See **SHARED APPRECIATION LOANS**)
Small claims courts
    Judgment   **CCP 116.820**
Trust deeds and mortgages, loans secured by (See **TRUST DEEDS AND MORTGAGES**)
Trusts (See **TRUSTS**)

INTEREST ON MONEY—Cont.
Unclaimed property
    Generally (See **UNCLAIMED PROPERTY**)
    Deposits unclaimed   **CCP 1513, 1513.5, 1516**
Usury (See **USURY**)
Variable interest rate loans (See **TRUST DEEDS AND MORT-GAGES**)
Waiver of   **CC 3290**
Wills, interest on legacies by (See **WILLS**)

INTERESTS OF JUSTICE
Attorney's fee award to prevailing party in action resulting in enforcement of right affecting public interest   **CCP 1021.5**
Disqualification of judges, grounds for   **CCP 170.1**
Preference, discretion of court to grant motion for   **CCP 36**
Stay or dismissal of action that should be heard in forum outside state   **CCP 410.30**

INTERLOCUTORY JUDGMENT
Family law rules (See **FAMILY RULES**)
Partition action   **CCP 872.720, 872.810**

INTERMENT (See **CEMETERIES**)

INTERNAL REVENUE DEPARTMENT
Estate tax (See **ESTATE TAX**)
Income tax (See **INCOME TAX**)
Marital deduction gifts (See **MARITAL DEDUCTION GIFTS**)
Will construction, application of Internal Revenue Code provisions to (See **WILL CONSTRUCTION**)

INTERNATIONAL COMMERCIAL ARBITRATION AND CONCILIATION
Appointment
    Arbitrators (See subhead: **Appointment of arbitrators**)
    Conciliators (See subhead: **Conciliation**)
Appointment of arbitrators
    Challenge to (See subhead: **Challenges to arbitrator**)
    Conciliator as arbitrator, appointment of   **CCP 1297.393**
    Court action
        Appealability of   **CCP 1297.117**
        Enforcement of appointment procedure   **CCP 1297.116**
        Factors for appointing arbitrator   **CCP 1297.118**
    Failure to agree on   **CCP 1297.114, 1297.115**
    Nationality requirements   **CCP 1297.111**
    Procedure for appointing tribunal   **CCP 1297.112**
    Substitute arbitrator, appointment of   **CCP 1297.152**
Arbitration agreement
    Defined   **CCP 1297.71**
    Writing requirements of   **CCP 1297.72**
Awards
    Additional award
        Generally   **CCP 1267.335, 1297.334**
        Extension of time for requesting   **CCP 1297.336**
        Form and content of   **CCP 1297.337**
    Correction or interpretation
        Generally   **CCP 1297.331 to 1297.333**
        Extension of time for requesting   **CCP 1297.336**
        Form and content of   **CCP 1297.337**
    Costs   **CCP 1297.318**
    Delivery of copy to parties   **CCP 1297.315**
    Enforcement of   **CCP 1297.316**
    Interest, award of   **CCP 1297.317**
    Interim award   **CCP 1297.316**
    Settlement, effect of   **CCP 1297.303, 1297.304**
    Statement of date and place of arbitration   **CCP 1297.314**
    Statement of reasons   **CCP 1297.313**
    Termination of proceedings on final award   **CCP 1297.321**
    Writing requirements   **CCP 1297.311**

Index

ISSUANCE

Bonds, procedure for validation of authorization, issuance, sale or exchange of   **CCP 349.4**

ISSUES

Fact issues for jury, referee or court   **CCP 592**
Joinder of issues (See **JOINDER OF ISSUES**)
Law, issues of   **CCP 591**
Notice of trial   **CCP 594**
Referees determining   **CCP 638**
Strike, motion to   **CCP 589**

ISSUE SANCTION

Case questionnaires under economic litigation provisions for limited civil cases, failure to obey order compelling response to   **CCP 93**

IUDS

Dalkon Shield claimants, extension of limitations statute in action for   **CCP 340.7**

J

JAILS (See **PRISONERS**)

JBSIS (See **JUDICIAL BRANCH STATISTICAL INFORMATION SYSTEM (JBSIS)**)

JENKINS ACT

Claims
　　Attorneys' fees and costs   **CCP 1021.10**

JEOPARDY WITHHOLDING ORDER

Taxes, earnings withholding orders for   **CCP 706.078**

JEWELRY AND JEWELERS

Assignment for benefit of creditors, property exempt from   **CCP 1801**
Common carrier's liability for transporting jewelry   **CC 2200**
Exempt property for purposes of enforcement of judgments   **CCP 704.040**
Lien for work performed in shops   **CC 3052a**

JOBBERS

Wholesale sales representatives, contractual relations with (See **WHOLESALE SALES REPRESENTATIVES**)

JOB LISTING SERVICES (See also **EMPLOYMENT AGENCIES; EMPLOYMENT COUNSELING SERVICES**)

Advertising requirements of   **CC 1812.520**
Bonding requirements   **CC 1812.515**
Defined   **CC 1812.501**
Exempt activities   **CC 1812.502**
Fees
　　Refund of fees to jobseeker   **CC 1812.516, 1812.518, 1812.523**
　　Schedule of job listing service fees   **CC 1812.517**
Fraud and misrepresentation, liability for   **CC 1812.520, 1812.523**
Job orders   **CC 1812.519**
Minors, job placement for   **CC 1812.521**
Nurses' registries (See **NURSES**)
Recordkeeping requirements   **CC 1812.522**
Refund of fees to jobseeker   **CC 1812.516, 1812.518, 1812.523**
Remedies available   **CC 1812.523**
Service agreements with jobseeker, requirements of   **CC 1812.516**
Union contract or labor troubles at jobsite, notice to jobseeker of   **CC 1812.521**

JOINDER OF ACTIONS

Cross-complaints (See **CROSS-COMPLAINTS**)
Exceptions to compulsory joinder requirement   **CCP 426.40**
Permissive joinder of causes of action   **CCP 427.10**
Wrongful death (See **WRONGFUL DEATH**)

JOINDER OF CAUSES (See **JOINDER OF ACTIONS**)

JOINDER OF ISSUES

Generally   **CCP 588**
Demurrer, law issues joined on   **CCP 589**
Fact issues joined on answer   **CCP 590**
Motion to strike, effect of   **CCP 589**

JOINDER OF PARTIES

Answer alleging defect of   **CCP 430.10**
Arbitration proceedings   **CCP 1281.2**
Compulsory joinder   **CCP 389**
Costs in absence of   **CCP 1022**
Creditor's action against third person, joinder of judgment debtor in   **CCP 708.220**
Cross-complaints, joinder of parties in (See **CROSS-COMPLAINTS**)
Demurrer alleging defect of   **CCP 430.10**
Dependent child or ward of court proceedings, joinder of government agency or private service provider in   **CRC 5.575**
Dismissal of action where person subject to compulsory joinder cannot be joined   **CCP 389**
Dissolution of marriage (See **DISSOLUTION OF MARRIAGE**)
Doubt as to person from whom plaintiff is entitled to redress   **CCP 379**
Eminent domain action   **CCP 1250.240**
Enforcement of judgments (See **ENFORCEMENT OF JUDGMENTS**)
Family law proceedings   **CRC 5.150 to 5.162**
Family law rules (See **FAMILY RULES**)
Identity theft, action involving   **CC 1798.94**
Interest in property, joinder of persons claiming   **CCP 389.5**
Interpleader   **CCP 386**
Intervention   **CCP 387**
Mechanic's liens, foreclosure of   **CC 3149**
Parent of injured child   **CCP 376**
Partition action   **CCP 872.510 to 872.550**
Partnership or other unincorporated association, joinder of member as party in action against   **CCP 369.5**
Permissive joinder
　　Defendants   **CCP 379**
　　Plaintiffs   **CCP 378**
Public works stop notice proceedings   **CC 3214**
Quieting title action   **CCP 762.040**
Quo warranto proceedings, defendants in   **CCP 808**
Separate trials   **CCP 379.5**
Surety bonds, joinder of surety and principal in action to enforce liability on   **CCP 996.430**
Unwilling plaintiff made defendant   **CCP 382**
Venue, improper joinder to fix   **CCP 395**
Ward of court proceedings
　　Joinder of government agency or private service provider in   **CRC 5.575**

JOINT ACCOUNTS (See **MULTIPLE-PARTY ACCOUNTS**)

JOINT AND SEVERAL LIABILITY   **CC 1430 to 1432**

Benefits under contract   **CC 1659**
Bond furnished by estate representative   **Pro 8480**
Contribution among joint tortfeasors   **CCP 875 to 880**
Covenant not to sue, effect on liability of joint tortfeasor   **CCP 877**
Dismissal of suit, effect on liability of joint tortfeasor   **CCP 877**
Execution of contract by several persons   **CC 1660**

Index

Index

JUDICIAL ADMINISTRATION STANDARDS—Cont.

Grand juries, guidelines for selection **CRC JudAdminStand 10.50**

Interpreters **CRC JudAdminStand 2.10, CRC JudAdminStand 2.11**

Judicial comments on verdict or mistrial, propriety of **CRC JudAdminStand 2.30**

Judicial education (See **JUDGES**)

Juror complaints

Receiving and responding to complaints **CRC JudAdminStand 10.51**

Jury (See **JURY**)

Jury selection

Master jury list, updating **CRC JudAdminStand 10.31**

Uninterrupted jury selection **CRC JudAdminStand 2.25**

Juvenile court matters (See **JUVENILE COURTS**)

Mediation

Alternative dispute resolution programs

Committees to oversee ADR programs **CRC JudAdminStand 10.71**

Coordination of ADR programs, judicial council guidelines for **CRC JudAdminStand 10.70**

Memorandum opinions by courts of appeal **CRC JudAdminStand 8.1**

Mistrial

Judicial comments on verdict or mistrial, propriety of **CRC JudAdminStand 2.30**

Telephones (See **TELEPHONES AND TELEGRAPHS**)

Traffic infraction procedures **CRC JudAdminStand 4.40 to CRC JudAdminStand 4.42**

Bail schedule adherence **CRC JudAdminStand 4.40**

Courtesy notice **CRC JudAdminStand 4.41**

Extensions of time **CRC JudAdminStand 4.40**

Scheduling trials **CRC JudAdminStand 4.42**

Trial court performance standards **CRC JudAdminStand 10.17**

Trial management standards **CRC JudAdminStand 2.20**

Trusts

Settlements or judgments in civil cases involving minors or persons with disabilities **CRC JudAdminStand 7.10**

Verdict

Judicial comments on verdict or mistrial, propriety of **CRC JudAdminStand 2.30**

Waste reduction and recycling programs for courts **CRC JudAdminStand 10.55**

JUDICIAL APPOINTMENTS, COMMISSION ON

Broadcasting of hearings *CRCSupp JudAppointGuide 5*

Chairperson, powers of *CRCSupp JudAppointGuide 3*

Commission on Judicial Nominees Evaluation, recommendations *CRCSupp JudAppointGuide 4*

Communications with commission *CRCSupp JudAppointGuide 4*

Conference before confirmation hearing *CRCSupp JudAppointGuide 5*

Confirmation hearings, scheduling *CRCSupp JudAppointGuide 4*

Decisions, announcement *CRCSupp JudAppointGuide 5*

Definitions *CRCSupp JudAppointGuide 1*

Files, access to *CRCSupp JudAppointGuide 7*

Headquarters of commission *CRCSupp JudAppointGuide 1*

Hearings

Absence of commission member at *CRCSupp JudAppointGuide 5*

Procedures *CRCSupp JudAppointGuide 5*

Public attendance and broadcasting *CRCSupp JudAppointGuide 5*

JUDICIAL APPOINTMENTS, COMMISSION ON—Cont.

Hearings—Cont.

Records *CRCSupp JudAppointGuide 5*

Membership *CRCSupp JudAppointGuide 2*

Nominees

Notice to *CRCSupp JudAppointGuide 4*

Witness lists, presentation of *CRCSupp JudAppointGuide 4*

Notice to nominee *CRCSupp JudAppointGuide 4*

Official records *CRCSupp JudAppointGuide 5*

Permissible testimony

Post-hearing procedures *CRCSupp JudAppointGuide 7*

Pre-hearing procedures *CRCSupp JudAppointGuide 4*

Publication and distribution of guidelines *CRCSupp JudAppointGuide 8*

Public attendance at hearings *CRCSupp JudAppointGuide 5*

Record of hearing *CRCSupp JudAppointGuide 5*

Requests to testify *CRCSupp JudAppointGuide 4*

Secretary to commission *CRCSupp JudAppointGuide 6*

Speakers and communications, release of lists of *CRCSupp JudAppointGuide 4*

Staff to commission *CRCSupp JudAppointGuide 6*

Testimony, permissible *CRCSupp JudAppointGuide 4*

Web site of official guidelines *CRCSupp JudAppointGuide 8*

Witnesses

List

Presentation of nominee's witness list *CRCSupp JudAppointGuide 4*

Order of hearing *CRCSupp JudAppointGuide 5*

Written presentations *CRCSupp JudAppointGuide 4*

JUDICIAL ARBITRATION **CRC 3.810 to 3.830**

Absence of party **CRC 3.821**

Actions subject to **CCP 1141.11, 1141.12, CRC 3.811**

Administrative costs, parties liable for payment of **CCP 1141.28**

ADR administrator

Designation **CRC 3.813**

ADR committee

Duties **CRC 3.813**

Panels

Duties of committee as to **CRC 3.814**

Amount in controversy **CCP 1141.11, 1141.12, CRC 3.811**

Awards in excess of **CCP 1141.26**

Determination of **CCP 1141.16**

Applicability of rules **CRC 3.810**

Appointments by court, nondiscrimination standard for **CRC 10.611, CRC JudAdminStand 10.21**

Arbitration generally (See **ARBITRATION**)

Arbitration under an agreement not in conformity to rules of **CRC 3.830**

Arbitrator's fees **CCP 1141.18, 1141.28, CRC 3.819**

Assignment of cases **CRC 3.815**

Assignment to arbitration **CRC 3.812**

At-issue memorandum **CCP 1141.16**

Attorney, representation by **CRC 3.821**

Authority of arbitrators **CRC 3.824**

Awards **CCP 1141.20, CRC 3.825**

Amount in controversy, effect of awards in excess of **CCP 1141.26**

Small claims court jurisdiction **CCP 116.220**

Vacation of awards **CCP 1141.22, CRC 3.827**

Bad-faith actions or tactics, award of expenses and attorney's fees incurred as result of **CCP 128.5, 128.6**

Case management conference **CRC 3.812**

Telephone appearance at case management conferences **CRC 3.670**

JUDICIAL NOTICE—Cont.

Administrative Procedure Act, judicial notice of agency regulations filed under　**Ev 451, Gov 11343.6, 11344.6**

Appeals court　**Ev 459**

Appellate rules

Briefs

Capital case　**CRC 8.630**

Motion requesting in court of appeal or supreme court　**CRC 8.252**

Habeas corpus　**CRC 8.386**

Attorneys, rules of conduct governing　**Ev 451**

Common knowledge, facts within　**Ev 451, 452**

Computer-generated official court records relating to criminal convictions　**Ev 452.5**

Demurrer　**CCP 430.30, 430.70**

Denial by court to take judicial notice　**Ev 456**

English language　**Ev 451**

Expert consultants

Generally　**Ev 454, 455, 459**

Appointment by court　**Ev 460**

Habeas corpus

Petition hearings　**CRC 4.551**

Return of writ to reviewing court　**CRC 8.386**

Jury, instructions to　**Ev 457**

Law and motion rules

Hearing, evidence at　**CRC 3.1306**

Moving papers, request associated with　**CRC 3.1113**

Legislative history materials

3rd Appellate District local rules　**CRCSupp *3rd App-Dist***

Mandatory judicial notice　**Ev 451, 453**

Parentage determinations　**CRC 5.635**

Permissive judicial notice　**Ev 452, 453**

Propriety of court taking judicial notice, determination of　**Ev 454, 455**

Requests for　**CRC 8.252, Ev 453, 456**

1st Appellate District local rules　**CRCSupp *1st App-Dist***

Habeas corpus　**CRC 8.386**

Restrictive covenants in recorded instruments　**CC 53**

Review courts, judicial notice by　**Ev 459**

Secretary of state, judicial notice of agency regulations filed with　**Ev 451, Gov 11343.6, 11344.6**

Submission of arguments prior to court decision for taking　**Ev 455**

Subsequent proceedings of trial, effect on　**Ev 458**

Summary judgments, support or opposition of motion for　**CCP 437c**

Supreme court or court of appeal, motion for judicial notice in case pending before　**CRC 8.252**

Habeas corpus　**CRC 8.386**

JUDICIAL OFFICERS (See **JUDGES**)

JUDICIAL PERFORMANCE, COMMISSION ON

Censure, removal, admonishment or retirement of judges

Additional evidence　**JudPerR 133**

Advisory letter to judge

Correction of errors of fact, law or both　**JudPerR 111.5**

Preliminary investigation　**JudPerR 111**

Staff inquiry　**JudPerR 110**

Amendment to pleadings　**JudPerR 128**

Amicus curiae briefs　**JudPerR 131**

Answer　**JudPerR 104, 119**

Amendments　**JudPerR 128**

Extension of time for　**JudPerR 108, 119**

Appearance before commission

Masters' report, appearance after　**JudPerR 132**

Modification of decision after formal proceedings　**JudPerPolicy 2.6**

JUDICIAL PERFORMANCE, COMMISSION ON—Cont.

Censure, removal, admonishment or retirement of judges—Cont.

Appearance before commission—Cont.

Notice of intended private admonishment, appearance after　**JudPerR 114**

Notice of intended public admonishment, appearance after　**JudPerR 116**

Attorney representing judge　**JudPerR 106, 126**

Briefs　**JudPerR 130**

Amicus curiae briefs　**JudPerR 131**

Characteristics of misconduct

Factors relevant to sanctions　**JudPerPolicy 7.1**

Commencement of commission action　**JudPerR 109**

Commission member's participation prohibited in proceedings involving own censure, removal or admonishment　**JudPerR 101**

Commission's own motion, staff inquiry or preliminary investigation on　**JudPerR 109**

Confidentiality of proceedings　**JudPerR 102, 122**

Conflicts of interest

Disqualification of commission member unless quorum prevented by disqualification　**JudPerR 134.5**

Consent

Amicus curiae briefs, consent to submission of　**JudPerR 131**

Discipline by　**JudPerPolicy 2.4**

Discipline by consent　**JudPerR 127**

One master to hear case, judge's consent to appointment of　**JudPerR 121**

Conservator

Appointment　**JudPerR 126**

Construction of rules governing　**JudPerR 138**

Cooperation, duty of

Factors relevant to sanctions　**JudPerPolicy 7.1**

Defamatory material　**JudPerR 103**

Defending against charges, opportunity for　**JudPerR 126**

Definitions　**JudPerR 138**

Demeanor of judge

Factors relevant to sanctions　**JudPerPolicy 7.1**

Depositions　**JudPerR 122**

Dereliction of duty　**JudPerR 109**

Disclosures concerning proceedings　**JudPerR 102**

Discovery　**JudPerR 122**

Extension of time　**JudPerR 108**

Dishonesty

Factors relevant to sanctions　**JudPerPolicy 7.1**

Dismissal of charge by examiner　**JudPerR 128**

Dismissal of proceedings　**JudPerR 134**

Disqualification pending further proceedings or appeal　**JudPerR 120**

Drug use　**JudPerR 109**

Duty to cooperate　**JudPerR 104**

Evidence

Additional evidence, hearing for taking　**JudPerR 133**

Hearings, evidence admissible at　**JudPerR 123, 125**

Exhibits at hearings　**JudPerR 125.5**

Extension of time in proceedings　**JudPerR 108, 119**

Failure to appear at hearing　**JudPerR 123**

Filing with Commission　**JudPerR 119.5**

Finality of commission determination　**JudPerR 136**

Former judges

Barring assignments to former judges　**JudPerPolicy 2.5**

Hearings

Additional evidence　**JudPerR 133**

Confidentiality　**JudPerR 102**

Index

Index

Index

JUSTICE COURTS

Chambers, powers and duties of judges at   **CCP 167**

Clerks

    Fees (See subhead: **Fees**)

Contempt orders (See **CONTEMPT**)

Costs

    Generally (See **COSTS**)

Fax machines, use of (See **FAX FILING AND SERVICE**)

Filing

    Fax machines, use of (See **FAX FILING AND SERVICE**)

    Fees for filing (See subhead: **Fees**)

Jury (See **JURY**)

Law and motion proceedings (See **LAW AND MOTION PRO-
CEEDINGS**)

Local rules

    Sanctions for noncompliance   **CCP 575.2**

Recycled paper, court's use of   **CRC 10.503**

Small claims courts (See **SMALL CLAIMS COURTS**)

Transcripts

    Court reporters generally (See **COURT REPORTERS**)

JUSTICE, DEPARTMENT OF

Check cashers, registration of   **CC 1789.37**

Conviction of crime, report by courts concerning   **CRC 4.320**

Domestic violence protective orders, notification of   **Fam 6380,
6385**

Information Practices Act procedures   **CC 1798.23**

JUSTICE OF THE PEACE

Generally (See **JUSTICE COURTS**)

JUSTICES

Courts of appeal (See **COURTS OF APPEAL**)

Supreme Court (See **SUPREME COURT, CALIFORNIA**)

JUVENILE COURTS   CCP 917.7

Adoption of child

    Interstate Compact on Placement of Children   **Fam 7900
to 7912**

        Children covered by compact   **Fam 7907.5**

    Juvenile rules (See **JUVENILE RULES**)

    Relative adoptions

        Generally   **Fam 8714.5**

        Kinship adoption agreement with birth parent   **CRC
5.400**

        Postadoption contact agreement with birth parent
Fam 8616.5

    Relinquishment by birth parent of child subject to depen-
dency proceedings, notice of   **Fam 8700**

    Reports submitted to court   **Fam 8715**

    Statewide exchange system, registration of approved family
with   **Fam 8710.3**

Appeals

    Extraordinary writ, petition for review by   **CRC 8.454,
8.456**

    Freedom from custody proceedings, review of (See **FREE-
DOM FROM PARENTAL CUSTODY AND CON-
TROL**)

    Juvenile case appeals   **CRC 5.585 to 5.600**

        Supreme court and courts of appeal   **CRC 8.400 to
8.474**

Attorneys

    Delinquency proceedings

        Responsibility of children's counsel in delinquency
proceedings   **CRC 5.663**

    Discrimination, prohibition against in appointments   **CRC
JudAdminStand 5.40**

    Representation and compensation standards   **CRC
JudAdminStand 5.40**

Certification to juvenile court

    Superior court to juvenile court   **CRC 4.116**

JUVENILE COURTS—Cont.

Child protection workers, extent of immunity of   **Gov 820.21**

Child welfare services case plan, effect of parent signing or
accepting services under   **Ev 1228.1**

Claims against public agencies (See **CLAIMS AGAINST
PUBLIC ENTITIES AND EMPLOYEES**)

Continuances

    Educational rights of children before juvenile court   **CRC
5.651**

Court-appointed counsel

    Child's counsel, responsibilities in delinquency proceedings
CRC 5.663

Court reporters   **CCP 274a**

Criminal prosecutions, certification to juvenile court   **CRC
4.116**

Custody of child

    Juvenile rules (See **JUVENILE RULES**)

Dependent child of court proceedings (See **DEPENDENT
CHILDREN**)

Detention

    Dependency (See **DEPENDENT CHILDREN**)

    Wardship (See **JUVENILE WARDSHIP PROCEED-
INGS**)

Disposition hearings

    Dependency (See **DEPENDENT CHILDREN**)

    Wardship (See **JUVENILE WARDSHIP PROCEED-
INGS**)

Domestic violence proceedings involving minor party, jurisdiction over   **CCP 374.5**

Educational rights of children   **CRC JudAdminStand 5.40**

Ethics code for court employees, adoption of   **CRC JudAdminStand 10.16**

Expert witnesses by court-appointment, compensation of   **Ev
731**

Fitness hearings

    Wardship (See **JUVENILE WARDSHIP PROCEED-
INGS**)

Forms

    Judicial council legal forms   **CRCAppx A**

Freedom from parental custody and control, proceedings for (See
**FREEDOM FROM PARENTAL CUSTODY AND CON-
TROL**)

Guardians

    Termination of   **CRC 5.620**

Harassment proceedings brought against or initiated by minor,
jurisdiction over   **CCP 374.5**

Hearing officers

    Law practice of subordinate judicial officers   **CRC 10.702**

        Ethical provisions   **CRCSupp JudEthicsCanon 6**

    Qualifications and education of subordinate judicial officers
CRC 10.701

Hearings

    Educational rights of children before juvenile court   **CRC
5.651**

    Juvenile rules (See **JUVENILE RULES**)

    Marsden hearings, transcript of   **CRC 8.328**

Immunity of social workers and child protection workers, extent
of   **Gov 820.21**

Initial hearing

    Dependency (See **DEPENDENT CHILDREN**)

Interpreters   **CRC 2.893**

Judges

    Judicial administration standards for judges assigned to
CRC JudAdminStand 5.40

Judicial administration standards

    Assignment of judges, guidelines for   **CRC JudAdmin-
Stand 5.40**

    Attorney representation, guidelines for   **CRC JudAdmin-
Stand 5.40**

Index

Index

Index

K

Index

Index

LAW AND MOTION PROCEEDINGS—Cont.

Support actions under Social Security Act Title IV-D, notice **CRC 5.315**

Supporting papers   **CRC 3.1112**

Telephone appearances   **CCP 367.5, CRC 3.670**

Temporary restraining order, application for order to show cause   **CRC 3.1150**

Tentative rulings   **CRC 3.1308**

    Procedure for issuance of   **CRC 3.1306**

Time

    Filing and service of papers   **CRC 3.1300**

    Hearing, time of   **CRC 3.1304**

    Motions to strike   **CRC 3.1322**

    Moving and supporting papers, filing and serving   **CRC 3.1300**

    Preparation of court orders by prevailing party   **CRC 3.1312**

    Proof of service, time for filing   **CRC 3.1300**

    Shortening time, application for order   **CRC 3.1300**

    Venue, moving to strike, demur or plead following denial of motion to transfer   **CRC 3.1326**

Transcript of law and motion proceedings, availability of   **CRC 3.1310**

Trial date

    Motion or application to advance, specially set or reset   **CRC 3.1335**

Unlawful detainer

    Quash or stay, motions in summary proceedings involving real property possession   **CRC 3.1327**

Venue, motion for change of   **CRC 3.1326**

Writs

    Administrative mandate cases, lodging of record   **CRC 3.1140**

    Driving license suspension, stay of   **CRC 3.1142**

LAW BOOKS

Presumptions of accuracy of   **Ev 645**

LAW CLERKS

Small claims court judges, law clerks assisting   **CCP 116.270**

LAW ENFORCEMENT AGENCIES

Domestic violence orders (See **DOMESTIC VIOLENCE**)

Harassment, enforcing protective orders against   **CCP 527.6**

Real Estate Fraud Prosecution Trust Fund, procedures for distributions from   **Gov 27388**

LAW ENFORCEMENT OFFICERS

Arbitration procedure in collective bargaining agreement (See **ARBITRATION, subhead: Firefighters and law enforcement officers**)

Arrest (See **ARREST**)

Claims against public entities and employees (See **CLAIMS AGAINST PUBLIC ENTITIES AND EMPLOYEES**)

Contempt orders, stay of execution of   **CCP 128**

Decedent's tangible personal property to surviving spouse, delivery of   **Pro 330**

Defamation action brought by   **CC 47.5**

Deprivation of individual's constitutionally protected rights, privileges or immunities, prohibition against   **CC 52.3**

Dogs

    Assignment of officer to canine unit outside jurisdiction

        Discrimination in lodging, eating, or transportation due to dog   **CC 54.25**

Domestic violence prevention orders (See **DOMESTIC VIOLENCE**)

Harassment, serving and enforcing protective orders against   **CCP 527.6**

Immunity (See **CLAIMS AGAINST PUBLIC ENTITIES AND EMPLOYEES**)

LAW ENFORCEMENT OFFICERS—Cont.

Injuries willfully inflicted on peace officers, responsibility for   **CC 1714.9**

Jury duty

    Criminal proceedings, exclusion as juror   **CCP 219**

    Scheduling accommodations   **CCP 219.5, CRC 2.1004**

Lost property, duties as to   **CC 2080.1 to 2080.5**

Missing persons, search for   **Pro 12406**

Resuscitative measures, requests regarding   **Pro 4780 to 4786**

    Health care providers   **Pro 4781**

Unemployment insurance administration, right to disclosure of information obtained through   **Ev 1040**

Warrants for arrest (See **ARREST**)

Witnesses, peace officers as (See **WITNESSES**)

Work-related death, health care benefits for survivors

    Continuity for survivors   **Pro 13600**

LAW SCHOOLS

Certified law students

    Practice under supervision   **CRC 9.42**

Examining committee, schools unaccredited with   **CRC 9.30**

Judges, teaching by   **CRCSupp JudEthicsCanons 4, 5**

Legal services programs

    Registered legal services attorneys   **CRC 9.45**

Small claims courts, law students assisting litigants in   **CCP 116.940, CRC 3.2120**

Unaccredited schools   **CRC 9.30**

    Study in unaccredited law schools   **CRC 9.30**

LAW STUDENTS

Certified law student program   **CRC 9.42**

Small claims courts, law students assisting litigants in   **CCP 116.940, CRC 3.2120**

Unaccredited law schools, study in   **CRC 9.30**

LAWYERS (See **ATTORNEYS**)

LAYAWAY PLANS   **CC 1749 to 1749.4**

Defined   **CC 1749.1**

LAYING FOUNDATION (See **EVIDENCE**)

LEASES

Abandonment by lessee   **CC 1951 to 1951.7, 1954, CCP 415.47**

Administration of estates (See **ADMINISTRATION OF ESTATES**)

Agricultural land, limitations on leasing   **CC 717**

Arbitration under   **CC 1942.1, 1942.5**

Asian language contracts, translations   **CC 1632**

Assignments

    Commercial real property leases, transfer of (See subhead: **Commercial real property leases**)

    Creditors, assignee occupying leased business premises subject to assignment for benefit of   **CC 1954.1**

    Subrogation, right of (See subhead: **Subrogation rights**)

    Trust deed or mortgage, assignment in connection with (See **TRUST DEEDS AND MORTGAGES**)

Attachments on   **CCP 487.010**

Automobiles (See **AUTOMOBILES**)

Blanket encumbrance, required notice to purchaser or lessee of   **CC 1133**

Blind persons, right to lease housing accommodations   **CC 54.1, 54.3, 54.4, 55**

    Construction or application of provisions in issue, solicitor general notified   **CC 55.2**

Breach of lease, statutes of limitations on action involving (See subhead: **Statutes of limitation**)

Broker's duty to inspect premises   **CC 2079 to 2079.5**

Change of term of lease period   **CC 827**

City property, lease of   **CC 719**

LEASES—Cont.

Subleases—Cont.

Lessor's remedies for abandoned lease subject to lessee's right to sublet property, availability of **CC 1951.4**

Subletting (See subhead: **Subleases**)

Subrogation rights

Lessee's remedies against assigns of lessor for breach **CC 823**

Lessor's remedies against assignee of lessee for breach **CC 822**

Surrender, landlord entering after **CC 1954**

Termination of lease

Inspection by landlord **CC 1950.5**

Notice requirements **CC 1946.1**

Rights of parties after **CC 1951 to 1951.7**

Statutes of limitation (See subhead: **Statutes of limitation**)

Victims of domestic violence, sexual assault or stalking

Termination of tenancy **CC 1946.7**

30 years after execution of instrument, invalidity of lease if possession does not commence within **CC 715**

Trust deeds, notification of foreclosure of **CC 2924b**

Trusts (See **TRUSTS**)

Unclaimed property (See **UNCLAIMED PROPERTY**)

Unlawful detainer (See **UNLAWFUL DETAINER**)

Use restrictions (See subhead: **Commercial real property leases**)

Vacation of premises, rights of parties after **CC 1951 to 1951.7**

Waiver

Clause in lease, requirements for **CC 1953**

Restrictions on right to **CC 1942.1**

Warranty protection for leased goods **CC 1791, 1795.4**

Water supply, requirements for furnishing **CC 1941.1**

Weather, protecting from **CC 1941.1**

Writing requirements **CC 1624, CCP 1971**

LEGAL AID

Registered legal services attorneys **CRC 9.45**

LEGAL DISABILITIES (See **STATUTES OF LIMITATION**)

LEGAL ESTATES PRINCIPAL AND INCOME LAW

Administrative expenses, allocation of **CC 731.15**

Animals, allocation of receipts for **CC 731.10**

Applicability of Act **CC 731.02, 731.04**

Bonds, allocation of **CC 731.08**

Citation of Act **CC 731**

Construction and interpretation **CC 731.05**

Continuation of business, use of principal for **CC 731.09**

Corporate assets, distribution of **CC 731.07**

Death of tenant, effect of **CC 731.06**

Definitions **CC 731.03**

Delayed income, allocation of **CC 731.13**

Depletion, allocation of property subject to **CC 731.12**

Management expenses, allocation of **CC 731.15**

Mortgage payments, apportionment of **CC 731.14**

Natural resources, allocation of receipts for **CC 731.11**

Sale of property, allocation of gain on **CC 731.14**

Saving clause of Act **CC 731.01**

Termination of tenant's right to income **CC 731.06**

LEGAL MALPRACTICE (See **MALPRACTICE**)

LEGAL RESEARCH

Small claims court judges, law clerks assisting **CCP 116.270**

LEGAL SEPARATION Fam 2000

Action for breach of fiduciary duty between spouses **Fam 1101**

Affidavit, proof of grounds by **Fam 2336**

Assets and liabilities, disclosure of **Fam 2100 to 2113**

Attorney's fees and costs **Fam 270 to 274, 2010, 2030 to 2034, 2040**

LEGAL SEPARATION—Cont.

Case management plan for allocation of attorneys' fees **Fam 2032, 2034**

Concealment of property **Fam 2040 to 2045**

Conciliation petition affecting stay on filing petition for separation **Fam 1840**

Consent required for judgment **Fam 2345**

Contempt **CCP 1218**

Conversion of proceeding to dissolution proceeding **Fam 2321**

Decision of court on **Fam 2338**

Declaration of assets and liabilities **Fam 2100 to 2113**

Default judgment

Procedure for **Fam 2335.5, 2338.5**

Proof required for **Fam 2336**

Waiver of final declaration of financial disclosure **Fam 2110**

Disclosure of assets and liabilities **Fam 2100 to 2113**

Division of property

Income tax liability, joint **Fam 2628**

Domestic partnerships **CRC 5.28**

Earnings and accumulations while living separate and apart are separate property **Fam 771, 772**

Encumbering property, restrictions on **Fam 754, 2040 to 2045**

Expenses and income, disclosure of **Fam 2100 to 2113**

Extension of time **Fam 2339**

Family law information centers for unrepresented low-income litigants **Fam 15000 to 15012**

Family rules

Domestic partnerships

Dissolution, legal separation, or annulment **CRC 5.28**

Parties

Husband and wife or domestic partners as parties **CRC 5.102**

Title IV-D support enforcement

Consolidation of support orders **CRC 5.365**

Fees

Superior court fees

First paper, filing **Gov 70670**

Financial assets and liabilities

Sealing pleadings concerning financial assets and liabilities **Fam 2024.6**

Forms

Judicial council legal forms **CRCAppx A**

Grounds for **Fam 2310**

Income and expenses, disclosure of **Fam 2100 to 2113**

Income tax liability, joint **Fam 2628**

Joinder of parties **Fam 2021**

Judgments **CRC 5.134, Fam 2338**

Consent required for **Fam 2345**

Final **Fam 2339, 2342**

Notice of entry of judgment **CRC 5.136**

Protective orders included in **Fam 2049, 6360, 6361**

Relief from **Fam 2120 to 2129**

Subsequent judgment for dissolution not barred by **Fam 2347**

Jurisdiction **Fam 2010 to 2013**

Military personnel, waiver of respondent's filing fees for **Gov 70673**

Notice of entry of judgment **CRC 5.134, 5.136**

Notice to parties advising review of wills, insurance policies, etc **Fam 2024**

Pendency of proceeding, recording notice of **Fam 754**

Petitions

Generally **Fam 2330**

Amendment to convert proceeding to dissolution proceeding **Fam 2321**

Contents of **Fam 2330**

LIENS—Cont.

Auctioned items, disclosure of liens on   **CC 1812.607**
Automobiles (See **AUTOMOBILES**)
Bankers' liens   **CC 3054**
Bankruptcy affecting   **CCP 493.030 to 493.050**
Blanket encumbrances, required notice to purchaser or lessee of   **CC 1133**
Blanket liens, priority of   **CC 2899**
Boarding houses   **CC 1861 to 1861.28**
Bonded stop notice   **CC 3083, 3156 to 3175**
Bottomry lien regulations applicable to   **CC 2877**
Breeders' liens   **CC 3062 to 3064.1**
Carriers' liens (See **COMMON CARRIERS**)
Cause of action, lien on   **CRC 3.1360**
Cessation, notice of
  Recordation
    Notice of recordation by owner   **CC 3259.5**
Child support (See **CHILD SUPPORT**)
Claims against decedents' estates (See **CLAIMS AGAINST ESTATES**)
Cleaners' lien   **CC 3066**
Common carriers' liens (See **COMMON CARRIERS**)
Common interest developments (See **COMMON INTEREST DEVELOPMENTS**)
Completion, notice of
  Recordation
    Notice of recordation by owner   **CC 3259.5**
Concurrent liens, priority between   **CC 2899**
Condominiums (See **COMMON INTEREST DEVELOPMENTS**)
Construction liens (See **IMPROVEMENTS**)
Contract, creation by   **CC 2881**
Conversion extinguishing   **CC 2910**
Damages for conversion   **CC 3338**
Decedents' estates (See subhead: **Administration of decedents' estates**)
Defined   **CC 2872, CCP 1180**
Deposits (See **DEPOSITS**)
Design professionals' liens   **CC 3081.1 to 3081.10**
Disclosures on purchase money liens on residential property   **CC 2956 to 2967**
Discriminatory clauses in lien instruments, prohibition against   **CC 53, 782**
Earnings assignment for support   **Fam 5242**
Eminent domain (See **EMINENT DOMAIN**)
Enforcement of judgments (See **ENFORCEMENT OF JUDGMENTS**)
Expenditures concerning lien, recovery of   **CC 2892**
Factors   **CC 3053**
Family law attorney's real property lien   **Fam 2033, 2034**
Family support
  Judgments, abstract of
    Digital form of lien record   **Fam 17523.5**
Farm workers, liens by   **CC 3061 to 3061.6**
Federal Lien Registration Act   **CCP 2100 to 2107**
Fixtures   **CC 1013.5**
Floating homes (See **FLOATING HOMES**)
Foreclosure
  Generally   **CCP 726**
  Apartment housekeepers' lien   **CC 1861a**
  Appraisal on   **CCP 726**
  Attorneys' fees   **CCP 730**
  Boarding housekeeper's liens   **CC 1861**
  Deficiency judgments   **CCP 726**
  Deposit, lien for   **CC 1857**
  Hospital liens   **CC 1862.5**
  Hotelkeeper's liens   **CC 1861**
  Judgments   **CCP 726**
  Partial sales   **CCP 728**
  Stay of proceedings   **CCP 917.2**

LIENS—Cont.

Foreclosure—Cont.
  Surplus on   **CCP 727**
Forfeiture agreement, validity of   **CC 2889**
Forms
  Service dealer lien notice   **CC 3052.5**
  Wages, liens securing   **CC 3061.5, 3061.6**
Future act secured by   **CC 2884**
Garnishment proceedings (See **GARNISHMENT**)
General liens defined   **CC 2873, 2874**
Harvester's liens   **CC 3061.5, 3061.6**
Health care liens   **CC 3040**
Home equity loans   **CC 2970 to 2971**
Homesteads (See **HOMESTEADS**)
Horses (See **HORSES**)
Hospital liens (See **HOSPITALS**)
Implied obligations   **CC 2890**
Improvements (See **IMPROVEMENTS**)
Income tax (federal), registration act for   **CCP 2100 to 2107**
Inferior liens
  Dwelling, lienholder served with notice of removal of occupant from   **CCP 700.080**
  Mobilehomes (See **MOBILEHOMES**)
  Priorities   **CC 2897 to 2899**
  Redemption   **CC 2904**
Information Practices Act, disclosure under   **CC 1798.67**
Jewelers' liens   **CC 3052a**
Judgment liens (See **JUDGMENTS**)
Junior liens (See subhead: **Inferior liens**)
Labor performed   **CC 3051, 3051a, 3052**
Law and motion rule of court regarding motion to grant lien on cause of action   **CRC 3.1360**
Livestock (See **LIVESTOCK**)
Loggers   **CC 3065 to 3065c**
Lottery prize, procedure for enforcement of lien against   **CCP 708.755**
Mechanics' liens (See **MECHANICS' LIENS**)
Mining liens   **CC 3060**
Mistakes, effect of   **CC 3261**
Mobilehomes (See **MOBILEHOMES**)
Mortgage foreclosure consultants taking   **CC 2945.4**
Mortgages (See **TRUST DEEDS AND MORTGAGES**)
New trial, procedure for   **CC 3259**
Oil and gas (See **OIL AND GAS**)
Operation of law, creation by   **CC 2881, 2882**
Option granted to secured party, priority of   **CC 2906**
Original obligation, security limited to   **CC 2891**
Parking facilities   **CC 3067 to 3074**
Partial performance, effect of   **CC 2912**
Partition (See **PARTITION**)
Pending actions or proceedings, liens in   **CRC 3.1360**
Performance of main obligation, effect of   **CC 2909, 2912**
Personal services secured by   **CC 3051**
Pledge transactions, lien regulations applicable to   **CC 2877**
Possession, lien dependent on   **CC 2913, 3051**
Postponed property taxes, notice of default on property subject to lien for   **CC 2924b**
Priorities
  Generally   **CC 2897 to 2899**
  Option granted to secured party, priority of   **CC 2906**
Procedure for enforcement   **CC 3259 to 3267**
Protective ex parte order determining payment of liens   **Fam 6324**
Publication of notice of   **CC 3052.5**
Public improvements (See **PUBLIC CONTRACTS AND WORKS**)
Purchase money liens on residential property, disclosures on   **CC 2956 to 2967**
Recreational vehicle parks (See **RECREATIONAL VEHICLE PARKS**)

MALPRACTICE—Cont.

Health care providers—Cont.

Death of judgment creditor, modification of periodic payments on **CCP 667.7**

Declaration of rights of insurers **CCP 1062.5**

Defined **CCP 340.5, 364**

Failure to comply with notice requirement **CCP 365**

Form for arbitration clause in medical services contract **CCP 1295**

Indemnification by state **Gov 827**

Insurance

Arbitration, applicability of **CCP 1295**

Declaration of rights of professional liability insurer **CCP 1062.5**

Indemnification **Gov 827**

Punitive damages award against insurer, special notice of **CC 3296**

Third-party cause of action for unfair claims settlement practices, applicability of provisions for **CC 2871**

Judgment liens against **CCP 697.320, 697.350, 697.380 to 697.400**

Multiphasic screening units, patients referred by **CC 43.9**

Noneconomic losses, recovery for **CC 3333.2**

Notice

Arbitration clause in medical services contract **CCP 1295**

Insurer, special notice of punitive damages award against **CC 3296**

Intention to commence action **CCP 364**

Periodic payment of future damages **CCP 667.7**

Preference, setting for trial on grant of motion for **CCP 36**

Professional negligence defined **CCP 364**

Punitive damages, claim for **CCP 425.13**

Recommendation of medical staff, limited immunity from liability for action taken on **CC 43.97**

Release of state from claim against **CC 1542.1**

Separate trial of defense of statutes of limitation **CCP 597.5**

Sexual harassment, civil action for

Construction or application of provisions in issue, solicitor general notified **CC 51.1**

Statutes of limitation

Actions for injury or death **CCP 340.5**

Punitive damages, time for filing amended pleading for **CCP 425.13**

Separate trial of defense of statutes of limitation **CCP 597.5**

Undertaking to secure costs in action against **CCP 1029.6**

Indemnification of health care providers by state **Gov 827**

Insurance (See subhead: **Health care providers**)

Legal malpractice (See subhead: **Attorneys**)

Medical malpractice (See subhead: **Health care providers**)

Professional negligence defined **CCP 340.5, 364**

Release of state from claim against health care provider **CC 1542.1**

Statutes of limitation

Architects (See **ARCHITECTS**)

Engineers (See **ENGINEERING**)

Health care providers (See subhead: **Health care providers**)

Legal malpractice **CCP 340.6**

Surveyors (See **SURVEYS AND SURVEYORS**)

Surveyors (See **SURVEYS AND SURVEYORS**)

Unlicensed person, treble damages for injury caused by **CCP 1029.8**

MANAGED HEALTH CARE (See HEALTH CARE SERVICE PLANS)

MANAGEMENT

Agent managing business **CC 2319**

Apartment houses, requirements for notice of manager of **CC 1961 to 1962.5**

Common interest developments (See **COMMON INTEREST DEVELOPMENTS**)

Mobilehome parks **CC 798.2**

Trustee **Pro 16227**

MANDAMUS

Abuse of discretion, administrative body **CCP 1094.5**

Adequacy of other remedy **CCP 1086**

Administrative orders or decision, review of (See **ADMINISTRATIVE ADJUDICATION**)

Alternative writs **CCP 1087, 1088**

Answer **CCP 1089, 1089.5**

Change of venue, petition for writ of mandate on grant or denial of motion for **CCP 400**

Claims against public entities and employees (See **CLAIMS AGAINST PUBLIC ENTITIES AND EMPLOYEES**)

Contents of writ **CCP 1087**

Coordination of actions **CCP 404.6**

Costs **CCP 1094.5, 1095**

Countervailing return **CCP 1091**

Damages, recovery of **CCP 1095**

Default judgments **CCP 585, 586**

Default, prohibition against granting writ by **CCP 1088**

Defined **CCP 1084**

Demurrer **CCP 1089**

Disobedience of writ **CCP 1097**

Disqualification of judge, review of determination re **CCP 170.3**

Emancipation of minors, petition for **Fam 7123**

Eminent domain proceedings **CCP 1245.255**

Food and Agriculture Department, special procedures for mandamus proceedings against **CCP 1085.5**

Hearings **CCP 1094, 1094.5, 1094.6**

Irrigation cases, appeal from **CCP 1110a**

Judgment on peremptory writ **CCP 1094**

Jurisdiction (See **JURISDICTION**)

Jury, trial by **CCP 1090**

Local agency decisions **CCP 1094.6**

New trial, motion for **CCP 1092**

Notice

Application on notice **CCP 1088**

Argument of application **CCP 1093**

Notice of pendency of action (See **PENDENCY OF ACTIONS**)

Peremptory writs **CCP 1087, 1088, 1097**

Pest control and eradication, special procedure for **CCP 1085.5**

Petition **CCP 1086**

Public entity, damages and costs where respondent is officer of **CCP 1095**

Reclassification of action, review of order granting or denying **CCP 403.080**

Record of proceedings

Local agency decisions, review of **CCP 1094.6**

Retention or destruction of **CCP 1094.5**

Return of writ **CCP 1089, 1108**

Service

Petition, service of **CCP 1088**

Prerogative writs, service of application for **CCP 1107**

Proof of service of petition **CCP 1088.5**

Writ, service of **CCP 1096**

Settlement in good faith, review of determination of **CCP 877.6**

Stay of proceedings

Administrative order or decision stayed pending judgment **CCP 1094.5**

When appeal does not stay **CCP 1110a, 1110b**

Summons, quashing service of **CCP 418.10**

MICROFILM—Cont.

Indexes accessible by   **CRC 10.851**

Judgments recorded on   **CCP 668.5**

Lost or destroyed writings   **Ev 1551**

MILEAGE

Depositions (See **DEPOSITIONS**)

Subpoena duces tecum, mileage costs for   **Ev 1563**

MILITARY

Absentees (See subhead: **Missing persons**)

Acknowledgment of instruments   **CC 1183.5**

Adoption proceedings, absence of adoptive parent serving in military   **Fam 8613**

Annulment of marriage or legal separation, waiver of respondent's filing fees in action for   **Gov 70673**

Attack shelters, governmental liability   **CC 1714.5**

Attorney representation by military counsel   **CRC 9.41**

Child support

    Arrears collection

        Compromise of arrears program   **Fam 17560**

    Modification of support

        Active duty   **Fam 3651, 3653**

        Government support enforcement services   **Fam 17440**

Consumer warranty protection

    Motor vehicle purchased in US   **CC 1791.8**

Custody of children

    Absence or relocation of parent from family residence as consideration for court in awarding custody or visitation

        Active service in military   **Fam 3047**

Discharge from service records, waiver of recording fees for   **Gov 27381**

Dissolution of marriage or legal separation, waiver of respondent's filing fees in action for   **Gov 70673**

Dogs used in police work, injuries inflicted by   **CC 3342, 3342.5**

Family support

    Modification of support

        Active duty   **Fam 3651, 3653**

Fiduciaries substituted during wartime (See **FIDUCIARIES' WARTIME SUBSTITUTION LAW**)

Infants (See **PARENT AND CHILD**)

Investigative agencies, military identification card as identification   **CC 1786.22**

Judge advocate, appearance in state court   **CRC 9.41**

Judges   **CRCSupp JudEthicsCanon 2**

Marriage

    Overseas personnel

        Attorney-in-fact may appear on behalf of personnel stationed overseas to solemnize marriage   **Fam 420**

Minor's enlistment in armed forces   **Fam 6950**

Missing persons

    Generally   **Pro 3700**

    Agency, revocation of   **CC 2357**

    Fiduciaries substituted during wartime (See **FIDUCIARIES' WARTIME SUBSTITUTION LAW**)

    Judicial proceedings to set aside personal property of   **Pro 3701 to 3708**

    Management of personal property without court proceeding   **Pro 3710 to 3712**

    Power of attorney   **Pro 3720 to 3722**

Paternity suit, waiver of filing fees for defendant in   **Gov 70673**

POWs (See subhead: **Missing persons**)

Small claims actions, appearance in   **CCP 116.540**

Spousal support

    Modification of support

        Active duty   **Fam 3651, 3653**

MILITARY—Cont.

Statutory violations in caring out orders of military commander   **CC 1714.6**

Veterans Administration (See **VETERANS ADMINISTRATION**)

Warranties

    Consumer warranty protection

        Motor vehicle purchased in US   **CC 1791.8**

MILK (See **DAIRIES AND DAIRY PRODUCTS**)

MINERALS AND MINERAL RIGHTS

Abandonment of mineral rights

    Generally   **CC 883.130**

        Lessee's responsibility after   **CC 883.140**

Applicability of chapter   **CC 883.120, 883.270**

Attachment (See **ATTACHMENT**)

Attorneys' fees in actions involving preservation of   **CC 883.250**

Definitions   **CC 883.110**

Dormant mineral rights (See subhead: **Termination of mineral rights**)

Easement rights   **CC 801, 802**

Enforcement of judgments (See **ENFORCEMENT OF JUDGMENTS**)

Expenses of litigation, late notice of intent to preserve mineral rights upon payment of   **CC 883.250**

Gas (See **OIL AND GAS**)

Intent to preserve mineral rights (See subhead: **Preservation of mineral rights**)

Municipal land leased for production of mineral   **CC 718, 718f**

Notices

    Entry on land by mineral rights owner, notice of   **CC 848**

    Preservation of mineral rights (See subhead: **Preservation of mineral rights**)

Oil (See **OIL AND GAS**)

Preservation of mineral rights

    General notice of intent to preserve mineral rights   **CC 883.230**

    Late notice of intent to preserve mineral rights upon payment of litigation expenses   **CC 883.250**

Principal and income allocations of investments in   **CC 731.11, Pro 16363**

Termination of mineral rights

    Generally   **CC 883.210, 883.240**

    Abandonment (See subhead: **Abandonment of mineral rights**)

    Conditions for dormant mineral right   **CC 883.220**

    Unenforceability of terminated mineral right   **CC 883.260**

Trust assets (See **TRUSTS**)

MINES AND MINING

Administration of estate (See **ADMINISTRATION OF ESTATES**)

Bill of sale for mining machinery   **CC 1631**

Continuance of trial concerning claims on   **CCP 595.3**

Co-owners failing to pay taxes   **CCP 850 to 856**

Customs, usages or regulations, admission of evidence of established   **CCP 748**

Entry on land

    Right of entry on mining lease, action to terminate   **CCP 772.010 to 772.060**

    To conduct survey   **CCP 742, 743**

Hearings for co-owners failing to pay taxes   **CCP 854**

Judgments on co-owners failing to pay taxes   **CCP 855**

Liens by miners   **CC 3060**

Machinery, sales of   **CC 1631**

Minerals and mineral rights (See **MINERALS AND MINERAL RIGHTS**)

Notice to co-owners failing to pay taxes   **CCP 851**

Index

Index

Index

NAMES—Cont.

Commercial blockage tort, pseudonyms used in civil proceedings for **CC 3427.3**

Complaint, names of parties in title **CCP 422.40**

Deeds (See **DEEDS**)

Dissolution of marriage, restoration of former name in proceedings for **Fam 2080 to 2082, 2401**

Doe defendants, generally (See **UNKNOWN PERSONS**)

Fictitious names (See **FICTITIOUS NAMES**)

Invasion of privacy, unauthorized use of name or likeness in advertising as **CC 3344, 3344.1**

Judgment lien on property of misidentified owner, release of **CCP 697.410, 697.660**

Juror personal information (See **JURY**)

Owner of property (See **TITLE AND OWNERSHIP**)

Pleadings, amendment of **CCP 473**

Prohibition against refusal to engage in business with person using birth or former name regardless of marital status **CCP 1279.6**

Restoration of former name **Fam 2080 to 2082, 2401**

Small claims court (See **SMALL CLAIMS COURTS**)

True name of defendant designated as unknown, amendment to add **CCP 474**

NARCOTICS AND DANGEROUS DRUGS

Abuse of (See **SUBSTANCE ABUSE**)

Custody of children

Substance abuse as custody determining factor

Testing for alcohol or controlled substance use ordered by court **Fam 3041.5**

Guardian and ward, custody of child

Substance abuse as custody determining factor

Testing for alcohol or controlled substance use ordered by court **Fam 3041.5**

Marriage license denied to persons under influence of **Fam 352**

Mobilehome tenancy terminated for conviction of use on premises **CC 798.56**

Nuisance actions (See **NUISANCES**)

Overdoses

Emergency medical care to treat

Naloxone hydrochloride, immunity from liability **CC 1714.22**

Pharmacists and pharmacies (See **PHARMACISTS AND PHARMACIES**)

Unlawful detainer proceedings based on tenant's drug-selling on premises **CCP 1161**

NATIONAL BANKS (See **BANKS AND BANKING**)

NATIONAL INFLUENZA PROGRAM

Public entity or employee participating in program, immunity of **Gov 856.6**

NATIONAL ORIGIN

Adoption proceedings, prohibited discrimination in **Fam 8708**

Discrimination **CC 51 to 53**

Foster care placement **Fam 7950**

Jury service exemption not allowed based on **CCP 204**

NATIONAL PARKS

Appropriation of water originating in **CC 1422**

NATIVE AMERICANS

Abandoned children

Transfer by parent of care, custody and control to Indian custodian as not constituting abandonment **Fam 7822**

Adoption (See **ADOPTION**)

Conservation easements held by tribes **CC 815.3**

Conservatorship proceedings for Indian children

Applicability of Indian Child Welfare Act **Pro 1459.5**

NATIVE AMERICANS—Cont.

Conservatorship proceedings for Indian children—Cont.

Attorneys

Inability to afford counsel **Pro 1474**

Involuntary placements

Indian Child Welfare Act, rules governing **CRC 5.480 to 5.487** (See **INDIAN CHILD WELFARE ACT INVOLUNTARY PLACEMENTS**)

Legislative findings and intent **Pro 1459**

Notice

Indian children as proposed conservatee **Pro 1460.2**

Custody of children (See **CUSTODY OF CHILDREN**)

Dependency proceedings

Generally (See **DEPENDENT CHILDREN**)

Placement under Indian Child Welfare Act **CRC 5.565, 5.570**

Rules governing involuntary placements **CRC 5.480 to 5.487** (See **INDIAN CHILD WELFARE ACT INVOLUNTARY PLACEMENTS**)

Tribal rights in **CRC 5.534**

Divorces, validity of **Fam 295**

Foster placements

Involuntary placements

Indian Child Welfare Act, rules governing **CRC 5.480 to 5.487** (See **INDIAN CHILD WELFARE ACT INVOLUNTARY PLACEMENTS**)

Gaming rights

Injunction to protect **CCP 1811**

Guardianship proceedings for Indian children

Applicability of Indian Child Welfare Act **Pro 1459.5**

Attorneys

Inability to afford counsel **Pro 1474**

Investigation and report **Pro 1513**

Involuntary placements

Indian Child Welfare Act, rules governing **CRC 5.480 to 5.487** (See **INDIAN CHILD WELFARE ACT INVOLUNTARY PLACEMENTS**)

Legislative findings and intent **Pro 1459**

Notices

Indian children as proposed ward **Pro 1460.2, 1511**

Petition, contents **Pro 1510**

Termination of guardianship **Pro 1601**

Indian Child Welfare Act

Involuntary placements, rules governing **CRC 5.480 to 5.487** (See **INDIAN CHILD WELFARE ACT INVOLUNTARY PLACEMENTS**)

Interstate compact on placement of children

Applicability to Indian children **Fam 7907.3**

Intestate succession **Fam 295**

Juvenile wardship proceedings

Involuntary placements, rules governing **CRC 5.480 to 5.487** (See **INDIAN CHILD WELFARE ACT INVOLUNTARY PLACEMENTS**)

Marriage, validity of **Fam 295**

Termination of parental rights

Indian children **Fam 7892.5**

Involuntary placements **CRC 5.480 to 5.487** (See **INDIAN CHILD WELFARE ACT INVOLUNTARY PLACEMENTS**)

NATURAL CATASTROPHES

Boundary reestablishment **CCP 751.50 to 751.65**

Business records destroyed by **CCP 1953.10 to 1953.13**

Contract performance prevented by **CC 1511**

Court record destroyed by **CCP 1953 to 1953.06**

Destroyed land records relief law **CCP 751.01 to 751.28**

NEWLY DISCOVERED EVIDENCE
New trial because of　CCP 657

NEWS MEDIA
Newspapers and magazines (See **NEWSPAPERS AND MAGA-ZINES**)
Radio and television (See **RADIO AND TELEVISION**)

NEWSPAPERS AND MAGAZINES
Administration of decedent's estate, publication of notice of petition for　**Pro 8121**
Attorneys
　　Advertising and solicitation restrictions　**ProfC 1-400**
　　Compensation for publicity for attorney or law firm, prohibition of　**ProfC 1-320**
　　Trial publicity, restrictions concerning　**ProfC 5-120**
Contempt
　　Disruption of proceedings　**CCP 1209**
　　Journalist in contempt for failure to testify, findings of court required for holding　**CCP 1986.1**
　　Privilege against disclosure of sources　**Ev 1070**
Court proceedings, media coverage　**CRC 1.150**
Indecency and obscenity (See **INDECENCY AND OBSCENITY**)
Journalists (See **JOURNALISTS**)
Judges' writings, Code of Judicial Ethics provisions concerning
　　CRCSupp JudEthicsCanons 2, 4
Levied property, advertising sale of　**CCP 701.545**
Libel
　　Correction demands　**CC 48a**
　　Fair comment doctrine　**CC 47**
　　Official proceedings published　**CC 47**
Missing person, notice of search for　**Pro 12406**
Official proceedings, privilege attaching report on　**CC 47**
Pornography (See **INDECENCY AND OBSCENITY**)
Presumption regarding publications purporting to be newspapers or periodicals　**Ev 645.1**
Privilege against disclosure of sources　**Ev 1070**
Seller assisted marketing plan defined　**CC 1812.201**
Telegrams for publication in newspapers, priority for transmitting
　　CC 2207
Trials
　　Attorney conduct relative to trial publicity　**ProfC 5-120**
　　Court proceedings, restrictions on media coverage of　**CRC 1.150**

NEWSREELS (See **MOTION PICTURES**)

NEW TRIAL
Administration of estates proceedings　**Pro 7220**
Affidavits
　　Grounds for new trial requiring filing of supporting affidavit
　　　CCP 658
　　Motion for new trial, affidavit in support of　**CCP 659a**
　　Time for service of　**CCP 659a**
Appeals　**CCP 906**
　　Order on motion for, appeal from
　　　Extension of time　**CRC 8.108**
　　　Superior courts, limited civil cases in appellate division
　　　　Motion for new trial　**CRC 8.823**
　　　Supreme court and courts of appeal
　　　　Notice of appeal, extension of time to file　**CRC 8.108**
Bifurcated trial, motion following　**CRC 3.1591**
Bill of exceptions, loss of　**CCP 663.1**
Court reporter (See subhead: **Reporter**)
Courts of appeal authorized to direct　**CCP 43**
Damages
　　Excessive or inadequate damages　**CCP 662.5**
　　Grounds for new trial　**CCP 657**
　　Reduction of　**CCP 662.5**

NEW TRIAL—Cont.
Death or disability of court reporter as grounds for　**CCP 657.1, 914**
Defined　**CCP 656**
Denial of motion, extension of time for appeal　**CRC 8.108**
Discretion abuse as ground for　**CCP 657**
Dismissal actions regarding　**CCP 583.320**
Dissolution of marriage (See **DISSOLUTION OF MARRIAGE**)
Evidence
　　Grounds for new trial　**CCP 657**
　　Motions, evidence supporting　**CCP 660**
Extensions of time　**CCP 659, 659a, 663a**
Fire destroying bill of exceptions　**CCP 663.1**
Grounds for　**CCP 657**
Hearings　**CCP 660, 663.2**
Judicial arbitration (See **JUDICIAL ARBITRATION**)
Jury misconduct as grounds for new trial　**CCP 657**
Law errors as grounds for　**CCP 657**
Lien enforcement proceedings　**CC 3259**
Mandamus　**CCP 1092**
Mandatory time to bring action to trial
　　Generally　**CCP 583.320**
　　Computation of　**CCP 583.340**
　　Extension of time　**CCP 583.330, 583.350**
　　Failure to obtain action within time limit, effect of　**CCP 583.360**
Mediation, new trial on grounds of irregular reference to　**CCP 1775.12, Ev 1128**
Motion for new trial
　　Affidavit in support of new trial motion　**CCP 659a**
　　Bifurcated trial, motion following　**CRC 3.1591**
　　Evidence considered on　**CCP 660**
　　Hearings on　**CCP 660, 663.2**
　　Memorandum in support of　**CRC 3.1600**
　　Notice of　**CCP 659**
　　Ruling on motion, alternatives　**CCP 662**
　　Time for filing　**CCP 659**
　　Trial judge determining　**CCP 661**
Natural catastrophe destroying bill of exceptions　**CCP 663.1**
Newly-discovered evidence as ground for　**CCP 657**
Nonjury cases　**CCP 662**
Reporter
　　Death or disability of court reporter, effect of　**CCP 657.1, 914**
　　Hearings on new trial motion, use of transcripts at　**CCP 660**
Reviewing court's authority to order new trial　**CCP 906**
Ruling on motion, alternatives　**CCP 662**
Service of papers
　　Motion for new trial　**CCP 659**
　　Supporting affidavit for new trial　**CCP 659a**
Special proceedings　**CCP 1110**
Supreme Court authorized to direct　**CCP 43**
Surprise as grounds for　**CCP 657**
Trial court rules
　　Notice of intention to move for
　　　Memorandum in support of　**CRC 3.1600**
Unlawful detainer　**CCP 1178**
Will probate proceedings　**Pro 7220**

NEXT BUSINESS DAY
Extension of time to next day which is not a holiday　**CCP 12a**
Postponing performance from holiday to　**CCP 13**

NIGHT SESSIONS
Small claims court sessions　**CCP 116.250**

99-YEAR LEASE
Validity of　**CC 718, 718f**

NO CONTEST CLAUSES (See **WILL PROBATE**)

NURSING HOMES—Cont.
Employment agencies, referrals from—Cont.
    Prevention of patient abuse, policies and procedures of
      employment agency for   **CC 1812.543**
Ombudsman or advocate for patient in skilled nursing facility,
  Health Care Decisions Law provision for   **Pro 4675**
Public administrator of death of patient, notification of   **Pro
7600.5**
Statutes of limitation for recovery or conversion of personal
  property left at   **CCP 341a**

O

OATHS
Generally   **CCP 2015.6, 2093 to 2094**
Administrative Procedure Act (See **ADMINISTRATIVE PRO-
  CEDURE ACT**)
Administrators (See **EXECUTORS AND ADMINISTRA-
  TORS**)
Arbitration   **CCP 1282.8**
    Judicial arbitration   **CRC 3.824**
Attachment (See **ATTACHMENT**)
Claims and delivery possession writ, application for   **CCP
512.010**
County recorder's fees for administering or certifying   **Gov
27379**
Declaration or certification of written instrument executed under
  penalty of perjury   **CCP 2015.5**
Dependent persons   **Ev 710**
Depositions
    Oath of deponent   **CCP 2025.330**
Executors (See **EXECUTORS AND ADMINISTRATORS**)
Form of   **CCP 2094**
Inclusions in definition   **CCP 17**
Innkeeper's liens, writ of possession on   **CC 1861.5**
Judges
    Temporary judges   **CRC 2.814**
        Request by parties for temporary judge   **CRC 2.831**
Jurors, oath sworn by   **CCP 232**
Jury commissioner's power to administer   **CCP 196**
Manner of administering oath or affirmation   **CCP 2094**
Parties administering   **CCP 2093**
Penalty of perjury, declaration or certification of written instru-
  ment executed under   **CCP 2015.5**
Power of court to administer   **CCP 128**
Power of judge to administer   **CCP 177**
Proofs of execution of instruments, officers administering oaths
  for   **CC 1201**
Public guardians appointed as guardian or conservator, oaths
  required for   **Pro 2922**
Receivers, faithful performance of   **CCP 567**
Shorthand reporters at deposition proceedings, oaths administered
  by   **CCP 2093**
State agency proceedings (See **ADMINISTRATIVE PROCE-
  DURE ACT**)
Statutory requirement   **Ev 710**
Temporary restraining order, certification of attempt to notify
  party of   **CCP 527**
Translators and interpreters in court proceedings   **Ev 751**
Witnesses   **Ev 710**

OATS
Storage regulations after sale of   **CC 1880 to 1881.2**

OBJECTIONS AND EXCEPTIONS
Administrators of decedents' estates (See **EXECUTORS AND
  ADMINISTRATORS**)
Answers, objection to allegations in   **CCP 430.20**
Appealable orders deemed excepted to   **CCP 647**
Arbitration (See **ARBITRATION**)

OBJECTIONS AND EXCEPTIONS—Cont.
Blood test, submission of evidence on technique of taking
  Ev 712
Complaints, objection to allegations in   **CCP 430.10, 430.30**
Conservatorship proceedings (See **CONSERVATORS**)
Court reporters to take down all objections and exceptions made
  CCP 269
Cross-complaints, objection to allegations in   **CCP 430.10,
430.30**
Demurrers (See **DEMURRERS**)
Economic litigation provision excluding evidence or witness not
  included in statement   **CCP 97**
Eminent domain, objections to right to take in   **CCP 1250.350
  to 1250.370, 1260.110, 1260.120**
Enforcement of judgments (See **ENFORCEMENT OF JUDG-
  MENTS**)
Evidence erroneously admitted   **Ev 353**
Exception defined   **CCP 646**
Executors of decedents' estates (See **EXECUTORS AND AD-
  MINISTRATORS**)
Guardian and ward (See **GUARDIAN AND WARD**)
Interlocutory orders deemed excepted to   **CCP 647**
Judges (See **JUDGES**)
Judicial arbitration, exceptions to   **CCP 1141.13, 1141.15**
Jurisdiction, objection to   **CCP 418.10, 418.11**
Orders and rulings, exceptions to   **CCP 646, 647**
Pleadings, objections to   **CCP 430.10 to 430.80**
Referee's statement of decision   **CCP 645**
Reversed without exceptions, orders and rulings   **CCP 647**
Sterilization proceedings, objections by party to be sterilized in
  Pro 1958
Striking out or refusing to strike out pleading   **CCP 647**
Summary judgment hearing, waiver of objections not raised in
  CCP 437c
Superior courts (See **SUPERIOR COURTS**)
Surety and fidelity bonds (See **SURETYSHIP, BONDS AND
  UNDERTAKINGS**)
Time to except   **CCP 646**
Verdicts deemed excepted to   **CCP 647**

OBLIGATIONS
Abstaining from injuring person or property of another   **CC
1708**
Civil actions, obligations as basis for   **CCP 26**

OBSCENITY AND INDECENCY (See **INDECENCY AND
  OBSCENITY**)

OCCUPANCY (See **ADVERSE POSSESSION**)

OCCUPATION
Jury service exemption not allowed based on   **CCP 204**

OFFAL (See **GARBAGE**)

OFFENSES (See **CRIMINAL ACTIONS AND PROCEED-
  INGS**)

OFFER
Contracts (See **CONTRACTS AND AGREEMENTS**)
Settlement offers (See **SETTLEMENT AND COMPROMISE**)
Tender, refused offer as   **CCP 2074**

OFFICE
Service of process at office of person being served   **CCP 415.20**

OFFICE OF ADMINISTRATIVE LAW (See **ADMINISTRA-
  TIVE PROCEDURE ACT**)

OFFICE OF INFORMATION PRACTICES (See **INFOR-
  MATION PRACTICES ACT**)

ORDER TO SHOW CAUSE—Cont.
Temporary restraining order
Application for show cause order **CRC 3.1150**
Use **CRC 3.1150**

ORDINANCES
Advertising realty for sale, restrictions on **CC 713**
Leases of city property subject to **CC 719**
Lost property, providing for disposition of **CC 2080.4**
Pleading **CCP 459**
Rent control ordinances (See **RENT CONTROL**)

ORGANIZATIONS AND CLUBS (See **ASSOCIATIONS**)

ORIENTATION
Juror orientation **CCP 214**

ORIGINAL PROCEEDINGS IN APPELLATE COURTS
Habeas corpus **CRC 8.380 to 8.388**
Mandate, certiorari and prohibition in supreme court or court of appeal **CRC 8.485 to 8.493**

ORIGINAL WRIT (See **ATTACHMENT**)

ORNAMENTS
Fixtures removable **CC 1019**

ORPHANS
Abandoned children (See **PARENT AND CHILD**)
Adoption (See **ADOPTION**)

OSTEOPATHS
Bond required to secure costs in action against **CCP 1029.6**
Malpractice (See **MALPRACTICE**)
Mandamus for review of administrative order of agency issuing licenses **CCP 1094.5**
Medical records, attorney's authorized inspection of **CCP 1985.7, Ev 1158**

OTHER STATES
Acknowledgment of instruments **CC 1182, 1189**
Adoption (See **ADOPTION**)
Affidavits taking in **CCP 2013, 2015**
Ancillary administration (See **ANCILLARY ADMINISTRATION**)
Attachment (See **ATTACHMENT**)
Attorneys (See **ATTORNEYS**)
Certification of state-law questions to California Supreme Court by courts of last resort in other states and territories **CRC 8.548**
Child support (See **UNIFORM INTERSTATE FAMILY SUPPORT ACT**)
Community property (See **COMMUNITY PROPERTY**)
Conflict of laws (See **CONFLICT OF LAWS**)
Conservatorship proceedings (See **CONSERVATORS**)
Cum testamento annexo (See **ADMINISTRATORS WITH WILL ANNEXED**)
Custody proceedings (See **CUSTODY OF CHILDREN**)
Declaration or certification of written instrument executed under penalty of perjury **CCP 2015.5**
Depositions
Generally (See **DEPOSITIONS**)
Interstate and international depositions and discovery act **CCP 2029.100 to 2029.900** (See **DISCOVERY**)
Discovery
Interstate and international depositions and discovery act **CCP 2029.100 to 2029.900** (See **DISCOVERY**)
Divorce obtained in other state by parties domiciled in California **Fam 2090 to 2093**

OTHER STATES—Cont.
Domestic partnership
Same sex unions formed in other jurisdiction
Recognition of legal unions as domestic partnership **Fam 299.2**
Earnings assignments for support (See **EARNINGS ASSIGNMENT FOR SUPPORT**)
Escheat of property subject to **CCP 1504**
Inconvenient forum as grounds for stay or dismissal of action **CCP 410.30, 418.10**
Injunctions staying proceedings in **CCP 526**
Interstate Compact on Placement of Children **CRC 5.616, Fam 7900 to 7912**
Children covered by compact **Fam 7907.5**
Home environment study request from another state **Fam 7901.1**
Custody of child in requesting state **Fam 7906.5**
Judgments (See **FOREIGN JUDGMENTS**)
Limitation of actions (See subhead: **Statutes of limitation**)
Marriages, validity of foreign **Fam 308**
Mechanics liens, serving preliminary notice **CC 3097, 3097.1, 3114**
Nonresidents (See **NONRESIDENTS**)
Paternity determinations (See **PATERNITY**)
Penalty of perjury, declaration or certification of written instrument executed under **CCP 2015.5**
Power of attorney (See **POWER OF ATTORNEY**)
Process, service of (See **PROCESS AND SERVICE OF PROCESS**)
Retail installment sales contracts **CC 1802.19**
Rules of professional conduct, geographic scope of **ProfC 1-100**
Sentence running consecutively with sentence imposed in **CRC 4.451**
Service of process (See **PROCESS AND SERVICE OF PROCESS**)
Statutes of limitation
Lapse of time for bringing action under laws of state where action has arisen, effect of **CCP 361**
Upon judgment or decree of court of sister state **CCP 337.5**
Stay or dismissal, inconvenient forum as grounds for **CCP 410.30, 418.10**
Support orders (See **UNIFORM INTERSTATE FAMILY SUPPORT ACT**)
Trusts (See **TRUSTS**)
Unclaimed deposits and payments (See **UNCLAIMED DEPOSITS AND PAYMENTS**)
Uniform Divorce Recognition Act **Fam 2090 to 2093**
Water rights **CC 1410a**
Witnesses (See **WITNESSES**)

OUSTER
Cotenant's right to establish **CC 843**

OVERDOSES
Emergency care and treatment
Opioid antagonists to treat **CC 1714.22**

OWNERSHIP (See **TITLE AND OWNERSHIP**)

P

PAIN AND SUFFERING
Assignment for benefit of creditors, compensatory payments exempt from **CCP 1801**
Damages for pain and suffering **CC 3333.2**
Voir dire examination re **CRC JudAdminStand 3.25**

PAINTINGS
Commissions for sale of **CC 986**

Index

Index

Index

PHYSICAL EXAMINATIONS—Cont.

Discovery procedure —Cont.

    Plaintiffs, personal injury cases   **CCP 2032.210 to 2032.260**

        Conditions for examination   **CCP 2032.220**

        Definitions   **CCP 2032.210**

        Failure to timely respond   **CCP 2032.240**

        Grounds for seeking examination   **CCP 2032.220**

        Motion for compliance with demand   **CCP 2032.250**

        Response to demand   **CCP 2032.230**

        Retention of demand, proof of service and response   **CCP 2032.260**

        Sanctions   **CCP 2032.240, 2032.250**

        Protective orders

            Suspension of examination pending motion   **CCP 2032.510**

        Recording examination   **CCP 2032.510**

        Reports of examination   **CCP 2032.610 to 2032.650**

            Attorney work product waived for demand for report   **CCP 2032.610, 2032.630**

            Demanding report   **CCP 2032.610**

            Existing and later reports of same condition, demand recipient's right to   **CCP 2032.640, 2032.650**

            Failure to timely deliver   **CCP 2032.620**

            Motion to compel   **CCP 2032.620, 2032.650**

        Right to discovery   **CCP 2032.020**

Economic litigation provisions for limited civil cases, permissible forms of discovery under   **CCP 94**

Interpreter during

    Generally   **Ev 755.5**

    Administrative adjudication (See **ADMINISTRATIVE ADJUDICATION**)

Judges, proceedings for removal of   **JudPerR 105**

Juvenile court, authorization of psychotropic medication for treatment of psychiatric disorder or illness of dependent child of   **CRC 5.640**

Sterilization proceedings   **Pro 1955**

PHYSICAL IMPAIRMENT

Disqualification of judges, grounds for   **CCP 170.1**

PHYSICALLY CHALLENGED PERSONS (See **DISABLED PERSONS**)

PHYSICAL THERAPISTS

Bond required to secure costs in action against therapists   **CCP 1029.6**

Malpractice (See **MALPRACTICE**)

Medical records, attorney's authorized inspection of   **CCP 1985.7, Ev 1158**

PHYSICIANS AND SURGEONS

Abortions (See **ABORTIONS**)

Administrative law proceedings (See **ADMINISTRATIVE ADJUDICATION**)

Artificial insemination, consent required for   **Fam 7613**

Bond required to secure costs in action against   **CCP 1029.6**

Chiropractors (See **CHIROPRACTORS**)

Commercial blockage tort affecting medical care facilities   **CC 3427 to 3427.4**

Complaints from public   **CC 43.96**

Conciliation court proceedings, testimony in   **Fam 1838**

Confidentiality of medical information   **CC 56.101, 56.104, 56 to 56.37**

Disciplinary proceedings (See **ADMINISTRATIVE ADJUDICATION**)

Discovery of medical records (See **DISCOVERY**)

Infants, treatment of (See **MINORS**)

Insurance

    Malpractice (See **MALPRACTICE**)

PHYSICIANS AND SURGEONS—Cont.

Insurance—Cont.

    Underwriting committee, liability of physician member of   **CC 43.7, 43.8**

Libel of physicians by communicating proceedings of peer review committees   **CC 43.7, 43.8**

Life sustaining procedures

    Physician orders for life sustaining treatment form   **Pro 4780**

        Conflicting instructions   **Pro 4781.4**

        Duties of health care providers to apply   **Pro 4781.2**

Limitation of actions (See **MALPRACTICE**)

Malpractice (See **MALPRACTICE**)

Medical treatment (See **MEDICAL TREATMENT**)

Minors, treatment of (See **MINORS**)

Morbidity and mortality studies, admissibility of   **Ev 1156, 1156.1**

Multiphasic screening units, immunity from liability for patients referred by   **CC 43.9**

Opticians and optometrists (See **OPTICIANS AND OPTOMETRISTS**)

Osteopaths (See **OSTEOPATHS**)

Peer review committees

    Disclosure of medical information to   **CC 56.10**

    Discovery or testimony, prohibition relating to   **Ev 1157, 1157.5**

    Liability of members of   **CC 43.7, 43.8**

Physical examinations

    Discovery procedure

        By whom performed   **CCP 2032.020**

Physical therapists (See **PHYSICAL THERAPISTS**)

Privileged communications (See **PRIVILEGED COMMUNICATIONS**)

Professional review committee (See subhead: **Peer review committees**)

Professional societies (See **PROFESSIONAL SOCIETIES**)

Psychotherapists (See **PSYCHOTHERAPISTS**)

Recommendation of medical staff, limited immunity from liability for action taken on   **CC 43.97**

Records of (See **MEDICAL RECORDS**)

Referral of complaints to appropriate board   **CC 43.96**

Review committee (See subhead: **Peer review committees**)

Wrongful death caused by physician (See **MALPRACTICE**)

PHYSICIAN'S PROFESSIONAL NEGLIGENCE (See **MALPRACTICE**)

PIANOS

Serial number destroyed or altered prior to sale   **CC 1710.1**

PICKETING (See **DEMONSTRATIONS, PARADES AND MEETINGS**)

PICNICS

Landowner liability for picnickers   **CC 846**

PICTURES

Motion pictures (See **MOTION PICTURES**)

Photographs (See **PHOTOGRAPHS AND PHOTOCOPIES**)

PIERS (See **WHARVES**)

PILOT AND DEMONSTRATION PROJECTS

Alternative dispute resolution   **CCP 1775**

Family law pilot projects (See **FAMILY LAW PILOT PROJECTS**)

Mediation of civil actions   **CCP 1730, 1742, 1775**

Small claims courts, public entity as party in   **CCP 116.232**

PISTOLS (See **FIREARMS AND OTHER WEAPONS**)

PLEADINGS—Cont.

Material allegation

Admission by failure to respond   **CCP 431.20, 431.30**

Defined   **CCP 431.10**

Mistakes

Amended pleadings   **CCP 473**

Demurrer (See **DEMURRERS**)

Disregard of nonprejudicial error   **CCP 475**

Variance in pleading and proof (See subhead: **Variance**)

Motion to strike (See **MOTION TO STRIKE**)

Nonprejudicial error, disregard of   **CCP 475**

Objections to pleadings   **CCP 430.10 to 430.80**

Permissible pleadings   **CCP 422.10**

Preemption of local rules for form and format   **CRC 3.20**

Privacy protection   **CRC 1.20**

Probate rules

Definitions   **CRC 7.3**

Execution and verification of amended or supplemental pleadings   **CRC 7.104**

Notice of hearing

Amended or supplemental pleadings   **CRC 7.53**

Description of pleadings in notice of hearing   **CRC 7.50**

Signature   **CRC 7.103**

Verification   **CRC 7.103**

Process and service of process

Time for service   **CRC 3.110**

Real property, recovery of   **CCP 455**

Related cases, notice to judge of   **CRC 3.300**

Relief from judgment application accompanied by pleading proposed to be filed therein   **CCP 473**

School districts, verification by   **CCP 446**

State, verification by   **CCP 446**

Statute of limitation, alleging cause of action barred by   **CCP 458**

Striking motion (See **MOTION TO STRIKE**)

Superior courts (See **SUPERIOR COURTS**)

Supplemental pleadings

Court to which action transferred, amended or supplemental pleadings necessary for determination in   **CCP 399**

Filing and service of   **CCP 465**

Motion for   **CCP 464**

Third party pleadings   **CCP 428.70**

Time after cross-complaint   **CCP 432.10**

Unpleaded cause, permission to assert   **CCP 426.50**

Variance

Distinguished from failure of proof   **CCP 471**

Immaterial variance   **CCP 470**

Material variance in pleading and proof   **CCP 469**

Verification of pleadings (See **VERIFICATION**)

Voided filing

Check for filing fees returned unpaid   **CCP 411.20**

Underpayment of filing fees   **CCP 411.21**

PLEAS

Court reporters to take down all arraignments, pleas and sentences in felony cases   **CCP 269**

Guilty plea (See **GUILTY PLEA**)

PLEDGES

Lien statutes applicable to   **CC 2877**

PLUMBERS AND PLUMBING

Inspection warrants to determine violations   **CCP 1822.50**

PLURAL

Construction of words used in code   **CCP 17**

Family code   **Fam 10**

P.O.DACCOUNTS (See **MULTIPLE-PARTY ACCOUNTS**)

PODIATRY AND PODIATRISTS

Administrative law disciplinary proceedings (See **ADMINISTRATIVE ADJUDICATION**)

Bond required to secure costs in action against podiatrists   **CCP 1029.6**

Communication of information, liability for   **CC 43.8**

Complaints from public   **CC 43.96**

Discovery prohibitions   **Ev 1157**

Malpractice (See **MALPRACTICE**)

Medical records, attorney's authorized inspection of   **CCP 1985.7, Ev 1158**

Referral of complaints to appropriate board   **CC 43.96**

Review committees, liability of   **CC 43.7, 43.8**

POINTS AND AUTHORITIES

Attachment   **CCP 484.070, 484.350, 484.360**

Claim and delivery hearings   **CCP 512.050**

Innkeeper's lien, writ of possession on   **CC 1861.9**

New trial, memorandum of points and authorities for (See **NEW TRIAL**)

POLICE OFFICERS (See **LAW ENFORCEMENT OFFICERS**)

POLITICAL AFFILIATION

Discrimination prohibited   **CC 51.7, 52**

Construction or application of provisions in issue, solicitor general notified   **CC 51.1**

POLITICAL SUBDIVISIONS

Bonds issued by (See **BONDS**)

Presentation of claims as prerequisite to commencement of actions against governmental agencies   **CCP 313**

Service of process on   **CCP 416.50**

POLITICS

Sale of political items   **CC 1739 to 1739.4**

POLLING JURY   **CCP 618**

POLLUTION (See **ENVIRONMENTAL HAZARDS**)

POLYGRAPH

Exclusion of polygraph evidence   **Ev 351.1**

POOLS

Juror pools (See **JURY**)

POOR PERSONS (See **INDIGENT PERSONS**)

POPULAR NAMES OF ACTS (See **CITATION OF ACTS**)

PORCELAIN PAINTING

Fine art, defined as   **CC 997**

PORTER-COLOGNE WATER QUALITY CONTROL ACT

Limitation of actions   **CCP 338**

POSSESSION

Action to recover for   **CC 3375, 3379, 3380**

Administrator having right of   **Pro 9650, 9651**

Adverse possession (See **ADVERSE POSSESSION**)

Attachment (See **ATTACHMENT**)

Bailment contract, transfer under   **CC 1925**

Bonds

Corporate executors, bond requirements for   **Pro 301**

Trust companies   **Pro 301**

Claim and delivery (See **CLAIM AND DELIVERY**)

Contempt for re-entry after removal from   **CCP 1210**

Damages for wrongful possession   **CC 3334 to 3336**

Domestic violence protective orders determining   **Fam 6324**

Easement, rights under   **CC 809, 810**

Index

Index

Index

Index

Index

PROCESS AND SERVICE OF PROCESS—Cont.
Servers—Cont.
Registration requirements, violation of **CCP 413.40**
Sheriff, service by (See **SHERIFF**)
Sheriff (See **SHERIFF**)
Action against, service of process in **CCP 262.7**
Service by (See **SHERIFF**)
Small claims courts **CRC 3.2102**
Spanish, legend in **CCP 412.20**
State of California **CCP 416.50**
Statute of limitation **CCP 583.210**
Statute, proof of service in manner prescribed by **CCP 417.10**
Stay of proceedings
Notice of court and others of stay
Duty of party requesting **CRC 3.650**
Substituted service
Small claims courts **CRC 3.2102**
Summons and complaint
Electronic filing and service
Issuance of electronic summons **CRC 2.259**
Service of
Forms **CRCAppx A**
Superior courts, process extending throughout state **CCP 71**
Telegraph, service of summons by **CCP 1017**
Time
Date of service, entry of **CCP 415.10**
Mailing summons **CCP 413.20**
Mandatory time for service of summons (See subhead: **Mandatory time for service of summons**)
Motion to quash service of process **CCP 418.10**
Transferred causes
Superior court appellate division case transferred to court of appeal
Briefs **CRC 8.1012**
Trial court rules
Proof of service
Computer-generated or typewritten proof of service forms, requirements for **CRC 2.150**
Unlawful detainer (See **UNLAWFUL DETAINER**)
Validation proceedings **CCP 861, 861.1, 863**
Will probate proceedings (See **WILL PROBATE**)

PRODUCTION DEMANDS (See **INSPECTION DEMANDS**)

PRODUCTION OF EVIDENCE
Burden of going forward (See **BURDEN OF GOING FORWARD**)
Demand for production for inspection of documents, tangible things, land or other property (See **INSPECTION DEMANDS**)
Depositions, production at (See **DEPOSITIONS**)
Subpoena duces tecum (See **SUBPOENA DUCES TECUM**)

PRODUCTS LIABILITY
Animal experimentations, inadmissibility of evidence in products liability actions involving motor vehicles based on **Ev 1159**
Inherently unsafe products, availability of products liability action for injury caused by **CC 1714.45**
Judicial council development and approval of pleading forms **CCP 425.12**

PROFESSIONAL CONDUCT
Attorneys (See **ATTORNEYS**)
Interpreters **CRC 2.890**

PROFESSIONAL CORPORATIONS
Small claims court, exceptions to restriction on representation by attorneys in **CCP 116.530**

PROFESSIONAL MALPRACTICE (See **MALPRACTICE**)

PROFESSIONAL SOCIETIES
Dental committee records subject to discovery **Ev 1156, 1157**
Immunity from liability of **CC 43.7, 43.91, 43.95**

PROFESSIONS
Exemption for purposes of enforcement of judgments of property used in **CCP 704.060**

PROFFERED EVIDENCE (See **ADMISSIBILITY OF EVIDENCE**)

PROFITS
Executors of decedents' estates liable for profits from sale of estate property **Pro 9657, 10005**
Limitation of actions (See **STATUTES OF LIMITATION**)
Trust deeds and mortgages (See **TRUST DEEDS AND MORTGAGES**)
Unclaimed deposits and payments escheated **CCP 1516**

PROFIT-SHARING
Employee pension benefit plan defined **Fam 80**

PRO HAC VICE
Application to appear as counsel pro hac vice **CRC 9.40**
Filing fee **Gov 70617**

PROHIBITION, WRIT OF **CRC 8.485 to 8.493**
Alternative writs **CCP 1104**
Appeals
Appellate division of superior court
Judgment involving mandamus or prohibition directed to superior court **CCP 904.3**
Writ proceedings within original jurisdiction of appellate division **CRC 8.930 to 8.936**
Applicability of code **CCP 1105**
Applicability of provisions **CRC 8.485**
Attorney general amicus brief **CRC 8.487**
Briefs **CRC 8.487**
Certificate of interested entities or persons **CRC 8.488**
Costs
Award and recovery **CRC 8.493**
Decisions **CRC 8.490**
Defined **CCP 1102**
Fees for issuance of writ
Superior court fees, specified services **Gov 70626**
Filing of decision **CRC 8.490**
Finality of decision **CRC 8.490**
Judicial holiday, issuance on **CCP 134**
Jurisdiction of issuing writs **CCP 1103**
Law and motion rules, applicability of **CRC 3.1103**
Modification of decision **CRC 8.490**
Notice if writ issues **CRC 8.489**
Notice of sanctions **CRC 8.492**
Opposition **CRC 8.487**
Sanctions **CRC 8.492**
Oral argument
Sanctions **CRC 8.492**
Original writs in reviewing courts **CRC 8.485 to 8.493**
Peremptory writs **CCP 1104**
Petition
Contents **CRC 8.486**
Supporting documents **CRC 8.486**
Remittitur **CRC 8.490**
Returns **CCP 1108**
Sanctions **CRC 8.492**
Sealed records **CRC 8.486**
Service **CCP 1107**
Petition and supporting documents **CRC 8.486**
Statute of limitation for commencement of action stayed by **CCP 356**

Index

Index

Index

REVERSAL OF JUDGMENT
Authority of Supreme Court and Courts of Appeal to affirm, reverse or modify judgment or order appealed from **CCP 43**
Costs on appeal **CRC 8.278**
Entering judgment of reviewing court in records of trial court **CCP 912**
General powers of reviewing court **CCP 906**
Restitution of rights on **CCP 908**
Review by supreme court, decision of cause on **CRC 8.528**
Statute of limitation, extension of **CCP 355**

REVERSE MORTGAGES (See TRUST DEEDS AND MORTGAGES)

REVERSION
Action for injury to estate **CC 826**
Attornment on transfer of **CC 1111**
Definition **CC 768**
Power of termination, applicability of **CC 885.015**

REVIEW, WRIT OF **CRC 8.495 to 8.499**
Certiorari
  Writs of mandate, certiorari and prohibition in supreme court or court of appeal **CRC 8.485 to 8.493**
Miscellaneous writs of review **CRC 8.495 to 8.499**
  Agricultural Labor Relations Board
    Judicial review of cases **CRC 8.498**
  Public Utilities Commission cases **CRC 8.496**
  Remittitur **CRC 8.499**
  Workers' Compensation Appeals Board cases, review of **CRC 8.495**

REVOCABLE TRUSTS (See TRUSTS)

REVOCATION
Administrators (See EXECUTORS AND ADMINISTRA-TORS)
Adoption (See ADOPTION)
Agency **CC 2356**
Conservator's letters (See CONSERVATORS)
Contract offer **CC 1586, 1587**
Executors (See EXECUTORS AND ADMINISTRATORS)
Gifts **CC 1148**
Guardian's letters (See GUARDIAN AND WARD)
Independent Administration of Estates Act, revoking authority for continued administration under **Pro 10454**
Letters of administration (See EXECUTORS AND ADMINIS-TRATORS)
Notaries public, registration of **Fam 535**
Orders made on subsequent application **CCP 1008**
Personal representative's letters (See EXECUTORS AND AD-MINISTRATORS)
Power of attorney (See POWER OF ATTORNEY)
Premarital agreements **Fam 1614**
Probate referees, revocation of authority of (See PROBATE REFEREES)
Summary dissolution of marriage, revocation of joint petition for **Fam 2342, 2401**
Trusts (See TRUSTS)
Wills (See WILLS)

REVOLVERS (See FIREARMS AND OTHER WEAPONS)

RICE
Storage regulations after sale of **CC 1880 to 1881.2**

RIGHT OF SURVIVORSHIP
Joint tenancy (See JOINT TENANCY)
Multiple-party accounts **Pro 5301 to 5306**

RIGHT OF WAY (See EASEMENTS)

RIGHTS OF ACCUSED
Appeal rights, notification of **CRC 4.305, 4.306**
  Determinate sentencing **CRC 4.470**

RIGHT TO PRIVACY (See INVASION OF PRIVACY)

RIPARIAN RIGHTS (See WATERS)

RIVERS AND STREAMS
Appropriation (See WATERS)
Appurtenances **CC 662**
Boundary, center of stream as **CCP 2077**
Declaratory judgments determining natural flow of **CCP 1060**
Easement rights to flow of water over land **CC 801**
Flooding (See FLOODS)
Injunction to prevent diversion of water **CCP 530, 532, 534**
Ownership of **CC 670**
Title
  Accretion **CC 1014 to 1017**
  Border land **CC 830**
  Erosion **CC 1015**
  Islands **CC 1016 to 1018**
  Nonnavigable streams **CCP 2077**
  Reclaiming land carried away by flooding **CC 1015**
  State **CC 670**
Venue in action for recovery of penalty imposed for offense committed on **CCP 393**

RIVERSIDE COUNTY
Senior citizen housing requirements **CC 51.10 to 51.12**

ROADS (See STREETS AND HIGHWAYS)

ROBES
Judges' robes **CRC 10.505**

ROCKS
Owner's liability for recreational land used for rock collecting **CC 846**
Real property, part of **CC 659**

ROOFING WARRANTIES
Duration or warranty, disclosure requirements for **CC 1797.93**
New homes **CC 1797.95**
Residences subject to warranty law **CC 1797.90**
Standardized warranties for multistate use **CC 1797.94**
Subsequent purchaser, enforceability by **CC 1797.92, 1797.94**
Writing requirement **CC 1797.91**

ROOMS
Tenant's possession of room rented **CC 1950**

ROSENTHAL FAIR DEBT COLLECTION PRACTICES ACT **CC 1788 to 1788.32**

ROSENTHAL-ROBERTI ITEM PRICING ACT **CC 7100 to 7106**

ROYALTIES
Artists **CC 986**
Judgment debtor, assignment of right to payment due **CCP 708.510 to 708.560**
Sound recordings
  Audits of royalty reporting parties **CC 2500, 2501**

RUBBISH (See GARBAGE)

RULE AGAINST PERPETUITIES (See PERPETUITIES AND RESTRAINTS ON ALIENATION)

RULE, PUTTING WITNESSES UNDER **Ev 777**

Index

Index

Index

Index

Index

SOLID WASTE RECOVERY AND RECYCLING
Paper and paper products
Courts, use in **CRC 10.503**

SONG-BEVERLY CONSUMER WARRANTY ACT CC 1790 to 1795.8 (See **WARRANTIES**)

SONG-BEVERLY CREDIT CARD ACT CC 1747 to 1748.95 (See **CREDIT CARDS**)

SORGHUM
Storage regulations after sale of **CC 1880 to 1881.2**

SOUND RECORDINGS (See **RECORDING OF SOUND**)

SOURCE OF INFORMATION (See **INFORMATION PRAC-TICES ACT**)

SOVEREIGN IMMUNITY (See **CLAIMS AGAINST PUB-LIC ENTITIES AND EMPLOYEES**)

SPACE
Real property, part of **CC 659**

SPANISH
Attorneys' fees, translation requirements in contracts for **CC 1632**
Contracts written in **CC 1632, 2991**
Cosigners of consumer credit contracts, notice of liability of **CC 1799.91**
Home solicitation sales contracts
Language used in negotiation to be used in written contract **CC 1689.7**
Membership camping contracts, language requirements for **CC 1812.303**
Summons, legend appearing on **CCP 412.20**
Title papers in Spanish relating to land claims, admissible evidence of **Ev 1605**

SPECIAL ADMINISTRATORS (See **EXECUTORS AND ADMINISTRATORS**)

SPECIAL AGENT (See **AGENCY**)

SPECIAL APPEARANCE (See **APPEARANCE**)

SPECIAL DEFENSE
Separate trial of **CCP 597**

SPECIAL DISTRICTS (See **PUBLIC ENTITIES**)

SPECIAL EDUCATION
Educational representative
Appointment **CRC 5.650**
Juvenile court proceedings **CRC 5.502, 5.534, 5.650**
Educational rights of children before juvenile court **CRC 5.651**
Qualifications **CRC 5.650**
Training **CRC 5.650**
Transfer of parent or guardian's educational rights to representative **CRC 5.650**
Limitations on parental control
Juvenile court proceedings **CRC 5.695, 5.790**
Surrogate parents
Juvenile court proceedings **CRC 5.650**

SPECIAL ISSUE
Jury, submitting special issue to **CCP 309**

SPECIAL LAWS (See **LOCAL OR SPECIAL LAWS**)

SPECIAL NEEDS TRUSTS
Claims of government agencies against **Pro 3605**

SPECIAL NEEDS TRUSTS—Cont.
Court supervision of **Pro 3604**
Disposition of funds to **Pro 3602, 3611**
Express consent of protected person to court orders, when required **Pro 3613**

SPECIAL OCCUPANCY PARKS
Danger imminent, requiring guests to move **CC 1867**
Eviction of overstaying guests **CC 1866**
Minors
Conditions for minors staying **CC 1866**

SPECIAL POWER OF APPOINTMENT (See **POWER OF APPOINTMENT**)

SPECIAL PROCEEDINGS
Agreed case (See **AGREED CASE**)
As class of judicial remedy **CCP 21**
Confession of judgments (See **CONFESSION OF JUDG-MENTS**)
Defined **CCP 23**
Forcible entry and detainer (See **FORCIBLE ENTRY AND DETAINER**)
Judgment creditor's lien (See **ENFORCEMENT OF JUDG-MENTS**)
Judicial arbitration (See **JUDICIAL ARBITRATION**)
Limitation periods prescribed, applicability of **CCP 363**
Mandamus (See **MANDAMUS**)
Prohibition, writ of (See **PROHIBITION, WRIT OF**)
Referees, appointment of **CCP 639**
Unlawful detainer (See **UNLAWFUL DETAINER**)
Writ of review (See **CERTIORARI**)

SPECIAL VERDICT (See **VERDICT**)

SPECIFIC DEVISES (See **WILLS**)

SPECIFIC PERFORMANCE
Adequate remedy at law, absence of **CC 3387**
Authority for action **CC 3384**
Conditions precedent, performance of **CC 3392**
Consideration, requirements for adequacy of **CC 3391**
Damages
Inadequate damages **CC 3387**
Liquidated damage provision **CC 3389**
Decedents' estates, conveyance or transfer of property in **Pro 850 to 859**
Defenses to action for **CC 3390 to 3394**
Denial of relief, grounds for **CC 3390**
Fraud
Generally **CC 3399**
Defense based on **CC 3391**
Good and sufficient title, requirements for **CC 3394**
Liquidated damages clauses affecting **CC 1680**
Mistake
Defense to actions **CC 3391**
Mutual mistakes **CC 3399**
Mutuality **CC 3386**
Parties bound by decree of **CC 3395**
Part performance **CC 3386, 3388, CCP 1972**
Penalties provided in contract **CC 3389**
Reasonableness of contract, requirements for **CC 3391**
Reformation of instruments **CC 3399 to 3402**
Revision of contract **CC 3399 to 3402**
Small claims court jurisdiction to grant equitable relief in lieu of or in addition to money damages **CCP 116.220**
Stay of **CCP 917.6**
Third party, denial of relief in actions involving **CC 3390**
Title requirements **CC 3394**

SPECIFIC RELIEF
Generally **CC 3366 to 3369**
Specific performance (See **SPECIFIC PERFORMANCE**)

Index

Index

Index

Index

STEPPARENTS
Adoption by (See **ADOPTION**)
Intestate succession (See **INTESTATE SUCCESSION**)
Visitation rights   Fam 3101, 3171, 3176, 3185

STEREO EQUIPMENT (See **PHONOGRAPHS AND PHO-NOGRAPH RECORDS**)

STERILIZATION
Appeals   **Pro 1962**
   Conservatee sterilization, judgment authorizing conservator to consent   **CRC 8.482**
   Stay of order pending appeal   **Pro 1965**
Appearance by party to be sterilized required at hearing   **Pro 1956**
Appointments
   Attorney, appointment of   **Pro 1954**
   Facilitator, appointment of   **Pro 1954.5**
   Limited conservators (See subhead: **Limited conservators**)
Attorneys
   Appointment of   **Pro 1954**
   Fees   **Pro 1963**
Attorney's fees   **Pro 1963**
Castrations, applicability of sterilization proceedings for procuring   **Pro 1961**
Consent
   Generally   **Pro 1951**
   Minor's consent   **Fam 6925**
   Rights of developmentally disabled persons capable of consent   **Pro 1969**
Conservators
   Limited conservators (See subhead: **Limited conservators**)
Costs   **Pro 1963**
Definitions   **Pro 1951**
Determinations by court for authorizing   **Pro 1958, 1959**
Facilitators
   Generally   **Pro 1954.5**
   Fees   **Pro 1963**
Fees   **Pro 1963**
Hearing
   Appearance by party to be sterilized required at   **Pro 1956**
   Notice of   **Pro 1953**
Hysterectomies, applicability of sterilization proceedings for procuring   **Pro 1961**
Interpreters (See subhead: **Facilitators**)
Investigations conducted by court   **Pro 1955**
Legislative intent   **Pro 1950**
Liability of parties   **Pro 1967**
Limited conservators
   Generally   **Pro 1960**
   Petition for appointment of   **Pro 1952**
Mental examinations of party to be sterilized   **Pro 1955**
Minor, consent required for sterilization of   **Fam 6925**
Notice of hearing   **Pro 1953**
Objections by party to be sterilized   **Pro 1958**
Orders
   Generally   **Pro 1962**
   Duration of   **Pro 1964**
   Stay of order pending appeal   **Pro 1965**
Other medical procedures resulting in sterilization, application of law to   **Pro 1968**
Petition
   Generally   **Pro 1952**
   Re-filing of petition after denial, grounds for   **Pro 1966**
Physical examinations of party to be sterilized   **Pro 1955**
Proof of findings beyond reasonable doubt, requirement of   **Pro 1958**
Reports by examiners   **Pro 1955**
Service of papers   **Pro 1953**
Statement of decision, requirement of   **Pro 1962**

STERILIZATION—Cont.
Stay of order pending appeal   **Pro 1965**
Translators (See subhead: **Facilitators**)
Witnesses
   Generally   **Pro 1955**
   Party to be sterilized, views of   **Pro 1957**

STEROIDS (See **ANABOLIC STEROIDS**)

STIPULATED JUDGMENTS (See **SETTLEMENT AND COMPROMISE**)

STIPULATIONS
Appellate rules, superior court appeals
   Attorneys
      Substitution   **CRC 8.814**
   Infraction case appeals
      Limited record on appeal   **CRC 8.910**
   Misdemeanor appeals
      Limited record on appeal   **CRC 8.860**
Appellate rules, supreme court and courts of appeal (See **APPELLATE RULES, SUPREME COURT AND COURTS OF APPEAL**)
Arbitration (See **ARBITRATION**)
Change of venue   **CCP 398**
Child support award, stipulated agreement for   **Fam 4057, 4065**
Dissolution of marriage, stipulation for retention of jurisdiction   **Fam 2343**
Family support   **Fam 4066**
Judgment by stipulation (See **SETTLEMENT AND COMPROMISE**)
Judgment reversal by stipulation of parties, appeal court's findings required for   **CCP 128**
Judicial arbitration (See **JUDICIAL ARBITRATION**)
Jurors, examination outside of judge's presence of   **CCP 222.5**
Reclassification of action, fees for   **CCP 403.050**
Retired judge not qualified to try criminal case, stipulation that   **CCP 170.65**
Reversal by stipulation of parties, appeal court's findings required for   **CCP 128**
Surety bonds (See **SURETYSHIP, BONDS AND UNDERTAKINGS**)

STOCK (See **CORPORATE SHARES AND SHAREHOLDERS**)

STOCK BONUS PLANS
Employee pension benefit plan defined   **Fam 80**

STOCK COOPERATIVES
Generally (See **COMMON INTEREST DEVELOPMENTS**)
Defined   **CC 783.1, 1351**

STOP NOTICES (See **BUILDING CONTRACTORS**)

STOP WORK ORDER
General discussion of original contractor's stop work order as remedy for nonpayment of contract   **CC 3260.2**

STORAGE
Aircraft liens   **CCP 1208.61**
Electronic recording reels for court proceedings   **CRC 2.952**
Landlord and tenant
   Commercial real property tenancies
      Disposition of property remaining upon termination, storage of property   **CC 1993.06**
Landlord's removal and storage of tenant's personal property (See **LANDLORD AND TENANT**)
Warehouses (See **WAREHOUSES**)

STORES AND STOREKEEPERS
Attachment proceedings   **CCP 481.120**

Index

Index

Index

Index

Index

TAXATION—Cont.

Internal revenue department—Cont.

Will construction, application of Internal Revenue Code provisions to (See **WILL CONSTRUCTION**)

Liens

Assessments (See subhead: **Assessments**)

Credit reports (See **CREDIT REPORTING**)

Federal tax lien registration **CCP 2100 to 2107**

State tax lien, notice of **CC 2885**

Mello-Roos Community Facilities Act, disclosure regarding special tax liens on transfer of property pursuant to **CC 1102.6b**

Mine co-owners failing to pay **CCP 850 to 856**

Mortgages (See **TRUST DEEDS AND MORTGAGES**)

Motion to tax costs (See **COSTS**)

Postponed property taxes, notice of default on property subject to lien for **CC 2924b**

Power of attorney, powers under statutory form of **Pro 4463**

Principal and income allocations **CC 731.14, Pro 6371, 6374, 6375**

Public entity's liability for tax law administration **Gov 860 to 860.4**

Quiet title to real property subject to public improvement assessment, action to **CCP 801.1 to 801.15**

Real property sales contract, payments received under **CC 2985.4**

Sales tax (See **SALES AND USE TAX**)

Special assessments (See subhead: **Assessments**)

Statutes of limitation on actions based on assessments (See subhead: **Assessments**)

Trust deeds (See **TRUST DEEDS AND MORTGAGES**)

Trusts (See **TRUSTS**)

Unclaimed property fund appropriations for payment **CCP 1325**

Validation proceedings on bonds for which tax revenue has been pledged by agency other than agency imposing tax, notice requirements for **CCP 870.5**

TAX COLLECTOR

Limitation of actions to recover goods seized by **CCP 341**

TAXING COSTS (See **COSTS**)

TAXIS

Blind persons having equal rights to use of **CC 54.1, 54.3, 54.4, 55**

Construction or application of provisions in issue, solicitor general notified **CC 55.2**

Disabled persons having equal rights to use of **CC 54.1, 54.3, 54.4, 55**

Construction or application of provisions in issue, solicitor general notified **CC 55.2**

Guide dogs permitted in **CC 54.2, 54.3**

Construction or application of provisions in issue, solicitor general notified **CC 55.2**

TAXPAYERS' SUITS

Public contracts enjoined **CCP 526a**

TEACHERS (See **SCHOOLS**)

TEAR GAS WEAPONS

Nuisance abatement

Unlawful weapons or ammunition purpose **CC 3485**

TEARING

Will revoked by **Pro 6120, 6121**

TECHNICAL LANGUAGE (See **CONSTRUCTION AND INTERPRETATION**)

TELECOMMUNICATIONS

Electronic commercial services (See **ELECTRONIC COMMERCIAL SERVICES**)

Radio and television (See **RADIO AND TELEVISION**)

Telephones and telegraphs (See **TELEPHONES AND TELEGRAPHS**)

TELEGRAPHS (See **TELEPHONES AND TELEGRAPHS**)

TELEMARKETING

Contracts

Unlawfulness of contracts generated by unlawful telemarketing **CC 1670.6**

TELEPHONE INFORMATION LIBRARY

Professional society referral service, liability of **CC 43.95**

TELEPHONES AND TELEGRAPHS

Accounts

Change of address requests

Notice to account holder **CC 1799.1b**

Administrative adjudication proceedings conducted by telephone (See **ADMINISTRATIVE ADJUDICATION**)

Appeals courts

Certiorari, mandate and prohibition

Notice by telephone **CRC 8.489**

Appearance of counsel by (See **APPEARANCE**)

Attorney-client privilege for cellular phone conversations **Ev 952**

Cancellation of utility, cable, etc, services on behalf of deceased person

In-person cancellation not to be required **Pro 217**

Cellular telephone conversations, attorney-client privilege for **Ev 952**

Change of number

Appeals

Service and filing notice of change **CRC 8.32**

Child support

Title IV-D support actions

Appearance by telephone **CRC 5.324**

Coin-operated telephone (See **VENDING MACHINES**)

Common interest developments, access to telephone wiring in **CC 1364**

Court appearances by telephone **CCP 367.5, CRC 3.670**

Conference call provider, designation of **CRC 3.670**

Hardware and procedure **CRC JudAdminStand 3.1**

Private vendor charges **CRC 3.670**

Unlawful detainer **CRC 3.670**

Credit reports, copies of **CC 1785.15**

Deaf or disabled persons

Equal access rights

Construction or application of provisions in issue, solicitor general notified **CC 55.2**

Debt collectors using telephones, regulation on **CC 1788.11**

Delivery of telegrams **CC 2161**

Depositions

Remote electronic means of taking depositions **CCP 2025.310**

Remote electronic means of taking oral depositions **CRC 3.1010**

Disabled persons, use of telephones by **CC 54.1**

Construction or application of provisions in issue, solicitor general notified **CC 55.2**

Discovery

Technology to conduct discovery in complex case **CCP 2017.710 to 2017.740**

Ex parte order enjoining annoying telephone calls **Fam 6320**

Denial of petition for ex parte order, reasons to be provided **Fam 6320.5**

Fax filing of legal documents (See **FAX FILING AND SERVICE**)

Index

TERMINATION OF PARENTAL RIGHTS—Cont.

Hearings

Setting termination hearing at disposition hearing   **CRC 5.705**

Indian children

Involuntary placements

Indian Child Welfare Act, rules governing   **CRC 5.480 to 5.487** (See **INDIAN CHILD WELFARE ACT INVOLUNTARY PLACEMENTS**)

Juvenile courts

Appellate review

Appeal from termination of parental rights   **CRC 8.416**

Extraordinary writ, petition for   **CRC 8.454, 8.456**

Juvenile case appeals in supreme court and courts of appeal   **CRC 8.400 to 8.474**

Order designating specific placement of dependent child, writ petition to review   **CRC 8.454, 8.456**

Orders setting hearing, writ petition to review   **CRC 8.450**

One parent, conditions to termination of rights of

Disposition hearings generally   **CRC 5.690 to 5.705**

Order for   **CRC 5.725**

Review of permanent placement orders   **CRC 5.600**

Writ petition, notice of intent to file   **CRC 5.600**

TERMITES AND PESTS

Common interest developments, liability for termite damages in   **CC 1364**

Conveyance of real property, requirement of pest control inspection report prior to   **CC 1099**

Home improvement goods and services   **CC 1689.8**

Inspection warrants for purposes of eradication of (See **INSPECTION WARRANTS**)

Landlord's duty to provide notice of pest control inspection to new tenant   **CC 1099**

Mandamus in actions involving state pest control and eradication, issuance of   **CCP 1085.5**

Structural pest control inspection

Landlord's duty to provide notice of pest control inspection to new tenant   **CC 1099**

Transfer of title, delivery to transferee of pest inspection report prior to   **CC 1099**

TERMS OF OFFICE

Congress of United States (See **CONGRESS**)

Probate referees   **Pro 403**

TERRORISM

Construction defects, actions for

Unforeseen act of nature

Defenses of builder   **CC 945.5**

September 11, 2001 terrorist attacks

Statute of limitations   **CCP 340.10**

TESTAMENTARY DISPOSITIONS (See **WILL CONSTRUCTION**)

TESTAMENTARY TRUSTS (See **TRUSTS**)

TESTATORS (See **WILLS**)

TESTIFY

Inclusions in definition   **CCP 17**

TESTIMONY (See **EVIDENCE; WITNESSES**)

TESTS (See **BLOOD TESTS**)

TEXTILE GOODS

Warranties   **CC 1790 to 1795.8**

TEXTURE COATING

Home improvement goods and services   **CC 1689.8**

THEATERS (See **MOTION PICTURES**)

THEFT (See also **EMBEZLEMENT**)

Attachments, real property destroyed   **CCP 488.060**

Automobile theft (See **AUTOMOBILE THEFT**)

Credit cards   **CC 1747.20**

False pretenses (See **FALSE PRETENSES**)

Fur-bearing animals   **CC 996**

Identity theft (See **IDENTITY THEFT**)

Landlord and tenant

Unduly influencing tenant to vacate   **CC 1940.2**

Public employee's liability for theft of money for employee's official custody   **Gov 822**

Repairs, theft of property deposited for   **CC 1858.2**

Statute of limitation for theft of articles of historic or artistic importance   **CCP 338**

THERAPY

Marriage and family counselors (See **MARRIAGE AND FAMILY COUNSELORS**)

Physical therapists (See **PHYSICAL THERAPISTS**)

Psychotherapists (See **PSYCHOTHERAPISTS**)

THING IN ACTION (See **CHOSE IN ACTION**)

THIRD PARTIES

Administrators, request for appointment as   **Pro 8465**

Adverse claims by   **CCP 1050**

Alcoholic beverages, social host's liability to third party after serving   **CC 1714**

Arbitration (See **ARBITRATION**)

Attachment (See **ATTACHMENT**)

Claim of property after levy   **CCP 514.050**

Contracts (See **CONTRACTS AND AGREEMENTS**)

Credit cards, termination of third party use of   **CC 1747.02**

Enforcement of judgments (See **ENFORCEMENT OF JUDGMENTS**)

Escheat, claims of ownership to prevent   **CCP 1352, 1353**

Escrow (See **ESCROW**)

Estate for life of   **CC 766**

Garnishment (See **GARNISHMENT**)

Genetic defects of child, action involving   **CC 43.6**

Husband and wife having transactions with   **Fam 721**

Improvements on land of another   **CCP 871.1 to 871.7**

Information Practices Act (See **INFORMATION PRACTICES ACT**)

Judgments (See **JUDGMENTS**)

Jury conversing with   **CCP 611**

Necessaries for child, recovery for   **Fam 6712**

Ownership or right of possession of property levied upon, third party claim of   **CCP 720.110 to 720.170**

Power of attorney (See **POWER OF ATTORNEY**)

Promise to answer for obligations of   **CC 2794**

Retail installment sales pursuant to loans by   **CC 1801.6, 1801.7, 1803.9**

Security interest in or lien on property levied upon, third party claim of   **CCP 720.210 to 720.290, 720.510 to 720.550**

Social host's liability after serving alcoholic beverages   **CC 1714**

Specific performance of contract to obtain consent of   **CC 3390**

Trusts (See **TRUSTS**)

Written contract to answer for default of   **CC 1624**

THIRD PARTY BENEFICIARIES (See **CONTRACTS AND AGREEMENTS**)

THREATS

Domestic violence protection orders

Denial of petition for ex parte order, reasons to be provided   **Fam 6320.5**

Duress (See **DURESS**)

TRANSLATORS AND INTERPRETERS—Cont.

Court interpreters—Cont.

    Instructions to interpreters   **CRC JudAdminStand 2.11**

    Periodic review of skills   **CRC 2.891**

    Preappearance interview, good cause for   **CRC JudAdminStand 2.10**

    Record of examination to determine need   **CRC JudAdminStand 2.10**

Court operations costs, salaries and benefits of court personnel as   **CRC 10.810**

Court proceedings   **Ev 750 to 754.5**

Cross-assignments for court interpreter employees   **CRC 10.762**

Custody of children, public provision of interpreters for proceedings to determine   **Fam 3032**

Deaf persons

    Administrative adjudicative proceeding   **Gov 11435.10**

    Court-appointed interpreters for   **Ev 754**

    Privileged communications of   **Ev 754.5**

Domestic violence cases (See **DOMESTIC VIOLENCE**)

Ethical violations, duty to report   **CRC 2.890**

Fees   **Ev 752**

    Administrative adjudicative proceeding (See **ADMINISTRATIVE ADJUDICATION**)

    Deaf persons, interpreter fees for   **Ev 754**

    Domestic violence proceedings   **Ev 755**

    Payment of   **Gov 68092**

Filing oath of translator or interpreter   **Ev 751**

Forms

    Judicial council legal forms   **CRCAppx A**

Functional budget categories   **CRC 10.810**

Harassment, translation of court orders concerning   **CCP 185**

Hard-of-hearing persons (See subhead: **Deaf persons**)

Instructions for   **CRC JudAdminStand 2.11**

Intermediary interpreters, court appointment of   **Ev 754**

Judicial Council standards for   **CRC JudAdminStand 2.10, CRC JudAdminStand 2.11**

Juror with physical disability, use of service provider for   **CCP 224**

Labor and employment relations

    Cross-assignments for court interpreter employees   **CRC 10.762**

    Regional court interpreter employment relations   **CRC 10.761**

Medical examination

    Generally   **Ev 755.5**

    Administrative law proceedings (See **ADMINISTRATIVE ADJUDICATION**)

Oath of   **Ev 751**

Privileged communications of hearing-impaired persons, use of interpreters facilitating   **Ev 754.5**

Professional conduct   **CRC 2.890**

Proof of execution of instruments, officers calling interpreters for   **CC 1201**

Qualified interpreters, court appointment of   **Ev 754**

Record of translator's or interpreter's oath   **Ev 751**

Sign language interpreters, generally (See subhead: **Deaf persons**)

Skills, review of   **CRC 2.891**

Small claims actions   **CCP 116.550**

State agency adjudicative proceedings (See **ADMINISTRATIVE ADJUDICATION**)

Sterilization proceedings, facilitator in (See **STERILIZATION**)

Will written in foreign language   **Pro 8002**

Workplace violence, translation of court orders concerning   **CCP 185**

TRANSMITTERS

Subcutaneous implanting of identification device, requiring of another   **CC 52.7**

TRANSMUTATION OF MARITAL PROPERTY (See **COMMUNITY PROPERTY**)

TRANSPORTATION

Aircraft and aviation (See **AIRCRAFT AND AVIATION**)

Automobiles (See **AUTOMOBILES**)

Bicycles (See **BICYCLES**)

Buses (See **BUSES**)

Common carriers (See **COMMON CARRIERS**)

Elevators (See **ELEVATORS**)

Motor carriers (See **MOTOR CARRIERS**)

Public Utilities Commission regulating (See **PUBLIC UTILITIES COMMISSION**)

Street railways (See **STREET RAILWAYS**)

Taxis (See **TAXIS**)

Trains (See **RAILROADS**)

Vessels (See **VESSELS**)

TRANSPORTATION DEPARTMENT

Eminent domain taking by   **CCP 1245.210**

TRASH (See **GARBAGE**)

TRAVELER'S CHECKS

Court clerks, payments to   **CRC 10.821**

Credit card number notation as condition of acceptance for negotiable instruments, prohibited use of   **CC 1725**

Escheat   **CCP 1511, 1513, 1542, 1581**

TRAVEL EXPENSES

Financial institutions commissioner, hearings on sale of savings and loan association properties in possession of   **CCP 73d**

Jury   **CCP 215, 631, 631.5**

Jury commissioner   **CCP 196**

Superior court appellate division, judges designated as members of   **CCP 77**

Visitation of child, travel expenses for   **Fam 4062**

TREASURER

Administration of decedent's estate (See **ADMINISTRATION OF ESTATES**)

Common carrier selling unclaimed property, disposition of proceeds   **CC 2081.3**

Credit denied because of marital status, distribution of fines for   **CC 1812.33**

Escheat (See **ESCHEAT**)

Public administrator depositing funds with   **Pro 7640 to 7644**

TREASURY

Artists, deposit of money owed to   **CC 986**

Deposits in court

    Deposit with treasury   **CCP 573**

Eminent domain compensation deposited in   **CCP 1255.070**

Expert testimony, payment of costs of   **Ev 731**

TREBLE DAMAGES

Adoption facilitators

    Enforcement of provisions   **Fam 8638**

Child support, assisting obligor in avoiding payment   **CC 1714.4, 1714.41**

Forcible entry   **CCP 735**

Human trafficking   **CC 52.5**

Public social services

    Unreasonable fees to assist applicants for public social services as deceptive practice   **CC 1780**

Trees or timber, liability for injuries to   **CCP 733, 734**

Unfair trade practices actions

    Public social services

        Unreasonable fees to assist applicants for public social services as deceptive practice   **CC 1780**

Unlawful detainer   **CCP 735**

Unlicensed person, action for injury caused by   **CCP 1029.8**

Usury   **CC 1916.12-3**

Waste, actions for recovery of treble damages for   **CCP 732**

Index

Index

Index

Index

VALUE—Cont.

Community property **Fam 2552**

Damages, measure of (See **DAMAGES**)

Deposit in lieu of surety bonds (See **SURETYSHIP, BONDS AND UNDERTAKINGS**)

Eminent domain, exchange of valuation data for **CCP 1258.210 to 1258.300, Ev 810 to 822**

Enforcement of judgments (See **ENFORCEMENT OF JUDGMENTS**)

Evidence rules for ascertaining value of property (See **EXPERT AND OPINION EVIDENCE**)

Expert testimony of (See **EXPERT AND OPINION EVIDENCE**)

Form for exchange of valuation data in eminent domain action **CCP 1258.210**

Opinion testimony of (See **EXPERT AND OPINION EVIDENCE**)

Ownership, value as affecting **CC 1027, 1028, 1032**

Peculiar value **CC 3355**

Small estates distributed without administration, value limitation **Pro 6602, 13100**

Spouse of owner, testimony by **Ev 813**

Surety bonds (See **SURETYSHIP, BONDS AND UNDERTAKINGS**)

VANDALISM

Graffiti as evidence of vandalism, admissibility of **Ev 1410.5**

VANS

15-passenger van rollover danger

Rental car companies to provide documentation **CC 1936.1**

VARIABLE INTEREST RATE LOANS (See **TRUST DEEDS AND MORTGAGES**)

VARIANCE (See **PLEADINGS**)

VAULTS (See **SAFES**)

VEHICLE LEASING ACT (See **AUTOMOBILES**)

VEHICLES

Automobiles (See **AUTOMOBILES**)

Bicycles (See **BICYCLES**)

Buses (See **BUSES**)

Mobilehomes (See **MOBILEHOMES**)

Recreational vehicles (See **RECREATIONAL VEHICLES**)

Street railways (See **STREET RAILWAYS**)

VENDING MACHINES

Seller assisted marketing plans **CC 1812.200 to 1812.221**

VENDOR AND PURCHASER (See also **SALE OF REALTY**)

AIDS, liability of owner regarding occupant afflicted with **CC 1710.2**

Blanket encumbrance, required notice to purchaser or lessee of **CC 1133**

Brokers (See **BROKERS**)

Consideration, measure of damages based on **CC 3353**

Contracts

Administrator's contract for purchase of estate property (See **ADMINISTRATION OF ESTATES**)

Construction of **CC 1662**

Damages for breach of contract **CC 3306 to 3307**

Decedent's estate, contract to purchase realty from (See **ADMINISTRATION OF ESTATES**)

Installment contracts (See **REAL PROPERTY SALES CONTRACTS**)

Liquidated damages clauses **CC 1675 to 1681**

Written contracts for sale **CC 1624**

Decedents' estates, sale of realty of (See **ADMINISTRATION OF ESTATES**)

VENDOR AND PURCHASER—Cont.

Destruction of property, party bearing loss from **CC 1662**

Disclosure requirements

AIDS, disclosures regarding occupant afflicted with **CC 1710.2**

Earthquake hazard

Generally **CC 1103 to 1103.14**

Consumer information booklets **CC 2079.8, 2079.9, 2079.11**

Environmental hazards, compliance with requirements to inform transferee of **CC 2079.7, 2079.11**

Explosive munitions in neighborhood area, written notice of **CC 1102.15**

Fire and flood hazards, disclosure requirements concerning **CC 1103 to 1103.14**

Home energy ratings, information regarding **CC 2079.10**

Industrial use zoning **CC 1102.17**

Mello-Roos Community Facilities Act, disclosure regarding special tax liens on transfer of property pursuant to **CC 1102.6b**

Purchase money liens on residential property **CC 2956 to 2967**

Registered sex offenders, notification concerning statewide database of locations of **CC 2079.10a**

Statements (See subhead: **Disclosure statements**)

Taxation

Supplemental property tax bills **CC 1102.6c**

Water conservation **CC 2079.10**

Window security bars and safety release mechanism **CC 1102.16**

Disclosure statements

Amendment of **CC 1102.9, 1103.9**

Applicability of requirement **CC 1102 to 1102.2, 1103**

Condominiums, newly converted **CC 1134**

Damages for noncompliance **CC 1102.13**

Delivery of **CC 1102.3, 1102.10, 1103.3, 1103.10, 1103.12**

Errors or omissions, liability for **CC 1102.4, 1102.5, 1103.4**

Escrow agents, effect on **CC 1102.11**

Forms

General form of transfer disclosure statement **CC 1102.6**

Local requirements, form of statement reflecting **CC 1102.6a**

Natural hazards, form of disclosure concerning **CC 1103.2**

Good faith requirement **CC 1102.7, 1103.7**

Legislative intent **CC 1102.1**

Other laws, effect of **CC 1102.8, 1103.8**

Earthquake hazard (See subhead: **Disclosure requirements**)

Eminent domain, alternative to **CCP 1240.120**

Enforcement liens **CCP 996.510 to 996.560**

Environmental hazards, compliance with requirements to inform transferee of **CC 2079.7, 2079.11**

Equity sales contracts (See **HOME EQUITY SALES CONTRACTS**)

Escrow (See **ESCROW**)

Explosive munitions in neighborhood area, disclosure of **CC 1102.15**

Fire hazard disclosure **CC 1103 to 1103.14**

Flood hazard disclosure **CC 1103 to 1103.14**

Fraud **CC 3343**

Guardian (See **GUARDIAN AND WARD**)

Home energy ratings, disclosure of information regarding **CC 2079.10**

Home equity sales contracts (See **HOME EQUITY SALES CONTRACTS**)

Homesteads (See **HOMESTEADS**)

VENUE—Cont.

Freedom from parental custody and control, petition for **Fam 7845**

Guardianship (See **GUARDIAN AND WARD**)

Guardian, venue in action against **CCP 395.1**

Health Care Decision Law, actions under **Pro 4763**

Improper joinder to fix venue **CCP 395**

Information Practices Act, action under **CC 1798.49**

Juvenile court proceedings **CRC 5.510**

Juvenile wardship proceedings **CRC 5.510**

Lake, river or stream, recovery of penalty imposed for offense committed on **CCP 393**

Law and motion proceedings
> Motions concerning pleading and venue **CRC 3.1320 to 3.1326**

Local agencies, actions by or against **CCP 394**

Negligence **CCP 395**

Parental relationship, proceedings to determine **CCP 395**

Partition, action for **CCP 872.110**

Penalty or forfeiture imposed by statute, actions for recovery of **CCP 393**

Personal, family or household use, action founded on obligation for goods or services intended primarily for **CCP 395, 396a**

Personal injury actions **CCP 395**

Petition for writ of mandate on grant or denial of motion for change of **CCP 400**

Power of attorney, venue in actions involving (See **POWER OF ATTORNEY**)

Property damage, actions for **CCP 395**

Public entities and employees, claims against (See **CLAIMS AGAINST PUBLIC ENTITIES AND EMPLOYEES**)

Public officers, actions against **CCP 393**

Quieting title action **CCP 760.050**

Recovery of real property, action for **CCP 392**

Rental-purchase contracts, actions involving **CC 1812.645**

Residence of defendant **CCP 395**

Retail installment sales contract, action on **CC 1812.10, CCP 396a**

Situs of subject matter **CCP 392**

Small claims courts **CCP 116.370, CRC 3.2106**

State, actions by or against **CCP 401**

Support obligation, actions to enforce **CCP 395**

Time
> Moving to strike, demur or plead following denial of motion to transfer venue **CRC 3.1326**

Title vesting in state **CCP 1410**

Transfer of venue (See subhead: **Change of venue**)

Trustee, venue in action against **CCP 395.1**

Trust estate **CCP 395.1, Pro 17005**

Uniform Parentage Act **Fam 7620**

Uniform Transfers to Minors Act, venue for hearing on petition filed under **Pro 3921**

Unincorporated association, action against **CCP 395.2**

Unlawful detainer actions **CCP 396a**
> Location nearest or most accessible to real property involved **CCP 392**
> Stay or dismissal of action for inconvenient forum **CRC 3.1327**

Where cause of action arose **CCP 393**

Will probate proceedings (See **WILL PROBATE**)

Wrong court, appeal or petition filed in
> Transfer to appropriate court **CCP 396**

Wrongful death action **CCP 395**

Wrong venue, transfer of action or proceeding to proper court where commenced in **CCP 396b**

VERDICT

Admission of erroneous evidence **Ev 353**

Conflict with special verdict **CCP 625**

Defective verdict, correction of **CCP 619**

VERDICT—Cont.

Directed verdict
> Generally **CCP 630**
> Costs on **CCP 1038**

Entry in minutes **CCP 628**

Exceptions, reserved without **CCP 647**

Exclusion of evidence, effect of **Ev 354**

General verdict **CCP 624**

Impeachment of **Ev 1150**

Judgment notwithstanding **CCP 629**

Judicial comments on verdict **CRC JudAdminStand 2.30**

Judicial holiday, receiving verdict on **CCP 134**

Mandamus **CCP 1093**

Minutes, entry in **CCP 628**

Mistake, correction of **CCP 618, 619**

Mistrial for jury failing to reach **CCP 616**

Money recovery, determining amount of **CCP 626**

Number of jurors required by **CCP 613**

Polling jury **CCP 618**

Post-trial discussions with jurors regarding **CCP 206**

Punitive damages action **CCP 625**

Receiving verdict **CCP 618**

Retrial of action where jury discharged without rendering verdict **CCP 616**

Sealed verdict **CCP 617**

Special verdict **CCP 624**
> Civil cases **CRC 3.1580**
> Entry **CCP 628**
> General verdict, control over **CCP 625**
> Referee's decision **CCP 645**

Writing requirements **CCP 618**

VERIFICATION

Accounts, pleadings alleging **CCP 454**

Administration of estates (See **ADMINISTRATION OF ESTATES**)

Administrative adjudicative proceedings (See **ADMINISTRATIVE ADJUDICATION**)

Affidavits, use of **CCP 2009**

Eminent domain action **CCP 1250.330**

Family law proceedings, verification of pleadings in **Fam 212**

Pleadings, in general **CCP 446**

Quieting title complaint **CCP 761.020**

Will probate proceedings (See **WILL PROBATE**)

VESSELS

Attachment (See **ATTACHMENT**)

Bail and penalty schedules **CRC 4.102**

Bill of lading (See **BILL OF LADING**)

Bill of sale **CC 1135**

Blind persons having equal rights to use of **CC 54.1, 54.3, 54.4, 55**
> Construction or application of provisions in issue, solicitor general notified **CC 55.2**

Bottomry (See **BOTTOMRY**)

Charter-party agreement **CC 1959**

Disabled persons having equal rights to use of **CC 54.1, 54.3, 54.4, 55**
> Construction or application of provisions in issue, solicitor general notified **CC 55.2**

Enforcement of judgments (See **ENFORCEMENT OF JUDGMENTS**)

Fines and civil penalties
> Bail schedule **CRC 4.102**

Floating homes (See **FLOATING HOMES**)

Fraudulent transfer provisions, applicability to vessel cargo **CC 3440**

Guide dogs permitted on **CC 54.2, 54.3**
> Construction or application of provisions in issue, solicitor general notified **CC 55.2**

Loans upon respondentia (See **LOANS UPON RESPONDENTIA**)

Index

WILL PROBATE—Cont.

Proof of will—Cont.

Former testimony of subscribing witnesses in subsequent will contests, admissibility of **Pro 8224**

Holographic wills **Pro 8222**

Lost or destroyed wills **Pro 8223**

Pro per court documents, interactive computer system authorized to prepare standardized **CCP 1062.20**

Publication (See subhead: **Notices**)

Recording requirements

Admission of will to probate, recordation of **Pro 8225**

Orders affecting real property **Pro 7263**

Response to petition for **Pro 1043, 8251**

Revocation of probate

Judgment, order of **Pro 8272**

Limitations period (See subhead: **Statutes of limitation**)

Petition for **Pro 8270**

Statute of limitation **Pro 8270**

Summons, service of **Pro 8271**

Search of will stored with clerk of court, fees for **Gov 70661**

Service of papers

Notices (See subhead: **Notices**)

Summons (See subhead: **Summons**)

Severance of matters associated with proceedings and actions under Probate Code **Pro 801**

Shortening time for giving notice **Pro 1203**

Small estates (See **SMALL ESTATES WITHOUT ADMINISTRATION**)

Special notice, request for **Pro 1250 to 1252**

Statutes of limitation

Before probate **Pro 8250**

Revocation of probate **Pro 8270**

Subscribing witnesses

Beneficiaries as **Pro 6112**

No contest clause, effect of will provision benefiting witnesses contested by party subject to forfeiture under **Pro 6112**

Production and examination of **Pro 8253**

Proof of will by **Pro 8220, 8224**

Summons

Contested will proceedings **Pro 8250**

Revocation of probate, proceedings for **Pro 8271**

Surviving spouse (See **SURVIVING SPOUSE**)

Time

Limitations period (See subhead: **Statutes of limitation**)

Will contest, time for **Pro 8250, 8270**

Titles of petition or pleading papers to identify relief sought or granted **CRC 7.102**

Transferee defined **Pro 81.5**

Transfer of documents to clerk of court, fees for **Gov 70660, 70661**

Trial **Pro 1000 to 1051**

Costs **Pro 1002**

Jury trial, right of **Pro 825**

New trial motions **Pro 7220**

Procedural rules of practice governing **Pro 1000, 1001**

Trusts (See **TRUSTS**)

United States as interested person for purposes of **Pro 7280**

Venue

Generally **Pro 7051**

Nondomiciliary decedent, venue for **Pro 7052**

Verification

Generally **Pro 1021**

Evidentiary use of verified petition **Pro 1022**

Waiver of notice requirements **Pro 1204**

Witnesses (See subhead: **Subscribing witnesses**)

WILLS

Abatement of bequests (See **ADMINISTRATION OF ESTATES**)

WILLS—Cont.

Abuse or neglect of elder or dependent testator by beneficiary, effect of **Pro 259**

Acceptance of documents for deposit, effect on attorney of **Pro 713**

Accounts defined **Pro 21 to 23, 46**

Acknowledgment (See subhead: **Subscribing witnesses**)

Ademption **Pro 6409, 21131 to 21139**

Administration of estates (See **ADMINISTRATION OF ESTATES**)

Administrators of (See **EXECUTORS AND ADMINISTRATORS**)

Advancements (See **ADVANCEMENTS**)

Advertising, transferable property rights in use of deceased personality's name or likeness for **CC 3344.1**

After-born heirs (See **POSTHUMOUS CHILDREN**)

Annuities, interest on **Pro 12004**

Annulment of marriage (See subhead: **Dissolution of marriage**)

Appellate rules, supreme court and courts of appeal

Construction of term will **CRC 8.10**

Will probate cases, costs on appeal of **CRC 8.278, Pro 1002**

Applicability of law **Pro 6103**

At-death transfers

Annuities **Pro 21117**

Anti-lapse **Pro 21110**

Class gifts **Pro 21114**

Classification of gifts **Pro 21117**

Defined **Pro 21104**

Demonstrative gifts **Pro 21117**

Failure of transfer, treatment **Pro 21111**

General gifts **Pro 21117**

General pecuniary gifts **Pro 21117**

Lifetime gifts in satisfaction of at-death transfer **Pro 21135**

Residuary gifts **Pro 21111, 21117**

Rules, intent **Pro 21139**

Securities **Pro 21132**

Specific gifts **Pro 21117, 21133**

Transfer of specific gift, rights of transferee **Pro 21134**

Survival of transferee **Pro 21109**

Attesting witnesses (See subhead: **Subscribing witnesses**)

Attorney in fact, authority of **Pro 4265**

Attorneys' fees for deposit of documents (See subhead: **Deposit of documents with attorney**)

Beneficiaries

Abatement of bequests (See **ADMINISTRATION OF ESTATES**)

Advancements (See **ADVANCEMENTS**)

Care custodian of dependent adult as disqualified person under provisions limiting donative transfers **Pro 21350**

Defined **Pro 24, 44**

Disclaimer of interest **Pro 260 to 295**

Drafter or associate as beneficiary, restrictions concerning **Pro 21350 to 21356**

Escheat for failure to claim distribution **Pro 11900 to 11904**

Governmental agencies **Pro 6102**

Homicide, effect of **Pro 250 to 258**

Judge as beneficiary **Pro 7060**

Neglect or abuse of elder or dependent testator by beneficiary, effect of **Pro 259**

Omitted child (See **HEIRS**)

Omitted spouse (See **SURVIVING SPOUSE**)

Posthumous children (See **POSTHUMOUS CHILDREN**)

Preliminary distribution to **Pro 11620 to 11624**

Representation, taking by **Pro 245 to 246**

Service of probate notice on **Pro 8110**

Settlement of accounts, distribution after **Pro 11641**

Index

Index

WRONGFUL DEATH

Administrative adjudicative proceedings, generally (See **AD-MINISTRATIVE ADJUDICATION**)

Arbitration clause in real estate contract, applicability of   **CCP 1298.7**

Arbitration proceedings   **CCP 1283.1**

Asbestos, limitation of actions based on exposure to   **CCP 340.2**

Assignment for benefit of creditors, compensatory payments exempt from   **CCP 1801**

Common interest developments, limited liability of volunteer officer or director of   **CC 1365.7**

Complaints for   **CCP 425.10 to 425.12**

Consolidation

    Action arising out of same wrongful act or neglect   **CCP 377.61**

    Minor child, actions for injury and for wrongful death of   **CCP 376**

Damages recoverable

    Generally   **CCP 377.61**

    Complaint or cross-complaint, demand for judgment in   **CCP 425.10**

    Punitive damages (See subhead: **Punitive damages**)

    Request for statement of damages   **CCP 425.11, 425.12**

Deceased person's statements against plaintiff   **Ev 1227**

Default judgment, reservation of right to seek punitive damages on   **CCP 425.12, 425.115**

Domestic partners

    Eligibility to bring action for wrongful death   **CCP 377.60**

Exemption for purposes of enforcement of judgment of cause of action or award for   **CCP 704.140**

Health care provider's professional negligence, limitation of actions based on   **CCP 340.5**

Heirs maintaining action for   **CCP 377.60**

Homicide

    Benefit from wrongful death action, homicide slayer not expected to   **Pro 258**

    Punitive damages   **CC 3294**

Joinder of actions (See subhead: **Consolidation**)

Married person liable for damages caused by other spouse   **Fam 1000**

Medical malpractice, death by (See **PHYSICIANS AND SUR-GEONS**)

Minors

    Consolidation of actions for wrongful death and injury to minor child   **CCP 376**

    Heirs for purposes of maintaining wrongful death action   **CCP 377.60**

Parent's liability for acts of minor child   **CC 1714.1, 1714.3**

Patent deficiencies in planning or construction of improvement to real property, limitation of actions for death from   **CCP 337.1**

Personal representatives maintaining action for   **CCP 377.60**

Physician-patient privilege, applicability of   **Ev 996**

Public entities, collateral source payments in claims against   **Gov 985**

Punitive damages

    Default judgment, reservation of right to seek punitive damages on   **CCP 425.12, 425.115**

WRONGFUL DEATH—Cont.

Punitive damages—Cont.

    Homicide   **CC 3294**

Putative spouse and children of putative spouse as heirs   **CCP 377.60**

Request for statement of damages being sought   **CCP 425.11, 425.12**

Reservation of right to seek punitive damages on default   **CCP 425.12, 425.115**

Statement of damages being sought, request for   **CCP 425.11, 425.12**

Statutes of limitation

    Generally   **CCP 335.1**

    Asbestos, actions based on exposure to   **CCP 340.2**

    Health care provider's professional negligence, actions based on   **CCP 340.5**

    Patent deficiencies in planning or construction of improvement to real property, actions for death from   **CCP 337.1**

Under age of 14, entitlement to preference of party who is   **CCP 36**

Venue   **CCP 395**

WRONGFUL LIFE

Parent, cause of action against   **CC 43.6**

Y

YEAR 2000 PROBLEM

Civil fines for violations by small businesses due to Year 2000 problems, protection against   **CC 3272 to 3272.9**

Dissemination of information concerning Year 2000 Problem, liability for   **CC 3269 to 3271**

State agencies' late payment of claims, reasonable cause for   **Gov 927.2, 927.5**

YOUTH AUTHORITY

Juvenile facilities generally (See **JUVENILE FACILITIES**)

Z

ZONES AND ZONING

Common interest developments (See **COMMON INTEREST DEVELOPMENTS**)

Eminent domain valuation data for   **CCP 1258.260**

Floating homes and floating home marinas, zoning change for   **CC 800.33**

Industrial use zoning, residential property seller's obligation to disclose   **CC 1102.17**

Inspection warrants to determine violations   **CCP 1822.50**

Mobilehome parks (See **MOBILEHOMES**)

ZOOS

Eminent domain statutes affecting property reserved for   **CCP 1240.670**

Guide dogs allowed in   **CC 54.7**

Index

Matthew Bender® Desktop California Codes

To order additional copies of this or any other **Matthew Bender® Desktop California Codes** publication, please contact your LexisNexis® Sales Representative or **call toll-free at 800.223.1940**, or order online at **www.lexisnexis.com/bookstore**.

Each Matthew Bender Desktop California Codes publication features:

- *A single consolidated index*—all the Codes, all in one place
- *Legislative and regulatory histories*—for every section
- *Notes*—containing pertinent portions of uncodified legislation

In addition, no other publications document changes to the Codes so thoroughly and accurately—and no other publications are available as soon as the amendments go into effect! All of the **Matthew Bender Desktop California Codes** publications are completely updated for 2009, ensuring that you are kept abreast of the latest changes in the Codes.

When you order multiple volumes of a single **Desktop California Codes** publication, you qualify for multiple-order discounting:

5 – 15 = 5%	**31 – 50 = 15%**	**76 – 100 = 25%**
16 – 30 = 10%	**51 – 75 = 20%**	**101 and above = 30%**

Standard California Codes: 6-IN-2™ $106
2 volumes, softbound, replaced and billed annually, Pub. #00700, ISBN 9781422454077
2 volumes, hardbound, replaced and billed annually, Pub. #00700, ISBN 9781422453575

Standard California Codes: Rules of Court $42
1 volume, softbound, replaced and billed annually, Pub. #01475, ISBN 9781422453599

Standard California Codes: 4-IN-1 ....$65
1 volume, softbound, replaced and billed annually, Pub. #00704, ISBN 9781422453582

Standard California Codes: Penal Code
  with Evidence Code $49
1 volume, softbound, replaced and billed annually, Pub. #00698, ISBN 9781422454060
1 volume, hardbound, replaced and billed annually, Pub. #00698, ISBN 9781422453551

Workers' Compensation Laws of California $69
1 volume, softbound, replaced and billed annually, Pub. #00840, ISBN 9781422427439

California Corporations Code and Commercial Code with
  Corporate Securities Rules and Releases $65
1 volume, softbound, replaced and billed annually, Pub. #00191, ISBN 9781422453537

California Intellectual Property Laws $93
1 volume, softbound, Pub. #00855, ISBN 9781422427606

Bernhardt's California Real Estate Laws $99
1 volume, softbound, replaced and billed annually, Pub. #21106, ISBN 9781422450918

California Juvenile Courts: Practice and Procedure $125
1 volume, softbound, replaced and billed annually, Pub. #00046, ISBN 9781422427569

California Federal Civil Rules: with Local
Practice Commentary $50
1 volume, softbound, replaced and billed annually, Pub. #01256, ISBN 9781422427583

Lawyer's Guide to the AMA Guides and
California Workers' Compensation $64
1 volume, softbound, replaced and billed annually, Pub. #01432, ISBN 9781422427613

Prices do not include sales tax, shipping or handling where applicable. Prices subject to change without notice. Satisfaction guaranteed. If not completely satisfied, return any publication within 30 days for refund of purchase price.

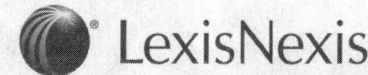

Standard California Codes, 6-IN-2™ $108

California Workers' Compensation $81

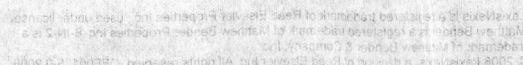